61005

BATTLE OVER BRITAIN

A history of the German air assaults on Great Britain, 1917-18 and July—December 1940, and of the development of Britain's air defences between the World Wars

FRANCIS K. MASON

F.R.Hist.S.,   F.C.G.A.,   A.M.R.Ae.S.,   R.A.F.(Retd).

By the same Author
Published by Aston Publications Limited

THE HAWKER HURRICANE (1987)
THE HAWKER TYPHOON AND TEMPEST (1988)
THE AVRO LANCASTER (1989)

_____

BATTLE OVER BRITAIN
First published by McWhirter Twins Ltd.,
September 1969

This edition published in 1990 by
Aston Publications Ltd.,
Bourne End House, Harvest Hill,
Bourne End, Bucks SL8 5JJ

British Library Cataloguing in Publication Data

Mason, Francis K. (Francis Kenneth) *1928–*
    Battle over Britain.–2nd. ed.
    1. World War 2. Battle of Britain
    I. Title
    940.54211

    ISBN 0-946627-15-0

Book typeset in 6pt, 7pt, 8pt and 9pt. Times New Roman by Francis K. Mason with Apple® Macintosh® SE, using Microsoft Word© and Aldus PageMaker©. Acknowledgement is made to C.A. Mason, CAM Design, Wensum Street, Norwich, Norfolk.

Sole distributors to the U.K. Book Trade,
Springfield Books Ltd., Norman Road,
Denby Dale, Huddersfield
West Yorkshire, HD8 8TH

Sole Distributors for the U.S.A.,
Motorbooks International
Osceola, Wisconsin 54020
United States of America

Printed in England by
The Amadeus Press Limited
Huddersfield

LIST OF CONTENTS

DEDICATION

To three Fighter Command groundcrewmen crushed to death when a bomb blew a hangar door down upon them; they had left the shelter trench under attack to save aircraft in the hangar

To the Hurricane pilot who crawled back into his cockpit to prevent his blazing fighter from falling in a densely populated area

To the two W.A.A.F. telephone operators who remained at their post in a bombed operations centre until further raids destroyed the building around them

To the bomb disposal squad who worked for more than four hours to remove a delayed action bomb embedded beneath an oil storage tank in a blazing tank farm

To the young German flight engineer who took the place of his dead pilot in the cockpit of a crippled Dornier over Biggin Hill, and successfully brought the wounded crew back to France

To the Post Office engineers who repaired the communications link to a fighter station three times in 24 hours, in craters full of water and escaping gas and in constant danger from repeated bombing attacks

To these men and women, and to the nameless thousands, this book is dedicated with respect and admiration.

INTRODUCTION

The conflict between nations is the greatest tragedy known to man. It represents the triumph of human failings over human reason; it is born of greed, jealousy, fear and hate; and it involves a terrible misappropriation of mankind's priceless assets. In modern times the harnessing of science in the production of machines of mass destruction has tended to relegate the human being to a position of obscurity and apparent insignificance, adding to the age-old horrors a new assault on human dignity and an ennervating environment of apprehension and despair.

In the pervading atmosphere of scepticism—often amounting to an open denial of man's finer qualities—there is an all too common tendency to discount the achievements of former generations. As the Second World War, with its forty million dead, fades into the history books, the men who took up arms—and indeed those who were its innocent victims—seem increasingly to be figures from a different world, the mere raw material for academic theorists. Yet these were *men*, individual identities whose involvement took the form of personal battles, ordeals, and wracking decisions; and so long as the capacity for physical aggression continues to be implanted in the human genes, their thoughts and deeds will be relevant to the history of our species.

Wars are composed of battles, large and small, fought in the light of current knowledge and ability. It is a feature of military history that subsequent accounts of such battles are written as chronological commentaries of tactics, often seeking to assess the decisions taken in a highly critical light. It is only by honest examination of past events that we can hope to build a philosophy for the future; but it is undeniable that certain critical exercises carried out in recent years have been less than honest, and have been prepared with a closer eye to the tides of social opinion than to a genuine desire for human truth. How many commanders, capable men who had risen to the highest ranks of their profession through sheer ability and battlefield prowess, have been pilloried by pens wielded in the safety and comfort of the peace they bought so dearly?

The cheap glorification of war is loathsome: the purpose of any legitimate study of war must be to increase our understanding of this most traumatic of human experiences. Yet no study can be honest without constant reminders of one of the central tragedies of the human condition—that the disease of war produces to a higher degree than any other stimulus the finest qualities of the human spirit; sublime courage, incredible sacrifice, and paradoxically, a sort of love between men that is rarely displayed in the absence of a common peril.

The Battle of Britain remains one of the classic chapters in the story of modern warfare. Its outcome was critical and clearly defined, and was innocent of political subtleties. Its conduct struck a balance between conventional strategy and courageous chance. Above all, it was fought by men who, in their own eyes at least, were taking up arms in the simple defence of their homes, and not as political adventurers. (Some readers may question this assessment of the motivation of German airmen—if so, I can only recommend them to a study of published diaries, and their fellow men. The higher echelons of Nazi authority provide numerous examples of sophisticated evil—the rank and file of the *Luftwaffe*, precious few.)

One of the recurring features of European history has been the periodic attempt by continental aggressors to invade and subjugate Great Britain, and the equally regular frustration of that attempt. For nearly nine hundred years the island nation, surrounded by that "blessed ditch", withstood the forces of would-be invaders; and then, in 1909, the faltering flight by Louis Blériot over twenty miles of water essentially cancelled out the might of the Home Fleet in a single day. The traditions of centuries withered quickly—notwithstanding the superfluous and bloody death-rattle of Jutland—and a new weapon fell upon the island, aimed not at soldiers and seamen but at the entire population and the agencies of day-to-day life.

The appearance in London skies of airships and Gothas during the 1914-18 war, though obviously of central concern to those among whom the bombs fell, was regarded as of no great significance in the overall progress of that war, being symptomatic only of the increasing horror of *la guerre totale*. To the rising generation of military strategists, however, it opened a whole new philosophy of international conflict—a philosophy which found its first major expression in the events of 1939 and 1940, and which colours international diplomacy to this day.

In this book I have based my central commentary on the actions of men, under increasing strain and forced to react to a rapidly changing environment. The products of science and their application to the Battle have been repeated and ably chronicled elsewhere by those best qualified to discuss them; but over the years I have been conscious that the feats of arms of the men who fought have been allowed to lapse into the mists of memory. Worse, a kind of clichéd and wholly spurious glamour has grown up around these events, which threaten to bring genuine achievement into discredit. There was no glamour; it was a merciless battle, and the men who took part in it, on both sides, deserve a better epitaph than the rag-ends of artificially created propaganda images. I have therefore attempted to portray the course of events with the Battle's classic structure by emphasis upon, and systematic reference to contemporary material.

Historical research in recent years has brought to light a wealth of material which, pieced together, has thrown the Battle and its wider implications into a more subtle perspective than hitherto—a perspective too often viewed from a British standpoint. Too many accounts have perceptibly been based upon retrospective despatches and official propaganda. This is not necessarily to suggest that facts have been wilfully misrepresented, rather that they have been rearranged to suit an accepted pattern. It has been the systematic study of contemporary records—the essential primary research for the writing of this book—which has brought to light the parts played by individuals of both sides, and it would have been all too easy to justify this or that decision by an analysis of secondary statistics.

Perhaps the most obtrusive example of this has been in the matter of battle casualties; in this respect it soon became obvious that if the victory claims of either side were to be believed, the Battle would have been lost and won long before the middle of September 1940. The actual casualties suffered were obviously a critical factor in the development of the campaign; and even an examination of captured German records went only a short way towards reconciling accepted figures with fact. When it emerged that the figures purporting to show British losses—too long a sacred cow of supposedly impeccable honesty—were based on an inconsistent definition of what constituted a "loss", it became adundantly clear that while it would be impossible to describe in detail each and every personal combat in the Battle (it is estimated that there were more than forty thousand individual confrontations), it would be necessary to quote "chapter and verse" of each action involving damage and/or casualties on a daily basis throughout the Battle. It has been in the preparation of these details that the true drama of the Battle has been disclosed.

It is to be hoped that the central narrative of this book can convey that drama adequately. In one essential area, the painstaking retrospective analysis of an historical event throws up its own barrier to understanding; every fact presented to the reader is unavoidably coloured by hindsight, and the conflict becomes a sterile thing of move and countermove. But the true heart of the story lies in the uncertainties of the day. The events of that remarkable summer were charged with a terrible tension, and for many, a terrible exhilaration. To the men and women involved in them, there was no way of knowing that this was not Armageddon; the fabric of their lives and of the society which had shaped them was in genuine peril, and they lived those days with a fierceness which a peacetime generation can never really share.

AUTHOR'S NOTE

It will be seen that this book falls conveniently into two parts: a brief commentary on the events which led to the arrival of the *Luftwaffe* on the French coast, and a detailed narrative of the three simultaneous air campaigns launched against and by Britain during the second half of 1940—namely the Battle of Britain itself, the Night Blitz, and the Battle of the Barges. The whole sequence of events which commenced with the limited attacks by Gothas in 1917 and which followed through the varying fortunes of the two air forces culminated in these critical campaigns. To have described events prior to 1940 in greater detail would have been to "unbalance" this book, and I have been at pains to keep the first part as brief as possible; reference to the Bibliography will disclose some of the wealth of further reading matter covering this preliminary period in greater detail and authority than is possible here.

The purpose of this book, as already explained in the Introduction, is to provide a source of detailed reference to the events which constituted the three air campaigns of July—December 1940. Although designed to appeal to the military specialist by offering fact and a fair degree of extrapolated opinion (whose origin of evidence is general quoted), it is hoped that the book will be acceptable to the general reader.

Fairly extensive recourse has been made to the use of Appendices, but the selection of matter included in these has largely been governed by a desire to present material directly concerned with the fighting men, rather than the tedium of statistical data. It is true of the Battle of Britain as it is of any other subject, that statistics can be made to prove anything; and numerous tables (generally of a secondary or derived nature) of aircraft production figures, losses sustained and units strengths have been published widely elsewhere. In many cases, even a cursory comparison with the primary matter presented here will disclose their weakness.

Finally, a word about the illustrations selected. Unfortunately it is the frustrating experience of every author to learn too late of the existence of material which he could or should have included. The decision to present a large number of illustrations—logically positioned to accompany text reference—was taken in the hope of strengthening the efforts of the pen to portray events. Had it been the sole purpose of this book to chronicle the destruction of men and machines, larger numbers of this type of picture would have been included. The selection has thus been a compromise, and an attempt to illustrate as widely as possible the many aspects of human achievement, courage, pathos, and destruction which constitute modern air warfare.

★　　★　　★　　★　　★

Special acknowledgement is made for the publication of certain passages from Official Records which are Crown Copyright Reserved. Lord Dowding's letter of 16th May 1940 is reproduced by permission of the Controller of Her Majesty's Stationery Office. The opinions expressed in this book are those of the Author alone—unless otherwise indicated—and do not necessarily reflect official views.

FOREWORD

**By Group Captain T.P. Gleave, C.B.E., F.R.Hist.S., F.C.G.A., R.A.F.(Retd),
Commanding Officer of No. 253 (Fighter) Squadron during the Battle
of Britain, later Cabinet Historian, and Deputy Chairman and Historian of the Battle of Britain Fighter Association.**

Though the task of the aviation historian is to search for the truth wherever he can find it, analyse it and interpret it for guidance in the future, he can also, in so doing, give immense pleasure to people who enjoy recalling events and things with which they were associated during times long past. This is undoubtedly so in the context of warfare, and military aviation can rightly claim a very large slice of this particular cake. For the benefit of readers of all kinds the Author has provided an immense wealth of encyclopædic information on the subject, but that would not in itself be so palatable if not nicely balanced between the historic and contemporary scenes. This the Author has done admirably.

It is a *sine qua non* that to give sound judgements on the potentials of opposing teams in any contest, those judgements must be unbiased and complete. In this context the Author has given generous space and consideration to both sides: to the pilots and members of aircrew, units and equipment of the *Luftwaffe* on the one hand, and to the fighter elements of the Royal Air Force, Commonwealth and Allied Air Forces on the other. He has therefore set the stage quite impartially for the first ever Battle in human history to be fought in the limitless space of the third dimension out of reach of land or sea, and on which the fate of a civilization depended.

Inherent in the Author's day-to-day chronicle of the Battle of Britain are those strands of thought which have a stake in the future as well as in the past. For example, each of the *Luftwaffe's* big bomber/fighter formations attracted a considerable number of Fighter Command's fighters, and this inevitably left gaps in Fighter Command's coastwise defences which could not be filled. Thus, if the enemy had persisted in simultaneously launching small raids spread widely on a large scale along the southern and eastern coasts of England, Fighter Command would have been stretched beyond endurance. As the Author has shown, comparatively great damage was inflicted by those few small enemy raids, which in the event did get through gaps in Fighter Command's air defences, but happily they remained few—the opportunities were not exploited by the *Luftwaffe*, to its enormous cost. It will also be noticed how inflexible were those big bomber/fighter formations which made them vulnerable to piecemeal attacks. But perhaps the most striking strand of thought to be evoked in this book is on the other side of the fence—the fallacy of using big defensive fighter wings composed of several squadrons with which to oppose the *Luftwaffe's* big bomber/fighter wings. These ponderous fighter formations rarely met the enemy because they were too slow to form up and climb to height. And, as is now known, the

claims made of enemy aircraft destroyed, were greatly exaggerated, an inevitable result when large numbers of aircraft are closely engaged. But the most serious penalty that had to be paid for operating big wings was the bleeding of the available total pool of fighters desperately needed elsewhere where they could be used more profitably to plug the gaps in Fighter Command's air defences.

All these strands and many others are part and parcel of the fabric of the Battle of Britain saga woven by the Author in his own inimitable style.

What of the men who were at the heart and soul of these gigantic forays into the heavens? Whether attacked in a fleece-lined valley amid the clouds, where the hunter stalked the hunted in a grim game of hide-and-seek, or "bounced" in clear air beneath a dazzling blue sky by someone with the edge in height, orange tracers gave warning of an unseen myriad of bullets and cannon shot criss-crossing the area like a vast net waiting for some unfortunate to collide with it. It gave no discount to friend or foe, or to the wary or unwary, for it could not be seen, and it treated all alike. From the Author's chronicle of day to day confrontations such as these, the reader can only hazard a guess as to what passed through the minds of pilots and members of aircrew on both sides when they found themselves in frantic struggles to stay alive; and for the fighters of the Royal Air Force, Commonwealth and Allied Air Forces there was the added knowledge of having to face unpredictable yet never less than heavy odds. To meet them many of Fighter Command's pilots and members of aircrew were mere boys. Pilot Officer Colin Francis, who died on 30th August when charging through a great flock of Me 109s at 17,000 feet over Kent, was nineteen years old, and there were many others who would not see their twentieth birthday before the end of the Battle.

The daily surveys of operations also give a detailed mental panoramic view of the whole Battle. On the other hand the daily tables of losses, including the personal details of pilots and members of aircrew lost, constitute a unique and tragic indicator of the progressive cost to each side in life and limb. It is proper and historically desirable that the Author in his wisdom should have given pride of place to these surveys and tables which, despite the excellent preamble and equally excellent appendices, are the quintessence of the whole saga of the Battle of Britain. In them the brutality of war provides each day with its own requiem, for friend and foe alike.

It is a privilege to be allowed to make these introductory comments on a magnificent work of historical importance which the reader will find both informative and captivating, and a source of pride in one's own kith and kin.

ACKNOWLEDGEMENTS AND INTRODUCTION
TO THIS EDITION

When this book was first published more than twenty years ago relatively few documentary accounts of the Battle of Britain had been published which had not tended to perpetuate the wartime publications; these were, by necessity, produced for "home consumption". They were, quite simply, propaganda documents prepared from carefully vetted material released to the Press. When I first began researching the Battle in the mid-1950s, with access to contemporary Fighter Command records, it was all too clear that the events of 1940 had only been superficially portrayed—and not always correctly. I had been fortunate to serve under quite a number of Battle of Britain participants, men who as line pilots a dozen years earlier were in the unique position of being able to speak from first-hand experience. They felt, for instance, that the "Battle of Britain pilot" had been artificially stereotyped—something that they bitterly resented; others felt that because a small number of men, whose names had been seized by the wartime media on account of their undoubted prowess in battle, reflected a particular image, all were of that image. Nothing could be further than the truth. It had, moreover, concealed countless other feats of skill and courage which, unless rectified—and rectified quickly and accurately—would never become known. And it was while serving under men like John Worrall, Charles Widdows, Bob Yule, John Ellacombe, Bird-Wilson, and others by then of lofty rank and whose recollections I inwardly digested, I decided to undertake a thorough study of the events that led up to and constituted the Battle of Britain.

Even so, after leaving the R.A.F., when I decided to write this book, many of the Battle participants whom I contacted, while being generous with their time to talk and write about their experiences, were still reluctant to allow me to quote their views, either out of modesty or unwillingness to be seen to contradict the "official" version. It should be remembered that in 1969, which this book's first edition was published, many of the wartime records were still subject to the 35-Year Rule, and were not readily available for unlimited scrutiny by the general public. However, being careful to observe caution with regard to obvious areas of sensitivity, I was—owing to the kindness of the Staff of the Air Historical Branch—given complete access to the R.A.F. records; furthermore, and I suspect at the behest of Group Captain Tom Gleave, then Cabinet Historian, I was able to transcribe and translate the wartime *Luftwaffe* records. Fortunately—from a purely selfish viewpoint—I was able to complete the latter chore before these records were returned to Germany, where access to them is now much more difficult. I am told that no one had ever been required to examine these in any depth.

As is so often the case, and is the lot of the historian, publication of the original edition of *BATTLE OVER BRITAIN* provided a signal for literally hundreds of Battle participants to write to me to record their own recollections. Fortunately these seldom identified errors of fact, but all contributed to a much more complete picture of the events described. Moreover, where I was reluctant to record the names of all those who had previously contributed to my researches, I now feel it is appropriate to do so. Alas, time has already taken many of them from us.

Those listed below, with stars against their names, were participants in the great Battle.

★ Wing Commander H.R. Allen, D.F.C. (No. 66 Sqn.)
★ Flight Lieutenant J.A. Anderson (No. 253 Sqn.)
★ Group Captain Sir Douglas Bader, C.B.E., D.S.O.✿, D.F.C.✿ (No. 242 Sqn.)
★ Wing Commander J.C.G. Barnes (No. 600 Sqn.)
★ Squadron Leader P.H. Beake, D.F.C. (No. 64 Sqn.)
★ Wing Commander R. P. Beamont, C.B.E., D.S.O.✿, D.F.C.✿ (No. 87 Sqn.)
★ Flight Lieutenant R.A. Beardsley, D.F.C. (Nos. 610 and 41 Sqns.)
★ Warrant Officer E.H. Bee (No. 29 Sqn.)
★ Squadron Leader G.H. Bennions, D.F.C. (No. 41 Sqn.)
★ Wing Commander M.V. Blake, D.S.O., D.F.C. (Nos. 238 and 234 Sqns.)
★ Flying Officer L.D. Bowman, D.F.M. (No. 141 Sqn.)
★ Air Chief Marshal Sir Harry Broadhurst, G.C.B., K.B.E., D.S.O.✿, D.F.C.✿ (No. 1 Sqn.)
★ Air Commodore P.M. Brothers, C.B.E., D.S.O., D.F.C.✿ (Nos. 32 and 257 Sqns.)
  Flight Lieutenant R. Brown
★ Flight Lieutenant B.M. Bush D.F.C. (No. 504 Sqn.)
  Sir Sydney Camm, C.B.E.
★ Squadron Leader D.F. Chadwick (No. 64 Sqn.)
★ Captain R.H.P. Carver, C.B.E., D.S.C., R.N. (No. 804 Sqn., R.N.)
★ Air Vice-Marshal G.P. Chamberlain, C.B., O.B.E. (F.I.U.)
★ Group Captain R.F.H. Clerke, D.F.C. (Nos. 32 and 79 Sqn.)
★ Sergeant J.W. Compton (No. 25 Sqn.)
  Peter Connon, Esq.
★ Wing Commander M.H. Constable-Maxwell, D.S.O., D.F.C. (No. 56 Sqn.)
★ Sgt. R.V. Cook (No. 219 Sqn.)
★ Flight Lieutenant A.R. Covington (No. 238 Sqn.)
★ Flight Lieutenant D.G.S.R. Cox, D.F.C.✿ (No. 19 Sqn.)
★ Group Captain J. Cunningham, C.B.E., D.S.O.✿✿, D.F.C.✿ (No. 604 Sqn.)
★ Squadron Leader R.W. Dalton, D.F.M. (No. 604 Sqn.)
  E.A. Davies, Esq.
★ Squadron Leader G.G.A. Davies (No. 222 Sqn.)
★ Squadron Leader P.F.McD. Davies (No. 56 Sqn.)
★ Wing Commander E.C. Deanesly, D.F.C. (No. 152 Sqn.)
★ Air Commodore A.C. Deere, D.S.O., O.B.E., D.F.C.✿ (No. 54 Sqn.)
★ Group Captain P.K. Devitt (No. 152 Sqn.)
★ Flight Lieutenant R.H. Dibnah, R.C.A.F. (Nos. 1 and 242 Sqns.)
★ Squadron Leader B. Drobinski, D.F.C. (No. 65 Sqn.)
★ Flight Lieutenant J.H. Duart (No. 219 Sqn.)
  Muriel, Lady Dowding
★ Air Commodore J.L.W. Ellacombe, C.B., D.F.C.✿ (No. 151 Sqn.)
  Don Everson, Esq.
★ Squadron Leader D. Fopp, A.F.C. (No. 17 Sqn.)
★ Wing Commander R.W. Foster, D.F.C. (No. 605 Sqn.)

- ★ Air Chief Marshal Sir Christopher Foxley-Norris, G.C.B., D.S.O., O.B.E. (No. 3 Sqn.)
- ★ General Adolf Galland (JG 26, *Luftwaffe*)
- Roger L. Geach, Esq.
- ★ Flying Officer A.W. Gear, D.F.C. (No. 32 Sqn.)
- ★ Group Captain D.E. Gillam, D.S.O.✿✿, D.F.C.✿ (Nos. 616 and 312 Sqns.)
- ★ Group Captain T.P. Gleave, C.B.E. (No. 253 Sqn.)
- Flight Lieutenant A. Grant, R.A.F.V.R.(T)
- ★ Major Gerhard Granz (ZG 2, *Luftwaffe*)
- ★ Wing Commander C.F. Gray, D.S.O., D.F.C.✿ (No. 54 Sqn.)
- Miss Helen Greenwood
- Mr. Peter M. Grosz
- ★ Flight Lieutenant R.M.D. Hall, D.F.C. (No. 152 Sqn.)
- ★ Squadron Leader H.J.L. Hallowes, D.F.C., D.F.M.✿ (No. 43 Sqn.)
- ★ Flight Lieutenant L.W. Harvey (Nos. 54 and 245 Sqns.)
- ★ Wing Commander R.E. Havercroft, A.F.C., D.F.M. (No. 92 Sqn.)
- ★ Wing Commander G.S. Hebron (No. 225 Sqn.)
- ★ Group Captain J.H. Hill C.B.E. (No. 222 Sqn.)
- K.B. Hiscock, Esq.
- ★ Warrant Officer A.J.B. Hithersay (No. 141 Sqn.)
- ★ Flight Lieutenant G.A. Holder (No. 236 Sqn.)
- Herr Fritz Hotzelmann
- ★ Wing Commander P.I. Howard-Williams, D.F.C. (No. 19 Sqn.)
- ★ Wing Commander G.L. Howitt, D.F.C.✿ (Nos. 245 and 615 Sqns.)
- ★ Air Vice-Marshal F.D. Hughes, C.B., C.B.E., D.S.O., D.F.C.✿✿, A.F.C. (No. 264 Sqn.)
- ★ Flight Lieutenant J.E. Hybler (No. 310 Sqn.)
- A.S. Ingram, Esq.
- ★ Flight Lieutenant R.H. James, D.F.M. (No. 29 Sqn.)
- ★ Flight Lieutenant E.W. Jereczek, A.F.C. (Nos. 42, 229 and 145 Sqns.)
- ★ Group Captain G.B. Johns, D.S.O., D.F.C., A.F.C. (No. 229 Sqn.)
- ★ Air Vice-Marshal J.E. Johnson, C.B., C.B.E., D.S.O.✿✿, D.F.C.✿ (No. 616 Sqn.)
- ★ Flight Lieutenant R.B. Johnson (No. 222 Sqn.)
- ★ Wing Commander J.R. Kayll, D.S.O., O.B.E., D.F.C. (No. 615 Sqn.)
- ★ Group Captain J.A. Kent, D.F.C.✿, A.F.C. (Nos. 303 and 92 Sqns.)
- ★ Flight Lieutenant J. Koukal (No. 310 Sqn.)
- ★ Pilot Officer J. Kucera (No. 238 Sqn.)
- ★ Flight Lieutenant T.L. Kumiega (No. 17 Sqn.)
- ★ Squadron Leader J.H. Lacey, D.F.M.✿ (No. 501 Sqn.)
- ★ Flight Lieutenant A. Laing (No. 151 Sqn.)
- ★ Flight Lieutenant F.C.A. Lanning, D.F.C. (No. 141 Sqn.)
- ★ Fg. Off. E.S. Lawler (No. 603 Sqn.)
- ★ Wing Commander E.F. Le Conte, O.B.E., D.F.C. (F.I.U.)
- L.T. Lee, Esq.
- ★ Flight Lieutenant M.E. Leng (No. 73 Sqn.)
- ★ Flight Lieutenant R.T. Llewellyn, D.F.M. (No. 213 Sqn.)
- ★ Air Commodore A.R.D. MacDonnell, C.B., D.F.C. (No. 64 Sqn.)
- ★ Wing Commander K.W. Mackenzie, D.F.C., A.F.C. (Nos. 43 and 501 Sqns.)
- ★ Wing Commander D.A.P. McMullen, D.F.C.✿✿✿ (Nos.

- 54 and 222 Sqns.)
- ★ Flight Lieutenant M.H. Maggs, D.F.C. (No. 264 Sqn.)
- ★ Squadron Leader M.J. Mansfeld, D.S.O., D.F.C., A.F.C. (No. 111 Sqn.)
- ★ Group Captain G.A.L. Manton (No. 56 Sqn.)
- ★ Flight Lieutenant L. Martel (Nos. 54 and 603 Sqns.)
- ★ Group Captain P.G.H. Matthews, D.F.C. (No. 1 Sqn.)
- ★ Squadron Leader J.G.P. Millard (Nos. 1 and 242 Sqn.)
- ★ Wing Commander R.R. Mitchell, M.B.E., D.F.C. (No. 222 Sqn.)
- ★ Air Commodore E.J. Morris, C.B., C.B.E., D.S.O., D.F.C. (No. 79 Sqn.)
- Peter Murton, Esq., R.A.F. Museum
- Don Myhill, Esq.
- Dipl.-Ing. Kurt Newald
- ★ Group Captain S.G. Nunn, O.B.E., D.F.C. (No. 236 Sqn.)
- Michael Ockenden, Esq.
- ★ Squadron Leader V.D. Page, D.F.C.✿ (Nos. 601 and 610 Sqns.)
- ★ Air Chief Marshal Sir Keith Park G.C.B., K.B.E., M.C., D.F.C. (A.O.C., No. 11 Group, R.A.F. Fighter Command)
- ★ Flight Lieutenant E.G. Parkin (No. 501 Sqn.)
- ★ Wing Commander P.L. Parrott, D.F.C.✿, A.F.C. (Nos. 145 and 605 Sqns.)
- ★ Flight Lieutenant F.S. Perkin (Nos. 600, 615 and 73 Sqns., and No. 421 Flt.)
- ★ Wing Commander L.F. Ralls, O.B.E. (No. 605 Sqn.)
- ★ Squadron Leader R.W. Richardson, A.F.C. (No. 610 Sqn.)
- ★ Flying Officer L.P.V.J. Ricks (No. 235 Sqn.)
- Brian Robinson, Esq.
- Richard H.M. Robinson, Esq.
- ★ Squadron Leader S.N. Rose (No. 602 Sqn.)
- ★ Air Chief Marshal Sir Frederick Rosier, G.C.B., C.B.E., D.S.O. (No. 229 Sqn.)
- ★ Flight Lieutenant A.K. Sandifer (No. 604 Sqn.)
- ★ Squadron Leader D.S. Scott, D.F.C. (No. 73 Sqn.)
- Peter Sharpe, Esq.
- ★ Flight Lieutenant T.B.A. Sherrington (No. 92 Sqn.)
- ★ Squadron Leader V.C. Simmonds (No. 238 Sqn.)
- ★ Wing Commander F.M. Smith, D.F.C. (No. 72 Sqn.)
- ★ Wing Commander R.L. Smith, O.B.E. (No. 151 Sqn.)
- ★ Flight Lieutenant R.H. Smyth, D.F.C. (Nos. 111 and 249 Sqns.)
- ★ Warrant Officer A. Spiers (No. 236 Sqn.)
- ★ Squadron Leader D.W.A. Stones, D.F.C.✿ (No. 79 Sqn.)
- ★ Squadron Leader P.H. Tew, A.F.C. (No. 54 Sqn.)
- ★ Squadron Leader L.A. Thorogood, D.F.C. (No. 87 Sqn.)
- ★ Wing Commander R.R.S. Tuck, D.S.O., D.F.C.✿✿ (Nos. 92 and 257 Sqn.)
- ★ Flight Lieutenant L.J. Tweed (No. 111 Sqn.)
- ★ Squadron Leader V.B.S. Verity, D.F.C. (No. 229 Sqn.)
- ★ Flying Officer A. Vrana (No. 312 Sqn.)
- ★ Wing Commander C. Warren, M.B.E., D.F.C. (No. 152 Sqn.)
- ★ Squadron Leader R. Watson (No. 87 Sqn.)
- Trevor M.L. Wayman, Esq.
- ★ Flight Lieutenant J. Weber (Nos. 1 and 145 Sqn.)
- ★ Wing Commander I.B. Westmacott, D.F.C. (No. 56 Sqn.)
- ★ Group Captain F.L. White (No. 74 Sqn.)
- ★ Squadron Leader D.C. Wilde (No. 236 Sqn.)
- ★ Wing Commander R.C. Wilkinson, O.B.E., D.F.M.✿ (No.

3 Sqn.)
G.F. Wilson, Esq.
★ Wing Commander E.C. Wolfe, D.F.C. (Nos. 219 and 141 Sqns.)
Squadron Leader E. Wormald

★ Air Vice-Marshal J. Worrall, C.B., D.F.C. (No. 32 Sqn.)
★ Squadron Leader J.R.C. Young, A.F.C. (No. 249 Sqn.)
★ Squadron Leader M.H. Young, D.F.C. (No. 264 Sqn.)

Of all those listed above I must single out the name of Group Captain Tom Gleave as representing the inspiration for my efforts for, not only has he done me the greatest honour by contributing the Foreword to this book, but has, year after year, kept me fully up-to-date with the researches of the Battle of Britain Fighter Association—that most august body of men of which he is Historian. Tom Gleave commanded a Hurricane squadron in the Battle and, as far as I can discover, was the only R.A.F. pilot to destroy four enemy aircraft, all Messerschmitt Bf 109s—Germany's best—in a single sortie. And a fifth may also have fallen to his guns. As a result of injuries he sustained the very next day, he was to become a member (one of the first) of the other select band of supremely courageous men, the Guinea Pig Club. Tom is today the Chief Guinea Pig. Need I say more?

PART ONE

PREPARATION FOR BATTLE

Hauptmann Rudolf Kleine, commander of *Kagohl 3*; on his office wall, a large scale map of South-East England (Photo: Peter M. Grosz)

CHAPTER 1

AN ISLAND NO MORE

Shortly after ten o'clock on the evening of 16th February 1918 a heavy explosion rocked the London borough of Chelsea. Overhead, above the inadequately blacked-out metropolis, droned a huge lone bomber which, having now completed its mission, swung on to a south-westerly course to begin a tortuous four-hour return flight to its base in Belgium. The aircraft commander, Hauptmann Richard von Bentivegni, had just released the first one-ton bomb to be dropped upon London—the heaviest dropped by any aircraft during the First World War[1], and the first of several dropped by *Reisenflugzeugabteilung* 501 before hostilities ended nine months later. If its delivery to London that evening had involved all the difficulties so characteristic of German attempts to raid England in those early years of Air Power, the relative immunity of the raider during its approach and return was hardly surprising, in view of the failure of the British armed forces to provide adequate protection against such incursions by the enemy. With such a failure in mind, well might Stanley Baldwin theorise fifteen years later that no defence existed against the bombing aeroplane[2]. Nor, for that matter could the British claim that the ability of the Germans to launch air attacks on this country came as any surprise; they had been doing so on a slowly increasing scale for three years.

Bentivegni's achievement heralded the climax of German air assaults on England, attacks which had started as long ago as Christmas Eve, 1914, when a single small bomb dropped harmlessly from a German aeroplane into a garden at Dover. In those early war months the whole concept of sending aircraft on raids against Britain was the subject of a constant battle involving the strategic dogmas of the German militarists and the conscience of the moderates: Kaiser Wilhelm—grandson of Queen Victoria—and his Chancellor, Theobald von Bethmann Hollweg. Portrayed as a rapist Hun descendant in then-current British propaganda, the Kaiser, mindful of his own ties with English royalty, forcefully deprecated a course of direct warfare against innocent women and children as well as priceless London landmarks and treasures, and went so far as to withhold approval from the Imperial Staff to conduct an offensive against targets in England.

It was the Imperial Naval Staff, headed by Admiral Hugo von Pohl, which prevailed upon the Kaiser to permit limited air attacks upon coastal targets in return for solemn assurances that only military targets would be raided. Thus naval and military facilities on the shores of the Thames Estuary came within the sphere of legitimate assault in January 1915, though London itself remained inviolable. Subsequent scattered night raids by airships of the Imperial Navy which roamed apparently aimlessly about the English countryside, though of some propaganda value in Germany, did little to reassure the Supreme War Lord as to the military or moral benefit of such forays, but brought forth a more detailed definition of what might or might not be attacked. Yet this new order now permitted raids upon the London docks and,

---

[1] The heaviest bomb to be dropped by the Royal Air Force weighed 1,650 pounds.

[2] "I think it well. . .for the man in the street to realise there is no power on earth that can protect him from bombing, whatever people may tell him. The bomber will always get through. . ." Stanley Baldwin, Prime Minister, House of Commons, 1932.

in view of the total lack of bomb-aiming equipment, endangered large areas of the City and residential suburbs.

The danger became reality when the German Army, anxious to display the superiority of its own airships and crews over those of the Navy, briefed its Commanders to attack any likely target in East London, without specifying waterside location. Only bad weather delayed the onset of these attacks. After a token objection to the new orders, the Kaiser himself finally relented to the extent that, in May 1915, he signed a directive permitting raids to the east of the Tower of London. The very next day, 31st May, the first bombs were dropped on the East End by an Army airship[3].

Bitter at having apparently lost the initiative, the Imperial Naval Staff—now headed by Admiral Gustav Backmann, who had replaced Pohl—now determined to persuade the Supreme War Lord to allow unrestricted attacks on London, arguing that to strike such targets as Government offices, the Bank of England and the railway termini was quite impossible without endangering surrounding areas. To support these arguments, the Kaiser was reminded of the indiscriminate nature of attacks upon Karlsruhe. Recognising the growing influence of the military grip upon German national politics in 1915, the Kaiser now permitted London to become the legitimate target for German bomber crews. It is perhaps ironic to reflect that while the Kaiser scarcely possessed adequate weapons with which to ravage London in 1914-15, Adolf Hitler, who possessed entirely suitable aircraft at the outbreak of the Second World War, also held his hand until the Royal Air Force had struck Berlin. The difference, of course, lies in the fact that whereas Kaiser Wilhelm was wholly dominated by the military Staffs at the beginning of the Great War, Hitler held absolute sway over both Germany's political and military strategies; indeed, Hitler's political deputy, Hermann Göring, was also head of the Air Force.

Airship attacks on England were not confined to London and, owing to their great range, the Zeppelins were able to roam over much of East Anglia and the Midlands as well as the South-East. Their raids were almost invariably carried out at night, yet despite a general laxity in black-out precautions in the provincial towns and cities their crews seldom identified military targets, and the bombing was of little more than of nuisance value. Their load-carrying capacity was high, however, and their heavy bombs (often 600-pounders) caused consternation in Parliament—not to mention the suffering among the humbler homes on which they so often fell. Preoccupied with the conduct of the war on the Western Front and its insatiable demands for men and munitions, the War Office spared precious little thought and effort for defence against the airship raids of 1915 and 1916, recognising that an enormous effort would be required to provide a worthwhile defence over so large an area. Isolated aeroplane patrols were sent up, but it was not until the night of 2nd/3rd September 1916 that the first enemy airship, a Schutte-Lanz, was destroyed over Britain. The successful pilot, Lieutenant W. Leefe Robinson of No. 39 (Home Defence) Squadron, Royal Flying Corps, was awarded the Victoria Cross two days afterwards. Almost three months later, during the early hours of

28th November, two airships of the Imperial German Navy were destroyed over the East Coast. Welcome news though this double victory was to the people of England, that date was seen in retrospect to have a far greater significance; for—unheralded and scarcely reported—a single German aeroplane managed to penetrate to London, and dropped six tiny bombs in broad daylight over the West End. Only in the light of subsequent events was this otherwise insignificant episode recognised for its true importance.

Although airships continued to raid England sporadically almost until the end of the War, the Germans had already realised in 1916 that the expense involved in the airships' manufacture and operation was in no way justifiable by the material damage they caused. Added to their mounting losses in the air were those sustained on the ground when, in raids of quite incredible daring, Allied airmen had destroyed several of the monster aircraft in their sheds in Germany. For many months the German High Command (O.H.L.[4]), had been formulating plans to launch aeroplanes against England—plans whose origins lay, like those of the airship raids, back in 1914.

It was in October 1914 that Major Wilhelm Siegert approached O.H.L. with a proposal to raid South-East England with aeroplanes based at Calais. At this time the German Army, in its sweep through Belgium, had reached the coast just south of Ostend, and there was nothing to suggest that it could not be prevented from "rolling up" the French Channel ports. Riding the wave-crest of pre-War commendation by O.H.L. for his success in the organisation of early German military aviation, Siegert was given command of a small formation of aircraft, based near Ostend[5], and instructed to make ready for flights against England. Unfortunately for the enthusiastic commander, the German Army failed to advance beyond Ostend, so that Siegert had to remain at his improvised airfield at Ghistelles; out of range of England, he simply had to content himself with bombing Calais and the other French ports instead. With hardening stalemate on the Western Front, Siegert and his crews were withdrawn to Metz in April 1915, to his bitter disappointment[6].

Nevertheless, the failure to reach England in force with Army aeroplanes in 1915 lent a motive (amongst others) for the design and testing of larger aircraft in Germany, the Grosskampfflugzeug or G-Type bombers and "battleplanes". Many manufacturers tendered designs, among them A.E.G., Friedrichshafen, Gotha, Albatros, Halberstadt and L.V.G., of which the Gothas were probably built in the greatest quantities. However, no single type was adopted to the exclusion of the others, and the force of roughly twenty machines which reached the German air arm in 1915 consisted of at least six different designs! These early G.Is and G.IIs were not destined to attack Britain owing to the situation which developed on the Western Front in 1916, claiming every possible Ger-

[3] The first airship raid on Britain was carried out by two Zeppelins which dropped bombs on King's Lynn, Norfolk, on the night of 19th/20th January 1915.

[4] O.H.L.= *Oberste Heeresleitung*
[5] Codenamed *Brieftauben-Abteilung Ostende* (=Carrier-Pigeon Flight, Ostend), this detachment flew aircraft of the *Taube* (Pigeon) varieties, which were machines of several pre-War designs; a great deal of experience gained on them was incorporated in the later, much larger C-Type aircraft.
[6] Wilhelm Siegert lived until 1929, having won respect as one of the great pioneer military airmen of Germany. At Metz he assisted in the establishment of a second "carrier-pigeon" detachment before leaving to become Inspector-General of the *Luftstreitkräfte* in 1916.

Gotha G.IVs at Gontrode, Belgium (Photos: Peter M. Grosz)

man squadron and almost resulting in their decimation over Verdun and the Somme.

Now realising the potential value of the aeroplane in the ground battle, O.H.L. set about a massive overhaul of the air arm, and placed it under the command of General Ernst von Hoeppner, the first officer of Field Rank to command the German air arm—now designated the *Luftstreitkräfte*. From all accounts von Hoeppner was an energetic administrator—despite his fifty-eight years of age—and quickly resurrected Siegert's old schemes for bombing England, now that aeroplanes of greater range existed. Before the end of 1916 he proposed to O.H.L. the formation of a squadron of 30 Gotha G.IV bombers, whose duty would be to raid London from bases in Belgium, commencing during the spring of 1917; shortly afterwards a second squadron would participate, flying even larger aircraft, the *Riesenflugzeugen* or R-Type Giant bombers[7].

Endorsed under the codename *Türkenkreuz* (Turk's Cross) by O.H.L., the campaign was delayed by late delivery of the bombers to the new squadron, which began to take shape early in 1917. Siegert's old Ostend squadrons, now re-named *Kagohl* 1[8], was called upon to supply three *Staffeln* (Flights) including a number of his veteran crews to form the nucleus of the new squadron. Once again they were to be based at Ghistelles, although three new airfields were being completed at Gontrode, St. Denis-Westrem and Mariakerke. The man chosen to lead the new squadron—indeed to play an important rôle in German aeronautics for fifteen years—was Hauptmann Ernst Brandenburg, an exceptional leader and administrator, and a man of striking appearance and bearing.

Deploying his bombers in six *Staffeln*, two at each base, with headquarters at Gontrode, Brandenburg set about training his crews to overfly large stretches of open sea, for his

mission was to be based on no established precedent. Possessing no military manuals to which he could refer, he was to learn that the whole concept of formation attacks by day across a hundred miles of sea was subject to weather criteria and accurate navigation ("dead reckoning" in latterday parlance), the mysteries whose depths had yet to be plumbed. Anxious that the full element of surprise should be his, Brandenburg conducted his training from Heligoland; yet considerable anxiety persisted that Allied reconnaissance would reveal the new Gothas at Ghistelles until in April the bombers were deployed at their new bases further away from the

---

[7] Cf. Major Freiherr Hilmer von Bülow. *Die Luftwacht: Die Angriffe des Bombengeschwader 3 auf England*, 1927

[8] *Kagohl* 1= *Kampfgeschwader* 1 of the O.H.L. Although the German word *Geschwader* is more usually translated as "Wing", it was, in the context of the First World War, closer to what was generally regarded as a "Squadron".

Hauptmann Ernst Brandenburg, commander of *Kagohl 3* until his flying accident in June 1917 (Photo: Peter M. Grosz)

Western Front. By mid-May Brandenburg reported to O.H.L. that his Squadron—*Kagohl* 3, inevitably dubbed *England Geschwader*—was ready for action: on Friday 25th May 1917 it was launched on its first raid.

The Gotha G.IV, with which *Kagohl* 3 was equipped, was an efficient aircraft by the standards of 1917, and conventional in its basic layout and structure. With a crew of three[9] the G.IV was powered by two 260-h.p. Mercedes D.IV a six-cylinder water-cooled engines which bestowed a top speed of 87.5 m.p.h. at 12,000 feet. The bomb-load varied with range between 600 and 1,000 pounds, and in the raids on England

was seldom more than six 110-lb. bombs, owing to the long distances to be flown. Single Parabellum machine guns were mounted in the nose and midships cockpits[10].

The raid of 25th May emphasised the difficulties faced by Brandenburg in his missions against England. Taking off from Gontrode and St. Denis-Westrem[11] with 23 Gothas, the German crews had to put down again at Nieuwmunster near the Belgian coast to refuel before setting course for England. One aircraft forcelanded in Belgium and another turned back soon after crossing out over the coast. Pressing on beyond the mouth of the Thames Estuary, the remaining 21 Gothas made landfall on the British coast near Burnham-on-Crouch, Essex, flying at about 12,000 feet. It was now that the lack of advance weather information became seriously evident as Brandenburg found his path to London obscured by towering cumulus clouds surmounting thick haze. Realising that it was pointless to attempt to bomb the capital without sight of the ground, the German commander reluctantly turned his formation south, crossing the Thames into Kent 20 miles east of the city. Occasionally dropping bombs on targets of opportunity[12], the Gothas regained the sea at Hythe on the South Coast, and then turned east.

The new course brought the German bombers directly over Folkestone, and it was upon this unfortunate town that Brandenburg signalled his crews to drop their bombs. Whether it was by design or chance is not clear from surviving records but, while a fair proportion of the raiders' bombs fell upon nearby Shorncliffe Camp (occupied by a Brigade of Canadian troops), the greater weight of explosive fell squarely upon the town itself. Casualties and damage were suffered in most areas of the town, although the greatest havoc was caused by six bombs which dropped on the crowded shopping arcade in Tontine Street. As the raiders passed on towards Dover, they left behind them 95 dead and 260 injured—higher casualty figures than in any previous air raid on Britain. Between them they had dropped less than five tons of bombs.

Now warned of the approaching Gothas, the Dover anti-aircraft gun batteries put up a heavy barrage; but it was clear that, unaccustomed to the size of the enemy bombers, the gun crews misjudged the raiders' height, for the shells burst

---

[9] The crew comprised Commander, pilot and midships gunner. The Commander was also responsible for navigation and bomb-aiming. Brandenburg was not a pilot himself, his aircraft being piloted by Oberleutnant Freiherr von Trotha.

[10] Cf. Gray and Thetford, German Aircraft of the First World War, p.132, Putnam, London.
[11] Mariakerke was not ready for Gotha operations until July 1917.
[12] At Wrotham, Marden, Ashford and Lympne airfield.

Left, Kagohl 3 armourers loading bombs on a Gotha G.IV. *Right*, preparing liquid oxygen equipment for the bomber crews before a raid over England (Photos: Peter M. Grosz)

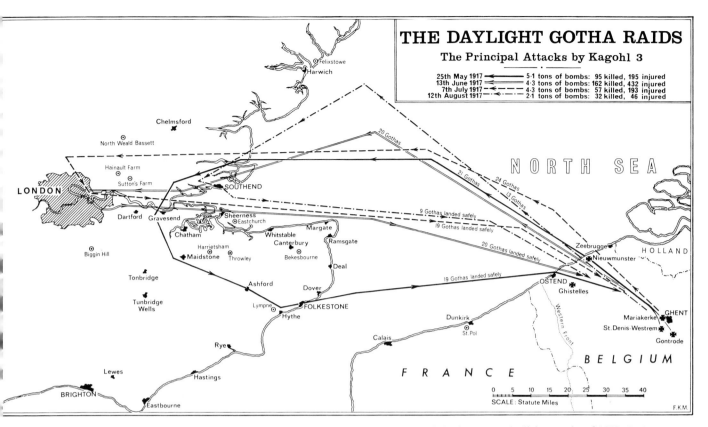

THE DAYLIGHT GOTHA RAIDS
The Principal Attacks by Kagohl 3

25th May 1917	5·1 tons of bombs:	95 killed, 195 injured
13th June 1917	4·3 tons of bombs:	162 killed, 432 injured
7th July 1917	4·3 tons of bombs:	57 killed, 193 injured
12th August 1917	2·1 tons of bombs:	32 killed, 46 injured

This map illustrates the raid tracks flown by the main Gotha formations in each of the four mass daylight attacks of 1917. It does not take account of minor raids carried out by bombers which broke away from the formations. The annotations stating the number of bombers which landed safely do not include several aircraft which crashed or force landed in Belgium for reasons other than combat damage.

ineffectually 4,000 feet below them. 74 British aircraft, which took off after the Germans were first sighted, were no more effective, although one of the raiders came down in the sea (probably as the result of engine trouble) and another crashed on landing.

The raid on Folkestone brought forth angry outbursts in Parliament by a group of hitherto discredited and ridicule "air enthusiasts", and the wolf-wolf cries of men like Noel Pemberton-Billing, M.P.[13] , were still being uttered among deaf ears when a second daylight raid was launched by *Kagohl* 3 on 5th June, this time against the naval dockyards at Sheerness on the Isle of Sheppey. Flown by 22 Gothas, this was a less spectacular raid than that on Folkestone, although the bombers—again led by Brandenburg—were caught by a small number of British scouts and lost one of their number to anti-aircraft gunfire. The bombing caused a total of 45 deaths, but little material damage. The shot-down Gotha was salvaged from the sea off Sheerness, but provided no infor-

mation of value; a rescued crew member, when interrogated, confirmed the existence of *Kagohl* 3—news that might reasonably have been expected to galvanise the British defence commanders from their inertia. The outcome, however, was to be no more than the withdrawal of Field Marshal Lord French's order banning many of his anti-aircraft guns from firing at enemy raiders![14]

The outcry that now arose as speculation about German daylight raids was published in the Press served to emphasise the astounding absence of organised defence against such raids. True, scores of British pilots had taken off, ostensibly to intercept the enemy, but few had come within ten miles of the Gothas; still fewer had the slightest idea of how to attack a heavily defended formation. On the ground, the gun defences were almost impotent, possessing instructions which were uncompromising only in the event of night raids—often summed up in such phrases as "Fire at source of sound".

Exactly one week after the Sheerness attack, Brandenburg set out from his Belgian bases with twenty Gothas on a raid

[13] Pemberton-Billing, though constantly heckled and vilified by his Parliamentary colleagues for his demands for the re-organisation of Britain's defences, was perhaps unfortunate in being thought prejudiced in his vocal outbursts. Among the most outspoken of the air enthusiasts, he had been one of the pioneer British aircraft constructors, but had failed to secure production contracts for his designs—a bureaucratic snub for which he never forgave the Government. It was later said, though probably with little justification, that his constant outbursts in the Commons, delayed rather than accelerated the creation of an independent Air Ministry on the grounds that the Establishment never likes to be proved wrong!

[14] Incredible though this order may seem, it should be explained that, sited as they were in and around densely-populated areas, the anti-aircraft gun batteries caused fairly heavy casualties among the civilian population through falling shell fragments. To civilians—unprepared for personal involvement in warfare—the noise and commotion of barrage firing was quite unnerving, and it was apprehension about the morale and material effects on the vital munition workers which led French to restrict many of his guns. Considering the enormous number of shells that were fired in barrage, with so little effect on the enemy, the ban was almost academic in significance.

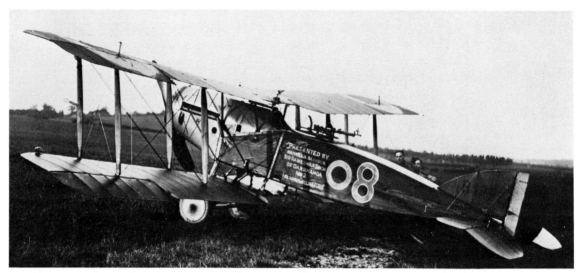

The Bristol Fighter F.2B was widely used by Home Defence squadrons of the Royal Air Force in 1918.

that was to mark the climax of the German commander's career and apparently demonstrate ample justification for all his efforts and preparations. By the time his formation crossed the English coast over Foulness three of his aircraft had turned back, and another three had swerved away to attack targets in the Thames Estuary, but the main formation pressed forward, arriving over the East End just after 11.30 hours. A few bombs fell on or near the Royal Group of docks at this time, as the Germans began their run-up to the great sprawling city. Below lay the targets whose suitability for attack was the very *raison d'être* of the Squadron. In almost cloudless skies the first aiming point—Liverpool Street railway station—was clearly visible, and almost two tons of bombs fell in this area, three bombs striking the terminus itself. Passing on beyond the City, Brandenburg's crews split into two formations, one flying north to attack other rail targets, the other to bomb dock and rail yards on the south bank of the river.

It was a random bomb, dropped by the latter group as it turned north to rejoin the first formation, which was to spark the powder of public reaction to the raid. The bomb, a 110-pounder, ploughed into an infants' school in Poplar, killing sixteen young children and injuring a further 30. By the time Brandenburg turned for home no fewer than 162 people had

been killed and 432 injured—the greatest toll from a single raid over Britain in the First World War. This time the anti-aircraft guns could not reach the raiders' altitude, and although some British fighters managed to attack the Germans, they met with no success, and Brandenburg brought his formation home intact. On the other hand a Bristol Fighter of No. 35 Squadron, which had succeeded in closing with the Gotha formation, landed at Northolt with a dead gunner.

Notwithstanding the relative immunity enjoyed by the German formations, this first dramatic raid on London not only represented the zenith of Brandenburg's own fortunes but marked an almost imperceptible change in the fortunes of *Kagohl* 3. Ernst Brandenburg was invested with the coveted *Pour le Mérite*. . .but within a week was lying in a hospital, badly injured in a flying accident far behind the Western Front. No other leader was to command the respect and affection enjoyed by Brandenburg, and when his place was taken by Hauptmann Rudolf Kleine much of the former *élan* had disappeared for ever from the men of *Kagohl* 3.

In Britain public clamour was also reaching a climax. Pemberton-Billing repeated his charges in the Commons until ordered from the Chamber. Realising the weakness of home defence squadrons, the Cabinet itself, largely as a gesture to public demands, ordered the recall of two veteran Squadrons (Nos. 56 and 66, equipped with S.E.5s and Sopwith Pups respectively) from the Western Front to join in home defence duties. Despite the undoubted prowess of No. 56 Squadron—only recently Captain Albert Ball, v.c., had served on this squadron—this meagre contribution reflected not so much the Cabinet's supercilious estimate of German air power, but rather its deference to the protests of Major General Hugh Trenchard, commanding the Royal Flying Corps in France. The strength of his forces was low, and the loss of two squadrons was, to him, critical. His arguments moreover prompted Haig to secure an undertaking that No. 56 Squadron would return to France within a fortnight, that is to say by 5th July.

Having regard to the previous raid tracks flown by *Kagohl* 3 in its attacks on South-East England, the choice of Bekesbourne in Kent as No. 56 Squadron's base during its brief return to home skies was logical. Ironically, the only daylight raid launched by Kleine before the return of the S.E.5s to

Rare air-to-air photograph of a Gotha G.IV, probably taken over Belgium in 1917. (Photo: Peter M. Grosz)

Accidents in Belgium due to bad weather were fairly frequent among Gotha formations returning from raids on England. (Photo: Peter M. Grosz)

France was flown against Felixstowe and Harwich far to the north, and neither 56 nor 66 Squadons made contact!

The irony of the situation was heightened when, only two days after the return of No. 56 Squadron to France, Kleine led 22 Gothas on a second raid on London. No doubt apprehensive about his squadron's continuing immunity, the German commander led his formation on a westerly course some miles north of the British capital before wheeling round to deliver his attack from the north-west. Once again it was the humble homes of the East End which bore the brunt of the raid. Once again a fighter squadron (No. 46 with Sopwith Pups) was returned to Britain—this time to Sutton's Farm on the outskirts of London—and once again the pilots were to return to France without combat. Now, however, there were ominous signs of unrest among the civilian population in outbreaks of arson and sporadic rioting. It was clear to the authorities that not even strict censorship of Press reports could contain the growing indignation at the military's incapacity for effective air defence.

Three other daylight attacks were carried out by Gothas on South-East England after the second raid on London of 7th July, the Germans losing a total of nine bombers—of which five were victims of crash landings in Belgium. And while these losses were being made good, and the value of daylight raids was being analysed by O.H.L., the shortcomings of the British air defences were undergoing a more reasoned study as the result of the first political realisation of the potential dangers posed by continued attacks upon the civilian population.

Pemberton-Billing's many charges had included one that the whole of Britain's air strength was being dissipated through a lack of control unity, for ever since the birth of military aviation both the War Office and Admiralty had resounded with the desk-pounding of Generals and Admirals jealously manœuvring to secure executive control of one or other of the numerous facets of the young Services. Quite apart from the chaotic military situation which resulted from this split command, there arose disagreeable circumstances within the aircraft industry which threatened to affect the smooth outflow of new aircraft—so urgently required by both home defence squadrons and by those in action over the Western Front. It only required for these quarrels to be aired in public and fanned into flame by civil unrest for the whole question of home defence to erupt into a major political firestorm. Such were the immediate but quite disproportionate results of *Kagohl* 3's sporadic daylight raids in mid-1917. The subsequent chain reaction established a fully autonomous Air Force, and in turn resulted in a coherently organised air defence system being evolved.

The Chief of the Imperial General Staff, Field Marshal Sir William Robertson, having personally witnessed the Gothas' flight over London on 7th July, recognised the need to amalgamate a single air force. Thus, with no opposition likely from Britain's senior soldier, Lloyd George seized the opportunity to attend the Cabinet with proposals for the establishment of a committee to formulate the basis upon which future air plans could be laid. It was perhaps a stroke of genius that prompted the Prime Minister to persuade General Jan Smuts, the dynamic and farsighted Boer leader turned Anglophile who was in London to attend a war conference, to chair the Committee on Air Organisation and Home Defence against Air Raids. The Committee came into being on 11th July, only four days after the last daylight raid on London by *Kagohl* 3.

Quickly realising the weakness of dispersed command, Smuts advocated a single defence command authority with control of all defences in the south-east of England. The London Air Defence Area (L.A.D.A.) was drawn up to co-ordinate control over all guns, observer corps (then a military body of only limited ability to recognise aircraft types), defence fighters and raid warning systems. The guns were to

Sopwith Camels of No. 44 Squadron at Hainault.

be re-deployed so as to form a barrier on the north, east and south of London; flight patrol lines behind these guns were organised to deal with enemy aircraft before they penetrated to the capital itself—where the Inner London gun defences were to be situated. Command of L.A.D.A. was vested in Brigadier General E.B. Ashmore, C.M.G., M.V.O., an artillery officer who was also a qualified pilot and had commanded an R.F.C. Wing in France. At his headquarters in Horse Guards Parade, Ashmore appointed Lieut. Col. C. Hankey as Chief of Staff, Lieut. Col. T.C.R. Higgins[15] as air commander, and Lieut. Col. M.St.L. Simon[16] as artillery commander. Three regular Home Defence Squadrons were assigned to be deployed in the vicinity of London; these were No. 44 with Camels at Hainault Farm, No. 61 with Pups at Rochford, and No. 112 at Throwley, also with Pups. In addition, Ashmore also fielded six other squadrons which, deployed the previous year to combat the Zeppelin threat, were still flying F.E.2Bs and Pups. Such was the urgency with which the new committee attended to the defences that the first stage of the new re-organisation was completed by the beginning of August 1917.

---

[15] Bearer of Royal Aero Club Certificate No. 88; later Air Commodore, C.B., C.M.G., R.A.F.

[16] Later Observer Corps, 1932-1942.

Lt.-General Sir David Henderson, Director General of Military Aeronautics.

Thus for the first time in more than a century London and its environs were transformed from a supposedly defenceless city into a fortified stronghold, intended to be impregnable from the ravages of German bombers. Fortunately the defence was not to be put to the test; only two more daylight raids were launched—on 12th and 22nd August—but neither penetrated beyond the coast. The strength of *Kagohl* 3 was being sapped; German losses were mounting and the realisation by Kleine's crews that the defences were alert and becoming increasingly effective led to a noticeable drop in morale.

O.H.L. therefore decided on a change of tactics. Accepting that further daylight raids could result in the decimation of *Kagohl* 3, the German bombers switched to night attacks and their crews set about hurried training in the new environment.

Smuts realised that the measures provided for in his initial defence proposals were inadequate in the face of prolonged assault and, by 17th August, had completed a second document outlining further proposals for the complete re-organisation of Britain's air forces. The great Field Marshal recognised that an air force, like an army and a navy, was capable of independent strategic use—the recent German attacks on London had provided ample evidence of this—and, with sufficient strength available, might well be used decisively in war. Nor was Smuts the first to discern this fundamental concept of Air Power: only the timing and the unusual authority vested in him enabled him to brush aside the customary partisan opposition from the Admiralty and War Office. During 1916 Lord Curzon, as President of the Air Board and a member of the Cabinet, had served in a subordinate rôle; for whatever proposals he placed before the Cabinet were subject to the decisions of the War Committee—almost wholly dominated by Arthur Balfour, First Lord of the Admiralty, and by Lord Kitchener, the War Minister.

As a means of breaking this deadlock, Smuts theorised in August 1917 that only a separate Air Ministry, with equal status and representation on the War Committee of the Cabinet could secure decisions in its favour on such vital matters as financial appropriations for new aircraft. Strong though his views were, he was scarcely dismayed when, in the course of canvassing support for the new Ministry, he encountered almost universal opposition. In particular Trenchard, fearful that his hard-won strength in France might be dissipated by re-organisation and up-grading of home defence priorities, was *against* the proposed independent air service, and went so far as to solicit support from Haig himself. As it has been generally fashionable to attribute the foundation of the Royal Air Force to the efforts of Trenchard, it is ironic to recall that this preoccupation with the air war in France

A unique photograph taken from a Gotha during the raid on London on 17th July 1917. The markings are the original annotations by German photographic interpreters and indicate among others, the fire started in the Central Telegraph Office (marked "O", "Post O") near St. Paul's Cathedral (Photo: Peter M. Grosz)

nurtured his pride in the Royal Flying Corps *as an integral part of the Army*, and strengthened his active opposition to the "separatists".

It was from another soldier—now seldom remembered, yet greatly admired by Trenchard—that Smuts gained his staunchest support. Lieutenant General Sir David Henderson, an Argyll and Sutherland Highlander, had been Director General of Military Aeronautics and had carefully steered the R.F.C. through continuing arguments ever since 1912, and it was certainly to his professional interest and personal attributes as an experienced pilot[17] that many adversaries bowed. To Henderson, no less than Smuts, must be credited the birth of the Air Ministry at a time when lethargy was the hallmark of Britain's military executive. If Trenchard later earned the sobriquet of "Father of the Royal Air Force", Smuts and Henderson were certainly its grandfathers.

---

[17] Henderson was taught to fly in 1911 and gained his *brevet* at Brooklands on 16th August that year under the tuition of C. Howard Pixton after only two hours' passenger flying. His Royal Aero Club Certificate (dated 18th August) was one of the earliest to be awarded to an Army officer and clearly afforded considerable encouragement to the junior officers who were later to provide the backbone of the R.F.C. and Royal Naval Air Service. (Cf. R. Dallas Brett, *The History of British Aviation, 1908-1914*, Chapter III (39—Army Activities).

An extraordinary picture of London's Central Telegraph Office burning during the raid of 7th July 1917. The horse-drawn fire pump and dense crowds of City spectators illustrate graphically the novelty held by air attacks for the civilian population.

The Night Raids

A Gotha G.IV over London, flying at about 8,000 feet. This was rather lower than the German bombers' normal altitude over the capital, which was usually between 12,000 and 16,000 feet.

Two days after the last daylight Gotha raid on 22nd August 1917, the Cabinet decided to set up yet another panel under Smuts—called the Air Organisation Committee—who promptly co-opted Henderson as a full-time member. Try as it might, however, this Committee made little headway for several weeks against constant prevarication and opposition from the professional staff officers, while it was deprived of active support from Lloyd George—usually energetic in this sphere of politics—who was at this time suffering ill health. His deputy, Bonar Law, anxious to avoid crisis in the Cabinet, would go no further than to provide passive arbitration.

In Belgium the German bomber crews of *Kagohl* 3 were completing their preparations for night attacks on Britain, and during the late evening of 3rd September four Gothas raided towns in North Kent under full moon conditions. One of four 110-pounders released over Chatham fell squarely upon the drill hall of the naval barracks crowded with sleeping ratings, killing 131 and injuring 90 others. No other bomb dropped on Britain in the First World War was to cause such loss of life.

Confusion on the ground prevented British fighters—of which a small number took off—from intercepting and, although anti-aircraft guns opened fire, the haze diffused the searchlight beams and the firing was erratic. The apparent lack of opposition confirmed Kleine in his view that night raids were worthwhile, and within the next thirty nights *Kagohl* 3 flew no fewer than 64 sorties over South-East England, reaching London on six occasions.

At the start of the Gotha night raids the defences were confused; apart from the fact that the guns were solely dependent upon visual reports for any degree of accuracy in aim, the pilots of the Pups and Camels were quite untrained in night flying—let alone night fighting[18]. But now, for the first time, there was an established defence command, enthu-

[18] During the night of 2nd September three pilots, Captain G.W. Murlis-Green, Captain C.J.Q. Brand and Lieutenant C.C. Banks, managed to take off from Hainault Farm and, although they failed to sight the raiders, their flight was regarded as something of an achievement and lent urgency to the preparation of aircraft and airfields for regular night flying. The two first-named pilots were to serve in the R.A.F. with continued distinction for many years and held senior appointments during the Battle of Britain in 1940. Murlis-Green was credited with 32 combat victories before the Armistice in 1918, and had by then been awarded the D.S.O. and Bar, and the M.C. with two Bars.

Two photographs which illustrate the great size of the German Giant (R-Type) bombers. *Above*, the six-engine Zeppelin-Staaken R.IV, in which a pair of engines was located in the nose, and a pair in each nacelle, each pair of engines being geared to drive a single propeller. The aircraft had a span of 138 feet—just 33 inches less than that of the Boeing B-29 Superfortress of 1944. Below, the four engine Zeppelin-Staaken R.VI at Scheldewindeke. (Photos: Peter M. Grosz)

Two views from the starboard engine nacelle of a Staaken R.IV bomber in flight, showing (*left*) five crewmen in the gunners' position and (*right*) another five in the pilots' cockpit and port engine nacelle. (Photos: Peter M. Grosz)

siastic for the active development of defence measures; and spurred by public clamour, the Air Board authorised numerous experiments to combat the night threat. Simon ordered an ingenious system of barrage firing in which, by reporting the position of enemy aircraft with reference to a squared grid, specified areas of the night sky could be saturated with barrage fire. Such fixed lines of fire were termed "curtains", and were referred to by code names; within two months the entire metropolis area was covered by closely defined barrage curtains.

Ashmore decided to introduce a balloon barrage and three Balloon Apron Squadrons were formed with headquarters at Barking and Woodford in Essex and at Shooters Hill in South-East London. The aprons consisted of a number of balloons which could be raised to heights of up to 10,000 feet and which carried aloft numerous steel wires suspended from cross cables joining adjacent balloons. So effective was this balloon screen considered to be—not so much as a means of destroying enemy aircraft but for forcing them to fly at predictable heights and thus also making accurate bomb aiming more difficult—that this form of defence was increased many hundred-fold in the Second World War, though the interconnected wire screen was abandoned in favour of a greatly increased number of balloons.

Realising that the German aircraft raiding London were operating at the extreme limit of their range and that the airship threat was steadily disappearing, Ashmore redeployed large numbers of anti-aircraft guns from the provinces to areas in the South-East, and sited them so as to allow well-defined corridors for fighter patrols.

A short lull in the night attacks followed in mid-September, during which Kleine brought the remainder of his crews up to the required degree of training proficiency to make the night flight to London. The raids were resumed on the 24th when a small number of German raiders penetrated to London, but it was on 28th September that the raids entered a new stage—though the defences were blissfully unaware of the fact. On that night the Gothas of *Kagohl* 3 were joined by another squadron, flying aircraft of such gargantuan proprtions that only three or four were required to lift the bomb-load of fifteen Gothas.

In 1916 German had established two Giant Aeroplane Squadrons, *Riesenflugzeugabteilungen* 500 and 501, for service on the Russian Front, and had equipped them with a variety of huge aircraft designated *Riesen*, or R-Type bombers. During the late summer months of 1917 O.H.L. decided

to redeploy one of these squadrons, No. 501, to Belgium to reinforce Kleine's night offensive against Britain. Commanded by Hauptmann Richard von Bentivegni, No. 501 Squadron moved to the West, collecting *en route* a number of new R-Types from airfields near Berlin; Bentivegni (not himself a pilot) was to be allotted a Staaken R.VI, the *R.39* [19].

The Squadron put down its mammoth aeroplanes at St Denis-Westrem early in September 1917, and within a fortnight were winging their way towards the British capital.

In the raid of 28th September the Giants did not reach London however, and *Kagohl* 3 now began to suffer heavy casualties. This raid cost the Squadron three aircraft shot down by British coastal A.A. guns, and a further five crashed on return to Belgium; yet another crashed in neutral Holland.

The following night the raiders came again, and this time one Giant and two Gothas reached London; two bombs from the former struck the railway track complex outside Waterloo Station [20], but generally there was no concentration and bombs fell over a wide area in South-East England. Obviously the size and sound of the Giants confused the defences, for although only four Gothas and three Giants reached the English coast a defence communiqué, issued afterwards, estimated the raid to have been carried out by eighteen aircraft. As yet the British were unaware of the Giant's existence.

It was as much the scattered nature of the bombing as the frequency with which the raiders were now visiting the capital that sent Londoners in their hundreds of thousands scurrying for shelter [21]. On Sunday 30th September the likelihood of an evening raid in fine weather and under a full moon brought the civilian population and A.A. gunners to such a state of nervous apprehension that the raid which *was* launched came as something of an anti-climax. Nevertheless

---

[19] The Zeppelin Staaken R.VI was the largest German aeroplane produced in quantity during the First World War, eighteen being built by four manufacturers. Powered by four 245-h.p. Maybach Mb IV or 260-h.p. Mercedes D IVa engines, they had a top speed of 84 m.p.h. and could carry about 5,000 pounds of bombs over fairly short distances. They were somewhat larger than the R.A.F.'s Handley Page V/1500 heavy bombers with which it was intended to attack Berlin in 1918-19 (but were prevented from doing so by the Armistice).

[20] Evidence of the damage caused by these bombs was still visible in 1969 in the gaunt shells of two Victorian rail-side slum dwellings.

[21] Fredette states in his book *The First Battle of Britain, 1917-1918*, that by the end of September 1917 300,000 Londoners were seeking refuge in the Underground stations.

Left, bomb damage at the Royal Mint. *Right*, the Eaglet public house in Seven Sisters Road.

the barrage that night consumed no fewer than 14,000 shells—without so much as a single hit![22] Such a consumption represented more than half a month's production and when, the following night, the barrage all but petered out through lack of ammunition it was scarcely surprising that the Cabinet sat up sharply and took renewed interest in the matter of air defence. Others, Winston Churchill included, drew attention to the damage and casualties caused by shrapnel falling from the enormous number of shells bursting over the city.

With one further raid on the evening of 1st October, the first concerted night campaign by German aeroplanes came to an end. The effects caused by about one hundred airmen in a score of aircraft were remarkable; apart from the subterranean existence sought by the civilian population, much of the normal, everyday life of the capital city had become disrupted and, worst of all, the London production of munitions had dropped by an alarming amount during the last week in September.

By now the German bases in Belgium were known by the British for what they were and, from 25th September on, the R.N.A.S. raided St. Denis-Westrem, and R.F.C. light bombers paid repeated visits to Gontrode. These relatively light raids, coming on top of the losses suffered in recent weeks, went a long way towards corroding the morale of Kleine's crews, and brought about a falling off of raids in the next three months.

The raids on the Belgian bases, though perhaps temporarily and locally effective, did not bring about the abandoning of the Gotha raids altogether, and such militarily-orientated reprisals cut precious little ice with the British people. Instead the pressure grew in London for the extension of raids upon Germany—a cry that was taken up in the Press and was heard by Lloyd George and the Cabinet.

Haig was immediately instructed to divert bombing effort from the immediate vicinity of the Western Front to towns in Germany itself, and Trenchard was ordered back to London to discuss the nature of this effort. Despite a background of demands for reprisals against Germany, Trenchard—who only possessed four bombing squadrons in France—once again opposed the diversion of his forces away from purely military operations. To him in France the trumpeting of the

Press was superficial, and the involvement of the civilian population in active warfare was superfluous to the conduct of the War. In any case plans for a strategic bombing force had already been laid with the formation of the first Handley Page O/400 squadrons, but these were not expected to be ready before the end of 1917[23]. Nevertheless, despite his voiced misgivings, Trenchard agreed to mount a small number of token raids, but was at pains to justify them militarily rather than countenance any idea of haphazard reprisal. The first such raid—by eight D.H.4 light bombers of No. 55 Squadron—was flown on 17th October against an iron works near Saarbrücken.

Meanwhile, as the Germans continued their night raids on London, occasionally supported by groups of airships, a new weapon was being delivered to the Belgian-based raiders. This was the ten-pound incendiary bomb, of which a large number could be carried by the Gotha and the Giant. The first "fire raid" was launched by Kleine on 31st October with 22 Gothas and, although damage was caused over a wide area, there were relatively few casualties in London and the Home Counties—due in part to the failure of many of the new bombs to ignite—and five of the bombers crashed on their return to Belgium. Furthermore the onset of winter brought adverse weather and, as it was practically impossible to provide an accurate weather forecast which would permit any certainty of suitable bombing conditions, wireless-equipped reconnaissance aircraft were sent out to report on the weather situation over South-East England before the Gothas were cleared to take off.

Bad weather prevented any raids by *Kagohl* 3 and *Rfa* 501 Squadron throughout November, and it was not until the early hours of 6th December that another fire raid was carried out. In this attack almost 20,000 pounds of bombs were scattered over London and the Kentish towns, and of this total a large proportion was incendiary. Only the magnificent efforts of London's Fire Brigade prevented the spread of major conflagrations—as it was, the damage caused was estimated at over £100,000.

---

[23] It was "A" Squadron, R.N.A.S., with four Handley Page O/400s, which, when transferred from Manston to Ochey to raid industrial targets in Southern Germany, represented the beginnings of the Independent Force, R.A.F. (cf. J.M. Bruce, *British Aeroplanes, 1914-1918.*

---

[22] Op. Cit., p.145.

An even more devastating raid was carried out on the night of 18th December by only thirteen Gothas and one Giant[24]. Although no more than twelve people were killed—two of them by barrage shrapnel—almost a quarter of a million pounds' worth of damage was caused to property. Eight Gothas failed to return—one of them brought down off Folkestone as the result of a lucky encounter by Murlis-Green.

The Defences are Strengthened

Largely as a result of increased priorities gained by the tactful Smuts for the needs of home defence, the strength of the air and ground forces in South-East England perceptibly improved during the winter of 1917-18, and continued to grow throughout the last twelve months of the War. Although the material results—in terms of enemy aircraft destroyed—were perhaps disappointing, the ultimate co-ordination of command and the benefit of training under this command were to lay the foundations of Britain's air defence for the next twenty years.

Theoretically the steps taken to improve the defences in 1918 may be summarised as follows although, as will be seen in due course, the effective realisation of these measures was to be long delayed:

Air Defences

(a) Replacement of outmoded aircraft by effective interceptors.
(b) Improvement in control of the interceptors.
(c) Build-up of squadrons (both in numbers and in unit strength) to provide a balanced defence over all areas.

Ground Defences

(d) Better co-ordination between guns, searchlights and aircraft.
(e) Improved raid warning communications.
(f) Improved training for visual observers.
(g) Improved and increased numbers of guns and searchlights.

Leaving aside for the moment the wider implications of the re-organisation of Britain's air forces, one can detect the emergence of an "independent" air force as the means by which success was achieved in the development of the home defences in the air. The Sopwith Camel—a tricky little aeroplane to fly by day, and positively treacherous to the less initiated night pilot—was joined by the Bristol Fighter. This was a two-seater with a forward-firing Vickers gun and one or two Lewis guns in the rear cockpit. Its place in the defences was to be with No. 141 Squadron, based at Biggin Hill and operating in the narrow gun-free lane between the Green Line

and the Inner London gun defences[25]. Furthermore the performance and equipment of the Bristol Fighter made it a useful night interceptor: with a speed margin of 40 m.p.h. over the operating speed of the Gothas and Giants, the new fighter could also climb to 20,000 feet—well above the operating altitude of the German raiders.

By mid-1918 the number of Home Defence squadrons in the South-East had increased to eleven, with an established strength of 264 Camels, Bristol Fighters, S.E.5s and S.E.5As, and a further five squadrons with 112 Bristol Fighters in the North.

With strength growing in aircraft, the greatest weakness in the defence system remained in the lack of aircraft control. The importance of ground-to-air radio telephony had been recognised by General Henderson as early as 1914, and from time to time this energetic officer had sought to accelerate development of the technique; however, owing to the pervading apathy and diluted priorities, little had been achieved in the issue of reliable wireless sets to R.A.F. squadrons. Efforts to rectify this situation were now redoubled, and in the meantime night patrol instructions were transmitted to the pilots by flashing searchlights. For daylight operations an elaborate system using large rotatable arrows was laid out at numerous locations in South-East England. From information provided by the observer network, these arrows were rotated so as to indicate to patrolling pilots the general direction of enemy raiders; of course the system had serious limitations, not least of which were the efficiency of the observer corps and the visibility existing in the area of the patrolling fighters.

The observer corps had hitherto consisted of soldiers of low medical category, and their training was, of necessity, rudimentary in the extreme. Identification of aircraft was not yet an art, let alone a science; it was, however, seldom important to achieve more than discrimination between a large hostile raider and a small British scout. It was in the ability to handle and report this information quickly and articulately that the soldiers were weakest, and from December 1917 their duties were assumed by Regular and Special Constables of the civil police force. This expedient showed that the police were well versed in local telephone communications and, with great ingenuity, they were often able to obtain message priorities quite outside the scope of the general public!

Efforts were made to improve communications between the defence headquarters in London and the gun batteries and searchlight companies; a new series of instructions was issued limiting arcs of fire so as to improve the patrol areas covered by the defending fighters. So detailed were these instructions that almost every gun crew's arc of fire was defined.

At the beginning of December, 150 anti-aircraft guns were assigned to London and a further one hundred guns covered Chatham, Dover, Harwich, Margate, Rochester and Sheerness. Just over 300 searchlights—of which the great majority

---

[24] Hauptmann Kleine had, in the meantime, been killed in action over the Western Front, shot down on 12th December by Capt. W.W. Rogers (of No. 1 Squadron, R.F.C.) over No Man's Land near Armentières. Brandenburg, partially recovered, returned to command of *Kagohl* 3.

[25] It is more than ironic that No. 141 Squadron was to fly the two-seat Defiant fighter—tactically a direct descendant of the Bristol Fighter— in the Battle of Britain of 1940, one of only two squadrons to do so, again with headquarters at Biggin Hill. The fundamentally flawed concept of the two-seat interceptor changed very little during the intervening years, taking no account of its inferiority to the manœuvrability of enemy fighters. The result for No. 141 Squadron was, as described in Chapter 6, nothing short of disastrous.

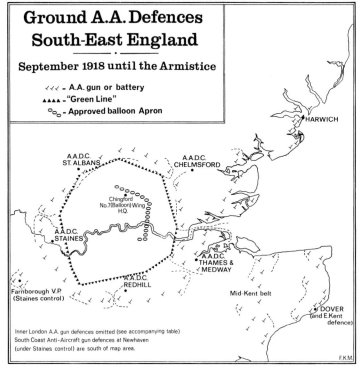

Royal Air Force Defences South-East England

September 1918 until the Armistice

Location of the Home Defence Airfields and Air Patrol Lines in relation to the established Gun Defended Areas

⊙ Elmswell
75 Sqdn.,'B'&'C' Flts.
Bristol Fighters

Hadleigh
75 Sqdn.,'A'Flt.
⊙ Bristol Fighters

HARWICH

37 Sqdn.,'C' Flt. F
Goldhanger
Camels
North Weald
BX Bassett
Stow Camels
39 Sqdn., Camels B
Maries
Hainault Farm
37 Sqdn.,'A&B'Flts.
44Sqdn.,Camels ⊙
Rochford
Sutton's Farm
6 Sqdn
78 Sqdn.,Camels
Camels
D
G
E
EX
Biggin Hill
Detling
141 Sqdn.,
143 Sqdn.,
Bristol Fighters
Camels
Throwley ⊙
112 Sqdn.,
Bekesbourne
M
Camels
50 Sqdn., Camels
H
K

Ref: Air Defence Operations Orders, Appendices & Schedules, L.A.D.A., IV Brigade, 10th September 1918

Ground A.A. Defences South-East England

September 1918 until the Armistice

⌄⌄⌄ - A.A. gun or battery
▲▲▲▲ - "Green Line"
°o₀ - Approved balloon Apron

HARWICH

A.A.D.C.
ST. ALBANS
A.A.D.C.
CHELMSFORD

Chingford
No.7(Balloon) Wing
H.Q.

A.A.D.C.
STAINES

A.A.D.C.
THAMES &
MEDWAY

Farnborough V.P.
(Staines control)

A.A.D.C.
REDHILL

Mid-Kent belt

DOVER
(and E.Kent
defence)

Inner London A.A. gun defences omitted (see accompanying table)
South Coast Anti-Aircraft gun defences at Newhaven
(under Staines control) are south of map area.

F.K.M.

HOME DEFENCE OPERATION ORDERS

(Extract from Operation Order No. 30 of 12th September 1918)

B. Aeroplane Patrols against Aeroplanes by Day

Fighting Patrols

1. On receiving the order "Patrol" the Squadrons concerned will go up and patrol on the lines laid down in Schedule II.

As far as is possible, machines should get their height and formation over their own aerodromes and then proceed on to their patrol lines.

In the case of No. 143 Squadron, whose patrol runs parallel to No. 141 Squadron's patrol, a height of 4,000 feet and formation will be formed over the aerodrome or its vicinity and the formation will proceed to their patrol line by way of the railway line running from SOUTHEND TO HORNCHURCH.

2. The G.O.C., VI Brigade, R.A.F., will issue from time to time such orders as are necessary as to the heights of patrols.

Priority of Action—A.A. Guns and Aeroplanes

4. During such time as any Hostile Formation is approaching LONDON all A.A. Guns outside the GREEN LINE will normally have priority of action, that is to say while crossing all gun areas any formation of our machines will fly to a flank to give unrestricted action to A.A. Guns. If, however, at any time the Hostile Formation is crossing these gun areas the Patrol Leader considers he has really favourable opportunity to attack he will do so and A.A. Guns will stop firing.

Inside the GREEN LINE our aeroplanes will always have priority of action, that is to say, all A.A. Guns will give preference to our machines, and will fire only up to that time when it becomes plain that our machines have seen the enemy and are in a position to attack him.

Attack

5. Fighting Squadrons will be prepared to attack as soon as possible after the Hostile Formation on its way to LONDON crossed the GREEN LINE.

If on the outward journey, the enemy is in good formation, Patrol Leaders should manœuvre to atttack when the guns of the barrage have had an opportunity of breaking up the enemy formation.

---

were of the "single 60-centimetre" type[26]—were deployed in the South-East.

While these important improvements were put in hand, the raiding squadrons suffered constant frustration from Lon-

don's famous winter fogs. On the evening of 28th January 1918, however, the skies over Belgium and England were clear; and before the North Sea mists rolled in over the bomber bases 13 Gothas had taken off for England. Seven of these persevered westward and three reached London, to be met by a barrage of 15,000 shells. One Gotha was destroyed at Wickford by two Camels, and the raid seemed to peter out long before midnight. As the Londoners retired to bed they realised from gunfire in the north-east that another raid was approaching.

---

[26] By mid-1918 the total number of searchlights in the United Kingdom had increased to 622, with approval gained to increase the establishment strength to 668, of which 240 were to be of the 120-centimetre type. It was proposed to equip all Companies with this or even larger types. Ref. *Schedule of Establishment, 6th Brigade*, dated 10th June 1918, pp. 169-170.

The appalling scene at the Odham's Printing Works in Long Acre. Thirty-eight people were killed in the basement when a bomb caused the upper floors to collapse, bringing down the huge presses.

shaking the foundations of the outer walls and setting huge rolls of newsprint afire. As the front wall crumbled and collapsed, the upper floors crashed down into the basement below—taking with them the massive printing presses. The bomb caused the deaths of 38 people and injured 85 others.

Formation of the Royal Air Force

This time it was a single Giant, *R.39*, with Bentivegni himself aboard. Briefly but vainly engaged by a Bristol Fighter, and scarcely damaged as it struck the balloon barrage near Chingford, the huge bomber approached the very heart of London. Here the German commander dropped his bombs, among them a 660-pounder—aimed at the Admiralty—which landed outside the Odham's Printing Works in Long Acre. This steel-framed concrete building had been scheduled as a public shelter and, as *R.39* arrived overhead, about 500 civilians crowded the basement. The bomb struck and exploded below the pavement hard by the cellar, severely On 29th November 1917 the Air Force (Constitution) Bill, which provided for the creation of the Royal Air Force, received the Royal Assent; thirty-four days later, on 2nd January 1918, the Air Ministry was formed. These two events came as the culmination of the single-minded efforts by the committees set up by Lloyd George, and in particular those chaired by Smuts. Yet only two months before receiving the Royal assent the Bill had faced abrogation at the hands of the Cabinet. The attitude of Trenchard, whose determination to retain all possible priorities for the Royal Flying Corps in

France as a natural branch of the Army ("the War will be won or lost in France") had had its effect on the Cabinet. Nor could any contrary support for a separate Air Ministry be said to have been contributed by members other than those with strictly partisan views.

It was at this time that news reached London of the existence of the Giant bombers[27] and, although the number said to be planned for production in Germany was greatly exaggerated, the circumstantial evidence suggested that such huge raiders were already operating and could cause devastation on an unprecedented scale. This Intelligence roused the Cabinet and clearly alarmed even the most ardent opponents of the proposed Air Ministry. As opposition thus crumbled, Lloyd George seized his chance to introduce the Bill to Parliament, and it fell to Bonar Law to announce on 16th October the Government's intention to set up an independent Air Ministry.

At once it seemed that the "air enthusiasts" had been vindicated; the Bill passed smoothly through both Chambers and, in so doing, brought to light some important aspects of Government policy not exposed in the Bill itself. For example, although clearly introduced as a War expedient, it was intended that the new Service should retain its autonomy alongside the Royal Navy and Army in times of peace.

Having attained the Royal assent it now remained to estab-

[27] The information reached Rear-Admiral Mark Kerr, a member of the Air Board, who addressed a memorandum to Lord Cowdray outlining the threat posed by the new bombers; Cf. Kerr, *Land, Sea and Air*, p.290, Longmans, Green, London, 1927.

lish political representation and the new chain of command. The manœuvres that followed were to display all the symptoms of temperament that had dogged the previous political evolutions and now brought forth a number of painful clashes of personality. As was to be expected, having achieved a successful conclusion to his brief, Smuts had anticipated that Henderson—his staunchest advocate of the independent air force—would be appointed the first Chief of the Air Staff. At the same time, and by the same token, Lord Cowdray, as president of the Air Board, had expected to become the new Air Minister. Lloyd George however, in the firm belief that the new Cabinet appointment demanded a man of wide popular influence, turned to Lord Northcliffe, powerful proprietor of an influential section of the British Press. For ten years Northcliffe, through his newspapers—particularly *The Times* and the *Daily Mail*—had campaigned to strengthen British achievement in the air and had, with offers of valuable cash prizes, provided constant encouragement to the early pioneers of aviation. Nonetheless Northcliffe had openly opposed Lloyd George's Government and now *publicly* declined the offer of the Cabinet appointment in no uncertain terms. Incensed by the public humiliation by the Prime Minister, Lord Cowdray promptly followed by resigning from the Air Board.

Lloyd George, with no outward display of political pride, blandly turned to Lord Northcliffe's younger brother, Lord Rothermere, and invited him to occupy the new Cabinet position. Closer perhaps to the military administration, Rothermere was also a fairly influential newspaper magnate and had been less critical of Government policies and personalities. His acceptance of the appointment was conditional, however, upon Lloyd George's securing the services of Trenchard as his Chief of the Air Staff. Fully aware of Trenchard's established favour among Cabinet members (an attribute that Trenchard would scarcely admit to being mutual), Lloyd George thankfully agreed and, abruptly brushing aside opposition from Haig, ordered Trenchard home in mid-December.

Thus on 3rd January 1918 Rothermere and Trenchard assumed their respective positions at the Hotel Cecil in the Strand. Simultaneously formed was the first Air Council, whose members were to be:

Secretary of State for Air and President of the Council: Rt. Hon. the Lord Rothermere, P.C.

Chief of the Air Staff: Major General Sir Hugh Trenchard, K.C.B., D.S.O. [28]

Master General of Equipment: Major General W. Sefton Brancker

Deputy Chief of the Air Staff: Rear Admiral M.E.F. Kerr, C.B., M.V.O.

Director General of Aircraft Production in the Ministry of Munitions: Sir William Weir

Administrator of Works and Buildings: Sir John Hunter, K.B.E.

Parliamentary Under-Secretary of State: Major John L. Baird

Additional Member of Council and Vice-President: Lieutenant General Sir David Henderson, K.C.B., D.S.O.

Secretary of the Council: W.A. Robinson, C.B.

Assistant Secretary: H.W.W. McAnally

---

[28] Trenchard was knighted in the 1918 New Year's Honours List.

From the outset, the first Air Council was doomed to self-destruction. Its members had been conscripted—often unwillingly—from widely differing backgrounds. The Service officers still persisted in their allegiance to the old Services, and Trenchard could not divest himself of lingering doubts as to whether he had betrayed the cause of the Royal Flying Corps in France. Rothermere, himself a man long practised in the exploitation of administrative power and reliance upon subordinate advisers, constantly provoked Trenchard's susceptibilities as a professional soldier. There were frequent angry confrontations during the first weeks of 1918, and enemies of the new Ministry played constantly upon the weaknesses displayed[29]. Moreover Trenchard claimed that his position and duties on the Air Council were never clearly defined; when he made so bold as to address a letter[30] to Rothermere suggesting that recent lapses of procedure—amounting to a lack of confidence in his professional ability and that of his own department at the Air Ministry—exposed Rothermere's insistence on his own right to seek advice other than that of his Chief of Staff, Trenchard determined to resign.

The letter of resignation, dated 19th March 1918, not unnaturally caused a bitter and immediate storm in the Cabinet. Rothermere complained of Trenchard's outspoken demands of absolute authority in air matters and even went on to imply that he had deposed him. Lloyd George, worried by the possibilities of a public scandal, once more called upon Smuts to enquire into the matter and, inevitably, Trenchard's resignation was accepted. For Trenchard the episode was filled with bitter irony: his successor—appointed on 14th April—was Major General Sir Frederick Sykes, a man "he distrusted as a colleague and despised as a man"[31].

A similar opinion was held by Henderson, who was so upset at having twice been passed over despite his "absolute" loyalty to the "Service" he had fostered since 1912, that he now resigned and abandoned all ties with military aviation. Admiral Kerr had also resigned from the Air Council after altercations with Trenchard.

Thus at the very moment on 1st April 1918, when the Royal Air Force came into being as Britain's unified air service, there was total *disunity* in its commanding body. Moreover the situation had been seriously complicated by events on the Western Front, where the massive German breakthrough had even suggested that the Royal Flying Corps might be on the

---

[29] An example of such enemies is afforded by the Rt. Hon. Sir Eric Geddes, G.B.E., K.C.B., M.P., First Lord of the Admiralty, Hon. Major General, Hon. Vice-Admiral, who had been a persistent opponent of the separatists and now discomfited the Air Council by pursuing a policy of driving a wedge between Rothermere and Trenchard by making impossible demands for naval aircraft.

[30] Dated 18th March 1918. Cf. Boyle, p.269 (see Bibliography)

[31] Op. Cit., p.125. By quoting from Trenchard's biographer is not to imply that the views expressed were widely held, but simply to demonstrate that Trenchard held them. In fact Sykes had achieved enormous strides in the development of the R.F.C. early in the War, especially in France; and it was while Sykes was in France, and Trenchard was at home in England, that the latter joined in the largely unwarrantable criticism of the R.F.C. in France. There is no doubt but that Sykes was mentally far more agile than Trenchard; and, unlike Trenchard, Sykes would not have indulged in public criticism of a brother officer. (Cf. Letter to the Author by the Cabinet Historian, dated 19th October 1975).

point of decimation[32].

The drama of the situation was not at an end. The affair reached the debating stage in the Commons on 25th April and Rothermere—verging on nervous collapse aggravated by the loss of a son—threw in his hand and resigned. His place as Secretary of State for Air was taken by the senior surviving Council member, Sir William Weir[33].

April 1918 has been described as the blackest month for Britain during the War. As disaster followed disaster for the British armies in France, the atmosphere at home was one of unmitigated gloom; and, had any concerted raid or series of raids been carried out at that moment by the Belgian-based bombers against London, there is no saying what pressures might have been brought to bear to shorten the War.

True to his loyalties, Trenchard used all his remaining influence—his resignation was not made public until 15th April—to rush every available pilot and machine to France, and by mid-May the situation on the Western Front was definitely showing encouraging signs of stabilising.

The fact that no raid was launched against Britain by the Gothas and Giants[34] can be attributed to the doubt expressed by the O.H.L. as to the strategic benefits being achieved by the bombers. Unwittingly sharing views held by Trenchard at that time, the O.H.L. was convinced that the main purpose of

the air arm was to support the ground operations, and accordingly the Gothas were thrown into the desperate battles being fought on the Western Front.

One last raid, however, was launched against London, on the night of 19th/20th May 1918. No fewer than 38 Gothas set out from Belgium and all but ten reached England, together with three Giants. For more than two hours the raiders straggled in over Kent and Essex to be met by an astonishing barrage of more than 30,000 shells and numerous patrolling fighters. One of the raiders was shot down over the Isle of Sheppey by Captain C.J.Q. Brand[35] flying a Camel of No. 112 Squadron from Throwley, and an S.E.5 of No. 143 Squadron shared with a Bristol Fighter of No. 141 Squadron in the destruction of another Gotha which crashed near Harrietsham airfield[36]. Three bombers were shot down by anti-aircraft guns that night, the German bombers falling off the coast at Foreness Point, Maplin Sands and Dover. A sixth Gotha was brought down by the combined attacks of a No. 78 Squadron Camel and a Bristol Fighter of No. 39 Squadron. Bentivegni's R.39 also raided England that night, but there are no records to indicate where his one-ton bomb landed. Always prone to overestimate the size of raiding forces, the British were unaware that the 20% casualties they had inflicted on the Germans represented a defeat for the Belgium-based raiders: they were not to know that they had been

---

[32] Boyle quotes Trenchard as recalling that Rothermere was anxious to withdraw the R.F.C. from France for the defence of the British Isles, thus leaving the Army to fend for itself; it is therefore not difficult to find the reasons for the animosity that existed between the two men. Cf. Boyle, p.273.

[33] Later Viscount Weir of Eastwood, P.C., G.C.B.

[34] The last airship raid to inflict casualties in Britain was launched on 12th April 1918.

[35] The same pilot who had accompanied Murlis-Green on the night patrol during the Chatham raid of 3rd September 1917. The remains of this Gotha were recovered during the early 1970s from the prison grounds at Eastchurch.

[36] This was the first of Biggin Hill's proud record of enemy aircraft destroyed—a record unlikely to have been equalled by any other fighter airfield anywhere in the world.

Devastation caused by Bentivegni's one-ton bomb at the Chelsea Hospital on 16th February 1918.

visited by hostile aeroplanes for the last time for 22 years.

The defence commanders on the other hand could only interpret the attack as a renewal of the campaign started the previous autumn, and continued with the strengthening of their forces—albeit encouraged by the joint successes of the guns and fighters.

To overcome the weakness in ground communications, it was decided to instal a comprehensive network of "tied" telephone lines between VI Brigade Headquarters in Horseguards Parade and all sub-control headquarters in the defence command, and between these headquarters and their gun batteries, searchlight companies, observer posts, aerodromes and balloon squadrons. Henderson's long-awaited ground-to-air wireless sets were ready for general use by June 1918[37].

By the end of the War—but too late to be put to practical test by hostile raids—an air defence control and reporting system had been constructed. There is little doubt that it would have stood the test had Brandenburg or Bentivegni persisted with their attacks after that last fateful raid of 19th May.

The losses inflicted upon the Gothas were only contributory to the discontinuation of the raids on England. O.H.L. now directed the crews against the British Army in the field as it advanced into Belgium and threatened the bases around Ghent. By October Brandenburg's squadron had been withdrawn to Evère, near Brussels; on the 30th of that month the Gothas made their last raid—against an army supply base at Menin. *Riesenflugzeugabteilung* 501 survived the Armistice and some of the crews carried on the fight against the Bolsheviks in the independent campaign of 1919.

The Reconciliation of Trenchard

It might be thought that the fortunes of Sir Hugh Trenchard, after his tempestuous departure from the Air Ministry in April 1918, could not influence the development of Britain's air defences. Far from being the proud parent of the infant Service, Trenchard had narrowly escaped a humiliating and

lasting defeat at the hands of the very politicians he had been at pains to avoid. There could be no question of a return to the R.A.F. in France—now commanded by Major General Sir John Salmond—and, having resigned from the senior appointment in the R.A.F., his future in wartime aviation posed something of a dilemma not only for himself but for the Air Council. Nor did the departure of Lord Rothermere commend his return to the Air Ministry.

It was perhaps the very youth of the new Service that enabled Weir to offer Trenchard a fairly wide selection of senior posts in the Royal Air Force. In the event, and despite misgivings, Trenchard opted for the independent command of the long range bombing force being built up in France. The Independent Air Force, advocated by Weir no less than twelve months previously for the long-range bombardment of Germany, was finally set up by Trenchard on 5th June 1918. And notwithstanding his early misgivings, it must be said that Trenchard suited his new appointment admirably and achieved considerable success despite relatively slender resources during the remaining months of the War. Moreover his close association with the new British strategic bombers, even in their infancy, brought about a profound change in his personal appreciation of an air force's primary responsibilities. From the the date of its eventual creation until the Armistice, the Handley Page O/400s, D.H.4s and, later, the D.H.9s—all based in France—flew against the towns of Western Germany. In contrast to the two German bomber squadrons in Belgium, Trenchard's force amounted to 120 bombers, the majority of which were the big O/400s. Such were the repercussions caused by, and the significance recognised in the establishment of the independent bombing force that Marshal Foch agreed to Trenchard's appointment to command an Inter-Allied Independent Air Force embodying British, French, Italian and American bombing squadrons. The new appointment took effect on 26th October, but no raids could be launched under the new command before the Armistice was signed with Germany on 11th November. Had the War persisted for a further six or nine months there is little doubt that Douhet[38] could have pointed to practical results in support of his philosophy of strategic bombing in the resolution of "total war". Trenchard certainly became reconciled to that philosophy.

---

[37] The Air Commander, Higgins, by now a Brigadier General, was able to pass instructions direct from the control room at Horseguards Parade to the pilots in the air, using a direct line to a high-power transmitter at Biggin Hill. At night, with less accuracy in raid reporting, Higgins passed instructions to his aerodromes whence they were relayed to the local flying pilots on less powerful transmitters.

[38] See Chapter 2.

A general view of aircraft assembled at Hendon for the 1920 R.A.F. Tournament. Apart from the Sopwith Snipes, Bristol Fighters, Avro 504s and a Blackburn Kangaroo, at least one German aircraft is visible—the fin of a Fokker D.VII can be seen to the left of the bus. (Photo: Flight International)

CHAPTER 2

THE RETREAT FROM WAR

It is questionable whether the air raids on Britain during the First World War attained any worthwhile results *for Germany*. In terms of damage and casualties they achieved precious little when compared with the carnage of the Western Front, and scarcely disrupted Britain's conduct of the War. The effort of launching the raids, it is true, was small; and, in relation to this, the efforts of the defence were costly in the extreme. Taking the much longer view, however, the expense to Britain was clearly justified when the Gotha and Giant raids brought about the establishment of an efficient defence system which provided the basis of Britain's shield for the next quarter-century. It may also be conjectured that, from the German viewpoint, more immediate benefits might have accompanied the launching of the Gothas and Giants *exclusively* against targets immediately behind the Allied lines on the Western Front. That such raids were carried out confirmed their feasibility, and the casualties caused among military units would certainly have provided ample justification. The fact was that the German militarists were determined to strike at the very fabric of the British nation, in the belief that undermining the population's morale could well erode the armed services' will to wage war. As would be learned 25 years hence, it would require more than a score of bombers, scattering fairly small bombs over a wide area, to bring a world Power to its knees. However, once it was realised by the British Government that to leave the civilian population unprotected was to risk an upsurge of civil disturbance, the Germans simply did not possess the necessary means by which to pursue their air offensive, and exploit their opportunity to bring the War to a successful conclusion.

Thus, justified or not, the very fact that Germany launched the raids, and that an organised defence system was evolved to counter the threat, must be considered—indeed was considered—in its broadest sense, and not simply in terms of effort and achievement. These attributes would be achieved in the fullness of time with the inevitable advance of technology. What was perhaps one of the saddest results of the air attacks on Britain was that not one other nation in Europe took note of the potential danger of the bombing aeroplane and took scarcely any measures against its use in the future, either in maintaining forces capable of deterring aggression against themselves or in seeking collective defence through treaty.

There is no doubt that the attacks of 1917-18 were recognised by Britain, not so much as a dress rehearsal for a possible future air offensive against the nation, but as a yardstick by which the vulnerability of the nation could be measured against a known state of technology and the known strength of an attacking nation. Such knowledge was scarcely comforting for British defence commanders, but the ramifications appear to have been lost on the rest of the world. Too many European nations donned the mantle of pacifism in the belief that, if they spoke in whispers, no one would notice them. They certainly raised their voices in anguish when the Nazis sought *Lebensraum*.

Of course the appearance of the embryonic strategic bomber during the Kaiser's war introduced a new dimension to the military interaction of nations, and extended the responsibilities of the fighting arms—in that the direction of hostilities embraced the employment of measures to protect the homes and families of the fighting men, and this fundamental extension in the concept of international warfare bestowed a new strategic philosophy upon every extrovert nation, and set the strategists to serious meditation. Remembering that Italian airmen had carried out some of the most audacious long range offensive sorties of the War[1], it is perhaps not altogether surprising that it was an Italian general, Giulio Douhet, who first crystallised the new strategic doctrine based upon air power by defining the ultimate object of the bombing aeroplane, and thereby creating what came to be known as the "Blue Sky" doctrine. In terms of world war, this philosophy is certainly as true in the closing years of the twentieth century as it was when it was first defined: That war will be won through power in the air, and that to win a war the major effort of a nation must be to secure air superiority—if not air supremacy. The traditional forces on land and sea, although necessary for the defence of bases and the ultimate occupation of conquered territories, would provide a shield behind which air power could be flexed and then launched. The Douhet doctrine was to be seized upon by the strategists of many nations, and even trumpeted by the defeated Germans,

" In future wars the initial hostile attack will be directed against the great nerve and communications centres of the enemy's territory, against the large cities, factory centres, ammunition areas, water, gas and light supplies; in fact, against every life artery of the country. . .Entire regions inhabited by peaceful populations will continually be threatened with extinction."[2]

This uncomfortable definition of reality came to be regarded as *Schrectlichkeit*—"frightfulness"—and, with care taken to resort to euphemism, was portrayed in reasoned works by farsighted strategists in the West, such as the American Brigadier General William Mitchell and the British Major General J.F.C. Fuller[3]. Trenchard, in his rôle as the Allies' bomber *patron* at the Armistice, was naturally cast as a protagonist with first hand experience. Mitchell, who became Director of Military Aeronautics in the United States on 10th March 1919, was to pursue his belief in the importance of the bomber—so dramatically as to offend the susceptibilities of the traditionalists[4].

Well might British strategists recognise in the Douhet doctrine vital ingredients of future planning for the continued security of Great Britain. The nation depended fundamentally upon trade routes to and from the four corners of the earth, and her dependence upon her far-flung Empire was mutual. Furthermore, the first 25 years of the century had witnessed an acceleration in the military development of several potentially influential nations—notably Japan and Italy.

At home, Britain was particularly vulnerable, once the Royal Navy was deprived of total control of her sea approaches. Already the nation had come within an ace of defeat at the hands of the U-boat during the Kaiser's war; if to this threat were now to be added the destruction of her deep sea ports, Britain could not long survive the depredations of another European war. Moreover the experience of the air raids had shown that any town or city could become a target either by accident or design. Little wonder that the strategists saw Britain's position—faced by foreign shores on two sides—as having materially changed with the new maturity of the bomber[5].

---

[1] Although primarily flown in leaflet-dropping and reconnaissance sorties, those undertaken by the *Aviazione Militare* were remarkable for the distances covered and the natural hazards overcome. For example, a single-engine S.V.A. scout flown by Captain N. Palli, airborne for almost six hours, covered 600 miles, of which 200 were over the sea.

Sir Hugh Trenchard, often referred to as the "Father of the Royal Air Force", became Chief of the Air Staff in 1919 but did little to advance the fighter defence of Great Britain, being more pre-occupied with the very survival of "his" Service. (Photo: Radio Times Hulton Picture Library).

---

[2] Cf. *Militär Wochenblatt*, General von Altrock.

[3] So prolific were authors in their views on Douhet and the Blue Sky school that it is only possible to quote representative references here. Analytical: Luftmacht: *Gegenwart und Zukunft im Urteil des Auslandes*, Fischer von Poturzyn, Berlin, 1938, pp. 57-58. In advocacy: *Sea Power in the Modern World*, Admiral Sir Herbert Richmond, London, 1934, pp. 100-101. *The Reformation of War*, Major General J.F.C. Fuller, London, 1922, p.148. In opposition: *The Navy and the Next War*, Capt. Bernard Acworth, London, 1934. *National Policy and Naval Strength*, lecture by Admiral Sir Herbert Richmond, R.U.S.I., February 1923. Letter to *The Times*, Earl Beatty, Admiral of the Fleet, 2nd May 1930. These references should be noted in conjunction with broader works listed in the Bibliography.

[4] Mitchell commanded a formation of Glenn Martin bombers which, in bombing trials off the coast of Virginia, sank the German dreadnought *Ostfriesland*, 22,800 tons, on 21st July 1921. He was later castigated for his outspoken criticism of the U.S. Army, Navy and air service and, on 17th December 1925, was found guilty by court martial of conduct likely to reflect discredit on the military service. Long after he had resigned his commission he became symbolised as the American *patron* of strategic warfare.

[5] Lord Northcliffe, in 1906—three years before Blériot flew the Channel—at the start of his newspaper campaign to make Britain "air minded", exclaimed that Britain was "no longer an island" in the environment of the flying machine. Cf. *Flying Witness*, Graham Wallace, Putnam, London, 1958, p.52.

The 1923 Salisbury Report led to a limited expansion of the R.A.F., and one of the designs ordered was the Gloster Grebe, a Jaguar-engined descendant of the wartime S.E.5. This Grebe was photographed at the 1923 Air Pageant. (Photo: Flight International)

The expression of these views in Britain not unnaturally fell upon deaf ears after the 1918 Armistice. The nation was economically exhausted and politically disenchanted. It had just survived "a war to end wars". The Liberal Government went to the country a month after peace was declared and Lloyd George was returned, this time leading a Coalition, on election tags of "Hang the Kaiser", "Make the Germans pay for the War until the lemon pips squeak", and "Make the country fit for heroes to live in". In short, the people had become devoted to a vision of retreat from war.

Notwithstanding this moral pacifism, Britain remained intensely patriotic and her armed forces could proudly proclaim their world supremacy. Yet, inevitably, the exhaustion of the economy aligned Lloyd George with the people in his determination to redress the nation's division of labour by swingeing reductions in her armed forces. The niceties of long term strategic defence were utterly lost on a government—whose political colour was, at least for the time being, immaterial—intent on re-aligning the nation for peace.

The fledgling R.A.F.—focal point of the developing strategic philosophies—was to suffer almost to the point of extermination, not only in the general atmosphere of post-War austerity, but under the arrogant vindictiveness of the Geddes "axe". Having suffered a number of rebuffs at the time of the new Service's creation, Sir Eric Geddes—wartime First Lord of the Admiralty under Lloyd George— was unquestionably motivated by a personal animosity towards the Royal Air Force, and a number of its senior officers; the upshot was that he was to achieve almost total emasculation in his assaults on the R.A.F's peacetime strength. Although the full effects of the Geddes reductions were not to be fully appreciated until 1922, the discharge of personnel and disestablishment of Service Units dated from 1920, as the following return of strengths indicates:

	November 1918	March 1920
Operational squadrons ...	188	25
Training squadrons ...	199	11
Fleet Air Arm squadrons ...	12	5
Airfields, landing grounds, etc.	700	101
Personnel ...	291,000	28,300

These figures were inclusive of all overseas R.A.F. forces

and, bearing in mind Britain's world-wide responsibilities and trade protection commitments, the application of Douhet's principles was clearly out of the question.

Yet one man—Hugh Trenchard—held fast to those principles. After the Armistice Sykes abandoned military aviation to become Controller-General of Civil Aviation at the Air Ministry, and Trenchard, his bomber appointment in France now terminated, returned willingly to London to become Chief of the Air Staff on 31st March 1919[6] —a position he was to occupy until 31st December 1929.

From the outset Trenchard faced continual sniping from Whitehall sharpshooters, intent not only on safeguarding the interests of the older Services but upon erosion of the R.A.F. After all, they argued, there was no evidence of justification for the up-grading of Britain's air arm to a fully-fledged peace-time Service; its value had been demonstrated simply as an extension of the fleet and of the army in the field. For home defence the air arm had commandeered large quantities of matériel and abducted squadrons of men and machines from the fighting fronts to meet the threat posed by perhaps a score of airships and fifty aeroplanes—and had achieved very little. If allowed to continue in the ascendant, this upstart Service would appropriate the entire output of the rapidly contracting aircraft industry.

To counter these forays, Trenchard possessed and could seek no ammunition at home; his course clearly lay in demonstrating the ability of his emaciated Service to stand beside the army and the navy on equal terms overseas, and in this fate played into his hands.

The extraordinary train of events which resulted in Britain finding herself an involuntary participant in the Turko-Greek War of 1922 do not warrant lengthy comment here. Since the Armistice with Turkey on 30th October 1918, the Allies had deployed forces of occupation on Turkish soil to safeguard the entrance to the Black Sea. Military adventures by Greece amounted to an invasion of Asia Minor before reaction by Kemal Ataturk, the Turkish leader, threw the Greeks into headlong retreat. In no mood to tolerate *any* forces of occupation, Kemal's army arrived at and threatened the gates of Chanak, the Allied garrison of occupation. As French and Italian detachments were moved away by sea, Britain deter-

---

[6] His appointment in fact dated from 11th January 1919.

mined to stand fast and defend what was, after all, a neutral position established by international treaty to withstand just such a threat as this. Almost overnight Britain came to the brink of war, a knife-edge situation immediately aggravated by the Cabinet's decision to send fairly substantial reinforcements. Among these was a Royal Air Force troopship which, *en route* for Iraq, was diverted to Chanak; it was widely felt that the arrival of the Braemar Castle with 1,000 R.A.F. men at the critical moment provided the necessary stabilising influence, and the crisis passed[7]. No shot had been fired, yet Trenchard could face his opponents with the view that the military commander at Chanak had been well disposed to accept the much-maligned R.A.F. as an effective element of reinforcement.

That Britain, unwilling and apparently unwarned, could be pitchforked into a war of this nature undoubtedly confirmed the British public in its dissatisfaction with Lloyd George's vacillating foreign policy, and in the General Election of October 1922 the Conservatives under Bonar Law were returned with a 75-seat majority.

If the resolution of the Chanak Crisis had been fortuitous for Trenchard, the successful application of air power in Iraq was decisive in the R.A.F.'s battle for survival. The whole area of the Middle East, since time immemorial, has been a desert of ill-defined national politics, racial and religious aggression and exploitation. More recently the opening of the Suez Canal and the discovery of oil had rendered the stability of an enormous territory essential to the economy of the Western World. After the conclusion of the wartime Turkish campaign in Mesopotamia, the British army had waged a long, costly and exhausting policing operation to maintain law and order throughout Iraq in the face of constant rampaging by tribesmen and the incursions of Kurdish bandits on the Eastern borders.

In 1920 an uprising in the Euphrates valley prompted the despatch from Egypt of a bomber squadron, which evidently played a major part in restoring the situation; this in turn caused Winston Churchill—then Colonial Secretary—to ask Trenchard to prepare a plan for the policing of the whole area by air. The result was the transfer of four squadrons to Iraq, and the gradual assumption of policing responsibilities by the Royal Air Force. Chief Staff Officer of the newly-established air command in Baghdad was a 40-year-old Air Commodore named Hugh Dowding[8]. It was largely in the policies advocated by Dowding that the success of the R.A.F.'s new rôle lay. A policy of indiscriminate bombing of Arab villages would have brought instant discredit, loss of respect for justice and inevitable failure; however, by dropping very small bombs upon villages known to be harbouring the offending tribesmen—always after due warning of the consequences—it proved possible to reduce the bloodshed to a minimum, and at the same time brought about a marked respect for the Royal Air Force. That the measures were successful at no great cost is reflected in the relative calm that existed in the area during the following fifteen years.

If these events served to safeguard the Royal Air Force's continued existence, its future also rested in the hands of a very small surviving band of Regular officers and men, spread thinly over the territories in which the R.A.F.'s presence was deemed necessary—so thinly indeed that at one time in 1920 the air defence of the United Kingdom rested upon a single squadron of Sopwith Snipes[9]. Nevertheless Trenchard, acutely conscious of the necessity to cultivate among his men a spontaneous pride in their Service no less than that of the nation in its air arm, determined to stage an annual pageant similar in concept to the tattoos of the army and navy. The first, known as the R.A.F. Tournament[10], was organised by Sir John Salmond and held at Hendon on 5th July 1920. By providing the public with a colourful display, the theme of successive pageants was to portray the Royal Air Force as an efficient, disciplined and enthusiatic Service capable of performing a wide range of duties both in the air and on the ground. There is no doubt but that these occasions were very popular with the public and succeeded in achieving Trenchard's aim, particularly in those difficult years; furthermore they inevitably provided a welcome spur to recruitment of the particular type of young man whom Trenchard was anxious to attract.

The Royal Air Force had benefitted from a valuable inheritance on its emergence from the old R.F.C. and R.N.A.S. The pilots were among the finest in the world, and had quickly bestowed upon the new Service a tradition and roll of battle honours which any veteran corps would be proud to possess. The ruthless and often random reductions applied after the Armistice inevitably deprived the R.A.F. of much *ésprit*, yet the survivors quickly displayed to Trenchard's Air Staff the particular qualities demanded by a *corps d'élite*, namely attraction to adventure, individualism and a pride in their uniform.

Of course the majority of the senior officers had spent their early service with the Colours in one of the older Services, and it was to ensure a constant stream of young Regular officers that Trenchard opened the Royal Air Force College at Cranwell in Lincolnshire in 1920[11]. Such was the devotion demanded by the Service that for thirteen years successive "generations" of cadets had to endure life at an establishment composed of an agglomeration of draughty wooden huts; not until 1932 were the Air Estimates sufficient to provide buildings of comparable dignity with those of Sandhurst and Dartmouth.

The Cautious Re-armament

The R.A.F.'s escape from extinction became absolute with the publication of the Salisbury Committee's report in June

---

[7] An ultimatum had been given by the British commander for the withdrawal of Kemal's troops; had the time limit expired, a major battle would have followed. The constant arrival of British reinforcements convinced the Turks that Britain "meant business".

[8] Early in 1920 a three-week campaign by the British-led Camel Corps in Somaliland had put an end to the mischief of Mahomed bin Abdullah Hassan—the Mad Mullah. This campaign was supported by D.H.9 bombers of "Z" Force, R.A.F., which certainly influenced the speedy conclusion of a nuisance that had preoccupied ground forces intermittently for twenty years. It would, however, be inaccurate to claim, as the Air Ministry did at the time, that air power alone had ended the campaign. Cf. *Memoirs of Lord Ismay*, Heinemann, London, 1960.

[9] No. 25 (Fighter) Squadron, R.A.F.

[10] Subsequent annual events were termed "Displays" or "Pageants"

[11] Cranwell's first Commandant was Air Commodore C.A.H. Longcroft, C.M.G., D.S.O., (later Air Vice-Marshal Sir Charles, K.C.B., C.M.G., D.S.O., A.F.C.) who had commanded the home air training division of the R.F.C. during 1917-18.

Hawker Woodcocks wearing No. 17 Squadron's distinctive zig-zag markings. The two Woodcock squadrons, Nos. 3 and 17, were based at Upavon for the night defence of the Midlands in the late 1920s.

1923. Precipitate moves to abolish the Royal Air Force by the Conservative Bonar Law the previous year had been overruled in favour of the appointment of a sub-committee chaired by Lord Salisbury, Lord President of the Council. The effect of the report was to confirm the Chief of the Air Staff in status equal to that of the Chief of the Imperial General Staff and the First Sea Lord; and it went on to recommend the strengthening of the R.A.F. so as to provide the nation with adequate defence against the strongest air force within striking distance. These proposals were in turn confirmed by Stanley Baldwin who, after the resignation of Bonar Law, led the short-lived Conservative Government from mid-1923 until the end of that year. Baldwin announced in the Commons on 20th June that following the recommendations of the Salisbury Committee the Home Air Defence Force was to be increased from eighteen squadrons to 52 "with as little delay as possible".

Well might Trenchard feel satisfied with this avowed display of confidence in the Royal Air Force, yet to attain such expansion was another matter, in the light of the parsimonious appropriations allotted to aviation. With regard to military aircraft scarcely any finance had been provided for technical development or applied research, and almost every fighter in service was of 1918 vintage—and with nothing much better on the horizon.

The absence of production contracts had all but brought the British aircraft industry to its knees. Manufacturers of the wartime bombers, notably de Havilland and Handley Page, had turned with some success to civil application of their designs but had been obliged to contract to a shadow of their former size. Britain's leading fighter manufacturer, the Sopwith Aviation Company, had gone into voluntary liquidation in 1920 largely through lack of work—only to be bailed out by the Company's Chief Test Pilot, Harry Hawker[12], under the name of H.G. Hawker Engineering Co. Ltd. Many other companies had disappeared for ever.

The fact that the aircraft industry survived at all can be attributed to a handful of men—some of whom had been in aviation since the pioneer days—who passionately believed that the technology recession of the early 'twenties would be shortlived. This was also a period in which very close ties between the Service and the Industry were established, for it should be explained that all equipment requirements were formulated within the Air Ministry, and contracts issued to Industry direct by the Royal Air Force. This close association between the manufacturer and the Service, which lasted until the Second World War, was undoubtedly responsible to a considerable extent for the progressive development of the fine aeroplanes which entered service with the R.A.F. during the nineteen-thirties.

By the end of 1923, although Sopwith Snipes still represented the in-service equipment of home-based fighter squadrons, new contracts had been issued for the first British fighter of post-War design[13]; namely the Armstrong Whitworth Siskin III. The Siskin's design represented the transition from the design practices adopted in the wartime fighters to those made possible by the easing of embargos on "strategic" materials. The original prototype had flown in 1921 as an all-wooden aircraft powered by the 340-h.p. A.B.C. Dragonfly radial engine but, in the absence of production contracts, the manufacturers had persevered with development of the basic design. A two-seat version had appeared in 1922, powered by the new Siddeley Jaguar, which represented a marked improvement over the Dragonfly. This Mark II seized the limelight by participating in the King's Cup Race that year. Also introduced in the Siskin at that time was a patent steel

---

[12] Hawker, an Australian, had built for himself the reputation of being one of Britain's foremost pilots. When he performed his rescue operation on the old Sopwith company he was, however, in failing health and died in an air crash before his company was a year old. T.O.M. Sopwith became Chairman after his death, but Hawker's name has been perpetuated in the huge industrial group of today—Hawker Siddeley—of which Sir Thomas Sopwith remained President until his death in 1989 in his 101st year. Cf. *Hawker Aircraft since 1920*, Mason, Putnam/Conway, 1990.

[13] Several prototypes had been built at private expense (notably by the Gloucestershire Aircraft Company) but these were little more than attempts to exploit wartime development, and were not supported by production contracts; in short, none promised any significant improvement over the Sopwith Snipe.

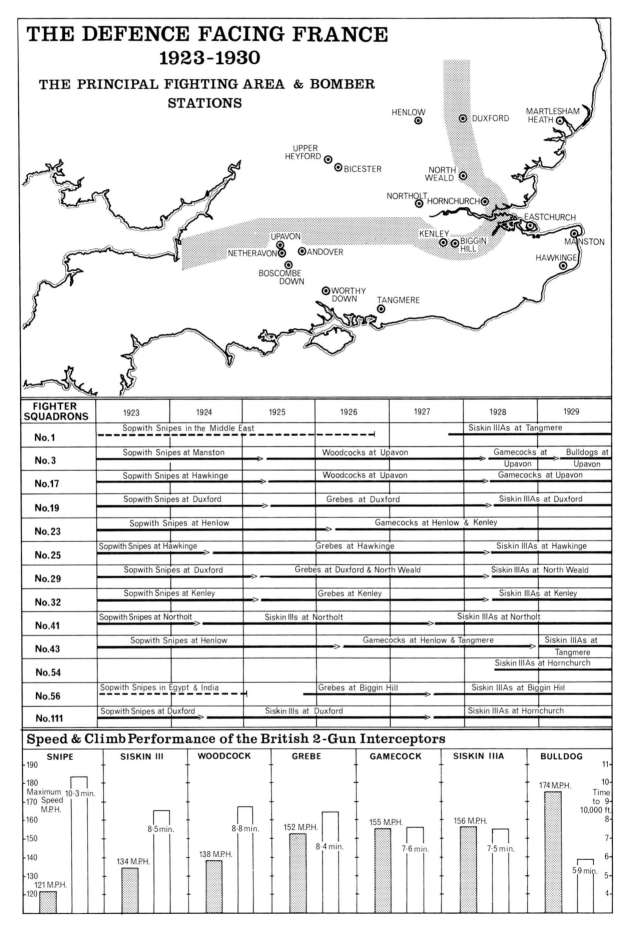

THE DEFENCE FACING FRANCE
1923-1930
THE PRINCIPAL FIGHTING AREA & BOMBER STATIONS

FIGHTER SQUADRONS	1923	1924	1925	1926	1927	1928	1929
No. 1	Sopwith Snipes in the Middle East					Siskin IIIAs at Tangmere	
No. 3	Sopwith Snipes at Manston			Woodcocks at Upavon		Gamecocks at Upavon	Bulldogs at Upavon
No. 17	Sopwith Snipes at Hawkinge			Woodcocks at Upavon		Gamecocks at Upavon	
No. 19	Sopwith Snipes at Duxford			Grebes at Duxford		Siskin IIIAs at Duxford	
No. 23	Sopwith Snipes at Henlow				Gamecocks at Henlow & Kenley		
No. 25	Sopwith Snipes at Hawkinge			Grebes at Hawkinge		Siskin IIIAs at Hawkinge	
No. 29	Sopwith Snipes at Duxford			Grebes at Duxford & North Weald		Siskin IIIAs at North Weald	
No. 32	Sopwith Snipes at Kenley			Grebes at Kenley		Siskin IIIAs at Kenley	
No. 41	Sopwith Snipes at Northolt		Siskin IIIs at Northolt			Siskin IIIAs at Northolt	
No. 43	Sopwith Snipes at Henlow				Gamecocks at Henlow & Tangmere		Siskin IIIAs at Tangmere
No. 54						Siskin IIIAs at Hornchurch	
No. 56	Sopwith Snipes in Egypt & India			Grebes at Biggin Hill		Siskin IIIAs at Biggin Hill	
No. 111	Sopwith Snipes at Duxford		Siskin IIIs at Duxford			Siskin IIIAs at Hornchurch	

Speed & Climb Performance of the British 2-Gun Interceptors

SNIPE	SISKIN III	WOODCOCK	GREBE	GAMECOCK	SISKIN IIIA	BULLDOG
121 M.P.H. / 10·3 min.	134 M.P.H. / 8·5 min.	138 M.P.H. / 8·8 min.	152 M.P.H. / 8·4 min.	155 M.P.H. / 7·6 min.	156 M.P.H. / 7·5 min.	174 M.P.H. / 5·9 min.

Maximum Speed M.P.H. — 190, 180, 170, 160, 150, 140, 130, 120

Time to 10,000 ft. — 11, 10, 9, 8, 7, 6, 5, 4

Capt. Howard Saint, chief test pilot of the Gloster Aircraft Company, taking off from Brockworth in a Gamecock. This Grebe derivative came into service in 1926. (Photo: Flight International)

strip form of construction, and so, with the production contracts of 1923, the Siskin became the R.A.F.'s first fighter of metal construction.

Early in 1924 further orders followed, this time for the Gloster Grebe II—an aggressive-looking little fighter whose ancestral lineage originated in the S.E.5, designed by H.P. Folland. Also powered by a Jaguar engine, the Grebe was 18 m.p.h. faster than the Siskin, with a top speed of 152 m.p.h. at sea level.

Third of those first-generation fighters to be ordered as a result of the 1923 expansion plans was the Hawker Woodcock. Like the Grebe, the Woodcock was of all-wooden construction and, in appearance was probably the most conservative of the trio—and that isn't saying much! Possibly reflecting the difficult times suffered by its manufacturers, the Woodcock had originally been designed by Captain B. Thomson[14] in 1921, but had later been developed under the direction of W.G. Carter. Despite its disappointing top speed of 138 m.p.h., it was, in its Mark II version, nevertheless a tractable aeroplane and, on account of this, came to be developed primarily as a night fighter, and as such came to be regarded as the R.A.F.'s first purpose-built night interceptor.

Bearing in mind that the Siskin, Grebe and Woodcock possessed a range of no more than about 200 miles (plus a small reserve in case of bad weather), it is as well to examine here the deployment of the R.A.F. interceptor squadrons.

Although friendly relations with France could not be questioned, it became British policy to align the defences to face the most powerful potential enemy within striking distance of London and the industrial Midlands. With this in mind the operational organisation of the Royal Air Force followed the establishment of a number of "combat areas". With regard to the interception of enemy raiders, in the absence of

over-sea warning facilities there was no alternative but to declare a "no man''s land"—a fifty-mile-deep coastal belt, behind which the main fighters patrolled, thus extended from the Bristol Channel south of Bristol, eastwards to Kent and then north to Cambridgeshire. Along and immediately behind this line was a zone known as the "fighting area". With the establishment of this system of defence, Britain at once acknowledged the vital weakness created by inadequate warning measures; moreover, lying so far ahead of the interception zone, the important naval bases at Portland and Portsmouth lay at the mercy of enemy bombers. With the resources available this defence structure—with a few minor exceptions—remained in being until the introduction of the R.A.F. Command organisation in 1936.

By the end of 1924 the R.A.F. possessed ten home-based fighter squadrons, of which seven still flew Sopwith Snipes and two had Siskin IIIs; No. 25 Squadron had received the first Grebes. Most of these squadrons were grouped around the approaches to London.

The next two years brought no fundamental improvement in R.A.F. equipment, and only a small increase in strength. No. 1 Squadron, which had flown Snipes in the Middle East and India since the end of the War, was disbanded overseas and re-formed at Tangmere with Siskin IIIAs[15]. A development of the Grebe, the Gamecock, had also appeared and, with a top speed of 155 m.p.h., was in service with Nos. 23 and 43 Squadrons at Henlow. No. 56 Squadron, another Middle East Unit, was also now re-established at home, flying Siskin IIIAs from Biggin Hill.

Included in the R.A.F.'s routine training was night flying, and all squadrons were expected to complete a monthly programme of night exercises. However the Air Ministry considered that any attack likely to be launched against the Midlands would *only* be flown at night owing to the long

---

[14] Captain Thomson, an ex-cavalry officer whose appointment as Hawker's chief designer has never been satisfactorily explained, possessed no known academic qualifications. It is thought that he may have joined the company as a "political expedient" as he seems to have occupied much of his time designing a "corps reconnaissance" aircraft, the Duiker—of which it was said that no sane pilot would fly a second time.

[15] This was a much improved version of the Mark III, which had been found to suffer from wing flutter—a fairly common malady among aircraft of the day, resulting from inadequate wing stiffness and unbalanced lateral control surfaces. The Siskin IIIA eventually equipped eleven fighter squadrons, but was nevertheless generally regarded as a somewhat pedestrian aeroplane.

overland flight involved. It was to meet this threat that the aerodrome at Upavon was specially prepared to accommodate two squadrons, Nos. 3 and 17, both of which flew Woodcocks as night interceptors.

Thus by the end of 1927 the R.A.F.'s home-based fighter strength had increased to twelve squadrons, all flying aeroplanes with top speeds in the 130-160 m.p.h. range, each armed with two Vickers rifle-calibre machine guns. Whatever improvements had been achieved in structural design since the Armistice were scarcely apparent in the performance and firepower of the fighters themselves. The reason for this lay in the finance made available in the annual Air Estimates for research. Such advance in technology as was achieved was wholly underwritten by the privately-owned aircraft industry[16].

The relatively slow build-up in the strength of the Royal Air Force was to a large extent the result of the political lethargy engendered by the "Ten Year Rule"—an expedient formulated by Lloyd George in 1919, and one which had been almost superfluous until 1923. This arbitrary theory suggested that at least ten years' notice of a threat of international war in Europe would be detectable and, by implication, that the progress of British defence development should be limited to a rate no more than sufficient to achieve war readiness within those ten years. While such a policy inevitably drew sharp and prolonged criticism from those ultimately responsible for accelerating re-armament when the "rule" was abolished in 1933, the policy certainly stood Britain in good stead during the years of depression, at least from an economic viewpoint. Moreover, it might be considered to have achieved exactly what it was designed to achieve—to balance Britain's forces against what she could afford. And when the "rule" fell into disrepute in 1930, the ten year estimate was not so very far from the mark.

By 1927 it seemed that technical development of the interceptor fighter had reached stalemate; each new fighter seemed doomed to conform to the age-old formula of air-cooled radial engine and twin-gun armament. Yet two years previously a remarkable light bomber had been produced in the Fairey Fox which, in the absence of a suitable British engine, used the American Curtiss D-12 liquid-cooled in-line engine. The slim contoured nose contributed so little drag that the Fox—which was capable of carrying 460 pounds of bombs—achieved 156 m.p.h. This was roughly the same as the fastest R.A.F. interceptor.

However Mr. Richard Fairey's resort to an American engine caused offence, not only in other parts of the British aircraft industry, but in the all-powerful Contracts Department of the Air Ministry. Even the R.A.F. expressed doubt as to whether it would be able, within its budget, to maintain the foreign engines—any difficulty in acquiring the spares for which could ground an entire squadron. In the event, only 28 production Foxes were built, attributed to an enthusiastic but impetuous Trenchard, and these served with only one squadron[17].

Whether the appearance of the Fox spurred engine development in Britain is open to doubt, yet it was only the following year that Rolls-Royce unveiled its F.XI engine—justifiably regarded as the most significant single milestone of the inter-War years. Quite likely the new engine possessed some features common to the Curtiss D-12, yet it was the adoption of cylinder banks cast in one component that made possible undreamed-of reductions in weight, as well as the low frontal area seen in the American engine.

The first manufacturer to seize upon the new British engine was the H.G. Hawker Engineering Company whose recently-appointed Chief Designer, Sydney Camm, had expressed frustration at the inadequacy of the traditional radial engines[18]. Recognising in the F.XI enormous potential, Camm proposed two separate but related aircraft designs, one for a light bomber ("to out-fox the Fox") and the other for an interceptor. When the bomber—the Hawker Hart—first flew, its performance astonished the R.A.F., for its top speed of 184 m.p.h. was ten miles per hour greater than that of the Bristol Bulldog interceptor which entered service in 1928.

By 1930 the Royal Air Force displayed a façade of high morale and efficiency with aircraft apparently second to none in Europe. Despite the Depression, these were the bright evening years of the old Empire, in whose environment successive Hendon Air Displays depicted the R.A.F. dealing firmly but paternally with recalcitrant tribesmen. With such terms of reference there is no doubt that for sheer economy of effort the R.A.F. was achieving a remarkable atmosphere of calm in the Middle East and the North-West Frontier Province of India, with such benevolent rectitude that the international verdict was one of admiration rather than of opportunist exploitation.

Nevertheless, in the environment of muskets and mules, any serviceable aeroplane represented a powerful instrument of influence and authority. Among European air forces, however, British Service aeroplanes at the beginning of 1930 were by no means outstanding, though not inferior. True, the

---

[16] Until 1924 it was Government policy to publish the appropriation Estimate for Research and Development, but thereafter the figure was contained in the appropriation for "warlike stores". The average sum set aside during the years 1921-24 was approximately £1.5m annually. The following table shows the total Annual Air Estimates between 1921 and 1938, including the Supplementary Estimates introduced to accommodate the various expansion programmes.

Year	Personnel	Estimate	Year	Personnel	Estimate
1921	30,880	£18.4m.	1930	32,000	£17.9m.
1922	33,000	£12.5m.	1931	32,000	£18.1m.
1923	33,000	£12.0m.	1932	32.000	£17.4m.
1924	35,000	£14.5m.	1933	31,000	£17.4m.
1925	35,500	£15.5m.	1934	31,000	£17.7m.
1926	35,500	£16.0m.	1935	45,000	£27.6m.
1927	33,000	£15.5m.	1936	55,000	£50.7m.
1928	32,500	£16.3m.	1937	70,000	£56.5m.
1929	32,000	£17.0m.	1938	83,000	£73.5m.

---

[17] Trenchard was present at a demonstration of the Fox in October 1925 and was so impressed that he promptly "ordered a complete squadron" (Cf. *Aircraft of the Royal Air Force*, Thetford, Putnam, London, p.204). It appears that his impetuosity found disapproval among the politicians, a *fait accompli* so unpopular that the Fox was doomed to be officially ignored (see *Trenchard*, Boyle, 1962, p.563).

[18] Camm had produced a prototype fighter, the Hornbill, which, powered by a 698-h.p. Rolls-Royce Condor in-line engine, possessed a top speed of about 194 m.p.h. in 1925. It was, however, a very tricky aeroplane to fly and its pilot was only accommodated with acute discomfort. It did not reach production, but the prototype contributed extremely useful research data on control at high speeds for half a dozen years.

No. 12 Squadron Fairey Foxes, photogrpahed in 1928. Trenchard's enthusiastic support for this remarkable light bomber, powered by an American Curtiss engine, caused ill-feeling which was reflected in the disinterested attitude adopted by the Air Ministry Contracts Department. (Photo: Flight International)

Hart was probably the finest light bomber in the world when it started coming into service at the end of 1929, and it was the breakthrough by this bomber—which was capable of out-stripping the Bulldog, whose service had been planned to continue far into the nineteen-thirties—that gave the Air Ministry Requirements Department seriously to consider what steps must be taken to ensure the performance superiority of R.A.F. interceptor fighters. If Britain did not maintain its lead, another nation would quickly take her place. And it was at this moment that Trenchard, the "Bomber Baron", retired from the helm of the Royal Air Force.

It was clear that if a fighter were to be introduced that could outstrip the Hart in speed, the whole concept of air fighting would undergo a radical change. Apart from the particular tactic of the "tail chase", dogfighting involving high-deflection firing would render fire from the traditional pair of machine guns that much less effective from any but the most accomplished marksman. It was therefore decided to formulate an "impossible" specification for a fighter capable of a speed of no less than 250 miles per hour and armed with four machine guns. The sponsor of this arbitrary target was none other than Air Chief Marshal Sir John Salmond, who succeeded Trenchard as Chief of the Air Staff at the beginning of 1930, and who had previously for four years commanded Air Defence of Great Britain—the R.A.F. fighter force[20].

Such an advance in technology implicit in the new Specification was deemed to be unheard-of, but the reward of very large production orders for the winning design was promised, in the belief that private finance in industry would be forth-coming to subsidise the necessary research. Bearing in mind the lengthy period likely to elapse before the nation would be called on to pay for large quantities of such an aeroplane, the F.7/30 Specification won approval from the Treasury of Ramsay Macdonald's Labour Government—elected in June 1929—which was firmly committed to a policy of supporting world disarmament.

Sydney Camm's other design based on the Rolls-Royce F.XI engine (now named the Kestrel) was the Hawker Fury fighter and, with a top speed of 207 m.p.h., it was natural that this should attract the Air Ministry's attention as a likely

Bulldog replacement, notwithstanding the ramifications of F.7/30 and the fact that the old two-gun armament had been retained. However, there could be no question in Government minds of replacing the Bulldog as this fighter was already in fairly extensive production and the whole re-equipment programme of R.A.F. fighter squadrons during the next five years was orientated about the Bristol design. Furthermore, cancellation of existing contracts would effectively double the cost of the already-expensive Fury through compensation, while the Labour Government viewed with concern the likely unemployment that would result from cancellation at the Filton factories[21]. After all, the Kingston and Brooklands

[21] Another of Ramsay Macdonald's election pledges had been to tackle the deteriorating problem of unemployment, yet it was later estimated that his Government's policies of trimming the armed forces by 10 % over two years and delaying orders for equipment for the armed forces worth £7m. alone contributed 25,000 to the national total.

Sir Frederick Henry Royce, director and chief engineer of Rolls-Royce Ltd., whose F.XI engine made possible great advances in aircraft design from 1928 onwards. (Photo: Radio Times Hulton Picture Library)

[20] It is now known that Salmond had discussed at length the matter of future R.A.F. interceptors with both Sopwith and Camm at the Hawker company on several occasions during 1929 and it is likely that the emphases evident in the new fighter Specification reflected the tenor of these discussions. They certainly influenced Camm's future direction of thought. Cf. *Records of meetings of the Board of Management, Hawker Engineering Co., Ltd.*, 1929-31.

factories of the Hawker company were already stocked with orders for the Hart, Horsley and Tomtit[22].

The result was a compromise. The Air Ministry gained approval to purchase sufficient Hawker Furies to equip first one squadron, and later two others; contracts were then raised in 1930 and 1931 for 24 and 48 aircraft respectively. And it was logical that, with the air defences still deployed to face France, the new fighters should form the spearhead of those defences; they were accordingly delivered to Tangmere, joining No. 43 (Fighter) Squadron ("The Fighting Cocks") under the command of Sqn. Ldr. L.H. Slatter[23] in May 1931. During the Air Exercises that year this handful of Furies achieved many more interceptions than the more numerous Bulldogs.

The following winter No. 25 (Fighter) Squadron, commanded by Sqn. Ldr. W.E.G. Bryant, M.B.E., at Hawkinge (another forward airfield) took delivery of Furies, to be followed by this squadron's traditional rivals, No. 1 (Fighter) Squadron at Tangmere. These three fighter squadrons, flying as they did the R.A.F.'s first combat aeroplane capable of more than 200 m.p.h., came to acquire the reputation of a *corps d'élite*—prestige that was to remain with them long after the Fury had disappeared from service. Before production of this splendid little fighter ceased in 1937, no fewer than 214 had been built for the R.A.F.

One other fighter was introduced at this time: the Hawker Demon. While negotiations were still underway with the Treasury to secure approval for the purchase of Furies, the Air Ministry acceded to a proposal submitted by Camm that an *interim* expedient could be achieved by "setting a Hart to catch a Hart". In other words, by uprating or supercharging the Kestrel engine, giving the pilot two forward guns and eliminating the bomb-carrying gear from the Hart, a fighter version of marginally superior performance could quickly be produced. Though acknowledged as no more than an interim remedy, the Demon project won approval from the Treasury on the grounds of economy and *six* aircraft were ordered; these equipped one Flight of No. 23 (Fighter) Squadron at Kenley. So popular did these aeroplanes prove to be that in 1933 the Squadron's remaining Bulldogs were disposed of and replaced by further Demons. A total of 244 Demons was built for the R.A.F. between 1932 and 1936, and these eventually equipped six R.A.F. fighter squadrons and five of the Auxiliary Air Force. Unfortunately their design, despite its intended makeshift nature, came to perpetuate a tactical theory which may have suited the realities of combat in the days of the old Bristol Fighter intercepting Gothas and Zeppelins—and one that was conceivably acceptable during the early 1930s (when the margin of speed between the Demon and the nimble Furies was no more than 20 m.p.h.), but was, in the long term a dead end and a dangerous tactical philosophy. However, so entrenched had this concept become among R.A.F. fighter tactics that, even when interceptors were far outperforming the Demon, replacement Speci-

fications were raised which ultimately sired the Boulton Paul Defiant— a fundamentally flawed aircraft whose tragic misfortunes in the presence of highly manœuvrable singleseaters were entirely predictable and of which more will be told later.

The Retreat is Halted

The year 1933 was a turning point in British military aviation. For fifteen years technology had to a great extent stagnated owing to a persistent witholding of financial assistance for basic research. The retreat from war had been a continuing process in which the armed forces were merely tolerated as *symbols* of influence among nations otherwise utterly preoccupied with successive economic and social upheavals.

For Britain the studied nonchalance with regard to national security diminished principally with the first rumblings of an extremist element in Germany. The slow emergence from the Depression brought a belief in Britain that she should now drag her head from the sand and take note of world events. In the Far East Japan was attempting to establish a puppet government in Manchukuo and, while the Sino-Japanese war had not directly endangered British interests in the area, the widespread use of air power by the Japanese had caused misgivings with regard to the safeguarding of worldwide British influence.

At home, the Royal Air Force had reached a crossroads both in terms of flying personnel and in the quality of their aircraft. The number of airmen who had survived the Geddes "axe" and upon whom the Service had leaned heavily during its first fifteen years was by now reduced to a relative handful of senior officers; the training establishments had maintained a steady trickle of well-trained and devoted men of high *ésprit*. Now, in 1933, the Royal Air Force was to formalise its officers' training college at Cranwell with an establishment entirely comparable in stature with its naval and military counterparts. The mere attendance at these proud buildings was enough in itself to enhance the respectability (if any had been lacking) of a professional career in the Royal Air Force.

Another era now ending in British military aviation was that of the biplane—a process that would continue henceforth for a further seven years or so. Just as the lean post-War years of 1919-21 had sounded the death-knell of several leading aircraft manufacturers, so the Depression further thinned their ranks. Those that had managed to secure contracts to "see them through" the austere years of 1929-32 were now on the threshold of a new age of prosperity. By far the most powerful was the H.G. Hawker Engineering Company which had secured orders for numerous variants of its successful Hart and Fury designs both for the R.A.F. and for foreign air forces[24]. The company's first step in consolidation was to issue shares on the public market, a brilliant coup by T.O.M. Sopwith which attracted an enormous influx of capital with which to underwrite massive new contracts (by peacetime

---

[22] Cf. *Records of meetings between the Board of Management, H.G. Hawker Engineering Co. Ltd., and the Contracts Department, Air Ministry, 1929-31.*

[23] Later Air Marshal Sir Leonard Slatter, K.B.E., C.B., D.S.C., D.F.C. This officer had formed and commanded the R.A.F. High Speed Flight and captained the British Schneider Trophy team at Venice in 1927; he also commanded Nos. 19 and 111 (Fighter) Squadrons during the years 1929-31.

[24] In long retrospect, the late Sir Sydney Camm ascribed the survival of the British aircraft industry to the extensive export orders which were gained during 1933-34. Not only was the high standard of the British aeroplanes immediately apparent to the foreign customers but established the industry as second to none in the world for quality of workmanship and efficient customer relations. This prestige was to stand Britain in good stead for another twenty years.

standards) and to undertake the necessary research to satisfy the radical demands made by the Air Ministry since 1930. Other companies, which had managed to retain their staffs— but in so doing were in effect so mortgaged as to be unable to underwrite any profitable work—therefore became ripe for take-over. One such company was Glosters, which had only managed to obtain limited prototype orders after the Gamecock production terminated, and this firm with its extensive factory was taken over in 1934 by Hawker. Supermarine Aviation Works (Vickers) Ltd., although it had acquired little revenue from its Schneider Trophy racing seaplanes, had produced a series of successful flying boats, but could not luxuriate in economic comfort until it merged fully with Vickers (Aviation) Ltd. in 1938. The Bristol Aeroplane Company and its associated aero-engine works had survived as the result of their heavy Bulldog fighter commitments, while Boulton and Paul were saved by the production of

Sidestrand and Overstrand bombers between 1928 and 1934. Rolls-Royce Ltd. had had few worries since 1927 as this eminent manufacturer had of course supplied almost every engine for the Hawker designs. Among the bomber manufacturers, Vickers and Handley Page enjoyed an almost total joint monopoly in the supply of these aeroplanes (such as the Vickers Virginia and the Handley Page Hinaidi) to the Royal Air Force, but were unable to enjoy any fruits of exporting such aircraft; after the departure of Trenchard, the British bomber was relegated to the wilderness as efforts were now made to repair the deficiencies of the interceptor fighter that had suffered something of an eclipse during his term of office.

Yet the survival of these great companies was to become progressively more critical in the coming years, for in their assembly shops were to take shape all the fighters and aero-engines on which Britain's own survival was to depend seven crowded years hence.

The Bristol Bulldog, backbone of Britain's fighter defences between 1929 and 1936. This No. 23 Squadron aircraft, photographed in 1931, was typical of the R.A.F. fighter squadrons which flew in this most colourful period of the Service's history. (Photo: Flight International)

CHAPTER 3

THE SECRET AIR FORCE

The rapidity with which the War reached its final act of Armistice in 1918 was certainly contributory to the ineptitude of the Allies when it came to convening an international body to decide the future of Germany. Furthermore the progress through the agenda (*sic*) of this assembly—the Versailles Convention—was constantly sidetracked by the French pre-occupation with troubles in Foch's army, and this led in turn to some recrimination among the Allies. The achievement of the Assembly was the Treaty of Versailles, an instrument designed to "squeeze Germany until the lemon pips squeak", signed in June 1919, which displayed all the hallmarks of hurried preparation; its vindictiveness, born of the horrors of war and in the popular view fully justified by recent history, was further evidence of the Allies' absolute inability to understand the German national circumstance—the dissolution of the German Empire and the fierce and almost frantic German nationalism. To the Allies' superficial view, the German danger lay in the long term projection of traditional Prussian militarism.

The Treaty imposed vicious and economically crippling punitive measures which took no account of the appalling social and economic upheaval which was tearing Germany apart from within. From these fatal shortcomings grew the unrest which nurtured the German determination to regain a position of national equality in Europe. And from this social and political instability it was but a short step to the precipice of totalitarian aggression.

The military clauses of Versailles deprived Germany of her proud and powerful navy, which sailed to an ignominious internment and ultimate scuttling in Scapa Flow; the latter event was almost certainly predictable, bearing in mind the seething discontent among the German crews and the lack of vigilance on the part of the Royal Navy, itself the result of severe post-War cutbacks in manpower. The German air service—a force of about 20,000 aircraft—was to be surrendered to the Allies, and more than 15,000 aircraft and 27,000 aero-engines were handed over under the ægis of the Allied Control Commission. Germany was permanently forbidden to support a military air force, or to import and manufacture military aircraft or their components. Yet so new and untried was commercial air transport in 1919 that its potentialities were virtually overlooked in the preparation of the Treaty, so that restrictions on the manufacture of civil aircraft were only applied for a period of six months. *Therein lay the fatal flaw and ultimate failure of the Treaty.* (After all, British manufacturers soon came to adapt military aircraft designs for commercial use; there was no practical impediment to prevent Germany from adapting commercial aircraft for military use—and so it transpired, in due course.)

This short-lived embargo upon civil aircraft enabled Germany to retain her industry in being and, when the statutory period lapsed, no time was lost in making plans for the future.

In the military sphere Germany was secretly careful to retain the services of her key officers. She had been permitted

General Hans von Seeckt, architect of the *Luftwaffe*. (Photo: Radio Times Hulton Picture Library)

even to retain a defence ministry in Berlin, the *Reichswehr Ministerium*, and this legitimised façade masked the *de facto* assembly of a German Staff under General Hans von Seeckt. And it is to von Seeckt (and not to Hermann Göring, as has been widely averred[1]) that the survival of the German air force should be attributed. Among this staff were men like Felmy, Kesselring, von Richthofen[2] , Sperrle, Stumpff and Wever, all of whom were to occupy senior command positions in the *Luftwaffe* of the 1930s and 1940s. It was among this Staff in 1923 that von Seeckt—an unwitting adherent to the Douhet doctrine—circulated a top secret memorandum which formulated the principle that the future German air force should be independent of the other two Services.

The Contribution of Commercial Aviation

Though it is true that many of the wartime aircraft manufac-

---

[1] Hermann Göring, who had been a relatively inconspicuous squadron commander during the War, spent the years 1920-21 and 1923-27 in Sweden—at times as a pilot of the *Flygvapnet* and at others—thoroughly dissipated—in hospital undergoing treatment as a drug addict.

[2] Wolfram Freiherr von Richthofen was a cousin of the famous wartime ace, Manfred Freiherr von Richthofen, who had been killed in action.

turers in Germany forsook aviation after the Armistice, others sought survival in a variety of expedients. Claude Dornier went into voluntary exile with factories in Italy and Switzerland, but returned later to set up a plant at Friedrichshafen to built the flying boats (and ultimately the bombers) for which his company attained such fame. Professor Hugo Junkers established his company and factory at Dessau in 1920 for the production of civil aircraft, and went on to set up facilities in Sweden and Turkey. In 1922 Ernst Heinkel began building a large factory at Warnemünde on the Baltic coast, and also extended his facilities into Sweden. In Bremen, Heinrich Focke and Georg Wulf together formed the Focke-Wulf company in 1924, and a year later the Bavarian Aircraft Company provided Willy Messerschmitt with the facilities with which to build fast sporting aircraft.

Even as early as 8th January 1919 the transitional Reich Aviation Department of the Transport Ministry authorised the formation of a new transport company, *Deutsche Luftreederei*. One month later the new company was flying mails between Berlin and Weimar.

Though Germany was prevented by the 1922 Paris Air Agreement[3] from building large commercial aeroplanes, the restrictions lapsed in 1926 so that the semi-dormant indigenous industry possessed a free licence to manufacture civil aircraft of any type and size it wished.

In the meantime Hans von Seeckt had discreetly engineered an astute manœuvre within the sphere of German aviation. Among his staff protégés in the *Reichswehr* was the familiar figure of Ernst Brandenburg—late of the *England Geschwader* and, in 1924, an Oberstleutnant; von Seeckt now arranged for the appointment of Brandenburg as head of the Civil Aviation Department at the Ministry of Transport, thereby safeguarding the development of civil aviation under the clandestine control of the *Reichswehr*.

With the lapse of the Paris restrictions in 1926, Germany established a State airline—the *Deutsche Lufthansa*—largely through the efforts of another ex-wartime pilot, Erhard Milch. Milch had left the *Luftstreitkräfte* on its dissolution in 1919,

[3] This was a "postscript" to the Paris Convention, signed on 13th October 1919, which, under the League of Nations, set down the fundamentals of regulations governing international commercial air services.

and had, since 1920, occupied a number of appointments in industry and commercial aviation, including a sales appointment with Junkers and the post of general manager of the Danzig Air Transport company. The original *Luftreederei* had prospered for some years by co-operation with various other European airlines, and something of a monopoly for the supply of Junkers-designed and built aircraft existed, to the extent that Professor Junkers was encouraged to subsidise the formation of two *Luftreederei* subsidiaries, *Junkers-Luftverkehr* and *Deutsche Aero-Lloyd*. At Government insistence, these two companies merged to become *Lufthansa* with 37.5 per cent State share holding. It was largely as a result of Milch's association with Junkers, himself influential in the creation of *Lufthansa*, that Milch now became chairman of the new state airline. He in turn was to exert considerable influence in the aircraft industry and set about the organisation of aircrew training and the setting up of extensive ground facilities, heavily subsidised by State funds. In his first year he established regular air line connections between Berlin and Moscow, and commenced route-proving flights with a Dornier *Wal* flying boat to South America. By 1928 *Lufthansa* had become the most efficient airline in Europe by a wide margin.

As an adjunct to this commercial activity, Germany had embarked on a policy of encouraging airmindedness by appeal to the sporting instincts of her people. The *Deutsche Luftsportverband* grew from its inception in 1920 to a membership of 20,000 in 1926, and to 50,000 three years later. Little wonder that Germany could quietly claim to be Europe's most air-minded nation; in Britain, not even the combined memberships of all its flying clubs and learned aeronautical bodies could come close to matching the German figures. For almost everywhere else in the world, sporting flying was still very much the recreation of the wealthy.

It was also during the early 1920s that the sport of gliding gained widespread popularity in Germany, for in this the limitations imposed at Versailles were superfluous, and large numbers of would-be pilots could learn the rudiments of flying without resort to more costly tuition in powered aeroplanes. It was also a means by which von Seeckt secretly evaded the strictures of the 1926 Paris Air Agreement which limited the number of German army and naval personnel

The growing airmindedness of pre-War Germany was nurtured by, and demonstrated in the popularity of gliding and other aviation sports. *Above*, Berlin students at a gliding school.

permitted to fly. Meanwhile *Lufthansa* was openly and quite legally training commercial aircrews, so that as early as 1928 Germany possessed many hundred of pilots who would, at short notice, provide the basis on which a military air force could be built.

Added to these legitimate training achievements von Seeckt had managed to exploit the favourable relationship which had evolved between Germany and Russia; accordingly, in great secrecy, he had in 1923 negotiated for the setting up of an illicit training establishment at Lipetsk, about 200 miles south-east of Moscow. Selected personnel were sent to the new centre and, undisturbed and undiscovered by the Western nations, underwent fairly sophisticated training, having been temporarily suspended from the German Services. The training received at Lipetsk was clearly regarded as of greater significance than a routine flying course would suggest, as contemporary records indicate that most of the officers who passed through it later rose to high rank in the *Luftwaffe*. Among them was Major Kurt Student, who had been largely responsible for the organisation of the German gliding schools in the early 'twenties and who, in 1940 and 1941, commanded the parachute forces in the aerial invasions of Holland and Crete. Sperrle, the German commander during the Spanish Civil War and in the Battle of Britain, also passed through Lipetsk, as did Wenninger—later German Air Attaché in London.

As economic depression spread through the world after October 1929—bringing with it an effective standstill in national and industrial enterprise—the German government

Hermann Göring, the drug addict whose much-touted but relatively undistinguished flying record, coupled with political opportunism, brought him the portfolio of Air Minister. (Photo: Topix)

subsidies in *Lufthansa* were halved, and it seemed that all Milch's preparations would have to mark time. It was now, however, that Göring was able to exert his new-found influence to maintain German preparations. Returning to Germany in 1927 from Sweden, Göring found that his support for Adolf Hitler's ill-fated *putsch* of 1923 now qualified him for nomination as a *Reichstag* deputy; and it was to Göring that Milch appealed—successfuly—to lobby for the continued government support of military preparation. Thus, while the other Air Forces in being were obliged to arrest their growth and severely restrict costly research, Germany continued her air training almost unaffected.

It must be emphasised that the nature of German aspirations in the air rendered her airmen no less a professional corps than those of established air forces elsewhere. It was the frustration fostered among these "professional" officers by the continuing denigration of Germany that inclined them toward any allegiance that promised to lead to the unification of their nation.

With the opening of the Geneva Disarmament Conference on 2nd February 1932 under the League of Nations, it soon emerged that powerful influences were still dedicated to perpetuating German humiliation. When on 27th March 1933 Japan walked out of the League following its refusal to recognise the puppet State of Manchukuo, the Geneva Conference was doomed.

In the meantime a general election in Germany on 31st July 1932 had returned the N.S.D.A.P.[4] as the strongest single party in the *Reichstag*, so that Hitler became Chancellor on 30th January the following year. Having regard to the advanced stage of military training secretly achieved by Germany in 1933, the air of injured innocence adopted by the German delegation at the Geneva Disarmament Conference can now be seen as an astute cover for Hitler's determination to accelerate the process of *re-armament* in Germany—as well as a means of allaying any suspicion that might arise as to his real intentions.

The prospect of an apparently unified and powerful Germany appealed to the regular officers, who were restless in their clandestine environment, and many threw in their lot with the Nazi party from the outset. When Hitler assumed the political leadership in 1933, the Ministry of Defence assumed control of the armed forces, and on 14th October Germany finally withdrew from the Disarmament Conference and from the League of Nations. She justified her actions—if she felt any justification was necessary—by her claim that the heavily-armed nations (*sic*) had shown no intention of disarming or of satisfying German claims to equality of rights.

The following year Hitler authorised the introduction of conscription—perhaps the first tangible evidence to the world at large that Germany had embarked on a violent return journey towards an armed presence in Europe. Simultaneously the post of Defence Minister was abolished, and in its place now came General Werner von Blomberg in the combined appointment of Minister of War and Commander-in-Chief of the Armed Forces (*Reichskriegminister und Oberbefehlshaber der Wehrmacht*). However, it was not until August 1934, when the old Chancellor von Hindenburg died, that Hitler assumed total control of the nation; and, although members of the armed forces took the oath of allegiance to the

[4] *National Sozialistische Deutsche Arbeiter Partei*

The aged Chancellor Hindenburg attends the 1933 May Day celebrations in Berlin. Behind him, eyes modestly cast down, is Adolf Hitler, with Goebbels in attendance; around them, the banners and salutes of the Berlin S.S. *Standarte*. (Photo: Topix)

law and people of Germany before Hitler in person, the new Chancellor remained aloof from military matters for the time being. It was not until the Nazis adopted an undisguised policy of armed domination towards their European neighbours in 1938 that Hitler assumed the title of Supreme Commander; Blomberg was made to suffer the indignity of a domestic intrigue and was dismissed, making way for General Keitel who was installed as Chief of the Supreme Command (*Oberkommando der Wehrmacht*, or O.K.W.)—a position he was to occupy until 1945.

Birth of the Luftwaffe

It is likely that the extreme nationalist posture, presented by the Nazi party to the world, to some extent cloaked Hitler's ultimate territorial ambitions and aims for political domination of Europe. Yet it is clear that, from the outset in 1933, the old Staff memorandum prepared by von Seeckt was still favoured as a means of providing Germany with a strategic air force—that is, an air force designed from scratch as an instrument of strategic attack rather than a support force for the army. Had such an aim been maintained throughout the next seven years, the events of 1939 and 1940 might have been very different in outcome. The one man who held firm in the strategic doctrine was to be Erhard Milch.

When Milch appealed to Göring to gain support for the continuation of military preparation in 1928, Göring addressed the *Reichstag* in secret to point to the inevitability of the formation of an air force. Although not of his own initiative, this intervention by Göring may be said to have marked the start of the portly airman's influence in German military aviation. When Hitler came to power four years later,

he recognised in Göring a link with the glorious heyday of German air power, and therefore one who could appeal to the great majority of German people.

However, it must be emphasised that Göring was no more than a figurehead; he had been a capable pilot and a junior commander of no more than average ability in the First World War. He had maintained a normal Service pilot's grasp of technical progress until about 1927, but attended no Senior Staff course at all. Thereafter his energies became almost entirely politically orientated. Yet upon this man Hitler bestowed no fewer than four senior Government appointments— including that of Special Commissioner for Aviation. Within three months the Air Commissariat had been abolished and Göring became Air Minister.

Milch, on the other hand, had been more cautious. Having only met Hitler for the first time in 1931, he had deferred joining the Nazi party until after its successful seizure of power two years later, when he agreed to become Göring's deputy at the Air Ministry. Due, however, to the Air Minister's political preoccupation, Milch was in effective control, not only of German commercial aviation—he was still head of *Lufthansa*—but also the shaping of the embryo air force.

It was one thing to compile statistics of fully-trained aircrews, but a very different matter to regard them as a military air force, and Milch was careful to present a cautious picture of the likely growth rate of the air force to a point of parity with Britain and France. He calculated that he would require eight to ten years in which to built a first rate air force. In the meantime responsibility for the vital acceleration of expansion fell squarely upon Milch who set about the extension of training facilities within *Lufthansa* and simultaneously increased the orders for new aircraft coming into airline service.

Outstanding among the new aircraft of 1933 was the Junkers Ju 52/3m—a passenger and transport aircraft so designed as to require little modification to enable it to carry bombs[5]. Also ordered in large numbers were trainers, the Arado Ar 66 and the Focke-Wulf Fw 44, and priority was given to the design preparation of the first generation of fighters and bombers.

To Milch fell the task of organising the structure of the new Air Ministry after the discontinuation of the old Air Commissariat. This structure was essentially straightforward for, unlike so many Service ministries elsewhere, the German example was not yet dogged by "vested interests" and sacred cows—they would come later. In effect the ministry was conceived *ab initio*.

It was constructed around a central administrative core which comprised five departments:

(1) A co-ordinating department to pool the air interests of the army and navy with the object of providing an Air Staff. By 1935 this was fully established and Generalmajor Wever was appointed the first Chief of the Air Staff.
(2) A technical supply department under Oberst Wimmer, reponsible for aircraft and equipment development and production.
(3) Aviation services department under Ministerialdirigent Fisch, responsible for civil aviation and a weather reporting network.
(4) Administration services including welfare, catering, clothing and works under Generalmajor Kesselring.
(5) Personnel department, later headed by Generalmajor Stumpff.

The organisation of this central administration, later to be accommodated in the massive *Leipzigerstrasse* building in Berlin, was completed in 1934 and was largely staffed by ex-army officers—there being as yet a marked deficiency of senior air force officers with staff experience. Milch was at this time quite unaware of Hitler's future ambitions, and he expected that the "eight to ten years" required to build the new air force would also see these positions gradually taken over by rising Air Force staff officers. So preoccupied was Göring elsewhere that Milch scarcely ever had the opportunity to meet his chief and acquaint himself with the Nazi plans.

The wider organisation of the air force was by means of territorial command or Air Offices (*Luftamt*) of which three were formed immediately—ostensibly for civil air traffic control—and another added later. Although this system has been widely criticised for its apparent inflexibility, before the Second World War, it proved to be astonishingly malleable and adaptable to the demands of territorial expansion between 1938 and 1943. The irony of these criticisms was that in 1936 the *Luftwaffe* adopted a regional defence system (within a functional Command structure) and it was the German Intelligence appreciation of 1940 which wrongly criticised R.A.F. Fighter Command for its inflexibility. It is certainly demonstrable that, given freedom and means of movement, a regionally-based organisation is more flexible than a functionally-organised structure. The strength of the German system lay in the self-sufficiency of the *Luftamt*, as will be clear in due course.

Milch's plans for the operational expansion of the air force were seen in 1934 as being the formation of eighteen Geschwader—six each for bomber, fighter and reconnaissance, each with 120 aircraft. Planned aircraft production was to be 4,021 aircraft by the end of September 1935, and the records of Wimmer's department indicate how this total was to be constituted and allocated:

Operational Land Aircraft

Dornier Do 11 and 18 bombers	...	372
Junkers Ju 52 (interim)	...	450
Heinkel He 45 (long-range reconnaissance)	...	320
Heinkel He 46 (short-range reconnaissance)	...	270
Arado Ar 64 and 65 and Heinkel He 51[*] (single-engine fighters)	...	251
Heinkel He 50 dive-bombers	...	51

Operational Coastal Aircraft

Heinkel He 60 (single-engine reconnaissance floatplanes)	...	81
Dornier Wal (long-range reconnaissance flying boats)	...	21
Heinkel He 38 and 51 (single-engine fighter seaplanes)	...	26
Heinkel He 59 general purpose floatplanes	...	21

Elementary trainers

Focke-Wulf Fw 44, Arado Ar 66, Heinkel He 72, etc.	...	1,760

Communications

Klemm Kl 31 and 32	...	89

Miscellaneous (including new prototypes)

Heinkel He 111, Dornier Do 17, Junkers Ju 86, etc.	...	309
Total ...		4,021

These aircraft were to be allocated as follows:

Lufthansa	...	...	...	115
Operational Echelons (*sic*)		...	...	1,085
Training Establishments		...	...	2,168
Research establishments		...	...	138
Air communications	...		...	156
A.A. training establishments	...		...	5
Target-towing establishments	...		...	48
Flying clubs	...	...	...	33
Reichsbank	...	...	...	12
Hitler	...	...	...	10
Miscellaneous	...	...	...	80
Wastage	...	...	...	171
Total ...				4,021

Bearing in mind that the average monthly output of the German aircraft industry in 1933 had been no more than 31 machines, some idea of the necessary expansion of production main be gained. In 1934 the figure rose to 164, and in 1935 to 265. This massive expansion, more than 800 per cent

---

[5] The first deliveries of the bomber version, the Ju 52/3mg3e, were made in 1934.

Junkers Ju 52/3m "Manfred von Richthofen" of *Deutsche Lufthansa*. After two years' service as a commercial transport both in Germany and abroad, the famous aircraft entered service with the new *Luftwaffe* in 1934 both as a bomber and a transport.

in two years—was achieved by the allocation of State funds in the form of loans to companies like Arado, Fieseler, Heinkel, Junkers and B.F.W. to increase their facilities, while other manufacturers[6] were attracted into the industry for the manufacture of components.

Notwithstanding the preparations that accompanied the Nazis' climb to power, Hitler was not yet ready to attract world attention to his resurgent policies for fear of armed intervention by the Western Powers before a measure of re-armament had been achieved.

The enormous expansion of aircraft production had been matched in the field of training. The *Verkehrsflieger Schule* had been formed in the early 1930s with bases at Brunswick, List, Schleissheim and Warnemünde to train commercial pilots and crews; in 1933 new syllabi were introduced to provide junior military staff training as well as *ab initio* flying courses for military personnel. Among those who passed from a gliding school through Schleissheim was a young man named Adolf Galland, a pilot whose notable career was to become linked with the Air Force he now joined. Ultimately, but within only ten years, he was to rise to the rank of *Generalmajor*, Inspector of Fighters in the *Luftwaffe*, and holder of the Oak Leaves with Swords and Diamonds to the

---

[6] Among these were Gotha, which had returned to the manufacture of rolling stock after the First World War, Henschel (a locomotive builder) and Blohm und Voss (a shipbuilding company at Hamburg)

Knight's Cross. Such was the life span of the German Air Force that no other military pilot was to achieve such a meteoric advance in professional status and rank.

Galland left Schleissheim in the summer of 1933 and, with about 60 other young German trainee pilots, was sent to complete his training at Grottaglie in Southern Italy—the fruits of sympathetic overtures that passed between Hitler and Mussolini. Galland recalls the frustration of this interlude by reference to the Italians' lack of professional application to military aviation; the official assessment, too, was that the course had little value, and it was not repeated.

With a flow of newly trained crews assured from the *Verkehrsflieger Schule*, and aircraft production now rapidly increasing, Hitler and Göring decided in March 1935 to proclaim to the world the foundation of the new German Air Force, the *Luftwaffe*. Göring was appointed its Commander-in-Chief and, in execution of von Seeckt's 1923 memorandum, the new Service was established as an independent branch of the Armed Forces subordinated to General Keitel. General Wever became the Chief of the Air Staff, though Milch, as Secretary of State for Air, remained largely in control. It was now, however, that Göring began to exercise his authority at Staff level by appointing First World War colleagues of the *Richthofen Geschwader* to senior posts—a move calculated to consolidate his own high position.

The means by which—overnight—the *Luftwaffe* emerged as an air force in being was unknown to the French and British

The ungainly Junkers Ju 86, another of the "disguised" military designs flown by *Lufthansa* during the 1930s. (Photo: DLH-Stocker)

governments, who refused to believe that a force could exist in sufficient strength to present a serious threat in the short term. Such an admission would be to acknowledge their own lack of control and vigilance during the past ten years. Flying clubs and "police" units (storm troops) were embraced into the *Luftwaffe* at impressive ceremonial parades, Hitler and Göring often attending in person to accept the allegiance of the new units. An Air Staff College was established to provide staff training for senior and middle-ranked officers; the anti-aircraft defence command (*Fliegerabwehrkanonen = Flak*) was incorporated into the *Luftwaffe* and greatly expanded, and a large-scale Signals Command was set up.

The *Luftamt* organisation was adapted to provide the basis of the new Regional Command deployment of the *Luftwaffe*. For operational control four regional Groups, *Gruppenkommandos*, were formed with headquarters at Berlin, Königsberg, Munich and Brunswick. Ten air districts, *Luftgaue*, were set up to administer supplies, maintenance, recruiting and training, airfield staffing and the operational signals network.

Thus the *Luftwaffe* at birth represented a nucleus of around 20,000 men and 1,888 aircraft, supported by an indigenous industry of between 30 and 40 factories supplying airframes, engines and equipment at a rapidly increasing rate. The output of German factories in 1935 rose from an average of 184 aircraft per month during the first half of the year to 303 during the second. Moreover the year 1935 found Milch implementing even more ambitious plans for increased output—production that would include such aircraft as the Dornier Do 17, the Messerschmitt Bf 109, the Junkers Ju 87 and the Heinkel He 111.

As these aircraft will feature constantly in the account hereafter, it is convenient to give a brief description of their early fortunes.

The Dornier Do 17[7]

Conceived early in 1934 as a high-speed mailplane, capable of carrying six passengers on an express air line network throughout Europe, the twin-engine Dornier Do 17 was clearly designed with a potential military application in mind. The extraordinarily slim fuselage was utterly inappropriate for passenger comfort and, after initial trials by the prototype late in 1934, the first three aircraft were relegated to storage at Löwenthal. There they might have languished, forgotten and abandoned, had not an R.L.M.[8] test pilot, Flugkapitän Untucht, put forward a proposal for the aircraft to be converted for operations as a high-speed bomber.

The *Schnellbomber* concept, though not original, appealed to the R.L.M. and three additional prototypes were ordered. The Do 17V4[9] flew in 1935 powered by a pair of 750-h.p. B.M.W. VI in-line engines, and this was similar to the version which was ordered into production as the Dornier Do 17E; it could carry a 2,200-lb. (1,000-kg.) bombload, had provision for three 7,9-mm. machine guns and possessed a top speed of 230 m.p.h.

The Messerschmitt Bf 109[10]

As will be shown in due course the Bf 109 single-seat interceptor was conceived and developed along similar lines to the British Hurricane and Spitfire eight-gun fighters, and was to all intents a contemporary of theirs—albeit protected by the secrecy of their early progress. When, in mid-1934, a requirement was conceived for the replacement of the He 51 and Ar 68 biplane fighters, relations between the *Bayerische Flugzeugwerke* at Augsburg and Milch were not of the best, and it was clear that Professor Willy Messerschmitt's design participation would be by way of a research contract only. Four prototypes were submitted, the Arado Ar 80V1, the Focke-Wulf Fw 159V1, the Heinkel He 112V1 and the Bf 109V1 from the *Bayerische Flugzeugwerke* (the last named having first flown in September 1935—two months before the British Hurricane). The first two entries were eliminated early in the trials and, only after prolonged evaluation at Travemünde was the Bf 109 declared the successful design and awarded an 0-series contract[11]. With enclosed cockpit, wing leading edge slats and narrow-track retractable undercarriage, the radical Messerschmitt design was regarded with a degree of distaste—and attitude which seemed entirely justified when the undercarriage collapsed on landing at the newly-established experimental station (*Erprobungstelle*) at Rechlin. It is interesting to record that the Ar 80, He 112 and the Bf 109 evaluation prototypes all used the 695-h.p. Rolls-Royce Kestrel engine—conveniently exported from Derby—as no equivalent powerplant was yet considered suitable or readily available in Germany.

The proposed armament of twin nose-mounted, synchronised 7,9-mm. machine guns was seen to be quite inadequate in the light of reports reaching Germany in 1936 relating to the almost unprecedented eight-gun armament of the British fighters, and it was only possible at this stage to increase the Bf 109's armament by one gun, mounted between the engine cylinder banks and firing through the propeller shaft. Later this gun would be replaced by a 20-mm. Oerlikon-type cannon.

Though no authentic figures have ever been traced relating to the performance of the prototype Bf 109s, it is unlikely that the Kestrel-powered Bf 109V1 exceeded 280 m.p.h. The first production variant—the Bf 109B-1—was powered by the 635-h.p. Junkers Jumo 210D which bestowed a top speed of 292 m.p.h. at 13,100 feet and a time to height of 9.8 minutes to 19,700 feet. In 1937 the *Richthofen Geschwader* was the first fighter unit to receive the new interceptors in place of the old He 51 biplane fighters.

The Junkers Ju 87[12]

Another of the famous German designs which first flew

---

[7] Cf. *Aircraft Profile No. 164. The Dornier Do 17 and 215*, Smith, Profile, Leatherhead, 1967. *German Aircraft of the Second World War*, Smith and Kay, Putnam, London, 1975.

[8] R.L.M. = *Reichsluftfahrtministerium*, literally "national air transport ministry".

[9] The German prototype nomenclature consisted of suffixing the aircraft designation with the letter "V" (=*Versuchs*) followed by the number of the prototype. Thus the first Do 17 prototype was designated the Do 17V1, the second Do 17V2 and so on.

[10] Cf. *Aircraft Profile No. 40, The Messerschmitt Bf 109E*, Windrow, Profile, Leatherhead, 1965. *German Aircraft of the Second World War*, Smith and Kay, Putnam, London, 1975.

[11] It was a German practice to order a batch of about 10-16 pre-production examples of a successful prototype tender. Referred to as 0-Series, these aircraft were distinguished by the numeral "0" in their designation, usually after the production variant had been decided. The Bf 109A was never completed, and the B-series was the first to achieve production, so the pre-production aircraft were referred to as the Bf 109B-0.

[12] Cf. *Aircraft Profile No. 76, The Junkers Ju 87A and B*, Smith, Profile, Leatherhead, 1966. *German Aircraft of the Second World War*, Smith and Kay, Putnam, London, 1975.

with a Derby-built Rolls-Royce Kestrel engine was the extraordinary Junkers Ju 87 dive-bomber (*Sturzkampfflugzeug*, contracted to "Stuka").

The Junkers company in Sweden, established under the name *Aktiebolaget Flygindustrie*, had in 1928 designed and built its first dive-bomber, the K-47, the testing of which was conducted in secret collaboration with the *Reichswehr* staff in Berlin. When the Nazis gained power in 1933 a biplane dive-bomber, the Henschel Hs 123[13], was chosen for immediate production and, in fact, remained in service long after the outbreak of the Second World War. However, on 27th September 1933, a new requirement was issued for a "second generation" dive-bomber design, and four companies tendered designs for evaluation at Rechlin in June 1936. Although the first prototype Ju 87V1 (which had been powered by a Kestrel V engine) crashed as the result of tail flutter[14], the V2 machine was ready for the *Erprobungstelle* trials, during which it faced competition from the Arado Ar 81, the Blohm und Voss Ha 137 and the Heinkel He 118. The Heinkel and Junkers designs quickly demonstrated their superiority, and only after the Heinkel had been crashed by Ernst Udet—of whom more anon—was the Ju 87 adjudged the winner.

Four prototype Ju 87s had been produced by the end of 1936, and the V4 aircraft foreshadowed the pre-production variant, the Ju 87A-0, which entered service as the A-1 in the spring of 1937.

With its grotesque, cranked-wing appearance, screaming sirens and nerve-shattering near-vertical dive, the Stuka was to epitomise the tactics of selective horror characteristic of Hitler's crushing invasion of Europe from 1939 onwards. After early doubts as to the real benefit to be derived from the dive-bomber, the success achieved by the Ju 87 during the invasion of Poland and the Low Countries seemed to justify the faith pinned on it in those early days of 1935 and 1936. Only the Battle of Britain would check the Stuka in its stride and point to its Achilles heel.

The Heinkel He 111[15]

Designed by Siegfried and Walter Günther during 1933-34, the Heinkel He 111 was originally the outcome of a *Lufthansa* requirement for a fast twin-engine mail/passenger aircraft coupled with provision for a bomb-carrying capability for military operations. The Heinkel He 111V1 prototype, which flew early in 1935 at Marienehe, was in fact a military aircraft capable of a top speed of 214 m.p.h., a range of 930 miles, and of carrying a 2,200-lb. bomb load. The He 111V3 was also a bomber, while the V2 and V4 were 10-seater *Lufthansa* commercial prototypes.

By the end of 1935 a pre-production batch of He 111A-0 bombers had been completed at Heinkel's Rostock plant, and by 1937 the new bomber was entering service with bomber *Geschwader* of the *Luftwaffe*. Between then and its appearance over the British Isles in 1939-40, however, it underwent considerable development by way of the B, D, E and F variants, to become virtually the mainstay of the German long-range bombing force during the Second World War.

* * * * *

Thus in March 1936 the *Erprobungstelle* at Rechlin was fully engaged in the evaluation of contenders for substantial production contracts which would, in three short years, place Germany's air force ahead of the world in terms of numbers and quality of aircraft.

It was at about this time that Milch's proposals for the long-term growth of the *Luftwaffe* came under open criticism from Göring. It now became clear that this tempo was inconsistent with Hitler's determination to win the arms race, which was an established fact now that Britain and France had embarked on a course of re-armament—with Germany as the named opponent. Hitler's demand for an accelerated expansion were made to Göring who, in turn, vested the responsibility for satisfying the demands in Milch. Milch, who enjoyed Hitler's respect and confidence, had in the meantime been transferred to the *Luftwaffe* with the rank of General, and this aroused Göring's enmity and spite. Throughout the next twelve months the Air Minister, fearing for the sanctity of his leadership, systematically deprived Milch of all his powers, including directorship of the R.L.M. Utterly oblivious of Milch's brilliance in organisation and technical prowess, Göring now called on men of inferior administrative qualities to attend his conferences. Among these was Colonel Ernst Udet, a long-standing friend of Göring, and one of the "aces" of the old *Luftstreite-krafte*[16]. Udet's enthusiasm for the German fighters and for the dive-bomber concept endeared him to the Air Minister, who bestowed upon him the title of Inspector of Fighters and Dive-Bombers in February 1936, and four months later awarded him the post of Director of the Technical Deptartment at the Air Ministry. Udet's rise to influence and command was undoubtedly popular among the flying echelons of the *Luftwaffe*, for here was a kindred spirit, a fine pilot and a familiar figure on German airfields during the inter-War years. Yet Udet lacked the vital attributes of broad leadership and administrative capacity demanded by Germany's critical expansion during 1937 and 1938. On him must rest the blame for the disorganisation which spread through German industry when the new aircraft were ordered into mass production, for it is unthinkable that Milch's organising genius and previous grasp of the situation would have failed to prevent the *deceleration* of production output that was a feature of Udet's administration.

The Strategic Bomber Fiasco

The antagonism that was first manifest between Göring and Milch in 1936 was symptomatic of the specific lack of purpose definition in the German Air Ministry—which, in turn, can only reflect the general ignorance of broad matters concerning aviation by the German Air Minister, an ignorance that was to become progressively more apparent throughout the next few years. It was, indeed, this lack of grasp that was to cost the *Luftwaffe* victory just four years hence in the Battle of Britain. While Milch was committing himself to a

---

[13] Henschel Flugzeugwerke A.G. was formed out of Henschel & Sohn, G.m.b.H., the locomotive manufacturers, early in 1933.

[14] The Junkers Ju 87V1 was originally fitted with twin fins and rudders; these were replaced by a single vertical tail surface.

[15] Cf. Aircraft Profile No. 15, The Heinkel He 111H, Windrow, Profile, Leatherhead, 1965. German Aircraft of the Second World War, Smith and Kay, Putnam, 1975.

[16] Born in 1896, Udet had entered the German Army on the outbreak of the First World War, but transferred to the air arm in June 1915. He rose to command *Jagdstaffeln* 37 and 11 before leaving the *Luftstreitekrafte* in 1918. He attained considerable international repute as an aerobatic, sporting and test pilot during the 'twenties and 'thirties, and entered the *Luftwaffe* in 1935.

long-term consolidation of the *Luftwaffe* on relatively orthodox lines, in ignorance of Hitler's political aims, others were seeking to achieve specialised capabilities, often of an untried nature, within the young service. Use of the dive-bomber—although not entirely new—was one such adventure, and one that owed its survival largely to Udet. Another was the strategic bomber.

Generalmajor Wever, as first Chief of the German Air Staff, had been the originator of the German strategic bomber even as early as 1934. As a pilot of considerable technical ability, and endowed with brilliant organising capacity, Wever saw the long-range bomber as the means by which Germany, as a "central" power, could exert her will by striking out at any corner of Europe. His specification, issued in 1934, called for a bomber able to reach the north of Scotland, or the Urals, from bases in Germany with a worthwhile bomb load. Both Junkers and Dornier took up the challenge and by mid-1935 both companies were busy building prototypes.

First to fly was the Dornier Do 19, a large four-engine bomber with a span of 114 ft. 10 in.—greater than that of the R.A.F.'s Stirling, Halifax and Lancaster, of Second World War fame. Powered in its prototype form by four 650-h.p. Bramo 322 H82 unsupercharged radial engines, the Do 19V1 returned a top speed of 199 m.p.h., and a still-air range of 994 miles. It had provision for four single-gun defensive positions and was designed to carry a maximum bomb load of 6,600 lb. (3,000 kg.). Construction of the V1 had started before the end of 1934, and that of the V2 and V3 commenced the following year. Only the first prototype ever flew—in mid-1936—before the venture was scrapped[17].

The second design was the Junkers Ju 89. Manufacture commenced in 1935 and two prototypes were completed before their career was likewise cut short. Powered by four Daimler-Benz DB600 supercharged in-line engines, the Ju 89V1, which flew in December 1936, had a top speed of 242 m.p.h., and had a range similar to that of the Do 19. Empty it weighed 37,437 lb., loaded 61,415 lb., and could carry a bomb load of approximately 8,800 lb. (4,000 lb.).

These two heavy bombers were remarkable, not so much for their performance and load-carrying capabilities—though impressive in all conscience—but for the fact that the German aircraft designers, so long isolated from free and open interchange of technical information, were able to produce aircraft more advanced than anything then under development for Western air forces.

There is no doubt but that had General Wever's plans for a strategic bomber force materialised, equipped with either of these large aircraft, Germany by 1939 would have been invincible, and probably capable of delivering a crushing weight of bombs on Great Britain before the end of 1940. However, Wever was to lose his life in a flying accident on 3rd June 1936, and with him died the driving force behind the *Luftwaffe*'s strategic bombing philosophy.

Wever's successor as Chief of Staff was Kesselring, an ex-Army staff officer whose air force career had only started in 1933[18], and it was not altogether surprising that he still tended to regard the *Luftwaffe* as a tactical support rather than a strategic striking force. Accordingly, together with Göring,

Kesselring carried out a survey of aircraft under development and, at a single stroke of the pen, struck the Dornier Do 19 and Junkers Ju 89 from the *Luftwaffe*'s inventory. Naturally, some of Wever's former staff protested that the prototypes should at least complete their test programme, but the Air Staff remained adamant[19].

Milch, who was abroad when the heavy bomber programme was cancelled, was astonished to find such a step had been so lightly and precipitately taken; more so as he had himself approved the original requirement. However, now resigned to the new accelerated expansion policy, Milch saw the inherent difficulties and disruption of the industry in the production of these large aircraft, and even came to endorse the Air Staff's decision.

The Spanish Civil War

The year 1936 has been called the first year of the Second World War. On 7th March Germany achieved an unopposed re-occupation of the Rhineland, and two months later, at the end of a six-month war, Mussolini's colonial army occupied Addis Ababa, and Abyssinia became annexed to Italy. Then, on 18th July, following many months of political unrest, Spain erupted into civil war.

Fundamentally and traditionally committed to oppose the Communist threat in Europe, Hitler's Nazi Party and Mussolini's Fascists regarded the danger of a Bolshevist foothold in Western Europe as absolute justification for active support of General Franco's Nationalist army. Germany's immediate act was to establish a semi-spurious air transport company, Hisma AG, and by means of this expedient was able in August to dispatch twenty Junkers Ju 52/3m bomber-transports with six Heinkel He 51 escort fighters, as well as 85 volunteer air and ground crews. Their first assignment was to ferry 10,000 Moorish soldiers from Tetuan across the Straits of Gibraltar to Seville. Franco's early successes included the capture of Badajóz, Irun and San Sebastian, and in November his forces reached the suburbs of Madrid to commence a siege which was to last for more than two years.

Meanwhile, despite the convening of a European non-intervention committee to preclude the likelihood of international participation in Spain, Germany quickly and secretly set about the organisation of a powerful, semi-autonomous air component for collaboration with General Franco. Called the *Legion Cóndor*—and occasionallly the "German Volunteer Corps"—this large force played a not-inconsiderable part in the Civil War, a part that has attracted denigration among political historians but which, in the longer-term military sphere, was to provide an invaluable "teething ring" for the youthful German air force. Certainly the German pilots who fought in Spain between November 1936 and December 1938 were to feature prominently in the Second World War, and the tactics—often of a radical nature—which

---

[17] The V2 and V3 were dismantled without ever having flown. The V1 was taken on charge by the *Luftwaffe* in 1939 and used as a transport in the Polish campaign.

[18] Generalmajor Albert Kesselring was born in 1885 and entered the German Army in 1904. He served as a Brigade Adjutant and on the General Staff during the First World War. As previously stated, he entered the new Air Ministry in 1933 as head of the Administrative Department.
[19] An oft-quoted remark, attributed to Göring, stated "The Führer will not ask how big the bombers are, but how many there are". Kesselring calculated the three twin-engine bombers could be built for the same cost and effort as two four-engine bombers.

The Heinkel He 51 bore the brunt of early fighter operations by the *Legion Cóndor* in Spain. (Photo: Hans Obert)

were evolved by the *Legion Cóndor* were among those which smashed half-a-dozen air forces in 1939-40.

Command of the *Legion* was given to Generalmajor Hugo Sperrle who, as already stated, had been one of the officers concerned in the Lipetsk training centre in the U.S.S.R. during the nineteen-twenties. His Chief of Staff was Oberstleutnant Wolfram Freiherr von Richthofen, later to take over command from Sperrle himself.

Recruiting for service in Spain was achieved by seeking volunteers in the *Luftwaffe*; these came forward readily enough for, political considerations aside, the rates of pay were good[20] and the chances of excitement high. Germany, anxious not to attract antagonism among her neighbours by direct intervention, adopted a shallow subterfuge in sending her airmen volunteers to Spain as civilians, ostensibly on "Strength through Joy" (*Kraft durch Freude*) cruises[21].

In May 1937 the *Legion Cóndor* was operating about 200 aircraft, including 50 Ju 52/3m bomber transports, between 40 and 50 fighters (mainly He 51s, but also a few Ar 68s) and a diverse force of ground-attack and short-range reconnaissance aeroplanes. The *Legion* also maintained an extensive ground organisation which included airfield staffs, *Flak* units, signals, supply and medical units. The air fighting units were deployed as one bomber and one fighter wing and a reconnaissance squadron, each accompanied by its own ground support echelons. Having regard to the extreme fluidity of the fighting fronts, the emphasis was on flexibility and mobility, and in these respects the *Legion* was unsurpassed.

Civil wars are almost invariably the bloodiest and most tragic of all conflicts, for revolutionary ideologies are usually pursued without restraint. Quarter is granted as seldom as it is expected. The general air of terror and confusion is further heightened by participation by foreign forces whose motives are often misunderstood. Nowhere was this more true than in Spain and, perhaps because the German intervention (*sic*) was seen by the world to be of a highly organised nature, the air operations by the *Legion Cóndor* inflamed the sensitivites of many Western nations. The name Guernica became an anathema on the German people until long after the outbreak of the Second World War[22].

In May 1937 reinforced the *Legion* by sending her latest aircraft. The implication must be that at this early stage the Spanish War was considered by the Nazi leaders to be an ideal testing ground for their new air force—and that intervention for political and ideological motives would simply provide moral justification. Moreover, service in Spain was already showing valuable results in the operational training of *Luftwaffe* flying personnel with the result that the volunteer system was abolished and replaced by the regular posting of promising young officers on a six-monthly rotational basis. At his trial at Nuremburg after the War, Hermann Göring still displayed a justifiable pride in the *Luftwaffe*. Referring to the Spanish Civil War, he stated that "with the permission of the Führer I sent a large part of my transport fleet and a number of experimental fighter units, bombers and anti-aircraft guns; in that way I had an opportunity to ascertain, under combat conditions, whether the equipment was equal to the task. In order that the personnel, too, might gather a certain experience, I saw to it that there was a continuous flow, new people

---

[20] German volunteers were promoted one rank for service in Spain.

[21] Adolf Galland, as a Leutnant in the *Luftwaffe*, was one such volunteer, and recalls that his passage from Hamburg to El Ferrol was one of extreme discomfort, cooped up with 370 fellow airmen in the holds of an ancient gun-running liner which had been commandeered by General Franco's navy. Cf. *Die Ersten und die Letzten*, Galland, Franz Schneekluth, 1953 (*The First and the Last*, Methuen, London, 1955).

[22] The town of Guernica was the seat of the Basque Government. Its tactically-important road bridge was attacked as a military target by the *Legion*'s bomber wing; bomb aiming equipment for such a pinpoint target was entirely inadequate, with the result that a considerable part of the town was devastated, and heavy casualties suffered among the civilian population. In view of its political and tactical significance, it would be difficult to justify Guernica as an "open" town; no one, however, was more sensitive than the men of the *Legion* to the horror and culpability of such a bombing error.

The Henschel Hs 123 ground attack biplane was to remain in limited service with the *Luftwaffe* well into the Eastern Front campaigns of the Second World War. (Photo: Gerhard Joos)

being constantly sent out and others recalled."[23]

As Hitler's European plans of domination for *lebensraum* would inevitably be achieved only by armed aggression (or the threat of such aggression), the superiority of German equipment and tactics in Spain would doubtless cultivate the seeds of powerful propaganda.

Already the Legion had embarked on a new phase in ground support operations. During March 1937 the He 51 fighter wing on the northern Republican front was ordered to support

Franco's offensive between Gijón and San Sebastian—its object being to gain control of the vital industrial area around Gijón. The small biplanes were accordingly fitted to carry six 20-lb. fragmentation bombs apiece and flown against fortified positions with outstanding success, releasing their bombs from 500 feet or less. Targets which remained immune from high level bombing—due to the lack of bomb-aiming equipment—could now be destroyed by calling upon the "fighter bombers". Such were the demands for this support that as many as seven sorties a day were being carried out by each aircraft.

[23] Cf. *Trial of the Major War Criminals*, Vol. IX, p.281.

The hated Stuka dive-bomber, the Junkers Ju 87. The early Ju 87A, seen here wearing Nationalist markings with the *Legion Cóndor* in Spain, laid the groundwork for later and improved versions which spearheaded the 1940 *blitzkrieg*. (Photo: Hans Obert)

Another wartime aircraft of the *Luftwaffe*, for which Spain provided a useful combat laboratory, was the Messerschmitt Bf 109B.

These early sorties marked the beginning of a whole new concept of air warfare[24], one which was already half-formed in the minds of Kesselring, Udet and others. Combat developments necessarily spurred the despatch of more modern aircraft to Spain and accordingly two *Staffeln* of Messerschmitt Bf 109Bs were activated to provide escort for the three He 51 close-support *Staffeln* now formed[25]. To supplement the Junkers Ju 52/3ms—and ultimately replace them— Heinkel He 111 bombers were now sent out to serve with *Kampfgruppe* 88. Next to arrive were Henschel Hs 123 and Junkers Ju 87A dive-bombers, and these were used to develop a refined application of close support by exploiting the great accuracy of pinpoint bombing achieved by steep diving attacks. Under the circumstances that prevailed—a secure local air superiority, achieved by the *Legion*'s fighters—the seeds of the Stuka's reputation as an effective terror weapon were sown. That reputation only foundered when the Stuka fell victim to misuse by its own commanders.

---

[24] A concept that was quickly recognised and developed by the Communists in Spain. The "benefits" were seen to be in the rapid introduction of close-support units to the Russian Air Force, and their subsequent widespread operation on the Eastern Front between 1942 and 1945.

[25] The arrival at the front of the Russian Polikarpov I-16 "*Rata*" monoplane fighter to reinforce the largely biplane-equipped Republican fighter groups was a factor in this situation. By the close of hostilities the He 51 biplanes had been completely phased out of the *Legion*'s fighter units, and early Messerschmitt Bf 109Es were in action in Spain.

A Heinkel He 111 of the *Legion Cóndor* after a landing mishap in Spain. (Photo: Hans Obert)

The *Luftwaffe* on the Eve of War

Notwithstanding the experience gained by the *Luftwaffe* during participation in the Spanish Civil War, the O.K.L. formed a Technical Development Flying Unit—the *Lehr Division*—at Greifswald in 1937. The purpose of this unit was to develop the operating techniques of the new air force and to integrate the lessons being learned in Spain into the *Luftwaffe* itself. As each new type of aircraft was ready for delivery to the Service a new sub-unit of the *Lehr Division* was established to prepare the aircraft for the *Luftwaffe*—and vice versa. Within two years, eight *Gruppen*, each with about 30 aircraft, had been established and covered the whole spectrum of fighters, bombers and reconnaissance aircraft.

The *Lehr Division* did vital work during the years 1937-39 and acquired staff pilots of superlative quality. As the new generation of operational aircraft passed out of the development stage, the *Lehr Division* was slowly deprived of its exclusive status and, in the guise of *Lehrgeschwader* 1 and 2, came to be regarded as a conventional combat unit. Within eighteen months these *Geschwader* had suffered battle casualties of almost 40 per cent among their most experienced crews.

Meanwhile Hitler's campaign for European domination was, in 1938, gathering pace. He had obtained control of the Saar basin by means of a plebiscite, and the Wehrmacht had marched unopposed into the Rhineland. His political achievements had secured almost universal support in Germany—as well as strengthening his own convictions of personal infallibility.

In March 1938 Germany annexed Austria, an occupation in which the *Luftwaffe* played a prominent part, 150 troop-carrying transport aircraft lifting more than 2,000 fully-equipped soldiers to Vienna. Moreover, the appearance in strength of modern German bombers added fuel to the propaganda campaign being waged, and which was fast becoming a major weapon in the Nazis' armoury.

Strategically the annexation of Austria provided Germany with a number of useful bases from the *Wehrmacht* would, eighteen months later, strike at Poland. The *Luftwaffe* formed a fourth *Luftflotte* to administer the operational activities in this area. Furthermore, acquisition of further factory space in Vienna enabled production of the Messerschmitt Bf 109 fighter to be expanded—and by September 1939 twenty such aircraft were being produced monthly in Austria.

Next to fall under Nazi influence were the Sudetan areas of Czechoslovakia; and by the instrument of the Munich agreement of September 1938 the world gained one year's respite from war. It is often implied that Britain was alone in her unpreparedness for the World War that now seemed inevitable. Germany herself was not yet ready for a world war and such was the atmosphere of prevailing interdependence among European nations that further aggression by Germany might well spark an armed confrontation with France and Britain.

At the time of Munich the *Luftwaffe* was experiencing temporary difficulties associated with the production and introduction into service of its second generation of combat aircraft. The first-line strength of aircraft in September 1938, at only 2,928, compared with about 2,500 a year earlier. With aircraft factories working a 60-hour week since June 1938 this strength was disappointing and was accounted for by the widespread re-tooling demanded by the new generation of aircraft entering production. By the end of 1938 the industry's monthly output had risen to 700 aircraft, but another year was to elapse before the 800 mark was passed.

If any doubt still existed as to the aggressive nature of the *Luftwaffe*'s intended rôle in support of the Nazis' determination to subjugate Europe, the following breakdown of aircraft strengths demonstrated a preponderance of assault forces clearly designed to support the Army.

Establishment, Strength and Serviceability of Operational Units of the Luftwaffe, 1st August 1938

Type of Operational Unit	Establishment	Strength	Aircraft Serviceable
Strategic Reconnaissance	228	197	136
Tactical Reconnaissance	297	285	164
Fighter	938	643	453
Bomber	1,409	1,157	582
Dive-bomber	300	207	159
Ground Attack	195	173	1
Transport	117	81	23
Coastal and Naval	230	185	151
Totals	3,714	2,928	1,669

In March 1939 Germany invaded and occupied the whole of Czechoslovakia and again mounted a massive display of air strength, landing airborne forces at Prague. Though the occupation was unopposed, the Czech nation reacted with great bitterness to its deprivation of freedom, and many supremely gallant men escaped the Nazi occupation forces to join *L'Armée de l'Air* and the British Royal Air Force.

And so the German territorial rampage went on. Despite protests from France and Britain, Hitler demanded from Lithuania and acquired the secession of Memel. Clearly war with the Western powers could not be long delayed and the *Luftwaffe* took the precaution of commencing synthetic air exercises simulating attacks upon British shipping and ports. Airfields were constructed and paved runways laid down in Western Germany. But despite all these preparations, Milch voiced his unease about the *Luftwaffe*'s capacity to withstand a prolonged war; his long-term plans for expansion of the air force—scarcely half completed—would be compromised by

a war of attrition with France and Britain, whereas it had been intended that Germany would engage in isolated campaigns between which time would be available to re-equip and make good losses in men and materials. By now, however, Milch had been relegated to the background since Ernst Udet had been appointed *Luftwaffe* Director General of Equipment (*Luftzeugmeister*)[26].

Thus one year after the signing of the Munich Agreement, Europe stood poised on the brink of war. The *Luftwaffe*'s operational strength was not increasing more rapidly, and at the beginning of September 1939 stood at 3,750 aircraft; this total was made up of the following:

Heinkel He 111 long-range bombers	...	...	780
Dornier Do 17 long-range bombers	...	...	470
Dornier Do 17 long-range reconnaissance		...	280
Junkers Ju 88 long-range bombers	...	...	20
Junkers Ju 87 dive-bombers	...	...	335
Messerschmitt Bf 109D fighters	...	...	235
Messerschmitt Bf 109E fighters	...	...	850
Messerschmitt Bf 110 fighters	...	...	195
Arado Ar 66 fighters	...	...	5
Arado Ar 68 fighters	...	...	35
Henschel Hs 126 tactical reconnaissance		...	195
Heinkel He 46 tactical reconnaissance	...	...	100
Coastal aircraft	...	...	...	205
Miscellaneous reconnaissance	...	...	45
Total			3,750

This force constituted the most advanced in Europe, the bombers being marginally superior in most respects to the Wellington, Hampden and Whitleys of R.A.F. Bomber Command—though possessing rather lighter defensive armament. The Bf 109E was considered to be superior to the Hawker Hurricane fitted with fixed-pitch propeller (except in manœuvrability), and outnumbered the Supermarine Spitfire by more than four to one in squadron service. The Bf 110 was approximately equivalent to the Bristol Blenheim fighter in rôle, but was superior both in armament and performance by a considerable margin. In reconnaissance aircraft the *Luftwaffe* possessed a massive numerical superiority over those of any other single air force.

In terms of armament the *Luftwaffe* tended to rely on bombs of relatively light weight (including the 1- and 2-kilo incendiary, 10-kilo fragmentation, 50-, 250- and 500-kilo general purpose and armour piercing weapons), although 1940 would see the 1,000-kilo (2,200-lb.) bomb introduced into service—at about the same time the R.A.F. first used the 2,000-pounder. German gas bombs were ready for use from the outset, stocks of "Green Cross" (irritant) and "Yellow Cross" (mustard) being maintained.

At the beginning of the War, German aircraft were armed with the 7,9-mm. M.G.15 or M.G.17 machine gun (equivalent to the British 0.303-inch gun), but the Messerschmitt Bf 109E also mounted the 20-mm. Oerlikon-type gun—which

---

[26] It was probably the mounting losses in men and material which Germany suffered in 1940-41 and with which Udet found the aircraft industry incapable of keeping pace that led to his suicide. On his death, Milch was recalled with the result that astonishing feats of production were achieved through the organising genius of this remarkable man.

the R.A.F. did not introduce until 1940. In gun mountings the *Luftwaffe* remained behind the R.A.F. throughout the War, relying on simple manually-rotatable single- and twin-gun cockpit mountings, while the British had almost completely abandoned these in favour of power-operated turrets.

In manpower the *Luftwaffe* was a powerful service with a strength of one and a half million men; of these 900,000 were serving with *Flak* regiments and other anti-aircraft units, about 25,000 in Air Ministry and headquarters staff, 50,000 as aircrew and other flying personnel, 100,000 in the air signals organisation, and 60,000 on airfield construction and other *Luftwaffe* labour projects, while 80,000 provided the maintenance and supply services. The remainder were personnel under training.

At the outbreak of war the *Luftwaffe*'s training organisation was producing pilots at the rate of nearly 15,000 a year—a figure rather in excess of requirements. The quality of training was at this stage very high (despite repeated statements to the contrary in contemporary British propaganda), that of the pilot occupying nearly two years, during which time he would complete between 250 and 300 hours' flying; after this he would be posted to an operational flying training school at which he would receive fighter, bomber or dive-bomber training according to his allocation. It is an interesting point to make in passing that—unlike the practice in R.A.F. bomber crews—in German bombers the pilot was seldom the aircraft's captain, this post being taken by the observer; yet the observer was also a fully-qualified pilot, and was thus the most experienced crew member. This practice did not long survive under wartime conditions of rapidly mounting losses[27].

Wartime Organisation of the Luftwaffe

Hitler's constant acquisition of territories beyond Germany's 1933 frontiers had placed something of a strain on the regionally-administered *Luftwaffe*, and it was in 1939 that major changes were made in the air force's command structure from the O.K.L. right down to field commands. The office of Secretary of State for Air was combined with that of the Inspector-General of the *Luftwaffe*, but remained under Milch. The position of the Chief of the Air Staff, held by General Wever until his death in 1936, passed to Kesselring who was in turn replaced by Stumpff in 1937. Now, with the creation of three operational Commands, or *Luftflotten* (Air Fleets), the senior Air Staff post passed to Generaloberst Hans Jeschonnek. This relatively young officer had joined an infantry regiment on the outbreak of the First World War at the age of fifteen. After transferring to the air force in 1933, he commanded the *Lehrgeschwader* at Greifswald and thus brought to the Air Staff a personal knowledge and appreciation of the new aircraft in service; his advocacy of the Junkers Ju 88 was clearly contributory to its huge production during the War.

As remarked above, three *Luftflotten* were created in February 1939. *Luftflotte 1*, commanded by Kesselring, covered North and East Germany, and had its headquarters in Berlin; *Luftflotte 2* was commanded by Felmy, with headquarters at Brunswick, and covered North-west Germany; and *Luftflotte 3*, commanded by Sperrle, covered South-west Germany and

had its headquarters in Munich. The last two *Luftflotten* were those which were to be the most involved in the Battle of Britain[28].

A month later a fourth *Luftflotte* was established to cover South-east Germany, Austria and the occupied parts of Czechoslovakia; it was commanded by General Löhr, an Austrian who had joined the *Luftwaffe* when his country was seized by the Nazis.

Within the *Luftflotte*, parallel administrative and operational hierarchies existed. There was a clear division of responsibility between the administrative *Luftgau* organisation, regionally based and operating through the airfield network; and the *Fliegerdivision*, a striking force made up of numbers of different types of flying unit. The strength of the *Fliegerdivision* (later redesignated as the *Fliegerkorps*) and its composition depended on current operational requirements; but a typical *Luftflotte* establishment might include two *Fliegerkorps*, each of which mustered three complete *Geschwader* (bomber and fighter units in combination) plus various specialised reconnaissance *Gruppen*, coastal units, and so forth. The main tactical unit within the *Fliegerdivision/Fliegerkorps* was the *Geschwader*.

The organisation of tactical units of the German air force evolved from the *Feldfliegerabteilungen* of 1915. The operation of those units, whose main function had been reconnaissance, were closely co-ordinated with the needs of "parent" ground formations of the German Army. Increasingly frequent encounters with Allied aircraft, and the availability of the new Fokker monoplanes, led to the allocation of one or two of these fighting scouts to each *Feldfliegerabteilung* for the protection of the two-seaters which formed their main equipment. Late in 1915 the *Kampfeinsitzer Kommandos* ("single-seater combat detachments") were formed; a rather loose control arrangement, superimposed on the continuing Fl. Abt. system, allowed an army commander to concentrate all his Fokkers in a given area if the need arose.

It was in the sumer of 1916 that the evolution of air warfare took a major step forward with the formation of the first *Jagdstaffeln*. Each *Jagdstaffel*, or *Jasta*, was to be a self-contained unit of single-seaters whose rôle was to destroy enemy aircraft on both sides of the lines. The ever-increasing scope of operations, and a pressing need to regain the initiative in the air during the late spring of 1917, led to the formation of the first *Jagdgeschwader*; this grouping of four *Jagdstaffeln* under one command (that of the senior *Staffelführer*) allowed a better co-ordinated and more flexible response to conditions at various points along the Front.

Thus it may be seen that, after the re-constitution of the German Air Force in 1933, conceived in the image of the fighting over the Western Front in the First World War and officered largely by men traditionally owing allegiance to the Army (either through training or combat, or both), the ponderous and complex organisation of the *Luftwaffe* was to

---

[27] Uninfluenced by the practices adopted by other air forces between the Wars, the German observer/captain system dated from the First World War.

[28] Unlike senior officers of the Royal Air Force, who usually preferred to retire from the Service rather than accept retrograde or junior appointments having achieved higher Staff levels, their *Luftwaffe* counterparts were given less chance to display similar pride. Both Kesselring and Stumpff were given command of *Luftflotten* after having served as Chief of the Air Staff. Kesselring was 55 when the War broke out. Jeschonnek, Chief of the Air Staff at that time, was only 40; he committed suicide in August 1943.

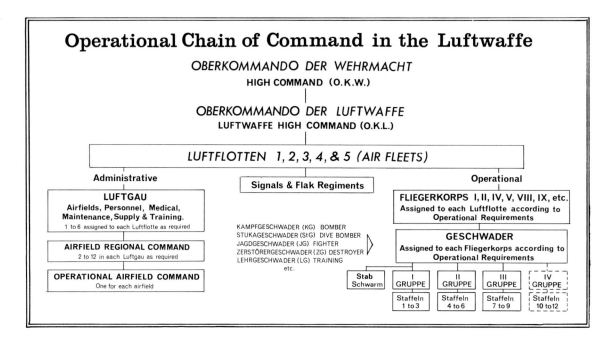

Operational Chain of Command in the Luftwaffe

OBERKOMMANDO DER WEHRMACHT
HIGH COMMAND (O.K.W.)

OBERKOMMANDO DER LUFTWAFFE
LUFTWAFFE HIGH COMMAND (O.K.L.)

LUFTFLOTTEN 1, 2, 3, 4, & 5 (AIR FLEETS)

Administrative

Signals & Flak Regiments

Operational

LUFTGAU
Airfields, Personnel, Medical,
Maintenance, Supply & Training.
1 to 6 assigned to each Luftflotte as required

AIRFIELD REGIONAL COMMAND
2 to 12 in each Luftgau as required

OPERATIONAL AIRFIELD COMMAND
One for each airfield

KAMPFGESCHWADER (KG) BOMBER
STUKAGESCHWADER (StG) DIVE BOMBER
JAGDGESCHWADER (JG) FIGHTER
ZERSTÖRERGESCHWADER (ZG) DESTROYER
LEHRGESCHWADER (LG) TRAINING
etc.

FLIEGERKORPS I, II, IV, V, VIII, IX, etc.
Assigned to each Luftflotte according to
Operational Requirements

GESCHWADER
Assigned to each Fliegerkorps according to
Operational Requirements

Stab Schwarm	I GRUPPE	II GRUPPE	III GRUPPE	IV GRUPPE
	Staffeln 1 to 3	Staffeln 4 to 6	Staffeln 7 to 9	Staffeln 10 to 12

some extent an anachronism. As the new air force "grew up" in a very short space of time, and the wider responsibilities of the modern fighting force came to be appreciated, so the antiquated administrative machinery underwent progressive adaptation, if not modernisation. Thus, such considerations as the suggested integration of a strategic bombing force, whose operations would be wholly divorced from the prime function of the *Luftwaffe*—support of the Army—were anathema to the diehard ex-Army staff officers now given command in the new Service.

The basic field unit in the *Luftwaffe* at the outbreak of war in 1939 was also termed the *Geschwader*, but it was a much larger and tighter-knit unit than its First World War predecessor. The numbered units were designated by a prefix according to their function: *Jagdgeschwader* (JG) signified single-seat fighters, *Kampfgeschwader* (KG) indicated bombers, *Stukageschwader* (StG) indicated dive-bombers, and so on. Each *Geschwader* was divided into a staff unit (*Stab*) and three or four *Gruppen*; these latter were indicated by Roman numerals, for instance II./JG 27 signified II.*Gruppe* of *Jagdgeschwader* 27. Each *Gruppe* was itself divided into three or four *Staffeln* of about ten or a dozen aircraft each, depending upon serviceability; these *Staffeln* were identified by Arabic numerals so that, for instance, 3./StG 77 signified 3.*Staffel* of *Stukageschwader* 77. Thus a full-strength *Geschwader* possessed about 90-120 aircraft. The *Gruppen* would operate from more or less dispersed bases in the field, but would remain under the control of the *Geschwader* staff. The commanding officers of these three echelons were referred to as *Geschwader Kommodore*, *Gruppenkommandeur* and *Staffelkapitän*, except when acting command passed to a subordinate—following the loss or posting away of the regular commander—when the term "*Führer*" (leader) was used, e.g. *Staffelführer*.

The Geschwader Staff (*Geschwaderstab*) establishment was included in a separate flight, usually of four aircraft, which were flown on operations by the *Geschwader Kommodore*, the Adjutant, the Staff Major and the operations officer (*Geschwader 1a*). Each *Gruppe* also included a *Stab* flight,

but at *Staffel* level the "specialist" officers tended to fly as component members of the unit.

From this it will be seen that no realistic comparison can be made with the Royal Air Force's fighting echelons, Group, Wing, Squadron and Flight. A *Staffel* was, in effect, something between a "Flight" and a "Squadron", both in size and administration. However a further clue to the disparity may be obtained from the relative command ranks. A Flight Lieutenant in the Royal Air Force is equivalent to Hauptmann in the German Air Force, a rank commonly held by the *Gruppenkommandeur*—commanding between 30 and 40 pilots or crews. The *Staffel* was commonly commanded by an Oberleutnant (equivalent to a Flying Officer in the R.A.F.).

Aircraft Identification Markings

The system of aircraft identification employed by the *Luftwaffe* was vastly more complex than the simple lettering sequence within a squadron favoured by the R.A.F. To detail all the known variations is unnecessary in a work of this type; however, a brief explanation of the main guidelines may be useful so as to understand the significance of German aircraft depicted in the many of the photographs, and to identify the importance of some of the German aircraft shot down in the Battle of Britain and listed in the daily loss tables.

Single-seat Fighters

Single-seat fighters were identified by a large numeral, usually between 1 and 16, painted ahead of the national marking on the fuselage side, the numbers being repeated in different colours for each *Staffel* within a *Gruppe*, in the sequence white—red—yellow. Thus in a *Geschwader* of three *Gruppen* each of three *Staffeln*, white numerals would be painted on aircraft of 1, 4 and 7 *Staffeln*; red numerals on aircraft of 2, 5 and 8 *Staffeln*; and yellow numerals of 3, 6 and 9 *Staffeln*. The *Gruppen* were differentiated by a symbol painted in the *Staffel* colour behind the national marking on the fuselage side; I *Gruppe* aircraft bore no marking, II *Gruppe* machines with a horizontal bar, and III *Gruppe* with a wavy line or a vertical bar. Where a fourth *Gruppe* existed in a *Jagdgeschwader* it was usually identified by a solid disc. (In this book the national marking is denoted by the symbol "+".)

Thus a Messerschmitt Bf 109E bearing the markings "red 9 + —" can be identified as a machine of the 5th *Staffel* of its *Geschwader*; similarly "yellow 9 +" indicates an aircraft of the 3rd *Staffel*.

Staff aircraft bore black and white symbols painted ahead of the fuselage cross in place of the numeral, these symbols being combinations of chevrons and bars. The significance of individual symbols occasionally varied from unit to unit, but some of the most commonly used were a single chevron for a *Gruppe* adjutant; a double chevron for a *Gruppenkommandeur*; and a single chevron followed by two vertical bars for a Staff Major.

Other Aircraft

All other types of unit (*Kampfgeschwader*, *Zerstörergeschwader*, *Stukageschwader*, etc.) identified their aircraft by a four-letter coding system painted on the fuselage sides and sometimes partially or entirely repeated under the wings. The first two characters, to the left of the fuselage cross, were an identification code peculiar to each *Geschwader*; e.g. G1 for KG 55, M8 for ZG 76, and so on. (The great majority of such codes, current at the time of the Battle of Britain, are given in Appendix B, relevant to each unit; however, study of the detailed *Luftwaffe* daily loss tables in the body of the text will reveal that these codes were not applied as rigidly as has frequently been supposed—newly delivered aircraft might serve for days or weeks with their previous unit's codes unchanged).

The third character, on the immediate right of the fuselage cross, was the individual aircraft letter; this was usually painted or outlined in the *Staffel* colour. The same sequence of white—red—yellow was followed, but as four-*Staffel Gruppen* were more common in the bomber arm, blue was

added for IV.*Gruppe*. Staff aircraft usually had the individual letter painted in green.

The fourth and final letter, on the extreme right of the code, identified the *Staffel*, according to a rigid sequence as follows:

Geschwader	Staff	... A	5 *Staffel* ...	...	N
I. *Gruppe*	Staff	... B	6 *Staffel* ...	...	P
II. *Gruppe*	Staff	... C	7 *Staffel* ...	...	R
III. *Gruppe*	Staff	... D	8 *Staffel* ...	...	S
IV. *Gruppe*	Staff	... E	9 *Staffel* ...	...	T
1 *Staffel*	...	... H	10 *Staffel* ...	...	U
2 *Staffel*	...	... K	11 *Staffel* ...	...	V
3 *Staffel*	...	... L	12 *Staffel* ...	...	W
4 *Staffel*	...	... M			

Where a V.*Gruppe* existed (for instance in the *Lehrgeschwader*), the letter F was used on Staff aircraft and X, Y and Z on the aircraft of 13, 14 and 15 *Staffeln* respectively.

Thus a Heinkel He 111 marked "G 1 + (red J) K" can be identified as serving with 2 *Staffel*, I.*Gruppe*, KG 55; similarly "M 8 + (yellow H) P" is the code that would be carried by a Messerschmitt Bf 110 of 6./ZG 76.

It should be emphasised that under field conditions these general practices were sometimes ignored.

The German reconnaissance units, or *Aufklärungsgruppen*, were more flexibly organised than the fighter and bomber units. Because the broad spectrum of reconnaissance duties was reflected in the diversity of their equipment, these units were established as autonomous *Gruppen*, each mustering a varying number of *Staffeln* according to operational requirements. The short or long range reconnaissance rôles of these *Staffeln* were indicated by the letters (H) or (F) respectively in the unit's title, e.g. 4.(F)/14 signified the 4th (long-range) *Staffel* of *Aufklärungsgruppe* 14. The aircraft carried four-character codes in the normal way.

Hawker Demons of No. 23 Squadron. The Demon was a three-gun fighter development of the famous Hawker Hart light bomber. (Photo: Flight International)

CHAPTER 4

THE AWAKENING

"Awake, arise, or be for ever fall'n!"
They heard, and were abashed, and up they sprung
Upon the wing, as when men wont to watch
On duty, sleeping found by whom they dread,
Rouse and bestir themselves ere well awake.

JOHN MILTON: *Paradise Lost*

If one accepts the accession to power by the N.S.D.A.P. under Adolf Hitler in 1933 as the first obtrusive event in the progressive subversion of European international relations, it is possible to trace and relate to the danger posed by Germany events and policies assumed thereafter by successive British administrations. As has already been related (in Chapter 2), Britain's home defences had been deployed for ten years against a possible attack by France—not so much for fear of an attack by France, but simply because she represented the most powerful neighbour within striking distance of England. So long as Germany remained disarmed, both France and Britain were content with this *status quo*, while the Locarno Treaty, ratified on 14th September 1926, had tended to foster an air of reassurance throughout Europe.

Rearmament in Britain, to which little more than lip service

had been paid during the late 'twenties, was further slowed by Ramsay MacDonald's Labour Government of 1929 by the extension of the current schedule by two years. The League of Nations had achieved precious little in its bid to reduce armaments and when, as has been shown in Chapter 3, Germany abandoned the Geneva Disarmament Conference, Europe became, in effect, committed to a policy of re-armament—so dangerous was the likely upset in the balance of power in Europe thought to be. It may thus be argued that in the long term the Treaty of Versailles was potentially destructive in itself for, while the powers to enforce it were progressively weakened by pacifist administrations, any act in violation of the Treaty perpetrated by one of the subject nations inevitably demanded massive and instant re-armament by the invigilating powers.

Nevertheless, since the formation of Ramsay MacDonald's National Government late in October 1931, Britain had been increasingly uneasy about the rapid deterioration of European affairs, the more so because of the appalling social and economic effects of the "slump". No nation would benefit more than Britain if international disarmament could be achieved, and it remained a partisan policy of National Labour members of MacDonald's government to "set the pace" of disarmament in their stated belief that other nations would follow Britain's example. In the light of Germany's covert preparations since the First World War, such a policy could be, and very nearly was disastrous. It is an unpleasant reality of human nature that a nation seldom follows a foreign example in *disarmament*, only in *re-armament*.

Though a member of the National Government, Stanley Baldwin remained convinced of the air threat to this nation by a resurgent Germany, as the famous Baldwinisms ("the Bomber will always get through", and "the frontier on the Rhine"[1]) demonstrated. Inherent in the Douhet doctrine was the precept that there was no defence against the bomber, and it had remained Trenchard's policy as Chief of the Air Staff until 1930 to invest the major part of Britain's air defence appropriations in a bomber force at the expense of other arms of the Royal Air Force. Yet few could pretend that the R.A.F. in 1932 boasted much in the way of a strategic bomber force, least of all one that could bomb Germany any more effectively than in 1918. The truth lay in the worldwide responsibilities vested in the R.A.F.—in the Middle East, India and the Far East—which accounted for a relatively large proportion of the annual Air Estimates. Britain may have been justified in her pride of achievement in "keeping the King's peace" in distant parts, but the metropolitan air force had sunk to a feeble shadow by the time Trenchard left the Air Staff.

In 1933, the last year in which Britain could justifiably set her face against European instability, her regular air force numbered 29,400 officers and men—just 1,100 more than the survivors of the Geddes "axe" which had fallen a dozen years before. To this figure were added 10,600 regular reservists and 1,480 members of the Special Reserve and Auxiliary Air Force; however, the true esteem in which these reserves were regarded may be seen in the total allocation of only £1.2m. from the Estimates over a period of five years!

Still determined to resist the demands for re-armament, and continuing to pay lip service to the crumbling Geneva Conference, MacDonald determined to resist increased expenditure and, despite his own Labour Government's undertaking to maintain expansion of the Royal Air Force as originally formulated ten years before—albeit with the 1929 two-year "stretch"—the R.A.F.'s strength was not increased by a single squadron between April 1932 and April 1934.

The lack of expansion was equalled by the absence of new equipment in the R.A.F.—again the result of the Government's overriding pacifism, but compounded by the effects of the Depression and the resulting Treasury parsimony. True, the Hawker Hart light bomber, first introduced in January 1930 (together with army co-operation, interceptor and fleet reconnaissance derivatives), had spread throughout the R.A.F.; yet the Bulldog interceptor, first issued in May 1929 and by

1933 thoroughly pedestrian by international standards, still provided the backbone of the A.D.G.B. fighter squadrons.

The years 1930-33 had brought the Salmond brothers to the top of the Royal Air Force. Air Chief Marshal Sir John Salmond had succeeded Trenchard as Chief of the Air Staff on New Year's Day, 1930, and a year later Sir Geoffrey Salmond was appointed Air Officer Commanding-in-Chief, Air Defence of Great Britain (A.D.G.B.). Air Marshal Sir Hugh Dowding became Air Member for Supply and Research on the Air Council on 1st September 1930. These three officers were therefore ultimately responsible for the re-equipment policies of the R.A.F. between 1930 and 1933; there was little doubt, however, that the spectre of the "bomber doctrine" still lingered after Trenchard's departure, to the detriment of the fighter defences. When Sir Geoffrey Salmond succeeded his brother as Chief of the Air Staff on 1st April 1933, he brought to the Cabinet first-hand knowledge of the fighter deficiencies of the A.D.G.B. Truth to tell, the apparently farsighted F.7/30 Specification, sponsored by Sir John and which was intended to accelerate British fighter technology, had made scarcely any progress, and the reasons why this was so will be related in due course.

Sir Geoffrey Salmond only served four weeks in the R.A.F.'s highest appointment, and his death on 27th April resulted in Air Chief Marshal Sir Edward Ellington succeeding to the post of Chief of the Air Staff. Nevertheless the bomber mystique, if not entirely dispelled, had been considerable weakened, and although development of new bombers (the Boulton & Paul Overstrand, the Handley Page Heyford and the Fairey Hendon in particular) continued at a reduced pace, priority was now given to the development of new interceptors, for which Dowding was able to provide the necessary encouragement and influence. Furthermore, continuity of administration—essential during a period of radical advance—was to benefit from Ellington's long tenure of office, for his appointment as C.A.S. was to continue until 1st September 1937[2].

The gathering clouds of 1933 were certainly recognised in their true nature by those to whom the pacifists referred to as "the prophets of doom". It was Winston Churchill[3] who, on 24th October 1933—only ten days after Germany withdrew from the Geneva Disarmament Conference—rose in the Commons to give the first of numerous warnings: "Germany is already well on her way to become, and must become, incomparably the most heavily armed nation in the world and the nation most ready for War. . .We cannot have any anxieties comparable to the anxiety caused by German re-armament."

Bearing in mind that Germany's forces had been maintained in great secrecy, such a warning was remarkable, and Churchill never disclosed the source of his detailed informa-

---

[1] "Since the day of the air the old frontiers are gone. When you think of the defence of England you no longer think of the chalk cliffs of Dover; you think of the Rhine. That is where our frontier lies." House of Commons, 30th July 1934.

[2] The principal Air Staff members during 1933-35 were: The Marquess of Londonderry, Secretary of State for Air (appointed 9th November 1931); Air Chief Marshal Sir Edward Ellington, Chief of the Air Staff (appointed 22nd May 1933); Air Marshal Sir Hugh Dowding, Air Member for Supply and Research (appointed 1st September 1930; changed to Research and Development, 14th January 1935); Air Chief Marshal Sir Cyril Newall, Air Member for Supply and Organisation (appointed 14th January 1935); Air Marshal Sir Frederick Bowhill, Air Member for Personnel (appointed 31st July 1933).

[3] Then Conservative Member of Parliament for the Epping Division of Essex.

tion. Be that as it may, uttered by a Government back-bencher—a distinguished and experienced politician who had served in almost every ministerial post but the most senior of all—the charges prompted the establishment early in 1934 of an *ad hoc* defence committee to make recommendations for the repair of Britain's cumulative defence deficiencies. Although this committee made strong representations for the maintenance of an armed expeditionary force to secure the Low Countries in the event of a war with Germany, the Government decided instead on the massive strengthening of the home-based R.A.F. Accordingly, on 19th July 1934, plans were announced to increase the total number of squadrons from 75[4] to 116 in five years, and to enlarge the home-based first-line strength of aircraft from 488 to 1,304 in the same period.

Described by its sponsors as no more than "modest", the plans brought forth a storm of protest and a motion for a vote of censure by the Labour Party with Liberal Support; Mr. Clement Attlee claimed to "deny the need for increased armaments". The historic Commons debate followed on 30th July.

Once again Churchill rose to repeat his warnings, expressing his belief that Germany already possessed an air force two-thirds as strong as the R.A.F.[5] It was times such as these—when national security and integrity were threatened—that the oratory of that famous figure roused his colleagues and discomfited his opponents. So vividly expressed was his portrayal of the dangers inherent in Germany's resurgence, in relation to subsequent events, that they are quoted here at some length:

"One would have thought that the character of His Majesty's Government and the record of its principal Ministers would have induced the Opposition to view the request for an increase in the national defence with some confidence and consideration. I do not suppose that there has ever been such a pacifist-minded Government. . .No one could have put forward a proposal in such extremely inoffensive terms. Meekness has characterised every word which they have spoken since this subject was first mooted. We are assured that the steps we are taking, although they may to some lower minds have associated with them some idea of national defence, are really only associated with the great principle of collective security, which, I understand, is the only principle that will induce Hon. Gentlemen opposite to make any preparation for the defence of this island. . .

"We are a rich and easy prey. No country is so vulnerable and no country would better repay pillage than our own. With our enormous Metropolis here, the greatest target in the world, a kind of tremendous fat cow, a valuable fat cow tied up to attract the beasts of prey, we are in a position in which we have never been before, and in which no other country in the world is at this present time. Let us remember this: our weakness does not only involve ourselves. . .

"Yet when this Government, this peace-loving Government, makes this modest demand upon Parliament, when these world-famous pacifist Ministers. . .feel driven by their duty to ask for additional security, what is the attitude of the Opposition? They have the same sort of look of pain and shocked surprise which came over the face of Mr. Bumble when Oliver Twist held out his little bowl and asked for more.

"I will venture. . .to assert some facts, and I hope the Government will be able to contradict them. I shall be delighted if the Government are able to contradict them. I first assert that Germany has already in violation of the treaty created a military air force which is nearly two-thirds as strong as our present home defence air force. . .Germany is rapidly increasing this air force. . .By the end of 1935 the German air force will be nearly equal in numbers and efficiency. . .to our own home defence air force at that date even if the present proposals are carried out. . .

". . .if Germany continues this expansion and if we continue to carry out our scheme, then, sometime in 1936, Germany will be definitely and substantially stronger in the air than Great Britain. . .Once they have got that lead we may never be able to overtake them."

No one could contradict this forecast of Germany's military growth, and it was carefully phrased so as to lay no stress upon the German air force's lack of readiness and operational experience in 1934[6]; Churchill evidently assumed that "Teutonic thoroughness and discipline" would ultimately provide for these necessary attributes.

The Upper House had already defeated the censure motion—albeit after outraged references to Germany's "unconditional offer to abolish air warfare"—by 54 votes to 9. The Commons were equally forthright and defeated the motion by 404 to 60. Britain had at last committed herself on the road to re-armament.

Yet armed though it was with a charter for expansion, the Air Staff realised that the danger of German re-armament—now established in fact—was no more than a threat, which might not have to be faced for another five years. There was no immediate scramble to order large quantities of new aircraft, nor to adopt measures to increase the manpower of the R.A.F.; it was one matter to authorise expansion, and another to pay for it. Despite Supplementary Air Estimates (which were to become annual symptoms of increasing European tension between 1934 and 1939), the Air Staff had to rest content with planning until the issue of the 1935 Air Estimates. Furthermore, before turning to the administration of expansion, it is necessary to examine in some detail the development progress which was now being achieved in the evolution of the equipment with which the "new" R.A.F. was to be supplied.

---

[4] The R.A.F. operational strength in 1934 was deployed as follows: 42 home-based squadrons, four flying-boat squadrons (for naval co-operations), five army co-operation squadrons, one squadron on Malta, six in Egypt, Palestine and the Sudan, five in Iraq, one at Aden, eight in India and three in the Far East.

[5] Owing to the lack of definition, it is not possible accurately to relate Churchill's estimate to the facts. Assuming he was referring to the Royal Air Force's home-based strength of 488 first-line aircraft, his estimate of about 320 German aircraft (also presumably first-line) was probably, if anything, optimistic by 50 %. In other words in terms of comparable first-line aircraft, Germany had probably already reached parity in numbers. The quality of equipment was also not dissimilar.

[6] "The object of oratory alone is not truth, but persuasion", *Essay on Athenian Orators (Works, 1898, vol. xi)*, Macaulay.

The Eight-gun Interceptors

In mid-1933 the A.D.G.B. fighter forces comprised thirteen squadrons[7], all based within one hundred miles of London:

Nine Squadrons of Bristol Bulldogs

Nos. 3 and 17 (at Kenley); No. 19 (at Duxford); Nos. 29 and 56 (at North Weald); No. 32 (at Biggin Hill); No. 41 and 111 (at Northolt); and No. 54 (at Hornchurch).

Bulldog: Single-seater with two-gun armament; top speed, 174 m.p.h.

Three Squadrons of Hawker Fury Is.

Nos. 1 and 43 (at Tangmere); and No. 25 (at Hawkinge)

Fury I: Single-seater with two-gun armament; top speed, 207 m.p.h.

One Squadron of Hawker Demons

No. 23 (at Kenley)

Demon: Two-seater with three-gun armament; top speed, 182 m.p.h.

The fact that the aged Bulldog had not been replaced by the splendid Fury must be attributed to the then-prevailing financial strictures for, apart from the normal cost of re-equipment, the Fury was unquestionably an expensive aeroplane[8].

Dowding's first achievement as Air Member for Supply and Research was, however, significant—the exclusion of wood in the main structure of first-line aircraft; the Gamecock finally disappeared from squadron service in 1931 and with it went the old woodworking trades. His main preoccupation was to examine the age-old formula of biplane fighters with twin-gun armament and see how best to enable the industry's designers to break free of the old formula, although of course Specification F.7/30 had already been issued in draft form by the time he arrived in his new appointment. Moreover, he was aware that some of the fighter designers were expressing misgivings about the Air Ministry's policy on fighter engines, although it was not beyond the bounds of possibility that these murmurings originated in the design offices at Bristol, rather than at Derby.

However, while numerous efforts were beginning to be made to satisfy F.7/30's demands for four-gun armament and a speed of 250 m.p.h. through the media of relatively orthodox biplane prototypes, attention was beginning to focus on the concept of the monoplane.

The monoplane had been almost entirely ignored in Britain as a realistic approach to high-performance military aircraft design since before the First World War when a pair of fatal accidents had caused a ban to be imposed on the cantilever wing[9] in R.F.C. aeroplanes. The unsupported belief that a single wing could not be designed to withstand flight loads comparable with those sustained by a biplane had persisted in numerous circles. Even the monoplane's dominance of the

---

[7] The Unit Establishment (U.E.) of a fighter squadron of the R.A.F. in 1933 was eighteen aircraft, i.e. three Flights of six aircraft; in practice, only two flights were regarded as operational, one Flight being used as a training reserve. In most instances two additional aircraft were held as "Immediate Reserve", to take the place of those grounded for repair or maintenance.

[8] The Fury in its early production form cost £4,800 fully-equipped, compared to £3,900 for the Bulldog. Ref: Appendices to Contract Nos. 40559/30 and 102468/31 (respectively).

[9] It is interesting to reflect upon the stigma which can attach to a ban, however shortlived or ill-advised. The edict banning R.F.C. pilots from flying military monoplanes was imposed by Colonel Seeley, Secretary of State for War, in October 1912, following the break-up of two monoplanes (one on 6th September over Hitchin, the other over Port Meadow, Oxford, on 10th September). The ban, in fact, only lasted five months; nor was it recognised by Winston Churchill who, as First Lord of the Admiralty, refused to so constrict naval aviation. Such was the stigma that succeeding generations of army officers continued, long after 1913, to look askance at monoplanes. Dowding—himself an ex-subaltern—was not so constrained.

The Supermarine S.5, Reginald Mitchell's superb Schneider Trophy seaplane; note the asymmetric mounting of the floats, adopted to counteract the engine's enormous torque. The aerodynamic advances of this and its successor, the S.6, spurred Mitchell in his efforts to produce a monoplane fighter—that would one day emerge as the classic Spitfire. (Photo: Flight International)

Classic view of No. 19 Squadron's Gloster Gauntlets, almost the final act in the R.A.F.'s colourful period of "flying wires and chequer-boards". (Photo: Flight International)

Schneider Trophy contests during the years 1927-31 had left the traditionalists unmoved.

It was Reginald Mitchell, designer of the victorious Schneider Trophy twin-float monoplane racers who sought to apply the monoplane formula to the F.7/30 Specification. The result was depressing and the Supermarine Type 224—a cumbersome gull-wing monoplane with fixed "trousered" undercarriage—achieved the disappointing speed of only 230 m.p.h.

The Type 224, failure though it proved to be, provided Mitchell with valuable experience in the design of high performance military aircraft—if only by demonstrating a "yardstick of mediocrity". The Specification had called for a low landing speed, and his seaplanes had not been thus restricted. His design had also been compromised by the unsuitable, but officially favoured, Rolls-Royce Goshawk steam-cooled engine[10].

Frank Barnwell of the Bristol Aeroplane Company produced several designs to F.7/30, including the Goshawk-powered Type 123, the last biplane built at the famous Filton factory. Most promising of Barnwell's designs was the Type 133, which was powered by Bristol's own Mercury radial engine. Capable of achieving 260 m.p.h., the four-gun Type 133 was superficially similar to the Supermarine Type 224 with its gull wing, although the landing gear retracted into underwing fairings. Bristol's Chief Test Pilot, Cyril Uwins, declared the prototype showed great promise—a view supported by its smooth progress through the early flight trials.

_____

[10] Cf. *Spitfire*, Robertson, Harborough, Letchworth, 1960.

However, when the sole prototype crashed on 8th March 1935, the old F.7/30 requirements were already history, and the issue of a new Specification (F.5/34, of which more anon) was already attracting Barnwell's attention[11].

So much for the radical approaches to the F.7/30 requirement; others, of a more orthodox nature (that is to say, biplanes such as the Hawker P.V.3, the Bristol Type 123, and designs from Blackburn and Westlands[12]), suffered from the inadequacies of the Goshawk engine and attracted no more than academic interest.

One company which had, however, remained aloof from the costly ramifications of F.7/30 was the Gloster Aircraft Company of Brockworth, near Gloucester. Since the acceptance of the Grebe and Gamecock fighters by the R.A.F., the company had been content to pursue privately sponsored development of the interceptor through an interesting line of prototypes whose relatively high performance was achieved by close attention to design detail, not least of which was an ingenious combination of high-lift upper wing and low-lift, low-drag lower wing. By the early 'thirties H.P. Folland (who had been responsible for the design of the S.E.5 fighters of the First World War) had evolved a promising fighter prototype, the Gloster S.S.19 which, with an armament of no fewer than six machine guns, outstripped the Bulldog by a clear margin of 14 m.p.h. Viewed with some scepticism by the Air Ministry, the armament was reduced to four guns and the S.S.19 was, with a top speed of 204 m.p.h., accepted as the basis of an interim interceptor by the R.A.F. Further improved by the installation of a Mercury IIA engine, the S.S.19B, named the Gauntlet, returned a maximum speed of 212 m.p.h. when flown by the Service in 1933.

This was the version ordered by the Air Ministry when a contract for 24 aircraft was received by Glosters in September 1933. Reversion, however, to the old two-gun formula was implicit in the Specification, so that when the Gauntlet appeared in squadron service in 1935, it might have represented little more than a cleaned-up Bulldog. Nevertheless, despite its two-gun armament, the Gauntlet (of which a total

_____

[11] Cf. *Bristol Aircraft since 1910*, Barnes, Putnam. London, 1964.

[12] The Westland design, although a biplane, was interesting in that the engine was situated *behind* the pilot, driving the propeller through an extension shaft. By adopting this layout and a fuselage-mounted upper wing, design emphasis was placed on providing the pilot with good all-round visibility. Unfortunately it deprived the aeroplane of a worthwhile top speed—only 185 m.p.h.

Gloster Gladiators at the 1937 Air Pageant. A Gauntlet "afterthought" development which owed its success to the delayed introduction of the monoplane designs, the Gladiator served with distinction during the first three years of the War. (Photo: Flight International)

of 228 was built for the R.A.F. and issued to no fewer than twenty-two fighter squadrons) came close to the zenith of biplane fighter design, and many experienced R.A.F. pilots came to regard it as unsurpassed for its near-perfect handling qualities.

Notwithstanding the qualities of the Gauntlet, it was clear to the Air Ministry and Gloster alike that this fighter fell far short of the demands of F.7/30 for, while it came within 20 m.p.h. of the speed requirements, the two-gun armament limited its rôle to that of a stopgap. To Glosters, who had watched other manufacturers floundering in a sea of expedients in their attempts to satisfy F.7/30 (and defeated by a steam-cooled engine), it seemed that their own Gauntlet had come within an ace of the required speed and that with relatively little "cleaning up" they might yet scoop the pool; moreover their own experience of four-gun installations also stood them in good stead.

So it was that a limited redesign was put in hand during the spring of 1934 with such urgency that a prototype was completed by September that year. Now fitted with single-bay wings, armed with four machine guns (two Vickers and two Lewis) and powered by a 645-h.p. Bristol Mercury VIS radial engine, the new prototype (S.S.37) returned a speed of 242 m.p.h. When the engine was changed to an 840-h.p. Mercury IX the speed was raised to 255 m.p.h., and the new aircraft—the Gladiator—was declared the winner. Once again Glosters had achieved the means of securing large production contracts (more than 600 Gladiators were built in five years), but although the Gauntlet and Gladiator occupied much of the Brockworth factory space up to the outbreak of War, by ignoring the chances of a radical break from the old biplane formula offered by F.7/30, the Gloster company forfeited the opportunity to enter the infinitely more rewarding contest to provide Britain with one of its first monoplane fighters. As it was, the company was preoccupied in 1934 with no more than a small production contract (for the first batch of Gauntlets) when it was taken over by T.O.M. Sopwith of Hawker Aircraft Ltd., to provide additional space for the manufacture of Hawker aeroplanes; ironically it was to be the Hawker Henley, Hurricane and Typhoon that filled the extensive production shops at Brockworth for much of the Second World War.

*   *   *   *   *

Almost every other member of the British aircraft industry had at some time studied the possibility of producing a monoplane interceptor prior to 1933. Several attempts had been made to produce such designs to meet F.7/30, notably those of the Bristol and Supermarine companies.

Sydney Camm, Hawker's Chief Designer, was in 1933 engaged in investigations into the possibility of developing the Fury fighter biplane into a monoplane. The Directorate of Technical Development (D.T.D.) at the Air Ministry was casting around for a ten per cent increase in speed over the 250 m.p.h. demanded by F.7/30, and it was thought possible at Kingston to achieve such an advance by adaptation of the Fury. Such a course was discussed by Camm and Major J.S. Buchanan at the D.T.D. in August that year, with the result that a preliminary scheme was evolved; known as the Fury Monoplane, the design employed the Goshawk steam-cooled engine—still favoured by the Air Ministry, despite increas-

ing technical problems—and featured fixed undercarriage, enclosed cockpit and four-gun armament. A similar scheme was being evolved by Mitchell, who was still determined to apply the object lessons provided by the aerodynamic advances provided by his superb Schneider Trophy seaplanes as well as the Type 224 essay.

It should be emphasised that the Hawker and Supermarine designs differed (and continue to differ throughout their lives) in one fundamental respect. The Hawker design, developed directly from the Fury, and manufactured in factories also engaged in the production of the older Hart and Fury biplanes, used a fabric-covered, fabricated steel tubular structure, and was therefore in effect of an older design concept than Mitchell's aircraft; the latter was entirely new and used metal stressed-skin monocoque structure—only the control surfaces being fabric-covered. As will be seen in due course, despite the older structural concept of the Hawker design, it was this very feature that rendered it such a vital element in the R.A.F.'s expansion plans of the next few years, and bestowed such important qualities in service during the first three years of the Second World War; by contrast, Mitchell's aeroplane, grace and beauty personified, was to be more difficult to build and required entirely new production techniques and standards.

As early detail design of the two projects continued during 1934—against a background of official interest, albeit without the support of government financing—it gradually became obvious to the Air Ministry that the steam-cooled Goshawk engine was quite unsuitable for installation in a compact interceptor fighter, and official preference for this engine was waived. However, since 1931 Rolls-Royce Ltd. had been privately at work on another engine, then referred to as the P.V.12, which was an enlarged derivative of the highly successful, conventional liquid-cooled Kestrel engine, and, with reports of bench tests suggesting brake horsepower output approaching 1,000 at relatively low power/weight ratio, both Camm and Mitchell altered their designs to accommodate the P.V.12—soon to be named the Merlin, and undoubtedly the most famous aero-engine of all time. By way of a bonus, choice of the Merlin permitted a cleaning up of both designs; the increased engine weight was balanced by moving the radiator aft, leaving the wing centresection clear for landing gear retraction on Camm's design, and for a very slim nose contour on the Supermarine project.

The other major development being undertaken in 1934 was in the sphere of aircraft armament. Almost since the dawn of military aviation, British fighting aeroplanes had been armed with fixed, synchronised Vickers rifle-calibre machine guns, firing forward, and with Lewis guns mounted on gunners' cockpits. The Vickers had been an adequate gun just so long as it continued to fire but, since time immemorial it had been prone to perpetual stoppage problems with the result that aircraft designers placed the guns within physical reach of the pilot—who often carried a hide-faced mallet with which to smite the offending gun to clear a stoppage. The location of the guns in the fuselage necessitated, in turn, the fitting of synchronising gear so as to prevent the bullets from striking the propeller when fired. This not only tended to reduce the rate of fire but constituted just another piece of equipment that could jam. In 1933 the Air Ministry's Armament Research Department, in deciding to look for a replacement for the old Vickers gun, staged a machine gun competition, evaluating the Vickers and Lewis against the Colt, Madsen, Spandau, Kiraleji, Darne and Hispano. Of these, the Colt emerged head and shoulders above the rest, although it fired 0.300-inch rimless ammunition. Negotiations were immediately put in hand with the Colt's Patent Fire Arm Manufacturing Company of Hartford, Connecticut, U.S.A., to build the gun under licence in Britain, adapted to fire 0.303-inch ammunition. Forthwith Wing Command Claude Keith of the Royal Arsenal Ordnance Board, and Major H.S.V. Thompson, a Principal Technical Officer of the D.T.D., visited Colt in the United States and successfully paved the way for licence agreements with the Birmingham Small Arms Company. (Under those agreements more than half a million machine guns were to be produced for the R.A.F. alone during the next ten years.)

Meanwhile a new Specification had been raised by the Air Ministry; this was F.5/34 which, though in its draft form did not attempt to embrace the overall requirements for an interceptor fighter, did call for design studies to be made for a machine gun battery of up to eight guns. The man behind this radical idea was Squadron Leader Ralph Sorley[13], who had had much to do with the preparation of F.7/30, and who was now seeking to extend his thesis on the need to increase fighter armament. It should be pointed out that up to the point at which final agreement was reached on the licence manufacture of the Colt gun (under the name of Browning), both Mitchell's and Camm's projected fighters were to be armed with synchronised machine guns mounted on the fuselage or in the wing roots. Moreover, although there was unlikely to be any difficulty in mounting a battery of eight guns in the Hawker fighter's wing (owing to its greater thickness), problems were foreseen in Mitchell's fighter, and it proved impossible to group the guns in a single gun bay—making for slower re-arming—as was to be found in service.

By August 1934 model tests of the two fighters at the National Physics Laboratory, Teddington, suggested that both aircraft would likely exceed 300 miles per hour in level flight, so that two Specifications, F.36/34 for the Hawker project and F.37/34 for the Supermarine design, were raised and issued in September that year. By the end of the year full-scale mock-ups had been started and early in 1935 these were studied by Air Commodore Lawrence Pattinson of the Air Ministry's Armament Research Department and Wing Commander Cyril Lowe of A.D.G.B., with a view to deciding on the practicability of installing the eight-gun wing batteries. It was upon these men that, under the direction of Sorley, a decision rested as to whether the design proposals now submitted by Hawker and Supermarine should be accepted. It was the very compactness and operating reliability of the American guns that inclined them to favour the idea, and there is little doubt that they were unaware of the extraordinary stakes at hazard; for had the installation of the guns themselves—in their adapted form—failed to live up to expectations, their failure would compromise the entire design concept of the two vital fighters.

First to be completed in prototype form was the Hawker F.36/34, *K5083*, built at Kingston-upon-Thames and moved by road to Brooklands for its first flight on 6th November 1935 in the hands of Flight Lieutenant P.W.S. Bulman, the company's chief test pilot. Shortly afterwards this aeroplane would be named the Hurricane.

Four months later, on 5th March 1936, the prototype Supermarine Type 300, *K5054*, was flown for the first time at Eastleigh airport, near Southampton, by Captain J. Summers, chief test pilot of the Vickers group; this, in turn, was to be named the Spitfire.

Before going on to describe the introduction of the new eight-gun fighters into service and the means by which they were brought to combat readiness, it is relevant here to outline the equipment strength of A.D.G.B. at the beginning of 1936. By January that year the thirteen home-based fighter squadrons were based and equipped as follows:

Six squadrons of Bristol Bulldogs
> Nos. 3 and 178 (at Kenley); No. 32 (at Biggin Hill); No. 54 (at Hornchurch); No. 56 (at North Weald); and No. 111 (at Northolt).

> *Bulldog*: Single-seater with two-gun armament and top speed of 174 m.p.h.

Three Squadrons of Hawker Fury Is
> Nos. 1 and 43 (at Tangmere); and No. 25 (at Hawkinge).

> *Fury I*: Single-seater with two-gun armament and top speed of 207 m.p.h.

Three Squadrons of Hawker Demons
> No. 23 (at Biggin Hill); No. 29 (at North Weald); and No. 65 (at Hornchurch)

---

[13] Later Air Marshal Sir Ralph Sorley, K.C.B., O.B.E., D.S.C., A.F.C.

The four-gun wing battery of the Hurricane. The licence agreement for the production of the reliable Colt gun in Britain was central to the success of the eight-gun fighters and had incalculable results in 1940. (Photo: Author's Collection)

Demon: Two-seater with three-gun armament and top speed of 182 m.p.h.

One squadron of Gauntlets
No. 19 (at Duxford)

Gauntlet: Single-seater with two-gun armament and top speed of 230 m.p.h.

At first glance it would seem that this strength was little greater than in 1933, excepting the introduction of the Gauntlet. Nevertheless the Abyssinian crisis of 1935 had resulted in the re-formation of two Squadrons with Demons (Nos. 64 and 74) at Heliopolis and Malta respectively, otherwise these would have been formed as home-based units—and were in any case to come home to the United Kingdon within fifteen months. Another Squadron, No. 41, also with Demons, had also been sent to the Middle East.

As thus implied, the improvement in Britain's air defences had hitherto been in the accelerated development of equipment rather than in the numerical strength of squadrons and aircraft. This was to be expected simply on account of the time taken to recruit and train the required numbers of aircrew and ground crews need to man additional squadrons. The year 1936 was, however, to bring forth the first results of numerical expansion.

Successive expansion schemes, designated in alphabetical order, had been planned, issued and superseded as the increasing danger presented by German re-armament came to be appreciated. In 1936, Scheme "F" was issued calling for the production of 500 Hurricanes and 300 Spitfires[14] within three years, the first scheme embodying the eight-gun interceptors—such was Sorley's implicit faith in their design potential. Already the largescale increase in the R.A.F.'s manpower was being achieved (see Chapter 2), and previous expansion schemes, notably "C" and "D", had provided for massive production contracts for interim aircraft which would provide relatively inexpensive media for operational training of the large number of new pilots[15]. By 1936 Hawker Aircraft Limited had sub-contracted production orders for 754 Hart bombers and trainers, 75 Fury fighters, 106 Demons, 422 Audaxes, 47 Hardys and 178 Hectors. The Company itself had built, or was engaged in building 214 Harts, 218 Furies, 133 Demons, 131 Ospreys, 209 Audaxes and 528 Hinds[16]. These contracts had been the saving of the British aircraft industry; worth roughly sixteen million pounds, they enabled factories up and down the country to expand, acquire plant and train the huge labour force soon to be needed to manufacture the new fighters and bombers about to be ordered into production. The Hawker sub-contracts were placed with the Gloster Aircraft Company, Sir W.G. Armstrong Whitworth Aircraft Ltd., and A.V. Roe & Co. Ltd., all of which companies were merged or purchased by T.O.M. Sopwith to form the Hawker Siddeley Group. Other orders were sub-contracted to Westland Aircraft Company, Boulton-Paul Aircraft Ltd., Vickers (Aviation) Ltd., the Bristol Aeroplane Company and the General Aircraft Company. It was estimated that seven-eighths of the industry's manpower was engaged in the manufacture of Hawker-designed aircraft.

On 17th March the Secretary of State for Air, Sir Philip Sassoon, presented his Air Estimates, showing that current plans were for the increase of the R.A.F.'s first-line strength to 1,500 aircraft by the end of that year, of which 270 were to be based overseas and about 220 in the Fleet Air Arm.

A complete re-organisation of the Royal Air Force was also undertaken during 1936. The age-old Inland and Fighter Areas were to disappear and a functional Command structure introduced. Air Marshal Sir Wilfred Freeman succeeded Dowding on 1st April as Air Member for Research and Development on the Air Council. The first of the new Commands, Training Command, came into being on 21st May under the Command of Air Marshal Sir Charles Burnett. On 14th July Air Chief Marshal Sir Hugh Dowding was appointed Air Officer Commanding-in-Chief of the newly formed Fighter Command; Air Chief Marshal Sir John Steel took charge of Bomber Command, and Air Marshal Sir Arthur Longmore of Coastal Command, which came into being on the same day[17].

Also authorised in 1936 was the construction of 26 operational aerodromes in the United Kingdom, of which nine were to be fighter airfields and incorporated into the structure of the new Fighter Command. This structure was to be formulated on a multiple Group basis, each Group being responsible for an area's defence. At the outset two Fighter Groups were formed, No. 11 covering the south of England, No. 12 the Midlands and the North. Later, No. 13 Group would be formed to take over the North, and yet a fourth, No. 10 Group, would come into being in 1940 to defend the South-West.

Each Group would incorporate a number of "master" fighter bases, each provided with an operations centre to control fighters for the defence of a Sector. These bases, known as Sector Stations, being long-established with extensive maintenance and repair facilities, would accommodate the Sector's fighter squadrons on a semi-permanent basis; in addition the Sector Station Commander would have at his disposal a small number of forward satellite landing grounds from which he could operate detachments of his fighters, either for re-fuelling or advanced-readiness purposes.

The principal benefit of the new defence structure was that, with the considerable increase in defending forces now planned, it provided for an organised, all-round guard with clearly defined local defence responsibilities vested in an operational chain of command. In itself, however, the new

[14] The differential in no way suggested any inferiority of the Spitfire, but simply that production techniques on this fighter were recognised as being slower to achieve than those of the Hurricane, and some difficulties were anticipated. This proved correct and the rate of delivery of Spitfires lagged by about nine months throughout 1938 and 1939; Hurricane production was also slowed, but to nothing like the same extent.

[15] The formation of the Royal Air Force Volunteer Reserve (R.A.F.V.R.) was announced on 30th July 1936.

[16] The Demon, Audax, Hardy and Hector were all variants of the Hart, being designed as fighter, army co-operation, general purpose (tropical) and army co-operation aircraft respectively. The Osprey was a fleet reconnaissance Hart derivative for the Fleet Air Arm, and the Hind was a light bomber development of the Hart which it replaced during 1936-37. A naval fighter, related to the Fury—though not developed from it—was the Nimrod, of which Hawker produced several batches during the mid-1930s.

[17] Sir Arthur Longmore was succeeded by Air Marshal P.B. Joubert de la Ferté as A.O.C.-in-C., Coastal Command, after only six weeks, on 1st September.

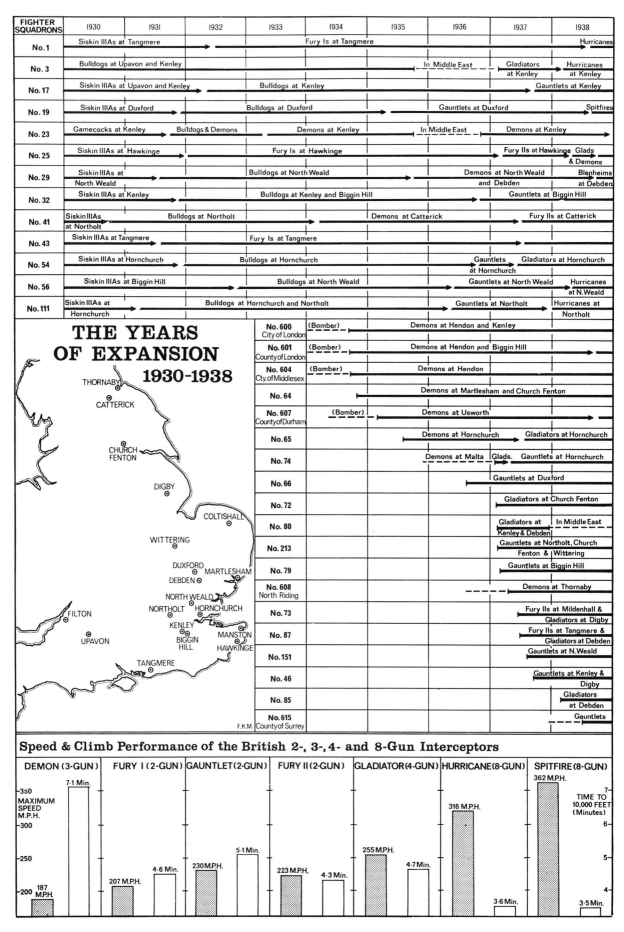

FIGHTER SQUADRONS	1930	1931	1932	1933	1934	1935	1936	1937	1938
No. 1	Siskin IIIAs at Tangmere →		Fury Is at Tangmere						Hurricanes
No. 3	Bulldogs at Upavon and Kenley →					In Middle East	Gladiators at Kenley	Hurricanes at Kenley	
No. 17	Siskin IIIAs at Upavon and Kenley →		Bulldogs at Kenley →					Gauntlets at Kenley	
No. 19	Siskin IIIAs at Duxford →		Bulldogs at Duxford →			Gauntlets at Duxford			Spitfires
No. 23	Gamecocks at Kenley →	Bulldogs & Demons	Demons at Kenley		In Middle East	Demons at Kenley →			
No. 25	Siskin IIIAs at Hawkinge →		Fury Is at Hawkinge				Fury IIs at Hawkinge	Glads & Demons	
No. 29	Siskin IIIAs at North Weald →		Bulldogs at North Weald →				Demons at North Weald and Debden	Blenheims at Debden	
No. 32	Siskin IIIAs at Kenley →		Bulldogs at Kenley and Biggin Hill →				Gauntlets at Biggin Hill		
No. 41	Siskin IIIAs at Northolt	Bulldogs at Northolt →			Demons at Catterick →			Fury IIs at Catterick	
No. 43	Siskin IIIAs at Tangmere →		Fury Is at Tangmere →						
No. 54	Siskin IIIAs at Hornchurch →		Bulldogs at Hornchurch →				Gauntlets at Hornchurch	Gladiators at Hornchurch	
No. 56	Siskin IIIAs at Biggin Hill →		Bulldogs at North Weald →				Gauntlets at North Weald	Hurricanes at N.Weald	
No. 111	Siskin IIIAs at Hornchurch →		Bulldogs at Hornchurch and Northolt →				Gauntlets at Northolt	Hurricanes at Northolt	

THE YEARS OF EXPANSION
1930-1938

No. 600 City of London	(Bomber) ---	Demons at Hendon and Kenley →
No. 601 County of London	(Bomber) ---	Demons at Hendon and Biggin Hill →
No. 604 Cty. of Middlesex	(Bomber) ---	Demons at Hendon →
No. 64		Demons at Martlesham and Church Fenton
No. 607 County of Durham	(Bomber) ---	Demons at Usworth →
No. 65		Demons at Hornchurch → Gladiators at Hornchurch
No. 74		Demons at Malta --- Glads. Gauntlets at Hornchurch
No. 66		Gauntlets at Duxford
No. 72		Gladiators at Church Fenton
No. 80		Gladiators at Kenley & Debden In Middle East ---
No. 213		Gauntlets at Northolt, Church Fenton & Wittering
No. 79		Gauntlets at Biggin Hill
No. 608 North Riding		Demons at Thornaby ---
No. 73		Fury IIs at Mildenhall & Gladiators at Digby
No. 87		Fury IIs at Tangmere & Gladiators at Debden
No. 151		Gauntlets at N.Weald
No. 46		Gauntlets at Kenley & Digby
No. 85		Gladiators at Debden
No. 615 County of Surrey		Gauntlets ---

F.K.M.

Map locations: THORNABY, CATTERICK, CHURCH FENTON, DIGBY, COLTISHALL, WITTERING, DUXFORD, MARTLESHAM, DEBDEN, NORTH WEALD, NORTHOLT, HORNCHURCH, FILTON, KENLEY, MANSTON, BIGGIN HILL, HAWKINGE, UPAVON, TANGMERE

Speed & Climb Performance of the British 2-, 3-, 4- and 8-Gun Interceptors

DEMON (3-GUN)	FURY I (2-GUN)	GAUNTLET (2-GUN)	FURY II (2-GUN)	GLADIATOR (4-GUN)	HURRICANE (8-GUN)	SPITFIRE (8-GUN)
7·1 Min.						362 M.P.H.
					316 M.P.H.	
		230 M.P.H.		255 M.P.H.		
		5·1 Min.				
			223 M.P.H. 4·3 Min.	4·7 Min.		
187 M.P.H.	207 M.P.H. 4·6 Min.				3·6 Min.	3·5 Min.

MAXIMUM SPEED M.P.H. — 350, 300, 250, 200

TIME TO 10,000 FEET (Minutes) — 7, 6, 5, 4

Fighter Command could not provide anything more than the old defence-in-depth system in which interception of incoming raids could only be achieved by the wasteful recourse to standing patrols, as well as leaving coastal targets vulnerable to attack. What was required—and indeed was about to be integrated into the defence system—was a means of providing warning of approaching raids, so that the fighters would be enabled to take off in readiness to meet the raid before it reached the coast. With modern bomber speeds (being demonstrated by the new Vickers Wellington (about 230 m.p.h.) and Handley Page Hampden (about 250 m.p.h.), whose prototypes flew on 15th and 21st June 1936 respectively), the old accoustic-location warning system was utterly inadequate, and it was now that a new scientific development was about to transform the entire concept of Britain's air defence

The Introduction of Radar[18]

The shortcomings of the air defence system of 1918 (see Chapter 1) had continued for sixteen years to occupy the thoughts of British scientists and the various research departments of the Air Ministry. Not least of these deficiencies was the inability of the fighter defences to meet hostile raiders before they crossed the coasts of Britain. The old aerodrome at Biggin Hill had been for many years the location of an experimental unit charged with the improvement of the various aspects of the ground control of fighters in the air and of the detection of approaching raids. Ground-to-air radio telephony had been to some extent developed at Biggin Hill, as had a rudimentary form of sound location. By 1934 sufficient funds had been accumulated to construct an enormous concrete acoustic mirror on Romney Marshes with which it was hoped to detect the sound of approaching aircraft; this proved virtually useless for, even if weather and other conditions (such as the absence of road and sea traffic) were ideal, it possessed a range of only about eight miles, while such vital information as the altitude and bearing of aircraft could not be obtained. The equipment, if such it can be termed, was brought into use during the Air Exercises of June-July 1934, but the R.A.F.'s then-standard heavy night bomber, the Vickers Virginia, penetrated the defences almost undetected. It may be remarked that this bomber possessed a cruising speed of less than 80 m.p.h.—not materially different from that of the Giants of 1918.

It was in the same month the Air Exercises were emphasising the critical weakness of the defences that a staff member of the Air Ministry's Directorate of Scientific Research, Mr. A.P. Rowe, prepared a memorandum for his Director, Mr. H.E. Wimperis, suggesting that unless this appalling deficiency was rectified, any war waged against Britain within ten years would result in the destruction of her vital centres by enemy bombers. Wimperis, in turn, proposed to the Secretary of State for Air, the Marquess of Londonderry, the setting up of a committee under Mr. Henry Tizard, a prominent scientist, to carry out a review of possible means by which scientific developments might be applied to strengthen the air

defences. The proposal was accepted and the committee was established, composed of Tizard (chairman), Rowe (secretary), Wimperis, Professor P.M.S. Blackett and Dr. A.V. Hill[19].

All manner of possibilities were explored, not least that of a "death ray". No one seriously considered this a realistic measure but, if only as a scientific means of eliminating it from the committee's agenda, Wimperis asked Mr. R.A. Watson-Watt of the National Physics Laboratories for relevant calculations to indicate the impracticability of the far-fetched idea. It was, however, one of Watson-Watt's staff, Mr. A.F. Wilkins who, after indicating that it was not possible to generate sufficient power in beams to harm human beings, suggested that radio beams themselves might well be affected by the presence of aircraft—and thus that, by use of radio beams, aircraft could be detected, and possibly located. Watson-Watt could point to two areas of experience which appeared to support Wilkins' suggestion. Ten years previously, the N.P.L. had employed radio waves to measure the height of the Heaviside Layer above the earth's surface; pulses had been transmitted and, as a proportion of the signal was reflected from the ionised layer, the signal's elapsed time could be measured.

It had also been shown that the passage of aircraft affected radio waves, and to some extent reflected them; such a phenomenon had occurred accidentally and a report of it had been filed by the Post Office in 1932.

On 12th February 1935 Watson-Watt submitted to the Air Ministry Wilkins' report entitled Detection and Loacation of Aircraft by Radio Methods, and within a week a meeting was arranged at the Royal Aircraft Establishment, Farnborough, between Dowding, Wimperis and Watson-Watt. Explaining that no realistic equipment had yet been evolved, Watson-Watt suggested that a simple demonstration might be sufficient for the theory to be proved. Accordingly, on 26th February, a Heyford bomber was flown along the centreline of the fifty-metre radio beam transmitted by the B.B.C.'s Daventry overseas station, and a receiver was linked to a cathode ray oscilloscope to display the beam's signal. As the aircraft passed within eight miles of the transmitter, the beam display was displaced by a measurable degree—thus confirming that aircraft detection *could* be achieved using radio signals.

Events now moved with surprising speed. A Radio Direction Finding experimental unit was established under Watson-Watt by the Radio Research Station, and a coastal site was set up on the Suffolk coast at Orfordness. By the first week in June 1935, a 75-foot radio aerial had been erected, together with transmitters and receivers, and trials commenced using a Vickers Valentia bomber-transport as "target". Early results showed some promise, although the 56-

---

[18] Between the years 1936 and 1942 the terms Radio Direction Finding and Radio Location were current in British terminology. The American contraction "Radar", which subsequently achieved universal acceptance, has however been adopted through this book so as to avoid repetitive explanation.

[19] These committee members were among the most brilliant of British scientists of their day. Tizard was knighted in 1937 and, apart from having served in the R.F.C., was the Rector of the Imperial College of Science and Technology from 1929 until 1942, serving on countless Councils and Committees charged with recommending improvements in the R.A.F.'s equipment. Professor Patrick Blackett, F.R.S., M.A., was in 1934 Professor of Physics at Birbeck College; he was awarded the Nobel Prize for Physics in 1948. Dr. Archibald Hill, O.B.E., F.R.S., M.A., was to become Secretary of the Royal Society in 1935 and had been awarded the Nobel Prize for Physiology and Medicine in 1922; he also served on many committees concerned with defence matters.

metre wavelength, initially selected, proved to be prone to atmospherics and commercial radio interference. By reducing the wavelength to 26 metres it was found possible to detect the Valentia at a range of 38 miles, and to follow it out to 42. On 24th July a much smaller aeroplane, a Westland Wallace, was followed out to 34 miles, while a formation of Hawker Harts was identified at twenty. Two months later the Orfordness station was able to track an aircraft out to 58 miles.

Meanwhile the secret progress of Watson-Watt's team was being closely watched in Whitehall, and a Sub-Committee of Imperial Defence on Air Defence had been set up to study all manner of defence projects. Viscount Swinton, the newly-appointed Secretary of State for Air, suggested that Winston Churchill should serve on the Sub-Committee—in deference to that statesman's constantly voiced apprehension at the nation's defence shortcomings. Nevertheless Churchill—for all his enthusiasm for scientific novelties and military expedients—possessed little capacity to understand complex technicalities and, in accepting Baldwin's invitation, stipulated that his friend and scientific adviser, Professor Frederick Lindemann[20], should accompany him on the Committee. The latter appointment was to prove embarrassing in the extreme, for Lindemann pursued his own ideas for aircraft location—using infra-red detectors. Though of basically sound concept, such a system was impracticable over the ranges being achieved using radio waves, yet such were Lindemann's powers of insistence, and his enhanced influence owing to his new appointment, that considerable effort and money was diverted on his ideas. Later, in 1936, his partisan behaviour led to disagreements with Tizard and Hill, resulting in their resignations. Only the tact of Baldwin's Secretary of State for Air saved the situation; Swinton promptly reconstituted the Sub-Committee by re-appointing Tizard and Hill, but omitted Lindemann; he also added the name of Professor Edward Appleton, F.R.S., M.A., D.SC. (who had in 1924 conducted the experiments to measure the height of the Heaviside Layer[21]).

Progress continued to be made at Orfordness and ranges of 50 miles were, by the end of 1935, becoming commonplace, though as yet accurate altitude and bearing information continued to elude the scientists. It was also clear that the 75-foot aerial was inadequate, while even this modest erection represented a flying hazard to pilots from nearby Martlesham Heath airfield. At the suggestion of Wimperis, the Air Ministry purchased Bawdsey Manor from Sir Cuthbert Quilter—a small seashore estate a few miles south of Orfordness. During the following six months a pair of 250-foot lattice masts was constructed. By mounting up to six directional aerials, operating on a six-metre wavelength, on the four cardinal points of the compass, direction finding could be achieved by signal-strength comparison using a manually-operated goniometer at the base of the aerial. Later this essential part of the fixed array aerial system was moved to the operations hut. Thus by applying established direction finding techniques, akin to the rotating loop aerial, Wimperis achieved a fair degree of bearing information. As with loop operation, however, ambiguity from back-signals (that is, a reciprocal bearing) was theoretically possible, but special relay sensing was intended to overcome this[22].

The next stage was to integrate the new developments into the regular defence system of the Royal Air Force. Having regard to the considerable ground yet to be covered and the fact that this could only be achieved by the civilian scientific staffs, fairly radical changes in policy would have to be accepted—not least the induction of such civilians into the secret air defence departments of the Service. That this was achieved smoothly and without acrimony can be attributed to Dowding and Swinton.

As already stated, Dowding, who as Air Member for Research and Development had been directly involved with the early radar proposals, was now appointed A.O.C.-in.-C. of Fighter Command, and thus brought to the top echelons of the air defences an intimate knowledge of the progress being made at Orfordness and Bawdsey; it was thus through Dowding (and his succesor, Sir Wilfred Freeman) that R.A.F. personnel, including Squadron Leader Raymund Hart[23], were posted to Bawdsey to establish the basis of a radar training school to produce a flow of trained personnel with which to man future coastal radar stations.

It was the attainment of 50-mile pick-up ranges in September 1935 that convinced the Air Defence Sub-Committee that in radar lay the whole basis of an air defence warning system, and it was in that month that the first proposals were drawn up for a chain of twenty coastal radar stations (termed Air Ministry Experimental Stations, Type 1, or A.M.E.S.1, and later Chain Home (C.H.) stations) to be constructed between Southampton and Newcastle—covering the likely over-sea approaches from Germany. As a first stage the R.A.F. asked that three stations at Bawdsey, Canewdon and Dover be activated in June 1936, and a further four in the next two months. This proved to be an impossible target due to the lack of trained operators and to delays in the ponderous Air Ministry equipment contracts departments, and in fact only the Bawdsey experimental station was operating during the air defence exercises of 24th-26th September 1936. Results were promising and Bawdsey was formally taken on Air Ministry charge in May 1937, followed by the Dover station in July, and Canewdon the next month. These stations participated in the Air Exercises of August 1937, and some idea of the advances hitherto made may be judged by the fact that pick-up ranges of 100 miles were being achieved, and trained operators were correctly identifying formation raids.

It was at Bawdsey that a prototype Group operations room was developed by G.P.O. engineers under Mr. E.J.C. Dixon and an R.A.F. equipment detachment under Warrant Officer Reginald Woodley[24]. An important innovation was currently being developed by Squadron Leader Hart (in addition to his

---

[22] Early in the War there were several instances of the "back cut-off" failing, with the result that quite innocuous domestic flights well inland were reported by the coastal radar as incoming raids. The famous "Battle of Barking Creek" of 6th September 1939, in which interceptor fighters were ordered off against non-existent raids and finished up attacking each other, was sparked off by such a failure.

[23] Raymund Hart, a multi-lingual Service interpreter and qualified signals specialist, was in fact an Acting Squadron Leader when posted to Bawdsey. A recipient of the M.C. in the First World War, he retired as Air Marshal Sir Raymund Hart K.B.E., C.B., M.C., and died on 16th July 1960

[24] Woodley was to be commissioned and retired in 1955 as a Wing Commander with the O.B.E.

[20] Later Viscount Cherwell, P.C., C.H., F.R.S.

[21] As Sir Edward Appleton, G.B.E., K.C.B., F.R.S., he was to be awarded the Nobel Prize for Physics in 1947.

vital school); this was a "filter room" through which all radar plots passed before appearing on the Group operations table. The filter room staff would ultimately decide—from knowledge of all friendly aircraft movements—which plots should be labelled as being friendly and which otherwise.

The limited successes achieved during the 1937 Air Exercises prompted the Air Ministry to put in hand the construction of the remaining seventeen stations forthwith. Owing to the great improvement in the performance of the radar, it was found possible to increase the distance between stations, with the result that the seventeen stations could be located over a rather longer stretch of coast, namely from Land's End to just north of Newcastle, and included the following:

Dry Tree (Cornwall)	Pevensey	West Beckham
West Prawle	Rye	Stenigot
Worth Matravers	Dunkirk (Kent)	Staxton Wold
Ventnor	Bromley	Danby Beacon
Poling	High Street	Ottercops Moss
Truleigh	Stoke Holy Cross	

To this list would be added another twelve stations, covering the West and the North, before February 1940.

Before leaving the subject of the introduction of radar, it is convenient here to describe briefly the procedures adopted by which the raid information provided by the coastal radar was made available to Group controllers, and thus to the intercepting pilots.

Generally speaking the CH radar stations were located on the coast, where possible on high ground to achieve long range; some stations (notably Stoke Holy Cross near Norwich, and Ottercops Moss, north-west of Newcastle) were, however, situated well inland. They consisted fundamentally of a number of 350-foot transmitter aerial masts, 250-foot receiver aerial masts, a transmitter and a receiver block and a watch office in which were situated the radar displays. Radio signals were transmitted in all directions by several stacks of aerials so that in the event of an aircraft entering the area so covered by the transmissions, a proportion of the signals

Masts on a typical Chain Home (Air Ministry Experimental Station, A.M.E.S. Type 1) radar station. The transmitter aerials were suspended between the larger masts, the receiver aerials from the smaller. The Bawdsey station was operational in 1936, and 28 others had been completed on the East and South Coasts by 1940.

would be reflected back and received by the CH receivers. By measuring on a calibrated cathode ray tube in the watch office the elapsed time between transmission and reception, the range of the target could be displayed; by use of the goniometer, already mentioned, the target's bearing could be derived, and by switching in and out various of the vertically stacked transmitter aerials (each of which possessed known but differing vertical coverage characteristics) a fairly accurate indication of the target's height could be assessed. It was the latter procedure which demanded the greatest skill as the coverage characteristics were to some extent affected by anomalous propagation (caused by variations in the height of the ionised layers), so that throughout the War altitude information from CH radar was often regarded with some suspicion. Before the introduction of the goniometer, a single CH radar could thus not provide the position of an incoming raid—only a range. However, by passing this range to the Group Filter Room, where other range details from neighbouring CH radars would be received, a "range cut" would provide a raid position.

On sighting an incoming signal, the officer or N.C.O. on watch at the CH station would commence telling its range, strength (i.e. the estimated number of aircraft) and altitude to his Group Filter Room by means of a direct telephone link; this information would continue to flow to a filter plotter who would be awaiting information about the raid from one or more neighbouring CH stations; by drawing an arc at the relevant ranges this plotter was able to pass an immediate position to the operations room, where W.A.A.F. plotters, seated round an large table map, translated this information into visual plaques placed on a miniature rack beside a coloured arrow showing the direction of flight and the position of the plot on the table map. The raid would be allocated a serial number in the Filter Room and in turn be prefixed by the raid's identity, i.e. friendly, hostile or X-raid. Such a plot might thus be told as: "Charlie George two, one, three, zero (*map grid position*), north-east (*direction of flight*), hostile four, five (*raid's identity serial number*), three plus (*raid strength*) at one, six (*raid altitude in thousands of feet*)."

As the plot appeared on the table map, a teller, seated at a balcony overlooking the table, passed the plot to Fighter Command Operations Room (in cases of hostile raids) and to Sector Operations Rooms simultaneously. In all these operations rooms were exactly synchronised clocks whose faces were segmented in various colours, each segment covering a period lasting three minutes. The colour of the arrow placed on the filter and operations rooms tables corresponded to the colour being indicated by the minute hand of the colour clock, so that wherever that plot was subsequently passed the arrow's colour remained the same; in this way all controllers would, by reference to their own clocks, know how fresh the information being displayed was. In practice, W.A.A.F. plotters usually achieved four of five plots every minute and this was about the limit that one CH radar operator could accurately define.

Of course, as time passed, Group and Sector Controllers came to recognise that some radar stations were more accurate than others, and it became one of the main purposes of the Filter Room to eliminate duplicated plots from adjacent CH stations. By 1940 a system of "mental triangulation" by filter personnel was producing raid pictures of quite remarkable accuracy.

It is worth remarking here that the old CH radar stations (and the Chain Overseas) continued to render essential service to Fighter Command well into the jet age, but were dismantled in the 1950s.

Overland Tracking of Aircraft—The Observer Corps

The origins of visual reporting of aircraft over Britain lie in the year 1914 when the civil police were instructed by the Admiralty to report the presence of any aircraft flying within sixty miles of London. A year later this was extended to apply over the entire country. As might be expected this led to widespread congestion of the civil telephone network, so that early in 1917 the Army assumed this responsibility for aircraft reporting. As already mentioned in Chapter 1, personnel of low medical category so employed proved unsuitable (usually on account of sight or speech defects) with the result that the responsibility passed back to the civil police later the same year. With the formation of L.A.D.A. an extensive network of telephone communications linking police stations with operations rooms was established in 1918, but within seven months the Armistice was signed and the entire system was abandoned and dismantled.

With the setting up of the Fighting Area Defence System in 1923-24, it was realised that in deciding to meet hostile raids over the coastal belt no means existed by which enemy raids could be tracked as they crossed the coast. A committee was set up to make proposals to overcome this deficiency, and it was L.A.D.A.'s old commander, Major General E.B. Ashmore, a member of the committee, who took charge of a limited pilot scheme, using a small number of observer posts in Kent, linked to a control centre in the village post office at Cranbrook. Results of tracking were so promising that Ashmore was authorised to organise a similar network covering the whole of Kent and Sussex, with control centres at Maidstone and Horsham respectively. These two county areas came to be referred to as Nos. 1 and 2 Areas (later Groups). The observer personnel were volunteers and were enrolled as unpaid special constables and wore no uniform. The control centres were linked by telephone to Air Defence of Great Britian headquarters—but not to the fighter airfields. In the following year Ashmore established two more Groups so that, by the 1925 Air Exercises, one hundred posts in the South-East were manned.

In 1929 the Air Ministry took over control of the Observer Corps from the War Office[25] and provided for the post of Commandant to be filled by a retired Air Commodore. The first such Commandant was Air Commodore E.A.D. Masterman who was appointed on 1st March 1929[26] and retained the post until 1936, when his place was taken by Air Commodore

[25] Major-General Edward Ashmore, C.B., C.M.G., M.V.O., retired on the transfer of the Observer Corps to the Air Ministry in 1929. During the Battle of Britain this 68-year-old veteran of the Boer War raised and commanded a battalion of the Home Guard.
[26] Air Commodore Edward Masterman, C.B., C.M.G., C.B.E., A.F.C., had been commissioned in the Royal Navy at the turn of the century, but transferred to the R.N.A.S. on formation, becoming involved with the development of British rigid airships. After relinquishing the post of Commandant of the Observer Corps in 1936, he went on to command the Corps' Western Area whose headquarters were at Gloucester, and occupied this post during the Battle of Britain. He died on 26th August 1957.

A.D. Warrington-Morris[27]. With the assumption of control by the R.A.F., the observer control centres were linked to the Fighting Area airfields as follows: No. 1 Group, Maidstone, linked to R.A.F. Biggin Hill; No. 2 Group, Horsham, linked to R.A.F. Kenley; No. 3 Group, Winchester, linked to Tangmere; and No. 18 Group, Colchester, linked to R.A.F. North Weald. A fifth Group, No. 17, centred in Watford, came into existence in 1931.

The economic stringencies of the early 'thirties prevented further exapnsion of the Corps until German re-armament spurred renewed growth in 1935. A new sub-committee, under Air Commodore O.T. Boyd, O.B.E., M.C., A.F.C.[28], recommended the formation of eleven further Groups by 1939. As events transpired no fewer than 31 Groups had been activated by June 1940, and posts throughout the remainder of the country were manned by the end of that year.

The main function of the Observer Corps was to report the position and direction of flight of aircraft flying over the land—in other words the Corps took over the reporting of raid tracks as they crossed the coast and could no longer be told by the CH radar. The Corps was essentially divided between post observers and centre personnel—all of whom stoutly defended their volunteer status and independence of Service discipline.

The Observer posts, of which there were upwards of fifty in each Group (arranged in "clusters"), were rudimentary in the extreme, often consisting of nothing more than an open sandbagged platform situated in the middle of an otherwise anonymous field. The post observers' sole equipment consisted of binoculars, earphones and chest-mounted telephone, and an extraordinary piece of apparatus reminiscent of a rudimentary sextant. In fact this gadget was extremely efficient, combining simplicity with—given a modicum of experience—accuracy. It consisted of a circular chart of the post's locality, suitably superimposed with grid reference squares, in the centre of which was mounted a vertical, rotatable triangular frame. By estimating the aircraft's altitude and setting this on the vertical member of the frame and sighting the aircraft along the oblique member, the position of the aircraft was indicated by the base of the vertical member on the chart. Even if the aircraft's altitude could not be judged accurately, triangulation of two posts' bearings on the aircraft could be effected at the Group centre.

Having regard to the fact that these posts were manned round the clock throughout the War, one can only pay tribute to those men who braved all manner of discomforts (from atrocious weather to enemy bombs and gunfire) without the benefits of Service pay and amenities.

Their other duties included blackout supervision and the lighting of flares at night for the guidance of friendly aircraft on patrol or in difficulties.

The Observer Group Centres, invariably located in some convenient large building in a town or city, resembled a miniature operations room with plotters seated round a table map and overlooked by Observer officers and tellers. Overland plots were told to the Group Operations Room and, in specified cases, to the local Sector Station Operations Room. The senior Observer officer on watch at the Group Centre was in direct contact with an Observer Corps Liaison Officer at Group Operations, so that two-way communication could be maintained on such matters as the whereabouts of friendly fighters.

The vital work performed by this remarkable volunteer Corps, especially during the Battle of Britain and the Blitz, was recognised in 1941 by the award of the prefix "Royal". During the War its membership rose to 32,000, of whom 4,300 were women.

The Expansion Gains Momentum

Prior to 1935 all R.A.F. pilots were trained at Service stations, their flying course occupying about eleven months. Advanced training, including night flying, bombing, gunnery and formation flying, was carried out on their squadrons. As a result of Expansion Schemes "D" and "E", thirteen civil flying schools were approved to provide elementary training for new pilots (four such schools had for some time been giving instruction to Reserve pilots). During 1935 and 1936 five regular Flying Training Schools were opened to bring the total to eleven. A new training course, introduced in 1936, enabled all pilots to receive their instruction (including the applied flying) before reaching their squadrons, thus relieving the squadron of non-operational effort. This in turn allowed some fighter squadrons to dispense with one of their Flights to provide the nucleus of a new squadron.

The greatly increased number of aircraft and squadrons scheduled for the R.A.F. demanded an increase of 2,500 pilots by the beginning of April 1937. These were obtained by offering short service commissions to pilots, and this alone attracted 1,700 entrants; a further 800 N.C.O. pilots were recruited, while Australia, Canada, New Zealand and South Africa all increased their contribution of pilots to the R.A.F.

The Blenheim light bomber prototype, "Britain First", presented to the nation by Lord Rothermere. A promising aircraft at the time of its introduction into service with the R.A.F., it was quickly rendered obsolescent by the new generation of monoplane fighters such as the Messerschmitt Bf 109. It was also introduced into Fighter Command as an interim night fighter, pending the arrival of the Bristol Beaufighter, but achieved little success.

---

[27] Air Commodore Alfred Warrington-Morris, C.B., C.M.G., O.B.E., (a former England rugby international player, 1909) was thus Commandant of the Observer Corps during the Battle of Britain.

[28] As an Air Vice-Marshal, Boyd was appointed to command R.A.F. Balloon Command in November 1938, and occupied that post during the Battle of Britain. Shortly afterwards, in December 1940, his promising career was cut short when, after his appointment as Deputy A.O.C.-in-C., R.A.F. Middle East, the aircraft in which he was flying from Britain to Egypt ran short of fuel and landed in Sicily instead of Malta, and he was taken prisoner. The second choice for the appointment then fell to Air Vice-Marshal Arthur Tedder.

As already mentioned, the Royal Air Force Volunteer Reserve was created in 1936. By the following year 800 men would be undergoing flying training annually at thirteen training airfields selected close to large population centres throughout the country. The pilots, volunteers between 18 and 25 years of age, would receive week-end training for an annual retainer of £25; they would start as N.C.O. pilots and aircrew, but would be given the opportunity to enter the R.A.F. Reserve and also to attain commissioned rank. By 1939 no fewer than 310 Volunteer Reserve members were fully trained pilots in Fighter Command—of whom more than 200 were to fight in the Battle of Britain.

Another expedient announced by Viscount Swinton in April 1936 was the "shadow factory" scheme, evolved to make possible the rapid build-up of new aircraft and aero-engines then being ordered in very large quantities. This scheme was intended to provide factory space as a back-up for the aircraft industry by using the massive facilities of the motor car industry. To begin with, arrangements were made for the factories of Austin, Rover, Humber, Standard and Daimler to manufacture components of the Bristol Mercury radial engine—which powered the Gladiator, Blenheim and Lysander aircraft. The Fairey Battle was to be manufactured by the Austin Motor Company, and Blenheims by the Rootes Group. Rolls-Royce Ltd. established its own shadow factories at Crewe and Glasgow for the manufacture of Merlins for Hurricanes, Spitfires, Battles, Henleys and Fulmars (and later for Beaufighters, Whitleys, Lancasters and Mosquitos). Other factories switched to the production of propellers, munitions and components, so that by 1938 an enormous network of sub-contractors, large and small, had come into being; it is estimated that in that year the labour force engaged in the aircraft and shadow industry exceeded two million.

In 1937 Viscount Swinton presented Air Estimates which, for the first time, exceeded those for the Army. During the years 1935-37 the Royal Air Force and Fleet Air Arm had grown from 91 squadrons to 169, of which 123 were home-based. The number of first-line aircraft had risen to 2,031; however, *more than 80 per cent of these were obsolescent.*

The presence in strength returns of so high a proportion of interim and outdated aircraft—like the similar situation that existed in the *Luftwaffe* at the end of 1937—was caused by the lengthy delays encountered in re-tooling for metal monocoque construction in the factories. Production of both the Hurricane and Spitfire had run into delays owing to the decision to abandon the Rolls-Royce Merlin I (in fighter aircraft[29]), it being decided to concentrate on the Merlin II—necessitating extensive re-design of the nose of each aircraft.

Early in 1938 the shadow factory scheme ran into problems—most of which were politically inspired as the result of uncertainty with regard to the contractual obligations should the international tension ease. Owing to the ponderous Whitehall procedures for raising production contracts, a great deal of work was undertaken upon receipt of "Instructions to Proceed", the contracts being raised retrospectively. Many of the car factories became so committed to aircraft production that unpremeditated loss of such work could result in financial ruin. The difficulties were temporarily overcome through the recommendations of a powerful committee[30] on which served Air Council members, Treasury officials and Sir Charles Bruce-Gardner Kt., chairman of the Society of British Aircraft Constructors. The committee in effect empowered the Air Ministry to purchase direct from industry without lengthy consultation among other Whitehall departments; this speeded up the process of ordering and reduced the period of uncertainty so costly to an industry that had become utterly committed to defence contracts. While this innovation was undoubtedly most beneficial during the pre-War period, it had within two years acquired its own web of stultifying bureaucracy, so that in May 1940 a separate Ministry of Aircraft Production was brought into being under the dynamic leadership of Lord Beaverbrook.

---

[29] The existing production run of Merlin Is was henceforth confined to the Fairey Battle light bomber.

[30] Air Council Committee on Supply, 1938-39.

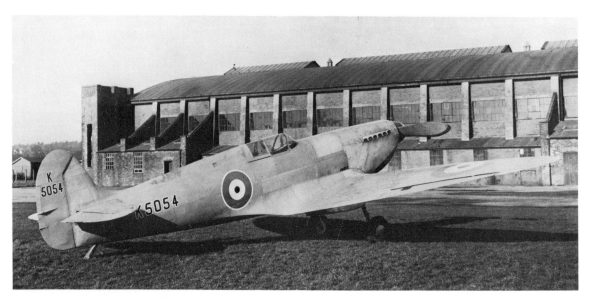

The prototype Spitfire, *K5054*, in a very early configuration; main undercarriage fairings have not been fitted and the aircraft features a tail skid. With its monocoque construction, it was "half a generation" later than the Hurricane, and joined the R.A.F. a year later than the Hawker fighter.

The first production Hurricane fighter, *L1547*. First flown in prototype form in November 1935, the Hurricane entered service with No. 111 Squadron at Northolt around Christmas, 1937. The aircraft pictured here actually flew in the Battle of Britain with a Czech squadron, and was lost in an accident on 10th October 1940. (Photo: Hawker Aircraft Ltd.)

Munich and the Eve of War

In September 1937 Fighter Command's most modern fighter was the four-gun Gladiator biplane, with which eight squadrons were fully equipped. The following month the British Government played host to the senior *Luftwaffe* staff officers, Milch, Udet and Stumpff, who were—astonishing to relate—given an official reception at Hornchurch, one of London's key defence airfields, where they were permitted to inspect Nos. 54 and 65 (Gladiator) Squadrons. Presumably no mention was made of the new generation of interceptors about to enter service with British fighter squadrons. Whether this was an extraordinary lapse of official security or a brilliantly-timed piece of deception will probably never be known.

As already mentioned, both the Hurricane and Spitfire had run into production delays. Moreover the Spitfire's brilliant designer, Reginald Mitchell, had died on 11th June 1937, his place as Chief Designer being taken by Joseph Smith. Development of the Merlin had been delayed through the demand to optimise the engine for conflicting power output requirements—for interceptors, long-range heavy bombers, dive-bombers and target tugs.

For all these setbacks, the first production Hurricane (*L1547*) emerged from the Brooklands assembly sheds on 12th October 1937, and was followed by a dozen more before the end of the year. With by far the greater bulk of Service development and clearance completed by using the prototype, four of these fighters were issued to the first Fighter Command Hurricane Squadron, No. 111, before Christmas. A further twelve were delivered during January and February 1938. No. 111 (Fighter) Squadron, commanded by Squadron Leader John Gillan, was based at Northolt; equipped with the first of the new generation of eight-gun monoplane fighters, it acquired an enviable reputation among Fighter Command pilots—its prestige further heightened when Gillan flew from Turnhouse, near Edinburgh, to Northolt in February at an average ground speed of 407.75 m.p.h., an achievement which, understandably, was far more widely publicised than

the strong tailwind enjoyed throughout the flight[31].

While five further squadrons (Nos. 3, 32, 56, 85 and 87) were converted to Hurricanes during the spring and summer of 1938, the parent company was hard at work improving the breed—investigating the development of metal stressed-skin wings, variable-pitch propellers, and even 20-mm. cannon armament. The first two of these developments were being incorporated in production aircraft before the outbreak of war, and two cannon-armed Hurricanes fought in the Battle of Britain, albeit with only modest success.

Despite all the efforts of the previous years, the Munich Crisis of September 1938 found Fighter Command still appallingly deficient in modern aircraft. The German staff officers had, in 1937, seen British squadrons wholly dependent upon biplane fighters, and the situation a year later was not substantially altered. Only three Hurricane squadrons were combat-ready, and the remaining sixteen operational squadrons were equipped with Gladiator, Gauntlet, Fury and Demon biplanes, while three other Hurricane squadrons were still engaged in converting to their new fighters and were not yet operational. One solitary Spitfire had been delivered to No. 19 Squadron at Duxford.

Whatever moral implications must be drawn from the political fiasco of Munich, and however shamefacedly one may regard the "accomplishment" of Neville Chamberlain, any fair judgement must be accompanied by an assessment of British fighter defences at that time; and that assessment must be made with the knowledge—which British politicians possessed at that time—of the current equipment of the *Legion Cóndor* and its combat experience in Spain. That is not to suggest that a German air attack could have, or would have been launched against Britain in the autumn of 1938; but had the events that took place over Southern England in the summer of 1940 been advanced by one year the results for Britain must have been catastrophic.

Deliveries of the long-awaited Spitfire, that most emo-

---

[31] Cf. *The Hawker Hurricane*, Mason, Aston, Bourne End, 1987.

tively-named fighter of all time, accelerated immediately after Munich, to the great satisfaction of Fighter Command and, indeed of the nation. No. 19 Squadron, commanded by Squadron Leader Henry Iliffe Cozens, had been equipped with Gauntlets longer than any other and, in deciding to re-equip this unit with Spitfires, it was also considered logical to concentrate all the new fighters at specific bases, rather than to mingle Hurricanes and Spitfires on the same airfield. By this policy it was intended that squadrons should benefit from mutual exchange of training and maintenance facilities. This designation of specific "Spitfire bases" was to establish a useful precedent in the short term, though one that was to impose a limit on the tactical deployment of the excellent fighter during the Battle of Britain, tending to concentrate, as it did, the repair and maintence facilities for a fighter with stressed-skin monocoque structure at a limited number of airfields. By contrast, the Hurricane, being much simpler to maintain and repair after battle, was free to operate from almost any R.A.F. airfield if the need arose.

No. 19 Squadron's Duxford partner, No. 66 Squadron, commenced deliveries of its Spitfires in October 1938, and by early the following year both were fully-equipped and well advanced in their efforts to become fully operational. It was intended that Hornchurch should be No. 11 Group's first Spitfire base but, as No. 41 Squadron at Catterick had been

warned of a possible move south, this was the next unit to be re-equipped. The move did not take place, and the next three Spitfire Squadrons, Nos. 74, 75 and 65 (equipped in that order during the spring of 1939) were all based at Hornchurch. It is significant that these first five squadrons were the Spitfire squadrons most heavily engaged in the Battle of Britain, and this probably reflects the length of time found necessary to work up to full combat proficiency on the new fighter. There were also still problems to be overcome with the Spitfire, and although these (principally concerned with gun heating and cockpit misting after descending from high altitude) did not cause delays in the delivery of aircraft, they tended to slow the process of reaching full operational proficiency. In the mean-time altitude restrictions were placed on gun-firing in the squadrons.

The Hurricane had also encountered problems of spin-recovery early in 1938, but these were fairly quickly over-come by incorporating a ventral spine fairing under the rear fuselage, and deliveries were not slowed for more than three weeks. By the end of 1938 eleven squadrons had received Hurricanes, and all but two, Nos. 43 and 151, had been declared "fully operational by day and night".

So smoothly was conversion training progressing (from the old biplanes to aircraft more than 100 m.p.h. faster) that it was decided to transfer most of the Auxiliary Air Force squad-rons—previously attached to Bomber and Army Co-opera-tion Commands—to Fighter Command. The first of these, Nos. 501 (County of Gloucester) and 504 (County of Notting-ham), received their Hurricanes early in 1939.

The Hurricane and Spitfire were thus Fighter Command's main weapons. There were, however, two other types of inter-ceptor which had retained their places in the defence system down the years—the two-seat fighter and the night fighter. Specifications for the former category, epitomised in turn by the Bristol Fighter and the Hawker Demon, had been issued to the aircraft industry in 1935. Several designs had been

The Defiant prototype, *K8310*. Repeated difficulties seriously delayed the turret fighter's introduction to squadron service and only three had been delivered by the outbreak of war. (Photo: Flight International). The only competitor at the design stage was the Hawker Hotspur (*top*), but this aircraft was compromised from the outset owing to the Air Ministry's insistence that nothing should "sidetrack" Hawker's production of the Hurricane; had the Hotspur been selected, it would have been built by A.V. Roe & Co., Ltd.

The pre-War years of expansion also witnessed the establishment of new fighter airfields. This picture of the airfield at Warmwell was taken in 1938, yet it was not declared fully operational until shortly after the beginning of the Battle of Britain when its value as a fighter station for the defence of the Portland naval base came to be appreciated.

tendered, and prototypes ordered from Hawker and Boulton-Paul; the latter company had taken over sub-contract production of the Demon. The design submitted by Sydney Camm at Hawker was for an aircraft named the Hotspur, intended to be capable of employing the same outer wings and other components as the Hurricane (and, indeed, the Henley dive-bomber[32]). It was, however, Hawker's pre-occupation with the Hurricane that critically delayed the Hotspur prototype,

[32] The Henley had been a promising aircraft intended to initiate close support tactics on the battlefield. It had few vices, and it has been suggested with some authority that it came to be relegated to target-towing simply on account of the anathema which attached to dive-bombing at the time. This official hysteria must seem extraordinary when written in the pages of history, and was sparked by current British revulsion against Japanese and German use of the weapon in China and Spain. The Fleet Air Arm Skua was to some extent a victim of the same self-righteous fantasy, yet went on to sink the German cruiser *Königsberg* in Bergen harbour in 1940!

and the Boulton-Paul Defiant two-seat turret fighter prototype flew first on 11th August that year. In the prevailing atmosphere of urgency (as well as some reluctance to divert any attention from the Hurricane at Kingston), the Defiant was accepted by the Air Ministry for production.

The two-seat Defiant was an anachronism—in effect the product of the ancient tactical thinking evolved through the interception of the slow, unescorted bombers and airships of the First World War; in those conditions it proved entirely possible to fly alongside the raiders while the rear-seat gunner raked them with his gun or guns. As time passed, no account was taken of the extreme manœuvrability of modern single-seaters and, unlike even the Demon, the Defiant possessed no forward-firing guns. The Defiant's tactics against bombers, painfully evolved by Fighter Command, depended upon complicated and ponderous converging, cross-over and diving beam attacks, and even the relatively heavy concentration of fire-power in the power-operated turret was so positioned

Hawker Furies of No. 43 Squadron (the "Fighting Cocks") at the time of the Munich Crisis. The aircraft feature the dark earth and green camouflage on their upper surfaces, and black and white undersurfaces. The officer pilots wore white overalls while the N.C.O. pilots were provided with Sidcot suits—a peacetime differential soon to disappear.

that no advantage could be achieved during the run-up to the target. More distressing was the difficulty experienced by the gunner in the event of his need to bale out; it was found that, if the aircraft's electrical system was damaged, the turret jammed in such a position as to render escape impossible. The first Defiants did not enter operational service until March 1940.

In the field of night fighting, Dowding's Command still relied in 1938 upon the age-old formula of training daylight line fighter squadrons to fly at night in conjunction with ground searchlights, although to some extent this expedient was extended by giving certain day squadrons a specific secondary rôle of night interception. Already, however, the Bristol Blenheim was under consideration as a night fighter— on introduction to Bomber Command in 1937 the Mark I had shown itself to be a tractable light bomber with a speed (260 m.p.h.) at least greater than that of the Gladiator. Perhaps the Blenheim has in the past been unfairly criticised and ridiculed as a fighter, yet it did represent a sensible expedient in the absence of foresight in the years 1935-36. And it should be remembered that the German air force—albeit unknown to the R.A.F.—had virtually ignored the matter of night fighting altogether, and continued to do so until 1940.

During 1938 the Blenheim was converted to the night fighting rôle by deletion of the bomb doors and substitution of a gun pack (manufactured by the Southern Railway Company at its Ashford workshops) containing four Browning 0.303-inch machine guns. In little more than a year this version had been issued to Nos. 23, 25, 29, 145, 219, 600 and 604 Squadrons as the Blenheim Mark IF. Perhaps its most lasting claim to fame was provided by its airborne radar

First Squadron to be equipped with Spitfires was No. 19, based at Duxford. Photographed in 1939, the aircraft carried the squadron number (in Flight colours) on their fins; by the outbreak of War these numerals had been replaced by Squadron code letters on the fuselage.

installation, four aircraft of No. 25 Squadron being equipped with rudimentary "breadboard"[33] interception sets in 1939— the world's first installation of airborne radar and forerunner of a whole new concept of air defence. It was not until the Battle of Britain, however, that the Blenheim intercepted and destroyed its first victim at night using radar.

Thus by mid-1939 Fighter Command was at last approaching the strength deemed necessary to defend Britain against an air attack by Germany. The introduction of its new fighters was proceeding smoothly, although running almost six months behind schedule. The amalgamation of Auxiliary Squadrons within Fighter Command had enhanced their prestige and recruiting had surged forward accordingly. The new fighter airfields were being activated at a most satisfactory rate, and the sector station network was virtually complete throughout Nos. 11 and 12 Groups (then commanded respectively by Air Vice-Marshal Ernest Leslie Gossage[34] and Air Vice-Marshal Trafford Leigh Leigh-Mallory[35]). The old-established coastal airfields at Hawkinge and Lympne were reduced in operational status, although the former would inevitably continue to represent a vital forward operating airfield for its sector station, Biggin Hill. Manston, with its extensive facilities, remained a fighter base although, being in an exposed position, was not designated as a sector station. The airfields at Tangmere, Biggin Hill, Hornchurch and Kenley were established as cornerstones of the defence system in the South-East, and remained as such throughout the Second World War.

As the international situation deteriorated during the late summer, the fighter squadrons redoubled their training efforts; armament practice camp—traditionally providing a fine spell of sport and flying recreation—assumed a new and earnest significance. A new ground syllabus was introduced in aircraft recognition—German aircraft recognition.

Yet Dowding remained ill at ease, haunted by an apparently extraneous defence responsibility he knew he could ill afford to assume—namely the defence of a British Expeditionary Force to be sent to France should war break out with Germany. Ever since the mid-'twenties, when such a force was mooted, the provision of continental based R.A.F. fighters— though mandatory by agreement—had been brushed aside during the planning of British defence Estimates. Now, with the reality of war facing both France and Britain, this demand for air cover overseas threatened to deprive Fighter Command of much of its hard-earned strength. And as Bomber Command engaged in a series of air raid exercises in collaboration with L'Armée de l'Air, the French High Command sought from Britain a firm assurance that a force of not less than six fighter squadrons would be despatched to France immediately war broke out. Nor yet had Fighter Command achieved the level of 52 squadrons calculated years before as being the strength necessary for the air defence of Great Britain. . .

[33] Latterday sobriquet for equipment assembled in exposed ad hoc fashion without recourse to "black boxes" and ordered layout.

[34] Later Air Marshal Sir Leslie Gossage, K.C.B., C.V.O., D.S.O., M.C. This officer, on appointment to the Air Council in 1940, was succeeded at No. 11 Group by the New Zealander, Air Vice-Marshal Keith Park, M.C., D.F.C., who was to command the key defence area during the Battle of Britain.

[35] Later Air Chief Marshal Sir Trafford Leigh Leigh-Mallory, K.C.B., C.B., D.S.O.

CHAPTER 5

THE WORLD AT WAR

> "I have done my best, in the past few years to make our *Luftwaffe* the largest and most powerful in the World. The creation of the Greater German Reich has been made possible largely by the strength and constant readiness of the Air Force. Born in the spirit of the German airmen of the First World War, inspired by faith in our Führer and Commander-in-Chief—thus stands the German Air Force today, ready to carry out every command of the Führer with lightning speed and undreamed-of might."
>
> *Reichsmarshall Hermann Göring,*
> *Order of the Day No. 130, August 1939*

Evil is a word which has lost its ancient strength in the environment of twentieth-century political adventures; yet the motives which spurred Adolf Hitler on in his treacherous depredations against his European neighbours were evil, and his means were brutal. Despite repeated denials of territorial ambition, and lip service to the cause of peace[1]—and despite a calculated risk of World War involving Britain and France—Hitler turned his attention in mid-1939 to the long-standing aggravation of Polish nationhood, demanding the cession of Danzig and an intermediate corridor on the pretext of liberating German subjects from Polish subjugation.

Not even the treaties of alliance between Poland, France and Britain deterred Hitler from ordering the deployment of five Armies on the eastern frontier towards the end of August; he simply didn't believe that the Western Powers would go to war over Poland. When Poland finally rejected the German demands, a cynical farce was played out involving a border incident faked by the *SD*, and the subsequent "discovery" of bodies in Polish uniforms[2]; and having made this brief gesture to public opinion, Hitler unleashed those five Armies, supported by *Luftflotten 1* and *4*, in an all-out attack and invasion of Poland along the entire length of her borders with Germany, Austria and Czechoslovakia on 1st September. In a forlorn gesture, Neville Chamberlain issued his ultimatum to Germany, and two days later declared war. The French Government followed suit immediately; and Europe was at war.

The Polish campaign realised the worst fears of the prophets of total war. What began as a textbook invasion and occupation swiftly deteriorated into an appalling exercise of Douhet's doctrines; the shape of warfare first seen in Spain was now projected on to a larger screen, and combined with the bitterest type of nationalist feelings.

Fundamental to the success of Germany's campaign was the devastating efficiency of the *Luftwaffe*. Early on the first day almost every Polish airfield was covered by reconnaissance, and this was quickly followed by massive attacks by Heinkel He 111s, Dornier Do 17s and Junkers Ju 87s on the

Under the watchful eyes of a Henschel Hs 126 short range reconnaissance aircraft, a column of German trucks and armour slashes through the French countryside.

airfields at Cracow, Lublin, Lwow, Radom, Kattowicz and Warsaw. Such a measure of surprise was achieved that scarcely any opposition was encountered, and the damage inflicted was crippling. Isolated attacks by Polish interceptors (obsolescent P.Z.L. P-11s) were easily brushed aside by the swarms of Messerschmitt Bf 109s. German air superiority was quickly raised to air supremacy, and this was never again seriously disputed.

Realising that to deploy their aircraft on the major airfields was to court disaster, the Poles dispersed their surviving fighters and bombers to much smaller fields, but in the absence of established communications their future resistance was necessarily disjointed, albeit of tremendous cour-

---

[1] Cf. Hitler's *Reichstag* speech of 28th April 1939 describing rumours of a planned invasion of Poland as "mere inventions of the international Press".

[2] A simulated attack on the Gleiwitz radio station near the Polish border, ordered by Reinhard Heydrich and executed by an *SD* agent named Alfred Naujocks.

(Top) A PZL P.11C fighter of the Polish Air Force's No. 141 "Wild Ducks" Squadron, shortly before the War. (Below) A German officer inspects the wreckage of a Polish P.23 *Karas* light bomber of No. 42 Squadron.

age and tenacity. Miracles of improvisation were performed, and a surprisingly high proportion of damaged fighters were put back into the air from the dispersed and ill-equipped airstrips. Post-War research showed that the fighters survived the early bombing attacks with fewer losses than other types of unit; of a total of 166 fighters of all types, no less than 116 were in fact destroyed in air combat during the first four or five days of fighting.

In the absence of powerful opposition, the *Luftwaffe* was able to demonstrate to the world the terrible efficiency of its weapons and tactics. By the third day, the day on which Britain declared war, the *Luftwaffe* considered the Polish Air Force to have been annihilated; this was not strictly accurate, but with a superiority of ten to one in numbers, and five years in quality, the German airmen had no need to avoid combat and could concentrate on support of the Army. While tactical formations of Ju 87s and Henschel Hs 123s bombed strong points and artillery batteries in direct support of advancing ground forces, escorted bombers roamed the Polish skies, raiding arms and fuel dumps, railway stations and bridges, factories and barracks. It was a campaign performed with unprecedented efficiency, with second-line *Luftwaffe* units transporting supplies for the rapidly advancing armoured divisions, as well as moving airfield staffs and ground crews forward to newly captured airstrips. The front line fighting was characterised by the constant swarms of German reconnaissance aircraft reporting Polish dispositions to the ground forces.

By 17th September the campaign seemed to be approaching its conclusion, with the Polish forces no longer offering a cohesive resistance, and the fall of Warsaw imminent. On this day the *Luftwaffe* began moving some operational units out of Poland to rest and refit in preparation for transfer to the West. Yet the Warsaw garrison refused to admit defeat, and for eight days withstood all German attacks. On 25th September, under cover of continuous bombing from the air, the final assault was launched. Two days later the city fell, and Poland's epic resistance ended—for a time. The front line

troops of the *Wehrmacht* were quickly replaced in many areas by second-line occupation units, including the sinister cohorts of the S.S. Police. The end of the fighting signalled the beginning of Poland's long crucifixion.

It must be stated at this point that the campaign had been opened with strict adherence to the principle of air attacks on military targets only; but, as has so often been demonstrated since, it is in the nature of modern warfare involving air support of swiftly advancing troops that the civilian population inevitably becomes the most tragic victim. Refugees in their tens of thousands flooded on to the roads and railways, and were thus exposed to the rain of bombs legitimately aimed at Polish lines of communication. One must therefore be cautious in apportioning blame for the horrors which undoubtedly accompanied this first demonstration of *blitzkrieg*—cautious, that is, when considering the assault phase of the invasion. The huge casualties among Polish civilians after the essential military objectives had been achieved are not open to question; they occurred in flagrant violation of all written and unwritten conventions of international conduct, and they are forever inexcusable.

The extraordinarily effective functioning of all arms of the *Luftwaffe* in the Polish campaign now provided a rich dividend of fear among Germany's other enemies. The dive-bomber units had been particularly remarkable, both in their military and psychological success. Without significant fighter opposition, they had been used with unnerving accuracy against small but vital targets in the path of the Panzer formations. However, the enormous propaganda effect of these operations actually back-fired on Germany; as will be shown in due course, Göring's supreme confidence in the dive-bomber blinded him to later developments. When the Stuka was thrown into action against targets defended by strong forces of interceptors, the *Reichsmarschall* was simply unable to believe that the scourge of Poland was in significant danger—until the lesson was brutally hammered home[3].

The Norwegian Campaign

After the conclusion of the Polish Campaign, the combat units of Löhr's *Luftflotte 4* and Kesselring's *Luftflotte 1* were withdrawn to their winter quarters to rest, re-equip and expand. In order to maintain the necessary rate of expansion for the proposed invasion of Western Europe during the spring of 1940, units based on the Western Front facing France's Maginot Line were forbidden to seek combat, while operations against Britain were limited to armed reconnaissance and occasional light attacks on ports and naval units.

Before this major westward assault, however, it was decided to secure Germany's northern flank by the occupation of Denmark and Norway. Political as well as strategic considerations influenced the decision to attack Norway, not least

---

[3] Total German aircraft and *Luftwaffe* personnel losses from all causes in the Polish campaign, as disclosed by *Oberbefehlshaber der Luftwaffe Genst.Gen.Qu./6 Abteilung/40.g.Kdos.IC*, were reported as being 203 aircraft, although as close an examination as possible of the individual losses indicates that 48 of these were subsequently classified as "less than 60% damaged", indicating that the aircraft were recovered and subsequently repaired. 221 aircrew were killed, 133 wounded and 218 listed as Missing. (See Introduction to Part 2 of this work).

the desire to safeguard vital supply routes from the far north for German iron ore shipments from Sweden via Narvik. It is perhaps ironic that at about the same time that German forces were moving against South Norway, Britain herself was assembling a task force to land at Narvik, with the object of depriving Germany of this port. Furthermore the R.A.F. was secretly investigating the possibility of using Norwegian airfields for operations against the enemy[4].

Although the Norwegian campaign scarcely extended the limited German forces employed—from all three Services—it is worth outlining the progress of the operation, as it brought British fighters into bitter confrontation with the *Luftwaffe* for the first time, as well as being the means by which Germany secured important bases for operations against Britain a few months hence. The nature of the German operation against Norway demanded complete integration of Army, Navy and Air Force planning; an integration which was achieved with considerable success. The air component was *Fliegerkorps X*, commanded by Generalleutnant Hans Geiseler and comprising approximately 1,000 aircraft:

Heinkel He 111, Dornier Do 17 bombers	290
Junkers Ju 52/3m, Ju 90 transport aircraft	500
Messerschmitt Bf 109E fighters	30
Messerschmitt Bf 110C *zerstörer*	70
Junkers Ju 87B and Ju 87R dive-bombers	40
Reconnaissance and maritime aircraft	70

The invasion was launched shortly after 05.00 hours on 9th April 1940 with the simultaneous advance by land forces into Denmark and seaborne landings on the Danish islands and in Norwegian ports. The Danish airfields of Aalborg East and Aalborg West fell to paratroops a few hours later; the carefully timed activities of a few strategically placed collaborators, and demonstrations by massed aircraft *en route* for Norway had the desired effect, and Denmark fell in a day with scarcely any resistance. The meagre and archaically equipped Danish forces could have done nothing but commit mass suicide even if warning had been forthcoming.

Also assaulted and captured on the first day were the vital airfields at Oslo-Fornebu, Oslo-Kjeller and Stavanger-Sola, on which German transports quickly landed with troops and supplies. The tiny Royal Norwegian Air Force was taken completely by surprise and was able to offer only token opposition; a pathetic handful of Gloster Gladiator pilots put up a gallant and desperate fight until, one by one, they were shot down or crashed. On the second day Trondheim-Vaernes airfield was captured, as was the small landing ground at Kristiansand; the latter airfield was quickly occupied by three *Staffeln* of Bf 109Es.

As stated above the British were already far advanced with their preparations for an expeditionary force, and this made an unopposed landing at Narvik on 15th April, which was followed by further landings at Namsos and Andalsnes in Central Norway during the next three days. Accompanying the landing forces at Andalsnes was a single R.A.F. Squadron

of Gladiators, No. 263, commanded by Squadron Leader John Donaldson. Benefiting from the survey work carried out by Straight, the Gladiators flew forward to the frozen Lake Lesjaskog and set up a base there to cover British infantry forces advancing inland to meet the Germans. Unfortunately the frozen lake was under constant scrutiny by German reconnaissance aircraft and it was not long before the bombs came raining down to smash the ice. Furthermore, appallingly undermanned and ill-equipped as it was, the British squadron was scarcely able to defend itself, let alone provide any cover for the local ground forces. Within three days the surviving Gladiators were dispersed to neighbouring makeshift landing grounds, and finally destroyed (owing to lack of fuel) to prevent their capture. The pilots returned home to re-equip; they had, at least, drawn blood in their brief operations against the *Luftwaffe*.[5]

Ill-planned and chaotic—partly redeemed by the courage of individuals—was to be the pattern for the whole Norwegian campaign; and this did not only apply to the Royal Air Force. With the evacuation of the small R.A.F. contingent from Central Norway, air cover for the withdrawal of the British ground forces was provided, to a limited extent by the Fleet Air Arm; and the fact that this withdrawal was accomplished without serious loss was largely attributable to the fact that the *Luftwaffe* was not yet fully experienced in night bombing. By early May the only British foothold in Norway was at Narvik, far to the north; and in view of their military commitments elsewhere, this presence was to cause the Germans some embarrassment.

As Norwegian resistance in the south of the country was overcome, and *Fliegerkorps* X established permanent operational bases at Oslo-Fornebu and Stavanger-Sola, so it became necessary to create an entirely new *Luftflotte* to man this new outpost of the German empire. *Luftflotte 5* was formed in northern Germany in mid-April, shortly afterwards moving its Staff to Oslo; command of this new Air Fleet was vested in Generaloberst Stumpff; he was to hold this appointment until January 1944.

It was with the German plan for the invasion of the Low Countries and France (timed for 10th May) in mind that Hitler personally ordered Stumpff to step up his air attacks on the Narvik enclave on 5th May; this task necessitated a 40 per cent increase in aircraft strength, including the acquisition of an additional *Kampfgeschwader* of Heinkel He 111s.

At this stage Britain had every intention of maintaining the stand at Narvik; and No. 263 (Fighter) Squadron, re-equipped with eighteen new Gladiators, embarked in H.M.S. *Glorious* which set sail on 14th May. They were followed ten days later by No. 46 (Fighter) Squadron, commanded by Squadron Leader Kenneth Cross, with Hawker Hurricanes. In the dull, cold Arctic light these few fighters flew guard over the Narvik perimeter in face of increasing German pressure, operating

---

[4] Whitney Straight, a well-known British sporting pilot, was working in secret collaboration with Norwegian Air Force authorities, and his work was turned to useful effect when the British landed in Central Norway. At this time given the acting rank of Squadron Leader, he reverted to Pilot Officer when afterwards posted to No. 601 Squadron, late in the Battle of Britain.

[5] Early in 1940 No. 263 Squadron had been preparing to embark for Finland to assist in the defence of that country against Russia. This squadron was selected as it, like the Finns, still flew Gladiators, and the spares and servicing situation would thus be eased. The preparations were incomplete when the Russo-Finnish War (the "Winter War") ended, and No. 263, partly equipped for operations in the Arctic Circle, was ordered to Norway; it was transported in the carrier H.M.S. *Glorious*. In this first expedition, its pilots destroyed six German aircraft for the loss of all eighteen Gladiators—all of which were destroyed on the ground. Cf. *The Gloster Gladiator*, Mason, Macdonald, London, 1963.

under extreme difficulties and suffering from inadequate supplies. It was a forlorn venture; despite numerous individual successes against German aircraft, the British fighters were obviously doomed to be overwhelmed by sheer weight of numbers, operating as they were far out of range of home-based bombers. Accordingly, on 3rd June the evacuation of Narvik began, covered by the Hurricanes and Gladiators. On the 7th the two squadron commanders were ordered to destroy their aircraft and embark their personnel; but arguing that they should be allowed to bring their aircraft home, they gained permission to fly them on to H.M.S. *Glorious*—a feat they accomplished despite the absence of deck landing gear and the fact that none of the pilots had made a deck landing before. Tragically, the carrier was forced by shortage of fuel to steer a direct course for home, which brought it face to face with the German capital ships, *Scharnhorst* and *Gneisenau*. Inside two hours the *Glorious* had disappeared below the waves, taking with her almost the entire crew, all the fighter aircraft and all but two of the pilots[6].

On 10th June the Norwegian campaign ended. Apart from the Narvik setback[7], the operation had once more proved the superiority of the German armed forces. The relative impunity with which the German Navy had operated off the Norwegian coast (again excepting Narvik) threw British claims of naval superiority open to question, while in the air a serious deficiency in equipment was displayed by the lack of long-range fighters. The British Army, too, had shown that while spirit and determination were high, training and equipment were wholly inadequate for any campaign involving amphibian operations at short notice. In all three Services the experience had been costly, at a time when every man, every gun and every machine were desperately needed at home.

For the Germans, the securing of Norway provided air and naval bases which were to play vital parts in the Battle of the Atlantic and the operations against the North Cape Convoys. To some extent they would also feature as flank bases in the Battle of Britain.

The Main Attack in the West

There is ample evidence to indicate that as early as the winter of 1939-40 Hitler entertained a determination to move against Soviet Russia; but having drawn both France and Britain into the War by his invasion of Poland, he dared not embark on simultaneous campaigns against powerful adversaries on two fronts. Therefore, while maintaining at least the semblance of non-aggressive intentions towards Stalin, the Führer ordered massive planning for the elimination of the potential threat to his western frontiers. It is certain that, while keeping an open mind on the best conduct of future operations against Great Britain, he was spurred on by an emotional determination to humiliate and crush France. Like many of his race, Hitler had a deep and cancerous grudge against his Continental neighbour which went back to French attitudes at Versailles.

Prior to May 1940, a general preoccupation with events in

Poland and Scandinavia had brought about a stagnation of the military situation in the West, with a tactical stalemate existing between the Siegfried and Maginot Lines. A straightforward frontal assault upon the latter was clearly out of the question, involving the appalling risk of a return to the static trench warfare which had claimed millions of lives twenty-five years earlier. In any case, the whole of Germany's new forces were built around the concept of mobility and flexible firepower, while France had to a large extent clung to the "fortress mentality", and would have an immediate advantage in operations of that type. Unencumbered by any moral misgivings about the violation of neutral territory, Hitler and his generals prepared a brilliantly audacious plan for a lightning armoured thrust through the Low Countries into Northern France, with the object of destroying the French and British armies north of the Somme and Aisne—thereby turning the flank of the Maginot defences—and driving south towards Paris.

The risks attending a thrust on such a narrow front were formidable, and success would depend to a large extent upon the use of air power in constant and crushing support of the ground forces—in effect, a 24-hour "creeping barrage" from the air. The German air forces employed were provided by *Luftflotte 2*, under the Generaloberst Kesselring, and *Luftflotte 3* commanded by Generaloberst Sperrle:

Luftflotte 2

Fliegerkorps I	In support of Army Group B
Fliegerkorps IV	in the North, commanded by
Fliegerdivision IX	General von Bock

Luftflotte 3

Fliegerkorps II	In support of Army Group C
Fliegerkorps V	on the Central Front, com-
Fliegerkorps VIII	manded by General von
	Rundstedt

Between them these air fleets mustered almost 4,000 aircraft, out of Germany's first line strength of nearly 5,000; their comparative strengths in the various arms were as follows:

Long-range bombers	1,120
Dive-bombers	358
Long-range fighters	248
Single-engine fighters	1,016
Long-range reconnaissance	300
Short-range reconnaissance	340
Transports	475
Gliders	45
	————
Total	3,902

In outlining the Allied air forces opposing this formidable array, it is necessary to digress briefly and return to September 1939. In accordance with Britain's agreement with France, the declaration of war on 3rd September led to the assembly of an expeditionary force, which sailed for France within the first week of hostilities. In support of this British Expeditionary Force (B.E.F.) the R.A.F. was called upon to provide two distinct air groups; the Air Component, based in the extreme North-East of France, whose purpose was to provide direct cover and support for the B.E.F.; and the Advanced Air

---

[6] Squadron Leader K.B.B. Cross and Flight Lieutenant P.G. Jameson survived many hours on a Carley float, to be rescued and brought home. Five other Hurricane pilots and six from No. 263 Squadron returned home safely aboard other ships.

[7] It is significant that throughout the War, *Narvik* was a jealously prized battle honour among the involved units of all three German Services.

Striking Force (A.A.S.F.), largely composed of medium-range light bombers—Fairey Battles and Bristol Blenheims—together with its own token fighter escort force.

Understandably, Dowding was reluctant to spare fighter squadrons from his own Command in view of the slow build-up achieved with the Hurricane and Spitfire. Nevertheless, in meeting the minimum requirement he despatched four Hurricane Squadrons during September, Nos. 85 and 87 forming the fighter element of the Air Component, and Nos. 1 and 73 accompanying the A.A.S.F. Choice of the Hurricane was fortuitous as it was soon evident that the poor airfield surfaces in France demanded sturdy, wide-track undercarriages—a characteristic of the Hurricane's design, but absent in the Spitfire.

The reluctance of the *Luftwaffe* to join battle over the Western Front during the early months of the War gave little opportunity for the Hurricane pilots to gain combat experience, and interceptions were rare. In deference to constant demands by the French Cabinet for the strengthening of British forces in France, Dowding was instructed to send further squadrons during the autumn; and two Auxiliary units, Nos. 607 (County of Durham) and 615 (County of Surrey) Squadrons, both equipped with Gladiators, were despatched from Croydon on 15th November to join the Air Component.

Thus, up to the beginning of May 1940, the average daily R.A.F. fighter strength in France was approximately forty Hurricanes and twenty Gladiators. Numerically this was indeed a small force compared with the strength of *Armée de l'Air* fighter units. The serviceable strength of French fighter squadrons on 10th May has been established as follows:

278 Morane-Saulnier MS 406

Standard French equipment, serving with eleven *Groupes de Chasse*. Top speed, 304 m.p.h.; armament of two machine guns and one 20-mm. cannon.

36 Dewoitine D.520

Serving with one *Groupe de Chasse*, this was unquestionably the best French fighter, with a top speed of 334 m.p.h.; armament of four machine guns and one 20-mm. cannon.

140 Bloch MB 151 and 152

A disappointing design, inadequately developed, the Bloch served with seven *Groupes de Chasse*; top speeds, 276 and 288 m.p.h., respectively; and armaments of four machine guns, or two machine guns and two 20-mm. cannon.

98 Curtiss Hawk 75A

Ordered from America during 1938, and serving with four *Groupes de Chasse*. Top speed, 313 m.p.h.; armament four machine guns.

By comparison with the R.A.F.'s Hurricane I (in its latest form, i.e., with metal wings and constant speed propeller), only the Dewoitine was of comparable combat quality, while the Morane-Saulnier was roughly equivalent to the early Hurricanes with 2-blade, fixed-pitch propellers—which had almost disappeared from the Squadrons in France by May 1940. The Bloch 152, however, despite its poor speed, proved to be an adequate "bomber destroyer" owing to its two cannon; nevertheless it was extremely vulnerable to the German fighter escorts, so the French pilots would have

One of the few *Luftwaffe* aircraft shot down over Britain during the "phoney war" —1H+EH, a Heinkel He 111H of 1./KG 26, brought down after raiding shipping in the Firth of Forth on 10th February 1940.

difficulty in reaching the enemy bombers. . .

The Dutch and Belgian air forces added small numbers of obsolescent Fokker D.XXIs, Gladiator Is, Hurricane Is and Fiat CR.42 biplanes to this total. Thus it will be clear that, of the 650-odd Allied fighters facing the *Luftwaffe* in May 1940, none could match the performance of the superb Messerschmitt Bf 109—while the German bombers could outstrip almost two-thirds of the Allied fighter force[8].

The blow fell at first light on 10th May, when more than 300 Heinkel and Dornier bombers of six *Kampfgeschwader* launched heavy co-ordinated raids on twenty-two airfields in Holland, Belgium and North-East France. Long-range attacks were carried out on French rail centres and on the bomber bases at Dijon, Lyon, Metz, Nancy and Romilly. Within hours, the Dutch and Belgian air forces had virtually ceased to exist.

In the Netherlands, eight Fokker G-1As (excellent twin-engine heavy fighters) managed to take off from Waalhaven to intercept the raiders, their pilots claiming the destruction of fourteen German aircraft; by that evening, however, only one Fokker survived. The little D.XXI single-seat monoplanes were flown with enormous courage by a handful of Dutch pilots, retreating across the country and mounting operations continuously until hostilities ended on the 14th; but after the first day they were never able to muster more than about a dozen aircraft, and their sacrifice could not alter the course of events. Everywhere the story was the same. Following the airfield attacks, the Germans launched crushing airborne landings, occupying key points throughout the country. Transport aircraft were flown into the three main airfields at The Hague, and airborne infantry were brought in by large Heinkel

[8] Cf. *No. 80, The Curtiss Hawk 75*, Bowers, Profile, Leatherhead, 1966; *No. 135, The Dewoitine 520*, Danel, Profile, Leatherhead, 1967; *No. 147, The Morane Saulnier 406*, Botquin, Profile, Leatherhead, 1967; *No. 201, The Bloch 151 & 152*, Cristesco, Profile, Leatherhead, 1968; *The Gloster Gladiator*, Mason, Macdonald, London, 1964; *The Hawker Hurricane*, Mason, Aston, 1987.

(Left to right, top to bottom) **Hurricane I of the Belgian 2nd** *Escadrille,* **based at Diest; a colourful Gladiator of the 1st** *Escadrille—* *"Escadrille Cométe"*; **German soldiers with a captured Belgian Fairey Fox; and a burned out Gladiator of No. 607 (County of Durham) Squadron, A.A.F., in France.**

He 59 seaplanes at Rotterdam. The vital Moerdijk bridge was captured intact by paratroopers and held for the advancing *Panzertruppen.* The planned capture of the Dutch Royal Family failed, however; they were hurriedly embarked in a British destroyer, H.M.S. *Codrington,* and brought safely to England.

Further south the forces of von Bock's Army Group B, supported by *Fliegerkorps* I, were thrusting across the Albert Canal north of Fort Eben Emael. This modern fortress, widely regarded as impregnable, fell in a matter of hours on the morning of 11th May to a brilliant glider assault by *Sturm Abteilung Koch*; only 55 men were involved in the whole attack, and the total casualties were five[9]—a light price indeed for this vital sector of the Belgian defence line.

Throughout the first five days of the offensive the Germans enjoyed unqualified air superiority over the Low Countries; and, in furtherance of years of carefully prepared propaganda, were at pains to demonstrate this superiority. Strike formations of dive-bombers roamed the skies at will, "taking out" points of resistance and systematically destroying communications and troop concentrations.

The final chapter in the elimination of "Fortress Holland" opened and closed with the murderous air assault on Rotterdam. Acknowledging that the Dutch Army had offered sterner

resistance than had been anticipated, Hitler directed an all-out assault to end the campaign without further delay[10]. He and Göring personally ordered the bombing of Rotterdam, and aircraft were accordingly made ready. Meanwhile, apparently unknown to O.K.L., negotiations for the surrender of the city were taking place between the commander of the German Army's XXXIX Corps and the Dutch garrison in the city. These negotiations had in fact been concluded when the German bombers (among them the aptly named "Death's Head" *Geschwader,* KG 54) arrived overhead. A recall signal had been transmitted to the aircraft but was not received by the leading formations, as their radio operators had left their sets to man their bombsights; only the rearmost crews heard the recall, or spotted "abandon raid" signals displayed on the ground by German troops, and broke away without bombing. The raid—one of the great tragedies of aviation history— wiped out the centre of Rotterdam, killing 814 people, of whom the vast majority were civilians, injuring several thousand, and rendering 78,000 homeless. The following day the Dutch Army laid down its arms.[11]

---

[10] Directive No. 11, issued on the morning of 14th May 1940.

[11] For many years the casualties were stated to be 25,000 dead; the figures quoted here are the amended particulars offered in evidence at Nuremburg by the Dutch Government. No convictions were obtained at Nuremburg on charges arising out of this raid, and the exact responsibility for the conflicting orders which led to the attack has never been satisfactorily fixed. Direct responsibility rests, of course, with Hitler and Göring. A lesser known incident illustrates the confusion existing among some German commanders at this time; General Kurt Student, the paratroop leader, was wounded by a stray bullet while supervising the laying down of arms by Dutch units in the city. The bullet was fired by *Waffen-S.S.* troops who drove through the streets firing wildly, although all fighting had ceased hours before.

---

[9] This fascinating operation was carried out by a mixed force drawn from *1 Kompanie, Fallschirmjäger Regiment 1,* and the parachute sapper detachment of *Fliegerkorps VII.* Amateur glider pilots were trained secretly at Hildesheim, and the gliders taken to Köln-Butzweilerhof, dismantled in furniture vans. Seven gliders carrying 55 troops reached the target. Supported by dive-bombers, 1./FJR 1 captured three bridges while the sappers penetrated the fort with grenades and satchel charges. Cf. *No. 177, The Junkers Ju 52,* Smith, Profile, Leatherhead, 1968.

Meanwhile the German Army was about to launch its second phase of attacks, to outflank the Maginot Line, sweep forward south of Namur, and reach the French coast in the area of Dunkirk. A feature of this most critical phase of operations was the continued use of German reconnaissance units, with Dornier Do 17s ranging almost unchallenged far behind the Allied lines, passing back clear reports of troop and air concentrations by day and night. Short-range Henschel Hs 126s accompanied the forward motorised and armoured columns, so that movement of British and French troops seldom passed unnoticed and quickly attracted the attention of von Richthofen's dive-bombers.

The British Expeditionary Force, commanded by General Lord Gort, had, at the commencement of the anticipated German offensive, moved forward into Belgium following the pre-determined Plan D; by chance, the Hurricanes of Nos. 1 and 73 Squadrons had escaped the airfield raids of 10th May with only light damage. By pre-arranged plan, four more Hurricane Squadrons—Nos. 3, 79, 501 (County of Gloucester) and 504 (County of Nottinham)—were sent to France, and one of these, No. 501, was in action against forty Heinkels within an hour of landing on the Continent. The Allied line was to be established at Meuse—Namur—Antwerp, held by the French Army in the south, with the Ninth on its left flank. The B.E.F. moved forward to take up positions on the River Dyle between Wavre and Louvain, its northern flank covered by the French Second Army, and its southern by the Ninth. A gap would exist between the B.E.F. and the Seventh, which would be filled by the retiring Belgian Army. With the crossing of the Albert Canal and the penetration of the

The eyes of the *Wehrmacht*—a Henschel Hs 126 short-range reconnaissance aircraft. Flying ahead of the armour, these spotters were able to report Allied dispositions in time for them to be neutralised by Stukas; this close co-ordination was one of the main strengths of *blitzkrieg*. (Photo: Hans Obert)

forward Belgian defences (in spite of the heroic but almost fruitless attacks at Maastricht and elsewhere by A.A.S.F. Blenheims and Battles, which suffered almost 100 per cent casualties), the Belgian Army was thrown into utter confusion; and it was at the weak spot between the B.E.F. and the French Seventh Army that von Rundstedt thrust on 13th May.

Raids by *Fliegerkorps* II and VIII were stepped up, roads, rail centres and airfields being the main targets. The attacks almost invariably opened with the appearance of *zerstören*, which strafed any visible target with cannon and machine guns. They were closely followed by low-flying bombers which dropped delayed-action loads. Immediately ahead of the *Panzer* columns flew the Ju 87s of *Fliegerkorps* VIII, eliminating any serious axis of resistance—and achieving a

The R.A.F. in France (left to right, top to bottom) Hurricanes of No. 85 Squadron; Hurricanes of No. 1 Squadron landing at Vassincourt; a Morane Saulnier 406 with an A.A.S.F. Fairey Battle; and a line-up of A.A.S.F. fighters during a visit by H.M. King George VI in December 1939.

The speed of the German advance through Belgium and France paralysed the Allied armies, and within a week of launching his main thrust von Runstedt had established bridgeheads across the Lower Somme. Here infantry and light mobile troops of General Rommel's 7th *Panzer* Division pass through the crossing areas.

degree of paralysed impotence which amazed even the Germans themselves. Often strongpoints and rearguard positions were so crippled and demoralised by the Stukas that the formidable PzKw III tanks could drive through the remains without firing a shot.

Within a week of von Rundstedt's main thrust, his leading *Panzer* units had established a bridgehead across the Lower Somme between Amiens and Abbeville, virtually isolating the Seventh Army and the B.E.F. from the remainder of France. The remnants of the A.A.S.F. fell back, leapfrogging from airfield to airfield in the face of the swiftly advancing German columns. Nos. 1 and 73 Squadrons managed to retain some semblance of cohesion, despite suffering the loss of nineteen aircraft and twelve pilots in seven days; but it was the Gladiator squadrons which suffered most. These two Squadrons had been on the point of exchanging their biplanes for Hurricanes when the storm broke, and about a dozen Hurricanes were taken on charge just as orders were received to move back. The experience of No. 607 Squadron was typical. Flying more than 70 sorties from Vitry-en-Artois on 10th May alone, the Squadron's Gladiators claimed the destruction of seven German aircraft. During the following week the commanding officer, Squadron Leader Launcelot Eustace Smith, A.A.F., was shot down and killed. His place was taken by a flight commander, who was shot down in his turn and taken prisoner; three other pilots were shot down and captured, and five killed. By 21st May the A.A.S.F. fighter squadrons were virtually without aircraft and were ordered to make for Boulogne, whence they sailed for England. Detachments from other squadrons, prevented from doing likewise, retreated westwards until they could go no further, and were evacuated—without aircraft—from St. Malo, Brest and St. Nazaire in early June.

To return to the plight of the northern armies and the Air Component squadrons, it was obvious that the tremendous pressure being exerted by von Rundstedt threatened to annihilate a French Army and a large proportion of the British Army. Despite Dowding's pleading (and in fact before the German breakthrough further south had been established) the British Cabinet had sanctioned the despatch of 32 Hurricanes to France. Many of these were in fact replacements for Nos.

607 and 615 Squadrons' Gladiators; and at least eight were captured intact by the Germans, underlining Dowding's objections with grim irony.

The French Prime Minister, Paul Reynaud, realising the gravity of the disaster on the Meuse, made strong representations to the British for the further despatch of ten fighter squadrons on the 14th; and the Cabinet, under Winston Churchill—who had become Prime Minister on the fateful 10th May—went so far as to give instructions for the despatch of these squadrons. At his own request, Dowding was allowed to plead his case in person before the Cabinet on 15th May, and with more logic than eloquence pointed to the critical wastage of fighters that had already taken place. If it was allowed to continue at this rate, with the effective loss of ten further squadrons, it would deprive Britain of her entire fighter defences within a fortnight. His letter, amounting to resignation if such forces were indeed sent across the Channel, stated his case without mincing words:

Sir,

I have the honour to refer to the very serious calls which have recently been made upon the Home Defence Fighter Units in an attempt to stem the German invasion of the Continent.

2. I hope and believe that our Armies may yet be victorious in France and Belgium, but we have to face the possibility that they may be defeated.

3. In this case I presume that there is no-one who will deny that England should fight on, even though the remainder of the Continent of Europe is dominated by the Germans.

4. For this purpose it is necessary to retain some minimum fighter strength in this country and I must request that the Air Council will inform me what they consider this minimum strength should be, in order that I may make my dispositions accordingly.

5. I would remind the Air Council that the last estimate which they made as to the force necessary to defend this country was 52 squadrons, and my strength has now been reduced to the equivalent of 36 squadrons.

6. Once a decision has been reached as to the limit on which the Air Council and the Cabinet are prepared to stake the existence of this country, it should be made clear to the Allied Commanders on the Continent that not a single aeroplane from Fighter Command beyond the limit will

German PzKw II and Czech-built PzKw 38 tanks of the 25th *Panzer* Regiment form up for an attack; France, May 1940.

Blenheim IF fighters of No. 29 Squadron landing at Digby early in 1940.

be sent across the Channel, no matter how desperate the situation may become.

7. It will, of course, be remembered that the estimate of 52 squadrons was based on the assumption that the attack would come from the eastwards, except insofar as the defences might be outflanked in flight. We now have to face the possibility that attacks may come from Spain or even from the north coast of France. The result is that our line is very much extended at the same time as our resources are reduced.

8. I must point out that within the last few days the equivalent of ten Squadrons have been sent to France, that the Hurricane Squadrons remaining in this country are seriously depleted, and that the more squadrons which are sent to France the higher will be the wastage and the more insistent the demand for reinforcements.

9. I must therefore request that as a matter of paramount urgency the Air Ministry will consider and decide what level of strength is to be left to Fighter Command for the defence of this country, and will assure me that when this level is reached, not one fighter will be sent across the Channel however urgent and insistent the appeals for help may be.

10. I believe that, if an adequate fighter force is kept in the country, if the fleet remains in being, and if Home Forces are suitably organised to resist invasion, we should be able to carry on the war single-handed for some time, if not indefinitely. But, if the Home Defence Force is drained away in desperate attempts to remedy the situation in France, defeat of France will involve the final, complete and irremediable defeat of this country.

The desperate situation brought Churchill to Paris on 16th May. At first unable to comprehend the measure of the catastrophe, the British statesman was soon shown that nothing short of a miracle could save France; her armies were in headlong retreat, morale had completely broken down (with the few inevitable and honourable exceptions), and a deadly and ennervating defeatism had apparently gripped French authorities at all levels of the administration. The reasons for this sudden and apparently inexplicable "cave in" were

complex in the extreme, and have been ably chronicled elsewhere by those qualified to comment on the psychological and social implications; the military situation was, however, simple and appalling.

Notwithstanding the extreme—even hysterical—pressures brought to bear on Churchill (who initially cabled London for the despatch of a further six squadrons) the Air Staff was now convinced by Dowding's lucid and brutal arguments; it was aware that no long time would pass before these same men and machines would be called upon to defend their own homes. The French collapse was beyond remedy; it had become a bottomless pit into which the precious squadrons, if ventured, would disappear forever. *It was Dowding's astonishingly accurate vision—that the critical battle would be fought over Britain, not France—which spelt survival for Fighter Command.*

The squadrons never departed; instead Dowding instructed Air Vice-Marshal Keith Park, commanding Fighter Command's No. 11 Group in South-East England, to render all

Combat damage to Hurricane YB-S of No. 17 Squadron over France, 19th May 1940. (Photo: R.A.F. Museum)

Exhausted Belgian horse artillery retreating on the Louvain-Brussels road.

possible assistance in covering the withdrawal of the British and French forces towards the coast—not twenty minutes' flying time away.

The Evacuation of Dunkirk

On the evening of 20th May the German 2nd *Panzer* Division reached Abbeville on the Channel Coast, effectively trapping the B.E.F., three French Armies, and the remnants of the Belgian Army. The speed of General Heinz Guderian's

tanks[12] astonished Hitler's headquarters staff. Fresh reserves of infantry were thrown into the battle to consolidate the wedge in anticipation of a fierce French counterattack. Such an attack was indeed ordered by General Maurice Gamelin the previous day, but his removal and replacement by the

---

[12] Guderian was later to become Inspector of Armoured Troops and Army Chief of Staff, and was widely regarded as the outstanding tank general and armoured tactician to emerge during the Second World War.

Wounded soldiers of the British Expeditionary Force come ashore from a destroyer during the Dunkirk evacuation, 31st May 1940.

Pilots of No. 17 Squadron retreating through Le Mans in late May or early June 1940.

ageing General Maxime Weygand caused the cancellation of the order and rendered hopes for the relief of the northern forces futile.

For the next four days Guderian's armour, constantly supported by a heavy umbrella of fighters and dive-bombers, advanced northwards, capturing Boulogne and isolating Calais. And then, on 24th May, as the *Panzer* battalions stood poised to eliminate the last seaports remaining open to the trapped armies, Hitler ordered a halt to the advance[13].

This provided the miraculous opportunity which Lord Gort had not dared to expect. Since 20th May the British Admiralty had been assembling a huge fleet of small vessels—tugs, motor launches, pleasure cruisers, lifeboats, drifters, paddle steamers, trawlers, yachts; any vessel, of any ownership, capable of crossing the Channel with a cargo of troops, no matter how few. These boats had been mustered in ports along the Kent coast against the slender chance that there might be an opportunity to rescue *some* of the trapped soldiers from the mainland. At 18.57 hours on the evening of 26th May the Admiralty signalled the commencement of Operation Dynamo—the evacuation of forces from Dunkirk. That night Guderian was ordered to resume his attack on the port; but the 72-hour delay had enabled Gort to set up a perimeter in the meantime. It was a tattered perimeter, made up of exhausted men in "scratch" units, short of every military necessity; but it held off the German assault, and continued to hold it off for

the next seven days. There was, after all, no reason to save ammunition; this was as far as the Army was carrying most of its equipment. Everything which could buy time was thrown into the defence of the perimeter—including human lives. There must have been many who knew that they themselves would never see the beach; but the perimeter held, conceding ground, yard by yard, only when further resistance was physically impossible.

Behind them the extraordinary armada of more than 800 vessels, a large number of them manned by civilian volunteers, commenced their epic and bizarre task of plying to and fro across the twenty-mile stretch of sea, loaded far beyond the limits of safety with exhausted soldiers who had waded out from the beaches, often standing up to their necks in water for hours on end awaiting their turn. On the first day, 27th May, 7,669 men were brought home; on the 28th, 17,804; on the 29th, 47,310; and on the 30th, no fewer than 53,823—a total of 126,606 British and French soldiers, already far in excess of the figure thought possible during the planning of Operation Dynamo.

Germany was, at this time, the victim of its own propaganda, which had proclaimed to the world at large that the Allied armies, trapped on the coast, were doomed. At last O.K.W. realised what was happening—that the vital pocket was emptying. At once Göring ordered an all-out attack on the beaches on 1st June; hitherto only sporadic attacks had been carried out, bad weather causing the grounding of the heavy bombers, while the dive-bombers were fully occupied elsewhere. On this day the *Luftwaffe* broke through the screen of home-based British fighters covering Dunkirk, and sank three destroyers and several transports, losing 30 aircraft in

---

[13] The origin of this order was the centre of controversy for many years. It was eventually established as emanating from von Rundstedt who determined to conserve his armour for future battles—preferring to feed new infantry reserves into the line. Hitler endorsed the order, despite protests from the General Staff.

the process. About the same number of British aircraft were destroyed, but fifteen pilots were saved. By the night of 3rd June only some 4,000 British troops remained within the perimeter, which was manned by 100,000 French soldiers who continued to cover the last stages of the evacuation. To the British forces the Dunkirk evacuation was nothing short of a miracle; 338,226 British and French troops had been brought back across the Channel. Such had been the nature of their ordeal, however, that almost every item of their equipment— from tanks to mess tins—now lay scattered along the roadsides of France and Belgium, or smashed and charred on the beaches.

That the *Luftwaffe* had not assaulted the beaches at Dunkirk in any strength before 1st June was not only the result of bad weather. Park had maintained a constant shuttle of fighter patrols from his Kent airfields—Biggin Hill, Manston, Lympne, Hawkinge and Kenley. The Spitfires, Hurricanes, Blenheims and Defiants had tended to keep clear of the beaches themselves, their pilots preferring to meet the enemy raids outside the perimeter of the beachhead before they could attack the concentrations of exhausted men. This fact, taken in conjunction with the heavy raids which broke through to the beaches on 1st June—the day on which the ground forces were probably most concentrated—gave rise to fairly widespread bitterness among the tormented soldiers, who wanted to know why the "Brylcreem Boys" had not protected them better. In truth Fighter Command's baptism had been costly in men and machines—far too costly for Dowding, to whom every pilot was vital. Moreover when Göring finally unleashed the *Luftwaffe* against Dunkirk the British fighter pilots fought desperately and with great effect, giving the German aircrews their first foretaste of the calibre of Dowding's men fighting on "interior lines".

Though it would be quite inaccurate to regard Fighter Command's successes over Dunkirk as decisive, the measure of experience gained in this first organised confrontation with the *Luftwaffe* cannot be overestimated. However, in at least one instance, that of the Defiants of No. 264 Squadron, whose crews claimed the destruction of about 60 enemy aircraft in the course of their first three days in action[14], the tactical experience was not only overestimated but misunderstood, to the extent that almost magical powers were ascribed to an aircraft whose tactical concept was utterly unsound. Yet the lessons learned by the squadrons which fought over France between 10th May and 3rd June were priceless; and, despite the heavy toll and exhaustion suffered by those squadrons— in particular Nos. 1, 32, 73, 79, 85, 87, 501 and 615 with Hurricanes, and No. 54 with Spitfires— these units were to become the very hardcore on which Dowding's defences would rely to a great extent in the following four months.

The tragedy of Dunkirk and the Battle of France—so far as Fighter Command was concerned—lay in the nature of the casualties suffered. The War was but eight months old, and the squadrons chosen to fight over France were of necessity front echelon units with pilots almost entirely composed of Regulars or peacetime trainees. Such men would, in the normal course of events, be those who would have risen quickly to command flights and squadrons as wartime expansion gathered momentum. The extent to which their losses were to become so keenly felt will be evident in later pages of this narrative.

---

[14] As far as can be ascertained from all relevant records, the actual number of German aircraft that fell to the Defiants' guns in this period was between fifteen and twenty.

Boulton Paul Defiants awaiting delivery from the factory. These two-seat turret fighters received their baptism of fire in the skies over Dunkirk, and their crews acquitted themselves well, their dorsal armament taking the Germans by surprise. The lesson was thoroughly digested by the *Luftwaffe*, and thereafter the Defiant was quickly recognised for what it was—a slow, ungainly fighter with no forward armament.

PART TWO
THE BATTLE

A Spitfire is armed while the pilot waits in his cockpit. (Right) Air Chief Marshal Sir Hugh Dowding, A.O.C.-in-C., Royal Air Force Fighter Command.

INTRODUCTION

"What General Weygand called the Battle of France is over. I expect that the Battle of Britain is about to begin. Upon this battle depends the survival of Christian civilisation. . . The whole fury and might of the enemy must very soon be turned on us. Hitler knows that he will have to break us in this Island or lose the War. If we can stand up to him, all Europe may be free and the life of the world may move forward into broad sunlit uplands. But if we fail, then the whole world, including the United States, including all that we have known and cared for, will sink into the abyss of a new Dark Age made more sinister, and perhaps more protracted, by the lights of perverted science. Let us therefore brace ourselves to our duties, and so bear ourselves that, if the British Empire and its Commonwealth last for a thousand years, men will still say 'This was their finest hour'."

The Rt. Hon. Winston Churchill, *Speech to the House of Commons*, 18th June 1940

As the Battle of France had dragged on for another fortnight after the Dunkirk evacuation ended, with all the agonies imposed by the marauding invader on that stricken country, British and Allied forces—including the remnants of several R.A.F. squadrons—continued to fall back on ports in Western France where ships waited to carry them to England. When the final cost was counted the losses were staggering. In forty dramatic days the R.A.F. had lost 959 aircraft in the Battle of France and sixty-six in the Norwegian campaign, of which 509 were fighters—or, expressed otherwise, the losses represented more than two-thirds of all aircraft delivered to the R.A.F. since the outbreak of War.

The spirit evoked by the Prime Minister's words epitomised and inspired the determination of Britain to shake off the lethargy which had characterised those early months, and apply herself to the awesome task which was now inescapable. There were many, at home and abroad, who summed up the evidence objectively—and despaired. At least the task was clear-cut, and involved no ennervating struggles of conscience; the goal was the oldest, simplest, and most fundamental known to intelligent life—bare survival. One of the natural consequences of Britain's imperial past had been an almost universal sense of confidence in the security of the country. Now, for the first time, the nation was forced to recognise that the unthinkable had become a distinct possibility—that within a matter of weeks Great Britain might very well cease to exist as a sovereign state. It was a traumatic but

extremely beneficial experience. As Samuel Johnson remarked, "When a man knows he is to be hanged in a fortnight, it concentrates his mind wonderfully".

The problems now facing the Royal Air Force were immense. For eight years the fighter force had been calculated as being that necessary to withstand an attack by Germany; that attack would now come, not from bases two hundred miles distant, but thirty. The world's largest target lay within one hours' flight of the world's most powerful bomber force. The enemy was no longer confined to attacks launched from a small sector of the compass, but from bases ranged along the entire northern coastline of continental Europe. The arbitrary strength of 52 fighter squadrons deemed necessary for the defence of the island had scarcely been achieved before it had begun to suffer from the running sores of Norway and France. Six first-line units had to be withdrawn to rest, and two others had been virtually destroyed; five more, equipped with Blenheims and only nominally operational, were grappling with the difficulties of night defence; while no less than eleven squadrons—also ostensibly operational—had been equipped with Spitfires so recently that weeks would elapse before they were truly ready for battle. Far from possessing 52 first-line operational interceptor squadrons, Dowding in fact had available only 28 fresh, combat-ready squadrons—of which just 23 were equipped with Hurricanes and Spitfires.

How long the Germans would have to pause before opening their attack was obviously unknown to the British commanders[1]; but balanced against the time required to deploy the *Luftwaffe* and assemble an invasion force was the rigid timetable of nature. Hitler must launch his invasion in the coming four months of fine weather, before autumn gales and winter storms rendered large-scale air operations and a surface crossing of the Channel militarily impossible. The *Wehrmacht*'s ace card in the invasion of the Low Countries had been the element of surprise; that card was now out of play, and the *Luftwaffe* would confront a fully alert defence system.

The nation as a whole now responded to the Prime Minister's Shakespearean phrases. The Local Defence Volunteers, composed largely of men over military age who were eager to prove that they had not forgotten the skills learned in Flanders a generation before, patrolled the countryside, manned ditches and threw up road blocks, and maintained a constant vigilance for enemy parachutists; small arms were intially in such short supply that the L.D.V. were frequently armed with shot guns and rabbit rifles, and even with pikes manufactured by jamming the hilt of a First World War bayonet into a five-foot length of iron pipe. Concrete pillboxes and barbed wire entanglements appeared in country lanes. Strangers were regarded with active suspicion and hostility, rather than the faintly amused indifference more normal in rural communities. Official sources and arm-chair experts vied with one another in the proliferation of advice on how to turn every field and street into a potential death-trap for invaders[2]. Posters appeared on every wall demanding "Is your journey really necessary?", in an attempt to free the transport facilities for military traffic, and warning that "Careless talk costs lives".

Fighter Command

For all the mystique which surrounded the achievements of the *Luftwaffe*, Dowding recognised that the forthcoming battle would be fought on strictly conventional lines, uncomplicated—until the launching of an invasion—by the intrusion of ground support and battlefield tactics.

The Hertfordshire Local Defence Volunteers on parade. This particular section seems to have a higher proportion of rifles— albeit of 1914 pattern—than was usual.

As previously described, Fighter Command was organised geographically by Groups, under the central operational control of Command Headquarters at Bentley Priory, Stanmore, Middlesex[3]. In the opening phases of the Battle there were three Groups, Nos. 11, 12 and 13, commanded respectively by Park, Leigh-Mallory and Air Vice-Marshal Richard Saul, D.F.C. A fourth Group, No. 10, had already been authorised for the defence of the South-West and would become operational in July. It was the realisation that the German occupation of the entire French Coast could result in the turning of Dowding's western flank which hastened the completion of this important Group[4].

There had been precious little opportunity to test the fighter defence system since the outbreak of war, owing to the preoccupation of the German air forces elsewhere. Occasional raids—seldom at more than *Staffel* strength and usually without fighter escort—had been detected and intercepted, and a few enemy aircraft had been shot down. There had also been the occasional breakdown of the defence system (without serious consequences), but increasing familiarity with the procedures and equipment involved was breeding confidence among Dowding's pilots.

The radar chain was perhaps the most valuable asset possessed by Fighter Command, for this alone could deprive the enemy of any element of surprise. By now 29 Chain Home stations had been erected and all but three were fully operational and integrated into the Command. The first of the fixed aeriel "low-looking" Chain Home Low stations had been activated, and seven others were awaiting calibration. By dint of feverish activity the radar cover on the East Coast had been greatly extended during the past eight months, and all ap-

---

[1] Although the British Intelligence services had acquired a working example of the German Enigma encoding/decoding apparatus and were therefore to intercept much of the enemy's secret signal traffic, it was to be some months before the full pattern of material thus gained could be fully understood. For instance, signals of a tactical nature were seldom transmitted—but sent by surface despatches. Moreover, Orders of the Day from Hitler, the Naval Staff, O.K.W. and O.K.L. seldom included details of forces or dates of attack, although these frequently outlined the strategic intentions of the German High Command. It became possible, however, by collating obscure information—such as the posting of specialist personnel to new units—to build up a remarkably detailed picture of the nature of intended enemy operations.

Notwithstanding, British Intelligence was all too aware that uncontrolled dissemination of valuable information gleaned from this signal interception could compromise the entire process, so that information thus gleaned and processed was invariably confined to the Cabinet, the Chiefs of Staff and the Commanders-in-Chief. By so doing, the British Intelligence was able to gain benefit from continuing Enigma traffic right up to the end of the War—wholly unsuspected by the Germans.

[2] Those inclined to parody this atmosphere by referring to the "How to Knock Out a Jerry Tank with Two Safety Pins and a Rubber Band" mentality should perhaps consider the events that took place in Budapest in 1956.

---

[3] On being created 1st Baron in 1943, the Lord Dowding chose for his territorial designation "of Bentley Priory in the County of Middlesex".

[4] No. 10 Group was to be commanded—brilliantly—by no less a man than Air Vice-Marshal Sir Christopher Quintin Brand, K.B.E., D.S.O., M.C., D.F.C., the South African who, as a Captain in the R.F.C., had shared with Murlis-Green the night combat hazards of 1917. Murlis-Green himself, by 1940 a Group Captain, commanded the R.A.F. Station at Aston Down.

(Left) Keith Park, the brilliant New Zealander who commanded No. 11 Group, covering the vital South-Eastern defence airfields and the approaches to London. A sensitive and popular commander, whose handling of his hard-pressed squadrons must rank among the outstanding feats of defensive generalship in this century, Park's immediate rewards were less than generous. (Right) Trafford Leigh-Mallory commanded No. 12 Group on Park's northern flank, and was an advocate of fighter Wing tactics which were not well suited for the particular conditions of the Battle of Britain and which are now generally accepted as having been fundamentally flawed.

proaches to the island between the Bristol Channel and Land's End and the Orkneys now covered out to 150 miles' range at 18,000 feet. Almost the entire South and East Coasts were covered down to 600 feet at forty miles' range.

In the vital matter of aircraft production, there was no disguising the fact that the British aircraft industry had never caught up on its planned schedules; when war broke out all aircraft factories were at least twenty per cent short of their targets, despite massive increases in the labour force. Moreover, when on the outbreak of war the production department of the Air Ministry under Lieutenant Colonel H.W.S. Outram, C.B.E., was moved to Harrogate, and a new "optimised"

production schedule was agreed with aircraft industry leaders in January 1940—the "Harrogate Programme"—the production of new aircraft continued to fall further and further behind; so much so that at the time of Dunkirk the total shortfall against contract amounted to more than one thousand aircraft![5]

When, on 10th May, Prime Minister Neville Chamberlain resigned and Winston Churchill formed a Coalition Government, Sir Archibald Sinclair succeeded Sir Samuel Hoare as Secretary of State for Air. Four days later the Ministry of Aircraft Production was established under Lord Beaverbrook, absorbing the Air Ministry's old Directorates of Research, Development and Production. Under the energetic leadership of the newspaper magnate, whose activities were characterised by a lively and outspoken contempt for administrative delays and bureaucratic inertia, the new Ministry soon began to produce the desired effect. From May 1940 until the end of the War, there was never a single month in which actual total aircraft production fell below the planned target.

A Marine sentry and a barrage balloon outside the Admiralty, Spring 1940.

---

[5] However, this shortfall was almost entirely composed of bombers and training aircraft. There was in fact a considerable surplus in fighters, such was the over-riding priority afforded to this type. The "Harrogate Programme" had in fact called for the production of 1,158 Hurricanes, Spitfires and Defiants between 1 January and 30 June 1940, and the actual figure achieved was 1,841; of this "surplus" of 683 aircraft, 531 were Hurricanes, 121 Spitfires and 37 Defiants. Among the factories which consistently beat their target production figures was the Brockworth factory of Gloster Air Company, which frequently beat its target by about 50 per cent each month.

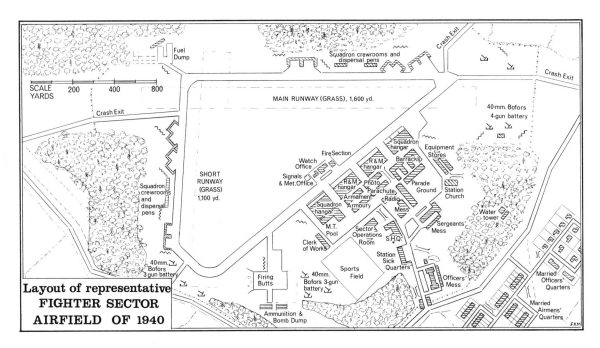

Layout of representative
**FIGHTER SECTOR
AIRFIELD OF 1940**

The Luftwaffe

In contrast to the simply-defined aim of Fighter Command—
that of continuing to maintain an effective defence of Great
Britain against air attack—the *Luftwaffe*'s objective was
complex, and as month followed month even this rather
vaguely formulated plan came to be blurred by constant
supplementary requirements demanded by the German Naval
Staff and O.K.W. Nevertheless, in anticipation of the customary Directive from Hitler for a landing operation against
Britain—an operation for which an obvious prerequisite
would be the destruction or emasculation of Fighter Command—the *Luftwaffe* units which had crushed France and the
Low Countries moved into position throughout the occupied
territories; *Luftflotte 2* occupied the area of Holland, Belgium
and North-East France, while *Luftflotte 3* established bases in
North-West France.

The successful campaigns in Poland, Norway and Western
Europe had confirmed the absolute faith of Hitler and Göring
in *blitzkrieg* tactics, and this blind faith was to cause a
dangerous delusion during the planning of the invasion of
Britain. While no element of strategic surprise was possible,
they persisted in seeing the forthcoming cross-Channel invasion in the light of a massive "river crossing under fire"—a
basic exercise in mobile warfare—with the dive-bomber
providing the necessary "artillery support". The analogy was
to prove utterly false, simply because the "river" was too
wide. The hitherto invincible Messerschmitt Bf 109 would
now be operating at its extreme range without any measure of
ground control, and even so could only be brought to bear on
the front line of defences. The so-called strategic bombers,
the Heinkels and Dorniers, would be unprotected in daylight
operations beyond the range of the Bf 109. The rôle of escort
fighter would fall to the Messerschmitt Bf 110, a rôle which
it had not hitherto been called upon to play to any great extent
and in which it was an unknown quantity, despite the confidence it inspired.

Notwithstanding these shortcomings in the German plan—
fundamental as they were to prove—the *Luftwaffe* possessed

commanders of outstanding ability; it is difficult to believe
that they were not fully aware of the limitations of their
equipment but, like the good generals they were, determined
to carry forward the overall plan as ordered. It is significant
that the few major blunders committed by the *Luftwaffe* were
the outcome of direct interference at subordinate level by
Göring, and by Hitler himself.

Without doubt the most able of the three *Luftflotte* commanders was Albert Kesselring, who would continue to
occupy a succession of high field appointments until his
capture by the Allies in 1945. Aged 55 at the time of the Battle
of Britain, he had served as an artillery officer early in his
career; and it is perhaps not surprising that he was a prominent
advocate of the dive-bomber, which he had used with bril-

**Albert Kesselring, commander of *Luftflotte 2* during the Battle,
and later C.-in-C. of all German forces in Italy, was a soldier
turned airman. Though an able commander, his grasp of the
situation in September 1940 was faulty. (Photo: Heinz Nowarra)**

liance as Commander of *Luftflotte 1* in Poland, and *Luftflotte 2* in France. Much later in the War he was to display his considerable prowess as an army commander, first as C.-in-C. South and later as C.-in-C. West, in command of all German air and ground forces opposing the invading Allies. The undeniably brilliant German defensive operations in Italy during 1943-44 were probably his greatest achievement.

Hugo Sperrle, commanding *Luftflotte 3*, was strictly an air force officer, whose career had begun in the *Luftstreitkrafte*. His experience of tactical air power was considerable, however; as stated in Chapter 3, he had commanded the *Legion Cóndor* during the first year of the Spanish Civil War. Aged 56 during the Battle, he retained command of *Luftflotte 3* until his transfer to the reserve in 1944. He too was captured by the Allies in 1945.

The third of the senior German commanders was Hans-Jürgen Stumpff, at the head of the Scandinavian-based *Luftflotte 5*; possessing only relatively light forces for operations against Britain, this command was to suffer disproportionately high losses early in the Battle, and thereafter launched only sporadic raids. Stumpff was a staff officer of long standing, having served in von Seeckt's *Reichswehr Ministerium* after the First World War. His name was not closely associated with the army support doctrine, and it may be significant that vigorous use of the dive bomber in conjunc-

Hugo Sperrle, one-time commander of the *Legion Cóndor*, who led *Luftflotte 3* during the Battle of Britain. (Photo: Heinz Nowarra)

Hermann Göring confers with his friend Ernst Udet, and with Oberst Josef (Beppo") Schmid, his chief of Intelligence. (Photo: Heinz Nowarra)

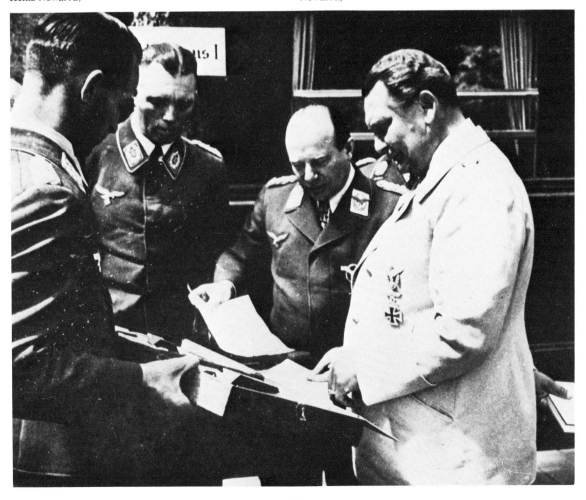

Oberst Schmid was largely responsible for the *Studie Blau* Intelligence appreciation of the R.A.F., a remarkably erroneous document which was to have disastrous consequences for the *Luftwaffe* during the Battle. It is reproduced as Appendix H. (Photo: *Gemeinschaft der Jagdflieger E.V.*)

tion with ground forces was not a feature of his campaign in Norway.

Among the dozen or so *Fliegerkorps* commanders involved in the Battle, one name stands above all others—the most famous surname in German military aviation. General (later Generalfeldmarschall) Wolfram, Freiherr von Richthofen, led *Fliegerkorps* VIII in *Luftflotte 2*. He had served in *Jagdgeschwader 1* (led by and named after his legendary cousin, Manfred) during the First World War, and in 1936 commanded the German expeditionary force in Spain, be-

coming Chief of Staff and later commander of the *Legion Cóndor*. Unquestionably the foremost advocate of close support tactics, von Richthofen was the "Stuka General", commanding *Fliegerkorps* VIII in Poland, France, the Balkans and Russia, and *Luftflotte 2* in the Mediterranran theatre in 1943. He became seriously ill in 1944, and died at the age of 50 from a brain tumor shortly after the War ended in Europe.

The German Aircraft

Reference to Appendix C of this book will indicate the relevant and individual characteristics of the various aircraft types employed by the *Luftwaffe* in the Battle. With regard to strengths of units and numbers of aircraft deployed, German records of this period are notoriously vague and inaccurate owing to the considerable movement by the *Gruppen* after the fall of France. The following approximate figures have been quoted as referring to the actual deployed strength on 20th July 1940:

Bombers	
He 111, Do 17 and Ju 88	1,200 (+ 115 in *Luftflotte 5*)
Dive-bombers	
Ju 87	280
Single-engine fighters	
Bf 109	760 (+ 30 in *Luftflotte 5*)
Zerstörer	
Bf 110 and Ju 88C ...	220 (+ 45 in *Luftflotte 5*)
Long-range reconnaissance	
Do 17, He 111, Bf 110 and Ju 88	50 (+ 30 in *Luftflotte 5*)
Short-range reconnaissance	
Hs 126	90
Total	2,600 (+ 220 in *Luftflotte 5*)

It has been estimated that due to the disruption caused by the redeployment of forces, which was still taking place well into July, the actual serviceable combat strength of the three *Luftflotten* on 1st July was slightly below 50 per cent of the figures quoted here. On that day Dowding's fighter states showed that a total of 591 aircraft were combat-ready throughout his Command, with a pilot availability of 1,200.

Daily Loss Tables

A note of explanation is necessary for the loss tables presented daily during the narrative on the Battle. These have been prepared exclusively from primary sources, and are in no way related to official statistics formerly issued for propaganda and other purposes. Because such published figures have not taken account of the widely differing definitions of "losses"— or for that matter what constituted a combat or operational sortie—fairly wide discrepancies will be apparent between the details quoted here and those published elsewhere which may purport to represent the true casualties.

Fighter Command Loss Tables

The columns in which the details are presented are as follows: Item No.; Squadron and base airfield at time of sortie; Combat or Not Combat (C or NC); details of incident and fate of crew; time of incident (A = approximately); crew name(s); aircraft type; serial number where known; and extent of damage to aircraft. Details are given, where known of aircraft losses on the ground. It must be emphasised that the losses do not include those suffered by R.A.F. units other than those of Fighter Command (unless stated).

It may be seen that at least one respect the losses shown in this edition differ marginally from those published in previous editions. A close study of Maintenance Command records (made available for public examination in 1976) indicates that a number of aircraft otherwise shown in Fighter Command records as "Category 3 Destroyed" have been found to have been salvaged, repaired and returned to service (evidently unknown to Fighter Command statisticians); such amended figures, relating to about a dozen days during the Battle, have thus had the effect of slightly reducing the loss rate suffered on those days; in any case, it is believed that the figures presented here are the most accurate ever to have been published for the Battle of Britain.

Luftwaffe Loss Tables

To some extent based upon losses quoted in the Luftwaffe *Quartermaster General's Returns (Oberbefehlshaber der Luftwaffe Genst. Gen. Qu./6 Abteilung/40.g.Kdos.IC) as notified to* Reichsmarschallstab, *these tables have been resolved to a form as nearly as possible comparable with those of Fighter Command, although it has not always been possible to establish with absolute certainty what losses were suffered as a direct result of combat. It has therefore been necessary simply to state whether or not the aircraft was on a combat mission—(CM) or (NCM) respectively.[6]*

The columns in which the details are presented are as follows: Item number; Unit (down to Staffel, where positively known); Combat Mission or Not Combat Mission; cause of loss or damage, target and time (where known); aircraft type, with Werkernummer *(Wkr.Nr. or Works Serial Number) and markings (where known), percentage damage[7], and fate of crew member(s).*

It should be mentioned in passing that as the Battle progressed and the casualties among men and aircraft began to assume major importance, German records became perceptibly less casual in presentation. Non-commissioned crew members, often anonymous in the opening stages of the Battle, soon became recorded by rank and name. The identification of aircraft types down to the most minute details of sub-variant was also undertaken as the importance of accurate replacement became critical; and in the last stages of the Battle aircraft markings, previously regarded as unimportant, were recorded with scrupulous care. The historian has reason to be grateful for this latter procedure, as it casts new light on German identification practices, showing them to be rather less rigid than previously supposed.

---

[6] The German raid records and loss returns used three different sortie definitions: *Feindflug* (= war flight); *bei Einsatz* (colloquially = war support flight, e.g. air/sea rescue); and *Heimat* (literally, domestic or local non-combat flight). It has become abundantly clear in the preparation of this book that in the compilation of official German loss details losses under the heading of *bei Einsatz* have not been accorded combat status—an absurd anomaly considering, for instance the number of *Luftwaffe* aircraft shot down while on air/sea rescue missions.

[7] The *Luftwaffe* used a system of percentage damage suffered when assessing losses of aircraft, assuming 100% as a total loss. 60% and over represented a write off with varying degrees of possible cannibalisation; 45-60%, aircraft severely damaged and requiring replacement of major components; 40-45%, aircraft damaged and requiring engine replacement with systems; 25-39%, aircraft suffered local damage, requiring major inspection on unit; 10-24%, aircraft suffered local damage from shrapnel or gunfire, requiring minor replacements; less than 10%, minor gunfire damage requiring local making good. It is believed that in preparation by British sources of German loss figures, the definition of a "destroyed aircraft" was taken as being "80% damaged"; this was clearly erroneous in view of the specific German assessment—"less than 60%"—of a salvageable aircraft. The cumulative progress of many false analyses by both sides, mentioned in this and the above footnote, goes a long way towards explaining the extraordinary discrepancies between pilots' claims and the so-called official figures published hitherto.

R.A.F. FIGHTER COMMAND ORDER OF BATTLE

09.00 hrs., 1st July 1940

Sector	Sqn.	Aircraft	Combat Ready (Unserviceable)	Base Airfield	Pilots on State	Commanding Officer
No. 11 Group, H.Q. Uxbridge, Middlesex						
Biggin Hill	32 Sqn.	Hurricanes	12 (4)	Biggin Hill	16	Squadron Leader J. Worrall
	79 Sqn. (1)	Hurricanes	12 (5)	Biggin Hill	14	Squadron Leader J.D.C. Joslin
	245 Sqn. (2)	Hurricanes	15 (1)	Hawkinge	16	Squadron Leader E.W. Whitley
	600 Sqn.	Blenheims	8 (6)	Manston	22	Squadron Leader D. de B. Clarke
	610 Sqn.	Spitfires	14 (3)	Gravesend	20	Squadron Leader A.T. Smith
North Weald	25 Sqn.	Blenheims	6 (10)	Martlesham	22	Squadron Leader K.A.K. McEwan
	56 Sqn.	Hurricanes	16 (2)	North Weald	20	Squadron Leader G.A.L. Manton
	85 Sqn.	Hurricanes	15 (3)	Martlesham	21	Squadron Leader P.W. Townsend
	151 Sqn.	Hurricanes	14 (4)	North Weald	20	Squadron Leader E.M. Donaldson
Kenley	64 Sqn.	Spitfires	10 (4)	Kenley	19	Squadron Leader N.C. Odbert
	111 Sqn.	Hurricanes	12 (4)	Croydon	17	Squadron Leader J.M. Thompson
	501 Sqn.	Hurricanes	10 (5)	Croydon	18	Squadron Leader H.A.V. Hogan
	615 Sqn.	Hurricanes	12 (6)	Kenley	21	Squadron Leader J.R. Kayll
Northolt	1 Sqn.	Hurricanes	10 (6)	Northolt	18	Squadron Leader D.A. Pemberton
	257 Sqn.	Hurricanes	13 (5)	Hendon	17	Squadron Leader D.W. Bayne
	604 Sqn.	Blenheims	10 (6)	Northolt	21	Squadron Leader M.F. Anderson
	609 Sqn.	Spitfires	15 (2)	Northolt	18	Squadron Leader H.S. Darley
Hornchurch	54 Sqn.	Spitfires	12 (3)	Rochford	18	Squadron Leader J.L. Leathart
	65 Sqn.	Spitfires	11 (5)	Hornchurch	16	Squadron Leader D. Cooke
	74 Sqn.	Spitfires	10 (7)	Hornchurch	20	Squadron Leader F.L. White
Tangmere	43 Sqn.	Hurricanes	13 (4)	Tangmere	18	Squadron Leader C.G. Lott
	145 Sqn.	Hurricanes	11 (7)	Tangmere	17	Squadron Leader J.R.A. Peel
	601 Sqn.	Hurricanes	15 (2)	Tangmere	19	Squadron Leader the Hon. M. Aitken
	F.I.U.	Blenheims	4 (4)	Tangmere	10	Wing Commander G.P. Chamberlain
Filton	92 Sqn.	Spitfires	11 (6)	Pembrey	19	Squadron Leader F.J. Sanders
	213 Sqn.	Hurricanes	14 (4)	Exeter	20	Squadron Leader H.D. McGregor
	234 Sqn.	Spitfires	9 (6)	St. Eval	21	Squadron Leader R.E. Barnett
Middle Wallop	236 Sqn.	Blenheims	11 (4)	Middle Wallop	19	Squadron Leader P.E. Drew
	238 Sqn. (3)	Hurricanes	10 (2)	Middle Wallop	17	Squadron Leader H.A. Fenton
Debden	17 Sqn.	Hurricanes	14 (4)	Debden	19	Squadron Leader R.I.G. MacDougall
No. 12 Group, H.Q. Watnall, Nottingham						
Duxford	19 Sqn.	Spitfires	8 (5)	Fowlmere	24	Squadron Leader P.C. Pinkham
	264 Sqn.	Defiants	11 (7)	Duxford	23	Squadron Leader P.A. Hunter
Coltishall	66 Sqn.	Spitfires	12 (4)	Coltishall	25	Squadron Leader R.H.A. Leigh
	242 Sqn.	Hurricanes	10 (4)	Coltishall	21	Squadron Leader D.R.S. Bader
Kirton-in-Lindsey	222 Sqn.	Spitfires	12 (4)	Kirton-in-Lindsey	21	Squadron Leader H.W. Mermagen
Digby	29 Sqn.	Blenheims	10 (5)	Digby	15	Flight Lieutenant J.S. Adams
	46 Sqn.	Hurricanes	15 (3)	Digby	17	Flight Lieutenant A.D. Murray
	611 Sqn.	Spitfires	3 (11)	Digby	21	Squadron Leader J.E. McComb
Wittering	23 Sqn.	Blenheims	10 (6)	Colly Weston	20	Squadron Leader L.C. Bicknell
	229 Sqn.	Hurricanes	14 (2)	Wittering	20	Squadron Leader H.J. Maguire
	266 Sqn.	Spitfires	8 (5)	Wittering	21	Squadron Leader J.W.A. Hunnard
No. 13 Group, H.Q. Newcastle, Northumberland						
Church Fenton	73 Sqn.	Hurricanes	8 (5)	Church Fenton	22	Squadron Leader J.W.C. More
	87 Sqn.	Hurricanes	14 (4)	Church Fenton	23	Squadron Leader J.S. Dewar
	249 Sqn.	Hurricanes	10 (4)	Leconfield	23	Squadron Leader J. Grandy
	616 Sqn.	Spitfires	11 (4)	Church Fenton	19	Squadron Leader M. Robinson
Catterick	41 Sqn.	Spitfires	11 (6)	Catterick	21	Squadron Leader H. West
	219 Sqn.	Blenheims	10 (4)	Catterick	19	Squadron Leader J.H. Little
Usworth	72 Sqn.	Spitfires	12 (4)	Acklington	19	Squadron Leader R.B. Lees
	152 Sqn.	Spitfires	8 (4)	Acklington	25	Squadron Leader P.K. Devitt
	607 Sqn.	Hurricanes	10 (6)	Usworth	17	Squadron Leader J.A. Vick
Turnhouse	141 Sqn.	Defiants	14 (5)	Turnhouse	20	Squadron Leader W.A. Richardson
	253 Sqn.	Hurricanes	13 (5)	Turnhouse	19	Squadron Leader T.P. Gleave
	602 Sqn.	Spitfires	12 (4)	Drem	19	Squadron Leader G.C. Pinkerton
	603 Sqn. (4)	Spitfires	10 (6)	Turnhouse	19	Squadron Leader E.H. Stevens
	605 Sqn. (5)	Hurricanes	8 (6)	Drem	17	Squadron Leader W.M. Churchill
Dyce	263 Sqn. (6)	Hurricanes	3 (2)	Grangemouth	7	Squadron Leader H. Eeles
Wick	3 Sqn.	Hurricanes	12 (2)	Wick	18	Squadron Leader S.F. Godden
	504 Sqn.	Hurricanes	12 (4)	Castletown	15	Squadron Leader J. Sample.

Notes:
(1) Squadron moving to Hawkinge. Non-operational during transit.
(2) Squadron ready to move to Turnhouse to rest and retrain.
(3) Squadron non-operational. Still working-up after recent formation.
(4) Flights detached at Dyce and Montrose.
(5) Squadron non-operational. Resting and re-training.
(6) One Flight only. Still working-up.

CHAPTER 6

THE SKIRMISHING OF JULY

In the broad sense the Battle of Britain can justifiably be said to have opened on the last day of June 1940, for on that day, with the landing of enemy troops on the Channel Island of Guernsey and the complete occupation of the Islands within twenty-four hours, unopposed German armed forces first set foot on sovereign territories of the British Isles. On Monday 1st July London announced that communications with the Islands had been severed. Within a month the *Luftwaffe* was to establish a landing ground on Guernsey from which fighter *Staffeln* would operate against England[1].

The suggestion that R.A.F. Fighter Command was granted a respite after the Dunkirk evacuation, in which to make good the heavy losses suffered, may be somewhat misleading, for it must be remembered that until 17th June six Hurricane squadrons were engaged in the defence of British and French forces elsewhere in France. Although stoutly maintaining that they ultimately left the mainland "in good order and discipline", these squadrons were in truth utterly exhausted, and many of the aircraft which managed to fly home were promptly consigned, if not actually to the scrap heap, to languish at Maintenance Units. Moreover, many of the groundcrews from these and other R.A.F. squadrons were unable to rejoin their units before mid-July, having travelled by all manner of routes to British ports.

The state of these squadrons at the beginning of the Battle must be qualified for, in numerous accounts of the air fighting, in which details of the forces deployed are quoted,

it is implied that the squadrons were fully operational. This was far from the truth.

For instance, No. 73 Squadron, sent north to Church Fenton to recover from its ordeal in France, had only seven pilots fully fit for operations, and every Hurricane was undergoing some measure of repair. Its ground personnel were only up to 45 per cent of establishment. No. 242 Squadron—also with Hurricanes—although not so heavily engaged as No. 73, was languishing at Coltishall, almost paralysed through lack of spares and equipment, incapable of putting sufficient aircraft

A German Army band marches down Smith Street, St. Peter Port, Guernsey, shortly after the occupation of the Channel Islands. (Photo: Carel Toms)

[1] Aircraft of Major Günther Freiherr von Maltzahn's II./JG 53 <Pik As>, and from JG 27, used the airstrip at different stages of the Battle.

Kriegsmarine flak ship in St. Peter Port harbour, apparently mounting a 20-mm. cannon. (Photo: Carel Toms)

into the air to ensure adequate combat training of replacement pilots. No. 87 Squadron at Church Fenton, although fully strengthed with 23 pilots, was down to only half its ground crew establishment and possessed no qualified armourers. No. 605 Squadron had recently been given an aged collection of fabric-winged Hurricanes as replacements for aircraft lost in France, and now, despite the extreme dilapidation of its aeroplanes, the Squadron was told that no chance existed of their replacement in the immediate future[2].

---

[2] This Squadron had brought home eight of the old L-series Hurricanes, of which four were promptly grounded and re-allocated as Ground Instruction machines; their replacements were equally old—but at least had not been ravished by combat.

Finally, both Nos. 245 (Hurricanes) and 611 (Spitfires) Squadrons were regarded as non-operational due to low strength of aircraft and other factors, and were withdrawn to Turnhouse and Digby, respectively—the former soon to be moved to Aldergrove in Northern Ireland where it remained until long after the Battle was over.

If the R.A.F. was licking its wounds after disengaging from France, the *Luftwaffe* was quickly making good its losses and moving up to its bases in Northern Europe. By 1st July the operational units of *Luftflotte 5* were almost fully deployed in Norway and Denmark, while a total of eleven bomber *Gruppen* had moved into their allotted bases in France and Belgium. Such was the supreme confidence imbued by their victorious campaign over the French that some of these bomber units had already commenced night training sorties *over Britain*—with precious little interference from the defences. The German ground echelons worked with extraordinary speed to establish the command and communications structures necessary to co-ordinate the strength of the two *Luftflotten* for the likely assault on Britain.

And all the while the British—now deprived of an Allied continental-based Intelligence for the first time in centuries—strove to operate a makeshift aerial photo reconnaissance over Germany's newly won territories in order to piece together a picture of the forces massing for the coming Battle.

Monday 1st July

As German forces gathered for the occupation of the Island of Jersey under cover of thick mist, which extended along the north French coast during the early morning hours, the day dawned clear and fine over Southern England. The night had been restless for much of the country for, although no more than twenty enemy bombers had been plotted over Britain, air raid warning sirens had been sounded in twenty counties. The night fighter Blenheims had also been up, and one, flown by Pilot Officer Sisman of No. 29 Squadron from Digby in Lincolnshire, had been diverted towards a raider. Unfortunately searchlights exposed the Blenheim and evidently blinded the pilot, for eyewitnesses reported seeing the aircraft roll on to its back and dive to the ground, bursting into flames on impact; it was also said that the enemy aircraft then bombed the wreckage and both crew members were killed.

The early morning mist over France prevented offensive operations by *Luftflotten 2* and *3*, although limited reconnaissance was undertaken by several *Aufklärungsgruppen* at first light, two Dornier Do 215s falling to anti-aircraft guns on the East Coast[3]. A Junkers Ju 88 of 3.(F)/121 also failed to return to its base, but it must be assumed that this suffered engine failure or fuel shortage over the sea as no such reconnaissance aircraft was engaged over Britain.

The mist also frustrated British reconnaissance of the French coast and it was not until later in the day that a successful sortie was flown by three Blenheims (escorted by six Hurricanes of No. 145 Squadron) over the Abbeville area,

---

[3] For a note on the use of Dornier Do 215 aircraft on reconnaissance missions, see Appendix C.

Bristol Blenheim IF fighter *L1336:WR-E* of No. 248 Squadron in 1940; note the ventral fairing with four 0.303-in. Browning machine guns.

Views of Oberleutnant Gillios' bullet-torn Dorner Do 17Z, 3Z+GS of 8./KG 77, in a Kentish hop field, shot down by fighters and the Dover defences on 1st July 1940.

although two earlier attempts had been made by other squadrons.

It was in the North that No. 72 Squadron at Acklington drew Fighter Command's first blood of the Battle. In gloomy early morning light and under threatening clouds, three Spitfires of Blue Section (Flt. Lt. Edward Graham, Fg. Off. Edgar John Wilcox and F/Sgt. Harry Steere)[4] were ordered off to investigate an aircraft in the vicinity of a convoy eight miles off Sunderland. This materialised as a Heinkel He 59 float biplane at 500 feet and displaying Red Cross markings. Quickly ordering line astern, Graham led his section into the traditional No. 1 Attack, firing more than 2,500 rounds at the hapless seaplane, which hurriedly put down on the water. The crew of four was rescued by an escorting cruiser as their aircraft sank[5].

This action took place shortly after 06.00 hours, and three hours later further action was joined over Yorkshire—but with rather different results. Three Spitfires of Yellow Section, No. 616 Squadron from Leconfield, were engaged on an air training flight; Fg. Off. Robert Miller was demonstrating "tail chase" tactics to two new pilots, Plt. Off. R.A. Smith[6] and Plt. Off. W.L.B. Walker, when they were warned to look out for an enemy raider in their vicinity. Catching sight of a Dornier Do 17, Miller ordered Walker to attack. No doubt the trainee pilot performed a model attack but, on pressing his firing button, discovered his guns were empty—the exercise had been a cine-gun sortie! The Dornier escaped. . .

In the South the morning remained relatively quiet and the small number of X-raids investigated turned out to be Sunderland flying boats. However, shortly after mid-day a deep-sea convoy, codenamed JUMBO, which was approaching Plymouth radioed that it was being dive-bombed, and at 12.31

hours three Hurricanes of No. 213 Squadron scrambled from Exeter to mount guard over the ships—only to find the raiders gone. The bombers were almost certainly Junkers Ju 87s of III./St.G 51 which had been among the first such units to report being operational from the airfields at Cherbourg.

In the early afternoon, returning R.A.F. reconnaissance aircraft reported improved weather conditions over France and, as a precaution, No. 11 Group increased its patrols over the Channel. No. 235 Squadron[7] also flew three offensive patrols over Guernsey on the look-out for German transport aircraft. During one of these, at about 14.00 hours, Fg. Off. W.J. Carr sighted and attacked a Dornier Do 17 and claimed it damaged.

The constant friendly "traffic" flying to and fro over the coast undoubtedly confused the radar picture[8] for, at about 15.00 hours reports started coming in from the Observer Corps of several German aircraft well inland. In the North a Junkers Ju 88 of KG 30 was claimed damaged by No. 602 Squadron's Blue Section at 15.15 hours near Dunbar, and an hour later a Heinkel He 111 of KG 26 was intercepted by Yellow Section (Fg. Off. R. Miller, Fg. Off. J.S. Bell and Plt. Off. J. Brewster) of No. 616 Squadron over Yorkshire; the German bomber, which had bombed Hull, was badly damaged and struggled south, only to ditch off the Suffolk coast. The crew of four was picked up and landed at Harwich.

Better luck attended the fighters of No. 11 Group later in the evening when a Dornier Do 17 of 2./KG 77 was plotted

---

[4] Detached from No. 19 Squadron.

[5] On interrogation the German crew members complained bitterly at the violation of the Red Cross. Graham's action was later fully vindicated with the issue of an order warning that enemy seaplanes found flying in the vicinity of convoys did so at their own risk. The absence of medical crew members in the great majority of the "ambulance/rescue" aircraft must have been significant.

[6] Pilot Officer Robert Allwyn Smith evidently never became fully operational; he was to be killed on a night flying training sortie on 7th August, and is not included in the official list of Battle of Britain participants; his presence during the confrontation with the Dornier would presumably have qualified him for the Battle of Britain Clasp, had it occurred after 10th July.

[7] A Blenheim squadron which at this time was attached to Coastal Command with a Flight at Bircham Newton in Norfolk, and the other at Thorney Island, near Portsmouth.

[8] I.F.F. radar (Identification of Friend or Foe) had still to be fitted in about 30 per cent of the R.A.F.'s operational aircraft; however, its installation in all Fighter Command aircraft was to be completed by 14th July.

Junkers Ju 87R, with long range fuel tanks under the wings; this variant was fairly widely used by the *Stukageschwader* on the Channel coast during the first half of the Battle of Britain.

approaching Kenley. Three Spitfires of No. 64 Squadron (Fg. Off. D.M. Taylor, Sub-Lt. F. Dawson-Paul, R.N., and Plt. Off. Milne) were ordered off to guard their airfield, and six Hurricanes of No. 145 Squadron diverted from patrol to cut off the enemy's line of retreat. All nine fighters engaged the German bomber and, after a lengthy chase, finally shot it down at 19.20 hours into the Channel 45 miles south of Beachy Head.

The first day's fighting had been confused, and such was the nature of enemy attacks that no strategic plan or aim could be deduced—other than its obvious need to engage in widespread reconnaissance. In truth the *Luftwaffe* had not as yet formulated any strategic plan. The east coast ports of Wick and Hull had been bombed (the former suffering 14 dead) and the convoy JUMBO had been singled out for a "set-piece" attack, and these raids might have suggested that British shipping and ports were to become main targets for a preliminary softening-up phase.

Fighter Command was still re-arranging its Order of Battle and during the day several fighter squadrons had moved up to Sector advanced airfields, among them the veterans of No. 79 Squadron who transferred from Biggin Hill to Hawkinge on the south coast of Kent.

R.A.F. FIGHTER COMMAND LOSSES — MONDAY 1st JULY 1940

1.	3 Sqn. Wick	NC	Flying accident; no casualties	Not known	Not known	Hurricane	—	Cat. 2 Damaged
2.	29 Sqn. Digby	C	During night interception over Lincolnshire, searchlights blinded pilot causing him to crash. Enemy aircraft bombed wreck and killed both crew.	00.40 hrs.	Plt.Off. Sisman Sgt. Reed	Blenheim I	*L1376*	Cat. 3 Destroyed

LUFTWAFFE LOSSES—MONDAY 1st JULY 1940

1.	Aufkl. Gr. Ob. d. L.	CM	Target Grimsby. Probably shot down by anti-aircraft gunfire.	Dornier Do 215	100 %	Ltn. Vockel + three crew missing.	
2.	Aufkl. Gr. Ob. d. L.	CM	Target Liverpool. Probably shot down by anti-aircraft gunfire.	Dornier Do 215	100 %	Oblt. Rothenberg, Ltn. Kikat + two crew missing.	
3.	3(F)/121	CM	Target not known. Aircraft not destroyed over the United Kingdom.	Junkers Ju 88A	100 %	Fate of crew not notified.	
4.	St. St./KG 1	NCM	Crashed near Kolberg. Not encountered by R.A.F. aircraft.	Heinkel He 111H-2	100 %	Crew unhurt.	
5.	3./KG 4	CM	Bombed oil tanks at Hull. Attacked by Spitfires of 616 Sqn., flown by Miller, Bell and Brewster, and ditched; crew picked up and landed at Harwich at 17.50 hrs.	Heinkel He 111H (5J+EL)	100 %	Ofw. Herman Diasbach, Oblt. Friedrich Wilhelm Koch, unhurt; Fw.Alfred Weber and Ofw. Rudolf Ernst wounded; all made P.O.W.	
6.	I./KG 51	CM	Damaged by Spitfires of 602 Sqn. near Dunbar at 15.45 hrs., and crashed at Melun-Villaroche.	Junkers Ju 88	60-70 %	Crew unhurt.	
7.	1./KG 77	CM	Target Harwich. Probably shot down by anti-aircraft gunfire.	Dornier Do 17Z	100 %	Oblt. Steiner + three crew missing.	
8.	2./KG 77	CM	Shot down by Spitfires of 64 Sqn., and Hurricanes of 145 Sqn. near Brighton at 19.30 hrs.	Dornier Do 17Z	100 %	Four crew missing; names not notified.	
9.	2./KG 77	CM	Target Dover. Probably shot down by anti-aircraft gunfire.	Dornier Do 17Z	100 %	Oblt. Kretzschman + three crew missing.	
10.	8./KG 77	CM	Damaged by fighters and shot down by A.A. near Dover.	Dornier Do 17Z	100 %	Oblt. Gillios + one killed; one missing.	
11.	8./KG 77	CM	Target Aldershot. Probably shot down by anti-aircraft gunfire.	Dornier Do 17Z	100 %	Four crew missing; names not notified.	
12.	9./KG 77	CM	Target Dover. Probably shot down by anti-aircraft gunfire	Dornier Do 17Z	100 %	Oblt. Kapsch + three missing.	
13.	*Seenot-flugkdo. 3*	CM	Shot down by Spitfires of Graham, Wilcox and Steere of 72 Sqn. near convoy 8 miles east of Sunderland at 06.01 hrs.	Heinkel He 59 (D-ASAM) (1)	100 %	Uffz. Ernst Ielsen, Ltn. Hans-Joachim Fehske and Ogefr. Erich Philipp rescued by R.N. unhurt; Uffz. Stuckmann severely wounded	

[(1) This aircraft was reported lost in German records during 2nd July; however, three independently-compiled contemporary British reports (R.A.F. Squadron and Group records, and Admiralty Day Report) all confirm the action took place as stated above. German records also suggest that the aircraft, engaged on a search/rescue operation, was not lost through enemy action.]

Tuesday 2nd July

In contrast to the previous day, 2nd July was cloudy with outbreaks of rain over much of Britain. Once again German air activity was on a small scale and, during the course of 340 operational sorties, Fighter Command shot down only one

German aircraft; this was a reconnaissance Dornier Do 215 of *Aufklärungsgruppe Oberbefehlshaber der Luftwaffe* which, at 08.45 hours, fell to the guns of three Spitfires (Flt. Lt. W.J. Leather, Plt. Off. J.R.G. Sutton and Plt. Off. J.W. Lund) of 611 Squadron off the east coast at Withernsea.

It was on this day that No. 238 Squadron, which had only been formed at Middle Wallop half-way through May with Hurricanes, was reported operational for the first time. On the same airfield, however, another Hurricane squadron was experiencing some difficulty in working up to combat status; this was No. 1 Squadron of the Royal Canadian Air Force, to whose pilots the English countryside seemed utterly crowded with confusing landmarks and to whom the radio "patter" of Fighter Command presented all the difficulties of a new language. Moreover, taking on charge a number of the new Canadian-built Hurricanes—at its own request—the Squadron soon discovered that two different sets of tools, one American and one British, were required for servicing each aircraft (the airframe being built to American standards, while the early Canadian Hurricanes were fitted with Merlins manufactured at Derby). In due course these hybrid Hurricanes were returned to the Maintenance Units and replaced by standard British-built aircraft.

Another Squadron, No. 19, on Duxford's satellite airfield at

Waiting in the wings. Although in action over Dunkirk a month earlier, No. 222 Squadron was not heavily committed in the Battle of Britain until the latter stages. Here three pilots (*left to right*), Sergeant John Burgess, Flying Officer Brian van Mentz and Pilot Officer Hilary Edridge, relax at Kirton-in-Lindsey between patrols. (Photo: Flt. Lt. R.B. Johnson)

Fowlmere—which had been the first to receive Spitfires in September 1938—was also experiencing problems with its aircraft. It was at the beginning of July that the first few cannon-armed Spitfires were issued to the Squadron, equipment which was received with great enthusiasm, until it was found that the guns suffered an appalling stoppage rate. Termed Spitfire Mark IBs, the new aircraft were armed with a single Hispano Mark I gun in each wing, but these early guns were dogged by unreliable feed mechanism and an ejector which, manufactured to very close tolerances, caused frequent jamming of spent cases and stoppages of the gun. Furthermore it was soon discovered that the cannon were markedly prone to icing at heights above 20,000 feet.

Squadron Leader Philip Campbell Pinkham—No. 19's commanding officer—while enthusiastic about the tremendous potential destructive power, accuracy and range of the guns, explained that one gun stoppage rendered the fighter useless as the asymmetric recoil of the remaining gun made it impossible to aim; he also deprecated the small quantity of ammunition carried (sufficient for only six seconds' firing time), suggesting that it was quite inadequate when intercepting enemy fighters[9]. As will be shown, No. 19 was to fight a losing battle—not so much against the *Luftwaffe* but against its own impotence—only meeting the enemy on more equal terms when the two-cannon Spitfires were eventually discarded in exchange for "conventional" eight-gun fighters.

It had been Lord Beaverbrook who, recognising the great potential of the 20-mm gun, had insisted that the cannon-armed Spitfires be rushed into service before completion of full trials at the Aeroplane and Armament Experiemtal Establishment, and the Air Fighting Development Unit. While this great exponent of administrative expediency gained a reputation for "getting things done", he had yet to learn that no alternative existed to thorough equipment testing and extensive development before general Service use—least of all in wartime. His early months in a difficult but vitally important appointment were to be punctuated by a series of similar headstrong and ill-advised decisions but—in the longer term these were to be far outweighed by the monumental achievements of accelerated production within Britain's aircraft industry.

---

[9] Cf. Form 540, No. 19 Squadron, July 1940.

R.A.F. FIGHTER COMMAND LOSSES — TUESDAY 2nd JULY 1940 — Nil

LUFTWAFFE LOSSES—TUESDAY 2nd JULY 1940

1.	Aufkl. Gr. Ob. d. L.	CM	Shot down by Spitfires of Leather, Sutton and Lund of 611 Sqn., off Withernsea at approx. 08.35 hrs.	Dornier Do 215	100 %	Four crew missing; names not notified.
2.	St./KG 2	CM	Damaged in combat with unknown R.A.F. fighters.	Dornier Do 17Z	90 %	Crew safe; aircraft crashed at base.
3.	I./KG 3	CM	Believed shot down by A.A. fire over England.	Dornier Do 17Z	100 %	Oblt. Scharpkowski + three missing.
4.	II./KG 51	CM	Damaged during landing at Evreux airfield.	Junkers Ju 88	10 %	Crew unhurt.
5.	II./KG 76	NCM	Damaged during landing at Münster-Handorf airfield.	Junkers Ju 88A-1	30 %	Crew unhurt.
6.	I./JG 2	CM	Crashed at Soesterberg; probably not the result of combat.	Messerschmitt Bf 109E-3	100 %	Pilot unhurt.
7.	Kurierstaffel 12	NCM	Crashed at Châteaudun; cause not known, but not enemy action.	Focke-Wulf Fw 58	100 %	Oberst Abernetty and Oberstltn. Lock killed.
8.	Transp. St. Fl. Korps V	NCM	Crashed at Rhein Main airfield. Not enemy action.	Junkers Ju 52	70 %	Three crew injured.

Wednesday 3rd July

With fine weather over most of Britain the *Luftwaffe* resumed its attacks against coastal targets, occasionally venturing overland under cover of darkness. Two more R.A.F. squadrons achieved operational status; the first, No. 249 with Hurricanes at Leconfield in Yorkshire, had assumed a limited night defence rôle, sending one Flight at a time to Prestwick to carry out night training. As yet it was only considered fully operational by day. At Croydon No. 501 (County of Gloucester) Squadron, Auxiliary Air Force, which had fought so hard in France—and suffered accordingly—was now declared fully fit once more for operations.

On the other side of the Channel all three *Gruppen* of KG 1, KG 2, KG 54 and KG 77 were ready for action, and in Norway KG 26 and KG 30 commenced fairly regular operations over Britain from Stavanger. It is estimated that the three *Luftflotten* commanders could operate between 400 and 500 "heavy" bombers, about 100 dive-bombers and three whole *Geschwader* of short-range fighters (about 300 aircraft). Perhaps more important were the relatively large numbers of reconnaissance aircraft being flown by the four *Aufklärungsgruppen* (Aufkl. Gr. 120, 121, 122 and 123), and it was among these units that Fighter Command did relatively heavy execution during July. The aircraft almost invariably flew singly, without fighter escort, and lacked the mutual crossfire protection afford in the formations of bombers. Unquestionably their heavy losses were in no small way contributory to the poor state of German Intelligence which was to be the cause of such wasted German effort later on.

It was estimated from raid plots that more than fifty enemy aircraft approached Britain's coasts on 3rd July, of which about a quarter were reconnaissance aircraft. A Dornier Do 17 was encountered off the Yorkshire coast by Fg. Off. G.E. Moberley, Fg. Off. H.S.L. Dundas and F/Sgt. Bernard of No. 616 Squadron, and although the enemy aircraft was clearly seen to have crashed into the sea, no such loss can be identified in German records. The fact that another similar aircraft was claimed damaged shortly afterwards—again

with no mention in German records—suggests that some *Luftwaffe* support units were operating against Britain while omitting to file the statutory returns of losses through their respective *Fliegerkorps* quartermaster staffs. (This administrative lapse was soon found to compromise the units' chance of obtaining replacement crews and aircraft, and a "consolidated return" was to be raised on 26th July which purported to list all aircraft losses which had not been subjects of daily returns—but only a single, incomplete copy of this return is known to survive.)[10]

The most successful pilots on 3rd July were those of No.

---

[10] The whole contentious matter of aircraft losses sustained by the *Luftwaffe* during the Battle of Britain has to a certain extent been resolved by a detailed analysis of claims, not previously undertaken in official circles. While numerous apparent anomalies have been explained by duplication of R.A.F. claims, others can only be attributed to omissions from German records. Such omissions can often be traced to specific units (particularly in instances in which crew members survived to be taken prisoner) and the constant omission by these units of their losses suggests that there existed other channels by which losses could be made good. It is also apparent that the notifiction of losses by some units was hampered by poor communications. As will be shown later, some units adopted a *weekly* return of losses, resulting in inaccurate dating of their casualties; numerous examples of this are evident (as denoted in the daily losses shown in this book) so that losses hitherto published, and which have been slavishly derived directly from the *Luftwaffe Quartermaster General*'s returns are clearly inaccurate—often by a considerable margin. The above remarks are particularly applicable to *Seenotflugkommando* (air/sea rescue units), *Wettererkundungsstaffeln* (weather reconnaissance flights), several of the *Küstenfliegergruppen* (coastal reconnaissance and minelaying units) and some of the specialist bomber units (such as *Kampfgeschwader* 40 and *Kampfgruppe* 100). Several other factors have been investigated to explain the inaccuracy of claims—on both sides—and these will be explained in the course of the narrative. However, still largely unresolved are the very wide discrepancies between the claims against the *Stukageschwader* and losses recorded in the German returns.

Waiting in the Wings. Another Squadron heavily committed during the last stages of the Battle of France, this time with Hurricanes, was No. 17, one of whose pilots is seen with *P3878:YB-W* at Debden during the first week in July 1940. (Photo: R.A.F. Museum)

603 (City of Edinburgh) Squadron which was, at this early stage of the Battle, operating Sections and Flights of Spitfires at Dyce, Montrose and Turnhouse. At 13.46 hours Green Section (Fg. Off. B.J.G. Carbury, Plt. Off. R. Berry and Plt. Off B. Stapleton) was ordered off to investigate an aircraft in the neighbourhood of Montrose and found a Junkers Ju 88A-2 of 8 *Staffel*, KG 30, which they shot down into the sea. Three of the crew were seen to survive the combat. At about 16.15 hours Red Section (Sqn. Ldr. G.L. Denholm, Plt. Off. Stewart-Clark and Sgt. I.K. Arber) intercepted another Ju 88 from the same *Staffel*, 25 miles north-east of Peterhead; in shooting down this aircraft, all three Spitfires suffered damage from the German gunners. Yet a third Ju 88 of 8./KG 30 was destroyed by No. 603 Squadron when Plt. Off. I.S. Ritchie, Plt. Off G.K. Gilroy and Sgt. J.R. Caister came upon the raider off Stonehaven; local coastguards confirmed that the enemy bomber crashed into the sea.

However, most of the day's activity was in the South. Numerous patrolling pilots caught fleeting glimpses of enemy aircraft. The civilian police at Holmbury St. Mary—a small village near Dorking in Surrey—identified a low-flying bomber and hurriedly phoned a sighting report to Biggin Hill before it was even sighted by the Observer Corps. Ten minutes later two heavy bombs fell on the outskirts of Guildford, killing fifteen people. A snap raid was carried out by a handful of Dornier Do 17s against the forward airfield at Manston, but the light bombs dropped caused no more harm than to destroy a gang mower. The raid was interrupted by the arrival of nine Spitfires of No. 54 Squadron which broke up the attack, claiming one Dornier damaged.

Several of the Manston raiders had not dropped their bombs and these aircraft fanned out over Kent, Surrey and Sussex, being spotted over Kenley, Edenbridge and West Malling. One of the Dorniers was caught by Flt. Lt. J.H. Coghlan in a Hurricane of No. 56 Squadron and, after a long chase, was shot down off Burnham at about 16.30 hours. Coghlan had in fact been directed towards another German bomber (plotted as Raid 34 by the Observer Corps) and this was finally caught and shot down at Wateringbury by Plt. Off. P.M. Gardner, Sgt. E.A. Bayley and Sgt. W.B. Higgins of No. 32 Squadron in Hurricanes from Biggin Hill. Although German records only include one Dornier Do 17 lost on this day, both raiders were seen from the ground to crash, survivors being rescued from the former, while wreckage of the latter was still visible at the scene of the crash more than ten years after the War.

Several electric storms added to flying hazards later in the afternoon, more than a dozen barrage balloons lining the Thames Estuary being destroyed by lightning. A Spitfire of No. 74 Squadron, on patrol from Hornchurch over Margate, was struck and the pilot, Sergeant White, was killed in the crash.

The day's total of five German aircraft shot down scarcely reflected the flying effort mounted by Fighter Command. Twenty-eight squadrons had flown more than 120 patrols at Flight or Section strength, involving 570 sorties. Apart from the light raid on Manston, scattered bombs had fallen on White Waltham (an airfield being used as a ferry pool), Kenley and Lympne. As darkness fell, enemy aircraft were reported flying at low level over the Thames Estuary and this was probably accounted for by minelaying by the German *Küstenfliegergruppen*—an explanation supported by reports of heavy explosions out to sea off the Isle of Sheppey, probably caused by premature detonation of air-dropped mines entering the water[11].

---

[11] The fusing of German mines, at this stage in the War, did not permit their sowing in water less than seven feet deep. The numerous sandbanks in the Thames Estuary caused a large number of air-dropped mines to detonate prematurely.

R.A.F. FIGHTER COMMAND LOSSES — WEDNESDAY 3rd JULY 1940

1.	74 Sqn., Hornchurch	NC	Struck by lightning and crashed near Margate killing the pilot.	17.00 hrs.	Sgt. White	Spitfire	K9928	Cat. 3 Destroyed
2.	238 Sqn., Middle Wallop	C	Aircraft damaged in combat with Ju 88 south of Middle Wallop; pilot returned unhurt to base.	16.50 hrs.	Flt. Lt. J.C. Kennedy	Hurricane	—	Cat. 1 Damaged
3.	603 Sqn., Dyce	C	Three aircraft damaged in combat with He 111 near Peterhead	16.00 hrs.	Sqn. Ldr. G.L. Denholm Plt. Off.D. Stewart-Clarke Sgt. I.K. Arber	Spitfire	—	Cat. 1 Damaged

LUFTWAFFE LOSSES—WEDNESDAY 3rd JULY 1940

1.	1(F)./123	CM	Damaged by Hurricane flown by Kennedy of of 238 Sqn. near Middle Wallop airfield at approx. 17.00 hrs.	Junkers Ju 88A	3 %	Ltn. Wachtel and crew returned safely.
2.	3(F)./123	CM	Crashed at Buc airfield; cause not known.	Junkers Ju 88A	20 %	Crew unhurt.
3.	8./KG 30	CM	Shot down by Spitfires of 603 Sqn. (Green Section), near Montrose at approx. 14.00 hrs.	Junkers Ju 88A-2	100 %	Four crew members missing.
4.	8./KG 30	CM	Shot down by Spitfires of 603 Sqn. (Red Section), near Stonehaven at approx. 19.15 hrs.	Junkers Ju 88A-2	100 %	Four crew members missing.
5.	8./KG 30	CM	Shot down by Spitfires of 603 Sqn. (Red Section), NE of Peterhead at approx. 16.15 hrs.	Junkers Ju 88A-2	100 %	Hptm. von Langsdorf, Ltn. Buroth + two crew members missing.
6.	II./KG 54	NCM	Taxying accident on Gütersloh airfield.	Junkers Ju 88A	20 %	No casualties notified.
7.	8./KG 77	CM	Shot down by Hurricane flown by Coghlan of 56 Sqn. off Burnham at approx. 16.30 hrs.	Dornier Do 17Z (3Z+GS)	100 %	Ogefr. Erich Hoffmann and Uffz. Waldemar Theilig killed; Uffz. Richard Brandes and Oblt. Hans-Georg Gallion, wounded, P.O.W.
8.	II./JG 52	NCM	Aircraft crashed at Böblingen; cause not known.	Messerschmitt Bf 109 E-3	100 %	Pilot killed; name not notified.
9.	I./KGzbV 172	NCM	Landing accident at Brest airfield.	Junkers Ju 52 (Nr.5515)	20 %	No casualties notified.
10.	II./St.G 77	NCM	Landing accident at Picauville airfield.	Junkers Ju 87	60 %	No casualties notified.

Thursday 4th July

This day marked the commencement of co-ordinated attacks by the *Luftwaffe* based throughout Northern France in concert with fighter units based in the Pas de Calais. If the British Government had been in any doubt as to the German target priorities, few doubts can have remained by the end of the day, for in both the major attacks by the *Luftwaffe* upon shipping targets Fighter Command was caught off guard and failed to score.

The first blow fell at 08.41 hours when 33 Junkers Ju 87s of *III.Gruppe, Stukageschwader 51* dived out of a misty sky to hit shipping and installations at the Portland naval base on the Dorset coast. No fighters were patrolling the area, and the raiders' task was completed in four short minutes. A merchant tanker, which had only arrived in Weymouth Bay twelve hours previously, was hit by a 500-kilo (1,100-lb.) bomb, set on fire and burned for 24 hours before the blaze was controlled. The largest vessel in the naval base itself became the Stukas' main target, and it was aboard this ship that the first Victoria Cross of the Battle of Britain was won—only the second in the entire history of the award to be won in or over Britain[12] When the enemy bombers arrived over the base there was present only one ship armed with anti-aircraft guns, the auxiliary anti-aircraft ship, H.M.S. *Foyle Bank*, 5,582 tons. Manning one of the "pom-pom" guns was Acting Seaman Jack Foreman Mantle. Early in the attack the *Foyle Bank* received a direct hit and Jack Mantle's left leg was shattered, but despite this he continued firing and operating his gun manually as the ship's power system had been put out of action. After further hits Mantle was repeatedly wounded in many places and, although he must have realised his life was now forfeit, he remained in action until the enemy left. As the stricken *Foyle Bank* began to sink, Jack Mantle fell dying by the gun he had so valiantly fought. His posthumous award of the Victoria Cross was gazetted on 3rd September 1940.

The principal weaknesses in the defence were twofold. The responsibilities of No. 11 Group, whose Headquarters at Uxbridge in effect faced the entire front of both *Luftflotten 2* and *3*, were too great, and it was clearly impossible to deploy fighter patrols from one operations centre over such a large front. It was for this reason that responsibility for local defence rested largely upon Sector operations rooms, and herein lay the weakness of some of the Sectors—and that of Middle Wallop, in which Portland was situated, in particular. Only on this day was construction work on the coastal satellie airfield at Warmwell considered adequately advanced to permit operations by Middle Wallop squadrons. By the time coastal patrols could be put up over the South Coast the Portland raiders had long since departed[13].

The other main attack of the day was launched against a convoy of about nine ships as it passed through the Straits of Dover shortly after about 14.00 hours. Sound plots in the vicinity of the convoy, recorded by numerous coastal Observer posts throughout the morning suggest that it had been shadowed by German reconnaissance aircraft, and the precision with which the raid (by two *Staffeln* of Dornier Do 17s escorted by 30 Messerschmitt Bf 109s) was timed to catch the convoy without fighter escort tends to confirm this. The bombers, however, lingered near the ships longer than was necessary so that eight Hurricanes of No. 79 Squadron, scrambled from Hawkinge at 14.05 hours, were in time to catch the enemy formation. The Hurricanes were in turn set upon by the German escort which shot down and killed Sgt. H. Cartwright, D.F.M., over St. Margaret's Bay. None of the raiders was claimed, and one of the ships which suffered a direct hit managed to beach on the coast near Deal.

German fighter pilots were at this stage beginning to get into their stride with "free chase" patrols over the Kent coast, joining in sweeps at medium altitude on the look-out for small numbers of British fighters on standing patrols. The apparently miraculous speed and accuracy with which Fighter Command intercepted raiders suggested to the Germans that the R.A.F. was resorting to the wasteful and exhausting practice of mounting precautionary standing patrols. The significance of the coastal radar chain was only slowly

An informal photograph of Adolf Galland, *Gruppenkommandeur* of III./JG 26 *<Schlageter>* until 22nd August 1940 when he was promoted *Geschwader Kommodore*. This legendary officer was one of the most popular and respected German fighter leaders; at 30, he was to become one of the youngest Generals in the German forces. He was to be awarded the Knight's Cross on 29th July 1940 after achieving 20 combat victories, this being followed by the Oakleaves on 24th September, the Swords on 1st July 1941 and the Diamonds on 28th January 1942. Later in the War he was appointed Inspector of Fighters and in the final months before Germany's defeat led a crack fighter unit (JV 44) flying Messerschmitt Me 262 jet fighters (Photo: Author's Collection).

---

[12] The first and only Victoria Cross to be won in or over Britain had been awarded to Lieutenant Leefe Robinson of the Worcester Regiment and Royal Flying Corps who, under conditions of great danger and difficulty, destroyed a German airship over Cuffley, Hertfordshire, during the night of 2nd/3rd September 1915.

[13] On 13th July No. 10 Group, with Headquarters at Box in Wiltshire, was fully activated with defence responsibilities for the South-West. Thereafter there were precious few instances of raids upon Portland escaping as lightly as that on 4th July.

The Messerschmitt Bf 109E, the *Luftwaffe*'s standard single-engine fighter during 1939-40. These E-4s have bomb racks under the fuselage, and display both early and late cockpit canopies and camouflage schemes. It has been said that the aircraft above belonged to 3./Erpr. Gr. 210, a special pathfinder fighter-bomber unit that came into being early in July 1940.

coming to be recognised by the enemy.

The relatively high R.A.F. casualties suffered throughout the Battle of Britain as a result of the *Jagdgeschwader* free chase tactics testifies to their undoubted success. The famous Adolf Galland has since recorded the frustration felt by German fighter pilots when Göring later tethered his short range fighters to the bomber formations as close escort. By doing so he unquestionably deprived his *Luftwaffe* of one of its most effective tactics, which could, in time, have destroyed Fighter Command—and very nearly did so.

During the evening of the 4th nine Hurricanes of No. 32 Squadron were ordered up from Biggin Hill to patrol off Dungeness. At 18.42 hours they were vectored towards an incoming plot (Raid 20) which—too late—materialised as three *Staffeln* of Bf 109 fighters, bent on a free chase. In the first thirty seconds two Hurricanes were shot down, Plt. Off. Douglas Grice force landing unhurt near Manston, and Plt. Off. K.R. Gillman on Hawkinge airfield. Plt. Off. R.F. Smythe claimed he shot down two of the Messerschmitts.

Later that evening, on airfields in Lincolnshire and East Anglia, R.A.F. Bomber Command was preparing to carry the battle back to the German homeland. Under cover of darkness twelve Hampdens attacked enemy naval installations at Kiel with 2,000-lb. bombs, while groups totalling twenty Welling-

tons and ten Whitleys ranged over northern Germany dropping bombs in raids on Hamburg, Emden, Wilhelmshaven and Bremen. These scattered raids seldom caused much damage, but their launching, announced to an apprehensive population of Britain, had a profound effect on morale. The R.A.F. bombing raids of 1940 have seldom been accorded due recognition for their morale benefit or for the great skill and bravery involved. Furthermore it must be recorded that Bomber Command suffered much greater casualties among its flying personnel during the period of the Battle of Britain than did Fighter Command.

R.A.F. FIGHTER COMMAND LOSSES — THURSDAY 4th JULY 1940

1.	32 Sqn. Biggin Hill	C	Forced down by Bf 109 at Manston; pilot unhurt	A19.00 hrs.	Plt.Off.D.H.Grice	Hurricane	—	Cat. 2 Damaged
2.	32 Sqn. Biggin Hill	C	Forced down by Bf 109 at Hawkinge; pilot unhurt	A19.00 hrs	Plt. Off. K.R. Gillman	Hurricane	—	Cat. 2 Damaged
3.	54 Sqn. Rochford	C	Damaged in combat with Bf 109s near Manston; pilot unhurt	A12.30 hrs.	Plt. Off. J.L.Kemp	Spitfire	—	Cat. 1 Damaged
4.	54 Sqn. Rochford	C	Damaged by Bf 109s near Manston; pilot unhurt	A12.30 hrs.	Fg. Off. D.A.P. Mullen	Spitfire	—	Cat. 1 Damaged

R.A.F. Losses, 4th July 1940—*continued*

5.	79 Sqn. Hawkinge	C	Shot down over St. Margaret's Bay by Bf 109s; pilot killed.	14.30 hrs.	Sgt. H. Cartwright	Hurricane	N2619	Cat. 3 Lost
6.	222 Sqn. Kirton-in-Lindsey	NC	Flying accident near Withernsea; pilot killed.	Evening	Sgt. Lewis	Spitfire	N3294	Cat. 3 Destroyed
7.	601 Sqn. Tangmere	NC	Pilot overcome by glycol fumes during training flight over Sussex; crashed but not hurt.	Not known	Not known	Hurricane	L1936	Cat. 3 Destroyed

LUFTWAFFE LOSSES—THURSDAY 4th JULY 1940

1.	4./KG 54	CM	Shot down by Spitfires of Fokes, Saunders and Edwards of 92 Sqn., at Mere, Wincanton	Heinkel He 111P (2480:B3+DM)	100 %	Ltn. Belz, Uffz. Gerhard Bischoff and Uffz. Hermann Krack killed; Uffz. Heinz Karwelat wounded and made P.O.W.
2.	III./St.G 1	CM	Shot down by A.A. gunfire from H.M.S. *Foyle Bank* in Portland harbour at 08.50 hrs.	Junkers Ju 87B	100 %	Ltn. Schwarz + one crew member missing.
3.	III./St.G 1	CM	Aircraft landed at Cherbourg with combat damage.	Junkers Ju 87B	less than 60 %	No casualties notified.
4.	1./JG 3	NCM	Flying accident at Grandeville airfield; cause not known.	Messerschmitt Bf 109 E-1	70 %	Pilot unhurt.
5.	7./JG 3	CM	Flying accident at Dargiesen airfield; cause not known.	Messerschmitt Bf 109	10-60 %	Pilot unhurt.
6.	III./JG 27	CM	Damaged in landing at Therville after combat with Hurricane flown by Smythe of 32 Sqn. near Hawkinge at 19.00 hrs.	Messerschmitt Bf 109 E-4	25 %	Pilot unhurt.
7.	4./LG 2	CM	Shot down by Hurricane flown by Smythe of 32 Sqn. into sea near Hawkinge at 19.00 hrs.	Messerschmitt Bf 109 E-4	100 %	Pilot missing; name not notified.
8.	KGzbV 106	—	Destroyed in bombing raid by R.A.F. at Evère.	Junkers Ju 52 (6296)	100 %	No casualties.
9.	Kurier-St.Ob.d.L—	—	Destroyed in bombing raid by R.A.F. at Evère.	Junkers Ju 52 (6881)	100 %	No casualties.

Friday 5th July

Once again weather was generally poor over Britain, with rain in the North and East Anglia, and threatening skies in the South. German air activity was accordingly on a reduced scale. A number of small enemy formations were evidently recalled to their bases as they were reported by South Coast CH radar stations, but they never crossed the Channel. A single Heinkel He 111 of 8.*Staffel*, KG 1, was intercepted over Dover at about 06.30 hours by nine Spitfires of No. 65 Squadron and shot down into the sea by Blue Section (Fg. Off. G.V. Proudman[14], Sgt. Joseph Kilner and Plt. Off. K.G. Hart).

In the late evening, at 19.55 hours, three Spitfires of No. 64 Squadron took off for a reconnaissance patrol over the Pas de Calais. Perhaps not surprisingly the Section, which flew at about 22,000 feet, was intercepted by Messerschmitt Bf 109s (of JG 51) and a fierce skirmish ensued, during which Pilot Officer Milne was shot down and killed. Sub-Lt. Dawson damaged one of the enemy and brought his own damaged Spitfire home to a crash landing at Hawkinge, while Fg. Off. Taylor returned safely to Kenley.

These reconnaissance patrols were being carried out fairly frequently at this stage of the Battle, but it was soon found that the pilots, pre-occupied with their look-out for enemy interceptors, were seldom able to provide worthwhile information about enemy ground dispositions. Moreover their constant passage over the Channel tended to confuse the all-important radar picture. The losses incurred soon prompted the discontinuation of reconnaissance patrols by Fighter Command Spitfire squadrons.

On the other hand, some Spitfires *were* carrying out photographic reconnaissance sorties—very successfully. These specially modified aircraft were sent out almost daily from their base at Heston on the western outskirts of London. Part of the Photographic Development Unit[15], these unarmed Spitfires (painted pale shades of blue or green) roamed the coasts of Northern Europe taking thousands of vital photographs of enemy preparations for the invasion of Britain. In the six months from July to December 1940 their pilots carried out 841 sorties, losing a total of ten aircraft.

[14] Flying Officer Proudman was killed two days later.

[15] Established and commanded by the eccentric but brilliantly inventive Wing Commander F.S. Cotton (who had as a civilian performed various illicit pre-War reconnaissance flights over Germany), the P.D.U. later became known as the Photographic Reconnaissance Unit. The early reconnaissance Spitfires (designated Type Cs) were equipped with a fuselage-mounted camera and others in the port wing. Extra fuel was also carried, enabling long endurance sorties to be flown.

R.A.F. FIGHTER COMMAND LOSSES — FRIDAY 5th JULY 1940

1.	23 Sqn., Digby	NC	Crashed during exercise near Digby; crew unhurt.	Not known	Not known	Blenheim	K7516	Cat. 3 Destroyed
2.	64 Sqn., Kenley	C	Shot down by Bf 109 near Rouen; pilot Missing.	A20.30hrs	Plt. Off. Milne	Spitfire	P9449	Cat. 3 Missing
3.	64 Sqn., Kneley	C	Damaged by Bf 109s near Rouen; pilot landed at Hawkinge, unhurt.	A20.30 hrs.	Sub-Lt. A. Dawson-Paul	Spitfire	P9507	Cat. 2 Damaged
4.	92 Sqn., Pembrey	NC	Force landed in bog near Cardiff after engine failure; pilot unhurt.	Not known	Plt. Off. A.C. Bartley	Spitfire	P9454	Cat. 2 Damaged
5.	238 Sqn., Middle Wallop	NC	Pilot flew into Pennings Hill, near Tidworth, in bad weather and was killed.	Not known	Plt. Off. B. Firminger	Hurricane	P3703	Cat. 3 Destroyed

LUFTWAFFE LOSSES—FRIDAY 5th JULY 1940

1.	5.(F)/122	NCM	Landing accident at Thury airfield.	Dornier Do 17P	5 %	No casualties.
2.	II./KG 1	NCM	Force landed at Amiens after engine failure.	Heinkel He 111H-2	35 %	No casualties.
3.	8./KG 1	CM	Shot down by Spitfires flown by Hart, Proudman, and Kilner of 65 Sqn., near Folkestone at approx. 06.30 hrs.	Heinkel He 111H-2 (V4+GS)	100 %	Uffz. Marcklovitz killed. Gefr. Burian and Gefr. Martinck both drowned; Ofw. Hermann Frischmuth and Uffz. Gottfried Wagner made P.O.W.
4.	III./KG 2	NCM	Flying accident at Darmstadt.	Junkers Ju 52	80 %	No casualties notified.
5.	Zerst.St./KG 30	NCM	Crashed at Ludwigslust following engine failure.	Junkers Ju 88C	100 %	No casualties notified.
6.	St./KG 53	NCM	Landing accident at Lille airfield	Heinkel He 111H-2	40 %	No casualties notified.
7.	II./KG 53	NCM	Taxying accident at Fellhausen airfield.	Heinkel He 111H-2	40 %	No casualties notified
8.	St./St.G 1	NCM	Crashed near Bapaume following engine failure.	Junkers Ju 87B	40 %	No casualties notified.
9.	II./LG 1	CM	Crashed at Limoges following combat (probably with Spitfires of 611 Sqn., near Spurn Head at 17.00 hrs.)	Junkers Ju 88	100 %	No casualties notified.
10.	I./JG 1	NCM	Flying accident at Plumetot airfield.	Messerschmitt Bf 109 E-4	45 %	Pilot unhurt.
11.	I./JG 2	NCM	Landing accident at Beaumont-le-Roger airfield.	Messerschmitt Bf 109 E-1	30 %	Pilot unhurt.
12.	2./JG 51	CM	Landing accident at Deksei (?) airfield.(1)	Messerschmitt Bf 109 E-4	30 %	Pilot unhurt.

[(1) Doubt still remains as to the cause and exact location of this accident, and owing to the time similarity it seems possibly that the aircraft may have been the Messerschmitt claimed by Sub-Lt. F. Dawson-Paul, R.N., of No. 64 Squadron, to have been damaged at approx. 21.00 hrs.]

Saturday 6th July

As more of Dowding's fighter squadrons regained their former operational status with the infusion of new pilots from the Operational Training Units, the Air Marshal undertook with his Group Commanders, Keith Park and Trafford Leigh-Mallory, a limited redeployment of squadrons. As it was now obvious that Fighter Command would face a growing weight of attack on its western flank, from *Kampfgeschwader* now seen to be established in western France, Park moved No. 609 (West Riding) Squadron with Spitfires from Northolt to Middle Wallop on Salisbury Plain[16], while No. 87 Squadron with Hurricanes commenced a move from Church Fenton in Yorkshire to Exeter to cover the vital Western Approaches to Plymouth and Bristol. Also at this time the night fighter Blenheim squadron, No. 236, was moved forward from Middle Wallop to Thorney Island to provide night patrols over the Solent, Southampton and Portsmouth. Dependent entirely upon ground control and visual sighting, this Blenheim squadron remained impotent throughout the Battle, failing to engage a single enemy aircraft successfully at night.

On 6th July it was the North's turn to enjoy fine weather, while Tangmere reported rain and low cloud throughout the day. Once again No. 603 Squadron was successful when at 12.29 hours its Red Section (Plt. Off. G.K. Gilroy, Plt. Off. D. Stewart-Clark and Sgt. J.R. Caister) was ordered off against a fleeting radar plot off the Scottish coast. After a long pursuit they finally caught and shot down a reconnaissance Messer-schmitt Bf 110 of *Aufklärungsgruppe Oberbefehlshaber der Luftwaffe* one hundred miles north-north-east of Aberdeen (tarnishing their feat by identifying it as a Dornier Do 215!).

On No. 72 Squadron Plt. Off. R.D. Elliott had a narrow escape during a sortie at 20,000 feet over Yorkshire when his oxygen supply failed. Unaware of the defect, Elliott passed out and his aircraft went into a dive; recovering consciousness only 1,000 feet above the Cheviots, the pilot regained control through sheer strength and so strained his Spitfire that it was written off charge on return to his airfield at Acklington. Though not classed as injured, Elliott was admitted to hospital for lengthy examination.

The *Luftwaffe* also suffered an unusual loss on this day when a reconnaissance Dornier Do 17P of 1./Aufkl. Gr. 120 was accidentally landed in neutral Sweden and its crew was interned.

While No. 19 Squadron struggled to overcome the gun stoppage problems with its cannon-armed Spitfires, one of No. 151 Squadron's flight commanders, Flt. Lt. R.L. Smith, was ordered to collect a two-cannon Hurricane, *L1750*, from Martlesham Heath—one of the only two cannon-armed Hurricanes flown in the Battle[17]

[16] The fortunes of No. 609 Squadron were graphically chronicled in the book *Spitfire Pilot* by the late Flight Lieutenant D.M. Crook, D.F.C. (Faber & Faber, London, 1942). Bearing in mind the stringent censorship imposed upon such wartime books, this must rank among the best eye-witness accounts of the Battle. Crook himself was killed in a flying accident in 1941.

[17] As will be recounted later, both cannon-armed Hurricanes were flown in combat. The two-gun version, referred to here, carried its guns *under* the wings and suffered relatively infrequently from stoppages. This had been the trials aircraft in which the original installation of cannon had been made early in 1939, and it was largely as the result of the success of these trials that it had been decided to arm Spitfires with the bigger guns. Only when the guns were placed *inside* the restricted gunbays of the Spitfire's rather thinner wing were difficulties with the ejection mechanism encountered.

R.A.F. FIGHTER COMMAND LOSSES — SATURDAY 6th JULY 1940

1.	242 Sqn., Coltishall	NC	Flying accident near Coltishall; pilot unhurt.	Not known	Sub-Lt. R.J. Cork	Hurricane	P3813	Cat. 3 Destroyed
2.	72 Sqn., Acklington	NC	Pilot fainted from lack of oxygen but landed safely; aircraft overstrained in dive and subsequently written off.	Not known	Plt. Off. (?) Elliott	Spitfire	P9444	Cat. 3 Destroyed

LUFTWAFFE LOSSES—SATURDAY 6th JULY 1940

1.	Aufkl. Gr. OB. d. L.	CM	Shot down by Spitfires of Gilroy, Stewart-Clarke and Caister of 603 Sqn. 100 miles ENE of Aberdeen at approx. 13.15 hrs.	Messerschmitt Bf 110	100 %	Ltn. Brix and Ltn. Kösters missing.
2.	1.(F)/20	NCM	Aircraft force landed in Sweden. Further details not known.	Dornier Do 17P	100 %	Two crew members interned in Sweden.
3.	III./KG 3	NCM	Totally destroyed by premature bomb explosion.	Dornier Do 17Z	100 %	No casualties notified.
4.	II./JG 26	CM	Landing accident at Marquise-Ost airfield.	Messerschmitt Bf 109 E-1	100 %	Hptm. Noack, Gr.Kdr., killed. (1)
5.	I./JG 27	CM	Landing accident at Cherbourg airfield.	Messerschmit Bf 109 E-1	100 %	Pilot unhurt.
6.	KGzbV 9	NCM	Landing accident at Oudenarde airfield.	Junkers Ju 52 (6097)	30 %	No casualties notified.

[(1) Several German sources record Hauptmann Noack's accident as having occurred on 24th July 1940. It must be assumed that this refers to the date of notification of Next of Kin as it is unlikely that the 6th Abteilung report (dated 8th July), reporting his death, would make an error of this nature concerning a *Gruppenkommandeur*. Moreover the details and location of the accident are accurate and agree in all other reliable reference sources.]

Sunday 7th July

Although there was little sign of an improvement in the weather, the *Luftwaffe* had begun to step up its operations over Britain, commencing with sharp raids the night before. Bombs had fallen on Godalming, Aldershot, Hazelmere and Farnborough, in each instance narrowly missing important military installations. Nevertheless four railways were either struck by bombs or blocked by debris, and a total of 62 people (including fourteen soldiers) were killed. Heavy anti-aircraft fire in the area had proved of little value.

If the R.A.F. had suffered frustration during the hours of darkness, the daylight hours of this Sunday were to bring fairly heavy losses to its fighter squadrons. The *Luftwaffe* started off in its accustomed manner with weather- and photo-reconnaissance sorties over the South and East Coasts. Sqn. Ldr. John Peel (C.O. of No. 145 Squadron with Hurricanes), flying a dawn patrol over a convoy off the Isle of Wight, spotted a Dornier Do 17P "cloud-hopping" about five miles away; ordering one of his Section to remain with the convoy, he and Plt. Off. E.C.J. Wakeham set off after the enemy and eventually shot it down twenty miles south of the Needles. A couple of hours later another Hurricane Squadron, No. 43 from Tangmere, shot down another reconnaissance Do 17P— also probably shadowing the east-bound convoy that Peel's section had been escorting.

Clearly the enemy intended to watch the progress of this convoy closely, putting up constant patrols by Dorniers throughout the morning, and it was 601 Squadron's commanding officer who shared in the destruction of a third such aircraft about fifteen miles north of Cherbourg after a long chase, the enemy falling to the guns of Sqn. Ldr. Max Aitken and Fg. Off. W.P. Clyde.

It was in mid-morning that Kesselring's *Luftflotte 2* began the day's fighter screen operations with two or three free chases along the South Coast between Bognor Regis and Dover. These sweeps were to continue throughout the day and, although several Sections of R.A.F. fighters were scrambled on information passed by the Observer Corps, the Messerschmitts had long since turned for home before the Spitfires and Hurricanes arrived; after all, anything up to twenty minutes would elapse between an observer reporting an enemy aircraft over the South Coast and the arrival of fighters ordered off from an airfield perhaps fifty miles distant. Moreover such were the fuel reserves of the Messerschmitt Bf 109s that free-chasing enemy pilots seldom re-

Squadron Leader John Peel, D.S.O., D.F.C., commanded No. 145 (Hurricane) Squadron during the first ten weeks of the Battle of Britain; in this time he shot down three enemy aircraft, shared several others, was shot down twice himself and was slightly wounded. He had entered Cranwell in 1930 and had flown with the Fleet Air Arm before the War. He retired from the R.A.F. in 1948 as a Group Captain.

mained over British soil for more than fifteen to twenty minutes.

These free chases nevertheless had the desired effect of advancing the readiness state at all Sector stations south of London. No. 54 Squadron's "B" Flight, which had been ordered forward to Manston during the early morning, was scrambled to investigate an X-raid and, in preparing to attack a lone Heinkel He 111, was set upon by a *Staffel* of Bf 109s which shot down Plt. Off. A.R.McL. Campbell and Plt. Off. E.J. Coleman, both of Green Section; both force landed near Deal with minor injuries, and their section leader, Fg. Off. Desmond McMullen, succeeded in landing his damaged Spitfire at Manston.

The convoy continued on its eastward course, arriving off Folkestone by early evening, it being planned to pass through

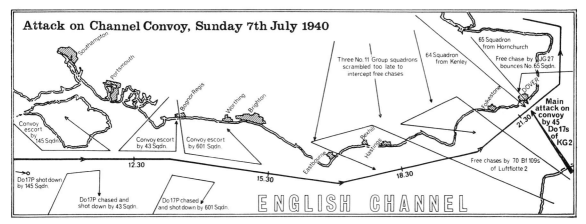

Attack on Channel Convoy, Sunday 7th July 1940

the Straits of Dover under cover of darkness. Throughout the afternoon Park maintained at least nine fighters overhead with orders to the pilots to avoid combat with enemy fighters if possible. Such was the state of apprehension that existed during the passage of this convoy that no fewer than 215 sorties were flown in its area between mid-day and 20.00 hours.

Meanwhile German reconnaissance petered out during the early evening, reliance probably being placed on sighting reports from free-chasing fighter pilots. These served to confirm the likely position of the ships by early evening so that a major attack by four *Staffeln* of I and II *Gruppen*, KG 2, could be launched at short range before darkness fell. These 45 Dornier Do 17Zs took off from their bases at Arras at 19.30 hours (British Time) and struck the convoy 55 minutes later, sinking one ship and damaging three others.

The CH radar at Pevensey, Rye and Dover had provided good warning of the approaching raid, so that seven Spitfires of No. 64 Squadron were ordered up from Kenley, together with six of No. 65 Squadron from Hornchurch, to intercept. The squadrons were slow taking off, however, and had too far to fly to intercept before bombs fell among the ships. Moreover, to meet just such a threat from intercepting fighters, a free chase by JG 27 was timed to sweep over Kent and Sussex at the time of the raid, and these Bf 109s caught No. 65 Squadron from above, shooting down and killing all three pilots of Green Section (Fg. G.V. Proudman, Plt. Off. N.J. Brisbane and Sgt. Hayes). Another pilot, F/Sgt. Franklyn, attacked and chased a 109 almost to France before shooting it down into the sea. Returning to the convoy, he found another Bf 109 and also claimed this destroyed[18].

No. 64 Squadron fared better, and caught up with the

[18] Neither of these aircraft, nor the Dornier claimed shot down by No. 43 Squadron earlier in the day, can be identified in German records.

Dorniers as they neared their own coast—albeit after they had dropped their bombs. Dawson-Paul, the Fleet Air Arm pilot, severely damaged a Do 17, causing it to crash land at Boulogne; another suffered some damage from an attack by Fg. Off. A.J.O. Jeffery, but this managed to put down safely at St. Omer.

As night descended on the English Channel, the convoy sailed on while night fighters took up the vigil and two destroyers put out from Dover to provide anti-aircraft guns in case of further attacks.

The considerable German efforts made against this convoy now left the British in no doubt whatsoever as to the *Luftwaffe*'s main targets. This confirmation brought no comfort, for at this very moment there were no fewer than seven coastal convoys in passage round Britain's coasts between Swanage and the Firth of Forth, discovery of which could now be expected to attract large enemy bomber formations. To these could be added three deep-sea convoys approaching the Channel from distant ports.

It was this type of wasteful defensive action that Dowding had feared, and the high rate of attrition could well sap the strength of Fighter Command before the real Battle was joined. This Sunday's fighting had been frustrating for the British pilots; their losses had amounted to six aircraft destroyed and two badly damaged, with four pilots killed. Five enemy aircraft were shot down, although at the time it was thought that about a dozen had fallen. Moreover the principal bombing raid of the day had escaped almost scot free.

However, the *Luftwaffe* had reason to be concerned at the loss of three reconnaissance Dorniers, two of them from 2.(F)/123. Seven such aircraft, with a high proportion of experienced officer crew members, had been lost over Britain in a week; orders were therefore given for some measure of fighter escort or cover to be provided for short range reconnaissance sorties whenever possible.

R.A.F. FIGHTER COMMAND LOSSES — SUNDAY 7th JULY 1940

1.	43 Sqn., Tangmere	NC	Pilot baled out after fire in the air 4 miles S.E. of Tangmere.	Not known	Not known	Hurricane	*L1849*	Cat. 3 Destroyed
2.	54 Sqn., Hornchurch	C	Shot down by Bf 109s near Deal; pilot slightly wounded.	A10.00 hrs.	Plt.Off.A.R.McL. Campbell	Spitfire	*R6711*	Cat. 3 Destroyed
3.	54 Sqn., Hornchurch	C	Shot down by Bf 109s near Deal; pilot slightly wounded.	A10.00 hrs.	Plt. Off. E.J. Coleman	Spitfire	—	Cat. 3 Destroyed
4.	54 Sqn., Hornchurch	C	Damaged by Bf 109s near Deal; pilot landed unhurt at Manston.	A10.00 hrs.	Fg. Off. D.A.P. McMullen	Spitfire	*P9390*	Cat. 2 Damaged
5.	65 Sqn., Hornchurch	C	Shot down by Bf 109s near Folkestone; pilot killed.	A20.50 hrs.	Fg. Off. G.V. Proudman	Spitfire	*N3129*	Cat. 3 Missing
6.	65 Sqn., Hornchurch	C	Shot down by Bf 109s near Folkestone; pilot killed.	A20.50 hrs.	Sgt. Hayes	Spitfire	*R6615*	Cat. 3 Missing

R.A.F. Losses, 7th July 1940—*continued*

7.	65 Sqn., Hornchurch	C	Shot down by Bf 109s near Folkestone; pilot killed.	A20.50 hrs.	Plt. Off. N.J. Brisbane	Spitfire	*R6609*	Cat. 3 Missing
8.	79 Sqn., Hawkinge	C?	Aircraft crashed at Chilberton Elms, near Folkestone; cause unknown. Pilot killed.	21.10 hrs.	Sqn. Ldr. J.D.C. Joslin	Hurricane	*P2756*	Cat. 3 Destroyed
9.	145 Sqn., Tangmere	NC	Pilot taxied into another Hurricane (Item 10), but unhurt.	A05.00 hrs.	Plt. Off. D.N. Forde	Hurricane	*P3545*	Cat. 1 Damaged
10.	145 Sqn., Tangmere	NC	Struck by another Hurricane on the ground (Item 9); no casualties.	A05.00 hrs.	Not known	Hurricane	*P2924*	Cat. 1 Damaged
11.	145 Sqn., Tangmere	NC	Crashed during take-off in coarsepitch; pilot unhurt.	A05.00 hrs.	Plt. Off. L.D.M. Scott	Hurricane	*N2497*	Cat.. 2 Damaged

LUFTWAFFE LOSSES—SUNDAY 7th JULY 1940

1.	2.(F)/11	NCM	Crashed at Rouen; believed due to technical fault.	Dornier Do 17P	100 %	Three crew members killed.
2.	4.(H)/31	NCM	Landing accident at Vitry-en-Artois airfield.	Henschel Hs 126	10 %	No casualties notified.
3.	3.(F)/121	CM	Damaged by Hurricanes of Brunner, Buck and Cruttenden of 43 Sqn. near Tangmere at 08.15 hrs. Aircraft crashed near Rouen.	Dornier Do 17P	60 %	No casualties notified.
4.	2.(F)/123	CM	Shot down by Hurricanes of Aitken and Clyde of 601 Sqn., 15 miles north of Cherbourg, at 10.25 hrs.	Dornier Do 17P	100 %	One crew member killed; two missing.
5.	2.(F)/123	CM	Shot down by Hurricanes of Peel and Wakeham of 145 Sqn. 20 miles SSW of the Needles at approx. 06.00 hrs.	Dornier Do 17P	100 %	Ltn. Nest, Ltn. Vedder and one other missing.
6.	II./KG 2	CM	Crash landed at Boulogne airfield after combat with Spitfire of Dawson-Paul of 64 Sqn. near Calais at approx. 21.00 hrs.	Dornier Do 17Z	80 %	Oblt. Seidel wounded; remainder of crew unhurt.
7.	III./KG 2	CM	Landing accident at St. Omer following combat with Spitfire of Jeffrey of 64 Sqn. near Calais at approx. 21.00 hrs.	Dornier Do 17Z	10 %	No crew casualties notified.
8.	9./KG 4	CM	Shot down by Spitfires of Boyd, MacLean and Coverley of 602 Sqn. (Yellow Section), off May Island at approx. 18.15 hrs.	Junkers Ju 88A-1	100 %	Hptm. Rohloff, *St.Kap.*, killed.
9.	1./KG 30	CM	Shot down by British fighters over Firth of Forth. R.A.F. pilots and squadron not identified.	Junkers Ju 88A-1	100 %	Ltn. Meinhold, Ltn. Wallenstein + two others killed.
10.	I./KG 51	NCM	Landing accident at Lechfeld airfield.	Junkers Ju 88A	15 %	No casualties notified.
11.	I./KG 76	NCM	Landing accident at Beauvais airfield.	Dornier Do 17Z	10 %	No casualties notified.
12.	III./JG 27	CM	Take-off accident at Therville airfield.	Messerschmitt Bf 109 E-1	80 %	Pilot unhurt.
13.	II./JG 77	CM	Landing accident at Vaernes airfield.	Messerschmitt Bf 109 E-4	70 %	Pilot unhurt.
14.	III./JG 77	CM	Landing accident at Vaernes airfield.	Messerschmitt Bf 109 E-4	100 %	Pilot injured.

Monday 8th July

With so many convoys at sea off the south and south-east coasts of England, Dowding's worst fears were to be realised on this day. The weather was perfect for attacks on shipping—fairly heavy cloud extending from around 1,500 up to 20,000 feet. A convoy sailing up the Bristol Channel was shadowed throughout the early morning hours, and a Section of No. 92 Squadron's Spitfires (Flt. Lt. R.R. Stanford Tuck, Plt. Off. R.H. Holland and Sgt. R.E. Havercroft), sent up from Hullavington, intercepted and claimed a Dornier Do 17 shot down over Bristol[19].

It was a large convoy, which had put out from the Thames Estuary in the small hours, that was to cause the defences most anxiety, for the ships were timed to pass Dover shortly after mid-day. The first German aircraft, a Heinkel He 111 found prowling near the convoy off the North Foreland, was attacked at 11.30 hours by three Spitfires of No. 74 Squadron, (Flt. Lt. W.E.G. Measures, Plt. Off. D.H.T. Dowding[20] and Sgt. Wilfred Skinner) and, although claimed destroyed at the time, appears to have managed to regain its base.

About an hour later the Kent CH radar stations reported considerable air activity over the Pas de Calais, and this

Digging out the remains of a Bf 109E shot down on 8th July; the insignia of 3./LG 2 is just visible, suggesting that this was the aircraft of Leutnant Striberny, shot down by Flying Officer Way of No. 54 Squadron.

[19] Not identified in German loss records.
[20] Son of Fighter Command's Commander-in-Chief.

prompted Park to order up patrols over Dover. The first two Sections returned home without seeing anything, but the

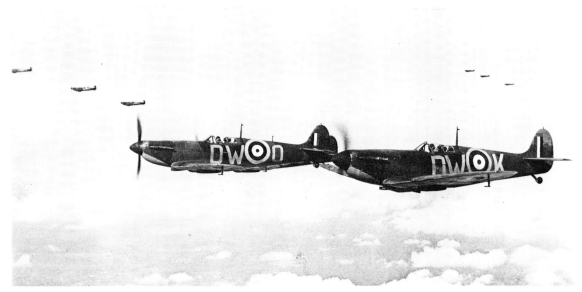

Spitfires of No. 610 (County of Chester) Squadron, flying in loose vics of three aircraft.

third, Blue Section of No. 610 Squadron, arriving over the convoy at about 14.00 hours, was in time to intercept a *Staffel* of unescorted Dornier Do 17s ten miles off the coast, forcing them to drop their bombs wide of the ships. Sergeant Peter Else claimed a Dornier damaged, but Plt. Off. Raven was caught in the crossfire from several bombers and shot down in flames. (Another member of his Section saw him swimming in the sea, but he evidently drowned before rescue craft could reach him.) No. 610 Squadron sent off another six aircraft on patrol at 14.56 hours over the convoy, which had by then reached Hythe, and although the pilots sighted a *Staffel* of Do 17s, escorted by a dozen Bf 109s, they were unable to attack; Plt. Off. C.O.J. Pegge, however, surprised a trio of Bf 109s in the area, and claimed one destroyed.

It was now the turn of No. 79 Squadron's Hurricanes. This Squadron had suffered heavily during the past two months and there is no doubt that, having remained in Kent continuously without the benefit of a rest, its pilots were suffering from acute fatigue—perhaps more noticeable at this early stage in the Battle of Britain than in any other Squadron, with the possible exception of No. 54[21]. Now nine No. 79 Squadron Hurricanes were ordered off from Hawkinge—almost in sight of the convoy—only to be "bounced" by enemy fighters which were free chasing between Dover and the convoy. Before the Squadron could react, Plt. Off. J.E.R. Wood was shot down in flames into the Channel and, although he baled out safely, he was found by the crew of a naval rescue launch to have died of burns. Fg. Off. E.W. Mitchell died in the cockpit of his blazing Hurricane which crashed at Temple Ewell, three miles north-east of Dover. The wreck burned for an hour, and identification of the pilot was only possible by checking the gun numbers.

Whether or not returning *Luftwaffe* bomber crews reported the fact that the convoy's merchant ships were sailing in

ballast (for such was the case), it was seen that enemy attacks petered out as the vessels rounded Dungeness. The scene of battle now shifted to the Western Approaches with the appearance of another convoy, and a number of unsuccessful attacks were launched by Junkers Ju 88s of KG 54. One such aircraft was claimed at 18.15 hours by a Section of No. 234 Squadron, flying from St. Eval, but the raider in fact made good its escape.

If the day's fighting in these major identifiable attacks appeared one-sided, the R.A.F. once again proved itself adept at "picking off" stragglers. For instance, F/Sgt. Geoffrey Allard of No. 85 Squadron, already among Fighter Command's top scoring pilots, spotted a Heinkel of KG 1 while on a morning patrol from Martlesham. Apparently catching the enemy unawares, Allard dived on the bomber from astern and, with two three-second bursts from his guns, sent the Heinkel crashing into the sea off Felixstowe[22].

A Junkers Ju 88 of LG 1 was attacked in turn by Nos. 41 and 249 Squadrons as it sought to escape the Yorkshire defences, finally falling to the guns of the latter's Green Section (Fg. Off D.G. Parnall, Plt. Off H.J.S. Beazley and Sgt. A,D.W. Main). Three of the German crew baled out but the pilot, Oberleutnant Meyer, died at his controls[23].

The shooting down of four Messerschmitt Bf 109s undoubtedly brought encouragement to No. 11 Group, to whom the scourge of free chasing fighters was causing some apprehension, not least to No. 54 Squadron's pilots (who shot down two near Dover). No. 65 Squadron's commanding officer had a narrow escape during the afternoon; flying alone at 15.45 hours, Squadron Leader Henry Sawyer was stalked by four free-chasing 109s of 4./JG 51. Arriving just in time—but unable to warn Sawyer—Red Section of No. 74 Squadron attacked and shot down one of the Messerschmitts. This fell at Elham and the pilot, Ltn. Johann Böhm, was taken prisoner. The timing of this action is perhaps interesting for Sqn. Ldr.

---

[21] Graphic witness of this fatigue has been provided by the New Zealander, Group Captain A.C. Deere (then a Flight Lieutenant on No. 54 Squadron) in his book *Nine Lives* (see Bibliography). No. 79 Squadron's fatigue can be sensed as much from the tone as from the contents of the combat reports (Forms 1151) submitted at the time.

[22] This was Allard's eleventh "confirmed" victory.
[23] One of the crew landed at Aldbrough where he was taken prisoner by a Mrs. Caldwell. She relieved the airman of his pistol and handed him over to the local police, subsequently being awarded the O.B.E. for her action.

Werner Mölders (centre), the remarkable commander of JG 51, and arguably Germany's greatest fighter ace. The *Geschwader* was heavily committed from the beginning of the Battle; on July 28th Mölders was himself wounded in a dogfight with the South African "Sailor" Malan of No. 74 Squadron.

Sawyer, who had been serving "supernumerary" on 65 Squadron for several days, was scheduled to take over command of the Squadron from Sqn. Ldr. Desmond Cooke on this day. It transired that Cooke never lived to hand over command, for at about 16.00 hours that same afternoon he disappeared near Dover and is thought to have been shot down by other Messerschmitts of JG 51.

Fighter Command at large had been slow to appreciate the tactics being employed by German fighter units. For years British fighter pilots had been educated in the "set piece" formation attack manœuvres, known as the "Fighting Area Attacks"—even this nomenclature dated the drill[24]. Almost universally adopted was the Flight formation of six aircraft, split into two Sections, each of three aircraft (so that a Squadron would operate four Sections, i.e. Blue, Red, Green and Yellow). On receiving take-off orders, depending on the number of aircraft ordered off, the Squadron would fly as a mass of relatively close-spaced aircraft with Sections in Vic or line astern, each Section with three aircraft in Vic formation. So inflexible was this system and so pre-occupied was each pilot with his formation keeping that only small arcs of sky could be searched for enemy aircraft by each pilot, with the result that the rear arc of the Squadron was highly vulnerable to attack from astern. Quite early in the War some squadrons adopted the practice of appointing a rear-guard

weaver, or "tail-end Charlie", but this often proved wasteful in fuel so that this pilot would have to return home early; moreover casualties among weavers were high at Dunkirk and most squadrons—with some notable exceptions—had discontinued this practice by July 1940.

It is true that some squadrons—principally those flying Hurricanes—had learned of the impracticability of the Fighting Area Attacks in France and over Dunkirk, but in the absence of new orders some retained the old tactics—until punishing losses prompted squadron commanders to improvise. Nos. 19 and 54 Squadrons were among the first to develop a looser formation, the former retaining the larger unit of six aircraft, while the latter—through losses—began flying in pairs. It was, however, No. 152 Squadron under Squadron Leader Peter Devitt, who in mid-July instituted a regular battle formation using "pairs" and "fours", A Flight consisting of Red, Yellow and White Sections, and B Flight of Blue, Green and Black. Each pair was a fighting unit, the leader responsible for taking offensive action and the No. 2 for defence against any possible stern attack.

While these tactics were developed to counter the depredations of the German free chases of 1940, they differed to some extent from the German practice. Because the *Staffel* usually flew as a group of eight or nine fighters, the *Luftwaffe* adopted two formations (*Schwarmen*) of about four aircraft, each flying well spaced out, with one formation covering the rear of the other. Each formation could, at will, break away and operate on its own, often breaking into pairs (*Rotten*). Rather later the R.A.F. also adopted the true "four" section—called the Finger Four for obvious reasons.

[24] Each attack was identified by a drill number, and the formation leader would specify which attack he considered suitable. This might entail a long line astern attack by twelve fighters each firing a snap burst on a single bomber.

R.A.F. FIGHTER COMMAND LOSSES — MONDAY 8th JULY 1940

1.	32 Sqn., Biggin Hill	C	Damaged by Bf 109s over convoy off Dungeness; pilot landed at Hawkinge unhurt	A15.20 hrs.	Fgt. Off. R.F. Smythe	Hurricane	—	Cat. 1 Damaged
2.	65 Sqn., Hornchurch	C?	Believed shot down by Bf 109s during climb near Dover; pilot killed.	A16.00 hrs.	Sqn. Ldr. D. Cooke	Spitfire	K9907	Cat. 3 Missing
3.	66 Sqn., Coltishall	C	Crashed with engine fire while landing at Coltishall after patrol; pilot unhurt.	Not known	Not known	Spitfire	K9114	Cat. 3 Destroyed
4.	74 Sqn., Manston	NC	Crashed while landing at Manston; pilot unhurt.	A16.45 hrs.	Plt. Off. P.C.F. Stevenson	Spitfire	P9465	Cat. 2 Damaged

R.A.F. Losses, 8th July 1940—*continued*

5.	79 Sqn., Hawkinge	C	Shot down in flames off Dover; pilot baled out but had died when picked up . Buried at Hawkinge.	15.40 hrs.	Plt. Off J.E.R. Wood	Hurricane	*P3461*	Cat. 3 Lost
6.	79 Sqn., Hawkinge	C	Shot down in flames at Temple Ewell, Kent; pilot killed; buried at Hawkinge.	15.50 hrs.	Fg. Off. E.W. Mitchell	Hurricane	*N2384*	Cat. 3 Destroyed
7.	141 Sqn., Turnhouse	NC	Collided with another Defiant (Item 8) on the ground; gunner injured.	15.20 hrs.	Plt. Off. A.N. Constantine Plt. Off. F.C.A. Lanning	Defiant	*L6998*	Cat. 2 Damaged
8.	141 Sqn., Turnhouse	NC	In collision with another Defiant (Item 7) on the ground; pilot injured.	15.20 hrs.	Plt. Off. R.E. Orchard Plt. Off. W. Weber	Defiant	*L6994*	Cat. 2 Damaged
9.	610 Sqn., Biggin Hill	C	Shot down by Do 17s over convoy 6 miles off Dover; pilot seen in the sea but believed to have drowned.	14.15 hrs.	Plt. Off. A.L.B. Raven	Spitfire	*L1075*	Cat. 3 Lost

LUFTWAFFE LOSSES—MONDAY 8th JULY 1940

1.	1.(F)/120	CM	Shot down by Spitfires of 602 Sqn. near Firth of Forth during the evening.	Heinkel He 111H-2	100 %	Ltn. Bank (photgraphic specialist) + two killed; three missing.
2.	Stab/KG 1	CM	Shot down by Hurricane of Allard, 85 Sqn., 6 miles SE of Felixstowe at approx. 10.30 hrs.	Heinkel He 111H-2	100 %	Oblt. Paulsen killed; four missing.
3.	5./KG 3	—	Damaged in R.A.F. raid on Laon airfield.	Dornier Do 17Z	5 %	Three crew members wounded
4.	St.St./LG 1	CM	Shot down by Hurricanes of Main, Parnall and Beazely of 249 Sqn., off Hornsea at 11.25 hrs.	Junkers Ju 88	100 %	Oblt. Meyer killed; three other crew members missing.
5.	I./St.G 2	NCM	Accident near Heiligenstadt; cause not known.	Junkers Ju 87B	100 %	Three civilian technicians killed.
6.	3./LG 2	CM	Shot down by Spitfire flown by Way of 54 Sqn. near Dover.	Messerschmitt Bf 109 E-3	100 %	Ltn. Striberny missing.
7.	4./JG 51	CM	Shot down by Spitfire flown by Mould of 74 Sqn. at Elham, Kent, at 15.45 hrs.	Messerschmitt Bf 109 E-3 (1162)	100 %	Ltn. Johann Böhm made P.O.W.
8.	II./JG 51	CM	Shot down by Spitfire flown by Franklin of 65 of 65 Sqn. 8 miles off Dover at 15.45 hrs.	Messerschmitt Bf 109 E-3	100 %	Pilot missing, believed killed.
9.	II./JG 51	CM	Force landed at St. Inglevert after combat with Spitfire of Pegge of 610 Sqn., 6 miles off Hythe at 15.20 hrs.	Messerschmitt Bf 109 E-3	12 %	Pilot wounded.
10.	III./JG 51	CM	Shot down by Spitfires of Way and Garton of 54 Sqn., over English Channel at 20.15 hrs	Messerschmitt Bf 109 E-1	100 %	Pilot killed.
11.	9./JG 52	NCM	Landing accident during test at Mannheim airfield.	Messerschmitt Bf 109 E-4	20 %	Pilot unhurt.
12.	3./Erpr.Gr. 210	NCM	Crashed and burned near Enehl (?); cause not known.	Messerschmitt Bf 109 E-3	100 %	Pilot killed.
13.	Kurier-St. 8	NCM	Landing accident at Evère airfield.	Focke-Wulf Fw 44	60 %	No casualties notified.

Tuesday 9th July

After an uneasy night, during which about a dozen enemy aircraft had been plotted over the Midlands, and incendiary bombs had fallen on the edge of Rochford airfield and near Battle in Sussex, first light brought low cloud and rain over almost the whole of Britain. Later in the day the cold front moved away to the east and a slow improvement in flying conditions was reported during the afternoon.

The operations which were to be mounted on this day were the continuing manifestation of Göring's interpretation of the German Naval Staff's insistence that priority be given to the destruction of British coastal shipping and naval installations. Neither Kesselring nor Sperrle deviated from this aim, seeing—and indeed demonstrating—that in thus attracting British fighters into the air, their own *Jagdgeschwader* were able to inflict fairly heavy losses, without undue cost. The fighting on this Tuesday was nevertheless to sound a harsh note to German ears for, in launching a heavy attack at rather longer range than hitherto, Kesselring committed the apparently élite *Zerstörergeschwader* to action in strength for the first time against the R.A.F., in the rôle of heavy escort fighters. Such were the losses among the Messerschmitt Bf 110s from the guns of the nimble interceptors that, in time, they themselves had to be covered by Bf 109s.

The first combat of the day accompanied a dawn patrol by

"Al" Deere, the well-known New Zealand pilot who flew with No. 54 Squadron during the Battle. Among his numerous narrow escapes was one from a head-on collision with a Bf 109 on 9th July.

three Hurricane pilots of No. 257 Squadron who, airborne from Northolt at 05.45 hours, caught a Dornier Do 17 of II./KG 3 over Kent on its return flight from the Midlands. Sergeant R.V. Forward fired all his ammunition at the enemy but, as he was not using tracer, he could not assess his aim. Although he entered no claim, the enemy was in fact severely hit and carried a dead crew member home to a crash landing near Antwerp.

As the cloud built up with the cold front, enemy air activity petered out during the morning. Convoy patrols at Section strength were ordered to be flown over six small coastal convoys, and Park seized the opportunity to move No. 609 Squadron forward from Middle Wallop to the nearly-completed coastal satellite at Warmwell. While use of forward satellites elsewhere was a daily expedient, 609 Squadron came to regard Warmwell as much a base as Middle Wallop, as it was found that the use of the coastal airfield offered the only means of effectively covering Portland.

From about 11.00 hours on, the south-east coastal radar reported a number of single-strength plots in the vicinity of convoys off Kent and Essex. Due to the thick cloud conditions none of the patrolling pilots sighted any of the intruders and were loath to wander from their charges lest they should lose contact. Clearly these lone Germans were particularly interested in the assembly of a large northbound convoy in the mouth of the Thames, and managed to radio position reports to their bases for, at 12.45 hours, Dover CH reported a heavy build-up of enemy forces well behind the Pas de Calais.

Faced with the possibility of a large raid approaching unseen under cloud cover and attacking the Thames convoy out of the trailing edge of the cold front, Park brought six No. 11 Group squadrons to Available, and shortly after 13.00 hours ordered six Hurricanes into the air from North Weald.

At this airfield the Station Commander, Wing Commander Victor Beamish, had listened with mounting impatience to the Sector Controller's commentary on the approaching raid plot over the airfield broadcast system; on hearing his Hurricanes ordered off, he dashed out of his office, calling for his own aircraft to be started up. Thus, at 13.36 hours, "A" Flight of No. 151 Squadron, with Beamish in the No. 2 position, was airborne climbing hard through scattered cloud on an easterly course. Without more than one or two instructions from the ground controller, the pilots suddenly found themselves confronted by the enemy—a huge mass of around one hundred fighters and bombers, stepped up from 12,000 to 20,000 feet. Quickly recognising the lower formations of Heinkel He 111s and Junkers Ju 88s, the six Hurricane pilots split into two sections, one diving on the bombers and the other turning to face the sixty Messerschmitt Bf 109s and 110s of the escort.

As it transpired, none of the interceptors managed to reach the bombers before the escort reacted, and all the Hurricanes were engaged by the Bf 109s. However, seizing an opportunity to disengage, Beamish, Fg. Off. A.D. Forster, and Plt. Off. J.R. Hamar singled out a Bf 110 of III./ZG 26 and shot it down. Meanwhile Flt. Lt. H.H.A. Ironside, Midshipman O.M. Wightman and Fg. Off. R.M. Milne tried to edge closer to the bombers, but were prevented from doing so by the Bf 109s, of which they claimed two shot down. Evidently unaware of the small number of British fighters engaging their escort, the German bomber pilots split into six sections, of which only one found the convoy. Bombing was scattered and no ship was hit.

Ironside received a shell in the cockpit which inflicted a bad wound in his face, but he managed to bring his aircraft home

(*Left*) Sqn. Ldr. E.M. ("Teddy") Donaldson, commander of No. 151 Squadron, with Wg. Cdr. Victor Beamish, the legendary Station Commander of North Weald, who "scrambled" with No. 151's "A" Flight on the afternoon of 9th July. Station Commanders were not, as a rule, expected to fly in combat, but there were several notable exceptions. Beamish, a 37-year-old Irishman, who had retired from the R.A.F. in 1933 suffering from tuberculosis but returned to the Colours in 1937. He destroyed at least eight enemy aircraft and shared in the destruction of many others before being killed in action on 28th March 1942.

D-ASUO, the Heinkel He 59 seaplane forced down on the Goodwins by Plt. Off. John Allen of No. 54 Squadron on 9th July.

safely[25]. Wightman was shot down but baled out into the sea; he was picked up by a trawler and reported back to his squadron the same evening, none the worse for his experience.

Unfortunately none of the other Sections sent up were able to intercept this raid, although a *Staffel* of III./ZG 26 had been caught by Red Section of No. 43 Squadron. This appears to have been a diversionary sortie as the Bf 110s were engaged over Folkestone shortly after mid-day. Two Messerschmitts were shot down and another damaged[26], but the British

---

[25] Ironside was admitted to hospital and did not recover from his wounds in time to fight in the Battle. As the "official definition" of the Battle of Britain only dated from the following day, he was not entitled to wear the coveted Clasp.

[26] The second crew member of this aircraft evidently baled out as the damaged aircraft struggled home with only the pilot aboard.

squadron commander, Sqn. Ldr. Charles Lott, was hit in the face by splinters from his windscreen and, blinded in the right eye, baled out at only 700 feet after trying to regain his base with a crippled Hurricane. Such was his disability that he had to hand over his command to Sqn. Ldr. J.V.C. Badger[27].

Dissatisfied—with some justification—at their efforts against the Thames convoy, the Germans mounted a second heavy raid, the 70-strong formation setting course north-westerly to pass the North Foreland at about 15.50 hours. Park, who had previously moved three Spitfire squadrons forward to Manston, was now well-equipped to meet the new threat in good time and, as a preliminary move, nine Spitfires

---

[27] Lott was also prevented from taking further part in the Battle and, although he did not qualify for the Battle Clasp, his action was recognised by the award of the D.S.O. on 30th August 1940. See Appendix A.

Views of D-ASUO after it had been towed ashore by the Walmer lifeboat; the crew were taken prisoner unhurt.

of No. 65 Squadron were ordered off. . .

At 15.35 hours three Sections were ordered off to intercept raiders off the North Foreland. One aircraft failed to start up, and another returned with engine trouble. The remaining seven pilots climbed to 10,000 feet and almost at once sighted about seventy enemy aircraft heading for the Thames Estuary. The enemy were in vics of five, seven and nine, stepped up from 8,000 to 14,000 feet, three vics abreast and in line astern. There was a layer of bombers well protected above and at the sides by 109s and 110s. Saunders, who was leading, climbed to 18,000 feet and found himself slightly above five 109s; he dived on one of them and opened fire with slight deflection at 400 yards. After a further short burst the enemy aircraft pulled up sharply into a half roll; a final burst from 100 yards and the enemy fell away and something appeared to break off from the tail. Grant damaged another aircraft but was unable to confirm it as he was attacked by two others. Walker (Red 1) sighted enemy aircraft over Margate and fired at one, but had to break off as his Section was being attacked by 109s. He attacked a 109 from below at about 200 yards and this aircraft went into a turning dive with smoke pouring from the fuselage. F/Sgt. Phillips (Red 2) fired at several enemy aircraft and eventually got in a 5-second burst at a 109 and saw it go into a vertical dive five miles north-east of Ramsgate; a 109 was subsequently found to have crashed near where the combat took place. All our aircraft returned safely.

Nine Hurricanes of No. 79 Squadron were also on patrol at this time and spotted some of the Bf 109s as they turned for home, short of fuel. The 109s were too fast and although Plt. Off. H.W. Millington, Midshipman M.A. Birrell and Plt. Off. D.A. Stones all filed claims for damaged aircraft, their quarry evidently escaped without much difficulty.

Bad weather and scattered interceptions again frustrated the would-be convoy attackers, which again broke up into *Staffeln* to search the British coast off Suffolk and Essex. A stray Heinkel He 111 of I./KG 53 was caught by Hurricanes of No. 17 Squadron, flown by Plt. Off. G.R. Bennette, Plt. Off. K. Manger and Sgt. G. Griffiths; the raider promptly dumped his bombs into the sea and set a speedy course for home, pursued by the fighters. All three closed to the attack and fired over 2,000 rounds from as close as 50 yards. With both engines on fire, the Heinkel crashed into the sea about 40 miles east of Harwich, overturned and sank nose first.

There followed sporadic probing by enemy aircraft all along the East Coast. Two Junkers Ju 88s of KG 30, flying from Aalborg in Denmark, were intercepted by three Spitfires of No. 602 Squadron twenty miles east of May Island but, although one was claimed destroyed, it evidently escaped.

Luftflotte 2, having lost six aircraft during the day, now alerted *Seenotflugkommando 1* at Boulogne to despatch several Heinkel He 59 ambulance seaplanes (each escorted by a *Staffel* of Bf 109s) to search for ditched airmen. Whether the crews of these aircraft were instructed to look for and report the position of a convoy off East Kent is not known; it was nevertheless unfortunate for the crew of one such aircraft that, finding themselves almost over the convoy, they were set upon by Spitfires of two Sections from No. 54 Squadron led by Plt. Off. J.L. Allen and Flt. Lt. A.C. Deere. The Heinkel was forced down by Allen while Deere's three aircraft tackled the fighter escort. . .

. . .Deere had an amazing experience in a head-on attack when neither l09 nor Spitfire would give way and a collision resulted, the 109 striking the Spitfire's propeller and cockpit hood. Deere, with engine stopped, managed to force land at Manston whereupon his aircraft caught fire. He broke his way out, uninjured save for slight burns on his hands[28].

The escort, though failing to protect the ambulance, gave good account of itself, for two other Spitfire pilots (Plt. Off. Garton and Plt. Off. A. Evershed) were shot down and killed. The Heinkel landed on the Goodwin Sands at 19.30 hours and was stranded at low tide; it was later towed off by the Walmer lifeboat and beached at Deal, the crew being taken prisoner[29].

The final assault was mounted that evening when 27 Junkers Ju 87 dive-bombers, escorted by a small number of Bf 109s, attacked the Portland naval base at about 19.00 hours. No. 609 Squadron, with some radar warning, had scrambled a patrol of Spitfires from its new base at Warmwell but was scarcely able to reach the Junkers before being engaged by the escort. Fg. Off D.M. Crook nevertheless attacked one of the dive-bombers (flown by a *Staffelkapitän* of I./St.G 77, Hauptmann Freiherr von Dalwigk—to be awarded a posthumous Knight's Cross) and shot it down into the sea. The score was evened when Fg. Off. Peter Drummond-Hay was shot down and killed.

Thus ended the most strenuous day's fighting yet experienced in the Battle of Britain. Three major attacks had developed, but Park had to some extent anticipated each move and deployed his forces to counter each threat. Nevertheless the relatively small intercepting formations, though skilfully controlled, had been all but overwhelmed and, despite causing the two convoy raids to break up, had been fortunate not to be annihilated in the air. It was, however, too early in the Battle for Park to decide how best to alter his tactics so as to meet the enemy with stronger fighter forces.

While the Luftwaffe had been preparing its battle orders for the day, R.A.F. Bomber Command's No. 2 Group had carried out an attack on *Luftflotte 5*'s principal base at Stavanger-Sola in Norway. For some days the crews had been awaiting favourable weather conditions and, with a forecast of fine weather ahead of the cold front, twelve Blenheims took off from Wick at dawn under clear skies. All went well on the journey to Stavanger and the bombing was carried out in the face of only moderate *flak*. However, as the Blenheims set course for home they were attacked by three Bf 110s of I./ZG 76 and three whole *Staffeln* of JG 77's Bf 109s. Before the formation could reach adequate cloud cover it had lost no fewer than seven of its number—and all the five surviving aircraft were classified as Cat. 2 Damaged on their return to Wick. The German records show that three Dornier Do 215s of *Aufklärungsgruppe Oberbefehlshaber der Luftwaffe* were hit by the Blenheims' bombs and these were provisionally classified as destroyed; one however was later repaired.

[28] Cf. Form 540, No. 54 Squadron, 9th July 1940. An excellent account of this action is given in Deere's own book *Nine Lives* (see Bibliography).

[29] This action, following upon that by No. 72 Squadron on 1st July, became the focus of Air Ministry deliberations as to whether German use of the Red Cross in close proximity to vital British convoys qualified for immunity under provision of the Geneva Convention. Only five days were to elapse before a decision was reached to attack such seaplanes. See entry for Sunday, 14th July.

R.A.F. FIGHTER COMMAND LOSSES — TUESDAY 9th JULY 1940

1.	19 Sqn., Duxford	NC	Taxying collision at Duxford (with Item 2); pilot unhurt.	Not known	Not known	Spitfire	—	Cat. 1 Damaged
2.	19 Sqn., Duxford	NC	Taxying collision at Duxford (with Item 1); pilot unhurt.	Not known	Not known	Spitfire	—	Cat. 1 Damaged
3.	43 Sqn., Tangmere	C	Pilot blinded in right eye during combat near Southampton; pilot baled out safely.	12.10 hrs.	Sqn. Ldr. C.G. Lott	Hurricane	P3464	Cat. 3 Lost
4.	43 Sqn., Tangmere	NC	Crashed on landing at Tangmere; pilot unhurt.	Not known	Plt. Off. J. Cruttenden	Hurricane	L1824	Cat. 3 Destroyed
5.	54 Sqn., Hornchurch	C	Collided with Bf 109 near Manston; pilot force landed at Manston, slightly burned.	A19.30 hrs.	Flt. Lt. A.C. Deere	Spitfire	P9398	Cat. 3 Destroyed
6.	54 Sqn., Hornchurch	C	Shot down near Manston; pilot killed.	A19.30 hrs.	Plt. Off. Garton	Spitfire	R6705	Cat. 3 Destroyed
7.	54 Sqn., Hornchurch	C	Shot down by Bf 109s south of Dover; pilot killed.	A19.15 hrs.	Plt. Off. A. Evershed	Spitfire	N3183	Cat. 3 Missing
8.	151 Sqn., North Weald	C	Pilot wounded in face during combat over convoy in Thames Estuary but returned safely.	A14.00 hrs.	Flt. Lt. H.H.A. Ironside	Hurricane	P3309	Cat. 1 Damaged
9.	151 Sqn., North Weald	C	Shot down over Thames Estuary; pilot baled out and picked up safely by trawler.	A14.00 hrs.	Midshipman O.M. Wightman	Hurricane	P3806	Cat. 3 Lost
10.	609 Sqn., Warmwell	C	Pilot missing after combat over Portland.	Evening	Fg. Off. P. Drummond-Hay	Spitfire	R6637	Cat. 3 Missing

LUFTWAFFE LOSSES—TUESDAY 9th JULY 1940

1.	Aufkl. Gr. Ob. d. L.	—	Aircraft damaged in raid on Stavanger-Sola by 12 Blenheims of 12 and 57 Sqns. (Seven Blenheims lost and remainder damaged.)	Dornier Do 215	100 %	No aircrew casualties notified.
				Dornier Do 215	60 %	
				Dornier Do 215	30 %	
2.	1.(H)/11	NCM	Flying accident at Châteaudun; cause not known.	Henschel Hs 126	100 %	Two crew members killed.
3.	II./KG 3	CM	Crashed near Antwerp after combat with Hurricane flown by Forward of 257 Sqn. over Kent at 067.30 hrs.	Dornier Do 17Z-2	100 %	One crew member killed and one wounded.
4.	I./KG 51	NCM	Landing accident at Villaroche airfield.	Junkers Ju 88A	15 %	No casualties notified.
5.	7./KG 51	CM	Crashed at Brie-Conte-Robert following engine failure.	Junkers Ju 88A	100 %	Lt. Heinrich killed.
6.	I./KG 53	CM	Shot down by Hurricanes of Manger, Griffiths and Bennette of 17 Sqn. off Harwich at 17.15 hrs.	Heinkel He 111H-3	100 %	Oblt. Kollmer, Oblt. Fritz + two killed; one other member missing.
7.	St.St./KG 76	CM	Force landed at Etaples after combat with six Spitfires of 610 Sqn. between Dungeness and Cap Gris Nez at 14.20 hrs.	Dornier Do 17Z	40 %	Two crew members wounded.
8.	I./St.G 77	CM	Shot down by Spitfire flown by Crook of 609 Sqn. at approx. 19.00 hrs. near Portland.	Junkers Ju 87B	100 %	Hptm. Frhr. von Dalwigk + one crew member missing.
9.	V./LG 1	CM	Shot down by Spitfires of 609 Sqn. near Portland.	Messerschmitt Bf 110C	100 %	Two rescued by Seenotflugkdo.
10.	2./JG 26	NCM	Landing accident on Bonninghardt airfield.	Messerschmitt Bf 109 E-1	40 %	No casualties notified.
11.	II./JG 51	CM	Shot down by Spitfire of Deere, 54 Sqn., south of Dover at 19.30 hrs. Escorting air/sea rescue operations.	Messerschmitt Bf 109 E-3	100 %	Pilot missing.
12.	II./JG 51	CM	Shot down by Spitfire of Phillips of 65 Sqn., 5 miles NE of Ramsgate at approx. 16.00 hrs.	Messerschmitt Bf 109 E-3	100 %	Ltn. Triebel missing.
13.	III./ZG 26	CM	Shot down by Hurricanes of Lott, Carey and Miller of 43 Sqn. into sea off Folkestone at approx. 12.05 hrs.	Messerschmitt Bf 110 C-2	100 %	Oblt. Siegmund + one crew member missing.
14.	III./ZG 26	CM	Shot down by Hurricanes of Lott, Carey and Miller of 43 Sqn. into sea off Folkestone at approx. 12.04 hrs.	Messerschmitt Bf 110 C-2	100 %	Two N.C.O. crew members missing.
15.	III./ZG 26	CM	Shot down by Hurricanes of Beamish, Foster and Hamar of 151 Sqn. over Thames Estuary at approx. 13.45 hrs.	Messerschmitt Bf 110 C-2	100 %	Two N.C.O. crew members missing.
16.	III./ZG 26	CM	Damaged in combat with Hurricanes of 43 Sqn. off Folkestone at approx. 12.00 hrs.	Messerschmitt Bf 110C	50 %	One crew member missing; pilot safe.
17.	Seenot- flugkdo. 1	CM	Shot down by Spitfire flown by Allen of 54 Sqn. off Ramsgate at 19.30 hrs. Aircraft engaged in air/sea rescue operations.	Heinkel He 59 (D-ASUO) (1)	100 %	Uffz. Helmut Bartmann, Uffz. Walter Anders, Uffz. Erich Schiele and Fw. Gunther Maywald made P.O.W.s, unhurt.

[(1) This aircraft was reported in *Abteilung* returns as being lost on 10th July; this is clearly incorrect as the Heinkel was brought ashore near Walmer Lifeboat Station, and photographs of the beached aircraft appeared in the British morning national newspapers on 10th July; some of the originals of these photographs bear the censor's date-stamp of the previous day.]

Wednesday 10th July

It is more than ironic that although the Battle of Britain has elsewhere been deemed to have opened on 10th July—indeed that is the official date from which eligibility for the R.A.F.'s "Battle Clasp" is deemed to begin—Fighter Command had in

Hermann Göring (*sixth from right*) with senior *Luftwaffe* officers and staff, photographed on the Channel coast near Calais during the Battle of Britain; the English coast is clearly visible on the horizon. This well-known picture was said to have been taken on 1st July; the visibility on that day, however, was quite insufficient for this to have been the case.

the previous few days been called on to meet more than a dozen raids, each by over fifty enemy aircraft, and had suffered the loss of eighteen fighters in combat—the equivalent of a whole squadron—together with thirteen pilots killed and six wounded. To some of the hard-pressed pilots of No. 11 Group such an anachronism would have bordered on the insulting, and a quotation from No. 54 Squadron's operational diary for 10th July is perhaps relevant: "As a result of the first phase of the Battle of Britain, the Squadron could only muster eight aircraft and thirteen pilots."

No. 79 Squadron's pilots had probably reached the stage of mental and physical exhaustion at which they were of minimal value to the defence, and represented a distinct danger to themselves. Accordingly Park ordered them north to Turnhouse to rest and train replacement pilots. (A couple of days later two of the pilots collided with training aircraft in a landing circuit—such accidents to experienced pilots certainly suggest extreme fatigue.)

No fewer than eight convoys were at sea in British coastal water as dawn broke on this day. Thick cloud and thundery rain covered most of the country, but these conditions did not prevent convoy patrols being flown in almost every Sector from Exeter to Wick. Even the Blenheims of No. 236 Squadron were withdrawn from offensive patrolling to mount guard over a convoy off the Cornish coast.

It was the large convoy BREAD, which had set sail in ballast from the Thames Estuary on the early morning tide, that was to attract the heaviest raid of the day. Rounding the North Foreland soon after 10.00 hours, the convoy came under scrutiny by a Dornier Do 17P of 4.(F)/121—heavily escorted by an entire *Gruppe* of Bf 109s (I./JG 51). Already six Spitfires of No. 74 Squadron had scrambled from nearby Manston and at about 10.50 hours battle was joined. The composition of the enemy formation at once indicated the Dornier's importance and, try as they might, the British pilots could not penetrate the escort in sufficient strength to destroy

the reconnaissance machine. It is not known who finally scored on this aircraft, for it struggled home carrying dead and wounded crew members. One of the escorting Bf 109s was damaged by Plt. Off. J.C. Freeborn, but he and Sgt. E.A. Mould had to force land their Spitfires with combat damage.

A covering free chase in the Dover area shortly afterwards by a *Staffel* of Bf 109s was met by nine Spitfires of No. 610 Squadron, scrambled from Biggin Hill at 10:51 hours. One of the Spitfires (Flt. Lt. E.B.B. Smith) was shot down and the intruders escaped unscathed.

The convoy's position was now known to the *Luftwaffe* and at 13.31 hours the first radar plots of heavy enemy build-up over the Pas de Calais were passed to No. 11 Group. To meet this threat one Flight of No. 32 Squadron's Hurricanes at Biggin Hill had been at Readiness for some time, and were ordered off at 13.15 hours to mount guard over the ships. Twenty minutes later their pilots sighted the approaching raid—about 26 Dornier Do 17s of I./KG 2 escorted by all three *Staffeln* of I./ZG 26's Bf 110s and two *Staffeln* of I./JG 3's Bf 109s. Mistaking the Bf 110s for more Dorniers, Fg. Off. J.B.B. Humpherson radioed a sighting report of "60 Dorniers" and called for reinforcements. These were already on their way in the shape of seven Hurricanes of "B" Flight, No. 56 Squadron (previously ordered from North Weald to Manston), nine Hurricanes of No. 111 Squadron from Croydon, and eight Spitfires of No. 74 Squadron, also from Manston.

A massive dogfight, involving more than one hundred aircraft, then followed. As the interceptors strove to upset the bombers' aim, they were attacked time and again by the escort. It was impossible to co-ordinate attacks as the radio became utterly jammed by the voices of excited pilots. No. 74 Squadron failed to score decisively but Plt. Off. P.C.B. St. John damaged a Bf 109 and Fg. Off. J.C. Mungo-Park claimed a Dornier severely damaged. Flt. Lt. W.E.G. Measures, leading the famous "Tiger" Squadron, reported that two enemy aircraft collided; he was mistaken as the following extract from No. 111 Squadron's diary explains:

> About twenty-four Do 17s were (sighted) flying in a series of Vics and the Squadron approached from head-on, flew past until astern and then made attacks from astern on the two rear sections. The bombers were diverted from their attacks on the convoy and at least two were destroyed (one by general attacks by the whole squadron, the occupants being seen to bale out; and one by Fg. Off. T.P.K. Higgs who rammed the enemy aircraft in the course of his attack. A launch was despatched immediately to the scene but no sign was found either of Higgs or the Dornier's crew.) Fg. Off. H.M. Ferris drove a 109 into the sea and was in turn attacked by three others who shot away an aileron control; he was persistently attacked for about twenty miles but managed to avoid further damage. Sgt. R. Carnall crashed on landing. (Ferris did not land at Hawkinge but returned to Croydon where he picked up a fresh Hurricane and immediately set off to join his Squadron.)

This extract highlights a feature that was characteristic of No. 111 Squadron's battle tactics—and those of No. 32 Squadron—and, as far as is known, was unique to these two Squadrons at the time. This was the opening head-on attack by the entire formation in shallow Vic or even in line abreast. Unnerving for the enemy crews, it was shown to be very effective in causing the bomber pilots to swerve out of formation and abandon their aim. However, as battle casualties on No. 111 Squadron mounted, so the number of experienced pilots dwindled and the head-on attacks (which demanded great courage) came to be abandoned. Indeed Fg. Off. Henry Ferris, the pilot who calmly landed his critically damaged Hurricane at base after a twenty-mile pursuit by enemy fighters and collected a "fresh aircraft", was to lose his life in a head-on collision with an enemy aircraft five weeks later[30].

The efforts of the R.A.F. fighters to upset the bombers' aim were largely successful in that only one direct hit was scored (sinking a 700-ton sloop) out of 150 bombs dropped. Flt. Lt. Gracie and Sgt. C. Whitehead of No. 56 Squadron together destroyed a Bf 110 off Dungeness, and No. 32 Squadron's Green Section (Sgt. E.A. Bayley and Sgt. L.H.B. Pearce led by Humpherson) severely damaged a Do 17 which subsequently crashed on its return to France.

Six Spitfires of No. 64 Squadron also managed to enter the fight before the enemy withdrew, having flown at maximum speed from Kenley. Their pilots arrived to find the Bf 110s breaking from a defensive circle[31] and harassed them all the way back to France, Dawson-Paul damaging one near Calais.

Far to the west, 63 Ju 88s of *Luftflotte 3* had just withdrawn from two raids without loss, having struck at Falmouth and the area around Swansea. In each instance the enemy bombers had approached their targets from the west and thus confused the radar; at Pembrey airfield, No. 92 Squadron's Spitfires were ordered off too late to intercept. A munitions factory nearby was struck by three heavy bombs which killed twelve people and injured fourteen. Elsewhere bombs fell upon anchored ships and on railways, causing more than 60 casualties.

An amusing anecdote is recalled by that fiery little Welshman, Wg. Cdr. Ira Jones, D.S.O., M.C., D.F.C., M.M., who at the time was Wing Commander (Flying) at Stormy Down, a training airfield. Fuming at the absence of British fighters during the raid upon his native land, the First World War veteran pilot took off in the only aircraft at his disposal—a Hawker Henley target tug—and intercepted a Ju 88. His sole weapon was a Verey signal pistol, which he discharged with considerably more feeling than effect[32].

In the North, patrols had been flown all day over several convoys and a minor alarm was caused when a KG 26 Heinkel was spotted and a radio message intercepted from it reporting the position of a convoy in the vicinity. However, due to bad weather, both the Heinkel and the convoy escaped unhurt.

With the withdrawal of No. 79 Squadron's Hurricanes from No. 11 Group, Fighter Command decided to move No. 141 Squadron—equipped with Boulton-Paul Defiant turret fighters—from Turnhouse to Biggin Hill during the next few days, and two transport aircraft[33] were accordingly sent north to collect the ground personnel.

---

[30] There have been several other instances quoted elsewhere of pilots apparently "ramming" enemy aircraft, the implication being that theirs were intentional tactics. Without exception these collisions were the result of "set piece" formation head-on attacks, and it is the opinion of most pilots that the deliberate act of ramming was entirely out of character with the R.A.F. pilot of 1940.

[31] Numerous references will be made during the course of this narrative to the defensive circle (the so-called "death circle") adopted by the Bf 110s and less frequently by the Bf 109s. There were in fact two distinctly different manœuvres, both expedients adopted when the formation was in danger of being overwhelmed by British fighters. The more common tactic employed was for all aircraft to enter a continuous circle over a fixed point, each aircraft thereby covering the tail of the fighter ahead. In theory this represented an impregnable formation, but in practice British pilots were able to take advantage of the enemy's preoccupation with his circling manœuvre, attacking from below the flanks and breaking away downwards to escape the Bf 110's rear gunner.

The other tactic, often mistaken by the R.A.F. for the "death circle" was a circular formation in which the whole group moved on a particular course. This was adopted under the same circumstances as above and for mutual defence, but enabled the formation to retire—perhaps to cloud cover. It was a difficult formation to maintain in combat conditions and seldom employed.

The fact that either manœuvre was adopted by German fighters was clear evidence of the Bf 110's weakness when confronted by British interceptors, and, as will become evident, Hurricanes in particular.

[32] Cf. *Tiger Squadron*, Ira Jones, W.H. Allen, London, 1954, pp. 224-225.

[33] A Bristol Bombay and a Handley Page 42 (an impressed ex-Imperial Airways airliner).

R.A.F. FIGHTER COMMAND LOSSES — WEDNESDAY 10th JULY 1940

1.	74 Sqn., Hornchurch	C	Force landed at Manston after combat with Uffz. Fritz Schupp of 8./ZG 26; pilot unhurt.	14.00 hrs.	Plt. Off. D.C. Cobden	Spitfire	*P9399*	Cat. 2 Damaged

R.A.F. Losses, 10th July 1940—*continued*

2.	74 Sqn., Hornchurch	C	Damaged in combat and landed at Manston; pilot unhurt.	A11.00 hrs.	Plt. Off. J.C. Freeborn	Spitfire	*K9863*	Cat. 2 Damaged
3.	74 Sqn., Hornchurch	C	Damaged in combat and landed at Manston; pilot unhurt.	A11.05 hrs.	Sgt. E.A. Mould	Spitfire	*P9446*	Cat. 2 Damaged
4.	111 Sqn., Croydon	C	Collided with Dornier during convoy attack; sea search failed to find pilot.	13.30 hrs.	Fg. Off. T.P.K. Higgs	Hurricane	*P3671*	Cat. 3 Lost
5.	111 Sqn., Croydon	C	Aileron controls damaged in combat off Folkestone; pilot landed safely at Croydon.	13.35 hrs.	Fg. Off. H.M. Ferris	Hurricane	—	Cat. 1 Damaged
6.	111 Sqn., Croydon	NC	Crashed on landing at Hawkinge; pilot unhurt.	A13.50 hrs.	Sgt. R. Carnall	Hurricane	—	Cat. 2 Damaged
7.	111 Sqn., Croydon	NC	Aircraft hit in fuel tank by Spitfire of No. 54 Sqn. over Kent, but landed safely; pilot unhurt.	A18.40 hrs.	Plt. Off. B. Fisher	Hurricane	—	Cat. 1 Damaged
8.	253 Sqn., Kirton-in-Lindsey	NC	Crashed while on patrol in Humber area; not attributed to combat. Pilot killed.	09.59 hrs.	Sgt. I.C.C. Clenshaw	Hurricane	*P3359*	Cat. 3 Destroyed

LUFTWAFFE LOSSES—WEDNESDAY 10th JULY 1940

1.	Aufkl. Gr. Ob. d. L.	CM	Shot down by Hurricanes of Dutton, Yule and Newling of 145 Sqn. over English Channel at 05.15 hrs. Crashed at Le Havre.	Dornier Do 215	100 %	Ltn. Blindow and one other killed; Ltn. Rack wounded.
2.	2.(F)/11	CM	Damaged landing at Cherbourg after combat with Hurricanes of 145 Sqn. south of the Isle of Wight at 05.30 hrs.	Dornier Do 17P	30 %	Crew unhurt.
3.	4.(F)/121	CM	Crashed at Boulogne after combat with Spitfires of 74 Sqn. over Margate at 10.50 hrs.	Dornier Do 17P	60 %	Oblt. Sombern killed; one other crew member wounded.
4.	2.(F)/122	NCM	Landing accident at Münster-Loddenheide airfield.	Junkers Ju 52 (5162)	35 %	No casualties notified.
5.	3./KG 2	CM	Collided in combat with Hurricane flown by Higgs of 111 Sqn. during raid on convoy off Dover at 13.20 hrs. Crashed near Dungeness.	Dornier Do 17Z (U5+FL)	100 %	Hptm. Walter Krieger, *St.Kap.*, and Ofw. Werner Thalman, wounded and made P.O.W. Fw. Umpkelmann and Fw. Osonsky killed.
6.	I./KG 2	CM	Shot down by 9 Hurricanes of 111 Sqn. during attack on convoy off Dover at 13.15 hrs.	Dornier Do 17Z	100 %	One crew member killed; one wounded and two missing.
7.	I./KG 2	CM	Force landed near Marquise after combat with Hurricanes of Bayley and Pearce of 32 Sqn., off Dungeness at 13.30 hrs.	Dornier Do 17Z	70 %	One crew member killed and two wounded.
8.	II./KG 3	CM	Shot down by Spitfires of Cooke, Studd and Robertson of 66 Sqn. off Winterton.	Dornier Do 17Z	100 %	Oblt. Bott and Ltn. Schröder killed; two other crew members missing.
9.	III./KG 51	NCM	Flying accident at Memmingen airfield.	Junkers Ju 88A	30 %	No casualties notified.
10.	III./KG 53	CM	Shot down by Hurricane of Sub-Lt. Gardner of 242 Sqn. off the Norfolk coast.	Heinkel He 111H-2	100 %	Ltn. Kupfer and one other killed; two other crew members missing.
11.	III./ZG 26	CM	Shot down by Hurricanes of Whitehead and Gracie of 56 Sqn. over convoy off Dungeness at 14.20 hrs.	Messerschmitt Bf 110 C-4	100 %	Ltn. Kuhrich + one killed.
12.	8./ZG 26	CM	Shot down by Hurricanes and crashed 3 miles east of Folkestone Gate Light.	Messerschmitt Bf 110C	100 %	Gefr. Willi Rohde killed; Ofw. Willi Meyer wounded, P.O.W.
13.	I./ZG 2	NCM	Bad weather flying accident near Bitsch.	Messerschmitt Bf 110C	100 %	Two crew members killed.
14.	III./ZG 26	CM	Damaged in combat with Hurricane of Dawson-Paul of 64 Sqn. near Calais at 13.50 hrs.	Messerschmitt Bf 110 C-2	5 %	No casualties notified.
15.	2./JG 3	CM	Shot down by Hurricane of Ferris of 111 Sqn. near Dieppe during raid on convoy at 13.20 hrs.	Messerschmitt Bf 109 E-1	100 %	Pilot wounded but rescued by *Seenotflugkommando.*
16.	I./JG 27	CM	Taxying accident at Mathieu airfield.	Messerschmitt Bf 109 E-1	25 %	Pilot unhurt.
17.	I./JG 27	CM	Landing accident at Mathieu airfield.	Messerschmitt Bf 109 E-4	30 %	Pilot unhurt.
18.	I./JG 51	CM	Damaged in combat with Spitfire of Freeborn of 74 Sqn. near Margate at 10.50 hrs.	Messerschmitt Bf 109 E-4	25 %	Pilot unhurt.
19.	II./JG 51	CM	Stated as being shot down by British fighters over Thames Estuary; no claimant traced.	Messerschmitt Bf 109 E-3	100 %	Pilot missing.
20.	III./JG 51	CM	Damaged by Spitfire of St. John of 74 Sqn. at	Messerschmitt Bf 109	30 %	Pilot unhurt.

[*Note*: German records state that a Messerschmitt Bf 110 of *Erprobungsgruppe 210* was lost to *flak* in an attack on Harwich on this day and the crew killed (ref. *Ob. d.L. Genst. Gen. Qu./6th Abteilung Nr. 3590.g.Kdos(Ic)*, dated 26th July 1940). No British records can be traced to confirm any attack in the Harwich area on this date; it also most certainly refers to the attack on 25th July—see *Luftwaffe* Losses, 25th July, Item No. 18.]

Thursday 11th July

After a night disturbed by about a score of enemy bombers which found no worthwhile target, but evidently aimed their bombs at flaws in the blackout, daylight found Britain once again covered by a blanket of cloud with outbreaks of rain in many places.

With reconnaissance information on the course and position of a convoy off the South Coast, *Fliegerkorps* VIII's dive-bombers set out from the Cherbourg peninsula on the first of several raids soon after 07.00 hours. No. 501 Squadron, whose Green Section (Plt. Off. E.J.H. Sylvester leading

R.A.F. personnel examining the wreck of G1+LK, a Heinkel of 2./KG 55 which crashed and burned on East Beach, Selsey, on 11th July. Two Heinkels collided and crashed after being damaged by F/Sgt. Arthur Pond of No. 601 Squadron. The fin damage clearly indicates that Pond attacked from astern. Even so, Pond did not claim either enemy bomber as being a victim of his guns.

Sgt. F.J.P. Dixon and Plt. Off. R.S. Don) flew escort over the convoy, was vectored towards the approaching raid, but before it could reach the ten Ju 87s was itself attacked by escorting Bf 109s which shot down Dixon. The pilot was seen to bale out, but was evidently drowned. At the first sign of the raid's approach, No. 609 Squadron's "Readiness" Flight was scrambled from Warmwell and these six Spitfires arrived just as the raiders were beginning their dives. While one Section straightway went for the Junkers, the other attempted to hold off the escort. Overwhelmed by odds of six to one, however, the Spitfires were routed and two pilots killed (Flt. Lt. P.H. Barran and Plt. Off. G.T.M. Mitchell). None of the enemy aircraft was destroyed and the defences would find comfort only in the fact that no damage was done to the merchant vessels of the convoy. The 36-year-old Armed Yacht, H.M.S. *Warrior II*, 1,124 tons, was, however, hit and sunk.

Throughout the morning all three *Luftflotten* sent a constant stream of reconnaissance aircraft to British coastal waters; it is estimated that no fewer than eighty such sorties were plotted by radar from the north of Scotland to Land's End. One such aircraft of *Wettererkundungsstaffel 261* was sent out on a met. flight to report the weather conditions off the Suffolk and Norfolk coasts shortly after dawn, but was intercepted by Sqn. Ldr. R.H.A. Leigh and Sgt. R.J. Hyde in Spitfires of No. 66 Squadron off Yarmouth at 06.00 hours. Leigh's oil tank was hit by fire from the Dornier which made off in the clouds, only to be intercepted and shot down ten minutes later off Cromer by a lone Hurricane; this was flown by that legendary pilot, the legless Sqn. Ldr. Douglas Bader, who commanded No. 242 Squadron based at Coltishall[34].

A third squadron commander was engaged in combat with a Dornier at about this time; Squadron Leader Peter Townsend of No. 85 Squadron, on a lone dawn patrol, found a Dornier 17 of II./KG 2 near Harwich, but in his attack stopped a burst of fire from the enemy gunner. With his engine on the point

of seizing up, Townsend baled out; he was picked up by a naval launch after twenty minutes in the water and landed safely at Harwich. The Dornier returned home with three wounded crew members.

Encouraged by the relative immunity enjoyed by his Stukas during the early morning raid over Lyme Bay, Sperrle ordered his dive-bombers to assemble for a follow-up attack. This time, however, Messerschmitt Bf 110s of III./ZG 76 were sent as escort in place of Bf 109s, and just before 11.00 hours the formation—consisting of two Staffeln from III./ St.G 2 and about forty Bf 110s—set course for Portland from the Cherbourg peninsula.

As almost all fighters in the Middle Wallop Sector were being refuelled when the raid was first reported by Ventnor CH, No. 11 Group Controller ordered off six Hurricanes of No. 601 Squadron from Tangmere. With more than fifty

---

[34] The personal courage and determination of this pilot must be almost without parallel in the history of the Royal Air Force. The book *Reach for the Sky* by Paul Brickhill (Collins, London, 1957) tells how Bader lost both legs in a flying accident in the early 'thirties and was invalided from the Service. Acquiring artificial legs and overcoming all manner of official opposition, he not only joined Fighter Command as a fully operational pilot, but commanded No. 242 Squadron throughout the Battle of Britain. This Squadron was in poor shape when Bader joined it, having been heavily engaged at the end of the French campaign. Under Bader's extraordinary leadership the Squadron quickly recovered its spirits and it was on 4th July that Bader sent his provoking signal to Air Ministry: "*Squadron operationally trained by day, but non-operational with regard to equipment*". Within 72 hours he had received his equipment and his pilots were in action.

miles to fly to Portland, these fighters arrived too late to prevent the bombing, and in fact found the enemy forces conveniently split, with the dive-bombers at low level and their escort high above—too high to interfere with the Hurricanes' first attack. Flt. Lt. Sir Archibald Hope[35] promptly led his Flight into the attack on the Junkers, and Fg. Off. Gordon Cleaver sent one crashing into the water close by Portland mole. As the bombers hurriedly jettisoned their remaining bombs into the sea and made off to the south, the Bf 110s now appeared and the Hurricane pilots split up, each endeavouring to manœuvre on to the tail of an enemy aircraft. Fg. Off. H.J. Riddle[36] shot one down and, seeing it crash land in marshy ground near Warmwell, circled while the two crew members climbed out. Two other Hurricanes (one flown by Plt. Off. P.C. Lindsey) shot down a second Bf 110 into the sea.

This successful action (from which all the No. 601 Squadron Hurricanes returned unscathed) was in fact the Squadron's second action of a most strenuous day. An hour earlier Fg. Off. W.H. Rhodes-Moorhouse had led the Squadron's other Flight into combat against a lone Do 17P of 2.(F)/121, and with Plt. Off. J.W. Bland, had shot down the enemy into the sea twenty miles south of the Isle of Wight.

Not to be caught unawares again, No. 11 Group ordered both Flights of No. 601 Squadron into the air again from Tangmere at 17.15 hours in good time to meet a smaller raid making for the naval base at Portsmouth. Sighting twelve He 111s[37] and a similar number of Bf 110s, Rhodes-Moorhouse led the attack on the bombers. This time the escort reacted quickly, and the running dogfight continued over the Solent and on up to Portsmouth where the Heinkels dropped their bombs. Perhaps not unnaturally the anti-aircraft gunners seeing the raid approaching apparently unchecked, opened

fire, and continued firing into the midst of the dogfight. Sgt. A.W. Woolley's aircraft was evidently hit by an anti-aircraft shell and the pilot had to bale out with burns and shrapnel wounds, his Hurricane falling in flames at Cranmore in the Isle of Wight. F/Sgt. Pond attacked one Heinkel with such ferocity that it swerved, struck its neighbour and blew up. Cleaver damaged a third. A Messerschmitt which crashed near Lymington (one crew having baled out) was shot down by Fg. Off. C.R. Davis, but was not included in German loss returns.

A fascinating incident occurred earlier in the day following a light raid over Exeter. German rescue seaplanes were evidently on patrol off the south Cornish coast on the look-out for ditched airmen when a Heinkel He 59 was forced down on the sea by engine failure, whereupon another He 59 alighted nearby to lend assistance. The fact was reported by a Cornish coastguard and two destroyers immediately put out from Plymouth in a bid to capture the enemy seaplanes, under cover provided by three Blenheims of No. 236 Squadron from St. Eval. Arriving in the area, the destroyers became the target of a Ju 88 which was shot down by the Blenheims; shortly afterwards a Heinkel He 111 of KG 55 appeared, and this was also chased away, severely damaged by Plt. Off. B.M. McDonough. As the German records indicate that a Heinkel He 59 was lost on this day, it seems likely that the second aircraft rescued the crew of the disabled seaplane which was

---

[35] Hope observed in his combat report that some of the German dive bombers were carrying long-range fuel tanks under the wings, confirming that St.G 2 was at that time operating the Ju 87R variant; this had first been encountered in small numbers during the Norwegian campaign.

[36] One of two brothers serving as Flying Officers on No. 601 Squadron at that time; both were peacetime Auxiliary pilots. Both survived the War and left the R.A.F. shortly after as Squadron Leaders. (See Appendix A).

[37] This is an interesting raid in that, from an examination of wreckage and analysis of German records, it appears to have included aircraft from KG 1 (of I *Fliegerkorps*) as well as I./KG 55 (of V *Fliegerkorps*). If this is correct, it is the only known instance of mixed bomber unit composition in such a small raid, and is inexplicable at this stage in the Battle of Britain; it is conceivable that the escort was also a mixed formation, and this may explain the absence of Davis' victim from the German loss returns.

Pilots and aircraft of No. 601 (County of London) Squadron, showing the "winged sword" emblem of the Auxiliary squadron painted on the aircraft's fin flash. No. 601 Squadron fought a successful action against a force of Ju 87s and Bf 110s over Portland on the morning of 11th July.

presumably scuttled[38].

If attacks against Britain and her coastal shipping had appeared to lack cohesion during the past fortnight, this was probably due to the delay in the issue of preliminary battle orders. As has been shown, Göring's instructions of 30th June misrepresented Hitler's strategic policies, and the relatively brief Directive No. 15 issued by the Führer on 2nd July called in effect for staff planning in preparation for the future assault

on Britain to be integrated between the Naval, Army and Air Staffs. The framework of the overall planning occupied O.K.W. until 10th July, so that it was not until the following day that O.K.L. was able to issue detailed instructions to *Luftflotten* staffs on which a co-ordinated air offensive could be developed. As will be seen later, the Führer's Directive, No. 16 of 16th July, was to further complicate the Air Staff's planning by demanding the annihilation of the R.A.F.'s Fighter Command as a prerequisite for the launching of invasion forces.

[38] Cf. diary kept by J.N. Llewellyn, Esq. Ref. also Form 540, No. 236 Sqn., 11th July 1940.

R.A.F. FIGHTER COMMAND LOSSES — THURSDAY 11th JULY 1940

No.	Sqn.		Details	Time	Pilot	Aircraft	Serial	Category
1.	66 Sqn., Coltishall	C	Hit in oil tank by Do 17 ten miles S.E. of Gt. Yarmouth; pilot landed safely unhurt.	06.00 hrs.	Sqn. Ldr. R.H.A. Leigh	Spitfire	—	Cat. 1 Damaged
2.	85 Sqn., Martlesham	C	Hit in cockpit and coolant tank by Do 17; pilot baled out, picked up by naval launch and landed unhurt at Harwich.	05.20 hrs.	Sqn. Ldr. P.W. Townsend	Hurricane	P2716	Cat. 3 Lost
3.	145 Sqn., Tangmere	C	Shot down near Selsey Bill; pilot picked up by Selsey lifeboat, semi-conscious but unwounded.	18.15 hrs.	Sqn. Ldr. J.R.A. Peel	Hurricane	—	Cat. 3 Lost
4.	242 Sqn., Coltishall	NC	Aircraft destgroyed in accident; pilot unhurt.	Not known	Plt. Off. R.D. Grassick	Hurricane	—	Cat. 3 Destroyed
5.	501 Sqn., Middle Wallop	C	Shot down off Portland Bill; pilot baled out but drowned.	A08.00 hrs.	Sgt. F.J.P. Dixon	Hurricane	N2485	Cat. 3 Lost
6.	601 Sqn., Tangmere	C	Shot down by A.A. fire over Cranmore, Isle of Wight; pilot baled out with burns and shrapnel wounds.	A17.45 hrs.	Sgt. A.W. Woolley	Hurricane	P3681	Cat. 3 Destroyed
7.	609 Sqn., Warmwell	C	Pilot Missing from combat over Portland.	Not known	Flt. Lt. P.H. Barran	Spitfire	L1069	Cat. 3 Missing
8.	609 Sqn., Warmwell	C	Pilot Missing from combat over Portland.	Not known	Plt. Off. G.T.M. Mitchell	Spitfire	L1095	Cat. 3 Missing

LUFTWAFFE LOSSES—THURSDAY 11th JULY 1940

No.	Unit		Details	Aircraft	%	Casualties
1.	Wekusta. 261	CM	Shot down by Hurricane of Bader of 242 Sqn. near Cromer at approx. 06.10 hrs.	Dornier Do 17	100 %	Reg. Rat. Belger + three crew members missing.
2.	2.(F)/111	CM	Shot down by Hurricanes of Rhodes-Moorhouse and Bland of 601 Sqn. 20 miles south of Isle of Wight at 10.14 hrs.	Dornier Do 17P	100 %	Three crew missing.
3.	1./KG 1	CM	Shot down by 12 Hurricanes of 145 Sqn. near Selsey Bill at 18.15 hrs.	Heinkel He 111H	100 %	Hptm. Behreus and Ltn. Wagner + fourn crew members missing.
4.	1./KG 1	CM	Shot down by Hurricane of Storrar of 145 Sqn. near Selsey Bill at 18.20 hrs.	Heinkel He 111H	100 %	Oblt. Grunwald + three crew members missing.
5.	1./KG 1	CM	Force landed at Montdidier airfield after combat with Hurricane of Cleaver of 601 Sqn. over Portsmouth at 17.40 hrs.	Heinkel He 111H	60-70 %	No casualties notified.
6.	II./KG 2	CM	Damaged by Hurricane flown by Townsend of 85 Sqn. on dawn patrol near Harwich.	Dornier Do 17Z	50 %	Ltn. Werner Borner and two crew members wounded.
7.	I./KG 3	CM	Damaged by Spitfires of Leigh and Hyde of 66 Sqn. 10 miles east of Yarmouth at 06.20 hrs.	Dornier Do 17Z	10-60 %	Ltn. Fischer wounded.
8.	II./KG 3	NCM	Landing accident at Schweinfurt airfield.	Dornier Do 17Z	10 %	No casualties notified.
9.	Zerst.St/KG 30	NCM	Landing accident at Schipol airfield.	Junkers Ju 88C-2	100 %	No casualties notified.
10.	I./KG 51	CM	Shot down by Blenheims of Peachment, Riley and McDonough of 236 Sqn.. during attack on destroyers off Start Point at approx. 12.10 hrs.	Junkers Ju 88A	100 %	Four crew members missing.
11.	3./KG 51	CM	Crashed at Verneuil following engine failure.	Junkers Ju 88A	100 %	Ofw. Josef Rattel killed.
12.	2./KG 55	CM	Two Heinkels collided in combat with Hurricane of Pond of 601 Sqn. over Portsmouth at 17.30 hrs.	Heinkel He 111H / Heinkel He 111H (2648:G1:LK)	100 % / 100 %	Uffz. Müller and Ofw. Schlüter killed; Ofw. Erich Slatosch, Oblt. Siegfried Schweinhagen and Fw. Herbert Steiner made P.O.W. Four other crew members missing.
13.	I./KG 55	CM	Damaged by Blenheim of McDonough of 236 Sqn. off Cornish coast at 12.50 hrs.	Heinkel He 111H	80 %	Two crew members missing.
14.	III./St.G 2	CM	Shot down by Hurricane of Cleaver of 601 Sqn. and crashed by Portsmouth Mole at 11.30 hrs.	Junkers Ju 87B	100 %	Two crew members missing.
15.	III./St.G 77	NCM	Landing accident at Flers airfield.	Junkers Ju 87B	100 %	No casualties notified.
16.	II./LG 1	CM	Cause of loss corrupt in German records.	Junkers Ju 88A	100 %	Oblt. Vitende + one killed.
17.	11./LG 1	CM	Shot down by Hurricane flown by Hope of 601 Sqn. near Portland at 11.30 hrs.	Junkers Ju 87B	100 %	One crew member killed and one one missing.
18.	11./LG 1	CM	Force landed at St. Inglevert after combat with Hurricane of Guy of 601 Sqn. near Portland at 11.30 hrs.	Junkers Ju 87B	10 %	No casualties notified.
19.	III./ZG 76	CM	Shot down by Hurricane of Walsh of 238 Sqn. south of Portland at approx. 12.05 hrs.	Messerschmitt Bf 110C (2N+EP)	100 %	Oblt. Gerhard Kadow wounded after landing; made P.O.W. (1) Gefr. Helmut Scholz also P.O.W.

20.	III./ZG 76	CM	Shot down by Hurricanes near Portland at 11.30 hrs., and crashed off Ney Breakwater.	Messerschmitt Bf 110C	100 %	Oblt. Göring made P.O.W.; one crew member missing.
21.	III./ZG 76	CM	Believed shot down by Hurricane of Riddle of 601 Sqn. near Warmwell at 11.30 hrs.	Messerschmitt Bf 110C	100 %	Ltn. Schröder + one missing.
22.	III./ZG 76	CM	Shot down by Hurricane of Dewar of 87 Sqn. near Exeter at 12.10 hrs.	Messerschmitt Bf 110C	100 %	Ltn. Castell + one missing.
23.	5./JG 3	NCM	Taxying accident on Baromesnil airfield.	Messerschmitt Bf 109 E-3	70 %	Pilot unhurt.
24.	II(Schl.)/LG 2	NCM	Force landed in bad weather at Öbisfelde.	Bücker Bü 131	60-70 %	No casualties notified.
25.	Seenotflug-kdo. 1	CM	Said to have been shot down by British fighters over English Channel. See text.	Heinkel He 59	100 %	Crew said to have been rescued by by *Seenotflugkommando*..

[(1) Oberleutnant Kadow, *Staffelkapitän* of 6./ZG 76, was shot and wounded by a British soldier when he attempted to burn his papers.]

Friday 12th July

The night had been considerably disturbed for the people of South-East England, not only by a sharp raid upon the Medway towns but also by the coming and going of enemy bombers over the capital around midnight. A warehouse in Camberwell had caught fire accidentally and was blazing out of control, attracting a score of enemy bombers to the scene. Such was the strictness of their orders not to bomb the capital that they resisted the temptation to add to the fire fighters' task; instead they dropped their loads on Rochester and Chatham, killing 36 people.

After the Auxiliary fighter squadrons' successes of the day before, the major share of this day's fighting was to fall to the Regulars. Under grey skies and occasional outbreaks of thundery rain, first light found two large convoys in the outer environs of the Thames Estuary, one named BOOTY, steaming southwards off the Essex coast, and the other, AGENT, off the North Foreland. The heaviest German attack was launched against the former.

At about 08.00 hours "A" Flight of No. 17 Squadron, having been ordered forward from Debden to Martlesham for the day's patrols, took off to fly escort over BOOTY. On the way the pilots were warned of an approaching raid, and simultaneously heavy reinforcements were ordered off, including three Hurricanes of No. 85 Squadron from Martlesham, three Hurricanes of No. 242 Squadron from Coltishall, six Defiants of No. 264 Squadron from Duxford and eleven Hurricanes of No. 151 Squadron from North Weald. Such heavy forces, sent piecemeal, although probably dictated by availability, were not characteristic of Leigh-Mallory's reaction to raids (as will be seen later on), and clearly the failure on this occasion of sizeable parts of his defending formations to make contact with the enemy, only served to strengthen his resolve in future to commit his interceptors to battle only after they had joined together in a cohesive "Wing" formation. It transpired, on this morning, that neither No. 242 nor 264 Squadrons made contact with the enemy.

The raiding formation—two *Staffeln* of II./KG 2's Dornier Do 17s and two *Staffeln* of III./KG 53's Heinkel 111s—was first sighted by No. 17 Squadron and attacked at 08.48 hours as the enemy dived out of the clouds and dropped the first bombs. Flying in Sections of paired Hurricanes, the Squadron went straight for about twelve Heinkels at 8,000 feet, Plt. Off. K. Manger of Yellow Section firing all his ammunition in a single 15-second burst while closing on a bomber from 350 yards to 50 yards; his No. 2, Sgt. G. Griffiths, followed up with a nine-second burst and left the Heinkel "generally falling to pieces". Griffiths then spotted

another straggling behind the main formation, fired all his remaining ammunition, and sent this spinning into the sea with both engines blazing. Meanwhile Red Section (Plt. Off. P.E. Pitman and Sgt. D. Fopp) were carrying out co-ordinated quarter attacks on the other Heinkel *Staffel*; they shot one bomber down near a trawler which, despite falling bombs, hove to and picked up three survivors. Shortly afterwards Fg. Off. Count Manfred Czernin and Plt. Off. David Hanson singled out the leader of one of the Dornier formations and, after a number of head-on and quarter-stern attacks, left the bomber wallowing badly and in obvious trouble just above the sea. It did not return to base and Hauptmann Mechetski, the *Staffelkapitän*, was reported missing by his unit.

The Dorniers depended on tight formation flying to afford mutual protection, and when No. 151 Squadron, led by Sqn. Ldr. "Teddy" Donaldson, attacked, the Hurricanes came under vicious crossfire. Fg. Off. J.H.L. Allen (from New Zealand) was seen to be badly hit, gliding down with a dead engine; he was not seen again. Wg. Cdr. Beamish severely damaged a Dornier, and this was finished off by the other pilots. Several Hurricanes returned home very much the worse for wear.

A Section of No. 85 Squadron's Hurricanes managed to intercept the Heinkels before the raid dispersed, and Plt. Off. J.L. Bickerdyke (another New Zealander) claimed to have destroyed one of the enemy; Sgt. L. Jowitt of his Section was however shot down and killed off Felixstowe.

This was the only major raid of the day, the *Luftwaffe* obviously deciding that weather conditions ruled out the possibility of further effective bombing on a large scale. That is not to say that "nuisance raids" did not continue, and several lone raiders played hide-and-seek with the defending forces. Three Hurricanes of No. 145 Squadron came across a small formation of Junkers Ju 88s and Messerschmitt Bf 110s, and Plt. Off R.D. Yule destroyed a Ju 88 in a fight that took place in and out of cloud patches which came as low as 700 feet. In the North, No. 603 Squadron's Yellow Section caught a Heinkel He 111 of 9.*Staffel*, KG 26 at 12.43 hours and Plt. Off. George Gilroy[39], Sgt. J.R. Caister and Sgt. I.K. Arber shot this down over Aberdeen; unfortunately the enemy bomber crashed into the town's newly completed ice rink.

---

[39] Gilroy was later to claim 21 victories, was wounded three times (once during the Battle of Britain) and was awarded three British gallantry decorations as well as the Croix de Guerre (Belge)— (see Appendix A).

126

Having missed its chance to attack the convoy AGENT as it rounded the east coast of Kent, the *Luftwaffe* made several efforts to locate it in the bad weather over the Channel. A Heinkel of KG 55's Staff Flight was caught at about 14.30 hours by six Hurricanes of No. 43 Squadron from Tangmere, led by Sqn. Ldr J.V.C. Badger, and was shot down at Southwick; the bomber crash landed with two of its crew dead and two wounded. The pilot was unhurt.

Later on, *Luftflotte 3* sent reconnaissance Dorniers at low level in search of another convoy, reported off Portland, and these were intercepted by six Hurricanes of No. 501 Squadron, scrambled from Middle Wallop; in driving the enemy off a Canadian pilot, Plt. Off. D.A. Hewett, misjudged his dive and was killed, crashing into the sea[40].

In preparation for the coming all-out offensive, the *Luftwaffe* embarked on an increasing scale of night raiding from the night of 12th/13th onwards. Greater emphasis in bomber crew briefing was given to the avoidance of known gun-defended areas on the way to the target; in a raid on Cardiff by a dozen Heinkels of Oberst Alois Stoeckl's KG 55 on this night, the bombers' flight plan took them far out to the southwest so as to round Land's End before their run-up to the target. Other fairly complicated flight plans were drawn up for raids against Bristol, Northumberland and Yorkshire towns. In thus confusing the defences—as well as avoiding them—the raids brought further frustration to the hardworking but ineffective night fighter crews.

[40] The day before his death, Hewett filed a combat report claiming the destruction of "an enemy Hurricane". No confirmation is available from German sources that *Luftwaffe* pilots ever flew any of the Hurricanes which were captured in France on operations against Britain. Indeed, those German survivors to whom the Author has spoken on this matter, categorically denied that any such aircraft were flown other than at experimental stations in Germany. The inference that Hewett may have shot down an R.A.F. fighter can be discounted as the circumstances relating to the loss of British fighters in the area clearly contradict this, so his claim must remain a mystery.

R.A.F. FIGHTER COMMAND LOSSES — FRIDAY 12th JULY 1940

1.	79 Sqn., In transit	NC	Collided with Miles Master at Sealand; pilot unhurt	Not known	Not known		Hurricane	N2609	Cat. 3 Destroyed
2.	79 Sqn., In transit	NC	Collided with Miles Master at Sealand; pilot unhurt	Not known	Not known		Hurricane	—	Cat. 3 Destroyed
3.	85 Sqn., Martlesham	C	Shot down by He 111s over convoy off Felixstowe; pilot killed.	A09.00 hrs.	Sgt. L. Jowitt		Hurricane	—	Cat. 3 Lost
4.	145 Sqn., Tangmere	NC	Force landed near Ringwood, Hants; not attributed to combat; pilot not hurt.	Not known	Not known		Hurricane	N2703	Cat. 3 Destroyed

No. 145 Squadron pilots enjoy a spot of relaxation. Sqn. Ldr. Peel (centre) had been shot down into the sea off Selsey on the 11th and was picked up only semi-conscious by the local lifeboat but returned to operations six days later. (Left) Flight Lieutenant Roy Dutton, "A" Flight Commander, shot down a Do 17 on 10th July, and a Heinkel He 111 the following day; he died as an Air Commodore in 1988. (Right) Flying Officer Antoni Ostowicz, a Polish pilot who joined No. 145 Squadron in mid-July but who was killed over the Isle of Wight on 11th August.

R.A.F. Losses, 12th July 1940—*continued*

5.	151 Sqn., North Weald	C	Damaged by Do 17s over convoy off Orfordness; pilot returned unhurt to base.	A09.00 hrs.	Sqn. Ldr.E.M. Donaldson	Hurricane	P3152	Cat. 2 Damaged
6.	151 Sqn., North Weald	C	Shot down by Do 17s over convoy off Orfordness; pilot believed drowned.	A09.00 hrs	Fg. Off. J.H.L. Allan	Hurricane	P3275	Cat. 3 Missing
7.	151 Sqn., North Weald	C	Damaged by Do 17s over convoy off Orfordness; pilot returned to base unhurt.	A09.00 hrs.	Wg. Cdr. F.V. Beamish	Hurricane	P3304	Cat. 2 Damaged
8.	257 Sqn., Northolt	NC	Landing accident at Northolt; pilot unhurt.	Not known	Plt. Off. G.H. Maffett	Hurricane	—	Cat. 2 Damaged
9.	257 Sqn., Northolt	NC	Landing accident at Northolt; pilot unhurt.	Not known	Plt. Off. The Hon. D.A. Coke	Hurricane	P3767	Cat. 3 Destroyed
10.	263 Sqn., Grangemouth	NC	Flying accident at Tatsfield, Kent; pilot killed. (1)	11.36 hrs.	Sgt. Watson-Parker	Hurricane	—	Cat. 3 Destroyed
11.	501 Sqn., Middle Wallop	C	Crashed off Portland; pilot killed.	A15.35 hrs.	Plt. Off. D.A. Hewett	Hurricane	P3084	Cat. 3 Lost
12.	610 Sqn., Biggin Hill	NC	Pilot dived into cloud during dogfight training, striking ground at Titsey Park.	11.36 hrs.	Sgt. S. Ireland	Spitfire	P9502	Cat. 3 Destroyed

[(1) The identical time at which Items 10 and 12 crashed in Kent suggests that the two aircraft collided, although No. 263 Squadron records stated that Watson-Parker's Hurricane was lost on 11th July; the date and time given here are taken from on-the-spot Observer Corps records and signals.]

LUFTWAFFE LOSSES—FRIDAY 12th JULY 1940

1.	II./KG 2	CM	Shot down by Hurricanes of Czernin and Hansen of 17 Sqn., near convoy BOOTY off Orfordness at 09.32 hrs.	Dornier Do 17Z	100 %	Hptm. Machetzki, St.Kap., Oblt. Röwe + two others missing.
2.	II./KG 2	CM	Shot down by eleven Hurricanes of 151 Sqn. near convoy BOOTY off Orfordness at 09.05 hrs.	Dornier Do 17Z	100 %	Four crew members missing.
3.	9./KG 26	CM	Shot down by Spitfires of Gilroy, Caister and Arber of 603 Sqn., over Aberdeen at 12.43 hrs. Aircraft crashed in town.	Heinkel He 111H-3	100 %	Ltn. Huck + three crew members missing.
4.	I./KG 51	CM	Severely damaged by Hurricane of Yule of 145 Sqn., off St. Catherine's Head at 18.45 hrs. Crashed at Villaroche.	Junkers Ju 88A	100 %	No crew casualties notified.
5.	III./KG 53	CM	Force landed at Kotwijk airfield following engine failure.	Heinkel He 111H-3	40 %	Crew unhurt.
6.	8./KG 53	CM	Shot down by Hurricanes of Manger and Griffiths of 17 Sqn., near convoy Booty off Orfordness at 08.54 hrs. Aircraft landed on sea 4 miles ENE of Shipwash Light vessel.	Heinkel He 111H-2	100 %	Uffz. Werner Weber killed; Fw. Peter Baumeister, Oblt. von Brocke and Gefr. Albert Mehringer wounded and made P.O.W.(1)
7.	III./KG 53	CM	Shot down by Hurricane flown by Griffiths of 17 Sqn., near convoy BOOTY off Orfordness at 08.58 hrs. Aircraft landed on sea 10 miles NNW of Aldeburgh Light Float.	Heinkel He 111H-2 (A1+ES)	100 %	Uffz. Heinz Zittwitz, Gefr. Helmuth Tonne and Gefr. Wagner killed or drowned; Uffz. Hans Bolte and Fw. Karl Hartmann made P.O.W.
8.	II./KG 53	CM	Shot down by Spitfires of Malan, Mould and Stevenson of 74 Sqn., into sea off Margate.	Heinkel He 111H-2	100 %	Three crew killed and two missing.
9.	St.St./KG 55	CM	Target not known. Shot down by six Hurricanes of 43 Sqn., at 14.30 hrs.; aircraft crashed at Hipley, Hants.·	Heinkel He 111P (G1+FA)	100 %	Oblt. Kleinhanns killed; Fw. John Möhn (2), Fw. Heinz Knecht and and Ofw. Philipp Müller , P.O.W.
10.	St.St./St.G 3	CM	Force landed near Cherbourg after combat with Spitfires of Lawrence and Gordon of 234 Sqn., at 15.45 hrs.	Heinkel He 111H	50 %	Three crew members wounded.
11.	III./St.G 77	NCM	Force landed near Breux after engine failure.	Junkers Ju 87B	35 %	No casualties notified.

[(1) Feldwebel Baumeister wore the *Eiserne Kreuze* (Iron Cross), 1st and 2nd Class.
(2) Feldwebel Möhn was the first German airman wearing the bronze wound badge to be taken prisoner in Britain; his wounds had been suffered in an action with twelve Morane fighters over France during April 1940.]

Saturday 13th July

Another overcast morning heralded a day of sporadic attacks against convoys in transit off the South Coast. As usual these attracted the inquisitive shadowing aircraft, and a Junkers Ju 88 of II./KG 51 was shot down by Hurricanes of Blue Section, No. 43 Squadron (Flt. Lt. T.P. Dalton-Morgan, Plt. Off D.G. Gorrie and Plt. Off. R.A. de Mancha) after a long chase from the Isle of Wight almost as far as Cherbourg.

The convoy being shadowed was sailing westwards and by early afternoon was entering the "unhealthy" area of Lyme Bay. Two squadrons were deployed at Warmwell and shortly before 15.00 hours twelve Hurricanes of No. 238 Squadron and three No. 609 Squadron Spitfires were ordered off to mount guard over the ships—expected to have arrived off Portland. However, owing to earlier zig-zagging, the convoy was about a dozen miles behind schedule, and the Hurricane pilots found no ships—only about fifty enemy aircraft, equally mystified by the non-arrival of the convoy. Seeing two apparently straggling Dorniers, the pilots of two Hurricane Sections (Red and Yellow) made off in pursuit; Flt. Lt. J.C. Kennedy (an Australian) shot down one off Chesil Bank, and the other was left losing height with one engine on fire (it survived a force landing at Caen); Kennedy seems to have suffered battle damage and was killed in a crash landing at base.

The pilots of the main formation—about 40 Bf 110C fighter-bombers of V./LG 1[41]—now deprived of their reconnaissance "eyes", were obviously undecided as to their course of action and, in the presence of intercepting fighters, promptly assumed the characteristic defensive circle about six miles south of Portland. Try as they might, the Hurricane pilots could not manœuvre to secure any kills, although they damaged two Messerschmitts. Another was severely damaged by the Spitfire Section led by Fg. Off. J.C. Dundas.

While convoy BREAD sailed on unscathed to the westward, yet another was running the gauntlet of the Dover Strait. Predictably, as the ships passed within sight of German observation posts on the French coast, the *Luftwaffe* reacted, this time sending a *Staffel* of Ju 87 dive-bombers from II./St.G 1 (now based in the Pas de Calais) escorted by at least three *Staffeln* of JG 51's Bf 109s. Eleven Hurricanes of No. 56 Squadron had been sent up at 15.30 hours from Rochford on a sweeping patrol between Dover and Calais, and ran into the enemy raid. As the intercepting pilots managed to get at the dive bombers before the Bf 109s could interfere, a bitter dogfight followed—all the while moving steadily closer to Dover. When the escort did join combat, it found the Hurricane pilots preoccupied and shot down two (Sgt. J.R. Cowsill and Sgt. J.J. Whitfield). The British pilots claimed the destruction of seven dive bombers, but in fact all returned home safely, though two were damaged.

It fell to the Spitfires of Nos. 54 and 64 Squadrons to avenge these losses, and a couple of hours later a JG 51 Messerschmitt Bf 109 was caught and finally shot down after a long chase at sea level by Plt. Off. Colin Gray of No. 54 Squadron[42]. The naval pilot, Dawson-Paul of No. 64, claimed another but this evidently escaped and reached base. In the latter action, which took place over Dover, the anti-aircraft guns also claimed a victim, for Sgt. A.E. Binham's Spitfire was hit and force landed at nearby Hawkinge airfield.[43]

The nature of *Luftwaffe* daylight operations being carried out at this time was undoubtedly having a serious effect upon

Mixed *Kriegsmarine/Luftwaffe* crews were a feature of maritime units; here a captured Oberleutnant zur See and a *Luftwaffe* Unteroffizier are shown under escort. (Photo: Topix)

Fighter Command; and while, on paper at any rate, losses sustained in action were by no means crippling, the attrition due to sustained patrolling (80 per cent of it over the sea) was certainly making itself felt. The poor weather conditions imposed considerable strain upon pilots, as well as slowing down the final training of new pilots on the squadrons. Added to this the frequent isolated enemy flights over the whole country also restricted flying training so that greater responsibility for interception fell upon the very pilots who should have been resting. In relation to the total number of pilots involved, Fighter Command could already see a disconcertingly high proportion of Squadron and Flight Commanders among the casualty lists; while it is true that most of them had escaped physical injury, the cumulative mental strain that accompanied force landings, ditchings, parachute descents and exhausting ordeals in the sea awaiting rescue[44], would inevitably take its toll among men whose skill and judgement would be vital in the heavy air battles of the coming weeks.

It is true that only one in three of all fighter squadrons had yet been in action in the past fortnight, yet so slowly was training proceeding on many others that it is perhaps not too difficult to understand Dowding's reluctance to embark on a policy of resting tired squadrons too early in the Battle.

---

[41] This was the first major effort by *Lehrgeschwader 1* in the Battle of Britain. A mixed unit of bombers, Stukas and *Zerstörer* staffed mainly by former instructors and personnel of the pre-War Technical Development Flying Unit, it acquired something of an élite reputation, and was to be heavily committed to many different types of mission during the Battle.

[42] This was Gray's first solo confirmed victory in the Battle of Britain; in the course of the next seven weeks he was to achieve a score of fourteen solo victories. (See Appendix A).

[43] Other accounts of the Battle suggest that the *Luftwaffe* also lost a four-engine Focke-Wulf Fw 200 long-range reconnaissance bomber on 13th July. As was frequently the practice, this loss was reported by *Kampfgeschwader 40* more than a week later (in *Obd. L. Genst. Gen. Qu./6th Abt. Nr. 3520*, dated 22nd July) and did in fact refer to an aircraft shot down by A.A. fire during the night of 19th/20th July (*q.v.*).

[44] For a sea-girt nation, Britain's air/sea rescue organisation in the summer of 1940 left much to be desired, with few established high-speed rescue launches yet available. In too many instances recourse was made to the devoted services of the National Lifeboat Assocation, and its use of relatively slow boats often resulted in the loss from drowning of an injured pilot. This is, of course, no reflection on the magnificent Lifeboat service, which rescued many R.A.F. and German airmen from the sea—often under fire—but rather the lack of preparedness for a Battle which, by the nature of the new air defence system, *was intended to be fought over the sea.*

R.A.F. FIGHTER COMMAND LOSSES — SATURDAY 13th JULY 1940

1.	19 Sqn., Duxford	NC	Pilot killed on training flight; circumstances not known	Not known	Sgt. Birch	Spitfire	R6688	Cat. 3 Destroyed
2.	25 Sqn., Martlesham	NC	Force landed at base folowing engine failure off Felixstowe; crew unhurt.	Not known	Fg. Off. A. Lyall	Blenheim	—	Cat. 2 Damaged
3.	56 Sqn., North Weald	C	Shot down (probably by Bf 109) over Dover Strait; pilot assumed killed.	A16.00 hrs.	Sgt. J.R. Cowsill	Hurricane	P2902	Cat. 3 Missing

R.A.F. Losses, 13th July 1940—*continued*

4.	56 Sqn., North Weald	C	Shot down (probably by Bf 109) over Dover Strait; pilot assumed killed.	A16.00 hrs.	Sgt. J.J. Whitfield	Hurricane	N2432	Cat. 3 Missing
5.	56 Sqn., North Weald	C	Force landed at Ditchling after combat over Dover Strait; pilot unhurt.	A16.00 hrs.	Sgt. R.D. Baker	Hurricane	—	Cat. 2 Damaged
6.	64 Sqn., Kenley	C	Hit by A.A. fire at Dover; pilot unhurt and landed at Hawkinge.	17.40 hrs.	Sgt. A.E. Binham	Spitfire	K9795	Cat. 2 Damaged
7.	238 Sqn., Middle Wallop	C	Crashed on landing at Warmwell after combat with Do 17 off Chesil Bank; pilot killed.	15.05 hrs.	Flt. Lt. J.C. Kennedy	Hurricane	P2950	Cat. 3 Destroyed
8.	263 Sqwn., Grangemouth	NC	Night flying accident at Grangemouth; cause not known. Pilot unhurt.	At night	Flt. Lt. W.O.L. Smith	Hurricane	P2991	Cat. 3 Destroyed

LUFTWAFFE LOSSES—SATURDAY 13th JULY 1940

1.	4.(F)/14	CM	Landed at Caen with damage from combat with Hurricanes of No. 238 Sqn., 5 miles south of Portland at 15.06 hrs.	Dornier Do 17M	10 %	No casualties notified
2.	4.(F)/122	CM	Target and circumstance of loss not known.	Junkers Ju 88	100 %	Four crew members missing.
3.	2.(F)/123	CM	Shot down by Hurricane of Kennedy of 238 Sqn., off Chesil Bank at 15.04 hrs.	Dornier Do 17P	100 %	Ltn. Weinbauer killed; Oblt. Graf von Kesselstadt + one missing.
4.	6./KG 51	CM	Shot down by Hurricanes of Dalton-Morgan, Gorrie and de Mancha of 43 Sqn., off Cherbourg at 09.35 hrs.	Junkers Ju 88A	100 %	Oblt Fritz Kesper killed; three others missing.
5.	7./KG 51	CM	Landed at Rouen with damage from South Coast A.A. gunfire.	Junkers Ju 88A-1 (7074: 9K+CR)	20 %	No casualties notified.
6.	I./KG 54	NCM	Force landed near Paris due to bad weather.	Junkers Ju 88A	25 %	No crew casualties.
7.	II./KG 76	NCM	Landing accident at Creil airfield.	Junkers Ju 88A-1	30 %	No casualties notified.
8.	II./St.G 1	CM	Force landed at Noorfontes with damage from combat with Hurricane of Cowsill of 56 Sqn., near Dover at 15.49 hrs.	Junkers Ju 87B	30 %	No casualties notified.
9.	II./St.G 1	CM	Forcelanded at Cap Gris Nez with damage from combat with Hurricane flown by Brooker of 56 Sqn., near Dover at 15.51 hrs.	Junkers Ju 87B	10-60 %	No crew casualties.
10.	Erpr. Gr. 210	CM	Landing accident at St. Omer with damage believed caused by A.A. guns over Margate.	Messerschmitt Bf 110C	45 %	No casualties notified.
11.	V./LG 1	CM	Damaged in combat with Spitfire of Dundas of 609 Sqn., near Portland at 15.02 hrs.	Messerschmitt Bf 110C	60 %	Ltn. Krebitz wounded.
12.	V./LG 1	CM	Damaged in combat with Hurricanes of 238 Sqn., near convoy BREAD off Portland at 15.12 hrs.	Messerschmitt Bf 110C	60-70 %	Ltn. Eiselert + one killed.
13.	V./LG 1	CM	Damaged in combat with Hurricanes of Walsh, Considine and Seabourne of 238 Sqn., near convoy BREAD at 15.12 hrs.	Messerschmitt Bf 110C	50 %	No casualties notified.
14.	11./LG 2	CM	Landing accident at Husum airfield.	Messerschmitt Bf 109 E-3	30 %	Pilot unhurt.
15.	II./JG 51	CM	Believed to have crashed at St. Inverser with damage from combat with Spitfires of 64 Sqn., south of Folkestone at 18.00 hrs.	Messerschmitt Bf 109 E-1	70 %	Pilot wounded.
16.	III./JG 51	CM	Shot down by Spitfire flown by Gray of 54 Sqn., off French coast near Calais at 17.53 hrs.	Messerschmitt Bf 109	100 %	Ltn. Lange killed.
17.	9./JG 51	CM	Shot down by Spitfire of Dawson-Paul of 64 Sqn., south of Folkestone at 17.58 hrs.	Messerschmitt Bf 109 E-4	100 %	Pilot killed; name not notified.
18.	9./JG 51	CM	Damaged by Hurricane of Page of 56 Sqn., south of Folkestone at 17.54 hrs.	Messerschmitt Bf 109 E-1	60 %	Pilot wounded.
19.	9./JG 51	CM	Damaged by Hurricane of Coghlan of 56 Sqn., south of Folkestone at 17.57 hrs.	Messerschmitt Bf 109 E-1	40 %	Pilot unhurt.
20.	3./906	CM	Believed hit A.A. gunfire over Thames Estuary during mining operations at night.	Heinkel He 115	100 %	Oblt. z. S. Hildebrand and Ltn.Dr. Steinert killed; one other missing.

Sunday 14th July

The aggravating problem posed by the frequent appearance of enemy ambulance rescue seaplanes off the British coasts had been referred to the Air Ministry, following the sighting of several Heinkel He 59s and the deliberate interception of at least two by R.A.F. fighters. It could be argued that the R.A.F. (which as yet possessed no established air/sea rescue organisation of its own) did not recognise as valid the enemy's right to rescue their crews to fight another day. Moreover, with so many convoys in passage round the coast, it was perhaps an easy argument to suggest that such aircraft were being—or could be used—for reconnaissance. Yet, equally valid, was the counter premise that with so many attacks being launched against these convoys it was natural that rescue aircraft would be seen in their vicinity, of all places.

Nevertheless the Air Ministry decided uncompromisingly that the enemy should not be allowed to acquire immunity through use of the Red Cross, and that shot-down airmen should take their chances of being rescued by a passing vessel, along with R.A.F. pilots in similar circumstances. Fighter Command was therefore on 14th July instructed to pass orders to all pilots to shoot down any enemy ambulance seaplane found—and later confirmed the British Government's view in Air Ministry Order No. 1254, dated 29th July:

"The Young Turks"—Adolf Galland (left) of *Jagdgeschwader 26 <Schlageter>* with Oberstleutnant Werner Mölders (centre) of JG 51; on the right is Generalmajor ("Uncle Theo") Osterkamp. Osterkamp, a First World War fighter-pilot who had won the coveted "Blue Max" as leader of *Marinejagdstaffel 2* in Flanders, formed and was the first commander of *Jagdgeschwader 51*. He became *Jafu 2* on 27th July 1940, and Mölders took over as *Geschwader Kommodore*. (Photo: Heinz Nowarra).

"It has come to the notice of His Majesty's Government in the United Kingdom that enemy aircraft bearing civil markings and marked with the Red Cross have recently flown over British ships at sea and in the vicinity of the British coast, and that they are being employed for purposes which H.M. Government cannot regard as being consistent with the privileges generally accorded to the Red Cross.

H.M. Government desires to accord to ambulance aircraft reasonable facilities for the transportation of the sick and wounded, in accordance with the Red Cross Convention, and aircraft engaged in the direct evacuation of sick and wounded will be respected, provided that they comply with the relevant provisions of the Convention.

H.M. Government is unable, however, to grant immunity to such aircraft flying over areas in which operarions arc in progress over land or at sea, or approaching British or Allied territory in British occupation, or British or Allied ship.

Ambulance aircraft which do not comply with the above requirements will do so at their own risk and peril."

The continuing poor weather served to protect almost all the nine small coastal convoys at sea on this Sunday. Fighter Command flew 597 sorties, almost all of them over the ships, but only encountered one sizeable raid—this on a convoy off Eastbourne in the afternoon. Again the forces employed were Ju 87s—all three *Staffeln* of IV./LG 1—escorted by about 30 Bf 109s of JG 3. Nine Hurricanes of No. 615 Squadron from Hawkinge, seven Hurricanes of No. 151 Squadron from Rochford, and twelve Spitfires of No. 610 Squadron from Biggin Hill intercepted the raid, destroying one Ju 87 and one of the escort. Plt. Off M.R. Mudie's Hurricane was set on fire and the pilot baled out over the sea; he was picked up by a naval vessel with terrible burns and rushed to hospital in Dover, but died the following day.

One of No. 151 Squadron's flight commanders, Flt. Lt. R.L. Smith, was flying the two-cannon Hurricane in combat for the first time and managed to get in a snap burst at a Messerschmitt of 8./JG 3; although he set the enemy fighter on fire, it survived only to crash land at Wissant.

R.A.F. FIGHTER COMMAND LOSSES — SUNDAY 14th JULY 1940

1.	111 Sqn., Croydon	NC	Crashed while taking off in coarse pitch; pilot unhurt.	A07.00 hrs.	Plt. Off. B.M. Fisher	Hurricane	P2958	Cat. 2 Damaged
2.	615 Sqn., Kenley	C	Shot down by Bf 109s over convoy off Dover. Pilot baled out and picked up by naval vessel badly wounded; died the following day in Dover Hospital.	Not known.	Plt. Off. M.R. Mudie	Hurricane	L1584	Cat. 3 Lost

LUFTWAFFE LOSSES—SUNDAY 14th JULY 1940

1.	3.(F)/121	CM	Crashed at Painpol; not believed the result of combat.	Junkers Ju 88A	100 %	Oblt. Specht killed; one missing.

R.A.F. Losses, 14th July 1940—*continued*

2.	11./LG 1	CM	Shot down by Hurricanes of Gayner, Collard and Hugo of 615 Sqn., near Dover at 15.09 hrs.	Junkers Ju 87B	100 %	Oblt. Sonnberg killed; one missing.
3.	III./JG 2	NCM	Landing accident of Rhein-Main airfield.	Messerschmitt Bf 109 E-1	30 %	Pilot unhurt.
4.	8./JG 3	CM	Damaged by Spitfire of Litchfield of 610 Sqn., over Channel convoy at 15.15 hrs and crashed at Boulogne.	Messerschmitt Bf 109 E-1	100 %	Pilot baled out wounded.
5.	8./JG 3	CM	Force landed at Wissant after combat with Hurricane of Smith of 151 Sqn., west of Dover at 15.11 hrs.	Messerschmitt Bf 109	40 %	Pilot unhurt.

Monday 15th July

After a quiet night, about a dozen enemy reconnaissance aircraft were plotted flying singly off the South and East Coasts, evidently searching for gaps in the 200-foot cloud base through which they might spot convoys; otherwise the morning was undisturbed. Shortly after 13.00 hours, however, Kent radar stations reported indications of a raid building up over the Continent. Thus warned, No. 11 Group ordered up three Hurricane Sections over convoys in the Thames Estuary and at 14.15 hours No. 56 Squadron's Blue Section suddenly spotted fifteen Dornier Do 17s (of KG 2, flying from Arras) as they emerged from low cloud on their bombing run. Although the fighters failed to hit any of the raiders, all the bombs fell wide of the ships.

A Heinkel He 111 of 2./KG 26 was less fortunate when, straying from thick cloud cover off Peterhead, it was spotted by two Spitfire pilots of No. 603 Squadron (Plt. Off. J.S. Morton and Plt. Off. D. Stewart-Clark) who carried out a hurried quarter attack before the enemy bomber disappeared

again. Their aim had been devastatingly accurate, however, for later that day four German airmen were picked up out of the North Sea, who confirmed that when they climbed out of their ditched aircraft they counted more than 200 bullet holes!

Bad weather considerably interfered with fighter patrols in the West Country and no aircraft were ordered off to meet a small raid by LG 1 which suddenly appeared out of the low clouds over Yeovil in the afternoon and dropped twelve bombs on the Westland Aircraft Company's factory and airfield—hitting a flight shed and pitting the grass runway, but without hitting any of the parked Whirlwind fighters.

On this day the first of a small but select and highly colourful band of Americans reached an operational Fighter Command unit with the arrival of Pilot Officer W.M.L. Fiske on No. 601 Squadron at Tangmere. This was an extraordinary group of young men, who had travelled all manner of strange and often exciting routes to find themselves dressed in Air Force Blue and wearing the thin sleeve band of Pilot Officer's

Three of the seven American volunteers who flew with Fighter Command during the Battle of Britain; (left to right) Plt. Off. "Andy" Mamedoff, Plt. Off. "Shorty" Keogh and Plt. Off. "Red" Tobin. All flew with No. 609 (West Riding) Squadron; all were to die later in the War.

rank and the R.A.F. pilot's brevet. Some were accomplished pilots, others possessed no more experience than that which Training Command had been able to given them; but those American pilots—volunteers as they were— possessed no less determination to fight Nazi Germany than their British colleagues. They were universally popular on the squadrons—affectionately being regarded as considerably larger than life! Of the seven who fought with Fighter Command during the Battle, six were to lose their lives in the defence of Britain.[45]

[45] Apart from Plt. Off. "Billy" Fiske (who died of wounds on 17th August 1940), the other American pilots were: Plt. Off. A.G. Donahue, D.F.C. (No. 64 Squadron, killed since the Battle, 11th September 1942); Plt. Off. J.K. Haviland, D.F.C. (No. 151 Squadron, survives); Plt. Off. V.C. ("Shorty") Keogh (No. 609 Squadron, killed since the Battle, 15th February 1941); Plt. Off. P.H. Leckrone (No. 616 Squadron, killed since the Battle, 5th January 1941); Plt. Off. A. ("Andy") Mamedoff (No. 609 Squadron, killed since the Battle, 8th October 1941); Plt. Off. E.Q. ("Red") Tobin (No. 609 Squadron, killed since the Battle, 7th September 1941).

R.A.F. FIGHTER COMMAND LOSSES — MONDAY 15th JULY 1940

1.	17 Sqn., Debden	NC	Crashed on patrol, not due to combat; pilot unhurt.	Not known	Plt. Off. D.L. Dawbarn	Hurricane	P3482	Cat. 3 Destroyed
2.	213 Sqn., Exeter	C	Believed shot down near Dartmouth; pilot survived.	A.13.20 hrs.	Sub-Lt. H.G.K. Bramah	Hurricane	N2541	Cat. 3 Lost
3.	249 Sqn., Church Fenton	NC	Night take-off accident at Church Fenton; pilot unhurt.	At night	Not known	Hurricane	—	Cat. 2 Damaged
4.	249 Sqn., Church Fenton	NC	Night landing accident at Church Fenton; pilot unhurt.	At night	Not known	Hurricane	—	Cat. 2 Damaged
5.	249 Sqn., Church Fenton	NC	Engine failure at night 8 miles north of Church Fenton; pilot killed in crash.	At night	Sgt. A.D.W. Main	Hurricane	—	Cat. 3 Destroyed

LUFTWAFFE LOSSES—MONDAY 15th JULY 1940

1.	1.(F)/121	CM	Crashed and burned in landing accident at Stavanger airfield.	Junkers Ju 88A-1	100 %	No casualties notified.
2.	2./KG 26	CM	Shot down by Spitfires of Morton and Stewart-Clark of 603 Sqn., near Peterhead at 12.14 hrs. Survivors picked up and taken to Fraserburgh on 17th July.	Heinkel He 111H-3 (1H+EK)	100 %	Oblt. Ottmar Hollmann and Ogefr. Heinrich Probst, Walz and Prefzger made P.O.W.s; Reinhardt (rank unknown) killed.
3.	III./KG 55	NCM	Force landed near Beauville; not combat.	Heinkel He 111P	25 %	No casualties notified.
4.	II./LG 1	CM	Shot down by Spitfire of Holland of 92 Sqn., near Cardiff.	Junkers Ju 88A	100 %	Two crew killed and two missing.
5.	4./JG 2	CM	Landing accident at Husum airfield; not the result of combat.	Messerschmitt Bf 109 E-3	20 %	Pilot unhurt.
6.	Schul.St./ KG 53	NCM	Force landing following engine failure; location not known.	Heinkel He 111H-2	90 %	No casualties notified.
7.	Ku.Fl.Gr.806	NCM	Taxying accident at Ütersen airfield.	Junkers Ju 88A	40 %	No casualties notified.
8.	2./406	CM	Crashed in Sq. 4282 after combat with fighters.	Dornier Do 18	100 %	No casualties notified.

Tuesday 16th July

" As England, despite her hopeless military situation, still shows no sign of willingness to come to terms, I have decided to prepare, and if necessary to carry out a landing operation against her.

The aim of this operation is to eliminate the English motherland as a base from which war against Germany can be continued, and, if necessary, to occupy the country completely."

With these words the Führer prefaced his Directive No. 16, "Preparing for a Landing Operation Against England", promulgated for O.K.W. on 16th July. While Luftflotten staffs had persevered with their plans for co-ordination of attacks upon the Royal Air Force and its supply industries, Adolf Hitler thus broadened the Luftwaffe's pre-invasion responsibilities. Clearly as the result of the apprehension felt by the German Naval Staff at the likely intervention by the Royal Navy in the coming invasion, Hitler now in effect demanded the destruction by air attack of all naval forces and coastal defence installations. The ability of the British Army to offer any significant opposition was discounted following

the known loss of huge quantities of materiel at Dunkirk[46].

Areas of operation were allocated to each Luftflotte. These were dictated solely by the range capabilities of the aircraft— not by the suitability of those aircraft to attack the targets listed within their sphere of operations. As will be shown in due course, the inadequacy of up-dated German Intelligence was to render a high proportion of this target allocation superfluous, and the reliance upon the two-year-old Studie Blau—whose fundamental premises had long since been overtaken by events—was a principal factor in the Luftwaffe's failure to achieve Hitler's aim as set forth in his July 16th Directive.

It thus became apparent that any all-out attack upon the industrial areas of Britain could only be achieved in daylight with fighter escort—and this, in the shape of the Messerschmitt Bf 110, was already displaying alarming symptoms

[46] The extent of the Luftwaffe's inability seriously to harm the Royal Navy during the period July—October 1940 can be seen by reference to Appendix L. The total tonnage sunk amounted to 39,670 tons, and no ship mounting guns larger than 4.7-inch was more than superficially damaged by air attack.

of extreme vulnerability to the determined attacks of defending fighters. It was therefore necessary to maintain the previously-stated aim of luring Fighter Command into the air and destroying it in the south and south-east of England.

In the event that destruction of the Royal Navy could not be achieved, all naval bases north of the English Channel were to be sealed by mining and, as far as possible, the Channel itself similarly isolated. The Channel ports were to remain unmined so as to be usable by German invasion forces. For the purpose of this large-scale mining programme numerous *Küstenfliegergruppen* had been deployed in Scandinavia and elsewhere, and were—almost nightly—hard at work in the Firth of Forth, Humber and Thames Estuary.

The area of operation allocated to *Luftflotte 3*, based in Western France, lay to the west of an arbitrary line running north from the eastern end of the Isle of Wight to Carlisle. That allotted to *Luftflotte 2* in North-East France and the Low Countries lay to the east of this line, and south of a line extending roughly from the Humber, north-west to Carlisle. The remaining area to the north of the latter would be covered by *Luftflotte 5* in Scandinavia. Such a theoretical inflexibility of operation was not in fact apparent in practice, and the three *Luftflotten* carried out their raids according to operational expediency, especially when launching attacks by specialist units such as *Erprobungsgruppe 210, Lehrgeschwader 1, Kampfgeschwader 40* and *Kampfgruppen 100* and *126*.

Meanwhile the almost nightly raids by R.A.F. Bomber Command upon Germany—scattered and materially uneconomic though they may have been—were beginning to cause embarrassment among the Nazi leaders. Scarcely any thought had been given to the night air defence of Germany; and to the German population the British Whitleys, Wellingtons and Hampdens seemed to have the night skies very much to themselves. Thus it was at about this time that the first steps were taken in the establishment of the first *Nachtjagdgeschwader* with the deployment of night fighter *Staffeln* of regular day *Jagdgeschwader*; and on the night of 15th/16th July the first German night fighter [*sic*] is believed to have been shot down by British bombers—an adapted Do 17Z of 5.(Nacht)/JG 1, which crashed near Krefeld, killing the crew of two.

Within about a month these *Staffeln* were to be assembled to form *Nachjagdgeschwader 1* (NJG 1), with small groups of fighters detached all over Germany.

During the daylight hours of 16th July bad weather again interfered with operations by the *Luftwaffe* over the English Channel, with extensive fog covering Northern France and South-East England. Most R.A.F. Squadrons were released from operations during the morning, the routine convoy patrols being taken over by Blenheims of the night fighter squadrons, although a partial improvement in the weather at mid-day allowed the Hurricanes of No. 242 Squadron to get off the ground at Coltishall to fly guard over a thirty-ship convoy off Great Yarmouth. Shortly after this three Bf 110s were sighted by No. 238 Squadron Hurricane pilots off Portland, but lost almost immediately in the haze.

The only action to be fought during the day occurred later in the afternoon at 17.05 hours when Fg. Off. W.H. Rhodes-Moorhouse[47], leading six Hurricanes of No. 601 Squadron from Tangmere, shot down into the sea a Junkers Ju 88 of II./KG 54, midway between the Needles and the mainland. Almost immediately after this he sighted another Ju 88 and although he attacked it the enemy bomber escaped.

With steadily growing reserves of Hurricanes accumulating at the Maintenance Units, most of the No. 11 Group squadrons had by this day attained strengths of at least eighteen aircraft apiece, which enabled most to "field" two whole Flights of six aircraft each when called upon to do so, leaving a Command Reserve of two, and others for repair or routine maintenance. Another Hurricane squadron was also formed on this day—No. 232 Squadron at Sumburgh in the Shetlands, formed from a nucleus provided by "B" Flight of No. 3 Squadron; initially the establishment was to be eight aircraft.

---

[47] Son of 2nd Lieut. William Barnard Rhodes-Moorhouse who won the Victoria Cross for his raid on Courtrai on 26th April 1915, but who died of his wounds shortly after. Fg. Off. William Henry Rhodes-Moorhouse, had been born in January 1914, and became a peace-time member of the Auxiliary Air Force. After an outstanding record in the Battle of Britain, he was to be shot down and killed in combat against great odds on 6th September 1940.

R.A.F. FIGHTER COMMAND LOSSES — TUESDAY 16th JULY 1940 — Nil

LUFTWAFFE LOSSES—TUESDAY 16th JULY 1940

1.	5.(F)/122	CM	Force landed at Haute Fontaine as the result of faulty servicing.	Dornier Do 17P	40 %	No casualties notified.
2.	II./KG 3	NCM	Landing accident at St. Niklas airfield.	Dornier Do 17Z	15 %	No casualties notified.
3.	II./KG 54	CM	Shot down by Hurricane of Rhodes-Moorhouse of 601 Sqn. between the Needles and the mainland.	Junkers Ju 88A (B3+GP)	100 %	Fw. Rudolf Fortmann and Gefr. Helmut Herbert, wounded, made P.O.W.s. Gefr. Otto Marb and Ogefr. Herbert Vetter killed
4.	5.(Nacht)/JG 1	CM	Believed shot down by R.A.F. bombers;	Dornier Do 17Z	100 %	Two crew killed.
5.	3./JG 21	NCM	Crashed during works test flight near Antwerp.	Messerschmitt Bf 109 E-1	100 %	Pilot killed.
6.	I./JG 27	NCM	Force landed at Arras due to bad weather.	Messerschmitt Bf 109 E-4	20 %	Pilot safe.

Wednesday 17th July

The continuing spell of poor flying weather, with drizzle falling almost everywhere except in East Anglia, confined German air activity to isolated reconnaissance sorties and light raids. The most significant attack was carried out by less than half-a-dozen Heinkel He 111s of Major Viktor von Lossberg's III./KG 26, flying from Stavanger in Norway, which bombed the Imperial Chemical Industries' factory at Ardeer, Ayrshire, during the afternoon. As the raiders straggled back, one was caught by three Spitfires of No. 603 Squadron (Plt. Off. I.S. Ritchie, Plt. Off. J.S. Morton and Plt. Off D. Stewart-Clark) and was shot down off Fraserburgh, two of the crew being seen to climb into their dinghy as their bomber sank.

In the South the *Luftwaffe* made skilful use of the cloud and during a patrol by twelve No. 64 Squadron Spitfires in the neighbourhood of Beachy Head the formation was "bounced" by enemy fighters which shot down Fg. Off. D.M. Taylor; he force landed near Hailsham with slight wounds. No one in the Squadron even caught a glimpse of the enemy aircraft.

At about the same time, three Blenheim fighters of No. 236 Squadron, flying along the coast between Selsey and Dungeness, happened upon three Ju 87s apparently having difficulty in finding their target in the bad visibility. Jettisoning their bombs forthwith, the dive-bombers hurriedly made for the nearest cloud and escaped.

In the evening a Ju 88 of I./KG 51, probably taking note of new shipping arrivals in the Bristol Channel, was caught by Plt. Off. C.H. Saunders of No. 92 Squadron and shot down over Bristol. Whether or not Oberleutnant Rechenberg, in the Ju 88, had managed to radio his report before being intercepted is not known, but within ninety minutes coastal radar plots were showing that Heinkel He 115s were on their way to mine the approaches to the port. Unfortunately R.A.F. night fighters as yet possessed no radar capable of distinguishing aircraft flying at low level.

R.A.F. FIGHTER COMMAND LOSSES — WEDNESDAY 17th JULY 1940

| 1. | 64 Sqn., Kenley | C | Shot down by Bf 109s and force landed at Hailsham; pilot wounded and admitted to Eastbourne Hospital. | A14.00 hrs. | Fg. Off. D.M. Taylor | Spitfire | P9507 | Cat. 2 Damaged |
| 2. | 603 Sqn., Dyce | C? | Pilot missing from patrol; circumstances of loss not known. | Not known | Fg. Off. C.D. Peel | Spitfire | K9916 | Cat. 3 Missing |

LUFTWAFFE LOSSES—WEDNESDAY 17th JULY 1940

1.	3.(F)/123	NCM	Crashed on take-off at Buc airfield.	Junkers Ju 88A	100%	Three crew members injured.
2.	St.St./KG 2	CM	Damaged in combat with Hurricane of Hugo of 615 Sqn., off Folkestone at 12.05 hrs. Force landed at St. Inglevert.	Dornier Do 17Z	10-60 %	No casualties notified.
3.	9./KG 26	CM	Shot down by Spitfire of Ritchie, Morton and Stewart-Clark of 603 Sqn., 25 miles east of Fraserburgh at 16.12 hrs.	Heinkel He 111H-3 (1H+KT)	100 %	Oblt. Gerhard Lorenz and Uffz. Heinz Beer made P.O.W.s. Uffz. Harri Liedtke and Gefr. Kurt Heimbach killed.
4.	I./KG 27	NCM	Crashed and burned at Luere/Vogesen.	Heinkel He 111P	100 %	Oberarzt Dr. Zobel + four killed.
5.	II./KG 27	CM	Force landing at Le Blanc; cause not known.	Heinkel He 111P	35 %	Crew unhurt.
6.	3./KG 51	CM	Shot down by Spitfire of Saunders of 92 Sqn., near Bristol at 19.25 hrs.	Junkers Ju 88A	100 %	Oblt. Dieter Rechenberg + two killed; one missing.

Thursday 18th July

As more *Luftwaffe* formations became activated in France and the Low Countries, the Air Staffs continued their planning for the coming assault. The Army's plans for Operation *Seelöwe*[48]—the invasion of Britain—were now complete in broad outline and the forces to cross the Channel nominated. A total of twelve "crack" divisions (plus elements of four others) were to be launched against the Sussex and Kent coasts under an impregnable air umbrella provided by *Luftflotten 2* and *3*, transported by a massive fleet of barges, construction and assembly of which now started. The fact that such a fleet would be integral with any invasion plan was naturally realised by the British, and a careful watch by R.A.F. reconnaissance aircraft was ordered; as yet there were few signs that German forces were moving up to the Channel ports, nor were there any indications as to what form the invasion fleet would take. Nevertheless the British—convinced that they would inevitably face a powerful seaborne assault, supported by airborne landings—were working feverishly on a whole range of anti-invasion measures, both active and passive in nature.

These ranged in sophistication from the installation of liquid-fuel pipelines in the sea off likely beaches (so that

Two captured German pilots in transit. A surprising number of *Luftwaffe* officers wore their breeches and top-boots while flying.

[48] Operation "Sealion"

approaching invasion craft could be enveloped in a holocaust of flame by "setting the sea on fire") to the removal of road signs so that enemy parachutists should not know their whereabouts! Such was the consciousness of the peril in which the nation stood that the postal districts were obliterated on all London street name plates. Of course Britain was hopelessly lacking in weapons with which to defend herself on the ground. With something like a quarter of a million men without arms and equipment after the Dunkirk evacuation, every available small-arms weapon was issued to the army. The Local Defence Volunteers (soon to be re-named, on Churchill's insistence, the Home Guard), a heterogeneous but determined army of men too old or too young for conscription, patrolled the countryside and manned thousands of road blocks, armed with all manner of makeshift weapons ranging from pikes and pitchforks to home-made bombs and shotguns.

Concrete "dragon's teeth" were installed at strategic places beside railway lines and roadways; the countryside was studded with countless machine gun pill-boxes and elaborate obstructions were set up by farmers in their fields to prevent landings by enemy troop-carrying aircraft. More than one hundred important road and rail bridges were sown with demolition charges, and extensive minefields were laid on every beach on the South Coast likely to be chosen by the Germans for their landings. Such was the R.A.F.'s preoccupation with active air operations against the enemy, that it was decided to provide patrols by light aircraft—to be flown by instructors from the numerous flying training schools up and down the country. Accordingly designs were prepared for the adaptation of Tiger Moth elementary trainers to carry small bombs for use against coastal craft.

Gone now were all signs of Britain's traditional lethargy. The image of a bestial invader was no longer just a creeping spectre whose depredations elsewhere were the subject of the "wireless" news bulletins every evening. The *Luftwaffe* was daily and nightly roaming British skies—already embarked on the now-familiar pattern of softening up Hitler's next victim. Only the British weather—otherwise exasperatingly unpredictable—now seemed determined to offer what protection it could to the apprehensive island race.

With no sign of significant improvement in the weather over Britain, air operations by the *Luftwaffe* on 18th July were yet again on a limited scale. Several dogfights occurred during the day's attacks on the South Coast convoys, and a new German tactic was used in an effort to combat British fighters. Now painfully aware that British radar could "see" German raids building up over France, Kesselring determined to lure the interceptors up and teach their pilots a lesson. Warned of the passage of a convoy through the Dover Strait and taking advantage of the low cloud, the Germans duly started assembling a raid behind the French coast. With reports of this build-up being passed to No. 11 Group shortly after 09.00 hours, Park ordered up twelve Spitfires of No. 610 Squadron from Biggin Hill to the Dover area. Arriving at the convoy's position and flying just below cloud, the Squadron was set upon by a *Staffel* of Bf 109s, which dived right through the formation, shooting down Plt. Off. P. Litchfield into the sea. In a moment of confusion the Spitfires broke in all directions, only two pilots managing to fire snap bursts at fleeting targets. The German "raid" had consisted solely of Bf 109 fighters.

In the North, Stumpff's *Luftflotte 5* began increasing the tempo of operations with an unopposed raid by three Heinkel He 111s of KG 26 on Montrose at 10.00 hours. Four hours later a convoy-spotting Do 215 was intercepted by three Spitfires of No. 603 Squadron, but their target escaped. Another small KG 26 formation was intercepted by No. 603 at 16.25 hours over Aberdeen, but this not only escaped but forced down Plt. Off. George Gilroy at Old Meldrum with strikes in his engine coolant system. To make matters worse, a student pilot taxied his Miles Master trainer into a No. 603 Squadron Spitfire, writing off both aircraft. Final retribution was in part achieved in the evening when Sgt. J.R. Caister caught one of Major Fritz Doensch's Ju 88s of I.*Gruppe*, KG 30, in the act of raiding a convoy off Aberdeen; the damaged enemy returned home with a wounded crew member.

The Blenheims of No. 235 Squadron at Bircham Newton in Norfolk, although not strictly listed in Fighter Command strength, were frequently called upon to fly defensive sorties. Their crews were ordered off to provide escort for a convoy in bad weather off the Norfolk coast during the morning, and one of their number failed to return; the other crews reported that they had been challenged by a Section of Hurricanes over the convoy . . .In the evening the hard-working Blenheim crews accompanied Hudson bombers on a raid over Emden.

In the South another Blenheim Squadron, No. 248 at Thorney Island, was transferred out of Fighter into Coastal Command while continuing to fly defensive sorties in addition to constant attacks on the French coast. One of the squadron's Blenheims failed to return from an escort mission over Le Havre.

A reconnaissance of Boulogne revealed the first indications of pre-invasion activity and a strike by eighteen Bomber Command Blenheims, escorted by 24 Hurricanes of Nos. 111 and 615 Squadrons, obtained bomb strikes on vessels and jetties. A Henschel Hs 126 of 2.(H)/21, which ventured into the area, was pounced on and damaged by the escort.

Throughout the day, convoy patrols along the South Coast continued to occupy the attention of the Tangmere and Middle Wallop pilots, who shot down an elderly Heinkel He 111 and a Junkers Ju 88. The Heinkel, destroyed by six Hurricanes of Sqn. Ldr. John Peel's No. 145 Squadron, twenty miles south of Bognor Regis, numbered among its occupants Oberst Georgi, *Geschwaderkommodore* of *Kampfgeschwader 27 "Boelcke"*, who was killed.

Notwithstanding this latter success (of whose import the R.A.F. was ignorant at the time), it must be apparent to the reader that so far Fighter Command had been suffering relatively heavy losses in relation to its ability to stem the *Luftwaffe*'s attacks which, in all conscience, had been little more than desultory. In truth the British commanders and pilots alike firmly believed that their claims reflected a serious erosion of enemy strength. They were not yet aware that the confusion which resulted from simultaneous combat by several squadrons in cloudy weather led to a fairly heavy exaggeration of combat claims. It is perhaps a significant observation to make at this point that if R.A.F. losses from all causes in pilots and aircraft were to continue to rise at the rate main attack had yet to be launched.

There is no evidence to suggest that anybody entertained such dismal forebodings at Fighter Command on this day—nor could anyone know that on the morrow the Command was to suffer its worst single-squadron defeat of the entire Battle.

apparent during the past fortnight, the Command would cease   to exist as a fighting force within six weeks. And the enemy's

R.A.F. FIGHTER COMMAND LOSSES — THURSDAY 18th JULY 1940

1.	145 Sqn., Tangmere	C	Damaged by He 111 south of Bognor Regis; pilot returned to base unhurt.	13.15 hrs.	Flt. Lt. A.H. McN. Boyd	Hurricane	P3381	Cat. 2 Damaged
2.	152 Sqn., Warmwell	C	Damaged by By 109s; pilot returned unhurt.	Not known	Plt. Off.T.N. Bayles	Spitfire	K9990	Cat. 1 Damaged
3.	235 Sqn., Bircham Newton	C	Aircraft failed to return from convoy patrol off East Coast; three crew Missing.	A11.00 hrs	Plt. Off. R.L. Patterson Sgt. F.D. Tucker Sgt. L.H.M. Reece	Blenheim	N3541	Cat. 3 Missing
4.	236 Sqn., Thorney Island	C	Failed to return from patrol escort over Le Havre; two crew Missing. Believed to have been *flak* victim.	A12.15 hrs.	Plt. Off. C.R.D. Thomas Sgt. H.D.B.Elsdon	Blenheim	L6639	Cat. 3 Missing
5.	236 Sqn., Thorney Island	C	Failed to return from patrol escort over Le Havre; two crew Missing. Believed to have been *flak* victim.	A12.15 hrs.	Plt. Off. R.H. Rigby Sgt. D.D. MacKinnon	Blenheim	L6779	Cat. 3 Missing
6.	266 Sqn., Wittering	NC	Collided with tractor while taxying; pilot unhurt.	Not known	Plt. Off. D.G. Ashton	Spitfire	N3170	Cat. 2 Damaged
7.	266 Sqn., Wittering	NC	Force landed due to engine failure; pilot unhurt.	Not known	Plt. Off. R.J.B. Roach	Spitfire	N3240	Cat. 2 Damaged
8.	603 Sqn., Dyce	C	Aircraft's coolant system hit by fire from He 111, and pilot force landed, unhurt, at Old Meldrum.	16.40 hrs.	Plt. Off. G.K. Gilroy	Spitfire	R6755	Cat. 2 Damaged
9.	603 Sqn., Dyce	NC	Miles Master taxied into parked Spitfire. No casualties.	Not known	None	Spitfire	—	Cat. 3 Destroyed
10.	609 Sqn., Middle Wallop	C	Shot down by Ju 88 near Swanage; force landed on Studland Beach. Pilot unhurt.	Not known	Fg. Off. A.R. Edge	Spitfire	R6636	Cat. 2 Damaged
11.	609 Sqn., Middle	C	Shot down by Ju 88 near Swanage; pilot baled out unhurt and picked up by naval vessel.	Not known	Flt. Lt. F.J. Howell	Spitfire	R6634	Cat. 3 Lost
12.	610 Sqn., Biggin Hill	C	Shot down by Bf 109s 10 miles off Calais; seen to dive vertically into the sea; pilot killed.	A10.10 hrs.	Plt. Off. P. Litchfield	Spitfire	R6765	Cat. 3 Lost

LUFTWAFFE LOSSES—THURSDAY 18th JULY 1940

1.	2.(H)/21	CM	Damaged by Hurricanes of 111Sqn.; crashed and burned at St. Sabine.	Henschel Hs 126	100 %	Two crew wounded.
2.	I./KG 3	NCM	Force landed at Lens after engine failure.	Heinkel He 111H-2	20 %	Crew unhurt.
3.	Stab/KG 27	CM	Shot down by six Hurricanes of 145 Sqn., 20 miles south of Bognor Regis at 13.15 hrs.	Heinkel He 111D	100 %	Oberst Georgi, *Geschw.Kdr.*, Oblt. Buss + one crew member killed.
4.	1./KG 30	CM	Damaged by Spitfire of Caister of 603 Sqn., over convoy off Aberdeen at 22.25 hrs. Crash landed at Aalborg, Denmark.	Junkers Ju 88	50 %	One crew member wounded
5.	I./KG 54	CM	Shot down by Spitfires of Howell, Feary and Edge of 609 Sqn. over convoy east of Swanage.	Junkers Ju 88A	100 %	Two crew killed; two missing.
6.	II./KG 54	CM	Damaged by Spitfires of Overton and Bisdee of 609 Sqn. over convoy east of Swanage and crashed at Coulommiers.	Junkers Ju 88A	35 %	Crew unhurt.
7.	II./LG 1	CM	Believed shot down by naval anti-aircraft guns over English Channel	Junkers Ju 88	100%	One crew member killed; Oblt. Pohl + two missing.
8.	Stab/St.G 77	CM	Shot down by Spitfire flown by Hogg of 152 Sqn., over Channel convoy; time not known.	Dornier Do 17M	100 %	Oblt. Strecker + one killed; one missing.
9.	2/606 Gen.d. L.b.Ob.d.M.	NCM	Crashed at Gabinkirchen following fire in the air.	Junkers Ju 52/3m	Not known	Three killed; Ltn.z.S. Krenzien and Ltn.z.S. Stock injured.

Friday 19th July

With no less than nine convoys off the coasts and a noticeable improvement in the weather, all Group Commanders moved stronger forced than hitherto up to forward satellite airfields in anticipation of trouble brewing during the daylight hours.

The day started relatively quietly. A Dornier Do 17P of 4.(F)/121 managed to slip unnoticed through the radar screen and penetrated as far as Croydon before being spotted and reported as Raid 15 by the Observer Corps at 06.40 hrs. The only conveniently placed fighters were a Section of No. 145 Squadron's Hurricanes (Sqn. Ldr. John Peel, Plt. Off. Ernest Wakeham and Plt. Off. R.D. Yule) who successfully inter-

cepted the Dornier and finally shot it down into the sea off Brighton at 07.40 hours[49].

An hour later far to the north, four Dornier Do 17s carried out a surprise raid on Glasgow, their crews approaching the city from the *west*; quickly identifying the Rolls-Royce

[49] This "victory" must be shared with two Hurricanes of No. 257 Squadron (Fg. Off. Lancelot Mitchell and Sgt. Donald Hulbert) who were ordered off from Northolt at 06.30 hours and also intercepted the Dornier near Hove. They joined in, claiming that John Peel's Section was firing wide! (Cf. Form 540, No. 257 Sqn., 19th July).

works, they made a perfect line astern attack from low level. Fairly heavy damage was caused and a number of casualties were reported. The bombers escaped unscathed[50].

Among the fighters which were moved forward during the morning were twelve Defiants of No. 141 Squadron, ordered from West Malling (an uncompleted airfield near Maidstone) to Hawkinge at 08.45 hours. Great hopes had been entertained for this squadron ever since its brother unit, No. 264 Squadron, had achieved considerable success over Dunkirk, six weeks before. No. 141 Squadron was as yet untried in battle, having only arrived in the South a week earlier with aircraft, many of which had lacked essential modifications. In order to improve the performance of the Defiants, constant speed propellers had been fitted during the last week, but this spell on the ground by the aircraft—although staggered—had deprived the crews of much-needed flying practice, as well as an opportunity to become acquainted with the various control procedures in No. 11 Group. Regarding the aircraft itself, apart from its lack of forward-firing armament and generally poor performance (as well as its anomalous fighting concept, to which reference has already been made), the Defiant bestowed a marked feeling of apprehension upon the gunners who, huddled and trussed in the confines of their turrets, were without means of speedily "abandoning ship" in a combat emergency.

The Squadron had flown a few uneventful patrols during the previous days at Section or Flight strength, but generally lacked practice in manœuvring in greater numbers. At 12.23 hours on this day, twelve Defiants were ordered off from Hawkinge to patrol twenty miles south of Folkestone. In the event three pilots could not take off owing to engine trouble so that nine crews, led by Sqn. Ldr. William Richardson, were left to continue to the patrol line. Suddenly, and apparently without warning from the Controller, the sky was filled with German fighters whose pilots had identified the Defiants for what they were and who immediately carried out co-ordinated attacks from below and astern. A *Staffel* of about ten Bf 109s from II./JG 2, the crack "*Richthofen Geschwader*", completely routed the squadron whose remnants now broke

to the flanks so as to allow the gunners to bring their guns to bear for bursts to the beam. As they swung their turrets in vain attempts to track the Messerschmitts breaking below them, a second *Staffel* struck the squadron in a high head-on attack. In less than sixty seconds the Defiants of Plt. Off. John Kemp, Plt. Off. Richard Howley, Plt. Off. Rudal Kidson and Plt. Off. John Gard'ner were shot down in flames. None of their gunners managed to extricate themselves from their turrets, and all died in their aircraft; of the pilots, only Gard'ner was rescued, wounded, from the sea.

The Squadron's remaining pilots sought escape in the clouds from the enemy snapping at the Defiants' heels of Achilles. Flt. Lt. Ian Donald's aircraft was set ablaze and the gunner, Plt. Off. Arthur Hamilton set about the laborious procedure for baling out; this he succeeding in doing, but with insufficient height and was drowned. Donald, presumably unable to control the aircraft, died in his cockpit when the Defiant crashed at Elmsvale Road in Dover.

As news of the combat was flashed to No. 141 Squadron's dispersal at Hawkinge, anxious pilots and gunners scanned the horizon for their friends. At length four Defiants straggled into the circuit, two in obvious difficulties. As three touched down on the airfield, the engine of the fourth cut out and Flt. Lt. Malcolm Loudon crashed on the outskirts of Hawkinge village; on being severely hit, Loudon had ordered Plt. Off. Eric Farnes to bale out, and this gunner was the only one to be picked up alive after abandoning his aircraft. Of the three that landed on Hawkinge airfield, Plt. Off Ian MacDougall's Defiant was so badly damaged that it was promptly written off charge; his gunner, Sgt. John Wise, had baled out, never to be seen again[51].

Although the inscrutable machinery of Fighter Command set about the immediate replacement of crews and aircraft on No. 141 Squadron, it was obvious that with the loss of twelve pilots and crew members and seven aircraft, the Squadron had lost all cohesion as a fighting unit. During the next few days the survivors were withdrawn to the North while Fighter Command contemplated the wisdon of ever again committing the Defiant to the risk of combat with enemy single-seat fighters. The result of those deliberations were as surprising as they were tragic.

As the pilots of No. 141 Squadron had sought to extricate themselves from combat, twelve Hurricanes of No. 111 Squadron, led by Sqn. Ldr. John Thompson, were flying to their rescue at top speed from Hawkinge. There is no doubt that but for their arrival in the nick of time the entire Defiant

---

[50] For some years the identity of the unit which carried out this raid remained unknown, for Glasgow lay squarely in *Luftflotte 5*'s area of responsibility and yet possessed no bomber unit equipped with Dornier Do 17s; recently obtained evidence suggests, though not conclusively, that the aircraft belonged to an independent *Staffel* based in the Brest peninsular, and staffed by naval pilots. Later to become a component of *Küstenfliegergruppe 606*, this bomber unit "specialised" in raids which involved long flights up the Irish Sea, and would have accounted for the approach to the Glasgow Rolls-Royce works from the west.

[51] Ian Neil MacDougall, a pre-War Cranwell graduate, served on in the Royal Air Force after the War, retiring as an Air Commodore in 1969; he died in 1987.

A line-up of No. 264 Squadron's Boulton Paul Defiant turret fighters.

No. 264 Squadron's aircraft in flight. On 19th July the other Defiant Squadron, No. 141, was almost annihilated by Bf 109Es of the "*Richthofen Geschwader*".

squadron would have been destroyed. As it was, Plt. Off. Peter Simpson destroyed one of the Messerschmitts—the pilot of which was rescued, wounded, from the sea. A destroyer, which later searched the area for survivors, was promptly attacked by German bombers, but was not hit.

With the effective loss of No. 141 Squadron, the Biggin Hill Sector Commander recalled No. 32 Squadron from Released to fill the Readiness rota, and this unit was soon in action from Hawkinge. Seeing a number of Ju 87s dive-bombing Dover harbour, Sqn. Ldr. John Worall led his squadron through the anti-aircraft barrage to the enemy aircraft which turned tail and fled. The Hurricanes were then set on by twelve Bf 109s and, in the dogfight that followed, F/Sgt. Guy Turner was shot down in flames. After baling out, Turner was rescued and admitted to Dover Hospital where he remained on the danger list for some days before starting a slow but successful recovery.

Not content with their early morning efforts, the pilots of No. 145 Squadron scored another success when their Red Section sighted and shot down a Heinkel He 111P of Major Schlemell's III.*Gruppe*, KG 55, off Shoreham at 17.55 hours; Plt. Off. Michael Newling's Hurricane stopped an enemy burst in the hydraulic system which resulted in a wheels-up landing on Shoreham airfield.

As No. 145 Squadron's pilots were taking off before this combat, Tangmere's other Hurricane squadron was just returning from a hard fight with Bf 109s off Selsey Bill. No. 43 Squadron's "A" Flight had lost its leader when Flt. Lt. John Simpson baled out and landed near Worthing with a bullet in his leg and a broken collar bone. Sgt. John Buck radioed that he had been wounded and baled out over the sea; later he was found to have drowned when his body was washed up at Shoreham. Apparently the squadron had failed to score.

To the west a Hurricane pilot of No. 87 Squadron found a *Staffel* of Ju 87s near Portland manœuvring for a down-sun attack on the naval base, and damaged one. A Heinkel He 115,

apparently attempting to sow mines in the Thames Estuary in broad daylight, was shot down by a Spitfire flown by Fg. Off. Alastair Jeffrey of No. 64 Squadron.

Notwithstanding these small successes, this had been a gloomy day indeed for Fighter Command. In the course of no fewer than 701 operational sorties the Command had lost five pilots and six Defiant gunners killed, and five pilots wounded, as well as eleven fighters destroyed in combat. It had shot down five of the enemy (although, at the time, pilots' claims amounted to thirteen). Such figures, seen in the light of losses suffered later in the War—indeed suffered by Fighter Command within the next month—may seem trifling and scarcely serious enough to cause the Group Commanders to lose much sleep. Yet they had been suffered in relatively small skirmishes, and in all conscience most of the enemy had been stragglers. In almost every instance of a major dogfight developing, the intercepting forces had been all but overwhelmed and had suffered accordingly.

No doubt encouraged by similar exaggerated claims by the *Luftwaffe*, Hitler on the 19th delivered his famous "last appeal to reason" as part of a speech to the Reichstag:

> " If this struggle continues it can only end in the annihilation of one of us. Mr. Churchill thinks it will be Germany. I know it will be Britain. I am not the vanquished begging for mercy. I speak as a victor. I see no reason why this war must go on. We should like to avert the sacrifices which must claim millions."

Hitler also took this opportunity to announce the promotion of Hermann Göring to the singular rank of *Reichsmarschall*, together with the elevation of four *Luftwaffe* generals to the rank of *Generalfeldmarschall*. Millions of copies of the Führer's speech were showered over Britain during the course of the next three weeks.

R.A.F. FIGHTER COMMAND LOSSES — FRIDAY 19th JULY 1940

1.	1 Sqn., Northolt	C	Shot down by He 111 near Brighton; pilot unhurt.	17.40 hrs.	Plt. Off. D.O.M. Browne	Hurricane	*P3471*	Cat. 3 Destroyed
2.	32 Sqn., Hawkinge	C	Shot down in flames near Dover; pilot, badly wounded, baled out and taken to Dover hospital. Aircraft crashed at Hougham.	15.50 hrs.	F/Sgt. G. Turner	Hurricane	*P3144*	Cat. 3 Destroyed
3.	43 Sqn., Tangmere	C	Shot down by Bf 109s near Worthing; pilot baled out with bullet wound in leg and broken collar bone.	17.30 hrs.	Flt. Lt. J.W.C. Simpson	Hurricane	*P3140*	Cat. 3 Destroyed

R.A.F. Losses, 15th July 1940—*continued*

4.	43 Sqn., Tangmere	C	Shot down by Bf 109s off Selsey Bill; pilot baled out, injured, but drowned.	17.26 hrs.	Sgt. J.A. Buck	Hurricane	*P3531*	Cat. 3 Destroyed
5.	43 Sqn., Tangmere	C	Damaged by Bf 109s off Selsey Bill; pilot unhurt.	17.35 hrs.	Sgt. J.L. Crisp	Hurricane	*P3468*	Cat. 1 Damaged
6.	141 Sqn., Hawkinge	C	Shot down by Bf 109s south of Folkestone; both crew killed.	A12.45 hrs.	Plt.Off.J.R. Kemp Sgt. R. Crombie	Defiant	*L6974*	Cat. 3 Lost
7.	141 Sqn., Hawkinge	C	Shot down by Bf 109s south of Folkestone; both crew killed.	A12.45 hrs.	Plt. Off. R.A. Howley Sgt. A.G. Curley	Defiant	*L6995*	Cat. 3 Lost
8.	141 Sqn., Hawkinge	C	Shot down by Bf 109s south of Folkestone; both crew killed.	A12.45 hrs.	Plt.Off.R.Kidson Sgt. F.P.J. Atkins	Defiant	*L7015*	Cat. 3 Lost
9.	141 Sqn., Hawkinge	C	Shot down by Bf 109s south of Folkestone. Gunner killed; pilot resued from the sea, wounded.	A12.45 hrs.	Plt. Off J.R. Gard'ner Sgt. D.M. Slatter	Defiant	*L7016*	Cat. 3 Lost
10.	141 Sqn., Hawkinge	C	Crashed at Dover after combat with Bf 109s. Pilot killed; gunner baled out but drowned, and buried at Hawkinge.	A12.50 hrs.	Flt. Lt. I.D.G. Donald Plt. Off. A.C. Hamilton	Defiant	*L7009*	Cat. 3 Destroyed
11.	141 Sqn., Hawkinge	C	Crashed at Hawkinge following engine failure after combat; pilot wounded, and gunner rescued unhurt from the sea.	A13.00 hrs.	Flt. Lt. M.J. Loudon Plt.Off. E. Farnes	Defiant	*L7001*	Cat. 3 Destroyed
12.	141 Sqn., Hawkinge	C	Damaged in combat with Bf 109s. Pilot unhurt, but gunner had baled out and was presumed to have drowned.	A13.00 hrs.	Plt. Off. I.N. MacDougall Sgt. J.F. Wise	Defiant	*L6983*	Cat. 2 Damaged
13.	145 Sqn., Tangmere	C	Damaged by He 111 off Shoreham; pilot slightly wounded and force landed at Shoreham.	A.18.20 hrs.	Plt. Off. M.A. Newling	Hurricane	—	Cat. 2 Damaged

LUFTWAFFE LOSSES—FRIDAY 19th JULY 1940

1.	4.(F)/121	CM	Shot down by Hurricanes of Peel, Yule and Wakeham of 145 Sqn. off Brighton at 07.04 hrs.	Dornier Do 17P	100 %	One crew member killed; Ltn. Thiele + one missing.
2.	3.(F)/123	NCM	Crash landing at Toussus-Buc; cause not known.	Farman	100 %	Hptm. Liebe-Piederit killed; one hurt.
3.	II./KG 51	NCM	Crash landing at Orly airfield; cause not known.	Junkers Ju 88A	40 %	Crew unhurt.
4.	III./KG 55	CM	Shot down by Hurricanes of Dutton, Ostowicz and Newling of 145 Sqn., 5 miles off Shoreham at 17.55 hrs.	Heinkel He 111P	100 %	Oblt. Westhaus + one killed; three missing.
5.	II./JG 51	CM	Shot down by Spitfires of 74 Sqn., and crashed near Chartres.	Messerschmitt Bf 109 E-1	100 %	Pilot wounded.
6.	3/906	CM	Shot down by Spitfire of Jeffrey of 64 Sqn. over Thames Estuary at approx. 16.00 hrs.	Heinkel He 115	100 %	Three crew missing.

[*Note.* It is also known that Leutnant Graf Erbo von Kageneck of III./JG 27 was wounded in action over Britain on this day, but the circumstances are not known; he was later to be awarded the Oakleaves to the Knight's Cross.]

The mighty Fw 200C-1 Condor was used in small numbers during the Battle on minelaying and night bombing missions. The aircraft show here, F8+EH, was shot down into the sea off Hartlepool on the night of 19th/20th July. (Photo: Hans Obert)

Saturday 20th July

If the World was in any doubt as to Britain's reply to Hitler's call for her surrender, events of 20th and 21st July must surely have dispelled any belief that Fighter Command was yet a spent force.

The first enemy aircraft to fall to the defences was a four-engine Focke-Wulf Fw 200 revealed by searchlights on the East Coast between Hartlepool and Sunderland at around midnight of 19th/20th July. This large aircraft, commanded by Hauptmann Roman Steszyn of 2./KG 40, had set out from Marx on a minelaying sortie but ventured too close inshore and, despite frantic manœuvring to evade the searchlights, was bracketed and shot down by anti-aircraft gunfire. The crew commander and two others lost their lives, but two men were rescued unwounded and made prisoners. The same *Staffel* was unfortunate to lose a second Fw 200 off the north coast of Ireland on this night—also whilst engaged in mine-laying[52].

In anticipation of the detailed Staff instructions setting down the anti-shipping priorities for the *Luftwaffe*, numerous units of all three *Luftflotten* were now visiting British coastal waters bent on mainlaying. The mines sown were of approximately 1,100 lb. weight and—depending on the range of the sortie—the Heinkel He 111H and Junkers Ju 88A usually carried two such weapons. The technique of aerial minelaying demanded extremely accurate navigation and flying at low speed and low altitude—a task entrusted only to the more experienced bomber pilots[53].

CH radar heralded the approach of a 40-plus raid to the Thames Estuary. Twelve No. 54 Squadron Spitfires were ordered off at 05.21 hours but failed to find the enemy. It appears likely that the raid had been triggered by inaccurate reports of a convoy in the Estuary and, finding no ships, split into several small formations to start a search. Although radar tracking was thus obviously confused, No. 56 Squadron's Blue Section (Fg. Off. Edward Gracie, Plt. Off. Alan Page and Fg. Off. Percy Weaver) ordered up from North Weald at 05.45 hours, spotted a small group of Junkers Ju 88s off Burham and forced one down at St. Osyth. Four prisoners were captured unhurt[54].

Meanwhile, fearful that enemy raiders might attack lightships off the East Coast—only the previous Thursday the East Goodwin lightship had been sunk by enemy bombers—both Park and Leigh-Mallory ordered Sections to patrol in the vicinity of such vessels. Normally radar would give warning of the approach of raiders, but in cloudy or half-light condi-

tions these small ships were particularly vulnerable. The courage of the Trinity House crews, anchored in one spot and unable to manœuvre, was of the highest order.

Reports of isolated enemy aircraft sightings flowed in all morning, from Scotland (where No. 603 Squadron Spitfires shot down a reconnaissance Do 17 off Peterhead at about 11.35 hours) to the Dorset coast. Hurricane pilots of No. 238 Squadron were ordered to maintain standing patrols over a convoy, named BOSOM, in Lyme Bay, and a Section chased off three Bf 109s found prowling in the area. Shortly afterwards, at 14.30 hours, the Squadron shot down a Heinkel He 59 seaplane which had been found to be flying near the convoy.

As convoy BOSOM steamed to the east, so its protection was taken over by the Hurricanes from Tangmere. Once again a Heinkel He 59 put in an appearance, but this time the enemy fought back effectively and shot down Fg. Off. Joseph Haworth of No. 43 Squadron before escaping in cloud. However, six Hurricanes of No. 601 Squadron had now arrived to take over the patrol and, on instructions from the Tangmere Controller, found and destroyed the enemy seaplane. The crew of four baled out, but were too low for their parachutes to open.

A couple of hours after this the convoy entered the Kenley and Biggin Hill Sectors and, with its presence now obviously compromised, Park ordered standing patrols of no less than 24 fighters from two Hurricane and two Spitfire squadrons. When, at roughly 18.00 hours, a formation of Ju 87 dive-bombers of Hauptmann Keil's II.*Gruppe, Stukageschwader 1*, escorted by upwards of 50 Bf 109s and 110s, approached the convoy, a big dogfight developed which spread over a wide area and, surprisingly, lasted for almost half an hour. The battle resulted in overwhelming victory for Fighter Command, for its pilots gained the element of surprise from the outset.

Flying a reciprocal course to that of the convoy, the German pilots faced the sun and did not see the powerful escort of Hurricanes which hurtled out of the glare, John Worrall leading eight aircraft of No. 32 Squadron straight through the 109s to shoot down two and cripple four of the dive-bombers below. As the escorting Bf 109s broke, they were engaged by eleven Hurricanes of No. 615 Squadron (which shot down three), and nine Spitfires of No. 610 Squadron. One Hurricane, flown by a Fleet Air Arm pilot attached to No. 32 Squadron, and a Spitfire of No. 610 Squadron were lost. The Bf 110s took no part in the fight, their pilots preferring to circle on seeing the strength of the opposition.

As darkness descended at the end of a day on which eleven fighter squadrons had been engaged in combat, Park could relax his weary pilots and reflect on their first significant victory. Clearly a high state of preparedness by strong fighter forces was demanded during the passage of convoys, and with something like parity in numbers his pilots had shown themselves more than a match for the enemy. Perhaps more agreeable was the fact that the Hurricane, given the choice of combat altitude, could certainly hold its own against enemy single-seat fighters. The filip to morale provided by this air battle was most welcome after weeks of frustrating and inconclusive operations.

---

[52] Although both these losses were reported in 6th *Abteilung* returns, the loss of Hptm. Steszyn's aircraft was recorded on 22nd July as having occurred on 13th July. The other, commanded by Hptm. Zenke, was stated in the return dated 28th July to have occurred on the 23rd. All crew interrogation records relating to the survivors from these aircraft, together with the Observer Corps and coastguard records (of the Sunderland area) confirm beyond any doubt that both losses occurred during the night of 19th/20th July.

[53] There is a story—possibly apocryphal—that one such parachute mine was accidentally released over land and exploded in a South Coast town. So awesome did the explosion appear to the low-flying German crew that their subsequent de-briefing report encouraged the *Luftwaffe* to adopt the parachute mine as a standard bombing weapon. Whether or not this anecdote is well-founded, the fact remains that 470 such weapons were dropped on British towns and cities before the end of 1940.

[54] No reference to this raid can be found in *Luftwaffe* records; nor is the loss of a Ju 88, attributable to this raid, recorded in 6th *Abteilung* returns. The exact time at which the German aircraft crashed was reported by the Observer Corps as 05.58 hours, and fragments, capable of confirming the aircraft's identity, were recovered from the ground in 1972. (See Item 4 in the *Luftwaffe* Loss Table for this day.)

R.A.F. FIGHTER COMMAND LOSSES—SATURDAY, 20th JULY 1940

1.	32 Sqn., Hawkinge	C	Shot down by Bf 109s of I./JG 51 five miles N.E. of Dover; pilot baled out over the sea but was drowned.	A18.20 hrs.	Sub-Lt. G.G.R. Bulmer	Hurricane	N2670	Cat. 3 Destroyed
2.	43 Sqn., Tangmere	C	Shot down by He 59 of Seenotfluflugkdo. 1 ten miles off Selsey Bill. Pilot baled out but was drowned.	A16.50 hrs.	Fg. Off. J.F.J. Haworth	Hurricane	P3964	Cat. 3 Lost
3.	152 Sqn., Warmwell	C?	Missing from patrol. (1)	Not known	Not known	Spitfire	K9380	Cat. 3 Missing
4.	236 Sqn., Thorney Island	C	Shot down by Bf 109s off Cherbourg. Crew believed to have been killed.	A18.30 hrs	Sgt. E.E. Lockton Sgt. H. Corcoran	Blenheim	L1300	Cat. 3 Missing
5.	238 Sqn., Warmwell	C	Shot down in flames over Lyme Bay; pilot baled out and was picked up by H.M.S. Acheron; however he died of his burns.	A13.30 hrs.	Sgt. C. Parkinson	Hurricane	P3766	Cat. 3 Lost
6.	263 Sqn., Grangemouth	NC	Crash landed near Grangemouth; pilot killed.	Not known	Plt. Off. Downer	Hurricane	—	Cat. 3 Destroyed
7.	501 Sqn., Warmwell	C	Pilot killed in combat over Lyne Bay.	A16.30 hrs.	Plt. Off. E.J.H. Sylvester	Hurricane	P3082	Cat. 3 Lost
8.	603 Sqn., Montrose	NC	Ferry pilot crashed during delivery flight.	Not known	Plt. Off. R.G. Manlove	Spitfire	R6752	Cat. 3 Destroyed
9.	610 Sqn., Biggin Hill	C	Pilot wounded in leg during combat with Bf 109s, baled out and was admitted to hospital.	18.20 hrs.	Plt. Off. G. Keighley	Spitfire	R6621	Cat. 3 Lost

[(1) The loss of this aircraft is something of a mystery. The Spitfire was reported to No. 11 Group as being Cat. 3 Missing, normally implying that its pilot was also Missing, yet no Spitfire nor pilot was reported shot down, or even Missing or Killed, on this date by No. 152 Squadron, a squadron whose records were notoriously badly kept during the early weeks of the Battle — probably with ample justification. Air Ministry records also showed this Spitfire as being "Missing in Action" and Struck off Charge on this date.]

LUFTWAFFE LOSSES—SATURDAY 20th JULY 1940

1.	1.(F)/20	CM	Shot down by Spitfires of Cunningham, Waterson and Stapleton of 603 Sqn. off Peterhead at 11.35 hrs.	Dornier Do 17P	100 %	Ltn. Heuer + two missing.
2.	5.(F)/122	NCM	Force landed at Roan following engine failure.	Dornier Do 17P	6 %	Crew safe.
3.	III./KG 2	CM	Damaged by Spitfire of Leathart of 54 Sqn. near Dover at 08.55 hrs; crash landed at Zeyenkerke.	Dornier Do 17Z	80 %	One crew member killed; Oblt. Davids wounded.
4.	KG 4	CM	Shot down by Hurricanes of Gracie, Page and Weaver of 56 Sqn. at St. Osyth.	Junkers Ju 88A	20 %	Four crew made P.O.W. un-wounded.
5.	III./KG 4	NCM	Crash landed at Zwischenahn; cause not known.	Junkers Ju 88A-1	20 %	Crew unhurt.
6.	St.St./KG 27	NCM	Crashed at Compeigne following engine failure.	Heinkel He 111P	100 %	Oblt. Pommerening + three injured.
7.	2./KG 40	CM	Shot down by A.A. guns while minelaying off Sunderland at approx. 00.15 hrs.	Focke-Wulf Fw 200 (F8+EH)	100 %	Hptm. Roman Steszyn (1), Fw. Meier and Fw. Zraunig drowned; Fw. Kulken and Fw. Nicolai made P.O.W.
8.	2./KG 40	CM	Lost off N. Ireland; cause not known.	Focke-Wulf Fw 200	100 %	Two crew killed; Hptm. Zenke and two others made P.O.W.
9.	II./St.G 1	CM	Shot down by Hurricane of Humpherson of 32 Sqn. over convoy BOSOM 10 miles off Dover at 17.58 hrs.	Junkers Ju 87B	100 %	Ltn. Roden + one killed.
10.	II./St.G 1	CM	Shot down by Hurricanes of 32 Sqn. as above.	Junkers Ju 87B	100 %	Both crew members killed.
11.	II./St.G 1	CM	Damaged by Hurricanes of 32 Sqn. as above.	Junkers Ju 87B	30 %	Crew unhurt.
12.	II./St.G 1	CM	Damaged by Hurricanes of 32 Sqn. as above.	Junkers Ju 87B	30 %	Crew unhurt.
13.	II./St.G 1	CM	Damaged by Hurricanes of 32 Sqn. as above.	Junkers Ju 87B-1	30 %	Crew unhurt.
14.	II./St.G 1	CM	Damaged by Hurricanes of 32 Sqn. as above.	Junkers Ju 87B-1	30 %	One crew member wounded.
15.	Stab/St.G. 1	CM	Crashed at Théville following combat (possibly with night fighter Blenheim of 25 Sqn.)	Dornier Do 17M	100 %	One crew member killed; Ltn. Schenkel + one wounded.
16.	Stab I./JG 27	CM	Shot down by Hurricane of Hugo of 615 Sqn. over convoy BOSOM at 18.03 hrs.	Messerschmitt Bf 109E	100 %	Maj. Helmut Riegel missing.
17.	3./JG 27	CM	Shot down by Hurricane of Eyre of 615 Sqn. over convoy BOSOM at 18.03 hrs.	Messerschmitt Bf 109 E-3	100 %	Ltn. Ulrich Scherer missing.
18.	I./JG 27	CM	Shot down by Hurricane of Gaunce of 615 Sqn. over convoy BOSOM at approx. 18.00 hrs.	Messerschmitt Bf 109 E-4	100 %	Ofw. Heinz Beusshausen killed.
19.	I./JG 51	CM	Shot down by Hurricane of Brothers of 32 Sqn. at 18.00 hrs and crashed at Audinghem.	Messerschmitt Bf 109E	100 %	N.C.O. pilot killed.
20.	II./JG 51	CM	Shot down by Spitfire of Olive of 65 Sqn. off Calais at 18.40 hrs.	Messerschmitt Bf 109 E-3	100 %	Pilot rescued safely.
21.	Seenotflug-kdo. 1	CM	Shot down by Hurricanes of Hubbard, Doulton and Grier of 601 Sqn. near convoy BOSOM off Selsey Bill at 17.50 hrs.	Heinkel He 59 (D-AKAR)	100 %	Four crew killed.
22.	Seenotflug-kdo. 4	CM	Shot down by Hurricane of Mann of 238 Sqn. 3 miles off Cherbourg at 14.10 hrs.	Heinkel He 59	100 %	Four crew missing.

[(1) Records of KG 51 indicate that Hptm. Roman Steszyn was in fact on the strength of that unit and lends evidence that KG 40 drew upon the ex-perienced members of other long-range bomber Geschwader.]

Sunday 21st July

In contrast to the previous day, this Sunday was fairly quiet, apart from an attack on a west-bound convoy in the Channel and scattered coastal reconnaissance over Southern England.

Profiting from recent experience, both Park and Brand (now commanding the newly-established No. 10 Group at Rudloe Manor, Box) determined to provide the Channel convoy with powerful cover, and maintained patrols of not less than twelve fighters throughout the day.

No. 238 Squadron scored first when its Red Section (Flt. Lt Donald Turner, Fg. Off. Charles Davis and Plt. Off. John Wigglesworth) intercepted a reconnaissance Bf 110C of 4.(F)/14 ten miles south of Middle Wallop at 10.30 hours and shot it down at Goodwood. Later, at 14.30 hours, the same pilots (now joined by Sqn. Ldr. Harold Fenton and Sgt. Leslie Batt) found a Dornier Do 17M of the same reconnaissance *Staffel* and destroyed it over Blandford.

The westbound convoy, which had passed through the Dover Strait during the night and whose heavy escort had evidently discouraged enemy interference all morning, came under heavy attack by a *Gruppe* of Dornier Do 17s escorted by some 50 Bf 109s and 110s about ten miles south of the Needles at 14.30 hours. Once again the Hurricanes of No. 43 Squadron, led by Sqn. Ldr. John Badger, were on the spot and broke up the bomber formations before being engaged by the escort. Unfortunately the Hurricane flown by Plt. Off. Ricardo de Mancha[55] collided with the Bf 109 of Ltn. Heinz Kroker of 7./JG 27, and both pilots were killed.

As the 109s disengaged and joined the Dorniers—which had dropped their bombs without effect and turned away south—No. 43 Squadron was relieved by further Hurricanes of No. 238 Squadron. Obviously the German fighter pilots had hoped to lure the escort away from the convoy and had not reckoned on the prompt arrival of reinforcements, for the new pilots were astonished to see the Bf 110s (which had previously taken up a defensive circle a few miles to the south) diving at the convoy and dropping bombs. The aircraft belonged to V.*Gruppe*, *Lehrgeschwader 1*, the first operational unit to use the Bf 110 as a fighter-bomber and of whose existence the R.A.F. had been unaware. The Irishman, Plt. Off. Brian Considine, singled out one of the enemy and went after it as it made off to escape southwards; only when it had almost reached the French coast was he able to hit and disable one of the enemy's engines. He was not to know that the Bf 110 crashed on landing at Theville, killing a crew member.

There were few other incidents involving enemy aircraft during the afternoon as thunderstorms developed all over Southern England. All through the day reports flooded in of barrage balloons being struck by lightning, one detachment in north Kent losing six in the space of half an hour.

It may be said that July was the first month in which Britain suffered widespread air raids since 1918. Accordingly thousands of men, women and children were suffering the ravages of total war for the first time in their lives, and all the intricate services were beginning to take the strain of bringing relief to those who suffered as a result. As was becoming all too familiar, it was the homes of ordinary people that were devastated, people least equipped to fend for themselves. As yet

Three views of the reconnaissance Messerschmitt Bf 110C-5, 2177:5F+CH, flown by Oberleutnant Friedrich of 4.(F)/14 and shot down by Turner, Wigglesworth and Davis of No. 238 Squadron at Goodwood at 10.30 hrs. on 21st July.

there were only the relatively isolated "incidents", each capable of being managed by local services. Nevertheless scarcely a bomb dropped that did not bring its own tale of domestic heroism.

For instance, it was during this period that one of the first awards of the George Cross was made to a civilian rescue worker at the Yorkshire coastal town of Bridlington—hit by bombers of KG 26 and 30 several times during July and August 1940[56]. Thomas Alderson was a part-time Rescue Detachment Leader in Bridlington where a pair of houses was

[55] Son of an English mother and an Italian father.

[56] Although one of the first group of three George Crosses gazetted on 30th September 1940, this award was chronologically the third to be won.

demolished by bombs. Hearing that a woman was trapped under a pile of rubble, Alderson tunnelled his way in and dragged her out. A few days later Alderson dug his way into the cellars of two five-storey buildings which had been reduced to rubble, and after several hours of working among severed gas and water mains, reached and rescued eleven survivors. Yet again, Alderson worked among falling bombs to tunnel his way to another cellar and brought out six trapped occupants. On another occasion he dug his way under debris to rescue two people—apparently oblivious of a wall, three storeys high, swaying in the wind directly over him. On this occasion Alderson worked for five hours—during which time further raids were heralded and enemy bombers passed overhead.

R.A.F. FIGHTER COMMAND LOSSES—SUNDAY 21st JULY 1940

1.	43 Sqn., Tangmere	C	Shot down by Bf 109s ten miles south of the Needles. Pilot killed.	14.45 hrs.	Plt. Off. R.A. de Mancha	Hurricane	P3973	Cat. 3 Lost
2.	43 Sqn., Tangmere	C	Damaged by Bf 109 ten miles south of the Needles. Pilot unhurt.	14.15 hrs.	Sqn. Ldr. J.V.C. Badger	Hurricane	P3971	Cat. 1 Damaged
3.	54 Sqn., Rochford	NC	Pilot baled out 15 miles east of Clacton after engine failure; picked up by destroyer unhurt.	Not known	Plt. Off. J.L. Kemp	Spitfire	N3184	Cat. 3 Lost
4.	238 Sqn., Middle Wallop	C	Damaged by Do 17 over Blandford; pilot landed safely at base.	15.00 hrs.	Plt. Off. C.T. Davis	Hurricane	P3767	Cat. 1 Damaged

LUFTWAFFE LOSSES—SUNDAY 21st JULY 1940

1.	4.(F)/14	CM	Shot down by Hurricanes of Fenton, Turner, Batt and Wigglesworth of 238 Sqn. at Blandford at 14.30 hrs.	Dornier Do 17M (5F+OM)	100 %	Oblt. Georg Thiele, Fw. Fritz Bohnen and Uffz. Alfred Werner wounded and made P.O.W.s.
2.	4.(F)/14	CM	Shot down by Hurricanes of Turner, Davis and Wigglesworth of 238 Sqn. at Goodwood at 10.30 hrs.	Messerschmitt Bf 110C (2177:5F+CM)	100 %	Oblt. Friedrich Kark Runde and Fw. Willi Baden made P.O.W.s.
3.	III./KG 3	NCM	Mid-air collision near Würzburg.	Dornier Do 17Z	100 %	Three crew killed.
4.	II./KG 51	NCM	Landing accident at Orly airfield.	Junkers Ju 88A	40 %	Crew unhurt.
5.	I./KG 54	CM	Crashed and burned on landing at Coulommiers. No claim by R.A.F.	Junkers Ju 88A	100 %	Four crew killed.
6.	V./LG 1	CM	Destroyed in crash landing at Théville after combat with Hurricane of Considine of 238 Sqn.	Messerschmitt Bf 110C	80 %	One crew member killed.
7.	I./St.G 2	NCM	Crashed on landing at Condé-sur-Ifa.	Junkers Ju 87B	100 %	Both crew members killed.
8.	I./JG 26	NCM	Force landed near Emmerich after engine failure.	Messerschmitt Bf 109 E-4	80 %	Pilot unhurt.
9.	9./JG 26	NCM	Formation of four aircraft force landed near Le Havre with fuel shortage after becoming lost in bad weather.	Messerschmitt Bf 109 (E-1s and E-4s)	All 40 %	All four pilots unhurt.
10.	7./JG 27	CM	Collided with Hurricane of de Mancha of 43 Sqn. over convoy 10 miles south of the Needles at 14.40 hrs.	Messerschmitt Bf 109 E-4	100 %	Ltn. Heinz Kroker killed.
11.	III./JG 77	CM	Believed shot down by R.A.F. bombers in Sq. 9589.	Messerschmitt Bf 109	100 %	Oblt. Weber missing.
12.	1./406	CM	Said by Germans to have been shot down by British fighters in Square 2697, but no R.A.F. claim.	Dornier Do 18	100 %	One crew member killed.
13.	2./106	NCM	Believed to have crashed at Caen.	Dornier Do 18	100 %	Ltn.z.S. Set killed; three crew in jured.
14.	1./606	CM	Shot down by A.A. guns on Scottish coast.	Dornier Do 17	100%	Ltn.z.S. Geschke + three missing.

Monday 22nd July

"Many of you will have read two days ago the speech in which Herr Hitler summoned Great Britain to capitulate to his will. I will not waste your time by dealing with his distortion of almost every main event since the War began. He says he has no desire to destroy the British Empire, but there was in his speech no suggestion that peace must be based on justice, no word of recognition that the other nations of Europe had any right to self-determination, the principle which he has so often invoked for Germans. His only appeal was to the base instinct of fear, and his only arguments were threats. . .

"Hitler has now made it plain that he is preparing to direct the whole weight of German might against this country. That is why in every part of Britain there is only one spirit, a spirit of indomitable resolution. Nor has anyone any doubt that if Hitler were to succeed it would be the end, for many besides ourselves, of all those things which make life worth living. We realise that the struggle may cost us everything, but just because the things we are defending are worth any sacrifice, it is a noble privilege to be the defenders of things so precious. We never wanted the War; certainly no one here wants the War to go on for a day longer than is necessary. But we shall not stop fighting till freedom, for ourselves and others, is secure."

Thus the British Foreign Secretary, Lord Halifax, in an unequivocal reply broadcast on this Monday to Hitler's call for Britain's surrender. Certainly no one in the country had expected any other reply, and such categorical rejection of the

Spitfire *R6597:GR-A* of No. 92 Squadron, flown by Sgt. R.H. Fokes, which suffered a night landing accident at Pembrey on 22nd July.

German appeal served to consolidate the nation's determination to withstand every assault by the enemy, be it on land or from the sea or air.

Coinciding with this statement of intent was the issue of the *Luftwaffe*'s detailed staff instructions for air operations to prepare for the invasion of Britain. On the previous day Göring had called Milch, the three *Luftflotte* commanders and their staffs to Karinhall to hear him outline the broad terms of these instructions. Once again it was clear that the Naval Staff was apprehensive about the impunity with which British shipping continued to sail up and down the Channel, and now called upon the *Luftwaffe* to seal off the ports of Dover, Plymouth, Portland and Portsmouth by mining and, if possible, to direct attacks on the Royal Navy in these ports. Other ports were to remain undamaged so as to be available for use by the invasion forces.

The broad aims of the forthcoming air offensive were based on the capacity of the forces already deployed in the three Luftflotten as well as that of units whose deployment was still incomplete; these forces, based on strength returns of 20th July, were as follows[57]:

	Luftflotten 2 & 3	Luftflotte 5
	On Strength (Serviceable)	On Strength (Serviceable)
Long-range Reconnaissance	67 (48)	67 (48)
Long-range Bombers	1,131 (769)	129 (95)
Dive-Bombers	316 (248)	—
Coastal Recce., Minelayers &c	82 (46)	28 (15)
Single-engine fighters	809 (656)	84 (69)
Twin-engine fighters	246 (168)	34 (32)
Totals ...	2,651 (1,935)	342 (259)

As the single-engine fighters of *Luftflotte 5* were out of range

---

[57] Cf. German Air Staff Historical Section (8th Abteilung) records. The figures do not include about ninety short-range reconnaissance (army co-operation) aircraft which would only have entered the battle after the invasion had started.

of the British Isles, the effective number of such aircraft available for the campaign was 656. The strength of Fighter Command in single-engine fighters on this day was 609, of which 531 were serviceable; this figure included 27 Defiants whose future value was now seriously in doubt.

Whether or not the *Luftwaffe*'s subordinate staffs were preoccupied with a study of the new Operations Order on 22nd July is not known, for there was a marked reduction in enemy activity over the Islands during daylight. The opportunity was taken to remove the remnants of No. 141 (Defiant) Squadron out of the battle area to Prestwick in the west of Scotland—a move made more difficult by the fact that only eight pilots had survived the ravages of combat.

Considerable night activity had occurred during the early hours and a KG 30 Junkers Ju 88 unloaded its bombs on a cemetary at Leith; ironically, they demolished the graves of German airmen who had participated in the War's first raid on the Firth of Forth.

Shortly after mid-day three Hurricanes of No. 145 Squadron (Flt. Lt. Adrian Boyd, Plt. Off. Archibald Weir and Plt. Off. Peter Dunning-White) were scrambled to Beachy Head and later diverted to Selsey Bill where they found and shot down a Dornier Do 17P of 4.(F)/121 at 13,00 hours.

As darkness came down on a score of *Luftwaffe* bomber bases from Stavanger to Lannions, bomber crews were emerging from briefings at which they had received instructions to lay mines in British ports. From radar and Observer Corps sound plots it is estimated that upwards of one hundred mining sorties were flown this night.

The pilot of one such aircraft was Hauptmann Hans-Joachim ("Hajo") Herrmann, *Staffelkapitän* of 7./KG 30, who set course from Zwischenahn in Germany with four Ju 88s, each to lay their magnetic mines in Plymouth South. His plan was to approach the Sound from the north-east at 16,000 feet and let down to about 300 feet, reducing speed to no more than 180 m.p.h. and dropping the weapons beside the breakwater. All went according to plan as the formation approached Plymouth and, with the moonlight throwing the details of the port into sharp relief, Herrman trimmed his aircraft into the steep descent. Suddenly he saw looming directly ahead the

145

great shining hulk of a barrage balloon; too late he struggled to turn aside, but at low speed his controls were sluggish and the German bomber squashed down on top of the balloon—coming virtually to a dead stop. Mercifully the engines continued to run without piercing the hydrogen-filled gasbag with the propellers, and now the two "aircraft" started falling, the Junkers riding the back of the balloon. Herrmann recalls:

"It only lasted for a few seconds, though it felt like an hour. Then I noticed that the British searchlights were shining from above—we had fallen off the balloon, and now we were upside down, with virtually no forward speed, and going down out of control. I felt as if I was playing a piano which was falling from a fifth storey!"

Finding that he could not regain control, Herrmann ordered his crew to bale out, and jettisoned the rear canopy; but before anyone left the bomber the pilot found that his aircraft was gradually righting itself and flying low over the city of Plymouth. In spite of the glare from the searchlights, which continued to hold the Junkers during its accelerated descent, Herrmann saw that he was making straight for the breakwater, and determined to complete his mission if humanly possible. Despite the fact that all the defences were now thoroughly alert and were firing with everything that had, Herrmann rammed his throttles wide open and dropped his mines in the prescribed position before thankfully setting course for more friendly skies. After landing at Soesterberg in Holland, an inspection of his aircraft revealed extraordinarily little damage—air brakes slightly bent and some loss of paint from the wings. . . but not a mark from flak[58].

[58] Hajo Herrmann, who was to survive the War, performed a number of quite exceptionally courageous feats and survived miraculous escapes from almost certain death, as well as becoming a holder of the Swords and Oakleaves to the Knight's Cross. He it was who, when bombing the Greek harbour at Piraeus at low level in 1941, scored a direct hit on an ammunition ship which blew up with such force that much of the port was destroyed; Herrmann managed to land his severely crippled bomber safely. In 1942 he led the most successful bombing attack on a North Cape convoy to Murmansk inside the Arctic Circle. It was he who led the volunteer *Rammkommando*—the fighter unit formed late in the War to destroy American B-17 Fortress bombers by ramming tactics; against all conceivable odds, Herrmann survived two such rammings. And in the summer of 1943 he played a leading part in the establishment and operations of 30 *Jagddivision* ; this was the *Wilde Sau* (Wild Boar) force of single-seat day fighters which flew freelance night interceptor sorties with considerable success against R.A.F. Bomber Command.

R.A.F. FIGHTER COMMAND LOSSES—MONDAY 22nd JULY 1940

1.	85 Sqn., Martlesham	NC	Pilot killed in night landing at Castle Camps.	At night	Plt. Off. J.L. Bickerdyke	Hurricane	P3895	Cat. 3 Destroyed
2.	92 Sqn., Pembrey	NC	Pilot unhurt in night landing accident at Pembrey	At night	Sgt. R.H. Fokes	Spitfire	R6597	Cat. 2 Damaged
3.	235 Sqn., Bircham Newton	NC	Force landed after engine failure at Horsham St. Faith, Norwich; crew unhurt.	Not known	Plt. Off. D.N. Woodger	Blenheim	P4835	Cat. 2 Damaged
4.	601 Sqn., Tangmere	NC	Force landed at Pagham after engine failure; pilot unhurt.	Not known	Plt. Off. J.K.U.B. McGrath	Hurricane	L1772	Cat. 3 Destroyed
5.	611 Sqn., Ternhill	NC	Landing accident at Ternhill; pilot unhurt.	Not known	Sgt. Burt	Spitfire	K9950	Cat. 2 Damaged
6.	611 Sqn., Ternhill	NC	Force landed on beach at Colwyn Bay following coolant failure; pilot unhurt.	Not known	Plt. Off. D.A. Adams	Spitfire	N3062	Cat. 2 Damaged

LUFTWAFFE LOSSES—MONDAY 22nd JULY 1940

1.	4.(F)/121	CM	Shot down by Hurricanes of Boyd, Weir and Dunning-White of 145 Sqn. off Selsey Bill at approx. 07.40 hrs.	Dornier Do 17P	100 %	Ltn. Georg Borman made P.O.W.; Ltn. Erwin Reichart, Fw. Rowe and Fw. Reinhard killed.
2.	2./KG 30	CM	Crashed near Narvik, not the result of combat.	Junkers Ju 88	100 %	Four crew members killed.
3.	III./KG 30	NCM	Crashed at Aalborg following engine failure.	Junkers Ju 88A-1	75 %	Crew unhurt.
4.	Stab/St.G 1	CM	Taxying accident on Quilly-le-Tesson airfield.	Dornier Do 17M	30 %	Crew unhurt.
5.	Stab/St.G 77	NCM	Crashed on landing at Caen airfield.	Junkers Ju 87B	60 %	Crew unhurt.

Tuesday 23rd July

As Hajo Herrmann made his way eastwards up the Channel, another drama was occupying the attention of the defences. After weeks of slow progress with their recalcitrant radar sets, the crews of Blenheims belonging to the Fighter Interception Unit (F.I.U.), based at Tangmere, had worked out an interception procedure that was at last to bring success.

A Dornier Do 17Z of 2./KG 3 was picked up by the CH radar at Poling and a Blenheim of the F.I.U. was diverted to intercept. While information of the raider's course was passed from Poling to the Tangmere operations room, the F.I.U.'s commanding officer, Wg. Cdr. George Chamberlain, "talked" his Blenheim to the spot. Radar contact was achieved by Sgt. Reginald Leyland (using one of the first A.I. Mark III sets delivered to the R.A.F.), who steered the pilot, Fg. Off. Glynn Ashfield, towards the bomber. Straining his eyes in the turret of the Blenheim was Plt. Off. Geoffrey Morris who suddenly caught sight of the Dornier crossing ahead, slightly above. Hearing the excited shout from the Observer to turn, Ashfield swung the Blenheim round and found the enemy almost dead ahead, silhouetted against the moon. Raising the nose of his aircraft, Ashfield fired a ten-second burst, setting the enemy's fuel tank on fire.

As the Dornier plummeted towards the waters of the Channel, Ashfield set course for home with the knowledge that he had just completed the very first successful interception using airborne radar. In the months and years to come such tactics were to revolutionise the entire concept of night and bad weather defence by fighters.

In an effort to foil the night raiders another innovation was tried at about this time. Codenamed LICORICE, this was an aerial smokescreen laid from about 6,000 feet over a town in which fires had been started by enemy bombers, in order to conceal the target from other raiders who might be uncertain of their whereabouts. In practice it was found that the screen could not be made thick enough to conceal the bright glare of fires on the ground and that the smoke only tended to diffuse it over a wider area. Trials were carried out over Slough by a Wellington bomber flying from Stradishall before the project was abandoned.

Daylight on 23rd July brought no return to heavy attacks, so Dowding and his Group Commanders continued to rearrange their lines of battle. No. 43 Squadron at Tangmere, which had been in action constantly for the past three weeks and had lost six pilots killed or wounded (including its squadron commander) was moved back to Northolt to train new pilots. Its place was taken by another famous Hurricane Squadron, No. 1, commanded by Sqn. Ldr. David Pemberton, D.F.C., which moved from Northolt to its old peacetime base at Tangmere. At the same time further reinforcements were sent to the extreme right flank with the transfer of the Gladiators of No. 247 Squadron from Sumburgh in the Shetland Islands to Exeter for the sole purpose of covering Plymouth. (It was soon decided to move the Gladiators to Roborough—a small

Firemen and a gaily-blazered civilian inspect the remains of a Bf 109E which crashed in a suburban street during the last week of July.

grass airfield nearer to Plymouth—so as to leave Exeter clear for the Hurricane squadrons.)

Convoy patrols continued throughout the day all round the South and East Coasts, and although there were signs of enemy interest in the convoy PILOT off Lincolnshire, only two enemy aircraft were shot down. These were a Junkers Ju 88 of 4.(F)/122, destroyed by Flt. Lt. George Powell-Sheddon of No. 242 Squadron off Great Yarmouth, and a Dornier Do 17 shot down by three Spitfires of No. 603 Squadron 75 miles east of Aberdeen.

R.A.F. FIGHTER COMMAND LOSSES—TUESDAY 23rd JULY 1940

1.	3 Sqn., Wick	NC	Pilot seriously injured in take-off collision with Hudson of No. 269 Sqn. (Bombs exploded, killing Hudson's crew of four.)	12.35 hrs.	Plt. Off. D.L. Bisgood	Hurricane	P2862	Cat. 3 Destroyed
2.	232 Sqn., Sumburgh	NC	Force landed in sea off Shetlands following engine failure; pilot rescued unhurt.	Not known	Sgt. A.F. Butterick	Hurricane	P2861	Cat. 3 Lost
3.	257 Sqn., Northolt	NC	Crashed while landing at Hendon; pilot unhurt.	Not known	Plt. Off J.A.G. Chomley	Hurricane	P3641	Cat. 3 Destroyed
4.	603 Sqn., Montrose	NC	Crashed while landing at Montrose; pilot unhurt.	Not known	Sqn. Ldr. G.L. Denholm	Spitfire	N3026	Cat. 2 Damaged

LUFTWAFFE LOSSES—TUESDAY 23rd JULY 1940

1.	3.(F)/122	NCM	Force landed at Zorge/Harz after engine failure.	Heinkel He 111H-2	100 %	One killed; Ltn. Scharper + two injured.
2.	4.(F)/122	CM	Shot down by Hurricane of Powell-Sheddon of 242 Sqn. at dawn SE of Yarmouth.	Junkers Ju 88	100 %	Two killed; two missing.
3.	Not known	CM	Shot down by Spitfires of Rushmer, Berry and Benson of 603 Sqn., 75 miles east of Aberdeen at 15.00 hrs.	Dornier Do 17P	100 %	Four crew members killed.
4.	2./KG 3	CM	Shot down by AI-equipped Blenheim of F.I.U. of Ashfield at night south of Brighton.	Dornier Do 17Z	100 %	Ltn. Kahlfuss wounded ; three believed rescued.
5.	III./JG 26	NCM	Damaged by trees while low flying.	Messerschmitt Bf 109	10 %	Pilot unhurt.
6.	Kü.Fl.Gr. 806	NCM	Crashed at Ütersen, not the result of combat.	Junkers Ju 88A-1	100 %	Three crew members killed.
7.	Transp.St. Fl.Korps 1	NCM	Crashed at Compeigne during training flight.	Bücker Bü 131	100 %	Two crew killed

Wednesday 24th July

The successful interception by Ashfield during the night of 22nd/23rd July serves to illustrate the degree of progress being made in the application of advanced science to the problems of war. For some months British scientists had been aware that the *Luftwaffe* raiders had been using radio beams, transmitted across Britain from continental stations, to assist

navigation towards their targets. Dr. R.V. Jones[59], a brillaint physicist attached to the Air Ministry's Directorate of Intelligence, had sifted numerous documents emanating from

---

[59] Later Professor R.V. Jones, C.B., C.B.E., F.R.S., later Director of Intelligence (Research).

enemy sources in efforts to learn about possible German "secret weapons". By an extraordinary chain of circumstantial evidence Jones learned of the German *Knickebein*[60], a system of narrow radio beams transmitted from stations in Germany placed wide apart so as to intersect over an intended target. Interrogation of a *Luftwaffe* prisoner in March 1940 revealed that the beams could reach London from Germany with a divergence of less than one mile—an achievement far beyond British scientific experience at the time. Subsequent examination of a shot down Heinkel He 111 revealed that the standard German *Lorenz* radio receiver was otherwise inexplicably more sensitive than equivalent British equipment.

In the face of apathy and disbelief by such powerful influences as Professor F.A. Lindemann[61], Jones set out to prove the existence of the enemy radio aid; for if such equipment did indeed exist, not only did it represent a particularly dangerous weapon in a night bombing offensive over Britain, but it might be so interfered with as to render enemy night bombers largely ineffective.

Examination of shot-down German bombers' radio log books continued to confirm Jones' theories and eventually revealed not only the operating frequencies of the beams, but the locations of the transmitting stations. During June a flight of Anson training aircraft, commanded by Sqn. Ldr. George Scott-Farnie, was established to listen on frequencies in the thirty-megacycle band, and in due course confirmed the existence of a transmission on 31.5 megacycles which, on a particular occasion, was found to represent a beam passing about a mile south of Spalding in Lincolnshire.

With such confirmation, Lindemann gave support for plans to interfere with the *Knickebein* beams, and this work was initiated by Air Commodore O.G.W.G. Lywood, Director of Signals at the Air Ministry, who in turn approached Dr. Robert Cockburn of the Telecommunications Research Establishment to develop a device for obliterating (or "jamming") the German radio signals. Such sophisticated equipment would take time to produce in quantity, but it was found that by suitably modifying electro-diathermy equipment (of the sort used in hospitals for surgical purposes) it was possible to obliterate the dots and dashes of the *Knickebein* signals. These sets were installed in scattered police stations throughout the country with instructions for switching on passed by the R.A.F. Signals Branch. At the same time, R.A.F. *Lorenz* transmitters were used to transmit spurious *Knickebein* signals to confuse enemy raiders.

The adapted electro-diathermy equipment was made ready for use during July 1940, and on the 24th other sets (known as "Meacons"), developed by the G.P.O. to mask enemy radio beacons, came into operation, the first being situated at Flimwell, near Tunbridge Wells in Kent.

As such "passive" defence measures continued under development to counter the night threat, the day battle raged on with a return to formation raids by the *Luftwaffe*. However, during the morning hours of the 24th the Germans continued with isolated reconnaissance and nuisance sorties. A Heinkel He 111 of KG 26 was damaged by No. 603 Squadron between Aberdeen and Peterhead, and a Junkers Ju 88 of 1./LG 1 was shot down in flames over Porthcawl by Flt. Lt. Brian King-

Two Spitfires approaching to land after patrol. Spitfires of Nos. 54, 92, 603 and 610 Squadrons had a particularly successful day on 24th July.

combe, Flt. Lt. James Paterson and Plt. Off John Bryson of No. 92 Squadron. One of the crew of this aircraft baled out at about 60 feet and was killed; the others stayed with their aircraft and escaped with severe burns when it crashed.

A convoy passing through the Dover Strait at around 08.00 hours was the target of two *Staffeln* of Dornier Do 17s which, being intercepted by No. 54 Squadron, were unable to make an accurate bombing run, and dropped their loads well clear of the ships. Nonetheless the Spitfire pilots were unable to claim any of the enemy aircraft destroyed.

A more dangerous raid developed later in the morning on a convoy which set sail from the Medway soon after 11.00 hours. Again about eighteen Dorniers appeard, this time escorted by about 40 Bf 109s of Adolf Galland's III./JG 26. With some warning of the raid's approach, No. 54 Squadron was ordered up at 11.20 hours and soon after was locked in combat with the escorting Bf 109s. At about the same time nine Spitfires of No. 610 Squadron took off from Biggin Hill with orders to patrol near Dover and perhaps cut off the retreat of the Estuary raid. While No. 54 Squadron was engaging the Bf 109s, six further Spitfires—this time of No. 65 Squadron from Manston—entered the fray and, seeing the escort preoccupied elsewhere, attempted to attack the Dorniers. Although they loosed off some long-range bursts they were unable to approach the bombers closely owing to the compactness of the enemy's formation and their extremely effective crossfire. The bombers escaped unscathed.

The German fighters were not so lucky, and lost two of their number, one to Sqn. Ldr. Henry Sawyer of No. 65 Squadron, and one to Plt. Off. Colin Gray of No. 54 Squadron. The Messerschmitt pilots were held in combat for so long that fear of fuel shortage compelled them to disengage and, knowing that they could out-dive the Spitfire, many sought this method of escape. These tactics undoubtedly misled some of the Spitfire pilots into believing that more of the enemy had been shot down; in contrast to the sole victim of Colin Gray's Spitfire, No. 54 Squadron pilots claimed to have destroyed six, probably destroyed eight and damaged two. . .

As III./JG 26 made good its escape at low level over Kent, III./JG 52 came in over Dover on a free chase to protect it— and ran straight into the nine Spitfires of No. 610 Squadron, who shot down two Messerschmitts of 7./JG 52 over Margate, killing both enemy pilots. British losses in these combats amounted to two Spitfires of No. 54 Squadron, flown by

---

[60] *Knickebein* = Crooked Leg
[61] Winston Churchill's Chief Scientific Adviser and later Lord Cherwell (see also Chapter 4).

Plt. Off John Allen D.F.C., killed when his aircraft crashed near North Foreland, and Sgt. George Collett who force landed, slightly wounded, near Orfordness.

An interesting attack was carried out by a single enemy aircraft during the afternoon. This aircraft managed to penetrate the Sussex coast in cloud and was fleetingly spotted by numerous observer posts over an area of about a thousand square miles, being variously identified as a Blenheim, Dornier, Heinkel and Ju 88. Sections of fighters were sent up from Kenley, Hornchurch and Biggin Hill to investigate, but all failed to sight the intruder. Eventually it appeared below the cloud at 15.16 hours near Weybridge and, putting its wheels down, made as if to land at the nearby Brooklands airfield. Realising too late that the aircraft was in fact a Dornier Do 17, the nearby observer post could only report the fall of bombs "in the direction of Weybridge". The enemy bomber dropped sixteen 50-kilo fragmentation bombs which in fact did little material damage. The Dornier then escaped.

R.A.F. FIGHTER COMMAND LOSSES—WEDNESDAY 24th JULY 1940

1.	46 Sqn., Digby	NC	Pilot killed in force landing near Digby.	Not Known	Plt. Off. A.M. Cooper-Slipper	Hurricane	P2685	Cat. 3 Destroyed
2.	54 Sqn., Rochford	C	Shot down by Bf 109s of JG 26 near Foreness; pilot killed.	A12.15 hrs.	Plt. Off. J.L. Allen	Spitfire	R6812	Cat. 3 Lost
3.	54 Sqn., Rochford	C	Force landed at Sizewell, near Orfordness, after combat; pilot slightly wounded.	A12.15 hrs.	Sgt. G.R. Collett	Spitfire	N3192	Cat. 2 Damaged
4.	66 Sqn., Coltishall	NC	Pilot baled out off the Norfolk coast following engine failure; rescued unhurt.	Not known	Not known	Spitfire	L3041	Cat. 3 Lost
5.	151 Sqn., North Weald	NC	Aircraft dived into ground after take-off; pilot killed.	Not known	Plt. Off. J.R. Hamar	Hurricane	P3316	Cat. 3 Destroyed
6.	610 Sqn., Biggin Hill	C	Crashed on landing after combat; pilot killed Aircraft burnt out.	A16.00 hrs.	Sqn. Ldr. A.T. Smith	Spitfire	R6976	Cat. 3 Destroyed

LUFTWAFFE LOSSES—WEDNESDAY 24th JULY 1940

1.	Weküsta. 1	CM	Shot down by Hurricanes of Rook, Frisby and Haw of 504 Sqn., 10 miles east of Wick at 09.05 hrs.	Heinkel He 111H-3	100 %	Three crew killed; two rescued and made P.O.W.s.
2.	1.(F)/123	CM	Crashed at Brest due to technical trouble.	Junkers Ju 88A	100 %	Oblt. Muhlbauer + three killed.
3.	3./KG 26	CM	Damaged by Spitfires of Gilroy, Haig and Read of 603 Sqn. off Aberdeen at approx. 07.00 hrs. and crashed on return to base.	Heinkel He 111H-3	100 %	Three crew members wounded.
4.	6./KG 26	NCM	Crashed near Moen following engine failure.	Heinkel He 111H-3	100 %	Two crew members killed.
5.	I./KG 27	NCM	Crashed near Münster following engine failure.	Heinkel He 111P	85 %	Ltn. Stadel killed.
6.	I./LG 1	CM	Shot down by Spitfires of Kingcombe, Bryson and Paterson of 92 Sqn., near Porthcawl at at 07.30 hrs.	Junkers Ju 88A	100 %	One killed; Hptm. von Maltitz + one missing.
7.	III./JG 26	CM	Shot down by Spitfire of Gray of 54 Sqn., near North Foreland at 11.48 hrs.	Messerschmitt Bf 109 E-1	100 %	Ltn. Schauff killed.
8.	III./JG 26	CM	Shot down by Spitfire of Collett of 54 Sqn. over Thames Estuary at 11.20 hrs.	Messerschmitt Bf 109 E-1	100 %	Pilot killed (name not known).
9.	III./JG 26	CM	Shot down by Spitfire of Sawyer of 65 Sqn. off North Kent at approx. 12.35 hrs.	Messerschmitt Bf 109 E-1	100 %	Ltn. Bartels wounded.
10.	7./JG 52	CM	Shot down by Spitfire of Smith of 610 Sqn. north of Dover at 11.25 hrs.	Messerschmitt Bf 109 E-1	100 %	Oblt. Fermer killed.
11.	7./JG 52	CM	Shot down by Spitfire of Ellis of 610 Sqn. near Margate at 11.28 hrs.	Messerschmitt Bf 109E	100 %	Pilot killed (name not known).
12.	8./JG 52	CM	Shot down by Spitfire of Gardner of 610 Sqn. over convoy west of Dover at 15.20 hrs.	Messerschmitt Bf 109E	100 %	Oblt. Ehrlich, St. Kap., killed.
13.	17./KGzbV.5	NCM	Collided with light beacon.	Heinkel He 46	100 %	Ltn. Tregl killed.
14.	Aufkl.St. Oberost	NCM	Crashed into group of soldiers at Radom, Poland.	Arado Ar 66	95 %	Pilot and eight soldiers of SS Regt. killed.

A crashed Bf 109E-3, "Red 13" of an unidentified unit, guarded by two soldiers. (Photo: Radio Times Hulton Picture Library)

Thursday 25th July

Sometimes dismissed as a day of only sporadic skirmishing, 25th July in fact witnessed further escallation of German attacks along the South and East Coasts and proved critical in the fortunes of several R.A.F. fighter squadrons. With clear early morning skies, reconnaissance pilots of *Luftflotte 2* took due note of a heavily-protected westbound convoy approaching the Dover Strait, with a result that carefully timed fighter and bomber sweeps were mounted throughout the day. The recurring German plan was to send out powerful fighter formations to exhaust the patrolling R.A.F. fighters so that, as these were returning to refuel and re-arm, a heavy bomber strike could be launched against the convoy before reinforcements arrived.

No. 65 Squadron's Spitfires were first in action at 12.20 hours when their pilots spotted some Bf 109s flying low over the water near Dover; F/Sgt. Franklin managed to manœuvre on to the tail of one before he sighted another diving on him from above. By "jinking" from side to side little more than a dozen feet above the waves, he evaded the enemy's fire to such good effect that the Messerschmitt struck the sea and crashed; Franklin had not fired a shot!

Nine Hurricanes of No. 32 Squadron were next in action at 12.46 hours and were quickly reinforced by eleven Hurricanes of No. 615 Squadron in a vicious dogfight against more than 40 Bf 109s. The enemy fighters were, however, running short of fuel and quickly disengaged after severely damaging Plt. Off. Victor Daw's aircraft.

As both sides withdrew, a mass attack by over 60 Ju 87s of three *Stukageschwader* developed, meeting only the gunfire from the convoy's escort. In answer to frantic calls for fighters, nine Spitfires of No. 54 Squadron made for the area, but were utterly overwhelmed by an avalanche of 109s which shot down Plt. Off. Douglas Turley-George and killed Basil Way, "B" Flight's popular flight commander. Although claims were entered for the destruction of several of the enemy, the raiders evidently escaped without loss.

Interpreting the enemy's intention to saturate the defences by mounting increasingly heavy attacks, the No. 11 Group Controller preferred to feed relatively light forces into the area of the convoy—until a main attack developed—so that when only eight Spitfires of No. 64 Squadron took off to fly guard over the ships at 14.30 hours their pilots found 30 Junkers Ju 88s of Hauptmann Bloedorn's III./KG 4, heavily escorted by more than fifty Bf 109s. As Sqn. Ldr. Aeneas MacDonnell (the squadron's newly-arrived commander[62]) radioed a hurried "tally-ho" and led his tiny formation to the attack, his three remaining Spitfires scrambled from Kenley, as did twelve Hurricanes of No. 111 Squadron from Hawkinge. Once again John Thompson's pilots entered the battle with their terrifying head-on charge and, beset by attacks from all sides, the Junkers broke and turned for home. So

confused was the fighting that the Hurricane pilots afterwards claimed that they had occasionally been fired on by Spitfires. On seeing the Ju 88s abandoning the attack, the Messerschmitt pilots disengaged and left the scene of battle.

As the attacks continued throughout the afternoon, the sorely-pressed men of the convoy must have realised that they were the *Luftwaffe*'s principal target, and three relatively harmless sweeps by low-flying formations of Messerschmitts served their purpose of aggravating the strain upon the ships' gunners—for their approach was not plotted on the coastal radar. As the ships left Dover astern and Folkestone lay on their starboard beam, 60 dive bombers struck at the convoy, diving out of the afternoon sun, and hit several ships, sinking five and damaging four, including the destroyers H.M.S. *Boreas* and *Brilliant*, which had sped to the convoy's rescue from Dover. The raid had caught the convoy between fighter patrols and the nine Hurricanes of No. 56 Squadron arrived as the bombing was in progress. Apparently oblivious of the Messerschmitt escort, Flt. Lt. John Coghlan flew straight to the assistance of the destroyers and engaged the Junkers, blunting their attack. The German chose this moment to launch a forey by nine E-boats which caused the ships to scatter, but not before a further three vessels had been hit by gunfire.

Three Spitfire pilots of No. 64 Squadron and ten of No. 54 Squadron, who were patrolling nearby, now joined the fray and engaged the Messerschmitts, but the enemy clearly had the upper hand for, every time the few British fighters managed to manœuvre into a favourable position, they were immediately forced to break away by other Bf 109s which fell on them from above. It was in this fight that that very gallant naval pilot, Sub-Lt. Francis Dawson-Paul was shot down, severely wounded; he was to be rescued by one of the German E-boats but died several days later in a hospital in France.

One further attack developed at 18.30 hours and on this occasion, for the second day running, the Biggin Hill pilots of No. 610 Squadron were able to shoot down two Messerschmitts of 7./JG 52 without loss. As darkness fell, the two destroyers were limping into Dover, one under tow.

While the Dover convoy had been the target for *Luftflotte 2*, Portland harbour had again attracted several raids, and three fighter squadrons had between them flown more than a hundred sorties. No. 152 Squadron had been the most successful—shooting down a Dornier 17 and a Junkers 87. A further Ju 87 was damaged by naval anti-aircraft gunfire over the base.

The day's fighting had brought fifteen Fighter Command squadrons into action and had cost them six Spitfires destroyed and four pilots killed (three of them highly experienced men). Nos. 54 and 64 Squadrons lost three aircraft apiece, and the cumulative pressure on the former was to cause its withdrawal to the North on the following day. Three weeks' fighting had cost it five pilots killed and three wounded, and twelve Spitfires destroyed. The pilots had flown 504 combat sorties in three weeks (a Command record) and flown just over 800 hours in the same period.

---

[62] Squadron Leader MacDonnell, the Hereditary Chief of Glengarry, had graduated from the R.A.F. College, Cranwell, in 1934; he was to be awarded the D.F.C. later in the Battle of Britain with a score of ten enemy aircraft destroyed. He retired from the Royal Air Force in 1964 on his 50th birthday as an Air Commodore.

R.A.F. FIGHTER COMMAND LOSSES—THURSDAY 25th JULY 1940

1.	32 Sqn., Hawkinge	C	Shot down by Bf 109s near Dover; pilot force landed, wounded in the leg.	A13.00 hrs.	Plt. Off. V.G. Daw	Hurricane	—	Cat. 2 Damaged
2.	43 Sqn., Northolt	NC	Night training accident; pilot unhurt.	At night	Plt. Off. R. Lane	Hurricane	N2665	Cat. 2 Damaged
3.	54 Sqn., Hornchurch	C	Shot down by Bf 109s near Dover; pilot killed.	Not known	Flt. Lt. B.H. Way	Spitfire	R6707	Cat. 3 Destroyed
4.	54 Sqn., Hornchurch	C	Shot down by Bf 109s near Dover; pilot unhurt.	Not known	Plt. Off. D.R. Turley-George	Spitfire	P9387	Cat. 3 Destroyed
5.	54 Sqn., Hornchurch	C	Shot down by Bf 109s off Dover; pilot killed.	16.30 hrs.	Plt. Off. A. Finnie	Spitfire	R6816	Cat. 3 Destroyed
6.	64 Sqn., Kenley	C	Shot down by Bf 109s off Dover; pilot killed.	15.05 hrs.	Fg. Off. A.J.O. Jeffrey	Spitfire	P9421	Cat. 3 Lost
7.	64 Sqn., Kenley	C	Aircraft severely damaged in combat with Ju 88s off Dover, but pilot landed safely, unhurt.	15.10 hrs.	Sqn. Ldr. A.R.D. MacDonnell	Spitfire	L1055	Cat. 2 Damaged
8.	64 Sqn., Kenley	C	Shot down by Bf 109s off Kent coast; pilot killed.	A18.00 hrs.	Sub-Lt. F. Dawson-Paul	Spitfire	L1035	Cat. 3 Lost
9.	152 Sqn., Warmwell	C	Shot down by Bf 109s twenty miles south of Portland; pilot baled out and was picked up	11.20 hrs.	Fg. Off. E.C. Deanesly	Spitfire	K9901	Cat. 3 Lost
10.	222 Sqn., Kirton-in-	NC	Force landed owing to fuel shortage; pilot unhurt.	Not known.	Plt. Off. J.W. Cutts.	Spitfire	—	Cat. 2 Damaged
11.	234 Sqn., St. Eval	NC	Crashed at night at Porthtowan; pilot killed.	23.45 hrs.	Plt. Off. G.K. Gout	Spitfire	P9493	Cat. 3 Destroyed

The wreckage of an elderly Do 17M flown by the Staff Flight of *Stukageschwader 1*; it was shot down on 25th July after a running fight with Deanesly, Wolton and Holmes of No. 152 Squadron.

LUFTWAFFE LOSSES—THURSDAY 25th JULY 1940

1.	Weküsta. 1	CM	Shot down by Hurricanes of Jones and Lonsdale of 3 Sqn., near Wick at 07.25 hrs.	Heinkel He 111H-3	100 %	Reg. Rat a. Kr. Franken + two missing; two killed.
2.	Stab/KG 3	CM	Possible damaged in combat with Spitfires of 54, 65 and 610 Sqns. Landed at Antwerp.	Dornier Do 17Z-3	10 %	Crew unhurt.
3.	4./KG 3	CM	Destroyed in crash landing at Combleux with fuel shortage.	Dornier Do 17Z-3	100 %	Oblt. Schrader wounded.
4.	1./KG 4	CM	Suffered explosion during mining sortie over the Bristol Channel. Crashed 9 miles north of Honiton.	Heinkel He 111H-4 (5J+AH)	100 %	Gefr. Helmuth Grabke, Uffz. Wilhelm Fommer, Ofw. Hermann Kessler and Uffz. Gerhard Hähnel killed; Uffz. Georg Strickstrock, wounded, made P.O.W.
5.	II./KG 51	CM	Fate not known. Not claimed by R.A.F.fighters.	Junkers Ju 88A	100 %	Ltn. Walter Theiner killed; one crew member missing.
6.	8./KG 76	CM	Take-off accident at Cormeilles-en-Vexin.	Dornier Do 17Z	30 %	Crew unhurt.
7.	Stab/St.G 1	CM	Shot down by Spitfires of Deanesly, Wolton and Holmes of 152 Sqn. near Fleet, Hants, at 11.23 hrs.	Dornier Do 17M (3620 : A5+EA)	100 %	Uffz. Kurt Lengenbrink killed. Fw. Bernard Erdmann and Fw. Erich Grossman made P.O.W.s.
8.	III./St.G 1	CM	Shot down by Spitfires of Wolton and Hogg of 152 Sqn. off Portland at 11.30 hrs.	Junkers Ju 87B	100 %	One killed and one missing.
9.	III./St.G 1	CM	Damaged by naval A.A. gunfire at Portland.	Junkers Ju 87B	30 %	Crew unhurt.
10.	11(Stuka)/LG 1	CM	Damaged by Hurricane of Maunsdon of 56 Sqn. during attack on Dover destroyers at 17.10 hrs.	Junkers Ju 87B	15 %	One crew member wounded.

Luftwaffe Losses, 25th July 1940—*continued*

11.	I.(Nacht)/ZG 1	CM	Possibly shot down by R.A.F. bombers; crashed at Coesfeld.	Messerschmitt Bf 110	100 %		Ltn. Back + one killed.
12.	I.(Nacht)/ZG 1	CM	Flying accident at Gütersloh.	Messerschmitt Bf 110 C-4	90 %		One crew member wounded
13.	III./JG 27	CM	Shot down by Hurricane of Goodman of 1 Sqn. into sea off Portland at 15.28 hrs.	Messerschmitt Bf 109 E-4	100 %		Oblt. Karl-Heinz Kirstein killed.
14.	III./JG 52	CM	Shot down by Spitfire of Else of 610 Sqn. off Folkesstone at 18.53 hrs.	Messerschmitt Bf 109E	100 %		Ltn. Schmidt missing.
15.	7./JG 52	CM	Shot down by Spitfires of Wilson and Ellis of 610 Sqn. off Folkestone at 18.53 hrs.	Messerschmitt Bf 109E	100 %		Oblt. Keidel, *St.Kap.*, missing.
16.	7./JG 52	CM	Shot down by Hurricane of Wilson of 111 Sqn. off Dover at 15.12 hrs.	Messerschmitt Bf 109E	100 %		Oblt. Bielefeld, *St. Führer*, killed.
17.	8./JG 52	CM	Forced down by Franklin in Spitfire of 65 Sqn. off Dover at 12.45 hrs.	Messerschmitt Bf 109E	100 %		Pilot missing.
18.	Erpr.Gr. 210	CM	Believed shot down by A.A. in Harwich area.	Messerschmitt Bf 110C	100 %		Oblt. Fallenbach + one killed.
19.	2./406	CM	Collision during night take-off at Stavanger.	Dornier Do 18	100 %		One crew member injured.
20.	2./406	CM	Collision (with Item 19) at Stavanger.	Dornier Do 18	100 %		No crew casualties.
21.	Seenotflug-kdo. 5	CM	Crashed on take-off at Norderny.	Heinkel He 59	100 %		No crew casualties.

Friday 26th July

After the spirited actions of the previous day, and with low cloud and heavy rain over much of Britain, there was a marked pause in German operations on the 26th.

Only relatively small groups of ships were moving in the Channel during the morning and, though these were the targets of several small dive-bomber formations which were not engaged, the vessels continued on their way unscathed. A pilot of No. 601 Squadron was "bounced" by a free chase and shot down south of St. Catherine's Point, but the score was evened when, after a short combat, Flt. Lt. Stuart Walch of No. 238 Squadron destroyed a Bf 109 of JG 27 off Portland. Spitfires of No. 65 Squadron damaged two reconnaissance aircraft off the Kent coast.

At night a Hurricane pilot (Plt. Off John Cock of No. 87 Squadron) flying a "cat's eye" patrol was lucky to catch sight of an enemy bomber over the Bristol Channel and shot it

down near Portishead Point. It transpired that this raider was part of a small force of Dornier Do 17s from KG 76—their crews briefed to raid Southampton. As a means of avoiding radar detection, the crews set course westerly from their base at Beauvais to fly round Land's End and up the Bristol Channel, attacking the south coast port from the north-west. Although the enemy raiders were plotted by Carnanton CH, it was little more than fortuitous that the Hurricane pilot caught sight of the Dornier—even more so that he managed to destroy it. (He mistakenly identified it as a Heinkel He 111.)

With the departure of Sqn. Ldr. James Leathart's No. 54 Squadron northwards for a well-earned rest at Catterick, Dowding ordered its place at Hornchurch to be taken by No. 41 Squadron—commanded by Sqn. Ldr. Hamish West. In little over 24 hours his squadron would be in action.

R.A.F. FIGHTER COMMAND LOSSES—FRIDAY 26th JULY 1940

1.	87 Sqn., Exeter	NC	Night landing accident at Hullavington; pilot killed.	At night	Sgt. J.H. Culverwell	Hurricane	P3596	Cat. 3 Destroyed
2.	92 Sqn., Pembrey	NC	Night landing accident at Pembrey; pilot unhurt.	At night	Sgt. S.M. Barraclough	Spitfire	N3167	Cat. 3 Destroyed
3.	266 Sqn., Wittering	NC	Landing accident in rain at Wittering; pilot unhurt.	Not known	Sqn. Ld. D.G.H. Spencer	Spitfire	N3118	Cat. 2 Damaged
4.	501 Sqn., Hawkinge	C	Believed shot down by Dover A.A. guns; pilot killed.	A17.50 hrs.	Flt. Lt. P.A.N. Cox	Hurricane	P3808	Cat. 3 Lost
5.	601 Sqn., Tangmere	C	Shot down by Bf 109s two miles south of St. Catherine's Point; pilot killed in aircraft.	10.05 hrs.	Plt. Off. P.C. Lindsey	Hurricane	P2753	Cat. 3 Lost
6.	603 Sqn., Dyce	NC	Damaged while landing in mud at Dyce; pilot unhurt.	Not known	Plt. Off G.K. Gilroy	Spitfire	N3288	Cat. 1 Damaged
7.	609 Sqn., Warmwell	NC	Crashed at Piddlehinton, Dorset, after pilot became blinded by glycol; otherwise unhurt.	Not known	Not known	Spitfire	K9815	Cat. 3 Destroyed
8.	616 Sqn., Leconfield	NC	Damaged in dawn landing at Leconfield; pilot unhurt.	05.10 hrs.	Not known	Spitfire	—	Cat. 2 Damaged

LUFTWAFFE LOSSES—FRIDAY 26th JULY 1940

1.	Aufkl.Gr. (H)/21	NCM	Taxiing accident at Lessay airfield.	Henschel Hs 126B	2 %		No crew casualties.
2.	3.(F)/121	CM	Damaged by Spitfires of 65 Sqn., near Folkestone at 16.55 hrs.	Junkers Ju 88A	10 %		One crew member killed.
3.	5.(F)/122	CM	Damaged by Spitfires of 65 Sqn., near Folkestone at 16.30 hrs.	Dornier Do 17P	5 %		No crew casualties.
4.	I./KG 55	NCM	Accident at Grandpré; cause unknown.	Heinkel He 111P	15 %		No crew casualties.
5.	3./KG 76	CM	Shot down by Cock in Hurricane of 87 Sqn. at night over Portishead Point.	Dornier Do 17Z	100 %		Four crew members missing.
6.	7./KG 77	NCM	Landing accident at Regensburg airfield.	Junkers Ju 88A (3131 : 3Z+AR)	12 %		No crew casualties.
7.	I./JG 27	NCM	Landing accident at Plumetot airfield.	Messerschmitt Bf 109B	50 %		Pilot unhurt.
8.	2./JG 27	CM	Shot down by Walsh in Hurricane of 238 Sqn. 25 miles south of Portsmouth at 11.55 hrs.	Messerschmitt Bf 109	100 %		Fw. Günther Böer missing.

Saturday 27th July

With the threat of thunder in the air, the early morning hours of this Saturday were undisturbed by enemy aircraft, yet news reached Sperrle's headquarters in Paris of the presence at dawn of a large convoy off Portland. Forthwith a strike of 30 Junkers Ju 87s of I./St.G 77 was despatched from Caen shortly before 08.00 hours, collecting its escort of JG 27 Messerschmitts *en route*.

As coastal radar reported the forty-plus raid approaching convoy BACON, No. 10 Group fighter states were hurriedly advanced and three Hurricanes scrambled from Middle Wallop, arriving just as the dive-bombers started to "peel off".

Although Fg. Off. Davis of No. 238 Squadron shot down one of the Ju 87s, the close attendance of the Bf 109s frustrated the main efforts of the three British pilots and the raiders withdrew without further loss shortly before 09.00 hours.

As the Stuka pilots flew off southwards, their course crossed that of a second wave of twenty Junkers Ju 87s from Caen, which struck the convoy off Swanage at 09.45 hours but found six Spitfires and three Hurricanes overhead. Once again the close escort of Bf 109s was effective in protecting the vulnerable dive-bombers and shot down a Spitfire of No. 609 Squadron, killing Plt. Off J.R. Buchanan.

The towering cumulonimbus clouds which had been building up all morning finally discharged a number of violent storms over Southern England during the afternoon, virtually halting all combat operations. Once again the balloon barrage suffered, with more than twenty balloons lining the Thames Estuary struck by lightning; also struck was a small building on which was perched an Observer Corps post—much to the discomfort of the crew on duty!

As the storms moved away to the east, and convoy BACON entered the Biggin Hill Sector, Park advanced his fighter state by moving three whole squadrons forward to Hawkinge and Manston. The precaution proved unnecessary as no enemy raid materialised, although just as the twelve Hurricanes of No. 615 Squadron were about to touch down at Hawkinge at 18.30 hours they were diverted to investigate an X-raid off Deal; here they found a Heinkel He 59 seaplane of *Seenotflugkommando 3* flying a few feet above the sea, and shot it down.

A number of small enemy formations had carried out convoy attacks off the East Coast, and heavy bombs from Heinkel He 111s struck and sank H.M. Destroyer *Wren*, 1,120 tons, off Aldeburgh, Suffolk. The destroyer flotilla leader H.M.S. *Codrington* (1,540 tons) was hit and sunk in Dover harbour[63].

Only the previous day R.A.F. reconnaissance had revealed that the Germans were preparing a battery of very heavy coastal guns on the French coast near Calais, and this news accompanying the loss of several naval vessels in the Dover area prompted the Admiralty to abandon Dover as a base for anti-invasion warships, and withdrew the remaining destroyers to Harwich and Sheerness. Sorely though the loss of two destroyers was felt, it did not substantially reduce the force of four flotillas (originally 36 ships) based between the Humber and Portsmouth. The withdrawal from Dover must, however, be acknowledged as a minor victory for Kesselring's *Luftflotte 2* in its prime objective of denying the Royal Navy freedom of the English Channel.

---

[63] H.M. Destroyer *Codrington* was the ship which conveyed the Dutch Crown Princess and her family from Ijmuiden to England on 12th May during the German invasion of the Netherlands. The ship had also evacuated numerous British soldiers in the Dunkirk evacuation.

R.A.F. FIGHTER COMMAND LOSSES—SATURDAY 27th JULY 1940

1.	87 Sqn., Exeter	NC	Take-off collision with another Hurricane (see Item 2); pilot injured.	Not known	Plt. Off. C.W.W. Darwin	Hurricane	—	Cat. 3 Destroyed
2.	87 Sqn., Exeter	NC	Take-off collision with another Hurricane (see Item 1); pilot unhurt.	Not known	Not known	Hurricane	—	Cat. 1 Damaged
3.	92 Sqn., Pembrey	NC	Pilot became lost at night and baled out near Exeter without injury.	At night	Plt. Off. T.S. Wade	Spitfire	N3287	Cat. 3 Lost
4.	232 Sqn., Sumburgh	NC	Aircraft hit by Blenheim taking off; no casualties.	Not known	None	Hurricane	P3411	Cat. 2 Damaged
5.	236 Sqn., Thorney Island	NC	Aircraft force landed in storm, short of fuel; crew unhurt.	12.06 hrs.	Sgt. N.P.G. Barron	Blenheim	L1119	Cat. 2 Damaged
6.	609 Sqn., Warmwell	C	Shot down over Weymouth Bay by Bf 109s; pilot killed	Not known	Plt. Off. J.R. Buchanan	Spitfire	N3023	Cat. 3 Lost.

LUFTWAFFE LOSSES—SATURDAY 27th JULY 1940

1.	I./KG 51	CM	Shot down by Hughes, Connor and Bailey in Hurricanes of 234 Sqn. 25 miles SE of Land's End at 15.09 hrs.	Junkers Ju 88A	100 %	Ltn. Ruckdeschel + three missing.
2.	III./KG 53	CM	Fate not confirmed; possibly shot down by Hurricanes of 504 Sqn., from Castletown.	Heinkel He 111H-2	100 %	One crew killed; four missing.
3.	II./KG 54	NCM	Landing accident at St. André airfield.	Junkers Ju 88A	15 %	No crew casualties.
4.	8./KG 55	CM	Shot down by flak north-west of Newbury at 02.00 hrs after raid north of Bristol.	Heinkel He 111H-2	100 %	Fw. Theodore Metzner, Fw. Josef Mankl, Uff. Kurt Böker, Gefr. Morganthal and Gefr. Ostheimer, made P.O.W.s.
5.	III./KG 77	NCM	Landing accident at Regensburg airfield.	Junkers Ju 88A	20 %	No crew casualties.
6.	I./St.G 77	CM	Shot down by Davis in Hurricane of 238 Sqn. over Convoy BACON in Weymouth Bay at 08.58 hrs.	Junkers Ju 87B	100 %	One crew member killed and one missing.
7.	V./LG 1	NCM	Flying accident at Théville.	Messerschmitt Bf 110C	10 %	No crew casualties.

8.	Seenotflug-kdo. 3	CM	Shot down by six Hurricanes of 615 Sqn., 10 miles north-east of Dover at 18.50 hrs.	Heinkel He 59	100 %	Oblt. Chudziak + three crew members missing.

Sunday 28th July

The summer storms of the previous day had cleared the air for fine weather over much of England on this Sunday, and No. 10 Group fighters were quickly off the mark when three Spitfires of No. 234 Squadron—Flt. Lt. Paterson Hughes (Australian), Plt. Off. Kenneth Dewhurst (British), and Plt. Off. Patrick Horton (New Zealander)—were ordered up from St. Eval to investigate a plot south of Plymouth and came across a Junkers Ju 88 of II./LG 1, which they shot down thirty miles out to sea at 15.32 hours.

In anticipation of heavy raids off the Kent coast, the Biggin Hill, Horchurch and North Weald Sector Controllers moved eight squadrons forward to Hawkinge, Manston and Martlesham. When, at 13.50 hours, a large raid was plotted approaching Dover, twelve Spitfires of No. 74 Squadron, led by Flt. Lt. "Sailor" Malan—the famous South African—were ordered off from Manston. Hurricanes were also scrambled from Hawkinge with orders to attack the bombers, leaving the Messerschmitts to the Spitfires—a judicious precaution re-

Sqn. Ldr. Adolphus "Salor" Malan, popular and widely respected C.O. of No. 74—"Tiger"—Squadron, who wounded Werner Mölders in a dogfight on 28th July. Malan, photographed here with his dog Peter, was a South African ex-merchant seaman; he was one of the handful of junior fighter commanders whose wartime exploits were to make them legends in their own lifetime.

sulting from combat confusion in previous days. For some unknown reason, however, the enemy bombers turned away and flew off to the south-east without dropping any bombs.

Above and behind them a sharp dogfight developed when Malan's Spitfires joined combat with four *Staffeln* from I and II.*Gruppen*, *Jagdgeschwader 51*, led by Major Werner Mölders[64]. Malan, after a determined assault on one of the Messerschmitts in the leading *Kette*, which he shot down, found himself beset by another enemy fighter turning on to his tail, and turned so sharply that he was able to rake the Messerschmitt from nose to tail; from detailed reconstruction of the fight from combat reports, there is no doubt but that the second Bf 109 was flown by Mölders himself, the wounded German commander managing to put down his failing aircraft in a crash landing at Wissant. Malan's pilots had acquitted themselves well and shot down three Bf 109s and damaged two others, for the loss of two Spitfires and one pilot killed (Plt. Off. James Young).

Shortly after this fight the Germans sent out a number of Heinkel He 59 rescue seaplanes to search the Dover Strait for ditched pilots. One of these aircraft was sighted by Pilot Officer Robert Wilson of No. 111 Squadron, and shot down by Sgt. James Robinson. A quarter of an hour later the same squadron spotted another He 59 riding on the sea only ten miles west of Boulogne, presumably engaged in picking up an enemy pilot; Fg. Off. Henry Ferris dived down and emptied more than 2,000 rounds into the hapless aircraft. . .

While this small drama was being enacted, No. 41 Squadron's Spitfires were in action with a *Staffel* of JG 53's Bf 109s near Dover; in a sharp engagement Plt. Off. G.H. ("Ben") Bennions shot down the aircraft of Ltn. Below—who was evidently rescued, wounded, by an enemy seaplane; the British pilot had just come to the aid of Fg. Off. Anthony Lovell, who was hit in the thigh by fire from the 109, but managed to crash land his Spitfire at Manston.

[64] Werner Mölders was the greatest German fighter pilot of the early War years. He was one of only three *Luftwaffe* fighter pilots to be awarded the Oakleaves to the Knight's Cross before the end of the Battle of Britain (the others were Galland of JG 26, and Helmut Wick of JG 2). Mölders won the Swords on 22nd June 1941 and, less than a month later, the Diamonds. He was to lose his life on 22nd November 1941. Such was the esteem in which he was held that his *Geschwader*, JG 51, carried his name as "honour title" after his death. His younger brother also served in JG 51 but was shot down and captured during the Battle of Britain.

R.A.F. FIGHTER COMMAND LOSSES—SUNDAY 28th JULY 1940

1.	41 Sqn., Manston	C	Pilot wounded in thigh during combat with Bf 109 flown by Ltn. Below of JG 53 near Dover, and crash landed at base.	A15.30 hrs.	Fg. Off. A.D.J. Lovell	Spitfire	*P9429*	Cat. 3 Destroyed
2.	74 Sqn., Manston	C	Shot down by Bf 109s near Dover; pilot killed	A14.30 hrs.	Plt. Off. J.H.R. Young	Spitfire	*P9547*	Cat. 3 Lost
3.	74 Sqn., Manston	C	Shot down by Bf 109s near Dover; pilot baled out, wounded, and admitted to Dover Military Hospital.	A14.30 hrs.	Sgt. E.A. Mould	Spitfire	*P9336*	Cat. 3 Lost

R.A.F. Losses, 28th July 1940—*continued*

4.	245 Sqn., Aldergrove	NC	Landing accident at Aldergrove after patrol; pilot seriously injured.	A07.30 hrs.	Sgt. P. Killick	Hurricane	—	Cat. 3 Destroyed
5.	257 Sqn., Northolt	C	Shot down by Bf 109 south of Maidstone; pilot baled out, slightly wounded.	18.40 hrs.	Sgt. R.V. Forward	Hurricane	*P3622*	Cat. 3 Destroyed
6.	611 Sqn., Digby	NC	Landed wheels-up at Digby; pilot unhurt.	Not known	Plt. Off. J.W. Lund	Spitfire	*K9970*	Cat. 2 Damaged

LUFTWAFFE LOSSES—SUNDAY 28th JULY 1940

1.	II./KG 2	NCM	Flying accident at Beyreuth.	Dornier Do 17Z	100 %	One killed; one technician injured.
2.	9./KG 4	CM	Damaged by A.A. fire in Thames Estuary and crashed at Théville.	Junkers Ju 88A-1	100 %	One crew member killed and three wounded.
3.	9./KG 4	CM	Damaged by A.A. fire in Thames Estuary and crashed at Schipol.	Junkers Ju 88A-1	100 %	Obly. Podbielski + three wounded.
4.	I./KG 51	CM	Force landed at Laroche after engine failure.	Junkers Ju 88A-1	40 %	No crew casualties.
5.	II./LG 1	CM	Shot down by Hughes, Dewhurst and Horton in Spitfires of 234 Sqn., 30 miles south of Plymouth at 15.32 hrs.	Junkers Ju 88A	100 %	Ltn. Pfanf + two missing; one wounded.
6.	3.(Nacht)/JG 1	CM	Not encountered by R.A.F. ; crashed at Ennigerloh.	Messerschmitt Bf 110	100 %	Two crew members killed.
7.	II./JG 27	CM	Damaged by Spitfires of 41 Sqn. near Dover at 13.05 hrs; force landed at Francker.	Messerschmitt Bf 109 E-3	60 %	Oblt. Karl Preiser wounded.
8.	Stab/JG 51	CM	Damaged by Malan in Spitfire of 74 Sqn., near Dover at 14.10 hrs.	Messerschmitt Bf 109 E-3	80 %	Maj. Mölders, *Gesch.Kdr.*, wounded.
9.	1./JG 51	CM	Damaged by Stevenson in Spitfire of 74 Sqn. near Dover at 14.15 hrs; landed at Wissant.	Messerschmitt Bf 109 E-1	20 %	Pilot unhurt.
10.	I./JG 51	CM	Shot down by Malan in Spitfire of 74 Sqn. near Dover at 14.08 hrs.	Messerschmitt Bf 109 E-1	100 %	Pilot missing.
11.	I./JG 51	CM	Shot down by Freeborn in Spitfire of 74 Sqn. near Dover, and crashed at Wissant.	Messerschmitt Bf 109 E-4	100 %	Hptm. Eichele killed.
12.	4./JG 51	CM	Damaged by St. John in Spitfire of 74 Sqn. near Dover and force landed in France with engine failure.	Messerschmitt Bf 109 E-3	50 %	Pilot unhurt.
13.	6./JG 51	CM	Shot down by Kelly in Spitfire of 74 Sqn. between Dover and Calais at 14.12 hrs.	Messerschmitt Bf 109 E-1	100 %	Uffz. Hemmerling killed.
14.	III./JG 53	CM	Shot down by Bennions in Spitfire of 41 Sqn. near Dover at approx. 15.00 hrs.	Messerschmitt Bf 109 E-1	100 %	Ltn. Below wounded.
15.	Seenotflug-kdo. 1	CM	Shot up on the water by Ferris in Hurricane of 111 Sqn. 10 miles west of Boulogne at 15.20 hrs.	Heinkel He 59	60 %	Ltn. Wölke + one wounded.
16.	Seenotflug-kdo. 3	CM	Shot down in mid-Channel by Robinson in Hurricane of 111 Sqn. at 15.05 hrs.	Heinkel He 59	100 %	Two killed; Ltn. Sandgaard + two wounded.

A wounded gunner being helped from a Heinkel He 111 on a French airfield after a raid over Britain. The officer on the left wears the cuff title of *Kampfgeschwader 4 "General Wever"*. (Photo: Hans Obert).

German bombs explode in the waters of Dover harbour during the early morning raid of 29th July.

Monday 29th July

With fine weather and cloudless skies following a misty dawn, Kent Sector Operations Rooms were soon receiving news of a large raid building up behind Calais. As there were two fairly sizeable convoys off No. 11 Group's coasts, the Controllers were reluctant to order up heavy formations until the enemy showed his hand. As the raid moved down the CH radar time bases at 07.20 hours, it suddenly became obvious that neither convoy was the target, but that it was aimed directly at Dover. Eleven Spitfires of No. 41 Squadron were therefore immediately ordered off from Manston, and were airborne within five minutes, climbing hard to attack the enemy's right flank. Twelve Hurricanes of No. 501 Squadron took off simultaneously from Hawkinge to strike the left. The Spitfires were the first to make contact and found 48 Junkers Ju 87s (drawn from six *Staffeln* of IV.(Stuka)/LG 1, II./St.G 1 and II./St.G 4), escorted by about 80 Bf 109s.

The German fighter commander had chosen to position his greatest strength high on the right flank so as to be looking down-sun at his charges. In fact, before No. 41 Squadron dived to attack the Ju 87s, the British pilots had not seen the Bf 109s in the sun, and were soon being viciously engaged. Hurriedly splitting his force, Flt. Lt. John Webster turned six Spitfires against the escort, leaving the others to deal with the dive bombers. Fg. Off. Douglas Gamblen was shot down and killed almost immediately near Deal. Four Spitfires were damaged and crashed on landing (fortunately without injury to their pilots). The Ju 87s were now being heavily assailed as No. 501 Squadron's Hurricanes waded in. As the waters of Dover harbour erupted under the storm of heavy bombs, four dive bombers were shot down into the sea. The score would almost certainly have been higher had not the Dover anti-aircraft guns persisted in firing barrage into the midst of the dogfight[65].

Notwithstanding this major attack on Dover (which caused

remarkably little damage), the two convoys already mentioned were not to escape the enemy's attention, and one of them was attacked by a small force of Junkers Ju 88s of II./KG 76 which approached at very low level. Eyewitness accounts vary as to the course of this raid and it is believed that the leading aircraft flew headlong into a balloon cable[66], while another was shot down by Oerlikon guns on one of the escort vessels. The low altitude at which the bombers attacked prevented their approach being spotted by shore radar and, when the twelve Spitfires of No. 610 Squadron eventually arrived, the raiders had long since departed. A Dornier Do 17 put in an appearance at this point and although the Spitfires pumped about 10,000 rounds in the enemy's direction, the bomber dumped its load and hurriedly took to its heels. As No. 610 Squadron was under orders to cover the ships, the pilots could not give chase.

The attack on the other convoy is graphically described in a German account taken from the diary of a Messerschmitt pilot of *Erprobungsgruppe 210* who was shot down and killed over Sussex on 15th August.

"My second War Flight[67]. A Dornier Do 17 has reported an English convoy of sixty ships sailing northwards from the Thames Estuary. *Erprobungsgruppe 210* starts off from St. Omer at 16.35 hours; eight Bf 110 bombers of the 2nd *Staffel* and three Bf 110C-6s of the 1st *Staffel* fly over Dunkirk and meet thirty Bf 110C-2s of *Zerstörergeschwader 26* who are acting as fighter escort on account of probable clear skies. Thirty minutes' flying northwards at sea level, then ten minutes climbing northwards to the clouds at 4,500 feet. The bombers attack at 17.15 hours just off Orfordness in position

---

[65] Almost since the advent of the bomb-dropping aeroplane, ships of the Royal Navy have been under uncompromising orders to fire at any aircraft, whether or not identified as an enemy, considered to be in a position to endanger the vessel. Considering the ordeal faced by the crews of the destroyers in Dover harbour—vital target of the *Luftwaffe* as they were—no blame can surely attach to the gun crews for their seeming "trigger-happiness".

[66] If this is correct, the aircraft carried to his death Oberstleutnant Genth, *Gruppenkommandeur* of III.*Gruppe*, KG 76.

[67] In this account all times have been converted to conform to British times. The reference to this being the pilot's "second war flight" is interesting. The British were as yet unaware of the existence of Erpr. Gr. 210, a special fighter-bomber unit formed less than a month before to pioneer pathfinding techniques. The only previous traceable operation by the unit was an attack on or near Harwich on 25th July. Erpr. Gr. 210 was commanded by Hauptmann Walter Rubensdörffer, presumably "the Chief" referred to here, about whom more will be told anon.

1219. At the same time two Hurricane squadrons approach from the left, one below us and one above. The Chief makes a tight climbing turn and I fall back a bit, then it is a flat-out climb. I have to abandon the idea of getting on the tail of one of the lower Englishmen because the upper formation comes at me from above and to the right. Straightening up for a moment I fire a short burst at a singleton who comes past me, but he doesn't fall. The next moment my gunner shouts something unintelligible and a hail of fire sears through my whole aircraft from the right. The intercom packs up completely, but in another two seconds I'm in the clouds; I circle to take stock and decide to beat it. Above the clouds I come across three Bf 110s, the Chief and two aircraft of ZG 26 who want to attack again. I feel inclined to join them but my gunner calls out: "I am wounded: let's go home". So I head for the Dutch coast, flying low. My trim tabs are shot away and oil spurts from the starboard engine. At last at 18.05 hours I land at St. Omer with tyres shot through. My aircraft has suffered about 30 hits; one shot struck an ammunition drum and exploded all the cartridges. Other hits in engines, cockpit, wings and flaps. Result of the attack—One hit on a 1,000-ton ship and one hit on an 8,000-ton ship. ZG 26 bagged four Hurricanes without loss."

In fact only one squadron of Hurricanes had been engaged; this was No. 151 Squadron, which split into Flights of six aircraft each. Casualties amounted to two aircraft which force landed at Rochford and Martlesham, but neither pilot was hit. An interesting point arising out of this German account is the reference to the reconnaissance Dornier which passed the sighting report on the convoy. Such a Dornier was sighted near the convoy by Fg. Off. Patrick Woods-Scawen of No. 85 Squadron, on patrol out of Martlesham at 15.00 hrs. Although he chased the enemy all the way to the Belgian coast and fired all his ammunition, the Dornier evidently managed to radio the size, position and course of the convoy. This aircraft, a Staff-crewed machine of Oberst Fink's KG 2, crash landed at St. Inglevert—not far from Erpr.Gr.210's base at St. Omer.

Among other operations on this day was a sudden raid launched at low level against a small group of ships off Portland, which caught the air defences off guard. Before No. 10 Group could put up adequate cover, H.M. Destroyer *Delight* (1,375 tons) had been struck by a bomb and sank shortly afterwards. The enemy raiders escaped without loss.

R.A.F. FIGHTER COMMAND LOSSES—MONDAY 29th JULY 1940

1.	41 Sqn., Manston	C	Shot down by Bf 109s near Dover; pilot killed.	A08.00 hrs.	Fg. Off. D.R. Gamblen	Spitfire	N3038	Cat. 3 Lost
2.	41 Sqn., Manston	C	Landing crash after combat with Bf 109s near Dover; pilot unhurt.	A08.20 hrs.	Flt. Lt. J.T. Webster	Spitfire	—	Cat. 2 Damaged
3.	41 Sqn., Manston	C	Landing crash after combat with Bf 109s near Dover; pilot unhurt.	A08.20 hrs.	Fg. Off. W.J.M. Scott	Spitfire	—	Cat. 2 Damaged
4.	41 Sqn., Manston	C	Landing crash after combat with Bf 109s near Dover; pilot unhurt.	A08.20 hrs.	Plt. Off. J.N. MacKenzie	Spitfire	—	Cat. 2 Damaged
5.	41 Sqn., Manston	C	Landing crash with damaged flaps after combat with Bf 109s near Dover; pilot unhurt.	A08.20 hrs.	Plt. Off. G.H. Bennions	Spitfire	—	Cat. 2 Damaged
6.	43 Sqn., Hawkinge	NC	Crashed during force landing in Kent after engine failure; pilot killed.	Not known	Plt. Off. K.C. Campbell	Hurricane	L1955	Cat. 3 Destroyed
7.	56 Sqn., Rochford	C	Shot down by Bf 109 over Dover; pilot killed	A08.10 hrs.	F/Sgt. C.J. Cooney	Hurricane	P3897	Cat. 3 Lost
8.	64 Sqn., Kenley	C	Force landed after combat with Bf 109s over St. Margaret's Bay; pilot unhurt.	A08.05 hrs.	Sgt. A.E. Binham	Spitfire	R6643	Cat. 2 Damaged
9.	66 Sqn., Coltishall	C	Crashed at Orfordness, probably following combat; pilot wounded.	A15.10 hrs.	Plt. Off. L.W. Collingridge	Spitfire	N3042	Cat. 3 Destroyed
10.	151 Sqn., North Weald	C	Force landed at Martlesham after combat with Bf 110s of ZG 26 over the Thames Estuary; pilot unhurt.	A17.15 hrs.	Fg. Off. C.D. Whittingham	Hurricane	P3119	Cat. 2 Damaged
11.	151 Sqn., North Weald	C	Force landed at Rochford after combat with Bf 110s of ZG 26 over the Thames Estuary; pilot unhurt.	A.17.15 hrs.	Fg. Off. R.M. Milne	Hurricane	P3307	Cat. 2 Damaged

LUFTWAFFE LOSSES—MONDAY 29th JULY 1940

1.	2.(F)/122	CM	Crashed in Square 3350 after engine failure.	Junkers Ju 88A	100 %	Ltn. Rabbow + three missing.
2.	Stab/KG 2	CM	Damaged by Hurricane of 85 Sqn. between Harwich and the Belgian coast at 15.10 hrs.	Dornier Do 17Z	60 %	Ltn. Hunger wounded.
3.	III./KG 4	NCM	Crashed at Schipol folowing engine failure.	Junkers Ju 88A-1	50 %	No crew casualties.
4.	7./KG 4	CM	Shot down by Hurricanes of 145 Sqn. south of Worthing at 14.10 hrs.	Junkers Ju 88A-1	100 %	Four crew members killed
5.	I./KG 27	CM	Crashed off Guernsey following engine failure.	Heinkel He 111H	100 %	Crew rescued unhurt.
6.	III./KG 51	CM	Crash landed after operations. No R.A.F. claim traced.	Junkers Ju 88A-1 (7081 : 9K+ER)	100 %	Gefr. Böhmisch, Fw.Wilhelm Jörg, Fw. Emil Kürzweg and Fw. Ewald Oschliess killed.
7.	I./KG 53	CM	Shot down by Spitfire of Campbell-Colquhoun, 66 Sqn., east of Hammond's Knoll at 15.30 hrs.	Heinkel He 111H-2	100 %	Ltn. Kliffken + two killed; two missing.
8.	I./KG 53	CM	Shot down by Spitfires of Oxspring, Studd and Pickering of 66 Sqn. off Lowestoft at 14.45 hrs.	Heinkel He 111H-2	100 %	Ltn. Schattka + four killed.
9.	III./KG 55	CM	Shot down by Hurricanes of Bayne, Wissler and Bird-Wilson of 17 Sqn., over the Thames Estuary at 15.30 hrs.	Heinkel He 111P	100 %	Five crew members missing.
10.	4./KG 76	CM	Shot down by naval A.A. gunfire off Dungeness at 13.12 hrs.	Junkers Ju 88A-1	100 %	Two crew killed; Maj.i.G. Donaubauer and Ltn. Nier missing.

Luftwaffe Losses, 29th July 1940—*continued*

11.	III./KG 76	CM	Believed to have collided with seaborne balloon cable off Dungeness at 13.16 hrs.	Junkers Ju 88A-1	100 %	Oberstlt. Genth, *Gr.Kdr.*, killed; three crew members missing.
12.	11.(Stuka)/LG 1	CM	Shot down by Spitfires of 41 Sqn., off Dover at 07.45 hrs.	Junkers Ju 87B	100 %	Ltn. Fürnwagner + one missing.
13.	11.(Stuka)/LG 1	CM	Shot down by Spitfires of 41 Sqn., off Dover at 07.45 hrs.	Junkers Ju 87B	100 %	Oblt. Köthe + one missing.
14.	II./St.G 1	CM	Shot down by Hurricane of Stoney of 501 Sqn. off Dover at 07.45 hrs.	Junkers Ju 87B	100 %	Crew believed rescued.
15.	II./St.G 1	CM	Shot down by 501 Sqn. Hurricane of Gibson off off Dover; crashed at St. Inglevert at 07.48 hrs.	Junkers Ju 87B	100 %	Crews unhurt.
16.	II./St.G 1	CM	Damaged by Hurricane of McKay of 501 Sqn. off Dover at 07.50 hrs.	Junkers Ju 87B	30 %	One crew member wounded.
17.	I./JG 27	NCM	Landing accident at Plumetot airfield.	Messerschmitt Bf 109E	30 %	Pilot unhurt.

Tuesday 30th July

With low cloud and continuous drizzle covering almost the whole of Britain, air activity on this day was very much reduced. Nevertheless Fighter Command, apprehensive that the enemy might use the cloud to cloak their attacks, put up numerous convoy and minesweeper escort patrols throughout the day.

The Norwegian-based KG 26 sent over a small number of He 111s on nuisance raids against Scotland and, just after mid-day, lost one aircraft to the guns of Flt. Lt. Frederick Rushmer, Plt. Off. Ronald Berry and Plt. Off. Arthur Pease of No. 603 Squadron; the bomber crashed into the sea south-east of Montrose, with no survivors.

The only other German aircraft destroyed by Fighter Command on this day was one of a pair of Bf 110s from *Erprobungsgruppe 210*, which appeared off a convoy near the Suffolk coast. After a spirited chase just above the wave tops, Flt. Lt. Harry Hamilton and Sgt. Geoffrey Allard managed to score the vital strikes which sent the Messerschmitt crashing into the sea.

Night raiders were active during the hours of darkness and a couple of sea mines were accidentally dropped over land at Guyzance, two miles from Acklington, by a Heinkel He 115 floatplane of *Küstenfliegergruppe 506*.

R.A.F. FIGHTER COMMAND LOSSES—TUESDAY 30th JULY 1940

1.	236 Sqn., Thorney Island	NC	Crashed in bad weather at Carew Cheriton, Hants. Pilot and crew unhurt.	In evening	Flt. Lt. R.M. Power	Blenheim	—	Cat. 3 Destroyed
2.	604 Sqn., Middle Wallop	—	Destroyed in bombing raid; no aircrew casualties. (Assumed to be hit-and-run raid.)	Not known	None	Blenheim	—	Cat. 3 Destroyed

LUFTWAFFE LOSSES—TUESDAY 30th JULY 1940

1.	6./KG 4	NCM	Flying accident at Mark, Friedland; not combat.	Heinkel He 111P	100 %	Four crew members killed.
2.	6./KG 4	NCM	Take-off accident at Mark, Friedland.	Heinkel He 111P	80 %	Ltn. Ziegler injured.
3.	9./KG 4	NCM	Landing accident at Pinnow airfield.	Heinkel He 111P	100 %	Four crew members killed.
4.	8./KG 26	CM	Shot down by 603 Sqn. Spitfires of Rushmer, Berry and Pease, 40 miles SE of Montrose at 12.05 hrs.	Heinkel He 111H-4	100 %	Four crew members missing.
5.	II./KG 27	CM	Shot down by A.A. near Bristol during evening.	Heinkel He 111P	100 %	Ltn. Wiedenhöft + three missing.
6.	II./KG 51	NCM	Force landed at Fontainebleu after engine failure.	Junkers Ju 88A-1	30 %	Crew unhurt.
7.	2./KG 76	NCM	Premature bomb explosion at La Boessie.	Dornier Do 17Z-1	100 %	Four crew members killed.
8.	6./KG 76	CM	Said to have been damaged by R.A.F. fighters, but no R.A.F. claim traced.	Junkers Ju 88A-1	30 %	No crew casualties.
9.	1./Erpr.Gr. 210	CM	Shot down by Hurricanes of Hamilton and Allard of 85 Sqn. off Harwich.	Messerschmitt Bf 110C	100 %	Ltn. Gerold + one killed.
10.	7./JG 27	CM	Landing accident at Caroubert airfield due to bad ground conditions.	Messerschmitt Bf 109 E-1	65 %	Pilot unhurt.
11.	5./196	CM	Crashed in Trondheim Fjord with engine failure.	Arado Ar 196	100 %	Ltn. Müller killed; Ltn.z.S. Behrmann missing.

Wednesday 31st July.

Although weather conditions improved considerably, this was to be a tiresome day for Fighter Command, operations being severely frustrated by haze. Enemy bombers attempted to penetrate the South Coast at dawn but were tracked in by the radar chain so that, at some risk, several Sections of fighters were scrambled in poor visibility. Observer Corps plots suggest that a few bombers did cross the coast, but these

were evidently unable to confirm any targets as only nine bombs fell—all in open countryside on the coast. It was not until after 07.00 hours that three Hurricane pilots of No. 111 Squadron spotted a Ju 88 of III./KG 76 and attacked it over mid-Channel. It was slightly damaged and carried a dead crew member home to its base. A Dornier Do 17 which approached the Isle of Wight in the mid-morning was luckier for, although three Hurricanes from Tangmere chased it for 60 miles and fired 5,600 rounds at it, it escaped untouched!

Enemy traffic appeared to build up during the afternoon but try as they might the R.A.F. pilots could find no targets until nearly 16.00 hours. Then 30 Spitfires and 24 Hurricanes from six squadrons were ordered to Dover where it was reported that Messerschmitts were indulging in strafing the balloon barrage—presumably in preparation for an attack on the harbour. Only the twelve Spitfires of No. 74 Squadron (already airborne from Manston) engaged the enemy—two *Staffeln* from Oberstleutnant Harry von Bülow's JG 2 "*Richthofen*". Although "A" Flight of Malan's Spitfires met the Bf 109s at equal height, "B" Flight was still climbing when the enemy fell on it from above, shooting down two aircraft of Blue Section; only Flt. Lt. Dillon Kelly managed to fire a snap burst at a 109 before he had to break off with a severely crippled aircraft, which he landed safely at Manston. Nevertheless his marksmanship had been effective and his fleeting shots wounded the German pilot who crashed at Fécamp. It

transpired that this was the only German aircraft destroyed by Fighter Command during the whole day.

One of the few German bombs to fall on British soil on 30th July landed on a bus station in Norwich. (Photo: Swains, Norwich).

R.A.F. FIGHTER COMMAND LOSSES—WEDNESDAY 31st JULY 1940

1.	74 Sqn., Manston	C	Shot down into Folkestone Harbour by Bf 109; pilot killed.	15.48 hrs.	Sgt. F.W. Eley	Spitfire	P9398	Cat. 3 Destroyed
2.	74 Sqn., Manston	C	Shot down in flames near Folkestone by Bf 109; pilot killed.	15.49 hrs.	Plt. Off. H.R. Gunn	Spitfire	P9379	Cat. 3 Destroyed
3.	74 Sqn., Manston	C	Damaged by Bf 109s near Folkestone; pilot unhurt and managed to regain base.	15.50 hrs.	Flt. Lt. D.P.D.G. Kelly	Spitfire	R6983	Cat. 2 Damaged
4.	234 Sqn., St. Eval	NC	Crashed in night landing at St. Eval; pilot injured	At night	Sgt. W.W. Thompson	Spitfire	P9365	Cat. 3 Destroyed
5.	501 Sqn., Gravesend	NC	Engine caught fire; pilot baled out but was injured on landing.	Not known	Plt. Off. R.S. Don	Hurricane	P3646	Cat. 3 Destroyed
6.	501 Sqn., Gravesend	NC	Landing accident at Gravesend; pilot badly injured.	Not known	Plt. Off. E.G. Parkin	Hurricane	—	Cat. 3 Destroyed

LUFTWAFFE LOSSES—WEDNESDAY 31st JULY 1940

1.	Aufkl.Gr. Ob.d.L.	CM	Collided with FH 104 on take-off at Neufchâteau. Do 215's crew unhurt.	Dornier Do 215	100 %	Oblt. Klein-Reschkampf killed; four others injured.
2.	III./KG 51	NCM	Damaged in bad weather landing at Orly airfield.	Junkers Ju 88A-1 (7068 : 9K+FT)	35 %	Two killed; one injured.
3.	Stab II./KG 76	CM	Damaged by Hurricanes of 111Sqn. in mid-Channel at 07.35 hrs.	Junkers Ju 88A-1	15 %	One crew member killed.
4.	I./KG 77	NCM	Flying accident at Rothenberg; cause unknown.	Junkers Ju 88A	100 %	Oblt. Röder + 2 killed.
5.	II./ZG 76	NCM	Crashed at Le Mans airfield after engine failure.	Messerschmitt Bf 110C	50 %	No crew casualties.
6.	I./LG 2	NCM	Landing accident at Jever airfield.	Messerschmitt Bf 109E	60 %	Pilot unhurt.
7.	JG 2	CM	Damaged by Spitfire of Kelly of 74 Sqn. south of Dover at 15.50 hrs. Crashed at Fécamp after engine failure.	Messerschmitt Bf 109E	100 %	Pilot wounded.

---

* * * * *

So ended the first month of the Battle of Britain, a month of constant sparring and thrusting. Although they had well-defined aims, the Germans had engaged in all manner of thrusts, attempting to discover particular weaknesses in the defences. Such weaknesses *had* been exposed, but such was the operational command structure of Fighter Command that Dowding and his Group Commanders were able to take immediate remedial steps to correct the failing, so that at no time was the German Air Force able to exploit local success.

Meanwhile both Bomber and Coastal Command had kept

up a constant, though necessarily diffuse pressure against enemy targets, both in Germany and her newly-won territories and, apart from inflicting some damage on the *Luftwaffe* and its bases, was already having the effect of keeping *Jagdgeschwader*—or parts thereof—tied up for defensive purposes. There is no doubt that at this stage of the Battle the enemy single-seat fighters presented the greatest potential danger to the continued existence of Britain's air defences—so long as they could continue to draw Fighter Command into the air over the South and South-East.

R.A.F. FIGHTER COMMAND ORDER OF BATTLE

09.00 hrs., 1st August 1940

Sector	Sqn.	Aircraft	Combat Ready (Unserviceable)		Base Airfield	Pilots on State	Commanding Officer
No. 10 Group, H.Q. Rudloe Manor, Box, Wiltshire							
Middle Wallop	152 Sqn.	Spitfires	10	(5)	Warmwell	20	Squadron Leader P.K. Devitt
	238 Sqn.	Hurricanes	12	(3)	Middle Wallop	18	Squadron Leader H.A. Fenton
	604 Sqn.	Blenheims	11	(5)	Middle Wallop	20	Squadron Leader M.F. Anderson
	609 Sqn.	Spitfires	10	(6)	Middle Wallop	18	Squadron Leader H.S. Darley
Filton	87 Sqn.	Hurricanes	13	(5)	Exeter	20	Squadron Leader T.G. Lovell-Gregg
	92 Sqn.	Spitfires	12	(4)	Pembrey	17	Squadron Leader P.J. Sanders
	213 Sqn.	Hurricanes	12	(5)	Exeter	19	Squadron Leader H.D. McGregor
	234 Sqn.	Spitfires	10	(6)	St. Eval	22	Squadron Leader R.E. Barnett
No. 11 Group, H.Q. Uxbridge, Middlesex							
Biggin Hill	32 Sqn.	Hurricanes	11	(4)	Biggin Hill	18	Squadron Leader J. Worrall
	501 Sqn.	Hurricanes	11	(5)	Gravesend	19	Squadron Leader H.A.V. Hogan
	600 Sqn.	Blenheims	9	(6)	Manston	20	Squadron Leader D. de B. Clarke
	610 Sqn.	Spitfires	12	(3)	Biggin Hill	18	Squadron Leader J. Ellis
North Weald	25 Sqn.	Blenheims	7	(7)	Martlesham	22	Squadron Leader K.A.K. McEwan
	56 Sqn.	Hurricanes	15	(2)	North Weald	24	Squadron Leader G.A.L. Manton
	85 Sqn.	Hurricanes	12	(6)	Martlesham	21	Squadron Leader P.W. Townsend
	151 Sqn.	Hurricanes	13	(5)	North Weald	19	Squadron Leader E.M. Donaldson
Kenley	64 Sqn.	Spitfires	12	(4)	Kenley	21	Squadron Leader A.R.D. MacDonnell
	111 Sqn.	Hurricanes	10	(2)	Croydon	20	Squadron Leader J.M. Thompson
	615 Sqn.	Hurricanes	14	(2)	Kenley	23	Squadron Leader J.R. Kayll
Northolt	43 Sqn. (1)	Hurricanes	18	(1)	Northolt	18	Squadron Leader J.V.C. Badger
	257 Sqn.	Hurricanes	10	(5)	Northolt	14	Squadron Leader H. Harkness
Hornchurch	41 Sqn.	Spitfires	10	(6)	Hornchurch	19	Squadron Leader H. West
	65 Sqn.	Spitfires	11	(5)	Hornchurch	19	Squadron Leader H.C. Sawyer
	74 Sqn.	Spitfires	12	(3)	Hornchurch	14	Squadron Leader F.L. White
Tangmere	1 Sqn. (2)	Hurricanes	13	(3)	Tangmere	19	Squadron Leader D.A. Pemberton
	145 Sqn.	Hurricanes	10	(7)	Westhampnett	21	Squadron Leader J.R.A. Peel
	266 Sqn.	Spitfires	13	(5)	Tangmere	20	Squadron Leader R.L. Wilkinson
	601 Sqn.	Hurricanes	14	(4)	Tangmere	23	Squadron Leader W.F.C. Hobson
	F.I.U.	Blenheims	4	(3)	Tangmere	11	Wing Commander G.P. Chamberlain
Debden	17 Sqn.	Hurricanes	14	(5)	Debden	19	Squadron Leader C.W. Williams
No. 12 Group, H.Q. Watnall, Nottingham							
Duxford	19 Sqn.	Spitfires	9	(6)	Fowlmere	25	Squadron Leader P.C. Pinkham
Coltishall	66 Sqn.	Spitfires	12	(4)	Coltishall	26	Squadron Leader R.H.A. Leigh
	242 Sqn.	Hurricanes	11	(5)	Coltishall	25	Squadron Leader D.R.S. Bader
Kirton-in-Lindsey	222 Sqn.	Spitfires	14	(3)	Kirton-in-Lindsey	16	Squadron Leader J.H. Hill
	264 Sqn.	Defiants	12	(4)	Kirton-in-Lindsey	21	Squadron Leader P.A. Hunter
Digby	29 Sqn.	Blenheims	8	(4)	Digby	16	Squadron Leader S.C. Widdows
	46 Sqn.	Hurricanes	12	(5)	Digby	23	Flight Lieutenant A.D. Murray
	611 Sqn.	Spitfires	6	(7)	Digby and Ternhill	20	Squadron Leader J.E. McComb
Wittering	23 Sqn.	Blenheims	9	(5)	Colly Weston	22	Squadron Leader L.C. Bicknell
	229 Sqn.	Hurricanes	14	(4)	Wittering and Bircham Newton	16	Squadron Leader H.J. Maguire
No. 13 Group, H.Q. Newcastle, Northumberland							
Church Fenton	73 Sqn.	Hurricanes	11	(5)	Church Fenton	20	Squadron Leader J.W.C. More
	249 Sqn.	Hurricanes	11	(5)	Church Fenton	21	Squadron Leader J. Grandy
	616 Sqn.	Spitfires	12	(4)	Leconfield	20	Squadron Leader M. Robinson
Catterick	54 Sqn.	Spitfires	11	(3)	Catterick	15	Squadron Leader J.L. Leathart
	219 Sqn.	Blenheims	10	(5)	Leèming	18	Squadron Leader J.H. Little
Usworth	72 Sqn.	Spitfires	10	(5)	Acklington	19	Squadron Leader A.R. Collins
	79 Sqn.	Hurricanes	10	(2)	Acklington	14	Squadron Leader J.H. Heyworth
	607 Sqn.	Hurricanes	12	(4)	Usworth	15	Squadron Leader J.A. Vick
Turnhouse	253 Sqn.	Hurricanes	12	(4)	Turnhouse	17	Squadron Leader T.P. Gleave
	602 Sqn.	Spitfires	11	(4)	Drem	17	Squadron Leader A.V.R. Johnstone
	603 Sqn.	Spitfires	11	(4)	Turnhouse	20	—
	605 Sqn.	Hurricanes	14	(4)	Drem	22	Squadron Leader W.M. Churchill
Dyce	263 Sqn. (3)	Hurricanes	4	(2)	Grangemouth	7	Squadron Leader H. Eeles
Wick	3 Sqn.	Hurricanes	10	(2)	Wick	20	Squadron Leader S.F. Godden
	232 Sqn.	Hurricanes	6	(4)	Sumburgh	9	Flight Lieutenant M.M. Stephens
	504 Sqn.	Hurricanes	13	(4)	Castletown	19	Squadron Leader J. Sample
	804 Sqn., F.A.A.	Gladiators	8	(6)	Wick	13+	Lieutenant Commander J.C. Cockburn, R.N.
	808 Sqn., F.A.A.	Fulmars	6	(6)	Castletown	15	—
(Prestwick)	141 Sqn.	Defiants	8	(4)	Prestwick	14	Squadron Leader W.A. Richardson
Aldergrove	245 Sqn.	Hurricanes	8	(2)	Aldergrove	15	Squadron Leader F.W. Whitley

Notes: (1) Squadron moved to Tangmere during this day (1st August).
(2) Squadron moved to Northolt during this day (1st August).
(3) One Flight only (used for local defence).

Re-arming a Spitfire IA of No. 19 Squadron at either Duxford or its satellite, Fowlmere, after a combat sortie—note the gun patches blown away. Note the necessity to replenish the ammunition from beneath the wing.

CHAPTER 7

AUGUST—THE MAJOR ASSAULT

The growing weight and fury of the air attacks during the last weeks of July had been weathered by Fighter Command, and the British commanders could face the future without serious misgivings—provided the scope and extent of the German assault were not much further increased. True, several squadrons had been exhausted by constant combat and had either been withdrawn to the North or were about to move. Less than a quarter of Fighter Command's squadrons had been fully extended for any length of time, so that Dowding could still feed entirely fresh units into the South and South-East should he so wish.

July's weather had not entirely favoured massive assaults by the *Luftwaffe*, yet as conditions gradually improved during the first week in August there was no increase in enemy pressure—indeed the German attacks all but petered out during this period. To some extent this respite was attributable to the British themselves who, aware that the sailing of Channel convoys invited heavy air attacks, now reduced the number of sailings to a mere fraction of the average July number. (They did not, as has been suggested elsewhere, stop them altogether—as will be shown.)

However, it was abundantly clear to Dowding and Park that, as they had not inflicted any major defeat on the enemy, no lasting encouragement could be derived from the *Luftwaffe*'s relative inactivity. Indeed, in line with Hitler's determination to "eliminate" Britain, there could be only one explanation for the pause of early August—that Göring's commanders were regrouping and flexing their muscles for an all-out offensive against Britain in preparation for the invasion which every islander firmly believed was inevitable.

While the air and field commanders of both sides were readying their forces for the coming invasion, certain influential factions in the *Reich* were seriously questioning the very desirability of launching a landing operation against Britain—quite apart from military considerations of the practical difficulties involved, remembering that neither the Royal Air Force nor the Royal Navy had been defeated decisively. An account, published in 1969, states that Major Reinhard Gehlen, A.D.C. to General Fritz Halder (Chief of the German General Staff) and one of the Reich's foremost Intelligence experts, prepared a long memorandum for his chief in which he advanced the view that even should the proposed invasion be successful, Germany would not reap the major benefit. In Gehlen's view the disintegration of the British Empire would follow and, in the long run, serve the best interests of Japan and the United States. This memorandum is known to survive, and with it a reply by Halder stating that the Führer had decided "that Russia's destruction must be made part of the struggle against England; with Russia smashed, England's hope would be shattered". The reply is supposedly dated 31st July. If an accurate report of Hitler's feelings, it indicates that only fifteen days after his issue of Directive No. 16, the Führer's faith in a decisive outcome of the Battle of Britain was, to say the least, wavering. This naturally poses the question as to whether Hitler was ever fully committed to an invasion of Britain[1].

If such misgivings existed in the Führer's mind, they were

---

[1] Reinhard Gehlen, an enigmatic figure in many respects, was totally committed to the struggle against Communism. At the end of the

Re-arming a Hurricane. Being grouped in a single gun bay in each wing and accessible from above, the gun magazines of the Hurricane could be replenished rather more quickly than those of the Spitfire.

R.A.F. strength and losses formulated by Oberst Josef Schmid, Göring's chief of Intelligence. Moreover, just as the R.A.F. had already displayed a tendency to overestimate their successes against German aircraft, German fighter pilots and bomber crews had filed claims which suggested that Schmid's original strength estimates were considerably deficient or that Fighter Command was almost exhausted.

In truth, as show in Appendix H, Schmid had *overestimated* the British strength by almost 50 per cent, but—victory claims aside—clearly *underestimated* the output and repair capacity of Britain's fighter factories. These substantiasl shortcomings in the German field Intelligence, apart from seriously and perhaps fatally influencing the progress of Göring's offensive, were to lead to growing apprehension and frustration among *Luftwaffe* aircrews who continued to encounter strong and determined intercepting fighter formations in spite of repeated assurances that Fighter Command was almost exhausted.

To the contrary, it was on 1st August that Dowding issued his formal authorisation to increase the established strength of each fighter squadron. Such was the recovery of his Command, allied with a marked improvement in fighter output[2], that the unit establishment (U.E.) was re-established at the pre-Dunkirk figure of 20 aircraft (plus two as Command Reserve)[3]. More important, Fighter Command, which had been struggling ever since Dunkirk to make good heavy deficiencies in combat-proficient pilots, had made good progress during July—increasing by an effective total of 214 pilots its strength of 1,200 on 1st July. It was the actual strength of 1,414 pilots, compared with the establishment of 1,454, that encouraged Dowding to increase the Command Establishment to 1,588. By so doing he thus established a large "paper" deficiency, and this has hitherto been widely quoted to indicate a shortage of pilots, whereas the Command was in fact more than making good its battle losses at this stage. Statistically, Fighter Command's strength was never to drop to the depths of the figures of early July.

It was, as will be seen in this chapter, in the calibre, proficiency and experience of his pilots that Dowding's anxieties lay. Even before the main battle had been joined, his Command had lost more than eighty Regular squadron and flight commanders, and their places were now necessarily being taken by pilots with little experience of handling formations of six or a dozen fighters, let alone leading them into battle.

If there was one vital lesson which the *Luftwaffe* should have learned from the early probing attacks of July—but patently failed to do so, despite all the evidence—it was of the

certainly not transmitted to the Military commanders, who were now ready with plans for the main air and land assaults on Britain. The invasion, fairly aptly codenamed *Unternehmen Seelöwe* (Operation Sealion) was expected to be launched two or three weeks after the all-out air assault by the *Luftwaffe*. This intended attack (*Adlerangriff*, Attack of the Eagles) would be hurled against Britain on a day to be nominated as *Adler Tag*, which would be decided by weather forecasts promising a subsequent spell of fine weather. Estimates varied enormously as to the likely period necessary to destroy Fighter Command; its length was clearly proportionate to the degree of reliability placed in the estimates of

War he handed over to the United States authorities an unparalleled archive of material garnered during his years as German Intelligence chief on the Russian Front, and an espionage and counter-espionage network which survived the collapse of Germany remarkably intact. He retired as Chief of the Federal German Intelligence Service in May 1968, having worked hand in glove with the American Central Intelligence Agency and its predecessors for 22 years; it is probable that this shadowy, self-effacing figure made the greatest single contribution to the Western Intelligence apparatus in the Cold War. (Cf. "*The Spy of the Century*", E.H.C. Cookridge, published in *The Daily Telegraph Magazine*, © European Copyright Company., 1969.)

[2] The planned fighter output for July of the three main interceptor aircraft (Hurricane, Spitfire and Defiant) of 410 had been bettered by 78. Of the surplus, 52 had been Hurricanes, and it must be to the credit of their manufacturers that since the outbreak of war they had consistently passed each monthly production target. Reserves of Hurricanes and Spitfires had dropped during July from 364 to 320, but this had been due to the formation of six new fighter squadrons. The generally good production figures for July are directly attributable to measures initiated by Lord Beaverbrook, the fruits of whose handling of adminisatrative inertia in the British Civil Service, as well as some of the aircraft manufacturers themselves, were beginning to be fully realised.

[3] After Dunkirk the U.E. of most fighter squadrons was dropped to 16+2, and even this low figure was only achieved after considerable "milking" of training units.

true value of launching numerous attacks simultaneously, each of lesser strength, rather than mounting one or two massive raids. Park's tactics of committing his squadrons piecemeal to battle against these huge formations—even if this was necessary owing to the distances over which they had to fly—gained much better results in terms of enemy aircraft shot down and, more important, had a marked tendency to sap the energy and morale of the bomber crew and their escorting fighter pilots. If, on the other hand, the *Luftwaffe* had adopted the free chase tactic universally from the outset, and even extended the tactic to such aircraft as the Messerschmitt Bf 110 fighter bomber and the Junkers Ju 88, the strain upon

Fighter Command would have been critical; it would have proved impossible to "plug all the holes". The weakness in *Luftwaffe* planning lay in the fact that there was no tactical thinking which lay between the massed bomber formation—which appeared to demand heavy fighter escorts—and the dive-bomber or "battlefield support" philosophy. Neither of these schools of thought had effective relevance to an attack on Britain's air defence system as it was in 1940. It was the growing frustration of the German fighter pilots in August that brought about a change in tactics towards the end of the month—a stepping up of the free chase tactics—that so nearly changed the course of the Battle.

Smoke rising from the Boulton Paul factory at Norwich after the raid by I./KG 4 on 1st August. (Photo: Swains, Norwich)

Thursday 1st August

With mist enveloping the coastal waters around Britain, the German minelaying effort was restricted to about half a dozen sorties by *Küstenfliegergruppen 106* and *506* to the approaches to Hull, Harwich and the Medway during the early morning hours of darkness. Two Heinkel He 115 seaplanes were lost over the North Sea, probably as a result of the bad weather. Two others crashed on landing at Schellingwoude.

The low cloud was slow to disperse over England and four coastal convoys sailed from East Coast ports. The swept channels were free of mines and the ships were not inconvenienced by recent enemy minelaying, so that by mid-day they were sailing off the Yorkshire, Lincolnshire, Suffolk and Kent coasts. No fewer than 14 squadrons took turns to fly escort patrols over the ships and, despite occasional warnings from the various Sector Controllers that radar plots suggested the approach of raiders, it was not until evening that any attack developed.

Meanwhile apart from the approach of a deep-sea convoy towards Plymouth, which was escorted by Hurricanes of Nos. 87 and 213 Squadrons during the early morning, the Channel skies were relatively free from the din of battle until the afternoon. Sqn. Ldr. John Peel's hard-worked No. 145 Squad-

ron sent up two Sections and one of these caught and turned away a Junkers Ju 88 off Beachy Head, but without apparently damaging it. The other Section found a Henschel Hs 126 (a short-range reconnaissance aircraft) of 4.(H)/31 wandering about 10 miles south of Hastings; it was shot down by Plt. Off. Ernest Wakeham, but not before a well-aimed burst from the enemy gunner had killed Sub-Lt. Ian Kestin, a Fleet Air Arm pilot seconded to No. 145 Squadron.

While the Coltishall Sector Controller (Wing Commander Walter Beisiegel[4]) was pre-occupied with providing escorts for two convoys during the mid-afternoon, a raid by about 30 Heinkel He 111s of Hauptmann Meissner's I.*Gruppe*, KG 4, penetrated the Norfolk coast undetected and un-intercepted and carried out a sharp raid on Norwich[5]. The target was

[4] Widely and affectionately known throughout the R.A.F. as "Bike".
[5] A likely explanation for the relative immunity enjoyed by raiders over Norfolk—during the Battle of Britain and for much of the remainder of the War—was the very bad siting of some of the CH stations, which were among the worst in the country. The author served for a short time at the CH station at Stoke Holy Cross (long since dismantled) on the southern outskirts of Norwich and well remembers the very poor radar "picture" obtained up to twenty miles' range, i.e. covering most of Norfolk.

again the Boulton Paul factory and this was slightly damaged, as were the Thorpe railway goods yard. A timber yard was also entirely burnt out. A total of 43 casualties were suffered, and the raiders made good their escape without interference from Nos. 66 and 242 Squadrons based not ten miles away.

The official figures issued to show German operational losses of five aircraft on 1st August are far from accurate, as the accompanying loss table shows. The Messerschmitt Bf 109s commanded by Hauptmann Werner Andres, caught at Leeuwarden by R.A.F. bombers, had been temporarily withdrawn from France but, after their losses had been made good, returned to their bases at Fiennes and Crépon within a week, only to suffer further heavy losses on their resumption of Channel sorties.

R.A.F. FIGHTER COMMAND LOSSES—THURSDAY 1st AUGUST 1940

1.	145 Sqn. West-hampnett	C	Shot down by Henschel Hs 126 ten miles south of Hastings; pilot killed.	A15.15 hrs.	Sub-Lt. I.H. Kestin	Hurricane	P3155	Cat. 3 Destroyed
2.	504 Sqn., Castletown	NC	Night landing accident at Wick; pilot unhurt.	At night	Plt. Off. H.N. Hunt	Hurricane	—	Cat. 2 Damaged
3.	602 Sqn., Drem	NC	Night landing accident at Drem; pilot unhurt.	01.30 hrs.	Plt. Off. H.M. Moody	Spitfire	K9892	Cat. 3 Destroyed

[Note: A Blenheim of No. 236 Sqn., flown by Plt. Off. B.M. McDonough, was also reported lost on this date, but the circumstances are not known. The Photographic Reconnaissance Unit reported losing Spitfire K9882, which dived into the ground at Crewkerne, Somerset, after the pilot lost consciousness owing to oxygen starvation.]

LUFTWAFFE LOSSES—THURSDAY 1st AUGUST 1940

1.	4.(H)/31	CM	Shot down by Hurricane of Wakeham of 145 Sqn. 10 miles south of Hastings at A15.30 hrs.	Henschel Hs 126	100 %	Two crew members missing.
2.	1./KG 2	CM	Crashed at Melovres; crew baled out.	Dornier Do 17Z	100 %	Crew unhurt.
3.	3./KG 4	CM	Landing accident at Soesterburg.	Heinkel He 111H-4	30 %	Crew unhurt.
4.	II./KG 4	NCM	Crashed and burned at Friedland, N. Germany.	Heinkel He 111P	100 %	Three crew killed; one injured.
5.	II./KG 4	NCM	Crash landed at Friedland, N. Germany.	Heinkel He 111P	80 %	Crew unhurt.
6.	9./KG 4	CM	Shot down by Hurricane of Richardson of 242 Sqn. over convoy off Norfolk at A18.55 hrs.	Junkers Ju 88A-1	100 %	Oblt. Geisler, Oblt. Wagner and and two others missing.
7.	KG 30	NCM	Engine failed on take-off at Stavanger-Sola.	Junkers Ju 88	40 %	No crew casualties.
8.	KG 30	NCM	Overturned on landing at Stavanger-Sola.	Junkers Ju 88	100 %	No crew casualties.
9.	1./KG 30	CM	Target Carlisle. Believed shot down by A.A. fire near Edinburgh.	Junkers Ju 88A-1	100 %	Four crew members missing.
10.	2./KG 30	CM	Damaged by Hurricane of Christie of 242 Sqn. off East Coast at 19.15 hrs; landed at Aalborg.	Junkers Ju 88A-1	70 %	Two crew memebrs killed and
11.	3./KG 30	NCM	Damaged in night landing at Aalborg, Denmark.	Junkers Ju 88A-1	60 %	No crew casualties.
12.	II./KG 53	CM	Crashed after engine failure at Vendeville.	Heinkel He 111H-2	80 %	Ltn. Buhmert + two injured.
13.	8./KG 53	NCM	Crashed near Giebelstadt; cause not known.	Heinkel He 111	100 %	Ltn. Seddvig and Ltn. Altaker killed
14.	I./KG 55	CM	Crashed at Tours after reported combat with fighters; no R.A.F. claim traced. Night sortie.	Heinkel He 111H	100 %	No crew casualties.
15.	I./KG 55	CM	Crashed after reported combat with fighters; no R.A.F. claim traced. Night sortie.	Heinkel He 111	100 %	No crew casualties.
16.	Erg.Zerst.St.	NCM	Aircraft broke up in the air near Ringstedt.	Messerschmitt Bf 110B	100 %	One killed; Ltn. Adametz injured.
17.	5./JG 27	CM	Shot down by R.A.F. bombers over Leeuwarden.	Messerschmitt Bf 109 E-4	95 %	Hptm. Albrecht von Ankum-Frank, *St. Kap.*, killed.
18.	II./JG 27	—	Bombed by R.A.F. aircraft at Leeuwarden.	Messerschmitt Bf 109 E-1	80 %	No aircrew casualties.
19.	II./JG 27	—	Bombed by R.A.F. aircraft at Leeuwarden.	Messerschmitt Bf 109 E-3	100 %	No aircrew casualties.
20.	II./JG 27	—	Bombed by R.A.F. aircraft at Leeuwarden.	Messerschmitt Bf 109 E-4	100 %	No aircrew casualties.
21.	3./106	CM	Landing accident at Schellingwoude after mining sortie.	Heinkel He 115C	100 %	No crew casualties.
22.	3./106	CM	Landing accident at Schellingwoude after mining sortie.	Heinkel He 115	100 %	No crew casualties.
23.	1./196	NCM	Landing accident at Schellingwoude.	Arado Ar 196	70 %	No crew casualties.
24.	3./506	CM	Missing on mining sortie over Thames Estuary.	Heinkel He 115	100 %	Ltn.z.S. Starke + two missing.
25.	3./506	CM	Crashed on mining sortie off British coast.	Heinkel He 115	100 %	Ltn.z.S. Richter + one killed; one other missing.
26.	Seenotzentrale Cherbourg	CM	Force landed in English Channel (not the result of combat).	Heinkel He 59	100 %	No crew casualties.

Friday 2nd August

While light enemy attacks served to keep the defences on their toes, Fighter Command's strengthening process continued, and on this day the second Polish fighter squadron, No. 303 (*Kosciuszko*) Squadron was formed with Hurricanes at Northolt with elements of the original No. 1 (Warsaw) Squadron of the *Lotnictwo Wojskowe*. Like the pilots of No. 302 (City of Poznan) Squadron, which had formed on 17th July, those of No. 303 had travelled an astonishing variety of arduous routes since the rape of their country, almost a year earlier, to join the R.A.F. Some had escaped through the

Balkans to the Middle East, while others had fought with *l'Armée de l'Air* in France. On arrival in the United Kingdom, the pilots were processed through No. 3 Polish Wing at Blackpool and sent to Operational Training Units before being posted to fighter and bomber squadrons. The earliest arrivals had been absorbed into Regular and Auxiliary squadrons, and several had already been in action with the R.A.F. by the end of July. It was only when their numbers had grown too large to be absorbed (bearing in mind all the difficulties encountered with the radio "patter" peculiar to Fighter Command) that it was decided to create special squadrons almost entirely composed of Poles and Czechs. A total of 154 Polish pilots served with Fighter Command during the Battle of Britain, and no fewer than 30 had lost their lives by 31st October. When it is further realised that neither of the Polish squadrons was fully operational much before the end of August, the exceptionally high casualties testify to the bitterness and fury with which the Poles hurled themselves at the *Luftwaffe*.

The record of No. 303 Squadron was truly remarkable. Formed under the joint command of Squadron Leaders Zdislav Krasnodebski and Ronald Kellett (an ex-Auxiliary pilot), the Squadron also possessed two outstanding R.A.F. flight commanders in John Kent and Athol Forbes. By the end of August the Squadron had assembled no fewer than fifteen holders of the *Virtuti Militari* and three of the Polish Military Cross. One of its original members, a Czech sergeant pilot named Josef Frantisek, was to achieve the highest individual score of victories during the Battle of Britain—in only about three weeks' fighting—but more of this later.

Rather better weather conditions during the night of 1st/2nd August brought out more minelayers to British coasts, but once again the Royal Navy minesweepers managed to keep the approach channels clear for the convoys. And once again these convoys attracted the *Luftwaffe*'s attention, with an attack by ten Heinkels of Oberstleutnant Robert Fuch's KG 26 on a small convoy off the east coast of Scotland. The spirited barrage put up by the ships not only served to disrupt the bombers' aim but destroyed two of the aircraft—one of which landed squarely on the deck of the steamship *Highlander*. It proved impossible to free the ship of the wreckage and the ship steamed into Leith later in the afternoon, proudly displaying the trophy of a successful battle.

In the South-East a sharp raid on a convoy off Harwich was slightly more successful for the *Luftwaffe* when H.M. Trawler *Cape Finisterre*, 590 tons, sank from a direct hit by a 250-kilo bomb; the enemy aircraft, believed to have been of a *Staffel* from *Erprobungsgruppe 210*, escaped, having surprised the defences between patrols.

On the German side, the final operational order for *Adler-angriff* was issued by O.K.L. to *Luftflotten 2, 3* and *5*, with *Adler Tag* provisionally set for 10th August—weather permitting.

In Britain, as much in recognition of the achievements of Lord Beaverbrook as an administrative spur to lend further weight to his authority, the Minister of Aircraft Production was appointed to full membership of the Cabinet.

R.A.F. FIGHTER COMMAND LOSSES—FRIDAY 2nd AUGUST 1940

1.	65 Sqn., Hornchurch	NC	Night take-off accident near Hornchurch; pilot killed.	23.40 hrs.	Sqn. Ldr. H.C. Sawyer	Spitfire	—	Cat. 3 Destroyed
2.	219 Sqn., Catterick	NC	Overshot on night landing at Catterick; crew unhurt.	23.30 hrs.	Plt. Off. W.G.M. Lambie LAC A.E. Gregory	Blenheim	L7118	Cat. 2 Damaged
3.	504 Sqn., Castletown	NC	Landing accident at Castletown; pilot unhurt.	17.55 hrs.	Sgt. D.A. Helcke	Hurricane	—	Cat. 2 Damaged
4.	603 Sqn., Turnhouse	NC	Crashed at Inkhorn, Aberdeenshire, during training flight; pilot died of injuries.	Not known	Sgt. I.K. Arber	Spitfire	—	Cat. 3 Destroyed

LUFTWAFFE LOSSES—FRIDAY 2nd AUGUST 1940

1.	3.(F)/121	CM	Crashed at Dinard after reconnaissance sortie.	Junkers Ju 88A-1	100 %	Oblt. Viefhues, Ltn. Taubertad + two others missing.
2.	8./KG 2	CM	Crashed at Guines after bombing sortie.	Dornier Do 17Z	60 %	No crew casualties.
3.	8./KG 2	CM	Crashed at Guines after bombing sortie.	Dornier Do 17Z	20 %	No crew casualties.
4.	KG 26	CM	Shot down by ss. *Highlander* off East Coast.	Heinkel He 111H	100 %	Five crew members killed.
5.	KG 26	CM	Shot down by naval A.A. guns off East Coast.	Heinkel He 111H	100 %	Five crew believed killed.
6.	II./KG 51	CM	Crashed on landing at Orly after bombing sortie.	Junkers Ju 88A-1	30 %	No crew casualties.
7.	I./KG 51	NCM	Damaged in force landing at Melun-Villaroche.	Junkers Ju 88A-1	30 %	No crew casualties.
8.	II./KG 55	CM	Damaged by Spitfires of 19 Sqn., believed north-east of London at approx. 11.30 hrs.	Heinkel He 111	20 %	No crew casualties.
9.	I./St.G 2	NCM	Crash landed at Ernes airfield.	Junkers Ju 87B-1	100 %	Both crew members killed.
10.	Stab/St.G 3	NCM	Crashed at Dinant following engine failure.	Dornier Do 17M	100 %	Oblt. Kusko + two killed.
11.	I./St.G 77	NCM	Force landed at Bayeux after engine failure.	Junkers Ju 87B-1	50 %	No crew casualties.
12.	5.(Nacht)/JG 1	CM	Night landing accident at Schipol airfield.	Dornier Do 17Z	45 %	No crew casualties.
13.	2./JG 3	NCM	Force landed at Poix after engine failure.	Messerschmitt Bf 109 E-4	40 %	Pilot unhurt.
14.	Seenotzentrale Boulogne	NCM	Broke loose from mooring buoy and struck breakwater at Boulogne.	Heinkel He 59	40 %	No aircrew casualties.

Saturday 3rd August

Despite only sporadic probing by isolated German aircraft over the British Isles during the night of 2nd/3rd August, Fighter Command suffered an unfortunate loss when No. 65 Squadron's commander, Sqn. Ldr. Henry Sawyer was killed in a night take-off accident near Hornchurch. The current fall-off of daylight operations by the *Luftwaffe* prompted many Fighter Command squadrons to seize the opportunity to combine limited night training with a system of "cat's eye" patrols. Experience was to show that the Spitfire was quite unsuitable for night flying, and with very little to show in the way of enemy aircraft shot down—despite the weight of traffic—the practice of employing the Spitfire in this rôle was now abandoned. The Fighter Command loss tables for the period 1st—7th August provide a dismal commentary in this respect. The Hurricane, however, continued both in the *ad*

hoc and regular night fighting rôle as well as a night intruder, for another three years.

It was during the night of 3rd/4th August that Plt. Off. Douglas Grice of No. 32 Squadron was ordered up as the air raid sirens sounded in the Medway towns. After wandering about for half an hour, during which the "all clear" was sounded, Grice was ordered to Canterbury but arrived too late to intercept the intruding Heinkel of KG 1 which had scattered bombs far and wide over Kent. One of these fell upon an Observer Corps post at Higham.

R.A.F. FIGHTER COMMAND LOSSES—SATURDAY 3rd AUGUST 1940—Nil

LUFTWAFFE LOSSES—SATURDAY 3rd AUGUST 1940

1.	3.(F)/14	CM	Believed crashed, not the result of combat.	Dornier Do 17P	100 %	Oblt. Volkel and Oblt. Schäfer killed.
2.	III./KG 55	CM	Reported to have been shot down by A.A. fire over the West Midlands.	Heinkel He 111P	100 %	One killed; four crew missing.
3.	IV./LG 1	NCM	Crashed at Tramecourt; cause not known.	Junkers Ju 87B	100 %	Two crew killed.
4.	5./JG 3	NCM	Force landed at Aumale following engine failure.	Messerschmitt Bf 109 E-1	60 %	Pilot safe.
5.	III./JG 27	NCM	Landing accident at Cherbourg airfield.	Messerschmitt Bf 109 E-1	25 %	Pilot safe.
6.	6./JG 51	NCM	Force landed at Devres airfield following engine failure.	Messerschmitt Bf 109 E-1	80 %	Pilot safe.
7.	3./506	CM	Shot down by Blenheim flown by Laughlin of 235 Sqn. over the North Sea.	Heinkel He 115	100 %	Oblt.z.S.Ballier + one killed; Ltn. Ducoffre missing.
8.	*Seenotzentrale Boulogne*	—	Broke loose from mooring buoy and struck breakwater at Boulogne.	Heinkel He 59	20 %	No casualties among flying personnel.

Sunday 4th August

While Fighter Command continued to suffer its minor epidemic of training accidents, the cloud and fog which covered much of Britain provided the *Luftwaffe* with adequate reason to further reduce its scale of operations. It is perhaps curious to note that the *Luftwaffe* was also suffering a spate of flying accidents at this time, and one of the casualties of 4th August was Hauptmann Douglas Pitcairn—a German-born descendant of Scottish great-grandparents—who was injured when his Messerschmitt collided with another aircraft during take-

off at Pihen. The accident occurred as a formation of Blenheims was reported to be approaching Le Havre on a reconnaissance sortie over the Channel ports, and the fighters of JG 51 were ordered off to intercept. In the event only four Messerschmitts made contact with the Blenheims and these were roughly treated by the escort, provided by No. 236 Squadron whose pilots shot down one Bf 109 and damaged another.

R.A.F. FIGHTER COMMAND LOSSES—SUNDAY 4th AUGUST 1940

1.	23 Sqn., Wittering	NC	Crashed after engine failure at Wittering.	At night	Not known	Blenheim	L1356	Cat. 3 Destroyed
2.	141 Sqn., Prestwick	NC	Night taxying accident; crew unhurt.	At night	Not known	Defiant	—	Cat. 3 Destroyed
3.	141 Sqn. Prestwick	NC	Night taxying accident; crew unhurt.	At night	Not known	Defiant	—	Cat. 2 Damaged
4.	232 Sqn., Sumburgh	NC	Taxying accident at Sumburgh; pilot unhurt.	Not known	Not known	Hurricane	N2911	Cat. 2 Damaged
5.	616 Sqn., Leconfield	NC	Aircraft spun and crashed in Yorkshire during dogfight practice; pilot killed.	Not known	Sgt. Walsh	Spitfire	N3271	Cat. 3 Destroyed

LUFTWAFFE LOSSES—SUNDAY 4th AUGUST 1940

1.	2.(F)/122	NCM	Force landed at Wissel; cause not known.	Heinkel He 111	70 %	Oblt. Sommerich + one wounded.
2.	7./KG 1	NCM	Force landed at Toul-Rosières; cause not known.	Heinkel He 111H-2	35 %	No crew casualties.
3.	8./KG 1	NCM	Force landed at Toul following engine failure.	Heinkel He 111H-2	50 %	No crew casualties.
4.	9./KG 1	NCM	Force landed at Toul-Rosières; cause not known.	Heinkel He 111H-2	35 %	No crew casualties.
5.	7./KG 3	NCM	Taxying accident at Altenburg.	Dornier Do 17Z	40 %	No crew casualties.
6.	9./KG 3	NCM	Crashed at Meinberg; cause not known.	Dornier Do 17Z	95 %	Four crew members killed.
7.	I./KG 51	NCM	Landing accident at Orly airfield.	Junkers Ju 88A-1	40 %	No crew casualties.
8.	2./KGr. 100	NCM	Crashed near Köthen; cause not known.	Heinkel He 111	100 %	Two crew members killed.
9.	2./LG 1	NCM	Crashed at Beverloo following engine failure.	Heinkel He 111	100 %	Six crew members injured.
10.	3./ZG 26	NCM	Crashed at Yvrench; cause not known.	Messerschmitt Bf 110	100 %	One crew member killed.

Luftwaffe Losses, 4th August 1940—*continued*

11.	2./Erpr.Gr.210	NCM	Crashed at Denain; cause not known.	Messerschmitt Bf 110	100 %	Ltn. Brokop + one killed.
12.	2./Erpr.Gr.210	NCM	Crashed at Denain during works test flight.	Messerschmitt Bf 110	100 %	One crew member killed.
13.	1./JG 51	CM	Take-off collision at Pihen.	Messerschmitt Bf 109	90 %	Hptm. Douglas Pitcairn injured.
14.	1./JG 51	CM	Shot down by Blenheim of 236 Sqn. while escorting reconnaissance sortie off Le Havre.	Messerschmitt Bf 109 E-4	100 %	Pilot killed.
15	8./JG 51	CM	Damaged by Blenheims of 236 Sqn, while escorting reconnaissance sortie off Le Havre.	Messerschmitt Bf 109E	40 %	Pilot unhurt

Monday 5th August

With cloudless skies and early morning haze, meteorological offices throughout the country forecast a fine and warm day, and accordingly Sector Controllers mounted fairly heavy patrols over the five convoys which were at sea between Plymouth and Newcastle. The *Luftwaffe* was, however, still preoccupied with consolidation of its battle order, and only appeared in any strength in the Dover area.

It had been No. 615 Squadron's turn to fly the regular dawn patrols over the Kent coast between Beachy Head and Dover and, as the last Section turned for home after an uneventful patrol, its place was taken at about 08.30 hours by six Spitfires of No. 64 Squadron, also flying from Kenley. No sooner had they arrived when a *Staffel* of Bf 109s from JG 54 appeared, and a sharp fight followed. As the German fighters had possessed a height advantage from the outset, Sqn. Ldr. Aeneas MacDonnell, leading the Spitfires, soon found himself in difficulties and called for reinforcements. Forthwith three more of his Squadron scrambled and just managed to join the fight before the Messerschmitt pilots disengaged. The British pilots claimed two of the enemy shot down, but unfortunately observers on the ground who lent confirmation were mistaken in their identification of the fallen fighters; they were in fact the Spitfires of Plt. Off. Arthur Donahue and Sgt. Lewis Isaac (the latter pilot being killed). The enemy had not escaped unscathed, and one of the damaged aircraft crashed on return to France.

It is not known whether the JG 54 pilots reported the presence of an eastbound convoy on their return but the fact that no major attack on it materialised only serves to confirm that Kesselring was determined to conserve his bomber crews for the all-out offensive, now less than a week away.

Nevertheless, as the convoy sailed through the Dover Strait during the early afternoon, several Junkers Ju 88s put in an

The Heinkel He 115 twin-engine floatplane, widely used for minelaying and coastal reconnaissance during the Battle. (Photo: Hans Obert).

appearance in company with a *Staffel* of JG 54's Messerschmitts. They were engaged by the Hurricanes of No. 151 Squadron whose pilots succeeded in shooting down one of the escort and damaged a Ju 88.

As darkness fell *Küstenfliegergruppe 506* seaplanes set out from their Stavanger base to continue their mining operations off the North-East Coast. By now the relatively haphazard sowing of mines was beginning to show limited results, as the loss of four naval trawlers in 24 hours indicates[6]

---

[6] These were all requisitioned trawlers. They were *Drummer*, 297 tons (mined off Brightlingsea, Essex), *Marsona*, 276 tons (mined off Cromarty, Scotland), and *Oswaldian* (mined in the Bristol Channel), all lost on 4th August. The *River Clyde*, 276 tons, was sunk by a mine off Aldeburgh, Suffolk, on 5th August. See Appendix L.

R.A.F. FIGHTER COMMAND LOSSES—MONDAY 5th AUGUST 1940

1.	41 Sqn., Manston	C	Crasahed on take-off at Manston; pilot unhurt.	Morning	Not known		Spitfire	N3234	Cat. 3 Destroyed
2.	64 Sqn., Kenley	C	Shot down by Bf 109s at Hawkinge; pilot unhurt.	A08.30 hrs.	Plt. Off. A.G. Donahue		Spitfire	K9991	Cat. 3 Destroyed
3.	64 Sqn., Kenley	C	Shot down by Bf 109s over Kent; pilot killed.	A08.40 hrs.	Sgt. L.R. Isaac		Spitfire	L1029	Cat. 3 Destroyed
4.	219 Sqn., Catterick	NC	Wheels-up landing accident; crew unhurt.	Not known	Sgt. H.K. Hodgkinson		Blenheim	—	Cat. 2 Damaged
5.	219 Sqn., Catterick	NC	Wheels-up landing accident; crew unhurt.	Not known	Sgt. T. Birkett		Blenheim	—	Cat. 2 Damaged

LUFTWAFFE LOSSES—MONDAY 5th AUGUST 1940

1.	3./Aufkl.Gr. Ob.d.L.	NCM	Landing accident at Berlin/Tempelhof airfield	Dornier Do 215	60 %	No crew casualties.
2.	3./KG 3	CM	Landing accident at Le Culot airfield.	Dornier Do 17Z	15 %	No crew casualties.
3.	III./KG 3	NCM	Crashed at Schweinfurth; cause not known.	Dornier Do 17	100 %	Four crew members killed.
4.	III./KG 30	NCM	Damaged in landing accident at Aalborg.	Junkers Ju 88A-1	25 %	No crew casualties.
5.	III./KG 51	NCM	Force landed near Berka after engine failure.	Junkers Ju 88A	30 %	No crew casualties.

Luftwaffe Losses, 5th August 1940—*continued*

6.	I./St.G 2	NCM	Take-off incident at Condé airfield.	Junkers Ju 87B-2	6 %	No crew casualties.
7.	5./JG 3	NCM	Landing incident at Orombon airfield.	Messerschmitt Bf 109 E-1	5 %	Pilot unhurt.
8.	I./JG 27	NCM	Landing accident at Plumetot airfield.	Messerschmitt Bf 109 E-1	20 %	Pilot unhurt.
9.	1./JG 54	CM	Damaged by Spitfire of Orchard of 65 Sqn. off Kent coast at 08.05 hrs. Landed at Beauvais.	Messerschmitt Bf 109	35 %	Pilot unhurt.
10.	1./JG 54	CM	Shot down by Hurricane of Blair of 151 Sqn. off Dover at 15.25 hrs; pilot rescued.	Messerschmitt Bf 109 E-4	100 %	Oblt. Seiler wounded.
11.	3./JG 54	NCM	Landing accident at Detmold.	Messerschmitt Bf 109 E-3	60 %	Pilot unhurt.
12.	1./196	NCM	Crashed while alighting in heavy seas near cruiser *Hipper* off Greenland coast.	Arado Ar 196	100 %	Crew unhurt.

Tuesday 6th August

No doubt encouraged by the recent lack of interference with the movement of shipping, the Admiralty saw no reason to prevent the sailing of eight convoys during the 24 hours ending at midnight on 6th/7th August. Two further deep sea convoys were also approaching the Cornish coast, and these were afforded strong protection by the fighter squadrons based in the South-West.

Not more than about half a dozen enemy aircraft, probably engaged in reconnaissance and navigation familiarisation, ventured near the British coasts and one, a Dornier Do 17 from Hauptmann Rathmann's III./KG 3, found itself in the dangerous vicinity of a convoy off Harwich shortly after dawn. Guard was at that time being provided by three sergeant pilots in Hurricanes of No. 85 Squadron, led by Geoffrey Allard. All three pilots attacked the Dornier, and shot it down

in flames near the convoy; a destroyer circled the spot, looking for survivors, but in vain. Allard was one of Fighter Command's most successful pilots at this time, having achieved considerable success during the Battle of France and at Dunkirk. He had already been awarded the Distinguished Flying Medal, and was to receive a Bar to the decoration later in August (one of the first such recipients). By the end of the month he had been commissioned as a Pilot Officer, and the following month was promoted to Flight Lieutenant and awarded the Distinguished Flying Cross. Like so many of the most successful fighter pilots, Allard attributed his high score to superlative eyesight; whether or not he was leading his formation, he was frequently the first to sight the enemy and warn his fellow pilots.

R.A.F. FIGHTER COMMAND LOSSES—TUESDAY 6th AUGUST 1940

1.	17 Sqn., Debden	NC	Crashed at Debden Park during air test; pilot killed.	Not known	Plt. Off. H.W.A. Britton	Hurricane	N2456	Cat. 3 Destroyed
2.	72 Sqn., Acklington	NC	Crashed on landing at Acklington after patrol; pilot unhurt.	Not known	Not known	Spitfire	L1078	Cat. 3 Destroyed
3.	219 Sqn., Catterick	NC	Struck high tension cables during searchlight exercise and crashed; crew slightly hurt.	At night	Plt. Off. J.C. Carriere Sgt. C. Beveridge	Blenheim	—	Cat. 3 Destroyed
4.	232 Sqn., Sumburgh	NC	Replacement aircraft crashed on delivery; pilot unhurt.	Not known	Not known	Hurricane	R4090	Cat. 3 Destroyed
5.	234 Sqn., St. Eval	NC	Night landing accident ; pilot unhurt.	23.05 hrs.	Plt. Off. P.W. Horton	Spitfire	P9366	Cat. 3 Destroyed

LUFTWAFFE LOSSES—TUESDAY 6th AUGUST 1940

1.	Aufkl.Gr.(H)/21	NCM	Landing accident at Lessay airfield.	Henschel Hs 126	60 %	No crew casualties.
2.	1./KG 3	NCM	Landing accident at Le Culot airfield.	Dornier Do 17Z	75 %	No crew casualties.
3.	7./KG 3	NCM	Landing accident at Le Trond airfield.	Dornier Do 17Z	30 %	No crew casualties.
4.	7./KG 3	CM	Shot down by Hurricanes of Allard, Ellis and Evans of 85 Sqn. off Harwich at 06.15 hrs.	Dornier Do 17Z	100 %	Oblt. Ullricht + three missing.
5.	7./KG 53	NCM	Crashed at Markheidenfeld after engine failure.	Heinkel He 111H-2	100 %	Four crew members killed.
6.	II./KG 54	NCM	Taxying accident at Erfurt-Bindersleben.	Junkers Ju 88	40 %	No crew casualties..
7.	II./KG 55	NCM	Force landed near Nancy after engine failure.	Heinkel He 111	25 %	No crew casualties.
8.	II./LG 2	NCM	Crashed at Dankmarshausen after engine failure.	Messerschmitt Bf 109	95 %	Pilot injured.
9.	II./ZG 2	NCM	Force landed at Verdun owing to bad weather.	Messerschmitt Bf 110 C-4	30 %	No crew casualties.
10.	I./JG 3	CM	Landing accident at St. Omer (not due to combat)	Messerschmitt Bf 109	40 %	Pilot unhurt.
11.	II./JG 53	NCM	Take-off accident at Dinant airfield.	Messerschmitt Bf 109 E-4	50 %	Pilot unhurt.
12.	II./JG 53	NCM	Take-off accident at Dinant airfield.	Messerschmitt Bf 109 E-4	40 %	Pilot unhurt.
13.	1./196	NCM	Accident at Schellingwoude; cause not known.	Arado Ar 196	100 %	Ltn.z.S. Nowrat injured; one killed.

Wednesday 7th August

Although air activity over Britain continued at low intensity, with scattered nuisance raids at night, it fell to R.A.F. Bomber Command to strike the heaviest blow at the *Luftwaffe*. In a well-executed daylight raid on Haamstede, the British bombers struck the airfield just as the 4th *Staffel* of JG 54 was scrambling to intercept. The bombs fell among the taxying Messerschmitts, killing three pilots, destroying two aircraft and seriously damaging five others; three further pilots were wounded. The *Staffel*, which was due to re-join its *Gruppe* at Guines later that day, was effectively *hors de combat* and was withdrawn from Kesselring's order of battle for more than a fortnight.

Another German loss of some significance on this date,

though not suffered in combat, was that of Hauptmann Valesi, *Staffelkapitän* of 3./Erpr.Gr. 210. As leader of this *Staffel*, Valesi was probably one of the most experienced exponents of fighter-bombing tactics with the Bf 109. *Erprobungsgruppe 210* was composed of two *Staffeln* of Bf 110s and one of Bf 109s, all fitted with bomb racks. In their often brilliantly executed "set piece" attacks on pinpoint targets it was usual for the 109s to go·into the attack first and, having dropped their bombs, climb up to fly guard over the slower 110 bombers. It is no doubt significant that Valesi had flown He 51s on ground-attack sorties during the Spanish Civil War. The cause of his crash at Denain remains a mystery to this day.

R.A.F. FIGHTER COMMAND LOSSES—WEDNESDAY 7th AUGUST 1940

1.	253 Sqn., Turnhouse	NC	Night landing accident at Turnhouse; pilot unhurt.	21.00 hrs.	Plt. Off. D.N.O. Jenkins	Hurricane	*P3457*	Cat. 2 Damaged
2.	263 Sqn., Grangemouth	NC	Crashed near Stirling on training flight; pilot unhurt.	Not known	Not known	Whirlwind	—	Cat. 3 Destroyed
3.	501 Sqn., Gravesend	NC	Landing collision in bad weather at Gravesend; pilot unhurt.	A09.15 hrs.	Sgt. E.F. Howorth	Hurricane	—	Cat. 3 Destroyed
4.	501 Sqn., Gravesend	NC	Landing collision in bad weather at Gravesend; pilot unhurt.	A09.15 hrs.	Sgt. W.A. Wilkinson	Hurricane	—	Cat. 3 Destroyed
5.	616 Sqn., Leconfield	NC	Night flying accident 3 miles from Leconfield; pilot killed.	02.53 hrs.	Plt. Off. R.A. Smith	Spitfire	—	Cat. 3 Destroyed
6.	616 Sqn., Leconfield	NC	Night landing accident at Leconfield; pilot unhurt.	At night	Sgt. T.E. Westmoreland	Spitfire	—	Cat. 3 Destroyed

LUFTWAFFE LOSSES—WEDNESDAY 7th AUGUST 1940

1.	5.(H)/13	NCM	Landing accident at Lessa airfield.	Henschel Hs 126B	15 %	No crew casualties.
2.	1.(F)/121	CM	Reported to have been lost over Britain; no claim traced to any R.A.F. unit.	Junkers Ju 88A-1	100 %	Three crew missing.
3.	9./LG 1	CM	Crashed at Châteaudun airfield; cause unknown.	Junkers Ju 88A	100 %	Ltn. Hartzog + three killed.
4.	3./ZG 26	CM	Air collision near Conteville (with Item 5).	Messerschmitt Bf 110	100 %	Two crew members injured.
5.	3./ZG 26	CM	Air collision near Conteville (with Item 4).	Messerschmitt Bf 110D	100 %	One crew member killed.
6.	7./ZG 26	NCM	Crashed at Böblingen; cause not known.	Messerschmitt Bf 110 C-4	90 %	One crew member killed.
7.	3./Erpr.Gr.210	NCM	Crashed at Denain; cause not known.	Messerschmitt Bf 109 E-4	100 %	Hptm. Valesi killed.
8.	4./JG 3	NCM	Landing accident at Samer; cause not known.	Messerschmitt Bf 109 E-1	45 %	Pilot unhurt.
9.	II./JG 52	NCM	Landing accident at Oldendorf airfield.	Messerschmitt Bf 109 E-1	60 %	Pilot injured.
10.	3./906	CM	Damaged by A.A. guns in Firth of Forth at night.	Heinkel He 115	20 %	One crew member wounded.

[Note. In the R.A.F. bombing raid on Haamstede the bombs landed among Bf 109s of 4./JG 54 while taking off; three pilots were killed and four wounded; two aircraft were classified as "over 60 % damaged" (written off), and five aircraft classifed as "below 60 %" damaged.]

Thursday 8th August

For several years after the War military historians selected 8th August as the opening day of the Battle of Britain, and with some justification, principally on the grounds of the weight of attacks launched by the *Luftwaffe* and the bitterness of the fighting[7]. The operations mounted on this day, however, were not directly associated with *Adlerangriff*, but more a continuation of the former skirmishing phase; it would undoubtedly be more accurate to regard the conflict of 8th August simply as the Battle of Convoy C.W.9.

This convoy, consisting of twenty merchant ships with nine naval escort vessels and codenamed PEEWIT by the R.A.F., had sailed on the previous evening's tide from the Medway and attempted to pass through the Dover Strait undetected under cover of darkness. Its approach was nevertheless spot-

ted on the newly-installed German *Freya* radar on the Calais coast and this led to a spirited attack by E-boats in the early morning half light which cost the convoy three merchantmen sunk and three damaged.

As full daylight developed and the cloud base lifted to around 2,500 feet, Sperrle ordered an all-out air assault by *Luftflotte 3*—and in particular by the dive-bombers of *Fliegerkorps VIII*—to destroy the convoy. Sporadic attacks by small dive-bomber formations during the morning were beaten back by patrolling fighters without further loss to the convoy which, by 10.00 hours, had reached a position south of Brighton. Such dive-bombers as had managed to penetrate the fighter screen found their quarry well covered by a balloon barrage—a fact no doubt reported on their return to base.

It was now on the airfields at Angers, Caen and St. Malo that feverish activity commenced. Crews of 57 Junkers Ju 87s

---

[7] See Royal Air Force, 1939—1945, D. Richards, H.M.S.O., London, 1953; page 164.

German photograph of a Spitfire diving inverted with engine ablaze. In all likelihood the pilot had rolled on to his back so as to drop out of his cockpit. The black and white undersurfaces were still in evidence on some R.A.F. fighters well into the Battle. (Photo: Heinz Nowarra)

from *Stukageschwader 2, 3* and *77* were briefed to hit the convoy as it passed south of the Isle of Wight shortly after mid-day (British time). Their escort was to be provided by about twenty Messerschmnitt Bf 110s of V./LG 1 which would accompany the dive-bomber force from Caen. They would also rendezvous with about thirty Bf 109s of II. and III.*Gruppen* of JG 27, flying from Crépon and Carquebut.

This large formation had scarcely reached mid-Channel when the magnificently-sited CH station at Ventnor in the Isle of Wight started reporting plots of the raiders' approach. The enemy's intentions had to some extent been anticipated and there were in the vicinity of the convoy a total of eighteen Hurricanes from three squadrons, with a further squadron of Spitfires (No. 609) on its way full-tilt from Warmwell. As far as can be ascertained, the first contact was made by Flt. Lt. Noel Hall at the head of nine Hurricanes of No. 257 Squadron. Moments later three Hurricanes from No. 145 Squadron dived out of the sun on to a flank formation of the escort and, passing through the screen of Messerschmitts, attacked and shot down two Ju 87s. Within minutes the leading formations of the enemy raid were being furiously engaged by 30 British fighters, and already bombs were falling among the ships below. By engaging all the intercepting Spitfires and Hurricanes as they arrived over the convoy, the pilots of JG 27 enabled the dive-bombers to reach and attack the ships, which promptly scattered; this manœuvre in turn drastically reduced the defence provided by the balloon barrage and within ten minutes four ships had been sunk (all merchantmen). A further seven ships were fairly badly damaged by near misses.

This tremendous dogfight, involving about 150 aircraft, lasted approximately twenty minutes and cost the raiders three Ju 87s, one Bf 110 and three Bf 109s shot down, as well as four Ju 87s, three Bf 110s and one Bf 109 damaged; several of the damaged aircraft were written off on their return to France. The R.A.F. losses amounted to three Hurricanes of No. 257 Squadron and two of No. 238 Squadron—all five pilots being killed.

No. 238 Squadron had made very good progress since it had been declared operational on 2nd July. Its pilots had in the past five weeks been in action a dozen times and, while acquiring skill and confidence in the air under the léadership of Squadron Leader Harold Fenton, had also achieved an eviable esprit. This extended not only among the flying personnel but throughout the ground members of the squadron. On hearing that two of his pilots were missing from the mid-day combat, Fenton took off again from Middle Wallop to search the area for possible survivors, and came across a Heinkel He 59 of *Seenotzentrale Cherbourg*, also obviously engaged in the same task. This aircraft Fenton promptly shot down, but in so doing was hit in the engine by return fire and had to ditch alongside H.M. Trawler *Basset*; unfortunately he had omitted to tighten his straps and, on touching down, he was catapulted out of the cockpit, injuring his legs, face and chest. His temper was scarcely improved when, instead of returning immediately to port, he heard the trawler's captain, Lieut. Nigel Herriot, R.N.R., give orders to make for a ditched and bellicose German pilot with whom he had to spend a thoroughly uncomfortable afternoon.

While the scattered remains of convoy PEEWIT re-assembled during the early afternoon south of St. Catherine's Point, No. 10 Group put up a constant umbrella of fighters. In France, hearing that the convoy was still struggling on, Baron von Richthofen ordered a further heavy strike by dive-bombers and again asked for an escort of Bf 109s from *Jafu 3*. By 16.00 hours 82 Ju 87s and 68 Bf 109s and Bf 110s were on their way to Weymouth Bay. Once again the coastal radar gave good warning of the raiders' approach so that two Squadrons of Hurricanes were ready in position to meet the attack well south of the convoy. John Peel, leading No. 145

Captured German aircrew N.C.O.s at a railway station somewhere in England. The Oberfeldwebel on the left wears the Observer's (navigator's) badge.

Officers of IV.(Stuka)/LG 1 play chess beside their aircraft as they wait for the order that will send them over England. The ten-day "battle of the Stuka" opened on 8th August. (Photo: Aero Publishers Inc.)

Squadron as usual, spotted the incoming mass of dive-bombers, but delayed his attack so as to sweep round and strike the Junkers with the sun behind him. The surprise was complete; not only had No. 145 Squadron achieved its first murderous charge before the escort reacted, but No. 43 Squadron, led by Flt. Lt. Thomas Morgan, was also well positioned for an attack. It was almost certainly Morgan himself who, attacking the lead formation of escorting Bf 109s with a fleeting burst, shot down Werner Andres—*Gruppenkommandeur* of II./JG 27. (No other R.A.F. pilot's combat report indicates an attack on an unbroken enemy fighter formation, while Andres has himself confirmed that he was taken by surprise by the Hurricanes' interception.) Flt. Lt. Roy Dutton of No. 145 Squadron had his engine cut out just as he was about to fire at a Bf 109 and had to break away; as he dived down he decided to put in a snap attack on a Ju 87, and having set one on fire he found that his engine was showing signs of coming back to life, so promptly attacked and destroyed a second dive-bomber.

It seems that the Bf 110s' pilots had been briefed to destroy all the remaining barrage balloons over the convoy; the spectacle of flaming aircraft and balloons in a sky flecked

The boats of the Royal National Lifeboat Institution played a major part in rescuing ditched airmen during the Battle. Here, the Dungeness boat brings in a wounded German N.C.O.

Rescue launches of the Royal Air Force (left) and the Royal Navy. At this point in the War the Air-Sea Rescue service was only an embryo of the large and well-organised network it was to become later; the R.A.F. relied heavily on range launches and Coastal Command tenders.

with clouds and drifting parachutes over burning ships must have presented a nightmare picture to be remembered for may a day. As the German aircraft retired from the scene of battle, upwards of thirty airmen drifted in the waters of the Channel, among them Werner Andres. He, as well as about a dozen others, were picked up before nightfall by *Luftwaffe* rescue units.

The convoy PEEWIT had been shattered. Of the twenty ships that had set sail the previous night, only four sailed into Swanage virtually unscathed; seven had gone to the bottom of the Channel and six had had to make for other ports in a critical condition. Four escort and rescue vessels had also been badly damaged. With such a heavy toll of shipping it is perhaps invidious to suggest that the intercepting fighters had been victorious; yet Sqn. Ldr. John Peel's Hurricane pilots of No. 145 Squadron had fought the fight of their lives. The Squadron had been in action three times during the day[8] and had claimed 21 enemy aircraft destroyed for the loss of five

pilots. While the actual score appears to have been eleven destroyed and six damaged, the success of the day's operations was immediately apparent as confirmation of individual victories was gathered, and messages of congratulation converged on Westhampnett[9].

While it is true that the heavy attacks upon convoy PEEWIT were not part of Göring's overall plan for Adlerangriff, they had followed the pattern of some of the heavy convoy attacks launched in July. Only the weight had increased. Yet, despite the heavy losses in shipping, as well as fairly heavy casualties among Fighter Command squadrons, Dowding and his Group Commanders could review the day's fighting with some satisfaction. It had shown, or at least suggested that the larger the enemy formation launched the better the radar picture and warning given. In every instance during the Channel battles the intercepting fighters had been scrambled in good time and had reached a favourable position to meet the raiders.

---

[8] The Squadron had intercepted an attack over a westbound convoy which had set sail from Weymouth Bay at about 09.00 hours; in this raid it had claimed the destruction of six Ju 87s and three Bf 110s, for the loss of two pilots.

[9] Telegram from the Secretary of State for Air, "Congratulations on your splendid achievements today". From the Chief of the Air Staff, "Well done 145 Squadron in your hard fighting today. Good work by all". From Air Officer Commanding No. 11 Group, "Group Commander sends warm congratulations to No. 145 Squadron on their outstanding success during three heavy engagements today and sincerely hopes that some of the missing

pilots will turn up as frequently happened in the past. Today's fighting demonstrated fine offensive spirit, good leadership and straight shooting which reflect great credit on the whole Squadron". H.R.H. The Duke of Gloucester visited the Squadron during the day and added his congratulations. On 12th August Winston Churchill directed that a telegram be sent by the Cabinet to Sir Hugh Dowding, "The War Cabinet would be glad if you would convey to the Fighter Squadrons of the R.A.F. engaged in Thursday's brilliant action their admiration of the skill and prowess which they displayed and congratulate them upon the defeat and heavy losses inflicted on a far more numerous enemy".

R.A.F. FIGHTER COMMAND LOSSES—THURSDAY 8th AUGUST 1940

No.	Squadron		Details	Time	Pilot	Aircraft	Serial	Category
1.	43 Sqn., Tangmere	C	Shot down by enemy fighters south of the Isle of Wight; pilot killed.	A16.20 hrs.	Plt. Off. J.R.S. Oelofse	Hurricane	*P3781*	Cat. 3 Lost
2.	43 Sqn., Tangmere	C	Shot down by enemy fighters south of the Isle of Wight; pilot killed.	A16.20 hrs.	Plt. Off. J. Cruttenden	Hurricane	*P3468*	Cat. 3 Lost
3.	43 Sqn., Tangmere	C	Shot down and crashed near Ventnor, Isle of Wight; pilot unhurt.	16.35 hrs.	Plt. Off. H.C. Upton	Hurricane	*R4102*	Cat. 3 Destroyed
4.	64 Sqn., Kenley	NC	Crashed at Capel, Surrey, following engine failure; pilot injured.	A11.15 hrs.	Sgt. J.W.C. Squier	Spitfire	*P9369*	Cat. 3 Destroyed
5.	64 Sqn., Kenley	C	Shot down by Bf 109s near Dover; pilot baled out seriously wounded but died of wounds on 10-8-40.	12.07 hrs.	Plt. Off. P.F. Kennard-Davis	Spitfire	*L1039*	Cat. 3 Destroyed

R.A.F. Losses, 8th August 1940—*continued*

6.	65 Sqn., Manston	C	Shot down in Dover area by Bf 109s; pilot killed.	A10.45 hrs	F/Sgt. N.T. Phillips	Spitfire	K9905	Cat. 3 Lost
7.	65 Sqn., Manston	C	Shot down in Dover area by Bf 109s; pilot killed.	A10.45 hrs.	Sgt. D.I. Kirton	Spitfire	K9911	Cat. 3 Lost
8.	145 Sqn., Westhampnett	C	Shot down by Bf 109s off the Isle of Wight; pilot killed.	A09.00 hrs.	Plt. Off. L.A. Sears	Hurricane	P3381	Cat. 3 Lost.
9.	145 Sqn., Westhampnett	C	Shot down in flames by Bf 109s over the English Channel; pilot killed.	A09.00 hrs.	Sgt. E.D. Baker	Hurricane	P2957	Cat. 3 Lost
10.	145 Sqn., Westhampnett	C	Shot down over convoy off the Isle of Wight; pilot killed.	A16.25 hrs.	Sub.-Lt. F.A. Smith, **R.N.**	Hurricane	P3163	Cat. 3 Lost
11.	145 Sqn., Westhampnett	C	Shot down over convoy off the Isle of Wight; pilot killed.	A.16.30 hrs.	Plt.Off. Lord R.U.P.Shuttleworth	Hurricane	P2955	Cat. 3 Lost
12.	145 Sqn., Westhampnett	C	Shot down over convoy off the Isle of Wight; pilot killed.	A.16.30 hrs.	Plt. Off.E.C. Wakeham	Hurricane	—	Cat. 3 Lost
13.	152 Sqn., Warmwell	C	Shot down by Bf 109s and force landed at Langton Matravers; pilot unhurt.	Not known	Sgt. D.N. Robinson	Spitfire	—	Cat. 2 Damaged
14.	152 Sqn., Warmwell	C	Shot down by Bf 109s and force landed; pilot unhurt.	Not known	Plt. Off. W. Beaumont	Spitfire	—	Cat. 2 Damaged
15.	234 Sqn., St. Eval	NC	Force landed (not the result of combat); pilot unhurt.	Not known	Sgt. J. Szlagowski	Spitfire	N3278	Cat. 3 Destroyed
16.	238 Sqn., Middle Wallop	C	Shot down over convoy PEEWIT south of the Needles; pilot killed.	12.34 hrs.	Flt. Lt. D.E. Turner	Hurricane	P3823	Cat. 3 Lost
17.	238 Sqn., Middle Wallop	C	Shot down over convoy PEEWIT south of the Needles; pilot killed.	12.30 hrs.	Fg. Off. D.C. MacCaw	Hurricane	P3617	Cat. 3 Lost
18.	238 Sqn., Middle Wallop	C	Shot down by He 59 off the Isle of Wight and crashed into the sea; pilot slightly hurt but rescued by H.M. Trawler *Basset.*	13.50 hrs.	Sqn. Ldr. H.A. Fenton	Hurricane	P2947	Cat. 3 Lost
19.	257 Sqn., Tangmere	C	Shot down by Bf 109s off St. Catherine's Point; pilot killed.	A12.30 hrs.	Flt. Lt. N.M. Hall	Hurricane	P2981	Cat. 3 Missing
20.	257 Sqn., Tangmere	C	Shot down by Bf 109s off St. Catherine's Point; pilot killed.	A12.30 hrs.	Fg. Off. B.W.J. D'Arcy-Irvine	Hurricane	P3058	Cat. 3 Missing
21.	257 Sqn., Tangmere	C	Shot down by Bf 109s off St. Catherine's Point; pilot killed.	A12.30 hrs.	Sgt. K.B. Smith	Hurricane	R4094	Cat. 3 Missing
22.	303 Sqn., Northolt	NC	Landing accident during training; pilot unhurt.	Not known	Sgt. M. Belc	Hurricane	—	Cat. 2 Damaged
23.	303 Sqn., Northolt	NC	Landing accident during training; pilot unhurt.	Not known	Sgt. J. Frantisek	Hurricane	—	Cat. 2 Damaged
24.	600 Sqn., Manston	C	Shot down (believed by enemy fighters) and crashed off Margate; three crew killed.	11.37 hrs.	Fg.Off. D.N.Grice Sgt. F.J. Keast AC J.B.W. Warren	Blenheim	L8665	Cat. 3 Lost
25.	610 Sqn., Biggin Hill	NCM	Crashed during forced landing at Wittersham; pilot unhurt.	Not known	Sgt. W.J. Neville	Spitfire	L1045	Cat. 3 Destroyed

LUFTWAFFE LOSSES—THURSDAY 8th AUGUST 1940

1.	9./KG 4	NCM	Crashed at Fassberg; cause not known.	Heinkel He 111P	100 %	Three crew killed.
2.	II./KG 54	NCM	Crashed at St. André after engine failure.	Junkers Ju 88A	95 %	One killed and two injured.
3.	I./KG 77	NCM	Landing accident at Regensburg airfield.	Junkers Ju 88A	25 %	No crew casualties.
4.	II./St.G 1	CM	Damaged by 145 Sqn. Hurricane near Swanage at 09.10 hrs.	Junkers Ju 87B	Under 60 %	Oblt. Ostmann + one wounded.
5.	III./St.G 1	CM	Shot down by Hurricane of Branch of 145 Sqn. near Swanage at A09.10 hrs.	Junkers Ju 87B	100 %	Two crew members missing.
6.	III./St.G 1	CM	Shot down by Hurricane of Branch of 145 Sqn. near Swanage at A09.19 hrs.	Junkers Ju 87B	100 %	Two crew members missing.
7.	I./St.G 2	CM	Damaged by Hurricane of 145 Sqn. off Isle of Wight at A12.30 hrs. Force landed on return.	Junkers Ju 87B	40 %	No crew casualties.
8.	III./St.G 2	CM	Damaged by Hurricane of 145 Sqn. off Isle of Wight at A12.30 hrs. Force landed in France.	Junkers Ju 87B	Under 60 %	Two crew members wounded.
9.	I./St.G 3	CM	Damaged by Spitfire of McArthur of 609 Sqn. over Channel at 12.30 hrs. Landed at Théville.	Junkers Ju 87B	10 %	One crew member wounded.
10.	I./St.G 3	CM	Shot down by Hurricane of 145 Sqn. off the Isle of Wight at A12.30 hrs.	Junkers Ju 87B	100 %	One killed; one missing.
11.	I./St.G 3	CM	Shot down by Hurricane of 145 Sqn. off the Isle of Wight at A12.30 hrs.	Junkers Ju 87B	100 %	One killed; one missing.
12.	I./St.G 3	CM	Shot down by Spitfire of McArthur of 609 Sqn. over mid-Channel at 12.25 hrs.	Junkers Ju 87B	100 %	Oblt. Müller + one killed.
13.	I./St.G 3	CM	Damaged by Spitfires of 609 Sqn. over Channel at A12.25 hrs. Landed at Wuilly-le-Tessin.	Junkers Ju 87B	45 %	One crew member wounded.
14.	II./St.G 77	CM	Shot down by 145 Sqn. Hurricane over convoy PEEWIT off Isle of Wight at A16.20 hrs.	Junkers Ju 87B	100 %	Hptm. Plewig made P.O.W.; one missing.
15.	II./St.G 77	CM	Shot down by 145 Sqn. Hurricane over convoy PEEWIT off Isle of Wight at A16.20 hrs.	Junkers Ju 87B	100 %	Hptm. Schmack + one missing.
16.	II./St.G 77	CM	Shot down by 145 Sqn. Hurricane over convoy PEEWIT off Isle of Wight at A16.20 hrs.	Junkers Ju 87B	100%	One killed and one missing.
17.	II./St.G 77	CM	Damaged by 43 Sqn. Hurricane of Woods-Scawen off Isle of Wight at 15.25 hrs.	Junkers Ju 87B	25 %	No crew casualties.
18.	II./St.G 77	CM	Intercepted by 43 Sqn. Hurricanes at 16.30 hrs.	Junkers Ju 87B	Nil	Two crew members wounded.
19.	II./St.G 77	CM	Damaged by 145 Sqn. Hurricanes over convoy PEEWIT at 16.25 hrs. Landed at Deauville.	Junkers Ju 87B	80 %	No crew casualties.
20.	II./St.G 77	CM	Damaged by 145 Sqn. Hurricane over convoy PEEWIT at 16.25 hrs. Landed at Bourgy.	Junkers Ju 87B	70 %	No crew casualties.
21.	II./St.G 77	CM	Damaged by 43 Sqn. Hurricane of Morgan off Isel of Wight at 16.30 hrs. Landed at Bourgy.	Junkers Ju 87B	20 %	No crew casualties.
22.	V./LG 1	CM	Damaged by 238 Sqn. Hurricanes of Domagola and Steborowski at A12.30 hrs. over Channel.	Messerschmitt Bf 110C	40 %	Two crew members wounded.
23.	V./LG 1	CM	Damaged by 238 Sqn. Hurricanes of Davis and Hughes off Isle of Wight at A12.30 hrs.	Messerschmitt Bf 110C	25 %	No crew casualties.
24.	V./LG 1	CM	Shot down by 609 Sqn. Spitfire of Appleby over convoy PEEWIT off Isle of Wight at 12.30 hrs.	Messerschmitt Bf 110C	100 %	Two crew members missing.
25.	V./LG 1	CM	Damaged by 609 Sqn. Spitfire of Darley over convoy PEEWIT off Isle of Wight at 12.25 hrs.	Messerschmitt Bf 110C	70 %	No crew casualties.
26.	V./LG 1	CM	Damaged by 145 Sqn. Hurricane over convoy PEEWIT off Isle of Wight at A12.25 hrs.	Messerschmitt Bf 110C	70 %	No crew casualties.
27.	V./LG 1	CM	Damaged by 145 Sqn. Hurricane over convoy PEEWIT off Isle of Wight at A12.25 hrs.	Messerschmitt Bf 110C	80 %	One crew member killed and one wounded.

Luftwaffe Losses, 8th August 1940—*continued*

28.	I./JG 3	CM	Take-off accident at Colombert; not combat.	Messerschmitt Bf 109E	30 %		Pilot injured.
29.	5./JG 3	CM	Landing accident at Samer; not result of combat.	Messerschmitt Bf 109 E-4	15 %		Pilot unhurt.
30.	III./JG 26	CM	Shot down by 64 Sqn. Spitfires of MacDonnell and Mann near Dover at A11.45 hrs.	Messerschmitt Bf 109 E-4	100 %		Oblt. Ohm missing.
31.	I./JG 27	CM	Shot down by 145 Sqn. Hurricane over Weymouth Bay at 09.10 hrs.	Messerschmitt Bf 109 E-1	100 %		Pilot rescued safely.
32.	1./JG 27	CM	Shot down by 145 Sqn. Hurricane of Boyd over Weymouth Bay at A09.10 hrs.	Messerschmitt Bf 109 E-3	100 %		Ltn Igor Birkenbach killed.
33.	1./JG 27	CM	Shot down by 145 Sqn. Hurricane of Boyd over Weymouth Bay at 09.08 hrs.	Messerschmitt Bf 109 E-3	100 %		Ltn. Karl-Heinz Bothfeld killed.
34.	II./JG 27	CM	Damaged by 43 Sqn. Hurricane of Hallowes over convoy off Isle of Wight at A16.30 hrs.	Messerschmitt Bf 109 E-2	60 %		Pilot safe.
35.	II./JG 27	CM	Shot down by 43 Sqn. Hurricane of Hallowes over convoy PEEWIT off the Isle of Wight at 16.30 hrs.	Messerschmitt Bf 109 E-4	100 %		Pilot rescued safely.
36.	II./JG 27	CM	Shot down by 238 Sqn. Hurricanes of Domagola and Seabourne over convoy at 12.30 hrs.	Messerschmitt Bf 109 E-4	100 %		Pilot rescued safely.
37.	6./JG 27	CM	Shot down by 43 Sqn. Hurricane of Morgan off Isle of Wight at A16.30 hrs.	Messerschmitt Bf 109 E-1	100 %		Uffz. Heinz Uebe wounded, but rescued.
38.	5./JG 27	CM	Shot down by 145 Sqn. Hurricane over convoy PEEWIT off Isle of Wight at A16.20 hrs.	Messerschmitt Bf 109 E-4	100 %		Ofw. Erich Krenzke wounded, but rescued.
39.	5./JG 27	CM	Shot down by 238 Sqn. Hurricanes of Domagola and Seabourne over convoy PEEWIT at 12.30 hrs.	Messerschmitt Bf 109 E-4	100 %		Uffz. Edgar Schulz killed.
40.	III./JG 27	CM	Damaged by 238 Sqn. Hurricanes of Cawse and Batt over convoy PEEWIT at A12.25 hrs.	Messerschmitt Bf 109 E-1	35 %		Gefr. Ernst Nittmann wounded.
41.	III./JG 27	CM	Shot down by 257 Sqn. Hurricane of Gundry off St. Catherine's Point at A12.25 hrs.	Messerschmitt Bf 109 E-4	100 %		Uffz. Ludwig Girrbach missing.
42.	III./JG 51	CM	Force landed in Wizernes—St. Omer area; not the result of combat.	Messerschmitt Bf 109E	40 %		Pilot unhurt.
43.	II./JG 53	CM	Damaged by 41 Sqn. Spitfires at A12.00 hrs.	Messerschmitt Bf 109 E-4	45 %		Pilot unhurt.
44.	III./JG 54	CM	Damaged by 41 Sqn. Spitfires at A12.00 hrs.	Messerschmitt Bf 109 E-4	40 %		Pilot unhurt.
45.	Seenotflugkdo. Cherbourg	CM	Shot down by Hurricane of Fenton of 238 Sqn. in mid-Channel at A13.50 hrs.	Heinkel He 59	100 %		Two crew missing.

Probably damaged in the engine or coolant system this Bf 109E-4, bearing staff markings and the III.*Gruppe* vertical bar of an unidentified *Geschwader*, made a good wheels-up forced landing and was later put on public display in Croydon, Surrey, during August. It was unusual for a German pilot not to have jettisoned his canopy and head armour before making his forced landing.

Friday 9th August

The previous day's heavy fighting over the Channel no doubt suggested to the British defence commanders that Germany's all-out air offensive had at last started and, with much the same sort of weather prevailing on the 9th, an apparent return to the lethargy of August's first week must have been puzzling. It was of course not realised that the convoy battle had been unpremeditated and formed no integral part of the planned German campaign.

The *Luftwaffe* nevertheless flew several hundred scattered sorties against Britain. KG 26 sent about half a dozen Heinkels against convoys off the North-East coast, but found none of them. Instead, they dropped their bombs on ports in Yorkshire and further north; one such aircraft was caught by Hurricanes of No. 79 Squadron and shot down into the sea—but not before it had dropped its bombs on the docks at Sunderland.

A Junkers Ju 88, which ventured over Falmouth, where a deep sea convoy had put in the evening before, was pounced on by Hurricanes of No. 234 and 601 Squadron and shot down before it could do any damage. Another Ju 88, engaged in reconnaissance over the aircraft factories at Filton and Yeovil, escaped with a dead crew member after a brief clash with a Hurricane of No. 213 Squadron.

Messerschmitts of JG 51 attempted to pursue their new-found sport of balloon strafing over Dover, but were turned away by Spitfires of No. 64 Squadron, one of which was damaged in the fight. They also found that the *flak* over Dover was accurately predicted for balloon height—so accurately that the guns brought down one of the balloons!

A young Leutnant pilot being assisted along an English quayside after being "fished out of the drink". One would imagine that during his enforced swim he bitterly regretted the vanity which prompted him to wear his jack-boots while flying. (Photo: Royal National Lifeboat Institution)

R.A.F. FIGHTER COMMAND LOSSES—FRIDAY 9th AUGUST 1940

1.	64 Sqn., Kenley	C	Damaged by Bf 109; location not known; pilot unhurt.	Not known	Sgt. J. Mann	Spitfire	—	Cat. 1 Damaged
2.	266 Sqn., Wittering	NC	Aircraft hit obstruction during landing; pilot unhurt.	Not known	Sgt. A.W. Eade	Spitfire	L1059	Cat. 2 Damaged
3.	303 Sqn., Northolt	NC	Aircraft damaged in taxying accident at Northolt; pilot unhurt.	Not known	Fg. Off. L.W. Paszkiewicz	Hurricane	—	Cat. 1 Damaged
4.	600 Sqn., Manston	NC	Engine failure near Margate and crew baled out; pilot picked up and gunner swam ashore.	Not known	Fg. Off. S. Le Rougetel Sgt. A. Smith	Blenheim	L8679	Cat. 3 Lost
5.	605 Sqn., Drem	NC	Dived into sea off Dunbar; pilot believed to have been asphyxiated from glycol leak. Body recovered by m.v. *Eunmara*.	Not known	Sgt. R.D. Ritchie	Hurricane	L2103	Cat. 3 Lost

LUFTWAFFE LOSSES—FRIDAY 9th AUGUST 1940

1.	3.(F)/11	NCM	Crashed on Oslo/Fornebu airfield; not combat.	Dornier Do 17P	100 %	Ltn. Roh and Ltn. Thiel unjured.
2.	3.(F)/123	CM	Damaged by 213 Sqn. Hurricane of Sizer near Yeovil at 06.55 hrs. Returned to base.	Junkers Ju 88A	25 %	One crew member killed.
3.	2./KG 4	CM	Shot down by A.A. guns in Humber Estuary.	Heinkel He 111H-4	100 %	Two crew killed and two missing.
4.	7./KG 26	CM	Shot down by three 79 Sqn. Hurricanes near Newcastle at 11.40 hrs.	Heinkel He 111H-3 (1H+ER)	100 %	Uffz. Otto Denner, Uffz. Gustav Karkos, Fw. Willi Haertel and Uffz. Fritz Feinekat made P.O.W.s.
5.	III./KG 51	CM	Take-off accident at Etampes; not combat.	Junkers Ju 88A (7052 : 9K+GS)	75 %	No crew casualties.
6.	III./KG 51	CM	Take-off accident at Etampes; not combat.	Junkers Ju 88A (5064 : 9K+DD)	50 %	No crew casualties.
7.	II./LG 1	CM	Crashed in Channel after combat with Hurricanes over Falmouth at 14.30 hrs. (Mortimer-Rose and Harker of 234 Sqn. and three Hurricanes of 601 Sqn.)	Junkers Ju 88A	100 %	Four crew members missing.
8.	I./JG 53	CM	Collided with flak tower at Guernsey, killing 3 and injuring 2 members of *Flakregiment*.	Messerschmitt Bf 109 E-1	80 %	Pilot severely injured.

Saturday 10th August

Originally scheduled by Göring as *Adler Tag*, 10th August was "scratched" as the result of unfavourable weather forecasts. These proved dismally correct, with successive thundery squalls sweeping much of North France, the Channel and England. The bad weather did not, however, deter R.A.F. Bomber Command, whose crews carried out a number of light raids over Belgium and Holland; three such crews found Schipol and bombed the airfield, slightly damaging two German bombers.

A Dornier Do 17 of KG 2 stalked in over the coast at Deal and, despite a cat-and-mouse chase by No. 501 Squadron's Red Section in the squall clouds over the length of Kent, made good its escape after dropping its load of light bombs in the vicinity of West Malling.

Messerschmitt Bf 110 fighter-bombers of *Erprobungsgruppe 210* were sent out from the Pas de Calais on one of their pinpoint raids against the Norwich factory of Boulton

Paul, but the weather frustrated them, and their bombing was scattered. No. 242 Squadron was again slow in reacting from nearby Coltishall, and the raiders had vanished when the Hurricane pilots arrived over Norwich. Again the poor radar picture was to blame.

After a day of constant patrols over convoys by Fighter Command, the minelayers of General Coeler's *Fliegerkorps* IX went to work against the British ports in the south, and accomplished almost one hundred sorties during darkness without loss.

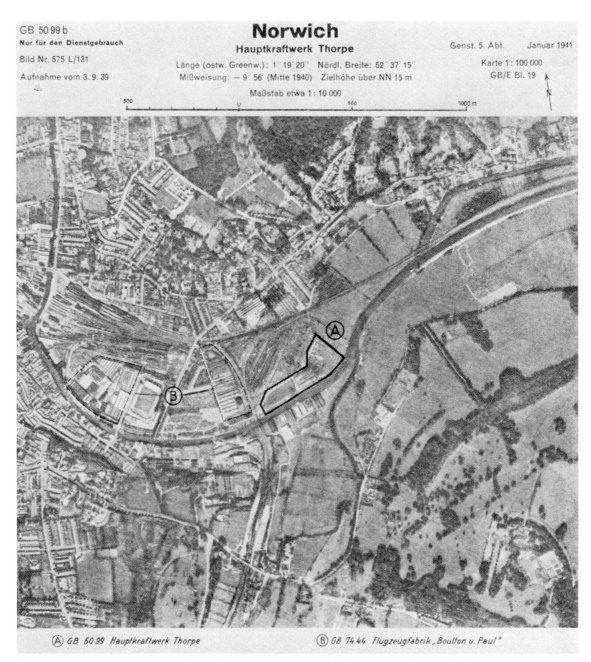

German target photo of Norwich, showing the Thorpe power station and the Boulton Paul factory. The date annotations show that this photo was prepared in September 1939, and was still in use in January 1941.

R.A.F. FIGHTER COMMAND LOSSES—SATURDAY 10th AUGUST 1940

1.	234 Sqn., St. Eval	NC	Wheels-up landing at St. Eval; pilot unhurt.	Not known	Sgt. A.S. Harker	Spitfire	P9468	Cat. 2 Damaged

LUFTWAFFE LOSSES—SATURDAY 10th AUGUST 1940

1.	Kü.Fl.Gr.806	NCM	Force landed at Brest-Sud; not combat action.	Junkers Ju 88A	60 %	No crew casualties.
2.	KGr.126	—	Damaged in bombing raid on Schipol airfield.	Heinkel He 111	35 %	No aircrew casualties.
3.	III./KG 4	—	Damaged in bombing raid on Schipol airfield.	Junkers Ju 88	2 %	No aircrew casualties.
4.	I./KG 4	CM	Crashed on Cairnsmoor, Kircudbrightshire, in night raid on Glasgow.	Heinkel He 111H-4	100 %	Ltn. Artur Zeiss, Uffz. Gernot von Turcheim and Uffz. Walter Meschner killed.
5.	7./KG 51	NCM	Landing accident at Beauvais; not combat.	Junkers Ju 88A-1 (7071 : 9K+JR)	20 %	Oblt. Simon and crew unhurt.
6.	St.St./LG 1	NCM	Crashed at Godshorn following engine failure.	Junkers Ju 88A-1	70 %	Two crew members injured.
7.	II./LG 2	NCM	Take-off accident at Beaumont-le-Roger airfield.	Messerschmitt Bf 109 E-4	100 %	Pilot killed.
8.	I/JG 27	—	Damaged by bomb splinters in R.A.F. raid on Cherbourg.	Messerschmitt Bf 109 E-4	25 %	No aircrew casualties.
9.	I/JG 27	NCM	Landing accident at Cherbourg; not combat.	Messerschmitt Bf 109 E-4	10 %	Pilot unhurt.

Sunday 11th August

Once again the *Luftwaffe* returned to the battle in force; yet once again, despite a day of ferocious combat, the operations still fell short of the planned Adlerangriff. The losses inflicted during this Sunday bear testimony to the growing weight and tempo of the Battle, but the near equality of casualties on both sides must have caused more than passing worry to Dowding, for such an attrition balance could only result in the destruction of his fighter squadrons long before that of the *Luftwaffe*.

Dawn brought fine weather almost everywhere and this deteriorated only slowly as the day wore on. Without serious complications enforced by weather conditions, the attacks launched can now be seen clearly as a dress rehearsal of carefully synchronised attacks against Nos. 10, 11 and 12 Groups.

With all radar stations between the Wash and Land's End "on the air", good warning of all attacks was afforded, and the first of these were a series of marauding free chases by Bf 109s in the Dover area. As if either to catch the dawn patrols

A favourite target of opportunity for German fighters was the balloon barrage. Here, a Bf 109 shoots up one of the Dover balloons during August. Although perhaps suggested as being a frivolous activity, it was fairly hazardous as the Dover guns in particular were often laid to fire to the height of the balloons which were sited to offer protection for the important harbour. The loss of half a dozen such balloons made the job of the bombers and dive bombers that much simpler.

Hauptmann Walter Rubensdörffer, the Swiss national and veteran of the Spanish Civil War, commanded the outstanding *Erprobungsgruppe 210* from its formation in July 1940 until his death in the massacre of his unit which followed the unintentional raid on Croydon of 15th August. (Photo: *Gemeinschaft der Jagdgeschwader E.V.*)

at the end of their fuel or to exhaust their reliefs, Hauptmann Walter Rubensdörffer of *Erprobungsgruppe 210* led his Messerschmitt fighter-bombers on a strafe over Dover; his single-seaters shot down three barrage balloons of No. 961 Balloon Squadron, and were closely followed by seventeen Bf 110s which swept over the harbour dropping about sixty light bombs, but without causing significant damage. This raid was not intercepted as it was anticipated that the attack on the balloons heralded a heavier attack by bombers.

Park reacted by ordering fighters from his Sector Stations to provide a fresh force with which to reinforce his dawn patrols, now nearing the end of their fuel reserves. No. 74 Squadron, with twelve Spitfires led by Malan, arrived from Manston too late to engage Rubensdörffer's aircraft, but ran straight into the first free chase by three *Staffeln* of Bf 109s; so rapidly did the two formations close that only fleeting bursts were fired before both sides became so dispersed that, as if by mutual consent, each drew away to reassemble. Several 109s were claimed as probably destroyed but in fact all returned home. Plt. Off. Peter Stevenson had to abandon

Views of Messerschmitt Bf 110Cs of *1.Staffel, Zerstörergeschwader 1*. These aircraft provided the escort for the raid on Portland on the morning of 11th August. The lower photo shows a pilot being assisted from the cockpit of his crash-landed aircraft. The *Geschwader*'s I *Gruppe* had four aircraft shot down and four damaged during the Portland raid; the *Gruppenkommandeur*, Major Ott, was killed. (Photos: Aero Publishers Inc.)

his Spitfire and was rescued unhurt from the sea.

Shortly after this a similar action was fought between Deal and Dover by twelve Hurricanes of No. 32 Squadron, led by Flt. Lt. Michael Crossley, and a *Staffel* of 109s. Again the interceptors failed to score, and a searchlight crew which passed a message to Hawkinge stating that it had seen an enemy fighter fall into the sea was unwittingly confirming the destruction of No. 74 Squadron's Spitfire.

Third of the free chases intercepted was one mounted by Bf 109s over Sussex at 09.45 hours and met by nine Spitfires of No. 64 Squadron, whose pilots shot down two without loss into the sea south-west of Bognor Regis.

By launching this series of fighter sweeps, Kesselring succeeded in drawing a high proportion of No. 11 Group's aircraft into the air and forward to the coastal airfields. It is possible that he also hoped to attract further reinforcements

into the area from other Groups. In this he failed, but now embarked on the second phase, using a large number of single *Staffeln* to saturate the Kent defences. Park refused to be drawn, and those combats which flared up were fought by Sections which had accidentally become separated from their Squadrons, in particular Nos. 32, 54 and 74.

The main target of the day's operations was again to be the naval base at Portland[10], and it was at 09.45 hours, while Park was busy restraining his squadrons from unnecessarily engaging fighter sweeps over Kent and Sussex, that Ventnor CH first reported what looked like a very heavy raid building up near the Cherbourg Peninsula. A hurried discussion between Park and Brand brought agreement that this was to be the enemy's main threat, and forthwith twelve Spitfires of No. 609 Squadron were ordered up to patrol over their base at Warmwell at the same time as nine Hurricanes of No. 1 Squadron were scrambled from Tangmere. Six other squadrons (involving 53 fighters) at Exeter, Middle Wallop, Tangmere and Warmwell were ordered to Readiness while the radar picture developed.

The enemy raid consisted in the main of 54 Junkers Ju 88s from I. and II.*Gruppen*, KG 54, led by Oberstleutnant Hoehne and Major Leonardi, accompanied by about twenty Heinkels from KG 27 led by Oberst Behrendt and Major Schlichting. Escort was provided by 61 Messerschmitt Bf 110s of I. and II.*Gruppen*, ZG 2, led by Oberstleutnant Friedrich Vollbracht and Major Ott. Thirty Bf 109s from III.*Gruppe*, JG 2, led by Hauptmann Dr. Erich Mix, accompanied the leading formations. This raid, amounting to about 165 aircraft approaching Portland on a front of more than five miles, was the largest yet sent against Britain. By ten o'clock (British time) it had reached mid-Channel.

At seven minutes past ten, three CH stations simultaneously amended the raid strength to "one hundred plus", so that Brand and Park ordered off their main fighter formations; these fighters were now vectored towards the raid as follows:

No. 152 Squadron (four Spitfires), up from Middle Wallop and headed for Warmwell, diverted at 10.04 hours,

No. 145 Squadron (twelve Hurricanes), up from Westhampnett at 10.06 hours,

No. 87 Squadron (six Hurricanes), up from Exeter at 10.08 hours,

No. 213 Squadron (eight Hurricanes), up from Middle Wallop at 10.14 hours, and

No. 238 Squadron (twelve Hurricanes), up from Middle Wallop at 10.14 hours.

In addition, nine Hurricanes of No. 1 Squadron (up at 09.45

---

[10] The significance of Portland as a main target during the Battle of Britain has never been emphasised adequately, yet it is statistically proved that, apart from London and Liverpool, this naval base was scheduled for more main formation raids than any other target during 1940. (Dover was hit more frequently, though more often than not as a target of opportunity.)

Portland, being outside but fairly close to the proposed invasion area, was regarded as being the Royal Navy's principal Channel base from which operations could be mounted against the German sea communications once the invasion had been launched. However, owing to the general efficiency of the fighter defences of No. 10 Group—harmonised with well-sited CH radar stations—only about half the German raids managed to reach the Portland base itself.

hours from Tangmere), eleven Hurricanes of No. 601 Squadron (up at 09.55 hours from Tangmere) and twelve Spitfires of No. 609 Squadron (up from Warmwell) were directed towards the raid at 10.05 hours.

The German fighter formations arrived well ahead of the bombers at a point five miles south-east of Portland at 10.09 hours and immediately formed a number of holding circles, as if to attract the intercepting fighters. Battle was joined at 23,000 feet about one minute later when Squadron Leader Horace Darley led his No. 609 Squadron Spitfires straight across the top of the hugh circle formed by the Bf 110s. By firing full deflection bursts and breaking down on the far side of the enemy circle, they were able to avoid the Messerschmitt's front guns, and no fewer than five Bf 110s were shot down in this initial charge; Major Ott's aircraft appears to have fallen to the guns of Plt. Off. Noel Agazarian's Spitfire. The Bf 109s were slow to react and only engaged Dundas and McArthur; the latter took evasive action by spinning down for 15,000 feet, after which he admitted to feeling "rather unwell".

Most of the British squadrons fell for the German "trap" and allowed themselves to become fully occupied by the escorting Messerschmitts, with the result that casualties were high on both sides (as the loss tables indicate). Only some of the Exeter-based Hurricane pilots and those of the four Spitfires of No. 152 Squadron, who arrived rather late in the battle, spotted the Ju 88s and He 111s as they made for Portland and Weymouth. The Heinkels commenced their level bombing runs at 15,000 feet just as the Ju 88s dived from 10,000 feet and struck the oil storage farm, hitting and setting two oil tanks on fire.

The massive dogfight which, by 10.40 hours, had spread across the width of Weymouth Bay, was dying out as the Bf 109s sought to cover the broken ranks of ZG 2 while they retired. Further Bf 109s (from JG 27) had arrived as reinforcements to assist in covering the withdrawal which continued until well after 11.00 hours.

German casualties were substantially fewer than were claimed, with six Bf 110s, five Ju 88s, one He 111 and six Bf 109s destroyed. Fighter Command lost sixteen Hurricanes— with thirteen pilots killed—and one Spitfire of No. 152 Squadron, whose pilot drowned after baling out.

More significant by far was the nature of the German losses. In this one raid Major Ott (*Gruppenkommandeur* of I./ZG 2), Major Schlichting (*Gruppenkommandeur* of II./KG 27) and Major Leonardi (*Gruppenkommandeur* of II./KG 54) and three other senior *Geschwader* staff members were shot down and killed or captured.

The heavy casualties suffered by both sides now prompted unit commanders to send out patrols and rescue vessels to the area. Wing Commander David Roberts, commanding Middle Wallop, whose station had lost six fighters, ordered two Blenheims of No. 604 Squadron, escorted by three Spitfires of No. 152 Squadron, to mid-Channel to look for ditched pilots. They came across a Heinkel He 59 ambulance seaplane riding on the sea thirty miles off Cherbourg with two German vessels recovering enemy airmen under the watchful care of six Bf 109s. The Spitfires held off the escort while the Blenheims destroyed the seaplane.

Another Heinkel He 59 of *Seenotzentrale Cherbourg*, detached at Calais, was ordered to the same area but was caught

A Spitfire photographed from the cockpit of a Heinkel He 111; it was originally suggested that this may have been a staged photograph but the print shows no evidence of this; though obscured by under-exposure, squadron code letters are painted on the Spitfire's fuselage. (Photo: Heinz Nowarra)

by twelve Spitfires of No. 610 Squadron before it had travelled twenty miles, and was shot down by Flt. Lt. Edward Smith; the Spitfire pilots were, however, themselves caught unawares by escorting 109s which shot down and killed F/Sgt. John Tanner and Sgt. William Neville.

One final phase in the day's attacks remained. This opened with a blistering attack by Rubensdörffer's Messerschmitts on the convoy BOOTY at sea off the Harwich—Clacton coast at 11.50 hours, in company with and leading about eight Dornier Do 17s of 9./KG 2, and escorted by twenty Bf 110s of ZG 26. The German formation had been spotted by the low-looking radar at Foreness, and eleven Spitfires of No. 74 Squadron (not led on this sortie by Malan) arrived as the attack on the convoy was developing. Six Hurricanes of No. 17 Squadron were already in action and shot down a Bf 110 as the Spitfires destroyed another three. Sqn. Ldr. Peter Townsend, leading a Section of No. 85 Squadron's Hurricanes, was also in action during this raid.

The withdrawal of Rubensdörffer's formation to some extent confused the radar picture and thus perhaps afforded cover for the next raids, which were so timed as to catch those fighters already committed at the end of their fuel. This time a convoy at the mouth of the Thames was the target for forty-five Dornier Do 17s and a *Staffel* of of Ju 87s, with a strong escort of Bf 109s. This time Malan was at the head of No. 74 Squadron, which successfully broke up the raid and damaged several of the enemy. Hurricanes of No. 111 Squadron and Spitfires of No. 54 Squadron were also ordered into action, but by now the cloud was beginning to build into towering masses over the Estuary and several pilots reported getting separated from their Squadrons; thus the interception effort became so dissipated as to be almost ineffective. Nevertheless Malan's Spitfires saved the convoy from substantial damage. (No. 74 Squadron's diary mentions wistfully that almost all the pilots had flown four sorties before lunch and that most had been in action three times.)

The continuing deterioration of the weather during the afternoon brought a comparative lull in air activity, an opportunity gladly seized by both sides to arrange for replacements on squadrons badly hit during the morning. Dowding was not to know that *Adler Tag* was now set for 13th August—a fact of which Hugo Sperrle was painfully aware as his quartermaster staffs made hurried arrangements to re-establish the strengths of *Kampfgeschwader 54*, *Zerstörergeschwader 2* and *Jagdgeschwader 2* and 27 in readiness for the great day.

Snapshots of scenes on the airfield at Soesterberg in Holland, used by I./KG 4 "*General Wever*" during the Battle; and an in-flight photo of a Feldwebel in the nose position of one of the unit's Heinkel He 111s. (Photo: Hans Obert)

R.A.F. FIGHTER COMMAND LOSSES—SUNDAY 11th AUGUST 1940

No.	Squadron		Description	Time	Pilot	Aircraft	Serial	Category
1.	1 Sqn., Tangmere	C	Shot down by Bf 109s and crashed near Sandown, Isle of Wight; pilot killed.	11.40 hrs.	Plt. Off. J.A.J. Davey	Hurricane	P3172	Cat. 3 Destroyed
2.	17 Sqn., Martlesham	C	Damaged by Bf 110 off Harwich and further damaged on landing; pilot unhurt.	A11.50 hrs.	Plt. Off D.W.H. Hanson	Hurricane	—	Cat. 2 Damaged
3.	17 Sqn., Martlesham	C	Missing after combat with Bf 110s over convoy off Harwich; pilot assumed killed.	A12.10 hrs.	Plt. Off. K. Manger	Hurricane	P3760	Cat. 3 Missing
4.	56 Sqn., North Weald	(C)	Reported to have been shot down by Spitfire on convoy patrol; pilot's body recovered.	A12.30 hrs.	Sgt. R.D. Baker	Hurricane	N2667	Cat. 3 Lost
5.	64 Sqn., Kenley	C	Damaged in combat with Bf 109s, believed in Dover area; pilot returned unhurt.	11.58 hrs.	Plt. Off C.J.D. Andreae	Spitfire	—	Cat. 2 Damaged
6.	74 Sqn., Manston	C	Shot down by Bf 109 off Dover; pilot baled out and rescued from the sea.	08.10 hrs.	Plt. Off. P.C.F. Stevenson	Spitfire	P9393	Cat. 3 Lost
7.	74 Sqn., Manston	C	Shot down by Bf 110s off Clacton; pilot killed.	12.04 hrs.	Plt. Off. D.G. Cobden	Spitfire	R6757	Cat. 3 Missing
8.	74 Sqn., Manston	C	Shot down by Bf 110s off Clacton; pilot killed.	12.09 hrs.	Plt. Off. D.N.E.	Spitfire	R6962	Cat. 3 Missing
9.	87 Sqn., Exeter	C	Shot down by Bf 109s ten miles south of Portland Bill; pilot killed.	A11.00 hrs.	Flt. Lt. R.V. Jeff	Hurricane	—	Cat. 3 Lost
10.	87 Sqn., Exeter	C	Shot down by Bf 109s south of Portland; pilot baled out and swan ashore wounded in arm.	A11.00 hrs.	Plt. Off J.R. Cock	Hurricane	—	Cat. 3 Lost
11.	87 Sqn., Exeter	C	Damaged by Bf 109s south of Portland. Force landed near Warmwell; pilot unhurt.	A11.10 hrs.	Plt. Off. A.C.R. McLure	Hurricane	—	Cat. 2 Damaged
12.	111 Sqn., Croydon	C	Shot down by Bf 109s off North Foreland; pilot killed.	13.10 hrs.	Plt. Off. R.R. Wilson	Hurricane	P3942	Cat. 3 Missing
13.	111 Sqn., Croydon	C	Shot down by Bf 109s off North Foreland; pilot killed.	13.10 hrs.	Plt. Off. J.W. McKenzie	Hurricane	P3922	Cat. 3 Lost
14.	111 Sqn., Croydon	C	Shot down by Bf 109s off North Foreland; pilot assumed drowned.	13.10 hrs.	Plt. Off. J.H.H. Copeman	Hurricane	—	Cat. 3 Lost
15.	111 Sqn., Croydon	C	Shot down by Bf 109s off North Foreland; pilot assumed drowned.	A13.15 hrs.	Sgt. R.B. Sim	Hurricane	P3105	Cat. 3 Lost
16.	111 Sqn., Croydon	C	Crash landed at Martlesham after combat off North Foreland with Bf 109s; pilot unhurt.	A13.25 hrs.	Sgt. H.S. Newton	Hurricane	—	Cat. 3 Destroyed
17.	145 Sqn., Westhampnett	C	Missing after combat with Bf 109s and 110s off Swanage; pilot assumed killed.	A10.05 hrs.	Fg. Off. G.R. Branch	Hurricane	—	Cat. 3 Missing
18.	145 Sqn., Westhampnett	C	Missing after combat with Bf 109s and 110s off Swanage; pilot assumed killed.	A10.05 hrs.	Fg. Off. A. Östowicz	Hurricane	P2951	Cat. 3 Missing
19.	145 Sqn., Westhampnett	C	Shot down and force landed on Isle of Wight after above combat; pilot slightly hurt.	A10.20 hrs.	Sqn. Ldr. J.R.A. Peel	Hurricane	—	Cat. 3 Destroyed
20.	145 Sqn., Westhampnett	C	Forced down in above combat and crashed near Christchurch; pilot unhurt.	A10.20 hrs.	Plt. Off. A.N.C. Weir.	Hurricane	—	Cat. 3 Destroyed
21.	152 Sqn., Middle Wallop	C	Shot down by Bf 109s off Portland; pilot seen to bale out, but drowned.	A10.50 hrs.	Plt. Off. J.S.B. Jones	Spitfire	—	Cat. 3 Lost
22.	213 Sqn., Exeter	C	Shot down by Bf 109s off Portland; pilot killed.	10.23 hrs.	Flt. Lt. R.D.G. Wight	Hurricane	N2650	Cat. 3 Missing
23.	213 Sqn., Exeter	C	Shot down by Bf 109s off Portland; pilot killed.	10.27 hrs.	Sgt. S.L. Butterfield	Hurricane	—	Cat. 3 Missing

R.A.F. Losses, 11th August 1940—*continued*

No.	Squadron/Base		Description	Time	Pilot	Aircraft	Serial	Category
24.	213 Sqn., Exeter	C	Damaged in above combat off Portland; force landed and pilot unhurt.	10.34 hrs.	Sgt. E.G. Snowden	Hurricane	—	Cat. 2 Damaged
25.	238 Sqn. Middle Wallop	C	Shot down by Bf 109s between Weymouth and Swanage; pilot killed.	A10.45 hrs.	Flt. Lt. S.C. Walch	Hurricane	P3819	Cat. 3 Lost
26.	238 Sqn. Middle Wallop	C	Shot down by Bf 109s between Weymouth and Swanage; pilot killed.	A10.45 hrs.	Fg. Off. M.J. Steborowski	Hurricane	R4097	Cat. 3 Lost
27.	238 Sqn. Middle Wallop	C	Shot down by Bf 109s between Weymouth and Swanage; pilot killed.	A10.45 hrs.	Sgt. G. Gledhill	Hurricane	P3222	Cat. 3 Lost
28.	238 Sqn. Middle Wallop	C	Shot down by Bf 109s between Weymouth and Swanage; pilot killed.	A10.45 hrs.	Plt. Off. F.N. Cawse	Hurricane	P2978	Cat. 3 Lost
29.	238 Sqn. Middle Wallop	C	Damaged by Bf 109s near Swanage, but retuned safely.	A10.50 hrs.	Sgt. L. Pidd	Hurricane	—	Cat. 2 Damaged
30.	601 Sqn., Tangmere	C	Shot down by Messerschmitts off Portland; pilot killed.	10.24 hrs.	Plt. Off. J. Gillan	Hurricane	P3783	Cat. 3 Destroyed
31.	601 Sqn., Tangmere	C	Shot down by Messerschmitts off Portland; pilot killed.	A10.30 hrs.	Plt. Off. W.G. Dickie	Hurricane	L2057	Cat. 3 Lost
32.	601 Sqn., Tangmere	C	Shot down by Messerschmitts off Portland; pilot killed.	A10.25 hrs.	Plt. Off. R.S. Demetriadi	Hurricane	R4092	Cat. 3 Lost
33.	601 Sqn., Tangmere	C	Shot down by Messerschmitts off Portland; pilot killed.	10.23 hrs.	Plt. Off. J.L. Smithers	Hurricane	P3885	Cat. 3 Destroyed
34.	609 Sqn., Warmwell	C	Damaged in combat with Bf 109s and 110s off Swanage; pilot returned unhurt.	A10.05 hrs.	Fg. Off. J.C. Dundas	Spitfire	R6769	Cat. 2 Damaged
35.	610 Sqn., Biggin Hill	C	Shot down by Bf 109s escorting He 59 off Calais; pilot killed.	11.09 hrs.	Sgt. J.H. Tanner	Spitfire	L1037	Cat. 3 Lost
36.	610 Sqn., Biggin Hill	C	Shot down by Bf 109s escorting He 59 off Calais; pilot killed.	11.09 hrs.	Sgt. W.J. Neville	Spitfire	—	Cat. 3 Lost
37.	615 Sqn., Kenley	NC	Struck fence while landing at Hawkinge and overturned; pilot unhurt.	Not known	Plt. Off. J.A.P. McClintock	Hurricane	N2337	Cat. 2 Damaged
38.	616 Sqn., Leconfield	NC	Take-off accident and subsequent crash landed; pilot unhurt.	18.28 hrs.	Plt. Off. L.H. Casson	Spitfire	—	Cat. 3 Destroyed

LUFTWAFFE LOSSES—SUNDAY 11th AUGUST 1940

No.	Unit		Description	Aircraft	%	Crew
1.	3./KG 2	CM	Crashed at St. Inglevert and bombs exploded.	Dornier Do 17Z	100 %	Three crew members wounded.
2.	4./KG 2	CM	Landing accident at St. Omer; not combat action.	Dornier Do 17Z	100 %	Two crew members injured.
3.	9./KG 2	CM	Damaged by 85 Sqn. Hurricane of Townsend over convoy off Harwich at A11.50 hrs.	Dornier Do 17Z	5 %	One crew member wounded.
4.	9./KG 2	CM	Damaged by 85 Sqn. Hurricane of Allard over convoy off Harwich at A11.50 hrs.	Dornier Do 17Z	5 %	Two crew members wounded.
5.	9./KG 2	CM	Damaged by 85 Sqn. Hurricane of Stevens over convoy off Harwich at A11.50 hrs.	Dornier Do 17Z	8 %	One crew member killed.
6.	9./KG 4	CM	Reported to have been shot down by fighters over Folkestone; R.A.F. unit not traced.	Dornier Do 17Z	100 %	Four crews members rescued; one wounded.
7.	Stab II./KG 27	CM	Shot down by 238 Sqn. Hurricanes of Bann and Marsh 5 miles south of Swanage at 11.45 hrs.	Heinkel He 111H-3 (1G+AC)	100 %	Maj.i.G. Hans-Jurgen Brehmer, Maj. Freidrich-Karl Schlichting, *Gr.Kdr.*, Ofw. Günther Löhneng, Ofw. Willi Bendrich, and Ofw. Herbert Frey all made P.O.W.s
8.	9./KG 53	CM	Force landed at Alphen and burned.	Heinkel He 111	95 %	No crew casualties.
9.	I./KG 54	CM	Shot down by 87 Sqn. Hurricane of David ten miles south of Portland at A11.00 hrs.	Junkers Ju 88A	100 %	One killed and three missing
10.	I./KG 54	CM	Shot down by 87 Sqn. Hurricane of Cock ten miles south of Portland at A11.00 hrs.	Junkers Ju 88A	100 %	Crew rescued safely
11.	I./KG 54	CM	Damaged by night fighter and crashed at Evreux.	Junkers Ju 88A	35 %	One crew member wounded.
12.	II./KG 54	CM	Shot down by 601 Sqn. Hurricanes off Portland at A10.30 hrs.	Junkers Ju 88A	100 %	Maj. Leonardi, Gr.Kdr., Oblt. Schott + one other killed; one missing.
13.	II./KG 54	CM	Shot down by 601 Sqn. Hurricanes off Portland at A10.30 hrs.	Junkers Ju 88A	100 %	Oblt. Schaden killed; three missing.
14.	II./KG 54	CM	Shot down by 601 Sqn. Hurricanes off Portland at A10.30 hrs.	Junkers Ju 88A	100 %	Oblt Welte, wounded, made P.O.W.; three others missing.
15.	II./St.G 1	CM	Believed shot down by 74 Sqn. Spitfires off Clacton at A12.00 hrs.	Junkers Ju 87B	100 %	One killed; one missing.
16.	IV./LG 1	CM	Shot down by 151 Sqn. Hurricanes off Clacton.	Junkers Ju 87B	100 %	Two crew members missing.
17.	Stab/ZG 2	CM	Shot down by 609 Sqn. Spitfire of Dundas off Portland at A10.10 hrs.	Messerschmitt Bf 110 C-2	100 %	Oblt. Hensel killed; Oblt. Schäfer wounded.
18.	I./ZG 2	CM	Shot down by 609 Sqn. Spitfire of Agazarian off Portland at A10.10 hrs.	Messerschmitt Bf 110C	100 %	Maj. Ott, *Gr.Kdr.*, + one killed.
19.	I./ZG 2	CM	Shot down by 609 Sqn. Spitfire of Crook off Portland at A10.10 hrs.	Messerschmitt Bf 110C	100 %	One killed; Ltn. Jess missing.
20.	I./ZG 2	CM	Shot down by 609 Sqn. Spitfire of Bisdee off Portland at A10.10 hrs.	Messerschmitt Bf 110C	100 %	Two crew members missing.
21.	I./ZG 2	CM	Shot down by 609 Sqn. Spitfire of McArthur off Portland at A10.10 hrs.	Messerschmitt Bf 110 C-4	100 %	Two crew members missing.
22.	I./ZG 2	CM	Damaged by 1 Sqn. Hurricanes of Chetham and Goodman in mid-Channel at A10.10 hrs.	Messerschmitt Bf 110D	10 %	Crew safe.
23.	I./ZG 2	CM	Damaged by 1 Sqn. Hurricane of Brown in mid-Channel at A.10.10 hrs.	Messerchmittt Bf 110C	10 %	Crew safe.
24.	I./ZG 2	CM	Damaged by 213 Sqn. Hurricanes off Portland at A10.20 hrs.	Messerschmitt Bf 110C	15 %	Crew safe.
25.	II./ZG 2	CM	Shot down by 145 Sqn. Hurricanes off Swanage at 10.35 hrs.	Messerschmitt Bf 100 D-0	100 %	Two crew members missing.
26.	II./ZG 2	CM	Damaged by 145 Sqn. Hurricanes off Swanage at 10.35 hrs.	Messerschmitt Bf 110D	10 %	Crew safe.
27.	I./ZG 2	CM	Damaged by 213 Sqn. Hurricane off Portland at A10.25 hrs.	Messerschmitt Bf 110C	20 %	Crew unhurt.
28	I./ZG 26	CM	Shot down by 74 Sqn. Spitfire of Mungo-Park over convoy BOOTY at A12.00 hrs.	Messerschmitt Bf 110D	100 %	Hptm. Kogler, *St.Kap.*, + one wounded, made P.O.W.s.
29.	1./ZG 26	CM	Shot down by 74 Sqn. Spitfire of Freeborn over convoy BOOTY at A12.00 hrs.	Messerschmitt Bf 110	100 %	Two crew members missing.
30.	2./ZG 26	CM	Damaged by 85 Sqn. Hurricanes of Townsend, Hampshire and Allgood at A11.45 hrs.	Messerschmitt Bf 110	20 %	Crew unhurt.
31.	2./ZG 26	CM	Damaged by 74 Sqn. Spitfire of Skinner over convoy BOOTY at 12.11 hrs.	Messerschmitt Bf 110C	70 %	Crew unhurt.
32.	Erpr.Gr. 210	CM	Shot down by 17 Sqn. Hurricane of Stevens over convoy BOOTY at 11.56 hrs.	Messerschmitt Bf 110 C-6	100 %	Two crew members killed.

Luftwaffe Losses, 11th August 1940—*continued*

33. Erpr.Gr. 210	CM	Shot down by 74 Sqn. Spitfire of Nelson over convoy Booty at 12.01 hrs.	Messerschmitt Bf 110 C-6	100 %	Ltn. Bertram + one killed..
34. I./JG 2	CM	Shot down by 64 Sqn. Spitfire of MacDonnell over South Coast at A10.00 hrs.	Messerschmitt Bf 109 E-4	100 %	Pilot, wounded, made P.O.W.
35. I./JG 2	CM	Shot down by 64 Sqn. Spitfire of King over South Coast at A10.00 hrs.	Messerschmitt Bf 109 E-4	100 %	Pilot killed.
36. II./JG 2	CM	Crashed into sea after fighter combat; victor not known.	Messerschmitt Bf 109 E-4	100 %	Oblt. Rempel, *St.Kap.*, killed.
37. II./JG 2	CM	Missing after fighter combat; victor not known.	Messerschmitt Bf 109 E-4	100 %	Pilot missing.
38. III./JG 2	CM	Shot down by 87 Sqn. Hurricane of David over South Coast at A11.05 hrs.	Messerschmitt Bf 109 E-4	100 %	Oble. Fricke killed.
39. III./JG 2	CM	Shot down by 87 Sqn. Hurricane of McLure over South Coast at A11.05 hrs.	Messerschmitt Bf 109 E-3	100 %	Pilot rescued, unhurt.
40. III./JG 2	CM	Missing from combat over South Coast; victor not traced.	Messerschmitt Bf 109 E-1	100 %	Pilot missing.
41. III./JG 2	CM	Crashed near Cherbourg after combat with 87 Sqn. Hurricane of Badger at 11.05 hrs.	Messerschmitt Bf 109	100 %	Oblt. Steidle killed.
42. III./JG 26	CM	Damaged by 74 Sqn. Spitfire of Malan near Cap Gris Nez at A10.30 hrs. Crashed at Calais.	Messerschmitt Bf 109 E-1	80 %	Pilot wounded.
43. I./JG 27	CM	Shot down by 152 Sqn. Spitfire of Wildblood.	Messerschmitt Bf 109 E-1	100 %	Pilot rescued, unhurt.
44. 5./JG 27	CM	Shot down by 238 Sqn. Hurricane of Mann 5 miles south of Swanage at 10.50 hrs.	Messerschmitt Bf 109 E-1	100 %	Uffz. Sigfreid Lackner killed.
45. II./JG 27	NCM	Landing accident at St. Mere Eglise airfield.	Messerschmitt Bf 109	5 %	Pilot unhurt.
46. III./JG 27	CM	Shot down by 145 Sqn. Hurricane off Swanage at A10.35 hrs.	Messerschmitt Bf 109 E-4	100 %	Uffz. Rüdiger Menz missing.
47. 5./JG 51	CM	Shot down by 54 Sqn. Spitfire of Deere near Dover.	Messerschmitt Bf 109 E-3	100 %	Pilot missing.
48. I./JG 54	NCM	Take-off accident at Compiegne.	Messerschmitt Bf 109 E-4	33 %	Pilot unhurt.
49. 6./JG 54	NCM	Crashed at Haamstede following engine failure.	Messerschmitt Bf 109 E-3	100 %	Ltn. Wagner injured.
50. Seenotzentrale Cherbourg	CM	Shot down by 610 Sqn. Spitfire of Smith off Calais at 11.05 hrs.	Heinkel He 59	100 %	No crew casualties.
51. Seenotzentrale Cherbourg	CM	Shot down by two Blenheims of 604 Sqn. 30 miles off French coast.	Heinkel He 59	100 %	No crew casualties.

Monday 12th August

With the great offensive scheduled for the morrow, it was with some anxiety that *Luftwaffe* operations staffs examined the forecast weather maps prepared from reports by *Wetter-erkundungsstaffeln 1* and *161*, and by *Kampfgeschwader 40*, whose crews had flown far and wide over the Atlantic and British Isles to collect weather data. These confirmed a likely spell of fine weather and clear skies in a substantial ridge of high pressure building up to the north-east from the Azores.

As it was, 12th August dawned fine and clear, and seemed ideal for a number of preparatory attacks against targets in Southern England. It was quite obvious from de-briefing reports made out by crews who returned from the previous day's big raid in the Portland area that British radar had given considerable warning of their approach, and it was therefore decided after earnest representations by General Wolfgang Martini (head of the *Luftwaffe* signals branch at O.K.L.) to try to put out of action all known radar stations between Portland and the Thames Estuary before *Adlerangriff*. The day's effort was thus designed with this aim in mind, and at the same time attacks would be made upon the R.A.F.'s coastal fighter stations by taking advantage of the likely radar blackout.

As on the previous day, free chases were sent over Kent soon after first light, the first being reported by Dover CH at 07.20 hours. Knowing that such small formations could turn away at the last moment, the No. 11 Group Controller waited ten minutes before scrambling twelve Spitfires of No. 610 Squadron from Biggin Hill. Airborne at 07.31 hours, Squadron Leader John Ellis led his pilots to New Romney where he found nine Bf 109s of II./JG 52. A spirited dogfight followed in which it was clear that the German pilots were trying to draw the Spitfires eastwards. Flt. Lt. Edward Smith (who had destroyed the Heinkel seaplane on the previous day) received

two cannon shells in his cockpit and had to bale out when his aircraft caught fire; he landed in the sea with burns on his

B.E. ("Paddy") Finucane flew as a Pilot Officer with No. 65 Squadron during the Battle; he was to be awarded the D.S.O. and D.F.C. with two Bars. On 12th August he was credited with shooting down a Bf 109, possibly an aircraft of III./JG 54. (Cuthbert Orde portrait, courtesy Imperial War Museum)

Shot-down Messerschmitt Bf 110C of Stab.I/ZG 26, said to have crash-landed in Kent. (Photo: R.A.F. Museum)

hands and face, but was picked up by a motor torpedo boat and landed at Dover. Four other Spitfires were damaged, but two Messerschmitts were destroyed.

The attacks on the radar stations undoubtedly caught Fighter Command unawares. Having regard to the relatively small size of the targets, it was natural that Kesselring should choose Rubensdörffer's *Erprobungsgruppe 210* to strike the blows. Taking off from Calais-Marck at 08.40 hours, Rubensdörffer led four sections each of four Bf 110s on a westerly course south of Dover at right angles to the radar stations' normal line of sight. One by one the sections broke towards the Kent and Sussex coast in a series of brilliantly executed strikes. Oberleutant Otto Hintze[11] was the first to go into the attack against the CH radar at Dover, followed two minutes later by Wilhelm Rössiger's section which dropped its bombs among the compound huts at Rye, but fortunately missed the vital T/R buildings. As Martin Lutz made on for Pevensey CH and smashed its power supply cables with 500-kilo bombs, Rubensdörffer himself turned his section to the north and streaked for the inland CH station at Dunkirk; although almost all his section's bombs fell within the compound perimeter, no vital damage was done and the radar remained "on the air". Dover, Pevensey and Rye were put out of action temporarily, but emergency measures were brought into effect, and all were reporting within six hours—albeit with some discomfort to the men and women personnel.

Although the difficulty experienced in destroying these radar installations was soon realised by Martini (whose detection equipment disclosed that the CH stations were operating again during the afternoon), its impotance during the morning permitted a brief but heavy attack on the airfield at Lympne, commanded by Sqn. Ldr. Denis Montgomery. Fortunately for Park, this had only been used as an emergency fighter satellite field since June, and the 141 bombs which were dropped, though causing considerable damage, did not

seriously affect operations in the Biggin Hill Sector. Far more important was a raid by Junkers Ju 88s of II./KG 76 on Hawkinge airfield—also launched while the radar was blind—which destroyed two hangars, the station's maintenance workshops and four fighters on the ground. Nevertheless, under the inspired leadership of the station commander, Sqn. Ldr. E.E. Arnold[12], the airfield personnel set to with a will and had restored all services within 24 hours, so that Hawkinge was not wholly out of action.

The next stage in the day's attacks began soon after Rubensdörffer's strike had returned home. Believing that the CH screen was out of action, Kesselring launched dive-bombing attacks against two small convoys, AGENT and ARENA, off the North Foreland and in the Thames Esturay respectively. The first was spotted by the Foreness CHL, but the six Spitfires of No. 65 Squadron arrived too late to prevent the bombing, and were in turn closely engaged by escorting Messerschmitts. As No. 65 Squadron landed back at Manston to re-fuel at 11.15 hours, another raid appeared over a convoy between Deal and Ramsgate. This time twelve Hurricanes of No. 501 Squadron and three of No. 151 were ready, and the dive-bombers were harried and chased away (albeit without loss), so that their bombing was quite ineffective. Four Hurricanes were lost, but two of their pilots were saved unhurt.

Meanwhile, unseen by the Kent and Sussex radar, a very large raid was building up over the French coast, composed of *Kampfgeschwader 51* (almost one hundred Ju 88s) and *Zerstörergeschwader 2* and *76* (120 Bf 110s) and 25 Bf 109s from JG 53. This huge formation was not spotted by Poling CH until 11.45 hours. It was then plotted for about five minutes approaching Brighton from the south, but then the signals became confused, and it seemed that the raid was

---

[11] Later to succeed to the leadership of *Erprobungsgruppe 210* after heavy casualties in the unit. His award of the Knight's Cross was promulgated by O.K.W. on 24th November 1940.

[12] Squadron Leader E.E. Arnold D.F.C. was born in 1894 and had retired from the R.A.F. in 1934 as a Flight Lieutenant. He rejoined the Service at the outbreak of war and was given command of this important fighter station. He retired again in 1945 with the rank of Wing Commander.

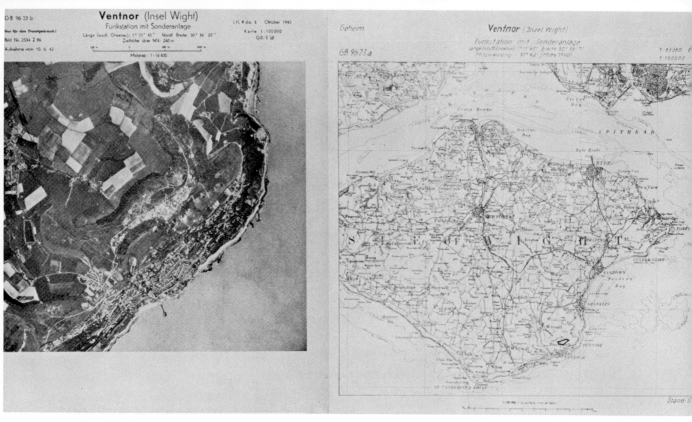

An aerial photograph dated June 1942, and a target map dated September 1940, demonstrate the close and continued interest of the *Luftwaffe* in the radar station at Ventnor in the Isle of Wight. The photograph shows cratering around the compound as a result of the bombing raids during the Battle. The station was badly damaged by Junkers Ju 88s on 12th August 1940.

turning away. A few minutes after mid-day the coastal posts of No. 2 Observer Corps area gave No. 11 Group its first indication of the raid's plan as the great armada swept westwards towards the Isle of Wight. Once again Brand and Park reacted with large forces, ordering 48 Hurricanes and ten Spitfires away from Tangmere, Middle Wallop, Warmwell and Exeter[13].

Once again the Messerschmitts formed up in their huge holding circle over the Nab to attract the British fighters, while the Ju 88s split into two well-defined groups. The larger, composed of more than 70 aircraft, made as if to pass on up the Solent but, when abreast the entrance to Portsmouth harbour, suddenly swung north through a gap in the balloon barrage and carried out a devastating attack on the dockyards and town, hitting and destroying many installations, including the railway station, some fuel storage tanks and three small vessels. Fires raged for several hours, and casualties

among civilians and naval personnel amounted to 96[14]. Every A.A. gun in the harbour—afloat and ashore—blazed away an impressive barrage and succeeded in destroying two of the bombers. The Junkers appear to have flown round the naval basin in *Staffeln*, following in line astern, and remained over Portsmouth for about fifteen minutes until 12.25 hours when they made their exit from the balloon perimeter over the entrance to the harbour. The R.A.F. pilots, who knew better than anyone the folly of venturing over Portsmouth's hair-triggered *flak* gunners, were waiting "outside"; No. 213 Squadron's Hurricanes were first to pounce on the bombers as they emerged, and it was to their guns that the leading aircraft of KG 51's *Geschwaderkommodore*, Oberst Dr. Fisser, fell.

Returning to the moment when Fisser swung his bombers into the attack on Portsmouth, a group of about fifteen Ju 88s turned port and made for the Isle of Wight instead. Arriving over the centre of the island, they broke downwards in a steep diving attack on the vital CH radar station situated on the heights above Ventnor. Despite an energetic defence put up by the three Bofors guns on the ground, the bombers were able to strike the signals site with fifteen 500-kilo bombs—an incredible concentration which demolished almost every building in the compound, and severely damaged the aerial lattice suspended between the transmitter towers[15].

---

[13] It is an important point worth emphasising here that the relatively large forces of fighters ordered up against the heavy Channel raids of 11th and 12th August were sent into battle as independent squadrons, and that no attempt was made to form them into Wings. Had such been the case, the delays involved would have been fatal. As it was, almost all the fighters made contact with the enemy and great execution was done. It is as well to bear this in mind when considering the controversy that arose in September, when Leigh-Mallory insisted that Wings of fighters inflicted much greater damage upon the enemy. No doubt his argument was born of a false premise, for it has been statistically demonstrated that interception by the Wing formation—on the very small number of occasions when indeed an interception occurred—resulted in numerous duplicated and therefore greatly exaggerated claims. What is certain is that, had either Brand or Park ordered their fighters up in Wings over the South Coast, the German bombing formations would have laid waste to their targets long before the fighters arrived.

[14] During the course of this heavy raid at least three SC1000 (2,200-lb.) bombs were dropped, these weapons being carried by the aircraft of the *Staffelkapitäne*. A photo taken by one of the raiders clearly shows that these bombs fell in the centre of Portsmouth town—well away from the dockyard.

[15] Contrary to some accounts, Ventnor CH was put out of action for no more than three days. The transmitting and receiving aerials were quickly repaired, and mobile generating plant and an operations van was on site within 72 hours enabling makeshift reporting to be resumed on 15th August.

As the Ventnor attackers made off over the south coast of the Island they were engaged by the Spitfires of Nos. 152 and 609 Squadrons, but when the Bf 109s of JG 53 came rushing to the Junkers' rescue the 609 pilots turned to meet the new threat and a dogfight developed over the Needles.

From the defenders' viewpoint the action fought off Portland and the Isle of Wight was more satisfactory in outcome than that over Portland on the previous day. The British pilots had for the most part tried to ignore the enemy fighters which, while they continued to circle high overhead, posed no immediate threat. One or two had ventured to attack them and were promptly shot down. By "feeding in" successive squadrons of Hurricanes to attack the Portsmouth raiders, the Controller deprived the Messerschmitts of a worthwhile target to justify breaking from their circle. Thus KG 51 lost ten bombers while the Messerschmitts continued to wait 10,000 feet above. Only when the Ventnor raiders were in imminent danger of annihilation did the Bf 109s come to their rescue.

Remembering the German tactic of introducing new formations of Bf 109s to cover the withdrawal of a large raid, Park was careful to keep back some fighters so that, when a free chase was reported flying west near Beachy Head, twelve Hurricanes of No. 615 Squadron were well placed to intercept the Messerschmitts which were at least prevented from upsetting the *status quo* over the Isle of Wight. It is possible that the two Bf 109s claimed shot down (by Flt. Lt. Lionel Gaunce, a Canadian, and Plt. Off. Petrus Hugo, a South African) were the two aircraft reported missing by JG 54 over the Channel.

While fitters, clerks and cooks—officers and men alike— toiled in the heat of a summer day amid the smoke and rubble of Hawkinge airfield, Kesselring's airmen were again on their way to another of Park's forward aerodromes. Manston, on the north-east tip of Kent, was the home base of No. 600 Squadron with Blenheim night fighters; apart from being a regular forward satellite in the Biggin Hill Sector, it was also frequented by all manner of fighter squadrons based at North Weald, Hornchurch, Kenley and Northolt owing to its strategic position at the mouth of the Thames Estuary. The airfield was now about to embark on an ordeal by bomb and shot that was to tax the nerves of the station personnel to the limit. Often misunderstood by visiting pilots—wearied by combat— Manston's singular ordeal was to result in an atmosphere of mutual acrimony and petulance that quickly undermined the morale of the station. At 12.50 hours on this Monday the Spitfires of No. 65 Squadron were on the point of taking off on patrol when, without warning, the Messerschmitts of Rubensdörffer's hard-worked *Gruppe* swept down on the airfield, bombing and gunning as they went; simultaneously eighteen Dornier Do 17s of KG 2 made a single pass at medium altitude dropping a dense pattern of 250-kilo and fragmentation bombs. At once all was utter confusion as the airfield erupted in a cloud of smoke and chalf dust. Scarcely any of the Spitfires managed to take to the air[16] and in any

case the enemy aircraft, their strike completed in less than five minutes, were already streaking for home. Several pilots from other squadrons, already airborne in the area, could only stare at the great mushroom cloud that now hung over Manston.

The German crews returned home to report that Manston had been destroyed, yet the spectacle of the raid had been deceptive. None of the Spitfires had been seriously damaged, and only one of No. 600 Squadron's Blenheims had been destroyed. The station workshops had been gutted and two hangars were hit. Although about 150 high explosive bombs were dropped, so that the aerodrome surface was badly cratered, only 24 hours were to elapse before the airfield was made operational again.

In the evening Kesselring maintained his pressure on No. 11 Group by sending three small raids by about twenty Do 17s against coastal towns in Kent. The rapidity with which these small raids were intercepted must have confirmed his worst fears that the British had managed to get their radar working again. There were already signs that Fighter Command pilots were beginning to avoid unnecessary combat with free chasing *Jagdstaffeln* and were concentrating on the bomber formations. This was soon to have important repercussions when, much against their instincts, the German fighter pilots were virtually withdrawn from free chasing patrols and ordered to stick close to the bomber formations. One may only speculate at the nature of the remarks made by the returning crews of Fisser's Ju 88s who, having suffered a fifteen minute ordeal by *flak* over Portsmouth, were then to be subjected to a vigorous onslaught of eager British interceptors as they emerged—while more than one hundred German fighters continued to circle high overhead. . .

As this most strenuous day drew to a close, Dowding took stock of his squadrons. Fearful that the *Luftwaffe* had embarked on a systematic process of destroying his coastal airfields, he ordered Peter Townsend's No. 85 Squadron from Martlesham back to its Sector base at Debden, a move that took place the following day. Signals were despatched to five squadrons in the North warning them to be ready to move southwards at a moment's notice. Correctly diagnosing that the minor raids upon the Thames convoys had been no more than feints designed to cover the *Luftwaffe*'s main aims, Dowding realised that the main assault on Britain was now about to open[17].

---

[16] One pilot who did manage to take off was Fg. Off. Jeffery Quill, the Supermarine test pilot, who was serving for a short spell with No. 65 Squadron to gain operational experience on the Spitfire.

[17] As a postscript to this day, the eve of the German attack, a minor event is worth recording here. This was the first delivery of the Bristol Beaufighter night fighter to the Fighter Interception Unit at Tangmere. Although some weeks were to elapse before this powerful new aircraft would be considered operational by the R.A.F., it represented the first of a generation of aircraft designed specifically to combat the German night raiders whose activities were to increase steadily throughout the coming month.

R.A.F. FIGHTER COMMAND LOSSES—MONDAY 12th AUGUST 1940

1.	32 Sqn., Biggin Hill	C	Shot down over Dover by Bf 109s and crashed near Hawkinge; pilot unhurt.	17.12 hrs.	Plt. Off. A.R.H. Barton	Hurricane	N2596	Cat. 3 Destroyed
2.	43 Sqn., Tangmere	NC	Crashed on landing at Tangmere (not the result of combat). Pilot safe.	Not known	Not known	Hurricane	R4108	Cat. 3 Destroyed
3.	54 Sqn., Hornchurch	C	Force landed at Lympne after combat with Bf 109s; pilot wounded.	A17.30 hrs.	Plt. Off. D.R. Turley-George	Spitfire	P6914	Cat. 3 Destroyed
4.	54 Sqn., Hornchurch	C	Force landed at Lympne after combat with Bf 109s ; oilot wounded.	A17.30 hrs.	Plt. Off. J.L. Kemp	Spitfire	R6815	Cat. 3 Destroyed

R.A.F. Losses, 12th August 1940—*continued*

5.	54 Sqn., Hornchurch	NC	Force landed in cornfield near Dartford (not the result of combat); pilot unhurt.	15.20 hrs.	Plt. Off. E.F. Edsall	Spitfire	N3160	Cat. 2 Damaged
6.	56 Sqn., Rochford	C	Shot down ten miles north of Margate; pilot baled out and rescued from sea with burns.	17.39 hrs.	Plt. Off. A.G. Page	Hurricane	P2970	Cat. 3 Lost
7.	64 Sqn., Kenley	C	Shot down by Bf 109; pilot baled out wounded.	A17.20 hrs.	Plt. Off A.G. Donohue	Spitfire	X4018	Cat. 3 Lost
8.	145 Sqn., Westhampnett	C	Shot down near the Isle of Wight; pilot killed.	A17.20 hrs.	Flt. Lt. W. Pankratz	Hurricane	R4176	Cat. 3 Lost.
9.	145 Sqn., Westhampnett	C	Shot down near the Isle of Wight; pilot killed.	A12.20 hrs.	Plt. Off. J.M. Harrison	Hurricane	P3391	Cat. 3 Lost
10.	145 Sqn., Westhampnett	C	Shot down near the Isle of Wight; pilot killed.	A12.20 hrs.	Sgt. J. Kwiecinski	Hurricane	R4180	Cat. 3 Lost
11.	151 Sqn., North Weald	C	Shot down by Bf 109s off North Foreland; pilot baled out slightly wounded.	Not known	Fg. Off. A.B. Tucker	Hurricane	P3302	Cat. 3 Lost
12.	151 Sqn., North Weald	C	Shot down in above combat; pilot picked up by launch but died from shock and wounds.	Not known	Plt. Off. R.W.G. Beley	Hurricane	P3304	Cat. 3 Lost
13.	151 Sqn., North Weald	C	Severely damaged in above combat; pilot returned to base unhurt.	Not known	Plt. Off. K.B.L. Debenham	Hurricane	P3780	Cat. 2 Damaged
14.	152 Sqn., Warmwell	C	Shot down by Ju 88 near St. Catherine's Point; pilot killed.	Not known	Flt. Lt. L.C. Withall	Spitfire	P9456	Cat. 3 Destroyed
15.	152 Sqn., Warmwell	C	Shot down by Ju 88s near St. Catherine's Point; pilot killed.	Not known	Plt. Off. D.C. Shepley	Spitfire	K9999	Cat. 3 Destroyed
16.	213 Sqn., Exeter	C	Shot down ten miles south of Bognor Regis; pilot killed.	12.35 hrs.	Sgt. S.G. Stuckey	Hurricane	P2854	Cat. 3 Missing
17.	213 Sqn., Exeter	C	Shot down ten miles south of Bognor Regis; pilot killed.	A12.35 hrs.	Sgt. G.N. Wilkes	Hurricane	P2802	Cat. 3 Missing
18.	257 Sqn., Northolt	C	Shot down near Portsmouth; pilot wounded.	Morning	Fg. Off. The Hon. D.A. Coke	Hurricane	P3776	Cat. 3 Destroyed
19.	257 Sqn., Northolt	C	Shot down near Portsmouth; pilot killed.	Morning	Plt. Off. J.A.G. Chomley	Hurricane	P3662	Cat. 3 Destroyed
20.	266 Sqn., Tangmere	C	Shot down over Portsmouth; pilot killed.	12.12 hrs.	Plt. Off. D.G. Ashton	Spitfire	P9333	Cat. 3 Destroyed
21.	266 Sqn., Tangmere	C	Shot down near Portsmouth and force landed at Bembridge, Isle of Wight; aircraft exploded, but pilot escaped unhurt.	12.18 hrs.	Plt. Off. W.S. Williams	Spitfire	N3175	Cat. 3 Destroyed
22.	303 Sqn., Northolt	NC	Wheels-up landing accident; pilot unhurt.	Not known	Sgt. P. Gallus	Hurricane	—	Cat. 2 Damaged
23.	501 Sqn., Hawkinge	C	Shot down and pilot killed by Bf 109s escorting Ju 87s off Dover.	11.33 hrs.	Plt. Off. K. Lukaszewicz	Hurricane	—	Cat. 3 Missing
24.	501 Sqn., Hawkinge	C	Force landed near Dover after above combat; pilot unhurt.	11.41 hrs.	Sqn. Ldr. A.L. Holland	Hurricane	—	Cat. 2 Damaged
25.	504 Sqn., Castletown	NC	Force landed at Evanton with oil trouble; pilot unhurt.	Not known	Fg. Off. M. Jebb	Hurricane	—	Cat. 1 Damaged
26.	600 Sqn., Manston	—	Destroyed in bombing raid on Manston; no aircrew casualties.	12.57 hrs.	Nil	Blenheim	—	Cat. 3 Destroyed
27.	600 Sqn., Manston	—	Damaged in bombing raid on Manston; no aircrew casualties.	12.57 hrs.	Nil	Blenheim	—	Cat. 1 Damaged
28.	610 Sqn., Biggin Hill	C	Shot down by Bf 109s near Dover; pilot baled out with burns to neck and face.	A07.50 hrs.	Flt. Lt. E.B.B. Smith	Spitfire	K9818	Cat. 3 Lost.
29.	610 Sqn., Biggin Hill	C	Damaged by Bf 109s near Dover; pilot wounded.	A08.05 hrs.	Sgt. B.G.D. Gardner	Spitfire	N3124	Cat. 2 Damaged
30.	610 Sqn., Biggin Hill	C	Damaged by Bf 109s off Dover; pilot unhurt but aircraft written off on landing.	A08.05 hrs.	Not known	Spitfire	L1044	Cat. 3 Destroyed
31.	610 Sqn., Biggin Hill	C	Damaged by Bf 109s near Dover; pilot unhurt.	A08.05 hrs.	Not known	Spitfire	—	Cat. 2 Damaged
32.	610 Sqn., Biggin Hill	C	Damaged by Bf 109s near Dover; pilot unhurt.	A08.05 hrs.	Not known	Spitfire	—	Cat. 2 Damaged

LUFTWAFFE LOSSES—MONDAY 12th AUGUST 1940

1.	4.(F)/121	CM	Crashed at Barfleur with *flak* damage.	Junkers Ju 88A-1	80 %	One crew member missing.
2.	Stab/KG 51	CM	Shot down by 213 Sqn. Hurricanes south of Bognor at A12.30 hrs.	Junkers Ju 88A-1	100 %	Oberst. Johann Fisser, *Geschw. Kdr.*, killed. Oblt. Luderitz, Ltn. Sched + one missing.
3.	I./KG 51	CM	Believed shot down by Spitfires of 266 Sqn.	Junkers Ju 88A-1	100 %	One killed; three missing.
4.	I./KG 51	CM	Believed shot down by Spitfires of 266 Sqn.	Junkers Ju 88A-1	100 %	One killed; three missing.
5.	3./KG 51	CM	Shot down by 213 Sqn. Hurricane south of Bognor at A12.30 hrs.	Junkers Ju 88A-1	100 %	Oblt. Hans Graf, Uffz. Walter Flocter and Gefr. Horst Czepik killed; one crew member missing.
6.	I./KG 51	CM	Damaged by 213 Sqn. Hurricane south of Bognor at A12.30 hrs.	Junkers Ju 88A-1	30 %	No crew casualties.
7.	II./KG 51	CM	Shot down by 145 Sqn. Hurricane near Ventnor, Isle of Wight, at 12.15 hrs.	Junkers Ju 88A-1	100 %	Oblt. Schlegel + three missing.
8.	Stab III./KG 51	CM	Damaged by British fighters near Portsmouth.	Junkers Ju 88A-1 (7073 : 9K+ED)	10-60 %	Ltn. Schweisgut and crew unhurt.
9.	7./KG 51	CM	Shot down by 43 Sqn. Hurricane of Carey near Portsmouth at 12.15 hrs.	Junkers Ju 88A-1 (5063 : 9K+AS)	100 %	Oblt. Wilhelm Nölken + two killed; one missing.
10.	III./KG 51	CM	Shot down by 152 Sqn. Spitfire of Boitel-Gill off St. Catherine's Point.	Junkers Ju 88A-1 (5072 : 9K+FS)	100 %	Oblt. Wildemuth, Oblt. Stern + one missing.
11.	8./KG 51	CM	Shot down by anti-aircraft guns at Portsmouth.	Junkers Ju 88A-1 (4078 : 9K+BS)	100 %	Ltn. Seidel, Sd.Fhr. Bigalke, Uffz. Fischer and Fw. Velten killed.
12.	9./KG 51	CM	Damaged by British fighters and crashed at Le Havre.	Junkers Ju 88A-1 (5042 : 9K+AT)	70 %	Ltn. Capesius and crew unhurt.
13.	III./KG 51	CM	Shot down by 152 Sqn. Spitfire of Bayles near St. Catherine's Point.	Junkers Ju 88A-1 (5052 : 9K+LT)	100 %	Four crew members missing.
14.	III./KG 51	CM	Shot down by anti-aircraft guns at Portsmouth.	Junkers Ju 88A-1 (7091 : 9K+KT)	100 %	Ltn. Heinrich Höchstetter + three missing.
15.	III./KG 51	CM	Damaged by 152 Sqn. Spitfire of Hogg off St. Catherine's Point.	Junkers Ju 88A-1	30 %	One crew member wounded.
16.	III./KG 51	CM	Damaged by 152 Sqn. Spitfire of Beaumont near St. Catherine's Point.	Junkers Ju 88A-1	10 %	No crew casualties.
17.	III./KG 55	CM	Damaged by 257 Sqn. Hurricane near Portsmouth; crashed at Mambervillier on return.	Heinkel He 111P	100 %	Two crew members killed and two wounded.
18.	III./KG 55	NCM	Forced landed at Villacoublay following engine failure.	Heinkel He 111P	25 %	No crew casualties.

19.	III./KG 77	NCM	Landing accident at Illesheim airfield.	Junkers Ju 88A	80 %	One killed; Oblt. Pfeiffer + two injured.
20.	II./St.G 77	NCM	Force landed at Lannion with airframe failure.	Junkers Ju 87R	40 %	No crew casualties.
21.	III./St.G 77	NCM	Landing accident at Brandville airfield.	Junkers Ju 87B	10 %	No crew casualties.
22.	I./LG 1	NCM	Engine failure on take-off at Bricy airfield.	Junkers Ju 88A-1	90 %	One crew member killed; three injured.
23.	III./LG 1	NCM	Engine failure on take-off at Chateaudun .	Junkers Ju 88A-1	50 %	Two crew members injured.
24.	I./ZG 2	CM	Shot down by 266 Sqn. Spitfire of Bazley over South Coast.	Messerschmitt Bf 110D	100 %	Hptm. Kulbel, St.Kap., + one killed.
25.	I./ZG 2	CM	Shot down by 213 Sqn. Hurricane of Atkinson over South Coast.	Messerschmitt Bf 110C	100 %	Oblt. Blume + one missing.
26.	I./ZG 2	CM	Landing accident at St. Aubin after combat.	Messerschmitt Bf 110D	35 %	No crew casualties.
27.	I./ZG 2	CM	Shot down by British fighters over South Coast.	Messerschmitt Bf 110 C-4	100 %	Crew rescued unhurt.
28.	II./ZG 2	CM	Shot down by 213 Sqn. Hurricane of Atkinson over South Coast.	Messerschmitt Bf 110 C-2	100 %	Two crew members missing.
29.	II./ZG 2	CM	Damaged by 257 Sqn. Hurricane of Beresford over the Isle of Wight at A12.30 hrs.	Messerschmitt Bf 110D	20 %	No crew casualties.
30.	II./ZG 2	CM	Damaged by British fighters over South Coast.	Messerschmitt Bf 110D	40 %	No crew casualties.
31.	III./ZG 26	CM	Landing accident at Calais after combat.	Messerschmitt Bf 110C	45 %	No crew casualties.
32.	III./ZG 26	CM	Shot down by 609 Sqn. Spitfires west of Isle of Wight, 12.26 hrs.	Messerschmitt Bf 110 C-2	100 %	Hptm. Graf Hoyen, St.Kap.,
33.	III./ZG 76	CM	Crashed on landing at Caen after fighter combat.	Messerschmitt Bf 110 C-2	35 %	Two crew members wounded.
34.	Erpr.Gr. 210	CM	Shot down by 54 Sqn. Spitfire (believed of Deere) near Manston at 17.45 hrs.	Messerschmitt Bf 110C	100 %	Both crew members rescued, one wounded.
35.	I./JG 2	CM	Overturned on landing at base.	Messerschmitt Bf 109 E-4	80 %	Pilot injured.
36.	1./JG 3	NCM	Landing accident at Folembert airfield.	Messerschmitt Bf 109 E-1	15 %	Pilot unhurt.
37.	3./JG 3	CM	Shot down by 54 Sqn. Spitfire of Gray over East Kent at A11.50 hrs.	Messerschmitt Bf 109 E-1	100 %	Pilot killed.
38.	3./JG 3	CM	Shot down by 54 Sqn. Spitfire of Matthews over East Kent at A11.55 hrs.	Messerschmitt Bf 109 E-1	100 %	Pilot killed.
39.	I./JG 26	CM	Shot down by 64 Sqn. Spitfire of Woodward over South Coast at A17.15 hrs.	Messerschmitt Bf 109 E-4	100 %	Ltn. Regenauer missing.
40.	I./JG 26	CM	Shot down by 54 Sqn. Spitfire of Deere over East Kent at A17.30 hrs.	Messerschmitt Bf 109 E-1	100 %	Oblt. Friedrich Butterweck killed, and buried at Hawkinge.
41.	II./JG 52	CM	Shot down by 610 Sqn. Spitfire of Ellis over New Romney at A08.00 hrs.	Messerschmitt Bf 109 E-1	100 %	Pilot killed.
42.	II./JG 52	CM	Shot down by 610 Sqn. Spitfire of Ellis over New Romney at A08.00 hrs.	Messerschmitt Bf 109 E-3	100 %	Ltn. Gelhalsis missing.
43.	III./JG 53	CM	Shot down by 609 Sqn. Spitfire of Crook west of the Needles at A12.35 hrs.	Messerschmitt Bf 109 E-4	100 %	Hptm. Harder, Gr.Kdr., killed.
44.	III./JG 53	CM	Shot down by 609 Sqn. Spitfire of Crook south of the Needles at A12.38 hrs.	Messerschmitt Bf 109 E-4	100 %	Pilot rescued unhurt.
45.	I./JG 54	CM	Landing accident at Compiègne airfield.	Messerschmitt Bf 109E	25 %	Pilot injured.
46.	III./JG 54	CM	Landing accident at Guines-Süd airfield.	Messerschmitt Bf 109E	60 %	Oblt. Schön wounded.
47.	III./JG 54	CM	Shot down by 32 Sqn. Hurricane of Crossley near Dover at 17.20 hrs.	Messerschmitt Bf 109 E-4	100 %	Oblt. Drewes missing.
48.	III./JG 54	CM	Shot down over the Channel; British action not traced.	Messerschmitt Bf 109 E-4	100 %	Pilot missing.
49.	III./JG 54	CM	Shot down over the Channel; British action not traced.	Messerschmitt Bf 109 E-4	100 %	Ltn. Eberle missing.
50.	I./JG 77	NCM	Force landing at Esbjoek after engine failure.	Messerschmitt Bf 109 E-1	40 %	Pilot unhurt.

Bf 109E bearing the markings of the *Gruppe Adjutant*, I./JG 2, shot down during August 1940; note the three "victory bars" on the rudder, decorated with R.A.F. roundels.

Tuesday 13th August 1940 *Adler Tag*

The quite extraordinary chain of events which constituted the much vaunted *Adlerangriff* were to trigger a reaction of recrimination and doubts among the German High Command as to whether it was pursuing the air campaign against Britain in such a way as to eliminate R.A.F. Fighter Command—or indeed whether it was equipped to do so. Though perhaps not sufficiently clear to Göring at the time, the fatal weakness in the plan for *Adlerangriff*, and perhaps for *Seelöwe* itself, was in the German Intelligence interpretation.

The fundamental inaccuracies of *Studie Blau*, prepared by Oberstleutnant Josef Schmid at Operations Staff IC at O.K.L. and issued on 16th July, have been mentioned. Subsequent data, amassed from constant reconnaissance sorties and from prisoner interrogation, had been used to *complement* the report rather than to correct it, such was the blind faith in its infallibility. Thus on the dawn of *Adler Tag*, the Germans were not yet fully aware of the operational structure of Fighter Command's airfield network, nor were they aware of the means by which the radar reporting chain was co-ordinated as a control apparatus for British fighter formations. Examples of the Germans' lack of attention to detail are afforded by the list of fighter airfield targets which included such old aerodromes as Eastchurch, Worthy Down and Upavon—airfields which had not accommodated regularly-based fighters for nearly ten years. Another extraordinary lapse was the *Luftwaffe*'s ignorance of the purpose of the Woolston factory at Southampton, surely one of the most vulnerable and vital targets imaginable; here, situated on the waterfront in the South of England, was the parent factory producing Spitfires. Yet the German raid briefing documents—shown in Chapter 8—show this factory to be labelled that of A.V. Roe & Co., a bomber manufacturer. True, the *Luftwaffe* later mounted a devastating raid upon the factory, but was plainly unaware that it might have struck a heavy blow against Spitfire production. Fortunately, by the time the raid was launched, the bulk of Spitfire production had been switched to the Midlands.

Under cover of the heavy attacks of the last two days, four *Aufklärungsgruppen* had flown more than two hundred reconnaissance sorties over Southern England, and some extraordinary interpretations had been placed on the photographs returned. The naval stations at Detling and Lee-on-Solent (labelled fighter stations) were said to have Hurricanes and obsolete Demon fighters dispersed on them, whereas in truth the aircraft were Skuas and Swordfish of the Fleet Air Arm. The pitfalls of inadequate Intelligence were demonstrated when photographs disclosed Blenheims at Tangmere, which were dismissed as bombers; they were in fact the radar-equipped Blenheim fighters of the Fighter Interception Unit. And so the commentary of inadequacy could go on. . .The result was that the targets listed for destruction on *Adler Tag*

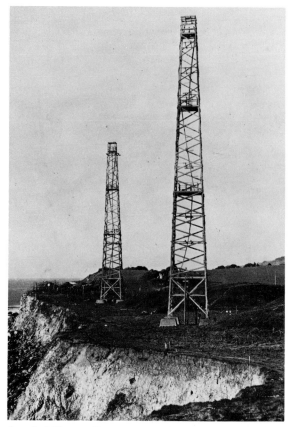

A typical "Remote Reserve" radar station. Constant pressure on the main radar chain, and damage to some stations, increased dependence on back-up aerial systems like this—the fruits of Fighter Command's accurate contingency planning.

contained *none* whose destruction would have impaired Fighter Command's operation for one moment.

Before dawn on this day the airfields at Arras, Epinoy and Cambrai in North-East France reverberated to the sound of 74 Dornier Do 17s of KG 2 running up their engines prior to take-off for an attack on the Isle of Sheppey in the Thames Estuary. Led by Oberst Johannes Fink, the bombers took off shortly after 05.00 hours and made for the French coast where they were to be joined by their escort of about sixty Bf 110s of ZG 26, led by the wooden-legged veteran Oberstleutnant Joachim Huth. Sure enough, some Messerschmitts appeared, but after some inexplicable manœuvres (which Fink simply ascribed to high spirits) the "escort" promptly disappeared.

Unknown to the bomber commander, orders had been passed directly from Göring postponing *Adlerangriff* until the afternoon. Overnight weather reports had indicated a temporary setback in the fine weather conditions over Southern England. Unfortunately owing to a hitch in the issue of radio crystals, it had been impossible to contact the bombers to recall them—only the fighters—so Fink, unaware that other covering operations had been withdrawn, led the big formation towards the Kent coast without the benefit of fighter cover.

The bad weather that had caused the German postponement to some extent protected Fink, and his crossing of the North Foreland was reported inaccurately by the Observer Corps, with the result that of the five squadrons scrambled, only No. 74 Squadron (led by Malan) intercepted the raid before it reached Sheppey. The Spitfires continued to harass Fink's

A police sergeant, a soldier and civilian wardens wade through the mud of the Thames Estuary at low tide on 13th August with the body of a Dornier crewman from III./KG 2, killed in the raid on Eastchurch.

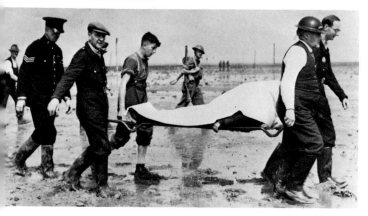

formation as it split over the island, one Gruppe making for the naval base at Sheerness, and the remainder bombing the coastal air base at Eastchurch. The Spitfire pilots claimed that the Dorniers were escorted by Bf 109s, though these can only have been the Hurricanes of Nos. 111 and 151 Squadrons which joined the fight over the island. The Dornier crews claimed the destruction of ten Spitfires on Eastchurch airfield and their claims have hitherto been held to some ridicule on the grounds that no such fighters were present. No. 266 (Fighter) Squadron's Form 540 records otherwise:

> **13th August.** Eastchurch bombed by two vics each of fifteen Dornier Do 17s at 07.50 hours until 07.20 hours, from South to East, which dropped over one hundred high explosive and incendiary bombs. Airmen's quarters were severely damaged, with sixteen killed. Plt. Off. H.H. Chandler injured in foot. Casualties to County Council Hospital at Minster. All hangars hit and 266 Squadron's hangar set on fire. Three Spitfires and two Magisters removed undamaged. One Spitfire destroyed (Cat. 3 Burnt). All squadron ammunition, ammunition tanks and much equipment destroyed. One bomb on Officers' Mess. Water supplies damaged.

It is true that No. 266 Squadron had been only temporarily moved to Eastchurch for possible anti-shipping operations, yet it was still a Fighter Command squadron, with normal defence responsibilities. Its presence at Eastchurch was purely coincidental and must have confirmed in German minds the airfield's air defence rôle. Apart from one Spitfire destroyed, No. 35 Squadron of Coastal Command lost five Blenheims[18]. The operations block was also destroyed and 48 people were injured but, notwithstanding the widespread damage and disrupted communications, the airfield was operational before the day's end.

Although Fink's raid had continued on its way without the benefit of a fighter escort (it lost five aircraft[19]), other sorties *were* flown, despite Göring's orders. No word of the postponement had reached Oberstleutnant Harry von Bülow at Beaumont-le-Roger, and three free chases were flown by the

Staffeln of I./JG 2, one of which was caught by some Hurricane pilots of No. 43 Squadron who shot down Oberleutnant Paul Temme between Petworth and Shoreham; the pilot was captured unwounded.

These free chases had been mounted to cover a raid by a *Gruppe* of Ju 88s from KG 54 against the army co-operation airfield at Odiham and the Royal Aircraft Esatblishment at Farnborough. This raid also took off without fighter escort and approached the South Coast, but the crews became so frustrated by the cloud conditions and harassed by British fighters that they did not persevere more than about ten miles inside the coast before the word was given to turn about and make what escape they could; in this they were successful and none was lost—as the British fighters were also recalled.

Although KG 54 suffered no aircraft loss in the abortive attack, a lone German airman, Gefreiter Neissl, was discovered wandering about the countryside just east of Tangmere—suggesting that a raider had in fact crashed nearby. On interrogation, however, he stated that his aircraft (a Junkers Ju 88, B3+TP of 6./KG 54 from St. André) had been attacked by fighters near the Isle of Wight, and when the engines started to fail the captain headed for the mainland and ordered the crew to bale out. The Bordmechaniker (flight engineer) promptly obeyed—too promptly as it transpired, for the pilot managed to regain control and successfully nursed his damaged aircraft back to base. It was Gefreiter Neissl's first and only operational sortie. . .

Three hours later to the south-west the *Zerstörergruppe*, I./ZG 2, which had been so roughly treated two days two days before, and had lost its leader, Major Ott, was heading for another fiasco. Now led by Hauptmann Heinlein, the *Gruppe* had been scheduled to meet other Ju 88s of KG 54 and escort them on a feint raid against Portland. By now, of course, KG 54 had been told of the postponement, yet no one evidently though it necessary to check that ZG 2 had received the signal. No such message had been received and the 28 Bf 110s duly set course for Portland without their charges! On arrival they found two squadrons of British fighters awaiting them and, before they could turn tail, lost one of their number to the guns of Fg. Off. David Hughes of No. 238 Squadron.

Adlerangriff was eventually launched in the middle of the afternoon and it was shortly after 15.30 hours that the CH radars at Worth Matravers and Hawks Tor reported a number of large raids approaching on a front of 40 miles from the direction of the Cherbourg Peninsula and the Channel Islands. These formations consisted of about 40 Ju 88s of KG 54 and 80 Ju 88s of I., II., and III. *Gruppen*, *Lehrgeschwader 1*, on the eastern flank, and 30 BF 110s of V. *Gruppe*, LG 1, flying as escort for the Ju 88s; on the western flank were 27 Ju 87s of II./St.G 2 led by Major Walter Ennecerus from Lannion in the Brest Peninsula. Thrusting ahead of the bombers were 30 Bf 109s of II./JG 53 led by Major Günther Freiherr von Maltzahn from Dinan and Guernsey. A second formation of 52 Ju 87s of Major Graf Schönborn's St.G 77 was provided with a close escort of Bf 109s from Oberstleutnant Max Ibel's JG 27. Thus advanced Göring's first massive attack, comprising some 300 bombers and fighters, intended to smash Brand's No. 10 Group defences.

It was the belief that Fighter Command would be ready for the incoming raid that had prompted General Kurt Pflugbeil, commanding IV *Fliegerkorps* to which LG 1 was assigned, to request Oberst Werner Junck to provide the fighter sweep by

---

[18] Six Spitfires of No. 19 Squadron (almost certainly the cannon-armed aircraft) were also detached to Eastchurch at the time of KG 2's raid, but none was damaged. It may be asked why the Spitfires present at Eastchurch were not ordered off to defend the airfield. The reason has been given that, being a Coastal Command airfield, no machinery existed to scramble or control fighters, and in all likelihood their pilots were "released".

[19] One of these was an aircraft of 7./KG 2, shot down by the only two-cannon Hurricane in the R.A.F. at that time (L1750) flown by Flt. Lt. Roddick Smith of No. 151 Squadron; this was one of the first enemy aircraft to be destroyed by the R.A.F. using the 20-mm. cannon, the Hispano version of which for fifteen years was to become the standard armament in British fighter aircraft. In Smith's own words, "I ordered the attack, telling the pilots (who I hoped were all there, although one Section was not visible in my mirror, and my No. 3 could not keep up) to dive through the enemy formation and on into the clouds, as I assumed the rear formation were Messerschmitt 110s and three-quarters of my pilots were new. I opened fire at about 300 yards with my cannon, firing into the general mass as the enemy were in exceptionally close formation. One immediately burst into flames and another started smoking when my windscreen front panel was completely shattered by enemy fire, and I broke away downwards and returned to North Weald."

JG 53. This made landfall just west of the Isle of Wight shortly before 16.00 hours, swept along the coast over Warmwell and made for the sea near Lyme Regis. As it did so, No. 152 Squadron's Spitfires scrambled under a welter of orders from Wg. Cdr. David Roberts, the Middle Wallop Controller, and promptly split into sections. Sergeant Denis Robinson caught the 109s and attacked them as they crossed out near Abbotsbury, but they were now short of fuel and did not stay to fight. In its attempt to draw the British fighters away to the west, JG 53's sweep failed; all it succeeded in achieving was to advance the fighter state by perhaps five critical minutes, so that when LG 1 and St.G 2 arrived over the coast 77 Hurricanes and Spitfires were climbing hard from their bases at Exeter, Warmwell, Middle Wallop and Tangmere.

Sheer weight of numbers enabled the larger part of LG 1 to penetrate up the Solent to Southampton at about 16.05 hours despite the efforts of the Hurricanes of Nos. 43 and 257 Squadrons, and this raid inflicted heavy damage and casualties in the port, both to dock facilities and in the residental areas. The important Spitfire factory escaped almost unscathed. Other Ju 88s had turned north and were making for Middle Wallop.

The Ju 88s of KG 54 were now attempting to make their feint attack on Portland (postponed from the morning), but interference by No. 152, 213 and 601 Squadrons not only upset their bombing runs but put the escorting Bf 110s to rout, three being shot down by No. 601 Squadron.

Meanwhile the Ju 87s had reached the coast near Lyme Regis and were just turning north-east towards their target at Middle Wallop when the Spitfires of No. 609 Squadron struck; unfortunately the escorting Bf 109s, which should have covered the Stukas' approach, had already turned for home, short of fuel. The result was a massacre of one *Staffel* from St.G 2 which alone lost six out of nine aircraft shot down by the guns of 609 Squadron, and another damaged. The remainder turned back. The other Stukas of St.G 77 escaped notice and pressed on over the Dorset countryside searching for Warmwell but, failing to find it, spread out and dropped their bombs at random. The two *Staffeln* of Ju 88s from LG 1 were also having difficulty finding Middle Wallop, and most them bombed Andover in mistake for their target; only one found Middle Wallop and dropped its bombs in the village— well clear of the airfield. Some damage was done at the grass airfield at Andover, but this was of no significance to Fighter Command.

In the South-East the dive-bombers of Hauptmann Anton Keil flew from their bases in the Pas de Calais to spearhead the other flank thrust by Kesselring's *Luftflotte 2* shortly after 17.00 hours. Their target was the airfield at Rochester and, although only the Hurricane pilots of No. 56 Squadron spotted the Ju 87s, Keil's pilots failed to find their target and turned back, scattering their bombs all over Kent; these fell on Ramsgate, Ashford, Canterbury and again at Lympne (though without inflicting any more damage)[20].

As the result of a well-timed free chase by Major Gotthardt Handrick's[21] JG 26 Messerschmitts, better fortune attended the other half of Kesselring's main thrust by Hauptmann von Brauchitsch's IV.(Stuka)/LG 1, whose forty Ju 87s made for the airfield at Detling, near Maidstone, Kent. At 17.16 hours the dive-bombers arched into their attacks and struck the airfield with a veritable storm of well-aimed bombs just as the station personnel were flocking to their canteens for their evening meal. Three messes were demolished, as were all the hangars; the operations block suffered a direct hit which killed the station commander, Group Captain Edward Davis. Sixty-seven Service and civilian personnel were killed; runways, tarmac taxyways and hardstandings were cratered, and twenty-two aircraft were totally destroyed.

Yet, catastrophic though the raid on Detling might have seemed—it was, however, soon repaired—it was not part of Dowding's Command, and its damage in no way affected the air defence of No. 11 Group.

As the Germans turned for home and Dowding's Group operations tables emptied of hostile plots around 18.00 hours, the weary R.A.F. pilots were recalled to their bases. If the *Luftflotte* was dismayed by the lack of cohesion in its great offensive, the British could only point to limited success. Too many enemy aircraft had roamed about Southern England without interception; true, several non-vital airfields had been heavily bombed, but the defence in cloudy conditions had been ragged to say the least. If the Germans intended to use such weather conditions for their assault the consequences could be extremely serious.

That evening, as combat claims were totted up by both sides, it was decided that the German casualties had amounted to 64 aircraft, while the O.K.L. claimed 84 R.A.F. fighters. The true figures emerged much later as 47 German aircraft destroyed, and thirteen British fighters lost in combat, three of whose pilots had been killed[22]. A further 47 aircraft (only one of them a fighter) were destroyed on six airfields.

---

[20] Hauptmann Keil was to be awarded the Knight's Cross six days later, although it seems unlikely that the award was in respect of the operation recorded above. He was to be killed almost exactly one year leter in the opening phase of Hitler's attack on Russia.

[21] Major Gotthardt Handrick was the Modern Pentathlon Gold Medallist in the 1936 Berlin Games; he had the "Olympic Rings" insignia painted on the nose of his Messerschmitt Bf 109 while flying with J.88 in Spain.

[22] To put these comparative loss figures into their true perspective, however, against the death of three British fighter pilots, the Germans lost 89 pilots and crew members killed or taken prisoner. Two other British pilots had been severely burned.

R.A.F. FIGHTER COMMAND LOSSES—TUESDAY 13th AUGUST 1940

1.	43 Sqn., Tangmere	C	Shot down near Petworth; pilot baled out and landing at Cocking slightly wounded.	06.40 hrs.	Flt. Lt. T.F.D. Morgan	Hurricane	*P3072*	Cat. 3 Destroyed
2.	43 Sqn., Tangmere	C	Shot down over Southampton; pilot baled out unhurt.	16.36 hrs.	Plt. O.F. C.A. Woods-Scawen	Hurricane	—	Cat. 3 Destroyed
3.	56 Sqn., North Weald	C	Shot down near Rochford; pilot baled out slightly wounded.	16.18 hrs.	Plt. Off. C.C.O. Joubert	Hurricane	*R4093*	Cat. 3 Lost
4.	56 Sqn., North Weald	C	Shot down near Rochford; pilot baled out severely burned.	16.15 hrs.	Fg. Off. P.F.McD. Davies	Hurricane	*P2693*	Cat. 3 Lost
5.	56 Sqn., North Weald	C	Shot down over Thames Estuary; pilot baled out and swam two miles to shore.	16.21 hrs.	Sgt. P. Hillwood	Hurricane	*P2690*	Cat. 3 Lost
6.	56 Sqn., North Weald	C	Shot down over Kent and crash landed at Hawkinge; pilot unhurt.	16.29 hrs.	Fg. Off. R.E.P. Brooker	Hurricane	—	Cat. 3 Destroyed

R.A.F. Losses, 13th August 1940—*continued*

7.	74 Sqn., Hornchurch	C	Shot down over East Kent by Do 17; pilot baled out unhurt.	A06.30 hrs.	Flt. Lt. S. Brzezina	Spitfire	K9871	Cat. 3 Destroyed
8.	87 Sqn., Exeter	C	Crashed after combat with Ju 88A 20 miles south of Selsey Bill; pilot killed.	Not known	Fg. Off. R.L. Glyde	Hurricane	—	Cat. 3 Missing
9.	151 Sqn., North Weald	C	Shot down off South Coast; pilot rescued and admitted to hospital with shock.	A06.40 hrs.	Sgt. G. Atkinson	Hurricane	P3310	Cat. 3 Lost
10.	152 Sqn., Warmwell	C	Damaged in combat over Portland; pilot wounded in the arm.	A08.00 hrs.	Fg. Off. R.F. Inness	Spitfire	—	Cat. 1 Damaged
11.	152 Sqn., Warmwell	C	Damaged in combat over Portland; pilot unhurt.	A11.00 hrs.	Flt. Lt. D.P.A. Boitel-Gill	Spitfire	—	Cat. 2 Damaged
12.	213 Sqn., Exeter	C	Missing after combat over Portland; pilot assumed killed.	15.42 hrs.	Sgt. P.P. Norris	Hurricane	P3348	Cat. 3 Missing
13.	238 Sqn., Middle Wallop	C	Forced landed near Tangmere with damage to oil tank; pilot unhurt.	06.55 hrs.	Sgt. L.G. Batt	Hurricane	—	Cat. 2 Damaged
14.	238 Sqn., Middle Wallop	C	Shot down by Bf 109s south of Isle of Wight; pilot rescued by destroyer with serious burns.	06.58 hrs.	Sgt. E.W. Seabourne	Hurricane	—	Cat. 3 Lost
15.	238 Sqn., Middle Wallop	C	Shot down by Messerschmitt near Portland; pilot assumed killed.	12.14 hrs.	Sgt. H.J. Marsh	Hurricane	—	Cat. 3 Missing
16.	238 Sqn., Middle Wallop	C	Shot down into sea by Messerschmitt near Portland; pilot picked up and landed unhurt.	12.12 hrs.	Sgt. R. Little	Hurricane	—	Cat. 3 Lost
17.	257 Sqn., Northolt	C	Damaged by Ju 88 south of Tangmere; pilot returned unhurt.	A07.15 hrs.	Sgt. D.J. Hulbert	Hurricane	—	Cat. 2 Damaged
18.	257 Sqn., Tangmere	C	Damaged by Ju 88 west of Selsey Bill; pilot returned unhurt.	A15.50 hrs.	Plt. Off. C.F.A. Capon	Hurricane	—	Cat. 2 Damaged
19.	266 Sqn., Eastchurch	—	Aircraft destroyed in bombing raid on Eastchurch; no aircrew casualties.	07.18 hrs.	Nil	Spitfire	—	Cat. 3 Burnt
20.	601 Sqn., Tangmere	C	Damaged in combat near Tangmere; pilot unhurt.	12.15 hrs.	Fg. Off. W.P. Clyde	Hurricane	P3393	Cat. 2 Damaged

LUFTWAFFE LOSSES—TUESDAY 13th AUGUST 1940

1.	3.(3)/22	CM	Shot down by Spitfire flown by Malan of 74 Sqn., off Kent coast at 06.19 hrs.	Dornier Do 17P	100 %	Ltn. Pannhas killed; two missing.
2.	Wekusta. 51	CM	Crashed at Guyancourt after instrument failure.	Heinkel He 111H-3	100 %	One killed; Ltn.Stickel + one wounded.
3.	Stab/KG 2	CM	Shot down by Hurricane of Walker of 111 Sqn., at Barham at approx. 07.10 hrs.	Dornier Do 17Z	100 %	Four crew members missing
4.	Stab/KG 2	CM	Damaged by Hurricanes of No. 111 Sqn., over the Thames Estuary at 07.09 hrs.	Dornier Do 17Z	35 %	Two crew members wounded
5.	7./KG 2	CM	Damaged by Spitfires of 74 Sqn., and Hurricanes of No. 111 Sqn., over Thames Estuary at 07.10 hrs.	Dornier Do 17Z	45 %	Crew unhurt.
6.	7./KG 2	CM	Shot down by cannon-armed Hurricane flown by Smith of 151 Sqn., over Kent at A.07.10 hrs.	Dornier Do 17Z (U5+ER)	100 %	Uffz. Georg Vogel, Uffz. Herbert Arndt, Uffz. Willi Mehringer, and Gefr. Helmuth Bahr made P.O.W.
7.	7./KG 2	CM	Shot down by 111Sqn. Hurricanes of Dymond and Craig near Herne Bay at A.07.10 hrs.	Dornier Do 17Z	100 %	One killed; Oblt. Müller and Oblr. Morch + one other missing.
8.	7./KG 2	CM	Shot down by 111Sqn. Hurricane flown by Thompson over Thames Estaury at 07.06 hrs.	Dornier Do 17Z	100 %	Oblt. Schlegel and Oblt. Oswald + two missing.
9.	7./KG 2	CM	Shot down by 111 Sqn. Hurricane of McIntyre and 64 Sqn. Spitfire of Woodward at St. Nicholas at Wade, Kent, at A.07.10 hrs.	Dornier Do 17Z	100 %	Three killed; Oblt. von der Broeben missing.
10.	7./KG 2	CM	Damaged by 74 Sqn. Spitfires over Kent.	Dornier Do 17Z	20 %	Crew unhurt.
11.	8./KG 2	CM	Damaged by 151 Sqn. Hurricanes over Kent.	Dornier Do 17Z	20 %	One crew member wounded.
12.	8./KG 2	CM	Damaged by 74 Sqn. Spitfires over Kent.	Dornier Do 17Z	5 %	One crew member wounded.
13.	III./KG 27	CM	Shot down by 87 Sqn. Hurricanes of Dewar, Jay and Glyde over Mid-Channel; pilot rescued.	Heinkel He 111	100 %	Three killed; pilot unhurt.
14.	1./KG 54	CM	Shot down by 213 Sqn. Hurricanes over Lyme Bay at A.16.00 hrs.	Junkers Ju 88A-1	100 %	Oblt. Östermann killed; three missing.
15.	I./KG 54	CM	Shot down by 92 Sqn. Spitfires of Tuck, Watling and Havercroft at A16.25 hrs.	Junkers Ju 88A-1	100 %	Oblt. Erdmann killed; Oblt. Meyer + two others missing.
16.	I./KG 54	CM	Damaged by 213 Sqn. Hurricanes over Lyme Bay at A.16.00 hrs.	Junkers Ju 88A-1	40 %	Crew unhurt.
17.	I./KG 54	CM	Damaged by British fighters over Lyme Bay at A.16.00 hrs.	Junkers Ju 88A-1	10—60 %	Crew unhurt.
18.	I./KG 54	CM	Damaged by British fighters over Lyme Bay at A.16.00 hrs.	Junkers Ju 88A-1	10—60 %	Crew unhurt.
19.	I./KG 54	CM	Damaged by British fighters over Lyme Bay at A.16.00 hrs.	Junkers Ju 88A-1	10—60 %	Crew unhurt.
20.	I./KG 54	CM	Damaged by British fighters over Lyme Bay at A.16.00 hrs.	Junkers Ju 88A-1	5 %	One crew member wounded.
21.	II./KG 54	CM	Shot down by 601 Sqn. Hurricanes near Portland A.16.00 hrs.	Junkers Ju 88A-1	100 %	Two crew killed; Oblt. Fredebeul + one missing.
22.	II./KG 54	CM	Shot down by 601 Sqnm. Hurricanes over Lyme Bay at A.16.00 hrs.	Junkers Ju 88A-1	100 %	Hptm. Strauch + one killed; Oblt. Rosse + one missing.
23.	II./KG 54	CM	Damaged by British fighters over Lyme Bay at A.16.00 hrs.	Junkers Ju 88A-1	40 %	Three crew unhurt; Gefr. Neissl later reported P.O.W.
24.	II./KG 54	CM	Damaged by British fighters over Lyme Bay at A.16.00 hrs.	Junkers Ju 88A-1	40 %	Crew unhurt.
25.	II./KG 54	CM	Damaged by British fighters over Lyme Bay at A.16.00 hrs.	Junkers Ju 88A-1	5 %	One crew member wounded.
26.	II./KG 54	CM	Damaged by British fighters over Lyme Bay at A.16.00 hrs.	Junkers Ju 88A-1	5%	One crew member wounded.
27.	I./KG 77	NCM	Landing accident at Regensburg; not combat.	Junkers Ju 88A-1	65 %	Crew unhurt.
28.	II./St.G 2	CM	Shot down by 609 Sqn. Spitfire of Staples, Lyme Bay, A.16.10 hrs. Crew rescued by boat.	Junkers Ju 87R	100 %	Crew rescued unhurt.
29.	II./St.G 2	CM	Shot down by 152 Sqn. Spitfire of Boitl-Gill, Lyme Bay, A.16.00 hrs.	Junkers Ju 87R	100 %	Two crew members killed.
30.	II./St.G 2	CM	Shot down by 609 Sqn. Spitfire of Feary over Lyme Bay, A.16.10 hrs.	Junkers Ju 87R	100 %	One crew member missing; one wounded.
31.	II./St.G 2	CM	Shot down by 609 Sqn. Spitfire of Goodwin over Lyme Bay, A.16.10 hrs.	Junkers Ju 87R	100 %	Two crew members killed.
32.	II./St.G 2	CM	Shot down by 609 Sqn. Spitfire of Dundas over Lyme Bay, A.16.10 hrs.	Junkers Ju 87R	100 %	One crew member missing; one killed.

191

Luftwaffe Losses, 13th August 1940—*continued*

33.	II./St.G 2	CM	Damaged by 609 Sqn. Spitfire, probably of Miller; caught fire and crashed off Guernsey.	Junkers Ju 87R	100 %	Two crew members killed.
34.	III./St.G 77	NCM	Accident on Argentan airfield; not combat.	Junkers Ju 87B	70 %	Crew unhurt.
35.	III./St.G 77	NCM	Accident on Tonneville airfield; not combat.	Junkers Ju 87B	50 %	Crew unhurt.
36.	I./LG 1	CM	Damaged by unknown British fighters and crashed at Cherbour-Ost airfield.	Junkers Ju 88A-1	70 %	Crew unhurt.
37.	II./LG 1	CM	Burnt after take-off crash at Bricy airfield.	Junkers Ju 88A-1	100 %	Four crew members killed.
38.	II./LG 1	CM	Take-off accident at Bricy airfield.	Junkers Ju 88A-1	50 %	Crew unhurt.
39.	III./LG 1	CM	Shot down by 257 Sqn. Hurricanes four miles west of Selsey Bill at 16.04 hrs.	Junkers Ju 88A-1	100 %	One killed; three missing.
40.	III./LG 1	CM	Shot down by 257 Sqn. Hurricane of Mitchell near Tangmere at 07.14 hrs.	Junkers Ju 88A-1	100 %	Hptm. Schenplein + two killed.
41.	7./LG 2	CM	Force landed at Wissant following engine failure.	Messerschmitt Bf 110 C-5	40 %	Crew unhurt.
42.	V./LG 1	CM	Damaged by 609 Sqn. Spitfire over Lyme Bay at A.16.15 hrs; force landed in France.	Messerschmitt Bf 110D	50 %	Two crew members wounded.
43.	V./LG 1	CM	Shot down by 601 Sqn. Hurricanes near Port-land at A.16.00 hrs.	Messerschmitt Bf 110D	100 %	Ltn. Beck killed; one missing.
44.	V./LG 1	CM	Shot down by 601 Sqn. Hurricanes near Port-land at A.16.00 hrs.	Messerschmitt Bf 110D	100 %	One killed; one missing.
45.	V./LG 1	CM	Damaged by 601 Sqn. Hurricanes near Portland at A.16.00 hrs; force landed on France.	Messerschmitt Bf 110D	80 %	Crew unhurt.
46.	13./LG 1	CM	Shot down by 601 Sqn. Hurricanes off Portland at A.16.00 hrs.	Messerschmitt Bf 110 C-4 (L1+BH)	100 %	Oblt. Glienke and Gefr. Stück missing.
47.	V./LG 1	CM	Damaged by 601 Sqn. Hurricanes off Portland at A.16.00 hrs. Force landed at Rocquancourt.	Messerschmitt Bf 110D	60 %	Crew unhurt.
48.	14./LG 1	CM	Shot down by 213 Sqn. Hurricanes over Port-land at A.16.00 hrs.	Messerschmitt Bf 110D	100 %	Ltn. Werner and Gefr. Klemm missing.
49.	V./LG 1	CM	Damaged by 213 Sqn. Hurricanes off Portland at A.16.00 hrs. Force landed at Rocquancourt.	Messerschmitt Bf 110D	10 %	Crew unhurt.
50.	II.(Schlacht)/ LG 2	NCM	Wing failure in bombing dive over the weapons range at Rohrau.	Messerschmitt Bf 109 E-7	100 %	Oblt. Rudolf Claus killed.
51.	1./ZG 2	CM	Shot down by 238 Sqn. Hurricane of Hughes and crashed at Baggesly, near Romsey.	Messerschmitt Bf 110 C-4	100 %	Ltn. Wolf Münchmeyer, wounded, P.O.W.; Uffz. Fritz Labusch killed
52.	I./ZG 2	CM	Shot down by 238 Sqn. Hurricanes near Portland at A.12.25 hrs. and crashed at Lulworth.	Messerschmitt Bf 110 C-4	100 %	Uffz. Kurt Schumichen and Ogefr. Otto Giglhuber made P.O.W.s
53.	I./ZG 2	CM	Damaged by 238 Sqn. Hurricanes near Portland at A.12.25 hrs.	Messerschmitt Bf 110 C-4	3 %	One crew member wounded.
54.	I./ZG 26	CM	Damaged by 56 Sqn. Hurricanes at A.16.15 hrs.	Messerschmitt Bf 110 C-4	25 %	Crew unhurt.
55.	I./ZG 26	CM	Damaged by 56 Sqn. Hurricanes at A.16.15 hrs. and crashed landed at St. Omer.	Messerschmitt Bf 110C	80 %	Crew unhurt.
56.	2./ZG 26	CM	Crash landed at Mollenburcel after combat with 56 Sqn. Hurricanes at A.16.15 hrs.	Messerschmitt Bf 110D	10—60 %	Crew unhurt.
57.	3./ZG 26	CM	Damaged by 56 Sqn. Hurricanes at A.16.16 hrs. Crashed at St. Omer.	Messerschmitt Bf 110C	80 %	Crew unhurt.
58.	3./ZG 26	CM	Shot down by 56 Sqn. Hurricane of Weaver near Rochford at A.16.15 hrs.	Messerschmitt Bf 110C	100 %	Oblt . Fuchs + one killed.
59.	7./ZG 26	CM	Damaged by 56 Sqn. Hurricanes at A.16.15 hrs. and force landed near Amsterdam.	Messerschmitt Bf 110	10—60 %	One crew member wounded.
60.	8./ZG 26	CM	Damaged by 56 Sqn. Hurricanes at A.16.15 hrs. and crashed at Vlissingen.	Messerschmitt Bf 110C	90 %	Crew unhurt.
61.	3./ZG 76	CM	Shot down by Spitfire and crashed at Warden Bay 5 miles SE of Sheerness at 16.05 hrs.	Messerschmitt Bf 110C	100 %	Uffz. Willi Ebben and one other killed.
62.	III./ZG 76	CM	Shot down by ground fire in raid on Manston.	Messerschmitt Bf 110C	100 %	One killed and one missing.
63.	III./ZG 76	CM	Shot down by ground fire in raid on Manston.	Messerschmitt Bf 110C	100 %	Two crew members missing.
64.	I./JG 2	CM	Damaged by 43 Sqn. Hurricane flown by Mills at Petworth at A.07.00 hrs.	Messerschmitt Bf 109 E-1	100 %	Oblt. Temme missing.
65.	I./JG 2	CM	Damaged by 609 Sqn. Spitfire of Nowierski over Lyme Bay at A.16.10 hrs.	Messerschmitt Bf 109 E-4	80 %	Pilot wounded.
66.	II./JG 26	CM	Reported in German records as shot down near Folkestone; British action not traced.	Messerschmitt Bf 109E	100 %	Pilot missing.
67.	III./JG 51	CM	Believed shot down by 65 Sqn. Spitfires in area of Manston at A.15.30 hrs.	Messerschmitt Bf 109 E-1	100 %	Pilot wounded.
68.	III./JG 51	CM	Believed damaged by 65 Sqn. Spitfires in area of Manston, and crashed at Calais.	Messerschmitt Bf 109 E-1	80 %	Pilot unhurt.
69.	III./JG 51	CM	Believed damaged by 65 Sqn. Spitfires in area of Manston, and crashed at Coquelles.	Messerschmitt Bf 109 E-4	80 %	Pilot unhurt.
70.	II./JG 53	CM	Shot down by 609 Sqn. Spitfire of Crook over Lyme Bay at A.16.10 hrs.	Messerschmitt Bf 109 E-1	100 %	Ltn. Pfannschmidt killed.
71.	II./JG 53	CM	Shot down by 609 Sqn. Spitfire of Nowierski over Lyme Bay at A.16.15 hrs.	Messerschmitt Bf 109 E-1	100 %	Pilot missing.
72.	II./JG 53	CM	Shot down by 238 Sqn. Hurricane of Seabourne over Lyme Bay at A.06.45 hrs.	Messerschmitt Bf 109 E-4	100 %	Pilot missing.
73.	II./JG 53	CM	Take-off collision at Guernsey.	Messerschmitt Bf 109 E-4	30 %	Pilot unhurt.
74.	II./JG 53	CM	Take-off accident at Dinant airfield.	Messerschmitt Bf 109 E-4	60 %	Pilot unhurt.
75.	KGzbV.9	NCM	Take-off accident at Erbenheim airfield.	Junkers Ju 52/3m(6894)	70 %	No casualties.

Wednesday 14th August

As darkness had fallen at the close of *Adler Tag*, Sperrle sent nine *Kampfgruppe 100* Heinkel He 111s to raid the Spitfire factory at Castle Bromwich, Birmingham, but, despite their navigational expertise, only four crews managed to find their target and the damage by the eleven 25-kilo bombs dropped was not sufficient to delay aircraft production. Better results were obtained by fifteen KGr. 100 Heinkels, led by the *Gruppenkommandeur*, Hauptmann Friedrich Carol Aschenbrenner, which flew up the Irish Sea from their base at Vannes in Brittany to strike the Short Bros. factory at Queen's Island,

Belfast, where five of the new R.A.F. Stirling heavy bombers were totally destroyed[23].

Other bombers, commencing the night stage of *Adlerangriff*, resolutely flew the length and breadth of England, Scotland and Wales, bombing Bristol, Cardiff, Swansea, Liverpool, Sheffield, Norwich, Edinburgh and Aberdeen. Very little damage was done, although several railway lines were cut and more than one hundred casualties were suffered.

As these bombers were landing back at their bases during the small hours of 14th August, British Whitley bombers were also returning from a long distance raid. Nine hours previously 36 of these aircraft had set out to fly more than 1,500 miles to Milan and Turin in Northern Italy to raid the Caproni and Fiat aircraft factories[24]. With only four 250-lb. bombs apiece, their crews could scarcely expect to achieve much material damage, yet the morale effect upon the Italian population must have been significant in the face of German propaganda, which gave little hint of an R.A.F. bomber force in being[25].

The *Luftwaffe* attacks during daylight on 14th August, though on a much reduced scale compared with those of the previous day, were again delivered in two main thrusts. The first was launched by Kesselring over Kent at around noon when heavy concentrations of enemy aircraft were reported by Dover CH to be building up over the Pas de Calais. Park ordered 42 Hurricanes and Spitfires of Nos. 32, 65, 610 and 615 Squadrons to take-off at 11.50 hours, and these met up with the three *Gruppen* of Handrick's energetic JG 26 Messerschmitt pilots escorting eighty Ju 87s of Keil's II./St.G 1 and von Brauchitsch's IV./LG 1. The resulting dogfight involved a massive mêlée of over 200 aircraft over Dover, and, operating at very short range, the German fighters were able to stay and fight it out as, one by one, the R.A.F. squadrons joined in. While the 30-odd Bf 109s of Hauptmann Fischer's I.*Gruppe* stuck close to the dive-bombers, Karl Ebbighausen's II.*Gruppe* claimed two Hurricanes of No. 32 Squadron— which force landed at Hawkinge— and Adolf Galland's III.*Gruppe* claimed to shoot down six British fighters (of which three were in fact destroyed).

It is perhaps worth recording here the individual claims by the German pilots as they were clearly fighting men of great repute, and JG 26 suffered no loss in this battle. Ebbighausen

himself shot down one Hurricane, but was to be killed two days later; the other II./JG 26 victim was claimed by Oberleutnant Hans Krug of 4.*Staffel*, who was to be shot down and captured on 7th September having achieved a personal score of seven victories. In III.*Gruppe*, Galland himself shot down one British fighter; one of his successful pilots on this day was Oblt. Jochen Müncheberg, who rose to Major and shot down 135 Allied aircraft before his death on 23rd March 1943, by which time he had won the Knight's Cross with Oakleaves and Swords. Oblt. Georg Beyer, who shot down a Hurricane of No. 615 Squadron, was himself shot down and captured on 28th August with two victories to his credit. Oblt. (later Major) Gerhard Schöpfel added to his score on this day and went on to accumulate a tally of 40 Allied aircraft destroyed. Ltn. Joseph Bürschgens probably shot down Sergeant Bernard Gardner's Spitfire of No. 610 Squadron, but was himself shot down and captured on 1st September with a score of ten. Ltn. Gerhard Müller-Dühe, the sixth victorious pilot of III./JG 26, was killed only four days later with a score of five British fighters.

So closely engaged were the R.A.F. squadrons that one of the German fighter *Staffeln* was able to take time to destroy eight of Dover's balloons, each pilot carefully selecting one and shooting it up almost at leisure. One bunch of Ju 87s dive-bombed and sank the Goodwin lightship, and it was over this unarmed vessel that No. 615 Squadron fought its battle with III./JG 26.

While Group Captain Richard Brice, the Biggin Hill Controller, was considering whether to send further reinforcements into battle over Dover, messages flashed in that Manston airfield was again under attack. Yet again Rubensdörffer's indefatigable Erpr.Gr. 210 had struck—this time using only the Bf 110s of the 1st and 2nd *Staffeln*. Four hangars went up in smoke and three Blenheims of No. 600 Squadron were destroyed on the ground; the dispersals were reduced to shambles but from one, where 600 Squadron personnel had rigged up a 20-mm. Hispano gun, ground fire brought down one of the raiders. The Royal Artillery, manning a Bofors 40-mm. gun on the edge of the airfield, destroyed another. No sooner had the hard-worked ground personnel filled in the craters caused by Rubensdörffer's last attack than they were out again filling another fifty.

Possibly somewhat dismayed by the casualties suffered on the previous day, Sperrle's thrust on the afternoon of the 14th took the form of no fewer than nine relatively small raiding formations which advanced on the South Coast on a front of one hundred miles. They certainly succeeding in dispersing Brand's defending squadrons, and it was probably inevitable that several groups of enemy bombers should achieve penetration. Three Heinkel He 111s of KG 55's *Stabskette*, led by Oberst Alois Stoeckl (the *Geschwaderkommodore*), managed to reach the Middle Wallop airfield where they bombed No. 609 Squadron's hangar and offices. At the height of the raid three airmen ran out to close the hangar door to afford some protection for the Spitfires inside. As they were doing so, the building was struck by a 500-kilo bomb which blasted the huge doors on top of the gallant men. David Crook and John Dundas managed to take off amid the smoke and soon caught up with the enemy raiders; singling out the leader, Crook made a long and careful pass, firing a ten seconds' burst down to 30 yards' range, and Dundas delivered the coup de grace. In the wreckage were found the bodies of Oberst

[23] These Stirlings were *N6025—N6028* and *N6031* (Cf. *The Short Stirling*, Norris, G., Profile, Leatherhead, 1966, No. 142, p.10).

[24] Light relief to the grim battles is provided by an amusing anecdote on this night (recalled by the late Air Vice-Marshal Foster MacNeece-Foster, then Station Commander at R.A.F. Abingdon). It was customary for British bombers, which had been unable to drop their bombs, to jettison their loads on a bombing range at Charlton-on-Otmoor, about five miles north-east of Oxford, before landing at base, against a long-standing barrage of complaints from nearby farm residents. On the night in question a Whitley from Abingdon had dropped its remaining 250-lb. bomb accurately in the centre of the range. Unfortunately a number of KG 55 Heinkel crews, unaware of the remote nature of the "target", spotted the bomb burst and unloaded all manner of fairly heavy bombs in the area—much to the indignation of the Oxfordshire farmers who deluged the Abingdon bomber station with a flood of infuriated telephone calls!

[25] These raids by the R.A.F. were contributory to Mussolini's offer to send a detachment of *Regia Aeronautica* aircraft and crews to join Göring's *Luftwaffe* in the Battle of Britain. Although Hitler was to decline the offer, the eventual despatch of such a force was the result of Italian outrage at continuing R.A.F. raids on Italy.

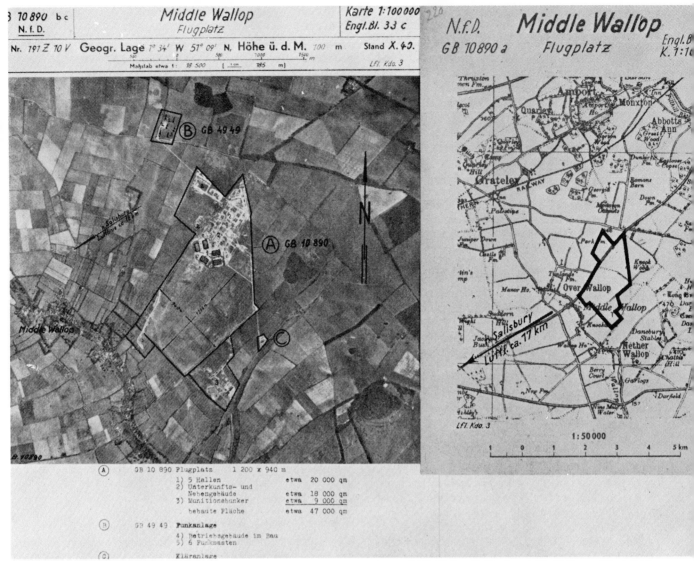

B 10 890 b c
N. f. D.
Middle Wallop
Flugplatz
Karte 1:100 000
Engl. Bl. 33 c

Nr. 191 Z 10 V   Geogr. Lage 1° 34' W 51° 09' N, Höhe ü. d. M. 100 m   Stand X. 43.
Maßstab etwa 1: 18 500   [1 cm = 185 m]   Lfl. Kdo. 3

N. f. D.   Middle Wallop
GB 10 890 a   Flugplatz
Engl. B
K. 1:1

Ⓐ GB 49 49

Ⓑ GB 10 890

ⒸⒸ

Ⓐ   GB 10 890 Flugplatz   1 200 x 940 m
   1) 5 Hallen   etwa 20 000 qm
   2) Unterkunfts- und
      Nebengebäude   etwa 18 000 qm
   3) Munitionsbunker   etwa 9 000 qm
      bebaute Fläche   etwa 47 000 qm

Ⓑ   GB 49 49 Funkanlage
   4) Betriebsgebäude im Bau
   5) 6 Funkmasten

Ⓒ   Kläranlage

German aerial photograph and target map of Brand's key sector station at Middle Wallop. Unlike those in No. 11 Group, this airfield was attacked by small enemy formations, but was never the target of a mass raid.

Stoeckl together with Oberst i.G. Frank (Chief of Staff, *Luftgau* VIII attached to V *Fliegerkorps*) and Oberleutnant Brossler, KG 55's navigation specialist. The loss of the formation's navigator deprived the two remaining crews of accurate information of their destination target, with the result that their pilots reported that they had bombed Netheravon—an old airfield a dozen miles to the north-west of Middle Wallop.

Meanwhile another raid had struck Southampton, where the main railway line was temporarily blocked. Three small formations of KG 27's Heinkels managed to penetrate Brand's fighter screen undetected and flew on northwards to the West Midlands. The airfield at Colerne (where the Hurricanes of the Maintenance Unit were understandably mistaken for operational fighters) was bombed, but no appreciable damage was caused. Three Heinkels even reached the airfield at Sealand in Cheshire (home of No. 30 Maintenance Unit), where rather more damage was caused—but of a temporary nature.

A direct hit on 14th August caused this damage to Pickfords premises in Southampton—typical of the growing proportion of damage now being suffered by the private and commercial sectors. (Photo: Southern Newspapers Ltd.)

As the German bombers flew northwards, anti-aircraft gunfire betrayed their presence to the flying instructors at No. 7 Operational Training Unit based at Hawarden, fifteen miles south of Birkenhead. Three staff pilots, belonging to an *ad hoc* local defence flight of Spitfires, took off and shot down one of the Heinkels near Chester[26].

Whether by an extraordinary flash of intuition or solely from necessity—or even from a more informed source, such as Enigma traffic—Dowding chose this day to re-arrange his order of battle, withdrawing some of his exhausted squadrons from the immediate battle area and bringing in fresh units. The remnants of John Peel's No. 145 Squadron were withdrawn to Drem in the north to rest and re-train. No. 238 Squadron, scarcely six weeks old but already a veteran unit, was moved west to the doubtful quiet of St. Eval in Cornwall. "Sailor" Malan's No. 74 Squadron was withdrawn to Wittering, and No. 266 Squadron was installed at Hornchurch in its place. No. 249 Squadron, with twenty Hurricanes, was transferred from Church Fenton to Boscombe Down at noon.

Notwithstanding these inspired moves, Dowding can scarcely have guessed that his pilots on the following day would face the heaviest fighting of the entire Battle. Nor could a stout Prussian have conceived that his vaunted *Luftwaffe* was to suffer losses that would shake that air force to its very foundations for the first time in its history.

---

[26] It is an extraordinary anomaly that at least six fighter pilots, who were not members of the officially designated Battle of Britain squadrons but who achieved confirmed victories against German aircraft over the United Kingdom during the Battle, were not made eligible for the Battle of Britain Clasp. The pilots involved in the above combat were Wg. Cdr. John Hallings-Pott (who retired as an Air Vice-Marshal, C.B.E., D.S.O., A.F.C. on 13th July 1957), Sqn. Ldr. John McLean (who retired as a Group Captain, O.B.E., D.F.C. on 19th August 1960), and Plt. Off. Peter Ayerst (who was still serving in the R.A.F. as a Squadron Leader, D.F.C. in 1965).

R.A.F. FIGHTER COMMAND LOSSES—WEDNESDAY 14th AUGUST 1940

No.	Squadron		Details	Time	Pilot	Aircraft	Serial	Category
1.	32 Sqn., Biggin Hill	C	Shot down and force landed at Hawkinge; pilot unhurt.	A13.00 hrs.	Plt. Off. R.F. Smythe	Hurricane	—	Cat. 2 Damaged
2.	32 Sqn., Biggin Hill	C	Shot down and force landed at Hawkinge; pilot unhurt.	A13.00 hrs.	Plt. Off. A.R.H. Barton	Hurricane	—	Cat. 2 Damaged
3.	32 Sqn., Biggin Hill	C	Shot down and force landed north of Dover; pilot unhurt.	A13.05 hrs.	Plt. Off. B. Wlasnowalski	Hurricane	P3171	Cat. 3 Destroyed
4.	43 Sqn., Tangmere	C	Shto down by He 111 forty miles south of Beachy Head; pilot killed.	A18.05 hrs.	Sgt. H.F. Montgomery	Hurricane	L1739	Cat. 3 Lost
5.	600 Sqn., Manston	—	Destroyed in raid on Manston; no aircrew casualties.	Not known	Nil	Blenheim	L1521	Cat. 3 Burnt
6.	600 Sqn., Manston	—	Destroyed in raid on Manston; no aircrew casualties.	Not known	Nil	Blenheim	—	Cat. 3 Burnt
7.	600 Sqn., Manston	—	Destroyed in raid on Manston; no aircrew casualties.	Not known	Nil	Blenheim	—	Cat. 3 Burnt
8.	610 Sqn., Biggin Hill	C	Shot down and force landed at Wye; pilot wounded.	12.40 hrs.	Sgt. B.D.G. Gardner	Spitfire	K9947	Cat. 3 Destroyed
9.	615 Sqn., Hawkinge	C	Damaged in combat with Bf 110 near Dover; pilot returned safely	12.12 hrs.	Fg. Off. J.R.H. Gayner	Hurricane	—	Cat. 2 Damaged
10.	615 Sqn., Hawkinge	C	Shot down by Bf 110s near Dover; pilot killed.	A12.15 hrs.	Fg. Off. P. Collard	Hurricane	P3109	Cat. 3 Missing
11.	615 Sqn., Hawkinge	C	Shot down by Bf 110s near Dover; pilot killed.	A12.15 hrs.	Plt. Off. C.R. Montgomery	Hurricane	P3160	Cat. 3 Missing

LUFTWAFFE LOSSES—WEDNESDAY 14th AUGUST 1940

No.	Unit		Details	Aircraft	%	Remarks
1.	I./KG 27	NCM	Crash landed at Villedieu with engine on fire.	Heinkel He 111P	100 %	Two crew members injured.
2.	8./KG 27	CM	Shot down by 7 O.T.U. Spitfire of Hallings-Pott near Chester.	Heinkel He 111P (1G+FS)	100 %	Oblt. Artur Weisemann, Fw. Heinrich Röder, Uffz. Hans Köchy, Uffz. Walter Schaum and Uffz. Gustav Ullman made P.O.W.
3.	9./KG 27	CM	Shot down by 92 Sqn. Spitfires of Williams and Wright at A.18.00 hrs, and crashed at Puriton between Highbridge and Bridewater.	Heinkel He 111P (1G+OT)	100 %	Ltn. Otto Uhland, Ogefr. Ramstetter, Uffz. Edfo Flick, Uffz. Josef Kremm and Gefr. Gerhard Rother made P.O.W.
4.	9./KG 27	CM	Shot down by 92 Sqn. Spitfires of Williams and Wright at A.18.15 hrs, and crashed in Mendip Hills, near Cheddar.	Heinkel He 111P (1G+NT)	100 %	Oblt. Ernst Uhlenschlager, Uffz. Kurt Sulzbach, Uffz. Adolf Blumenthal, Fw. Nikolaus and Gefr. Kurt Kupsch made P.O.W.
5.	III./KG 27	CM	Shot down by four Hurricanes of 43 Sqn. off Beachy Head at 18.17 hrs.	Heinkel He 111P	100 %	One killed; Hptm. Riedel + three missing.
6.	8./KG 27	CM	Shot down by seven Hurricanes of 43 Sqn., south of the Needles at 20.30 hrs.	Heinkel He 111P (1G+CS)	100 %	Uffz. Heinrich Schrage killed; Fw. Franz Knoblich and Fw. Tom Wiesmeyer missing; Fw. Walter Gietz and Fw. Oscar Dubral made P.O.W.s.
7.	III./KG 53	NCM	Force landed at Bouillon after engine failure.	Heinkel He 111H-1	50 %	Crew unhurt
8.	III./KG 53	NCM	Force landed at Bouillon; reason not known.	Heinkel He 111H-1	40 %	Crew unhurt.
9.	II./KG 54	NCM	Crashed near Wesel in bad weather.	Junkers Ju 88A-1	100 %	Oblt. Gerlin + two killed.
10.	St.St./KG 55	CM	Shot down by 609 Sqn. Spitfires of Crook and Dundas after raid on Middle Wallop; crashed at Eastdene at 18.30 hrs.	Heinkel He 111P (2898 : G1+AA)	100 %	Oberst Alois Stoeckl, *Geschw.Kdr.* Oberst.i.G. Frank (*Ch.de Lg.VIII*), Oblt. Bruno Brossler killed; two other missing.
11.	II./KG 55	NCM	Crashed at Merzhausen after engine failure.	Heinkel He 111P	Over 60 %	Tr.Arzt Dr. Frhr. von Liebenstein, Ltn. Wandfrie + one killed; two injured.
12.	I./LG 1	CM	Shot down by 92 Sqn. Spitfire of Tuck at A.18.10 hrs.	Junkers Ju 88A-1	100 %	One killed; Oblt. Heinrich + two missing.
13.	I./LG 1	CM	Shot down by 92 Sqn. Spitfire of Tuck over Bristol Channel at A.18.15 hrs.	Junkers Ju 88A-1	100 %	Four crew members missing.
14.	I./LG 1	CM	Shot down by 43 Sqn. Hurricanes 20 miles S.W. of St. Catherine's Point at 16.50 hrs.	Junkers Ju 88A-1	100 %	One killed; Ltn. Stahl + 2 missing.
15.	10./LG 1	CM	Shot down by 615 Sqn. Hurricane of Lofts over Folkestone at A.12.10 hrs.	Junkers Ju 87B	100 %	Obly. Gramling + 1 missing.

Luftwaffe Losses, 14th August 1940—*continued*

16.	10./LG 1	CM	Shot dowen by 615 Sqn. Hurricanes of Eyre and Porter over Folkestone at 12.10 hrs.	Junkers Ju 87B	100 %	One crew member wounded.
17.	10./LG 1	CM	Shot down by 610 Sqn. Spitfires over Folkestone at A.12.15 hrs.	Junkers Ju 87B	100 %	Both crew members missing.
18.	10./LG 1	CM	Shot down by 610 Sqn. Spitfires over Folkestone at A.12.15 hrs.	Junkers Ju 87B	100 %	Both crew members missing.
19.	2./ZG 26	CM	Damaged by Spitfires (probably of 610 Sqn.) over Folkestone; landed at St. Omer.	Messerschmitt Bf 110 C-4	10 %	Crew unhurt.
20.	Erpr.Gr. 210	CM	Shot down by Bofors gunfire during attack on Manston at 12.10 hrs.	Messerschmitt Bf 110D (S9+NK)	100 %	Ltn. Heinrich Brinkmann + one killed.
21.	Erpr.Gr. 210	CM	Shot down by machine gun fire during attack on Manston at 12.10 hrs.	Messerschmitt Bf 110D (S9+MK)	100 %	Uffz. Hans Steding killed; Gefr. Ewald Schank, wounded, P.O.W.
22.	III./JG 3	CM	Shot down over English Channel; R.A.F. action not known.	Messerschmitt Bf 109E	100 %	Pilot killed.
23.	I./JG 26	CM	Shot down by 32 Sqn. Hurricane of Smythe near Dover at A.12.45 hrs.	Messerschmitt Bf 109 E-1	100 %	Pilot missing.
24.	4./JG 52	CM	Shot down by 151 Sqn. Hurricane of Gordon over Kent at 16.20 hrs.	Messerschmitt Bf 109 E-1	100 %	Pilot missing.
25.	4./JG 52	CM	Shot down by 151 Sqn. Hurricane of Beggs over Kent at 16.24 hrs.	Messerschmitt Bf 109 E-1	100 %	Pilot missing.
26.	5./JG 52	CM	Shot down by 65 Sqn. Spitfire over East Kent at 12.20 hrs.	Messerschmitt Bf 109 E-3	100 %	Pilot missing.
27.	6./JG 52	NCM	Overturned on take-off at Peuplingne airfield.	Messerschmitt Bf 109E	60 %	Pilot unhurt.
28.	3./JG 54	NCM	Taxying accident at Campagne airfield	Messerschmitt Bf 109 E-4	17 %	Pilot unhurt.

Messerschmitt Bf 110Cs of II./ZG 76—known as the "*Haifisch Gruppe*", the Shark Group, for obvious reasons—shown here carrying underwing long-range fuel tanks. No fewer than eight of the unit's aircraft were destroyed on 15th August over the South Coast of England. (Photo: R.A.F. Museum)

Thursday 15th August

One can detect an atmosphere of seething frustration among the German High Command following the abortive launching of *Adlerangriff* on 13th August. Despite carefully synchronised attacks in the South of England, which had clearly achieved a high degree of success, the fury with which these attacks had been met had emphasised several weaknesses in the *Luftwaffe*'s plan, and there was already a hint that some of the German aircraft, if not entirely unsuitable for the tasks allotted to them, were not being employed correctly. Rendezvous between bombers and their escorts had been delayed or missed altogether, and communications between subordinate headquarters had left much to be desired. Continuing forecasts of bad weather on the 15th therefore prompted Reichsmarschall Göring to summon his senior Air Corps commanders back to Karinhall on this day to perform an autopsy on the *Adler Tag* assaults. In the absence of these staff

officers from the scene of battle, it is scarcely surprising that such lessons as had been learned in the past few days were not applied on the 15th—which was to witness the bitterest fighting of the whole Battle, and which came to be referred to as Black Thursday throughout the *Luftwaffe*.

After bad weather on the previous day, the 24-hour forecast suggested that it would hardly clear the United Kingdom in time to mount any worthwhile attack during daylight on the 15th. However, plans to include synchronised raids by *Luftflotte 5*, based in Denmark and Norway, in the *Adlerangriff* had been part of the overall strategy (*sic*) and detailed sortie plans were authorised on the evening of the 14th[27], so that when early morning reconnaissance suggested a slow clear-

---

[27] See *Luftwaffe War Diaries*, p.156.

ance over Scotland and Northern England it was decided to make preparations for formation attacks by this Air Fleet. Likewise, despite the adverse forecast in the South, and the absence of Lörzer, Kesselring, Sperrle, Grauert and Osterkamp from their headquarters, almost all units in *Luftflotte 2* and *3* were brought to readiness, and received precautionary briefing for operations similar in concept to those of *Adler Tag.*

As dawn broke, the weather forecasts appeared correct, returning German night raiders reporting fairly extensive cloud all over Britain. A small number of Blenheim night fighters of Nos. 25, 600 and 604 Squadrons (some of them radar-equipped) had groped about ineffectually over much of Southern England during the early hours, but without any contact. A Heinkel He 115 seaplane of 3./506, flying from Stavanger in Norway was exposed by searchlights on the Scottish coast and, flying low to confirm his landfall the pilot, Oberfeldwebel Hoffert, was evidently so blinded that he crashed into a lonely hilltop. The aircraft disintegrated over three fields and two of the crew were killed instantly, and the third was seriously injured. There was no fire and the absence of mines suggested a sortie purpose other than mining[28]

Sporadic reconnaissance flights had been tracked using sound plots by the Observer Corps during the early daylight hours over the Southern Counties, but only three enemy aircraft were positively identified—due mainly to cloud, but also to the fact that no fewer than six CH radars were off the air for maintenance and raid damage repair[29]. A Dornier Do 17 and a Junkers Ju 88 were, however, accurately plotted flying eastwards along the South Coast and six Spitfires, ordered up from the mist-shrouded airfield at Westhampnett to patrol Brighton at 06.50 hours, were vectored to intercept. They came upon the enemy south of Portsmouth and in a brisk running fight the Dornier was sent crashing into the sea about five miles south of Ventnor[30]. About 8,000 rounds were fired by the Spitfires at this aircraft (from 3.(F)/31, so that no claim was entered by any individual pilot.

Although the Ju 88 escaped from this combat, a similar aircraft was sighted over the Medway at about the same time and was engaged by anti-aircraft fire to such effect that it turned back over the Estuary and was last seen losing height. A Ju 88 of 5.(F)/122 was subsequently reported lost by the *Luftwaffe* and as its briefed target was Rochester it must be assumed that this was the same aircraft[31]. No record of crew rescue can be traced.

Thus far the morning had passed with little to suggest that any major attack was impending. By 10.00 hours all plotting tables were clear of enemy aircraft and most of the CH radars were back on the air in the South. Weather reports showed that

The Bf 110D, 3155:M8+CH flown by Oblt. Ketling of *1.Staffel, Zerstörergeschwader 76*, which was shot down by Pilot Officer "Ben" Bennions of No. 41 Squadron and crashed three miles east of Barnard Castle at 13.36 hrs on 15th August. (Photos: By courtesy of No. 41 Squadron and Flt. Lt. Robin Brown)

---

[28] Subsequent examination of a chart recovered from the wreckage revealed a track drawn from Stavanger to Montrose. Apart from a theory that this aircraft was engaged on weather reconnaissance (*Luftflotte 5* was notoriously ill-served by established *Wettererkundungsstaffeln*) for the day's planned raids, a postulation is held that this was a timing rehearsal for a feint scheduled to be undertaken by seaplanes of *Küstenfliegergruppe 506* later in the day.

[29] Cf. No. 11 Group O.C.L.O. Signals Log, 06.00 hours.

[30] Confirmed by Culver Cliff Station and Ventnor lifeboat crew.

[31] Observer Corps records (Bromley Centre) suggest that other reconnaissance aircraft had already overflown Rochester several times during the previous two hours.

overland cloud was clearing in the North and West, and it was obvious that this fact would have been reported by enemy reconnaissance. As a precaution one squadron of fighters in each of No. 11 Group's Sectors was moved forward to the coastal satellites, and single Sections ordered to Readiness.

On the other side of the Channel, the reported clearance of the skies over Britain was accompanied by a rapid improvement in visibility over Northern France. In the absence of General Lörzer, comanding II *Fliegerkorps*, executive authority rested with his Chief of Staff, Oberst Paul Deichmann, in the Corps Headquarters at Bonningues. Upon him now rested the responsibility to decide whether to launch the massive synchronised assault on Britain that was timed to saturate the defences over an 800-mile front from Edinburgh to Exeter. Despite Göring's "proposal" that no large-scale attack should be launched on this day, it was clear to Deichmann that the Reichsmarschall's reservations were dependent solely upon weather conditions and, as already remarked, all operational units were standing by ready for take-off.

Primary targets for all units were to be Fighter Command airfields, with little effort to be exerted against radar stations as it was now abundantly clear that no lasting damage could be caused without incurring heavy loss.

Nevertheless the inclusion of such airfields as Driffield (a bomber station in Yorkshire), Worthy Down and Eastchurch among the targets yet again displayed the Germans' ragged knowledge of the British defence structure. One may ask whether, in view of this, any detailed plans for the forthcoming invasion could be wholly realistic.

The fighter state in No. 11 Group was, between 10.00 and 11.00 hours, well balanced between squadrons available on the ground and in the air, with other aircraft refuelling after uneventful morning patrols. After the previous day's relative lack of combat, most squadrons were reporting a serviceable strength of twelve aircraft. There was no vulnerable concentration:

On patrol

  56 Squadron: 12 Hurricanes patrolling from Rochford,
  85 Squadron: 12 Hurricanes patrolling from Martlesham,
615 Squadron: 12 Hurricanes patrolling near Dungeness.

Landed

501 Squadron: 12 Hurricanes at Hawkinge, refuelling after
            patrol.

On State

  54 Squadron: 12 Spitfires "Available" at Manston,
  64 Squadron: 12 Spitfires "Available" at Kenley,
  65 Squadron: 9 Spitfires "Available" at Hornchurch,
111 Squadron: 12 Hurricanes "Available" at Croydon,
151 Squadron: 12 Hurricanes "Available" at North Weald,
257 Squadron: 12 Hurricanes "Available" at North Weald,
266 Squadron: 12 Spitfires "Available" at Hornchurch.

Other squadrons

  1 Squadron: 9 Hurricanes ordered to fly to North Weald
           by noon,
17 Squadron: 6 Hurricanes flying forward to Martlesham
           for convoy patrols,
32 Squadron: "Released" during morning at Biggin Hill
           (Hurricanes),
610 Squadron: "Released" during morning at Biggin Hill
           (Spitfires).

(All night fighter squadrons "Released")

A few minutes after 11.00 hours reports from Kent CH radars suggested a build-up of activity south of the Pas de Calais. This was the gathering of two Ju 87 *Staffeln* of von Brauchitsch's IV.(Stuka)/LG 1 which had taken off from Tramecourt. A few minutes later 26 more Ju 87s from Keil's II./St.G 1 were airborne in the Pas de Calais, joining up with a veritable umbrella of Bf 109s from neighbouring fields.

So massive were the raid signals displayed on the CH displays that it was impossible to direct fighters to a specific

The scattered remains of a Junkers Ju 87 flown by Uffz. Hermann Weber of 10./LG 1, which crashed in Folkestone at 17.30 hrs. on 15th August. Crippled by Hurricanes of No. 501 Squadron, the German aircraft hit the high tension cables, seen in the background; Weber and his gunner, Kraus, died in the crash.

raid[32]. If the Group or Sector Controllers were holding their hand until the raids developed, they were to be overtaken by events as the Ju 87s of LG 1 spilled out of the bright hazy sky over Hawkinge. By a stroke of luck—it can only otherwise be ascribed to the intuition of Group Captain Grice at Biggin Hill—eleven Hurricanes of No. 501 Squadron had been ordered off from Hawkinge 25 minutes earlier at 11.10 hours, to be followed by the twelve Spitfires of No. 54 Squadron led by Sqn. Ldr. James Leathart. Both squadrons were patrolling an area ten miles to the west of Dover just as the Ju 87s were taking up their pre-dive echelon over Hawkinge itself. The Hurricanes, being rather lower than the Spitfires, were in a better position to attack the dive-bombers and claimed ten "probably destroyed". In fact only two were shot down, one flown by Hauptmann Münchenhagen falling to the guns of Sgt. Paul Farnes; the other, crippled by several Hurricanes, struck some high tension cables on the outskirts of Folkestone and plunged into some houses. As the two R.A.F. squadrons tried to get at the dive-bombers, the top cover fell on them from above, shooting down Sergeants Norman Lawrence and Wojciech Klozinski of No. 54 Squadron[33]; No. 501 Squadron also lost two aircraft but the pilots escaped unhurt.

Intervention by the two fighter squadrons over Hawkinge undoubtedly prevented the destruction of the airfield (reported to have been achieved once again by the German crews on their return). A direct hit by a 500-kilo bomb demolished a hangar, and a 250-kilo bomb smashed one end of a barrack block. The predominant use of 50-kilo fragmentation bombs would have resulted in great damage to grounded aircraft—had there been any. Far more serious were four bomb strikes outside the airfield which severed sub-area cables carrying power to the CH radar stations at Dover and Rye, and the low-looking CHL station at Foreness. These radars were only brought back on state much later that day[34].

[32] Form 540, No. 54 Squadron, 15th August 1940, remarks: "By now the order *Patrol behind Dover and engage enemy fighters* is becoming as familiar as the old convoy patrols. . ."

[33] Both pilots recovered in hospital, Lawrence at Dover and Klozinski at Ashford.

[34] Too late to provide any reliable information during daylight, cf. O.C.L.O. Log, No. 11 Group.

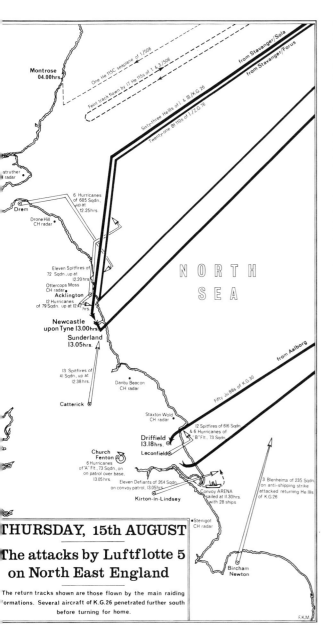

Montrose 04.00hrs.

One He 115C seaplane of 1/506

Feint track flown by 17 He 115s of 1, 4 & 3/506

from Stavanger/Sola

from Stavanger/Forus

Sixty-three Heills of I, & III/K.G 26

Twenty-one Bf 110s of I/Z.G 76

N O R T H

S E A

struther radar

6 Hurricanes of 605 Sqdn., up at 12.25hrs.
Drem

Drone Hill CH radar

Eleven Spitfires of 72 Sqdn.,up at 12.20 hrs.
Ottercops Moss CH radar
Acklington
12 Hurricanes of 79 Sqdn. up at 12.47 hrs.

Newcastle upon Tyne 13.00hrs.
Sunderland 13.05hrs.

from Aalborg

13 Spitfires of 41 Sqdn., up at 12.38 hrs.

Danby Beacon CH radar

Catterick

Staxton Wold CH radar

Fifty Ju 88s of K.G.30

12 Spitfires of 616 Sqdn. & 6 Hurricanes of "B" Flt., 73 Sqdn.

Driffield 13.18hrs.
Leconfield

Church Fenton
6 Hurricanes of "A" Flt., 73 Sqdn., on patrol over base, 13.05hrs.

Eleven Defiants of 264 Sqdn. on convoy patrol, 13.05hrs.

Kirton-in-Lindsey

Convoy ARENA sailed at 11.30hrs. with 28 ships

3 Blenheims of 235 Sqdn. on anti-shipping strike attacked returning He IIIs of K.G.26

Stenigot CH radar

Bircham Newton

F.K.M.

THURSDAY, 15th AUGUST

The attacks by Luftflotte 5 on North East England

The return tracks shown are those flown by the main raiding formations. Several aircraft of K.G.26 penetrated further south before turning for home.

cannon and machine gun fire. Sixteen casualties were inflicted upon the long suffering station personnel, and two Spitfires which had landed earlier in the morning were destroyed. It is believed that this attack was carried out by II./ZG 76, flying its first raid with bomb-carrying Bf 110s.

While Park anxiously scanned his operations table for signs of further raid build-up after mid-day, it was to the North that the battle now moved. Conscious that since the fall of Norway his flank could be turned by heavy attacks on the industrial North of England, Dowding had steadfastly resisted the temptation to concentrate all his fighter resources in the South, preferring to rely upon a system of mutual re-inforcement between Groups and Sectors, and to use the airfields in the North as bases for squadrons resting and re-forming—knowing that many a pilot almost resented being taken out of the battle area at this stage. As it happened, there were in the North a number of first-rate fighter squadrons which, though heavily committed at Dunkirk, were now well rested and fighting fit.

The deployment of three *Luftflotten*, including *Luftflotte 5* in Denmark and Norway, was such that under certain favourable circumstances almost the entire British Isles were within range of *Luftwaffe* bombers carrying worthwhile bomb-loads. Already all three Air Fleets had contributed raids on Britain—but not simultaneously in strength, *Luftflotte 5* in particular staging only isolated attacks by single aircraft or small formations.

The circumstances that may be said to have contributed to bring about the widespread air attacks on 15th August focus attention once more on the shortcomings of German Intelligence both in the short and long term senses. The effective resistance to raids mounted against the South by day during July and the first two weeks of August convinced O.K.L. that the British had deprived the North of its fighters and anti-aircraft guns to provide this resistance. There is no evidence available to suggest that Germany acquired any field Intelligemnce (from agents in Britain, from aircraft unit identification or from prisoner interrogation) to confirm this concentration; moreover, even had identification of fresh squadrons in the South been forthcoming, the Germans would most likely have interpreted these signs as confirmation of their own ill-founded beliefs. The truth lay in Fighter Command's newly-

If von Brauchitsch's dive-bombers had to some extent been frustrated over Hawkinge, those of Keil had things much their own way and were able to strike the forward airfield at Lympne unopposed by fighters. Considerable concentration was achieved and few of the remaining buildings, untouced by the previous raid, were left unscathed. A direct hit on the sick quarters led to requisition of several house near the airfield—which was not made operational again until the evening of the 17th. Once again the use of fragmentation bombs indicated the *Luftwaffe*'s determination to destroy grounded aircraft—and again there were none.

As reports came in from Observer posts that enemy raids had cleared the coast, the Sector Controllers were anxious to recover their fighters and refuel them without delay as recent experience had shown that, with so much of the radar chain out of action, it was necessary to bring a high proportion of the Available fighters up to Readiness. It was perhaps fortunate that No. 54 Squadron did not return to Manston to refuel as it would almost certainly have been caught on the ground by a snap raid by a dozen Bf 110s which swept the airfield with

A Heinkel He 111 of *Kampfgeschwader 26*—the lion badge and motto *Vestigium Leonis* are visible on the nose. On 15th August KG 26 flew from its Norwegian bases to a severe mauling over Britain's North-East Coast.

introduced practice of "rotating" squadrons to and from the rugged atmosphere of the South. Such flexibility was quite unimagined in the German appreciation of R.A.F. fighter operations[35].

What the German High Command did *not* know was that there were in the North a number of fighter squadrons which, if not fully acclimatised to the atmosphere of the South, were at least battle-tested veterans of the Battle of France and Dunkirk. Events of this Thursday were to leave General Hans-Jürgen Stumpff, commanding *Luftflotte 5*, under no delusions as to the weakness of German Intelligence.

It has been suggested that the absence of heavy enemy air activity against the North might have resulted in a lack of vigilance in the radar chain, the existence of which was amply clear to the *Luftwaffe* by now. If the German planners had placed any store in such a belief, they were sadly optimistic. Whether or not they knew of the existence of the important convoy ARENA which was to put out from Hull at about mid-day, they were certainly unaware of the special vigilance ordered in all coastal radar stations during the convoy's passage northwards[36].

Shortly after 10.00 hours (British time) on the bleak, windswept airfield at Stavanger/Sola on the Norwegian coast, the engines of KG 26's Heinkel He 111s came to life. Seventy-two crews had just completed their briefing for attacks on airfields in the North of England—notably Dishforth and Usworth—with secondary targets at Newcastle, Sunderland and Middlesbrough, each of their aircraft being loaded with 3,000 pounds of bombs consisting of 500- and 250-kilo H.E. bombs.

About 30 minutes previously two *Staffeln* of Heinkel He 115 seaplanes[37] had taken off from the neighbouring anchorage and set course for Dundee as a feint to attract northwards any defending fighter squadrons that might be based around Edinburgh.

Immediately after take-off by the Heinkel He 111 bombers came 21 Messerschmitt Bf 110s of I *Gruppe*, *Zerstörergeschwader 76*, led by *Gruppenkommandeur* Hauptmann Werner Restemeyer, which were to accompany the raid, flying above and on the sunward side of the bombers.

Unfortunately, and disastrously as events were to prove, owing to a three-degree error in navigation the Heinkel bombers followed a track which carried them almost along that flown by the feinting seaplanes. The illusion was thus utterly ruined and the heavy raid responses which suddenly appeared on the Anstruther CH radar were caused by a conglomeration of harmless seaplanes (which turned back about forty miles from the Scottish coast), 63 Heinkel bombers—several had also turned back, thereby *adding to* the raid strength picture—and the escorting Messerschmitts. In the course of five minutes after mid-day, Anstruther reported a raid of 3-plus, quickly amending this to 30-plus. Whatever lack of accuracy existed—resulting from inexperience in recognising mass raids—it was clear to the No. 13 Group

Controller that a major raid was approaching.

Faced with radar information suggesting a heavy raid aimed at Edinburgh, the Controller immediately ordered the whole of No. 72 Squadron (twelve Spitfires) to Readiness at Acklington at 12.10 hours, and five minutes later scrambled it to patrol over base when the raid appeared to swing south. In a moment of truth Oberstleutnant Fuchs' Heinkel crews had realised their navigation error and hurriedly altered course away from the area to which they expected British fighters had been lured by the feinting seaplanes.

Now that indications were that many more than 30 aircraft were approaching, the fighter defences of the North were alerted, and No. 72 Squadron was now ordered north to meet the threat; the Hurricane pilots of No. 79 Squadron, "resting" at Acklington, were recalled from Released and ordered to Available at 12.15 hours. At the same time two Flights of Hurricanes from No. 605 Squadron at Drem were scrambled and were airborne at 12.25 hours, climbing hard and making for a rendezvous with the raid 50 miles south-east of their base. Had they known it, the pilots were racing on a converging course with the enemy, but now the CH radar at Ottercops Moss was "on the air", having been brought hurriedly off maintenance, and the radar picture was being confused by friendly fighters. The Controller was therefore reluctant to turn a squadron into a quarter attack while it was still climbing for, even had it managed to attain the necessary altitude, any inaccuracy or delay in radar plotting might place the fighters irrevocably far astern.

As it was, Sqn. Ldr. Edward Graham arrived with eleven Spitfires off the Farne Islands at 18,000 feet and sighted not 30, but about one hundred enemy aircraft. Approaching almost head-on at a closing speed of about 400 m.p.h., and with about 3,000 feet height advantage, the squadron commander had to react quickly; passing a hurried sighting report of "about a hundred bandits" to the Controller, he led his formation to the seaward side so that he would have the sun behind him, and then dived on the Messerschmitts and carried on downwards towards the Heinkels below and beyond.

Precisely which of the Spitfire pilots scored in that initial dive will never be known as none was using a cine gun, but two Bf 110s fell, that flown by Restemeyer himself—his aircraft torn apart by an explosion of petrol gas in his exhausted ventral tank[38], and the other flown by the I.*Gruppe* Adjutant, Oberleutnant Loobes, crashing on the Durham coast.

---

[35] Cf. *Luftwaffe Operations Staff IC Intelligence Survey*, Appendix K: "(The R.A.F. possesses). . . little strategic flexibility in operations as ground personnel are usually permanently stationed at home bases."

[36] Cf. No. 13 Group O.C.L.O. Log , 18.00 hours, 14th August 1940).

[37] These were *1.* and *3.Staffeln* of *Küstenfliegergruppe 506*, the same *Gruppe* that had lost an aircraft several hours previously over the Scottish coast.

[38] Several of the intercepting pilots reported considerable radio interference from what appeared to be *en clair* German. Almost as Graham's Spitfires went into the attack, this interference stopped. This may be explained by the fact that Restemeyer's aircraft was equipped as a flying control position, loaded with radio monitoring equipment to intercept R.A.F. fighter control orders. His crew companion was Hauptmann Hartwich, X *Fliegerkorps* radio Intelligence expert. *The Luftwaffe War Diaries* speculate that Restemeyer was unable to jettison his long range fuel tank when the Spitfires attacked; however a more likely explanation was that Restemeyer may have been flying a Bf 110D-0, a version that featured a large, *fixed* fuel tank fairing under the nose; it is now known that about ten such aircraft were flown by operational units during the Battle of Britain, and although German records only refer to Restemeyer's aircraft being a "Bf 110D", the D-0 would have been an obvious choice on this occasion.

Pilot Officer Bennions of No. 41 Squadron. One of the truly outstanding young pilots of 1940 who never sought or acquired the limelight of some other British pilots yet, only commissioned three months before the Battle, frequently found himself leading his squadron after the loss of its C.O. and his flight commander. He survived severe wounds and is living in quiet retirement at the time of writing.

Fearful of being isolated from the protection of the main formation's guns, several straggling bomber crews lightened their loads, while others, left helpless with little defence, prudently jettisoned their bombs and dived at full throttle for the scanty cloud cover that existed on the seaward side. These manœuvres, suggesting to the Spitfire pilots that the enemy bombers were stricken by damage, undoubtedly caused some to believe their victims had fallen, and No. 72 Squadron claimed the destruction of eleven aircraft; it is now clear that in this initial attack only three aircraft fell[39]. No. 72 Squadron's fight lasted five short minutes between 12.30 and 12.35 hours. Five minutes later it was No. 605 Squadron's turn, just north of Blyth. However, because the Heinkel formation had by now split into several groups, the Controller had divided 605 Squadron into two Flights and only five Hurricane pilots of "B" Flight made contact.

Two other squadrons were closing with the Heinkels; thirteen Spitfires of No. 41 Squadron had been scrambled and were airborne from Catterick at 12.38 hours, and twelve Hurricanes of No. 79 Squadron took off from Acklington at 12.42 hours as it now seemed that thier own base was threatened by attack. The raid, however, passed to the east of the airfield and both squadrons fell upon the enemy bombers as

they approached Newcastle. By now another four Heinkels had fallen—to No. 605 Squadron's guns—and two more were to fall in the coastal area between Sunderland and Bridlington before the raiders turned for home[40]; several stragglers were pursued south over Yorkshire before they too made off to the east between 13.00 and 13.20 hours. The Messerschmitts had retired at about 12.40 hours having lost no less than a third of their number. One further Heinkel was to be lost when it was unlucky enough to run into a shipping strike by Blenheims of No. 235 Squadron over the North Sea and was shot down by Plt. Off. Norman Smith.

As the plotting tables in No. 13 Group were showing the Heinkels of KG 26 over Newcastle and Sunderland, the No. 12 Group fighter state was being advanced as some of the northern raiders looked likely to fly down the coast. At 13.05 hours eleven Defiants of No. 264 Squadron at Kirton-in-Lindsey were ordered off to guard the convoy ARENA which had sailed from Hull with sixteen merchantmen, eight escort vessels and four minesweepers. As the Defiants were taking off, first reports were just being plotted of a 40-plus raid approaching Staxton Wold CH radar station from the northeast. Aimed directly at the fighter airfields of Church Fenton and Leconfield, the raid—composed of 50 Junkers Ju 88s of *Kampfgeschwader 30* apparently flying without conventional escort from Aalborg in Denmark—crossed the coast at Flamborough Head and was simultaneously intercepted by twelve Spitfires of No. 616 Squadron and six Hurricanes of "B" Flight, No. 73 Squadron, scrambled in great haste from Leconfield at about 13.07 hours. It is now known that only about half the German aircraft carried bombs, being the familiar Ju 88A-1 aircraft—their crews under orders to fly at full throttle after crossing the English coast; the other aircraft in the formation were Ju 88 "fighters", the Ju 88C *Zerstörer* version, whose pilots were tasked with covering the bombers and screening them from fighter attack. The enemy formation held on a south-westerly course over the land and then suddenly swung south over the Bomber Command airfield at Driffield whose four heavy and sixteen Bofors gun crews were ready warned and put up a heavy fire. The enemy's approach coincided with a practice exercise at Driffield, so that when the enemy bombers arrived overhead most of the station personnel were already in shelter trenches and the gun defences fully manned. Despite this the numerous H.E. and fragmentation bombs caused very heavy damage on the bomber base; several Whitley bombers were hit by fragmentation bombs, and one blew up with such force that the explosion destroyed two others; one hangar was severely damaged together with the aircraft inside, and a direct hit wrecked the Officers's Mess. All told, ten Whitleys were totally destroyed and six others badly damaged—the greatest single blow of the day for the R.A.F. The raiders also suffered heavily before they turned for home, two bombers and five *Zerstörer* Ju 88Cs being shot down; one of the latter became isolated from its formation and was hounded westwards,

---

[39] The Messerschmitts of Restemeyer and Loobes, and a Heinkel He 111 of the 9th *Staffel*, KG 26.

[40] Contrary to strongly-held beliefs in the *Luftwaffe*, only one casualty was suffered by Fighter Command in these air battles; this was Plt. Off. Kennith Schadtler-Law of No. 605 Squadron who managed to bring his badly damaged Hurricane back over the coast to a crash landing near Hartley railway station, five miles north of Tynemouth. This pilot later changed his name to Law, having retired from the R.A.F. as a Wing Commander in 1968; he died in 1986.

Scenes at the Bomber Command airfield at Driffield after the raid by Junkers Ju 88s of *Kampfgeschwader 30* at lunchtime on 15th August. Hangars were hit and badly damaged (*top*), ten Whitleys were destroyed (*centre*) and part of the officers' mess was wrecked (*bottom*). (Photos: R.A.F. Museum)

finally to crash in Lancashire. Three others, with combat damage, crashed on their return, one of them in Holland.

So ended the first—and as it transpired the last—flank attack in strength in daylight by *Luftflotte 5*. Subsequent German analyses have sought to play down the significance of the attack and have denied that the air combat was as one-sided as the results might suggest. Yet with losses amounting to almost twenty per cent (from the Germans' own casualty returns and which also give details of 81 aircrew losses in killed and missing from the one *Luftflotte*), it was obvious, from the presence of strong fighter defences in the North of England, that mounting an attack in strength over the expanse of the North Sea without the protection of single-seat fighters must be accompanied by the risk of crippling losses. It transpired that, unknown to the British until long after, some of the Scandinavian-based bombers were now to be redeployed to strengthen *Luftflotten 2* and *3*; had the passing of the danger in the North been recognised by Fighter Command, it is open to conjecture whether Dowding might also have felt inclined to redeploy some of the northern fighters to strengthen Nos. 10, 11 and 12 Groups.

As the surviving Junkers Ju 88s of KG 30 returned to Denmark, the scene of battle again shifted southwards, and at 14.15 hours the Kent and Essex CH stations reported a build-up of enemy forces beyond the Pas de Calais and over Belgium. This was to be one of the most difficult threats posed during the day, cleverly confused by feint attacks and dog-legs in the bomber tracks. It was mounted by all three *Gruppen* of KG 3, flying Dornier Do 17s from St. Trond and Antwerp, their crews briefed to raid airfields in North Kent. As the raid plots approached, the radar picture became confused by the appearance of a fighter screen which rose from the Pas de Calais to cover the bombers, so that the No. 11 Group Controller was once more justifiably reluctant to order patrols until certain of the likely area of attack.

It was during this short period of uncertainty that very brief warning was flashed of a fast raid, labelled Raid 22, approaching Harwich[41]. No. 17 Squadron, which had been moved forward for the day to Martlesham from Debden to fly convoy patrols, was ordered off and three pilots (Flt. Lt. William Harper, Plt. Off. Geoffrey Pittman and Sgt. Glyn Griffiths) managed to get airborne before the raid swung in over the airfield. This was a superbly executed attack—once again flown by Rubensdörffer's *Erprobungsgruppe 210*— the Bf 110s streaking very low across Martlesham to drop about 30 bombs, of which eighteen landed among the station buildings. A fragmentation bomb struck a Fairey Battle bomber which exploded with such violence that it demolished the watch office, severely damaged two hangars and wrecked No. 25 Squadron's equipment store. Also hit were the station workshops, the Officers' Mess, and water and telephone services. The airfield was not to become fully operational again for 48 hours after the raid, which was carried out by no more than 25 fighter-bombers. Some reports suggest that a nearby signals site was attacked by Ju 87 dive bombers—and Ju 87Rs would certainly have possessed the range to reach Martlesham; however, no mention is made of

a Ju 87 unit in German reports of the raid and no such sightings were recorded by British pilots. In any case it is unlikely that the slow dive-bombers would have accompanied the faster fighter-bombers; more likely is the explanation that the Bf 109s of 3./Erpr.Gr. 210 opened the raid with steep diving attacks—as was their wont—and that these aircraft were mistaken for Ju 87 dive-bombers.

Apart from the three pilots of No. 17 Squadron, nine Hurricanes of No. 1 Squadron were also directed against Raid 22, but were surprised by the Bf 109s which—having dropped their bombs—were giving top cover for the Bf 110s. Flt. Lt. Mark Brown, leading the squadron, was shot down off Harwich but was rescued from the sea with minor wounds. Two other pilots, Plt. Off. Dennis Browne and Sgt. Martin Shanahan, were shot down and killed. Rubensdörffer's formation returned home unscathed; fortunately for him, twelve Spitfires (about half of them cannon-armed) of No. 19 Squadron, ordered off from Fowlmere, arrived too late to intercept the raid, and arrived over Martlesham only to find an ominous pall of smoke—but no sign of the raiders.

Meanwhile the 88 Dornier Do 17s, which constituted the entire serviceable strength of *Kampfgeschwader 3*, led by Oberst Wolfgang von Chamier-Glisczinski, had collected their escort, provided by more than 130 Messerschmitt Bf 109s from JG 51, JG 53 and JG 54 and were approaching Deal at 15.30 hours. Simultaneously more than 60 Bf 109s from JG 26 swept in over Kent on either side of Dover. Against this massive array Grice, at Biggin Hill, could only divert three airborne squadrons (twelve Hurricanes of No. 111 Squadron[42], twelve Hurricanes of No. 151 Squadron and twelve Spitfires of No. 64 Squadron), but four more quickly scrambled and attempted to engage. The enemy fighter screen was, however, virtually impregnable and KG 3 itself only suffered two losses from British fighters (as no R.A.F. pilot filed a combat report claiming to have shot down any aircraft in this raid, it must be assumed that whoever did so was immediately shot down and killed by the escort). Once again JG 26 had a field day, victories being claimed by Hptm. Karl Ebbighausen, Oblt. Eberhard Henrici, Ltn. Hans Krug, Oblt. Kurt Ebersberger, Oblt Georg Beyer, Ltn. Joseph Bürschgens, Ltn. Walter Blume and Ltn. Gerhard Müller-Dühe.

The Dorniers reached Faversham and then split, the *Stabskette*, I. and II.*Gruppen* continuing westwards to Rochester, and III.*Gruppe*, led by Hptm. Rathmann, turning north-west to attack Eastchurch once more. Von Chamier-Glisczinski led his formation on a devastating raid on Rochester where more than 300 bombs—many of them delayed action—fell on the airfield and upon the Short Bros. factory. Once again the Short Stirling bomber production was severely disrupted when the component stores were struck, reducing delivery schedules to the R.A.F. for the next three months.

Raids at *Staffel* strength by aircraft of KG 1 and KG 2— closely covered by Messerschmitts of Major Hans Trübenbach's I.*Gruppe, Lehrgeschwader 2*—were now exploiting the disrupted fighter defences and fanned out over Kent,

---

[41] This German formation had passed within twenty miles of the North Foreland CHL low-looking radar on the "tip" of Kent; however, owing to the power failure caused earlier, the equipment was still off the air.

[42] The commanding officer of No. 1 Squadron, R.C.A.F., Sqn. Ldr. Ernest McNab R.C.A.F., was invited to fly with No. 111 Squadron by John Thompson on this occasion to gain first hand experience of Fighter Command's combat tactics. He later claimed the destruction of a KG 2 Dornier Do 17 over the marshes off Westgate.

attacking Hawkinge airfield, Maidstone, Dover, Rye and the Foreness CHL radar. A few lucky interceptions were made, but generally the British fighters were closely marked and casualties mounted quickly.

Once again the battle switched to the West and at about 17.00 hours the depleted radar system on the Sussex and Hampshire coasts reported the distant approach of two heavy raids. Twenty minutes later these were sighted by the pilots of Nos. 43 and 234 Squadrons south-east of the Isle of Wight and of Portland respectively.

The raid intercepted by No. 43 Squadron—and shortly after by Nos. 249, 601 and 609 Squadrons—consisted of about 60 Junkers Ju 88s of LG 1, escorted by forty Bf 110s of ZG 2 led by Oberstleutnant Vollbracht. Despite determined attacks by the Hurricanes and Spitfires over Southampton and the Solent, the Ju 88 pilots forced their way through the defences, thirty aircraft making for Middle Wallop and the remaining bombers attacking Worthy Down. Very little damaged was done at either airfield and some aircraft, which broke away from the Middle Wallop raid, attacked the airfield at Odiham—but reported on their return home that they had attacked Andover.

The raiders which attacked Worthy Down were severely handled by the interceptors, one *Staffel* alone—4./LG 1, led by Hptm. Jochen Helbig—losing five out of seven Ju 88s to the guns of No. 601 Squadron's Hurricanes.

Further west, Portland was again under attack by Stukas—about forty Junkers Ju 87s of I./St.G 1 led by Hauptmann Hozzel and II./St.G 2 led by Hptm. Eneccerus, heavily escorted by 60 Messerschmitt Bf 109s of JG 27 and JG 53, and twenty Bf 110s of V./LG 2. As two Hurricane Squadrons (Nos. 87 and 213 from Exeter) engaged the *Zerstörer* and dive-bombers, the fourteen Spitfire pilots of No. 234 Squadron went for the enemy single-seaters. Their meeting was vicious and, although they gave a good account of themselves, they were overwhelmed by sheer weight of numbers.

Those who chose, and were able to disengage, escaped, but three pilots were hemmed in, and two (Plt. Off. Vincent Parker, an Australian, and Plt. Off Cecil Hight, a New Zealander) were shot down. The third aircraft, flown by Plt. Off. Richard Hardy, was hit by machine gun fire far out to sea and force landed near Cherbourg, the pilot being taken prisoner.

It was during the combat fought by the Hurricanes that there occurred one of those superb feats of airmanship that were the hallmark of long flying experience and great courage. Squadron Leader John Dewar had led the Hurricanes of No. 213 Squadron's "B" Flight into action against the Bf 110s southeast of Portland but had been frustrated from scoring when the enemy fighters took up their customary defensive circle. When he decided to climb above the circle to attempt a diving attack, he was himself attacked by a whole *Staffel* of Bf 109s:

". . .my cockpit filled with smoke and fumes, and I realised I had been hit. I dived steeply away; it was difficult to see but I knew from the sun that I was going north. I saw I was being pursued but it turned out to be Fg. Off. Strickland who, at considerable risk to himself, had come to protect me and watch where I fell. I found it impossible to sit in the cockpit and prepared to bale out; half out of the cockpit, however, my head was clear of the fumes; there was no fire and the engine was running, so I decided to make for land, flying on the stick alone. Having reached Weymouth Bay the Hurricane was still flying splendidly, so I followed a Spitfire back

Views of the Spitfire flown by Richard Hardy of No. 234 Squadron, *N3277*: AZ-H, guarded by German soldiers near Cherbourg. In combat with German aircraft far out over the English Channel, the Spitfire was badly damaged and had its radio smashed (note damage aft of cockpit); running short of fuel, Hardy force landed in France and was taken prisoner. (Photos: Hans Obert)

SIGNAL OFFICE DIARY.

DATE *Aug 15th 1940* STATION *Bromley*

Watch Times.	*A Crew Cont*	REMARKS.	Signature.

16   11·33   *L/O R.2 post reported air raid warning sounded.*

17   11·42   *From L/O Requested us to ask Maidstone to ring them*

18   12·06   *To L/O Reported that a H/E with fuselage badly shot away was making for Biggin Hill and being told to them. Fighters Designation F.G.*

19   12·25   *To L/O. R.2 post reported all clear sounded.*

At about 11.30 hrs. on the morning of 15th August, Plt. Off. Anthony Truran of No. 615 Squadron was involved in a dogfight with Bf 109Es over the sea off Dungeness when his Hurricane, KW-W, was hit in the rear fuselage by cannon fire; the wings and fuselage were peppered with machine gun bullets, and he himself was later wounded. He dropped out of the fight, and half an hour later the Bromley Observer Corps signal office received a report that he had been sighted limping across the sky towards Biggin Hill; the log extract above reads "To L/O (*liaison officer*) Reported that a H/c (*Hurricane*) with fuselage badly shot away was making for Biggin Hill and being told to them." Despite his wounds and the massive damage to his aircraft, Truran flew on to his own base at Kenley and landed safely. These photographs provide eloquent testimony to the Hurricane's ability to withstand extensive battle damage.

to Warmwell. By holding my breath I managed to lower the undercarriage and flaps and make a landing, which was very fortunate as the aircraft is not seriously hit except in the engine and wings. . ."[43]

One other group of raids was to be launched on this most critical day. While various formations of Dorniers penetrated the Kent coast at about 18.20 hours under cover of free chases by Bf 109s of JG 26, fifteen bomb-carrying Bf 110s of eight Bf 109s of the extraordinary *Erprobungsgruppe 210* —yet again led by Rubensdörffer—swept in near Dungeness and made for its target at the Kenley Sector Station. The Dornier pilots had been briefed to attack Biggin Hill, thereby dividing the defences.

Rubensdörffer had had a difficult decision to make. He had missed the rendezvous with his Bf 109 escort from JG 52 over France and, knowing that the Dorniers would face the whole defence alone if he abandoned his attack, decided to carry on without close fighter cover. Hoping to confuse the defences he led his Messerschmitts in a wide sweep over Sevenoaks and started a diving turn which would bring him over Kenley from the north. Sure enough at 18.59 hours and airfield loomed up ahead and at once the raiders dropped their bombs and raked the buildings around the aerodrome with cannon and machine guns. But the airfield was Croydon—not Kenley.

Moments earlier John Thompson had scrambled with nine Hurricanes and just had time to go into line astern and turn about when the bombs came crashing down. The bombing was murderous and effective, for it was a characteristic of Erpr.Gr. 210's bombing accuracy that its loads invariably fell among buildings rather than merely cratering the grass surfaces. Several small aircraft factories (including Rollasons, which was engaged in repairing Hurricanes) were hit, as were the famous commercial airport terminal buildings, several hangars on the north of the airfield and the equipment stores of No. 1 (Canadian) Squadron. Some of the bombs were of the delayed action type and the detonation of these, added to the constant noise of exploding ammunition in the burning armouries, gave rise to considerable panic among the civilian population on the outskirts of the airfield. Of the 68 fatalities suffered, only six were servicemen on the airfield itself. 192 others were injured. It was more than quarter of an hour after the attack started that the air raid sirens were sounded. . .

As the black smoke boiled up over the stricken airfield, Thompson's pilots pinned the raiders into a "circle of death" while some Hurricanes of No. 32 Squadron (which had arrived from Biggin Hill) engaged the Bf 109s. As if on a radioed command from their leader, the Bf 110s suddenly broke into two or three groups, each making for cloud cover to the south. It was the Staff Flight which Thompson and three other pilots chose to pursue, and it was Rubensdörffer himself who fell to the Squadron Leader's guns[44]—his Messerschmitt cleaving the evening sky over Rotherfield in Sussex with a fearsome trail of fire. The end had come at last for the brilliant and supremely courageous Swiss-born pilot. His Staff Flight was almost entirely destroyed[45].

These evening raids were something of an anti-climax for the *Luftwaffe*, for while *Erprobungsgruppe 210* had struck Croydon (and in so doing had contravened Hitler's specific orders against raids on Greater London[46]) instead of Kenley, the Dornier *Gruppe* which had set out to raid Biggin Hill in fact bombed West Malling—a new airfield not yet fully integrated as an operational part of the air defences.

So ended Dowding's greatest test. The German air force had flown something over 2,000 sorties[47], and Fighter Command 974. Claims by the R.A.F. for enemy aircraft destroyed amounted to 182 but, as the following loss table indicates, this was a substantial exaggeration; as on almost all days on which the heaviest fighting took place, such over-estimates were understandable, for there was simply no time to eliminate the inevitable duplication of claims.

Two incontrovertible facts emerged from the battle of the 15th. The Germans had not detected any major weakness in Britain's air defences—least of all in the North—and Stumpff's Scandinavian-based *Luftflotte 5* was never again committed in any substantial force to the assault on Britain.

Less obvious to Göring than to Dowding was the extraordinary degree of wasted effort expended against relatively unimportant airfields. True, Croydon, Martlesham, Manston and Hawkinge *were* important fighter bases; but all the vital Sector Stations had escaped serious damage, while nearly fifty German aircraft had fallen in raids on airfields quite irrelevant to the defence.

---

[43] Sqn. Ldr. John Dewer, then aged 33, had graduated from Cranwell in 1927 with "exceptional" flying ratings. He had been a test pilot at Martlesham Heath between 1936 and 1938, and commanded No. 87 Squadron during the Battle of France, and on 31st May 1940 had been one of the first group of four officers to receive the D.S.O. and D.F.C. simultaneously (he had continued flying despite a broken shoulder). He was to be posted Missing on 12th September 1940, and his body was recovered from the sea to be buried at North Baddesley, Hampshire; his final victory score was eight enemy aircraft destroyed.

[44] The author recalls being fortunate to examine a number of surviving wartime cine-gun combat films while serving in Fighter Command in the 1950s; among these was Thompson's film of 15th August showing his attack on a Bf 110 in which the enemy aircraft's code letters (S9+AB) were clearly visible on the starboard side of the fuselage. Such clarity of film was extremely rare, and was made possible by the fact that the enemy aircraft was flying south, and the evening sun was fairly low in the west as Thompson carried out a rear quarter attack down to close range on the starboard side with the sun behind him.

[45] Several erroneous accounts have been written of this raid. It has been said that No. 66 Squadron was responsible for the destruction of *Erprobungsgruppe 210*'s Staff Flight; that Squadron was in fact at that moment engaged in a convoy patrol off the Norfolk coast more than one hundred miles away!

[46] Yet the posthumous award of the Knight's Cross to Walter Rubensdörffer was promulgated four days later on 19th August.

[47] The oft-quoted figure of 1,786 sorties refers only to those flown by *Kampfgeschwader, Jagdgeschwader* and *Zerstörergeschwader* of *Luftflotten 2* and *3*; it does not include the raids of *Lehrgeschwader 1* and *2*, nor those by *Luftflotte 5*.

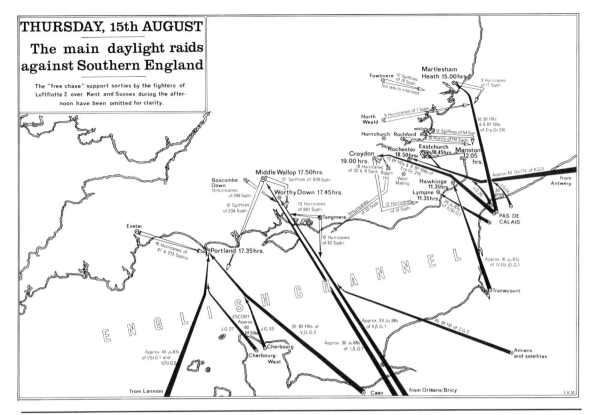

THURSDAY, 15th AUGUST
The main daylight raids against Southern England

The "free chase" support sorties by the fighters of Luftflotte 2 over Kent and Sussex during the afternoon have been omitted for clarity.

R.A.F. FIGHTER COMMAND LOSSES—THURSDAY 15th AUGUST 1940

No.	Sqn.		Description	Time	Pilot	Aircraft	Serial	Category
1.	1 Sqn., Northolt	C	Shot down south of Harwich; pilot baled out injured but picked up by trawler and landed at Harwich; admitted to hospital.	A14.30 hrs.	Flt. Lt. M.H. Brown	Hurricane	P3047	Cat. 3 Lost
2.	1 Sqn., Northolt	C	Shot down south of Harwich; pilot killed.	A14.30 hrs.	Plt. Off. D.O.M. Browne	Hurricane	P3043	Cat. 3 Lost
3.	1 Sqn., Northolt	C	Shot down south of Harwich; pilot killed.	A14.30 hrs.	Sgt. M.M. Shanahan	Hurricane	R4075	Cat. 3 Lost
4.	17 Sqn., Martlesham	C	Shot down and force landed near Felixstowe; pilot wounded in leg and face and admitted to Felixstowe hospital.	A15.00 hrs.	Flt. Lt. W.J. Harper	Hurricane	—	Cat. 3 Destroyed
5.	32 Sqn., Biggin Hill	C	Shot down in flames 15 miles east of Harwich and pilot baled out with burns to face and wrists; rescued by M.T.B.	A15.00 hrs.	Plt. Off. D.H. Grice	Hurricane	N2459	Cat. 3 Lost
6.	32 Sqn., Biggin Hill	C	Force landed in Essex; pilot unhurt.	A15.00 hrs.	Plt. Off. B. Wlasnowalski	Hurricane	—	Cat. 1 Damaged
7.	32 Sqn., Biggin Hill	C	Damaged in combat in the vicinity of Tangmere; required engine change; pilot unhurt.	18.45 hrs.	Sgt. B. Henson	Hurricane	—	Cat. 1 Damaged
8.	54 Sqn., Hornchurch	C	Shot down off Folkestone; pilot stayed with aircraft and picked up by naval vessel; admitted to hospital.	A11.30 hrs.	Sgt. N.A. Lawrence	Spitfire	—	Cat. 3 Lost
9.	54 Sqn., Hornchurch	C	Shot down near Ashford; pilot stayed with aircraft and admitted to Ashford hospital.	A11.45 hrs.	Sgt. W. Klosinski	Spitfire	—	Cat. 3 Destroyed
10.	54 Sqn., Hornchurch	C	Shot down near Deal; pilot baled out safely but sprained ankle.	A19.45 hrs.	Flt. Lt. A.C. Deere	Spitfire	—	Cat. 3 Destroyed
11.	54 Sqn., Hornchurch	C	Shot down and force landed at West Malling; pilot unhurt.	Not known.	Sgt. H.K.F. Matthews	Spitfire	N3097	Cat.3 Destroyed
12.	64 Sqn., Kenley	C	Shot down near Dungeness; pilot killed.	A15.00 hrs.	Plt. Off. C.J.D. Andreae	Spirfire	R6990	Cat. 3 Lost
13.	64 Sqn., Kenley	C	Shot down over Calais Marck and taken prisoner.	A15.15 hrs.	Plt. Off. R. Roberts	Spitfire	K9964	Cat. 3 Lost
14.	79 Sqn., Acklington	C	Damaged but landed safely at base; pilot unhurt.	A13.15 hrs.	Not known	Hurricane	—	Cat. 1 Damaged
15.	87 Sqn., Exeter	C	Shot down off Portland. Pilot killed; body recovered and buried at Warmwell.	A18.00 hrs.	Sqn. Ldr. T.G. Lovell-Gregg	Hurricane	P3215	Cat. 3 Lost
16.	87 Sqn., Exeter	C	Shot down off Portland. Pilot killed.	A18.00 hrs.	Plt. Off. P.W. Comeley	Hurricane	P3465	Cat. 3 Lost
17.	87 Sqn., Exeter	C	Shot down and force landed near Portland;	A18.00 hrs.	Sgt. J. Cowley	Hurricane	P2872	Cat. 2 Damaged
18.	87 Sqn., Exeter	C	Damaged in combat near Portland and force landed near Weymouth; pilot unhurt.	A18.00 hrs.	Plt. Off. D.T. Jay	Hurricane	P2687	Cat. 2 Damaged
19.	111 Sqn., Croydon	C	Shot down in flames over Selsey Bill; pilot did not bale out and was killed.	Afternoon	Plt. Off. B.M. Fisher	Hurricane	P3944	Cat. 3 Destroyed
20.	111 Sqn., Croydon	C	Damaged in combat but landed safely at Hawkinge; pilot unhurt.	A15.00 hrs.	Flt. Lt. H.M. Ferris	Hurricane	P3595	Cat. 1 Damaged
21.	111 Sqn., Croydon	NC	Pilot experienced control difficulties and abandoned the aircraft; unhurt.	Not known	Not known	Hurricane	R4193	Cat. 3 Destroyed
22.	151 Sqn., North Weald	C	Damaged in combat west of Dover but landed safely at Rochford; pilot unhurt.	A15.30 hrs.	Plt. Off. K.B.L. Debenham	Hurricane	P3273	Cat. 1 Damaged
23.	151 Sqn., North Weald	C	Shot down over sea west of Dover; pilot baled out but when picked up was found to be dead. Buried at Hawkinge.	A19.15 hrs.	Plt. Off. J.T. Johnston	Hurricane	P3941	Cat. 3 Lost
24.	151 Sqn., North Weald	C	Shot down west of Dover but pilot (attached to Sqn. from No. 56 Sqn) baled out safely.	A19.15 hrs.	Plt. Off. G. Radwanski	Hurricane	—	Cat. 3 Lost

R.A.F. Losses, 15th August 1940—*continued*

25.	151 Sqn., North Weald	C	Damaged over East Kent and force landed; pilot, slightly wounded, admitted to hospital.	A19.15 hrs.	Plt. Off. J.L.W. Ellacombe	Hurricane	*L1975*	Cat. 2 Damaged
26.	151 Sqn., North Weald	C	Shot down over West Kent; pilot wounded.	A19.15 hrs.	Sub-Lt. H.W. Beggs	Hurricane	*P3065*	Cat. 3 Destroyed
27.	151 Sqn., North Weald	C	Damaged in action over Kent; pilot landed at Rochford, wounded in back of head and in leg, and admitted to hospital.	A19.15 hrs.	Sqn. Ldr. J.A.G. Gordon	Hurricane	*P3940*	Cat. 1 Damaged.
28.	234 Sqn., Middle Wallop	C	Shot down into Channel south of Swanage; rescued by Germans and made P.O.W.	A17.30 hrs.	Plt. Off. V. Parker	Spitfire	*R6985*	Cat. 3 Lost
29.	234 Sqn., Middle Wallop	C	Damaged in combat south of Swanage and force landed near Cherbourg; pilot P.O.W.	A17.30 hrs.	Plt. Off. R. Hardy	Spitfire	*N3277*	Cat. 3 Lost
30.	234 Sqn., Middle Wallop	C	Shot down near Swanage; pilot killed.	A17.30 hrs.	Plt. Off. C.H. Hight	Spitfire	*R6988*	Cat. 3 Lost
31.	257 Sqn., Northolt	NC	Crashed in street near Harrow-on-the-Hill after engine fire; pilot baled out unhurt.	12.00 hrs.	Plt. Off. C.G. Frizell	Hurricane	*L1703*	Cat. 3 Destroyed
32.	266 Sqn. Hornchurch	C	Shot down by He 115 twelve miles east of Deal; pilot killed.	A16.30 hrs.	Sgt. F.B. Hawley	Spitfire	*N3189*	Cat. 3 Lost
33.	266 Sqn. Hornchurch	C	Shot down by Bf 109s at Teston, Kent; pilot's body recovered from R. Medway.	A19.00 hrs.	Plt. Off. F.W. Cale	Spitfire	*N3168*	Cat. 3 Destroyed
34.	303 Sqn., Northolt	NC	Damaged in ground accident; pilot unhurt.	Not known	Sgt. M. Wojciechowski	Hurricane	—	Cat. 1 Damaged
35.	303 Sqn., Northolt	NC	Damaged in ground accident; pilot unhurt.	Not known	Fg. Off. L. Paszkiewicz	Hurricane	—	Cat. 1 Damaged
36.	303 Sqn., Northolt	NC	Damaged in ground accident; pilot unhurt.	Not known	Plt. Off. W. Lokuciewski	Hurricane	—	Cat. 1 Damaged
37.	501 Sqn., Gravesend	C	Shot down south of Folkestone; pilot baled out and rescued unhurt.	A11.30 hrs.	Flt. Lt. A.R. Putt	Hurricane	*P3582*	Cat. 3 Lost
38.	501 Sqn., Gravesend	C	Shot down south of Folkestone but crashed on land; pilot unhurt.	A11.30 hrs.	Flt. Lt. J.A.A. Gibson	Hurricane	*P3040*	Cat. 3 Destroyed
39.	601 Sqn., Tangmere	C	Shot down and crashed at Selsey; pilot unhurt.	A17.40 hrs.	Plt. Off. J.K.U.B. McGrath	Hurricane	—	Cat. 3 Destroyed
40.	601 Sqn., Tangmere	C	Shot down over Winchester; pilot baled out with severe facial injuries.	A17.45 hrs.	Plt. Off. G.N.S. Cleaver	Hurricane	*P3232*	Cat. 3 Destroyed
41.	605 Sqn., Drem	C	Shot down and crashed at Hartley, near Newcastle; pilot wounded.	A12.45 hrs.	Plt. Off. K.S. Law	Hurricane	*P2717*	Cat. 3 Destroyed
42.	615 Sqn., Kenley	C	Shot down by Bf 109s near Folkestone; pilot killed.	Morning	Sgt. D.W. Halton	Hurricane	*P2581*	Cat. 3 Lost
43.	615 Sqn., Kenley	C	Damaged near Dungeness but returned safely to Kenley; pilot wounded.	Morning	Plt. Off. A.J.J. Truran	Hurricane	—	Cat. 2 Damaged

Other aircraft losses recorded:

Ten Whitley bombers destroyed on ground at Driffield
Two Spitfires destroyed on ground at Manston
One Battle bomber destroyed on ground at Martlesham
Three Blenheims destroyed on ground at Middle Wallop
One Blenheim fighter (Squadron unknown) shot down and force landed at Driffield

LUFTWAFFE LOSSES—THURSDAY 15th AUGUST 1940

1.	5.(F)/122	CM	Recce. target Rochester. Fate not known.	Junkers Ju 88A-1	100 %	Three crew members missing.
2.	3.(F)/31	CM	Shot down by 602 Sqn. Spitfires five miles south of Ventnor at A.07.40 hrs.	Dornier Do 17P	100 %	Ltn. Raasch, Oblt. Horn + one missing.
3.	I./KG 3	NCM	Landing accident at Wisand. Not combat.	Dornier Do 17Z-3	60 %	Oberstlt. Frhr. von Wechmar, *Gr. Kdr.,* and Oblt Kohnke injured.
4.	2./KG 3	CM	Damaged by British fighters near Dover.	Dornier Do 17Z-2	8 %	One crew member wounded.
5.	6./KG 3	CM	Shot down by R.A.F. fighters over Kent.	Dornier Do 17Z-2	100 %	Ltn. Walter + three missing.
6.	6./KG 3	CM	Shot down by R.A.F. fighters over Kent.	Dornier Do 17Z-2	100 %	Ltn. Kringler + two killed.
7.	6./KG 3	CM	Damaged by *flak* and R.A.F. fighters over Thames Estuary.	Dornier Do 17Z-2	8 %	One crew member wounded.
8.	6./KG 3	CM	Damaged by *flak* and R.A.F. fighters over Thames Estuary.	Dornier Do 17Z-2	8 %	Two crew members wounded.
9.	6./KG 3	CM	Damaged by fighters over Thames Estuary.	Dornier Do 17Z-2	8 %	One crew member wounded.
10.	6./KG 3	CM	Damaged by fighters over Thames Estuary.	Dornier Do 17Z-3	60 %	Crew unhurt.

Two eagles that failed to return from *Adlerangriff*. (*Left*) The wreckage of Leutnant Kringler's Dornier of 6./KG 3, shot down at Sevenoaks. (*Right*) The scattered debris of Leutnant Walter's aircraft of the same *Staffel*, at Paddock Wood; the bomb load exploded 90 minutes after the crash.

Luftwaffe Losses, 15th August 1940—*continued*

11.	I./KG 26	CM	Shot down by 79 Sqn. Hurricane of Millington near Middlesbrough at A.13.45 hrs.	Heinkel He 111H-4	100 %	Oblt. Koch + four missing.
12.	8./KG 26	CM	Believed shot down by *flak* near Dishforth.	Heinkel He 111H-4	100 %	Oblt. von Lübke + four missing.
13.	8./KG 26	CM	Shot down by 79 Sqn. Hurricane of Millington into sea off Middlesbrough at A.13.45 hrs.	Heinkel He 111H-4	100 %	Oblt. Riedel + four missing.
14.	8./KG 26	CM	Believed shot down by *flak* near Dishforth.	Heinkel He 111H-4	100 %	Oblt. von Besser + four missing.
15.	8./KG 26	CM	Shot down by fighters near Middlesbrough.	Heinkel He 111H-4	100 %	Ltn. Burk + four missing.
16.	8./KG 26	CM	Shot down by 79 Sqn. Hurricane of Millington in Middlesbrough area at A.13.45 hrs.	Heinkel He 111H-4	100 %	Ltn. Renner + four missing.
17.	9./KG 26	CM	Shot down by 235 Sqn. Blenheim of Jackson-Smith about 150 miles off East Coast at A.14.15 hrs.	Heinkel He 111H-4	100 %	Five missing; no names notified.
18.	9./KG 26	CM	Shot down by R.A.F. fighters and crashed in field near Bridlington at A.13.40 hrs.	Heinkel He 111H-4	100 %	Five missing; no names notified.
19.	I./KG 30	CM	Shot down by 73 Sqn. Hurricane of Griffiths near Flamborough Head at 13.15 hrs.	Junkers Ju 88C	100 %	Four crew members missing.
20.	I./KG 30	CM	Shot down by 73 Sqn. Hurricane of McNey near Flamborough Head at 13.15 hrs.	Junkers Ju 88C	100 %	Four crew members missing.
21.	3./KG 30	CM	Shot down by 73 Sqn. Hurricane of Carter near Flamborough at 13.20 hrs; crashed, Bridlington.	Junkers Ju 88A-5 (4D+KL)	100 %	Four crew members missing.
22.	4./KG 30	CM	Shot down by 616 Sqn. Spitfire and crashed near Hunmanby at 13.25 hrs.	Junkers Ju 88A-5 (4D+?M)	100 %	Four crew killed; one body recovered.
23.	II./KG 30	CM	Crashed at Oldenburg with combat damage.	Junkers Ju 88A-5	40 %	Crew unhurt.
24.	III./KG 30	CM	Shot down by 73 Sqn. Hurricane of Scott near Flamborough Head at 13.20 hrs.	Junkers Ju 88C	100 %	Oblt. Rachmann + three missing.
25.	III./KG 30	CM	Shot down by 73 Sqn. Hurricane of Lovett near Flamborough Head at 13.15 hrs.	Junkers Ju 88C	100 %	Ltn. Riede + three missing.
26.	III./KG 30	CM	Crashed on landing at Aalborg after combat.	Junkers Ju 88C	75 %	Crew unhurt.
27.	III./KG 30	CM	Crash landed in Holland as result of combat.	Junkers Ju 88C	less than 60 %	Crew unhurt.
28.	7./KG 30	CM	Shot down by fighters and crashed at Hornby.	Junkers Ju 88C(4D+DR)	100 %	Three crew members missing.
29.	II./KG 53	CM	Shot down by R.A.F. fighters over Channel.	Heinkel He 111H-2	100 %	Two crew killed; one rescued.
30.	9(Erg.)/KG 54	NCM	Landing accident at Fassberg airfield.	Junkers Ju 88A	80 %	Crew unhurt.
31.	I./KG 55	NCM	Landing accident at Granville airfield.	Heinkel He 111	70 %	Ltn. Göpel and crew unhurt.
32.	Stab./KG 76	NCM	Landing accident at Colonie airfield.	Dornier Do 17Z	30 %	Crew unhurt.
33.	Stab./KG 76	CM	Damaged by R.A.F. fighters over Redhill.	Dornier Do 17Z	5 %	Oblt. Lommatzich and crew unhurt.
34.	III./KG 77	NCM	Landing accident at Regensberg airfield.	Junkers Ju 88A	5 %	Crew unhurt.
35.	3./KGr. 100	CM	Crashed at St. Brieux; not result of combat.	Heinkel He 111H-3	100 %	Crew unhurt.
36.	3./KGr. 100	CM	Night landing accident at Bordeaux; not combat.	Heinkel He 111H-1	100 %	Crew unhurt.
37.	I./LG 1	CM	Shot down by R.A.F. fighters over Channel; crew rescued by *Seenotflugkommando*	Junkers Ju 88A-1	100 %	Four crew members rescued unhurt.
38.	II./LG 1	CM	Shot down by 266 Sqn. Spitfires of Armitage and Eade south-east of Dover at A.18.45 hrs.	Junkers Ju 88A	100 %	Fate of crew not known.
39.	II./LG 1	CM	Missing from sortie over Britain; fate not known.	Junkers Ju 88	100 %	Oblt. Müller and crew missing.
40.	II./LG 1	CM	Shot down by 601 Sqn. Hurricane of Davis north-west of Petersfield at A.17.45 hrs.	Junkers Ju 88A	100 %	Three crew members missing.
41.	II./LG 1	CM	Shot down by 601 Sqn. Hurricane of Pond off Isle of Wight at 17.45 hrs.	Junkers Ju 88A	100 %	Crew of three rescued by *Seenotflugkommando*.
42.	II./LG 1	CM	Shot down by 601 Sqn. Hurricanes of Clyde and Doulton south of Winchester at 17.45 hrs..	Junkers Ju 88A	100 %	Oblt. Suin de Boutemard + three crew members made P.O.W.s.
43.	II./LG 1	CM	Shot down by 601 Sqn. Hurricanes of Hope and Guy north-west of Petersfield at 17.45 hrs.	Junkers Ju 88A	100 %	Two crew members killed and and two made P.O.W.s.
44.	II./LG 1	CM	Missing from sortie over Britain; fate not known.	Junkers Ju 88A-1	100 %	Fate of crew not known.
45.	10./LG 1	CM	Aircraft hit ground near Folkestone; caught fire and burned out; both crew killed.	Junkers Ju 87B	100 %	Uffz. Hermann Weber and Uffz. Heinrich Kraus killed; both buried at Hawkinge.
46.	10./LG 1	CM	Shot down by 501 Sqn. Hurricane of Farnes near Folkestone at A.11.40 hrs.	Junkers Ju 87B	100 %	Hptm. Münchenhagen + one killed.
47.	V./LG 1	CM	Damaged in combat; force landed at Cherbourg.	Messerschmitt Bf 110C	60 %	Crew unhurt.
48.	I./St.G 1	CM	Shot down in Lympne/Hawkinge area.	Junkers Ju 87R	100 %	Two crew members missing.
49.	II./St.G 2	CM	Shot down by 54 Sqn. Spitfires over Hawkinge at A.11.45 hrs.	Junkers Ju 87R	100 %	Ltn. von Rosen + one missing.
50.	II./St.G 2	CM	Shot down by 54 Sqn. Spitfire of Lawrence into sea off Hawkinge at 11.45 hrs.	Junkers Ju 87R	100 %	One crew member rescued by Seenotflugkommando; one missing.
51.	II./St.G 2	CM	Shot down by 54 Sqn. Spitfire of Lawrence over Hawkinge at A. 11.45 hrs.	Junkers Ju 87R	100 %	Two crew members missing.
52.	II./St.G 2	CM	Shot down by fighters in Hawkinge area.	Junkers Ju 87R	100 %	Crew made P.O.W.s; one wounded.
53.	II./ZG 2	CM	Missing from sortie over Britain; fate unknown.	Messerschmitt Bf 110C	100 %	Both crew members missing.
54.	I./ZG 76	CM	Shot down by 72 Sqn. Spitfires off Durham coast; crashed into sea.	Messerschmitt Bf 110D	100 %	Hptm. Restmeyer, *Gr.Kdr.*, + one crew member killed.
55.	I./ZG 76	CM	Shot down by 72 Sqn. Spitfires over Durham coast; crashed on land.	Messerschmitt Bf 110D	100 %	Oblt. Loobes, *Gr.Adj.*, + one crew member killed.
56.	1./ZG 76	CM	Shot down by 41 Sqn. Spitfire of Bennions three miles east of Barnard Castle at 13.36 hrs.	Messerschmitt Bf 110D (3155 : M8+CH)	100 %	Oblt. Ketling + one crew member missing.
57.	2./ZG 76	CM	Shot down by fighters off the Durham coast and crashed into the sea.	Messerschmitt Bf 110D (M8+EK)	100 %	Both crw members killed.
58.	2./ZG 76	CM	Shot down by fighters and crashed on land; crew did not bale out.	Messerschmitt Bf 110D	100%	One crew member killed and one wounded.
59.	3./ZG 76	CM	Shot down by fighters over North-East England.	Messerschmitt Bf 110D	100 %	Ltn. Kohler + one killed.
60.	3./ZG 76	CM	Shot down by fighters over North-East England.	Messerschmitt Bf 110D	100 %	Two crew wounded, made P.O.W.
61.	II./ZG 76	CM	Shot down by fighters over South-East England.	Messerschmitt Bf 110C	100 %	Fate of crew not known.
62.	II./ZG 76	CM	Shot down by fighters over South-East England.	Messerschmitt Bf 110C	100 %	Fate of crew not known.
63.	II./ZG 76	CM	Shot down by 213 Sqn. Hurricane of Phillipart and crashed near Ashey Down, Isle of Wight.	Messerschmitt Bf 110C (M8+BP)	100 %	Both crew members killed.
64.	II./ZG 76	CM	Shot down by fighters over South-East England.	Messerschmitt Bf 110C	100 %	One killed and one missing.
65.	II./ZG 76	CM	Shot down by 213 Sqn. Hurricane of Phillipart and crashed in Weymouth Bay.	Messerschmitt Bf 110C (2N+BC)	100 %	Both crew members missing.
66.	II./ZG 76	CM	Shot down by 213 Sqn. Hurricane of Phillipart and crashed off Dorset coast.	Messerschmitt Bf 110 C-4	100 %	Oblt. Bremer + one missing.
67.	II./ZG 76	CM	Shot down by fighters off South Coast.	Messerschmitt Bf 110C	100 %	Oblt. Wien killed; one missing.
68.	II./ZG 76	CM	Damaged by fighters off South Coast.	Messerschmitt Bf 110C	80 %	Ltn. Hahn unhurt.
69.	III./ZG 76	CM	Shot down by fighters over South Coast.	Messerschmitt Bf 110C	100 %	Hptm. Dickore, *Gr.Kdr.* killed, and one missing.
70.	III./ZG 76	CM	Shot down by fighters over South Coast.	Messerschmitt Bf 110C	100 %	Two crew members missing.
71.	III./ZG 76	CM	Shot down by fighters over South Coast.	Messerschmitt Bf 110C	100 %	Ltn.Miakich killed; one missing.
72.	Stab/ZG 76	CM	Shot down by fighters over South-East England.	Messerschmitt Bf 110C	100 %	Oblt. Knop missing.

Two views of Croydon during the Battle of Britain. No amount of camouflage netting could disguise the famous airport terminal tower, and could not save the airfield from Rubensdörffer's chance raid on the evening of 15th August. The Blenheims are probably of No. 600 Squadron.

Luftwaffe Losses, 15th August 1940—*continued*

73.	Stab/Erpr. Gr. 210	CM	Shot down by 111 Sqn. Hurricane of Thompson after raid on Croydon and crashed at Mayfield.	Messerschmitt Bf 110D (S9+AB)	100 %	Hptm. Walter Rubensdörffer, *Gr. Kdr.*, and Fw. Richard Ehekercher killed.
74.	Stab/Erpr. Gr. 210	CM	Shot down by 111 Sqn. Hurricane of Craig after raid on Croydon and crashed at A.19.10 hrs on Redhill airfield.	Messerschmitt Bf 110D (S9+BB)	100 %	Oblt. Fiedeler, Gr.Adj., killed and one missing.
75.	Stab/Erpr. Gr. 210	CM	Shot down by 111 Sqn. Hurricanes of Connors and Wallace and crashed 6 miles NNW of Bexhill at 19.19 hrs.	Messerschmitt Bf 110D (S9+CB)	100 %	Ltn. Koch, Gr.TO., + one missing.
76.	1./Erpr.Gr. 210	CM	Shot down by 111 Sqn. Hurricane of Thompson and crashed at Broadbridge Farm, Horley, at A.19.05 hrs.	Messerschmitt Bf 110 C-6 (S9+TH)	100 %	Ltn. Beuel + one killed.
77.	2./Erpr.Gr. 210	CM	Shot down by 32 Sqn. Hurricane of Crossley and crashed at Ightham, near Sevenoaks, at A.19.10 hrs.	Messerschmitt Bf 110 C-6 (S9+BK)	100 %	Ltn. Ortner + one missing.
78.	2./Erpr.Gr. 210	CM	Shot down by 111 Sqn. Hurricane of Dymond and crashed at Hawkhurst at A.19.10 hrs.	Messerschmitt Bf 110 C-6 (S9+CK)	100 %	Oblt. Habisch + one missing.
79.	3./Erpr.Gr. 210	CM	Shot down by 32 Sqn. Hurricane of Barton at A.19.05 hrs. after raid on Croydon.	Messerschmitt Bf 109 E-4	100 %	Ltn. Marx missing.
80.	I./JG 3	CM	Damaged by R.A.F. fighters and force landed at Colombert.	Messerschmitt Bf 109 E-4	25 %	Pilot unhurt.
81.	I./JG 51	CM	Damaged by R.A.F. fighters and crashed at Pihen.	Messerschmitt Bf 109 E-4	100 %	Hptm. Brustellin, *Gr.Kdr.*, wounded.
82.	5./JG 51	CM	Believed shot down by 32 Sqn. Hurricane of Wlasnowalski south of Harwich at A.15.00 hrs.	Messerschmitt Bf 109 E-4	100 %	Pilot missing.
83.	7./JG 51	CM	Crashed at Wissant after combat with fighters.	Messerschmitt Bf 109 E-3	15 %	Pilot wounded.
84.	II./JG 53	NCM	Crashed at Binan; not the result of combat.	Messerschmitt Bf 109 E-1	60 %	Pilot unhurt.
85.	2./JG 54	CM	Shot down by 266 Sqn. Spitfire of Greenshields south-east of Dover at A.18.45 hrs.	Messerschmitt Bf 109 E-4	100 %	Pilot missing.
86.	2./JG 54	CM	Shot down by 615 Sqn. Hurricanes of Eyre and Lofts off Folkestone at A.11.00 hrs.	Messerschmitt Bf 109 E-4	100 %	Ltn. Gorlach missing.
87.	I./JG 77	CM	Missing from intercept sortie over Denmark; no details known.	Messerschmitt Bf 109 E-1	100 %	Oblt. Hauck missing.
88.	1./196	CM	German records state aircraft was shot down by R.A.F. fighters while on air/sea rescue sortie; no British claim traced.	Arado Ar 196	100 %	Ltn.z.S. Schlenker killed; Hptm. Wiegmink missing.
89.	*Seenotflug-kommando 4*	CM	Shot down by six Spitfires of 266 Sqn., 12 miles east of Deal at A.16.25 hrs.	Heinkel He 59	100 %	Ltn.z.S. Börner killed; one crew member wounded.
90.	1./506	CM	Struck ground on coast near Montrose (pilot possibly blinded by searchlights); aircraft disintegrated.	Heinkel He 115B-1	100 %	Ltn.z.S. Hans-Eberhardt Tonne, Ofw. Hoffert and Uffz. Schroers missing.

Friday 16th August

If the scale of battle losses inflicted on the *Luftwaffe* during "Black Thursday" had been considered critical by the three *Luftflotte* commanders, there was no sign to indicate to Fighter Command that they were crippling for—apart from an absence of attacks by *Luftflotte 5*—the raids in the South continued with unabated fury. It was in fact at this stage in the Battle that the scale and frequency of German assaults, including the increasing use of the nerve-racking Stuka, engendered a new grimness in the character of the British. Hitherto Fighter Command had gone about its business with

A Heinkel He 111 which crashed in the grounds of Aldro School, Eastbourne, on 16th August.

little more than a professional determination to defeat the *Luftwaffe*; one could not regard its determination as light-hearted (as has so often been suggested), but, except in isolated instances, the enemy had been fought off to some extent "at arm's length". The growing toll of enemy aircraft which fell over the English countryside, the increasing numbers of German airmen baling out amongst a population keyed up to meet an imminent invasion, the disruption of long-established civil amenities by enemy raids—all these pressures upon the English now quite suddenly gave birth to a startling and perhaps frightening atmosphere of hatred for the German people as a whole. A wave of total loathing blinded the population to the difference between natural patriotism on the part of the German airmen, and the extremes of Nazi ideology; to a people suffering under constant air raids and expecting invasion in the near future, such a distinction was academic indeed. Henceforward there would be growing evidence of this murderous attitude—a dangerous growth, concealed and controlled as far as possible by the authorities, who correctly considered that to indulge this mood would be to condone the abandonment of "accepted codes of warfare". Mercifully the Government reacted swiftly and harshly to the few incidents of "lynch law" which did occur; it was recognised that weakness in this field would invite immediate and unrestricted terror assaults on the civilian population. Such conduct was not contemplated by the German leaders until the launching of *Seelöwe*.

The *Luftwaffe* delayed sending raids against England on the 16th until early morning mists had cleared the Channel

Karl Borris, in August 1940 a Leutnant with the Staff Flight of II/JG 26 <*Schlageter*>, and the type of steady professional pilot who formed the backbone of the *Luftwaffe*'s *Jagdverband*. For the last two years of the War he commanded I./JG 26. (Photo: Heinz Nowarra)

coasts, and took this opportunity to replenish some of its units which had suffered heavy casualties on the previous day. Fighter Command spent much of the morning maintaining light patrols over the South Coast and moving squadrons forward to their advanced airfields.

At about 10.45 hours three small raids were reported by CH radar to be approaching Kent from the south and east. Park, presumably suspecting that these were feints, reacted by sending only small forces to intercept, while advancing his fighter state on the ground. Unfortunately, of the 30-odd fighters vectored to meet the raiders, only two Sections made contact, and they failed to score. The enemy formations split off the North Foreland and two *Staffeln* of KG 2's Dorniers penetrated the coast to attack the airfield at West Malling; after the previous day's raid on this partly-completed aerodrome, repair teams were still in the process of clearing rubble and filling bomb craters when the new raid swept in from the north-east. More than 80 high-explosive and fragmentation bombs fell, destroying a Lysander and ensuring that the airfield would remain out of action for a further four days[48].

As these raids withdrew shortly after 11.15 hours, the Sector Controllers ordered their patrols back to base to refuel. Half an hour later reports of large enemy raids started coming in all round the South and South-East coasts. By 12.15 hours these were identified as three groups totalling more than 300 aircraft; a total of 86 fighters were climbing hard to meet the threat.

The first raid to be encountered was flown by 24 Dornier Do 17s of II./KG 2, apparently making for the fighter airfield at Hornchurch, and was intercepted by nine Spitfires of No. 54 Squadron as it flew up the Thames Estuary at 12.25 hours. The main raid was prevented from reaching its target and the Spitfires engaged the escort all the way back to the French coast, Colin Gray claiming two Bf 109s destroyed; one of these crashed on the airfield at St. Inglevert.

A more serious threat was posed by the 150 enemy aircraft which crossed the Kent coast near Dover and fanned out in several formations to the north and north-west. Park ordered 30 Spitfires of Nos. 64, 65 and 266 Squadrons and 21 Hurricanes of Nos. 32 and 111 Squadrons against this raid. The two Hurricane formations went into action with furious head-on attacks over the coast and succeeded in breaking up several groups of Dorniers before their escort could intervene. It was in this initial attack that Flt. Lt. Henry Ferris met his death when his Hurricane collided head-on with a Dornier of 3./KG 2, the two aircraft falling in flames at Marden.

Bombing by the Dorniers was scattered, several aircraft managing to penetrate undetected to the large airfield at Harwell in Berkshire, while others found and bombed the Royal Aircraft Establishment at Farnborough. Casualties were suffered at Wimbledon and at Esher in Surrey where bombs fell on the railway station and among shops. Light attacks were carried out on Gravesend and the dock area at Tilbury. A total of 66 civilian casualties was suffered, of whom fifteen were killed.

---

[48] West Malling was not yet a regular fighter station. Lysander army co-operation aircraft based on the airfield were at this time engaged on an *ad hoc* basis to "spot" and report large fields in the South-East on which enemy troop transport aircraft might land. Instructions were issued for such fields to be obstructed by the erection of numerous concrete posts.

No. 266 Squadron's Spitfires were flown into battle led by Sqn. Ldr. Rodney Wilkinson, and managed to surprise a *Staffel* of II./JG 26's Messerschmitt Bf 109s near Deal. At first the British pilots gained the upper hand, but when nine more Bf 109s joined in the tables were turned. One of the German pilots, Leutnant Karl Borris, recorded in his diary:

> **16th August.** Air battle between seven Spitfires and five aircraft of our Staff Flight. I was flying at about 21,000 feet behind our *Staffelführer* and Eckhardt Roch, Leibing and März. Seven Spitfires suddenly attacked us, diving from high on the left forward quarter. . .and we break up. Over the Channel I spot a Spitfire on the tail of a Bf 109; the 109 reacted with a quick half loop and roll out (*Abschwung*). . .it was Waldi März. I don't think my warning call reached him as the radio was damaged; März landed with twenty bullet holes and an overheating engine. I saw one (Spitfire) shot down by Eckhardt Roch, but our Section Leader, Hauptmann Ebbighausen, did not return[50].

---

[50] *Author's translation.* Priller, in his *Die Luftschlacht um England*, states that Ebbighausen had scored seven victories at the time of his death in this combat. Another Spitfire was shot down by Feldwebel Wilhelm Philipp of II./JG 26 who, retaining his N.C.O. rank, ultimately destroyed no less than 81 Allied aircraft and was awarded the Knight's Cross. Leutnant Roch was to be killed in action on 3rd September 1940.

Tangmere airfield, devastated by Stukas on 16th August, blazes fiercely; every one of the hangars was hit and badly damaged; parked aircraft included 600 Squadron's Blenheims.

No. 266 Squadron was overwhelmed in this combat. Sqn. Ldr. Wilkinson was shot down in flames at Eastry, near Deal; Plt. Off. Nigel Bowen's body was found at Adisham, near Canterbury; Flt. Lt. Sydney Bazley baled out of his blazing aircraft nearby and was rushed to hospital with severe burns, and Plt. Off. John Soden force landed with leg wounds. Sub-Lt. Henry Greenshields did not return and is thought to have been shot down by Leutnant Gerhard Müller-Dühe of III./JG 26 over the Channel.

The third of the noontide raids crossed the Channel further west and consisted of more than one hundred aircraft—Junkers Ju 87s of *Stukageschwader 2*, and Messerschmitt Bf 109s of *Jagdgeschwader 2*. Following behind were twelve Junkers Ju 88s of KG 54 and some Bf 110s of III./ZG 76.

As much of Park's strength was being deployed to meet the raids in the South-East, eight squadrons were scrambled from Tangmere and airfields to the west to meet the attack. At exactly 13.00 hours the German raid reached the Nab at the

Two photos of the Fighter Interception Unit's first Beaufighter, *R2055*, taken at Tangmere, probably a day or two before 16th August when it was slightly damaged in the German dive bombing attack. Note the aircraft's black and white undersurfaces, and that only the nose cannon are fitted. (Photos: R.A.F. Museum)

eastern end of the Isle of Wight, whereupon, as signal flares fell from the leading aircraft, the formation split into four—the largest, consisting of the Ju 87s, making straight for Tangmere. Most of the airfield's fighters had been scrambled but were unable to approach the enemy before the dive-bombers cascaded out of the sun to carry out a textbook assault. As the Hurricanes of No. 1, 43 and 601 Squadrons waded into the Stukas, No. 602 Squadron's Spitfires went headlong for the escort, which they successfully warded off.

As massive fires broke out all over the aerodrome, and more and more bombs thundered down, a damaged Hurricane appeared over the boundary fence, its pilot obviously having difficulty in picking a landing path between the bomb craters. Miraculously it rolled to a stop without turning over, but at once became the target of several strafing attacks. Before the pilot could leave his cockpit the aircraft had become an inferno, and it was only by extraordinary feats of gallantry that ground crewmen were able to extricate the terribly burned man; he was rushed to hospital but succumbed to his wounds the following day. So died Pilot Officer William Mead Lindsley Fiske—the first American volunteer pilot to lose his life defending Britain[51].

Although the Hurricanes had dealt faithfully with the dive bombers (destroying seven and damaging three) the raid on Tangmere had been highly successful, every one of the hangars being hit, together with the station workshops, stores, water plant, sick quarters, Officers' Mess and transport section. Every one of the Fighter Interception Unit's aircraft (including the R.A.F. first Beaufighter night fighter) was destroyed or damaged; seven Hurricanes and several Spitfires, which were undergoing maintenance or repair, were initially classified as damaged, but later written off as irreparable. Fourteen servicemen and six civilians were killed and 41 severely injured.

Elsewhere five Ju 87s again went for the Ventnor CH radar and their 22 bombs further damaged the station, with the result that it again went off the air, this time for seven days. The gap in the radar screen was filled by setting up a mobile installation at nearby Bembridge, but the performance of this was initially so inferior that its picture only confused the defences, a situation that was alleviated after painstaking calibration. The Spitfires of No. 152 Squadron interrupted

this raid but were forestalled by escorting Bf 109s.

Another section of the German raid attacked the naval station at Lee-on-Solent and, although it was intercepted by Hurricanes of No. 213 Squadron which had flown at top speed from Exeter, the bombing and strafing destroyed half a dozen naval aircraft as well as three hangars.

The last of the four formations—composed of twelve Ju 88s and eighteen Bf 110s—carried out a sharp raid on another naval airfield, at Gosport, causing some damage and killing six servicemen. Against this threat Brand sent Spitfires of No. 234 Squadron, but these failed to make contact; it was three Hurricane pilots of No. 249 Squadron who, on patrol over the eastern outskirts of Southampton, sighted the raiders.

No. 249 Squadron which, only two days previously had moved to the main battle area from the north, had been brought to Readiness at Boscombe Down at mid-day and scrambled soon afterwards to patrol between Poole and Southampton. Catching sight of the raid developing over Gosport, the pilots of Red Section (Flt. Lt. James Nicolson leading Sqn. Ldr. Eric King—supernumerary on the Squadron—and Plt. Off. Martyn King) were detached to attack the

Flt. Lt. James Nicolson, Fighter Command's first and only recipient of the Victoria Cross who, on 16th August, remained at the controls of his blazing Hurricane to continue his attack on an enemy aircraft; he then baled out, only to be fired on by L.D.V. and Army riflemen. He was to be awarded a D.F.C. in 1944 but was killed while flying in a Liberator bomber in the Far East on 2nd May 1945.

---

[51] "Billy" Fiske, aged 29 at the time of his death, came of a wealthy banking family. Ten years earlier he had driven a Stutz in the Le Mans 24-hour motor race, and in 1932 captained the victorious American Olympic bobsleigh team on the Cresta Run. In 1941 a memorial plaque, with the words *An American citizen who died that England might live*, was unveiled in St. Paul's Cathedral.

Bf 110s. As the Section was about to open fire, it was suddenly bounced from above and astern by a *Staffel* of Bf 109s which hit all three Hurricanes. Sqn. Ldr. King, least badly hit, broke off his attack and dived away, bringing his aircraft back to Boscombe Down. Plt. Off. King abandoned his flaming aircraft and took to his parachute. Nicolson, his aircraft on fire, continued his diving attack on the Bf 110s, before being forced to bale out with severe wounds and burns to face and hands, descending not a quarter mile from Plt. Off. King.

There followed one of those tragic events so often sparked by the high emotions of battle. Seeing two parachutes falling together (at a time when enemy aircraft were known to be in the area), an officer of a Royal Artillery detachment ordered his men to take up positions and open fire with their rifles at the two airmen—ostensibly under the impression that they were enemy parachutists. Some Local Defence Volunteers joined in the fusillade. Whether King himself was hit is not known, but some of his parachute shrouds parted, the canopy collapsed and the young pilot plunged to his death. Nicolson, in great pain from his burns, landed alive—albeit further wounded by shotgun pellets. Only when the mistake was discovered was the pilot rushed to the Royal Southampton Hospital and later made a full recovery, to receive Fighter Command's first and only Victoria Cross[52].

In the late afternoon Kesselring and Sperrle launched three more raids in conjunction with a number of free chases over Kent which were intended to tie down the No. 11 Group squadrons. One of the latter (by eight Bf 109s), after feinting in the mouth of the Thames and avoiding combat, suddenly swung south over the North Foreland and swept over Manston, raking airfield buildings and parked aircraft with machine gun fire; they destroyed a Spitfire and a Blenheim.

As a raid by Heinkel He 111s of KG 27, escorted by Bf 110s, crossed the Sussex coast near Brighton shortly after 17.00 hours and was intercepted by Hurricanes of Nos. 1 and 615 Squadrons and Spitfires of No. 64, another raid was turning south from the Thames Estuary and making for Biggin Hill. Grice had been watching its approach and had ordered his own squadrons into the air in good time, so that the Ju 88s were intercepted and turned away by the Hurricanes of Nos. 32, 56 and 501 Squadrons and Spitfires of No. 610 Squadron.

Perhaps one of the most audacious raids of the day was a remarkable set-piece attack by two Junkers Ju 88s (whose unit is not known) which penetrated in broad daylight as far as Brize Norton in Oxfordshire. This attack has sometimes been ascribed to a lucky chance, yet German briefing material indicates that it was a carefully premeditated raid, whose

Stukageschwader 2 **paid a heavy price for its attack on Tangmere on 16th August. The aircraft is T6+HL, a 3 Staffel machine which crash-landed near Selsey. The Stuka crewman fell from his aircraft during the raid—without a parachute; the distortion of his body tells its own grim story.**

flight plan was designed to overfly areas previous covered by fighters which would probably be back on the ground refuelling. The two German bombers appeared in the circuit at Brize Norton during the evening with their wheels down as if to land—their pilots hoping that in the haze they would be mistaken for Blenheims. As they reached the airfield perimeter the pilots raised the wheels and made straight for the large hangars on which they dropped thirty-two bombs, including two of 250 kilos. As one of the hangars was hit, fuelled-up aircraft inside blew up, destroying 46 aircraft and damaging seven others. The majority of the aircraft were trainers belonging to No. 2 Service Flying Training School, but eleven Hurricanes of the resident Maintenance Unit were also damaged in another hangar. One of the 250-kilo bombs, dropped from very low level, skidded off the hard-standing and finished up within yards of the ammunition store. . .but failed to explode. The raiders escaped unscathed.

The pattern of the day's raids had remained much the same as that of the previous day, with the greatest efforts made by the *Luftwaffe* directly against the R.A.F. Again, much of this effort had been wasted against airfields (such as Brize Norton, Gosport, Lee, Farnborough and West Malling) which were not vital to the defence system, in further demonstration of German Intelligence weakness.

---

[52] The unhappy circumstances surrounding this episode were of course concealed from the public during the War. The author is grateful to Mr. N.C. Parker, who has undertaken research into the history of No. 249 Squadron, for having disclosed a quantity of documentary material (among it depositions from some of those personally involved) which partly confounds the officially perpetuated version—issued to support the award citation. It is likely that the award for valour (London Gazette, 15th November 1940) was endorsed by H.R.H. The Duke of Kent who paid a visit to No. 249 Squadron shortly afterwards. Nicolson rose to the rank of Wing Commander and commanded No. 27 Squadron with Mosquitos in Burma during 1944 (D.F.C., 11th August 1944). On 2nd May 1945 he was accompanying the crew of a Liberator as an observer on a bombing raid when the aircraft crashed at sea following an engine fire, and he was not among the survivors.

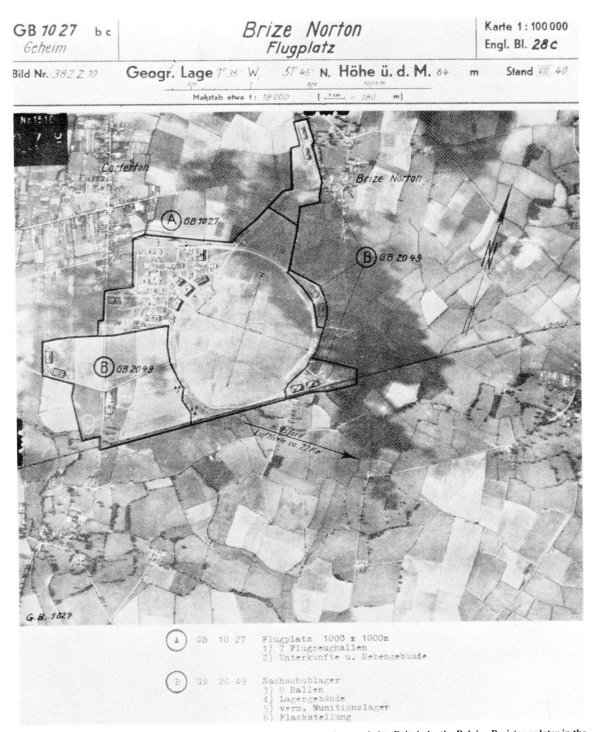

GB 10 27   b c
Geheim

Brize Norton
Flugplatz

Karte 1 : 100 000
Engl. Bl. **28 c**

Bild Nr. *382 Z 10*   **Geogr. Lage** *1° 35'* W, *51° 45'* **N, Höhe ü. d. M.** *84* m   Stand *VIII. 40*

Maßstab etwa 1 : *18 000*   [*1 cm* = *180* m]

One of a set of aircrew briefing documents stolen from the Germans and smuggled to Britain by the Belgian Resistance later in the War. This aerial photograph, dated August 1940, is fairly conclusive evidence of the planning that went into the small, set-piece raid on Brize Norton on 16th August. The numbered annotations are: "A. Airfield, 1000 X 1000 metres. (1) Seven aircraft hangars. (2) Shelters and associated buildings. B. Camp. (3) Eight hangars. (4) Camp buildings. (5) Ammunition storage. (6) Anti-aircraft position." It is worth recording that, after the War, Brize Norton became a massive United States Air Force Base, and on return to the R.A.F. formed an important Transport Command facility. (Photo: Author's Collection)

R.A.F. FIGHTER COMMAND LOSSES—FRIDAY 16th AUGUST 1940

1.	1 Sqn., Northolt	C	Hit by Portsmouth A.A. guns; pilot baled out over Thorney Island, wounded.	A13.05 hrs.	Plt. Off. J.F.D. Elkington	Hurricane	P3173 Cat. 3 Destroyed
2.	1 Sqn., Northolt	C	Damaged in combat with He 111 over West Sussex; pilot returned unhurt.	17.08 hrs.	Sqn. Ldr. D.A. Pemberton	Hurricane	P2571 Cat. 1 Damaged
3.	1 Sqn., Northolt	C	Damaged by He 111s over West Sussex; pilot force landed on Hog's Back, unhurt.	17.11 hrs.	Fg. Off. P.V. Boot	Hurricane	P3653 Cat. 2 Damaged
4.	19 Sqn., Coltishall	C	Damaged in combat east of Harwich; pilot unhurt.	A17.50 hrs.	Sgt. H.A.C. Roden	Spitfire	— Cat. 1 Damaged

R.A.F. Losses, 16th August 1940—*continued*

5.	43 Sqn., Tangmere	C	Glycol leak from battle damage near Tangmere; pilot baled out but broke thigh.	13.05 hrs.	Sgt. J.L. Crisp	Hurricane	*L1736*	Cat. 3 Lost
6.	43 Sqn., Tangmere	C	Crash landed ar Parkhurst, I.o.W., after combat near Tangmere; pilot slightly wounded.	13.15 hrs.	Plt. Off. C.A. Woods-Scawen	Hurricane	*N2521*	Cat. 3 Destroyed
7.	56 Sqn., Rochford	C	Shot down in flames over Manston; pilot baled out slightly wounded	A13.15 hrs.	Plt. Off. L.W. Graham	Hurricane	*P3547*	Cat. 3 Destroyed
8.	56 Sqn., Rochford	C	Damaged by Bf 109s off Eastchurch; burnt after force landing at Rochford; pilot unhurt.	A17.25 hrs.	F/Sgt. F.W. Higginson	Hurricane	*P3043*	Cat. 3 Destroyed
9.	64 Sqn., Kenley	C	Force landed at Hawkinge after combat with Bf 109s over South Coast; pilot wounded.	12.45 hrs.	Sgt. J. Mann	Spitfire	*L1038*	Cat. 2 Damaged
10.	64 Sqn., Kenley	C	Shot down by He 111; pilot baled out unhurt.	17.25 hrs.	Sqn. Ldr. A.R.D. MacDonnell	Spitfire	*P9554*	Cat. 3 Lost
11.	64 Sqn., Kenley	C	Hit by A.A. gunfire (Dover?); pilot unhurt.	A17.30 hrs.	Plt. Off. P.J. Simpson	Spitfire	*L1068*	Cat. 2 Damaged
12.	65 Sqn., Manston	C	Missing after combat near Manston; pilot assumed killed.	Afternoon	Plt. Off. L.L. Pyman	Spitfire	*K9915*	Cat. 3 Missing
13.	111 Sqn., Hawkinge	C	Head-on collision with Do 17 over Marden; pilot killed.	12.18 hrs.	Flt. Lt. H.M. Ferris	Hurricane	—	Cat. 3 Destroyed
14.	111 Sqn., Hawkinge	C	Shot down in flames by Bf 109 near Dungeness; pilot baled out with burns.	12.22 hrs.	Sgt. R. Carnall	Hurricane	—	Cat. 3 Lost
15.	213 Sqn., Exeter	C	Shot down over Portland; pilot killed.	A13.10 hrs.	Fg. Off. J.E.P. Laricheliere	Hurricane	—	Cat. 3 Missing
16.	234 Sqn., Middle Wallop	C	Shot down near Southampton by Bf 109s; pilot baled out unhurt at Gosport.	A17.30 hrs.	Plt. Off. K.S. Dewhurst	Spitfire	*R6967*	Cat. 3 Lost
17.	234 Sqn., Middle Wallop	C	Shot down off Isle of Wight by Bf 109s; pilot baled out and picked up by launch unhurt.	A17.30 hrs.	Fg. Off. F.H.P. Connor	Spitfire	*X4016*	Cat. 3 Lost
18.	249 Sqn., Boscombe Down	C	Shot down by Bf 109 over Southampton; pilot baled out burned and wounded.	A12.45 hrs.	Flt. Lt. J.B. Nicolson	Hurricane	*P3576*	Cat. 3 Destroyed
19.	249 Sqn., Boscombe Down	C	Shot down by Bf 109 over Southampton; pilot baled out but fired on from the ground; parachute collapsed and pilot killed.	A.12.45 hrs.	Plt. Off. M.A. King	Hurricane	*P3616*	Cat. 3 Destroyed
20.	266 Sqn., Hornchurch	C	Shot down near Deal; pilot found dead at Eastry; died from wounds.	A12.45 hrs.	Sqn. Ldr. R.L. Wilkinson	Spitfire	*R6768*	Cat. 3 Destroyed
21.	266 Sqn., Hornchurch	C	Shot down near Deal; pilot killed.	A12.45 hrs.	Sub-Lt. H. la Fore Greenshields	Spitfire	*N3240*	Cat. 3 Missing
22.	266 Sqn., Hornchurch	C	Shot down at Adisham, Kent; pilot killed.	A12.45 hrs.	Plt. Off. N.G. Bowen	Spitfire	*N3095*	Cat. 3 Destroyed
23.	266 Sqn., Hornchurch	C	Shot down near Canterbury; pilot baled out with burns.	A12.45 hrs.	Flt. Lt. S.H. Bazley	Spitfire	*P9312*	Cat. 3 Destroyed
24.	266 Sqn., Hornchurch	C	Shot down and force landed at Faversham; pilot wounded in the leg.	A12.45 hrs.	Plt. Off. J.F. Soden	Spitfire	*K9864*	Cat. 2 Damaged
25.	600 Sqn., Manston	—	Destroyed in raid on Manston; no casualties.	17.45 hrs.	Nil	Blenheim	—	Cat. 3 Burnt
26.	600 Sqn., Manston	—	Damaged in raid on Manston; no casualties.	17.45 hrs.	Nil	Blenheim	—	Cat. 1 Damaged
27.	600 Sqn., Manston	—	Damaged in raid on Manston; no casualties.	17.45 hrs.	Nil	Blenheim	—	Cat. 1 Damaged
28.	601 Sqn., Tangmere	C	Landed damaged at Tangmere; pilot rescued but died the next day from burns suffered.	A13.05 hrs.	Plt. Off. W.M.L. Fiske	Hurricane	*P3358*	Cat. 3 Burnt
29.	602 Sqn., Tangmere	—	Destroyed in raid on Tangmere; no casualties.	13.01 hrs.	Nil	Spitfire	—	Cat. 3 Destroyed
30.	602 Sqn., Tangmere	—	Damaged in raid on Tangmere; no casualties.	13.01 hrs.	Nil	Spitfire	—	Cat. 1 Damaged
31.	610 Sqn., Hawkinge	C	Shot down by Bf 109s near Dungeness; pilot killed.	16.54 hrs.	Flt. Lt. W.H.C. Warner	Spitfire	*R6802*	Cat. 3 Missing
32.	F.I.U., Tangmere	—	Destroyed in raid on Tangmere; no casualties.	13.01 hrs.	Nil	Blenheim	—	Cat. 3 Destroyed
33.	F.I.U., Tangmere	—	Destroyed in raid on Tangmere; no casualties.	13.01 hrs.	Nil	Blenheim	—	Cat. 3 Destroyed
34.	F.I.U., Tangmere	—	Destroyed in raid on Tangmere; no casualties.	13.01 hrs.	Nil	Blemheim	—	Cat. 3 Destroyed
35.	F.I.U., Tangmere	—	Destroyed in raid on Tangmere; no casualties.	13.01 hrs.	Nil	Blenheim	—	Cat. 3 Destroyed
36.	F.I.U., Tangmere	—	Destroyed in raid on Tangmere; no casualties.	13.01 hrs.	Nil	Blenheim	—	Cat. 3 Destroyed
37.	F.I.U., Tangmere	—	Damaged in raid on Tangmere; no casualties.	13.01 hrs.	Nil	Blenheim	—	Cat. 2 Damages
38.	F.I.U., Tangmere	—	Damaged in raid on Tangmere; no casualties.	13.01 hrs.	Nil	Blenheim	—	Cat. 1 Damaged
39.	F.I.U., Tangmere	—	Damaged in raid on Tangmere; no casualties.	13.01 hrs.	Nil	Beaufighter	*R2055*	Cat. 1 Damaged.
40.	Manston	—	Destroyed in raid on Manston; no casualties.	17.45 hrs.	Nil	Spitfire	—	Cat. 3 Burnt

LUFTWAFFE LOSSES—FRIDAY 16th AUGUST 1940

1.	2.(F)/122	CM	Force landed at Lille following combat.	Junkers Ju 88A-1	70 %	Two crew members wounded.
2.	3./KGr. 126	CM	Shot down by *flak* in Humber Estuary.	Heinkel He 111H-4	100 %	Oblt. Volkmann + two killed; two missing.
3.	3./KG 2	CM	Shot down by 111 Sqn. Hurricane of Thompson between Tonbridge and Ashford at 12.22 hrs.	Dornier Do 17Z	100 %	Ltn. Möllenbock + one killed; two missing.
4.	3./KG 2	CM	Collided with Hurricane flown by Ferris of 111 Sqn., near Marden at 12.18 hrs.	Dornier Do 17Z-3	100 %	One killed; Oblt. Brandenburg + two missing.
5.	3./KG 2	CM	Shot down by 111 Sqn. Hurricane of Craig near Tonbridge at 12.24 hrs.	Dornier Do 17Z-3	100 %	Crew made P.O.W.; two wounded.
6.	I./KG 27	CM	Shot down by 615 Sqn. Hurricane of Young ten miles south-east of Bognor Regis at 17.20 hrs.	Heinkel He 111P	100 %	All crew members (one wounded) rescued by *Seenotflugkdo.*
7.	II./KG 27	CM	Shot down by 615 Sqn. Hurricane of Lofts near Stayning, Shoreham, at 17.35 hrs.	Heinkel He 111P	100 %	Four crew members missing.
8.	II./KG 51	CM	Force landed at Orly with mechanical failure.	Junkers Ju 88A-1	30 %	Crew unhurt.
9.	III./KG 51	CM	Landing accident at Etampes; not combat.	Junkers Ju 88A-1	25 %	Crew unhurt.
10.	II./KG 55	CM	Shot down by 1 Sqn. Hurricane of Pemberton over Sussex at A.17.30 hrs.	Heinkel He 111P	100 %	Two killed, one wounded; Oblt. Weiland + one missing.
11.	II./KG 55	CM	Shot down by 602 Sqn. Spitfire flown by Boyd at 17.28 hrs.	Heinkel He 111P	100 %	Hptm. Sabler + four killed.

Stukageschwader 2 paid a heavy price for its attack on Tangmere on 16th August. The aircraft is T6+HL, a 3 Staffel machine which crash-landed near Selsey. The Stuka crewman fell from his aircraft during the raid—without a parachute; the distortion of his body tells its own grim story.

Luftwaffe Losses, 16th August 1940—*continued*

12.	II./KG 55	CM	Damaged by 615 Sqn. Hurricane of McClintock off Bognor Regis at 17.33 hrs.	Heinkel He 111P	15 %	Crew safe.
13.	III./KG 55	CM	Shot down by 64 Sqn. Spitfires of MacDonnell and Simpson, and 1 Sqn. Hurricane of Goodman over Sussex coast at 17.30 hrs.	Heinkel He 111P	100 %	Two killed; Ltn. Theobald + two missing.
14.	III./KG 55	CM	Damaged by 64 Sqn. Spitfire of MacDonnell over Sussex coast at 17.40 hrs.	Heinkel He 111P	80 %	Crew unhurt.
15.	III./KG 55	CM	Damaged by 64 Sqn. Spitfires of Laing and Jones at A.17.30 hrs.; crashed on landing.	Heinkel He 111P	100 %	Three crew members wounded.
16.	II./KG 77	NCM	Crashed in Starnbergersee; cause not known.	Junkers Ju 88	100 %	Three crew members killed
17.	7./KG 76	CM	Shot down by Hurricanes of 501 Sqn. at A.17.15 hrs.	Dornier Do 17Z-2	100 %	Two killed; two missing.
18.	III./LG 1	CM	Crashed at Châteaudun following engine failure.	Junkers Ju 88A-1	80 %	Fate of crew not known.
19.	4./ZG 2	CM	Shot down by 1 Sqn. Hurricane of Matthews and crashed at Aldro School, Eastbourne 17.30 hrs.	Messerschmitt Bf 110C	100 %	Oblt. Ernst Hollekamp and Fw. Schurk killed.
20.	II./ZG 2	CM	Shot down by 32 Sqn. Hurricane of Brothers at 17.25 hrs.	Messerschmitt Bf 110D	100 %	Maj. Karl, Gr.Kdr., + one killed.
21.	2./ZG 26	CM	Shot down by 19 Sqn. Spitfire of Unwin off Harwich at 18.10 hrs.	Messerschmitt Bf 110C	100 %	One killed and one missing.
22.	Stab/ZG 26	CM	Damaged by 19 Sqn. Spitfire of Unwin off Harwich at A.18.15 hrs.	Messerschmitt Bf 110 C-2	80 %	Crew unhurt.
23.	II./ZG 76	CM	Shot down by 19 Sqn. Spitfire of Potter off Harwich at A. 18.10 hrs.	Messerschmitt Bf 110C	100 %	Ltn. Lemmer killed; one missing.
24.	III./ZG 76	CM	Shot down by 602 Sqn. Spitfires over the Isle of Wight at 16.45 hrs.	Messerschmitt Bf 110C	100 %	Oblt. Schlaffer, *St.Kap.*, + one missing.
25.	III./ZG 76	CM	Shot down by 602 Sqn. Spitfires and crashed at Lee Farm, near Clapham, near Worthing at 16.45 hrs.	Messerschmitt Bf 110C (2N+AP)	100 %	Ltn. Marchfelder + one missing.
26.	III./ZG 76	CM	Shot down by fighters off the Isle of Wight.	Messerschmitt Bf 110C	100 %	Crew rescued by *Seenotflugkdo.*
27.	I./St.G 2	CM	Shot down by 43 Sqn. Hurricanes at A.13.05 hrs. near Tangmere.	Junkers Ju 87B	100 %	One wounded and one missing.
28.	I./St.G 2	CM	Shot down by 43 Sqn. Hurricanes at A.13.05 hrs. near Tangmere.	Junkers Ju 87B	100 %	Both crew members missing.
29.	I./St.G 2	CM	Shot down by 43 Sqn. Hurricanes at A.13.05 hrs. near Tangmere.	Junkers Ju 87B	100 %	Both crew members killed.
30.	I./St.G 2	CM	Shot down by 43 Sqn. Hurricanes at A.13.05 hrs. near Tangmere.	Junkers Ju 87B	100 %	Both crew members missing.
31.	I./St.G 2	CM	Shot down by 43 Sqn. Hurricanes at A.13.05 hrs. near Tangmere.	Junkers Ju 87B	100 %	One killed; one picked up unhurt.
32.	I./St.G 2	CM	Damaged by 43 Sqn. Hurricanes at A.13.05 hrs. near Tangmere.	Junkers Ju 87B	50 %	Crew unhurt.
33.	I./St.G 2	CM	Damaged by 43 Sqn. Hurricanes at A.13.05 hrs. near Tangmere.	Junkers Ju 87B	10 %	Crew unhurt.
34.	I./St.G 2	CM	Damaged by 43 Sqn. Hurricanes at A.13.05 hrs. near Tangmere.	Junkers Ju 87B	10 %	Crew unhurt.
35.	III./St.G 2	CM	Shot down by *flak* at Tangmere at A.13.05 hrs.	Junkers Ju 87B	100 %	Ltn. Kühn + one missing.
36.	III./St.G 2	CM	Shot down by 43 Sqn. Hurricanes at A.13.05 hrs. near Tangmere.	Junkers Ju 87B	100 %	One killed and one missing.
37.	III./St.G 2	CM	Shot down by 43 Sqn. Hurricanes at A.13.05 hrs. near Tangmere.	Junkers Ju 87B	100 %	One killed and one missing.
38.	III./St.G 2	CM	Shot down by 602 Sqn. Spitfire of Boyd near Tangmere at 13.08 hrs.	Junkers Ju 87B	100 %	Both crew members missing.
39.	I./St.G 77	NCM	Force landed at St. Carrentan after engine failure.	Junkers Ju 87B	10 %	Crew unhurt.
40.	II./JG 2	CM	Shot down by 601 Sqn. Hurricanes near Portsmouth at A.13.00 hrs.	Messerschmitt Bf 109 E-1	100 %	Oblt. Moeckel missing.
41.	II./JG 2	CM	Shot down by 601 Sqn. Hurricanes near Portsmouth at A.13.00 hrs.	Messerschmitt Bf 109 E-1	100 %	Pilot missing.
42.	II./JG 2	CM	Landing accident at Maneville after combat with British fighters at 13.15 hrs.	Messerschmitt Bf 109 E-4	40 %	Pilot unhurt.

Luftwaffe Losses, 16th August 1940—*continued*

43.	4./JG 3	CM	Shot down by 601 Sqn. Spitfires and ditched off Wirrer au Bois; pilot picked up by boat.	Messerschmitt Bf 109 E-4	100 %	Hptm. Müller, St.Kap., wounded.
44.	4./JG 3	CM	Shot down by 601 Sqn. Spitfires and ditched off Wirrer au Bois; pilot picked up by boat.	Messerschmitt Bf 109 E-4	100 %	Pilot unhurt.
45.	7./JG 3	CM	Damaged in combat and force landed at Desvres.	Messerschmitt Bf 109 E-4	100 %	Pilot unhurt.
46.	II./JG 26	CM	Shot down by 266 Sqn. Spitfires near Deal at A.12.35 hrs.	Messerschmitt Bf 109 E-4	100 %	Hptm. Ebbighausen, Gr.Kdr.,
47.	6./JG 27	CM	Damaged in combat and crashed near Cherbourg.	Messerschmitt Bf 109 E-1	100 %	Uffz. Paul Wilbert killed.
48.	III./JG 27	CM	Collided with Item 49 in combat over Isle of Wight.	Messerschmitt Bf 109 E-4	100 %	Oblt. Hans-Volkert Rosenboom killed.
49.	III./JG 27	CM	Collided with Item 48 in combat over Isle of Wight.	Messerschmitt Bf 109 E-4	100 %	Pilot rescued by Seenotflugkdo.
50.	4./JG 51	CM	Shot down by 111 Sqn. Hurricane of Walker off Dover at 12.28 hrs.	Messerschmitt Bf 109 E-3	100 %	Pilot missing.
51.	4./JG 51	CM	Shot down by 111 Sqn. Hurricane of Wallace off Calais at 12.33 hrs.	Messerschmitt Bf 109 E-1	100 %	Pilot missing.
52.	I./JG 53	CM	Shot down by 234 Sqn. Spitfire of Doe off Isle of Wight at 17.10 hrs.	Messerschmitt Bf 109 E-4	100 %	Pilot missing.
53.	II./JG 53	CM	Shot down by 234 Sqn. Spitfire of Hughes off Isle of Wight at 17.08 hrs.	Messerschmitt Bf 109 E-1	100 %	Pilot wounded, but rescued.
54.	II./JG 53	CM	Shot down by 234 Sqn. Spitfire of Horton off Isle of Wight at 17.10 hrs.	Messerschmitt Bf 109 E-4	100 %	Pilot rescued unhurt.
55.	II./JG 53	CM	Damaged by 152 Sqn. Spitfires of Beaumont and Thomas over the Isle of Wight.	Messerschmitt Bf 109 E-1	50 %	Pilot unhurt.
56.	Stab/JG 53	CM	Landing accident at Rennes; not the result of combat.	Messerschmitt Bf 109 E-4	35 %	Pilot unhurt.
57	I./JG 54	CM	Damaged by 54 Sqn. Spitfires at 12.45 hrs. and crashed at St. Inglevert.	Messerschmitt Bf 109 E-1	100 %	Pilot wounded.
58.	3./JG 54	CM	Shot down by 54 Sqn. Spitfires at A.12.45 hrs.	Messerschmitt Bf 109 E-4	100 %	Pilot missing.
59.	7./JG 54	NCM	Crashed at Guines-Süd on works test flight.	Messerschmitt Bf 109 E-4	100 %	Pilot injured.
60.	9./JG 54	CM	Shot down by 54 Sqn. Spitfires south-east of London at A.12.50 hrs.	Messerschmitt Bf 109 E-4	100 %	Pilot killed.
61.	Seenotflug- Kommando	CM	Wrecked in sea landing during air/sea rescue sortie (at German Grid square 6997).	Dornier Do 24	100 %	Crew rescued unhurt.

Saturday 17th August

The past eight days' fighting had cost Fighter Command the lives of 78 pilots, and another 27 had been severely wounded. Of these, more than 60 per cent had been men of experience whose places on the squadrons could only be taken by newly-trained youngsters, freshly posted from an abbreviated flying course at an Operational Training Unit. What was more disturbing was that at this stage the O.T.U.s were unable to keep pace with Fighter Command's requirements—let alone the needs of new squadrons being formed. It is true that the four Polish and Czech squadrons would be manned by pilots of these nations, but it was deemed necessary to provide R.A.F. personnel in key positions, and on these units the squadron and flight command was duplicated—placing a further strain on Dowding's slender reserves.

For some time the Air Staff had been deliberating on the question of whether to divert pilots from other Commands in answer to appeals by Dowding. Dire though his need was seen to be, it could be argued that when the invasion was launched it would be the coastal and bomber pilots whose operations would be critical in its defeat. Nevertheless it was seen that the recent high rate of losses in Fighter Command, if not made good, could result in unopposed enemy raids on coastal and bomber airfields. It was on 17th August that the Air Staff sanctioned the transfer of twenty volunteer pilots from Fairey Battle (light bomber) squadrons and twelve from Lysander units to Fighter Command after a brief conversion course at an O.T.U. These pilots began to join the fighter squadrons before the end of August.

Despite the fine weather on 17th August, the *Luftwaffe* flew few sorties during the day, having carried out only minor raids over the Midlands during the night. The day was spent by Fighter Command flying numerous convoy patrols, but without contact with the enemy. In the English Channel an Arado seaplane ventured too close to a trawler of the Royal Navy, mistaking the Red Ensign for a Red Cross flag, and was hit by machine gun fire; it made off, but was wrecked while alighting on the sea off Boulogne.

During the night of the 17th/18th a Blenheim of No. 29 Squadron scored a well-deserved victory over a Heinkel He 111 of II./KG 53:

> Plt. Off. Rhodes and Sgt. Gregory (gunner) in Blenheim *L6741*, flying from Ternhill, took off at 01.32 hours to patrol the Medway area. They were vectored on to an enemy aircraft identified as a Heinkel He 111, and at 02.28 hours Rhodes sighted the bandit about fifteen miles south-west of Chester. After flying south and chasing the enemy for two hours, during which the enemy turned east and north, Rhodes finally caught up with the He 111 about 25 miles off Spurn Head, opened fire at 400 yards' range with his front guns and fired all his ammunition. The Heinkel slowed down, enabling Rhodes to fly alongside so that his gunner could fire. Gregory emptied a drum into the raider, which continued to lose height and finally landed on the sea about ten miles west of Cromer Knoll[53].

Among the six members of the crew of this Heinkel who were killed was Major Tamm, *Gruppenkommandeur* of II./KG 53.

---

[53] Cf. Form 540, No. 29 Squadron, 18th August 1940.

R.A.F. FIGHTER COMMAND LOSSES—SATURDAY 17th AUGUST 1940

1.	235 Sqn., Bircham Newton	NC	Night landing accident; no crew casualties.	At night	Sgt. S.J. Hobbs	Blenheim	—	Cat. 3 Destroyed
2.	302 Sqn., Leconfield	NC	Crashed at Wheel, Beverley, after fire in the air; pilot badly burned.	Not known	Plt. Off. Glowczynski	Hurricane	P3927	Cat. 3 Destroyed

LUFTWAFFE LOSSES—SATURDAY 17th AUGUST 1940

1.	III./LG 1	NCM	Take-off accident at Châteaudun airfield.	Junkers Ju 88A-1	15 %	Crew unhurt.
2.	1./196	CM	Shot down by small vessel of Royal Navy; flew too close, mistaking Red Ensign for Red Cross flag; aircraft ditched in see off Boulogne.	Arado Ar 196	100 %	Crew unhurt.

Sunday 18th August

Whatever material achievement was gained by either side on this day, 18th August must be recorded as the date of the first decisive defeat of the Stuka dive-bomber. Two weeks previously the number of these aircraft available for operations with eight *Stukagruppen* based in France amounted to 281, yet in the course of those weeks they had flown fourteen major raids and, according to *Luftwaffe* records had suffered the loss of 39 aircraft—all but a handful to the guns of fighters. In this one day's fighting, one *Stukageschwader* alone would lose seventeen more.

In preparation for the day's raids Kesselring sent over a small number of high-flying reconnaissance machines to discover if possible what forward airfields were still occupied by Park's fighters. Five Spitfires of No. 54 Squadron on patrol over the Thames Estuary caught a Bf 110 of 7.(F)/LG 2 at 31,000 feet and shot it down over Manston at 10.54 hours.

Shortly after mid-day Dover CH reported the heaviest build-up of enemy foces yet seen on the radar displays, causing the No. 11 Group Sector Controllers to bring every serviceable aircraft to Readiness by 12.30 hours. The first fighters—twelve Spitfires of No. 54 Squadron at Hornchurch—were scrambled at 12.38 to meet about 300 enemy aircraft over Kent. Within minutes seventy more fighters from nine squadrons were taking off.

At about 13.00 hours Biggin Hill was attacked by nine Dornier Do 17s of 9./KG 76. It had been intended that about 30 Junkers Ju 88s of II./KG 76 would attack the airfield at medium altitude as the Dorniers swept in from low level, but owing to a missed rendezvous over France the Dorniers attacked alone at about 100 feet; they were met by the Hurricanes of Nos. 32 and Spitfires of No. 610 Squadrons whose pilots shot down two, including the lead aircraft flown by Oberleutnant Lamberty with Hauptmann Roth (the *Staffelkapitän*) on board. Of the seven remaining aircraft two were so badly damaged that they crashed in the Channel—their crews being rescued—and three force landed in France. In one of the two which landed safely, the pilot had been killed over Biggin Hill and the aircraft was flown back to Cormeilles-en-Vexin by Feldwebel Wilhelm-Freidrich Illg, the young flight engineer. He succeeded in making a normal wheels-down landing, and was to be awarded the Knight's Cross (on 1st October) for his devotion to duty; he was, however, soon to be shot down over London and taken prisoner.

After the departure of the Dorniers, the Ju 88s made their belated appearance over Biggin Hill, but did little more than crater the airfield surface. One of the two Ju 88s shot down in this raid was destroyed by Flt. Lt. Stanford Tuck, who was on a flying visit to No. 11 Group from Pembrey; his victim fell

Stuka over English rooftops. This aircraft did not recover from its dive. (Photo: Topix)

near Tonbridge, but the return fire from the enemy bomber caused the Spitfire pilot to abandon his aircraft and take to his parachute.

Meanwhile the nearby Sector Station at Kenley was under heavy attack by a similar force of Dorniers, the airfield defences this time being successfully distracted by fifty bombers at medium altitude while a *Staffel* of low-flying aircraft came in from the east. Both formations were intercepted, though No. 111 Squadron—detailed for the low fliers—was unable to engage until the raiders had cleared the airfield. Despite an effective barrage by the local Parachute

Burnt-out Dornier Do 17Z near Biggin Hill on 18th August. This is F1+DT, the lead aircraft flown by Oberleutnant Lamberty of 9./KG 76.

A study in contrasts. A hay wain crosses a Kent field, framed by the tail (already stripped by souvenir hunters) of Oberleutnant Lamberty's Dornier.

and Cable installations, which destroyed two aircraft[54], the airfield suffered considerable damage from about one hundred high explosive bombs which destroyed all ten hangars, the equipment stores, ten Hurricanes (of which six belonged to No. 615 Squadron), two Blenheims, and damaged five other aircraft. Though the operations block itself narrowly escaped being hit, all communications were cut, as were water and gas mains outside the camp. A shelter trench was hit, and among the casualties were the station medical officer and one of the squadron engineering officers. 32 casualties were suffered by the station, of whom twelve were killed. Urgent calls for assistance were made after a despatch rider was sent to a nearby Observer Post, and so many ambulances and fire engines responded that all entrances to the station became blocked.

No. 615 Squadron fought a bitter battle to defend its base but was caught by a Gruppe of Bf 109s which arrived to cover the withdrawal of the bombers. Five more of the Squadron's Hurricanes were shot down, although four of the pilots escaped with their lives[55].

The destruction at Kenley had an immediately but short-lived effect on the capabilities of No. 11 Group as a whole. Although No. 605 Squadron's survivors were ordered to land at Croydon, No. 64 Squadron's Spitfires managed to return to their own airfield and landed on a crater-free strip marked out on the field by white flags. The Sector operations staff moved to a local shop and by characteristic ingenuity the G.P.O. had transferred almost all the vital telephone lines to the improvised centre within 60 hours.

Not all the Dorniers and Junkers were able to drop their bombs on Kenley and several of the raiders made for Croydon, where about eleven bombs were dropped, hitting one of the

undamaged hangars and destroying one Hurricane and damaging another. West Malling was also hit.

As the German raiders straggled eastwards in more than a dozen groups—each well covered by Bf 109s and 110s—the eight R.A.F. squadrons were recovered to whatever airfield was immediately serviceable. Owing to widespread disruption to ground telephone lines it was more than two hours before all Sector Controllers were able to report their states to Fighter Command or to No. 11 Group—an uncomfortable situation which led Park seriously to review his standing instructions regarding the necessity of enlisting support from neighbouring Groups at times of enemy raid saturation. Within 24 hours he had issued explicit orders aimed at avoiding a repetition of the situation in which London lay at the mercy of enemy raids simply because Controllers had lost contact with their forces through disrupted communications or by saturation of the reporting network.

---

[54] The local police, being unaccustomed to the P.A.C. weapon, telephoned a report to London that a large number of parachutists were dropping in the vicinity of Kenley. A signal is known to have been sent by a member of the Cabinet enquiring to know "how the invasion is going".

[55] During the course of these battles no less than four aircraft force landed on golf courses in the neighbourhood, and the fact calls to mind an amusing anecdote which reflects the gravity with which the serious-minded golfing fraternity viewed these events. The belligerent activities of aircraft over golf courses was allowed for in the issue of temporary provisions in the *Golfers' Handbook*:

"(i) Players are asked to collect bomb and shell splinters to save these causing damage to the mowing machines.

"(ii) In competition, during gunfire or while bombs are falling, players may take cover without penalty for ceasing play.

"(iii) The position of known delayed-action bombs are marked by red and white flags placed at a reasonably, but not guaranteed, safe distance.

"(iv) A ball lying in a crater may be lifted and dropped not nearer the hole without penalty.

"(v) A ball moved by enemy action may be replaced as near as possible to where it lay, or if lost or destroyed a ball may be dropped not nearer the hole without penalty.

"(vi) A player whose stroke is affected by the simultaneous explosion of a bomb or shell, or by machine-gun fire, may play another ball from the same place. Penalty, one stroke."

While No. 11 Group was pulling itself together, it was granted a respite by the shifting of enemy pressure to the west. Four distinct formations were reported shortly after 14.00 hours approaching the Isle of Wight from the south and southeast. These raids were composed of 28 Junkers Ju 87s of Hauptmann Meisel's I.*Gruppe, Stukageschwader 77*, 27 of II.*Gruppe*, and 30 of III.*Gruppe*; the fourth raid consisted of 25 Junkers Ju 88s of KG 54.

Fearing a repetition of the disastrous Tangmere raid of the 16th, the South Coast Sector Controllers ordered all their fighters off the ground to fly guard over their airfields. Though undoubtedly justified, this action enabled the German bombers to reach their targets which were quickly revealed, not as the R.A.F. fighter fields but as the CH radar station at Poling near Littlehampton, the naval air station at Ford, the naval airfield at Gosport and the Coastal Command airfield at Thorney Island.

As the Ju 88s made an unopposed raid in three waves on Gosport, in which further heavy damage was inflicted on airfield facilities and aircraft, Meisel's Ju 87 pilots were wasting precious seconds forming up to approach the Poling radar station down sun. Not three miles distant the pilots of No. 43 Squadron's Hurricanes spotted the dive-bombers and flew straight into the attack, catching the German aircraft at their most vulnerable attitude—that is to say, just as they were committed to their dives. By the same token the escorting Bf 109s (of I. and II.*Gruppen*, JG 27) were unable to cover all the dive-bombers simultaneously throughout their dives and preferred to remain at 15,000 feet, while the Hurricanes clung desperately to the Stukas, to some extent disrupting their aim and sticking closely to them as they made for the sea at low level. The massacre was impressive indeed, and when the three St.G 77 *Gruppen* attempted to join forces after their raids on Ford and Thorney Island (where they hit hangars, a fuel dump and aircraft), they merely brought upon themselves a concentration of Hurricanes and Spitfires from Nos. 152, 601 and 602 Squadrons, while No. 234 Squadron's

Hauptmann Horst "Jakob" Tietzen, *Staffelführer* of 5./JG 51. A seven-victory veteran of the Spanish Civil War, he died on 18th August, and his body was later washed ashore at Calais. (Photo: *Gemeinschaft der Jagdflieger E.V.*)

Spitfires held the Bf 109s at bay. No fewer than sixteen of the dive-bombers were shot down, and two crashed on their return home; four others were damaged. The escort, in shooting down four Spitfires and two Hurricanes, lost eight aircraft.

The Poling radar was extensively damaged and was not

Günther Lützow, *Kommodore* of JG 3 <*Udet*> from mid-August, with his III.*Gruppe Kommandeur* Hauptmann Wilhelm Balthasar (centre) and Leutnant Egon Troha (right) (Photo: *Gemeinschaft der Jagdflieger E.V.*)

restored to full-time watch for more than a week, during which time a "remote site" was brought into operation in conjunction with a mobile watch office and transmitter deployed nearby.

An evening attack phase by Kesselring's *Luftflotte 2* was preceded by a snap strafing raid at 15.30 hours by twelve hedge-hopping Messerschmitt Bf 109s on Manston. Using cannon and machine gun fire, they destroyed two Spitfires and killed one groundcrew man; fifteen others, mostly in the Servicing Flight, were wounded.

At about 17.00 hours a total of five separate formations converged on Kent, and one of these flew up the Thames Estuary before wheeling round in the direction of Croydon. Fearing for the safety of his airfield, Beamish had ordered his aircraft up from North Weald (accompanying them himself) and these Hurricanes caught up with the enemy formation just as the Hornchurch Spitfires also made contact. In the face of such opposition, the Germans missed Croydon and dropped their bombs over a wide area of Kent and Surrey. Again the warning sirens sounded late, and 59 casualties were reported in the Medway towns alone.

As darkness fell at the end of yet another day of deperate fighting, both Kesselring and Sperrle kept up the pressure by sending over about 50 bombers in widespread nuisance raids, but achieved very little in the way of material damage. Heinkel He 115s were again active, sowing mines in the Bristol Channel.

It has been affirmed that 18th August witnessed the hardest fighting of the entire Battle of Britain, but the postulation is debatable. Certainly Fighter Command installations had suffered heavy damage at Poling and Kenley, and more R.A.F. fighters than hitherto had been ordered into the air to meet the various threats. Moreover the much-vaunted Stuka had suffered a significant defeat. Yet the tempo of air combat did not match that of the 15th and 16th, largely owing to considerable confusion among the British fighters following the disruption of control communications, while the "swatting" of the German dive-bombers had been achieved in the classic situation of an escort being isolated from its charges. The actual number of British fighters which was engaged in air combat on this day was exceeded on at least half a dozen other occasions during the Battle.

The heavy casualties suffered by the *Stukaverband*, following on previous days' losses, prompted the Germans to withhold this weapon from the main battle henceforth, though—contrary to suggestions elsewhere—the Ju 87 was *not* wholly withdrawn from the *Kanalfront*. There were still to be more than a score of dive-bombing raids by these aircraft before the end of the Battle, some of them achieving serious damage to British installations. Nevertheless the *raison d' être* of the German Stuka was as "long range artillery" and its main rôle was intended to be played out in the invasion assault itself. The devastation achieved at Kenley demonstrated that carefully planned and co-ordinated attacks by conventional bombers could, where necessary, do anything the dive-bombers could do. Moreover, so long as Fighter Command still possessed sharp teeth, the use of Stukas in main raids exposed them to crippling losses.

R.A.F. FIGHTER COMMAND LOSSES—SUNDAY 18th AUGUST 1940

1.	17 Sqn., Debden	C	Force landed at Manston after combat; aircraft destroyed in raid; pilot unhurt.	A15.30 hrs.	Sgt. G. Griffiths	Hurricane	—		Cat. 3 Burnt
2.	17 Sqn., Debden	C	Missing after combat near Dover; pilot killed.	13.30 hrs.	Plt. Off. N.D. Solomon	Hurricane	L1921		Cat. 3 Missing
3.	32 Sqn., Biggin Hill	C	Shot down by Bf 109 near Biggin Hill; pilot wounded	13.10 hrs.	Plt. Off. J.F. Pain	Hurricane	V6535		Cat. 3 Destroyed
4.	32 Sqn., Biggin Hill	C	Shot down in flames by Bf 110 near Biggin Hill; pilot baled out severely wounded.	13.12 hrs.	Flt. Lt. H. a'B. Russell	Hurricane	—		Cat. 3 Destroyed
5.	32 Sqn., Biggin Hill	C	Force landed after combat near Biggin Hill; pilot slightly wounded.	13.28 hrs.	Sgt. B. Henson	Hurricane	—		Cat. 2 Damaged
6.	32 Sqn., Biggin Hill	C	Shot down by Bf 109s near Herne Bay; pilot baled out unhurt near Detling.	17.42 hrs.	Flt. Lt. M.N. Crossley	Hurricane	N2461		Cat. 3 Lost

Officers of *Zerstörergeschwader 26 <Horst Wessel>*, one of the most prominent Bf 110 units in the Battle. (Left) Oberstleutnant Joachim-Friedrich Huth, one-legged First World War veteran and *Kommodore* of ZG 26 throughout the Battle. (Centre) Ralph von Rettberg, who commanded II./ZG 26 in the Battles of France and Britain, the Balkan campaign and the early stages of the fighting in Russia. (Right) Johann Schalk, who led III./ZG 26 during the Battle of Britain and later took over the *Geschwader* command. (Photos: *Gemeinschaft der Jagdflieger E.V.*)

R.A.F. Losses, 18th August 1940—*continued*

No.	Squadron/Base		Description	Time	Pilot	Aircraft	Serial	Category
7.	32 Sqn., Biggin Hill	C	Shot down by Bf 109s near Herne Bay; pilot baled out with burns and wounds.	17.46 hrs.	Plt. Off. R.C.C. De Grunne	Hurricane	P3147	Cat. 3 Lost
8.	32 Sqn., Biggin Hill	C	Shot down by Bf 109s at Chartham Hatch; pilot baled out with burns.	17.48 hrs.	Sgt. L.H.B. Pearce	Hurricane	R4106	Cat. 3 Lost
9.	43 Sqn., Tangmere	C	Damaged by Bf 109s near Portsmouth; pilot wounded and crashed on landing at base.	14.29 nrs.	Flt. Lt. F.R. Carey	Hurricane	R4109	Cat. 2 Damaged
10.	65 Sqn., Rochford	C	Missing after combat over Kent; pilot killed.	13.30 hrs.	Fg. Off. F. Gruszka	Spitfire	—	Cat. 3 Missing
11.	85 Sqn., Debden	C	Collided with enemy aircraft; pilot returned unhurt, aircraft minus wingtip.	17.45 hrs.	Plt. Off. J.E. Marshall	Hurricane	—	Cat. 2 Damaged
12.	85 Sqn., Debden	C	Shot down by Ju 88s twelve miles east of Clacton; pilot baled out and rescued by Lightship 81; landed at Felixstowe by MTB.	17.51 hrs.	Plt. Off. A.G. Lewis	Hurricane	—	Cat. 3 Lost
13.	85 Sqn., Debden	C	Missing after combat with Bf 109s north of Foulness Point; pilot assumed killed.	17.54 hrs.	Flt. Lt. R.H.A. Lee	Hurricane	P2923	Cat. 3 Missing
14.	92 Sqn., Pembrey	C	Shot down by Ju 88 near Beachy Head; pilot baled out unhurt.	14.15 hrs.	Flt. Lt. R.S.S. Tuck	Spitfire	N3040	Cat. 3 Destroyed
15.	111 Sqn., Croydon	C	Shot down by Kenley A.A. guns ; pilot killed.	13.30 hrs.	Flt. Lt. S.D.P. Connors	Hurricane	N2340	Cat. 3 Destroyed
16.	111 Sqn., Croydon	C	Shot down by Ju 88 near Kenley; pilot baled out unhurt.	13.35 hrs.	Sgt. A.H. Deacon	Hurricane	P3943	Cat. 3 Destroyed
17.	111 Sqn., Croydon	C	Shot down near Kenley; pilot baled out wounded.	13.38 hrs.	Sgt. H.S. Newton	Hurricane	R4187	Cat. 3 Destroyed
18.	111 Sqn., Croydon	C	Shot down by Do 17s and force landed on Woodcote Bank Golf Course; pilot unhurt.	13.38 hrs.	Plt. Off. P.J. Simpson	Hurricane	—	Cat. 2 Damaged
19.	111 Sqn., Croydon	—	Destroyed in raid on Croydon; no pilot casualties.	A13.45 hrs.	Nil	Hurricane	—	Cat. 3 Destroyed
20.	111 Sqn., Croydon	—	Damaged in raid on Croydon; no pilot casualties.	A13.45 hrs.	Nil	Hurricane	—	Cat. 2 Damaged
21.	151 Sqn., North Weald	C	Damaged by Ju 88 near Chelmsford; pilot safe.	17.35 hrs.	Wg. Cdr. F.V. Beamish	Hurricane	—	Cat. 1 Damaged
22.	151 Sqn., North Weald	C	Shot down south of Chelmsford; pilot baled out with burns and admitted to hospital.	17.37 hrs.	Sqn. Ldr. J.A.G. Gordon	Hurricane	P3940	Cat. 3 Lost
23.	151 Sqn., North Weald	C	Shot down off Essex coast; pilot killed.	17.37 hrs.	Plt. Off. J.B. Ramsay	Hurricane	R4181	Cat. 3 Missing
24.	152 Sqn., Warmwell	C	Damaged in combat near Portsmouth; pilot unhurt.	A14.30 hrs.	Not known	Spitfire	—	Cat. 1 Damaged
25.	152 Sqn., Warmwell	C	Damaged in combat near Portsmouth; pilot unhurt.	A14.30 hrs.	Not known	Spitfire	—	Cat. 1 Damaged.
26.	257 Sqn., Debden	C	Shot down by He 111 over Thames Estuary; pilot baled out wounded in foot but rescued.	17.26 hrs.	Sgt. A.G. Girdwood	Hurricane	P3708	Cat. 3 Lost
27.	266 Sqn., Manston	—	Destroyed on the ground at Manston by Bf 109s; no pilot casualties.	Afternoon	Nil	Spitfire	X4066	Cat. 3 Destroyed
28.	501 Sqn., Hawkinge	C	Shot down in flames by Bf 109s over Kent; pilot baled out with sight burns	A11.00 hrs.	Sgt. D.N.E. McKay	Hurricane	R4219	Cat. 3 Destroyed
29.	501 Sqn., Hawkinge	C	Shot down by Bf 109s of JG 26 near Canterbury; pilot killed.	A13.00 hrs.	Plt. Off. J.W. Bland	Hurricane	P3208	Cat. 3 Destroyed
30.	501 Sqn., Hawkinge	C	Shot down by Bf 109s of JG 26 near Canterbury; pilot seriously wounded.	A13.00 hrs.	Plt. Off. F. Kozlowski	Hurricane	P3815	Cat. 3 Destroyed
31.	501 Sqn., Hawkinge	C	Shot down by Bf 109s of JG 26 near Canterbury; pilot wounded in the knee.	A13.00 hrs.	Plt. Off. K.N.T. Lee	Hurricane	P2549	Cat. 3 Destroyed
32.	501 Sqn., Hawkinge	C	Shot down by Bf 109s of JG 26 near Canterbury; pilot unhurt.	A13.00 hrs.	F/Sgt. P.F. Morfill	Hurricane	N2617	Cat. 3 Destroyed
33.	501 Sqn., Hawkinge	C	Shot down near Biggin Hill; pilot baled out unhurt.	17.30 hrs.	Plt. Off. R.C. Dafforn	Hurricane	P3270	Cat. 3 Destroyed
34.	501 Sqn., Hawkinge	C	Shot down by Bf 110s near Hawkinge; pilot killed.	A17.40 hrs.	Flt. Lt. G.E.B. Stoney	Hurricane	P3059	Cat. 3 Destroyed
35.	504 Sqn., Castletown	NC	Pilot became lost and force landed near St. Fergus, Dyce.	Not known	Sgt. H.D.B. Jones	Hurricane	—	Cat. 3 Destroyed
36.	601 Sqn., Tangmere	C	Shot down by Bf 109s near Portsmouth; pilot killed. Aircraft crashed at Pagham.	14.28 hrs.	Sgt. R.P. Hawkings	Hurricane	L1990	Cat. 3 Destroyed
37.	601 Sqn., Tangmere	C	Shot down by Bf 109s near Portsmouth; pilot killed.	14.36 hrs.	Sgt. L.N. Guy	Hurricane	V7253	Cat. 3 Destroyed
38.	602 Sqn., Westhampnett	C	Shot down by Bf 109s over Solent; pilot baled out, wounded in the foot.	14.34 hrs.	Flt. Lt. J.D. Urie	Spitfire	X4110	Cat. 3 Destroyed
39.	602 Sqn., Westhampnett	C	Damaged in combat near Southampton; pilot crashed through HT cables; admitted to hospital with severe shock.	14.41 hrs.	Fg. Off. P.J. Ferguson	Spitfire	K9969	Cat. 3 Destroyed
40.	602 Sqn., Westhampnett	C	Shot down by Bf 109s near Portsmouth; pilot unhurt.	14.37 hrs.	Sgt. B.E.P. Whall	Spitfire	L1019	Cat. 3 Destroyed
41.	602 Sqn., Westhampnett	C	Shot down by Bf 109s near Portsmouth; pilot baled out unhurt.	14.39 hrs.	Plt. Off. H.M. Moody	Spitfire	X4161	Cat. 3 Destroyed
42.	615 Sqn., Kenley	C	Shot down in flames by BF 109s at Croydon; pilot admitted to hospital with severe shock.	A13.10 hrs.	Plt. Off. D.J. Looker	Hurricane	L1592	Cat. 3 Destroyed
43.	615 Sqn., Kenley	C	Shot down by Bf 109 on Morden Park golf course; pilot killed.	13.12 hrs.	Sgt P K. Walley	Hurricane	P2768	Cat. 3 Destroyed
44.	615 Sqn., Kenley	C	Shot down by Bf 109 near Sevenoaks; pilot unhurt.	13.15 hrs.	Flt. Lt. L.M. Gaunce	Hurricane	P2966	Cat. 3 Destroyed
45.	615 Sqn., Kenley	C	Shot down near Orpington; pilot admitted to Orpington hospital with leg wounds.	13.17 hrs.	Plt. Off. P.H. Hugo	Hurricane	R4221	Cat. 3 Destroyed
46.	615 Sqn.	—	Destroyed in raid on Kenley; no casualties.	13.03 hrs.	Nil	Hurricane	R4186	Cat. 3 Destroyed
47.	615 Sqn.	—	Destroyed in raid on Kenley; no casualties.	13.03 hrs.	Nil	Hurricane	P3158	Cat. 3 Destroyed
48.	615 Sqn.	—	Destroyed in raid on Kenley; no casualties.	13.03 hrs.	Nil	Hurricane	P3488	Cat. 3 Destroyed
49.	615 Sqn.	—	Destroyed in raid on Kenley; no casualties.	13.03 hrs.	Nil	Hurricane	P3487	Cat. 3 Destroyed
50.	615 Sqn.	—	Destroyed in raid on Kenley; no casualties.	13.03 hrs.	Nil	Hurricane	—	Cat. 3 Destroyed
51.	615 Sqn.	—	Destroyed in raid on Kenley; no casualties.	13.03 hrs.	Nil	Hurricane	—	Cat. 3 Destroyed

LUFTWAFFE LOSSES—SUNDAY 18th AUGUST 1940

No.	Unit		Description	Aircraft	%	Casualties
1.	1./KG 1	CM	Target Biggin Hill; damaged by unknown R.A.F. fighters; later crashed.	Heinkel He 111H-3	100 %	One killed; one wounded.
2.	2./KG 1	CM	Shot down by 65 Sqn. Spitfires over Kent at A.13.00 hrs.	Heinkel He 111H-3	100 %	One killed; Ltn. Ahrens + three
3.	6./KG 2	CM	Damaged by 46 Sqn. Hurricanes over Thames Estuary at A.17.45 hrs.	Dornier Do 17Z-3	3 %	Hptm. Lindemann wounded

Luftwaffe Losses, 18th August 1940—*continued*

4.	6./KG 4	CM	Landing accident at Eindhoven after combat.	Heinkel He 111P	35 %	Crew unhurt.
5.	III./KG 4	CM	Force landed at Vlaardingen with engine failure.	Junkers Ju 88A-4	70 %	Crew unhurt.
6.	III./KG 4	CM	Force landed near Rotterdam with fuel shortage.	Junkers Ju 88A-1	50 %	Crew unhurt.
7.	II./KG 27	CM	Force landed at Laval following engine failure.	Heinkel He 111P	90 %	Three crew members injured.
8.	II./KG 27	CM	Shot down by 610 Sqn. Spitfire of Ellis 8 miles off Dungeness at 13.40 hrs.	Heinkel He 111P	100 %	Two killed; two wounded.
9.	III./KG 27	CM	Landing accident at Rennes airfield.	Heinkel He 111P	40 %	Crew unhurt.
10.	III./KG 51	NCM	Force landed at Orly following engine failure.	Junkers Ju 88A-1	10 %	Crew unhurt.
11.	II./KG 53	CM	Shot down by 29 Sqn. Blenheim night fighter of Rhodes and Gregory off Norfolk coast at A.04.00 hrs.	Heinkel He 111H-3	100 %	Major Tamm, *Gr.Kdr.*, Ltn. Ludmann + one killed; three missing. (Six in crew).
12.	III./KG 53	CM	Shot down by 615 Sqn. Hurricane of Sanders south of Kenley at 13.28 hrs.	Heinkel He 111H-2	100 %	Ltn. Leber + three missing.
13.	III./KG 53	CM	Shot down by 85 Sqn. Hurricanes of Hamilton and Marshall 10 miles off Foulness at 17.43 hrs.	Heinkel He 111H	100 %	Ltn. Woldmann + four missing.
14.	III./KG 53	CM	Shot down by 257 Sqn. Hurricane of Beresford off Foulness at A.17.50 hrs.	Heinkel He 111H-2	100 %	Oblt. Zipse + four missing.
15.	1./KG 76	CM	Shot down by 111Sqn. Hurricanes of Connors and Simpson near Kenley at 13.12 hrs.	Dornier Do 17Z	100 %	Oblt. Stodt + one killed; thre missing.
16.	2./KG 76	CM	Damaged by 111 Sqn. Hurricanes over Sussex coast at A.13.25 hrs.	Dornier Do 17Z	20 %	One wounded.
17.	3./KG 76	CM	Damaged by 111Sqn. Hurricane of Brown between Biggin Hill and South Coast at 13.25 hrs.	Dornier Do 17Z	3 %	One wounded.
18.	5./KG 76	CM	Shot down by 92 Sqn. Spitfire of Tuck near Tonbridge at 13.25 hrs.	Junkers Ju 88A-1	100 %	Four crew members killed.
19.	5./KG 76	CM	Damaged by 32 Sqn. Hurricane of Barton near Tonbridge at 13.25 hrs.	Junkers Ju 88A-1	40 %	Crew unhurt.
20.	6./KG 76	CM	Shot down by 111Sqn. Hurricane of Dymond near Biggin Hill at 13.14 hrs.	Junkers Ju 88A-1	100 %	Sd.Fhr. Berchemeier + three missing.
21.	8./KG 76	CM	Shot down by 610 Sqn. Spitfires and 615 Sqn. Hurricanes near Sevenoaks at 13.18 hrs.	Dornier Do 17Z	100 %	Ltn. Leder + two killed; two missing.
22.	8./KG 76	CM	Damaged by 615 Sqn. Hurricanes at A.13.20 hrs. and crash landed at Calais.	Dornier Do 17Z-2	50 %	Crew unhurt.
23.	9./KG 76	CM	Shot down by 610 Sqn. Spitfire of Parsons and 32 Sqn. Hurricane of Flinders over Kent coast at A.13.25 hrs.	Dornier Do 17Z-2	100 %	Oblt. Ahrends + three killed; Oberst Dr. Sommer missing.
24.	9./KG 76	CM	Damaged by 615 Sqn. Hurricanes and ditched in Channel at A.13.25 hrs; crew rescued.	Dornier Do 17Z-2	100 %	Crew unhurt.
25.	9./KG 76	CM	Shot down by 615 Sqn. Hurricanes near Biggin Hill at 13.09 hrs.	Dornier Do 17Z-2	100 %	Hptm. Roth, *St.Kap.*, Oblt. Lamberty, Hptm. Peters + two missing.
26.	9./KG 76	CM	Damaged by 32 Sqn. Hurricanes over north Kent coast; landed safely at Norrent-Fontes.	Dornier Do 17Z-2	5 %	Oblt. Magin killed.
27.	9./KG 76	CM	Damaged by 111 and 615 Sqn. Hurricanes at 13.20 hrs. Landed at Cormeilles-en-Vexin.	Dornier Do 17Z-2	10—60 %	Crew unhurt.
28.	9./KG 76	CM	Damaged by 32 Sqn. Hurricanes near Biggin Hill at A.13.20 hrs.; landed at Abbeville.	Dornier Do 17Z-3	60 %	Crew unhurt.
29.	9./KG 76	CM	Damaged by *flak* and 111 Sqn. Hurricanes near Biggin Hill; landed at Cormeilles-en-Vexin.	Dornier Do 17Z-2	50 %	One killed; two wounded.
30.	KGr. 100	CM	Force landed at Dinard; not due to combat.	Heinkel He 111H-1	100 %	No crew casualties.
31.	I./St.G 77 (1)	CM	Shot down by 43 Sqn. Hurricanes over Selsey Bill at 14.25 hrs.	Junkers Ju 87B-1	100 %	Two crew members missing.
32.	I./St.G 77	CM	Shot down by 43 Sqn. Hurricanes over Selsey Bill at 14.25 hrs.	Junkers Ju 87B-1	100 %	Hptm. Meisel + one missing.
33.	I./St.G 77	CM	Damaged by 43 Sqn. Hurricanes over Selsey Bill at 14.25 hrs.	Junkers Ju 87B-1	60 %	One crew member wounded.
34.	I./St.G 77	CM	Shot down by 602 Sqn. Spitfires at A.14.30 hrs.	Junkers Ju 87B-1	100 %	Oblt.Schmidt killed; one wounded.
35.	I./St.G 77	CM	Damaged by 43 Sqn. Hurricanes at 14.25 hrs.	Junkers Ju 87B-1	5 %	Oblt Scheffel + one wounded.
36.	I./St.G 77	CM	Damaged by 43 Sqn. Hurricanes at 14.25 hrs.	Junkers Ju 87B-1	10 %	Two crew members wounded.
37.	I./St.G 77	CM	Shot down by 43 Sqn. Hurricanes at 14.25 hrs.	Junkers Ju 87B-1	100 %	One killed; Oblt. Sailer missing.
38.	I./St.G 77	CM	Shot down by 152 Sqn. Spitfire of Boitel-Gill in Selsey Bill area at 14.25 hrs.	Junkers Ju 87B-1	100 %	One killed; Ltn. Sinn missing.
39.	I./St.G 77	CM	Shot down by 152 Sqn. Spitfires off Isle of Wight at A.14.30 hrs.	Junkers Ju 87B-1	100 %	Oblt. Wilhelm + one missing.
40.	I./St.G 77	CM	Shot down by 43 Sqn. Hurricanes at 14.25 hrs.	Junkers Ju 87B-1	100 %	Oblt. Schäffer + one missing.
41.	I./St.G 77	CM	Shot down by 152 Sqn. Spitfires off Isle of Wight at A.14.30 hrs.	Junkers Ju 87B-1	100 %	Two crew members missing.
42.	I./St.G 77	CM	Shot down by 152 Sqn. Spitfires off Isle of Wight at A.14.30 hrs.	Junkers Ju 87B-1	100 %	Both crew members killed.
43.	I./St.G 77	CM	Shot down by 152 Sqn. Spitfires off Isle of Wight at A.14.30 hrs.	Junkers Ju 87B-1	100 %	One killed; one missing.
44.	I./St.G 77	CM	Shot down by 152 Sqn. Spitfires off Isle of Wight at A.14.30 hrs.	Junkers Ju 87B-1	100 %	Both crew members missing.
45.	I./St.G 77	CM	Damaged by 601 Sqn. Hurricanes at 14.25 hrs.	Junkers Ju 87B-1	70 %	One killed; one wounded.
46.	II./St.G 77	CM	Shot down by 602 Sqn. Spitfires over Poling CH.	Junkers Ju 87B-1	100 %	Oblt. Sonntag + one missing.
47.	II./St.G 77	CM	Shot down by 602 Sqn. Spitfires over Poling CH at 14.20 hrs; believed crashed in sea.	Junkers Ju 87B-1	100 %	One killed; one missing.
48.	II./St.G 77	CM	Damaged by 602 Sqn. Spitfires over Poling at 14.20 hrs. Crash landed at Barfleur.	Junkers Ju 87B-1	100 %	Crew unhurt.
49.	III./St.G 77	CM	Damaged by 602 Sqn. Spitfires over Poling at 14.25 hrs. Force landed at Caen.	Junkers Ju 87B-1	35 %	One crew member wounded.
50.	III./St.G 77	CM	Damaged by 602 Sqn. Spitfires over Poling at 14.25 hrs. Crashed on Argentan airfield.	Junkers Ju 87B-1	100 %	Both crew members killed.
51.	III./St.G 77	CM	Damaged by 602 Sqn. Spitfires over Poling at 14.25 hrs. Crashed on Argentan airfield.	Junkers Ju 87B-1	35 %	Crew unhurt.
52.	III./St.G 77	CM	Shot down by 602 Sqn. Spitfire of Boyd over Littlehampton at 14.29 hrs.	Junkers Ju 87B-1	100 %	Both crew members killed.
53.	I./ZG 26	CM	Shot down by 46 Sqn. Hurricane of Ragabliati over Thames Estuary at 17.45 hrs.	Messerschmitt Bf 110 C-4	100 %	Oblt. Proske + one missing.
54.	I./ZG 26	CM	Shot down by 85 Sqn. Hurricane over Thames Estuary at A.17.45 hrs.	Messerschmitt Bf 110C	100 %	Both crew members missing.
55.	1./ZG 26	CM	Shot down by 151 Sqn. Hurricane of Blair and crashed at Lydd at 13.45 hrs.	Messerschmitt Bf 110 C-2 (U8+BB)	100 %	Both crew members missing.
56.	2./ZG 26	CM	Damaged by 46 Sqn. Hurricane over Thames Estuary at 17.45 hrs. Landed at Hermalingen.	Messerschmitt Bf 110 D-0	40 %	Crew unhurt.
57.	2./ZG 26	CM	Damaged by 56 Sqn. Hurricane over Thames Estuary at 17.45 hrs. Crashed at Ypern.	Messerschmitt Bf 110 D-0	85 %	Crew unhurt.

Luftwaffe Losses, 18th August 1940—*continued*

58.	2./ZG 26	CM	Damaged by 151 Sqn. Hurricane over Thames Estuary at 17.45 hrs. Landed at Dunkirk.	Messerschmitt Bf 110 C-2	10—60 %	Hptm. Kaminski, *St.Kap.*, + one wounded.
59.	3./ZG 26	CM	Damaged by 54 Sqn. Spitfire over Thames Estuary at A.17.45 hrs. Landed at Clairmarais.	Messerschmitt Bf 110 C-4	10 %	Crew unhurt.
60.	3./ZG 26	CM	Damaged by 54 Sqn. Spitfire over Thames Estuary at A.17.45 hrs. Crashed at Le Nieppe.	Messerschmitt Bf 110 D-0	100 %	Crew unhurt.
61.	3./ZG 26	CM	Shot down by 54 Sqn. Spitfires at A.17.45 hrs.	Messerschmitt Bf 110C	100 %	Both crew members killed.
62.	3./ZG 26	CM	Shot down by 54 Sqn. Spitfires over Thames Estuary at A.17.465 hrs.	Messerschmitt Bf 110 D-0	100 %	Oblt. Kirchhof and Ltn. Mader missing.
63.	4./ZG 26	CM	Shot down by 501 Sqn. Hurricanes off North Foreland at 19.20 hrs.	Messerschmitt Bf 110C (3U+CM)	100 %	One killed; one missing.
64.	4./ZG 26	CM	Shot down by 501 Sqn. Hurricanes 2 miles east of Eastchurch at 19.20 hrs.	Messerschmitt Bf 110C (3U+AM)	100 %	One killed; Hptm. Ludtke, *St.Kap.*, missing.
65.	4./ZG 26	CM	Damaged by 501 Sqn. Hurricane over Kent coast at 19.20 hrs; force landed at Wizernes.	Messerschmitt Bf 110C	30 %	One crew member killed.
66.	6./ZG 26	CM	Shot down by 56 Sqn. Hurricane over Ashford.	Messerschmitt Bf 110C	100 %	Ltn. Kastner + one missing.
67.	6./ZG 26	CM	Shot down by 56 Sqn. Hurricane of Weaver over Ashford.	Messerschmitt Bf 110C	100 %	One killed; one missing.
68.	6./ZG 26	CM	Shot down by 56 Sqn. Hurricanes of Whitehead and Westmacott at Newchurch at 13.00 hrs.	Messerschmitt Bf 110C (3U+EP)	100 %	Both crew members killed.
69.	6./ZG 26	CM	Shot down by 56 Sqn. Hurricane of Mounsdon and crashed at Lydd at A.13.00 hrs.	Messerschmitt Bf 110C	100 %	Oblt. Helmut + one killed.
70.	8./ZG 26	CM	Shot down by 56 Sqn. Hurricane of Robinson over Ashford.	Messerschmitt Bf 110C	100 %	Both crew members missing.
71.	8./ZG 26	CM	Damaged in combat with R.A.F. fighters; force landed at Arques.	Messerschmitt Bf 110C	30 %	Crew unhurt.
72.	1./LG 2	NCM	Pilot became lost and force landed at Ligecourt.	Messerschmitt Bf 109 E-3	35 %	Pilot unhurt.
73.	1./LG 2	NCM	Pilot became lost and force landed at Ligecourt.	Messerschmitt Bf 109 E-4	40 %	Pilot unhurt.
74.	7.(F)/LG 2	CM	Shot down by five 54 Sqn. Spitfires at 31,000 ft. over Manston at 10.54 hrs.	Messerschmitt Bf 110B	100 %	One killed; Oblt. Werdin missing.
75.	II./JG 2	CM	Shot down by 601 Sqn. Hurricanes over Isle of Wight at 14.20 hrs.	Messerschmitt Bf 109 E-4	100 %	Oblt. Möller missing.
76.	II./JG 2	CM	Damaged by 601 Sqn. Hurricanes over Isle of Wight at 14.20 hrs. Crashed near Cherbourg.	Messerschmitt Bf 109 E-1	100 %	Pilot wounded.
77.	2./JG 3	CM	Struck ground in combat with 54 Sqn. Spitfire of Tew over East Kent.	Messerschmitt Bf 109 E-4	100 %	Oblt. Tiedtmann, *St.Kap.*, missing.
78.	II./JG 3	CM	Force landed in France; no further details.	Messerschmitt Bf 109E	60 %	Pilot unhurt.

Camouflaged with corn to prevent destruction by other German aircraft before R.A.F. Intelligence staff could examine it, the Bf 109E-4 of Oberleutnant Tiedtmann of 2./JG 3, who flew into the ground while chasing Tew's Spitfire at "nought feet"—see Item 77 of the German loss table on this day.

79.	III./JG 3	CM	Shot down by 266 Sqn. Spitfires over Dover at 14.05 hrs.	Messerschmitt Bf 109 E-4	100 %	Ltn. von Fonderen killed.
80.	6./JG 3	CM	Crashed at Boulogne after combat with damage.	Messerschmitt Bf 109E	70 %	Pilot wounded.
81.	6./JG 3	CM	Crashed at Marquise after combat with damage.	Messerschmitt Bf 109E	80 %	Pilot killed.
82.	8./JG 3	CM	Shot down by 602 Sqn. Spitfire of Boyd at 14.35 hrs.	Messerschmitt Bf 109 E-4	100 %	Pilot killed.
83.	III./JG 26	CM	Shot down by 54 Sqn. Spitfire of Gribble near Canterbury at A.13.00 hrs.	Messerschmitt Bf 109 E-4	100 %	Ltn. Blume, wounded, made P.O.W.
84.	III./JG 26	CM	Shot down by 54 Sqn. Spitfire of Campbell over East Kent at A.13.45 hrs.	Messerschmitt Bf 109 E-1	100 %	Ltn. Müller-Dühe killed.
85.	1./JG 27	CM	Shot down by 234 Sqn. Spitfires over the Solent at 14.35 hrs.	Messerschmitt Bf 109 E-1	100 %	Oblt. Martin Trümpelmann killed.
86.	1./JG 27	CM	Shot down by 234 Sqn. Spitfires over the Solent at 14.35 hrs.	Messerschmitt Bf 109 E-4	100 %	Ltn. Gerhard Mitsdörfer made P.O.W.
87.	2./JG 27	CM	Shot down by 234 Sqn. Spitfires over the Solent at 14.35 hrs.	Messerschmitt Bf 109 E-4	100 %	Fw. Otto Sawallisch missing.
88.	6./JG 27	CM	Shot down by 43 Sqn. Hurricane of Hallowes over the Solent at A.14.35 hrs.	Messerschmitt Bf 109 E-4	100 %	Oblt. Julius Neumann made P.O.W.

Luftwaffe Losses, 18th August 1940—*continued*

89.	6./JG 27	CM	Shot down bh 234 Sqn. Spitfires over the Solent at 14.35 hrs.	Messerschmitt Bf 109 E-4	100 %	Uffz. Karl Nolte killed.
90.	II./JG 27	CM	Shot down by 601 Sqn. Hurricane off the Isle of Wight at A.14.35 hrs.	Messerschmitt Bf 109 E-4	100 %	Pilot rescued, unhurt, by *Seenot- flugkommando.*
91.	I./JG 51	CM	Minor collision over St. Inglevert; not combat.	Messerschmitt Bf 109E	30 %	Pilot unhurt.
92.	3./JG 51	CM	Shot down by 1 Sqn. Hurricane of Pemberton at Tenterden, Kent, at 13.54 hrs.	Messerschmitt Bf 109 E-3	100 %	Ltn. Lessing killed.
93.	6./JG 51	CM	Shot down by 85 Sqn. Hurricane (possibly of Townsend) over Thames Estuary at A.17.50 hrs.	Messerschmitt Bf 109E	100 %	Hptm. Tietzen, *St.Kap.*, killed;
94.	II./JG 54	—	Two aircraft damaged in raid on Vlissingen.	Messerschmitt Bf 109E	Less than 60%	No pilot casualties.
95.	7./JG 54	CM	Take-off accident at Guines-West airfield.	Messerschmitt Bf 109E	60 %	Pilot unhurt.
96.	Stab/JG 53	NCM	Landing accident at Rennes airfield; not combat.	Junkers Ju 52/3m	15 %	No casualties.

[(1) In the dive bombing attack on the Poling CH radar station at 14.12 hrs the evidence of combat nd victory claims is tenuous, though better than circumstantial. The order and manner in which losses were reported through 6th *Abteilung* staffs is consistent with losses suffered by nine *Staffeln* within the three *Gruppen* of *Stukageschwader* 77. It is also apparent from analysis of the chronolgy (*sic*)of losses and claims in relation to crash sites shows that I.*Gruppe* struck first, and suffered accordingly. However, only one aircraft's destruction can with any certainty be attributed to a specific R.A.F. pilot. German records refer to the target as Littlehampton, (three miles from the Poling CH station.)]

Monday 19th August

The results of the grim air battles of 15th, 16th and 18th August were far-reaching, though indecisive—apart from the crushing defeat of the Stuka. On three out of four days the *Luftwaffe* had lost more than fifty aircraft in a single day, and despite sanguine claims by the combat units it was clear to Göring that little lasting impression had yet been made on Fighter Command's strength. For the second time in a week Göring summoned his *Luftflotte* commanders away from the battlefield and forcefully expressed his contempt for their failure to produce the spectacular results of previous campaigns.

He faced his *Jagdgeschwader Kommodore* with the heavy bomber losses and attributed these to a lack of aggression on the part of the fighter forces—no doubt quoting certain instances in which they had apparently failed to cover the vulnerable Ju 87s. Such criticisms were scarcely justified, for the nature of the Stukas' diving tactics made close escort virtually impossible to achieve. Furthermore, apart from the psychological strain of flying single-seat fighters over the sea, there was a growing tendency among the bomber hierarchy to demand close escort for sorties against targets at the fighters' extreme range, so that at best they could scarcely afford to linger with the ponderous bomber formations. Time and again German fighter pilots had to disengage from air combat so as to have some chance of reaching their bases before their fuel ran out—and scarcely a pilot did not experience the harrowing ordeal of watching a fuel warning light indicate that his tanks were almsot dry, with miles of sea yet to cross.

The Reichsmarschall's petulant ranting begged the question. His blind faith in the *Zerstörer*—the Messerschmitt Bf 110 and the Junkers Ju 88C—was unshaken, and their losses only provided fuel for his criticism of their crews' incompetence. He would brook no argument and refused to accept that the weakness lay in faulty planning concepts—that both the Bf 110 and Ju 87 were critically vulnerable in the presence of Hurricanes and Spitfires. Forthrightly he ordered a complete re-organisation and re-deployment of the *Jagdgeschwader*, dismissing several *Kommodore* whom he regarded as too old or lacking in fighting *élan*, and appointing in their place "the young Turks"—men like Galland, Trautloft, Lützow and Schellmann.[56] Brushing aside their objections that the fault lay in shackling the Bf 109s as close escort instead of allowing them free rein, he went further and demanded even closer attendance upon the bombers. It must have been obvious to these accomplished pilots that, in the *Luftwaffe*'s principal task of defeating Fighter Command, it was to the guns of free-chasing Bf 109s that the great majority of British casualties were falling. *This was the first critical error committed by the Luftwaffe High Command.*

While voicing the belief that the pilots were to blame, Göring could hardly ignore the serious rising scale of casualties—whatever the reason—and ordered the Ju 87 to be omitted from all main-raid operations and conserved for close-support duties when the invasion was launched. Another decree issued at this time forbade the inclusion of more than a single commissioned officer in each aircraft's crew (although photo and maritime reconnaissance units were exempt from this edict)—ten days' fighting had, after all, cost the *Luftwaffe* one *Geschwaderkommodore*, two *Fliegerkorps* Chiefs of Staff, seven *Gruppenkommandeure*, thirteen *Staffelkapitäne* and 149 other officers killed, seriously wounded or missing.

In the matter of the Bf 110, Göring did not bother to offer any truly constructive remedy, other than to instruct senior operations officers to allocate Bf 109s to cover the *Zerstörer*—an extraordinary expedient of providing the escort itself with an escort. This was of course in itself an admission of failure. Moreover it placed an intolerable strain upon the Bf 109 units—so much so that units were withdrawn from other theatres (for example JG 77 from Scandinavia) to bolster the forces on the Channel Coast.

Concluding his tirade, Göring gave free rein to his *Luftflotte* Staffs to select their own targets—reserving for himself the sole right of sanction for raids upon London and Liverpool; each sanction was to be given with increasing frequency during the next two months.

With the benefit of long hindsight, and the knowledge of operational policy on both sides, it is possible to detect the seeds of defeat for the *Luftwaffe* at this meeting between Göring and his field commanders. Royal Air Force Fighter Command as yet had suffered no catastrophic weakening of its system of defence; indeed it was frustrating the day-by-

---

[56] Long term results were to vindicate the policy of rapid promotion of junior flight leaders to positions of responsibility; nevertheless, it should not be assumed that Göring's opinions of the command qualities of the men they replaced were justified. More than one had been wounded in combat shortly before this "reshuffle".

day efforts of the *Luftwaffe* to overwhelm the defences, no matter how powerful the raiding formations. However, any fundamental shift in the *Luftwaffe*'s offensive tactics could be decisive, one way or the other, such was the fine balance between success and failure. Such was the ill-considered and turbulent nature of Göring's command of his Air Force that he had already on more than one occasion flouted the time-honoured principles of war, and paid the traditional penalty.

No one was more conscious of this balance of fortunes than Dowding and Park, and Fighter Command was also carrying out a reappraisal of the battle situation on 19th August, for now sufficient experience had been gained during ten days' heavy fighting to assess the enemy's apparent strategy and tactics. In some instances the fighter forces had fallen prey to enemy tactics and had suffered accordingly, and as it was now clear that the main weight of attacks had switched from the coastal shipping as a means of attracting British fighters into the air and was now directed against the defence system itself, Park drafted and issued a new Instruction, No. 4, for the guidance of No. 11 Group Sector Controllers:

(a) Despatch fighters to engage large enemy formations over land or within gliding distance of the coast. During the next two or three weeks we cannot afford to lose pilots through forced landings in the sea.

(b) Avoid sending fighters out over the sea to chase reconnaissance aircraft or small formations of enemy fighters.

(c) Despatch a pair of fighters to intercept single reconnaissance aircraft that come inland. If clouds are favourable, put a patrol of one or two fighters over an aerodrome which enemy aircraft are approaching in clouds.

(d) Against mass attacks coming inland despatch a minimum number of squadrons to engage enemy fighters. Our main objective is to engage enemy bombers, particularly those approaching under the lowest cloud layer.

(e) If all our squadrons around London are off the ground engaging enemy mass attacks, ask No. 12 Group or Command Controller to provide squadrons to protect Debden, North Weald and Hornchurch aerodromes.

(f) If heavy attacks have crossed the coast and are proceeding towards aerodromes, put a squadron, or even a sector training flight, to patrol under clouds over each sector aerodrome.

(g) No. 303 (Polish) Squadron can provide two sections for patrol of inland aerodromes, especially while the older squadrons are on the ground refuelling, when enemy formations are flying over land.

(h) No. 1 (Canadian) Squadron can be used in the same manner by day as other fighter squadrons.

In contrast to the previous day, 19th August was mainly cloudy, and although several large formations of enemy aircraft were reported assembling over the Pas de Calais and further west, it is likely that the *Luftwaffe* was anticipating favourable weather reports from the dozen reconnaissance aircraft previousaly despatched. In any event the only major formations to approach the English coast (about one hundred Bf 109s of Osterkamp's *Jafu 2* from the Pas de Calais) between mid-day and 13.00 hours were ignored by the defences. Further to the west Sperrle sent thirty escorted Junkers Ju 88s of KG 51 to the Southampton area, while other aircraft of the same *Geschwader* attacked Pembroke Dock and set several oil storage tanks on fire. Accompanying the latter raid were several Ju 88s which bypassed the targets in South Wales and carried on up the Bristol Channel, fanning out in the Bristol and Gloucester area. The airfield at Bibury, which was used by a night flying detachment from No. 92 Squadron, was strafed by a lone raider which destroyed one Spitfire, damaged another and killed an airman. Rushing out to their aircraft, Flt. Lt. Trevor Wade and Flt. Lt. James Peterson took off in hot pursuit and finally shot the Junkers down over the Solent. Wade's aircraft was badly hit by return fire and he had hurriedly to force land nearby—only just getting clear before it blew up[57].

In return for a fairly heavy day's flying Fighter Command only managed to destroy four enemy aircraft, although German casualties from other causes were surprising high, and the crack pathfinder unit, *Kampfgruppe 100*, suffered three aircraft casualties—two from crashes following fuel shortage.

[57] Universally known as "Wimpey", Wade was later to become Chief Test Pilot with Hawker Aircraft Ltd., but lost his life in a flying accident on 3rd April 1951.

R.A.F. FIGHTER COMMAND LOSSES—MONDAY 19th AUGUST 1940

1.	1 Sqn., Northolt	C	Struck balloon cable during night patrol; pilot abandoned aircraft at Finsbury Park.	At night	Not known	Hurricane	P3684	Cat. 3 Destroyed
2.	66 Sqn., Coltishall	C	Shot down by He 111 off East Coast; pilot baled out but drowned.	A18.10 hrs.	Plt. Off J.A.P. Studd	Spitfire	N3182	Cat. 3 Lost
3.	92 Sqn., Bibury	—	Destroyed in raid by Ju 88 on Bibury; no pilot casualties.	14.40 hrs.	Nil	Spitfire	—	Cat. 3 Burnt
4.	92 Sqn., Bibury	—	Damaged in the above raid; no casualties.	14.40 hrs.	Nil	Spitfire	—	Cat.1 Damaged
5.	92 Sqn., Bibury	—	Damaged in the above raid; no casualties.	14.40 hrs.	Nil	Spitfire	—	Cat. 1 Damaged
6.	92 Sqn., Bibury	—	Damaged in the above raid; no casualties.	14.30 hrs.	Nil	Spitifre	—	Cat. 1 Damaged
7.	92 Sqn., Bibury	C	Shot down by Ju 88 over Solent; force landed and exploded; pilot got clear, unhurt.	15.20 hrs.	Plt. Off. T.S. Wade	Spitfire	R6703	Cat. 3 Destroyed
8.	248 Sqn., Sumburgh	C	Missing from reconniassance sortie over Norwegian coast; crew missing.	Not known	Sgt. J.H. Round Sgt. W.H. Want Sgt. M.P. Digby-Worsley	Blenheim	—	Cat. 3 Missing
9.	602 Sqn., Westhampnett	C	Shot down by Ju 88 near Westhampnett; pilot baled out with burns to hands.	14.28 hrs.	Plt. Off. H.M. Moody	Spitfire	P9423	Cat. 3 Destroyed

LUFTWAFFE LOSSES—MONDAY 19th AUGUST 1940

1.	4.(F)/121	CM	Landing accident at Condé; cause not known.	Junkers Ju 88A-1	90 %	Ltn. Bürkow + three wounded.
2.	7./KG 2	CM	Shot down by 19 Sqn. Spitfires over Essex at 18.40 hrs.	Dornier Do 17Z-2	100 %	Ltn. Hamp + three missing.
3.	II./KG 4	NCM	Crashed near Heringsdorf; not result of combat.	Heinkel He 111P-2	100 %	Oblt. Steiner + three killed.
4.	III./KG 27	CM	Target Liverpool. Shot down by 66 Sqn. Spitfire of Studd off East Coast at 18.10 hrs.	Heinkel He 111P	100 %	One killed; Oblt. Siegel + two missing.
5.	I./KG 51	CM	Damaged near St. Catherine's Point by Spitfires of 602 Sqn. at 16.45 hrs. Force landed at Caen.	Junkers Ju 88A-1	10—60 %	Crew unhurt.
6.	7./KG 51	CM	Shot down by 92 Sqn. Spitfires of Paterson and Wade over the Solent at 15.20 hrs. Aircraft had attacked Bibury.	Junkers Ju 88A-1 (7069 : 9K+FR)	100 %	Fw. Max Schachtner, Fw. Haag, Fw. Bachauer and Fw. Johann Moser killed.
7.	KGr. 100	CM	Night pathfinding over Midlands. Force landed at Vertou, short of fuel.	Heinkel He 111H-3	80 %	Ltn. Zetzsche + one wounded.
8.	KGr. 100	CM	Night pathfinding over Midlands. Crashed near Crozon with *flak* damage and engine failure.	Heinkel He 111H-2	100 %	Crew unhurt.
9.	KGr. 100	CM	Night pathfinding over Midlands. Force landed at Les Sables, short of fuel.	Heinkel He 111H-2	10—60 %	Crew unhurt.
10.	4./JG 3	NCM	Crash landed at Brombes; cause not known.	Messerschmitt BF 109E	70 %	Pilot unhurt.
11.	5./196	NCM	Crashed in bad weather in Molderfjord, Norway.	Arado Ar 196	100 %	Ltn.z.S. Burk + one killed.
12.	5./196	NCM	Struck HT cable while searching for Item 11.	Arado Ar 196	100 %	Ltn.z.S. Hirschberg + one killed.
13.	Seenotflug-kommando 4	NCM	Crashed at Bergen, Norway; cause not known.	Heinkel He 59	100 %	Ltn. Jahnke + two killed. One wounded.

Scenes on a *Luftwaffe* fighter airfield; these snapshots of the pilots and aircraft of 3./JG 1 were in fact taken shortly after the end of the Battle, but are typical of the period. The pilots sprawling on the grass with dogs and deck chairs while awaiting further orders underline the similarity between life on operational squadrons in the *Luftwaffe* and R.A.F. Fighter Command during the Battle of Britain. The close-ups (*right*) show a certain Uffz. Schubert posing for pictures in his Bf 109E-4. The grinning pilot at *bottom left* points to a patched bullet hole; the practice of marking such patches with the insignia of the enemy who made them necessary dated from the First World War. (Photo: Hans Obert)

Tuesday 20th August

Throughout the hours of darkness the long-range German bombers had kept up a steady stream of flights across the southern half of Britain. Heinkel He 111 crews of KG 27 were briefed to attack the Liverpool docks (with Göring's sanction) and at least 30 tracks were reported over Lincolnshire and Nottinghamshire. Some of these crews did not persevere right across the country, preferring to unload their bombs on Bomber Command's flarepaths exposed for returning British bombers; five such airfields were hit and six bombers destroyed. Apart from Liverpool (attacked by twelve Heinkels), Sheffield, Nottingham, Hull, Derby and Leicester were raided by small numbers, and in these towns and cities a total of 112

casualties were reported. Night fighter Blenheims were active but without exception their rudimentary radar equipment was unequal to the task of locating the enemy, and many a frustrated crew retired to bed at dawn.

A further deterioration in the weather reduced German air activity during daylight on the 20th. The morning was spent in sending reconnaissance aircraft over the Home Counties and South Midlands. The difficult cloud conditions gave these aircraft adequate protection from Fighter Command, and a number of important targets were photographed—including the Spitfire repair depot at Cowley, Oxford, and the Morris Radiator Works in North Oxford. It is one of the mysteries of the period that neither was subsequently attacked. The burning oil tanks at Pembroke Dock attracted a small number of raiders shortly before mid-day, though most of their bombs fell wide.

Curiosity as to the state of repair of No. 11 Group's fighter airfields brought a dozen reconnaissance aircraft over the stations in the South-East, and again it is clear from targets covered that German Intelligence was not yet aware of what airfields were vital to the defence system. Notwithstanding, *Erprobungsgruppe 210*, led by its new commander Hauptmann von Boltenstern, launched an attack on Martlesham, and although the raid clearly took the defences by surprise, many of the bombs fell outside the airfield perimeter. Flt. Lt. Kenneth Gillies of No. 66 Squadron from Coltishall, leading six Spitfires, caught the Bf 110s as they sped for home and shot one down.

It was at 14.20 hours that a formation of enemy bombers (27 Dornier Do 17s of KG 3 escorted by about 30 Bf 109s of I./JG 51) was reported flying up the Thames Estuary. Possibly as the result of the morning's heavy reconnaissance activity and in anticipation of afternoon raids, Park's Controllers had maintained a high state of readiness so that within eight minutes more than 40 fighters from six squadrons had scrambled. The Hurricanes of No. 615 Squadron were first in action, Sqn. Ldr. Joseph Kayll and Plt. Off. Brian Young destroying a Dornier of 9./KG 3 over its target at Eastchurch. As the escorting Bf 109s entered the fray, Flt. Lt. Gerald Saunders led six Spitfires of No. 65 Squadron into action and harried the raiders in their withdrawal along the North Kent coast. Although German records only mention the loss of three aircraft, it is clear from prisoners taken that two other Bf 109s and a Dornier also fell at this time[58].

A significant combat was fought later on this day off the Yorkshire coast when six Hurricanes of No. 302 (Polish) Squadron shot down a Junkers Ju 88 of 8./KG 30. This Polish fighter squadron had been declared operational two days previously at Leconfield, and it had been only with the greatest difficulty that its British C.O., Sqn. Ldr. Bill Satchell, had restrained the vengeful Poles from flying south in search of German aircraft. In this action Satchell led his formation on a patrol off Flamborough Head and spotted the Junkers flying at only 3,000 feet, and shot it down into the sea six miles

Hauptmann Otto Bertram, a former *Legion Cóndor* veteran with eight Spanish victories to his name, commanded III.*Gruppe*, JG 2 <*Richthofen*> during the Battle of Britain. "Otsch" was subsequently withdrawn from combat flying as a "last surviving son" under the unique German regulation after his brothers Hans and Kurt died in action as fighter pilots on the Channel Front. (Photo: *Gemeinschaft der Jagdflieger E.V.*)

south-west of Withernsea. The crew of four was rescued and made prisoner. It transpired that the enemy aircraft had been coast-hopping northwards to attack the airfield at Thornaby.

It was during this relative lull in the Battle that Winston Churchill chose to immortalise the handful of Allied pilots in their ordeal, rising in the House of Commons to announce:

> "The gratitude of every home in our Island, in our Empire, and indeed thoughout the world, except in the abodes of the guilty, goes out to the British airmen who, undaunted by odds, unwearied in their constant challenge and mortal danger, are turning the tide of world war by their prowess and devotion. Never in the field of human conflict was so much owed by so many to so few."

---

[58] Though by no means conclusive, the capture of these airmen suggests that bombs which fell at West Malling and Manston at about this time were dropped by Dorniers of KG 2, and that a free chase mounted by another *Gruppe* of JG 51 was intended to cover the withdrawal of the two bomber formations.

On an English beach, oily smoke riseas in a pall from a bullet-riddled Dornier Do 17Z of *Kampfgeschwader 3*.

R.A.F. FIGHTER COMMAND LOSSES—TUESDAY 20th AUGUST 1940

1.	65 Sqn., Rochford	C	Shot down by Bf 109s over Thames Estuary; pilot rescued unhurt from the sea.	A15.20 hrs.	Plt. Off. K.G. Hart	Spitfire	—	Cat. 3 Lost
2.	242 Sqn., Coltishall	C?	Crashed into sea 5 miles off Winterton during patrol; pilot killed.	A15.30 hrs	Midshipman P.J. Patterson	Hurricane	P2976	Cat. 3 Lost
3.	600 Sqn., Manston	—	Damaged in raid on Manston; no aircrew casualties.	15.00 hrs.	Nil	Blenheim	—	Cat. 2 Damaged

LUFTWAFFE LOSSES—TUESDAY 20th AUGUST 1940

1.	7./KG 2	CM	Damaged by 257 Sqn. Hurricane of Mitchell off Southwold at A.18.20 hrs.	Dornier Do 17Z-2	25 %	One crew member wounded.
2.	9./KG 2	CM	Shot down by 65 Sqn. Spitfires and 257 Sqn. Hurricanes near Eastchurch at 15.05 hrs.	Dornier Do 17Z-3	100 %	Two wounded, P.O.W.s, and
3.	9./KG 3	CM	Shot down by 615 Sqn. Hurricanes of Kayll and Young at Eastchurch at 15.09 hrs.	Dornier Do 17Z-3	100 %	One killed; three missing.
4.	III./KG 27	NCM	Crashed near Rennes airfield; cause not known.	Heinkel He 111	100 %	Four crew members killed.
5.	8./KG 30	CM	Target Thornaby. Shot down by 302 Sqn. Hurricane of Satchell six miles SW of Withernsea.	Junkers Ju 88A-1	100 %	Four crew made P.O.W.
6.	I./KG 40	CM	Missing from sortie off Northern Ireland; fate not known.	Focke-Wulf Fw 200	100 %	Oblt. Mollenhauser, Reg.Rat.Dr. Krüger + four others missing.
7.	III./KG 77	NCM	Landing accident at Obertraubling airfield.	Junkers Ju 88A-1	30 %	Crew unhurt.
8.	2./Erpr.Gr. 210	CM	Target convoy off Aldeburgh. Shot down by 66 Sqn. Spitfire of Gillies at A.11.00 hrs.	Messerschmitt Bf 110D	100 %	Both crew members missing.
9.	II./JG 27	NCM	Landing accident at Carquebut airfield.	Messerschmitt Bf 109E	70 %	Pilot unhurt.
10.	1./JG 51	CM	Shot down by 615 Sqn. Hurricane of Lofts near Eastchurch at 14.59 hrs.	Messerschmitt Bf 109 E-4	100 %	Pilot missing.
11.	I./JG 53	CM	Landing accident at Rennes. Not combat.	Messerschmitt Bf 109E	35 %	Pilot unhurt.
12.	5./196	—	Damaged by storm at Narvik; beached and salvaged.	Arado Ar 196 (0073 : 6W+QN)	20 %	No crew casualties.
13.	5./196	—	Destroyed in storm at Narvik. No salvage attempted.	Arado Ar 196 (0056 : 6W+IN)	100 %	No crew casualties.
14.	Seenotflug-kommando 3	NCM	Damaged in take-off accident in mid-Channel.	Heinkel He 59	50 %	Crew unhurt.

Wednesday 21st August

There is little doubt that Göring's demand for re-organisation of the *Luftwaffe*'s fighter arm was to some extent disrupting the operations of *Luftflotten 2* and *3*. The promotion of three fighter *Gruppenkommandeure* led to *Staffelkapitäne* being promoted to command *Gruppen*, while steps were already being taken to re-deploy certain fighter units. Major Schellmann's *Jagdgeschwader 2* received orders to leave the Cherbourg Peninsula and integrate with *Jafu 2* in the Pas de Calais. Oberst Werner Junck, commanding *Jafu 3*, was himself about to be ordered to transfer his headquarters from Cherbourg to Wissant under the command of Kesselring. Whether this deployment already foreshadowed a German intention to commence heavy raiding of London is open to conjecture; what is unarguable is that, in obeying Göring's directive to concentrate his single-engine fighter forces (by implication in the Pas de Calais), the comparative scarcity of such fighters in *Luftflotte 3* resulted in a sharp increase in losses among the *Zerstörergeschwader* when the *Luftwaffe* launched daylight raids over South-East Engalnd in September.

The continuing poor weather over Britain gave added justification for the low scale of effort by the *Luftwaffe*. It was nevertheless important to give the R.A.F. as little respite as possible, and both Sperrle and Kesselring ordered scattered raids over a wide front, each to be carried out by not more than about three aircraft. One such raid was flown by three Dornier Do 17s of II./KG 3 over Norfolk, the formation penetrating to the airfield at Horsham St. Faith before being detected. Forthwith two sections of No. 611 Squadron's Spitfires were scrambled from Digby, but owing to the apparently aimless behaviour of the German formation it was difficult to vector the fighters accurately, and it took more than an hour to find and destroy all three aircraft.

At just about the same time in the far West, the airfield at St. Eval was under attack by a single Junkers Ju 88, which dropped six bombs, one of which destroyed the hangar. Although Hurricane pilots of No. 238 Squadron took off and gave chase, this raider escaped. Retribution was exacted later when three Hurricanes (flown by Plt. Off. John Urwin-Mann, Plt. Off. John Wigglesworth and Flt. Lt. Minden Blake) came across three Ju 88s of *Kampfgruppe 806* off Trevose Head and destroyed two of them[59]. A chart which was subsequently washed ashore with wreckage from one of these aircraft indicated that their targets included Newquay (which had been raided the night before) and Penzance.

---

[59] The inclusion of naval officers among the crews of the above aircraft (see loss tables for this date) is evidence of *Kampfgruppe 806*'s coastal attack rôle, its designation having only recently been changed from that of a *Küstenfliegergruppe*.

R.A.F. FIGHTER COMMAND LOSSES—WEDNESDAY 21st AUGUST 1940

1.	56 Sqn., North Weald	C	Shot down by Do 17 and burned in force landing; pilot slightly burned.	18.32 hrs.	Fg. Off. R.E.P. Brooker	Hurricane	P3153	Cat. 3 Burnt
2.	236 Sqn., St. Eval	—	Destroyed in raid on St. Eval; no casualties.	13.52 hrs.	Nil	Blenheim	—	Cat. 3 Destroyed
3.	236 Sqn., St. Eval	—	Destroyed in raid on St. Eval; no casualties.	13.52 hrs.	Nil	Blenheim	—	Cat. 3 Destroyed
4.	236 Sqn., St. Eval	—	Destroyed in raid on St. Eval; no casualties.	13.52 hrs.	Nil	Blenheim	—	Cat. 3 Destroyed
5.	236 Sqn., St. Eval	—	Damaged in raid on St. Eval; no casualties.	13.52 hrs.	Nil	Blenheim	—	Cat. 2 Damaged

R.A.F. Losses, 21st August 1940—*continued*

6.	236 Sqn., St. Eval	—	Damaged in raid on St. Eval; no casualties.	13.52 hrs.	Nil	Blenheim	—	Cat. 2 Damaged
7.	236 Sqn., St. Eval	—	Damaged in raid on St. Eval; no casualties.	13.52 hrs.	Nil	Blenheim	—	Cat. 2 Damaged
8.	604 Sqn., Middle Wallop	—	Damaged in raid on Middle Wallop; no aircrew casualties.	Not known	Nil	Blenheim	—	Cat. 2 Damaged
9.	611 Sqn., Digby	C	Damaged by Do 215 near Downham Market; pilot unhurt.	12.35 hrs.	Fg. Off. D.H. Watkins	Spitfire	P7290	Cat. 1 Damaged
10.	611 Sqn., Digby	C	Damaged by Do 215 near Downham Market; pilot unhurt.	12.35 hrs.	Plt. Off. J.W. Lund	Spitfire	P7303	Cat. 1 Damaged
11.	611 Sqn., Digby	C	Damaged by Do 215 near Downham Market; pilot unhurt.	12.35 hrs.	Plt. Off. M.P. Brown	Spitfire	P7304	Cat. 1 Damaged
12.	611 Sqn., Digby	C	Damaged by Do 17 off Mablethorpe; pilot unhurt.	13.45 hrs.	Sgt. A.D. Burt	Spitfire	P7314	Cat. 2 Damaged
13.	611 Sqn., Digby	(C)	Landing accident (chock on runway) after the above combat; pilot unhurt.	14.21 hrs.	Sgt. A.S. Darling	Spitfire	P7305	Cat. 1 Damaged

LUFTWAFFE LOSSES—WEDNESDAY 21st AUGUST 1940

1.	2./KG 2	CM	Missing from sortie over England; fate unknown.	Dornier Do 17Z-3	100 %	Ltn. Ermecke killed; three missing.
2.	8./KG 2	CM	Shot down by 56 Sqn. Hurricane of Brooker at 18.20 hrs. near Ipswich.	Dornier Do 17Z-3	100 %	Ltn. Kzienzyk + three missing.
3.	4./KG 3	CM	Shot down by 242 Sqn. Hurricane of Gardner near Norwich at A.12.20 hrs.	Dornier Do 17Z-3	100 %	Two killed and two missing.
4.	6./KG 3	CM	Shot down by 611 Sqn. Spitfires of McComb, Burt and Darling near Mablethorpe at 13.40 hrs.	Dornier Do 17Z-2	100 %	Two killed; one wounded. Oblt. Matschoss missing.
5.	6./KG 3	CM	Shot down by 611 Sqn. Spitfires of Watkins, Lund and Brown 8 miles north of Burnham Market at 12.35 hrs.	Dornier Do 17Z-3	100 %	Ltn. Krüger + three killed.
6.	6./KG 3	CM	Shot down by 611 Sqn. Spitfires of McComb, Burt and Darling near Mablethorpe at 13.46 hrs.	Dornier Do 17Z-3	100 %	Oblt. Schwartz, *St.Kap.*, + three made P.O.W.s.
7.	9./KG 30	CM	Target Edinburgh; shot down by A.A. defences.	Junkers Ju 88A-1	100 %	Five crew members missing.
8.	9./KG 30	CM	Landing accident at Aalborg airfield, Denmark.	Junkers Ju 88A-1	15 %	Crew unhurt.
9.	III./KG 53	NCM	Missing from sortie over England; fate unknown.	Heinkel He 111H-2	100 %	Hptm.Pfeiffer,*St.Kap.*, + four missing.
10.	I./KG 54	CM	Shot down by 234 Sqn. Spitfires of Doe, Page and O'Brien off Cornish coast at 13.20 hrs.	Junkers Ju 88A-1	100 %	Oblt. Birkenstock + three missing.
11.	II./KG 54	CM	Shot down by 17 Sqn. Hurricane of Bird-Wilson off the Isle of Wight during afternoon.	Junkers Ju 88A-1	100 %	Ltn. Kiefer + three missing.
12.	II./KG 54	CM	Shot down by 17 Sqn. Hurricane of Czernin, Chew and Bartless off I.O.W. during afternoon.	Junkers Ju 88A-1	100 %	Hptm. Mainwald + three missing.
13.	KGr. 806	CM	Shot down by 238 Sqn. Hurricane of Urwin-Mann off Trevose Head, Cornwall, at 17.30 hrs.	Junkers Ju 88A-1	100 %	Ltn.z.S.von Davidson + three missing.
14.	KGr. 806	CM	Shot down by 238 Sqn. Hurricane of Blake off Trevose Head, Cornwall, at A.17.30 hrs.	Junkers Ju 88A-1	100 %	Ltn.z.S. Miehr + two missing; one
15.	1./NJG 1	NCM	Accident due to brake failure on Bonninghardt airfield.	Messerschmitt Bf 110	60 %	Crew unhurt.
16.	II./JG 54	NCM	Engine failure on Xaffevillers airfield.	Messerschmitt Bf 109 E-3	5 %	Pilot unhurt.
17.	7./JG 54	CM	Landing accident at Vlissingen airfield; not the result of combat.	Messerschmitt Bf 109 E-1	20 %	Pilot unhurt.
18.	III./JG 54	NCM	Take-off accident at Guines-Süd airfield.	Messerschmitt Bf 109 E-4	70 %	Pilot unhurt.

Junkers Ju 88A bomber, believed to be that flown by Hauptmann Schaumann, a *Staffelführer* on III./LG 1; it was shot down by anti-aircraft fire near Portsmouth during 22nd August. Although all four crew members were listed as Missing, it is thought that all four were taken prisoner unhurt.

Thursday 22nd August

Park's reference in his instructions of 19th August to the loss of fighter pilots through drowning had brought forth a number of observations by his squadron commanders—at least five of whom had experienced landings in the sea, and who had been lucky to survive. The point they made was that too much *luck* was involved in rescuing pilots from the sea. It

An air/sea rescue Westland Lysander of No. 277 Squadron. Army Co-operation Lysanders were diverted to these duties during late August. Note the smoke floats carried on racks under the rear fuselage, used to mark the position of airmen in the water for the benefit of rescue launches.

must be remarked that in all the planning that had gone into the air defence of the island nation, virtually nothing had been done to provide an organisation to rescue pilots from the sea, apart from providing a limited rescue capability within Coastal Command. Traditionally, the British sought to rely upon the long-established, voluntary life-boat service which, magnificent though its record was, was clearly inadequate to provide extensive search facilities for ditched airmen. It was on 22nd August that Air Marshal Harris[60] chaired an Air Ministry conference to outline the basis of an R.A.F. air/sea rescue organisation embracing the use of suitable aircraft for search purposes (elements of two Lysander squadrons were transferred from army co-operation duties and stationed on airfields in the South) and organise the re-deployment of range and rescue launches at frequent intervals around the South and East Coasts. These launches would join those of the Naval Auxiliary Patrol under local naval control. Although these measures were put into immediate effect, their benefit to Fighter Command was scarcely felt during the Battle; however, they did result in the rescue of a dozen of so bomber crews (British *and* German) from the Channel.

August 22nd was notable for the outbreak of shelling by the heavy gun battery installed by the Germans near Cap Gris Nez. The passage of convoy TOTEM through the Dover Strait between 08.00 and 09.00 hours had been noted by the battery crews and about one hundred shells were fired—without scoring a hit. To the ships' crews, unaware that they were under shellfire, it appeared that the convoy was under air attack by aircraft flying above the cloud base, and they reported accordingly. Hurricanes of No. 32 Squadron were

scrambled from Biggin Hill, but of course encountered nothing. Perhaps, fittingly, five aircraft from the same squadron were sent off in the evening to escort an Anson engaged in spotting for the British guns at Dover which carried out a forty-minute retaliatory bombardment.

Frustrated by the guns' failure to damage convoy TOTEM, Kesselring despatched a light striking force composed of *Erprobungsgruppe 210*'s Bf 110s with an escort of 27 Bf 109s to attack the ships soon after mid-day. Interference by Nos. 54 and 610 Squadrons' Spitfires upset the purpose of the fighter-bombers, although the latter squadron was itself "bounced" by the German top cover, which shot down Sgt. Douglas Corfe; he managed to reach Hawkinge where he put down—only just getting clear of the aircraft before it blew up. Sgt. George Collett of No. 54 Squadron was, however, shot down and killed off Deal.

As if to make up for his failure to damage the convoy, von Boltenstern led *Erprobungsgruppe 210* to Manston at 18.50 hours in the evening under cover of two flanking free chases over Dover and Herne Bay. Following the depredations of previous raids, No. 600 Squadron (with Blenheim night fighters) had been withdrawn from Manston to Hornchurch on 21st August, and when the Messerschmitts swept in from the sea, over Manston's East Camp, the squadron's ground personnel were still engaged in loading stores and equipment into lorries. The half dozen heavy bombs dropped struck hangars, radio stores and squadron offices; but the station personnel, by now well aware of the need for quick reactions, had scattered with commendable speed and gone to ground. There were no casualties.

No. 616 Squadron, which had scrambled the unusually large number of fourteen Spitfires at 18.45 hours, arrived over Dover just as the second free chase was about to leave the Kent coast, and was bounced by about a dozen Bf 109s whose guns claimed Fg. Off. Hugh Dundas' aircraft, wounding the pilot in the leg and arm.

As the evening light faded, the coastal radar stations reported numerous enemy aircraft approaching the coast in small extended groups. Daylight reconnaissance by the Germans had disclosed the presence of a small convoy (code-named TOPAZ) off the Scottish coast, and this came under attack by five Ju 88s of KG 30, but no hits were scored. At the other end of the country another Ju 88 visited St. Eval and scored a lucky hit on the pyrotechnics store; the effect was startling as all manner of flares and rockets exploded in the darkness. No doubt the German crew considered they had obliterated the airfield! Scattered bombing was reported in eleven counties, but fewer than thirty casualties were reported.

---

[60] Later Marshal of the Royal Air Force Sir Arthur Harris, Bomber Command's famous Commander-in-Chief.

R.A.F. FIGHTER COMMAND LOSSES—THURSDAY 22nd AUGUST 1940

1.	32 Sqn., Hawkinge	NC	Landing accident at Hawkinge; pilot unhurt.	09.45 hrs.	Plt. Off. J.P. Pfeiffer	Hurricane	*P3205*	Cat. 3 Destroyed
2.	54 Sqn., Hornchurch	C	Shot down by Messerschmitts off Deal; pilot killed; buried at Bergen-op-Zoom, Holland.	A13.00 hrs.	Sgt. G.R. Collett	Spitfire	*R6708*	Cat. 3 Lost
3.	65 Sqn., Manston	C	Shot down by Bf 109s near Dover; pilot killed; buried at Bazinghen, France.	A19.20 hrs.	Sgt. M. Keymer	Spitfire	*K9909*	Cat. 3 Missing
4.	152 Sqn., Warmwell	C	Damaged by Ju 88 off The Needles; pilot unhurt.	16.50 hrs.	Plt. Off. R.M. Hogg	Spitfire	—	Cat. 1 Damaged
5.	610 Sqn., Biggin Hill	C	Shot down by Bf 109s near Folkestone and crashed near Hawkinge; pilot unhurt.	A13.15 hrs.	Sgt. D.F. Corfe	Spitfire	*R6695*	Cat. 3 Destroyed
6.	615 Sqn., Kenley	(C)	Believed damaged by another Hurricane near Deal; pilot unhurt.	A13.30 hrs.	Plt. Off. D.H. Hone	Hurricane	—	Cat. 2 Damaged
7.	616 Sqn., Kenley	C	Shot down by Bf 109s near Dover; pilot baled out slightly wounded in leg and arm.	A19.30 hrs.	Fg. Off. H.S.L. Dundas	Spitfire	—	Cat. 3 Destroyed

LUFTWAFFE LOSSES—THURSDAY 22nd AUGUST 1940

1.	3.(F)/121	CM	Shot down by 152 Sqn. Spitfires of Cox, Hogg and Holmes off the Needles at A.17.10 hrs.	Junkers Ju 88A-1	100 %	Ltn. Baudler + two mising; one killed.
2.	1./KG 2	CM	Crashed at Escoudreuvres. Cause not known.	Dornier Do 17Z-2	100 %	Hptm. von Winterfeld + three killed.
3.	7./KG 30	CM	Damaged by 302 Sqn. Hurricanes off Yorkshire coast, and further damaged on landing.	Junkers Ju 88A-1	20 %	Crew unhurt.
4.	8./KG 30	CM	Damaged by 302 Sqn. Hurricanes off Yorkshire coast; further damaged on landing at Aalborg.	Junkers Ju 88A-1	20 %	Crew unhurt.
5.	III./LG 1	CM	Shot down by 213 Sqn. Hurricane of Phillipart near Portsmouth.	Junkers Ju 88A-1	100 %	Hptm. Schaumann, *Staffelführer*, + three missing.
6.	5./JG 52	NCM	Crashed on Stade airfield; cause not known.	Messerschmitt Bf 109E	100 %	Pilot killed.
7.	1./NJG 1	NCM	Landing accident at Bonninghardt airfield.	Messerschmitt Bf 110	50 %	Oblt. Berger + one injured.
8.	Seenotflugkdo.3	—	Damaged by storm and high seas at Boulogne.	Heinkel He 59	50 %	No aircrew casualties.
9.	Seenotflugkdo.3	—	Damaged by storm and high seas at Boulogne.	Heinkel He 59	50 %	No aircrew casualties.

Friday 23rd August

While weather forecasters on both sides waited for the extension of a massive anti-cyclone from the Azores to bring fine weather to the British Isles, conditions over Northern Europe were still unsuitable for widespread daylight raids. Manston was again bombed and although low cloud interfered with the raiders' aim, four bombs which fell just outside the station smashed the main telephone lines (both operational and domestic) and burst a sewer.

In the far North, following accurate radar reporting, a lone weather reconnaissance Heinkel He 111 was caught by three Spitfires of No. 232 Squadron (flown by Flt. Lt. Michael Stephens, Plt. Off. Joseph Hobbs and Plt. Off. Charles Jefferies) and shot down eight miles west of Fair Isle. The Heinkel's gunner damaged Stephens' aircraft quite badly. A little later Blenheims of No. 248 Squadron set out to search the area for survivors, but found none.

Isolated raids were reported elsewhere, including a sneak raid in the evening by three Ju 88s on the Coastal Command airfield at Thorney Island; little damage was caused and there were no casualties. The Ju 88s were chased in and out of the low cloud by Spitfires of No. 602 Squadron from nearby Westhampnett, but when two of the British fighters collided the sortie was abandoned.

During the day, attacks were made on Tangmere, Portsmouth, Cromer and Harwich, and bombs were jettisoned over Outer London, Maidstone and Colchester (causing forty casualties). The *Luftwaffe* maintained its pressure after dark as the weather improved from the west, *Luftflotte 3* sending eighteen Heinkel He 111s against Cardiff and Pembroke Dock. The Fort Dunlop rubber works near Birmingham were also hit—this difficult target was accurately marked by Heinkel pathfinders of *Kampfgruppe 100* flying from Vannes in the Brest Peninsula. The *Luftwaffe* attempted several raids on this important factory during 1940 but, following the introduction of a smoke screen installation at the works premises, little damage was done.

R.A.F. FIGHTER COMMAND LOSSES—FRIDAY 23rd AUGUST 1940

1.	32 Sqn., Hawkinge	C	Landing accident at Hawkinge following combat; pilot unhurt.	Not known	Plt. Off. J.P. Pfeiffer	Hurricane	—	Cat. 2 Damaged
2.	85 Sqn., Croydon	—	Destroyed in night raid on Croydon; no pilot casualties.	At night	Nil	Hurricane	—	Cat. 3 Burnt
3.	85 Sqn., Croydon	—	Damaged in night raid on Croydon; no pilot casualties.	At night	Nil	Hurricane	—	Cat. 1 Damaged
4.	85 Sqn., Croydon	—	Damaged in night raid on Croydon; no pilot casualties.	At night	Nil	Hurricane	—	Cat. 1 Damaged
5.	232 Sqn., Sumburgh	C	Damaged in combat with He 111 eight miles east of Fair Isle; pilot unhurt.	09.18 hrs.	Flt. Lt. M.M. Stephens	Hurricane	P3104	Cat. 2 Damaged
6.	602 Sqn., Westhampnett	C	Collided with another Spitfire during combat; pilot returned unhurt.	18.05 hrs.	Plt. Off. T.G.F. Ritchie	Spitfire	X4160	Cat. 2 Damaged

LUFTWAFFE LOSSES—FRIDAY 23rd AUGUST 1940

1.	St.St./KG 2	CM	Shot down by 257 Sqn. Hurricanes over Thames Estuary at A.08.30 hrs.	Dornier Do 17Z-2	100 %	Oblt. Hellmers, *St.Kap.*, + three missing.
2.	I./KG 27	NCM	Landing crash at Avord; cause not known.	Heinkel He 111P	100 %	Ltn. Ginzinger + three killed.
3.	Ausb.St./KG 40	NCM	Crashed near Reichenberg; cause not known.	Heinkel He 111H-4	100 %	Oblt. Eschmann, Ltn.z.S. Meinhold + two killed.
4.	I./KG 55	CM	Damaged by British fighters near Le Havre.	Heinkel He 111P	10 %	One killed and one wounded.
5.	I./KG 55	CM	Damaged by British fighters near Le Havre.	Heinkel He 111H-2	25 %	Two wounded and one missing.
6.	7./KG 76	CM	Crashed at Cormeilles after combat sortie.	Dornier Do 17Z-2	70 %	Crew unhurt.
7.	II./ZG 76	CM	Taxying accident on Jersey airfield.	Messerschmitt Bf 110C	40 %	Crew unhurt.
8.	I./JG 26	CM	Air collision with another Bf 109.	Messerschmitt Bf 109E	100 %	Pilot killed.
9.	II./JG 26	NCM	Landing accident at Marquise.	Messerschmitt Bf 109E	30 %	Pilot unhurt.
10.	1./106	NCM	Landing accident at Mariensiel airfield.	Junkers W 34Hi	50 %	One crew member injured.
11.	Wettererkundungsstaffel 1	CM	Shot down by 232 Sqn. Hurricanes of Stephens, Hobbs and Jefferies 8 miles west of Fair Isle at 09.30 hrs. No survivers seen.	Heinkel He 111H-3	100 %	Three killed; Reg. Rat a.Kr. Knauf + one missing.
12.	IV./KGzbV 1	NCM	Force landed on Jersey airfield; cause not known.	Junkers Ju 52/3m (6324 : 1Z+AA)	70 %	Crew unhurt.

Saturday 24th August

Many accounts of the Battle of Britain, which adhere to the identification of specific phases in the Battle, point to August 24th as the beginning of the third phase—a phase supposedly devoted to the destruction of Fighter Command, and one that was to last until 6th September. While the entire Battle was waged by the *Luftwaffe* with this aim uppermost in mind, the period was indeed critical for Fighter Command. It would, however, be more accurate to define the operations of this "phase" as being mounted in such strength as to attempt a break-through of the defences in daylight. In so doing it was hoped to force the R.A.F. to abandon its airfields in the extreme South and South-East and entice its remaining forces into the air in defence of inland targets—including London. Fighter Command's continuing ability to put large fighter forces into the air did not so much suggest that the *Luftwaffe*'s victory claims were exaggerated as that the British aircraft industry's output of new aircraft had been underestimated. Göring had therefore decreed that factories in this industry were to be raided, if necessary calling for intricate feint raids in order to ensure the success of such attacks.

The movement of Bf 109 units from North-West France to the Pas de Calais continued for the next three or four days, it being argued that the width of the Channel north of the Cherbourg Peninsula deprived the single-seaters of a worthwhile combat endurance over Southern England—in turn making them of little value as escort fighters. The coming mass attacks against the South-East would require the largest possible number of Bf 109s to accompany the huge bomber formations envisaged. By providing an increased number of aircraft in North-East France it was now decided to introduce a new tactic to increase the strain upon Fighter Command— that of maintaining an almost constant stream of German aircraft flying parallel to the Sussex coast, about twenty miles out to sea, occasionally turning in towards the radar stations before making off. In this way it was hoped to attract the fighters up from their bases, and then launch crushing attacks while these squadrons were back on the ground refuelling.

Life in Fighter Command, meanwhile, was harrowing to say the least. Few airfields had escaped the enemy's attention with the result that the services had been disrupted and countless makeshift expedients employed. Occasionally the fighter pilots, warned that their squadron would be "released" on the following day, would make their way into London to enjoy a few hours relaxation—often high-spirited. Such excursions were rare, however, and most of the young men were by now so affected by the constant physical and mental strain of combat, and the likelihood of combat, that they were only too thankful to retreat into the doubtful solace of sleep. Too many of them had witnessed the horrors of violent death, and suffered the agonies of watching a friend spinning to earth in a blazing fighter, for relaxation to come easily.

Fatigue was the common enemy in Fighter Command. While the pilots suffered the wearying demands of long hours at Readiness and Available, their groundcrews toiled to repair and maintain their aircraft, often working through the night in draughty hangars, performing intricate repairs in rigid blackout conditions. Essential repairs to airfields made extra demands of fitters and other personnel—so that the aircraft that had been so carefully repaired could take the air on the morrow. Added to this was the constant worry that the families of the fighting men might be in danger from German attacks elsewhere in Britain.

The short respite between the 20th and 24th August was seized by all Group and Sector Commanders as an opportunity to stand down as many squadrons as possible, merely maintaining sufficient states to meet any likely scale of attack in the existing weather conditions.

When dawn broke clear and fine on Saturday the 24th, it was obvious to the commanders on both sides that the lull was over. Park had not long to wait for the attack to come. At 08.30 hours Pevensey reported a build-up of enemy forces along a wide front of the French coast. Within fifteen minutes this had contracted into a dense raid formation of about forty Do 17s and Ju 88s escorted by sixty-six Bf 109s from three *Jagdgeschwader*. So compact was the enemy formation that, of the twelve squadrons scrambled against it, only two managed to penetrate the fighter screen. One of these, No. 85 Squadron, had flown from Croydon and was about to make a series of quarter attacks on the bombers when the Dover anti-aircraft barrage opened up and forced the pilots to break away. Geoffrey Allard, on turning away, found himself being stalked by a lone Bf 109, which he promptly shot down into the sea off Ramsgate.

At about 10.00 hours the German raid, which had retired to the south-east, broke up and disappeared from the radar screens, although two free chases swept in west of Dover in the hope of catching isolated British fighters short of fuel. They found none.

Bombs had fallen on Dover, but damage had been confined to residential areas—from which much of the civilian population had been evacuated.

One of the squadrons which had been engaged (albeit without effect) had been No. 264, equipped with Defiants. This was the squadron that had fought so successfully with the turret fighter over Dunkirk, when the novelty of the dorsal armament had taken German pilots by surprise and had brought about the destruction of a fairly large number of enemy aircraft. The extraordinary decision to deploy the Defiants of No. 264 Squadron in No. 11 Group on 22nd August after the destruction of the other similarly-equipped squadron (No. 141) a month previously has never been explained nor justified. They were based at Hornchurch (an established Spitfire base with no personnel experienced in the maintenance of such aircraft, so that the squadron had to be entirely self-sufficient, and were therefore ordered forward to operate on a daily basis from Manston; experinced gained during the next few days was to show the folly of operating the Defiant (with its two-man crew and ponderous boarding procedure) under conditions that demanded scrambling at very short notice.

Shortly after mid-day No. 264 Squadron was on the ground being refuelled when hurried warning was given of the approach of hostile aircraft. Hastily taking off as the first bombs were falling, the Defiants had no time to form up to make their co-ordinated attacks and were thus at the mercy of the German fighter escort. Three of the turret fighters were shot down, the squadron commander, Philip Hunter, being last seen pursuing a Ju 88 towards France. The futility of pursuing a bomber of roughly similar top speed and a worthwhile rearward defence in a stern chase by a fighter which lacked any forward-firing armament must have dawned upon the Defiant pilot too late. . .

The remaining crews returned to Hornchurch only to snatch a hurried lunch before being ordered off to meet another attack—this time on Hornchurch itself. Once again the formation took off as the first bombs began to fall, and once again the squadron was unable to form up, so that its fire power was dissipated over too great an area.

Squadron Leader Philip Hunter of No. 264 Squadron (extreme left) with some squadron pilots and gunners beside one of the unit's Defiants. Hunter was killed on 24th August; in four days the squadron lost or wrote off twelve aircraft, four more being badly damaged.

Meanwhile Manston had been subjected to yet another raid, this time rendering the airfield virtually useless for operations other than those of a forward refuelling satellite. Living quarters were destroyed, seventeen casualties suffered, and three aircraft badly damaged. Unexploded bombs which fell among the station buildings forced the evacuation of all administrative personnel so that only those required for ground defence and servicing remained. All communications had been cut, so that No. 11 Group lost touch with the situation at one of its vital forward bases. When contact was established with a local Observer Post through the Maidstone centre, an Observer volunteered to cycle to the airfield and report on the situation. Post Office engineers were hurriedly called in and under conditions of extreme difficulty and danger from the large number of unexploded bombs these men repaired the essential cables within two hours—and had restored all lines by the following day.

German crews who had carried out the raid on Manston reported that the bombs from the first wave created so much smoke and chalk dust that they had been unable to define their target and so attacked another airfield nearby. This was the small flying club field at nearby Ramsgate, which had no military value whatsoever—but the town itself also suffered heavily, 26 casualties being reported.

While Hornchurch was being attacked by a fairly large formation of Heinkel He 111s and Junkers Ju 88s, bombing from about 12,000 feet, yet another raid by 46 Dornier Do 17s and Heinkel He 111s was appoaching North Weald. Three squadrons met this raid and succeeded in turning away a proportion of the bombers. The escorting Bf 109s were flying too high and too far astern of the main force to prevent No. 151 Squadron's Hurricanes from attacking the He 111s just as Flt. Lt. Herbert Giddings led nine Hurricanes of No. 111 Squadron in the traditional head-on attack on the Dorniers. The attack was broken up and upwards of fifty fighters set about harrying the straggling groups of German bombers as they sought to escape across the Thames Estuary. On this occasion the *Zerstörer* escort provided welcome cover, and certainly prevented a massacre for, long before the massive dogfight had dissolved, the Bf 109s (which had been flying at their extreme range) disengaged and made for home.

About twenty bombers had succeeded in reaching North Weald and their bombs fell squarely upon the station buildings, hitting two Messes, married quarters and stores—but scarcely affecting the operational capabilities of the airfield.

With virtually all his squadrons airborne and engaged in combat shortly before 16.00 hours, Park called upon Leigh-Mallory to provide cover for the airfields of No. 11 Group north of the Thames, but only No. 19 Squadron appeared on the scene. The No. 12 Group commander had attempted to assemble his squadrons into a Wing over Duxford, but the orders had been misunderstood and no such formation materialised. Instead Flt. Lt. Brian Lane led six cannon-armed Spitfires of No. 19 Squadron into action against the Bf 110s near North Weald and claimed three destroyed; unfortunately only two aircraft managed to fire their complete armament— the others were plagued by infuriating gun stoppages.

Leigh-Mallory's other fighters arrived over Essex too late to see any of the German aircraft; had any doubt remained in their pilots' minds as to the ordeal being suffered by their colleagues in the South, they were dispelled by the sight that met their eyes as they approached the outskirts of London. With fierce fires raging at Hornchurch and North Weald, and numerous columns of smoke caused by jettisoned bombs, the otherwise cloudless summer sky had taken on a depressing greyness that seemed to foreshadow impending disaster.

While Park and Leigh-Mallory voiced their recriminations—which were eventually to lead to an open conflict of opinions—Sir Quintin Brand, commanding No. 10 Group in the South-West, was fully occupied by his own problems. At 15.40 hours the Ventnor radar (which was still experiencing difficulty in providing range information owing to the prob-

Werke Nr. 5587, a Messerschmitt Bf 109E of 6 *Staffel*, JG 51, shot down by Pilot Officer Bryan Wicks of No. 56 Squadron on 24th August, seen here posing with his victim. As was usual practice, the German pilot had jettisoned his canopy and head armour before force landing; the engine had evidently stopped before the aircraft hit the ground—as witness only two propeller blades buckled. The painting of *Staffelabzeichen* on the rear fuselage was not common.

lem of calibrating new receivers after the damage caused in mid-August) reported a large formation of enemy aircraft approaching the Isle of Wight. Remembering the success of previous tactics against dive-bombers, and not yet aware that these aircraft had been largely withdrawn by the *Luftwaffe*, the Tangmere and Middle Wallop controllers ordered their fighters to remain too low. The result was that when the raid, consisting of about fifty Junkers Ju 88s of *Lehrgeschwader 1*, escorted by a similar number of Bf 110s, appeared somewhat earlier than the radar had predicted, the Spitfire pilots of No. 609 Squadron found themselves over Ryde in the Isle of Wight, 5,000 feet directly below the enemy fighter escort, down-sun and right in the midst of an anti-aircraft barrage! The Squadron was extremely fortunate to escape, only two aircraft being damaged—one of which was flown by Plt. Off. "Andy" Mamedoff, the American pilot. LG 1 was therefore able to continue its course untroubled, save by anti-aircraft gunfire, and arrived over the naval base at Portsmouth where it dropped more than two hundred 250-kilo bombs in the space of no more than four minutes. Considerable damage was caused in the city as well as to the naval installations. The toll of casualties was the highest in a single raid yet suffered in the War, with 104 civilians killed and 237 injured, and upwards of 50 casualties among naval personnel. A fuel oil store, hit in this raid, continued to burn for almost 36 hours before it was finally extinguished.

For many towns in the South and South-East dusk fell prematurely on 24th August, the sky darkened by smoke that served to emphasise that all had not gone well for the defences. It was clear to Dowding that the raids on Hornchurch

and North Weald foreshadowed a renewed attack on his defence system. Was there anything sinister in the switch from attacks on his airfields south of London? If there was any suggestion that Göring might be about to mount an assault upon London itself, the events of the night tended to confirm it. From 22.00 hours onwards more than one hundred bombers were tracked in over Kent, Sussex and Surrey, and these made their way almost unopposed to the capital. These raids, however, were ill-defined and were not launched against specific targets (apart for the oil storage farm at Thameshaven, which escaped damage), and fires sprang up all over the great sprawling city—for the first time since the raids of 1918. Sticks of bombs fell in the City and the neighbouring boroughs of Bethnal Green, East Ham, Stepney and Finsbury. According to Fire Service records there were 76 "incidents", of which eleven demanded the services of more than half a dozen pumps. The location of these incidents foreshadowed a depressing feature of London's bombardment during the coming autumn and winter; it was to be the rows of humble dwellings and tenements inhabited by the poorest members of the population which were to crumble under the growing weight of German bombs—just as it had been in the previous War. No one yet had the slightest idea of just what horror lay in store. . . .

R.A.F. FIGHTER COMMAND LOSSES—SATURDAY 24th AUGUST 1940

1.	32 Sqn., Hawkinge	C	Shot down by Bf 109 over South London; pilot injured and admitted to Royal Masonic Hospital, Hamersmith.	15.27 hrs.	Fg. Off. R.F. Smythe		Hurricane	*V6568*	Cat. 3 Destroyed
2.	32 Sqn., Hawkinge	C	Shot down by Bf 109; pilot injured in knee and ankle, but returned to Squadron; aircraft crashed at Rhodes Minnis, near Lyminge.	15.17 hrs.	Plt. Off. K. Pniak		Hurricane	*V6572*	Cat. 3 Destroyed
3.	32 Sqn., Hawkinge	C	Crashed after combat with Bf 109s near Hawkinge. (No further injury).	16.30 hrs.	Plt. Off. K. Pniak		Hurricane	—	Cat. 3 Destroyed

R.A.F. Losses, 24th August 1940—*continued*

	Squadron/Base		Remarks	Time	Pilot/Crew	Aircraft	Serial	Category
4.	32 Sqn., Hawkinge	C	Shot down by Bf 109s and crashed at Tedders Leas, near Eltham; pilot rescued from sea.	16.30 hrs.	Plt. Off. E.G.A. Seghers	Hurricane	V6567	Cat. 3 Destroyed
5.	32 Sqn., Hawkinge	C	Shot down at Lyminge; pilot unhurt.	16.30 hrs.	Flt. Lt. M.N. Crossley	Hurricane	P3481	Cat. 3 Destroyed
6.	54 Sqn., Hornchurch	C	Damaged in combat with Bf 109s near Manston; pilot unhurt.	09.59 hrs.	Plt.Off.A.R.McL. Campbell	Spitfire	—	Cat. 2 Damaged
7.	54 Sqn., Hornchurch	C	Shot down by Bf 109s south of Dover; pilot picked up slightly wounded.	Afternoon	Plt. Off. C. Stewart	Spitfire	P9389	Cat. 3 Lost
8.	73 Sqn., Leconfield	(C)	Shot down by Leeds A.A. gunfire at night; pilot baled out near Beverley, unhurt.	01.25 hrs.	Sgt. M.E. Leng	Hurricane	P3758	Cat. 3 Destroyed
9.	85 Sqn., Croydon	(C)	Damaged by Dover A.A. gunfire; pilot force landed at Hawkinge.	08.34 hrs.	Plt. Off. J. Lockhart	Hurricane	—	Cat. 1 Damaged
10.	151 Sqn., North Weald	C	Damaged in combat with Bf 109s; pilot unhurt.	Morning	Plt. Off. I.S. Smith	Hurricane	—	Cat. 1 Damaged
11.	151 Sqn., North Weald	C	Shot down by Bf 109s over Ramsgate; pilot wounded; aircraft crashed at Ospringe.	A11.00 hrs.	Sgt. G.T. Clarke	Hurricane	P3273	Cat. 3 Missing
12.	151 Sqn., North Weald	C	Shot down by Bf 109s over Ramsgate; pilot severely wounded and burned.	A11.00 hrs.	Plt. Off. K.B.L. Debenham	Hurricane	R4183	Cat. 3 Burnt
13.	151 Sqn., North Weald	C	Propeller shot off by Bf 109; pilot force landed at North Weald, unhurt.	Afternoon	Sqn. Ldr. E.B. King	Hurricane	—	Cat. 2 Damaged
14.	234 Sqn., Middle Wallop	C	Shot down and crashed on Isle of Wight; pilot unhurt.	16.55 hrs.	Plt. Off. J. Zurakowski	Spitfire	N3239	Cat. 3 Destroyed
15.	235 Sqn., Thorney Island	(C)	Shot down by Hurricanes of No. 1 (Canadian) Sqn., near Portsmouth ; both crew members killed.	17.05 hrs.	Plt. Off. D.N. Woodger Sgt. D.L. Wright	Blenheim	T1804	Cat. 3 Lost
16.	235 Sqn., Thorney Island	(C)	Damaged by Hurricanes of No. 1 (Canadian) Sqn., near Portsmouth; crashed on landing but crew unhurt.	17.05 hrs.	Sgt. K.E. Naish Sgt. W.G. Owen	Blenheim	Z5730	Cat. 3 Destroyed
17.	235 Sqn., Thorney Island	(C)	Damaged by Hurricanes of No1. 1 (Canadian) Sqn., near Portsmouth; landed safely and crew unhurt.	17.05 hrs.	Flt. Lt. F.W. Flood (Observer not known)	Blenheim	N3531	Cat. 1 Damaged
18.	264 Sqn., Manston	C	Assumed shot down by Ju 88 south-east of Manston; neither of crew's bodies ever re-covered.	A13.20 hrs.	Sqn. Ldr. P.A. Hunter L.A.C. F.H. King	Defiant	N1535	Cat. 3 Missing
19.	264 Sqn., Manston	C	Shot down by Bf 109 (said to be flown by Major Lützow of JG 3) east of Manston; neither of crew's bodies ever recovered.	A13.15 hrs.	Plt.Off. J.T.Jones Plt. Off. W.A. Ponting	Defiant	L6966	Cat. 3 Missing
20.	264 Sqn., Manston	C	Shot down by Bf 109 (possibly of Major Lützow of JG 3) east of Manston; neither of crew's bodies ever recovered.	A13.18 hrs.	Fg.Off. I.G. Shaw Sgt. A. Berry	Defiant	L7027	Cat. 3 Missing
21.	264 Sqn., Hornchurch	C	Collided with Item 22 prior to scramble; crew unhurt.	15.40 hrs.	Plt. Off. G.H. Hackwood	Defiant	—	Cat. 3 Destroyed
22.	264 Sqn., Hornchurch	C	Collided with Item 21prior to scramble; crew unhurt.	15.40 hrs.	Not known	Defiant	—	Cat. 2 Damaged
23.	264 Sqn., Hornchurch	C	Shot down by Bf 109 near Hornchurch; pilot pilot baled out, slightly wounded, but gunner died of his wounds.	A16.10 hrs.	Plt. Off. R.S. Gaskell Sgt. W.H. Machin	Defiant	L6965	Cat. 3 Destroyed
24.	302 Sqn., Leconfield	C	Damaged by Ju 88 and force landed near Leconfield; pilot unhurt.	Not known	Plt. Off. S.J. Chalupa	Hurricane	P3933	Cat. 2 Damaged
25.	501 Sqn., Gravesend	C	Shot down by Bf 109s off Kent coast near Hawkinge. Pilot assumed killed.	A09.00 hrs.	Plt. Off. P. Zenker	Hurricane	P3141	Cat. 3 Missing
26.	501 Sqn., Gravesend	C	Shot down by Bf 109s near Dover; pilot baled out at Ryarth sustaining a broken arm.	A16.00 hrs.	Plt. Off. K.R. Aldridge	Hurricane	L1865	Cat. 3 Destroyed
27.	604 Sqn., Middle Wallop	NC	Crashed at Odiham (not the result of combat); crew unhurt.	Not known	Fg. Off. H. Speke Sgt. S.H.J. Shirley	Blenheim	L6681	Cat. 3 Destroyed
28.	609 Sqn., Middle Wallop	C	Shot down by Bf 109 near Ryde; pilot unhurt.	A16.24 hrs.	Plt. Off. A. Mamedoff	Spitfire	L1082	Cat. 3 Destroyed
29.	610 Sqn., Biggin Hill	C	Shot down by Bf 109 near Deal; pilot baled out but sustained a broken ankle.	08.27 hrs.	Sgt. S.J. Arnfield	Spitfire	K9975	Cat. 3 Destroyed
30.	610 Sqn., Biggin Hill	C	Shot down by Bf 109; crash landed at Shepherswell, near Dover; pilot wounded.	11.12 hrs.	Plt. Off. D.McI. Gray	Spitfire	X4102	Cat. 3 Destroyed
31.	610 Sqn., Biggin Hill	C	Shot down by Bf 109s and crashed at Fyfield; wounded pilot admitted to Ongar Hospital.	16.19 hrs.	Plt. Off. C. Merrick	Spitfire	L1037	Cat. 3 Destroyed
32.	615 Sqn., Kenley	C	Shot down by Do 17 and crash landed near Meopham; pilot unhurt.	16.03 hrs.	Plt. Off. D.H. Hone	Hurricane	—	Cat. 2 Damaged

LUFTWAFFE LOSSES—SATURDAY 24th AUGUST 1940

	Unit		Remarks	Aircraft	%	Casualties
1.	Aufkl.Gr.d. Ob. d. L.	CM	Shot down by Hurricane of Beamish flying with 151 Sqn. north of Sheppey at A.16.00 hrs.	Messerschmitt Bf 110	100 %	Ltn. Hofer + two missing (note three-man crew).
2.	1.(F)/122	CM	Damaged by A.A. near Dover and crashed near Boulogne.	Junkers Ju 88A-1	70 %	Crew unhurt.
3.	5.(F)/122	CM	Shot down by 501 Sqn. Hurricane off Kent coast at A.13.00 hrs.	Junkers Ju 88A-1	100 %	One killed; Ltn. Hellermann and Ltn. Hurck + one missing.
4.	Stab/KG 4	—	Damaged in R.A.F. raid on Schipol airfield.	Messerschmitt Bf 108	15 %	No aircrew casualties.
5.	Stab I./KG 27	CM	Crashed at Cherbourg following engine failure.	Heinkel He 111P	100 %	Crew unhurt.
6.	I./KG 51	CM	Landing accident on Villaroche airfield.	Junkers Ju 88A-1	40 %	Crew unhurt.
7.	7./KG 51	CM	Shot down by 501 Sqn. Hurricane off Kent coast at A.13.15 hrs.	Junkers Ju 88A-1 (7072 : 9K+BR)	100 %	Uffz. Maurer, Uffz. Schulz and Gefr. Pfaff killed.
8.	III./KG 53	CM	Shot down by 56 Sqn. Hurricane of Weaver over	Heinkel He 111H-2	100 %	One killed; Hptm. von Lonicer
9.	9./KG 53	CM	Shot down by 615 Sqn. Hurricanes of Kayll and McClintock near Hornchurch at A.15.50 hrs.	Heinkel He 111H-3 (A1+KT)	100 %	Ltn. Willi Lüttigen, Fw. Alfred Fraas, Uffz. Oscar Lackher, Uffz. Karl Platzer and Uffz. Herbert Hermans all made P.O.W.s.
10.	9./KG 53	CM	Shot down by 151 Sqn. Hurricane of Blair west of North Weald at A.15.30 hrs.	Heinkel He 111H-2 (A1+LT)	100 %	Oblt Gerhard Winter, Uffz. Otto Wieck, Fw. Adolf Angelhardt, Uffz. Hans Schmidt and Gefr. Willi Maurer all made P.O.W.s.
11.	III./KG 53	CM	Shot down by 151 Sqn. Hurricane of Ellacombe west of North Weald at A.15.55 hrs.	Heinkel He 111H-2	100 %	Oblt. Huhn + three killed; one missing.
12.	Stab III./KG 53	CM	Shot down by 151 Sqn. Hurricane of Dymond near North Weald at 15.50 hrs. Crashed at South Essex Waterworks, near Colchester.	Heinkel He 111H-2	100 %	Major Karl Ritscherle missing; Uffz. Alfred Kramer, Flg. Erich Salvino, Ogefr.Erwin Gleissner and Uffz. Gerhard Schaffner P.O.W.s.

Luftwaffe Losses, 24th August 1940—*continued*

13.	III./KG 53	CM	Shot down by 29 Sqn. Blenheim night fighter of Braham and Wilsdon at 01.30 hrs and crashed in the Humber.	Heinkel He 111P	100 %	One killed; Ltn . Jerusel + three missing.
14.	Stab II./KG 76	CM	Shot down by 264 Sqn. Defiant of Banham and Baker south of Manston at 12.55 hrs.	Junkers Ju 88A-1	100 %	Major Moricke, *Gr.Kdr.*, Oblt. Schulte + two killed.
15.	Stab II./KG 76	CM	Shot down by 264 Sqn. Defiant of Garvin and Ash south of Manston at 12.55 hrs.	Junkers Ju 88A-1	100 %	One killed and three missing..
16.	4./KG 76	CM	Shot down by 264 Sqn. Defiant of Whitley and Turner near Manston at A. 13.05 hrs.	Junkers Ju 88A-1	100 %	Ltn. Grell + two missing; one killed.
17.	4./KG 76	CM	Shot down by 264 Sqn. Defiant of Thorn and Barker south of Manston at A.13.05 hrs.	Junkers Ju 88A-1	100 %	One kiled and three missing.
18.	4./KG 76	CM	Possibly damaged by 264 Sqn. Defiant at A.13.20 hrs.	Junkers Ju 88A-1	60 %	Crew unhurt.
19.	II./ZG 2	CM	Reported in German records as shot down by fighter off Cherbourg Peninsula; no R.A.F. claim traced.	Messerschmitt Bf 110 C-4	100 %	Ltn. Meyer killed; one missing.
20.	I./LG 2	CM	Shot down by 54 Sqn. Spitfire of Gray near Manston at 10.05 hrs.	Messerschmitt Bf 109 E-1	100 %	Pilot killed.
21.	I./LG 2	CM	Damaged by 54 Sqn. Spitfire of McMullen near Manston at 10.05 hrs..	Messerschmitt Bf 109 E-4	60 %	Pilot unhurt.
22.	I./LG 2	CM	Shot down by 54 Sqn. Spitfire of Robbins near Manston at A.10.10 hrs.	Messerschmitt Bf 109 E-4	100 %	Pilot missing.
23.	II./JG 2	CM	Shot down by 249 Sqn. Hurricanes of Wynn and Barton off Isle of Wight at 16.40 hrs.	Messerschmitt Bf 109 E-4	100 %	Pilot killed.
24.	II./JG 2	CM	Damaged by 249 Sqn. Hurricanes over English Channel, and crashed near Le Havre	Messerschmitt Bf 109 E-4	75 %	Pilot wounded.
25.	I./JG 3	CM	Reported damaged by Bf 109 near Calais.	Messerschmitt Bf 109E (1649)	10—60 %	Pilot unhurt.
26.	III./JG 3	CM	Crashed on landing at Colombert; not combat.	Messerschmitt Bf 109E	90 %	Pilot injured.
27.	III./JG 3	CM	Shot down by 32 Sqn. Hurricane of Gillman off Folkestone at 16.20 hrs.	Messerschmitt Bf 109 E-4	100 %	Ltn. Achleitner missing.
28.	III./JG 3	CM	Shot down by 32 Sqn. Hurricane of Brothers off Folkestone at 15.10 hrs.	Messerschmitt Bf 109 E-1	100 %	Pilot missing.
29.	III./JG 3	CM	Damaged by 32 Sqn. Hurricane of Barton off French coast and force landed at Desvres.	Messerschmitt Bf 109 E-4	25 %	Pilot unhurt.
30.	7./JG 3	CM	Damaged by 32 Sqn. Hurricane of Pniak over Kent at 15.08 hrs.	Messerschmitt Bf 109 E-4	25 %	Pilot unhurt.
31.	III./JG 26	CM	Believed damaged by 151 Sqn. Hurricane of Smith.	Messerschmitt Bf 109 E-4 (5020)	65 %	Pilot unhurt.
32.	7./JG 26	CM	Shot down by 85 Sqn. Hurricane of Allard near Margate at 08.30 hrs.	Messerschmitt Bf 109 E-4	100 %	Pilot, wounded, made P.O.W.
33.	9./JG 26	CM	Damaged by R.A.F. fighters and crashed near St. Inglevert.	Messerschmitt Bf 109 E-3	100 %	Fw. Beese unhurt.
34.	1./JG 51	CM	Shot down by 264 Sqn. Defiant of Barwell and Martin over sea near Margate and collided with another Messerschmitt (see Item 35)	Messerschmitt Bf 109 E-4	100 %	Pilot killed.
35.	5./JG 51	CM	Collided with another Bf 109 (see Item 34) near Margate.	Messerschmitt Bf 109 E-1	100 %	Pilot injured.
36.	II./JG 51	CM	Crashed at Marquise following engine failure.	Messerschmitt Bf 109E	75 %	Pilot unhurt.
37.	6./JG 51	CM	Shot down by 56 Sqn. Hurricane of Wicks over Thames Estuary.	Messerschmitt Bf 109 E-4 (5587)	100 %	Pilot, unwounded, made P.O.W.
38.	8./JG 51	CM	Shot down by 56 Sqn. Hurricane of Manton over Thames Estuary at A.15.15 hrs.	Messerschmitt Bf 109 E-4	100 %	Pilot missing.
39.	8./JG 51	CM	Shot down by 56 Sqn. Hurricane of Marston over Thames Estuary at A.15.15 hrs.	Messerschmitt Bf 109 E-1	100 %	Uffz. Wilhelm Kaiser made P.O.W.
40.	9./JG 51	CM	Shot down by 32 Sqn. Hurricane of Higgins off Folkestone at 16.25 hrs.	Messerschmitt Bf 109 E-1	100 %	Pilot killed.
41.	JG 51	CM	Crashed in English Channel after engine failure.	Messerschmitt Bf 109E	100 %	Pilot unhurt.
42.	I./JG 52	CM	Crashed in Thames Estuary after engine failure.	Messerschmitt Bf 109E	100 %	Pilot missing.
43.	II./JG 53	NCM	Crashed at Dinant following technical failure.	Messerschmitt Bf 109E	100 %	Pilot unhurt.
44.	Stab/JG 54	—	Destroyed in R.A.F. raid on Schipol airfield.	Aradao Ar 66 (6601)	100 %	No casualties.
45.	2./506	—	Severely damaged in storm at Trondheim.	Heinkel He 115	Over 60 %	No casualties.
46.	2./506	—	Severely damaged in storm at Trondheim.	Heinkel He 115	Over 60 %	No casualties.
47.	1./196	—	Damaged in R.A.F. raid on Boulogne.	Arado Ar 196	20 %	No casualties.
48.	1./196	—	Damaged in R.A.F. raid on Boulogne.	Arado Ar 196	25 %	No casualties.

Sunday 25th August

The bombing of London and towns in Surrey and Kent had continued until the early hours of this Sunday, giving little chance of sleep—especially among the tired pilots of No. 11 Group. Some experienced day pilots had been ordered up during the night to fly "cat's eye" patrols, among them Flt. Lt. James Sanders flying a Hurricane of No. 615 Squadron from Kenley. Taking off at ten minutes past midnight he "toured the South Coast", waiting to see if any raider was exposed by searchlights. After half an hour he caught sight of an enemy aircraft which he stalked, putting down his undercarriage so as not to overshoot or collide. Firing more than 2,000 rounds, he saw strikes on both the Heinkel's engines, and the enemy aircraft half-rolled and dived into the sea off Hastings shortly after 01.00 hours.

Kesselring felt disinclined to launch any major attacks during the morning of the 25th, although fine weather covered the whole of Southern England. He did however embark on his plan to erode the defenders' nerves by flying several formations at *Staffel* strength up and down the Channel. Neither Park nor Brand reacted by ordering fighters into the air, but preferred to keep the squadrons on the ground at Available. Only one Section—three Hurricanes of No. 501 Squadron on a standing patrol near Folkestone—caught sight of one of the enemy formations, but were too low to engage.

It was late afternoon before a change in these tactics became evident when, at about 16.00 hours, Ventnor reported a number of groups of enemy aircraft forming up to the west of the Cherbourg Peninsula. When, characteristically, this raid was "seen" to join up with another group near Cherbourg, it was reported as a 100-plus raid and plotted approaching

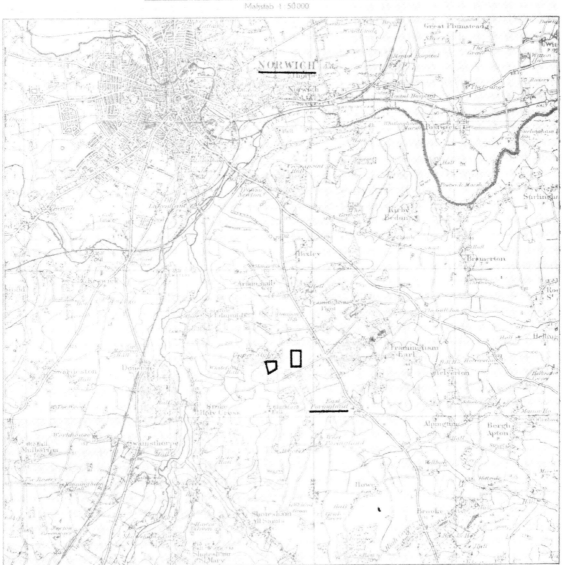

GB 96 7 a

Nur für den Dienstgebrauch!

Norwich - Poringland
Funkstation mit Sonderanlage
Länge (ostw. Greenw.): 1° 20'   Nördl. Breite: 52° 34' 30"
Zielhöhe über NN: 61 m

LII. Kdo. 3   Oktober 1942
Karte 1:100000
GB/E 19

Maßstab 1:50000

German target map, still on file in October 1942, showing the CH radar station at Stoke Holy Cross, south of Norwich. The German use of a British Ordnance Survey map has resulted in naming the station "Poringland", after a village about a mile south-east of the compound. Several raids were launched against this station during the second half of 1940, including at least one by *Erprobungsgruppe 210*; however, owing to the remote nature of the target, and wide dispersal of installations, little significant damage was caused. Because of its poor performance it was not regarded as a vital part of the radar chain after mid-September 1940, but its weakness was keenly felt when German night intruders began to roam the skies of East Anglia soon after the Battle of Britain.

Weymouth Bay. It was in fact composed of nearly 300 aircraft. Determined not to repeat the previous day's mistake of ordering the interceptors to remain low—the absence of dive bombers had been duly noted—the Tangmere, Exeter, Middle Wallop and Warmwell squadrons were scrambled in good time with orders to make all possible altitude.

As the raid neared Weymouth Bay, the Junkers Ju 88s of II./KG 51 and II./KG 54 and Messerschmitt Bf 110s of I./ZG 2, II./ZG 2 and V./LG 1 split into three formations, each of about thirty bombers and forty *Zerstören*, and commenced running up to attack Portland, Weymouth and Warmwell airfield. As Wg. Cdr. John Dewar led his twelve 87 Squadron Hurricanes against the Ju 88s over Portland, Sqn. Ldr. Horace Darley with twelve 609 Squadron Spitfires went for the escorting Bf 110s—only to be surprised by the sudden appearance of a *Gruppe* of Bf 109s from JG 53, the "Ace of Spades" *Geschwader*.

The formation which made to attack Warmwell found its

way barred by No. 17 Squadron's Hurricanes led by Sqn. Ldr. Cedric Williams; only seven bombers got through, hitting two hangars and the station's sick quarters. As at Manston on the previous day, it was a bomb which fell just outside the station perimeter that severed all the station's telephone and teleprinter lines.

As the Hurricanes blunted the attack, the Ju 88s veered away to the east and made as if to attack Southampton. Seeing the danger, Darley detached some of his Spitfires from the fight over Weymouth Bay and joined in the pursuit with No. 17 Squadron. One of the most successful pilots was Fg. Off. Count Manfred Czernin who, finding himself in a position to "cut the corner", turned in and delivered a head-on attack, breaking downwards and pulling up, half-rolling and bearing down on the Messerschmitts again from above and astern. He destroyed three of the enemy[61]. Sqn. Ldr. Williams' aircraft was seen to be hit by a withering hail of fire which severed the port wing and undoubtedly also killed the pilot. . . . Flt. Lt. Alfred Bayne was shot down into the sea, but was picked up an hour or so later. A Bf 110 pilot, who force landed in a field under the watchful eye of a circling 609 Squadron pilot,

climbed out and set fire to his aircraft.

There was to be no pause. As *Luftflotte 3*'s huge raid retired to the south soon after 18.00 hours, more than 100 aircraft were forming up behind the Pas de Calais, and Park ordered six of his squadrons into the air over Dover at around 18.15 hours. Of these, No. 32 Squadron, which was beginning to display the now-familiar symptoms of over-fatigue, was in action first, engaging a *Gruppe* of Dornier Do 17s marginally before the accompanying Bf 109s fell on it. The squadron's loss of Plt. Off. Keith Gillman reduced the strength to no more than eight pilots—scarcely adequate to ensure the availability of a single Flight. Forty-eight hours later the tattered remains of this redoubtable Squadron were withdrawn from the battle area, and its commanding officer, John Worrall, assumed control of the Biggin Hill Sector.

When Park ordered up 42 further fighters against the raid over Kent, the attack was already turning away, and few pilots reported having made contact.

The precipitate attacks on London the previous night had not been part of Göring's expressed plan and were producing a minor flurry of recriminations among the Staff of *Luftflotte 2*. No less quick to react, the British Cabinet sanctioned what amounted to a reprisal against Berlin, and this was mounted by 80 British twin-engine bombers on the night of 25th/26th August. From all accounts little material damage was caused, but the morale effect was tremendous, not only to the weary people of Britain but upon the growing complacency of the German nation—to whom the appearance of British bombers over the Reich's capital came as a severe shock. After all, Hitler had implied that the War was almost won.

---

[61] Count Czernin, son of an Austrian diplomat and English mother, and educated at Oundle, had a distinguished War record; after destroying thirteen German aircraft during the Battles of France and Britain, and sharing in the destruction of half a dozen others, he joined the Special Operations Executive and undertook two hazardous parachute drops behind the enemy lines in Italy, finishing the War with a D.S.O., M.C., and D.F.C. He was to die in his sleep on 6th October 1962.

R.A.F. FIGHTER COMMAND LOSSES—SUNDAY 25th AUGUST 1940

No.	Squadron & Base		Details	Time	Pilot	Aircraft	Serial	Category
1.	17 Sqn., Tangmere	C	Shot down in head-on attack on Bf 110 south of Tangmere; pilot killed.	17.20 hrs.	Sqn. Ldr. C.W. Williams	Hurricane	R4199	Cat. 3 Destroyed
2.	17 Sqn., Tangmere	C	Shot down by Bf 109 south of Tangmere; pilot baled out but rescued from sea unhurt.	17.25 hrs.	Flt. Lt. A.W.A. Bayne	Hurricane	V7407	Cat. 3 Lost
3.	29 Sqn., Wellingore	C	Believed shot down by enemy aircraft near Wainfleet; crew killed.	Not known	Plt. Off. R.A. Rhodes Sgt.R.J.Gouldstone A.C.1 N. Jacobson	Blenheim (radar equipped)	L1330	Cat. 3 Lost
4.	32 Sqn., Biggin Hill	C	Shot down by Bf 109s off Dover; pilot baled out and rescued unhurt from the sea.	18.38 hrs.	Plt. Off. J. Rose	Hurricane	V6547	Cat. 3 Lost
5.	32 Sqn., Biggin Hill	C	Shot down by Bf 109s near Dover; pilot assumed killed.	18.35 hrs.	Plt. Off. K.R. Gillman	Hurricane	P2755	Cat. 3 Missing
6.	54 Sqn., Hornchurch	C	Shot down by Bf 109s and force landed near Manston; pilot severely wounded.	Evening	Plt. Off. M.M. Shand	Spitfire	—	Cat. 2 Damaged
7.	87 Sqn., Exeter	C	Shot down off Portland. Pilot killed; body recovered and buried at Warmwell.	17.25 hrs.	Sgt. S.R.E. Wakeling	Hurricane	P3093	Cat. 3 Missing
8.	92 Sqn., Pembrey	C	Force landed after combat with Do 17 off St. Gowan's Head; pilot wounded in leg.	18.20 hrs.	Flt. Lt. R.S.S. Tuck	Spitfire	N3268	Cat. 2 Damaged
9.	152 Sqn., Warmwell	C	Shot down by Bf 109s west of Portland; pilot assumed killed.	17.22 hrs.	Plt. Off. R.M. Hogg.	Spitfire	—	Cat. 3 Lost
10.	152 Sqn., Warmwell	C	Shot down by Bf 109s west of Portland; pilot assumed killed.	17.28 hrs.	Plt. Off. T.S. Wildblood	Spitfire	R6994	Cat. 3 Lost
11.	213 Sqn., Exeter	C	Shot down by Bf 109s near Portland. Pilot killed; body recovered from the sea.	A17.30 hrs.	Plt. Off. H.D. Atkinson	Hurricane	P3200	Cat. 3 Lost
12.	213 Sqn., Exeter	C	Shot down by Bf 109 of Hptm. Mayer of I./JG 53 near Portland; pilot killed, and buried at Exeter; later re-interred in Belgium.	A17.30 hrs.	Plt. Off. J.A.L. Philippart	Hurricane	P2766	Cat. 3 Lost
13.	263 Sqn., Grangemouth	NC	Pilot baled out after fire in the air and landed in Grangemouth docks; arrested but later released.	Not known	Plt. Off. D. Stein	Hurricane	L1803	Cat. 3 Burnt
14.	602 Sqn., Westhampnett	C	Shot down by Bf 110s near Dorchester; pilot baled out unhurt.	17.47 hrs.	Fg. Off. W.H. Coverley	Spitfire	P9381	Cat. 3 Destroyed
15.	602 Sqn., Westhampnett	C	Shot down by Bf 110s off Portland; pilot baled out unhurt.	17.51 hrs.	Sgt. M.H. Sprague	Spitfire	N3226	Cat. 3 Lost
16.	609 Sqn., Middle Wallop	C	Badly damaged by Bf 110 over Swanage; pilot returned slightly wounded but crashed on landing at Warmwell.	A17.15 hrs.	Fg.Off. P. Ostaszewski- Ostoja	Spitfire	R6986	Cat. 3 Destroyed
17.	609 Sqn., Middle Wallop	C	Damaged in combat with Bf 110s; pilot returned unhurt.	A17.10 hrs.	Not known	Spitfire	—	Cat. 1 Damaged
18.	610 Sqn., Biggin Hill	C	Crashed at Sandwich after combat with Bf 109s over Dover; pilot wounded and admitted to Waldershore Hospital.	19.33 hrs.	Plt. Off. F.T. Gardiner	Spitfire	P9451	Cat. 3 Destroyed
19.	616 Sqn., Kenley	C	Shot down in flames by Bf 109 south of Canterbury; pilot assumed killed.	A18.45 hrs.	Sgt. T.E. Westmoreland	Spitfire	R6966	Cat. 3 Destroyed
20.	616 Sqn., Kenley	C	Shot down over Dover Straits; pilot rescued by Germans and made P.O.W.; escaped later.	18.50 hrs.	Sgt. P.T. Wareing	Spitfire	K9819	Cat. 3 Missing.

LUFTWAFFE LOSSES—SUN DAY 25th AUGUST 1940

	Unit		Cause	Aircraft	%	Remarks
1.	3./KG 4	CM	Crashed into Zuider See after engine failure on take-off.	Heinkel He 111H-4	100 %	Crew rescued unhurt.
2.	9./KG 55	CM	Shot down by 615 Sqn. Hurricane of Sanders near Hastings at 01.20 hrs.	Heinkel He 111P (G1+CT)	100 %	Four crew killed, and one missing; pilot survived.
3.	II./KG 51	CM	Damaged by 87 Sqn. Hurricane of Dewar near Portland at 17.30 hrs. and crashed at Cherbourg.	Junkers Ju 88A-1	100 %	Two crew members wounded
4.	II./KG 51	CM	Shot down by 87 Sqn. Hurricane of Thorogood near Portland at 17.30 hrs.	Junkers Ju 88A-1	100 %	Ltn. Walter Roy and Flt. Emil Rückert killed. Two made P.O.W.
5.	3./KG 76	CM	Shot down by 32 Sqn. Hurricane of Crossley between Dover and Calais at 18.26 hrs.	Dornier Do 17Z-2	100 %	Crew rescued by Seenotflugkdo. two members wounded.
6.	I./St.G 77	NCM	Landing accident at Maltot airfield.	Junkers Ju 87B	25 %	Crew unhurt.
7.	III./St.G 2	NCM	Engine failure on take-off at Ernes airfield.	Junkers Ju 87B	90 %	Crew unhurt.
8.	I./ZG 2	CM	Shot down by 17 Sqn. Hurricane of Czernin at A.18.00 hrs. and crashed at Wareham.	Messerschmitt Bf 110 C-4	100 %	Oblt Gerard Götz and Uffz. Kurt Haupt badly wounded and made P.O.W.s.
9.	I./ZG 2	CM	Shot down by 17 Sqn. Hurricane of Czernin at 18.00 hrs. and crashed near Warmwell.	Messerschmitt Bf 110 C-4 (3M+CH)	100 %	Ltn. Westphal and Ogefr. Josef Brief killed.
10.	I./ZG 2	CM	Shot down by 17 Sqn. Hurricane of Czernin at A.18.00 hrs. and crashed near Wareham.	Messerschmitt Bf 110 C-4 (3M+KH)	100 %	Uffz. Siegfried Becker and Ogefr. Walter Wöpzel made P.O.W.s.
11.	I./ZG 2	CM	Shot down by 17 Sqn. Hurricanes of Pitman and Williams off Portsmouth at A.17.15 hrs.	Messerschmitt Bf 110 C-4	100 %	Two crew members missing.
12.	II./ZG 2	CM	Damaged by 17 Sqn. Hurricanes near Portsmouth at A.17.15 hrs..	Messerschmitt Bf 110 C-4	20 %	Crew unhurt.
13.	II./ZG 2	CM	Damaged by 609 Sqn. Spitfires near Portsmouth at A.17.15 hrs.	Messerschmitt Bf 110D	65 %	Crew unhurt.
14.	II./ZG 2	CM	Damaged by 609 Sqn. Spitfires near Portsmouth at A.17.15 hrs.	Messerschmitt Bf 110 C-4	25%	Crew unhurt.
15.	II./ZG 2	CM	Damaged by 609 Sqn. Spitfires near Portsmouth at A.17.15 hrs.	Messerschmitt Bf 110 D-0	20 %	Crew unhurt.
16.	III./ZG 76	CM	Missing from combat sortie; fate not known.	Messerschmitt Bf 110C	100 %	Two crew missing.
17.	V./LG 1	CM	Shot down by 609 Sqn. Spitfires near Portsmouth at A.17.15 hrs.	Messerschmitt Bf 110 C-2	100 %	Oblt Glienke + one missing.
18.	V./LG 1	CM	Damaged by 609 Sqn. Spitfires near Portsmouth at A.17.15 hrs., and crashed at Roquancourt.	Messerschmitt Bf 110 C-2	60 %	One crew member wounded.
19.	V./LG 1	CM	Damaged by 609 Sqn. Spitfires near Portsmouth at A.17.15 hrs., and force landed at Barfleur.	Messerschmitt Bf 110 C-1	10—60 %	Crew unhurt.
20.	V./LG 1	CM	Shot down by 609 Sqn. Spitfires near Portsmouth at A.17.15 hrs.	Messerschmitt Bf 110 C-4	100 %	Two crew missing.
21.	III./JG 2	CM	Shot down by 609 Sqn. Spitfires off the Isle of Wight.	Messerschmitt Bf 109 E-1	100 %	Pilot, wounded, made P.O.W.
22.	III./JG 2	CM	Shot down by 609 Sqn. Spitfires off the Isle of Wight.	Messerschmitt Bf 109 E-1	100 %	Pilot, wounded, made P.O.W.
23.	III./JG 2	CM	Damaged during sortie over Southern England.	Messerschmitt Bf 109E	10—60 %	Pilot unhurt.
24.	II./JG 26	CM	Landing accident at Blecqueneques; not combat.	Messerschmitt Bf 109E (815)	20 %	Pilot unhurt.
25.	Stab II./JG 27	NCM	Force landed Colombiers after engine failure.	Messerschmitt Bf 109E	40 %	Pilot unhurt.
26.	I./JG 53	CM	Shot down by 17 Sqn. Hurricanes of Bayne and Leary near Portsmouth at A.17.15 hrs.	Messerschmitt Bf 109 E-1	100 %	Pilot missing.
27.	II./JG 53	CM	Shot down by 87 Sqn. Hurricane of David near Portland at 17.30 hrs.	Messerschmitt Bf 109 E-4	100 %	Hptm. Maculan missing.
28.	II./JG 53	CM	Shot down by 87 Sqn. Hurricane of Tait near Portland at 17.30 hrs.	Messerschmitt Bf 109 E-4	100 %	Pilot missing.
29.	II./JG 53	CM	Shot down by 87 Sqn. Hurricane of Mitchell near Portland at 17.30 hrs.	Messerschmitt Bf 109 E-4	100 %	Pilot, wounded, made P.O.W.
30.	I./KG 54	CM	Shot down by 32 Sqn. Hurricane of Proctor off Cap Gris Nez at 18.52 hrs.	Messerschmitt Bf 109 E-4	100 %	Oblt. Hild killed.
31.	I./JG 54	CM	Damaged by 54 Sqn. Spitfire of Gray at A.19.00 hrs. and force landed near Wissant.	Messerschmitt Bf 109 E-3 (6135)	15 %	Pilot unhurt.
32.	3./106	NCM	Landing accident at Schellingwoude; cause not known.	Heinkel He 115	100 %	Crew unhurt.
33.	1./606	CM	Shot down by 92 Sqn. Spitfire of Tuck 15 miles S.W. of St. Gowan's Head at 18.15 hrs.	Dornier Do 17P	100 %	Three crew killed; one missing.

Bombs exploding on Folkestone during the mid-day raid on 26th August.

241

Monday 26th August

Though the British Air Staff could not possibly have been aware of the possibility, the reprisal raid upon Berlin, carried out on the night of 25th/26th August, was to contribute to a chain of events that would swing the course of the Battle of Britain irrevocably in Fighter Command's favour. Yet, as it has been related, neither of the German attacks on the evening of 15th August and the night of 24th/25th had been premeditated, and it was ironic or fortuitous—according to the point of view—that these should have led to the raid on Berlin. Henceforth, and with increasing bitterness, the bomber forces of each nation would strike at the other's capital city. Unfortunately London—the great fat cow of Churchill's earlier oratory—was no more than an hour's flying time from Kesselring's bases, whereas the flight to Berlin from the bomber bases in Lincolnshire involved a long and arduous journey of perhaps four hours. With the need to carry so much fuel, it was little wonder that the bomb loads of the Wellingtons and Whitleys were so puny.

The pattern of the daylight raids on the 26th was much the same as on the previous day—except that whereas Park's Sector Stations south of London had escaped attention on the 25th, both Biggin Hill and Kenley were listed for attack on this Monday morning. From first light single Dornier Do 17 and Junkers Ju 88 reconnaissance aircraft flew back and forth over No. 11 Group's entire area, and it may have been the unusually large number of fighters concentrated at Biggin Hill and Kenley that prompted Kesselring to attack these targets. It had been the pattern of the two previous days' attacks (when the raiding formations had flown up the Thames Estuary instead of attempting to cross the Kent peninsula) that decided Park to hold most of his strength around London rather than deploy it forward at the coastal satellites. In any case, with Manston, Lympne and Hawkinge now operating at much reduced capacity, the No. 11 Group Controllers had little option but to use these airfields sparingly.

The first large raid, consisting of about 40 Heinkel He 111s and twelve Dornier Do 17s escorted by 80 Bf 109s and some Bf 110s, crossed the coast north of Dover at about 11.30 hours and, while the main force continued to press westwards, some of the 109s embarked on tactics of aggravation, strafing small towns and villages in East Kent and shooting up the Dover balloon barrage. Some of the Heinkels turned south and dropped bombs on Folkestone.

Already Park had deduced that his Sector Stations were in danger and had scrambled about 40 Hurricanes and 30 Spitfires to intercept the bombers—and a long drawn-out battle raged all the way from Canterbury to Maidstone. No. 616 Squadron suffered badly in this action. Scrambled from Available at Kenley, only seven Spitfires managed to get away quickly and, although directed against the raid over Dungeness at about 11.40 hours, they arrived too late to attack the Heinkels, and turned north again—only to run straight into about fifty Bf 109s. For something like fifteen minutes the Spitfires jockeyed to gain height up-sun of the enemy formations and just as five more members of the Squadron joined up—having been delayed on the ground—they were bounced by about 30 more Bf 109s which in less than thirty seconds shot down six of their number, killing two pilots and wounding four.

Meanwhile the luckless Defiant crews of No. 264 Squad-

The most successful Defiant crew of the War, Sgt. Edward Thorn (left) and his gunner, Sgt. Frederick Barker, of No. 264 Squadron. Each had won D.F.M.s over Dunkirk. On 26th August they destroyed three enemy aircraft before being shot down and slightly wounded, victories for which each man was awarded a Bar to the D.F.M. Both were later commissioned, and Thorn won a D.F.C. and Bar, only to be killed in a flying accident after the War on 12th February 1946.

ron, scrambled from Hornchurch, were tackling the formation of Dorniers alone near Herne Bay. Just as they were getting ready to perform their complicated cross-over attacks they were also set on by two *Gruppen* of Bf 109s. They lost three more aircraft, but this time were able to give a good account of themselves:

"Flt. Lt. Banham, after destroying a Dornier 17, received an explosive shell in his cockpit which set fire to the aircraft. He rolled on to his back calling to his gunner to bale out, and then baled out himself. He was picked up after one and a half hours in the sea; his gunner, Sgt. Baker, is missing. Plt. Off. Goodall was attacked by a Bf 109 and after beating off the attack made an overtaking attack on a Do 17 which he saw catch fire, and also saw two of the crew bale out. Plt. Off. Hughes, in his first engagement with the enemy, successfully destroyed two Do 17s by converging attacks. Sgt. Thorne and Sgt. Barker put up a magnificent show by destroying two of the Do 17s, and while attacking a third were in turn attacked by a Bf 109 and their machine developed oil and glycol leaks. Taking evasive action they spun away and were preparing to make a crash landing near Herne Bay when the Bf 109 attacked them again at 500 feet. The aircraft caught fire, but before crashing Sgt. Barker fired his remaining ammunition into the enemy which crashed a few fields away. Both Sergeants Thorne and Barker escaped with minor injuries. Campbell-Colquhoun, after attacking a Do 17 which dived smoking from both engines, was attacked by a Bf 109 and was unable to confirm the destruction of the Dornier. Fg. Off. Stephenson's Defiant was set on fire by a Bf 109; the pilot baled out and was picked up from the sea and later taken to Canterbury Hospital with minor injuries. His gunner, Sgt. Maxwell, is missing."

Both Thorne and Barker had won D.F.M.s for their actions over Dunkirk, and both were to receive Bars to these decorations for their combat on this day. Hughes went on to pursue a distinguished career in the Royal Air Force, destroying a total of seventeen enemy aircraft in various two-seat fighters and retiring from the Service in 1974 as an Air Vice-Marshal with C.B., C.B.E., D.S.O., three D.F.C.s and the A.F.C.

As the Defiants effectively drew off the escorting Bf 109s, the Hurricane pilots of No. 1 (Canadian) Squadron charged in and attacked the Dorniers, but ran into a withering cross-fire which accounted for three aircraft (including that of the squadron commander, Sqn. Ldr. Ernest McNab) and killed one pilot. However, the continuous pressure against the bombers, as three more squadrons joined the battle, succeeded in turning away the enemy formation before it reached Biggin Hill; the escorting Bf 109s, in joining battle with 264 and 616 Squadrons—notwithstanding their successes—had consumed too much fuel and were now disengaging, becoming separated from the bombers which broke into *Staffeln* and hurried to cross the coast as best they could, jettisoning their bombs on any worthwhile target.

As Park's fighters withdrew to refuel and re-arm, more German fighters from *Jafu 2* swept in over Deal, Dover and Folkestone and, finding no British aircraft, resorted to their favourite sport of balloon strafing in the area. This was probably a tactical error, for Kesselring was already assembling his next bombing wave—comprising 40 Dorniers from KG 2 and KG 3 over south-west Belgium with orders to attack

Hon. Vincent Massey, Canadian High Commissioner, with pilots of No. 1 (Canadian) Squadron at Northolt. This squadron had attacked a formation of Dorniers on 26th August, whose escort had been drawn off by the Defiants of No. 264 Squadron. The Canadians were, however, caught by the bombers' crossfire and lost three Hurricanes; one pilot was killed but the other two—including Sqn. Ldr. E.A. McNab, seen here with the High Commissioner—were unhurt.

the airfields at Debden and Hornchurch. Despite the provision of a fighter escort of eighty Bf 110s and forty Bf 109s the raid proved abortive, simply because the relatively light screen of Bf 109s was operating at the limit of its fuel and was used to protect the Bf 110s!

The approach of the raid was watched closely on the Essex radar screens as it flew north-west across the mouth of the Thames Estuary (see accompanying map), but when the larger part of the enemy formation broke away to port the radar picture at Canewdon became so confused for five vital minutes that it appeared that a far greater raid was approaching London. The result was that Park ordered almost all his squadrons against this raid—including the Hurricanes of No. 111 Squadron from Martlesham.

The raid, which continued on its north-westerly course, managed to penetrate the coast before being intercepted and met with considerable *flak* opposition in the Colchester area. In the event most of this raid turned south long before it reached its target at Debden, only about half a dozen unescorted Dorniers persisting in their efforts to attack the airfield. Three of the bombers managed to release their bombs accurately; three airmen of No. 257 Squadron were killed when a bomb struck their shelter trench. Sqn. Ldr. Bill Harkness and Fg. Off. Frank Bolton (No. 257 Squadron's engineering officer) had close shaves, as they were both in the same trench when the bomb hit. The three sticks of bombs made tracks from east to west; a bomb fell between the first and second hangars and one aircraft was severely damaged. The Sergeants' Mess, transport yard and stores were all hit.

The successful Dorniers turned and made for the coast at top speed and, as far as can be ascertained, escaped. Their colleagues in the main formation were less lucky and ran up against seven squadrons of Hurricanes and Spitfires. Their Bf 109 escort, now seriously short of fuel, could not defend the formation and avoided combat. Several Dorniers and Bf 110s were shot down and it was obvious that as more interceptors made contact the bombers would be overwhelmed if they persisted in their course towards Hornchurch. Eyewitnesses state that a number of signal flares were dropped from the leading raiders, whereupon the entire formation wheeled about and retreated—a few small groups breaking away over Kent and jettisoning their bombs over Rochester, Maidstone, Ashford, Canterbury and Dungeness.

This raid was a major failure, and one that led to recriminations on both sides. In *Luftflotte 2* it was realised that the wastage of free-chasing Bf 109s immediately prior to the launching of KG 2 and KG 3 had deprived the raid of adequate cover, and this in turn led to further demands by the bomber commanders for a reduction in free chasing.

Once again Park had been obliged to deploy all his available forces against what appeared to be a heavy raid making for London, and had called on Leigh-Mallory to cover his northern airfields. This cover yet again failed to materialise, with the result that a small number of enemy bombers had reached Debden, caused some damaged and escaped. The cannon-armed Spitfires were slow off the ground, and arrived over Debden long after the raiders had departed.

The Hurricanes flown by the Free Czechs of No. 310 Squadron took off from Duxford (about seven miles from Debden) and, despite chaotic air-to-air communications resulting from the wrong radio crystals being fitted in some aircraft, managed to intercept the main northern formation.

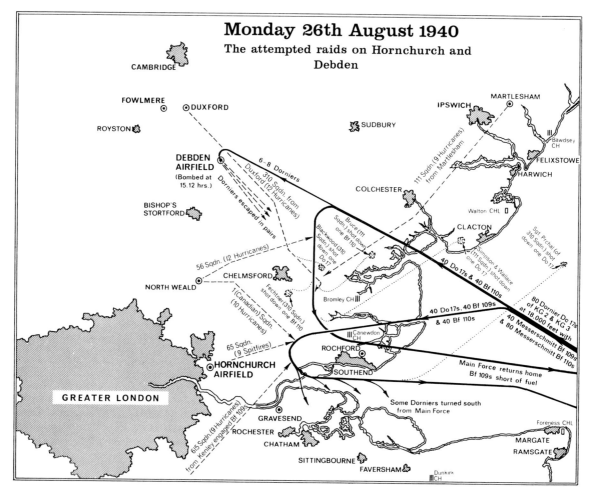

Monday 26th August 1940
The attempted raids on Hornchurch and Debden

Several successful combats followed and one, by Sgt. Edward Prchal, involved a thirty-mile chase of a Dornier 17, which he shot down only to be set upon by a prowling Bf 109 which almost blew off one of his wings. He force landed unhurt near Upminster. In this, No. 310 Squadron's first combat, three enemy aircraft were claimed destroyed for the loss of three Hurricanes, all of whose pilots escaped unhurt.

Following the accepted pattern, the *Luftwaffe* launched a third major attack in the Isle of Wight area at around 16.00 hours when Sperrle sent about fifty Heinkel He 111s of KG 55 against Portsmouth with an escort of 107 Bf 109s and 110s. Against this Park and Brand ordered eight squadrons, but only the twelve Hurricanes of No. 43 Squadron, ten Hurricanes of No. 615 Squadron and ten Spitfires of No. 602 Squadron managed to intercept, between them destroying four He 111s and four Bf 109, for the loss of two Hurricanes and two Spitfires. Three of the pilots were wounded, one of whom, Plt. Off. Harold North of No. 43 Squadron, wrote the following dramatic combat report:

"I was Yellow Leader and on the Tally Ho being given I echeloned my Section to port and attacked head-on a formation of six He 111s. They were the lower layer of a much larger mass stepped up. I could only fire the briefest of bursts and broke away below without noticing any results. I was nearly hit by some of the shower of bombs that were being jettisoned wholesale into the sea. I climbed back to the attack and got in two long quarter astern bursts (on a He 111). Quantities of smoke were emitted, the undercarriage dropped, one person at least baled out and the enemy was last seen diving, but I got hit by an explosive shell which went into my shoulder and arm, and pieces of perspex scratched my face so I could not see very well. I wiped my face, checked over my machine and when I felt better I looked up and saw three Heinkels passing overhead. I turned and attacked one who was lagging behind a bit—expending all my ammunition. Smoke belched from one of the engines—and the aircraft was diving steeply in a northern direction overland when I was forced to bale out, my aircraft having been hit from behind. I landed at Birdham near West Wittering and understand a Heinkel crashed at Waterlooville."

The 20-year-old New Zealander was admitted to hospital but was flying again with his Squadron about a fortnight later.

This raid by KG 55 proved to be the last major daylight raid launched by *Luftflotte 3* for about three weeks, for most of the Air Fleet's bomber *Geschwader* were transferred to night raiding of the industrial Midlands.

As the Heinkels were repulsed—without having reached either of their targets at Portsmouth and Southampton in any strength—*Seenotflugkommando 2* sent out several Heinkel He 59s to look for ditched crews, and one of these seaplanes was caught and shot down by five Spitfires of No. 602 Squadron twenty miles south of St. Catherine's Point.

Nightfall brought little respite, with upwards of 200 German bombers raiding Bournemouth, Plymouth, Coventry and Birmingham. Twenty aircraft raided the last-named town, evidently hoping to find the Spitfire factory at Castle Bromwich—but, in the absence of a pathfinding force on this occasion, little damage was done. Numerous raids were carried out by bombers operating singly but, apart from five railways reported damaged, little else was achieved.

R.A.F. FIGHTER COMMAND LOSSES—MONDAY 26th AUGUST 1940

No.	Unit		Details	Time	Pilot	Aircraft	Serial	Category
1.	1 (Canadian) Sqn., Northolt	C	Shot down by Do 17s; pilot killed. Aircraft crashed at Little Bardfield, Essex.	15.26 hrs.	Fg. Off. R.L. Edwards	Hurricane	P3874	Cat. 3 Destroyed
2.	1 (Canadian) Sqn., Northolt	C	Shot down by Do 17s ; pilot force landed unhurt.	15.24 hrs.	Sqn. Ldr. E.A. McNab	Hurricane	—	Cat. 2 Damaged
3.	1 (Canadian) Sqn., Northolt	C	Shot down by Do 17s ; pilot force landed unhurt.	15.27 hrs.	Fg. Off. J-P. J. Desloges	Hurricane	N2530	Cat. 3 Destroyed
4.	43 Sqn., Tangmere	C	Shot down near Portsmouth; pilot baled out wounded. Aircraft crashed near Birdham.	16.25 hrs.	Plt. Off. H.L. North	Hurricane	V7259	Cat. 3 Destroyed
5.	43 Sqn., Tangmere	C	Damaged in combat and crashed near Tangmere; pilot unhurt.	16.30 hours.	Not known	Hurricane	P3202	Cat. 3 Destroyed
6.	43 Sqn., Tangmere	C	Shot down and crashed near West Wittering, Sussex; pilot safe, believed unhurt.	16.30 hrs.	Not known	Hurricane	P3220	Cat. 3 Destroyed
7.	56 Sqn., North Weald	C	Shot down by Bf 109; pilot baled out unhurt near Canterbury.	12.20 hrs.	Plt. Off. B.J. Wicks	Hurricane	V7340	Cat. 3 Lost.
8.	56 Sqn., North Weald	C	Shot down by Bf 109; pilot force landed unhurt at Foulness.	A12.30 hrs.	Sgt. G. Smythe	Hurricane	P3473	Cat. 3 Destroyed
9.	85 Sqn., Croydon	C	Shot down by Bf 109; pilot baled out unhurt on Pitsea Marshes.	A13.35 hrs.	Sgt. J.A. Hemingway	Hurricane	P3966	Cat. 3 Lost
10.	111 Sqn., Martleham	C	Damaged in combat with Bf 110s; pilot returned unhurt.	A15.30 hrs.	Flt. Lt. D.C. Bruce	Hurricane	—	Cat. 1 Damaged
11.	111Sqn., Martlesham	C	Shot down and crashed near Martlesham; pilot slightly wounded.	A15.40 hrs.	Sgt. R.F. Sellars	Hurricane	R4096	Cat. 3 Destroyed
12.	234 Sqn., Middle Wallop	C	Force landed after combat with Bf 109s near Portsmouth; pilot unhurt.	16.30 hrs.	Sgt. M.C.B. Boddington	Spitfire	P9494	Cat. 2 Damaged
13.	234 Sqn., Middle Wallop	C	Damaged by Bf 109s near Portsmouth; pilot landed wheels-up at base, but unhurt.	16.40 hrs.	Plt. Off. P.W. Horton	Spitfire	X4023	Cat. 2 Damaged
14.	257 Sqn., Debden	—	Damaged in enemy raid on Debden; no pilot casualties.	15.30 hrs.	Nil	Hurricane	—	Cat. 2 Damaged
15.	264 Sqn., Hornchurch	C	Shot down by Bf 109 near Herne Bay. Pilot baled out and rescued unhurt from the sea, but gunner assumed killed; body not found.	12.08 hrs.	Flt. Lt. A.J. Banham Sgt. B. Baker	Defiant	L6985	Cat. 3 Destroyed
16.	264 Sqn., Hornchurch	C	Shot down by Bf 109 and crashed in North Kent; both crew members slightly wounded.	12.10 hrs.	Sgt. E.R. Thorn Sgt. F.J. Barker	Defiant	L7005	Cat. 3 Destroyed
17.	264 Sqn., Hornchurch	C	Shot down by Bf 109 off North Kent coast; pilot baled out and rescued from the sea, wounded. Gunner assumed killed.	12.27 hrs.	Fg. Off. I.R. Stephenson Sgt. W. Maxwell.	Defiant	L7025	Cat. 3 Lost
18.	310 Sqn., Duxford	C	Shot down by Bf 110; pilot baled out at Wickham Bishop, near Maldon, unhurt.	A15.30 hrs.	Sqn. Ldr. G.D.M. Blackwood	Hurricane	P3887	Cat. 3 Destroyed
19.	310 Sqn., Duxford	C	Shot down by Bf 110; pilot baled out at Southminster, unhurt.	A15.30 hrs.	Plt. Off. V. Bergman	Hurricane	P3960	Cat. 3 Destroyed
20	310 Sqn., Duxford	C	Shot down and force landed near Upminster; pilot unhurt.	A15.40 hrs.	Sgt. E.M. Prchal	Hurricane	P3517	Cat. 3 Destroyed
21.	602 Sqn., Westhampnett	C	Shot down by Bf 109s; pilot, badly wounded, crashed and had left foot amputated.	16.38 hrs.	Fg. Off. C.H. MacLean	Spitfire	X4187	Cat. 2 Damaged
22.	602 Sqn., Westhampnett	C	Shot down by Bf 109s off Bognor Regis; pilot rescued by Bognor lifeboat, unhurt.	16.43 hrs.	Sgt. C.F. Babbage	Spitfire	X4188	Cat. 3 Lost
23.	610 Sqn., Hawkinge	C	Shot down by Bf 109s; pilot baled out over Hawking, wounded; left arm amputated.	A12.00 hrs.	Sgt. P. Else	Spitfire	P9496	Cat. 3 Lost
24.	610 Sqn., Hawkinge	C	Crashed at Hawking after combat with Bf 109s off Folkestone; pilot killed.	A12.00 hrs.	Plt. Off. F.K. Webster	Spitfire	X4011	Cat. 3 Destroyed
25.	615 Sqn., Kenley	C	Shot down by Bf 109 off North Kent; pilot baled out and rescued from sea with shock.	15.10 hrs.	Flt. Lt. L.M. Gaunce	Hurricane	R4111	Cat. 3 Lost
26.	615 Sqn., Kenley	C	Shot down by Bf 109 off Sheerness; pilot baled out unhurt.	15.08 hrs.	Plt. Off. J.A.P. McClintock	Hurricane	R4121	Cat. 3 Lost
27.	615 Sqn., Kenley	C	Shot down and crashed on Rochester airfield; pilot wounded in the legs.	A15.30 hrs.	Plt. Off. D.H. Hone	Hurricane	—	Cat. 3 Destroyed
28.	615 Sqn., Kenley	C	Shot down near Rowlands Castle; pilot slightly wounded.	A16.50 hrs.	Fg. Off. J.R.H. Gayner	Hurricane	P2878	Cat. 3 Destroyed
29.	616 Sqn., Kenley	C	Shot down and killed by Bf 109s off Dungeness; body recovered from the sea.	11.40 hrs.	Fg. Off. G.E. Moberley	Spitfire	N3275	Cat. 3 Destroyed
30.	616 Sqn., Kenley	C	Shot down and killed by Bf 109s near Dungeness; pilot buried at Hawkinge.	11.49 hrs.	Sgt. M. Ridley	Spitfire	—	Cat. 3 Destroyed
31.	616 Sqn., Kenley	C	Shot down by Bf 109s and force landed at Eastchurch; pilot wounded and admitted to Minster Hospital.	12.04 hrs.	Fg. Off. E.F. St. Aubin	Spitfire	R7018	Cat. 3 Destroyed
32.	616 Sqn., Kenley	C	Shot down and force landed after combat with Bf 109s; pilot slightly wounded.	A12.10 hrs.	Plt. Off. R. Marples	Spitfire	—	Cat. 3 Destroyed
33.	616 Sqn., Kenley	C	Pilot baled out, wounded, after combat with Bf 109s near Dungeness.	A12.12 hrs.	Plt. Off. W.L.B. Walker	Spitfire	R6701	Cat. 3 Lost
34.	616 Sqn., Kenley	C	Force landed after combat with Bf 109s near Dungeness; pilot unhurt.	A12.20 hrs.	Sgt. P. Copeland	Spitfire	K9827	Cat. 3 Destroyed

LUFTWAFFE LOSSES—MONDAY 26th AUGUST 1940

No.	Unit		Details	Time	Aircraft	%	Crew
1.	4.(F)/121	CM	Struck Bf 110 while landing at Caen-Carpiquet.		Junkers Ju 88A-1	20 %	Vrew unhurt.
2.	2./KG 2	CM	Shot down by 85 Sqn. Hurricanes of Allard and Worrall and force landed on Rochford airfield.		Dornier Do 17Z-3	100 %	Oblt. Heidereich + one killed; two missing.
3.	2./KG 2	CM	Shot down by 85 Sqn. Hurricanes and crashed near Eastchurch.		Dornier Do 17Z-3	100 %	Maj. Gutzmann, Gr.Kdr., Oblt. Siegfried Hertel + two missing.
4.	3./KG 2	CM	Damaged by 65 Sqn. Spitfire over Thames Estuary at A.15.20 hrs.		Dornier Do 17Z-2	10—60 %	Oblt. Bucholz, St.Kap., and Oblt. Konrad wounded.
5.	4./KG 2	CM	Crashed at Namur with combat damage.		Dornier Do 17Z-2 (U5+MM)	100 %	Crew unhurt.
6.	7./KG 2	CM	Shot down by 111Sqn. Hurricanes of Simpson and Wallace near Clacton at A.15.30 hrs.		Dornier Do 17Z-3	100 %	Hptm. Böse + three missing.
7.	7./KG 2	CM	Shot down by 310 Sqn. Hurricane of Prchal 15 miles south-east of Harwich.		Dornier Do 17Z-3	100 %	One killed and three missing.

245

Luftwaffe Losses, 26th August 1940—*continued*

8.	7./KG 2	CM	Shot down by 310 Sqn. Hurricane of Blackwood north-east of Chelmsford.	Dornier Do 17Z-2	100 %		Ltn. Krieger + three missing.
9.	2./KG 3	CM	Crashed near Tirlemont with fuel shortage.	Dornier Do 17Z-2 (2541)	80 %		One killed and two wounded.
10.	III./KG 3	CM	Damaged by 264 Sqn. Defiant and crashed at Calais/Marck.	Dornier Do 17Z-3 (3602)	70 %		One wounded.
11.	7./KG 3	CM	Shot down by 264 Sqn. Defiant of Banham and Baker over North Foreland at A. 12.15 hrs.	Dornier Do 17Z-3 (2646)	100 %		Ltn. Eggert + two killed; one missing.
12.	7./KG 3	CM	Shot down by 610 Sqn. Spitfire of Lamb near Dover at A.12.30 hrs.	Dornier Do 17Z-2 (1160)	100 %		One killed and three missing.
13.	7./KG 3	CM	Damaged by R.A.F. fighters and force landed at St. Merville.	Dornier Do 17Z-3 (2822)	10—60 %		Two wounded.
14.	7./KG 3	CM	Shot down by 264 Sqn. of Hughes over East Kent at A.12.15 hrs.	Dornier Do 17Z-2 (5K+GR)	100 %		Ltn. Sachse killed; three missing.
15.	8./KG 4	CM	Take-off collision with another Ju 88 (Item 16).	Junkers Ju 88A-1	100 %		Oblt. Meissner, *St.Kap.*, + three killed.
16.	8./KG 4	CM	Take-off collision with another Ju 88 (Item 15).	Junkers Ju 88A-1	100 %		One crew member injured.
17.	6./KG 30	CM	Missing from sortie over Northern England.	Junkers Ju 88A-1(3103)	100 %		One killed + three wounded.
18.	III./KG 53	NCM	Crashed near Brügge following faulty servicing.	Heinkel He 111H-2	100 %		Ltn. Weber + three killed.
19.	I./KG 55	CM	Shot down by 17 and 43 Sqn. Hurricanes south of Portsmouth at A.16.20 hrs.	Heinkel He 111P	100 %		Oblt. Krenn + four missing.
20.	II./KG 55	CM	Shot down by 43 Sqn. Hurricanes and crashed near Waterlooville at A.16.30 hrs.	Heinkel He 111P	100 %		Four killed; Ltn. Metzger missing.
21.	II./KG 55	CM	Shot down by 602 Sqn. Spitfire off Selsey Bill and crashed in Channel; crew rescued.	Heinkel He 111P	100 %		Three wounded; crew P.O.W.s.
22.	II./KG 55	CM	Shot down by 43 Sqn. Hurricanes of Badger and Hallowes near Portsmouth at A.16.20 hrs.	Heinkel He 111P	100 %		One killed; Ltn. Walter + three missing.
23.	I./KG 77	NCM	Force landed at Illesheim; cause not known.	Junkers Ju 88A-1	40 %		Crew unhurt.
24.	I./LG 1	NCM	Landing accident at Orléans-Bricy airfield.	Junkers Ju 88A-1(3090)	30 %		Crew unhurt.
25.	II./ZG 2	CM	Crashed at St. Pierre Eglise following combat.	Messerschmitt Bf 110	60 %		Crew unhurt.
26.	4./ZG 26	CM	Shot down by 111 Sqn. Hurricane of Bruce at A.15.30 hrs. and crashed one mile west of Great Tey, Essex.	Messerschmitt Bf 110 D-0 (3U+CM)	100 %		Uffz. Herbert Heinrich + one other killed
27.	9./ZG 26	CM	Shot down by 310 Sqn. Hurricane of Fechtner near Chelmsford at A.15.30 hrs.	Messerschmitt Bf 110 C-4	100 %		Two crew members killed.
28.	9./ZG 26	CM	Shot down by fighters in Chelmsford area; no R.A.F. claim traced.	Messerschmitt Bf 110 C-4 (3299)	100 %		One killed and one missing.
29.	2./ZG 76	CM	Dived vertically into the ground at Crabtree Farm, Great Bentley, Essex, at 15.25 hrs.	Messerschmitt Bf 110 C-4 (2N+AK)	100 %		Both crew members killed.
30.	III./JG 2	CM	Missing from sortie over English South Coast.	Messerschmitt Bf 109 E-4 (3702)	100 %		Ltn. Hoffman killed.
31.	4./JG 3	CM	Damaged by 56 Sqn. Hurricane of Mounsdon and crashed near Calais.	Messerschmitt Bf 109 E-4 (5132)	20 %		Pilot unhurt.
32.	4./JG 3	CM	Shot down by 615 Sqn. Hurricane near Canterbury.	Messerschmitt Bf 109 E-1 (6221))	100 %		Pilot missing.
33.	4./JG 3	CM	Shot down by 56 Sqn. Hurricane of Marston in Canterbury area.	Messerschmitt Bf 109 E-4 (5289)	100 %		Oblt. Heinrich Held killed; buried
34.	5./JG 3	CM	Force landed at Ossendrecht after engine failure.	Messerschmitt Bf 109	10 %		Pilot unhurt.
35.	6./JG 3	CM	Shot down by 56 Sqn. Hurricane of Marston over North Kent coast.	Messerschmitt Bf 109 E-1 (3874)	100 %		Uffz. Wilhelm Finker made P.O.W.
36.	8./JG 3	CM	Damaged by 610 Spitfire and force landed near Calais.	Messerschmitt Bf 109 E-4	20 %		Pilot safe.
37.	III./JG 27	CM	Missing from sortie over English South Coast.	Messerschmitt Bf 109E	100 %		Uffz. Erich Ackmann missing.
38.	I./JG 52	CM	Shot down by 54 Sqn. Spitfire near Ramsgate.	Messerschmitt Bf 109 E-1	100 %		Pilot missing.
39.	I./JG 52	CM	Shot down by 610 Sqn. Spitfire of Ellis near Folkestone	Messerschmitt Bf 109 E-4	100 %		Pilot missing.
40.	I./JG 52	CM	Shot down by 610 Sqn. Spitfires near Dover.	Messerschmitt Bf 109 E-1	100 %		Pilot missing.
41.	I./JG 52	CM	Shot down by British fighters near Ramsgate.	Messerschmitt Bf 109 E-1	100 %		Pilot missing.
42.	I./JG 52	CM	Shot down by British fighters near Ramsgate.	Messerschmitt Bf 109 E-1	100 %		Pilot missing.
43.	I./JG 53	CM	Shot down by 234 Sqn. Spitfires near Portsmouth.	Messerschmitt Bf 109 E-4	100 %		Pilot killed.
44.	II./JG 53	CM	Shot down by 43 Sqn. Hurricanes south of Portsmouth and crashed into English Channel.	Messerschmitt Bf 109 E-4	100 %		Ltn. Roos missing.
45.	II./JG 53	CM	Shot down by 234 Sqn. Spitfire near Portsmouth.	Messerschmitt Bf 109 E-4	100 %		Ltn. Berwanger missing.
46.	II./JG 53	CM	Shot down by 610 Sqn. Spitfires and crashed off coast of Cherbourg Peninsula.	Messerschmitt Bf 109 E-1	100 %		Pilot killed.
47.	III./JG 53	NCM	Crashed near Brest following technical failure.	Messerschmitt Bf 109 E-1	80 %		Pilot unhurt.
48.	II./JG 54	NCM	Force landed on Beveland Island after engine failure.	Messerschmitt Bf 109 E-1 (3639)	30 %		Pilot safe.
49.	1./506	—	Destroyed in R.A.F. bombing raid on Tromsö.	Heinkel He 115	100 %		No aircrew casualties.
50.	1./506	—	Destroyed in R.A.F. bombing raid on Tromsö.	Heinkel He 115	100 %		No aircrew casualties.
51.	Seenotflug-kommando 2	CM	Shot down by five Spitfires of 602 Sqn., twenty miles south of St. Catherine's Point.	Heinkel He 59 (935)	100 %		Ltn.z.S. Mietlin + one killed; two missing.

Tuesday 27th August

In contrast to the previous day, most Fighter Command squadrons reported little activity on this Tuesday. Early drizzle and low cloud over much of the country gave place to clear skies and warm sunshine later, but no major attack materialised. The *Luftwaffe* was drawing breath before renewing its final and major attack upon Fighter Command, and while reconnaissance activity was reported over much of the South-East, new plans were being drawn up to ensure still closer ties between the bomber formations and their escorting Bf 109s.

Of the small number of German aircraft intercepted on this day, one was of particular importance. This was a Heinkel He

A Spitfire of No. 19 Squadron taxies out for take-off. This unit was one of the components of the "Duxford Wing", subject of heated controversy during the Battle—and ever since.

111 of *Stab* III./KG 1 which was intercepted near Portland and shot down by the Spitfires of Fg. Off. Peter O'Brian[62] and Plt. Off. William Beaumont. The latter was also shot down in this engagement, but not before the Heinkel's destruction had been confirmed; with it fell Major Fanelsa, *Gruppenkommandeur* of III./KG 1. A Dornier Do 17P of 3.(F)/31 was shot down near St. Eval and in the wreckage was found a large reconnaissance camera; it had evidently been engaged in photographing damage caused in a raid by eight bombers the previous night. (62 bombs had been dropped on the dummy flarepath some distance from the airfield.) The Dornier crashed near Tavistock and three prisoners were taken.

Dowding took the opportunity during the day's lull to relieve some of his worst-hit squadrons. No. 65 Squadron, down to nine aircraft and twelve exhausted pilots, was ordered to leave Hornchurch to rest and re-train at Church Fenton. No. 32 Squadron was moved north to Acklington, its place at Biggin Hill being taken once more by an invigorated No. 79 Squadron.

The vexed problem facing Park at this time was the apparent lack of co-operation by Leigh-Mallory's squadrons on his northern flank. Clearly a difference of opinion between the

---

[62] Peter O'Brian, a Canadian in the Royal Air Force, had been a peacetime flight cadet at the Royal Air Force College, Cranwell, and Graduated with the Sword of Honour in December 1937—the only Canadian ever to do so. He retired from the R.A.F. as a Group Captain in July 1959.

The pilot of this Bf 109E attempted to crash land his damaged aircraft on what had appeared to be a large unobstructed field in Kent, only to discover too late that it was studded with tree trunks—distributed all over fields in South-East England as an anti-invasion measure to prevent the landing of German troop-carrying gliders. The poles made short work of the Messerschmitt.

two commanders existed as how best to handle defensive fighter forces, although the No. 12 Group Commander's true convictions were not to become evident for another few days. Basically it may be said that Park was only able to control his squadrons singly owing to the shortage of warning of a raid's approach. To waste time assembling a Wing of fighters would simply allow the enemy raids to penetrate the defences. Being situated further north No. 12 Group squadrons might have adequate to time form up in a Wing before intercepting hostile bombers in strength. Although no opportunity had yet presented itself to throw such a Wing into battle, Sqn. Ldr. Douglas Bader (commanding No. 242 Squadron) had suggested the tactic to Leigh-Mallory and found sympathy for the idea. However, the very nature and urgency of Park's calls for assistance had prevented the Wing from forming up quickly and efficiently, so that when the squadrons arrived piecemeal over No. 11 Group's airfields they were invariably too late. This deficiency further strengthened Park's opinion that wing formations were unwieldy and relatively inefficient. Rather later in the Battle, Park *was* able to operate paired squadrons in certain favourable conditions, but there is no reliable evidence to show that the Duxford Wing (so-called from the rendezvous for Leigh-Mallory's squadrons) ever achieved combat results commensurate with the number of aircraft employed. To the contrary, it is recorded that of the 28 occasions on which a "Wing" was ordered, there were nine instances when the Wing failed to form up at all, and only seven resulted in combat; only once did the Wing intercept a raid before other fighters appeared, and on this occasion the pilots claimed the destruction of 57 German aircraft, when in truth only eight had fallen—of which just four fell to the guns of the Wing. On two well documented occasions the Wing was itself "bounced" by a large number of enemy aircraft, occasions which together cost the Wing a total of eighteen Hurricanes and Spitfires. Needless to say, it was fortunate indeed that Leigh-Mallory never had to face the frequency and weight of enemy attacks thrown against No. 11 Group, for if he had, and had attempted to meet them with laboriously assembled Wings he could only have offered a very poor fighter defence, and his airfields would have been bombed to rubble.

As already remarked, Leigh-Mallory was not yet ready to employ full Wing tactics before the end of August 1940, but already the embryo of his plan was causing Park acute discomfort. Park, for his part, believed the fault lay at Squadron level and, rather than precipitate a head-on quarrel with Leigh-Mallory advised his Sector Commanders to appeal direct to the Fighter Command Controller for the provision of fighter cover for their airfields.

R.A.F. FIGHTER COMMAND LOSSES—TUESDAY 27th AUGUST 1940

1.	72 Sqn., Acklington	NC	Landing accident at Acklington; pilot unhurt.	Not known	Not known		Spitfire	K9922	Cat. 3 Destroyed
2.	92 Sqn., Bibury	NC	Pilot became lost on night patrol; crash landed at Martlesham, but unhurt.	At Night	Plt. Off. F.N. Hargreaves	Spitfire	P9548	Cat. 3 Destroyed
3.	152 Sqn., Warmwell	C	Shot down by Ju 88 west of Portland; pilot baled out and rescued unhurt.	Not known	Plt. Off. W. Beaumont	Spitfire	R6831	Cat. 3 Lost
4.	213 Sqn., Exeter	NC	Struck sea during patrol and assumed to have been killed.	Not known	Sub-Lt. W.J.M. Moss	Hurricane	N2336	Cat. 3 Lost

LUFTWAFFE LOSSES—TUESDAY 27th AUGUST 1940

1.	4.(F)/14	CM	Landing accident at Cherbourg airfield.	Messerschmitt Bf 110 C-5	15 %	Crew unhurt.
2.	3.(F)/31	CM	Shot down by 238 Sqn. Hurricanes of Considine and Blake and crashed at Tavistock at 10.13 hrs.	Dornier Do 17P	100 %	Ltn. Haffan + two missing.
3.	Stab III./KG 1	CM	Shot down by 152 Sqn. Spitfires near Portland.	Heinkel He 111H-2 (5376)	100 %	Maj. Fanelsa, *Gr.Kdr.*, + four missing.
4.	5./KG 2	CM	Reported to have been damaged by 222 Sqn. Spitfires and crashed at Slyge.	Dornier Do 17Z-2 (4188)	100 %	Three wounded.
5.	6./KG 2	CM	Force landed near St. André short of fuel.	Dornier Do 17Z-3 (2784)	35 %	Crew unhurt.
6.	Ausb.St./KG 3	NCM	Crashed at Schweinfurth after engine failure.	Dornier Do 17	90 %	Two crew members injured.
7.	7./KG 4	CM	Missing from sortie over England; fate unkown.	Junkers Ju 88A-5 (0284)	100 %	Ltn. Annis + two killed; Ltn.z.S. von Athens missing.
8.	II./KG 27	CM	Landing accident at Bourges airfield.	Heinkel He 111P	28 %	Crew unhurt.
9.	6./KG 30	CM	Landing accident at Aalborg airfield.	Junkers Ju 88A-1(4033)	100 %	Ltn. Kiessner + three killed.
10.	9./KG 30	NCM	Take-off accident at Aalborg airfield.	Junkers Ju 88A-1(4076)	50 %	Crew unhurt.
11.	II./KG 55	CM	Landing accident at Chartres airfield.	Heinkel He 111P	35%	Crew unhurt.
12.	KGr. 806	NCM	Accident on Nantes airfield; details not known.	Junkers Ju 88A-1	50 %	Crew unhurt.
13.	KGr. 806	NCM	Accident on Nantes airfield; details not known.	Junkers Ju 88A-1	10 %	Crew unhurt.
14.	II./LG 1	CM	Crashed at Cherbourg after combat with R.A.F. fighters; British unit not traced.	Junkers Ju 88A-1	50 %	Crew unhurt.
15.	V./LG 1	NCM	Taxying accident on Roquancourt airfield.	Messerschmitt Bf 110 C-2	70 %	Crew unhurt.
16.	6./JG 3	NCM	Landing accident at Samer airfield.	Messerschmitt Bf 109 E-4 (1471)	75 %	Pilot unhurt.
17.	I./JG 52	CM	Take-off accident at Calais-Marck airfield.	Messerschmitt Bf 109 E-1 (6215)	65 %	Pilot unhurt.
18.	3./106	CM	Damaged by night fighter in Grid Square 4330. R.A.F. claim not traced.	Heinkel He 115C (2782)	30 %	Ltn. Arnim + two wounded.

Wednesday 28th August

As will be seen from the accounts of the battles fought over Southern England since the 24th, both Park and Brand had on numerous occasions ordered large numbers of fighters into the air to meet massed formations of German aircraft approaching the Kent, Sussex and Hampshire coasts. Although the first fighters to take off usually intercepted the raids successfully over the coast, the German tactics of splitting their formations once over the land so confused the Observer Corps—and therefore the overland plotting tables at the sector operations centres—that it had proved impossible to guide subsequent fighters on to the enemy formations with any accuracy. The result had been for upwards of two-thirds of the fighter forces to miss the enemy altogether, and this caused Park to instruct his fighter leaders to pass a coherent sighting report back to their controller before going into the attack, giving the traditional "Tally-ho" and the position, course, strength and height of the enemy. This procedure, although taking effect from the 27th, was to be used to great advantage for the first time on the 28th.

With *Luftflotte 3* now effectively withdrawn from the daylight battle—at least temporarily—with the transfer of almost all its Bf 109s into Kesselring's *Luftflotte 2*, the weight of attacks was now applied almost exclusively against No. 11 Group, and while the daily attacks continued to follow the familiar three-phase pattern there was to be no respite for Park through flank attacks against No. 10 Group. Now, more than ever, the survival of No. 11 Group depended upon the assistance rendered by reinforcements provided by its neighbouring Group commanders.

After isolated sparring with reconnaissance Dorniers shortly after first light, Dover CH reported a heavy raid building up over the Pas de Calais shortly after 08.00 hours. Thirty-two Hurricanes of 79, 501 and 615 Squadrons, and twelve Defiants of 264 Squadron were ordered off, and all made contact with the enemy just as two heavily escorted formations (one of Dorniers, the other of Heinkels) crossed the Kent coast near Deal. Once again the raiding formations split, twenty-three Dorniers of I./KG 3 making for Eastchurch airfield and 27 Heinkels from II. and III./KG 53 for Rochford. Fortuitously the Hurricane pilots of No. 79 Squadron, who were flying forward to Hawkinge, sighted the Heinkels and passed a sighting report before going into the attack. They were prevented from achieving any conclusive results, as they were overwhelmed by the large number of escorting Bf 109s. They were lucky to escape without loss.

Taking the opportunity to attack while the escort's attention was diverted, the Defiants, led by Sqn. Ldr. George Garvin with Flt. Lt. Robert Ash as gunner[63], launched what was to be the last daylight squadron attack by these aircraft. Their pilots did not see another *Gruppe* of Bf 109s waiting in the sun. . .

"The Squadron attacked but was split up by Bf 109s and the cross-fire from the Heinkels. One of the Heinkels was destroyed by Plt. Off. William Carnaby in this, his first combat, and one was damaged by Sgt. Lauder. Sqn. Ldr. Garvin had a turret fuse blow and while Flt. Lt. Ash was replacing it his aircraft was hit by a cannon shell and caught fire; both baled out but Flt. Lt. Ash was dead when found. . .Plt. Off. Whitley and Sgt. Turner, one of the most successful crews on the Squadron, were killed when their machine crashed and burst into flames. Plt. Off. Kenner and Plt. Off. Johnson crashed and were killed. Plt. Off Bailey made a forced landing after being shot down by a Bf 109; both he and his gunner, Sgt. Hardy, were unhurt. Eight Defiants returned to Hornchurch, but of these only three were serviceable."

Despite the efforts of these two squadrons, the Heinkels got through to the Rochford area, but thanks to fairly accurate *flak* around the airfield little material damage was inflicted. Meanwhile the Dorniers had forced their way through—their escort of about sixty Bf 109s from I. and III./JG 51 warding off attacks by Hurricanes of Nos. 501 and 615 Squadrons— and dropped more than one hundred bombs on the airfield at Eastchurch a few minutes after 09.00 hours. Despite the destruction of several light bombers and extensive damage to the grass surface, the airfield was not put out of action.

The next phase again involved an attack against Rochford—presumably when it was learned that little damage had been caused by KG 53. This time 30 Dorniers of II. and III./ KG 3 flew up the Thames Estuary at 18,000 feet and reached their target at 12.35 hours.

At nearby Hornchurch the crews of the three remaining Defiants pleaded for permission to scramble (it was being reported that Flight Lieutenant Ash had been fired on and killed by enemy fighters as he descended by parachute, and feelings were running high in the Squadron), but this was refused until the bombs began to fall, and by then it was too late. Eleven Hurricanes of No. 1 Squadron did manage to intercept, and destroyed a Dornier of 6./KG 3 which crashed on Rochford airfield; the crew of four was captured.

This second raid on Rochford was also intercepted by twelve Spitfires of No. 54 Squadron, which destroyed an escorting Bf 109. Yet again Flt. Lt. Alan Deere had to bale out, this time having apparently been attacked by a Spitfire![64]

Scarcely had Park's fighters returned and been refuelled when the South Kent radar stations reported a number of high flying enemy formations approaching from the south and south-east. In anticipation of a follow-up attack, the No. 11 Group Controllers had ordered several Flights to cover the Sector airfields, and six groups of fighters were vectored on to the incoming raids. Unfortunately these turned out to be five *Gruppen* of Bf 110s and six of Bf 109s. As successive waves of enemy fighters approached, No. 11 Group became involved in exactly the type of combat—fighter versus fighter—which Park was anxious to avoid. First in action were eleven Hurricanes of No. 85 Squadron, led by Sqn. Ldr. Peter Townsend (who claimed a Bf 109 north-west of

---

[63] Flight Lieutenant Ash had, until just before the War been an equipment officer, but volunteered for flying duties. At 31 he was the senior ranking—though not the oldest—Defiant gunner at the time of the Battle of Britain and had hitherto contributed much advice on the development of turret fighting tactics. The oldest Defiant gunner, indeed the oldest flying participant in Fighter Command during the Battle of Britain was Pilot Officer Sydney Carlin, also of No. 264 Squadron, who at the age of 51 already held the M.C., D.F.C. and D.C.M. Born in 1889, Carlin had lost a leg in the trenches during the First World War before joining No. 74 Squadron as an S.E.5 pilot, shooting down eleven enemy aircraft. He was the only member of a Fighter Command squadron in the Battle of Britain entitled to wear the R.F.C. pilot's "wings" *and* R.A.F. Observer's brevet. He survived the Battle only to be killed in May 1941 while attempting to run to his Defiant to fire at enemy aircraft attacking his airfield. Throughout his service with the R.F.C. and R.A.F., he was affectionately known as "Timbertoes".

[64] This was the first combat in which No. 54 Squadron's newly appointed C.O. participated. Donald Finlay was famous as Britain's Olympic Silver Medallist in the 1936 Games' 110 metres Hurdles. See also below.

Lympne). His pilots gave a good account of themselves, claiming five other 109s without loss. Among the ground spectators was Winston Churchill, who was on this day paying a visit to the hard-pressed defences of the South-East.

No. 85 Squadron was more fortunate than others committed in this phase. Nos. 56 and 151 Squadrons each lost two Hurricanes and No. 54 Squadron lost a Spitfire, the latter when the squadron commander-to-be, Donald Finlay, had to bale out with minor wounds.

The heavy fighting of the mid-afternoon achieved Kesselring's aim, and the loss of the equivalent of almost two squadrons in a single day was clearly more than Park could afford. It is true that about a quarter of these losses were suffered by the Defiant squadron (which was now removed from the daylight battle for good), yet the conduct of the afternoon battle was strictly contrary to Park's instructions—a fact to which his Controllers' attention was sharply drawn. German losses had also been fairly heavy, especially among the fighters. Curiously enough, not one Bf 110 was lost on this day, despite more than 60 being committed to battle. The

inference must be that the *Zerstörer* was itself being afforded close protection by the Bf 109s.

An interesting loss on this day occurred in the late evening when a small communications aircraft, a Gotha Go 145 belonging to JG 27, touched down on Lewes racecourse when the pilot apparently "lost his way *en route* for Germany". The mail which he was carrying home from the *Jagdgeschwader* fell into British hands. There is now, however, some evidence to suggest that this was a deliberate ruse by the Germans to conceal the fact that JG 27 had in reality moved away eastwards from the Cherbourg peninsula, something that Kesselring would have been at pains to conceal from the British—so as not to encourage the R.A.F. to move fighters from the west to reinforce the defences in the South-East. The loss of a small communications aircraft and a single pilot would have been small price to pay for such a ruse to succeed. The excuse given that the pilot had lost his way and followed an incorrect course over a hundred miles of Channel in fine weather is scarcely credible!

R.A.F. FIGHTER COMMAND LOSSES—WEDNESDAY 28th AUGUST 1940

1.	54 Sqn., Hornchurch	C	Shot down by Spitfire during combat with Bf 109s; pilot baled out unhurt.	A13.15 hrs	Flt. Lt. A.C. Deere	Spitfire	R6832	Cat. 3 Lost
2.	54 Sqn., Hornchurch	C	Shot down by Bf 109s near Canterbury; pilot baled out wounded.	16.50 hrs.	Sqn. Ldr. D.O. Finlay	Spitfire	X4053	Cat. 3 Destroyed
3.	56 Sqn., North Weald	C	Shot down by Bf 109 over Thames Estuary; pilot slightly wounded.	13.20 hrs.	Plt. Off. M.C. Constable-Maxwell	Hurricane	—	Cat. 3 Lost
4.	56 Sqn., North Weald	C	Shot down by Bf 109s over Thames Estuary; pilot unhurt.	13.20 hrs.	Fg. Off. P.S. Weaver	Hurricane	R4117	Cat. 3 Lost.
5.	56 Sqn., North Weald	C	Shot down by Bf 109 at Acrise, near Folkestone; pilot baled out unhurt.	16.47 hrs.	Sgt. G. Smythe	Hurricane	N2524	Cat. 3 Destroyed
6.	56 Sqn., North Weald	C	Shot down, possibly by a Spitfire; pilot baled out with serious burns.	A16.50 hrs	Plt. Off. F.B. Sutton	Hurricane	R4198	Cat. 3 Destroyed
7.	151 Sqn., North Weald	C	Shot down in flames by Bf 109 at Godmersham; pilot baled out badly burned.	A16.30 hrs.	Plt. Off. J.W.E. Alexander	Hurricane	L2005	Cat. 3 Destroyed
8.	151 Sqn., North Weald	C	Force landed on Eastchurch airfield after combat; pilot wounded.	A16.40 hrs.	Sgt. L. Davies	Hurricane	P3320	Cat. 2 Damaged
9.	219 Sqn., Catterick	NC	Night landing accident at Catterick in bad weather; crew unhurt.	01.45 hrs.	Sgt. E.G. Grubb Sgt. S. Austin	Blenheim	L1524	Cat. 3 Destroyed
10.	264 Sqn., Hornchurch	C	Shot down by Bf 109 in flames on Luddenham Marsh; pilot baled out slightly wounded, but gunner baled out, and possibly shot during parachute descent.	09.30 hrs.	Sqn. Ldr. G.D. Garvin Flt. Lt. R.C.V. Ash	Defiant	L7021	Cat. 3 Destroyed
11.	264 Sqn., Hornchurch	C	Shot down by Bf 109s near Manston; crew baled out but both were killed.	09.30 hrs.	Plt. Off. D. Whitley Sgt. R.C. Turner	Defiant	N1574	Cat. 3 Destroyed
12.	264 Sqn., Hornchurch	C	Shot down by Bf 109s at Hinxhill, near Ashford; crew did not bale out and both were killed. Gunner buried at Hawkinge.	09.35 hrs.	Plt. Off. P.L. Kenner Plt. Off. C.E. Johnson	Defiant	L7026	Cat. 3 Destroyed
13.	264 Sqn., Hornchurch	C	Shot down by Bf 109s and force landed at Court Lodge Farm, Petham, near Canterbury; neither crew member hurt.	09.45 hrs.	Plt. Off. J.R.A. Bailey Sgt. O.A. Hardy	Defiant	N1569	Cat. 3 Destroyed
14.	264 Sqn., Hornchurch	C	Damaged in combat with Bf 109s; crew unhurt.	09.35 hrs.	Crew not known	Defiant	—	Cat. 2 Damaged
15.	264 Sqn., Hornchurch	C	Damaged in combat with Bf 109s; crew unhurt.	09.35 hrs.	Crew not known	Defiant	—	Cat. 1 Damaged
16.	264 Sqn., Hornchurch	C	Damaged in combat with Bf 109s; crew unhurt.	09.35 hrs.	Crew not known	Defiant	—	Cat. 1 Damaged
17.	603 Sqn., Hornchurch	C	Shot down in combat with Bf 109s over Dover; pilot assumed killed.	Not known	Flt. Lt. J.L.G. Cunningham	Spitfire	N3015	Cat. 3 Missing
18.	603 Sqn., Hornchurch	C	Damaged in combat with Bf 109s off Dover, wounded; returned to base but aircraft written off.	Not known	Flt. Lt. I.S. Ritchie	Spitfire	R6989	Cat. 3 Destroyed
19.	603 Sqn., Hornchurch	C	Shot down by Bf 109s over Dover and pilot aircraft assumed lost over the sea.	Not known	Plt. Off. D.K. MacDonald	Spitfire	L1046	Cat. 3 Lost
20.	603 Sqn., Hornchurch	C	Shot down by Bf 109s near Dover; pilot assumed killed.	Not known	Plt. Off. N.J.V. Benson	Spitfire	—	Cat. 3 Lost
21.	610 Sqn., Biggin Hill	C	Shot down by Bf 109s near Deal; pilot killed and aircraft crashed into house at Stelling Minnis, north-west of Folkestone.	16.04 hrs.	Plt. Off. K.H. Cox	Spitfire	P9511	Cat. 3 Destroyed
22.	615 Sqn., Kenley	C	Shot down and force landed near Ashford, pilot with slightly injuries to face.	Morning	Plt. Off. S.J. Madle	Hurricane	R4116	Cat. 3 Destroyed

LUFTWAFFE LOSSES—WEDNESDAY 28th AUGUST 1940

1.	Stab II/KG 1	CM	Damaged by 79 Sqn. Hurricane of Nelson-Edwards at 08.45 hrs and crashed at Calais.	Heinkel He 111H-2 (5588)	50 %	One wounded.
2.	4./KG 1	CM	Bomb fell off during take-off at Montdidier and detonated.	Heinkel He 111H-2 (5587)	100 %	Ltn. Beck + one killed; two wounded.
3.	3./KG 3	CM	Crashed and burned near Malmedyn; not combat.	Dornier Do 17Z-2(3378)	100 %	Four killed.
4.	3./KG 3	CM	Damaged by 615 Sqn. Hurricane of Kayll and crashed near Marche.	Dornier Do 17Z-3(2807)	100 %	Oblt. Graf von Platen-Hallermund + one killed; two wounded.

Luftwaffe Losses, 28th August 1940—*continued*

5.	6./KG 3	CM	Shot down by 615 Sqn. Hurricane of Eyre off Folkestone during the morning.	Dornier Do 17Z-3(4251)	100 %	Four wounded. and made P.O.W.s.
6.	6./KG 3	CM	Damaged by R.A.F. fighter (squadron unkown)) but landed safely at Mardyck.	Dornier Do 17Z-2 (3411 : 5K+DP)	3 %	Crew unhurt.
7.	II./KG 30	CM	Force landed; cause and location not known.	Junkers Ju 88 (6055)	Under 60 %	Crew unhurt.
8.	II./KG 53	CM	Force landed near Wesel owing to fuel shortage.	Heinkel He 111H-3 (5560 : A1+LM)	50 %	Crew unhurt.
9.	3./KG 53	CM	Crashed near Vitry-en-Artois after structural failure.	Heinkel He 111H-2 (6878)	100 %	Five crew members killed.
10.	4./KG 53	CM	Collided on take-off at Vendeville with Item 11.	Heinkel He 111H-2 (5346)	100 %	Ltn. Simon + four killed.
11.	5./KG 53	CM	Collided on take-off at Vendeville with Item 10.	Heinkel He 111H-3 (6815)	100 %	Hptm. Neumann + three killed; one injured.
12.	6./KG 53	CM	Crashed on take-off at Vendeville; cause unkown.	Heinkel He 111H-2 (2770)	100 %	Five crew members killed.
13.	III./St.G 1	NCM	Air collision at Deauville with Item 14.	Junkers Ju 87B-1 (479)	100 %	Oblt. Kathe killed.
14.	III./St.G 1	NCM	Air collision at Deauville with Item 13.	Junkers Ju 87B-1(5236)	100 %	Ltn. Mühltaler + one killed.
15.	Stab/KGr. 806	CM	Crashed at Rennes with engine failure after night raid on Britain.	Junkers Ju 88A-1(5075)	100 %	Four crew members killed.
16.	I./LG 1	CM	Crashed at Masserac; cause not known.	Junkers Ju 88A-1(3124)	100 %	Three killed; one injured.
17.	3./Erpr.Gr. 210	NCM	Landing accident at Cologne-Ostheim.	Messerschmitt Bf 109 E-4 (3741)	15 %	Pilot injured.
18.	3./Erpr.Gr. 210	NCM	Crashed at Calais-Marck; cause not known.	Messerschmitt Bf 109E (1208)	60 %	Pilot unhurt.
19.	I./JG 2	CM	Missing from combat sortie over England; cause not known.	Messerschmitt Bf 109 E-4 (5383)	100 %	Oblt. Grüsech missing.
20.	I./JG 2	NCM	Landing accident at Fécamp; cause not known.	Messerschmitt Bf 109 E-1 (3337)	20 %	Pilot unhurt.
21.	Stab I./JG 3	CM	Shot down by 56 Sqn. Hurricane of Down over Thames Estuary at 13.21 hrs.	Messerschmitt Bf 109 E-4 (0941)	100 %	Ltn. Landry killed.
22.	II./JG 3	CM	Shot down by 501 Sqn. Hurricanes over Channel at A.09.35 hrs.	Messerschmitt Bf 109 E-4 (5142)	100 %	Pilot wounded; made P.O.W.
23.	II./JG 3	CM	Shot down by 501 Sqn. Hurricanes over Channel at A.09.35 hrs.	Messerschmitt Bf 109 E-4 (1449)	100 %	Pilot rescued unhurt.
24.	II./JG 3	CM	Shot down by 501 Sqn. Hurricanes over Channel at A.09.35 hrs.	Messerschmitt Bf 109 E-1 (6611)	100 %	Pilot wounded; made P.O.W.
25.	Stab III./JG 3	CM	Missing after combat with fighters over Channel; British squadron involved not known.	Messerschmitt Bf 109 E-4 (5146)	100 %	Pilot killed.
26.	7./JG 3	CM	Shot down by 54 Sqn. Spitfire of Gribble over Dover at 16.50 hrs.	Messerschmitt Bf 109 E-1 (3553)	100 %	Pilot rescued by *Seenotflugkdo.*, unhurt.
27.	Stab/JG 26	CM	Shot down by 610 Sqn. Spitfire of Hamlyn near Deal at A.16.00 hrs.	Messerschmitt Bf 109E (2743)	100 %	Oblt. Beyer missing.
28.	Stab/JG 26	CM	Shot down by 610 Sqn. Spitfire of Pegge near Deal at A.16.00 hrs.	Messerschmitt Bf 109E (1353)	100 %	Pilot missing.
29.	Stab/JG 27	NCM	Pilot became lost between Cherbourg and Germany and force landed on Lewes racecourse in error.	Gotha Go 145 (1115)	100 %	Pilot missing.
30.	2./JG 27	NCM	Landing accident at Leulingen; cause not known.	Messerschmitt Bf 109 E-1 (3284)	40 %	Pilot unhurt.
31.	2./JG 27	NCM	Landing accident at Leulingen; cause not known.	Messerschmitt Bf 109 E-4 (6234)	15 %	Pilot unhurt.
32.	III./JG 27	NCM	Force landed at Cherbourg; not result of combat.	Messerschmitt Bf 109 E-4 (2782)	35 %	Pilot unhurt.
33.	Stab/JG 51	CM	Shot down by 85 Sqn. Hurricane of Allard off Dymchurch at 16.39 hrs.	Messerschmitt Bf 109 E-4 (5395)	100 %	Oblt. Kircheis missing.
34.	I./JG 51	CM	Shot down by 85 Sqn. Hurricane of Woods-Scawen off Folkestone at 16.35 hrs.	Messerschmitt Bf 109 E-4 (1436)	100 %	Pilot missing.
35.	1./JG 51	CM	Landing accident at Pihen; cause not known.	Messerschmitt Bf 109 E-1 (6154)	50 %	Pilot unhurt.
36.	III./JG 51	CM	Shot down by 85 Sqn. Hurricane of Townsend 12 miles north-west of Lympne at 16.30 hrs.	Messerschmitt Bf 109 E-4 (1523)	100 %	Pilot missing.
37	III./JG 51	CM	Damaged by 85 Sqn. Hurricane of Allard off the French coast at A.13.48 hrs.	Messerschmitt Bf 109 E-4 (1984)	60 %	Oblt. Lignitz wounded.
38.	I./JG 54	CM	Shot down by 56 Sqn. Hurricane of Weaver near Dover at 16.46 hrs.	Messerschmitt Bf 109 E-1 (6204)	100 %	Fw. Schöttle missing.
39.	II./JG 54	CM	Shot down by 56 Sqn. Hurricane of Maxwell near Dover at 16.48 hrs.	Messerschmitt Bf 109 E-4 (2759)	100 %	Uffz. Kleeman missing.
40.	II./JG 54	CM	Landing accident at Soesterberg; cause not known.	Messerschmitt Bf 109 E-1 (3538)	35 %	Pilot unhurt.
41.	Seenotflug-kommando 3	CM	Shot down by 79 Sqn. Hurricanes of Bryant-Fenn, Morris and Mayhew in Square 1116 at 11.48 hrs.	Heinkel He 59 (1528)	100 %	One killed; Ltn.z.S. Sprenger + two missing.
42.	Seenotflug-kommando 3	CM	Shot down by 79 Sqn. Hurricane of Clerke in grid square 1285 at 11.30 hrs.	Heinkel He 59 (1512)	100 %	Four rescued, all wounded.
43.	KGzbV. 108	NCM	Collided with He 59 while landing at Stavanger-Sola.	Heinkel He 59 (1820 : BV+MH)	55 %	Crew unhurt.
44.	5./196	NCM	Force landed following engine failure near Nest.	Arado Ar 196 (0077 : 6W+DN)	50 %	Crew unhurt.

Thursday 29th August

It was at this stage of the Battle that all three *Luftflotten* began to step up the night offensive against Britain—particular attention being paid to the industrial Midlands and the North. The progressive improvement of German radio beam flying procedures was beginning to show promising results with line *Geschwader* crews flying in clearly-defined streams behind the KGr. 100 pathfinders. The impotence of the British night fighter squadrons was, it seemed, ample justification for the withdrawal of such units as KG 55 and their application to a night offensive. Accordingly, with Göring's sanction, Liverpool was selected for a series of heavy night attacks and the Merseyside area was raided by about 150 bombers on the

GB 49 16 (96 4) bc

Bawdsey Manor

Funkanlage

Lfl. Kdo. 3   Juli 1942

Nur für den Dienstgebrauch

Bild Nr. 2274 Z 49 V.

Aufnahme vom 11. 4. 42

Länge (ostw. Greenw.): 1° 24′ 30″   Nördl. Breite: 51° 59′ 30″
Zielhöhe über NN: 15 m

Karte 1:100000
GB/E 25

Maßstab: 1:15000

n.Harwich
Luftlinie ca 10 km

1. 4 freistehende Funkmasten mit Richtstrahlereinrichtung	etwa	80 m	hoch
2. 4 freistehende Funkmasten	etwa	60 m	hoch
3. 6 freistehende Funkmasten	etwa	28 m	hoch
4. Betriebs- und Unterkunftsgebäude	etwa	2 000 qm	
Gesamtfläche	etwa	254 000 qm	

Bawdsey Manor, first prototype of the CH radar stations, never lost its experimental status, despite being integrated into Fighter Command's defence chain. Throughout the War it was the site of development work, a fact of which the *Luftwaffe* was evidently unware; this aerial photo, dated 1942, shows very little damage beyond some cratering south of the river mouth. The station was never heavily attacked and never put out of action for any length of time. (Photo: Author's Collection)

night of 28th/29th August, the units employed being two *Gruppen* of KG 27, three of KG 55 and *Kampfgruppe 806*. This raid was the heaviest yet experienced by Great Britain, with widespread damage in the dock area and more than 470 casualties reported in the Liverpool area alone. Other bombers, usually at one or two *Staffel* strength, raided Birmingham, Bristol, Bournemouth, Coventry, Derby, Manchester and Sheffield, from which towns and cities more than 550 casualties were notified. The Observer Corps centres struggled to

sort out the mass of sound plots up and down the country, while five Blenheim night fighter squadrons flew more than eighty patrols, but with only one sighting of an enemy aircraft; this proved too fast for the Blenheim (flown by Flt. Lt. Charles Pritchard of No. 600 Squadron), and the bombers escaped.

So frustrated were the Blenheim crews that Sqn. Ldr. Charles Widdows, C.O. of No. 29 Squadron at Wellingore (the night satellite of Digby in Lincolnshire), acquired a

Hurricane and personally resorted to a nightly vigil over the Midlands and East Anglia. If persistence had been the yardstick of combat success, this much-respected officer would have destroyed the *Luftwaffe* singlehanded; sad to relate he only twice spotted enemy raiders in the course of more than forty sorties, and on both occasions he was unable to score.

Apart from the material damage caused by this new phase of night attacks, it was soon realised that the system of air raid warnings, though possibly acceptable during daylight, was unwieldy and unnecessarily cautious when applied at night. There were three stages of warning; *Yellow*, a precautionary degree of warning issued by Fighter Command to civil defence authorities in areas over which approaching enemy aircraft might pass; *Purple*, a night precautionary warning to all authorities, factories and defence establishments in areas on the raiders' direct course; and *Red*, the "raid likely or imminent" warning, on receipt of which the sirens would be sounded. The constant tracking to and fro across the country of enemy bombers, almost invariably by sound plots, on the night of the 28th/29th resulted in almost 70 per cent of all towns being placed in the Red warning category, with countless thousands of people unnecessarily disturbed and seeking shelter below ground. Lights in factories and on railways were extinguished for a long period with enormous consequent loss of vital industrial activity.

With the arrival of daylight on the 29th the radar screens in the South-East were completely clear of enemy activity, so that once again Dowding seized the opportunity to re-shuffle some of his weary squadrons. The remains of No. 264 Squadron were moved out of Hornchurch to Kirton-in-Lindsey, their place being taken by nineteen Spitfires of No. 222 Squadron (commanded by Sqn. Ldr. John Hill) from the same airfield. The ten remaining Hurricanes of No. 615 Squadron flew north from Kenley to Prestwick, changing places with eighteen Hurricanes of No. 253 Squadron, commanded by Sqn. Ldr. Harold Starr[65].

Despite reasonable weather conditions, the morning remained quiet and it was not until shortly after 15.00 hours that radar reports showed a build-up of enemy activity over the French coast. Park, as a precaution, ordered off nine squadrons to join four already airborne, entreating his controllers to avoid committing them to combat should the enemy be repeating his previous day's fighter offensive. This time, however, a small number of Heinkels and Dorniers were sighted ahead of and below a huge array of fighters (more than 500 Bf 109s of JG 3, 26, 51, 52 and 54, and 150 Bf 110s of ZG 26 and ZG 76) approaching the coast between Beachy Head and Hastings. Sqn. Ldr. Townsend's No. 85 Squadron was again most conveniently placed, and he obtained permission for his twelve Hurricanes to attack. . . .

"Although at a serious height disadvantage, the Squadron began to chase the enemy aircraft, most of which started to climb to 16,000 feet. Large numbers of enemy aircraft were then seen. After something of a cat and mouse game in which enemy fighters evidently tried to lure the Hurricanes into a trap, Townsend managed to single out a Bf 109 and shot it down in mid-Channel. Ellis and Walker-Smith were both forced to bale out, the latter pilot wounded in the foot."[66]

This was indeed a trap, with the cautious use of a small number of bombers as bait. As No. 85 Squadron was ordered to disengage, it immediately became clear to the German commanders that the absence of further interceptions confirmed that the fighter defences were now studiously avoiding the attrition that would inevitably accompany such massive fighter-versus-fighter combats.

Switching tactics once more, Kesselring momentarily reverted to a short evening phase of free chases, but in only two instances were British fighters seen. On one such sortie a *Staffel* of Bf 109s caught twelve Hurricanes of No. 501 Squadron unawares and shot down Flt. Lt. John Gibson and Sgt. William Green.

The fine weather which had spread over England during the day continued through the night so that once again Sperrle was able to pursue his offensive, sending nearly two hundred bombers from fourteen *Gruppen* to the Liverpool and Birkenhead area for the second night running. In cloudless skies most of these aircraft had no difficulty in finding the target area and dropped a large number of incendiary bombs on dock areas still smouldering from the previous night's raid. Among the aircraft which participated in this raid were the Dornier Do 17Zs of KGr. 606, still almost exclusively officered by naval personnel.

---

[65] Also accompanying the Squadron was Sqn. Ldr. Tom Gleave, who had until recently been its C.O. Receiving a posting to No. 14 Group, Gleave had been granted permission to remain with the Squadron as supernumerary until his posting took effect. More will be told shortly of this officer's continuing service with No. 253 Squadron.

[66] On a later sortie that evening, Flt. Lt. Harry Hamilton, a Canadian pilot, was bounced by three Bf 109s and killed when his Hurricane crashed at Winchelsea.

R.A.F. FIGHTER COMMAND LOSSES—THURSDAY 29th AUGUST 1940

1.	85 Sqn., Croydon	C	Shot down by Bf 109s; pilot baled out 12 miles east of Battle unhurt.	16.05 hrs.	Sgt. J.H.M. Ellis	Hurricane	V6623	Cat. 3 Destroyed
2.	85 Sqn., Croydon	C	Shot down by Bf 109s; pilot, wounded in the foot, baled out at Hawkhurst.	16.01 hrs.	Sgt. F.R. Walker-Smith	Hurricane	V7530	Cat. 3 Destroyed
3.	85 Sqn., Croydon	C	Shot down by Bf 109s; pilot did not bale out and was killed when aircraft crashed. Buried at Hawkinge.	18.50 hrs.	Flt. Lt. H.R. Hamilton	Hurricane	L1915	Cat. 3 Destroyed
4.	151 Sqn., Stapleford	C	Shot down over Essex; pilot baled out and fractured ribs; admitted to Epping Hospital.	19.15 hrs.	Plt. Off. A.G. Wainwright	Hurricane	P3882	Cat. 3 Destroyed
5.	501 Sqn., Gravesend	C	Shot down by Bf 109s; pilot baled out unhurt.	18.40 hrs.	Flt. Lt. J.A.A. Gibson	Hurricane	P3102	Cat. 3 Destroyed
6.	501 Sqn., Gravesend	C	Shot down by Bf 109s; pilot baled out near Hawkinge unhurt.	18.44 hrs.	Sgt. W.J. Green	Hurricane	R4223	Cat. 3 Destroyed
7.	603 Sqn., Hornchurch	C	Aircraft damaged in combat; pilot slightly wounded. Aircraft believed to have crashed on landing.	Not known	Fg. Off. J.C. Boulter	Spitfire	—	Cat. 3 Destroyed
8.	610 Sqn., Biggin Hill	C	Shot down by Bf 110s over Mayfield; pilot killed.	15.54 hrs.	Sgt. E. Manton	Spitfire	P9433	Cat. 3 Destroyed
9.	610 Sqn., Biggin Hill	C	Shot down and crash landed at Gatwick; pilot unhurt.	15.59 hrs.	Sgt. A.C. Baker	Spitfire	X4011	Cat. 3 Destroyed

LUFTWAFFE LOSSES—THURSDAY 29th AUGUST 1940

1.	1.(H)/14	NCM	Landing accident at airfield in Northern France.	Henschel Hs 126B (4066 : 5H+BH)	40 %	Crew unhurt.
2.	II./KG 2	CM	Damaged by R.A.F. fighter at night and crashed at Selis-Persan.	Dornier Do 17Z-3 (2839 : U5+PF)	80 %	Two killed; Oblt. Kindler wounded and Uffz. Matusseck missing.
3.	6./KG 3	CM	Collided with radio mast, crashed and burned.	Dornier Do 17Z-3 (3480 : 5K +FP)	100 %	Ltn. Zein + two killed.
4.	Stab/KG 40	NCM	Communications aircraft; forced landed at Ahlhorn.	Gotha Go 145 (0928 : KB+OU)	70 %	Reg. Rat Dr. Hermström + one injured.
5.	I./KG 40	CM	Force landed near Bordeaux short of fuel.	Focke-Wulf Fw 200C-2 (0014)	10 %	Crew unhurt.
6.	Erg.St./KG 51	NCM	Landing accident at Lechfeld; not combat.	Heinkel He 111 (1723)	20 %	Crew unhurt.
7.	Erg.St./KG 51	NCM	Suffered accident on training flight.	Junkers Ju 88A-1(8018)	40 %	Crew unhurt.
8.	I./KG 53	CM	Crashed at Vitry-en-Artois after combat sortie.	Heinkel He 111H-2 (2613 : A1+FH)	85 %	Two killed and two wounded.
9.	III./KG 55	CM	Shot down by 92 Sqn. Spitfire of Wright on "cat's eye" patrol at 22.35 hrs.	Heinkel He 111P (2151)	100 %	Five crew members killed.
10.	III./KG 55	CM	Force landed at Sens, short of fuel, after night sortie over Britain.	Heinkel He 111P-2 (2858)	30 %	Crew unhurt.
11.	5./KG 77	NCM	Collided with another Ju 88 (Item 12) at Hornisgrinde.	Junkers Ju 88A-1 (7090 : 3Z+AN)	100 %	Hptm. Büs, St.Kap., + three killed.
12.	5./KG 77	NCM	Collided with another Ju 88 (Item 11) at Hornisgrinde.	Junkers Ju 88A-1 (4131 : 3Z+EN)	100 %	Four crew members killed.
13.	KGr. 100	CM	Force landed at Chateaudun short of fuel.	Heinkel He 111H-3 (6891)	40 %	Crew unhurt.
14.	KGr. 806	CM	Damaged by *flak* over the Midlands at night; crashed at Vannes.	Junkers Ju 88A-1 (3116)	100 %	Four crew members killed.
15.	Stab II/ZG 26	CM	Damaged by 610 Sqn. Spitfire of Lamb near Mayfield at 15.50 hrs.	Messerschmitt Bf 110 C-2 (2121 : 3U+CC)	25 %	Ltn. Thüring wounded.
16.	Stab/JG 3	CM	Shot down by 501 Sqn. Hurricane of Lacey near Hawkinge at 18.30 hrs.	Messerschmitt Bf 109 E-3 (1166)	100 %	Oblt. Floorke killed.
17.	2./JG 3	CM	Shot down by 501 Sqn. Hurricanes near Hawkinge at 18.35 hrs.	Messerschmitt Bf 109 E-4 (5338)	100 %	Ofw. Lampskemper missing.
18.	4./JG 3	CM	Shot down by 85 Sqn. Hurricane of Townsend near Hastings at 15.50 hrs.	Messerschmitt Bf 109 E-4 (5464)	100 %	Uffz. Gericke killed.
19.	4./JG 3	CM	Shot down by 85 Sqn. Hurricane of Hamilton near Hastings at 15.52 hrs.	Messerschmitt Bf 109 E-1 (1134)	100 %	Oblt. Wipper killed.
20.	III./JG 3	CM	Damaged by 85 Sqn. Hurricane of Booth and foce landed at Colombert.	Messerschmitt Bf 109 E-1 (2675)	45 %	Pilot unhurt.
21.	III./JG 3	CM	Crashed on take-off at Desvres airfield.	Messerschmitt Bf 109 E-4 (0964)	60 %	Pilot unhurt.
22.	III./JG 3	CM	Shot down by fighters over Channel; R.A.F. squadron not identified.	Messerschmitt Bf 109 E-1 (4031)	100 %	Pilot, unhurt, rescued by *Seenotflugkommando*.
23.	III./JG 3	CM	Shot down by 603 Sqn. Spitfire of Boulter.	Messerschmitt Bf 109 E-1 (6335)	100 %	Uffz. Pfeifer missing.
24.	I./JG 26	CM	Shot down by 610 Sqn. Spitfire of Baker near Mayfield.	Messerschmitt Bf 109 E-4 (1181)	100 %	Ofw. Treuberg missing.
25.	I./JG 26	CM	Shot down by Spitfire, probably of 610 Sqn., over Channel, but combat report not traced.	Messerschmitt Bf 109 E-1 (3634)	100 %	Pilot , unhurt, rescued by *Seenotflugkommando*.
26.	5./JG 52	NCM	Crashed in bad weather near Jever, Germany.	Messerschmitt Bf 109 E-3 (1974)	100 %	Pilot killed.
27.	III./JG 54	NCM	Force landed at Le Bortel after engine failure.	Messerschmitt Bf 109 (1547)	20 %	Pilot unhurt.
28.	6./JG 54	CM	Landing accident at Vlissingen airfield.	Messerschmitt Bf 109 E-3 (1266)	10 %	Pilot unhurt.
29.	II./NJG 1	NCM	Crashed at Elsdorf; cause not known.	Junkers Ju 88Z-2 (*sic*) (0256)	100 %	Ltn. Bregand + two killed.
30.	3./106	CM	Reported to have suffered double engine failure and crashed in grid square 3376.	Heinkel He 115 (3263 : M2+LL)	100 %	One killed; Ltn.z.S. Kinzel, Uffz. Brommen and Gefr. Hennigsen missing.
31.	3./506	CM	Landing accident at Stavanger-Sola, probably after mining sortie.	Heinkel He 115 (2771 : S4+DL)	80 %	Oblt.z.S. Raether killed.
32.	1./606	CM	Missing from night raid on Liverpool; fate not known.	Dornier Do 17Z-3 (2878 : 7T+GH)	100 %	Ltn.z.S. Rees missing; three killed.

Friday 30th August

With an extensive anti-cyclone covering North-West Europe and weather conditions likely to remain fine for several days to come, the Battle now entered its critical phase, with the tempo of operations increasing daily to an undreamed-of climax—intended by the Germans to coincide with the launching of *Seelöwe*. It was to be the very nature of this climax, enacted nine days hence, that deprived the *Luftwaffe* of victory in the Battle. Those nine days were, however, to sap the resources and energy of Fighter Command to a point of near exhaustion.

The tactics employed by *Luftflotten 2* and *3* must have come as something of a shock to the defences, and their very nature must have suggested to Dowding and Park that the German conduct of the Battle had indeed entered its critical phase.

Soon after dawn Kesselring launched a number of probing attacks, ostensibly against a north-bound convoy in the Thames Estuary, in an effort to discover what fighter forces would react and from what direction. Nine Hurricanes of No. 111 Squadron, which had by chance been scrambled to investigate an incoming raid (which materialised as three Blenheims of No. 25 Squadron), were vectored towards Manston and ran into one of these early raids consisting of a *Gruppe* of Do 17s covered by about thirty Bf 110s of III./ZG 76, one of which was damaged by the Hurricanes. The sighting report radioed by Flt. Lt. Herbert Giddings, leading the Hurricanes, brought three of No. 54 Squadron's Spitfires(flown by Flt. Lt. Deere, Plt. Off. Eric Edsall and Fg. Off. Desmond McMullen) into action, and these damaged two of the bombers.

This relatively light skirmishing gave no hint of the next phase of Kesselring's attack, which was launched in three waves, crossing the Kent coasts on three sides at half-hourly intervals from 10.30 hours onwards. The first wave consisted

Two pre-War views of the airfield at Hawkinge. At the beginning of the Battle this airfield was a forward satellite in the Biggin Hill Sector, but it was soon realised that its exposed position on the South Coast rendered it exceedingly vulnerable to enemy fighter and bomber attacks; indeed, it was largely destroyed in attacks during August. Nevertheless, owing to the tireless efforts by the station personnel, it remained in use as a forward field, and in the desperate days at the end of August and early September many a British fighter "lobbed in" at Hawkinge to replenish fuel and ammunition, and even to effect hasty repairs. Within forty years of the end of the War the airfield had all but disappeared, swallowed up by housing developments—yet the name Hawkinge lives on as a fond memory of many Allied airmen, struggling with a faltering engine after life or death combat over the Channel.

of three *Gruppen* of Bf 109s (about sixty aircraft) which crossed in at different points but against which Park did not react, save to advance his fighters states at Kenley, Biggin Hill, Northolt, Croydon, North Weald, Rochford and Hornchurch, believing that the enemy fighter sweeps foreshadowed a second wave flown by bombers. In this he was proved correct when, at 11.00 hours, reports from the coastal Observer Corps posts showed that raids totalling 40 Heinkels, 30 Dorniers, 60 Bf 109s and 30 Bf 110s were converging on Kent. Twelve Hurricanes of No. 151 Squadron had been ordered off from Stapleford to patrol the mouth of the Thames just previously and were ordered to split into Flights; Sqn.

Ldr. Eric King[67] evidently became separated from his formation and was attacked by enemy aircraft; his body was later found in the burned out remains of his Hurricane at Rochester. The rest of No. 151 Squadron intercepted a group of about seventy Heinkels and Bf 110s at about 11.20 hours and claimed the destruction of three bombers for the loss of two more Hurricanes and Sgt. Feliks Gmur, a Polish pilot, who was posted missing.

---

[67] The same pilot who had survived the combat of 16th August in which Flt. Lt. Nicolson of No. 249 Squadron had won the Victoria Cross over Southampton.

The same raid was now attacked over Kent by eleven Hurricane pilots of No. 85 Squadron, who opened with a withering head-on assault; this utterly smashed the enemy formation and resulted in numerous dogfights over most of Surrey and Kent. Two Bf 110s fell to the guns of Sgt. Geoffrey Allard and Fg. Off. Patrick Woods-Scawen. Plt. Off. James Marshall was shot down but baled out unhurt at Ashford.

The raid situation over Kent and Surrey had become so confused by 11.45 hours that it was impossible to identify with any certainty what raids had been intercepted; no less than 48 Oberver Posts reported combats overhead. All of Parks fighters were now airborne and ten squadrons were in action; he had called for reinforcements and two No. 12 Group squadrons had flown south from Duxford to cover Kenley and Biggin Hill. Notwithstanding this the fighters over the latter airfield failed to spot a *Staffel* of Ju 88s which had detached from the third attack wave and which dropped more than thirty 250-kilo delayed action bombs from about 18,000 feet. These did little damage to the airfield—a high proportion falling on the neighbouring villages of Biggin Hill and Keston.

No. 222 Squadron, fresh from the North only the day before, was on patrol over Gravesend at this time when ten Bf 109s dived straight through "B" Flight, shooting down Sgt. Iain Hutchinson. It is clear from the tactics being employed by this squadron (i.e. close formation with a weaver) that the lessons learned in the South were not being passed on to other squadrons as they worked up to operational status. No. 222 Squadron would, by the end of this day, have learned the hard way.

At Kenley the pilots of the other newly-arrived squadron, No. 253, had had a frustrating morning. Eleven Hurricanes had taken off at 10.50 hours when it looked as though Kenley might be bombed. When no attack materialised, the squadron was vectored south to meet part of the third wave of Kesselring's bombers which were crossing in near Hove (and were being harried by the Hurricanes of No. 43 Squadron from Tangmere). As Starr turned to meet this threat, three further Hurricanes from the squadron, flown by Sqn. Ldr. Tom Gleave, Flt. Lt. George Brown and Plt. Off. Douglas Francis, took off at Kenley and were ordered to climb hard towards the east. They had just passed close to Maidstone at about 17,000 feet when suddenly a great mass of Bf 109s passed across their front about 500 feet above; in Gleave's own words: "Shown up clearly by the sun, and stretching fore and aft as far as the eye could see were rows of 109s riding above the haze, each row flying in line astern and well spaced out—all of them heading south-south east. It was a fantastic sight." With the sun over their right shoulders these three pilots "drove straight into the enemy flank", or so Gleave thought; Brown, however, had spotted a straggler at the last moment and went after this, only to be jumped by other enemy fighters and shot down near Maidstone. He was only slightly hurt.

Gleave's account of his astonishing encounter with the enemy "Balbo"[68] is so graphic that nothing less than verbatim reproduction can do justice:

"Amid the rows of 109s I turned with the tide and took a bead on the nearest aircraft. Flying at about twenty degrees to starboard of his line of flight and slightly above, I fired at about 175 yards' range on a slight right hand turn. The thin streaks of yellow tracer flame ran parallel for what appeared to be about seventy-five yards and then bent away to the left in a rapid succession of curves. The hiss of pneumatics, the smell of cordite in the cockpit and the feel of the nose dipping slightly under the recoil all lent excitement to the first real combat in my short-lived career at Kenley. Most of my shot appeared to be going into the engine cowling and cockpit. It was the tracer, fired on a turn, which produced the strange illusion of the shot entering at right angles. The Hun flew straight for a while and then turned gently on to his back. After a short burst of about four seconds I stopped firing and as I did so I saw sunlit pieces of shattered perspex spiralling aft like a shower of tracer. The Hun slewed slightly while on his back, his nose dropped and he dived beneath out of my sight—going straight down.

"Suddenly tracers whistled over my head. A glance in my mirror told me that there was a 109 on my tail and about 200 yards astern. I jinked, dipping and turning to starboard and then pulling up again in a sharp climbing turn to port. There were no signs of my No. 1 or No. 2, but by then it was impossible to tell friend from foe at a distance, for the Hun fighters were flying at a variety of levels and there was a lot of firing going on—at what, it was difficult to see.

"As I came up to the centre of the formation again, another Hun crossed my sights from left to right—it must have been about 120 yards off and flying steady, as though completely ignoring the fracas going on behind. I gave him a short burst as I turned with him, and a column of black smoke burst from what appeared to be the leading edge of his starboard plane, about a yard from the wing root—from the path of the tracers I thought my shot had gone slap into the fuselage. The Hun turned across my path, and his nose dropped as he went into a dive, leaving a long column of smoke in his wake. I quickly lost sight of him, for I had to pull up to avoid a collision with another 109. This flew past me only a few yards out, obviously unaware that I was there, and quickly gained distance on me. At about sixty yards he turned slightly across my sights, and I turned with him to port as I fired. It was too good to be true. I gave him a three-second burst, holding fire as he pulled the nose up; he then appeared to lose speed rapidly and fell out of the sky into a dive. At that point I gave him another short burst for luck. I could see through the cockpit canopy into the cockpit and I remember my astonishment that it appeared to be empty. It was an illusion of course.

"I seemed now to be in the midst of a mass of 109s. They were all over the place but still trying to keep some semblance of formation. Tracers passed above and below, curving downwards and giving the impression of flying in a gigantic cage of gilt wire. I looked for another target and as I turned towards the sun a Hun passed just to the right of me and slightly above. I raised the nose, turning slightly with him, and at about seventy-five yards' range

---

[68] R.A.F. jargon for a mass formation, so-called after Marshal Balbo, the Italian Minister for Air during the 1930s who in July 1933 had commanded a formation of 24 Savoia-Marchetti flying boats in a trans-Atlantic flight. As Governor of Libya Balbo was shot down and killed by his own anti-aircraft guns near Tobruk on 28th June 1940.

opened fire. My shots appeared to be going into the lower part of the fuselage and belly, but after about two or three seconds the steady rhythm of the Hurricane's eight Browning machine guns turned to a series of feeble clicks as the last Prideaux links holding the ammunition together slid through the chutes into free air. And almost simultaneously the Hun rolled on to his back, flew inverted for a second or two and then dropped into a dive—to streak down at full bore. A quick glance in the mirror showed three more 109s on my tail in neat line astern, so I flicked the Hurricane on its side at the same time, sticking the nose well and truly down, skidding and turning until I was going flat out."[69]

Kesselring now changed his phasing tactics. Instead of waiting his customary two or three hours before launching the next series of attacks, he gave Fighter Command little time to draw breath and started to mount his next assault shortly after 13.00 hours with successive waves of bombers, *Zerstörer* and Bf 109s crossing the South Kent coast at twenty minute intervals from 13.30 hours onwards. Owing to a lucky hit on the main electricity grid during the morning, the CH and CHL radars at Beachy Head, Dover, Fairlight, Foreness, Pevensey, Rye and Whitstable were off the air at this critical time, with the result that only five fighter squadrons made contact. No. 222 Squadron was again in action, but lost one Spitfire destroyed and two badly damaged by Bf 110s of II./ZG 2. Plt. Off. Timothy Vigors (who was in action three times during this day) claimed a Bf 110D-O of this unit. During four combats during this day, No. 222 Squadron was to lose eight Spitfires, of which five were destroyed; one pilot was killed and two wounded.

This phase of attacks continued until 16.00 hours when, again without pause, the third and most serious group of raids was reported approaching. During the course of two hours no fewer than nineteen *Gruppen* of enemy aircraft forged in over Kent and the Thames Estuary, their targets situated at Luton, Radlett, Oxford, Slough, North Weald, Kenley and Biggin Hill. At the last-named airfield another *Staffel* of Ju 88s swept in at under 1,000 feet and dropped sixteen well-aimed 500-kilo bombs, all of which fell among the station buildings, destroying one of the four remaining hangars, workshops, armoury, barrack blocks, stores, the W.A.A.F. quarters and the transport yard. Most of the telephone lines were again severed, as were gas, water and electricity mains. Hornchurch took over temporary control of the Biggin Hill Sector. 65 casualties were suffered, of whom 39 were killed—one bomb struck a crowded shelter trench. Six Hurricanes of No. 79 Squadron managed to take off at the height of the raid and

German groundcrewman inspecting flak damage to a Heinkel He 111 of 4.*Staffel* KG 1 <*Hindenburg*>. (Photo: Aero Publishers Inc.)

their pilots claimed two of the attackers, without loss to themselves.

While the formations briefed to attack Oxford were turned back over Surrey, another raid succeeded in its attack. A group of 60 Heinkel He 111s of II./KG 1 and I. and II./KG 53 with an escort of Bf 110s came in over the coast north of the Thames shortly after 16.20 hours. It was heavily engaged by the Hurricanes of No. 242 Squadron (ordered south from No. 12 Group), and by those of No. 56 Squadron, ordered up from North Weald. Despite the onslaught by British fighters, the raid split, the KG 1 bombers turning towards Luton where ten heavy bombs hit the Vauxhall works, causing 113 casualties—of whom 53 were killed. The larger part of the formation, which survived attacks by Nos. 1, 56, 222, 242 and 501 Squadrons (losing five aircraft), flew doggedly on to its target, which turned out to be the Handley Page factory at Radlett. With ten miles still to go the fighters were forced to break off, low on either fuel or ammunition, and the raiders were left with only anti-aircraft gunfire to contend with. This however probably saved the factory to a considerable extent for the damage caused was not substantial and, as far as is known, production of the new Halifax bomber was not affected, and no completed aircraft were damaged.[70]

The fighting on 30th August had been the heaviest so far

---

[69] The author is greatly indebted to Group Captain Gleave for permission to quote the above passage. He entered a claim for five Bf 109s destroyed in this combat but, possibly on account of the number of claims submitted in relation to the number of wrecked enemy aircraft found, he was officially credited with "one Bf 109 destroyed and four probably destroyed". Extensive post-War research, both by Tom Gleave and by others, have conclusively indicated that all five Bf 109s claimed in fact fell; examination of wreckage of an aircraft, which fell in the area at the time stated, disclosed an aircraft's Works Number that was not included in the Luftwaffe's statement of losses; it is now clear that all five casualties suffered by I.Gruppe, JG 27 (the Geschwader that had moved from the Cherbourg peninsula to the Pas de Calais only a few days earlier), fell to Gleave's guns.

[70] Details of this raid have been difficult to research owing to the tight restrictions imposed for security reasons at the time, as well as confusion in surviving Observer Corps logs. The Halifax bomber, on which so much importance was attached at the time, was surrounded by considerable secrecy and it was assumed that the choice of Radlett as the target on this evening was on account of a German determination to disrupt *Hampden* production rather than any knowledge of the Halifax. No mention of the effects of the raid has been found in any R.A.F. records (the fighters squadrons involved having drawn off before the German bombers reached their target), and it must be assumed that no efforts were made to attack the bombers on their escape to the coast.

experienced by Dowding's pilots, as the total of 1,054 sorties indicated. Even the great events of 15th August—in which the fighting had been spread over four Group areas—had come nowhere near matching the intensity of effort on this Friday. Altogether twenty-two squadrons had been in action, some of them as many as four times—and almost all at least twice.

And yet again the French-based Heinkels and Dorniers of

Luftflotte 3 made their way northwards after dark, with some 130 aircraft again striking Liverpool. Eleven smaller groups were plotted coming in over the South and South-East to carry out diversionary attacks upon Birmingham, Sheffield, Norwich, Colchester, Southampton, Bristol and Cardiff. Isolated attacks were also made on a number of airfields, although generally little damage was inflicted.

R.A.F. FIGHTER COMMAND LOSSES—FRIDAY 30th AUGUST 1940

1.	32 Sqn., Biggin Hill	—	Destroyed on the ground in raid on Biggin Hill; no pilot casualties.	A17.00 hrs.	Nil		Hurricane	N2540	Cat. 3 Burnt
2.	43 Sqn., Tangmere	C	Shot down near Hove; pilot killed.	11.58 hrs.	Sgt. D. Noble		Hurricane	V6548	Cat. 3 Lost
3.	43 Sqn., Tangmere	C	Shot down near Hove; pilot wounded and admitted to Ashford Hospital.	A17.10 hrs.	Sqn. Ldr. J.V.C. Badger		Hurricane	P3179	Cat. 3 Destroyed
4.	56 Sqn., North Weald	C	Believed shot down and crashed; pilot unhurt.	Not known	Fg. Off. R.E.P. Brooker		Hurricane	N2668	Cat. 3 Destroyed
5.	66 Sqn., Coltishall	C	Shot down by Do 17 off Norfolk coast; pilot baled out and picked up by lightship.	16.49 hrs.	Plt. Off. J.H. Pickering		Spitfire	—	Cat. 3 Lost
6.	85 Sqn., Croydon	C	Shot down near Ashford; pilot baled out unhurt.	11.13 hrs.	Plt. Off. J.E. Marshall		Hurricane	P3166	Cat. 3 Destroyed
7.	151 Sqn., Stapleford	C	Shot down in flames near Rochester; pilot's body found in burnt out aircraft.	11.50 hrs.	Sqn. Ldr. E.B. King		Hurricane	V7369	Cat. 3 Burnt
8.	151 Sqn., Stapleford	C	Shot down by Bf 110s; pilot killed.	16.00 hrs.	Sgt. F. Gmur		Hurricane	R4213	Cat. 3 Lost.
9.	151 Sqn., Stapleford	C	Shot down and force landed; pilot unhurt.	16.50 hrs.	Plt. Off. J.L.W. Ellacombe		Hurricane	P3119	Cat. 2 Damaged
10.	222 Sqn., Hornchurch	C	Shot down by Bf 109 and force landed near Hornchurch; pilot wounded.	A11.25 hrs.	Sgt. I. Hutchinson		Spitfire	R6719	Cat. 3 Destroyed
11.	222 Sqn., Hornchurch	C	Shot down and force landed near Bekesbourne, Kent; pilot unhurt.	A14.55 hrs.	Plt. Off. W.R. Assheton		Spitfire	R6720	Cat. 3 Destroyed
12.	222 Sqn., Hornchurch	C	Shot down and force landed at Eastchurch; pilot unhurt.	A15.05 hrs.	Sgt. S. Baxter		Spitfire	P9325	Cat. 3 Destroyed
13.	222 Sqn., Hornchurch	C	Shot down near Rochford; pilot baled out unhurt.	15.15 hrs.	Plt. Off. J.M.V. Carpenter		Spitfire	P9378	Cat. 3 Destroyed
14.	222 Sqn., Hornchurch	C	Shot down and crashed at West Malling; pilot killed.	18.05 hrs.	Sgt. J.I. Johnson		Spitfire	R6628	Cat. 3 Destroyed
15	222 Sqn., Hornchurch	C	Shot down and crash landed at Sittingbourne; pilot slightly wounded; aircraft burnt out.	18.07 hrs.	Flt. Lt. G.C. Matheson		Spitfire	P9443	Cat. 3 Burnt
16.	222 Sqn., Hornchurch	C	Shot down in flames near Barham, Kent; pilot escaped with slight burns to face.	18.15 hrs.	Plt. Off. H.P.M. Edridge		Spitfire	K9826	Cat. 3 Destroyed
17.	222 Sqn., Hornchurch	C	Shot down over the Isle of Sheppey; pilot baled out unhurt	A18.15 hrs.	Sgt. A.W.P. Spears		Spitfire	P9323	Cat. 3 Destroyed
18.	253 Sqn., Kenley	C	Shot down near Redhill; pilot baled out but parachute did not open.	A11.45 hrs.	Plt. Off. D.N.O. Jenkins		Hurricane	P3921	Cat. 3 Destroyed
19.	253 Sqn., Kenley	C	Shot down south of Maidstone; pilot killed.	A11.45 hrs.	Plt. Off C.D. Francis		Hurricane	L1965	Cat. 3 Destroyed
20.	253 Sqn., Kenley	C	Shot down by Bf 109s over South Kent; pilot shot dead while descending by parachute.	A17.20 hrs.	Sgt. J.H. Dickenson		Hurricane	P2946	Cat. 3 Destroyed
21.	253 Sqn., Kenley	C	Shot down by Bf 109s near Maidstone; pilot wounded.	A11.45 hrs	Flt. Lt. G.A. Brown		Hurricane	P3802	Cat. 3 Destroyed
22.	501 Sqn., Kenley	C	Aircraft forced down in combat with damaged radiator; pilot unhurt.	16.50 hrs.	Sgt. J.H. Lacey		Hurricane	—	Cat. 2 Damaged
23.	603 Sqn., Hornchurch	NC ?	Pilot experienced control difficulties and abandoned aircraft safely.	Not known	Not known		Spitfire	L1067	Cat. 3 Destroyed
24.	616 Sqn., Kenley	C	Shot down by Bf 109s at West Malling; pilot killed.	11.50 hrs.	Fg. Off. J.S. Bell		Spitfire	X4248	Cat. 3 Destroyed
25.	616 Sqn., Kenley	C	Crashed at Kenley on landing after combat; pilot unhurt.	A12.25 hrs.	Sgt. J. Hopewell		Spitfire	—	Cat. 3 Destroyed

LUFTWAFFE LOSSES—FRIDAY 30th AUGUST 1940

1.	4./Aufkl.Gr.	CM	Shot down by 66 Sqn. Spitfires off Norfolk coast at 16.45 hrs.	Dornier Do 215 (0036 : G2+JH)	100 %	Oblt. Sonnleitner killed; Ofw. Weise, Fw. Neubauer and Ogefr. Hefman missing.
2.	3.(F)/22	CM	Reported shot down by flak over Scotland in early morning.	Dornier Do 17P (1119 : 4N+AL)	100 %	Ltn. von Seebeck, Fw. Aigner and Uffz. Schobert missing.
3.	5./KG 1	CM	Shot down by 151 Sqn. Hurricane of Surma south of Southend at 14.50 hrs.	Heinkel He 111H-2 (2720 : V4+BV)	100 %	Hptm. Baess, *St.Kap.*, and Oblt. Foelisch missing; three others killed.
4.	5./KG 1	CM	Shot down by 242 Sqn. Hurricanes north of London at 14.49 hrs.	Heinkel He 111H-2 (5444 :V4+GV)	100 %	Oblt. Wächter and Gefr. Mahlbeck killed; three others missing.
5.	5./KG 1	CM	Shot down by 242 Sqn. Hurricane of Hart north of London at 14.55 hrs.	Heinkel He 111H-2 (5125 :V4+HV)	100 %	Uffz. Burger, Gefr. Hildebrand, Gefr. Fierbend, Gefr. Roggeman and Gefr. Klappholz missing.
6.	5./KG 1	CM	Shot down by 56 Sqn. Hurricane of Gracie during raid on Luton at A.16.30 hrs.	Heinkel He 111H-2 (3305 : V4+MV)	100 %	Gefr. Walter Reis killed; Fw. Schnabel, Uffz. Päslack, Uffz. Stärk and Gefr. Groth missing.
7.	6./KG 1	CM	Shot down by 253 Sqn. Hurricane of Greenwood near Redhill at A.11.50 hrs.	Heinkel He 111H-2 (2750 : V4+DW)	100 %	Ofw. Rauschert and Flg.Zinoegger killed (buried at Uckfield cemetery); Fw. Ester and Uffz. Stein made P.O.W.s
8.	9./KG 2	CM	Crashed near Brügge after combat with unknown British fighters.	Dornier Do 17Z-3 (2868 : U5+FT)	100 %	Ltn. Wittmann + two killed; one wounded.
9.	III./KG 27	CM	Shot down by 601 Sqn. Hurricanes led by Rhodes-Moorhouse off South Coast at 17.10 hrs.	Heinkel He 111H-2 (3438)	100 %	Oblt. Hünerbein, Uffz. Schlesser, Uffz. Siebers and Ogefr. Walpert wounded and made P.O.W.s

Luftwaffe Losses, 30th August 1940—*continued*

10.	III./KG 27	CM	Damaged by flak over Midlands at night and force landed at Rennes.	Heinkel He 111P (1697)	30 %	Crew unhurt.
11.	III./KG 51	NCM	Landing accident at Montdésir airfield.	Junkers Ju 88A-1 (7076 : 9K+DS)	15 %	Crew unhurt.
12.	3./KG 53	CM	Shot down by 1 Sqn. Hurricane of Merchant during raid on Radlett, and crashed in Lisstan Way, Southend-on-Sea at 17.15 hrs.	Heinkel He 111H-2 (5532 : A1+JL)	100 %	Uffz.Johann Erhard von Kühnheim, Ogefr.Fischer and Uffz. Adolf Sam killed; Ltn. Wolf Rössler and Uffz. Helmut Gall made P.O.W.s
13.	4./KG 53	CM	Shot down by 242 Sqn. Hurricane of Crowley-Milling during afternoon raid on Radlett.	Heinkel He 111H-2 (2711 : A1+JM)	100 %	Ofw. Ostertrag, Uffz. Brock and Uffz. Franck killed; Fw. Bettert and Gefr. Schiedel missing.
14.	5./KG 53	CM	Shot down by 222 Sqn. Spitfires of Cutts and Davies at Colne Engaine, near Halstead, Essex, at 16.30 hrs. Target, Radlett, Herts.	Heinkel He 111H-2 (3142 : A1+BN)	100 %	Ofw. Thomas Ditrich killed; Fw. Fritz Steinberg, Fw. Andreas Fellner, Fw. Alois Hummel and Uffz. Theo Hugenschütz missing.
15.	6./KG 53	CM	Shot down by 242 Sqn. Hurricanes of Ball and Stansfeld at 13,000 feet over Essex. Target, Radlett, Herts.	Heinkel He 111H-2 (2782 : A1+JP)	100 %	Fw.Eckert killed. Gefr.Hans-Georg Köhler wounded and died later. Gefr. Alberrt Klapp, Fw. Kurt Stock and Gefr. Friedrich Glück made P.O.W.s.
16.	6./KG 53	CM	Shot down by 501 Sqn. Hurricanes off the Isle of Sheppey at 16.30 hrs.; aircraft ditched and crew took to dinghy.	Heinkel He 111H-2 (6818 : A1+GP)	100 %	Uffz. Rascher, Uffz. Römpert, Uffz. Wagner, Uffz. Schall and Uffz. Feuerleber made P.O.W.s
17.	7./KG 53	CM	Shot down by 56 Sqn. Hurricanes at A.16.30 hrs. and crashed at Hunsdon Rectory, near Bishops Stortford, in raid on Radlett.	Heinkel He 111H-2 (2624 : A1+CR)	100 %	Gefr. Stilp and Gefr. Fritz Reiss killed; Ltn. Ernst Fischbach, Fw. Wilhlem Kusserow and Fw. Georg Distler made P.O.W.s.
18.	III./KG 55	CM	Damaged by 43 Sqn. Hrricanes over Hove at A.17.00 hrs., and crashed at Nantes.	Heinkel He 111P (2813)	80 %	Oblt. Nedden, Ltn. Wrenski and three others wounded.
19.	Erg.St./KG 55	NCM	Suffered air collision with Item 20 at Chartres.	Heinkel He 111 (1629)	100 %	Five crew members killed.
20.	Erg.St./KG 55	NCM	Suffered air collision with Item 19 at Chartres.	Heinkel He 111 (1703)	100 %	Five crew members killed.
21.	I./St.G 77	NCM	Suffered landing accident at Maltot airfield.	Junkers Ju 87B (0355)	20 %	Crew unhurt.
22.	Stuka Erg.St./ Fliegerkorps VIII	NCM	Crashed during training flight near Lippstadt.	Junkers Ju 87B (5345 : T6+HZ)	90 %	Oblt. Jäger killed.
23.	I./LG 2	CM	Shot down by 610 Sqn. Spitfire of Hamlyn and crashed near Calais.	Messerschmitt Bf 109 E-4 (2043)	100 %	Hptm. Nielke missing.
24.	II./ZG 2	CM	Shot down by 253 Sqn. Hurricane of Cambridge near Redhill at A.11.55 hrs.	Messerschmitt Bf 110 D-0 (3315 : A2+HK)	100 %	Hptm. Schuldt and Uffz. Dyroff
25.	I./ZG 26	CM	Shot down by 85 Sqn. Hurricane of Goodman over the English Channel.	Messerschmitt Bf 110 C-4 (3583 : E8+CX)	100 %	Both crew members rescued unhurt from the sea.
26.	3./ZG 26	CM	Shot down by 85 Sqn. Hurricane of Hodgson and crashed at Cap Gris Nez.	Messerschmitt Bf 110 C-4 (3583 : K8+AL)	90 %	Crews escaped unhurt.
27	6./ZG 26	CM	Shot down by 56 Sqn. Hurricane of Westmacott at 16.30 hrs. and crashed at Mill Hill Farm, Rettenden, Essex.	Messerschmitt Bf 110 C-2 (3496 : 3U+KP)	100 %	Uffz. Rudolf Franke and Uffz. Willi Hubner made P.O.W.s.
28.	II./ZG 76	CM	Shot down by 85 Sqn. Hurricane of Woods-Scawen near Dover at 11.20 hrs.	Messerschmitt Bf 110C (3257 : M8+BM)	100 %	Hptm. Wagner and Stabfw. Schmidt killed.
29.	II./ZG 76	CM	Shot down by 85 Sqn. Hurricane of Allard at A.16.30 hrs. and crashed at Barley Beans Farm, Kimpton, Herts.	Messerschmitt Bf 110C (2615 : M8+MM)	100 %	Ofw. Georg Anthony killed. Uffz. Heinrich Normeyer, paralysed with fractured spine, made P.O.W.
30.	III./ZG 76	CM	Damaged by 111 Sqn. Hurricane of Dymond near Manston at A.07.10 hrs.	Messerschmitt Bf 110 C-2 (3235 : 2N+LM)	30 %	Crew unhurt.
31.	II./JG 2	CM	Shot down by 616 Sqn. Spitfire of Gillam in Eastchurch area at 16.45 hrs.	Messerschmitt Bf 109 E-4 (2765)	100 %	Ofw. Harbauer killed.
32.	II./JG 2	CM	Shot down by 616 Sqn. Spitfire of Hopewell in Eastchurch area at A. 16.45 hrs.	Messerschmitt Bf 109 E-4 (2753)	100 %	Pilot, unhurt, made P.O.W.
33.	III./JG 2	CM	Shot down by 610 Sqn. Spitfire of Chandler over Biggin Hill at A.16.50 hrs.	Messerschmitt Bf 109 E-4 (2782)	100 %	Uffz. Reih missing.
34.	II./JG 3	NCM	Suffered landing accident at Wierre-au-Bois.	Messerschmitt Bf 109 E-1 (3350)	15 %	Pilot unhurt.
35.	III./JG 3	NCM	Suffered landing accident at Desvres airfield.	Messerschmitt Bf 109 E-1 (6622)	70 %	Pilot unhurt.
36.	I./JG 26	CM	Ditched in Channel after combat with fighters (probably Hurricanes of 85 Sqn.)	Messerschmitt Bf 109E (5650)	100 %	Pilot, wounded, rescued by *Seenot-flugkommando.*
37.	II./JG 26	CM	Shot down near Folkestone (probably by Hurri-canes of 85 Sqn.) and crashed in sea.	Messerschmitt Bf 109 E-4 (0804)	100 %	Pilot, unhurt, rescued by *Seenot-flugkommando.*
38.	II./JG 26	CM	Ditched in Channel after combat with fighters (probably Hurricanes of 85 Sqn.)	Messerschmitt Bf 109 E-4 (6298)	100 %	Pilot, unhurt, rescued by *Seenot-flugkommando.*
39.	I./JG 27	CM	Shot down by 616 Sqn. Spitfire of Smith over Thames Estuary at A. 1145 hrs.	Messerschmitt Bf 109 E-1 (6123)	100 %	Pilot, unhurt, rescued and made P.O.W.
40.	3./JG 27	CM	Shot down by 253 Sqn. Hurricane of Gleave south-east of Maidstone at A.11.55 hrs.	Messerschmitt Bf 109 E-1 (3771)	100 %	Fw. Ernst Arnold, unhurt, made P.O.W.
41.	3./JG 27	CM	Shot down by 253 Sqn. Hurricane of Gleave near Maidstone at A.11.55 hrs.	Messerschmitt Bf 109 E-1 (6270)	100 %	Oblt. Erwin Axthelm, unhurt, made P.O.W.
42.	I./JG 27	CM	Shot down by 253 Sqn. Hurricane of Gleave near Maidstone at A.11.55 hrs.	Messerschmitt Bf 109 E-4	100 %	Pilot missing, believed killed.
43.	III./JG 27	CM	Shot down by 253 Sqn. Hurricane of Gleave near Maidstone at A.11.55 hrs.	Messerschmitt Bf 109 E-1 (6330)	100 %	Pilot , unhurt, made P.O.W.
44.	III./JG 27	CM	Shot down by 253 Sqn. Hurricane of Gleave south-east of Maidstone at A.11.55 hrs.	Messerschmitt Bf 109 E-4 (1623)	100 %	Fw. Georg Lehmann killed.
45.	5./JG 51	CM	Taxying accident at Jever, probably at night.	Messerschmitt Bf 109 E-1 (6219)	20 %	Pilot unhurt.
46.	I./JG 52	CM	Reported to have suffered engine failure over Dover; ultimate fate not known.	Messerschmitt Bf 109 E-1 (1973)	100 %	Ltn. Geller missing.
47.	4./JG 54	CM	Struck the tail of Item 48 during combat with Hurricanes; pilot baled out , unhurt, at Oxted, Surrey, at A.11.50 hrs.	Messerschmitt Bf 109 E-4 (1643: "White 5")	100 %	Ltn. Rudolf Ziegler made P.O.W.
48.	4./JG 54	CM	Air collision with Item 47 during combat with Hurricanes; pilot baled out, unhurt, at Ledgers Farm, Chelsham, near Croydon, at A.11.50 hrs..	Messerschmitt Bf 109 E-4 (6072: "White 6")	100 %	Oblt. Hans Rath made P.O.W.
49.	3./606	CM	Reported to have struck high ground at Bilbao, Northern Spain, after becoming lost.	Dornier Do 17Z-3 (2838 : 7T+GL)	100 %	Ltn.z.S. Hanschke and three crew killed.

Saturday 31st August

If previous experience had suggested to the defenders that the *Luftwaffe* might be unable to sustain heavy pressure against Britain over a number of days (and nights), Fighter Command was now to learn otherwise—to its cost.

With more than eighty per cent of the Bf 109s in Northern Europe now concentrated in the Pas de Calais under Kessel-ring's command, it was to be expected that these superb fighters would be used on every possible occasion, both in the escort and free chase rôles. With power supplies now restored to the radar stations on the Kent coast, reports came in just before 08.00 hours to the Fighter Command operations room at Bentley Priory of four waves of enemy aircraft, one approaching Dover and the other three flying up the Thames Estuary. When observers reported that the Dover raid consisted solely of Bf 109s, Park's controllers tried to withdraw the two Hurricane squadrons which were on their way to intercept. No. 501 Squadron turned away, but before the Canadians of No. 1 Squadron, R.C.A.F., could follow suit a *Staffel* of Bf 109s dived out of the sun and shot down Flt. Lt. Vaughan Corbett, Fg. Off. George Hyde and Fg. Off. William Sprenger; all three pilots baled out, but Corbett and Hyde suffered burns to face and hands. Finding no further fighter opposition, the Messerschmitt pilots again indulged themselves in shooting at the Dover balloons—this time destroying every one!

When Dunkirk and Canewdon radar reported the approach of an estimated force of 200 enemy aircraft, Park scrambled thirteen squadrons from seven airfields around London. Twelve Hurricanes of No. 257 Squadron climbed from Martlesham and encountered a screen of about fifty Bf 110s near Clacton; the Germans went into a defensive circle on being attacked head-on, losing two of their number. The Hurricanes of Plt. Offs. Gerald Maffett and James Henderson were shot down and the former pilot was killed. As one of the raids approached North Weald, twelve Hurricanes of No. 56 Squadron met the German formation near Colchester, but were heavily engaged by the escort; without scoring, the squadron lost four aircraft, the pilot of one, Flt. Lt. Percy Weaver[71], being killed, and two others wounded.

As part of this raid penetrated to North Weald, another formation of Dorniers was making its way with heavy Bf 110 escort north-westwards to the No. 12 Group Sector Station at Duxford. Neither of the resident fighter squadrons had been brought up to state and Wg. Cdr. Alfred Woodhall, controlling at the time, urgently requested cover for his airfield. Park promptly diverted nine Hurricanes of No. 111 Squadron (which had been on patrol since 08.10 hours) to intercept the raid; as luck would have it, their pilots were so positioned as to be able to deliver a head-on attack at the outset, and did so, first on the Dorniers and then on the Messerschmitts—claiming one of each destroyed—for the loss of one Hurricane, whose pilot, Sergeant John Craig, baled out wounded near Felixstowe. The vigour with which the Hurricanes engaged this formation resulted in the escort adopting the familiar defensive circle, so that the Dornier crews, now irrevocably scattered, turned for home at full speed, lighten-ing their loads without further thoughts of targets.

The third part of this attack—in fact part of the Duxford raid which had escaped detection—was carried out by a *Gruppe* of Dorniers on the airfield at Debden. About one hundred 250-kilo bombs fell within the aerodrome perimeter, demolishing part of the station sick quarters and damaging three barrack blocks. Eighteen casualties were suffered and four Hurricanes were badly damaged on the ground, but the serviceability of the airfield was not seriously impaired.

The cannon-Spitfires of No. 19 Squadron had scrambled from Fowlmere and intercepted the Debden raid. Two Sections engaged the Bf 110s, but two Spitfires were shot down, Fg. Off. James Coward baling out with a severely wounded foot, but Fg. Off. Francis Brinsden escaping unhurt. Plt. Off. Raymond Aeberhardt's Spitfire was hit in the hydraulics and when he returned to his airfield he had to land without flaps; the aircraft turned over and caught fire; the nineteen-year-old pilot died in the flames.

Shortly after 09.00 hours two groups of aircraft, one composed of about twenty escorted Dornier Do 17s, and the other a mixed group of Bf 109s and 110s, were reported over the north Kent coast. The former made for Eastchurch, where eighty bombs caused limited damage but none critical to the continued working of the airfield. The fighter sweep, which it is believed was intended to provide an outer screen for the bombers attacking Eastchurch, turned its attention on the airfield at Detling, carrying a succession of very low strafing runs, seeking in vain to find parked aircraft as targets for their guns.

After a number of free chases over Kent, which served to keep the controllers on the alert for larger raids, but against which they refrained from committing fighters, Kesselring sent two waves of Dorniers and Heinkels, escorted by Bf 109s and 110s, to attack Croydon and Biggin Hill. The former almost reached its target at 12.55 hours, flying at 2,000 feet, before the defences reacted; Peter Townsend's twelve Hurricanes of No. 85 Squadron were only just taking off as the first bombs from twelve Dorniers landed on the east side of the aerodrome. Climbing at full throttle the Squadron caught up with the enemy over Tunbridge Wells and went for the Bf 110s just as the 109s fell on them from above. Townsend was hit in the foot and baled out, landing at Hawkhurst and being taken to hospital where a shell nose cap was removed from his foot and his left big toe was amputated; his parachute was put on display by the local police and raised £3 for the local Spitfire fund. The squadron claimed the destruction of two Bf 109s and one Bf 110 for the loss of two Hurricanes, both of whose pilots were slightly wounded. Croydon suffered some damage (including the destruction of a hangar) and a number of casualties.

The raid on Biggin Hill was carried out by two *Staffeln* of Heinkel He 111s which bombed from 12,000 feet, hitting two of the three remaining hangars[72], messes, living quarters and

---

[71] The award of the D.F.C. to this popular Flight Commander was announced on this day—only a few hours after his death in action had been confirmed.

[72] The Station Commander, Gp. Capt. Richard Grice, believed that, so long as the remaining hangar still stood untouched, the *Luftwaffe* would continue to raid the airfield, inevitably inflicting serious damage to the rest of his station. He accordingly ordered the hangar to be demolished—an act which later brought a Court Martial upon himself, but at which he was exonerated of all culpability.

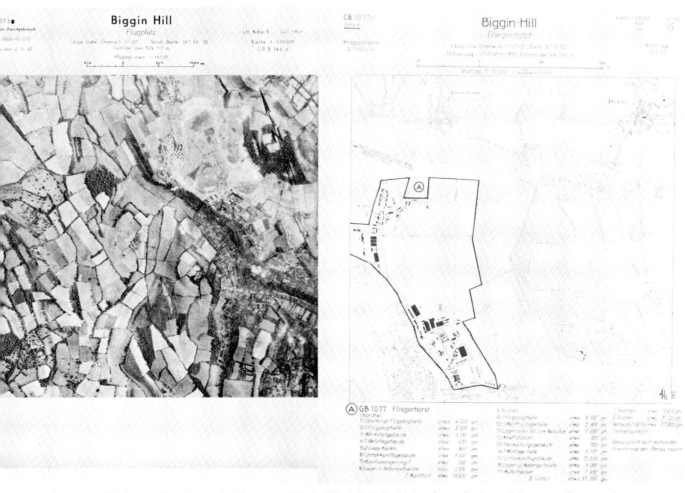

German aerial photograph and target briefing map of Biggin Hill airfield, Park's key Sector Station and the target of heavy and repeated raids during late August and early September 1940; the photograph shows evidence of heavy cratering on the airfield and in the village. The map makes a clear distinction between North and South Camps.

the all-important operations room. Once again all the telephone lines—so tediously repaired since the previous day's raid—were smashed. As the Heinkels made off to the southeast they ran into seven Hurricanes of No. 253 Squadron who shot down one of their number. The British pilots returned to base independently, but Sqn. Ldr. Tom Gleave was jumped and shot down by an unseen fighter near Biggin Hill. He was seriously wounded and burned, but baled out safely[73].

---

[73] The C.O. of No. 253 Squadron, Sqn. Ldr. Harold Starr, had been shot down during the morning of this day, but after baling out was apparently shot at and killed by enemy aircraft. Command of the Squadron then reverted to Sqn. Ldr. Gleave who, it will be recalled was serving supernumerary with No. 253. For many years he remained uncertain as to how and by what fighter he had been shot down early that afternoon. However in 1966 the fragmented remains of his Hurricane were found, and an examination of the surviving sternpost by the author disclosed a 20-mm. shell hole which had penetrated from astern and below, evidence that he had been shot down by a Bf 109 (no Bf 110 was reported in the area at the time), positioned in the Hurricane's blind spot under the tail. Gleave was very severely burned to the face and limbs and was in due course admitted to the Queen Victoria Hospital at East Grinstead; here, under the direction of Archibald McIndoe, he underwent plastic surgery, and in less than a year began flying once more. He later became Station Commander at Manston. During the 1970s, as a Founder-Member of the Guinea Pig Club (whose members were those who had survived serious burns and who had been treated by the Serious Burns Unit under Sir Archibald McIndoe), he succeeded to the title of Chief Guinea Pig.

The Biggin Hill raiders, unlike those of the previous day, had flown in over the Kent coast west of Folkestone as part of a two-wave mass, the second part of which split near Maidstone and flew on to the airfield at Hornchurch. Heat haze east of London prevented the Observer Corps from passing accurate plots on this raid so that the Dornier *Gruppe* almost reached the airfield before the Spitfires of No. 54 Squadron started to take off:

"**13.15 hours**. A large formation of enemy bombers—a most impressive sight in vic formation at 15,000 feet—reached the aerodrome and dropped their bombs (probably sixty in all) in a line from our original dispersal pens to the petrol dump and beyond into Elm Park. Perimeter track, dispersal pens and barrack block windows suffered, but no other damage to buildings was caused, and the aerodrome, in spite of its ploughed condition, remained serviceable. The squadron was ordered off just as the first bombs were beginning to fall and eight of our machines safely cleared the ground; the remaining section, however, just became airborne as the bombs exploded. All three machines were wholly wrecked in the air, and the survival of the pilots is a complete miracle. Sgt. Davis, taking off towards the hangars was thrown back across the River Ingrebourne two fields away, scrambling out of his machine unharmed. Flt. Lt. Deere had one wing and his prop torn off; climbing to about 100 feet, he turned over and, coming down, slid along the aerodrome for a hundred yards upside down. He was rescued from this unenviable position by Plt. Off. Edsall, the third member of the section, who had suffered a similar fate except that he landed the right way up. Dashing across the aerodrome with bombs still dropping, he extricated Deere from his machine. All three pilots were ready again for battle by the next morning."[74]

A disturbing turn of events occurred during the afternoon when *Erprobungsgruppe 210* returned to the fray and carried out a series of snap raids from low level on the CH radar stations in Kent and Sussex, and the CHL installation at Foreness. All were damaged but were back on the air by the end of the day.

Both Hornchurch and Biggin Hill were raided for a second time at around 17.30 hours when *Erprobungsgruppe 210* ac-

companied three *Staffeln* of Ju 88s and Bf 110s to drop about thirty bombs on each target. Two Spitfires were destroyed at Hornchurch, but both Nos. 54 and 222 Squadrons were away over Kent in action against the Biggin Hill raiders.

The night offensive was maintained by more than 160 German bombers, three-quarters of which visited Liverpool for the fourth consecutive night. Fairly large numbers of single aircraft roamed the countryside apparently aiming bombs at flaws in the blackout. No major target was hit—or could be identified by the bomb plots—apart from Liverpool. Still the night fighters were virtually powerless to interfere with these night raids, and this fact must have clinched Fighter Command's decision, reached on 31st August, to withdraw the Defiant from daylight operations (save in the absence of enemy fighters) and train the two squadrons in night fighting. Months later the Defiant would emerge as a useful weapon in the hands of trained crews.

[74] Cf. Form 540, No. 54 Squadron, 31st August 1940.

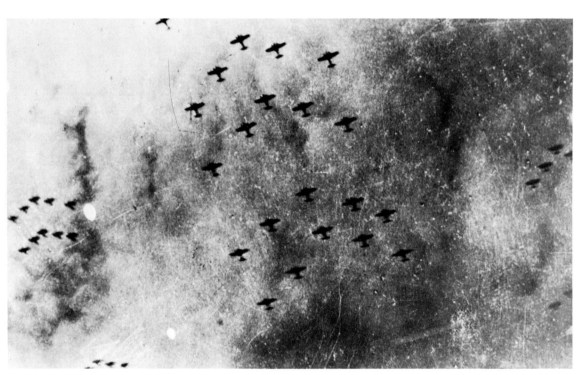

Dorniers over Biggin Hill during one of the raids late in August. The textbook Staffel formation is clearly defined.

R.A.F. FIGHTER COMMAND LOSSES—SATURDAY 31st AUGUST 1940

1.	1 Sqn., Northolt	C	Shot down by Bf 110 over Chelmsford; pilot baled out with burns.	09.05 hrs.	Sgt. H.J. Merchant	Hurricane	V7375	Cat. 3 Destroyed
2.	1 (Canadian) Northolt	C	Shot down by Bf 109 near Dover; pilot baled out with burns to face and hands.	A09.20 hrs.	Flt. Lt. V.B. Corbett	Hurricane	P3858	Cat. 3 Destroyed
3.	1 (Canadian) Northolt	C	Shot down by Bf 109 near Dover; pilot baled out with burns to face and hands.	A09.20 hrs.	Fg. Off. G.G. Hyde	Hurricane	P2971	Cat. 3 Destroyed
4.	1 (Canadian) Northolt	C	Shot down by Bf 109 near Dover; pilot baled out unhurt.	A09.20 hrs.	Fg. Off. W.P. Sprenger	Hurricane	N2530	Cat. 3 Destroyed
5.	17 Sqn., Tangmere	C	Shot down bf Bf 109s near Maidstone and destroyed in force landing; pilot unhurt.	A15.05 hrs.	Sgt. G.A. Steward	Hurricane	—	Cat. 3 Destroyed
6.	19 Sqn., Fowlmere	C	Shot down by Bf 109 near Little Shelford, Essex; pilot baled out wounded in the foot.	A09.00 hrs.	Fg. Off. T.J.B. Coward	Spitfire	X4231	Cat. 3 Destroyed
7.	19 Sqn., Fowlmere	C	Damaged by Bf 109s; crashed on landing and burnt out; pilot killed.	A09.35 hrs.	Plt. Off. R.C. Aeberhardt	Spitfire	R6912	Cat. 3 Burnt
8.	19 Sqn., Fowlmere	C	Shot down by Bf 109s near North Weald; pilot baled out unhurt.	A09.10 hrs.	Fg. Off. F.N. Brinsden	Spitfire	R6958	Cat. 3 Destroyed
9.	54 Sqn., Hornchurch	C	Aircraft caught by bomb blast during take-off at Hornchurch; pilot unhurt.	13.17 hrs.	Sgt. J. Davis	Spitfire	X4236	Cat. 3 Destroyed
10.	54 Sqn., Hornchurch	C	Aircraft caught by bomb blast during take-off at Hornchurch; pilot slightly hurt.	13.17 hrs.	Flt. Lt. A.C. Deere	Spitfire	N3110	Cat. 3 Destroyed
11.	54 Sqn., Hornchurch	C	Aircraft caught by bomb blast during take-off at Hornchurch; pilot unhurt.	13.17 hrs.	Plt. Off E.F. Edsall	Spitfire	—	Cat. 2 Damaged
12.	54 Sqn., Hornchurch	C	Shot down by Hurricane near Tonbridge, Kent; pilot baled out unhurt.	17.55 hrs.	Sgt. D.G. Gibbins	Spitfire	X4054	Cat. 3 Destroyed

R.A.F. Losses, 31st August 1940—*continued*

13.	56 Sqn., North Weald	C	Shot down by Bf 110s near North Weald; pilot killed.	A09.10 hrs.	Flt. Lt. P.S. Weaver	Hurricane	*R4197*	Cat. 3 Destroyed
14.	56 Sqn., North Weald	C	Shot down by Bf 110s over Blackwater Estu- ary; pilot baled out badly burned.	A09.10 hrs.	Fg. Off. I.B. Westmacott	Hurricane	—	Cat. 3 Destroyed
15.	56 Sqn., North Weald	C	Shot down by Bf 110s near Colchester; pilot wounded.	A09.15 hrs.	Plt. Off. M.H. Mounsdon	Hurricane	—	Cat. 3 Destroyed
16.	56 Sqn., North Weald	C	Shot down by Bf 110s over Colchester; pilot baled out unhurt.	A09.15 hrs.	Sgt. C. Whitehead	Hurricane	*V6628*	Cat. 3 Destroyed
17.	72 Sqn., Biggin Hill	C	Shot down by Bf 109s near Dungeness and crashed near Staplehurst; pilot killed.	18.20 hrs.	Plt. Off. E.J. Wilcox	Spitfire	*P9457*	Cat. 3 Destroyed
18.	72 Sqn., Biggin Hill	C	Shot down by Bf 109s near Tenterden, Kent; pilot baled out, wounded and badly burned.	18.25 hrs.	Flt. Lt. F.M. Smith	Spitfire	*P9438*	Cat. 3 Destroyed
19.	85 Sqn., Croydon	C	Shot down near Hawkhurst by Bf 109; pilot baled out at Hawkhurst, wounded in left foot.	A13.45 hrs.	Sqn. Ldr. P.W. Townsend	Hurricane	*P3166*	Cat. 3 Destroyed
20.	85 Sqn., Croydon	C	Shot down by Bf 110 at Newenden; pilot blaed out slightly wounded in thigh.	A13.40 hrs.	Plt. Off. P.A. Worrall	Hurricane	*V6581*	Cat. 3 Destroyed
21.	85 Sqn., Croydon	C	Shot down by Bf 109 and force landed near Shotgate, Essex; pilot unhurt.	A13.40 hrs.	Plt. Off. W.T. Hodgson	Hurricane	—	Cat. 3 Burnt
22.	111 Sqn., Debden	C	Shot down by Bf 110 over Felixstowe; pilot baled out wounded.	A09.10 hrs.	Sgt. J.T. Craig	Hurricane	*P2888*	Cat. 3 Destroyed
23.	151 Sqn., Stapleford	C	Force landed at Foulness after combat with Bf 109s; pilot wounded in the shoulder.	10.40 hrs.	Plt. Off. F. Czajkowski	Hurricane	*P3301*	Cat. 2 Damaged
24.	151 Sqn., Stapleford	C	Shot down by Ju 88 over Essex; pilot baled out near Southend with burns.	13.30 hrs.	Plt. Off J.L.W. Ellacombe	Hurricane	*P3312*	Cat. 3 Burnt
25.	222 Sqn., Hornchurch	C	Shot down by Bf 109 and crash landed at Eastchurch; pilot slightly wounded.	A18.00 hrs.	Flt. Lt. A.I. Robinson	Spitfire	*N3233*	Cat. 3 Destroyed
26.	222 Sqn., Hornchurch	C	Shot down by Bf 109s near Ashford; aircraft caught fire and pilot received burns.	18.08 hrs.	Plt. Off. C.G.A. Davies	Spitfire	*P9337*	Cat. 3 Burnt
27.	253 Sqn., Kenley	C	Shot down by Bf 109 near Biggin Hill; pilot baled out with serious wounds and burns.	A13.30 hrs.	Sqn. Ldr. T.P. Gleave	Hurricane	—	Cat. 3 Destroyed
28.	253 Sqn., Kenley	C	Shot down at Eastry by Bf 109s; pilot baled out and killedby Bf 109s while descending.	A11.30 hrs.	Sqn. Ldr. H.M. Starr	Hurricane	*L1830*	Cat. 3 Destroyed
29.	257 Sqn., Martlesham	C	Shot down by bf 110s near North Weald; pilot baled out unhurt.	A09.10 hrs.	Plt.Off. J.A.McD. Henderson	Hurricane	*P3708*	Cat. 3 Destroyed
30.	257 Sqn., Martlesham	C	Shot down by Bf 110s over Clacton and crashed at Walton-on-the-Naze; pilot killed.	A09.15 hrs.	Plt. Off. G.H. Maffett	Hurricane	*P3175*	Cat. 3 Destroyed
31.	310 Sqn., Duxford	C	Shot down by Do 17s over Thames Estuary; pilot killed. (Had been on Sqn. for 3 hours)	A13.40 hrs.	Plt. Off. J. Sterbacek	Hurricane	*P3159*	Cat. 3 Destroyed
32.	310 Sqn., Duxford	C	Shot down by Do 17s over the Thames Estu- ary; pilot baled out unhurt.	A13.35 hrs.	Plt. Off. M. Kredba	Hurricane	*P8814*	Cat. 3 Lost
33.	601 Sqn., Debden	C	Shot down by Bf 110s near Debden; pilot unhurt.	09.02 hrs.	Plt. Off. T. Grier	Hurricane	*P5208*	Cat. 3 Destroyed
34.	601 Sqn., Debden	C	Shot down by Bf 109 near Colchester; pilot baled out unhurt.	13.36 hrs.	Sgt. N. Taylor	Hurricane	*P3735*	Cat. 3 Destroyed
35.	601 Sqn., Debden	C	Shot down near Gravesend by Bf 109s; pilot baled out with burns.	13.42 hrs.	Sgt. A.W. Woolley	Hurricane	*N2602*	Cat. 3 Burnt
36.	601 Sqn., Debden	C	Shot down over Thames Estuary by Bf 110; pilot baled out unhurt.	13.45 hrs.	Plt. Off. H.T. Gilbert	Hurricane	*V7260*	Cat. 3 Destroyed
37.	601 Sqn., Debden	C	Assumed shot down over the Thames Estuary; pilot posted Missing and body not recovered.	A13.45 hrs.	Fg. Off. M.D. Doulton	Hurricane	*P3383*	Cat. 3 Missing
38.	602 Sqn., Westhampnett	C	Damaged by Bf 109 near Dungeness; pilot returned unhurt.	A18.25 hrs.	Sgt. D.W. Elcombe	Spitfire	*L1040*	Cat. 2 Damaged
39.	603 Sqn., Hornchurch	C	Shot down and crashed at Woolwich; pilot killed when aircraft broke up in the air.	Not known	Fg. Off. R.McG. Waterston	Spitfire	*X4273*	Cat. 3 Destroyed
40.	603 Sqn., Hornchurch	C	Shot down and crashed at Wanstead, Essex; pilot safe.	Not known	Not known	Spitfire	*X4271*	Cat. 3 Destroyed

[*Note:* No. 32 Squadron at Acklington reported the loss of a Hurricane (*N2345*) on this date, probably in an accident; no details are known.]

LUFTWAFFE LOSSES—SATURDAY 31st AUGUST 1940

1.	4./Aufkl.Gr. Ob.d.L.	CM	Shot down by 66 Sqn. Spitfires of Gillies, Bodie and Hunt over Suffolk at 15.03 hrs.	Dornier Do 215 (0028 : G2+LH)	100 %	Fw. Maurer and Uffz. Vogel killed; Uffz. Goebbels and Uffz. Kamolz missing.
2.	Aufkl.Gr.21	NCM	Crashed following engine failure near Illes.	Henschel Hs 126 (3246)	100 %	Crew unhurt.
3.	II./KG 2	CM	Shot down by 19 Sqn. Spitfires of Clouston and Burgoyne south of Duxford at A.09.00 hrs.	Dornier Do 17Z-2 (3483 : U5+CN)	100 %	One crew member wounded.
4.	Stab III./KG 2	CM	Damaged by 111 Sqn. Hurricane of Giddings near Felixstowe at 09.05 hrs.	Dornier Do 17Z-2 (3356 : U5+AD)	5 %	Maj. Fuchs, *Gr. Kdr.*, wounded.
5.	Stab I./KG 3	NCM	Landing accident at St. Inglevert airfield.	Junkers Ju 52/3m (12353 : N3+AQU)	15 %	Crew unhurt.
6.	I./KG 3	CM	Crashed at St. Omer after combat with 72 Sqn. Spitfires at A.18.00 hrs.	Dornier Do 17Z-2 (1178 : 5K+KL)	100 %	One killed; three wounded.
7.	II./KG 3	CM	Shot down by 151 Sqn. Hurricane of Blair near Hornchurch at 13.20 hrs.	Dornier Do 17Z-2 (3456 : 5K+BC)	100 %	Five missing, including Ltn. Schopper.
8.	II./KG 3	CM	Damaged by 310 Sqn. Hurricanes near Horn- church at 13.20 hrs.	Dornier Do 17Z-2 (3458 : 5K+EM)	8 %	One wounded.
9.	II./KG 3	CM	Shot down by 310 Sqn. Hurricane near Horn- church at A.13.20 hrs.	Dornier Do 17Z-2 (3414 : 5K+GN)	100 %	Uffz. Blasche, Fw. Nickel, Fw. Gutat and Uffz. Sonntag missing.
10.	II./KG 3	CM	Shot down by 310 Sqn. Hurricane of Jefferies near Hornchurch at A.13.20 hrs.	Dornier Do 17Z-2 (3264 : 5K+KM)	100 %	Uffz.Bock killed, Oblt.Gahtz, Ofw. Bulach, Gefr. Neumann missing.
11.	II./KG 3	CM	Shot down by 310 Sqn. Hurricane near Horn- church at A. 13.20 hrs.	Dornier Do 17Z-2 (2669 : 5K+LM)	100 %	Ofw.Lange, Uffz.Kostropetsch, Fw. Berndt and Fw. Wunsche missing.
12.	7./KG 27	NCM	Accident following engine failure at Rennes.	Hreinkel He 111P(1418)	40 %	Crew unhurt.
13.	II./KG 51	CM	Landing accident at Orly following combat.	Junkers Ju 88A-1(6075)	30 %	Crew unhurt.
14.	II./KG 51	NCM	Accident on Orly airfield; not recalled.	Junkers Ju 88A-1(5028)	30 %	Crew unhurt.
15.	III./KG 51	NCM	Landing accident on Etampes airfield.	Junkers Ju 88A-1(7051)	10 %	Crew unhurt.
16.	II./KG 76	CM	Shot down by 151 Sqn. Hurricane of Pattullo over Thames Estuary at A.18.00 hrs.	Dornier Do 17Z-2 (3316 : F1+BK)	100 %	Ltn.Klepmeier, Fw.Fähler, Uffz. Boss and Ofw. Lang missing.
17.	KGr. 806	CM	Crashed at Nantes with *flak* damage after com- bat sortie.	Junkers Ju 88A-1 (4061)	100 %	Oblt.Jansen, Ogefr. Horst Müller, Fw. Duschelka, Fw. Erdmann missing.
18.	I./LG 1	CM	Crashed near Provins following combat (possi- bly with 253 Sqn. Hurricane of Gleave).	Junkers Ju 88A-1 (2113)	90 %	Crew unhurt.

Luftwaffe Losses, 31st August 1940—*continued*

19. III./LG 1	CM	Landing accident at Chateaudun after combat.	Junkers Ju 88A-1 (2079 : L1+AR)	30 %	Crew unhurt.
20. 13./LG 1	CM	Shot down by British fighters near Croydon; R.A.F. squadron not identified.	Messerschmitt Bf 110 (0958 : L1+CH)	100 %	Ofw. Kobert and Fw. Meinig missing.
21. 14./LG 1	CM	Shot down by 257 Sqn. Hurricane of Beresford in London area.	Messerschmitt Bf 110 (3617 : L1+BK)	100 %	Ltn. Karl-Joachim Eichorn made P.O.W. Uffz. Gröwe killed.
22. 14./LG 1	CM	Shot down by British fighters and crashed near the Nore Lightship at 09.10 hrs.	Messerschmitt Bf 110 (3805 : L1+AK)	100 %	Fw. Fritz Gottlob and Ogefr. Karl Döpfer made P.O.W.s.
23. 15./LG 1	CM	Shot down by British fighters near Edenbridge.	Messerschmitt Bf 110 C-1 (3558 : L1+KV)	100 %	Fw. Jäckel killed; Fl. Rösler missing.
24. I./LG 2	NCM	Crashed at Calais-Marck after engine failure.	Messerschmitt Bf 109E	60 %	Pilot unhurt.
25. I./LG 2	CM	Damaged by 17 Sqn. Hurricane over Kent at A.18.15 hrs.	Messerschmitt Bf 109 E-4 (1399)	60 %	Pilot unhurt.
26. I./LG 2	CM	Shot down by 17 Sqn. Hurricane of Bird-Wilson near Maidstone at 18.15 hrs.	Messerschmitt Bf 109 E-7 (5600)	100 %	Oblt. von Perthes killed.
27. I./ZG 2	NCM	Landing accident on Grandeville airfield.	Messerschmitt Bf 110 C-2 (3083)	30 %	Crew unhurt.
28. Stab/ZG 26	CM	Force landed at Wizernes after fighter combat.	Messerschmitt Bf 110 (3280 : U8+JH)	15 %	Crew unhurt.
29. Stab III./ZG 26	CM	Crashed at Arques after combat with 19 Sqn. Spitfires at A.09.00 hrs.	Messerschmitt Bf 110 C-4 (2167 : 3U+CD)	38 %	One crew member wounded.
30. 8./ZG 26	CM	Shot down by 19 Sqn. Spitfire of Cox over Essex at A.09.00 hrs.	Messerschmitt Bf 110D (3396 : 3U+HS)	100 %	Oblt. von Bergen and Uffz. Becker missing.
31. II./ZG 76	CM	Crashed at St. Inglevert after combat.	Messerschmitt Bf 110C (3603 : M8+KM)	100 %	Hptm. Nacke + one wounded.
32. 2./Erpr.Gr. 210	CM	Shot down by 85 Sqn. Hurricane of Worrall at 13.32 hrs., and crashed on Wrotham Hill.	Messerschmitt Bf 110D (3381 : S9+GK)	100 %	Ogefr. Konrad Schweda killed; Fw. Ernst Gläske made P.O.W.
33. 2./Erpr.Gr. 210	CM	Damaged by 85 Sqn. Hurricane of Booth near Croydon and force landed at Calais-Marck.	Messerschmitt Bf 110 D-0 (3370 : S9+DK)	30 %	Crew unhurt.
34. 3./Erpr.Gr. 210	CM	Damaged by 85 Sqn. Hurricanes near Croydon at 13.38 hrs. and force landed at Calais-Marck.	Messerschmitt Bf 110 D-0 (3368 : S9+EK)	25 %	Crew unhurt.
35. II./JG 2	CM	Shot down by British fighters over the Channel. R.A.F. squadron not identified.	Messerschmitt Bf 109 E-1 (3510)	100 %	Pilot, unhurt, rescued by *Seenot-flugkommando.*
36. I./JG 3	CM	Shot down by 151 Sqn. Hurricanes at A.09.00 hrs.	Messerschmitt Bf 109 E-4 (5339)	100 %	Oblt. Loidolt missing.
37. I./JG 3	CM	Shot down by British fighters over Kent; R.A.F. squadron not identified.	Messerschmitt Bf 109 E-4 (1503)	100 %	Oblt. Walter Binder killed.
38. I./JG 3	CM	Shot down by British fighters over Kent; R.A.F. squadron not identified.	Messerschmitt Bf 109 E-4 (1082)	100 %	Oblt. Rau missing.
39. 4./JG 3	CM	Shot down by 1(Canadian) Sqn. Hurricane of Christmas near Gravesend at A.18.00 hrs.	Messerschmitt Bf 109 E-1 (3175)	100 %	Ltn. Larisch killed.
40. 6./JG 3	CM	Shot down by 1(Canadian) Sqn. Hurricane of Little near Gravesend at A.18.00 hrs.	Messerschmitt Bf 109 E-4 (1475)	100 %	Oblt. Westerhof missing.
41. III./JG 3	CM	Landing accident at Desvres after combat with British fighters.	Messerschmitt Bf 109 E-1 (3549)	25 %	Pilot unhurt.
42. I./JG 26	CM	Shot down by 222 Sqn. Spitfire of Vigors near Biggin Hill at 13.20 hrs.	Messerschmitt Bf 109 E-1 (4806)	100 %	Ltn. Hafer killed.
43. II./JG 26	CM	Shot down by 54 Sqn. Spitfire of Gray near Manston at 17.45 hrs.	Messerschmitt Bf 109 E-4 (5393)	100 %	Ogefr. Heyer missing.
44. III./JG 26	CM	Shot down over Channel by British fighters; R.A.F. squadron not identified.	Messerschmitt Bf 109 E-4 (3712)	100 %	Pilot, unhurt, rescued by *Seenot-flugkommando.*
45. III./JG 26	CM	Shot down by 54 Sqn. Spitfires of Gribble and Norwell after Hornchurch raid at 13.55 hrs.	Messerschmitt Bf 109 E-1 (6309)	100 %	Gefr. Liebeck missing.
46. III./JG 26	CM	Shot down by 85 Sqn. Hurricane of Hodgson over Thameshaven at 17.40 hrs.	Messerschmitt Bf 109 E-4 (1184)	100 %	Ltn. Fronhöfer missing.
47. III./JG 26	CM	Shot down by 85 Sqn. Hurricane of Woods-Scawen east of London at A.17.40 hrs.	Messerschmitt Bf 109 E-1 (3464)	100 %	Fw. Klar wounded.
48. 3./JG 27	CM	Force landed at Lendlingen after combat with British fighters.	Messerschmitt Bf 109 E-1 (1486)	35 %	Pilot unhurt.
49 4./JG 27	NCM	Accident of Guines airfield following tyre burst.	Messerschmitt Bf 109 E-4 (1425)	30 %	Pilot unhurt.
50. 3./JG 51	CM	Suffered air collision (with Item 51) over Calais. Pilot baled out safely.	Messerschmitt Bf 109 E-4 (5355)	100 %	Pilot unhurt.
51. 3./JG 51	CM	Suffered air collision (with Item 50) over Calais. Pilot baled out safely.	Messerschmitt Bf 109 E-4 (4837)	100 %	Pilot unhurt.
52. Stab/JG 53	CM	Force landed at Etaples after combat with British fighters.	Messerschmitt Bf 109 E-4 (5053)	40 %	Pilot unhurt.
53. I./JG 77	CM	Shot down by 87 Sqn. Hurricanes over Channel at A.19.40 hrs.	Messerschmitt Bf 109 E-1 (6092)	100 %	Fw. Kramer missing.
54. I./JG 77	CM	Shot down by 87 Sqn. Hurricane of Allard over Channel at A.19.40 hrs.	Messerschmitt Bf 109 E-1 (4448)	100 %	Ltn. Petrenko missing.
55. 1./JG 77	CM	Shot down by 85 Sqn. Hurricanes over Channel at A.19.40 hrs.	Messerschmitt Bf 109 E-1 (4068)	100 %	Uffz. Keck missing.
56. 1./JG 77	CM	Shot down by 85 Sqn. Hurricane of Lewis over Kent at approx. 19.25 hrs.	Messerschmitt Bf 109 E-1 (3652)	100 %	Fw. Walter Evers died in hospital and buried at Maidstone cemetery.
57. 2./JG 77	CM	Shot down by 222 Sqn. Spitfire of Van Mantz over south Kent at A.18.15 hrs.	Messerschmitt Bf 109 E-4 (5105)	100 %	Oblt. Erick missing.
58. 2./JG 77	CM	Shot down by 222 Sqn. Spitfire of Hutchinson over south Kent at 18.15 hrs.	Messerschmitt Bf 109 E-1 (4076)	100 %	Oblt. Priebe missing.
59. 3./JG 77	CM	Damaged in combat with British fighters over the Channel during the evening.	Messerschmitt Bf 109 E-1 (3642)	35 %	Pilot unhurt.
60. 3./JG 77	CM	Shot down by 222 Sqn. Spitfire of Broadhurst over the Channel; pilot baled out safely.	Messerschmitt Bf 109 E-1 (5408)	100 %	Pilot, unhurt, rescued by *Seenot-flugkommando.*

R.A.F. FIGHTER COMMAND ORDER OF BATTLE
09.00 hrs., 1st September 1940

Sector	Sqn.	Aircraft	Combat Ready (Unserviceable)	Base Airfield	Pilots on State	Commanding Officer
No. 10 Group, H.Q. Rudloe Manor, Box, Wiltshire						
Pembrey	92 Sqn.	Spitfires	12 (4)	Pembrey	19	Squadron Leader F.J. Sanders
Filton	87 Sqn.	Hurricanes	9 (6)	Exeter	18	Squadron Leader R.S. Mills
	213 Sqn.	Hurricanes	8 (7)	Exeter	19	Squadron Leader H.D. McGregor
St. Eval	236 Sqn.	Blenheims	12 (5)	St. Eval	22	Squadron Leader G.W. Montagu
	238 Sqn.	Hurricanes	11 (4)	St. Eval	20	Squadron Leader H.A. Fenton (absent wounded)
Middle Wallop	152 Sqn.	Spitfires	12 (4)	Warmwell	19	Squadron Leader P.K. Devitt
	234 Sqn.	Spitfires	12 (5)	Middle Wallop	19	Squadron Leader J.S. O'Brien
	249 Sqn. (1)	Hurricanes	15 (1)	Boscombe Down	18	Squadron Leader J. Grandy
	604 Sqn.	Blenheims	11 (3)	Middle Wallop	20	Squadron Leader M.F. Anderson
	609 Sqn.	Spitfires	11 (5)	Middle Wallop	20	Squadron Leader H.S. Darley
No. 11 Group, H.Q. Uxbridge, Middlesex						
Biggin Hill	79 Sqn.	Hurricanes	10 (5)	Biggin Hill	17	Squadron Leader J.H. Heyworth
	501 Sqn.	Hurricanes	12 (5)	Gravesend	22	Squadron Leader H.A.V. Hogan
North Weald	25 Sqn. (2)	Blenheims	14 (2)	Martlesham	24	Squadron Leader W.W. Loxton (acting)
	56 Sqn. (3)	Hurricanes	9 (5)	North Weald	18	*(Temporarily unfilled)*
	151 Sqn. (4)	Hurricanes	9 (4)	Stapleford	17	*(Temporarily unfilled)*
Kenley	72 Sqn. (5)	Spitfires	15 (3)	Croydon	20	Squadron Leader A.R. Collins
	85 Sqn.	Hurricanes	13 (3)	Croydon	17	Squadron Leader P.W. Townsend
	253 Sqn.	Hurricanes	10 (4)	Kenley	17	*(Temporarily unfilled)*
	616 Sqn.	Spitfires	12 (4)	Kenley	20	Squadron Leader M. Robinson
Northolt	1 Sqn.	Hurricanes	10 (3)	Northolt	14	Squadron Leader D.A. Pemberton
	1 (Can.) Sqn.	Hurricanes	13 (4)	Northolt	24	Squadron Leader E.A. McNab, R.C.A.F.
	303 (Polish) Sqn.	Hurricanes	13 (5)	Northolt	24	Squadron Leader R.G. Kellett and Squadron Leader Z. Krasnodebski
Hornchurch	54 Sqn.	Spitfires	11 (5)	Hornchurch	14	*(Temporarily unfilled)*
	222 Sqn.	Spitfires	12 (3)	Hornchurch	18	Squadron Leader J.H. Hill
	600 Sqn.	Blenheims	9 (5)	Hornchurch	23	Squadron Leader D. de B. Clarke
	603 Sqn.	Spitfires	13 (3)	Hornchurch	18	*(Temporarily unfilled)*
Tangmere	17 Sqn.	Hurricanes	12 (5)	Tangmere	19	Squadron Leader A.G. Miller
	43 Sqn.	Hurricanes	10 (4)	Tangmere	19	Squadron Leader C.B. Hull
	602 Sqn.	Spitfires	12 (4)	Westhampnett	19	Squadron Leader A.V.R. Johnstone
Debden	111 Sqn.	Hurricanes	11 (5)	Debden	19	Squadron Leader J.M. Thompson
	257 Sqn.	Hurricanes	12 (5)	Debden	20	Squadron Leader M. Harkness
	601 Sqn.	Hurricanes	12 (5)	Debden	22	Squadron Leader Sir Archibald Hope, Bt.
No. 12 Group, H.Q. Watnall, Nottingham						
Duxford	19 Sqn.	Spitfires	11 (4)	Fowlmere	22	Squadron Leader P.C. Pinkham
	310 (Czech) Sqn.	Hurricanes	10 (4)	Duxford	24	Squadron Leader G.D.M. Blackwood
Coltishall	66 Sqn.	Spitfire	10 (6)	Coltishall	19	Squadron Leader R.H.A. Leigh
	242 Sqn.	Hurricanes	11 (4)	Coltishall	21	Squadron Leader D.R.S. Bader
Kirton-in-Lindsey	264 Sqn.	Defiants	8 (7)	Kirton-in-Lindsey	18	Squadron Leader G.D. Garvin
Digby	29 Sqn. (6)	Blenheims	10 (4)	Wellingore	23	Squadron Leader S.C. Widdows
	46 Sqn. (7)	Hurricanes	15 (2)	Digby	20	Flight Lieutenant A.D. Murray
	611 Sqn.	Spitfires	12 (6)	Digby	23	Squadron Leader J.E. McComb
Wittering	23 Sqn.	Blenheims	11 (6)	Wittering	26	Squadron Leader G.F.W. Heycock
	74 Sqn.	Spitfires	11 (5)	Wittering	20	Squadron Leader A.G. Malan
	229 Sqn.	Hurricanes	12 (4)	Bircham Newton	18	Squadron Leader H.J. Maguire
	266 Sqn.	Spitfires	8 (4)	Wittering	17	*(Temporarily unfilled)*
No. 13 Group, H.Q. Newcastle, Northumberland						
Church Fenton	64 Sqn.	Spitfires	12 (6)	Leconfield	22	Squadron Leader A.R.D. MacDonnell
	73 Sqn.	Hurricanes	11 (4)	Church Fenton	19	Squadron Leader M.W.S. Robinson
	302 (Polish) Sqn.	Hurricanes	12 (4)	Leconfield	26	Squadron Leader W.A.J. Satchell and Squadron Leader M. Mumler
Catterick	32 Sqn.	Hurricanes	8 (6)	Acklington	15	Squadron Leader M.N. Crossley
	41 Sqn.	Spitfires	14 (3)	Catterick	20	Squadron Leader H. West
	219 Sqn.	Blenheims	8 (5)	Leeming	18	Squadron Leader J.H. Little
	607 Sqn. (8)	Hurricanes	16	Usworth	22	Squadron Leader J.A. Vick.
	610 Sqn.	Spitfires	9 (2)	Acklington	18	Squadron Leader J. Ellis
Turnhouse	141 Sqn.	Defiants	9 (7)	Turnhouse	22	Squadron Leader W.A. Richardson
	605 Sqn.	Hurricanes	12 (5)	Drem	19	Squadron Leader W.M. Churchill
Dyce	145 Sqn.	Hurricanes	9 (5)	Montrose and Dyce	18	Squadron Leader J.R.A. Peel
	263 Sqn. (9)	Hurricanes	5 (3)	Grangemouth	10	Flight Lieutenant T.P. Pugh
Wick	3 Sqn. (10)	Hurricanes	15 (2)	Wick	22	Squadron Leader S.F. Godden
	504 Sqn. (11)	Hurricanes	14 (2)	Castletown	21	Squadron Leader J. Sample

Notes
(1) Squadron moved to North Weald later on this day.
(2) Squadron moved to North Weald later on this day.
(3) Squadron moved to Boscombe Down later on this day
(4) Squadron withdrawn to Digby later on this day.
(5) Squadron had moved from Biggin Hill to Croydon at 07.45 hrs. on this day.
(6) Squadron also possessed one Hurricane (*P3201*) on strength.
(7) Squadron moved to Stapleford later on this day.
(8) Squadron moved to Tangmere later on this day.
(9) One Flight only.
(10) Squadron under orders to move to Castletown, Caithness.
(11) Squadron under orders to move to Catterick *en route* for No. 11 Group.

Raid devastation at Inner Avenue, Southampton, on the afternoon of 24th September 1940, after a visit by Erprobungsgruppe 210 and II.*Gruppe*, *Zerstörergeschwader 76*. (Photo: Southern Newspapers Ltd.)

CHAPTER 8

INVASION IN SEPTEMBER ?

In many minds 1940 was characterised by a blazing summer. This was perhaps understandable, though not strictly accurate, for the finest weather occurred at just the time when such conditions would have most favoured the forces of the German invasion—and when such forces were supposedly making ready to embark for England. And as each sultry day passed, and no German army came, it must have seemed to the British—and to Fighter Command in particular—that this was indeed an unnaturally long summer.

Despite the heavy losses inflicted on the British fighters during the last few days of August, the defence's ability to put an apparently inexhaustible supply of aircraft into the air was suggesting to the Germans that the output of British factories and repair units had been seriously underestimated. There is no evidence in German records or accounts to suggest that *Luftwaffe* aircrews had detected any deterioration of British strength, courage or skill—the raids were still intercepted efficiently and, generally speaking, the attacks by Fighter Command were pressed home with determination. After two months of hard fighting, such determination was difficult to reconcile with repeated assurances by Göring that the British were almost exhausted.

Göring, however, was in part correct in his assessment, in that Fighter Command's aircraft reserves fell to their lowest level during the during the first week in September—in relation to the number of first-line squadrons now in existence—though in fact they still remained adequate to make good losses in Nos. 10, 11 and 12 Groups throughout the period. The critical problem facing Dowding at the beginning of September concerned not aircraft but the men to fly them. The two months of hard fighting had taken an appalling toll of his Command. Of the 46 squadron commanders who had led their men into battle in this period eleven had been killed or seriously wounded; of his 96 flight commanders, 27 had been killed, twelve seriously wounded and seven promoted to take command of squadrons. It was the loss of half of this core of infra-squadron leadership which was placing an intolerable strain upon the experienced survivors on the squadrons. And these experienced men—on whom Dowding and the nation now depended, and of whom there were not more than five hundred officers and sergeant pilots at any one time— were veterans at the age of twenty years or less. Nor was it uncommon for these young men to go into battle two, three or even four times a day. Added to the physical strain imposed by such combat was the psychological burden of responsibility for ensuring the survival of their squadrons.

Replacements were arriving on the squadrons at about 90 per cent of the required rate, but successive abbreviations of training courses now often resulted in young pilots having no more than twenty hours' experience on Spitfires and Hurricanes; they had acquired no proficiency in formation, night or simulated combat flying. Even the volunteer pilots who had transferred from Battle and Lysander squadrons were quite inexperienced in the swiftly changing tactics of the dogfight. It was a tragic and all too frequent occurrence for the fledgling pilot, posted to a squadron in the thick of the Battle, to be shot down on his first combat sortie—before any instructional time could be devoted to demonstrating the rudiments of air fighting. Often the squadron or flight commander would order a new pilot to fly as his own No. 2—imploring him to stick close and keep his eyes open. If he survived he would have at least learned the first essentials of combat.

No. 85 (Fighter) Squadron was one of those units which had suffered punishing losses during the latter half of August; on 1st September it was to lose two pilots killed and two badly wounded, with four aircraft shot down and another damaged. Not surprisingly it was one of the first Class C squadrons ordered north by Dowding under his scheme to rest his exhausted pilots at the beginning of September. This photograph was taken later in the month, showing Sqn. Ldr. Peter Townsend with some of his N.C.O. pilots; he had been wounded in the left foot—hence the walking stick.

Sunday 1st September

Some measure of Dowding's dilemma may be deduced from the redeployment of squadrons which took place on 1st September. No. 151 Squadron, which was down to ten aircraft and twelve pilots, and was without a squadron commander, was transferred to Digby to re-form. No. 46 Squadron, now fully re-constituted after its destruction at the end of the Norwegian campaign, was moved from Digby to Stapleford, and was in action within 24 hours.

No 56 Squadron, also without a C.O. and down to seven aircraft, was moved from North Weald to the relative quiet of Boscombe Down, changing places with No. 249 Squadron. No. 43 Squadron, which had lost two commanding officers, four flight commanders and fourteen pilots, now acquired a colourful and legendary figure in Sqn. Ldr. Caesar Hull[1].

The cumulative damage suffered by Biggin Hill prompted the transfer of No. 72 Squadron from that airfield to Croydon, while No. 79 Squadron remained behind to provide local airfield defence. No. 504 Squadron, which had been stationed

[1] This indefatigable 27-year-old South African, of whom it had been said that every night in the Mess was a Guest Night, had been one of only seven surviving pilots—albeit wounded—of the Norwegian campaign, flying Gladiators. He had since been engaged in working up No. 263 Squadron on the recalcitrant Whirlwind fighter, and in answer to constant pleas for a combat posting was, on 1st September, given command of No. 43 Squadron. One week later he was killed.

at several bases in the North, was now ordered to make ready to move into No. 11 Group; its assembly at Catterick commenced on 1st September, but the move south occupied five days.

Several other squadrons re-grouped on 1st September, and the temptation to move more must have been strong, but Park realised that without descending to suicide tactics he must retain a hard core of experienced units. It transpired that there was little to choose between the casualties suffered by exhausted but experienced squadrons and those newly-arrived in the south: the one had "too much" experience, the other not enough. The next seven days would bring about the effective destruction of no fewer than six squadrons.

It was at 10.20 hours on the 1st that Kent radar stations reported the first signs of enemy raids assembling over France. These eventually advanced along a five-mile front over Dover at 10.55 hours, and split into two groups each of about thirty bombers and a similar number of fighters. A quarter of an hour later, as these two groups again divided, No. 11 Group squadrons struck, but scarcely anywhere were they able to break through the escorting Bf 109s and 110s. The targets of this phase emerged as the airfields at Biggin Hill, Detling and Eastchurch, and the London Docks. At the long-suffering Biggin Hill aerodrome, No. 79 Squadron had not been brought on state and did not take-off; No. 610 Squadron, whose main body had already left to re-form in the North, was still engaged in packing up stores. One of the pilots, waiting in a slit trench while his Hurricane was made ready for the flight north, watched helplessly as his aircraft received a direct hit and was blown to smithereens.

No. 85 Squadron, which had been in action seven times in four days, had lost nine aircraft and whose squadron commander was in hospital wounded, was to fight twice on 1st September and suffer heavy losses. For this squadron the battle had reached its climax:

"At 11.05 hours twelve Hurricanes took off from Croydon and were vectored to Hawkinge to meet Raid 23. Nine Bf 109s were sighted at 11.30 hours at 17,000 feet attacking the Dover balloon barrage. All the aircraft had white circles round their black crosses. Allard led the squadron into the attack from the sun and shot one Bf 109 down into the sea ten miles off Cap Gris Nez. Goodman (with only port guns firing) attacked and claimed another destroyed."[2]

The pattern of attack was repeated in Kesselring's next phase which commenced soon after 13.00 hours, about 170 German aircraft crossing the Kent coast at about 13.40 hours. Again No. 85 Squadron took off:

"Squadron again airborne at 13.50 hours to intercept enemy formation approaching Tunbridge Wells/Kenley area. At about 13.55 hours about 150-200 aircraft (Do 17, Bf 109

and Bf 110) were sighted near Biggin Hill at 15,0000 feet. When sighted the Squadron was still about 5,000 feet lower, and while climbing were attacked continuously by the 109s and 110s. Allard attacked a straggling Do 17 whose rear gunner baled out and whose pilot attempted a force landing near the railway line at Lydd. Allard's oil pressure dropped so he switched off and landed at Lympne, but while the aircraft was being serviced the airfield was bombed and his aircraft was hit (one groundcrewman killed and another seriously wounded). Plt. Off. English carried out two quarter attacks on a Do 17, stopping its starboard engine; the enemy aircraft landed between Ham Street and Hythe and two crew were seen to emerge. Evans attacked and destroyed a Bf 109 with a seven-second burst, and a Bf 109 with a five-second burst but was unable to identify location of crashes. Howes attacked and shot down a Do 17 just south of Tunbridge Wells, two crew members baling out; he also damaged a Bf 109. Gowers was hit by a cannon shell and baled out with severe burns on hands, and wounds in hands and face; his Hurricane crashed at Oxted. Booth's aircraft was hit by cannon shells; he baled out near Purley, and his aircraft crashed at Sanderstead. His parachute did not open properly and he suffered a broken back, leg and arm. Patrick Woods-Scawen was posted Missing and his body was found near Kenley on 6th September—his parachute unopened. Sgt. Ellis was also killed in this fight. Six Hurricanes—all that remained of the Squadron—landed at Croydon between 14.30 and 15.00 hours, and Lewis had to land wheels-up."

No. 253 Squadron, veterans after only two days in the South, and also without a squadron commander—Sqn. Ldr. Starr killed and Sqn. Ldr. Gleave badly wounded on the last day of August—attacked the same large formation, going for stragglers all over Kent and Sussex.

In Kesselring's last phase of attacks, launched at around 17.30 hours, most of the seven distinct formations were composed of fighters which swept in over the Kent coast; finding that Park's squadrons would not react, they set about strafing attacks in an effort to needle the defences. It was a small group of Dorniers, which penetrated under cover of these fighter sweeps, which reached and bombed Biggin Hill for the third time on this day. It was a disastrous attack for, apart from the customary cratering of the runways, the vital operations room received a direct hit. Two W.A.A.F. telephone operators, Sergeant Helen Turner and Corporal Elspeth Henderson, who remained at their switchboard throughout the raid, survived all manner of debris when a 250-kilo bomb struck and brought down the heavy concrete ceiling; their devotion to duty earned them the award of the Military Medal.

The attack on Biggin Hill, as well as destroying the the sector operations room, also broke all communications lines. Post Office engineers had been at work restoring cables after the raids of 30th and 31st August, persevering in constant danger from further bombs and in craters filled with water and escaping gas. Throughout 1st September these engineers had worked on, and succeeded in restoring the main London-Westerham cables. Then shortly after six in the evening they were called on to patch lines to a makeshift operations room in a local village shop; within an hour they had rigged up some measure of communication and by working through the night had provided the temporary centre with adequate switch-

---

[2] Three points of interest emerge from the above account (from the Squadron's Form 540). Geoffrey Allard, only this day promoted to Flight Lieutenant, henceforth frequently led the Squadron. The reference to the white circles is interesting and reflects the Luftwaffe's hope that it would lead to confusion in aircraft identification (it was a practice not widely adopted by the Germans during the Battle of Britain). Lastly, when Goodman's Hurricane was subsequently examined, it was found that matchsticks had been forced into the airlines of his guns. . .

board facilities. And not only did they again repair the main cable—which was cut once more during the night—but also re-connected a number of local observer posts which had lost their telephone lines. These men, as much as any wearing uniform, contributed to the survival of Dowding's fighter forces.

R.A.F. FIGHTER COMMAND LOSSES—SUNDAY 1st SEPTEMBER 1940

1.	1 Sqn., Northolt	NC	Aircraft crashed (believed accidentally); pilot unhurt.	Not known	Sgt. G.F. Berry	Hurricane	P3276	Cat. 3 Destroyed
2.	1 (Canadian) Sqn.,Northolt	C	Shot down by Bf 110 over Biggin Hill; pilot baled out near Maidstonewith burns to hands and face.	14.30 hrs.	Fg.Off. B.V. Kerwin	Hurricane	P3963	Cat. 3 Destroyed
3.	1 (Canadian) Sqn.,Northolt	C	Shot down by Bf 109 near West Malling; pilot baled out unhurt.	14.40 hrs.	Fg.Off. A. Yuile	Hurricane	R4171	Cat. 3 Destroyed
4.	1 (Canadian) Sqn.,Northolt	C	Damaged by Bf 109 near Biggin Hill and crashed on landing at Northolt; pilot unhurt.	14.35 hrs.	Fg. Off. E.W.B. Beardmore	Hurricane	P3068	Cat. 2 Damaged
5.	72 Sqn., Croydon	C	Shot down by Bf 109 over Kent; pilot killed.	11.30 hrs.	Fg. Off. O.St.J. Pigg	Spitfire	P9458	Cat. 3 Destroyed
6.	72 Sqn., Croydon	C	Shot down by Bf 109 and force landed; pilot wounded by shell splinters.	11.25 hrs.	Fg. Off. R.A. Thompson	Spitfire	P9448	Cat. 2 Damaged
7.	72 Sqn., Croydon	C	Shot down by Bf 110 and force landed at West Malling; pilot wounded in leg and arm.	13.40 hrs.	Sgt. M.H. Pocock	Spitfire	L1056	Cat. 2 Damaged
8.	79 Sqn., Biggin Hill	C	Crashed on landing after combat with Bf 109s; pilot unhurt.	A14.30 hrs.	Flt. Lt. G.D.L. Haysom	Hurricane	—	Cat. 3 Destroyed
9.	79 Sqn., Biggin Hill	C	Shot down by Bf 109s and Do 17s near Biggin Hill; pilot baled out wounded in leg.	A14.30 hrs.	Plt. Off. L.T. Bryant-Fenn	Hurricane	W6670	Cat. 3 Destroyed
10.	79 Sqn., Biggin Hill	C	Shot down by Bf 109s near Biggin Hill; pilot baled out wounded and burned.	A14.30 hrs.	Plt. Off. B.R. Noble.	Hurricane	L2062	Cat. 3 Destroyed
11.	85 Sqn., Croydon	C	Pilot landed at Lympne with engine trouble after combat; aircraft bombed and destroyed at Lympne but pilot unhurt.	A14.40 hrs.	Sgt. G. Allard	Hurricane	—	Cat. 3 Destroyed
12.	85 Sqn., Croydon	C	Shot down by Bf 109 near Oxted; pilot baled out badly burned.	A14.45 hrs.	Fg. Off. A.V. Gowers	Hurricane	V7343	Cat. 3 Destroyed
13.	85 Sqn., Croydon	C	Shot down by Bf 109 near Purley; pilot baled out but parachute failed to open fully and he suffered broken back, leg and arm.	14.48 hrs	Sgt. G.B. Booth	Hurricane	P3150	Cat. 3 Destroyed
14.	85 Sqn., Croydon	C	Shot down by Bf 109 near Kenley; pilot baled out but was killed when parachute failed to open.	A14.45 hrs.	Fg. Off. P.P. Woods-Scawen	Hurricane	P2673	Cat. 3 Destroyed
15.	85 Sqn., Croydon	C	Shot down by enemy fighters near Kenley; pilot killed.	A14.50 hrs.	Sgt. J.H.M. Ellis	Hurricane	L2071	Cat. 3 Destroyed
16.	85 Sqn., Croydon	C	Damaged by Bf 109s over Biggin Hill and landed wheels-up at base; pilot unhurt.	A15.00 hrs.	Plt. Off. A.G. Lewis	Hurricane	—	Cat. 2 Damaged
17.	222 Sqn., Hornchurch	C	Damaged on landing at Manston.	A14.00 hrs.	Fg. Off. B. Van Mantz	Spitfire	P9360	Cat. 2 Damaged
18.	253 Sqn., Kenley	C	Shot down by Bf 109s and Do 17s north of Dungeness; pilot killed.	14.25 hrs.	Plt. Off. J.K.G. Clifton	Hurricane	P5185	Cat. 3 Destroyed
19.	603 Sqn., Hornchurch	C	Shot down by Bf 109s over Woolwich; pilot killed.	18.08 hrs.	Fg. Off. R.McG. Waterson	Spitfire	X4273	Cat. 3 Destroyed
20.	603 Sqn., Hornchurch	C	Shot down by Bf 109s over Ilford; pilot baled out wounded.	18.17 hrs.	Plt. Off. G.K. Gilroy	Spitfire	X4271	Cat. 3 Destroyed
21.	616 Sqn., Kenley	C	Damaged in combat with Do 17 over Kenley; pilot landed unhurt.	14.10 hrs.	Plt. Off. L.H. Casson	Spitfire	—	Cat. 1 Damaged

LUFTWAFFE LOSSES—SUNDAY 1st SEPTEMBER 1940

1.	1.(F)/22	CM	Crashed on landing at Ostend; not combat.	Messerschmitt Bf 110 (2206 : 4N+CH)	40 %	Crew unhurt.
2.	6./KG 1	CM	Damaged by British fighters over Ashford; R.A.F. squadron not identified.	Heinkel He 111H-2 (2433 : V4+GW)	60 %	Two crew members killed.
3.	III./KG 27	CM	Crash landed near Cherbourg with fuel shortage.	Heinkel He 111P (2628 : 1G+GS)	60 %	Crew unhurt.
4.	III./KG 27	CM	Crashed while taking-off at Rennes on operational sortie.	Heinkel He 111H-2 (1577 : 1G+GT)	100 %	Oblt. Stössel + three killed.
5.	1./KGr. 100	CM	Crash landed at St. Briyonné with fuel shortage.	Heinkel He 111H-3 (5687 : 6N+OH)	30 %	Crew unhurt.
6.	2./KGr. 100	CM	Crash landed at Vannes airfield; probably the result of battle damage.	Heinkel He 111H-1 (5100 : 6N+MK)	60 %	Crew unhurt.
7.	III./LG 1	CM	Crash landed on Chateaudun airfield, and aircraft burned.	Junkers Ju 88A-1 (7009 : L1+FR)	100 %	Oblt. Hirsch + one killed; two injured.
8.	14./LG 1	CM	Damaged by three Hurricanes of 501 Sqn. near Tunbridge Wells at A.14.45 hrs.	Messerschmitt Bf 110 (3544 : L1+DK)	50 %	Crew unhurt.
9.	14./LG 1	CM	Shot down by numerous aircraft at Tarpot Farm, Ham Street, south of Ashford, at A.14.00 hrs.	Messerschmitt Bf 110 (L1+OH)	100 %	Ofw. Rudolf Kobert and Fw. Werner Meinig made P.O.W.s.
10.	III./ZG 76	CM	Damaged by British fighters; R.A.F. squadron not identified.	Messerschmitt Bf 110 C-4 (3071 : 2N+EM)	50 %	Crew unhurt.
11.	I./ZG 2	NCM	Suffered air collision at Conchez with Item 12.	Focke-Wulf Fw 58 (0089 : DB+CR)	100 %	Oblt. Blume + two killed.
12.	I./ZG 2	NCM	Suffered air collision at Conchez with Item 11.	Messerschmitt Bf 109 E-4 (1968)	100 %	Pilot killed.
13.	II./JG 53	NCM	Suffered take-off accident at Dinan airfield.	Messerschmitt Bf 109 E-1 (6020)	60 %	Pilot unhurt.
14.	III./JG 53	NCM	Force landed near Boulogne after engine failure.	Messerschmitt Bf 109 E-4 (3237)	100 %	Pilot unhurt.
15.	III./JG 53	CM	Shot down by 85 Sqn. Hurricane of Goodman off North Foreland at 11.30 hrs.	Messerschmitt Bf 109 E-4 (4020)	100 %	Oblt. Bauer killed.
16.	III./JG 53	CM	Shot down by 85 Sqn. Hurricane of Allard 10 miles off Cap Gris Nez at A.11.30 hrs.	Messerschmitt Bf 109 E-4 (5087)	100 %	Ltn. Strasser missing.
17.	III./JG 53	CM	Crashed at Benylong (?) with engine failure after combat with 222 Sqn. Spitfires.	Messerschmitt Bf 109 E-4 (5155)	50 %	Pilot unhurt.
18.	3./NJG 1	CM	Crashed at Lippborg due to fuel shortage.	Messerschmitt Bf 110 (3510 : G9+BL)	100 %	Ltn. Schmitz injured.

Monday 2nd September

The night of the 1st/2nd had brought a comparative lull in raids by concentrated streams of German bombers, although six *Kampfgruppen* sent more than 120 aircraft against scattered towns and targets from Glasgow to Exeter. It was noticeable from the pattern of bombing that the Germans were experimenting with the use of mixed indendiary and high explosive bombs, although some towns were repeatedly raided with one type of bomb to the exclusion of the other. In Liverpool there had been no attempt to phase attacks with different types of bombs; the result had been that the fire services had managed to deal with most outbreaks of fire fairly quickly. At Sheffield and Birmingham, however, there had been signs that raids were carried out in three phases, the first being a marking attack using 250-kilo incendiary bombs; this was followed by an incendiary attack, intended to involve a large proportion of the fire fighting forces and produce a skyglow for the benefit of the last raiders who would drop high explosive bombs; the latter would smash water mains and probably destroy many of the fire appliances tackling the incendiaries. (It has frequently been suggested that R.A.F. Bomber Command later pioneered this "planned method of attack" two years later; certainly in the R.A.F.'s raids being carried out in 1940-41 there was little attention paid to phasing of incendiary and high explosive bomb loads; nor did Bomber Command's Pathfinder Force come into existence until the late summer of 1942. These bombing tactics, together with radio aids to bombing and the use of a bomber stream, were all pioneered by the Germans in 1940.)

The slowly emerging pattern of night attacks was being examined with considerable interest, and nowhere more avidly than at Fighter Command. It is more than likely that both Dowding and Park considered heavy attacks on London itself to be imminent, and by the evening of 1st September Park had re-grouped his two night fighter Squadrons, Nos. 25 and 600, closer to the capital with the movement of the former from Martlesham to North Weald; the latter had by now extricated its surviving equipment from Manston and settled into Hornchurch.

It was on 2nd September that the Beaufighter night fighter was given limited clearance for delivery to Fighter Command, and six such aircraft were delivered to squadrons, though not yet fitted with their full armament and only carrying certain control components of their radar equipment. The Fighter Interception Unit, now at Shoreham, which had been battling with unserviceability with its first Beaufighter since mid-August, now took delivery of its second aircraft.

Determined to maintain heavy pressure against Park's airfields, Kesselring launched the first of his now-customary daily four-phase attacks early on the morning of 2nd September, assembling one *Gruppe* of KG 3's Dorniers and one *Geschwader* of Bf 109s at around 07.00 hours behind Calais. As this raid, labelled Raid 49 on R.A.F. operations room tables, approached Deal, Park scrambled sixty fighters, but of these only about twenty made contact owing to controllers

maintaining standing patrols over the sector airfields. No. 253 Squadron was, however, ordered forward but could not penetrate the enemy fighter screen. The Dorniers split in the Maidstone area and attacked Biggin Hill, Rochford, Eastchurch and North Weald, while a few bombs landed on the edge of Gravesend, slightly wounding two soldiers. While nine Spitfires were busy engaging Dorniers and Bf 110s at 13,000 feet over Maidstone, nine more bombers swept in far below to carry out a sharp raid on Biggin Hill at low level.

No. 603 Squadron was scrambled at Hornchurch but when it was realised that the airfield was in no immediate danger the Spitfires were ordered forward and caught the Bf 109s as they withdrew over Kent. One of the pilots who claimed the destruction of a Messerschmitt was Plt. Off. Richard Hillary[3].

At about noon a larger concentration of enemy aircraft was plotted approaching Dover; this time Park's controllers sent their squadrons forward at the outset and were correspondingly more successful—if not necessarily in the number of German aircraft destroyed, at least in the breaking up of the raiding formations. However, sensing that this raid might overwhelm his fighters, the senior Biggin Hill Controller, Sqn. Ldr. John Worrall, asked for reinforcements and four squadrons were vectored in from neighbouring Sectors. Altogether more than seventy Hurricanes and Spitfires intercepted the 250 German fighters and bombers over Kent. One of the Squadrons was No. 43 from Tangmere, which claimed two Bf 109s destroyed near Ashford[4].

---

[3] Author of *The Last Enemy*—see Bibliography. This book faithfully projects the singularly introspective nature of the 21-year-old ex-undergraduate Australian pilot; as such, Hillary was perhaps more sensitive than the vast majority of British pilots and when, the following day, he suffered ghastly burns in action his subsequent fight for recovery was the result of a ponderously reasoned philosophy of life rather than a determination to re-enter the war against Nazism. That he *did* return to flying must be evidence of great courage—an attribute not easily identified in his self-effacing book.

Another No. 603 Squadron pilot had had a harrowing escape on the previous day. Plt. Off. George ("Sheep") Gilroy had been shot down and baled out of his blazing Spitfire near Ilford, Essex. On reaching the ground the young wounded pilot was given thoroughly harsh treatment when the Home Guard—who apparently jumped to the conclusion that this was an enemy parachutist—threatened to lynch him. By good fortune he was rescued and was admitted to hospital where he made a complete recovery.

[4] One of the enemy fell to the guns of Flt. Lt. Dick Reynell, Hurricane test pilot from Hawker Aircraft Ltd., and a pre-War member of the R.A.F. Reserve of Officers, who had voluntarily joined the Squadron during his leave to gain first hand experience of the Hurricane in combat; he was to be shot down and killed in the fight which also cost the life of Caesar Hull on 7th September.

The fight over Ashford in the morning of 2nd September involved the death of Plt. Off. Tony Woods-Scawen, the younger brother of Patrick who, with No. 85 Squadron, had been killed the previous day, but the whereabouts of whose body was not to be discovered until 6th September—the day on which Tony's award of the D.F.C. was announced.

Spitfires of No. 92 (Fighter) Squadron at Pembrey in South Wales. This squadron, with some of the best-known pilots of the Battle (such as Stanford Tuck, "Wimpey" Wade and Brian Kingcome), had been kept out of the thick of the Battle until September, although its members had adopted a policy of "looking for trouble" and scored a number of successes while roaming the skies of the West Country. Early in September the squadron was moved to Biggin Hill where the pilots more than made up for their period of relative inactivity—but in doing so suffered very heavy losses.

Both the two following attack phases were aimed at Park's airfields, and both saturated the available fighter forces. Kesselring still possessed sufficient reserves to throw more than 250 aircraft against Kent, crossing the coast near Dover shortly after 17.00 hours; and one of the biggest dogfights of the day developed—again near Ashford—when elements of ten squadrons (about 70 Hurricanes and fifteen Spitfires) ran into about 160 Bf 109s. Waiting directly in the path of the enemy were twelve Hurricane pilots of No. 303 (Polish) Squadron, who managed to attack a flank *Staffel* of 109s head-on. The Messerschmitt pilots turned back towards Dover and climbed, knowing the Hurricanes would lose distance. In following, they were led directly into a trap set by another *Staffel* which dived out of the evening sun and shot down Fg. Off. Miroslaw Feric. This fight was broken off (as if by mutual consent) when the Dover barrage commenced firing into the melée.

The same story could be told by numerous squadrons which attacked the bombers or close escort, only to be surprised by a high-flying top cover diving out of the sun. Used in such widespread fashion, these tactics represented a new departure by the *Luftwaffe*, in that sanction was now apparently forthcoming to permit a high proportion of the escort to fly considerably further from the bomber formations. There was in fact a mistaken belief in Fighter Command that they represented a return to widespread free chasing, and for some days this prompted sector controllers to withhold a proportion of their forces accordingly. Although such tactical deployment was contrary to Park's instructions it was—quite fortuitously—to result in some profitable encounters, as will be seen during the next few days.

The afternoon raids of 2nd September were successful in reaching seven airfields including Biggin Hill, Kenley and

Hornchurch. The Brooklands airfield—at which were situated the Hawker and Vickers factories—received the first of several attacks[5].

The airfield at Detling was attacked by a *Gruppe* of Do 17s which dropped about one hundred H.E. bombs without causing much damage. At Eashchurch, however, a smaller raid hit the bomb dump in which 350 bombs exploded, virtually demolishing every building within 400 yards as well as five aircraft. Drainage mains and power cables were cut, as were almost all telephone and teleprinter lines.

The Brooklands raid confirmed in Dowding's mind that it would not be long before all-out attacks would be launched against the aircraft factories, for it was logical to believe that, as his combat losses mounted, the enemy would strike at the sources of Fighter Command's replenishment. Park shared this premonition, and for several days past a standing patrol had been maintained by fighters from Tangmere (and, less frequently, from Boscombe Down) over a line drawn from Weybridge (Brooklands) through Guildford to the South Coast. Several squadrons had been on duty over Guildford on 2nd September, but in each case they had been drawn off over Kent—so the Brooklands raid got through.

---

[5] It has often been stated that in raiding Brooklands the *Luftwaffe* was aiming to attack the Vickers works—in which Wellington bombers were assembled. These they hit and caused fairly heavy damage and casualties. However, post-War examination of German briefing documents discloses that, without exception during the Battle of Britain, the primary target was the Hawker assembly sheds on the other side of the famous airfield motor race track. Production of the vital fighters gave the factory high priority for a balloon barrage, and these fifteen balloons effectively saved the Hawker plant.

R.A.F. FIGHTER COMMAND LOSSES—MONDAY 2nd SEPTEMBER 1940

#	Squadron/Base		Details	Time	Pilot	Aircraft	Serial	Category
1.	43 Sqn., Tangmere	C	Shot down by Bf 109s over Ashford; pilot killed. Buried at Hawkinge.	13.12 hrs.	Plt. Off. C.A. Woods-Scawen	Hurricane	P3903	Cat. 3 Destroyed
2.	43 Sqn., Tangmere	C	Shot down by Bf 109s over Ashford; pilot baled out severely burned and wounded by shell fragments in thigh and chest.	13.15 hrs.	Fg. Off. M.K. Carswell	Hurricane	—	Cat. 3 Destroyed
3.	43 Sqn., Tangmere	C	Shot down by Bf 109s over Kent; pilot baled out unhurt.	A13.20 hrs.	Not known	Hurricane	P3786	Cat. 3 Destroyed
4.	46 Sqn., Stapleford	C	Shot down by Bf 109 near Eastchurch; pilot crash landed at Detling but died afterwards. Buried at Maidstone.	17.30 hrs.	Plt. Off. J.C.L.D. Bailey	Hurricane	P3067	Cat. 2 Damaged
5.	46 Sqn., Stapleford	C	Shot down and force landed near Sittingbourne; pilot unhurt.	17.35 hrs.	Flt. Lt. A.C. Rabagliati	Hurricane	P3957	Cat. 2 Damaged
6.	65 Sqn., Hornchurch	C	Crashed on scramble; pilot unhurt.	Not known	Not known	Spitfire	N3128	Cat. 3 Destroyed
7.	72 Sqn., Biggin Hill	C	Shot down by Bf 110 near Herne Bay; pilot baled out, believed unhurt.	12.25 hrs.	Not known	Spitfire	K9938	Cat. 3 Destroyed
8.	72 Sqn., Biggin Hill	C	Shot down by Bf 110s near Herne Bay; pilot baled out, believed unhurt.	12.30 hrs.	Not known	Spitfire	X4262	Cat. 3 Destroyed
9.	72 Sqn., Biggin Hill	C	Shot down by Bf 110s near Herne Bay; pilot baled out, believed unhurt.	12.30 hrs.	Not known	Spitfire	—	Cat. 3 Destroyed
10.	72 Sqn., Biggin Hill	C	Shot down by Bf 110s near Herne Bay; pilot baled out, believed unhurt.	12.30 hrs.	Not known	Spitfire	—	Cat. 3 Destroyed
11.	72 Sqn., Biggin Hill	C	Damaged in combat near Chatham; pilot slightly wounded.	A17.30 hrs.	Sqn. Ldr. A.R. Collins	Spitfire	—	Cat. 2 Damaged
12.	111 Sqn., Debden	C	Force landed at Detling after combat with He 111s over the Thames Estuary, but aircraft bombed on the ground; pilot unhurt.	12.55 hrs.	Flt. Lt. H.S. Giddings	Hurricane	—	Cat. 3 Destroyed
13.	111 Sqn., Debden	C	Shot down by Bf 110s over the Thames Estuary. Pilot assumed killed.	A13.00 hrs.	Sgt. W.L. Dymond	Hurricane	P3875	Cat. 3 Lost
14.	222 Sqn., Hornchurch	C	Force landed after combat with Bf 110; pilot slightly wounded in the leg.	A13.00 hrs.	Flt. Lt. A.I. Robinson	Spitfire	—	Cat. 3 Destroyed
15.	222 Sqn., Hornchurch	C	Damaged in combat near Hornchurch; pilot unhurt.	A13.15 hrs.	Not known	Spitfire	—	Cat. 2 Damaged
16.	222 Sqn., Hornchurch	C	Damaged in combat near Hornchurch; pilot unhurt.	A13.15 hrs.	Not known	Spitfire	—	Cat. 2 Damaged
17.	249 Sqn., North Weald	C	Shot down by Bf 109 and crash landed near Chartham, Kent; pilot wounded by bullet in the neck.	07.40 hrs.	Plt. Off. R.E.N. Wynn	Hurricane	V7352	Cat. 3 Destroyed
18.	249 Sqn., North Weald	C	Shot down by Bf 109 near Gravesend; pilot baled out unhurt.	07.45 hrs.	Plt. Off. H.J.S. Beazley	Hurricane	P2988	Cat. 3 Destroyed
19.	249 Sqn., North Weald	C	Shot down and force landed on Gravesend airfield; pilot unhurt.	07.48 hrs.	Plt. Off. P.R-F. Burton	Hurricane	—	Cat. 3 Destroyed
20.	253 Sqn., Kenley	C	Shot down by Bf 109s ten miles north of Dover; pilot slightly wounded.	07.50 hrs.	Sgt. J. Metham	Hurricane	P2946	Cat. 3 Destroyed
21.	253 Sqn., Kenley	NC	Crashed, not due to enemy action; pilot unhurt.	Afternoon	Not known	Hurricane	V6640	Cat. 3 Destroyed
22.	253 Sqn., Kenley	NC	Crashed, not due to enemy action; pilot unhurt.	Afternoon	Not known	Hurricane	P3610	Cat. 3 Destroyed
23.	303 Sqn., Northolt	C	Shot down by Bf 109s and force landed north of Dover; pilot unhurt.	18.10 hrs.	Plt. Off. M. Feric	Hurricane	—	Cat. 3 Destroyed
24.	501 Sqn., Gravesend	C	Shot down by Bf 109s near Gravesend; pilot wounded.	A17.50 hrs.	Sgt. W.B. Henn	Hurricane	P3803	Cat. 3 Destroyed
25.	501 Sqn., Gravesend	C	Shot down and force landed near Gravesend; pilot wounded.	A17.55 hrs.	Plt. Off. S. Skalski	Hurricane	—	Cat. 3 Destroyed
26.	501 Sqn., Gravesend	C	Shot down near Dungeness and pilot killed; this was his first day on the squadron.	A17.00 hrs.	Plt. Off. A.T. Rose-Price	Hurricane	L1758	Cat. 3 Destroyed
27.	501 Sqn., Gravesend	C	Shot down by Bf 109s south of Ashford, Kent; pilot force landed and was unhurt.	A17.00 hrs.	Sgt. H.C. Adams	Hurricane	V7234	Cat. 2 Damaged
28.	603 Sqn., Hornchurch	C	Landed wheels-up at base after combat with Do 17s and Bf 109s; pilot unhurt.	A12.30 hrs.	Plt. Off. J.G.E. Haig	Spitfire	R6752	Cat. 2 Damaged
29.	603 Sqn., Hornchurch	C	Shot down in flames by Bf 109s near Maidstone; pilot baled out severely burned.	16.25 hrs.	Sgt. J. Stokoe	Spitfire	N3056	Cat. 3 Destroyed
30.	616 Sqn., Kenley	C	Shot down by Bf 110s near Tonbridge, Kent; pilot baled out unhurt.	16.30 hrs.	Flt. Lt. D.E. Gillam	Spitfire	X4181	Cat. 3 Destroyed

LUFTWAFFE LOSSES—MONDAY 2nd SEPTEMBER 1940

#	Unit		Details	Aircraft	%	Crew
1.	2.(H)/32	NCM	Suffered accident on Konstanz airfield.	Henschel Hs 126 (3033)	20 %	Crew unhurt.
2.	2.(F)/122	CM	Missing from sortie over Britain; fate not known.	Junkers Ju 88A-1 (0276 : F6+DK)	100 %	Oblt. Schmid, Fw. Jahnke, Ogefr. Rochstroh and Gefr. Kronberg missing.
3.	9./KG 3	CM	Damaged by 72 Sqn. Spitfires over Maidstone at 08.15 hrs.; crashed on landing at St. Trond.	Dornier Do 17Z-2 (1187 : 5K+MT)	100 %	Two crew members killed and three wounded.
4.	9./KG 3	CM	Shot down by 249 Sqn. Hurricanes near Chatham at A.08.00 hrs.	Dornier Do 17Z-2 (3269 : 5K+HT)	100 %	Uffz. Hilbrecht killed; Fw. Seidel wounded; Oblt Rohr and Fw. Spring missing.
5.	9./KG 3	CM	Damaged by 72 Sqn. Spitfires over Maidstone at 08.15 hrs.; crashed on landing at St. Omer.	Dornier Do 17Z-3 (3390 : 5K+GT)	65 %	Crew unhurt.
6.	II./KG 77	NCM	Crashed at Stuttgart-Untertürkheim following engine failure.	Junkers Ju 88B (7097 : 3Z+BN)	100 %	Four crew members killed.
7.	IV./LG 1	NCM	Suffered air collision with Item 8 at Tramecourt; aircraft landed safely.	Junkers Ju 87B-2 (5773 : L1+AV)	20 %	Crew unhurt.
8.	IV./LG 1	NCM	Suffered air collision with Item 7 at Tramecourt; crew baled out safely.	Junkers Ju 87B-2	100 %	Crew unhurt.
9.	I./LG 2	CM	Suffered landing accident at Calais-Marck; not the result of combat.	Messerschmitt Bf 109E (3579)	50 %	Pilot unhurt.
10.	I./ZG 2	CM	Shot down by 249 Sqn. Hurricanes near Gravesend at A.16.15 hrs.	Messerschmitt Bf 110 C-4 (3622 : 3M+HK)	100 %	Ltn. Schippen and Gefr. Schockenhoff missing.
11.	I./ZG 2	CM	Missing from sortie over the Thames Estuary; fate of aircraft not known.	Messerschmitt Bf 110 D-0 (3193)	100 %	Crew, unhurt, made P.O.W.s.

Luftwaffe Losses, 2nd September 1940—*continued*

No.	Unit		Cause	Aircraft	%	Crew
12.	II./ZG 2	CM	Shot down by 249 Sqn. Hurricanes near Gravesend at A.16.15 hrs.	Messerschmitt Bf 110 D-0 (3197)	100 %	Uffz. Deuker and Uffz. Knapp missing.
13.	II./ZG 2	CM	Shot down by 249 Sqn. Hurricanes near Gravesend at A.16.15 hrs.	Messerschmitt Bf 110 D-0 (3269 : A2+KR)	100 %	Fw. Beil and Ogefr. Oehl killed.
14.	2./ZG 26	CM	Shot down by four Spitfires (squadron not known) over Thames Estuary at 08.10 hrs.	Messerschmitt Bf 110 D-1 (3309 : E8+DK)	100 %	Fw. Karl Schutz killed; Fw. Herbert Stüwe made P.O.W.
15.	5./ZG 26	CM	Following combat with British fighters, crashed at Wizernes with engine failure.	Messerschmitt Bf 110 C-4 (3045 : 3U+BN)	100 %	Two crew members wounded.
16.	5./ZG 26	CM	Shot down by Hurricanes and crashed near the Nore Lightship at A.09.00 hrs.	Messerschmitt Bf 110 C-4 (3536 : 3U+GN)	100 %	Ofw. Kurt Rochel and Uffz. Willi Schözler made P.O.W.s.
17.	7./ZG 26	CM	Damaged by 111 Sqn. Hurricane of Hampshire over Thames Estuary at A.13.00 hrs; crashed at Arques on return.	Messerschmitt Bf 110 C-4 (2191 : 3U+BR)	45 %	One crew member wounded.
18.	II./ZG 76	CM	Shot down by unknown British fighters near London.	Messerschmitt Bf 110C (3226 : M8+DM)	100 %	Oblt. Wrede and Uffz. Lukawke killed.
19.	III./ZG 76	CM	Damaged in action with British fighters and crashed near Calais.	Messerschmitt Bf 110 C-4 (2095 : 2N+GM)	50 %	Crew unhurt.
20.	Stab I/JG 3	CM	Take-off accident at Colombert; not combat.	Messerschmitt Bf 109 E-4 (1979)	30 %	Pilot unhurt.
21.	4./JG 3	CM	Crashed on landing at Wierre; believed not a result of combat.	Messerschmitt Bf 109 E-4 (5136)	10 %	Pilot unhurt.
22.	5./JG 3	CM	Crashed at Marquise with battle damage following combat with British fighters.	Messerschmitt Bf 109 E-4 (1443)	75 %	Pilot unhurt.
23.	6./JG 3	CM	Crash landed at Sanoutte following combat with British fighters.	Messerschmitt Bf 109 E-4 (1469)	30 %	Pilot unhurt.
24.	9./JG 3	CM	Crashed at Le Portel; possibly the result of faulty servicing.	Messerschmitt Bf 109 L-2 (3609)	95 %	Pilot unhurt.
25.	1./JG 51	CM	Shot down by 603 Sqn. Spitfires of Berry and Haig over Kent at A.07.50 hrs.	Messerschmitt Bf 109E (4807)	100 %	Ltn. Ruttkowski killed.
26.	1./JG 51	CM	Shot down by 603 Sqn. Spitfires over Kent at A.07.50 hrs.	Messerschmitt Bf 109 E-1 (4850)	100 %	Ltn. Thorl missing.
27.	1./JG 51	CM	Shot down by 603 Sqn. Spitfires over Kent coast at A.07.50 hrs.	Messerschmitt Bf 109 E-4 (3714)	100 %	Pilot, unhurt, rescued by *Seenotflugkommando*.
28.	8./JG 51	CM	Shot down by Spitfires (possibly of 603 Sqn.) over the English Channel.	Messerschmitt Bf 109 E-4 (1632)	100 %	Pilot, unhurt, rescued by *Seenotflugkommando*.
29.	I./JG 52	CM	Shot down by *flak* in Eastchurch area.	Messerschmitt Bf 109 E-4 (1261)	100 %	Fw. Urlings missing.
30.	1./JG 51	CM	Shot down by 43 Sqn. Hurricane of Reynell at A.13.10 hrs. over Ashford.	Messerschmitt Bf 109E (6276)	100 %	Ltn. Riegel missing,
31.	I./JG 53	CM	Shot down by 43 Sqn. Hurricane of Jeffreys at A.13.10 hrs. near Ashford.	Messerschmitt Bf 109E (3584)	100 %	Uffz. Karl missing.
32.	I./JG 53	CM	Shot down by British fighters (reported as Hurricanes) over Kent at A.13.00 hrs.	Messerschmitt Bf 109 E-4 (1167)	100 %	Ofw. Kuhlmann missing.
33.	I./JG 53	CM	Shot down by British fighters between Dover and Calais; pilot baled out.	Messerschmitt Bf 109 E-4 (1569)	100 %	Pilot, unhurt, rescued by *Seenotflugkommando*.
34.	I./JG 53	CM	Crashed at Boulogne after combat with British fighters.	Messerschmitt Bf 109E (3494)	50 %	Pilot wounded.
35.	II./JG 54	CM	Suffered air collision with Item 36 over Calais; not involved in combat.	Messerschmitt Bf 109 E-4 (1940)	100 %	Oblt. Elsing killed.
36.	II./JG 54	CM	Suffered air collision with Item 35 over Calais; not involved in combat.	Messerschmitt Bf 109 E-1 (6225)	100 %	Pilot killed.
37.	Stab III./JG 54	CM	Shot down by 303 Sqn. Hurricane of Feric at A.18.25 hrs.	Messerschmitt Bf 109 E-4 (1574)	100 %	Oblt. Schelcher killed.
38.	Stab III./JG 54	CM	Damaged by 303 Sqn. Hurricane of Henneberg at A.18.25 hrs., and crashed at Audembert.	Messerschmitt Bf 109 E-4 (5292)	60 %	Pilot unhurt.
39.	7./JG 54	CM	Suffered landing accident at Guines-Sud, probably as a result of battle damage.	Messerschmitt Bf 109 E-4 (1335)	50 %	Pilot unhurt.
40.	8./JG 54	CM	Shot down by 46 Sqn. Hurricane of Ambrose at A.17.30 hrs., south-east of Herne Bay.	Messerschmitt Bf 109 E-1 (3470)	100 %	Uffz. Elbers missing.
41.	I./JG 77	CM	Suffered take-off accident at Marquise-West airfield.	Messerschmitt Bf 109 E-1 (3503)	50 %	Pilot unhurt.
42.	3./JG 77	CM	Damaged by 303 Sqn. Hurricane of Rogowski at A.18.30 hrs., and crashed near Wissant.	Messerschmitt Bf 109 E-1 (2695)	80 %	Pilot unhurt.
43.	II./JG 2	CM	Missing from sortie over Southern England; fate not known.	Messerschmitt Bf 109 E-1 (6115)	100 %	Uffz. Glomb missing.
44.	II./JG 2	CM	Missing from sortie over Southern England; fate not known.	Messerschmitt Bf 109 E-4 (1452)	100 %	Uffz. von Stein missing.
45.	1./KGzbV. 172	NCM	Crashed during parachute training drop at Pritzwalk.	Junkers Ju 52/3M (6925 : N3+CB)	95 %	Three crew and seven paratroopers killed.
46.	1./806	CM	Crashed while landing at Nantes; possibly the result of combat.	Junkers Ju 88A-1 (5069 : M7+HH)	25 %	Crew unhurt.
47.	1./806	CM	Crashed at Pontivy following engine fire.	Junkers Ju 88A-1 (5111 : M7+AH)	100 %	Hptm. Schwenger killed.
48.	3./906	CM	Crashed on landing at Lymuiden after minelaying sortie, probably with *flak* damage.	Heinkel He 115 (2218 : 8L+LL)	100 %	Uffz. Bock killed; Ltn.z.S. Anderson + one wounded.

Tuesday 3rd September

Scattered raids on Birmingham, Cardiff, Castle Bromwich, Liverpool and Manchester by about 50 bombers during the night had caused little damage and few casualties. Bomber Command, on the other hand, again flew all the way to Italy to attack Turin and Milan, while an incendiary raid was flown by Wellingtons against the Black Forest; although the latter attack undoubtedly caused some damage, it is difficult to understand what importance was attached to that particular target[6].

An assessment of fighter squadron strengths had again been undertaken the previous evening, and as a result Dowding

---

[6] Plans for a similar fire raid on the Black Forest, suggested a year earlier, had been turned down, with some asperity, by the Chamberlain administration on the grounds that much of the target area was private property. . . .

German pilots and groundcrew gather round a young Unteroffizier (sergeant pilot) of III./JG 51 newly returned from a sortie over Southern England. (Photo: *Gemeinschaft der Jagdflieger E.V.*)

was reluctantly forced to adopt a new classification of his Squadrons, whereby certain units in the North would be "milked" of their more experienced pilots to make good losses on the Squadrons in the South. Although this scheme was not brought into full operation until 8th September—it met with anguished opposition from squadron commanders desperately struggling to build up morale and team efficiency in their units—Park was forced to re-arrange his battle order once again. The exhausted remnants of No. 85 Squadron, down to eleven pilots and eight aircraft, were withdrawn from Croydon and moved to Castle Camps in Cambridgeshire. No. 111 Squadron, which had by no means been resting at Debden, was brought to Croydon. No. 41 Squadron, which had been re-forming at Catterick since 8th August, now returned to Hornchurch, its place being taken by No. 504 Squadron which, as already stated, was staging a slow move to the South. No. 66 Squadron brought thirteen Spitfires from Coltishall to Kenley, changing places with No. 616 Squadron, one of whose Flight Lieutenants now assumed command of the Squadron.

The main attack of this day was the first, which commenced building up behind the Pas de Calais in full view of British radar at 08.30 hours. Whether by accident or design a large proportion of the enemy force delayed its approach to Kent rather longer than usual, and this allowed three fighter squadrons to move forward to the Dover area in good time. When it became apparent that the formation was composed of enemy fighters the British squadrons were ordered to avoid combat and disengage northwards.

Meanwhile a group of 54 Dorniers, escorted by about 80 Bf 110s, was flying up the Thames Estuary at 20,000 feet. Uncertain whether this raid (now labelled Raid 45) was bent on returning to the assault on the north Kent airfields, or was turning northwards—or indeed continuing on its course for London, Park's controllers ordered all remaining fighters to the area and called for reinforcements from No. 12 Group. By 09.40 hours, sixteen squadrons—totalling 122 fighters—had

been ordered into the air to patrol specific positions in Essex and Kent.

At 09.45 hours the enemy turned northwards, just west of Southend, crossing the northern shore of the Thames and making directly for North Weald. As fighters scrambled from airfields all round, the Dorniers had time to sweep round and carry out, from 15,000 feet, a text book pattern bombing attack in open formation from the north-east. More than 200 bombs, of which a high proportion were delayed action, fell on the airfield; all the hangars were hit, and fire gutted two of them; messes and administrative buildings were damaged, and the vital operations block struck—though fortunately not destroyed. The runways were heavily cratered but, despite some casualties (four killed), the airfield remained operational.

The controllers had delayed too long before scrambling the fighters, and it was only as the raiders turned for home that the interceptors managed to attain the necessary altitude. Eight cannon-armed Spitfires of No. 19 Squadron found themselves ideally positioned to attack but were closely engaged by the Bf 110s; but when *six* of the Spitfires suffered gun stoppages, the pilots disgustedly disengaged and left the arena to wave after wave of Hurricanes of Nos. 1, 17, 46, 249, 257 and 3210 Squadrons, and eight Spitfires of No. 603 Squadron. As the bombers strove to reach the coast, the escorting Bf 110s performed magnificently; although they lost heavily, they took a surprising toll of the British fighters. The sky around Colchester was streaked with the dirty trails of stricken aircraft and mottled with parachutes. Fg. Off. David Hanson of No. 17 Squadron was seen by observers on Foulness Island to shoot down a Dornier into the River Crouch, but his aircraft caught fire and he was killed trying to bale out at 100 feet. Sub-Lt. Jack Carpenter of No. 46 Squadron shot down a Bf 110 and circled as the two crewmen crawled out of the crumpled wreckage. The Czech pilots of No. 310 Squadron had had something of a field day, but had not been controlled accurately, with the result that they had to break off the fight short of fuel. Their victims fell between North Weald and Chelmsford.

As the German formation withdrew and the harrassed controllers struggled to marshal their scattered fighters, three Blenheim pilots of No. 25 Squadron, who had scrambled from North Weald just before the end of the raid and had endeavoured to climb to the west, now returned to their airfield—and were promptly attacked out of the sun by Hurricanes of No. 46 Squadron.

"Plt. Off Douglas Hogg was killed; Plt. Off. Ernest Cassidy force landed at Hatfield, and Sqn. Ldr. Wilfred Loxton returned safely to base. Sgt. Edward Powell, who was Hogg's rear gunner, was instructed to jump by the pilot before he died. Powell crawled to the cockpit, found the

pilot dead over the controls, returned aft and jumped. The aircraft crashed about a mile from North Weald."[7]

Back at Fowlmere the raging pilots of No. 19 Squadron were greeted with the news that their cannon-armed Spitfires were to be replaced forthwith. The following day they were fascinated by the arrival of eight elderly Spitfires, which taxied up to dispersal; "and what wrecks, but at least their guns fire" was the Squadron's qualified judgement.

[7] As evidence of the confusion that could arise under combat conditions, three No. 46 Squadron pilots claimed one Ju 88 destroyed and three damaged between them. There were no Ju 88s in the area, and an examination of times and locations clearly shows that their victims were the No. 25 Squadron Blenheims.

An eight-gun Spitfire IA of No. 19 Squadron; this aircraft, *X4474,* was not among the batch delivered early in September about which the squadron spoke so deprecatingly.

R.A.F. FIGHTER COMMAND LOSSES—TUESDAY 3rd SEPTEMBER 1940

1.	1 Sqn., Northolt	C	Aircraft and pilot missing from patrol; fate not known.	A10.30 hrs.	Flt. Lt. H.B.L. Hillcoat	Hurricane	*P3044*	Cat. 3 Missing
2.	1 Sqn., Northolt	C	Aircraft and pilot missing from patrol; fate not known.	A10.30 hrs.	Plt. Off. R.H. Shaw	Hurricane	*P3782*	Cat. 3 Missing
3.	17 Sqn., Debden	C	Shot down in flames by Bf 110 near Ingrave, Essex; pilot baled out badly burned.	A10.30 hrs.	Sgt. D. Fopp	Hurricane	*P3673*	Cat. 3 Destroyed
4.	17 Sqn., Debden	C	Shot down by Bf 110 and force landed at North Weald; pilot unhurt.	A10.30 hrs	Sqn. Ldr. A.G. Miller	Hurricane	*R4224*	Cat. 3 Destroyed
5.	17 Sqn., Debden	C	Shot down (probably by Do 17) and crashed on Foulness Island; pilot baled out too low and was killed.	A10.35 hrs	Fg. Off. D.H.W. Hanson	Hurricane	*P3539*	Cat. 3 Destroyed
6.	25 Sqn., North Weald	(C)	Shot down by Hurricanes near North Weald; pilot killed; gunner baled out unhurt.	Not known	Plt.Off.D.W.Hogg Sgt. E. Powell	Blenheim	*L1409*	Cat. 3 Destroyed
7.	25 Sqn., North Weald	(C)	Shot down by Hurricanes and force landed near Hatfield; crew unhurt.	Not known	Plt.Off.E.Cassidy Gunner not known.	Blenheim	*L1512*	Cat. 3 Destroyed
8.	46 Sqn., Stapleford	C	Shot down north of Southend (probably by Bf 110); pilot killed.	A10.30 hrs.	Sgt. G.H. Edworthy	Hurricane	*P3064*	Cat. 3 Destroyed
9.	46 Sqn., Stapleford	C	Shot down near Rochford; pilot baled out unhurt. Aircraft crashed at Canewdon.	A10.30 hrs.	Plt. Off. H. Morgan-Gray	Hurricane	*P3063*	Cat. 3 Destroyed
10.	46 Sqn., Stapleford	C	Shot down near Canewdon, Essex; pilot baled with slight burns to face; aircraft crashed at South Fambridge.	A10.30 hrs.	Sgt. E. Bloor	Hurricane	*P3024*	Cat. 3 Destroyed
11.	46 Sqn., Stapleford	C	Crashed at base on landing after combat; pilot unhurt.	A10.45 hrs.	Not known	Hurricane	*P3066*	Cat. 3 Destroyed
12.	141 Sqn., Turnhouse	NC	Suffered landing accident; crew unhurt.	At night.	Not known	Defiant	—	Cat. 2 Damaged
13.	222 Sqn., Hornchurch	NC	Aircraft developed glycol leak; pilot baled out unhurt over Burnham.	A07.30 hrs.	Sgt. R.B. Johnson	Spitfire	*L1010*	Cat. 3 Lost
14.	238 Sqn., St. Eval	NC	Landing accident at St. Eval; pilot unhurt.	Not known	Sgt. F.A. Sibley	Hurricane	*R2680*	Cat. 2 Damaged

R.A.F. Losses, 3rd September 1940—*continued*

15.	249 Sqn., North Weald	C	Damaged by A.A. gun defences at Dover; pilot unhurt.	Afternoon	Sgt. P.A. Rowell	Hurricane	—	Cat. 2 Damaged
16.	253 Sqn., Kenley	NC	Crashed at Nonnington (not combat); pilot unhurt.	Not known	Plt. Off. L.C. Murch	Hurricane	P3610	Cat. 3 Destroyed
17.	257 Sqn., Martlesham	C	Shot down in flames by Bf 110 near Chelmsford; pilot baled out with burns and admitted to Billericay Hospital.	10.30 hrs.	Plt. Off. D.W. Hunt	Hurricane	—	Cat. 3 Burnt
18.	257 Sqn., Martlesham	C	Shot down by Bf 110s at Ingatestone; pilot baled out, but landed dead.	A10.35 hrs.	Plt. Off. C.R. Bonseigneur	Hurricane	P3518	Cat. 3 Lost
19.	257 Sqn., Martlesham	C	Port tailplane shot off near Chelmsford by Bf 110, but pilot landed unhurt at base.	A10.40 hrs.	Plt. Off. K.C. Gundry	Hurricane	P3704	Cat. 2 Damaged
20.	257 Sqn., Martlesham	C	Shot down in combat with Bf 110s; pilot baled out unhurt.	A10.40 hrs.	Not known	Hurricane	L1585	Cat. 3 Lost
21.	257 Sqn., Martlesham	C	Damaged in combat with Bf 110s; pilot, slightly wounded, landed safely at base.	A10.40 hrs.	Sgt. R.C. Nutter	Hurricane	P3706	Cat. 1 Damaged
22.	303 Sqn., Northolt	C	Shot down by Bf 109 and force landed at Woodchurch, near Tenterden.	10.41 hrs.	Sgt. S. Wojtowicz	Hurricane	R2688	Cat. 3 Destroyed
23.	303 Sqn., Northolt	C	Damaged by Bf 109s near Dungeness; pilot unhurt.	10.45 hrs.	Fg. Off. Z. Henneberg	Hurricane	—	Cat. 2 Damaged
24.	310 Sqn., Duxford	C	Shot down by Bf 110s over Essex; pilot baled out unhurt.	10.15 hrs.	Sgt. J. Kopriva	Hurricane	P8811	Cat. 3 Destroyed
25.	603 Sqn., Hornchurch	C	Shot down by enemy fighters over Thames Estuary off Essex coast, and admitted to Chelmsford General Hospital (1)	09.45 hrs	Plt. Off. D. Stewart-Clark	Spitfire	X4185	Cat. 3 Destroyed
26.	603 Sqn., Hornchurch	C	Shot down in flames off North Foreland; pilot baled out with grievous burns; rescued by the Margate Lifeboat. (1)	09.55 hrs.	Plt. Off. R.H. Hillary	Spitfire	X4277	Cat. 3 Destroyed

[(1) It has sometimes been suggested that Hauptmann Böde of II./JG 26 shot down both Stewart-Clark and Hillary; however, even allowing for a time difference of one hour between British and German times, Böde's reported combat does not correspond in time, altitude or location; his victim or victims—reported shot down at 11.30 hrs (German time)—may have been one or more No. 46 Squadron Hurricanes further west which were lost at about that time.]

LUFTWAFFE LOSSES—TUESDAY 3rd SEPTEMBER 1940

1.	5./KG 2	CM	Shot down by 17 Sqn. Hurricane of Hanson into River Crouch at 10.55 hrs.; Hanson was shot down .	Dornier Do 17Z-2 (3450 : U5+AN)	100 %	Ltn. Schildt, Uffz. Swientsch and Gefr. Nigisch killed; Fw. Kriegel missing.
2.	5./KG 26	NCM	Suffered taxying accident at Gilje-Rijen.	Heinkel He 111H-3 (6825 : 1H+KN)	20 %	Crew unhurt.
3.	5./KG 26	NCM	Crashed after air collision with Item 4 at Venlo.	Heinkel He 111H-3 (3252)	100 %	Oblt. Wandered + two killed.
4.	5./KG 26	NCM	Crashed after air collision with Item 3 at Venlo.	Heinkel He 111H-3 (3164)	100 %	Ltn. Zobernig + two killed.
5.	8./KG 77	NCM	Crashed at Mons-Soignes following engine fire.	Junkers Ju 88A-1 (4016 : 4D+DS)	70 %	One crew member injured.
6.	8./KG 77	NCM	Crashed at Laon airfield; cause not notified.	Junkers Ju 88A-1 (5108 : 3Z+KS)	55 %	Crew unhurt.
7.	1./KGr. 100	CM	Damaged by 87 Sqn. Hurricane of Beamont on "cat's eye" night patrol near Wells.	Heinkel He 111H-3 (6873 : 6N+BH)	45 %	Crew unhurt.
8.	3./KGr. 100	CM	Suffered landing collision at Vannes with Item 9 on return from night sortie over Britain.	Heinkel He 111H-2 (5455 : 6N+ML)	80 %	No crew casualties notified.
9.	3./KGr. 100	CM	Suffered landing collision at Vannes with Item 8 on return from night sortie over Britain.	Heinkel He 111H-2 (5475 : 6N+AL)	50 %	Two crew members injured.
10.	1./LG 2	CM	Landing accident at Calais-Marck.	Messerschmitt Bf 109 E-7 (5572)	35 %	Pilot unhurt.
11.	4./LG 2	NCM	Precautionary landing after pilot became lost.	Messerschmitt Bf 109E (6313)	15 %	Pilot unhurt.
12.	I./ZG 2	CM	Shot down by 310 Sqn. Hurricane of Fechtner south-east of North Weald at A.10.55 hrs.	Messerschmitt Bf 110 C-4 (2133 : 3M+HL)	100 %	Uffz. Korn killed; Oblt. Müller missing.
13.	I./ZG 2	CM	Shot down by 310 Sqn. Hurricane of Jeffries near North Weald at A.10.55 hrs.	Messerschmitt Bf 110 C-4 (2065 : 3M+EK)	100 %	Uffz. Schuberth and Fw. Wagenbreth killed.
14.	I./ZG 2	CM	Shot down by 310 Sqn. Hurricane of Sinclair near North Weald at A.10.55 hrs.	Messerschmitt Bf 110 C-4 (3113 : 3M+EL)	100 %	Ofw. Winkler and Gefr. Weiler missing.
15.	I./ZG 2	CM	Shot down by 46 Sqn. Hurricane of Carpenter south-east of North Weald at A.10.40 hrs.	Messerschmitt Bf 110 C-4 (2146 : 3M+BF)	100%	Oblt. Gottschalk and Uffz. Hoffmann missing.
16.	I./ZG 2	CM	Shot down by 310 Sqn. Hurricane of Maly near North Weald at A.10.50 hrs.	Messerschmitt Bf 110 (3120 : 3M+CB)	100 %	Oblt. Messner and Uffz. Santoni missing.
17.	I./ZG 26	CM	Damaged by 17 Sqn. Hurricane of Czernin and crashed near Fontend; one baled out.	Messerschmitt Bf 110 C-4 (3294 : U8+KL)	70 %	Uffz. Klatt killed.
18.	6./ZG 26	CM	Shot down by 19 Sqn. cannon-Spitfire of Haines near North Weald at 10.48 hrs.	Messerschmitt Bf 110D (3310 : 3U+EP)	100 %	Ltn. Manhard and Uffz. Driews missing.
19.	7./ZG 26	CM	Shot down by 19 Sqn. cannon-Spitfire of Unwin near North Weald at 10.48 hrs.	Messerschmitt Bf 110 C-2 (3225 : 3U+KR)	100 %	Uffz. Ucker killed; Fw. Grau, wounded, made P.O.W.
20.	9./ZG 26	CM	Damaged by 19 Sqn. cannon-Spitfire of Blake at A.10.45 hrs., and crashed at Wissant.	Messerschmitt Bf 110 C-2 (3378 : 3U+GT)	80 %	No crew casualties.
21.	Stab/JG 26	CM	Shot down by 603 Sqn. Spitfire of Pease off Margate at 10.55 hrs.	Messerschmitt Bf 109 E-4 (0823)	100 %	Ltn. Roch missing.
22.	3./JG 27	CM	Shot down by 603 Sqn. Spitfire of Caister off Dunkirk at 10.40 hrs.	Messerschmitt Bf 109 E-1 (6231)	100 %	Fw. Wilhelm Harting, wounded, rescued.
23.	4./JG 27	NCM	Suffered serious taxying collision with Item 24 on Fiennes airfield.	Messerschmitt Bf 109 E-1 (6336)	95 %	Uffz. Wilhelm Morgenstern injured.
24.	5./JG27	NCM	Suffered serious taxying collision involving Item 23 on Fiennes airfield.	Messerschmitt Bf 109 E-1 (2689)	70 %	Pilot unhurt.
25.	9./JG 51	CM	Shot down by 303 Sqn. Hurricane of Frantisek into the sea off Dover at 14.45 hrs.	Messerschmitt Bf 109 E-1 (6290)	100 %	Pilot, wounded, rescued.
26.	II./JG 53	NCM	Landing accident at Sempy airfield; not the result of combat.	Messerschmitt Bf 109 E-4 (1244)	55 %	Pilot unhurt.
27.	I./JG 54	NCM	Landing accident near Lillers involving *Staffel* communications aircraft.	Arado Ar 66 (2234 : BA+HQ)	45 %	Crew unhurt.
28.	KGzbV. 106	NCM	Air collision involving Item 29 at Sachau.	Junkers Ju 52/3m (6923 · KC+CU)	100 %	Ltn. Engler + two killed.

Luftwaffe Losses, 3rd September 1940—*continued*

29.	KGzbV. 172	NCM	Air collision involving Item 28 at Sachau.	Junkers Ju 52/3m (5355 : N3+FK)	100 %	Three killed.
30.	Korps- Führungskette VIII Fl.Korps.	NCM	Taxying accident at St. Mards airfield.	Messerschmitt Bf 109E (3893 : GA+GI)	50 %	Pilot unhurt.
31.	3./406	CM	Shot down by British aircraft in grid square 8229; probably shot down by Fleet Air Arm.	Dornier Do 18 (0868 : K6+DL)	100 %	Ltn.z.S. Logier + one killed; two rescued by *Seenotflugkdo*.

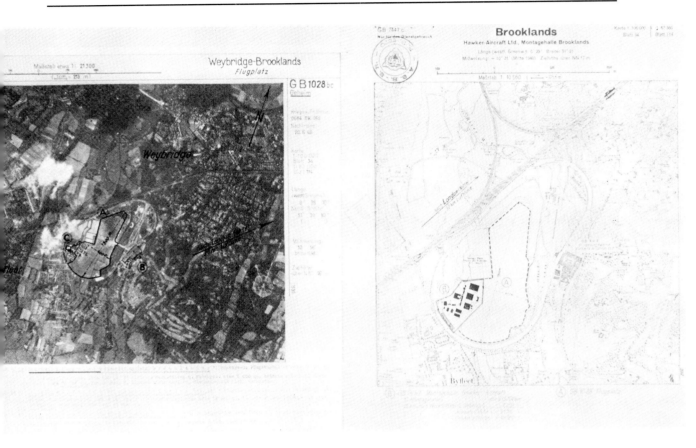

Two of the briefing documents (dated 20th June 1940) issued to *Luftflotte 2* for the attacks on the Hawker Aircraft factory at Brooklands, Surrey. The specific primary annotation of the Hawker premises leaves no doubt but that these were the primary target, rather than the Vickers works. The circular stamp impression in the top left-hand corner of the chart was an endorsement indicating that these documents passed through the hands of the Belgian underground resistance movement; they were smuggled out of Belgium early in 1944.

Wednesday 4th September

No. 25 Squadron's excitements had not ended with the previous day's tragic fiasco; when night fell on the 3rd, three pilots took off to search for Kesselring's elusive bombers. Plt. Off. Bernard Rofe sighted one and closed to the attack; he had scarcely opened fire (apparently damaging the bomber) when anti-aircraft guns opened up, hitting the Blenheim's tail and throwing it into a spin. Only by great skill was Rofe able to recover and bring his crippled fighter home. By way of comfort he learned that two other German night raiders had been claimed by his squadron; both were shot down by the New Zealander, Plt. Off. Michael Herrick, with Sgt. John Pugh as gunner, and the first of his victims, a Heinkel He 111H of *Stab* I./KG 1, carried the German *Gruppenkomman- deur* to his death.

Sperrle had returned to Liverpool, sending in a force of

about 80 Heinkel He 111s of KG 55 and Dornier Do 17s of KGr. 606, as usual flying with geometrical precision from Cherbourg in a stream which crossed the Dorset coast near Portland on a northerly course. Try as they might, Brand's controllers could not succeed in vectoring night fighters into the right position at the right time, and the rudimentary radar in the handful of Blenheims was so unreliable that it was a chance in a thousand if a set were to function throughout an operational sortie—the odds lengthening considerably against a set which happened to be working if an enemy aircraft conveniently entered the patrol area. Nearly two months were to elapse before the recalcitrant equipment could be mastered and squadron aircrews made proficient in its use. Even the Beaufighters, of which eight had now been distributed among Fighter Command night fighter squadrons, were still without their full equipment and armament[8].

Dowding's fear for the safety of his fighter factories were justified on 4th September, although he could not have known that O.K.L. had in fact issued orders for their destruction four days previously unless, conceivably, some indication of this order had been obtained from Enigma signals. Although the attacks on this morning consisted of the familiar assault upon the airfields in Kent—Lympne and Eastchurch being attacked with bombs and gunfire—the mid-day phase was a complicated operation designed to conceal what was in appearance a small and insignificant formation of Bf 110s streaking northwards over Sussex from the coast at Littlehampton.

As seventy-odd Heinkels and Dorniers, with an escort of over 200 Bf 109s, approached the Kent coast between Dover and Hastings and split up to attack Canterbury, Faversham, Reigate, Redhill and Eastchurch, about twenty Bf 110s of V.(*Zerstörer*)/LG 1, carrying bombs on fuselage racks, were reported by the Observer Corps at 13.15 hours to be flying north over Guildford at about 6,000 feet. Nine Hurricane pilots of No. 253 Squadron, led by Flt. Lt. William Cambridge, had been ordered off from Kenley at 13.00 hours to patrol the area, found themselves in a perfect position to attack the enemy:

"Leader turned the formation ninety degrees starboard... and dived to attack out of the sun. The enemy was then flying in sections of vic and the formation was broken up. No enemy evasive tactics nor escort were encountered...visibility was not good owing to haze, but the sky was cloudless. Cambridge delivered his attack on a Bf 110 from high on its beam, expended all his ammunition in one burst and saw the enemy's port engine catch fire; the enemy dived and Cambridge saw it crash in flames in a field. Plt. Off. W.M.C. Samolinski (Polish) attacked a Bf 110 and saw a fire in the cockpit after which the enemy turned port and went into a dive. Sgt. A.S. Dredge attacked a Bf 110 from above, giving it a ten-second burst from 300 yards down to 25 yards; both engines caught fire and a red glow was seen in the cockpit; the enemy was seen to crash in flames (this was confirmed by Fg. Off. Jefferson Woodward). Plt. Off. Tadeusz Nowak (Polish) attacked a Bf 110 , saw it catch fire and crash. Wedgewood managed to get on the tail of a 110 and fired a ten-second burst from 250 yards to point blank range; the enemy caught fire, climbed steeply for a moment, and was then seen to crash into a wood. Plt. Off. Alan Corkett attacked a Bf 110 which was flying on the starboard side of the enemy vic formation; after two bursts the enemy broke formation, climbed 500 feet, turned over and dived straight down, exploding in a field. Sgt. Ernest Kee

delivered a head-on attack, closing from 250 to 50 yards and saw small pieces ripping off the 110's fuselage and tail. Fg. Off. Roy Watts and Fg. Off. Robert Innes silenced the rear gunners of two Bf 110s. Nine Hurricanes landed back at Kenley at 13.35 hrs. Claims, six Bf 110s destroyed, one damaged. Nil casualties."[9]

This combat was so clearly defined that the claims were almost accurate, the enemy aircraft all falling just south of Weybridge, two at East Clandon, two at East Horsley and one near Ripley[10]. Despite the Hurricane's onslaught, the survivors of the German formation managed to reach Brooklands, but were obviously so confused and disorientated that they swept over not the Hawker factory, but the Vickers works, dropping six 500-kilo bombs on the machine shops and Wellington assembly sheds which inflicted no fewer than 700 casualties—of whom 88 were killed. The scene in the factory was appalling, with shattered machines and their dead and dying operators buried under the rubble of the collapsed roofs and walls. It took four days to clear before some degree of production could be re-started. The Hawker factory—the briefed target for the attack—escaped untouched.[11]

Among the feint raids carried out to cover the Brooklands attack was one by *Erprobungsgruppe 210* on the Poling CH station, so timed as to enable the formation of Bf 109s and Bf 110s to rid themselves of their bombs before acting as fighters to cover V./LG 1's withdrawal from the north. Unfortunately for this *Gruppe*, it was itself set upon by Hurricanes and Spitfires flying eastwards to attack the large formations over Kent, and the *Gruppenkommandeur*, Hauptmann Boltenstern, was among those shot down and killed.

Meanwhile the Kent raids were being successfully engaged by nine squadrons, which turned some of the enemy formations away before the escorts could interfere. However, No. 222 Squadron, in meeting the raid on Canterbury, became involved with the Bf 109s and lost two pilots killed. Plt. Off. John Carpenter's Spitfire was hit by *flak* after he had just attacked an enemy fighter; he was literally blown out of his cockpit, but landed at Renton by parachute with only slight injuries. For Tim Vigors this was his eleventh combat sortie in five days.

One of the mid-day raids penetrated to Rochester where the Short Bros. factory producing Stirling bombers was slightly damaged.

---

[8] Owing to the heavy drain upon stocks of Browning machine guns for Spitfires and Hurricanes, it was decided to deliver the first Beaufighters armed with cannon only. Had their radar functioned to good effect the four-cannon armament would have been adequate to destroy any German raider. Only one Beaufighter, *R2059*, delivered to the F.I.U., was fully armed and equipped, and this aircraft was lost on operations on 13th September.

[9] Cf. Form 540, No. 253 Sqn., 4th September 1940

[10] The craters and scars made by the above aircraft could all be seen as recently as the late-1970s. A sixth Bf 110 *may* have fallen in this fight, although only five aircraft were reported missing by 14.*Staffel*, LG 1. There was a crater made by a crashed wartime aircraft beside the railway line near West Clandon which was clearly visible in 1969.

[11] The fact that all the casualties suffered by the German formation were on 14.*Staffel*, LG 1, suggests that No. 253 Squadron unwittingly attacked the escorting *Staffel*, while the other *Staffel* were the only aircraft to have been carrying bombs; none of the Hurricane pilots mentioned their victims as carrying or jettisoning bombs, and it seems almost certain that while the above combat was taking place, the bomber *Staffel* made straight for Brooklands and carried out its devastating attack.

R.A.F. FIGHTER COMMAND LOSSES—WEDNESDAY 4th SEPTEMBER 1940

1.	46 Sqn., Stapleford	C	Shot down by Bf 109s near Southend; pilot baled out severely wounded and died on 15-9-40.	13.25 hrs.	Fg. Off. R.P. Plummer	Hurricane	P3052	Cat.3 Destroyed
2.	46 Sqn., Stapleford	C	Shot down by Bf 109s near Rochford; pilot baled out unhurt.	13.25 hrs.	Plt. Off. C.F. Ambrose	Hurricane	P3026	Cat. 3 Destroyed
3.	46 Sqn., Stapleford	C	Shot down by Bf 109 and force landed at Heybridge, but in doing so injured his spine and fractured his jaw.	13.35 hrs.	Plt. Off. R.H. Barber	Hurricane	V7201	Cat. 3 Destroyed
4.	66 Sqn., Kenley	C	Shot down in flames by Bf 109s; pilot baled out slightly wounded; aircraft crashed at Aldington, Kent.	Not known	Plt. Off. D.A. Cooke	Spitfire	R6689	Cat. 3 Destroyed
5.	66 Sqn., Kenley	C	Shot down by Bf 109 over Thames Estuary and force landed near Canterbury with superficial wounds.	Not known	Flt. Lt. G.P. Christie	Spitfire	X4052	Cat. 3 Destroyed
6.	66 Sqn., Kenley	C	Shot down over Thames Estuary and baled out slightly wounded; aircraft crashed at Howe Green Farm, Purleigh.	Not known	Plt.Off. A.N.R.L. Appleford	Spitfire	P9316	Cat. 3 Destroyed
7.	66 Sqn., Kenley	C	Shot down by Bf 109s and force landed near Billericay, slightly wounded.	Not known	Flt. Lt. F.P.R. Dunworth	Spitfire	N3044	Cat. 3 Destroyed
8.	66 Sqn., Kenley	C	Shot down and pilot baled out over Ashford grievously wounded; he succumbed to his wounds on 6-9-40. Aircraft fell at Mersham.	Not known	Sgt. A.D. Smith	Spitfire	N3048	Cat. 3 Destroyed
9.	79 Sqn., Biggin Hill	C	Severely damaged by Bf 110s over Biggin Hill and crashed at Surbiton; pilot grievously wounded and died the following day.	A13.25 hrs.	Sgt. J. Wright	Hurricane	P3676	Cat. 3 Destroyed
10.	111 Sqn., Croydon	C	Shot down by Bf 109 east of Folkestone; pilot killed.	09.25 hrs.	Flt. Lt. D.C. Bruce	Hurricane (1)	Z2309	Cat. 3 Lost
11.	111 Sqn., Croydon	C	Shot down by Bf 109 east of Folkestone; pilot killed, believed shot by enemy fighters during parachute descent.	09.25 hrs.	Plt. Off. J. Macinski	Hurricane	R4172	Cat. 3 Lost
12.	141 Sqn., Turnhouse	NC	Taxying accident; crew unhurt.	At night	Crew not known.	Defiant	—	Cat. 2 Damaged
13.	141 Sqn., Turnhouse	NC	Taxying accident; crew unhurt.	At night	Crew not known.	Defiant	—	Cat. 2 Damaged
14.	152 Sqn., Warmwell	C	Shot down by Do 17 twenty-five miles SSE of Bognor; body washed up in France and buried in cemetery at Etaples.	Not known	Sgt. J.K. Barker	Spitfire	—	Cat. 3 Lost
15.	222 Sqn., Hornchurch	(C)	Shot down by A.A. defences at Dover; pilot blown out of cockpit but landed safely by parachute at Renton with minor injuries.	13.30 hrs.	Plt. Off. J.M.V. Carpenter	Spitfire	P9398	Cat. 3 Destroyed
16.	222 Sqn., Hornchurch	C	Shot down by Bf 109s near West Malling, and crashed at Yalding; pilot died before reaching hospital.	13.35 hrs.	Sgt. J.W. Ramshaw	Spitfire	P9962	Cat. 3 Destroyed
17.	222 Sqn., Hornchurch	C	Shot down by Bf 109s; crashed and burnt out at Chart Sutton, Kent. Pilot killed.	13.35 hrs.	Fg. Off. J.W. Cutts	Spitfire	X4278	Cat. 3 Burnt
18.	234 Sqn., Middle Wallop	C	Damaged by Bf 110 near Haselmere; pilot unhurt.	13.20 hrs.	Sgt. Z. Olenski	Spitfire	X4182	Cat. 1 Damaged
19.	253 Sqn., Kenley	C	Shot and killed in combat over Kenley; aircraft crashed at Banstead, Surrey.	09.45 hrs.	Fg. Off. A.A.G. Trueman	Hurricane	V6638	Cat. 3 Destroyed
20.	264 Sqn., Kirton-in-Lindsey	NC	Suffered take-off accident at night; both crew members killed.	At night	Fg.Off.D.H.C. O'Malley Sgt. L.A.W. Rasmussen	Defient	N1628	Cat. 3 Destroyed
21.	601 Sqn., Tangmere	C	Shot down and force landed near Worthing; pilot slightly wounded.	A14.00 hrs.	Fg. Off. J. Jankiewicz	Hurricane	R4214	Cat. 2 Damaged
22.	602 Sqn., Westhampnett	C	Landing accident after combat 15 miles south of Beachy Head; pilot unhurt.	A13.45 hrs.	Sgt. G.A. Whipps	Spitfire	K9855	Cat. 3 Destroyed
23.	603 Sqn., Hornchurch	NC	Force landed near Ashford after engine failure; pilot unhurt.	Not known	Sgt. A.R. Sarre	Spitfire	—	Cat. 3 Destroyed

[(1) This was the first Hurricane Mark II to be lost on operations.]

LUFTWAFFE LOSSES—WEDNESDAY 4th SEPTEMBER 1940

1.	3.(F)/10	NCM	Believed to have struck high ground and crashed while low flying.	Messerschmitt Bf 110 (2175 : T1+TL)	100 %	Oblt. Ellerlage killed.
2.	Stab. I/KG 1	CM	Shot down by 25 Sqn. Blenheim night fighter of Herrick and Pugh at 02.15 hrs.	Heinkel He 111H-3 (3324 : V4+AB)	100 %	Maj. Maier, Oblt. von Rittberg, Ofw. Stockert and Uffz. Bendig all killed; Oblt. Biebrach missing.
3.	4./KG 26	CM	Shot down by 25 Sqn. Blenheim night fighter of Herrick and Pugh at 02.45 hrs.	Heinkel He 111H-4 (3287 : 1H+AM)	100%	Fw. Ewerts, Ofw. Süssman, Fw. Handwerker and Uffz. Mahlmann missing.
4.	I./KG 51	NCM	Force landed at Melun-Villaroche airfield following technical failure.	Junkers Ju 88A-1 (2054)	25 %	Crew unhurt.
5.	I./KG 51	NCM	Accident following tyre burst at Villeneuf-Orly.	Junkers Ju 88A-1(2057)	15 %	Crew unhurt.
6.	I./KG 55	NCM	Landing accident on Dreux airfield.	Heinkel He 111P (3016)	50 %	Crew unhurt.
7.	I./LG 1	CM	Damaged by 1(Canadian) Sqn. Hurricane west of East Grinstead, and crashed at Dinard.	Junkers Ju 88A-1 (4034 : L1+AK)	40 %	Crew unhurt.
8.	III./LG 1	NCM	Landing accident at Chateaudun airfield; not the result of combat.	Junkers Ju 88A-1 (7004 : L1+BR)	60 %	Crew unhurt.
9.	V./LG 1	CM	Damaged by 253 Sqn. Hurricane at A.13.35 hrs. near Effingham; crashed near Abbeville.	Messerschmitt Bf 110 C-1 (2803)	50 %	Crew unhurt.
10.	14./LG 1	CM	Shot down by 253 Sqn. Hurricanes at 13.30 hrs. and crashed at East Horslay.	Messerschmitt Bf 110D (3303 : L1+BK)	100 %	Fw. Rörung killed; Uffz. Joachim Jäckel, wounded, made P.O.W.
11.	14./LG 1	CM	Shot down by 253 Sqn. Hurricanes at 13.25 hrs. and crashed at Washington, near Pulborough.	Messerschmitt Bf 110 C-2 (3541 : L1+CK)	100 %	Ogefr. Krischewski killed; Ltn. Braukmeier missing.
12.	14./LG 1	CM	Shot down by 253 Sqn. Hurricanes at 13.30 hrs. and crashed at East Clandon.	Messerschmitt Bf 110 C-4 (2212 : L1+FL)	100 %	Uffz. Neumann killed; Uffz. Speier missing.
13.	14./LG 1	CM	Shot down by 253 Sqn. Hurricanes at 13.30 hrs. and crashed at West Horsley.	Messerschmitt Bf 110D (3306 : L1+FK)	100 %	Oblt. Michael Junge and Uffz. Bremser, unhurt, made P.O.W.s.
14.	14./LG 1	CM	Shot down by 253 Sqn. Hurricanes at 13.30 hrs. and crashed south-east of Ripley.	Messerschmitt Bf 110D (L1+FM)	100 %	Both crew members believed killed.
15.	II./LG 2	CM	Damaged in landing accident at Monchy-Breton airfield; not the result of combat.	Messerschmitt Bf 109 E-7 (5564)	50 %	Pilot unhurt.

279

Luftwaffe Losses, 4th September 1940—*continued*

16.	II./LG 2	NCM	Damaged in landing accident at Calais-Marck airfield; not the result of combat.	Messerschmitt Bf 109 E-7 (5572)	35 %	Pilot unhurt.
17.	Stab/ZG 2	CM	Shot down by 234 Sqn. Spitfire of Doe south of Haselmere at A.13.30 hrs.; crashed at Mill Hill, north of Shoreham-by-Sea.	Messerschmitt Bf 110 C-4 (2116 : 3M+AA)	100 %	Oblt. Wilhelm Schäfer and Uffz. Heinz Bendjus made P.O.W.s.
18.	I./ZG 76	CM	Shot down by 79 Sqn. Hurricaneof Peters south of Biggin Hill; crashed north of Worthing.	Messerschmitt Bf 110 C-4 (3254 : 2N+BM)	100 %	Oblt. Walter Schiller and Fw. Helmut Winkler made P.O.W.s.
19.	Stab II./ZG 76	CM	Shot down by 72 Sqn. Spitfire and crashed at Little Bull Farm, Cousleywood, at 13.50 hrs.	Messerschmitt Bf 110C (3602 : M8+AC)	100 %	Oblt. Herbert Weber and Uffz. Max Michael made P.O.W.s.
20.	II./ZG 76	CM	Shot down by 72 Sqn. Spitfires at Cowden, 7 miles west of Tunbridge Wells at 13.45 hrs.	Messerschmitt Bf 110C (2089 : M8+CP)	100 %	Obly. Gunther Piduhn and Gefr. Rudolf Conde both killed.
21.	II./ZG 76	CM	Shot down by 72 and 234 Sqn. Spitfires near Tenterden and crashed into sea off Pevensey.	Messerschmitt Bf 110C (3287 : M8+JN)	100 %	Oblt. Freiherr Ernst Hartmann von Schlothem and Uffz. Georg Hommel rescued and made P.O.W.
22.	III./ZG 76	CM	Shot down by 43 Sqn. Hurricane of Ayling north-west of Pulborough at A.13.25 hrs.	Messerschmitt Bf 110 C-4 (2104 : 2N+KP)	100 %	Oblt. Kurt Rätsch and Ogefr. Hempel both killed.
23.	III./ZG 76	CM	Shot down by three 43 Sqn. Hurricanes and crashed at Black Patch, NE of Angmering.	Messerschmitt Bf 110 C-4 (3101 :2N+CN)	100 %	Oblt. Han s Münich and Uffz. Adolf Käser made P.O.W.
24.	III./ZG 76	CM	Probably shot down by 234 Sqn. Spitfires over Sussex; wreckage not located.	Messerschmitt Bf 110 C-4 (3545 : 2N+AC)	100 %	Ofw. Daun and Uffz. Mayer missing, believed killed.
25.	III./KG 76	CM	Shot down by 43 Sqn. Hurricane of Upton and crashed at Stayning, Sussex at 13.30 hrs.	Messerschmitt Bf 110 C-4 (3563 : 2N+HM)	100 %	Uffz. Wilhelm Schultis and Uffz. Richard Bilek made P.O.W.s.
26.	Erpr.Gr. 210	CM	Shot down by 601 Sqn. Hurricanes between Tangmere and Littlehampton at 13.40 hrs.	Messerschmitt Bf 110 D-0 (3390 : S9+AB)	100 %	Hptm. von Boltenstern, *Gr.Kdr.*, and Fw. Schneider killed.
27.	JG 2	NCM	Crashed near Nuremburg after engine failure.	Heinkel He 70 (1347 : CF+BF)	15 %	Pilot injured.
28.	II./JG 2	CM	Believd shot down by 602 Sqn. Spitfire south of Beachy Head at A.13.25 hrs.	Messerschmitt Bf 109 E-1 (2678)	100 %	Oblt. Müller missing.
29.	III./JG 3	CM	Intercepted by 222 Sqn. Spitfires near Canterbury at A.13.00 hrs.	Messerschmitt Bf 109E	—	Hptm. Wilhelm Balthasar, *Gr.Kdr.*, wounded.
30.	I./JG 26	CM	Force landed at Audembert following engine failure; not the result of combat.	Messerschmitt Bf 109 E-1 (3884)	45 %	Pilot unhurt.
31.	II./JG 26	CM	Accident following tyre burst on Marquise-Ost airfield	Messerschmitt Bf 109 E-4 (0825)	70 %	Pilot injured.
32.	2./JG 51	CM	Damaged by unknown R.A.F. fighters and crashed at Pihen.	Messerschmitt Bf 109 E-4 (2760)	80 %	Pilot unhurt.
33.	3./JG 54	CM	Shot down by 111Sqn. Hurricane of Giddings over Folkestone at A.09.30 hrs.	Messerschmitt Bf 109 E-4 (5026)	100 %	Oblt. Witt missing.
34.	3./JG 54	CM	Shot down by 111 Sqn. Hurricane of Wallace five miles east of Folkestone at A.09.30 hrs.	Messerschmitt Bf 109 E-1 (4839)	100 %	Pilot, unhurt, rescued by *Seenotflugkommando.*
35.	I./JG 77	CM	Shot down by unknown R.A.F. fighters over the English Channel.	Messerschmitt Bf 109 E-4 (5807)	100 %	Pilot wounded but rescued.

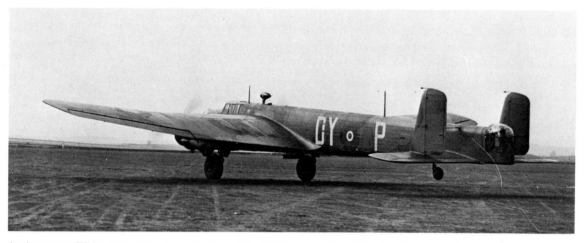

An Armstrong Whitworth Whitley heavy bomber of No. 102 Squadron, R.A.F. Bomber Command. These ungainly, but robust workhorses, with Wellingtons and Hampdens, constituted the generation of British heavy bombers which, with relatively little publicity, carried the night air war back to Berlin in 1940.

Thursday 5th September

It is perhaps a fundamental observation to make of any battle that, in fluid operations, the ability of the attacking forces to choose their time, place, frequency and strength of assault earns them an enormous dividend in the physical fatigue, nervous exhaustion and demoralising uncertainty which is the lot of the defenders. The defenders can counter and rise above these pressures only so long as they possess unlimited reserves with which to meet these initiatives, and replace exhausted forces. Had Göring but known it, Fighter Com-

mand was now reaching the point at which nervous and physical exhaustion among the squadrons could no longer be offset adequately by replacements of men and machines.

Nor, apparently was he wholly aware of the growing exhaustion—born largely of frustration and continuing heavy losses—among his own men. In every type of *Geschwader* (excepting perhaps those engaged in the night raids) this fatigue was becoming daily more apparent. The daylight bombers continued to pay a daily toll in men and aircraft, as

Scene at the back of a terraced house in Maidstone after a Messerschmitt Bf 109 had crashed; the engine penetrated to the cellar. The author visited the house in the early 1970s to find it fully repaired and bearing few signs of its ordeal. However, in the garden stood a bird table constructed from one of the Messerschmitt's propeller blades, and a wheelbarrow employing the fighter's tailwheel, visible here—still fully inflated with "1940 air". (Photo: The Kent Messenger, Neg No. 3763/2)

the Hurricanes and Spitfires managed to penetrate the escorts again and again; the effect on morale was aggravated by a growing realisation that the figures of British fighters destroyed, touted by their own rear echelon services, had been wildly exaggerated. The escorting Bf 109 pilots were frustrated by their orders to stick close to the bombers—bombers now frequently operating north of the Thames, at the extreme limit of the Messerschmitt's fuel endurance—and were also suffering a mounting scale of losses. The *Zerstörer* crews were fully aware that their aircraft were no match for the British interceptors, and spent far more time over England defending themselves than protecting the bombers.

It is pertinent to observe at this point that statistically (though at the time there was no way of deducing accurate figures) the *Luftwaffe* was winning the battle of aircraft attrition; it will be seen from the daily loss tables that on several days during the first week in September British combat losses were running at a higher rate than German. But this fact would have brought no comfort to the rank and file of the *Luftwaffe*; after all, the "official version" was that this was nothing new. And colouring the attitude of the airmen based south of the Channel was one overriding thought, infinitely more abrasive to the nerves than mere tactical setbacks. They were ignorant of the fate of their missing comrades, but they knew with complete certainty that when an aircraft slipped down out of formation, their friends would not return. To the British pilot, it was a great comfort to know that a short journey by parachute would, more often than not, return him to familiar surroundings and sympathetic friends.

Thus, on both sides of the Channel—a Channel which by this stage was feared and hated by most German aircrew more

fiercely than their human enemy—the airmen were reaching a crisis of efficiency. It is probable that neither side fully appreciated the predicament of the other; and in this the R.A.F. pilots were paradoxically strengthened. Their situation involved no uncertainty of purpose; they knew that no matter what transpired, they *had* to maintain their effort. In a desperate environment, a clear and unremitting purpose is of incalculable value.

*   *   *   *   *

The tactics employed on 5th September presented something of an enigma to Park as his controllers attempted to identify specific attack phases. However, Kesselring had in fact decided to abandon his pattern, and launched no fewer than 22 separate formations over a period of eight hours. Given good reporting and tracking by radar and Observer Corps, most of these raids were intercepted. No. 79 Squadron, scrambled to cover its base at Biggin Hill at 10.00 hours, broke up a raid by 30 escorted bombers, Flt. Lt. Geoffrey Haysom being forced to land with shot-up ailerons. He promptly ran to another aircraft and took off to re-join the fight.

No. 19 Squadron, on patrol over Hornchurch with eleven Spitfires, intercepted a raid by more than a hundred aircraft, but lost its commanding officer, Philip Pinkham, shot down in flames and killed. Fg. Off. Benjamin Bowring, an Auxiliary pilot who had recently been transferred to No. 111 Squadron, now led eight Hurricanes against more than a hundred enemy aircraft north of Dungeness. He singled out a Bf 109 and attacked it, but did not score a lethal hit. No doubt gripped by the excitement of the battle, which does not make for logical reasoning, he then drew alongside the damaged enemy twice and signalled the German pilot to land; the enemy airman shook his fist, throttled back and opened fire; the indignant Bowring had little difficulty in manœuvring to the attack and shooting the Messerschmitt down into the sea ten miles off Dungeness.

No 46 Squadron on this day included an unfamiliar aircraft—the first four-cannon Hurricane, flown by Flt. Lt. Alexander Rabagliati. During the afternoon this squadron joined up with No. 249 Squadron and began a patrol over Rochford; as they were climbing to intercept a large formation of enemy aircraft at 20,000 feet, they spotted some Bf 109s just below, over the mouth of the Thames:

"I sighted one 109 diving towards the ground straight past us; I fired at him but as he was drawing away only a short burst was delivered from astern (my Nos. 2 and 3 continued the attack right down to sea level). I climbed back to 12,000 feet and spotted a 109 on the tail of a Spitfire; I gave this enemy aircraft a three-second burst and he blew up in the air. He took no evasive action. . ."[12]

No. 43 Squadron pilots, hurriedly ordered south from Church Fenton to Debden, landed at 10.05 hours and within four hours were ordered off against a raid over the Thames Estuary; four of their Hurricanes were destroyed, one pilot killed and another wounded. The objective of this raid, carried out by Heinkels and Ju 88s, was the oil storage farm at Thameshaven, where five tanks were set ablaze. Once again, No. 303 (Polish) Squadron gave a good account of itself.

The arrival of darkness brought increased night activity by Sperrle's bombers, which once more set precise course northwards from Cherbourg; their targets were, however, distributed all over England. At Shoreham, the F.I.U.'s second Beaufighter was at long last ready; as reports of the raiders started coming in, the new aircraft was ordered off on its first operational patrol with Flt. Lt. Glynn Ashfield (the pilot who had scored the first A.I. night victory in a Blenheim on 22nd/ 23rd July) at the controls. At the critical moment when he was approaching the position of an oncoming enemy aircraft, his radar operator reported that the equipment had failed. . .once more the night defences had been frustrated.

[12] Flt. Lt. Roddick Smith of No. 151 Squadron had been detailed to fly the cannon-Hurricane on operations, and had on several occasions flown the old two-gun *L1750* (with Oerlikon guns) from North Weald during August. Persistent trouble with these guns—which demanded greased ammunition—caused this aircraft to be withdrawn, and the first four-cannon aircraft, *V7360* (with Hispano cannon which were entirely reliable with "dry" shells), was delivered to North Weald on 3rd September. Smith and No. 151 Squadron had already left for their rest, and when Rabagliati, who had been shot down on the previous day, was casting about for another aircraft he was granted permission to take over *V7360*. Although the guns of this Hurricane damaged more than half a dozen enemy aircraft, the Bf 109 shot down in the above engagement was its only confirmed victory. Contrary to other accounts, the 20-mm. Oerlikon was *not* adopted by the R.A.F.—owing to the necessity for "greasing"—and its service was confined to the Royal Navy, and the Hispano came to be adopted as the standard armament in countless R.A.F. fighter aircraft.

R.A.F. FIGHTER COMMAND LOSSES—THURSDAY 5th SEPTEMBER 1940

1.	19 Sqn., Fowlmere	C	Shot down by Bf 109 near Hornchurch; pilot killed.	A10.10 hrs.	Sqn. Ldr. P.C. Pinkham	Spitfire	P9422	Cat. 3 Destroyed
2.	19 Sqn., Fowlmere	C	Aircraft severely damaged in combat with Bf 109s near Hornchurch; pilot returned unhurt.	A10.15 hrs.	Plt. Off W.J. Lawson.	Spitfire	—	Cat. 2 Damaged
3.	19 Sqn., Fowlmere	C	Aircraft severely damaged in combat with Bf 109s; pilot returned unhurt.	A10.20 hrs.	Plt. Off.E. Burgoyne	Spitfire	—	Cat. 2 Damaged
4.	41 Sqn., Hornchurch	C	Shot down and force landed at Stanford-le-Hope; pilot unhurt.	A10.00 hrs.	Sgt. R.A. Carr-Lewtry	Spitfire	—	Cat. 3 Destroyed
5.	41 Sqn., Hornchurch	C	Collided with Item 6 during combat against Do 17s over Thames Estuary; aircraft said to have disintegrated over Wickford, Essex. Pilot killed.	A15.30 hrs.	Sqn. Ldr. H.R.L. Hood	Spitfire	P9428	Cat. 3 Destroyed
6.	41 Sqn., Hornchurch	C	Collided with Item 5 during combat against Do 17s over Thames Estuary; pilot killed.	A15.30 hrs.	Flt. Lt. J.T. Webster	Spitfire	R6635	Cat. 3 Destroyed
7.	41 Sqn., Hornchurch	C	Shot down during combat against Do 17s over Thames Estuary; pilot baled out with shell wound in leg at Rawreth, Essex.	A15.40 hrs.	Fg. Off. R.W. Wallens	Spitfire	X4021	Cat. 3 Destroyed
8.	41 Sqn., Hornchurch	C	Shot down in the above combat and baled out unhurt; aircraft crashed at South Benfleet.	A15.35 hrs.	Fg. Off. A.D.J.	Spitfire	R6885	Cat 3 Destroyed
9.	64 Sqn., Ringway	NC	Aircraft crashed at Hartington (not combat); pilot unhurt.	Not known	Sgt. D.E. Lloyd	Spitfire	R9563	Cat. 3 Destroyed
10.	66 Sqn., Kenley	C	Shot down by Bf 109s over Rochester; pilot baled out but killed when parachute failed.	Afternoon	Plt. Off. P.J.C. King	Spitfire	N3060	Cat. 3 Destroyed
11.	66 Sqn., Kenley	C	Shot down and force landed; pilot unhurt.	Afternoon	Plt. Off. H.R. Allen	Spitfire	—	Cat. 3 Destroyed
12.	66 Sqn., Kenley	C	Shot down and force landed; pilot unhurt.	Afternoon	Plt. Off. R.J. Mather	Spitfire	K9944	Cat. 3 Destroyed
13.	72 Sqn., Biggin Hill	C	Shot down by Bf 109s over Kent; pilot baled out too low and was killed; aircraft crashed at Elham.	13.20 hrs.	Plt. Off. D.C. Winter	Spitfire	X4013	Cat. 3 Destroyed
14.	72 Sqn., Biggin Hill	C	Shot down by Bf 109s and crashed at Elham; pilot killed.	13.20 hrs.	Sgt. M. Gray	Spitfire	N3093	Cat. 3 Destroyed
15.	72 Sqn., Biggin Hill	C	Shot down by Bf 109s over Hawkinge; pilot escaped unhurt.	13.20 hrs.	Not known	Spitfire	X4034	Cat. 3 Destroyed
16.	73 Sqn., Debden	C	Crashed landed after combat with He 111 and Ju 88; pilot unhurt.	A16.00 hrs.	Sqn. Ldr. M.W.S. Robinson	Hurricane	P2815	Cat. 3 Destroyed
17.	73 Sqn., Debden	C	Shot down (said to have been by a Ju 88) over Burnham; pilot assumed killed.	A15.30 hrs.	Sgt. A.L. McNay	Hurricane	P3224	Cat. 3 Missing
18.	73 Sqn., Debden	C	Shot down by Bf 109s near Billericay; pilot baled out with shell wound in the ankle.	A15.30 hrs.	Plt. Off. R.D. Rutter.	Hurricane	P3110	Cat. 3 Destroyed
19.	73 Sqn., Debden	C	Shot down by enemy fighters near Burnham; pilot baled out unhurt.	A.15.30 hrs.	Flt. Lt. R.E. Lovett	Hurricane	P3204	Cat. 3 Destroyed

R.A.F. Losses, 5th September 1940—*continued*

20.	79 Sqn., Biggin Hill	C	Ailerons damaged in combat over Biggin Hill; pilot returned safely.	10.20 hrs.	Flt. Lt. G.D.L. Hawsom	Hurricane	—	Cat. 1 Damaged
21.	111 Sqn., Biggin Hill	C	Shot down and force landed near Lulling-stone Castle; pilot slightly wounded.	10.15 hrs.	Sgt. F.H. Silk	Hurricane	—	Cat. 2 Damaged
22.	222 Sqn., Hornchurch	C	Shot down by Dover A.A. defences; pilot baled out unhurt at Pineham.	15.43 hrs.	Sgt. D.J. Chipping	Spitfire	X4057	Cat. 3 Destroyed
23.	249 Sqn., North Weald	C	Shot down near Shellhaven; pilot baled out unhurt.	A15.00 hrs	Flt. Lt. R.A. Barton	Hurricane	V6625	Cat. 3 Destroyed
24.	303 Sqn., Northolt	C	Shot down near Rochford; pilot baled out with broken broken arm.	A15.30 hrs.	Fg. Off. W. Lapkowski	Hurricane	P2985	Cat. 3 Destroyed
25.	501 Sqn., Gravesend	C	Shot down between Canterbury and Herne Bay by Bf 109s; pilot wounded.	09.55 hrs.	Plt. Off. S. Skalski	Hurricane	V6644	Cat. 3 Destroyed
26.	603 Sqn., Hornchurch	C	Missing from combat near Biggin Hill with Bf 109s; fate of aircraft and location of pilot's body never established.	09.50 hrs.	Flt. Lt. F.W. Rushmer	Spitfire	X4261	Cat. 3 Missing
27.	603 Sqn., Hornchurch	C	Shot down by Bf 109s near Maidstone; pilot baled out, wounded, and admitted to Maidstone West Kent Hospital.	09.55 hrs.	Plt. Off. W.P.H. Rafter	Spitfire	X4264	Cat. 3 Destroyed

LUFTWAFFE LOSSES—THURSDAY 5th SEPTEMBER 1940

1.	3.(H)/12	NCM	Overturned on landing; airfield not notified.	Henschel Hs 126B (4153)	80 %	Crew unhurt.
2.	3.(F)/121	NCM	Engine failure on take-off at Chateaudun.	Junkers Ju 88A-1 (2124 : 7A+BL)	40 %	Ltn. Zander + two injured.
3.	4.(F)/122	NCM	Take-off accident at Melsbroeck airfield.	Focke-Wulf Fw 44 (0468 : CA+SN)	50 %	Crew unhurt.
4.	Geschw.Erg.St/ KG 1	NCM	Engine failure on take-off at Münster airfield.	Heinkel He 111H-1 (5740 : V4+GR)	88 %	Crew unhurt.
5.	6./KG 2	CM	Damaged by 41 Sqn. Spitfires over Thames Estuary at A.10.00 hrs. Crashed near Calais.	Dornier Do 17Z-2 (1134 : U5+FP)	20 %	Two crew members wounded.
6.	6./KG 2	CM	Damaged by 41 Sqn. Spitfires over Thames Estuary at A.10.00 hrs. Crashed at St. Omer.	Dornier Do 17Z-3 (2828 : U5+KP)	20 %	One crew member wounded.
7.	II./KG 26	CM	Shot down by 17 Sqn. Hurricanes of Czernin and Chew near Chatham at A.15.00 hrs.	Heinkel He 111H-3 (6896 : 1H+BC)	100 %	Uffz. Stenzel, Fw. Wilde + two missing.
8.	II./KG 26	CM	Take-off collision at Gilze-Rijen airfield.	Heinkel He 111H-3 (3193 : 1H+CC)	20 %	Crew unhurt.
9.	4./KG 26	CM	Crashed near Amsterdam; probably the result of combat.	Heinkel He 111H-4 (5707 : 1H+JM)	100 %	Uffz. Henningsen and Fw. Höper killed; three wounded.
10.	4./KG 26	NCM	Taxying accident at Gilze-Rijen airfield.	Heinkel He 111H-4 (5703 : 1H+CM)	20 %	Crew unhurt.
11.	4./KG 26	NCM	Taxying accident at Gilze-Rijen airfield.	Heinkel He 111H-4 (3316 : 1H+LM)	20 %	Crew unhurt.
12.	5./KG 26	CM	Crashed near Calais; probably the result of combat.	Heinkel He 111H-3 (3295 : 1H+GN)	50 %	Crew unhurt.
13.	6./KG 26	CM	Take-off collision with Item 8 at Gilze-Rijen airfield.	Heinkel He 111H-3 (6872 : 1H+CP)	20 %	Crew unhurt.
14.	6./KG 26	CM	Take-off accident at Gilze-Rijen, followed by fire.	Heinkel He 111H-4 (3318 : 1H+FP)	100 %	Ltn. Baltes + three killed.
15.	Ausb.St./KG 40	NCM	Landing accident at Unterstedt airfield.	Heinkel He 111H-4 (3263 : JZ+FL)	30 %	Crew unhurt.
16.	II./KG 53	CM	Damaged by 73 Sqn. Hurricanes near Burnham at 15.30 hrs. Force landed at Vendeville.	Heinkle He 111H-2 (3143 : A1+CC)	20 %	One wounded.
17.	III./KG 53	CM	Shot down by 17 Sqn. Hurricanes near Gravesend at A.15.20 hrs.	Heinkel He 111H-3 (3388 : A1+CR)	100 %	Fw. Waier, Ltn. Anger, Uffz. Lenger, Uffz. Armbruster and Gefr. Nowotny missing.
18.	III./KG 53	CM	Shot down by 17 Sqn. Hurricanes near Gravesend at A.15.20 hrs.	Heinkel He 111H-2 (2632 : A1+GR)	100 %	Fw. Bohn killed; Uffz. Bolz, Uffz. Rosenberger, Gefr.Hack, and Uffz. Bickl missing.
19.	Ausb.St./KG 54	NCM	Crashed following engine fire at Lechfeld airfield.	Junkers Ju 88A-1 (8025)	40 %	Crew unhurt.
20.	II./KG 54	CM	Accident at St. André; nature not notified.	Junkers Ju 88A-1 (4122)	90 %	Crew unhurt.
21.	I./KG 55	NCM	Landing accident at Illesheim airfiled.	Heinkel He 111P-4 (2885 : CC+KF)	25 %	Crew unhurt.
22.	Stab/St.G 1	NCM	Crashed at St. Pol; local training flight.	Junkers Ju 87B (5447 : A5+HA)	100 %	Two crew killed.
23.	II./LG 2	NCM	Landing accident at Calais-Marck airfield.	Messerschmitt Bf 109 E-7 (2001)	45 %	Pilot unhurt.
24.	II./LG 2	NCM	Landing accident at Calais-Marck airfield.	Messerschmitt Bf 109 E-7 (6315)	40 %	Pilot unhurt.
25.	1./JG 3	CM	Shot down by 303 Sqn. Hurricane of Kellett over Thames Estuary at 15.20 hrs.	Messerschmitt Bf 109 E-1 (3612)	100 %	Oble. Lammer missing.
26.	I./JG 3	CM	Shot down by 303 Sqn. Hurricane of Frantisek over Thames Estuary at 15.20 hrs.	Messerschmitt Bf 109 E-4 (1985)	100 %	Ltn. Schnabel missing.
27.	2./JG 3	CM	Damaged by 303 Sqn. Hurricane over Kent at A.15.15 hrs.	Messerschmitt Bf 109 E-1 (3882)	50 %	Pilot unhurt.
28.	2./JG 3	CM	Shot down by 234 Sqn. Spitfire of Zurakowski over south Kent coast at 15.30 hrs.	Messerschmitt Bf 109 E-4 (5342)	100 %	Ltn. Klöber killed.
29.	3./JG 3	CM	Shot down by 234 Sqn. Spitfire of Doe over Kent at A.15.25 hrs.	Messerschmitt Bf 109 E-4 (0750)	100 %	Uffz. Grabow missing.
30.	II./JG 3	CM	Shot down by 234 Sqn. Spitfire of Hughes over Kent at A.15.25 hrs.	Messerschmitt Bf 109 E-4 (1480)	100 %	Oblt. von Werra missing.
31.	5./JG 3	CM	Shot down by 111Sqn. Hurricane of Bowring south-west of Dungeness; pilot rescued.	Messerschmitt Bf 109 E-4 (1464)	100 %	Pilot, unhurt, made P.O.W.
32.	8./JG 3	CM	Landing accident at Desvres; probably the result of combat.	Messerschmitt Bf 109 E-4 (0818)	30 %	Pilot unhurt.
33.	5./JG 27	CM	Shot down by 43 Sqn. Hurricane of Hurry at Elham, Kent, at 16.15 hrs.	Messerschmitt Bf 109 E-1 (3627)	100 %	Ltn. Helmut Strobl missing.
34.	I./JG 52	CM	Shot down by 501 Sqn. Hurricane of Lacey north of Folkestone at A. 15.10 hrs.	Messerschmitt Bf 109 E-4 (1949)	100 %	Uffz. Kind killed.
35.	Stab/JG 53	CM	Missing from sortie over England; fate not known.	Messerschmitt Bf 109 E-1 (5375)	100 %	Pilot missing.
36.	II./JG 53	CM	Landing accident at Sempy following combat sortie.	Messerschmitt Bf 109 E-1 (4053)	25 %	Pilot unhurt.

Luftwaffe Losses, 5th September 1940—*continued*

37.	II./JG 53	CM	Landing accident at Sempy following combat sortie.	Messerschmitt Bf 109 E-1 (3429)	40 %	Pilot unhurt.
38.	7./JG 53	CM	Shot down by unknown British fighters south-east of London.	Messerschmitt Bf 109 E-1 (4017)	100 %	Ltn. Deutsch missing.
39.	7./JG 53	CM	Crashed at Wissant following combat with British fighters south-east of London.	Messerschmitt Bf 109 E-1 (6064)	100 %	Pilot unhurt.
40.	9./JG 53	CM	Shot down by unknown British fighters south-east of London.	Messerschmitt Bf 109 E-1 (6252)	100 %	Fw. Oxenkühn missing.
41.	I./JG 54	CM	Shot down by cannon-armed Hurricane flown by Rabagliati near Southend at A.15.30 hrs.	Messerschmitt Bf 109 E-4 (1096)	100 %	Uffz. Hotzelmann missing.
42.	II./JG 54	CM	Shot down by 46 Sqn. Hurricane of Carpenter in Southend area at 15.22 hrs.	Messerschmitt Bf 109 E-4 (1098)	100 %	Pilot, unhurt, made P.O.W.
43.	II./JG 54	CM	Shot down by 41 Sqn. Spitfire of Ryder over Thames Estuary at A.10.00 hrs.	Messerschmitt Bf 109 E-4 (5353)	100 %	Uffz. Behse killed.
44.	II./JG 54	CM	Shot down by 41 Sqn. Spitfire of Boyle over Thames Estuary at A.10.00 hrs.	Messerschmitt Bf 109 E-4 (5291)	100 %	Hptm. Ultsch killed.
45.	3./406	CM	Crashed on return to Calais after combat with 235 Sqn. Blenheim of Westlake, Wordsworth and Sutton off Norfolk coast.	Dornier Do 18 (0874 : K6+KL)	Over 60 %	Oblt. Dietrich + one wounded.

Friday 6th September

Further rearrangement of the defences had taken place on 5th September with the eventual arrival of No. 504 Squadron at Hendon after five days in transit from Castletown via Catterick. No. 85 Squadron, temporarily moved to Castle Camps, was now ordered to Church Fenton, reluctantly assuming the category of Class C Squadron (see below) for training purposes. It had been in the thick of the battle for almost four months and had by this time claimed 141 enemy aircraft destroyed and a further 64 damaged. In the same period the Squadron had lost eighteen pilots killed. Its pilots had already won two D.S.O.s, ten D.F.C.s, two D.F.M.s, a Bar to the D.F.C., and a Bar to the D.F.M.; the Squadron's engineering officer, Fg. Off. Stephen Newton, had been awarded the M.B.E.

With no hint of the massive change of fortune that would occur on the following day, the raids over South-East England on this Friday waxed as furious as ever, as Kesselring reverted to phased attacks. The appearance of reconnaissance aircraft suggested a return to previous targets, and Park appealed to the ever-willing Brand for fighters to cover his Weybridge factory. No. 609 Squadron's Spitfires performed this duty throughout the day, but were absent refuelling when a small raid penetrated to Brooklands and at last succeeded in hitting the Hawker works; the damage was very slight and production was unaffected.

The oil tanks at Thameshaven, still blazing from the previous day's raid, attracted a heavy formation which escaped detection by the patrolling fighters by approaching at 12,000 feet through the huge smoke haze from the fires raging below. Part of the formation consisted of a *Staffel* of Ju 87s, which was only seen and attacked by a lone Hurricane flown by Wg. Cdr. Victor Beamish; he had taken off by himself from North Weald, and claimed two probably shot down.

No. 303 (Polish) Squadron, which had recently displayed such high courage and determination in its efforts to smash enemy attacks, was this day to meet its match. Led by the three famous "Ks"—Kellett, Krasnodebski and Kent[13]—nine Hurricanes were ordered off at 08.40 hours to engage an enemy formation over Kent. Unfortunately they were too late to gain height before sighting the Heinkels and Dorniers, and as they struggled to climb at no more than 140 m.p.h., they were attacked by Bf 109s. Krasnodebski was hit before he could go into action and baled out of his blazing aircraft with terrible burns. Kellett managed to attack a Do 17Z before he was wounded, and force landed at Biggin Hill. Sergeant Stanislaw Karubin destroyed a Heinkel and was in turn shot down by a Bf 109. Altogether the squadron lost five Hurricanes, as well as both squadron commanders wounded. An interesting phenomenon which was reported several times by this squadron probably stemmed from German radio monitors learning to identify the call-sign of No. 303 Squadron—

[13] Sqn. Ldr. Ronald Kellett shared command of the Squadron with Sqn. Ldr. Zdislav Krasnodebski. Flt. Lt. John Kent, the Canadian who was to become one of the great figures of the Battle, and later commanded the Polish Wing, was a flight commander at this time.

Although held shortly before the Battle of Britain (27th June 1940) a field investiture ceremony at Hornchurch was attended by—*left to right*— Plt. Off. J.L. Allen, Flt. Lt. R.S. Stanford Tuck, Flt. Lt. A.C. Deere, Flt. Lt. A.G. Malan and Sqn. Ldr. J.A. Leathart, seen here cheering H.M. King George VI after receiving their decorations. Allen was to be killed on 24th July, but the other pilots were to survive the War.

"Apany"—from the accents of the Polish pilots on the R/T. There were instances when a voice broke in on their headphones ordering "all Apany aircraft to pancake"—that is, to return to base. On return they found that no controller had passed any such order.

It was losses such as those suffered by No. 303 Squadron which finally defeated the objections to Dowding's plan to classify exhausted squadrons as training units. His plan was now carried into effect; it was to classify the squadrons as follows:

Class A All squadrons which were based in No. 11 Group, and those in Nos. 10 and 12 Groups which might be called on by Park to provide first line reinforcement.

Class B Squadrons of all Groups (other than No. 11 Group) which were fully established in men and machines, which the Southern Groups could call into action with consideration of fatigue and lack of combat experience.

Class C All remaining squadrons which, although possessing combat experience, had suffered crippling losses in action and were clearly overdue for rest and training of new pilots.

Experienced survivors would be "milked" from these squadrons after a short respite to provide replacements for those in Classes A and B.

Misfortunes in battle tend to foster strong, even belligerent ties of comradeship within units of any armed service; and it is entirely understandable that Squadrons such as Nos. 85, 145, 151 and 615, which had achieved so much together and had together paid such a heavy price, should object to wholesale dispersal of their most respected colleagues. But at such a critical stage in the Battle, even this risk of lowering morale had to be faced. The truth lay not in any remote Command disdain for the personal feelings of the pilots, but in Dowding's realisation that the introduction of whole new squadrons to Park's battle area was no answer; hard-won experience now counted for so much in the cauldron of No. 11 Group that a fresh unit, composed of inexperienced pilots, was in very great danger of incurring catastrophic losses before it could make a worthwhile contribution. He had to try to strengthen his best squadrons by feeding them experienced and refreshed veterans. If they could only hang on, they might just win through. . . .

R.A.F. FIGHTER COMMAND LOSSES—FRIDAY 6th SEPTEMBER 1940

No.	Squadron	Class	Description	Time	Pilot	Aircraft	Serial	Category
1.	72 Sqn., Croydon	C	Shot down in head-on attack on a Bf 109 over Maidstone; pilot baled out unhurt.	A13.00 hrs.	Plt. Off. R.D. Elliott	Spitfire	N3070	Cat. 3 Destroyed
2.	72 Sqn., Croydon	C	Damaged by Bf 109s near Maidstone; pilot unhurt.	A13.00 hrs.	Not known	Spitfire	—	Cat. 1 Damaged
3.	73 Sqn., Debden	C	Shot down by Bf 109s over Thames Estuary; pilot baled out with burns and admitted to Twickenhurst Hospital.	09.15 hrs.	Plt. Off. H.W. Eliot	Hurricane	P2875	Cat. 3 Destroyed
4.	111 Sqn., Croydon	C	Windscreen shattered by fire from Ju 88 near Kenley; pilot returned unhurt.	09.05 hrs.	Fg. Off. B.H. Bowring	Hurricane	—	Cat. 1 Damaged
5.	111 Sqn., Croydon	C	Shot down by Ju 88s near Kenley; pilot baled out wounded.	09.08 hrs.	Sgt. L.J. Tweed	Hurricane	L1892	Cat. 3 Destroyed
6.	111 Sqn., Croydon	C	Shot down by Bf 109s near Dartford; pilot wounded in the arm.	18.10 hrs.	Fg. Off. B.H. Bowring	Hurricane	—	Cat. 3 Destroyed
7.	234 Sqn., Middle Wallop	C	Shot down by Bf 109 over Sussex and crashed near Hadlow Down; pilot unhurt.	Afternoon	Not known	Spitfire	X4035	Cat. 3 Destroyed
8.	234 Sqn., Middle Wallop	C	Shot down by enemy fighters over Weymouth; pilot baled out unhurt.	Afternoon	Not known	Spitfire	N3061	Cat. 3 Lost
9.	234 Sqn., Middle Wallop	C	Shot down by Bf 109 near Northiam, Sussex; pilot believed unhurt.	Afternoon	Not known	Spitfire	X4183	Cat. 3 Destroyed
10.	249 Sqn., North Weald	C	Shot down by Bf 109s near Maidstone; pilot baled out slightly wounded.	09.25 hrs.	Sqn. Ldr. J. Grandy	Hurricane	R4229	Cat. 3 Destroyed
11.	253 Sqn., Kenley	C	Pilot suffered engine trouble during patrol; he baled out but was killed.	A09.00 hrs.	Flt. Lt. W.P. Cambridge	Hurricane	P3032	Cat. 3 Destroyed
12.	303 Sqn., Northolt	C	Engine caught fire during patrol; pilot landed safely at base.	A13.30 hrs.	Flt. Lt. J.A. Kent	Hurricane	R2685	Cat. 2 Damaged
13.	303 Sqn., Northolt	C	Shot down by Do 17 and force landed at Biggin Hill; pilot slightly wounded.	09.15 hrs.	Sqn. Ldr. R.G. Kellett	Hurricane	—	Cat. 3 Destroyed
14.	303 Sqn., Northolt	C	Damaged on combat with Bf 109s and crashed on landing at base; pilot slightly hurt.	09.35 hrs.	Flt. Lt. A.S. Forbes	Hurricane	—	Cat. 3 Destroyed
15.	303 Sqn., Northolt	C	Damaged in combat with Bf 109; pilot unhurt.	09.30 hrs.	Sgt. J. Frantisek	Hurricane	—	Cat. 1 Damaged
16.	303 Sqn., Northolt	C	Shot down by Bf 109 over Farnborough, Kent; pilot baled out with grievous burns.	09.20 hrs.	Sqn. Ldr. Z. Krasnodebski	Hurricane	P3974	Cat. 3 Destroyed
17.	303 Sqn., Northolt	C	Shot down by He 111 and force landed at Pembury, Kent. Pilot suffered severe bullet wound in thigh.	09.20 hrs.	Sgt. S. Karubin	Hurricane	—	Cat. 3 Destroyed
18.	303 Sqn., (with 1 (Canadian) Sqn.)	C	Shot down by Bf 109 at Lenham, Kent; pilot unhurt.	Not known	Fg. Off. W. Januszewicz	Hurricane	—	Cat. 3 Destroyed
19.	501 Sqn., Gravesend	C	Shot down by Bf 109 near Elham, Kent; pilot killed. (Pilot was Commissioned on this day).	09.10 hrs.	Sgt. H.C. Adams	Hurricane	V6612	Cat. 3 Destroyed
20.	501 Sqn., Gravesend	C	Shot down near Maidstone; pilot killed. Aircrashed at Charing.	09.12 hrs.	Sgt. O.V. Houghton	Hurricane	V6646	Cat. 3 Destroyed
21.	501 Sqn., Gravesend	C	Shot down near Ashford; pilot killed; aircraft fell at Hothfield.	09.15 hrs.	Sgt. G.W. Pearson.	Hurricane	P3516	Cat. 3 Destroyed
22.	601 Sqn., Tangmere	C	Shot down by Bf 109s over Mayfield, Kent; pilot baled out wounded.	09.30 hrs.	Plt. Off. H.T. Gilbert	Hurricane	V6647	Cat. 3 Destroyed
23.	601 Sqn., Tangmere	C	Shot down by Bf 109s over Mayfield, Kent; pilot baled out wounded.	09.30 hrs.	Fg. Off. J. Topolnicki	Hurricane	P3382	Cat. 3 Destroyed
24.	601 Sqn., Tangmere	C	Shot down by Bf 109s and crashed at Brenchley, near Tunbridge Wells, Kent; pilot died in the aircraft.	09.35 hrs.	Fg. Off. C.R. Davis	Hurricane	P3363	Cat. 3 Destroyed

R.A.F. Losses, 6th September 1940—*continued*

25.	601 Sqn., Tangmere	C	Shot down in flames near Tunbridge Wells, Kent. Pilot killed; aircraft crashed at High Brooms Viaduct, Southborough.	09.35 hrs.	Fg. Off. W.H. Rhodes-Moorhouse	Hurricane	*P8818*	Cat. 3 Destroyed
26.	602 Sqn., Westhampnett	C	Shot down by Bf 109s over Hailsham; pilot baled out slightly wounded in the legs.	13.28 hrs.	Plt. Off. T.G.F. Ritchie	Spitfire	*R6834*	Cat. 3 Destroyed
27.	602 Sqn., Westhampnett	C	Shot down by Bf 109s over Hailsham; pilot baled out unhurt; aircraft crashed at Peasmarsh, East Sussex.	13.25 hrs.	Sgt. G.A. Whipps	Spitfire	*N3227*	Cat. 3 Destroyed
28.	602 Sqn., Westhampnett	C	Shot down by Bf 109s near Hailsham; pilot baled out unhurt.	13.26 hrs.	Not known	Spitfire	—	Cat. 3 Destroyed
29.	603 Sqn., Hornchurch	C	Shot down by Bf 109s of JG 54 in combat off Manston; pilot landed in France and taken prisoner.	13.45 hrs.	Plt. Off.J.R. Caister	Spitfire	*X4260*	Cat. 3 Missing

LUFTWAFFE LOSSES—FRIDAY 6th SEPTEMBER 1940

1.	4.(F)/121	CM	Landing accident at Caen airfield; not combat.	Junkers Ju 88A-1 (2127)	5 %	Crew unhurt.
2.	4./KG 4	NCM	Crashed near Stettin following instrument failure.	Heinkel He 111P-2 (1543 : 5J+SM)	100 %	One crew member killed.
3.	6./KG 4	CM	Aircraft lost in grid square 8271; probably crashed with *flak* damage.	Heinkel He 111P (3065 : 5J+JP)	100 %	Oblt. Schröder, Uffz. Reitz and Ogefr. Marten killed; Gefr. Wick missing.
4.	2./KG 26	CM	Shot down by 303 Sqn. Hurricane of Karubin in London area.	Heinkel He 111H-3 (6902 : 1h+HK)	100 %	One killed;Uffz. Fass, Fw. Jessen, and Gefr. Haslache missing.
5.	II./KG 26	CM	Target, Newcastle-on-Tyne; damaged by Tyneside A.A. defences at night.	Heinkel He 111H-3 (5682 : 1h+NK)	38 %	Crew unhurt.
6.	4./KG 26	CM	Target, Newcastle-on-Tyne; damaged by Tyneside A.A. defences and crashed at Gilze-Rijen.	Heinkel He 111H-3 (6966 : 1H+FH)	80 %	Crew unhurt.
7.	4./KG 26	CM	Target, Derby; shot down by *flak* over Midlands and crashed in Lincolnshire.	Heinkel He 111H-5 (3516 : 1H+EM)	100 %	Uffz. Stut, Ogefr. Hubrig, Gefr. Schneider killed; Oblt. Kuckeld and Gefr. Kisling missing.
8.	4./KG 26	CM	Target, Newcastle-on-Tyne; damaged by Tyneside *flak* and crashed at Schipol.	Heinkel He 111H-4 (3294 : 1H+BM)	100 %	Oblt. Bischoff and Uffz. Kohlhopp killed.
9.	4./KG 26	CM	Target, Newcastle-on-Tyne; damaged by Tyneside flak and crashed near Koppern.	Heinkel He 111H-4 (5704 : 1H+FM)	100 %	One killed and one wounded.
10.	6./KG 26	CM	Target, Newcastle-on-Tyne; shot down by Tyneside *flak* and crashed, killing whole crew.	Heinkel He 111H-3 (3258 : 1H+HP)	100 %	Uffz. Bartels, Ofw. Staffeldt, Fw. Markuse, Gefr. Meier and Uffz. Schweizer killed.
11.	9./KG 26	NCM	Crashed at Schwerin-Neumühle; cause unknown. Killed a woman and a child, and injured a child.	Heinkel He 111H-3 (7173 : 1H+LT)	100 %	Three crew members killed.
12.	III./KG 27	NCM	Crashed at Rennes airfield; cause not known.	Heinkel He 111P (1380 : 1K+LR)	40 %	Crew unhurt.
13.	I./KG 30	NCM	Crashed at Sorau airfield; cause not known.	Junkers Ju 88A-1 (4D+NF)	75 %	Crew unhurt.
14.	II./KG 55	CM	Shot down by *flak* at night over Britain; location of crash not known.	Heinkel He 111P-2 (1532)	100 %	One crew member killed; four others made P.O.W.
15.	6./KG 76	CM	Damaged by 41 Sqn. Spitfire of Lock at 09.25 hrs., and crashed at Evére on return.	Junkers Ju 88A-1 (8078 : F1+DP)	Under 60 %	Crew unhurt.
16.	6./KG 76	CM	Shot down by 111Sqn. Hurricane of Bowering near Kenley at 09.01 hrs.	Junkers Ju 88A-1 (8104 : F1+HP)	100 %	Ltn. Kernbach, Fw. Schumacher, Uffz. Agel and Gefr. Reisel missing.
17.	6./KG 76	CM	Target reported as "Littlestone". Believed shot down by fighters and *flak* but units not traced.	Junkers Ju 88A-1 (3176 : F1+LP)	100 %	Uffz. Haenel, Ogefr. Kohn killed. Oblt.Wagner, Uffz.Geyer missing.
18.	III./KG 77	NCM	Landing accident at Cambrai; cause not known.	Junkers Ju 88A-1 (3159 : 3Z+AD)	6 %	Crew unhurt.
19.	2./St.G 77	NCM	Landing accident at Maltot; cause not known.	Junkers Ju 87B (5097 : S2+LK)	15 %	Crew unhurt.
20.	8./St.G 77	NCM	Force landed at Argentan after engine failure.	Junkers Ju 87B (5638 : F1+CN)	50 %	Crew unhurt.
21.	1./KGr. 806	CM	Crashed on Nantes airfield after combat sortie.	Junkers Ju 88A-1 (6043 : M7+BH)	40 %	Crew unhurt.
22.	Stab/ZG 26	CM	Target, Hawker factory at Brooklands; shot down by 1 Sqn. Hurricane of Dibnah near Kenley at 09.01 hrs.	Messerschmitt Bf 110 C-4 (2145 : 3U+CA)	100 %	Uffz. Roth killed; Oblt. Virtel missing.
23.	I./ZG 26	CM	Target, Hawker factory at Brooklands; shot down by 1 Sqn. Hurricane of Goodman west of Kenley at 09.24 hrs.	Messerschmitt Bf 110 C-4 (2146 : U8+CL)	100 %	Uffz. Kiehn killed; Uffz. Neuss missing.
24.	7./ZG 26	CM	Target, Hawker factory at Brooklands; possibly shot down by flak in the Epsom area.	Messerschmitt Bf 110 D-0 (3405 : 3U+HR)	100 %	Gefr. Schumann killed; Fw. Kaufmann missing.
25.	1./Erpr.Gr. 210	CM	Target, Redhill. Shot down by three Hurricanes and crashed south of Oxted at 09.15 hrs.	Messerschmitt Bf 110 D-0 (3373 : S9+BH)	100 %	Uffz. Gerhard Rüger killed; Gefr. Edmund Ernst, wounded, P.O.W. Fw. Werner Gottschalk missing.
26.	II./LG 2	CM	Shot down by fighters in Canterbury area, but landed intact at Hawkinge at 18.14 hrs.	Messerschmitt Bf 109 E-7 (5567)	100 %	
27.	II./LG 2	CM	Shot down by fighters into the sea off Herne Bay.	Messerschmitt Bf 109 E-7 (3736)	100 %	Ltn. Dürtgen missing.
28.	1./JG 2	CM	Shot down by 222 Sqn. Spitfire of Hutchinson over Thames Estuary at A.18.00 hrs.	Messerschmitt Bf 109 E-4 (5044)	100 %	Ltn. Schimmelheller missing.
29.	II./JG 26	CM	Shot down by 501 Sqn. Hurricanes near Ashford at 09.05 hrs.	Messerschmitt Bf 109 E-4 (5385)	100 %	Ltn. Krug, *St.Kap.*, missing.
30.	II./JG 26	CM	Shot down by 501 Sqn. Hurricanes near Ashford at 09.05 hrs.	Messerschmitt Bf 109 E-4 (0735)	100 %	Uffz. Braun missing.
31.	7./JG 26	CM	Shot down by fighters in the Kenley area at A.09.30 hrs.	Messerschmitt Bf 109 E-4 (2781)	100 %	Ltn. Christinecke missing.
32.	7./JG 26	CM	Shot down by fighters in the Kenley area at A.09.30 hrs.	Messerschmitt Bf 109 E-1 (3877)	100 %	Gefr. Holzapfel missing.
33.	7./JG 26	CM	Shot down by 73 Sqn. Hurricane of Marchand near Kenley at A.09.20 hrs.	Messerschmitt Bf 109 E-1(3578)	100 %	Gefr. Bickir killed.
34.	9./JG 26	CM	Damaged by 73 Sqn. Hurricane near Maidstone at 09.20 hrs., and crashed at Pihen.	Messerschmitt Bf 109E (6033)	30 %	Pilot wounded.
35.	I./JG 27	CM	Damaged by 303 Sqn. Hurricane of Feric over NW Kent at 09.15 hrs., and crashed at Guines.	Messerschmitt Bf 109 E-4 (5296)	25 %	Pilot unhurt.
36.	1./JG27	CM	Shot down east of Tilbury docks by unknown British fighters.	Messerschmitt Bf 109E (6318)	100 %	Gefr. Ernst Nittmann made P.O.W.

Luftwaffe Losses, 6th September—*continued*

37. 3./JG 27	CM	Shot down by 303 Sqn. Hurricane of Feric over Thames Estuary at 09.13 hrs.	Messerschmitt Bf 109 E-1 (3225)	100 %	Oblt. Werner Schüller made P.O.W. and later exchanged.
38. 3./JG 27	CM	Crashed on landing at Guines after combat.	Messerschmitt Bf 109 E-1 (3180)	100 %	Fhr. Otto Kargl wounded.
39. 5./JG 27	CM	Shot down by 43 Sqn. Hurricanes off Dungeness at 09.24 hrs.	Messerschmitt Bf 109 E-4 (2762)	100 %	Fw. Erich Braun made P.O.W.
40. 5./JG 27	CM	Shot down by 43 Sqn. Hurricanes off Dungeness at A.09.25 hrs.	Messerschmitt Bf 109 E-1 (3894)	100 %	Ltn. Heinz Halbach , wounded, made P.O.W.
41. Stab III./JG 27	CM	Suffered landing accident at Guines after combat.	Messerschmitt Bf 109 E-4 (1577)	25 %	Pilot unhurt.
42. III./JG 27	CM	Suffered landing accident at Cherbourg-West after combat.	Messerschmitt Bf 109 E-4 (0929)	30 %	Pilot unhurt.
43. III./JG 27	CM	Shot down by 303 Sqn. Hurricane of Urbanowicz over Kent at 09.12 hrs.	Messerschmitt Bf 109E (1380)	100 %	Hptm. Schlichting, *Gr.Kdr.*, made P.O.W.
44. 3./JG 52	CM	Shot down by 72 Sqn. Spitfires in the Maidstone area at A.13.00 hrs.	Messerschmitt Bf 109 E-4 (1138)	100 %	Oblt. Waller missing.
45. III./JG 52	CM	Landing accident at Coquelles; cause not known.	Messerschmitt Bf 109 E-4 (5064)	100 %	Pilot unhurt.
46. I./JG 53	CM	Shot down by 602 Sqn. Spitfires north of Hastings at 13.25 hrs.	Messerschmitt Bf 109 E-4 (5347)	100 %	Pilot, wounded, made P.O.W.
47. 3./JG 53	CM	Shot down by unknown British fighters in the Tilbury dock area.	Messerschmitt Bf 109 E-4 (1216)	100 %	Oblt. Riegel missing.
48. II./JG 53	CM	Damaged by unknown British fighters over Kent.	Messerschmitt Bf 109 E-4 (3571)	35 %	Oblt. Schulz-Blank wounded.
49. II./JG 53	NCM	Suffered landing accident at Senty airfield.	Focke-Wulf Fw 58 (3579)	30 %	No casualties.
50. 7./JG 53	CM	Shot down by unknown British fighters in the Tilbury dock area.	Messerschmitt Bf 109 E-4 (1506)	100 %	Uffz. Scchulte missing.
51. 8./JG 53	CM	Shot down by unknown British fighters in the Tilbury dock area.	Messerschmitt Bf 109 E-4 (1129)	100 %	Fw. Hempel killed.
52. *Korps-Führungskette* VIII.	NCM	Crashed at Toutoinoille; cause not notified.	Messerschmitt Bf 109 E-5 (3889 : GA+GH)	100 %	Oblt. Tettenborn killed.
53. 1./106	CM	Crashed on take-off at Norderney seaplane base. (Probably flying a mining sortie).	Heinkel He 115 (2730 : M2+EH)	100 %	Two crew members injured.

The Spitfire, *R6800*, of Squadron Leader R.H.A. Leigh, commanding No. 66 Squadron, with a Hurricane of No. 501 (County of Gloucester) Squadron at Gravesend. This airfield lay directly in the path of the huge German bomber formations which made for London in the late afternoon of Saturday 7th September. Note the groundcrewmen wearing steel helmets.

Saturday 7th September

Though not accorded a grandiloquent codename, the German operations of 7th September, both in their nature and their motivation, were as decisive as any ever launched by the *Luftwaffe* in the Second World War. Göring's personal command of these operations moreover implied that the *Reichsmarshall* had been goaded into personal action by his frustration at the lack of identifiable progress in the annihilation of R.A.F. Fighter Command. The arrival of the porcine warlord in the Pas de Calais, complete with his retinue of personal Staff Officers and his Ruritanian uniforms and impedimenta, was accomplished by all the pomp and flamboyance of a State Visit. The feelings of the grimy and exhausted squadron officers may readily be imagined.

The concentrations of invasion barges which had been assembling at an increasing rate along the Channel Coast implied to British Intelligence authorities that the landing assault could not be far off; indeed the Air Ministry issued to Commands its Invasion Alert No. 1 ("Attack Imminent"[14]) while Blenheims, Hampdens, Whitleys, Wellingtons and Battles of Bomber Command kept up their pressure against the invasion fleet. Coastal Command and the Fleet Air Arm also carried out numerous sorties. Bearing in mind the heavy

---

[14] The classification of invasion warnings was as follows: Alert 3, "Invasion probable within three days"; Alert 2, ". . . .within two days"; and Alert 1, "Imminent".

Condensation trails from Göring's fighters point the way to London in the late afternoon of 7th September. (Photo: Radio Times Hulton Picture Library)

concentration of fighters—present on the coast for other purposes—it was to be expected that casualties among these bombers were appalling; preoccupation with the immediate battle did not permit Fighter Command to provide more than token escorts.

Oblivious to the day's historic portents, Park must have realised that his difficulty lay not so much in the correct recognition of the enemy's tactics as in the successful interpretation of orders given to counter them. One suspects that by this stage he had come to regard the doctrinaire insistence of his northern colleague on the Wing formation as beyond his influence; he could, after all, do little to interfere with the method of application of another Group's forces. He was, however, more than a little aggravated by controllers and squadron commanders who seemed to modify combat instructions summarily to suit what they believed to be tactically necessary. For example, in the past, owing to frequent inaccuracy of height estimation by radar and Observer Corps of enemy raids, fighters had been ordered to too low an altitude and had in consequence been "bounced" from above by Messerschmitt Bf 109s. Following the age-old fighter dictum, "to have height is to have the upper hand", controllers and formation leaders (and many have admitted their "guilt") now adopted the practice of taking the fighters that much higher than the specified altitude so as to meet the enemy on more even terms. The result had been two-fold; the enemy was penetrating further due to the longer climbing time before interception, and on an increasing number of occasions the bombers, which seldom flew above 18,000 feet anyway, were getting through altogether while the opposing fighters were engaged in dogfights far overhead. As already stated, this was the form of battle which Dowding's fighters *had* to avoid if they were to survive. With his accustomed asperity Park instructed his subordinates to follow orders from Group operations without anticipatory modifications,

leaving formation leaders free to decide their course of action in the light of *observed* tactical conditions. That this timely rebuke went home is clearly demonstrated by the mounting destruction of enemy bombers henceforward.

Daylight operations by the *Luftwaffe* opened quietly enough on 7th September, with the customary early reconnaissance sorties over the previous night's targets. A Dornier Do 215 of Aufkl.Gr. 123, which had been engaged in noting raid damage at Liverpool, was intercepted by Spitfires of No. 266 Squadron shortly before 09.00 hours on its return flight over East Anglia and chased by Plt. Off. Wycliffe Williams, Plt. Off. Robert Roach and the New Zealander, Plt. Off. Richard Trousdale all the way to Walcheren island, where it was shot down in flames.[15]

There then followed an enigmatic lull for six hours—no less puzzling than welcome to Fighter Command in view of the continuing fine, warm weather. The radar screens remained empty of enemy plots, and the sector controllers relaxed their

---

[15] This was the first recorded combat by Spitfire Mark IIs—the Squadron had been re-equipped during the previous two days. It is worth mentioning here that up to the beginning of September the R.A.F. pilots had been instructed that while both Dornier Do 17s and Do 215s were in service with the *Luftwaffe*, it was assumed that the four-year old "flying pencil"—the pre-War nickname for early variants of the Do 17—had almost disappeared from service; not until late August, when British Intelligence had collated the mass of information derived from crashed enemy aircraft, did the R.A.F. fully realise that in fact the Do 17 was still the most numerous of *Luftwaffe* bombers; and it had yet to become evident that as yet the Do 215 was used solely by reconnaissance *Gruppen*. The fighter squadrons were accordingly informed that claims for destroying "Do 215s" should henceforth be for "Do 17s". Paradoxically the three No. 266 Squadron pilots claimed that their victim *was* a Do 17, whereas it was in fact one of the relatively small number of Do 215s serving with the *Aufklärungsgruppen*.

fighter states. To many, with the ominous invasion warning uppermost in their minds, those six hours of sinister quiet must have been unnerving in the extreme. No hint yet came as to what form the storm would take, yet few can have doubted that a storm was coming. The atmosphere on that sunny Saturday afternoon all over Southern England was charged with foreboding.

It was at 15.54 hours that the first track plotter at Bentley Priory reached forward to place an initial raid counter on the table map. Showing a strength of twenty-plus over the Pas de Calais, it was quickly followed by others of growing size, until it must have become appallingly clear to Dowding that this was the largest raid he had yet faced. As the full situation was flashed to Group and Sector controllers, fighters of all three southern Groups were frantically brought to state.

The first coastal Observer Corps report of the enemy formation reached the Maidstone centre at 16.16 hours, and told of "many hundreds" of aircraft approaching the coast between Deal and the North Foreland. Half an hour previously Hermann Göring, a bloated figure ridiculously bedecked in pale blue and gold, had stood on the cliffs near Calais and, posed no doubt with an eye on the fawning photographers, watched wave upon wave of his bombers and fighters set course for England—their target, London. Göring had exercised his stated privilege of taking command of the air assault on Britain's ancient capital, and had launched 348 bombers and 617 fighters in the greatest aerial armada yet seen. Almost the entire strength of five *Kampfgeschwader*—1, 2, 3, 26 and 76—was accompanied by the *Zerstörer* of ZG

2 and the Bf 109s of I. and II./LG 2, JG 2 «*Richthofen*», JG 3 «*Udet*», JG 51, JG 52, JG 54 «*Grünherz*» and I./JG 77. . . nearly one thousand aircraft massed in a single huge phalanx stepped from 14,000 to 23,000 feet, advancing inexorably on a twenty-mile front towards the Thames Estuary.

At 16.17 hours Park ordered eleven squadrons into the air, and six minutes later brought all remaining Spitfires and Hurricanes to Readiness; by 16.30 hours all 21 squadrons based within 70 miles of London were in the air or under take-off orders.

At this moment the first British pilots were experiencing a sight which would haunt the survivors for the rest of their lives. Breaking out of a layer of haze east of Sheppey, they found themselves on the edge of a tidal wave of aircraft, towering above them rank upon rank, more than a mile and a half high and covering 800 square miles, blotting out the sky like some vast irresistible migration. Together the first four squadrons of fighters hurled themselves at the southern flank of Göring's juggernaut, and the awesome mass of aircraft shuddered under the impact.

To Dowding and Park the approach of so mighty a force could indicate but one target—London. No worries now for the safety of their airfields; squadrons and flights patiently on guard over Guildford, Biggin Hill, Croydon and North Weald were urgently ordered to Thameshaven and Tilbury. As the fighters strove to break through the massive escort, bombers faltered and broke away with blazing engines, twisting streaks of pale tracer patterned the air, condensation trails from the fighters high above wheeled and curved, parachutes drifted

The awesome spectacle of London's docks ablaze, 7th September 1940.

German target briefing photograph used for the raids on the London docks, which started in earnest on 7th September. This reconnaissance photograph, taken during the first nine months of the War, clearly shows about 20 large merchant vessels in the dock area, countless smaller ships in the Thames itself, the Beckton gasworks (in the top right-hand corner), the tanker terminal in Silvertown and the gun and balloon defences in Woolwich.

down towards the green world below, and columns of smoke roiled darkly up to meet them from the first funeral pyres.

The people of London now began their months-long ordeal; to them was to fall the doubtful privilege of the first capital city of the Western world to survive the horrors of all-out air attack undefeated. Since half-past four there had been the sound of guns; this was nothing new. But as the man-made thunder grew closer and louder, and the black curtains spread and thickened in the east, they looked up and saw the sky filling with tiny silhouettes sharp and clear against the blanket of contrails spun by the scores of circling fighters. The whine and crash of bombs, the constant rattle of gunfire, the murderous rain of shrapnel—all the special terrors for a close-packed city under air attack—now London's East End faced the reality of them at last. The bombs thundered down upon the docks at Rotherhithe, on Limehouse and Millwall, on Woolwich Arsenal, on the Surrey Docks and those hard by Tower Bridge. The vast gasworks at Beckton and the West Ham Power Station shook and erupted under the storm of explosive. In a wave of fire and ruin Kesselring's bombers swept across the city, reaching Westminster and Kensington;

but it was the vital docks that felt the full-weight of Göring's frustration and fury that afternoon, and it was in the crushed streets of poor dockland terraces that the deafened, scorched, bewildered men and women now saw the sun's glare wane to a blood-red glow under the huge black shroud that spread across the evening sky.

It is tempting to wonder at the thoughts of an elderly, partially crippled German civilian named Ernst Brandenburg as he listened to the strident claims of that evening's new bulletin, somewhere in Germany. It is impossible that he did not see in his mind's eye the sunlit map of London laid out before him; but though the target remained much as it had been twenty-three years before, it is unlikely that the old veteran could have imagined the fury of the transformed defences. Where he had known empty skies, twenty squadrons of Hurricanes and Spitfires now ripped into the stately formations of bombers.

High above the burning city the Bf 109s weaved and circled, striving to keep the British fighters away from their charges—and with considerable success. The *Zerstörer* had broken away to the south and had formed a circle over

Croydon, evidently waiting to cover the bombers' with-drawal; they were attacked by nine Hurricanes of John Thompson's No. 111 Squadron which in the confusion of scramble orders found themselves too low to intercept the main raid. No. 41 Squadron's Spitfires hit the northern flank of bombers but were pinned down by 109s and lost three aircraft. On Brian Lane's No. 19 Squadron about eight pilots went for one Bf 110 and "had fun shooting it to pieces". Rabagliati again took his four-cannon Hurricane into combat but could do no more than damage a Do 17. No. 249 Squadron struck the southern flank of bombers over North-East London but were quickly hemmed in on all sides by about sixty Bf 109s; Plt. Off. Robert Fleming was killed, Sgt. Fred Killing-back baled out wounded, Sgt. Richard Smithson crashed wounded at Eastchurch, and Fg. Off. Patrick Wells was shot down, also wounded; Barclay and Beard baled out unhurt, the latter's Hurricane hit by *flak*. Six aircraft lost, one pilot killed and three wounded, in a single combat, without scoring. . .

Flt. Lt. James McArthur led the Spitfires of No. 609 Squadron all the way from Middle Wallop at full speed to catch the enemy bombers as they turned south-west of Lon-don, claiming the destruction of three Bf 110s, two Do 17s and one Bf 109 without loss. From Tangmere came nine Hur-ricanes of No. 43 Squadron led by Caesar Hull, which ran into 109s over North Kent and Sheppey; the fight cost them the lives of their popular South African leader and of Dick Reynell, the Hawker test pilot.

The Duxford Wing once more wasted time trying to join up and, in frustration, the component squadrons eventually made their way independently towards the Isle of Sheppey, arriving as a loose mass of aircraft with Spitfires about 3,000 feet above the Hurricanes of No. 242 and 310 (Czech) Squadron. Without warning an entire *Jagdgeschwader* of 109s dived through the Wing shooting down three aircraft immediately and damaging others. In a running fight two more Hurricanes were shot down; Plt. Off. Denis Crowley-Milling of No. 242 Squadron survived a crash landing near Chelmsford with slight injuries, but his Canadian colleague, Plt. Off. John Benzie, was killed. The Czech pilot, Sgt. Josef Koukal of No. 310 Squadron, was blown out of his burning Hurricane when a wing tank exploded; delaying opening his parachute for fear that his burning clothes would damage the shrouds, he landed dreadfully burned at the eastern end of Sheppey. Not a hundred yards away the Hurricane of Flt. Lt. Hugh Beresford from No. 257 Squadron (which arrived from Martlesham) hurtled into the ground, the pilot almost certainly dead long before impact.[16] It has been deduced that the clash of arms above the Isle of Sheppey involved more than 1,100 British and German aircraft during a period of twenty minutes.

By 17.45 hours the German formations had turned south and east for home, scattered and disordered, but still largely intact. The huge vics had lost their impeccable patterns; here the Dorniers were bunched together, one of their number trailing smoke from a mangled engine and struggling to keep

---

[16] The writer was present when the remains of Koukal's and Beresford's Hurricanes were discovered and identified in August 1972. By great coincidence Josef Koukal returned from Czecho-slovakia to be the guest of honour at the Battle of Britain Pilot's Association annual reunion about a week later when he was presented with a component from his aircraft suitably mounted and inscribed. The following day he visited the farm house close to where his Hurricane had crashed to meet the woman who had been with him before he was rushed off to hospital, and who visited him there. Koukal was later admitted to the serious burns unit at East Grinstead where he occupied the bed next to Tom Gleave. He survived over 70 per cent third-degree burns and 28 major skin grafts, but went back to flying in 1943, and was appointed a State test pilot in his native Czechoslovakia after the War.

View looking east along Cube Street, Shadwell, in East London during the early evening of 7th September.

within the protection of the formation's other guns; there, a *Staffel* of 110s manœuvred into a new pattern to fill a suddenly empty place in the formation. Around them the tireless Bf 109s weaved and shepherded, their pilots constantly twisting in their narrow cockpits on the look-out for new hunting parties of Hurricanes and Spitfires. But there was little need; the British fighters were returning to their fields, low on fuel and with ammunition spent. In ones and twos they landed the pilots silently aghast as they remembered the sight of London obliterated by fire and rolling banks of smoke, and the incredible size of the enemy formations.[17]

In London's dockland firemen fought to control the spread-

[17] Correctly assuming that the attack on London would attract fighters from the South Coast airfields, Kesselring sent *Erprobungsgruppe 210* in a snap raid against Southampton. This was not intercepted, but lost one Bf 109 to the Portsmouth gun defences; the pilot was picked up from the Channel by the German Air/Sea Rescue service.

A Heinkel He 111 over London's Surrey Commercial Docks at the start of the raid on 7th September.

ing flames along the waterfront, as warehouses and granaries collapsed into the river and street. As every firefighting appliance for miles around was sent into the wharves and alleys of the East End: as ambulance drivers sought out the centres of tragedy in well-known streets whose geography had been suddenly and brutally altered; as Heavy Rescue squads struggled to free those trapped under the shambles of bricks, glass and timber—there came from the east the distant rumble of gunfire.[18]

Flying up the Estuary towards the vast pall of smoke which prematurely darkened the western sky were the leading pilots of Göring's second wave of bombers—318 Heinkels and Dorniers of eight *Kampfgruppen* and *Kampfgeschwader 53 «Legion Cóndor»*, their bomb loads composed of a high proportion of incendiaries. from 20.10 hours until 04.30 hours the following morning the *Luftwaffe* streamed in from the east and south, stoking the fires which now raged scarcely

Dorniers over the Docks. The yellow or white wingtip marking was intended to identify a particular *Gruppe*'s position in the bombing formations and to assist stragglers to regain their own formation; the practice of painting these markings came to be employed increasingly by the Germans in the coming weeks.

[18] It was as this moment that a young girl, cycling home from visiting a friend the other side of London, arrived at the end of her street in East London and caught sight of a barrage ballon drifting above the roofs; from it dangled an airman whose parachute shrouds had snagged the gasbag's fins and who was too high to release his harness. She always wondered about the fate and nationality of the man. Numerous enquiries elicited the information that the airman was a Dornier gunner who had baled out high over London and whose parachute became entangled with the balloon. Seeing the predicament of the man stranded on their balloon, the winch crew hurriedly began to wind it down but when it was no more than about 250 feet up the cable parted and the balloon drifted away over London. As it drifted eastwards towards the Estuary, the stranded airman, seeing the open sea ahead decided to release his harness; fortunately at the moment of release he was no more than about 50 feet up and fell in marshy ground on the north shore of the Thames and lived. He was found by some members of the Home Guard who summoned an ambulance. He was found to have suffered more than a dozen bone fractures but made a complete recovery; he was later to shipped to Canada as a prisoner of war.

checked along nine miles of waterfront. Huge areas of flame merged, to daunt the most hardened London fireman; this was the greatest incendiary raid that had even been launched. Eighty per cent of the firemen involved on this night were auxiliaries with no previous experience of anything remotely approaching the ordeal they now faced.

It is the practice among fire services to measure the size of fires by the number of appliances required to control the blaze; and one demanding thirty pumps is generally regarded as a very large fire. By midnight on 7th/8th September London firemen were fighting nine fires rated at over one hundred pumps each; and in Quebec Yard of the Surrey Docks raged the fiercest single fire ever recorded in Britain, arbitrarily rated as a three-hundred-pump conflagration. Vast in area, moving and spreading at frightening speed, uncontrolled and unsurrounded, it was said to have been more than thirty times greater than London's largest recent blaze, that in the Barbican in 1938. As more property was devoured the growing heat dragged a fierce draught of cold air into the base of the fire to feed the storm, and yards-long beams of timber, incandescent before the flames even touched them, rose like straws on the wind to be tossed down in streets hundreds of yards distant, starting fresh fires behind the frantic A.F.S. teams. Thames fireboats, creeping past three hundred yards

away under the lee of the opposite shore, had every square inch of paint blistered off by the blast of superheated air. The wooden blocks which formed the surface of many of the older dockside streets, drenched with fire hoses, dried, smouldered and burst into spontaneous flame again in minutes. This was the bomber's first fire storm.

At Woolwich Arsenal a two-hundred-pump fire was fought among cases of nitroglycerine and live ammuntion; in the docks, rum barrels exploded flinging sheets and tongues of blazing spirit in all directions. Paint and rubber warehouses sent columns of flame hundreds of feet into the sky. . .flour and pepper exploded into flame by their own deadly chemistry. . .huge rats scurried into the open in their scores, driven from their centuries-old hiding places beneath the old city. The surface of the Thames itself was on fire, covered in places by a sheet of blazing, liquid sugar. It was a scene from a Bosch painting brought to reality.

The loss of life was, by the standards of the time, heavy— by far the heaviest yet experienced by any British city in an air attack—306 killed and 1,337 seriously injured in the capital itself, and a further 142 killed in the suburbs. Only a minority of these were victims of direct hits by bombs; most had been killed or mangled by fire, by collapsing walls and roof timbers, or by murderous shards of glass.

The start of the Surrey Docks fire storm as seen from the roof of The Daily Sketch offices. This conflagration attracted more than 300 fire appliances before it was abandoned to burn itself out. (Photo: Topix)

* * * * *

Notwithstanding the evidence baldly presented by the comparative loss tables below, the London raids of 7th September marked the irretrievable turning point of the Battle of Britain.

Hermann Göring had descended on his front-line commanders in his chosen rôle as *deus ex machina*, and had committed the one fateful error that would deprive the *Luftwaffe* of victory in the skies of Britain—a victory for which, let it be said, they had fought as skilfully, cleanly and courageously as any air force in the world. His mistake would start the downhill progress which would, in time, place Germany in the predicament she most feared: war on two fronts. Within reach of the goal for which he had spent German lives for two gruelling months—the pounding of Dowding's fighters into final exhaustion—*the Reichsmarschall had shifted his aim from the military target to the civil and commercial life of Britain.* Thus he lost (and by the unforgiving laws of generalship, deserved to lose) the initiative to dictate the course of battle. Though many months would pass before the *Luftwaffe* abandoned its heavy assaults on Britain, the cessation of concentrated attacks on his airfields gave Dowding the vital respite he so badly needed to fill the depleted ranks of his squadrons, build up his reserves, and send his veterans back into action refreshed at least to that minimum point at which they were no longer a danger to themselves.

The reasons on which Göring based his decision were muddled. From a military point of view, he argued that the time had come to attack the most important target in England—and London was, after all, the administrative and commercial hub of the Empire, as well as Britain's most vital port. His mind was already made up when he puts his views to Sperrle and Kesselring and invited their comments. Sperrle was uneasy, and wished to continue the scourging of the southern airfields. Kesselring, however, supported his chief, and stated his belief that the airfield raids were not of central importance. He considered that even if they were knocked out, the fighter force would simply move back to the fields north of London and continue their fight from there; indeed he could not understand why such a transfer had not been carried out already, unless the holding of the coastal belt was considered to be vital to morale. He also recorded his view that British reserves had by this point been so far depleted that a campaign against London could be carried out without undue risk to the bomber force. The position which Kesselring adopted thus embodies the whole failure of German Intelligence to appreciate the structure and strength of R.A.F. Fighter Command[19]. It must be emphasised, however, that he was preaching to the converted; and this leads to the second reason for Göring's mistake.

For political reasons, it had been judged inadvisable to bomb London during the early stages of the Battle. Isolated damage had been caused, often through navigational error; but the reaction by R.A.F. Bomber Command had been, in the view of the Führer, unreasonably vigorous. By the standards of three years later the R.A.F. raids on Berlin of 25th/26th August and subsequent nights were pin-pricks, but they represented a sturdy defiance which was as aggravating to the Nazi hierarchy as it was heartening to the British public. Göring had stated, with great public bombast, that no enemy 'plane would ever fly over the Reich. In the expressive American phrase, he had been made to "eat crow", and was hot for revenge. Kesselring's support and the wish to draw the "the last fifty Spitfires" into battle protecting a target they could not possibly abandon confirmed Göring in his determination.

It has been said that the issue of personal and national prestige is too simplistic and superficial an argument to be considered seriously in an assessment of events of this gravity; but the unnatural character of the Nazi power structure should not be dismissed lightly. The whole system was founded upon propaganda, the manipulation of opinion and belief, and the fostering of an image of invincibility. Further, the upper echelons of Nazi authority were entirely peopled by ruthless, ambitious, self-seeking men to whom personal power and the prestige of the Führer's favour were the driving factors in life. The preservation of "face" was of almost Oriental importance to Göring and his sinister contemporaries; and in this atmosphere Churchill's warning of the danger of the "new dark age" faced by Europe was more than usually apt. The brief and terrible Nazi age was a denial of everything so painfully attained by European man over the last thousand years; and among its other ludicrous atrocities was this return to the policy-making processes and motivations not just of the Hapsburgs and the Bourbons, but of the Angevins and the Franks.

One other result of the assault on London must be mentioned here, intangible though it was. This first stunning experience of all-out warfare waged on British civil life brought with it an inevitable appreciation of just what the Royal Air Force had been warding off over the past months, and a new feeling of warmth and identification between civilian and serviceman. For every voice which resented the inability of the fighter pilots to turn back the enemy before they reached the cities, there were three which spoke with a new kind of proprietary pride in "the boys up there". This conviction that "We're all in the front line now" was yet another element in a new and vital sense of unity. The "London can take it" spirit, ridiculed by the self-styled academic cynic as a plebeian cliché, was nevertheless a vital reality in 1940; it was a kind of splendid bloodymindedness which led to a tacit and temporary armistice between social and political factions in the face of common danger.

[19] Cf. *The Luftwaffe War Diaries.*

R.A.F. FIGHTER COMMAND LOSSES—SATURDAY 7th SEPTEMBER 1940

1.	41 Sqn., Hornchurch	C	Shot down in combat over Hornchurch and forced landed at Great Wakering, Essex; pilot unhurt.	Afternoon	Plt. Off. O.B. Morrogh-Ryan	Spitfire	*X4318*	Cat. 3 Destroyed
2.	41 Sqn., Hornchurch	C	Shot down in combat over Hornchurch and force landed at West Hanningfield, Essex; pilot unhurt.	Afternoon	Sgt. R.C. Ford	Spitfire	—	Cat. 3 Destroyed
3.	41 Sqn., Hornchurch	C	Shot down and crashed near Rayleigh, Essex; pilot unhurt.	Afternoon	Sgt. J. McAdam	Spitfire	*P9430*	Cat. 3 Destroyed

An ambulance steamer passes blazing Thames-side warehouses (*top*). *Below*, a timber barge still blazing, a burnt-out fire engine, a partly capsized vessel and melted building frames—a scene near what had been the heart of the fire storm. (Photos: Topix)

R.A.F. Losses, 7th September 1940—*continued*

4.	43 Sqn., Tangmere	C	Shot down by Bf 109s over S.E. London; pilot baled out but killed when parachute failed; aircraft crashed at Blackheath.	17.12 hrs.	Flt. Lt. R.C. Reynell	Hurricane	V7257	Cat. 3 Destroyed
5.	43 Sqn., Tangmere	C	Shot down by Bf 109 while attacking Do 17s over S.E. London; pilot killed. Aircraft fell at Purley High School.	17.13 hrs.	Sqn. Ldr. C.B. Hull	Hurricane	V6541	Cat. 3 Destroyed
6.	54 Sqn., Catterick	NC	Crashed on training flight; pilot killed.	Not known	Plt. Off. D.J. Sanders	Spitfire	—	Cat. 3 Destroyed
7.	54 Sqn., Catterick	C	Crashed into sea off Flamborough Head during patrol; pilot killed.	Not known	Plt. Off. W. Krepski	Spitfire	R6901	Cat. 3 Lost
8.	66 Sqn., Coltishall	C	Damaged by enemy fighters and force landed; pilot unhurt.	Not known.	Plt. Off. C.A.W. Bodie	Spitfire	X4321	Cat. 1 Damaged
9.	72 Sqn., Croydon	C	Shot down over Thames Estuary and crash landed at Biggin Hill severely wounded in shoulder and knee.	A17.00 hrs.	Fg. Off. T.A.F. Elsdon	Spitfire	X4254	Cat. 3 Destroyed
10.	72 Sqn., Croydon	C	Shot down by Bf 110 at Eynsford, Kent; pilot slightly hurt.	A17.00 hrs.	Sgt. J. White	Spitfire	R7022	Cat. 3 Destroyed
11.	73 Sqn., Debden	C	Damaged by Bf 110 near Chelmsford; force landed on Burnham Marshes after engine failed; pilot unhurt.	A17.35 hrs.	Sgt. A.E. Marshall	Hurricane	P3863	Cat. 2 Damaged
12.	79 Sqn., Biggin Hill	C	Shot down by Bf 109 and force landed at West Malling; pilot wounded in the leg.	17.20 hrs.	Plt. Off. D.W.A. Stones	Hurricane	—	Cat. 2 Damaged

R.A.F. Losses, 7th September 1940—*continued*

13.	111 Sqn., Croydon	C	Damaged by Bf 109 over Channel; pilot reached coast and baled out near Ashford slightly wounded.	A17.45 hrs.	Sgt. T.Y.Wallace	Hurricane	P3025	Cat. 3 Destroyed
14.	234 Sqn., Middle Wallop	C	Shot down by Bf 109s near Biggin Hill and pilot killed; buried at Orpington.	17.20 hrs.	Sqn. Ldr. J.S. O'Brien	Spitfire	P9466	Cat. 3 Destroyed
15.	234 Sqn., Middle Wallop	C	Shot down by Bf 109s S.E. of London and crashed at Bessels Green.	A17.25 hrs.	Flt. Lt. P.C. Hughes	Spitfire	X4009	Cat. 3 Destroyed
16.	242 Sqn., Coltishall	C	Shot down near North Weald; pilot assumed killed, but location of crash not established.	17.15 hrs.	Plt. Off. J. Benzie	Hurricane	P2962	Cat. 3 Missing
17.	242 Sqn., Coltishall	C	Shot down and crashed near Chelmsford; pilot unhurt.	17.20 hrs.	Plt. Off. D.W. Crowley-Milling	Hurricane	P3715	Cat. 2 Damaged
18.	249 Sqn., North Weald	C	Shot down by Bf 109 near Maidstone and crashed at Hollingbourne; pilot killed.	A17.00 hrs.	Plt. Off. R.D.S. Fleming	Hurricane	R4114	Cat. 3 Destroyed
19.	249 Sqn., North Weald	C	Shot down by Bf 109s near Maidstone; pilot baled out wounded; aircraft probably crashed at Eastling.	A17.00 hrs.	Sgt. F.W.G. Killingback	Hurricane	R4230	Cat. 3 Destroyed
20.	249 Sqn., North Weald	C	Shot down by Bf 109s north of Maidstone and crashed at Eastchurch; pilot wounded.	A17.15 hrs.	Sgt. R. Smithson	Hurricane	V6574	Cat. 3 Destroyed
21.	249 Sqn., North Weald	C	Shot down by He 111 north of Maidstone and pilot baled out, wounded, at Dunkirk, Kent.	17.18 hrs.	Fg. Of. P.H.V. Wells	Hurricane	P3594	Cat. 3 Destroyed
22.	249 Sqn., North Weald	C	Shot down by Bf 109s over north Kent; pilot unhurt.	17.24 hrs.	Plt. Off. R.G.A. Barclay	Hurricane	V6610	Cat. 3 Destroyed
23.	249 Sqn., North Weald	(C)	Shot down by ground defences over N.E. London; pilot baled out unhurt.	17.50 hrs.	Sgt. J.M.B. Beard	Hurricane	N2440	Cat. 3 Destroyed
24.	257 Sqn., Martlesham	C	Shot down over the Isle of Sheppey; pilot killed.(Location of crash established in 1972)	17.35 hrs.	Flt. Lt. H.R.A. Beresford	Hurricane	P3049	Cat. 3 Missing
25.	257 Sqn., Martlesham	C	Shot down over the Isle of Sheppey; pilot killed.	17.35 hrs.	Fg. Off. L.R.G. Mitchell	Hurricane	V7254	Cat. 3 Missing
26.	257 Sqn., Martlesham	C	Shot down over the Isle of Sheppey and force landed at Sittingbourne; pilot unhurt.	17.40 hrs.	Sgt. D.J. Hulbert	Hurricane	V7317	Cat. 2 Damaged
27.	257 Sqn., Martlesham	C	Damaged in the wings during combat over the Isle of Sheppey; landed unhurt at Debden.	17.45 hrs.	Sgt. P.T. Robinson	Hurricane	P3709	Cat. 2 Damaged
28.	303 Sqn., Northolt	C	Shot down by Bf 109s over Essex and force landed; pilot slightly hurt.	17.08 hrs.	Flt. Lt. A.S. Forbes	Hurricane	—	Cat. 2 Damaged
29.	303 Sqn., Northolt	C	Shot down in flames by Bf 109; pilot baled out unhurt at Loughton, Essex.	17.12 hrs.	Fg. Off. M. Pisarek	Hurricane	R4173	Cat. 3 Destroyed
30.	303 Sqn., Northolt	C	Shot down by Bf 109s; pilot baled out badly wounded in the thigh. Admitted to Waldershire Hospital, Selstead, Kent.	17.12 hrs.	Plt. Off. J. Daszewski	Hurricane	P3890	Cat. 3 Destroyed
31.	303 Sqn., Northolt	C	Damaged by Bf 109s over Essex; pilot returned to base unhurt.	17.09 hrs.	Not known	Hurricane	—	Cat. 2 Damaged
32.	310 Sqn., Duxford	C	Shot down in flames by Bf 109s over the Isle Sheppey and crashed at Harty Ferry. Pilot baled out grievously burned, but recovered.	17.45 hrs.	Sgt. J. Koukal	Hurricane	V7437	Cat. 3 Destroyed
33.	504 Sqn., Hendon	C	Shot down by Bf 109s over Isle of Sheppey, and crashed at Graveney, Faversham; pilot killed, and buried in Faversham Cemetery.	A17.05 hrs.	Plt. Off. K.V. Wendle	Hurricane	L1615	Cat. 3 Destroyed
34.	504 Sqn., Hendon	C	Damaged in combat over the Isle of Sheppey, and force landed at Eastchurch; pilot unhurt.	A17.05 hrs.	Sgt. B.M. Bush	Hurricane	P3021	Cat. 1 Damaged
35.	600 Sqn. Hornchurch	NC	Suffered landing accident at Rainham during training flight.	16.00 hrs.	—Saunders (1) —Davies (1)	Blenheim	—	Cat. 3 Destroyed
36.	602 Sqn., Westhampnett	C	Shot down in flames by Bf 109 near Biggin Hill; pilot baled out; body not located until 16-9-40. Aircraft crashed near Tonbridge.	17.45 hrs.	Fg. Off. W.H. Coverley	Spitfire	N3198	Cat. 3 Destroyed
37.	602 Sqn., Westhampnett	C	Shot down by Bf 109s in the Biggin Hill area. Pilot killed.	A17.45 hrs.	Plt. Off. H.M. Moody	Spitfire	X4256	Cat. 3 Lost
38.	602 Sqn., Westhampnett	C	Damaged by Bf 109s near Biggin Hill; pilot returned unhurt.	A17.45 hrs.	Plt. Off. O.V. Hanbury	Spitfire	N3228	Cat. 2 Damaged
39.	602 Sqn., Westhampnett	C	Shot down by Bf 109 and force landed near Wrotham; pilot unhurt.	A17.45 hrs.	Plt. Off. E.W. Aries	Spitfire	K9839	Cat. 3 Destroyed
40.	603 Sqn., Hornchurch	C	Damaged in wing by Bf 109 and force landed at base; pilot unhurt.	17.05 hrs.	Sqn. Ldr. G.L. Denholm	Spitfire	X4250	Cat. 1 Damaged
41.	603 Sqn., Hornchurch	C	Shot down by Bf 109; pilot baled out slightly wounded.	17.08 hrs.	Sgt. A.R. Sarre	Spitfire	X4263	Cat. 3 Destroyed
42.	603 Sqn., Hornchurch	C	Shot down by enemy fighters over north Kent; force landed at Sutton Valence, Maidstone.	A17.25 hrs.	Plt. Off. B.G. Stapleton	Spitfire	N3196	Cat. 2 Damaged
43.	609 Sqn., Middle Wallop	C	Force landed after combat; pilot unhurt.	A18.00 hrs.	Not known	Spitfire	P9467	Cat. 3 Destroyed
44.	610 Sqn., Duxford	C	Shot down over Sussex; pilot unhurt (nature and location of combat not known.)	A18.15 hrs.	Not known	Spitfire	X4168	Cat. 3 Destroyed

[(1) Rank and initials not known; neither crew member had achieved operational status at the time of his death.]

LUFTWAFFE LOSSES—SATURDAY 7th SEPTEMBER 1940

Note: Owing to the very large number of aircraft in simultaneous combat (more than 1,000 aircraft in an area of 800 square miles) it has proved almost impossible to sort claims against losses even down to squadron level, and only in isolated instances when pilots became detached from the main combat have aircraft, British or German, been identified with any certainty.

1.	4.(F)/14	CM	Missing from reconnaissance sortie over England; probably during the morning.	Messerschmitt Bf 110 C-5 (2205: 5F+MM)	100 %	Ltn. Gödsche and Oblt. Russel killed.	
2.	4.(F)/14	CM	Crashed at Cherbourg after combat with British fighters.	Messerschmitt Bf 110 C-5 (2211)	20 %	Ltn. Felix wounded.	
3.	1.(F)/22	CM	Crashed near Vlissingen after combat with British fighters.	Messerschmitt Bf 110C (2207 : 4N+DH)	35 %	Two crew members wounded.	
4.	3.(F)/123	CM	Intercepted by 266 Sqn. Spitfires near Norwich and shot down over Scheldt Estuary.	Dornier Do 215	100 %	Oblt. Hans Kauter, Ltn. Erich Böhle, Uffz. Leisner and Fw. Kobold missing.	
5.	3./KG 1	CM	Crashed at Dieppe after combat with British fighters in the London area.	Heinkel He 111H-3 (8664 : V4+AT)	100 %	Three crew members killed.	
6.	II./KG 1	CM	Aircraft interecepted by British fighters; undamaged, but crew member wounded.	Heinkel He 111H	Nil	Oberstltn. Koch, *Gr.Kdr.*, wounded.	
7.	4./KG 1	CM	Crashed at Bixchaete after combat with British fighters.	Heinkel He 111H-2 (2745 : V4+FU)	100 %	Three crew members killed.	

Luftwaffe Losses, 7th September 1940—*continued*

8.	Stab/KG 2	CM	Damaged by fighters near London during the evening.	Dornier Do 17Z-2 (2764 : U5+CA)	10 %	Two crew members wounded.
9.	4./KG 2	CM	Shot down by 41 Sqn. Spitfires near London during the evening.	Dornier Do 17Z (2830 : U5+FM)	100 %	Uffz. Christoph, Uffz. Greiner, Uffz. Treuer and Gefr. Pilz killed.
10.	Stab/KG 3	CM	Reported to have been shot down by *flak* in the London area during the evening.	Dornier Do 17Z-3 (2619 : 5K+DA)	100 %	Hptm. Ötting, *St.Kap.*, Ofw. Kleine killed; Uffz. Völkert and Fw. Hubert missing.
11.	5./KG 3	CM	Crashed at Calais following combat with British fighters during the evening.	Dornier Do 17Z (2840 : 5K+FN)	50 %	Ltn. Leitner + one wounded.
12.	5./KG 4	CM	Crashed near Clermont; probably not combat.	Heinkel He 111P	Not notified	Oblt. Wiegand killed.
13.	6./KG 4	CM	Missing from sortie over London; reported as being shot down by fighters.	Heinkel He 111P-2 (3078 : 5J+JP)	100 %	Oblt. Walter Klotz and Uffz. Wolf killed; Uffz. Klein, Uffz. Knoll and Gefr. Beckmann missing.
14.	2./KG 26	CM	Damaged by *flak* and fighters over London.	Heinkel He 111H-3 (6865 : 1H+DK)	10 %	Crew unhurt.
15.	3./KG 26	CM	Damaged by *flak* and fighters over London.	Heinkel He 111H-3 (6937 : 1H+FL)	10 %	Crew unhurt.
16.	6./KG 26	CM	Force landed at Gilze-Rijen after combat sortie over London.	Heinkel He 111H-3 (5706 : 1H+JP)	10 %	Crew unhurt.
17.	4./KG 30	CM	Shot down by fighters over London.	Junkers Ju 88 (0105 : 4D+KM)	100 %	One crew member killed; three made P.O.W.s.
18.	8./KG 30	CM	Force landed at Vendeville with engine failure after combat with fighters over London.	Junkers Ju 88A-5 (0351 : 4D+NS)	30 %	Crew unhurt.
19.	Stab/KG 40	CM	Missing from night sortie over England; probably shot down by *flak*.	Heinkel He 111H-5 (3515 : 1T+HH)	100 %	Oberstltn.Geisse, *Geschw.Kdr.*, Oblt. Schwengke, Fw. Köpplin missing.
20.	I./KG 51	NCM	Landing accident at Melun-Villaroche airfield.	Junkers Ju 88A-1 (6076)	50 %	Crew unhurt.
21.	II./KG 51	NCM	Landing accident at Villeneuf airfield following hydraulics failure.	Heinkel He 111P-2 (2815)	10 %	Crew unhurt.
22.	III./KG 51	NCM	Landing accident at Melun-Villaroche airfield following tyre burst.	Junkers Ju 88A-1 (2167 : 9K+CD)	30 %	Crew unhurt.
23.	I./KG 53	CM	Aircraft shot down by British fighters in London area.	Heinkel He 111H-3 (6912 : A1+AB)	100 %	Ofw.Müller, Fl.Hönig killed; Oblt. Weber, Ofw. Winter and Fw. Kempgen missing.
24.	II./KG 53	CM	Crashed at Brugges following combat with British fighters in the London area.	Heinkel He 111H-2 (2722 : A1+AP)	40 %	One crew member wounded.
25.	II./KG 53	CM	Reported to have been shot down by British fighters near London in the evening.	Heinkel He 111H-2 (2777 : A1+DN)	100 %	Ogefr. Neumann killed; Oblt. Breuer. Ofw. Pitzkar, Gefr. Uhrich and Uffz. Bergmann missing.
26.	I./KG 54	NCM	Landing accident at Meaulte airfield, not combat.	Heinkel He 111P (2650)	15 %	Crew unhurt.
27.	II./KG 54	CM	Shot down by cannon-armed Spitfire of Pilkington of No. 7 O.T.U. near Hoylake.	Junkers Ju 88A-1 (6032 : B3+AM)	100 %	Ofw. Schmitz, Ofw. Brehmer and Fw. Kalucza killed; Fw. Liebernecht killed.
28.	II./KG 54	NCM	Landing accident at St. André airfield.	Junkers Ju 88A-1 (4143)	40 %	Crew unhurt.
29.	III./KG 55	CM	Crashed following engine failure near Laigle.	Heinkel He 111P (1731)	100 %	Oblt. Wolf-Witte wounded.
30.	I./KGr. 806	CM	Crashed on Nantes airfield; cause not known.	Junkers Ju 88A-1 (4094 : M7+JK)	100 %	Four crew members killed.
31.	II./LG 1	NCM	Landing accident at Orléans airfield; not combat.	Junkers Ju 88A-1 (7041 : L1+AM)	50 %	Crew unhurt.
32.	II./LG 1	CM	Engine failure on take-off at Orléans airfield.	Junkers Ju 88A-1 (2044 : L1+EM)	50 %	Crew unhurt.
33.	I./LG 2	CM	Missing from free chase sortie over Southern England.	Messerschmitt Bf 109 E-1 (5798)	100 %	Uffz. Gotting missing.
34.	II./LG 2	CM	Landing accident on Marck airfield after combat.	Messerschmitt Bf 109 E-4 (2016)	20 %	Pilot safe.
35.	II./LG 2	CM	Landing accident on Marck airfield after combat.	Messerschmitt Bf 109 E-4 (2026)	20 %	Pilot safe.
36.	3./ZG 2	CM	Shot down by fighters of the Duxford Wing and crashed at Eythorne 8 miles SW of Deal at 17.50 hrs.	Messerschmitt Bf 110 C-4 (3117 : 3M+FL)	100 %	Ofw. Ernst Otterbach and Hptfw. Ohligschläger killed.
37.	I./JG 2	CM	Shot down by fighters of the Duxford Wing and crashed at Nokes Hill, Billericay, at 17.30 hrs.	Messerschmitt Bf 110 C-4 (3246 : 3M+BB)	100 %	Oblt. Gerhard Granz, P.O.W., and Fw. Willi Schutel missing.
38.	I./ZG 2	CM	Shot down by 73 Sqn. Hurricane of Beytagh 2 miles SE of Herne Bay at 17.20 hrs.	Messerschmitt Bf 110 C-4 (2216 : 3M+LM)	100 %	Ltn. Kisslinger killed; Uffz. Reinhold Dahnke made P.O.W.
39.	II./ZG 2	CM	Shot down by British fighters and crashed at Bullers Farm, Little Burstead, Essex, 17.30 hrs.	Messerschmitt Bf 110 D-0 (3328 : A2+FH)	100 %	Ltn. Carl Stix made P.O.W.; Gefr. Heinrich Fiez killed.
40.	II./ZG 2	CM	Shot down by Spitfires and crashed into sea 5 miles off Burchington, Thanet, at A.18.00 hrs.	Messerschmitt Bf 110 (3570 : A2+ML)	100 %	Uffz. August Galla drowed; Oblt. Willi Brede made P.O.W.
41.	II./ZG 2	CM	Shot down by 73 Sqn. Hurricane of Langham-Hobart during evening raid.	Messerschmitt Bf 110 D-0 (3334 : A2+NH)	100 %	Ltn. Schönemann and Uffz. Mescheden killed.
42.	II./ZG 2	CM	Shot down by British fighters and crashed at Ramsden Bell House, near Wickford, Essex.	Messerschmitt Bf 110 D-0 (3185 : A2+BH)	100 %	Ltn. Hans-Dietrich Abert and Uffz. Hans Scharf killed.
43.	3./Erpr.Gr. 210	CM	Shot down by flak near Portsmouth; pilot baled out over the Channel and rescued.	Messerschmitt Bf 109 E-4 (5390)	100 %	Pilot , unhurt, made P.O.W.
44.	I./JG 2	CM	Missing from sortie over England; no details as to pilot's fate.	Messerschmitt Bf 109 E-4 (3909)	100 %	Oblt. Gotz missing.
45.	II./JG 2	CM	Missing from sortie over England; no details as to pilot's fate.	Messerschmitt Bf 109 E-5 (3320)	100 %	Uffz. Melchert missing.
46.	Stab III./JG 3	CM	Shot down by British fighters over the Thames Estuary.	Messerschmitt Bf 109 E-4 (5249)	100 %	Oblt. Göttmann killed.
47.	6./JG 3	NCM	Landing accident at Vierre-au-Bois airfield.	Messerschmitt Bf 109 E-2 (6236)	10 %	Pilot unhurt.
48.	8./JG 3	CM	Shot down into Channel; pilot baled out.	Messerschmitt Bf 109 E-1 (6271)	100 %	Pilot, unhurt, rescued by *Seenotflugkommando*.
49.	1./JG 27	CM	Shot down by British fighters in London area.	Messerschmitt Bf 109 E-4 (5390)	100 %	Ltn. Günther Genske made P.O.W.
50.	1./JG 51	CM	Shot down by British fighters in London area.	Messerschmitt Bf 109 E-1 (4840)	100 %	Uffz. Zurlage missing.
51.	2./JG 51	CM	Shot down by British fighters in London area.	Messerschmitt Bf 109 E-1 (6342)	100 %	Ofe. Ströhlein missing.
52.	3./JG 51	CM	Shot down by British fighters in London area.	Messerschmitt Bf 109 E-3 (5091)	100 %	Gefr. Werner missing.
53.	9./JG 51	CM	Shot down by British fighters south of London.	Messerschmitt Bf 109 E-4 (4097)	100 %	Uffz. Koch missing.

Luftwaffe Losses, 7th September 1940—*continued*

54.	9./JG 51	CM	Shot down by fighters over South Coast; pilot baled out over the Channel and rescued.	Messerschmitt Bf 109 E-4 (2046)	100 %	Pilot, unhurt, rescued by *Seenotflugkommando*.
55.	5./JG 53	NCM	Suffered take-off accident at Dinan airfield.	Messerschmitt Bf 109 E-4 (0672)	80 %	Pilot unhurt.
56.	2./JG 54	CM	Suffered take-off accident at Guines airfield.	Messerschmitt Bf 109E (1153)	60 %	Pilot unhurt.
57.	Stab I./JG 77	CM	Shot down by British fighters off Dungeness; pilot baled out over the Channel and rescued.	Messerschmitt Bf 109 E-4 (5129)	100 %	Pilot, unhurt, rescued by *Seenotflugkommando*.
58.	I./JG 77	CM	Shot down by British fighters south of London.	Messerschmitt Bf 109 E-4 (5811)	100 %	Ofw. Goltzsche missing.
59.	*Wettererkundungsstaffel Kette Luftflotte 5*	CM	Suffered landing accident at Vaernes airfield.	Heinkel He 111H-2 (2724 : DE+GS)	65 %	Crew unhurt.
60.	1./106	CM	Reported shot down by R.A.F. Hudson in grid Square 6779; no British claim traced.	Heinkel He 115 (2724 : M2+FH)	100 %	One crew member wounded.
61.	*Seenotflugkommando 3*	CM	Landing accident in rough sea during rescue operation in grid Square 1114.	Heinkel He 59 (0840 : DA+WT)	100 %	Crew unhurt.
62.	Stab KGzbV 2	NCM	Crashed on Johannisthahl airfield following engine failure.	Junkers Ju 52/3m (6517 : KD+GO)	85 %	One crew member injured.

Sunday 8th September

As dawn broke on this Sunday—the 25th anniversary of Germany's first heavy airship raid upon London—first light revealed streets blocked by rubble and burned out fire engines, and pathetic groups of men, women and children staring in dazed silence at the smoking shambles which had been their homes before the sirens had sounded twelve long hours before. This was the new scarred face which London would wear for five years to come.

To the people of Kent, Surrey and Sussex the night had been one of fearful apprehension, as bomber after bomber droned overhead from the spreading glow which lit the northern skyline. As 28,000 anti-aircraft shells crashed high overhead the night had come alive with the steel rain of shrapnel. And many of the menfolk had been away all night manning roadblocks, for the invasion codeword had been broadcast to defence commanders in the South the previous evening. The church bells had sounded,[20] and the men had left their homes and scattered to their posts to watch for the expected swarms of parachutists.

The alarm had been entirely false, and no invasion fleet had set sail—a fact confirmed by early morning reconnaissance. The previous evening's heavy fighting had taken a considerable toll among Dowding's men and machines. The first and most famous Hurricane Squadron, "Treble One", was taken out of the line at last, seven remaining Hurricanes being led north by John Thompson—disheartened by the news that their job henceforth would be to train replacements for Park's other squadrons. Another veteran unit withdrawn to the north was No. 43 Squadron, the now leaderless "Fighting Cocks"; it took eight days to repair and fly from Tangmere to Usworth the tattered remains of eleven Hurricanes.

As the majority of German bomber crews slept late on this Sunday morning, Kesselring sent over two small raids each composed of about 30 Dorniers of II. and III. *Gruppen*, KG 2, to attack airfields and suburbs south of London; these crossed the South Coast west of Dungeness at 11.45 hours. While the majority of Park's squadrons were kept at a low state of readiness, five were scrambled and four (the Hurricanes of Nos. 46, 253, 504 and 605 Squadrons) made contact between Maidstone and Rochester. Possibly as a result of recent experience in meeting British fighters at high altitude

the escort were on this occasion positioned too high to protect the bombers; several Dorniers fell before the Bf 109s and Bf 110s could interfere.

At this point in contemporary accounts it is possible to trace a relaxation of tension on this, the first occasion in ten days when Park's squadrons were not held at Readiness throughout the daylight hours. In the early morning Park and Dowding conferred on what was clearly the beginning of a shift in enemy pressure. While Park still insisted that his particular field of battle was unsuitable for the assembly of fighter Wings, he readily agreed to compromise whenever his controllers could be given adequate warning of an enemy raid in the issue of instructions to operate his squadrons in pairs. The mid-day action confirmed the feasibility of this course when one pair of squadrons, Nos. 253 and 605 Squadrons, had entered combat together and penetrated the escort screen in some strength.

Dowding was now able to give Park a transfusion of fresh blood with the movement of No. 92 Squadron from Pembrey to Biggin Hill. This Spitfire squadron, hitherto based in South Wales (with a Flight detached at Bibury for night defence of the Midlands, much as Nos. 3 and 17 Squadrons had been stationed at Upavon a dozen years before) had acquired something of a reputation in Fighter Command without being in the thick of the fighting. Fretting at its relative inactivity, its pilots had flown far and wide looking for enemy aircraft, and had achieved a fair success. This type of sortie had fostered a particular brand of individualism among the pilots, who included such figures as Stanford Tuck, Wimpey Wade, Brian Kingcombe and Don Kingaby. The energy and dash displayed by this Squadron was to be reflected in the record of its first fortnight at Biggin Hill: sixteen enemy aircraft claimed destroyed for the loss of five pilots killed, five wounded and nineteen Spitfires lost.

The relative lull in the daylight battle on 8th September was followed by a further night assault on London of almost the same proportions as those of the previous night, confirming to Dowding that the *Luftwaffe* had indeed embarked on a wholly revised pattern of operations. This in turn led to increasingly urgent pressure for deliveries of the Beaufighter to be accelerated; six more aircraft were handed over to Fighter Command during the period 8th-12th September.

At 19.30 hours on this Sunday the sirens sounded in East London as the ominous, ragged drone of Sperrle's bombers

---

[20] During the War the ringing of church bells was forbidden, being reserved as the signal of the coming of invasion.

was heard in the Medway Towns. Once again Göring had unleashed the *Luftwaffe* in a devastating raid which lasted for nine and a half hours, during which time 207 Heinkels, Junkers and Dorniers of eleven *Kampfgruppen* rained more than 1,700 high explosive bombs and countless thousands of incendiaries on the docks and City. The great conflagrations which had blazed almost unchecked since the previous night were fed afresh, and by first light on Monday morning twelve new areas of fire were raging out of control. During the night 412 more civilians had died in the flames, and 747 had been maimed. Factories and private houses, railways and docks had all suffered, as had six hospitals and blocks of flats—one bomb killed fifty people in one such block. Every railway line out of London to the South and South-East was out of operation after four termini, including Waterloo and Victoria, had been hit.

Mercifully, the people of London could not know the truth; they regarded this simply as the second raid in two nights. In fact it was to be only the second in *fifty-seven consecutive nights* of raids on the British capital.

R.A.F. FIGHTER COMMAND LOSSES—SUNDAY 8th SEPTEMBER 1940

1.	41 Sqn., Hornchurch	C	Shot down in flames near Dover, probably by Bf 109s, during patrol; pilot killed.	12.05 hrs.	Fg. Off. W.J.M. Scott	Spitfire	*R6576*	Cat. 3 Lost
2.	46 Sqn., Stapleford	C	Shot down by Bf 109s over Sheerness; pilot baled out but was dead on landing.	12.15 hrs.	Sub-Lt. J.C. Carpenter	Hurricane	*P3201*	Cat. 3 Missing.
3.	46 Sqn., Stapleford	C	Shot down near Maidstone by Bf 109s; pilot baled out unhurt.	12.20 hrs.	Not known	Hurricane	*P3053*	Cat. 3 Destroyed
4.	46 Sqn., Stapleford	C	Shot down over Isle of Sheppey and crash landed at Hollingbourne, slightly wounded.	A12.25 hrs.	Fg. Off. N.W. Burnett	Hurricane	*V6631*	Cat. 3 Destroyed
5.	600 Sqn., Hornchurch	NC	Became lost on training flight; crew baled at Basingstoke.	Not known	Plt. Off. H.B.L. Hough	Blenheim	*L1111*	Cat. 3 Destroyed
6.	605 Sqn., Croydon	C	Shot down in flames by Bf 109 while attacking bombers over Tunbridge Wells; pilot baled out severely burned and shocked.	12.30 hrs.	Plt. Off. J. Fleming	Hurricane	*L2061*	Cat. 3 Destroyed

LUFTWAFFE LOSSES—SUNDAY 8th SEPTEMBER 1940

1.	II./KG 2	CM	Shot down by flak east of London at A.12.40 hrs; crew baled out near Gravesend and taken to Woolwich Military Arsenal.	Dornier Do 17Z-2 (2662 : U5+BN)	100 %	Oblt. Schneider, Uffz. Schumacher Ogefr. Hoffmann and Fl. Kohl made P.O.W.s.
2.	II./KG 2	CM	Shot down by 46 Sqn. Hurricane of Andrews over the Isle of Sheppey at A. 12.30 hrs.	Dornier Do 17Z-1 (3415 : U5+LN)	100 %	Oblt. Ziems, Uffz. Selter killed. Uffz. Flisk, Uffz. Trost missing.
3.	II./KG 2	CM	Shot down by *flak* east of London at A.12.40 hrs. At least one crew member known to have baled out and been rescued.	Dornier Do 17Z-1 (1130 : U5+FN)	100 %	Ltn.Landenberger. Gefr. Lotter and Fl. Schütze killed; Ofw. Ströbl missing.
4.	III./KG 2	CM	Damaged by 46 Sqn. Hurricanes over north Kent at A12.40 hrs.	Dornier Do 17Z-3 (2758 : U5+CP)	100 %	Crew unhurt.
5.	3./KG 3	CM	Air collision with Item 6 at Ertvelde-Gent; not combat.	Dornier Do 17Z-2 (3321 : 5K+CL)	100 %	Hptm. Kükens, *St.Kap.*, + two killed.
6.	3./KG 3	CM	Air collision with Item 5 at Ertvelde-Gent; not combat.	Dornier Do 17Z-2 (3426 : 5K+GL)	60 %	Crew unhurt.
7.	Geschw.Erg.St./ KG 4	NCM	Landing accident at Fassburg airfield; details not known.	Heinkel He 111P (2474 : 5J+KU)	8 %	Crew unhurt.
8.	Geschw.Erg.St./ KG 4	NCM	Accident at Fassburg airfield; possibly involving Item 7.	Heinkel He 111P (2508 : 5J+NU)	5 %	Crew unhurt.
9.	II./KG 27	CM	Take-off accident at Brest airfield.	Heinkel He 111P (2839 : 1G+NN)	100 %	Two killed; one wounded.
10.	Ausb.St./KG 53	NCM	Crashed during night flight at Giebelstadt.	Heinkel He 111H-1 (5250 : A1+NR)	100 %	One killed; one injured.
11.	I./KG 54	CM	Missing from night sortie over England; probably shot down by *flak* over the Midlands.	Junkers Ju 88A-1 (4032 : B3+BK)	100 %	Hptm. Brisch, Fw.Ofschonka, Ofw. Zingel and Fl. Kudina killed.
12.	III./KG 55	CM	Crash landed at night at Villacoublay with *flak* damage suffered over England.	Heinkel He 111P-2 (3353)	50 %	Ltn. Richter + one wounded.
13.	Stab/KGr. 806	CM	Night crash at St. Clementin following bombing sortie over England.	Junkers Ju 88A-1 (6136 : M7+EA)	100 %	Four crew members killed.
14.	I./LG 1	CM	Take-off accident near Orléans; aircraft burned.	Junkers Ju 88A-1 (2122 : L1+BB)	100 %	Major Kanus + three crew killed.
15.	II./LG 1	CM	Crashed after engine failure near Orléans.	Junkers Ju 88A-1 (2044 : L1+EM)	60 %	Crew unhurt.
16.	II./LG 1	CM	Crashed after engine failure near Orléans-Bricy.	Junkers Ju 88A-1 (2102 : L1+JM)	60 %	Crew unhurt.
17.	III./LG 1	CM	Crashed near Chateaudun following engine fire.	Junkers Ju 88A-1 (6060 : L1+DS)	100 %	Two killed; one injured.
18.	I./St.G 77	NCM	Taxying accident on Maltot airfield.	Junkers Ju 87B-1 (0472 : S2+BL)	20 %	Crew unhurt.
19.	I./St.G 77	NCM	Minor landing accident at Maltot airfield.	Junkers Ju 87B-2 (5589 : S2+CB)	5 %	Crew unhurt.
20.	3./Erpr.Gr.210	NCM	Take-off accident at Denain airfield.	Messerschmitt Bf 109 E-4 (1998)	30 %	Pilot unhurt.
21.	I./JG 53	CM	Shot down by 501 Sqn. Hurricane near Hawkinge at A13.00 hrs.	Messerschmitt Bf 109 E-4 (0867)	100 %	Uffz. Adelwart killed.
22.	I./JG 53	CM	Air collision with Item 23 over English Channel. Pilot baled out.	Messerschmitt Bf 109 E-1 (3478)	100 %	Oblt. Witmeier, injured, rescued.
23.	I./JG 53	CM	Air collision with Item 22 over English Channel.	Messerschmitt Bf 109 E-7 (1171)	100 %	Oblt. Kuhnert, *St. Kap.*, killed.
24.	1./106	CM	Assumed shot down by British coastal *flak*; crew rescued by *Seenotflugkommando*.	Heinkel He 115 (2088 : M2+JH)	100 %	Ltn.z.S. Molis wounded.
25.	1./706	NCM	Destroyed by storm in Aalborg anchorage.	Arado Ar 196 (0095 : CK+FJ)	100 %	No casualties.

Monday 9th September

It is difficult to equate Göring's new policy of night attacks on London with preparations for the forthcoming invasion.

Simply to suggest that the erosion of civilian morale and the destruction of the nation's fighting spirit was the central aim is to imply that the defences were already beaten or that the quick destruction of the capital would render invasion unnecessary. Clearly neither supposition held good, and there is documentary evidence that the German High Command was well aware of this. In the first place the daylight raiding crews already detected a renewed vigour in Fighter Command's response, and, partly as a result of Park's new tactic of using paired squadrons, Kesselring's bomber formation leaders were again uncompromising in their demands for heavier and closer fighter escort. It was now the *Luftwaffe* that was ordered to disengage in the event of substantial fighter opposition. In this order lay the first open admission of failure to overwhelm Fighter Command; to many south of the *Kanalfront* the long term inplications must have been obvious.

The second significant step was the order issued by O.K.L. on 9th September on Göring's personal instructions, detailing a systematic "round-the-clock" destruction of the British capital. Kesselring's *Luftflotte*—using escorted bombers—would carry out daylight raids principally against key military and commercial targets in Greater London, while Sperrle's night raiding formations would pursue area attacks against the central and dock areas, employing bomber streams throughout the hours of darkness:

> "The city has been divided into two areas: Area A includes the eastern part with its extensive dock installations. Area B, to the west, contains the major power supplies, commercial and domestic installations."

And as if to justify this scarcely concealed switch to attacks on the civilian population, the instruction continued

> "The destruction raids on London will be accompanied wherever possible by raids upon the armament areas and harbour facilities throughout England as hitherto."

These priorities cannot be seen to constitute any sort of realistic preparations for an invasion. Seen in relation to the progress of the Battle up to this point, they smack of a fatal blurring of aim. Yet the extraordinary fact remains that Hitler, at least, saw no inconsistency. It is this gulf between the trends which must have been apparent on the Channel Coast, and the blinkered view maintained by Hitler, which gives this short period in the Battle its strange air of vagueness and unreality. Hitler still clung to the hope that massive destruction in the streets of London would shatter the morale of the British and bring about internal collapse; simultaneously, he allowed the invasion timetable to stand. With all the instances of continuing successful interception by Fighter Command, Göring still insisted that Britain was down to a handful of fighters which could be drawn into the cauldron over London and annihilated. The faulty assessment of Britain's physical resources still went hand in hand with a total inability to understand the mood of the country at large. To the observer looking back over the years, this flabby indecision seems to amount almost to wilful self-deception. Yet the moment was soon coming when the Führer would have to grasp the nettle; for the preliminary stages of *Seelöwe* were now only 48 hours away.

The timetable of events to which O.K.W. had been working was as follows.

11th September:Orders for the launching of *Seelöwe* to be given. This warning order would have included instructions for the laying of a minefield path across the Channel and a final disposition of certain support units, notably *Flakartillerie*.

18th September:Final operational orders to be distributed.

19th September: Embarkation of seaborne forces, and launching of deception manœuvre, codenamed *Herbstreise*.[21]

20th September:Invasion fleet to sail; repetition of *Herbstreise*.

21st September:Landing assault.

27th September:Phase I of *Seelöwe* completed.

11th October: Phase II of *Seelöwe* completed.

The first actual amendment to the timetable was to be made largely as a result of operations on 9th September.

*   *   *   *   *

Daylight operations on the 9th were devoted to a spate of raids during the late afternoon against targets situated in the South London suburban area. Enemy briefing documents refer to Weybridge, Kingston, Rochester and Croydon, and it may be deduced that aircraft factories were again the centre of attention. Park's squadrons, ready briefed to fight in pairs, were scrambled in good time to meet five enemy formations as they approached over Kent and Sussex, and fierce fights developed over Surrey. Three Dorniers of KG 2 penetrated to Kingston and Surbiton where, instead of attempting to identify specific targets, their pilots flew straight along the railway line, dropping their loads from low level. This necessitated considerable filling of craters, but remarkably little damage was done to the permanent way. As was becoming increasingly common, it was the huge suburban residential areas which were to suffer most from the large number of bombs jettisoned hurriedly over South London.

The biggest single raid of this afternoon was flown by 26 Heinkel He 111s of II./KG 1, escorted by twenty Bf 110s of III./ZG 76 and 60 Bf 109s of JG 3. Said to have been briefed to attack the Royal Aircraft Establishment at Farnborough, this raid was tracked south of London on a westerly course, and therefore had to run the gauntlet of fighter squadrons from Biggin Hill, Kenley, Croydon and Northolt; in the event nine squadrons engaged, eight of which attacked simultaneously in pairs as the formation passed over Croydon. This determined charge by some 70 British fighters utterly dismayed the German escort, a large part of which promptly took up a defensive circle, which left the Heinkels vulnerable. One *Staffel* of bombers immediately turned south and dumped its bombs over Purley and Epsom. These aircraft then joined up with another raid, by about 40 Junkers Ju 88s of KG 30, which was being heavily attacked by nine Hurricanes of No. 253 Squadron and twelve of No. 303 (Polish) Squadron, the pilots

---

[21] "Autumn Cruise", a feint to draw British forces away from the South by despatching fourteen empty merchant vessels (including four liners) and four cruisers from Scandinavian ports towards the North-East Coast between Tynemouth and Aberdeen. They would turn back at night and repeat the manœuvre on 20th September.

Left: No. 242 Squadron pilots (*left to right*), Flt. Lt. G.E. Ball, Sqn. Ldr. D.R.S. Bader, Plt. Off. W.L. McKnight (Canadian). *Right*: No. 303 (Polish) Squadron pilots (*left to right*), Fg. Off. Z. Henneberg (Polish), Flt. Lt. J.A. Kent (Canadian), Plt. Off. M. Feric (Polish). Kent destroyed a Bf 110 of III./ZG 76 on 9th September.

of the former unit claiming five Junkers.

Somewhere in this area the Duxford Wing, led by Sqn. Ldr. Douglas Bader, attacked a formation of Dornier Do 17s and claimed nineteen destroyed. None is in fact confirmed as lost in German records. Nor can any confirmatory sighting of Dorniers crashing be traced in Observer Corps records[22]. The Wing, which was already short of fuel when it engaged, lost five Hurricanes destroyed, a Spitfire damaged and two pilots killed.

Sergeant Josef Frantisek, the top-scoring pilot, joined the fight against KG 1 and KG 30, destroying a Heinkel and a Bf 109 before he ran out of fuel and force landed in a cabbage field near the Downs Hotel at Woodingdrine, Brighton. John Kent shot down a Bf 110 into the Channel, and remained over the wreckage long enough the see the crew launch their dinghy.

As weary pilots climbed from their cockpits in the gathering dusk, and others made their way back to their stations by rail after force landing, the air raid sirens were already heralding yet another night attack on London. At 18.06 hours 195 bombers began to cross the Sussex coast at 18,000 feet on a

northerly course which would bring them directly over the centre of the capital; bombing continued thereafter for eight hours. O.K.L.'s "Area B" now began to feel the weight of German bombs, and such metropolitan landmarks as St. Thomas's Hospital, Somerset House and the Royal Courts of Justice were among the casualties. Three more main line railways stations were temporarily put out of action; 370 Londoners were killed and more than 1,400 injured.

As the morning light of 10th September revealed the dockland fires still raging unabated, a German broadcaster in Bremen announced: "It is only a question of time—a few short weeks, then this conflagration will have reached its natural end." Such an empty threat unintentionally pointed up the German inability to do more to Britain than set fire to her cities at night.

---

[22] Such an extraordinary discrepancy is impossible to reconcile, and can only realistically be explained by incomplete Luftflotte 2 records for this day. Unfortunately, some of the squadron records are also missing, and it must be assumed that the Wing flew too far south before its combat as it seems that several aircraft had to land at No. 11 Group airfields, almost out of fuel.

R.A.F. FIGHTER COMMAND LOSSES—MONDAY 9th SEPTEMBER 1940

No.	Squadron		Details	Time	Pilot	Aircraft	Serial	Category
1.	1(Canadian) Sqn.,Northolt	C	Shot down by Bf 109s south of Northolt; pilot baled out with burns and leg wounds.	Not known	Fg.Off.W.B.McD. Millar	Hurricane	—	Cat. 3 Destroyed
2.	19 Sqn., Fowlmere	C	Damaged by Bf 109 of 5./JG 27 near Maidstone; pilot unhurt.	A17.50 hrs.	Sgt. D.G.S.R. Cox	Spitfire	K9815	Cat. 2 Damaged
3.	66 Sqn., Kenley	C	Shot down by Bf 109 over Cowden, Kent; pilot baled out slightly wounded.	17.45 hrs.	Plt. Off. G.H. Corbett	Spitfire	L3049	Cat. 3 Destroyed
4.	92 Sqn., Biggin Hill	C	Crash landed at Midley, Rye, after combat over Biggin Hill; pilot suffered leg wounds.	A17.00 hrs.	Plt. Off. C.H. Saunders	Spitfire	L1077	Cat. 3 Destroyed
5.	92 Sqn., Biggin Hill	C	Shot down by Bf 109s near Biggin Hill; pilot baled out with severe to face and hands.	A17.00 hrs.	Plt. Off. W.C. Watling	Spitfire	P9372	Cat. 3 Destroyed
6.	222 Sqn., Hornchurch	C	Shot down by Bf 109 and force landed at Dartford. Pilot unhurt.	17.35 hrs.	Plt. Off. T.A. Vigors.	Spitfire	—	Cat. 3 Destroyed
7.	222 Sqn., Hornchurch	C	Shot down by Bf 109 and force landed at Rochford. Pilot unhurt.	A17.40 hrs.	Plt. Off. J.W. Broadhurst	Spitfire	—	Cat. 3 Destroyed
8.	242 Sqn., Coltishall	C	Shot down by Do 17s and Bf 110s over Thameshaven and crashed at Marden Park Farm, Caterham; pilot killed.	17.45 hrs.	Plt. Off. K.M. Sclanders	Hurricane	P3087	Cat. 3 Destroyed
9.	242 Sqn., Coltishall	C	Shot down by Do 17 and pilot baled out at Caterham, unhurt; aircraft crashed in Kenley.	17.45 hrs.	Sgt. R.V.H. Lonsdale	Hurricane	P2831	Cat. 3 Destroyed
10.	253 Sqn., Kenley	C	Shot down and crashed landed at Cobham Park Farm; pilot unhurt.	17.50 hrs.	Not known	Hurricane	—	Cat. 2 Damaged
11.	303 Sqn., Northolt	C	Shot down and force landed near Brighton; pilot unhurt..	18.10 hrs.	Sgt. J. Frantisek	Hurricane	—	Cat. 2 Damaged
12.	303 Sqn., Northolt	C	Shot down by Bf 109s near Beachy Head; pilot baled out with burns. Aircraft crashed at Poynings, north of Brighton.	18.15 hrs.	F/Sgt. K. Wunsche	Hurricane	P3700	Cat. 3 Destroyed
13.	310 Sqn., Duxford	C	Shot down by Bf 109 near Croydon; pilot baled out near Purley, little hurt.	17.45 hrs.	Fg. Off. G.L. Sinclair	Hurricane	R4084	Cat. 3 Destroyed
14.	310 Sqn., Duxford	C	Crashed near Oxted having exhausted fuel in combat with Bf 109s; pilot unhurt.	17.58 hrs.	Plt. Off. F. Rypl	Hurricane	P3142	Cat. 3 Destroyed
15.	310 Sqn., Duxford	C	Collided with Hurricane (Item 13) and He 111; pilot lost control, crashed at Woodmanstern and was killed.	17.44 hrs.	Plt. Off. J.E. Boulton	Hurricane	P3888	Cat. 3 Destroyed

R.A.F. Losses, 9th September 1940—*continued*

16.	602 Sqn., Westhampnett	C	Crashed on landing after combat with Do 17s; pilot wounded.	A18.00 hrs.	Fg. Off. P.C. Webb	Spitfire	K9910	Cat. 3 Destroyed
17.	602 Sqn., Westhampnett	C	Damaged by Do 17s; pilot returned slightly wounded.	18.20 hrs.	Sgt. B.E.P. Whall	Spitfire	N3282	Cat. 1 Damaged
18.	605 Sqn., Croydon	C	Shot down by Bf 110 near Borden; pilot baled out slightly wounded.	A17.30 hrs.	Plt. Off. J.S. Humphreys	Hurricane	P2765	Cat. 3 Destroyed
19.	605 Sqn., Croydon	C	Shot down by crossfire from He 111s of KG 53 over Farnborough and, in falling, struck another and crashed near Alton; pilot killed.	A17.30 hrs.	Plt. Off. G.M. Forrester	Hurricane	L2059	Cat. 3 Destroyed
20.	607 Sqn., Tangmere	C	Shot down in Mayfield area by Bf 109s. Aircraft crashed at Goudhurst; pilot killed.	A17.15 hrs.	Plt. Off. S.B. Parnall	Hurricane	P3574	Cat. 3 Destroyed
21.	607 Sqn., Tangmere	C	Shot down in Mayfield area by Bf 109s. Aircraft crashed at Cranbrook; pilot killed.	A17.15 hrs.	Plt. Off. J.D. Lenaham	Hurricane	P3117	Cat. 3 Destroyed
22.	607 Sqn., Tangmere	C	Shot down in Mayfield area by Bf 109s. Aircraft crashed at Goudhurst; pilot killed.	A17.15 hrs.	Plt. Off. G.J. Drake	Hurricane	P2728	Cat. 3 Destroyed
23.	607 Sqn., Tangmere	C	Shot down and force landed at Knockholt, near Biggin Hill; pilot slightly wounded.	A17.35 hrs.	Sgt. P.A. Burnell-Phillips	Hurricane	P2912	Cat. 3 Destroyed
24.	607 Sqn., Tangmere	C	Shot down by Bf 109s while attacking Do 17s, and crashed at Stilstead Farm, East Peckham; pilot slightly wounded.	17.30 hrs.	Sgt. R.A. Spyer	Hurricane	P2680	Cat. 3 Destroyed
25.	607 Sqn., Tangmere	C	Shot down by Bf 109s over Surrey; pilot baled out unhurt.	A17.35 hrs.	Not known.	Hurricane	—	Cat. 3 Destroyed
26.	611 Sqn., Digby	NC	Ran out of fuel and force landed near Henlow; pilot unhurt.	19.00 hrs.	Sgt. F.E.R. Sheppherd	Spitfire	P7320	Cat. 2 Damaged

LUFTWAFFE LOSSES—MONDAY 9th SEPTEMBER 1940

1.	1.(H)/32	NCM	Taxying accident on Rebstock airfield.	Henschel Hs 126A (2982 : V7+LA)	10 %	Crew unhurt.
2.	3./KG 1	CM	Shot down by 19 Sqn. Spitfire of Blake and crashed at Sundridge, Sevenoaks, at 17.50 hrs.	Heinkel He 111H-3 (5713 : V4+BL)	100 %	Uffz. Erich Marck, Ofw. Alfred Heidrich, Gefr. Heinrich Reinecke, Oblt. Erich Kiunka and Uffz. Anton Stumbaum P.O.W.s.
3.	4./KG 1	NCM	Crashed at Mezieres following technical failure.	Heinkel He 111H-2 (5460 : V4+GU)	60 %	Crew unhurt.
4.	6./KG 1	CM	Crashed with engine failure after combat.	Heinkel He 111H-2 (V4+AU)	Under 60 %	Crew unhurt.
5.	6./KG 1	CM	Crashed at Glissy with *flak* damage.	Heinkel He 111H-2 (2729 : V4+KW)	35 %	Crew unhurt.
6.	Erg.St./KG 4	NCM	Crashed and burned on take-off at Sorau.	Heinkel He 111P-4 (2864 : 5J+CL)	100 %	One crew member killed.
7.	Stab/KG 30	CM	Shot down by 253 Sqn. Hurricanes south of Biggin Hill at A.18.00 hrs.	Junkers Ju 88A-1 (0274 : 4D+AA)	100 %	Oblt. Heil, Uffz. Beck, Fw. Fuss and Uffz. Paustian missing.
8.	Stab II./KG 30	CM	Shot down by 253 Sqn. Hurricanes south of Biggin Hill at A.18.00 hrs.	Junkers Ju 88A-1 (5074 : 4D+KK)	100 %	Uffz.Diebler killed; Oblt.Golnitsch Uffz.Rolf, Uffz.Hamerla missing.
9.	Stab II./KG 30	CM	Shot down by 253 Sqn. Hurricanes south of Biggin Hill at A.18.00 hrs.	Junkers Ju 88A-1 (8032 : 4D+FB)	100 %	Uffz.Stahl, Uffz.Fecht, Uffz. Hallert and Gefr.Görth missing.
10.	Stab III./KG 30	CM	Shot down by 253 Sqn. Hurricanes south of Biggin Hill at A.18.00 hrs.	Junkers Ju 88A-1 (0333 : 4D+AD)	100 %	Maj. Hackbarth, *Gr.Kdr.*, Uffz. Sawallisch and Gefr. Petermann killed; Ofw. Manger missing.
11.	8./KG 30	CM	Shot down by 253 Sqn. Hurricanes south of Biggin Hill at A.18.00 hrs.	Junkers Ju 88A-1 (3195 : 4D+LS)	100 %	Uffz. Hettinger and Ogefr. Baumgarten killed; Fw. Jung and Uffz. Vetter missing.
12.	II./KG 51	CM	Landing accident at Villeneuve after combat.	Junkers Ju 88 (0307)	30 %	Crew unhurt.
13.	III./KG 51	CM	Landing accident at Villaroche after combat.	Junkers Ju 88A-1(7063)	15 %	Crew unhurt.
14.	III./KG 53	CM	Struck by 310 Sqn. Hurricane of Boulton which was falling after collision with another Hurricane south of Croydon at A.18.00 hrs.	Heinkel He 111H-2 (2630 : A1+ZD)	100 %	Fw. Endorf, Fw.Wenninger and Fw. Dorig killed; Oblt Meinecke and Fw. Broderich missing.
15.	III./KG 53	CM	Damaged by flak over north Surrey at A.18.00 hrs.	Heinkel He 111H-2 (3306 : A1+AS)	10 %	Two crew members wounded.
16.	III./KG 53	CM	Damaged by 303 Sqn. Hurricane of Frantisek over Sussex coast at A.18.15 hrs.	Heinkel He 111H-2 (5548 : A1+DS)	22 %	One killed; two wounded.
17.	I./KG 54	CM	Force landed near Paris after combat sortie.	Junkers Ju 88A-1(7086)	40 %	Crew unhurt.
18.	Geschw.Erg.St./ KG 76	NCM	Taxying accident at Beaumont airfield.	Dornier Do 17Z-3 (2560 : F1+JH)	30 %	Crew unhurt.
19.	Stab/LG 1	CM	Crashed and burned on Orléans airfield.	Junkers Ju 88A-1 (5093 : L1+DA)	100 %	Four crew members killed.
20.	II./LG 1	CM	Crashed and burned on take-off at Orléans.	Junkers Ju 88A-1 (7078 : L1+JP)	100 %	Four crew members killed.
21.	II./LG 1	CM	Landing accident on Orléans airfield.	Junkers Ju 88A-1 (5106 : L1+BM)	40 %	Crew unhurt.
22.	15./LG 1	CM	Shot down by two Hurricanes and crashed on the Maori Sports Club, Old Malden Lane, Worcester Park, Surrey at 17.45 hrs.	Messerschmitt Bf 110 C-3 (L1+DL)	100 %	Uffz. Pfafflhuber and Uffz. Kramp killed.
23.	III./ZG 76	CM	Shot down by 310 Sqn. Hurricane of Blackwood at Borden, Sittingbourne, at 17.40 hrs.	Messerschmitt Bf 110C (2137 : 2N+FM)	100 %	Uffz. Georg Bierling and Uffz. Weiher killed.
24.	6./ZG 76	CM	Shot down by 303 Sqn. Hurricane of Kent over Channel 5 miles off Newhaven, 18.00 hrs.(1)	Messerschmitt Bf 110C (3108 : 2N+EP)	100 %	Uffz. Karella killed; Fw. Hermann Koops rescued and made P.O.W.
25.	III./ZG 76	CM	Shot down by 310 Sqn. Hurricane of Bergman near Croydon at 17.50 hrs.	Messerschmitt Bf 110C (3207 : 2N+EP)	100 %	Fw. Ostermüncher and Gefr. Zimmermann killed.
26.	III./ZG 76	CM	Damaged by fighters over Surrey at A.18.00 hrs. and crash landed on Quoeux airfield.	Messerschmitt Bf 110C (2081 : 2N+CP)	60 %	Crew unhurt.
27.	II./NJG 1	NCM	Crashed near Ingolstadt after technical failure.	Messerschmitt Bf 110D (3136)	100 %	Both crew members killed.
28.	III./JG 2	CM	Landing accident at Beaumont-le-Roger airfield.	Messerschmitt Bf 109 E-1 (2947)	30 %	Pilot unhurt.
29.	4./JG 3	CM	Shot down by 41 Sqn. Spitfire of Bennions at A.18.00 hrs.	Messerschmitt Bf 109E (6138)	100 %	Ofw. Müller missing.
30.	7./JG 3		Shot down by British fighters near London.	Messerschmitt Bf 109 E-4 (5451)	100 %	Fw. Bauer missing.
31.	7./JG 3		Shot down by British fighters near London.	Messerschmitt Bf 109 E-1 (6316)	100 %	Uffz. Massmann missing.
32.	Stab I./JG 27	CM	Shot down by 19 Sqn. Spitfire of Cunningham near London 17.50 hrs.	Messerschmitt Bf 109 E-4 (1394)	100 %	Oblt Günther Bode made P.O.W.

302

Luftwaffe Losses, 9th September 1940—*continued*

33.	5./JG 27	CM	Shot down by 19 Sqn. Spitfire of Cox north of Maidstone at A.18.00 hrs.	Messerschmitt Bf 109 E-1 (3488)	100 %		Oblt. Erwin Daig made P.O.W.
34.	6./JG 27	CM	Shot down by 222 Sqn. Spitfire of Whitbread east of London at 17.30 hrs.	Messerschmitt Bf 109 E-1 (6280)	100 %		Uffz. Georg Rauwolf made P.O.W.
35.	7./JG 27	CM	Shot down by 222 Sqn. Spitfire of Vigors over East London at 17.30 hrs.	Messerschmitt Bf 109 E-4 (1617)	100 %		Uffz. Karl Born killed.
36.	1./JG 51	CM	Force landed at Abbeville short of fuel after combat.	Messerschmitt Bf 109 E-1 (3614)	80 %		Pilot unhurt.
37.	I./JG 53	CM	Shot down by British fighters over Kent.	Messerschmitt Bf 109 E-4 (1508)	100 %		Fw. Höhnisch missing.
38.	4./JG 53	CM	Shot down by 303 Sqn. Hurricane of Zumbach near Hastings at A.18.00 hrs.	Messerschmitt Bf 109 E-4 (0963)	100 %		Oblt.Schulze-Blank,*St.Kap.*, killed.
39.	8./JG 53	CM	Shot down by 303 Sqn. Hurricane of Frantisek bear Brighton at A.18.00 hrs.	Messerschmitt Bf 109E (6139)	100 %		Gefr. Peter Becker killed.
40.	1./JG 54	CM	Shot down by British fighters over South Coast.	Messerschmitt Bf 109 E-1 (6103)	100 %		Fw. Biber missing.
41.	3./JG 54	CM	Shot down by British fighters over South Coast; pilot baled out over the sea.	Messerschmitt Bf 109 E-1 (3906)	100 %		Pilot, unhurt, rescued by *Seenotflugkommando.*
42.	I./JG 77	CM	Force landed at Fécamp short of fuel after combat.	Messerschmitt Bf 109E (4055)	30 %		Pilot unhurt.
43.	1./JG 77	CM	Force landed at Fécamp short of fuel after combat.	Messerschmitt Bf 109 E-4 (3753)	30 %		Pilot unhurt.
44.	Kurierstaffel 10	CM	Force landed at Oldenburg after engine failure.	Junkers W.34hau (1352 : GB+NT)	40 %		Crew unhurt.
45.	*Luftdienst- kommando 64*	(CM)	Shot down by R.A.F. bomber (sic) over Rövar Island; crew rescued by Norwegian fishing vessel.	Junkers W.34 (1377 : BB+MG)	100 %		One crew member wounded.

[(1) Feldwebel Koops, on being interrogated, stated that he had been attacked by Spitfires near London which had wounded his gunner; while trying to return to France, he was attacked by a Hurricane (Kent's) and shot down. He ditched in the sea and was rescued; his gunner had however succumbed.]

The scene at Platform 2, Liverpool Street Station, London, on 10th September 1940 after a direct hit by a 100-kilo bomb. Little damage was done to the main fabric of the station. (Photo: British Rail, Eastern Region).

Tuesday 10th September

With dull weather covering much of Northern Europe and little chance to repeat the previous day's raids, the German High Command continued to deliberate on the achievements of the last few days. Having regard to the momentum which had been gained in the preparations for *Seelöwe*, with more than 2,000 barges and other craft already assembled, it was, as already stated, an integral stage of the operation to issue warning instructions, giving ten days' notice to the forces involved in the assault. With *Seelöwe* planned for 21st September, the issue of that warning order was but 24 hours away.

As more and more evidence became available—provided by the early evening battles of 9th September—it was clear that Fighter Command had already embarked on remedial tactics designed to counter the mass raids on London, made possible by the respite gained in the absence of attack upon the fighter defences themselves. Furthermore, bearing in mind that between the issue of the invasion warning instructions and the landing itself there would be a period of all-out air assault, the weather forecast for the coming ten days suggested conditions insufficiently settled for such operations. On Hitler's orders, therefore, the timetable for *Seelöwe* was retarded by three days, the Führer reserving his decision until the 14th.

Enemy air activity during daylight on the 10th was limited to widespread nuisance raids by single aircraft and small formations. Several Dorniers of KG 2 roamed over East Anglia, and bombs fell on the outskirts of Great Yarmouth and Norwich; the cloud conditions were such, however, that effective raid reporting was impossible and the R.A.F. fighters at Coltishall did not react.

In the evening about a dozen Ju 88s crossed the coast singly between Dover and Southampton, and dropped bombs in Portsmouth dockyard, at Littlehampton, Farnborough and Bognor Regis; a pair of enemy aircraft which had passed over Kenley was spotted over Kingston by Spitfire pilots of No. 72 Squadron, and one of the enemy was shot down near Weybridge, the other falling at East Grinstead.

The daylight raiding honours on 19th September undoubtedly went to R.A.F. Bomber Command for an excellent and damaging attack by Blenheims on *Kampfgeschwader 4*'s base at Eindhoven in Holland, which destroyed nine Heinkels He 111s of the unit's II.*Gruppe*, and damaged two others.

R.A.F. FIGHTER COMMAND LOSSES—TUESDAY 10th SEPTEMBER 1940

1.	141 Sqn., Turnhouse	NC	Suffered landing accident at dusk; crew unhurt.	A21.00 hrs.	Not known	Defiant	—	Cat. 2 Damaged
2.	232 Sqn., Croydon	NC	Crashed during Sector flight from Manston	Not known	Sgt. F. Butterick	Hurricane	—	Cat. 2 Damaged.
3.	312 Sqn., Duxford	NC	Aircraft caught fire in the air; pilot baled out unhurt.	Not known	Not known	Hurricane	L1644	Cat. 3 Burnt
4.	602 Sqn., Westhampnett	NC	Crashed on Bognor golf course; pilot, with no night flying experience, unhurt.	21.05 hrs	Plt. Off. O.V. Hanbury	Spitfire	L1002	Cat. 2 Damaged.
5.	602 Sqn., Westhampnett	NC	Crashed at Tangmere after dusk patrol; pilot, with no night flying experience, unhurt.	20.56 hrs.	Fg. Off. C.J. Mount	Spitfire	X4270	Cat. 2 Damaged
6.	602 Sqn., Westhampnett	NC	Crashed at Tangmere after dusk patrol; pilot, with no night flying experience, unhurt.	20.57	Sgt. D.W. Elcombe	Spitfire	L1040	Cat. 3 Destroyed

LUFTWAFFE LOSSES—TUESDAY 10th SEPTEMBER 1940

1.	2.(H)/32	NCM	Force landed on local flight; details not notified.	Henschel Hs 126B (3156)	45 %	Crew unhurt.
2.	II./KG 4	CM	Landing accident on Soesterberg airfield.	Heinkel He 111P-4 (2919)	20 %	Crew unhurt.
3.	II./KG 4	CM	Crashed at Eindhoven after bombing sortie.	Heinkel He 111P-4 (2869)	100 %	Ltn. Arnold + two killed; one wounded.
4.	II./KG 4	—	Destroyed in R.A.F. bombing raid on Eindhoven.	Heinkel He 111P-4 (2972)	100 %	No aircrew casualties.
5.	II./KG 4	—	Destroyed in R.A.F. bombing raid on Eindhoven.	Heinkel He 111P-4 (2939)	100 %	No aircrew casualties.
6.	II./KG 4	—	Damaged in R.A.F. bombing raid on Eindhoven.	Heinkel He 111P-4 (2935)	90 %	No aircrew casualties.
7.	II./KG 4	—	Damaged in R.A.F. bombing raid on Eindhoven.	Heinkel He 111P-4 (3933)	90 %	No aircrew casualties.
8.	II./KG 4	—	Damaged in R.A.F. bombing raid on Eindhoven.	Heinkel He 111P-4 (3080)	90 %	No aircrew casualties.
9.	II./KG 4	—	Damaged in R.A.F. bombing raid on Eindhoven.	Heinkel He 111P-4 (3079)	90 %	No. aircrew casualties.
10.	II./KG 4	—	Damaged in R.A.F. bombing raid on Eindhoven.	Heinkel He 111P-2 (2792)	50 %	No aircrew casualties.
11.	II./KG 4	—	Damaged in R.A.F. bombing raid on Eindhoven.	Heinkel He 111P-2 (2637)	85 %	No aircrew casualties.
12.	II./KG 4	—	Damaged in R.A.F. bombing raid on Eindhoven.	Heinkel He 111P-2 (2635)	85 %	No aircrew casualties.
13.	II./KG 4	—	Damaged in R.A.F. bombing raid on Eindhoven.	Heinkel He 111P-2 (2140)	30 %	No aircrew casualties.
14.	II./KG 54	CM	Possibly shot down by 72 Sqn. Spitfires at East Grinstead at A.17.30 hrs.	Junkers Ju 88A-1 (4146 : B3+DP)	100 %	Oblt. John , Uffz. Schauer, Gefr. Weiler and Uffz. Flamm killed.
15.	II./KG 54	CM	Crashed and burned on St. André airfield after engine failure.	Junkers Ju 88A-1 (3093)	100 %	Ltn. Fischer + one killed; two injured.
16.	9./KG 76	CM	Shot down by 72 Sqn. Spitfires at Weybridge, Surrey, at 17.30 hrs.	Dornier Do 17Z-3 (2778 : F1+ET)	100 %	Oblt. Domenik and Uffz. Stralendorf killed; Gefr. Greza and Uffz. Nümber missing.
17.	I./JG 2	CM	Take-off accident at Le Havre airfield.	Messerschmitt Bf 109E	40 %	Pilot unhurt.
18.	III./KGzb. 1	NCM	Landing accident at Guines airfield.	Junkers Ju 52/3m (5589 : 1Z+FU)	35 %	No casualties.
19.	Aufkl.St.Ob.d.L.	NCM	Engine failure on take-off at Værløse airfield.	Heinkel He 116 (3058 : D-ANYW)	95 %	Ltn. Rading + one injured.
20.	*Seenotflug-kommando 4*	NCM	Taxying accident at Wesermünde airfield.	Focke-Wulf Fw 58 (0002 : KP+AB)	5 %	No casualties.

Wednesday 11th September

The night of 10th/11th September had been tiresome for the populations of both London and Berlin. Bomber Command attacked the German capital and at last caused the Germans to admit "considerable damage"; the Postdamer station, Brandenburger Tor and the Reichstag were all hit, and severe fires started in the Potsdamerplatz, Dorotheenstrasse and Hermann Göringstrasse; elsewhere in Germany the Focke-Wulf factory at Bremen, naval barracks at Wilhelmshaven and the railway centre at Duisberg were hit.

Meanwhile the *Luftwaffe* was busy bombing London again, striking at Thames-side factories and warehouses, but also hitting a number of buildings in the central area—including a church (which was gutted) and Buckingham Palace.

Daylight brought a deterioration in the weather and there was little enemy activity during the morning, a few reconnaissance aircraft being spotted over the Southern Counties. One

Two famous Battle pilots. *Left*, **Plt. Off. E.S. Lock, of No. 41 (Fighter) Squadron. Right, Stanford Tuck, seen here as a Squadron Leader, commanding No. 257 Squadron late in the Battle.**

such plot was tracked over six counties and three Spitfire squadrons searched in vain among the clouds for almost an hour before it was discovered to be a Blenheim—which landed at Thorney Island.

The afternoon's weather improved and both Kesselring and Sperrle launched heavy co-ordinated attacks lasting two hours. Bomber formations were reported to be building up over the Pas de Calais shortly before 15.00 hours and soon afterwards, accompanied by more than 200 fighters, flew up the Thames Estuary towards London. Nine fighter squadrons attacked from about 15.30 hours but could not get close to the bombers until the bombs began falling in the dock area. Once again the *Zerstörer* forces pulled away to the south (as they had done on the 9th) and formed up in circles in the Croydon

area to cover the withdrawal of the bombers. This time, however, the Bf 109s had wasted too much fuel on the approach to the target and had to break off for their return to base.

The Heinkels of I. and II.*Gruppen*, KG 26 were thus left entirely shorn of protection fairly early in their run-up over London, and upon them fell more than 60 Hurricanes and Spitfires of Nos. 17, 56, 73, 222, 249 and 303 Squadrons. No fewer than ten bombers were shot down, and twelve others were damaged, as they struggled to reach the coast; and the Bf 110s were so effectively hounded by the Hurricanes that they could provide no effective cover. The two bomber *Gruppen* lost about 50 aircrew killed or missing, with another dozen men wounded.

The Heinkel He 111Hs of KG 26 suffered particularly heavy casualties on 11th September, seven aircraft being shot down; ten men were killed, seventeen missing and seven wounded. The aircraft shown here was shot down and the pilot succeeded in making a good forced landing, but once again the anti-invasion posts proved effective obstacles, probably rupturing a fuel tank and causing the bomber to catch fire; the fate of the crew is not known.

In the confusion of battles, however, some squadrons—in particular the Spitfires of Nos. 41 and 92 Squadrons, and the Hurricanes of No. 1 (Canadian) Squadron—were ordered to engage too low and were attacked by enemy fighters—a free chase arrived at the critical moment—which shot down about four Hurricanes and eight Spitfires. Wimpey Wade of No. 92 Squadron had to force land at Gravesend. The Bf 110s of ZG 26 were also given a hard time by the British fighters, and lost five of their number.

Meanwhile, further west, Brand had been unable to reinforce Park as he was hurriedly ordering up squadrons to meet a raid flying towards the Isle of Wight. This was closely covered by Bf 109s and 110s, and these effectively protected the bombers as they flew in over Portsmouth and Southampton. Relatively little damage was done, and as the raid turned south several of No. 10 Group's squadrons were diverted over Sussex to join in the battle south of London.

Later in the evening, following reports from reconnaissance aircraft of continuing assembly of invasion barges in the Channel ports, Bomber and Coastal Commands mounted concerted raids by every available aircraft. In the space of three hours more than one hundred aircraft dropped about 80 tons of bombs on the docks of Calais, Dunkirk, Le Havre and Boulogne, destroying upwards of one hundred barges. The *Luftwaffe* reacted violently against each raid, putting up at least 60 Bf 109s. Six Blenheims of No. 235 Squadron were ordered to escort a formation of the Fleet Air Arm's new Albacores which were bombing Calais; they were attacked by the Messerschmitts of Galland's JG 26 and lost two aircraft— those of Flt. Lt. Frederick Flood and Plt. Off. Peter Wickings-Smith. The loss of fifteen aircraft over the Channel ports that evening more than balanced the day's losses in the Germans' favour.

R.A.F. FIGHTER COMMAND LOSSES—WEDNESDAY 11th SEPTEMBER 1940

#	Squadron		Details	Time	Pilot	Aircraft	Serial	Category
1.	1 (Canadian) Sqn.(Northolt)	C	Shot down by He 111s over Tunbridge Wells; pilot baled out with burns and wounds. Aircrashed at Lakestreet Manor, Mayfield.	16.12 hrs.	Fg. Off. T.B. Little	Hurricane	P3534	Cat. 3 Destroyed
2.	1 (Canadian) Sqn.(Northolt)	C	Shot down by He 111s near Tunbridge Wells; aircraft crashed near Romney; pilot unhurt.	16.19 hrs.	Fg. Off. P.W. Lochnan	Hurricane	V6670	Cat. 3 Destroyed
3.	17 Sqn., Debden	C	Damaged in combat with Bf 110; pilot landed at base, unhurt.	A16.10 hrs.	Sgt. L.H. Bartlett	Hurricane	—	Cat. 1 Damaged
4.	19 Sqn., Fowlmere	C	Believed damaged by Bf 110 east of London and force landed; pilot unhurt.	A15.50 hrs.	F/Sgt. G.C. Unwin	Spitfire	—	Cat. 2 Damaged
5.	41 Sqn., Hornchurch	C	Damaged by Bf 110s over the Thames Estuary; pilot landed at base would by shell splinter in left heel. (1)	16.10 hrs.	Plt. Off. G.H. Bennions	Spitfire	—	Cat. 3 Destroyed
6.	41 Sqn., Hornchurch	C	Shot down by Bf 110s and crashed at Sevenoaks, Kent; pilot unhurt.	A15.50 hrs.	Not known	Spitfire	X4325	Cat. 3 Destroyed
7.	46 Sqn., Stapleford	C	Shot down by Bf 109 north of Dungeness and force landed; pilot slightly wounded.	A16.00 hrs.	Plt. Off. P.R. McGregor	Hurricane	P3094	Cat. 3 Destroyed
8.	46 Sqn., Stapleford	C	Missing after combat over the Thames Estuary; pilot assumed lost at sea.	Not known	Sgt. W.A. Peacock	Hurricane	V7232	Cat. 3 Lost
9.	46 Sqn., Stapleford	C	Shot down by Bf 110 over Hawkhurst, Kent; pilot baled out at Bodiam, slightly wounded. Aircraft crashed at Sandhurst, Kent.	15.48 hrs.	Sgt. R.E.de C. d'Hamale	Hurricane	V6549	Cat. 3 Destroyed
10.	66 Sqn., Gravesend	C	Shot down by He 111 and force landed near Ashford. Pilot unhurt.	Not known	Plt. Off. I.J.A. Cruickshanks	Spitfire	—	Cat. 2 Damaged
11.	72 Sqn., Croydon	C	Damaged in action with Bf 109s over Gravesend; pilot landed at base slightly wounded.	A16.05 hrs.	Plt. Off. B. Douthwaite	Spitfire	R6710	Cat. 1 Damaged
12.	73 Sqn., Debden	C	Shot down by Bf 110 near Detling; pilot baled out unhurt.	16.13 hrs.	Sgt. H.G. Webster	Hurricane	P2796	Cat. 3 Destroyed
13.	73 Sqn., Debden	C	Damaged by Bf 110 over the Isle of Sheppey; pilot returned to base unhurt.	16.15 hrs.	Sgt. R.V. Ellis	Hurricane	P3868	Cat. 1 Damaged
14.	92 Sqn., Biggin Hill	C	Shot down by Bf 109s near Dungeness and assumed lost with pilot at sea.	16.10 hrs.	Plt. Off. F.N. Hargreaves	Spitfire	K9793	Cat. 3 Missing
15.	92 Sqn., Biggin Hill	C	Shot down by Bf 109s and force landed at Hawkinge; pilot unhurt.	16.20 hrs.	Plt. Off. T.S. Wade	Spitfire	P9513	Cat. 2 Damaged
16.	92 Sqn., Biggin Hill	C	Shot down by Bf 109s east of London; crash landed, but pilot unhurt.	18.15 hrs.	Plt. Off. A.J.S. Pattinson	Spitfire	R6613	Cat. 3 Destroyed
17.	92 Sqn., Biggin Hill	C	Shot down by Bf 109s between Hythe and Asford. Aircraft crashed at Smeeth; pilot killed, and buried at Hawkinge.	18.14 hrs.	Plt. Off. H.D. Edwards	Spitfire	P9464	Cat. 3 Destroyed
18.	92 Sqn., Biggin Hill	C	Shot down by Bf 109s and force landed at Gravesend; pilot unhurt.	18.23 hrs.	Plt. Off. T.S. Wade	Spitfire	—	Cat. 2 Damaged
19.	213 Sqn., Exeter	C	Shot down by Bf 110s into sea one mile off Selsey; pilot and aircraft missing.	16.30 hrs.	Sgt. A. Wojcicki	Hurricane	W6667	Cat. 3 Missing
20.	213 Sqn., Exeter	C	Shot down by Bf 110s into sea off Selsey; pilot baled out unhur and rescued.	16.30 hrs.	Flt. Lt. J.E.J. Sing	Hurricane	P3780	Cat. 3 Missing
21.	222 Sqn., Hornchurch	C	Shot down by Bf 109 and force landed at Parsonage Farm, Fletching, East Sussex; pilot unhurt.	16.01 hrs.	Plt. Off. W.R. Assheton	Spitfire	R6638	Cat. 2 Damaged
22.	229 Sqn., Northolt	C	Shot down by enemy fighters over Biggin Hill; pilot baled out and admitted to Langley Hospital, Shorncliffe, with shock.	16.14 hrs.	Plt. Off. M. Ravenhill	Hurricane	P3038	Cat. 3 Destroyed
23.	229 Sqn., Northolt	C	Shot down while attacking He 111s over Maidstone; baled out at Flimwell with burns to face and wrists.	16.18 hrs.	Plt. Off. K.M. Carver	Hurricane	N2466	Cat. 3 Destroyed
24.	229 Sqn., Northolt	C	Attacked by Bf 109 over Maidstone which shattered windscreen causing facial injuries to pilot; aircraft was landed safely however.	16.21 hrs.	Flt. Lt. R.F. Rimmer	Hurricane	P3463	Cat. 1 Damaged
25.	235 Sqn., Thorney Island	C	Shot down over Calais by Bf 109s while escorting Albacores on bombing raid; crew killed.	20.10 hrs.	Plt. Off. P.C. Wickings-Smith Plt. Off. A.W.V. Green Sgt. R.D.H. Watts	Blenheim	—	Cat. 3 Destroyed
26.	235 Sqn., Thorney Island	C	Shot down over Calais by Bf 109s while escorting Albacores on bombing raid; crew killed.	20.21 hrs.	Flt.Lt.F.W. Flood Plt. Off. N.B. Shorrocks Sgt. B.R. Sharp	Blenheim	Z5725	Cat. 3 Destroyed

R.A.F. Losses, 11th September 1940—*continued*

27.	238 Sqn., Middle Wallop	C	Shot down by Ju 88 near Brooklands, near Rye; pilot baled out with burns and admitted to Tunbridge Wells Hospital.	16.05 hrs.	Plt. Off. W. Tower-Perkins	Hurricane	*P3906*	Cat. 3 Destroyed
28.	238 Sqn., Middle Wallop	C	Missing after interception of Ju 88s near Tunbridge Wells; pilot assumed killed.	A16.10 hrs	Flt. Lt. D.P. Hughes	Hurricane	*V7240*	Cat. 3 Missing
29.	238 Sqn., Middle Wallop	C	Missing after interception of Ju 88s near Tunbridge Wells. (Wreckage located in 1973 at Little Scotney Farm, Lydd, proved to be this Hurricane.)	A16.10 hrs.	Sgt. S. Duszinski	Hurricane	*R2682*	Cat. 3 Missing
30.	249 Sqn., North Weald	C	Shot down in flames by He 111; pilot baled out unhurt at Benenden, Kent.	15.58 hrs.	Sgt. W.L. Davis	Hurricane	*V6682*	Cat. 3 Destroyed
31.	266 Sqn., Wittering	C	Shot down by He 111 near Billericay and pilot baled out unhurt.	A17.10 hrs.	Plt. Off. R.J.B. Roach	Spitfire	*P7313*	Cat. 3 Destroyed
32.	303 Sqn., Northolt	C	Shot down by Bf 109 over Pembury, Kent; pilot, grievously wounded, died on 19-9-40.	16.00 hrs.	Fg. Off. A. Cebrzynski	Hurricane	*V6665*	Cat. 3 Destroyed
33.	303 Sqn., Northolt	C	Shot down by Bf 109 over Kent; pilot killed. Aircraft fell at Hogtrough Hill, Westerham.	16.04 hrs.	Sgt. S. Wojtowicz	Hurricane	*V7242*	Cat. 3 Destroyed
34.	303 Sqn., Northolt	C	Damaged by Bf 109 over Kent; pilot, wounded, landed safely at Heston.	16.10 hrs.	Flt. Lt. A.S. Forbes	Hurricane	—	Cat. 2 Damaged
35.	501 Sqn., Kenley	C	Shot down by Bf 109s over Maidstone; pilot baled out unhurt.	16.01 hrs.	Sgt. T.G. Pickering	Hurricane	*P5200*	Cat. 3 Destroyed
36.	504 Sqn., Hendon	C	Shot down by Bf 109s near Newchurch, Kent; pilot died in his cockpit.	16.05 hrs.	Plt. Off. A.W. Clarke	Hurricane	*P3770*	Cat. 3 Destroyed
37.	504 Sqn., Hendon	C	Suffered take-off accident when undercarriage collapsed; pilot unhurt.	15.10 hrs.	Plt. Off. M. Rook	Hurricane	*P3249*	Cat. 2 Damaged
38.	504 Sqn., Hendon	C	Force landed after take-off with oil trouble; pilot unhurt.	15.12 hrs.	Plt. Off. J.V. Gurteen	Hurricane	*N2471*	Cat. 2 Damaged
39.	602 Sqn., Westhampnett	C	Shot down by Bf 110 over Selsey Bill; pilot's body recovered from sea at Brighton on 10-10-40.	16.10 hrs.	Sgt. M.H. Sprague	Spitfire	*N3282*	Cat. 3 Missing
40.	602 Sqn., Westhampnett	C	Shot down by Bf 110 over Sussex; pilot slightly wounded.	16.14 hrs.	Plt. Off. S.N. Rose	Spitfire	*L1027*	Cat. 3 Destroyed
41.	602 Sqn., Westhampnett	C	Shot down by Bf 110 over Sussex; pilot baled out unhurt.	A16.15 hrs.	Not known	Spitfire	—	Cat. 3 Destroyed
42.	611 Sqn., Fowlmere	C	Shot down by Bf 109 near Croydon; pilot baled out with parachute on fire and was dead on landing at Farleigh, Surrey; aircraft fell in Shirley.	15.52 hrs.	Sgt. F.E.R. Shepherd	Spitfire	*P7298*	Cat. 3 Destroyed
43.	611 Sqn., Fowlmere	C	Shot down by Bf 109 and force landed near Kenley; pilot unhurt.	15.55 hrs.	Sgt. S.A. Levenson	Spitfire	*P7321*	Cat. 3 Destroyed

[(1) Plt. Off. Bennions managed to force land his damaged Spitfire at Hornchurch despite a shell splinter in his left heel; his parachute was smouldering from the impact of an incendiary bullet, and his back armour plate had been penetrated by an armour-piercing shell.]

LUFTWAFFE LOSSES—WEDNESDAY 11th SEPTEMBER 1940

1.	Stab/KG 1	CM	Shot down by 303 Sqn. Hurricane of Frantisek near Horsham at 16.16 hrs.	Heinkel He 111H-3 (5606 : V4+FA)	100 %	Ltn. Behn, Fw. Sommer, Uffz. Möck, Uffz. Arndt and Gefr. Männich missing.
2.	KG 1	CM	Shot down by 303 Sqn. Hurricane of Henneberg south-east of London at 16.10 hrs.	Heinkel He 111H-2 (5364 : V4+RW)	100 %	Uffz. Hanzen, Uffz. Markert, Uffz. Wildehopf, Uffz. Krall and Fl. Wilhelm missing.
3.	3./KG 1	CM	Shot down by *flak* south of London at A.16.05 hrs.	Heinkel He 111H-3 (3233 : V4+KL)	100 %	Uffz. Steinicke, Uffz. Hirsch, Uffz. Kramer, Gefr. Pfeiffer and Gefr. Pümpel missing.
4.	3./KG 1	CM	Damaged by British fighters south of London and crashed at Amiens on return.	Heinkel He 111H-3 (6852 : V4+AL)	60 %	One killed and one wounded.
5.	6./KG 1	CM	Damaged by British fighters south of London and force landed at Boisville on return.	Heinkel He 111H-2 ((2733 : V4+BW)	10 %	Two wounded.
6.	I./KG 26	CM	Damaged by British fighters over Thames Estuary and crashed at Wevelghem on return.	Heinkel He 111H-4 (6965 : 1H+AB)	15 %	Crew unhurt.
7.	I./KG 26	CM	Damaged by fighter over Thames Estuary and force landed at Wevelghem on return.	Heinkel He 111H-3 (5616 : 1H+BB)	40 %	One crew member wounded.
8.	I./KG 26	CM	Shot down by 222 Sqn. Spitfire of Baxter near Hornchurch at A.16.20 hrs.	Heinkel He 111H-3 (5680 : 1H+CB)	100 %	Fw. Friedrich, Fw. George, Uffz. Hoffmann, Uffz. Dreyer, Uffz. Stirnemann missing.
9.	1./KG 26	CM	Shot down by 303 Sqn. Hurricane of Brzozowski near Horsham at 16.20 hrs.	Heinkel He 111H-4 (6962 : 1H+AH)	100 %	Uffz. Schang and Fw. Schäfer killed; Hptm. Künstler, *St.Kap.*, Uffz.Schmidt, Fw.Büttner missing.
10.	1./KG 26	CM	Damaged by British fighters near London.	Heinkel He 111H-4 (6977 : 1H+EH)	15 %	One crew member wounded.
11.	1./KG 26	CM	Damaged by British fighters near London.	Heinkel He 111H-4 (3214 : 1H+HH)	40 %	Oblt. Lensch killed.
12.	1./KG 26	CM	Damaged by British fighters, and pilot baled out near London; bombardier flew aircraft home and force landed near Dieppe.	Heinkel He 111H-4 (6981 : 2H+KH)	100 %	Fw. Jabusch missing; one crew member wounded.
13.	2./KG 26	CM	Damaged by British fighters near London.	Heinkel He 111H-3 (5603 : 1H+FK)	15 %	Crew unhurt.
14.	2./KG 26	CM	Shot down by British fighters into Channel; four crew members baled out.	Heinkel He 111H-3 (3215 : 1H+JK)	100 %	Fw. Horn killed; four crew (one wounded) rescued by *Seenotflug-kommando*.
15.	3./KG 26	CM	Damaged by British fighters south of London.	Heinkel He 111H-3 (6854 : 1H+BL)	25 %	Crew unhurt.
16.	3./KG 26	CM	Shot down by 222 Sqn. Spitfire of Scott near Hornchurch at A.16.20 hrs.	Heinkel He 111H-3 (3157 : 1H+ML)	100 %	Fw. Westfalen, Uffz. Herms, Gefr. Zähle killed; Oblt. Abenhausen and Fw. Hauswald missing.(1)
17.	II./KG 26	CM	Damaged by British fighters east of London.	Heinkel He 111H-3 (6856 : 1H+AC)	25 %	One crew member wounded.
18.	4./KG 26	CM	Damaged by British fighters near London.	Heinkel He 111H-5 (3540 : 1H+CM)	30 %	One killed and two wounded.
19.	5./KG 26	CM	Shot down by 249 Sqn. Hurricanes east of London at 14.48 hrs.	Heinkel He 111H-3 (6903 : 2H+JN)	100 %	Ofw. Kramer killed; Oblt. Bertram, Gefr. Schröder and Gefr.Entrich missing.

Luftwaffe Losses, 11th September 1940—*continued*

20.	5./KG 26	CM	Shot down by 249 Sqn. Hurricanes east of London at 14.48 hrs.	Heinkel He 111H-5 (3545 : 1H+BC)	100 %	Uffz.Meusel killed;Ltn.Wesemann, Fw. Gutacker, Fw. Geiss missing.
21.	5./KG 26	CM	Damaged by 249 Sqn. Hurricanes east of London at A.16.00 hrs., and crashed at Gilze-Rijen.	Heinkel He 111H-3 (6936 : 1H+EN)	40 %	Crew unhurt.
22.	5./KG 26	CM	Damaged by British fighters east of London.	Heinkel He 111H-3 (3935 : 1H+FN)	40 %	Crew unhurt.
23.	II./KG 54	NCM	Landing accident at St. André airfield.	Junkers Ju 88A-1(6092)	30 %	Crew unhurt.
24.	St.St./KG 55	NCM	Landing accident at Villacoublay airfield.	Heinkel He 111P (2683)	100 %	Three killed and one injured.
25.	2./St.G 77	NCM	Air collision with Item 26 at Curfeulles.	Junkers Ju 87B-1 (5162 : S2+KP)	100 %	Two crew members killed.
26.	2./St.G 77	NCM	Air collision with Item 25 at Curfeulles.	Junkers Ju 87B-1 (5521 : S2+JK)	100 %	One crew member killed.
27.	3./St.G 77	NCM	Taxying accident at Maltot airfield.	Junkers Ju 87B-1 (0472 : S2+BL)	20 %	Crew unhurt.
28.	3./St.G 77	NCM	Air collision with Item 29 at Curfeulles.	Junkers Ju 87B-2 (5739 : S2+HL)	100 %	One killed and one injured.
29.	3./St.G 77	NCM	Air collision with Item 28 at Curfeulles.	Junkers Ju 87B-2 (5630 : S2+FL).	100 %	Crew unhurt.
30.	I./ZG 2	CM	Missing from combat sortie over Southern England.	Messerschmitt Bf 110 C-4 (3376 : A2+MH)	100 %	Gefr. Kling and Gefr. Sossner missing.
31.	I./ZG 2	CM	Damaged by British fighters over Southern England and force landed at St. Aubin.	Messerschmitt Bf 110 C-4 (3623)	50 %	Crew unhurt.
32.	1./ZG 26	CM	Damaged by 46 Sqn. Hurricane of Johnson over Kent at 15.45 hrs.	Messerschmitt Bf 110 C-4 (2190 : U8+KH)	20 %	One crew member killed.
33.	2./ZG 26	CM	Shot down by Spitfire and crashed at Cobham Farm, Charing, Kent , at 17.00 hrs.	Messerschmitt Bf 110 C-3 (1372 : U8+HL)	100 %	Fw. Hermann Brinkmann and Uffz. Erwin Krusphow, P.O.W.s.
34.	Stab II./ZG 26	CM	Shot down by 17 Sqn. Hurricane of Czernin over Thames Estuary at 16.15 hrs.	Messerschmitt Bf 110 C-4 (3625 : 3U+HM)	100 %	Oblt. Henken and Fw. Radelmeier killed.
35.	4./ZG 26	CM	Shot down by 73 Sqn. Hurricane of Smith over the Isle of Sheppey at 16.12 hrs.	Messerschmitt Bf 110 D-2 (3392 : 3U+DM)	100 %	Uffz. Kleiber killed; Oblt. Birkner missing.
36.	6./ZG 26	CM	Shot down by 17 Sqn. Hurricane of Bayne over Margate Sands at A.16.15 hrs.	Messerschmitt Bf 110 D-2 (3400 : 3U+HP)	100 %	Ogefr. Hofman killed; Ltn. Volk missing.
37.	9./ZG 26	CM	Shot down by 73 Sqn. Hurricane of Robinson five miles east of Herne Bay at 16.20 hrs.	Messerschmitt Bf 110 C-4 (3231 : 3U+LT)	100 %	Oblt. Junghans and Gefr. Eckert missing.
38.	II./ZG 76	CM	Force landed in the sea off Etaples (?) after combat.	Messerschmitt Bf 110C (3286 : M8+KC)	100 %	Both crew members, unhurt, rescued by *Seenotflugkommando.*
39.	I./LG 2	CM	Said to have collided with British fighter near London; R.A.F. pilot not identified.	Messerschmitt Bf 109 E-7 (2029)	100 %	Uffz. Heckmeier killed.
40.	I./LG 2	CM	Damaged in combat with British fighters and crashed on return to Wissant.	Messerschmitt Bf 109 E-7 (5797)	75 %	Pilot unhurt.
41.	II./LG 2	NCM	Landing accident at Calais-Marck; not combat.	Messerschmitt Bf 109 E-4 (2020)	50 %	Pilot unhurt.
42.	1./JG 3 (2)	CM	Collided with Item 43 over the Channel; pilot baled out.	Messerschmitt Bf 109 E-4 (5276)	100 %	Pilot, unhurt, rescued by *Seenotflugkommando.*
43.	1/.JG 3	CM	Collided with Item 42 over the Channel but returned to base safely.	Messerschmitt Bf 109 E-4 (5341)	25 %	Pilot unhurt.
44.	6./JG 3	CM	Landing accident at Wierre-au-Bois airfield.	Messerschmitt Bf 109 E-4 (5056)	45 %	Pilot unhurt.
45.	2./JG 51	CM	Shot down by 303 Sqn. Hurricane of Frantisek over Sussex at A.16.30 hrs.	Messerschmitt Bf 109 E-4 (1641)	100 %	Hptm. Wiggers, *St.Kap.*, killed.
46.	8./JG 51	CM	Shot down by 66 Sqn. Spitfire of Bodie over Sussex during the afternoon.	Messerschmitt Bf 109 E-1 (6293)	100 %	Fw. Siemer killed.
47.	5./196	NCM	Caught fire during gunnery practice on the Holtenau air firing range.	Arado Ar 196 (0067 : 6W+KN)	75 %	One crew member injured.
48.	*Seenotsonder-kommando Wesermünde*	NCM	Landing accident on Rheims airfield.	Focke-Wulf Fw 58 (2033)	90 %	One crew member injured.
49.	*Korps-Führ-ungskette X Fliegerkorps*	CM	Engine failure while returning from operational sortie over the Moray Firth.	Heinkel He 111H-3 (3253 : P4+BA)	30 %	Hptm. Kowalewski wounded.

[Notes. (1) This aircraft was pursued by Scott and finally crashed at Dormansland, near Lingfield, Surrey. Fw. Heinrich Westfalen, Uffz. Bruno Herms and Gefr. Zähle were killed and were buried in Dormansland churchyard. Oblt. Abenhausen and Fw. Hauswald were saved by their parachutes and made prisoners.
(2) At least three other Bf 109s of I./JG 3 (not mentioned in the German loss returns) are known to have been destroyed on this day. Wreckage was examined and prisoners taken at Wadhurst and Newhaven at around 16.30 hrs.]

Thursday 12th September

As reports from reconnaissance squadrons and the P.R.U. continued to indicate a steady build-up of invasion forces along the French coast, Bomber Command added a number of rail centres in France and Germany to its list of vital targets.

German activity over Britain was again on a reduced scale with isolated reconnaissance sorties being flown over the South, and it must be assumed that by now the *Luftwaffe* was being ordered to keep watch for any obvious movement of British troops towards the South Coast. A number of nuisance raids was mounted by LG 1 crews against coastal targets, and bombs fell close to several radar stations in Kent, Sussex and Hampshire. Plt. Off. Tom Cooper-Slipper in a Hurricane of No. 605 Squadron caught sight of a reconnaissance Junkers

Ju 88 of 1.(F)/122 in the afternoon and chased it almost to the French coast before shooting it down. Further north No. 12 Group intercepted a radio message from a Junkers Ju 88 of KG 54 informing its base that it had been attacked by British fighters and was returning home; the British pilots were Flt. Lt. Roddick Smith and Fg. Off. Kenneth Blair of No. 151 Squadron. The Ju 88 managed to reach its base, though with a dead crew member.

The night raids on London, though lighter than of late, dropped bombs over a wide area of the City and the West End. A delayed action bomb fell within yards of St. Paul's Cathedral, and its removal by Lt. Robert Davies and Sapper George Cameron Wylie not only earned them the award of the first

George Crosses but also undoubtedly saved the historic building from serious damage[23]. In another incident on this day an important piece of equipment was brought into use for the first time to deal with an unexploded bomb which was lying in London's Regent Street outside the Ford show-rooms[24]. This was the "steam sterilizer", which was introduced through a hole cut in the bomb casing, well away from the sensitive electrical condenser resistance fuse; steam was forced into the relatively inert main explosive to emulsify it, allowing it to be drained away.

---

[23] The introduction of this medal, to be awarded to civilians for supreme acts of valour, and ranking immediately after the Victoria Cross, was announced on 23rd September. It is significant that a need for a supreme civilian gallantry award was now recognised.

[24] This bomb was dropped during the night of 11th/12th September, and was neutralised by Arthur Douglas Merriman; his George Cross citation indicates that his act was performed *prior* to that of Davies and Wylie.

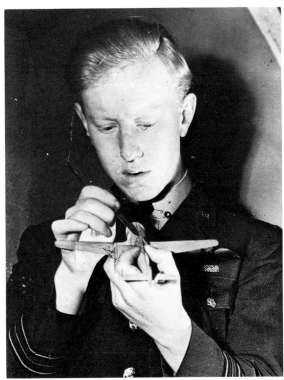

J.H. ("Ginger") Lacey who, as a sergeant pilot in the Battle of Britain, was one of the top-scoring Allied pilots, and shot down a Heinkel He 111 of III./KG 27 on 13th September. The photograph shows him as a Squadron Leader later in the War.

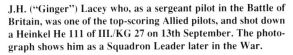

R.A.F. FIGHTER COMMAND LOSSES—THURSDAY 12th SEPTEMBER 1940

1.	46 Sqn., Stapleford	C	Aircraft crashed during patrol; not combat.	Not known	Sgt. S. Andrew	Hurricane	*P3525*	Cat. 3 Destroyed
2.	87 Sqn., Exeter	C	Aircraft and pilot missing on flight from Exeter to Tangmere; pilot's body recovered from the sea on the Sussex coast on 30-9-40.	Not known	Wg. Cdr. J.S. Dewar	Hurricane	—	Cat. 3 Missing

LUFTWAFFE LOSSES—THURSDAY 12th SEPTEMBER 1940

1.	3.(H)/14	NCM	Suffered landing accident at Malines airfield.	Henschel Hs 126 (4204)	40 %	Crew unhurt.
2.	4.(F)/121	NCM	Suffered take-off accident at Boblingen airfield.	Dornier Do 17P (3530)	100 %	Two crew members killed.
3.	1.(F)/122	CM	Shot down by three 605 Sqn. Hurricanes 8 miles south-east of Cap Gris Nez at 14.40 hrs.	Junkers Ju 88A-1 (0318 : F6+NH)	100 %	Ltn.Krautwurst, Fw.Bibers, Ogefr. Plänge, Fw.Kaltenbach missing.
4.	II./KG 4	CM	Crashed with engine failure on take-off at Eindhoven.	Heinkel He 111P-4 (2924 : 5J+FN)	90 %	Crew unhurt.
5.	I./KG 51	CM	Crash landed near Melun-Villaroche; cause not notified.	Junkers Ju 88A-1 (2089)	100 %	Uffz. Wilhelm Hölzner, Uffz. Helmut Kirsch, Gefr. Köhler and Uffz. Fritz Wöhler killed.
6.	I./KG 51	CM	Damaged by 238 Sqn. Hurricanes of Davis and Simmonds 4 miles east of Boscombe Down.	Junkers Ju 88A-1 (4052)	40 %	Uffz. Karl Hennike killed, and two other crew members wounded.
7.	I./KG 54	CM	Damaged by 151 Sqn. Hurricanes of Blair and Smith. (Confirmed by intercepted signal.)	Junkers Ju 88A-1 (6131)	17 %	Crew unhurt.
8.	II./LG 1	CM	Crash landed, short of fuel, near Romorantin.	Junkers Ju 88A-1 (2062 : L1+EM)	100 %	Hptm. Ehrenfordt killed.
9.	9./ZG 26	NCM	Force landed at Teuteburger-Wald; cause not notified.	Messerschmitt Bf 110 (3628)	15 %	Crew unhurt.
10.	II./ZG 76	NCM	Crashed near Camrai; cause not notified.	Messerschmitt Bf 110C (3610 : M8+MN)	100 %	Both crew members injured.
11.	6./JG 27	CM	Taxying accident of Rennes airfield.	Messerschmitt Bf 109E (3859)	30 %	Pilot unhurt.
12.	2./JG 52	NCM	Crashed near Calais; cause not notified.	Messerschmitt Bf 109 E-1 (3182)	100 %	Pilot killed.
13.	II./JG 53	NCM	Landing accident at St. Malo airfield.	Arado Ar 68 (0362 : DK+QE)	15 %	Pilot injured.

Friday 13th September

The mounting pressure exerted by Bomber and Coastal Commands against the "Invasion Coast" was now causing the German forces to concentrate increasing numbers of anti-aircraft guns in the various embarkation port areas, while the fighter defences were increased by the withdrawal of a further six *Staffeln* from offensive operations. Bomber Command therefore introduced a series of tactics aimed at improving the effect of the bombing and reducing losses; these included co-ordinated low and medium level attacks over a wide area, lasting throughout the hours of darkness. Such attacks were made on the nights of 12th/13th and 13th/14th on Boulogne, Calais and Antwerp, in which ports more than 70 landing barges were destroyed. Two bombers were lost to *flak*.

Among the Fighter Command night losses was an aircraft

of the Fighter Interception unit, always previously recorded as having been the Beaufighter *R2059*, lost off the coast of France. The aircraft was in fact a Blenheim Mark IV night fighter equipped with A.I. radar and I.F.F. equipment; there was some anxiety that this secret equipment might have fallen into German hands intact. These fears were allayed with the arrival of a postcard addressed to "Uncle Joe" (Wg. Cdr. George Chamberlain's nickname, the C.O. of the F.I.U.) from Sgt. Edward Byrne, the radar operator, in a German prison camp, in which he successfully contrived to disclose that the aircraft had been destroyed by fire and that the destructor charges had been activated.

R.A.F. FIGHTER COMMAND LOSSES—FRIDAY 13th SEPTEMBER 1940

1.	248 Sqn., Sumburgh	C	Shot down by enemy fighters while on reconnaissance sortie over Norwegian coast; crew killed.	Not known	Sgt. W.J. Garfield Sgt. B.W. Mesner Sgt. A. Kay	Blenheim	—	Cat. 3 Missing
2.	501 Sqn., Kenley	C	Shot down by He 111; pilot baled out unhurt. Aircraft fells at Abbey Farm, Leeds, Kent.	11.45 hrs.	Sgt. J.H. Lacey	Hurricane	P2793	Cat. 3 Destroyed
3.	F.I.U. Shoreham	C	Missing from night patrol over Channel; aircraft crashed into sea off Calais; crew taken prisoner. (1)	At night	Flt. Lt. R.G. Ker-Ramsay Sgt. G. Dixon AC E.L. Byrne	Blenheim IV	Z7251	Cat. 3 Missing

[(1) Previously recorded as having been a Beaufighter, this aircraft was indeed a Blenheim equipped with Mark IV A.I. radar and the latest I.F.F. equipment; a coded message from the P.O.W.s to the F.I.U. provided reassurance that the destruction charges had prevented any risk of this equipment falling into enemy hands.]

LUFTWAFFE LOSSES—FRIDAY 13th SEPTEMBER 1940

1.	2./KG 1	CM	Crashed at Montdidier airfield; cause not known.	Heinkel He 111H-3 (5458 : V4+OK)	100 %	Oblt. Eisenbrandt + one killed; two crew members wounded.
2.	III./JG 27	CM	Shot down by 501 Sqn. Hurricane of Lacey over Kent at A.12.00 hrs.	Heinkel He 111P (2670 : 1G+DS)	100 %	Uffz. Bernd, Ofw. Elster, Uffz. Okunek killed; Oblt. Harry Wappler missing.
3.	9./KG 51	CM	Crashed at Rouen, possibly as the result of combat with 607 Sqn. Hurricane of Blackadder.	Junkers Ju 88A-1 (5053 : 9K+DT)	100 %	Ogefr. Rueba and Uffz. Gutberlet killed.
4.	III./KG 55	CM	Crashed at Etretat, possibly following combat.	Heinkel He 111P-2 (2910)	100 %	Ltn. Helmut Rockenhäuser + four other crew members killed.
5.	III./LG 1	CM	Damaged by three Hurricanes of 238 Sqn. over Wiltshire at A..15.45 hrs.; crashed on return.	Junkers Ju 88A-1 (6112 : L1+DD)	100 %	One crew member wounded.
6.	II./NJG 1	NCM	Landing accident at Lechfeld airfield.	Junkers Ju 88C (0260)	35 %	Crew unhurt.
7.	3./JG 53	NCM	Overturned on landing at Neuville airfield.	Messerschmitt Bf 109 E-4 (6275)	30 %	Pilot unhurt.
8.	5./JG 77	CM	Struck obstacle on the runway at Vaernes; five Norwegian labourers killed.	Messerschmitt Bf 109E (5262)	100 %	Pilot unhurt.
9.	*Seenotflug-kommando 3*	—	Destroyed in R.A.F. raid on Boulogne.	Heinkel He 59 (0932 : TV+HM)	100 %	No aircrew casualties.
10.	*Kurierstaffe¹*	NCM	Force landed in bad weather at Etaples le Touquet; Generalmajor Cantzler (Heer) injured.	Focke-Wulf Fw 58 C-2 (0251 : TD+HK)	60 %	Two crew members injured.

Saturday 14th September

Despite a temporary deterioration in the weather, German daylight operations over Britain on this day showed a distinct increase, and six *Luftwaffe* aircraft were destroyed[25]. Again London was the target for about twenty Heinkels of KG 4, most of which managed to reach the southern outskirts under cover of cloud, but were prevented by the weather from attacking any important target; random bombs did, however, inflict 49 fatal casualties in the Kingston and Wimbledon areas.

[25] The frequently quoted figure of fourteen (derived from post-War official British examination of German aircraft loss reports), is an example of a superficial understanding of the German definition of what constituted a "combat" loss. For instance the crash in fog of a Henschel Hs 126 (labelled *Feindflug* or "war flight" in German records) has hitherto been ascribed as a Battle of Britain casualty. Examination of the German loss table for this day will indicate that the figure of fourteen was reached by including all aircraft suffering 60 % or greater damage—irrespective of the nature of the loss.

Oberleutnant Joachim Müncheberg, *Staffelkapitän* of 7th *Staffel*, JG 26, during August and September 1940. On 14th September he claimed his twentieth victory, and was awarded the Knight's Cross. He later rose to become *Kommodore* JG 77, but was killed in action on his 500th combat sortie on 23rd March 1943 as a Major with Oakleaves, Swords and Diamonds to his Knight's Cross. (Photo: via Martin Windrow).

Following raids by Junkers Ju 88s of KG 1 on the South Coast radar stations—intended to "blind" Fighter Command—small formations of Dorniers and Heinkels carried out sharp attacks on Brighton and Eastbourne where substantial damage was caused among residential areas, and about sixty people were killed or injured. Fighter Command, whose radar stations were scarcely affected by the earlier attacks, was nevertheless handicapped by jamming. Only eleven fighter pilots reported contact with the enemy, and eight of these claimed the destruction of two raiders! That Nos. 72 and 247 Squadrons managed to intercept at all was extremely lucky, as the jamming was causing fairly heavy interference at all four CH stations in the area. The technique had only been introduced a few days earlier, and was in its infancy; due to the Germans' lack of high powered transmitting equipment, it was only effective at relatively short ranges. Later, of course, the whole science of radio and radar countermeasures was to grow into into a highly effective form of "passive" warfare whose steady development would create major prob-

lems in the conduct of bomber operations throughout the remainder of the War[26].

Meanwhile Hitler still prevaricated on the all-important decision to invade Britain. The air situation over Britain had shown little or no change since the evening of 9th September, a fact which O.K.L. ascribed to continuing adverse weather conditions over the island. Although crew reports of a lack of co-ordination in fighter reaction were reported to Göring and his Führer, Hitler remained unconvinced, and once more put off his decision for the final preparation of *Seelöwe* until 17th September. Whether or not the events of the 15th were an attempt by Göring to prove that Fighter Command was indeed down to its "last fifty Spitfires" was immaterial. The result brooked no further compromise in the mind of the Führer; the *Luftwaffe* had failed in its allotted task.

---

[26] See *Instruments of Darkness*, A. Price, William Kimber, London, 1966.

R.A.F. FIGHTER COMMAND LOSSES—SATURDAY 14th SEPTEMBER 1940

No.	Squadron		Details	Time	Pilot	Aircraft	Serial	Category
1.	19 Sqn., Fowlmere(1)	NC	Crashed at Orford, Sussex, after oxygen system failure; pilot killed.	A16.20 hrs.	Sgt. F. Marek	Spitfire	R6625	Cat. 3 Destroyed
2.	41 Sqn., Hornchurch	C	Pilot bounced and shot down by a Bf 109; pilot baled out, slightly wounded.	A18.30 hrs.	Sqn. Ldr. R.C.F. Lister	Spitfire	—	Cat. 3 Destroyed
3.	66 Sqn., Gravesend	C	Shot down by Bf 109s over Maidstone; pilot seriously wounded.	A16.30 hrs	Plt. Off. R.H. Robbins	Spitfire	X4327	Cat. 3 Destroyed
4.	66 Sqn., Gravesend	C	Force landed with engine failure near Gravesend (possibly after combat). Pilot unhurt.	A16.30 hrs.	Sgt. P.H. Willcocks	Spitfire	—	Cat. 3 Destroyed
5.	73 Sqn., Castle Camps	C	Shot down by Bf 109s and force landed near Dover CH station; aircraft wrecked but pilot unhurt.	16.25 hrs.	Sgt. A.E. Marshall	Hurricane	—	Cat. 3 Destroyed
6.	73 Sqn., Castle Camps	(C)	Shot down (reported as being by a Spitfire) and force landed at Gravesend; pilot unhurt.	16.15 hrs.	Sgt. M.E. Leng	Hurricane	P3209	Cat. 3 Destroyed
7.	73 Sqn., Castle Camps	C	Shot down near Tonbridge; pilot slightly injured while baling out.	16.28 hrs.	Sqn. Ldr. M.W.S. Robinson	Hurricane	—	Cat. 3 Destroyed
8.	73 Sqn., Castle Camps	C	Shot down near Maidstone; pilot baled out with dislocated shoulder; aircraft crashed at Staplehurst.	16.27 hrs.	Sgt. J.J. Griffin	Hurricane	—	Cat. 3 Destroyed
9.	73 Sqn., Castle Camps	C	Shot down by Bf 109s near Tonbridge; pilot killed. Aircraft crashed at Chart Sutton.	16.24 hrs.	Sgt. J.J. Brimble	Hurricane	P2542	Cat. 3 Destroyed
10.	73 Sqn., Castle Camps	(C)	Aircraft hit in radiator by fire from Spitfire, and force landed at West Malling; pilot unhurt.	16.30 hrs.	Flt. Lt. M.L.ff. Beytagh	Hurricane	V7209	Cat. 1 Damaged
11.	73 Sqn., Castle Camps	C	Damaged in combat over Kent, but pilot landed safely at base.	16.40 hrs.	Plt. Off. R.A. Marchand	Hurricane	P2869	Cat. 1 Damaged
12.	92 Sqn., Biggin Hill	C	Shot down and force landed at Biggin Hill; pilot slightly wounded.	18.28 hrs.	Sgt. J. Mann	Spitfire	X4051	Cat. 2 Damaged
13.	92 Sqn., Biggin Hill	C	Shot down by Bf 109s and pilot baled out wounded. Aircraft crashed at Faversham.	18.24 hrs.	Sgt. H.W. McGowan	Spitfire	R6624	Cat. 3 Destroyed
14.	222 Sqn., Hornchurch	C	Severely damaged by Bf 110 near Gravesend; pilot attempted to land at Rochford but crashed and was killed.	15.56 hrs.	Sgt. S. Baxter	Spitfire	X4275	Cat. 3 Burnt
15.	222 Sqn., Hornchurch	C	Shot down by Bf 110 and force landed at Detling; pilot unhurt.	15.55 hrs.	Sgt. I. Hutchinson	Spitfire	X4265	Cat. 2 Damaged
16.	222 Sqn., Hornchurch	C	Shot down by Bf 109; pilot baled out slightly wounded at Aveley, Essex.	16.03 hrs.	Sgt. R.B. Johnson	Spitfire	X4249	Cat. 3 Destroyed
17.	229 Sqn., Northolt	C	Shot down by Bf 109 and force landed at Heston; pilot unhurt.	16.35 hrs.	Plt. Off. J.W. Hyde	Hurricane	N2592	Cat. 2 Damaged
18.	253 Sqn., Kenley	C	Shot down by Bf 109 near Faversham; pilot severely wounded and admitted to Faversham Cottage Hospital.	A16.00 hrs.	Sgt. J.A. Anderson	Hurricane	P3804	Cat. 3 Destroyed
19.	253 Sqn., Kenley	C	Shot down by Bf 109s over Isle of Sheppey; aircraft crashed in flames at Bredgar, near Sittingbourne.	A16.00 hrs.	Sgt. W.B. Higgins	Hurricane	P5184	Cat. 3 Burnt
20.	605 Sqn., Croydon	C	Missing after combat; circumstances not known.	Not known	Not known	Hurricane	L2118	Cat. 3 Missing

LUFTWAFFE LOSSES—SATURDAY 14th SEPTEMBER 1940

No.	Unit		Details	Aircraft	%	Crew
1.	2.(H)/12	CM	Crash landed in fog at Quimper.	Henschel Hs 126 (4255 : H1+NK)	70 %	Crew unhurt.
2.	2.(F)/22	CM	Crashed following tyre burst at Stavanger-Sola.	Dornier Do 17P (3519 : 4N+CK)	70 %	Crew unhurt.
3.	3./KG 4	CM	Shot down by unknown British fighters in the London area.	Heinkel He 111H-4 (3294 : 5J+BL)	100 %	Uffz. Müller-Wernscheid and Uffz. Töpfer killed; Oblt. Hermann Kell and Fw. Hobe missing.
4.	I./KG 54	CM	Engine failure on take-off at Evreux-Fauville.	Junkers Ju 88A-1(7083)	30 %	Crew unhurt.
5.	II./KG 54	CM	Landing accident at St. André airfield.	Junkers Ju 88A-1(4092)	30 %	Crew unhurt.
6.	St.St./KG 55	CM	Shot down by 72 Sqn. Spitfires off Eastbourne at A.16.00 hrs.	Heinkel He 111H (5357 : G1+HA)	100 %	Ltn. Hans Parei, Ltn. Friedrich Schlink, Gefr.Wanger, Uffz. Geiger and Ogefr. Petersen killed.

Luftwaffe Losses, 14th September 1940—*continued*

7.	2./KGr. 126	CM	Shot down by 257 Sqn. Hurricane of Mortimer at Harkstead at A.15.30 hrs.	Heinkel He 111H-4 (5710 : 1T+GK)	100 %	Ltn. Friedrich Viet, Oblt. Paul Mesche, Uffz. Schräder and Uffz. Schröder missing.
8.	1./KGr. 606	CM	Damaged by British fighters and crash landed at Cherbourg-West airfield.	Dornier Do 17Z-3 (2815 : 7T+NH)	50 %	Crew unhurt.
9.	1./KGr. 606	CM	Damaged by British fighters and crash landed at Cherbourg-West airfield.	Dornier Do 17Z-1 (1216 : 7T+FN)	80 %	Crew unhurt.
10.	1./KGr. 606	CM	Damaged by British fighters and force landed at Cherbourg-West airfield.	Dornier Do 17Z-2 (1213 : 7T+BH)	15 %	Crew unhurt.
11.	Stab/KGr. 806	CM	Pilot became lost, ran out of fuel and force landed near Caen.	Junkers Ju 88A-1 (5071 : M7+BA)	70 %	Crew unhurt.
12.	III./JG 2	NCM	Crashed at Le Havre as a result of faulty servicing.	Focke-Wulf Fw 58 (2984 : SE+VK)	100 %	Ltn. Schäfer + three killed.
13.	9./JG 3	CM	Force landed at Ampleteuse with combat damage.	Messerschmitt Bf 109 E-4 (0746)	45 %	Pilot unhurt.
14.	Stab/JG 26	CM	Shot down by 46 Sqn. Hurricane of Rabagliati near Maidstone at 18.40 hrs.	Messerschmitt Bf 109 E-1 (5813)	100 %	Oblt. Kurt Dähm, *Adj.*, killed.
15.	9./JG 26	CM	Shot down by 222 Sqn. Spitfire of McMullen and crashed near St. Inglevert at A.16.15 hrs.	Messerschmitt Bf 109 E-4 (1491)	60 %	Pilot unhurt.
16.	Stab I./JG 77	CM	Shot down by 603 Sqn. Spitfire of Carbury east of London at A.16.00 hrs.	Messerschmitt Bf 109 E-4 (3759)	100 %	Oblt. Herbert Kunze, *Adj.*, killed. Buried at Hawkinge.
17.	I./JG 77	CM	Shot down by 603 Sqn. Spitfire of Boulter over Kent at A.16.00 hrs.	Messerschmitt Bf 109 E-1 (3854)	100 %	Fw. Ettler missing.
18.	1./406	—	Damaged in storm at Thiestedt.	Dornier Do 18 (0875 : K6+KH)	35 %	No aircrew casualties.
19.	2./606	NCM	Destroyed in landing accident at Cherbourg-West airfield.	Dornier Do 17 (2687 : 7T+FK)	100 %	Ltn.z.S. Sibeth + three killed.
20.	*Seenotflug-kommando 3*	CM	Force landed in the sea off Boulogne after air-sea rescue sortie.	Heinkel He 59 (1513 : TV+HO)	100 %	No casualties.

Sunday 15th September

The tremendous air battles fought between Fighter Command and the *Luftwaffe* on this memorable Sunday represented the climax of the entire Battle of Britain and, as will be seen in due course, amounted to a crushing defeat of Göring's bomber forces. Thus the day can only be regarded as that on which the Battle of Britain was won and lost; for whatever qualifications may be added to the *degree* of damage done to Germany's principal long-range weapon, the *nature* of the defeat was uncompromising. It is logical, therefore, that in Britain this date has been celebrated ever since as Battle of Britain Day.

Before describing the events that occurred on this day, one should perhaps examine the environment of the Battle at this stage. To the British, Hitler's invasion was imminent—several false alarms had sounded in the past week, and observers at Dover had recorded the passage of a number of large landing vessels on their way down Channel. In line with recent events in Europe, the *Luftwaffe* had embarked on heavy attacks on the civilian population, apparently supporting the popular belief that such attacks were the traditional curtain-raiser for invasion.

One of the most significant factors identifiable in contemporary documents of this second week of September, however, was the renewed *élan* of Fighter Command. Less than a fortnight previously the British line of defence had undoubtedly been on the verge of a major setback, although whether this would have taken the form of wholesale redeployment of all remaining reserves in No. 11 Group, or the abandoning of the airfields south of London, is matter for conjecture. It is not unlikely that Dowding—already loath to overtax exhausted squadrons, and determined to preserve the system of squadron and pilot rotation as far as possible—would have favoured the latter alternative.

Since that first heavy daylight raid on London on 7th September, the situation had changed with dramatic speed. The R.A.F. fighter pilots had at no time during the period 8th—14th September been extended to the degree which had been commonplace during the previous ten days. Dowding's redeployment had taken effect immediately, so that for the first time since mid-July there were no exhausted squadrons in No. 11 Group, and most of the fighter units had enjoyed day-long rest periods without being called to State. Many of them had even managed to organise training sorties to help acclimatise newly-arrived pilots—an unheard-of luxury in the terrible days so recently past. Apart from the practical value of these sorties to teenage pilots with only a bare twenty hours' experience on Spitfires or Hurricanes (some of them had never used a reflector gunsight when they arrived on an operational squadron), the psychological value of this breathing space was enormous. With the resilience of the very

View in a London street towards St. Paul's Cathedral on 15th September. The condensation trails, persistent on this day at 28,000 feet, indicate the presence of fighters.

Two of No. 249 Squadron's successful pilots on 15th September. *Left*, Plt. Off. Thomas Neil, who was credited with two Dornier Do 17s (probably of KG 2), and, *right*, Plt. Off. Richard Barclay, who also destroyed a Dornier.

young, Park's pilots felt the terrible burden of combat fatigue ease a little from their shoulders; so that at dawn on 15th September, Fighter Command stood stronger and better equipped for battle than ever before.

In remarkable contrast stood the main force of the *Luft-waffe*, whose crews were by this time dogged by doubts as to the wisdom of continued daylight attacks, and whose field commanders were by no means confident regarding the real value of such attacks in view of the High Command's prevarication over *Seelöwe*. The deteriorating morale among the attacking forces must have been responsible, to some extent at least, for the picture that unfolded during Sunday 15th September.

The day started quietly enough, although the fine weather, with only scattered early autumn mist, suggested to Dowding's controllers that the enemy might return in force. Accordingly, from first light, the three southern Groups maintained a number of standing patrols at Section or Flight strength on constant coastal patrol between Harwich and Land's End; at each Sector station at least one whole squadron was retained at Readiness from about 07.00 hours. For more than two hours these patrols were vectored against reconnaissance aircraft but without conclusive results.

The first indications of heavy enemy raid build-up came with a report from Rye CH at 10.50 hours of a twenty-plus concentration about ten miles south-east of Boulogne, quickly followed by unfiltered plots of fifteen-plus, thirty-plus and ten-plus in the same area. Five minutes later Park ordered all his squadrons to Readiness, even recalling three from Released, and simultaneously warned Brand and Leigh-Mallory of the raid indications. At this moment only three sections of Spitfires were airborne over Kent; two of these were ordered to return to base for refuelling while No. 92 Squadron and seven Spitfires of No. 72 Squadron were scrambled from Biggin Hill at 11.03 hours to await the enemy raid between Canterbury and Dungeness.

The formation, assembled and launched in full view of British radar, consisted of about one hundred Dornier Do 17s drawn principally from Oberst von Chamier-Glisczinski's *Kampfgeschwader 3 «Blitz-Geschwader»* which had taken off from the Antwerp area and flown westwards to pick up its massive escort behind the Pas de Calais. This was in direct contrast to the earlier practice of making for the mouth of the Thames Estuary and allowing the escort to join formation *en route*. The outcome of several missed rendezvous in the past,

this diversion not only allowed the defences to "examine" the raid while it assembled, but was also an implied mark of respect for Fighter Command.

The result on this Sunday morning was that Kesselring's main bomber formation was struck first by about twenty Spitfires as it crossed the coast at Dungeness at about 11.35 hours, and by progressively heavier concentrations of fighters as it struggled north-westwards towards London. By 11.55 hours London was in sight, and at this moment no fewer than nine squadrons struck simultaneously, four Hurricane squadrons of 43 aircraft engaging head-on as the Duxford Wing (two Spitfire and three Hurricane squadrons, led by Sqn. Ldr. Bader) wheeled in on the flank and burst through the close escort. The withering shock of this tremendous assault smashed the formation of the Dorniers irrevocably; despite the determination of the escort pilots to shield the bombers, their task was made all but impossible by the dispersal of their shaken charges. The bomber crews, suddenly deprived of the comforting presence of rank upon rank of Bf 109s to left and right, fought desperately for survival under the guns of more than 160 Hurricanes and Spitfires. The Dorniers steered a broad, curving sweep over Central London and dropped their bombs at random before easing into a long powered dive to escape as best they could over the Kent coast.

Not unnaturally, the huge battle developed into a series of individual fights, of straggler versus straggler, and squadron versus squadron. It was to be expected that a fighter or a bomber pilot who became detached from his formation would become the target for any prowling enemy, and it was a feature of this day's combat that many an R.A.F. pilot who was posted Missing before evening had strayed from his comrades and become the victim of wandering Bf 109s far from the main battle. The British pilots, whose combat reports themselves reflect the marked upsurge in confidence and morale, had the fight of their lives, but the true nature of the battle clearly did not dawn upon them until after the next and much heavier raid in the afternoon.

The Dornier Do 17Z-2 flown by Hauptmann Ernst Püttmann, *Staffelkapitän* of 5th *Staffel*, KG 3, which was shot down by Sergeant Raymond Holmes of No. 504 Squadron and crashed on the forecourt of Victoria Station, London, at about mid-day on 15th September.

The damage inflicted upon London at mid-day was of little significance owing to its complete lack of concentration; bombs fell in Battersea, Lambeth, Clapham, Victoria, Camberwell, Kensington, Chelsea, Crystal Palace, Lewisham, Wandsworth and Westminster. Two large unexploded bombs fell on Buckingham Palace and in its grounds, but their Majesties were not in residence at the time.

One Hurricane pilot, Sgt. Raymond Holmes of No. 504 Squadron, attacked several Dorniers and finally destroyed one which blew up with such force that it sent the Hurricane spinning down out of control. The Dornier crashed in the forecourt of Victoria Station, its crew baling out over the Oval cricket ground; Holmes baled out over Chelsea, and landed in a dustbin!

As Kesselring's bombers fled south-eastwards, Park's controllers ordered a quick turn-round of all fighters as they landed. While sandwiches and mugs of tea were handed round to grimy, jubilant pilots on airfields all over the South-East, a second wave of *Luftflotte 2* bomber *Geschwader* was already taking off to assemble over North-East France. This raid, consisting of three waves of more than 150 Dorniers and Heinkels from Oberst Fink's KG 2 «*Holzhammer*», Oberst Stahl's KG 53 «*Legion Cóndor*» and Oberstleutnant Frölich's KG 76, was escorted by Bf 109s of Adolf Galland's veteran JG 26 «*Schlageter*», and Hannes Trautloft's JG 54 «*Grünherz*». The massive formation advanced on London shortly after 14.00 hours on a ten-mile front over North Kent.

Obviously encouraged by the early reports of the mid-day rout of von Chamier-Glisczinski's bombers, the British pilots were quickly airborne after the orders to scramble were passed between 13.50 hours and 14.20 hours. After tremendous efforts by groundcrews of all three Groups, almost every squadron was able to put up two full Flights—despite the earlier losses in missing and damaged aircraft. Even the veteran Station Commander of Northolt, Gp. Capt. Stanley Vincent[27], took off in his Hurricane and charged head-on at a *Staffel* of eight Dorniers— and watched in astonishment as they broke and wheeled away to the south.

A total of 170 Hurricanes and Spitfires met the German bombers over Kent and although the escort managed to engage these for more than ten minutes without any widespread disruption of the bomber formations, their reception over East London finally doomed any hope of keeping the Dornier and Heinkel vics intact and concentrated. It was there that the five-squadron Duxford Wing fell on them; instants later six No. 11 Group and two No. 10 Group squadrons charged in head-on, scattering all three enemy formations beyond hope of re-assembly. Once again the massive fighter charge completely demoralised the German crews, who hurriedly unloaded their bombs over Lewisham, Stepney, East and West Ham, Erith, Penge and Hackney; and, under whatever degree of cover the harassed Messerschmitt pilots could provide, they made off to the south-east as fast as their straining engines could propel them.

It was probably about this moment in time that the full significance of the day's fighting began to dawn on the airmen, British and German alike. For the sweat-soaked,

Hannes Trautloft was transferred from III./JG 51 to lead the new *Grünherz* (Green Heart) *Geschwader*, JG 54, in August 1940. He was to lead it for three years, winning for himself a high reputation as a thoughtful and intelligent commander, and a "pilot's pilot". His outspoken championing of the front line airmen led him, like Galland, into eventual disfavour with the upper echelons of command. Trautloft survived the War, to hold high rank in the post-War *Luftwaffe* in the 1960s.

exhilarated pilots of the R.A.F., the smashing and pursuit of this armada of bombers was a supreme achievement. As they watched the scattered, uneven groups of Heinkels and Dorniers streaming south in disorder, with the deadly Messerschmitts following in apparent impotence, many must have felt a new swell of confidence. A happy series of events had placed their enemy in their sights in the most perfect possible combination of circumstances, and they had not wasted the opportunity.

The Messerschmitt pilots were primarily concerned with the red lights that now winked on their instrument panels, the hated signal that they would once more face a twenty-mile flight over the sea with no certainty of reaching the other side. Desperately short of fuel, each had to make his own decision; to turn and protect some hard-pressed bomber, and use up precious litres, or to fly hard and straight for the safety of France. They were dedicated and courageous men, and the frustration of their hopeless task was very galling. That endless trip back across the Channel must have given rise to many cheerless thoughts of the future.

For the German bomber crews the appalling shock of meeting upwards of three hundred fighters in twenty minutes can scarcely be imagined. It is impossible to believe that

---

[27] Later Air Vice-Marshal, C.B., D.F.C., A.F.C., Stanley Vincent was born in 1897 and commissioned in the Royal Flying Corps in 1915. His distinguished career in the R.A.F. culminated in command of No. 11 Group, Fighter Command, in 1948-50.

many of them felt any great optimism, as bomber after bomber faltered and slid out of formation with stopped propellers and smoking engines, with wings and tailplanes tattered by gunfire, with perspex starred and blood-smeared. At the beginning of a campaign, fresh and confident, they might have been able to bury the experience in their minds as an isolated disaster; but they had been crossing and re-crossing the hungry Channel for more than two months now. They were the cream of their nation, young, healthy, confident, and proud of their skill and their equipment; but they were very tired, and they were becoming very cynical. For too long they had been told that the Royal Air Force had been swept from the sky, that they faced only "the last fifty Spitfires". It is too much to ask of a young man to feel confidence in his leaders when he is limping south again on a summer afternoon, wrists aching from the drag of distorted controls, watching for the first sign of fire with the stink of a ruptured fuel tank filling the cockpit, perhaps with a dead friend lolling hideously in his harness inches away—and knowing that tomorrow there will still be three hundred fighters waiting for him.

Whether as the result of an impassioned radio call from the bombers for further assistance, or as a premeditated tactic, there now swept in over Kent two small formations of Bf 109s and Bf 110s, whose obvious task was to occupy the attention of the jubilant British pilots. They crossed the coast shortly after 15.30 hours; but they were too late, and were scarcely noticed.

From 15.00 hours onwards it was the turn of Brand's western flank, and so willingly had he met the need for fighters over London that he only managed to meet the more direct threat with two squadrons. This raid, mounted by 27 Heinkels of Major Schlemell's III./KG 55 «Greifen-Gesch-wader» from Villacoublay, steered as if to attack Southampton, but turned away to the west to bomb Portland; they were intercepted by six Spitfires of "B" Flight, No. 152 Squadron from Warmwell, whose pilots destroyed one bomber and damaged a second. The raid was of only minor significance and only five bombs fell among naval installations at Portland, causing little damage.

As KG 55's raid disappeared from the CH screens, Ventnor reported the approach from the south of a fast raid shortly after 17.00 hours. Having by now recovered most of their fighters from the London area, the Tangmere and Middle Wallop Sector controllers[28], suspecting that this was a free chase from the Cherbourg area, put up six squadrons. These were ordered to make for the area between the Isle of Wight and Portland, on the suspicion that this raid might again turn west. It eventually materialised as eighteen Bf 110 fighters and fighter-bombers of *1* and *2 Staffeln, Erprobungsgruppe 210*, led by Hauptmann Martin Lutz—*Gruppenkommandeur* since von Ahrenhein's death in action on 4th September. Making good use of cloud cover, this formation rounded the Nab and made straight for Southampton, avoiding the balloon barrage and carrying out a sharp attack on the Wollston factory producing Spitfires. Heavily engaged by anti-aircraft fire over the Solent, they were frustrated in their attack and the vital factory escaped damage.[29]

---

[28] Wg. Cdr. John Boret, M.C., A.F.C., and Wg. Cdr. David Roberts, A.F.C., respectively.

[29] This raid has some unexplained features. For some time Erpr. Gr. 210 had been based at Denain in Eastern France while its 3rd *Staffel* exchanged its bomb-carrying Bf 109s for Bf 110Cs. At about this time the unit moved to Cherbourg and it is possible that the above raid on Southampton was the first carried out from the new base. Regarding the attack on the Woolston Works, it is hard to equate the choice of this unit for the attack with a belief that the factory was producing bombers—i.e. a relatively low priority target; yet all relevant briefing documents confirm the target as being the A.V. Roe & Company factory. Finally, an interesting point emerges from the combat reports of No. 607 Squadron, whose pilots were the only ones to attack Erpr.Gr.210 as it made off west of the Needles. Erpr.Gr. 210 was one of the few units which flew the rare Bf 110D-0, and certainly flew at least three of these aircraft on this occasion; none of the No. 607 Squadron pilots mention Bf 110s with a prominent bulged fairing under the nose. On almost every other occasion on which these distinctive aircraft were encountered, the R.A.F. pilots concerned "positively" identified the enemy aircraft as Do 17s! The adjustment of such confused claims goes a long way towards explaining reports of interception of "Dornier" raids which were in fact flown by *Zerstörergeschwader* or Erp.Gr.210 with Bf 110D-0s.

Although barrage balloons perhaps did not bring about the destruction of a large number of enemy aircraft, their main function was to prevent German bombers from attacking important targets from low level—indeed to force them to fly so high as to lessen the chance of accurate bombing. These photos show balloon crews undergoing training in the country, and the barrage located around Buckingham Palace in Central London.

The evening raid on Southampton was the final attack in a day of mounting tension. The excited claims by British fighter pilots were hurriedly totted up and issued to the Press and B.B.C. The score of 185 enemy aircraft destroyed brought a storm of acclamation for Dowding's men, as well it might. Later, however, the figure was drastically cut to 60. Yet, lest it be thought that the extraordinary tonic to civilian morale provided by the huge victory was cynically engineered, it must be stated that the initial exaggerated figure was arrived at in absolute good faith. One has only to examine the combat reports, to count the individual claims, and to remember the nature of the fighting in those two huge battles over London to realise that in every pilot's estimation each aircraft that fell to his guns was a personal victory. Added to this, countless pilots were entirely justified in believing that an aircraft with both engines on fire would never reach home—unaware that the same machine had already been claimed as fatally damaged by a previous attacker, and might finally disintegrate under the fire of a third or fourth.

The "Wing" controversy now took a new turn; complaints were voiced by the pilots, led by Douglas Bader, that the Wing had not been ordered into the attack soon enough, with the result that the bombers were already scattered and scarcely presented an adequate target for a concentrated force of fifty fighters. The reason for this late interception on this occasion lay in Park's reluctance to feed in reinforcements from other Groups while there remained a chance that the raid would still attack targets north of London. As it was, there can be no doubt of the devastating effect of the Wing's impact on the German bombers over London itself.

Winston Churchill, with his uncanny sense of the dramatic, had during the day paid an unexpected visit to Park's operations room at Uxbridge, and had witnessed the inexorable saturation of the vital No. 11 Group fighter defences as the great armada made its way across Kent. Park's famous reply to the Prime Minister's query about reserves ("There are none") was scarcely reflected in the message of congratulation sent by Churchill to Dowding that evening, and obviously intended for wide circulation:

> "...aided by Czech and Polish squadrons, and using only a small proportion of their total strength, the Royal Air Force cut to rags and tatters separate waves of murderous assault upon the civil population of their native land."

The figures were unimportant: the sense was everything. Sunday 15th September had seen the defeat of Germany's daylight bombing offensive; did they but know it, the island race no longer stood in the shadow of Hitler's invasion.

R.A.F. FIGHTER COMMAND LOSSES—SUNDAY 15th SEPTEMBER 1940

1.	1(Canadian) C Sqn., Northolt	Shot down by Bf 109 and pilot baled out over Tunbridge Wells with head wound.	12.04 hrs.	Fg. Off. A.D. Nesbitt	Hurricane	P3080	Cat. 3 Destroyed
2.	1(Canadian) C Sqn., Northolt	Shot down by Bf 109s over Tunbridge Wells; pilot killed.	A12.00 hrs.	Fg. Off. R. Smither	Hurricane	P3876	Cat. 3 Missing
3.	1(Canadian) C Sqn., Northolt	Damaged by He 111 south of London; pilot landed at base, wounded in shoulder.	14.13 hrs.	Fg. Off. A.M. Yuile	Hurricane	L1973	Cat. 2 Damaged
4.	19 Sqn., C Fowlmere	Hit in glycol tank and force landed; pilot unwounded.	14.50 hrs.	Sgt. H.A.C. Roden	Spitfire	P9431	Cat. 2 Damaged
5.	19 Sqn., C Fowlmere	Damaged by Bf 109 and force landed; pilot unwounded.	A14.50 hrs.	Sub-Lt. A.G. Blake	Spitfire	—	Cat. 2 Damaged
6.	19 Sqn., C Fowlmere	Missing after combat with Bf 109s; ditched off French coast; pilot, wounded, taken prisoner.	A15.00 hrs.	Sgt. J.A. Potter	Spitfire	X4070	Cat. 3 Missing
7.	25 Sqn., NC North Weald	Suffered accident at night near Biggin Hill; pilot survived.	At night	Plt. Off. B.G. Hooper	Beaufighter	R2067	Cat. 3 Destroyed
8.	41 Sqn., C Hornchurch	Shot down by Bf 109 near Gravesend and crashed at Bulpham, Essex; pilot killed.	12.20 hrs.	Plt. Off. G.A. Langley	Spitfire	P9324	Cat. 3 Destroyed
9.	73 Sqn., C Castle Camps	Shot down at Lynsted, near Sittingbourne; pilot killed.	11.50 hrs.	Plt. Off. R.A. Marchand	Hurricane	P3865	Cat. 3 Destroyed
10.	92 Sqn., C Biggin Hill	Shot down by He 111s over Staplehurst, Kent; pilot baled out but was injured on landing.	A15.00 hrs.	Plt. Off. R.H. Holland	Spitfire	R6606	Cat. 3 Destroyed
11.	229 Sqn., C Northolt	Shot down in combat with Bf 110s; pilot, wounded in legs, baled out at Sevenoaks.	12.04 hrs.	Plt. Off. R.R. Smith	Hurricane	V6616	Cat. 3 Destroyed
12.	229 Sqn., C Northolt	Shot down by Do 17; pilot killed and aircraft crashed on Staplehurst railway station.	12.07 hrs.	Plt. Off. G.L.J. Doutrepont	Hurricane	N2537	Cat. 3 Destroyed
13.	238 Sqn., C Middle Wallop	Shot down by Bf 110 near Kenley; pilot baled out but killed when parachute failed to open.	A15.00 hrs.	Sgt. L. Pidd	Hurricane	P2836	Cat. 3 Destroyed
14.	238 Sqn., C Middle Wallop	Damaged by Bf 110s over Kent; pilot unhurt.	A15.00 hrs.	Plt. Off. V.C. Simmonds	Hurricane	L2089	Cat. 2 Damaged
15.	238 Sqn., C Middle Wallop	Damaged in action over South London; no details of combat, but pilot unhurt.	A14.50 hrs.	Not known	Hurricane	P3462	Cat. 2 Damaged
16.	238 Sqn., C Middle Wallop	Damaged in action over South London; no details of combat, but pilot unhurt.	A14.50 hrs.	Not known	Hurricane	P3833	Cat. 2 Damaged
17.	242 Sqn., C Coltishall	Shot down by Do 17 over Kent coast; pilot baled out with dislocated shoulder; aircraft crashed at Udimore, East Sussex.	A14.15 hors	Plt. Off. G.ff. Powell-Sheddon	Hurricane	P2884	Cat. 3 Lost
18.	253 Sqn., C Kenley	Damaged by fire from Do 17 over the English Channel and force landed at Hawkinge; pilot unhurt.	15.10 hrs.	Plt. Off. A.R.H. Barton	Hurricane	R6698	Cat. 2 Damaged
19.	303 Sqn., C Northolt	Damaged in action with Bf 109s over Kent coast; pilot, wounded in leg, returned safely.	12.01 hrs.	Plt. Off. W. Lokuciewski	Hurricane	—	Cat. 1 Damaged
20.	303 Sqn., C Northolt	Shot down by enemy fighters over Thames Estuary; pilot and aircraft missing.	A14.55 hrs.	Sgt. M. Brzezowski	Hurricane	P3577	Cat. 3 Missing
21.	303 Sqn., C Northolt	Shot down by Bf 109s over Dartford; pilot baled out unhurt; aircraft crashed at Lower Stoke, Isle of Grain.	14.51 hrs.	Sgt. T. Andruszkow	Hurricane	P3939	Cat. 3 Destroyed
22.	310 Sqn., C Duxford	Shot down by enemy fighters over Billericay; pilot baled out unhurt.	14.55 hrs.	Sqn. Ldr. A. Hess	Hurricane	R4085	Cat. 3 Destroyed
23.	310 Sqn., C Duxford	Shot down by Bf 109 near Chatham; pilot baled out slightly wounded in leg.	14.54 hrs.	Sgt. J. Hrbacek	Hurricane	R4087	Cat. 3 Destroyed
24.	501 Sqn., C Kenley	Shot down by Bf 109 near Maidstone; pilot baled out unhurt.	12.04 hrs.	Sqn. Ldr. H.A.V. Hogan	Hurricane	V7433	Cat. 3 Destroyed
25.	501 Sqn., C Kenley	Aircraft damaged by Bf 109s and exploded over Maidstone; pilot killed.	12.05 hrs.	Plt. Off. A.E. van den Hove	Hurricane	P2760	Cat. 3 Destroyed

R.A.F. Losses, 15th September 1940—*continued*

26.	504 Sqn., Kenley	C	Aircraft hit by return fire from Do 17 over Central London and crashed in Buckingham Palace Road; pilot baled out and landed, un-hurt, in Chelsea High Street.	11.53 hrs.	Sgt. R.T. Holmes	Hurricane	P2725	Cat. 3 Destroyed
27.	504 Sqn., Kenley	C	Shot down by Do 17s over south-east London and crashed at Longfield, Kent; pilot killed.	A12.00 hrs.	Plt. Off. J.V. Gurteen	Hurricane	N2481	Cat. 3 Destroyed
28.	504 Sqn., Kenley	C	Shot down by Do 17s at Dartford; pilot baled out with grievous burns, and died on 19-9-40.	A14.00 hrs.	Fg. Off. M. Jebb	Hurricane	N2705	Cat. 3 Destroyed
29.	602 Sqn., Westhampnett	C	Shot down by Do 17 over Beachy Head and crashed landed; pilot unhurt.	15.24 hrs.	Sgt. C.F. Babbage	Spitfire	X4412	Cat. 3 Destroyed
30.	603 Sqn., Hornchurch	C	Shot down by Bf 109s and crashed at Kings-wood, south-east of Maidstone; pilot killed.	15.07 hrs	Plt. Off. A.P. Pease	Spitfire	X4324	Cat. 3 Destroyed
31.	603 Sqn., Hornchurch	C	Shot down by Do 17 over Sussex coast; pilot baled out, unhurt, at Guestling Green, near Hastings; aircraft crashed at Fairlight.	A15.10 hrs.	Sqn. Ldr. G.L. Delholm	Spitfire	R7019	Cat. 3 Destroyed
32.	605 Sqn., Croydon	C	Shot down during attack on Do 17s over Croydon; pilot baled out slightly wounded; aircraft crashed at Plaxtol, east of Sevenoaks.	11.56 hrs.	Plt. Off. R.E. Jones	Hurricane	L2122	Cat. 3 Destroyed
33.	605 Sqn., Croydon	C	Collided with Do 17 over Marden, Kent; pilot baled out slightly hurt.	14.40 hrs.	Plt. Off. T.P.M. Cooper-Slipper	Hurricane	L2012	Cat. 3 Destroyed
34.	607 Sqn., Tangmere	C	Collided with Do 17 over Appledore, Kent; pilot baled out slightly wounded.	14.51 hrs.	Plt. Off. P.J.T. Stephenson	Hurricane	V6688	Cat. 3 Destroyed
35.	609 Sqn., Middle Wallop	C	Shot down by Do 17s over London; crashed and burnt near Kenley; pilot killed.	12.12 hrs.	Plt. Off. G.N. Gaunt	Spitfire	R6690	Cat. 3 Destroyed
36.	611 Sqn., Duxford	C	Damaged by Bf 110 over west London; pilot returned unhurt.	14.50 hrs.	Not known	Spitfire	P7303	Cat. 2 Damaged

LUFTWAFFE LOSSES—SUNDAY 15th SEPTEMBER 1940

1.	1./KG 1	CM	Crashed with battle damage at Le Houdrel after combat with British fighters.	Heinkel He 111H-3 (3245 : V4+EH)	100 %	Three crew members wounded.
2.	5./KG 2	CM	Shot down into English Channel by 607 Sqn. Hurricanes at A.18.00 hrs.	Dornier Do 17Z-3 (2678 : U5+CN)	100 %	Oblt. Ullrich Latz, Uffz. Reinisch, Ofw. Hafner and Fw. Hasse missing.
3.	5./KG 2	CM	Shot down by 19 Sqn. Spitfires in London area at A.15.00 hrs.	Dornier Do 17Z-3 (2304 : U5+HN)	100 %	Uffz. Böhmel and Uffz. Huber killed. Uffz. Möbius and Gefr. Birg missing.
4.	4./KG 2	CM	Damaged by 19 Sqn. Spitfires in London area at A.15.00 hrs.	Dornier Do 17Z-2 (1135 : U5+MN)	7 %	Crew unhurt.
5.	7./KG 2	CM	Damaged by 17 Sqn. Hurricanes in London area at 14.58 hrs.	Dornier Do 17Z (2539 : U5+ER)	5 %	Oblt. Rolf Schweitring killed.
6.	7./KG 2	CM	Damaged by 17 Sqn. Hurricanes in London area at 14.58 hrs.	Dornier Do 17Z (1153 : U5+KR)	2%	One crew member wounded.
7.	8./KG 2	CM	Shot down by 242 Sqn. Hurricanes in London area at A.15.00 hrs.	Dornier Do 17Z-3 (2549 : U5+FS)	100 %	Fw. Simon killed; Uffz. Flemming Fw. Hirsch, Gefr. Sandmann missing.
8.	8./KG 2	CM	Shot down by 242 Sqn. Hurricanes over Kent at A.15.00 hrs.	Dornier Do 17Z-2 (3401 : U5+DS)	100 %	Gefr. Ertl killed; Fw. Dürtmann missing. Two crew rescued by *Seenotflugkommando*.
9.	8./KG 2	CM	Damaged by British fighters in the London area at A.15.00 hrs.	Dornier Do 17Z (3432 : U5+JS)	2 %	One crew member wounded.
10.	8./KG 2	CM	Shot down by British fighters south-east of London at A.15.10 hrs.	Dornier Do 17Z-3 (3440 : U5+PS)	100 %	Oblt. Werner Kittmann, Uffz. Stampfer and Uffz. Langer missing.
11.	8./KG 2	CM	Shot down by 607 Sqn. Hurricane of Bowen over Sussex coast at A.15.20 hrs.., and crashed into Channel; pilot rescued by *Seenotflugkommando*	Dornier Do 17Z-2 (4245 : U5+GS)	100 %	Oblt. Hugo Holleck-Weitmann killed; Uffz. Lindemeier missing; Uffz. Schweighart wounded.
12.	9./KG 2	CM	Shot down by British fighters and crashed on Sussex coast at 15.19 hrs.	Dornier Do 17Z (3230 : U5+JT)	100 %	Uffz. Krummheuer, Fw. Glaser, and Uffz. Lenz killed; Uffz. Sehrt missing.
13.	9./KG 2	CM	Shot down by British fighters and crashed into Channel off Sussex coast at 15.27 hrs.	Dornier Do 17Z-2 (3405 : U5+FT)	100 %	Ofhr. Staib, Uffz. Hoppe killed; Gefr. Zierer and Gefr. Hoffmann missing.
14.	4./KG 3	CM	Shot down by 501 Sqn. Hurricanes south-east of London at 11.50 hrs.	Dornier Do 17Z-3 (3294 : 4K+DM)	100 %	Oblt. Kurt Dümler, Uffz. Horst Maskolus, Fw. August Vogel killed; Uffz. Friebel missing.
15.	4./KG 3	CM	Shot down by 501 Sqn. Hurricanes south-east of London at 11.50 hrs.	Dornier Do 17Z-3 (2881 : 4K+CM)	100 %	Fw. von Goertz, Uffz. Wien, Gefr. Schild, Gefr. Weymar missing.
16.	4./KG 3	CM	Damaged by 501 Sqn. Hurricanes south-east of London at A.11.50 hrs., and landed at Calais.	Dornier Do 17Z-3 (2879 : 5K+AM)	40 %	Two crew members wounded.
17.	4./KG 3	CM	Shot down by 501 Sqn. Hurricanes south-east of London at A.12.00 hrs.	Dornier Do 17Z-2 (3457 : 5K+JM)	100 %	Uffz. Hansburg, Uffz. Burballa killed; Ltn. Herbert Michaelis and Fl. Bormann missing.
18.	5./KG 3	CM	Damaged by 19 Sqn. Spitfires over East London at 12.05 hrs.	Dornier Do 17Z-3 (2649 : 5K+HN)	3 %	One crew member wounded.
19.	5./KG 3	CM	Shot down by 504 Sqn. Hurricanes over Central London at 12.10 hrs.	Dornier Do 17Z-2 (4200 : 5K+JN)	100 %	Ofw. Erich Rilling killed; Ofw. Howind, Ofw. Höbel, and Fw, Zimmermann missing.
20.	5./KG 3	CM	Shot down by 504 Sqn. Hurricanes over Central London at 12.10 hrs.	Dornier Do 17Z-3 (3458 : 5K+GN)	100 %	Oblt. Helmuth Becker-Ross, Fw. Hansen, Ofw. Brückner killed; Fw. Brinkmann missing.
21.	5./KG 3	CM	Shot down by 504 Sqn. Hurricane of Holmes over Central London at 12.10 hrs.; crashed on Victoria Station.	Dornier Do 17Z-2 (1176 : 5K+DN)	100 %	Hptm. Ernst Püttman, *St.Kap.*, Fw. Franke killed; Oblt. Adolf Langen-haim and Fw. Falke missing.
22.	6./KG 3	CM	Damaged by British fighters in Great London area shortly after mid-day.	Dornier Do 17Z-2 (3470 : 5K+CP)	50 %	One crew member killed.
23.	6./KG 3	CM	Damaged by British fighters south-east of Lon-don at around mid-day.	Dornier Do 17Z-3 (4237 : 5K+EM)	15 %	One crew member wounded.
24.	II./KG 4	CM	Damaged by British fighters and force landed at Eindhoven.	Heinkell He 111P-4 (3086 : 5J+HP)	30 %	Crew unhurt.
25.	I./KG 26	CM	Damaged by flak and fighters near London.	Heinkel He 111H-3 (5612 : 1H+GL)	20 %	Crew unhurt.
26.	I./KG 26	CM	Damaged by flak and fighters near London.	Heinkel He 111H-3 (5609 : 1H+EL)	20 %	Crew unhurt.

A fighter's cine-gun record of an attack on three Heinkel He 111s from two o'clock high (a starboard quarter attack).

Luftwaffe Losses, 15th September 1940—*continued*

27. I./KG 26	CM	Shot down by 72 Sqn. Spitfire near Dartford.	Heinkel He 111H-4 (6985 : 1H+JH)	100 %	Fw. Marenbach and Uffz. Domes wounded; Ltn. Heinrich Streubel, Fw. Schwartz, Fw.Pottenberg missing.
28. 6./KG 26	CM	Damaged by British fighters over Sussex and crashed in France on return.	Heinkel He 111H-3 (6849 : 1H+AP)	50 %	Two crew members wounded.
29. 6./KG 30	CM	Damaged by fighters; force landed at St. Omer.	Junkers Ju 88A-1 (4020: 4D+BH)	40 %	One crew member wounded.
30. 6./KG 30	NCM	Suffered engine failure and crashed in France.	Junkers Ju 88A-1 (0101 : 4D+KH)	60 %	Crew unhurt.
31. I./KG 51	CM	Suffered landing accident at Melun-Villaroche airfield after combat sortie.	Junkers Ju 88A-1 (7056)	80 %	Two crew members wounded.
32. I./KG 51	CM	Shot down by British fighters south of London (probably in afternoon raid).	Junkers Ju 88A-1 (3071 : 9K+AH)	100 %	Ltn. Willi Richter, Uff. Heinz Breuker, Uffz. Hirschfeld and Uffz. Konrad Schubert killed.
33. II./KG 51	CM	Shot down by British fighters south of London (probably in afternoon raid).	Junkers Ju 88A-1 (9K+KM)	100 %	Oblt. Horst de Vivanco, Uffz. Walter Kupfernagel, Gefr. Stelzner killed; Fw. Vogel missing.
34. Stab/KG 53	CM	Shot down by British fighters south of London during the afternoon raid.	Heinkel He 111H-2 (3140 : A1+DA)	100 %	Fw. Alois Schweiger, Uffz. Heinrich Meyer, Fw. Arnold Benz and Uffz. Georg Geiger killed; Fw. Cionber missing.
35. I./KG 53	CM	Shot down by British fighters south of London during the afternoon raid.	Heinkel He 111H-2 (5120 : A1+EL)	100 %	Fw. Ortzki killed; Uffz. Altmann wounded; Ltn.Hermann Böck,Uffz. Gerding,Ogefr.Kurzawski missing.
36. 3./KG 53	CM	Shot down by 92 Sqn. Spitfires near Hornchurch at 14.32 hrs.	Heinkel He 111H-2 (5481 : A1+GL)	100 %	Uffz. Lehner, Uffz. Rütig killed; Oblt.Gerhard Büchler, Gefr.Stamminger, Gefr. Richter missing.
37. 3./KG 53	CM	Force landed with battle damage at Boulogne after fighter combat near London in afteroon.	Heinkel He 111H 2 (5494 : A1+JL)	35 %	Two crew members wounded.
38. II./KG 53	CM	Shot down by 92 Sqn. Spitfires near Hornchurch at 14.35 hrs.	Heinkel He 111H-2 (5718 : A1+LN)	100 %	Fw.Meier, Gefr.Hoffmann killed; Ltn. Helmut Bäusch, Fw. Bauer and Uffz. Buttler missing.
39. II./KG 53	CM	Shot down by British fighters in the Greater London area during the afternoon raid.	Heinkel He 111H-1 (2771 : A1+AN)	100 %	Uffz.Lange, Gefr.Sailer killed; Fw. Behrends, Fw. Lichenhagen and Uffz. Zilling missing.
40. II./KG 53	CM	Shot down by British fighters in the Greater London area during the afternoon raid.	Heinkel He 111H-3 (6843 : A1+GM)	100 %	Fw.Grassi killed; Maj.Max Gruber, Gr.Kdr., Oblt. Hans Schirning, Fw. Nagel and Ofw.Schmittborn, made P.O.W.s.
41. ·III./KG 53	CM	Force landed at Armentiers following fighter combat.	Heinkel He 111H-3 (3340 : A1+BT)	40 %	Two crew members wounded.
42. III./KG 55	CM	Shot down by British fighters into the English Channel. (Two crew believed baled out.)	Heinkel He 111P-2 (1586)	100 %	Three crew members killed.
43. III./KG 53	CM	Damaged by British fighters over the Sussex coast.	Heinkel He 111P-2 (2815)	25 %	One crew member killed and one wounded.
44. 1./KG 76	CM	Crashed at Cap Gris Nez following fighter combat.	Dornier Do 17Z (2364 : F1+EH)	60 %	One crew member killed and two wounded.
45. 1./KG 76	CM	Shot down by Hurricanes (probably of 303 Sqn.) south of London during afternoon raid.	Dornier Do 17Z (2361 : F1+FH)	100 %	Oblt.Robert Zehbe, Uffz.Goschenhofer, Uffz. Hubel killed; Uffz. Amameister and Ogefr.Armbruster missing.

Luftwaffe Losses, 15th September 1940—*continued*

46.	2./KG 76	CM	Crashed near Poix following fighter combat.	Dornier Do 17Z (2524 : F1+JK)	60 %	Oblt. Martin Florian wounded.
47.	3./KG 76	CM	Shot down by Hurricanes (probably of 303 Sqn.) south of London during afternoon raid.	Dornier Do 17Z (2651 : F1+FL)	100 %	Fw. Niebler, Fw. Wissmann, Uffz. Schatz killed; Oblt. Walter Wilke wounded; Fw. Zremer missing.
48.	8./KG 76	CM	Probably shot down by 66 Sqn. Spitfire of Bodie during afternoon raid.	Dornier Do 17Z-2 (2555 : F1+FS)	100 %	Fw. Stephan Schmidt killed; Fw. Sauter, Fw. Heitsch, and Fw. Pfeiffer missing.
49.	8./KG 76	CM	Shot down by 66 Sqn. Spitfire of Bodie during during afternoon raid.	Dornier Do 17Z-2 (2578 :F1+BS)	100 %	Fw.Keck, Uffz.Osenau killed;Uffz. Zahn, Uffz.Heitmann missing.
50.	9./KG 76	CM	Shot down by 19 Sqn. Spitfires during afternoon raid.	Dornier Do 17Z (2814 : F1+AT)	100 %	Ofhr.Wagner, Ogefr.Böhme, Gefr. Holdenreit, Gefr.Kottusch killed.
51.	9./KG 76	CM	Shot down by 66 Sqn. Spitfire south of London and believed crashed off Sussex coast.	Dornier Do 17Z (3322 : F1+DT)	100 %	Uffz. Malter killed; Fw.Teufert wounded; Fw. Raab and Ofw. Streit missing.
52.	13./LG 1	CM	Shot down by 303 Sqn. Hurricane of Feric and crashed at Hothfield Farm, Hothfield, near Ashford, at 15.50 hrs.	Messerschmitt Bf 110 C-3	100 %	Oblt. Müller and Fw. Andreas Hoffmann killed.
53.	13./LG 1	CM	Shot down by 303 Sqn. Hurricane of Kellett at A.15.50 hrs., over North Kent.	Messerschmitt Bf 110 C-3	100 %	Ltn. ErnstGorisch killed; Uffz. Gerick missing.
54.	14./LG 1	CM	Shot down by 257 Sqn. Hurricane of Tuck over Kent during afternoon.	Messerschmitt Bf 110 C-3	100 %	Ltn. Hugo Adametz and Ogefr. Stief missing.
55.	I./LG 2	CM	Shot down by British fighters south of London and believed crashed in Kent.	Messerschmitt Bf 109 E-7 (2058)	100 %	Uffz. Klick missing.
56.	I./LG 2	CM	Shot down by British fighters south-east of London during late afternoon.	Messerschmitt Bf 109 E-7 (2061)	100 %	Uffx. Streibing missing.
57.	Stab/JG 3	CM	Believed shot down by Dover ground defences.	Messerschmitt Bf 109 E-4 (5205)	100 %	Oberstlt. Hasso von Wedel made P.O.W.
58.	I./JG 3	CM	Shot down into Channel by British fighters.	Messerschmitt Bf 109 E-4 (1563)	100 %	Pilot, unhurt, rescued by *Seenotflugkommando*.
59.	1./JG 3	CM	Shot down by British fighters over Sussex.	Messerschmitt Bf 109 E-4 (0945)	100 %	Fw. Volmer missing.
60.	2./JG 3	CM	Shot down by British fighters over Sussex.	Messerschmitt Bf 109 E-4 (1606)	100 %	Oblt. Helmuth Reumschüssel, *St.Kap.*, missing.
61.	1./JG 27	CM	Shot down by British fighters south-east of London.	Messerschmitt Bf 109 E-4 (6232)	100 %	Oblt. Werner Ahrens missing.
62.	1./JG 27	CM	Force landed near Lille, short of fuel, after combat.	Messerschmitt Bf 109 E-4 (6249)	30 %	Pilot unhurt.
63.	2./JG 27	CM	Ran out of fuel and pilot baled out over the English Channel.	Messerschmitt Bf 109 E-1 (6147)	100 %	Uffz. Andreas Walburger rescued and made P.O.W.
64.	2./JG 27	CM	Crashed at Guined-West, short of fuel after combat.	Messerschmitt Bf 109 E-1 (3875)	80 %	Gefr. Franz Elles wounded.
65.	7./JG 51	CM	Shot down by 605 Sqn. Hurricane of Currant near Maidstone at A.14.40 hrs.	Messerschmitt Bf 109 E-4 (3266)	100 %	Ltn. Bildau missing.
66.	9./JG 51	CM	Shot down by 41 Sqn. Spitfire of Bennions near Ashford; pilot baled out.	Messerschmitt Bf 109 E-4 (2803)	100 %	Fw. Klotz, wounded, made P.O.W.
67.	Stab I./JG 52	CM	Shot down by British fighters over Margate.	Messerschmitt Bf 109 E-4 (3182)	100 %	Ltn. Hans Berthol, *Adj.*, missing.
68.	I./JG 53	CM	Shot down by 603 Sqn. Spitfire of Bailey over North Kent.	Messerschmitt Bf 109 E-4 (6160)	100 %	Uffz. Schersand killed.
69.	i./JG 53	CM	Force landed at Etaples with battle damage after combat over Kent.	Messerschmitt Bf 109 E-4 (5111)	15 %	Pilot unhurt.
70.	I./JG 53	CM	Shot down by 603 Sqn. Spitfire of Denholm near the Isle of Sheppey at A.12.05 hrs.	Messerschmitt Bf 109 E-4 (1345)	100 %	Ofw. Alfred Müller, wounded, made P.O.W.
71.	1./JG 53	CM	Shot down by 603 Sqn. Spitfire of Macphail near the Isle of Sheppey at A.12.05 hrs.	Messerschmitt Bf 109 E-4 (5197)	100 %	Fw. Tschopper missing.
72.	3./JG 53	CM	Missing from sortie over England; believed shot down over Kent.	Messerschmitt Bf 109 E-4 (1590)	100 %	Oblt. Julius Jase, *St.Kap.*, killed.
73.	3./JG 53	CM	Missing from sortie over south-east England.	Messerschmitt Bf 109 E-1 (3619)	100 %	Uffz. Feldmann missing.
74.	III./JG 53	CM	Force landed at Etaples after combat; aircraft caught fire and burnt out.	Messerschmitt Bf 109 E-4 (1174)	100 %	Pilot unhurt/
75.	III./JG 53	CM	Pilot baled out over Channel after running out of fuel.	Messerschmitt Bf 109 E-4 (5251)	100 %	Pilot, unhurt, rescued by *Seenotflugkommando*.
76.	1./JG 77	CM	Force landed in France with engine failure after combat near Dungeness.	Messerschmitt Bf 109 E-1 (4847)	25 %	Pilot unhurt.
77.	3./JG 77	CM	Missing from sortie involving combat near Dungeness.	Messerschmitt Bf 109 E-4 (4802)	100 %	Uffz. Meixner missing.
78.	*Wettererkun-dungsstaffel 51*	CM	Shot down by 87 Sqn. Hurricanes of David and Jay off Bolt Head at A.09.00 hrs.	Heinkel He 111H-3 (6938 : 4T+DH)	100 %	Reg.Insp.a.Kr. Erwin Franzreb, Ofw. Schweizer, Uffz. Baume, Uffz.M.Müller, Gefr. F.Müller,
79.	3./406	CM	Crashed while take-off from the sea off the south coast of Ireland; crew rescued.	Dornier Do 18 (0810 : K6+FL)	100 %	Crew unhurt.

Monday 16th September

The heavy fighting of the 15th caused the commanders on both sides to reflect at some length on the tactical implications. The German losses, though obviously of great concern to the field commanders, were initially brushed aside by Göring, who returned once more to his favourite theme—that the R.A.F. would be annihilated "in four or five days". And, as if to support this bland and meaningless prophecy, he ordered a return to attacks on Fighter Command and the factories supplying it. Such an extraordinary refusal to face the fact that Dowding's forces were now gaining strength daily was equalled in stupidity only by the continuing failure of German Intelligence to understand the British fighter supply system; for on the morning of 16th September there were at Maintenance Units in England no fewer than 160 new Hurricanes and Spitfires available as reinforcements, and upwards of 400 aircraft available elsewhere for delivery within one week. Within a fortnight this reserve would grow by almost 50 per cent, while most of the new fighters now

This Heinkel He 115C minelayer of the 3rd *Staffel*, *Küstenfliegergruppe 506*, 32610:S4+CL, suffered a double engine failure off Britain's north-east coast at 01.00 hrs. on 16th September; the pilot, Hauptmann Hans Kriependorf, ditched in the sea but the aircraft capsized. The crew was rescued by a fishing boat and brought ashore, the aircraft being towed into Eyemouth harbour, near Berwick.

being completed at the factories were of the improved Hurricane and Spitfire Mark II variety. Furthermore six new fighter squadrons had been formed and these would achieve operational status in the coming weeks. Even the pilot supply situation had eased as it became possible to bring men back into operational squadrons who, after their punishing ordeal in France had been "rested" as flying instructors for much of the Battle, were successfully pleading to be allowed "back on ops". 28 such battle-hardened pilots returned to Fighter Command during the second half of September.

At No. 11 Group Park examined reports of the Sunday's fighting, and the claim figures were undergoing drastic revision—due principally to the relative absence of crashed enemy aircraft on British soil. Park was still far from satisfied with the conduct of the defences; he felt that logically, with more than three hundred fighters scrambled in good time and in good weather against an equal number of German aircraft, of which half were bombers, results should have been even better. He therefore issued his Instruction No. 18 to his Sector controllers outlining the main tactical errors as he saw them. These may be summed up as the inefficient handling of paired squadrons—in that too much time was wasted in joining up, that some squadrons did not even bother to join up, and that others preferred to make for the enemy formation hoping that the "pair" would join up *en route*. One suspects that while Park clearly realised the value of operating squadrons in pairs, he was being over-critical, in view of his stated misgivings about the wisdom of unwieldy defence formations.

So as to avoid any mistakes in the future, Park now detailed the Spitfire squadrons from Biggin Hill and Hornchurch to confine their attention to the enemy top cover of Bf 109s, but not necessarily operating as paired squadrons. The Hurricanes (operating *only if time allowed* in groups of up to three squadrons each from Tangmere and Northolt) were to attack the bombers at medium altitude.

The night of 15th/16th September had again seen six *Gruppen* of Kesselring's bombers over London, where they dropped more than 200 tons of bombs, hitting Shell-Mex House and Woolwich Arsenal and causing more than one hundred casualties in the boroughs of Battersea, Brixton, Camberwell, Clapham and Chelsea. One of the raiders was shot down by Flt. Lt. Charles Pritchard (an Auxiliary pilot) in a Blenheim night fighter of No. 600 Squadron off the coast at Bexhill shortly after midnight.

Also during the hours of darkness No. 25 Squadron suffered the loss of its first Beaufighter, *R2067*, as well as a Blenheim.

Handley-Page Hampden bombers of No. 44 Squadron, R.A.F. Bomber Command. (Photo: R.A.F. Museum)

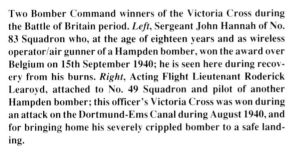

Two Bomber Command winners of the Victoria Cross during the Battle of Britain period. *Left*, Sergeant John Hannah of No. 83 Squadron who, at the age of eighteen years and as wireless operator/air gunner of a Hampden bomber, won the award over Belgium on 15th September 1940; he is seen here during recovery from his burns. *Right*, Acting Flight Lieutenant Roderick Learoyd, attached to No. 49 Squadron and pilot of another Hampden bomber; this officer's Victoria Cross was won during an attack on the Dortmund-Ems Canal during August 1940, and for bringing home his severely crippled bomber to a safe landing.

It has always been suggested that the two aircraft collided near Biggin Hill, although some circumstances of their loss have never come to light.

The R.A.F. had been particularly active over Northern Europe, carrying out more than 200 bombing sorties against barge concentrations at Antwerp, Ostend, Boulogne, Flushing, Calais and Dunkirk. It was during the raid by Hampdens of No. 83 Squadron on the Antwerp docks that Sergeant John Hannah won the Victoria Cross. His aircraft was hit by flak and the fuel tanks pierced, starting a severe fire which enveloped the after cabin and forced the rear gunner to bale out. Although the great heat was melting the cabin floor, Hannah attacked the fire with two fire extinguishers, and when they were exhausted he went to work on the blaze with his logbook. When the flames were smothered the slight,

eighteen-year-old sergeant, badly burned about the face and hands, crawled forward to find that the navigator had also baled out; so he remained with his pilot, passing him charts and log and helping him to bring the charred Hampden safely back to base.

When daylight came, much of the country was covered by rain clouds, and only isolated sorties were flown by the *Luftwaffe*. One of these resulted in the loss of a reconnaissance Ju 88 of *Aufklärungsgruppe 122* to the guns of Fg. Off. Colin MacFie and Plt. Off. Phillip Leckrone (the American who flew with No. 616 Squadron) off the Lincolnshire coast. The destruction of this aircraft was interesting in that, contrary to O.K.L.'s month-old order, the crew included two officers as well as (inexplicably) a member of the *Luftwaffe*'s medical corps.

R.A.F. FIGHTER COMMAND LOSSES—MONDAY 16th SEPTEMBER 1940

1.	25 Sqn., North Weald	NC	Flying accident, possibly involving Beaufighter *R2067* (see Item 7, R.A.F. Losses, 15th September)	A01.00 hrs.	Fg. Off. H.M.S. Lambert	Blenheim	—	Cat. 3 Destroyed
2.	151 Sqn., Digby	NC	Force landed and crashed following engine failure; pilot unhurt.	Not known	Not known	Hurricane	*R4185*	Cat. 3 Destroyed
3.	257 Sqn., Martlesham	NC	Crash landed following engine failure; pilot unhurt.	A11.00 hrs.	Sgt. D.J. Hulbert	Hurricane	*P3642*	Cat. 2 Damaged
4.	605 Sqn., Croydon	C	Shot down by Maj. Werner Mölders of JG 51 and force landed at Detling, Kent; pilot wounded.	07.40 hrs.	Plt. Off. E.J. Watson	Hurricane	—	Cat. 2 Damaged
5.	616 Sqn., Kirton-in-	C	Ditched in sea 20 miles north of Cromer after running out of fuel while pursuing Ju 88; pilot, unhurt, rescued by launch.	10.40 hrs.	Sgt. T.C. Iveson	Spitfire	*L1036*	Cat. 3 Lost

LUFTWAFFE LOSSES—MONDAY 16th SEPTEMBER 1940

1.	2.(H)/32	NCM	Crashed in bad weather near Kassel; not combat.	Henschel Hs 126 (4109)	90 %	Crew unhurt.
2.	4.(F)/122	CM	Shot down by 616 Sqn. Spitfires of MacFie and Leckrone over convoy off Lincolnshire coast at A.09.40 hrs.	Junkers Ju 88A-1 (0374 : F6+HM)	100 %	Oblt. Hans Starkloff, Hptm. Kurt Lüdke, Uffz.Pawletta, Oberarzt.Dr. Ulrich Guizetti missing.

Luftwaffe Losses, 16th September 1940—*continued*

3.	I./KG 27	CM	Take-off accident at Tours airfield.	Heinkel He 111P (2847 : 1G+DH)	30 %		Crew unhurt.
4.	III./KG 51	CM	Take-off accident at Villeneuf airfield.	Junkers Ju 88A-1 (7065 : 9K+JT)	25 %		Crew unhurt.
5.	Geschw.Erg.St./	NCM	Landing accident; location not notified.	Heinkel He111P-2 (1578 : A1+WK)	45 %		Crew unhurt.
6.	I./KG 54	CM	Shot down by 600 Sqn. Blenheim night fighter of Pritchard, Jacobs and Smith off South Coast at Bexhill at A.00.30 hrs.	Junkers Ju 88A-1 (7087 : B3+HH)	100 %		Hptm. Willi Henke and Uffz. Rattay killed; Fw. Perleberg and Fw. Baur missing.
7.	II./KG 54	CM	Crashed near Evreux; cause not known.	Junkers Ju 88A-1(6050)	100 %		Four crew members killed.
8.	I./KG 55	CM	Suffered landing accident at Dreux.	Heinkel He111H (5370)	35 %		Crew unhurt.
9.	4./KG 76	CM	Crashed near Arlon, probably after operational sortie. Crew baled out.	Junkers Ju 88A-1 (3123 : F1+BM)	100 %		One crew member wounded.
10.	KGr. 806	NCM	Crashed at Köln-Ostheim airfield due to faulty maintenance.	Junkers Ju 88A-1 (7131)	25 %		Crew unhurt.
11.	II./LG 1	NCM	Landing accident at Orléans airfield following tyre burst..	Junkers Ju 88A-1 (6135 : L1+GP)	40 %		Crew unhurt.
12.	7.(F)/LG 2	NCM	Take-off accident at Karlsruhe airfield.	Dornier Do 17P	35 %		Crew unhurt.
13.	3./NJG 2	CM	Missing from night intruder sortie over Lincolnshire; assumed shot down by R.A.F. bomber or airfield *flak*.	Junkers Ju 88C-2 (0190 : R4+AH)	100 %		Fw. Pahn killed; Gefr. Reinisch and Gefr. Haberland missing.
14.	1./JG 3	CM	Missing from sortie over Southern England.	Messerschmitt Bf 109E (2685)	100 %		Ofw. Gessel missing.
15.	7./JG 26	CM	Missing from sortie over London.	Messerschmitt Bf 109 E-1 (6294)	100 %		Uffz. Bock made P.O.W.
16.	5./JG 77	CM	Struck obstacle on runway at Vaernes, Norway; two Norwegian labourers killed and three injured.	Messerschmitt Bf 109 E-1 (6294)	90 %		Pilot unhurt.
17.	3./506	CM	Both engines failed during night sortie and ditched 7 miles north-east of Eyemouth, near Berwick, at 01.00 hrs. Crew rescued by fishing boat; aircraft capsized and towed into Eyemouth harbour.	Heinkel He 115C (3261 : S4+CL)	100 %		Hptm. Han Kriependorf, Oblt. Clemens Lucas, Hptm. Ernst Wilhelm Bergmann and Fw. Erich Kalinowski, all unwounded, made P.O.W.s
18.	Seenotflug-kommando 2	CM	Crashed after engine failure on take-off at Boulogne.	Heinkel He 59 (0529 : DA+MG)	100 %		One killed; Maj. Ulrich Klintzsch, Oblt. Dr. Arnold von Vogel and two others wounded.

Tuesday 17th September

As Blenheims of Coastal and Bomber Commands returned to Thorney Island, Eastchurch and Bircham Newton with reports and photographs of the invasion ports in Belgium and Northern France, photographic interpreters set about the intricate task of estimating the rate of assembly of landing craft. At Boulogne the concentration of barges had increased from 102 to 150 in forty-eight hours; at Calais the number had reached 266. Altogether the Channel ports harboured more than one thousand such craft, with a further 600 on their way down river to Antwerp. It was as much the continued pressure maintained against these targets by an enemy air force very

much in being[30] as the continued effective defence by Fighter Command which once again delayed Hitler's decision to launch *Seelöwe*. By this day, clearly, he must have felt considerable misgivings over the chances of launching the invasion at all, with any hope of success.

In keeping with Göring's instructions of the previous day, Kesselring contented himself with a single multi-wave attack phase of fighter formations, which crossed the South Kent

---

[30] An estimated 12 per cent of the invasion barges were destroyed by Bomber and Coastal Command attacks during September 1940.

An unarmed Spitfire of the Photographic Reconnaissance Unit; flying from Heston aircraft of this type flew numerous sorties high over France and the Low Countries during the Battle of Britain to bring back photos which told the story of the Germans' preparations to invade Britain—and of the dispersal of landing craft after Hitler's decision to postpone Operation Seelöwe.

coast between 15.00 and 16.00 hours. Each formation consisted of about two *Gruppen* of Bf 109s, their pilots ordered to engage weaker R.A.F. formations whenever possible. In the main the British preferred to avoid combat—being well aware of the enemy's intentions—and only II. and III.*Gruppen* of JG 53 were intercepted in any strength. This formation of the «*Pik As*» *Geschwader* dealt harshly with the Hurricanes of No. 501 Squadron near Ashford, but was then engaged by Spitfires of No. 41 Squadron over East Kent, and shortly afterwards by squadrons of the Duxford Wing. In this combat German losses amounted to three destroyed and two damaged, against an R.A.F. loss of one Spitfire and two Hurri-

canes destroyed and two Spitfires damaged. One of the Hurricane pilots, Sgt. Edward Egan (who had started in the Battle of Britain flying Blenheims with No. 600 Squadron) was killed, his Hurricane falling at Tuesnoad Farm, Bethersden, near Ashford.

If this was to be representative of forthcoming fighter-versus-fighter combats, then little or no advantage could be gained by the *Luftwaffe*; for though parity in aircraft losses was achieved on this occasion, once again the loss of three Bf 109s over England meant the loss of all three pilots—one of whom was the *Staffelkapitän* of 9./JG 53.

R.A.F. FIGHTER COMMAND LOSSES—TUESDAY 17th SEPTEMBER 1940

No.	Squadron		Details	Time	Pilot	Aircraft	Serial	Category
1.	17 Sqn., Debden	NC	Crashed after engine failure on take-off; pilot unhurt.	15.00 hrs.	Flt. Lt. A.W.A. Bayne	Hurricane	P3027	Cat. 3 Destroyed
2.	41 Sqn., Hornchurch	C	Shot down by Bf 109 at Spelling Minnies; pilot unhurt.	15.25 hrs.	Plt. Off. H.C. Baker	Spitfire	X4409	Cat. 3 Destroyed
3.	41 Sqn., Hornchurch	C	Damaged by Bf 109s over Kent; pilot unhurt.	A15.20 hrs.	Not known	Spitfire	—	Cat. 2 Damaged
4.	41 Sqn., Hornchurch	C	Damaged by Bf 109s over Kent; pilot unhurt.	A15.20 hrs.	Not known	Spitfire	—	Cat. 2 Damaged
5.	151 Sqn., Digby	C	Pilot flew into high ground during combat with He 111; pilot injured.	A18.00 hrs.	Sgt. J. Winstanley	Hurricane	R4185	Cat. 3 Destroyed
6.	152 Sqn., Warmwell	C	Damaged in combat with Ju 88 over Shepton Mallet; pilot landed, unhurt, at Colerne.	13.50 hrs.	Plt. Off. E.S. Marrs	Spitfire	—	Cat. 1 Damaged
7.	257 Sqn., Martlesham	—	Taxying accident in high wind; pilot unhurt.	14.40 hrs.	Sgt. R.H.B. Fraser	Hurricane	P3705	Cat. 1 Damaged
8.	501 Sqn., Kenley	C	Shot down by Bf 109 near Ashford; crashed in Daniels Wood, Bethersden; pilot killed.	A15.25 hrs.	Sgt. E.J. Egan	Hurricane	P3820	Cat. 3 Destroyed
9.	501 Sqn., Kenley	C	Shot down near Ashford by Bf 109; pilot baled out unhurt.	A15.25 hrs.	Sgt. J.H. Lacey	Hurricane	V7357	Cat. 3 Destroyed
10.	504 Sqn., Hendon	NC	Pilot experienced difficulties during training dogfight; baled out but struck tailplane and was killed. Aircraft fell at Selling, Kent.	Not known	Sgt. D.A. Helcke	Hurricane	V7529	Cat. 3 Destroyed
11.	607 Sqn., Tangmere	C	Shot down by Bf 109s near Gravesend; pilot killed. Aircraft crashed at Beltring, near Paddock Wood, Kent.	15.36 hrs.	Sgt. J. Landesdell	Hurricane	P3860	Cat. 3 Destroyed
12.	607 Sqn., Tangmere	C	Shot down by Hptm. Neumann of I./JG 27, and force landed at Tuesnoad Farm, Bethersden, Kent. Pilot slightly wounded.	15.42 hrs.	Plt. Off. G.H.E. Welford	Hurricane	—	Cat. 3 Destroyed
13.	611 Sqn., Duxford	NC	Suffered landing collision at Duxford in bad weather; pilot unhurt.	Not known	Plt. Off. J.W. Lund	Spitfire	P7305	Cat. 2 Damaged

LUFTWAFFE LOSSES—TUESDAY 17th SEPTEMBER 1940

No.	Unit		Details	Aircraft	%	Casualties
1.	8./KG 4	CM	Shot down by 141 Sqn. Defiant of Lawrence and Chard near Barking at 23.50 hrs.	Junkers Ju 88A-1 (2126 : 5J+BS)	100 %	Fw.Gebser and Ogefr.Krauss killed; Uffz. Borchardt and Uffz. Guldenburg wounded.
2.	7./KG 30	CM	Damaged by British fighters and force landed at Vlissingen on return.	Junkers Ju 88A-1 (0220 : 4D+BR)	40 %	Three crew members wounded.
3.	I./KG 54	CM	Damaged by 141 Sqn. Defiant and by A.A. fire, and crashed in Maidstone at A.23.30 hrs.	Junkers Ju 88A-1 (2152 : B3+OL)	100 %	Ltn. Rudolf Ganslmeyr, Uffz.Ernst Bauer, Uffz. Karl Schlösser and Ofw.Willi Fachinger killed.
4.	7./KG 77	CM	Crashed on take-off at Laon; cause not notified.	Junkers Ju 88A-1 (5089 : 3Z+CR)	100 %	Two crew members killed; Ltn. Josef Zimmer + one wounded.
5.	II./LG 1	CM	Shot down by 151 Sqn. Spitfires of Holland, Marrs and O'Brien over Shepton Mallet and crashed at Chitterne at 13.50 hrs.	Junkers Ju 88A-1 (3188 : L1+XC)	100 %	Ltn. Otto Heinrich killed; Fw. Franz Schultz wounded; Maj.Heinz Cramer and Ofw.Stützel missing.
6.	III./LG 1	CM	Engine failure following *flak* damage and force landed near Le Havre.	Junkers Ju 88A-1 (5012 : L1+KT)	10 %	Crew unhurt.
7.	III./ZG 76	NCM	Landing accident at Laval airfield due to faulty maintenance.	Messerschmitt Bf 110C (3513 : NZ+HN)	60 %	Crew unhurt.
8.	9./JG 3	NCM	Wheels-up landing at Desvres airfield; cause not notified.	Messerschmitt Bf 109 E-1 (3561)	35 %	Pilot unhurt.
9.	6./JG 27	NCM	Take-off accident at Crépon airfield.	Messerschmitt Bf 109 E-1 (3544)	60 %	Pilot unhurt.
10.	Stab II./JG 53	CM	Damaged by 41 Sqn. Spitfires over East Kent at 15.40 hrs., and force landed at Wissant.	Messerschmitt Bf 109 E-4 (1313)	15 %	Pilot unhurt.
11.	Stab II./JG 53	CM	Damaged by 41 Sqn. Spitfires over East Kent at 15.40 hrs, but landed safely at Wissant.	Messerschmitt Bf 109 E-4 (1644)	5%	Pilot unhurt.
12.	9./JG 53	CM	Shot down by 19 Sqn. Spitfire of Blake east of London at 15.45 hrs.	Messerschmitt Bf 109 E-4 (5141)	100 %	Oblt. Jakob Stoll, *St.Kap.*, missing.
13.	9./JG 53	CM	Shot down by 19 Sqn. Spitfire of Blake east of London at A.15.45 hrs.	Messerschmitt Bf 109 E-4 (1228)	100 %	Oblt. Herbert Seliger missing.
14.	9./JG 53	CM	Shot down by 303 Sqn. Hurricane of Wojciechowski over the Thames Estuary atA.16.30 hrs.	Messerschmitt Bf 109 E-1 (3177)	100 %	Uffz. Langer killed.
15.	1./906	CM	Missing from mining sortie over English East Coast; fate not known.	Heinkel He 115 (2754 : 8L+GH)	100 %	Ltn.z.S. Otto Aldus, Hptm. Heinrich Kothe, Uffz.Meissner missing.
16.	Wekusta. 1	NCM	Force landed with engine failure at Lichtenfelde.	Heinkel He 111 (5175)	35 %	Crew unhurt.
17.	Seenotflug-kommando 3	—	Damaged in storm at Boulogne.	Heinkel He 59 (1848 : NE+TA)	30 %	No aircrew casualties.

Wednesday 18th September

Yet again, while the *Luftwaffe* spent its night raiding forces— 193 sorties over London, Bristol, Liverpool, Southampton and elsewhere—in almost fruitless and undiscriminating attacks, Bomber Command sent more than one hundred Whitleys, Wellingtons and Hampdens against barge concentrations and other shipping at Ijmuiden, Dunkirk, Boulogne, Ostend, Zeebrugge, Antwerp and Cherbourg. Dawn reconnaissance revealed that more than 150 barges had been destroyed, while considerable dockside destruction had been inflicted at Dunkirk and Antwerp; at the former port 500 tons of ammunition had blown up, causing immense destruction to quays and warehouses.

Kesselring's high altitude fighter sweeps started out fairly early in the morning, two formations each of about *Gruppe* strength crossing in over East Kent at 09.15 hours. Park's controllers scrambled fifteen squadrons (totalling 90 Hurricanes and Spitfires) but only six engaged—the Biggin Hill and Hornchurch "pairs". Once again the losses on each side were roughly balanced, with three Bf 109s falling, as against five Spitfires—only one of whose pilots was killed. Shortly after this phase of attacks closed, Plt. Off. Tony Bartley of No. 92 Squadron caught and shot down a reconnaissance Dornier Do 215 of *Aufklärungsgruppe Oberbefehlshaber der Luftwaffe* over Gravesend.

The next phase, composed of a small number of Ju 88s escorted by more than one hundred Bf 109s, came in north of Dover and carried out a sharp raid in the Chatham and Rochester area. Now fully aware of the enemy's tactics, Park refused to be drawn and no squadrons were scrambled. Kesselring must have realised that such intentional avoidance of combat could only be countered by sending more bombers, as had been the case a month earlier, for he now mounted a fast raid by the Ju 88s of III./KG 77—which had only very recently been brought into the Battle. The relatively inexperienced crews were treated to a brutal baptism. Recognised by the Observer Corps as they flew in two formations along the North Kent coast, they drew a violent reaction from Park, who ordered fourteen squadrons up to meet the threat. As the Junkers neared their target at Gravesend more than one hundred Hurricanes and Spitfires attacked, shooting down nine bombers in short order. The 8th *Staffel* alone lost five aircraft, and among the dead was the *Gruppenkommandeur*, Major Maxim Kless.

Once again the Duxford Wing was in action, claiming no less than 30 of the enemy destroyed; in fact its pilots shot down four bombers and suffered damage to three of their aircraft.

The R.A.F. had been drawn into the air; but to what purpose? No fighter sweep followed the sacrificial bombers to exploit the situation; it must appear that they were thrown away for nothing. And the days were past when Kesselring could afford to send a fresh bomber *Gruppe* to destruction without some very clear return on the investment.

R.A.F. FIGHTER COMMAND LOSSES—WEDNESDAY 18th SEPTEMBER 1940

1.	3 Sqn., Turnhouse	NC	Force landed due to mishandling of fuel cock; pilot unhurt.	Not known	Plt. Off. P. Kennett	Hurricane	P3020	Cat. 2 Damaged
2.	17 Sqn., Debden	NC	Minor air collision with Item 3; pilot unhurt.	Not known	Sqn. Ldr. A.G. Miller	Hurricane	L1808	Cat. 1 Damaged
3.	17 Sqn., Debden	NC	Minor air collision with Item 2; pilot unhurt.	Not known	Sgt. L.H. Bartlett	Hurricane	V7241	Cat. 1 Damaged
4.	19 Sqn., Fowlmere	NC	Force landed following engine failure; pilot unhurt.	Not known	Plt. Off. F. Hradil	Spitfire	N3265	Cat. 2 Damaged
5.	19 Sqn., Fowlmere	C	Aircraft hit in glycol tank during combat and force landed at Eastchurch; pilot unhurt.	A13.35 hrs.	Plt. Off. W.J. Lawson	Spitfire	X4170	Cat. 2 Damaged
6.	25 Sqn., North Weald	C	Hit by return fire from enemy aircraft intercepted at night; crew unhurt.	At night	Plt. Off. B.J. Rofe.	Blenheim	—	Cat. 2 Damaged
7.	46 Sqn., Stapleford	C	Shot down by Bf 109s over Clacton; pilot baled out but killed when parachute failed.	12.45 hrs.	Sgt. G.W. Jefferys	Hurricane	V7442	Cat. 3 Lost
8.	46 Sqn., Stapleford	C	Shot down by Bf 109s near Chatham; pilot baled out, wounded in the le and with burns to face and hands.	12.50 hrs.	Sgt. C.A.L. Hurry	Hurricane	P3816	Cat. 3 Destroyed
9.	46 Sqn., Stapleford	C	Shot down by Bf 109s near Chatham; pilot baled out slightly wounded. Aircraft crashed at Walderslade, near Gillingham, Kent.	12.52 hrs.	Plt. Off. P.W. Lefevre	Hurricane	V6554	Cat. 3 Destroyed
10.	66 Sqn., Gravesend	C	Shot down by Bf 109s and crashed at Petham, south of Canterbury; pilot wounded.	A13.25 hrs.	Sgt. D.F. Corfe	Spitfire	R6603	Cat. 3 Destroyed
11.	66 Sqn., Gravesend	C	Shot down over the Thames Estuary; pilot baled out unhurt. Aircraft said to have crashed at Coldred near Dover.	16.30 hrs.	Plt. Off. R.J. Mather	Spitfire	R6925	Cat. 3 Destroyed
12.	72 Sqn., Biggin Hill	C	Damaged by Bf 109s near Dover and pilot force landed, wounded.	A09.40 hrs.	Plt. Off. J.P. Lloyd	Spitfire	P9368	Cat. 2 Damaged
13.	72 Sqn., Biggin Hill	C	Shot down by Bf 109s near Gravesend; pilot baled out badly wounded.	A09.30 hrs.	Sgt. H.J. Bell-Walker	Spitfire	R6704	Cat. 3 Destroyed
14.	92 Sqn., Biggin Hill	C	Shot down by Bf 109s over the Medway and crashed at Hollingbourne, near Maidstone.	09.55 hrs.	Plt. Off. R. Mottram	Spitfire	N3193	Cat. 3 Destroyed
15.	92 Sqn., Biggin Hill	C	Shot down by Bf 109s near Gravesend; pilot unhurt.	09.48 hrs.	Plt. Off. A.C. Bartley	Spitfire	N3283	Cat. 3 Destroyed
16.	302 Sqn., Kenley	C	Suffered landing accident after combat; pilot unhurt.	17.30 hrs.	Not known	Hurricane	—	Cat. 2 Damaged
17.	501 Sqn., Kenley	C	Shot down by Bf 109s over Tonbridge, and pilot baled out unhurt; aircraft crashed at Staplehurst.	09.30 hrs.	Sgt. C.J. Saward	Hurricane	V6600	Cat. 3 Destroyed
18.	501 Sqn., Kenley	C	Shot down in combat with He 111 and Bf 109s over West Malling; pilot baled out, unhurt, and aircraft crashed near Charing.	A13.00 hrs	Sqn. Ldr. H.A.V. Hogan	Hurricane	V6620	Cat. 3 Destroyed
19.	603 Sqn., Hornchurch	C	Shot down by Bf 109s near Ashford; pilot killed; aircraft crashed at Kennington.	09.40 hrs.	Plt. Off. P. Howes	Spitfire	X4323	Cat. 3 Destroyed
20.	603 Sqn., Hornchurch	C	Damaged in combat with Bf 109s near Ashford; pilot returned unhurt.	09.36 hrs.	Sgt. G.J. Bailey	Spitfire	K9803	Cat. 2 Damaged

LUFTWAFFE LOSSES—WEDNESDAY 18th SEPTEMBER 1940

1.	Aufkl.Gr.	CM	Shot down by 19 Sqn. Spitfire of Bartley near Gravesend at A.10.00 hrs.	Dornier Do 215 (0038 : G2+KH)	100 %	Fw. Helmut Schütz killed; Ltn. Hans Poser, Uffz. Wiesen and Uffz. Linsner missing.
2.	3.(F)/10	CM	Damaged by British fighters near Dover but returned safely to base.	Dornier Do 17P (1063 : T1+EL)	12 %	Crew unhurt.
3.	3.(F)/10	CM	Damaged by 64 Sqn. Spitfire of Taylor near Manchester at 19.55 hrs.	Dornier Do 17P (1105 : T1+HL)	30 %	Crew unhurt.
4.	3.(H)/32	NCM	Landing accident; location and details not notified.	Henschel Hs 126B (4202)	40 %	Crew unhurt.
5.	I./KG 30	NCM	Take-off accident at Ludwiglust; aircraft burnt out.	Junkers Ju 88A-1 (8015 :4D+JP)	98 %	Two crew members injured.
6.	I./KG 54	CM	Landing accident at Schellingwoude airfield.	Junkers Ju 88A-1(4058)	100 %	One crew member killed.
7.	II./KG 54	CM	Shot down by 213 Sqn. Hurricanes over South Coast convoy.	Junkers Ju 88A-1 (0226 : B3+CP)	100 %	Oblt. Max Winkler, Fw. Gödecke, Üffz.Pettau and Uffz.Schwenzfeier missing.
8.	Stab/KG 55	CM	Accident following engine failure at Evreux.	Heinkel He 111P (2503)	30 %	Crew unhurt.
9.	Stab III./KG 77	CM	Aircraft missing from bombing sortie over London; fate not traced.	Junkers Ju 88A-1 (3173 : 3Z+ED)	100 %	Maj. Max Kless,Gr.Kdr., and Oblt. Fritz Lauth killed; Fw. Himsel and Fw. Pröbst missing.
10.	7./KG 77	CM	Aircraft missing from bombing sortie over London; fate not traced.	Junkers Ju 88A-1 (5098 : 3Z+KR)	100 %	Fw.Wursche, Fw.Nolte, Fw.Friedel killed; Uffz. Stammnite missing.
11.	8./KG 77	CM	Shot down by 92 Sqn. Spitfire of Kingcombe over Tenterden, Kent, at 16.35 hrs.	Junkers Ju 88A-1 (5100 : 3Z+HS)	100 %	Oblt. Hans-Ludwig Weber, Fw. Kripmann and Gefr.Neumeg killed; Fw. Gorn missing.
12.	8./KG 77	CM	Shot down by 92 Sqn. Spitfire of Kingcombe near Tenterden , Kent, at A.16.35 hrs.	Junkers Ju 88A-1 (5097 : 3Z+ES)	100 %	Fw. Heinz Damschen and Uffz. Eggert killed; Ofw. Simerau and Gefr. Treutmann missing.
13.	8./KG 77	CM	Shot down by 92 Sqn. Spitfire of Hill over Kent at A.16.30 hrs.	Junkers Ju 88A-1 (3147 : 3Z+AS)	100 %	Ofw. Brendel, Uffz. Künkl and Uffz. Weidemüller missing. (1)
14.	8./KG 77	CM	Shot down by 302 Sqn. Hurricanes over the Thames Estuary at 16.50 hrs.	Junkers Ju 88A-1 (3162 : 3Z+FS)	100 %	Oblt. Georg Fuchs killed; Fw . Stier wounded; Ogefr. Baumann and Gefr. Folinger missing.
15.	8./KG 77	CM	Shot down by 302 Sqn. Hurricanes over the Thames Estuary at 16.50 hrs.	Junkers Ju 88A-1 (3142 : 3Z+BS)	100 %	Crew (one member wounded) made P.O.W.s.
16.	9./KG 77	CM	Target Tilbury Docks. Shot down by 19 Sqn. Spitfires of Lawson, Cunningham and Lloyd east of London at A.13.15 hrs.	Junkers Ju 88A-1 (3168 : 3Z+FT)	100 %	Fw. Wahl, Gefr. Hans Buschbeck and Gefr. Lesker killed; Fw. Graf missing.
17.	9./KG 77	CM	Target Tilbury Docks. Shot down by 19 Sqn. Spitfires east of London at A.13.15 hrs.	Junkers Ju 88A-1 (5104 : 3Z+DT)	100 %	Uffz. Alfons Kurz killed; Fw. Burkant wounded; Gefr. Rudulf Kühn and Uffz. Gläseker missing.
18.	3./JG 3	CM	Force landed at Calais following engine failure.	Messerschmitt Bf 109 E-1 (0897)	50 %	Pilot wounded.
19.	1./JG 27	NCM	Take-off accident at Cherbourg-West airfield.	Messerschmitt Bf 109 E-7 (5574)	100 %	Gefr. Günther Poppek killed.
20.	1./JG 27	CM	Shot down by British fighters over Sussex.	Messerschmitt Bf 109 E-4 (5388)	100 %	Oblt. Rudolf Krafftschick made P.O.W.
21.	2./JG 27	CM	Damaged in combat but returned safely to Guines.	Messerschmitt Bf 109 E-1 (5366)	30 %	Pilot unhurt.
22.	9./JG 27	CM	Shot down by 41 Sqn. Spitfire of Bennions near Maidstone at A.13.15 hrs.	Messerschmitt Bf 109 E-1 (2674)	100 %	Gefr. Walter Glöckner made P.O.W.
23.	9./JG 27	CM	Shot down by 41 Sqn. Spitfires near Maidstone at A.13.15 hrs.	Messerschmitt Bf 109 E-1 (6327)	100 %	Fw. Ernst Schulz, wounded, made P.O.W.; died of wounds,12-12-40.
24.	4./JG 53	CM	Shot down by British fighters near Dover.	Messerschmitt Bf 109 E-1 (4842)	100 %	Ltn. Erich Dodendiek missing.
25.	1./JG 54	CM	Shot down by British fighters into the Channel.	Messerschmitt Bf 109 E-1 (6220)	100 %	Pilot, unhurt, rescued by *Seenotflugkommando*.
26.	9./JG 54	CM	Force landed at Guines-Süd following engine failure.	Messerschmitt Bf 109 E-4 (0972)	20 %	Pilot unhurt.
27.	1./JG 77	CM	Shot down by British fighters near Ramsgate.	Messerschmitt Bf 109 E-1 (2669)	100 %	Gefr. Still killed.

[(1) This crew also carried a Sonderführer, Uffz. Smorlatzy, of Lw.Kr.Ber.Kp.4; his unit was subsequently notified that he met his death on this sortie.]

Thursday 19th September

It is not possible to identify any specific event which so influenced Adolf Hitler in his deliberations on 19th September that he finally abandoned his plans to launch the invasion of Britain in 1940. The overwhelming probability is that he could no longer ignore the combination of factors which now threatened *Seelöwe*. The continued resistance of Fighter Command must have destroyed his belief in Göring's wide-ranging claims for the invincibility of "his" *Luftwaffe*—a betrayal of faith which was to be repeated more than once in the coming years. To the Naval Staff's vocal misgivings about its ability to keep an invasion lane open across the Channel must now have been added complaints by the *Wehrmacht* that the *Luftwaffe* seemed unable to protect the assembly ports, let alone the eventual beachheads. The summer was drawing to a close, and the approach of uncertain autumn weather must have put the final seal on *Seelöwe*'s fate—only

Scene of raid damage in Oxford Street in London's West End on the morning of 19th September (Photo: Topix)

48 hours before the date originally planned for its launching. Whatever the most telling of those factors, the decision was taken; Hitler shelved the project indefinitely on 19th September, and only two days later British reconnaissance pilots reported a noticeable decrease of activity in the invasion ports.

Air operations on the 19th were much reduced by rain showers which spread across Britain from the west.

Kampfgeschwader 77's I.*Gruppe* was sent against London and was met by the paired Hurricane Squadrons, Nos. 249 and 302 (Polish), losing one Junkers to each squadron without inflicting any damage on their attackers. That indefatigable Hurricane pilot, Count Manfred Czernin, led two colleagues in an attack on a reconnaissance Dornier of 4.(F)/121 off Harwich, and shot it down into the sea. Elsewhere the *Luftwaffe* lost two *Staffelkapitäne*—one killed and one wounded.

R.A.F. FIGHTER COMMAND LOSSES—THURSDAY 19th SEPTEMBER 1940

1.	257 Sqn., Martlesham	NC	Pilot force landed at Bawdsey following engine failure during convoy patrol.	14.45 hrs.	Flt. Lt. P.M. Brothers	Hurricane	—	Cat. 1 Damaged

LUFTWAFFE LOSSES—THURSDAY 19th SEPTEMBER 1940

1.	4.(F)/121	CM	Shot down by 17 Sqn. Hurricanes of Czernin, Griffiths and Bartlett off the Suffolk coast at 11.15 hrs.	Junkers Ju 88A-1 (0362 : 7A+FM)	100 %	Ltn. Helmut Knab, Uffz. Zscheket, Uffz. Thöring and Ogefr. Bresch missing.
2.	5.(F)/122	CM	Damaged by 92 Sqn. Spitfires near Biggin Hill and force landed on return.	Junkers Ju 88A-6 (0400 : F6+ZA)	50 %	One crew member killed; Hptm. Böhm, St.Kap., Oblt. Hans von Vleuten wounded.
3.	7./KG 2	CM	Landing accident near Cambrai following combat.	Dornier Do 17Z (4242 : U5+JR)	65 %	Crew unhurt.
4.	2./KG 3	CM	Landing accident after combat; location not notified.	Dornier Do 17Z-2 (3429 : 5K+LK)	30 %	Oblt. Richard Geissler wounded.
5.	6./KG 3	CM	Force landed after engine failure; location not notified.	Dornier Do 17Z-2 (2535 : 5K+BP)	50 %	Two crew members wounded.
6.	9./KG 3	CM	Landing accident near St. Albert; cause not notified.	Dornier Do 17Z-3 (2647 : 5K+GT)	50 %	Crew unhurt.
7.	4./KG 4	CM	Damaged by 504 Sqn. Hurricane (probably flown by Lacey) at A.09.00 hrs.	Heinkel He 111P-4 (3087 : 5J+DM)	20 %	Crew unhurt.
8.	9./KG 4	CM	Landing accident at Schipol following combat.	Junkers Ju 88A-1 (5055 : 5J+LT)	18 %	Crew unhurt.
9.	III./KG 27	CM	Wheels-up landing on Rennes airfield following combat.	Heinkel He 111P (1985 : 1G+GT)	25 %	Crew unhurt.
10.	3./KG 51	CM	Believed shot down by British fighters over south-west England; R.A.F. unit not identified.	Junkers Ju 88A-1 (7058 : 9K+DL)	100 %	Ofw. Heinrich Luckhardt, Uffz. Waldemar Henker, Fw. Wilhelm Walter and Gefr. Röder killed.
11.	II./KG 51	CM	Damaged by British fighters (probably Spitfires of 151 Sqn.) and force landed at Cherbourg.	Junkers Ju 88A-1 (3076)	20 %	No casualties notified.
12.	II./KG 51	CM	Crashed on landing at Orly with combat damage.	Junkers Ju 88A-1(7124)	65 %	One crew member wounded.
13.	II./KG 54	CM	Believed shot down by *flak* over Southern England.	Junkers Ju 88A-1 (4148 : B3+HM)	100 %	Ofw. Rörig, Fw. Fischer, and Gefr. Neumann killed.; Fw. Schlake missing.
14.	I./KG 55	CM	Shot down (believe by *flak* at night) over the English Midlands.	Heinkel He 111P-2 (2146 : G1+GL)	100 %	Uffz. Goliath, Fw. Albert, Uffz. Pohl killed; Uffz. Gers missing.
15.	1./KG 77	CM	Shot down by 249 Sqn. Hurricanes of Beazley and Burton over Greater London.	Junkers Ju 88A-1 (6141 : 3Z+CH)	100 %	Gefr. Möckel killed; Uffz Kunz, Ofw. Strahl anf Fw. Winkelmann missing.
16.	1./KG 77	CM	Shot down by 302 Sqn. Hurricanes of Riley and Kowalski, 4 miles north-east of Brandon at 12.15 hrs.	Junkers Ju 88A-1 (2151 : 3Z+GH)	100 %	Uffz. Dorawa, Gefr. Schulz and Gefr. Scholz killed; Uffz. Etzold missing.
17.	1./KGr. 806	CM	Damaged by British fighters and force landed at Carpiquet airfield.	Junkers Ju 88A-1 (6100 : M7+BL)	20 %	Crew unhurt.
18.	1./KGr. 806	CM	Shot down by 152 Sqn. Spitfires of Williams and Holland over the English Channel.	Junkers Ju 88A-1 (4065 : M7+EH)	100 %	Ofw. Sowade, Uffz. Dresen, Gefr. Springfeld and Uffz. Weigand missing.
19.	3./106	CM	Landing accident at Hofden (?) after mining sortie in British coastal waters.	Heinkel He 115C (3259 : M2+CL)	100 %	Hptm.Hans Kannengiesser,St.Kap., Obit. JoachimLohse and Ogefr. Kirschwehn killed.
20.	IV./KGzbV 1	NCM	Engine failure on take-off at St. Denis Westrem.	Junkers Ju 52/3m (5516 : 1Z+CX)	80 %	Two crew members injured.

Friday 20th September

German air activity on this day was confined to a single powerful sweep in two waves, each of about thirty Bf 109s, which crossed the Kent coast at 14,000 feet over Dungeness and Dover between 10.45 and 11.15 hours, and set course for the Medway Towns. The Biggin Hill and Hornchurch Spitfire squadrons scrambled at 11.15 hours and a dogfight developed in the Maidstone area. From the British viewpoint this was a disappointing combat; for just as No. 72 Squadron was attacking the Bf 109s of *Jagdgeschwader 3 «Udet»* over Ashford, No. 92 Squadron lost contact with the enemy and broke away to the south-east. The Hornchurch squadrons,

which had been vectored into the area in which No. 72 was fighting, were bounced by the second wave of the German sweep and lost three Spitfires. As the Germans retired between 11.30 and 12.00 hours the four British Squadrons (Nos. 41, 72, 92 and 222) continued to engage all the way to the coast, but only succeeded in shooting down two Bf 109s. British losses totalled seven Spitfires, four pilots losing their lives. It was a salutary reminder of the competence of the German *Jagdflieger* when they were released from the cares of close bomber escort over long distances.

R.A.F. FIGHTER COMMAND LOSSES—FRIDAY 20th SEPTEMBER 1940

1.	41 Sqn., Hornchurch	C	Shot down by Ju 88 and force landed at Lympne; pilot unhurt.	A10.55 hrs.	Plt. Off. G.H. Bennions	Spitfire	—	Cat. 2 Damaged (1)

R.A.F. Losses, 20th September 1940—*continued*

2.	56 Sqn., Boscombe Down	NC	Crashed on local flight; pilot killed.	A11.10 hrs.	Sgt. C.V. Meeson	Hurricane	—	Cat. 3 Destroyed
3.	72 Sqn., Biggin Hill	C	Shot down by Bf 109s and crashed near Sittingbourne, Kent. Pilot killed.	10.48 hrs.	Plt. Off. D.F. Holland	Spitfire	*X4410*	Cat. 3 Destroyed
4.	72 Sqn., Biggin Hill	C	Shot down by Bf 109s near Canterbury; pilot unhurt.	10.46 hrs.	Plt. Off. A.I. Lindsay	Spitfire	*R6881*	Cat. 3 Destroyed
5.	92 Sqn., Biggin Hill	C	Shot down in flames near Dover by Bf 109s of JG 51 and crashed at West Hougham, west of Dover; pilot killed.	11.55 hrs.	Plt. Off. H.P. Hill	Spitfire	*X4417*	Cat. 3 Destroyed
6.	92 Sqn., Biggin Hill	C	Shot down by Bf 109s of JG 51 into the sea between Dungeness and Dover; pilot killed.	11.55 hrs.	Sgt. P.R. Eyles	Spitfire	*R6840*	Cat. 3 Lost
7.	222 Sqn., Hornchurch	C	Shot down by Bf 109s at Rochester, Kent. Aircraft crashed at Higham; pilot killed.	A11.45 hrs.	Plt. Off. H.L. Whitbread	Spitfire	*N3203*	Cat. 3 Destroyed
8.	222 Sqn., Hornchurch	C	Damaged in combat with Bf 109s over the Thames Estuary, but crashed on landing at base.	12.05 hrs.	Plt. Off. E.F. Edsall	Spitfire	*R6840*	Cat. 3 Destroyed
9.	222 Sqn., Hornchurch	C	Shot down by Bf 109s over the Thames Estuary. Pilot baled out with slight burns at Latchingdon; aircraft crashed at West Hanningfield, Essex.	11.50 hrs.	Plt. Off. W.R. Assheton	Spitfire	*K9993*	Cat. 3 Destroyed
10.	605 Sqn., Croydon	C	Damaged in combat with Bf 109s ; pilot returned unhurt.	11.40 hrs.	Plt. Off. W.J. Glowacki	Hurricane	*V6722*	Cat. 2 Damaged

LUFTWAFFE LOSSES—FRIDAY 20th SEPTEMBER 1940

1.	4.(F)/121	CM	Damaged by British fighters over Southern England and force landed at Caen airfield.	Dornier Do 17P (1102)	60 %	One crew member wounded.
2.	1.(F)/123	CM	Damaged by 41 Sqn. Spitfire of Bennions over Southern England and crashed near Pont de Briques.	Junkers Ju 88A-1 (0379 : 4U+EH)	100 %	One killed; Oblt. Hoffmann, Ltn. Rommel and one other wounded.
3.	3./KG 4	CM	Force landed, short of fuel, after combat sortie.	Junkers Ju 88A-1 (1337 : 5J+CT)	30 %	Crew unhurt.
4.	I./KG 27	CM	Shot down by *flak* at night, believed west of London; location of crash not known.	Heinkel He 111P (1683 : 1G+FP)	100 %	Hptm. Josef Fellinger, Uffz. Spazier, Uffz. Nonnemann and Ogefr. Schwerb missing.
5.	7./KG 30	CM	Landing accident at Melsbrück; cause not notified.	Junkers Ju 88A-1 (7048 : 4D+MR)	25 %	Crew unhurt.
6.	9./KG 30	CM	Landing accident at Melsbrück; cause not notified.	Junkers Ju 88A-1 (4075 : 4D+IT)	65 %	Crew unhurt.
7.	III./KG 51	CM	Landing accident at Lille-Nord; cause not notified.	Junkers Ju 88A-1 (7092 : 9K+MR)	45 %	Crew unhurt.
8.	3./KGr. 606	CM	Damaged by *flak* over Liverpool at night; crashed on return.	Dornier Do 17Z (1211 : 7T+ML)	80 %	Crew unhurt.
9.	8./JG 3	CM	Damaged by 72 Sqn. Spitfires between Ashford and Canterbury at 10.55 hrs.; crashed at Cap Gris Nez.	Messerschmitt Bf 109 E-1 (1435)	90 %	Pilot wounded.
10.	9./JG 27	CM	Shot down by 92 Sqn. Spitfire of Sanders near Dover at A.11.50 hrs.	Messerschmitt Bf 109 E-4 (2789)	100 %	Uffz. Erich Clauser missing.
11.	5./JG 53	CM	Take-off accident at Dinan airfield.	Messerschmitt Bf 109 E-1 (3427)	80 %	Pilot unhurt.
12.	7./JG 53	CM	Force landed near Boulogne with slight combat damage.	Messerschmitt Bf 109 E-1 (5175)	5 %	Pilot unhurt.
13.	1./706	CM	Struck submerged object while taxying at Aalborg, Denmark.	Heinkel He 59 (2598 : 6T+CK)	25 %	Crew unhurt.

Saturday 21st September

The emerging pattern of large high-flying fighter sweeps posed a serious problem for Park: how were such sweeps to be positively identified without previously committing unnecessarily vulnerable Hurricane formations against them? In hazy or cloudy conditions these Messerschmitt formations were virtually invisible to the coastal Observer Corps, and such sighting reports as did pass would be too late to enable even Spitfires to gain sufficient altitude to intercept—with the result that they would probably be bounced on the climb, as No. 222 Squadron had been on the 20th. Now that his Command reserves were increasing rapidly, Dowding saw every reason to engage these sweeps even though it involved the risk of incurring disproportionately high losses. By the same token he was equally anxious to avoid missing the chance of intercepting an enemy bomber formation through excessive caution about an ambiguous sighting report.

This clear appreciation of the enemy's tactics, coupled with the extraordinarily flexible nature of the operational branch of the R.A.F., prompted Dowding to authorise the formation of two Spotting Flights (Nos. 421 and 422)[31] of Spitfires, whose task it would be to maintain fairly constant patrols at high altitude over the Kent and Sussex coasts to pass sigthing reports of any approaching enemy formations. As these patrols would consist of only two or three pilots, their position in the event of their being attacked themselves was extremely hazardous; but from the commencement of their operations in early October, Park had frequent cause to be thankful for their courageous work.

After reduced night activity over London, daylight sorties by the *Luftwaffe* amounted to only scattered raids by isolated aircraft. *Lehrgeschwader 1* was principally engaged in nuisance attacks, and one of its aircraft flew up the railway line north of Guildford to attack Brooklands at low level. Three of its bombs exploded harmlessly in open ground but the fourth, a 250-kilo delayed-action weapon, fell in the main Hurricane assembly shop. A Canadian engineer, Lt. J.M.S. Patton, finding the bomb too badly distorted to defuse *in situ*, loaded it on to a makeshift sled, towed it out and tipped it into a crater left by one of the other bombs; shortly afterwards it exploded harmlessly. Patton was awarded a richly-deserved George Cross.

Early in the afternoon another of LG 1's Junkers Ju 88s flew

---

[31] These Flights later formed the nuclei of Nos. 91 and 96 Squadrons.

over Middle Wallop and was caught by two Hurricanes of No. 238 Squadron; it was shot down as it approached Tangmere on its way back to the coast.

As a preliminary to the night's attack on Liverpool the Germans sent a small number of Dornier Do 215s of Aufkl.Gr.Ob.d.L. to reconnoitre the port, and one of these was intercepted during the evening by Plt. Off. Dennis Adams of No. 611 Squadron flying from Ternhill, who shot it down at Dolgellau, Merioneth.

At about this time Kesselring launched some half-dozen small raids on Park's airfields south of London. Although six squadrons were scrambled from these airfields, and Leigh-Mallory's Duxford Wing was summoned from the north, only Biggin Hill's No. 92 Squadron managed to engage, and that without success.

R.A.F. FIGHTER COMMAND LOSSES—SATURDAY 21st SEPTEMBER 1940

1.	29 Sqn., Ternhill	NC	Aircraft had been engaged by Merseyside gun defences and struck floodlight while landing at base.	21.05 hrs.	Sgt. V.H. Skillen AC D.W. Isherwood	Blenheim	L1507	Cat. 1 Damaged
2.	92 Sqn., Biggin Hill	C	Damaged by Bf 109s near Dover; pilot force landed at Manston, unhurt.	18.15 hrs.	Plt. Off. T.B.A. Sherrington	Spitfire	N3032	Cat. 2 Damaged
3.	601 Sqn., Exeter	NC	Aircraft struck machine gun post while taking off; pilot believed unhurt.	Not known	Not known	Hurricane	L1894	Cat. 3 Destroyed

LUFTWAFFE LOSSES—SATURDAY 21st SEPTEMBER 1940

1.	Aufkl.Gr. Ob.d.L.	CM	Crashed on landing on return from reconnaissance sortie over England; cause not known.	Junkers Ju 88A-6 (0246 : K9+IH)	100 %	Crew unhurt.
2.	Aufkl.Gr. Ob.d.L.	CM	Shot down by 611 Sqn. Spitfire of Adams during reconnaissance sortie over Liverpool.	Dornier Do 215 (0023 : VB+KK)	100 %	Ltn. Book, Fw. Jensen and Fw. Kühl, P.O.W.; Uffz.Pelzer missing.
3.	5./KG 2	NCM	Suffered landing accident at St. Leger airfield.	Dornier Do 17Z-2 (3454 : U5+FN)	80 %	Crew unhurt.
4.	1./KG 40	CM	Ran short of fuel and force landed at Brest.	Focke-Wulf Fw 200 C-1 (0023 : F8+EM)	30 %	Crew unhurt.
5.	5./KG 40	CM	Engine failure on take-off; crashed and burned.	Heinkel He 111P-4 (2868 : 5J+EN)	100 %	Ltn. Willi Diesel + one killed; two crew members injured.
6.	3./KG 77	CM	Crashed during low flying near Laon, France.	Junkers Ju 88A-1 (2158 : 3Z+DS)	100 %	Oblt. Heinz Urban + three killed.
7.	1./KGr. 606	CM	Crashed at Sizun following combat with fighters.	Dornier Do 17 (3497 : 7T+LH)	100 %	Crew unhurt.
8.	3./KGr. 606	CM	Crashed at Landernecq following fighter combat.	Dornier Do 17 (3471 : 7T+CL)	100 %	Oblt.z.S. Eberhardt von Krosigk + two killed.
9.	1./KGr. 806	CM	Shot down by *flak* over the Midlands at night.	Junkers Ju 88A-1 (3079 : M7+CH)	100 %	Ltn.Günter Grunwald, Fw.Baasch, Fw.Strube, Fw. Krüger missing.
10.	1./LG 1	CM	Shot down by 238 Sqn. Hurricanes of Davis and Bann over Tangmere at 14.50 hrs.	Junkers Ju 88A-1 (2088 : L1+AL)	100 %	Oblt. Kurt Sodemann, Fw. Berg-strasser, Fw. Lorenz, Gefr. Bossert missing.
11.	5./LG 2	CM	Shot down by *flak* near Dover; pilot rescued.	Messerschmitt Bf 109 E-4 (3716)	100 %	Pilot, unhurt, rescued by *Seenotflugkommando*.
12.	6./LG 2	NCM	Landing accident at Calais-Marck; not combat.	Messerschmitt Bf 109E (5899)	100 %	Pilot unhurt.
13.	2./506	—	Destroyed in storm at Trondheim anchorage.	Heinkel He 115 (2765 : S4+LK)	100 %	No loss of life.
14.	NCM	—	Force landed near Roubaix with engine failure in bad weather.	Junkers W.34 (0498 : TI+NI)	5 %	Crew unhurt.

Sunday 22nd September

In direct contrast to the previous Sunday, this dull and foggy day brought less than a score of raiders to the English skies. The only enemy aircraft encountered—a solitary Junkers Ju 88 of *Aufklärungsgruppe 121*—was caught by a No. 234 Squadron Spitfire flown by Sgt. Alan Harker 50 miles out over the Channel, south-east of Start Point, and sent down into the sea at about 17.00 hours.

Clearing skies in the evening brought out Kesselring's night raiders, and four *Gruppen* of bombers attacked the capital dropping more than one hundred tons of high explosive and fifty of incendiary bombs. Some enemy aircraft, including intruder Junkers Ju 88Cs of the newly established *Nachtjagdgeschwader*, mingled with No. 5 Group's Hampdens returning to Lincolnshire from raids on Northern Germany, and carried out brief bombing and strafing attacks at Waddington, Scampton and Digby.

R.A.F. FIGHTER COMMAND LOSSES—SUNDAY 22nd SEPTEMBER 1940

1.	19 Sqn., Duxford	—	Destroyed in enemy bombing raid on Duxford; no aircrew casualties.	Not known.	Nil	Spitfire	X3451	Cat. 3 Destroyed
2.	64 Sqn., Leconfield	NC	Landing accident at Catfoss after patrol, pilot unhurt.	19.40 hrs.	Sgt. G.D. Goodwin	Spitfire	R6683	Cat. 1 Damaged
3.	232 Sqn., Castletown	NC	Landing accident at Castletown; pilot unhurt.	Not known.	Flt. Lt. M.M. Stephens	Hurricane	P3738	Cat. 2 Damaged

LUFTWAFFE LOSSES—SUNDAY 22nd SEPTEMBER 1940

1.	3.(F)/11	CM	Shot down by own *flak* near Mardyck and force landed.	Messerschmitt Bf 110 C-5 (2231 : MJ+ZE)	15 %	Crew unhurt.
2.	4.(F)/121	CM	Shot down by 234 Sqn. Spitfire of Harker 50 miles south-east of Start Point at A.17.00 hrs.	Junkers Ju 88A-1 (0352 : 7A+AM)	100 %	Ltn. Helmut Böttcher, Fw. Vater, Uffz.Willi Müller, and Uffz. Rabe missing.
3.	7./KG 2	CM	Crash landed near Cambrai; cause not known.	Dornier Do 17Z-3 (2858 : U5+FR)	65 %	Crew unhurt.

Luftwaffe Losses, 22nd September 1940—*continued*

4.	8./KG 76	CM	Minor landing incident at Clermont airfield.	Dornier Do 17Z-2 (2809 : F1+HS)	3 %	Crew unhurt.
5.	1./KGr. 100	CM	Crashed during take-off at Vannes due to faulty maintenance.	Heinkel He 111H-1 (5247 : 6N+MH)	90 %	Three crew members killed and one injured.
6.	I./LG 1	CM	Take-off accident at Orleans-Bricy; crashed and burned.	Junkers Ju 88A-1 (3121: L1+JK)	100 %	All four crew members killed.
7.	IV./LG 1	CM	Engine failure and force landing at Hilversum.	Junkers Ju 87B-1 (5586 : L1+LV)	40 %	Crew unhurt.
8.	3./JG 27	NCM	Take-off accident at Guines-West; cause not notified.	Messerschmitt Bf 109 E-1 (3381)	20 %	Pilot unhurt.
9.	8./JG 53	NCM	Landing accident at Etaples; cause not notified.	Messerschmitt Bf 109 E-1 (3519)	100 %	Pilot injured.
10.	2./506	—	Damaged by storm at Trondheim anchorage.	Heinkel He 115 (3267 : S4+FK)	25 %	No aircrew casualties.
11.	2./506	—	Damaged by storm at Trondheim anchorage.	Heinkel He 115 (1197 : S4+GK)	25 %	No aircrew casualties.
12.	3./906	NCM	Crashed at Schellingwoude due to faulty maintenance.	Heinkel He 115B-1 (2412 : 8L+EL)	100 %	Crew unhurt.

Monday 23rd September

"Many and glorious are the deeds of gallantry done during these perilous but famous days. In order that they should be worthily and promptly recognised I have decided to create at once a new mark of honour for men and women in all walks of civilian life. I propose to give my name to this new distinction, which will consist of the George Cross, which will rank next to the Victoria Cross, and the George Medal for wider distribution."

Extract from broadcast by H.M. King George VI, 23rd September 1940 [32]

The constant bombardment of civilian property not only brought about the issue of the Royal Warrant for the institution of the George Cross, but had moved the British Cabinet

---

[32] See Appendix J. Although the Cross was announced on the 23rd, and formally instituted by Royal Warrant the next day, a number of qualifying acts had been performed prior to these dates which led to subsequent gazetting and award of the Cross and Medal. The George Cross also superseded the Empire Gallantry Medal.

An unidentified Leutnant poses by his Messerschmitt Bf 109E of 3rd *Staffel*, *Lehrgeschwader 2*; and a close-up of this *Staffel*'s insignia on the rear fuselage. Three aircraft of the *Staffel* were lost or written off after combat on 23rd September, and another damaged.

under Winston Churchill to order the Air Staff to commence what in later years would be known as "area bombing". Suggesting the use of naval parachute sea mines, the Cabinet presumably overlooked the fact that no aircraft could yet carry such a weapon as far as the German capital, although the day was not far off. In any case, the policy of indiscriminate bombing was not favoured by the Air Staff—not from any moral considerations but merely in the belief that far more could be achieved for military ends by aiming the bombs at military targets.[33]

---

[33] The Air Staff had, moreover, less than a month previously announced that henceforth it would be Bomber Command's aim to re-equip heavy bomber squadrons exclusively with four-engine aircraft, this despite that fact that the twin-engine Manchester was only then undergoing its acceptance trials by the Royal Air Force. From the Manchester was already being evolved the Lancaster—which would enter service in 1941 and, under the direction of Sir Arthur Harris, would spearhead Bomber Command's devastating "area bombing" attacks in the last three years of the Second World War and contribute more than any other aircraft to Germany's final defeat.

As was subsequently shown, it was not so much poor bomb aiming as weakness in navigation which saved not only the enemy targets, but sometimes the towns in which they lay. . As it was, the force of 119 British bombers which set out for Berlin on the evening of 23rd September carried a mixed load of 1,000-lb. high explosive bombs and incendiary canisters. They hit the Neukölln and Danzigerstrasse gasworks, the Rangsdorf, Potsdamer and Grunewald railway stations, five power stations, the aero-engine factory at Spandau and the Tempelhof airport. Meanwhile London and Merseyside again suffered heavy raids by forces totalling more than 300 aircraft.

The daylight operations over Britain had again been devoted largely to German fighter sweeps which had crossed in high over the Dover area in the early morning and late evening. Park reacted powerfully but ineffectually, and few of his pilots managed to intercept the sweeps. A particularly pointless piece of enemy bombing was an attack on Eastbourne by a single aircraft which unloaded 28 incendiaries on the residential area, causing some slight damage but few casualties.

R.A.F. FIGHTER COMMAND LOSSES—MONDAY 23rd SEPTEMBER 1940

1.	3 Sqn., Turnhouse	NC	Suffered taxying accident at Turnhouse; pilot unhurt.	Not known	Plt. Off. A.M.W. Scott	Hurricane	P2693	Cat. 1 Damaged
2.	72 Sqn., Biggin Hill	C	Shot down by Bf 109 over Gravesend; pilot baled out unhurt at Eastchurch.	09.40 hrs.	Plt. Off. B.W. Brown	Spitfire	X4063	Cat. 3 Destroyed
3.	73 Sqn., Debden	C	Shot down by Bf 109s over Isle of Sheppey; pilot baled out and was injured on landing. Aircraft crashed near Rodmersham.	09.55 hrs.	Sgt. M.E. Leng	Hurricane	P8812	Cat. 3 Destroyed
4.	73 Sqn., Debden	C	Shot down by Bf 109s near Sittingbourne; aircraft crashed in the Swale near Harty ferry.	19.55 hrs.	Sgt. F.S. Perkin	Hurricane	V7445	Cat. 3 Destroyed
5.	73 Sqn., Debden	C	Shot down by Bf 109s over the Thames Estuary; pilot ditched near Lightship 93 severely burned; rescued by the Navy and admitted the Chatham Hospital.	10.02 hrs.	Plt. Off. N.G. Langham-Hobart	Hurricane	L2036	Cat. 3 Lost
6.	73 Sqn., Debden	C	Shot down in the above combat and ditched near Lightship 93 with severe burned; rescued and admitted to Chatham Hospital.	10.03 hrs.	Plt. Off. D.S. Kinder	Hurricane	P3226	Cat. 3 Lost
7.	74 Sqn., Coltishall	C	Shot down by unknown enemy aircraft while on patrol; pilot baled out south-east of Southwold, but body not recovered until 4-10-40.	11.20 hrs.	Sgt. D.H. Ayers	Spitfire	P7362	Cat. 3 Lost
8.	92 Sqn., Biggin Hill	C	Crash landed at Biggin Hill after combat with Bf 109s; pilot severely wounded in the thigh.	A10.00 hrs.	Plt. Off. A.J.S. Pattinson	Spitfire	P9371	Cat. 3 Destroyed
9.	111 Sqn., Drem	NC	Force landed during training flight. Pilot unhurt.	11.20 hrs.	Sgt. A.D. Page	Hurricane	R4226	Cat. 1 Damaged
10.	229 Sqn., Northolt	C	Shot down over Thames Estuary by enemy fighters; pilot baled out, wounded at Westcliff; aircraft crashed near St. Mary's Hoo.	10.05 hrs.	Plt. Off. P.O.D. Allcock	Hurricane	P2789	Cat. 3 Destroyed
11.	232 Sqn., Castletown	NC	Landing accident (tyre burst) at Castletown; pilot unhurt.	Not known	Sgt. E.A. Redfern	Hurricane	P3664	Cat. 2 Damaged
12.	234 Sqn., St. Eval	C	Missing from patrol over Channel; shot down by Bf 109s. Pilot baled out off the French coast, rescued and traken prisoner.	Morning	Plt. Off. T.M. Kane	Spitfire	R6896	Cat. 3 Missing
13.	257 Sqn., Castle Camps	C	Shot down by Bf 109 at Detling; pilot baled out with burns. Aircraft crashed at Grove, near Eastchurch.	10.08 hrs.	Sgt. D.J. Aslin	Hurricane	P2960	Cat. 3 Destroyed

LUFTWAFFE LOSSES—MONDAY 23rd SEPTEMBER 1940

1.	3.(F)/123	CM	Missing from reconnaissance sortie over England.	Junkers Ju 88A-1 (0130 : 4U+CL)	100 %	Four crew members missing.
2.	6./KG 26	CM	Target, Beckton Gasworks. Shot down by flak over Surrey at night, before reaching target and crashed at West End, Chobham, at 01.37 hrs. on 24-9-40.	Heinkel He 111H-3 (3322 : 1H+GP)	100 %	Uffz. Niemeyer, Gefr. Leibnitz, Gefr. Weinlich and Gefr. Jenreck made P.O.W.s
3	Geschw.Erg.St./ KG 26	NCM	Crashed and burned at Lübeck-Blankensee; cause not notified.	Heinkel He 111 (5391 : 1H+BM)	100 %	Ltn. Ölerich + one killed.
4.	I./KG 51	CM	Suffered landing accident at Villaroche airfield.	Junkers Ju 88A-1 (2188)	25 %	Crew unhurt.
5.	II./KG 54	CM	Take-off accident at St.André; aircraft burned.	Junkers Ju 88A-1 (7098)	100 %	Three dead and one injured.
6.	I./LG 1	CM	Engine fire on take-off at Orléans-Bricy.	Junkers Ju 88A-1 (2084)	30 %	Crew unhurt.
7.	3./LG 2	CM	Damaged by British fighters over South-East England, and crash landed at Calais-Marck.	Messerschmitt Bf 109 E-7 (2042)	45 %	Pilot unhurt.
8.	3./LG 2	CM	Shot down by 257 Sqn. Hurricane of Tuck 10 miles off Cap Gris Nez at 10.05 hrs.	Messerschmitt Bf 109 E-7 (5094)	100 %	Pilot, unhurt, rescued by Seenotflugkommando.
9.	3./LG 2	CM	Damaged by British fighters over South-East England and crashed at Calais-Marck.	Messerschmitt Bf 109 E-7 (2057)	90 %	Pilot unhurt.
10.	3./LG 2	CM	Damaged by British fighters over South-East England and crashed at Calais-Marck.	Messerschmitt Bf 109 E-7 (5803)	65 %	Pilot unhurt.
11.	4./JG 2	CM	Shot down by 41 and 603 Sqn. Spitfires near Rochford at 09.50 hrs.	Messerschmitt Bf 109 E-4 (1969)	100 %	Uffz. Dilthey missing.
12.	Stab/JG 3	CM	Shot down by 303 Sqn. Hurricane of Kent over Kent coast at A.10.20 hrs.	Messerschmitt Bf 109 E-1	100 %	Oblt. Willi Hopp killed.

Luftwaffe Losses, 23rd September 1940—*continued*

13.	3./JG 3	NCM	Suffered landing accident at St. Omer airfield.	Messerschmitt Bf 109 E-1 (6367)	15 %	Pilot unhurt.
14.	7./JG 3	CM	Shot down by 603 Sqn. Spitfire of Boulter over Kent at A.10.20 hrs.	Messerschmitt Bf 109 E-1 (6304)	100 %	Uffz. Elbing missing.
15.	8./JG 26	CM	Shot down by 72 Sqn. Spitfires near Gravesend at A.09.50 hrs.	Messerschmitt Bf 109 E-4 (5817)	100 %	Ofw. Grzymalla killed.
16.	8./JG 26	CM	Shot down by 92 Sqn. Spitfires near Gravesend at A.09.50 hrs.	Messerschmitt Bf 109 E-4 (3735)	100 %	Fw. Küppa killed.
17.	Stab III./JG 53	CM	Shot down by 41 Sqn. Spitfires off Calais at 13.20 hrs.	Messerschmitt Bf 109 E-4 (5894)	100 %	Pilot rescued unhurt.
18.	9./JG 53	CM	Suffered engine failure off Boulogne after combat over South-East England.	Messerschmitt Bf 109 E-1 (6279)	100 %	Pilot rescued unhurt.
19.	3./JG 54	CM	Shot down by 92 Sqn. Spitfires near Dover at A.10.05 hrs.	Messerschmitt Bf 109 E-4 (1516)	100 %	Ofw. Knippscheer killed.
20.	*Wekusta. 2*	CM	Shot down by 236 Sqn. Blenheim of Innes, Russell and Smith in position 48°5'N., 10°15'W (270 miles from Land's End) (1)	Heinkel He 111 (5396 : TG+KA)	100 %	Reg. Rat.Dr. Reinhardt plus one killed.
21.	*Seenotzentrale Boulogne*	NCM	Aircraft missing on local flight; possibly air collision with Item 22. Crew rescued.	Heinkel He 59 (2596)	100 %	Crew rescued unhurt.
22.	*Seenotzentrale Boulogne*	NCM	Aircraft missing on local flight; possibly air collision with Item 21. Crew rescued.	Heinkel He 59 (2792)	100 %	Crew rescued unhurt.

[(1) The Blenheim pilot reported seeing three crew members emerge from the ditched Heinkel, and threw his own dinghy down to them; the loss of two crew members, reported a week later in German records, suggests that these three crew members were later rescued, the assumption being that the Heinkel carried its normal crew of five.]

Tuesday 24th September

The daylight operations on this day included an incident which marked the beginning of a new phase in the German air attack on Britain. In line with Göring's new orders for attacks on the British aircraft industry, the Woolston factory at Southampton was again singled out for a set-piece attack by Martin Lutz's crack *Erprobungsgruppe 210*, which was now fully established in the Cherbourg Peninsula. The raid, seen in retrospect, also foreshadowed a renewal of attacks on the West Country.

Approaching on a direct course from Cherbourg in two *Staffeln* each of nine Bf 110s (*1 Staffel* with Bf 110D fighters and *2 Staffel* with Bf 110C bombers led by Lutz himself, under cover of further Bf 110s provided by ZG 76) the raid made straight for the aircraft factory situated on the very waterfront, and commenced diving individually to drop their 250-kilo bombs. Five direct hits were scored on the factory without causing serious damage, but a sixth struck a works shelter, killing ninety-eight senior employees and wounding more than 40 others. The raid occupied just eight minutes, after which the bombers and fighters joined up and made off to the south—losing one of their number to the defences[34].

Further east two phases of raids had been launched during the morning by Kesselring's bombers under heavy fighter escort, but although they penetrated to within twenty miles of London they did not persevere in the face of growing opposition and, rather than risk unnecessary losses, Park's controllers recalled their fighters when the German raids turned back. Once again, Biggin Hill's No. 92 Squadron was heavily engaged by the Messerschmitt escort, losing two Spitfires and one pilot killed over Swanley; Sqn. Ldr. Robert Lister was badly wounded in the wrists and legs, but brought his badly damaged aircraft back to base. It transpired that too

German aircrew using a model of Southampton during their pre-raid briefing. (Photo: Hans Obert)

much time had again been spent by Biggin Hill's three squadrons in trying to form up into a Wing, with the result that when it attempted to attack the enemy raid the Spitfires were still well below the escorting fighters.

[34] Martin Lutz was killed three days later, but his posthumous award of the Knight's Cross, promulgated on 1st October, was undoubtedly in respect of the above raid on the Woolston Works.

R.A.F. FIGHTER COMMAND LOSSES—TUESDAY 24th SEPTEMBER 1940

1.	17 Sqn., Debden	C	Shot down by Bf 109 of JG 26 (said to be of Maj. Adolf Galland) over Thames Estuary; pilot baled out with burns and rescued from the sea by naval launch.	Not known	Plt. Off. H.A.C. Bird-Wilson	Hurricane	*P3978*	Cat. 3 Lost

St. Barnabas Church, Southampton, totally destroyed in the raid on the afternoon of 24th September (Photo: Radio Times Hulton Picture Library)

R.A.F. Losses, 24th September 1940—*continued*

2.	17 Sqn., Debden	C	Crashed on landing after combat with Bf 109s; pilot wounded in the left arm.	Not known	Plt. Off. D.H. Wissler	Hurricane	*P3168*	Cat. 3 Destroyed
3.	41 Sqn., Rochford	C	Shot down by Bf 109s near Dover; pilot baled out, wounded, and rescued from the sea.	13.40 hrs.	Sgt. J. McAdam	Spitfire	*N3118*	Cat. 3 Lost
4.	41 Sqn., Rochford	C	Shot down and crashed near Dover; pilot unhurt.	A13.40 hrs.	Sgt. E.V. Darling	Spitfire	*R6604*	Cat. 3 Destroyed
5.	72 Sqn., Biggin Hill	C	Damaged by Ju 88s over Swanley; pilot unhurt.	A09.00 hrs.	Not known	Spitfire	—	Cat. 2 Damaged
6.	92 Sqn., Biggin Hill	C	Shot down by Bf 109s at North Weald. Pilot killed; buried at North Weald.	A09.10 hrs.	Plt. Off. J. Bryson	Spitfire	*X4037*	Cat. 3 Destroyed
7.	92 Sqn., Biggin Hill	C	Shot down over Maidstone by Bf 109 and crash landed on Higham Marshes.	09.20 hrs.	Sgt. W.T. Ellis	Spitfire	*X4356*	Cat. 3 Destroyed
8.	92 Sqn., Biggin Hill	C	Damaged by Bf 109s near Swanley; pilot wounded in wrists and legs.	09.10 hrs.	Sqn. Ldr. R.C.F. Lister	Spitfire	*X4427*	Cat. 2 Damaged
9.	141 Sqn., Gatwick	NC	Night landing accident; crew unhurt.	03.00 hrs.	Plt. Off. A.W. Smith Sgt. A.E.Ashcroft	Defiant	*N1563*	Cat. 3 Destroyed
10.	151 Sqn., Digby	NC	Air collision with Item 11; pilot force landed, unhurt, at Waddington	10.20 hrs.	Plt. Off. J.K. Haviland	Hurricane	*V7432*	Cat. 3 Destroyed
11.	151 Sqn., Digby	NC	Air collision with Item 10; pilot baled out unhurt.	10.20 hrs.	Sgt. J. McPhee	Hurricane	*P3306*	Cat. 3 Destroyed
12.	601 Sqn., Exeter	NC	Overturned on landing; pilot unhurt.	Not known	Plt. Off. D.B. Ogilvie	Hurricane	*R4120*	Cat. 2 Damaged
13.	605 Sqn., Croydon	C	Chased a Do 17 over French coast but was jumped by Bf 109s and shot down; pilot killed. Buried in Guines cemetery.	A16.30 hrs.	Plt. Off. W.J. Glowacki	Hurricane	*P3832*	Cat. 3 Missing
14.	615 Sqn., Prestwick	NC	Ditched in sea having run out of fuel; pilot, slightly hurt, rescued.	Not known	Sgt. Finch	Hurricane	—	Cat. 3 Lost
15.	616 Sqn., Kirton-in-Lindsey	NC	Force landed when lost and out of fuel; pilot unhurt.	Not known	Plt. Off. J.H. Rowden	Spitfire	—	Cat. 2 Damaged

LUFTWAFFE LOSSES—TUESDAY 24th SEPTEMBER 1940

1.	2.(H)/32	CM	Landing accident at Deulemont; cause unknown.	Henschel Hs 126B (3063)	40 %	Crew unhurt.
2.	8./KG 1	CM	Suffered take-off accident at Handorf airfield.	Junkers Ju 88A-1 (3206 : V4+DT)	35 %	Crew unhurt.
3.	1./KG 3	CM	Damaged by fighters and crashed at Antwerp.	Dornier Do 17Z-3 (2633 : 5K+JH)	60 %	Three crew members wounded.
4.	7./KG 51	CM	Shot down by 72 Sqn. Spitfires over Rochester at A.09.00 hrs.	Junkers Ju 88A-1 (4144 : 9K+FR)	100 %	Ltn. Gustav Maier, Fw. Eimers, Gefr. Herich and Gefr. Altmann killed.
5.	I./KG 54	CM	Force landed at Evreux with *flak* damage.	Junkers Ju 88A-1(4099)	35 %	Crew unhurt.
6.	I./KG 54	CM	Take-off accident at Evreux-Fauville airfield.	Junkers Ju 88A-1(4038)	35 %	Crew unhurt.
7.	1./KG 76	CM	Landing accident at Beauvais airfield.	Dornier Do 17Z (1184 : F1+BH)	30 %	Crew unhurt.
8.	2./KG 76	CM	Shot down by 605 Sqn. Hurricanes of Muirhead and Glowacki 5 miles SW of Boulogne at A.16.15 hrs.	Dornier Do 17Z (3317 : F1+GK)	100 %	Crew, one member wounded, rescued.
9.	4./KG 77	CM	Landed at Couvron with combat damage from fighters.	Junkers Ju 88A-1 (7120 : 3Z+KM)	30 %	Crew unhurt.
10.	5./KG 77	CM	Landed at St. Armand with combat damage from fighters.	Junkers Ju 88A-1 (7107 : 3Z+FN)	35 %	Crew unhurt.
11.	6./KG 77	CM	Landed at St. Omer with combat damage from fighters.	Junkers Ju 88A-1 (7108 : 3Z+BP)	80 %	Crew unhurt.
12.	1./KGr. 126	CM	Shot down by 66 Sqn. Spitfires of Oxspring and Reilly near Gravesend at A.17.00 hrs.	Heinkel He 111H-4 (6964 : 1T+GH)	100 %	Ltn.z.S. Hans Drews, Uffz. Mellin, Gefr.Blau, Fl.Saal missing.
13.	II./St.G 2	NCM	Crashed following engine failure near Bangan.	Junkers Ju 87B (5492)	70 %	Crew unhurt.

Luftwaffe Losses, 24th September 1940—*continued*

14.	II./LG 1	NCM	Landing accident at Orléans; cause not notified.		Junkers Ju 88A-1(6126)	35 %	Crew unhurt.
15.	III./LG 1	CM	Crashed and burned on take-off at Caen airfield.		Junkers Ju 88A-1(2076)	100 %	Ltn.Elmar Rintelen + three killed.
16.	II./ZG 76	CM	Damaged by *flak* in Portsmouth-Southampton area at A.14.30 hrs.		Messerschmitt Bf 110 C-2 (2638)	10 %	One crew member wounded.
17.	II./ZG 76	CM	Damaged by *flak* near Southampton at A.14.30 hrs.		Messerschmitt Bf 110 C-4 (2159)	10 %	Ltn. Calame wounded.
18.	III./ZG 76	CM	Shot down by *flak* near Portsmouth at A.14.30 hrs.		Messerschmitt Bf 110 C-4 (3534 : 2N+DN)	100 %	Uffz. Helwig and Uffz. Mirow missing.
19.	III./ZG 76	CM	Shot down by *flak* near Portsmouth at A.14.30 hrs. Crew rescued from Channel.		Messerschmitt Bf 110 C-4 (3251)	100 %	Crew, unhurt, rescued by *Seenotflugkommando*.
20.	Erpr.Gr. 210	CM	Shot down by *flak* near Southampton at A.14.15 hrs.		Messerschmitt Bf 110 D-0 (3384 : S9+HH)	100 %	Ltn. Ulrich von der Horst and Ogefr. Öllers missing.

Wednesday 25th September

The reduction in the daylight raids upon London enabled the *Luftwaffe* to redistribute a number of its bomber units along the French coast in readiness to resume day and night attacks in the West, and with them returned the fighter and *Zerstörer* units which had contributed to the concentration of strength in North-East France associated with the projected invasion. Much of this activity—involving the movement of more than 200 aircraft westwards along the coast—occurred on the morning of 25th September, and was watched with considerable interest at Fighter Command, whose radar screens told much of the story. Added to this dispersal of air strength came the morning reconnaissance photographs, which disclosed a forty per cent reduction in the number of barges docked at Calais, Dunkirk and Boulogne. This was the moment when the British commanders dared to believe that the imminent danger of invasion had passed.

Yet this day also brought renewed attacks in strength, and a particularly heavy raid on Filton caught the defences wrong-footed. It had of course been no secret that the Bristol factory at Filton had been the key manufacturer not only of the Blenheim bomber (and indirectly of the night fighter version) but also of a range of widely-used aero-engines—the Mercury, Pegasus, Perseus, Taurus and Hercules—which powered the Blenheim, Botha, Beaufort, Gladiator, Hampden, Wellington and Lysander. To what extent the Germans were yet aware of the existence of the new Beaufighter is not known, but a former *Luftwaffe* pilot has testified that, while at Rechlin before the end of 1940, he examined an example of this aircraft, though it is not clear whether it was a damaged or airworthy aircraft[35].

German reconnaissance during the 23rd and 24th had disclosed to the *Luftwaffe* that no interceptor fighters were based at Filton, and at 11.00 hours on the 25th a set-piece attack was launched along the front of Brand's No. 10 Group. With minor diversionary raids attacking Plymouth, Falmouth, Swanage and Southampton on the flanks, 58 Heinkel He 111s from all three *Gruppen* of *Kampfgeschwader 55 «Greifen»*

crossed the Dorset coast at 11.15 hours on a northerly course, at the same moment as an attack on Portland was mounted by a small number of *Lehrgeschwader 1* Junkers Ju 88s.

With the sighting report showing that the main raid was accompanied by Bf 110s, Brand considered the Yeovil works of Westland Aircraft (manufacturers of the Whirlwind fighter) to be the probably target, and ordered three squadrons of fighters to that area. The raid, however, passed ten miles to the east, and reached Filton scarcely opposed at 11.45 hours, the Bf 110s of Erpr.Gr. 210 preceding the main force with diving attacks to mark the factory area. The raid was fairly well concentrated and the damage caused production to be halted; more than 250 casualties were suffered in the factory area and 107 elsewhere. The neighbouring railway line to South Wales was blocked and vital telephone lines cut. Eight newly-built Beauforts and Blenheims were totally destroyed and more than a dozen others badly damaged.

Kampfgeschwader 55 dropped about a hundred tons of bombs (including twenty-four oil bombs[36]) before turning south. They now met the Hurricanes of No. 238 Squadron and the Spitfires of No. 152 Squadron, whose pilots between them destroyed five bombers and damaged another between Yeovil and mid-Channel.

The attacks on No. 10 Group persisted throughout the remainder of the day, with a further attack by Erpr.Gr. 210 in the Plymouth area at 16.30 hours (once more the unit's Bf 110D-0s were mis-identified as Dornier Do 215s), and a sweep by the *Zerstörer* of ZG 26 «*Horst Wessel*» near the Isle of Wight. A Blenheim of No. 236 Squadron, which had for some days been carrying out hazardous patrols near the Channel Islands as part of the anti-invasion watch, came across a Dornier Do 18 flying boat of 2./106 between Ushant and Guernsey, and shot it down.

---

[35] Efforts to establish beyond doubt the identity of this aircraft have not been successful.

[36] Used quite frequently at this stage of the War, the German 250-kilo oil bomb did little damage owing to frequent mis-ignition. The author remembers one such weapon which fell in a Kent orchard; there was no crater, and only a dozen trees lost their harvest, but the unpleasant smell persisted for weeks.

R.A.F. FIGHTER COMMAND LOSSES—WEDNESDAY 25th SEPTEMBER 1940

1.	23 Sqn., Middle Wallop	NC	Crashed during night patrol; three crew members killed. Aircraft crashed near Stourbridge.	At night	Plt. Off. E. Orgias Sgt. L.R. Karasek (One not known)	Blenheim	L8369	Cat. 3 Destroyed
2.	85 Sqn., Church Fenton	NC	Crashed near Church Fenton; pilot believed unhurt.	Not known.	Not known	Hurricane	L1854	Cat. 3 Destroyed
3.	152 Sqn., Warmwell	C	Shot down by enemy fighters and crash landed near Bath; pilot unhurt.	A11.50 hrs.	Sqn. Ldr. P.K. Devitt	Spitfire	N3173	Cat. 3 Destroyed
4.	152 Sqn., Warmwell	C	Shot down by Bf 109s over Somerset; pilot killed.	A12.00 hrs.	Sgt. W.G. Silver	Spitfire	P9463	Cat. 3 Destroyed
5.	152 Sqn., Warmwell	C	Shot down by enemy bombers near Frome and crashed near Woolverton; pilot killed.	A11.50 hrs.	Sgt. K.C. Holland	Spitfire	—	Cat. 3 Destroyed

R.A.F. Losses, 26th September 1940—*continued*

6.	234 Sqn., St. Eval	NC	Crashed five miles east of Newquay; pilot baled out but was seriously injured.	Not known	Sgt. R. MacKay	Spitfire	*X4182*	Cat. 3 Destroyed
7.	238 Sqn., Middle Wallop	C	Shot down by Bf 110s and force landed at Charmey Down. Pilot unhurt.	A12.20 hrs.	Sgt. F.A. Sibley	Hurricane	*N2597*	Cat. 3 Destroyed
8.	238 Sqn., Middle Wallop	NC	Suffered landing accident at base; pilot unhurt. Not combat.	17.15 hrs.	Plt. Off. D.S. Harrison	Hurricane	*P3223*	Cat. 2 Damaged
9.	607 Sqn., Tangmere	C	Shot down by Bf 109; pilot baled out unhurt over Kaylthorpe, Isle of Wight.	16.15 hrs.	Flt. Lt. C.E. Bowen	Hurricane	—	Cat. 3 Lost
10.	609 Sqn., Middle Wallop	NC	Crashed near Glastonbury, Somerset; pilot unhurt	Not known.	Not known	Spitfire	*L1009*	Cat. 3 Destroyed

LUFTWAFFE LOSSES—WEDNESDAY 25th SEPTEMBER 1940

1.	1.(F)/121	NCM	Crashed and burned while landing at Stavanger-Sola airfield.	Heinkel He 111H-3 (2704 : 7A+EH)	100 %	Oblt. Wölz + three killed.
2.	4./KG 1	CM	Landing accident at Amiens after combat.	Heinkel He 111H-2 (2639 : V4+MU)	50 %	Crew unhurt.
3.	5./KG 26	CM	Crashed at Amiens-Glicy; cause not notified.	Heinkel He 111H-3 (5645 : 1H+AN)	100 %	One killed and three injured.
4.	7./KG 53	CM	Shot down by 238 Sqn. Hurricane of Urwin-Mann over Dorset coast at 12.10 hrs.	Heinkel He 111H-2 (5307 : A1+HR)	100 %	Crew, unhurt, made P.O.W.
5.	I./KG 55	CM	Shot down by 238 Sqn. Hurricane of Urwin-Mann south of Yeovil at A.11.50 hrs.	Heinkel He 111H-3 (6305 : G1+BH)	100 %	Uffz. Altrichter killed; Hptm. Karl Köthke, Fw. Jürges, Gefr.Weissbach, Fl. Otto Müller missing.
6.	II./KG 55	CM	Shot down by 152 Sqn. Spitfires six miles north of Frome at A.11.20 hrs.	Heinkel He 111P (1525 : G1+EP)	100 %	Oblt. Hans Bröcker, Oblt. Heinz-Harry Scholz, Uffz. Günther Weidner, Uffz. Josef Hanft killed; Uffz. Scharps missing.
7.	II./KG 55	CM	Shot down by A.A. fire over Bristol and crashed at Racecourse Farm, Portbury, Somerset.	Heinkel He 111H (2126 : G1+DN)	100 %	Fw. Gerdsmeier wounded; Oblt. Gottfried Weigel, Ofw. Narres, Fw. Engel and Gefr. Geib missing.
8.	II./KG 55	CM	Damaged by 238 Sqn. Hurricane of Simmonds south of Yeovil at A.12.00 hrs.	Heinkel He 111P (1579)	50 %	Crew unhurt.
9.	II./KG 55	CM	Shot down by 238 Sqn. Hurricane of Little south of Yeovil at A.11.50 hrs.	Heinkel He 111H (1525 : G1+EP)	100 %	Ofw. Witzkamp, Ofw.Kirschhoff, Uffz. Mertz, Gefr. Beck killed; Hptm. Helmut Brand missing.
10.	I./KGr. 100	CM	Landing accident at Vannes ; cause not notified.	Heinkel He 111H (2768)	30 %	Crew unhurt.
11.	I./St.G 1	NCM	Engine failure on take-off at Angers airfield.	Junkers Ju 87R (5461)	50 %	Crew unhurt.
12.	7.(F)/LG 2	CM	Intercepted over Enfield and shot down over Tunbridge Wells at A.11.00 hrs. by 229 Sqn. Hurricane of Dewar.	Messerschmitt Bf 110 (2185 : L2+ER)	100 %	Oblt. Weyergang and Fw. Nelson killed.
13.	II./ZG 76	NCM	Crashed at Würzburg; probably technical failure.	Messerschmitt Bf 110 C-2 (3111)	100 %	Ltn. Pistor killed.
14.	III./ZG 26	CM	Shot down by 152 Sqn. Spitfire of Williams 30 miles north of Poole at A.11.30 hrs.	Messerschmitt Bf 110 C-4 (3591 : 3U+GS)	100 %	Gefr. Schuhmacher killed; Fw. Scherer killed.
15.	III./ZG 26	CM	Shot down by 607 Sqn. Hurricanes off the Isle of Wight at 16.15 hrs.	Messerschmitt Bf 110C (3263)	100 %	Crew, unhurt, rescued by *Seenotflugkommando.*
16.	III./ZG 16	CM	Damaged by fighters off the South Coast and and crash landed on return to Theville.	Messerschmitt Bf 110 C-4 (2194)	60 %	Crew unhurt.
17.	III./ZG 26	CM	Damaged by fighters off the South Coast and and force landed on return to France.	Messerschmitt Bf 110 C-4 (2130)	20 %	Crew unhurt.
18.	3./JG 27	CM	Shot down by 607 Sqn. Hurricane off the Isle of Wight at 16.15 hrs.	Messerschmitt Bf 109 E-1 (6061)	100 %	Pilot, unhurt, rescued by *Seenotflugkommando.*
19.	7./JG 27	CM	Force landed at Philippi following engine failure.	Messerschmitt Bf 109E (5097)	5 %	Pilot unhurt.
20.	I./JG 53	CM	Crashed near Cherbourg following engine failure.	Messerschmitt Bf 109E (6981)	100 %	Pilot wounded.
21.	1./506	CM	Crashed at grid Square 2843 after engine failure.	Heinkel He 115 (3265 : S4+AH)	100 %	Maj. Wilhelm Rentsch, Ltn. Bock and Ofw.Josef Schmidt missing.
22.	2./106	CM	Shot down by 236 Sqn. Blenheim of Russell between Ushant and Guernsey at 16.05 hrs. Five crew members seen to inflate dinghy. (1)	Dornier Do 18 (0881 : M2+EK)	100 %	Oblt.z.S. Steele, Oblt. Heuveldop, Uffz. Kahlfeld and Fw. Brasch missing, believed drowned.

[(1) This aircraft loss was reported (in 6th *Abteilung* Return No. 4440, dated 28th September 1940) to have occurred on 26th September. This is clearly in error as Russell's combat report was filed the evening before. It must be assumed that the four crew members, reported drowned, met their deaths in their dinghy. If Russell was correct in believing he saw five men in the sea, the fifth man evidently survived.]

Thursday 26th September

The scarcely opposed and devastating raid by KG 55 on the Filton factory brought immediate reaction from Dowding, who ordered No. 504 Squadron with Hurricanes from Hendon to Filton—which was in fact a No. 10 Group Sector station, but whose squadrons were deployed "forward" to Exeter for the defence of Plymouth and the Devon radar stations. This squadron arrived, with seventeen aircraft, on the 26th.

The Heinkels of KG 55 were again in action on this day, this time in an attack on the Woolston factory—repeatedly shown to have escaped serious damage from numerous local attacks. Covered by a heavy screen of 70 Messerschmitt Bf 110s of ZG 26, which approached at 16.30 hours and flew ahead of the main force on a five mile front, 59 Heinkels made their way up the Solent and delivered a precision "carpet attack" in a single run across the factory. Despite the intervention of the Hurricanes of Nos. 229, 238 and 303 (Polish) Squadrons, which destroyed one Heinkel and damaged another, the raid was highly successful; the seventy tons of bombs dropped brought production to a standstill, destroyed three completed Spitfires and damaged more than twenty others. 37 people died in the factory and 52 in the surrounding areas.

Though Woolston was at this time still the principal producer of the Spitfire, the shadow factory at Castle Bromwich, Birmingham, was just coming into full production (a fact of which the *Luftwaffe* was by now aware) and although deliveries of the fighter slowed perceptibly for about three weeks, the immediate dispersal of production facilities ordered after

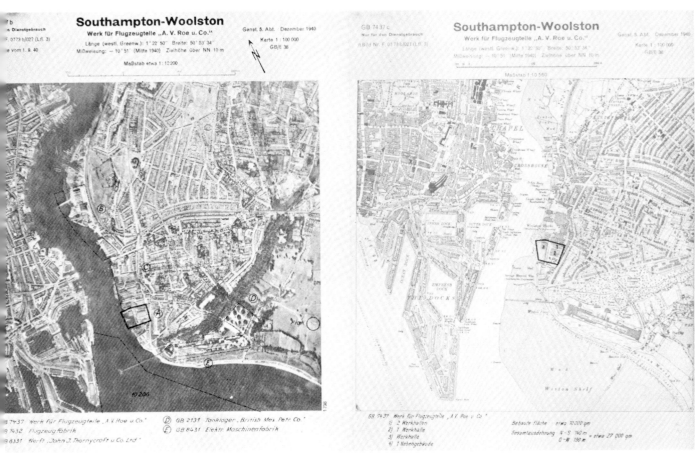

Southampton-Woolston
Werk für Flugzeugteile „A. V. Roe u. Co."

Southampton-Woolston
Werk für Flugzeugteile „A. V. Roe u. Co."

The briefing documents used by the *Luftwaffe* for raids on Southampton. Endorsed with the dates 1.9.40 and December 1940, both documents indicate the Supermarine factory area as that of "A.V. Roe u. Co." Also clearly defined, presumably as raid targets, were the Thornycroft boatbuilding premises, the "British Mex Petroleum Co." storage tank farm and the elctrical switchgear factory. Also indicated are several *flak* positions. Although the military targets are fairly concentrated around the dock area, the widespread damage suffered throughout Southampton suggests that the port's balloon barrage and gun defences forced most raiders to drop their bombs from relatively high altitude.

the raid of the 26th restored the rate well before the end of October. With almost one hundred Spitfires at Maintenance Units and a further 60 in dispersed repair sites, the raid by KG 55 caused no crisis of supply in Fighter Command[37].

[37] For Schedule of Fighter Production, see Appendix E.

R.A.F. FIGHTER COMMAND LOSSES—THURSDAY 26th SEPTEMBER 1940

1.	152 Sqn., Warmwell	C	Shot down by Bf 109s to the west of the Isle of Wight; pilot picked up dead from the sea.	A16.40 hrs.	Sgt. J.McB. Christie	Spitfire	K9882	Cat. 3 Lost
2.	152 Sqn., Warmwell	C	Shot down by Bf 109s south of the Isle of Wight; pilot rescued wounded from the sea.	A16.40 hrs.	Fg. Off. E.C. Deanesly	Spitfire	K9982	Cat. 3 Lost
3.	229 Sqn., Northolt	C	Shot down by Bf 110 over Southampton and force landed at Hambledon; pilot slightly wounded with cuts and burns to face.	A16.25 hrs.	Sgt. S.W. Merryweather	Hurricane	V6745	Cat. 2 Damaged
4.	238 Sqn., Middle Wallop	C	Shot down by Bf 110s and force landed at Lee-on-Solent; pilot unhurt.	16.40 hrs.	Sqn. Ldr. H.A. Fenton	Hurricane	P2920	Cat. 2 Damaged
5.	238 Sqn., Middle Wallop	C	Shot down by Bf 110s over the Isle of Wight; pilot baled out unhurt.	A16.40 hrs.	Plt. Off. R.A. Kings	Hurricane	V6792	Cat. 3 Destroyed
6.	238 Sqn., Middle Wallop	C	Shot down by Bf 110s off the north coast of Isle of Wight; pilot missing, believed killed.	A16.45 hrs.	Sgt. V. Horsky	Hurricane	P3098	Cat. 3 Missing
7.	253 Sqn., Kenley	C	Shot down into the English Channel; pilot baled out and rescued unhurt.	A16.30 hrs.	Not known	Hurricane	P2958	Cat. 3 Lost

LUFTWAFFE LOSSES—THURSDAY 26th SEPTEMBER 1940

1.	4.(F)/14	CM	Shot down by 92 Sqn. Spitfires of Wright, Oldfield and Lewis at Hailsham at 16.30 hrs.	Messerschmitt Bf 110 C-5 (2187 : 5F+CM)	100 %	Ltn. Wilhelm Pank and Uffz. Schmidt missing.
2.	5.(F)/14	NCM	Force landed at Bad Liebenwerder.	Dornier Do 17P (1092)	10 %	Crew unhurt.
3.	Stab/KG 3	CM	Pilot became lost and force landed at Maastricht.	Dornier Do 17Z-3 (2591 : 5K+FA)	100 %	Two crew members injured.
4.	I./KG 27	CM	Force landed at Gijon, Spain, during patrol; crew and aircraft handed back to *Luftwaffe* without internment.	Heinkel He 111H (6871)	—	Crew unhurt.
5.	I./KG 27	NCM	Crashed near Tours due to faulty maintenance.	Heinkel He 111H (5406)	100 %	Oblt.Horst Fock injured; two killed.

The Messerschmitt Bf 110C-5 which landed almost intact on 26th September. Flown by Leutnant Wilhelm Pank of 4.(F)/14, the aircraft force landed at Hailsham and is here seen at the R.A.E., Farnborough, where it was extensively evaluated by the British.

Luftwaffe Losses, 26th September 1940—*continued*

6.	7./KG 51	CM	Air collision with Item 7 near Etampes.	Junkers Ju 88A-1 (6153 : 9K+BR)	100 %	Uffz. Maier, Fw. Conrad and Fw. Brünningsen killed.
7.	7./KG 51	CM	Air collision with Item 6 near Etampes.	Junkers Ju 88A-5 (2174 : 9K+IR)	100 %	Gefr. Kurt Israel, Gefr. Jung, Gefr. Erwin Keinbauer, Uffz. Emil Bender killed.
8.	I./KG 54	CM	Landing accident at Evreux airfield.	Junkers Ju 88A-1(6071)	35 %	One crew member injured.
9.	I./KG 55	CM	Force landed at Dreux; cause not known.	Heinkel He 111P (3098)	40 %	Oblt. Karbe + one injured.
10.	2./KG 55	CM	Shot down by 607 Sqn. Hurricanes near Southampton at 17.45 hrs.	Heinkel He111H (5314 : G1+BL)	100 %	Oblt. Graf Schweinitz, Uffz. Widmann, Uffz. Schob and Gefr. Wastian missing.
11.	KGr. 100	CM	Landing accident at Vannes; cause not known.	Heinkel He 111H (5291)	30 %	Crew unhurt.
12.	I./ZG 26	CM	Shot down by 238 Sqn. Hurricane of Simmonds near Southampton at A.16.35 hrs.	Messerschmitt Bf 110 C-4 (3028 : U8+HH)	100 %	Fw. Rhode and Fw. Feder missing.
13.	III./JG 26	CM	Shot down by 238 Sqn. Hurricane of Mann near Southampton at A.16.35 hrs.	Messerschmitt Bf 110 C-4 (3094 : 3U+AR)	100 %	Ltn. Konopka and Uffz. Eiberg killed.
14.	3./JG 51	CM	Shot down by 602 Sqn. Spitfire of Boyd at A.16.30 hrs.	Messerschmitt Bf 109 E-4 (5369)	100 %	Fw. Meudner missing.
15.	5./JG 77	NCM	Caught fire on take-off at Fornebu, Oslo.	Messerschmitt Bf 109 E-3 (5369)	60 %	Pilot unhurt.
16.	Wettererkundungskette, Luftflotte 5	NCM	Landing accident at Vaernes airfield; cause not notified.	Heinkel He 111H-3 (6942 : 1B+CH)	45 %	Crew unhurt.
17.	II./KGzbV. 1	NCM	Crashed near Willingen; cause not notified.	Junkers Ju 52/3m (6937 : 1Z+DS)	100 %	Two killed and four injured.

Friday 27th September

As the night *blitz* continued to pound away at British towns and cities, and R.A.F. bombers dropped their loads on German arms and railway centres, the *Luftflotten* commanders on the French coast reverted to phased daylight attacks against Nos. 10 and 11 Groups. These started with the customary reconnaissance sorties, ranging over fourteen counties between 06.00 and 08.30 hours, but neither Park nor Brand reacted with much vigour against them, preferring to conserve their pilots' strength for what promised, with fine weather, to be a busy day.

Sure enough, at 08.15 hours, the Kent and Sussex CH stations reported a number of fast raids approaching on a fifty-mile front, and these quickly materialised as six groups of Bf 110 fighter-bombers of V./LG 1 and II./ZG 76, together with Bf 109s from *Jafu 2*. Crossing in between Dover and Brighton, these formations were repeatedly hit by Park's fighters, and although the Germans made no apparent effort to attack specific targets they remained over Kent and Surrey for almost an hour, some penetrating to London. Their object was to exhaust the magazines and fuel tanks of the defending fighters so that a subsequent heavy raid could reach London without interference.

This raid, which was intended to approach under a heavy escort of Bf 109s, met with disaster; it was late in the assembly

Squadron Leader Brian Lane, the energetic and outspoken leader of No. 19 Squadron. The exhaustion in this officer's face speaks for itself.

area off the French coast, and crossed the Channel almost entirely exposed. It was composed of the Junkers Ju 88s of I. and II.*Gruppen* of *Kampfgeschwader 77*, whose III.*Gruppe* had taken such a thrashing nine days before. Now the 55 bombers were at the mercy of some 120 Hurricanes and Spitfires, whose pilots promptly set about the two immaculate formations of Junkers. Frantic calls for assistance brought large numbers of Bf 109s and 110s to the scene, and British losses were fairly heavy; but not before twelve of the bombers had been sent down to destruction.

In the West, Sperrle decided to repeat the previous formula in another attack on the Bristol factory—which German reconnaissance had incorrectly reported as having been only lightly damaged. A single *Gruppe* of thirty KG 55 Heinkels was preceded by nineteen bomb-carrying Bf 110s of Erpr.Gr. 210 and covered by 27 Bf 110s of II./ZG 26. This time, however, Brand was waiting; and five squadrons met the raid, including the freshly deployed No. 504 Squadron. The fighters went straight for the Heinkels over Yeovil, and forced them to turn away, scattering their loads in the Sherbourne area before racing for the coast and the protection of other Messerschmitts which had taken up holding circles near Portland to await their return.

As might be expected, the hard-flying crews of *Erprobungsgruppe 210* forced their way through to the Bristol area alone. They were beset on all sides by Brand's fighters, and lost four aircraft—more than twenty percent of their formation. Among the dead were Martin Lutz, their leader, and Wilhelm Rössiger, *Staffelkapitän* of the 2nd *Staffel*. Lutz died at his controls after a fifty-mile fight, and crashed at Cranbourne Chase at mid-day.

The true nature of this crack German *Gruppe*'s extraordinary rôle in the Battle only began to dawn on the British on this day, with the capture and interrogation of an N.C.O. pilot during the Bristol raid. In action almost continuously since July, its crews had been called upon to carry out a wide range of daring pinpoint attacks. These were originally against shipping targets, but more recently against radar installations, aircraft factories and port installations; each Bf 110 carried two 500-kilo bombs, and they were covered in the early raids by the Bf 109s of the 3rd *Staffel*. It was estimated that in ninety days the unit flew sixty raids, often against heavily defended targets and, until the latter stages of the Battle, without

Oberleutnant Wilhelm-Richard Rössiger, who led the 2nd *Staffel* of *Erprobungsgruppe 210* in strikes against British shipping, radar, airfields and other pinpoint targets during the Battle of Britain until he met his death in action on 27th September 1940. (Photo: *Gemeinschaft der Jagdflieger E.V.*)

additional escort. Losses had been exceptionally heavy in relation to the unit's total strength—never more than 33 pilots; it had lost three *Gruppenkommandeure* and four *Staffelkapitäne* in a period of six weeks, and would lose two more before the end of the Battle—yet the morale and efficiency of the crews seemed to be unimpaired. Their skill was a worthy memorial to their brilliant and courageous first commander.

R.A.F. FIGHTER COMMAND LOSSES—FRIDAY 27th SEPTEMBER 1940

1.	19 Sqn., Duxford	C	Shot down by Bf 109s at Wye, near Ashford, Kent; pilot wounded.	A12.30 hrs.	Sgt. D.G.S.R. Cox	Spitfire	X4237	Cat. 3 Destroyed
2.	19 Sqn., Duxford	C	Shot down by Bf 109s and crashed at Coldred, north-west of Dover; pilot killed.	A12.30 hrs.	Plt. Off. A. Burgoyne	Spitfire	X4352	Cat. 3 Destroyed
3.	41 Sqn., Rochford	C	Shot down by Bf 109s at Yalding, near Maidstone; pilot wounded in leg.	A12.20 hrs.	Sgt. F. Usmar	Spitfire	R5884	Cat. 3 Destroyed
4.	41 Sqn., Rochford	C	Shot down by Bf 109s over West Malling; pilot baled out wounded in the shoulder.	A12.25 hrs.	Sgt. E.V. Darling	Spitfire	—	Cat. 3 Destroyed
5.	41 Sqn., Rochford	C	Shot down by Bf 109s and crashed at East Malling; pilot baled out unhurt.	15.40 hrs.	Flt. Lt. E.N. Ryder	Spitfire	R6755	Cat.3 Destroyed
6.	46 Sqn., Stapleford	C	Force landed at Rochester after combat with Bf 109s at Biggin Hill; pilot unhurt.	A12.30 hrs.	Plt. Off. K. Mrazak	Hurricane	P3756	Cat. 2 Damaged
7.	64 Sqn., Leconfield	C	Aircraft missing from routine local patrol; no details known, and pilot assumed killed.	A10.30 hrs.	Sgt. L.A. Dyke	Spitfire	X4032	Cat. 3 Missing
8.	66 Sqn., Gravesend	C	Aircraft hit by A.A. gunfire south of London; crashed landed at Orpington; pilot unhurt.	A15.40 hrs	Plt. Off. G.A. Corbett	Spitfire	P9515	Cat. 3 Destroyed
9.	72 Sqn., Biggin Hill	C	Shot down by Bf 109 at Sevenoaks; pilot baled out but landed dead.	09.20 hrs.	Plt. Off. P.J. Davies-Cooke	Spitfire	N3068	Cat. 3 Destroyed
10.	72 Sqn., Biggin Hill	C	Shot down by Bf 109 at Shadwell Dock, Stepney, London; pilot killed.	A09.20 hrs.	Plt. Off. E.E. Males	Spitfire	X4340	Cat. 3 Destroyed
11.	73 Sqn., Debden	C	Damaged by Bf 110s over Kenley but pilot, unwounded, force landed at Kenley.	09.40 hrs.	Sgt. A.E.Marshall	Hurricane	—	Cat. 2 Damaged
12.	73 Sqn., Debden	C	Damaged by Bf 110s over Kenley; pilot force landed, unhurt, near Limpsfield.	09.50 hrs.	Sgt. P. O'Byrne	Hurricane	P3209	Cat. 2 Damaged
13.	92 Sqn., Biggin Hill	C	Shot down in flames near Maidstone by Bf 109s; pilot killed. Crashed at Farningham.	09.40 hrs.	Flt. Lt. J.A. Paterson	Spitfire	X4422	Cat. 3 Destroyed

R.A.F. Losses, 27th September 1940—*continued*

14.	92 Sqn., Biggin Hill	C	Shot down in flames by Bf 109s and crashed in Kingston-upon- Thames; pilot killed.	09.45 hrs.	F/Sgt. C. Sydney	Spitfire	R6767	Cat. 3 Destroyed
15.	92 Sqn., Biggin Hill	C	Shot down by enemy fighters and crashed in flames at Dartford. Pilot killed.	A15.25 hrs.	Sgt. T.G. Oldfield	Spitfire	R6622	Cat. 3 Destroyed
16.	92 Sqn., Biggin Hill	C	Aircraft probably hit by fire from Ju 88; pilot crashed at base with damage, but unhurt.	A15.35 hrs.	Sgt. H. Bowen-Morris	Spitfire	R6760	Cat. 3 Destroyed
17.	152 Sqn.	C	Damaged in combat near Poole; pilot unhurt.	12.30 hrs.	Not known.	Spitfire	—	Cat. 1 Damaged
18.	152 Sqn	C	Damaged in combat near Poole; pilot unhurt.	12.30 hrs.	Not known.	Spitfire	—	Cat. 1 Damaged
19.	152 Sqn.	C	Damaged in combat near Poole; pilot unhurt.	12.30 hrs.	Not known.	Spitfire	—	Cat. 1 Damaged
20.	152 Sqn.	C	Damaged in combat near Poole; pilot unhurt.	12.30 hrs.	Not known.	Spitfire	—	Cat. 1 Damaged
21.	152 Sqn.	C	Damaged in combat near Poole; pilot unhurt.	12.30 hrs.	Not known.	Spitfire	—	Cat. 1 Damaged
22.	222 Sqn., Hornchurch	C	Shot down by Bf 109s at Wennington, East London; pilot seriously wounded in spine.	A12.10 hrs.	Sgt. R.H. Gretton	Spitfire	R6720	Cat. 3 Destroyed
23.	229 Sqn. Northolt	C	Shot down by Bf 109s and aircraft exploded over Burwash, East Sussex; pilot killed.	A15.30 hrs.	Flt. Lt. R.F. Rimmer	Hurricane	V6782	Cat. 3 Destroyed
24.	229 Sqn. Northolt	C	Shot down by Ju 88s and crashed landed at Lingfield, Surrey; pilot unhurt.	A15.30 hrs.	Flt. Lt. W.A. Smith	Hurricane	P3603	Cat. 3 Destroyed
25.	242 Sqn., Coltishall	C	Shot down in flames over North Kent at Milstead, near Sittingbourne; pilot killed.	12.30 hrs.	Fg. Off. M.G. Homer	Hurricane	P2967	Cat. 3 Destroyed
26.	249 Sqn. North Weald	C	Crashed in combat with Bf 110 of V./LG 1 at Hailsham, Sussex; pilot killed.	10.30 hrs	Plt. Off. P.R.F. Burton	Hurricane	V6683	Cat. 3 Destroyed
27.	249 Sqn., North Weald	C	Damaged by Bf 110 near Gatwick; pilot returned wounded in the foot.	A10.30 hrs.	Plt. Off. H.J.S. Beazley	Hurricane	V6559	Cat. 1 Damaged
28.	249 Sqn. North Weald	C	Shot down in combat with Bf 110s over Sussex; pilot crash landed but was unhurt.	A10.30 hrs.	Flt. Lt. R.A. Barton	Hurricane	V6729	Cat. 3 Destroyed
29.	249 Sqn., North Weald	C	Shot down by return fire from Ju 88 at Dallington, East Sussex; pilot baled out but landed dead at nearby Brightling.	15.20 hrs.	Plt. Off. J.R.B. Meaker	Hurricane	P3834	Cat. 3 Destroyed
30.	249 Sqn., North Weald	C	Shot down by Bf 109s south-east of London, and force landed, unhurt, at West Malling.	15.27 hrs.	Plt. Off. R.G.A. Barclay	Hurricane	V6622	Cat. 2 Damaged
31.	253 Sqn., Kenley	C	Damaged in action with Bf 109s north of Hastings; pilot unhurt.	10.15 hrs.	Not known	Hurricane	—	Cat. 2 Damaged
32.	253 Sqn., Kenley	C	Damaged in action with Bf 109s north of Hastings; pilot unhurt.	10.15 hrs.	Not known	Hurricane	—	Cat. 1 Damaged
33.	302 Sqn., Duxford	C	Damaged by return fire from He 111; pilot, unhurt, force landed near Chelmsford.	Not known	Sgt. E. Paterek	Hurricane	—	Cat. 1 Damaged
34.	303 Sqn., Northolt	C	Shot down by Bf 109s at Crowhurst Farm, Borough Green, Kent. Pilot killed.	09.55 hrs.	Fg. Off. L.W. Paszkiewicz	Hurricane	L1696	Cat. 3 Destroyed
35.	303 Sqn., Northolt	C	Shot down by Bf 109s over Horsham, Sussex, and crashed at Cowden; pilot killed.	A10.00 hrs.	Sgt. T. Andruszkow	Hurricane	V7246	Cat. 3 Destroyed
36.	303 Sqn., Northolt	C	Shot down by enemy fighters near Horsham; pilot baled out with burns.	A10.00 hrs.	Fg. Off. W. Zak	Hurricane	—	Cat. 3 Destroyed
37.	310 Sqn., Duxford	C	Shot down by Bf 109 near Chilham, Kent; pilot baled out unhurt.	A13.25 hrs.	Fg. Off. G.L. Sinclair	Hurricane	V6608	Cat. 3 Destroyed
38.	501 Sqn., Kenley	C	Shot down by Bf 110 near Godstone; pilot baled out wounded and admitted to Sevenoaks Hospital.	A09.30 hrs.	Sgt. V.H. Ekins	Hurricane	V6672	Cat. 3 Destroyed
39.	501 Sqn., Kenley	C	Shot down in combat with Do 17s; pilot baled out near Sittingbourne but was killed when his parachute failed.	12.05 hrs.	Plt. Off. E.M. Gunter	Hurricane	V6645	Cat. 3 Destroyed
40.	504 Sqn., Filton	C	Shot down in combat with Bf 110 and force landed at Axminster; pilot unhurt.	A12.10 hrs.	Sgt. C. Haw	Hurricane	P3415	Cat. 2 Damaged
41.	602 Sqn., Westhampnett	C	Hit in the coolant tank by Bf 109 and force landed near Mayfield; pilot unhurt.	09.20 hrs.	Plt. Off. D.H. Gage	Spitfire	X4414	Cat. 3 Destroyed
42.	603 Sqn., Hornchurch	C	Shot down by Bf 109s off coast at Folkestone; pilot baled out wounded into the sea, but was dead when a boat reached him.	A12.20 hrs.	Plt. Off. P.M. Cardell	Spitfire	N3244	Cat. 3 Lost
43.	603 Sqn., Hornchurch	C	Force landed on Folkestone beach in effort to organise rescue of pilot (Item 42 above).	A12.30 hrs	Plt. Off. P.G. Baxter	Spitfire	X4250	Cat. 3 Destroyed
44.	609 Sqn., Middle Wallop	C	Collided with Bf 110 near Kingcombe, Dorset; pilot killed.	Not known	Plt. Off. R.F.G. Miller	Spitfire	X4107	Cat. 3 Destroyed
45.	616 Sqn., Duxford	C	Shot down by Bf 109s near Faversham, Kent; pilot baled out grievously wounded and died the following day in Faversham Hospital.	A12.30 hrs.	Plt. Off. D.S. Smith	Spitfire	X4328	Cat. 3 Destroyed

LUFTWAFFE LOSSES—FRIDAY 27th SEPTEMBER 1940

1.	3.(F)/123	CM	Shot down by 152 Sqn. of Marrs over North Devon at A.09.00 hrs.	Junkers Ju 88A-1 (0393 : 4U+RL)	100 %	Oblt.Willi Rude, Fw.Ackenhausen, Fw.Riehle and Fl. Reuhl missing.
2.	8./KG 2	NCM	Crashed at Remilly; cause not notified.	Dornier Do 17Z (2871: A5+ES)	100 %	Ltn. Landhorst + three killed.
3.	I./KG 53	CM	Landing accident at Vitry-en-Artois airfield.	Heinkel He 111H-5 (3556 : A1+EH)	25 %	Crew unhurt.
4.	5./KG 53	CM	Force landed near Calais; cause not notified.	Heinkel He 111H-3 (3344 : A1+DR)	40 %	One crew member wounded.
5.	I./KG 54	CM	Landing accident at Evreux; cause not notified.	Junkers Ju 88A-1(4029)	35 %	Crew unhurt.
6.	Geschw.Erg.St./ KG 55	NCM	Taxying accident at Landsberg airfield.	Heinkel He 111P (1398)	25 %	Crew unhurt.
7.	1./KG 77	CM	Losses incurred by I. and II. *Gruppen, Kampfgeschwader 77,* during the afternoon raid on South London. Owing to the confined area and short duration of combat it has proved impossible to analyse individual combats and indentify individual claims; the following Squadrons and pilots scored "kills":	Junkers Ju 88A-1 (8090 : 3Z+DH)	100 %	Gefr. Zabel killed; Ofw. Herbert Müller, Uffz. Köllmannsmäger and Ofw. Robert Müller missing.
8.	2./KG 77	CM		Junkers Ju 88A-1 (2164 : 3Z+IK)	100 %	Uffz.Hertlein and Fw.Krebs killed; Fw. Sergocke wounded; Uffz. Gerhard Schmidt missing.
9.	2./KG 77	CM		Junkers Ju 88A-1 (8095 : 3Z+HK)	100 %	Uffz. Menningmann killed; Uffz. Schumann, Uffz. Tenholt and Uffz. Ackermann missing.
10.	3./KG 77	CM	46 Sqn., Rabagliati, one Junkers Ju 88 66 Sqn., Cameron, one Junkers Ju 88 66 Sqn., Parsons, one Junkers Ju 88	Junkers Ju 88A-1 (5103 : 3Z+CL)	100 %	Uffz.Helmut Damerius, Uffz.Franz Hastrich killed; Uffz. Mershen and Uffz. Ludwig missing.
11.	3./KG 77	CM	92 Sqn., seven Junkers Ju 88s 229 Sqn., two Junkers Ju 88s 249 Sqn., Lewis, one Junkers Ju 88	Junkers Ju 88A-1 (8099 : 3Z+EL)	100 %	Uffz. Ruhlandt, Uffz. Gerhard Richter, Uffz. Erich Richter and Gefr. Reiner missing.

Luftwaffe Losses, 27th September 1940—*continued*

12.	3./KG 77	CM		Junkers Ju 88A-1 (8109 : 3Z+BL)	100 %	Fw. Precht, Uffz. Kasing and Uffz. Winkelmann killed; Fw. Bräutigam missing.
13.	Stab II./KG 77	CM	Losses incurred by I. and II. *Gruppen, Kampfgeschwader 77*, during the afternoon raid on South London. Owing to the confined area and short duration of combat it has proved impossible to analyse individual combats and indentify individual claims; the following Squadrons and pilots scored "kills":	Junkers Ju 88A-5 (0293 : 3Z+DC)	100 %	Oblt. Karl-Heinz Lutz, Fw. Adler, and Fw.Zeller killed; Uffz. Brodbeck, wounded, made P.O.W.
14.	4./KG 77	CM		Junkers Ju 88A-1 (4140 : 3Z+LM)	100 %	Fw. Nölp, Fw. Scheibner, Uffz. Ganter and Ogefr. Möttig missing.
15.	5./KG 77	CM		Junkers Ju 88A-1 (7112 : 3Z+HN)	100 %	Ogefr. Kühn killed; Hptm.Günther Zetzsche, *St.Kap.*, Fw. Marl and Ogefr. Burkardt missing.
16.	5./KG 77	CM	46 Sqn., Rabagliati, one Junkers Ju 88 66 Sqn., Cameron, one Junkers Ju 88 66 Sqn., Parsons, one Junkers Ju 88 92 Sqn., seven Junkers Ju 88s 229 Sqn., two Junkers Ju 88s 249 Sqn., Lewis, one Junkers Ju 88	Junkers Ju 88A-1 (4117 : 3Z+DN)	100 %	Oblt. Friedrich Ziel, Fw. Niederer and Uffz. Isensee killed; Gefr. Teichtmeyer missing.
17.	5./KG 77	CM		Junkers Ju 88A-1 (7109 : 3Z+GN)	100 %	Gefr. Reinhardt and Gefr. Zott killed; Ltn. Walter Pflüger and Uffz. Grönke missing.
18.	6./KG 77	CM		Junkers Ju 88A-1 (4118 : 3Z+DP)	100 %	Oblt.Horst Sief, Fw. Adolf Eichinger and Uffz. Gebhardt killed; Fw. Zinsmeister missing.
19.	III./LG 1	CM	Landing accident on Chateaudun airfield.	Junkers Ju 88A-5(3183)	15 %	Crew unhurt.
20.	III./LG 1	CM	Shot down by 249 Sqn. Hurricane of Barclay	Junkers Ju 88A-5 (4153 : L1+BR)	100 %	Gefr. Lorenz and Fw. Söchting killed; Oblt. Richard Strasser and Uffz. Forster missing.
21.	III./LG 1	CM	Shot down by 602 Sqn. Spitfire of Babbage during mid-day raid on South London.	Junkers Ju 88A-5 (3197 : L1+DR)	100 %	Uffz. Wächtler killed; Fw. Krings, Uffz. Wurm and Ofhr. Vanselow missing.
22.	V./LG 1	CM	Shot down by 249 Sqn. Hurricane of Burton over Hailsham, Sussex, at A.10.30 hrs.	Messerschmitt Bf 110 C-2 (3560 : L1+XB)	100 %	Hptm. Horst Linsberger, *Gr.Kdr.*, and Uffz. Körpe killed.
23.	13./LG 1	CM	Shot down by 17 Sqn. Hurricane of Hogg and crashed on Duxford airfield at 09.55 hrs.	Messerschmitt Bf 110 D-0 (3304 : L1+CH)	100 %	Fw. Bruns and Gefr. Gröwel killed.
24.	13./LG 1	CM	Target London. Shot down by 72 Sqn. Spitfires near Sevenoaks at 09.38 hrs.	Messerschmitt Bf 110 D-0 (3333 : L1+BH)	100 %	Gefr. Welz killed; Gefr. Swietlik missing.
25.	14./LG 1	CM	Target London. Shot down by 72 Sqn. Spitfires near Sevenoaks at 09.35 hrs.	Messerschmitt Bf 110 C-2 (3548 : L1+CK)	100 %	Fw. Lindemann and Ogefr. Hübner killed.
26.	15./LG 1	CM	Target London. Shot down by 46 Sqn. Hurricane of Rabagliati 10 miles south of Rye at 09.30 hrs.	Messerschmitt Bf 110 C-2 (3489 : L1+GL)	100 %	Uffz. Koch killed; Uffz. Berchtold missing.
27.	15./LG 1	CM	Target London. Shot down by 46 Sqn. Hurricane of Pattullo near Penshurst at 09.25 hrs.	Messerschmitt Bf 110 C-2 (3533 : L1+LL)	100 %	Oblt. OttoWeckeisser and Uffz. Brügow missing.
28.	15./LG 1	CM	Target London. Shot down by 46 Sqn. Hurricane south-west of Maidstone at 09.19 hrs.	Messerschmitt Bf 110 D-0 (3147 : L1+BL)	100 %	Oblt. Frhr.Ulrich von Grafenreuth, *St.Kap.*, and Fw. Otto Reinhold killed.
29.	1./LG 2	CM	Target London. Shot down by 46 Sqn. Hurricanes of Pattullo and Tyrer south-east of Biggin Hill.	Messerschmitt Bf 109 E-7 (2062)	100 %	Oblt. Adolf Bühl, *St.Kap.*, missing.
30.	2./LG 2	CM	Landing accident at Calais-Marck following combat.	Messerschmitt Bf 109 E-7 (5592)	10 %	Pilot unhurt.
31.	2./LG 2	CM	Force landed at Wissant following fighter combat.	Messerschmitt Bf 109 E-7 (2039)	20 %	Pilot unhurt.
32.	I./ZG 26	CM	Shot down by 56 Sqn. Hurricane of Maxwell south of Bristol at A.11.40 hrs.	Messerschmitt Bf 110 C-4 (2162 : U8+FK)	100 %	Ofw. Tipelt and Uffz. Brosig killed.
33.	3./ZG 26	CM	Shot down by 56 Sqn. Hurricane of Marston south of Bristol at A.11.40 hrs.	Messerschmitt Bf 110 C-4 (3571 : U8+CL)	100 %	Uffz. Johann Schmidt killed; Ltn. Joachim Köpsel missing.
34.	II./ZG 26	CM	Shot down by 152 Sqn. Spitfires of Watson and Hall near Lulworth Cove at A.11.55 hrs.	Messerschmitt Bf 110 C-7 (3629 : 3U+SM)	100 %	Oblt. Artur Niebuhr and Uffz. Klaus Theisen killed. Both men buried at Wareham, Dorset.
35.	III./ZG 26	CM	Shot down by 152 Sqn. Spitfire of Watson near Poole at A.12.20 hrs.	Messerschmitt Bf 110 C-4 (3297 : 3U+FT)	100 %	Gefr. Lidtke killed; Gefr. Jackstedt missing.
36.	III./ZG 26	CM	Shot down by 609 Sqn. Spitfire of Bisdee over Dorset in raid on Bristol.	Messerschmitt Bf 110 C-4 (2168 : 3U+BD)	100 %	Oblt.Hans Barschel and Uffz.Klose missing.
37.	III./ZG 26	CM	Shot down by two 152 Sqn. Spitfires and crashed near Kimmeridge, 6 miles south-east of Wareham.	Messerschmitt Bf 110 C-4 (3290 : 3U+DS)	100 %	Uffz. Fritz Schupp and Gefr. Karl Nechwatal, wounded, made P.O.W.
38.	III./ZG 26	CM	Damaged by British fighters during raid on Bristol and force landed on Cherbourg airfield.	Messerschmitt Bf 110 C-4 (3098)	40 %	Crew unhurt.
39.	II./ZG 76	CM	Shot down by 17 Sqn. Hurricane of Czernin east of Redhill at 09.40 hrs.	Messerschmitt Bf 110 D-3 (4215 : M8+XE)	100 %	Uffz. Bartmus killed; Oblt. Wilfred von Eichborn missing.
40.	9./ZG 76	CM	Damaged by 249 Sqn. Hurricane of Lewis at A.10.30 hrs., and crash landed near Dieppe.	Messerschmitt Bf 110 (3584 : 2N+DP)	70 %	One crew member wounded.
41.	Stab/Erpr.Gr. 210	CM	Shot down by Spitfires in Yeovil area during raid on Britsol; crashed 5 miles S.E. of Shaftesbury.	Messerschmitt Bf 110 D-3 (3378 : S9+DH)	100 %	Hptm. Martin Lütz, *Gr.Kdr..*, and Uffz. Schön killed.
42.	1./Erpr.Gr. 210	CM	Shot down by Spitfires in Yeovil area during raid on Bristol; crashed at Preston Hill, Iwerne Minster at A.12.00 hrs.	Messerschmitt Bf 110 D-3 (3888 : S9+JH)	100 %	Ltn. Gerhard Schmidt and Fw. Richter killed.
43.	2./Erpr.Gr. 210	CM	Shot down by Spitfires over the Dorset coast after raid on Bristol; believed to have fallen in the sea.	Messerschmitt Bf 110 D-0 (2248 : S9+GK)	100 %	Oblt. Wilhelm Rössiger, *St.Kap.*, killed; Ofw. Marx missing.
44.	2./Erpr.Gr. 210	CM	Shot down by two Spitfires in Yeovil area during raid on Bristol; crashed near Preston Hill, Iwerne Minster, at A.12.00 hrs.	Messerschmitt Bf 110 D-0 (4270 : S9+DU)	100 %	Fw. Fritz Ebner, unhurt, and Gefr. Werner Zwick, severely wounded, made P.O.W.s.
45.	6./JG 3	CM	Shot down by 17 Sqn. Hurricane of Griffiths into the English Channel.	Messerschmitt Bf 109 E-4 (4141)	100 %	Pilot, unhurt, rescued by *Seenotflugkommando.*
46.	III./JG 3	CM	Shot down by British fighters into the English Channel.	Messerschmitt Bf 109 E-4 (5340)	100 %	Oblt. Horst Rech, wounded, rescued by *Seenotflugkommando.*
47.	8./JG 3	CM	Damaged by British fighters and crashed at Wissant.	Messerschmitt Bf 109 E-4 (1283)	100 %	Pilot unhurt.
48.	8./JG 3	CM	Shot down by British fighters into the English Channel.	Messerschmitt Bf 109 E-1 (6197)	100 %	Uffz. Struwe missing.
49.	9./JG 3	CM	Shot down by 310 Sqn. Hurricane of Kominek 5 miles south-west of Dover at 12.44 hrs.	Messerschmitt Bf 109 E-1 (3217)	100 %	Pilot missing.
50.	3./JG 27	CM	Shot down by 222 Sqn. Spitfire of Broadhurst off Dungeness at A.12.20 hrs.	Messerschmitt Bf 109 E-4 (5333)	100 %	Pilot, unhurt, rescued by *Seenotflugkommando.*
51.	5./JG 27	CM	Shot down by 19 Sqn. Spitfire of Lawson near Tonbridge at 12.28 hrs.	Messerschmitt Bf 109 E-1 (3369)	100 %	Gefr. Hans-Dieter John killed.
52.	6./JG 27 (1)	CM	Shot down by 19 Sqn. Spitfire of Blake near Tonbridge at 12.31 hrs.	Messerschmitt Bf 109 E-4 (1447)	100%	Uffz. Josef Scheidt killed.

Luftwaffe Losses, 27th September 1940—*continued*

53.	3./JG 51	CM	Damaged by British fighters over Kent and crash landed at St. Inglevert.	Messerschmitt Bf 109 E-4 (5582)	75 %	Pilot unhurt.
54.	II./JG 52	CM	Shot down by 249 Sqn. Hurricane of Lewis near Chatham, Kent.	Messerschmitt Bf 109 E-1 (3907)	100 %	Oblt. Karl Treiber, wounded, made P.O.W.
55.	4./JG 52	CM	Shot down by 222 Sqn. Spitfire of Scott near Maidstone at 12.18 hrs.	Messerschmitt Bf 109 E-1 (3442)	100 %	Gefr. Bosch missing.
56.	4./JG 52	CM	Shot down by 249 Sqn. Hurricane of Lewis near Chatham, Kent.	Messerschmitt Bf 109 E-4 (5181)	100 %	Fw. Bogasch, wounded, made P.O.W.
57.	4./JG 52	CM	Shot down by 249 Sqn. Hurricanes near Gravesend.	Messerschmitt Bf 109 E-1 (6245)	100 %	Ltn. Hans Geist missing.
58.	5./JG 52	CM	Shot down by 242 Sqn. Hurricane of Brimble north of Dover at A.12.30 hrs.	Messerschmitt Bf 109 E-1 (3431)	100 %	Fw. Hoffmann missing.
59.	6./JG 52	CM	Damaged by British fighters and crashed at Peuplinghen.	Messerschmitt Bf 109 E-4 (5152)	70 %	Pilot unhurt.
60.	6./JG 52	CM	Shot down by British fighters over the English Channel.	Messerschmitt Bf 109 E-1 (6162)	100 %	Pilot, wounded, rescued by *Seenotflugkommando*.
61.	II./JG 53	CM	Damaged by British fighters but landed safely at base.	Messerschmitt Bf 109 E-4 (1168)	10 %	Pilot unhurt.
62.	II./JG 53	CM	Damaged by British fighters but landed safely at base.	Messerschmitt Bf 109 E-4 (1644)	15 %	Pilot unhurt.
63.	II./JG 53	CM	Damaged by British fighters but landed safely at Wissant.	Messerschmitt Bf 109 E-4 (1164)	15 %	Pilot unhurt.
64.	6./JG 53	CM	Damaged by British fighters and crashed at Berck.	Messerschmitt Bf 109 E-4 (1169)	100 %	Pilot unhurt.
65.	8./JG 54	CM	Shot down by 19 Sqn. Spitfires near Tilbury Docks.	Messerschmitt Bf 109E (1538)	100 %	Oblt. Anton Schön killed.
66.	*Corpo Aereo Italiano*	NCM	Crashed near Spa following engine failure.	Fiat BR. 20	Not known	Crew unhurt.
67.	*Corpo Aereo Italiano*	NCM	Crashed at Brussels-Evère airfield; cause not notified.	Fiat BR. 20	70 %	One crew member injured.

[(1) Gefr. Werner, a Bf 109 pilot of 9./JG 27, was also wounded in combat over Britain on this date.]

Saturday 28th September

After two substantial defeats inflicted by Park and Brand on Göring's bombers on the previous day, the operations of this Saturday came as an unpleasant anti-climax to Dowding, whose fighters only destroyed four of the enemy for the loss of four Spitfires, eleven Hurricanes and nine pilots killed.

The high percentage of Hurricane losses suggests that these aircraft engaged enemy fighter formations—and that is exactly what occurred. Realising from the painful experience of KG 77 that British fighters were still concentrating on their bombers, both Kesselring and Sperrle now mounted enormous escort formations of Bf 109s over relatively light bombing raids. By using the faster Bf 110s as bombers, together with the fairly speedy Ju 88s, they ensured that their Bf 109 pilots would not have to fly wastefully throttled back, and would therefore be able to spend more time over Southern England.

Thus it was that when two raids crossed the Kent coast on this Saturday Hurricane pilots, scrambled to deal with a single *Gruppe* of Ju 88s, were confronted not by forty or fifty Bf 109s—which could be occupied without much difficulty by three or four Spitfire squadrons—but by three entire *Jagdgeschwader*, numbering well over 200 fighters. The Junkers were nevertheless prevented from reaching Central London, but eighteen squadrons of fighters were pinned down by massive German escort groups over Kent, with inevitably high casualties.

R.A.F. FIGHTER COMMAND LOSSES—SATURDAY 28th SEPTEMBER 1940

1.	29 Sqn., Ternhill	C	Aircraft hit by A.A. fire over the Midlands but returned to base safely; crew unhurt.	19.30 hrs	Plt. Off. J. Buchanan	Blenheim	L1317	Cat. 1 Damaged
2.	41 Sqn., Rochford	C	Shot down in flames by Bf 109 and crashed at Lynstead, Kent; pilot died in aircraft.	10.10 hrs.	Fg. Off. J.G. Boyle	Spitfire	X4426	Cat. 3 Burnt
3.	41 Sqn., Rochford	C	Shot down by Bf 109s near Chilham, Kent; pilot baled out severely wounded.	10.10 hrs.	Plt. Off. H.H. Chalder	Spitfire	X4409	Cat. 3 Destroyed
4.	41 Sqn., Rochford	C	Shot down by Bf 109s near Charing, Kent; crashed at Pluckley, pilot slightly wounded.	A10.10 hrs.	Plt. Off. E.S. Aldous	Spitfire	X4345	Cat. 3 Destroyed
5.	41 Sqn., Hornchurch	C	Damaged by Bf 109s near Hornchurch; pilot unhurt.	A13.30 hrs.	Not known.	Spitfire	—	Cat. 2 Damaged
6.	41 Sqn., Hornchurch	C	Damaged by Bf 109s near Hornchurch; pilot unhurt.	A13.30 hrs.	Not known	Spitfire	—	Cat. 2 Damaged
7.	66 Sqn., Gravesend	C	Shot down by Bf 109s near Mayfield; pilot baled out with wounds to leg and shoulder.	Not known	Plt. Off. A.B. Watkinson	Spitfire	X4322	Cat. 3 Destroyed
8.	66 Sqn., Gravesend	C	Damaged by Bf 109s over Kent; pilot force landed, unhurt (but location not known).	Not known	Sgt. B. Wright	Spitfire	N3170	Cat. 1 Damaged
9.	141 Sqn., Gatwick	NC	Night landing accident at Gatwick; crew unhurt.	21.45 hrs.	Plt. Off. J. Waddingham Sgt. A.B. Cumbers	Defiant	L7014	Cat. 3 Destroyed
10.	238 Sqn., Middle Wallop	C	Shot down by Bf 110 over Fareham, Hants; pilot killed when parachute failed to open.	14.40 hrs.	Sgt. E.S. Bann	Hurricane	N2400	Cat. 3 Lost
11.	238 Sqn., Middle Wallop	C	Shot down by Bf 109s over the Solent and both pilot and aircraft are assumed to have been lost at sea.	A14.40 hrs.	Plt. Off. D.S. Harrison	Hurricane	V6776	Cat. 3 Missing
12.	238 Sqn., Middle Wallop	C	Shot down by Bf 109s over the Isle of Wight and both pilot and aircraft are assumed to have been lost at sea.	A14.40 hrs.	Sgt. R. Little	Hurricane	P3836	Cat. 3 Missing
13.	249 Sqn., North Weald	C	Shot down by Bf 109s over Faversham; pilot baled out with severe burns; aircraft crashed at Tonge Corner, near Sittingbourne.	A14.00 hrs.	Plt. Off. A.G. Lewis	Hurricane	V6617	Cat. 3 Destroyed
14.	501 Sqn., Kenley	C	Shot down by Bf 109s near Deal; pilot baled out unhurt; aircraft crashed at East Sutton.	10.25 hrs.	Plt. Off. E.B. Rogers	Hurricane	V7497	Cat. 3 Destroyed

R.A.F. Losses, 28th September 1940—*continued*

15.	501 Sqn., Kenley	C	Shot down by Bf 109s and crashed at Ul-combe, near Sutton Valence; pilot killed.	A10.40 hrs.	Plt. Off. F.C. Harrold	Hurricane	*P3417*	Cat. 3 Destroyed
16.	501 Sqn., Kenley	C	Crashed on landing at base after combat over Kent; pilot unhurt.	A11.00 hrs.	Fg. Off. D.A.E. Jones	Hurricane	*P3605*	Cat. 3 Destroyed
17.	603 Sqn., Hornchurch	C	Bounced and shot down by Bf 109s over Gillingham; pilot killed; aircraft crashed on Brompton Barracks.	09.40 hrs.	Flt. Lt. H.K. MacDonald	Spitfire	*L1076*	Cat. 3 Destroyed
18.	605 Sqn., Croydon	C	Shot down by Bf 109s at Ticehurst; pilot baled out unhurt; aircraft crashed at Lamber-hurst.	13.50 hrs.	Fg. Off. R. Hope	Hurricane	*P3828*	Cat. 3 Destroyed
19.	605 Sqn., Croydon	C	Shot down by Bf 109s at Ticehurst; pilot baled out but killed when parachute failed.	A13.50 hrs.	Fg. Off. P.G. Crofts	Hurricane	*V6699*	Cat. 3 Destroyed
20.	607 Sqn., Tangmere	C	Shot down by Bf 109s east of Selsey Bill, and both aircraft and pilot assumed lost at sea.	14.50 hrs.	Flt. Lt. W.E. Gore	Hurricane	*P3108*	Cat. 3 Lost
21.	607 Sqn., Tangmere	C	Shot down by Bf 109s east of Selsey Bill, and both aircraft and pilot assumed lost at sea.	14.50 hrs.	Flt. Lt. M.M. Irving	Hurricane	*R4189*	Cat. 3 Lost
22.	611 Sqn., Ternhill	NC	Suffered landing accident at Ternhill after routine night patrol.	Not known	Plt. Off. N. Sutton	Spitfire	*P7369*	Cat. 3 Destroyed

LUFTWAFFE LOSSES—SATURDAY 28th SEPTEMBER 1940

1.	5./KG 2	CM	Crashed at St. Leger; cause not notified.	Dornier Do 17Z (3355 : U5+3N)	100 %	Oblt. Hubert Roch + three killed.
2.	8./KG 4	CM	Missing from night bombing sortie over England; probably shot down by *flak*.	Junkers Ju 88A-1 (4071 : 5J+GS)	100 %	Ltn. Fritz Lange, Ofw. Camp, and Ogefr.Kieg killed;Gefr.Marschardt missing.
3.	1./KG 26	CM	Crashed near Douai; cause not notified.	Heinkel He 111H-4 (6977 : 1H+EH)	100 %	Ltn. Werner Kose + three killed.
4.	II./KG 26	CM	Crashed on return from operational sortie over Britain; location not notified.	Heinkel He 111H-3 (5621 : 1H+EP)	100 %	Four crew members killed.
5.	5./KG 26	CM	Crashed at St. Germain on return from night bombing sortie, probably with *flak* damage.	Heinkel He 111H-3 (3190 : 1H+LN)	100 %	Four crew members killed.
6.	6./KG 76	NCM	Crashed at Le Lavissière following engine failure; not the result of combat.	Junkers Ju 88A-1 (4162 : F1+HP)	100 %	One killed; Oblt. Mölinnus + two injured.
7.	KGr. 806	CM	Crashed near Caen on return from night bombing sortie over Britain, probably with *flak* damage.	Junkers Ju 88A-1 (5078)	90 %	Ltn.z.S. Quedenau + one killed; two crew members injured.
8.	I./ZG 2	NCM	Crashed near Seilham having run short of fuel.	Messerschmitt Bf 110	100 %	Hptm. Heinlein killed; one injured.
9.	I./LG 2	CM	Crashed at Theville following engine failure.	Messerschmitt Bf 109 E-7 (4091)	35 %	Pilot unhurt.
10.	I./JG 2	CM	Crashed at Theville following engine failure.	Messerschmitt Bf 109 E-1 (6165)	95 %	Pilot unhurt.
11.	I./JG 26	CM	Shot down by 249 Sqn. Hurricane of Beard over the English Channel at A.14.00 hrs.	Messerschmitt Bf 109 E-4 (3756)	100 %	Pilot, unhurt, rescued by *Seenotflugkommando*.
12.	3./JG 26	CM	Shot down by 72 Sqn. Spitfire near Hastings at A.14.20 hrs.	Messerschmitt Bf 109 E-1 (6273)	100 %	Fw. Schür killed.
13.	2./406	CM	Shot down by 248 Sqn. Blenheim of Bennett, Clarke and Brash, over the North Sea.	Dornier Do 18 (0884 : K6+JK)	100 %	Crew rescued unhurt.

Sunday 29th September

Operations on this Sunday were subdued over much of Britain, providing a welcome break for Dowding's pilots, for whom the recent intensity of combat had come near to matching the exhausting days of early September. Yet despite the heavy losses of the previous day, all but No. 41 Squadron were operating with pilot strengths of the order of twenty.

One engagement which took place on this day is, however, worthy of note. Oberstleutnant Hans Korte's KG 55 was among those units briefed to raid the Merseyside area during the night of 29th/30th September; and, mindful of the *Geschwader*'s bitter experience of No. 10 Group's fighter defences, the planning staff determined to avoid following the customary route which would take the Heinkels straight through the area in which heavy losses had been suffered recently. Accordingly the three *Staffeln* of III./KG 55 set off at 18.00 hours

to fly up the Irish Sea hugging the coast of neutral Ireland. They were nevertheless spotted by the Cornish radar, and eleven Hurricanes of No. 79 Squadron were ordered off from Pembrey to attempt an interception. The 7th and 8th *Staffeln* slipped past unseen; but far out over the sea, against the setting sun, the Hurricane pilots spotted the nine Heinkels of the 9th *Staffel*. The Squadron went into the attack; Plt. Off. Paul Mayhew and Plt. Off. George Nelson-Edwards together destroyed one of the Heinkels, and two more were so badly damaged that they were forced to turn back. No less than three Hurricanes were shot down by the unusually well-directed crossfire of the other bombers; Plt. Off. George Peters was killed, Nelson-Edwards was later rescued from the sea and landed at Milford Haven, and Mayhew force landed in Ireland, to be returned to Britain later.

R.A.F. FIGHTER COMMAND LOSSES—SUNDAY 29th SEPTEMBER 1940

1.	79 Sqn., Pembrey	C	Shot down by He 111s of KG 55 off coast of Eire; pilot interned in Eire but returned later.	Evening	Plt. Off. P.F. Mayhew	Hurricane	*P5178*	Cat. 3 Missing (Interned in Eire)
2.	79 Sqn., Pembrey	C	Shot down into the sea off Eire by He 111s of KG 55; pilot killed.	Evening	Plt. Off. G.C.B. Peters	Hurricane	*P5177*	Cat. 3 Lost
3.	79 Sqn., Pembrey	C	Shot down into the sea off Eire by He 111s of KG 55; pilot rescued by ss *Dartford* and landed at Milford Haven.	Evening	Plt. Off. G.H. Nelson-Edwards	Hurricane	—	Cat. 3 Lost
4.	145 Sqn., Dyce	NC	Taxying accident involving another Hurricane (Item 5); pilot unhurt.	Not known	Sgt. J. McConnell	Hurricane	—	Cat. 1 Damaged
5.	145 Sqn., Dyce	NC	Taxying accident involving Item 4 above; pilot unhurt.	Not known	Not known	Hurricane	—	Cat. 2 Damaged

R.A.F. Losses, 29th September 1940—*continued*

6.	253 Sqn., Kenley	C	Shot down in flames by another Hurricane near Haywards Heath; pilot baled out with burns; aircraft crashed at Chailey.	16.40 hrs.	Plt. Off. R.C. Graves	Hurricane	*V6621*	Cat. 3 Destroyed
7.	504 Sqn., Exeter	C	Hit by A.A. fire near Nuneaton, Warwicks; pilot baled out unhurt.	At night	Not known.	Hurricane	*L1913*	Cat. 3 Destroyed
8.	601 Sqn., Exeter	NC	Suffered landing acident after patrol; pilot unhurt.	Not known	Sgt. F.H.R.	Hurricane	—	Cat. 2 Damaged
9.	615 Sqn., Prestwick	NC	Crashed during training flight; pilot killed.	Not known	Plt. Off. J. McGibbon	Hurricane	—	Cat. 3 Destroyed

LUFTWAFFE LOSSES—SUNDAY 29th SEPTEMBER 1940

1.	4.(F)/14	CM	Crashed during night take-off at Plumetot.	Dornier Do 17P (1096)	100 %	Ltn. von Nissen, Ltn. Breitenbach + one killed.
2.	3./KG 1	CM	Crashed at Montdidier; cause not notified.	Heinkel He 111H-3 (3336 : V4+FL)	100 %	Five crew members killed.
3.	3./KG 1	CM	Force landed at Hendricourt following engine failure.	Heinkel He 111H-3 (5468 : V4+EL)	40 %	Crew unhurt.
4.	5./KG 1	CM	Crashed at Dillingen; crew had baled out.	Heinkel He 111H-2 (2714 : V4+AV)	100 %	Crew unhurt.
5.	5./KG 1	CM	Force landed at Marin; cause not notified.	Heinkel He 111H-2 (2736 : V4+DV)	30 %	Crew unhurt.
6.	Stab/KG 2	NCM	Force landed near Fürth following engine failure.	Messerschmitt Bf 108 (1924)	15 %	Occupants unhurt.
7.	I./KG 54	CM	Crash landed at Lisieux following engine failure.	Junkers Ju 88A-1 (4051)	100 %	One crew member killed.
8.	III./KG 55	CM	Shot down by 79 Sqn. Hurricanes of Mayhew and Nelson-Edwards off Irish coast in evening.	Heinkel He 111P (2822 : G1+DT)	100 %	Fw. Birkholz, Uffz. Firchau and Gefr. Günther killed; Oblt. Hans Köhler and Fw. Lippert missing.
9.	III./KG 55	CM	Crashed at St. Lô, probably with battle damage, on return from night bombing sortie.	Heinkel He 111P (2820)	100 %	Five crew members killed.
10.	III./KG 55	CM	Force landed near Brest with engine failure, on return from night bombing sortie.	Heinkel He 111P (2148)	50 %	Crew unhurt.
11.	Stab II./KG 76	CM	Force landed at Calais-Marck following bombing sortie over Britain.	Junkers Ju 88A-1 (8088 : F1+EC)	25 %	Crew unhurt.
12.	Stab I./LG 1	CM	Crashed in France after bombing sortie; three crew baled out but pilot remained at controls.	Junkers Ju 88A-5 (3135 : L1+AB)	100 %	Ofw. Heinz killed.
13.	III./ZG 26	NCM	Crashed at St. Aubin; cause not notified.	Messerschmitt Bf 110C (3422)	80 %	Crew unhurt.
14.	II./LG 2	NCM	Force landed at Monchy Breton; cause not notified.	Messerschmitt Bf 109 E-4 (3719)	40 %	Pilot unhurt.
15.	II./LG 2	CM	Force landed at Berck, short of fuel.	Messerschmitt Bf 109 E-4 (5576)	40 %	Pilot unhurt.
16.	2./JG 26	CM	Force landed at Cap Gris Nez following engine	Messerschmitt Bf 109 E-4 (2767)	15 %	Pilot unhurt.
17.	4./JG 54	CM	Force landed at Berck-sur-Mer short of fuel.	Messerschmitt Bf 109 E-4 (3185)	50 %	Pilot unhurt.
18.	2./JG 77	CM	Shot down by 253 Sqn. Hurricane of Graves near Haywards Heath at 16.40 hrs.	Messerschmitt Bf 109 E-4 (3746)	100 %	Oblt. Walter Leyerer killed.

Monday 30th September

The widespread raids of this last day of September were remarkable for the variety of tactics employed by the *Luftwaffe*, some of which had been logically discarded owing to the high losses suffered. When again employed on this day—presumably to confuse the defences—they drew the same lesson as before from Fighter Command. Moreover, Park and Brand were now on the alert to avoid the trap sprung on them during the massive fighter sweeps of two days previously. Be that as it may, bitter fighting took place on this Monday, and both sides suffered heavy casualties.

After a solitary reconnaissance Ju 88 had been shot down by three Hurricanes of No. 151 Squadron led by Fg. Off. Kenneth Blair 90 miles off the Lincolnshire coast at 07.15 hours, the day's attacks opened with a two-wave raid totalling 200 aircraft which crossed the Kent coast west of Dover soon after 09.00 hours and made for London. Met by eight squadrons of Hurricanes and four of Spitfires, the bombers were generally turned away as they reached the Maidstone area, three Ju 88s and four Bf 109s falling for the loss of three Hurricanes.

The Messerschmitt Bf 109E-1 flown by Oberleutnant Karl Fischer of 7./JG 27 on 30th September. This pilot dived to attack two Anson training aircraft, misjudged a steep turn and stalled, crashing in Windsor Great Park.

An hour later Sperrle tried a free chase using a mixed formation of Bf 109s of JG 2 and 5./JG 53, and Bf 110s of ZG 26. This force flew from the Cherbourg Peninsula in the direction of Weymouth Bay, and met with little success; the range was long for the Bf 109s, and a strong force of 60 Hurricanes and eighteen Spitfires barred their way and prevented any penetration.

Between mid-day and mid-afternoon Kesselring sent upwards of one hundred bombers and two hundred fighters over the Sussex coast in an effort to reach London. One *Gruppe* of KG 30's Junkers Ju 88s reached the outskirts of the city, together with a formation of Bf 109s from JG 27; this *Jagdgeschwader* suffered heavily on the 30th, losing eight aircraft and five pilots.

One final major attack was launched on this day. While the crews of III./KG 55 rested after their long night raid on Liverpool, I. and II.*Gruppen*, KG 55 were briefed for an attack on the Westland factory at Yeovil. Forty Heinkels escorted by Bf 110s crossed the Dorset coast near Weymouth shortly after 16.30 hours, and were met by twenty Hurricanes and Spitfires of Nos. 56 and 152 Squadrons. As the raid approached Yeovil the Hurricanes of No. 504 Squadron joined the fight and the Heinkels turned back. They were unable to identify their target through the scattered cloud, and jettisoned their bombs, many of which again fell on Sherbourne. The Bf 110 crews fought well on this mission and, suffering damage to only one of their number, shot down five Hurricanes and one Spitfire. *Kampfgeschwader 55*, which had been worked extremely hard over the past week, lost another four Heinkels and seventeen men.

R.A.F. FIGHTER COMMAND LOSSES—MONDAY 30th SEPTEMBER 1940

1.	41 Sqn., Rochford	C	Shot down by Bf 109s and force landed at Hawkinge on fire; pilot (unknown) unhurt.	13.40 hrs.	Not known		Spitfire	—	Cat. 3 Burnt
2.	41 Sqn., Rochford	C	Landed damaged at Hornchurch after combat with Bf 109s over Dungeness; pilot unhurt.	13.55 hrs.	Not known	Spitfire	—	Cat. 1 Damaged
3.	56 Sqn., Boscombe Down	C	Shot down by enemy fighters over Bournemouth; crashed at East Knighton, pilot with slight wounds.	A11.30 hrs.	Fg. Off. K.J. Marston	Hurricane	P2866	Cat. 3 Destroyed
4.	56 Sqn., Boscombe Down	C	Shot down by enemy fighters over Portland; pilot crash landed with broken arm.	17.00 hrs.	Sgt. R.W. Ray	Hurricane	P3655	Cat. 3 Destroyed
5.	56 Sqn., Boscombe Down	C	Shot down by Bf 110s over Portland; pilot believed to have baled out, unhurt.	17.00 hrs.	Flt. Lt. R.S.J. Edwards	Hurricane	P3088	Cat. 3 Destroyed
6.	56 Sqn., Boscombe Down	C	Shot down by Bf 110s over Portland; crash landed on Chesil Bank; pilot unhurt.	17.00 hrs.	Plt. Off. M.H. Constable-Maxwell	Hurricane	L1764	Cat. 3 Destroyed
7.	56 Sqn., Boscombe Down	C	Shot down by Bf 110s over Portland; pilot baled out with leg wounds. Aircraft crashed at Okeford Fitzpaine N.E. of Bladford Forum.	A16.50 hrs.	Sgt. P.H. Fox	Hurricane	N2434	Cat. 3 Destroyed
8.	56 Sqn., Boscombe Down	C	Damaged by Bf 110s near Portland; pilot force landed, unhurt, at Warmwell.	A16.50 hrs.	Flt. Lt. H.M. Pinfold	Hurricane	P2910	Cat. 2 Damaged
9.	56 Sqn., Boscombe Down	C	Damaged by Bf 110s near Portland; pilot force landed, unhurt, at Warmwell.	A16.50 hrs.	Plt. Off. B.J. Wicks	Hurricane	P3870	Cat. 2 Damaged
10.	92 Sqn., Biggin Hill	C	Force landed at Shoreham after combat with Bf 109s near Brighton; pilot slightly wounded	16.50 hrs.	Plt. Off. A.R. Wright	Spitfire	X4069	Cat. 1 Damaged
11.	151 Sqn., Digby	C	Damaged by fire from Ju 88 off Lincolnshire coast; pilot unhurt.	07.15 hrs.	Fg. Off. K.H. Blair	Hurricane	P2826	Cat. 1 Damaged
12.	151 Sqn., Digby	C	Damaged by fire from Ju 88 off Lincolnshire coast; pilot unhurt.	07.15 hrs.	Sgt. D.B.F. Nicholls	Hurricane	P5182	Cat. 1 Damaged
13.	152 Sqn., Warmwell	C	Shot down by Bf 110s over Portland and believed crashed into the sea; pilot killed.	A17.00 hrs.	Sgt. L.A.E. Reddington	Spitfire	L1072	Cat. 3 Missing
14.	152 Sqn.	C	Damaged by Bf 110s at Portland; pilot unhurt.	A17.00 hrs.	Not known	Spitfire	—	Cat. 2 Damaged
15.	152 Sqn.	C	Damaged by Bf 110s at Portland; pilot unhurt.	A17.00 hrs.	Not known	Spitfire	—	Cat. 2 Damaged
16.	152 Sqn.	C	Damaged by Bf 110s at Portland; pilot unhurt.	A17.00 hrs.	Not known	Spitfire	—	Cat. 2 Damaged
17.	152 Sqn.	C	Damaged by Bf 110s at Portland; pilot unhurt.	A17.10 hrs.	Not known	Spitfire	—	Cat. 1 Damaged
18.	219 Sqn., Catterick	NC	Night take-off accident; aircraft disintegrated, killing entire crew.	21.40 hrs.	Sgt. C. Goodwin Sgt. G.E. Sheppherd LAC J.P. McCaul	Blenheim	L1261	Cat. 3 Destroyed
19.	222 Sqn., Hornchurch	C	Shot down by Bf 109 and crash landed at Denham; pilot badly wounded.	13.40 hrs.	Sgt. I. Hutchinson	Spitfire	P9492	Cat. 3 Destroyed
20.	229 Sqn., Northolt	C	Shot down by Bf 109s over Kent; pilot baled out at West Malling, wounded in the leg.	09.35 hrs.	Plt. Off. F.A. Robshaw	Hurricane	P3227	Cat. 3 Destroyed
21.	229 Sqn., Northolt	C	Shot down by Bf 109s and pilot baled out at Edenbridge, wounded in the leg.	09.37 hrs.	Plt. Off. N.K. Stansfeld	Hurricane	N2652	Cat. 3 Destroyed
22.	229 Sqn., Northolt	C	Damaged by Bf 109s near Maidstone; pilot returned unhurt.	09.40 hrs.	Plt. Off. R.A.L. Duvivier	Hurricane	P3422	Cat. 2 Damaged
23.	229 Sqn., Northolt	C	Slightly damaged by Bf 109s near Maidstone; pilot returned with foot wound.	09.43 hrs.	Sgt. R.J. Ommaney	Hurricane	N2647	Cat. 1 Damaged
24.	229 Sqn., Northolt	C	Shot down in flames by Bf 109s at Ightham, Kent; pilot died in his cockpit.	09.43 hrs.	Plt. Off. M. Ravenhill	Hurricane	P2815	Cat. 3 Burnt
25.	229 Sqn., Northolt	C	Hit by return fire from Do 17 over Kent; pilot force landed on beach at Lydd, unhurt.	13.45 hrs.	Plt. Off. V. Ortmans	Hurricane	R4112	Cat. 2 Damaged
26.	229 Sqn., Northolt	C	Pilot baled out; location and circumstances not recorded.	A17.00 hrs.	Plt. Off. L.B.R. Way	Hurricane	P3037	Cat. 3 Destroyed
27.	229 Sqn., Northolt	C	Pilot baled out with nose wound; location and circumstances not recorded. (Pilot on attachment from No. 1 Squadron)	A17.00 hrs.	Sgt. C.G. Hodson	Hurricane	V7411	Cat. 3 Destroyed
28.	238 Sqn., Middle Wallop	NC	Air collision with Item 29; pilot baled out unhurt, north of Shaftesbury.	11.45 hrs.	Plt. Off. V.C. Simmonds	Hurricane	L1702	Cat. 3 Destroyed
29.	238 Sqn., Middle Wallop	NC	Air collision with Item 28; pilot baled out unhurt, north of Shaftesbury.	11.45 hrs.	Plt. Off. R.A. Kings	Hurricane	N2474	Cat. 3 Destroyed
30.	302 Sqn., Leconfield	—	Taxying collision with Item 31; pilot unhurt.	Not known	Sgt. J. Zaluski	Hurricane	P3935	Cat. 1 Damaged
31.	302 Sqn., Leconfield	—	Taxying collision with Item 30; unmanned.	Not known	Nil	Hurricane	P3924	Cat. 1 Damaged
32.	303 Sqn., Northolt	C	Crashed at Lydd after combat with Do 17, possibly shot down by Bf 109; pilot unhurt.	13.30 hrs.	Plt. Off. J. Radomski	Hurricane	P3663	Cat. 3 Destroyed
33.	501 Sqn., Kenley	C	Damaged by Bf 109s; pilot, unhurt, force landed at Pembury, Kent.	09.35 hrs.	Fg. Off. N.J.M. Barry	Hurricane	L1657	Cat. 2 Damaged
34.	504 Sqn., Filton	C	Shot down and crash landed south of Yeovil; pilot unhurt.	A17.00 hrs.	Sgt. B.M. Bush	Hurricane	P3021	Cat. 3 Destroyed

35.	504 Sqn., Filton	C	Shot down and force landed south of Yeovil; pilot unhurt.	A17.00 hrs.	Plt. Off. E.M. Frisby	Hurricane	*P2987*	Cat. 2 Damaged
36.	504 Sqn., Filton	C	Shot down and force landed south of Yeovil; pilot unhurt.	A17.00 hrs.	Sgt. W.H. Banks	Hurricane	*P3774*	Cat. 2 Damaged
37.	504 Sqn., Filton	C	Shot down south of Weymouth; pilot killed. Body recovered from the sea at Yarmouth, Isle of Wight, 10-10-40, and buried at Fawley.	A17.15 hrs.	Fg. Off. J.R. Hardacre	Hurricane	*P3414*	Cat. 3 Lost.

LUFTWAFFE LOSSES—MONDAY 30th SEPTEMBER 1940

1.	1.(F)/123	CM	Shot down by 151 Sqn. Hurricanes of Blair, Ingle-Fince and Nicholls 90 miles off the Lincolnshire coast at 07.20 hrs.	Junkers Ju 88A-1 (0385 : 4U+MH)	100 %	Fw. Waak, Uffz. Essmann and Uffz. Obermayer killed; Ltn. Walter Frenzel missing.
2.	4./KG 2	CM	Force landed at Orléans after bombing sortie.	Dornier Do 17Z-2 (3420 : U5+EM)	15 %	Crew unhurt.
3.	8./KG 2	CM	Crashed at Bertincourt after bombing sortie.	Dornier Do 17Z-3 (2861 : U5+BS)	100 %	Ltn. Günther Scheffel + three killed.
4.	Stab III./KG 3	CM	Force landed at St. Omer after bombing sortie.	Dornier Do 17Z-2 (3360 : 5K+AD)	50 %	Crew unhurt.
5.	7./KG 3	CM	Crash landed at Boulogne after bombing sortie.	Dornier Do 17Z-3 (2822 : 5K+GR)	70 %	Crew unhurt.
6.	8./KG 3	CM	Shot down by British fighters over South-East England.	Dornier Do 17Z-3 (4227 : 5K+HR)	100 %	Fw. Schierling, Fw. Bauer, Uffz. Schonn, Uffz. Schroff and Fw. Salomo missing.
7.	3./KG 30	CM	Crashed on landing at Gilze-Rijen after bombing sortie.	Junkers Ju 88A-1 (0233 : 4D+DL)	100 %	Four crew members killed.
8.	II./KG 30	CM	Force landed at Gilze-Rijen after bombing sortie.	Junkers Ju 88A-1 (6074 : 4D+AM)	40 %	Crew unhurt.
9.	II./KG 30	CM	Landed damaged at Gilze-Rijen after bombing sortie.	Junkers Ju 88A-1 (0280 : 4D+FL)	15 %	Two crew members wounded.
10.	II./KG 30	CM	Damaged by British fighters over South-East England.	Junkers Ju 88A-1 (0164 : 4D+GM)	5 %	Crew unhurt.
11.	5./KG 30	CM	Landing accident at Lombartzyde after bombing sortie over Southern England.	Junkers Ju 88A-1 (4030 : 4D+GK)	50 %	Crew unhurt.
12.	III./KG 30	CM	Crashed at Kamenz; not the result of combat.	Junkers Ju 88A-1 (5062 : 4D+AT)	100 %	Four crew members killed.
13.	9./KG 30	CM	Missing from bombing sortie over South-East England; fate not known.	Junkers Ju 88A-1 (3067 : 4D+BZ)	100 %	Oblt. Julius Richter, Uffz. Fuchs and Fw. Läge missing.
14.	I./KG 51	CM	Shot down by British fighters south of London; location of crash not known.	Junkers Ju 88A-1 (2063 : 9K+DH)	100 %	Fw. Fritz Paczinski, Gefr. Peuka, Gefr. Roppert, Gefr. Eduard Dürrschmidt killed.
15.	6./KG 53	CM	Crashed on landing at Vendeville airfield on return from bombing sortie with battle damage.	Heinkel He 111H-3 (3312 : A1+ER)	60 %	Crew unhurt.
16.	I./KG 54	CM	Shot down by 602 Sqn. Spitfires off Selsey Bill at 16.10 hrs.	Junkers Ju 88A-1 (7090)	100 %	Crew, unhurt, rescued by *Seenotflugkommando.*
17.	St.St./KG 55	CM	Shot down by British fighters into English Channel; three crew seen to bale out.	Heinkel He 111P-2 (2836 : G1+JA)	100 %	Uffz. Barabas killed; Maj. Ernst Kühl + 2, wounded, rescued by *Seenotflugkommando.*
18.	I./KG 55	CM	Shot down by 238 Sqn. Hurricane of Doe south of Portland at 16.40 hrs.	Heinkel He 111P-2 (1616 : G1+AL)	100 %	Oblt. Hans Mössner, Uffz. Reiter, Uffz. Trenkmann, Fl. Geist and Gefr. Thümel missing.
19.	II./KG 55	CM	Shot down by 238 Sqn. Hurricane of Kucera south of Portland at 16.40 hrs.	Heinkel He 111P-2 (1545 : G1+AM)	100 %	Uffz. Kübler killed; Uffz. Eggert Ogefr.Geyer, Gefr. Rösel and Gefr. Biedmann missing.
20.	II./KG 55	CM	Shot down by 504 Sqn. Hurricanes near Portland at A.16.55 hrs.	Heinkel He 111P-2 (2643 : G1+CM)	100 %	Ogefr.Schocke killed; Gefr.Rudek, Ofw. Gittler, Gefr. Bauer and Gefr. Strauss missing.
21.	Stab I./KG 77	CM	Landing accident at Chamby airfield; cause not notified.	Junkers Ju 88A-1 (4050 : 3Z+DB)	15 %	Crew unhurt.
22.	2./KG 77	CM	Shot down by 501 Sqn. Hurricane of Farnes and crashed at Gatwick at A.17.00 hrs.	Junkers Ju 88A-1 (2142 : 3Z+DK)	100 %	Uffz. Georg Klasing killed; Oblt. Friedrich Oeser, Gefr. Hülsmann and Ofw. Görke missing.
23.	III./LG 1	NCM	Force landing near Illesheim; cause not known.	Junkers Ju 88A-1(6061)	20 %	Crew unhurt.
24.	12./LG 1	NCM	Crashed at Antricourt with engine failure; one crew member baled out too low for parachute to open.	Junkers Ju 87B-1 (0217 : L1+JW)	100 %	One crew member killed.
25.	2./ZG 26	CM	Damaged by 56 Sqn. Hurricane of Higginson over South Coast at 11.15 hrs.	Messerschmitt Bf 110 D-0	60 %	Two crew members wounded.
26.	I./JG 2	CM	Shot down by British fighters over Southern England.	Messerschmitt Bf 109 E-4 (0847)	100 %	Fw. Hermes missing.
27.	II./JG 2	CM	Shot down by British fighters over Southern England.	Messerschmitt Bf 109 E-4 (3447)	100 %	Gefr. Schuhmacher missing.
28.	II./JG 2	CM	Shot down by British fighters over Southern England.	Messerschmitt Bf 109 E-4 (4861)	100 %	Uffz. Dollinger killed.
29.	II./JG 2	CM	Minor landing accident at Calais-Marck after combat.	Messerschmitt Bf 109 E-4 (5391)	5 %	Pilot unhurt.
30.	III./JG 2	CM	Suffered take-off collision with Item 31 at Octeville airfield.	Messerschmitt Bf 109 E-4 (4831)	100 %	Pilot killed.
31.	III./JG 2	CM	Suffered take-off collision with Item 30 at Octeville airfield.	Messerschmitt Bf 109 E-4 (3338)	100 %	Pilot killed.
32.	Stab/JG 26	CM	Shot down by 222 Sqn. Spitfire of Edsall over South-West London at A.13.30 hrs.	Messerschmitt Bf 109 E-4 (5818)	100 %	Hptm. Walter Kienzle, wounded, made P.O.W.
33.	3./JG 26	CM	Force landed at Audembert after fighter combat.	Messerschmitt Bf 109 E-1 (6346)	40 %	Pilot unhurt.
34.	II./JG 26	CM	Shot down by British fighter over Southern England.	Messerschmitt Bf 109 E-4 (1190)	100 %	Uffz. Perez missing.
35.	6./JG 26	CM	Damaged by British fighters and force landed at Coquelles.	Messerschmitt Bf 109 E-1 (2688)	30 %	Pilot unhurt.
36.	7./JG 26	CM	Shot down by British fighters south-east of London.	Messerschmitt Bf 109 E-4 (3645)	100 %	Gefr. Ziemenz killed.
37.	9./JG 26	CM	Shot down by 66 Sqn. Spitfires over Thames Estuary at A.09.40 hrs.	Messerschmitt Bf 109 E-1 (4820)	100 %	Gefr. Hornatschet killed.
38.	9./JG 26	CM	Crash landed at Caffiers after fighter combat.	Messerschmitt Bf 109 E-4 (3891)	100 %	Pilot wounded.

Luftwaffe Losses, 30th September 1940—*continued*

39.	1./JG 27	CM	Serious taxying accident at Guines-West airfield (collided with wreckage of Item 40).	Messerschmitt Bf 109 E-1 (4878)	70 %	Uffz. Fritz Neef injured.
40.	2./JG 27	CM	Crash landed at Guines-West after fighter combat.	Messerschmitt Bf 109 E-4 (2801)	70 %	Ltn. Willi Kothmann wounded.
41.	2./JG 27	CM	Shot down by 303 Sqn. Hurricane of Frantisek near Croydon at 17.10 hrs.	Messerschmitt Bf 109 E-4 (3763)	100 %	Oblt. Hans Bertram, *Adj.*, killed.
42.	3./JG 27	CM	Shot down by 303 Sqn. Hurricane of Urbano-wicz near Croydon at A.17.10 hrs.	Messerschmitt Bf 109 E-4 (3630)	100 %	Uffz. Richard Sander killed.
43.	4./JG 27	CM	Shot down by 41 Sqn. Spitfire of Baker near Dungeness at 13.45 hrs.	Messerschmitt Bf 109 E-1 (6306)	100 %	Uffz.Robert Hammer made P.O.W.
44.	6./JG 27	CM	Shot down by 92 Sqn. Spitfire of Wright over Channel off Shoreham at A.17.00 hrs.	Messerschmitt Bf 109 E-1 (3859)	100 %	Ltn. Herbert Schmidt, wounded, made P.O.W.
45.	7./JG 27	CM	Shot down by 92 Sqn. Spitfire of Fokes over South Coast at A.17.00 hrs.	Messerschmitt Bf 109 E-1 (4851)	100 %	Oblt. Karl Fischer made P.O.W.
46.	9./JG 27	CM	Force landed at Marquise after fighter combat.	Messerschmitt Bf 109 E-4 (1577)	70 %	Pilot unhurt.
47.	7./JG 51	CM	Landing accident at Clairmarais after combat.	Messerschmitt Bf 109 E-4 (1544)	50 %	Pilot unhurt.
48.	7./JG 51	CM	Shot down by 303 Sqn. Hurricane of Karubin in the London area.	Messerschmitt Bf 109 E-1 (3391)	100 %	Uffz. Hubel killed.
49.	7./JG 51	CM	Shot down by British fighters over south London.	Messerschmitt Bf 109 E-1 (4856)	100 %	Uffz. Limpert killed.
50.	9./JG 51	CM	Crashed into the English Channel after running out of fuel.	Messerschmitt Bf 109 E-4 (1331)	100 %	Ltn. Gerhard Canier killed.
51.	i./JG 52	CM	Shot down by 603 Sqn. Spitfire of Boulter over south-east England.	Messerschmitt Bf 109 E-1 (1391)	100 %	Oblt. Kurt Kirchner missing.
52.	3./JG 52	CM	Missing after combat in the Tonbridge area.	Messerschmitt Bf 109 E-4 (1262)	100 %	Uffz. Wolf missing.
53.	4./JG 52	CM	Missing after combat over South London.	Messerschmitt Bf 109 E-4 (3417)	100 %	Gefr. Mommert missing.
54.	6./JG 52	CM	Missing after combat over South London.	Messerschmitt Bf 109 E-1 (3192)	100 %	Gefr. Strasser missing.
55.	I./JG 53	CM	Shot down by 213 Sqn. Hurricane of Atkinson over Southern England.	Messerschmitt Bf 109 E-4 (1325)	100 %	Fw. Schulz missing.
56.	II./JG 53	CM	Shot down off Sussex coast; pilot baled out.	Messerschmitt Bf 109 E-1 (2693)	100 %	Pilot, unhurt, rescued by *Seenotflugkommando*.
57.	II./JG 53	CM	Missing after combat off Sussex coast.	Messerschmitt Bf 109 E-1 (6384)	100 %	Uffz. Bogel missing.
58.	III./JG 53	CM	Missing after combat in the Haywards Heath area.	Messerschmitt Bf 109 E-1 (5175)	100 %	Uffz. Poschenrieder missing.
59.	7./JG 54	CM	Missing after fighter combat over Southern England.	Messerschmitt Bf 109 E-1 (6050)	100 %	Uffz. Marks missing.
60.	9./JG 54	CM	Missing after fighter combat over Southern England.	Messerschmitt Bf 109 E-4 (5116)	100 %	Uffz. Braats missing.

So ended September 1940, a supremely fateful month in the history of Britain. Hitler's planned invasion had been thwarted, and the *Luftwaffe* defeated by day. It may be asked what measure of defeat the German Air Force had suffered that it could still hurl 200 aircraft at a time against British targets? Yet the fact remains that while, at the beginning of the month, it could launch massive raids on almost any target within range of its escort fighters and bomb those targets with relative impunity, at the close of the month it could no longer expect to do so. Local air superiority over Southern England, previously achieved on many occasions by Göring's *Jagdflieger*, now rested firmly in the grasp of Park, Brand and Leigh-Mallory.

September's battles had cost the *Luftwaffe* dearly in men and aircraft; and for all the prohibitions laid against multiple-officer crews, Germany still lost four *Geschwaderkommodore*, thirteen *Gruppenkommandeure* and 31 *Staffelkapitäne* killed, missing or taken prisoner in the space of 30 days. This scale of losses among field commanders was unacceptable when set against the results achieved.

Göring's favourite weapon, the Stuka—whose value in the Battle of Britain had clearly been overplayed—had taken virtually no part in the month's operations, having shown itself incapable of living in the English skies. The *Zerstörer* had suffered disastrously time and time again when deprived of single-seater company, yet still soldiered on by virtue of its range and useful light bombing capability. Nor had the German bombers fared much better in daylight. First, the

now-elderly Dornier Do 17s of KG 2, KG 3 and KG 76 had fallen in the raids on and around London early in the month and on the memorable 15th, and by the end of the month were far less frequent visitors to the British shores in daylight. Then it had been the turn of the Heinkels of KG 1 and KG 55—and each one that fell took with it a crew of five or six men. Finally, in an attempt to seek safety in speed, Göring had placed more reliance upon the excellent Junkers Ju 88—but a single *Geschwader*, KG 77, had suffered the loss of 40 aircraft in fifteen days—some thirty per cent casualties, and another 160 trained airmen were lost to the *Luftwaffe*.

While the *Luftwaffe* lost its strategic purpose, and indulged in a welter of confused tactics to very little military advantage, Dowding had continued to defend the British Isles with scarcely any deviation from the now firmly established system of defence. In the all-important Groups, both Park and Brand had worked well together as partners, identifying the enemy's changing tactics and adapting their own with great flexibility to meet changing situations. The wracking decision to "milk" and dismember some of the very best squadrons at the beginning of the month had proved absolutely correct, so that the defence stood firmer than ever before. Only the increasingly vociferous "Wing" controversy between Park and Leigh-Mallory threatened the otherwise smooth running of Fighter Command.

It was fitting that on this last day of September Dowding should be named by H.M. King George VI as Knight Grand Commander of the Order of the Bath.

A Hurricane taking off on a night patrol. The continuing inability of the regular night fighter squadrons to get to grips with the German night raiders prompted Dowding to order several Hurricane squadrons to assume night fighting duties—but with little immediate success.

CHAPTER 9

OCTOBER ANTI-CLIMAX

Tuesday 1st October

Though German tactics were once again to change drastically during the course of the coming week, there was little evidence of this during the first two days of the month.

The first raid of the day, which was reported by Ventnor to be approaching from the south, turned in over the Nab and carried out a swift attack on the Portsmouth area in the face of determined interceptions by squadrons from Tangmere and Middle Wallop. Although only one of the raiders was shot down, the enemy's aim was severely upset and little significant bomb damage was suffered. The one aircraft destroyed was a Bf 110D of ZG 26, shot down by Plt. Off. Robert Doe of No. 238 Squadron, one of Fighter Command's top scoring pilots during the Battle. He reported that among the raiders he saw a couple of Focke-Wulf Fw 200 four-engine bombers; this has since been authenticated, and it is now known that KG 40, Sperrle's long-range maritime reconnaissance bomber unit equipped with these aircraft in Western France, accompanied bombing raids over Southern and Western Britain on at least half a dozen occasions. Other aircraft of this *Geschwader* had from time to time carried out lone sorties from Norway against targets in Scotland, flying on southwards over Wales and the Irish Sea to their base near Brest.

On this day *Lehrgeschwader 1*'s Messerschmitt Bf 109s joined in several free chases which were sent in over Kent,

Surrey and Sussex; some of these aircraft were of the newly-introduced Bf 109E-7 version, equipped to carry a single 250-kilo bomb or a long-range fuel tank on shackles under the belly. As will become evident, these aircraft were to come into widespread use; however, unlike the specially-trained pilots of 3./Erpr.Gr. 210, the majority of *Jagdgeschwader* personnel were unable to achieve more than nuisance value with the bomb-carrying single-seaters.

One of the pilots shot down on this day was Plt. Off. "Ben" Bennions of No. 41 Squadron who, in the past month had shot down eight enemy aircraft—seven of them fighters—despite being wounded in the foot. Following the loss of his C.O. and flight commander, he had frequently led the squadron in action, even though he was only newly commisioned. In the afternoon of 1st October his Spitfire was shot down over Henfield in Sussex, and Bennions baled out with terrible wounds, blinded in one eye and with a head wound that left part of his brain exposed. He later underwent plastic surgery by McIndoe at East Grinstead. He nevertheless recovered and returned to flying Spitfires in the Mediterranean in 1943, and left the R.A.F. in 1946 as a Squadron Leader. He received just one gallantry award, the D.F.C., announced on the day he was finally shot down—1st October 1940.

R.A.F. FIGHTER COMMAND LOSSES—TUESDAY 1st OCTOBER 1940

1.	3 Sqn., Turnhouse	NC	Force landed at Chryston, Lanarkshire, due to mishandling of fuel cock; pilot unhurt.	Not known	Plt. Off. J. Lonsdale	Hurricane	P3261	Cat. 2 Damaged
2.	41 Sqn., Hornchurch	C	Shot down by Bf 109s over Horsham, Sussex; pilot baled out grievously wounded.	14.30 hrs.	Plt. Off. G.H. Bennions	Spitfire	X4559	Cat. 3 Destroyed
3.	238 Sqn., Middle Wallop	C	Crashed on return from combat with Bf 109s; pilot unhurt.	11.40 hrs.	Plt. Off. A.R. Covington	Hurricane	R4099	Cat. 3. Destroyed

R.A.F. Losses, 1st October 1940—*continued*

4.	238 Sqn., Middle Wallop	C	Missing after combat with Bf 110s over Poole; pilot assumed killed, lost at sea.	11.30 hrs.	Sgt. F.A. Sibley	Hurricane	*P3599*	Cat. 3 Missing
5.	248 Sqn., Sumburgh	C	Missing from reconnaissance sortie over Norwegian coast; crew reported killed.	Not known	Plt. Off. C.C. Bennett, Sgt. G.S. Clarke, Sgt. G.B. Brash	Blenheim	*R3626*	Cat. 3 Missing
6.	302 Sqn., Duxford	NC	Froce landed at Bramcote when gun panel came adrift; pilot unhurt.	Not known	Plt. Off. W.E. Karwowski	Hurricane	—	Cat. 2 Damaged
7.	607 Sqn., Tangmere	C	Shot down by enemy fighters near Swanage; pilot killed.	11.20 hrs.	Flt. Lt. C.E. Bowen	Hurricane	*V6686*	Cat. 3 Missing
8.	607 Sqn., Tangmere	C	Shot down by enemy fighters near Swanage; pilot killed.	11.20 hrs.	Sgt. N. Brumby	Hurricane	*P2900*	Cat. 3 Missing

LUFTWAFFE LOSSES—TUESDAY 1st OCTOBER 1940

1.	I./KG 2	NCM	Crashed at Mons-au-Chausée; cause not known.	Dornier Do 17Z-2 (1177 : U5+BH)	100 %	Two crew members killed.
2.	9./KG 30	CM	Said to have been shot at by night fighter (German ?) and crashed at Kloppenburg.	Junkers Ju 88A-1 (5343 : 4K+FZ)	100 %	Crew baled out unhurt.
3.	I./KG 51	CM	Take-off accident at Corbeil; crashed and burned.	Junkers Ju 88A-1 (3085)	100 %	Oblt.Günther Heinig, Fw. Alois Kaltenhauser, Fw. Helmut Muche, Fw. Hans Kussin killed.
4.	II./KG 53	CM	Shot down by *flak* during night bombing sortie over Britain.	Heinkel He 111H-2 (5546 : A1+LN)	100 %	Uffz. Wagner, Gefr. Möhlenhoff, Gefr. Günther, Uffz. König and Gefr. Petroll missing.
5.	I./LG 1	CM	Engine failure on take-off at Chateaudun.	Junkers Ju 88A-1 (2154)	20 %	Crew unhurt.
6.	I./ZG 26	CM	Shot down by 238 Sqn. Hurricane of Doe south of Poole at 11.20 hrs.	Messerschmitt Bf 110D (4212)	100 %	Ltn. Scharnhorst + 1 killed.
7.	4./JG 26	CM	Probably shot down by 41 Sqn. Spitfire of Bennions over Sussex at A.14.30 hrs.	Messerschmitt Bf 109 E-1 (1190)	100 %	Uffz. Blüder killed.
8.	1./JG 51	CM	Shot down by 303 Sqn. Hurricane of Kent over South Coast at 14.20 hrs.	Messerschmitt Bf 109 E-4 (5814)	100 %	Uffz. Garneth missing.
9.	5./196	—	Destroyed in storm at Cherbourg anchorage.	Arado Ar 196	100 %	No aircrew casualties.
10.	5./196	—	Destroyed in storm at Cherbourg anchorage.	Arado Ar 196	100 %	No aircrew casualties.
11.	5./196	—	Destroyed in storm at Cherbourg anchorage.	Arado Ar 196	100 %	No aircrew casualties.
12.	5./196	—	Destroyed in storm at Cherbourg anchorage.	Arado Ar 196	100 %	No aircrew casualties.
13.	*Luftflotten-res.3*	NCM	Crashed near Nancy following engine failure.	Junkers Ju 88A-1 (7159)	100 %	One killed and one injured.
14.	*Korpsfugrungskette* X *Fliegerkorps*	CM	Damaged by *flak* over East Coast of Scotland.	Heinkel He 111H-4 (3257 : P4+BA)	50 %	Two crew members wounded.

Wednesday 2nd October

The *Luftwaffe* took advantage of the clear skies to send numerous high-flying fighters and fighter-bombers of *Jafu 2* to attack London and Biggin Hill throughout the day. Flying for the most part at nearly 30,000 feet, they were effectively beyond the reach of Park's Hurricanes, but the Spitfires of No. 603 Squadron had something of a field day, shooting down three Bf 109s of 8./JG 53 «*Pik As*» over the Thames Estuary during the morning.

Over the north of the Estuary a Dornier of KG 2 had been the subject of a fiasco. Four Hurricanes, which had already been on patrol for 90 minutes, were vectored on to the lone raider; however, three ran out of fuel in the course of their attack, and had to force land. The last pilot (Flt. Lt. Alfred Bayne) did manage to shoot down the Dornier near Pulham; he landed beside it, inspected it, saw that the crew was taken prisoner, and took off again only to run out of fuel. He managed to put down safely at Martlesham, insisting that the enemy aircraft be credited to all four pilots!

Dowding's foresight in authorising the formation of the Spotting Flights (see 21st September) was now to be fully vindicated. He did not yet know that an instruction had been issued in *Luftflotte 2* for one *Gruppe* in each *Jagdgeschwader* to fit bomb racks to its "Emils", and it was these fighter-bombers which were beginning to appear high over Kent. Within a fortnight Kesselring would possess more than 200 of these "*Jabos*"[1] —a formidable raiding force, bearing in mind that only one-third of Park's fighters—perhaps six

Luftwaffe personnel loading a 250-kilo bomb under a Bf 109E-7 during the final stages of the Battle of Britain; it says much for the qualities of this German fighter that it could operate at altitudes of 30,000 feet or over while carrying this load. By the middle of October one *Gruppe* in each of Kesselring's *Jagdgeschwader* had been equipped entirely with "*Jabos*" (Photo: R.A.F. Museum)

squadrons of No. 11 Group—could reach their altitude before they dropped their bombs.

---

[1] "*Jabo*" = *Jagdbomber,* or fighter-bomber.

347

R.A.F. FIGHTER COMMAND LOSSES—WEDNESDAY 2nd OCTOBER 1940

1.	17 Sqn., Debden	C	Force landed near Pulham, short of fuel; pilot unhurt.	10.05 hrs.	Fg. Off. H.P. Blatchford	Hurricane	—	Cat. 1 Damaged
2.	17 Sqn., Debden	C	Force landed near Pulham, short of fuel; pilot unhurt.	10.05 hrs.	Plt. Off. F. Fajtl	Hurricane	—	Cat. 1 Damaged
3.	41 Sqn., Hornchurch	C	Collided with parked aircraft during scramble; pilot slightly injured.	16.35 hrs.	Sgt. J.K. Norwell	Spitfire	X4545	Cat. 3 Destroyed
4.	41 Sqn., Hornchurch	—	Struck by aircraft in Item 3 above; no pilot.	16.35 hrs.	Nil	Spitfire	—	Cat. 3 Destroyed
5.	603 Sqn., Hornchurch	C	Shot down by Bf 109 over Croydon; pilot baled out but suffered severe leg injuries.	10.30 hrs.	Plt. Off. P.G. Dexter	Spitfire	P9553	Cat. 3 Destroyed

LUFTWAFFE LOSSES—WEDNESDAY 2nd OCTOBER 1940

1.	3.(H)/21	NCM	Crash landed at Moerbecke; cause not notified.	Henschel Hs 126B (4029)	70 %	Crew unhurt.
2.	Stab/KG 2	CM	Shot down by 17 Sqn. Hurricanes of Blatchford, Fajtl and Ross near Pulham, South Norfolk, at 09.50 hrs.	Dornier Do 17Z-3 (3423 : U5+FA)	100 %	Oblt. Hans Langer, St.Kap., Oblt. Erich Eitze, Uffz. Seidel and Uffz. Bellmann made P.O.W.s.
3.	4./KG 2	CM	Crashed near Paris with combat damage; crew baled out.	Dornier Do 17Z-3	100 %	Crew unhurt.
4.	9./KG 3	CM	Crashed at Le Culot; cause not notified.	Dornier Do 17Z-2 (3270 : 5K+CT)	100 %	Ltn. Rudolf Schulze + three killed.
5.	8./KG 4	CM	Shot down by 602 Sqn. Spitfires of Barthropp and Boyd 35 miles south of Shoreham at 08.50 hrs.	Junkers Ju 88A-5 (8128 : 5J+US)	100 %	Uffz. Meierhofer, Gefr. Scholz, Ogefr. Hansmeier and Ogefr. Preugscha missing.
6.	9./KG 4	CM	Landing accident at Schipol, cause not notified.	Junkers Ju 88A-5 (6138 : 5J+KT)	40 %	Crew unhurt.
7.	1./KG 53	CM	Shot down by 151 Sqn. Hurricane of Smith 10 miles north of Skegness during late afternoon. Crew of five seen to enter dinghy.	Heinkel He 111H-5 (3554 : A1+CH)	100 %	Oblt. Hans Seidel, Ofw. Ziller, Ofw. Zickler, Fw. Weidner and Uffz. Kreuzer made P.O.W.s.
8.	1./KG 53	CM	Became lost; crew baled out and aircraft crashed near Nancy.	Heinkel He 111H-3 (3334 : A1+DB)	100 %	Crew unhurt.
9.	6./KG 3	CM	Landing accident on Vendeville airfield.	Heinkel He 111H-2 (2635 : A1+CP)	10 %	Crew unhurt.
10.	Gesch.Erg.St./	NCM	Struck high ground in the Eifel Mountains in fog.	Dornier Do 17U (2427 : 3Z+FD)	100 %	Six crew members killed.
11.	1./KGr. 126	CM	Shot down by 234 Sqn. Spitfires of Blake and Hookway near Newquay (time not confirmed).	Heinkel He 111H-4 (6948 : 1T+KH)	100 %	Ltn. Kurt-Fritz Schreyer, Gefr. Weger, Uffz. Greeven missing; Ltn.z.s.Günter Grünewald and Uffz. Plenert killed.
12.	7.(F)/LG 2	NCM	Air collision with Item 13 near Brussels.	Messerschmitt Bf 110 C-5 (2263 : L2+DR)	100 %	Oblt. Eckert + one killed.
13.	7.(F)/LG 2	NCM	Air collision with Item 12 near Brussels.	Messerschmitt Bf 110 (2188 : L2+FK)	100 %	Crew unhurt (baled out).
14.	6./JG 27	CM	Landing accident at Bonningues airfield; cause	Messerschmitt Bf 109 E-1 (6351)	60 %	Pilot unhurt.
15.	Stab III./JG 53	CM	Shot down by 66 Sqn. Spitfire of Kendal over the Thames Estuary at 10.16 hrs.	Messerschmitt Bf 109 E-1 (6291)	100 %	Oblt. Walter Radlick killed.
16.	8./JG 53	CM	Shot down by 603 Sqn. Spitfire of Hartas over the Thames Estuary at 10.20 hrs.	Messerschmitt Bf 109 E-4 (5901)	100 %	Oblt. Ludwig Fiel missing.
17.	8./JG 53	CM	Shot down by 603 Sqn. Spitfire of Carbury over the Thames Estuary at 10.20 hrs.	Messerschmitt Bf 109 E-4 (5374)	100 %	Oblt. Siegfried Stronk killed.
18.	8./JG 53	CM	Shot down by 603 Sqn. Spitfire of Dexter over the Thames Estuary at 10.20 hrs.	Messerschmitt Bf 109 E-1 (6370)	100 %	Gefr. Zag missing.
19.	1./506	CM	Shot down by 145 Sqn. Hurricane of de Hemptinne 5 miles south of Kinnaird's Head at 19.20 hrs.	Heinkel He 115 (2095 : 8L+DL)	100 %	Oblt.z.S. Gottfried Lenz, Uffz. Schweetke and Ogefr. Neuberg missing.
20.	Seenotflug-kommando 4	CM	Aircraft landed in minefield in area of grid Sq. 8166—8241; crew took to dinghy, but this evidently struck mine and all were killed.	Heinkel He 59 (1510 : NO+FU)	100 %	Ltn. Philipp Barbinger killed; Ofw. Niess, Gefr. Brand and Fw. Horr assumed killed.

Thursday 3rd October

The night had brought heavy and widespread raids over Britain, with four *Gruppen* of Sperrle's bombers crossing the Sussex coast to attack London's northern suburbs. Others, at *Staffel* strength or less, had orders to attack airfields, and delayed action bombs landed on or around more than a dozen bases. Once again it was the intrepid members of the bomb disposal squads who stepped into the front line of defence.

Daylight found low cloud with drizzle covering much of the country, and Fighter Command was virtually grounded. Sneak raiders penetrated at some points, but only two aircraft were brought down—both by anti-aircraft fire. One of the sneak raids carried out on this day was by a Junkers Ju 88, almost certainly of *Lehrgeschwader 1*, which swept in at fifty feet over the de Havilland factory at Hatfield in Hertfordshire and "skip-bombed" four 250-kilo weapons off the wet grass of the

airfield into the plant buildings. There were 21 fatalities and 71 people injured, and a sheet-metal shop was destroyed. The bombs also destroyed 80 per cent of the materials assembled for the brilliant new Mosquito bomber. However, the Germans were evidently unaware that the prototype of this aeroplane—even if they were aware of its existence—was, for safety's sake, being manufactured at Salisbury Hall about half a dozen miles from Hatfield. It would fly for the first time about six weeks hence.

The *Luftwaffe* returned during the next night, but much of the bombing was blind, and the only significant target hit was the General Aircraft Company's factory at Feltham, where only minor damage was caused. Two more raiders were brought down by anti-aircraft fire, one of them a pathfinder Heinkel of KGr. 100 (see loss table for 4th October).

The *Werke Nr. 4136* on the tail of this Junkers Ju 88A-1 clearly identifies it as Item 10 in the German loss table for 3rd October—Oberleutnant Siegward Fiebig's aircraft of I.*Gruppe*, KG 77, which fell at Hertingfordbury, Hertfordshire. The light-coloured bars on the fin and wing tip were intended to provide quick air-to-air identification of the bomber's unit.

R.A.F. FIGHTER COMMAND LOSSES—THURSDAY 3rd OCTOBER 1940

| 1. | 600 Sqn., Hornchurch | NC | Aircraft crashed at night at Forrest Row in heavy rain during patrol; entire crew killed. | 03.45 hrs. | Plt. Off. C.A. Hobson
Sgt. D.E. Hughes
Sgt. C.F. Cooper | Blenheim | *L4905* | Cat. 3 Destroyed |

LUFTWAFFE LOSSES—THURSDAY 3rd OCTOBER 1940

1.	1.(F)/122	CM	Believed shot down by Spitfires during the early morning.	Junkers Ju 88A-1 (0328 : F6+BH)	100 %	Ofw. Spanke, Fw. Peters, Ofw. Adler and Uffz. Wabnitz missing.
2.	I./KG 1	CM	Take-off accident at Montdidier airfield.	Heinkel He 111H-3 (6923)	100 %	Oblt. Göhler + three killed.
3.	I./KG 1	CM	Take-off accident at Montdidier airfield.	Heinkel He 111H-3 (6824)	60 %	Crew unhurt.
4.	III./KG 1	NCM	Suffered landing accident at Handorf airfield.	Junkers Ju 88A-1 (6107 : V4+BT)	20 %	Crew unhurt.

Luftwaffe Losses, 3rd October 1940—*continued*

5.	1./KG 2	CM	Became lost and force landed when fuel ran out.	Dornier Do 17Z-2 (2579 : U5+DH)	40 %	Crew unhurt.
6.	2./KG 2	CM	Crashed near Marquise owing to faulty maintenance.	Dornier Do 17Z-3 (2638 : U5+AK)	95 %	One killed and two injured.
7.	5./KG 30	CM	Missing from bombing sortie over England; believed shot down by London *flak*.	Junkers Ju 88A-5 (4169 : 4D+FK)	100 %	Fw. Bunker killed; Uffz. Brandmüller, Gefr. Gerard and Gefr. Balt missing.
8.	7./KG 30	CM	Crashed into sea off Schouwen Island, Holland, following double engine failure.	Junkers Ju 88A-1 (7024 : 4D+AR)	100 %	Oblt. Otto Bieger, Fw. Heilmeier, Gefr.Bauer, Gefr.Herndeck killed.
9.	I./KG 55	CM	Crashed at Le Havre with *flak* damage.	Heinkel He 111H (2749)	100 %	Crew unhurt.
10.	I./KG 77	CM	Missing from bombing sortie over England.	Junkers Ju 88A-1 (4136 : 3Z+BB)	100 %	Oblt. Siegward Fiebig, Fw. Ruthof, Ofw.Göbel, Uffz. Seiffert missing.
11.	Kü.Fl.Gr. 606	CM	Shot down by *flak* defences over West Midlands at night.	Dornier Do 17Z (3491 : 7T+EL)	100 %	Ltn.z.S. Max-Dieter Schmidt and Hgefr. Dorkschmidt killed; Fw. Wilm, Uffz. Seidenstahl missing.
12.	Kü.Fl.Gr. 606	NCM	Landing accident at Brest-Süd; not combat.	Dornier Do 17Z (2530)	20 %	Crew unhurt.
13.	Wekusta. Ob.d.L.	CM	Crashed after combat with unknown British fighters in German grid Square 0070.	Dornier Do 17Z-2 (2547 : T5+IU)	100 %	Reg. Rat a. Kr. Heinrich wounded.

Friday 4th October

Although the poor weather continued to prevent widespread air activity, Park's pilots destroyed three enemy bombers off the south-east coast. *Kampfgeschwader 77* lost another Junkers Ju 88, this time to the guns of Stanford Tuck—now commanding No. 257 Squadron, flying Hurricanes. *Lehrgeschwader 1* sent two *Staffeln* of Ju 88s on dive-bombing attacks against Hythe and Folkestone around mid-day, causing more than fifty casualties and losing one aircraft to the Hurricanes of No. 605 Squadron.

The "official" British figures purporting to show enemy losses on this day (twelve) are misleading in that they include several which were in no way attributable to R.A.F. action; for instance, they include a Dornier which was shot down by German fighters, and a Heinkel He 59 seaplane which capsized while being towed into port!

After due consideration of the new high flying tactics, Park was at pains to emphasise once again that the Bf 109s were to be tackled by Spitfires only, and took the opportunity to explain the purpose of the introduction of the Spotter Flights; the first of these took delivery of its aircraft at Gravesend on this day.

During the night of 4th/5th several raids were mounted against arms factories in the London area, using large bombs and air mines at Lewisham, Enfield and Woolwich; all in fact fell on residential property.

Another Ju 88, said to have been shot down early in October, being dismantled by technical personnel for removal to a scrap depot.

R.A.F. FIGHTER COMMAND LOSSES—FRIDAY 4th OCTOBER 1940

1.	66 Sqn., Gravesend	C	Missing after intercepting He 111 off the East Coast. Pilot's body recovered from the sea at Covehithe on 21-10-40.	A15.35 hrs	Flt. Lt. K.McL. Gillies	Spitfire	X4320	Cat. 3 Missing
2.	266 Sqn., Wittering	NC	Force landed at Little Bytham due to bad weather; pilot unhurt.	Not known	Sgt. S.A. Goodwin	Spitfire	P7296	Cat. 2 Damaged
3.	501 Sqn., Kenley	C	Force landed at Cuckfield, Sussex, due to bad weather after combat; pilot unhurt.	A12.00 hrs.	Fg. Off. D.A.E. Jones	Hurricane	V6733	Cat. 2 Damaged
4.	501 Sqn., Kenley	C	Force landed at Hassocks, Brighton, due to bad weather after combat; pilot unhurt.	A11.55 hrs.	Sgt. J.H. Lacey	Hurricane	V7498	Cat. 2 Damaged
5.	605 Sqn., Croydon	C	Force landed at Limpsfield, Surrey, due to bad weather after combat; pilot unhurt.	17.15 hrs.	Plt. Off. C.E. English	Hurricane	V6784	Cat. 2 Damaged

LUFTWAFFE LOSSES—FRIDAY 4th OCTOBER 1940

1.	II./KG 2	CM	Landing accident at Bouly airfield.	Dornier Do 17Z (4201 : U5+EP)	70 %	Crew unhurt.
2.	5./KG 3	NCM	Shot down by German fighters off the Dutch coast, and crashed on land.	Dornier Do 17Z-2 (3343 :5K+KN)	80 %	Three crew members wounded.
3.	I./KG 26	CM	Shot down by 607 Sqn. Hurricanes off Beachy Head at A.12.25 hrs.	Heinkel He 111H-3 (5609 : 1H+EL)	100 %	Ltn.Hans Kingel,Uffz.Winter,Uffz. Reinelt and Uffz. Blasius killed.
4.	I./KG 51	CM	Landing accident (tyre burst) at Villacoublay.	Junkers Ju 88A-1(6084)	30 %	Crew unhurt.
5.	I./KG 54	CM	Damaged by 229 Sqn. Hurricanes of Bary and Dewar over Channel and crashed at Le Havre at A.11.00 hrs.	Junkers Ju 88A-1 (6101)	50 %	Crew unhurt.
6.	Stab/KG 76	CM	Crashed at St. Pol after running out of fuel in bad weather.	Dornier Do 17Z (2610)	100 %	Crew unhurt.

Luftwaffe Losses, 4th October 1940—*continued*

7.	II./KG 76	CM	Crashed near Abbeville after combat with un-identified British fighters.	Junkers Ju 88A-1 (8076)	80 %	One crew member wounded.
8.	II./KG 76	CM	Crashed near Calais after combat with fighters (probably 605 Sqn. Spitfires) at 13.00 hrs.	Junkers Ju 88A-1	100 %	One crew member wounded.
9.	III./KG 76	CM	Crashed near Henonville; cause not notified.	Dornier Do 17Z (1136)	100 %	Oblt. Altenmüller + three killed.
10.	III./KG 76	CM	Crashed landing in bad weather at Cormeilles.	Dornier Do 17Z (2887)	50 %	Crew unhurt.
11.	III./KG 76	NCM	Crashed at Haudivilliers due to faulty servicing.	Dornier Do 17Z (2888)	100 %	Ltn. Meister killed; three injured.
12.	I./KG 77	CM	Shot down by 257 Sqn. Hurricane of Tuck 10 miles off Southwold at A.10.10 hrs.	Junkers Ju 88A-1 (3160 : 3Z+HL)	100 %	Uffz. Herold killed; St.Fw. Hart-mann, Ogefr. Hackmann, and Gefr. Einbrick missing.
13.	I./KGr. 100	CM	Missing from night bombing sortie over Britain; believed shot down by *flak*.	Heinkel He 111H-3 (6831 : 6N+FH)	100 %	Uffz. Stock, Uffz. Krische, Fw. Tomuschat, Gefr. Perkel missing.
14.	Kü.Fl.Gr. 606	CM	Missing from night bombing sortie over West Midlands of Britain.	Dornier Do 17Z-3 (3617 : 7T+CH)	100 %	Uffz. Fuchs killed; Ltn.z.S. Paul Vollbrecht, Uffz. David and Uffz. von Postel missing.
15.	Stab/St.G 3	NCM	Landing accident at Dinard; cause not known.	Dornier Do 17Z (2832)	40 %	Crew unhurt.
16.	I./LG 1	CM	Force landed at Vallery with *flak* damage.	Junkers Ju 88A-1(6113)	40 %	Crew unhurt.
17.	II./LG 1	CM	Force landed at Berck-sur-Mer with combat damage.	Junkers Ju 88A-1 (6165 : L1+EM)	45 %	One crew member wounded.
18.	II./LG 1	CM	Shot down by 605 Sqn. Hurricanes of Currant and Milne off Dungeness at 12.50 hrs.	Junkers Ju 88A-1 (6116 : L1+EP)	100 %	Gefr. Jahn and Gefr. Schöffmann killed; Uffz. Kross and Uffz. Kirchbaur missing.
19.	II./JG 51	NCM	Landing accident; location not known.	Messerschmitt Bf 109 E-3 (0991)	15 %	Pilot unhurt.
20	*Seenotflug-kommando 4*	CM	Capsized under tow after force landing in sea.	Heinkel He 59 (2602 : NE+UX)	100 %	No crew casualties.

Saturday 5th October

Despite poor weather conditions, Kesselring's fighters and bombers returned in considerable strength on this day, with five phases of attack lasting until mid-afternoon. At the same time Sperrle threw in three small diversionary raids against the South-West for good measure.

The curtain raiser consisted of three *Staffeln* of bomb-carrying Bf 109s which aimed for South London at around 09.00 hours, and against which Park did not react in strength. Instead the Poles of No. 303 Squadron were ordered up on patrol to await another raid approaching Dungeness from Calais shortly afterwards. On crossing the coast this split into two formations, one of which comprised eighteen bombers of *Erprobungsgruppe 210* (which had recently moved back to the Pas de Calais from Cherbourg), and the other of Bf 110s of II./ZG 76.

Led by its new acting *Gruppenkommandeur*, Oblt. Werner Weimann, Erpr.Gr. 210 had been briefed to attack the newly-completed airfield at West Malling, near Maidstone, and the formation of Bf 110s ran straight into the guns of the waiting Poles. Although eight bombs landed among the airfield's buildings and caused about twenty casualties, the raid was broken up and the Messerschmitts were harried and chased back across the Sussex Downs. Weimann himself fell in this battle, his aircraft falling not five miles from the village where Walter Rubensdörffer had died.

The raid by the other formation, on Detling, was unopposed but caused little damage due to ragged bombing. It was followed by six sweeps between 11.00 hours and mid-day; the mixture of high and medium altitude raids so confused the picture at No. 11 Group operations room that interceptions were untidy, and only five of the eleven squadrons scrambled managed to make contact with the enemy. Five Bf 109s were shot down—one of them by No. 92 Squadron which had just finished blasting away at a wandering Henschel Hs 126 spotter aircraft that had strayed over the Channel; although the observer of this hapless aircraft took to his parachute,

Hauptmann Hermann-Friedrich Joppien (*left*) led I./JG 51 during the later stages of the Battle; he was credited with destroying 25 British aircraft by October 1940. Joppien died on the Russian Front late in August 1941. (Photo: Heinz Nowarra)

prompting the Spitfire pilots to claim a victory, the wounded German pilot managed to limp back to a crash landing in France.

The main raid of the afternoon was an attack by two *Gruppen* of Ju 88s on Southampton, and the bombers escaped with only slight damage from the Portsmouth gun defences.

R.A.F. FIGHTER COMMAND LOSSES—SATURDAY 5th OCTOBER 1940

#	Sqn.		Details	Time	Pilot	Aircraft	Serial	Category
1.	41 Sqn., Hornchurch	C	Suffered damage in wing from Bf 109 near Dungeness; pilot returned unhurt.	11.55 hrs.	Fg. Off. A.D.J. Lovell	Spitfire	N3225	Cat. 1 Damaged
2.	66 Sqn., Gravesend	C	Damaged by Bf 109s over Kent; pilot unhurt.	11.15 hrs.	Sgt. B. Wright	Spitfire	X4543	Cat. 1 Damaged
3.	66 Sqn., Gravesend	C	Damaged by Bf 109s over Kent; pilot slightly wounded.	11.50 hrs.	Plt. Off. J.B. Kendal	Spitfire	X4473	Cat. 1 Damaged
4.	66 Sqn., Gravesend	C	Damaged by Bf 109s over Kent; pilot unhurt.	12.00 hrs.	Plt. Off. C.A.W. Bodie	Spitfire	—	Cat. 1 Damaged
5.	72 Sqn., Biggin Hill	C	Collided with Item 6 on scramble; pilot killed.	09.35 hrs.	Plt. Off. N. Sutton	Spitfire	X4544	Cat. 3 Destroyed
6.	72 Sqn., Biggin Hill	C	Collided with Item 5 on scramble; pilot landed unhurt.	09.35 hrs.	Sgt. R.C.J. Staples	Spitfire	K9989	Cat. 3 Destroyed
7.	72 Sqn., Biggin Hill	C	Damaged by Bf 109s over the Channel; pilot returned unhurt.	10.20 hrs.	F/Sgt. H. Steere	Spitfire	K9935	Cat. 1 Damaged
8.	238 Sqn., Middle Wallop	C	Shot down by Bf 109s over Dorset; pilot baled out with multiple burns and admitted to Shaftesbury Hospital.	14.25 hrs.	Sgt. J.W. McLaughlin	Hurricane	P3611	Cat 3. Destroyed
9.	303 Sqn., Northolt	C	Shot down in flames by Bf 109s between Ashford and Folkestone and crashed at Stowting. Pilot killed.	Not known	Fg. Off. W. Januszewicz	Hurricane	P3892	Cat. 3 Destroyed
10.	603 Sqn., Hornchurch	C	Shot down by Bf 109s near Dover and crashed near Chilham; pilot baled out with burns.	11.50 hrs.	Plt. Off. J.S. Morton	Hurricane	K9807	Cat. 3 Destroyed
11.	607 Sqn., Tangmere	C	Shot down by Bf 109s near Swanage; pilot forced landed unhurt.	A13.50 hrs.	Not known	Hurricane	P3554	Cat. 3 Destroyed
12.	607 Sqn., Tangmere	C	Shot down by Bf 109s near Swanage; pilot force landed unhurt.	A13.50 hrs.	Not known	Hurricane	—	Cat. 3 Destroyed
13.	607 Sqn., Tangmere	C	Shot down by Bf 109s near Swanage; pilot force landed unhurt.	A13.50 hrs.	Not known	Hurricane	—	Cat. 3 Destroyed
14.	607 Sqn., Tangmere	C	Shot down by Bf 109s near Swanage; pilot force landed unhurt.	A13.50 hrs.	Not known	Hurricane	—	Cat. 2 Damaged
15.	616 Sqn., Kirton-in-Lindsey.	NC	Undercarriage collapsed on landing; pilot unhurt.	Not known	Sgt. K.A. Wilkinson	Spitfire	—	Cat. 1 Damaged

LUFTWAFFE LOSSES—SATURDAY 5th OCTOBER 1940

#	Unit		Details	Aircraft	%	Crew
1.	4.(H)/31	CM	Damaged by 92 Sqn. Spitfires over Channel at 10.59 hrs.	Henschel Hs 126 (3423 : 5D+FM)	70 %	Ltn. Hans-Joachim von Kläden missing; pilot wounded.
2.	II./KG 1	CM	Missing after night bombing sortie over England; fate not known.	Heinkel He 111H-2 (5586 : V4+FW)	100 %	Uffz. Hildebrand, Gefr. Tschop and Uffz. Bauer killed; Gefr. Zuckriegel missing.
3.	Geschw.Erg.St./ KG 1	NCM	Force landed near Goldberg after engine failure.	Heinkel He 111H-1 (2316 : V4+FM)	30 %	Crew unhurt.
4.	1./KG 2	CM	Became lost and crashed at Krefeld.	Dornier Do 17Z-2 (1212 : U5+GH)	100 %	Three crew members injured.
5.	2./KG 3	CM	Crashed near Hammemille; cause not known.	Dornier Do 17Z-2 (2537 : 5K+AK)	100 %	Ltn. Berghahn + three killed.
6.	I./KG 26	CM	Force landed near Amiens with combat damage.	Heinkel He 111H (6933)	25 %	Crew unhurt.
7.	7./KG 30	CM	Landing accident at Eindhoven after combat.	Junkers Ju 88A-4 (4040 : 4D+ER)	20 %	Crew unhurt.
8.	II./KG 76	CM	Missing from night bombing sortie over Britain.	Junkers Ju 88A-1 (6156 : F1+LP)	100 %	Oblt.Johann Hölzer,Fw.Kolb,Gefr. Graf and Uffz. Beiseroth killed.
9.	I./KG 77	CM	Force landed at Ligeschout with flak damage.	Junkers Ju 88A-1(2160)	50 %	One killed and one wounded.
10.	KGr. 806	CM	Force landed at Le Havre with damage from fighter combat.	Junkers Ju 88A-1(7138)	50 %	One crew member killed.
11.	II./LG 1	CM	Shot down by 253 Sqn. Hurricanes of Corkett and Kee off Beachy Head at 08.40 hrs.	Junkers Ju 88A-1 (4134 : L1+JN)	100 %	Ltn. Ottfried Hoffmann, Gefr. Neuenberg, Gefr. Steiner and Uffz. Worbanger killed.
12.	6./LG 2	CM	Shot down by 66 Sqn. Spitfire of Oxspring near Dover at A.11.30 hrs.	Messerschmitt Bf 109 E-4 (3726)	100 %	Fw. Pankratz missing.
13.	1./Erpr.Gr. 210	CM	Shot down by 303 Sqn. Hurricane near Maidstone.	Messerschmitt Bf 110 D-0 (3382 : S9+FH)	100 %	Oblt. Werner Weimann, Acting Gr. Kdr., and Uffz. Hübner missing.
14.	1./Erpr.Gr. 210	CM	Shot down by 303 Sqn. Hurricane of Bele and crashed on Industrial School, Milbank Place, 3 miles south of Ashford at 11.30 hrs.	Messerschmitt Bf 110 D-3 (3383 : S9+GH)	100 %	Fw. Fritz Dünsnig and Fw. Helmut Keppitsch killed. Both men buried at Hawkinge.
15.	1./Erpr.Gr. 210	CM	Damaged by 303 Sqn. Hurricanes over Kent and force landed near Calais at A.12.00 hrs.	Messerschmitt Bf 110 D-0 (3598 : S9+EH)	15 %	One crew member wounded.
16.	2./Erpr.Gr. 210	CM	Damaged by 303 Sqn. Hurricanes over Kent and force landed at Calais-Marck airfield.	Messerschmitt Bf 110 C-2 (4209 : S9+EK)	40 %	One crew member wounded.
17.	1./JG 3	CM	Shot down by 41 Sqn. Spitfire of Lock near Canterbury at 14.27 hrs.	Messerschmitt Bf 109 E-1 (4865)	100 %	Fw. von Bittenfeld missing.
18.	II./JG 3	CM	Landing accident at St. Inglevert airfield.	Messerschmitt Bf 109 E-4 (3554)	20 %	Pilot unhurt.
19.	9./JG 3	CM	Shot down by 41 Sqn. Spitfire of Mackenzie over English Channel at 14.30 hrs.	Messerschmitt Bf 109 E-4 (3876)	100 %	Pilot, unhurt, rescued by Seenotflugkommando.
20.	I./JG 26	NCM	Crashed at Marquise-West; not due to combat.	Messerschmitt Bf 109 E-4 (5384)	100 %	Pilo killed.
21.	Stab I./JG 51	CM	Landed at Pihen with damage from fighter combat.	Messerschmitt Bf 109 E-4 (4102)	25 %	Pilot unhurt.
22.	3./JG 51	NCM	Force landed at St. Omer after engine failure.	Messerschmitt Bf 109 E-4 (3502)	30 %	Pilot unhurt.
23.	8./JG 51	CM	Force landed at Audembert with fuel shortage.	Messerschmitt Bf 109 E-4 (3883)	30 %	Pilot unhurt.
24.	1./JG 53	CM	Shot down by 41 Sqn. Spitfire of Mileham south of Chatham at 11.50 hrs.	Messerschmitt Bf 109 E-4 (1804)	100 %	Uffz. Gehsla missing.
25.	1./JG 53	CM	Shot down by 41 Sqn. Spitfire of Bamberger north of Dungeness at 12.00 hrs.	Messerschmitt Bf 109 E-4 (1564)	100 %	Ltn. Alfred Zweis missing.
26.	7./JG 53	CM	Damaged by British fighters of Kent; pilot baled out safely over Cap Gris Nez.	Messerschmitt Bf 109 E-4 (5372)	100 %	Pilot unhurt.
27.	2./JG 77	CM	Shot down by 92 Sqn. Spitfires over the Channel at 11.04 hrs. Pilot baled out.	Messerschmitt Bf 109 E-1 (4073)	100 %	Pilot, wounded, rescued by Seenotflugkommando.

Sunday 6th October

Another dismal day of continuous rain over the whole country permitted only scattered enemy attacks. These were confined to raids by single or small groups of aircraft on airfields in Southern England. Eight bombs fell at Middle Wallop and twelve at Northolt; in the latter raid, one of several flown by KG 30 «Adler-Geschwader», a 500-kilo bomb fell between two hangars, striking a taxying Hurricane of No. 303 (Polish) Squadron, blowing it and its pilot to shreds. The bomber, a Ju 88 of the Geschwader's 4th Staffel, was shot down shortly afterwards by a No. 229 Squadron Hurricane flown by the New Zealander, Plt. Off. Victor Verity. At Biggin Hill bombs from another KG 30 Ju 88 destroyed three barrack blocks and on this occasion the raider was struck by the airfield's P.A.C. defences; the aircraft was seen making off with one engine stopped and must be assumed to have crashed in the Channel as the Geschwader's 9th Staffel reported that the aircraft whose target had been Biggin Hill failed to return.

Four parachute mines dropped at Uxbridge, and one of them, a delayed-action weapon, greatly endangered the No. 11 Group Headquarters. The brilliant work of Sub-Lieutenant Horace Taylor in de-fusing the mine saved the situation and, as the culmination of ten days' supremely hazardous work, earned for him the award of the George Cross.

R.A.F. FIGHTER COMMAND LOSSES—SUNDAY 6th OCTOBER 1940

1.	64 Sqn., Leconfield	NC	Crashed into the sea off Yorkshire coast during routine patrol; pilot killed.	14.30 hrs.	Sgt. E.F. Vinyard	Spitfire	R6683	Cat. 3 Lost
2.	229 Sqn., Northolt	NC	Force landed on patrol at Leatherhead, out of fuel and with radio failure; pilot unhurt.	12.20 hrs.	Flt. Lt. W.A. Smith	Hurricane	P3716	Cat. 3 Destroyed
3.	303 Sqn., Northolt	—	Aircraft struck by bomb while taxying during air raid; pilot killed.	Not known	Sgt. A. Suidak	Hurricane	R4175	Cat. 3 Destroyed
4.	303 Sqn., Northolt	—	Aircraft destroyed in raid on Northolt; no pilot casualty.	Not known	Nil	Hurricane	P3120	Cat. 3 Destroyed

LUFTWAFFE LOSSES—SUNDAY 6th OCTOBER 1940

1.	1.(F)/123	CM	Tyre burst on landin at Buc airfield.	Junkers Ju 88A-1 (0383 : 4U+KH)	30 %	Crew unhurt.
2.	3./KG 1	NCM	Take-off accident at Münster-Handorf airfield.	Junkers Ju 88A-1(3220)	45 %	Crew unhurt.
3.	10./KG 2	NCM	Crashed at Osnabrück due to faulty servicing.	Dornier Do 17Z (2664 :U5+AZ)	100 %	Ltn. Obermayer + three wounded.
4.	KG 3	CM	Shot down by 253 Sqn. Hurricanes of Duke-Woolley and Murch at Hayfield at A.11.00 hrs.	Dornier Do 17Z-3	100 %	Four crew members missing.
5.	II./KG 4	CM	Landing accident at Soesterberg; cause unknown.	Heinkel He 111P-4 (2932 : 5J+FN)	40 %	Crew unhurt.
6.	5./KG 4	CM	Landing accident at Soesterberg; cause unknown.	Heinkel He 111P-4 (2970 : 5J+JN)	20 %	Crew unhurt.
7.	I./KG 27	CM	Crashed and burned at Tours after combat.	Heinkel He 111P (1520)	100 %	Oblt. Mahnke + four killed.
8.	4./KG 30	CM	Shot down by 229 Sqn. Hurricane of Verity after lone raid on Northolt at 12.25 hrs.	Junkers Ju 88A-5 (8045 : 4D+HM)	100 %	Fw. Koschella, Uffz.Phel, Fw.Wilhenig and Uffz. Benderen missing.
9.	III./KG 30	CM	Landing accident at Eindhoven after combat.	Junkers Ju 88A-1 (2111 : 4D+GR)	30 %	Crew unhurt.
10.	9./KG 30	CM	Missing from bombing sortie over Biggin Hill; probably shot down by ground defences.	Junkers Ju 88A-1 (0176 : 4D+DT)	100 %	Gefr. Böbel killed; Ofw. Ortlepp, Uffz. Röder and Uffz. Holzmeier missing.
11.	I./KG 54	CM	Crashed at Les Andelys following engine failure.	Junkers Ju 88A-1(4079)	100 %	Crew baled out unhurt.
12.	III./KG 76	CM	Shot down by 17 Sqn. Hurricanes of Steward and Ross near Debden at A.13.00 hrs. (also claimed by pilots of 249 Sqn. Hurricanes).	Dornier Do 17Z-3	100 %	Uffz. Wagner killed; Ltn. Fritz Morr, Uffz. Mroszinski and Fw. Pohl missing.
13.	II./NJG 1	NCM	Crashed following engine fire at Könen.	Messerschmitt Bf 110 D-0 (3174 : G9+CC)	98 %	Hptm. Graf Stillgried, Gr.Kdr., and one other killed.
14.	10./NJG 1	CM	Take-off accident at Vlissingen airfield.	Messerschmitt Bf 109 E-1 (3660)	90 %	Pilot unhurt.

Servicing Hurricane *P3886* of No. 601 (County of London) Squadron at Exeter. Although deployed far to the west of the main area of battle, the Exeter squadrons had a large area of defence responsibility, covering Plymouth, Bristol and Portland; on occasion they were scrambled to assist in the defence of Southampton, and even London.

Monday 7th October

With improving weather, *Jafu 2* sent an almost continuous stream of Bf 109s over Kent during the morning, and the Spitfire Squadrons were hard-pressed to meet the threat; in fact, on this occasion, it was the Hurricane pilots of Nos. 501 and 605 Squadrons who enjoyed the greatest success. Flt. Lt. Archie McKellar shot down two Bf 109s within three minutes near Westerham[2]. Another Scot, whose exploits on this day earned the immediate award of the D.F.C., was Plt. Off.

---

[2] McKellar, of No. 605 Squadrion, was the most successful of the Auxiliary Air Force fighter pilots in the Battle of Britain, and claimed the confirmed destruction of fourteen aircraft, plus one shared. He was to be killed on 1st November—the day after the Battle "officially" ended. Sergeant "Ginger" Lacey, also a member of an Auxiliary Squadron, No. 501, who claimed fifteen confirmed victories in the Battle, was a member of the R.A.F. Volunteer Reserve, not the Auxiliary Air Force. Both were, of course, Hurricane pilots.

Kenneth MacKenzie, a newly-joined No. 501 Squadron pilot who, having used up all his ammunition on a Bf 109 south of Folkestone, closed with another and banged its tail with his wing—forcing the enemy to crash into the sea. He brought his Hurricane back to a successful crash landing on the coast—even though the aircraft had to be written off.

The main single raid of the day was mounted against the Westland Aircraft plant at Yeovil by 25 Ju 88s of II./KG 51, escorted by about fifty Bf 110s of II. and III./*Gruppe*, ZG 26. It was met by five of Brand's squadrons, which shot down seven of the *Zerstörer* and two of the bombers. This afternoon raid inflicted relatively light damage on the factory but caused more than a hundred casualties, many of them in a shelter which received a direct hit. The tally of enemy aircraft would probably have been greater but for the timely intervention of 30 Bf 109s which appeared over the Dorset coast to cover the raiders' withdrawal.

R.A.F. FIGHTER COMMAND LOSSES—MONDAY 7th OCTOBER 1940

	Squadron		Details	Time	Pilot	Aircraft	Serial	Category
1.	41 Sqn., Hornchurch	C	Shot down by Do 17 or 215 near Folkestone; pilot baled out unhurt at Douglas Farm, Postling.	11.30 hrs.	Plt. Off. D.A. Adams	Spitfire	N3267	Cat. 3 Destroyed
2.	56 Sqn., Boscombe Down	C	Shot down by enemy bombers near Yeovil; pilot baled out but badly injured on landing.	A16.10 hrs.	Sgt. D.H. Nichols	Hurricane	P3154	Cat. 3 Destroyed
3.	66 Sqn., Gravesend	C	Damaged in combat with Bf 109; pilot returned unhurt.	13.20 hrs.	Plt. Off. H.M.T. Heron	Spitfire	X4326	Cat. 2 Damaged
4.	152 Sqn., Warmwell	C	Shot down by enemy fighters and force landed near Worthy Down; pilot unhurt.	16.30 hrs.	Plt. Off. R.M.D Hall	Spitfire	—	Cat. 3 Destroyed
5.	152 Sqn., Warmwell	C	Shot down by enemy fighters and crashed at Shillingstone, Blandford Forum; pilot grievously burned and died the next day.	A16.30 hrs.	Plt. Off. H.J. Akroyd	Spitfire	N3039	Cat. 3 Destroyed
6.	222 Sqn., Hornchurch	C	Shot down by enemy bombers at Salehurst, East Sussex; pilot baled out, but was dead on landing.	16.45 hrs.	Plt. Off. J.W. Broadhurst	Spitfire	P9469	Cat. 3 Destroyed
7.	238 Sqn., Middle Wallop	C	Shot down by Bf 109s near Yeovil and crashed at Winterbourne Houghton; pilot baled out at Blandford, slightly burned.	16.15 hrs.	Plt. Off. A.R. Covington	Hurricane	V6777	Cat. 3 Destroyed
8.	245 Sqn., Aldergrove	NC	Crashed on landing after engine failure; pilot killed.	17.30 hrs.	Plt. Off. J.J. Beedham	Hurricane	N2707	Cat. 3 Destroyed
9.	264 Sqn., Luton	NC	Suffered collision on take-off; both crew members injured.	Not known	Plt. Off. G.H. Hackwood Fg. Off. A. O'Connell	Defiant	N1578	Cat. 3 Destroyed
10.	501 Sqn., Kenley	C	Shot down by Bf 109 at Wrotham, Kent; pilot baled out at Wilmington but was dead on landing; aircraft crashed at Darenth, Dartford.	10.01 hrs.	Fg. Off. N.J.M. Barry	Hurricane	V6800	Cat. 3 Destroyed
11.	501 Sqn., Kenley	C	Force landed at Folkestone after destroying a Bf 109 by striking it with his wing; pilot suffered slight injuries to his face.	10.14 hrs.	Plt. Off. K.W. Mackenzie	Hurricane	V6799	Cat. 3 Destroyed
12.	601 Sqn., Exeter	C	Hit in coolant tank during combat and force landed south of Axminster; pilot slightly hurt.	16.30 hrs.	Plt. Off. H.C. Mayers	Hurricane	R4218	Cat. 2 Damaged
13.	602 Sqn., Westhampnett	C	Shot down by Ju 88 near Seaford; pilot grievously wounded and died the next day.	A16.00 hrs.	Sgt. B.E.P. Whall	Spitfire	X4160	Cat. 3 Destroyed
14.	605 Sqn., Croydon	C	Shot down by Bf 109s near London; pilot baled out unhurt; aircraft crashed at Bexley.	A10.00 hrs.	Plt. Off. I.J. Muirhead	Hurricane	V7305	Cat. 3 Destroyed
15.	605 Sqn., Croydon	C	Shot down by Bf 109 over Westerham and crashed at Brasted; pilot killed.	13.20 hrs.	Plt. Off. C.E. English	Hurricane	P3677	Cat. 3 Burnt
16.	607 Sqn., Tangmere	C	Collided with Item 17. Pilot remained in aircraft and was killed when it crashed.	Not known	Fg. Off. I.B. Difford	Hurricane	L1728	Cat. 3 Destroyed
17.	607 Sqn., Tangmere	C	Collided with Item 16. Pilot baled out unhurt at Slindon, West Sussex.	Not known	Plt. Off. A.M.W. Scott	Hurricane	P3860	Cat. 3 Destroyed
18.	609 Sqn., Warmwell	C	Shot down by Bf 109s over Dorset; pilot baled out unhurt.	Afternoon	Not known	Spitfire	N3231	Cat. 3 Destroyed

LUFTWAFFE LOSSES—MONDAY 7th OCTOBER 1940

	Unit		Details	Aircraft	%	Crew
1.	4.(F)/11	NCM	Take-off accident near Le Bourget airfield.	Dornier Do 17P (3527 : 6M+HM)	100 %	One killed and two injured.
2.	5.(H)/14	NCM	Landing accident at Vron airfield; cause not notified.	Henschel Hs 126B-1 (4296 : C2+LK)	40 %	Crew unhurt.
3.	Stab/KG 1	NCM	Landing accident at Amiens following trouble with undercarriage.	Heinkel He 111H-3 (5646 : V4+CA)	40 %	Crew unhurt.
4.	II./KG 51	CM	Shot down by 152 Sqn. Spitfire of Shepphred near Dorchester at A.16.20 hrs.	Junkers Ju 88A-1 (8064 : 9K+SN)	100 %	Oblt.Sigmund Heye,Ltn.Fritz Bein, Ofw. König and Ofw.Krell killed.
5.	4./KG 51	CM	Shot down by 238 Sqn. Hurricane of Doe near Yeovil at A.16.30 hrs.	Junkers Ju 88A-1 (6115 : 9k+DM)	100 %	Ltn.Gottfried Döttlinger, Gefr. Diegbert Köhne, Gefr. Hans Büttner and Uffz. Gerhard Semper killed.
6.	Stab/St.G 3	NCM	Wheels-up landing at St. Michel airfield.	Dornier Do 17Z (2877)	40 %	Crew unhurt.
7.	II./ZG 26	CM	Shot down by British defences during raid on Yeovil at A.16.30 hrs.	Messerschmitt Bf 110 E-1(3427 : 3U+FM)	100 %	Ofw. Gensler and Uffz. Häfner missing.

Luftwaffe Losses, 7th October 1949—*continued*

8.	8./ZG 26	CM	Shot down by 609 Sqn. Spitfire of Bisdee during raid on Yeovil at A.16.30 hrs.	Messerschmitt Bf 110 D-2 (3416 :3U+HN)	100 %	Ofw. Stahl and Uffz. Mauer missing.
9.	II./ZG 26	CM	Shot down by 238 Sqn. Hurricane of Fenton south of Yeovil at A.16.30 hrs.	Messerschmitt Bf 110 C-7 (3418 : 3U+JP)	100 %	Ofw. Hertzog and Uffz. Schilling missing.
10.	III./ZG 26	CM	Shot down by British defences during raid on Yeovil at A.16.30 hrs.	Messerschmitt Bf 110 C-4 (3283 : 3U+BT)	100 %	Ltn. Kurt Sidow and Gefr. Repik killed.
11.	III./ZG 26	CM	Shot down by 601 Sqn. Hurricanes north of Portland at A.16.20 hrs.	Messerschmitt Bf 110 C-4 (3640 : 3U+GT)	100 %	Oblt. Herbert Grisslich and Uffz. Obermayer missing.
12.	III./ZG 26	CM	Shot down by 601 Sqn. Hurricanes north of Portland at A.16.20 hrs.	Messerschmitt Bf 110 C-4 (3564 : 3U+JT)	100 %	Ogefr. Bachmann killed; Gefr. Demmig missing.
13.	Stab III./ZG 26	CM	Shot down by 601 Sqn. Hurricanes east of Portland at A.16.20 hrs.	Messerschmitt Bf 110 E-1 (3421 :3U+DD)	100 %	Ltn. Bodo Sommer and Uffz. Paul Preuler made P.O.W.s
14.	9./NJG 1	CM	Engine failure on take-off at Stendal; aircraft crashed.	Messerschmitt Bf 110 D-1 (3308 : G9+GT)	80 %	Crew unhurt.
15.	4./LG 2	CM	Shot down by 605 Sqn. Hurricane of Foster near Biggin Hill at A.16.20 hrs.	Messerschmitt Bf 109 E-4 (5391)	100 %	Uffz. Ley missing.
16.	4./LG 2	CM	Shot down by 603 Sqn. Spitfire of Carbury over Kent at A.16.20 hrs.	Messerschmitt Bf 109 E-4 (5566)	100 %	Uffz. Mörschel missing.
17.	5./LG 2	CM	Crash landed near Calais-Marck after combat.	Messerschmitt Bf 109 E-4 (3717)	60 %	Pilot unhurt.
18.	5./LG 2	CM	Crash landed at Calais-Marck after combat.	Messerschmitt Bf 109 E-4 (2013)	50 %	Pilot unhurt.
19.	5./JG 27	CM	Shot down by 605 Sqn. Hurricane of McKellar between Westerham and Maidstone at A.13.30 hrs.	Messerschmitt Bf 109 E-1 (3665)	100 %	Uffz. Paul Lederer made P.O.W.
20.	5./JG 27	CM	Shot down by 605 Sqn. Hurricane of McKellar between Westerham and Maidstone at A.13.30 hrs.	Messerschmitt Bf 109 E-1 (3881)	100 %	Uffz. Paul Lege killed.
21.	9./JG 27	CM	Destroyed by 501 Sqn. Hurricane of Mackenzie over Kent by striking the German aircraft with his wing, at 10.55 hrs.	Messerschmitt Bf 109 E-4 (0751)	100 %	Fhr. Lothar Bartsch made P.O.W.
22.	9./JG 27	CM	Shot down by 501 Sqn. Hurricane over the south Kent coast at 10.50 hrs.	Messerschmitt Bf 109 E-1 (6131)	100 %	Pilot, unhurt, rescued by *Seenotflugkommando*.
23.	2./JG 51	CM	Crash landed at Calais after combat with British fighters.	Messerschmitt Bf 109 E-4 (5805)	65 %	Pilot wounded.
24.	2./JG 51	CM	Shot down by 501 Sqn. Hurricane of Holden near Ashford at 10.20 hrs.	Messerschmitt Bf 109 E-4 (4853)	100 %	Ltn. Erich Meyer missing.
25.	2./JG 51	CM	Shot down by 303 Sqn. Hurricane of Belc over south Kent at A.10.30 hrs.	Messerschmitt Bf 109 E-4 (4103)	100 %	Oblt. Viktor Mölders, *St.Kap.*, made P.O.W.
26.	9./JG 53	CM	Crashed near Boulogne after combat with R.A.F. fighters; pilot baled out safely.	Messerschmitt Bf 109 E-4 (1593)	100 %	Pilot unhurt.
27.	1./196	CM	Crashed at Schellingwoude; cause not known.	Arado Ar 196A-2 (0069 : T3+BK)	100 %	Ltn. Stelter + one killed.
28.	*Flugbereitsch. Luftflotte 2*	NCM	Taxying accident at Evére airfield.	Junkers Ju 52/3m (5890 : BT+AJ)	30 %	No casualties.

Tuesday 8th October

Still not entirely satisfied with the efforts being made to counter the high-flying Messerschmitt raids, Park issued further instructions to his controllers outlining his plan to use a "forward" squadron to cover the London front while other squadrons climbed in the rear of attacking formations:

> "When a Spitfire squadron is ordered to. . .patrol on the Maidstone line, its function is to cover the area Biggin Hill—Maidstone—Gravesend, while other squadrons are gaining height, and protect them from the enemy screen. The form of attack which should be adopted on the high enemy fighters is to dive repeatedly on them and climb again each time to regain height. . .
> When other squadrons have gained their height and the course of the engagement is clear, the Group Controller will take a suitable opportunity to put (the original) Spitfire squadron on to the enemy raids where its height can be used to advantage."

It is clear that Park's instructions hitherto were intended to counter enemy raids apparently approaching at between 24,000 and 28,000 feet, at which altitude Spitfires could deal effectively with the bomb-carrying Bf 109s, and where Hurricanes had a fair chance (as had been demonstrated the previous day). However, some sighting reports from pilots of No. 420 Flight now indicated that the Bf 109 *Jabos* were being covered by unencumbered comrades flying as high as 32,000 feet, and it was these latter which were to inflict

Sergeant Josef Frantisek, the Czech pilot who served on No. 303 (Polish) Squadron and was the top-scoring R.A.F. pilot of the Battle of Britain. Dated 19th September 1940, the Cuthbert Orde portrait was executed during the short period of this gallant pilot's short but prolific combat spell. He was to be killed on 8th October when his Hurricane crashed at Ewell, Surrey.

increasing casualties on the British squadrons.

The destruction of a lone reconnaissance Junkers Ju 88 of 3.(F)/121 over Merseyside by the Czechs of No. 312 Squadron focuses attention on the growing confidence and efficiency of the "Free European" pilots in the R.A.F. By this date Fighter Command had ingested more than 240 Polish, Czech, Belgian and French pilots into its operational squadrons, and four special units (Nos. 302 and 303 Polish, and Nos. 310 and 312 Czech Squadrons) were now fully operational. No one who witnessed the magnificent courage of these men—almost all of whom had left far behind them families and loved ones in lands now bitterly oppressed by Nazi Germany—could dismiss their fight simply as fanaticism. They had more reason than any other group to feel a cold, implacable hatred of Germany, and their great contribution to the Battle must never be forgotten.

It was on 8th October that Josef Frantisek died, the Czech sergeant who flew with the Poles of No. 303 Squadron and whose seventeen confirmed victories, all won during the crucial thirty days of September, made him the R.A.F.'s top-scoring pilot of the Battle of Britain. His sole British gallantry award, the Distinguished Flying Medal—the only permissible award under the terms of Royal Warrant at the time—was never more richly deserved. The circumstances of his death have never been firmly established, and he was flying alone when his Hurricane crashed at Cuddington Way, Ewell, Surrey.

R.A.F. FIGHTER COMMAND LOSSES—TUESDAY 8th OCTOBER 1940

1.	66 Sqn., Gravesend	C	Crashed at Rochester after combat; pilot unhurt.	Not known	Not known	Spitfire	N3043	Cat. 3 Destroyed
2.	72 Sqn., Biggin Hill	C	Force landed at Holstead with engine trouble after combat; pilot unhurt.	10.35 hrs.	Sgt. N.V. Glen	Spitfire	K9847	Cat. 1 Damaged
3.	72 Sqn., Biggin Hill	C	Damaged by Bf 109s; landed at base, pilot unhurt.	10.30 hrs.	Not known	Spitfire	—	Cat. 1 Damaged
4.	72 Sqn., Biggin Hill	C	Damaged by Bf 109s; landed at base, pilot unhurt.	10.30 hrs.	Not known	Spitfire	—	Cat. 1 Damaged
5.	229 Sqn., Northolt	NC	Aircraft blew up in the air over Bovingdon (probably oxygen system); pilot killed.	Not known	Sgt. J.R. Farrow	Hurricane	V6820	Cat. 3 Destroyed
6.	264 Sqn., Luton	NC	Night flying accident at Marlow; both crew members killed.	22.30 hrs.	Plt. Off. H.I. Goodall LAC R.B.M.Young	Defiant	N1627	Cat. 3 Destroyed
7.	303 Sqn., Northolt	C	Crashed at Ewell, Surrey, during patrol; pilot killed. Circumstances not established.	Not known	Sgt. J. Frantisek	Hurricane	R4175	Cat. 3 Destroyed
8.	312 Sqn., Speke	C	Damaged in combat with Ju 88 over Merseyside; pilot unhurt.	16.25 hrs.	Flt. Lt. D.E. Gillam	Hurricane	—	Cat. 1 Damaged
9.	312 Sqn., Speke	C	Damaged in combat with Ju 88 over Merseyside; pilot unhurt.	16.25 hrs.	Plt. Off. A. Vasatko	Hurricane	L1926	Cat. 1 Damaged
10.	312 Sqn., Speke	C	Damaged in combat with Ju 88 over Merseyside; pilot unhurt.	16.25 hrs.	Sgt. J . Stehlik	Hurricane	L1807	Cat. 1 Damaged
11.	604 Sqn., Middle Wallop	NC	Night landing accident (overshot flarepath); crew unhurt.	At night	Plt. Off. D. Bayliss	Blenheim	L1218	Cat. 3 Destroyed

LUFTWAFFE LOSSES—TUESDAY 8th OCTOBER 1940

1.	2.(F)/22	CM	Believed shot down by 41 Sqn. Spitfire near Folkestone at 11.25 hrs.	Dornier Do 17 (3576 : 4N+GK)	100 %	Ltn. Egon von Eichstedt, Hptm. Konrad Barth and Ofw. Hubert Freund missing.
2.	3.(F)/121	CM	Shot down by 312 Sqn. Hurricanes of Gillam, Vasatko and Stehlik over Merseyside at 16.20 hrs.	Junkers Ju 88A-5 (0412 : 7A+JL)	100 %	Uffz. Walter Bender, Gefr. Paul Nikutta killed; Ltn. Wilhelm Schedemund and Fw. Wilhelm Nippel missing.
3.	3./KG 4	CM	Force landed at Schipol after bombing sortie.	Junkers Ju 88A-1 (4125 : 7A+JL)	30 %	Crew unhurt.
4.	I./KG 27	CM	Crashed on Tours airfield after bombing sortie.	Heinkel He 111H-2 (5442 : 1G+CL)	90 %	Crew unhurt.
5.	III./KG 27	CM	Crashed with engine failure at Rennes airfield.	Heinkel He 111P-1 (1460 : 1G+ER)	100 %	Four crew members killed.
6.	II./KG 30	CM	Crashed and burned at Dörenberg due to faulty maintenance.	Junkers Ju 88A-1 (4164 : 4D+EP)	100 %	Hptm. von Symonski, Gr.Kdr., + three killed.
7.	4./KG 30	CM	Force landed at Gilze-Rijen after bombing sortie.	Junkers Ju 88A-1 (4067 : 4D+CM)	20 %	Crew unhurt.
8.	8./KG 30	CM	Landing accident at Eindhoven after combat.	Junkers Ju 88A-1 (4081 : 4D+AS)	50 %	Crew unhurt.
9.	8./KG 30	CM	Landing accident at Eindhoven after combat.	Junkers Ju 88A-1 (5032 : 4D+HS)	15 %	Crew unhurt.
10.	I./KG 40	CM	Damaged by anti-aircraft gunfire from British warship and force landed near Brest.	Focke-Wulf Fw 200 C-2 (0022 : F8+AK)	20 %	One crew member wounded.
11.	5./KG 53	NCM	Landing accident at Oberweisenfeld airfield.	Heinkel He 111H-2 (2772 : A1+GN)	35 %	Crew unhurt.
12.	6./KG 53	CM	Force landed at Vendeville following engine failure.	Heinkel He 111H-2 (2790 : A1+KP)	20 %	One crew member injured.
13.	Stab/KG 54	NCM	Landing accident at Lechfeld; cause not known.	Junkers Ju 88A-1 (7093 : VK+VU)	35 %	Crew unhurt.
14.	III./KG 55	CM	Believed shot dowm by flak during night raid on London.	Heinkel He 111P-2 (1715 : G1+MS)	100 %	Ltn. Ulrich Flug, Fw. Ernst Enns, Uffz. Johann Ernstberger, Uffz. Ernst Herber and Gefr. Hans Pewlik killed.
15.	III./KG 55	CM	Landed with flak damage at Villacoublay.	Heinkel He 111P(1619)	5 %	One crew member wounded.
16.	6./KG 55	CM	Landed with flak damage at Villacoublay.	Heinkel He 111P(2809)	5 %	Crew unhurt.
17.	2./KGr. 806	CM	Missing from bombing sortie over London area.	Junkers Ju 88A-1 (4068 : M7+DK)	100 %	Oblt. Helmut Brückmann, Uffz. Helmut Weth and Ltn.z.S. Herbert Schlegel missing.
18.	12./LG 1	NCM	Suffered air collision with Item 19 at Marles.	Junkers Ju 87B (5086 : L1+MW)	100 %	Ltn. Schlegel + one killed.
19.	12./LG 1	NCM	Suffered air collision with Item 18 at Marles.	Junkers Ju 87B (0395 : L1+AW)	90 %	Ltn. Kuhn + one injured.
20.	I./ZG 26	NCM	Suffered taxying accident at Trecquile airfield.	Messerschmitt Bf 110 C-3 (1373)	10 %	Crew unhurt.

Luftwaffe Losses, 8th October 1940—*continued*

21.	4./JG 3	CM	Shot down by British fighters over the Channel.	Messerschmitt Bf 109 E-4 (1656)	100 %	Oblt. Werner Vogt, *St.Kap.*, missing.
22.	6./JG 3	CM	Take-off accident at Arques; cause not known.	Messerschmitt Bf 109 E-4 (1145)	20 %	Pilot unhurt.
23.	7./JG 3	CM	Landing accident at Desvres; cause not known.	Messerschmitt Bf 109 E-4 (1178)	40 %	Pilot unhurt.
24.	Erg.St./ JG 26	NCM	Engine caught fire while landing at Domayle.	Messerschmitt Bf 109 E-1 (3612)	70 %	Pilot unhurt.
25.	8./JG 51	CM	Force landing after engine failure at Ramecourt.	Messerschmitt Bf 109 E-4 (5282)	30 %	Pilot unhurt.
26.	4./JG 52	CM	Missing from combat sortie in the London area.	Messerschmitt Bf 109 E-1 (3465)	100 %	Fw. Boche missing.
27.	3./JG 53	NCM	Landing accident at Etaples; cause not known.	Messerschmitt Bf 109 D-4 (0977)	40 %	Pilot unhurt.
28.	4./JG 53	CM	Suffered take-off accident at Berck-sur-Mer.	Messerschmitt Bf 109 E-1 (6200)	65 %	Pilot unhurt.
29.	*Seenotflug-kommando 2*	CM	Shot down by 235 Sqn. Blenheims of Fenton and Gonay over Channel off Cherbourg at A.08.00 hrs.	Heinkel He 59 (0534 : TW+HH)	100 %	Ltn.z.S.Siegfried Stelzner, Uffz. Karl Hirschmann, Uffz. Helmuth Fischer and Uffz. Karl Wischer missing.
30.	*Seenotflug-kommando 2*	CM	Shot down by 235 Sqn. Blenheim of Prevot over Channel off Cherbourg at A.08.00 hrs. (1)	Heinkel He 59 (0541 : DA+MJ)	100 %	Ltn.z.S. Bernhard Schulz, Fw. Nicolai Bridi, Ogefr. Karl Kampf and Uffz. Stargnet missing.

[(1) In German records this loss is shown as "presumed air collision"; as none of the eight crew members is believed to have survived when the Heinkels were shot down, it is of course impossible to state which aircraft was destroyed by which R.A.F. pilots. It is, however, known that Fenton and Gonay "shared" in the destruction of one.]

Between August and November 1940 III.*Gruppe* of Mölders' *Jagdgeschwader 51* was led by Hauptmann Walter Oesau, another of the old "Spanish hands". After a distinguished career, which included command of both JG 2 *<Richthofen>* and JG 1, "Gulle" Oesau was killed in action with American P-38 Lightnings over the Eifel Mountains in May 1944. (Photo: Heinz Nowarra)

Oberleutnant Hans "Assi" Hahn, one of the best-known pilots of the *Luftwaffe*'s Fighter Arm, who led the 4th *Staffel* of JG 2 *<Richthofen>* during the Battle of Britain; in October 1940 he was promoted to command III./JG 2. He was awarded the Knight's Cross on 24th September on scoring his 20th victory. This deadly pilot (who ultimately gained 108 victories) and irrepressible "comedian" did not return from Russian captivity until 1950, but it was said that his sense of humour survived the ordeal intact. (Photo: *Gemeinschaft der Jagdflieger E.V.*)

Wednesday 9th October

With line squalls sweeping in quick succession over Southern England, Park's pilots were at some disadvantage in their efforts to intercept the German fighter-bombers which concentrated their attacks in three phases against the fighter airfields in Kent. Widespread damage was caused, but not of a nature that impaired the operational efficiency of the de-

fences. Plt. Off. Eric ("Sawn-off") Lock, the diminutive pilot who was to become the R.A.F.'s second-highest scoring pilot in the Battle of Britain, claimed a Bf 109 near Rochester during the afternoon—his fourteenth victory claim in five weeks.

At night the *Luftwaffe* sent a constant stream of bombers

over the whole country, resulting in the longest and most widespread alert of the War thus far. More than one hundred bombers kept up a steady but diffused raid over the capital; one land mine struck a hospital block housing geriatric patients, killing more than fifty. And it was announced on this day that in a recent raid the London University College Library had received a direct hit, losing more than 100,000 of its priceless books.

R.A.F. FIGHTER COMMAND LOSSES—WEDNESDAY 9th OCTOBER 1940

1.	1 Sqn., Wittering	C	Missing from patrol over the Wash; possibly shot down by Ju 88 reported in the area.	11.30 hrs.	Sgt. S. Warren	Hurricane	V7376	Cat. 3 Missing
2.	41 Sqn., Hornchurch	C	Landed wheels-up after combat with Bf 109s; pilot unhurt.	A15.35 hrs.	Sqn. Ldr. D.O. Finlay	Spitfire	X4558	Cat. 2 Damaged
3.	74 Sqn., Coltishall	C	Suffered air collision with Item 4 during practice attacks and crashed at Gillingham, near Beccles; pilot killed.	Not known.	Plt. Off. D. Hastings	Spitfire	P7329	Cat. 3 Destroyed
4.	74 Sqn., Coltishall	C	Suffered air collision with Item 3; pilot killed.	Not known	Plt. Off. Buckland	Spitfire	—	Cat. 3 Destroyed
5.	92 Sqn., Biggin Hill	C	Shot down by Bf 109s near Dungeness; pilot baled out badly burned, but died on 17-10-40. Aircraft crashed at Smeeth, near Brabourne.	A12.20 hrs.	Sgt. E.T.G. Frith	Spitfire	X4597	Cat. 3 Destroyed
6.	235 Sqn., Thorney Island	C	Shot down over the Channel by Bf 109s; all crew members killed.	Not known	Plt. Off. J.C. Kirkpatrick Plt. Off. R.C. Thomas Sgt. G.E. Keel	Blenheim	N3530	Cat. 3 Missing

LUFTWAFFE LOSSES—WEDNESDAY 9th OCTOBER 1940

1.	4.(H)/12	NCM	Force landed at Blankenberghe airfield.	Fieseler Fl 156 (4281)	40 %	Occupants unhurt.
2.	3.(F)/121	CM	Force landed at St. Brieux with engine failure.	Junkers Ju 88A-5 (0433 : 7A+KL)	40 %	Crew unhurt.
3.	III./KG 1	NCM	Taxied into Bf 110 (Item 18 below) at Handorf.	Junkers Ju 88A-5 (3230 : V4+KS)	50 %	Crew unhurt.
4.	III./KG 27	CM	Damaged by 601 Sqn. Hurricanes north of Dartmouth and crashed at Tours.	Heinkel He 111P (1633 : 1K+CT)	100 %	Ltn. Fritz Friele + two killed. One crew member wounded.
5.	III./KG 27	CM	Landing accident at Tours after bombing sortie.	Heinkel He 111P-2 (2166)	30 %	Crew unhurt.
6.	6./KG 30	CM	Shot down by 1 Sqn. Hurricanes of Elkington and Davies over Thames Estuary at 11.30 hrs.	Junkers Ju 88A-5 (0311 : 4D+EP)	100 %	Four crew members missing.
7.	I./KG 51	CM	Undercarriage collapsed at Villaroche airfield.	Junkers Ju 88A-1(4154)	35 %	No aircrew casualties.
8.	I./KG 51	CM	Landing accident at Villaroche airfield after bombing sortie.	Junkers Ju 88A-1 (6131)	45 %	One crew member killed; Ltn. Wilhelm Haberl + one wounded.
9.	III./KG 51	CM	Accident on Etampes-Mondesir airfield; details not known.	Junkers Ju 88A-1 (2104 : 9K+CD)	25 %	Crew unhurt.
10.	III./KG 51	CM	Target Crewe.Hit by flak over the Midlands and crashed in River Roach, Horseshoe Corner, Foulness Island at 04.00 hrs. on 10-10-40.	Junkers Ju 88A-1 (0299 : 9K+HS)	100 %	Uffz. Karl Kafka and Fw. Hans Wolff killed; Uffz. Richard Metschuldt and Uffz. Albrecht Schragl made P.O.W.s
11.	4./KG 53	CM	Landing accident at Monteville after bombing sortie.	Heinkel He 111H-2 (5479 : A1+AM)	25 %	Crew unhurt.
12.	I./KG 54	CM	Missing from night bombing sortie over Britain (target Crewe).	Junkers Ju 88A-1 (8039 : B3+KH)	100 %	Ofw. Heinrich Matzel, Gefr. Otto Lockowandt, Gefr. Johann Hasreiter and Uffz. August Klinkmann missing.
13.	I./KG 55	CM	Crashed at St. Sabens following engine failure.	Heinkel He 111P (2866)	100 %	Crew unhurt.
14.	II./KG 55	CM	Force landed at Chartres with flak damage.	Heinkel He 111P (2139)	40 %	One crew member wounded.
15.	Kü.Fl.Gr. 606	CM	Missing from night bombing sortie over Britain (target Crewe).	Dornier Do 17Z-3 (2771 : 7T+HL)	100 %	Ltn.z.S. Harbou, Fw. Hans Langer, and Ogefr. Albert Rübesam killed. Fw. Kurt Göhlisch missing.
16.	I./St.G 1	NCM	Suffered landing accident at Evrecy airfield.	Junkers Ju 87R-1 (5291 : A5+CL)	15 %	Crew unhurt.
17.	III./ZG 76	CM	Suffered taxying accident on Laval airfield.	Messerschmitt Bf 110 D-0 (3330 : 2N+EM)	10 %	Crew unhurt.
18.	Stab/NJG 1	NCM	Involved in taxying accident (with Item 3 above) at Handorf airfield.	Messerschmitt Bf 110 D-0(N)(3360 : G9+CA)	45 %	Crew unhurt.
19.	I./JG 2	NCM	Force landed at Brecquebec, short of fuel; not involved in combat.	Messerschmitt Bf 109 E-4 (4028)	40 %	Pilot unhurt.
20.	4./JG 3	CM	Force landed at Arques following engine failure.	Messerschmitt Bf 109 E-4 (1463)	35 %	Pilot unhurt.
21.	2./JG 26	CM	Crashed and burned at Sangatte after combat.	Messerschmitt Bf 109 E-1 (6264)	100 %	Pilot wounded.
22.	5./JG 51	CM	Crashed and burned at Calais after combat.	Messerschmitt Bf 109 E-1 (3492)	100 %	Pilot killed.
23.	7./JG 54	CM	Shot down by 41 Sqn. Spitfire of Lock near Rochester at 15.30 hrs.	Messerschmitt Bf 109 E-4 (5327)	100 %	Fw. Fritz Schweser missing.
24.	9./JG 54	CM	Shot down by 41 Sqn. Spitfire of Walker near Rochester at 15.35 hrs.	Messerschmitt Bf 109 E-4 (1573)	100 %	Ltn. Josef Eberle killed.
25.	1./JG 77	CM	Shot down by 222 Sqn. Spitfire of Thomas west of Hawkinge; pilot crashed, set fire to aircraft and then surrendered to civilians.	Messerschmitt Bf 109 E-4 (0966)	100 %	Ltn. Heinz Eschwerhaus made P.O.W.

Thursday 10th October

It is difficult to ascribe to the German daylight tactics of this period of the Battle any other purpose than that of creating nuisance and fatigue among the British pilots. Whether this could constitute a worthwhile military aim is highly questionable, but the attempt certainly succeeded. British pilots, like those of any other dedicated air force, were never wont to complain of the amount of flying which they were called upon to do; but the long periods spent in cramped cockpits under the blinding glare of the sun on the autumn carpets of cumulous clouds, added to the burning sensation of constant oxygen breathing at high altitude, and were taking their toll. This was reflected in the growing number of accidents caused by sheer fatigue—accidents which under other circumstances would be judged the results of stupidity or negligence. No such harsh judgement can be applied to these tired men—any more than to the men of the *Luftwaffe* who returned to their bases in France with aircraft shot through by *flak*, after long hours of battling against the onset of English winter weather. A glance at the loss table will indicate the degree to which the *Luftwaffe* itself was suffering.

R.A.F. FIGHTER COMMAND LOSSES—THURSDAY 10th OCTOBER 1940

1.	56 Sqn., Warmwell	C	Shot down by Bf 109s at Wareham and crashed at Worgret; pilot killed.	A12.40 hrs.	Sgt. J. Hlavac	Hurricane	P3421	Cat. 3 Destroyed
2.	92 Sqn., Biggin Hill	C	Collided with Item 3 east of Brighton in combat with Do 17; pilot baled out, wounded, but was too low and was killed.	07.45 hrs.	Plt. Off. J.F. Drummond	Spitfire	R6616	Cat. 3 Destroyed
3.	92 Sqn., Biggin Hill	C	Collided with Item 2 east of Brighton in combat with Do 17; pilot killed when aircraft broke up in the air.	07.45 hrs.	Plt. off D.G. Williams	Spitfire	X4038	Cat. 3 Destroyed
4.	92 Sqn., Biggin Hill	C	Damaged by fire from Do 17 over Brighton and crash landed at Poynings; pilot unhurt.	07.48 hrs.	Sgt. W.T. Ellis	Spitfire	X4553	Cat. 3 Destroyed
5.	238 Sqn., Middle Wallop	C	Shot down near Poole; pilot baled out, wounded in the leg and shoulder, over Brownsea Island; aircraft crashed near Corfe Castle.	A12.50 hrs.	Plt. Off. R.F.T. Doe	Hurricane	P3984	Cat. 3 Destroyed
6.	249 Sqn., North Weald	NC	Crashed due to oxygen failure at Cooling, 7 miles ENE of Gravesend; pilot killed.	A16.00 hrs.	Sgt. E.A. Bayley	Hurricane	V6878	Cat. 3 Destroyed
7.	253 Sqn., Kenley	NC	Crashed due to oxygen failure during patrol at Maidstone; pilot killed.	A16.00 hrs.	Sgt. H.H. Allgood	Hurricane	L1928	Cat. 3 Destroyed
8.	312 Sqn., Speke	NC	Crashed beside the River Mersey after fire in the air; pilot baled out but was killed.	14.15 hrs.	Sgt. O. Hanzlicek	Hurricane	L1547 (1)	Cat. 3 Destroyed

[(1) *L1547* was the very first production Hurricane, first flown in 1937.]

LUFTWAFFE LOSSES—THURSDAY 10TH OCTOBER 1940

1.	1./KG 2	CM	Damaged by 92 Sqn. Spitfires east of Brighton at A.08.00 hrs; returned safely to base.	Dornier Do 17Z (3442 : U5+CH)	10 %	Ltn. Walter Dilcher killed.
2.	4./KG 2	CM	Crashed at St. Leger following engine failure.	Dornier Do 17Z-2 (1201 : U5+BM)	70 %	Crew unhurt.
3.	7./KG 3	CM	Became lost and crashed at Borkum; crew baled out.	Dornier Do 17Z (3293 : 5K+AR)	100 %	One crew member injured.
4.	1./KG 30	NCM	Landing accident at Ludwiglust; cause unknown.	Junkers Ju 88A-1 (7020)	40 %	Crew unhurt.
5.	1./KG 30	NCM	Landing accident at Ludwiglust; cause unknown.	Junkers Ju 88A-1 (8021)	10 %	Gefr. Suppick injured.
6.	Geschw.Erg.St./	NCM	Take-off accident at Lechfeld; detailed not notified.	Junkers Ju 88A-1 (5007 : 9K+FA)	30 %	Crew unhurt.
7.	6./KG 53	CM	Landed at Holt (Holland) with combat damage.	Heinkel He 111H-3 (5716 : A1+FP)	25 %	Crew unhurt.
8.	II./KG 55	CM	Force landed at Chartres following engine failure.	Heinkel He 111P-2 (3132)	20 %	Crew unhurt.
9.	Kü.Fl.Gr. 606	CM	Suffered landing accident at Brest following bombing sortie over Britain.	Dornier Do 17Z-3 (3618 : 7T+KL)	15 %	Crew unhurt.
10.	3./St.G 2	NCM	Suffered air collision with Item 11 over Fôret de Bretonne.	Junkers Ju 87B-2 (0513 : T6+FL)	100 %	One crew member killed.
11.	3./St.G 2	NCM	Suffered air collision with Item 10 over Fôret de Bretonne.	Junkers Ju 87B-2 (0557 : T6+JL)	100 %	Ltn. Rolf Brücker + one killed.
12.	III./LG 1	NCM	Crashed at Telgte following engine failure.	Junkers Ju 88A-1 (6061 : CF+WD)	70 %	One crew member injured.
13.	II./LG 2	CM	Landing accident at Breton after combat.	Messerschmitt Bf 109 E-4 (3722)	60 %	Pilot unhurt.
14.	6./JG 27	NCM	Minor accident at Bonningues; details not known.	Messerschmitt Bf 109 E-1 (1312)	15 %	Pilot unhurt.
15.	1./JG 51	NCM	Take-off accident at Pihen; details not known.	Messerschmitt Bf 109 E-1 (6238)	80 %	Pilot unhurt.
16.	III./JG 52	NCM	Suffered air collision (with Item 17) at Schonwalde; pilot baled out.	Messerschmitt Bf 109 E-1 (5200)	100 %	Pilot unhurt.
17.	III./JG 52	NCM	Suffered air collision (with Item 16) at Schonwalde; pilot baled out.	Messerschmitt Bf 109 E-3 (6333)	100 %	Pilot unhurt.
18.	4./JG 53	CM	Shot down by 603 Sqn. Spitfire of Carbury near Ramsgate at A.11.00 hrs.	Messerschmitt Bf 109 E-1 (4143)	100 %	Oblt. Richard Vogel, *St. Kap.*, missing.
19.	I./JG 54	CM	Force landed at Groningen short of fuel after combat.	Messerschmitt Bf 109E (5238)	5 %	Pilot unhurt.
20.	*Luftwaffen-Kontroll-Inspektion*	NCM	Accident involving total loss of aircraft; nature and location not divulged.in records.	Junkers Ju 52/3m	100 %	Oberst.von Floten (pilot),Ltn.Weiss (2nd pilot), Hptm. Dr. Schweitzer, Uffz. Mauss, Uffz. Merten, Gefr. Thiel and Fl. Stingl killed. Major Augustini missing.

Friday 11th October

Park's fears were to be realised on this day as successive groups of bomb-carrying Bf 109s came in during the morning, with top cover extending to well above 30,000 feet. Bombs were scattered over Ashford, Canterbury and Folkestone, causing more than fifty casualties. In the afternoon Biggin Hill and Kenley received some hits, and the Spitfires of No. 41 Squadron chased and caught a *Staffel* of JG 27; Eric Lock shot down a Bf 109 into the sea off Deal, its pilot being rescued later in the evening by an enemy seaplane. No. 41 Squadron lost three aircraft, two of which collided.

In the gathering dusk the Spitfires of No. 611 Squadron and the Hurricanes of No. 312 (Czech) Squadron were scrambled to meet the first of the night raiders making for Liverpool and the Midlands. Sgt. Kenneth Pattison shot one down, and the Squadron shared another, while a third (two of whose crew baled out) limped home to crash land at Brest. The quasi-

No. 312 (Czech) Squadron made a tentative start on operations early in October while based at Speke near Liverpool, sharing in the destruction of a Dornier Do 17Z-3 of the 1st *Staffel*, *Küstenfliegergruppe 606* on the 11th. Here, the British C.O., Squadron Leader Frank Tyson, is flanked by his two R.A.F. flight commanders.

naval unit, *Küstenfliegergruppe 606* had now lost more than a dozen Dorniers in its night attacks on Merseyside and the industrial West Midlands.

It was at about this time that an Air Ministry Intelligence Unit, whose task was to examine enemy aircraft which crashed in Britain, began to circulate reports of its findings. Staffed with only a pair of investigation teams at this stage of the Battle, it had proved possible only to visit a small proportion of the crash sites during the hectic days of September (although many German aircraft, which it had not yet proved possible to move, were now being methodically examined). A vast amount of information was now being collated, enabling British Intelligence to build up an astonishingly complete picture of the *Luftwaffe*, its aircraft, deployment of units and personnel. This Department, A.I.1(g), headed by Wing Commander James Alfred Easton (a General Duties pilot and a qualified armament specialist), gradually trained new teams to visit crash sites all over Britain, and by the end of October 1940 had issued reports on more than 300 German aircraft, reports which, equated with the results of prisoner interrogation and collated by A.D.I.K. provide a fascinating insight into the life and workings of the wartimne *Luftwaffe*. A *résumé* of A.I.1(g)'s reports is reproduced in Appendix M.

R.A.F. FIGHTER COMMAND LOSSES—FRIDAY 11th OCTOBER 1940

1.	41 Sqn., Hornchurch	C	Suffered air collision with Item 2. Aircraft crashed near West Kingsdown; pilot killed when his parachute failed to open.	16.30 hrs.	Fg. Off. D.H. O'Neill	Spitfire	X4052	Cat. 3 Destroyed
2.	41 Sqn., Hornchurch	C	Air collision with Item 1. Pilot baled out and landed unhurt.	16.30 hrs.	Sgt. L.R. Carter	Spitfire	X4554	Cat. 3 Destroyed
3.	41 Sqn., Hornchurch	C	Shot down by Bf 109s and crashed at Preston Hall, Maidstone; pilot baled out but was dead on landing.	16.35 hrs.	Plt. Off J.G. Lecky	Spitfire	P9447	Cat. 3 Destroyed
4.	66 Sqn., Gravesend	NC	Force landed at Eastchurch in bad weather; pilot unhurt.	Not known	Sgt. P.H. Willcocks	Spitfire	N3121	Cat. 1 Damaged
5.	66 Sqn., Gravesend	C	Shot down by Bf 109s of JG 51near Canterbury and crashed in Covert Wood, Elham. Pilot injured.	11.20 hrs.	Plt. Off. J.H. Pickering	Spitfire	X4562	Cat. 3 Destroyed
6.	66 Sqn., Gravesend	C	Shot down by Bf 109s and crash landed at Hawkinge; pilot slightly concussed.	11.25 hrs.	Plt. Off. H.R. Allen	Spitfire	X4255	Cat. 3 Destroyed
7.	72 Sqn., Biggin Hill	C	Shot down in flames by Bf 109s over a convoy off Deal; pilot baled out wounded.	08.10 hrs.	Plt. Off. P.D. Pool	Spitfire	K9870	Cat. 3 Destroyed
8.	73 Sqn., Debden	C	Shot down while flying as weaver by Bf 109s; pilot baled out woundedover the Medway Estuary; aircraft fell at Frindsbury, Rochester.	11.10 hrs.	Sgt. R. Plenderleith	Hurricane	V6857	Cat. 3 Destroyed
9.	249 Sqn., North Weald	NC	Pilot omitted to lower wheels before landing; was unhurt.	15.25 hrs.	Plt. Off. J.J. Solak	Hurricane	V6728	Cat. 1 Damaged
10.	253 Sqn., Kenley	C	Shot down by Bf 109s near Tunbridge Wells; pilot baled out and sustained a broken arm.	11.35 hrs.	Plt. Off. L.C. Murch	Hurricane	V6570	Cat. 3 Destroyed
11.	253 Sqn., Kenley	C	Crashed while on patrol, cause unknown; pilot unhurt.	16.55 hrs.	Sgt. R.A. Innes	Hurricane	L1666	Cat. 3 Destroyed
12.	312 Sqn., Speke	C	Damaged in combat near Chester; pilot unhurt.	18.15 hrs.	Plt. Off. J.A. Jaske	Hurricane	L1807	Cat. 1 Damaged
13.	611 Sqn., Ternhill	C	Hit by return fire from Do 17; aircraft crashed at Cooksey Green, near Kidderminster. Pilot grievously injured and died on 13-10-40.	19.45 hrs.	Sgt. K.C. Pattison	Spitfire	P7323	Cat. 3 Destroyed

LUFTWAFFE LOSSES—FRIDAY 11th OCTOBER 1940

1.	4.(H)/22	NCM	Suffered minor landing accident at St. Martin.	Henschel Hs 126 (0305 : CH+AM)	10 %	Crew unhurt.
2.	2.(H)/32	NCM	Accident due to faulty servicing at Roth airfield.	Henschel Hs 126A (3042 : V7+AD)	12 %	Crew unhurt.
3.	1.(F)/121	CM	Missing from reconnaissance sortie over Scotland	Junkers Ju 88A-1 (0414 : 7A+NH)	100 %	Maj. Wilhelm Gerlach, Uffz. Kurt Koltermann, Gefr. Hermann Eha and Uffz. Kurt Mehle missing.
4.	II./KG 1	CM	Crashed at Maarten following technical failure.	Heinkel He 111H-2 (2754 : V4+EW)	100 %	Uffz. Erich Linke killed.
5.	5./KG 2	NCM	Became lost on navigation training flight and crashed into the River Aisne.	Dornier Do 17Z-2 (2893 : U5+AN)	100 %	Ltn. Johannes Hübner, Gefr. Adolf Schreiner, Ogefr. Willi Zechner and Fl. Oskar Brüske killed
6.	I./KG 55	CM	Force landed at Dreux airfield in bad weather.	Heinkel He 111P (2928)	40 %	Crew unhurt.
7.	1./Kü.Fl.Gr.606	CM	Shot down by 312 Sqn. Hurricanes and 611 Sqn. Spitfires near Chester; target Liverpool.	Dornier Do 17Z-3 (2772 : 7T+EH)	100 %	Ltn.z.S. Jürgen von Krause, Fw. Josef Vetterl,Ogefr.Helmut Sundermann and Fw. Heinrich Arpert missing.
8.	1./Kü.Fl.Gr.606	CM	Attacked by 611 Sqn. Spitfires during raid on Liverpool; aircraft set on fire and two crew baled out. Aircraft returned safely to Brest.	Dornier Do 17Z-3 (2787 : 7T+HH)	45 %	Uffz. Heinz Johanssen killed; Fw. Hans Starf made P.O.W.
9.	2./Kü.Fl.Gr.606	CM	Target Crewe. Shot down by 611 Sqn. Spitfire of Pattinson near Kidderminster at19.45 hrs.	Dornier Do 17Z-3 (3475 : 7T+EK)	100 %	Ltn.z.S. Horst Felber, Oblt. Friedrich Wilhelm Richter and Gefr. Walter Hoppmann killed; Uffz. Jürgen Weber missing.

Luftwaffe Losses, 11th October 1940—*continued*

10.	II./LG 1	CM	Take-off accident at Orléans-Bricy airfield.	Junkers Ju 88A-5 (3187 : L1+YC)	25 %	Crew unhurt.
11.	5./JG 27	CM	Shot down by 41 Sqn. Spitfire of Lock near Deal at 16.20 hrs.; pilot baled out into the seas.	Messerschmitt Bf 109 E-1 (6267)	100 %	Uffz. Wiemann, wounded, rescued by *Seenotflugkommando*.
12.	1./JG 51	CM	Damaged by 66 Sqn. Spitfire of Bodie, and force landed at Sangatte.	Messerschmitt Bf 109 E-4 (5357)	20 %	Pilot unhurt.
13.	4./JG 53	CM	Crashed on take-off at Berck-sur-Mer airfield.	Messerschmitt Bf 109 E-4 (3751)	85 %	Pilot unhurt.
14.	6./JG 53	NCM	Force landed at Berck-sur-Mer; not combat.	Messerschmitt Bf 109 E-1 (4832)	30 %	Pilot unhurt.
15.	1./JG 77	CM	Force landed at Cap Gris Nez after combat over Kent.	Messerschmitt Bf 109 E-4 (5109)	70 %	Pilot unhurt.
16.	2./406	—	Force landed off Vardoen and damaged beyond repair while under tow by steamship *Stralsund*.	Dornier Do 18 (0848 : K6+LK)	100 %	No casualties notified.
17.	Kurierstaffel 110	NCM	Take-off accident at Ypenburg; details not notified.	Junkers Ju W.34Hi (0589 : SD+DV)	60 %	No casualties notified.

Saturday 12th October

Bad weather once again reduced air defence operations over Britain, although Lehrgeschwader 2 sent a *Staffel* of bomb-carrying Bf 109E-7s on snap raids over Kent; at least three penetrated to Central London, where a 250-kilo bomb, dropped from 20,000 feet, killed five people in Piccadilly Circus. Squadron Leader Stanford Tuck, visiting his old Squadron—No. 92—at Biggin Hill, took off in a Spitfire and shot down one of the LG 2 fighter-bombers during the morning. Another fighter-bomber raid was flown by I./JG 52 and, although it is said that three of its aircraft were shot down, they have not been identified in German records.

R.A.F. FIGHTER COMMAND LOSSES—SATURDAY 12th OCTOBER 1940

1.	3 Sqn., Montrose	NC	Suffered taxiing accident at Montrose; pilot unhurt.	Not known	Sgt. J. Biel	Hurricane	R4077	Cat. 1 Damaged
2.	29 Sqn., Wellingore	NC	Suffered engine failure on take-off for air test at Wellingore and crashed; pilot unhurt.	15.50 hrs.	Plt. Off. J. Buchanan	Blenheim	L1472	Cat. 3 Destroyed
3.	41 Sqn., Hornchurch	NC	Crashed landed near Romford following engine failure; pilot unhurt.	A16.40 hrs.	Sgt. J. McAdam	Spitfire	P9512	Cat. 3 Destroyed
4.	72 Sqn., Biggin Hill	C	Crashed near Folkestone after breaking away from formation; cause not established. Pilot killed.	A10.00 hrs.	Plt. Off. H.R. Case	Spitfire	P9338	Cat. 3 Destroyed
5.	92 Sqn., Biggin Hill	C	Shot down by Bf 109s over Hawkinge; pilot killed. Aircraft crashed at Postling, Hythe.	16.30 hrs.	Plt. Off. A.J.S. Pattinson	Spitfire	X4591	Cat. 3 Destroyed
6.	145 Sqn., Tangmere	C	Shot down by Bf 109s over Hastings; pilot baled out, wounded, at Coghurst; aircraft crashed at Guestling.	A10.30 hrs.	Sgt. P. Thorpe	Hurricane	P3896	Cat. 3 Destroyed
7.	145 Sqn., Tangmere	C	Shot down by Bf 109s over Hastings; aircraft crashed at Chittenden. Pilot killed.	A10.30 hrs.	Sgt. J.V. Wadham	Hurricane	V7426	Cat. 3 Destroyed
8.	219 Sqn., Redhill	C	Crashed at night during patrol near Ewhurst, Hastings; pilot and radar operator baled out.	At night	Sgt. D.M. Head Sgt. C. Browne	Blenheim	L1113	Cat. 3 Destroyed
9.	249 Sqn., North Weald	C	Shot down by Bf 109s near Eastchurch; pilot baled out slightly wounded.	A10.00 hrs.	Adj. C. Perrin	Hurricane	V6854	Cat. 3 Destroyed
10.	257 Sqn., North Weald	C	Shot down by Bf 109s near Faversham; pilot, unwounded, force landed at Selling.	09.50 hrs.	Plt. Off. J. Redman	Hurricane	P3704	Cat. 3 Destroyed
11.	257 Sqn., North Weald	C	Damaged by Bf 109s over East Kent; pilot, unhurt, force landed at Detling.	09.58 hrs.	Plt. Off. K.C. Gundry	Hurricane	P3775	Cat. 2 Damaged
12.	257 Sqn., North Weald	C	Shot down by Bf 109 over Dungeness; pilot baled out slightly wounded; aircraft crashed at Stone, near Appledore, Kent.	A16.40 hrs.	Plt. Off. C.F.A. Capon	Hurricane	V7298	Cat. 3 Destroyed
13.	602 Sqn., Westhampnett	C	Damaged by Ju 88 over Channel; crash landed at Iford, Sussex, but overturned; pilot unhurt.	15.36 hrs.	Sgt. C.F. Babbage	Spitfire	X4541	Cat. 3 Destroyed
14.	602 Sqn., Westhampnett	C	Damaged by Ju 88 over Channel near Beachy Head; pilot returned unhurt.	15.36 hrs.	Plt. Off J.S. Hart	Spitfire	P9446	Cat. 2 Damaged
15.	605 Sqn., Croydon	C	Shot down and pilot killed in combat with Bf 109s near Dungeness; aircraft crashed at Littlestone golf course, near New Romney.	A13.00 hrs.	Sgt. P.R.C. McIntosh	Hurricane	P3022	Cat. 3 Destroyed
16.	615 Sqn., Northolt	NC	Force landed at Selling, Kent, with engine trouble during patrol; pilot unhurt.	16.05 hrs.	Plt. Off. N.D. Edmond	Hurricane	—	Cat. 2 Damaged

LUFTWAFFE LOSSES—SATURDAY 12th OCTOBER 1940

1.	4.(F)/14	CM	Struck the ground while low flying near Caen.	Messerschmitt Bf 110 C-5 (2243 : 5F+MM)	100 %	Oblt. Doffek + one killed.
2.	7./KG 51	CM	Suffered take-off accident at Montdidier airfield.	Junkers Ju 88A-1 (7075 : 9K+DR)	100 %	Fw. Bruno Torprzisseck killed; Oblt. Simon, Ofw. Strauss and Fw. Baader injured.
3.	II./LG 1	CM	Damaged by 602 Sqn. Spitfires of Babbage and Hart and crashed at Orléans-Bricy.	Junkers Ju 88A-1 (3075 : L1+HN)	75 %	Crew unhurt.
4.	2./LG 2	CM	Shot down by Spitfire of Tuck (flying with 92 Sqn.) over Kent, and crashed at Chantry Farm, Hollingbourne.	Messerschmitt Bf 109 E-7 (5793)	100 %	Pilot made P.O.W.
5.	2./LG 2	CM	Shot down by 605 Sqn. Hurricane of Ingle and crashed at Bean's Hill, Harrietsham, near Maidstone.	Messerschmitt Bf 109 E-7	100 %	Pilot made P.O.W.
6.	2./LG 2	CM	Shot down by 145 Sqn. Hurricane of Rabone and crashed Weeke's Lane, West Brabourne, near Ashford.	Messerschmitt Bf 109 E-3	100 %	Pilot made P.O.W.
7.	2./LG 2	CM	Shot down by unknown aircraft and crashed at Chapel Holding, Small Hythe, Tenterden, Kent.	Messerschmitt Bf 109 E-3 (<+I)	100 %	Pilot made P.O.W.
8.	2./LG 2	CM	Force landed at Calais-Marck airfield after engine failure.	Messerschmitt Bf 109 E-4 (5563)	15 %	Pilot unhurt.

Luftwaffe Losses, 12th October 1940—*continued*

9.	8./JG 51	NCM	Take-off accident at Clairmarais airfield.	Messerschmitt Bf 109 E-1 (3313)	60 %	Pilot unhurt.
10.	II./JG 77	CM	Crashed at Stavanger-Sola; cause not known.	Messerschmitt Bf 109 E-1 (3309)	100 %	Pilot killed.
11.	1./196	CM	Shot down by 145 Sqn. Hurricanes during the evening.	Arado Ar 196 (0088 : 6W+FN)	100 %	Hptm. Karl Thewaldt, *St.Kap.*, killed; UJffz. Willi Kottwitz missing.

Sunday 13th October

The fog and low cloud that had covered much of Southern England for the past two days now spread over the Low Countries, and probably accounted for some of the flying accidents reported by *Luftwaffe* units.

The sirens sounded three times in London after mid-day as formation after formation of high-flying intruders—each of about *Gruppe* strength—fought their way past the Spitfires scrambled from Biggin Hill and Hornchurch. Combat casualties were relatively light, although undoubtedly in the Germans' favour—probably as a result of the British fighters being bounced while climbing to tackle the top cover Bf 109s.

R.A.F. FIGHTER COMMAND LOSSES—SUNDAY 13th OCTOBER 1940

1.	17 Sqn., Martlesham	(C)	Shot down by Chatham A.A. guns; pilot baled out unhurt.	14.30 hrs.	Plt. Off. J.H. Ross	Hurricane	P3536	Cat. 3 Destroyed
2.	29 Sqn., Ternhill	(C)	Shot down into the sea by Hurricanes of No. 312 (Czech) Sqn., 10 miles NW of Liverpool; all three crew members killed.	A18.00 hrs.	Sgt. R.E. Stevens Sgt. O.K. Sly AC A. Jackson	Blenheim	L6637	Cat. 3 Lost
3.	29 Sqn., Ternhill	(C)	Damaged by Hurricanes of No. 312 (Czech) Sqn., and written off on landing; crew safe.	A18.00 hrs.	Plt. Off. J.D. Humphreys Sgt. E.H. Bee AC J.F. Fizell	Blenheim	L7135	Cat. 3 Destroyed
4.	46 Sqn., Stapleford	C	Bounced by Bf 109s over Dungeness; pilot, wounded in arm, force landed at Biggin Hill.	A13.00 hrs.	Sgt. L.H.B. Pearce	Hurricane	—	Cat. 1 Damaged
5.	66 Sqn., Gravesend	C	Shot down by Bf 109s near Maidstone and force landed at Hornchurch; pilot unhurt.	A13.00 hrs.	Sgt. H. Cook	Spitfire	X4543	Cat. 3 Destroyed
6.	66 Sqn., Gravesend	C	Damaged by Bf 109s and force landed at Burnham; pilot unhurt.	A15.40 hrs.	Sqn. Ldr. R.H.A. Leigh	Spitfire	X4479	Cat. 2 Damaged
7.	66 Sqn., Gravesend	C	Damaged in combat with Bf 109s; pilot returned unhurt.	A16.40 hrs.	Plt. Off. C.A.W. Bodie	Spitfire	N3285	Cat. 1 Damaged

LUFTWAFFE LOSSES—SUNDAY 13th OCTOBER 1940

1.	II./KG 54	CM	Take-off accident at St. André; details not notified.	Junkers Ju 88A-1 (5122 : B3+GN)	20 %	Crew unhurt.
2.	Stab/KG 76	NCM	Hit ground in fog near Rheinbollen.	Junkers W.34 (2749 : DA+ZX)	75 %	One occupant injured.
3.	II./KG 76	CM	Landed at Rheims airfield with combat damage after bombing sortie.	Junkers Ju 88A-1 (2136 : F1+JM)	30 %	Two crew members wounded.
4.	Stab/KGr. 126	CM	Force landed at Wittmundhafen with combat damage after bombing sortie.	Heinkel He 111H-4 (3265 : 1T+CB)	30 %	Crew unhurt.
5.	2./KGr. 126	NCM	Landing accident at Delmenhorst; no details notified.	Heinkel He 111H-4 (6978 : 1T+DK)	70 %	Crew unhurt.
6.	2./KGr. 126	NCM	Landing accident at Bremen; no details notified.	Heinkel He 111H-4 (6983 : 1T+FK)	30 %	Crew unhurt.
7.	III./LG 1	CM	Crashed at Rouen with engine failure after combat.	Junkers Ju 88A-1 (7018 : L1+KT)	100 %	Crew unhurt.
8.	II./ZG 76	NCM	Force landed at Le Cateau on local flight.	Messerschmitt Bf 110D (3401)	25 %	Crew unhurt.
9.	7./JG 3	CM	Shot down by 92 Sqn. Spitfire of Kingcombe at A.13.30 hrs. and crashed at Robert's Dane, Wye, Kent.	Messerschmitt Bf 109 E-4 (0860 : White 7)	100 %	Gefr. Hubert Rungen made P.O.W.
10.	4./JG 27	CM	Crashed following engine failure at Bonningues.	Messerschmitt Bf 109 E-1 (6310).	70 %	Pilot unhurt.
11.	II./JG 53	CM	Crashed following engine failure at St. Inglevert.	Messerschmitt Bf 109 E-7 (5932)	80 %	Pilot unhurt.
12.	7./JG 54	CM	Take-off accident at Guines-Süd airfield.	Messerschmitt Bf 109 E-4 (5066)	35 %	Pilot unhurt.

Monday 14th October

Although involving each side in only a fraction of the number of combat sorties mounted a month previously, this stage of the Battle saw the *Luftwaffe* achieving almost as great a strain on Fighter Command, as the defence commanders and controllers struggled to meet each local variation of tactics. Now that Göring's medium bombers were almost wholly withdrawn from the daylight fighting, the Bf 109 pilots, whose depredations in English skies had always caused Fighter Command acute discomfort, were once more on the verge of gaining air superiority over the South-East.

Such an achievement would not, however, have counted for much at this stage in the Battle. While well-loved landmarks and ancient treasures were blasted by the Messerschmitts by day, and incinerated by the Heinkels and Dorniers by night, the strength of Fighter Command continued to grow. True, the British fighters could not reach the high-flying Bf 109s; but the day was drawing nearer when the new variants of the Hurricane and Spitfire would reach the squadrons, and give them the muscle to guard the skies again—to say nothing of crossing the Channel and meeting the Messerschmitts over their own territory.

After a day of high altitude raids, in which airfields as far north as North Weald were bombed, Kesselring and Sperrle stepped up the night attacks on London and the Midlands. Despite more than fifty night sorties by seven squadrons of Blenheims, Hurricanes and Defiants, not one of the 300 German raiders was spotted. While Coventry suffered its first severe raid by more than 60 Dorniers, about 200 Heinkels and Ju 88s dropped over a thousand high explosive bombs on London, including fifty land mines; this raid, which has sometimes been referred to as the beginning of the "Blitz", killed 591 civilians and injured 2,300. As has been shown, the night assault on Britain had been in progress almost continuously since early September, and it was Kesselring's determination to exploit the full moon that led to this, the first really devastating raid for almost a month.

R.A.F. FIGHTER COMMAND LOSSES—MONDAY 14th OCTOBER 1940

1.	601 Sqn., Exeter	NC	Suffered landing accident during training flight. Pilot unhurt.	Not known	Sgt. R.A. Milburn	Hurricane	P3393	Cat. 2 Damaged
2.	605 Sqn., Croydon	C	Pilot flew into Inner Artillery Zone during combat with He 111; aircraft either struck ballon cable or was shot down, and crashed at South Norwood; pilot killed.	Not known	Fg. Off. R. Hope	Hurricane	P3107	Cat. 3 Destroyed
3.	616 Sqn., Kirton-in-Lindsey	NC	Pilot experienced undercarriage trouble; aircraft slightly damaged on landing; pilot unhurt.	Not known	Sgt. R.V. Hogg	Spitfire	—	Cat. 1 Damaged

LUFTWAFFE LOSSES—MONDAY 14th OCTOBER 1940

1.	4.(F)/121	NCM	Landing accident at Caen; not combat.	Junkers Ju 88A-1 (0314 : 7A+DM)	40 %	Crew unhurt.
2.	9./KG 2	CM	Force landed at Cambrai-Süd airfield after combat.	Dornier Do 17Z (2556 : U5+BT)	25 %	Crew unhurt.
3.	2./KG 3	CM	Engine failure on take-off at Le Culot airfield.	Dornier Do 17Z-2 (5K+FK)	45 %	Crew unhurt.
4.	Stab II./KG 76	NCM	Crashed near Creil after engine failure; crew baled out.	Focke-Wulf Fw 44 (2672 : RG+AW)	100 %	One occupant injured.
5.	III./KG 77	CM	Night landing accident at Reims airfield.	Junkers Ju 88A-1 (0314 : 7A+DM)	40 %	Crew unhurt.
6.	I./NJG 2	CM	Believed to have been attacked and damaged by 17 Sqn. Hurricane of Czernin while on dusk intruder sortie over Suffolk.	Dornier Do 17Z (2815 : R4+DK)	80 %	Three crew wounded.
7.	III./JG 2	CM	Reported as having been shot down by fighters over Selsey Bill. No British claim trace.	Messerschmitt Bf 109 E-7 (0720 : White 12)(1)	100 %	Ogefr. Lux missing.
8.	4./JG 3	NCM	Landing accident at Arques; not combat.	Messerschmitt Bf 109 E-4 (5359)	25 %	Pilot unhurt.
9.	3./506	CM	Landing accident at Stavanger after mining sortie.	Heinkel He 115 (2677 : S4+LL)	100 %	Crew unhurt.
10.	Geschw.Erg.St./ JG 52	NCM	Force landed at Grubbensort after engine failure.	Messerschmitt Bf 109 E-1 (6147)	10 %	Pilot unhurt.

[(1) At about this date the German fighter units began to include in their loss returns the individual code markings of their aircraft casualties to bring them into line with those of other operational units.]

Tuesday 15th October

Despite all that Park's ingenuity could devise, Messerschmitt Bf 109 *Jabos*, attacking soon after first light, broke through to London where a 250-kilo bomb struck the railway concourse just outside Waterloo station, bringing almost all services to a standstill; nevertheless, all but two lines had been repaired within six hours. Factories on the South Bank were also badly hit, and in this and another raid, an hour later, more than fifty people died.

During the course of the day's attacks the squadron commanders at Biggin Hill and Hornchurch pleaded to be allowed to take off and climb before the raids crossed the coast; and on several occasions the predictable regularity with which the raids appeared enabled the Spitfire pilots to climb early and manoeuvre into the sun, delivering the very type of diving attack which Park had advocated some days before. The result was that four Bf 109s fell over Kent, and another over the Channel.

With the evenings drawing in, the *Luftwaffe* arrived over London shortly before 19.00 hours and carried out another heavy raid, losing only two bombers in the process. Few of the bombs dropped were incendiaries, and the numerous high explosive weapons caused important damage in the dock area and at the Paddington, Waterloo, Victoria and Liverpool Street rail termini. The Beckton gasworks and the Battersea power station were again badly hit, and two subway stations were demolished by land mines. Once again the City was heavily damaged, and the narrow streets became easily blocked, hindering the fire services. During this night 512 people were killed in Greater London; nearly 1,000 were badly injured, and 11,000 rendered homeless—many of the latter in the eastern boroughs.

R.A.F. FIGHTER COMMAND LOSSES—TUESDAY 15th OCTOBER 1940

1.	29 Sqn., Ternhill	—	Destroyed in bombing raid on Ternhill; no aircrew casualties.	Not known	Nil	Blenheim	L7135	Cat. 3 Destroyed
2.	29 Sqn., Ternhill	—	Damaged in bombing raid on Ternhill; no aircrew casualties.	Not known	Nil	Blenheim	L6741	Cat. 1 Damaged
3.	41 Sqn., Hornchurch	C	Shot down by Bf 109s of JG 51 off north Kent coast; pilot killed and his body recovered from the sea at Herne Bay on 27-10-40.	09.08 hrs.	Sgt. P.D. Lloyd	Spitfire	X4178	Cat. 3 Lost
4.	46 Sqn., Stapleford	C	Bounced by Bf 109s over the Thames Estuary and crashed at Little Thurrock, Essex; pilot killed.	A12.55 hrs.	Plt. Off. P.S. Gunning	Hurricane	N2480	Cat. 3 Destroyed

R.A.F. Losses, 15th October 1940—*continued*

5.	46 Sqn., Stapleford	C	Bounced by Bf 109s and crashed at Gravesend; pilot killed.	A12.55 hrs.	F/Sgt. E.E. Williams	Hurricane	V6550	Cat. 3 Destroyed
6.	46 Sqn., Stapleford	C	Bounced by Bf 109s and crashed at Gravesend; pilot baled out slightly wounded.	A12.55 hrs.	Sgt. A.T. Gooderham	Hurricane	V6789	Cat. 3 Destroyed
7.	92 Sqn., Biggin Hill	C	Shot down by Bf 109s over the Thames Estuary; pilot killed and body recovered from the sea off the Dutch coast.	A09.20 hrs.	Sgt. K.B. Parker	Spitfire	R6838	Cat. 3 Missing
8.	92 Sqn., Biggin Hill	C	Shot down by Bf 109s and crashed into sea; pilot rescued, unwounded, by naval vessel.	A12.00 hrs.	Plt. Off. J. Lund	Spitfire	R6642	Cat. 3 Lost
9.	92 Sqn., Biggin Hill	C	Shot down by Bf 109s near the Medway Estuary; pilot baled out wounded. Aircraft crashed at High Halstow, north-east of Rochester.	A09.20 hrs.	Flt. Lt. C.B.F. Kingcombe	Spitfire	X4418	Cat. 3 Destroyed
10.	145 Sqn., Tangmere	C	Shot down by Bf 109s over Christchurch Bay; pilot baled out wounded at New Milton. Aircraft assumed to have crashed at sea.	A12.30 hrs.	Plt. Off.J. Machacek	Hurricane	V7337	Cat. 3 Lost
11.	213 Sqn., Tangmere	C	Shot down by Bf 109 near Swanage and crash landed; pilot unhurt.	A12.35 hrs.	Flt. Lt. J.M. Strickland	Hurricane	V6726	Cat. 3 Destroyed
12.	222 Sqn., Hornchurch	NC	Crashed at Terling, Essex, following engine failure; pilot unhurt.	16.30 hrs.	Plt. Off. H.P.M. Edridge	Spitfire	K9795	Cat. 3 Destroyed
13.	229 Sqn., Northolt	C	Shot down in flames and crashed near Stockbury; pilot baled out severely burned.	A10.00 hrs.	Flt. Lt. A.J. Banham	Hurricane	P3124	Cat. 3 Destroyed
14.	229 Sqn., Northolt	C	Damaged by Bf 109s near Winchelsea; pilot returned unhurt.	A10.10 hrs.	Flt. Lt. W.A. Smith	Hurricane	P3456	Cat. 2 Damaged
15.	253 Sqn., Kenley	C	Shot down by Bf 109s at Dunton Green, Sevenoaks, Kent; pilot unhurt.	08.35 hrs.	Sgt. E.H.C. Kee	Hurricane	V6756	Cat. 3 Destroyed
16.	257 Sqn., North Weald	C	Shot down by Bf 109s and force landed at Hawkinge; pilot unhurt.	A11.40 hrs.	Plt. Off. G. North	Hurricane	V7351	Cat. 2 Damaged
17.	302 Sqn., Duxford	C	Shot down near Chatham; pilot unhurt.	A09.30 hrs.	Not known	Hurricane	P2752	Cat. 3 Destroyed
18.	312 Sqn., Speke	NC	Pilot baled out, thinking he was out of fuel, near Dalton-in-Furness, unhurt.	Not known	Major J.K. Ambrus	Hurricane	V6846	Cat. 3 Destroyed
19.	312 Sqn., Speke	NC	Pilot baled out, thinking he was out of fuel, near Dalton-in-Furness, unhurt.	Not known	Plt. Off. T. Vybiral	Hurricane	V6811	Cat. 3 Destroyed
20.	312 Sqn., Speke	NC	Pilot ran out of fuel and force landed, unhurt, at Carnforth.	Not known	Flt. Lt. H.A.G. Comerford	Hurricane	V6542	Cat. 2 Damaged
21.	501 Sqn., Kenley	C	Shot down by Bf 109s near Redhill; pilot killed. Aircraft crashed at Godstone, Surrey.	08.33 hrs.	Sgt. S.A. Fenemore	Hurricane	V6722	Cat. 3 Destroyed
22.	501 Sqn., Kenley	C	Shot down over Isle ofSheppey and force landed at Rochford; pilot wounded.	A13.10 hrs.	Sgt. R.W.E. Jarrett	Hurricane	P5194	Cat. 3 Destroyed
23.	501 Sqn., Kenley	C	Damaged by Bf l09s over Sheppey and force landed at Rochford; pilot unhurt.	A13.20 hrs.	Fg. Off. R.C. Dafforn	Hurricane	V6787	Cat. 1 Damaged
24.	601 Sqn., Exeter	NC	Suffered landing accident at Exeter; pilot unhurt.	Not known	Plt. Off. J.W. Seddon	Hurricane	P8886	Cat. 1 Damaged
25.	605 Sqn., Croydon	C	Shot down by Bf 109s near Maidstone and crashed at Darland, near Gillingham; pilot killed.	09.20 hrs.	Plt. Off. I.J. Muirhead	Hurricane	N2546	Cat. 3 Destroyed

LUFTWAFFE LOSSES—TUESDAY 15th OCTOBER 1940

1.	3.(F)/123	CM	Landing accident at Buc airfield; no details notified.	Junkers Ju 88A-5 (0429 : 4U+CL)	40 %	Crew unhurt.
2.	I./KG 26	CM	Damaged by 92 Sqn. Spitfire of Fokes over Kent and force landed at Beauvais airfield.	Heinkel He 111H-3 (5637 : 1H+JL)	20 %	Three crew members wounded.
3.	III./KG 27	NCM	Force landed at Rennes airfield after engine failure.	Heinkel He 111P (1734 : 1G+MS)	20 %	Crew unhurt.
4.	8./KG 30	NCM	Suffered taxying accident at Eindhoven airfield.	Junkers Ju 88A-5 (0271 : 4D+CS)	20 %	Crew unhurt.
5.	6./KG 53	CM	Force landed at Arendonk after fighter combat.	Heinkel He 111H-2 (6814 : A1+EP)	45 %	Crew unhurt.
6.	II./KG 55	CM	Damaged by 145 Sqn. Hurricanes over Christchurch Bay at 12.30 hrs. and force landed at Cherbourg.	Heinkel He 111P-2 (1542 : G1+DM)	40 %	Ltn. Wolfgang Hansen + one wounded.
7.	Geschw.Erg.St./ KG 76	NCM	Crashed near Stuttgart due to faulty servicing.	Dornier Do 17Z (3368 : F1+BR)	95 %	Four crew members killed.
8.	I./LG 1	CM	Shot down by 234 Sqn. Spitfires of Harker and Sharpley over Falmouth and crashed into the English Channel	Junkers Ju 88A-1 (3138 : L1+CK)	100 %	Fw. Rudi Döscher, Uffz. Karl Osterried, Gefr. Rudi Annerl and Uffz. Heinz Weiske missing.
9.	NJG 1	CM	Shot down by R.A.F. bombers at night over Gardelegen.	Messerschmitt Bf 110D (3620 : G9+FK)	100 %	Ltn. Mangersdorf + one killed.
10.	4./NJG 2	CM	Shot down by R.A.F. bombers at night; crew baled out.	Messerschmitt Bf 110D (3812 : 2A+BL)	100 %	One crew member injured.
11.	Stab I./LG 2	CM	Shot down by 92 Sqn. Spitfire of Kingaby over Kent at 09.20 hrs.	Messerschmitt Bf 109 E-7 (3734)	100 %	Ltn. Ludwig Lenz killed. (Buried in Hawkinge Cemetery.)
12.	II./LG 2	CM	Landing accident at Calais-Marck after fighter combat.	Messerschmitt Bf 109 E-4 (5569)	25 %	Pilot unhurt.
13.	I./JG 2	CM	Shot down by 145 Sqn. Hurricane of Boyd over Christchurch Bay at A.13.00 hrs., and crashed at Bowcombe Down, Isle of Wight.	Messerschmitt Bf 109 E-4 (1588 : Yellow 8)	100 %	Fw. Horst Hellriegel made P.O.W.
14.	II./JG 2	CM	Missing from combat over Christchurch Bay at A.12.30 hrs.	Messerschmitt Bf 109 E-1 (3279)	100 %	Gefr. Alois Pollach missing.
15.	II./JG 2	CM	Crashed at Beaumont-le-Roger with battle damage sustained in combat over Christchurch Bay.	Messerschmitt Bf 109 E-4 (1412)	100 %	Pilot wounded.
16.	II./JG 3	CM	Crashed at Outrau following engine failure.	Messerschmitt Bf 109 E-4 (6100)	100 %	Pilot injured.
17.	5./JG 3	CM	Landing accident at Arques following combat.	Messerschmitt Bf 109 E-1 (3279)	20 %	Pilot unhurt.
18.	5./JG 3	CM	Take-off accident at Arques on combat sortie.	Messerschmitt Bf 109 E-1 (3251)	60 %	Pilot unhurt.
19.	8./JG 3	CM	Shot down by 229 Sqn. Hurricane of Brown east of Canterbury at 10.15 hrs. and crashed on Sandwich Beach.	Messerschmitt Bf 109 E-4 (1294 : Black 7)	100 %	Ofw. Wilhelm Bauer made P.O.W.
20.	Geschw.Erg.St./ JG 26	NCM	Take-off accident at St. Omer; further details not recorded.	Messerschmitt Bf 109 E-1 (3910)	60 %	Pilot unhurt.

21.	6./JG 27	CM	Shot down by 92 Sqn. Spitfire of Fokes off Cap Gris Nez at 09.45 hrs.	Messerschmitt Bf 109 E-1 (3456)	100 %	Ofw. Gotthardt Freis killed.
22.	9./JG 27	CM	Shot down by Spitfires near Maidstone; time not recorded.	Messerschmitt Bf 109 E-1 (6341)	100 %	Oblt. Günther Deicke made P.O.W.
23.	4./JG 51	CM	Shot down by 92 Sqn. Spitfire of Fokes near Sevenoaks and crashed at Lamberhurst at 12.05 hrs.	Messerschmitt Bf 109 E-1 (3535)	100 %	Uffz. Erich Höhn made P.O.W.
24.	9./JG 51	CM	Landing accident at St. Omer after combat sortie.	Messerschmitt Bf 109 E-1 (6341)	25 %	Pilot unhurt.
25.	Geschw.Erg.St./ JG 52	NCM	Force landed at Krefeld following technical failure.	Messerschmitt Bf 109 E-1 (3363)	50 %	Pilot unhurt.
26.	Stab/JG 53	NCM	Take-off accident at Neuerburg; cause not notified.	Focke-Wulf Fw 58 C (2204 : NF+NV)	90 %	Occupants unhurt.
27.	2./JG 77	CM	Force landed at Cap Gris Nez following combat.	Messerschmitt Bf 109 E-4 (1189)	95 %	Pilot unhurt.

Wednesday 16th October

While London suffered under the bombs of *Kampfgeschwader 26*, twenty Dorniers of Kü.Fl.Gr. 606 were on course for Birmingham, which they raided just before dawn. One evidently missed its way, stumbled across the airfield at Ternhill in Shropshire, and unloaded a single GG mine which struck a hangar demolishing it and the twenty training aircraft inside. One of No. 29 Squadron's Blenheim night fighters was also destroyed. The enemy aircraft made off safely in the early morning gloom.

After one of the relatively few daylight combats over the South-East, the Polish pilots of No. 302 Squadron—now flying from Northolt—stumbled into the balloon barrage guarding the Hawker Aircraft factory at Langley in Buckinghamshire. Miraculously none was killed, but Sgt. Wilhelm Kosarz struck a cable and lost fourteen inches of his starboard wing; he experienced some difficulty in recovering from the subsequent spin without the benefit of ailerons, but brought his Hurricane down to a perfect landing at Heston.

Close-up view of a KG 77 Junkers Ju 88; just visible is part of its external bomb load. This *Kampfgeschwader* suffered punishing losses during the last six weeks of the Battle of Britain. (Photo: Hans Obert)

R.A.F. FIGHTER COMMAND LOSSES—WEDNESDAY 16th OCTOBER 1940

1.	1 Sqn., Wittering	NC	Force landed following engine trouble; pilot unhurt.	A14.30 hrs.	Sgt. J. Prihoda	Hurricane	P3318	Cat. 2 Damaged
2.	264 Sqn., Luton	C	Overshot on landing in fog after night combat; crew unhurt.	A02.30 hrs.	Plt. Off. F.D. Hughes	Defiant	—	Cat. 1 Damaged
3.	302 Sqn., Duxford	NC	Force landed following engine trouble; pilot unhurt.	Not known	Plt. Off. J.L. Malinski	Hurricane	R2684	Cat. 2 Damaged
4.	302 Sqn., Duxford	C	Shot down in flames by Bf 109 near Chatham and crashed at Stoke; pilot wounded.	A11.00 hrs.	Sgt. M. Wedzik	Hurricane	P2752	Cat. 3 Destroyed
5.	302 Sqn., Duxford	C	Aircraft struck balloon cable, losing 14 inches of starboard wingtip; pilot landed unhurt at Heston.	Not known	Sqt. W. Kosarz	Hurricane	P3935	Cat. 2 Damaged
6.	310 Sqn., Duxford	NC	Crashed on training flight near Ely; pilot killed	Not known	Plt. Off. S.J. Chalupa	Hurricane	P3143	Cat. 3 Destroyed
7.	504 Sqn., Filton	NC	Force landed at Whitchurch while on patrol; aircraft ran into pond, but pilot unhurt.	Not known	Plt. Off. R.E. Tongue	Hurricane	R4178	Cat. 2 Damaged
8.	601 Sqn., Exeter	NC	Suffered landing accident when pilot swerved to avoid an aircraft landing downwind.	Not known	Sqn. Ldr. Sir Archibald Hope,Bt.	Hurricane	V6649	Cat. 1 Damaged

LUFTWAFFE LOSSES—WEDNESDAY 16th OCTOBER 1940

1.	1.(H)/21	NCM	Crashed at Bergen op Zoom; cause not notified.	Messerschmitt Bf 110 E-1 (6300)	60 %	Fw. Pülke and Fw. Wehner wounded.
2.	3.(F)/121	CM	Crashed at Brest airfield due to faulty servicing.	Junkers Ju 88A-5 (0390 : 7A+BL)	30 %	Crew safe.
3.	1.(F)/122	CM	Force landed at Vendeville following combat sortie.	Junkers Ju 88A-1 (5047 : F6+LH)	60 %	One crew member wounded.
4.	6./KG 2	CM	Force landed at St. Leger following combat	Dornier Do 17Z-3 (3352 : U5+CC)	40 %	one crew member wounded.
5.	6./KG 3	NCM	Force landed at Antwerp due to faulty servicing.	Dornier Do 17Z (4252)	30 %	Crew safe.
6.	II./KG 26	CM	Shot down by 164 Sqn. Defiant night fighter of Hughes and Gash at Brentwood, Essex, at 01.30 hrs.	Heinkel He 111H-3 (3310 : 1H+DN)	100 %	Oblt. Karl Sommer, Uffz. Willi Bräutigam, Uffz. Willi Kaublau and Gefr. Josef Felleger killed.
7.	Stab II./KG 40	CM	Shot down by *flak* and crashed at Bishops Stortford; bombs exploded on impact.	Junkers Ju 88A-5 (0317 : 4D+DM)	100 %	Hptm.Erich Haas,Gr.Kdr., Fw. Günter Suhr and Fw. Josef Kessels killed. (Only three crew members.)
8.	9./KG 30	CM	Crashed at Eindhoven on return from bombing sortie.	Junkers Ju 88A-1 (0170 : 4D+KT)	100 %	Crew safe.
9.	I./KG 53	NCM	Landing accident at Antwerp; cause not known.	Junkers Ju 52 (5323)	30 %	No casualties.
10.	Geschw.Erg.St./ KG 54	NCM	Landing accident at Augsburg; cause not known.	Heinkel He 111P (2486)	80 %	Crew unhurt.

The remains of Heinkel He 111H, said to have been Wkr.Nr. 5709:1T+KL, which crashed at Cressey Farm, Hutton, near Brentwood, shot down by the Defiant night fighter flown by Fg. Off. Desmond Hughes (gunner Sgt. Fred Gash) at 02.15 hrs. on the night of 15th/16th October. Information about this aircraft is conflicting as the German records state that the pilot, Uffz. Konrad Gläser, was flying a different Heinkel, hence the discrepancy in the loss table. (See Report No. 4/72 in Appendix M).

Luftwaffe Losses, 16th October 1940—*continued*

11.	II./KG 55	CM	Suffered taxying accident at Chartres airfield.	Heinkel He 111P-2 (2840 : G1+SN)	15 %	Crew unhurt.
12.	I./KG 76	CM	Crashed and burned at Beauvais on return from bombing sortie.	Dornier Do 17Z (3448 : F1+FH)	100 %	Four crew members killed.
13.	I./KG 77	CM	Crashed at Beauvais due to technical failure.	Junkers Ju 88A-1 (2149 : 3Z+HH)	100 %	Crew unhurt.
14.	I./KG 77	CM	Crashed near Sevres after engine failure on return from bombing sortie.	Junkers Ju 88A-1 (2162)	90 %	Oblt. Otto Krauss, Ogefr. Ernst Sonntag, Uffz. Johann Klinger, and Uffz. Ludwig Jörn injured.
15.	II./KG 77	CM	Crashed at Neufchatel on return from bombing sortie.	Junkers Ju 88A-1 (7094 : 3Z+AP)	100 %	Oblt. Ernst Berbecker + three killed.
16.	III./KG 77	CM	Crashed at Amiens on return from bombing sortie.	Junkers Ju 88A-1 (5139 : 3Z+DT)	100 %	Oblt. Georg Reiss + three killed.
17.	2./KGr. 126	CM	Missing from night bombing sortie over England; fate not known.	Heinkel He 111H-4 (6955 : 1T+BB)	100 %	Uffz. Konrad Gläser, Gefr. Johann Tordik killed; Ltn. Kurt Newald, Gefr. Hans Granetz missing.
18.	3./KGr. 126	CM	Shot down by night fighters and crashed at Cressey Farm, Brentwood, at 02.15 hrs.	Heinkel He 111H-3 (5709 : 1T+LK)	100 %	Two crew killed; two crew members made P.O.W.s.
19.	2./Kü.Fl.Gr.606	CM	Suffered engine failure at night over Somerset and crashed at Masbury Ring, near Wells, at 23.50 hrs.	Dornier Do 17Z (2691 : 7T+HK)	100 %	Oblt.z.S. Erwin Blank, Fw. Heinrich Faupel, Fw. Erhard Steppat, Ogefr.Wilhelm Schnacke killed.
20.	3./Kü.Fl.Gr.606	CM	Shot down by night fighter and crashed near Nantglynn, Denbigh, at 19.20 hrs.	Dornier Do 17Z (2682 : 7T+LL)	100 %	Ltn.z.S. Heinz Havemann, Uffz. Gerhard Söcknitz, Uffz. Karl Hölscher, Gefr. Rudi Fährmann killed.
21.	7./NJG 1	CM	Force landed near Mecheln following technical failure.	Messerschmitt Bf 110C (2634 : G9+FR)	80 %	Crew unhurt.
22.	I./NJG 3	NCM	Force landed near Perleberg due to bad weather.	Messerschmitt Bf 110 (3302 : L1+AK) (1)	90 %	Oblt. Ernst Zobel + one wounded.

[(1) *Nachtjagdgeschwader 3* had only just been formed by this date (the third of the German night fighter Wings to be created to counter the growing R.A.F. raids over Germany); the appearance of the above Bf 110 in the loss list still carrying *Lehrgeschwader 1* code letters suggests the speed and urgency with which these night fighter units were being formed.]

Thursday 17th October

It is clear that Dowding regarded the problem of the continuing *Jabo* attacks as being the responsibility of his able Group Commander; and, as was demonstrated in the instance of Park's request for the Spotter Flights' aircraft, he was always ready to provide whatever force of authority was necessary to support him. Nevertheless, he was at this time giving much thought and attention to night defence, and urged greater efforts to speed Beaufighter delivery. Apart from the F.I.U., only one Squadron, No. 219, was flying regular operational night patrols with the new aircraft, and seldom did its radar function satisfactorily. Fewer than 30 aircraft had been delivered to the squadrons, and none had achieved any success. As a possible means of improving the situation Dowding demanded increased deliveries of the American Douglas Bos-

ton and, though this aeroplane turned out to be generally unsuitable for night fighting operations (and far inferior to the Beaufighter, once its radar had been mastered), the first such aircraft was undergoing trials as a night fighter with No. 600 Squadron at Catterick.

After a day of sharp raids over Kent and Greater London, the night's raiding opened with an attack on Kenley, where four Hurricanes of No. 501 Squadron were damaged by bomb splinters. A fire station was also among the buildings hit early in the evening, and eighteen members of the Auxiliary Fire Service were killed. Liverpool and Birmingham were again raided by Kü.Fl.Gr. 606, whose Dorniers now changed to bomb loads almost entirely composed of incendiaries.

R.A.F. FIGHTER COMMAND LOSSES—THURSDAY 17th OCTOBER 1940

1.	46 Sqn., Stapleford	NC	Became lost in bad weather and force landed at Chipping Ongar; pilot unhurt.	Morning	Sgt. R.E. de Cannaert d'Hamale	Hurricane	—	Cat. 2 Damaged
2.	66 Sqn., Gravesend	C	Shot down by Major Werner Mölders of JG 51 over Westerham; pilot killed.	15.20 hrs.	Plt. Off. H.W. Reilley	Spitfire	R6800	Cat. 3 Destroyed
3.	74 Sqn., Biggin Hill	C	Shot down over Maidstone and crashed near Southborough; pilot killed.	15.40 hrs.	Fg. Off. A.L. Ricalton	Spitfire	P7360	Cat. 3 Destroyed
4.	213 Sqn., Tangmere	C	Shot down by Bf 109s and crashed at Pluckley, Kent; pilot killed.	A17.00 hrs.	Plt. Off. R. Atkinson	Hurricane	P3174	Cat. 3 Destroyed
5.	213 Sqn., Tangmere	C	Shot down and crashed near Ashford, Kent; pilot unhurt.	A17.10 hrs.	Sgt. G. Stevens	Hurricane	V6866	Cat. 3 Destroyed
6.	242 Sqn., Coltishall	C	Shot down, probably by Do 17, off East Coast near Great Yarmouth; pilot killed.	09.25 hrs.	Plt. Off. N.N. Campbell	Hurricane	V6575	Cat. 3 Lost
7.	242 Sqn., Coltishall	C	Aircraft hit in throttle quadrant by return fire from Do 17 near Gt. Yarmouth; pilot unhurt.	09.25 hrs.	Plt. Off. M.K. Brown	Hurricane	P3207	Cat. 1 Damaged
8.	253 Sqn., Kenley	NC	Crashed near Gain Hill, near Paddock Wood, Kent, following engine failure; pilot unhurt.	Not known	Plt. Off. T. Nowak	Hurricane	P3537	Cat. 3 Destroyed
9.	266 Sqn., Wittering	NC	Suffered landing accident; pilot unhurt.	Not known	Sgt. C.E. Ody	Spitfire	X4164	Cat. 2 Damaged
10.	302 Sqn., Duxford	NC	Pilot killed when aircraft overturned during force landing at Colliers End, Herts.	09.05 hrs.	Sgt. J. Zalusky	Hurricane	V7417	Cat. 3 Destroyed
11.	609 Sqn., Warmwell	C	Bounced and shot down by Bf 109s over Weymouth; pilot baled out too low and was killed. Aircraft crashed at Watercombe Farm, near Warmwell.	Afternoon	Sgt. A.N. Feary	Spitfire	N3238	Cat. 3 Destroyed

LUFTWAFFE LOSSES—THURSDAY 17th OCTOBER 1940

1.	3.(H)/14	NCM	Landing accident at Keerbergen airfield.	Henschel Hs 126B (3116)	25 %	Crew unhurt.
2.	2.(H)/21	NCM	Crashed on Bergen airfield; details not notified.	Henschel Hs 126B (3331 : P2+HK)	100 %	One killed; Ltn. Friedrich Rutkowski injured.
3.	I./KG 1	CM	Force landed at Crequy (?) with *flak* damage after bombing sortie.	Heinkel He 111H-2 (5563)	60 %	Crew unhurt.
4.	II./KG 1	CM	Crashed at Mons with flak damage and engine failure after bombing sortie.	Heinkel He 111H-2 (2728)	100 %	Crew unhurt.
5.	Stab/KG 2	CM	Crashed at Eroillers after night bombing sortie.	Dornier Do 17Z (3379 : U5+EA)	100 %	Four crew members killed.
6.	I./KG 27	CM	Crashed at Ecommoy short of fuel after night bombing sortie.	Heinkel He 111H (5564)	80 %	Oblt.Eduard Sickmann killed; Ofw. Klaus Eims, Fw. Rudolf Gebhardt, and Uffz. Ernst Jannsen wounded.
7.	I./JG 55	CM	Landing accident at Dreux airfield; details not notified.	Heinkel He 111P-4 (2867)	80 %	Crew unhurt.
8.	2./KGr. 126	CM	During night bombing sortie over England the aircraft struck balloon cable and crashed at Shotley at A.22.00 hrs.	Heinkel He 111H-5 (3510 : 1T+JU)	100 %	Oblt.z.S. Wilhelm Stender, Fw. Heinz Günther and Ogefr. Hans Irrgang killed.
9.	I./LG 1	CM	Crashed short of fuel near Le Havre after night bombing sortie.	Junkers Ju 88A-1 (2095)	100 %	Oblt. Heinz Päckl killed.
10.	III./ZG 76	CM	Force landed at St. Aubin airfield with battle damage.	Messerschmitt Bf 110 D-2 (3391)	20 %	Crew unhurt.
11.	I./NJG 2	CM	Landing accident at Gilze-Rijen; further details not notified.	Junkers Ju 88C-2 (0251 : R4 +EL)	20 %	Crew unhurt.
12.	4./NJG 2	CM	Crashed and burned on landing at Capelle after night intercept sortie.	Messerschmitt Bf 110D (3385 : 3M+AH)	100 %	Oblt. Paul Zimmermann + one killed.
13.	II./LG 2	CM	Landing accident at Breton airfield; cause not notified.	Messerschmitt Bf 109E (5569)	20 %	Pilot unhurt.
14.	III./JG 2	NCM	Crashed near Lorient; not the result of combat.	Messerschmitt Bf 109 E-7 (1445)	90 %	Pilot safe.
15.	4./JG 3	CM	Landing accident at Arques after combat sortie.	Messerschmitt Bf 109 E-1 (4830)	10 %	Pilot unhurt.
16.	Geschw.Erg.St./ JG 3	NCM	Suffered take-off accident at Wizernes airfield.	Messerschmitt Bf 109 E-1 (3900)	12 %	Pilot unhurt.
17.	3./JG 27	NCM	Crashed at Dollern; not the result of cambat.	Messerschmitt Bf 109E (5346)	100 %	Gefr. Eugen Wels killed.
18.	4./JG 27	CM	Take-off accident at Bonningues airfield; cause not notified.	Messerschmitt Bf 109 E-4 (5346)	90 %	Pilot unhurt.
19.	Geschw.Erg.St./ JG 52	NCM	Suffered taxying accident at Krefeld airfield.	Messerschmitt Bf 109 E-1 (3023).	5 %	Pilot unhurt.
20.	Stab I./JG 53	CM	Shot down by 603 Sqn. Spitfires over Kent at A.17.30 hrs.	Messerschmitt Bf 109 E-7 (4138).	100 %	Hptm.Hans Meyer, *Gr.Kdr.*, killed.
21.	3./JG 53	CM	Shot down by 222 Sqn. Spitfire of McMullen over Kent and crashed on Manston airfield at A.15.30 hrs.	Messerschmitt Bf 109 E-4 (1106 : Yellow 1)	100 %	Oblt. Walter Rupp, *St.Kap.*, unwounded, made P.O.W.
22.	8./JG 53	CM	Shot down by 41 Sqn. Spitfire of Wells off Boulogne at A.16.30 hrs; pilot baled out.	Messerschmitt Bf 109 E-7 (5923)	100 %	Pilot, unwounded, rescued.
23.	I./JG 77	CM	Ditched in the sea off Cap Gris Nez after combat at A.17.00 hrs. Pilot rescued.	Messerschmitt Bf 109 E-4 (2050)	100 %	Pilot, unwounded, rescued by *Seenotflugkommando*.
24.	1./KGzbV. 101	NCM	Landing accident at Buc airfield; cause not notified.	Junkers Ju 52/3m (6379)	12 %	No casualties notified.
25.	III./Luft-landegesch. 1	NCM	Crashed; cause and location not notified.	Henschel Hs 126 (4359)	100 %	Ogefr. Odenwald and Gefr. Bienecke injured.

[Note. According to retrospective unit records, *3.Staffel, Jagdgeschwader 27*, lost four further aircraft on this day, but these do not feature in casualty returns. Much doubt must exist as to the authenticity of the these unit records as the pilots' names are quoted as Sickmann, Eilers, Gerhard and Jannsen, almost exactly the same names quoted as the crew of the Heinkel He 111 of I./KG 27 which crashed at Ecommoy on this date (Item 6 above).]

Friday 18th October

As Park continued to display the calmness and flexibility of thought which had characterised his conduct throughout the Battle, Göring chose this moment to address his airmen in terms of such fatuous bombast that any lengthy assessment is superfluous:

*   *   *   *   *

"In the past few days and nights you have caused the British world enemy disastrous losses by your constant destructive blows. Your indefatigable attacks at the heart of the British Empire, the City of London, with its population of eight and a half millions, have reduced the British plutocracy to fear and terror. Those losses which you have inflicted upon the much-vaunted Royal Air Force with your determined fighter combat are irreplaceable."

Memories are notoriously short; yet there were certainly many among the *Luftwaffe*'s fighter pilots who would remember those words three long years later, as they fought in the day and night skies over their own homes.

Fog on the 18th again brought air operations over Britain almost to a standstill, and brought disaster to a patrol by Hurricanes of No. 302 (Polish) Squadron. Hopelessly lost and short of fuel over the Surrey hills, the Section leader sighted the Sandown Park race course and ordered his pilots to force land on it; one overshot and crashed in the village of Thames Ditton, losing his life; another attempted to bale out at 50 feet; a third attempted to land at 200 miles per hour simply by putting down the nose of his aircraft. The fourth was already dead in the wreckage of his Hurricane, scattered over a hillside to the south-east.

R.A.F. FIGHTER COMMAND LOSSES—FRIDAY 18th OCTOBER 1940

1.	3 Sqn., Castletown	NC	Suffered taxying accident (involving Item 2) at Castletown; pilot unhurt.	Not known	Sgt. Weston	Hurricane	R4078	Cat. 1 Damaged
2.	3 Sqn., Castletown	NC	Suffered taxying accident (involving Item 1) at Castletown; pilot unhurt.	Not known	Plt. Off. J. Lonsdale	Hurricane	P3261	Cat. 1 Damaged
3.	145 Sqn., Tangmere	NC	Overshot runway on landing at Tangmere and crashed; pilot unhurt.	10.35 hrs.	Plt. Off. M.A. Newling	Hurricane	V6856	Cat. 3 Destroyed
4.	249 Sqn., North Weald	NC	Ran out of fuel and force landed at Thornwood Common near base; pilot unhurt.	15.50 hrs.	Adj. H. Bouquillard	Hurricane	P3463	Cat. 2 Damaged
5.	302 Sqn., Duxford	NC	Ran out of fuel on patrol; pilot killed in force landing at Thames Ditton, Surrey.	Not known	Plt. Off. S. Wapniarek	Hurricane	P3872	Cat. 3 Destroyed
6.	302 Sqn., Duxford	NC	Ran out of fuel on patrol; pilot killed when he baled out at 50 feet at Sandown racecourse, Esher, Surrey.	Not known	Plt. Off. P.E.G. Carter	Hurricane	P3930	Cat. 3 Destroyed
7.	302 Sqn., Duxford	NC	Ran out of fuel on patrol; pilot killed when he crashed at Sandown racecourse, Esher.	Not known	Plt. Off. J. Borowski	Hurricane	P3930	Cat. 3 Destroyed
8.	302 Sqn., Duxford	NC	Ran out of fuel on patrol and crashed at Bluebell Hill, Horsley, Surrey; pilot killed.	Not known	Plt. Off. A. Zukowski	Hurricane	V6571	Cat. 3 Destroyed
9.	616 Sqn., Kirton-in-Lindsey	NC	Force landed short of fuel at Broughton; pilot unhurt.	Not known	Sgt. R. Ivey	Spitfire	N3066	Cat. 3 Destroyed

LUFTWAFFE LOSSES—FRIDAY 18th OCTOBER 1940

1.	5.(F)/122	CM	Landing accident near Laon; details not notified.	Junkers Ju 88A-5(0409)	50 %	Crew unhurt.
2.	Geschw.Erg.St./	NCM	Crash landed at Münster following engine failure.	Heinkel He 111H-1	65 %	Uffz. Goetzel injured.
3.	Stab/KG 2	CM	Crashed at Kalkar; cause not notified.	Dornier Do 17Z (2674)	100 %	Ltn.Eberhard Steudel, Fw.Heinrich Brey, Ogefr.Friedrich Lintz, Ogefr. Herbert Grabner killed.
4.	8./KG 2	CM	Force landed at St. Romain; cause not notified.	Dornier Do 17Z-3(2876)	40 %	Crew unhurt.
5.	Stab II./KG 4	CM	Landing accident at Eindhoven after bombing sortie.	Heinkel He 111P-4 (3081)	15 %	Crew unhurt.
6.	II./KG 51	CM	Missing from bombing sortie over London; probably the victim of the ground defences.	Junkers Ju 88A-1 (7160 : 9K+EC)	100 %	Ofw. Anto Stegmüller, Ltn. Siegfried Sonntag, Oblt. Helmut von Claer killed.
7.	I./KG 54	CM	Crashed on landing at Vierville in bad weather.	Junkers Ju 88A-1(4062)	100 %	Fl. Karl Feldmann injured.
8.	I./KG 54	CM	Crashed on landing at Vierville in bad weather.	Junkers Ju 88A-1(6152)	100 %	Crew unhurt.
9.	I./KG 54	CM	Suffered landing accident at Evreux; cause not notified.	Junkers Ju 88A-1 (7095)	45 %	Uffz. Rudolf Streitz and Uffz. Heinz Meissner injured.
10.	I./KG 54	CM	Crashed on landing at Caen in bad weather.	Junkers Ju 88A-1(7152)	100 %	Four crew members killed.
11.	II./KG 54	CM	Crashed on landing at Orléans in bad weather.	Junkers Ju 88A-1(7064)	100 %	Crew unhurt.
12.	II./KG 54	CM	Crashed in bad weather at Bagnols; crew baled out.	Junkers Ju 88A-1 (6098)	100 %	Crew unhurt.
13.	I./KG 55	CM	Suffered landing accident at Dreux after bombing sortie over Britain.	Heinkel He 111P-4 (3105)	60 %	Crew unhurt.
14.	II./KG 76	CM	Crashed at Calais after combat with fighters; R.A.F. fighter unit not identified.	Junkers Ju 88A-1 (8070)	60 %	Crew unhurt.
15.	KGr. 806	CM	Crashed on landing at Deauville in bad weather.	Junkers Ju 88A-1(7121)	90 %	Fw. Kunert injured.
16.	KGr. 806	CM	Suffered minor accident at Evreux.	Junkers Ju 88A-1(7133)	20 %	Crew unhurt.
17.	III./LG 1	CM	Target London; shot down by 229 Sqn. Hurricanes of Bright, Ortmans and Barry over Kent.	Junkers Ju 88A-1 (8050 : L1+NT)	100 %	Four crew members missing.
18.	III./LG 1	CM	Crashed near Fécamp following fighter combat.	Junkers Ju 88A-5(3177)	100 %	Gefr. Stefan Külin wounded.
19.	III./LG 1	CM	Force landed at Grafville after engine failure.	Junkers Ju 88A-5(2207)	30 %	Crew safe.
20.	II./ZG 2	NCM	Suffered landing accident at the Hague; cause not notified.	Messerschmitt Bf 110 (3637)	30 %	Crew unhurt.
21.	III./NJG 1	CM	Crashed during landing at Standal; cause not notified.	Messerschmitt Bf 110C	60 %	Crew unhurt.
22.	I./JG 2	NCM	Crashed at Brieuc; not the result of combat.	Messerschmitt Bf 109E (0748)	100 %	Fhr. Hans-Eduard Siebold killed.
23.	III./JG 2	CM	Crashed at Grandcamp; not the result of combat.	Messerschmitt Bf 109 E-4 (5348)	100 %	Oblt. Walter Falting killed.
24.	II./JG 53	CM	Crashed on fire at Morleaux; cause not known.	Messerschmitt Bf 109 E-4 (1343)	100 %	Pilot killed.

Saturday 19th October

On this, one of the quietest days of the whole Battle, Kesselring sent no more than a pair of Bf 109 *Staffeln* over Kent. Park was unable to react against the first, owing to bad visibility on his airfields; but in the evening No. 92 Squadron was ordered up against enemy fighters near Folkestone, only to lose a Spitfire flown by Sgt. Leslie Allton—who was killed.

Far away in Holland the redoubtable Hajo Herrmann, now a *Staffelkapitän* in III./KG 4, was slightly injured when the undercarriage of his Ju 88 collapsed while landing at Schipol.

R.A.F. FIGHTER COMMAND LOSSES—SATURDAY 19th OCTOBER 1940

1.	3 Sqn., Castletown	NC	During local exercise pilot crashed and was killed during aerobatics over gun post.	Not known	Fg. Off. G.F. McAvity RCAF	Hurricane		P3260	Cat. 3 Destroyed
2.	92 Sqn., Biggin Hill	?	Crashed at Tuesnoad Farm, Smarden, Kent; pilot killed. Cause not established.	Not known	Sgt. L.C. Allton	Spitfire		R6922	Cat. 3 Destroyed
3.	249 Sqn., North Weald	NC	Force landed (probably due to engine trouble) during convoy patrol; pilot unhurt.	18.05 hrs.	Plt. Off. A.R.F. Thompson	Hurricane		V6635	Cat. 2 Damaged

LUFTWAFFE LOSSES—SATURDAY 19th OCTOBER 1940

1.	8./KG 2	NCM	Crashed at Cambrai; cause not notified.	Dornier Do 17Z-2 (1153)	75 %	Ltn. Josef Steudel, Ofw. Otto Waldemann, Uffz. Gotthard Wachtel, Gefr. Heinz Köhler injured.
2.	II./KG 4	CM	Suffered landing accident at Soesterburg; cause not notified.	Heinkel He 111P-4 (2923)	30 %	Crew unhurt.
3.	7./KG 4	CM	Undercarriage collapsed during landing at Schipol after bombing sortie.	Junkers Ju 88A-1 (5128)	80 %	Oblt. Hajo Herrmann, *St.Kap.*, and Ofw. Helmut Stiefelhagen injured.
4.	9./KG 30	CM	Suffered landing accident at Schipol after bombing sortie.	Junkers Ju 88A-1 (7160)	70 %	Crew unhurt.
5.	III./KG 77	CM	Crashed at Cansau after bombing sortie owing to fuel shortage.	Junkers Ju 88A-1 (5102)	100 %	Crew unhurt.
6.	Kü.Fl.Gr. 606	CM	Landing accident at Brest after bombing sortie.	Dornier Do 17Z (1210)	30 %	Crew unhurt.
7.	I./St.G 3	NCM	Suffered taxying accident at Bary.	Junkers Ju 87B-1(0237)	10 %	Crew unhurt.
8.	8./St.G 77	NCM	Suffered air collision with Item 9 at Occagnes.	Junkers Ju 87B (5617)	100 %	Both crew members killed.
9.	8./St.G 77	NCM	Suffered air collision with Item 8 at Occagnes.	Junkers Ju 87B (5628)	100 %	Both crew members killed.

Sunday 20th October

More than 300 sorties were flown by the fighter-bomber pilots of *Jafu 2* on this day, elements of five *Jagdgeschwader* flying a sweep in the morning and another in the afternoon. JG 27, 52, 54 and 77 all suffered casualties, but far below the number claimed at the time by the R.A.F.—in several identifiable instances the result of duplicated claims by pilots flying at greatly separated heights. Once again, however, the skill of

Plt. Off. Eric Lock prevailed; his sixteenth victim fell on this day, a Bf 109 which crashed near Biggin Hill from a great height.

London and Coventry were the main targets at night, with nine *Gruppen* raiding the capital. St. Dunstan's Hospital for the blind was hit, but mercifully there were no fatal casualties.

R.A.F. FIGHTER COMMAND LOSSES—SUNDAY 20th OCTOBER 1940

1.	74 Sqn., Biggin Hill	C	Shot down by Bf 109s over Maidstone; pilot baled out grievously wounded and died on 27-7-41.	14.40 hrs.	Sgt. T.B. Kirk	Spitfire	P7370	Cat. 3 Destroyed
2.	74 Sqn., Biggin Hill	C	Shot down by Bf 109s over Maidstone and crashed at Cowden; pilot baled out wounded.	14.44 hrs.	Sgt. C.G. Hilken	Spitfire	P7426	Cat. 3 Destroyed
3.	248 Sqn., Sumburgh (1)	C	Shot down by Bf 109s over Norwegian coast; pilot and two crew members survived and made P.O.W.s; Observer (Copcutt) drowned.	09.30 hrs.	Plt.Off.G.H.Baird Sgt. R. Copcutt Sgt. L. Burton Sgt. S.V. Wood	Blenheim	P6952	Cat. 3 Lost
4.	248 Sqn., Sumburgh (1)	C	Missing from search (for Item 3) off Norwegian coast; crew assumed killed.	A11.30 hrs.	Plt.Off.S.R.Gane Plt.Off.M.D.Green Sgt. N.J. Stocks	Blenheim	L9453	Cat. 3 Missing
5.	605 Sqn., Croydon	C	Damaged by Bf 109s over Ashford; pilot returned unhurt.	10.15 hrs.	Plt. Off. P.D. Thompson	Hurricane	V6844	Cat. 2 Damaged
6.	605 Sqn., Croydon	C	Damaged by Bf 109s over Ashford; pilot returned unhurt.	10.15 hrs.	Plt. Off. J.H. Rothwell	Hurricane	V6755	Cat. 2 Damaged

[(1) These two aircraft losses are included as the sorties were ordered by Fighter Command, although No. 248 Squadron was at this time in Coastal Command; all seven members had already flown on operations in the Battle of Britain (see Appendix A).]

LUFTWAFFE LOSSES—SUNDAY 20th OCTOBER 1940

1.	4.(F)/121	CM	Landing accident at Caen after bombing sortie.	Junkers Ju 88A-5 (0415)	75 %	Uffz. Fritz Rickershausen killed; Uffz. Kurt Sauslikat injured.
2.	I./KG 27	CM	Force landed at Tours following engine failure.	Heinkel He 111P (2452)	50 %	Crew safe.
3.	Geschw.Erg.St./ KG 51	NCM	Crashed near Lechfeld following fire in the air.	Heinkel He 111H (1726)	100 %	Fw. Johannes Apelbeck, Uffz. Hermann Reisach killed; Fw. Oskar Kirchberger wounded.
4.	Geschw.Erg.St./	NCM	Suffered taxying accident at Lechfeld airfield.	Junkers Ju 88A-1(2055)	40 %	Crew unhurt.
5.	III./KG 55	CM	Suffered taxying accident at Villacoublay.	Heinkel He 111P-2	25 %	Crew unhurt.
6.	II./KG 76	CM	Suffered landing accident at Cormeissel airfield.	Junkers Ju 88A-5(6124)	60 %	Crew unhurt.
7.	III./KG 77	CM	Crashed at Abbeville following engine fire.	Junkers Ju 88A-1(3152)	100 %	Gefr. Werner Hollstein killed.
8.	1./KGr. 100	CM	Crashed on take-off at Vannes airfield.	Heinkel He 111H-2 (2726)	100 %	Four crew members killed.
9.	1./Kü.Fl.Gr.606	CM	Crew baled out near Salisbury; aircraft crashed at Ness Point, near Shotley, Essex.	Dornier Do 17Z-3 (2783 : 7T+AH)	100 %	Ltn.z.S. Würdemann, Ltn. Stirnar, Uffz. Schörich and Uffz. Küttner baled out and made P.O.W.s.
10.	KGr. 806	NCM	Landing accident at Caen airfield; not combat.	Junkers Ju 88A-1(5068)	10 %	Crew unhurt.
11.	3./NJG 2	CM	Landing accident at Eindhoven airfield.	Junkers Ju 88C-2(0278)	60 %	Fw. Schlicht injured.
12.	3./LG 2	CM	Crashed at Calais after combat, possibly with 41 Sqn. Spitfire of Lovell.	Messerschmitt Bf 109E (5084)	75 %	Pilot unhurt.

Luftwaffe Losses, 20th October 1940—*continued*

13.	3./LG 2	CM	Shot down by 605 Sqn. Hurricane of McKellar at Lenham Heath at A.10.00 hrs.; pilot baled out but parachute failed.	Messerschmitt Bf 109E (2059 : Yellow 8)	100 %	Uffz. Franz Mairl killed.
14.	3./LG 2	CM	Landed at base with combat damaged after raid over London.	Messerschmitt Bf 109 E-1 (5598)	20 %	Pilot unhurt.
15.	7.(F)/LG 2	CM	Shot down by 92 Sqn. Spitfires of Villa and Saunders, and 66 Sqn. Spitfires, crash landed at Bockingford, Horsmonden, at 12.50 hrs.	Messerschmitt Bf 110 C-5 (2228 : L2+MR)	100 %	Oblt. Roland Lemmerich made P.O.W. Uffz. Rudolf Ebeling killed.
16.	7./JG 27	NCM	Landing accident at Guines-West; not combat.	Messerschmitt Bf 109 E-1 (6350)	50 %	Pilot unhurt.
17.	5./JG 52	CM	Shot down by 41 Sqn. Spitfire of Lock near Biggin Hill at 13.50 hrs.	Messerschmitt Bf 109 E-7 (5930 : Black 4)	100 %	Fw. Ludwig Bielmaier missing.
18.	6./JG 52	CM	Shot down by 41 Sqn. Spitfire of Brown and crashed at Plumstead, Woolwich, at 13.45 hrs.	Messerschmitt Bf 109 E-4 (2780 : Yellow 1)	100 %	Ofw. Walter Friedemann killed.
19.	Stab/JG 53	CM	Landing accident at St. Inglevert after combat.	Messerschmitt Bf 109 E-1 (4112)	2 %	Pilot unhurt.
20.	9./JG 54	CM	Shot down by 603 Sqn. Spitfires near Maidstone at 13.30 hrs. and crashed at Mereworth.	Messerschmitt Bf 109 E-4 (1525 : Yellow 6)	100 %	Fw. Adolf Jowig made P.O.W.
21.	3./JG 77	CM	Shot down by 603 Sqn. Spitfires near Eastbourne at 13.40 hrs. and crashed at Waldron, Sussex.	Messerschmitt Bf 109E (4007 : Yellow 11)	100 %	Fw. Heinz Wilhelm made P.O.W.
22.	3./JG 77	CM	Shot down by 603 Sqn. Spitfires and crashed at North Fording, near New Romney.	Messerschmitt Bf 109E (0316)	100 %	Pilot, wounded, made P.O.W.

Monday 21st October

With low cloud and mist persisting over the South-East, but better weather in the West Country, Sperrle mounted a number of reconnaissance sorties over the western ports, and subsequently sent single bombers against targets in pinpoint attacks. From the poor bomb plots obtained, it was not possible to deduce what most of these targets were, but one Junkers Ju 88 of 8./KG 51 entirely missed its briefed target—the Gloster Aircraft Company at Brockworth, location of the very large Hurricane production line—and finished up strafing the Army Co-operation airfield at Old Sarum, near Salisbury. Spitfires from nearby Middle Wallop successfuly caught the raider and shot it down between Christchurch and Lymington.

R.A.F. FIGHTER COMMAND LOSSES—MONDAY 21st OCTOBER 1940

1.	245 Sqn., Aldergrove	NC	Aircraft dived into Lough Neagh during battle climb practice; cause unknown; pilot killed.	Not known	Sgt. E.G. Greenwood	Hurricane	P3657	Cat. 3 Lost
2.	266 Sqn., Wittering	NC	Aircraft crashed at Stradishall during training flight; cause unknown; pilot killed.	Not known	Plt. Off. W.S. Williams	Spitfire	X4265	Cat. 3 Destroyed
3.	600 Sqn., Catterick	NC	Flew into hill in cloud near Kirkby Malzeard, North Yorks. Pilot (only occupant) killed.	11.20 hrs.	Plt. Off. P.R.S. Hurst	Blenheim	L1272	Cat. 3 Destroyed

LUFTWAFFE LOSSES—MONDAY 21st OCTOBER 1940

1.	2.(H)/14	NCM	Take-off accident at Hastenrath; cause unknown.	Bücker Bu 131	40 %	Crew unhurt.
2.	3.(F)/123	CM	Take-off accident at Brest; cause not notified.	Junkers Ju 88A-1 (0403)	100 %	Uffz. Willi Ruschenburg, Uffz. Martin Bachmann, Oblt. Heinz Jasper injured; Ofw. Martin Hering killed.
3.	II./KG 1	CM	Landing accident at Rosieres airfield.	Heinkel He 111H-2 (5467)	20 %	Crew unhurt.
4.	III./KG 1	CM	Damaged by 253 Sqn. Hurricane of Duke-Woolley and crash landed at Bapaume on return.	Junkers Ju 88A-1 (2212)	30 %	Crew unhurt.
5.	1./KG 51	CM	Target Brockworth. Shot down by 609 Sqn. Spitfires of Howell and Hill at Old Sarum and crashed between Christchurch and Lymington.	Junkers Ju 88A-5 (8116 : 9K+BH)	100 %	Oblt. Max Fabian, Uffz. Max Scolz, Uffz. Ernst Wilhelm and Gefr. Franz Stadelbauer killed.
6.	Stab/KG 53	CM	Crashed on landing at Vendeville after combat during bombing sortie.	Heinkel He 111H-3 (3160)	70 %	Crew unhurt.
7.	3./KG 3	CM	Force landed at Hesdin with fuel shortage.	Heinkel He 111H-5 (3758)	25 %	Crew unhurt.
8.	III./KG 55	CM	Caught fire and crashed at Villacoublay; crew baled out.	Heinkel He 111H-2 (2663)	100 %	Crew unhurt.
9.	III./KG 76	CM	Shot down by 253 Sqn. Hurricane of Edwards near Mayfield at 13.50 hrs.	Dornier Do 17Z (3397 : F1+LS)	100 %	Fw. Georg Stösser killed; Ltn. Heinz Wildhagen + two missing.
10.	KGr. 806	CM	Landing accident at Caen; cause not notified.	Junkers Ju 88A-1 (4172)	50 %	Crew unhurt.
11.	Erpr.Gr. 210	NCM	Landing accident at St. Leger; cause not notified.	Messerschmitt Bf 110C (3367)	80 %	Uffz. Werner Hesse and Uffz. Eckhard Stäler injured.
12.	8./NJG 1	CM	Take-off accident at Stendal airfield.	Messerschmitt Bf 110D (3143)	100 %	Oblt. Arno Walther, *St. Kap.*, and Uffz. Horst Hoffmann killed.
13.	Stab/JG 1	NCM	Force landed at Charleville with fuel shortage.	Focke-Wulf Fw 58 (2670)	20 %	Crew unhurt.
14.	*Seenotflug-kommando 1*	NCM	Aircraft struck Arado Ar 66 on Buc airfield.	Junkers W.34 H-1 (1400)	2 %	Crew unhurt.

Tuesday 22nd October

Once again fog restricted operations over England until the afternoon, when convoys off the Kent coast were attacked without success. German casualties were not confined to those inflicted by Fighter Command, and, as the loss table indicates, were not suffered by flying personnel alone. *Kampfgeschwader 27 «Boelcke»*, with the loss of a *Gruppenkommandeur*, three officers, eleven other aircrew and thirteen groundcrew, would long remember this day in the "quiet" period of the Battle of Britain.

This Dornier Do 17Z-3 (2783: 7T+AH of the 1st *Staffel, Küstenfliegergruppe 606*) had been flying on a raid over Liverpool during the night of 20th/21st October when it developed engine trouble over Salisbury Plain. The crew, Leutnant Stirnar, Leutnant zur See Würdemann, Uffz. Schörnich and Uffz. Küttner, baled out near Salisbury and were taken prisoner; a search of the immediate area failed to disclose any trace of their aircraft. It had in fact continued flying for about 120 miles on an easterly course before finally executing a graceful landing of its own accord on the mud flats at Shotley in Essex.

R.A.F. FIGHTER COMMAND LOSSES—TUESDAY 22nd OCTOBER 1940

1.	74 Sqn., Biggin Hill	C	Shot down by Bf 109s and crashed at South Nutfield, near Redhill; pilot killed.	14.10 hrs.	Plt. Off. P.C.B. St. John	Spitfire	*P7431*	Cat. 3 Destroyed
2.	74 Sqn., Biggin Hill	C	Aircraft broke up during combat with Bf 109s near Tonbridge; pilot baled out unhurt.	14.13 hrs.	Plt. Off. R.L. Spurdle	Spitfire	*P7364*	Cat. 3 Destroyed
3.	249 Sqn., North Weald	NC	Force landed near Hornchurch after engine failure; pilot unhurt.	Not known	Plt. Off. A.R.F. Thompson	Hurricane	*V6855*	Cat. 2 Damaged
4.	257 Sqn., North Weald	C	Aircraft hit by A.A. fire while in combat over Folkestone; pilot killed in crash at Lydd.	A16.30 hrs.	Plt. Off. N.B. Heywood	Hurricane	*R4195*	Cat. 3 Destroyed
5.	257 Sqn., North Weald	C	Shot down by Bf 109s over Folkestone and crashed at Shadoxhurst, near Ashford; pilot did not bale out and was killed.	A16.30 hrs.	Sgt. R.H.B. Fraser	Hurricane	*V6851*	Cat. 3 Destroyed
6.	605 Sqn., Croydon	C	Shot down by Bf 109s over Dorking; pilot force landed and dislocated his hip.	A14.35 hrs.	Plt. Off. J.A. Milne	*Hurricane*	*V6783*	Cat. 3 Destroyed

[Note: No. 46 Squadron at Stapleford reported the loss of Hurricane *R4074* on this date, but the identity of the pilot, his fate and the circumstances of the loss are not known.]

LUFTWAFFE LOSSES—TUESDAY 22nd OCTOBER 1940

1.	KG 27	NCM	Crashed landed at Avord airfield; cause not notified.	Junkers Ju 52/3m (1339)	70 %	Fw. Wilhelm Beck killed; Ltn. Gerhard Neuziel injured.
2.	I./KG 27	CM	Crashed at Tours airfield after bombing sortie; aircraft struck barrack block, killing crew and thirteen occupants of building and injuring eleven others (all KG 27 ground personnel).	Heinkel He 111H-2 (5443)	100 %	Ltn. Wolfgang Wilhelm; Uffz. Ernst Bautz, Uffz. Wilhelm Forster and Uffz. Alfons Jenau killed.
3.	III./KG 27	CM	Crashed at Rennes airfield following fire in the air during bombing sortie.	Heinkel He 111P-4 (2626)	100 %	Maj. Frhr. Manfred Speck von Sternberg, *Gr.Kdr.*, Ltn. Rudolf Jansen, Fw. Max Kramwinkel and Uffz. Erwin Schmidt killed.
4.	III./KG 27	CM	Crashed at Tours airfield following fire in the air during bombing sortie.	Heinkel He 111P-4 (1392)	100 %	Fhr. Kurt Schmiedfelden, Oblt. Kurt Walther, Uffz. Ernst Tauss-mann, Uffz.Hanns Moosbauer killed.
5.	8./KG 30	CM	Force landed at Eindhoven in bad weather and crashed.	Junkers Ju 88A-5 (2180)	60 %	Crew unhurt.
6.	I./KG 40	CM	Missing from weather reconnaissance off the coast of Ireland; fate not determined.	Focke-Wulf Fw 200C (0024 : F8+OK)	100 %	Oblt. Theo Schuldt, Fw. Walter Berghaus, Fw. Fritz Grüber, Gefr. Walter Gressle, Fw. Friedrich Plöger, Meteorologe Dr. Hans Sturm missing.
7.	2./KG 53	CM	Crashed at Vitry-en-Artois following bombing sortie.	Heinkel He 111H-5 (3571)	100 %	Oblt. Karl Müller + three killed; Ofw. Jakob Kraft injured.
8.	I./KG 54	CM	Suffered minor landing accident at Evreux.	Junkers Ju 88A-1(7158)	10 %	Crew unhurt.
9.	II./KG 77	CM	Take-off accident at Reims; cause not notified.	Junkers Ju 88A-1(0301)	80 %	Crew unhurt.
10.	II./KG 77	CM	Landing accident at Reims after bombing sortie.	Junkers Ju 88A-5(0327)	30 %	Crew unhurt.
11.	KGr. 806	CM	Crashed and burned at Caen airfield; whether before or after bombing sortie not known.	Junkers Ju 88A-1 (7130)	100 %	Oblt.z.S. Günther Reischle + three killed.
12.	2./JG 26	CM	Shot down by British fighters and crashed at Littlestone, near New Romney, at 15.30 hrs.	Messerschmitt Bf 109 E-4 (1124 : Black 10)	100 %	Uffz. Heinrich Arp killed; buried at Hawkinge. (See Appendix M)
13.	5./JG 27	CM	Suffered taxying accident at Bonningues airfield.	Messerschmitt Bf 109 E-1 (6285)	40 %	Pilot unhurt.
14.	7./JG 27	CM	Shot down by 257 Sqn. Hurricane of Coke off Dungeness at A.16.30 hrs.	Messerschmitt Bf 109 E-4 (5581)	100 %	Pilot, unhurt, rescued by *Seenotflugkommando.*
15.	1./JG 51	NCM	Landing accident at Pihen airfield; not combat.	Messerschmitt Bf 109 E-1 (5362)	60 %	Pilot unhurt.
16.	3./JG 51	CM	Missing from sortie over England; fate unknown.	Messerschmitt Bf 109 E-1 (4822 : Yellow 10)	100 %	Fhr. Kurt Müller missing.
17.	6./JG 51	CM	Suffered minor landing accident at Mardyck.	Messerschmitt Bf 109 E-1 (0686)	10 %	Pilot unhurt.
18.	Geschw.Erg.St./ JG 52	NCM	Suffered landing accident at Krefeld; not combat.	Messerschmitt Bf 109 E-1 (3187)	40 %	Pilot unhurt.

Wednesday 23rd October

As if to underline Fighter Command's impotence at night, orders were issued on this day for No. 73 Squadron, flying Hurricanes, to converted completely to the night fighting rôle. Although in retrospect seen as a hasty decision (for the practice of operating single-seaters at night was as wasteful as it was hazardous), the order reflected the growing anger and frustration felt throughout the Command at its continuing helplessness in the face of Göring's night raiders.

Even on this night, with scarcely a night fighter station clear of fog or low cloud, the *Luftwaffe* bombed London in force; and II./KG 26 made the long and dismal journey across the North Sea to bomb Glasgow.

R.A.F. FIGHTER COMMAND LOSSES—WEDNESDAY 23rd OCTOBER 1940

1.	145 Sqn., Tangmere	C	Shot down by Bf 109 and crashed at Burwash; pilot wounded in the leg.	Not known	Plt. Off. R.D. Yule	Hurricane	*P3926*	Cat. 3 Destroyed
2.	145 Sqn., Tangmere	C	Force landed on Haywards Heath golf course with engine failure after combat; pilot unhurt.	Not known	Plt. Off. B.M.G. de Hemptinne	Hurricane	*P2696*	Cat. 2 Damaged
3.	616 Sqn., Kirton-in-Lindsey	NC	Suffered landing accident during training sortie; pilot unhurt.	Not known	Sgt. Wilson	Spitfire	—	Cat. 2 Damaged

LUFTWAFFE LOSSES—WEDNESDAY 23rd OCTOBER 1940

1.	1.(F)/120	CM	Force landed at Groix; cause not notified.	Heinkel He 111H-2 (5280)	30 %	Crew unhurt.
2.	9./KG 3	CM	Crashed at Esneux short of fuel; crew baled out.	Dornier Do 17Z-2(3362)	100 %	Crew safe.
3.	KG 27	NCM	Landing accident at Avord; cause not notified.	Junkers Ju 52/3m (5054)	60 %	Gefr. Willi Wunderlich injured.
4.	II./KG 77	CM	Crashed near Laon, not the result of combat.	Junkers Ju 88A-1 (3158)	70 %	Fw. Erhard Kretschmer and Uffz. Josef Meyer injured.
5.	III./KG 77	CM	Crashed at Neuilly-Hopital after bombing sortie.	Junkers Ju 88A-1(3151)	100 %	Fw.Erich Kissel killed; two injured.
6.	III./KG 77	CM	Missing from night bombing sortie over London; probably destroyed by ground defences	Junkers Ju 88A-1 (5107 : 3Z+HT)	100 %	Ltn.Walter Spaar + three missing.
7.	2./JG 77	NCM	Suffered landing accident at Oslo-Fornebu airfield; cause not notified.	Messerschmitt Bf 109 E-1 (5011)	10 %	Pilot unhurt.

Thursday 24th October

While non-operational accidents continued to figure prominently in the loss records of both air forces, Kesselring and Sperrle kept sending the occasional fighter sweep and lone raiders to maintain pressure on the defence system. Another item of loss on the other side of the Channel (not included in the loss table) was the destruction of three Italian Fiat BR.20 bombers of "KG 13"—the *Regia Aeronautica's 13° Stormo B.T.*—which crashed during final familiarisation flights in bad weather at Houthem, Lustin and Reisel, killing six and injuring six aircrew.

R.A.F. FIGHTER COMMAND LOSSES—THURSDAY 24th OCTOBER 1940

1.	43 Sqn., Usworth	NC	Dusk landing accident at Usworth; pilot killed.	19.25 hrs.	Sgt. D.R. Stoodley	Hurricane	*V7307*	Cat. 3 Destroyed
2.	87 Sqn., Exeter	NC	Air collision with Item 3; pilot baled out but was killed after his parachute snagged aircraft.	Not known	Plt. Off. D.T. Jay	Hurricane	*P3404*	Cat. 3 Destroyed
3.	87 Sqn., Exeter	NC	Suffered air collision with Item 2; pilot force landed with extensive damage to aircraft's tail unit.	Not known	Plt.Off. J.R. Cock	Hurricane	—	Cat. 2 Damaged
4.	111 Sqn., Montrose	NC	Suffered take-off accident ; pilot unhurt.	Not known	Sgt. M.J. Mansfeld	Hurricane	*P3046*	Cat. 3 Destroyed
5.	141 Sqn., Cottesmore	NC	Suffered landing accident at Cottesmore during training flight; pilot unhurt.	Not known	Plt. Off. Edwards	Defiant	—	Cat. 2 Damaged
6.	151 Sqn., Digby	NC	Crashed during training flight; pilot unhurt.	18.30 hrs.	Fg. Off. C.D. Whittingham	Hurricane	—	Cat. 3 Destroyed

LUFTWAFFE LOSSES—THURSDAY 24th OCTOBER 1940

1.	3./Aufkl.Gr. Ob.d.L.	CM	Shot down by 1 Sqn. Hurricanes of Brown, Clowes and Kershaw, and 17 Sqn. Hurricanes of Czernin, Fajtl and Hogg and crashed near St. Neots at 12.35 hrs.	Dornier Do 215B-1 (0016 : L2+KS)	100 %	Ltn. Erwin Meyer, Uffz. Erhard Hofmann, Uffz. Helmut Brönig killed; Ogefr. Max Dorr made P.O.W. (See Appendix M)
2.	2.(F)/22	NCM	Suffered taxying accident at Lübeck airfield.	Heinkel He 111H-2 (5306)	35 %	Crew unhurt.
3.	1.(H)/41	NCM	Ditched off Frech Atlantic coast; crew picked up by French fishing vessel.	Henschel Hs 126B (4130 : C2+DH)	100 %	Crew safe.
4.	III./KG 1	NCM	Crashed at Bapaume-Greville; cause not known.	Junkers Ju 88A-5(3221)	90 %	Crew unhurt.
5.	1./KG 2	CM	Crashed on fire at Le Clouse; cause not known.	Dornier Do 17Z (2591)	100 %	Uffz. Hans Meyer; Ogefr. Wilhelm Welf, Uffz. Wilhelm Schermann and Gefr. Kurt Faust killed.
6.	1./KG 2	CM	Crashed at St. Court; cause not notified.	Dornier Do 17Z (3444)	100 %	Fw. Robert Dillger, Ogefr. Karl Kunze, Ogefr. Helmut Fürst and Gefr. Kurt Maas killed.
7.	9./KG 2	CM	Damaged by 229 Sqn. Hurricanes of Smith and Dewar over Hayes, Middlesex, at 14.30 hrs.	Dornier Do 17Z-2 (2863)	80 %	Gefr. Günther Schinz killed; Fw. Martin Bohnhof and Gefr. Wilhelm Elbert wounded.
8.	5./KG 30	CM	Crashed at Gilze-Rijen after engine failure suffered during bombing sortie.	Junkers Ju 88A-5 (0265)	90 %	Oblt. Werner Baumbach, Uffz. Heinz Menz, Fw. Heinrich Thies and Fw. Martin Köhler wounded.
9.	II./KG 51	CM	Suffered landing accident at Orly airfield.	Junkers Ju 88A-1(3171)	20 %	Crew unhurt.
10.	II./KG 55	NCM	Crashed at Halberstadt; cause not notified.	Heinkel He 111P-4 (3100)	100 %	Ofw. Jesuiter and Fw. Gass killed.

Luftwaffe Losses, 24th October 1940—*continued*

11.	Geschw.Erg.St./ KG 55	NCM	Crashed on fire at Camens; cause not known.	Heinkel He 111H-2 (5330)	100 %	Oblt. Erich Wamser + four killed.
12.	IV./LG 1	NCM	Suffered landing accident at Courtrai airfield.	Junkers Ju 87 (5200)	30 %	Crew unhurt.
13.	8./JG 27	CM	Suffered landing accident at Guines-West.	Messerschmitt Bf 109 (E-4 (3703)	35 %	Pilot unhurt.
14.	8./JG 27	CM	Crashed off Cap Gris Nez after engine failure following fighter combat.	Messerschmitt Bf 109 E-4 (1558 : Black 2)	100 %	Uffz. Ulrich Linke missing.
15.	Geschw.Erg.St./ JG 54	NCM	Take-off accident at Bergen airfield. Further details not notified.	Messerschmitt Bf 109 E-1 (6071)	100 %	Fw. Brixel killed.
16.	4./JG 77	NCM	Crashed in Sweden; pilot believed interned.	Messerschmitt Bf 109E (0820 : White 3)	100 %	Uffz. Fröba missing.

Friday 25th October

Notwithstanding the accidental loss of three Belgian-based Italian bombers on the previous day, sixteen Fiats took off to raid Harwich at night; as discussed in Chapter 10, the crews and performance of these aircraft were hardly up to Northern European standards of daylight bombing. From the small number of bombs reported to have landed in the area, it is estimated that fewer than half the force reached the target area; two crews baled out over the Belgian coast after running out of fuel, and a third suffered a take-off accident.

With the slight improvement in the weather, daylight activity increased and a number of sharp fighter clashes occurred over Kent and South London. At dusk four He 111s of II./KG 26 found and bombed the airfield at Montrose, demolishing the Officers' Mess, two hangars and seven Hurricanes of No. 111 Squadron. Six airmen were killed and 21 wounded. Sub-Lt. Thomas Worrall took off and gave chase in the gathering darkness, but failed to find the raiders; he crashed on return to the airfield, fortunately without injury.

R.A.F. FIGHTER COMMAND LOSSES—FRIDAY 25th OCTOBER 1940

1.	46 Sqn., Stapleford	C	Damaged by Bf 109s and struck house when force landing at Romford; pilot grievously injured and died the next day.	Afternoon	Plt. Off. W.B. Patullo	Hurricane	V6804	Cat. 3 Destroyed
2.	66 Sqn., Gravesend	C	Shot down by Bf 109 over Tunbridge Wells; pilot baled out slightly wounded.	09.10 hrs.	Plt. Off. R.W. Oxspring	Spitfire	X4170	Cat. 3 Destroyed
3.	79 Sqn., Pembrey	C	Crashed at Carew Cheriton on patrol; pilot killed. Cause of crash not known.	Not known	Plt. Off. S. Piatkowski	Hurricane	N2708	Cat. 3 Destroyed
4.	92 Sqn., Biggin Hill	C	Shot down by Bf 109s and crashed at Penshurst; pilot unhurt.	13.45 hrs.	Plt. Off. J. Mansel-Lewis	Spitfire	—	Cat. 3 Destroyed
5.	111 Sqn., Montrose	NC	Suffered night landing accident at Montrose; pilot unhurt.	A20.00 hrs.	Sub-Lt. T.V. Worrall RNVR	Hurricane	V6539	Cat. 3 Destroyed
6.	151 Sqn., Digby	NC	Suffered night landing accident at Digby; pilot unhurt.	21.45 hrs.	Sgt. I.A.C. Grant	Hurricane	L2047	Cat. 3 Destroyed
7.	238 Sqn., Middle Wallop	NC	Struck hedge on airfield during beat-up; pilot unhurt. Subject of Court of Enquiry.	18.00 hrs.	Plt. Off. J.S. Wigglesworth	Hurricane	—	Cat. 2 Damaged
8.	249 Sqn., North Weald	C	Shot down by Bf 109s over North Kent; pilot baled out, wounded, at Pembury.	A12.00 hrs.	Sgt. J.M.B. Beard	Hurricane	P3615	Cat. 3 Destroyed
9.	249 Sqn., North Weald	C	Shot down by Bf 109s and force landed on Rochester airfield; pilot wounded.	A12.00 hrs.	Adj. H. Bouquillard	Hurricane	V7409	Cat. 3 Destroyed
10.	302 Sqn., Duxford		Aircraft seen to leave formation and glide toward enemy coast; pilot posted Missing.	Not known	Flt. Lt. F. Jastrzebski	Hurricane	P3932	Cat. 3 Missing
11.	501 Sqn., Kenley	C	Collided with Item 12 during combat with Bf 109s and crashed at Staplehurst; pilot killed.	15.13 hrs.	Plt. Off. V. Göth	Hurricane	P2903	Cat. 3 Destroyed
12.	501 Sqn., Kenley	C	Collided with Item 11 during combat with Bf 109s; pilot baled out unhurt.	15.13 hrs.	Plt. Off. K.W. Mackenzie	Hurricane	V6806	Cat. 3 Destroyed
13.	501 Sqn., Kenley	C	Shot down by Bf 109s near Cranbrook; pilot, unhurt, believed to have baled out.	15.15 hrs.	Sgt. S.A.H. Whitehouse	Hurricane	P5193	Cat. 3 Destroyed
14.	501 Sqn., Kenley	C	Shot down by Bf 109s near Cranbrook; pilot baled out unhurt.	15.15 hrs.	Fg. Off. V.R. Snell	Hurricane	N2438	Cat. 3 Destroyed
15.	601 Sqn., Exeter	NC	Collided with Item 15 during formation practice off Exmouth; pilot killed.	Not known	Sgt. May	Hurricane	V6917	Cat. 3 Lost
16.	601 Sqn., Exeter	NC	Collided with Item 16 during formation practice off Exmouth; pilot killed.	Not known	Sgt. Mills-Smith	Hurricane	P3709	Cat. 3 Lost
17.	604 Sqn., Middle Wallop	NC	Lost propeller on landing and aircraft crashed; pilot unhurt.	Not known	Plt. Off. N.R. Wheatcroft	Blenheim	L8373	Cat. 3 Destroyed

[Note: Also notified as lost on this day were seven Hurricanes of No. 111 Squadron, all Destroyed (Cat. 3) by bombs dropped by four Heinkel He 111s at Montrose at dusk.]

LUFTWAFFE LOSSES—FRIDAY 25th OCTOBER 1940

1.	3.(F)/11	CM	Suffered accident at Zutkerque; cause unknown.	Dornier Do 17P (4073)	30 %	Crew unhurt.
2.	3.(H)/12	NCM	Suffered landing accident at Denain airfield.	Henschel Hs 126B (3439)	60 %	Crew unhurt.
3.	4.(F)/14	CM	Crashed at Plumetot airfield after combat.	Dornier Do 17P (4158)	100 %	Ltn. Helmut Höcker + two killed.
4.	2.(F)/122	CM	Shot down by 72 Sqn. Spitfire of Norfolk 15 miles north-east of Great Yarmouth at 14.05 hrs. Pilot rescued by H.M.S. Widgeon.	Messerschmitt Bf 110 C-5 (2257 : F6+MC)	100 %	Gefr. Gerhard Gneist killed; Ltn. Conrad Wacker rescued and made P.O.W.
5.	II./KG 1	CM	Crashed near Arras short of fuel after bombing sortie.	Heinkel He 111H-2 (5325)	100 %	Uffz. Hans Siefert wounded.
6.	II./KG 54	CM	Suffered landing accident at Dreux airfield.	Junkers Ju 88A-1(6095)	35 %	Crew unhurt.
7.	III./KG 55	CM	Force landed at Villacoublay with engine failure suffered on bombing sortie.	Heinkel He 111P-2 (1528)	30 %	Crew unhurt.
8.	II./KG 76	CM	Suffered taxiing accident at Cormeilles airfield.	Junkers Ju 88A-1(3081)	15 %	Crew unhurt.
9.	III./KG 76	CM	Crashed on fire at Cormeilles airfield.	Dornier Do 17Z (2882)	100 %	Ofw. Richard Jöckel + three killed.
10.	I./KG 77	CM	Suffered landing accident at Reims airfield.	Junkers Ju 88A-1(2140)	40 %	Crew unhurt.
11.	II./KG 77	CM	Missing from night bombing sortie over London; probably destroyed by ground defences.	Junkers Ju 88A-1 (4135 : 3Z+ES)	100 %	Fw. Rudi Müller, Fw. Anton Höhn, Fw. Erich Carnet, Gefr. Wilhelm Tschentke missing.

Luftwaffe Losses, 25th October 1940—*continued*

12.	III./KG 77	CM	Missing from night bombing sortie over London; probably destroyed by ground defences.	Junkers Ju 88A-1 (6140 : 3Z+KT)	100 %	Uffz. Wilhelm Hekers, Uffz. Kurt Pirschan, Ogefr. Harmut Hofmann and Ogefr. Fritz Gurnkranz killed.
13.	Erg.Kette/ KGr. 100	NCM	Suffered take-off accident at Lüneburg airfield.	Heinkel He 111H-2 (5469)	100 %	Ltn. Heinz Nachtmann + two killed.
14.	1./KGr. 126	CM	Crashed and burned at Nantes; cause not known.	Heinkel He 111H-4 (3228)	100 %	Obfhr. Ernst Mayer, Uffz. Hans Reith, Ogefr. Walter Löwe and Gefr. Robert Kirchner killed.
15.	8./KGr. 806	CM	Suffered take-off accident at Caen; cause not notified.	Junkers Ju 88A-5 (4185)	100 %	Oblt. Wilhelm Neumann, Oblt.z.S. Otto Metzner + two killed.
16.	II./ZG 26	NCM	Crashed at St. Autin; cause not notified.	Messerschmitt Bf 110 C-7 (3630)	65 %	Crew safe.
17.	3./Erpr.Gr. 210	CM	Suffered minor landing accident at Calais-Marck airfield.	Messerschmitt Bf 109 E-4 (3765)	20 %	Pilot unhurt.
18.	II./LG 2	CM	Suffered taxying accident at Calais-Marck.	Messerschmitt Bf 109 E-4 (3718)	40 %	Pilot unhurt.
19.	II./LG 2	CM	Crashed at Mont-de-Marsan; cause not notified.	Messerschmitt Bf 109 E-4 (4860)	70 %	Pilot unhurt.
20.	Geschw.Erg.St./ JG 3	NCM	Suffered take-off accident at St. Omer airfield.	Messerschmitt Bf 109 E-3 (0946)	100 %	Gefr. Walter Schuck injured.
21.	2./JG 26	CM	Force landed at Boulogne after fighter combat.	Messerschmitt Bf 109E (3631)	20 %	Pilot unhurt.
22.	II./JG 26	CM	Force landed at Marquise after fighter combat.	Messerschmitt Bf 109 E-1 (3601)	40 %	Pilot unhurt.
23.	5./JG 26	CM	Shot down by 257 Sqn. Hurricane of Tuck near London.	Messerschmitt Bf 109 E-4 (3724 : Black 12)	100 %	Oblt. Kurt Eichstädt killed.
24.	8./JG 26	CM	Shot down by 222 Sqn. Spitfire of Thomas in the Maidstone area at 13.35 hrs.	Messerschmitt Bf 109 E-4 (5185 : Black 7)	100 %	Fw. Josef Gärtner missing.
25.	8./JG 26	CM	Shot down by 222 Sqn. of McMullen over the South Coast at 13.43 hrs.	Messerschmitt Bf 109 E-4 (5795 : Black 2)	100 %	Ltn. Hermann Ripke killed.
26.	Stab/JG 51	CM	Shot down by 66 Sqn. Spitfire of Baker.	Messerschmitt Bf 109 E-4 (3737)	100 %	Hptm. Hans Asmus missing.
27.	6./JG 51	CM	Suffered minor landing accident at Calais-Marck after fighter combat.	Messerschmitt Bf 109 E-4 (5724)	10 %	Pilot unhurt.
28.	7./JG 51	CM	Shot down by 41 Sqn. Spitfire of Beardsley near Maidstone.	Messerschmitt Bf 109 E-1 (6281)	100 %	Fw. Willi Koslowski missing.
29.	7./JG 51	CM	Shot down over Kent (probably by 501 Sqn. Hurricanes) at A.15.15 hrs.	Messerschmitt Bf 109 E-1 (3548 : White 4)	100 %	Fw. Leonhard Birg missing.
30.	9./JG 51	CM	Damaged by *flak* over Dover but returned to base safely.	Messerschmitt Bf 109 E-4 (4098)	30 %	Pilot unhurt.
31.	9./JG 51	CM	Damaged by *flak* over Dover but returned to base safely.	Messerschmitt Bf 109 E-4 (4099)	50 %	Pilot unhurt.
32.	9./JG 51	CM	Shot down by 41 Sqn. Spitfire of McAdam off Kent coast near Dover at 09.45 hrs.	Messerschmitt Bf 109 E-4 (4100)	100 %	Pilot, unhurt, rescued by *Seenotflugkommando*.
33.	6./JG 53	CM	Shot down by 66 Sqn. Spitfires near Tunbridge Wells at 09.10 hrs.	Messerschmitt Bf 109 E-4 (1080 : Yellow 2)	100 %	Uffz. Karl Schulz missing.
34.	5./JG 54	CM	Shot down by 41 Sqn. Spitfire of Brown near Tunbridge Wells at A.10.00 hrs.	Messerschmitt Bf 109 E-4 (1988 : Black 7)	100 %	Oblt. Joachim Schypek missing.
35.	5./JG 54	CM	Believed shot down by Spitfires near Chatham.	Messerschmitt Bf 109 E-4 (5178 : Black 2)	100 %	Ltn. Ernst Wagner missing.
36.	3./JG 77	CM	Shot down by British fighters during sweep towards London.	Messerschmitt Bf 109 E-4 (5104 : Yellow 13)	100 %	Gefr. Karl Raisinger missing.
37.	3./JG 77	CM	Suffered landing accident at St. Andeyelle following fighter combat.	Messerschmitt Bf 109 E-1 (5812)	25 %	Pilot unhurt.
38.	1./KGzbV. 108	NCM	Crashed at Hommelvik; cause not notified.	Junkers Ju 52/3m (6945)	80 %	Crew unhurt.

Saturday 26th October

The *Luftwaffe*'s greatest coup on this day was the finding and bombing of the liner *Empress of Britain*, 42,000 tons, by a Focke-Wulf Fw 200C *Condor* captained by Hptm. Bernhard Jope of *2.Staffel, Kampfgeschwader 40*, off the north-west coast of Ireland. Set on fire by Jope's bombs 150 miles from land, the great liner limped slowly eastwards under constant fighter cover provided by Hurricanes of No. 245 Squadron from Aldergrove. Then a U-boat torpedoed her, and she was abandoned and taken under tow. Shortly afterwards she blew up and sank. 45 of the 643 persons on board perished during the initial attack; all were passengers. It was Bernhard Jope's first operational sortie. . .

Hauptmann Bernhard Jope of *Kampfgeschwader 40*, the Fw 200 Condor pilot who, on his first operational sortie, bombed the liner *Empress of Britain* on 26th October. His award of the Knight's Cross on 30th December 1940 was in respect of this operation. He was subsequently awarded the Oakleaves on 24th March 1944, and after the War became a senior pilot with *Lufthansa*. (Photo: Hans Obert)

R.A.F. FIGHTER COMMAND LOSSES—SATURDAY 26th OCTOBER 1940

1.	29 Sqn., Ternhill	NC	Suffered night landing accident at Ternhill; crew unhurt.	20.00 hrs.	Plt. Off. J.D. Humphreys	Blenheim	*L1375*	Cat. 3 Destroyed
2.	151 Sqn., Digby	NC	Crashed during night take-off accident at Coleby Grange; pilot died in hospital soon afterwards	20.40 hrs.	Sgt. D.O. Stanley	Hurricane	*V7434*	Cat. 3 Destroyed
3.	151 Sqn., Digby	NC	Crashed during night take-off at Coleby Grange; pilot killed.	20.45 hrs.	Sgt. R. Holder	Hurricane	*R4184*	Cat. 3 Destroyed
4.	222 Sqn., Hornchurch	NC	Crashed at Latchingden, Essex, after engine fire in the air; pilot unhurt.	17.45 hrs.	Sgt. P.O. Davis	Spitfire	*R6773*	Cat. 3 Destroyed
5.	229 Sqn., Northolt	C	Shot down by Bf 109s off the French coast; pilot assumed lost at sea.	A11.25 hrs.	Plt. Off. G.M. Simpson	Hurricane	*W6669*	Cat. 3 Missing
6.	229 Sqn., Northolt	C	Shot down off French coast and later reported to be a prisoner of war.	A11.25 hrs.	Plt. Off. D.B.H. McHardy	Hurricane	*V6704*	Cat. 3 Missing
7.	234 Sqn., St. Eval	C	Force landed near the Lizard after combat with Ju 88; pilot unhurt.	Not known	Plt. Off. E.B. Mortimer-Rose	Spitfire	*X4355*	Cat. 2 Damaged
8.	302 Sqn., Duxford	NC	Force landed at Sittingbourne with fuel shortage; pilot unhurt.	Not known	Plt. Off. S. Kleczkowski	Hurricane	*V6735*	Cat. 2 Damaged
9.	602 Sqn., Westhampnett	C	Reported missing after routine patrol; pilot assumed lost at sea.	A12.45 hrs.	Sgt. D.W. Elcombe	Spitfire	*R6839*	Cat. 3 Missing
10.	605 Sqn., Croydon	C	Damaged in combat with Bf 109s and crash landed at Marks Cross, Sussex; pilot unhurt.	12.10 hrs.	Fg. Off. C.W. Passy	Hurricane	*P3737*	Cat. 3 Destroyed
11.	605 Sqn., Croydon	C	Shot down by Bf 109s near Cranbrook; pilot baled out unhurt.	16.10 hrs.	Plt. Off. J.C.F. Hayter.	Hurricane	*V6943*	Cat. 3 Destroyed

LUFTWAFFE LOSSES—SATURDAY 26th OCTOBER 1940

1.	2.(F)/123	CM	Damaged by *flak* during sortie over England.	Junkers Ju 88A-1 (0348)	5 %	Uffz. Karl Grünmüller and Fw. Werner Fischer wounded.
2.	III./KG 1	CM	Crashed at Rosières with fuel shortage.	Junkers Ju 88A-5	100 %	Crew baled out unhurt.
3.	I./KG 26	CM	Missing from bombing sortie over Lossiemouth; assumed shot down by *flak*.	Heinkel He 111H-3 (6854 : 1H+BL)	100 %	Oblt. Georg Imhof, Fw. Walter Bastin, Uffz. Ebhardt Radloff, Uffz. Hermann Weniger killed.
4.	I./KG 26	CM	Returned with *flak* damage from bombing sortie over Scotland.	Heinkel He 111H-3 (3319)	20 %	Uffz. Heinz Krüger wounded.
5.	I./KG 26	CM	Returned with *flak* damage from bombing sortie over Scotland.	Heinkel He 111H-3 (6937)	20 %	Fw. Harald Jessen wounded.
6.	2./KG 53	CM	Missing from bombing sortie over London; assumed shot down by ground defences.	Heinkel He 111H-5 (3637 : A1+LK)	100 %	Ltn. Günther Hanau, Ltn. Hans Cichi + three missing.
7.	St.St./KG 55	CM	Crashed and burned at Versailles; circumstances not known.	Heinkel He 111P-2 (2653)	100 %	Oblt. Bodo Eitner, Ltn. Franz Oberhofer + three killed.
8.	St.St./KG 55	CM	Suffered landing accident at Villacoublay after bombing sortie.	Heinkel He 111P-2 (2666)	70 %	Crew unhurt.
9.	II./KG 76	CM	Landing accident at Creil airfield.	Junkers Ju 88A-5(6159)	50 %	Crew unhurt.
10.	II./KG 77	CM	Force landed at Soissons after engine failure.	Junkers Ju 88A-1(7111)	50 %	Crew unhurt.
11.	I./NJG 1	NCM	Collided with Item 12 at Schipol airfield.	Messerschmitt Bf 110 C-2 (3599)	35 %	Crew unhurt.
12.	II./NJG 2	NCM	Collided with Item 11 at Schipol airfield.	Messerschmitt Bf 110 C-2 (3538)	35 %	Crew unhurt.
13.	8./JG 27	NCM	Force landed at Guines-West; not combat.	Messerschmitt Bf 109E	20 %	Pilot safe.
14.	Geschw.Erg.St./ JG 52	NCM	Take-off accident at Krefeld airfield; circumstances not known.	Messerschmitt Bf 109E (3474)	35 %	Pilot unhurt.
15.	1./JG 53	CM	Shot down by 92 Sqn Spitfire of Holland near Maidstone at A.10.30 hrs.	Messerschmitt Bf 109 E-7 (5929 : White 6)	100 %	Ofw. Oskar Strack missing.
16.	4./JG 53	CM	Shot down by 92 Sqn Spitfire of Fokes into the English Channel; pilot baled out.	Messerschmitt Bf 109 E-1 (6180)	100 %	Pilot, unwounded, rescued by *Seenotflugkommando*.
17.	6./JG 53	CM	Damaged in fighter combat over Tonbridge.	Messerschmitt Bf 109E	20 %	Pilot unhurt.
18.	6./JG 53	CM	Damaged in fighter combat over Tonbridge.	Messerschmitt Bf 109 E-4 (1099)	40 %	Pilot unhurt.
19.	6./JG 53	CM	Shot down by 92 Sqn Spitfire of Mottram near Maidstone at A.10.30 hrs.	Messerschmitt Bf 109 E-1 (6391 : Yellow 8)	100 %	Uffz. Geiswinckler missing.
20.	II./JG 77	CM	Minor damage reported at Herdla; circumstances not notified.	Messerschmitt Bf 109E (6090)	1 %	Ltn. Jacob Arnoldy injured.
21.	II./JG 77	CM	Minor damage reported at Herdla; circumstances not notified.	Messerschmitt Bf 109E (6202)	2 %	Uffz. Niemeyer injured.

A post-Battle group photo of No. 92 Squadron's pilots; those in flying kit are (left to right) Plt. Off. R.H. Holland, Plt. Off. B. Wright, Flt. Lt. C.B.F. Kingcome, Sqn. Ldr. J.A. Kent, Sgt. H. Bowen-Morris, Sgt. D.E. Kingaby, Plt. Off. R. Mottram and Sgt. R.E. Havercroft. At the end of the Battle of Britain this Squadron was based at Biggin Hill.

Luftwaffe Losses, 26th October 1940—*continued*

22.	1./506	CM	Missing from sort over the North Sea; fate not known.	Heinkel He 115B (1889 : S4+AH)	100 %		Ltn.z.S. Karl-Heinz Kemper + two missing.
23.	Seenotflug-kommando 3	CM	Shot down by 229 Sqn. Hurricanes off Boulogne at A.11.00 hrs.	Heinkel He 55 (1984)	100 %		Ltn. Heinrich Hilke, Gefr.Wolfgang Michels,Uffz.Karl Bachmeier killed

Sunday 27th October

An extraordinary statistic reflecting the strain imposed on the defences by hit-and-run daylight raiding at this stage was the total of 1,007 sorties flown by Fighter Command on this Sunday—in comparison with the 974 flown on the memorable 15th August. It was a measure of the considerable growth of Dowding's Command in ten weeks, and the efficiency of No. 11 Group control, that so many sorties could be mounted, the great majority of them in the South-East. In contrast to the enormous battles of 15th August, however, 27th October saw the destruction of fewer than a dozen German aircraft.

The principal targets were once again airfields, and Coltishall, Feltwell, Driffield, Leconfield, Martlesham, Kirton-in-Lindsey and Hawkinge were all hit during the day and night by bombers of KG 1, 3, 4 and 76, which owed their relative immunity during the day to the fact that they attacked singly or in small groups under cover of heavy clouds.

R.A.F. FIGHTER COMMAND LOSSES—SUNDAY 27th OCTOBER 1940

1.	43 Sqn., Usworth	NC	Aircraft crashed at Edmondsley during aerobatics; pilot killed.	10.25 hrs.	Sgt. L.V. Toogood	Hurricane	L1963	Cat. 3 Destroyed
2.	66 Sqn., Gravesend	C	Pilot crashed at Hildenborough, near Tonbridge, during routine patrol; pilot killed.	08.40 hrs.	Plt. Off. R.J. Mather	Spitfire	P7539	Cat. 3 Destroyed
3.	74 Sqn., Biggin Hill	C	Shot down by Bf 109s over Maidstone and crashed at Elsted; pilot killed.	A09.00 hrs	Sgt. J.A. Scott	Spitfire	P7526	Cat. 3 Destroyed
4.	145 Sqn., Tangmere	C	Force landed at Hollington, near Hastings, short of fuel after combat with Bf 109s; pilot unhurt.	A12.30 hrs.	Fg. Off. D.S.G. Honor	Hurricane	V7422	Cat. 2 Damaged
5.	145 Sqn., Tangmere	C	Shot down by Bf 109s five miles south of Bembridge, Isle of Wight; pilot killed.	17.15 hrs.	Plt. Off. A.R.I. Jottard	Hurricane	P3167	Cat. 3 Lost
6.	145 Sqn., Tangmere	C	Force landed near Amersham after combat with Bf 109s and out of fuel; pilot unhurt.	A12.30 hrs.	Sgt. D.B. Sykes	Hurricane	N2494	Cat. 2 Damaged
7.	145 Sqn., Tangmere	C	Shot down off the Isle of Wight by Bf 109s; pilot baled out and rescued, unhurt, by M.T.B.	17.15 hrs.	Sgt. J. Weber	Hurricane	V7592	Cat. 3 Lost
8.	145 Sqn., Tangmere	C	Shot down off the Isle of Wight by Bf 109s; pilot ditched, and waded ashore unhurt.	17.15 hrs.	Sgt. J.K. Haire	Hurricane	V6888	Cat. 3 Lost
9.	222 Sqn., Hornchurch	C	Crashed at Hailsham, Sussex, short of fuel after combat; pilot severely wounded.	Not known	Plt. Off. E.F. Edsall	Spitfire	X4548	Cat. 3 Destroyed
10.	603 Sqn., Hornchurch	C	Bounced by Bf 109s near Maidstone and shot down near Waltham; pilot grievously wounded and died the following day.	14.05 hrs.	Fg. Off. C.W. Goldsmith	Spitfire	P7439	Cat. 3 Destroyed
11.	603 Sqn., Hornchurch	C	Bounced by Bf 109s near Maidstone and shot down at Chartham Hatch, near Canterbury; pilot killed.	14.09 hrs.	Plt. Off. R.B. Dewey	Spitfire	P7365	Cat. 3 Destroyed
12.	603 Sqn., Hornchurch	C	Bounced by Bf 109s near Maidstone; aircraft shot down and pilot baled out unhurt.	A.14.05 hrs.	Plt. Off. D.A. Maxwell	Spitfire	P7286	Cat. 3 Destroyed

LUFTWAFFE LOSSES—SUNDAY 27th OCTOBER 1940

1.	3.(H)/32	NCM	Damaged in force landing near Amiens.	Fieseler Fi 156 (0689)	35 %		Crew unhurt.
2.	3.(F)/121	CM	Force landed at Morlaix following engine failure.	Junkers Ju 88A-5(0452)	20 %		Crew unhurt.
3.	I./KG 1	CM	Shot down by 85 Sqn. Hurricane of Marshall at Salt Fleet, Norfolk, at 18.10 hrs.	Heinkel He 111H-2 (5541 : V4+HW)	100 %		Gefr. Karl Bosenberg, Uffz. Matthew Behres, Gefr. Rudi Hartlieb, Fw. Walter Saumsiegel, Uffz. Richard Heinhold missing.
4.	III./KG 1	NCM	Crashed on landing at Greville airfield.	Junkers Ju 88A-5(2194)	100 %		Crew unhurt.
5.	3./KG 2	CM	Landed with combat damage after bombing sortie; circumstances not notified.	Dornier Do 17Z-2 (3443)	5 %		Uffz. Hans Rutkowski wounded.
6.	7./JG 3	CM	Damaged by 1 Sqn. Hurricanes near Feltwell.	Dornier Do 17Z	Nil.		Fw. Passler killed.
7.	9./KG 3	CM	Damaged by 1 Sqn. Hurricanes near Feltwell.	Dornier Do 17Z	Nil.		Fw. Karl Heese wounded.
8.	7./KG 4	CM	Shot down by light A.A. fire and crashed at Kirby Grindalythe, Malton, Yorks, at 18.10 hrs.	Junkers Ju 88A-5 (6129 : 5J+ER)	100 %		Uffz. Otto Piontek killed; Oblt. Friedrich Podbielski, St. Kap., Fw. Hans Heier, Ofw. Karl Kiedrowski made P.O.W.s.
9.	8./KG 4	CM	Missing from bombing sortie over Britain: fate not established.	Junkers Ju 88A-1 (6048 : 5J+HS)	100 %		Oblt. Dietrich Marlwitz, Ofw. Werner Ehrbach, Gefr. Karl Herold and Uffz. Hubert Schmitz missing.
10.	II./KG 26	CM	Pilot encountered difficulties during bombing sortie, and three crew baled out.	Heinkel He 111H-3 (3326)	70 %		Obly. Helmut Küne and Uffz. Albert Lehmann injured.
11.	5./KG 53	CM	Suffered landing accident at Vendeville after bombing sortie; cause not notified.	Heinkel He 111H-2 (5500)	65 %		Crew unhurt.
12.	Geschw.Erg.St./	NCM	Suffered landing accident at Berleberg; details not notified.	Junkers Ju 88A-1 (3099)	80 %		Crew unhurt.
13.	III./KG 77	CM	Target Martlesham. Shot down by 17 Sqn. Hurricane of Ross into the River Stour at 18.50 hrs.	Dornier Do 17Z (1150 : F1+HR)	100 %		Uffz. Erich Johannes missing; Uffz. Friedrich Ebele, Uffz. Karl Fritz, Uffz. Richard Karl and Ogefr. Gustav Wilpern killed.
14.	III./LG 1	CM	Suffered landing accident at Manneville.	Junkers Ju 88A-1(6150)	50 %		Crew unhurt.
15.	3./NJG 2	CM	Suffered take-off accident at Gilze-Rijen airfield.	Junkers Ju 88A-1(6144)	60 %		Crew unhurt.
16.	Geschw.Erg.St./ ZG 26	NCM	Suffered landing accident at Guyancourt airfield.	Messerschmitt Bf 110 C-4 (3625)	20 %		Crew unhurt.
17.	Stab/JG 3	CM	Shot down by 501 Sqn. Hurricane of Mackenzie at 12.30 hrs., and crashed at Addington.	Messerschmitt Bf 109 E-7 (4124 : < + —)	100 %		Ltn. Wilhelm Busch, Signals Officer, made P.O.W.
18.	6./JG 27	NCM	Suffered take-off accident at Denain airfield.	Messerschmitt Bf 109 E-1 (1329)	60 %		Pilot unhurt.
19.	8./JG 27	CM	Force landed at Cap Gris Nez with battle damge after fighter combat.	Messerschmitt Bf 109E	20 %		Pilot unhurt.

Luftwaffe Losses, 27th October 1940—*continued*

20.	8./JG 27	CM	Missing after combat sortie over South-East England.	Messerschmitt Bf 109 E-4 (1604 : Black 10)	100 %	Oblt. Anton Pointer, *St.Kap.*, missing.
21.	9./JG 27	CM	Force landed at Calais after fighter combat over Kent.	Messerschmitt Bf 109 E-1 (4818)	40 %	Gefr. Albert Busenkeil wounded.
22.	2./JG 52	CM	Missing from fighter combat over Kent; fate not established.	Messerschmitt Bf 109 E-4 (1268 : Black 5)	100 %	Gefr. Karl Bott missing.
23.	3./JG 52	CM	Missing from fighter combat over Kent; fate not established.	Messerschmitt Bf 109 E-4 (2798 : Yellow 2)	100 %	Oblt. Ulrich Steinhilper missing.
24.	3./JG 52	CM	Shot down by 605 Sqn. Hurricane of Ingle over Kent.	Messerschmitt Bf 109 E-4 (3525 : Yellow 4)	100 %	Fw. Lothar Schieverhöfer missing.
25.	2./JG 53	CM	Suffered taxying accident at Etaples airfield.	Messerschmitt Bf 109 E-1 (1504)	25 %	Pilot unhurt.
26.	4./JG 53	CM	Shot down by 66 Sqn. Spitfire of Cook near Tonbridge at 08.50 hrs.	Messerschmitt Bf 109 E-4 (5243 : White 5)	100 %	Uffz. Hermann Schlitt missing.
27.	7./JG 54	CM	Shot down by 74 Sqn. Spitfire of Nelson and crashed near Lydd at A.09.30 hrs.	Messerschmitt Bf 109 E-1 (3576 : White 13)	100 %	Uffz. Arno Zimmermann made P.O.W.
28.	5./JG 77	NCM	Force landed on Hitra Island on transit flight.	Messerschmitt Bf 109E (3590)	20 %	Pilot unhurt.
29.	5./JG 77	NCM	Force landed on Hitra Island on transit flight.	Messerschmitt Bf 109E (1407)	20 %	Pilot unhurt.
30.	*Flugbereitschaft Luftgau Kdo. Belge/Nordfr.*	NCM	Suffered landing accident at Calais-Marck; details not notified.	Henschel Hs 126 (5279)	20 %	Crew unhurt.

Monday 28th October

The autumn weather was now seriously hampering the daylight activities of *Luftflotte 2* and *3*, and morning mist persisted over many of the enemy's coastal airfields. Resuming the attacks on British shipping, Göring ordered a number of bomber units to hit coastal and deep-sea convoys. For this purpose two *Gruppen* of Ju 87s, which had been languishing in idleness on Breton airfields for more than two months, were warned to be ready for shipping strikes if the call came.

In the event they were not required for another fortnight; and when they were once again ordered into British skies, they were to suffer severe punishment at the hands of British interceptors—once again.

During the afternoon of the 28th, Osterkamp's energetic *Jafu 2* units sent eight *Gruppen* of Bf 109s over Kent and the Thames Estuary, losing four Emils without scoring against Fighter Command.

R.A.F. FIGHTER COMMAND LOSSES—MONDAY 28th OCTOBER 1940

1.	616 Sqn., Kirton-in-Lindsey	NC	Downwind landing; aircraft overturned on overshooting, but pilot unhurt.	13.13 hrs.	Plt. Off. Heppell	Spitfire	—	Cat. 3 Destroyed

LUFTWAFFE LOSSES—MONDAY 28th OCTOBER 1940

1.	2.(F)/123	NCM	Suffered take-off accident at Saarbrücken.	Messerschmitt Bf 110 C-5 (2241)	60 %	Maj. Gunther Obernitz and Hptm. Georg Deehand injured.
2.	Geschw.Erg.St./ KG 1	NCM	Crashed at Nordhausen following engine failure.	Heinkel He 111H-2 (2788)	90 %	Crew unhurt.
3.	1./KG 3	CM	Shot down by ground defences and crashed at Boughton Malherbe, Kent, at 02.00 hrs.	Dornier Do 17Z-2 (2544 : 5K+CH)	100 %	Fw. Kurt Vosshagen, wounded, made P.O.W. Uffz. Harald Hausdorf, Fw. Alwin Schreiber, and Fw. Rudi Nitzsche killed.
4.	8./KG 3	CM	Engaged by British fighter over the Channel; undamaged but two crew members wounded.	Dornier Do 17Z	Nil	Gefr. Walter Büttner and Fl. Josef Ziebursch wounded.
5.	I./KG 51	CM	Landing collision with Item 6 at Villaroche.	Junkers Ju 88A-1(5112)	20 %	Crew unhurt.
6.	I./KG 51	CM	Landing collision with Item 5 at Villaroche.	Junkers Ju 88A-1(5125)	25 %	Crew unhurt.
7.	III./KG 51	CM	Missing from bombing sortie over London; fate not established.	Junkers Ju 88A-1 (8040 : 9K+MR)	100 %	Gefr.Erich König killed. Uffz.Ernst Krämer, Gefr. Arnold Hauff, Gefr. Helmut Zimmermann missing.
8.	I./KG 53	NCM	Crashed at Oppy/Arras following engine failure.	Heinkel He 111H(3536)	30 %	Crew unhurt.
9.	9./KG 53	CM	Crew became lost; believing they were over Holland, they baled out and the aircraft crashed in the River Stour, near Parkstone at 01.50 hrs. on 29-10-40.	Heinkel He 111H-2 (5536 : A1+LT)	100 %	Ofw. Karl Panzel, Ofw. Heinrich Metzger, Uffz. Forian Sigger, Uffz. Hans Klitscher and Uffz. Harry Lüdecke made P.O.W.s.
10.	II./KG 76	CM	Suffered landing accident; location not notified.	Junkers Ju 88A-1(8078)	70 %	Crew unhurt.
11.	I./KG 77	NCM	Crashed at St. Dizier; cause not notified.	Junkers Ju 88A-1 (2146)	100 %	Ogefr. Walter Schmitt injured; Ltn. Heinz Wagner + two killed.
12.	Gruppe Erg. Kette/KGr. 100	NCM	Crashed and burned at Lüneburg; cause not notified..	Heinkel He 111H-1 (2420)	100 %	Three crew members killed.
13.	Kü.Fl.Gr. 606	CM	Landing accident at Brest; cause not known.	Dornier Do 17Z (3437)	40 %	Crew unhurt.
14.	4./ZG 26	CM	Crashed at Jever following technical failure.	Messerschmitt Bf 110 C/D (3429)	80 %	Hptm. Hoppe injured.
15.	7./NJG 1	CM	Crashed and burned at Rendburg; cause not notified.	Messerschmitt Bf 110D (3356)	100 %	Uffz. Karl Bertram and Ofw. Kurt Lorenz killed.
16.	5./JG 27	CM	Shot down by 257 Sqn. Hurricane of Tuck in Gravesend area and crashed at Leybourne.	Messerschmitt Bf 109 E-8 (4906 : Black 2)	100 %	Uffz. Artur Gonschorek made P.O.W.
17.	Stab II./JG 51	CM	Shot down by British fighters and crashed at Fielding Lane, Dymchurch, at 17.10 hrs.	Messerschmitt Bf 109 E-4 (5095)	100 %	Ltn. Werner Knittel, *Adj.*, killed.
18.	4./JG 51	CM	Shot down by British fighters over the English South Coast.	Messerschmitt Bf 109 E-4 (1420 : White 10)	100 %	Fw. Hans John killed.
19.	1./JG 53	CM	Crash landed at Boulogne after fighter combat off the Sussex coast.	Messerschmitt Bf 109 E-8 (6395)	80 %	Pilot unhurt.
20.	4./JG 53	CM	Shot down by A.A. guns and crashed at North Common, Chailey, at 16.45 hrs.	Messerschmitt Bf 109 E-4 : 1531 : White 3)	100 %	Fw. Alfred Berg made P.O.W.
21.	*Seenotflug- kommando 1*	NCM	Crashed after enfine failure at Nordwyk.	Dornier Do 24 (0075)	80 %	Ltn.z.S.Unterhorst, Uffz.Friedrich Kruse injured; Ltn. Wilhelm Scheel killed.

Tuesday 29th October

If the fighter combats of the past weeks had proved disappointing for Park's frustrated pilots, the battle which occurred at around mid-day on 29th October was to reassure them.

After a brief phase of reconnaissance during the early daylight hours, a *Gruppe* of Bf 109s was intercepted at 11.10 hours as it crossed the coast near Deal. While two fighter *Staffeln* held the attention of the Spitfire pilots, a fighter-bomber *Staffel* disengaged and made for London, where two of its bombs landed close to the approach to Charing Cross station.

As these Messerschmitts turned for home, Park's controllers scrambled five Spitfire and four Hurricane squadrons in readiness for the next wave, which was already showing on the plotting tables. This materialised as about one hundred Bf 109s of I. and II.*Gruppen*, JG 51, escorting the *Jabos* of I. and II.*Gruppen, Lehrgeschwader 2.*

Park's premeditated tactics worked to perfection. As the Spitfires climbed to 28,000 feet, the Hurricane squadrons positioned themselves in pairs on the flanks of the enemy formation at 22,000 feet. Four squadrons attacked simultaneously, the Spitfires arching down on the 109s from out of the sun. Within six minutes, eleven Messerschmitts were falling in flames, and the remainder of the raiders had dumped their bombs and were heading for the Sussex coast at full speed.

Apart from two raids—one on Portsmouth during the morning by twelve Junkers Ju 88s of I./LG 1, escorted by two *Gruppen* of JG 2's Bf 109s, and one on Ramsgate by fifteen Italian BR.20s escorted by CR.42 biplanes—there was one other operation on this day which is worthy of note. This was a dive bombing attack on North Weald by the 3rd *Staffel* of *Erprobungsgruppe 210*, for this occasion once more specially equipped with bomb-carrying Bf 109Es. Operating at the very limit of their range with three 100-kilo bombs apiece, the crack pilots were led on this extremely hazardous mission by the veteran *Staffelkapitän* Otto Hintze. The attack, predictably, was brilliantly executed. As the Messerschmitts appeared flying low over the airfield at 16.45 hours, the Hurricanes of Nos. 249 and 257 Squadrons were in the process of taking off; two Hurricanes were destroyed and one pilot killed. On the ground, nineteen people were killed and 42 injured. The remaining Hurricanes gave chase, and one Messerschmitt fell to the guns of Flt. Lt. Robert Barton—the aircraft of Otto Hintze himself. He baled out safely and was taken prisoner, and a month later was awarded the Knight's Cross *in absentia*. Thus fell the last of the key quartet of brilliant pilots who had guided one of the *Luftwaffe*'s outstanding flying units into being, and flown some of the most hazardous operations imaginable.

R.A.F. FIGHTER COMMAND LOSSES—TUESDAY 29th OCTOBER 1940

#	Squadron		Details	Time	Pilot	Aircraft	Serial	Category
1.	1 Sqn., Wittering	C	Crashed on landing at base after combat with Do 17 near Wittering; pilot unhurt.	12.50 hrs.	Plt. Off. E. Cizek	Hurricane	V7302	Cat. 3 Destroyed
2.	1 Sqn., Wittering	NC	Suffered landing accident at Wittering; pilot unhurt.	10.30 hrs.	Sgt. J. Dygryn	Hurricane	P5187	Cat. 3 Destroyed
3.	19 Sqn., Duxford	C	Shot down, probably by Bf 109 over London, and crashed at Chelmsford; pilot killed.	16.50 hrs.	Sub-Lt. A.G. Blake RN	Spitfire	P7423	Cat. 3 Destroyed
4.	19 Sqn., Duxford	C	Force landed at Rochford, short of fuel after patrol; pilot unhurt.	17.05 hrs.	Sgt. A.N. McGregor	Spitfire	P7379	Cat. 1 Damaged
5.	29 Sqn., Ternhill	NC	Crashed into tree during night take-off; pilot (the only occupant) unhurt.	21.00 hrs.	Sgt. A.J.A. Roberts	Blenheim	L1503	Cat. 2 Damaged
6.	46 Sqn., Stapleford	C	Shot down by Bf 109s near Ashford; pilot badly burned and wounded, and died on the following day.	Not known	Sgt. H.E. Black	Hurricane	—	Cat. 3 Destroyed
7.	92 Sqn., Biggin Hill	NC	Suffered taxying accident (with Item 8); pilot unhurt.	Not known	Sgt. H. Bowen-Morris	Spitfire	—	Cat. 1 Damaged
8.	92 Sqn., Biggin Hill	NC	Suffered taxying accident (with Item 7); pilot unhurt.	Not known	Sgt. D.E. Kingaby	Spitfire	—	Cat. 1 Damaged
9.	213 Sqn., Tangmere	C	Pilot baled out after combat off Selsey Bill, but was dead when picked up by Selsey life boat. Buried at Tangmere.	A15.00 hrs.	Plt. Off. R.R. Hutley.	Hurricane	V7622	Cat. 3 Lost
10.	232 Sqn., Drem	NC	Landed wheels-up with undercarriage trouble; pilot unhurt.	Not known	Sgt. E.A. Redfern	Hurricane	V6848	Cat. 2 Damaged
11.	249 Sqn., North Weald	C	Aircraft damaged while taking off among falling bombs during raid on base; pilot unhurt.	A16.45 hrs.	Plt. Off. K.T. Lofts	Hurricane	V6727	Cat. 2 Damaged
12.	257 Sqn., North Weald	C	Aircraft struck by bomb while taking off during raid on base, and set on fire; pilot burned to death.	A16.45 hrs.	Sgt. A.G. Girdwood	Hurricane	V6852	Cat. 3 Destroyed
13.	257 Sqn., North Weald	C	Aircraft damaged on take-off during raid; pilot baled out at 3,000 feet, unhurt.	A16.45 hrs.	Plt. Off. F. Surma	Hurricane	P3893	Cat. 3 Destroyed
14.	302 Sqn., Duxford	NC	Air collision with Item 15 near Brooklands; pilot baled out slightly injured; aircraft crashed at Chobham.	Not known	Flt. Lt. J.A. Thompson	Hurricane	P3085	Cat. 3 Destroyed
15.	302 Sqn., Duxford	NC	Air collision with Item 14 near Brooklands; aircraft damaged but pilot returned unhurt.	Not known	Flt. Lt. J.T. Czerny	Hurricane	V6923	Cat. 2 Damaged
16.	310 Sqn., Duxford	NC	Air collision with Item 17 near Duxford; pilot killed.	A15.00 hrs.	Plt. Off. E. Fechtner	Hurricane	P3889	Cat. 3 Destroyed
17.	310 Sqn., Duxford	NC	Air collision with Item 16; pilot force landed near Duxford, slightly injured.	A15.00 hrs.	Plt.Off.J.M. Maly	Hurricane	—	Cat. 2 Damaged
18.	615 Sqn., Northolt	C	Shot down by Bf 109 and pilot severely wounded.	Not known	Fg. Off. N.D. Edmond	Hurricane	—	Cat. 3 Destroyed

LUFTWAFFE LOSSES—TUESDAY 29th OCTOBER 1940

#	Unit		Details	Aircraft		Remarks
1.	3.(F)/31	NCM	Landing accident at Orléans; cause not known.	Dornier Do 17P (3553)	50 %	Crew unhurt.
2.	5.(F)/122	NCM	Suffered taxying accident at Haute-Fontaine.	Junkers Ju 88A-1(0364)	8 %	Crew unhurt.
3.	I./KG 1	CM	Missing from bombing sortie over England; target West Raynham, Norfolk.	Heinkel He 111H-3 (3296 : V4+DH)	100 %	Gefr. Josef Overkäping killed; Oblt. Ernst Süss + two missing.
4.	III./KG 1	NCM	Crashed on landing at Bapaume airfied.	Junkers Ju 88A-5(2210)	60 %	Crew unhurt.
5.	8./KG 4	CM	Missing from bombing sortie over Britain; fate not established.	Junkers Ju 88A-1 (5014 : 5J+US)	100 %	Oblt.z.S. Johann Schubert + three missing.

No. 615 Squadron, two of whose Hurricanes are shown landing, moved back south in October to Northolt after its period of re-equipping and resting at Prestwick. (Photo: R.A.F. Museum)

Luftwaffe Losses, 29th October 1940—*continued*

6.	II./KG 77	NCM	Crashed at Rheims; cause not notified.	Junkers Ju 88A-1 (6127 : 3Z+JP)	100 %	Ofw. Heinz Gehring + three killed.
7.	I./LG 1	NCM	Crashed at Orléans-Bricy after engine failure.	Junkers Ju 88A-1(2082)	100 %	Fw. Werner Heyden + three killed.
8.	III./ZG 76	NCM	Crashed at Denain airfield; cause not notified.	Messerschmitt Bf 110 D-3 (4218)	100 %	Fw. Hocheder and Ogefr. Sengbusch killed.
9.	2./Erpr.Gr. 210	CM	Crashed at St. Inglevert following engine failure.	Messerschmitt Bf 110 DB (3655)	100 %	Uffz. Otto Büttner and Fw. Tröppel killed.
10.	3./Erpr.Gr. 210	CM	Shot down by Hurricane of 219 Sqn., probably flown by Barton, after raid on North Weald at A.17.10 hrs.	Messerschmitt Bf 109 E-4 (2024 : Yellow 6)	100 %	Oblt. Otto Hintze, *St.Kap.*, missing.
11.	3./LG 2	CM	Crashed at Wissant after fighter combat.	Messerschmitt Bf 109 E-7 (2032)	25 %	Pilot safe.
12.	4./LG 2	CM	Shot down and crashed near Langham Hoe, Colchester, Essex, at 17.10 hrs.	Messerschmitt Bf 109 E-4 (5593 : 3X+N)	100 %	Ofw.Harmeling, slightly wounded, made P.O.W.
13.	4./LG 2	CM	Shot down by British fighters over Essex at A.17.15 hrs.	Messerschmitt Bf 109 E-4 (5562 : 3X+B)	100 %	Fw. Max Rank killed.
14.	5./LG 2	CM	Shot down by 501 Sqn. Hurricane of Mackenzie and crashed near Goldhanger, Essex, 16.55 hrs.	Messerschmitt Bf 109 E-4 (4145 : 3X+S)	100 %	Oblt. Benno von Schenk, *St.Kap.*, killed.
15.	I./JG 2	CM	Crashed at Cherbourg with *flak* damage.	Messerschmitt Bf 109 E-1 (4063)	80 %	Uffz. Walter Bader wounded.
16.	III./JG 2	CM	Shot down by *flak* over the Isle of Wight.	Messerschmitt Bf 109 E-4 (3657)	100 %	Oblt. Erich Wolf, *Adj.*, killed.
17.	Geschw.Erg.St./ JG 2	NCM	Crashed and burned at Octeville; pilot baled out.	Messerschmitt Bf 109 E-1 (3273)	100 %	Pilot unhurt.
18.	Geschw.Erg.St./	NCM	Crashed and burned at Manneville.	Messerschmitt Bf 109 E-4 (1451)	95 %	Gefr. Karl Dietrich killed.
19.	5./JG 3	NCM	Crashed at Arques; cause not notified.	Messerschmitt Bf 109 E-1 (4873)	95 %	Ofw. Horst Götz killed.
20.	9./JG 3	CM	Shot down by British fighters over the Channel; pilot baled out.	Messerschmitt Bf 109 (5341)	100 %	Pilot, unwounded, rescued by *Seenotflugkommando*.
21.	9./JG 3	CM	Shot down by 253 Sqn. Hurricane of Marsland at A.16.30 hrs. and crashed at Shepherdswell,	Messerschmitt Bf 109 E-4(5153 : 1+Yellow 3)	100 %	Oblt. Egon Troha, *St.Kap.*, made P.O.W.
22.	8./JG 26	CM	Shot down by 17 Sqn. Hurricanes of Hogg and Kumiega and crashed near Tillingham, Essex, at 17.15 hrs.	Messerschmitt Bf 109 E-4 (5794 : Black 1)	100 %	Fw. Konrad Jäckel missing.
23.	Stab I./JG 51	CM	Shot down by 602 Sqn. Spitfires south of London at A.13.30 hrs.	Messerschmitt Bf 109 E-4 (5334 : White 2)	100 %	Oblt. Ernst Terry, *Adj.*, missing.
24.	3./JG 51	CM	Shot down by 602 Sqn. Spitfires south of London at A.13.30 hrs.	Messerschmitt Bf 109 E-1 (4816 : Yellow 13)	100 %	Fw. Karl Bubenhofer missing.
25.	4./JG 51	CM	Shot down by unidentified British fighters at 17.20 hrs., and crashed at Langton Green, Tunbridge Wells, Kent.	Messerschmitt Bf 109 E-4 (5370 : White 9)	100 %	Ltn. Heinrich Tornow killed.
26.	4./JG 51	CM	Shot down by 249 Sqn. Hurricane of Macie-jowski at 17.15 hrs., and crashed at Plummers Plain, Horsham, Sussex.	Messerschmitt Bf 109 E-1 (4828 : White 5)	100 %	Uffz. Alfred Lenz killed.
27.	5./JG 51	CM	Shot down by 602 Sqn. Spitfires south of London at A.13.30 hrs.	Messerschmitt Bf 109 E-4 (1397 : Black 2)	100 %	Fhr. Otto Brunk missing.
28.	6./JG 52	CM	Shot down by British fighters over the Channel; pilot baled out and rescued.	Messerschmitt Bf 109 E-7 (5933 : Yellow 2)	100 %	Pilot, unhurt, rescued by *Seenotflugkommando*.
29.	3./506	NCM	Crashed on Jan Mayen Island; cause not notified.	Heinkel He 115C(2762)	100 %	Crew safe.
30.	3./506	NCM	Details of accident not recorded.	Heinkel He 115C(2788)	100 %	Crew safe.
31.	1./196	CM	Missing in German grid Square 8259. Fate not established.	Arado Ar 196 (0063)	100 %	Ofw. Hans Eich and Fw. Helmut Stamp missing.

Wednesday 30th October

In contrast to the excitement of the 29th, the last two days of October saw comparatively little air activity, with only two engagements to the east of London and one to the south. On each occasion the capital was the target, but few aircraft broke through the cordon of fighters put up by Park, Brand and Leigh-Mallory. Even the night raiders seem to have been discouraged by the poor weather, and London enjoyed an unusually early "all clear".

R.A.F. FIGHTER COMMAND LOSSES—WEDNESDAY 30th OCTOBER 1940

1.	41 Sqn., Hornchurch	C	Shot down by Bf 109s at Postling, near Hythe; pilot remained in aircraft, slightly wounded.	16.15 hrs.	Plt. Off. G.G.F. Draper	Spitfire	P7282	Cat. 3 Destroyed
2.	41 Sqn., Hornchurch	C	Shot down by Bf 109s near Ashford and fell at Stanford, near Hythe; pilot killed.	16.18 hrs.	Sgt. L.A. Garvey	Spitfire	P7375	Cat. 3 Destroyed
3.	66 Sqn., Gravesend	C	Suffered landing accident at West Malling; pilot unhurt.	Not known	Sgt. W.J. Corbin	Spitfire	P7446	Cat. 1 Damaged
4.	222 Sqn., Hornchurch	C	Shot down by Bf 109s; pilot attempted a force landing at Ewhurst, but died soon after being released from the wreckage.	12.05 hrs.	Plt. Off. H.P.M. Edridge	Spitfire	K9939	Cat. 3 Burnt
5.	222 Sqn., Hornchurch	C	Shot down by Bf 109s near Crowhurst and pilot killed.	12.05 hrs.	Plt. Off. A.E. Davies	Spitfire	N3119	Cat. 3 Destroyed
6.	222 Sqn., Hornchurch	C	Damaged in combat with Bf 109s near Battle; pilot returned unhurt.	12.20 hrs.	Plt. Off. J.M.V. Carpenter	Spitfire	P3434	Cat. 2 Damaged
7.	249 Sqn., North Weald	C	Shot down by Bf 109s over the English Channel, and pilot assumed killed.	Not known	Fg. Off. W.H. Millington	Hurricane	—	Cat. 3 Lost
8.	253 Sqn., Kenley	C	Shot down by Bf 109s; force landed at Newbarn Farm, Northfleet, Kent; pilot unhurt.	A15.45 hrs.	Sgt. P.J. Moore	Hurricane	V7301	Cat. 2 Damaged
9.	602 Sqn., Westhampnett	C	Bounced by Bf 109s over Dungeness and force landed at Newchurch; pilot unhurt.	16.25 hrs.	Plt. Off. D.H. Gage	Spitfire	X4269	Cat. 3 Destroyed
10.	602 Sqn., Westhampnett	C	Bounced by Bf 109s over Dungeness and force landed on beach near Lydd; pilot wounded.	16.25 hrs.	Sgt. W.B. Smith	Spitfire	X4542	Cat. 3 Destroyed
11.	602 Sqn., Westhampnett	C	Bounced by Bf 109s over Dungeness and damaged; pilot returned unhurt.	16.30 hrs.	Plt. Off. A. Lyall	Spitfire	P9515	Cat. 1 Damaged

LUFTWAFFE LOSSES—WEDNESDAY 30th OCTOBER 1940

1.	3.(F)/10	CM	Damaged by Dover A.A. gun defences.	Dornier Do 17P	5 %	Fw. Ernst Baucks wounded.
2.	3.(H)/14	CM	Crashed at St. Pierre; cause not notified.	Henschel Hs 126 (3197)	100 %	Oblt.Obenhuber and Fw. Hartmann killed.
3.	4.(H)/23	NCM	Suffered landing accident at Schipol.	Henschel Hs 126 (3293)	45 %	Crew unhurt.
4.	2./KG 3	CM	Crashed at Herenthal having run out of fuel; crew baled out.	Dornier Do 17Z-3 (2617)	100 %	Crew unhurt.
5.	3./KG 4	CM	Suffered landing accident at Soesterberg.	Heinkel He 111H-4	50 %	Crew unhurt.
6.	Stab III./LG 1	CM	Crashed near Orléans having run out of fuel; crew baled out safely.	Junkers Ju 88A-5 (2199)	100 %	Crew unhurt.
7.	III./LG 1	CM	Shot down by 1 Sqn. Hurricanes of Lewis and Jicha and crashed at Stuntly, near Ely, at A.14.30 hrs.	Junkers Ju 88A-1 (5008 : L1+GS)	100 %	Four crew members made P.O.W.s.
8.	I./St.G 1	NCM	Collided with Dornier Do 215 near Brest.	Junkers Ju 87R-1(5541)	20 %	Crew unhurt.
9.	III./JG 2	—	Damaged by R.A.F. attack on Le Havre airfield.	Messerschmitt Bf 109 E-4 (4854)	10 %	No aircrew casualties.
10.	4./JG 3	CM	Force landed at Wissant after fighter combat.	Messerschmitt Bf 109 E-4 (1126)	30 %	Pilot unhurt.
11.	6./JG 3	CM	Shot down by 17 Sqn. Hurricane of Czernin near Maidstone at A.14.00 hrs., and crashed at Leylands, near Wrotham.	Messerschmitt Bf 109 E-4 (6360 : Yellow 9)	100 %	Uffz. Fahrian, wounded, made P.O.W.
12.	6./JG 3	CM	Shot down by 17 Sqn. Hurricane of Griffiths near Maidstone at A.16.05 hrs, and crashed at Court Lodge Farm, East Farleigh.	Messerschmitt Bf 109 E-4 (1474 : Yellow 1)	100 %	Gefr. Schuller made P.O.W.
13.	7./JG 26	CM	Shot down by 41 Sqn. Spitfire of Mackenzie at 11.40 hrs., and crashed at Brook Farm, Marden, Kent.	Messerschmitt Bf 109 E-4 (5242 : White 8)	100 %	Uffz. Kurt Töpfer killed.
14.	8./JG 26	CM	Shot down by 32 Sqn. Hurricane of Eckford over the Channel; pilot baled out.	Messerschmitt Bf 109 E-4 (5912)	100 %	Pilot, unwounded, rescued by *Seenotflugkommando.*
15.	Geschw.Erg.St./ JG 26	NCM	Suffered take-off accident at St. Omer.	Messerschmitt Bf 109 E-4 (1137)	20 %	Pilot unhurt.
16.	1./JG 77	CM	Crashed landed with battle damage at Marquise after fighter combat.	Messerschmitt Bf 109 E-1 (3250)	55 %	Pilot unhurt.
17.	2./JG 77	CM	Force landed with battle damage at Cap Gris Nez after fighter combat.	Messerschmitt Bf 109 E-4 (2053)	35 %	Pilot unhurt.

Thursday 31st October

As if to symbolise the "official" closing of the Battle of Britain, the last day of October was the quietest for four months. Although a small number of enemy aircraft dropped scattered bombs in East Anglia and in Scotland, not a single aeroplane of either air force was lost in combat.

R.A.F. FIGHTER COMMAND LOSSES—THURSDAY 31st OCTOBER 1940

1.	219 Sqn., Redhill	C	Crashed at night during landing at Redhill in bad weather; aircraft hit ground and exploded, killing both crew members.	02.30 hrs.	Plt. Off. K.W. Worsdell Sgt. E.C. Gardiner	Beaufighter	R2065	Cat. 3 Destroyed
2.	601 Sqn., Exeter	NC	Landing accident during training flight; pilot unhurt.	Not known	Sgt. Fearn	Hurricane	V6781	Cat. 1 Damaged

LUFTWAFFE LOSSES—THURSDAY 31st OCTOBER 1940

1.	4.(H)/21	NCM	Suffered landing accident at Theville.	Henschel Hs 126B (3436)	20 %	Crew unhurt.
2.	III./KG 76	CM	Ran out of fuel and crashed at Sedan; crew baled out.	Dornier Do 17Z (2886)	100 %	Crew unhurt.
3.	III./KG 76	CM	Ran out of fuel and crashed at Compiègne; crew baled out.	Dornier Do 17Z (2367)	100 %	Crew unhurt.
4.	I./KG 77	CM	Suffered take-off accident at Laon.	Junkers Ju 88A-1(2144)	25 %	Crew unhurt.

So ended the clearly defined period of four months during the which the survival of Britain had hung on the outcome of an air battle that had raged in her daylight skies. It had seen the frustration of Germany's aims, and the blunting of her finest weapon. Throughout October German airmen had penetrated the British defences and dropped bombs on British cities and airfields; but always, and by definition, their penetrations had been by numbers too small to threaten the overall military integrity of the country. The *Luftwaffe*'s fighter pilots, even after the bloody exhaustion of August and September, had proved that when released from the shackles of bomber escort and allowed to make the best use of their magnificent equipment, they were second to none in the world; but the fundamental lesson of October was that it did not *matter*. Isolated groups of Messerschmitts roaming at 28,000 feet could hold the attention of Fighter Command, could slip through gaps in the defences, could exhaust and infuriate the pilots, and could kill—a few people; but they could not destroy those defences, and they could not damage Britain's capacity for war. They had no strategic purpose; despite Göring's grandiloquent ravings, they were no more than nuisance raiders. In four months Royal Air Force Fighter Command had so won the balance of power in the skies over England that it had reduced the proud eagles of *Blitzkrieg* to so many thieves in the shadows.

But though England was now secure from invasion, and though Fighter Command's very existence was no longer in peril, there was still one weapon which Britain could not yet counter. For many weary months, Göring's bombers would roam over British towns and cities in the darkness, taking vengeance on those who had no way to protect themselves.

The first "Eagle" Squadron of the R.A.F., No. 71—though formed on 19th September 1940—was not declared operational before the end of the Battle of Britain, although several of its founder member pilots had flown and fought with other Fighter Command squadrons. Among the group of American volunteers who switched from R.A.F. line squadrons to the new unit was Plt. Off. Phillip H. Leckrone of Salem, Illinois, who had previously flown with No. 616 Squadron on Spitfires. He moved to No. 71 Squadron on 12th October to fly Hurricanes but, sad to record, became the unit's first fatal casualty when he was killed in a flying accident on 5th January 1941.

One of the German units widely engaged in the night bombing of British cities was *Kampfgeschwader 55 <Griefen-Geschwader>*—identified here by the codes "G1" on the fuselage of a Heinkel He 111H.

CHAPTER 10

THE NIGHT BLITZ

Just as the daylight operations of the Gotha crews of *Kagohl 3* had been abandoned in 1917 in favour of night raids when London's defences were brought to a reasonable standard of efficiency, so Göring committed his bombers to a night *blitz* in the winter of 1940-41. Just as in 1917-18, these raids could be justified militarily only in the attention and resources which they forced Britain to focus on the task of night defence. They also served to ensure that Germany herself would reap the whirlwind. As the distinction between military and civilian targets became an increasingly academic exercise, so the foundations were laid for the appalling "carpet bombing" which would devastate Germany's cities four years later.

Yet, as has been shown, the gradual easing by the *Luftwaffe* of the daylight pressures on Fighter Command, and its inability to strike hard, accurately and decisively at the major centres of war production, allowed the R.A.F. to consolidate and replenish its strength; the time was not far off when an outward-looking policy of carrying the War over German-occupied territory could realistically be considered.

The decrease in pilot and aircraft wastage in Fighter Command which commenced in September, and had continued throughout October—coupled with the long-awaited increase in fighter production, particularly in improved Hurricanes and Spitfires—allowed for the formation of twelve new squadrons by the beginning of November, and even for the despatch of a small number of fighter squadrons to the Middle East.[1]

More important still was the improvement in the night defences, and November saw the beginning of the gradual removal of the Blenheim night fighter from operational status and its replacement by the Beaufighter, of which almost fifty had been delivered to R.A.F. charge by the end of October. Yet despite continued efforts to overcome the tedious problems of the early airborne radar sets in the remaining Blenheims and the new Beaufighters, there had been precious little to show for all the hard work put in by the crews. Now, however, just as Dowding—who had had so much to do with the introduction of this radical equipment into Fighter Command—was replaced at the head of Britain's fighter defences (of which more anon), a slow but definite improvement in night 'kills' by radar-equipped fighters now became apparent. It must be emphasised that this improvement was in no way relative to the scale of enemy activity over Britain; rather, ordinary squadron crews were now succeeding in

---

[1] Lest any doubt be cast on the fact that Britain was at no time critically short of fighter aircraft during the Battle of Britain, it should be recorded that as early as June a trickle of Hurricane fighters had started to flow to the Mediterranean theatre; by the end of August a total of 110 Hurricanes had been flown, shipped or were awaiting shipment to Malta and Egypt. By the end of September an average of 30 Hurricanes were being shipped from Britain to Takoradi in West Africa *each week*. Furthermore, the hard-worked No. 73 Squadron (which had prematurely been warned to convert to the night fighting rôle on 23rd October) was to be one of the first Hurricane squadrons sent to the Middle East, leaving the United Kingdon on 13th November.

locating enemy aircraft using radar at night—and this was, of course, the sole purpose of those early radar sets. It was a long and intricate process to work out procedures by which these "sightings" could be integrated into an attack pattern. During 55 nights of November and December 1940, when these night fighters operated, out of 606 operational sorties flown, seventy-one radar contacts were obtained on enemy night raiders—but only four of them were destroyed.

On the other hand, six squadrons of Hurricanes and two of Defiants flew regular night patrols in collaboration with searchlight batteries and without the benefit of radar. Their 491 sorties (flown on 46 nights) resulted in the confirmed destruction of eleven German night bombers.

More dramatic perhaps were the achievements of the oft-maligned and under-estimated anti-aircraft artillery and balloon defences over Britain, which together destroyed thirty-nine enemy aircraft (with the expenditure of just over half a million shells in sixty-one nights). As had been the case during the earlier War, a large measure of their value had been in forcing bomber formations and streams to operate at high altitude—and this fact should be borne in mind when deploring the apparently wanton manner in which bombs fell upon so many buildings of no military significance.

What did this achievement of the defences amount to? These casualties, totalling 54 enemy aircraft destroyed—to which should be added a further twelve which crashed in Britain owing to self-inflicted misfortune (such as fuel shortage, bad navigation and collisions)—amounted to an overall loss rate of about one per cent of the forces employed, a level of attrition easily supported by any bomber force for an indefinite period.

The *Luftwaffe* persisted night after night in its offensive against British cities, with London and the industrial Midlands bearing the brunt of the attack. The intensity of the attack on London, which lasted without respite from the night of 7th/8th September until that of 13th/14th November, has never been equalled since—although of course Bomber Command's assault on Berlin later in the War, although more sporadic in nature, was more destructive by far.

By the end of October Göring had withdrawn all but four *Kampfgruppen* (about one hundred aircraft—mostly Junkers Ju 88s) from the daylight battle against Britain, and now deployed ten *Kampfgeschwader* (KG 1, 3, 26, 27, 30, 51, 54, 55, 76 and 77) and ten other *Kampfgruppen* in Holland, Belgium and France; this force, amounting to more than 1,150 bombers, now stood poised to carry out the systematic destruction of British cities. For the next sixty-one nights it would send an average force of 200 bombers each night to drop a total of 13,900 tons of bombs.

*　　*　　*　　*　　*

Night of 1st/2nd November. Targets Birmingham and London. As 80 aircraft of KG 55 approached the capital and drew the night fighter defences southwards, 58 other bombers, led by the Heinkel pathfinders of KGr. 100, made an almost unopposed raid on Birmingham. Total casualties, 123 killed and 382 injured.

Night of 4th/5th November. A switch to new tactics, temporarily dispensing with pathfinders, whereby a force of 231 aircraft crossed the South Coast on a wide front between Portland and Brighton, swamping the raid reporting organisation, and then formed two clearly defined streams which raided Liverpool and London, dropping 130 tons of incendiaries and 41 parachute mines. Total casualties, 401 killed and over 900 injured.

Fiat CR.42 fighters of the *85° Squadriglia, 18° Gruppo C.T.*, based at Maldegen, Belgium, during November 1940; and (bottom right), Italian groundcrew re-arming a Fiat G.50 bearing the black cat insignia of the *51° Stormo* painted on the fin. The aircraft of this famous unit's *351°, 352°* and *353° Squadriglie* were based at Ursel. The monoplane G.50s were seldom encountered by British fighters during their brief service on the Channel Front. (Photos: C. Milani-Gallieni, *Aeronautica Militare*)

The Fiat BR.20M, bomber equipment of the *Corpo Aereo Italiano*. (Photo: Giorgio Apostolo)

Night of 5th/6th November. Raid by 126 aircraft on London led by 70 aircraft of KG 77. Scattered raids by KG 55 over the Midlands. Two aircraft shot down and five others crashed in France, Belgium and Holland.

Night of 6th/7th November. Total of 317 aircraft over Britain. After an afternoon raid by 71 bombers on Southampton, the pathfinders of KGr. 100 led 40 aircraft to the difficult target of Birmingham, where smoke haze always presented problems of target identification. The ex-naval *Küstenfliegergruppe 606* made for Liverpool where eleven heavy delayed-action bombs and mines were dropped in the dock area. More than 70 Junkers Ju 88s of KG 51 raided the northern suburbs of London. Total number of dead exceeded 300.

Night of 8th/9th November. London raided by 90 aircraft of I. and III.*Gruppen*, KG 1, and I.*Gruppe*, KG 77. Twenty-two land mines dropped, causing more than 300 casualties. The gun barrage in the South-East fired 22,000 shells, destroying three raiders and damaging three others. R.A.F. Bomber Command carried out a 1,600-mile flight to Northern Italy to raid the Fiat works at Turin and the Pirelli factory at Milan. *Stukageschwader 77* carried out a daylight attack on a convoy in the Thames Estuary but suffered the loss of six aircraft, two to the guns of H.M. Destroyer *Winchester*.

Night of 10th/11th November. London and Liverpool again raided, London by 82 aircraft of KG 54, and Liverpool by 22 from *Küstenfliegergruppe 606*, which lost one aircraft.

*   *   *   *   *

It was at this point in the winter *blitz* that Germany's ally, Italy, re-appeared in English skies—in the climax of an extraordinary train of events. Displaying an outstanding talent for opportunist aggression, Mussolini had led Italy into the War on 10th/11th June at a moment when the Battle of France was drawing to a close and just in time to strike France in the South, with an eye to maximum territorial spoils at minimum cost. Simultaneously the *Duce*, believing Great Britain also to be doomed, struck towards the Suez Canal with the ground forces stationed in his North African empire.

Britain, for her part, saw in Italy a real threat to her ocean lifeline through the Mediterranean, a threat posed by the great numerical strength of the Italian air force—the *Regia Aeronautica*. It was largely against the aircraft factories in Northern Italy that R.A.F. Bomber Command had continued to strike throughout the Battle of Britain—raids, involving flights of considerable natural hazard, which infuriated the *Duce*. He had, of course, not considered the possibility of enemy aircraft violating his own air space.

As already stated, Mussolini had, as early as July, offered to assist in the daylight air assault on Britain, an offer which was at first politely refused by Hitler and Göring. Nevertheless, with the continuation of British night raids (which, let it be said, inflicted more than superficial damage, being almost completely unopposed) and, fearful of an erosion of morale in the industrial area of the North, the Italian dictator pressed his offer to operate an autonomous force against Britain. One suspects that it was with an air of tolerance, rather than eagerness, that Göring finally acceded to the request and, from mid-September on, a force of fighters and bombers assembled in Belgium under Kesselring's *Luftflotte 2* command.

This force, the *Corpo Aereo Italiano*, consisted of a total of 80 Fiat BR.20 medium bombers, 50 Fiat CR.42 biplane fighters and 48 Fiat G.50 monoplane fighters. The units involved were *13°* and *43° Stormi*, based at with their bombers at Melsbroek and Chievres; *18° Gruppo* with CR.42s; and *20° Gruppo* with G.50s, these fighters being based at Maldegen and Ursel respectively. A small detachment of CANT Z.1007Bis aircraft also accompanied this force.

All had not gone well with the Italians since they had assembled in Belgium, and about eight of the bombers had suffered forced landings *en route* for their new bases, due to bad weather and poor navigation. A number of light raids was

A Fiat BR.20 which was shot down in a fir planation during the Italian raid in the Harwich area of 11th November. (Photo: Giorgio Apostolo).

attempted against South-East England during October; but the Italian crews, unaccustomed to the vicissitudes of weather in these northern skies, seldom achieved any concentration, often turned tail at the appearance of British fighters, and caused a certain frustration among the *Luftwaffe* fighter pilots assigned to their escort. The Italian formations were ponderously slow and quite unsuited for joint operations with the speedy Messerschmitts.

It was on 11th November that the *Corpo Aereo Italiano* launched its heaviest (and, as it transpired, only) major daylight attack on Britain; up to this point the R.A.F. was only vaguely aware that an Italian force had been assembled against it.

At 13.30 hours on this day the Essex CH radar stations reported the approach of an apparently heavy raid making towards Harwich and about 30 Hurricanes were scrambled from Martlesham and North Weald in good time to intercept the raid before it crossed the British coast. The Italian formation consisted of about a dozen BR.20 bombers escorted by a similar number of CR.42s and possibly some G.50s. The Hurricanes attacked, and a rather one-sided combat followed during which about half a dozen of the bombers and three fighters were destroyed without loss. Flt. Lt. Peter Blatchford, leading No. 257 Squadron, ran out of ammunition, and successfully attacked one of the CR.42s by striking its upper wing with his propeller. The other two Squadrons involved were Nos. 17 and 46.[2]

Although of fairly minor significance in the Battle of Britain, with regard to the weight of attack launched, the

---

[2] To his chagrin, Sqn. Ldr. Stanford Tuck was not flying on 11th November, and so missed the opportunity to take part in this interception, which was later described by the pilots of No. 257 Squadron as a "turkey shoot".

defeat of the Italian formation clearly demonstrated that the then-current training and equipment of the *Regia Aeronautica* was wholly inadequate to meet a resurgent British metropolitan fighter defence, and a daylight raid of this size was never repeated. The outcome of this action also suggested the degree of confidence and ability now displayed by the pilots of Fighter Command—clearly masters of the daylight situation over the British Isles.

*   *   *   *   *

Night of 11th/12th November. Further German raids, mainly upon London, were carried out during the evening but, owing to poor weather, most had petered out by 22.00 hours. For the first time in two months the total number of civilian casualties fell below twenty.

Night of 13th/14th November. London raided by 77 Heinkel He 111s of KG 26 which dropped more than twenty land mines and a large quantity of incendiaries; Birmingham was raided by 63 aircraft of KG 55. Total casualties exceeded 300 dead.

Night of 14th/15th November. For the first time since the night of 7th/8th September, London was not attacked by German bombers at night. Instead, 437 aircraft flew to the city of Coventry—the industrial city in the Midlands. Although it caused a barrage of outraged public clamour against an indiscriminate assault against an ancient cathedral city—the 14th century cathedral itself was hit and destroyed—this raid was the first of several carried out on British provincial towns and cities; raids which were in fact minutely planned for the specific destruction of targets of considerable military importance.

The Coventry raid of 14th/15th November was preceded by a formation of about a dozen Heinkels of *Kampfgruppe 100*, which crossed the South Coast at Lyme Bay at 18.17 hours. Flying northwards along the radio beam of their specialised *X-Gerät* navigation aid[3], these highly trained pathfinder crews reached Coventry at 20.15 hours and unloaded more than a thousand incendiary bombs. The fires quickly took hold, and lit the sky for the main bomber forces which converged on the city in three streams from the Lincolnshire coast, Portland and Dungeness. The attack continued all

---

[3] The discovery by the British of the German *Knickebein* radio aid, and it subsequent jamming, led to a general loss of confidence in the device; and the new *X-Gerät* equipment was developed and brought into service with the pathfinder aircraft of KGr. 100. Basically it consisted of a narrow radio beam aimed directly at the intended target, along which the pathfinder flew. The beam was intersected by other radio signals which gave warning of the approach to the target area, and also warned the aircraft's observer when to set in motion a device which, after a further predetermined time interval, automatically released the target-marking bombs.

Coventry, November 1940. Despite the fact that the German bomber crews were briefed to attack specific industrial targets in the city, widespread destruction of commercial and residential property—as well as the cathedral—was suffered in the first major raid of 14th/15th November. Coventry came to symbolise the suffering of provincial cities during the winter *blitz*. (Photo: Radio Times Hulton Picture Library)

Surrealist effects of heat and explosive on a Birmingham factory damaged on the night of 22nd/23rd November. (Photo: Topix)

night; 394 tons of high explosive and 56 tons of incendiary bombs were dropped, as were 127 parachute mines.

The bomber units involved were KG 1, 3, 26, 27, 51, 55, LG 1 and Kü.Fl.Gr. 606, and a measure of the detailed nature of the planning that preceded the execution of the raid can be understood from some of the individual target assignments: The Alvis aero-engine factory to be attacked by II./KG 27, the Standard Motor Company by I./LG 1, the British Piston Ring Company by I./KG 51, the Daimler Works by II./KG 55, and the Hill Street Gas Works by Kü.Fl.Gr. 606. However, the nature of British city development down the centuries had been to integrate industrial sites with residential areas, and in the English industrial Midlands the huge slum areas occupied every yard of space between the factories engaged in essential war production. The bomb damage was colossal, with every railway line out of the city hit, twelve aircraft factories and nine other major plants damaged, and more than 500 retail shops in the extensive commercial area destroyed. 380 civilians were killed and 800 injured.

Night of 15th/16th November. Following a day on which several reconnaissance aircraft flew over Coventry to collect evidence of the night's devastating raid, Göring's bombers returned in force to the British capital with 247 aircraft, KG 76 forming the main force. The following night London was raided by 78 aircraft of KG 1.

17th and night of 17th/18th November. Following a sharp raid in the "old" tradition by the fighter-bombers of *Erprobungsgruppe 210* on Ipswich, the night bombers raided London and Southampton. Isolated daylight attacks by small numbers of Bf 109E-7s, which had dropped bombs on coastal towns in the South-East and made off out to sea before the defences had time to react, the raid on Ipswich was referred

to as a "hit-and-run" attack; it was in fact a full set-piece strike, with Bf 109s of the 3rd *Staffel* providing top cover. The hit-and-run attacks proper were only just getting into their stride, the tactics employed being little more than a modification of the old free chases, now performed by bomb-carrying Bf 109E-4/Bs and E-7s.

Night of 19th/20th November. On this night it was Birmingham's turn for a heavy attack, *Kampfgruppe 100* leading 369 bombers of KG 26, KG 54, KG 55 and Kü.Fl.Gr. 606. Five night raiders were shot down—falling near Nuneaton, East Wittering, Beckton and off the Norfolk and Dorset coasts; this last was destroyed by a radar-equipped Beaufighter.

Night of 22nd /23rd November. After two nights of raids, Birmingham was again hit, this time by KG 76, led by KGr. 100. Considerable damage was done in this important arms manufacturing town, more than 900 people being killed and nearly 2,000 injured.

Night of 23rd/24th November. A raid by about 60 aircraft on Southampton was followed by an attack by 62 aircraft of KG 53 on London.

Night of 24th/25th November. While 50 aircraft from KG 55 were over Bristol and Avonmouth, a relatively light raid was carried out by a single *Gruppe* of KG 26 on London. It was announced that in the past three weeks civilian casualties from air attacks amounted to 4,720 killed and 6,100 injured; a further 22,000 had been rendered homeless.

November 25th 1940 marked the end of an era for R.A.F. Fighter Command; for on that day Air Chief Marshal Sir Hugh Dowding, G.C.B., G.C.V.O., C.M.G., A.D.C., left his appointment, his place as Commander-in-Chief being taken by Air Chief Marshal William Sholto Douglas. Dowding, at the age of 58 and already retained on the Active List beyond the normal age of retirement, presented the Air Staff with something of a problem—being of greater seniority even than the Chief of the Air Staff, Air Chief Marshal Sir Charles Portal—and to a great many people his retirement to a relatively obscure appointment constituted nothing short of a scandal, and one that has been widely deprecated ever since. For here was a man who had served with the utmost distinction for ten years in high office; he had fought a brilliant campaign—no less fundamental to the survival of Britain than those of Nelson and Wellington—against a hitherto-victorious nation and had thereby won, not just a victory in a decisive campaign but survival for the whole western world. As befitted a man of his character and stature, Dowding left without rancour, conscious that his own previous high offices within the Air Staff did indeed pose problems of precedent. Nevertheless the three-year delay before the creation of his barony must forever reflect an extraordinary lack of gratitude—or, at best, an inertia that he himself never displayed during that fateful summer of 1940.

It was perhaps ironic that at this time Air Marshal Keith Park, unquestionably the most able of Dowding's Group Commanders during the Battle of Britain, was "moved sideways" to command a Training Group, his place in command of the all-important No. 11 Group being taken by Leigh-Mallory. Although now generally accepted as having been fundamentally flawed, Leigh-Mallory's defensive tactical philosophy had drawn some support from the Air Staff—not least from Sholto Douglas himself, who had been an instructor at the Imperial Defence College in the early 1930s at a time when Leigh-Mallory attended—*and at a time when Dowding was actively building the fighter defences that he had so brilliantly led to victory.*

The remaining nights of November brought only comparatively light raids by the *Luftwaffe*, London being attacked four times in five nights by forces averaging about 60 aircraft. Salisbury was raided by *Lehrgeschwader 1* on the 29th, and on the following night one hundred aircraft attacked Southampton, causing considerable damage in the centre of the port.

*   *   *   *   *

Night of 1st/2nd December. Southampton raided for the second night running, the total number of casualties amounting to 370. Considerable damage was caused in the commercial areas and residential suburbs; several cinemas, churches and two hospitals received direct hits. London raided by about 60 aircraft.

Night of 2nd/3rd December. Bristol raided by about one hundred aircraft which caused severe damage throughout the city; a children's hospital was hit, but the 80 young occupants were evacuated safely.

Night of 3rd/4th December. Birmingham, the night's main target, was raided by about 50 aircraft, led by *Kampfgruppe 100.*

Night of 6th/7th December. Bristol was again raided, this time by fifty aircraft of KG 27.

7th December. For the first time since 7th August twenty-four hours elapsed without the appearance of a single enemy aircraft over the British Isles.

Flight Lieutenant John Dundas, D.F.C. AND BAR, with seven Battle of Britain victories to his name, as well as two over Dunkirk and one on 28th November 1940. On that day, with other Spitfires of No. 609 (West Riding) Squadron, he engaged a group of Bf 109s off the Isle of Wight. He shot one down, but was immediately killed by another Messerschmitt. His last victim was Major Helmut Wick (below), the brilliant fighter pilot who rose from *Staffelkapitän* 3./JG 2 to *Geschwader Kommodore* of JG 2 in four months, and died with 56 victories and the Oakleaves to the Knight's Cross at the age of 25. (Photos: Aero Publishers Inc.)

Night of 8th/9th December. London suffered a heavy raid by 135 aircraft of KG 77 (carrying land mines) and LG 1. Among the many buildings destroyed were seven hospitals, four churches, two hotels, a block of flats (in which 45 deaths occurred), and numerous large stores and shops. Two German bombers were destroyed (both by *flak*), falling at Waltham Cross and West Thurrock.

Night of 11th/12th December. After two quiet nights, the *Luftwaffe* returned in strength, raiding Birmingham with about 200 aircraft (from KG 3, II./KG 26, KG 27 and KG 77), and Coventry with 80 aircraft. London was bombed by a force of approximately *Gruppe* strength. The raid on Birmingham

A Southampton tram burned out on 30th November. These vehicles tended to become welded to the tramlines during fire raids, thereby further hindering the emergency services. (Photo: Southern Newspapers Ltd.)

Dawn reveals the smoking rubble left by a night raid on Southampton during December 1940. (Photo: Radio Times Hulton Picture Library)

inflicted heavy casualties, and six churches, eleven schools, two cinemas, a crowded air raid shelter and a hospital were among the many buildings hit.

Night of 12th/13th December. Sheffield was raided by 150 aircraft and Birmingham by 77 bombers of KG 3. In the Sheffield raid, the damage caused in the highly concentrated attack was aggravated by the relatively large number of tramcars which became welded to their tracks and thus prevented fire appliances from reaching the main fires. According to the Chief Constable of Sheffield, the defences destroyed five German bombers, of which three can be identified in German records.

Night of 13th/14th December. Bristol and Avonmouth were bombed by 61 aircraft of KG 27.

Night of 15th/16th December. Sheffield was again raided by 150 aircraft, and again five bombers were destroyed (two by fighters).

Night of 20th/21st December. Fifty aircraft, led by Kü.Fl.Gr. 606, raided Liverpool and Merseyside where considerable

damage was suffered in the dock areas. One German bomber, a Focke-Wulf Fw 200 of KG 40, was destroyed by a night fighter (believed to be a radar-equipped Beaufighter of No. 25 Squadron) over Lincolnshire.

Night of 21st/22nd December. For the second consecutive night, Liverpool was bombed, this time by 150 aircraft led by Kü.Fl.Gr. 606, which lost five aircraft—three of them to night fighters, and all confirmed in German records. On this occasion the German bomber crews were briefed to attack targets well behind the dock area, resulting in very heavy loss of life in the homes of dock workers. Leicester was attacked by 31 aircraft of II./KG 2, which unit lost two bombers.

Night of 22nd/23rd December. 250 aircraft raided Manchester and Liverpool throughout the night; this was Manchester's heaviest raid to date and the entire fire services for miles around were called in to cope with the many large fires started. Five hospitals, twenty churches, three hotels, a theatre, a large block of stores and two public air raid shelters received direct hits. Railway lines throughout the Midlands were put temporarily out of operation with the destruction of eleven key bridges. A German bomber was shot down off

Temple Meads and (*right*) Cannon's Marsh railway stations, Bristol, damaged in raids on the night of 2nd/3rd December. (Photos: British Rail, Western Region).

One that got home... This Heinkel He 111H (B3+AN) of the 5th *Staffel, Kampfgeschwader 54 <Totenkopf>*, struck a balloon cable but, despite severe damage to the wing, the pilot succeeded in bringing his bomber home to a safe landing at St. André-de-L'Eure. Note the death's head insignia just visible above the port engine.

...and one that didn't. A Heinkel He 111, which attacked the bomber airfield at Watton in Norfolk during the winter *blitz*, was struck by the local parachute and cable defences, causing the bomber to crash at nearby Merton. A feature of this aircraft was that every vestige of insignia and national markings had been completely obscured by several coats of matt black paint.

Blackpool, and another over Sussex.

Night of 23rd/24th December. Manchester again attacked by one hundred aircraft of KG 1, led by *Kampfgruppe 100*. Less damage suffered than on the previous night.

Night of 29th/30th December. Representing the climax—though by no means the end—of the winter *blitz*, this night will go down in history as the most disastrous for the City of London since the Great Fire of 1666.

It has been conjectured that the choice of this Sunday evening was made for two principal reasons, namely the likely absence at the weekend of many City firewatchers, and the abnormally low tide reached by the Thames during the period of the attack, between 19.00 and 20.00 hours on 29th December. Carried out by about 130 aircraft operating at short range and heavily loaded almost exclusively with incendiary bombs, the *Luftwaffe* raid struck directly at the City area itself, causing six huge conflagrations and sixteen major fires. At one time St. Paul's Cathedral was ringed by fire and there were fears that huge embers blown by the strong wind would set fire to Wren's great edifice. As it was, eight of his other priceless churches suffered grievously.[4]

The whole area between St. Paul's and the historic Guildhall was impassable because of blazing buildings which burned for many hours. A conflagration which had attracted almost two hundred fire appliances around Fore Street was abandoned to burn itself out. The half-square-mile bordered by Moorgate, Aldersgate, Old Street and Cannon Street erupted into an inferno of huge flames approaching in size the fire storm of the Surrey Docks on 7th September. The priceless Guildhall was almost irrevocably damaged when showers of sparks from the blazing church of St. Lawrence Jewry nearby were blown on to its roof. At 20.30 hours this roof caught fire just above the Lord Mayor's screen; just as it was almost extinguished the water supply failed and the wind strengthened . . . within minutes the Hall was ablaze and the roof fell in. Only the walls were saved—but these provided the foundation for a magnificent restoration. As in the Great Fire of 1666, engineers were called in to blow up areas of buildings to provide fire breaks and to prevent the movement of conflagrations.

As remarked, this devastating fire raid on London was the climax of Göring's attack on Britain during 1940. Mercifully it progressed for only three of the nine hours scheduled. At 22.00 hours the weather started to deteriorate in Northern France, and succeeding bomber streams were recalled. History had come the full circle since 1917 when the Kaiser's air

---

[4]See Appendix J

The junction of Milton Street and Fore Street in the City of London, photographed on the morning of 31st December after the capital's worst fire since 1666. Had the weather not deteriorated over French airfields at about 22.00 hours, which led to many bombers being recalled, the damage would have been immeasurably worse. (Photo: Radio Times Hulton Picture Library)

commanders had struck at this very target—but with microscopic effect by comparison—and had to some extent been frustrated by weather.

*   *   *   *   *

Perhaps the most extraordinary feature of the night *blitz* was the manner in which the civilian population withstood the seemingly endless ordeal of bombing; it can only be described as superb. In this age of nuclear weapons, when the world has come to accept the possibility of such unspeakable horrors as the "doomsday" bomb if not with equanimity, then at least with a certain cynical resignation, the impact of prolonged conventional and terrorist bombing on an urban population has become something of a commonplace. Yet the *blitz* of 1940/41 was history's first example of this type of sustained assault on civilians; the psychological strain on the population was appalling, and its bearing was magnificent.

Assault by fire alone would have been bad enough; assault by high explosive is sudden, unexpected and terrorising, and if prolonged, desperately unnerving. The calm courage of men, women and children under nightly attack was beyond

praise. With precious few, and wholly understandable exceptions, there was no panic; each new attack strengthened a quiet, sullen resolve to survive the worst the *Luftwaffe* could do until such time as Britain was in a position to strike back. There was also, let it be said, a growing appetite for revenge.

Just as the Battle of Britain had destroyed forever the R.A.F.'s image of a socially élite yet happily dedicated band of individuals, so the *blitz* sparked the slow fuse of social change in Britain. There can be no doubt but that throughout the War there were those who used their commercial or social privileges to avoid personal risk and hardship; but not even a profiteer could avoid the consequences of a 500-kilo bomb or a shower of incendiaries. The bombs broke windows of the rich and the poor with a fine impartiality of malice. Five years of war were to lay far more solid foundations of social equality than all the doctrinaire ramblings of political factions in peacetime.

When an army is under fire in the field, given circumstances provoke specific and identifiable acts of courage and devotion to duty. The quiet heroism of thousands of civilians sharing a common ordeal is harder to identify. To describe, or indeed to uncover the countless examples of self-discipline and unselfishness that followed in the wake of Göring's bombers would occupy many volumes; to describe only a few would be invidious, but certain specific sections of the population ought to be mentioned in view of the contributions they made during the terrible winter of 1940-41.

The civilian population was in effect mobilised in the face of almost certain invasion; and later, as the night bombing campaign increased in intensity, that mobilisation was widened. There was, of course, the para-military Home Guard,

A group of London firemen take a tea-and-cigarette break, December 1940. Many of these men were auxiliaries, only partly trained when called upon to face some of the most catastrophic fires for centuries—and under direct enemy bombardment. (Photo: Topix)

The work of the bomb disposal teams probably provides the most awesome record of courage to come out of the *blitz*. Undermanned and constantly overworked, the Army, Navy and Air Force squads worked under appalling conditions and in constant peril from many types of anti-handling devices fitted to the German weapons. These pictures show (*above, left*) an unexploded 500-kilo (1,100-lb.) bomb being removed in Theatre Street, Norwich; (*above, right*) the heaviest type of bomb dropped during the *blitz*, a 1,000-kilo (2,200-lb) weapon, safely de-fuzed; (*left*), and an unexploded 2,000-lb. parachute mine which, an adaptation of the German magnetic sea mine, was potentially the most destructive of all "bombs" dropped.

deployed to operate locally in concert with fully established military units in the event of actual invasion. The civil police force—which never quite divested itself of its image of benevolent rectitude despite the onset of war—assumed a whole host of duties which ranged from population control under air raid conditions to the active search for and detention of enemy agents in Britain. They also provided and maintained the basis of air raid precautions (A.R.P.), working with and advising the veritable army of civilian air raid wardens and fire watchers both in the passive rôle of securing an effective black-out and in the very active ordeal of fight-fighting and directing the fire fighting and ambulance services.[5]

Surely the most cold-blooded courage was that displayed in the presence of unexploded and delayed-action bombs and mines—both by civilians, utterly untrained in their handling and motivated purely by unselfishness, and by the regular teams trained to render these weapons harmless. Details of

rewarded acts of courage by these men and teams are listed in Appendix J, yet countless others, enacted in the confusion and stress of battle, went unseen, unrewarded and unrecorded.[6]

This was equally true of the various volunteer sections of the Civil Defence organisation. People from all walks of life and every kind of social background, motivated in the most part by an unselfconscious determination to "do their bit" for the war effort, risked (and in too many cases, lost) their lives as wardens, drivers, first aid orderlies, auxiliary firemen, messengers and lookouts. The Heavy Rescue Squads saved many hundreds of civilians trapped in the ruins of their bombed homes, often under conditions of extreme danger to the rescuers; their self-sacrificing determination to help those in danger and distress while any hope remained was awe-inspiring.

Revival in the Air

Lest it might be thought that the respite bought so dearly by Fighter Command was spent solely in resting and retraining during the autumn of 1940, it is worthwhile to outline the substantial measures adopted to consolidate the air defences. Elsewhere it has been stated that Fighter Command underwent total reorganisation in order to take the offensive, once the *Luftwaffe*'s daylight campaign petered out. In fact, although it would be quite wrong to suggest that British fighters

[5] Contrary to the widely-held belief that large numbers of enemy agents were captured in 1940, only four were arrested during the period July-December 1940, and tried under the Defence Regulations, the Official Secrets Act and/or the newly-instituted Treachery Act of 1940. They were Jose Waldeberg, a German, and Karl Meier, a Dutch subject of German birth, both of whom were landed surreptitiously in Britain and who were found in possession of a portable radio transmitter; and Charles van den Kieboom, a Japanese-born Dutch subject, also equipped with a radio. These three agents were convicted of espionage and executed by hanging at Pentonville Prison on 9th December 1940. The fourth person, Dorothy Pamela O'Grady, described as a housewife, was sentenced to death on 22nd November following conviction under all three Acts, being found guilty of making *in the Isle of Wight*, a plan likely to be of assistance to military operations to the enemy, and of cutting a military telephone wire with intent to assist the enemy. There was an appeal and O'Grady did not suffer the death penalty.

[6] One of the more macabre incidents involved a civilian who, on returning home to his flat one night, found an unexploded 100-lb. bomb lodged in his ceiling. Aggravated by, but not in the least apprehensive of the likely incovenience posed by the bomb, he dislodged it, and carried it on his shoulder to a place where is later exploded harmlessly. He was charged and convicted under the Explosives Act, and fined £100. He appealed and the fine was reduced to £5!

4.7-inch anti-aircraft gun emplacement in Hyde Park, London; and (right) a victim of A.A. fire—an unknown Junkers Ju 88 night bomber brought down near Godstone, Surrey. (Photos: Topix)

achieved any real freedom of movement over Northern France during the Battle of Britain—save in the *ad hoc* pursuit of enemy fighters too short of fuel to fight back—they had carried out numerous premeditated patrols over the area ever since the fall of France whenever they could be spared from the vital defence of Southern England. During the period 1st July-31st October R.A.F. fighters flew a total of 1,321 sorties over France—the equivalent of about one squadron sweep every day. In terms of enemy aircraft destroyed their achievements were perhaps a little disappointing (about 30 shot down for the loss of 35 Hurricanes, Spitfires and Blenheims). Yet their presence or likely appearance forced on the *Luftwaffe* the necessity to withhold at least one *Jagdgruppe* in the Pas de Calais, and another in the Cherbourg area, for defence purposes. Nor must one forget the work of the Photographic Reconnaissance Unit which, throughout the Battle and the subsequent *Blitz*, sent daily (and often twice-daily) Spitfires on long, lonely and dangerous high-altitude sorties over Northern Europe to reconnoitre Hitler's territories. Not only did those very special pilots, some of whose religious beliefs forbade their bearing arms—but who did not flinch from

undertaking supremely hazardous flights in the unarmed Spitfires—bring back photographs of Bomber Command's targets before and after raids, but also kept watch on the progress of Hitler's preparations for the invasion of Britain.

It was in the nature and strength of Fighter Command's operations that the conduct of fighting across the Channel underwent radical changes. By the end of December, Fighter Command consisted of six Groups, between them deploying 71 squadrons with 1,467 fighters on strength:

Group No.	Group Headquarters	No. of Squadrons	No. of Aircraft
9	Barton Hall, Preston, Lancs	5	108
10	Rudloe Manor, Box, Wilts	13	249
11	Hillingdon House, Uxbridge, Middx.	26	507
12	Wattnall, Nottingham	15	261
13	Blakelaw Estate, Newcastle-on-Tyne	12	238
14	Drunmossie Hotel Inverness	5	104

Victors of the daylight skies: a formation of Hurricanes of No. 601 (County of London) Squadron, photographed late in 1940. When all the records and statistics had been sifted and examined long after the Battle, it was found that the pilots of Sydney Camm's Hurricane fighters had destroyed more enemy aircraft than all other British fighters and ground defences combined—by a considerable margin.

The majority of these aircraft had been delivered since mid-October and included a high proportion of the improved Hurricane IIs and Spitfire IIs, while six night fighter squadrons were now equipped and fast gaining experience with the Beaufighter. Furthermore, what had begun as a trickle of fighters manufactured in the Canada and the United States was now a steady flow.

The build up of squadrons in Fighter Command was also aided by the constant arrival of men from the British Commonwealth as well as a continuing in-flow of "Free Europeans" who, now fully trained, were assembled into squadrons—just as the first pioneers had formed Nos. 302, 303, 310 and 312 Squadrons before the end of the Battle. The gradual assumption of night defence duties by Beaufighters and Douglas Havocs[7] led to Hurricanes being released for night intruder operations over the French bases of Göring's bombers; small groups of fighters lurked near these airfields to destroy the night raiders on their return from England. These tactics were attended by considerable success—both physical and psychological—and were to continue until the end of the War, in varying forms.

By day Fighter Command embarked on a new spectrum of operations, ranging from the escort of daylight raids over France to low-level sweeps over enemy airfields and ports. Designed as much to achieve the destruction of ground targets as to lure German fighters into air combat, the sweeps themselves embraced numerous variations, ranging in size from several Wings of fighters, escorting one or two light bomber squadrons, down to a pair of free-lancing fighters. The fighter Wings came to be based at the airfields made famous in the Battle of Britain—Kenley, Biggin Hill, Hornchurch, North Weald and the rest—and they were led at the outset by men whose names were now famous, men like Douglas Bader, Bob Stanford Tuck and "Sailor" Malan. Yet, as if to drive home the lesson, taught and learned during the Battle of Britain, it was to be the tiny formations of roving fighters—known in Fighter Command as "Rhubarbs"—that achieved by far the highest number of victories over the *Luftwaffe* when Fighter Command went over to the offensive. The fighter pilot is an individualist and, as had been so often shown by the Emil pilots of 1940, were never so dangerous as adversaries as when they were free chasing in their *Staffeln*.

Bomber Command also continued to expand apace and by the end of 1940 was operating forty-five fully equipped squadrons of Whitleys, Wellingtons, Hampdens and Blenheims, while the first two squadrons (Nos. 7 and 207) had taken delivery of their quota of Short Stirling and Avro Manchester heavy bombers respectively—aircraft whose bomb loads eclipsed any carried by *Luftwaffe* aircraft.

These then were the principal areas of revival—or rather, perhaps, the areas in which the necessary preparations had been accomplished. Although it would be many months before Britain's new aggressive posture would offer any serious hindrance to Hitler's wider military ambitions, the foundations could now be laid—behind the sure shield of proven defences.

Assumption of the leadership of Fighter Command by Sholto Douglas must have been accompanied by a general feeling of profound relief that the air defence sy*stem* was demonstrably sound. The integration of all facets of defence was complete, tested to the limit and wholly justified. With occasional modifications to meet short-lived tactical circumstances[8], the system remained unchanged for eighteen years; fighters would improve, speeds would double, and radar cover would grow in area and accuracy, but the fundamental skeleton needed no improvement. This consolidated basis for defence, proved in battle, represented a firm and constant factor for the remainder of the War, a factor whose importance cannot be overstated. It stood as a fitting tribute to its architect.

In Germany the daylight defeat of the *Luftwaffe*—for there can be no other description—had serious results. The continued assault on British cities by night, which was maintained until May 1941, and which many German commentators insisted was "just another phase of the Battle of Britain" ceased after September 1940 to further any realistic military aim. (If, indeed, there *was* any aim by night, the *Luftwaffe* failed in its achievement just as surely as it had by day.)

The opportunity for invasion had been lost forever, although this was not admitted at the time; and Hitler applied his energies to preparations for his long-planned attack on Soviet Russia. Already his Italian ally was being checked and turned in Greece and North Africa; in time, German troops would have to be committed to these areas to complete the tasks bungled by Mussolini, and a proportion of the *Luftwaffe*'s striking force was switched from Western Europe to the Mediterranean and Balkan theatres in the early spring of 1941. Had the whole strength of the *Wehrmacht* and *Luftwaffe* been available to begin the march to Moscow six weeks before the eventual launching of *Barbarossa*, the results might have been incalculable.

It is probable that Hitler preferred not to think too deeply about the undefeated island to the West while he threw himself into the planning of his anti-Bolshevist crusade. It would be left to wither in isolation; the unrestricted activities of Doenitz's U-boats would throttle it, and a token *Luftwaffe* force would contain it. Even the night-raiding *Kampfgeschwader* were soon moved eastwards, and from May 1941 only two *Jagdgeschwader* faced the Royal Air Force across the narrow seas. When Russia was broken forever, and all Europe lay under the satraps of the Thousand Year Reich, from the Atlantic to the Urals—then surely Britain would despair, and sue for an end to the hopeless struggle.

But Russia would not break, and Britain would not starve; and four years later, in an empire reduced by the armies of two-score nations to a few acres of charred rubble, he poisoned his wife and his dog, and set a gun to his head.

---

[7] The Havoc was an American heavy fighter version of the Boston light bomber; its performance and armament was much inferior to that of the Beaufighter but, until production of the latter increased considerably, the Havoc was to be flown by a total of fifteen R.A.F. squadrons—with relatively little success.

---

[8] Such as the onset of the flying bomb and rockets attacks of 1944.

SURVIVAL

In concluding this history, it is legitimate to speculate on exactly what Britain avoided by denying Germany victory in the Battle of Britain.

Despite the uncertainty and vaccilation which surrounded plans for Operation *Seelöwe*, it is undeniable that those plans were far advanced in early September 1940, and that the timetable for invasion quoted in Chapter 8 was still the basis of German plans until its first postponement on 11th September. True, the relative merits of broad-front and narrow-front landings were vigorously argued by the Naval War Staff and the Army High Command. The Navy doubted its ability to prevent serious interference by the undefeated Royal Navy if operations took place on a wide front, involving the maintenance of several safe lanes across the Channel. The Army, on the other hand, feared that the British possessed forces adequate to contain, and possibly eliminate a small beachhead. In the event Admiral Otto Schneiwind (Chief of the Naval War Staff, and in these matters acting on behalf of Admiral Raeder) prevailed on Hitler, and the broad-front scheme was abandoned on 16th August. On that day Hitler issued two Directives, and specifically defined the landing area as the beaches between Brighton and Ramsgate. The date of *Seelöwe* was set for 15th September, and then amended to 21st September.

The commencement of the assembly of the invasion fleet in Channel ports was set for 1st September. It was argued, and has been argued since, that it would have required 3,300 barges, motor vessels and tugs to transport the quarter-million men deemed necessary to consolidate a beachhead, and that this would have deprived Germany of a large part of the inland waterway transport which played a vital rôle in the overall transport system of the Reich. Nevertheless, the concentration of these vessels *did* commence; numerous aerial photographs supply the proof. Had the events of late August and early September 1940 been different, there seems to be no convincing reason to doubt that the fleet would have put to sea.

The invasion would have involved the landing of 260,000 men in forty-one divisions, including six *Panzer*, three motorised and two airborne divisions. The central theme of the Battle of Britain was that in order to launch this huge force with a likelihood of success, it was essential for the *Luftwaffe* to achieve the destruction of the Royal Air Force as an effective weapon. As has been demonstrated throughout this narrative, the factors which prevented this conclusion sprang initially from the extraordinary weakness of German field Intelligence. The continued resistance of Fighter Command, and the defeat of the *Luftwaffe* by day, led to a new conduct of German operations which was basically non-productive.

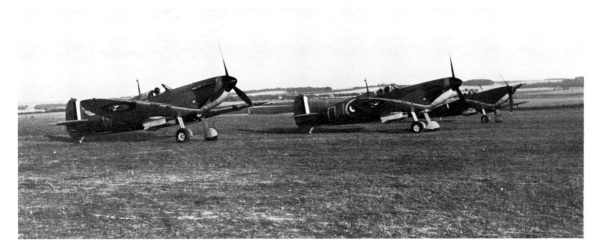

From 7th September, when pressure from the air was directed against domestic targets rather than against the fabric of the defence system, the over-strained fighter defences commenced their steady revival. The adoption of night raiding was an admission of defeat; the *Luftwaffe* could no longer endure the punishing losses attendant upon daylight operations, and was forced to adopt a type of operations from which no real damage to Britain's military strength—least of all to the fighter defences—could reasonably be expected to result.

It is not within the scope of this book to enter a lengthy discussion on the likelihood of success which might have attended an attempt by the *Wehrmacht* to launch *Seelöwe*, assuming that the direct pressure upon Fighter Command had been maintained to a point where such an invasion was militarily feasible. A few general observations, however, are perhaps in order.

When the British Army collected together the survivors of Dunkirk, it became apparent that it could field no more than six combat-ready divisions (about 120,000 men) with practically no artillery or armour. Yet by the middle of September, when *Seelöwe* was supposedly entering its crucial committal stage, the Army had staged a phenomenal recovery; no less

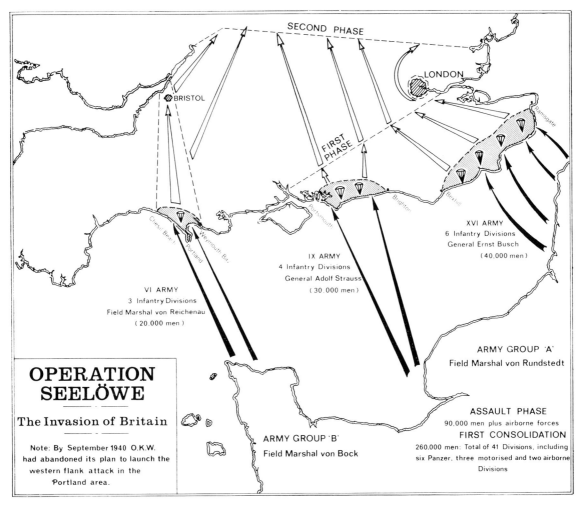

VI ARMY
3 Infantry Divisions
Field Marshal von Reichenau
(20,000 men)

IX ARMY
4 Infantry Divisions
General Adolf Strauss
(30,000 men)

XVI ARMY
6 Infantry Divisions
General Ernst Busch
(40,000 men)

ARMY GROUP 'A'
Field Marshal von Rundstedt

ARMY GROUP 'B'
Field Marshal von Bock

ASSAULT PHASE
90,000 men plus airborne forces
FIRST CONSOLIDATION
260,000 men: Total of 41 Divisions, including
six Panzer, three motorised and two airborne
Divisions

OPERATION SEELÖWE

The Invasion of Britain

Note: By September 1940 O.K.W. had abandoned its plan to launch the western flank attack in the Portland area.

Fallen Eagle. Young R.A.F. pilots examine a shot-down Junkers Ju 88A of I.*Gruppe*, *Kampfgeschwader 30* <*Adler-Geschwader*> (Eagle Wing) near the fighter station at Wittering in November 1940.

The pilots of No. 19 Squadron gather for an alfresco sortie briefing at their Fowlmere dispersal.

than sixteen combat-ready divisions (about 300,000 men) were available, of which three were armoured. The time bought so painfully by Fighter Command had not been wasted; well might the *Wehrmacht* commanders regard the prospect of a narrow-front landing with some alarm.

Assuming, again, that the *Wehrmach* had secured an established foothold on British soil, the fate of the occupied areas might have eclipsed even that of Poland. It should never be believed that during the assault phase of the invasion Hitler would have modified the conduct of his forces in any way, to accord with his proclaimed desire for an Anglo-Saxon *entente*. Had Germany occupied large areas of the country, the established Nazi policy of setting up a puppet collaborationist regime would no doubt have been put into effect; but puppet governments were the sop thrown to territories whose teeth had been drawn, and until all fighting ceased any part of England swallowed up by the Nazi empire would have felt the full weight of general and specific terror.

There has been a continuing tendency in recent years for sophisticates to ridicule the rag-tag of civilian and para-military organisations which awaited the invasion of 1940; and, indeed, the idea of an elderly bank clerk or farm labourer awaiting the finest mechanised army in the world armed only with a 1914 rifle or even a pike cannot help but be ridiculous. But had matters ever come to a confrontation, there would have been little cause for laughter. Although the picture of a population standing utterly united to face invasion is probably exaggerated, there can be little doubt but that a large majority had genuinely accepted and absorbed the attitude summed up by that most uncompromising and realistic of all pre-invasion slogans—"You can always take one with you". There would almost certainly have been prolonged, bitter and

bloody resistance by both officially sponsored and "freelance" groups. It should also be borne in mind that despite a very real shortage of arms, especially of automatic weapons, considerable preparations had been made for the concealment and sustaining of well-equipped resistance groups behind enemy lines; this underground network established *before* invasion would have been unique among Germany's conquests, and might have achieved unique results.

Regular armed forces engaged in active operations traditionally give short shrift to para-military groups attempting to hinder their activities; and apart from the predictably harsh response from the German Army, Britain would have had to suffer the attentions of the specialised apparatus of terror for which Nazi Germany will always be infamous. A very detailed programme had been prepared for the subjugation of the country by Reinhard Heydrich's Reich Central Security Office (R.S.H.A.), and an overlord had been chosen: *SS* Colonel Professor Franz Six, one of that clutch of perverted academics which the Nazis had a genius for harnessing to their cause. Under Six's direction the *SS*, and the even more sinister *SD*, would have moved into action immediately behind the advancing front line; the lessons of history have shown that England would not have been spared their attentions even during a fairly early stage of the fighting. They would have applied themselves enthusiastically to their traditional task: the removal of all leaders or potential leaders from the British scene, both political and intellectual; the cowing of the population at large; and the elimination of all active resistance by unsparing applications of the machine pistol, the flame thrower, the torture-chamber and the gallows.

Had widespread occupation been achieved, the R.S.H.A. planned to set up *Einsatzgruppen* ("Action Groups"—in

practice, mass murder squads) in London, Bristol, Birmingham, Liverpool, Manchester and Edinburgh. Prominent figures in civic and intellectual circles, especially those listed in Himmler's *Sonderfahndungsliste G.B.* , would have been rounded up and delivered into the horrifying embrace of the *Gestapo*. All organisations which might offer a nucleus for "non co-operation", however innocent in nature, would have been proscribed and purged; these included the Masonic movement, the Church, the public schools, the Boy Scouts, the trade unions and, naturally, all Jewish communities. There would have been massive deportation of men of military age to continental Europe.

Even if the invasion had failed, the price paid by the South-East would have been appalling. If the Royal Navy had successfully isolated the bridgehead and cut German supply lines across the Channel—the circumstances most feared by German professional military opinion—then the shrinking areas under German occupation would have provided a classically fertile ground for atrocity. Guerilla activity is invariably greatest behind and on the flanks of a failing front line; and the

Nazi machine of terror was invariably at its most rampant in the face of military set-backs. Encouraged by the turning tide of events, the official and unofficial resistance groups would have stepped up their attacks on communications and on isolated groups of invaders as the German forces, exhausted and short of supplies, fought their way back through the Home Counties. The *SS* formations, penned in a shrinking perimeter, would certainly have taken a terrible revenge on the population, in an orgy of mass executions. It requires no great effort of imagination to conjure up the picture; recorded history provides endless examples. Let no one doubt that Surrey would have had its Lidice.

Apart from this immediate ordeal, the long term effects of even a temporary occupation of part of the country would have been crippling. As it is, Britain's economic recovery from the Second World War was a prolonged and wavering process. If the cost of an actual clash of ground forces on British soil had been added to the monumental drain on every type of national resource, life in Britain in the next fifty years might have been very different.

*   *   *   *   *

It has frequently been averred that Great Britain "muddled through" all her early battles; too often in those first two years of the Second World War there rose the cry of beaten and exhausted men—"Too little, too late"—as Britain reeled from defeat to defeat, giving ground and ostensibly gaining time for ultimate recovery.

The Battle of Britain, perhaps alone among those early campaigns, was not a battle of improvisation and muddled logistics. It was a pitched battle fought on prepared lines in the classic pattern. Against the most powerful air force on earth was ranged a defence system which had been evolved against

this specific eventuality for twenty-three years. It was evolved, not under the aegis of a dictator's authority, or in the promise of spoils of war, but by dedicated men, members of an air force no more than tolerated by successive pacifist administrations, in an environment of almost universal lethargy.

In no less classic tradition, that battle was sharply defined in purpose for both sides; and one side, composed of just 3,080 men—the equivalent of a Brigade Group, or the complement of a single capital warship—achieved their purpose: the survival of the Free World.

APPENDIX A

ROYAL AIR FORCE FIGHTER COMMAND FLYING PERSONNEL
1st July—31st October 1940

The following list sets down the names of all flying personnel who were on the strength returns of home-based operational squadrons of R.A.F. Fighter Command between 01.00 hours on 1st July 1940 and 23.59 hours on 31st October 1940, and who carried out at least one operational sortie under Fighter Command control or instruction. The list is thus slightly longer than the official Roll as maintained by the Battle of Britain Pilots' Association owing to the earlier defined opening of the Battle adopted by this book. Those personnel, included in this list, who for one reason or another did not qualify for the award of the Battle of Britain Clasp to the 1939-45 Star, are annotated by "¶" to the left of their name.

Ranks
The ranks indicated are those of the personnel at the commencement of the Battle (if they were already in Fighter Command on 1st July) or at the time they arrived on their first operational squadron. Subsequent promotion and/or commissioning is included under "Operational and Service Summary". Most "Free European" pilots and aircrew acquired R.A.F. ranks equivalent to their seniority in their own national armed forces; exceptions to this were several French pilots. Some confusion resulted in Polish and Czech pilots being ranked "junior" to their assumed entitlement in the R.A.F., but this was quickly rectified.

Fleet Air Arm pilots retained their naval ranks when seconded to the R.A.F. (One of the anomalies of the entitlement to wear the Battle of Britain Clasp is the omission of Fleet Air Arm Observers who flew operational patrols in Fulmars during the Battle of Britain).

Most previously published lists of Battle participants have omitted Aircraftmen (L.A.C., A.C.1 and A.C.2). It was assumed that such airmen were automatically granted Acting Sergeant rank once they achieved operational status. This was not the case, and Wynn (see Bibliography) has identified eight airmen who were never granted Acting Sergeant rank before they were Killed in Action, flying on operations without flying badge and for three shillings per day (including one shilling flying pay).

Aircrew Status
In the column headed Aircrew Status only two categories—Pilot or Aircrew—are included. In the instances of Nos. 141 and 264 Squadrons, with two-man crews, the term "Aircrew" is qualified as meaning Gunner. However, in the various Blenheim squadrons, two- or three-man crews were flown either with or without a gunner or navigator. As re-mustering in different aircrew categories was fairly widespread, it has often proved difficult to differentiate between Observer, Wireless Operator/Air Gunner, etc. The introduction of radar in Blenheims and Beaufighters further complicated crew member identification, and there were certain instances in which *civilians* (ostensibly ranked as Aircraftmen) participating as radar operators on operational sorties. This may account in one or two instances for the absence of full service details being traced.

Squadrons
The squadrons on which the pilots and aircrew served are entered in the order of postings or attachment. Occasionally pilots were de-tached to serve with other squadrons, returning after a short period to their old unit. For reasons of space the original squadron is not listed twice.

No. 1 Squadron, R.C.A.F., was so designated throughout the Battle of Britain and is therefore abbreviated to 1(Canadian) Sqn. The Squadron was not re-designated No. 401 Squadron until early in 1941 and reference to this in the context of the Battle is incorrect.

Service Details
As explained elsewhere the date 1st July is convenient as an administrative datum, and thus enables aircrew postings to be defined with respect to this date. The use of any other datum presupposes that no movement of personnel was taking place at that time and has hitherto led to minor inaccuracies in squadron strength returns for, say, 10th July.

The word "joined" is used to denote arrival on a squadron, having been posted into Fighter Command for the first time. The word "posted" is used to indicate transfer from one fighter squadron to another. "Posted away" is used to denote movement away from an operational Fighter Command fighter squadron.

Victory Claims
Contrary to general belief, the Royal Air Force has never officially promulgated lists of personal scores of enemy aircraft destroyed. The victories claimed or unofficially listed in various records are, however, shown here. In previous editions of this book, the destruction of an enemy aircraft which was shared by more than one pilot, was shown as a "half victory"; this was clearly inaccurate, and in this list such victories are simply shown as "shared". (In 1940 there was no smaller fraction than a half share, even when the whole squadron attacked and destroyed a single aircraft!)

Owing to confusion by R.A.F. pilots regarding the spurious Heinkel He 112, reference to this in contemporary records has been altered to read "Bf 109"—as the Messerschmitt was the only single-engine German fighter encountered in the Battle. The letters "u.e.a." refer to Unidentified Enemy Aircraft.

Only victories achieved during the period 1st July—31st October 1940 are included.

Subsequent Service and Decorations
As far as has been possible from reference to the *London Gazette* all decorations awarded have been included (with the date of the L.G. accompanying them). This is because numerous awards, made long after the Battle, referred to service in 1940. However, no correlation between the decorations and the victory claims should necessarily be sought.

A Bar to a decoration is denoted by a rosette ❀.

Deceased Column
Entries for airmen who were killed during the Battle of Britain are accompanied by the words "Killed in Action", with the date of death. It has not always been possible to determine the circumstances of death since the Battle, although "Died since Battle" invariably refers to death from illness or natural causes. However, it does *not* follow that death was not the result of war.

Name	Rank	Aircrew Status	Squadrons	Operational and Service Summary	If Deceased	Nationality
ADAIR Hubert Hastings	Sgt.	Pilot	151-213	Joined 151 Sqn., 4-9-40; posted to 213 Sqn., 16-9-40	✟ Killed since Battle (6-11-40)	British
ADAMS Dennis Arthur ("Fanny")	Plt. Off.	Pilot	611-41	On 611 Sqn., 1-7-40; posted to 41 Sqn., 29-9-40; ✠ **1 Do 215, 21-9-40.**		British
ADAMS Eric Henry	Sgt.	Aircrew	236	On 236 Sqn., 1-7-40; survived War.		British
ADAMS Hugh Charles	Sgt.	Pilot	501	Joined 501 Sqn., 17-7-40; Commissioned as Plt. Off., 8-40; ✠ **1 Bf 109, 2-9-40.**	**Killed in Action** (6-9-40)	British
ADAMS Jack Sylvester	Flt. Lt.	Pilot	29	On 29 Sqn., 1-7-40; awarded D.F.C.✸. Retired from R.A.F. as Group Captain, 1958.		British
ADAMS Reginald Thomas	Sgt.	Aircrew	264	Defiant gunner. Joined 264 Sqn., 13-9-40.	✟ Killed since Battle (30-6-42)	British
¶ **ADAMS**	A.C.1	Aircrew	604	On 604 Sqn., 1-7-40; later promoted Sergeant.		British
ADDISON William Nathan	A.C.1	Aircrew	23	Joined 23 Sqn., 14-8-40; later promoted Sergeant.		British
AEBERHARDT Raymond Charles	Plt. Off.	Pilot	19	On 19 Sqn., 1-7-40.	✟ **Killed in Action** (31-8-40)	British
AGAZARIAN Noel le Chevalier	Plt. Off.	Pilot	609	Joined 609 Sqn., 8-7-40; ✠ **1 Bf 110, 11-8-40**; ✠ **1 Bf 110(shared), 25-8-40**; ✠ **1 He 111(shared), 25-9-40**; ✠ **1 Bf 109, 26-9-40**; ✠ **1 Bf 110, 27-9-40.**	✟ Killed since Battle (16-5-41)	British
AINDOW Charles Robert	A.C.1	Aircrew	23	Joined 23 Sqn., 25-8-40; later promoted Sergeant.		British
AINGE Eric Douglas	Sgt.	Aircrew	23	Joined 23 Sqn., 3-10-40.	✟ Died since Battle (30-11-79)	British
AINSWORTH Sidney	A.C.1	Aircrew	23	Joined 23 Sqn., 20-9-40; later promoted Sergeant.	✟ Died since Battle (20-10-79)	British
¶ **AIRES, E.H.**	Plt. Off.	Pilot	263-600	On 263 Sqn., 1-7-40. Posted to 600 Sqn., 3-7-40.		British
AITKEN Arthur	Sgt.	Aircrew	219	Joined 219 Sqn., early 9-40.		British
AITKEN Henry Aloysius	Sgt.	Pilot	54	Joined 54 Sqn., 6-10-40.		British
AITKEN, The Hon. John William Maxwell	Sqn. Ldr.	Pilot	601	Commanded 601 Sqn. at beginning of Battle. Posted away, 20-7-40; promoted Wing Commander, 7-40. Awarded D.S.O., D.F.C., Czech War Cross.		British
AKROYD Harold John	Plt. Off.	Pilot	152	On 152 Sqn., 1-7-40. ✠ **1 Ju 87, 15-8-40.**	✟ **Died of Wounds** (8-10-40)	British
ALBERTINI Anthony Victor	Sgt.	Pilot	600	Joined 600 Sqn., 14-7-40. Commissioned 1942.		British
ALDOUS Eric Stanley	Plt. Off.	Pilot	610-41	Joined 610 Sqn., 27-7-40. Posted to 41 Sqn., 12-9-40. ✠ **1 He 111, 30-8-40.**	✟ Killed since Battle (16-10-41)	British
ALDRIDGE Frederick Joseph	Plt. Off.	Pilot	610-41	Joined 610 Sqn., 3-9-40. Posted to 41 Sqn., 1-10-40. ✠ **1 Bf 109, 17-10-40**; ✠ **1 Bf 109, 30-10-40.**		British
ALDRIDGE Keith Russell	Plt. Off.	Pilot	32-501	On 32 Sqn., 1-7-40. Posted to 501 Sqn., 12-7-40; Wounded, 24-8-40. ✠ **1 Ju 88, 24-8-40.**		British
ALDWINCKLE Aylmer James Martinus	Plt. Off.	Pilot	601	Joined 601 Sqn., 11-9-40. Promoted Wing Commander, 1945.		British
ALEXANDER Edward Ariss	Sgt.	Pilot	236	On 236 Sqn., 1-7-40. Commissioned 11-40.	✟ Killed since Battle (25-2-41)	British
ALEXANDER John William Edward	Plt. Off.	Pilot	151	Joined 151 Sqn., 1-7-40. Severely wounded, 28-8-40. Serving Officer, 1965.		British
ALLARD Geoffrey ("Sammy")	Sgt.	Pilot	85	On 85 Sqn., 1-7-40. Commissioned Plt. Off., 8-40; Flt. Lt. 9-40. Awarded D.F.C., D.F.M.✸. ✠ **1 Bf 110 (shared), 30-7-40**; ✠ **1 Do 17 (shared), 6-8-40**; ✠ **1 Bf 109, 24-8-40**; ✠ **1 Do 215, 26-8-40**; ✠ **2 Bf 109, 28-8-40**; ✠ **2 He 111, 30-8-40**; ✠ **1 Bf 109, 31-8-40**; ✠ **1 Bf 109, 1-9-40**; ✠ **1 Do 17, 1-9-40.**	✟ Killed since Battle (13-3-41)	British
ALLCOCK Peter Owen Denys	Plt. Off.	Pilot	229	On 229 Sqn., 1-7-40. Wounded, 23-9-40.	✟ Killed since Battle (17-12-41)	British
ALLEN Hubert Raymond ("Dizzy")	Plt. Off.	Pilot	66	On 66 Sqn., 1-7-40. Awarded D.F.C. Serving Officer, 1965. ✠ **1 Do 17 (shared), 30-8-40**; ✠ **1 He 111, 9-9-40**; ✠ **1 He 111, 15-9-40**; ✠ **1 Bf 109, 18-9-40.**	✟ Died since Battle (31-5-87)	British
ALLEN James Henry Leslie	Fg. Off.	Pilot	151	On 151 Sqn., 1-7-40.	✟ **Killed in Action** (12-7-40)	New Zealander
ALLEN John Laurence	Plt. Off.	Pilot	54	On 54 Sqn., 1-7-40. Awarded D.F.C. ✠ **1 He 59 (shared), 9-7-40.**	✟ **Killed in Action** (24-7-40)	British
ALLEN John Watson	Sgt.	Pilot	266	Joined 266 Sqn., 7-10-40.		British
ALLEN Kenneth Mervyn	Sgt.	Pilot	257-43-253	Joined 257 Sqn., 21-9-40. Posted to 43 Sqn., 11-9-40. Posted to 253 Sqn., 28-9-40.	✟ Died since Battle (1984)	British
ALLEN Leslie Henry	Sgt.	Aircrew	141	Defiant gunner. Joined 141 Sqn., 13-9-40.		British
¶ **ALLEN**	Sgt.	Aircraft	29	On 29 Sqn., 1-7-40; posted away 9-7-40.		British
ALLGOOD Harold Henry	Sgt.	Pilot	85-253	Joined 85 Sqn., 7-40. Posted to 253 Sqn., 28-9-40. ✠ **1 Bf 109, 11-8-40.**	**Killed in Action** (10-10-40)	British
ALLISON Jack Whitwell	Sgt.	Pilot	41-611-92	On 41 Sqn., 1-7-40. Posted to 611 Sqn., end of 9-40. Posted to 92 Sqn., 27-10-40. ✠ **1 Ju 88 (shared), 8-7-40.**	✟ Killed since Battle (15-10-41)	British
ALLSOP Harold Gordon Leach	Sqn. Ldr.	Pilot	66	Flew at least one operational sortie. Retired as Wing Commander, 1956.		British
ALLTON Leslie Charles	Sgt.	Pilot	266-92	Joined 266 Sqn., 16-9-40. Posted to 92 Sqn., 30-9-40.	**Killed in Action** (19-10-40)	British
¶ **ALLSOP, E.R.**	Sgt.	Pilot	238	On 238 Sqn., 1-7-40. Posted away, 17-7-40.		British
AMBROSE Charles Francis	Plt. Off.	Pilot	46	On 46 Sqn., 1-7-40. Awarded D.F.C., A.F.C. ✠ **1 Bf 109, 2-9-40**; ✠ **1 Bf 109, 29-10-40.** Appointed C.B.E., 6-68. Retired, 1-72, as Group Captain.	✟ Died since Battle (1986)	British
AMBROSE Richard	Plt. Off.	Pilot	25-151	Joined 25 Sqn., 18-8-40. Posted to 151 Sqn., 26-8-40.	✟ **Killed in Accident** (4-9-40)	British
AMBRUS Jan	Sqn. Ldr.	Pilot	312	Joined 312 (Czech) Sqn., 9-9-40, to command.		Czech
ANDERSON Donald John	Plt. Off.	Pilot	29	Joined 29 Sqn., 7-7-40. Released from Service, 6-46.		British
ANDERSON James Alexander ("Andy")	Sgt.	Pilot	253	On 253 Sqn., 1-7-40. Severely wounded, 14-9-40.	✟ Died since Battle (28-5-78)	British
ANDERSON John Denis	A.C.2	Aircrew	604	Joined 604 Sqn., c.25-7-40; promoted Sergeant (1941). Commissioned, 1955, and retired, 1-73, as Squadron Leader.		British
ANDERSON Michael Frederick	Sqn. Ldr.	Pilot	604	In command of 604 Sqn., 1-7-40. Awarded D.F.C. (3-41). Retired, 10-45, as Wing Commander. Flew first squadron operational patrol in Beaufighter, 30-10-40.		British
¶ **ANDERTON**	Sgt.	Aircrew	219	On 219 Sqn., 1-7-40. Posted away, 4-7-40.		British
ANDREA Christopher John Drake	Plt. Off.	Pilot	64	Joined 64 Sqn., c.23-7-40.	✟ **Killed in Action** (15-8-40)	British
ANDREW Stanley	Sgt.	Pilot	46	On 46 Sqn., 1-7-40. ✠ **1 Do 17, 8-9-40.**	✟ **Killed in Action** (11-9-40)	British
ANDREWS Maurice Raymond	Sgt.	Aircrew	264	Defiant gunner. Joined 264 Sqn., 8-9-40.	✟ Died since Battle (24-3-71)	New Zealander
ANDREWS Sydney Ernest	Plt. Off.	Pilot	32-257	Joined 32 Sqn., early 9-40. Posted to 257 Sqn., 22-9-40 (Shared 1 BR.20, 11-11-40). (Previously awarded D.F.M.)	✟ Killed since Battle (9-8-42)	British
ANDRUSZKOW Tadeusz	Sgt.	Pilot	303	Joined 303 (Polish) Sqn., 21-8-40. ✠ **1 Do 17 (shared), 15-9-40**; ✠ **1 He 111 26-9-40.**	✟ **Killed in Action** (27-9-40)	Polish
ANGUS James	A.C.1	Aircrew	23	Joined 23 Sqn., c.3-8-40; later promoted Sergeant.	✟ Died since Battle (14-10-84)	British
ANGUS Robert Alexander	Sgt.	Pilot	611	Joined 611 Sqn., 29-9-40.	✟ Killed since Battle (20-2-41)	British

Name	Rank	Role	Sqn.	Notes	Fate	Nationality
APPLEBY Michael John	Plt. Off.	Pilot	609	On 609 Sqn., 1-7-40. ✠ 1 Bf 110, 8-8-40; ✠ 1 Do 17, 15-9-40; ✠ 1 Bf 109, 30-9-40.		
APPLEFORD Alexander Nelson Robin Langley	Plt. Off.	Pilot	66	On 66 Sqn., 1-7-40. Slightly wounded, 4-9-40.		
ARBER Ivor Kenneth	Sgt.	Pilot	603	On 603 Sqn., 1-7-40. ✠ 1 He 111, 3-7-40; ✠ 1 He 111 (shared), 12-7-40. Commissioned later (8-43), and awarded the A.F.C. (1-45).	✞ Died since Battle (1-9-52)	British
ARBON Paul Wade	Plt. Off.	Pilot	85	Joined 85 Sqn., 26-9-40. Awarded D.F.C. (14-4-44).	✞ Died since Battle (21-11-68)	British
ARBUTHNOT John	Sgt.	Pilot	1-229	On 1 Sqn., 1-7-40. Posted to 229 Sqn. later.	✞ Killed since Battle (4-2-41)	British
ARCHER Harold Thorpe	Sgt.	Aircrew	23	Joined 23 Sqn., 1-10-40.	✞ Killed since Battle (30-6-41)	British
ARCHER Samuel	Sgt.	Aircrew	236	Joined 236 Sqn., 19-7-40.	✞ Died since Battle (1980)	British
ARIES Ellis Walter	Plt. Off.	Pilot	602	Joined 602 Sqn., 5-7-40. ✠ 1 Do 17, 26-8-40; ✠ 1 Do 17, 7-9-40. Awarded A.F.C. (1-45).	✞ Died since Battle (1976)	British
ARMITAGE Dennis Lockhart	Flt. Lt.	Pilot	266	On 266 Sqn., 1-7-40. ✠ 1 Ju 88, 12-8-40. Awarded D.F.C., 18-7-41.		British
ARMITAGE Joseph Fox	Sgt.	Pilot	242	On 242 Sqn., 1-7-40. Posted away, 8-40.	✞ Killed since Battle (17-6-41)	British
ARMSTRONG William	Plt. Off.	Pilot	54-74	On 54 Sqn., 1-7-40. Posted to 74 Sqn., 28-10-40.	✞ Died since Battle (18-2-43)	British
ARNFIELD Stanley John	Sgt.	Pilot	610	On 610 Sqn., 1-7-40. ✠ 2 Bf 109s, 18-8-40. Slightly injured, 24-8-40. Commissioned, 1941. Awarded D.F.C. (30-6-44). Retired as Squadron Leader, 1951.	✞ Died since Battle (24-9-54)	British
ARTHUR Charles Ian Rose ("Duke")	Plt. Off.	Pilot	141	On 141 Sqn., 1-7-40. Awarded D.F.C. ✸ (9-6-44 and 29-12-44).		Canadian
ARTHUR Charles John	Plt. Off.	Pilot	248	On 248 Sqn., 1-7-40.	✞ **Killed in Action** (27-8-40)	British
ASH Robert Clifford Vacy	Flt. Lt.	Aircrew	264	Defiant gunner. On 264 Sqn., 1-7-40.	✞ **Killed in Action** (28-8-40)	British
ASHCROFT Alfred Edward	Sgt.	Aircrew	141	Defiant gunner. Joined 141 Sqn., 7-40. Commissioned, 11-41. Awarded D.F.C. (22-2-44).	✞ Killed since Battle (6-10-44)	British
ASHFIELD Glynn ("Jumbo")	Fg. Off.	Pilot	F.I.U.	On F.I.U., 1-7-40. Promoted to Flt. Lt. (Acting), 8-9-40; (War Subst.), 27-9-41. Awarded D.F.C. (4-12-42), A.F.C. (17-3-41). ✠ 1 Do 17 (shared), 22/23-7-40.	✞ Died since Battle (12-12-42)	British
ASHTON Dennis Garth	Plt. Off.	Pilot	266	On 266 Sqn., 1-7-40.	✞ **Killed in Action** (12-8-40)	British
ASHTON Dennis Kenneth	Sgt.	Pilot	32	Joined 32 Sqn., 12-7-40.	✞ Killed in Action (26-11-40)	British
ASHWORTH Jack	Sgt.	Aircrew	29	Joined 29 Sqn., early 8-40.		British
ASLETT Arthur Thomas Rayner	Sgt.	Aircrew	235	Joined 235 Sqn., 23-9-40. Severely wounded, 23-11-40. Commissioned (1943). Survived the War.		British
ASLIN Donald James	Sgt.	Pilot	32-257	Joined 32 Sqn., 4-8-40. Posted to 257 Sqn., 22-9-40. Wounded, 23-9-40. Commissioned, 7-41.	✞ Died since Battle (3-7-88)	British
ASSHETON William Radclyffe	Plt. Off.	Pilot	222	On 222 Sqn., 1-7-40. Suffered burns in action, 20-9-40. Retired from R.A.F. as Squadron Leader, 22-11-57.		British
ATKINS Frederick Peter John	Sgt.	Aircrew	141	Defiant gunner. On 141 Sqn., 1-7-41.	✞ **Killed in Action** (19-7-40)	British
ATKINSON Allan Arthur	Plt. Off.	Aircrew	23	On 23 Sqn., 1-7-40.	✞ **Killed in Action** (30-10-40)	British
¶ **ATKINSON, C.F.**	Fg. Off.	Pilot	151	On 151 Sqn., 1-7-40. Posted away, 8-7-40. Service Officer, R.A.F., 1965.		British
ATKINSON George	Sgt.	Pilot	151	On 151 Sqn., 1-7-40. Awarded D.F.M. (7-3-41). Commissioned, 11-41.	✞ Killed since Battle (1-3-45)	British
ATKINSON Gordon Barry	Plt. Off.	Pilot	248	On 248 Sqn., 1-7-40. Awarded D.F.C. (14-12-43); appointed M.B.E. (1-1-63). Retired from R.A.F. as Wing Commander, 18-3-76.		British
ATKINSON Harold Derrick	Plt. Off.	Pilot	213	On 213 Sqn., 1-7-40. ✠ 2 Bf 110s, 12-8-40; ✠ 1 Bf 109, 13-8-40; ✠ 1 He 111, 14-8-40; ✠ 1 Bf 109, 16-8-40; ✠ 1 Bf 109, 18-8-40. Awarded D.F.C., 25-6-40.	✞ **Killed in Action** (25-8-40)	British
ATKINSON Matthew Richard	Flt. Lt.	Pilot	43	Joined 43 Sqn., 20-9-40	✞ Killed since Battle (26-6-42)	British
ATKINSON Ronald	Plt. Off.	Pilot	242-600-111-213	On 242 Sqn., 1-7-40. Posted to 600 Sqn., 10-8-40. Posted to 111 Sqn., 16-8-40. Posted to 213 Sqn., 19-9-40. ✠ 1 Bf 109, 30-9-40.	✞ **Killed in Action** (17-10-40)	British
AUSTIN	Plt. Off.	Pilot	151	No details traced of this pilot.		British
AUSTIN Albert Lawrence	L.A.C.	Aircrew	604	On 604 Sqn., 1-7-40. Blenheim radar operator.	✞ **Killed in Action** (26-8-40)	British
AUSTIN Anthony Thomas	A.C.1	Aircrew	29	On 29 Sqn., 1-7-40. Promoted Sergeant, 7-40. Commissioned, 1942. Survived the War.		British
AUSTIN Frederick	Fg. Off.	Pilot	46	Joined 46 Sqn., 16-8-40.	✞ Killed since Battle (17-3-41)	British
AUSTIN Sydney	Sgt.	Aircrew	219	Joined 219 Sqn., 8-8-40. Awarded D.F.M. (30-5-41). Commissioned, 7-41.	✞ Killed since Battle (30-10-41)	British
AYERS David Hart	Sgt.	Pilot	600-74	On 600 Sqn., 1-7-40. Posted to 74 Sqn., 8-40.	✞ **Killed in Action** (23-9-40)	British
AYLING Charles Albert Henry	Sgt.	Pilot	43-66-421 Flt.	On 43 Sqn., 1-7-40. Posted to 66 Sqn., 10-9-40. Posted to 421 Flt., 8-10-40.	✞ **Killed in Action** (11-10-40)	British
¶ **AYRE, H.W.**	Sgt.	Pilot	266	Joined 266 Sqn., c.8.7.40		British
BABBAGE Cyril Frederick	Sgt.	Pilot	602	On 602 Sqn., 1-7-40. Awarded D.F.M., 25-10-40. ✠ 1 Ju 87, 18-8-40; ✠ 1 Do 17 and 1 Bf 110, 25-8-40; ✠ 1 Bf 110, 11-9-40; ✠ 1 He 111, 26-9-40; ✠ 1 Ju 88, 27-9-40.		British
BACHMANN Jack Henry	Plt. Off.	Pilot	145	Joined 145 Sqn., 20-8-40.	✞ Killed since Battle (9-4-43)	British
BACON Charles Harvey	Plt. Off.	Pilot	610	Joined 610 Sqn., 16-9-40.	✞ **Killed in Accident** (30-9-40)	British
BADDELEY Douglas Hiram	Sgt.	Aircrew	25	Joined 25 Sqn., c.4-10-40.	✞ Killed since Battle (26-6-42)	British
BADER Douglas Robert Steuart ("Douggie")	Sqn. Ldr.	Pilot	242	In command of 242 Sqn., 1-7-40. Later promoted Group Captain. ✠ 1 Do 17, 11-7-40; ✠ 1 Do 17, 21-8-40; ✠ 1 Bf 110 (shared), 30-8-40; ✠ 1 Do 17 (shared), 15-9-40; ✠ 1 Bf 109, 27-9-40. Appointed K.B.E.; awarded D.S.O.✸, D.F.C.✸. Also appointed to *Légion d'Honneur*, and awarded *Croix de Guerre* (French).	✞ Died since Battle (5-9-82)	British
BADGER Ivor James ("Pete")	F/Sgt.	Pilot	87	On 87 Sqn., 1-7-40. Later commissioned (6-41). Awarded D.F.C. (18-9-42). ✠ 1 Bf 109, 11-8-40. Retired from R.A.F., 12-8-61, retaining rank of Squadron Leader.		British
BADGER John Vincent Clarence ("Tubby")	Sqn. Ldr.	Pilot	43	Supernumerary on No. 43 Sqn., 1-7-40. Assumed command, 9-7-40. Awarded D.F.C. (6-9-40). ✠ 1 Ju 88 (shared) 14-8-40; ✠ 1 Ju 88, 15-8-40; ✠ 3 Ju 87, 16-8-40; ✠ 1 He 111 (shared), 26-8-40. Grievously wounded on 30-8-40, and died of these wounds ten months later.	✞ **Died of Wounds** (30-6-41)	British
BAILEY Colin Cyril	A.C.1	Aircrew	23	Joined 23 Sqn., 23-7-40. Promoted Sergeant. Commissioned 7-41. Awarded D.F.C. 30-11-43. Survived the War.		British
BAILEY Charles Gordon	Plt. Off.	Pilot	152	No details traced of this pilot.		British
BAILEY Graham George	Plt. Off.	Pilot	79-56	Joined 79 Sqn., 13-9-40. Posted to 56 Sqn., 15-10-40.	✞ Killed since Battle (9-11-41)	British
BAILEY George John ("Bill")	Sgt.	Pilot	234-603	On 234 Sqn., 1-7-40. Posted to 603 Sqn., 8-9-40. ✠ 1 Ju 88 (shared), 8-7-40; ✠ 1 Ju 88 (shared), 27-7-40; ✠ 1 Bf 109, 15-9-40; ✠ 1 Bf 109, 2-10-40.		British
BAILEY Henry Noel Dawson	Plt. Off.	Pilot	54	Joined 54 Sqn., 28-9-40.		British
BAILEY John Cyril Lindsay Dyson	Plt. Off.	Pilot	46	Joined 46 Sqn., 8-40.	✞ **Killed in Action** (2-9-40)	British

402

Name	Rank	Role	Sqn.	Details	Fate	Nationality
BAILEY James Richard Abe ("Jim")	Fg. Off.	Pilot	264-85	On 264 Sqn., 1-7-40. Posted to 85 Sqn., c.3-9-40. Awarded D.F.C. (8-9-44).		British
BAILLON Paul Abbott	Plt. Off.	Pilot	609	Joined 609 Sqn., c.11-10-40.	✟ Killed since Battle (28-11-40)	British
BAIN George Stobie Preston	Plt. Off.	Pilot	111	Joined 111 Sqn., c.5-10-40. Severely wounded, 1941, and withdrawn from flying duties. Survived the War.		British
BAINES Cyril Edgar Joseph	Sqn. Ldr.	Pilot	238	In command of 238 Sqn., 1-7-40. Posted away, 15-7-40. Appointed C.B.E. (1-6-53). Retired from R.A.F. as Group Captain, 1-3-58.		British
BAIRD George Maurice	Plt. Off.	Pilot	248	On 248 Sqn., 1-7-40. (Note. Doubt exists as to whether this pilot flew a qualifying operational sortie under orders from Fighter Command.)	✟ **Killed in Action** (20-10-40)	New Zealander
BAKER Aubrey Cyril	Sgt.	Pilot	610-41	Joined 610 Sqn., 27-7-40. Posted to 41 Sqn., 29-9-40. ✠ **1 Bf 109, 24-8-40**; ✠ **1 Bf 109, 29-8-40.** Commissioned, 4-41. Awarded D.F.C. (4-12-42).	✟ Died since Battle (1978)	British
BAKER Barrie	Sgt.	Aircrew	264	Defiant gunner. Joined 264 Sqn., c.24-7-40.	✟ **Killed in Action** (26-8-40)	British
BAKER Clive Conrad Mahoney	Plt. Off.	Pilot	23	On 23 Sqn., 1-7-40. Appointed O.B.E. Retired from the R.A.F. as Air Commodore, 7-71.		British
BAKER Eric Debnam		Pilot	145	On 145 Sqn., 1-7-40.	✟ **Killed in Action** (8-8-40)	British
BAKER Henry Collingham ("Butch")	Fg. Off.	Pilot	19-41- 421 Flt.	On 19 Sqn., 1-7-40. Posted to 41 Sqn., late 8-40. Posted to 421 Flt., 10-40. ✠ **1 He 111 (shared), 15-9-40;** ✠ **1 Bf 109, 30-9-40.**		British
BAKER Louis Victor	Sgt.	Aircrew	236	Joined 236 Sqn., end of 8-40. Commissioned later and left R.A.F. in 1945 as Flight Lieutenant.		British
BAKER, P.	Plt. Off.	Pilot	600	Joined 600 Sqn., 9-7-40. Further details not established.		British
BAKER Ronald David	Sgt.	Pilot	56	On 56 Sqn., 1-7-40. ✠ **1 Ju 87, 13-7-40.**	✟ **Killed in Action** (11-8-40)	British
BAKER Stanley	Plt. Off.	Pilot	54-66	Joined 54 Sqn., 18-8-40. Posted to 66 Sqn., c.24-9-40. ✠ **1 Bf 110, 27-9-40;** ✠ **1 Bf 109, 25-10-40.**	✟ Killed since Battle (11-2-41)	British
¶ **BALDEN, D.W.**	Flt. Lt.	Pilot	266	Joined 166 Sqn., 4-7-40, but posted away shortly after.		British
BALL George Eric	Fg. Off.	Pilot	242	On 242 Sqn., 1-7-40. Awarded D.F.C. (1-10-40). ✠ **1 He 111 (shared), 30-8-40;** ✠ **1 Bf 110, 7-9-40;** ✠ **1 Bf 109, 9-9-40;** ✠ **1 Ju 88, 18-9-40.**	✟ Killed since Battle (1-2-46)	British
BAMBERGER Cyril Stanley ("Bam")	Sgt.	Pilot	610-41	Joined 610 Sqn., 27-7-40. Posted to 41 Sqn., 9-40. Commissioned later (2-42) and awarded D.F.C.✿ (28-9-43 and 14-11-44). Retired from R.A.F., 1-59, as Squadron Leader. ✠ **1 Bf 109, 5-10-40.**		British
BANDINEL James Julius Frederic Henry	Fg. Off.	Pilot	3	Joined 3 Sqn., mid-7-40.	✟ Killed since Battle (12-12-41)	British
BANHAM Arthur John	Flt. Lt.	Pilot	264-229	On 264 Sqn., 1-7-40. Promoted to Sqn. Ldr. and posted to 229 Sqn., 11-9-40, to command. Severely wounded, 15-10-40. ✠ **1 Do 17, 26-8-40.**	✟ Died since Battle (1987)	British
BANISTER Thomas Henry	Sgt.	Aircrew	219	Joined 219 Sqn., c.5-8-40. Awarded D.F.M. (24-9-40). Commissioned later (3-42).		British
BANKS William Henry	Sgt.	Pilot	245-32-504	On 245 Sqn., 12-7-40. Posted to 32 Sqn., 18-9-40. Posted to 504 Sqn., 24-9-40. Commissioned later (10-41), and retired from the R.A.F., 5-58, as Squadron Leader.	✟ Died since Battle (16-1-80)	British
BANN Eric Samuel	Sgt.	Pilot	238	On 238 Sqn., 1-7-40.✠ **1 He 111, 11-8-40.**	✟ **Killed in Action** (28-9-40)	British
BARALDI Ferdinand Henry Raphael ("Jimmy")	Plt. Off.	Pilot	609	Joined 609 Sqn., 22-10-40. Released from R.A.F. in 1946 as Squadron Leader.	✟ Died since Battle (1988)	British
BARANSKI Wienczyslaw	Flt. Lt.	Pilot	607	Joined 607 Sqn., 9-10-40.		Polish
BARBER Robert Hugh	Fg. Off.	Pilot	46	Joined 46 Sqn., 15-8-40. Severely wounded, 4-9-40. Awarded A.F.C. (1-1-43).		British
BARCLAY Richard George Arthur	Fg. Off.	Pilot	249	On 249 Sqn., 1-7-40. Awarded D.F.C. (26-11-40). ✠ **1 Bf 109, 7-9-40;** ✠ **1 Do 17, 15-9-40;** ✠ **1 Ju 88, 19-9-40;** ✠ **1 Bf 109, 27-9-40;** ✠ **1 Ju 88, 27-9-40.**	✟ Killed since Battle (17-7-42)	British
BARKER Frederick James	Sgt.	Aircrew	264	Defiant gunner (of Sgt. E.R. Thorn, q.v.). On 264 Sqn., 1-7-40. Awarded D.F.M.✿ (14-6-40 and 11-2-41 respectively). Commissioned later (4-44).		British
BARKER George Leonard	Sgt.	Aircrew	600	Awarded D.F.M., 13-9-40. Commissioned as Plt. Off.	✟ Killed since Battle (18-7-40)	British
BARKER John Keeth	Sgt.	Pilot	152	On 152 Sqn., 1-7-40. ✠ **1 Ju 87, 18-8-40;** ✠ **1 Bf 109, 25-8-40.**	✟ **Killed in Action** (4-9-40)	British
BARNARD Eric Charles	A.C.2	Aircrew	600	On 600 Sqn., 1-7-40. Promoted Sergeant. Commissioned, 4-44.		British
BARNES John Guy Cardew	Fg. Off.	Pilot	600	On 600 Sqn., 1-7-40. Promoted Flt. Lt., 8-40. Left the R.A.F. in 1946 as Wing Commander.		British
BARNES Leslie Denis	Sgt.	Pilot	257-615-607	On 257 Sqn., 1-7-40. Posted to 615 Sqn., 4-9-40. Posted to 607 Sqn., 21-9-40. (✠ **1 CR.42, 11-11-40**). Commissioned, 1-41.		British
BARNES Wilkinson	Plt. Off.	Pilot	504	Joined 504 Sqn., 1-7-40. No further Service details traced.	✟ Died since Battle (believed 1980)	British
BARNETT Richard Edgar ("Dicky")	Sqn. Ldr.	Pilot	234	In command of 234 Sqn., 1-7-40; posted away, 13-8-40. Resigned Commission, 11-8-41, on account of ill health.	✟ Died since Battle (2-1-70)	British
BARON Ruper Victor	Plt. Off.	Aircrew	219	On 219 Sqn., 1-7-40.	✟ **Killed in Accident** (12-10-40)	British
¶ **BARON**	A.C.1	Aircrew	604	On 604 Sqn., 1-7-40. Promoted Sergeant, c.7-7-40, and posted away.		British
BARRACLOUGH Ronald George Victor	Sgt.	Pilot	266	On 266 Sqn., 1-7-40. Commissioned, 5-41.		British
BARRACLOUGH Stanley Michael	Sgt.	Pilot	92	On 92 Sqn., 1-7-40. Commissioned, 6-41. Retired from R.A.F. as Squadron Leader, 28-5-58.		British
BARRAN Philip Henry ("Pip")	Flt. Lt.	Pilot	609	On 609 Sqn., 1-7-40.	✟ **Killed in Action** (11-7-40)	British
BARRETT, W.E.	Sgt.	Pilot	25	Joined 25 Sqn., early 9-40. Awarded D.F.M.		British
BARRON Norman Percy Gerald	Sgt.	Pilot	236	On 236 Sqn., 1-7-40. Commissioned later (11-40). Survived the War.		British
BARROW Hector Jack Raymond	Sgt.	Pilot	607-43-213	On 607 Sqn., 1-7-40. Posted to 43 Sqn., 8-40. Posted to 213 Sqn., c.20-9-40. ✠ **1 Bf 110 (shared), 27-9-40.**	✟ Killed since Battle (28-11-40)	British
BARRY Nathaniel John Merriman	Fg. Off.	Pilot	3-501	On 3 Sqn., 1-7-40. Posted to 501 Sqn., 26-9-40.	✟ **Killed in Action** (7-10-40)	South African
BARTHROPP Patrick Peter Colum ("Paddy")	Fg. Off.	Pilot	602	Joined 602 Sqn., 8-9-40. Awarded D.F.C. (26-9-41), A.F.C. (10-6-54). ✠ **1 He 111 (shared), 27-9-40;** ✠ **1 Ju 88 (shared), 2-10-40.**		British
BARTLETT Leonard Harold	Sgt.	Pilot	17	Joined 17 Sqn., 15-7-40. Commissioned, 7-41. Awared D.S.O. (3-3-44). Retired from R.A.F. as Group Captain, 20-6-66. ✠ **1 Ju 88 (shared), 21-8-40;** ✠ **1 Ju 88 (shared), 19-9-40.**		British
BARTLEY Anthony Charles	Plt. Off.	Pilot	92	On 92 Sqn., 1-7-40. Awarded D.F.C.✿ (25-10-40 and 16-2-43). ✠ **1 Do 17, 18-9-40;** ✠ **1 Ju 88, 27-9-40.**		British
¶ **BARTLEY**	Plt. Off.	Aircrew	604	On 604 Sqn., 1-7-40. Posted away, c. 12-7-40.		British
BARTON Anthony Richard Henry	Plt. Off.	Pilot	32-253	Joined 32 Sqn., 5-8-40. Posted to 253 Sqn., 10-9-40. Seriously wounded, 20-9-40. Awarded D.F.C.✿ (10-4-42 and 7-7-42 respectively). ✠ **1 Bf 109, 11-8-40;** ✠ **1 Ju 88, 18-8-40;** ✠ **1 Do 215, 15-9-40.**	✟ Killed since Battle (4-4-43)	British
BARTON Robert Alexander ("Butch")	Flt. Lt.	Pilot	249	On 249 Sqn., 1-7-40. Promoted Sqn. Ldr. to command Sqn., 12-40. Awarded D.F.C.✿ (20-10-40 and 31-10-41 respectively); appointed O.B.E. (14-6-45). Retired from R.A.F. as Wing Commander, 27-2-59. ✠ **1 Bf 109, 15-8-40;** ✠ **1 Do 215 (shared), 2-9-40;** ✠ **1 Bf 110, 27-9-40;** ✠ **1 Bf 109, 29-10-40.**		Canadian
BARTOS Jindrich	Plt. Off.	Pilot	312	Joined 312 (Czech) Sqn., 5-9-40.	✟ Killed since Battle (13-2-41)	Czech
BARWELL Eric Gordon ("Auntie Bee")	Plt. Off.	Pilot	264	On 264 Sqn., 1-7-40. Awarded D.F.C.✿ 11-2-41 and 15-8-44 respectively). Released from R.A.F., 2-9-45, as Squadron Leader. ✠ **1 Bf 109, 24-8-40.**		British
BARWELL Philip Reginald	Wg. Cdr.	Pilot	(242)	Commanded R.A.F., Coltishall, and flew three operational sorties with No. 242 Sqn.	✟ Killed since Battle (1-7-42)	British
BARY Ronald Edward	Plt. Off.	Pilot	229	On 229 Sqn., 1-7-40. Awarded D.S.O. (12-2-46), D.F.C. (7-4-42). ✠ **1 Ju 88 (shared), 27-9-40.**	✟ Killed since Battle (11-4-45)	New Zealander
BASHFORD Henry	Sgt.	Aircrew	248	On 248 Sqn., 1-7-40. Commissioned later (1-43).		British

Name	Rank	Role	Sqn.	Service details	Fate	Nationality
BASSETT Francis Bernard	Plt. Off.	Pilot	222	On 222 Sqn., 1-7-40.	† Killed since Battle (14-11-42)	British
BATCHELOR Gordon Herbert	Plt. Off.	Pilot	54	Joined 54 Sqn., 14-10-40.	† Killed since Battle (15-4-42)	British
BATT Leslie Gordon	Sgt.	Pilot	238	On 238 Sqn., 1-7-40. Commissioned later (3-43). ✠ 1 Do 17 (shared), 21-7-41; ✠ 1 Bf 109, 8-8-40. Released from R.A.F. in 1945 as Flight Lieutenant.		British
BAXTER Sidney ("Sludge")	Sgt.	Pilot	222	On 222 Sqn., 1-7-40. ✠ 1 He 111, 11-9-40.	† Killed in Action (14-9-40)	British
BAYLES Ian Norman	Plt. Off.	Pilot	152	On 152 Sqn., 1-7-40. Promoted to Fg. Off., 8-40. Awarded D.F.C. (2-10-45). ✠ 1 He 111 (shared), 25-9-40; ✠ 1 Ju 88, 25-9-40.		British
BAYLEY Edward Alan ("Scruf")	Sgt.	Pilot	32-249	On 32 Sqn., 1-7-40. Posted to 249 Sqn., 9-40. ✠ 1 Do 17 (shared), 3-7-40; ✠ 1 Do 215, 18-8-40.	† Killed in Accident (10-10-40)	British
BAYLISS Derek	Plt. Off.	Pilot	604	On 604 Sqn., 1-7-40.		British
BAYLISS Ernest John	Sgt.	Aircrew	248	On 248 Sqn., 1-7-40.	† Killed since Battle (3-11-40)	British
BAYLY James	Sgt.	Pilot	111	Joined 111 Sqn., 28-9-40.		New Zealander
BAYNE Alfred William Alexander	Flt. Lt.	Pilot	17	On 17 Sqn., 1-7-40. Awarded D.F.C. (26-11-40). ✠ 1 He 111 (shared), 29-7-40; ✠ 1 Bf 109, 31-8-40; ✠ 1 Bf 109, 5-9-40; ✠ 1 Do 17 (shared), 2-10-40.	† Died since Battle (28-5-63)	British
BAYNE David Walter	Sqn. Ldr.	Pilot	257	In command of 257 Sqn., 1-7-40; posted away, 22-7-40. Retired from the R.A.F. as Group Captain.		British
BAYNHAM Geoffrey Theodore	Plt. Off.	Pilot	234-152	Joined 234 Sqn., c.14-9-40. Posted to 152 Sqn., 5-10-40. Awarded D.F.C. (10-9-43).		British
BAZIN James Michael	Flt. Lt.	Pilot	607	Joined 607 Sqn., 10-8-40. Awarded D.S.O. (21-9-45), D.F.C. (25-10-40). ✠ 1 Do 215, 15-9-40; ✠ 1 Ju 88, 30-9-40.	† Died since Battle (1985)	British
BAZLEY Sydney Howarth ("Kidney Bean")	Flt. Lt.	Pilot	266	On 266 Sqn., 1-7-40. Wounded, 16-8-40. ✠ 1 Bf 110, 12-8-40.	† Killed since Battle (2-3-41)	British
BEAKE Percival Harold	Fg. Off.	Pilot	64	Joined 64 Sqn., 22-9-40. Awarded D.F.C. (5-9-44). Released from R.A.F. as Squadron Leader, 21-1-46.		British
BEAMISH Francis Victor	Wg. Cdr.	Pilot	(151-249)	Was in command of R.A.F. North Weald, 1-7-40. Flew operational sorties with Nos. 17, 46, 56, 151, 249 and 257 Sqns. Awarded D.S.O. ❀ (23-7-40 and 25-9-41); D.F.C. (11-8-40), A.F.C. (1-1-38). ✠ 1 Do 17, 12-7-40; ✠ 1 Ju 87, 6-9-40; ✠ 1 Bf 109, 18-9-40; ✠ 1 Bf 109, 30-10-40.	† Killed since Battle (28-3-42)	Irish
BEAMISH Ronald	Sgt.	Pilot	601	Joined 601 Sqn., 11-9-40. Commissioned later (6-42).		British
BEAMONT Roland Prosper ("Bee")	Plt. Off.	Pilot	87	On 87 Sqn., 1-7-40. Promoted Fg. Off., 9-40. Appointed C.B.E. (1969); awarded D.S.O.❀ (6-5-43 and 25-7-44), D.F.C.❀ (6-6-41 and 29-1-43). ✠ 1 Bf 110, 15-8-40; ✠ 1 Bf 109, 25-8-40. Retired from R.A.F. as Wg. Cdr., 1-46.		British
BEARD John Maurice Bentley	Sgt.	Pilot	249	On 249 Sqn., 1-7-40. Awarded D.F.M. (22-10-40). Commissioned later (12-40). Awarded A.F.C. (1-1-45). ✠ 1 Bf 110, 18-9-40; ✠ 1 Bf 110, 27-9-40; ✠ 2 Bf 109s, 27-9-40; ✠ 1 Bf 109, 28-9-40.		British
BEARDMORE Eric Walter	Fg. Off.	Pilot	1(Canadian)	On 1 (Canadian) Sqn. on arrival in U.K., 20-6-40. Slightly wounded, 18-9-40. Released from R.C.A.F. as Wing Commander, 18-10-45.	† Died since Battle (23-8-40)	Canadian
BEARDSLEY Robert Arthur	Sgt.	Pilot	610-41	Joined 610 Sqn., 27-7-40. Posted to 41 Sqn., 18-9-40. Commissioned, 6-41. Awarded D.F.C. (17-10-41). Retired from R.A.F. as Flt. Ltn., 31-7-70. ✠ 1 Bf 109, 25-8-40; ✠ 1 He 111, 30-8-40; ✠ 1 Bf 109, 25-10-40.		British
BEATTY Marcus Alfred	Sgt.	Pilot	266	Joined 266 Sqn., 30-9-40. Commissioned, 6-41. Left R.A.F. as Flt. Ltn., 1946.		British
BEAUMONT Stephen Gerald	Flt. Lt.	Pilot	609	On 609 Sqn., 1-7-40. Appointed O.B.E., 1-1-45. Released from R.A.F. as Group Captain in 1945.		British
BEAZLEY Hugh John Sherard	Plt. Off.	Pilot	249	On 249 Sqn., 1-7-40. Promoted to Fg. Off., 25-9-40. Wounded 27-9-40. Awarded D.F.C. (7-3-44). ✠ 1 Bf 110, 15-8-40; ✠ 1 Do 215 (shared), 7-9-40; ✠ 1 Do 215, 15-9-40.		British
BEDA Antoni ("Tony")	Sgt.	Pilot	302	Joined 302 (Polish) Sqn., 20-8-40.	† Died since Battle (1960)	Polish
BEE Ernest Horace	Sgt.	Aircrew	29	On 29 Sqn., 1-7-40. Left R.A.F. in 1946 as a Warrant Officer.	† Died since Battle (1987)	British
BEECHEY Alfred Francis	Sgt.	Aircrew	141	Defiant gunner. On 141 Sqn., 1-7-40. Commissioned, 12-40. Awarded D.F.C. (12-1-43)		British
¶ **BEEDHAM, J.J.**	Plt. Off.	Pilot	245	Joined 245 Sqn., 30-9-40. Did not become operational.	† Killed in Accident (7-10-40)	British
BEER Cyril Sidney Frank ("Hoppy")	Sgt.	Aircrew	235	Joined 235 Sqn., 23-8-40. (Was killed flying with a Coastal Command Squadron)	† Killed in Action (19-9-40)	British
BEGGS Henry William	Sub-Lt.	Pilot	151	Fleet Air Arm. Joined 151 Sqn., 1-7-40. Wounded, 15-8-40. ✠ 1 Bf 109, 14-8-40.	† Killed since Battle (15-11-42)	British
¶ **BEHAL, F.**	Plt. Off.	Pilot	1	Joined 1 Sqn., 14-10-40. Did not become operational.		?
BELC Marian	Sgt.	Pilot	303	Joined 303 (Polish) Sqn., on formation, 2-8-40. Commissioned later, and awarded D.F.C., 15-11-42. ✠ 1 Bf 109, 26-9-40; ✠ 1 Bf 110, 5-10-40; ✠ 1 Bf 109, 7-10-40.	† Killed since Battle (27-8-42)	Polish
BELCHEM Lawrence George	Sqn. Ldr.	Pilot	264	Flew with No. 264 Sqn., on 18-7-40.	† Killed since Battle (14-7-42)	British
BELEY Robert Wilfred Garth	Plt. Off.	Pilot	151	Joined 151 Sqn., 14-7-40.	† Killed in Action (12-8-40)	Canadian
BELL Charles Algernon	Fg. Off.	Aircrew	29	On 29 Sqn., 1-7-40. No further service details established.		British
BELL Charles Henry	Sgt.	Pilot	234	Joined 234 Sqn., 9-40. ✠ 1 Do 17, 9-10-40.	† Killed since Battle (2-3-41)	British
BELL Derek	Sgt.	Aircrew	23	On 23 Sqn., 1-7-40.	† Killed since Battle (27-12-41)	British
BELL John Swift	Fg. Off.	Pilot	616	On 616 Sqn., 1-7-40. ✠ 1 He 111, 1-7-40.	† Killed in Action (30-8-40)	British
BELL Ralph	Sgt.	Aircrew	219	On 219 Sqn., 1-7-40. No further service details established.		British
BELL-SALTER David Basil ("Bell-Pusher")	Fg. Off.	Pilot	253	On 253 Sqn., 1-7-40. Severely injured, 2-9-40.	† Died since Battle (1985)	British
BELL-WALKER Howard John	Sgt.	Pilot	72	Believed with 72 Sqn., 1-7-40. Severely wounded, 18-9-40. Commissioned later, 8-41. Appointed M.B.E. (30-4-54). Retired from R.A.F. as Sqn. Ldr., 1-12-67.		British
BENN Gordon William	Sgt.	Aircrew	219	On 219 Sqn., 1-7-40. Left the R.A.F. as a Warrant Officer, 10-54.		British
BENNETT Clarence Charles	Plt. Off.	Pilot	248	On 248 Sqn., 1-7-40.	† Killed in Action (1-10-40)	Australian
BENNETT Hector Ernest	Sgt.	Pilot	43	No details of operations during the Battle established.	† Killed since Battle (4-2-41)	British
BENNETTE Geoffrey Ryding	Plt. Off.	Pilot	17	On 17 Sqn., 1-7-40. ✠ 1 He 111 (shared), 9-7-40.	† Killed since Battle (19-8-42)	British
BENNIONS George Herman ("Ben")	Plt. Off.	Pilot	41	On 41 Sqn., 1-7-40. Wounded, 11-9-40. Awarded D.F.C. (1-10-40). ✠ 1 Bf 109, 28-7-40; ✠ 1 Bf 110, 15-8-40; ✠ 2 Bf 109s, 6-9-40; ✠ 1 Bf 109, 15-9-40; ✠ 1 Bf 109, 18-9-40; ✠ 1 Ju 88, 20-9-40; ✠ 1 Bf 109, 23-9-40; ✠ 1 Bf 109, 1-10-40. Severely wounded, 1-10-40. Released from the R.A.F., 1946, as Squadron Leader.		British
BENNISON Alan	Sgt.	Aircrew	25	Joined 25 Sqn., 21-9-40. Commissioned, 2-44.		New Zealander
BENSON James Gillies	Plt. Off.	Pilot	141	Joined 141 Sqn., 24-7-40. Awarded D.S.O. (13-3-45), D.F.C.❀ (2-10-42 and 20-10-44).	† Died since Battle	British
BENSON Noel John Victor	Plt. Off.	Pilot	603	On 603 Sqn., 1-7-40.	† Killed in Action (28-8-40)	British
BENT Benjamin	L.A.C.	Aircrew	25	Joined 25 Sqn., 6-8-40. Promoted Sergeant, 27-9-40. Commissioned, 4-43. Awarded D.F.C. (26-5-44). Retired from R.A.F., 5-12-70, as Flight Lieutenant.		British

Name	Rank	Role	Sqn	Details	Fate	Nationality
BENZIE John	Plt. Off.	Pilot	242	On 242 Sqn., 1-7-40.	✠ **Killed in Action** (7-9-40)	Canadian
BERESFORD Hugh Richard Aden	Flt. Lt.	Pilot	257	On 257 Sqn., 1-7-40. ✠ 1 He 111 (shared), 18-8-40; ✠ 1 Bf 110, 31-8-40.	✠ **Killed in Action** (7-9-40)	British
BERGMAN Vaclav	Plt. Off.	Pilot	310	Joined 310 (Czech) Sqn., 12-7-40. Awarded D.F.C. Retired from R.A.F., 30-4-69, as Squadron Leader. ✠ 1 Bf 110, 9-9-40; ✠ 1 Do 215, 18-9-40.		Czech
BERKLEY Thomas Colqhoun Edmonds	Sgt.	Pilot	85	Joined 85 Sqn., 2-9-40.	✠ Killed since Battle (14-6-41)	British
¶ **BERNARD**	F/Sgt.	Pilot	616	On 616 Sqn., 1-7-40. Believed posted away shortly after.		British
BERNARD Frantisek Antonin	Sgt.	Pilot	238-601	Joined 238 Sqn., 8-40. Posted to 601 Sqn., 6-9-40. Returned to 238 Sqn., 8-10-40. Commissioned, 4-42. Awarded A.F.C. (1-1-57). Retired from R.A.F., 23-7-64.		Czech
BERNAS Bronislaw	Plt. Off.	Pilot	302	Joined 302 (Polish) Sqn., 23-9-40.	✠ Died since Battle (3-9-80)	Polish
BERRIDGE Horace Walter William	Sgt.	Aircrew	219	Commissioned, 1-42. Awarded D.S.O. (17-8-45), D.F.C. (23-6-42). Survived the War.		British
BERRY	Sgt.	Aircrew	264	Defiant gunner. On 264 Sqn., 1-7-40.	✠ **Killed in Action** (24-8-40)	British
¶ **BERRY, A.E.**	Plt. Off.	Pilot	3	Joined 3 Sqn., 27-9-40. Awarded D.F.C. Did not fly qualifying sortie.		British
BERRY Frederick George	F/Sgt.	Pilot	1	On 1 Sqn., 1-7-40.	✠ **Killed in Action** (1-9-40)	British
BERRY Ronald ("Ras")	Plt. Off.	Pilot	603	On 603 Sqn., 1-7-40. Awarded D.S.O. (1-6-43), D.F.C.✪ (25-10-40 and 2-3-43). Apointed C.B.E., 1-1-46. ✠ 1 Ju 88 (shared), 3-7-40; ✠ 1 He 111 (shared), 30-7-40; ✠ 3 Bf 109s, 31-8-40; ✠ 1 Bf 109, 2-9-40; ✠ 1 Do 17, 15-9-40; ✠ 1 + 1(shared) Bf 109, 27-9-40; ✠ 2 Bf 109s, 30-9-40. Retired, 29-1-69.		British
BERWICK Robert Charles	Sgt.	Aircrew	25	On 25 Sqn., 1-7-40.	✠ Killed since Battle (19-6-41)	British
BEVERIDGE Charles	Sgt.	Aircrew	219	Joined 219 Sqn., 1-8-40. Awarded A.F.M. (1-1-43). Commissioned, 8-43. Retired from R.A.F. as Flight Lieutenant, 1-9-52.	✠ Died since Battle (18-12-84)	British
BEYTAGH Michael Leo ffrench	Flt. Lt.	Pilot	73	Joined 73 Sqn., 24-7-40. Awarded D.F.C. (1-10-43). ✠ 1 Bf 110, 7-9-40. Retired from R.A.F., 10-1-46, as Squadron Leader.	✠ Died since Battle (12-8-52)	British
BICKERDIKE John Laurance	Plt. Off.	Pilot	85	On 85 Sqn., 1-7-40. ✠ 1 He 111, 12-7-40.	✠ **Killed in Accident** (22-7-40)	New Zealander
BICKNELL	Sgt.	Aircrew	23	Joined 23 Sqn., c.12-7-40. No other service details established.		British
BICKNELL Leslie Charles	Sqn. Ldr.	Pilot	23	In command of 23 Sqn., 1-7-40. Posted away, 9-8-40. Retired from the R.A.F. as Wing Commander, 20-6-49.		British
BIDGOOD Eric George	Plt. Off.	Pilot	253	On 253 Sqn., 1-7-40.	✠ Killed since Battle (16-11-40)	British
BIDGOOD Ivor Kenneth Jack	Sgt.	Pilot	213	Known to have served on 213 Sqn., during Battle, but no other service details traced.		British
BIGGAR Arthur James	Sqn. Ldr.	Pilot	111	Assumed command of 111Sqn., 10-40. Appointed C.B.E. (2-1-56), and retired from the R.A.F., 1-6-58, as Group Captain.	✠ Died since Battle (1975)	British
BIGNALL John Edward	Sgt.	Aircrew	25	Joined 25 Sqn., 20-7-40.	✠ Killed since Battle (4-9-41)	British
BINHAM Arthur Edward	Sgt.	Pilot	64	On 64 Sqn., 1-7-40. Posted away, 24-9-40. Awarded A.F.C., 14-6-45.		British
BIRCH Colin Norman	Plt. Off.	Pilot	1	On 1 Sqn., 1-7-40. Awarded A.F.C., 8-6-44. ✠ 1 He 111, 30-8-40; ✠ 1 Bf 109, 1-9-40. Retired from R.A.F., 28-3-58, as Squadron Leader.		British
BIRD Ronald Arthur	Lieut.	Pilot	804	Fleet Air Arm. Joined 804 Sqn., 1-7-40. Awarded D.S.C.✪ (26-6-45 and 7-8-45).	✠ Killed since Battle (10-4-46)	British
BIRD-WILSON Harold Arthur Cooper ("Birdie")	Fg. Off.	Pilot	17	On 17 Sqn., 1-7-40. Appointed C.B.E. (1962); awarded D.S.O. (9-1-45), D.F.C.✪ (24-9-40 and 29-10-43), A.F.C.✪ (1-1-46 and 1-1-55). ✠ 1 He 111 (shared), 29-7-40; ✠ 1 Bf 109, 25-8-40; ✠ 1 Bf 109, 31-8-40. Retired from R.A.F., 1-6-74, as Air Vice-Marshal.		British
BIRKETT Thomas	Plt. Off.	Pilot	219	On 219 Sqn., 1-7-40. Commissioned, 9-40.	✠ Killed since Battle (13-11-40)	British
BIRRELL Maurice Andrew	Mid/Ship.	Pilot	79-804	Fleet Air Arm. Joined 79 Sqn., 1-7-40. Returned to 804 Sqn., mid-7-40. Awarded D.S.C. (30-10-52). Retired from Royal Navy, 1972, as Commander.		British
BISDEE John Derek	Fg. Off.	Pilot	609	On 609 Sqn., 1-7-40. Appointed O.B.E. (14-6-45), D.F.C. (11-7-41). ✠ 1 Bf 110, 11-8-40; ✠ 1 Bf 110, 7-9-40; ✠ 1 Bf 110, 27-9-40; ✠ 1 Bf 110, 7-10-40. Released from the R.A.F., 1945, as Group Captain.		British
BISGOOD Douglas Leonard	Plt. Off.	Pilot	3	On 3 Sqn., 1-7-40. Severely injured, 23-7-40. Awarded D.F.C. (2-1-42).	✠ Killed since Battle (18-4-47)	British
BITMEAD Ernest Ralph ("Bitters")	Sqn. Ldr.	Pilot	29-266-310-253-229-611	Joined 29 Sqn. to command, 8-7-40. Posted to 266 Sqn., 14-7-50. Attached to 310 (Czech) Sqn., 8-40. Posted to 253 Sqn., early 9-40. Attached to 229 Sqn., mid-9-40. Posted to 611 Sqn., 19-10-40, to command. Awarded D.F.C. (21-11-44).	✠ Died since Battle (1955)	British
BLACK Allan	Sgt.	Pilot	54	Joined 54 Sqn., 28-9-40. Commissioned, 9-41.	✠ Killed since Battle (1-2-44)	British
BLACK Herbert Ernest	Sgt.	Pilot	32-257-46	Joined 32 Sqn., early 9-40. Posted to 257 Sqn., c.20-9-40. Posted to 46 Sqn., mid-10-40. Grievously wounded in action on 29-10-40, and died later.	✠ **Died of wounds** (9-11-40)	British
BLACKADDER William Francis ("Blackie")	Flt. Lt.	Pilot	607	On 607 Sqn., 1-7-40. Awarded D.S.O. (4-6-40), O.B.E. (1-1-45). ✠ 1 Ju 88 (shared), 14-9-40; ✠ 1 He 111, 26-9-40. Released from R.A.F. as Wing Commander, 19-11-45.		British
BLACKWOOD George Douglas Morant	Flt. Lt.	Pilot	310	In command of No. 310 (Czech) Sqn., on formation, 18-7-40. ✠ 1 Do 17, 26-8-40. Released from the R.A.F., 1945, as Wing Commander.		British
BLAIR Charles Edward	Plt. Off.	Aircrew	600	On 600 Sqn., 1-7-40.	✠ Killed since Battle (25-4-41)	British
BLAIR Kenneth Hughes	Flt. Lt.	Pilot	151	On 151 Sqn., 1-7-40. Awarded D.F.C.✪ (31-5-40 and 23-5-44). ✠ 1 Bf 109, 5-8-40; ✠ 1 Bf 110, 18-8-40; ✠ 1 He 111, 30-8-40; ✠ 1 Do 215, 31-8-40; ✠ 1 Ju 88 (shared), 30-9-40.	✠ Died since Battle (31-10-52)	British
BLAIZE Pierre Michel	Sous-Lt.	Pilot	111	Joined 111 Sqn., 9-40.	✠ Killed since Battle (15-4-41)	French
BLAKE Arthur Giles ("The Admiral")	Sub-Lt.	Pilot	19	Fleet Air Arm. On 19 Sqn., 1-7-40. ✠ 1 He 111, 9-9-40; ✠ 1 Bf 109, 15-9-40; ✠ 1 He 111 (shared), 15-9-40; ✠ 2 Bf 109s, 17-9-40; ✠ 2 Bf 109s, 27-9-40.	✠ **Killed in Action** (29-10-40)	British
BLAKE Minden Vaughan ("Mindy")	Flt. Lt.	Pilot	238-234	Joined 238 Sqn., 16-8-40. Promoted Sqn. Ldr., and posted to 234 Sqn., to command. Awarded D.S.O. (27-7-42), D.F.C. (20-12-40). ✠ 1 Ju 88, 21-8-40; ✠ 1 Do 17 (shared), 27-8-40; ✠ 1 Ju 88, 11-9-49; ✠ 1 He 111, 15-9-40. Retired from the R.A.F. as Wing Commander, 28-1-58.	✠ Died since Battle (30-11-81)	New Zealander
BLAND John Wellburn	Plt. Off.	Pilot	601-501	On 601 Sqn., 1-7-40. Postedto 501 Sqn., 12-7-40. ✠ 1 Do 215 (shared), 11-7-40; ✠ 1 Ju 87, 29-7-40.	✠ **Killed in Action** (18-8-40)	British
BLANE William Higgins	A.C.2	Aircrew	604	Joined 604 Sqn., 20-7-40. No further details known.		British
BLATCHFORD Howard Peter ("Cowboy")	Flt. Lt.	Pilot	17-257	Joined 17 Sqn., 30-9-40. Posted to 257 Sqn., 10-40. Awarded D.F.C. (6-12-40). ✠ 1 Do 17 (shared), 2-10-40. (✠ 1+1 Shared BR 20, 11-11-40).	✠ Killed since Battle (3-5-43)	Canadian
BLAYNEY Adolf Jarvis	Plt. Off.	Pilot	609	On 609 Sqn., 1-7-40. Posted away, 14-8-40. Awarded A.F.C. (2-4-43).		British
BLENKHARN Frank	Sgt.	Aircrew	25	Joined 25 Sqn., 9-40.		British
¶ **BLISS**	Sgt.	Pilot	604	On 604 Sqn., 1-7-40; posted away shortly after.		British.
BLOMELEY David Henry	Fg. Off.	Pilot	151	On 151 Sqn., 1-7-40. Awarded D.F.C. (26-10-43), A.F.C. (10-6-54). Retired from R.A.F. as Squadron Leader, 20-2-58.		British
BLOOR Ernest	Sgt.	Pilot	46	On 46 Sqn., 1-7-40. Slightly wounded, 3-9-40.	✠ Killed since Battle (27-8-41)	British
BLOW Kenneth Leslie Owen	Sgt.	Aircrew	235	On 235 Sqn., 1-7-40. Awarded D.F.C. as Warrant Officer (15-6-43).	✠ Killed since Battle (10-12-43)	British
BODDINGTON Michael Christopher Bindloss	Sgt.	Pilot	234	On 234 Sqn., 1-7-40. Awarded D.F.M. (26-11-40), D.F.C. (10-9-43). Commissioned, 10-40. Released from R.A.F., 13-2-46, as Squadron Leader. ✠ 1 Ju 88, 14-8-40; ✠ 2 Bf 110s, 4-9-40; ✠ 1 Bf 109, 5-9-40; ✠ 1 Bf 109, 6-9-40; ✠ 1 Ju 88 (shared), 28-10-40.	✠ Died since Battle (1977)	British

Name	Rank	Role	Sqn.	Details	Fate	Nationality
BODIE Crelin Arthur Walford ("Bogle")	Plt. Off.	Pilot	66	On 66 Sqn., 1-7-40. Awarded D.F.C. (8-11-40). ✠ 1 Bf 110 (shared), 20-8-40; ✠ 1 Do 215 (shared), 31-8-40; ✠ 1 He 111 (shared), 2-9-40; ✠ 1 He 111 11-9-40; ✠ 4 Do 17, 15-9-40; ✠ 1 He 111, 18-9-40; ✠ 1 Bf 109, 11-11-40.	♰ Killed since Battle (24-2-42)	British
BOITEL-GILL Derek Pierre Aumale	Flt. Lt.	Pilot	152	On 152 Sqn., 1-7-40. Awarded D.F.C. (22-10-40). ✠ 1 Ju 88, 12-8-40; ✠ 2 Bf 110 and 1 Ju 87, 15-8-40; ✠ 1 Ju 87, 18-8-40; ✠ 1 Ju 88, 25-9-40; ✠ 1 Bf 109, 25-9-40; ✠ 1 Ju 88, 26-9-40.	♰ Killed since Battle (18-9-41)	British
BOLTON Henry Albert	Sgt.	Pilot	79	Joined 79 Sqn., c.18-8-40.	♰ **Killed in Action** (31-8-40)	British
¶ **BOMFORD**	Sgt.	Pilot	601	Joined 601 Sqn., 25-8-40. Did not fly operational sortie before being posted away.		British
¶ **BOND**	Plt. Off.	Pilot	604-151	On 604 Sqn., 1-7-40. Posted to 151 Sqn., 4-9-40. Posted away soon after.		British
BONSEIGNEUR Camille Robespierre	Plt. Off.	Pilot	257	On 257 Sqn., 1-7-40. ✠ 1 Do 17 (shared), 19-7-40.	♰ **Killed in Action** (3-9-40)	Canadian
BOOT Peter Victor	Plt. Off.	Pilot	1	On 1 Sqn., 1-7-40. Awarded D.F.C. (1-10-40). Posted away, 18-10-40. ✠ 1 Bf 109, 1-9-40. Released from R.A.F. in 1946 as Flight Lieutenant.	♰ Died since Battle (1984)	British
BOOTH Glendon Bulmer	Sgt.	Pilot	85	Joined 85 Sqn., 15-7-40. ✠ 1 Bf 109, 28-8-40. Died from injuries received on 1-9-40.	♰ **Died of Wounds** (7-2-41)	British
BOOTH John James	A.C.1	Aircrew	600-23	On 600 Sqn., 1-7-40. Posted to 23 Sqn., 22-8-40, and promoted Sergeant. Commissioned, 1-44. Survived the War.		British
BORET Robert John	Plt. Off.	Pilot	41	On 41 Sqn., 1-7-40. Posted overseas, 10-40.	♰ Killed since Battle (16-11-40)	British
BOROWSKI Jan	Plt. Off.	Pilot	302	Joined 302 (Polish) Sqn., 17-10-40.	♰ **Killed in Accident** (18-10-40)	Polish
BOSWELL Reginald Arthur	Sgt.	Pilot	266-19	Joined 266 Sqn., 16-9-40. Posted to 19 Sqn., 25-9-40.		British
BOULDING Roger John Eric	Fg. Off.	Pilot	74	Joined 74 Sqn., 21-8-40. ✠ 1 Do 215 (shared), 5-10-40. Retired from R.A.F., 29-11-66, as Wing Commander.		British
BOULTER John Clifford	Flt. Lt.	Pilot	603	On 603 Sqn., 1-7-40. Slightly wounded, 29-8-40. Awarded D.F.C. (6-12-40). ✠ 1 Bf 109, 29-8-40; ✠ 1 Bf 109, 14-9-40; ✠ 1 Bf 109, 23-9-40.	♰ Killed since Battle (17-2-41)	British
BOULTON John Eric	Fg. Off.	Pilot	603-310	On 603 Sqn., 1-7-40. Posted to 310 (Czech) Sqn., on formation, 10-7-40.	♰ **Killed in Action** (9-9-40)	British
BOUQUILLARD Henri Jacques	Adj.	Pilot	245-615-249	Joined 245 Sqn., 12-9-40. Posted to 615 Sqn., 18-9-40. Posted to 249 Sqn., 1-10-40. Wounded in action, 25-10-40. Commissioned, 2-41.	♰ Killed since Battle (10-3-41)	French
BOWEN Charles Earle	Flt. Lt.	Pilot	607	On 607 Sqn., 1-7-40. ✠ 1 Do 215, 15-9-40; ✠ 1 Do 215 (shared), 15-9-40.	♰ **Killed in Action** (1-10-40)	British
BOWEN Nigel Greenstreet	Plt. Off.	Pilot	266	On 266 Sqn., 1-7-40. ✠ 1 Ju 88, 12-8-40.	♰ **Killed in Action** (16-8-40)	British
BOWEN Peter Duncan	Plt. Off.	Pilot	264	On 264 Sqn., 1-7-40.	♰ Killed since Battle (13-2-44)	British
BOWEN-MORRIS Hugh	Sgt.	Pilot	92	Joined 92 Sqn., 12-9-40. ✠ 1 Ju 88 (shared), 27-9-40.		British
BOWERMAN Oswald Robert	Sgt.	Pilot	222	Joined 222 Sqn., c.10-7-40. Posted away, c.20-7-40.	♰ Killed since Battle (24-10-42)	British
BOWMAN Leonard Douglas ("Butch")	Sgt.	Aircrew	141	Defiant gunner. Joined 141 Sqn., c.10-9-40. Awarded D.F.M. (27-4-43). Commissioned, 4-44.		British
BOWRING Benjamin Harvey	Sgt.	Pilot	600-111	On 600 Sqn., 1-7-40. ✠ 1 Bf 109, 4-9-40; ✠ 1 Bf 109, 5-9-40; ✠ 1 Ju 88, 6-9-40. Released from R.A.F. as Squadron Leader in 1945.		British
BOWYER Walter Stafford	Flt. Lt.	Pilot	257	On 257 Sqn., 1-7-40.	♰ Killed since Battle (24-1-42)	British
BOYD Adrian Hope	Flt. Lt.	Pilot	145	On 145 Sqn., 1-7-40. Awarded D.S.O. (2-12-41), D.F.C.✸ (21-6-40 and 20-8-40). ✠ 1 He 111, 18-7-40; ✠ 1 Do 17 (shared), 22-7-40; ✠ 2 Bf 109s, 2 Bf 110s and 1 Ju 87, 8-8-40; ✠ 1 He 111, 23-8-40; ✠ 1 Ar 196 (shared), 12-10-40; ✠ 1 Bf 109, 15-10-40. Retired from R.A.F. as Wing Commander 1947.	♰ Died since Battle (21-1-75)	British
BOYD Archibald Douglas McNeill	Fg. Off.	Pilot	600	On 600 Sqn., 1-7-40. Awarded D.S.O. (3-3-44), D.F.C. (9-1-42). Flew Squadron's first operational Beaufighter patrol, 30-9-40. Left R.A.F., 2-46, as Squadron Leader.		British
BOYD Robert Findlay	Flt. Lt.	Pilot	602	On 602 Sqn., 1-7-40. Awarded D.S.O. (10-4-42), D.F.C. ✸ (24-9-40 and 25-10-40). ✠ 1 Do 215, 15-8-40; ✠ 1 Ju 87, 16-8-40; ✠ 1 He 111, 16-8-40; ✠ 1 Ju 87 and 1 Bf 109, 18-8-40; ✠ 2 Bf 109s, 25-8-40; ✠ 1 Bf 109 and 1 Do 17, 4-9-40; ✠ 1 Bf 109, 11-9-40; ✠ 1 Bf 109, 26-9-40; ✠ 1 Ju 88 (shared), 2-10-40. Released from R.A.F. in 1945 as Group Captain.	♰ Died since Battle (4-75)	British
BOYLE Cyril	Sgt.	Aircrew	236	Served on 236 Sqn. during Battle. Commissioned, 1-43.	♰ Died since Battle (6-7-71)	British
BOYLE John Greer	Fg. Off.	Pilot	41	On 41 Sqn., 1-7-40. ✠ 1 Ju 88 (shared), 11-8-40; ✠ 1 Bf 109, 5-9-40; ✠ 1 Bf 109 and 1 Do 17 (shared), 15-9-40; ✠ 2 Bf 109s, 17-9-40.	♰ **Killed in Action** (28-9-40)	Canadian
¶ **BOZEK, W.**	Plt. Off.	Pilot	302	Joined 302 (Polish) Sqn., 6-8-40. Flew no operations before posted away, 15-8-40.		Polish
BRACTON	Sgt.	Pilot	602	Flew with 602 Sqn. during Battle, but no record of operations traced.		British
BRAHAM John Randall Daniel ("Bob")	Fg. Off.	Pilot	29	On 29 Sqn., 1-7-40. Awarded D.S.O.✸✸ (9-10-42, 24-9-43 and 13-6-44), D.F.C.✸✸ (17-1-41, 25-10-41 and 15-6-43), A.F.C. (1-1-51). Also *Croix de Guerre (Belge)*. ✠ 1 Do 17, 24-8-40. Retired from R.C.A.F., 1970, as Group Captain.	♰ Died since Battle (1973)	Canadian
BRAMAH Henry George Kenelm	Sub-Lieut.	Pilot	213	Fleet Air Arm. Joined 213 Sqn., 1-7-40. ✠ 1 Do 17, 15-7-40. Wounded, 15-7-40. Retired from Royal Navy, 1955, as Commander.	♰ Died since Battle (1973)	British
BRANCH Guy Raustrom	Fg. Off.	Pilot	145	On 145 Sqn., 1-7-40. (Had been awarded the E.G.M., 25-3-39; changed to G.C., 9-40.) ✠ 2 Ju 87s, 8-8-40.	♰ **Killed in Action** (11-8-40)	British
BRASH George Brown	Sgt.	Aircrew	248	Joined 248 Sqn., 7-40.	♰ **Killed in Action** (1-10-40)	British
BREEZE Reginald Arthur	Sgt.	Pilot	266-222	Joined 266 Sqn., 16-9-40. Posted to 222 Sqn., 1-10-40. Commissioned, 9-43.	♰ Killed since Battle (28-1-45)	British
BREJCHA Vaclav	Sgt.	Pilot	43	Served with 43 Sqn. during Battle. No other details traced.	♰ Killed since Battle (19-6-41)	Czech
BRENNAN Jack Stephen	Sgt.	Aircrew	23	Joined 23 Sqn., 6-7-40. This airman lost his life in an accident on the ground.	♰ **Killed in Accident** (21-8-40)	New Zealander
BRETT Colin Peter Noel	Fg. Off.	Pilot	29-17	On 29 Sqn., 1-7-40. Posted to 17 Sqn., 12-7-40. Posted away, 16-8-40. Released from R.A.F. in 1945 as Flight Lieutenant.		British
BREWSTER John	Plt. Off.	Pilot	615-616	On 615 Sqn., 1-7-40. Posted to 616 Sqn., c.6-8-40. ✠ 1 Bf 109, 1-9-40.	♰ Killed since Battle (6-4-41)	British
BRIERE Yves	Adj.	Pilot	232	Joined 232 Sqn., 14-9-40.	♰ Killed since Battle (13-5-41)	French
BRIESE Carl E.	Fg. Off.	Pilot	1(Canadian)	On 1(Canadian) Sqn. on arrival in U.K., 6-6-40. Flew operations in Battle.	♰ Died since Battle (20-11-83)	Canadian
BRIGGS Dennis Rushworth	Sgt.	Aircrew	236	Joined 236 Sqn., 24-7-40.	♰ Killed since Battle (21-12-40)	British
BRIGGS Michael Featherstone	Plt. Off.	Pilot	234	Joined 234 Sqn., 6-10-40.	♰ Killed since Battle (2-4-41)	British
BRIGHT Vernon Maxwell	Fg. Off.	Pilot	229	On 229 Sqn., 1-7-40. ✠ 1 He 111, 11-9-40; ✠ 1 He 111 (shared), 15-9-40; ✠ 1 He 111 and 1 Ju 88 (shared), 27-9-40.	♰ Killed since Battle (24-9-42)	British
BRIMBLE George William	Sgt.	Pilot	242	On 242 Sqn., 1-7-40. ✠ 1 Bf 110, 30-8-40; ✠ 1 Do 17, 18-9-40.	♰ Killed since Battle (1-12-40)	British
BRINSDEN Francis Noel ("Frankie")	Fg. Off.	Pilot	19-303	On 19 Sqn., 1-7-40. Posted to 303 (Polish) Sqn., 10-40. Retired from R.A.F. as Wing Commander, 31-12-66.		New Zealander
¶ **BRISBANE, N.J.**	Plt. Off.	Pilot	65	On 65 Sqn., 1-7-40.	♰ Killed in Action (7-4-40)	British
BRITTON Allan Walter Naylor	Fg. Off.	Pilot	263	On 263 Sqn., 1-7-40. Flew operational patrols in Hurricanes during Battle.	♰ Killed since Battle (12-10-40)	British
BRITTON Henry Wilfred Arthur	Plt. Off.	Pilot	17	On 17 Sqn., 1-7-40.	♰ **Killed in Accident** (6-8-40)	British
BROADHURST Harry	Wg. Cdr.	Pilot	1	Flew sorties with 1 Sqn. during Battle, but no record of date(s). Retired (1-3-61) as Air Chief Marshal Sir Harry Broadhurst, G.C.B. (1960), K.B.E. (1945), D.S.O.✸ (4-7-41 and 19-12-41), D.F.C.✸ (2-1-40 and 29-3-42), A.F.C. (1-32-37).		British

Name	Rank	Role	Sqn.	Details	Fate	Nationality
BROADHURST John William	Plt. Off.	Pilot	222	On 222 Sqn., 1-7-40. ✢ 1 Bf 109, 31-8-40; ✢ 1 Bf 109, 4-9-40; ✢ 1 Bf 109, 7-9-40; ✢ 1 Bf 109, 27-9-40.	✟ Killed in Action (7-10-40)	British
BROOKER Richard Edgar Peter	Fg. Off.	Pilot	56	On 56 Sqn., 1-7-40. Acting Flt. Lt., 1-9-40. Awarded D.S.O.⊛ (1-12-44 and 12-2-46), D.F.C.⊛ (30-5-41 and 27-3-42). ✢ 1 Ju 87, 13-7-40; ✢ 1 Do 17, 21-8-40.	✟ Killed since Battle (16-4-45)	British
BROOKMAN Richard Waller	Sgt.	Aircrew	235	Joined 253 Sqn., c.10-10-40.	✟ Killed since Battle (22-2-41)	New Zealander
BROOM Philip William ("Basher")	Sgt.	Aircrew	25	On 25 Sqn., 1-7-40. Commissioned, 1942. Released from R.A.F. as Flight Lieutenant, 1949.		British
¶ **BROTCHIE, G.F.**	Fg. Off.	Pilot	73	On 73 Sqn., 1-7-40. Posted away, 10-7-40.		British
BROTHERS Peter Malam	Flt. Lt.	Pilot	32-257	On 32 Sqn., 1-7-40. Posted to 257 Sqn., 9-9-40. Appointed C.B.E. (1964); awarded D.S.O. (3-11-44), D.F.C.⊛ (13-9-40 and 15-6-43). ✢ 1 Bf 109, 20-7-40; ✢ 1 Bf 110, 16-8-40; ✢ 1 Do 215 and 1 Bf 109, 18-8-40; ✢ 1 Bf 109, 24-8-40; ✢ 1 Do 17 (shared), 15-9-40. Retired, 4-4-73, as Air Commodore.		British
BROWN Archibald Wilkinson	Plt. Off.	Aircrew	25	Rejoined 25 Sqn., 27-8-40, after detachment away. Released from R.A.F. in 1945 as Flight Lieutenant.		British
BROWN Bernard Walter	Plt. Off.	Pilot	610-72	Joined 610 Sqn., c.23-8-40. Posted to 72 Sqn., 20-9-40. Wounded 23-9-40.		New Zealander
BROWN Cyril Bob	Sgt.	Pilot	245	Joined 245 Sqn., 9-40. Commissioned, 10-41. Appointed C.B.E. (1966); awarded A.F.C. (1-1-46). Retired as Air Commodore, 17-1-72.		British
BROWN Charles Walter Dryburgh	Sgt.	Aircrew	236	On 236 Sqn., 1-7-40.	✟ Killed since Battle (30-6-41)	British
BROWN De Peyster	Plt. Off.	Pilot	1(Canadian)	Joined 1(Canadian) Sqn., 30-8-40. ✢ 1 Do 215 and 1 Ju 88 (shared), 27-9-40. Transferred to U.S.A.A.F., 25-5-42.		American
BROWN Frederick Sydney	Fg. Off.	Pilot	79	On 79 Sqn., 1-7-40. Commissioned, 9-41. Retired from R.A.F., 9-12-46, as Flight Lieutenant.	✟ Died since Battle (14-12-56)	British
BROWN George Alfred ("Bruno")	Fg. Off.	Pilot	253	On 253 Sqn., 1-7-40. Wounded, 30-8-40. Posted away, 10-40. Awarded D.F.C. (26-12-41). Retired from R.A.F., 6-7-62, as Group Captain.		British
BROWN James Wood	Sgt.	Pilot	600	Joined 600 Sqn., 1-7-40. Commissioned, 5-43.	✟ Killed since Battle (22-12-43)	British
BROWN Mark Henry ("Hilly")	Flt. Lt.	Pilot	1	On 1 Sqn., 1-7-40. Awarded D.F.C.⊛ (30-7-40 and 23-5-41). ✢ 1 Bf 110, 11-8-40; ✢ 1 Do 17 (shared), 24-10-40.	✟ Killed since Battle (12-11-41)	Canadian
BROWN Marvin Kitchener	Plt. Off.	Pilot	242	Rejoined 242 Sqn., 13-7-42, after recovering from wounds.	✟ Killed since Battle (21-2-41)	Canadian
BROWN Maurice Peter ("Sneezy")	Fg. Off.	Pilot	611-41	On 611 Sqn., 1-7-40. Posted to 41 Sqn., 29-9-40. Awarded A.F.C. (1-1-46). Retired from R.A.F., 1946, as Squadron Leader. ✢ 1 Bf 109, 20-10-40.		British
BROWN Peter George Fleming	Sgt.	Pilot	234	Joined 234 Sqn., 11-9-40. Commissioned, 3-42.	✟ Killed since Battle (18-4-44)	British
BROWN Ronald Clifford	Fg. Off.	Pilot	229	On 229 Sqn., 1-7-40. ✢ 1 Bf 109, 15-10-40. Released from R.A.F., 1945, as Squadron Leader.	✟ Died since Battle (19-3-88)	British
BROWN Ronald John Walker	Plt. Off.	Pilot	111	Rejoined 111 Sqn. as Sergeant, 15-8-40, after recovering from wounds. Appointed M.B.E. (post-War). ✢ 1 Do 17 (shared), 18-8-40.		British
BROWNE Charles	Sgt.	Aircrew	219	On 219 Sqn., 1-7-40. Commissioned, 8-42 (in R.A.F. Regiment). Released from R.A.F., 26-10-45, as Flying Officer.		British
BROWNE Dennis Owen Matthew	Plt. Off.	Pilot	1	On 1 Sqn., 1-7-40.	✟ Killed in Action (15-8-40)	British
BRUCE David Campbell	Fg. Off.	Pilot	111	On 111 Sqn., 1-7-40. Promoted Acting Flt. Lt., 25-8-40. ✢ 1 Bf 110, 26-8-40; ✢ 1 He 111 (shared), 2-9-40.	✟ Killed in Action (4-9-40)	British
BRUMBY Norman	Sgt.	Pilot	615-607	Joined 615 Sqn., 4-9-40. Posted to 617 Sqn., 21-9-40.	✟ Killed in Action (1-10-40)	British
BRUNNER Geoffrey Clifford	Plt. Off.	Pilot	43	On 43 Sqn., 1-7-40. Wounded, 26-8-40. Awarded A.F.C.⊛ (1-1-42 and 21-7-43). Retired from R.A.F., 1-7-66, as Group Captain.		British
¶ **BRYANT, R.F.**	Sub-Lt.	Pilot	263-219-245	Fleet Air Arm. On 263 Sqn., 1-7-40; posted to 219 Sqn., 10-7-40; posted to 245 Sqn., 13-7-45. Posted away, c.20-7-40. May not have flown operationally.		British
BRYANT-FENN Leofric Trevor	Fg. Off.	Pilot	79	On 79 Sqn., 1-7-40. Wounded, 1-9-40. Awarded D.F.C. (3-9-43). ✢ 1 He 59, (shared), 28-8-40. Retired from R.A.F., 19-10-68, as Group Captain.		British
BRYSON John	Plt. Off.	Pilot	92	On 92 Sqn., 1-7-40. ✢ 1 Ju 88 (shared), 24-7-40.	✟ Killed in Action (24-9-40)	Canadian
BRZEZINA Stanislaw	Flt. Lt.	Pilot	74	Joined 74 Sqn., 5-8-40. ✢ 1 Do 17, 13-8-40. Posted away, 25-9-40.	✟ Killed since Battle (13-2-46)	Polish
BRZEZOWSKI Michal	Sgt.	Pilot	303	Joined 303 (Polish) Sqn., 21-8-40. ✢ 2 He 111s, 11-9-40.	✟ Killed in Action (15-9-40)	Polish
BUCHANAN Jack	Plt. Off.	Pilot	29	On 29 Sqn., 1-7-40.	✟ Killed since Battle (15-2-41)	British
BUCHANAN James Richebourg ("Buck")	Plt. Off.	Pilot	609	On 609 Sqn., 1-7-40.	✟ Killed in Action (27-7-40)	British
BUCHIN Maurice Simon Henri Charles	Plt. Off.	Pilot	213	Joined 213 Sqn., 23-7-40. ✢ 1 Ju 88, 11-8-40.	✟ Killed in Action (15-8-40)	Belgian
BUCK James Alan	Sgt.	Pilot	43	On 43 Sqn., 1-7-40.	✟ Killed in Action (19-7-40)	British
¶ **BUCKLAND**	Plt. Off.	Pilot	74	Joined 74 Sqn., 28-9-40. Did not fly operationally before death.	✟ Killed in Accident (9-10-40)	British
BUCKNOLE John Stanley	Sgt.	Pilot	54	Joined 54 Sqn., 29-9-40.	✟ Killed since Battle (24-7-41)	British
BUDD George Oliver	Flt. Lt.	Pilot	604	On 604 Sqn., 1-7-40. Awarded D.F.C. (4-7-41). Retired from R.A.F., 8-9-45, as Wing Commander.		British
BUDZINSKI Jan	Sgt.	Pilot	145-605	Joined 145 Sqn., 12-8-40. ✢ 1 Bf 109, 11-9-40; ✢ 1 Bf 110, 27-9-40; ✢ 1 Bf 109 (shared), 7-10-40. Left R.A.F., 1945, as Warrant Officer.		Polish
BULL Cecil Halford	Flt. Lt.	Pilot	25	On 25 Sqn., 1-7-40. Killed in shooting accident whilst on leave.	✟ Killed in Accident (8-8-40)	British
BULL John Cecil	Plt. Off.	Aircrew	600	On 600 Sqn., 1-7-40. Retired from the R.A.F., 19-11-62, retained rank of Squadron Leader.	✟ Died since Battle (1965)	British
BULMER Geoffrey Gordon Robson	Sub-Lieut.	Pilot	32	Joined 32 Sqn., 1-7-40.	✟ Killed in Action (20-7-40)	British
BUMSTEAD Ronald Frederick	Sgt.	Pilot	29-111	On 29 Sqn., 1-7-40. Posted to 111 Sqn., 26-8-40. Commissioned, 10-43. Awarded A.F.C. (1-1-46). Released from R.A.F., 6-46, as Flight Lieutenant.	✟ Died since Battle (1-10-77)	British
BUNCH Douglas Campbell	Sgt.	Aircrew	219	Joined 219 Sqn., 2-8-40. Commissioned, 1-42. Awarded D.S.O. (21-9-45), D.F.C.⊛ (13-7-43 and 9-3-45). Retired from R.A.F., 1-5-68, retaining rank of Wing Commander.	✟ Died since Battle (1972)	British
BUNCH Samuel Hoskin	Sub-Lieut.	Pilot	804	Fleet Air Arm. On 804 Sqn., 1-7-40.	✟ Killed since Battle (11-5-41)	British
BUNGEY Robert Wilton	Flt. Lt.	Pilot	145	Joined 145 Sqn., 20-9-40. Awarded D.F.C. (7-10-41).	✟ Died since Battle (10-6-43)	Australian
BURDA Frantisek	Plt. Off.	Pilot	310	Joined 310 (Czech) Sqn., end of 8-40.	✟ Died since Battle (2-88)	Czech
BURDEKIN Alan George	Sgt.	Aircrew	600	Joined 600 Sqn., 6-7-40. Posted away 21-9-40. Commissioned, 1-43. Released from R.A.F., 29-12-45, as Flying Officer.		British
BURGESS John Henry Bateman	Sgt.	Pilot	222	Joined 222 Sqn., 29-7-40. ✢ 1 Bf 109, 7-9-40; ✢ 1 Bf 109, 15-9-40; ✢ 1 Bf 109, 29-10-40. Released from R.A.F., 23-11-45, as Flight Lieutenant.	✟ Died since Battle (1988)	British
BURGOYNE Eric	Plt. Off.	Pilot	19	On 19 Sqn., 1-7-40.	✟ Killed in Action (27-9-40)	British
BURLEY Peter Slater	Sgt.	Aircrew	600	Joined 600 Sqn., 16-9-40. Record of operations not traced.	✟ Died since Battle (1978)	British
BURNARD Fred Percy	F/Sgt.	Pilot	616-74	On 616 Sqn., 1-7-40. Posted to 74 Sqn., 27-10-40. Commissioned, 3-41. Released from R.A.F. in 1947 as Squadron Leader.		British
BURNELL-PHILLIPS Peter Anthony	Sgt.	Pilot	607	Joined 607 Sqn., 7-40. Slightly wounded, 9-9-40. Awarded D.F.M. (1-11-40). Commissioned, 11-40. ✢ 1 Bf 110, 15-8-40; ✢ 1 Do 17, 9-9-40; ✢ 1 Do 215, 26-9-40; ✢ 1 Bf 110, 30-9-40.	✟ Killed since Battle (9-2-41)	British
BURNETT Norman Whitmore	Fg. Off.	Pilot	266-46	On 266 Sqn., 1-7-40. Posted to 46 Sqn., 25-7-40. Wounded, 8-9-40.	✟ Killed since Battle (11-6-41)	British
BURNS Owen Valentine	Sgt.	Aircrew	235	On 235 Sqn., 1-7-40. Commissioned, 2-43. Retired from R.A.F. in 1949 as Flight Lieutenant.		British

Name	Rank	Aircrew/Pilot	Sqn.	Details	Fate	Nationality
BURNS William Richard	Sgt.	Aircrew	236	Joined 236 Sqn., 6-7-40. Commissioned, 12-43. Released from R.A.F. as Flight Lieutenant.	✝ Died since Battle (23-5-49)	New Zealander
BURT Alfred Denmark	Sgt.	Pilot	611-603	On 611 Sqn., 1-7-40. Commissioned, 8-42. Awarded A.F.C.✧ (14-6-45 and 1-1-55). Retired from the R.A.F., 27-7-58, as Squadron Leader. ✠ 1 Do 17 (shared), 21-8-40.	✝ Died since Battle (17-3-80)	British
BURTENSHAW Allan Anthony	Sgt.	Pilot	54	Joined 54 Sqn., 29-9-40.	✝ Killed since Battle (12-3-41)	British
BURTON Cyril George	F/Sgt.	Pilot	23	On 23 Sqn., 1-7-40. Commissioned, 5-41. Released from the R.A.F. in 1945 as a Flight Lieutenant.		British
BURTON Douglas Lawrence	Sgt.	Aircrew	248	Joined 248 Sqn., 12-10-40. Wounded and made P.O.W., 20-10-40.	✝ Died since Battle (20-11-74)	New Zealander
BURTON Howard Frizelle	Flt. Lt.	Pilot	66-616	On 66 Sqn., 1-7-40. Promoted to Sqn. Ldr., and posted to 616 Sqn., 3-9-40, to command. Awarded D.S.O. (6-4-43), D.F.C.✧ (19-9-41 and 23-2-43).	✝ Killed since Battle (3-6-43)	British
BURTON Leslie Gilbert	Plt. Off.	Aircrew	236	Joined 236 Sqn., 19-7-40.	✝ Killed since Battle (24-12-40)	British
BURTON Percival Ross-Frames	Plt. Off.	Pilot	249	Joined 249 Sqn., 21-7-40. ✠ 1 Bf 110, 27-9-40.	✝ **Killed in Action** (27-9-40)	South African
BUSH Basil Martin	Sgt.	Pilot	504	On 504 Sqn., 1-7-40. Commissioned, 7-41. Awarded D.F.C. (23-3-45). Released from R.A.F., 1945, as Flight Lieutenant.		British
BUSH Charles Roy	Plt. Off.	Pilot	242	On 242 Sqn., 1-7-40. Awarded D.F.C. (30-9-41). ✠ 1 Bf 110, 9-9-40; ✠ 1 Bf 109, 27-9-40. Transferred to R.N.Z.A.F., 3-46.	✝ Killed since Battle (30-11-48)	New Zealander
BUSHELL George Downs	Sgt.	Pilot	213	On 213 Sqn., 1-7-40. ✠ 2 Bf 110s, 12-8-40; ✠ 1 Bf 110, 14-8-40.	✝ Killed since Battle (31-12-40)	British
BUTTERFIELD Samuel Leslie	Sgt.	Pilot	213	On 213 Sqn., 1-7-40. Had been awarded the D.F.M. (14-6-40).	✝ **Killed in Action** (11-8-40)	British
BUTTERICK Alec Frank	Sgt.	Pilot	3-232	On 3 Sqn., 1-7-40. Posted to 232 Sqn., 18-7-40, of formation of Squadron. Commissioned, 9-45, and served in R.A.F. post-War as Flying Officer. No record of operational flying traced.		British
BUTTERWORTH Kenneth	Sgt.	Aircrew	23			British
BYNG-HALL Percy	Plt. Off.	Aircrew	29	Joined 29 Sqn., 7-7-40. No record of operational flying traced.		British
BYRNE Edward Lawrence	A.C.1	Aircrew	F.I.U.	On F.I.U., 1-7-40. Crashed in Channel, 13-9-40, and taken prisoner. Left the R.A.F. in 1945 as Warrant Officer.		British
CAIN Anthony Richard	Sgt.	Aircrew	235	On 235 Sqn., 1-7-40. Flew operational sorties during the Battle of Britain.	✝ Killed since Battle (15-6-41)	British
CAISTER James Russell	Plt. Off.	Pilot	603	On 603 Sqn., 1-7-40. Commissioned, 8-40. Awarded D.F.M. (13-9-40). ✠ 1 Ju 88 (shared), 3-7-40; ✠ 1 Do 215 (shared), 6-7-40; ✠ 1 He 111 (shared), 12-7-40; ✠ 1 Bf 109, 3-9-40.		British
CALDERHEAD George Douglas	Plt. Off.	Pilot	54	Joined 54 Sqn., 28-9-40.	✝ Killed since Battle (12-1-42)	British
CALDERWOOD Thomas Morrow	Sgt.	Pilot	85	Joined 85 Sqn., 23-9-40. Commissioned 7-41. Released from R.A.F. in 1946 as Flight Lieutenant.	✝ Died since Battle (28-9-57)	British
CALE Francis Walter	Plt. Off.	Pilot	266	On 266 Sqn., 1-7-40.	✝ **Killed in Action** (15-8-40)	Australian
¶ **CALTHORPE**	Sgt.	Aircrew	25	Joined 25 Sqn., c.25-7-40. No record of operations traced.		British
CAMBRIDGE William Percival ("Bill")	Flt. Lt.	Pilot	253	On 253 Sqn., 1-7-40. Assumed temporary command of Squadron, 1-9-40.	✝ **Killed in Accident** (6-9-40)	British
CAMERON James Douglas	Sgt.	Aircrew	604	Known to have flown on operations with 604 Sqn. during Battle.	✝ Killed since Battle (9-5-42)	British
CAMERON Matthew	F/Sgt.	Pilot	66	On 66 Sqn., 1-7-40. Commissioned, 3-41. ✠ 1 Bf 110, 20-8-40; ✠ 1 Ju 88, 27-9-40. Released from R.A.F., 1945, as Flight Lieutenant.		British
CAMERON Neil	Sgt.	Pilot	1-17	Joined 1 Sqn., 26-9-40. Posted to 17 Sqn., 15-10-40. Commissioned, 7-41. Created life peer (1-1-83) as Marshal of the Royal Air Force Baron Cameron of Balhousie, K.T. (1983), G.C.B. (1976), C.B.E.(1967), D.S.O.(2-10-45), D.F.C. (21-11-44).	✝ Died since Battle (29-1-85)	British
CAMPBELL Alan	L.A.C.	Aircrew	264	Defiant gunner. Joined 264 Sqn., c.16-7-40. Promoted Sergeant, c.30-7-40.	✝ Killed since Battle (29-7-42)	New Zealander
CAMPBELL Alan Roberts McLeod	Plt. Off.	Pilot	54	On 54 Sqn., 1-7-40. Slightly wounded, 7-7-40. ✠ 1 Bf 109, 18-8-40. Joined R.C.A.F., 8-51. Retired, 17-10-56, as Wing Commander.	✝ Died since Battle (9-74)	Canadian
CAMPBELL Alexander Middleton	Flt. Lt.	Pilot	29	On 29 Sqn., 1-7-40. Retired as Wing Commander, 17-10-56.	✝ Died since Battle (1979)	British
CAMPBELL David Baillie	Sgt.	Aircrew	23	Joined 23 Sqn., 6-10-40. Took discharge from Service, 8-4-44.	✝ Died since Battle (6-84)	New Zealander
CAMPBELL Donald Cairnie Ogilvie	Sgt.	Pilot	66	Served on 66 Sqn. during Battle; no record of operations traced.		British
CAMPBELL Gillian Lorne	Plt. Off.	Pilot	236	Joined 236 Sqn., 5-8-40. Awarded D.F.C. (30-1-42)	✝ Killed since Battle (23-12-42)	British
CAMPBELL Norman Neil	Plt. Off.	Pilot	242	On 242 Sqn., 1-7-40. ✠ 1 Ju 88 (plus two Ju 88s shared), 18-9-40.	✝ **Killed in Action** (17-10-40)	Canadian
CAMPBELL-COLQUHOUN Ernest William	Flt. Lt.	Pilot	66-264	On 66 Sqn., 1-7-40. Posted to 264 Sqn., 21-8-40. Left the R.A.F. in 1946 as a Squadron Leader.	✝ Died since Battle (1989)	British
CANDY Robert John ("Jack")	Plt. Off.	Aircrew	25	On 25 Sqn., 1-7-40. Posted overseas, end of 7-40. Left the R.A.F. in 1945 as a Flight Lieutenant.		British
CANHAM Arthur William	Sgt.	Aircrew	600	On 600 Sqn., 1-7-40. Flew on night patrols in Blenheims. Medically discharged from R.A.F., 9-2-43.		British
CANNON Bernard	A.C.2	Aircrew	604	Joined 604 Sqn., 20-7-40. Promoted Sergeant later. Awarded D.F.M. (24-6-41). Released from the R.A.F. in 1945 as Warrant Officer.	✝ Died since Battle (17-9-83)	British
CAPEL Bernard	Sgt.	Aircrew	23	On 23 Sqn., 1-7-40. Awarded D.F.M. (15-8-41)		British
CAPON Cardale Frederick Alexander	Plt. Off.	Pilot	257	On 257 Sqn., 1-7-40. ✠ 1 He 111, 12-8-40; ✠ 1 Ju 88, 13-8-40. Slightly wounded, 12-10-40.	✝ Killed since Battle (1-1-41)	British
CAPSTICK Herbert	Plt. Off.	Aircrew	236	Joined 236 Sqn., 15-7-40. Released from the R.A.F. in 1946 as Squadron Leader.		Jamaican
CARBURY Brian John George	Fg. Off.	Pilot	603	On 603 Sqn., 1-7-40. Awarded D.F.C.✧ (24-9-40 and 25-10-40). ✠ 1 Ju 88 (shared), 3-7-40; ✠ 1 Bf 109, 29-8-40; ✠ 1 Bf 109, 30-8-40; ✠ 5 Bf 109s, 31-8-40; ✠ 1 Bf 109, 2-9-40; ✠ 2 Bf 109s, 7-9-40; ✠ 1 Bf 109, 14-9-40; ✠ 1 Bf 109, 2-10-40; ✠ 1 Bf 109, 7-10-40; ✠ 2 Bf 109s, 10-10-40.	✝ Died since Battle (7-62)	New Zealander
CARDELL Philip Melville	Plt. Off.	Pilot	263-603	On 263 Sqn., 1-7-40. Posted to 603 Sqn., 3-7-40. ✠ 1 Bf 109, 27-9-40.	✝ **Killed in Action** (27-9-40)	British
CARDNELL Charles Frederick	Plt. Off.	Pilot	23	On 23 Sqn., 1-7-40.	✝ **Killed in Action** (8-8-40)	British
CAREY Frank Reginald	Plt. Off.	Pilot	43	On 43 Sqn., 1-7-40. ✠ 1 Bf 110, 9-7-40; ✠ 1 Ju 88, 12-8-40; ✠ 1 Ju 88, 13-8-40; ✠ 2 Ju 87s, 16-8-40. Appointed C.B.E. (11-6-60); awarded D.F.C.✧✧ (31-5-40, 31-5-40 and 24-3-42), A.F.C. (1-1-45), D.F.M. (1-3-40). Retired from the R.A.F. as Group Captain, 2-6-60.		British
CARLIN Sydney ("Timbertoes")	Plt. Off.	Aircrew	264	Had won the M.C., D.F.C. and D.C.M. during First World War (losing a leg). Joined 264 Sqn., 8-40, as Defiant gunner.	✝ Killed since Battle (9-5-41)	British
CARNABY William Fleming	Fg. Off.	Pilot	264-85	On 264 Sqn., 1-7-40. Posted to 85 Sqn., 9-40.	✝ Killed since Battle (5-2-43)	British
CARNALL Ralph	Sgt.	Pilot	111	On 111 Sqn., 1-7-40. Badly wounded, 16-8-40. Commissioned, 3-42. Retired from R.A.F., 24-8-63, as Squadron Leader.	✝ Died since Battle (1984)	British
CARPENTER Jack Conway	Sub-Lieut.	Pilot	229-46	Fleet Air Arm. Joined 229 Sqn., 9-7-40. Posted to 46 Sqn., 23-7-40. ✠ 1 Bf 110, 3-9-40; ✠ 1 Bf 109, 5-9-40.	✝ **Killed in Action** (8-9-40)	British
CARPENTER John Michael Vowles	Plt. Off.	Pilot	222	On 222 Sqn., 1-7-40. Awarded D.F.C.✧ (2-1-42 and 7-7-44). Wounded, 9-40. ✠ 1 Bf 109, 1-9-40; ✠ 1 Bf 110, 3-9-40; ✠ 1 Bf 109, 4-9-40.		British

Name	Rank	Role	Sqn	Details	Status	Nationality
CARR William Joseph	Fg. Off.	Pilot	235	On 235 Sqn., 1-7-40. Awarded A.F.C. (1-7-41).	✝ Killed since Battle (26-8-42)	British
CARRIERE Jean Charles	Fg. Off.	Pilot	219	On 219 Sqn., 1-7-40. Slightly injured, 6-8-40. Released from R.C.A.F., 28-11-45, as Flight Lieutenant.		Canadian
CARR-LEWTY Robert Albert	Sgt.	Pilot	41	On 41 Sqn., 1-7-40. Commissioned, 6-41. Awarded A.F.C. (1-1-45). ✠ **1 Bf 109, 29-7-40.** Left the R.A.F. in 1946.		British
CARSWELL Malcolm Keith	Fg. Off.	Pilot	43	On 43 Sqn., 1-7-40. Wounded, 2-9-40. Promoted Flight Lieutenant, 5-10-40. Released from R.A.F., 26-1-46, as Squadron Leader.		New Zealander
CARTER Charles Albert William	Fg. Off.	Pilot	611	No record of flying operations traced. Released from R.A.F., 1946.	✝ Died since Battle (1960)	British
CARTER Leslie Raymond	Sgt.	Pilot	66-610-41	Joined 66 Sqn., 28-8-40. Posted to 610 Sqn., 10-9-40. Posted to 41 Sqn., 1-10-40.	**Killed in Action** (11-10-40)	British
CARTER Peter Edward George	Plt. Off.	Pilot	73-302	On 73 Sqn., 1-7-40. Posted to 302 (Polish) Sqn., 24-8-40. ✠ **2 Ju 88, 15-8-40.**	✝ Killed in Action (18-10-40)	British
CARTER Victor Arthur	Plt. Off.	Pilot	607	Joined 607 Sqn., 10-40. Released from R.A.F., 1945, as Flight Lieutenant.		British
CARTHEW Gerald Charles Trewalla	Plt. Off.	Pilot	253-85-145	On 253 Sqn., 1-7-40. Posted to 85 Sqn., 20-9-40. Posted to 145 Sqn., 14-10-40. Released from R.A.F., 1946, as Flight Lieutenant.		British
CARVER John Champion	Plt. Off.	Pilot	87	Joined 87 Sqn., 1-10-40. Awarded D.F.C. (10-4-42).	✝ Killed since Battle (6-6-42)	British
CARVER Kenneth Maltby	Plt. Off.	Pilot	29-229	On 29 Sqn., 1-7-40. Posted to 229 Sqn., 17-7-40. Wounded, 11-9-40. Released from R.A.F., 1946, as Squadron Leader.		British
CARVER Rodney Harold Power	Lieut.	Pilot	804	Fleet Air Arm. Appointed C.B.E., (13-6-59). Awarded D.S.C., (10-11-42). Retired from Royal Navy, 1-3-66, as Captain.		British
CASE Herbert Robert	Plt. Off.	Pilot	64-72	Joined 64 Sqn., 28-8-40. Posted to 72 Sqn., c.20-9-40.	**Killed in Action** (12-10-40)	British
CASSIDY Ernest	Plt. Off.	Pilot	25-249	On 25 Sqn., 1-7-40. Posted to 249 Sqn., 21-10-40. Awarded D.F.C. (2-1-42), A.F.C. (5-6-52). Retired from R.A.F., 1-6-58, retaining rank of Wing Commander.		British
CASSON Lionel Harwood ("Buck")	Plt. Off.	Pilot	616	On 616 Sqn., 1-7-40. Awarded D.F.C. (16-9-41), A.F.C. (1-6-53, with R.Aux.A.F.). ✠ **1 Do 17, 1-9-40.** Released from R.A.F., 12-11-45; joined R.Aux.A.F., 3-5-47.		British
CASTLE Colin Edward Patrick	Aircrew		219	On 219 Sqn., 1-7-40.	✝ Killed since Battle (13-11-40)	British
CAVE John Geoffrey	Fg. Off.	Pilot	600	On 600 Sqn., 1-7-40. Posted away, 11-8-40. Promoted Flt. Lt., 3-9-40.	✝ Died since Battle (1962)	British
CAWSE Frederick Norman	Plt. Off.	Pilot	238	Joined 238 Sqn., 7-7-40.	✝ Killed in Action (11-8-40)	British
CEBRZYNSKI Arsen	Fg. Off.	Pilot	303	Joined 303 (Polish) Sqn., 21-8-40. Shot down and mortally wounded, 11-9-40.	✝ Died of Wounds (19-9-40)	Polish
CHABERA Frantisek	Sgt.	Pilot	312	Joined 312 (Czech) Sqn., 5-9-40. Commissioned later. Released from R.A.F., 1945, as Squadron Leader.	✝ Died since Battle (1973)	Czech
CHADWICK Dennis Frederick	Sgt.	Pilot	64	Served on 64 Sqn. during Battle of Britain, but no details traced. Commissioned, 7-41. Released from R.A.F., 1945, as Squadron Leader.	✝ Died since Battle (1973)	British
CHAFFE Ronald Ivor	Plt. Off.	Pilot	245-43	On 245 Sqn., 1-7-40. Posted to 43 Sqn., 18-9-40.	✝ Killed since Battle (22-2-42)	British
CHALDER Harry Hutchinson	Plt. Off.	Pilot	266-41	On 266 Sqn., 1-7-40. Posted to 41 Sqn., 15-9-40. Wounded, 13-8-40. Shot down and mortally wounded, 28-9-40.	✝ Died of Wounds (10-11-40)	British
CHALLONER-LINDSEY Patrick	Plt. Off.	Pilot	601	On 601 Sqn., 1-7-40. ✠ **1 Bf 110, 11-7-40.**	✝ Killed in Action (27-7-40)	British
CHALUPA Stanislaw Jozef	Plt. Off.	Pilot	302	Joined 302 (Polish) Sqn., 23-7-40. ✠ **1 Do 17, 15-9-40.**		Polish
CHAMBERLAIN George Philip ("Joe")	Wg. Cdr.	Pilot	F.I.U.	In command of F.I.U., 1-7-40. Appointed C.B. (13-6-46), O.B.E. (24-9-41). Retired from R.A.F., 25-9-60, as Air Vice-Marshal.		British
CHAMBERLAIN Joseph Thomas Ronald	Plt. Off.	Pilot	235	Joined 235 Sqn., 5-8-40. Released from R.A.F., 1946, as Flight Lieutenant.		British
CHANDLER Horatio Herbert	Sgt.	Pilot	610	On 610 Sqn., 1-7-40. Commissioned, 6-41. Awarded A.F.C. (2-4-43), D.F.M. (22-10-40). ✠ **1 Bf 109, 25-7-40; ✠ 1 Bf 109, 14-8-40; ✠ 1 Do 215, 18-8-40; ✠ 1 Bf 109, 30-8-40.**		British
CHAPMAN Victor Ronald	Sgt.	Aircrew	264	Defiant gunner. Joined 264 Sqn., 7-40.		British
CHAPPELL Alan Kingsley	Plt. Off.	Pilot	236	Joined 236 Sqn., 15-8-40. Promoted Flight Lieutenant, 2-6-42. No further Service details traced.		British
CHAPPELL Charles Gordon	Plt. Off.	Pilot	65-609	Joined 65 Sqn., 19-8-40. Posted to 609 Sqn., 9-10-40. Promoted Flying Officer, 3-9-40. Released from R.A.F., 1945, as Squadron Leader.		British
CHAPPLE Douglas William Ernest	Sgt.	Aircrew	236	Joined 236 Sqn., 19-7-40.	✝ Killed since Battle (28-6-41)	British
CHARD Wilfred Thomas	Sgt.	Aircrew	141	Defiant gunner. On 141 Sqn., 1-7-40. Survived Battle of Britain.		British
CHARLES Edward Francis John	Fg. Off.	Pilot	54	Joined 54 Sqn., 3-9-40. Awarded D.S.O. (29-10-43), D.F.C.✠ (15-7-41 and 16-7-43). Transferred to R.C.A.F., 14-4-44.		Canadian
CHARNOCK Gerard	A.C.1	Aircrew	25	Joined 25 Sqn., c.25-9-40. Promoted Sergeant, 10-40.		British
CHARNOCK Harry Walpole	Sgt.	Pilot	64-19	On 64 Sqn., 1-7-40. Posted to 19 Sqn., 10-40. Commissioned, 1-43. Awarded D.F.C. (26-2-43), D.F.M. (7-4-42).	✝ Died since Battle (24-5-74)	British
CHATER George Frederick	Flt. Lt.	Pilot	247-3	In command of 247 Sqn., 1-8-40, on formation. Promoted Squadron Leader, 1-9-40, and post to No. 3 Sqn. to command, 22-9-40. Awarded D.F.C., 13-9-40.		South African
CHEETHAM John Cowper	Sgt.	Aircrew	23	On 23 Sqn., 1-7-40. Commissioned, 7-41.	✝ Killed since Battle (15-7-44)	British
CHELMECKI Marian	Plt. Off.	Pilot	56-17	Joined 56 Sqn., 31-8-40. Posted to 17 Sqn., 9-9-40. Released from R.A.F., 8-8-46, as Flight Lieutenant.	✝ Died since Battle (28-3-88)	Polish
CHESTERS Peter	Plt. Off.	Pilot	74	Joined 74 Sqn., 28-9-40. ✠ **1 Bf 109, 27-10-40.**	✝ Killed since Battle (10-4-41)	British
CHETHAM Charles Arthur Copeland	Plt. Off.	Pilot	1	On 1 Sqn., 1-7-40. ✠ **1 Bf 110 (shared), 11-8-40; ✠ 1 Bf 109, 1-9-40.**	✝ Killed since Battle (15-4-41)	British
CHEVRIER Joseph Armand Jacques	Plt. Off.	Pilot	1-1(Canadian)	Joined 1 Sqn., 3-10-40. Posted to 1 (Canadian) Sqn., 21-10-40.	✝ Killed since Battle (6-7-42)	Canadian
CHEW Clifford Archibald	Sgt.	Pilot	17	Joined 17 Sqn., 15-7-40. Commissioned, 1-42. Awarded A.F.C. (25-8-44). ✠ **1 Ju 88 (shared), 21-8-40.**	✝ Killed since Battle (24-3-45)	British
CHIGNELL Robert Alexander	Sqn. Ldr.	Pilot	145	Not on strength of 145 Sqn., though assumed to have flown at least one operational sortie. Promoted Wing Commander, 1-9-40.	✝ Killed since Battle (14-2-42)	British
CHILTON Patrick Charles Stuart	Sub-Lt.	Pilot	804	Fleet Air Arm. Joined 804 Sqn., 1-7-40. Awarded A.F.C. (1-1-59). Retired from Royal Navy, 5-4-71, as Captain.		British
CHIPPING Douglas James	Sgt.	Pilot	222	Joined 222 Sqn., c.28-7-40. Wounded, 5-9-40. Commissioned, 5-41. Awarded A.F.C. (1-1-46). Released from R.A.F., 1946, as Flight Lieutenant.	✝ Died since Battle (1985)	British
CHISHOLM Roderick Aeneas ("Rory")	Fg. Off.	Pilot	604	On 604 Sqn., 1-7-40. Appointed C.B.E. (1-1-46); awarded D.S.O. (14-1-44), D.F.C.✠ (11-4-41 and 10-2-42). Released from R.A.F., 1-1-46, as Air Commodore.		British
CHLOPIK Tadeusz	Flt. Lt.	Pilot	302	Joined 302 (Polish) Sqn., 3-8-40. ✠ **1 Do 17 (shared), 15-9-40.**	✝ Killed in Action (15-9-40)	Polish
CHOMLEY John Allison George	Plt. Off.	Pilot	257	Joined 257 Sqn., 7-7-40.	✝ Killed in Action (12-8-40)	Rhodesian
CHORON Maurice Philipe Cesar	Adj.	Pilot	64	Joined 64 Sqn., 11-10-40.	✝ Killed since Battle (10-4-42)	French
CHRISTIE George Patterson	Fg. Off.	Pilot	242-66	Joined 242 Sqn., 21-7-40. Posted to 66 Sqn., 3-9-40. Awarded D.F.C.✠ (21-8-40 and 14-1-41). ✠ **1 He 111, 30-8-40; ✠ 1 Bf 109, 4-9-40.** Wounded, 5-9-40.	✝ Killed since Battle (6-7-42)	Canadian
CHRISTIE John McBean	Sgt.	Pilot	152	Joined 152 Sqn., 1-7-40.	✝ Killed in Action (26-9-40)	British
CHRISTMAS Beverley E.	Plt. Off.	Pilot	1(Canadian)	On 1(Canadian) Sqn., 20-6-40, on arrival in U.K. ✠ **1 Bf 109, 30-8-40; ✠ 1 Ju 88 (shared), 27-9-40; ✠ 1 Bf 109, 5-10-40.** Retired from R.C.A.F., 5-7-73, as Colonel.	✝ Died since Battle (17-5-88)	Canadian
CHRYSTALL Colin	Sgt.	Aircrew	235	On 235 Sqn., 1-7-40. Commissioned, 3-8-41. Awarded D.F.C. (15-1-45). Transferred to R.N.Z.A.F., 1-7-45; released, 20-7-46.	✝ Died since Battle (28-7-61)	New Zealander

CHURCHES Edward Waler Gilles	Plt. Off.	Pilot	74	Joined 74 Sqn., 21-8-40. ✠ **1 Bf 109, 30-10-40.**	♀	Killed since Battle (19-4-41)	New Zealander
CHURCHILL Walter Myers	Sqn. Ldr.	Pilot	605	In command of 605 Sqn., 1-7-40. Posted away, 29-9-40. Awarded D.S.O. (31-5-40), D.F.C. (31-5-40). Was Group Captain at time of death.	♀	Killed since Battle (26-8-42)	British
CIZEK Evzen	Plt. Off.	Pilot	1	Joined 1 Sqn., 14-10-40. Was Group Captain at time of death.	♀	Killed since Battle (26-11-42)	Czech
CLACKSON David Laurence	Flt. Lt.	Pilot	600	On 600 Sqn., 1-7-40. Appointed M.B.E. (14-6-45). Released from R.A.F., 1946, as Wing Commander.			British
CLANDILLON James Albert	Sgt.	Pilot	219	Joined 219 Sqn., 22-8-40. Commissioned, 3-42.	♀	Killed since Battle (18-2-43)	British
CLARK Colin Anthony Gordon ("Nobby")	Plt. Off.	Pilot	F.I.U.	On F.I.U., 1-7-40.	♀	Killed since Battle (30-10-41)	South African
CLARK David de Brassey	Sqn. Ldr.	Pilot	600	In command of 600 Sqn., 1-7-40. Posted away, 14-9-40. Appointed C.B.E. (1-1-45). Released from R.A.F., 1945, as Group Captain.			British
CLARK Godfrey Percival	Sgt.	Aircrew	604	Joined 604 Sqn., 16-8-40. Commissioned, 3-43. Awarded D.F.C. (13-10-44) Released from R.A.F., 1947, as Flight Lieutenant.			British
CLARK Hugh Desmond	Fg. Off.	Pilot	213	Joined 213 Sqn., 19-8-40. Retired from R.A.F., 1-10-60, as Wing Commander.			British
CLARK William Terence	Sgt.	Aircrew	219	Joined 219 Sqn., 10-8-40. Awarded D.F.M. (8-7-41). Commissioned, 18-5-42. Released from R.A.F., 11-45, as Flight Lieutenant.			British
CLARKE Arthur William	Plt. Off	Pilot	504	On 504 Sqn., 1-7-40.	♀	**Killed in Action** (11-9-40)	British
CLARKE Gordon Stuart	Sgt.	Aircrew	248	On 248 Sqn., 1-7-40. Flew on reconnaissance sorties during Battle.	♀	**Killed in Action** (1-10-40)	British
CLARKE Gordon Thomas	Sgt.	Pilot	151	Joined 151 Sqn., 15-7-40. Wounded, 24-8-40. Commissioned, 5-3-53. Awarded A.F.C. (7-9-45). Remained in R.A.F. after War.	♀	Killed since Battle (11-8-53)	British
CLARKE Henry Reginald	Sgt.	Pilot	66-610	Joined 66 Sqn., 28-8-40. Posted to 610 Sqn., 12-9-40. Commissioned, 8-41. Released from R.A.F., 2-5-47, as Flight Lieutenant.			British
CLARKE Ronald Neville ("Nobby")	Sqn. Ldr.	Pilot	235	In command of 235 Sqn., 1-7-40. Awarded D.F.C. (17-1-41)	♀	Died since Battle (4-3-41)	British
CLARKE Raymond Walker	Plt. Off.	Pilot	79-238	Joined 79 Sqn., c.23-9-40. Posted to 238 Sqn., 3-10-40. ✠ **1 He 111 (shared), 27-9-40.**	♀	Killed since Battle (16-11-40)	British
¶ **CLAYTON**	Plt. Off.	Pilot	600	On 600 Sqn., 1-7-40. Posted away before 10-7-40.			British
CLEAVER Gordon Neil Spencer ("Mouse")	Fg. Off.	Pilot	601	On 601 Sqn., 1-7-40. Awarded D.F.C. (13-9-40). Severely wounded, 15-8-40. Released from R.A.F., 1943, as Flight Lieutenant.			British
CLENSHAW Ian Charles Cooper	Sgt.	Pilot	253	On 253 Sqn., 1-7-40. Was first R.A.F. casualty in the Battle of Britain.	♀	**Killed in Action** (10-7-40)	British
CLERKE Rupert Francis Henry	Flt. Lt.	Pilot	32-79	On 32 Sqn., 1-7-40. Posted to 79 Sqn., 25-7-40. Awarded D.F.C. (23-7-43). ✠ **1 He 111 (shared), 9-7-40; ✠ 1 Do 17 and 1 Bf 110 (both shared), 28-8-40; ✠ 1 He 59 (shared), 28-8-40; ✠ 1 He 111 (shared), 27-9-40.** Retired from R.A.F., 9-8-65, as Group Captain.			British
CLIFT Douglas Gerald	Plt. Off.	Pilot	79	On 79 Sqn., 1-7-40. ✠ **1 Bf 109, 15-8-40; ✠ 1 He 111 (shared), 30-8-40.** Retired from R.A.F., 2-7-74, as Squadron Leader.			British
CLIFTON John Kenneth Grahame ("Curly")	Plt. Off.	Pilot	253	On 253 Sqn., 1-7-40.	♀	**Killed in Action** (1-9-40)	British
¶ **CLIVE**	Plt. Off.	Pilot	264	Joined 264 Sqn., 9-40. Did not fly any operational sortie.			British
CLOUSTON Arthur Edmund	Sqn. Ldr.	Pilot	219	Flew with the R.A.E. during Battle, and attached to 219 Sqn., 18-10-40. Appointed C.B.; awarded D.S.O. (14-4-44), D.F.C. (1-10-43), A.F.C.✱ (1-1-38 and 1-1-42). Retired from R.A.F., 7-4-60, as Air Commodore.			New Zealander
CLOUSTON Wilfrid Greville	Fg. Off.	Pilot	19	On 19 Sqn., 1-7-40. Awarded D.F.C. (24-6-40). ✠ **1 Do 17 (shared), 31-8-40; ✠ 1 Bf 110 and 1 Do 17, 15-9-40; ✠ 1 Ju 88, 18-9-40.**	♀	Died since Battle (24-5-80)	New Zealander
CLOWES Arthur Victor	Sgt.	Pilot	1	On 1 Sqn., 1-7-40. Commissioned, 11-9-40. Awarded D.F.C. (13-5-41), D.F.M. **(20-8-40).** ✠ **1 Ju 88, 11-8-40; ✠ 1 He 111 and 1 Ju 88, 16-8-40; ✠ 1 Bf 110, 7-9-40; ✠ 1 Do 17 (shared), 24-10-40.** Served in R.A.F., post-War.	♀	Died since Battle (7-12-49)	British
CLYDE William Pancoast ("Billie")	Fg. Off.	Pilot	601	On 601 Sqn., 1-7-40. Awarded D.F.C. (31-5-40). ✠ **1 Ju 88 (shared), 7-7-40; ✠ 2 Bf 110s, 13-8-40; ✠ 1 Ju 88 (shared), 15-8-40; ✠ 1 Ju 87, 16-8-40; ✠ 1 Do 17, 31-8-40; ✠ 1 Bf 110, 7-10-40.** Released from R.A.F., 1945, as Group Captain.			British
COATES James Patrick	Lieut.	Pilot	808	Fleet Air Arm. On 808 Sqn., 1-7-40.	♀	Killed since Battle (26-11-40)	British
COBDEN Donald Gordon	Plt. Off.	Pilot	74	On 74 Sqn., 1-7-40.	♀	**Killed in Action** (11-8-40)	New Zealander
COCHRANE Arthur Charles ("Cocky")	Plt. Off.	Pilot	257	On 257 Sqn., 1-7-40. Awarded D.F.C. (30-3-43). ✠ **1 Bf 109, 8-8-40; ✠ 1 Bf 110, 31-8-40; ✠ 1 Do 215, 7-9-40; ✠ 1 He 111 (shared) and 1 Do 17, 15-9-40.**	♀	Killed since Battle (31-3-43)	Canadian
COCK John Reynolds	Plt. Off.	Pilot	87	On 87 Sqn., 1-7-40. Promoted Fg. Off., 3-9-40. Awarded D.F.C. (25-10-40). ✠ **1 Ju 88, 11-8-40; ✠ 1 Ju 88, 30-9-40.**	♀	Died since Battle (29-8-88)	Australian
COCKBURN John Clayton	Lt. Cdr.	Pilot	804	Fleet Air Arm. In command of 804 Sqn., 1-7-40. Awarded D.S.C. (23-5-44). Retired from Royal Navy, 1960, as Captain.			British
COCKBURN Richard Cockburn	Sub-Lt.	Pilot	808	Fleet Air Arm. On 808 Sqn., 1-7-40. Promoted Lieutenant, 3-10-40. Awarded D.S.O. (25-11-41). Retired from the Royal Navy, 1-46, as Lieutenant Commander.			British
COGGINS John	Plt. Off.	Pilot	235	On 235 Sqn., 1-7-40. Had been awarded D.F.M.✱ (22-11-38 and 14-4-39); awarded M.B.E. (21-1-41).	♀	Killed since Battle (16-12-40)	British
COGHLAN John Hunter	Fg. Off.	Pilot	56	On 56 Sqn., 1-7-40. Awarded D.F.C. (30-7-40). Posted away, 7-8-40. (Note: This pilot was killed while serving with a training unit)	♀	**Killed in Accident** (17-8-40)	British
COKE The Hon. David Arthur	Fg. Off.	Pilot	257	On 257 Sqn., 1-7-40. Slightly wounded, 12-8-40. Awarded D.F.C. (26-12-41). ✠ **1 Bf 109, 22-10-40.**	♀	Killed since Battle (9-12-41)	British
COLE Charles Frederick John	Sgt.	Aircrew	236	Joined 236 Sqn., 3-9-40. No details of operations traced.			British
COLEBROOK Christopher	Plt. Off.	Pilot	54	Joined 54 Sqn., 14-10-40.	♀	Killed since Battle (20-4-41)	British
COLEMAN Edward Jack	Plt. Off.	Pilot	54	On 54 Sqn., 1-7-40. Slightly wounded, 7-7-40, but flew with squadron during Battle.	♀	Killed since Battle (17-2-41)	British
COLLARD Peter	Plt. Off.	Pilot	615	On 615 Sqn., 1-7-40. Awarded D.F.C. (23-8-40). ✠ **1 Ju 87, 14-7-40; ✠ 1 He 59 (shared), 27-7-40.**	♀	**Killed in Action** (14-8-40)	British
COLLETT George Richard	Sgt.	Pilot	54	Joined 54 Sqn., 15-7-40. Slightly wounded, 24-7-40. ✠ **1 Bf 109, 24-7-40.**	♀	**Killed in Action** (22-8-40)	British
COLLINGRIDGE Leon William	Plt. Off.	Pilot	66	On 66 Sqn., 1-7-40. Slightly wounded, 29-7-40. Retired from R.A.F., 25-8-63, retaining rank of Squadron Leader.			British
COLLINS Anthony Roland	Sqn. Ldr.	Pilot	72-46	On 72 Sqn., 1-7-40, and appointed to command. Slightly wounded, 2-9-40. Posted to command No. 46 Sqn., 6-10-40. Retired from R.A.F., 22-6-55, as Wg. Cdr.	♀	Died since Battle (21-2-76)	British
COLLYNS Basil Gordon	Plt. Off.	Pilot	238	Joined 238 Sqn., 28-9-40.	♀	Killed since Battle (20-8-44)	New Zealander
COMELY Peter Woodruff	Plt. Off.	Pilot	87	On 87 Sqn., 1-7-40. ✠ **1 Ju 88, 11-8-40; ✠ 1 Bf 110, 15-8-40.**	♀	**Killed in Action** (15-8-40)	British
COMERFORD Harry Alfred George	Flt. Lt.	Pilot	312	Joined 312 (Czech) Sqn., 1-10-40. Awarded A.F.C. (30-9-41). Resigned commission, 10-4-43.			British
COMPTON John William	A.C.1	Aircrew	25	Joined 25 Sqn., c.10-10-40. Promoted Sergeant, c.20-10-40.			British
CONNELL William Charles	Plt. Off.	Pilot	32	Joined 32 Sqn., 7-10-40. Released from R.C.A.F., 16-6-46, as Flight Lieutenant.			Canadian
CONNOR Francis Hebblethwaite Powell	Fg. Off.	Pilot	234	Joined 234 Sqn., 6-7-40. ✠ **1 Ju 88 (shared), 27-7-40.** Seriously wounded, 16-8-40. Released from R.A.F., 1946, as Squadron Leader.	♀	Died since Battle (1-5-82)	British
CONNORS Stanley Dudley Pierce	Fg. Off.	Pilot	111	On 111 Sqn., 1-7-40. Awarded D.F.C.✱ (31-5-40 and 6-9-40). ✠ **1 Bf 109, 19-7-40; ✠ 1 Ju 88, 28-7-40; ✠ 1 Bf 109, 11-8-40; ✠ 1 Ju 88, 15-8-40; ✠ 1 Bf 110 (shared), 15-8-40; ✠ 1 Ju 88, 18-8-40.**	♀	**Killed in Action** (18-8-40)	British
CONSIDINE Brian Bertram	Plt. Off.	Pilot	238	On 238 Sqn., 1-7-40. ✠ **1 Bf 110, 21-7-40; ✠ 1 Do 17 (shared), 28-8-40.** Released from R.A.F., 12-45, as Flight Lieutenant.			Irish
CONSTABLE-MAXWELL Michael Hugh	Fg. Off.	Pilot	56	Re-joined 56 Sqn., 28-7-40, after recovering from wounds. Awarded D.S.O.(22-9-44), D.F.C. (18-5-43). ✠ **1 Do 17, 27-9-40.** Retired from R.A.F., 3-6-64, as Wg. Cdr.			British

CONSTANTINE Alexander Noel	Fg. Off.	Pilot	141	On 141 Sqn., 1-7-40.	✟ Killed since Battle (29-7-47)	British
COOK Arthur Willson	Sgt.	Aircrew	604	Joined 604 Sqn., 20-8-40. Awarded D.F.M. (2-6-42). Commissioned, 16-7-42. Released from R.A.F., 12-45, as Flight Lieutenant.		British
COOK Harry	Sgt.	Pilot	266-66	Joined 266 Sqn., 26-8-40. Posted to 66 Sqn., 12-9-40. Commissioned, 18-6-42. ✠ **1 Bf 110, 27-9-40; ✠ 1 Bf 109, 27-10-40.**		British
COOK Robert Vincent	Sgt.	Aircrew	219	Joined 219 Sqn., 12-8-40. No record of operations traced.		British
COOKE Charles Alfred	Plt. Off.	Pilot	66	On 66 Sqn., 1-7-40. Awarded D.F.C. (13-10-42). ✠ **1 Do 17 (shared), 10-7-40; ✠ 1 Bf 110 (shared), 20-8-40.** Retired from R.A.F., 11-7-58, as Sqn. Ldr.	✟ Died since Battle (28-1-85)	British
¶ **COOKE** Desmond	Sqn. Ldr.	Pilot	65	In command of 65 Sqn., 1-7-40. (Killed before Battle of Britain opened.)	✟ Killed in Action (8-7-40)	British
COOKE Herbert Reginald	Sgt.	Aircrew	23	On 23 Sqn., 1-7-40. Commissioned, 29-3-43. Awarded D.F.C. (10-12-43). Released from R.A.F., 1946, as Flying Officer.		British
COOMBES Eric	Sgt.	Aircrew	219	Joined 219 Sqn., 1-8-40.		British
COOMBS Robert Johnson	Sgt.	Pilot	600	On 600 Sqn., 1-7-40. Commissioned, 15-1-41. Released from R.A.F., 1947, as Flight Lieutenant.	✟ Died since Battle (1951)	British
COONEY Cecil John	F/Sgt.	Pilot	56	On 56 Sqn., 1-7-40.	✟ **Killed in Action** (29-7-40)	British
COOPE William Edwin	Sqn. Ldr.	Pilot	17	Flew as supernumerary with 17 Sqn. from 20-8-40.	✟ Killed since Battle (4-6-41)	British
COOPER Charles Frederick	A.C.2	Aircrew	600	Joined 600 Sqn., 26-9-40. Had not been promoted Sergeant by time of death.	✟ **Killed in Accident** (3-10-40)	British
COOPER Douglas Clifford	Sgt.	Aircrew	235	Joined 235 Sqn., 13-8-40. Commissioned, 9-6-43. Transferred to Reserve, 1954, as Flight Lieutenant.		British
COOPER James Enerton	Sgt.	Pilot	610	Joined 610 Sqn., 6-10-40.	✟ Killed since Battle (9-9-41)	British
COOPER Roy Norman	Sgt.	Pilot	610-65	Joined 610 Sqn., 6-10-40. Posted to 65 Sqn., 11-10-40. Commissioned, 18-7-44.	✟ Killed since Battle (28-10-45)	British
COOPER Sydney Frederick	Sgt.	Pilot	253	On 253 Sqn., 1-7-40. Commissioned, 28-6-43. Awarded A.F.C. (10-6-48). Retired from R.A.F., 29-6-58, as Flight Lieutenant.		British
COOPER Thomas Arthur	Sgt.	Pilot	266-92	Joined 266 Sqn., 30-9-40. Posted to 92 Sqn., 30-10-40. Commissioned, 3-3-45. Released from the R.A.F., 1946, as Flying Officer.		British
COOPER-KEY Aston Maurice	Plt. Off.	Pilot	46	On 46 Sqn., 1-7-40.	✟ **Killed in Action** (24-7-40)	British
COOPER-SLIPPER Thomas Paul Michael	Fg. Off.	Pilot	605	On 605 Sqn., 1-7-40. Awarded D.F.C. (26-11-40). ✠ **1 Bf 109, 8-9-40; ✠ 1 Do 17, 15-9-40.** Released from R.A.F., 1946, as Squadron Leader.		British
COOTE Leonard Edward Morgan	Sgt.	Aircrew	600	Joined 600 Sqn., 18-7-40. Commissioned, 13-10-42.	✟ Killed since Battle (3-10-43)	British
COPCUTT Richard	Sgt.	Aircrew	248	On 248 Sqn., 1-7-40. Flew on reconnaissance sorties over Norwegian coast.	✟ **Killed in Action** (20-10-40)	British
COPELAND Norman Downey	Sgt.	Aircrew	235	On 235 Sqn., 1-7-40. Commissioned, 12-43. Released from R.A.F., 1-46, as Flight Lieutenant.		British
COPELAND Percy	Sgt.	Pilot	616-66-73	On 616 Sqn., 1-7-40. Posted to 66 Sqn., 14-10-40. Posted to 73 Sqn., 24-10-40. Wounded 26-8-40. Commissioned, 10-11-41.	✟ Killed since Battle (26-6-42)	British
COPEMAN Jack Harry Hamilton	Plt. Off.	Pilot	111	On 111 Sqn., 1-7-40. ✠ **1 Bf 109, 19-7-40.**	✟ Killed in Action (11-8-40)	British
CORBETT George Henry	Plt. Off.	Pilot	66	Joined 66 Sqn., 26-7-40. Slightly wounded, 9-9-40. ✠ **1 Ju 88, 27-9-40.**	✟ **Killed in Action** (8-10-40)	Canadian
CORBETT Vaughan Bowerman	Flt. Lt.	Pilot	1(Canadian)	On 1 (Canadian) Sqn., 20-6-40, on arrival in U.K. Wounded, 31-8-40. Awarded D.F.C. (13-2-42).	✟ Killed since Battle (20-2-45)	Canadian
CORBIN William James ("Binder")	Sgt.	Pilot	66-610	Joined 66 Sqn., 26-8-40. Posted to 610 Sqn., 10-9-40. Commissioned, 6-42. Awarded D.F.C. (27-7-43). Released from R.A.F., 12-45, as Flight Lieutenant.		British
CORCORAN Henry	Sgt.	Aircrew	236	Joined 236 Sqn., 19-7-40.	✟ **Killed in Action** (20-7-40)	British
CORDELL Horace Arthur	Sgt.	Pilot	64-616	Joined 64 Sqn., 6-10-40. Posted to 616 Sqn., 13-10-40. Commissioned, 6-41. Released from R.A.F., 1947, as Flight Lieutenant.		British
CORFE Douglas Frederick	Sgt.	Pilot	73-610-66	On 73 Sqn., 1-7-40. Posted to 610 Sqn., 25-7-40. Posted to 66 Sqn., 10-9-40. Wounded, 18-9-40. ✠ **1 Bf 109, 14-8-40.**	✟ Killed since Battle (25-4-42)	British
CORK Richard John	Sub-Lt.	Pilot	242	Joined 242 Sqn., 1-7-40. Awarded D.S.O. (10-11-42), D.S.C. (18-10-40, commuted from D.F.C.). ✠ **1 Bf 110, 30-8-40; ✠ 1 Bf 110 and 1 Do 215, 7-9-40; ✠ 2 Do 17s, 15-9-40.**	✟ Killed since Battle (14-4-44)	British
CORKETT Allan Henry ("Corky")	Plt. Off.	Pilot	253	On 253 Sqn., 1-7-40. ✠ **1 Bf 110, 4-9-40; ✠ 1 Ju 88 (shared), 5-10-40.** Retired from R.A.F., 15-1-62, retaining rank of Squadron Leader.		British
CORNER Malcolm Charles	Plt. Off.	Aircrew	264	Defiant gunner. Joined 264 Sqn., 9-40. Was Squadron Leader at time of death.	✟ Died since Battle (23-4-45)	British
CORRY Noel Henry	Plt. Off.	Pilot	25	On 25 Sqn., 1-7-40. Awarded D.F.C. (8-12-44, with Bomber Command). Released from R.A.F., 11-45, as Squadron Leader.		British
CORY Guy Webster	Plt. Off.	Pilot	41	On 41 Sqn., 1-7-40. Promoted Fg. Off., 3-9-40. Awarded A.F.C., 1-1-43. Retired from R.A.F., 24-7-54, as Wing Commander.	✟ Died since Battle (20-6-81)	British
COSBY Eric Thomas	Sgt.	Pilot	3-615	Joined 3 Sqn., 31-7-40. Posted to 615 Sqn., 14-10-40. ✠ **1 Bf 109, 29-10-40.** Commissioned, 9-43. Retired from R.A.F., 3-3-67, as Flight Lieutenant.	✟ Died since Battle (26-4-78)	British
COSBY Ivor Henry	Plt. Off.	Pilot	610-72-222	Joined 610 Sqn., 8-40. Posted to 72 Sqn., c.6-9-40. Posted to 222 Sqn., 10-40. Awarded D.F.C. (4-8-44). ✠ **1 Bf 109 (shared), 23-9-40.** Retired from the R.A.F., 19-8-74, as Wing Commander.		British
COTES-PREEDY Digby Vawdre Cartmel ("Digger")	Plt. Off.	Pilot	236	On 236 Sqn., 1-7-40. Awarded D.F.C.✤, G.M. (5-5-41). Released from R.A.F. as Squadron Leader, 1946.	✟ Died since Battle (1972)	British
COTTAM Gerald	L.A.C.	Pilot	25	Joined 25 Sqn., c.3-10-40. Promoted Sergeant, 10-40.		British
COTTAM Hubert Weatherby	Plt. Off.	Pilot	213	On 213 Sqn., 1-7-40. ✠ **1 Bf 110, 12-8-40; ✠ 1 Bf 110, 15-8-40.**	✟ Died since Battle (5-12-41)	British
COURTIS Jack Burall	Sgt.	Pilot	111	Joined 111 Sqn., 28-9-40.	✟ Killed since Battle (5-12-40)	New Zealander
COURTNEY Ronald Noel Hamilton	Plt. Off.	Pilot	151	Rejoined 151 Sqn., 18-7-40, after recovery from wounds. Appointed C.B. (1-1-67); awarded D.F.C.✤ (8-9-44 and 29-1-46), A.F.C. (1-1-54). Retired from R.A.F., 6-1-68, as Group Captain.		British
COUSSENS Herbert William	Sgt.	Pilot	601	Joined 601 Sqn., 11-9-40. Commissioned, 3-42. Retired from R.A.F., 18-5-63, as Flight Lieutenant.		British
COUZENS George Walter	Plt. Off.	Pilot	54	On 54 Sqn., 1-7-40. Awarded A.F.C. (14-6-45). Retired from R.A.F., 8-9-46, retaining the rank of Squadron Leader.		British
COVERLEY William Hugh	Fg. Off.	Pilot	602	On 602 Sqn., 1-7-40. ✠ **1 Ju 88 (shared), 7-7-40.**	✟ **Killed in Action** (7-9-40)	British
COVINGTON Aubrey Richard	Plt. Off.	Pilot	238	Joined 238 Sqn., 20-8-40. Slightly wounded, 7-10-40. ✠ **1 Bf 110, 15-9-40; ✠ 2 Bf 110s, 1-10-40.** Retired from R.A.F., 22-1-64, as Flight Lieutenant.		British
COWARD James Baird	Fg. Off.	Pilot	19	On 19 Sqn., 1-7-40. Severely wounded, 31-8-40. Promoted Flight Lieutenant, 3-9-40. Awarded A.F.C., 1-1-54. Retired from R.A.F., 8-9-69, as Air Commodore.		British
COWEN William	Sgt.	Aircrew	25	Joined 25 Sqn., c.25-8-40.	✟ Died since Battle (29-6-79)	British
COWLEY James	Sgt.	Pilot	87	On 87 Sqn., 1-7-40. Wounded, 15-8-40. Posted away, 14-10-40. Commissioned, 2-7-42. Released from R.A.F., 1946, as Flight Lieutenant.		British
COWSILL James Roy	Sgt.	Pilot	56	On 56 Sqn., 1-7-40.	✟ **Killed in Action** (13-7-40)	British
COX Davis George Samuel Richardson	Sgt.	Pilot	19	On 19 Sqn., 1-7-40. Commissioned, 17-7-41. Awarded D.F.C.✤ (16-2-43 and 9-7-43). Released from R.A.F., 11-3-46. ✠ **1 Bf 110, 19-8-40; ✠ 1 Bf 109, 9-9-40; ✠ 1 Bf 109, 15-9-40.**		British
COX Gilbert Parish	Sgt.	Aircrew	236	Joined 236 Sqn., 20-9-40. No operational details traced.		British

Name	Rank	Role	Sqn	Notes	Fate	Nationality
COX Graham James	Plt. Off.	Pilot	152	On 152 Sqn., 1-7-40. Promoted Fg. Off., 2-10-40. Awarded D.S.O. (10-10-44), D.F.C. (16-2-43). ✠ **1 Ju 88 (shared), 12-8-40; ✠ 1 Bf 109, 18-8-40; ✠ 1 Ju 88 (shared); ✠ 1 Bf 110, 27-9-40.** Released from R.A.F., 1946, as Squadron Leader.		British
COX Kenneth Henry	Plt. Off.	Pilot	610	Joined 610 Sqn., 27-7-40. ✠ **1 Bf 109, 12-8-40; ✠ 1 Bf 109, 18-8-40.**	♱ Killed in Action (28-8-40)	British
COX Philip Anthony Neville	Fg. Off.	Pilot	501	On 501 Sqn., 1-7-40. ✠ **1 Bf 109 (shared) and 1 Bf 109 (solo), 20-7-40.**	♱ Killed in Action (27-7-40)	British
COX Ralph Cyril Rupert	Sgt.	Aircrew	248	On 248 Sqn., 1-7-40. Flew on reconnaissance sorties over Norwegain coast.	♱ Killed in Action (27-8-40)	British
COX Walter Edward	Sgt.	Aircrew	264	Defiant gunner. On 264 Sqn., 1-7-40. No details of operations traced.	♱ Died since Battle (1953 ?)	British
COXON John Harry	Sgt.	Aircrew	141	Defiant gunner. Joined 141 Sqn., 20-8-40.	♱ Killed since Battle (6-6-42)	British
CRABTREE Douglas Barker	Sgt.	Pilot	501	On 501 Sqn., 1-7-40. Later taken prisoner but escaped and return to U.K. Commissioned, 4-6-42. Released from R.A.F., 1946, as Flight Lieutenant.	♱ Killed since Battle (24-6-50)	British
CRAIG George Dudley	Flt. Lt.	Pilot	607	On 607 Sqn., 1-7-40. Appointed O.B.E., 26-7-46. Released from R.A.F., 1945.	♱ Died since Battle (1974)	British
CRANWELL Edward William	Sgt.	Pilot	610	Joined 610 Sqn., 6-10-40. Commissioned 6-2-43. Awarded D.F.C. (13-8-43). Released from R.A.F., 1945, as Flight Lieutenant.		British
CRAWFORD Hector Hugh ("Hank")	Plt. Off.	Pilot	235	Joined 235 Sqn., 18-8-40.	♱ Killed since Battle (6-2-42)	New Zealander
CRESSWELL Denis George	Sgt.	Aircrew	141	Defiant gunner. Joined 141 Sqn., 10-9-40.	♱ Killed since Battle (30-8-41)	British
CREW Edward Dixon	Fg. Off.	Pilot	604	Joined 604 Sqn., 8-7-40. Appointed C.B. (1-1-73); awarded D.S.O.✠ (26-9-44 and 10-3-50), D.F.C.(29-7-41). Retired from R.A.F., 3-3-73, as Air Vice-Marshal.		British
CRISP John Lawrence	Sgt.	Pilot	43	Joined 43 Sqn., 6-7-40. Injured in accident 16-8-40. Commissioned, 21-41.	♱ Killed since Battle (8-6-42)	British
CROCKETT Ronald Frederick	Plt. Off.	Aircrew	236	Joined 236 Sqn., 15-7-40.	♱ Killed since Battle (17-9-42)	British
CROFTS Peter Guerin	Fg. Off.	Pilot	615-605	Joined 615 Sqn., 4-9-40. Posted to 605 Sqn., 13-9-40.	♱ Killed in Action (28-9-40)	British
CROKER Eric Eugene	Sgt.	Pilot	111	Joined 111 Sqn., 28-9-40.	♱ Killed since Battle (1-6-41)	New Zealander
CROMBIE Robert	Sgt.	Aircrew	141	Defiant gunner. On 141 Sqn., 1-7-40.	♱ Killed in Action (19-7-40)	British
CROOK David Moore	Plt. Off.	Pilot	609	On 609 Sqn., 1-7-40. Awarded D.F.C. (1-11-40). ✠ **1 Ju 87, 9-7-40; ✠ 1 Bf 13-8-40; ✠ 1 He 111 (shared), 14-8-40; ✠ 1 Bf 109 (shared), 27-9-40; ✠ 2 Bf 109s, 30-9-40.**	♱ Killed since Battle (18-12-44)	British
CROOK Harold Kay	Sgt.	Pilot	219	On 219 Sqn., 1-7-40. Commissioned, 9-4-41. Transferred to R.A.F.O. as Squadron Leader, 1-8-47.	♱ Died since Battle (20-3-88)	British
CROOK Valton William James	L.A.C.	Aircrew	264	Defiant gunner. On 264 Sqn., 1-7-40. Promoted Sergeant, 7-40. Transferred to R.A.A.F., 6-44. Discharged 2-45.	♱ Died since Battle (1950)	Australian
CROSKELL Michael Ernest	Sgt.	Pilot	213	On 213 Sqn., 1-7-40. ✠ **1 Ju 88, 1 Bf 109 and 1 Bf 110, 11-8-40.** Commissioned, 5-42. Released from R.A.F., 3-47, as Flight Lieutenant.		British
CROSSEY James Terence	Plt. Off.	Pilot	249	On 249 Sqn., 1-7-40. Released from R.A.F., 1946, as Flight Lieutenant.		British
CROSSLEY Michael Nicholson ("Red Knight")	Flt. Lt.	Pilot	32	On 32 Sqn., 1-7-40. Awarded D.S.O. (20-8-40), O.B.E. (1-1-46), D.F.C. (21-6-40). ✠ **1 Bf 109 and 1 Bf 110, 20-7-40; ✠ 2 Bf 109s, 12-8-40; ✠ 1 Do 17 (shared), 1 Do 17 (solo) and 2 Ju 88s, 15-8-40; ✠ 1 Bf 109 and 1 Ju 88, 16-8-40; ✠ 1 Bf 109 and 1 Ju 88, 18-8-40; ✠ 1 Bf 109 and 1 Do 215, 25-8-40.** Promoted Sqn. Ldr., 11-8-40. Released from R.A.F., 1946, as Wg. Cdr.	♱ Died since Battle (9-87)	British
CROSSMAN John Dallas	Plt. Off.	Pilot	46	Joined 46 Sqn., 9-9-40.	♱ Killed in Action (30-9-40)	Australian
CROSSMAN Richard George	Sgt.	Aircrew	25	Joined 25 Sqn., c.4-10-40.	♱ Killed since Battle (8-7-41)	British
CROWLEY Harold Reginald	Plt. Off.	Aircrew	219-600	On 219 Sqn., 1-7-40. Detached to 600 Sqn., 9-40. Retired from R.A.F., 1-7-65, as Group Captain.	♱ Died since Battle (1984)	British
CROWLEY-MILLING Denis	Pilot Plt. Off.		242	On 242 Sqn., 1-7-40. Appointed K.C.B. (1973), C.B.E. (1-1-63); awarded D.S.O. (24-12-43), D.F.C.✠ (11-4-41 and 22-9-42). ✠ **1 He 111, 30-8-40; ✠ 1 Bf 110, 7-9-40; ✠ 1 Do 17, 14-9-40; ✠ 1 Bf 109, 15-9-40.** Retired from the R.A.F., 29-7-75, as Air Marshal.		British
CRUICKSHANKS Ian James Alexander	Plt. Off.	Pilot	66	On 66 Sqn., 1-7-40. ✠ **1 Bf 110 (shared), 20-8-40; ✠ 1 He 111 (shared), 9-9-40.** Slightly injured, 11-9-40.	♱ Killed since Battle (8-6-45)	British
CRUTTENDEN John	Plt. Off.	Pilot	43	On 43 Sqn., 1-7-40.	♱ Killed in Action (8-8-40)	British
CRYDERMAN Lawrence Elwood	Fg. Off.	Pilot	242	Joined 242 Sqn., 31-8-40.	♱ Killed since Battle (8-2-41)	Canadian
CUDDIE William Arthur	Plt. Off.	Pilot	141	Joined 141 Sqn., 19-8-40.	♱ Killed since Battle (3-10-43)	British
CUKR Vaclav Eric	Sgt.	Pilot	43-253	Joined 43 Sqn., 10-9-40. Posted to 253 Sqn., c.28-9-40. Awarded D.F.C. (1941). Commissioned, 1941. Left R.A.F., 4-46, as Flight Lieutenant. Changed name to Cooper.		Czech
CULLEN Reginald Walker	Sgt.	Aircrew	23	On 23 Sqn., 1-7-40. No records of operations traced.		British
CULMER James Douglas	Sgt.	Aircrew	25	On 25 Sqn., 1-7-40. Awarded D.F.M. (24-12-40). Commissioned, 24-8-44. Retired from R.A.F., 15-3-63, as Flight Lieutenant.		British
CULVERWELL John Henry	Sgt.	Pilot	87	On 87 Sqn., 1-7-40.	♱ Killed in Accident (25-7-40)	British
CUMBERS Alfred Bernard	Sgt.	Aircrew	141	Defiant gunner. Joined 141 Sqn., c.14-7-40. Awarded D.F.M. (18-3-41). Commissioned, 17-3-42. Released from R.A.F., 1945, as Flight Lieutenant.	♱ Died since Battle (28-12-85)	British
CUNNINGHAM James	L.A.C.	Aircrew	29	Joined 29 Sqn., c.26-9-40. Promoted Sergeant, 10-40. Commissioned later.		British
CUNNINGHAM John	Flt. Lt.	Pilot	604	On 604 Sqn., 1-7-40. Appointed C.B.E. Awarded D.S.O.✠✠ (8-8-41, 24-7-42 and 3-3-44), D.F.C.✠ (28-1-41 and 19-9-41). Released from R.A.F., 1945, as Group Captain.		British
CUNNINGHAM John Laurence Gilchrist	Flt. Lt.	Pilot	603	On 603 Sqn., 1-7-40. ✠ **1 Do 17 (shared), 20-7-40.**	♱ Killed in Action (28-8-40)	British
CUNNINGHAM Wallace	Plt. Off.	Pilot	19	On 19 Sqn., 1-7-40. Awarded D.F.C. (8-10-40). ✠ **1 Bf 110, 16-8-40; ✠ 1 He 111, 7-9-40; ✠ 1 Bf 109, 9-9-40; ✠ 1 Ju 88 (shared), 18-9-40.** Released from R.A.F., 1946, as Flight Lieutenant.		British
CUNNINGTON William George	Sgt.	Pilot	607	On 607 Sqn., 1-7-40. ✠ **1 Ju 88 (shared), 14-9-40.**	♱ Killed since Battle (17-11-40)	British
CUPITT Thomas	A.C.1	Aircrew	29	Joined 29 Sqn., c.26-9-40. Promoted Sergeant, 10-40.		British
CURCHIN John	Plt. Off.	Pilot	609	On 609 Sqn., 1-7-40. Awarded D.F.C. (1-11-40). ✠ **1 Bf 110, 8-8-40. ✠ 1 Bf 109, 25-8-40; ✠ 1 Bf 109, 7-9-40; ✠ 2 Do 17s (both shared), 15-9-40; ✠ 1 Bf 110, 24-9-40; ✠ 2 He 111s, 25-9-40; ✠ 1 He 111, 26-9-40.**	♱ Killed since Battle (4-6-41)	Australian
CURLEY Albert George	Sgt.	Aircrew	141	Defiant gunner. On 141 Sqn., 1-7-40.	♱ Killed in Action (19-7-40)	British
CURRANT Christopher Frederick ("Bunny")	Plt. Off.	Pilot	605	On 615 Sqn., 1-7-40. Awarded D.S.O. (7-7-42), D.F.C.✠✠ (8-10-40 and 15-11-40). ✠ **1 He 111 (solo) and 1 He 111 (shared), 15-8-40; ✠ 1 Bf Bf 109 and 1 Bf 110 (both shared), 9-9-40; ✠ 1 He 111, 11-9-40; ✠ 1 He 111 (shared), 12-9-40; ✠ 2 Do 17s and 1 Bf 109, 15-9-40; ✠ 1 Bf 110, 27-9-40; ✠ 1 Bf 109, 28-9-40; ✠ 1 Ju 88 (shared), 4-10-40; ✠ 1 Ju 88 (shared), 8-10-40; ✠ 1 Bf 109, 15-10-40.** Retired from the R.A.F., 11-1-59, as Wing Commander.		British
CURTIS Frank William	Sgt.	Aircrew	25	Joined 25 Sqn., c.26-9-40. Awarded D.F.M. (16-2-43)		British

Name	Rank	Role	Sqn	Details	Status	Nationality
CUTTS John Wintringham	Fg. Off.	Pilot	222	On 222 Sqn., 1-7-40. ✠ **1 Bf 109, 3-9-40.**	✟ **Killed in Action** (4-9-40)	British
CZAJKOWSKI Franciszek	Plt. Off.	Pilot	151	Joined 151 Sqn., early 8-40. Wounded, 31-8-40.	✟ Killed since Battle (25-10-42)	Polish
CZERNIAK Jerzy Michal	Plt. Off.	Pilot	302	Joined 302 (Polish) Sqn., 20-8-40.	✟ Killed since Battle (9-8-41)	Polish
CZERNIN Count Manfred Beckett	Fg. Off.	Pilot	17	On 17 Sqn., 1-7-40. Awarded D.S.O. (2-11-45), M.C. (1-12-44), D.F.C. (1-10-40). ✠ **2 Do 17s, 12-7-40;** ✠ **1 Ju 88 (shared), 21-8-40;** ✠ **2 Bf 110s (solo) and 1 Bf 110 (shared), 25-8-40;** ✠ **1 Bf 109, 5-9-40;** ✠ **1 He 111 (shared), 5-9-40;** ✠ **1 Bf 110, 11-9-40;** ✠ **1 Ju 88 (shared), 19-9-40;** ✠ **1 Bf 110, 27-9-40;** ✠ **1 Do 17 (shared), 24-10-40.** Released from R.A.F., 2-10-45, as Squadron Leader.	✟ Died since Battle	British
CZERNY Jan Tadeusz	Flt. Lt.	Pilot	302	Joined 302 (Polish) Sqn., 20-8-40. Awarded A.F.C., 9-2-45. Left the R.A.F., 1946, as Squadron Leader.		Polish
CZERWINSKI Tadeusz	Plt. Off.	Pilot	302	Joined 302 (Polish) Sqn., 23-7-40. ✠ **1 Do 17, 15-9-40.**	✟ Killed since Battle (22-8-42)	Polish
CZTERNASTEK Stanislaw	Plt. Off.	Pilot	32	Joined 32 Sqn., 12-10-40.	✟ Killed since Battle (5-2-41)	Polish
DAFFORN Robert Chippindall	Plt. Off.	Pilot	501	On 501 Sqn., 1-7-40. Awarded D.F.C. (17-1-41). ✠ **1 Ju 87, 12-8-40;** ✠ **1 Ju 88, 24-8-40;** ✠ **1 Do 17 (shared), 11-9-40;** ✠ **1 Bf 109, 30-10-40.**	✟ Killed since Battle (9-9-43)	British
DALTON Robert William ("Hank")	Sgt.	Aircrew	604	Joined 604 Sqn., 8-40. Awarded D.F.M. (2-12-41). Commissioned, 27-1-42. Retired from R.A.F., 31-3-58, as Squadron Leader.		British
DALY John J.	Sgt.	Pilot	141	On 141 Sqn., 1-7-40. No other details of service known.		British
¶ **DANIEL, W.J.**	Plt. Off.	Pilot	263	On 263 Sqn., 1-7-40. Posted away, 8-7-40.		British
DANN James Edwin	Sgt.	Pilot	23	On 23 Sqn., 1-7-40. Commissioned, 16-6-42. Awarded D.F.C. (23-3-45). Retired from R.A.F., 1949, as Flight Lieutenant.	✟ Died since Battle (1986)	British
DANNATT Alexander George	Sgt.	Aircrew	29	No details of operations traced.	✟ Died since Battle (16-12-82)	British
D'ARCY-IRVINE Brian William Jesse	Fg. Off.	Pilot	257	On 257 Sqn., 1-7-40.	✟ **Killed in Action** (8-8-40)	British
DARGIE Albert McDonald Smith	L.A.C.	Aircrew	23	On 23 Sqn., 1-7-40. Later promoted Sergeant.	✟ Killed since Battle (13-7-41)	British
DARLEY Horace Stanley	Sqn. Ldr.	Pilot	609	In command of 609 Sqn., 1-7-40. Posted away (to command R.A.F. Exeter, 4-10-40). Awarded D.S.O. (22-10-40). ✠ **1 Bf 110, 8-8-40;** ✠ **1 Bf 110; 25-8-40;** ✠ **1 Do 17, 25-9-40.** Retired from R.A.F., 15-6-59, as Group Captain.		British
DARLING Andrew Smitton ("Dimmy")	Sgt.	Pilot	611-603	On 611 Sqn., 1-7-40. Posted to 603 Sqn., 27-9-40. ✠ **1 Do 17 (shared), 21-8-40;** ✠ **1 Bf 109, 28-8-40.**	✟ Killed since Battle (26-4-41)	British
DARLING Edward Vivian ("Mitzi")	Sgt.	Pilot	41	On 41 Sqn., 1-7-40. Commissioned, 15-1-41. Awarded D.F.C. (17-10-41). ✠ **1 Ju 88 (shared), 11-8-40;** ✠ **1 Bf 109, 18-9-40.** Wounded, 27-9-40.	✟ Killed since Battle (2-6-42)	British
DARWIN Christopher William Wharton	Plt. Off.	Pilot	87	On 87 Sqn., 1-7-40.	✟ Killed since Battle (7-8-42)	British
DASZEWSKI Jan Kazimierz Daszewski	Plt. Off.	Pilot	303	Joined 303 (Polish) Sqn., on formation, 2-8-40. ✠ **1 Do 17, 7-9-40.** Severely wounded, 7-9-40.	✟ Killed since Battle (4-4-42)	Polish
DAVEY Brian	Plt. Off.	Pilot	32-257	Joined 32 Sqn., c.18-9-40. Posted to 257 Sqn., 23-9-40. (✠ **1 BR.20, shared, 11-11-40).**	✟ Killed since Battle (12-6-41)	British
DAVEY John Arthur Joseph	Plt. Off.	Pilot	1	Joined 1 Sqn., 15-7-40.	✟ **Killed in Action** (11-8-40)	British
DAVID William Dennis	Plt. Off.	Pilot	87-213	On 87 Sqn., 1-7-40. Appointed C.B.E. (1-1-60). Awarded D.F.C.✱ (31-5-40 and 4-6-40), A.F.C. (1-1-43). Promoted Fg. Off., 3-9-40. ✠ **1 Bf 109 and 1 Ju 88, 11-8-40;** ✠ **1 Ju 87, 15-8-40;** ✠ **1 Ju 88 and 1 Bf 109, 25-8-40;** ✠ **1 He 111 (shared), 15-9-40;** ✠ **1 Ju 88, 19-10-40.** Retired from R.A.F., 26-5-67, as Group Captain.		British
DAVIDSON Henry John	Sgt.	Pilot	249	On 249 Sqn., 1-7-40. Commissioned, 5-3-41. ✠ **1 Do 17, 7-8-40;** ✠ **1 Bf 110, 2-9-40;** ✠ **1 Bf 110 (shared) and 1 Ju 88, 27-9-40.**	✟ Killed since Battle (6-10-42)	British
DAVIES Alfred Eric	Plt. Off.	Pilot	610-222	Joined 610 Sqn., 3-9-40. Posted to 222 Sqn., 28-9-40.	✟ **Killed in Action** (30-10-40)	British
DAVIES Graham Gordon Ayerst	Plt. Off.	Pilot	222	On 222 Sqn., 1-7-40. Wounded, 1-9-40. Retired from R.A.F., 17-6-59, as Sqn. Ldr.		British
DAVIES John Alfred	Flt. Lt.	Pilot	604	On 604 Sqn., 1-7-40. Promoted Sqn. Ldr., 1-9-40. Posted away, 9-9-40.	✟ **Killed in Accident** (16-10-40)	British
DAVIES Leonard	Sgt.	Pilot	151	Joined 151 Sqn., 15-7-40. Wounded, 28-8-40. Commissioned, 2-12-42. Released from R.A.F., 1946, as Flight Lieutenant.		British
DAVIES Maurice Peter	Sgt.	Pilot	213-1	On 213 Sqn., 1-7-40. Posted to 1 Sqn., mid-9-40. Posted away, 10-10-40. Commissioned, 13-1-42. Released from R.A.F., 1946, as Flight Lieutenant.	✟ Died since Battle (22-7-53)	British
DAVIES Peter Frederick McDonald	Fg. Off.	Pilot	56	On 56 Sqn., 1-7-40. Wounded, 13-8-40. Left the R.A.F., 11-8-58, as Sqn. Ldr.		British
DAVIES Roy Blackburne	Fg. Off.	Pilot	29	On 29 Sqn., 1-7-40. Promoted Fg. Off., 3-9-40. Released from R.A.F., 1946, as Squadron Leader.	✟ Died since Battle (1972)	British
DAVIES-COOKE Paul John	Fg. Off.	Pilot	610-72	Joined 610 Sqn., 3-9-40. Posted to 72 Sqn., 20-9-40.	✟ **Killed in Action** (27-9-40)	British
DAVIS Alfred Stewart	Sgt.	Aircrew	235	Joined 235 Sqn., 18-7-40. No record of operations traced.		British
DAVIS Carl Raymond	Fg. Off.	Pilot	601	On 601 Sqn., 1-7-40. Awarded D.F.C. (30-8-40). ✠ **1 Bf 110, 11-7-40;** ✠ **2 Bf 110s, 11-8-40;** ✠ **3 Bf 110s, 13-8-40;** ✠ **1 Ju 87, 16-8-40;** ✠ **1 Bf 109, 1 Ju 87, and 1 Ju 87 (shared), 18-8-40;** ✠ **1 Bf 110, 4-9-40.**	✟ **Killed in Action** (6-9-40)	American
DAVIS Charles Trevor	Plt. Off.	Pilot	238	On 238 Sqn., 1-7-40. Awarded D.F.C. (25-10-40). ✠ **1 Do 17 (shared), 13-7-40;** ✠ **1 Bf 109, 20-7-40;** ✠ **1 Do 17 (Shared), 21-7-40;** ✠ **1 Ju 87, 27-7-40;** ✠ **1 Bf 110, 8-8-40;** ✠ **2 Bf 110s, 13-8-40;** ✠ **1 He 111, 15-9-40;** ✠ **1 Ju 88, 21-9-40.**	✟ Killed since Battle (26-3-41)	British
DAVIS Jack	Sgt.	Pilot	54	Joined 54 Sqn., 9-8-40. Commissioned, 28-10-42. Awarded A.F.C. (3-4-45). Retired from the R.A.F., 6-6-59, as Squadron Leader.		British
DAVIS, J.N.	Sgt.	Aircrew	600	On 600 Sqn., 1-7-40. No record of operations traced.		British
DAVIS Peter Edgar	Sgt.	Aircrew	236	Joined 236 Sqn., 24-10-40. No record of operations traced.		British
DAVIS Phillip Oscar	Sgt.	Pilot	222	Joined 222 Sqn., 24-10-40. Commissioned, 1-43.	✟ Killed since Battle (10-8-43)	British
DAVIS William L.	Sgt.	Pilot	249	Joined 249 Sqn., 5-8-40. Wounded, 11-9-40. Commissioned, 2-41 (Shot down and taken prisoner, 10-2-41).	✟ Died since Battle (1984)	British
DAVISON John Tregonwell	Plt. Off.	Pilot	235	Joined 235 Sqn., 25-8-40. Awarded O.B.E. (1-1-48), G.M. (13-3-41). Transferred to R.N.Z.A.F., c.1944. Retired from R.N.Z.A.F., 24-6-41, as Wing Commander.	✟ Died since Battle (9-10-81)	New Zealander
DAVY Thomas Daniel Humphrey	Fg. Off.	Pilot	266-72	Joined 266 Sqn., 28-8-40. Posted to 72 Sqn., 28-9-40. Had been awarded D.F.C., (31-5-40).	✟ Killed since Battle (13-9-42)	British
DAW Victor George ("Jackdaw")	Plt. Off.	Pilot	32	On 32 Sqn., 1-7-40. Had been awarded D.F.C. (25-6-40). Slightly wounded, 25-7-40. Awarded A.F.C. (1-1-45). Remained in R.A.F. after the War.	✟ Killed since Battle (24-3-53)	British
DAWBARN Peter Leslie	Plt. Off.	Pilot	17	On 17 Sqn., 1-7-40. Seriously injured in accident, 15-7-40. Released from R.A.F., 1946, as Squadron Leader.		British
DAWICK Kenneth	Sgt.	Pilot	111	Joined 111 Sqn., 30-9-40. Commissioned, 7-2-42. Released from R.N.Z.A.F., 14-11-45, as Flight Lieutenant.		New Zealander
DAWSON Thomas	Sgt.	Aircrew	235	On 235 Sqn., 1-7-40. No record of operations traced.		British
DAY Frank Samuel	Sgt.	Aircrew	248	On 248 Sqn., 1-7-40. Commissioned, 4-5-42.	✟ Killed since Battle (24-7-42)	British
DAY Robert Lionel Frank	Fg. Off.	Pilot	141	On 141 Sqn., 1-7-40. Awarded D.F.C. (6-6-41)	✟ Killed since Battle (18-6-44)	British
DEACON Albert Henry	Sgt.	Pilot	85-111	On 85 Sqn., 1-7-40. Posted to 111 Sqn., 18-8-40. Posted away, 16-9-40. Released from R.A.F., 1948, as Flight Lieutenant.		British

DEADMAN Sgt. Aircrew 236
Henry George
On 236 Sqn., 1-7-40. (Later changed name by deed poll to Stewart) — British

DEANESLY Fg. Off. Pilot 152
Edward Christopher
On 152 Sqn., 1-7-40. Slightly wounded, 25-7-40. Wounded again, 26-9-40. Awarded D.F.C. (30-5-41). Released from the R.A.F., 1945, as Wing Commander. — British

DEBENHAM Plt. Off. Pilot 151
Kenneth Barry Lempriere
Joined 151 Sqn., 15-7-40. ✠ 1 Bf 109, 15-8-40; ✠ 1 Bf 110 (shared), 18-8-40. Seriously wounded, 24-8-40. — ♱ Killed since Battle (16-12-43) — British

DE CANNAERT D'HAMALE Pilot 46
Roger Emile
Joined 46 Sqn., 13-8-40. Slightly wounded, 11-9-40. — ♱ Killed since Battle (1-11-40) — Belgian

DE CHERADE DE MONTBRON 64-92
Xavier Sgt. Pilot
Joined 64 Sqn., 19-8-40. Posted to 92 Sqn., 2-10-40. Commissioned, 16-3-41. — ♱ Killed since Battle (21-4-55) — French

DEE Sgt. Aircrew 235
Orlando John
Joined 235 Sqn., 13-9-40. — ♱ Killed since Battle (28-5-41) — British

DEERE Fg. Off. Pilot 54
Alan Christopher ("Al")
On 54 Sqn., 1-7-40. Awarded D.S.O. (15-7-43), O.B.E. (1-6-45), D.F.C.✪ (12-6-40 and 6-9-40). Slightly injured, 9-7-40. Again slightly injured, 15-8-40. ✠ 1 Bf 109, 9-7-40; ✠ 1 Bf 109, 11-8-40; ✠ 2 Bf 109s and 1 Bf 110; ✠ 1 Bf 109, 15-8-40; ✠ 1 Do 17, 30-8-40; ✠ 1 Bf 110, 3-9-40. Retired from R.A.F., 12-12-67, as Air Commodore. — New Zealander

DE HEMPTINNE Plt. Off. Pilot 145
Baudouin Marie Ghislain
Joined 145 Sqn., 17-8-40. ✠ 1 He 115, 2-10-40. — ♱ Killed since Battle (5-5-42) — Belgian

DE HEMRICOURT DE GRUNNE 32
Comte Rudolphe Ghislain Charles
Plt. Off. Pilot
Joined 32 Sqn., 15-8-40. ✠ 1 Bf 109, 16-8-40; ✠ 1 Bf 109, 17-8-40; ✠ 1 Do 17, 18-8-40. Seriously wounded, 18-8-40. — ♱ Killed since Battle (25-5-41) — Belgian

DEJACE Plt. Off. Pilot 236
Leopold Joseph
Joined 236 Sqn., 5-8-40. — ♱ Killed since Battle (26-7-42) — Belgian

DE LABOUCHERE Adj. Pilot 85
Francois Henri EdmondJoseph Andre
Joined 85 Sqn., 13-9-40. Commissioned, 1941. — ♱ Killed since Battle (5-9-42) — French

DE LA PERELLE Plt. Off. Pilot 245
Victor Breton
Joined 245 Sqn., 7-9-40. Retired, 1958, as Squadron Leader. — ♱ Killed since Battle (11-6-83) — New Zealander

DELLER Sgt. Pilot 43
Alan Lawrence Martin
Joined 43 Sqn., 3-8-40. Commissioned, 27-2-43. Released from R.A.F., 1946, as Flight Lieutenant. — British

DEMETRIADI Fg. Off. Pilot 601
Richard Stephen
On 601 Sqn., 1-7-40. — ♱ **Killed in Action** (11-8-40) — British

DEMOULIN Sgt. Pilot 235
Rene Jean Ghislain
Joined 235 Sqn., 5-8-40. Commissioned, 16-8-41. Was Squadron Leader when killed. — ♱ Killed since Battle (6-4-44) — Belgian

DEMOZAY Lieut. Pilot 1
Jean ("Moses")
Joined 1 Sqn., 16-10-40. Awarded D.S.O. (12-42), D.F.C.✪ (11-41 and 7-42) — ♱ Killed since Battle (19-12-45) — French

DENBY Plt. Off. Pilot 600
Gordon Alfred
Joined 600 Sqn., 9-7-40. Awarded D.F.C. (22-4-41). Was Squadron Leader when killed. — ♱ Killed since Battle (12-12-42) — British

DENCHFIELD Sgt. Pilot 610
Herbert David
Joined 610 Sqn., 7-10-40. Later taken prisoner, 2-41. — British

DENHOLM Flt. Lt. Pilot 603
George Lovell ("Uncle George")
On 603 Sqn., 1-7-40. Promoted Sqn. Ldr., 1-9-40, and appointed to command 603 Sqn. Awarded D.F.C. (22-10-40).✠ 1 Ju 88 (shared), 3-7-40; ✠ 1 Bf 109, 28-8-40; ✠ 1 Bf 109, 15-9-40; ✠ 1 Bf 109 (shared), 27-9-40. Released from R.A.F., 1947, as Group Captain. — British

DENISON Fg. Off. Pilot 236
Richard Warren
On 236 Sqn., 1-7-40. Promoted Flt. Lt., 6-8-40. Awarded A.F.C. (1-1-45). Released from R.A.F., 1945, as Wing Commander. — ♱ Killed since Battle (6-2-51) — British

DENTON Sgt. Aircrew 236
Denis Austin
Joined 236 Sqn., 24-7-40. Was Warrant Officer when killed. — ♱ Killed since Battle (30-8-44) — British

DERBYSHIRE Plt. Off. Pilot 236
John Montague
On 236 Sqn., 1-7-40. Later seriously injured (5-11-40). Released from R.A.F., 5-46, as Squadron Leader. — British

DERMOTT Plt. Off. Aircrew 236
Joined 236 Sqn., 12-7-40. (Neither forenames nor initials known.) — British

DE SCITIVAUX DE GREISCHE 245
Charles Jean Marie Philippe
Capt. Pilot
Joined 245 Sqn., 14-10-45. Awarded D.F.C. Later rose to rank of Vice-Admiral in France. — ♱ Died since Battle (10-8-86) — French

DESLOGES Fg. Off. Pilot 1(Canadian)
Jean-Paul Joseph
On 1(Canadian) Sqn., 20-6-40, on arrival in U.K. Severely wounded, 31-8-40. Was Wing Commander at time of death. — ♱ Killed since Battle (8-5-44) — Canadian

DE SPIRLET Plt. Off. Pilot 87
Francois Xavier Egenoff
Joined 87 Sqn., 12-8-40. — ♱ Killed since Battle (26-6-42) — Belgian

DEUNTZER Sgt. Pilot 79-247
Derrick Canut
Joined 79 Sqn., 30-9-40. Posted to 247 Sqn., 26-20-40. Commissioned, 29-10-41. Released from R.A.F., 1946, as Flight Lieutenant. — British

DEVITT Sqn. Ldr. Pilot 152
Peter Kenneth
In command of 152 Sqn., 1-7-40. — British

DEWAR Plt. Off. Pilot 229
John Michael Firth
Joined 229 Sqn., 10-8-40. ✠ 1 Bf 110, 25-9-40; ✠ 1 Bf 109, 26-9-40. — ♱ Killed since Battle (30-3-41) — British

DEWAR Wg. Cdr. Pilot 87-213
John Scatliff
Commanded 87 Sqn., 1-7-40. Had been awarded D.S.O. and D.F.C.(both 31-5-40). ✠ 2 Bf 110, 11-7-40; ✠ 1 Ju 88, shared, 13-8-40; ✠ 1 Ju 88, 25-8-40. — ♱ **Killed in Action** (12-9-40) — British

DEWEY Plt. Off. Pilot 611-603
Robert Basil ("Senator")
On 611 Sqn., 1-7-40. Posted to 603 Sqn., 27-9-40. ✠ 1 Bf 109, 20-10-40. — ♱ **Killed in Action** (27-10-40) — British

DEWHURST Plt. Off. Pilot 234
Kenneth Shortland ("Dewie")
On 234 Sqn., 1-7-40. Awarded A.F.C. (3-4-45). ✠ 1 Ju 88 (shared), 28-7-40; ✠ 1 Bf 109, 16-8-40; ✠ 1 Ju 88 (shared), 28-10-40. Released from R.A.F., 1946, as Squadron Leader. — British

DEXTER Plt. Off. Pilot 603-54
Peter Grenfell
On 603 Sqn., 1-7-40. Promoted Fg. Off., 30-9-40. Awarded D.F.C. (23-7-40). Wounded, 2-10-40. ✠ 1 Bf 109, 27-9-40; ✠ 1 Bf 109, 2-10-40. — ♱ Killed since Battle (14-7-41) — British

DIBNAH Plt. Off. Pilot 1-242
Roland Harold
On 1 Sqn., 1-7-40. Posted to 242 Sqn., 21-9-40. ✠ 1 Bf 110, 5-9-40. Transferred to R.C.A.F., 18-1-45. Released, 21-10-47, as Flight Lieutenant. — Canadian

DICKIE Plt. Off. Pilot 601
William Gordon
On 601 Sqn., 1-7-40. ✠ 1 Do 17 (shared) 7-7-40. — ♱ **Killed in Action** (11-8-40) — British

DICKINSON Sgt. Pilot 253
John Holt ("Dickie")
On 253 Sqn., 1-7-40. — ♱ **Killed in Action** (30-8-40) — British

DIEU Plt. Off. Pilot 236
Giovanni
Joined 236 Sqn., 5-8-40. Awarded A.F.C. Released from R.A.F., 1946, as Squadron Leader. — Belgian

DIFFORD Fg. Off. Pilot 85-607
Ivor Benison
Joined 85 Sqn., 23-9-40. Posted to 607 Sqn., 2-10-40. — ♱ **Killed in Action** (7-10-40) — South African

DIGBY-WORSLEY Sgt. Aircrew 248
Maxwell Paul
On 248 Sqn., 1-7-40. — ♱ **Killed in Action** (19-8-40) — British

DITZEL Sgt. Aircrew 235
John William ("Ditty")
On 25 Sqn., 1-7-40. Commissioned, 4-5-42. Released from the R.A.F., 1946, as Flight Lieutenant. — British

DIXON Sgt. Pilot 601
Christopher Alexander Wilfred
Joined 601 Sqn., 4-9-40. Commissioned, 9-4-42. Released from R.A.F., 1944. — ♱ Died since Battle (1977) — British

DIXON Sgt. Pilot 501
Frederick John Powell
On 501 Sqn., 1-7-40. — ♱ **Killed in Action** (11-8-40) — British

DIXON Sgt. Pilot F.I.U.
George
On F.I.U., 1-7-40. Taken prisoner, 13-9-40. Commissioned, 26-6-46. Retired from R.A.F., 5-6-48. — ♱ Died since Battle (28-2-72) — British

DIXON Fg. Off. Pilot 1
John Anthony
On 1 Sqn., 1-7-40. Posted away, 10-8-40. Awarded A.F.C. (9-6-49). Retired from R.A.F., 3-5-73, as Flight Lieutenant. — British

DIXON Sgt. Aircrew 600
Lawrence
Joined 600 Sqn., 25-7-40. Commissioned, 21-11-41. Awarded D.F.C.✪ (13-4-43 and 28-9-43). Released from R.A.F., 1947, as Squadron Leader. — British

DOBREE Fg. Off. Aircrew 264
Nicholas Robert
Defiant gunner. Joined 264 Sqn., 18-9-40. Retired from the R.A.F., 1945, as Group Captain. — British

DODD Plt. Off. Pilot 248
John Dodgson
Joined 248 Sqn., 29-9-40. — ♱ Killed since Battle (13-12-40) — British

DODGE Sgt. Aircrew 219
Charles William ("Chota")
On 219 Sqn., 1-7-40. — ♱ Died since Battle (1982) — British

DOE Plt. Off. Pilot 234-238
Robert Francis Thomas ("Bob")
On 234 Sqn., 1-7-40. Posted to 238 Sqn., 27-9-40. Awarded D.S.O. (Indian, 2-10-45); D.F.C.✪ (22-10-40 and 26-11-40). ✠ 2 Bf 110s, 15-8-40; ✠ 1 Bf 109, 16-8-40; ✠ 1 Bf 109, 18-8-40; ✠ 1 Ju 88, 21-8-40; ✠ 1 Bf 109, 26-8-40; ✠ 3 Bf 110s, 4-9-40; ✠ 1 Bf 109, 5-9-40; ✠ 1 Bf 109, 6-9-40; ✠ 1 He 111, 7-9-40; ✠ 1 Bf 109, 1-10-40; ✠ 1 Ju 88, 7-10-40. Wounded, 10-10-40, and again, 3-1-41. Retired from R.A.F., 1-1-66, as a Wing Commander. — British

414

Name	Rank	Duty	Sqn.	Service details	Fate	Nationality
DOLEZAL Frantisek ("Dolly")	Plt. Off.	Pilot	19	Attached to 32 Sqn., from 310 (Czech) Sqn., 8-40. Wounded, 11-9-40. ✠ **1 Bf 110, 7-9-40; ✠ Bf 109, 10-9-40; ✠ 1 He 111, 18-9-40.** Awarded D.F.C. (1942).	✝ Killed since Battle (3-3-45)	Czech
DOMAGALA Marian Boguslaw	Sgt.	Pilot	238	Joined 238 Sqn., 5-8-40. Commissioned, 1-6-42. ✠ **1 Bf 109 and 1 Bf 110, 8-8-40; ✠ 1 Bf 109, 11-8-40.** Released from R.A.F., 12-46, as Flight Lieutenant.		Polish
DON Ralph Stidson	Plt. Off.	Pilot	501	On 501 Sqn., 1-7-40. Awarded D.F.C. (11-12-45). Wounded, 31-7-40.	✝ Killed since Battle (22-1-45)	British
DONAHUE Arthur Gerald	Plt. Off	Pilot	64	Joined 64 Sqn., 3-8-40. Wounded, 12-8-40. Posted away to No. 71 Sqn., 29-9-40, but rejoined 64 Sqn., 23-10-40. Awarded D.F.C. (27-3-42).	✝ Killed since Battle (11-9-42)	American
DONALD Ian David Grahame	Fg. Off.	Pilot	141	On 141 Sqn., 1-7-40.	✝ **Killed in Action** (19-7-40)	British
DONALDSON Edward Mortlock ("Teddy")	Sqn. Ldr.	Pilot	151	In command of 151 Sqn., 1-7-40. Posted away, 5-8-40. Appointed C.B. (1-1-60), C.B.E. (1-6-53), D.S.O. (31-5-40), A.F.C.✺ (30-9-41 and 12-6-47). ✠ **1 Bf 109, 14-7-40.** Retired from R.A.F., 21-3-61, as Air Commodore.		British
¶ DONIGER	Sgt.	Pilot	56	Joined 56 Sqn., 5-9-40; posted away, 18-9-40; did not fly operations.		British
DOSSETT William Stanley	Sgt.	Aircrew	29	On 29 Sqn., 1-7-40. Posted away, 27-7-40. Awarded D.F.M., 22-9-42. Commissioned, 10-8-42. Retired from R.A.F., 22-5-54, as Flight Lieutenant.		British
DOUGHTY Neville Anthony Richard	Plt. Off.	Pilot	247	On 247 Sqn., 1-7-40. Promoted Fg. Off., 30-9-40. Retired from R.A.F., 6-1-58, as Squadron Leader.		British
DOUGLAS William Anderson	Plt. Off.	Pilot	610	Joined 610 Sqn., 16-9-40. Awarded D.F.C.✺ (4-12-42 and 26-9-44). Released from R.A.F., 17-12-45, as Wing Commander.		British
DOULTON Michael Duke	Fg. Off.	Pilot	601	On 601 Sqn., 1-7-40. ✠ **1 Do 17 (shared), 11-7-40; ✠ 1 He 59, 20-7-40; ✠ 1 Ju 88 (shared), 15-8-40; ✠ 1 Ju 87, 16-8-40.**	✝ **Killed in Action** (31-8-40)	British
DOUTHWAITE Basil	Sgt.	Pilot	72	On 72 Sqn., 1-7-40. Commissioned, 21-8-40. ✠ **1 Bf 109, 1-9-40.** Wounded, 11-9-40. Released from R.A.F., 1945, as Flight Lieutenant.		British
DOUTREPONT Georges Louis Joseph	Plt. Off.	Pilot	229	Joined 229 Sqn., 4-8-40. ✠ **1 Do 17 (solo), and 1 He 111 (shared), 11-9-40.**	✝ **Killed in Action** (15-9-40)	Belgian
DOWDING Derek Hugh Tremenheere	Plt. Off.	Pilot	74	On 74 Sqn., 1-7-40. Promoted, Fg. Off., 3-9-40. ✠ **1 He 111 (shared), 8-7-40.** Retired from R.A.F., 17-11-56, as Wing Commander.		British
DOWN John Knight	Sgt.	Pilot	64-616	Joined 64 Sqn., 7-10-40. Posted to 616 Sqn., 13-10-40. Commissioned, 18-9-42. Released from R.A.F., 30-11-45, as Flight Lieutenant.		British
DOWN Peter Derrick McLeod	Plt. Off.	Pilot	56	On 56 Sqn., 1-7-40. Posted away, 26-9-40. ✠ **1 Bf 110, 18-8-40; ✠ 1 Bf 109, 19-8-40.** Released from R.A.F., 1945, as Squadron Leader.		British
DRABY	A.C.1	Aircrew	25	Joined 25 Sqn., c.30-9-40. Promoted Sergeant, 10-40. (Forenames not known)		British
DRAKE Billy	Fg. Off.	Pilot	421 Flt.	Joined 421 Flt., 22-10-40. Awarded D.S.O. (4-12-42), D.F.C.✺ (7-1-41 and 28-7-42). Retired from R.A.F., 1-7-63, as Group Captain.		British
DRAKE George James	Plt. Off.	Pilot	607	Joined 607 Sqn., 10-8-40.	✝ **Killed in Action** (9-9-40)	South Afric
DRAPER Bryan Vincent	Plt. Off.	Pilot	74	On 74 Sqn., 1-7-40. Awarded D.F.C. (24-12-40).✠ **1 Ju 88, 14-9-40; ✠ 1 Bf 109, 17-10-40.**	✝ Killed since Battle (28-2-45)	British
DRAPER Gilbert Graham Fairley	Plt. Off.	Pilot	610-41	Joined 610 Sqn., 3-9-40. Posted to 41 Sqn., 29-9-40. Slightly injured, 30-10-40. Taken prisoner, 7-8-41. Released from R.A.F., 1945, as Flight Lieutenant.		British
DRAPPER, R.A.	Sgt.	Pilot	232	On 232 Sqn., injured in accident, 5-9-40.		British
DREDGE Allan Sydney	Sgt.	Pilot	253	On 253 Sqn., 1-7-40. Commissioned, 12-3-41. Awarded D.S.O. (5-12-44), D.F.C. (27-7-43). ✠ **2 Bf 109s, 30-8-40; ✠ 1 Bf 110, 4-9-40; ✠ 1 Bf 109, 14-9-40.**	✝ Killed since Battle (18-5-45)	British
DREVER Nigel George	Plt. Off.	Pilot	610	Joined 610 Sqn., 22-9-40. Released from the R.A.F., 1946, as Flight Lieutenant.		British
DREW Peter Edward	Sqn. Ldr.	Pilot	236	In command of 236 Sqn., 1-7-40.	✝ **Killed in Action** (1-8-40)	British
DROBINSKI Boleslaw ("Gandi")	Plt. Off.	Pilot	65	Joined 65 Sqn., 11-9-40. Awarded D.F.C. (30-10-41). Released from R.A.F., 1948, as Squadron Leader.		Polish
DRUMMOND John Fraser	Plt. Off.	Pilot	46-92	On 46 Sqn., 1-7-40. Promoted Fg. Off., 3-9-40. Awarded D.F.C. (26-7-40) ✠ **1 Bf 109, 23-9-40; ✠ 1 Ju 88 (solo) and 1 He 111 (shared), 27-9-40; ✠ 1 Bf 109 and 1 Hs 126, 5-10-40.**	✝ **Killed in Action** (10-10-40)	British
¶ DRUMMOND-HAY Peter	Fg. Off.	Pilot	609	On 609 Sqn., 1-7-40.	✝ Killed in Action (9-7-40)	British
DUART John Howard	Plt. Off.	Aircrew	219	On 219 Sqn., 1-7-40. Released from R.A.F., 23-11-45, as Flight Lieutenant.		British
DUBBER Ronald Edwin	Petty Off.	Pilot	808	Fleet Air Arm. On 808 Sqn., 1-7-40. Commissioned 1-1-43.	✝ Died since Battle (10-9-51)	British
DUCKENFIELD Byron Leonard	Plt. Off.	Pilot	74-501	On 74 Sqn., 1-7-40. Posted to 501 Sqn., 22-7-40. Awarded A.F.C. (24-9-41). ✠ **1 Ju 87, 29-7-40; ✠ 1 Do 17, 15-8-40; ✠ 1 Bf 109, 28-8-40; ✠ 1 Bf 109, 8-9-40.** Retired from R.A.F., 28-6-69, as Group Captain.		British
DUDA Josef	Plt. Off.	Pilot	312	Joined 312 (Czech) Sqn., 5-9-40. Appointed C.B.E. (1945). Released from R.A.F., 1945, as Group Captain.	✝ Died since Battle (c.1973)	Czech
DUFF Stanley Sutherland	Plt. Off.	Pilot	23	Joined 23 Sqn., 23-7-40. Awarded D.F.C. (20-8-43). Released from R.A.F., 1-12-45, as Squadron Leader.		British
DUKE-WOOLLEY Raymond Miles Beecham Duke ("Baron")	Flt. Lt.	Pilot	23-253	On 23 Sqn., 1-7-40. Posted to 253 Sqn., 12-9-40. Awarded D.S.O. (8-1-43), D.F.C.✺ (24-12-40 and 29-5-42). Promoted Acting Sqn. Ldr., 27-9-40. ✠ **1 Do 17, 6-10-40.** Retired from R.A.F., 30-1-61, as Group Captain.		British
DULWICH William Howard	Sgt.	Aircrew	235	Joined 235 Sqn., 24-8-40.	✝ Killed since Battle (2-8-41)	British
DUNDAS Hugh Spencer Lisle	Plt. Off.	Pilot	616	On 616 Sqn., 1-7-40. Awarded D.S.O.✺ (3-3-44 and 20-3-45), D.F.C. (5-8-41). Promoted Fg. Off., 2-10-40. ✠ **1 Do 17 (shared), 3-7-40; ✠ 1 Ju 88 (solo) and 1 Ju 88 (shared), 15-8-40.** Wounded, 22-8-40. Retired from R.A.F., 25-1-47, as Wing Commander.		British
DUNDAS John Charles	Fg. Off.	Pilot	609	On 609 Sqn., 1-7-40. Awarded D.F.C.✺ (22-10-40 and 7-1-41). ✠ **1 Bf 110, 13-7-40; ✠ 1 Bf 110, 19-7-40; ✠ 2 Bf 110s, 11-8-40; ✠ 1 Ju 87, 13-8-40; ✠ 1 Do 17 (solo) and 1 Ju 88 (shared), 14-8-40; ✠ 1 Do 17 (shared) 15-9-40; ✠ 1 Bf 110, 24-9-40; ✠ 1 Do 17, 25-9-40; ✠ 1 Bf 109, 26-9-40; ✠ 1 Bf 110, 27-9-40; ✠ 1 Bf 109, 15-10-40.**	✝ Killed since Battle (27-11-40)	British
DUNMORE Jack Townley	Sgt.	Pilot	266-222	Joined 266 Sqn., 16-9-40. Posted to 222 Sqn., 1-10-40. ✠ **1 Bf 109 (shared), 15-10-40.**	✝ Killed since Battle (17-5-41)	British
DUNN Ian Love	Sgt.	Aircrew	235	On 235 Sqn., 1-7-40. Commissioned, 11-6-42. Retired from R.A.F., 23-12-64, as Wing Commander.		British
DUNNING-WHITE Peter William	Plt. Off.	Pilot	145	Joined 145 Sqn., 2-7-40. Awarded D.F.C. (6-6-41). ✠ **1 He 111 (shared), 18-7-40; ✠ 1 Do 17 (shared), 22-7-40; ✠ 1 Bf 110 and 1 Ju 87, 8-8-40; ✠ 1 Bf 109, 11-8-40.** Released from R.A.F., 8-10-45, as Wing Commander.		British
DUNSCOMBE Raymond Douglas	Sgt.	Pilot	213-312	On 213 Sqn., 1-7-40. Posted to 312 (Czech) Sqn., c.28-8-40. Commissioned, 16-10-40. ✠ **1 Bf 110, 15-8-40.** Injured, 17-9-40.	✝ Killed since Battle (31-5-41)	British
DUNWORTH Felix Patrick Raphael	Flt. Lt.	Pilot	66-54	On 66 Sqn., 1-7-40. Slightly wounded, 4-9-40. Promoted Acting Sqn. Ldr., and posted to 54 Sqn., 9-9-40, to command. Awarded A.F.C. (3-4-45). Released from R.A.F., 1946, as Wing Commander.		British
DUPEE Oswald Arthur	Sgt.	Pilot	219	On 219 Sqn., 1-7-40. Commissioned, 9-5-42. Awarded D.F.C. (21-1-44), D.F.M. (24-9-40). Served with the R.A.F. after the War.		British
DURRANT Carroll Arnold	Sgt.	Aircrew	23	Joined 23 Sqn., 21-9-40. Commissioned, 10-6-42.	✝ Killed since Battle (28-10-42)	New Zealander
DURYASZ Marian	Plt. Off.	Pilot	213	Joined 213 Sqn., 17-8-40. Awarded D.F.C. ✠ **1 Bf 110, 11-9-40; ✠ 1 Do 17, 15-9-40.** Released from R.A.F., 12-46, as Squadron Leader.		Polish
DUSZYNSKI Stanislaw	Sgt.	Pilot	238	Joined 238 Sqn., 2-9-40.	✝ **Killed in Action** (11-9-40)	Polish
DUTTON, G.W.	Sgt.	Aircrew	604	Joined 604 Sqn., c.10-7-40. No further records traced.		British
DUTTON Roy Gilbert	Fg. Off.	Pilot	145	On 145 Sqn., 1-7-40. Appointed C.B.E. and awarded D.S.O. (8-6-45), D.F.C.✺ (31-5-40 and 20-8-40). ✠ **1 Do 17 (shared), 1-7-40; ✠ 1 Do 17 (shared), 10-7-40; ✠ 1 He 111, 11-7-40; ✠ 1 He 111 (shared), 19-7-40; ✠ 3 Ju 87s, 8-8-40; ✠ 2 Bf 110s, 11-8-40; ✠ 1 Ju 88, 12-8-40.** Retired from R.A.F., 3-12-70, as Air Commodore.	✝ Died since Battle (14-9-88)	British

Name	Rank	Category	Squadron	Notes	Status	Nationality
DUVIVIER, Reginal Albert Lloyd	Plt. Off.	Pilot	229	On 229 Sqn., 1-7-40.	Killed since Battle (30-3-41)	British
DVORAK, Alois	Sgt.	Pilot	310	Joined 310 (Czech) Sqn., 19-9-40.	Killed since Battle (24-9-41)	Czech
DYE, Bertram Ernest	Sgt.	Aircrew	219	On 219 Sqn., 1-7-40. Awarded D.F.M.✿ (2-5-41 and 6-6-41). Commissioned, 17-12-41.	Killed since Battle (31-8-43)	British
DYER, Henry David Patrick	Sgt.	Aircrew	600	Joined 600 Sqn., 20-9-40.	Killed since Battle (16-7-41)	New Zealan
DYGRYN, Josef	Sgt.	Pilot	1	Joined 1 Sqn., 22-10-40. Awarded D.F.M. (3-42)	Killed since Battle (4-6-42)	Czech
DYKE, Leslie Arthur	Sgt.	Pilot	64	Joined 64 Sqn., 9-40.	**Killed in Action (27-9-40)**	British
DYMOND, William Lawrence	Sgt.	Pilot	111	On 111 Sqn., 1-7-40. ✠ **1 Do 17 (shared) 13-8-40; ✠ 1 Do 17 and 1 Bf 110, 15-8-40; ✠ 1 Do 17, 18-8-40; ✠ 1 He 111, 24-8-40.**	**Killed in Action (2-9-40)**	British
EADE, Arthur William	Sgt.	Pilot	266-602	On 266 Sqn., 11-7-40. Posted to 602 Sqn., 13-9-40. Awarded A.F.C. (2-6-43). Released from R.A.F., 9-47, as Warrant Officer.		British
EARP, Richard Llewellyn	Sgt.	Pilot	46	On 46 Sqn., 1-7-40. Commissioned, 20-8-53. Retired from R.A.F., 4-1-67, as Flight Lieutenant.		British
EASTON, David Albert	Sgt.	Pilot	248	Joined 248 Sqn., 25-9-40. Commissioned, 19-7-42. Released from R.A.F., 1945, as Flight Lieutenant.		British
ECKFORD, Alan Francis ("Shag")	Plt. Off.	Pilot	242-32-253	On 242 Sqn., 1-7-40. Posted to 32 Sqn., 29-7-40. Posted to 253 Sqn., 12-9-40. Awarded D.F.C. (24-12-40). Promoted Fg. Off., 3-9-40. ✠ **1 Do 17 and 1 Bf 109, 18-8-40; ✠ 1 Bf 109, 27-9-40; ✠ 1 Bf 109, 30-10-40.** Released from R.A.F., 1946, as Squadron Leader.		British
EDGE, Alexander Rothwell	Fg. Off.	Pilot	609	On 609 Sqn., 1-7-40. Posted away, 2-8-40. Promoted Flt. Lt., 3-9-40. Awarded A.F.C., 1-1-43. Released from R.A.F., 1945, as Squadron Leader.	Died since Battle (1985)	British
EDGE, Gerald Richmond	Flt. Lt.	Pilot	605-253	On 615 Sqn., 1-7-40. Promoted Acting Sqn. Ldr., and posted to 253 Sqn., 5-9-40, to command. Awarded O.B.E. (1-1-45), D.F.C. (13-9-40). ✠ **1 Bf 109, 11-9-40.** Released from the R.A.F., 1945, as Group Captain.		British
EDGLEY, Alwyn	Sgt.	Pilot	601-253	Joined 601 Sqn., 4-9-40. Posted to 253 Sqn., 14-9-40. Wounded, 29-9-40. Commissioned, 4-4-42. Released from R.A.F., 1946, as Flight Lieutenant.		British
EDMISTON, Guy Arthur Fownes	Plt. Off.	Pilot	151	Joined 151 Sqn., 29-9-40. Released from the R.A.F., 1946, as Flight Lieutenant.	Died since Battle (1989)	British
EDMOND, Norman Douglas	Plt. Off.	Pilot	615	Joined 615 Sqn., 24-9-40. Wounded, 29-10-40.	Killed since Battle (20-4-41)	Canadian
EDMUNDS, Eric Ralph	Plt. Off.	Pilot	245-615	On 245 Sqn., 1-7-40. Posted to 615 Sqn., c.5-10-40. Severely wounded, 29-10-40. Transferred to R.N.Z.A.F., 1946, and released as a Flight Lieutenant.		New Zealander
EDRIDGE, Hilary Patrick Michael	Plt. Off.	Pilot	222	On 222 Sqn. Wounded, 30-8-40. ✠ **1 Bf 110 (shared), 20-10-40.**	**Killed in Action (30-10-40)**	British
EDSALL, Eric Frank	Plt. Off.	Pilot	54-222	Joined 54 Sqn., 1-8-40. Posted to 222 Sqn., 19-9-40. Awarded D.F.C. (16-1-42). Severely wounded, 27-10-40. ✠ **1 Bf 110, 18-8-40; ✠ 1 Bf 109, 24-8-40; ✠ 1 Bf 109, 30-9-40.**	Died since Battle (12-4-42)	British
EDWARDS	Sgt.	Pilot	247	Joined 247 Sqn., c.2-9-40. No record of operations traced.		British
EDWARDS, A.J.	L.A.C.	Aircrew	604	On 604 Sqn. Promoted Sergeant, 7-40. No record of operations traced.		British
EDWARDS, Frederick	A.C.1	Aircrew	29	On 29 Sqn., 1-7-40. Promoted Sergeant. No record of operations traced.		British
EDWARDS, Harry Davies	Plt. Off.	Pilot	92	On 92 Sqn., 1-7-40. ✠ **1 He 111 (shared), 4-7-40.**	**Killed in Action (11-9-40)**	Canadian
EDWARDS, Harold Harding	Sgt.	Aircrew	248	On 248 Sqn., 1-7-40. Commissioned, 12-5-42. Released from R.A.F., 1945, as Flight Lieutenant.		British
EDWARDS, Ivor Herbert	Plt. Off.	Pilot	234	Joined 234 Sqn., c.13-9-40. Awarded D.F.C. (22-9-42). Released from R.A.F., 1946, as Flight Lieutenant.		British
EDWARDS, Kenneth Charles	Plt. Off.	Aircrew	600	On 600 Sqn., 1-7-40. Commissioned, 8-40. Made P.O.W., 7-41. Released from R.A.F., 5-45, as Flight Lieutenant.		British
EDWARDS, Robert Leonard	Fg. Off.	Pilot	1(Canadian)	On 1(Canadian) Sqn., on arrival in U.K., 20-6-40.	**Killed in Action (26-8-40)**	Canadian
EDWARDS, Robert Sydney James	Flt. Lt.	Pilot	56	Joined 56 Sqn., 10-9-40. Awarded D.F.C. (21-11-41 with Bomber Command). Retired from R.A.F., 12-2-63, as Wing Commander.	Died since Battle (2-5-74)	Irish
EDWORTHY, Gerald Henry	Sgt.	Pilot	46	On 46 Sqn., 1-7-40.	**Killed in Action (3-9-40)**	British
EDY, Allen Laird	Plt. Off.	Pilot	602	Joined 602 Sqn., 8-9-40. Promoted Fg. Off., 3-9-40. Awarded D.F.C. (5-14-40). ✠ **1 Do 17, 15-9-40.**	Killed since Battle (16-6-41)	Canadian
EGAN, Edward James	Sgt.	Pilot	600-615-501	On 600 Sqn., 1-7-40. Posted to 615 Sqn., 27-8-40. Posted to 501 Sqn., 13-9-40. ✠ **1 Bf 109, 15-9-40.**	**Killed in Action (17-9-40)**	British
EIBY, William Thorpe	Plt. Off.	Pilot	245	Joined 245 Sqn., 28-9-40. Released from R.N.Z.A.F., 12-2-47, as Flight Lieutenant.		New Zealander
EKINS, Victor Howard	Sgt.	Pilot	111-501	Joined 111 Sqn., 18-7-40. Posted to 501 Sqn., 21-9-40. Commissioned, 2-4-41. Awarded D.F.C. (23-6-42), M.B.E. (1-1-46). ✠ **1 Bf 109, 5-9-40.**		British
ELCOME, Douglas William	Sgt.	Pilot	602	On 602 Sqn., 1-7-40. ✠ **1 Bf 109, 31-8-40.**	Killed in Action (26-10-40)	British
ELEY, Frederick William	Sgt.	Pilot	74	On 74 Sqn., 1-7-40.	**Killed in Action (31-7-40)**	British
ELGER, Frank Richard Charles	Plt. Off.	Pilot	248	On 248 Sqn., 1-7-40. Released from the R.A.F., 1946, as Flight Lieutenant.		Canadian
ELIOT, Hugh William ("Chubby")	Plt. Off.	Pilot	73	On 73 Sqn., 1-7-40. Wounded, 6-9-40. Awarded D.S.O. (23-5-44), D.F.C. (26-9-41). Was Squadron Leader at time of death.	Killed since Battle (4-3-45)	British
ELKINGTON, John Francis Durham	Plt. Off.	Pilot	1	Joined 1 Sqn., 15-7-40. Wounded, 16-8-40. ✠ **1 Bf 109, 15-8-40.** Retired from R.A.F., 23-12-75, as Wing Commander.		British
ELLACOMBE, John Lawrence Wemyss	Plt. Off.	Pilot	151	Joined 151 Sqn., 13-7-40. Wounded, 31-8-40. Appointed C.B. (1970); awarded D.F.C.✿ (7-4-42 and 29-12-44). ✠ **1 He 111, 24-8-40.** Retired from R.A.F., 16-4-73, as Air Commodore.		British
ELLERY, Cyril Charles	Plt. Off.	Aircrew	264	Defiant gunner. Joined 264 Sqn., 14-7-40. Released from R.A.F., 1945, as Squadron Leader.	Died since Battle (20-3-77)	British
ELLIOTT, G.J.	Plt. Off.	Pilot	607	Joined 607 Sqn., c.9-10-40. Released from R.C.A.F., 4-6-46, as Squadron Leader.		Canadian
ELLIOTT, Robert Deacon	Plt. Off.	Pilot	72	On 72 Sqn., 1-7-40. Awarded D.F.C. (17-10-41). ✠ **1 Bf 110, 4-9-40; ✠ 1 Bf 109, 6-9-40; ✠ 1 Bf 109, 9-9-40; ✠ 1 He 111, 11-9-40.** Retired from R.A.F., 27-9-68, as Air Vice-Marshal.		British
ELLIS, Gordon Eric	Plt. Off.	Pilot	64	Joined 64 Sqn., 12-7-40. No record of operations traced.		British
ELLIS, John	Fg. Off.	Pilot	610	On 610 Sqn., 1-7-40. Promoted Flt. Lt., 3-9-40 (commanded 610 Sqn. from 26-8-40). Appointed C.B.E., 11-6-60; awarded D.F.C.✿ (13-8-40 and 2-5-41). ✠ **1 Do 17 (shared), 3-7-40; ✠ 1 Bf 109, 24-7-40; ✠ 3 Bf 109s, 25-7-40; ✠ 1 Bf 109, 12-8-40; ✠ 1 He 111, 18-8-40; ✠ 1 Bf 109, 26-8-40; ✠ 1 Bf 109, 27-8-40.**		British
ELLIS, John Hugh Mortimer ("Cock Sparrow")	Sgt.	Pilot	85	On 85 Sqn., 1-7-40. ✠ **1 Do 17 (shared), 6-8-40; ✠ 1 Bf 109, 18-8-40.**	**Killed in Action (1-9-40)**	British
ELLIS, Ronald Vernon	F/Sgt.	Pilot	73	On 73 Sqn., 1-7-40. Commissioned, 14-10-41. Awarded A.F.C. (1-1-46), D.F.M. (2-1-42). ✠ **1 Bf 109 (shared), 27-9-40.** Retired from R.A.F., 11-10-66, as Flight Lieutenant.		British
ELLIS, Walter Thomas	Sgt.	Pilot	266-92	Joined 266 Sqn., 26-8-40. Posted to 92 Sqn., 21-9-40. Commissioned, 15-10-41. ✠ **1 Ju 88 (shared), 27-9-40.** Awarded A.F.C. (2-1-50). Retired from R.A.F., 8-6-63, as Wing Commander.		British
ELSDON, Harry Donald Buchanan	Sgt.	Aircrew	236	On 236 Sqn., 1-7-40.	**Killed in Action (18-7-40)**	British
ELSDON, Thomas Arthur Francis ("Jimmie")	Fg. Off.	Pilot	72	On 72 Sqn., 1-7-40. Promoted Flt. Lt., 3-9-40. Awarded O.B.E. (14-6-45), D.F.C. (8-10-40). ✠ **1 Bf 110, 15-8-40; ✠ 2 Bf 109s, 1-9-40; ✠ 1 Ju 87 and 1 Bf 110, 4-9-40; ✠ 1 Bf 109, 7-9-40.** Retired from R.A.F., 22-10-59, as Group Captain.		British

Name	Rank	Role	Sqn.	Notes	Fate	Nationality
ELSE Peter	Sgt.	Pilot	610	On 610 Sqn., 1-7-40. ✠ 1 Bf 109, 25-7-40. Severely wounded, 26-7-40. Discharged from R.A.F., 2-4-41, on medical grounds.		British
EMENY Clifford Stanley	L.A.C.	Aircrew	264	Defiant gunner. On 264 Sqn., 1-7-40. Promoted Sergeant, 27-7-40. Commissioned, 29-11-41. Released from R.N.Z.A.F., 1946, as Flight Lieutenant.		New Zealander
EMMETT Geoffrey	Sgt.	Aircrew	236	Joined 236 Sqn., 16-8-40. Commissioned, 18-5-43. Released from R.A.F., 23-11-45, as Flight Lieutenant.		British
EMMETT William Alexander Coote	Fg. Off.	Pilot	25	On 25 Sqn., 1-7-40. Promoted Flt. Lt., 15-10-40. Retired from R.A.F., 30-4-58, as Wing Commander.		British
ENGLISH Charles Edward ("Honk")	Plt. Off.	Pilot	85-605	On 85 Sqn., 1-7-40. Posted to 605 Sqn., 12-9-40. ✠ 1 Bf 110, 30-8-40; ✠ 1 Do 215, 1-9-40.	✝ Killed in Action (7-10-40)	British
ENSOR Philip Stephen	Plt. Off.	Pilot	23	On 23 Sqn., 1-7-40. Promoted Fg. Off., 3-9-40. Awarded D.F.C. (18-2-41)	✝ Killed since Battle (8-9-41)	British
ETHERINGTON Wilfred John	Sgt.	Pilot	17	On 17 Sqn., 1-7-40. Commissioned, 21-2-42. Released from the R.A.F., 8-45, as Squadron Leader.		British
EVANS Cecil Roy	Sgt.	Pilot	235	Joined 235 Sqn., 26-9-40.	✝ Killed since Battle (23-3-41)	British
EVANS David	Plt. Off.	Pilot	615-607	On 615 Sqn., 1-7-40. Posted to 607 Sqn., 8-9-40. Was a Squadron Leader at the time of his death.	✝ Killed since Battle (28-5-43)	British
EVANS George John	Sgt.	Aircrew	604	On 604 Sqn., 1-7-40. Awarded D.F.M. (4-7-41). Commissioned, 1-5-42. Released from R.A.F., 1946, as Flight Lieutenant.		British
EVANS Harold Arthur Charles	Plt. Off.	Aircrew	236	Joined 236 Sqn., 15-7-40. Released from R.A.F., 1947, as Flight Lieutenant.	✝ Died since Battle (10-84)	British
EVANS Walter Reginald	Sgt.	Pilot	85-249	On 85 Sqn., 1-7-40. Posted to 249 Sqn., 11-9-40. ✠ 1 Do 17 (shared) 6-8-40; ✠ 1 Bf 109 and 1 Bf 110, 1-9-40. Commissioned, 5-6-41. Released from R.A.F., 9-46, as Squadron Leader.		British
EVERETT Alfred Douglas	Sgt.	Aircrew	235	On 235 Sqn., 1-7-40.	✝ Died since Battle (1953)	British
EVERITT Geoffrey Charles	Sgt.	Aircrew	29	On 29 Sqn., 1-7-40.	✝ Killed since Battle (6-8-42)	British
¶ EVERSHED, A.	Plt. Off.	Pilot	54	On 54 Sqn., 1-7-40.	✝ Killed in Action (9-7-40)	British
EVLES Peter Raoul	Sgt.	Pilot	92	On 92 Sqn., 1-7-40. ✠ 1 He 111, 11-9-40.	✝ **Killed in Action** (20-9-40)	British
EYRE Anthony	Fg. Off.	Pilot	615	On 615 Sqn., 1-7-40. Awarded D.F.C. (30-8-40). ✠ 1 Bf 109, 2-7-40; ✠ 1 Ju 87 (solo) and 1 Ju 87 (shared), 14-8-40; ✠ 1 Bf 109 (shared), 15-8-40; ✠ 1 Do 17, 20-8-40; ✠ 1 Bf 109, 26-8-40; ✠ 1 Do 17, 28-8-40.	✝ Killed since Battle (16-2-46)	British
FAJTL Frantisek	Plt. Off.	Pilot	310-17	Joined 310 (Czech) Sqn., 6-8-40. Posted to 17 Sqn., 25-9-40. ✠ 1 Do 17 (shared), 2-10-40; ✠ 1 Do 17, 24-10-40. Awarded D.F.C. (1942) Volunteered for service in Russia, 2-44.		Czech
FALKOWSKI Jan Pawel	Fg. Off.	Pilot	32	Joined 32 Sqn., 12-9-40. Awarded D.F.C. (15-11-42). Survived the War.		Polish
FARLEY Walter Ronald	Flt. Lt.	Pilot	151-46	Flew operational sorties with both squadrons during Battle. Awarded D.F.C. (7-3-41) Was Wing Commander at time of death.	✝ Killed since Battle (21-4-42)	British
FARMER James Nigel Watts	Flt. Lt.	Pilot	302	Joined 302 (Polish) Sqn., 15-7-40, as flight commander. Awarded D.F.C. (7-3-41). Retired from R.A.F., 6-2-60, retaining rank of Air Commodore.		British
FARNES Eric	Plt. Off.	Aircrew	141	Defiant gunner. On 141 Sqn., 1-7-40. Released from R.A.F., 1947, as Squadron Leader.	✝ Died since Battle (23-9-85)	British
FARNES Paul Caswell Powe	Sgt.	Pilot	501	On 501 Sqn., 1-7-40. Awarded D.F.M. (22-10-40). ✠ 1 Ju 87, 12-8-40; ✠ 2 Ju 87s, 15-8-40; ✠ 1 Bf 110, 18-8-40; ✠ 1 Bf 109, 28-8-40; ✠ 1 Ju 88, 30-9-40. Commissioned, 27-11-40. Retired from R.A.F., 27-6-58, as Wg. Cdr.		British
FARQUHAR Andrew Douglas	Wg. Cdr.	Pilot	257	Commanded Martlesham Heath during Battle; flew operational sorties with 257 Sqn., 1-9-40 and 18-9-40. Awarded D.F.C., (1-3-40). Released from R.A.F., 1945, as a Group Captain.	✝ Died since Battle (c.1966)	British
FARROW John Robinson	Sgt.	Pilot	229	Joined 229 Sqn., 9-40.	✝ **Killed in Action** (8-10-40)	British
FARTHING John	Sgt.	Pilot	235	On 235 Sqn., 1-7-40. Awarded M.B.E.(1-1-46)		British
FAWCETT Derek R.	Sgt.	Aircrew	29	Joined 29 Sqn., c.5-10-40.	✝ Killed since Battle (15-9-41)	British
FAYOLLE Emile Francois Marie Leonce	Plt. Off.	Pilot	85	Joined 85 Sqn., 13-9-40.	✝ Killed since Battle (19-8-42)	French
FEARY Alan Norman	Sgt.	Pilot	609	On 609 Sqn., 1-7-40. ✠ 1 Ju 88 (shared), 18-7-40. ✠ 1 Bf 109, 12-8-40; ✠ 1 Ju 87, 13-8-40; ✠ 1 Ju 88, 14-8-40; ✠ 1 Bf 110, 25-8-40; ✠ 1 Do 17, 24-9-40.	✝ **Killed in Action** (17-10-40)	British
FEATHER John Leslie	Sgt.	Aircrew	235	Joined 235 Sqn., 2-8-40. (Killed while flying with No. 22 Sqn.)	✝ **Killed in Action** (18-9-40)	British
FECHTNER Emil	Plt. Off.	Pilot	310	Joined 310 (Czech) Sqn., 12-7-40. Awarded D.F.C. (10-40). ✠ 1 Bf 110, 26-8-40; ✠ 1 Do 17, 31-8-40; ✠ 1 Bf 110, 3-9-40; ✠ 1 Do 17, 18-9-40.	✝ **Killed in Action** (29-10-40)	Czech
FEJFAR Stanislav	Plt. Off.	Pilot	310	Joined 310 (Czech) Sqn., 6-8-40. ✠ 1 Bf 110, 9-9-40; ✠ 1 Do 17, 15-9-40; ✠ 1 Do 17 (shared), 18-9-40.	✝ Killed since Battle (17-5-42)	Czech
FENEMORE Stanley Allen	Sgt.	Pilot	245-501	Joined 245 Sqn., 17-7-40. Posted to 501 Sqn., 9-40.	✝ **Killed in Action** (15-10-40)	British
FENN Cecil Francis	Sgt.	Aircrew	248	On 248 Sqn., 1-7-40. Commissioned, 20-5-42. Released from R.A.F., 1945, as Flight Lieutenant.	✝ Died since Battle (27-12-87)	British
FENTON Harold Arthur	Sqn. Ldr.	Pilot	238	In command of 238 Sqn., 1-7-40. Appointed C.B.E. (1-1-46); awarded D.S.O. (16-2-43), D.F.C. (28-7-42). ✠ 1 Do 17 (shared), 21-7-40; ✠ 1 Bf 110, 7-10-40. Released from R.A.F., 1945, as Group Captain.		British
FENTON John Ollis	Plt. Off.	Pilot	235	Joined 235 Sqn., 5-8-40. ✠ 1 He 59 (shared), 8-10-40.	✝ Killed since Battle (28-5-41)	British
FENTON Walter Gordon	Sgt.	Aircrew	604	Joined 604 Sqn., 6-7-40. Slightly wounded, 15-8-40. Commissioned, 1-1-42. Released from Service on medical grounds, 15-11-43.		New Zealander
FENWICK Charles Raymond	Plt. Off.	Pilot	610	Joined 610 Sqn., 29-9-40. Released from R.A.F., 1946, as Squadron Leader.		British
FENWICK Samuel Green	Plt. Off.	Pilot	601	Joined 601 Sqn., 1-10-40. Released from R.A.F., 1946, as Flight Lieutenant.		British
FERDINAND Roy Frederick	Plt. Off.	Pilot	263	On 263 Sqn., 1-7-40.	✝ Killed since Battle (12-6-41)	British
FERGUSON Eric Hannah	Sgt.	Aircrew	141	Defiant gunner. Joined 141 Sqn., 17-9-40. Commissioned, 9-2-42.	✝ Killed since Battle (11-4-43)	British
FERGUSON Peter John	Fg. Off.	Pilot	602	On 602 Sqn., 1-7-40. Promoted Flt. Lt., 3-9-40. ✠ 1 Ju 87, 18-8-40. Wounded, 18-8-40. Released from R.A.F., 1945, as Wing Commander.		British
FERIC Miroslaw	Plt. Off.	Pilot	303	Joined 303 (Polish) Sqn., 2-8-40. Awarded D.F.C. (30-10-41). ✠ 1 Bf 109, 6-9-40; ✠ 1 Bf 109 and 1 Bf 110, 15-9-40; ✠ 1 Bf 109 and 1 Bf 110, 27-9-40; ✠ 1 Bf 110, 5-10-40.	✝ Killed since Battle (14-2-42)	Polish
FERRISS Henry Michael	Fg. Off.	Pilot	111	On 111Sqn., 1-7-40. Awarded D.F.C. (21-6-40). ✠ 1 Do 17 (shared) and 1 Bf 109, 10-7-40; ✠ 1 He 59 (shared) 28-7-40; ✠ 1 Do 215, 13-8-40; ✠ 1 Do 17, 16-8-40.	✝ **Killed in Action** (16-8-40)	British
FILDES Frank	Sgt.	Aircrew	25	Joined 25 Sqn., 10-40. Commissioned, 17-2-44. Released from R.A.F., 1945, as Flying Officer.		British
FINCH, T.R.H.	Fg. Off.	Pilot	151	✠ 1 Ju 88 (shared), 30-9-40. No further details of service known.		British
FINLAY Donald Osborne	Sqn. Ldr.	Pilot	54-41	Joined 54 Sqn., 26-8-40, to command. Posted to 41 Sqn., 9-40, to command. Awarded D.F.C. (10-4-42), A.F.C. (1-9-44).✠ 1 Bf 109, 23-9-40; ✠ 1 Do 17 (shared), 7-10-40. Wounded, 28-8-40. Retired from R.A.F., 23-2-59, as Group Captain.	✝ Died since Battle (1970)	British
FINNIE Archibald	Plt. Off.	Pilot	54	Joined 54 Sqn., 8-7-40.	✝ **Killed in Action** (25-7-40)	British
FINNIS John Frederick Fortescue	Flt. Lt.	Pilot	1-229	Ex-Southern Rhodesian Air Force. Joined 1 Sqn., 2-9-40. Posted to 229 Sqn., 10-40. Returned to S.R.A.F., 8-9-45.		British

Name	Rank	Duty	Sqn.	Details	Fate	Nationality
FINUCANE Brendon Eamonn Fergus ("Paddy")	Plt. Off.	Pilot	65	Joined 65 Sqn., 13-7-40. Promoted Fg. Off., 3-9-40. Awarded D.S.O. (21-10-41), D.F.C.✠✠ (13-5-41, 9-9-41 and 26-9-41). ✠ 1 Bf 109, 12-8-40; ✠ 1 Bf 109, 13-8-40. Was Acting Wing Commander at time of death.	✟ Killed since Battle (15-7-42)	Irish
¶ **FIRMINGER, B.**	Plt. Off.	Pilot	238	On 238 Sqn., 1-7-40. (Believed youngest Fighter Command pilot)	✟ Killed in Accident (5-7-40)	British
FISHER Anthony George Anson	Plt. Off.	Pilot	111	On 111 Sqn., 1-7-40. Posted away, 24-8-40. Awarded A.F.C. (1-9-44). Released from R.A.F., 1945, as Squadron Leader. Knighted, 6-88.	✟ Died since Battle (7-88)	British
FISHER Basil Mark	Fg. Off.	Pilot	111	On 111 Sqn., 1-7-40. (Brother of Fg. Off. G. Fisher)	✟ Killed in Action (15-8-40)	British
FISHER Gerald	Plt. Off.	Pilot	602	Joined 602 Sqn., 8-9-40. Promoted Fg. Off., 3-9-40. ✠ 1 Bf 109, 29-10-40. (Brother of Fg. Off. B.M. Fisher).	✟ Died since Battle (1973)	British
FISKE William Meade Lindsley ("Billy")	Plt. Off.	Pilot	601	Joined 601 Sqn., 12-7-40. ✠ 1 Ju 88, 13-8-40. (Died of wounds sustained on 16-8-40).	✟ Died of Wounds (17-8-40)	American
FITZGERALD Thomas Bernard	Fg. Off.	Pilot	141	Joined 141 Sqn., 10-8-40. Awarded D.F.C. (13-6-40). Later test pilot, Hawker Aircraft Ltd. Transferred to R.N.Z.A.F., 2-46, and released, 15-12-47.		New Zealander
FIZEL Joseph Francis	A.C.1	Aircrew	29	Joined 29 Sqn., 8-40. Promoted Sergeant, 9-40. No further Service details established.	✟ Died since Battle (29-8-76)	British
FLEMING John ("Jack")	Fg. Off.	Pilot	605	On 605 Sqn., 1-7-40. Severely wounded, 8-9-40. Awarded M.B.E. (1944). Retired from R.A.F., 5-2-59, as Wing Commander.		New Zealander
FLEMING Robert Davis Spittal	Plt. Off.	Pilot	249	On 249 Sqn., 1-7-40.	**Killed in Action** (7-9-40)	British
FLETCHER Andrew William	Flt. Lt.	Pilot	235	On 235 Sqn., 1-7-40. Promoted Sqn. Ldr., 1-9-40. Awarded D.F.C.✠ (22-10-40 and 31-10-41). Released from R.A.F., 1946, as Wing Commander.		Canadian
FLETCHER John Gordon Bowley	Sgt.	Aircrew	604	On 604 Sqn., 1-7-40.	**Killed in Action** (25-8-40)	British
FLETCHER Walter Thomas	Sgt.	Aircrew	23	Joined 23 Sqn., 21-9-40. Released from R.N.Z.A.F., 5-4-45.		New Zealander
FLETCHER	Sgt.	Pilot	3	No record of service or operations traced. Initials and forenames not known.		British
FLINDERS John ("Polly")	Plt. Off.	Pilot	32	On 32 Sqn., 1-7-40. ✠ 1 Do 17, 18-8-40. Released from R.A.F., 1946, as Squadron Leader.		British
FLOOD Frederick William	Flt. Lt.	Pilot	235	On 235 Sqn., 1-7-40.	**Killed in Action** (11-9-40)	Australian
FLOWER Hubert Juiz	Sgt.	Aircrew	248	Joined 248 Sqn., c.26-7-40.	✟ Died since Battle (23-8-41 ?)	British
FOGLAR Vaclav	Sgt.	Pilot	245	Joined 245 Sqn., 18-10-40. Commissioned, 25-5-42. Released from R.A.F., 1946.	✟ Killed since Battle (12-47 ?)	Czech
FOIT Emil Antonin	Plt. Off.	Pilot	310	Joined 310 (Czech) Sqn., 21-8-40. Awarded D.F.C. (1944). Released from R.A.F., 1946, as Squadron Leader.	✟ Died since Battle (1976)	Czech
FOKES Ronald Henry	Sgt.	Pilot	92	On 92 Sqn., 1-7-40. Commissioned, 19-11-40. Awarded D.F.C. (10-3-44), D.F.M. (15-11-40). ✠ 1 He 111 (shared), 4-7-40; ✠ 1 Do 17 (shared), 10-9-40; ✠ 2 Bf 109s and 1 He 111, 15-10-40; ✠ 1 Bf 109, 26-10-40.	✟ Killed since Battle (12-6-44)	British
FOLLIARD James Henry	Sgt.	Aircrew	604	Joined 604 Sqn., 14-9-40. Commissioned, 7-7-43. Released from R.A.F., 1945, as Flight Lieutenant.	✟ Died since Battle (c.1982)	British
FOPP Desmond	Sgt.	Pilot	17	On 17 Sqn., 1-7-40. Commissioned, 3-11-41. Awarded A.F.C. (29-9-44). ✠ 1 He 111 (shared), 12-7-40. Wounded, 3-9-40. Retired from R.A.F., 13-3-75, as Squadron Leader.		British
FORBES Athol Stanhope	Flt. Lt.	Pilot	303-66	Joined 303 (Polish) Sqn., 2-8-40, on formation. Promoted to Acting Sqn. Ldr., and posted to 66 Sqn., 17-10-40, to command. Awarded O.B.E. (1-1-44), D.F.C.✠ (22-10-40 and 4-11-41). ✠ 1 Ju 88, 5-9-40; ✠ 1 Bf 109, 6-9-40; ✠ 1 Do 17, 7-9-40; ✠ 2 Do 17s, 11-9-40; ✠ 1 He 111, 26-9-40; ✠ 1 He 111, 27-9-40. Released for the R.A.F., 1948, as Group Captain.	✟ Died since Battle (1981)	British
FORD Ernest George	Plt. Off.	Pilot	3-232	On 3 Sqn., 1-7-40. Posted to 232 Sqn., 17-7-40. Returned to 3 Sqn., 10-9-40. Returned to Canada, 1941.	✟ Killed since Battle (12-12-42)	Canadian
FORD Roy Clement	Sgt.	Pilot	41	On 41 Sqn., 1-7-40. Commissioned, 6-11-40. Released from R.A.F., 23-10-45, as Flight Lieutenant. Commissioned in R.A.F.V.R. until 11-5-52.		British
FORDE Derek Nigel	Plt. Off.	Pilot	145-605	On 145 Sqn., 1-7-40. Posted to 605 Sqn., 26-9-40. Promoted Fg. Off., 3-9-40. Awarded D.F.C. (26-2-43). Retired from R.A.F., 8-2-53, as Squadron Leader.	✟ Died since Battle (16-1-79)	British
FORREST Dudley Henry	Sgt.	Pilot	66-421 Flt.	On 66 Sqn., 1-7-40. Posted to 421 Flt., 7-10-40. Commissioned, 31-12-41. ✠ 1 Do 17 (shared), 27-9-40. Released from R.A.F., 1947, as Flight Lieutenant.		British
FORRESTER George Mathwin	Plt. Off.	Pilot	605	Joined 605 Sqn., 5-8-40.	**Killed in Action** (9-9-40)	British
FORSHAW Terence Henry Trimble	Fg. Off.	Pilot	609	Promoted Flt. Lt., 3-9-40. Joined 609 Sqn., 8-9-40. Retired from R.A.F., 29-11-57, as Squadron Leader.		British
FORSTER Anthony Douglas	Fg. Off.	Pilot	151-607	On 151 Sqn., 1-7-40. Posted to 607 Sqn., 12-8-40. Awarded D.F.C. (30-7-40). ✠ 1 Bf 110 (shared), 9-7-40. Retired from R.A.F., 24-4-62, as Wg. Cdr.		British
FORSYTH Colin Leo Malcolm	Sgt.	Aircrew	23	Joined 23 Sqn., 21-9-40. Commissioned, 3-12-42. Awarded D.F.C. (12-4-45), D.F.M. (15-11-42).	✟ Killed since Battle (8-5-44)	New Zealander
FORWARD Ronald Victor	Sgt.	Pilot	257	On 257 Sqn., 1-7-40. Commissioned, 16-3-44. Released from R.A.F., 1946, as Flying Officer.		British
FOSTER Robert William	Plt. Off.	Pilot	605	Joined 605 Sqn., 9-7-40. Awarded D.F.C. (13-8-43). ✠ 1 Bf 109, 7-10-40. Released from R.A.F., 27-2-47, as Wing Commander.		British
FOTHERINGHAM Alan Cook	Sgt.	Pilot	3	Flew with No. 3 Sqn. during Battle of Britain; dates of service not known. Made P.O.W., 1941. Released from R.A.F., 1945, as Warrant Officer.		British
FOWLER Alfred Lawrence	Plt. Off.	Pilot	248	On 248 Sqn., 1-7-40. Awarded D.F.C. (24-1-41).	✟ Killed since Battle (23-8-41)	New Zealander
FOWLER Reginald John	Sgt.	Pilot	247	Joined 247 Sqn., 15-8-40. Commissioned 22-3-42. Released from R.A.F., 1946, as Flight Lieutenant.		British
FOX Lawrence	A.C.1	Aircrew	29	Joined 29 Sqn., 4-10-40. Promoted Sergeant, 10-40.		British
FOX Peter Hutton	Sgt.	Pilot	56	Joined 56 Sqn., 17-9-40. Wounded, 30-9-40. Made P.O.W., 10-41. Released from R.A.F., 1946.		British
FOXLEY-NORRIS Christopher Neil	Fg. Off.	Pilot	3	Joined 3 Sqn., 27-9-40. Retired from R.A.F., 22-4-74, as Air Chief Marshal, G.C.B. (1973; K.C.B., 1969; C.B., 1966), D.S.O. (25-9-45), O.B.E. (2-1-56).		British
FOX-MALE Dennis Humbert ("Foxy")	Plt. Off.	Pilot	152	Joined 152 Sqn., 29-9-40. Released from the R.A.F., 1946, as Flight Lieutenant.	✟ Died since Battle (1986)	British
FRANCIS Clarence William	Sgt.	Pilot	74	On 74 Sqn., 1-7-40. Commissioned, 6-1-42. Released from R.A.F., 1946, as Flight Lieutenant.		British
FRANCIS Colin Dunstan	Plt. Off.	Pilot	253	On 253 Sqn., 1-7-40.	**Killed in Action** (30-8-40)	British
FRANCIS Douglas Norman	Sgt.	Pilot	257	Joined 257 Sqn., 13-9-40. Record of operations not traced.	✟ Died since Battle (7-1-61)	British
FRANCIS John	Cpl.	Aircrew	23	Joined 23 Sqn., c.8-7-40. Promoted Sergeant, 7-40. Record of operations not traced.		British
FRANCIS Noel Inglis Chalmers	Plt. Off.	Pilot	247	Joined 247 Sqn., 1-8-40. Promoted Fg. Off., 3-9-40.	✟ Killed since Battle (9-12-41)	British
FRANCIS	Sgt.	Pilot	3	Flew with No. 3 Sqn. during Battle of Britain. Record of operations not traced. Initials and forenames not known.		British
FRANKLIN Walter Derrick Kerr	Fg. Off.	Pilot	74	Joined 74 Sqn., 21-8-40. Resigned from R.A.F., 1947, as Flight Lieutenant.		British
FRANKLIN William Henry	Sgt	Pilot	65	On 65 Sqn., 1-7-40. Commissioned, 18-9-40. ✠ 2 Bf 109s, 7-7-40; ✠ 1 Bf 109, 8-7-40; ✠ 1 Bf 109, 26-7-40; ✠ 1 Bf 109, 5-8-40; ✠ 2 Bf 109s, 16-8-40. Awarded D.F.M.✠ (9-7-40 and 13-8-40).	✟ Killed since Battle (12-12-40)	British
FRANTISEK Josef	Sgt.	Pilot	303	Joined 303 (Polish) Sqn., 2-8-40, on formation. ✠ 1 Bf 109, 2-9-40; ✠ 1 Bf 109, 3-9-40; ✠ 1 Bf 109, 5-9-40; ✠ 1 Ju 88, 5-9-40; ✠ 1 Bf 109, 6-9-40; ✠ 1 He 111, 9-9-40; ✠ 1 Bf 109, 9-9-40; ✠ 2 Bf 109, 11-9-40; ✠ 1 He 111, 11-9-40; ✠ 1 Bf 110, 15-9-40; ✠ 1 Bf 109, 18-9-40; ✠ 2 He 111s, 26-9-40; ✠ 1 He 111, 27-9-40; ✠ 1 Bf 110, 27-9-40; ✠ 1 Bf 109, 30-9-40. Awarded D.F.M. (1-10-40); also awarded *Croix de Guerre* (Fr.), *Virtuti Militari* (5th Class), *Krzyz Walecznych* and three Bars, and the Czech Military Cross.	**Killed in Action** (8-10-40)	Czech

FRASER   Sgt.   Pilot   257
Robert Henry Braund
On 257 Sqn., 1-7-40.   ✠ Killed in Action (22-10-40)   British

FREEBORN   Plt. Off.   Pilot   74
John Connell
On 74 Sqn., 1-7-40. Promoted Fg. Off., 3-9-40. Awarded D.F.C.✿ (13-8-40 and 25-2-41).✠ 1 Bf 109, 10-7-40; ✠ 1 Bf 109, 28-7-40; ✠ 2 Bf 109s and 2 Bf 110s, 11-8-40; ✠ 1 Do 17, 13-8-40; ✠ 1 Do 17, 11-9-40. Released from the R.A.F., 1946, as Wing Commander.   British

FREEMAN   Sgt.   Aircrew   29
Richard Powell
Joined 29 Sqn., 7-8-40. No other service details traced.   British

FREER   Sgt.   Pilot   29
Peter Foster
On 29 Sqn., 1-7-40. Commissioned, 24-4-41.   ✠ Killed since Battle (11-5-41)   British

FREESE   Sgt.   Pilot   611-74
Laurence Eric
Joined 611 Sqn., 29-9-40. Posted to 74 Sqn., 26-10-40.   ✠ Killed since Battle (10-1-41)   British

FRENCH   Sgt.   Pilot   29
Thomas Lennox
Joined 29 Sqn., 8-7-40. Commissioned, 24-4-41.   ✠ Killed since Battle (14-12-42)   British

FREY   Flt. Lt.   Pilot   607
Juliusz
Joined 607 Sqn., 11-10-40. Released from R.A.F., 1946, as Squadron Leader.   Polish

FRIEND   Sgt.   Aircrew   25
Jack Richard
Joined 25 Sqn., c.5-10-40.   ✠ Killed since Battle (7-12-40)   British

FRIENDSHIP   Plt. Off.   Pilot   3
Alfred Henry Basil
On 3 Sqn., 1-7-40. Had been awarded D.F.M.✿ (31-5-40 and 4-6-40). Released from R.A.F., 1947, as Squadron Leader.   British

FRIPP   Sgt.   Pilot   248
Joffre Harry
On 248 Sqn., 1-7-40. Commissioned, 8-4-42. Released from R.A.F., 1945, as Flight Lieutenant.   ✠ Died since Battle (1973)   British

FRISBY   Plt. Off.   Pilot   504
Edward Murray
On 504 Sqn., 1-7-40. Promoted Fg. Off., 3-9-40.   ✠ Killed since Battle (5-12-41)   British

FRITH   Sgt.   Pilot   611-92
Eric Thomas George
Joined 611 Sqn., 29-7-40. Posted to 92 Sqn., 21-9-40. (Died from wounds received on 9-10-40).   **Died of wounds (17-10-40)**   British

FRIZELL   Plt. Off.   Pilot   257
Charles George
On 257 Sqn., 1-7-40. Injured in ground accident, 15-9-40. Released from R.A.F., 6-3-46, as Squadron Leader.   Canadian

FROST   Sgt.   Aircrew   600
Jack Lynch
On 600 Sqn., 1-7-40. Commissioned, 8-8-40. No further Service details traced.   British

FULFORD   Sgt.   Pilot   64-19
David
On 64 Sqn., 1-7-40. Posted to 19 Sqn., 25-9-40. Commissioned, 10-3-41. Awarded D.F.C. (4-11-41)   ✠ Killed since Battle (2-11-42)   British

FUMERTON   Plt. Off.   Pilot   32
Robert Carl
Joined 32 Sqn., 5-10-40. Awarded D.F.C.✿ (27-3-42 and 21-7-42), A.F.C. (1945). Released from R.C.A.F., 6-45.   Canadian

FURNEAUX   Sgt.   Pilot   3-73
Rex Horton
On 3 Sqn., 1-7-40. Posted to 73 Sqn., 25-9-40. Commissioned 31-7-41. Released from R.A.F., 1946, as Flight Lieutenant.   British

FURST   Sgt.   Pilot   310-605
Bohumir
Joined 310 (Czech) Sqn., mid-8-40. Posted to 605 Sqn., 19-10-40. ✠ 1 Bf 110, 3-9-40; ✠ 1 Bf 109, 7-9-40; ✠ 1 He 111, 15-9-40. Released from R.A.F., 1946, as Flight Lieutenant.   ✠ Died since Battle (c.1976 ?)   Czech

GABSZEWICZ   Plt. Off.   Pilot   607
Aleksander Klemens
Joined 607 Sqn., 11-10-40. Awarded D.S.O. (15-5-44), D.F.C. (20-8-42). Released from R.A.F., 1-47, as Group Captain.   Polish

GADD   Sgt.   Pilot   611
James Edward
Joined 611 Sqn., 12-10-40. Released from R.A.F., 11-45, as Warrant Officer.   British

GAGE   Plt. Off.   Pilot   602
Douglas Hugh
Joined 602 Sqn., 21-9-40.   ✠ Killed since Battle (6-6-41)   British

GALLUS   Sgt.   Pilot   303-3
Pawel Piotr
Joined 303 (Polish) Sqn., 2-8-40, on formation. Posted to 3 Sqn., 27-9-40. Awarded D.F.C. (26-5-45). Released from P.A.F., 1948, as Warrant Officer.   Polish

GAMBLEN   Fg. Off.   Pilot   41
Douglas Robert
On 41 Sqn., 1-7-40.   **Killed in Action (29-7-40)**   British

GANE   Plt. Off.   Pilot   248
Sydney Russell
On 248 Sqn., 1-7-40.   **Killed in Action (20-10-40)**   British

GANT   Sgt.   Aircrew   236
Ernest
Joined 236 Sqn., 3-9-40. Commissioned, 18-3-43. Released from R.A.F., 1946, as Flight Lieutenant.   British

GARDINER   Fg. Off.   Pilot   610
Frederick Thomas
On 610 Sqn., 1-7-40. Awarded D.F.C. (10-3-44). ✠ 1 Bf 110, 18-8-40. Wounded, 25-8-40. Released from the R.A.F., 1946, as Squadron Leader.   British

GARDINER   Sgt.   Pilot   3
William Nairn
On 3 Sqn. during Battle of Britain. Commissioned, 22-3-42. Nothing further known.   British

GARDNER   Sgt.   Pilot   610
Bernard George Derry
Joined 610 Sqn., 27-7-40. ✠ 3 Bf 109s, 12-8-40; ✠ 1 Bf 109, 14-8-40. Wounded, 14-8-40.   ✠ Killed since Battle (28-6-41)   British

GARD'NER   Plt. Off.   Pilot   141
John Rushton
On 141 Sqn., 1-7-40. Wounded, 19-7-40. Retired from R.A.F., 14-6-65, as Group Captain.   New Zealander

GARDNER   Plt. Off.   Pilot   32
Peter Melvill
On 32 Sqn., 1-7-40. Promoted Fg. Off., 29-8-40. Awarded D.F.C. (30-8-40). ✠ 1 Do 17 (shared), 3-7-40; ✠ 2 Bf 109s, 12-8-40; ✠ 1 Ju 88, 15-8-40; ✠ 1 Bf 109, 16-8-40. Retired from R.A.F., 1948, as Squadron Leader.   ✠ Died since Battle (23-5-84)   British

GARDNER   Sub-Lieut.   Pilot   242
Richard Exton ("Jimmy")
Fleet Air Arm. Joined 242 Sqn., 1-7-40. Awarded D.S.C. (29-7-41); O.B.E. (14-6-65) ✠ 1 He 111, 10-7-40; ✠ 1 Do 17 (shared), 21-8-40; ✠ 1 Do 215, 7-9-40; ✠ 1 Do 17, 18-9-40. Retired from Royal Navy, 13-3-46, as Commander.   British

GARFIELD   Sgt.   Pilot   248
Walter James
On 248 Sqn., 1-7-40.   **Killed in Action (13-9-40)**   British

GARRAD   Plt. Off.   Pilot   248
Anthony Hugh Hamilton
On 248 Sqn., 1-7-40.   ✠ Killed since Battle (3-11-40)   British

GARTON   Sgt.   Pilot   73
Geoffrey William
On 73 Sqn., 1-7-40. Commissioned, 26-4-41. Awarded D.S.O. (21-8-45), D.F.C. (28-7-42). ✠ 1 Bf 110, 27-9-40. Retired from R.A.F., 13-2-63, as Wg. Cdr.   ✠ Died since Battle (11-76)   British

¶ **GARTON**   Plt. Off.   Pilot   54
Jack Wallace
On 54 Sqn., 1-7-40. ✠ 1 Bf 109, 8-7-40.   ✠ Killed in Action (9-7-40)   British

GARVEY   Sgt.   Pilot   41
Leonard Arthur
Flew with 41 Sqn. in Battle of Britain. Few details traced.   **Killed in Action (30-10-40)**   British

GARVIN   Flt. Lt.   Pilot   264
George Desmond
Joined 264 Sqn., 8-8-40. Promoted Sqn. Ldr., 1-9-40.✠ 2 Ju 88s, 24-8-40. Appointed C.B.E., 13-6-57. Retired from R.A.F., 28-6-61, as Air Commodore.   British

GASH   Sgt.   Aircrew   264
Fred
Defiant gunner. Joined 264 Sqn., 8-40. ✠ 2 Do 17s, 26-8-40; ✠ 1 He 111, 16-10-40. Awarded D.F.M. (18-4-41). Commissioned, 6-5-43. Released from R.A.F., 1945, as Flight Lieutenant.   British

GASKELL   Plt. Off.   Pilot   264
Richard Stuart
On 264 Sqn., 1-7-40. Slightly wounded, 24-8-40. Retired from R.A.F., 1-4-63, as Flight Lieutenant.   British

¶ **GATES**   Sgt.   Pilot   29
On 29 Sqn., 1-7-40. Posted away, 13-7-40. No operations recorded. Initials not known.   British

GAUNCE   Fg. Off.   Pilot   615
Lionel Manley
On 615 Sqn., 1-7-40. Promoted Flt. Lt., 6-8-40. Awarded D.F.C. (23-8-40). ✠ 1 Bf 109, 20-7-40;✠ 1 Bf 109, 25-7-40; ✠ 1 Bf 109, 12-8-40; ✠ 1 Bf 109, 26-8-40 (✠ 1 CR.42, 11-11-40). Promoted Acting Sqn. Ldr., 30-10-40.   ✠ Killed since Battle (19-11-41)   Canadian

GAUNT   Plt. Off.   Pilot   609
Geoffrey Norman
Joined 609 Sqn., 16-8-40. ✠ 1 Bf 110, 25-8-40.   **Killed in Action (15-9-40)**   British

GAUNT   Sgt.   Aircrew   23
William Edwin
Joined 23 Sqn., 16-9-40. Commissioned, 27-1-42. Retired from R.A.F., 29-5-65, as Flight Lieutenant.   British

GAVAN   Sgt.   Pilot   54
Arthur
Joined 54 Sqn., 17-9-40. Commissioned, 26-12-41. Released from R.A.F., 1946.   ✠ Died since Battle (22-6-67)   British

GAWITH   Plt. Off.   Pilot   23
Alan Antill
On 23 Sqn., 1-7-40. Promoted Fg. Off., 3-9-40. Awarded D.F.C. (15-5-41).   New Zealander

GAYNER   Fg. Off.   Pilot   615
John Richard Hensman
On 615 Sqn., 1-7-40. Promoted Flt. Lt., 3-9-40. Awarded D.F.C. (9-6-44). ✠ 1 Ju 87 (shared), 14-7-40. Released for R.A.F., 1946, as Wing Commander.   ✠ Died since Battle (1987)   British

GEAR   Sgt.   Pilot   32
Alan Walter
Joined 32 Sqn., 1-10-40. Commissioned, 11-1-43. Awarded D.F.C. (27-7-43) Discharged from R.A.F., 1945, on medical grounds.   British

GEDDES   Plt. Off.   Pilot   604
Keith Irvine
Joined 604 Sqn., 8-7-40. Promoted Fg. Off., 3-9-40. Awarded D.F.C. (4-7-41). Released from R.A.F., 25-11-45, as Squadron Leader.   British

GEE   Sgt.   Pilot   219
Victor David
Joined 219 Sqn., 7-7-40.   ✠ Killed since Battle (21-3-41)   British

GENNEY   Plt. Off.   Aircrew   604
Terence
On 604 Sqn., 1-7-40. (Had been awarded M.C. in 1914-18 War). Aged 44 at time of death.   ✠ Killed since Battle (6-2-41)   British

GENT   Sgt.   Pilot   32-501
Raymond John Kitchell
On 32 Sqn., 1-7-40. Posted to 501 Sqn., c.28-8-40. ✠ 1 Bf 109, 25-10-40.   ✠ Killed since Battle (2-1-41)   British

Name	Rank	Role	Sqn.	Details	Fate	Nationality
GIBBINS Dudley Guy	Sgt.	Pilot	54-222	Joined 54 Sqn., 10-8-40. Posted to 222 Sqn., 11-9-40. Commissioned, 20-11-41. ✠ 1 Bf 109, 31-8-40; ✠ 1 Bf 109 (shared), 15-10-40. Released from R.A.F., 12-45, as Flight Lieutenant.		British
GIBBONS Charles Martin	Sgt.	Aircrew	236	Joined 236 Sqn., 19-7-40. Commissioned, 12-2-41. Retired from R.A.F., 1954, as Squadron Leader.		British
GIBSON John Albert Axel	Plt. Off.	Pilot	501	On 501 Sqn., 1-7-40. Promoted Fg. Off., 3-9-40. Awarded D.S.O. (11-3-45), D.F.C. (30-8-40). ✠ 1 Do 17, 13-7-40; ✠ 1 Ju 87, 29-7-40; ✠ 1 Ju 87, 12-8-40; ✠ 1 Bf 109, 12-8-40; ✠ 1 Ju 87, 15-8-40; ✠ 1 Ju 88, 24-8-40; ✠ 1 Bf 109, 29-8-40; ✠ 1 Bf 109, 7-9-40. Retired from R.A.F., 1954, as Flight Lieutenant.		New Zealander
GIDDINGS Herbert Selwyn	Flt. Lt.	Pilot	615-111	On 615 Sqn., 1-7-40. Posted to 111Sqn., 18-8-40. ✠ 1 Do 17, 31-8-40; ✠ 2 Bf 109s, 4-9-40.	✟ Killed since Battle (23-1-43)	British
GIL Jozef	Plt. Off.	Pilot	229-145	Joined 229 Sqn., 9-40. Posted to 145 Sqn., 30-10-40.	✟ Killed since Battle (31-12-42)	Polish
GILBERT Ernest George	Plt. Off.	Pilot	64	On 64 Sqn., 1-7-40. Commissioned, 26-8-40. ✠ 1 He 111 (shared), 18-8-40. Retired from R.A.F., 4-11-62, as Squadron Leader.		British
GILBERT Humphrey Trench	Plt. Off.	Pilot	601	Joined 601 Sqn., 16-8-40. Awarded D.F.C. (29-5-42). ✠ 1 Ju 87 (shared), 18-8-40; ✠ 1 He 111 (shared), 30-8-40; ✠ 1 Bf 110, 31-8-40; ✠ 1 Bf 110, 4-9-40.	✟ Killed since Battle (2-5-42)	British
GILBERT Peter Robert Joseph	Midshipman	Pilot	111	Fleet Air Arm. Joined 111 Sqn., 22-9-40. Released by the Royal Navy, 11-9-46, as Lieutenant.		British
GILDERS John Stanley	Sgt.	Pilot	72	On 72 Sqn., 1-7-40. ✠ 1 Bf 110, 4-9-40; ✠ 1 Do 17 (shared), 10-9-40; ✠ 1 Bf 110, 11-9-40; ✠ 1 Bf 109 and 1 Ju 88, 27-9-40.	✟ Killed since Battle (21-2-41)	British
GILL James Vivian	Sgt.	Aircrew	23	Joined 23 Sqn., 29-9-40.	✟ Killed since Battle (2-7-41)	British
GILLAM Denys Edgar	Flt. Lt.	Pilot	616-312	On 616 Sqn., 1-7-40. Awarded D.S.O.✸✸ (12-12-41, 11-8-44 and 23-1-45), D.F.C.✸ (12-11-40 and 21-10-41), A.F.C. (9-6-38). ✠ 1 Ju 88, 15-8-40; ✠ 1 Bf 109, 26-8-40; ✠ 1 Bf 110, 29-8-40; ✠ 1 Bf 109, 30-8-40; ✠ 1 Bf 109, 31-8-40; ✠ 1 Do 17, 1-9-40; ✠ 1 Bf 110, 2-9-40; ✠ 1 Ju 88, 8-10-40. Released from the R.A.F., 10-45, as Group Captain.		British
GILLAM Ernest	Sgt.	Aircrew	248	On 248 Sqn., 1-7-40.	✟ Killed since Battle (19-10-41)	British
GILLAN James	Fg. Off.	Pilot	601	Joined 601 Sqn., 5-8-40.	✟ **Killed in Action** (11-8-40)	British
GILLEN Thomas William	Fg. Off.	Pilot	247	Joined 247 Sqn., 1-8-40. Released from R.A.F., 1948, as Wing Commander.	✟ Died since Battle (1969)	British
GILLESPIE James Lyon	Plt. Off.	Aircrew	23	Joined 23 Sqn., 12-8-40. (Died of natural causes)	✟ Died (1-10-40)	British
GILLIES James	F/Sgt.	Pilot	602-421 Flt.	Joined 602 Sqn., 18-9-40. Commissioned, 17-11-41. Awarded M.C. (13-2-45), D.F.M. (30-5-41). ✠ 1 Ju 88 (shared), 21-9-40; ✠ 1 Bf 110, 26-9-40.	✟ Killed since Battle (21-4-44)	British
GILLIES Kenneth McLeod	Fg. Off.	Pilot	66	On 66 Sqn., 1-7-40. Promoted Flt. Lt., 9-9-40. ✠ 1 Bf 110 (shared), 20-8-40; ✠ 1 Do 215 (shared), 31-8-40; ✠ 1 Do 17, 15-9-40; ✠ 1 He 111, 18-9-40; ✠ 3 Do 17s (all shared), 27-9-40.	✟ **Killed in Action** (4-10-40)	British
GILLMAN Keith Reginald	Plt. Off.	Pilot	32	On 32 Sqn., 1-7-40. ✠ 1 Bf 109, 19-7-40.	✟ **Killed in Action** (25-8-40)	British
GILROY George Kemp ("Sheep")	Plt. Off.	Pilot	603	On 603 Sqn., 1-7-40. Promoted Fg. Off., 3-9-40. Awarded D.S.O. (2-3-43), D.F.C.✸ (13-9-40 and 23-6-42). Wounded, 31-8-40. ✠ 1 Ju 88 (shared), 3-7-40; ✠ 1 Do 215 (shared), 6-7-40; ✠ 1 He 111 (shared), 12-7-40; ✠ 1 Bf 109, 28-8-40; ✠ 1 Bf 109, 31-8-40; ✠ 1 Bf 109, 28-10-40. Released from R.A.F., 1945, as Group Captain. Commanded No. 603 Sqn., R.Aux.A.F., 6-46 until 9-49.		British
GILYEAT	A.C.1	Aircrew	29	Joined 29 Sqn., 9-40. Promoted Sergeant, 9-40. Initials not known.		British
GIRDWOOD Alexander George	Sgt.	Pilot	257	On 257 Sqn., 1-7-40. ✠ 1 Ju 88, 13-8-40; ✠ 1 He 111 (shared), 18-8-40; Wounded, 18-8-40.	✟ **Killed in Action** (29-10-40)	British
GLASER Ernest Derek	Plt. Off.	Pilot	65	Joined 65 Sqn., 13-7-40. Awarded D.F.C. (25-8-42). Retired from R.A.F., 26-6-53, as Squadron Leader.		British
GLEAVE Thomas Percy	Sqn. Ldr.	Pilot	253	Commanded 253 Sqn., 2-6-40 to 9-8-40, and 31-8-40. Wounded, 31-8-40. Appointed C.B.E., 1944. ✠ 5 Bf 109s, 30-8-40; ✠ 1 Ju 88, 31-8-40. Retired from R.A.F., 14-11-53, on medical grounds as Group Captain.		British
GLEDHILL Geoffrey	Sgt.	Pilot	238	Joined 238 Sqn., 4-8-40.	✟ **Killed in Action** (11-8-40)	British
GLEED Ian Richard	Fg. Off.	Pilot	87	On 87 Sqn., 1-7-40. Promoted Flt. Lt., 3-9-40. Awarded D.S.O. (22-5-42), D.F.C. (13-9-40). ✠ 2 Bf 110s, 15-8-40; ✠ 2 Bf 110, 25-8-40.	✟ Killed since Battle (16-4-43)	British
GLEGG Alexander Joseph	Plt. Off.	Aircrew	600	Joined 600 Sqn., 18-9-40. Awarded D.F.C. (9-1-42). Released from R.A.F., 1945, as Squadron Leader.		British
GLENDINNING John Nixon	Sgt.	Pilot	54-74	Joined 54 Sqn., 16-9-40. Posted to 74 Sqn., 21-10-40.	✟ Killed since Battle (12-3-41)	British
GLEW Norman	Sgt.	Pilot	72	On 72 Sqn., 1-7-40. Commissioned, 22-8-41. ✠ 1 Bf 109 (shared), 23-9-40; ✠ 1 Do 17, 27-9-40.	✟ Killed since Battle (17-5-44)	British
GLOWACKI Antoni	Sgt.	Pilot	501	Joined 501 Sqn., 4-8-40. Commissioned later. Awarded D.F.C. (15-11-42), D.F.M. (30-10-41). ✠ 1 Ju 87, 15-8-40; ✠ 3 Bf 109s and 2 Ju 88s, 24-8-40; ✠ 1 Bf 109, 28-8-40; ✠ 1 Do 215, 31-8-40. Transferred to R.N.Z.A.F., 1954.	✟ Died since Battle (5-80)	Polish
GLOWACKI Witold Jozef	Plt. Off.	Pilot	145-605	Joined 145 Sqn., 12-8-40. Posted to 605 Sqn., 31-8-40. ✠ 1 Bf 110, 11-9-40.	✟ **Killed in Action** (24-9-40)	Polish
¶ **GLOWCZYNSKI**	Plt. Off.	Pilot	302	Joined 302 (Polish) Sqn., c.2-8-40. Did not fly operational sortie before being injured in accident on 17-8-40.		Polish
GLYDE Richard Lindsay	Fg. Off.	Pilot	87	On 87 Sqn., 1-7-40. Awarded D.F.C. (4-6-40). ✠ 1 Bf 110, 11-7-40.	✟ **Killed in Action** (13-8-40)	Australian
GMUR Feliks	Sgt.	Pilot	151	Joined 151 Sqn., 21-8-40.	✟ **Killed in Action** (30-8-40)	Polish
GNYS Wladyslaw	Plt. Off.	Pilot	302	Joined 302 (Polish) Sqn., 28-7-40. Released from Polish Air Force, 1947.	✟ Died since Battle (1983)	Polish
GODDARD Henry Gordon	Fg. Off.	Pilot	219	On 219 Sqn., 1-7-40. Awarded D.S.O. (14-11-44), D.F.C. (18-2-41), A.F.C., (11-6-42). Released from R.A.F., 1945, as Wing Commander.	✟ Died since Battle (1972)	British
GODDARD William Bernard	Fg. Off.	Pilot	235	On 235 Sqn., 1-7-40. Promoted Flt. Lt., 3-9-40. Awarded D.F.C. (6-12-40).	✟ Killed since Battle (15-6-41)	British
GODDEN Stephen Frederick	Sqn. Ldr.	Pilot	3	In command of 3 Sqn., 1-7-40. Posted away, 6-9-40. Retired from R.A.F., 2-9-57, as Wing Commander.	✟ Died since Battle (8-66)	British
GOLDSMITH Claude Waller	Fg. Off.	Pilot	603-54	On 603 Sqn., 1-7-40. Posted to 54 Sqn., 3-9-40. Returned to 603 Sqn., 28-9-40. (Died of wounds received on 27-10-40)	✟ **Died of Wounds** (28-10-40)	South African
GOLDSMITH John Ernest	Sgt.	Aircrew	236	On 236 Sqn., 1-7-40. ✠ 1 He 111, 23-9-40; ✠ 1 Do 18, 25-9-40. (Both shot while flying with Plt. Off. G.H. Russell).	✟ Killed since Battle (27-4-41)	British
GONAY Henri Alphonse Clement	Plt. Off.	Pilot	235	Joined 235 Sqn., 5-8-40. ✠ 1 He 59 (shared), 8-10-40.	✟ Killed since Battle (14-6-44)	Belgian
GOODALL Harold Ingham	Plt. Off.	Pilot	264	On 264 Sqn., 1-7-40. ✠ 1 Ju 88 (shared), 24-8-40; ✠ 1 Do 17, 26-8-40.	✟ **Killed in Action** (8-10-40)	British
GOODERHAM Albert Thomas	Sgt.	Pilot	151-46	Joined 151 Sqn., 26-8-40. Posted to 46 Sqn., 15-9-40. Slightly wounded, 15-10-40.	✟ Killed since Battle (2-11-41)	British
GOODMAN Geoffrey	Sgt.	Pilot	85	Re-joined 85 Sqn., c.26-7-40 (after recovery from injuries). ✠ 1 Bf 110, 30-8-40; ✠ 1 Bf 109, 1-9-40. Commissioned, 12-3-41. Awarded D.F.C. (26-10-43), O.B.E. (13-6-59). Retired from R.A.F., 1-6-69, as Wing Commander.	✟ Died since Battle (1976)	British
GOODMAN George Ernest	Plt. Off.	Pilot	1	On 1 Sqn., 1-7-40. Awarded D.F.C. (26-11-40). ✠ 1 Bf 109, 25-7-40; ✠ 1 Bf 110, 11-8-40; ✠ 1 He 111, 16-8-40; ✠ 1 Bf 110 (solo) and 1 Do 17 (shared), 18-11-40; ✠ 1 Bf 110, 6-9-40; ✠ 1 Ju 88 (shared), 8-10-40; ✠ 1 Do 17, 27-10-40.	✟ Killed since Battle (14-6-41)	Palestinian
GOODMAN Maurice Venning	Sgt.	Aircrew	604	On 604 Sqn., 1-7-40. Commissioned, 23-10-42. Awarded D.F.C. (12-11-43). Released from R.A.F., 1946, as Flight Lieutenant.	✟ Died since Battle (8-1-88)	British
GOODWIN Charles	Sgt.	Pilot	219	Joined 219 Sqn., 20-8-40.	✟ **Killed in Action** (30-9-40)	British

Name	Rank	Role	Sqn.	Service record	Fate	Nationality
GOODWIN Henry MacDonald	Fg. Off.	Pilot	609	On 609 Sqn., 1-7-40. ✠ **1 Bf 110, 12-8-40; ✠ 2 Ju 87s, 13-8-40.**	✞ **Killed in Action** (14-8-40)	British
GOODWIN Roy Daniel	Sgt.	Pilot	64	Flew with 64 Sqn. in Battle of Britain. Commissioned, 13-4-42. Released from R.A.F., 1946, as Flight Lieutenant.	✞ Died since Battle (1983)	British
GOODWIN Stanley Albert	Sgt.	Pilot	266-66	Joined 266 Sqn., 30-9-40. Posted to 66 Sqn., 14-10-40. Commissioned, 22-12-43. Released from R.A.F., 1946, as Flight Lieutenant.	✞ Died since Battle (7-3-82)	British
GORDON John Arthur Gerald	Sqn. Ldr.	Pilot	151	Joined 151 Sqn., 5-8-40, to command. ✠ **1 Bf 109, 14-8-40.** Wounded, 18-8-40.	✞ Killed since Battle (1-6-42)	Canadian
GORDON Stanley	Sgt.	Aircrew	235	Joined 235 Sqn., 25-10-40.	✞ Killed since Battle (28-5-41)	British
GORDON William Hugh Gibson	Plt. Off.	Pilot	234	On 234 Sqn., 1-7-40. ✠ **1 Bf 109, 24-8-40.**	✞ **Killed in Action** (6-9-40)	British
GORE William Ernest	Fg. Off.	Pilot	607-54	On 607 Sqn., 1-7-40. Posted to 54 Sqn., 6-8-40. Returned to 607 Sqn., 9-40. Awarded D.F.C. (31-5-40). Promoted Flt. Lt., 3-9-40.	✞ **Killed in Action** (28-9-40)	British
GORRIE David George	Plt. Off.	Pilot	43	Joined 43 Sqn., 1-7-40. ✠ **1 He 111 (shared), 12-7-40; ✠ 1 Bf 109, 6-9-40.**	✞ Killed since Battle (4-4-41)	British
GORZULA Mieczyslaw	Plt. Off.	Pilot	607	Joined 607 Sqn., 10-40. Released from Polish Air Force, 1-47.		Polish
GOSLING Reginald Clive	Plt. Off.	Pilot	266	Joined 266 Sqn., 28-9-40. Released from R.A.F., 31-12-45, as Flight Lieutenant.		British
GOTH Vilem	Plt. Off.	Pilot	310-501	Joined 310 (Czech) Sqn., 10-7-40, on formation. Posted to 501 Sqn., 8-40. ✠ **2 Bf 110, 7-9-40.**	✞ **Killed in Action** (25-10-40)	Czech
GOTHORPE	Sgt.	Aircrew	25	Joined 25 Sqn., c.12-10-40. (Initials and forenames not known)		British
GOULD Derrick Leslie	Plt. Off.	Pilot	607-601	On 607 Sqn., 1-7-40. Posted to 601 Sqn., 5-10-40. Promoted Fg. Off., 3-9-40. Awarded D.F.C. (18-9-42). Released from R.A.F., 1946, as Squadron Leader.		British
GOULD Gordon Leslie	Sgt.	Aircrew	235	Joined 235 Sqn., 27-9-40.		British
GOULDSTONE Ronald Joseph	Sgt.	Aircrew	29	Joined 29 Sqn., 7-8-40.	✞ **Killed in Action** (25-8-40)	British
GOUT Geoffrey Kenneth	Plt. Off.	Pilot	234	On 234 Sqn., 1-7-40.	✞ **Killed in Action** (25-7-40)	British
GOWERS Arthur Vincent	Plt. Off.	Pilot	85	On 85 Sqn., 1-7-40. Promoted Fg. Off., 3-9-40. Awarded D.F.C. (1-7-41). ✠ **1 Bf 110, 30-8-40; ✠ 1 Bf 109, 31-8-40.** Badly wounded, 1-9-40.	✞ Killed since Battle (24-10-43)	British
GRACIE Edward John ("Jumbo")	Fg. Off.	Pilot	56	On 56 Sqn., 1-7-40. Awarded D.F.C. (1-10-40). ✠ **1 Bf 110, 10-7-40; ✠ 1 Ju 88, 20-7-40; ✠ 1 Ju 87, 25-7-40; ✠ 1 Bf 110, 18-8-40; ✠ 1 Do 17, 27-8-40; ✠ 1 Do 17, 28-8-40; ✠ 1 He 111, 30-8-40.** Wounded, 30-8-40.	✞ Killed since Battle (15-2-44)	British
GRAHAM Edward ("Ted")	Flt. Lt.	Pilot	72	On 72 Sqn., 1-7-40. ✠ **1 He 59 (shared), 1-7-40.** Retired from R.A.F., 27-12-58, as Group Captain.		British
GRAHAM James	Sgt.	Aircrew	236	Joined 236 Sqn., 3-9-40. Awarded D.F.M. (4-7-41). Commissioned, 19-2-42.	✞ Killed since Battle (26-6-42)	British
GRAHAM Kenneth Alfred George	Plt. Off.	Pilot	600-111	On 600 Sqn., 1-7-40. Posted to 111 Sqn., 24-8-40.	✞ Killed since Battle (8-2-41)	British
GRAHAM Leslie William	Plt. Off.	Pilot	56	Joined 56 Sqn., 29-7-40. Slightly wounded, 16-8-40. Posted away, 19-8-40. Released from R.A.F., 1946, as Squadron Leader.		South African
GRANDY John	Sqn. Ldr.	Pilot	249	In command of 249 Sqn., 1-7-40. Slightly wounded, 6-9-40. Awarded D.S.O. (19-10-45). Became Marshal of the R.A.F. Sir John Grandy, G.C.B. (1967), (K.C.B. [1964], C.B.[1956]), K.B.E.(1961). Appointed Constable and Governor of Windsor Castle, 1978.		British
GRANT Donald	Sub-Lieut.	Pilot	804	Fleet Air Arm. On 804 Sqn., 1-7-40. Released from Royal Navy, 1946, as Lieutenant.		British
GRANT Edwin John Forgan	Sgt.	Aircrew	600	Joined 600 Sqn.,	✞ Killed since Battle (1-12-41)	British
GRANT Ian Allan Charles	Sgt.	Pilot	151	Joined 151 Sqn., 21-9-40. Commissioned, 27-10-41.	✞ Killed since Battle (13-2-43)	New Zealander
GRANT Stanley Bernard	Fg. Off.	Pilot	65	On 65 Sqn., 1-7-40. Awarded D.F.C.✠ (5-6-42 and 29-1-43). Appointed C.B. (1969). Retired from R.A.F., 6-6-70, as Air Vice-Marshal.	✞ Died since Battle (7-87)	British
GRASSICK Robert Davidson	Plt. Off.	Pilot	242	On 242 Sqn., 1-7-40. Injured in ground accident, 8-40. Promoted Fg. Off., 3-9-40. Awarded D.F.C., 15-7-41. Transferred to R.C.A.F., 1945.		Canadian
GRAVES Edward Arthur	Sgt.	Aircrew	235	Joined 235 Sqn., 23-8-40.	✞ **Killed in Accident** (30-8-40)	British
GRAVES Richard Courtney	Plt. Off.	Pilot	253-85	Joined 253 Sqn., 3-9-40. Posted to 85 Sqn., 14-9-40. Returned to 253 Sqn., 28-9-40. Wounded, 29-9-40. Released from R.A.F., 1947, as Flight Lieutenant.	✞ Died since Battle (1978)	British
GRAY Anthony Philip	Flt. Lt.	Pilot	615	Joined 615 Sqn., 15-7-40. ✠ **1 Bf 109, 26-8-40.** Released from R.A.F., 1946, as Squadron Leader.	✞ Died since Battle (1986)	British
GRAY Colin Falkland	Plt. Off.	Pilot	54	On 54 Sqn., 1-7-40. Promoted Fg. Off., 23-10-40. Awarded D.S.O.(15-5-43), D.F.C.✠✠ (15-8-40, 20-9-41 and 15-11-43). ✠ **1 Bf 109, 13-7-40; ✠ 2 Bf 109s, 24-7-40; ✠ 2 Bf 109s, 12-8-40; ✠ 2 Bf 109s, 15-8-40; ✠ 1 Bf 110, 18-8-40; ✠ 1 Bf 110, 24-8-40; ✠ 1 Bf 109, 25-8-40; ✠ 1 Bf 109, 31-8-40; ✠ 1 Bf 109, 1-9-40; ✠ 1 Bf 109 and 1 Bf 110, 2-9-40; ✠ 1 Bf 109 (solo) and 1 Bf 110 (shared), 3-9-40.** Retired from R.A.F., 31-3-61, as Group Captain.		New Zealander
GRAY Clifford Kempson	Plt. Off.	Pilot	43	Joined 43 Sqn., 2-8-40. Awarded D.F.C. (17-8-45). ✠ **1 Ju 87, 16-8-40; ✠ 1 Ju 87, 18-8-40.** Retired from R.A.F., 1-8-63, as Wing Commander.		British
GRAY Donald McIntosh	Plt. Off.	Pilot	610	Joined 610 Sqn., 27-7-40. Wounded, 24-8-40.	✞ Killed since Battle (5-11-40)	British
GRAY Kenneth William	Sgt.	Pilot	85	Joined 85 Sqn., 16-9-40. Commissioned, 26-6-42.	✞ Killed since Battle (9-6-44)	British
GRAY Malcolm	Sgt.	Pilot	72	On 72 Sqn., 1-7-40.	✞ **Killed in Action** (9-12-40)	British
GRAY Trevor	Plt. Off.	Pilot	64	Joined 64 Sqn., 16-9-40. Released from R.A.F., 1946, as Flight Lieutenant.		British
GRAYSON Charles	F/Sgt.	Pilot	213	On 213 Sqn., 1-7-40. Commissioned, 21-6-41. ✠ **1 Bf 110, 18-8-40.**	✞ Killed since Battle (8-7-45)	British
GREEN Alexander William Valentine	Plt. Off.	Aircrew	235	Joined 235 Sqn., 11-7-40.	✞ **Killed in Action** (11-9-40)	British
GREEN Charles Patrick ("Paddy")	Fg. Off.	Pilot	421 Flt.	Promoted Flt. Lt., 3-9-40. Commanded 421 Flt., 1-10-40, on formation. Awarded D.S.O. (20-8-43), D.F.C. (18-4-41). Wounded, 12-10-40. Released from R.A.F., 1947, as Group Captain.		British
GREEN Frederick William Woodridge	Sgt.	Aircrew	600	On 600 Sqn., 1-7-40. Served throughout the Battle of Britain with this Squadron.		British
GREEN George Graham	Sgt.	Aircrew	236	On 236 Sqn., 1-7-40.		British
GREEN Herbert Edward	Sgt.	Pilot	141	On 141 Sqn., 1-7-40. Commissioned, 9-11-42. Awarded M.B.E. (31-5-56). Retired from R.A.F., 1-5-65, as Squadron Leader.		British
GREEN Maurice David	Plt. Off.	Aircrew	248	On 248 Sqn., 1-7-40. Flew on reconnaissance sorties over Norway during Battle of Britain.	✞ **Killed in Action** (20-10-40)	British
GREEN William James	Sgt.	Pilot	501	Joined 501 Sqn., 1-7-40. Commissioned, 30-10-42. Released from R.A.F., 11-45, as Flight Lieutenant. Served with R.A.F.V.R., 6-47 until 7-53.		British
GREENSHIELDS Henry la Fone	Sub-Lieut.	Pilot	266	Fleet Air Arm. Joined 266 Sqn., 1-7-40. ✠ **1 Bf 109, 15-8-40.**	✞ **Killed in Action** (16-8-40)	British
GREENWOOD John Peter Bowtell	Plt. Off.	Pilot	253	On 253 Sqn., 1-7-40. ✠ 1 He 111, 30-8-40. Released from R.A.F., 6-47, as Flight Lieutenant.		British
GREGORY Albert Edward	Sgt.	Aircrew	219	On 219 Sqn., 1-7-40. Commissioned, 31-8-42. Awarded D.F.C. (13-7-43). Released from R.A.F., 1947, as Flight Lieutenant.		British
GREGORY Alfred Henry	Sgt.	Pilot	111	Joined 111 Sqn., 28-9-40.	✞ Killed since Battle (23-7-41)	British
GREGORY Felix Stafford	Plt. Off.	Pilot	65	Joined 65 Sqn., 6-7-40. ✠ **1 Bf 109, 12-8-40.**	✞ **Killed in Action** (13-8-40)	British
GREGORY William James	Sgt.	Aircrew	29	On 29 Sqn., 1-7-40. Commissioned, 22-1-42. Awarded D.S.O.(17-7-45), D.F.C.✠ (4-8-42 and 16-7-43), D.F.M.(17-10-41). Retired from R.A.F., 1-6-64, as Wg. Cdr.		British

Name	Rank	Role	Sqn	Details	Status	Nationality
GRELLIS Horace Eustace	Plt. Off.	Aircrew	23	On 23 Sqn., 1-7-40. Released from R.A.F., 1946, as Flight Lieutenant.	✝ Died since Battle (7-3-50)	British
GRESTY Kenneth Gaston	Sgt.	Aircrew	219	On 219 Sqn., 1-7-40.	✝ Killed since Battle (17-4-41)	British
GRETTON Reginald Henry	Sgt.	Pilot	266-222	On 266 Sqn., 1-7-40. Posted to 222 Sqn., 12-9-40. Seriously wounded, 27-9-40. Awarded D.F.C. (2-42, as Warrant Officer). Released from R.A.F., 1-46.		British
GRIBBLE Dorian George	Plt. Off.	Pilot	54	On 54 Sqn., 1-7-40. Promoted Fg. Off., 3-9-40. Awarded D.F.C.(13-8-40). ✠ 1 Bf 109, 24-7-40; ✠ 1 Bf 109, 15-8-40; ✠ 1 Bf 109 (solo) and 1 Bf 110 (shared), 18-8-40; ✠ 1 Bf 109, 24-8-40; ✠ 2 Bf 109s, 28-8-40; ✠ 1 Bf 109 (shared), 31-8-40.	✝ Killed since Battle (4-6-41)	British
GRICE Dennis Neve	Fg. Off.	Pilot	600	Joined 600 Sqn., 9-7-40.	✝ **Killed in Action** (8-8-40)	British
GRICE Douglas Hamilton ("Grubby")	Plt. Off.	Pilot	32	On 32 Sqn., 1-7-40. Promoted Fg. Off., 26-9-40. Awarded D.F.C., 25-6-40. ✠ 1 Do 17, 12-8-40; ✠ 1 Bf 109, 15-8-40. Seriously wounded, 15-8-40. Awarded M.B.E., 1-1-46. Retired from R.A.F., 4-47, as Wing Commander.		British
GRIDLEY Robert Victor	Sgt.	Aircrew	235	Joined 235 Sqn., 3-8-40. Commissioned, 4-6-41.	✝ Killed since Battle (13-1-42)	British
GRIER Thomas	Plt. Off.	Pilot	601	On 601 Sqn., 1-7-40. Promoted Fg. Off., 3-9-40. Awarded D.F.C.(1-10-40) ✠ 1 Do 17 (shared), 7-7-40; ✠ 1 Ju 88 (shared), 16-7-40; ✠ 1 He 59 (shared), 20-7-40; ✠ 2 Bf 110s and 1 Ju 88 (solo), and 1 Ju 88 (shared); ✠ 2 Ju 87s, 18-8-40; ✠ 1 He 111 (shared), 30-8-40; ✠ 1 Bf 110, 31-8-40; ✠ 2 Bf 109s, 6-9-40; ✠ 1 Ju 88, 25-9-40.	✝ Killed since Battle (5-12-41)	British
GRIFFIN John James	Sgt.	Pilot	73	Joined 73 Sqn., early 7-40. ✠ 1 Ju 88, 15-8-40. Wounded, 14-9-40.	✝ Killed since Battle (7-4-42)	British
GRIFFITHS Glyn	Sgt.	Pilot	17	On 17 Sqn., 1-7-40. Awarded, D.F.M.(26-11-40). Commissioned, 4-4-42. ✠ 1 He 111 (shared), 9-7-40; ✠ 1 He 111 (solo) and 1 He 111 (shared), 12-7-40; ✠ 1 Bf 110 (shared), 11-8-40; ✠ 1 Ju 88 (shared), 19-9-40; ✠ 1 Bf 109 and 1 Bf 110, 27-9-40.	✝ Died since Battle (1983)	British
GRIFFITHS	Sgt.	Pilot	32	Joined 32 Sqn., 7-10-40. (Initials and forenames not known).		British
GROGAN George Jacques	Plt. Off.	Aircrew	23	On 23 Sqn., 1-7-40. Retired from R.A.F., 1-11-56, as Squadron Leader.	✝ Died since Battle (1983)	British
GROSZEWSKI Bernard	Plt. Off.	Pilot	43	Joined 43 Sqn., 26-10-40.	✝ Killed since Battle (12-12-41)	Polish
GROVE Harry Cyril	Sgt.	Pilot	3-501	Joined 3 Sqn., end of 8-40. Posted to 501 Sqn., 29-9-40.	✝ Killed since Battle (8-11-40)	British
GRUBB Ernest George	Sgt.	Pilot	219	On 219 Sqn., 1-7-40. Commissioned, 25-5-42. Released from R.A.F., 1945, as Flight Lieutenant. (Brother of Flight Lieutenant H.F. Grubb).		British
GRUBB Henry Frank	Sgt.	Pilot	219	On 219 Sqn., 1-7-40. Commissioned, 25-5-42. Released from R.A.F., 1945, as Flight Lieutenant. (Brother of Flight Lieutenant E.G. Grubb).	✝ Died since Battle (1981)	British
GRUSZKA Franciszek	Fg. Off.	Pilot	65	Joined 65 Sqn., 7-8-40.	✝ **Killed in Action** (18-8-40)	Polish
GRZESZCZAK Bohdan	Fg. Off.	Pilot	303	Joined 303 (Polish) Sqn., 21-8-40.	✝ Killed since Battle (28-8-41)	Polish
GUÉRIN Charles Paul	Adj.	Pilot	232	Joined 232 Sqn., 14-9-40.	✝ Killed since Battle (8-5-41)	French
GUEST Thomas Francis	Plt. Off.	Pilot	79-56	Joined 79 Sqn., 17-9-40. Posted to 56 Sqn., 8-10-40. Released from R.A.F., 1945, as Flight Lieutenant.		British
GUNDRY Kenneth Cradock	Plt. Off.	Pilot	257	Joined 257 Sqn., 3-8-40. Slightly wounded, 12-10-40.	✝ Killed since Battle (22-5-42)	British
GUNN Harold Raymond	Plt. Off.	Pilot	74	On 74 Sqn., 1-7-40. ✠ 1 Bf 109, 28-7-40.	✝ **Killed in Action** (31-7-40)	British
GUNNING Peter Stackhouse	Plt. Off.	Pilot	46	On 46 Sqn., 1-7-40.	✝ **Killed in Action** (15-10-40)	British
GUNTER Edward Maurice	Plt. Off.	Pilot	43-501	Joined 43 Sqn., 10-9-40. Posted to 501 Sqn., 22-9-40.	✝ **Killed in Action** (27-9-40)	British
GURTEEN John Vinter	Plt. Off.	Pilot	504	On 504 Sqn., 1-7-40.	✝ **Killed in Action** (15-9-40)	British
GUTHRIE Giles Connop McEacharn	Lieut.	Pilot	808	Fleet Air Arm. On 808 Sqn., 1-7-40. Awarded D.S.C. (25-11-41), O.B.E. (1-1-46). Released from Royal Navy, 30-1-46, as Lieutenant Commander (A).	✝ Died since Battle (31-12-79)	British
GUTHRIE Norman Henry	Sgt.	Aircrew	604	On 604 Sqn., 1-7-40. Awarded D.F.M.(24-6-41). Commissioned, 8-9-42. Released from R.A.F., 1946, as Flight Lieutenant.	✝ Died since Battle (17-2-81)	British
GUY Leonard Northwood	Sgt.	Pilot	601	On 601 Sqn., 1-7-40. ✠ 2 Bf 110s, 11-8-40; ✠ 1 Bf 110 (solo) and 1 Bf 110 (shared), 13-8-40; ✠ 1 Ju 88 (shared), 15-8-40; ✠ 2 Ju 87s, 16-8-40.	✝ **Killed in Action** (18-8-40)	British
GUY Peter	Midshipman	Pilot	808	Fleet Air Arm. On 808 Sqn., 1-7-40.	✝ Killed since Battle (28-1-42)	British
GUYMER Eric Norman Laurence	Sgt.	Pilot	238	Joined 238 Sqn., 7-9-40. Commissioned, 15-1-42. Released from R.A.F., 1945, as Flight Lieutenant.		British
HACKWOOD Gerald Henry ("Hackers")	Plt. Off.	Pilot	264	On 264 Sqn., 1-7-40.	✝ Killed since Battle (20-11-40)	British
HAIG John Galloway Edward	Fg. Off.	Pilot	603	On 603 Sqn., 1-7-40. ✠ 1 Bf 109, 2-9-40. Released from R.A.F., 1945, as Squadron Leader.		British
HAIGH Cyril	Sgt.	Pilot	604	On 604 Sqn., 1-7-40.	✝ **Killed in Action** (25-8-40)	British
HAINE Richard Cummins	Plt. Off.	Pilot	600	On 600 Sqn., 1-7-40. Awarded O.B.E.(1-1-62), D.F.C.(9-7-40). Retired from the R.A.F., 1-10-70, as Group Captain.		British
HAINES Leonard Archibald	Fg. Off.	Pilot	19	On 19 Sqn., 1-7-40. Awarded D.F.C., 8-10-40. ✠ 1 Bf 110 (shared) 19-8-40; ✠ 1 Bf 110, 3-9-40; ✠ 1 Bf 109, 5-9-40; ✠ 1 Bf 110, 11-9-40; ✠ 1 Bf 109 and 1 Bf 110, 15-9-40; ✠ 1 Ju 88 (shared), 18-9-40.	✝ Killed since Battle (30-4-41)	British
HAIRE John Keatinge	Sgt.	Pilot	145	Joined 145 Sqn., 11-9-40.	✝ Killed since Battle (6-11-40)	British
HAIRS Peter Raymond	Plt. Off.	Pilot	501	On 501 Sqn., 1-7-40. Posted away, 13-10-40. ✠ 1 Bf 109, 5-9-40. Released from R.A.F., 30-10-45, as Flight Lieutenant. Made M.B.E., 1-1-46.		British
HALL Noel Mudie	Flt. Lt.	Pilot	257	On 257 Sqn., 1-7-40. Had been awarded A.F.C.(2-1-39).	✝ **Killed in Action** (8-8-40)	British
HALL Rosswell Clifford	Plt. Off.	Aircrew	219	On 219 Sqn., 1-7-40. Served with squadron during Battle of Britain.		British
HALL Roger Montagu Dickenson	Plt. Off.	Pilot	152	Joined 152 Sqn., 1-9-40. Awarded D.F.C.(24-11-42). Transferred from flying duties on medical grounds and released from R.A.F., 1944, as Flight Lieutenant.		British
HALL William Clifford	Plt. Off.	Pilot	248	On 248 Sqn., 1-7-40. Flew reconnaissance sorties over Norway during Battle of Britain.	✝ Killed since Battle (14-4-41)	British
HALL	Sgt.	Aircrew	235	On 235 Sqn., 1-7-40. (Forenames and initials not known)		British
HALL	Sgt.	Aircrew	29	On 29 Sqn., 1-7-40. (Forenames and initials not known)		British
HALLAM Ian Lewis McGregor	Fg. Off.	Pilot	610-222	Joined 610 Sqn., 3-9-40. Posted to 222 Sqn., 30-9-40. Promoted Flt. Lt., 15-10-40. Was Squadron Leader at time of death.	✝ Killed since Battle (10-5-52)	British
HALLIWELL Antony Burton	Plt. Off.	Aircrew	141	Defiant gunner. On 141 Sqn., 1-7-40. ✠ 1 Bf 109, 19-7-40.	✝ Died since Battle (1974)	British
HALLOWES Herbert James Lempriere ("Jim")	Plt. Off.	Pilot	43	On 43 Sqn., 1-7-40. Awarded D.F.M.※ (both 6-9-40). Commissioned, 18-9-40. Awarded D.F.C. (19-1-43). ✠ 2 Bf 109s, 8-8-40; ✠ 1 Ju 88, 13-8-40; ✠ 3 Ju 87s, 16-8-40; ✠ 3 Ju 87s, 18-8-40; ✠ 1 He 111 (shared), 26-8-40. Retired from R.A.F., 8-7-56, as Wing Commander.	✝ Died since Battle (20-10-87)	British
HALTON Derrick Wilson	Sgt.	Pilot	615	On 615 Sqn., 1-7-40.	✝ **Killed in Action** (15-8-40)	British
HAMAR Jack Royston	Plt. Off.	Pilot	151	On 151 Sqn., 1-7-40. ✠ 1 Bf 110 (shared), 9-7-40; ✠ 1 Bf 109, 14-7-40. Awarded D.F.C. (30-7-40).	✝ **Killed in Action** (24-7-40)	British

Name	Rank	Role	Sqn.	Notes		Status	Nationality
HAMBLIN Richard Kaye	Wg. Cdr.	Pilot	17	Flew a single sortie with 17 Sqn. on 29-10-40. Appointed C.B.E. (1-1-46), and retired from R.A.F., 25-5-56, as Air Commodore.			British
HAMER Russel Chapman	Sgt.	Pilot	141	On 141 Sqn., 1-7-40.	✙	Killed since Battle (8-9-42)	British
HAMILL John Warren	Fg. Off.	Pilot	229	On 229 Sqn., 1-7-40.	✙	Killed since Battle (24-12-40)	New Zealander
HAMILTON Alexander Lewis ("Black")	Plt. Off.	Pilot	248	On 248 Sqn., 1-7-40. Flew reconnaissance sorties of enemy-held coasts during Battle of Britain. Retired from R.A.F., 5-4-61, as Wing Commander.			Australian
HAMILTON Arthur Charles ("Arch")	Plt. Off.	Aircrew	141	Defiant gunner. On 141 Sqn., 1-7-40.	✙	**Killed in Action** (19-7-40)	British
HAMILTON Charles Blackley	Sgt.	Aircrew	219	Joined 219 Sqn., c.1-9-40. Commissioned, 22-2-44. Awarded D.F.C. (26-9-44)	✙	Killed since Battle (13-4-45)	British
HAMILTON Claud Eric	Plt. Off.	Pilot	234	Joined 234 Sqn., 12-9-40.	✙	Killed since Battle (14-5-41)	British
HAMILTON Harry Raymond ("Hammy")	Flt. Lt.	Pilot	85	On 85 Sqn., 1-7-40. ✙ **1 Bf 110 (shared), 30-7-40; ✙ 1 Bf 110 (solo) and 1 He 111 (shared), 18-8-40; ✙ 1 Bf 109, 29-8-40.**	✙	**Killed in Action** (29-8-40)	Canadian
HAMILTON James Sutherland	Sgt.	Pilot	248	Joined 248 Sqn., 25-9-40. Flew reconnaissance sorties over Norwegian coast during Battle of Britain.	✙	Killed since Battle (13-12-40)	British
HAMLYN Ronald Fairfax	Sgt.	Pilot	610	On 610 Sqn., 1-7-40. Awarded D.F.M.(13-9-40). Commissioned, 29-1-41. Awarded A.F.C.(1-1-43). ✙ **1 Do 17 (shared), 3-7-40; ✙ 1 Bf 109, 14-8-40; ✙ 1 Ju 88 and 4 Bf 109s, 24-8-40; ✙ 1 Bf 109, 26-8-40; ✙ 1 Bf 109, 27-8-40; ✙ 1 Bf 109, 28-8-40; ✙ 1 Bf 109, 30-8-40.** Retired from R.A.F., 19-10-57, as Squadron Leader.			British
HAMMERTON Jack	Sgt.	Pilot	3-615	Joined 615 Sqn., 10-40, from 3 Sqn.	✙	Killed since Battle (6-11-40)	British
HAMMOND Derek John	Plt. Off.	Pilot	54-245-253	Joined 54 Sqn., 9-40. Posted to 245 Sqn., 27-9-40. Posted to 253 Sqn., 16-10-40. Released from R.A.F., 1947, as Squadron Leader.			British
HAMPSHIRE Cyril Edward	Sgt.	Pilot	85-111-249-422 Flt.	On 85 Sqn., 1-7-40. Posted to 111 Sqn., 17-8-40. Posted to 249 Sqn., 10-9-40. Posted to 422 Flt., 10-40. ✙ **1 Bf 110, 11-8-40.** Commissioned, 2-7-42. Released from R.A.F., 1-46, as Flying Officer.			British
HANBURY Bruce Alexander	Plt. Off.	Pilot	1-1(Canadian)	Joined 1 Sqn., 3-10-40. posted to 1 (Canadian) Sqn., 21-10-40.	✙	Killed since Battle (27-3-42)	Canadian
HANBURY Osgood Villiers	Plt. Off.	Pilot	602	Joined 602 Sqn., 3-9-40. Awarded D.S.O.(30-4-43), D.F.C.❦ (22-5-42 and 28-7-42). ✙ **1 Do 17, 15-9-40; ✙ 1 Ju 88 (shared), 21-9-40; ✙ 1 Ju 88, 30-9-40; ✙ 1 Bf 109, 30-10-40.**	✙	Killed since Battle (3-6-43)	British
HANCOCK Ernest Lindsay	Fg. Off.	Pilot	609	Joined 609 Sqn., 23-9-40. Awarded D.F.C.(16-11-45). Released from R.A.F., 1945, as Squadron Leader.			British
HANCOCK Norman Edward	Plt. Off.	Pilot	65-152	Joined 65 Sqn., 3-9-40. Posted to 152 Sqn., 10-10-40. Awarded D.F.C.(23-6-44). Released from R.A.F., 3-46, as Flight Lieutenant.			British
HANCOCK Norman Patrick Watkins	Plt. Off.	Pilot	1	On 1 Sqn., 1-7-40. Awarded D.F.C.(29-12-42). Retired from R.A.F., 12-8-58, as Squadron Leader.			British
HANNAN George Henry	Plt. Off.	Aircrew	236	On 236 Sqn., 1-7-40.	✙	Killed since Battle (21-12-40)	British
HANSON David Harry Wellsted	Fg. Off.	Pilot	17	On 17 Sqn., 1-7-40. ✙ **1 Do 17 (shared), 12-7-40; ✙ 1 Do 17, 3-9-40.**	✙	**Killed in Action** (3-9-40)	British
HANUS Josef Jan	Plt. Off.	Pilot	310	Joined 310 (Czech) Sqn., early 9-40. Awarded D.F.C.(26-5-43). Retired from R.A.F., 19-9-68, as Squadron Leader.			Czech
HANZLICEK Otto	Sgt.	Pilot	312	Joined 312 (Czech) Sqn., 19-9-40.	✙	**Killed in Action** (10-10-40)	Czech
HARDACRE John Reginald	Plt. Off.	Pilot	504	On 504 Sqn., 1-7-40. Promoted Fg. Off., 3-9-40. ✙ **1 Bf 110, 7-9-40; ✙ 1 Do 215, 15-9-40.**	✙	**Killed in Action** (30-9-40)	British
HARDCASTLE Jack	Sgt.	Aircrew	219	Joined 219 Sqn., 13-7-40. Posted away, c.9-40. (Was serving with bomber squadron at time of death).	✙	Killed in accident (28-10-40)	British
HARDIE	Sgt.	Pilot	232	Joined 232 Sqn., 26-9-40. (Initials and forenames not known).			British
HARDING Nelson Maxwell	Fg. Off.	Pilot	23	Joined 23 Sqn., 23-10-40. Promoted Flt. Lt., 21-9-40.	✙	Killed since Battle (16-9-44)	British
HARDING Noel Douglas	Sgt.	Aircrew	29	On 29 Sqn., 1-7-40. Commissioned, 9-2-42. Released from R.A.F., 1945, as Fg. Off.			British
HARDMAN Harry Gordon	Plt. Off.	Pilot	111	On 111 Sqn., 1-7-40. Posted away, 9-40. Released from R.A.F., 1945, as Squadron Leader.			Australian
HARDWICK William Robert Harrold	Sgt.	Aircrew	600	On 600 Sqn., 1-7-40. Commissioned in R.A.F.V.R.(T), 1945.			British
HARDY Oswald Anthony	Sgt.	Aircrew	264	Defiant gunner. Joined 264 Sqn., early 8-40. Commissioned, 31-8-42. Awarded D.F.C.(23-3-45). Released from R.A.F., 1947, as Squadron Leader.			British
HARDY Richard	Plt. Off.	Pilot	234	On 234 Sqn., 1-7-40. Taken prisoner, 15-8-40. Released from R.A.F., 1946.			British
HARE Maxwell	Sgt.	Pilot	245	Joined 245 Sqn., 4-10-40.	✙	Killed since Battle (30-6-41)	British
HARGREAVES Frederick Norman	Plt. Off.	Pilot	92	On 92 Sqn., 1-7-40.	✙	**Killed in Action** (11-9-40)	British
HARKER Alan Stuart ("Budge")	Sgt.	Pilot	234	On 234 Sqn., 1-7-40. Awarded D.F.M.(22-10-40). Commissioned, 19-3-41. ✙ **2 Bf 109s, 18-8-40; ✙ 1 Bf 110, 4-9-40; ✙ 2 Bf 109s, 6-9-40; ✙ 1 Bf 109, 7-9-40; ✙ 1 Ju 88, 22-9-40.** Released from R.A.F., 11-45, as Flight Lieutenant.			British
HARKNESS Hill	Sqn. Ldr.	Pilot	257	Joined 257 Sqn., 22-7-40, to command. ✙ **1 Ju 88, 13-8-40.** Posted away, 12-9-40. Resigned commission, 4-12-43.			Irish
HARNETT Thomas Patrick	Fg. Off.	Pilot	219	On 219 Sqn., 1-7-40. Transferred to R.C.A.F., 11-11-43. Awarded D.F.C. (19-10-45). Released from R.C.A.F., 10-9-46, as Wing Commander.	✙	Died since Battle (19-12-85)	Canadian
HARPER William John	Fg. Off.	Pilot	17	On 17 Sqn., 1-7-40. Wounded, 15-8-40.			British
HARRIS Patrick Arthur	Plt. Off.	Pilot	3	Joined 3 Sqn., 30-9-40.	✙	Killed since Battle (17-6-41)	British
HARRISON Anthony Robert James	Sgt.	Aircrew	219	Joined 219 Sqn., late 7-40.	✙	Killed since Battle (2-7-41)	British
HARRISON David Stewart	Plt. Off.	Pilot	238	Joined 238 Sqn., 12-9-40.	✙	**Killed in Action** (28-9-40)	British
HARRISON John Howard	Plt. Off.	Pilot	145	Joined 145 Sqn., c.6-8-40.	✙	**Killed in Action** (12-8-40)	British
HARROLD Frederick Cecil	Plt. Off.	Pilot	501-151	On 501 Sqn., 1-7-40. Posted to 151 Sqn., 26-8-40. Rejoined 501 Sqn., 26-9-40.	✙	**Killed in Action** (28-9-40)	British
HART John Stewart	Plt. Off.	Pilot	54-602	Joined 54 Sqn., early 9-40. Posted to 602 Sqn., mid-9-40. ✙ **1 Bf 109, 29-10-40.** Promoted Fg. Off., 2-10-40. Awarded D.F.C.(22-6-45). Released from R.A.F., 1946, as Squadron Leader.			Canadian
HART Kenneth Graham	Plt. Off.	Pilot	65	On 65 Sqn., 1-7-40. Awarded D.F.C.(20-1-42). ✙ **1 He 111 (shared), 5-7-40; ✙ 1 Bf 109, 12-8-40.** Was Squadron Leader at time of death.	✙	Killed since Battle (28-12-44)	British
HART Norris	Plt. Off.	Pilot	242	Joined 242 Sqn., 18-7-40. ✙ **1 He 111, 30-8-40; ✙ 1 Bf 109, 15-9-40; ✙ 2 Ju 88s, 18-9-40.**	✙	Killed since Battle (5-11-40)	Canadian
HARTAS Peter McDonnell	Plt. Off.	Pilot	603-421 Flt.	Joined 603 Sqn., 24-9-40. Posted to 421 Flt., 2-10-40. ✙ **1 Bf 109, 2-10-40.** Promoted Fg. Off., 3-9-40.	✙	Killed since Battle (10-2-41)	British
HARVEY Leslie Walter	Sgt.	Pilot	54-245	Joined 54 Sqn., 22-8-40. Posted to 245 Sqn., 27-9-40. Commissioned, 5-4-44. Released from R.A.F., 1946, as Flight Lieutenant.			British
HASTINGS Douglas	Plt. Off.	Pilot	74	On 74 Sqn., 1-7-40. ✙ **1 Bf 109, 11-8-40; ✙ 1 Do 17, 13-8-40.**	✙	**Killed in Accident** (9-10-40)	British
HATTON	Sgt.	Aircrew	604	Joined 604 Sqn., 8-8-40. (Initials and forenames not known)			British
HAVERCROFT Ralph Edward ("Titch")	Sgt.	Pilot	92	On 92 Sqn., 1-7-40. Commissioned, 17-11-41. Awarded A.F.C., 1-1-49. ✙ **1 Ju 88 (shared), 13-8-40.** Retired from R.A.F., 4-6-63, as Wing Commander.			British
HAVILAND John Kenneth	Plt. Off.	Pilot	151	Joined 151 Sqn., 23-9-40. Awarded D.F.C.(16-2-45).			American
HAVILAND Richard	Plt. Off.	Pilot	248	On 248 Sqn., 1-7-40.	✙	**Killed in Accident** (28-8-40)	South African

HAW Charlton ("Wag")	Sgt.	Pilot	504	On 504 Sqn., 1-7-40. Awarded D.F.M.(23-1-42). Commissioned, 6-3-42. Awarded D.F.C.(17-10-44). ✠ **1 Bf 110, 27-9-40.** Retired from R.A.F., 19-9-51, as Squadron Leader.			British
HAWKE Peter Sydney	Sgt.	Pilot	64-19	Joined 64 Sqn., 27-7-40. Posted to 19 Sqn., 20-9-40. Commissioned, 1-6-42. Awarded A.F.C.(1-1-46). ✠ **1 He 111, 18-8-40.** Released from R.A.F., 1946, as Flt. Lt.	✞	Died since Battle (12-5-88)	British
HAWKE Stanley Nelson	Sgt.	Aircrew	604	On 604 Sqn., 1-7-40.	✞	Killed since Battle (29-5-41)	British
HAWKINGS Redvers Percival	Sgt.	Pilot	601	On 601 Sqn., 1-7-40. ✠ **1 Do 17 (shared), 7-7-40.**	✞	**Killed in Action (18-8-40)**	British
HAWLEY Frederick Bernard	Sgt.	Pilot	266	On 266 Sqn., 1-7-40.	✞	**Killed in Action (15-8-40)**	British
HAWORTH Joseph Frederick John	Fg. Off.	Pilot	43	On 43 Sqn., 1-7-40.	✞	**Killed in Action (20-7-40)**	British
HAY Ian Bruce David Erroll ("Haybag")	Fg. Off.	Pilot	611	On 611 Sqn., 1-7-40. Discharged from R.A.F. as Wing Commander, 1945, on medical grounds.			South African
HAY Ronald Cuthbert	Lieut.	Pilot	808	Royal Marine in Fleet Air Arm. On 808 Sqn., 1-7-40. Awarded D.S.O.(1-5-45), D.S.C.✾ (25-11-41 and 31-7-45). Transferred to Royal Navy, 1947, and retired as Commander, 11-66.			British
HAYDEN Lawrence Hamilton	Sgt.	Aircrew	264	Defiant gunner. On 264 Sqn., 1-7-40. Awarded D.F.M.(11-2-41). Commissioned, 17-5-41. Released from R.A.F., 1945, as Flight Lieutenant.			British
HAYES Herbert Leonard	Sqn. Ldr.	Pilot	242	Flew at least one operational sortie with 242 Sqn., during Battle of Britain.			British
¶ **HAYES, P.S.**	Sgt.	Pilot	65	On 65 Sqn., 1-7-40.	✞	Killed in Action (7-7-40)	British
HAYES Thomas	Fg. Off.	Pilot	600	On 600 Sqn., 1-7-40. Promoted Flt. Lt., 3-9-40. Awarded D.F.C.(24-5-40). Released from R.A.F., 1945, as Wing Commander. Re-joined R.Aux.A.F., 1946, and commanded 600 Sqn., 7-46 until 7-48.			British
HAYLOCK Robert Arthur	Sgt.	Pilot	236	Joined 236 Sqn., 9-40. Commissioned, 22-11-41. Released from R.A.F., 1946, as Flight Lieutenant.			British
HAYSOM Geoffrey David Leybourne	Fg. Off.	Pilot	79	On 79 Sqn., 1-7-40. Promoted Flt. Lt., 11-10-40. Awarded D.S.O.(16-2-43), D.F.C.(29-4-41). ✠ **1 Bf 110, 15-8-40;** ✠ **1 Bf 109, 31-8-40.** Released by the R.A.F., 1946, as Group Captain.	✞	Died since Battle (1979)	South African
HAYTER James Chilton Francis	Plt. Off.	Pilot	615-605	Joined 615 Sqn., 4-9-40. Posted to 605 Sqn., 18-9-40. Awarded D.F.C.✾ (17-10-41 and 26-1-45). Transferred to R.N.Z.A.F. Reserve, 28-12-45.			New Zealander
HAYWOOD Douglas	Sgt.	Pilot	151-504	Joined 151 Sqn., 3-9-40. Posted to 504 Sqn., 21-9-40. Commissioned, 19-7-41. Retired from R.A.F., 1-6-55, as Squadron Leader.			British
HEAD Frederick Arthur Percy	Sgt.	Aircrew	236	On 236 Sqn., 1-7-40.	✞	**Killed in Action (1-8-40)**	British
HEAD Geoffrey Mons	Plt. Off.	Pilot	219	On 219 Sqn., 1-7-40.	✞	Killed since Battle (8-2-41)	British
HEAL Philip William Dunstan	Fg. Off.	Pilot	604	On 604 Sqn., 1-7-40. Promoted Flt. Lt., 3-9-40. Awarded A.F.C.(8-6-44). Retired from R.A.F., 24-2-62, as Group Captain.			British
HEALY Terence William Richard	Sgt.	Pilot	41-611	Joined 611 Sqn., 29-9-40, from 41 Sqn. Commissioned, 28-6-41.	✞	Killed since Battle (2-3-44)	British
HEATH Barrie	Fg. Off.	Pilot	611	On 611 Sqn., 1-7-40. Promoted Flt. Lt., 3-9-40. Awarded D.F.C.(29-4-41). Released from R.A.F., 1946, as Wing Commander.	✞	Died since Battle (22-2-88)	British
HEBRON George Stephen	Plt. Off.	Aircrew	235	On 235 Sqn., 1-7-40. Released from R.A.F., 6-46, as Wing Commander.			British
HEDGES Alan Lindsay	Plt. Off.	Pilot	245-257	On 245 Sqn., 1-7-40. Posted to 257 Sqn., 10-9-40. ✠ **1 Do 17 (shared), 15-9-40.** Released from R.A.F., 1945.			British
HEIMES Leopold	Sgt.	Pilot	235	Joined 235 Sqn., 26-8-40. Remained in R.A.F. after the War.			Belgian
HELCKE Denis Arnold	Sgt.	Pilot	504	On 504 Sqn., 1-7-40. ✠ **1 He 111, 7-9-40.**	✞	**Killed in Action (17-9-40)**	British
HELLYER Richard Owen	Flt. Lt.	Pilot	616	On 616 Sqn., 1-7-40. Released from R.A.F., 24-10-45, as Flight Lieutenant.			British
HEMINGWAY John Allman	Fg. Off.	Pilot	85	On 85 Sqn., 1-7-40. Promoted Fg. Off., 3-9-40. Awarded D.F.C.(1-7-41). Retired from R.A.F., 12-9-69, as Group Captain.			Irish
HENDERSON James Alan MacDonald	Plt. Off.	Pilot	257	Joined 257 Sqn., 7-7-40. ✠ **2 Bf 110s, 31-8-40.** Promoted Fg. Off., 3-9-40. Wounded, 31-8-40. Released from R.A.F., 1946, as Flight Lieutenant.			British
HENDRY David Oswald	Sgt.	Aircrew	219	Joined 219 Sqn., 2-9-40. Commissioned, 25-7-42. Awarded D.F.C. Released from R.A.F., 1946, as Flight Lieutenant.			British
HENN William Bryan	Sgt.	Pilot	501	Joined 501 Sqn., c.18-8-40. ✠ **1 He 111, 30-8-40.** Commissioned, 16-9-42. Awarded A.F.C.(1-1-45). Released from R.A.F., 1947, as Flight Lieutenant.	✞	Died since Battle (1979)	British
HENNEBERG Zdzislaw Karol	Fg. Off.	Pilot	303	Joined 303 (Polish) Sqn., 2-8-40, on formation. Awarded D.F.C.(30-10-40). ✠ **1 Bf 109, 31-8-40;** ✠ **1 He 111 and 1 Bf 109, 11-9-40;** ✠ **1 Do 17 and 1 Bf 109, 15-9-40;** ✠ **1 Bf 109, 27-9-40;** ✠ **1 Bf 110, 5-10-40.**	✞	Killed since Battle (12-4-41)	Polish
HENSON Bernard	Sgt.	Pilot	32-257	Joined 32 Sqn., 2-7-40. Posted to 257 Sqn., 9-40. Slightly wounded, 18-8-40. ✠ **1 Ju 87, 19-7-40;** ✠ **1 Do 215, 18-8-40.**	✞	Killed since Battle (17-11-40)	British
HENSTOCK Lawrence Frederick	Fg. Off.	Pilot	64	On 64 Sqn., 1-7-40. Promoted Flt. Lt., 3-9-40. Released from R.A.F., 1946, as Squadron Leader.	✞	Died since Battle (1981)	British
HERON Hugh Michael Turretin	Plt. Off.	Pilot	266-66	On 266 Sqn., 1-7-40. Posted to 66 Sqn., 15-9-40. ✠ **1 Bf 109, 30-9-40.** Awarded A.F.C.(7-9-45). Released from R.A.F., 9-46, as Squadron Leader.			British
HERRICK Brian Henry	Plt. Off.	Pilot	236	On 236 Sqn., 1-7-40. (Brother of Plt. Off. M.J. Herrick.)	✞	Killed since Battle (1-11-40)	New Zealander
HERRICK Michael James	Plt. Off.	Pilot	25	On 25 Sqn., 1-7-40. Awarded D.F.C.✾ (24-9-40 and 10-2-44). ✠ **2 He 111s, 4-9-40.**	✞	Killed since Battle (16-6-44)	New Zealander
HESLOP Victor William	Sgt.	Pilot	56	Joined 56 Sqn., 5-9-40. Commissioned, 10-2-43. Retired from R.A.F., 9-5-63, as Flight Lieutenant.			British
HESS Alexander	Flt. Lt.	Pilot	310	Supernumerary Acting Sqn. Ldr., with 310 (Czech) Sqn. from 10-7-40. ✠ **1 Bf 109 and 1 Do 215, 31-8-40.** Awarded D.F.C. Appointed Czech Air Attaché to the U.S.A., 1942, as Acting Group Captain.	✞	Died since Battle (1981)	Czech
HETHERINGTON Erik Lawson	Sgt.	Pilot	601	Joined 601 Sqn., 9-9-40. Commissioned, 17-7-41.	✞	Killed since Battle (31-10-42)	British
HEWETT Gordon Arthur	Sgt.	Pilot	607	On 607 Sqn., 1-7-40. Commissioned, 9-8-41. Assumed to have left R.A.F. in 1944 as Flight Lieutenant.			British
HEWITT Duncan Alexander	Plt. Off.	Pilot	501	On 501 Sqn., 1-7-40.	✞	**Killed in Action (12-7-40)**	Canadian
HEWLETT Colin Roy	Sgt.	Pilot	65	Joined 65 Sqn., 7-8-40. Commissioned, 26-6-41. Awarded D.F.C.(3-11-42).	✞	Killed since Battle (12-12-42)	British
HEWSON John Minchin	Fg. Off.	Pilot	616	Joined 616 Sqn., 19-8-40. Awarded D.F.C.(6-8-40). Promoted Flt. Lt., 3-9-40. Released from R.A.F., 1946, as Squadron Leader.			Australian
HEYCOCK George Francis Wheaton	Sqn. Ldr.	Pilot	23	Joined 23 Sqn., 9-8-40, to command. Appointed C.B. (8-6-63); awarded D.F.C. (29-9-42). Retired from R.A.F., 1-5-64, as an Air Commodore.	✞	Died since Battle (1983)	British
HEYWOOD Norman Bagshaw	Plt. Off.	Pilot	32-607-257	Joined 32 Sqn., early 9-40. Posted to 607 Sqn., 22-9-40. Posted to 257 Sqn., early 10-40.	✞	**Killed in Action (22-10-40)**	British
HEYWORTH John Harvey	Sqn. Ldr.	Pilot	79	Joined 79 Sqn., 12-7-40, to command. ✠ **1 He 111 (shared), 27-9-40.** Awarded A.F.C.(1-1-46). Released from R.A.F., 1945, as a Wing Commander.	✞	Died since Battle (21-9-59)	British
HICK David Thornhill	Sgt.	Pilot	32	Joined 32 Sqn., c.28-9-40.	✞	Died since Battle (26-7-73)	British
HIGGINS William Burley	Sgt.	Pilot	32-253	Joined 32 Sqn., 2-7-40. Posted to 253 Sqn., 9-9-40. ✠ **1 Do 17 (shared), 3-7-40;** ✠ **1 Bf 110, 20-7-40;** ✠ **1 Bf 109, 12-8-40;** ✠ **1 Bf 109, 24-8-40;** ✠ **1 Bf 109, 11-9-40.**	✞	**Killed in Action (14-9-40)**	British
HIGGINSON Frederick William ("Taffy")	Sgt	Pilot	56	On 56 Sqn., 1-7-40. Commissioned, 18-9-40. Awarded D.F.C.(9-2-43), D.F.M. (30-7-40). ✠ **1 Do 17, 12-8-40;** ✠ **1 Do 17, 16-8-40;** ✠ **1 Do 215, 18-8-40;** ✠ **1 Bf 110, 25-8-40;** ✠ **1 Bf 109, 28-8-40;** ✠ **1 Bf 109, 31-8-40;** ✠ **1 Do 17, 14-9-40;** ✠ **2 Bf 110s, 30-9-40.** Awarded O.B.E. and retired from R.A.F., 5-4-56, as a Wing Commander.			British

HIGGS Thomas Peter Kingsland	Fg. Off.	Pilot	111	On 111 Sqn., 1-7-40.	✝ Killed in Action (10-7-40)	British
HIGHT Cecil Henry	Plt. Off.	Pilot	234	On 234 Sqn., 1-7-40.	✝ Killed in Action (15-8-40)	New Zealander
HILES Arthur Herbert	Plt. Off.	Aircrew	236	Joined 236 Sqn., 24-9-40.	✝ Killed since Battle (15-3-42)	British
HILKEN Clive Geoffrey	Sgt.	Pilot	74	Joined 74 Sqn., mid-8-40. Wounded, 20-10-40. Taken prisoner by Germans, 27-6-41. Released by R.A.F., 1945, as Warrant Officer.		British
HILL Archibald Edmund	Plt. Off.	Pilot	248	On 248 Sqn., 1-7-40. Flew reconnaissance sorties over enemy-held coasts during Battle of Britain.	✝ Killed since Battle (15-4-41)	British
HILL Arnold Maurice	Sgt.	Aircrew	25	On 25 Sqn., 1-7-40. Commissioned, 1-5-42. Awarded D.F.C.(2-2-43). Released from R.A.F., 1945, as Flight Lieutenant.		British
HILL Charles Richard	Sgt.	Aircrew	141	Defiant gunner. Commissioned, 24-11-41. Awarded D.F.C.(30-4-43). Retired from R.A.F., 13-4-59, as Squadron Leader.	✝ Died since Battle (20-10-85)	British
HILL Geoffrey	Sgt.	Pilot	65	On 65 Sqn., 1-7-40. Commissioned, 27-11-40. Taken prisoner by Germans, 6-40. Awarded M.B.E. Released from R.A.F., 1945, as Flight Lieutenant.		British
HILL George Edward	Plt. Off.	Pilot	245	On 245 Sqn., 1-7-40.	✝ Killed since Battle (31-3-44)	British
HILL Howard Perry	Plt. Off.	Pilot	92	On 92 Sqn., 1-7-40. ✠ 1 Ju 88 (shared), 26-7-40; ✠ 2 Do 17s, 15-9-40; ✠ 1 Ju 88, 18-9-40.	✝ Killed in Action (20-9-40)	New Zealander
HILL Sqn. Ldr.	Sqn. Ldr.	Pilot	222	Joined 222 Sqn., 31-7-40, to command. Appointed C.B.E., 1-1-46. ✠ 1 Bf 109, 1-9-40. Retired from R.A.F., 1-2-60, as Group Captain.		British
HILL Michael Rowland	Plt. Off.	Pilot	266	Promoted Fg. Off., 9-8-40. Joined 266 Sqn., 28-9-40.	✝ Killed since Battle (12-3-45)	South African
HILL Sydney Jenkyn	Plt. Off.	Pilot	609	Joined 609 Sqn., mid-10-40. ✠ 1 Ju 88 (shared), 21-10-40.	✝ Killed since Battle (18-6-41)	British
HILLARY Richard Hope ("Dicks")	Plt. Off.	Pilot	603	Joined 603 Sqn., 6-7-40. Promoted Fg. Off., 3-10-40. ✠ 1 Bf 109, 29-8-40; ✠ 1 Bf 109, 31-8-40; ✠ 2 Bf 109s, 2-9-40; ✠ 1 Bf 109, 3-9-40. Severely wounded, 3-9-40.	✝ Killed since Battle (8-1-43)	Australian
HILLCOAT Harry Bryan Lillie	Fg. Off.	Pilot	1	On 1 Sqn., 1-7-40. ✠ 1 Do 17 (shared), 18-8-40; ✠ 1 Bf 109, 1-9-40.	✝ Killed in Action (3-9-40)	British
HILLMAN Ralph Walter	Sgt.	Aircrew	235	Joined 235 Sqn., 1-8-40.	✝ Killed since Battle (6-4-41)	British
HILLOCK Frank William	Plt. Off.	Pilot	1(Canadian)	Joined 1(Canadian) Sqn., 21-10-40. Retired from R.C.A.F., 21-11-65, as Wing Commander.		Canadian
HILLWOOD Peter	Sgt.	Pilot	56	On 56 Sqn., 1-7-40. Commissioned, 23-1-42. Awarded D.F.C.(24-11-44). ✠ 1 Ju 87, 13-7-40. Released from R.A.F., 1946, as Flight Lieutenant.	✝ Died since Battle (1966)	British
HIMR Jaroslav	Plt. Off.	Pilot	79-56	Joined 79 Sqn., 11-9-40. Posted to 56 Sqn., 8-10-40.	✝ Killed since Battle (24-9-43)	Czech
HINDRUP Frederick George	Sgt.	Aircrew	600	Joined 600 Sqn., 21-9-40.	✝ Killed since Battle (20-4-41)	New Zealander
HINE Merrick Hubert	Sgt.	Pilot	65	Joined 65 Sqn., 19-8-40.	✝ Killed since Battle (12-12-40)	British
HIRD Leonard	Sgt.	Aircrew	604	Joined 604 Sqn., 14-8-40.	✝ Killed since Battle (28-6-41)	British
HITCHINGS Bryan Albert Harold	Plt. Off.	Pilot	3	Joined 3 Sqn., 2-10-40. Promoted Fg. Off., 30-9-40. Retired from R.A.F., 1-10-63, as Squadron Leader.		British
HITHERSAY Arthur James Beaumont	Sgt.	Aircrew	141	Defiant gunner. On 141 Sqn., 1-7-40. Released from R.A.F., 1946, as Warrant Officer.		British
HLAVAC Jaroslav	Sgt.	Pilot	79-56	Joined 79 Sqn., 11-9-40. Posted to 56 Sqn., 8-10-40.	✝ Killed in Action (10-10-40)	Czech
HLOBIL Alois	Plt. Off.	Pilot	312	Joined 312 (Czech) Sqn., 5-9-40.		Czech
HOARE-SCOTT James Hammond	Plt. Off.	Pilot	601	Joined 601 Sqn., 1-9-40.	✝ Killed since Battle (21-11-40)	British
HOBBIS Dudley Ormston	Plt. Off.	Pilot	219	Joined 219 Sqn., 13-7-40. Awarded D.F.C.(8-7-41)	✝ Killed since Battle (25-11-43)	British
HOBBS Joseph Bedo	Plt. Off.	Pilot	3-232	On 3 Sqn., 1-7-40. On 232 Sqn., 17-7-40, on formation.	✝ Killed since Battle (7-12-41)	British
HOBBS Sydney John	Sgt.	Pilot	235	On 235 Sqn., 1-7-40.	✝ Killed since Battle (14-8-41)	British
HOBSON Colin Anthony	Plt. Off.	Pilot	600	On 600 Sqn., 1-7-40.	✝ Killed in Action (3-10-40)	British
HOBSON Desmond Bogan	Fg. Off.	Pilot	64	On 64 Sqn., 1-7-40. Promoted Flt. Lt., 3-9-40. Released from R.A.F., 1945, as Squadron Leader.		British
HOBSON William Francis Cripps	Sqn. Ldr.	Pilot	601	Posted to 601 Sqn., 17-7-40, to command. Posted away, 10-8-40. Retired from R.A.F., 23-5-56, as Group Captain.		British
HODDS William Henry	Sgt.	Aircrew	25	Served on 25 Sqn. during Battle of Britain.		British
HODGE John Stephen Arthur	Sgt.	Aircrew	141	Defiant gunner. Joined 141 Sqn., 19-8-40.	✝ Killed since Battle (15-7-42)	British
HODGKINSON Arthur John	Sgt.	Pilot	219	On 219 Sqn., 1-7-40. Commissioned, 19-2-41. Awarded D.S.O.(23-7-43), D.F.C.✿ (11-4-41 and 6-6-41).✠ 1 Do 17, 10-7-40.	✝ Killed since Battle (10-7-43)	British
HODGSON William Henry ("Ace")	Plt. Off.	Pilot	85	On 85 Sqn., 1-7-40. Awarded D.F.C.(25-10-40). ✠ 1 Bf 109, 18-8-40; ✠ 2 Do 17s (shared), 26-8-40; ✠ 1 Bf 109, 28-8-40.	✝ Killed since Battle (13-3-41)	New Zealander
HODSON Claude Gordon	Plt. Off.	Pilot	229-1	Joined 1 Sqn., mid-9-40, from 229 Sqn. Commissioned, 6-12-41. Transferred to the Southern Rhodesian Air Force, 26-8-45.		Rhodesian
HOGAN Henry Algernon Vickers	Sqn. Ldr.	Pilot	501	In command of 501 Sqn., 1-7-40. Appointed C.B.(1955); awarded D.F.C.(25-10-40). ✠ 1 Bf 109, 20-7-40; ✠ 1 Do 215, 27-8-40; ✠ 1 Bf 110 (shared), 27-9-40; ✠ 1 Bf 110, 5-10-40; ✠ 1 Bf 109 (shared), 7-10-40; ✠ 1 Bf 109, 12-10-40; ✠ 1 Bf 109, 15-10-40. Retired from R.A.F., 29-4-62, as an Air Vice-Marshal.		British
HOGG Douglas William	Plt. Off.	Pilot	25	Joined 25 Sqn., 1-9-40.	✝ Killed in Action (3-9-40)	British
HOGG Edward Sydney	Fg. Off.	Pilot	152	On 152 Sqn., 1-7-40. Promoted Flt. Lt., 3-9-40. ✠ 1 Ju 88 (shared), 23-8-40. Posted away, 10-40. Released from R.A.F., 1945, as a Wing Commander.	✝ Died since Battle (1986)	British
HOGG John Henry	Sgt.	Pilot	141	Joined 141 Sqn., 21-8-40.	✝ Killed since Battle (23-7-42)	British
HOGG Ralph Vincent	Sgt.	Pilot	616	Joined 616 Sqn., 6-10-40.	✝ Killed since Battle (12-12-40)	British
HOGG Richard Malzard	Plt. Off.	Pilot	152	On 152 Sqn., 1-7-40. ✠ 1 Ju 88 (shared), 12-8-40; ✠ 1 Ju 88 (shared), 21-8-40.	✝ Killed in Action (25-8-40)	British
HOGG Robert Dudley	Sgt.	Pilot	56-17	Joined 56 Sqn., c.3-9-40. Posted to 17 Sqn., 11-9-40. ✠ Bf 110, 27-8-40; ✠ 1 Do 17 (shared), 24-10-40; ✠ 1 Bf 109 (shared), 29-10-40.	✝ Killed since Battle (11-11-40)	British
HOLDEN Eustace ("Gus")	Fg. Off.	Pilot	501	On 501 Sqn., 1-7-40. Promoted Flt. Lt., 3-9-40. Awarded D.F.C.(16-8-40). ✠ 1 Bf 109, 5-10-40; ✠ 1 Bf 109, 7-10-40; ✠ 1 Bf 109, 12-10-40; ✠ 1 Bf 109, 25-10-40. Retired from R.A.F., 28-12-64, as Wing Commander.		British
HOLDEN Kenneth	Plt. Off.	Pilot	616	On 616 Sqn., 1-7-40. Promoted Fg. Off., 3-9-40. Awarded D.F.C.(15-7-41). ✠ 1 Bf 109, 27-9-40. Released from R.A.F., 1945, as Wing Commander.		British
HOLDER Gerald Arthur	Plt. Off.	Aircrew	236	Joined 236 Sqn., 18-7-40. Released from R.A.F., 1946, as Flight Lieutenant.		British
HOLDER Robert	Sgt.	Pilot	151	Joined 151 Sqn., 30-9-40. (In R.N.Z.A.F.)	✝ Killed in Accident (26-10-40)	British
HOLDERNESS John Browning	Fg. Off.	Pilot	1-229	Attached to R.A.F. from Southern Rhodesian Air Force. Joined 1 Sqn., 8-40, from 248 Sqn. Posted to 248 Sqn., 17-10-40. Promoted Flt. Lt., 3-9-40. ✠ 1 Do 215, 7-9-40. Returned to S.R.A.F., 26-8-45.		Rhodesian
HOLLAND Arthur Lawrence	Sqn. Ldr.	Pilot	501-65	Attached, 501 Sqn., 6-8-40. Posted to 65 Sqn., 14-8-40, to command. Appointed C.B.E. (1-1-55). Retired from R.A.F., 25-10-60, as Group Captain.		British
HOLLAND Dennis Frederick	Plt. Off.	Pilot	72	On 72 Sqn., 1-7-40. ✠ 1 Bf 110, 4-9-40; ✠ 1 Bf 109, 5-9-40; ✠ 1 He 111, 15-9-40. (Died in hospital from wounds suffered).	✝ Killed in Action (20-9-40)	British

425

Name	Rank	Role	Squadron	Details	Fate	Nationality
HOLLAND Kenneth Christopher	Sgt.	Pilot	152	On 152 Sqn., 1-7-40. ✠ **1 Ju 88 (shared), 17-9-40;** ✠ **1 Ju 88, 19-9-40;** ✠ **1 He 111, 25-9-40.**	✠ **Killed in Action** (25-9-40)	Australian
HOLLAND Robert Hugh	Plt. Off.	Pilot	92	On 92 Sqn., 1-7-40. Promoted Fg. Off., 23-10-40. Awarded D.F.C.(26-11-40) ✠ **1 Do 17 (shared), 8-7-40;** ✠ **1 Ju 88, 15-7-40;** ✠ **1 Ju 88, 25-7-40;** ✠ **1 Bf 109, 26-10-40.**	✠ Died since Battle 17-11-54	British
HOLLAND Robert Meredith	Sgt.	Aircrew	600	Served on 600 Sqn. during Battle of Britain.		British
HOLLIS Ernest James ("Gus")	Sgt.	Aircrew	25	Joined 25 Sqn., 30-9-40. Awarded D.F.C.(12-12-44, as Warrant Officer). Released from R.A.F., 1945.	✠ Died since Battle (27-1-75)	British
HOLLOWAY Sydney Victor	Sgt.	Pilot	25	Joined 25 Sqn., 6-7-40. Commissioned, 1-5-42. Awarded O.B.E.(6-9-49). Retired from R.A.F., 2-3-68, as Squadron Leader.		British
HOLLOWELL Kenneth Bruce	Sgt.	Pilot	25	On 25 Sqn., 1-7-40. Commissioned, 25-11-40. Awarded A.F.C.(8-6-44). Released from R.A.F., 1945, as Flight Lieutenant.		British
HOLMES Eric Leonard	Sgt.	Pilot	248	On 248 Sqn., 1-7-40. Flew sorties over enemy coasts during Battle of Britain.	✠ Killed since Battle (12-6-41)	British
HOLMES Frederick Henry	Plt. Off.	Pilot	152	On 152 Sqn., 1-7-40. ✠ **1 Do 17 (shared), 25-7-40;** ✠ **1 Ju 87, 18-8-40;** ✠ **1 Ju 88 (shared), 21-8-40.**	✠ Killed since Battle (4-12-44)	British
HOLMES George Henry	Sgt.	Aircrew	600	On 600 Sqn., 1-7-40. Awarded D.F.M.(24-5-40). Commissioned, 18-8-40.	✠ Killed since Battle (20-12-40)	British
HOLMES Raymond Towers ("Basher")	Sgt.	Pilot	504	On 504 Sqn., 1-7-40. Commissioned, 10-6-41. ✠ **1 Do 17, 15-9-40.** Released from R.A.F., 4-10-45, as Flight Lieutenant.		British
HOLROYD Wilfred Barwell	Sgt.	Pilot	501-151	Joined 501 Sqn., early 10-40. Posted to 151 Sqn., later in 10-40. Commissioned, 12-7-41. Released from R.A.F., 1946, as Flight Lieutenant.		British
HOLTON Arthur Gerald Vaughan	Sgt.	Aircrew	141	Defiant gunner. Joined 141 Sqn., 19-8-40. Released from R.A.F., 1945, as Warrant Officer.		British
HOMER Michael Giles	Plt. Off.	Pilot	1-242	Joined 1 Sqn., c.3-9-40. Had been awarded D.F.C.(6-4-40). Posted to 242 Sqn., 21-9-40.	✠ **Killed in Action** (27-9-40)	British
HONE Douglas Harold	Plt. Off.	Pilot	615	Joined 615 Sqn., 6-7-40. ✠ **1 He 59 (shared), 27-7-40;** ✠ **1 Do 17, 29-7-40.** Wounded, 26-8-40. Retired from R.A.F., 30-9-75, as Flight Lieutenant.		British
HONOR Dudley Sandry Garton	Fg. Off.	Pilot	145	Joined 145 Sqn., 28-8-40. Awarded D.F.C.✿ (5-11-40 and 10-6-41). ✠ **1 Ar 196 (shared), 12-10-40.** Released from R.A.F., 1947, as Group Captain.	✠ Died since Battle (Date not known)	British
HOOD Hilary Richard Lionel	Sqn. Ldr.	Pilot	41	In command of 41 Sqn., 1-7-40. ✠ **1 Bf 109 and 1 Ju 87, 29-7-40.**	✠ **Killed in Action** (5-9-40)	British
HOOK Archie	Sgt.	Aircrew	248	Joined 248 Sqn., 10-9-40.	✠ Killed since Battle (13-12-40)	British
HOOKWAY Douglas Newcombe	Plt. Off.	Pilot	234	Joined 234 Sqn., 20-9-40. Awarded A.F.C.(1-1-46). Released from R.A.F., 1-46, as Squadron Leader.		British
HOOPER Beresford Gwynne	Plt. Off.	Pilot	25	On 25 Sqn., 1-7-40. Promoted Fg. Off., 3-9-40. Continued to serve in the R.A.F. after the War.		British
HOPE Sir Archibald Philip, Bt. ("Archie")	Flt. Lt.	Pilot	601	On 601 Sqn., 1-7-40. Promoted Acting Sqn. Ldr., 19-8-40. to command squadron. Awarded D.F.C.(1-10-40). ✠ **1 Ju 88 (shared), 15-8-40;** ✠ **1 Bf 110, 16-8-40.** Released from the R.A.F., 1945, as Group Captain.	✠ Died since Battle (6-87)	British
HOPE Ralph	Fg. Off.	Pilot	605	On 605 Sqn., 1-7-40.	✠ **Killed in Action** (14-10-40)	British
HOPEWELL James	Sgt.	Pilot	616-66	Joined 616 Sqn., mid-7-40. Posted to 66 Sqn., 14-10-40. Awarded D.F.M.(24-6-41). ✠ **1 Ju 88, 15-8-40;** ✠ **1 Bf 109, 30-8-40;** ✠ **1 Do 215, 1-9-40;** ✠ **1 Bf 110, 2-9-40.**	✠ Killed since Battle (21-1-42)	British
HOPGOOD Charles Leonard	Sgt.	Pilot	64	Joined 64 Sqn., 29-9-40.	✠ Killed since Battle (5-12-40)	British
HOPKIN William Pelham ("John Willie")	Plt. Off.	Pilot	54-602	On 54 Sqn., 1-7-40. Posted to 602 Sqn., 12-9-40. Awarded D.F.C.(9-9-41). ✠ **1 Do 17 (solo) and 1 Bf 110 (shared); 18-8-40;** ✠ **1 Bf 110, 22-8-40;** ✠ **1 He 111, 26-9-40;** ✠ **1 Bf 110, 27-9-40.** Retired from the R.A.F., 1-8-67, as Wing Commander.		British
HOPTON Bernard Walter	Sgt.	Pilot	600-615- 73-66	On 600 Sqn., 1-7-40. Posted to 615 Sqn., 17-8-40. Posted to 73 Sqn., 1-10-40. Posted to 66 Sqn., 23-10-40.	✠ Killed since Battle (6-8-41)	British
HORNBY William Henry	Sgt.	Pilot	234	On 234 Sqn., 1-7-40. Commissioned, 22-1-41. ✠ **1 Bf 109, 26-8-40;** ✠ **1 Bf 110, 4-9-40.** Released from R.A.F., 1945, as Flight Lieutenant.		British
HORNER Frank George	Sgt.	Pilot	610	Joined 610 Sqn., 16-9-40. Commissioned, 12-6-41. Released from the R.A.F., 1947, as Flight Lieutenant.		British
HORROX James Michael	Plt. Off.	Pilot	151	Joined 151 Sqn., 10-40.	✠ Killed since Battle (16-11-40)	British
HORSKY Vladimir	Sgt.	Pilot	238	Joined 238 Sqn., 12-9-40.	✠ **Killed in Action** (25-9-40)	Czech
HORTON Patrick Wilmot	Plt. Off.	Pilot	234	On 234 Sqn., 1-7-40. ✠ **Ju 88 (shared), 28-7-40;** ✠ **1 Bf 109, 16-8-40;** ✠ **1 Bf 109, 26-8-40;** ✠ **1 Bf 110, 4-9-40.**	✠ Killed since Battle (16-11-40)	New Zealander
HOUGH Harold Basil Lincoln	Plt. Off.	Pilot	600	On 600 Sqn., 1-7-40.	✠ Killed since Battle (16-8-41)	British
HOUGHTON Cyril George	Plt. Off.	Pilot	141	Joined 141 Sqn., 18-8-40. Seconded from R.A.F. to B.O.A.C., 1945.	✠ Died since Battle (22-5-69)	British
HOUGHTON Oliver Vincent	Sgt.	Pilot	32-501	On 615 Sqn., 1-7-40. Posted to 501 Sqn., 27-8-40.	✠ **Killed in Action** (6-9-40)	British
HOWARD John	Plt. Off.	Pilot	54-74	Joined 54 Sqn., 10-40. Posted to 74 Sqn., 24-10-40.	✠ Killed since Battle (6-5-41)	British
HOWARD	Sgt.	Aircrew	235	Flew with 235 Sqn. during Battle of Britain. No further details traced.		British
HOWARD-WILLIAMS Peter Ian	Plt. Off.	Pilot	19	On 19 Sqn., 1-7-40. Awarded D.F.C.(4-11-41). Retired from R.A.F., 11-6-58, as Wing Commander.		British
HOWARTH Eric Francis	Sgt.	Pilot	501	On 501 Sqn., 1-7-40.	✠ Killed since Battle (5-9-41)	British
HOWE Bernard	Plt. Off.	Pilot	25	Joined 25 Sqn., early 9-40.	✠ Killed since Battle (20-4-41)	British
HOWE Donald Charles	Plt. Off.	Aircrew	235	On 235 Sqn., 1-7-40. Released from R.A.F., 1945, as Flight Lieutenant.		British
HOWELL Francis Vincent ("Perky")	Sgt.	Pilot	87	On 87 Sqn., 1-7-40. Transferred from R.A.F. to Civil Service, 5-47.	✠ Died since Battle (5-3-84)	British
HOWELL Frank Jonathan	Fg. Off.	Pilot	609	On 609 Sqn., 1-7-40. Promoted to Flt. Lt., 3-9-40. Awarded D.F.C.✿ (25-10-40 and 4-11-41). ✠ **1 Ju 87, 13-8-40;** ✠ **1 Ju 88, 15-8-40;** ✠ **1 Bf 110, 25-8-40;** ✠ **1 Bf 110, 7-9-40;** ✠ **1 Do 17, 15-9-40;** ✠ **1 Bf 110, 7-10-40;** ✠ **1 Ju 88 (shared), 25-10-40.** Served in R.A.F. after the War as Squadron Leader.	✠ Killed since Battle (9-5-48)	British
HOWES Harold Norman	Sgt.	Pilot	85-605	On 85 Sqn., 1-7-40. Posted to 605 Sqn., 12-9-40. Awarded D.F.M.(25-10-40). ✠ **2 Bf 110s, 18-8-40;** ✠ **1 Do 215, 26-8-40;** ✠ **1 Do 215, 1-9-40;** ✠ **1 Do 17, 15-9-40;** ✠ **1 Bf 109, 12-10-40.**	✠ Killed since Battle (22-12-40)	British
HOWES Peter	Plt. Off.	Pilot	54-603	Joined 54 Sqn., 8-7-40. Posted to 54 Sqn., 11-9-40.	✠ **Killed in Action** (18-9-40)	British
HOWITT Geoffrey Leonard	Plt. Off.	Pilot	245-615	On 245 Sqn., 1-7-40. Posted to 615 Sqn., 9-10-40. Awarded D.F.C.✿ (30-9-41 and 26-10-43). Released from R.A.F., 6-10-45, as Wing Commander.		British
HOWITT Isaac Edward	Sgt.	Pilot	41	On 41 Sqn., 1-7-40. Commissioned, 15-10-41. Released from R.A.F., 1945, as Flight Lieutenant.		British
HOWLEY Richard Alexander	Plt. Off.	Pilot	141	On 141 Sqn., 1-7-40.	✠ **Killed in Action** (19-7-40)	New-foundlander
HOYLE George Vincent	Sgt.	Pilot	232	Joined 232 Sqn., 14-9-40.	✠ Killed since Battle (21-5-41)	British
HOYLE Henry Nuttall	Sgt.	Pilot	32-257	Joined 32 Sqn., 3-9-40. Posted to 257 Sqn., 16-9-40. Commissioned, 31-10-41. Released from R.A.F., 1-46, as Flight Lieutenant.		British
HRADIL Frantisek	Plt. Off.	Pilot	310-19	Joined 310 (Czech) Sqn., 28-8-40. Attached, 19 Sqn., 29-8-40.	✠ Killed since Battle (5-11-40)	Czech
HRUBY Otakar	Plt. Off.	Pilot	111	Joined 111 Sqn., 16-10-40. Awarded D.F.C.(1943).		Czech
HUBACEK Josef	Sgt.	Pilot	310	Joined 310 (Czech) Sqn., 6-8-40. Slightly wounded, 15-8-40.		Czech

Name	Rank	Role	Sqn.	Details	Status	Nationality
HUBBARD Brian Frederick Robert	Sgt.	Aircrew	235	On 235 Sqn., 1-7-40.	✠ Killed since Battle (9-11-40)	British
HUBBARD Thomas Edward	Fg. Off.	Pilot	601	On 601 Sqn., 1-7-40. Promoted Flt. Lt., 3-9-40. ✠ **1 Ju 88(shared), 16-7-40; ✠ 1 He 59 (shared), 20-7-40.** Left R.A.F. in 1943 as Squadron Leader.		British
HUCKIN Philip Edward	Sgt.	Pilot	600	On 600 Sqn., 1-7-40. Commissioned, 10-1-43. Awarded D.F.C. (7-3-44). Released from R.A.F., 1945, as Flight Lieutenant.		British
HUGHES, A.J.	Sgt.	Pilot	245	Joined 245 Sqn., 30-9-40. Other details not traced.		British
HUGHES David Ernest	Sgt.	Aircrew	600	Joined 600 Sqn., 21-9-40.	✠ **Killed in Action** (3-10-40)	New Zealander
HUGHES David Price	Fg. Off.	Pilot	238	Joined 238 Sqn., 4-8-40. Promoted Flt. Lt., 17-8-40. ✠ **1 Bf 110, 8-8-40; ✠ 1 Bf 109, 11-8-40; ✠ 2 Bf 110s and 1 Do 17, 13-8-40.**	✠ **Killed in Action** (11-9-40)	British
HUGHES Dennis Lawrence	Plt. Off.	Pilot	141	Joined 141 Sqn., 19-8-40. Awarded D.F.C.(8-12-44). Released from R.A.F., 1946, as a Squadron Leader.		British
HUGHES Frederick Desmond	Plt. Off.	Pilot	264	On 264 Sqn., 1-7-40. Promoted Fg. Off., 29-10-40. ✠ 2 Do 17s, 26-8-40; ✠ 1 He 111, 16-10-40. Appointed C.B.(1972), C.B.E.(1-1-62); awarded D.S.O.(23-3-45), D.F.C.✠✠ (18-4-41, 13-4-43 and 28-9-43), A.F.C. (1-1-54). Retired from the R.A.F., 6-6-74, as an Air Vice-Marshal.		British
HUGHES John McCulloch Middlemore	Fg. Off.	Pilot	25	Joined 25 Sqn., 16-9-40. Had been awarded D.F.C.(21-6-40). Promoted Flt. Lt., 3-9-40.	✠ Killed since Battle (7-12-40)	British
HUGHES Paterson Clarence	Fg. Off.	Pilot	234	On 234 Sqn., 1-7-40. Awarded D.F.C.(22-10-40).✠ **1 Ju 88 (shared), 8-7-40; ✠ 1 Ju 88 (shared), 27-7-40; ✠ 1 Ju 88 (shared), 28-7-40; ✠ 2 Bf 110s, 14-8-40; ✠ 2 Bf 109s, 16-8-40; ✠ 2 Bf 109s, 18-8-40; ✠ 2 Bf 109s, 26-8-40; ✠ 3 Bf 110s, 4-9-40; ✠ 2 Bf 109s, 5-9-40; ✠ 1 Bf 109, 6-9-40.**	✠ **Killed in Action** (7-7-40)	Australian
HUGHES William Robert Kent	F/Sgt.	Aircrew	23	Joined 23 Sqn., 17-8-40. Commissioned, 11-11-42. Awarded D.F.C.(8-8-41). Released from R.A.F., 3-46, as Flight Lieutenant.		British
HUGO Petrus Hendrik ("Dutch")	Plt. Off.	Pilot	615	On 615 Sqn., 1-7-40. Promoted Fg. Off., 21-10-40. Awarded D.S.O. (29-5-42), D.F.C.✠✠ (23-8-40, 25-11-41 and 16-2-43). ✠ 1 Ju 87 (shared), 14-7-40; ✠ 2 Bf 109s, 20-7-40; ✠ 1 He 59 (shared), 27-7-40; ✠ 1 Bf 109, 12-8-40. Wounded on 16-8-40 and 18-8-40. Retired from R.A.F., 19-2-50, retaining the rank of Group Captain.		South African
HULBERT Donald James	Sgt.	Pilot	257-501	On 257 Sqn., 1-7-40. Posted to 501 Sqn., 10-40. Commissioned, 26-4-44. Released from R.A.F., 1946, as Flying Officer.		British
HULBERT Frank Horace Raymond	Sgt.	Pilot	601	Joined 601 Sqn., late 8-40. Commissioned, 8-5-42. Awarded A.F.C.(2-6-43). Joined R.A.F.V.R., 3-47, and retired, 1957, as Flight Lieutenant.		British
HULL Caesar Barrand	Flt. Lt.	Pilot	263-43	On 263 Sqn., 1-7-40. Joined 43 Sqn., 31-8-40, to command. Had been awarded D.F.C.(21-6-40). ✠ **1 Bf 109, 6-9-40.**	✠ **Killed in Action** (7-9-40)	South African
HUMPHERSON John Bernard William	Fg. Off.	Pilot	32-607	On 32 Sqn., 1-7-40. Posted to 607 Sqn., 23-8-40. Promoted to Flt. Lt., 3-9-40. Awarded D.F.C.(30-8-40). ✠ **1 Do 17, 10-7-40; ✠ 1 Ju 87, 20-7-40; ✠ 1 Bf 109, 12-8-40; ✠ 1 Ju 88, 15-8-40.**	✠ Killed since Battle (22-6-41)	British
HUMPHREY Andrew Henry	Plt. Off.	Pilot	266	Joined 266 Sqn., 16-9-40. Appointed G.C.B.(1974; K.C.B.,1958; C.B., 1959); awarded O.B.E.(1-1-51), D.F.C.(30-5-41), A.F.C.✠ (1-1-43 and 1-1-45). Became Marshal of the R.A.F., 8-76, and appointed Chief of the Air Staff, 1974-76.	✠ Died since Battle (24-1-77)	British
HUMPHREYS Jack David	Plt. Off.	Pilot	29	On 29 Sqn., 1-7-40. Promoted Fg. Off., 3-9-40. Awarded D.F.C.(21-10-41).	✠ Killed since Battle (2-8-42)	British
HUMPHREYS James Samuel	Plt. Off.	Pilot	605	On 605 Sqn., 1-7-40. Wounded, 9-9-40. Released from R.A.F., 12-7-46, as Squadron Leader.	✠ Died since Battle (1986)	New Zealander
HUMPHREYS Peter Cecil	Plt. Off.	Pilot	32	Joined 32 Sqn., 18-10-40. Released from R.A.F., 1945, as a Flight Lieutenant.		British
HUMPHREYS Peter Harry	Plt. Off.	Pilot	152	Joined 152 Sqn., 29-9-40. Awarded D.F.C.(1-10-43). Remained in the R.A.F. until his death as a Squadron Leader.	✠ Killed since Battle (11-11-47)	British
¶ **HUNNARD** John William Arthur	Sqn. Ldr.	Pilot	266	In command of 266 Sqn., 1-7-40. Posted away, 6-7-40. Retired, 1955, as Group Captain.		British
HUNT Douglas Alfred Charles	Sgt.	Pilot	66	On 66 Sqn., 1-7-40. ✠ **1 Do 215 (shared), 31-8-40.** Commissioned, 11-11-41. Retired from R.A.F., 1-10-58, retaining rank of Wing Commander.		British
HUNT David Walter	Plt. Off.	Pilot	257	On 257 Sqn., 1-7-40. Severely wounded, 3-9-40. Released from R.A.F., 9-45, as Flight Lieutenant.		British
HUNT Henry Norman	Plt. Off.	Pilot	263-504	On 263 Sqn., 1-7-40. Posted to 504 Sqn., 11-7-40.	✠ Killed since Battle (13-5-41)	British
HUNTER Alastair Stuart	Fg. Off.	Pilot	604	On 604 Sqn., 1-7-40. Promoted Flt. Lt., 3-9-40.	✠ Killed since Battle (6-2-41)	British
HUNTER Douglas John	Sgt.	Aircrew	29	On 29 Sqn., 1-7-40. Commissioned, 24-6-41. Released from R.A.F., 1947, as Flight Lieutenant.	✠ Died since Battle (7-84)	British
HUNTER Philip Algernon	Sqn. Ldr.	Pilot	264	In command of 264 Sqn., 1-7-40. Awarded D.S.O.(14-6-40).	✠ **Killed in Action** (24-8-40)	British
HUNTER-TOD John Hunter	Fg. Off.	Aircrew	23	On 23 Sqn., 1-7-40. (Technical Officer who flew on a number of operational sorties). Appointed K.B.E.(1-1-71; O.B.E.[1957]), C.B.(14-6-69). Retired, 30-4-73, as an Air Marshal.		British
HURRY Charles Alexander Lyall	Sgt.	Pilot	43-46	On 43 Sqn., 1-7-40. Posted to 46 Sqn., 10-9-40. Wounded, 18-9-40. ✠ **1 Bf 109, 5-9-40; ✠ 1 Bf 109, 6-9-40; ✠ 1 Do 215 (shared), 15-9-40.** Commissioned, 7-3-42. Awarded A.F.C.(1-1-46). Released from R.A.F., 1-46, as Flight Lieutenant.		British
HURST Peter Richard Scott	Plt. Off.	Pilot	600	Joined 600 Sqn., 9-40.	✠ **Killed in Accident** (23-10-40)	British
HUTCHINSON Iain	Sgt.	Pilot	222	On 222 Sqn., 1-7-40. Commissioned, 5-8-41. ✠ **1 Bf 109, 6-9-40; ✠ 1 Bf 109, 7-9-40; ✠ 1 Bf 109, 14-9-40.** Wounded, 30-9-40. Retired from R.A.F., 1-12-57, as Squadron Leader.		British
HUTCHISON David Alexander	Sub-Lieut.	Pilot	74-804	Fleet Air Arm. Joined 74 Sqn., 6-7-40. Posted to 804, 20-7-40. Awarded D.S.C. (10-3-42).	✠ Killed since Battle (15-11-42)	British
HUTLEY Richard Ralph	Plt. Off.	Pilot	32-213	Joined 32 Sqn., c.25-9-40. Posted to 213 Sqn., 10-40.	✠ **Killed in Action** (29-10-40)	British
HUTTON Robert Scott	Sgt.	Pilot	85	Joined 85 Sqn., 16-9-40.	✠ Killed since Battle (12-12-40)	British
HYBLER Josef Emil ("Joe")	Plt. Off.	Pilot	310	Joined 310 Sqn., 15-10-40. Released from R.A.F., 8-45, as Flight Lieutenant.	✠ Died since Battle (9-1-84)	Czech
HYDE George Gordon	Fg. Off.	Pilot	1(Canadian)	On 1(Canadian) Sqn., 20-6-40, on arrival in U.K. Wounded, 31-8-40.	✠ Killed since Battle (17-5-41)	Canadian
HYDE Reginald Jack ("Lobber")	Sgt.	Pilot	66	On 66 Sqn., 1-7-40. Posted away, 18-7-40. Awarded A.F.C.(1-1-45). Transferred to Reserve in New Zealand, 12-45.	✠ Died since Battle (23-3-85)	New Zealander
IEVERS Norman Lancelot	Fg. Off.	Pilot	312	Promoted Flt. Lt., 3-9-40. Joined 312 (Czech) Sqn., 19-10-40. Released from R.A.F., 1944, as Squadron Leader.		Irish
IGGLESDEN Charles Patrick	Fg. Off.	Pilot	234	On 234 Sqn., 1-7-40. Removed from flying duties, 7-8-40. Left R.A.F., 27-9-41. Commissioned in Royal Navy, 2-43. Released from R.N., 30-3-46, as Lieutenant.		British
IMRAY Horace Stanley	Sgt.	Aircrew	600	On 600 Sqn., 1-7-40.		British
INGLE Alec	Plt. Off.	Pilot	605	On 605 Sqn., 1-7-40. Awarded D.F.C.(17-8-43), A.F.C.(1-1-43). ✠ **1 Bf 109, 12-10-40; ✠ 1 Bf 109, 26-10-40; ✠ 1 Bf 109, 10-40.** Taken prisoner by Germans, 9-43. Retired from R.A.F., 6-5-66, as Group Captain.		British
INGLE-FINCH Michael Roscoe	Plt. Off.	Pilot	151-607-56	Joined 151 Sqn., 18-9-40. Posted to 607 Sqn., 3-10-40. Posted to 56 Sqn., 13-10-40. Awarded D.F.C.✠ (25-7-44 and 23-1-45), A.F.C.(1-1-43). Released from R.A.F., 1946, as Wing Commander.		British
INNES Robert Alexander	Sgt.	Pilot	253	Joined 253 Sqn., early 8-40. Commissioned, 5-3-41. ✠ **1 Bf 110, 30-8-40; ✠ 1 Do 17, 15-9-40.** Retired from R.A.F., 31-8-61, as Squadron Leader.		British
INNESS Richard Frederick	Plt. Off.	Pilot	152	On 152 Sqn., 1-7-40. Promoted Fg. Off., 3-9-40. ✠ **1 Ju 88, 26-9-40; ✠ 1 Bf 109, 27-9-40.** Released from R.A.F., 1946, as Squadron Leader.		British
INNISS Aubrey Richard de Lisle	Plt. Off.	Pilot	236	On 236 Sqn., 1-7-40. Awarded D.F.C.(9-7-43). ✠ **1 He 111, 23-9-40.** Retired from R.A.F., 18-12-57, as Wing Commander.		British
IRELAND, S.	Sgt.	Pilot	610	On 610 Sqn., 1-7-40. Did not achieve operational status before death.	✠ **Killed in Accident** 12-12-40	British

Name	Rank	Role	Sqn.	Details	Fate	Nationality
IRVING Maurice Milne	Fg. Off.	Pilot	607	On 607 Sqn., 1-7-40. ✠ 1 Ju 88 (shared), 14-9-40.	Killed in Action (28-9-40)	British
ISAAC Lewis Reginald	Sgt.	Pilot	64	Joined 64 Sqn., c.30-7-40.	Killed in Action (5-8-40)	British
ISHERWOOD Donald William	L.A.C.	Aircrew	29	On 29 Sqn., 1-7-40. Promoted Sergeant, 7-40. Discharged from R.A.F., 21-11-41, on medical grounds (following wounds received in action).		British
IVESON Thomas Clifford	Sgt.	Pilot	616	Joined 616 Sqn., 11-9-40. Commissioned, 5-42. Awarded D.F.C.(16-3-45, with Bomber Command). Retired from R.A.F., 12-7-49, as Flight Lieutenant.		British
IVEY Reginald	Sgt.	Pilot	248-616	Joined 248 Sqn., 7-40. Posted to 616 Sqn., 6-10-40. Commissioned, 2-5-42. Awarded D.F.C., 19-5-44. Released from R.A.F., 1946, as Flight Lieutenant.		British
JACK Donald MacFarlane	Fg. Off.	Pilot	602	On 602 Sqn., 1-7-40. Promoted Fg. Off., 3-9-40. ✠ 1 Bf 110, 25-8-40; ✠ 1 Bf 109, 26-8-40. Released from R.A.F., 9-45, as Wing Commander.		British
JACKSON Arthur	A.C.2	Aircrew	29	Joined 29 Sqn., 10-8-40. Promoted Sergeant, 9-40.	Killed in Action (13-10-40)	British
JACKSON Peter Frederic	Sgt.	Pilot	604	On 604 Sqn., 1-7-40. Awarded D.F.M.(14-1-41). Commissioned, 11-4-41.	Killed since Battle (29-5-41)	British
JACOBS Henry	Plt. Off.	Aircrew	219-600	Joined 219 Sqn., 9-40. Posted to 600 Sqn., 10-40. Awarded D.F.C.✸ (9-10-42 and 5-11-43), A.F.C.(3-4-45). Retired from R.A.F., 29-12-58, as Squadron Leader.	Died since Battle (9-10-78)	British
JACOBSON Norman	A.C.2	Aircrew	29	Joined 29 Sqn., 25-8-40.	Killed in Action (25-8-40)	British
JAMES Richard Harwood	Sgt.	Aircrew	29	Joined 29 Sqn., 20-10-40. Awarded D.F.M.(2-9-41). Commissioned, 10-2-42. Released from R.A.F., 1945, as Flight Lieutenant.		British
JAMES Robert Stuart Seymour	Sgt.	Aircrew	248	On 248 Sqn., 1-7-40. Flew on reconnaissance sorties over enemy-held coasts during Battle of Britain.	Killed since Battle (29-5-42)	British
JAMESON Patrick Geraint	Fg. Off.	Pilot	266	Promoted Flt. Lt., 3-9-40. Posted to 266 Sqn., 17-9-40, to command. Awarded D.S.O.(10-3-43), D.F.C.✸ (19-7-40 and 7-10-41). Retired from R.A.F., 6-8-60, retaining the rank of Air Commodore.		New Zealander
JANICKI Zbigniew	Plt. Off.	Pilot	32	Joined 32 Sqn., 12-10-40.	Killed since Battle (13-6-44)	Polish
JANKIEWICZ Jerzy	Plt. Off.	Pilot	601-303	Joined 601 Sqn., 18-8-40. Posted to 303 (Polish) Sqn., 22-10-40. ✠ 1 Bf 109, 25-9-40. Awarded D.F.C., 30-10-41.	Killed since Battle (25-5-42)	Polish
JANOUCH Svatopluk	Plt. Off.	Pilot	310	Joined 310 (Czech) Sqn., 10-7-40. ✠ 1 Bf 110, 7-9-40; ✠ 1 Do 215, (shared), 18-9-40. Released from R.A.F. as a Squadron Leader after the War.		Czech
JANUSZEWICZ Wojciech	Fg. Off.	Pilot	303	Joined 303 (Polish) Sqn., 2-9-40.	Killed in Action (5-10-40)	Polish
JARRETT Raymond Walter Emlyn	Sgt.	Pilot	245-501	On 245 Sqn., 1-7-40. Posted to 501 Sqn., 9-40. Commissioned, 6-4-45. Retired from R.A.F., 17-4-46, as Flying Officer.	Died since Battle (10-8-84)	British
JASKÉ Josef Antonin	Plt. Off.	Pilot	312	Joined 312 (Czech) Sqn., 5-9-40. Remained in R.A.F. after the War, and retired, 31-5-68, as a Flight Lieutenant.		Czech
JASTRZEBSKI Franciszek	Flt. Lt.	Pilot	302	Joined 302 (Polish) Sqn., 23-7-40. ✠ 1 Do 17 (shared), 15-9-40.	Killed in Action (25-10-40)	Polish
JAVAUX Lucien Leon Gustav	Sgt.	Aircrew	235	Joined 235 Sqn., 5-8-40. Commissioned as Plt. Off., 18-8-40.	Killed since Battle (18-10-43)	Belgian
JAY Dudley Trevor	Plt. Off.	Pilot	87	On 87 Sqn., 1-7-40. ✠ 1 He 111, 10-7-40; ✠ 1 Bf 110, 11-7-40; ✠ 1 Ju 88 (shared), 13-8-40. ✠ 2 Ju 87s and 1 Bf 109, 15-8-40.	Killed in Action (24-10-40)	British
JEBB Michael	Fg. Off.	Pilot	504	Joined 504 Sqn., 7-40. (Died of injuries sustained on 15-9-40).	Died of Wounds (19-9-40)	British
JEFF Robert Voase	Fg. Off.	Pilot	87	On 87 Sqn., 1-7-40. Had been awarded D.F.C.✸ (8-3-40 and 4-6-40).	Killed in Action (11-8-40)	British
JEFFCOAT Harry Jeffrey	Plt. Off.	Aircrew	236	On 236 Sqn., 1-7-40. Posted away, 1-8-40.	Killed since Battle (13-12-41)	British
JEFFERIES Jerrard	Fg. Off.	Pilot	85-310	On 85 Sqn., 1-7-40. Posted to 310 (Czech) Sqn., 12-7-40. Awarded D.F.C. (1-10-40). ✠ 1 Do 17, 31-8-40; ✠ 1 Bf 110, 3-9-40; ✠ 1 Bf 109 (solo) and 3 Do 17s (shared); ✠ 1 Do 17, 18-9-40. Changed name to **LATIMER** by deed poll.	Killed since Battle (5-4-43)	British
JEFFERSON George	Sgt.	Pilot	43	Joined 43 Sqn., 8-40. Commissioned, 12-8-42. Released from the R.A.F., 1946, as a Flight Lieutenant.		British
JEFFERSON Stanley Francis	Plt. Off.	Aircrew	248	Joined 248 Sqn., 30-9-40. Released from R.A.F., 1945, as Flight Lieutenant.		British
JEFFERY-CRIDGE Hugh Ronald	Sgt.	Aircrew	236	Joined 236 Sqn., 26-9-40. Commissioned, 26-11-43. Released from the R.A.F., 1946, as a Flight Lieutenant.		British
JEFFERYS George Willian	Sgt.	Pilot	43-46	Joined 43 Sqn., 8-40. Posted to 46 Sqn., 15-9-40. ✠ 1 Bf 109, 2-9-40; ✠ 1 Bf 110, 4-9-40; ✠ 1 Bf 109, 6-9-40; ✠ 1 Do 17 (shared), 9-9-40.	Killed in Action (18-9-40)	British
JEFFREY Alistair John Oswald	Fg. Off.	Pilot	64	On 64 Sqn., 1-7-40. Awarded D.F.C.(13-8-40). ✠ 1 Bf 110, 7-7-40; ✠ 1 He 115, 19-7-40.	Killed in Action (25-7-40)	British
JEFFRIES Charles Gordon St. David	Plt. Off.	Pilot	3-232	On 3 Sqn., 1-7-40. Joined 232 Sqn., 17-7-40. ✠ 1 He 111 (shared), 23-7-40. Awarded D.F.C.✸✸ (26-9-41, 25-1-44 and 22-3-55). Retired from R.A.F., 1-10-67, as Wing Commander.	Died since Battle (1-85)	British
JEKA Jozef	Sgt.	Pilot	238	Joined 238 Sqn., 2-9-40. Awarded D.F.M.(19-2-42). Commissioned, 1-11-41. ✠ 1 Bf 110, 15-9-40; ✠ 2 He 111s, 26-9-40; ✠ 1 Bf 110 (shared), 27-9-40; ✠ 1 Ju 88, 7-10-40.		Polish
JENKINS David Nicholas Owen ("Jenks")	Plt. Off.	Pilot	253	On 253 Sqn., 1-7-40.	Killed in Action (30-8-40)	British
JENNINGS Bernard James	Sgt.	Pilot	19	On 19 Sqn., 1-7-40. Awarded D.F.M.(4-4-41). Commissioned, 30-12-41. ✠ 1 Bf 110, 11-9-40; ✠ 1 Bf 109, 29-9-40. Retired from R.A.F., 21-3-62, as a Wing Commander.		British
JERAM Dennis Mayvore	Sub-Lieut.	Pilot	213	Fleet Air Arm. Joined 213 Sqn., 5-7-40. ✠ 1 Ju 88, 11-8-40; ✠ 1 Bf 110, 12-8-40; ✠ 1 Bf 110, 15-8-40; ✠ 1 Do 17, 15-9-40. Retired from Royal Navy in 1954 as Lieutenant-Commander.	Died since Battle (24-3-77)	British
JERECZEK Edmund Wincenty	Plt. Off.	Pilot	43-229	Joined 43 Sqn., 9-40. Posted to 229 Sqn., 10-40. Awarded A.F.C.(26-5-45). Released from Polish Air Force, 12-46.	Died since Battle (26-8-84)	Polish
JESSOP Ernest Robert	Sgt.	Pilot	257-43-253	Joined 257 Sqn., 1-9-40. Posted to 43 Sqn., 10-9-40; Posted to 253 Sqn., 28-9-40.	Killed since Battle (15-11-41)	British
JICHA Vaclav	Plt. Off.	Pilot	1	Joined 1 Sqn., 9-40. Awarded D.F.C. and A.F.C.	Killed since Battle (1-2-45)	Czech
JIROUDEK Miroslav	F/Sgt.	Pilot	310	Joined 310 (Czech) Sqn., 8-40. ✠ 1 Do 215 (shared), 18-9-40. Survived the War.		Czech
JOHNS George Binmore ("Johnnie")	Sgt.	Pilot	229	On 229 Sqn., 1-7-40. Commissioned, 26-3-41. Awarded D.S.O.(29-12-44), D.F.C.(7-4-42), A.F.C.(2-1-46). Retired from R.A.F., 24-3-72, as Group Captain.		British
JOHNSON Alfred Ernest	Sgt.	Aircrew	23	On 23 Sqn., 1-7-40. Commissioned, 29-7-42. Released from R.A.F., 1945, as Fg. Off.	Died since Battle (23-10-59)	British
JOHNSON Allan Everitt	Plt. Off.	Pilot	46	On 46 Sqn., 1-7-40. ✠ 1 Bf 109, 5-9-40; ✠ 1 Ju 88, 15-9-40; ✠ 1 Bf 110, 27-9-40.	Died since Battle (4-7-43)	British
JOHNSON Charles Alexander	Sgt.	Aircrew	25	Joined 25 Sqn., 26-9-40. Commissioned, 15-11-43.	Died since Battle (5-5-45 ?)	British
JOHNSON Charles Edward	Plt. Off.	Aircrew	264	Defiant gunner. Joined 264 Sqn., mid-8-40.	Killed in Action (28-8-40)	British
JOHNSON Gerald Bruce	Sgt.	Aircrew	23	Joined 23 Sqn., 6-7-40.	Killed since Battle (28-5-41)	New Zealander
JOHNSON James Edgar ("Johnnie")	Plt. Off.	Pilot	616	Joined 616 Sqn., 5-9-40. Appointed C.B.(1-1-65), C.B.E.(1-1-60), D.S.O.✸✸ (4-6-43, 24-9-43 and 7-7-44), D.F.C.✸ (30-9-41 and 26-6-42). Retired from R.A.F., 15-3-66, as an Air Vice-Marshal.		British
JOHNSON Joseph Inkerman	Sgt.	Pilot	222	On 222 Sqn., 1-7-40.	Killed in Action (30-8-40)	British
JOHNSON Reginald Bernard	Sgt.	Pilot	222	On 222 Sqn., 1-7-40. Commissioned, 29-6-42. Released from R.A.F., 1945, as a Flight Lieutenant.		British
JOHNSON Richard Kenneth Howard	Sgt.	Pilot	235	Joined 235 Sqn., 10-40. Commissioned, 12-7-41. Awarded D.F.C.(7-7-44). Was Acting Wing Commander at date of death.	Killed since Battle (31-1-45)	British

Name	Rank	Duty	Sqn.	Details	Fate	Nationality
JOHNSON Ronald Arthur	Sgt.	Pilot	43	Joined 43 Sqn., 12-40. Commissioned, 12-1-42. Awarded D.F.C.(25-7-44). Released from R.A.F., 1946, as Flight Lieutenant.		British
JOHNSON Sydney Frederick Farquhar	Plt. Off.	Pilot	600	On 600 Sqn., 1-7-40.	✠ Killed since Battle (26-2-41)	British
JOHNSON William John	Sgt.	Pilot	85-145	Joined 85 Sqn., early 10-40. Posted to 145 Sqn., 18-10-40. Commissioned, 7-1-42. Awarded D.F.C.✠ (22-1-43 and 1-12-44). Retired from R.A.F., 6-2-59, as Squadron Leader.		British
JOHNSTON James Thomas	Plt. Off.	Pilot	151	Joined 151 Sqn., 13-7-40.	✠ **Killed in Action** (15-8-40)	Canadian
JOHNSTONE Alexander Vallance Riddell ("Sandy")	Flt. Lt.	Pilot	602	On 602 Sqn., 1-7-40. Commanded 602 Sqn. from 12-7-40. Promoted Sqn. Ldr., 1-9-40. Appointed C.B.(1966); awarded D.F.C.(1-10-40).✠ **1 Ju 88 (shared), 19-8-40;** ✠ **1 Bf 109 and 1 Bf 110, 25-8-40;** ✠ **1 Bf 109, 1 Ju 88 and 1 He 111, 7-9-40;** ✠ **1 Do 17 (shared), 9-9-40;** ✠ **1 Ju 88, 30-9-40.** Retired from R.A.F., 14-12-68, as Air Vice-Marshal.		British
JOLL Ian Kenneth Sefton	Plt. Off.	Pilot	604	On 604 Sqn., 1-7-40. Awarded D.F.C.(29-10-43). Released from R.A.F., 1946, as Squadron Leader.		British
JONES Cyril Arthur Trevor ("Dizzy")	Plt. Off.	Pilot	611-616	On 611 Sqn., 1-7-40. Posted to 616 Sqn., 4-9-40. Awarded D.F.C.(14-4-44). Released from R.A.F., 1946, as Wing Commander.		British
JONES Denys Allan Evan	Fg. Off.	Pilot	3-501	On 3 Sqn., 1-7-40. Posted to 501 Sqn., 26-9-40. ✠ **1 He 111 (shared), 25-7-40.**		British
JONES Edwin	Sgt.	Aircrew	29	On 29 Sqn., 1-7-40.	✠ Killed since Battle (19-12-40)	British
JONES Herbert Daniel Baynton	Sgt.	Pilot	504-85	On 504 Sqn., 1-7-40. Posted to 85 Sqn., 16-10-40. ✠ **1 Bf 110, 27-9-40;** ✠ **2 He 111s, 30-9-40.**	✠ Killed since Battle (6-7-41)	British
JONES John Ferdinand Read	Sgt.	Aircrew	25	On 25 Sqn. during Battle of Britain. Commissioned, 25-7-42. Released from R.A.F., 1946, as a Flight Lieutenant.		British
JONES John Sinclair Bucknall	Plt. Off.	Pilot	152	On 152 Sqn., 1-7-40.	✠ **Killed in Action** (11-8-40)	British
JONES Joseph Trevor	Plt. Off.	Pilot	264	Joined 264 Sqn., early 7-40.	✠ **Killed in Action** (24-8-40)	British
JONES Kenneth Harold	Sgt.	Pilot	85-605	Joined 85 Sqn., 14-9-40. Posted to 605 Sqn., 19-10-40. (Shot down, 2-2-41, and taken prisoner; released 9-5-45).		British
JONES Richard Leoline	Plt. Off.	Pilot	64-19	Joined 64 Sqn., late 7-40. Posted to 19 Sqn., 10-40. Released from R.A.F., 1946, as Flight Lieutenant.		British
JONES Robert Eric	Plt. Off.	Pilot	605	On 605 Sqn., 1-7-40. Slightly wounded, 15-9-40. ✠ **1 He 111, 15-8-40;** ✠ **1 He 111 (shared), 11-9-40.** Released from R.A.F., 1945, as Flight Lieutenant.		British
JONES William Ross	Sgt.	Pilot	266-602	On 266 Sqn., 1-7-40. Commissioned, 2-9-40. Posted to 602 Sqn., 13-9-40. Awarded A.F.C.(1-1-46). ✠ **1 He 115 (shared), 15-8-40.** Retired from R.A.F., 28-1-59, retaining rank of Squadron Leader.		British
JOTTARD Alexis Rene Isidore Ghislain	Plt. Off.	Pilot	145	Joined 145 Sqn., 17-8-40.	✠ **Killed in Action** (27-10-40)	Belgian
JOUBERT Charles Cecil Oliver ("Scruffy")	Plt. Off.	Pilot	56	Joined 56 Sqn., 15-7-40. Slightly wounded, 13-8-40. Released from R.A.F., 1946, as a Flight Lieutenant.		British
JOWITT Leonard	Sgt.	Pilot	85	On 85 Sqn., 1-7-40.	✠ **Killed in Action** (12-7-40)	British
JULEFF John Rushworth	Plt. Off.	Aircrew	600	Joined 600 Sqn., 11-7-40. Released from R.A.F., 1946, as Squadron Leader.	✠ Died since Battle (1977)	British
KAHN Arthur Harold Evans	Plt. Off.	Aircrew	248	Joined 248 Sqn., 29-9-40. Flew on reconnaissance sorties over enemy-held coasts.	✠ Killed since Battle (15-6-44)	British
KANE Terence Michael	Fg. Off.	Pilot	234	Joined 234 Sqn., **14-9-40.** ✠ **1 Ju 88 (shared), 22-9-40;** ✠ **1 Bf 109, 23-9-40.** Shot down, 23-9-40, and taken prisoner by Germans. Retired from the R.A.F., 29-5-74, as a Wing Commander.		British
KANIA Josef	F/Sgt.	Pilot	303	Joined 303 (Polish) Sqn., 21-8-40. Released from Polish Air Force, 1946, as Warrant Officer.		Polish
KARASEK Laurence Robert	Sgt.	Aircrew	23	Joined 23 Sqn., 30-7-40.	✠ **Killed in Action** (25-9-40)	British
KARUBIN Stanislaw	Sgt.	Pilot	303	Joined 303 (Polish) Sqn., 2-8-40, on formation. Awarded D.F.M. (30-10-41). ✠ **1 Bf 109, 31-8-40;** ✠ **2 Bf 109s, 5-9-40;** ✠ **1 He 111, 6-9-40;** ✠ **1 Bf 109, 30-9-40;** ✠ **1 Bf 109, 5-10-40.**	✠ Killed since Battle (12-8-41)	Polish
KARWOWSKI Wlodzimierz Eugeniusz	Plt. Off.	Pilot	302	Joined 302 (Polish) Sqn., 8-40. ✠ **1 Ju 88, 18-9-40.** Released from Polish Air Force, 23-12-47, as Squadron Leader.	✠ Died since Battle (29-5-78)	Polish
KAUCKY Jan	Sgt.	Pilot	310	Joined 310 (Czech) Sqn., late 8-40. ✠ **2 Do 17s (shared), 15-9-40.** Released from R.A.F., 1946, as Flight Lieutenant.	✠ Died since Battle (c.1973)	Czech
KAWALECKI Tadeusz Wilhelm	Plt. Off.	Pilot	151	Joined 151 Sqn., 8-8-40. Released from the Polish Air Force, 5-46, as a Squadron Leader.		Polish
KAY Archibald	Sgt.	Aircrew	248	Joined 248 Sqn., 7-40. Flew on reconnaissance sorties over Norwegian coast during Battle of Britain.	✠ **Killed in Action** (13-9-40)	British
KAY Desmond Hayward Sidley	Plt. Off.	Pilot	264	On 264 Sqn., 1-7-40. Awarded D.F.C.✠ (14-6-40 and 13-10-44).	✠ Killed since Battle (19-10-44)	British
KAY Jack Kininmonth	Plt. Off.	Pilot	111-257	Joined 111 Sqn., 12-9-40. Posted to 257 Sqn., 28-9-40. Released from R.A.F., 1946, as Flight Lieutenant.	✠ Died since Battle (18-9-81)	British
KAYLL Joseph Robert	Flt. Lt.	Pilot	615	In command of 615 Sqn. (as Acting Sqn. Ldr.), 1-7-40. Promoted Sqn. Ldr., 1-9-40. Awarded D.S.O.(31-5-40), O.B.E.(26-6-46), D.F.C.(31-5-40). ✠ **1 He 59, 27-7-40;** ✠ **1 He 111, 16-8-40;** ✠ **1 Do 17, 20-8-40;** ✠ **1 He 111 (shared), 24-8-40.** Released from R.A.F., 1945, as Wing Commander.		British
KEARD John Alexander	Plt. Off.	Pilot	235	Joined 235 Sqn., 27-9-40.	✠ Killed since Battle (4-5-44)	British
KEARSEY Albert Wallace	Sgt.	Pilot	152	Joined 152 Sqn., 8-40. Commissioned, 22-1-41. ✠ **1 Bf 110, 30-9-40.** Released from R.A.F., 1946, as Flight Lieutenant.		British
KEARSEY Philip James	Plt. Off.	Pilot	607-213	Joined 607 Sqn., 9-10-40. Posted to 213 Sqn., 26-10-40.	✠ Killed since Battle (26-2-41)	British
KEAST Francis John	Sgt.	Aircrew	600	On 600 Sqn., 1-7-40.	✠ **Killed in Action** (8-8-40)	British
KEATINGS John	Sgt.	Aircrew	219	On 219 Sqn., 1-7-40. Released from R.A.F., 1945, as Warrant Officer.		British
KEE Ernest Henry Clarke	Sgt.	Pilot	253	On 253 Sqn., 1-7-40. Commissioned, 10-6-41. Awarded D.F.C. (21-12-45).	✠ Killed since Battle (20-4-44)	British
KEEL George Ernest	Sgt.	Aircrew	235	Joined 235 Sqn., 13-8-40.	✠ **Killed in Action** (9-10-40)	British
KEELER Rob Roy Gibbons	Sgt.	Aircrew	236	Joined 236 Sqn., 9-40. Commissioned, 14-5-42. Released from R.A.F., 1946, as Flight Lieutenant.		British
KEIGHLEY Geoffrey	Plt. Off.	Pilot	610	On 610 Sqn., 1-7-40. Slightly wounded, 20-7-40. Promoted Fg. Off., 17-9-40. Made O.B.E.(1-1-45). Released from R.A.F., 1946, as Wing Commander.		British
KELLETT Michael	Plt. Off.	Pilot	111	Joined 111 Sqn., 1-10-40. Awarded D.F.C.(21-11-44). Retired from R.A.F., 19-6-56, retaining the rank of Wing Commander.	✠ Died since Battle (28-8-75)	British
KELLETT Ronald Gustave	Sqn. Ldr.	Pilot	249-303	On 249 Sqn., 1-7-40. Posted to 303 (Polish) Sqn., on formation, to command. Awarded D.S.O.(25-10-40); D.F.C.(1-10-40). ✠ **1 Bf 109, 21-8-40;** ✠ **1 Bf 109, 5-9-40;** ✠ **1 Bf 110, 15-9-40;** ✠ **1 Bf 109, 26-9-40.** Released from R.A.F., 1945, as a Wing Commander.		British
KELLITT William Henry	Sgt.	Aircrew	236	Joined 236 Sqn., 3-9-40. Commissioned, 1-5-42. Released from R.A.F., 1945 as Flight Lieutenant.	✠ Died since Battle (1-84)	British
KELLOW Raymond Alan ("Granfer")	Fg. Off.	Pilot	213	On 213 Sqn., 1-7-40. Promoted Flt. Lt., 1-10-40. ✠ **1 Bf 110, 11-9-40;** ✠ **1 Bf 110, 28-9-40;** ✠ **1 Bf 110, 30-9-40.**		British
KELLS Lionel George Hosford	Plt. Off.	Pilot	29	On 29 Sqn., 1-7-40. Promoted Fg. Off., 22-8-40.	✠ Killed since Battle (21-2-41)	British
KELLY Dillon Piers Denis Gerald	Flt. Lt.	Pilot	74	Joined 74 Sqn., 15-7-40. Promoted Sqn. Ldr., 1-9-40. Awarded D.F.C.(21-5-43). ✠ **1 Bf 109, 28-7-40.** Posted away, 8-9-40. Retired from R.A.F., 7-10-61, as Group Captain.	✠ Died since Battle (11-2-87)	British

Name	Rank	Role	Sqn.	Notes	Fate	Nationality
KELSEY Eric Norman	Sgt.	Pilot	611	Joined 611 Sqn., 1-7-40. Posted away, late 7-40.	✠ Killed since Battle (19-1-41)	British
KEMP John Leslie	Plt. Off.	Pilot	54	On 54 Sqn., 1-7-40. Promoted Fg. Off., 17-7-40. Posted away, 10-40. Released from R.A.F., 1946, as Flight Lieutenant.		British
KEMP John Richard	Plt. Off.	Pilot	141	On 141 Sqn., 1-7-40.	✠ Killed in Action (19-7-40)	New Zealander
KEMP Nigel Leslie Digby	Plt. Off.	Pilot	85-242	Joined 85 Sqn., 29-9-40. Posted to 242 Sqn., 18-10-40. Awarded D.F.C. (17-10-41). Retired from R.A.F., 31-8-66, as Flight Lieutenant.		British
KENDALL John Bedford	Plt. Off.	Pilot	66	Joined 66 Sqn., 29-9-40. Slightly wounded, 2-10-40. ✠ 1 Bf 109, 2-10-40.	✠ Killed since Battle (25-5-42)	British
KENNARD Hugh Charles	Plt. Off.	Pilot	66	On 66 Sqn., 1-7-40. Promoted Fg. Off., 25-7-40. ✠ 1 Bf 110 (shared), 20-8-40. Awarded D.F.C.(30-6-42). Released from R.A.F., 6-46, as a Wing Commander.		British
KENNARD-DAVIS Peter Frank	Plt. Off.	Pilot	64	Joined 64 Sqn., 3-8-40. (Died of wounds sustained in action on 8-8-40).	✠ Died of Wounds (10-8-40)	British
KENNEDY John Connelly	Fg. Off.	Pilot	238	On 238 Sqn., 1-7-40. ✠ 1 Do 17 (shared), 13-7-40.	✠ Killed in Action (13-7-40)	Australian
KENNEDY Ronald William	Sgt.	Aircrew	604	On 604 Sqn., 1-7-40. Commissioned, 25-10-43.	✠ Killed since Battle (26-3-44)	British
KENNER Peter Lewis	Plt. Off.	Pilot	264	Joined 264 Sqn., mid-8-40.	✠ Killed in Action (28-8-40)	British
KENNETT Peter	Plt. Off.	Pilot	3-605	Joined 3 Sqn., early 9-40. Posted to 605 Sqn., 30-9-40.	✠ Killed since Battle (11-4-41)	British
KENSALL George	Sgt.	Aircrew	25	Joined 25 Sqn., early 10-40.	✠ Killed since Battle (20-12-43)	British
KENT John Alexander	Flt. Lt.	Pilot	303-92	Joined 303 (Polish) Sqn., 2-8-40, on formation. Awarded D.F.C.✠ (25-10-40 and 21-10-41), A.F.C.(2-1-39). Posted to 92 Sqn., 26-10-40, to command.✠ 1 Bf 109, 14-9-40; ✠ 1 Bf 109, 23-9-40; ✠ 1 Ju 88, 27-9-40; ✠ 1 Bf 109, 1-10-40. Retired from R.A.F., 1-12-56, as a Group Captain.	✠ Died since Battle (7-10-85)	Canadian
KENT Raymond Dugdale	Plt. Off.	Aircrew	235	Joined 235 Sqn., 11-7-40. Released for the R.A.F., 1945, as a Flight Lieutenant.		British
KEOUGH Vernon Charles ("Shorty")	Plt. Off.	Pilot	609	Joined 609 Sqn., 8-8-40. ✠ 1 Do 215 (shared), 15-9-40. Posted away, 19-9-40.	✠ Killed since Battle (15-2-41)	American
KEPRT Josef	Sgt.	Pilot	312	Joined 312 (Czech) Sqn., 5-9-45. Commissioned, 25-5-41. Awarded D.F.C.	✠ Died since Battle (c. 1974)	Czech
KER-RAMSAY Robert Gerald	Flt. Lt.	Pilot	25-F.I.U.	On 25 Sqn., 1-7-40. Posted to F.I.U., 13-7-40. Crashed in Blenheim off French coast, 13-9-40, and taken prisoner by the Germans. Awarded M.B.E. Retired from R.A.F., 1948, as a Squadron Leader.		British
KERSHAW Anthony	Plt. Off.	Pilot	1	Joined 1 Sqn., 20-9-40.	✠ Killed since Battle (1-1-41)	British
KERWIN Basil Virgil	Plt. Off.	Pilot	1(Canadian)	Joined 1(Canadian) Sqn., 8-40. ✠ 1 Do 17, 31-8-40; ✠ 1 Bf 110 and 1 Do 17, 1-9-40. Wounded, 1-9-40. Awarded D.F.C.(11-10-55). Retired from R.A.F., 1-1-58, as Squadron Leader.		Canadian
KESTIN Ian Herbert	Sub-Lieut.	Pilot	145	Fleet Air Arm. Joined 145 Sqn., 1-7-40.	✠ Killed in Action (1-8-40)	British
KESTLER Oldrich	Sgt.	Pilot	111	Joined 111 Sqn., 19-10-40.	✠ Killed since Battle (7-4-41)	Czech
KEYMER Michael	Sgt.	Pilot	65	Joined 65 Sqn., 7-8-40. ✠ 1 Bf 109 (shared), 14-8-40.	✠ Killed in Action (22-8-40)	British
KEYNES John Douglas	Sgt.	Pilot	236	Joined 236 Sqn., 27-9-40.	✠ Killed since Battle (4-6-43)	British
KIDSON Rudal	Plt. Off.	Pilot	141	On 141 Sqn., 1-7-41.	✠ Killed in Action (19-7-40)	New Zealander
KILLICK Peter	Sgt.	Pilot	245	Joined 245 Sqn., 17-7-40. Severely injured, 28-7-40. Retired from R.A.F., 27-9-70, as a Squadron Leader.	✠ Died since Battle (c.1982)	British
KILLINGBACK Frederick William George	Sgt.	Pilot	249	On 249 Sqn., 1-7-40. Wounded, 7-9-40. Commissioned, 21-8-41. Released from the R.A.F., 1948, as a Flight Lieutenant.		British
KILMARTIN John Ignatius ("Iggie")	Fg. Off.	Pilot	43	After rest period, rejoined No. 43 Sqn., 4-9-40. Awarded O.B.E. (1-1-45), D.F.C. (8-10-40). ✠ 1 Bf 110, 6-9-40; ✠ 1 Bf 109, 7-9-40. Retired from R.A.F., 8-7-58, as a Wing Commander.		Irish
KILNER Joseph Richard	Sgt.	Pilot	65	On 65 Sqn., 1-7-40. ✠ 1 He 111 (shared), 5-7-40; ✠ 2 Bf 109s, 16-8-40; ✠ 2 Bf 109s, 20-8-40. Awarded D.F.C., 5-9-44. Released from R.A.F., 1946, as a Squadron Leader.	✠ Died since Battle (11-5-86)	British
KINDER Douglas Steele	Plt. Off.	Pilot	615-73	Joined 615 Sqn., 14-9-40. Posted to 73 Sqn., 15-9-40. Severely wounded, 23-9-40. Awarded D.F.C., 7-12-43. Released from R.A.F., 1947, as a Flight Lieutenant.		British
KINDER Maurice Craig	Plt. Off.	Pilot	85-607-92	Promoted Fg. Off., 3-9-40. Joined 85 Sqn., 14-9-40. Posted to 607 Sqn., 29-9-40. Posted to 92 Sqn., 13-10-40. Awarded A.F.C.(1-1-44). Transferred to the Reserve in New Zealand, 18-10-46.		New Zealander
KINDERSLEY Anthony Thomas James	Lieut.	Pilot	808	Fleet Air Arm. On 808 Sqn., 1-7-40.	✠ Killed since Battle (25-7-41)	British
KING Eric Bruce	Sqn. Ldr.	Pilot	253-249-151	Posted supernumerary to 253 Sqn., 17-7-40. Posted supernumerary to 249 Sqn., 5-8-40. Posted to 151 Sqn., 21-8-40, to command.	✠ Killed in Action (30-8-40)	British
KING Frederick Harry	Plt. Off.	Aircrew	264	Defiant gunner. On 264 Sqn., 1-7-40. Had been awarded D.F.M.(14-6-40)	✠ Killed in Action (24-8-40)	British
KING Leonard Frank Douglas	Plt. Off.	Pilot	64	On 64 Sqn., 1-7-40. (Was a Squadron Leader at time of death.)	✠ Killed since Battle (19-3-45)	British
KING Martyn Aurel	Plt. Off.	Pilot	249	On 249 Sqn., 1-7-40.	✠ Killed in Action (16-8-40)	British
KING Peter James Christopher	Plt. Off.	Pilot	66	On 66 Sqn., 1-7-40. ✠ 1 Bf 109, 4-9-40.	✠ Killed in Action (5-9-40)	British
KING William Laurence	Plt. Off.	Pilot	236	On 236 Sqn., 1-7-40.	✠ Killed since Battle (22-1-43)	British
KINGABY Donald Ernest	Sgt.	Pilot	266-92	On 266 Sqn., 1-7-40. Posted to 92 Sqn., 25-9-40. Commissioned, 15-11-41. Awarded D.S.O.(9-3-43), A.F.C.(5-6-52), D.F.M.✠✠ (6-12-40, 29-7-41 and 11-11-41). ✠ 1 Bf 109, 12-10-40; ✠ 1 Bf 109, 15-10-40; ✠ 1 Bf 109 (shared), 20-10-40; ✠ 1 Do 17, 24-10-40. Retired from the R.A.F., 29-9-58, as a Squadron Leader.		British
KINGCOME Charles Brian Fabris	Fg. Off.	Pilot	92	On 92 Sqn., 1-7-40. Awarded D.S.O.(15-12-42), D.F.C.(15-10-40).✠ 1 Ju 88 (shared), 10-7-40; ✠ 1 Ju 88 (shared), 24-7-40; ✠ 1 He 111, 11-9-40; ✠ 1 Ju 88 (shared), 18-9-40; ✠ 1 Bf 109, 23-9-40; ✠ 1 Ju 88, 27-9-40; ✠ 1 Bf 109, 11-10-40; ✠ 1 Bf 109, 12-10-40; ✠ 1 Bf 109, 13-10-40. Invalided from R.A.F., 26-1-54, retaining rank of Group Captain.		British
KINGS Robert Austin	Plt. Off.	Pilot	238	Joined 238 Sqn., 27-8-40. Injured, 30-9-40. Retired from the R.A.F., 27-10-64, retaining rank of Squadron Leader.		British
KIRK Thomas Brian	Sgt.	Pilot	74	Joined 74 Sqn., 26-8-40. ✠ 1 Bf 110, 11-9-40. (Died of wounds sustained in action on 20-10-40).	✠ Died of wounds (22-7-41)	British
KIRKPATRICK James Charles	Plt. Off.	Pilot	235	Joined 235 Sqn., 5-8-40.	✠ Killed in Action (9-10-40)	Belgian
KIRKWOOD Mark Tyzack	Fg. Off.	Pilot	610	Promoted Flt. Lt., 3-9-40. Joined 610 Sqn., 22-9-40.	✠ Killed since Battle (8-11-40)	British
KIRTON David Ian	Sgt.	Pilot	65	Joined 65 Sqn., 7-40.	✠ Killed in Action (8-8-40)	British
KITA Szymon	Sgt.	Pilot	85-253	Joined 85 Sqn., 2-9-40. Posted to 253 Sqn., 30-9-40. Released from R.A.F., 3-46, as a Flight Sergeant.		Polish
KITSON Thomas Roy	Plt. Off.	Pilot	245	Rejoined 245 Sqn., 18-7-45 (after sick leave).	✠ Killed since Battle (10-3-41)	British
KLECZKOWSKI Stefan	Plt. Off.	Pilot	302	Joined 302 (Polish) Sqn., 23-9-40. Released from R.A.F., 5-6-46, as a Flight Lieutenant.		Polish
KLEIN Zygmunt ("Klug")	Sgt.	Pilot	234-152	Joined 234 Sqn., 6-8-40. Posted to 152 Sqn., 5-10-40. ✠ 1 Bf 109, 7-8-40.	✠ Killed since Battle (28-11-40)	Polish

Name	Rank	Role	Sqn.	Notes	Status	Nationality
KLOZINSKI Wojciech	Sgt.	Pilot	54	On 54 Sqn., 1-7-40. ✠ 1 Bf 109, 12-8-40. Severely wounded, 15-8-40. Moved to Canada, 8-45, and changed his name to **V.K. STEWART.**		Polish
KNIGHT Roland Anthony Lee	Fg. Off.	Pilot	23	On 23 Sqn., 1-7-40. Promoted to Flt. Lt., 3-9-40. Awarded D.F.C.(5-8-41)	♱ Killed since Battle (27-9-41)	British
KNOCKER William Rodney Alexander ("Roddy")	Plt. Off.	Pilot	264	On 264 Sqn., 1-7-40. Promoted to Fg. Off., 26-9-40. ✠ 1 Ju 88, 24-8-40. Released from R.A.F., 1946, as Wing Commander.		British
KOMAROFF Lennert Axel	Sgt.	Aircrew	141	Defiant gunner. On 141 Sqn., 1-7-40. Commissioned, 11-3-42.	♱ Killed since Battle (19-9-44)	British
KOMINEK Josef	F/Sgt.	Pilot	310	Joined 310 (Czech) Sqn., 10-7-40, on formation. ✠ 1 Do 17, 15-9-40; ✠ 1 Bf 109, 27-9-40.	♱ Killed since Battle (8-6-41)	Czech
KOPECKY Vaclav August	Sgt.	Pilot	111-253	Joined 111 Sqn., 12-9-40. Posted to 253 Sqn., 25-9-40. Commissioned, 1-3-41. Released from the R.A.F., 1946, as a Flight Lieutenant.	♱ Died since Battle (during 1970s)	Czech
KOPRIVA Josef	Sgt.	Pilot	310	Joined 310 (Czech) Sqn., 10-7-40, on formation. Commissioned, 20-8-41; Released from R.A.F., 1946, as Flight Lieutenant. Died (date unknown) in Czechoslovakia.	♱ Died since Battle	Czech
KORBER Karel	Sgt.	Pilot	32	Joined 32 Sqn., 14-10-40.	♱ Killed since Battle (3-5-43)	Czech
KORDULA Frantisek	Plt. Off.	Pilot	1-17	Joined 1 Sqn., late 8-40. Posted to 17 Sqn., 25-9-40. (Died in Britain after the War).	♱ Died since Battle	Czech
KOSARZ Wilhelm	Sgt.	Pilot	302	Joined 302 (Polish) Sqn., 20-8-40.	♱ Killed since Battle (8-11-40)	Polish
KOSINSKI Bronislaw Kazimierz	Flt. Lt.	Pilot	32	Joined 32 Sqn., 22-10-40.	♱ Killed since Battle (26-1-42)	Polish
KOUKAL Josef	Sgt.	Pilot	310	Joined 310 (Czech) Sqn., 7-40. Grievously burned during combat on 7-9-40. Was commissioned later, and released from the R.A.F. as a Flight Lieutenant.	♱ Died since Battle (23-2-80)	Czech
KOWALSKI Jan	Sgt.	Pilot	303	Joined 303 (Polish) Sqn., 21-8-40. ✠ 1 Bf 109, 25-9-40. Commissioned, 1-6-42. Awarded D.F.C.(10-4-46). Released from Polish Air Force, 1948, as Flt. Lt.		Polish
KOWALSKI Julian	Fg. Off.	Pilot	302	Joined 302 (Polish) Sqn., 26-7-40. ✠ 1 Do 17, 15-9-40; ✠ 1 Ju 88, 19-9-40; ✠ 1 Bf 109, 26-9-40. Awarded D.F.C.(20-8-42). Released from the Polish Air Force, 1-47, as a Wing Commander, and settled in Britain.		Polish
KOZLOWSKI Franciszek	Plt. Off.	Pilot	501	Joined 501 Sqn., 7-8-40. Seriously wounded, 18-8-40.	♱ Killed since Battle (13-3-43)	Polish
KRAMER Marcus	Plt. Off.	Aircrew	600	On 600 Sqn., 1-7-40. Awarded D.F.C.(9-7-40)	♱ Killed since Battle (21-5-41)	British
KRASNODEBSKI Zdzislaw	Flt. Lt.	Pilot	303	Joined 303 (Polish) Sqn., 2-8-40, as joint C.O. Severely wounded, 6-9-40. Released from Polish Air Force, 12-46, as Group Captain. (Settled and died in Canada).	♱ Died since Battle (1980)	Polish
KRATKORUKY Bedrich	Sgt.	Pilot	1	Joined 1 Sqn., 4-10-40. Commissioned, 1-11-41.	♱ Killed since Battle (16-1-43)	Czech
KREDBA Miroslav	Plt. Off.	Pilot	310	Joined 310 (Czech) Sqn., 10-7-40, on formation.	♱ Killed since Battle (14-2-42)	Czech
KREPSKI Walenty	Plt. Off.	Pilot	54	Joined 54 Sqn., 23-8-40.	♱ **Killed in Action** (7-9-40)	Polish
KROL Waclav Szczepan	Fg. Off.	Pilot	302	Joined 302 (Polish) Sqn., 21-8-40. Awarded D.F.C.(15-2-44). ✠ 1 Bf 109, 15-10-40. Released from Polish Air Force, 1946, as Wing Commander.		Polish
KRUML Tomas	Plt. Off.	Pilot	312	Flew with 312 (Czech) Sqn. during Battle of Britain. Returned to Czechoslovakia after the War.		Czech.
KUCERA Jaroslav	Sgt.	Pilot	245	Flew with 245 Sqn. during the Battle of Britain.	♱ Killed since Battle (19-12-41)	Czech
KUCERA Jiri	Sgt.	Pilot	238	Joined 238 Sqn., 12-9-40. Commissioned, 13-8-41. ✠ 1 Bf 110, 26-9-40; ✠ 1 He 111, 30-9-40. Returned to Czechoslovakia after the War.	♱ Died since Battle (24-1-80)	Czech
KUCERA Otmar	Sgt.	Pilot	111	Joined 111 Sqn., 6-10-40. Commissioned, 1942. Awarded D.F.C., 1943. Released from R.A.F., 8-45, and returned to Czechoslovakia.		Czech
KUMIEGA Tadeusz Leon	Plt. Off.	Pilot	17	Joined 17 Sqn., 1-9-40.✠ 1 Bf 109 (shared), 29-10-40. Remained in the R.A.F. after the War. Retired, 1-6-66, as Flight Lieutenant.		Polish
KUSTRZYNSKI Zbigniew	Fg. Off.	Pilot	607	Joined 607 Sqn., 1-9-40. Was later taken prisoner by the Germans, but escaped in 1945. Released by R.A.F., 1947, as Flight Lieutenant.		Polish
KUTTELWASCHER Karel Miroslav ("Kut")	Sgt.	Pilot	1	Joined 1 Sqn., 3-10-40. Commissioned, 7-10-41. Awarded D.F.C.✪ (20-5-42 and 1-7-42). (Destroyed 18 German aircraft after Battle of Britain.)	♱ Died since Battle (17-8-59)	Czech
KWIECINSKI Josef	F/Sgt.	Pilot	145	Joined 145 Sqn., 4-8-40.	♱ **Killed in Action** (12-8-40)	Polish
LACEY Edward Richard	Sgt.	Pilot	219	Joined 219 Sqn., 20-7-40. Commissioned, 30-10-42. Awarded D.S.O. (with Bomber Command, 20-4-43), O.B.E. (13-6-70). Retired from R.A.F, 18-8-75, as Wing Commander.	♱ Died since Battle (10-3-80)	British
LACEY James Harry ("Ginger")	Sgt.	Pilot	501	On 501 Sqn., 1-7-40. Commissioned, 15-1-41. Awarded D.F.M.✪ (23-8-40 and 26-11-40).✠ 1 Bf 109 (solo) and 1 Bf 109 (shared), 20-7-40; ✠ 1 Bf 110 and 1 Ju 87, 12-8-40; ✠ 1 Ju 88, 24-8-40; ✠ 1 Bf 109, 29-8-40; ✠ 1 He 111, 30-8-40; ✠ 1 Bf 109, 31-8-40; ✠ 2 Bf 109s, 2-9-40; ✠ 2 Bf 109s, 5-9-40; ✠ 1 He 111, 13-9-40; ✠ 2 Bf 109s and 1 He 111, 15-9-40; ✠ 1 Bf 109, 27-9-40; ✠ 1 Bf 109, 12-10-40; ✠ 1 Bf 109, 26-10-40; ✠ 1 Bf 109, 30-10-40. Retired from the R.A.F., 5-3-67, as a Squadron Leader.	♱ Died since War	British
LACKIE William Leckie	Sgt.	Aircrew	141	Defiant gunner. Joined 141 Sqn., 20-8-40.		British
LAFONT Henri G.	Adj.	Pilot	245-615	Joined 245 Sqn., 11-9-40. Posted to 615 Sqn., 18-9-40. Survived the War.		French
LAGUNA Piotr	Flt. Lt.	Pilot	302	Joined 302 (Polish) Sqn., 23-7-40.	♱ Killed since Battle (27-6-41)	Polish
LAING Alan	Sgt.	Pilot	151	Joined 151 Sqn., 30-9-40. Commissioned, 9-11-43. Retired from R.A.F., 8-5-55, as Flight Lieutenant.		British
LAING Alexander Lames Alan	Fg. Off.	Pilot	64	On 64 Sqn., 1-7-40. Believed posted away, late 7-40.		British
LAKE Donald Millar	Plt. Off.	Pilot	219	On 219 Sqn., 1-7-40.	♱ Killed since Battle (4-9-41)	British
LAMB Albert	Sgt.	Aircrew	25	Joined 25 Sqn., early 10-40.	♱ Died since Battle (5-1-48)	British
LAMB Owen Edward	Plt. Off.	Pilot	151	Joined 151 Sqn., mid-9-40.	♱ Killed since Battle (14-4-41)	New Zealander
LAMB Peter Gilbert	Fg. Off.	Pilot	610	On 610 Sqn., 1-7-40. Promoted Flt. Lt., 25-10-40. Posted away, 28-10-40. Awarded A.F.C.(26-10-43). ✠ 1 Bf 109, 24-8-40; ✠ 1 Bf 109, 26-8-40; ✠ 1 Bf 110, 29-8-40; ✠ 1 He 111, 30-8-40. Released from R.A.F., 1945, as Squadron Leader. Joined R.Aux.A.F. and commanded No. 610 Sqn., 7-46 until 3-50.		British
LAMB Robert Lionel	Plt. Off.	Aircrew	600	Joined 600 Sqn., 17-7-40. Shot down with Bomber Command, 2-44, and taken prisoner. Released from R.A.F., 1947, as Squadron Leader.		British
LAMB Roderick Russell	Sub-Lieut.	Pilot	804	Fleet Air Arm. On 804 Sqn., 1-7-40.	♱ Killed since Battle (24-8-42)	British
LAMBERT Hugh Michael Stanford	Fg. Off.	Pilot	25	Joined 25 Sqn., 4-9-40.	♱ **Killed in Action** (15-9-40)	British
LAMBIE William Gavin Mein	Plt. Off.	Pilot	219	On 219 Sqn., 1-7-40.	♱ Killed since Battle (15-11-40)	British
LAMMER Alfred	Plt. Off.	Aircrew	141	Defiant gunner. Joined 141 Sqn., late 7-40. Awarded D.F.C.✪ (16-2-43 and 29-10-43). Released from R.A.F., 7-11-45, as Squadron Leader.		British
LANDELS Leslie Ninian	Plt. Off.	Pilot	32-3-615	Joined 32 Sqn., 19-9-40. Posted to 3 Sqn., 27-9-40. Posted to 615 Sqn., 10-40.	♱ Killed since Battle (20-1-42)	British
LANDSDELL John	Sgt.	Pilot	607	On 607 Sqn., 1-7-40.	♱ **Killed in Action** (17-9-40)	British
LANE Brian John Edward	Flt. Lt.	Pilot	19	On 19 Sqn., 1-7-40. Took command of 19 Sqn., 5-9-40. Awarded D.F.C.(30-7-40). ✠ 1 Bf 110, 24-8-40; ✠ 1 Bf 110, 5-9-40; ✠ 1 Bf 110, 11-9-40.	♱ Killed since Battle (13-12-42)	British
LANE Roy	Plt. Off.	Pilot	43	Joined 43 Sqn., 13-7-40. ✠ 1 Ju 87, 18-8-40. Severely wounded, 26-8-40.	♱ Killed since Battle (c.20-6-44)	British

Name	Rank	Role	Sqn.	Details	Fate	Nationality
LANGDON Charles Edward	Plt. Off.	Pilot	43	Joined 43 Sqn., 21-9-40. Posted away, 10-40.	✠ Killed since Battle (26-2-41)	New Zealander
LANGHAM-HOBART Neville Charles	Plt. Off.	Pilot	73	On 73 Sqn., 1-7-40. ✠ 1 Bf 110, 7-9-40. Severely wounded, 23-9-40. Released from R.A.F., 9-45, as a Squadron Leader.		British
LANGLEY Gerald Archibald	Plt. Off.	Pilot	41	Joined 41 Sqn., late 8-40.	✠ **Killed in Action** (15-9-40)	British
LANGLEY Leonard	Sgt.	Aircrew	23	Joined 23 Sqn., 9-7-40. Awarded D.F.M.(30-5-41). Commissioned, 12-7-41. Re-released from R.A.F., 1946, as Flight Lieutenant, but rejoined, 1947.	✠ Died since Battle (26-9-53)	British
LANNING Francis Charles Anthony ("Tank")	Plt. Off.	Aircrew	141	Defiant gunner. On 141 Sqn., 1-7-40. Awarded D.F.C.(6-6-41). Released from the R.A.F., 2-11-46, as a Flight Lieutenant.		British
LAPKA Stanislaw	Plt. Off.	Pilot	302	Joined 302 (Polish) Sqn., 13-7-40. Released from Polish Air Force, 1947, as a Squadron Leader. Remained in Britain.	✠ Died since Battle (1978)	Polish
LAPKOWSKI Waclaw	Plt. Off.	Pilot	303	Joined 303 (Polish) Sqn., 2-8-40, on formation. ✠ 1 Ju 88, 5-9-40. Wounded, 5-9-40. Was Squadron Leader at time of death.	✠ Killed since Battle (2-7-41)	Polish
LARBALESTIER Basil Douglas	Plt. Off.	Aircrew	600	On 600 Sqn., 1-7-40. Released from R.A.F., 2-9-45, as a Flight Lieutenant.		British
LARICHELIERE Joseph Emile Paul	Plt. Off.	Pilot	213	On 213 Sqn., 1-7-40. ✠ 2 Bf 110s and 1 Bf 109, 13-8-40; ✠ 2 Bf 110s and 1 Ju 87, 15-8-40.	✠ **Killed in Action** (16-8-40)	Canadian
LATTA John Blandford	Plt. Off.	Pilot	242	On 242 Sqn., 1-7-40. Awarded D.F.C.(8-11-40). ✠ 1 Do 215 (shared), 21-8-40; ✠ 1 Bf 109, 9-9-40; ✠ 1 Bf 109, 15-9-40; ✠ 2 Bf 109s, 27-9-40.	✠ Killed since Battle (12-1-41)	Canadian
LAUDER Arnold John	Sgt.	Pilot	264	On 264 Sqn., 1-7-40. Commissioned, 1-5-42. Released from R.A.F., 1947, as a Flight Lieutenant.		British
LAUGHLIN John Hamilton ("Bodsie")	Fg. Off.	Pilot	235	On 235 Sqn. (23-3-45), M.B.E.(21-1-41). ✠ 1 He 115, 3-8-40. Released from the R.A.F., 1946, as a Squadron Leader.		British
LAURENCE George	Sgt.	Pilot	141	On 141 Sqn., 1-7-40. Awarded D.F.M.(30-5-41). ✠ 1 Ju 88, 17-9-40. Commissioned, 1-12-41.	✠ Killed since Battle (9-11-44)	British
LAW, K.S.	Plt. Off.	Pilot	605	On 605 Sqn., 1-7-40. Wounded, 15-8-40. Remained in R.A.F. after the War (was Wing Commander in 1965).		British
LAWFORD Derek Napier	Sgt.	Pilot	247	Joined 247 Sqn., 6-9-40. Commissioned, 23-10-41. Released from the R.A.F., 4-10-45, as a Flight Lieutenant.		British
LAWLER Edgar Stanley ("Tubby")	Sgt.	Aircrew	604	On 604 Sqn., 1-7-40. Commissioned, 27-7-44. Released from the R.A.F., 1945, as Flying Officer.	✠ Died since Battle (1984)	British
LAWRENCE John Thornett	Sgt.	Pilot	235	Joined 235 Sqn., 5-10-40. Commissioned, 5-8-41. Awarded A.F.C.(14-6-45). Released from R.A.F., 1946, as Flight Lieutenant.		British
LAWRENCE Keith Ashley	Plt. Off.	Pilot	234-603-421 Flt.	On 234 Sqn., 1-7-40. Posted to 603 Sqn., 9-9-40. Posted to 421 Flt., 8-10-40. Awarded D.F.C.(12-9-42). ✠ 1 Ju 88 (shared), 8-7-40; ✠ 1 Bf 109, 7-9-40; ✠ 1 Bf 109, 15-9-40. Transferred to Reserve in New Zealand, 2-9-46.		New Zealander
LAWRENCE Norman Anthony	Sgt.	Pilot	54	On 54 Sqn., 1-7-40. Commissioned, 4-12-40. ✠ 1 Bf 109, 9-7-40; ✠ 3 Ju 87s, 15-8-40. Left the R.A.F., 1943, as Flying Officer.	✠ Died since Battle (22-8-58)	British
LAWS Adrian Francis	Sgt	Pilot	64	On 64 Sqn., 1-7-40. Commissioned, 27-9-40. ✠ 1 Bf 109, 29-7-40; ✠ 1 Bf 109, 15-8-40; ✠ 1 Bf 110 (solo) and 1 He 111 (shared), 18-8-40. Awarded D.F.M.(1-10-40).	✠ **Killed in Action** (30-9-40)	British
LAWS George Godfrey Stone	Sgt.	Pilot	151-501	Joined 151 Sqn., 27-9-40. Posted to 501 Sqn., 10-40.	✠ Killed since Battle (28-3-41)	British
LAWSON Richard Chester	Plt. Off.	Pilot	601	Joined 601 Sqn., 9-9-40.	✠ Killed since Battle (10-2-41)	British
LAWSON Walter John ("Farmer")	Plt. Off.	Pilot	19	On 19 Sqn., 1-7-40. Awarded D.F.C.(26-11-40). ✠ 1 Bf 110, 9-9-40; ✠ 1 He 111, 11-9-40; ✠ 1 Ju 88 (shared), 18-9-40; ✠ 1 Bf 109, 27-9-40.	✠ Killed since Battle (28-8-41)	British
LAWSON-BROWN John	Plt. Off.	Pilot	64	Joined 64 Sqn., 14-9-40.	✠ Killed since Battle (12-5-41)	British
LAWTON Philip Charles Fenner	Fg. Off.	Pilot	604	On 604 Sqn., 1-7-40. Promoted Flt. Lt., 3-9-40. Awarded D.F.C.(11-11-41). Released from the R.A.F., 1945, as Group Captain.		British
LAYCOCK Herbert Keith	Plt. Off.	Pilot	79-56	Joined 79 Sqn., 27-7-40. Posted to 56 Sqn., 8-10-40.	✠ Killed since Battle (26-8-43)	British
LAYCOCK	Fg. Off.	Pilot	87	Flew with 87 Sqn. during Battle of Britain. No further details known.		British
LAZORYK Wlodzimierz	Fg. Off.	Pilot	607	Joined 607 Sqn., 9-10-40. Released from Polish Air Force, 5-46, as Squadron Leader.		Polish
LEARY David Cooper	Plt. Off.	Pilot	17	On 17 Sqn., 1-7-40. Awarded D.F.C.(26-11-40). ✠ 1 Bf 109, 25-8-40; ✠ 1 Do 17 (solo) and 1 Bf 110 (shared).	✠ Killed since Battle (28-12-40)	British
LEATHART James Anthony ("Prof")	Fg. Off.	Pilot	54	In command of 54 Sqn., 1-7-40. Promoted Flt. Lt., 24-8-40. Appointed C.B.(11-6-60); awarded D.S.O.(11-6-40). ✠ 1 Do 17, 28-8-40; ✠ 1 Bf 109, 2-9-40. Posted away, 18-10-40. Retired from the R.A.F., 24-7-62, as an Air Commodore.		British
LEATHEM Ernest George Cuthbert	Plt. Off.	Aircrew	248	On 248 Sqn., 1-7-40. Awarded D.F.C.(25-5-43). Served in the R.A.F. after the War.		British
LEATHER William Johnson ("Jack")	Flt. Lt.	Pilot	611	On 611 Sqn., 1-7-40. Awarded D.F.C.(8-10-40). ✠ 1 Do 17 (shared), 2-7-40; ✠ 1 Do 17 (solo) and 1 Do 17 (shared), 15-9-40; ✠ 2 Do 17s (shared), 11-10-40. Released from R.A.F., 1945, as Group Captain. Commanded 611 Sqn., R.Aux.A.F., 1946-49.	✠ Died since Battle (1965)	British
LE CHEMINANT Jerrold	Sgt.	Pilot	616	Joined 616 Sqn., 14-10-40. Awarded O.B.E.(13-6-70), D.F.C.(21-5-43). Commissioned, 9-5-42. Retired from R.A.F., 1-11-72, as a Wing Commander.		British
LECKRONE Phillip Howard	Plt. Off.	Pilot	616	Joined 616 Sqn., 2-9-40. (Posted to 71 Sqn., 12-10-40).	✠ Killed since Battle (5-1-41)	American
LECKY John Gage	Plt. Off.	Pilot	610-41	Joined 610 Sqn., 8-40. Posted to 41 Sqn., 1-10-40.	✠ **Killed in Action** (11-10-40)	British
LE CONTE Edgar Francis	Sgt.	Aircrew	F.I.U.	On F.I.U., 1-7-40. Commissioned, 24-6-43. Awarded O.B.E.(1-1-72). Retired from R.A.F., 8-3-75.	✠ Died since Battle (4-5-81)	British
LEDGER Leslie	Sgt.	Aircrew	236	Joined 236 Sqn., 19-7-40. Awarded D.F.M.(12-1-43). Commissioned, 8-11-44. Re-leased from the R.A.F., 1946, as Flying Officer.		British
LE DONG Terry	Sgt.	Aircrew	219	Joined 219 Sqn., 1-9-40.	✠ Killed since Battle (8-2-41)	British
LEE Kenneth Norman Thomson ("Hawkeye")	Plt. Off.	Pilot	501	On 501 Sqn., 1-7-40. Promoted to Fg. Off., 3-9-40. Awarded D.F.C.(22-10-40). ✠ 1 Ju 87, 12-8-40. Shot down and captured, 1943. Released from R.A.F., 1945 as Squadron Leader.		British
LEE Maurice Alexander William	Sgt.	Pilot	72-421 Flt.	Joined 72 Sqn., 15-9-40. Posted to 421 Flt., 3-10-40. Injured, 15-10-40. ✠ 1 He 111, 27-9-40.	✠ Killed since Battle (31-12-40)	British
LEE Richard Hugh Anthony	Fg. Off.	Pilot	85	On 85 Sqn., 1-7-40. Had been awarded the D.S.O.(31-5-40), D.F.C.(8-3-40).	✠ **Killed in Action** (18-8-40)	British
LEES Alan Farquhar Young	Plt. Off.	Pilot	236	Joined 236 Sqn., 11-8-40. Awarded D.F.C.(27-10-41). Invalided from R.A.F., 1946, as a Flight Lieutenant.	✠ Died since Battle (27-10-87)	British
LEES Ronald Beresford	Sqn. Ldr.	Pilot	72	In command of 72 Sqn., 1-7-40. Posted away, 26-7-40. (Flew with the squadron, 2-9-40, and was wounded). Appointed K.C.B.(10-6-61); C.B., 1-1-46), C.B.E. (2-6-43), D.F.C.⊛ (22-10-40 and 26-12-41). Retired from R.A.F., 3-2-66, as an Air Marshal.		Australian
LEFEVRE Peter William ("Pip")	Plt. Off.	Pilot	46	On 46 Sqn., 1-7-40. Promoted Fg. Off., 3-9-40. ✠ 1 Ju 88, 3-9-40. Slightly wounded, 18-9-40.	✠ Killed since Battle (6-2-44)	British
LEGG Richard James	Wg. Cdr.	Pilot	601	Believed to have flown an operational sortie with No. 601 Sqn., probably on 16-10-40. Retired from the R.A.F., 4-11-53, retaining the rank of Air Commodore.	✠ Died since Battle (1959)	British
LEGGETT Percival Graham	Plt. Off.	Pilot	615-245-46	Joined 615 Sqn., early 9-40. Posted to 245 Sqn., 28-9-40. Posted to 46 Sqn., 18-10-40. Retired from the R.A.F., 23-5-58, as a Squadron Leader.		British
LEIGH Arthur Charles	Sgt.	Pilot	64-72	Joined 64 Sqn., 9-40. Posted to 72 Sqn., 11-10-40. Commissioned, 10-11-41. Awarded D.F.C.(19-9-44), D.F.M.(9-9-41). Released from R.A.F., 1945, as a Flight Lieutenant.		British
LEIGH Rupert Henry Archibald	Sqn. Ldr.	Pilot	66	In command of 66 Sqn., 1-7-40. ✠ 1 He 111, 9-9-40; ✠ 1 u.e.a., 11-9-40. Posted away, 18-10-40. Retired from the R.A.F., 7-12-54, retaining the rank of Air Commodore.		British
LEJEUNE, O.G.	Sgt.	Pilot	235	Joined 235 Sqn., 5-8-40. Posted away, 30-10-40. Commissioned, 25-5-42.	✠ Died since Battle (10-4-47)	Belgian
LENAHAN John Desmond	Plt. Off.	Pilot	607	Joined 607 Sqn., 12-8-40.	✠ **Killed in Action** (9-9-40)	British

Name	Rank	Role	Sqn.	Details		Nationality
LENG Maurice Equity	Sgt.	Pilot	73	On 73 Sqn., 1-7-40. Injured, 23-9-40. Commissioned, 26-4-41. (Shot down and taken prisoner by the Germans, 30-9-42). Released from R.A.F., 3-46, as Flt. Lt.		British
LENNARD Paul Leonard	Midshipman	Pilot	501	Fleet Air Arm. Joined 501 Sqn., 8-7-40. Posted away, 20-7-40.	✝ Killed since Battle (26-3-42)	British
LENTON Edwin Claude	Plt. Off.	Pilot	56	Joined 56 Sqn., 6-8-40. Promoted Fg. Off., 3-9-40. Posted away, 7-9-40. Released from R.A.F., 1947, as a Squadron Leader.		British
LE ROUGETEL Stanley Paul	Fg. Off.	Pilot	600	On 600 Sqn., 1-7-40. Promoted Flt. Lt., 3-9-40. Retired from the R.A.F., 11-2-58, retaining the rank of Wing Commander.		British
LE ROY DU VIVIER Daniel Albert Raymond Charles Plt. Off.		Pilot	43	Commissioned on entry to R.A.F., 20-7-40. Joined 43 Sqn., 4-8-40. ✠ 1 Ju 87, 16-8-40. Wounded, 2-9-40, but returned to squadron, 22-10-40. Awarded D.F.C.✠ (30-1-42 and 15-9-42). Released from Air Force, 16-9-46. (Killed in road accident in the U.S.A.)	✝ Died since Battle (2-9-81)	Belgian
LERWAY Frederick Thomas	Sgt.	Aircrew	236	Joined 236 Sqn., 3-9-40. Commissioned, 15-1-43. Released from R.A.F., 1-46, as Flight lieutenant.		British
LESLIE George Mennie	Sgt.	Aircrew	219	Joined 219 Sqn., 2-8-40.	✝ Killed since Battle (17-12-40)	British
LEVENSON Stephen Austin	Sgt.	Pilot	611	On 611 Sqn., 1-7-40. ✠ 1 Ju 88, 11-9-40; ✠ 1 Do 17, 15-9-40.	✝ Killed since Battle (17-9-42)	British
LEWIS Albert Gerald	Plt. Off.	Pilot	85-249	On 85 Sqn., 1-7-40. Posted to 249 Sqn., 14-9-40. Awarded D.F.C.✠ (25-6-40 and 22-10-40). ✠ 1 Bf 109, 31-8-40; ✠ 1 He 111, 15-9-40; ✠ 1 Bf 109, 18-9-40; ✠ 3 Bf 109s, 2 Bf 110s and 1 Ju 88, 27-9-40. Released from the R.A.F., 1946, as a Squadron Leader.		South African
LEWIS Charles Sydney	Sgt.	Aircrew	600	On 600 Sqn., 1-7-40. Commissioned, 19-10-44. Released from the R.A.F., 1945, as a Flying Officer.	✝ Died since Battle (1954)	British
¶ LEWIS, E.I.	Sgt.	Pilot	222	On 222 Sqn., 1-7-40.	✝ Killed in Action (4-7-40)	British
LEWIS Raymond Grant	Plt. Off.	Pilot	1	Joined 1 Sqn., 21-10-40. Promoted, Fg. Off., 23-10-40. ✠ 1 Ju 88 (shared), 30-10-40.	✝ Killed since Battle (5-2-41)	Canadian
LEWIS William George	Sgt.	Aircrew	25	Joined 29 Sqn., 29-9-40.	✝ Killed since Battle (14-7-41)	British
LEYLAND Reginal Harry	Sgt.	Aircrew	F.I.U.	On F.I.U., 1-7-40. Was crew member of Blenheim which destroyed Do 17 on night of 22/23-7-40. Commissioned, 21-3-43. Released from R.A.F., 1946, as Flying Officer.		British
LILLE, P.	Sgt.	Aircrew	264	Defiant gunner. Record of operations not traced.		British
LILLEY Robert	Sgt.	Aircrew	29	On 29 Sqn., 1-7-40. Awarded D.F.C. (3-9-43, as Warrant Officer).	✝ Killed since Battle (28-4-44)	British
LIMPENNY Eric Ronald	Sgt.	Pilot	64	Joined 64 Sqn., c.29-9-40. Commissioned, 5-1-45. Released from R.A.F., 1946, as a Flying Officer.		British
LINDSAY Alec Ian	Plt. Off.	Pilot	72	Joined 72 Sqn., 11-9-40.	✝ Killed since Battle (23-10-42)	British
LINES Arthur Peter	Fg. Off.	Pilot	17	Joined 17 Sqn., 9-7-40. Posted away, 21-8-40. Released from R.A.F., 1947, as a Flight Lieutenant.		British
LINGARD John Granville	Sgt.	Pilot	25-219	On 25 Sqn., 1-7-40. Commissioned, 4-10-40. Posted to 219 Sqn., 24-10-40. Awarded D.F.C.(25-7-44). Retired from the R.A.F., 31-3-58, as a Wing Commander.		British
LINNEY Anthony Stuart	Plt. Off.	Pilot	229	On 229 Sqn., 1-7-40. Promoted Fg. Off., 3-10-40, and posted away. Awarded O.B.E., 2-6-43. Released from R.A.F., 1945, as a Wing Commander.	✝ Died since Battle (1983)	British
LIPSCOMBE Alfred John	Sgt.	Aircrew	600	Joined 600 Sqn., 8-10-40.	✝ Killed since Battle (20-9-41)	British
LISTER Robert Charles Franklin	Sqn. Ldr.	Pilot	41-92	Temporary C.O., 41 Sqn., 8-9-40. Slightly wounded, 14-9-40. Posted super-numerary to 92 Sqn., 22-9-40. Severely wounded, 24-9-40. Retired from R.A.F, 31-10-54, retaining the rank of Group Captain.		British
LITCHFIELD Peter	Plt. Off.	Pilot	610	On 610 Sqn., 1-7-40. ✠ 1 Bf 109, 14-7-40.	✝ **Killed in Action** (18-7-40)	British
LITSON Frederick William Ronald	Sgt.	Aircrew	141	Defiant gunner. Commissioned, 2-5-43. Released from R.A.F., 1946, as Flight Lieutenant. Rejoined R.A.F. later.		British
LITTLE Arthur Guthrie	Plt. Off.	Aircrew	235	On 235 Sqn., 1-7-40. Released from R.A.F., 1945, as a Flight Lieutenant.		British
LITTLE Bernard Williamson	Fg. Off.	Pilot	609	On 609 Sqn., 1-7-40. Promoted Fg. Off., 3-9-40. Released from R.A.F., 1945, as Squadron Leader. Made O.B.E.(1-1-46).	✝ Died since Battle (1986)	British
LITTLE James Hayward	Flt. Lt.	Pilot	219	Acting Sqn. Ldr. In command of 219 Sqn., 1-7-40. Awarded D.F.C.(18-3-41) Was Wing Commander at time of death.	✝ Killed since Battle (12-6-43)	British
LITTLE, P.	Sqn. Ldr.	Pilot	600	Joined 600 Sqn., c.28-9-40. No other details traced.		British
LITTLE Ronald	Sgt.	Pilot	238	On 238 Sqn., 1-7-40.	✝ **Killed in Action** (28-9-40)	British
LITTLE Thomas Burgess	Fg. Off.	Pilot	1(Canadian)	With 1(Canadian) Sqn., 20-6-40, on arrival in U.K. Wounded, 11-9-40.	✝ Killed since Battle (27-8-41)	Canadian
LLEWELLYN Arthur John Alexander	Fg. Off.	Pilot	29	On 29 Sqn., 1-7-40.	✝ Killed since Battle (7-2-42)	British
LLEWELLYN Reginald Thomas	Sgt.	Pilot	213	On 213 Sqn., 1-7-40. Awarded D.F.M.(22-10-40). Commissioned, 11-11-41. ✠ 1 Bf 109, 11-8-40; ✠ 1 Ju 88, 13-8-40; ✠ 3 Bf 109s, 15-8-40; ✠ 1 Ju 88, 19-8-40; ✠ 1 Ju 88, 20-8-40; ✠ 1 Bf 110 (solo) and 1 Bf 109 (shared); ✠ 2 Bf 110s, 11-9-40. Retired from R.A.F., 24-3-57, as Flight Lieutenant.		British
LLOYD David Edward	Sgt.	Pilot	19-64	Joined 64 Sqn., 28-8-40, from 19 Sqn. Commissioned, 13-1-42. ✠ 1 Ju 88 (shared), 18-9-40.	✝ Killed since Battle (17-3-42)	British
LLOYD John Phillip	Plt. Off.	Pilot	64-72	Joined 72 Sqn., 11-9-40, from 64 Sqn. Severely wounded, 18-9-40. Awarded A.F.C.(1-1-43). Released from R.A.F., 1945, as Squadron Leader.	✝ Died since Battle (1971)	British
LLOYD Philip David	Sgt.	Pilot	41	Joined 41 Sqn., early 9-40.	✝ **Killed in Action** (15-10-40)	British
LLOYD	A.C.1	Aircrew	29	Joined 29 Sqn., c.5-8-40. Promoted Sergeant. No further details traced.		British
LOCHNAN Peter William	Fg. Off.	Pilot	1(Canadian)	Joined 1(Canadian) Sqn., 30-8-40. ✠ 1 He 111, 15-9-40; ✠ 1 Bf 110 (shared), 27-9-40; ✠ 1 Bf 109, 7-10-40.	✝ Killed since Battle (21-5-41)	Canadian
LOCK Eric Stanley ("Sawn Off")	Plt. Off.	Pilot	41	Joined 41 Sqn., 8-40. Awarded D.S.O.(1-10-40), D.F.C.✠ (1-10-40 and 22-10-40). ✠ 1 Bf 110, 15-8-40; ✠ 2 Bf 109s and 2 He 111s, 5-9-40; ✠ 1 Ju 88, 6-9-40; ✠ 2 Bf 109s, 9-9-40; ✠ 1 Ju 88 and 1 Bf 110, 11-9-40; ✠ 2 Bf 109s, 14-9-40; ✠ 1 Bf 109 (solo) and 1 Do 17 (shared); ✠ 1 Bf 109, 18-9-40; ✠ 1 Bf 109 and 1 Hs 126, 20-9-40; ✠ 1 Bf 109, 5-10-40; ✠ 1 Bf 109, 9-10-40; ✠ 1 Bf 109, 11-10-40; ✠ 1 Bf 109, 20-10-40. Severely wounded, 17-11-40.	✝ Killed since Battle (3-8-41)	British
LOCKHART James	Plt. Off.	Pilot	85-213	On 85 Sqn., 1-7-40. Posted to 213 Sqn., 16-9-40. Promoted Fg. Off., 3-10-40.	✝ Killed since Battle (5-4-42)	British
LOCKTON Eric Edward	Sgt.	Pilot	236	Joined 236 Sqn., 3-7-40.	✝ **Killed in Action** (20-7-40)	British
LOCKWOOD Joseph Charles	Sgt.	Pilot	54	Joined 54 Sqn., 22-8-40.	✝ Killed since Battle (3-3-41)	British
LOFTS Keith Temple	Plt. Off.	Pilot	615-249	On 615 Sqn., 1-7-40. Promoted Fg. Off., 3-9-40. Awarded D.F.C.✠ (22-10-40 and 26-1-45). ✠ 1 Ju 87, 14-8-40; ✠ 1 Bf 109 (shared), 15-8-40; ✠ 1 He 111, 16-8-40; ✠ 2 Bf 109s, 20-8-40; ✠ 1 Bf 109, 27-9-40. Released from the R.A.F., 1946, as Wing Commander. Commanded 604 Sqn., R.Aux.A.F., from 1948 until death in flying accident, 1951.	✝ Killed since Battle (20-5-51)	British
LOGAN Colin	Plt. Off.	Pilot	266	Joined 266 Sqn., 20-8-40.	✝ Killed since Battle (27-3-41)	British
LOGIE Ormonde Arthur	Plt. Off.	Aircrew	29	On 29 Sqn., 1-7-40. Reliquished commission, 30-4-41, on medical grounds.		British
LOKUCIEWSKI Witold	Plt. Off.	Pilot	303	Joined 303 (Polish) Sqn., 2-8-40, on formation. ✠ 1 Do 17, 7-9-40; ✠ 1 Do 17 and 1 Bf 109, 11-9-40; ✠ 1 Bf 109, 15-9-40. Wounded, 15-9-40. Retired from Polish Air Force, 1974.		Polish
LONG	Sgt.	Aircrew	236	Said to have flown an operational sortie with 236 Sqn., 22-7-40. No details traced.		British
LONSDALE John	Plt. Off.	Pilot	3	Joined 3 Sqn., early 7-40. ✠ 1 He 111 (shared), 25-7-40.	✝ Killed since Battle (26-11-40)	British

433

LONSDALE Robert Henry	Sgt.	Pilot	46-242-501	On 46 Sqn., 1-7-40. Posted to 242 Sqn., 20-7-40. Posted to 501 Sqn., 12-10-40. ✠ 1 He 111, 30-8-40; ✠ 1 Do 17, 9-9-40.			British
LOOKER David John	Plt. Off.	Pilot	615	On 615 Sqn., 1-7-40. Promoted Fg. Off., 3-9-40. Wounded, 18-8-40. Released from the R.A.F., 1945, as Flight Lieutenant.			British
LOUDON Malcolm John	Flt. Lt.	Pilot	141	On 141 Sqn., 1-7-40. Wounded, 19-7-40. Awarded D.F.C.(26-12-41). Released from R.A.F., 1946, as a Wing Commander.			British
LOVELL Anthony Desmond Joseph	Fg. Off.	Pilot	41	On 41 Sqn., 1-7-40. Awarded D.S.O.✣ (3-11-42 and 23-2-45), D.F.C.✣ (26-11-40 and 10-2-42). ✠ 1 Ju 88, 8-7-40.✠ 1 Bf 110, 15-8-40; ✠ 1 Bf 110, 6-9-40; ✠ 1 Bf 109, 15-9-40; ✠ 1 Bf 109, 20-10-40. Was a Wing Commander at the time of his death.	✟	Killed since Battle (17-8-45)	British
LOVELL GREGG Terence Gunion	Sqn. Ldr.	Pilot	87	Took command of 87 Sqn., 12-7-40.	✟	**Killed in Action** (15-8-40)	New Zealander
LOVERSEED John Eric	Sgt.	Pilot	501	Joined 501 Sqn., 19-7-40. Awarded A.F.C.(1-1-43, as Warrant Officer)			British
LOVETT Reginald Eric	Flt. Lt.	Pilot	73	Re-joined 73 Sqn. (after recovery from wounds), 23-7-40. Awarded D.F.C.(16-7-40). ✠ 1 Ju 88, 15-8-40.	✟	**Killed in Action** (7-9-40)	British
LOWE Joseph	Sgt.	Aircrew	236	On 236 Sqn., 1-7-40. Awarded D.F.M.(22-9-42).	✟	Died since Battle (1973)	British
LOWETH Phillip Anthony	Plt. Off.	Pilot	249	On 249 Sqn., 1-7-40. Released from R.A.F., 1950, as a Flight Lieutenant.			British
LOWTHER Walter	Sgt.	Aircrew	219	On 219 Sqn. during Battle of Britain. No further details traced.			British
LOXTON Wilfred William	Sqn. Ldr.	Pilot	25	In command of 25 Sqn., 1-7-40; posted away, 24-9-40. Awarded A.F.C.(1-1-45). Retired from R.A.F., 31-5-57, as a Wing Commander.			British
LUCAS Robin Morton McTaggart Delight	Plt. Off.	Pilot	141	Joined 141 Sqn., 19-8-40. Released from R.A.F., 2-46, as Flight Lieutenant.			British
LUCAS Sidney Edward	Sgt.	Pilot	32-257	Joined 32 Sqn., mid-9-42. Posted to 257 Sqn., 15-10-40. Commissioned, 9-2-44. (✠ 1 CR.42, 11-11-40). Awarded D.F.C.(8-8-44). Released from R.A.F., 1946, as Flying Officer.			British
LUKASZEWICZ Kazimierz	Fg. Off.	Pilot	303-501	Joined 303 (Polish), 26-11-40. Posted to 501 Sqn., 7-8-40.	✟	**Killed in Action** (12-8-40)	Polish
LUMSDEN Dugald Thomas Moore	Plt. Off.	Pilot	236	On 236 Sqn., 1-7-40. Shot down and taken prisoner by Germans, 11-7-42. Awarded M.B.E.(1-6-53). Retired from R.A.F., 16-5-64, as Wing Commander.			British
LUMSDEN John Clapperton	Sgt.	Aircrew	248	Joined 248 Sqn., 5-10-40. Discharged from R.A.F., 1942.			British
LUND John Wilfred ("Thomas")	Plt. Off.	Pilot	611-92	On 611 Sqn., 1-7-40. ✠ 1 Do 17 (shared), 2-7-40. ✠ 1 Do 17 (shared), 21-7-40. Posted to 92 Sqn., 2-10-40.	✟	Killed since Battle (2-10-41)	British
LUSK Harold Stewart	Plt. Off.	Pilot	25	On 25 Sqn., 1-7-40. Promoted Fg. Off., 10-10-40. Transferred to R.N.Z.A.F., 1-1-44. To Reserve, 10-1-46.			New Zealander
LUSTY Kenneth Roy	Sgt.	Aircrew	25	On 25 Sqn., 1-7-40. Commissioned, 16-5-41. Released from R.A.F., 1947, as Squadron Leader.			British
LYALL Alastair McLaren	Fg. Off.	Pilot	25	On 25 Sqn., 1-7-40. Promoted Flt. Lt., 3-9-40. Posted away, 14-9-40. Released from R.A.F., 1946, as Flight Lieutenant.			British
LYALL Archibald	Plt. Off.	Pilot	602	On 602 Sqn., 1-7-40. ✠ 1 Bf 109 and 1 Do 17, 9-9-40; ✠ 1 Do 17, 15-9-40; ✠ 1 Ju 88 (shared), 21-9-40; ✠ 1 Bf 109, 29-10-40.	✟	Killed since Battle (18-11-40)	British
LYNCH James	Sgt.	Aircrew	25	Joined 25 Sqn., late 9-40.	✟	Killed since Battle (22-1-44)	British
LYONS Emanuel Barnett	Plt. Off.	Pilot	65	Joined 65 Sqn., 2-9-40. Awarded D.F.C.(8-5-45). Released from R.A.F., 1946, as Flight Lieutenant.			British
LYSEK Antoni	Sgt.	Pilot	302	Joined 302 (Polish) Sqn., 20-8-40. Commissioned, 31-5-42.	✟	Killed since Battle (5-6-42)	Polish
McADAM John	Sgt.	Pilot	41	On 41 Sqn., 1-7-40. ✠ 1 Do 17, 7-9-40; ✠ 1 Bf 109, 25-10-40.	✟	Killed since Battle (20-2-41)	British
McADAM William David	Sgt.	Aircrew	23	On 23 Sqn., 1-7-40.	✟	Killed since Battle (1-9-41)	British
McALLISTER, P.J.	A.C.1	Aircrew	23-29	Joined 23 Sqn., c.1-10-40. Promoted Sergeant. Posted to 29 Sqn., c.20-10-40.			British
McARTHUR James Henry Gordon	Flt. Lt.	Pilot	239-609	On 238 Sqn., 1-7-40. Posted to 609 Sqn., 1-8-40. Awarded D.F.C.(22-10-40) ✠ 2 Ju 87s, 8-8-40; ✠ 1 Bf 110, 11-8-40; ✠ 2 Bf 110s, 15-8-40; ✠ 1 Bf 110, 25-8-40; ✠ 1 Do 17, 7-9-40; ✠ 1 Bf 110, 25-9-40. Released from R.A.F., 1947, as Wing Commander. Transferred to R.C.A.F.	✟	Killed since Battle (5-61)	British
MacARTHUR Malcolm Robert	Fg. Off.	Pilot	236	On 236 Sqn., 1-7-40. Awarded D.F.C.(25-4-41). Released from R.A.F., 1946, as a Group Captain.			British
McCALL, S.V.	Plt. Off.	Pilot	607	Joined 607 Sqn., 9-10-40.			British
McCANN Thomas Andrew	Sgt.	Pilot	601	Joined 601 Sqn., 9-9-40. Commissioned, 19-2-42.	✟	Killed since Battle (27-7-42)	British
McCARTHY James Patrick	Sgt.	Aircrew	235	On 235 Sqn., 1-7-40. Commissioned later.			British
McCARTHY Thomas Francis	Sgt.	Aircrew	235	On 235 Sqn., 1-7-40.	✟	Killed since Battle (6-10-42)	British
McCAUL John Patrick	A.C.2	Aircrew	219	Joined 219 Sqn., 16-8-40. Was not promoted to Sergeant before death.	✟	**Killed in Action** (30-9-40)	British
McCAW Derek Charles	Fg. Off.	Pilot	238	On 238 Sqn., 1-7-40.	✟	**Killed in Action** (8-8-40)	British
McCHESNEY Robert Ian	Sgt.	Aircrew	236	Joined 236 Sqn., 6-7-40. Commissioned, 10-6-41.	✟	Killed since Battle (6-12-42)	New Zealander
McCLINTOCK John Arthur Peter	Plt. Off.	Pilot	615	On 615 Sqn., 1-7-40. ✠ 1 He 111 (shared), 24-8-40.	✟	Killed since Battle (25-11-40)	British
McCOMB James Ellis	Sqn. Ldr.	Pilot	611	In command of 611 Sqn., 1-7-40. Awarded D.F.C.(22-11-40). ✠ 1 Do 17 (solo) and 1 Do 17 (shared), 21-8-40; ✠ 1 Do 17, 15-9-40. Posted away, 19-10-40. Released from R.A.F., 1945, as a Wing Commander.	✟	Died since Battle (8-82)	British
McCONNELL John	Sgt.	Pilot	145	Joined 145 Sqn., 11-9-40. Slightly wounded, 7-11-40. Commissioned, 17-10-42. Retired from R.A.F., 29-1-58, as a Flight Lieutenant.	✟	Died since Battle (1965)	British
McCONNELL William Winder	Plt. Off.	Pilot	245-607-249	Joined 245 Sqn., 6-7-40. Posted to 607 Sqn., 24-9-40. Posted to 249 Sqn., 16-10-40. ✠ 1 Ju 88 (shared), 28-10-40. Awarded D.F.C.✣ (30-6-42 and 22-9-42). Released from R.A.F., 1945, as a Squadron Leader.			Irish
McCORMACK John Bernard ("Paddy")	Sgt.	Aircrew	25	On 25 Sqn., 1-7-40. Commissioned, 23-5-42.	✟	Killed since Battle (10-9-42)	British
McDERMOTT John Alexander	Sgt.	Aircrew	23	Joined 23 Sqn., 24-9-40. Commissioned, 19-11-42. Transferred to the Reserve in New Zealand, 22-11-44.	✟	Died since Battle (2-1-70)	New Zealander
MacDONALD Alexander Stewart	Sgt.	Pilot	601	Joined 601 Sqn., 16-7-40. No details of operations traced.			British
MacDONALD Donald Kennedy	Plt. Off.	Pilot	603	On 603 Sqn., 1-7-40. (Brother of Flt. Lt. H.K. MacDonald)	✟	**Killed in Action** (28-8-40)	British
MacDONALD Duncan Stuart	Flt. Lt.	Pilot	213	Joined 213 Sqn., 28-8-40, as Acting Squadron Leader, to command. Awarded D.S.O. (21-8-45), D.F.C.(17-12-40). Changed name to WILSON-MacDONALD.			British
MacDONALD Harold Kennedy	Flt. Lt.	Pilot	603	On 603 Sqn., 1-7-40. ✠ 1 Bf 109, 31-8-40; ✠ 1 Bf 109, 18-9-40; ✠ 1 Bf 109, 27-9-40. (Brother of Flt. Lt. D.K. MacDonald)	✟	**Killed in Action** (28-9-40)	British
MacDONNELL Aeneas Ranald Donald	Sqn. Ldr.	Pilot	64	Joined 64 Sqn., c.18-7-40, to command. Appointed C.B.(1-1-64); awarded D.F.C. (6-9-40). ✠ 1 Ju 87, 25-7-40; ✠ 1 Bf 109 and 1 Ju 87, 29-7-40; ✠ 1 Bf 109, 5-8-40; ✠ 1 Bf 109, 11-8-40; ✠ 1 Bf 109, 15-8-40; ✠ 1 Bf 109 (solo) and 1 He 111 (shared), 16-8-40; ✠ 1 Bf 110, 18-8-40. Retired from R.A.F., 15-11-64, as an Air Commodore.			British
McDONOUGH Bryan Martin	Plt. Off.	Pilot	236	On 236 Sqn., 1-7-40.	✟	**Killed in Action** (1-8-40)	Australian
MacDOUGAL Charles White	Sgt.	Pilot	111	On 111 Sqn., 1-7-40.	✟	Killed since Battle (5-3-41)	British
MacDOUGALL Ian Neil	Plt. Off.	Pilot	141	On 141 Sqn., 1-7-40. Awarded D.F.C.(15-5-42)	✟	Died since Battle (8-87)	British

Name	Rank	Role	Squadron	Notes	Status	Nationality
MacDOUGALL Ralph Ian George	Sqn. Ldr.	Pilot	17	In command of 17 Sqn., 1-7-40. Posted away, 18-7-40. Retired from R.A.F., 9-8-66, retaining rank of Wing Commander.		British
McDOUGALL Roy	Plt. Off.	Pilot	3-232	Joined 3 Sqn., 20-8-40. Posted to 232 Sqn., 8-9-40. Released from R.A.F., 1946, as Flight Lieutenant.		British
McDOWALL Andrew	Sgt.	Pilot	602	On 602 Sqn., 1-7-40. Awarded D.F.M.✻ (8-10-40 and 17-12-40). Commissioned, 29-11-40. ✤ 1 He 111, 24-7-40; ✤ 1 Bf 109, 18-8-40; ✤ 1 He 111, 26-8-40; ✤ 1 Bf 109, 9-9-40; ✤ 1 Bf 110, 11-9-40; ✤ 2 Ju 88s, 30-9-40; ✤ 1 Ju 88, 27-10-40; ✤ 2 Bf 109s, 29-10-40; ✤ 1 Bf 109, 30-10-40.	✝ Died since Battle (1981)	British
McFADDEN Aubrey	Plt. Off.	Pilot	73	On 73 Sqn., 1-7-40. ✤ 1 Bf 110, 27-9-40.	✝ Killed since Battle (5-4-42)	British
MacFIE Colin Hamilton ("Crow Hawk Mac")	Plt. Off.	Pilot	611-616	On 611 Sqn., 1-7-40. Promoted Fg. Off., 3-9-40. Posted to 616 Sqn., 7-9-40. Awarded D.F.C.(8-8-41). Retired from R.A.F., 18-10-63, as Squadron Leader.	✝ Died since Battle (1982)	British
McGAW Charles Alexander	Plt. Off.	Pilot	73-66	On 73 Sqn., 1-7-40. Posted to 66 Sqn., 23-10-40.	✝ Killed since Battle (1-10-43)	British
McGIBBON James	Plt. Off.	Pilot	65	Joined 615 Sqn., 23-9-40.	✝ Killed in Accident (29-9-40)	British
McGLASHAN Kenneth Butterworth	Plt. Off.	Pilot	245	On 245 Sqn., 1-7-40. Awarded A.F.C.(8-6-50). Retired from R.A.F., 29-8-58, as Squadron Leader.		British
McGOWAN Herbert Walter	Plt. Off.	Pilot	92	Joined 92 Sqn., late 8-40. Wounded, 14-9-40. Released from R.A.F., 1944, as Flight Lieutenant.		British
McGOWAN Roy Andrew	Plt. Off.	Pilot	46	On 46 Sqn., 1-7-40. Promoted Fg. Off., 3-9-40. Wounded, 15-9-40. Released from R.A.F., 11-45, as Squadron Leader.		British
McGRATH John Keswick Ulick Blake	Plt. Off.	Pilot	601	On 601 Sqn., 1-7-40. Awarded D.F.C.(27-8-40). ✤ 2 Bf 109s, 8-8-40; ✤ 2 Bf 110s, 11-8-40; ✤ 1 Ju 88 and 1 Bf 109, 13-8-40. Released from R.A.F., 1946, as a Squadron Leader.		British
McGREGOR Alan James	Plt. Off.	Pilot	504	On 504 Sqn., 1-7-40. Awarded D.S.O.(19-10-45). Retired from R.A.F., 23-11-76, as a Wing Commander.		British
MacGREGOR Alexander Noel	Sgt.	Pilot	266-19	Joined 266 Sqn., 14-9-40. Posted to 19 Sqn., 27-9-40. Commissioned, 8-10-41. Released from R.A.F., 1945, as a Flight Lieutenant.		British
McGREGOR Gordon Roy	Flt. Lt.	Pilot	1(Canadian)	With 1(Canadian) Sqn., 20-6-40, on arrival in U.K. Awarded O.B.E.(1-1-43), D.F.C.(25-10-40). ✤ 1 Do 17, 26-8-40; ✤ 1 He 111, 11-9-40; ✤ 1 Bf 109, 30-9-40; ✤ 1 Bf 109, 5-10-40. Released from R.C.A.F., 27-11-45, as Wing Commander.	✝ Died since Battle (8-3-71)	Canadian
McGREGOR Hector Douglas	Sqn. Ldr.	Pilot	213	In command of 213 Sqn., 1-7-40. ✤ 1 Ju 88, 11-8-40; ✤ 1 Bf 110, 12-8-40. Retired from R.A.F., 27-9-64, as Air Marshal Sir Hector McGregor, K.C.B., C.B.E., D.S.O.	✝ Died since Battle (11-4-73)	New Zealander
McGREGOR Peter Reginald	Plt. Off.	Pilot	46	On 46 Sqn., 1-7-40. Promoted Fg. Off., 3-9-40. Wounded, 11-9-40. Released from R.A.F., 15-12-46, as a Squadron Leader.		British
McGUGAN Robert	Sgt.	Aircrew	141	Defiant gunner. On 141 Sqn. Commissioned, 5-1-42. Retired from R.A.F., 17-5-69, as a Squadron Leader.		British
MACHACEK Jiri	Plt. Off.	Pilot	310-145	Joined 316 (Czech) Sqn., 6-8-40. Posted to 145 Sqn., 11-9-40. Wounded, 15-10-40.	✝ Killed since Battle (8-7-41)	Czech
McHARDY Donald Ballantine Hardy	Plt. Off.	Pilot	229	On 229 Sqn., 1-7-40. Promoted Fg. Off., 3-9-40. ✤ 1 He 111, 27-9-40. Shot down, 26-10-40, and taken prisoner by the Germans. Released from the R.A.F., 1946, as a Flight Lieutenant.	✝ Died since Battle (1967)	British
McHARDY Edric Hartgill	Plt. Off.	Pilot	248	On 248 Sqn., 1-7-40. Flew reconnaissance sorties over Norwegian coast during the Battle of Britain. Awarded D.S.O.(22-8-44), D.F.C.✻ (10-3-41 and 15-6-42). Retired from R.A.F., 7-5-58, as a Squadron Leader.		New Zealander
MACHIN William Howard	Sgt.	Aircrew	264	Defiant gunner. Joined 264 Sqn., 22-8-40.	✝ Killed in Action (24-8-40)	British
MACIEJOWSKI Michal	Sgt.	Pilot	249	Joined 249 Sqn., 10-40. Awarded D.F.M.(30-10-41). Commissioned, 1-6-42. Awarded D.F.C.(15-11-42). Shot down and made prisoner, 9-8-43. Released from Polish Air Force, 1947, as a Flight Lieutenant. Changed name to MANSON.		Polish
McINNES Archibald	Plt. Off.	Pilot	601-238	Joined 601 Sqn., 17-9-40. Posted to 238 Sqn., 8-10-40. Released from the R.A.F., 1946, as a Flight Lieutenant.		British
MACINSKI Janusz	Plt. Off.	Pilot	111	Joined 111 Sqn., 31-8-40.	✝ Killed in Action (3-9-40)	Polish
McINTOSH Peter Roy Charles	Sgt.	Pilot	151-605	Joined 151 Sqn., 7-7-40. Posted to 605 Sqn., 13-9-40.	✝ Killed in Action (12-10-40)	British
McINTYRE Athol Gordon	Plt. Off.	Pilot	111	Joined 111 Sqn., mid-7-40. ✤ 1 Do 17 (shared), 13-8-40. Slightly wounded, 15-8-40. Awarded A.F.C.(1-1-58). Retired from R.A.F., 30-1-59, as Sqn. Ldr.		New Zealander
McKAY Donald Alistair Stewart	Sgt.	Pilot	501-421 Flt.	On 501 Sqn., 1-7-40. Posted to 421 Flt., 22-10-40. Awarded D.F.M.✻ (7-1-41 and 18-3-41). Commissioned, 7-10-41. ✤ 2 Ju 87s, 15-8-40; ✤ 1 Do 17, 12-10-40. Slightly wounded, 18-8-40. Released from the R.A.F., 1947, as Flight Lieutenant.	✝ Died since Battle (30-9-59)	British
MacKAY Ronald	Plt. Off.	Pilot	234	Joined 234 Sqn., 9-9-40. Seriously injured, 25-9-40. Released from the R.A.F., 1-46, as a Flight Lieutenant.		British
McKELLAR Archibald Ashmore	Flt. Lt.	Pilot	605	On 605 Sqn., 1-7-40. Awarded D.S.O.(26-11-40), D.F.C.✻ (13-9-40 and 8-10-40). ✤ 3 He 111s, 15-8-40; ✤ 3 He 111s and 1 Bf 109, 9-9-40; ✤ 1 He 111 (shared), 11-9-40; ✤ 2 Bf 109s and 1 Do 17; ✤ 1 He 111, 16-9-40; ✤ 5 Bf 109s, 7-10-40; ✤ 1 Bf 109, 20-10-40; ✤ 1 Bf 109, 26-10-40; ✤ 1 Bf 109, 27-10-40.	✝ Killed since Battle (1-11-40)	British
MACKENZIE Donald Carr	Plt. Off.	Pilot	56	Joined 56 Sqn., 5-9-40. Awarded D.F.C.(20-7-43). Transferred to Bomber Command.	✝ Killed since Battle (12-6-43)	New Zealander
MACKENZIE John Noble	Plt. Off.	Pilot	41	On 41 Sqn., 1-7-40. Promoted Fg. Off., 3-9-40. Awarded D.F.C.(15-11-40). ✤ 1 Ju 88, 15-8-40; ✤ 1 Bf 109, 6-9-40; ✤ 1 He 111, 11-9-40; ✤ 1 Bf 109, 5-10-40; ✤ 1 Bf 109, 30-10-40. Retired from R.A.F., 18-12-57, as a Squadron Leader.		New Zealander
McKENZIE John Woffenden	Plt. Off.	Pilot	111	On 111 Sqn., 1-7-40.	✝ Killed in Action (11-8-40)	British
MACKENZIE Kenneth William	Sgt.	Pilot	43-501	Commissioned, 24-8-40. Joined 43 Sqn., 21-9-40. Posted to 501 Sqn., 29-9-40. Awarded D.F.C.(25-10-40), A.F.C.(1-1-53). ✤ 1 Ju 88 (shared), 4-10-40; ✤ 1 Bf 109, 5-10-40; ✤ 1 Bf 109 (solo) and 1 Bf 109 (shared), 7-10-40; ✤ 1 Bf 109 (solo) and 1 Bf 109 (shared), 25-10-40; ✤ 1 Bf 109, 27-10-40; ✤ 1 Bf 109, 29-10-40; ✤ 1 Bf 109, 30-10-40. Retired from the R.A.F., 1-7-67, as a Wing Commander.		British
McKIE Ernest John	Sgt.	Aircrew	248	Joined 248 Sqn., 4-9-40. Flew reconnaissance sorties over the Norwegian coast during the Battle of Britain. Commissioned, 8-4-42. Released from the R.A.F., 1945, as a Flight Lieutenant.	✝ Died since Battle (1981)	British
MacKINNON Adam McLeod	Lieut.	Pilot	804	Fleet Air Arm. On 804 Sqn., 1-7-40. Retired from Royal Navy, 1958, as Lieutenant Commander.		British
MacKINNON Donald Duncan	Sgt.	Aircrew	236	On 236 Sqn., 1-7-40. Killed during reconnaissance sortie over Le Havre.	✝ Killed in Action (18-7-40)	British
McKNIGHT William Lidstone	Plt. Off.	Pilot	242	On 242 Sqn., 1-7-40. Awarded D.F.C.✻ (4-6-40 and 8-10-40). ✤ 3 Bf 110s, 30-8-40; ✤ 2 Bf 109s, 9-9-40; ✤ 1 Do 17 (solo) and 1 Ju 88 (shared), 18-9-40.	✝ Killed since Battle (12-1-41)	Canadian
MacLACHLAN Alan Moncrieff	Flt. Lt.	Pilot	92	Commanded 92 Sqn., 26-9-40 until 25-10-40. Released from the R.A.F., 1945, as a Wing Commander.		British
MacLACHLAN James Archibald Findlay	Fg. Off.	Pilot	73-145	On 73 Sqn., 1-7-40. Posted to 145 Sqn., 20-8-40. Promoted Flt. Lt., 1-10-40. Awarded D.S.O.(29-5-42), D.F.C.✻✻ (16-7-40, 11-2-41 and 30-7-43). Shot down and taken prisoner by Germans, 18-7-43; died in German hospital.	✝ Died since Battle (31-7-43)	British
MacLACHLAN James Robert	Sqn. Ldr.	Pilot	46	In command of 46 Sqn., 1-7-40. Posted away, 6-10-40. Retired from the R.A.F., 1-9-56, as a Group Captain.		British
MacLAREN Archibald Colin	Plt. Off.	Pilot	604	On 604 Sqn., 1-7-40. Released from R.A.F., 1946, as a Flight Lieutenant.	✝ Died since Battle (21-3-71)	British
McLAUGHLIN John William	Sgt.	Pilot	238	Joined 238 Sqn., 9-40. Severely wounded, 5-10-40. Commissioned, 22-4-43. Released from the R.A.F., 1946, as a Flight Lieutenant.		British
MacLEAN Charles Hector	Fg. Off.	Pilot	602	On 602 Sqn., 1-7-40. Promoted Flt. Lt., 3-9-40. ✤ 1 Ju 88 (shared), 7-7-40. Severely wounded, 26-8-40. Released from R.A.F., 1945, as Wing Commander.		British

Name	Rank	Role	Sqn.	Service details	Fate	Nationality
MacLEOD George Sutherland Murray	Sgt.	Aircrew	235	Joined 235 Sqn., 26-9-40.	✝ Killed since Battle (23-3-41)	British
McLURE Andrew Crawford Rankin	Plt. Off.	Pilot	87	On 87 Sqn., 1-7-40. ✠ 1 Bf 109, 11-8-40; ✠ 1 Bf 110, 30-9-40.	✝ Killed since Battle (20-7-42)	British
McMAHON John Reginald	Sgt.	Aircrew	235	On 235 Sqn., 1-7-40. Commissioned, 27-6-42. Released from R.A.F., 1946, as a Flight Lieutenant.		British
McMULLEN Desmond Annesley Peter	Fg. Off.	Pilot	54-222	On 54 Sqn., 1-7-40. Posted to 222 Sqn., 11-9-40. Awarded D.F.C.✱✱ (1-10-40, 7-3-41 and 12-12-41). ✠ 1 Bf 109, 24-7-40; ✠ 1 Bf 109, 16-8-40; ✠ 1 Bf 109, 24-8-40; ✠ 1 Bf 109, 26-8-40; ✠ 1 Do 17 (shared), 3-8-40; ✠ 1 Do 215 (shared), 2-9-40; ✠ 1 Bf 109, 14-9-40; ✠ 1 Bf 109, 15-9-40; ✠ 1 Bf 109 (shared), 15-10-40; ✠ 1 Bf 109, 17-10-40; ✠ 1 Bf 110 (shared), 20-10-40; ✠ 1 Bf 109, 25-10-40; ✠ 1 Bf 109, 28-10-40. Retired from R.A.F., 16-12-57, retaining the rank of Wing Commander.	✝ Died since Battle (1-7-85)	British
McNAB Ernest Archibald	Sqn. Ldr.	Pilot	1(Canadian)	In command of 1 Canadian) Sqn., on arrival in U.K., 20-6-40. Made O.B.E.(1946) and awarded D.F.C.(22-10-40). ✠ 1 Do 17, 15-8-40 (flying with 111 Sqn.); ✠ 1 Do 17, 26-8-40; ✠ 1 He 111, 15-9-40. ✠ 1 Bf 110 (solo) and 1 Ju 88 (shared), 27-9-40. Retired from the R.C.A.F., 10-57, as Group Captain.	✝ Died since Battle (10-1-77)	Canadian
McNAIR Robin John	Sgt.	Pilot	3-249	Joined 3 Sqn., 28-7-40. Posted to 249 Sqn., 27-9-40. Commissioned, 26-11-41. Awarded D.F.C.✱ (22-9-42 and 26-9-44). Released from the R.A.F., 1-46, as a Squadron Leader.		British
MacNAMARA Brian Radley	Fg. Off.	Pilot	603	Joined 603 Sqn., 1-9-40. Appointed C.B.E. (13-6-57) and awarded D.S.O.(4-6-46). ✠ 1 He 111 (shared), 7-9-40; ✠ 1 Bf 109, 14-9-40. Retired from the R.A.F., 4-6-65, as an Air Commodore.		British
McNAY Alexander Logan	Sgt.	Pilot	73	Joined 73 Sqn., 21-7-40. ✠ 2 Ju 88s, 15-8-40; ✠ 2 Ju 88s, 16-8-40.	✝ **Killed in Action** (5-9-40)	British
MACONOCHIE Alfred Rippon Duke	Sgt.	Aircrew	235	Joined 235 Sqn., 16-7-40. Commissioned, 27-10-40. Retired from R.A.F., 2-3-60, retaining the rank of Squadron Leader.		British
MacPHAIL James Frederick John	Plt. Off.	Pilot	603	Joined 603 Sqn., 31-8-40. ✠ 1 He 111, 11-9-40; ✠ 1 Bf 109, 15-9-40. Released from R.A.F., 1945, as a Flight Lieutenant.	✝ Died since Battle (1963)	British
McPHEE James	Sgt.	Pilot	151-249	Joined 151 Sqn., 17-9-40. Posted to 249 Sqn., 29-9-40. Commissioned, 16-10-42. Awarded A.F.C.(1-1-43). Retired from R.A.F., 1-6-68, as a Flight Lieutenant.		British
MacPHERSON Robert Reid	F/Sgt.	Pilot	65	On 65 Sqn., 1-7-40. Commissioned, 27-11-40. ✠ 1 Bf 109, 12-8-40; ✠ 1 Bf 109 (shared), 14-8-40; ✠ 1 Bf 109, 20-8-40.	✝ Killed since Battle (13-10-41)	British
MacRAE Ian Nicholson	Sgt.	Aircrew	F.I.U.	No details of service traced.		British
MacRORY Harry Ian	Sgt.	Aircrew	23	Joined 23 Sqn., 5-8-40.	✝ Killed since Battle (3-1-41)	British
MADLE Sydney James	Plt. Off.	Pilot	615-605	On 615 Sqn., 1-7-40. Posted to 605 Sqn., 25-9-40. Wounded, 28-8-40. Released from R.A.F., 1947, as Flight Lieutenant.	✝ Died since Battle (31-1-84)	British
MAFFETT Gerald Hamilton	Plt. Off.	Pilot	257	Joined 257 Sqn., 7-7-40.	✝ **Killed in Action** (31-8-40)	British
MAGGS Mervyn Henry	Plt. Off.	Aircrew	264	Had served as pilot with R.F.C. in First World War. On 264 Sqn., 1-7-40. Awarded D.F.C. (9-3-43).	✝ Died since Battle (11-87)	British
MAGUIRE Harold John	Sqn. Ldr.	Pilot	229	In command of 229 Sqn., 1-7-40. Posted away, 8-9-40. Made prisoner by Japanese, 2-42. Created K.C.B.(1966; C.B., 1958); awarded D.S.O.(1-10-46), O.B.E.(2-1-50). Retired, 28-9-68, as an Air Marshal.		British
MAHONEY Timothy Joseph	Petty Off.	Pilot	804	Fleet Air Arm. On 804 Sqn., 1-7-40. Commissioned, 1-1-46. Retired from the Royal Navy, 1958, as Lieutenant Commander.	✝ Died since Battle (1-8-77)	British
MAIN Alistair David William	Sgt.	Pilot	249	On 249 Sqn., 1-7-40. ✠ 1 Ju 88 (shared), 8-7-40.	✝ **Killed in accident** (16-7-40)	British
MAIN Hedley Ronald	Sgt.	Aircrew	25	Joined 25 Sqn., 8-8-40.	✝ Killed since Battle (27-8-41)	British
MAITLAND-WALKER	Fg. Off.	Pilot	65	On 65 Sqn., 1-7-40. Promoted Flt. Lt., 3-9-40. Posted away, 19-9-40. Retired from R.A.F., 15-6-56, retaing the rank of Group Captain.	✝ Died since Battle (1969)	British
MAKINS	Sgt.	Pilot	247	On 247 Sqn., 1-7-40. No details of service traced.		British
MALAN Adolph Gysbert ("Sailor")	Fg. Off.	Pilot	74	Promoted Flt. Lt., 6-7-40. Awarded D.S.O.✱ (24-12-40 and 22-7-41); D.F.C.✱ (11-6-40 and 13-8-40). Assumed command of 74 Sqn., 8-8-40. ✠ 1 He 111 (shared), 12-7-40; ✠ 1 Bf 109, 28-7-40; ✠ 2 Bf 109s, 11-8-40; ✠ 1 Do 17, 13-8-40; ✠ 1 Ju 88, 11-9-40; ✠ 1 Bf 109, 22-10-40. Released from the R.A.F., 1946, as Group Captain.	✝ Died since Battle (17-9-63)	British South African
MALENGREAU Roger	Plt. Off.	Pilot	87	Joined 87 Sqn., 12-8-40. Released from Belgian Air Force, 1945. Appointed C.B.E.		Belgian
MALES Ernest Edward	Plt. Off.	Pilot	72	On 72 Sqn., 1-7-40. ✠ 1 Bf 109, 2-9-40; ✠ 1 Do 215 (shared), 10-9-40; ✠ 1 Bf 109, 14-9-40.	✝ **Killed in Action** (27-9-40)	British
MALINOWSKI Bronislaw	Sgt.	Pilot	43	Joined 43 Sqn., 25-10-40. Commissioned, 9-6-45. Awarded D.F.C.(25-9-45). Released from Polish Air Force, 1-47.	✝ Died since Battle (5-82)	Polish
MALINSKI Jan	Plt. Off.	Pilot	302	Joined 302 (Polish) Sqn., 20-8-40. Released from R.A.F., 1946, as Flight Lieutenant.		Polish
MALLETT Ronald Spencer	Sgt.	Aircrew	29	On 29 Sqn., 1-7-40. Commissioned 1-10-43. Awarded D.F.C.(9-6-44).	✝ Killed since Battle (28-6-44)	British
MALY Jaroslav Maria	Plt. Off.	Pilot	310	Joined 310 (Czech) Sqn., 10-7-40, on formation. ✠ 1 Bf 109, 31-8-40. Injured, 29-10-40.	✝ Died since Battle (5-6-41)	Czech
MAMEDOFF Andrew ("Andy")	Plt. Off.	Pilot	609	Joined 609 Sqn., 8-8-40. Posted away (to No. 71 Sqn.), 19-9-40.	✝ Killed since Battle (8-10-41)	American
MANGER Kenneth	Plt. Off.	Pilot	17	On 17 Sqn., 1-7-40. Awarded D.F.C.(25-6-40). ✠ 1 He 111 (shared), 9-7-40; ✠ 1 He 111 (shared), 12-7-40.	✝ **Killed in Action** (11-8-40)	British
MANN Harold John	Plt. Off.	Pilot	1	On 1 Sqn., 1-7-40. ✠ 1 Bf 109, 15-8-40. Released from R.A.F., 1950, as a Flight Lieutenant.		British
MANSEL-LEWIS John	Plt. Off.	Pilot	92	Joined 92 Sqn., 16-9-40. ✠ 1 Do 17, 27-9-40.	✝ Killed since Battle (4-4-41)	British
MANSFELD Miroslav Jan	Sgt.	Pilot	111	Joined 111 Sqn., 6-10-40. Commissioned, 9-6-41. Awarded D.S.O.(21-5-45), D.F.C.(10-7-42), A.F.C.(1-1-53). Retired from R.A.F., 30-9-58, as Squadron Leader.		Czech
MANSFIELD Bernard Martin	Sgt.	Aircrew	236	Joined 236 Sqn., late 9-40.	✝ Killed since Battle (25-2-41)	British
MANSFIELD David Ernest	Sgt.	Aircrew	236	Joined 236 Sqn., 24-8-40. Released from R.A.F., 1946, as a Flight Lieutenant.		British
MANTON Edward	Sgt.	Pilot	610	Joined 610 Sqn., 27-7-40.	✝ **Killed in Action** (29-8-40)	British
MANTON Graham Ashley Leonard	Sqn. Ldr.	Pilot	56	In command of 56 Sqn., 1-7-40. ✠ 1 Ju 87, 13-7-40; ✠ 1 Bf 110, 18-7-40; ✠ 1 Bf 109, 24-7-40. Promoted Wing Commander and posted away to command R.A.F. Manston, 9-40. Retired from R.A.F., 26-6-60, as Group Captain.		British
MARCHAND Roy Achille	Plt. Off.	Pilot	73	On 73 Sqn., 1-7-40. ✠ 1 Bf 109, 6-9-40.	✝ **Killed in Action** (15-9-40)	British
MARCINKOWSKI Mieczyslaw	Sgt.	Pilot	501	Joined 501 Sqn., 10-40.	✝ Killed since Battle (1-11-40)	Polish
MAREK Frantisek	Sgt.	Pilot	310-19	Joined 310 (Czech) Sqn., 6-8-40; attached to 19 Sqn., 29-8-40.	✝ **Killed in Action** (14-9-40)	Czech
MARKIEWICZ Antoni	Sgt.	Pilot	302	Joined 302 (Polish) Sqn., 6-8-40. Released from Polish Air Force, 11-45, as Warrant Officer.		Czech
MARLAND Rainford Gent	Sgt.	Pilot	222	Joined 222 Sqn., 1-9-40. ✠ 1 Bf 109, 7-9-40; ✠ 1 Ju 88, 11-9-40; ✠ 1 Bf 110, 14-9-40. Commissioned, 19-3-41.	✝ Killed since Battle (17-12-41)	British
MARPLES Roy	Plt. Off.	Pilot	616	On 616 Sqn., 1-7-40. ✠ 1 Ju 88 (shared), 15-8-40. Wounded, 15-8-40. Promoted Fg. Off., 3-9-40. Awarded D.F.C.✱ (17-10-41 and 5-1-43).	✝ Killed since Battle (26-4-44)	British
MARRS Eric Simcox	Plt. Off.	Pilot	152	On 152 Sqn., 1-7-40. Awarded D.F.C.(7-1-41). ✠ 1 Bf 109, 13-8-40; ✠ 1 Ju 87, 18-8-40; ✠ 1 Do 17 (shared), 22-8-40; ✠ 1 Bf 110, 25-8-40; ✠ 1 Ju 88 (shared), 17-9-40; ✠ 1 Ju 88, 27-9-40.	✝ Killed since Battle (24-7-41)	British
MARSH Alan Edward	Lieut.	Pilot	804	Royal Marine with Fleet Air Arm. On 804 Sqn., 1-7-40. Retired from Royal Marines, 30-9-53, as Captain.		British
MARSH Edward Howard	Sgt.	Pilot	152	Joined 152 Sqn., 29-9-40. Commissioned, 22-7-43. Released from R.A.F., 1945, as Flight Lieutenant.		British

MARSH   Sgt.   Pilot   238
Henry James
On 238 Sqn., 1-7-40. ✠ **1 He 111, 11-8-40; ✠ 1 Bf 110, 13-8-40.**   ✞ Killed in Action (13-8-40)   British

MARSH   Sgt.   Aircrew   236
William Charles
Joined 236 Sqn., 19-7-40. Commissioned, 26-3-42. Released from R.A.F., 1945, as a Flight Lieutenant.   British

MARSHALL   Sgt.   Pilot   73
Alfred Ernest
On 73 Sqn., 1-7-40. Slightly injured, 7-9-40. Awarded D.F.M.(6-6-41). Commissioned, 11-8-41. Awarded D.F.C.(6-10-42).   ✞ Killed since Battle (27-11-44)   British

MARSHALL   Plt. Off.   Pilot   85
James Eglington
On 85 Sqn., 1-7-40. Promoted Fg. Off., 3-9-40. Awarded D.F.C.(29-4-41). ✠ **1 He 111, 18-8-40; ✠ 1 Bf 109, 29-8-40; ✠ 1 He 111, 27-10-40.**   ✞ Killed since Battle (18-4-42)   British

MARSHALL   Plt. Off.   Pilot   232
John Victor
Joined 232 Sqn., 14-9-40. Awarded D.F.C.(18-2-44). Retired from the R.A.F., 3-9-70, as a Group Captain.   ✞ Died since Battle (24-6-84)   British

MARSHALL   Sgt.   Pilot   235
Thomas Brian
Joined 235 Sqn., 19-9-40. Commissioned, 12-7-41. Awarded D.F.C.(20-4-45). Released from R.A.F., 1945, as a Flight Lieutenant.   British

MARSHALL   Sgt.   Aircrew   219
Thomas Robson
Joined 219 Sqn., 8-40.   ✞ Killed since Battle (29-6-41)   British

MARSLAND   Plt. Off.   Pilot   245-253
Guy
On 245 Sqn., 1-7-40. Posted to 253 Sqn., 24-9-40. ✠ **1 Bf 109, 29-10-40.** Retired from R.A.F., 1-10-58, retaining the rank of Wing Commander.   ✞ Died since Battle (1983)   British

MARSTON   Plt. Off.   Pilot   56
Kenneth John
Joined 56 Sqn., 28-7-40. ✠ **1 Bf 109, 24-8-40; ✠ 2 Bf 109s, 26-8-40; ✠ 1 Bf 110, 25-9-40.** Wounded, 30-9-40.   ✞ Killed since Battle (12-12-40)   British

MARTEL   Plt. Off.   Pilot   54-603
Ludwik
Joined 54 Sqn., mid-9-40. Posted to 603 Sqn., 28-9-40. Released from the Polish Air Force, 1-47, as Flight Lieutenant.   Polish

MARTIN, A.   Sgt.   Aircrew   264
Defiant gunner. On 264 Sqn., 1-7-40. No other details traced.   British

MARTIN   Plt. Off.   Aircrew   235
Allan William
On 235 Sqn., 1-7-40. Awarded D.F.C.(7-12-43). Released from the R.A.F., 1945, as a Squadron Leader.   British

MARTIN   Fg. Off.   Pilot   257
John Claverly
Joined 257 Sqn., 17-9-40.   ✞ Killed since Battle (27-8-41)   New Zealander

MARTIN   Sub-Lieut.   Pilot   808
Richard Maurice Scott
Fleet Air Arm. On 808 Sqn., 1-7-40. Accompanied the Squadron aboard H.M.S. *Ark Royal*, 22-10-40.   ✞ Killed since Battle (27-11-40)   British

MASLEN   Sgt.   Aircrew   235
Thomas Arthur
On 235 Sqn., 1-7-40.   ✞ Killed since Battle (25-10-41)   British

MASON   Sgt.   Pilot   235
William
Joined 235 Sqn., 2-10-40.   ✞ Killed since Battle (14-2-41)   British

MASSEY   Sgt.   Aircrew   248
Kenneth
Joined 248 Sqn., 25-7-40. Commissioned, 24-1-42. Released from the R.A.F., 1946, as a Flight Lieutenant.   British

MATHER   Plt. Off.   Pilot   66
John Romney
On 66 Sqn., 1-7-40. ✠ **1 Do 17 (shared), 10-7-40; ✠ 1 He 111 (shared), 2-9-40.**   ✞ Killed in Action (27-10-40)   British

MATHERS   Sgt.   Aircrew   23-29
James W.
Joined 23 Sqn., 26-9-40. Posted to 29 Sqn., 10-40.   British

MATHESON   Fg. Off.   Pilot   222
Geoffrey Charles
On 222 Sqn., 1-7-40. Promoted Flt. Lt., 3-9-40. ✠ **1 Bf 109, 30-8-40.** Badly injured, 30-8-40.   ✞ Killed since Battle (24-8-43)   British

MATHEWS   Plt. Off.   Pilot   23
Kenneth
Joined 23 Sqn., late 8-40.   ✞ Killed since Battle (25-1-43)   British

MATTHEWS   Sgt.   Aircrew   236
Henry George
Joined 236 Sqn., 3-9-40. Awarded D.F.M.(25-11-41). Commissioned, 4-6-42. Retired from the R.A.F., 30-1-69, as Squadron Leader.   British

MATTHEWS   Fg. Off.   Pilot   54-603
Henry Key Fielding
On 54 Sqn., 1-7-40. Posted to 603 Sqn., 30-9-40. ✠ **1 He 59 (shared), 9-7-40; ✠ 1 Bf 109, 25-8-40.**   ✞ Killed in Action (7-10-40)   British

MATTHEWS   Sgt.   Pilot   64
Ian Walter
Joined 64 Sqn., 22-9-40. Commissioned, 17-7-41.   ✞ Killed since Battle (1-9-42)   British

MATTHEWS   Fg. Off.   Pilot   1
Peter Gerald Hugh
On 1 Sqn., 1-7-40. Awarded D.F.C., 13-5-41. ✠ **1 Bf 110, 16-8-40.** Retired from R.A.F., 8-5-66, as a Group Captain.   British

MAXWELL   Plt. Off.   Pilot   611-603
David Alexander
Joined 611 Sqn., 29-9-40. Posted to 603 Sqn., 10-40.   ✞ Killed since Battle (14-2-41)   British

MAXWELL   Sqn. Ldr.   Pilot   600
Hugh Lockhart
Posted to 600 Sqn., 15-9-40, to command. Awarded D.S.O.(22-11-40). Appointed C.B.E.(1-1-45). Retired from R.A.F., 10-6-56, retaining rank of Air Commodore.   British

MAXWELL   Sgt.   Aircrew   264
Walter
Defiant gunner. Joined 264 Sqn., 4-8-40.   ✞ Killed in Action (26-8-40)   British

MAYERS   Plt. Off.   Pilot   601
Howard Clive
Joined 601 Sqn., 2-8-40. Awarded D.S.O.(28-7-42), D.F.C.✠ (1-10-40 and 13-2-42). ✠ **1 Bf 109, 8-8-40; ✠ 1 Ju 88, 13-8-40; ✠ 2 Ju 87s, 16-8-40; ✠ 1 Do 17, 31-8-40; ✠ 1 Do 17, 4-9-40; ✠ 1 Bf 110, 25-9-40.**   ✞ Killed since Battle (c.20-7-42)   Australian

MAYHEW   Plt. Off.   Pilot   79
Paul Francis
Joined 79 Sqn., 8-40. Promoted Fg. Off., 26-9-40. ✠ **1 He 59 (shared), 28-8-40; ✠ 1 He 111, 30-8-40; ✠ 1 Do 17, 1-9-40.**   ✞ Killed since Battle (19-2-42)   British

MAYNE   W/Off.   Pilot   74
Ernest
Served in the R.F.C. in the First World War. On 74 Sqn., 1-7-40. Awarded A.F.C. (1-1-42). ✠ **2 Bf 110s (shared), 11-8-40.** Commissioned, 21-8-41. Retired from the R.A.F., 4-12-45, retaining the rank of Squadron Leader.   ✞ Died since Battle (24-3-78)   British

MEAKER   Plt. Off.   Pilot   249
James Reginald Bryan
On 249 Sqn., 1-7-40. ✠ **1 Bf 110, 12-8-40; ✠ 1 Bf 109, 24-8-40; ✠ 1 Do 17 and 1 Bf 110 (both shared), 2-9-40; ✠ 2 Do 17s, 15-9-40; ✠ 1 Bf 110 (shared), 27-9-40.**   ✞ Killed in Action (27-9-40)   British

MEARES   Flt. Lt.   Pilot   54
Stanley Thomas
Flew one operational sortie with 54 Sqn., 12-8-40.   ✞ Killed since Battle (15-11-41)   British

MEASURES   Fg. Off.   Pilot   74-238
William Edward Geoffrey
On 74 Sqn., 1-7-40. Posted away, 24-7-40. Joined 238 Sqn., 12-10-40. ✠ **1 He 111, 6-7-40; ✠ 1 He 111 (shared), 8-7-40.** Awarded A.F.C.(1-9-44). Retired from the R.A.F., 23-11-57, retaining the rank of Wing Commander.   British

MEDWORTH   Sgt.   Aircrew   25
John Charles Oswald
Joined 25 Sqn., late 9-40. Commissioned, 25-4-43. Released from the R.A.F., 1946, as a Flight Lieutenant.   British

MEESON   Sgt.   Pilot   56
Charles Victor
Joined 56 Sqn., late 8-40.   ✞ Killed in Accident (20-9-40)   British

MELVILL   Plt. Off.   Pilot   264
James Cosmo
Joined 264 Sqn., 1-9-40. Promoted Fg. Off., 3-10-40. Awarded A.F.C.(1-9-44). Released from the R.A.F., 1946, as a Squadron Leader.   British

MELVILLE-JACKSON   Pilot   236
George Holmes   Plt. Off.
Joined 236 Sqn., 9-7-40. Awarded D.F.C.(20-4-43). Retired from the R.A.F., 29-9-68, as a Wing Commander.   British

MENAGE   Sgt.   Aircrew   29
Thomas Nathan
Joined 29 Sqn., 9-40. Transferred to Bomber Command.   ✞ Killed since Battle (10-5-41)   British

MERCER   Sgt.   Pilot   609
Robert Turner Deighton
Joined 609 Sqn., 16-10-40.   ✞ Killed since Battle (9-5-41)   British

MERCHANT   Sgt.   Pilot   1
Hanry James
On 1 Sqn., 1-7-40. ✠ **1 He 111, 30-8-40; ✠ 1 Bf 110, 31-8-40.** Wounded, 31-8-40. Commissioned 13-8-41. Released from R.A.F., 1945, as Flight Lieutenant.   British

MEREDITH   Sgt.   Pilot   242-141
Arthur Douglas
On 242 Sqn., 1-7-40. Posted to 141 Sqn., 10-8-40. Commissioned, 12-3-41. Awarded A.F.C.(8-6-44). Released from the R.A.F., 16-10-45, as a Flight Lieutenant.   British

MERMAGEN   Sqn. Ldr.   Pilot   222-266
Herbert Waldemar ("Tubby")
In command of 222 Sqn., 1-7-40. Commanded 266 Sqn. from 12-9-40 to 17-9-40. Appointed C.B.(11-6-60), C.B.E.(1-1-45), O.B.E., 24-9-41), A.F.C.(11-7-40). Retired from the R.A.F., 14-11-60, as an Air Commodore.   British

MERRETT   Sgt.   Aircrew   235
John Charles
On 235 Sqn., 1-7-40. Commissioned, 19-8-41. Released form the R.A.F., 1946, as a Flight Lieutenant.   ✞ Died since Battle (1984)   British

MERRICK   Plt. Off.   Pilot   610
Claude
Joined 610 Sqn., 27-7-40. Slightly wounded. 24-8-40. Awarded D.F.C.(14-7-44). Released from the R.A.F., 1946, as a Wing Commander.   ✞ Killed since Battle (5-6-42)   British

MERRYWEATHER   Sgt.   Pilot   229
Sydney William
On 229 Sqn., 1-7-40. Slightly wounded, 26-9-40. Awarded D.F.M.(26-6-42).   ✞ Killed in Action (13-9-40)   British

MESNER   Sgt.   Aircrew   248
Bertram William
On 248 Sqn., 1-7-40. Flew on reconnaissance sorties over Norwegian coast during Battle of Britain.   British

METCALFE   Sgt.   Aircrew   604
Arthur Charles
Joined 604 Sqn., 10-7-40.   ✞ Killed since Battle (21-9-42)   British

METHAM   Sgt.   Pilot   253
James
On 253 Sqn., 1-7-40. Slightly wounded, 2-9-40. Commissioned, 29-10-40.   ✞ Killed since Battle (9-2-44)   British

MEYER   Sgt.   Pilot   236
Reginald Henry Rowe
Joined 236 Sqn., 20-10-40. Commissioned, 3-7-41.   ✞ Died since Battle (16-7-44)   Belgian

MICHIELS   Sgt.   Aircrew   235
Albert Charles Antoine
Joined 235 Sqn., 26-9-40. Commissioned, 9-1-43.   British

MIDDLEMISS   Sgt.   Aircrew   235
William
Joined 235 Sqn., 26-9-40. Awarded A.F.C.(1-1-46, as Warrant Officer). Served in the R.A.F. after the War.   ✞ Killed since Battle (27-8-41)   New Zealander

MIDDLETON   Plt. Off.   Pilot   266
William Arthur
Joined 266 Sqn., 26-8-40.

Name	Rank	Role	Sqn.	Notes	Status	Nationality
MIERZWA Boguslaw	Plt. Off.	Pilot	303	Joined 303 (Polish) Sqn., 21-8-40.	✠ Killed since Battle (16-4-41)	Polish
MIKSA Wlodzimierz	Plt. Off.	Pilot	303	Joined 303 (Polish) Sqn., 23-10-40. Awarded D.F.C.(26-5-45). Released from Polish Air Force, 2-46, as a Flight Lieutenant. Changed name to **PILKINGTON-MIKSA.**		Polish
MILBURN Reginald Alan	Sgt.	Pilot	601-87	Joined 601 Sqn., 10-40. Posted to 87 Sqn., 31-10-40. Assumed to have flown operational sorties with 601 Sqn.	✠ Died since Battle (19-12-83)	British
MILDREN Peter Raymond	Plt. Off.	Pilot	54-66	Joined 54 Sqn., early 10-40. Posted to 66 Sqn., 14-10-40.	✠ Killed since Battle (11-2-41)	British
MILEHAM Denys Edgar	Plt. Off.	Pilot	610-41	Joined 610 Sqn., 3-9-40. Posted to 41 Sqn., 29-9-40. ✠ 1 Bf 109, 5-10-40.	✠ Killed since Battle (15-4-42)	British
MILES Ernest Edwin	Sgt.	Aircrew	236	Joined 236 Sqn., c.28-9-40. No records of operations traced.		British
MILES Stanley Frederick	Sgt.	Aircrew	23	On 23 Sqn., 1-7-40. Commissioned, 25-11-42. Released from R.A.F., 5-50, as Flight Lieutenant.		British
MILEY Miles John	Fg. Off.	Pilot	25	On 25 Sqn., 1-7-40. Killed in Beaufighter.	✠ **Killed in Action** (15-9-40)	British
MILLAR William Bruce MacDougal	Fg. Off.	Pilot	1(Canadian)	Joined 1(Canadian) Sqn., 30-8-40. Wounded, 9-9-40. Retired from R.C.A.F., 10-7-64, as Wing Commander.	✠ Died since Battle (8-1-69)	Canadian
MILLARD Jocelyn George Power	Plt. Off.	Pilot	1-242	Joined 1 Sqn., early 10-40. Posted to 242 Sqn., 17-10-40. Released from R.A.F., 1947, as Squadron Leader.		British
MILLER Alfred John	Sgt.	Aircrew	23	Joined 23 Sqn., 4-10-40. No record of operations traced.		British
MILLER Anthony Garforth	Flt. Lt.	Pilot	F.I.U.-17	On F.I.U., 1-7-40. Assumed command of 17 Sqn., 29-8-40. Promoted Sqn. Ldr., 1-9-40. Awarded D.F.C.(3-3-42). Released from R.A.F., 8-46, as Group Captain.		British
MILLER Arthur Charles	Sgt.	Aircrew	604	On 604 Sqn., 1-7-40. Commissioned, 21-3-42. Awarded D.F.C.(26-2-43). Released from R.A.F., 1945, as Squadron Leader.		British
MILLER Robert	Flt. Lt.	Pilot	3	Joined 3 Sqn., mid-8-40.	✠ Killed since Battle (24-4-42)	British
MILLER Rogers Freeman Garland	Plt. Off.	Pilot	609	On 609 Sqn., 1-7-40. ✠ 1 Ju 87, 13-8-40.	✠ **Killed in Action** (27-9-40)	British
MILLER Thomas Henry	Sgt.	Aircrew	25	Joined 25 Sqn., early 10-40.	✠ Killed since Battle (17-12-42)	British
MILLINGTON William Henry	Plt. Off.	Pilot	79-249	On 79 Sqn., 1-7-40. Posted to 249 Sqn., 19-9-40. ✠ 1 Bf 109, 9-7-40; ✠ 3 He 111s, 15-8-40; ✠ 1 He 111, 30-8-40; ✠ 2 Bf 109s and 1 Bf 109, 31-8-40; ✠ 1 Ju 88 (solo) and 1 Ju 88 (shared), 27-9-40; ✠ 1 Ju 88 (shared), 28-10-40. Wounded, 31-8-40. Awarded D.F.C.(1-10-40).	✠ **Killed in Action** (30-10-40)	Australian
MILLIST Kenneth Milton	Plt. Off.	Pilot	615-73	Joined 615 Sqn., 3-9-40. Posted to 73 Sqn., 18-9-40. Awarded D.F.C.(4-11-41).	✠ Killed since Battle (7-4-41)	British
MILLS Jack Baillie	Sgt.	Aircrew	23	Joined 23 Sqn., 1-10-40. No record of operations traced.		British
MILLS Jack Percival ("Dusty")	Sgt.	Pilot	43-249	Joined 43 Sqn., early 7-40. Posted to 249 Sqn., 13-9-40. ✠ 1 Bf 109, 13-8-40; ✠ 1 Ju 87, 18-8-40; ✠ 1 Bf 109, 6-9-40; ✠ 1 Ju 88 (shared), 27-9-40. Commissioned, 24-4-41. Awarded D.F.C.(7-4-44). Released from R.A.F., 1947, as Squadron Leader.		British
MILLS Randolph Stuart	Flt. Lt.	Pilot	263-87	On 263 Sqn., 1-7-40. Posted to 87 Sqn., 24-8-40, to command (promoted Sqn. Ldr., 1-12-40). Awarded D.F.C.(10-5-40). Retired from R.A.F., 20-10-56, retaining rank of Group Captain.		British
MILNE John Archibald	Plt. Off.	Pilot	605	On 605 Sqn., 1-7-40. ✠ 1 Bf 110, 27-9-40. Slightly wounded, 22-10-40. Released from R.A.F., 7-46, as Flight Lieutenant.		Canadian
MILNE Richard Maxwell	Fg. Off.	Pilot	151	On 151 Sqn., 1-7-40. Awarded D.F.C.✧ (30-8-40 and 11-11-41).✠ 1 Bf 109, ✠ 2 Do 17s, 13-8-40; ✠ 1 Bf 109, 15-8-40; ✠ 1 He 111, 18-8-40. Shot down and made prisoner by the Germans, 14-3-43. Released by the R.A.F., 1946, as a Wing Commander.		British
¶ **MILNE**	Plt. Off.	Pilot	64	On 64 Sqn., 1-7-40.	✠ **Killed in Action** (5-7-40)	British
MILNES Ambrose Henry	Sgt.	Pilot	32	Joined 32 Sqn., late 9-40. Commissioned, 5-7-41. Retired from R.A.F., 24-4-58, as a Squadron Leader.		British
¶ **MITCHELL** Edward William	Fg. Off.	Pilot	79	On 79 Sqn., 1-7-40.	✠ **Killed in Action** (8-7-40)	British
MITCHELL George	Sgt.	Aircrew	23	Joined 23 Sqn., 7-40. Commissioned, 12-7-41. Retired from the R.A.F., 3-10-53, as a Flight Lieutenant.	✠ Died since Battle (1969)	British
MITCHELL Gordon Thomas Manners	Plt. Off.	Pilot	609	On 609 Sqn., 1-7-40.	✠ **Killed in Action** (11-7-40)	British
MITCHELL Harry Thorne	Plt. Off.	Pilot	87	On 87 Sqn., 1-7-40. ✠ 1 Ju 87, 14-8-40; ✠ 1 Bf 110, 15-8-40; ✠ 1 Bf 109, 25-8-40. Awarded, D.F.C.(11-2-41). Released from R.A.F., 1946, as a Squadron Leader.		Canadian
MITCHELL Henry Maynard	Flt. Lt.	Pilot	25	Promoted Sqn. Ldr., as assumed command of 25 Sqn., 25-9-40. Awarded D.F.C. (22-10-40). Released from the R.A.F., 1946, as a Wing Commander.		British
MITCHELL Herbert Robert	Sgt.	Pilot	3	Joined 3 Sqn., 4-10-40. Commissioned, 5-1-42.	✠ Killed since Battle (12-5-42)	New Zealander
MITCHELL Lancelot Robert George	Fg. Off.	Pilot	257	On 257 Sqn., 1-7-40. ✠ 1 Do 17 (shared), 19-7-40; ✠ 1 Bf 110, 31-8-40.	✠ **Killed in Action** (7-9-40)	British
MITCHELL Peter	Sgt.	Pilot	65	Joined 65 Sqn., 19-8-40.	✠ Killed since Battle (26-7-42)	British
MITCHELL Phillip Henry Gurrey	Plt. Off.	Pilot	266	On 266 Sqn., 1-7-40. Released from R.A.F., 1948, as a Flight Lieutenant.		British
MITCHELL Richard Ronald	Sgt.	Pilot	229	On 229 Sqn., 1-7-40. Commissioned, 29-11-40. Awarded D.F.C.(19-9-44), M.B.E. (1-1-46). Retired from R.A.F., 24-4-61, as a Wing Commander.		British
MOBERLEY George Edward	Fg. Off.	Pilot	616	On 616 Sqn., 1-7-40. ✠ 1 Do 17 (shared), 3-7-40.	✠ **Killed in Action** (26-8-40)	British
MOLSON Hartland de Montarville	Fg. Off.	Pilot	1(Canadian)	With 1(Canadian) Sqn., 20-6-40, on arrival in U.K. ✠ 1 He 111, 11-9-40. Wounded, 5-10-40. Retired from R.C.A.F., 1945, as Group Captain. Made O.B.E. (1-1-46).		Canadian
MONK Denis Aubrey	Sgt.	Aircrew	236	Joined 236 Sqn., early 9-40. Commissioned, 9-2-43. Released from R.A.F., 1946, as a Flight Lieutenant.		British
MONK Ernest William John	Plt. Off.	Pilot	25	Joined 25 Sqn., 12-8-40.	✠ Killed since Battle (21-11-40)	British
MONTAGU George Wroughton	Sqn. Ldr.	Pilot	236	Assumed command of 236 Sqn., 15-8-40.	✠ Killed since Battle (12-12-40)	British
MONTAGU-SMITH Arthur ("Monty")	Flt. Lt.	Pilot	264	Joined 264 Sqn., 11-9-40. Retired from R.A.F., 1-1-61, as Group Captain.		British
MONTGOMERY Cecil Robert	Plt. Off.	Pilot	615	On 615 Sqn., 1-7-40.	✠ **Killed in Action** (14-8-40)	British
MONTGOMERY Herbert Francis	Sgt.	Pilot	43	Joined 43 Sqn., 3-8-40.	✠ **Killed in Action** (14-8-40)	British
MOODY Dennis George	Sgt.	Aircrew	604	On 604 Sqn., 1-7-40. Commissioned, 20-3-42. Released from the R.A.F., 1945, as a Flight Lieutenant.		British
MOODY Henry Wollaston	Plt. Off.	Pilot	602	On 602 Sqn., 1-7-40. Wounded, 19-8-40. ✠ 1 Ju 87, 18-8-40; ✠ 1 Do 17, 4-9-40.	✠ **Killed in Action** (7-9-40)	British
MOORE Arthur Robert	Sgt.	Pilot	615-245-3	Joined 245 Sqn., 28-9-40, from 615 Sqn. Posted to 3 Sqn., 10-40. Commissioned, 18-7-42. Awarded D.F.C.(21-7-44). Released from the R.A.F., 1946, as a Squadron Leader.	✠ Died since Battle (1989)	British
MOORE Peter John	Sgt.	Pilot	253	Joined 253 Sqn., 10-40. Commissioned, 8-11-41.	✠ Killed since Battle (3-6-42)	British
MOORE William Roy	Plt. Off.	Aircrew	264	Defiant gunner. Joined 264 Sqn., mid-7-40. Released from the R.A.F., 1945, as a Flight Lieutenant.	✠ Died since Battle (1984)	British
MOORE William Storey	Fg. Off.	Pilot	236	On 236 Sqn., 1-7-40.	✠ Killed since Battle (24-12-43)	British
MORE James Winter Carmichael	Sqn. Ldr.	Pilot	73	In command of 73 Sqn., 1-7-40. Awarded D.F.C.(30-7-40); made O.B.E.(1-1-42). Posted away, 8-8-40. (Was a Group Captain at the time of his death).	✠ Killed since Battle (12-9-44)	British

Name	Rank	Role	Sqn.	Notes	Fate	Nationality
MOREWOOD, Roger Edward Guy	Fg. Off.	Pilot	248	On 248 Sqn., 1-7-40. Promoted Flt. Lt., 3-9-40. Retired from R.A.F., 9-57, as a Wing Commander.		British
MORFILL, Percy Frederick ("Splash")	F/Sgt.	Pilot	501	On 501 Sqn., 1-7-40. Awarded D.F.M.(22-10-40). ✠ 1 Bf 109, 29-7-40; ✠ 1 Bf 109, 24-8-40; ✠ 1 He 111 (shared), 11-9-40; ✠ 1 Do 17, 15-9-40. Commissioned, 15-1-42. Retired from R.A.F., 4-2-58, as a Squadron Leader.		British
MORGAN, Peter Jacques	Plt. Off.	Pilot	79-238	Joined 79 Sqn., 17-9-40. Posted to 238 Sqn., 5-10-40. Released from the R.A.F., 1946, as a Flight Lieutenant.	✠ Died since Battle (1977)	British
MORGAN, Thomas Frederick Dalton	Flt. Lt.	Pilot	43	On 43 Sqn., 1-7-40. ✠ 1 He 111 (shared), 12-7-40; ✠ 1 Bf 109, 21-7-40; ✠ 1 Bf 109 and 1 Ju 87, 8-8-40; ✠ 1 He 111, 13-8-40; ✠ 2 Bf 110s, 4-9-40; ✠ 1 Bf 109, 6-9-40. Wounded, 13-8-40 and 6-9-40. Awarded D.F.C. (6-9-40). Awarded D.S.O.(25-5-43), O.B.E.(14-6-45). Retired from the R.A.F., 4-11-52, as a Wing Commander.		British
MORGAN-GRAY, Hugh	Fg. Off.	Pilot	46	On 46 Sqn., 1-7-40. Wounded, 3-9-40.	✠ Killed since Battle (22-2-41)	British
MORRIS, Edward James ("Teddy")	Fg. Off.	Pilot	79	On 79 Sqn., 1-7-40. ✠ 1 He 59 (shared), 28-8-40; ✠ 1 He 111, 30-8-40; Wounded, 31-8-40. Awarded D.S.O.(7-4-42), D.F.C. (1-1-66), C.B.E.(1-1-59). Retired from the R.A.F., 16-7-68, as Air Commodore.		British
MORRIS, Geoffrey Edward	Plt. Off.	Aircrew	F.I.U.	On F.I.U., 1-7-40. Participated in destruction of Do 17, 22/23-7-40. Retired from the R.A.F., 29-5-70, as a Wing Commander.		British
MORRIS, John	Plt. Off.	Pilot	248	Joined 248 Sqn., late 10-40. Released from R.A.F., 1946, as a Squadron Leader.		British
MORRISON, Joseph Pearson	Sgt.	Pilot	43-46	Joined 46 Sqn., 17-9-40, from 43 Sqn.	✠ Killed in Action (22-10-40)	British
MORRISON, Neil	Sgt.	Pilot	54-72-74	Joined 54 Sqn., late 9-40. Posted to 72 Sqn., 4-10-40; Posted to 74 Sqn., 26-10-40.	✠ Killed since Battle (22-4-41)	British
MORROGH-RYAN, Oliver Bertram	Plt. Off.	Pilot	41	On 41 Sqn., 1-7-40. Promoted Fg. Off., 3-9-40. ✠ 1 Bf 109, 5-9-40.	✠ Killed since Battle (26-7-41)	British
MORTIMER, Percival Alexander	Plt. Off.	Pilot	85-257	Joined 85 Sqn., 4-9-40. Posted to 257 Sqn., 11-9-40. ✠ 1 Do 17 and 1 He 111 (both shared), 15-9-40. (✠ 1 Fiat BR.20, 11-11-40).	✠ Killed since Battle (7-11-42)	British
MORTIMER-ROSE, Edward Brian ("Mortie")	Plt. Off.	Pilot	234	On 234 Sqn., 1-7-40. ✠ 1 Bf 110, 15-8-40; ✠ 1 Bf 109, 18-8-40; ✠ 1 Bf 109, 26-8-40; ✠ 1 Ju 88 (shared), 9-10-40. Awarded D.F.C.✻ (6-6-41 and 12-12-41).	✠ Killed since Battle (28-1-43)	British
MORTON, James Storrs ("Black")	Plt. Off.	Pilot	603	On 603 Sqn., 1-7-40. Promoted Fg. Off., 3-9-40. ✠ 1 He 111 (shared), 15-7-40; ✠ 1 He 111 (shared), 16-7-40; ✠ 1 Bf 109, 28-8-40; ✠ 1 Do 17, 31-8-40; ✠ 1 Bf 109, 1-9-40; ✠ 1 Bf 109 (solo) and 1 Bf 109 (shared), 30-9-40. Wounded, 5-10-40. Awarded D.F.C.✻ (10-40 and 30-11-43). Released from R.A.F., 1946, as a Wing Commander. Commanded 603 Sqn., R.Aux.A.F., 11-46 until 3-51.	✠ Died since Battle (1982)	British
MOSS, Raymond Christopher	Sgt.	Aircrew	29	Joined 29 Sqn., 1-7-40. Awarded D.F.C.(19-2-43, as Warrant Officer). Commissioned, 29-3-44. Released from R.A.F., 1946, as a Flight Lieutenant.		British
MOSS, William James March	Sub-Lieut.	Pilot	213	Fleet Air Arm. Joined 213 Sqn., 1-7-40.	✠ Killed in Action (27-8-40)	British
MOTT, Walter Henry	Sgt.	Aircrew	141	Defiant gunner. Joined 141 Sqn., 21-8-40. Commissioned, 14-12-42. Retired from the R.A.F., 30-5-64, as a Squadron Leader.		British
MOTTRAM, Roy	Plt. Off.	Pilot	92	On 92 Sqn., 1-7-40. ✠ 1 He 111, 15-9-40. ✠ 1 Bf 110, 20-10-40. Slightly wounded, 18-9-40.	✠ Killed since Battle (31-8-41)	British
MOUCHOTTE, Rene Gaston Octave Jean	Adj	Pilot	245-615	Joined 245 Sqn., 11-9-40. Posted to 615 Sqn., 18-9-40. Awarded D.F.C.(1-9-42)	✠ Killed since Battle (27-8-43)	French
MOULD, Edward Anthony	Sgt.	Pilot	74	On 74 Sqn., 1-7-40. ✠ 1 Bf 109, 8-7-40. Wounded, 28-7-40. Commissioned, 22-5-41.	✠ Killed since Battle (20-1-43)	British
MOULTON, Eric Walter	Sgt.	Aircrew	600	Joined 600 Sqn., 20-7-40. Record of operations not traced.		British
MOUNSDON, Maurice Hewlett	Plt. Off.	Pilot	56	On 56 Sqn., 1-7-40. ✠ 1 Ju 87, 25-7-40; ✠ 1 Bf 110, 13-8-40; ✠ 1 Bf 110 (shared), 18-8-40; ✠ 1 Bf 109, 26-8-40. Wounded, 31-8-40. Released from R.A.F., 22-2-46, as a Flight Lieutenant.		British
MOUNT, Christopher John ("Micky")	Flt. Lt.	Pilot	602	On 602 Sqn., 1-7-40. ✠ 1 Bf 109, 29-10-40. Appointed C.B.E.(2-1-56); awarded D.S.O. (1-10-43), D.F.C.(26-11-40). Retired from R.A.F., 26-12-66, as an Air Commodore.		British
MOWAT, Noel Joseph	Plt. Off.	Pilot	245	Promoted Fg. Off., 18-7-40. On 245 Sqn., 1-7-40. Awarded D.S.O.(16-3-42).	✠ Killed since Battle (7-11-46)	New Zealander
MOWAT, Robert Innes	Sgt.	Aircrew	248	Joined 248 Sqn., 9-10-40. Released from the R.A.F., 30-10-45, as a Warrant Officer.		British
MOYNHAM, Harold Frederick John	Sgt.	Aircrew	248	Joined 248 Sqn., late 7-40. Flew on reconnaissance sorties over Norwegian coasts during the Battle of Britain.	✠ Killed since Battle (3-11-40)	British
MRAZEK, Karel	Plt. Off.	Pilot	43-46	Joined 43 Sqn., 10-9-40. Posted to 46 Sqn., 17-9-40. Awarded D.S.O., D.F.C. released from the R.A.F., 1946, as a Group Captain. Returned to Czechoslovakia.		Czech
MUCHOWSKI, Konrad Antoni	Sgt.	Pilot	85-501	Joined 85 Sqn., 10-9-40. Posted to 501 Sqn., 23-10-40. Commissioned, 15-4-43. Released from the Polish Air Force, 11-46, as a Flight Lieutenant.	✠ Died since Battle (1988)	Polish
MUDIE, Michael Robert	Plt. Off.	Pilot	615	On 615 Sqn., 1-7-40. (Died of wounds sustained on 14-7-40)	✠ Died of Wounds (15-7-40)	British
MUDRY, Wlodzimierz	Sgt.	Pilot	79	Joined 79 Sqn., 11-9-40. Released from the Polish Air Force, 1-46, and joined the R.A.F. as a Master Pilot, 1948.		Polish
MUIRHEAD, Ian James	Plt. Off.	Pilot	605	On 605 Sqn., 1-7-40. Awarded D.F.C.(28-6-40). ✠ 1 He 111, 15-8-40; ✠ 1 Do 17 (shared), 24-8-40.	✠ Killed in Action (15-10-40)	British
MÜMLER, Mieczyslaw	Sqn. Ldr.	Pilot	302	Appointed joint C.O. of 302 (Polish) Sqn., 23-7-40. ✠ 1 Do 17, 18-9-40. Appointed C.B.E.(9-2-45). Released from the Polish Air Force, 1946, as Gp. Capt.	✠ Died since Battle (1985)	Polish
MUNGO-PARK, John Colin	Fg. Off.	Pilot	74	On 74 Sqn., 1-7-40. ✠ 1 Do 17, 10-7-40; ✠ 1 Bf 109 and 1 Bf 110, 11-8-40; ✠ 1 He 111, 11-9-40; ✠ 1 Bf 110, 14-9-40; ✠ 1 Bf 109, 20-10-40; ✠ 1 Bf 109 (shared), 22-10-40; ✠ 2 Bf 109s, 29-10-40. Awarded D.F.C.(11-7-41).	✠ Killed since Battle (27-6-41)	British
MUNN, Wellesley Spencer	F/Sgt.	Pilot	29	On 29 Sqn., 1-7-40. Awarded D.F.M.(17-1-41). Commissioned, 22-1-41. Retired from R.A.F., 29-1-60, as Squadron Leader.	✠ Died since Battle (1982)	British
MURCH, Leonard Charles	Plt. Off.	Pilot	253	On 253 Sqn., 1-7-40. ✠ 1 He 111, 7-9-40; ✠ 1 Do 17 (shared), 6-10-40. Wounded, 11-10-40.	✠ Killed since Battle (16-9-43)	British
MURLAND, William John	L.A.C.	Aircrew	264	Defiant gunner. Joined 264 Sqn., 7-40. Posted away, 27-7-40. Promoted Sergeant. Returned to New Zealand, 5-44, and transferred to Reserve on medical grounds.	✠ Died since Battle (15-11-78)	New Zealander
MURRAY, Alan Duncan ("Ginger")	Flt. Lt.	Pilot	46-501-73	Joined 46 Sqn., 7-40. Attached to 501 Sqn., 9-40. Promoted Sqn. Ldr., 1-9-40. Posted to 73 Sqn., 21-9-40, to command. Awarded D.F.C.(28-3-41). Retired from the R.A.F., 15-1-58, retaining the rank of Group Captain.		British
MURRAY, James	Sgt.	Pilot	610-74	Joined 610 Sqn., 16-9-40. Posted to 74 Sqn.	✠ Killed since Battle (3-4-43)	British
MURRAY, Patrick Hatton	Sgt.	Aircrew	23	Joined 23 Sqn., 9-7-40. Transferred to Bomber Command.	✠ Killed since Battle (8-12-42)	British
MURRAY, Thomas Burnley	Plt. Off.	Pilot	616	On 616 Sqn., 1-7-40. ✠ 2 Ju 88s, 15-8-40. Awarded A.F.C.(13-6-46). Released from the R.A.F., 1946, as a Flight Lieutenant.	✠ Died since Battle (1984)	British
NAISH, Kenneth Edward ("Skipper")	Sgt.	Pilot	235	On 235 Sqn., 1-7-40. Commissioned, 19-2-41. Awarded D.F.C., 19-5-44. Released from the R.A.F., 1945, as Squadron Leader, but re-joined in 1946 as Flying Officer.		British
NARUCKI, Aleksander Ryszard	Plt. Off.	Pilot	607	Joined 607 Sqn., 9-10-40.	✠ Killed since Battle (11-5-41)	Polish
NAUGHTIN, Harold Thomas	Sgt.	Aircrew	235	Joined 235 Sqn., 5-8-40.	✠ Killed since Battle (28-5-41)	British
NEER, N.	Sgt.	Aircrew	29	Joined 29 Sqn., 7-40.		British
NEIL, Thomas Francis ("Ginger")	Plt. Off.	Pilot	249	On 249 Sqn., 1-7-40. ✠ 1 Bf 109, 7-9-40; ✠ 1 He 111, 11-9-40; ✠ 2 Do 17s, 15-9-40; ✠ 1 Bf 110, 1 Ju 88 (solo) and 1 Ju 88 (shared); ✠ 1 Bf 109, 25-10-40; ✠ 1 Ju 88 (shared), 28-10-40. Awarded D.F.C.✻ (8-10-40 and 26-11-40), A.F.C.(2-1-56). Retired from the R.A.F., 1964, as a Wing Commander.		British
NELSON, Dick	F/Sgt.	Pilot	235	On 235 Sqn., 1-7-40. Commissioned, 5-1-42. Retired from the R.A.F., 26-2-67, as a Wing Commander.	✠ Died since Battle (26-6-72)	British

Name	Rank	Role	Sqn.	Notes	Status	Nationality
NELSON William Henry	Fg. Off.	Pilot	74	Joined 74 Sqn., 20-7-40. Had been awarded D.F.C.(4-6-40). ✠ **1 Bf 109 and 1 Bf 110, 11-8-40; ✠ 1 Bf 109, 15-10-40; ✠ 1 Bf 109, 17-10-40; ✠ 1 Bf 110, 27-10-40; ✠ 1 Bf 109, 29-10-40.**	♰ Killed since Battle (1-11-40)	Canadian
NELSON-EDWARDS George Hassall ("Neddy")	Plt. Off.	Pilot	79	Joined 79 Sqn., 1-8-40.✠ **1 He 59 (shared), 28-7-40.** Promoted Fg. Off., 26-9-40. Awarded D.F.C.(26-2-43). Retired from R.A.F., 30-9-60, as Wing Commander.		British
NESBITT Arthur Deane	Fg. Off.	Pilot	1(Canadian)	With 1(Canadian) Sqn., 20-6-40, on arrival in U.K. ✠ **1 Bf 110, 4-9-40;** ✠ **1 Bf 109, 15-9-40.** Slightly wounded, 15-9-40. Awarded O.B.E.(1-1-46), D.F.C.(23-9-41). Released from the R.C.A.F., 1946, as a Wing Commander.	♰ Died since Battle (1979)	Canadian
NEVILLE William John	Sgt.	Pilot	610	Joined 610 Sqn., 27-7-40.	♰ **Killed in Action** (30-7-40)	British
NEWBERY John Charles	Fg. Off.	Pilot	609	Joined 609 Sqn., 8-7-40. Seriously injured, 25-9-40. Released from the R.A.F., 1945, as a Wing Commander.		British
NEWHAM Edward Arnold	Sgt.	Aircrew	235	Joined 235 Sqn., 23-9-40. Commissioned, 18-11-43. Released from the R.A.F., 1944, as a Flying Officer.	♰ Died since Battle (14-2-76)	British
NEWLING Michael Alan	Plt. Off.	Pilot	145	On 145 Sqn., 1-7-40. ✠ **1 He 111 (shared), 19-7-40.** Promoted Fg. Off., 23-10-40. Awarded D.F.C.(4-2-41).	♰ Killed since Battle (6-7-41)	British
NEWPORT Douglas Victor	Sgt.	Aircrew	235	On 235 Sqn., 1-7-40. No record of operations traced.		British
NEWTON Edwin Frank	Sgt.	Aircrew	29	Joined 29 Sqn., 13-9-40. No record of operations traced.		British
NEWTON Harry Snow	Sgt.	Pilot	111	On 111 Sqn., 1-7-40. ✠ **1 Do 17, 16-8-40; ✠ 1 Do 17, 18-8-40.** Awarded A.F.C.(1-9-44). Retired from R.A.F., 13-7-45, as Squadron Leader.		British
NICHOLAS John Beville Howard	Fg. Off.	Pilot	65	On 65 Sqn., 1-7-40. Retired from R.A.F., 7-49, as a Flight Lieutenant.		British
NICHOLLS Douglas Benjamin Fletcher	Sgt.	Pilot	85-242-151	Joined 151 Sqn., 9-40, after serving on 85 and 242 Sqns. ✠ **Ju 88 (shared), 30-9-40.** Awarded D.F.C.(19-5-44). Released from the R.A.F., as Flt. Lt.		British
NICHOLLS Thomas George Frank	Sgt.	Aircrew	23	Served with 23 Sqn. during the Battle of Britain.	♰ Killed since Battle (10-4-41)	British
NICHOLS Dennis Hugh	Sgt.	Pilot	56	Joined 56 Sqn., 15-9-40. Severely injured, 7-10-40. Released from R.A.F., 1946, as a Flight Lieutenant.		British
NICOLSON James Brindley	Fg. Off.	Pilot	249	On 249 Sqn., 1-7-40, as Acting Flt. Lt. Severely wounded, 16-8-40, and awarded **V.C.**(15-11-40). Awarded D.F.C.(11-8-44).	♰ Killed since Battle (2-5-45)	British
NICOLSON Peter Bethune	Sgt.	Pilot	232	Joined 232 Sqn., 17-7-40, on formation.	♰ Killed since Battle (29-5-41)	British
NIEMIEC Pawel	Plt. Off.	Pilot	17	Joined 17 Sqn., 1-9-40. Released from Polish Air Force, 12-46, as a Squadron Leader.		Polish
NIGHTINGALE Frederick George	Sgt.	Pilot	219	On 219 Sqn., 1-7-40. Commissioned, 9-10-40.	♰ Killed since Battle (17-12-40)	British
NIVEN Hugh Glen ("Nuts")	Plt. Off.	Pilot	601-602	Joined 601 Sqn., 4-9-40. Posted to 602 Sqn., 21-9-40. Invalided out of R.A.F., 12-3-42, as a Flying Officer.		Canadian
NIXON William	Sgt.	Pilot	23	Joined 23 Sqn., 24-9-40. Commissioned, 28-5-43. Transferred to Bomber Command.	♰ Killed since Battle (30-8-44)	British
NOBLE Brian Robert	Plt. Off.	Pilot	79	On 79 Sqn., 1-7-40. ✠ **1 He 59 (shared), 28-8-40.** Severely wounded, 1-9-40. Retired from R.A.F., 1-5-69, as Wing Commander.		British
NOBLE Dennis	Sgt.	Pilot	43	Joined 43 Sqn., 3-8-40. ✠ **1 Ju 87, 16-8-40.**	♰ **Killed in Action** (30-8-40)	British
NOBLE William John	Sgt.	Pilot	54	Joined 54 Sqn., 22-9-40. Commissioned, 17-11-41. Released from the R.A.F., 1946, as a Flight Lieutenant.	♰ Died since Battle (1979)	British
NOKES-COOPER Benjamin	Plt. Off.	Aircrew	236	On 236 Sqn., 1-7-40.	♰ **Killed in Action** (1-8-40)	British
NORFOLK Norman Robert	Sgt.	Pilot	72	On 72 Sqn., 1-7-40. Commissioned, 21-8-40. ✠ **1 Do 17, 7-9-40; ✠ 1 Do 17, 11-9-40; ✠ 1 Bf 110, 25-10-40.** Awarded D.F.C.(7-1-41). Released from the R.A.F., 1945, as a Flight Lieutenant.		British
NORRIS Philip Purchall	Sgt.	Pilot	213	On 213 Sqn., 1-7-40.	♰ **Killed in Action** (13-8-40)	British
NORRIS Robert Wilson	Fg. Off.	Pilot	1(Canadian)	Joined 1(Canadian) Sqn., 17-8-40. Released from R.C.A.F., 28-11-45, as a Wing Commander. Rejoined, 1951, and retired, 6-11-63, as Flight Lieutenant.		Canadian
NORRIS Stanley Charles	Plt. Off.	Pilot	610	On 610 Sqn., 1-7-40. Promoted Fg. Off., 29-8-40. ✠ **2 Bf 109s, 25-7-40; ✠ 2 Ju 87s, 14-8-40; ✠ 1 Bf 109, 24-8-40.** Awarded D.F.C.❋ (24-9-40 and 23-5-44). Released from the R.A.F., 9-47, as a Wing Commander.		British
NORTH Gerald	Plt. Off.	Pilot	85-257	Joined 85 Sqn., 2-9-40. Posted to 257 Sqn., 11-9-40.	♰ Killed since Battle (10-2-43)	British
NORTH Harold Leslie ("Knockers")	Plt. Off.	Pilot	43	On 43 Sqn., 1-7-40. Promoted Fg. Off., 3-9-40. ✠ **1 Ju 87, 18-8-40; ✠ 1 He 111, 26-8-40.** Slightly wounded, 26-8-40. Awarded D.F.C.(15-6-42).	♰ Killed since Battle (1-5-42)	New Zealander
NORTH-BOMFORD David John	Sgt.	Pilot	229-17-111	On 229 Sqn., 1-7-40. Posted to 17 Sqn., 29-7-40. Posted to 111 Sqn., 28-8-40. Released from the R.A.F., 1947, as a Warrant Officer. (Note. Had held Commission prior to War.)		British
NORWELL John King ("Jock")	Sgt.	Pilot	54-41	On 54 Sqn., 1-7-40. ✠ **1 Do 17 (shared), 3-7-40; ✠ 1 Bf 110 (shared), 18-8-40; ✠ 1 Bf 109, 22-8-40; ✠ 1 Bf 109 (shared), 31-8-40.** Posted to 41 Sqn., early 9-40. ✠ 1 Bf 109, 27-9-40. Commissioned, 2-7-42. Awarded A.F.C. (1-1-45). Released from the R.A.F., 1946, as a Flight Lieutenant.		British
NORWOOD Robin Keith Collen	Plt. Off.	Pilot	65	Joined 65 Sqn., 2-9-40. Released from the R.A.F., 1946, as a Flight Lieutenant.	♰ Died since Battle (2-4-70)	British
NOSOWICZ Zbigniew	Plt. Off.	Pilot	56	Joined 56 Sqn., 31-8-40. Injured, 12-12-40. Invalided from R.A.F., 1946.		Polish
NOWAK Tadeusz ("No-how")	Plt. Off.	Pilot	253	Joined 253 Sqn., 10-7-40. ✠ **1 He 111, 31-8-40; ✠ 1 Bf 110, 4-9-40; ✠ 1 Do 17, 29-10-40.**	♰ Killed since Battle (21-9-41)	Polish
NOWAKIEWICZ Eugeniusz Jan Adam	Sgt.	Pilot	302	Joined 302 (Polish) Sqn., 20-8-40. Commissioned, 1-6-42. Shot down, 23-7-42, and taken prisoner by the Germans. Released from Polish Air Force, 1947, as Flight Lieutenant.		Polish
NOWELL William Ronald	Sub-Lieut.	Pilot	804	Fleet Air Arm. On 804 Sqn., 1-7-40. Sailed in H.M.S. *Argus* for Gibraltar, 23-7-40. Retired from Royal Navy, 29-7-58, as a Lieutenant Commander.	♰ Died since Battle (2-12-76)	British
NOWIERSKI Tadeusz ("Novi")	Fg. Off.	Pilot	609	Joined 609 Sqn., 5-8-40. ✠ **1 Bf 109, 13-8-40; ✠ 1 He 111, 25-8-40; ✠ 1 Bf 109, 30-8-40; ✠ 1 Bf 109, 10-10-40.** Awarded D.F.C.(30-10-41).	♰ Died since Battle (2-4-83)	Polish
NUNN Stanley George	Plt. Off.	Pilot	236	Joined 236 Sqn., 5-8-40. Made O.B.E.(1-1-67); awarded D.F.C.(5-9-44). Retired from R.A.F., 25-7-75, as a Group Captain.		British
NUTE Romilly Ronald James	Sgt.	Aircrew	23	On 23 Sqn., 1-7-40.	♰ Killed since Battle (10-3-41)	British
NUTTER Reginald Charles	Sgt.	Pilot	257	On 257 Sqn., 1-7-40. Commissioned, 21-6-41. Awarded D.F.C.(14-9-45). Released from R.A.F., 4-46, as Squadron Leader.		British
OAKS Trevor Walter	Sgt.	Aircrew	235	Joined 235 Sqn., 3-10-40. Commissioned, 9-4-44. Released from R.N.Z.A.F., 6-2-45, as a Flying Officer.		New Zealander
O'BRIAN Peter Geoffrey St. George	Flt. Lt.	Pilot	152-247	Joined 152 Sqn., mid-8-40. ✠ **1 He 111 (shared), 27-8-40; ✠ 1 Ju 88 (shared), 17-9-40.** Awarded O.B.E.(1-1-54), D.F.C.❋ (2-12-41 and 6-8-43). Retired from the R.A.F., 18-7-59, as a Group Captain.		Canadian
O'BRIEN Joseph Somerton ("Spike")	Sqn. Ldr.	Pilot	92-234	Joined 92 Sqn., 1-7-40, supernumerary. Awarded D.F.C.(30-7-40). Posted to command 234 Sqn., 17-8-40. ✠ **1 Ju 88 (shared), 21-8-40; ✠ 1 Bf 109, 24-8-40; ✠ 2 Bf 109s, 6-9-40.**	♰ **Killed in Action** (7-9-40)	British
O'BYRNE Peter	Sgt.	Pilot	73-501	On 73 Sqn., 1-7-40. Posted to 501 Sqn., 29-10-40.		British
O'CONNELL Anthony	Plt. Off.	Aircrew	264	Defiant gunner. On 264 Sqn., 1-7-40. Injured in ground accident, 7-10-40. Retired from R.A.F., 9-9-58, as a Flight Lieutenant.	♰ Died since Battle (17-12-76)	British
ODBERT Norman Cyril	Sqn. Ldr.	Pilot	64	In command of 64 Sqn., 1-7-40. Posted away, late 7-40. Made O.B.E.(13-6-46). Retired from the R.A.F., 29-1-57, as a Group Captain.		British
OELOFSE Johannes Roelof Stephanus	Plt. Off.	Pilot	43	On 43 Sqn., 1-7-40.	♰ **Killed in Action** (8-8-40)	South African
OFFENBERG Jean Henri Marie ("Peiker")	Plt. Off.	Pilot	145	Joined 145 Sqn., 17-8-40. Awarded D.F.C.(6-41).	♰ Killed since Battle (22-1-42)	Belgian

Name	Rank	Role	Sqn.	Notes	Status	Nationality
OGILVIE Alfred Keith	Plt. Off.	Pilot	609	Joined 609 Sqn., 20-8-40. ✠ 1 Bf 109, 7-9-40; ✠ 1 Do 17 (shared), 15-9-40; ✠ 1 Bf 110, 27-9-40. Awarded D.F.C.(11-7-41). Transferred to R.C.A.F., 1946, and retired, 14-9-62.		Canadian
OGILVIE Donald Bruce	Plt. Off.	Pilot	601	Joined 601 Sqn., 31-8-40. Slighly injured in accident, 24-9-40. Invalided from the R.A.F., 7-45.		British
OLDFIELD Trevor Guest	Sgt.	Pilot	64-92	Joined 64 Sqn., early 9-40. Posted to 92 Sqn., mid-9-40.	✟ Killed in Action (27-9-40)	British
O'LEARY Arthur Alexander	L.A.C.	Aircrew	604	Joined 604 Sqn., 1-7-40. Wounded in Action, 20-12-40. Promoted sergeant, 12-40. Severely wounded, 1-5-41. Awarded D.F.M.(30-5-41). Awarded D.F.C.✪ (16-2-43 and 14-5-43, as Warrant Officer). Commissioned, 9-4-44. Awarded second Bar to D.F.C.(14-11-44, as Flying Officer). Released from R.A.F., 1946, as Fg. Off.		British
OLENSKI Zbigniew ("Bee")	Fg. Off.	Pilot	234-609	Joined 234 Sqn., 14-8-40. ✠ 1 Bf 110, 4-9-40. Posted to 5-9-40. Released from R.A.F., 3-47, as Flight Lieutenant.	✟ Died since Battle (20-6-70)	Polish
OLESON Wilfrid Pallasen	Plt. Off.	Pilot	607	On 607 Sqn., 1-7-40. Transferred to Technical Branch, 1941, and served until his death as a Wing Commander.	✟ Died since Battle (6-7-50)	British
OLEWINSKI Boleslaw	Sgt.	Pilot	111	Joined 111 Sqn., 19-10-40.	✟ Died since Battle (3-11-40)	Polish
OLIVE Charles Gordon Chaloner	Fg. Off.	Pilot	65	On 65 Sqn., 1-7-40. Promoted Flt. Lt., 19-8-40. ✠ 1 Bf 109, 20-7-40; ✠ 2 Bf 109s, 13-8-40; 1 Bf 110, 26-8-40. Awarded D.F.C.(24-9-40).	✟ Died since Battle (1987)	Australian
OLIVER George Dixon	Sgt.	Aircrew	23	On 23 Sqn., 1-7-40.	✟ Killed since Battle (8-9-41)	British
OLVER Peter	Plt. Off.	Pilot	603	Joined 603 Sqn., 10-40. Wounded, 25-10-40. Awarded D.F.C.(5-1-43). Released from the R.A.F., as a Squadron Leader.		British
O'MALLEY Derek Keppel Coleridge	Fg. Off.	Pilot	264	On 264 Sqn., 1-7-40.	✟ **Killed in Action** (4-9-40)	British
O'MEARA James Joseph ("Orange")	Plt. Off.	Pilot	64-72-421 Flt.	On 64 Sqn., 1-7-40. Promoted Fg. Off., 3-9-40. Posted to 72 Sqn., 20-9-40. Posted to 421 Flt., 3-10-40. ✠ 1 Bf 109, 19-7-40; ✠ 1 Bf 109, 15-8-40; ✠ 1 Ju 88 (solo) and 1 Ju 88 (shared); ✠ 1 Do 17, 27-9-40. Awarded D.S.O.(27-10-44), D.F.C.✪ (24-9-40 and 18-3-41). Retired from R.A.F., 31-7-59, as Squadron Leader.		British
OMMANEY Rupert John	Sgt.	Pilot	229	On 229 Sqn., 1-7-40. ✠ 1 Bf 110 (solo) and 1 Do 215 (shared), 15-9-40.	✟ Killed since Battle (12-2-42)	British
O'NEILL Desmond Hugh ("Peggy")	Fg. Off.	Pilot	611-41	Joined 611 Sqn., 20-8-40. Posted to 41 Sqn., 29-9-40.	✟ **Killed in Action** (11-10-40)	British
O'NEILL John Anthony	Fg. Off.	Pilot	601-238	Joined 601 Sqn., 4-10-40. Posted to 238 Sqn., 21-10-40. Awarded D.F.C.(30-7-40). Retired from the R.A.F., 29-11-57, retaining the rank of Group Captain.		British
ORCHARD Harold Charles	Sgt.	Pilot	65	On 65 Sqn., 1-7-40.	✟ Killed since Battle (5-2-41)	British
ORGIAS Eric	Plt. Off.	Pilot	23	On 23 Sqn., 1-7-40.	✟ **Killed in Action** (25-9-40)	New Zealander
ORTMANS Victor ("Vicky")	Plt. Off.	Pilot	229	Joined 229 Sqn., 10-8-40. ✠ 1 Do 17 (shared), 15-9-40; ✠ 1 He 111, 27-9-40; ✠ 1 Do 17, 30-9-40. Awarded D.F.C.(9-41).	✟ Killed since Battle (1948)	Belgian
ORZECHOWSKI Jerzy	Flt. Lt.	Pilot	615-607	Joined 615 Sqn., 3-10-40. Posted to 607 Sqn., 16-10-40. Awarded D.F.C.(15-5-44). Released from the Polish Air Force, 1-47, as a Wing Commander.	✟ Died since Battle (1988)	Polish
OSMAND Alexander Gordon	Plt. Off.	Pilot	213-3	On 213 Sqn., 1-7-40. Posted to 3 Sqn., 14-9-40. ✠ 1 Bf 109, 13-8-40.	✟ Killed since Battle (20-10-43)	British
OSTASZEWSKI-OSTOJA Piotr	Fg. Off.	Pilot	609	Joined 609 Sqn., 5-8-40. ✠ 1 Bf 110, 15-8-40. Slightly wounded, 25-8-40. Released from R.A.F., 12-46, as Wing Commander. Changed name to **RAYMOND**.		Polish
OSTOWICZ Antoni	Fg. Off	Pilot	145	Joined 145 Sqn., 16-7-40. ✠ He 111 (shared), 19-7-40.	✟ **Killed in Action** (11-8-40)	Polish
OVERTON Charles Nevil	Plt. Off.	Pilot	609	On 609 Sqn., 1-7-40. ✠ 1 Bf 109, 12-8-40; ✠ 2 Ju 87s, 13-8-40. Promoted Fg. Off., 3-9-40. Released from the R.A.F., 6-46, as Wing Commander.		British
OWEN Arthur Edward	Sgt.	Aircrew	600	Joined 600 Sqn., 19-7-40. Transferred to Bomber Command after the Battle.	✟ Killed since Battle (24-7-41)	British
OWEN Henry	Sgt.	Aircrew	219-235	On 219 Sqn., 1-7-40. Posted to 235 Sqn., 9-40. Commissioned, 20-9-44. Retired from R.A.F., 15-7-55, as a Flight Lieutenant.		British
OWEN William Gethin	Sgt.	Aircrew	235	On 235 Sqn., 1-7-40. Commissioned, 31-7-41. Awarded D.F.C.(20-7-45). Released from R.A.F., 1946, as a Flight Lieutenant.		British
OXSPRING Robert Wardlow ("Bobby")	Plt. Off.	Pilot	66	On 66 Sqn., 1-7-40. Promoted Fg. Off., 3-9-40. ✠ 1 He 111 (shared), 29-7-40; ✠ 1 He 111, 11-9-40; ✠ 1 Do 17, 15-9-40; ✠ 1 Bf 109, 18-9-40; ✠ 1 He 111, 24-9-40; ✠ 1 Bf 110, 27-9-40; ✠ 1 Bf 109, 30-9-40; ✠ 1 Bf 109, 5-10-40; ✠ 1 Bf 109, 13-10-40. Slightly wounded, 25-10-40. Awarded D.F.C.✪✪ (8-11-40, 18-9-42 and 16-2-43), A.F.C.(1-1-49). Retired from the R.A.F.. 29-2-68, as a Group Captain.		British
PAGE Alan Geoffrey	Plt. Off.	Pilot	56	On 56 Sqn., 1-7-40. Promoted Fg. Off., 3-10-40. ✠ 1 Bf 109, 13-7-40; ✠ 1 Ju 88 (shared), 20-7-40; ✠ 1 Ju 87 (shared), 25-7-40. Severely wounded, 12-8-40. Again severely wounded, 9-44. Awarded D.S.O.(29-12-44), D.F.C. (30-7-43). Retired from the R.A.F., 1-12-48, as a Squadron Leader.		British
PAGE Anthony Durrant	Sgt.	Pilot	111-257	Joined 111 Sqn., 31-8-40. Posted to 257 Sqn., 28-9-40.	✟ Killed since Battle (8-11-40)	British
PAGE Arthur John	Sgt.	Pilot	257	Joined 257 Sqn., 1-9-40. Transferred to Bomber Command later.	✟ Killed since Battle (24-10-41)	British
PAGE Cyril Leslie	Flt. Lt.	Pilot	234-145	On 234 Sqn., 1-7-40. Attached to 145 Sqn., 31-7-40 until 19-8-40, then returned to 234 Sqn. Released from the R.A.F., 1947, as a Squadron Leader.		British
PAGE Vernon Douglas	Sgt.	Pilot	601-610	Joined 610 Sqn., 17-10-40, from 601 Sqn. Commissioned, 9-4-41. Awarded D.F.C.✪ (19-5-44 and 3-4-45). Released from the R.A.F., 1946, as a Squadron Leader.		British
PAGE Wilfrid Thomas	Sgt.	Pilot	1	Joined 1 Sqn., 1-10-40. Commissioned, 1-5-41.	✟ Killed since Battle (16-11-43)	British
PAIN John Francis	Plt. Off.	Pilot	32	Joined 32 Sqn., 2-8-40. ✠ 1 Ju 88, 16-8-40; ✠ 1 Do 17, 18-8-40. Wounded, 18-8-40. Released from the R.A.F., 1944, as a Flight Lieutenant. Changed name to **BROOKER-PAIN**.	✟ Died since Battle (12-9-80)	Australian
PAISEY Frederick George	Plt. Off.	Pilot	235	On 235 Sqn., 1-7-40. Awarded D.F.C.(17-7-45). Released from the R.A.F., 1947, as a Wing Commander.		British
PALAK Jan	Sgt.	Pilot	302-303	Joined 302 (Polish) Sqn., 24-7-40. Posted to 303 (Polish) Sqn., 23-9-40. ✠ 1 Do 17 (shared), 15-9-40; ✠ 1 Bf 109, 5-10-40. Awarded D.F.C. as Warrant Officer, 10-4-46.		Polish
PALLISER George Charles Calder ("Tich")	Sgt.	Pilot	17-43-249	Joined 17 Sqn., 3-8-40. Posted to 43 Sqn., 18-8-40. Posted to 249 Sqn., 14-9-40. ✠ 1 Do 17 (shared), 15-9-40; ✠ 2 Bf 110s, 27-9-40. Commissioned, 24-4-42. Awarded D.F.C.(30-1-42). Released from the R.A.F., 1947, as Flt. Lt.		British
PALMER Norman Nelson	Sgt.	Aircrew	248	Joined 248 Sqn., 9-40. Flew reconnaissance sorties over Norwegian coast during Battle of Britain.	✟ Killed since Battle (8-2-42)	British
PALUSINSKI Jerzy Hipolit	Plt. Off.	Pilot	303	Joined 303 (Polish) Sqn., 21-8-40. Released from the Polish Air Force, 1-47, as Flight Lieutenant.	✟ Died since Battle (1984)	Polish
PANKRATZ Wilhelm	Flt. Lt.	Pilot	145	Joined 145 Sqn., 16-7-40.	✟ **Killed in Action** (12-8-40)	Polish
PANNELL Geoffrey Charles Russell	Sgt.	Pilot	3	Joined 3 Sqn., 29-9-40. Commissioned, 17-8-41. Awarded D.F.C.(29-6-42). Transferred to the Reserve in New Zealand, 25-1-46, as a Flight Lieutenant.	✟ Died since Battle (3-5-80)	New Zealander
PARKE Thomas Robert Verner	Sub-Lieut.	Pilot	804	Fleet Air Arm. On 804 Sqn., 1-7-40.	✟ Killed since Battle (7-7-41)	British
PARKER Denis Keith	Sgt.	Pilot	616-66	Joined 616 Sqn., 20-9-40. Posted to 66 Sqn., 30-9-40. Commissioned, 7-7-42. Released from the R.A.F., 11-45, as a Flight Lieutenant.		British
PARKER Ian Robertson	Wg. Cdr.	Pilot	611	Flew an operational sortie with 611 Sqn., 21-8-40. Released from the R.A.F., 1945, as a Group Captain. Made O.B.E., 1-1-46.		British
PARKER Kenneth Bruce	Sgt.	Pilot	64-92	Joined 64 Sqn., mid-9-40. Posted to 92 Sqn., 24-9-40.	✟ **Killed in Action** (15-10-40)	British
PARKER Thomas Campbell	Plt. Off.	Pilot	79	On 79 Sqn., 1-7-40. Promoted Fg. Off., 3-9-40. ✠ 1 He 59 (shared), 28-8-40. Released from the R.A.F., 1945, as Wing Commander. Made O.B.E.(1-1-46).		British
PARKER Vincent ("Bush")	Plt. Off.	Pilot	234	On 234 Sqn., 1-7-40. Shot down and taken prisoner by the Germans, 15-8-40. (Killed while flying with the R.A.F. after the War.)	✟ Killed since Battle (29-1-46)	Australian
PARKES William Bert	Sgt.	Pilot	74	Joined 74 Sqn., 17-8-40. Commissioned, 18-2-43. Resigned commission and left the R.A.F., 3-5-50.		British

Name	Rank	Role	Sqn.	Details	Fate	Nationality
PARKIN Eric Gordon	Plt. Off.	Pilot	501	On 501 Sqn., 1-7-40. Injured in flying accident, 31-7-40. Retired from R.A.F., 21-4-72, as a Flight Lieutenant.		British
PARKINSON Cecil	Sgt.	Pilot	238	On 238 Sqn., 1-7-40. ✠ **1 Do 17 (shared), 13-7-40.** (Died of injuries sustained on 20-7-40).	✟ **Died of Wounds** (21-7-40)	British
PARNALL Denis Geach	Fg. Off.	Pilot	249	On 249 Sqn., 1-7-40. ✠ **1 Ju 88 (shared), 8-7-40; ✠ 1 Bf 110, 15-8-40; ✠ 1 Bf 110, 2-9-40; ✠ 1 He 111 (shared), 7-9-40; ✠ 1 He 111 (shared), 11-9-40.**	✟ **Killed in Action** (18-9-40)	British
PARNALL Stuart Boyd	Plt. Off.	Pilot	607	On 607 Sqn., 1-7-40.	✟ **Killed in Action** (9-9-40)	British
PARR Douglas John	Sgt.	Aircrew	29	Joined 29 Sqn., early 10-40.	✟ Killed since Battle	British
PARR Leslie Alfred	Sgt.	Pilot	79	Joined 79 Sqn., 6-7-40. ✠ **1 He 111 (shared), 30-8-40.** Commissioned, 25-5-41. Retired from R.A.F., 14-3-69, as a Wing Commander.	✟ Died since Battle (1986)	British
PARROTT Dennis Thomas	Fg. Off.	Pilot	19-421 Flt.	Joined 19 Sqn., 31-7-40. Posted to 421 Flt., c.3-10-40. ✠ **1 Bf 109, 27-9-40.** Slightly injured, 19-10-40.	✟ Killed since Battle (22-6-41)	British
PARROTT Peter Lawrence	Plt. Off.	Pilot	145-605	On 145 Sqn., 1-7-40. Promoted Fg. Off., 3-9-40. Posted to 605 Sqn., 27-9-40. ✠ **1 He 111 (shared), 18-7-40; ✠ 1 Bf 109 and 1 Ju 87, 8-8-40; ✠ 1 Ju 88, 12-8-40.** Awarded D.F.C.✦ (22-10-40 and 20-3-45), A.F.C. (1-1-52). Retired from the R.A.F., 10-7-65, as a Wing Commander.		British
PARROTT Reginald James	Sgt.	Pilot	32	Joined 32 Sqn., late 9-40. (✠ **1 Fiat BR.20, 11-11-40**).	✟ Killed since Battle (5-5-41)	British
PARRY Emlyn	Sgt.	Aircrew	23	Joined 23 Sqn., 6-10-40. Commissioned, 28-11-42. Transferred to Bomber Command.	✟ Killed since Battle (4-4-44)	British
PARRY Montague Edward	Sgt.	Aircrew	604	Joined 604 Sqn., 4-9-40.		British
PARSONS Claude Arthur	Sgt.	Pilot	610-66	On 610 Sqn., 1-7-40. Poasted to 66 Sqn., 10-9-40. ✠ **1 u.e.a., 18-8-40; ✠ 1 He 111, 15-9-40; ✠ 1 Ju 88, 27-9-40.**	✟ Killed since Battle (8-11-41)	British
PARSONS Edwin Ernest	Sgt.	Aircrew	23	Joined 23 Sqn., 24-9-40. Transferred to the Reserve in New Zealand, 16-10-43.	✟ Died since Battle (4-10-77)	New Zealander
PARSONS John Graham	Sgt.	Aircrew	235	On 235 Sqn., 1-7-40. Commissioned, 26-1-43. Released from the R.A.F., 26-1-46, as a Flight Lieutenant.		British
PARSONS Phillip Trevor	Plt. Off.	Pilot	504	On 504 Sqn., 1-7-40. Promoted Fg. Off., 3-9-40. ✠ **1 Do 17 (solo) and 1 He 111 (shared), 15-9-40.**	✟ Killed since Battle (2-10-42)	British
PASSY Cyril Woolrich	Fg. Off.	Pilot	605	On 605 Sqn., 1-7-40. ✠ **1 Bf 109 (shared), 7-10-40.** Wounded, 1-12-40. Awarded D.F.C.(12-2-43). Made O.B.E.(14-6-45). Retired from the R.A.F., 4-6-47, as a Wing Commander.	✟ Died since Battle (1971)	British
PASZKIEWICZ Ludwik Witold ("Paszko")	Fg. Off.	Pilot	303	Joined 303 (Polish) Sqn., 2-8-40, on formation. ✠ **1 Do 17, 30-8-40; ✠ 2 Do 17s (7-9-40); ✠ 1 Bf 110, 11-9-40; ✠ 1 Bf 109, 15-9-40; ✠ 1 He 111 26-9-40.** Awarded D.F.C.(30-10-41).	✟ **Killed in Action** (26-9-40)	Polish
PATEREK Edward	Sgt.	Pilot	302-303	Joined 302 (Polish) Sqn., 23-7-40. ✠ **1 Ju 88, 18-9-40.** Posted to 303 (Polish) Sqn., 23-9-40.	✟ Killed since Battle (28-3-41)	Polish
PATERSON Brian	Lieut.	Pilot	804	Fleet Air Arm. On 804 Sqn., 1-7-40. Made M.B.E.(16-2-54); awarded D.F.C. (31-5-55). Retired from the Royal Navy, 1959, as a Lieutenant Commander.		British
PATERSON James Alfred	Fg. Off.	Pilot	92	Joined 92 Sqn., 7-40. ✠ **1 Ju 88 (shared), 24-7-40; ✠ 1 Ju 88 (shared), 19-8-40; ✠ 1 Bf 110, 11-9-40.** Severely wounded, 11-9-40. Posthumous award of M.B.E.(1-1-41) in respect of operations in France early in 1940.	✟ **Killed in Action** (27-9-40)	New Zealander
PATRICK Leon Fred	Sgt.	Pilot	222	Joined 222 Sqn., late 8-40. Commissioned, 1-5-42. Released from R.A.F., 1947, as a Flight Lieutenant.	✟ Died since Battle (23-10-85)	British
PATSTON Arthur George	L.A.C.	Aircrew	604	Joined 604 Sqn., 10-7-40. Flew on operations throughout the Battle as an L.A.C. Commissioned, 14-7-41. Awarded D.F.C.(9-11-43). Released from the R.A.F., 1945, as a Flight Lieutenant.		British
PATTEN Hubert Paul Frederick	Fg. Off.	Pilot	64	On 64 Sqn., 1-7-40. ✠ **1 Bf 110, 10-7-40.** Posted away, 15-9-40. Retired from the R.A.F., 28-5-64, retaining the rank of Squadron Leader.		British
PATTERSON Leonard John	Sgt.	Pilot	501	Joined 501 Sqn., 2-9-40.	✟ Killed since Battle (28-11-40)	British
PATTERSON Norris Henry	Sub-Lieut.	Pilot	804	Fleet Air Arm. On 804 Sqn., 1-7-40.	✟ Killed since Battle (22-12-41)	British
PATTERSON Peter John	Midshipman	Pilot	242	Fleet Air Arm. Joined 242 Sqn., 1-7-40.	✟ **Killed in Action** (20-8-40)	British
PATTERSON Robert Lawson	Plt. Off.	Pilot	235	On 235 Sqn., 1-7-40.	✟ **Killed in Action** (18-7-40)	British
PATTINSON Aberconway John Sefton	Plt. Off.	Pilot	23-92	On 23 Sqn., 1-7-40. Posted to 92 Sqn., 5-9-40.	✟ **Killed in Action** (12-10-40)	British
PATTISON John David	Fg. Off.	Pilot	1(Canadian)	Joined 1(Canadian) Sqn., 30-8-40. Awarded D.F.C.(6-11-42). Released from the R.C.A.F., 5-9-45, as a Wing Commander.		Canadian
PATTISON John Gordon	Plt. Off.	Pilot	266-92	Joined 266 Sqn., 27-8-40. Posted to 92 Sqn., 14-9-40. Wounded, 23-9-40. Awarded D.S.O.(20-3-45), D.F.C.(16-5-44). Released from R.N.Z.A.F., 1-46, as Squadron Leader.		New Zealander
PATTISON Kenneth Clifton	Sgt.	Pilot	611	Joined 611 Sqn., 26-9-40. ✠ **1 Do 17, 11-10-40.** Mortally wounded, 11-10-40.	✟ **Died of Wounds** (13-10-40)	British
PATTULLO William Blair	Plt. Off.	Pilot	46-151-249	On 46 Sqn., 1-7-40. Posted to 151 Sqn., 26-8-40. Posted to 249 Sqn., 10-9-40. Returned to 46 Sqn., 15-9-40. ✠ **1 Do 17, 31-8-40; ✠ He 111 (shared), 15-9-40; ✠ 1 Bf 110 (solo) and 1 Bf 109 (shared), 27-9-40.** (Mortally injured, 25-10-40).	✟ **Died of Wounds** (26-10-40)	British
PAUL Francis Dawson	Sub-Lieut.	Pilot	64	Fleet Air Arm. Joined 64 Sqn., 1-7-40. ✠ **1 Do 17 (shared), 1-7-40; ✠ 1 Bf 109, 5-7-40; ✠ 1 Bf 110, 7-7-40; ✠ 2 Bf 110s, 10-7-40; ✠ 1 Bf 109, 13-7-40; ✠ 1 Do 17, 24-7-40; ✠ 1 Bf 109, 25-7-40.** (Shot down and mortally wounded, 25-7-40; rescued by the Germans but died in captivity four days later.)	✟ **Died of Wounds** (29-7-40)	British
PAVITT Harold John	Sgt.	Aircrew	235	Joined 235 Sqn., 18-9-40. Commissioned, 16-9-42. Retired from the R.A.F., 10-1-50, as a Squadron Leader.	✟ Died since Battle (1972)	British
PAVLU Otto	Sgt.	Pilot	1	Joined 1 Sqn., 4-10-40. Commissioned, 3-3-42.	✟ Killed since Battle (28-4-43)	Czech
PAYNE Alec Dawson	F/Sgt.	Pilot	501-610	On 501 Sqn., 1-7-40. Posted to 610 Sqn., 23-9-40.		British
PAYNE Roy Ainley	Plt. Off.	Pilot	602	Joined 602 Sqn., 3-9-40.		British
PAYNE Reginald Irving	A.C.2	Aircrew	23	Joined 23 Sqn., 3-9-40. At time of death he had not been granted his due rank of Temporary Sergeant.	✟ **Killed in Action** (25-9-40)	British
PEACHMENT Charles Barton Gower	Plt. Off.	Pilot	236	On 236 Sqn., 1-7-40. Released from the R.A.F., 1947, as a Squadron Leader.	✟ Died since Battle (1979)	British
PEACOCK Denis Charles	Sgt.	Pilot	605	Served on 605 Sqn. during the Battle of Britain.	✟ Killed since Battle (15-9-42)	British
PEACOCK Reginal John	Plt. Off.	Pilot	235	Served on 235 Sqn. during the Battle of Britain. Promoted Fg. Off., 23-9-40.	✟ Killed since Battle (5-2-43)	British
PEACOCK William Albert	Sgt.	Pilot	46	On 46 Sqn., 1-7-40. ✠ **1 Bf 109, 8-9-40.**	✟ **Killed in Action** (11-9-40)	British
PEACOCK-EDWARDS Spencer Ritchie	Fg. Off.	Pilot	615-253	Joined 605 Sqn., 10-7-40. Posted to 253 Sqn., 15-9-40. Awarded D.F.C.(29-12-42). Retired from R.A.F., 14-2-58, as a Squadron Leader.	✟ Died since Battle (1983)	British
PEARCE Leonard Hilary Borlase	Sgt.	Pilot	32-249-46	On 32 Sqn., 1-7-40. Posted to 249 Sqn., 18-9-40. Posted to 46 Sqn., 10-40. Wounded, 18-8-40 and 13-10-40.	✟ Killed since Battle (9-4-41)	British
PEARCE Peter Griffin	Sgt.	Aircrew	600	On 600 Sqn., 1-7-40.	✟ Killed since Battle (15-12-41)	British
PEARCE Roy	Sgt.	Aircrew	29	Joined 29 Sqn., 10-40. Commissioned, 17-1-43. Released from the R.A.F., 1946, as a Flight Lieutenant.		British
PEARCE William John	Sgt.	Aircrew	236	Joined 236 Sqn., 24-9-40.	✟ Killed since Battle (5-11-41)	British
PEARCY Dennis Jack	Sgt.	Aircrew	219	Flew with 219 Sqn. during the Battle of Britain.	✟ Killed since Battle (15-11-40)	British
PEARMAN Stanley James	Plt. Off.	Aircrew	141	Defiant gunner. On 141 Sqn., 1-7-40. Released from R.A.F., 1947, as a Flight Lieutenant.		British

Name	Rank	Role	Squadron	Details		Fate	Nationality
PEARSE Leslie Lewis	Sgt.	Aircrew	236	Joined 236 Sqn., 10-10-40. Commissioned, 9-11-42. Awarded D.F.C.(21-9-45). Released from the R.A.F., 1945, as a Flight Lieutenant..			British
PEARSON Dennis Edward	Sgt.	Aircrew	236	Joined 236 Sqn., 21-7-40. Wounded, 6-11-40.			British
PEARSON Geoffrey Wilberforce	Sgt.	Pilot	501	Joined 501 Sqn., late 8-40.	✠	**Killed in Action** (6-9-40)	British
PEARSON Philip	Sgt.	Pilot	238	Joined 238 Sqn., mid-10-40. Slightly wounded, 5-11-40.	✠	Killed since Battle (29-5-42)	British
PEASE Arthur Peter	Fg. Off.	Pilot	603	Joined 603 Sqn., 6-7-40. ✠ **1 He 111 (shared), 30-7-40; ✠ 1 Bf 109, 3-9-40.**	✠	**Killed in Action** (15-9-40)	British
PEEBLES William	Sgt.	Aircrew	235	On 235 Sqn., 1-7-40.	✠	Killed since Battle (7-5-41)	British
PEEL Charles David	Fg. Off.	Pilot	603	On 603 Sqn., 1-7-40.	✠	**Killed in Action** (17-7-40)	British
PEEL John Ralph Alexander	Sqn. Ldr.	Pilot	145	In command of 145 Sqn., 1-7-40. ✠ **1 Do 17 (shared), 7-7-40; ✠ 1 Do 17 (shared), 19-7-40; ✠ 1 Ju 88 (shared), 29-7-40; ✠ 2 Ju 87s and 1 Bf 109, 8-8-40.** Slightly wounded, 11-8-40. Awarded D.S.O.(5-8-41), D.F.C.(13-8-40). Retired from the R.A.F., 20-1-48, retaining the rank of Group Captain.			British
PEGGE Constantine Oliver Joseph	Plt. Off.	Pilot	610	On 610 Sqn., 1-7-40. Promoted Fg. Off. 3-9-40. ✠ **1 Bf 109, 8-8-40; ✠ 2 Bf 109s, 12-8-40; ✠ 1 Bf 109 and 1 He 111, 18-8-40; ✠ 1 Bf 109, 28-8-40; ✠ 1 He 111, 30-8-40.** Awarded D.F.C.⊛ (22-10-40 and 29-1-46). Died while still serving in the R.A.F. as a Squadron Leader.	✠	Died since Battle (9-5-50)	British
PEMBERTON David Alwyne	Sqn. Ldr.	Pilot	1	In command of 1 Sqn., 1-7-40. ✠ **1 He 111, 16-8-40; ✠ 1 Bf 109, 18-8-40.** Awarded D.F.C.(1-10-40).	✠	Killed since Battle (3-11-40)	British
PENFOLD Paul Eric	Plt. Off.	Aircrew	29	On 29 Sqn. 1-7-40. Released from the R.A.F., 1945, as a Squadron Leader.			British
PENFOLD William David	Sgt.	Aircrew	236	Joined 236 Sqn., 12-10-40. Commissioned, 26-1-42. Awarded M.B.E. and released from the R.A.F., 1947, as a Squadron Leader.			British
PENFORD Vernon William Fox	F/Sgt.	Pilot	23	On 23 Sqn., 1-7-40. Commissioned, 22-2-43. Retired from the R.A.F., 1-9-50, as a Squadron Leader.	✠	Died since Battle (1976)	British
PENNINGTON Denis Arthur	Plt. Off.	Pilot	245-253	On 245 Sqn., 1-7-40. Posted to 253 Sqn., 13-10-40. Awarded D.F.C.(5-3-43). Released from the R.A.F., 1946, as a Squadron Leader.			British
PENNINGTON-LEGH Alan William	Fg. Off.	Pilot	248-232	On 248 Sqn., 1-7-40. Promoted Flt. Lt., 3-9-40. Posted to 232 Sqn., 1-10-40, to command, as Acting Sqn. Ldr.	✠	Killed since Battle (1-6-43)	British
PENNYCUICK Bruce	Sgt.	Aircrew	236	Joined 236 Sqn., late 9-40. Commissioned, 1-5-42. Released from R.A.F., 1946, as a Squadron Leader.			British
PERCY Hugh Harold	Plt. Off.	Pilot	264	On 264 Sdn., 1-7-40. Promoted Fg. Off., 3-10-40.	✠	Killed since Battle (22-5-44)	British
PERKIN Frederick Stanley ("Polly")	Sgt.	Pilot	600-615-73-421 Flt.	Joined 600 Sqn., 16-8-40. Posted to 615 Sqn., 25-8-40. Posted to 73 Sqn., 15-9-40. Posted to 421 Flt., 25-10-40. Commissioned, 21-8-41. Released from the R.A.F., 5-46, as a Flight Lieutenant.	✠	Died since Battle (1988)	British
PERRIN George Camille	Adj.	Pilot	615-249	Joined 615 Sqn., 19-9-40. Posted to 249 Sqn., 1-10-40. Wounded, 12-10-40.	✠	Died since Battle (1981)	French
PERRY Henry Thomas	A.C.	Aircrew	23	Joined 23 Sqn., 18-7-40. Had not been granted his due rank of Temporary Sergeant at the time of his death.	✠	**Killed in Action** (24/25-9-40)	British
PETERS George Charles Boyce	Fg. Off.	Pilot	79	Joined 79 Sqn., early 8-40. ✠ **1 Bf 110, 15-8-40; ✠ 1 He 111, 30-8-40; ✠ 1 Bf 110, 4-9-40.**	✠	**Killed in Action** (29-9-40)	British
PETERSON Otto John	Plt. Off.	Pilot	1(Canadian)	With 1(Canadian) Sqn., 20-6-40, on arrival in U.K. ✠ **1 Bf 109, 9-9-40; ✠ 1 Do 17 (shared), 25-9-40.**	✠	**Killed in Action** (27-9-40)	American
PETTET Alexander Henry	Plt. Off.	Aircrew	248	Joined 248 Sqn., 29-9-40.	✠	Killed since Battle (13-12-40)	British
PETTIT Henry William	Sgt.	Pilot	1-605	Joined 1 Sqn., 9-40. Posted to 605 Sqn., 20-10-40.	✠	Killed since Battle (2-2-41)	British
PEXTON Richard Dunning	Fg. Off.	Pilot	615	On 615 Sqn., 1-7-40. Promoted Flt. Lt., 15-9-40. Awarded D.F.C.(16-2-45), A.F.C. (26-10-43). Released from the R.A.F., 1945, as a Wing Commander.			British
PFEIFFER Jan Piotr	Plt. Off.	Pilot	32-257	Joined 32 Sqn., 18-8-40. Posted to 257 Sqn., 16-9-40. Posted away, 28-9-40.	✠	Killed since Battle (20-10-43)	Polish
PHILIPPART Jacques Arthur Laurent	Plt. Off.	Pilot	213	Joined 213 Sqn., 23-7-40. ✠ **1 Ju 88, 11-8-40; ✠ 3 Bf 110s, 15-8-40; ✠ 1 Ju 88, 22-8-40; ✠ 1 Ju 88, 25-8-40.**	✠	**Killed in Action** (25-8-40)	Belgian
PHILLIP James	Sgt.	Aircrew	25	Joined 25 Sqn., early 10-40.	✠	Killed since Battle (17-5-42)	British
PHILLIPS Austin	Sgt.	Aircrew	604	Joined 604 Sqn., 12-10-40.			British
PHILLIPS Ernest Russell	Plt. Off.	Pilot	235	Joined 235 Sqn., 14-8-40.	✠	Killed since Battle (14-2-41)	British
PHILLIPS Randall Frederick Prenter	Sgt.	Pilot	602	On 602 Sqn., 1-7-40. Commissioned, 16-2-42. Released from the R.A.F., 9-45, as a Flight Lieutenant.			British
PHILLIPSON John Ross	L.A.C.	Aircrew	604	Joined 604 Sqn., 10-7-40. Awarded D.F.C. as a Warrant Officer (19-2-43).	✠	Killed since Battle (19-2-43)	British
PHILO Robert Ferguson	Plt. Off.	Pilot	151	Joined 151 Sqn., 18-9-40. Released from the R.A.F., 1945, as a Flight Lieutenant.			British
PIATKOWSKI Stanislaw	Plt. Off.	Pilot	79	Joined 79 Sqn., 11-9-40.	✠	**Killed in Action** (25-10-40)	Polish
PICKERING James	Sgt.	Pilot	64	Joined 64 Sqn., early 7-40. Posted away, c. 16-7-40. Commissioned, 29-1-42. Released from the R.A.F., 1945, as a Flight Lieutenant. Awarded A.F.C.(1-1-46).			British
PICKERING John Harcourt	Plt. Off.	Pilot	66	On 66 Sqn., 1-7-40. ✠ **1 He 111 (shared), 29-7-40; ✠ 1 He 111 (shared), 30-8-40; ✠ 1 Bf 109, 24-9-40.** Wounded, 24-9-40.	✠	Killed since Battle (15-2-42)	British
PICKERING Tony Garforth	Sgt.	Pilot	32-501	Joined 32 Sqn., 27-7-40. Posted to 501 Sqn., 28-8-40. ✠ **1 Bf 109, 29-10-40.** Commissioned, 13-12-41. Released from R.A.F., 12-45, as a Squadron Leader.			British
PICKFORD James Thomas	Sgt.	Aircrew	604	On 604 Sqn., 1-7-40, Later transferred to Bomber Command. Awarded D.F.M. (29-12-42). Commissioned, 15-2-44. Released from R.A.F., 1946, as Fg. Off.			British
PIDD Leslie	Sgt.	Pilot	238	Joined 238 Sqn., 18-7-40. ✠ **1 Bf 109, 11-8-40.** Slightly wounded, 11-8-40.	✠	**Killed in Action** (15-9-40)	British
PIGG Oswald St. John	Fg. Off.	Pilot	72	On 72 Sqn., 1-7-40. ✠ **1 Bf 109, 15-9-40.**	✠	**Killed in Action** (1-9-40)	British
PILCH Edward Roman	Plt. Off.	Pilot	302	Joined 302 (Polish) Sqn., 16-7-40. ✠ **1 Do 17, 15-9-40; ✠ 1 Ju 88, 19-9-40.**	✠	Killed since Battle (20-2-41)	Polish
PILKINGTON Alfred	Sgt.	Aircrew	23	Joined 23 Sqn., 20-9-40.			British
PINCKNEY David John Colin	Fg. Off.	Pilot	603	Joined 603 Sqn., 6-7-40. ✠ **1 Bf 109, 29-8-40; ✠ 1 Bf 109, 17-10-40; ✠ 1 Bf 109, 19-10-40.** Awarded D.F.C.(8-5-42).	✠	Killed since Battle (23-1-42)	British
PINFOLD Herbert Moreton	Flt. Lt.	Pilot	56	Posted to 56 Sqn., 25-8-40, to command. Promoted Sqn. Ldr., 1-9-40. Retired from R.A.F., 1-10-58, as a Group Captain.			British
PINKHAM Philip Campbell	Flt. Lt.	Pilot	19	In command of 19 Sqn., 1-7-40, as Acting Sqn. Ldr. Awarded A.F.C.(11-7-40).	✠	**Killed in Action** (5-9-40)	British
PIPA Josef	Sgt.	Pilot	43	Joined 43 Sqn., 4-10-40. Commissioned, 2-2-43. Released from the R.A.F., 1946, as a Flight Lieutenant.	✠	Died since Battle (1977)	Czech
PIPER Arthur Howard	Sgt.	Aircrew	236	On 236 Sqn., 1-7-40. Posted away (to Bomber Command), 10-40. Commissioned, 5-6-41. Awarded D.F.C.(10-3-44). Retired from the R.A.F., 24-1-58, as a Squadron Leader.			British
PIPPARD Harold Alfred	Plt. Off.	Aircrew	29	Joined 29 Sqn., 7-40. Retired from the R.A.F., 5-9-58, as a Squadron Leader.			British
PIPPET John Gilbert	Plt. Off.	Pilot	64	Joined 64 Sqn., 16-10-40.	✠	Killed since Battle (23-2-41)	British
PISAREK Marian	Fg. Off.	Pilot	303	Joined 303 (Polish) Sqn., 21-8-40. ✠ **1 Bf 109, 7-9-40; ✠ 1 Bf 109, 15-9-40; ✠ 1 Bf 109, 5-10-40; ✠ 1 Bf 109, 7-10-40.** Awarded D.F.C.(30-10-41)	✠	Killed since Battle (29-4-42)	Polish
PITCHER Paul Brooks	Fg. Off.	Pilot	1(Canadian)	With 1(Canadian) Sqn., 20-6-40, on arrival in U.K. ✠ **1 Bf 109, 5-10-40.** Released from R.C.A.F., 28-11-44, as a Wing Commander.			Canadian
PITTMAN Geoffrey Edward	Plt. Off.	Pilot	17	On 17 Sqn., 1-7-40. ✠ **1 He 111 (shared), 12-7-40; ✠ 1 Bf 110 (shared), 11-8-40; ✠ 1 Bf 110 (shared), 25-8-40.** Released from R.A.F., 1-46, as a Squadron Leader.			British

Name	Rank	Role	Sqn.	Notes	Fate	Nationality
PLANT Ronald Eric	Sgt.	Pilot	72-611	Joined 72 Sqn., 11-7-40. Posted to 611 Sqn., 10-10-40.	✠ Killed since Battle (21-11-40)	British
PLEDGER Geoffrey Frank Colman	Plt. Off.	Aircrew	141	Defiant gunner. On 141 Sqn., 1-7-40.	✠ Killed since Battle (4-4-41)	British
PLENDERLEITH Robert	Sgt.	Pilot	73	On 73 Sqn., 1-7-40. ✠ 1 Bf 110, 27-9-40. Slightly wounded, 11-10-40. Commissioned, 21-11-42. Awarded D.F.C.(7-7-44). Released from the R.A.F., 21-7-47, as Flight Lieutenant.		British
PLUMMER Richard Pryer	Fg. Off.	Pilot	46	On 46 Sqn., 1-7-40. Mortally wounded, 4-9-40.	**Died of wounds** (14-9-40)	British
PLZAK Stanislaw ("Stando")	Sgt.	Pilot	310-19	Joined 310 (Czech) Sqn., 10-7-40, on formation. Attached to 19 Sqn., 29-8-40. ✠ 1 He 111, 18-9-40; ✠ 1 Bf 109, 27-9-40. Commissioned, 6-8-41.	✠ Killed since Battle (7-8-41)	Czech
PNIAK Karol	Plt. Off.	Pilot	32-257	Joined 32 Sqn., 8-8-40. Posted to 257 Sqn., 16-9-40. ✠ 1 Bf 109, 12-8-40; ✠ 1 Bf 109, 15-8-40; ✠ 2 Bf 109s, 18-8-40. Slightly injured, 25-8-40. On 11-11-40, ✠ 1 Fiat BR.20 (solo) and 1 BR.20 (shared). Awarded D.F.C. (1-6-42). Released from Polish Air Force, 12-46, as a Flight Lieutenant.	✠ Died since Battle (1980)	Polish
POCOCK Maurice Henry	Sgt.	Pilot	72	On 72 Sqn., 1-7-40. Wounded, 1-9-40. Commissioned, 16-5-42. Released from R.A.F., 19-12-46, as a Flight Lieutenant.		British
POLLARD Joseph Kenneth	Sgt.	Pilot	232	Joined 232 Sqn., 17-7-40, on formation.	✠ Killed since Battle (12-12-41)	British
POLLARD Philip Selwyn Covey ("Polly")	Plt. Off.	Pilot	611	On 611 Sqn., 1-7-40. ✠ 1 Do 17 (shared), 15-9-40; ✠ 2 Do 17s (shared), 11-11-40.	✠ Killed since Battle (22-6-41)	British
POND Arthur Herbert Dorrien	F/Sgt.	Pilot	601	On 601 Sqn., 1-7-40. ✠ 1 Ju 87, 18-8-40. Commissioned, 1-12-42. Awarded A.F.C.(1-1-46). Retired from R.A.F., 17-12-63, as a Squadron Leader.		British
PONTING William Alan	Plt. Off.	Aircrew	264	Defiant gunner. Joined 264 Sqn., 9-7-40.	**Killed in Action** (24-8-40)	British
POOL Peter Desmond	Plt. Off.	Pilot	266-72	Joined 266 Sqn., 26-8-40. Posted to 72 Sqn., 3-10-40. Wounded, 11-10-40.	✠ Killed since Battle (19-8-42)	British
POOLE Eric Leonard Ronald	Sgt.	Pilot	604	Joined 604 Sqn., 15-7-40. Commissioned, 30-7-43. Released from R.A.F., 1947, as a Flying Officer.		British
POPLAWSKI Jerzy	Plt. Off.	Pilot	111-229	Joined 111 Sqn., 10-9-40. Posted to 229 Sqn., 26-9-40. Released from the Polish Air Force, 2-47, as a Flight Lieutenant.		Polish
PORTER Edward Francis	Sgt.	Aircrew	141	Defiant gunner. Joined 141 Sqn., 20-8-40. Transferred to Bomber Command.	✠ Killed since Battle (2-7-41)	British
PORTER John Anthony ("Jackie")	Sgt.	Pilot	242-615	On 242 Sqn., 1-7-40. Posted to 615 Sqn., 10-8-40. ✠ 1 Ju 88 (solo) and 1 Ju 87 (shared), 14-8-40. Posted away, 23-9-40. Commissioned, 19-11-41. Released from the R.A.F., 1947, as a Flight Lieutenant.		British
PORTER Owen Wells	Sgt.	Pilot	111	Joined 111 Sqn., 31-8-40. Commissioned, 1-2-43.	✠ Killed since Battle (31-7-44)	British
POSENER Frederick Hyam	Plt. Off.	Pilot	152	On 152 Sqn., 1-7-40.	✠ Killed in Action (27-7-40)	South African
POTTER John Alfred	Sgt.	Pilot	19	On 19 Sqn., 1-7-40. ✠ 1 Bf 110, 16-8-40; ✠ 1 Bf 110, 18-8-40. Shot down and taken prisoner by the Germans, 15-9-40. Released from the R.A.F., 1946, as a Warrant Officer.	✠ Died since Battle (1977)	British
POULTON Harry Robert Godfrey	Plt. Off.	Pilot	616-64	Joined 616 Sqn., 23-9-40. Posted to 64 Sqn., 12-10-40. Awarded D.F.C.(25-5-43). Taken prisoner by the Germans, wounded, 1-44. Released from the R.A.F., 9-46, but rejoined, 9-51. Retired, 19-7-68, as a Flight Lieutenant.		British
POUND Reginald Robert Charles	Sgt.	Aircrew	25	Joined 25 Sqn., early 10-40.		British
POWELL Edwin ("Doc")	Sgt.	Aircrew	25	Joined 25 Sqn., 9-40.	✠ Killed since Battle (21-11-40)	British
POWELL Ronald James	Plt. Off.	Pilot	248	Joined 248 Sqn., 29-9-40. Flew reconnaissance sorties over Nowegian coast during 10-40.	✠ Killed since Battle (2-7-41)	British
POWELL Robin Peter Reginald	Flt. Lt.	Pilot	111	On 111 Sqn., 1-7-40. Awarded D.F.C.✿ (31-5-40 and 24-7-42). Retired from the R.A.F., 6-11-63, as a Group Captain.	✠ Died since Battle (28-1-70)	British
POWELL-SHEDDEN George ffolliott	Flt. Lt.	Pilot	242	On 242 Sqn., 1-7-40. ✠ 1 Do 17 (shared), 21-8-40; ✠ 1 Bf 109, 9-9-40; ✠ 1 Do 17, 9-9-40; ✠ 1 Do 17 (solo) and 1 Do 17 (shared), 15-9-40. Wounded, 15-9-40. Awarded D.S.O.(27-4-45), D.F.C.(12-12-41). Retired from the R.A.F., 20-3-61, as a Group Captain.		British
POWER Richard Maurice	Fg. Off.	Pilot	236	On 236 Sqn., 1-7-40. Injured, 26-7-40. Promoted Flt. Lt., 3-9-40. Released from the R.A.F., 1946, as a Wing Commander.		Australian
PRCHAL Edward Maximillian	Sgt.	Pilot	310	Joined 310 (Czech) Sqn., 10-7-40, on formation. ✠ 1 Do 17, 26-8-40. Slightly wounded, 26-8-40. Commissioned, 20-12-41. Lived in the U.S.A. after the War.	✠ Died since Battle (12-12-84)	Czech
PREATER Stanley George	Sgt.	Aircrew	235	Joined 235 Sqn., 13-7-40.		British
PREVOT Leon	Plt. Off.	Pilot	235	Joined 235 Sqn., 26-9-40. ✠ 1 He 59, 8-10-40. Awarded the D.F.C. and survived the War.		Belgian
PRICE Arthur Owen	Plt. Off.	Aircrew	236	On 236 Sqn., 1-7-40. Transferred to Bomber Command. Awarded D.F.C.(15-9-44). Released from the R.A.F., 1945, as a Squadron Leader.	✠ Died since Battle (1982)	British
PRICE James	Sgt.	Aircrew	29	Joined 29 Sqn., 14-9-40. Awarded D.F.M.(6-10-42). Commissioned, 12-4-42. Retired from the R.A.F., 12-7-74, as a Flight Lieutenant.	✠ Died since Battle (16-3-88)	British
PRICE Norman Albert Joseph	Sgt.	Pilot	236	Joined 236 Sqn., early 9-40. Taken prisoner by the Italians, 11-41, badly wounded. Medically discharged from the R.A.F., 10-45, as a Warrant Officer.		British
PRICE Robert Buckton	Sgt.	Pilot	245-73-222	Joined 245 Sqn., 27-9-40. Posted to 73 Sqn., 14-10-40. Posted to 222 Sqn., 23-10-40.	✠ Killed since Battle (15-11-41)	British
PRIESTLEY John Sinclair	Plt. Off.	Pilot	235	Joined 235 Sqn., 22-8-40.	**Killed in Accident** (30-8-40)	New Zealander
PRIHODA Josef	Sgt.	Pilot	1	Joined 1 Sqn., 5-10-40. Commissioned and awarded D.F.C. in 1941.	✠ Killed since Battle (6-3-43)	Czech
PRITCHARD Charles Arthur	Fg. Off.	Pilot	600	On 600 Sqn., 1-7-40; Promoted Flt. Lt., 3-9-40. ✠ 1 Ju 88, 15/16-9-40. Awarded D.F.C.(24-6-41). Released from R.A.F., 1945, as Squadron Leader.		Australian
PROCTOR Jack	Sgt.	Pilot	602	On 602 Sqn., 1-7-40. ✠ 1 Ju 88, 31-8-40; ✠ 1 Bf 109, 6-9-40; ✠ 1 Bf 110, 7-9-40; ✠ 1 Bf 110, 11-9-40.	✠ Killed since Battle (18-4-41)	British
PROCTOR John Ernest	Plt. Off.	Pilot	32	Joined 32 Sqn., 10-7-40. ✠ 1 Bf 110 (solo) and 1 Bf 110 (shared), 20-7-40; ✠ 1 Bf 109, 12-8-40; ✠ 1 Bf 109, 24-8-40. Awarded D.F.C.✿ (18-3-41 and 1944?). Retired from the R.A.F., 15-10-57, as a Wing Commander.		British
PROSSER Percy Rollo	Sgt.	Aircrew	235	On 235 Sqn., 1-7-40.	✠ Killed since Battle (16-12-40)	British
PROUDMAN Douglas Harry	Sgt.	Aircrew	248	Joined 248 Sqn., mid-7-40.	✠ Died since Battle (27-4-41)	British
PROWSE Harry Arthur Robin	Plt. Off.	Pilot	266-603	Joined 266 Sqn., 16-9-40. Posted to 603 Sqn., 20-10-40. Shot down and taken prisoner by the Germans, 4-7-41. Released by the R.A.F., 1947, as Flight Lieutenant.		British
PTACEK Rudolf	Sgt.	Pilot	43	Joined 43 Sqn., 4-10-40.	✠ Killed since Battle (28-1-41)	Czech
PUDA Raimund	Sgt.	Pilot	310-605	Joined 310 (Czech) Sqn., 8-40. ✠ 1 Do 17 (shared), 15-9-40; ✠ 1 Do 17 (shared), 18-9-40. Posted to 605 Sqn., 19-10-40. Commissioned, 24-6-41. Released from the R.A.F., 1946, as a Flight Lieutenant.		Czech
PUDNEY Geoffrey Bruce	Sub-Lieut.	Pilot	64	Fleet Air Arm. Joined 64 Sqn., 1-7-40.	✠ Killed since Battle (26-8-41)	British
PUGH John Stewart	Sgt.	Aircrew	29	On 29 Sqn., 1-7-40. As gunner with Plt. Off. M.J. Herrick: ✠ 2 He 111s, 4-9-40; ✠ 1 He 111, 15-9-40. Commissioned, 13-3-42. Awarded D.F.C.(21-9-45).		British
PUGH Thomas Patrick	Fg. Off.	Pilot	263	On 263 Sqn., 1-7-40. Awarded D.F.C.(21-10-41)	✠ Killed since Battle (2-8-43)	British
PUSHMAN George Rupert	Plt. Off.	Pilot	23	On 23 Sqn., 1-7-40. Awarded D.F.C.(17-10-44). Transferred to R.C.A.F., 3-45.		Canadian
PUTT Alan Robert	Flt. Lt.	Pilot	501	Joined 501 Sqn., 5-8-40. Released from the R.A.F., 1946, as Wing Commander.	✠ Died since Battle (1977)	British
PUXLEY William George Vernon	Sgt.	Aircrew	236	Joined 236 Sqn., 20-9-40. Commissioned, 7-3-42. Released from the R.A.F., 1946, as a Flight Lieutenant.	✠ Died since Battle (1984)	British
PYE John Walter	Sgt.	Aircrew	25	On 25 Sqn., 1-7-40. Commissioned, 16-5-41. Transferred to to the Reserve in New Zealand, 28-1-46, as a Flight Lieutenant.		New Zealander

Name	Rank	Duty	Sqn	Details	Fate	Nationality
PYMAN Laurence Lee	Plt. Off.	Pilot	65	Joined 65 Sqn., 20-7-40. Promoted Fg. Off., 31-7-40. ✠ 1 Bf 109, 14-8-40.	✟ Killed in Action (16-8-40)	British
PYNE Colin Campbell	Sgt.	Aircrew	219	Joined 219 Sqn., 6-7-40. Injured in ground accident, 7-9-42, and returned to New Zealand on medical grounds. Released from R.N.Z.A.F., 27-7-43.	✟ Died since Battle (19-2-75)	New Zealander
QUELCH Basil Herbert	Sgt.	Pilot	235	On 235 Sqn., 1-7-40. Commissioned, 30-12-41. Awarded D.F.C.(6-2-45). Released from the R.A.F., 1946, as a Flight Lieutenant.		British
QUILL Jeffery Kindersley	Fg. Off.	Pilot	65	Chief Test Pilot, Vickers (Aviation) Ltd. Attached to 65 Sqn., during 8-40. ✠ 1 Bf 109, 16-8-40. Awarded A.F.C.(23-6-36).		British
QUINN James	Sgt.	Pilot	236	Joined 236 Sqn., 10-10-40. Commissioned, 12-8-41. Awarded D.F.C.✸ (1-9-42 and 1944?). Retired from the R.A.F., 20-10-69, as a Group Captain.		British
RABAGLIATI Alexander Coultate ("Ratbag")	Flt. Lt.	Pilot	46	On 46 Sqn., 1-7-40. ✠ 1 Bf 110, 14-8-40; ✠ 1 Bf 109, 5-9-40; ✠ 1 Bf 109, 14-9-40; ✠ 1 Ju 88, 27-9-40; ✠ 1 Bf 109, 29-10-40. Awarded D.F.C.✸ (22-10-40 and 31-10-41).	✟ Killed since Battle (6-7-43)	British
RABONE John Henry Michael	Fg. Off.	Pilot	604	On 604 Sqn., 1-7-40. Promoted Flt. Lt., 3-9-40. Posted away, 24-9-40. Released from the R.A.F., 1945, as a Flight Lieutenant.		British
RABONE Paul Wattling	Plt. Off.	Pilot	145-422 Flt.	Joined 145 Sqn., 19-8-40. ✠ 1 Bf 109, 12-10-40. Posted to 422 Flt., 28-10-40. Awarded D.F.C.(25-1-44).	✟ Killed since Battle (24-7-44)	New Zealander
RADOMSKI Jerzy	Plt. Off.	Pilot	303	Joined 303 (Polish) Sqn., 21-8-40. ✠ 1 Do 17 (shared), 30-9-40. Released from the Polish Air Force, 11-46, and joined the R.A.F., 1951. Retired, 18-7-73, as Flight Lieutenant.	✟ Died since Battle (1978)	Polish
RADWANSKI Gustaw	Plt. Off.	Pilot	56	Joined 56 Sqn., 15-9-40. Released from the Polish Air Force, 1946, as a Flight Lieutenant.		Polish
RAFTER William Pearce Haughton	Plt. Off.	Pilot	603	Joined 603 Sqn., 31-8-40. Wounded, 5-9-40.	✟ Killed since Battle (29-11-40)	British
RAINE Woodrow	Sgt.	Pilot	610	Joined 610 Sqn., 5-10-40.	✟ Killed since Battle (21-8-41)	British
RAINS Douglas Norman	Sgt.	Aircrew	248	Joined 248 Sqn., 7-40. Flew on reconnaissance sorties over Norwegian coast during the Battle of Britain.	✟ Killed since Battle (12-8-42)	British
RALLS Leslie Francis	Sgt.	Pilot	605	On 605 Sqn., 1-7-40. Commissioned, 13-5-42. Made O.B.E.(1-1-71). Retired from the R.A.F., 20-12-72, as a Wing Commander.	✟ Died since Battle (1976)	British
RAMSAY John Basil	Plt. Off.	Pilot	151	Joined 151 Sqn., 29-7-40.	✟ Killed in Action (18-8-40)	British
RAMSAY John Strachan	Sgt.	Aircrew	235	Joined 235 Sqn., 18-8-40.	✟ Killed since Battle (27-4-41)	British
RAMSAY Norman Hugh Donald	Sgt.	Pilot	610-222	On 610 Sqn., 1-7-40. ✠ 1 Bf 110, 14-8-40. Posted to 222 Sqn., 15-9-40. Commissioned, 19-3-41. Awarded D.F.C.(28-9-43). Retired from the R.A.F., 29-7-62, as a Flight Lieutenant.		British
RAMSHAW John William	Sgt.	Pilot	222	On 222 Sqn., 1-7-40.	✟ Killed in Action (4-9-40)	British
RASMUSSEN Lauritz Andrew Woodney	Sgt.	Aircrew	264	Joined 264 Sqn., 29-8-40.	✟ Killed in Action (4-9-40)	New Zealander
RAVENHILL Malcolm	Plt. Off.	Pilot	229	On 229 Sqn., 1-7-40. Slightly wounded, 11-9-40.	✟ Killed in Action (30-9-40)	British
RAWLENCE Anthony James	Fg. Off.	Pilot	600	On 600 Sqn., 1-7-40. Released from the R.A.F., 1945, as a Squadron Leader.		British
RAWNSLEY Cecil Frederick ("Jimmy")	Sgt.	Aircrew	604	On 604 Sqn., 1-7-40. Commissioned, 14-7-41. Awarded D.S.O.(26-10-43), D.F.C. (19-9-41), D.F.M.✸ (4-4-41 and 23-5-41). Released from the R.A.F., 1946, as a Squadron Leader.	✟ Died since Battle (12-2-65)	British
RAY Ronald Wilfred	Sgt.	Pilot	56	Joined 56 Sqn., 5-9-40. Wounded, 30-9-40. Released from the R.A.F., 1946, as a Warrant Officer.	✟ Died since Battle (1985)	British
RAYNER Roderick Malachi Seaburne	Fg. Off.	Pilot	87	On 87 Sqn., 1-7-40. ✠ 1 Bf 110, 15-8-40. Awarded D.F.C.(11-2-41). Released from the R.A.F., 1946, as a Wing Commander.	✟ Died since Battle (1982)	British
READ William Albert Alexander ("Tannoy")	Plt. Off.	Pilot	603	Joined 603 Sqn., 7-7-40. Awarded A.F.C.(11-6-42). Released from the R.A.F., 3-46, as a Flight Lieutenant.		British
REAM Charles Alfred	Sgt.	Pilot	235	Joined 235 Sqn., 22-9-40.	✟ Died since Battle (1947)	British
REARDON-PARKER John	Sub-Lieut.	Pilot	804	Fleet Air Arm. On 804 Sqn., 1-7-40. Commission terminated, 28-11-41. (Death details speculative.)	✟ Killed since Battle (7-6-44)	British
RECHKA Joseph	Sgt.	Pilot	310	Joined 310 (Czech) Sqn., 10-7-40, on formation. ✠ 1 He 111 (shared), 15-9-40.	✟ Died since Battle (1984)	Czech
REDDINGTON Leslie Arthur Edwin	Sgt.	Pilot	152	Joined 152 Sqn., 8-40.	✟ Killed in Action (30-9-40)	British
REDFERN Eric Redfern	Sgt.	Pilot	607-232	On 607 Sqn., 1-7-40. Posted to 232 Sqn., 27-8-40.	✟ Killed since Battle (17-8-41)	British
REDMAN John	Plt. Off.	Pilot	245-43-257	On 245 Sqn., 1-7-40. Posted to 43 Sqn., 16-9-40. Posted to 257 Sqn., 10-40.	✟ Killed since Battle (20-4-43)	British
REECE Lawrence Hugh Murrell	Sgt.	Aircrew	235	On 235 Sqn., 1-7-40.	✟ Killed in Action (18-7-40)	British
REED Horace	Sgt.	Aircrew	600	Joined 600 Sqn., 11-7-40. Released from R.A.F., 13-9-45, as a Corporal.		British
REES Brian Victor	Fg. Off.	Pilot	610	On 610 Sqn., 1-7-40. ✠ 1 Bf 109, 12-8-40; ✠ 1 Do 17 and 1 Bf 109, 18-8-40. Believed released from R.A.F., 1944.	✟ Died since Battle (1979)	British
REES, J.A.	Sgt.	Pilot	601	Joined 601 Sqn., 11-9-40.		British
REID Robert	Plt. Off.	Pilot	46	On 46 Sqn., 1-7-40. ✠ 1 Bf 109, 18-9-40; ✠ 1 Bf 109, 15-10-40. Was a Squadron Leader at the time of death.	✟ Killed since Battle (23-3-45)	British
REILLEY Hugh William	Plt. Off.	Pilot	64-66	Joined 64 Sqn., early 9-40. Posted to 66 Sqn., 15-9-40. ✠ 1 Bf 109, 27-9-40.	✟ Killed in Action (17-10-40)	American
REILLEY Charles Christopher	Sgt.	Aircrew	23	Joined 23 Sqn., 21-9-40. Commissioned, 10-6-42.	✟ Killed since Battle (28-10-42)	New Zealander
RENVOIZE James Verdun	Sgt.	Pilot	247	Joined 247 Sqn., 14-8-40. Commissioned, 23-10-41. Released from the R.A.F., 1-46, as a Flight Lieutenant.		British
REYNELL Richard Carew	Flt. Lt.	Pilot	43	Test pilot with Hawker Aircraft Ltd. Attached to 43 Sqn., 26-8-40. ✠ 1 Bf 109, 2-9-40.	✟ Killed in Action (7-9-40)	Australian
REYNO Edwin Michael	Flt. Lt.	Pilot	1(Canadian)	With 1(Canadian) Sqn., 20-6-40, on arrival in U.K. Awarded A.F.C.(8-6-44). Retired from Canadian Forces, 30-10-72, as Lieutenant General.	✟ Died since Battle (10-2-82)	Canadian
RHODES Richard Arthur	Plt. Off.	Pilot	29	On 29 Sqn., 1-7-40. ✠ 1 He 111, 18-8-40.	✟ Killed in Action (25-8-40)	British
RHODES-MOORHOUSE William Henry	Fg. Off.	Pilot	601	On 601 Sqn., 1-7-40. ✠ 1 Do 17 (shared), 7-7-40; ✠ 1 Do 17 (shared), 11-7-40. Awarded D.F.C.(30-7-40). ✠ 1 Ju 88, 16-8-40; ✠ 2 Bf 109s, 11-8-40; ✠ 1 Bf 109, 18-8-40; ✠ 1 He 111 (shared), 30-8-40; ✠ 1 Do 17, 4-9-40. (Was the son of W.B. Rhodes-Moorhouse, the first recipient of the Victoria Cross for aerial combat, 26-4-15.)	✟ Killed in Action (6-9-40)	British
RICALTON Alan Leslie	Plt. Off.	Pilot	74	Promoted Fg. Off., 17-8-40. Joined 74 Sqn., 21-8-40.	✟ Killed in Action (17-10-40)	British
RICH Peter Geoffrey	Sgt.	Aircrew	25	Joined 25 Sqn., early 10-40.		British
RICHARDS Duncan Hamilton	Sub-Lieut.	Pilot	111	Fleet Air Arm. Joined 111 Sqn., 22-9-40. Was still serving with the Royal Navy at the time of his death as a Lieutenant Commander.	✟ Died since Battle (2-9-55)	British
RICHARDS William Charles	Sgt.	Pilot	235	Joined 235 Sqn., early 10-10-40. Commissioned, 5-7-41.	✟ Killed since Battle (11-8-41)	British
RICHARDSON Eric	Sgt.	Pilot	242	On 242 Sqn., 1-7-40. ✠ 1 Ju 88, 1-8-40; ✠ 1 Do 17, 9-9-40. Posted away, 18-9-40. Commissioned, 19-2-41. Awarded D.F.C.(9-9-41). Retired from the R.A.F., 1-10-58, as a Squadron Leader.	✟ Died since Battle (2-9-73)	British
RICHARDSON Roland Wharrier	Sgt.	Pilot	610	Joined 610 Sqn., 14-10-40. Commissioned, 3-12-41. Awarded A.F.C.(13-6-59). Retired from the R.A.F., 2-5-63, as a Squadron Leader.	✟ Died since Battle (18-11-88)	British
RICHARDSON Ronald William	Sgt.	Aircrew	141	Defiant gunner. On 141 Sqn., 1-7-40. Commissioned, 9-9-43. Released from the R.A.F., 1946, as a Flying Officer.	✟ Died since Battle (12-70)	British

Name	Rank	Role	Sqn.	Details	Fate	Nationality
RICHARDSON William Arthur	Sqn. Ldr.	Pilot	141	In command of 141 Sqn., 1-7-40. Posted away, 9-40. Retired from the R.A.F., 19-7-55, as a Wing Commander.	Died since Battle (1970)	British
RICKETTS Herbert Wain	Sgt.	Aircrew	235	On 235 Sqn., 1-7-40. Commissioned, 21-3-44.	Killed since Battle (31-3-45)	British
RICKETTS Victor Anthony	Plt. Off.	Pilot	248	On 248 Sqn., 1-7-40. Flew reconnaissance sorties over Norwegain coast during the Battle of Britain. Awarded D.F.C.(2-6-42)	Killed since Battle (12-7-42)	British
RICKS Leo Patrick Vincent John	Sgt.	Aircrew	235	On 235 Sqn., 1-7-40. Transferred to R.C.A.F., 14-2-45. Commissioned later, and retired as a Flying Officer.	Died since Battle (8-1-85)	Canadian
RIDDELL-HANNAM John Derrick	Sgt.	Aircrew	236	Joined 236 Sqn., 16-9-40. Commissioned in R.A.F. Regiment, 13-6-44. Retired, 1-55, as a Flight Lieutenant. Changed name to **HANNAM**.		British
RIDDLE Christopher John Henry	Fg. Off.	Pilot	601	On 601 Sqn., 1-7-40. ✠ **1 Do 17 (shared), 4-9-40**. Promoted Flt. Lt., 14-10-40. Released from the R.A.F., 1946, as Squadron Leader. Brother of Flt. Lt. H.J. Riddle.		British
RIDDLE Hugh Joseph	Fg. Off.	Pilot	601	On 601 Sqn., 1-7-40. ✠ **1 Bf 110 (shared), 11-7-40**. Promoted Flt. Lt., 3-9-40. Released from R.A.F., 1945, as Squadron Leader. Brother of Flt. Lt. C.J.H. Riddle.		British
RIDLEY Marmaduke	Sgt.	Pilot	616	On 616 Sqn., 1-7-40.	**Killed in Action** (26-8-40)	British
RIGBY Robert Harold	Plt. Off.	Pilot	236	On 236 Sqn., 1-7-40. Killed during photo reconnaissance sortie over France.	**Killed in Action** (18-7-40)	British
RILEY Frederick	Plt. Off.	Pilot	236	On 236 Sqn., 1-7-40.	Killed since Battle (7-12-42)	British
RILEY William	Flt. Lt.	Pilot	263-302-145	On 263 Sqn., 1-7-40. Posted to 302 (Polish) Sqn., 13-7-40. ✠ **1 Ju 88, 18-9-40; ✠ 1 Bf 109, 15-10-40**. Posted to 145 Sqn., 30-10-40. Awarded D.F.C.(31-10-41)	Killed since Battle (16-7-42)	British
RIMMER Reginald Frank	Fg. Off.	Pilot	229	On 229 Sqn., 1-7-40. ✠ **1 Do 17 (solo) and 1 He 111 (shared), 15-9-40**.	**Killed in Action** (27-9-40)	British
RINGWOOD Eric Alfred	Sgt.	Aircrew	248	Joined 248 Sqn., mid-7-40. Was killed during reconnaissance sortie over Norwegian coast.	**Killed in Action** (27-8-40)	British
RIPLEY William George	Sgt.	Aircrew	604	Joined 604 Sqn., 20-8-40. Awarded D.F.M.(13-5-41). Commissioned.(12-1-43.	Died of wounds (16-11-43)	British
RIPPON Anthony John	Plt. Off.	Pilot	601	Joined 601 Sqn., 26-9-40. Awarded D.F.C.(5-9-40).	Killed since Battle (25-8-44)	British
RISELEY Arthur Harry	Sgt.	Aircrew	600	On 600 Sqn., 1-7-40. Qualified as pilot, 1941. Commissioned, 3-9-41. Awarded D.S.O.(14-1-44). Released from R.A.F., 1-4-46, as Squadron Leader.		British
RITCHER Geoffrey Louis	Plt. Off.	Pilot	234	Joined 234 Sqn., mid-9-40. Released from R.A.F., 1946, as Squadron Leader.		British
RITCHIE Ian Small	Fg. Off.	Pilot	603	On 603 Sqn., 1-7-40. ✠ **1 Ju 88 (shared), 3-7-40; ✠ 1 He 111 (shared), 16-7-40**. Wounded, 28-8-40. Promoted Fg. Off., 3-9-40. Released from R.A.F., 1945, as a Wing Commander.		British
RITCHIE James Ritchie	Plt. Off.	Pilot	600-111-72	Joined 600 Sqn., 1-7-40. Posted to 111 Sqn. Posted to 72 Sqn., 10-9-40. Awarded A.F.C.(13-6-46). Retired from R.A.F., 3-6-72, as Wg. Cdr.		British
RITCHIE John Millar	Plt. Off.	Aircrew	141	Defiant gunner. On 141 Sqn., 1-7-40. Posted away, 30-8-40. Retired from the R.A.F., 20-1-59, as a Squadron Leader.		British
RITCHIE Robert Douglas	Sgt.	Pilot	605	On 605 Sqn., 1-7-40.	**Killed in Action** (9-8-40)	British
RITCHIE Thomas Glyn Finlayson	Plt. Off.	Pilot	602	On 602 Sqn., 1-7-40. ✠ **1 Ju 88 (shared), 19-8-40; ✠ 1 Bf 110, 25-8-40**.	Killed since Battle (3-7-41)	British
ROACH Robert James Bain	Plt. Off.	Pilot	266	On 266 Sqn., 1-7-40. ✠ **1 He 115 (shared), 15-8-40; ✠ 1 Do 17 (shared), 7-9-40**. Retired from R.A.F., 25-10-65, retaining rank of Squadron Leader.		British
ROBB Robert Andrew Lindsay	Plt. Off.	Pilot	236	Joined 236 Sqn., 26-9-40.		British
ROBBINS Robert Horley	Sgt.	Pilot	54-66	On 54 Sqn. Posted to 66 Sqn., 11-9-40. Severely wounded, 14-9-40. Commissioned, 24-10-43. Released from R.A.F., 1947, as a Flight Lieutenant.		British
ROBERTS Arthur John Alan	Sgt.	Pilot	29	On 29 Sqn., 1-7-40. Commissioned, 24-4-41. Awarded D.F.C.(20-8-43). Retired from the R.A.F., 23-12-57, as a Squadron Leader.		British
ROBERTS David Francis	Sgt.	Aircrew	25	Joined 25 Sqn., 8-40.	Killed since Battle (3-4-41)	British
ROBERTS David Neal	Wg. Cdr.	Pilot	238-609	Station and Sector Commander, Middle Wallop, during Battle. Flew operational sorties with 238 and 609 Sqns. Retired from R.A.F., 29-5-58, as Air Commodore, C.B.E.(1-1-54); O.B.E., 24-9-41), A.F.C.(9-6-38).		British
ROBERTS Elwyn Cooper	Sgt.	Aircrew	23	On 23 Sqn., 1-7-40. Commissioned, 4-2-42. Resigned commission, 1947.		British
ROBERTS George William	Midshipman	Pilot	808	Fleet Air Arm. On 808 Sqn., 1-7-40. Embarked in H.M.S. *Ark Royal*, 22-10-40.	Killed since Battle (30-5-46)	British
ROBERTS Ralph	Plt. Off.	Pilot	615-64	On 615 Sqn., 1-7-40. Joined 64 Sqn., 8-40. ✠ **1 Do 17, 13-8-40**. Shot down andtaken prisoner by the Germans, 15-8-40. Released from the R.A.F., 9-3-46, as a Flight Lieutenant.		British
ROBERTSON Basil Lionel	Sgt.	Pilot	54	Joined 54 Sqn., 22-8-40.	Killed since Battle (12-2-42)	British
ROBERTSON Frederick Neal	Sgt.	Pilot	66	On 66 Sqn., 1-7-40. ✠ **1 Do 17 (shared), 10-7-40**. Posted away, 18-7-40. Awarded D.F.M.(18-3-41). Commissioned, 30-3-42.	Killed since Battle (31-8-43)	British
ROBINSON Andrew Ian	Fg. Off.	Pilot	222	On 222 Sqn., 1-7-40. ✠ **1 Bf 109, 31-8-40; ✠ 1 Bf 109, 2-9-40**. Wounded, 2-9-40. Promoted Flt. Lt., 3-9-40. Released from R.A.F., 1946, as Squadron Leader.	Died since Battle (1958)	British
ROBINSON Denis Norman	Sgt.	Pilot	152	On 152 Sqn., 1-7-40. ✠ **1 Bf 109, 5-8-40; ✠ 1 Bf 109, 15-8-40; ✠ 1 Ju 87, 17-8-40; ✠ 1 Ju 88, 4-9-40**. Commissioned, 15-1-41. Released from the R.A.F., 1946, as a Flight Lieutenant.		British
ROBINSON Gerald	Plt. Off.	Aircraft	264	Defiant gunner. On 264 Sqn., 1-7-40. Made M.B.E.(1-1-45). Released from R.A.F., 1945, as a Flight Lieutenant.		British
ROBINSON James	Sgt.	Pilot	111	Re-joined 111 Sqn., 18-7-40 (after recovery from wounds). ✠ **1 He 59 (shared), 28-7-40**. Commissioned, 2-1-42. Awarded A.F.C.(8-6-44). Released from R.A.F., 1945, as a Flight Lieutenant.	Died since Battle (2-7-56)	British
ROBINSON James Clifton Edmeston	Plt. Off.	Pilot	1	Joined 1 Sqn., late 9-40. Promoted Fg. Off., 3-10-40. ✠ **1 Do 17, 29-10-40**.	Killed since Battle (21-5-41)	British
ROBINSON Marcus	Sqn. Ldr.	Pilot	616	In command of 616 Sqn., 1-7-40. Posted away, 9-40. Awarded A.F.C.✿ (30-9-41 and 1-1-44). Released from R.A.F., 2-46, as Group Captain. Commanded 602 Sqn., R.Aux.A.F., 9-46 until 1951. Appointed C.B.(31-5-56)		British
ROBINSON Michael Lister	Flt. Lt.	Pilot	601-238-609	Joined 601 Sqn., 16-8-40. Posted to 238 Sqn., 28-9-40. Posted to 609 Sqn., 4-10-40. ✠ **1 Bf 109, 18-8-40; ✠ 1 Bf 109, 6-9-40; ✠ 2 Bf 110s, 28-9-40; ✠ 2 Bf 110s, 7-10-40**. Awarded D.S.O.(5-8-41), D.F.C.(26-11-40)	Killed since Battle (10-4-42)	British
ROBINSON Maurice Wilbraham Sandford	Sqn. Ldr.	Pilot	73	Joined 73 Sqn., 8-8-40, to command. ✠ **1 Bf 110, 7-9-40; ✠ 1 Bf 110, 11-9-40**. Wounded, 14-9-40. Appointed C.B.E.(1-1-46). Retired from R.A.F., 1-3-58, as an Air Commodore.	Died since Battle (1977)	British
ROBINSON Peter Beverley	Fg. Off.	Pilot	601	On 601 Sqn., 1-7-40. ✠ **1 Bf 109, 6-9-40; ✠ 1 Bf 110, 25-9-40**. Released from the R.A.F., 1945, as a Wing Commander.		British
ROBINSON Peter Ethelbert Merrick	Sgt.	Pilot	56	Joined 56 Sqn., 25-7-40. ✠ **1 Bf 110, 18-8-40**. Commissioned 5-6-41.	Killed since Battle (17-6-41)	British
ROBINSON Peter Trevor	Sgt.	Pilot	257	Joined 257 Sqn., 3-8-40.	Died since Battle (3-10-75)	British
ROBSHAW Frederick Aspinall	Plt. Off.	Pilot	85-229	Joined 85 Sqn., 16-9-40. Posted to 229 Sqn., 27-9-40. Slightly wounded, 30-9-40. Released from the R.A.F., 1946, as a Flight Lieutenant.		British
ROBSON Norman Charles Harold	Plt. Off.	Pilot	72	On 72 Sqn., 1-7-40. Promoted Fg. Off.. 17-8-40. ✠ **1 He 111, 15-8-40; ✠ 1 Do 17 (shared), 10-9-40; ✠ 1 Do 17 (shared), 27-9-40**. Was still serving at the time of his death as a Squadron Leader.	Killed since Battle (18-1-54)	British
RODEN Henry Adrian Charles	Sgt.	Pilot	19	On 19 Sqn., 1-7-40. Slightly wounded, 15-9-40. (Died of wounds suffered on 15-11-40).	Died of wounds (16-11-40)	British
ROFE Bernard John	Plt. Off.	Pilot	25	On 25 Sqn., 1-7-40. Promoted Fg. Off., 1-9-40.	Killed since Battle (12-1-42)	British
ROGERS Bruce Arthur	Fg. Off.	Pilot	85-242	Joined 85 Sqn., 15-9-40. Posted to 242 Sqn., 28-9-40.	Killed since Battle (17-6-41)	British
ROGERS Everett Bryan	Plt. Off.	Pilot	615-501	Joined 615 Sqn., 4-8-40. Posted to 501 Sqn., 13-9-40. ✠ **1 Do 17, 15-9-40**. Transferred to Bomber Command. Awarded D.F.C.(27-3-45). Released from the R.A.F., 1945, as a Squadron Leader.	Died since Battle (1960)	British

Name	Rank	Role	Sqn.	Details		Fate	Nationality
ROGERS George Wade	Sgt.	Pilot	234	Joined 234 Sqn., 9-40.	✠	Killed since Battle (16-1-41)	British
ROGOWSKI Jan Aleksander	Sgt.	Pilot	303	Joined 303 (Polish) Sqn., 19-8-40. ✠ **1 Bf 109, 2-9-40.**	✠	Killed since Battle (28-5-43)	Polish
ROHACEK Rudolf Bohumil	Plt. Off.	Pilot	238-601	Joined 238 Sqn., 8-40. Posted to 601 Sqn., 9-9-40, but returned to 238 Sqn., 8-10-40.	✠	Killed since Battle (27-4-42)	Czech
ROLLS William Thomas Edward	Sgt.	Pilot	72	On 72 Sqn., 1-7-40. ✠ **1 Bf 110 and 1 Do 17, 2-9-40;** ✠ **2 Ju 88s, 4-9-40;** ✠ **1 Do 17, 8-9-40;** ✠ **1 Bf 109, 14-9-40;** ✠ **1 Bf 109, 20-9-40.** Awarded D.F.M.(8-11-40). Commissioned, 6-1-42. Awarded D.F.C.(4-12-42). Released from the R.A.F., 1-46, as a Flight Lieutenant.	✠	Died since Battle (7-88)	British
ROMAN Charles	Plt. Off.	Pilot	236	Joined 236 Sqn., 5-8-40. Awarded D.S.O. and D.F.C. Released from the R.A.F., 1946, as a Squadron Leader.	✠	Died since Battle (1951)	Belgian
ROOK Anthony Hartwell	Fg. Off.	Pilot	504	On 504 Sqn., 1-7-40. Promoted Flt. Lt., 3-9-40. ✠ **1 Bf 110, 27-9-40.** Awarded D.F.C.(3-3-42), A.F.C.(8-6-44). Released from the R.A.F., 1945, as a Wing Commander. Commanded 504 Sqn., R.Aux.A.F., 1946-48.	✠	Died since Battle (1976)	British
ROOK Michael	Plt. Off.	Pilot	504	On 504 Sqn., 1-7-40. Promoted Fg. Off., 8-8-40. ✠ **1 Do 17 (shared), 15-9-40;** ✠ **1 Bf 110, 27-9-40.** Awarded D.F.C., 16-2-43. Released from the R.A.F., 1946, as a Wing Commander.	✠	Killed since Battle (13-3-48)	British
ROSCOE Geoffrey Lawrence	Plt. Off.	Pilot	79-87	Joined 79 Sqn., 17-9-40. Posted to 87 Sqn., 8-10-40.	✠	Killed since Battle (24-2-42)	British
ROSE Jack	Plt. Off.	Pilot	3-32	On 3 Sqn., 1-7-40. Posted to 32 Sqn., 20-8-40. Promoted Fg. Off., 3-9-40. Awarded D.F.C.(9-10-42). Released from the R.A.F., 1946, as a Wing Commander. Later made C.M.G., M.B.E.			British
ROSE James Stanley	Sgt.	Pilot	23	On 23 Sqn., 1-7-40.	✠	Killed since Battle (4-3-41)	British
ROSE Stuart Nigel	Plt. Off.	Pilot	602	On 602 Sqn., 1-7-40. ✠ **1 Bf 110, 25-8-40;** ✠ **1 Bf 109, 29-10-40.** Released from the R.A.F., 2-46, as a Squadron Leader.			British
ROSE-PRICE Arthur Thomas	Fg. Off.	Pilot	501	Joined 504 Sqn., 2-9-40. (Killed later on this day).	✠	**Killed in Action** (2-9-40)	British
ROSIER Frederick Ernest ("Hettie")	Flt. Lt.	Pilot	229	Assumed command of 229 Sqn., 19-10-40. Awarded D.S.O.(13-2-42). Retired from the R.A.F., 3-9-73, as Air Chief Marshal, G.C.B.(3-6-72; K.C.B., 11-6-61; C.B., 31-12-60), C.B.E.(1-1-55; O.B.E., 2-6-43).			British
ROSS Alexander Richard	Plt. Off.	Pilot	610	Joined 610 Sqn., 22-9-40.	✠	Killed since Battle (15-4-41)	British
ROSS Jack Kenneth	Plt. Off.	Pilot	17	On 1-7-40. ✠ **1 Do 17 (shared), 2-10-40;** ✠ **1 Do 17 (shared), 6-10-40.** ✠ **1 Do 17, 27-10-40.** Awarded D.F.C.(25-11-41).	✠	Killed since Battle (6-1-42)	British
ROTHWELL John Hedley	Plt. Off.	Pilot	601-32-605	Joined 601 Sqn., 28-8-40. Posted to 32 Sqn., 24-9-40. Posted to 605 Sqn., 12-10-40.	✠	Killed since Battle (22-4-41)	British
ROUND James Henry	Sgt.	Pilot	248	On 248 Sqn., 1-7-40. Killed while flying a reconnaissance sortie over Norwegain coast.	✠	**Killed in Action** (3-8-40)	British
ROURKE John	Sgt.	Aircrew	248	Flew with 248 Sqn. during Battle of Britain on reconnaissance sorties over the Norwegian coast. Commissioned, 26-1-45. Released from R.A.F., 1946, as Fg. Off.	✠	Died since Battle (1966)	British
ROUSE Geoffrey Walter	Sgt.	Pilot	236	Joined 236 Sqn., 12-9-40. Commissioned, 12-8-42. Awarded D.F.C.(5-12-44). Released from the R.A.F., 1946, as a Flight Lieutenant.			British
ROWDEN John Hampton	Plt. Off.	Pilot	616-64	Joined 616 Sqn., 2-9-40. Posted to 64 Sqn., 13-10-40.	✠	Killed since Battle (9-4-41)	British
ROWELL Peter Archibald	Sgt.	Pilot	249	On 249 Sqn., 1-7-40. Commissioned, 6-1-42. Awarded A.F.C., 1-1-47. Retired from R.A.F., 1-4-50, as a Flight Lieutenant.			British
ROWLEY Richard Michael Bernard	Fg. Off.	Pilot	145	On 145 Sqn., 1-7-40. Promoted Flt. Lt., 3-9-40.	✠	Killed since Battle (1941?)	British
ROYCE Michael Elliott Appelbee ("Scruffy")	Fg. Off.	Pilot	504	On 504 Sqn., 1-7-40. ✠ **1 Do 17 (shared), 15-9-40;** ✠ **1 Bf 110, 27-9-40.** Released from the R.A.F., 1946, as Squadron Leader. Brother of W.B. Royce.			British
ROYCE William Barrington	Fg. Off.	Pilot	504	On 504 Sqn., 1-7-40. Awarded D.F.C.(31-5-40). Promoted Flt. Lt., 24-8-40. Released from the R.A.F., 1945, as Wing Commander. Brother of M.E.A. Royce.	✠	Died since Battle (1979)	British
ROZWADOWSKI Mieczyslaw	Plt. Off.	Pilot	151	Joined 151 Sqn., 8-8-40.	✠	**Killed in Action** (15-8-40)	Polish
ROZYCKI Wladyslaw	Plt. Off.	Pilot	238	Joined 238 Sqn., 19-8-40. ✠ **1 He 111, 11-9-40;** ✠ **1 He 111, 25-9-40;** ✠ **1 Bf 110, 28-9-40.** Awarded D.F.C.(15-11-42). Released from the Polish Air Force, 9-46, and returned to Poland.			Polish
RUDDOCK Wilfred Shepherd	Sgt.	Aircrew	23	Joined 23 Sqn., 18-7-40.	✠	Died since Battle (6-11-80)	British
RUDLAND Clifford Percival	Sgt.	Pilot	263	On 263 Sqn., 1-7-40. Commissioned, 8-5-41. Awarded D.F.C.✠ (19-9-41 and 15-5-45). Released from the R.A.F., 11-45, as a Wing Commander.			British
RUSHMER Frederick William	Flt. Lt.	Pilot	603	On 603 Sqn., 1-7-40. ✠ **1 He 111 (shared), 30-7-40.** Slightly wounded, 29-8-40.	✠	**Killed in Action** (5-9-40)	British
RUSSEL Blair Dalzel	Fg. Off.	Pilot	1(Canadian)	With 1(Canadian) Sqn., 20-6-40, on arrival in U.K. ✠ **1 Do 17, 26-8-40;** ✠ **1 Do 17 (shared), 21-9-40;** ✠ **1 Do 17 (shared), 25-9-40;** ✠ **1 Bf 110 (solo), 1 Bf 109 (solo), and 1 Bf 109 (shared), 27-9-40.** Awarded D.S.O.(3-10-44), D.F.C.✠ (25-10-40 and 16-11-43). Released from the R.C.A.F., 7-45.			Canadian
RUSSELL Anthony Gerald	Sgt.	Pilot	43	Joined 43 Sqn., 28-9-40. Commissioned, 13-4-42. Released from the R.A.F., 1946, as a Flight Lieutenant.			British
RUSSELL Godfrey Frederick	Lieut.	Pilot	804	Fleet Air Arm. On 804 Sqn., 1-7-40.	✠	Killed since Battle (13-12-40)	British
RUSSELL Graham Herbert	Plt. Off.	Pilot	236	On 236 Sqn., 1-7-40. Awarded D.F.C., 26-11-40. Left the R.A.F., 31-8-42, as a Flight Lieutenant.	✠	Died since Battle (1981)	British
RUSSELL Humphrey a'Beckett ("Humph")	Flt. Lt.	Pilot	32	Joined 32 Sqn., 17-8-40. ✠ **1 Bf 110, 18-8-40.** Severely wounded, 18-8-40. Awarded D.F.C.(19-5-44). Shot down and taken prisoner by the Germans, 5-44. Retired from the R.A.F., 17-2-58, as a Wing Commander.	✠	Died since Battle (15-2-83)	British
RUSSELL Leslie Plimmer	Sgt.	Aircrew	264	Defiant gunner. On 264 Sqn., 1-7-40. ✠ **1 He 111, 24-8-40** (with Plt.Off. M.H. Young as pilot). Transferred to Bomber Command, 11-41.	✠	Killed since Battle (19-5-42)	New Zealander
RUSSELL	Plt. Off.	Aircrew	141	Defiant gunner. (Forenames and initials not known). Joined 141 Sqn., 2-10-40.			British
RUST Charles Alan	Sgt.	Pilot	85-249	On 85 Sqn., 1-7-40. Posted to 249 Sqn., 11-9-40.			British
RUSTON Paul	Flt. Lt.	Pilot	604	Joined 604 Sqn., 12-7-40. Released from the R.A.F., 1945, as a Wing Commander.	✠	Died since Battle (11-1-54)	British
RUTTER Robert Durham	Plt. Off.	Pilot	73	On 73 Sqn., 1-7-40. Wounded, 5-9-40. Awarded D.F.C.(1-9-44). Invalided from the R.A.F., 1947, as a Squadron Leader.			British
RYALLS Derrick Lang	Sgt.	Aircrew	29-F.I.U.	On 29 Sqn., 1-7-40. Commissioned, 26-8-40. Posted to F.I.U., 26-8-40. Was an Acting Squadron Leader at the time his death.	✠	Killed since Battle (26-12-44)	British
RYDER Edgar Norman	Fg. Off.	Pilot	41	On 41 Sqn., 1-7-40. Promoted Flt. Lt., 3-9-40. ✠ **1 Bf 109, 5-9-40;** ✠ **1 Bf 109, 6-9-40;** ✠ **1 Do 17 (shared) 15-9-40.** Appointed C.B.E.(1-1-58); awarded D.F.C.✠ (18-4-40 and 29-7-41). Retired from the R.A.F., 28-10-60, as a Group Captain.			British
RYPL Frantisek	Plt. Off.	Pilot	310	Joined 310 (Czech) Sqn., 10-7-40, on formation. Survived the War and returned to Czechoslovakia.			Czech
SADLER Herbert Samuel ("Sadie")	Sgt.	Pilot	611-92	On 611 Sqn., 1-7-40. Posted to 92 Sqn., 5-9-40. ✠ **1 Bf 110, 11-9-40;** ✠ **1 Do 17 (shared), 15-9-40.** Commissioned, 30-10-40.	✠	Killed since Battle (5-2-41)	British
SADLER Norman Alfred ("Butch")	Plt. Off.	Aircrew	235	Joined 235 Sqn., 6-9-40.	✠	Killed since Battle (16-12-40)	British
St. AUBIN Edward Fitzroy	Fg. Off.	Pilot	616	Rejoined 616 Sqn., early 8-40, after training. Wounded, 26-8-40. Promoted Flt. Lt., 3-9-40.	✠	Killed since Battle (27-5-43)	British
St. JAMES-SMITH Ronald Godfrey	Sgt.	Aircrew	600	Joined 600 Sqn., 9-40.	✠	Killed since Battle (13-4-41)	British
St. JOHN Peter Cape Beauchamp	Fg. Off.	Pilot	74	On 74 Sqn., 1-7-40. ✠ **1 Bf 109, 29-7-40;** ✠ **1 He 111, 11-9-40;** ✠ **1 Bf 109, 15-10-40;** ✠ **1 Bf 109, 17-10-40.**	✠	**Killed in Action** (22-10-40)	British
SALMON Harold Nigel Egerton	Fg. Off.	Pilot	1-229	On 1 Sqn., 1-7-40. ✠ **1 Bf 110, 16-8-40.** Posted to 229 Sqn., 10-40. Transferred to Air Transport Auxiliary, 1942, as Captain.	✠	Killed since Battle (6-12-43)	British

Name	Rank	Role	Sqn.	Details		Nationality
SALMOND William Noel Compton	Plt. Off.	Pilot	64	Joined 64 Sqn., 26-10-40. Made one operational flight, 30-10-40.	† Died since Battle (26-9-85)	British
SALWAY Ernest	Sgt.	Aircrew	141	Defiant gunner. On 141 Sqn., 1-7-40. Transferred to Bomber Command later.	† Killed since Battle (21-6-42)	British
SAMOLINSKI Wlodzimierz Michal Czech ("Sammy")	Plt. Off.	Pilot	253	Joined 253 Sqn., 16-7-40. ✠ 1 Bf 110, 30-8-40; ✠ 1 Bf 110, 4-9-40.	**Killed in Action** (26-9-40)	Polish
SAMPLE John	Flt. Lt.	Pilot	504	In command of 504 Sqn., 1-7-40, as Acting Sqn. Ldr. (Promoted Sqn. Ldr., 1-9-40). ✠ 1 Do 17 (solo) and 1 He 111 (shared), 15-9-40. Awarded D.F.C.(4-6-40).	† Killed since Battle (28-10-41)	British
SAMPSON Arthur	Sgt.	Aircrew	23	Served as Air Gunner on 23 Sqn. during Battle of Britain. Awarded B.E.M.(11-6-42) while with Bomber Command.		British
SANDERS James Gilbert	Fg. Off.	Pilot	615	On 615 Sqn., 1-7-40. ✠ 1 Ju 88, 25-8-40. Promoted Flt. Lt., 25-8-40. Awarded D.F.C.(4-6-40). Released from the R.A.F., 1947, as a Wing Commander.		British
SANDERS Phillip James	Sqn. Ldr.	Pilot	92	In command of 92 Sqn., 1-7-40. ✠ 1 He 111 and 1 Bf 109, 11-9-40; ✠ 1 Do 17, 15-9-40; ✠ 1 Bf 109, 20-9-40. Severely injured, 20-9-40, on the ground. Awarded D.F.C.(8-10-40). Retired from the R.A.F., 3-4-62, retaining the rank of Air Commodore.	† Died since Battle (11-1-89)	British
SANDIFER Alfred Kemp ("Gandi")	Sgt.	Aircrew	604	Joined 604 Sqn., 7-40. Commissioned, 27-7-43. Released from the R.A.F., 1945, as a Flight Lieutenant.		British
SARGENT Robert Edward Butler	Sgt.	Pilot	219	Joined 219 Sqn., 20-7-40. Commissioned, 1-5-42. Awarded A.F.C.(3-4-45). Released from the R.A.F., 1945, as a Flight Lieutenant.		British
SARRE Alfred Richard	Sgt.	Pilot	603	Joined 603 Sqn., 8-40. ✠ 1 Bf 109, 30-8-40. Slightly wounded, 7-9-40. Commissioned, 25-2-45. Released from R.A.F., 1945, as a Flying Officer.	† Died since Battle (1980)	British
SASAK Wilhelm	Sgt.	Pilot	32	Joined 32 Sqn., late 9-40.	† Killed since Battle (30-11-40)	Polish
SATCHELL William Arthur John	Sqn. Ldr.	Pilot	302	Assumed command of 302 (Polish) Sqn., 13-7-40, on formation. ✠ 1 Ju 88, 20-8-40; ✠ 1 Do 17, 15-9-40; ✠ 1 Do 17, 18-9-40. Awarded D.S.O. (6-10-42). Retired from the R.A.F., 1-7-56.	† Died since Battle (3-86)	British
SAUNDERS Cecil Henry	Plt. Off.	Pilot	92	On 92 Sqn., 1-7-40. ✠ 1 He 111 (solo) and 1 He 111 (shared), 4-7-40; ✠ 1 Bf 109, 29-10-40. Slightly wounded, 9-9-40. Awarded D.F.C.(4-12-42). Retired from R.A.F., 5-5-58, as a Wing Commander.		British
SAUNDERS Gerald Alfred Wellesley	Fg. Off.	Pilot	65	On 65 Sqn., 1-7-40. ✠ 1 Bf 109, 7-7-40; ✠ 1 Bf 109, 9-7-40; ✠ 1 Do 17, 26-8-40. Promoted Flt. Lt., 28-7-40. Assumed command of 65 Sqn., 30-10-40. Awarded D.F.C.(4-4-41). Released from the R.A.F., 1945, as a Wing Commander.		British
SAVAGE Thomas Wood	Sgt.	Pilot	64	Joined 64 Sqn., 14-10-40. Commissioned, 2-8-41.	† Killed since Battle (10-7-43)	British
SAVILL Joseph Ernest	Sgt.	Pilot	151-242-501	On 151 Sqn., 1-7-40. ✠ 1 Do 17, 13-8-40. Posted to 242 Sqn., 21-9-40. Posted to 501 Sqn., 12-10-40.		British
SAWARD Cyril Joseph	Sgt.	Pilot	615-501	Joined 615 Sqn., 30-7-40. Posted to 501 Sqn., 13-9-40. Commissioned, 19-10-42. Released from the R.A.F., 3-46, as a Flight Lieutenant.	† Died since Battle (1988)	British
SAWICZ Tadeusz	Fg. Off.	Pilot	303	Joined 303 (Polish) Sqn., 20-10-40. Awarded D.F.C., 20-10-43. Released from the Polish Air Force, 1-47, as a Wing Commander, and returned to Poland.		Polish
SAWYER Henry Cecil	Sqn. Ldr.	Pilot	65	Joined 65 Sqn., 2-7-40, and assumed commanded, 8-7-40.	**Killed in Action** (2-8-40)	British
SAYERS James Edwards	F/Sgt.	Pilot	41	On 41 Sqn., 1-7-40. Reverted to ground trade, 3-10-40. Discharged from R.A.F., 5-1-53, as a Warrant Officer.		British
SCHADTLER-LAW Kennith	Plt. Off.	Pilot	605	On 605 Sqn., 1-7-40. Severely wounded, 15-8-40. Retired from the R.A.F., 1-7-68, as a Wing Commander. Changed his name to LAW.	† Died since Battle	British
SCHOLLAR Edward Cranston	Plt. Off.	Aircrew	248	Flew with 248 Sqn. throughout the Battle of Britain on reconnaissance sorties over the Norwegian coast. Released from the R.A.F., 1945, as a Squadron Leader.		British
SCHUMER Francis Herbert	Plt. Off.	Pilot	600	Joined 600 Sqn., 24-9-40.	† Killed since Battle (12-7-41)	British
SCHWIND Lionel Harold	Fg. Off.	Pilot	257-43-213	Joined 257 Sqn., 1-9-40. Posted to 43 Sqn., 10-9-40; Posted to 213 Sqn., 20-9-40.	**Killed in Action** (27-9-40)	British
SCLANDERS Kirkpatrick MacLure	Plt. Off.	Pilot	242	Joined 242 Sqn., 26-8-40.	**Killed in Action** (26-8-40)	Canadian
SCOTT Alex Maxtone Wright	Plt. Off.	Pilot	3-607-605	On 3 Sqn., 1-7-40. Posted to 607 Sqn., 27-9-40. Posted to 605 Sqn., 15-10-40.	† Killed since Battle (2-1-41)	British
SCOTT Alfred Enoch	Sgt.	Pilot	73-422 Flt.	On 73 Sqn., 1-7-40. Posted to 422 Flt., 17-10-40. Commissioned, 26-2-42.	† Killed since Battle (19-8-42)	British
SCOTT Donald Stuart	Plt. Off.	Pilot	73	On 73 Sqn., 1-7-40. ✠ 1 Ju 88, 15-8-40; ✠ 1 Bf 109, 15-9-40. Promoted Fg. Off., 3-9-40. Awarded D.F.C.(24-9-40). Released from R.A.F., 1945, as a Squadron Leader.		British
SCOTT Douglas Reginald	Flt. Lt.	Pilot	605	On 605 Sqn., 1-7-40. Posted away, 29-8-40. (Promoted Sqn. Ldr., 1-9-40). Awarded A.F.C.(15-1-43, backdated to 9-10-41)	† Killed since Battle (8-11-41)	British
SCOTT Ernest	Sgt.	Pilot	222	On 222 Sqn., 1-7-40. ✠ 1 Bf 109 and 1 Do 17, 3-9-40; ✠ 1 Bf 110, 5-9-40; ✠ 1 Bf 110, 7-9-40; ✠ 1 He 111, 11-9-40; ✠ 1 Bf 109, 27-9-40.	**Killed in Action** (27-9-40)	British
SCOTT George Wardrop	Sgt.	Pilot	64-19	Joined 19 Sqn., 25-9-40, from 64 Sqn. Commissioned, 5-3-41. Awarded A.F.C. (8-6-44). Released from the R.A.F., 1945, as a Squadron Leader. Made M.B.E. (1-6-53).	† Died since Battle (1986)	British
SCOTT John Alan	Sgt.	Pilot	611-74	Joined 611 Sqn., 27-9-40. Posted to 74 Sqn., 23-10-40.	**Killed in Action** (27-10-40)	British
SCOTT Ronald Hamilton	Fg. Off.	Pilot	604	On 604 Sqn., 1-7-40. Promoted Flt. Lt., 3-9-40. Released from the R.A.F., 1945, as a Wing Commander.		British
SCOTT William Jack	Sgt.	Aircrew	264	On 264 Sqn., 1-7-40 (though absent on gunnery course, rejoined 5-9-40). Posted away, 19-10-40. Awarded D.F.M.(29-5-41). Commissioned, 24-11-41. Transferred to the Reserve in New Zealand, 31-7-44.		New Zealander
SCOTT William John Moir	Fg. Off.	Pilot	41	On 41 Sqn., 1-7-40. ✠ 1 Bf 109, 7-9-40.	**Killed in Action** (8-9-40)	British
SCOTT-MALDEN Francis David Stephen ("Scottie")	Plt. Off.	Pilot	611-603	On 611 Sqn., 1-7-40. Promoted Fg. Off., 3-10-40. Posted to 603 Sqn., 3-10-40. Awarded D.S.O.(11-9-42), D.F.C.✶ (19-8-41 and 5-6-42). Retired from the R.A.F., 25-9-66, as an Air Vice-Marshal.		British
SCRASE George Edward Thomas	Fg. Off.	Pilot	600	On 600 Sqn., 1-7-40.	**Killed since Battle** (28-9-41)	British
SEABOURNE Eric William	Sgt.	Pilot	238	On 238 Sqn., 1-7-40. ✠ 1 Bf 110 (shared), 13-7-40; ✠ 1 Bf 109, 8-8-40; ✠ 2 Bf 109s, 13-8-40. Severely wounded, 13-8-40. Commissioned, 12-8-41. Awarded D.F.C.(23-6-42). Retired from the R.A.F., 2-12-60, as a Squadron Leader.		British
SEARS Lionel Argent	Plt. Off.	Pilot	145	On 145 Sqn., 1-7-40. ✠ 1 Do 17 (shared), 1-7-40.	**Killed in Action** (8-8-40)	British
SECRETAN Dennis	Plt. Off.	Pilot	54-72	Joined 54 Sqn., 3-9-40. Promoted Fg. Off., 23-9-40. Posted to 72 Sqn., 27-9-40. Awarded D.F.C.(26-2-43). Released from R.A.F., 1946, as a Wing Commander.		British
SEDA Karel	Sgt.	Pilot	310	Joined 310 (Czech) Sqn., 8-40. Commissioned later. Released from the R.A.F., 1945, as a Flight Lieutenant and returned to Czechoslovakia.		Czech
SEDDON Wilfrid John	Plt. Off.	Pilot	601	Joined 601 Sqn., 1-10-40. Promoted Fg. Off., 3-10-40.	† Killed since Battle (31-3-41)	British
SEGHERS Eugene George Achilles ("Strop")	Plt. Off.	Pilot	46-32	Joined 46 Sqn., 10-8-40. Posted to 32 Sqn., 18-8-40. Awarded D.F.C.	† Killed since Battle (26-7-44)	Belgian
SELLERS Raymond Frederick	Sgt.	Pilot	111-46	Joined 111 Sqn., 17-8-40. Slightly wounded, 26-8-40. Posted to 46 Sqn., 15-9-40. ✠ 1 Bf 110 (shared), 27-9-40. Commissioned, 29-10-41. Awarded A.F.C.(8-6-44). Released from the R.A.F., 10-12-45, as a Flight Lieutenant.		British
SELWAY John Barry	Fg. Off.	Pilot	604	On 604 Sqn., 1-7-40. Awarded D.F.C.(31-12-43). Released from the R.A.F., 1946, as a Wing Commander.		British
SENIOR Benjamin	Sgt.	Aircrew	600	Joined 600 Sqn., 1-7-40. No other details traced.		British
SENIOR John Norman	Sgt.	Pilot	23	Joined 23 Sqn., late 8-40.	† Killed since Battle (21-3-41)	British
SEREDYN Antoni	Sgt.	Pilot	32	Joined 32 Sqn., 12-10-40.		Polish
SERVICE Arthur	Sgt.	Aircrew	29	Joined 29 Sqn., late 9-40. Transferred to Bomber Command, 1941.	† Killed since Battle (15-10-41)	British
SEWELL Donald Alec	Sgt.	Pilot	17	On 17 Sqn., 1-7-40. ✠ 1 Bf 109, 25-8-40. Commissioned, 25-11-41. Transferred to Bomber Command.	† Killed since Battle (19-3-44)	British

Name	Rank	Role	Sqn.	Details	Fate	Nationality
SHANAHAN Martin Michael	Sgt.	Pilot	1	Joined 1 Sqn., 5-8-40.	✟ **Killed in Action** (15-8-40)	British
SHAND Michael Moray ("Mick")	Plt. Off.	Pilot	54	Joined 54 Sqn., 22-8-40. Severely wounded, 25-8-40. Awarded D.F.C.(16-9-42). Shot down and taken prisoner by the Germans, 28-11-42. Returned to New Zealand and transferred to the Reserve, 10-4-46.		New Zealander
SHARMAN Herbert Ronald	Plt. Off.	Aircrew	248	On 248 Sqn., 1-7-40. Flew on reconnaissance sorties over Norwegian coast during Battle of Britain. Awarded A.F.C.(7-9-45). Released from the R.A.F., 9-45, as a Squadron Leader.		British
SHARP Bruce Robertson	Sgt.	Aircrew	235	On 235 Sqn., 1-7-40. (Killed on escort sortie during raid on Calais.)	✟ **Killed in Action** (11-9-40)	British
SHARP Leslie Mark	Plt. Off.	Pilot	111	Joined 111 Sqn., 2-10-40.	✟ Killed since Battle (28-12-40)	British
SHARP Ronald James	Sgt.	Pilot	236	On 236 Sqn., 1-7-40. Commissioned 10-7-42. Released from the R.A.F., 1945, as a Flight Lieutenant.		British
SHARPLEY Hugh	Sgt.	Pilot	234	On 234 Sqn., 1-7-40. ✠ 1 Ju 88, 19-10-40.	✟ Killed since Battle (16-11-40)	British
SHARRATT William Gordon	Sgt.	Aircrew	248	Joined 248 Sqn., 5-10-40. Flew on reconnaissance sorties over enemy-held coasts.	✟ Killed since Battle (2-7-41)	British
SHAW Frederick James	Petty Officer	Pilot	804	Fleet Air Arm. On 804 Sqn., 1-7-40.	✟ Killed since Battle (2-8-42)	British
SHAW Ian Garstin	Fg. Off.	Pilot	264	Joined 264 Sqn., 7-40.	✟ **Killed in Action** (24-8-40)	British
SHAW Robert Henry	Plt. Off.	Pilot	1	On 1 Sqn., 1-7-40.	✟ **Killed in Action** (3-9-40)	British
SHEAD Harold Frederick William	Sgt.	Pilot	32-257	Joined 32 Sqn., 23-9-40. Posted to 257 Sqn., 15-10-40. Commissioned, 3-3-43. Awarded D.F.C.(3-9-43). Released from the R.A.F., 10-45, as a Flight Lieutenant.	✟ Died since Battle (1981)	British
SHEARD Horace	Sgt.	Aircrew	236	Joined 236 Sqn., 24-7-40.	✟ Killed since Battle (21-3-41)	British
SHEEN Desmond Frederick Burt	Fg. Off.	Pilot	72	Joined 72 Sqn., late 7-40. ✠ 1 Bf 110 and 1 Ju 88, 15-8-40. Promoted Flt. Lt., 3-9-40. Wounded, 5-9-40. Awarded D.F.C.✼ (7-5-40 and 21-10-41). Retired from the R.A.F., 2-1-71, as a Group Captain.		British
SHEPHERD Francis William	Sgt.	Aircrew	264	Defiant gunner. On 264 Sqn., 1-7-40. Commissioned, 8-1-43.	✟ Killed since Battle (27-7-44)	British
SHEPHERD Frederick Ernest Richard	Sgt.	Pilot	611	Joined 611 Sqn., 17-8-40.	✟ **Killed in Action** (11-9-40)	British
SHEPHERD John Bean	Sgt.	Pilot	234	Joined 234 Sqn., 13-9-40. Commissioned, 21-8-41. Awarded D.F.C.✼✼ (22-9-42, 27-8-43 and 1945). Killed in flying accident in Germany.	✟ Killed since Battle (22-1-46)	British
SHEPLEY Douglas Clayton	Plt. Off.	Pilot	152	On 152 Sqn., 1-7-40. ✠ 1 Bf 109, 8-8-40; ✠ 1 Bf 109, 11-8-40.	✟ **Killed in Action** (12-8-40)	British
SHEPPARD Walter John Patrick	Sgt.	Aircrew	236	Joined 236 Sqn., 4-10-40. Taken prisoner by the Germans, 4-12-40. Served in the post-War R.A.F. until c.1964.		British
SHEPPERD Edmund Eric	Sgt.	Pilot	152	On 152 Sqn., 1-7-40. ✠ 1 Bf 109, 25-7-40; ✠ 1 Ju 88, 12-8-40; ✠ 1 Ju 87, 18-8-40; ✠ 1 Ju 88, 7-10-40.	✟ **Killed in Action** (18-10-40)	British
SHEPPERD George Edward	Sgt.	Aircrew	219	On 219 Sqn., 1-7-40.	✟ **Killed in Action** (30-9-40)	British
SHERIDAN Stephan	Sgt.	Aircrew	236	Joined 236 Sqn., 7-40. Released from R.A.F., 1-46, as a Warrant Officer.		British
SHERRINGTON Thomas Baldwin Aloysius	Plt. Off.	Pilot	92	On 92 Sqn., 1-7-40. ✠ 1 Ju 88 (shared), 27-9-40; ✠ 1 Bf 109, 25-10-40. Released from the R.A.F., 1947, as a Flight Lieutenant		British
SHEWEL	Sgt.	Aircrew	236	Joined 236 Sqn., 3-9-40. No record of operations traced. Initials not known.		British
SHIPMAN Edward Andrew	Plt. Off.	Pilot	41	On 41 Sqn., 1-7-40. ✠ 1 Bf 110, 15-8-40; ✠ 1 He 111, 21-8-40. Posted away, 21-10-40. Awarded A.F.C.(1-1-45). Retired from the R.A.F., 9-12-59, retaining the rank of Wing Commander.		British
SHIRLEY Sidney Harry James	Sgt.	Aircrew	604	Joined 604 Sqn., early 7-40. Transferred to Bomber Command, 5-41.	✟ Killed since Battle (27-7-41)	British
SHORROCKS Norman Basil	Plt. Off.	Aircrew	235	On 235 Sqn., 1-7-40. Killed while on escort sortie for raid on Calais.	✟ **Killed in Action** (11-9-40)	British
SHUTTLEWORTH Lord (2nd Baron)	Fg. Off.	Pilot	145	On 145 Sqn., 1-7-40. ✠ 1 He 111 (shared), 11-7-40; ✠ 1 Ju 88 (shared) 27-7-40. (Born as Richard Ughtred Paul Kay-Shuttleworth, 30-10-13).	✟ **Killed in Action** (8-8-40)	British
SIBLEY Frederick Albert	Sgt.	Pilot	238	Joined 238 Sqn., 19-8-40.	✟ **Killed in Action** (1-10-40)	British
SIKA Jaroslav	Sgt.	Pilot	43	Joined 43 Sqn., 6-10-40. Commissioned, 23-7-43. Released from R.A.F., 1945, and returned to Czechoslovakia.	✟ Died since Battle (?)	Czech
SILK Frank Harry	Sgt.	Pilot	111	Joined 111 Sqn., early 8-40. Slightly wounded, 5-9-40. Posted away, 24-9-40. Commissioned, 21-11-41. Awarded D.F.C.(10-4-45). Retired from the R.A.F., 25-2-58, as a Flight Lieutenant.	✟ Died since Battle (25-8-70)	British
SILVER William Gerald	Sgt.	Pilot	152	On 152 Sqn., 1-7-40.	✟ **Killed in Action** (25-9-40)	British
SILVESTER George Frederick	Sgt.	Pilot	245-229	Joined 245 Sqn., 28-9-40. Posted to 229 Sqn., 16-10-40. Commissioned, 4-12-41. Awarded D.F.C.(17-10-44). Transferred to the Reserve, 1-50.		British
SIM Robert Black	Sgt.	Pilot	111	Joined 111 Sqn., early 7-40.	✟ **Killed in Action** (11-8-40)	British
SIMMONDS Vernon Churchill	Plt. Off.	Pilot	238	Joined 238 Sqn., 29-7-40. ✠ 1 Bf 110, 13-8-40; ✠ 1 He 111, 15-9-40; ✠ 1 He 111, 25-9-40; ✠ 1 Bf 110, 26-9-40. Released from the R.A.F., 1946, as a Squadron Leader.		British
SIMPSON Geoffrey Mervyn	Plt. Off.	Pilot	229	On 229 Sqn., 1-7-40.	✟ **Killed in Action** (26-10-40)	New Zealander
SIMPSON John William Charles	Fg. Off.	Pilot	43	On 43 Sqn., 1-7-40. Promoted Flt. Lt., 6-7-40. ✠ 1 Bf 109, 19-7-40. Wounded, 19-7-40. Awarded D.F.C.✼ (25-6-40 and 30-5-41). Died while still serving in the R.A.F. as a Wing Commander.	✟ Died since Battle (12-8-49)	British
SIMPSON Leslie William	Plt. Off.	Aircrew	264-141	Defiant gunner. Joined 264 Sqn., 12-7-40. Posted to 141 Sqn., 29-7-40. Released from the R.A.F., 1945, as a Flight Lieutenant.		British
SIMPSON Peter James	Plt. Off.	Pilot	111-64	On 111 Sqn., 1-7-40. ✠ 1 Bf 109, 19-7-40. Posted to 64 Sqn., c.10-8-40. ✠ 1 Bf 109 (solo), and 1 He 111 (shared), 16-8-40. Returned to 111 Sqn., 17-8-40. ✠ 1 Do 27 (shared), 26-8-40. ✠ 1 Bf 109, 4-9-40. Awarded D.F.C.✼ (17-12-40 and 29-8-44). Retired from the R.A.F., 5-3-68, retaining the rank of Group Captain.	✟ Died since Battle (1987)	British
SIMS Ivor Reginald	Sgt.	Aircrew	248	On 248 Sqn., 1-7-40. Commissioned, 8-4-42. Awarded D.F.M.(22-9-42, relating to service before commissioning).	✟ Killed since Battle (13-1-45)	British
SIMS James Ayscough	Plt. Off.	Pilot	3-232	On 3 Sqn., 1-7-40. Posted to 232 Sqn., 17-7-40, on formation. Retired from the R.A.F., 25-3-59, retaining the rank of Squadron Leader.	✟ Died since Battle (1977)	British
SINCLAIR Gordon Leonard	Fg. Off.	Pilot	310	Became Flight Commander with 310 (Czech) Sqn., 1-7-40, on formation. ✠ 1 Do 17, 31-8-40; ✠ 1 Do 17 and 1 Bf 110, 3-9-40; ✠ 1 Do 17, 9-9-40. Awarded D.F.C.(25-6-40). Retired from the R.A.F., 23-12-57, as a Wing Commander.		British
SINCLAIR John	Plt. Off.	Pilot	219	Joined 219 Sqn., 7-7-40. Retired from the R.A.F., 4-8-61, as Flight Lieutenant.		British
SING John Eric James	Fg. Off.	Pilot	213	On 213 Sqn., 1-7-40. Promoted Flt. Lt., 21-7-40. ✠ 1 Bf 109, 8-8-40. ✠ 2 Bf 110s, 12-8-40; ✠ 1 Bf 109, 12-8-40; ✠ 1 Bf 110 and 2 Ju 87s, 15-8-40; ✠ 1 Do 17, 15-9-40; ✠ 1 Bf 110 (shared), 27-9-40. Awarded D.F.C. (22-10-40). Retired from the R.A.F., 23-10-62, as a Wing Commander.		British
¶ **SISMAN, P.**	Plt. Off.	Pilot	29	On 29 Sqn., 1-7-40.	✟ Killed in Action (1-7-40)	British
SIUDAK Antoni	Sgt.	Pilot	302-303	Joined 302 (Polish) Sqn., 23-7-40. Posted to 303 (Polish) Sqn., 23-9-40. ✠ 1 Do 17 (shared), 15-9-40; ✠ 2 Bf 109s (solo) and 1 Bf 110 (shared), 5-10-40. (Was killed in his aircraft on the ground during bombing raid on Northolt.)	✟ **Killed in Action** (6-10-40)	Polish
SIZER Wilfred Max	Plt. Off.	Pilot	213	On 213 Sqn., 1-7-40. ✠ 1 Ju 88, 11-8-40; ✠ 1 Bf 110, 12-8-40; ✠ 2 Ju 87s, 15-8-40. Awarded D.F.C.(8-11-40). Retired from the R.A.F., 23-2-63, retaining the rank of Wing Commander.		British

Name	Rank	Role	Sqn.	Details	Fate	Nationality
SKALSKI Stanislaw	Plt. Off.	Pilot	302-501	Joined 302 (Polish) Sqn., 3-8-40. Posted to 501 Sqn., 12-8-40. ✠ **1 He 111, 30-8-40; ✠ 1 Bf 109, 31-8-40; ✠ 2 Bf 109s, 2-9-40.** Wounded, 5-9-40. Awarded D.S.O.(26-5-45), D.F.C.✿✿ (19-2-42, 15-11-42 and 20-10-43). Returned to Poland, 1-47.		Polish
SKILLEN Victor Hall	Sgt.	Pilot	29	Joined 29 Sqn., 7-40.	✝ Killed since Battle (11-3-41)	British
SKINNER Charles David Evelyn	Fg. Off.	Pilot	604	On 604 Sqn., 1-7-40. Promoted Flt. Lt., 28-9-40. Released from the R.A.F., 1946, as a Squadron Leader.		British
SKINNER Stanley Hewitt	Flt. Lt.	Pilot	604	On 604 Sqn., 1-7-40.	✝ Killed since Battle (19-8-42)	British
SKINNER Wilfred Malcolm ("Bill")	Sgt.	Pilot	74	On 74 Sqn., 1-7-40. ✠ **1 He 111 (shared), 8-7-40; ✠ 1 Bf 109, 31-7-40; ✠ 1 Bf 110 (solo) and 2 Bf 110s (shared), 11-8-40; ✠ 1 Do 17, 13-8-40; ✠ 1 Bf 109, 27-10-40.** Awarded D.F.M.(24-12-40). Commissioned, 17-5-41. Shot down and taken prisoner, 6-7-41. Released by the R.A.F., 1946, as a Flight Lieutenant.		British
SKOWRON Henryk	Sgt.	Pilot	303	Joined 303 (Polish) Sqn., 23-10-40.	✝ Killed since Battle (18-7-41)	Polish
SLADE John William	Sgt.	Pilot	64	Joined 64 Sqn., 9-40. Commissioned, 17-7-41. Awarded D.F.C.(22-1-43). (Was Squadron Leader at time of death)	✝ Killed since Battle (19-9-45)	British
SLATTER Dudley Malins	Plt. Off.	Aircrew	141	Defiant gunner. Joined 141 Sqn., 10-7-40.	✝ **Killed in Action (19-7-40)**	British
SLEIGH James Wallace	Lieut.	Pilot	804	Fleet Air Arm. On 804 Sqn., 1-7-40. Awarded D.S.O.(30-5-40), O.B.E.(6-11-53), D.S.C.(10-3-42). Retired from Royal Navy, 29-1-58, as a Commander.		British
SLOUF Vaclav	Sgt.	Pilot	312	Joined 312 (Czech) Sqn., 5-9-40. Commissioned, 26-11-41. Awarded D.F.C. Released from the R.A.F., 1945, as a Squadron Leader.		Czech
SLY Oswald Kenneth	Sgt.	Aircrew	29	Joined 29 Sqn., 7-8-40. (Shot down in error by Hurricanes and killed.)	✝ **Killed in Action (13-10-40)**	British
SMALLMAN James	A.C.2	Aircrew	236-23	On 236 Sqn., 1-7-40. Posted to 23 Sqn., early 9-40. Was not granted his due rank of Acting Sergeant during the Battle of Britain. Transferred to marine craft, 1941.		British
SMART Thomas	Fg. Off.	Pilot	65	On 65 Sqn., 1-7-40. ✠ **1 Bf 109, 13-8-40; ✠ 1 Do 17, 26-8-40.** Awarded D.F.C.✿ (4-2-41 and 18-9-45, back-dated to 11-4-43).	✝ Killed since Battle (12-4-43)	British
SMITH Alexander	Sgt.	Aircrew	600	On 600 Sqn., 1-7-40.	✝ Killed since Battle (22-8-41)	British
SMITH Andrew Thomas	Flt. Lt.	Pilot	610	In command of 610 Sqn., 1-7-40 (as Temporary Acting Sqn. Ldr.).	✝ **Killed in Action (25-7-40)**	British
SMITH Arthur Dumbell	Sgt.	Pilot	66	On 66 Sqn., 1-7-40. ✠ **1 Do 17 (shared), 30-8-40.** (Died from wounds suffered in combat on 4-9-40).	✝ **Died of Wounds (6-9-40)**	British
SMITH Arthur Joseph	Plt. Off.	Pilot	74	Joined 74 Sqn., 30-9-40. Posted away, 29-10-40. Released from R.A.F., 1946, as a Flight Lieutenant.		British
SMITH Arthur William	Plt. Off.	Pilot	141	On 141 Sqn., 1-7-40. Promoted Fg. Off., 3-9-40.	✝ Killed since Battle (28-3-41)	Canadian
SMITH Christopher Dermont Salmond	Flt. Lt.	Pilot	25	Joined 25 Sqn., 20-9-40. Awarded D.F.C.(7-5-40).	✝ Killed since Battle (22-12-41)	British
SMITH Denis Norman Evelyn	Plt. Off.	Pilot	74	Joined 74 Sqn., 20-7-40.	✝ **Killed in Action (11-8-40)**	British
SMITH Donald Sydney	Plt. Off.	Pilot	616	On 616 Sqn., 1-7-40. ✠ **1 Ju 88 (shared), 15-8-40; ✠ 1 Bf 109, 30-8-40.** (Died from wounds suffered in action on 27-9-40).	✝ **Died of Wounds (28-9-40)**	British
SMITH Edward Brian Bretherton	Fg. Off.	Pilot	610	On 610 Sqn., 1-7-40. ✠ **1 Bf 109, 24-7-40; ✠ 1 Bf 109, 25-7-40.** Wounded, 12-8-40. Awarded D.F.C.(30-8-40). Promoted Flt. Lt., 3-9-40. Released from the R.A.F., 1946, as a Squadron Leader.		British
SMITH Edward Stanley	Fg. Off.	Pilot	600	On 600 Sqn., 1-7-40. Promoted Flt. Lt., 3-9-40. Awarded D.F.C.(2-10-45), A.F.C. (2-6-43). Released from the R.A.F., 1945, as a Squadron Leader.		British
SMITH Eric Claude	Sgt.	Aircrew	600	On 600 Sqn., 1-7-40. Commissioned, 27-4-45. Retired from the R.A.F., 3-6-66, as a Flight Lieutenant.		British
SMITH Eric Leigh	Plt. Off.	Aircrew	604	On 604 Sqn., 1-7-40. Released from the R.A.F., 1945, as a Flight Lieutenant.	✝ Died since Battle (5-11-78)	British
SMITH Forgrave Marshall	Plt. Off.	Fg. Off.	72	On 72 Sqn., 1-7-40. Promoted Flt. Lt., 6-8-40. ✠ **1 He 111, 15-8-40.** Badly wounded, 31-8-40. Awarded D.F.C.(30-10-45). Retired from the R.A.F., 13-10-57, as a Wing Commander.		Canadian
SMITH Francis Alan	Sub-Lieut.	Pilot	145	Fleet Air Arm. Joined 145 Sqn., 2-7-40.	✝ **Killed in Action (8-8-40)**	British
SMITH Frank	A.C.2	Aircrew	604	Joined 604 Sqn., late 7-40. Flew throughout the Battle of Britain without being granted his due rank of Acting Sergeant.	✝ Killed since Battle (6-3-42)	British
SMITH Godfrey Ernest	Sgt.	Aircrew	264	Defiant gunner. Joined 264 Sqn., early 10-40. Commissioned, 1-5-42. Released from the R.A.F., 1946, as a Flight Lieutenant.	✝ Died since Battle (1980)	British
SMITH Irving Stanley ("Black")	Plt. Off.	Pilot	151	Joined 151 Sqn., 13-7-40. ✠ **2 Bf 109s, 15-8-40; ✠ 1 He 111, 24-8-40; ✠ 1 Bf 109 (shared), 30-8-40; ✠ 1 Do 17, 31-8-40; ✠ 1 He 111, 2-10-40.** Awarded D.F.C.✿ (7-3-41 and 16-7-42). Made O.B.E., 1953, and appointed C.B.E., 1960. Retired from the R.A.F., 2-2-66, as a Group Captain.		New Zealander
SMITH James Duncan ("Smudger")	Plt. Off.	Pilot	73	On 73 Sqn., 1-7-40. ✠ **1 Bf 110, 11-9-40; ✠ 1 Bf 109, 15-9-40.**	✝ Killed since Battle (14-4-41)	Canadian
SMITH Kenneth Barton	Sgt.	Pilot	257	On 257 Sqn., 1-7-40.	✝ **Killed in Action (8-8-40)**	British
SMITH Laurence Edward	Sgt.	Pilot	234	Joined 234 Sqn., 15-10-40. Commissioned, 17-10-41. Released from the R.A.F., 1945, as a Flight Lieutenant. Served with R.A.F.V.R. and R.Aux.A.F. until 1963. Changed name to **HOOPER-SMITH.**		British
SMITH Leonard	A.C.2	Aircrew	219	Joined 219 Sqn., 21-7-40. (Promoted to Sergeant, 11-40, back-dated). Released from the R.A.F., 16-11-46, as a Flight Lieutenant.		British
SMITH Norman Henry Jackson ("Jerker")	Plt. Off.	Pilot	235	On 235 Sqn., 1-7-40. Awarded D.F.C.(27-5-41). Retired from the R.A.F., 29-3-58, retaining the rank of Wing Commander. Changed name to **JACKSON-SMITH.**		British
SMITH Percy Ronald	Sgt.	Pilot	236	On 236 Sqn., 1-7-40.	✝ Killed since Battle (24-11-40)	British
SMITH Phillip Richard	Sgt.	Pilot	25	On 25 Sqn., 1-7-40. Commissioned, 18-12-40.	✝ Killed since Battle (4-4-43)	British
SMITH Reginald Cyril	Sgt.	Pilot	236	On 236 Sqn., 1-7-40.	✝ Killed since Battle (19-7-41)	British
SMITH Robert Rutherford	Plt. Off.	Pilot	229	On 229 Sqn., 1-7-40. Promoted Fg. Off., 3-9-40. Awarded D.F.C.(23-2-43). Shot down and taken prisoner, 10-3-43. Released from the R.A.F., 1945, as a Flt. Lt.	✝ Died since Battle (c.1963)	Canadian
SMITH Roddick Lee	Flt. Lt.	Pilot	151	On 151 Sqn., 1-7-40. ✠ **1 Do 17, 13-8-40.** Made O.B.E., 12-6-58. Retired from the R.A.F., 23-6-62, as a Wing Commander.		British
SMITH William Alexander	Fg. Off.	Pilot	229	On 229 Sqn., 1-7-40. ✠ **1 He 111, 11-9-40.** Awarded D.F.C.(17-3-42). Retired from the R.A.F., 24-11-62, as a Wing Commander.		British
SMITH William Bruce	Sgt.	Pilot	602	Joined 602 Sqn., 6-10-40. ✠ **1 Bf 109, 29-10-40.** Wounded, 30-10-40, and withdrawn from flying duties.	✝ Died since Battle (17-6-75)	British
SMITH Wynford Ormonde Leoni	Flt. Lt.	Pilot	263	On 263 Sqn., 1-7-40.	✝ Killed since Battle (29-12-40)	British
SMITHER Ross	Fg. Off.	Pilot	1(Canadian)	With 1(Canadian) Sqn., 20-6-40, on arrival in U.K. ✠ **1 Bf 110, 4-9-40.**	✝ **Killed in Action (15-9-40)**	British
SMITHERS Julian Langley	Plt. Off.	Pilot	601	On 601 Sqn., 1-7-40.	✝ **Killed in Action (11-8-40)**	British
SMITHSON Richard	Sgt.	Pilot	249	On 249 Sqn., 1-7-40. Wounded, 7-9-40. Commissioned, 17-7-41.	✝ Killed since Battle (22-7-41)	British
SMYTH Ronald Henry	Sgt.	Pilot	111-249	Joined 111 Sqn., 21-8-40. Posted to 249 Sqn., 2-10-40. Transferred to photo reconnaissance duties, 1943. Awarded D.F.C.(27-7-45). Released from the R.A.F., 1-46, as a Flight Lieutenant.		British
SMYTHE Derek Miles Altamont	Plt. Off.	Aircrew	264	Defiant gunner. Joined 264 Sqn., 12-7-40. Awarded D.F.C.(14-11-44). Released from the R.A.F., 3-46, as a Flight Lieutenant.		British
SMYTHE George	Sgt.	Pilot	56	On 56 Sqn., 1-7-40. ✠ **1 Ju 87, 13-7-40; ✠ 1 Bf 109, 12-8-40; ✠ 1 Bf 109, 28-8-40.** Awarded D.F.M.(30-8-40). Commissioned, 27-1-42. Made M.B.E., 13-6-46. Retired from the R.A.F., 24-11-61, as a Wing Commander.		British

Name	Rank	Role	Sqn.	Notes	Fate	Nationality
SMYTHE Rupert Frederick	Plt. Off.	Pilot	32	On 32 Sqn., 1-7-40. Promoted Fg. Off., 25-7-40. ✠ 2 Bf 109s, 4-7-40; ✠ 1 Bf 109, 19-7-40; ✠ 1 Do 17, 12-8-40; ✠ 1 Bf 109, 14-8-40. Wounded and withdrawn from operational flying. Released from R.A.F., 1946, as Flt. Lt.		British
SNAPE William George	W/Off.	Aircrew	25	On 25 Sqn., 1-7-40. Commissioned, 14-7-42. Released from the R.A.F., 1946, as a Flying Officer.	✟ Died since Battle (22-8-55)	British
SNELL Vivian Robert	Plt. Off.	Pilot	151-501	Promoted Fg. Off., 3-9-40. Joined 151 Sqn., 5-9-40. Posted to 501 Sqn., 26-9-40. ✠ 1 Bf 109, 25-10-40. Released from the R.A.F., 1946, as a Wing Commander.		British
SNOW William George	Plt. Off.	Pilot	236	Joined 236 Sqn., 9-40. Released from the R.A.F., 1945, as a Flight Lieutenant.		British
SNOWDEN Ernest George	Sgt.	Pilot	213	On 213 Sqn., 1-7-40. ✠ 1 Bf 110, 11-8-40; ✠ 1 Ju 88, 25-8-40; ✠ 1 Bf 110, 15-8-40; ✠ 1 Ju 88, 9-10-40. Commissioned, 28-6-41. Released from the R.A.F., 1946, as a Flight Lieutenant.	✟ Died since Battle (20-11-47)	British
SOARS Harold John	Sgt.	Pilot	74	Joined 74 Sqn., 20-8-40. Wounded, 1-11-40. Commissioned, 5-10-42. Released from the R.A.F., 1947, as a Flight Lieutenant.	✟ Died since Battle (1975)	British
SOBEY Philip Alfred	Sgt.	Aircrew	235	Joined 235 Sqn., 22-8-40.	✟ Killed since Battle (9-11-40)	British
SODEN John Flewelling	Plt. Off.	Pilot	266-603	On 266 Sqn., 1-7-40. ✠ 1 He 115 (shared), 15-8-40; ✠ 1 Bf 109, 30-9-40; ✠ 1 Bf 109, 10-10-40. Wounded, 25-10-40. (Lost in sinking of troopship *Laconia*).	✟ Killed since Battle (12-9-42)	British
SOLAK Jerzy Jakub ("Jeray")	Plt. Off.	Pilot	151-249	Joined 151 Sqn., 28-8-40. Posted to 249 Sqn., 27-9-40. Released from Polish Air Force, 1946.		Polish
SOLOMON Neville David	Plt. Off.	Pilot	17	Joined 17 Sqn., 19-7-40.	✟ **Killed in Action** (18-8-40)	British
SONES Lawrence Charles	Sgt.	Pilot	605	On 605 Sqn., 1-7-40. Commissioned, 11-7-42. Released from the R.A.F., 13-9-45, as a Flight Lieutenant.		British
SOUTHALL George	Sgt.	Aircrew	23	Joined 23 Sqn., 5-10-40.	✟ Killed since Battle (22-12-40)	British
SOUTHORN George Albert	Sgt.	Aircrew	235	Joined 235 Sqn., 18-8-40. Commissioned, 24-4-43. Released from the R.A.F., 1945, as a Flight Lieutenant.		British
SOUTHWELL John Sydney	Plt. Off.	Pilot	245	On 245 Sqn., 1-7-40.	✟ Killed since Battle (22-3-41)	British
SPEARS Arthur William Peter	Sgt.	Pilot	222-421 Flt.	On 222 Sqn., 1-7-40. Posted to 421 Flt., 4-10-40. Commissioned 16-10-42. Retired from R.A.F., 13-12-70, as a Squadron Leader.		British
SPEKE Hugh	Fg. Off.	Pilot	604	On 604 Sqn., 1-7-40. Promoted Flt. Lt., 3-9-40. Awarded D.F.C.(29-7-40).	✟ Killed since Battle (26-7-41)	British
SPENCE Douglas James	Plt. Off.	Pilot	245	On 245 Sqn., 1-7-40.	✟ Killed since Battle (30-4-41)	New Zealander
SPENCER Desmond Gerard Heath	Sqn. Ldr.	Pilot	266	On 266 Sqn., 1-7-40, and assumed command, 18-8-40. Posted away, 9-40. Had been made M.B.E.(1-1-40). Made C.B.E.(1-1-65). Retired from R.A.F., 22-3-67, as a Group Captain.		British
SPENCER Gordon Hamilton	Sgt.	Pilot	504	Joined 504 Sqn., 9-40. Commissioned, 18-3-44. Released from the R.A.F., 1947, as a Flight Lieutenant.		British
SPIERS Aubrey	Sgt.	Aircrew	236	On 236 Sqn., 1-7-40. Released from the R.A.F., 1946, as a Warrant Officer.	✟ Died since Battle (1988)	British
SPIRES John Henry	Sgt.	Aircrew	235	On 235 Sqn., 1-7-40. Awarded D.F.M.(17-6-41). Commissioned, 1-5-42. Awarded D.F.C.(7-11-44). Released from the R.A.F., 1946, as a Flight Lieutenant.		British
SPRAGUE Henry Arnold	Plt. Off.	Pilot	3	Joined 3 Sqn., 10-10-40. Shot down and taken prisoner by the Germans, 22-11-41. Released from R.C.A.F., 23-8-45, as a Flight Lieutenant.		Canadian
SPRAGUE Mervyn Herbert	Sgt.	Pilot	602	On 602 Sqn., 1-7-40.	✟ **Killed in Action** (11-9-40)	British
SPRENGER William Paterson	Fg. Off.	Pilot	1(Canadian)	With 1(Canadian) Sqn., 20-6-40, on arrival in U.K.	✟ Killed since Battle (26-11-40)	Canadian
SPURDLE Robert Lawrence	Plt. Off.	Pilot	74	Joined 74 Sqn., 21-8-40. Awarded D.F.C.✠ (14-8-42 and 26-1-45). Transferred to the Reserve in New Zealand, 18-4-46, as a Squadron Leader.		New Zealander
SPYER Richard Alfred	Sgt.	Pilot	607	On 607 Sqn., 1-7-40. Slightly wounded, 9-9-40.	✟ Killed since Battle (22-3-41)	British
SQUIER John William Copous	Sgt.	Pilot	64	Joined 64 Sqn., 28-7-40. Severely wounded, 15-8-40. Commissioned, 15-6-42. Released from the R.A.F., 1-9-46, as a Flight Lieutenant.		British
STANGER Noel Mizpah	Sgt.	Aircrew	235	Joined 235 Sqn., 11-10-40.	✟ Killed since Battle (14-2-41)	New Zealander
STANLEY Donald Arthur	Plt. Off.	Pilot	64	Joined 64 Sqn., 9-40.	✟ Killed since Battle (25-2-41)	British
STANLEY Douglas Owen	Sgt.	Pilot	151	Joined 151 Sqn., 30-9-40.	✟ **Killed in Accident** (26-10-40).	New Zealander
STANSFELD Noel Karl	Plt. Off.	Pilot	242-229	On 242 Sqn., 1-7-40. ✠ 1 He 111 (shared), 30-8-40; ✠ 1 Do 17, 7-9-40; ✠ 1 Do 17, 15-9-40; ✠ 1 He 111, 27-9-40. Posted to 229 Sqn., 29-9-40. Wounded, 30-9-40. Awarded D.F.C.(8-10-40). Transferred to R.C.A.F., 12-2-45, but invalided from the Service, 1947.		Canadian
STAPLES Lionel	Sgt.	Pilot	151	Joined 151 Sqn., 10-40. Commissioned, 28-2-42. Released from the R.A.F., 1945, as a Flight Lieutenant.		British
STAPLES Michael Edmund	Plt. Off.	Pilot	609	Joined 609 Sqn., 8-7-40. ✠ 1 Bf 110, 12-8-40; ✠ 1 Ju 87, 13-8-40; ✠ 1 Do 17 (shared), 15-9-40; ✠ 1 Do 17, 24-9-40; ✠ 1 Bf 109, 29-9-40; ✠ 1 Bf 109, 30-9-40. Wounded, 7-10-40.	✟ Killed since Battle (9-11-41)	British
STAPLES Robert Charles John	Sgt.	Pilot	72	On 72 Sqn., 1-7-40. Commissioned, 1-12-41. Retired from the R.A.F., 26-3-48, as a Flight Lieutenant.	✟ Died since Battle (1986)	British
STAPLETON Basil Gerard ("Stapme")	Plt. Off.	Pilot	603	On 603 Sqn., 1-7-40. Promoted Fg. Off., 21-10-40. ✠ 1 Ju 88 (shared), 3-7-40; ✠ 1 Do 17 (shared), 20-7-40; ✠ 1 Do 17, 3-9-40; ✠ 1 Bf 109, 5-9-40; ✠ 1 Do 17, 15-9-40. Awarded D.F.C.(15-11-40). Released from R.A.F., 1946, as a Squadron Leader, and returned to South Africa.		South African
STARLL	Sgt.	Pilot	601	Joined 601 Sqn., 10-10-40. No further Service record traced. (Initials not known).		British
STARR Harold Morley	Sqn. Ldr.	Pilot	245-253	Joined 245 Sqn., 21-7-40. Posted to 253 Sqn., 8-8-40, to command.	✟ **Killed in Action** (31-8-40)	British
STAVERT Charles Michael	Plt. Off.	Pilot	1-504	On 1 Sqn., 1-7-40. ✠ 1 He 111, 16-8-40; ✠ 1 Do 17 (shared), 18-8-40; ✠ 1 Ju 88, 5-9-40. Posted to 504 Sqn., mid-9-40. Awarded A.F.C.(1-6-53). Retired from the R.A.F., 10-8-64, as a Squadron Leader.		British
STEADMAN Dennis James	Sgt.	Pilot	54-245	Joined 54 Sqn., 22-8-40. Posted to 245 Sqn., 27-9-40. Commissioned, 12-3-41. Released from the R.A.F., 1946, as a Flight Lieutenant.		British
STEBOROWSKI Michal Jan	Fg. Off.	Pilot	238	Joined 238 Sqn., 5-8-40. ✠ 1 Bf 110, 8-8-40.	✟ **Killed in Action** (11-8-40)	Polish
STEELE Rodney Murrey	Sgt.	Aircrew	235	Joined 235 Sqn., 5-9-40. Commissioned, 15-2-42. Released from the R.A.F., 1946. as a Flight Lieutenant.	✟ Died since Battle (8-2-86)	British
STEERE Harry	F/Sgt.	Pilot	19	On 19 Sqn., 1-7-40. Awarded D.F.M.(25-6-40). ✠ 1 Bf 110 (shared), 19-8-40; ✠ 1 Bf 110, 9-9-40; ✠ 1 Do 17, 15-9-40; ✠ 1 Ju 88 and 1 He 111 (both shared), 18-9-40; ✠ 1 Bf 109 (27-9-40). Commissioned, 26-6-41. Awarded D.F.C.(23-6-44). (Brother of F/Sgt. J. Steere)	✟ Killed since Battle (9-6-44)	British
STEERE Jack	F/Sgt.	Pilot	72	On 72 Sqn., 1-7-40. Commissioned, 5-1-42. Awarded A.F.C.(13-6-46). Retired from R.A.F., 16-7-61, as a Squadron Leader. (Brother of F/Sgt. H. Steere)		British
STEFAN Jan	Sgt.	Pilot	1	Joined 1 Sqn., 6-10-40. Commissioned, 16-10-44 Released from the R.A.F., 1946, as a Flying Officer.		Czech
STEGMAN Stefan	Plt. Off.	Pilot	229	Joined 229 Sqn., 26-9-40.	✟ Killed since Battle (17-6-43)	Polish
STEHLIK Josef	Sgt.	Pilot	312	Joined 312 Sqn., 5-9-40. ✠ 1 Ju 88 (shared), 8-10-40. Commissioned, 6-8-41. Released from the R.A.F., 1946, as a Flight Lieutenant.		Czech
STEIN David	Plt. Off.	Pilot	263	Joined 263 Sqn., 1-8-40.	✟ Killed since Battle (30-10-41)	British
STEPHEN Harbourne Mackay ("Baby Tiger")	Plt. Off.	Pilot	74	On 74 Sqn., 1-7-40. ✠ 1 Bf 109, 28-7-40; ✠ 2 Bf 109s and 3 Bf 110s, 11-8-40; ✠ 1 Ju 88, 11-9-40; ✠ 1 Do 17 (shared), 5-10-40; ✠ 1 Bf 109, 20-10-40; ✠ 1 Bf 109, 27-10-40. Awarded D.S.O.(24-12-40), D.F.C.✠ (27-8-40 and 15-11-40). Released from the R.A.F., 1945, as a Wing Commander.		British
STEPHENS Cyril	Sgt.	Aircrew	23	On 23 Sqn., 1-7-40.	✟ **Killed in Action** (8-8-40)	British

Name	Rank	Role	Sqn.	Details	Status	Nationality
STEPHENS Maurice Michael	Plt. Off.	Pilot	3-232	On 3 Sqn., 1-7-40. Promoted Fg. Off., 20-8-40. Assumed command of 232 Sqn., 17-7-40, on formation. ✠ **1 He 111 (shared), 23-8-40.** Awarded D.S.O.(20-1-42), D.F.C.✠✠ (31-5-40, 31-5-40 and 3-11-42). Retired from the R.A.F., 10-11-60, as a Group Captain.		British
STEPHENSON Ian Raitt	Fg. Off.	Pilot	264	On 264 Sqn., 1-7-40. Wounded, 26-8-40. (Was a Wing Commander at time of death).	♱ Killed since Battle (26-11-43)	British
STEPHENSON Patrick Joseph Thomas ("Paddy")	Plt. Off.	Pilot	607	On 607 Sqn., 1-7-40. Slightly wounded, 15-9-40. Awarded D.F.C.(10-9-43). Retired from the R.A.F., 31-7-55, as a Squadron Leader.		British
STEPHENSON Stanley Philip	Fg. Off.	Pilot	85	On 85 Sqn., 1-7-40. Posted away, 4-8-40. Released from the R.A.F., 1947, as a Squadron Leader.		British
STERBACEK Jaroslav	Plt. Off.	Pilot	310	Joined 310 (Czech) Sqn., 31-8-40 (and killed the same day).	♱ **Killed in Action** (31-8-40)	Czech
STEVENS Eldred John	Plt. Off.	Pilot	141	Joined 141 Sqn., 24-7-40. Released from the R.A.F., 1946, as a Squadron Leader.		British
STEVENS Geoffrey	Sgt.	Pilot	151-213	Joined 151 Sqn., late 8-40. Posted to 213 Sqn., 14-9-40. Commissioned, 16-1-43. Invalided from the R.A.F., 4-5-68, as a Flight Lieutenant.		British
STEVENS Leonard Walter	Plt. Off.	Pilot	17	On 17 Sqn., 1-7-40. ✠ **1 Bf 110, 11-8-40;** ✠ **1 Do 17 (shared), 2-10-40.**	♱ Killed since Battle (21-5-41)	British
STEVENS Richard Playne	Plt. Off.	Pilot	151	Joined 151 Sqn., 4-9-40. Awarded D.S.O.(12-12-41), D.F.C.✠ (4-2-41 and 2-5-41).	♱ Killed since Battle (15/16-12-41).	British
STEVENS Robert Edward	Sgt.	Pilot	29	Joined 29 Sqn., 7-40. (Killed when shot down by R.A.F. fighters)	♱ **Killed in Action** (13-10-40)	British
STEVENS William Ronald	Sgt.	Aircrew	23	Joined 23 Sqn., 23-7-40. Awarded D.F.M. No further details traced.		British
STEVENSON Peter Charles Fasken	Plt. Off.	Pilot	74	On 74 Sqn., 1-7-40. ✠ **1 Bf 109, 8-7-40;** ✠ **1 Bf 109, 10-7-40;** ✠ **1 He 111 (shared), 12-7-40;** ✠ **1 Bf 109, 19-7-40;** ✠ **1 Bf 109, 28-7-40;** ✠ **1 Bf 109, 11-8-40.** Awarded D.F.C.(27-8-40). Posted away, 20-9-40.	♱ Killed since Battle (13-2-43)	British
STEWARD George Arthur	Sgt.	Pilot	17	On 17 Sqn., 1-7-40. ✠ **1 Bf 110, 27-7-40.** Awarded D.F.M.(17-12-40). Commissioned, 19-2-41.	♱ Killed since Battle (23-10-41)	British
STEWART Charles	Plt. Off.	Pilot	54-222	Joined 54 Sqn., 22-8-40. Posted to 222 Sqn., 1-10-40.	♱ Killed since Battle (11-7-41)	New Zealander
STEWART Charles Noel Douglas	Sgt.	Aircrew	604	On 604 Sqn., 1-7-40.	♱ Killed since Battle (31-5-42)	British
STEWART Donald George Alexander	Plt. Off.	Pilot	615	On 615 Sqn., 1-7-40. Promoted Fg. Off., 3-9-40.	♱ Killed since Battle (15-2-41)	British
STEWART-CLARK Dudley ("Duds")	Plt. Off.	Pilot	603	On 603 Sqn., 1-7-40. ✠ **1 Ju 88 (shared), 3-7-40;** ✠ **1 Do 17 (shared), 6-7-40;** ✠ **1 He 111 (shared), 15-7-40;** ✠ **1 He 111 (shared), 16-7-40.** Wounded, 3-9-40.	♱ Killed since Battle (19-9-41)	British
STICKNEY Phillip Ambrose Meynell	Flt. Lt.	Pilot	235	Joined 235 Sqn., 28-7-40. Released from the R.A.F., 1947, as a Flight Lieutenant.		British
STILLWELL Ronald Leslie	Sgt.	Pilot	65	Joined 65 Sqn., 19-8-40. Commissioned, 25-6-42. Awarded D.F.M.(16-6-42), D.F.C.(17-11-44). Invalided from the R.A.F., 15-9-47, as a Squadron Leader.		British
STOCK Eric	A.C.2	Aircrew	604	Joined 604 Sqn., 10-7-40. Flew as Radar Operator without being granted due rank of Acting Sergeant.		British
STOCKS Norman James	Sgt.	Aircrew	248	Joined 248 Sqn., 7-40. Was killed during photo reconnaissance sortie over Norwegian coast.	♱ **Killed in Action** (20-10-40)	British
STOCKWELL William Eric John	Petty Officer	Pilot	804	Fleet Air Arm. On 804 Sqn., 1-7-40. Taken prisoner by Italians, 17-11-40. Retired from Royal Navy as a Commissioned Pilot, 9-12-50.		British
STODDART Kenneth Maxwell ("Kenny")	Fg. Off.	Pilot	611	On 611 Sqn., 1-7-40. Promoted Flt. Lt., 3-9-40. Released from the R.A.F., 1945, as a Wing Commander.		British
STOKES Richard William ("Dickie")	Plt. Off.	Pilot	264	On 264 Sqn., 1-7-40.	♱ Killed since Battle (29-5-42)	British
STOKOE Jack	Sgt.	Pilot	263-603	On 263 Sqn., 1-7-40. Posted to 603 Sqn., 3-7-40. ✠ **1 Bf 109, 31-8-40;** ✠ **1 Bf 109, 1-9-40.** Wounded, 2-9-40. Commissioned, 26-1-41. Awarded D.F.C.(6-6-44). Released from R.A.F., 21-8-46, as a Squadron Leader.		British
STOKOE Sydney	Sgt.	Pilot	29	Joined 29 Sqn., 9-40.	♱ Killed since Battle (19-12-40)	British
STONE Cedric Arthur Cuthbert ("Bunny")	Fg. Off.	Pilot	263-245	On 263 Sqn., 1-7-40. Awarded D.F.C.✠ (31-5-40 and 10-4-42). Posted to 245 Sqn., 13-7-40. Released from the R.A.F., 1946, as a Wing Commander.		British
STONES Donald William Alfred ("Dimsie")	Plt. Off.	Pilot	79	On 79 Sqn., 1-7-40. ✠ **1 Bf 109, 9-7-40;** ✠ **1 Do 17, 31-8-40;** ✠ **1 He 111, 29-9-40.** Awarded D.F.C.✠ (4-6-40 and 10-4-42). Released from the R.A.F. as a Squadron Leader, and served on in the Malayan Auxiliary Air Force.		British
STONEY George Edward Bowes	Flt. Lt.	Pilot	501	On 501 Sqn., 1-7-40. ✠ **1 Ju 87, 29-7-40;** ✠ **1 Ju 87, 11-8-40.**	♱ **Killed in Action** (15-8-40)	British
STOODLEY Donald Raymond	Sgt.	Pilot	43	Joined 43 Sqn., 29-9-40.	♱ **Killed in Accident** (24-10-40)	British
STORIE John Munro	Plt. Off.	Pilot	615-607	Joined 615 Sqn., 30-9-40. Posted to 607 Sqn., 7-10-40. Released from the R.A.F., 1946, as a Flight Lieutenant.		British
STORRAR James Eric	Plt. Off.	Pilot	145-73-421 Flt.	On 145 Sqn., 1-7-40. ✠ **1 He 111 (shared), 16-7-40;** ✠ **1 He 111 (shared), 18-7-40;** ✠ **1 He 111 (shared), 20-7-40;** ✠ **1 Do 17 (shared), 21-7-40;** ✠ **1 Bf 109, 22-7-40;** ✠ **1 Ju 88 (shared), 29-7-40;** ✠ **1 Bf 109, 30-7-40;** ✠ **1 Ju 87, 8-8-40;** ✠ **1 Bf 110, 12-8-40.** Awarded D.F.C.✠ (20-8-40 and 29-10-43). Released from the R.A.F., 4-47, as a Wing Commander. Commanded 610 Sqn., R.Aux.A.F., 1954 until 10-3-57.		British
STORRIE Alexander James	Plt. Off.	Aircrew	264	Defiant gunner. On 264 Sqn., 1-7-40.	♱ Killed since Battle (20-11-40)	British
STRAIGHT Whitney Willard	Plt. Off.	Pilot	601	After special duties, re-joined 601 Sqn., 28-9-40. Promoted Fg. Off., 3-9-40. Awarded M.C.(1-1-41), D.F.C.(8-8-41). Released from the R.A.F., 11-45, retaining the rank of Air Commodore. Appointed C.B.E.(8-6-44).	♱ Died since Battle (5-4-79)	British
STRANG John Talbot	Plt. Off.	Pilot	253	On 253 Sqn., 1-7-40. Promoted Fg. Off., 3-9-40. Returned to New Zealand, 4-45, and transferred to the Reserve, 3-11-45.	♱ Died since Battle (17-7-69)	New Zealander
STREATFEILD Victor Charles Frederick	Sqn. Ldr.	Pilot	248	In command of 248 Sqn., 1-7-40. Flew photo reconnaissance sorties over Norwegian coast during Battle of Britain. Made O.B.E., 29-10-48. Released from the R.A.F., 1950, as a Squadron Leader.		British
STRETCH Reginald Robert	Sgt.	Aircrew	235	Joined 235 Sqn., 8-40. Released from the R.A.F., 18-12-45, as a Warrant Officer.		British
STRICKLAND Claud Dobree	Plt. Off.	Pilot	615	Joined 615 Sqn., 9-40.	♱ Killed since Battle (27-10-41)	British
STRICKLAND James Murray	Fg. Off.	Pilot	213	On 213 Sqn., 1-7-40. Promoted Flt. Lt., 21-9-40. ✠ **1 Ju 88, 11-8-40;** ✠ **1 Bf 109, 12-8-40;** ✠ **1 Bf 110 and 1 Ju 87, 15-8-40;** ✠ **1 Bf 109, 25-8-40;** ✠ **1 Bf 110 (shared), 27-9-40.** Awarded D.F.C.(22-10-40).	♱ Killed since Battle (14-8-41)	British
STRIHAVKA Jaromir	F/Sgt.	Pilot	310	Served with 310 (Czech) Sqn., during the Battle of Britain. Released from the R.A.F., 1946, as a Flight Lieutenant. Changed name to **SCOTT.**		Czech
STROUD George Alfred	Sgt.	Pilot	504-32-249	Served on 504 and 32 Sqns. before joining 249 Sqn., 9-40. Commissioned, 5-1-43. Released from the R.A.F., 1-47, as a Flight Lieutenant.		British
STUART Michael	A.C.1	Aircrew	23	Flew three operational sorties as an air gunner with 23 Sqn. during 10-40. Released from the R.A.F. as a Flight Sergeant on 13-11-45.		British
STUCKEY Sydney George	Sgt.	Pilot	213	Joined 213 Sqn., 7-40.	♱ **Killed in Action** (12-8-40)	British
STUDD John Alnod Peter	Plt. Off.	Pilot	66	On 66 Sqn., 1-7-40. ✠ **1 He 111 (shared), 29-7-40.**	♱ **Killed in Action** (9-8-40)	British
SULMAN John Edward	Plt. Off.	Pilot	607	On 607 Sqn., 1-7-40. ✠ **1 Do 17, 15-9-40.**	♱ Killed since Battle (23-11-41)	British
SUMMERS Richard Gordon Battensby	Sgt.	Aircrew	219	On 219 Sqn., 1-7-40. Posted away, 28-9-40. Awarded A.F.M.(1-1-42). Commissioned, 1-5-42. Made O.B.E.(6-3-56). Retired from the R.A.F., 8-10-68, as a Wing Commander.		British
SUMNER Frank	Sgt.	Aircrew	23	Joined 23 Sqn., 23-7-40. Transferred to Bomber Command.	♱ Killed since Battle (30-11-41)	British
SUMPTER Claude Harry Sidney	Sgt.	Aircrew	604	Served on 604 Sqn., during Battle of Britain, but no details traced.		British

Name	Rank	Role	Sqn.	Notes	Fate	Nationality
SURMA Franciszek	Plt. Off.	Pilot	151-607-257	Joined 151 Sqn., 8-7-40. Posted to 607 Sqn., 11-9-40. Posted to 257 Sqn., 20-10-40. ✠ 1 Bf 109, 26-9-40.	✝ Killed since Battle (8-11-41)	Polish
SUTCLIFFE William Alfred	Sgt.	Pilot	610	Joined 610 Sqn., 23-9-40.	✝ Killed since Battle (17-12-40)	British
SUTHERLAND Ian Welsh	Plt. Off.	Pilot	19	On 19 Sqn., 1-7-40.	✝ Killed on Active Service (4-8-40)	British
SUTTON Fraser Barton ("Barry")	Plt. Off.	Pilot	56	On 56 Sqn., 1-7-40. ✠ 1 Ju 87, 25-7-40; ✠ 1 Bf 110, 13-8-40; ✠ 1 Bf 109, 16-8-40; ✠ 1 Bf 110, 26-8-40. Seriously wounded, 28-8-40. Promoted Fg. Off., 3-9-40. Awarded D.F.C., 17-8-45. Retired from the R.A.F., 23-4-66, as a Group Captain.	✝ Died since Battle (16-3-88)	British
SUTTON Frederick Charles	Plt. Off.	Aircrew	264	Defiant gunner. Joined 264 Sqn., 13-7-40. ✠ 1 Bf 109, 28-8-40. Released from R.A.F., 1945, as a Flight Lieutenant.	✝ Died since Battle (1981)	British
SUTTON Harold Robert	Sgt.	Pilot	235	On 235 Sqn., 1-7-40. ✠ 1 He 60, 16-10-40. Commissioned, 15-6-42. Retired from the R.A.F., 28-11-53, as a Flight Lieutenant.		British
SUTTON James Ronald Gabert	Plt. Off.	Pilot	611	On 611 Sqn., 1-7-40. ✠ 1 Do 17 (shared), 2-7-40; ✠ 2 Do 17s (both shared), 11-10-40.	✝ Killed since Battle (23-7-41)	British
SUTTON Kenwyn Roland	Plt. Off.	Pilot	264	Joined 264 Sqn., 3-9-40, after training. Awarded D.F.C.(27-3-42). Severely wounded, 2-4-43. Released from the R.N.Z.A.F., 1-8-47.		New Zealander
SUTTON Norman	Plt. Off.	Pilot	611-72	Joined 611 Sqn., 9-9-40. Posted to 72 Sqn., 29-9-40.	✝ Killed in Action (5-10-40)	British
SWANWICK George William	Sgt.	Pilot	54	Joined 54 Sqn., 7-9-40. Commissioned 7-10-41. Retired from the R.A.F., 30-4-70, as a Wing Commander.		British
SWANWICK	Sgt.	Aircrew	141	Defiant gunner. Joined 141 Sqn., 7-40. Subsequent Service records not traced.		British
SWITON Leon	Sgt.	Pilot	54-303	Joined 54 Sqn., 9-8-40. Posted to 303 (Polish) Sqn., 16-8-40. Released from the R.A.F., 1946, as a Warrant Officer.		Polish
SWORD-DANIELS Albert Thomas	Plt. Off.	Aircrew	25	On 25 Sqn., 1-7-40. Released from the R.A.F., 1947, as a Squadron Leader.		British
SYDNEY Charles	F/Sgt.	Pilot	19-266-92	Joined 19 Sqn., 18-8-40. Posted to 266 Sqn., 24-8-40. Posted to 92 Sqn., 10-9-40.	✝ **Killed in Action** (27-9-40)	British
SYKES Duncan Broadford	Sgt.	Pilot	145	Joined 145 Sqn., 20-8-40. Released from the R.A.F., 1946, as a Warrant Officer.		British
SYKES John Humphrey Charlesworth	Sub-Lieut.	Pilot	64	Fleet Air Arm. Joined 64 Sqn., 8-7-40. Retired from the Royal Navy, 29-7-58, as a Lieutenant Commander.		British
SYLVESTER Edmund John Hillary	Plt. Off.	Pilot	501	On 501 Sqn., 1-7-40.	✝ **Killed in Action** (20-7-40)	British
SYMONDS John Edward	Sgt.	Aircrew	236	Joined 236 Sqn., 9-40. Commissioned, 19-8-41. Released from the R.A.F., 1947, as a Flight Lieutenant.		British
SZAFRANIEC Wilhelm	Sgt.	Pilot	151-607-56	Joined 151 Sqn., 12-9-40. Posted to 607 Sqn., 29-9-40. Posted to 56 Sqn., 14-10-40.	✝ Killed since Battle (23-11-40)	Polish
SZAPOZNIKOW Eugeniusz	Sgt.	Pilot	303	Joined 303 (Polish) Sqn., 2-8-40, on formation. ✠ 1 Bf 109, 31-8-40; ✠ 1 Do 17 and 1 Bf 109, 7-9-40; ✠ 2 Bf 110s, 11-9-40; ✠ 1 Bf 109, 23-9-40; ✠ 1 Bf 109, 27-9-40; ✠ 1 Bf 109, 7-10-40. Awarded D.F.M.(30-10-41). Commissioned, 1-11-41. Released from the Polish Air Force, 1946, as a Flight Lieutenant. Settled in Britain and changed his name to SHARMAN.		Polish
SZCZESNY Henryk ("Sneezy")	Plt. Off.	Pilot	74	Joined 74 Sqn., 6-8-40. ✠ 1 Do 17, 13-8-40; ✠ 1 Bf 110, 11-9-40; ✠ 1 Do 17 (shared), 5-10-40. Awarded D.F.C.(30-10-41). Remained in the R.A.F. after the War, and retired as a Squadron Leader, 27-3-65.		Polish
SZLAGOWSKI Jozef ("Slag")	Sgt.	Pilot	234-152	Joined 234 Sqn., 3-8-40. Posted to 152 Sqn., 21-10-40. ✠ 1 Bf 110 and 1 Do 17, 4-9-40. Released from the Polish Air Force, 11-46, as a Warrant Officer, and settled in Britain.		Polish
SZULKOWSKI Wladyslaw	Plt. Off.	Pilot	65	Joined 65 Sqn., 5-8-40. ✠ 1 Bf 109, 22-8-40.	✝ Killed since Battle (27-3-41)	Polish
TABOR George William	Sgt.	Pilot	65-152	Joined 65 Sqn., 2-9-40. Posted to 152 Sqn., 9-10-40.	✝ Killed since Battle (23-7-41)	British
TAIT Kenneth William	Fg. Off.	Pilot	87	On 87 Sqn., 1-7-40. ✠ 1 Bf 110, 15-8-40; ✠ 1 Bf 109 and 1 Bf 110, 25-8-40. Awarded D.F.C.(4-2-41)	✝ Killed since Battle (4-8-41)	New Zealander
TALMAN James MacGill	Plt. Off.	Pilot	213-145	Joined 213 Sqn., 9-40. Posted to 145 Sqn., 30-10-40.	✝ Killed since Battle (10-7-44)	British
TAMBLYN Hugh Norman	Fg. Off.	Pilot	141-242	On 141 Sqn., 1-7-40. Posted to 242 Sqn., 8-8-40. ✠ 1 Bf 109, 19-7-40; ✠ 1 Bf 110, 7-9-40; ✠ 2 Bf 110s, 9-9-40; ✠ 1 Do 17 (shared), 15-9-40; ✠ 1 Do 17, 18-9-40. Awarded D.F.C.(7-1-41).	✝ Killed since Battle (3-4-41)	Canadian
TANNER John Henry	F/Sgt.	Pilot	610	On 610 Sqn., 1-7-40.	✝ Killed in Action (11-8-40)	British
TATE	Sgt.	Aircrew	604	Flew with 604 Sqn. during the Battle of Britain. No Service records traced.		British
TATNELL Reginald Frederick	Sgt.	Pilot	235	Joined 235 Sqn., 20-9-40.	✝ Killed since Battle (18-5-41)	British
TAYLOR Dennis Edward	Petty Officer	Pilot	808	Fleet Air Arm. On 808 Sqn., 1-7-40. Embarked in H.M.S. *Ark Royal* for passage to the Mediterranean, 22-10-40. Commissioned, 1-5-43. Retired later as a Lieutenant. Killed while flying a light civil aircraft.	✝ Killed since Battle (7-10-78)	British
TAYLOR Donald Murray	Fg. Off.	Pilot	64	On 64 Sqn., 1-7-40. ✠ 1 Do 17 (shared), 1-7-40. Wounded, 17-7-40. Awarded D.F.C.(5-9-44). Retired from the R.A.F., 29-10-57, as a Squadron Leader.	✝ Died since Battle (1977)	British
TAYLOR Edgar Francis	Sgt.	Aircrew	29-600	On 29 Sqn., 1-7-40. Posted to 600 Sqn., late 9-40. Transferred to Bomber Command.	✝ Killed since Battle (22-10-43)	British
TAYLOR George Stringer	Sgt.	Pilot	3	Joined 3 Sqn., 29-9-40. (Died from injuries sustained on 9-2-43)	✝ Died of Wounds (10-2-43)	New Zealander
TAYLOR Graham Neville	Sgt.	Aircrew	236	Joined 236 Sqn., 21-7-40. Commissioned, 12-2-41. Released from the R.A.F., 1946, as a Flight Lieutenant.		British
TAYLOR Kenneth	Sgt.	Aircrew	29	On 29 Sqn., 1-7-40. Commissioned, 3-4-44. Awarded D.F.C.(1-6-45). Retired from the R.A.F., 7-6-71, as a Squadron Leader.		British
TAYLOR Norman	Sgt.	Pilot	601	Joined 601 Sqn., 7-8-40. ✠ 1 Ju 87, 18-8-40; ✠ 1 He 111 (shared), 30-8-40; ✠ 1 Bf 109, 31-8-40. Commissioned, 29-6-40. Awarded D.F.M.(29-7-41); D.F.C.(15-12-42). Remained in the R.A.F. after the War.	✝ Killed since Battle (29-4-48)	British
TAYLOR Reginald	Plt. Off.	Aircrew	235	Joined 235 Sqn., 14-8-40. Released from the R.A.F., 1947, as a Flight Lieutenant.	✝ Died since Battle (10-6-50)	British
TAYLOR Ronald Henry William	Sgt.	Aircrew	604	On 604 Sqn., 1-7-40.	✝ Killed since Battle (26-11-40)	British
TAYLOUR Edward Winchester Tollemache	Lieut.	Pilot	808	Fleet Air Arm. On 808 Sqn., 1-7-40. Awarded D.S.C.✠ (both on 9-10-40). Embarked in H.M.S. *Ark Royal* for passage to the Mediterranean.	✝ Killed since Battle (13-9-42)	British
TEARLE Francis Joseph ("Mike")	Sgt.	Aircrew	600	Joined 600 Sqn., 1-7-40. Commissioned, 28-5-42. Awarded D.F.C.(19-2-43). Released from the R.A.F., 1947, as a Flight Lieutenant.		British
TEMLETT Cyril Bernard	Plt. Off.	Pilot	3	Joined 3 Sqn., 27-9-40. Had been awarded D.F.C.(6-8-40).	✝ Killed since Battle (3-7-42)	British
TERRY Patrick Hugh Richard Runciman	Sgt.	Pilot	72-603	Joined 72 Sqn., 3-10-40. Posted to 603 Sqn., mid-10-40. (Had relinquished a short service commission before the War. No further service details traced.)		British
TEW Phillip Harry	F/Sgt.	Pilot	54	On 54 Sqn., 1-7-40. ✠ 1 Bf 109 (solo) and 1 Bf 110 (shared), 8-8-40. Commissioned, 17-5-42. Awarded A.F.C.(10-6-48). Retired from the R.A.F., 19-2-63)	✝ Died since Battle (1984)	British
THACKER David John	Plt. Off.	Pilot	32	Joined 32 Sqn., 10-40. Awarded A.F.C.(8-6-44). Released from R.A.F., 1946, as a Squadron Leader.		British
THEASBY Alec John	Sgt.	Aircrew	25	Joined 25 Sqn., 10-40.	✝ Killed since Battle (16-11-40)	British
THEILMANN John Graham	Fg. Off.	Pilot	234	On 234 Sqn., 1-7-40. Withdrawn from operational flying duties, 7-8-40, on medical grounds. Released from R.A.F., 1946, as a Squadron Leader.		British
THOM Alexander Henry	Sgt.	Pilot	79-87	Joined 79 Sqn., 6-10-40. Posted to 87 Sqn., 31-10-40. Commissioned, 3-12-41. Awarded D.F.C.(14-8-42). Released from the R.A.F., 4-12-45, as Flight Lieutenant.		British
THOMAS Charles Raymond Delauney	Fg. Off.	Pilot	236	On 236 Sqn., 1-7-40. Killed during reconnaissance sortie over Le Havre.	✝ **Killed in Action** (18-7-40)	British

Name	Rank	Role	Sqn.	Details	Fate	Nationality
THOMAS Eric Hugh	Fg. Off.	Pilot	222-19-266	On 222 Sqn., 1-7-40. Posted to 19 Sqn., 19-8-40. Posted to 266 Sqn., 24-8-40. Promoted to Flt. Lt., 3-9-40. Returned to 222 Sqn., 15-9-40. ✠ **1 Do 17 (shared), 15-9-40;** ✠ **1 Bf 109, 9-10-40;** ✠ **1 Bf 109, 25-10-40;** ✠ **1 Bf 109, 29-10-40.** Awarded D.S.O.(2-2-43), D.F.C.✾ (25-11-41 and 18-9-42). Released from the R.A.F., 1944, as a Wing Commander.	♱ Died since Battle (1972)	British
THOMAS Frederick Mytton	Flt. Lt.	Pilot	152	On 152 Sqn., 1-7-40. Retired from the R.A.F., 29-12-58, as a Wing Commander.		British
THOMAS Gordon Sinclair	Sgt.	Aircrew	604	On 604 Sqn., 1-7-40. Commissioned, 24-3-44. Released from the R.A.F., 1946, as a Flying Officer.		British
THOMAS Richard Ceredig	Plt. Off.	Aircrew	235	Joined 235 Sqn., 16-8-40.	♱ Killed in Action (9-10-40)	British
THOMAS Robert Tudor	Sgt.	Pilot	247	Joined 247 Sqn., 14-8-40.	♱ Killed since Battle (21-11-40)	British
THOMAS Samuel Richard	Plt. Off.	Pilot	264	On 264 Sqn., 1-7-40. Awarded D.F.C.(29-5-42), A.F.C.(2-6-43). Continued to serve in the R.A.F. after the War.		British
THOMAS	Sgt.	Aircrew	236	On 236 Sqn., 8-40. No further service details traced. (Initials not known).		British
THOMPSON Antony Robert Fletcher	Plt. Off.	Pilot	85-249	On 85 Sqn., 29-9-40. Posted to 249 Sqn., 17-10-40. ✠ **1 Ju 88 (shared), 28-10-40;** ✠ **1 Bf 109, 30-10-40.** Awarded D.F.C.(23-3-43). Released from R.A.F., 26-1-46, as a Flight Lieutenant. Flew with B.O.A.C. thereafter.		British
THOMPSON Frank Noble	Plt. Off.	Aircrew	248	On 248 Sqn., 1-7-40. Released from the R.A.F., 1946, as a Flight Lieutenant.		British
THOMPSON James Robert	Sgt.	Aircrew	236	Joined 236 Sqn., 8-40.	♱ Killed since Battle (10-3-41)	British
THOMPSON John Marlow	Sqn. Ldr.	Pilot	111	In command of 111 Sqn., 1-7-40. ✠ **1 Do 17, 13-8-40;** ✠ **1 Bf 110 and 1 Do 17, 15-8-40;** ✠ **1 Do 17, 16-8-40;** ✠ **1 He 111, 7-9-40.** Awarded D.S.O. (14-5-43), D.F.C.✾ (6-9-40 and 4-12-42), A.F.C.(1-1-52). Retired from the R.A.F., 14-9-66, as an Air Commodore.		British
THOMPSON Joseph Beckett	Sgt.	Pilot	25	On 25 Sqn., 1-7-40. (Killed in collision with Blenheim of 29 Sqn.)	♱ Killed in Accident (31-7-40)	British
THOMPSON Peter Douglas	Plt. Off.	Pilot	32-605	Joined 32 Sqn., early 8-40. Posted to 605 Sqn., 20-9-40. Posted away, 30-10-40. Awarded D.F.C.(30-1-42). Retired from R.A.F., 7-9-75, retaining the rank of Group Captain.		British
THOMPSON William Watson	Sgt.	Pilot	234	On 234 Sqn., 1-7-40. Severely injured, 31-7-40. Withdrawn from flying duties. Commissioned, 27-5-42. Released from the R.A.F., 1946, as a Flight Lieutenant.	♱ Died since Battle (1986)	British
THOMSON James Anderson ("Jock")	Flt. Lt.	Pilot	245-302	On 245 Sqn., 1-7-40. Posted to 302 (Polish) Sqn., 13-7-40. Slightly injured, 29-10-40. Released from the R.A.F., 18-12-57, retaining the rank of Wing Commander.		British
THOMSON Ronald Alexander	Fg. Off.	Pilot	72	On 72 Sqn., 1-7-40. Wounded, 1-9-40. Promoted Flt. Lt., 3-9-40. Transferred to the R.N.Z.A.F., 1945, and released, 6-47, as a Squadron Leader.		New Zealander
THOMSON Thomas Russell	Plt. Off.	Pilot	607-213	Joined 607 Sqn., 9-10-40. Posted to 213 Sqn., 21-10-40. Released from the R.A.F., 16-8-46, as a Wing Commander. Made O.B.E.(1-1-72).		British
THORN Edward Roland	Sgt.	Pilot	264	On 264 Sqn., 1-7-40. ✠ **2 Do 17s and 1 Bf 109, 26-8-40.** Awarded D.F.M.✾ (14-6-40 and 11-2-41). Commissioned, 11-10-41. Awarded D.F.C.✾ (22-9-42 and 8-12-44).	♱ Killed since Battle (12-2-46)	British
THOROGOOD Laurence Arthur	Sgt.	Pilot	87	On 87 Sqn., 1-7-40. ✠ **1 Ju 88, 25-8-40.** Commissioned, 14-8-41. Awarded D.F.C.(4-6-46). Retired from R.A.F., 1-6-64, retaining rank of Squadron Leader.		British
THORPE Peter	Sgt.	Pilot	145	Joined 145 Sqn., 22-8-40. Wounded, 12-10-40. No further service records traced.		British
TIDMAN Alfred Roberts	Plt. Off.	Pilot	64	Joined 64 Sqn., 11-10-40.	♱ Killed since Battle (17-9-41)	British
TILL John	Sgt.	Aircrew	248	Joined 248 Sqn., mid-7-40. Flew on reconnaissance sorties over the Norwegian coast during the Battle of Britain.	♱ Killed since Battle (12-6-41)	British
TILLARD Rupert Claude	Lieut.	Pilot	808	Fleet Air Arm. In command of 808 Sqn., 1-7-40. Embarked in H.M.S. *Ark Royal*, for passage to the Mediterranean, 22-10-40. Awarded D.S.C.(1941).	♱ Killed since Battle (8-5-41)	British
TILLETT James	Plt. Off.	Pilot	238	Joined 238 Sqn., 7-9-40.	♱ Killed since Battle (6-11-40)	British
TITLEY Edward George	Plt. Off.	Pilot	609	Joined 609 Sqn., 20-10-40. (Was Squadron Leader at time of death.)	♱ Killed since Battle (17-7-43)	British
TOBIN Eugene Quimby ("Red")	Plt. Off.	Pilot	609	Joined 609 Sqn., 8-8-40. ✠ **1 Bf 110 (shared), 25-8-40;** ✠ **1 Do 17 (shared), 15-9-40.** Posted away (to No. 71 Sqn.), 19-9-40.	♱ Killed since Battle (7-9-41)	American
TOMLINSON Paul Anthony	Plt. Off.	Pilot	29	Joined 29 Sqn., 29-8-40. Retired from the R.A.F., 31-3-45, retaining the rank of Squadron Leader.		British
TONGUE Reginald Ellis ("Reggie")	Plt. Off.	Pilot	3-504	Joined 3 Sqn., 27-7-40. Posted to 504 Sqn., 28-9-40. Released from the R.A.F., 14-12-45, as a Flight Lieutenant.		British
TOOGOOD Leonard Vivian	Sgt.	Pilot	43	Joined 43 Sqn., 28-9-40.	♱ Killed in Accident (27-10-40)	British
TOOMBS John Richard ("Two-pint")	Sgt.	Aircrew	264-236	On 264 Sqn., 1-7-40, as Defiant gunner. Posted to 236 Sqn., 8-40. Commissioned, 12-7-44. Released from the R.A.F., 1946, as a Flight Lieutenant.		British
TOPHAM John Groves	Plt. Off.	Pilot	219	On 219 Sqn., 1-7-40. Promoted to Fg. Off., 3-9-40. Awarded D.S.O.(1-9-44), D.F.C.✾ (3-3-42 and 14-7-42). Retired from R.A.F., 20-8-68, as Air Commodore.	♱ Died since Battle (1987)	British
TOPOLNICKI Juliusz	Fg. Off.	Pilot	601	Joined 601 Sqn., 18-8-40. ✠ **1 Bf 109 (shared), 6-9-40.** Wounded, 6-9-40.	♱ Killed in Action (21-9-40).	Polish
TOUCH Donald Frank	Sgt.	Pilot	235	Joined 235 Sqn., early 10-40. Commissioned, 5-11-41. Awarded A.F.C.(3-4-45). Released from the R.A.F., 1946, as Flight Lieutenant.	♱ Died since Battle (10-4-48)	British
TOWERS-PERKINS William	Plt. Off.	Pilot	238	Joined 238 Sqn., 13-7-40. Wounded, 11-9-40. Released from the R.A.F., 1946, as a Flight Lieutenant.		British
TOWNSEND Peter Wooldridge	Flt. Lt.	Pilot	85	In command of 85 Sqn., 1-7-40, as Acting Sqn. Ldr. (promoted Sqn. Ldr., 1-9-40). ✠ **1 Do 17, 11-8-40;** ✠ **2 Bf 109s and 1 Bf 110, 18-8-40;** ✠ **2 Do 17s (both shared), 26-8-40;** ✠ **1 Bf 109, 28-8-40;** ✠ **1 Bf 109, 30-8-40;** ✠ **1 Bf 109, 31-8-40.** Wounded, 31-8-40. Awarded D.S.O.(13-5-41), D.F.C.✾ (30-4-40 and 6-9-40). Made C.V.O.(1947). Retired, 18-11-56, as a Group Captain.		British
TOWNSHEND Thomas William	Sgt.	Aircrew	600	Joined 600 Sqn., c.8-7-40.		British
¶ **TOYNE** William Arthur	Flt. Lt.	Pilot	17	On 17 Sqn., 1-7-40. Posted away, 4-7-40. Awarded D.F.C.		British
TRACEY Owen Vincent	Plt. Off.	Pilot	79	Joined 79 Sqn., 6-7-40. ✠ **1 He 111, 15-8-40;** ✠ **1 Do 17, 28-8-40;** ✠ **1 He 111, 30-8-40;** ✠ **1 Do 17, 31-8-40.** Awarded D.F.C.(6-10-42, back-dated).	♱ Killed since Battle (8-12-41)	New Zealander
TREVENA Charles Warren	Fg. Off.	Pilot	1(Canadian)	Joined 1(Canadian) Sqn., 1-9-40. Retired from R.C.A.F., 9-10-43, on medical grounds, as an Acting Squadron Leader.		Canadian
TROUSDALE Richard Macklow	Plt. Off.	Pilot	266	On 266 Sqn., 1-7-40. ✠ **1 Bf 109, 16-8-40;** ✠ **1 Do 17 (shared), 7-9-40;** ✠ **1 Bf 109, 29-10-40.** Awarded D.F.C.✾ (4-3-41 and 8-5-42).	♱ Killed since Battle (16-5-47)	New Zealander
TRUEMAN Alec Albert Gray ("Handlebars")	Plt. Off.	Pilot	253	Joined 253 Sqn., 20-7-40.	♱ Killed in Action (4-9-40)	Canadian
TRUHLAR Jan	Sgt.	Pilot	312	Joined 312 (Czech) Sqn., 5-9-40. Commissioned, 1-3-41. Shot down and captured by the Germans, 9-6-41. Returned to Czechoslovakia after the War.	♱ Died since Battle (25-10-73)	Czech
TRUMBLE Anthony John	Fg. Off.	Pilot	264	On 264 Sqn., 1-7-40. Posted away, 18-7-40. Captured by Germans in Greece, 1-41, and made prisoner. Made O.B.E.(28-12-45). Retired from R.A.F., 3-5-66, as a Group Captain.		British
TRURAN Anthony John Jamieson	Plt. Off.	Pilot	615	Joined 615 Sqn., early 7-40. Slightly injured, 15-8-40.	♱ Killed since Battle (25-11-40)	British
TUCK Robert Roland Stanford ("Bob")	Fg. Off.	Pilot	92-257	On 92 Sqn., 1-7-40. Promoted Flt. Lt., 3-9-40. ✠ **1 Ju 88 (shared), 13-8-40;** ✠ **2 Ju 88s, 14-8-40;** ✠ **1 Ju 88, 18-8-40;** ✠ **1 Ju 88, 25-8-40;** ✠ **1 Bf 110, 15-9-40;** ✠ **1 Ju 88, 23-9-40;** ✠ **1 Ju 88, 4-10-40;** ✠ **1 Bf 109, 12-10-40;** ✠ **1 Bf 109, 25-10-40;** ✠ **1 Bf 109, 28-10-40.** Awarded D.S.O. (7-1-41), D.F.C.✾✾ (11-6-40, 25-10-40 and 11-4-41). Shot down and taken prisoner by the Germans, 28-1-42. Escaped from captivity, 1-2-45. Retired from the R.A.F., 13-5-49, as a Wing Commander.	♱ Died since Battle (5-5-87)	British
TUCKER Aidan Boys	Plt. Off.	Pilot	151	On 151 Sqn., 1-7-40. Wounded, 12-8-40. Retired from the R.A.F., 10-2-58, as a Flight Lieutenant.	♱ Died since Battle (1987)	British
TUCKER Bernard Eric	Plt. Off.	Pilot	266-66	Joined 266 Sqn., 7-10-40. Posted to 66 Sqn., 25-10-40. Released from the R.A.F., 1946, as a Flight Lieutenant.		British

TUCKER Frank Day	Sgt.	Aircrew	236	Joined 236 Sqn., 21-7-40. Commissioned, 12-2-41. Released from the R.A.F., 1946, as a Flight Lieutenant.	✞ Died since Battle (5-82)	British
TUCKER Ronald Yeaman	Sgt.	Aircrew	235	Joined 235 Sqn., 12-7-40.	✞ **Killed in Action** (18-7-40)	British
TURLEY-GEORGE Douglas Richard	Plt. Off.	Pilot	54	Joined 54 Sqn., 15-7-40. Wounded, 12-8-40. Promoted Fg. Off., 3-9-40. Awarded D.F.C.(3-10-44). Transferred to the R.A.F.O., 11-49, as a Squadron Leader.		British
TURNBULL Robert Nesbit	Sgt.	Aircrew	25	Joined 25 Sqn., 27-9-40. Awarded D.F.C.(25-5-43) as a Warrant Officer. Commissioned, 20-1-44. Released from the R.A.F., 1945, as a Flying Officer.	✞ Died since Battle (18-9-80)	British
TURNER Donald Eric	Flt. Lt.	Pilot	238	Joined 238 Sqn., 13-7-40. ✠ **1 Bf 109, 20-7-40; ✠ 1 Bf 110 (shared), 21-7-40.**	✞ **Killed in Action** (8-8-40)	British
TURNER Guy	F/Sgt.	Pilot	32	On 32 Sqn., 1-7-40. Severely wounded, 19-7-40. Commissioned, 19-11-42. Retired from the R.A.F., 18-1-61, retaining the rank of Squadron Leader.	✞ Died since Battle (5-12-82)	British
TURNER Percival Stanley	Plt. Off.	Pilot	242	On 242 Sqn., 1-7-40. ✠ **2 Do 17s, 15-9-40.** Awarded D.S.O.(23-5-44), D.F.C.✱ (8-10-40 and 5-8-41). Retired from the R.C.A.F., 1965.	✞ Died since Battle (23-7-85)	Canadian
TURNER Robert Charles	Sgt.	Aircrew	264	On 264 Sqn., 1-7-40.	✞ **Killed in Action** (28-8-40)	British
TWEED Leslie John	Sgt.	Pilot	111	Joined 111 Sqn., 27-7-40. Wounded, 6-9-40. Commissioned, 19-6-42. Retired from R.A.F., 21-10-72, as a Flight Lieutenant.	✞ Died since Battle (4-2-85)	British
TWITCHETT Francis John ("Twitch")	Sgt.	Pilot	43-229	Joined 43 Sqn., mid-9-40. Posted to 229 Sqn., 10-40. Commissioned, 7-1-42. Transferred to the R.A.F.O., 8-50, as a Flight Lieutenant.		British
TYRER Edward	Sgt.	Pilot	46	Joined 46 Sqn., early 7-40. ✠ **1 Do 17 (shared), 15-9-40; ✠ 1 Bf 109 (shared) 27-9-40.** Commissioned, 29-11-41. Released from the R.A.F., 1945, as a Flight Lieutenant.	✞ Died since Battle (1-4-46)	British
TYSON Frank Hastings	Sqn. Ldr.	Pilot	3-312	On 3 Sqn., 1-7-40, as supernumerary Sqn. Ldr. Posted to command 312 (Czech) Sqn., on formation. Retired from R.A.F., 14-2-62, as a Group Captain.	✞ Died since Battle (30-12-79)	British
UNETT John Windsor	Sgt.	Aircrew	235	Joined 235 Sqn., 4-8-40.	✞ Killed since Battle (27-12-40)	British
UNWIN George Cecil ("Grumpy")	F/Sgt.	Pilot	19	On 19 Sqn., 1-7-40. ✠ **1 Bf 109 and 1 Bf 110, 16-8-40; ✠ 1 Bf 110, 3-9-40; ✠ 2 Bf 109s, 7-9-40; ✠ 3 Bf 109s, 15-9-40; ✠ 1 Bf 110, 18-9-40; ✠ 1 Bf 109, 27-9-40.** Commissioned, 31-7-41. Awarded D.S.O.(21-3-52), D.F.M.✱ (1-10-40 and 6-12-40). Retired from the R.A.F., 18-1-61, as a Wing Commander.		British
UPTON Hamilton Charles	Plt. Off.	Pilot	43-607	On 43 Sqn., 1-7-40. ✠ **1 He 111 (shared), 12-7-40; ✠ 2 Ju 87s, 8-8-40; ✠ 1 Do 17, 13-8-40; ✠ 1 Ju 88, 15-8-40; ✠ 3 Ju 87s, 16-8-40; ✠ 1 Bf 109 and 1 Ju 87, 18-8-40; ✠ 1 Bf 110, 4-9-40.** Awarded D.F.C.(29-4-41). Transferred to the R.C.A.F., 1945, until 1953.	✞ Died since Battle (1965 ?)	British
URBANOWICZ Witold	Fg. Off.	Pilot	145-303	Joined 145 Sqn., 4-8-40. ✠ **1 Bf 109, 8-8-40; ✠ 1 Ju 88, 12-8-40.** Posted to 303 (Polish) Sqn., 21-8-40. ✠ **1 Bf 110, 6-9-40; ✠ 1 Do 17, 7-9-40; ✠ 2 Do 17s, 15-9-40; ✠ 1 He 111, 26-9-40; ✠ 2 Ju 88s, 1 Do 17 and 1 Bf 109, 27-9-40; ✠ 3 Bf 109s and 1 Do 17, 30-10-40.** Awarded D.F.C. (30-10-41). Released from the Polish Air Force, 18-10-45, and settled in America.	✞ Died since Battle (1987)	Polish
URIE John Dunlop	Flt. Lt.	Pilot	602	On 602 Sqn., 1-7-40. Promoted Sqn. Ldr., 1-9-40. Released from the R.A.F., 1945, as a Wing Commander.		British
URWIN-MANN John Ronald ("Jackie")	Plt. Off.	Pilot	238	On 238 Sqn., 1-7-40. ✠ **1 He 59, 20-7-40; ✠ 1 Bf 109, 11-8-40; ✠ 1 Bf 109, 13-8-40; ✠ 1 Ju 88, 21-8-40; ✠ 1 He 111, 15-9-40; ✠ 2 He 111s, 25-9-40; ✠ 1 Bf 110, 26-9-40; ✠ 1 Ju 88, 7-10-40.** Awarded D.S.O. (14-5-43), D.F.C.✱ (26-11-40 and 7-4-42). Retired from the R.A.F., 15-3-59, retaining the rank of Squadron Leader.		Canadian
USMAR Frank	Sgt.	Pilot	41	On 41 Sqn., 1-7-40. ✠ **1 He 111, 15-8-40; ✠ 2 Bf 109s, 18-9-40.** Wounded, 27-9-40. Commissioned, 15-12-41. Retired from the R.A.F., 16-9-64, as a Squadron Leader.		British
VAN DEN HOVE d'ERTSENRIJCK Albert Emanuel Alix Dieudonne Jean Ghislain	Plt. Off.	Pilot	43-501	Joined 43 Sqn., 5-8-40. ✠ **1 Ju 87, 16-8-40; ✠ 1 Bf 109, 26-8-40; ✠ 1 Bf 110, 4-9-40.** Posted to 501 Sqn., 11-9-40. (Killed on first patrol with Squadron.)	✞ **Killed in Action** (15-9-40)	Belgian
VAN LIERDE Willi	Plt. Off.	Pilot	87	Joined 87 Sqn., 12-8-40. No other details of service during the Battle of Britain traced.		Belgian
VAN MENTZ Brian	Fg. Off.	Pilot	222	Joined 222 Sqn., 8-8-40. ✠ **1 Bf 109, 3-9-40; ✠ 1 Ju 88, 11-9-40; ✠ 1 Bf 110, 23-9-40.** Awarded D.F.C.(25-10-40)	✞ Killed since Battle (26-4-41)	South African
VAN WAYENBERGHE Arthur Albert Leopold	Plt. Off.	Pilot	236	Joined 236 Sqn.	✞ Killed since Battle (10-3-41)	Belgian
VARLEY George Wallace	Plt. Off.	Pilot	79-247	Joined 79 Sqn., early 10-40. Posted to 247 Sqn., 26-10-40. Awarded D.F.C.(29-6-45). Released from the R.A.F., 1946, as a Flight Lieutenant.	✞ Died since Battle (11-2-82)	British
VASATKO Alois	Plt. Off	Pilot	312	Joined 312 (Czech) Sqn., 5-9-40. ✠ **1 Ju 88 (shared), 8-10-40.** Awarded D.F.C.	✞ Killed since Battle (23-6-42)	Czech
VELEBNOVSKY Antonin	Plt. Off.	Pilot	1	Joined 1 Sqn., 22-10-40.	✞ Killed since Battle (16-7-41)	Czech
VENESOEN Francois Auguste	Sgt.	Pilot	235	Joined 235 Sqn., 27-8-40. Commissioned, 17-7-41. Awarded D.F.C.	✞ Killed since Battle (6-6-44)	Belgian
VENN Jack Albert Charles	Plt. Off.	Aircrew	236	Joined 236 Sqn., 1-7-40. Posted away, 1-9-40. Released from the R.A.F., 9-45, as a Flight Lieutenant.		British
VERITY Victor Bosanquet Strachan	Plt. Off.	Pilot	229	On 229 Sqn., 1-7-40. ✠ **1 He 111, 11-9-40; ✠ 1 Ju 88, 4-10-40.** Awarded D.F.C.(2-8-41). Transferred to the Reserve in New Zealand, 1-46.	✞ Died since Battle (2-2-79)	New Zealander
VESELY Vlastimil	Plt. Off.	Pilot	312	Joined 312 (Czech) Sqn., 5-9-40. Awarded D.F.C., A.F.C.(10-6-54). Retired from the R.A.F., 3-10-68, as a Squadron Leader.		Czech
VICK James Anderson	Sqn. Ldr.	Pilot	607	In command of 607 Sqn., 1-7-40. Released from the R.A.F., 1942, to take up appointment with B.O.A.C.		British
VIGORS Timothy Ashmead	Plt. Off.	Pilot	222	On 222 Sqn., 1-7-40. ✠ **1 Bf 109, 31-8-40; ✠ 1 Bf 109, 1-9-40; ✠ 1 Bf 110, 3-9-40; ✠ 1 Bf 109, 9-9-40; ✠ 1 Ju 88, 8-10-40.** Awarded D.F.C. (1-10-40). Retired from the R.A.F., 8-11-46, retaining the rank of Wing Commander.		British
VILES Leslie William	Sgt.	Aircrew	236	Joined 236 Sqn., 8-40. Commissioned, 22-5-42. Released from the R.A.F., 1945, as a Flight Lieutenant.		British
VILLA John Wolferstan ("Pancho")	Flt. Lt.	Pilot	72-92	On 72 Sqn., 1-7-40. ✠ **1 Bf 110, 2-9-40; ✠ 1 Bf 110, 4-9-40; ✠ 1 Do 215 (shared), 10-9-40; ✠ 1 He 111 (shared), 14-9-40; ✠ 1 Do 17 (solo) and 1 He 111 (shared), ✠ 1 He 111, 27-9-40; ✠ 1 Bf 109, 28-9-40; ✠ 1 Do 17, 11-10-40; ✠ 1 Bf 110 (shared), 20-10-40; ✠ 1 Bf 109, 25-10-40; ✠ 1 Bf 110, 29-10-40.** Posted to 92 Sqn., 13-9-40. Awarded D.F.C.✱ (8-10-40 and 26-11-40). Released from the R.A.F., 1946, as a Squadron Leader.	✞ Died since Battle (1983)	British
VINCENT Stanley Flamank	Gp. Capt.	Pilot	257-229	Station Commander at R.A.F. Northolt during the Battle of Britain. Flew solo sorties with Nos. 257 and 229 Sqns. ✠ **1 Bf 109, 30-9-40.** Awarded D.F.C.(25-10-40); had been awarded A.F.C.(1-1-19). Retired from the R.A.F., 6-2-50, as an Air Vice-Marshal.	✞ Died since Battle (13-3-76)	British
VINDIS Frantisek	Sgt.	Pilot	310	Joined 310 (Czech) Sqn., 10-40. Commissioned, 20-6-43. Awarded D.F.C. Transferred to the R.A.F.O., as a Flight Lieutenant, 1962.		Czech
VINYARD Frederick Fenton	Sgt.	Pilot	64	Joined 64 Sqn., 9-40.	✞ **Killed in Action** (6-10-40)	British
VOKES Arthur Frank	Plt. Off.	Pilot	19	On 19 Sqn., 1-7-40.	✞ Killed since Battle (5-9-41)	British
VOPALECKY Josef	W/Off.	Pilot	310	Joined 310 (Czech) Sqn., 12-7-40, on formation. Commissioned, 1941.		Czech
VRANA Adolf	Plt. Off.	Pilot	312	Joined 312 (Czech) Sqn., 5-9-40.		Czech
VYBIRAL Tomas	Plt. Off.	Pilot	312	Joined 312 (Czech) Sqn., 5-9-40. Awarded D.S.O.(12-44), D.F.C.(7-44). Released from the R.A.F., 1946, as a Wing Commander.	✞ Died since Battle (2-81)	Czech
VYKOUKAL Karel Jan	Plt. Off.	Pilot	111-73	Joined 111 Sqn., 12-9-40. Posted to 73 Sqn., 25-9-40.	✞ Killed since Battle (21-5-42)	Czech

Name	Rank	Role	Sqn.	Details	Status	Nationality
WADDINGHAM John	Plt. Off.	Pilot	141	On 141 Sqn., 1-7-40. Promoted Fg. Off., 3-9-40. ✠ 1 He 111, 16-9-40. Awarded D.F.C.(18-3-41).	Killed since Battle (27-9-42)	British
WADE Trevor Sidney ("Wimpey")	Plt. Off.	Pilot	92	On 92 Sqn., 1-7-40. ✠ 1 Ju 88 (shared), 19-8-40; ✠ 1 Do 17 (shared), 10-9-40; ✠ 1 He 111, 11-9-40; ✠ 1 Do 17, 27-9-40; ✠ 1 Bf 109, 12-10-40. Awarded D.F.C.(15-7-41), A.F.C.(1-9-44). Released from R.A.F., 1946, as a Squadron Leader. Became test pilot with Hawker Aircraft Ltd.; killed in Hawker P.1081.	Killed since Battle (3-4-51)	British
WADHAM John Victor	Sgt.	Pilot	601-145	Joined 601 Sqn., 3-8-40. Posted to 145 Sqn., 20-8-40.	Killed in Action (12-10-40)	British
WAGHORN Peter Harry	Sgt.	Pilot	249-111	Joined 111 Sqn., 21-8-40, from 249 Sqn.	Killed since Battle (11-4-41)	British
WAGNER Alan Derek	Sgt.	Pilot	151	Joined 151 Sqn., 10-40. Commissioned, 1-5-41. Awarded D.F.C.✠ (5-3-43 and 28-4-41).	Killed since Battle (17-7-44)	British
WAINWRIGHT Alex George	Plt. Off.	Pilot	151	Joined 151 Sqn., 8-40. Injured, 29-8-40.	Killed since Battle (21-1-41)	British
WAINWRIGHT Michael Terry	Fg. Off.	Pilot	64	Joined 64 Sqn., 27-9-40. Awarded A.F.C.(1-1-51). Retired from the R.A.F., 31-3-58, as a Squadron Leader.		British
WAKE Frederick William	Sgt.	Aircrew	264	Defiant gunner. Joined 264 Sqn., 9-40. Awarded D.F.M.(8-8-41).		British
WAKEFIELD Herbert Kenneth	Plt. Off.	Aircrew	235	On 235 Sqn., 1-7-40. ✠ 1 Bf 109, 11-8-40; ✠ 1 Ju 87, 18-8-40. Awarded D.F.C.(22-10-40). Released from the R.A.F., 1946, as a Flight Lieutenant.		British
WAKEHAM Ernest Cecil John	Plt. Off.	Pilot	145	On 145 Sqn., 1-7-40. ✠ 1 Ju 88 (shared), 7-7-40; ✠ 1 He 111, 11-7-40; ✠ 1 Do 17 (shared), 19-7-40; ✠ 1 Ju 88 (shared), 29-7-40; ✠ 1 Hs 126, 1-8-40.	Killed in Action (8-8-40)	British
WAKELING Sidney Richard Ernest	Sgt.	Pilot	87	On 87 Sqn., 1-7-40.	Killed in Action (25-8-40)	British
WALCH Stuart Crosby	Fg. Off.	Pilot	238	On 238 Sqn., 1-7-40. ✠ 1 Bf 110, 11-7-40; ✠ 1 Bf 109 (shared), 20-7-40; ✠ 1 Bf 110, 21-7-40; ✠ 1 Bf 109, 26-7-40.	Killed in Action (11-8-40)	Australian
WALKER George Arthur	Sgt.	Pilot	232	Joined 232 Sqn., 14-9-40. Commissioned, 20-9-40. Released from the R.A.F., 1946, but rejoined later. Retired, 4-6-72, as a Squadron Leader.		British
WALKER James Arthur	Plt. Off.	Pilot	111	On 111 Sqn., 1-7-40. Promoted Fg. Off., 3-9-40. ✠ 1 Do 17, 13-8-40; ✠ 1 Bf 109, 16-8-40. Awarded D.F.C.(6-9-40).	Killed since Battle (8-2-44)	Canadian
WALKER James Ian Bradley	Sgt.	Aircrew	600	Joined 600 Sqn., 10-7-40. Transferred to Bomber Command, 1941. Released from R.N.Z.A.F., 15-3-44, as a Warrant Officer.		New Zealander
WALKER James Richard ("Hiram-J")	Plt. Off.	Pilot	611-41	Joined 611 Sqn., 27-7-40. Promoted to Fg. Off., 3-9-40. Posted to 41 Sqn., 29-9-40. ✠ 1 Bf 109, 7-10-40; ✠ 1 Bf 109, 9-10-40.	Killed since Battle (16-11-40)	Canadian
WALKER John Harold Gilbert	Fg. Off.	Pilot	25	On 25 Sqn., 1-7-40. Served throughout Battle of Britain with 25 Sqn.	Killed since Battle (9-5-42)	British
WALKER Norman MacDonald	Sgt.	Pilot	615	Joined 615 Sqn., 30-9-40.	Killed since Battle (12-6-41)	British
WALKER Robert James	Fg. Off.	Pilot	72	On 72 Sqn., 1-7-40. Awarded D.S.O.(12-6-45). Retired from R.A.F., 28-11-65, as a Group Captain.		British
WALKER Stanley	Sgt.	Aircrew	236	Joined 236 Sqn., early 8-40.	Killed since Battle (12-2-42)	British
WALKER William Louis Buchanan	Plt. Off.	Pilot	616	On 616 Sqn., 1-7-40. Wounded, 26-8-40. Released from R.A.F., 1-9-45, as a Flight Lieutenant.		British
WALKER-SMITH Francis Richard	Sgt.	Pilot	85	On 85 Sqn., 1-7-40. ✠ 2 Bf 110s, 18-8-40; ✠ 1 Do 17, 26-8-40; ✠ 1 Bf 109, 28-8-40. Wounded, 29-8-40.	Killed since Battle (13-3-41)	British
WALLACE Clarence Alfred Blake	Plt. Off.	Pilot	3	Joined 3 Sqn., 1-40.	Killed since Battle (27-10-41)	Canadian
WALLACE Thomas Young	Sgt.	Pilot	610-111	On 610 Sqn., 1-7-40. Posted to 111 Sqn., 17-7-40. ✠ 1 Bf 110 (solo) and 1 Bf 110 (shared), 15-8-40; ✠ 1 Do 17, 18-8-40; ✠ 1 Do 17 (shared), 26-8-40; ✠ 1 Bf 110, 31-8-40; ✠ 1 Bf 109, 4-9-40. Slightly wounded, 7-9-40. Awarded D.F.M.(25-10-40). Commissioned, 10-3-43.	Killed since Battle (11-11-44)	South African
WALLEN Dennis Stanley	Fg. Off.	Aircrew	604	On 604 Sqn., 1-7-40. Made O.B.E.(1-1-46). Released from the R.A.F., 1946, as a Wing Commander.		British
WALLENS Ronald Walter	Plt. Off.	Pilot	41	On 41 Sqn., 1-7-40. Promoted Fg. Off., 7-7-40. ✠ 3 Bf 109s, 8-8-40; ✠ 1 Ju 88 (shared), 11-8-40; ✠ 1 Bf 109, 5-9-40. Severely wounded, 5-9-40. Awarded D.F.C.(15-8-44). Released from the R.A.F., 1946, as a Squadron Leader.		British
WALLER George Alfred	Sgt.	Aircrew	29	Joined 29 Sqn., c.10-7-40. Commissioned, 24-6-43. Awarded D.F.C.(20-10-44). Released from the R.A.F., 1950, as a Flight Lieutenant.	Died since Battle (1983)	British
WALLEY Peter Kenneth	Sgt.	Pilot	615	Joined 615 Sqn., 6-8-40.	Killed in Action (18-8-40)	British
WALLIS Donald Sylvester	Sgt.	Pilot	235	Joined 235 Sqn., 19-9-40.	Killed since Battle (22-1-41)	British
WALMSLEY Harold William	Sgt.	Aircrew	248	On 248 Sqn., 1-7-40. Flew on reconnaissance sorties over Norwegian coast during the Battle of Britain.	Killed since Battle (13-12-40)	British
WALSH Edmund	Sgt.	Aircrew	141	Joined 141 Sqn., early 9-40. Commissioned, 26-8-42. Released from the R.A.F., 23-1-46, as a Flight Lieutenant.		British
WALSH John Joseph	Plt. Off.	Pilot	615	Joined 615 Sqn., 23-9-40.	Died since Battle (2-3-41)	Canadian
WALSH Robert William Meade	Sub-Lieut.	Pilot	111	Fleet Air Arm. Joined 111 Sqn., 22-9-40. Retired from the Royal Navy, 10-2-58, as a Lieutenant Commander.		British
WALTON Herbert	Sgt.	Pilot	87	On 87 Sqn., 1-7-40. Slightly wounded, 30-9-40. Commissioned, 25-1-43. Released from the R.A.F., 1946, as a Flight Lieutenant.		British
WANT William Hudson	Sgt.	Aircrew	248	On 248 Sqn., 1-7-40. Flew on reconnaissance sorties over the Norwegian coast during the Battle of Britain.	Killed in Action (19-8-40)	British
WAPNIAREK Stefan	Plt. Off.	Pilot	302	Joined 302 (Polish) Sqn., 30-7-40. ✠ 1 Ju 88, 18-9-40.	Killed in Action (18-10-40)	Polish
WARD Derek Harland	Fg. Off.	Pilot	87	On 87 Sqn., 1-7-40. ✠ 1 Bf 110, 15-8-40. Awarded D.F.C.✠ (17-10-41 and 22-5-42).	Killed since Battle (17-6-42)	New Zealander
WARD The Hon. Edward Frederick	Sqn. Ldr.	Pilot	601	Attached to 601 Sqn., 28-7-40. Assumed command, 10-8-40. Posted away, 19-8-40. Released from the R.A.F., 1945, as a Group Captain.	Died since Battle (4-87)	British
WARD John Lewis	Plt. Off.	Pilot	32	Joined 32 Sqn., late 9-40.	Killed since Battle (20-3-42)	British
WARD Rufus Arthur	Sgt.	Pilot	616-66	Joined 616 Sqn., 5-9-40. Posted to 66 Sqn., 29-9-40.	Killed in Action (8-10-40)	British
WARD William Barlow	Sgt.	Aircrew	604	No record of operational service traced.		British
WARDEN Noel Proctor	Sgt.	Pilot	610	Joined 610 Sqn., 6-10-40. Commissioned, 12-6-41.	Killed since Battle (1-10-41)	British
WARD-SMITH Peter	Sgt.	Pilot	610	Joined 610 Sqn., 16-9-40. Commissioned, 19-6-41. Released from the R.A.F., 1946, as a Flight Lieutenant.		British
WARE Ralph Taverham	Sgt.	Pilot	3	On 3 Sqn., 1-7-40. Commissioned, 18-6-43.	Killed since Battle (21-1-45)	British
WAREHAM Michael Percy	Plt. Off.	Pilot	1-242	Joined 242 Sqn., 17-10-40, from 1 Sqn. Awarded D.F.C.(12-12-41).	Died since Battle (16-11-48)	British
WAREING Phillip Thomas	Sgt.	Pilot	616	On 616 Sqn., 1-7-40. ✠ 1 Bf 109, 22-8-40. Shot down, 25-8-40, and made prisoner by the Germans. Escaped from captivity and returned to Britain, 1943. Commissioned, 13-7-43. Awarded D.C.M.(14-12-43). Released from the R.A.F., 1946, as a Flight Lieutenant.	Died since Battle (5-87)	British
WARING William	Sgt.	Aircrew	23	Joined 23 Sqn., 8-40. No other service details traced.		British
WARNER William Henry Cromwell	Fg. Off.	Pilot	610	On 610 Sqn., 1-7-40.	Killed in Action (16-8-40)	British
WARREN Charles	Plt. Off.	Pilot	152	On 152 Sqn., 1-7-40. ✠ 1 Do 17 (shared), 22-8-40. Promoted Fg. Off., 1-10-40. Awarded D.F.C.(10-9-43), and made M.B.E.(12-6-47). Retired from the R.A.F., 14-12-57, retaining the rank of Wing Commander.		British
WARREN Douglas Albert Palmer	Plt. Off.	Aircrew	248	Joined 248 Sqn., 26-8-40. Flew on reconnaissance sorties over the Norwegian Coast.	Killed since Battle (9-2-41)	British
WARREN John Benjamin William	A.C.1	Aircrew	600	Joined 600 Sqn., 7-40. (Killed in action while still holding A.C.1 rank.)	Killed in Action (8-8-40)	British

WARREN Stanley	Sgt.	Pilot	1	Joined 1 Sqn., mid-9-40.	✞	**Killed in Action** (9-10-40)	British
WARREN Thornton Arrowsmith	Sgt.	Aircrew	236	Joined 236 Sqn., late 9-40. Commissioned 12-2-41. Released from the R.A.F., 1945, as a Squadron Leader.			British
WATERSTON Robin McGregor	Fg. Off.	Pilot	603	On 603 Sqn., 1-7-40. ✠ **1 Do 17 (shared), 20-7-40; ✠ 1 Bf 109, 30-8-40.**	✞	**Killed in Action** (31-8-40)	British
WATKINS Douglas Herbert ("Dirty")	Fg. Off.	Pilot	611	On 611 Sqn., 1-7-40. ✠ **1 Do 17, 21-8-40.** Promoted Flt. Lt., 21-9-40. ✠ **1 Do 17, 11-10-40.** Awarded D.F.C.(29-4-41). Released from the R.A.F., 1945, as a Wing Commander.	✞	Died since Battle (1969)	British
WATKINSON Arthur Basil ("Watty")	Plt. Off.	Pilot	66	Joined 66 Sqn., 26-7-40. ✠ **1 Do 17, 11-9-40.** Wounded, 28-9-40. Released from the R.A.F., 1945, as a Flight Lieutenant.	✞	Died since Battle (18-10-85)	South African
WATLING William Charles	Plt. Off.	Pilot	92	Joined 92 Sqn., 15-7-40. ✠ **1 Ju 88 (shared), 13-8-40.** Wounded, 9-9-40.	✞	Killed since Battle (7-2-41)	British
WATSON Arthur Roy	Plt. Off.	Pilot	152	Joined 152 Sqn., 1-7-40. ✠ **1 He 111, 15-9-40; ✠ 1 Ju 88 and 1 Bf 110, 27-9-40.**	✞	Killed since Battle (28-11-40)	British
WATSON Edward James	Plt. Off.	Pilot	605	Joined 605 Sqn., 5-8-40. Wounded, 16-9-40.	✞	Killed since Battle (26-2-42)	British
WATSON Frederick Stanley	Plt. Off.	Pilot	3-1(Canadian)	Joined 1(Canadian) Sqn., 21-10-40, from 3 Sqn.	✞	Killed since Battle (11-10-41)	Canadian
WATSON John Gordon	A.C.2	Aircrew	604	Joined 604 Sqn., 7-40, and flew throughout the Battle without being granted rank or flying badge.			British
WATSON Lionel George	Plt. Off.	Aircrew	29	On 29 Sqn., 1-7-40. Transferred to the Administrative Branch and released from the R.A.F., 1945, as a Squadron Leader.			British
WATSON Rafael	Plt. Off.	Pilot	87	On 87 Sqn., 1-7-40. Promoted to Fg. Off., 3-9-40. Released from the R.A.F., 1947, as a Squadron Leader.	✞	Died since Battle (1986)	British
WATSON	Plt. Off.	Pilot	64	Joined 64 Sqn., 15-10-40. (Initials and forenames not known)			British
WATTERS Joseph	Plt. Off.	Pilot	236	Joined 236 Sqn., 27-8-40. Transferred to the Reserve in New Zealand, 2-7-46.	✞	Died since Battle (18-4-81)	New Zealander
WATTS Edwin Leslie	Sgt.	Aircrew	248	On 248 Sqn., 1-7-40. Flew on reconnaissance sorties over Norway during Battle.	✞	Killed since Battle (13-4-43)	British
WATTS Reginald Douglas Haig	Sgt.	Aircrew	235	On 235 Sqn., 1-7-40. (Killed on escort sortie during raid on Calais.)	✞	**Killed in Action** (11-9-40)	British
WATTS Roy Frederick	Fg. Off.	Pilot	253	Joined 253 Sqn., 1-7-40. Promoted Flt. Lt., 3-9-40. Retired from the R.A.F., 4-10-64, as a Group Captain.			British
WAY Basil Hugh ("Wonky")	Fg. Off.	Pilot	54	On 54 Sqn., 1-7-40. ✠ **1 Do 215 (shared), 3-7-40. ✠ 1 Bf 109 (solo) and 1 Bf 109 (shared), 8-7-40; ✠ 1 Bf 109, 11-7-40; ✠ 1 Bf 109, 25-7-40.**	✞	**Killed in Action** (25-7-40)	British
WAY Lewis Beniamin Roger	Plt. Off.	Pilot	229	Joined 229 Sqn., 23-9-40. Released from the R.A.F., 1946, as a Squadron Leader.			British
WCZELIK Antoni	Plt. Off.	Pilot	302	Joined 302 (Polish) Sqn., 20-8-40.	✞	Killed since Battle (14-4-42)	Polish
WEAVER Percy Stevenson	Fg. Off.	Pilot	56	On 56 Sqn., 1-7-40. ✠ **1 Ju 88 (shared), 20-7-40; ✠ 1 Bf 109, 29-7-40. ✠ 1 Do 17, 12-8-40; ✠ 1 Bf 110, 13-8-40; ✠ 1 Do 215 (shared), 16-8-40; ✠ 1 He 111 and 1 Bf 110, 18-8-40; ✠ 1 He 111, 24-8-40; ✠ 1 Bf 109, 28-8-40.** Awarded D.F.C.(1-10-40).	✞	**Killed in Action** (31-8-40)	British
WEBB Paul Clifford	Fg. Off.	Pilot	602	On 602 Sqn., 1-7-40. Promoted Flt. Lt., 3-9-40. ✠ **1 Bf 110, 16-8-40. ✠ 2 Bf 110s, 25-8-40; ✠ 1He 59, 26-8-40; ✠ 1 Bf 110, 7-9-40; ✠ 1 u.e.a., 9-9-40.** Wounded, 9-9-40. Awarded D.F.C.(17-10-44). Appointed C.B.E.(1-1-63). Retired from the R.A.F., 18-3-73, retaining the rank of Air Commodore.			British
WEBBER Wyndham Frederick Peirson	Plt. Off.	Aircrew	141	Defiant gunner. On 141 Sqn., 1-7-40. Transferred to the R.A.F.O., 1954, as a Squadron Leader.			British
WEBER Frantisek	Plt. Off.	Pilot	145	Joined 145 Sqn., 11-9-40. Released from the R.A.F., 1946, as a Squadron Leader.			Czech
WEBER Jack	Sgt.	Pilot	1-145	Joined 1 Sqn., 23-9-40. Posted to 145 Sqn., 13-10-40. Commissioned, 7-1-42. Released from the R.A.F., 11-45, as a Flight Lieutenant.	✞	Died since Battle (1988)	British
WEBSTER Ernest Reginald	Sgt.	Pilot	85	On 85 Sqn., 1-7-40. Commissioned, 4-10-43. Released from the R.A.F., 1947, as a Flying Officer.			British
WEBSTER Frank Kinnersley	Plt. Off.	Pilot	610	Joined 610 Sqn., 28-7-40.	✞	Killed in Action (26-8-40)	British
WEBSTER Herbert Garth	Sgt.	Pilot	73	On 73 Sqn., 1-7-40.	✞	Killed since Battle (14-4-41)	British
WEBSTER John Terrance	Fg. Off.	Pilot	41	On 41 Sqn 1-7-40. ✠ **1 Bf 109, 27-7-40; ✠ 1 Bf 109, 29-7-40; ✠ 4 Bf 109s, 8-8-40; ✠ 2 Bf 109s, 5-9-40.** Awarded D.F.C.(30-8-40).	✞	**Killed in Action** (5-9-40)	British
WEDGWOOD Jefferson Heywood ("Colonel")	Fg. Off.	Pilot	253	On 253 Sqn., 1-7-40. Promoted Flt. Lt., 6-7-40. ✠ **1 Bf 110, 4-9-40.** Posted away, 26-9-40. Awarded D.F.C.✠ (2-10-42 and 5-2-43).	✞	Killed since Battle (17-12-42)	British
WEDLOCK Gordon Victor	Sgt.	Aircrew	235	On 235 Sqn., 1-7-40. Awarded D.F.M.(17-1-41). Commissioned, 22-1-42. Released from the R.A.F., 1946, as a Squadron Leader.			British
WEDZIK Marian	Sgt.	Pilot	302	Joined 302 (Polish) Sqn., 23-7-40. ✠ **1 Do 17, 15-9-40.** Wounded, 15-10-40. Commissioned, 31-5-42. Awarded D.F.C.(1-6-45). Returned to Poland, 1946.	✞	Died since Battle (10-10-77)	Polish
WEIR Archibald Nigel Charles	Plt. Off.	Pilot	145	On 145 Sqn., 1-7-40. ✠ **1 He 111 (shared), 18-7-40; ✠ 1 Do 17 (shared), 22-7-40; ✠ 2 Bf 109s and 1 Ju 87, 8-8-40.** Awarded D.F.C.(30-8-40).	✞	Killed since Battle (7-11-40)	British
WELCH Eric	A.C.2	Pilot	604	Joined 604 Sqn., 7-40. Promoted Sergeant, 11-40..	✞	Killed since Battle (17-12-41)	British
WELFORD George Henry Ettrick	Plt. Off.	Pilot	607	On 607 Sqn., 1-7-40. Slightly wounded, 17-9-40. Released from the R.A.F., 1945, as a Squadron Leader.			British
WELLS Edward Preston ("Hawk")	Plt. Off.	Pilot	266-41	Joined 266 Sqn., 26-8-40. Posted to 41 Sqn., 2-10-40. ✠ **1 Bf 109, 17-10-40.** Awarded D.S.O.(28-7-42), D.F.C.✠ (7-8-41 and 6-11-41). Released from the R.N.Z.A.F., 13-2-47, and transferred to the R.A.F., from which he retired, 15-6-60, as a Group Captain.			New Zealander
WELLS Malcolm Leslie	Plt. Off.	Aircrew	248	On 248 Sqn., 1-7-40. Awarded D.F.C.(26-9-41). Released from the R.A.F., 1945, as a Squadron Leader.	✞	Died since Battle (1983)	British
WELLS Patrick Hardy Vesey	Fg. Off.	Pilot	249	On 249 Sqn., 1-7-40. Wounded, 7-9-40. Awarded D.S.O.(23-5-44). Released from the R.A.F., 1946, as a Squadron Leader.			British
WELLUM Geoffrey Harris Augustus	Plt. Off.	Pilot	92	On 92 Sqn., 1-7-40. ✠ **1 He 111, 11-9-40; ✠ 1 Ju 88 (shared), 27-9-40.** Awarded D.F.C.(5-8-41). Retired from the R.A.F., 30-6-61, as a Squadron Leader.			British
WELSH Terence Deane	Plt. Off.	Pilot	264	On 264 Sqn., 1-7-40. ✠ **1 Ju 88, 24-8-40.** Awarded D.F.C.(11-2-41). Released from the R.A.F., 1945, as a Flight Lieutenant.	✞	Died since Battle (1980)	British
WENDEL Kenneth Victor	Plt. Off.	Pilot	504	On 504 Sqn., 1-7-40. Promoted Fg. Off., 3-9-40.	✞	**Killed in Action** (7-9-40)	New Zealander
WEST Donal Rock	Plt. Off.	Pilot	141	Joined 141 Sqn., 24-7-40. Awarded D.F.C.(8-9-44). Retired from the R.A.F., 1-12-61, retaining the rank of Squadron Leader.			British
WEST Hamish	Sqn. Ldr.	Pilot	41-151	On 41 Sqn., 1-7-40, supernumerary. Posted to 151 Sqn., 8-9-40, to command. Released from the R.A.F., 1947, as a Wing Commander.			British
WESTCOTT William Henry James	Sgt.	Aircrew	235	On 235 Sqn., 1-7-40. Commissioned, 26-7-43. Released from the R.A.F., 1946, as a Flight Lieutenant.			British
WESTLAKE George Herbert	Plt. Off.	Pilot	43-213	Joined 43 Sqn., 21-9-40. Posted to 213 Sqn., 29-9-40. Awarded D.S.O.(22-6-45), D.F.C.(18-9-42). Retired from the R.A.F., 25-7-69, as a Group Captain.			British
WESTLAKE Richard Douglas	Plt. Off.	Pilot	235	Joined 235 Sqn., 1-8-40. Released from the R.A.F., 1945, as a Squadron Leader.			British
WESTMACOTT Innes Bentall	Fg. Off.	Pilot	56	Joined 56 Sqn., 3-8-40. ✠ **1 Bf 110 (shared), 18-8-40; ✠ 1 Bf 110, 26-8-40; ✠ 1 Do 17 (shared), 27-8-40; ✠ 1 Bf 110, 30-8-40.** Wounded, 31-8-40. Retired from the R.A.F., 1-5-58, as a Wing Commander.			British
WESTMORELAND Thomas Emrys	Sgt.	Pilot	616	On 616 Sqn., 1-7-40. ✠ **1 Ju 88, 15-8-40.**	✞	**Killed in Action** (25-8-40)	British
WHALL Basil Ewart Patrick	Sgt.	Pilot	602	Joined 602 Sqn., 5-7-40. ✠ **1 Do 17 (shared), 15-8-40; ✠ 2 Ju 87s, 18-8-40; ✠ 2 He 111s, 26-8-40; ✠ 1 Bf 109, 7-9-40; ✠ 1 Do 17, 9-9-40; ✠ 1 Ju 88 (shared), 30-9-40.**	✞	**Killed in Action** (7-10-40)	British
WHEATCROFT Nigel Ronald	Plt. Off.	Pilot	604	Joined 604 Sqn., 8-7-40.	✞	Killed since Battle (26-11-40)	British
WHEELER Norman John	Plt. Off.	Pilot	600-615	Joined 600 Sqn., 7-40. Posted to 615 Sqn., 28-8-40. Awarded A.F.C.(11-6-42). Released from the R.A.F., 1945, as a Flight Lieutenant.			British

Name	Rank	Aircrew	Sqn.	Details	Fate	Nationality
WHELAN John ("Spungy")	Sgt.	Pilot	64-19	On 64 Sqn., 1-7-40. Posted to 19 Sqn., 10-40. Commissioned, 5-6-43. Awarded A.F.C.(14-6-45); made M.B.E.(1-1-59). Retired from the R.A.F., 15-9-66, as a Wing Commander.		British
WHINNEY Maurice Toller	Plt. Off.	Pilot	3	Joined 3 Sqn., 21-8-40. Transferred to Bomber Command. Made O.B.E.(15-6-45). Released from the R.A.F., 1945, as a Squadron Leader.		British
WHIPPS George Albert	Sgt.	Pilot	602	Joined 602 Sqn., 21-6-40. ✠ 1 Bf 109, 29-10-40.	✟ Killed since Battle (26-8-41)	British
WHITBREAD Herbert Laurance ("Hops")	Plt. Off.	Pilot	222	On 222 Sqn., 1-7-40. ✠ 1 Bf 109, 9-9-40.	✟ **Killed in Action** (20-9-40)	British
WHITBY Alfred ("Bull")	Sgt.	Pilot	79	On 79 Sqn., 1-7-40. Awarded D.F.M.(28-6-40). ✠ 1 He 111(shared), 30-8-40. Commissioned, 1-5-41. Retired from the R.A.F., 29-6-62, as a Squadron Leader.		British
WHITE Blair Eustace Galloway	Plt. Off.	Pilot	504	Joined 504 Sqn., 7-8-40. ✠ 1 Do 17, 15-9-40; ✠ 1 Bf 110, 27-9-40.	✟ Killed since Battle (5-7-43)	British
WHITE Francis Lawrence ("Chalky")	Sqn. Ldr.	Pilot	74	On 74 Sqn., 1-7-40. Posted away, 8-8-40. Retired from the R.A.F., 9-9-52, as a Group Captain.		British
WHITE Jack	Sgt.	Aircrew	248	On 248 Sqn., 1-7-40. Flew on reconnaissance sorties over the Norwegian coast . Commissioned, 31-8-44. (Died while still a serving Officer.)	✟ Died since Battle (16-3-45)	British
WHITE John	Sgt.	Pilot	72	On 72 Sqn., 1-7-40. ✠ 1 Do 17, 2-9-40; ✠ 1 Do 17, 11-9-40; ✠ 1 He 111 (shared), 14-9-40; ✠ 1 He 111 (solo) and 1 He 111 (shared), 15-9-40. Awarded D.F.M.(24-12-40).	✟ Killed since Battle (14-6-41)	British
WHITE John Sidney ("Snowy")	Sgt.	Pilot	32	On 32 Sqn., 1-7-40. Commissioned, 15-7-42. Released from the R.A.F., 1946, as a Flying Officer.	✟ Died since Battle (1985)	British
WHITE John William	Plt. Off.	Pilot	3-F.I.U.	Joined 3 Sqn., 1-7-40. Posted to F.I.U., 5-9-40. Lost flying category on medical grounds, 1-41. Made M.B.E.(1-1-45). Retired from the R.A.F., 12-11-66, as a Group Captain.		British
WHITE Robert	Sgt.	Aircrew	235	Joined 235 Sqn., 16-9-40. Released from the R.A.F., 31-1-49.		British
WHITEHEAD Clifford	F/Sgt.	Pilot	56	On 56 Sqn., 1-7-40. ✠ 1 Bf 110, 10-7-40; ✠ 1 Do 215 (shared), 16-8-40; ✠ 1 Bf 110, 18-8-40. Awarded D.F.M.(30-8-40). Commissioned, 22-1-41.	✟ Killed since Battle (4-7-42)	British
WHITEHEAD Robert Oliver	Sgt.	Pilot	151-253	Joined 151 Sqn., 26-8-40. Posted to 253 Sqn., 9-40. Commissioned, 25-11-41. Released from the R.A.F., 1946, as a Flight Lieutenant.		British
WHITEHOUSE	Plt. Off.	Pilot	32	Joined 32 Sqn., 22-8-40. No details of service traced. (Initials not known)		British
WHITEHOUSE Sidney Anthony Hollingsworth	Sgt.	Pilot	501	Joined 501 Sqn., 26-8-40. Commissioned, 27-11-40. Released from the R.A.F., 1946, as a Wing Commander.		British
WHITFIELD Joseph James	Sgt.	Pilot	56	On 56 Sqn., 1-7-40.	✟ **Killed in Action** (13-7-40)	British
WHITLEY David ("Bull")	Plt. Off.	Pilot	264	On 264 Sqn., 1-7-40.	✟ **Killed in Action** (28-8-40)	British
WHITLEY Eric William	Sqn. Ldr.	Pilot	245	In command of 245 Sqn. throughout the Battle of Britain. Awarded D.S.O. (18-9-42), D.F.C.(30-7-40). Retired from the R.A.F., 25-10-73, as a Group Captain.	✟ Died since Battle (25-10-73)	New Zealander
WHITNEY Douglas Mitchell	Plt. Off.	Pilot	245	Joined 245 Sqn., 28-9-40. Transferred to the Reserve in New Zealand, 15-11-45.	✟ Died since Battle (1981)	New Zealander
WHITSON Alfred Daniel	Sgt.	Aircrew	236	Joined 236 Sqn., 19-7-40.	✟ Killed since Battle (6-5-41)	British
WHITTICK Harry George	Sgt.	Aircrew	604	Joined 604 Sqn., 8-40. Commissioned, 2-2-42. Released from the R.A.F., 1946, as a Flight Lieutenant.		British
WHITTINGHAM Charles Derek	Fg. Off.	Pilot	151	On 151 Sqn., 1-7-40. Released from the R.A.F., 1945, as a Squadron Leader.	✟ Died since Battle (8-4-58)	British
WHITTY William Hubert Rigby	Fg. Off.	Pilot	607	On 607 Sqn., 1-7-40. Promoted Flt. Lt., 7-9-40. Awarded D.F.C.(26-10-45). Released from the R.A.F., 1946, as a Squadron Leader.		British
WHITWELL Peter Coulson	Sgt.	Aircrew	600	In R.N.Z.A.F. Joined 600 Sqn., 18-9-40. Transferred to Bomber Command. Awarded D.F.M.(16-12-41).	✟ Killed since Battle (6/7-11-42)	British
WICKINGS-SMITH Peter Claude	Plt. Off.	Pilot	235	Joined 235 Sqn., 5-8-40. (Killed during escort sortie for raid on Calais).	✟ **Killed in Action** (11-9-40)	British
WICKINS Arthur Stanley	Sgt.	Pilot	141	On 141 Sqn., 1-7-40. Commissioned, 28-2-42. Awarded D.F.C.(9-1-45). Retired from the R.A.F., 12-4-61, as a Squadron Leader.		British
WICKS Bryan John	Plt. Off.	Pilot	56	On 56 Sqn., 1-7-40. ✠ 1 Bf 109, 24-8-40. Promoted Fg. Off., 1-9-40. Awarded D.F.C.(6-6-41).	✟ Killed since Battle (12-10-42)	British
WIDDOWS Stanley Charles	Sqn. Ldr.	Pilot	29	Joined 29 Sqn., 16-7-40, to command. Awarded D.F.C.(4-4-41). Made C.B.(1-1-59). Retired from the R.A.F., 29-12-58, as an Air Commodore.		British
WIGG Ronald George	Plt. Off.	Pilot	65	On 65 Sqn., 1-7-40. Promoted Fg. Off., 3-9-40. Released from the R.N.Z.A.F., 14-4-46, as a Squadron Leader.	✟ Died since Battle (4-8-76)	New Zealander
WIGGLESWORTH John Spencer	Plt. Off.	Pilot	238	On 238 Sqn., 1-7-40. ✠ 1 Do 17 (shared), 21-7-40; ✠ 1 He 111, 25-9-40; ✠ 1 Bf 110, 26-9-40.	✟ Died since Battle (6-2-42)	British
WIGHT Ronald Derek Gordon	Flt. Lt.	Pilot	213	On 213 Sqn., 1-7-40. Awarded D.F.C.(21-6-40).	✟ **Killed in Action** (11-8-40)	British
WIGHTMAN Owen Maurice	Midshipman	Pilot	151	Joined 151 Sqn., 1-7-40. ✠ 1 Bf 109, 9-7-40.	✟ **Killed in Action** (30-6-41)	British
WILCOCK Charles	Sgt.	Aircrew	248	Joined 248 Sqn., mid-7-40. Flew on reconnaissance sorties over Norwegian coast during the Battle of Britain. Commissioned, 3-7-41.	✟ Died since Battle (21-5-42)	British
WILCOX Edgar John	Fg. Off.	Pilot	72	On 72 Sqn., 1-7-40. ✠ 1 He 59 (shared), 1-7-40.	✟ **Killed in Action** (31-8-40)	British
WILDBLOOD Tomothy Seddon	Plt. Off.	Pilot	152	On 152 Sqn., 1-7-40. ✠ 1 Bf 109, 11-8-40. ✠ 1 Bf 109, 12-8-40; ✠ 1 Ju 87 (solo) and 1 Ju 87 (shared), 18-8-40.	✟ **Killed in Action** (25-8-40)	British
WILDE Denis Clifton ("Jimmy")	Plt. Off.	Aircrew	236	On 236 Sqn., 1-7-40. Transferred to Transport Command. Released from the R.A.F., 8-46, as a Squadron Leader.	✟ Died since Battle (1989)	British
WILKES Geoffrey Norman	Sgt.	Pilot	213	On 213 Sqn., 1-7-40.	✟ **Killed in Action** (12-8-40)	British
WILKINSON Kenneth Astill ("Wilkie")	Sgt.	Pilot	616-19	Joined 616 Sqn., 1-10-40. Posted to 19 Sqn., 17-10-40. Commissioned, 4-2-44. Released from the R.A.F., 11-45, as a Flying Officer.		British
WILKINSON Rodney Levett	Sqn. Ldr.	Pilot	266	Posted to 266 Sqn., 6-7-40, to command. ✠ 1 Do 17, 12-8-40; ✠ 1 Ju 88, 15-8-40.	✟ **Killed in Action** (16-8-40)	British
WILKINSON Royce Clifford	Plt. Off.	Pilot	3	On 3 Sqn., 1-7-40. Awarded D.F.M.✸ (both on 31-5-40). Promoted Fg. Off., 15-8-40. Posted away (to 71 Sqn.), 10-40. Made O.B.E. and released from the R.A.F., 4-46, as a Wing Commander.		British
WILKINSON Wilfred Arthur	Sgt.	Pilot	501	On 501 Sqn., 1-7-40. Posted away, 12-8-40. Commissioned, 14-8-42. Retired from the R.A.F., 10-8-70, as a Squadron Leader.		British
WILLANS Derek Alan	Plt. Off.	Pilot	23	Joined 23 Sqn., 24-7-40. Promoted Fg. Off., 3-9-40. Awarded D.F.C.(18-2-41).	✟ Killed since Battle (28-5-41)	British
WILLCOCKS Peter Hamilton	Sgt.	Pilot	610-66	Joined 610 Sqn., 27-7-40. Posted to 66 Sqn., 10-9-40. Slightly wounded, 29-9-40.	✟ Killed since Battle (28-11-40)	British
WILLIAMS Cedric Watcyn	Sqn. Ldr.	Pilot	17	Joined 17 Sqn., 18-7-40, to command. ✠ 1 Do 17, 18-8-40; ✠ 1 Ju 88, 21-8-40.	✟ **Killed in Action** (25-8-40)	British
WILLIAMS Dennis Conon	Plt. Off.	Pilot	141	On 141 Sqn., 1-7-40. Promoted Fg. Off., 3-9-40.	✟ Killed since Battle (4-4-41)	British
WILLIAMS Desmond Gordon	Plt. Off.	Pilot	92	On 92 Sqn., 1-7-40. ✠ 1 He 111, 10-7-40; ✠ 1 Ju 88 (shared), 26-7-40; ✠ 1 He 111, 14-8-40; ✠ 1 He 111, 11-9-40; ✠ 1 He 111 (solo) and 1 Do 17 (shared), 15-9-40.	✟ **Killed in Action** (10-10-40)	British
WILLIAMS Eric Edward	F/Sgt.	Pilot	46	On 46 Sqn., 1-7-40. Wounded, 3-9-40.	✟ **Killed in Action** (15-10-40)	British
WILLIAMS Gwilym Trevor	Sgt.	Aircrew	219	On 219 Sqn., 1-7-40. Awarded D.F.M.(30-5-41). Commissioned, 1-5-42. Made O.B.E.(13-6-46). Retired from the R.A.F., 11-10-72, as a Squadron Leader.		British
WILLIAMS Mark Alan	Plt. Off.	Pilot	604	On 604 Sqn., 1-7-40. Further service records not traced.		British
WILLIAMS Thomas Draper	Plt. Off.	Pilot	611	On 611 Sqn., 1-7-40. ✠ 1 Do 17 (shared), 11-10-40. Awarded D.F.C.(15-7-41). Released from the R.A.F., 1946, as a Squadron Leader.		British
WILLIAMS William Dudley	Plt. Off.	Pilot	152	On 152 Sqn., 1-7-40. ✠ 1 Bf 110 and 1 Ju 88, 25-9-40; ✠ 1 Bf 110, 27-9-40; ✠ 1 Bf 110 (solo) and 1 Bf 110 (shared). Awarded D.F.C.(7-1-41). Released from the R.A.F., 1945, as a Squadron Leader.	✟ Died since Battle (4-76)	British

Name	Rank	Role	Sqn.	Service	Fate	Nationality
WILLIAMS Wycliff Stuart	Plt. Off.	Pilot	266	On 266 Sqn., 1-7-40. ✠ **1 Bf 109, 18-8-40;** ✠ **1 Do 17 (shared), 7-9-40.**	♱ Killed in Accident (21-10-40)	New Zealander
WILLIS Ronald Frank	Sgt.	Aircrew	219	Joined 219 Sqn., 10-40.	♱ Killed since Battle (8-2-41)	British
WILLIS William Owen	Sgt.	Aircrew	600	Joined 600 Sqn., 21-9-40. Commissioned, 3-9-42. Discharged from R.N.Z.A.F., 7-12-43, on medical grounds.	♱ Died since Battle (23-4-69)	New Zealander
WILLS William Claude	Sgt.	Pilot	3-73	Joined 3 Sqn., early 7-40. Posted to 73 Sqn., 25-9-40.	♱ Killed since Battle (12-4-41)	British
WILSDON Albert Alfred	Sgt.	Aircrew	29	Joined 29 Sqn., 9-8-40. ✠ **1 Do 17, 24-8-40.**	♱ Killed since Battle (19-12-40)	British
WILSON Donald Fraser	Plt. Off.	Pilot	141	On 141 Sqn., 1-7-40. Promoted Fg. Off., 3-9-40. Made O.B.E. and retired from the R.A.F., 1-4-58, as a Squadron Leader.		New Zealand
WILSON Douglas Strachan	Fg. Off.	Pilot	610	On 610 Sqn., 1-7-40. ✠ **1 Bf 109, 25-7-40;** ✠ **1 Bf 109, 26-8-40.** Promoted to Flt. Lt., 3-9-40. Released from the R.A.F., 1945, as a Wing Commander.	♱ Died since Battle (1985)	British
WILSON Leonard Donald	Plt. Off.	Aircrew	29	On 29 Sqn., 1-7-40. Retired from the R.A.F., 30-3-48, as a Flight Lieutenant.	♱ Died since Battle (1987)	British
WILSON Robert Roy	Plt. Off.	Pilot	111	On 111 Sqn., 1-7-40. ✠ **1 Bf 109, 25-7-40.**	♱ **Killed in Action** (11-8-40)	Canadian
WILSON William	Sgt.	Aircrew	235	Joined 235 Sqn., 13-7-40. Service No. 553328. No further record of service traced.		British
WILSON William Charles	Sgt.	Aircrew	29	Joined 29 Sqn., mid-7-40. Service No. 910832. No further record of service traced.		British
WINGFIELD Victor John	Sgt.	Aircrew	29	Joined 29 Sqn., late 7-40.	♱ Killed since Battle (11-5-41)	British
WINN Charles Vivian	Plt. Off.	Pilot	29	On 29 Sqn., 1-7-40. Promoted Fg. Off., 29-8-40. Retired from the R.A.F., 1-7-74, as an Air Vice-Marshal, C.B.E.(1-1-63); O.B.E., 1-1-51), D.S.O.(3-7-45), D.F.C. (29-9-42).		British
WINSKILL Archibald Little	Sgt.	Pilot	72-603	Commissioned, 15-8-40. Joined 72 Sqn., 4-10-40. Posted to 603 Sqn., 17-10-40. Was shot down, 8-41, but evaded capture and returned to Britain. Retired from the R.A.F., 18-12-68, as an Air Commodore, C.B.E.(11-6-60), D.F.C.✱ (6-1-42 and 27-7-43). Appointed K.C.V.O.(1980; C.V.O., 1973).		British
WINSTANLEY John	Sgt.	Pilot	151	Joined 151 Sqn., 4-9-40. Wounded, 17-9-40. Commissioned, 29-4-43. Retired from the R.A.F., 26-7-66, as a Flight Lieutenant.		British
WINTER Douglas Cyril	Plt. Off.	Pilot	72	On 72 Sqn., 1-7-40. ✠ **2 Bf 110s, 15-8-40;** ✠ **1 Bf 109, 1-9-40.**	♱ **Killed in Action** (5-9-40)	British
WINTER Richard Arthur	Plt. Off.	Pilot	247	On 247 Sqn., 1-7-40. Promoted Fg. Off., 3-9-40. Released from the R.A.F., 1945, as a Squadron Leader.	♱ Died since Battle (1970)	British
WISE John Francis	Sgt.	Aircrew	141	Defiant gunner. On 141 Sqn., 1-7-40.	♱ **Killed in Action** (19-7-40)	British
WISEMAN William Douglas	Plt. Off.	Aircrew	600	On 600 Sqn., 1-7-40. Released from the R.A.F., 1946, as a Squadron Leader.		British
WISSLER Denis Heathcote	Plt. Off.	Pilot	17	On 17 Sqn., 1-7-40. ✠ **1 He 111 (shared), 29-7-40.** Wounded, 24-9-40.	♱ Killed since Battle (11-11-40)	British
WITHALL Latham Carr	Flt. Lt.	Pilot	152	On 152 Sqn., 1-7-40.	♱ **Killed in Action** (12-8-40)	Australian
WITORZENC Stefan	Plt. Off.	Pilot	501	Joined 501 Sqn., 6-8-40. ✠ **2 Ju 87s, 15-8-40;** ✠ **1 Bf 109, 18-8-40;** ✠ **1 Do 17, 2-9-40;** ✠ **1 Do 215 (shared), 11-9-40.** Awarded D.F.C.(1-6-42). Released from the Polish Air Force, 1-47, and returned to Poland.		Polish
WLASNOWOLSKI Boleslaw Andrzej ("Slogger")	Plt. Off.	Pilot	32-607-213	Joined 32 Sqn., 8-8-40. Posted to 607 Sqn., 13-9-40. Posted to 213 Sqn., 17-9-40. ✠ **1 Bf 109, 15-8-40;** ✠ **1 Bf 109 and 1 Do 215, 18-8-40;** ✠ **1 Do 17, 15-9-40;** ✠ **1 Bf 109, 15-10-40.**	♱ Killed since Battle (1-11-40)	Polish
WOJCICKI Antoni ("Tony")	Sgt.	Pilot	213	Joined 213 Sqn., 19-8-40.	♱ **Killed in Action** (11-9-40)	Polish
WOJCIECHOWSKI Miroslaw	Sgt.	Pilot	303	Joined 303 (Polish) Sqn., 15-8-40. ✠ **2 Bf 109s (solo) and 1 Do 17 (shared), 15-9-40;** ✠ **1 Bf 109, 17-9-40.** Released from the Polish Air Force, 1946.		Polish
WOJTOWICZ Stefan	Sgt.	Pilot	303	Joined 303 (Polish) Sqn., 2-8-40, on formation. Slightly wounded, 3-9-40. ✠ **2 Do 17, 7-9-40;** ✠ **1 Bf 109, 11-9-40.**	♱ **Killed in Action** (11-9-40)	Polish
WOLFE Edward Chatham	Fg. Off.	Pilot	219-141	On 219 Sqn.,1-7-40. Promoted Fg.Off., 3-9-40. Posted to 141 Sqn., 9-40, to command. Awarded D.F.C.(30-5-41). Released from the R.A.F., 1946, as a Wing Commander.		British
WOLTON Ralph	Sgt.	Pilot	152	On 152 Sqn., 1-7-40. ✠ **1 Do 17, 25-7-40;** ✠ **1 Ju 88, 26-9-40.** Commissioned, 12-3-41. Retired from the R.A.F., 4-9-48, as a Flight Lieutenant.		British
¶ **WOOD, J.E.R.**	Plt. Off.	Pilot	79	On 79 Sqn., 1-7-40.	♱ Killed in Action (8-7-40)	British
WOOD Kenneth Russell	Sgt.	Aircrew	23	Joined 23 Sqn., 1-10-40.	♱ Killed since Battle (10-7-41)	British
WOOD Stanley Victor	Sgt.	Aircrew	248	Joined 248 Sqn., 9-40. Shot down and captured by Germans during reconnaissance sortie over Norway, 20-10-40. Released from the R.A.F., 1946, as a Warrant Officer.		British
WOODGATE Joseph Eric	Sgt.	Aircrew	141	Defiant gunner. On 141 Sqn., 1-7-40. Transferred to Bomber Command and commissioned, 6-7-43.	♱ Killed since Battle (24-8-43)	British
WOODGER David Noel	Plt. Off.	Pilot	235	On 235 Sqn., 1-7-40. (Killed when his Blenheim was shot down by British fighters.)	♱ **Killed in Action** (24-8-40)	British
WOODLAND Norman Naylor	Sgt.	Aircrew	236	Joined 236 Sqn., 8-8-40. Transferred to Coastal Command. Released from the R.A.F., 1945, as a Warrant Officer.		British
WOODS-SCAWEN Charles Anthony ("Wombat")	Plt. Off.	Pilot	43	On 43 Sqn., 1-7-40. ✠ **1 Bf 110, 8-8-40.** Wounded, 8-8-40. ✠ **2 He 111s, 13-8-40;** ✠ **1 He 111, 15-8-40;** ✠ **2 Ju 87s, 16-8-40.** Slightly wounded, 16-8-40. ✠ **1 Bf 109, 30-8-40.** Awarded D.F.C.(6-9-40). (Was younger brother of Fg.Off. P.P. Woods-Scawen.)	♱ **Killed in Action** (2-9-40)	British
WOODS-SCAWEN Patrick Philip	Fg. Off.	Pilot	85	On 85 Sqn., 1-7-40. Awarded D.F.C.(25-6-40). ✠ **2 Do 17s (shared), 26-8-40;** ✠ **1 Bf 109, 28-8-40;** ✠ **1 Bf 110, 30-8-40;** ✠ **3 Bf 109s, 31-8-40.** (Was elder brother of Plt. Off. C.A. Woods-Scawen.)	♱ **Killed in Action** (1-9-40)	British
WOODWARD Herbert John	Fg. Off.	Pilot	64-23	On 64 Sqn., 1-7-40. ✠ **1 Bf 109, 5-8-40;** ✠ **1 Bf 109, 8-8-40;** ✠ **1 Bf 109, 12-8-40;** ✠ **1 Do 215, 13-8-40.** Posted to 23 Sqn., 10-40. Awarded D.F.C. (30-1-10-40).	♱ **Killed in Action** (30-10-40)	British
WOODWARD Robert Sinckler	Plt. Off.	Pilot	600	Joined 600 Sqn., 25-9-40. Promoted Fg. Off., 3-10-40. Awarded D.F.C.(29-8-41)	♱ Killed since Battle (7-12-42)	British
WOOLLEY Arthur William	Sgt.	Pilot	601	Joined 601 Sqn., 5-7-40. Wounded, 11-7-40, and again 31-8-40. Commissioned, 27-5-41. Released from the R.A.F., 1948, as a Flight Lieutenant.		British
WOOTTEN Ernest Waite ("Bertie")	Plt. Off.	Pilot	234	Joined 234 Sqn., late 8-40. ✠ **Ju 88, (shared), 9-10-40.** Awarded D.F.C.✱ (29-8-41 and 4-6-43), A.F.C.(2-1-50). Appointed C.B.E.(1-1-71). Retired from the R.A.F., 5-11-73, as an Air Commodore.		British
WORDSWORTH Douglas Kenneth Alfred	Plt. Off.	Pilot	235	Joined 235 Sqn., 1-8-40. Promoted Fg. Off., 3-9-40. Awarded D.F.C.(28-7-42).	♱ Killed since Battle (30-10-41)	British
WORRALL John ("Baron")	Sqn. Ldr.	Pilot	32	In command of 32 Sqn., 1-7-40. Awarded D.F.C.(6-8-40). ✠ **1 Do 17 (shared), 15-8-40.** Posted away, 8-40. Appointed C.B.(1963), and retired from the R.A.F., 5-8-63, as an Air Vice-Marshal.	♱ Died since Battle (14-1-88)	British
WORRALL Pyers Arthur	Plt. Off.	Pilot	85-249	Joined 85 Sqn., 21-7-40. ✠ **1 Do 17 (shared), 26-8-40;** ✠ **1 Bf 110, 31-8-40.** Slightly wounded, 31-8-40. Posted to 249 Sqn., 13-9-40. ✠ **1 Bf 109, 25-10-40.**	♱ Killed since Battle (8-6-42)	British
WORRALL Thomas Victor	Sub-Lieut.	Pilot	111	Fleet Air Arm. Joined 111 Sqn., 22-9-40.	♱ Killed since Battle (21-2-41)	British
WORSDELL Kenneth Wilson	Plt. Off.	Pilot	219	On 219 Sqn., 1-7-40.	♱ **Killed in Action** (30-10-40)	British
WORTHINGTON Alec Sillavan	Fg. Off.	Pilot	219	On 219 Sqn., 1-7-40. Released from the R.A.F., 1946, as a Squadron Leader.		British
WOTTON Harold John	Sgt.	Pilot	234	Joined 234 Sqn., 19-8-40. (Killed in enemy air raid.)	♱ Killed since Battle (25-1-41)	British
WRIGHT Alexander James	Lieut.	Pilot	804	Royal Marine with Fleet Air Arm. On 804 Sqn., 1-7-40. Retired from the Royal Marines as a Major, 15-8-49.		British

Name	Rank	Role	Sqn.	Details	Fate	Nationality
WRIGHT Allan Richard	Plt. Off.	Pilot	92	On 92 Sqn., 1-7-40. ✠ 1 Bf 109 (solo) and 1 He 111 (shared), 14-8-40; ✠ 1 He 111, 29-8-40; ✠ 1 He 111, 11-9-40; ✠ 1 Ju 88, 26-9-40; ✠ 1 Ju 88 (solo) and 1 He 111 (shared), 27-9-40. Promoted Fg. Off., 23-10-40. Awarded D.F.C.✠ (22-10-40 and 15-7-41). A.F.C.(1-9-44). Retired from the R.A.F., 12-2-67, retaining the rank of Group Catain.		British
WRIGHT, B.	Sgt.	Pilot	616-66	Joined 616 Sqn., 2-9-40. Posted to 66 Sqn., 17-9-40. No further details traced.		British
WRIGHT Daniel Leslie	Sgt.	Aircrew	235	On 235 Sqn., 1-7-40. (Killed when his Blenheim was shot down by British fighters)	✟ Killed in Action (24-8-40)	British
WRIGHT Eric William ("Ricky")	Sgt.	Pilot	605	Joined 605 Sqn., 8-7-40. ✠ 1 Bf 110 (shared), 9-9-40; ✠ 1 Do 17 (shared), 12-9-40; ✠ 1 Do 17, 15-9-40. Awarded D.F.M.(26-11-40). Commissioned, 18-12-40. Awarded D.F.C.(1-10-46). Appointed C.B.E.(1-1-64). Retired from the R.A.F., 21-7-73, as an Air Commodore.		British
WRIGHT John	Sgt.	Pilot	79	Joined 79 Sqn., 9-7-40. (Died from wounds sustained in action on 4-9-40)	✟ Died of Wounds (5-9-40)	British
WRIGHT Robert Ronald	Sgt.	Pilot	248	Joined 248 Sqn., 5-9-40. Commissioned, 8-1-41. Awarded D.F.C.(14-4-44). Released from the R.A.F., 1946, as a Flight Lieutenant.		British
WRIGHT William	Plt. Off.	Aircrew	604	On 604 Sqn., 1-7-40.	✟ Killed since Battle (26-8-41)	British
WROBLEWSKI Zbigniew	Plt. Off.	Pilot	302	Joined 302 (Polish) Sqn., 23-8-40. Released from the Polish Air Force, 12-45, as a Flight Lieutenant.		Polish
WUNSCHE Kazimierz	F/Sgt.	Pilot	303	Joined 303 (Polish) Sqn., 12-8-40, on formation. ✠ 1 Bf 109, 31-8-40; ✠ 1 Bf 109, 5-9-40; ✠ 1 Bf 109, 6-9-40. Slightly wounded, 9-9-40. Commissioned, 31-12-42. Released from the Polish Air Force, 12-46, and returned to Poland.	✟ Died since Battle (1980)	Polish
WYATT John Pile	L.A.C.	Aircrew	25	Joined 25 Sqn., late 7-40.	✟ Killed in Action (15-9-40)	British
WYATT-SMITH Peter	Plt. Off.	Pilot	263	On 263 Sqn., 1-7-40. Promoted Fg. Off., 23-9-40.	✟ Killed since Battle (5-1-45)	British
WYDROWSKI Bronislaw	Plt. Off.	Pilot	615-607	Joined 615 Sqn., 9-49. Posted to 607 Sqn., 9-10-40. Left the Polish Air Force, 10-42, and entered the Polish Army. Returned to Poland, 1946.		Polish
WYNN Richard Edward Ney	Plt. Off.	Pilot	249	Joined 249 Sqn., 4-8-40. Wounded, 2-9-40.	✟ Killed since Battle (7-4-41)	British
YAPP Derek Sydney	Plt. Off.	Pilot	245-253	On 245 Sqn., 1-7-40. Posted to 253 Sqn., 1-10-40. Awarded D.F.C.(29-9-42). Released from the R.A.F., 11-44, as a Squadron Leader.		British
YATES Gordon	Sgt.	Aircrew	248	Joined 248 Sqn., late 7-40. Released from the R.A.F. after the War as a Warrant Officer.		British
YATES William	A.C.2	Aircrew	604	Joined 604 Sqn., 2-8-40. Served throughout the Battle of Britain without being granted aircrew rank or badge. Promoted Sergeant, 1941. Invalided from the R.A.F., 1941.		British
YORK Ronald Lewis	Sgt.	Pilot	610	Joined 610 Sqn., 23-9-40.	✟ Killed since Battle (28-3-42)	British
YOUNG Cecil Reginald	Plt. Off.	Pilot	615-607-46	On 615 Sqn., 1-7-40. ✠ 1 He 111, 16-8-40; ✠ 1 Do 17, 18-8-40. Posted to 607 Sqn., 13-9-40. Posted to 46 Sqn., 16-10-40.	✟ Killed since Battle (5-12-40)	British
YOUNG James Harold	Plt. Off.	Pilot	234	Joined 234 Sqn., c.17-9-40. No further service details traced.		British
YOUNG James Hugh Roumieu	Plt. Off.	Pilot	74	On 74 Sqn., 1-7-40.	✟ Killed in Action (28-7-40)	British
YOUNG John Reginald Cass	Fg. Off.	Pilot	249	On 249 Sqn., 1-7-40. Awarded A.F.C.(1-1-42). Reverted to the Reserve, 4-45, as a Wing Commander.		British
YOUNG John Stewart ("Stew")	Fg. Off.	Pilot	234	Promoted Flt. Lt., 3-9-40. Joined 234 Sqn., c.17-9-40. Retired from the R.C.A.F., 10-62, as a Squadron Leader.		Canadian
YOUNG Michael Hugh	Plt. Off.	Pilot	264	On 264 Sqn., 1-7-40. ✠ 1 He 111, 24-8-40. Awarded D.F.C.(11-2-41). Released from the R.A.F., 1946, as a Squadron Leader.		British
YOUNG Randolph Charles	Sgt.	Pilot	23	On 23 Sqn., 1-7-40. Commissioned, 17-9-42. Retired from the R.A.F., 4-9-60, as a Squadron Leader.		British
YOUNG Robert Bett Mirk	Sgt.	Aircrew	264	Defiant gunner. On 264 Sqn., 1-7-40. ✠ 1 Ju 88, 24-8-40.	✟ Killed in Action (8-10-40)	New Zealander
YUILE Arthur McLeod	Plt. Off.	Pilot	1(Canadian)	With 1(Canadian) Sqn., 20-6-40, on arrival in Britain. Promoted to Fg. Off., 12-7-40. ✠ 1 He 111, 11-9-40. Wounded, 15-9-40. Resigned commissioned in R.C.A.F., 13-9-44.		Canadian
YULE Robert Duncan	Plt. Off.	Pilot	145	On 145 Sqn., 1-7-40. ✠ 1 Do 17 (shared), 1-7-40; ✠ 1 Do 17 (shared), 10-7-40; ✠ 1 Ju 88, 12-7-40; ✠ 1 Do 17 (shared), 19-7-40. Wounded, 25-10-40. Awarded D.S.O.(16-3-44), D.F.C.✠ (17-4-42 and 20-11-42). Was killed in flying accident while still flying with the R.A.F. after the War.	✟ Killed since Battle (11-9-53)	New Zealander
ZAK Walerian	Fg. Off.	Pilot	303	Joined 303 (Polish) Sqn., 21-8-40. ✠ 1 Do 17, 15-9-40; ✠ 1 He 111, 26-9-40. Wounded, 27-9-40. Awarded D.F.C.(15-5-44). Returned to Poland after the War.		Polish
ZALUSKI Jerzy	Sgt.	Pilot	302	Joined 302 (Polish) Sqn., 23-9-40.	✟ Killed in accident (17-10-40)	Polish
ZAORAL Vladimir	Plt. Off.	Pilot	310	Joined 310 (Czech) Sqn., 10-40. ✠ 1 Bf 109, 25-10-40.	✟ Killed since Battle (19-11-41)	Czech
ZAVORAL Antonin	Sgt.	Pilot	151-1	Joined 151 Sqn., late 9-40. Posted to 1 Sqn., 6-10-40.	✟ Killed since Battle (31-10-41)	Czech
ZENKER Pawel	Plt. Off.	Pilot	501	Joined 501 Sqn., 7-8-40. ✠ 1 Ju 87, 12-8-40; ✠ 1 Bf 109, 18-8-40.	✟ Killed in Action (24-8-40)	Polish
ZIMA Rudolf	Sgt.	Pilot	310	Joined 310 (Czech) Sqn., 6-8-40. No service details traced. Known to have returned to Czechoslovakia after the War.		Czech
ZIMPRICH Stanislav	Plt. Off.	Pilot	310	Joined 310 (Czech) Sqn., 10-7-40, on formation. ✠ 1 Do 17, 9-9-40.	✟ Killed since Battle (12-4-42)	Czech
ZUKOWSKI Aleksiej	Plt. Off.	Pilot	302	Joined 302 (Polish) Sqn., 20-8-40.	✟ Killed in Action (18-10-40)	Polish
ZUMBACH Jan Eugenius Ludwik	Plt. Off.	Pilot	303	Joined 303 (Polish) Sqn., 2-8-40, on formation. ✠ 2 Do 17s, 7-9-40; ✠ 1 Bf 109, 9-9-40; ✠ 1 Bf 109, 11-9-40; ✠ 1 Bf 109, 15-9-40; ✠ 1 Bf 109 and 1 He 111, 26-9-40; ✠ 1 Bf 109, 27-9-40. Awarded D.F.C.✠ (30-10-41 and 15-11-42).	✟ Died since Battle (1986)	Polish
ZURAKOWSKI Janusz ("Zura")	Plt. Off.	Pilot	234-609	Joined 234 Sqn., early 8-40. ✠ 1 Bf 110, 15-8-40; ✠ 1 Bf 109, 5-9-40; ✠ 1 Bf 109, 6-9-40. Became test pilot with Gloster Aircraft Co. and Avro (Canada) after the War.		Polish

APPENDIX B

KNOWN LUFTWAFFE PARTICIPANTS IN THE BATTLE OF BRITAIN

Due to the fact that, to the author's knowledge, no compilation of *Luftwaffe* participants in the Battle of Britain has ever been published elsewhere, and that all research has necessarily been confined to the surviving fragmentary primary sources, it has not proved possible to present the following list in the same form as in Appendix A. Known participants have been arranged alphabetically under the unit in which they are known to have served. In the few cases where transfers are known to have taken place, cross references appear in the list. The basic sources for the list are largely unit-orientated, e.g. *6th Abteilung* casualty returns. These have been supplemented by reference to award citations, surviving diaries and correspondence with *Luftwaffe* veterans. The volume of detail in surviving unit returns varies sharply, and this variation is reflected in this Appendix. Since it was first published in 1969 it has grown by about 20 per cent.

Ranks

The ranks indicated are those that appear in personnel returns of July—October 1940; in a few instances ranks have been deduced from award citations of a later date.

Command Status

In a number of instances two or more officers appear in the roll of a single unit as *Geschwader Kommodore, Gruppenkommandeur, Staffelkapitän*, etc. These entries naturally refer to successive holders of the same appointment. In some cases it has proved impossible to verify the exact dates of transfer of these commands. This difficulty has been aggravated by the practice followed in various German Orders of Battle, whereby a unit commander was still listed in his appointment many days after being posted Missing. Temporary command passed to another officer in the unit in such cases, and fairly long periods might elapse before a new commander was confirmed in his appointment. This is believed to explain cases of a *Staffelkapitän* and a "*Staffelführer*" of the same *Staffel* being listed as missing or killed on the same day; the latter designation was applied to the acting commander immediately on the disappearance of the official commander.

Casualties

The annotation of death and capture should not be taken as a comprehensive guide. They have only been included where the actual date of death or capture is known. The majority of *Luftwaffe* casualty notifications during the Battle concerned airmen posted Missing. In many cases it is not possible to determine the exact fate of these aircrew, and to avoid confusion and possible distress to surviving relatives such annotations have been omitted from this Appendix. The dated annotation "P.O.W." is only used where relevant British documents survive.

Decorations

Luftwaffe personnel were awarded a fairly wide range of decorations, the majority of which could be in respect of both efficient service and deeds of gallantry. Although the Knight's Cross (*Ritterkreuz*) was generally regarded as the highest award for gallantry, this was not strictly accurate and, from the number of such awards made, it would perhaps be more accurately compared with the British Distinguished Service Order (and in many instances was awarded for "distinguished service"). There were in 1940 three senior grades of the Knight's Cross, and a number of German participants in the Battle of Britain were to receive these higher grades. They are annotated as follows:

★★★★ Holders of the Oakleaves with Swords and Diamonds to the Knight's Cross of the Iron Cross (*Träger des Eichenlaubs mit Schwertern und Brillanten zum Ritterkreuz des Eisernen Kreuzes*).

★★★ Holders of the Oakleaves with Swords to the Knight's Cross of the Iron Cross (*Träger des Eichenlaubs mit Schwertern zum Ritterkreuz des Eisernen Kreuzes*).

★★ Holders of the Oakleaves to the Knight's Cross of the Iron Cross (*Träger des Eichenlaubs zum Ritterkreuz des Eisernen Kreuzes*)

★ Holders of the Knight's Cross of the Iron Cross (*Träger des Ritterkreuzes des Eisernen Kreuzes*)

Rank Equivalents

The following list of *Luftwaffe* and R.A.F. rank equivalents is necessarily speculative in some cases; various German ranks existed which have no exact British parallel

Flieger	. . .	Aircraftman (2)
Gefreiter.	. . .	Aircraftman (1)
Obergefreiter	. . .	Leading Aircraftman
Hauptgefreiter	. . .	Corporal
Unteroffizier, Unterfeldwebel	. . .	Sergeant
Feldwebel	. . .	Flight Sergeant
Oberfeldwebel, Stabsfeldwebel	. . .	Warrant Officer
Leutnant	. . .	Pilot Officer
Oberleutnant	. . .	Flying Officer
Hauptmann	. . .	Flight Lieutenant
Major	. . .	Squadron Leader
Oberstleutnant	. . .	Wing Commander
Oberst	. . .	Group Captain
Generalmajor	. . .	Air Commodore
Generalleutnant . . .		Air Vice-Marshal
General	. . .	Air Marshal
Generaloberst, Generalfeldmarschall		Air Chief Marshal
Reichsmarschall . . .		Marshal of the Royal Air Force

461

AUFKLÄRUNGSGRUPPE OBERBEFEHLSHABER DER LUFT-WAFFE
(Aufkl.Gr.Ob.d.L.)

Special reconnaissance *Gruppe* equipped with Dornier Do 215Bs (the only unit regularly flying these aircraft during the Battle of Britain) with small detached *Staffeln* widely dispersed in Scandinavia, the Low Countries and Northern France. Unit Codes, G2.

Bisping, Oberleutnant Josef ★22-10-41	4Staffel
Blindow, Leutnant	Staffel not known
Book, Leutnant	Staffel not known
Brix, Leutnant	Staffel not known
Brönig, Unteroffizier Helmut	3 Staffel, ✟ 24-10-40
Dorr, Obergefreiter Max	3 Staffel
Goebbels, Unteroffizier	4 Staffel
Hefman, Obergefreiter	4 Staffel
Hofer, Leutnant	Staffel not known
Hofmann, Unteroffizier Erhard	3 Staffel, ✟ 24-10-40
Jensen, Feldwebel	Staffel not known
Kamolz, Unteroffizier	4 Staffel
Kikat, Leutnant	Staffel not known
Klein-Reschkampf, Oberleutnant	Staffel not known,✟ 31-7-40
Krauss, Leutnant Walter ★★29-7-40 and 3-1-44	Staffel not known
Kühl, Feldwebel	Staffel not known
Linsner, Unteroffizier	Staffel not known
Maurer, Feldwebel	4 Staffel
Meyer, Leutnant Erwin	3 Staffel,✟ 24-10-40
Neubauer, Feldwebel	4 Staffel
Pelzer, Unteroffizier	Staffel not known, ✟ 21-9-40
Poser, Leutnant Hans	Staffel not known
Rack, Leutnant	Staffel not known
Rading, Leutnant	Staffel not known
Rothenberg, Oberleutnant	Staffel not known
Schütz, Feldwebel	Staffel not known, ✟ 18-9-40
Sonnleitner, Oberleutnant	4 Staffel, ✟ 30-8-40
Vockel, Unteroffizier	Staffel not known
Weise, Oberfeldwebel	4 Staffel
Wiesen, Unteroffizier	Staffel not known

AUFKLÄRUNGSGRUPPE 10
(Aufkl.Gr.10 <Tannenberg>)
Reconnaissance *Gruppe* equipped with Dornier Do 17Ps. Unit Codes T1.

Baucks, Oberfeldwebel Ernst	3 Staffel
Ellerläge, Oberleutnant,	3 Staffel, ✟ 4-9-40

AUFKLÄRUNGSGRUPPE 11
(Aufkl.Gr.11)
Reconnaissance *Gruppe* equipped with Messerschmitt Bf 110C-5s and Dornier Do 17Ps, based in Le Bourget area. Unit Codes, MJ (Bf 110s) and 6M (Do 17s)

Roh, Leutnant	3 Staffel
Thiel, Leutnant	3 Staffel

AUFKLÄRUNGSGRUPPE 13
(Aufkl.Gr.13)

Horn, Oberleutnant	3 Staffel
Raasch, Leutnant	3 Staffel

AUFKLÄRUNGSGRUPPE 14
(Aufkl.Gr.14)

Mixed reconnaissance *Gruppe* equipped with Messerschmitt Bf 110C-5s and Dornier Do 17P aircraft at Caen, Cherbourg and Plumetot. Also Henschel Hs 126B aircraft in the Malines area. Unit Codes, 5F. [4.(F)/14 was named <*Münchhausen-Staffel*>]

Baden, Feldwebel Willi	4 Staffel, P.O.W., 21-7-40
Bohnen, Feldwebel Fritz	4 Staffel, P.O.W., 21-7-40
Breitenbach, Leutnant	4 Staffel, ✟ 29-9-40

Doffek, Oberleutnant	4 Staffel, ✟ 12-10-40
Felix, Leutnant	4 Staffel
Friedrich, Oberleutnant	4 Staffel
Godsche, Leutnant von	4 Staffel
Hartmann, Feldwebel	3 Staffel, ✟ 30-10-40
Höcker, Leutnant Helmut	4 Staffel, ✟ 25-10-40
Nissen, Leutnant von	4 Staffel ✟ 29-9-40
Obenhuber, Oberleutnant	3 Staffel, ✟ 30-10-40
Pank, Leutnant Wilhelm	4 Staffel, ✟ 26-9-40
Runde, Oberleutnant Fredrich-Karl	4 Staffel, P.O.W., 21-7-40
Russel, Oberleutnant	4 Staffel, ✟ 7-9-40
Schafer, Oberleutnant	3 Staffel, ✟ 3-8-40
Schmidt, Unteroffizier	4 Staffel, ✟ 26-9-40
Thiele, Oberleutnant Georg	4 Staffel, P.O.W., 21-7-40
Volkel, Oberleutnant	3 Staffel, ✟ 3-8-40
Werner, Unteroffizier Alfred	4 Staffel, P.O.W., 21-7-40

AUFKLÄRUNGSGRUPPE 21
(Aufkl.Gr.21)
Mixed reconnaissance *Gruppe* equipped with Dornier Do 17Ps and Henschel Hs 126s, believed based at Bergen with *Luftflotte 5*. Unit Codes P2.

Krauss, Leutnant Walter, ★★ (29-7-40 and 3-1-44)	2 Staffel
Pülke, Feldwebel	1 Staffel
Rutkowski, Leutnant Friedrich	2 Staffel
Wehner, Felfwebel	1 Staffel

AUFKLÄRUNGSGRUPPE 22
(Aufkl.Gr. 22)
Reconnaissance *Gruppe* with Messerschmitt Bf 110C-5 *Staffel(n)* at Vlissingen, Holland, and Dornier Do 17P *Staffel(n)* at Stavanger, Norway. Unit Codes 4N.

Aigner, Feldwebel	3 Staffel
Barth, Hauptmann Konrad	2 Staffel
Eichstedt, Leutnant Egon	2 Staffel
Freund, Oberfeldwebel Herbert	2 Staffel
Hartmann, Gefreiter Helmut	1 Staffel, ✟ 1-11-40
Kröplin, Feldwebel Paul	1 Staffel, ✟ 1-11-40
Pannhas, Leutnant	3 Staffel, ✟ 13-8-40
Seebeck, Leutnant von	3 Staffel
Schobert, Unteroffizier	3 Staffel

AUFKLÄRUNGSGRUPPE 31
(Aufkl. Gr. 31)
Reconnaissance *Gruppe* with Dornier Do 17Ps and Henschel Hs 126s in Northern France. Unit Codes 5D.

Brixen, Oberleutnant Alexander von	3 Staffel
Burmeister, Leutnant Walter	3 Staffel
Haffan, Leutnant Walter	3 Staffel, P.O.W., 27-8-40
Kläden, Leutnant Hans-Joachim von	4 Staffel
Klaushenke, Feldwebel Gustav	3 Staffel, P.O.W., 27-8-40
Schlesjel, Gefreiter Johannes	3 Staffel, P.O.W., 27-8-40

AUFKLÄRUNGSGRUPPE 120
(Aufkl. Gr. 120)

Bank, Leutnant (*Bildoffizier*)	1 Staffel, ✟ 8-7-40
Heuer, Leutnant	1 Staffel

AUFKLÄRUNGSGRUPPE 121
(Aufkl. Gr. 121)

Reconnaissance *Gruppe* equipped with Dornier Do 17Ps, Junkers Ju 88A-1s and A-5s, and Heinkel He 111H-3s. Three *Staffeln* operational during the Battle of Britain: *1 Staffel*, with Junkers Ju 88A-1s and A-5s at Stavanger-Sola, Norway; *3 Staffel*, with Junkers Ju 88A-1s and A-5s, and Dornier Do 17Ps at Brest and Caen, France, and a detachment at Stavanger during October 1940; *4 Staffel*, with Dornier Do 17Ps and

Junkers Ju 88A-1s at Caen, France, and a detachment in Holland. Unit Codes 7A.

Baudler, Leutnant	3 Staffel
Bender, Unteroffizier Walter	3 Staffel, ✝ 8-10-40
Bormann, Leutnant Georg	4 Staffel, P.O.W., 22-7-40
Böttcher, Leutnant Helmut	4 Staffel
Bresch, Obergefreiter	4 Staffel
Burkow, Leutnant	4 Staffel
Eha, Gefreiter Hermann	1 Staffel
Gerlach, Major Walter	1 Staffel
Knab, Leutnant Helmut	4 Staffel
Koltermann, Unteroffizier Kurt	1 Staffel
Mehle, Unteroffizier Kurt	1 Staffel
Müller, Unteroffizier Willi	4 Staffel
Nikutta, Gefreiter Paul	3 Staffel. ✝ 8-10-40
Nippel, Feldwebel Wilhelm	3 Staffel
Rabe, Unteroffizier	4 Staffel
Reichardt, Leutnant Erwin	4 Staffel, ✝ 22-7-40
Rickershausen, Unteroffizier Fritz	4 Staffel, ✝ 20-10-40
Rowe, Feldwebel Reinhard	4 Staffel, ✝ 22-7-40
Sauslikat, Unteroffizier Kurt	4 Staffel
Schedemund, Leutnant Wilhelm	3 Staffel
Sombern, Oberleutnant	4 Staffel, ✝ 10-7-40
Specht, Oberleutnant	3 Staffel, ✝ 14-7-40
Taubertad, Leutnant	3 Staffel, ✝ 2-8-40
Thiele, Leutnant	4 Staffel
Thoring, Unteroffizier	4 Staffel
Wolz, Oberleutnant	1 Staffel, ✝ 25-9-40
Vater, Feldwebel	4 Staffel
Viefhues, Oberleutnant	3 Staffel, ✝ 2-8-40
Zander, Leutnant	3 Staffel
Zscheket, Unteroffizier	4 Staffel

AUFKLÄRUNGSGRUPPE 122
(Aufkl. G. 122)

Reconnaissance *Gruppe* equipped with Junkers Ju 88A-1s and Messerschmitt Bf 110C-5s, based at Vendeville, France. Unit Codes F6.

Adler, Oberfeldwebel	1 Staffel
Bibers, Feldwebel	1 Staffel
Böhm, Hauptmann	*St.Kap.*, 5 Staffel
Gneist, Gefreiter Gerhard	2 Staffel, ✝ 25-10-40
Guizetti, Oberarzt Dr. Ulrich	4 Staffel
Hellermann, Leutnant	5 Staffel
Hurck, Leutnant	5 Staffel
Jahnke, Feldwebel	2 Staffel
Kaltenbach, Feldwebel	1 Staffel
Koehler, Oberstleutnant Fritz, ★ (4-11-41)	*Gr.Kdr.*
Krautwurst, Feldwebel	1 Staffel
Kronberg, Gefreiter	2 Staffel
Ludke, Hauptmann Kurt	4 Staffel
Pawletta, Unteroffizier	4 Staffel
Peters, Feldwebel	1 Staffel
Plange, Obergefreiter	1 Staffel
Rabbow, Leutnant	2 Staffel
Rochstroh, Obergefreiter	2 Staffel
Scharper, Leutnant	3 Staffel
Schmid, Oberleutnant	2 Staffel
Sommerich, Oberleutnant	2 Staffel
Spanke, Oberfeldwebel	1 Staffel
Starkloff, Oberleutnant Hans	4 Staffel
Taubert, Leutnant Richard, ★ (28-11-42)	5 Staffel
Vleuten, Oberleutnant Hans von	5 Staffel
Wabnitz, Unteroffizier	1 Staffel
Wacker, Leutnant Conrad	2 Staffel, P.O.W., 25-10-40

AUFKLÄRUNGSGRUPPE 123
(Aufkl. Gr. 123)

Reconnaissance *Gruppe* flying Junkers Ju 88As, Messerschmitt Bf 110Cs and Dornier Do 17Ps from Buc and Bordeaux; detachment at Brest. Some Dornier Do 215s delivered before the end of the Battle of Britain. One of the most heavily committed of all *Aufklärungsgruppen* in 1940.

Ackenhausen, Feldwebel	3 Staffel
Bachmann, Unteroffizier Martin	3 Staffel
Böhle, Leutnant Erich	3 Staffel, P.O.W., 7-9-40
Deehand, Hauptmann Georg	3 Staffel
Essmann, Unteroffizier	1 Staffel, ✝ 30-9-40
Euler, Obergefreiter	3 Staffel
Fischer, Felwebel Werner	2 Staffel
Frenzel, Leutnant Walter	1 Staffel
Götz, Oberfeldwebel	3 Staffel
Gran, Gefreiter Hans	3 Staffel
Grünmüller, Unteroffizier Karl	2 Staffel
Hauber, Leutnant Elman	3 Staffel
Hering, Oberfeldwebel Martin	3 Staffel, ✝ 21-10-40
Höfer, Oberleutnant	1 Staffel
Hoffman, Oberleutnant	1 Staffel
Hollstein, Leutnant Herbert	3 Staffel
Jasper, Oberleutnant Heinz	3 Staffel
Kauter, Oberleutnant Hans	3 Staffel, P.O.W., 7-9-40
Keller, Leutnant Karl	3 Staffel
Kesselstadt, Oberleutnant Graf von	2 Staffel
Kobold, Feldwebel Walter	3 Staffel, P.O.W., 7-9-40
Koch, Unteroffizier Gustav	3 Staffel
Leisner, Unteroffizier Gotthard	3 Staffel, P.O.W., 7-9-40
Liebe-Piederit, Hauptmann	3 Staffel, ✝ 19-7-40
Maetzel, Oberleutnant	1 Staffel
Mühlbauer, Oberleutnant	1 Staffel, ✝ 24-7-40
Nest, Leutnant	2 Staffel
Obermayer, Unteroffizier	1 Staffel, ✝ 30-9-40
Obernitz, Major Gunther	*Gr.Kdr.*
Reichelt, Feldwebel	1 Staffel
Reuhl, Flieger	3 Staffel
Riehl, Feldwebel	3 Staffel
Rommel, Leutnant	1 Staffel
Ruck, Oberfeldwebel	1 Staffel
Rude, Oberleutnant Willi	3 Staffel
Ruschenburg, Unteroffizier Willi	3 Staffel
Schingshackel, Feldwebel Helmut	3 Staffel
Vedder, Leutnant	2 Staffel
Wachtel, Leutnant	1 Staffel
Weinbauer, Leutnant	2 Staffel, ✝ 13-7-40

KAMPFGESCHWADER 1
(KG 1 < Hindenburg >)

Long-range bomber *Geschwader* of I. *Fliegerkorps*. Staff flight, I. and II. *Gruppen* equipped with Heinkel He 111s; III. Gruppe equipped with Dornier Do 17Zs. Based at Rosières-en-Santerre and Montdidier, and later moved to Clairmont and Nijmegen. Unit Codes V4.

Ahrens, Leutnant	2 Staffel
Appelbeck, Feldwebel Johann	*Geschw.Erg.Staffel*, ✝ 20-10-40
Angerstein, Oberst Karl, ★ (2-11-40)	*Geschw.Kdr.*
Arndt, Unteroffizier	*Stab*
Baess, Hauptmann	*St. Kap.*, 5 Staffel
Bauer, Unteroffizier	II. Gruppe, ✝ 4-10-40
Beck, Leutnant	4 Staffel, ✝ 28-8-40
Behres, Unteroffizier Matthew	I. Gruppe
Behreus, Hauptmann	I. Gruppe, ✝ 11-7-40
Behn, Leutnant	*Stab*
Bendig, Unteroffizier	I. Gruppe
Biebrach, Oberleutnant	I. Gruppe
Burger, Unteroffizier	5 Staffel
Bosenberg, Gefreiter Karl	I. Gruppe
Burian, Gefreiter	8 Staffel, ✝ 5-7-40
Dürbeck, Hauptmann Wilhelm, ★ (2-12-40)	*St. Kap.*
Eisenbrandt, Oberleutnant	2 Staffel, ✝ 30-9-40
Ester, Feldwebel	6 Staffel
Exss, Oberstleutnant	*Geschw. Kdr.*
Fanelsa, Major Willibald	*Gr. Kdr.*, III. Gruppe
Feierabend, Gefreiter	5 Staffel
Foelisch, Oberleutnant	5 Staffel
Frischmuth, Oberfeldwebel Hermann	8 Staffel, P.O.W., 5-7-40
Goetzel, Unteroffizier	*Stab*, II. Gruppe

Göhler, Oberleutnant	I. Gruppe, ♱ 3-10-40
Groth, Gefreiter	5 Staffel
Grunwald, Oberleutnant	1 Staffel, ♱ 11-7-40
Hanzen, Unteroffizier	Gruppe not known
Hartlieb, Gefreiter Rudi	I. Gruppe
Heidrich, Oberfeldwebel	3 Staffel
Heimel, Gefreiter	5 Staffel, ♱ 30-8-40
Heinhold, Unteroffizier Richard	I. Gruppe
Hildebrand, Unteroffizier Emil	5 Staffel, ♱ 4-10-40
Hirsch, Unteroffizier	3 Staffel
Hofer, Gefreiter	5 Staffel
Hornick, Oberfeldwebel	5 Staffel, ♱ 30-8-40
Kirchberger, Feldwebel Oskar	Geschw.Erg.Staffel
Kiunka, Oberleutnant Erich	3 Staffel, P.O.W., 9-9-40
Klappholz, Gefreiter	5 Staffel
Kosch, Oberstleutnant Benno	Gr.Kdr., II. Gruppe
Krall, Unteroffizier	Gruppe not known
Kramer, Unteroffizier	3 Staffel
Linke, Unteroffizier Erich	II. Gruppe
Mahlbeck, Gefreiter	5 Staffel, ♱ 30-8-40
Maier, Major	I. Gruppe, ♱ 4-9-40
Männich, Gefreiter	Stab
Marck, Unteroffizier	3 Staffel
Marcklowitz, Unteroffizier Rudolf	8 Staffel, ♱ 5-7-40
Martinck, Gefreiter	8 Staffel, ♱ 5-7-40
Mock, Unteroffizier	Stab
Morninghoff, Obergefreiter	5 Staffel
Overkäping, Gefreiter Josef	1 Staffel, ♱ 29-10-40
Päslack, Unteroffizier	5 Staffel
Paulson, Oberleutnant	Stab, ♱ 8-7-40
Pfeiffer, Gefreiter	3 Staffel
Püpmel, Gefreiter	3 Staffel
Rauschert, Oberfeldwebel	6 Staffel, ♱ 30-8-40
Reineke, Gefreiter	3 Staffel
Reis, Gefreiter	5 Staffel, ♱ 30-8-40
Reisache, Unteroffizier Hermann	Geschw.Erg.Staffel, ♱ 20-10-40
Riemann, Oberfeldwebel	6 Staffel
Rittberg, Oberleutnant von	I. Gruppe, ♱ 4-9-40
Roogemann, Gefreiter	5 Staffel
Saumsiegel, Gefreiter	I. Gruppe
Schnabel, Feldwebel	5 Staffel
Siefert, Unteroffizier Hans	II. Gruppe
Sommer, Feldwebel	Stab
Stahlberg, Feldwebel	5 Staffel, ♱ 30-8-40
Stärk, Unteroffizier	5 Staffel
Steinicke, Unteroffizier	3 Staffel
Stockert, Oberfeldwebel	I. Gruppe
Struger, Gefreiter	5 Staffel
Stumbaum, Unteroffizier Anton	3 Staffel, P.O.W., 9-9-40
Süss, Oberleutnant Ernst	1 Staffel
Tschop, Gefreiter Willi	II. Gruppe, ♱ 4-10-40
Wachter, Oberleutnant	5 Staffel, ♱ 30-8-40
Wagner, Leutnant	1 Staffel, ♱ 11 -7-40
Wagner, Unteroffizier Gottfried	8 Staffel, P.O.W., 5-7-40
Wildehopf, Unteroffizier	Gruppe not known
Zinoegger, Oberfeldwebel	6 Staffel, ♱ 30-8-40
Zuckriegel, Gefreiter Fritz	II. Gruppe, P.O.W., 4-10-40

KAMPFGESCHWADER 2
(KG 2 < Holzhammer >)

Long-range bomber *Geschwader* **of II.***Fliegerkorps*, *Luftflotte 2*, **equipped with Dornier Do 17Zs. Headquarters and II.***Gruppe* **based at Arras, I.** *Gruppe* **at Epinoy and III.***Gruppe* **at Cambrai. Unit Codes U5. Commanded by Oberst Johannes Fink, this** *Geschwader* **was heavily committed throughout the Battle of Britain, especially in raids over South-East England; casualties were particularly heavy on 13th and 26th August, the latter being the occasion of the raid on Debden.**

Arndt, Unteroffizier Herbert	7 Staffel, P.O.W., 13-8-40
Babbe, Obergefreiter Gustav	Stab, P.O.W., 13-8-40
Bahr, Gefreiter Helmuth	7 Staffel., P.O.W., 13-8-40
Birg, Gefreiter	5 Staffel
Bellmann, Unteroffizier	Stab, II.Gruppe
Bernschein, Unteroffizier	II.Gruppe

Bohmel, Unteroffizier	5 Staffel, ♱ 15-9-40
Bohnhof, Feldwebel Martin	9 Staffel
Borner, Leutnant Werner	II.Gruppe
Böse, Hauptmann Hans	St.Kap., 2 Staffel, P.O.W., 26-8-40
Brandenburg, Oberleutnant	3 Staffel
Brey, Feldwebel Heinrich	Stab, ♱ 18-10-40
Brudern, Leutnant Hans-Joachim	3 Staffel
Brüske, Flieger Oskar	5 Staffel, ♱ 11-10-40
Bucholz, Oberleutnant Hans, ★ (24-3-41)	St.Kap.,3 Staffel, ♱ 19-5-41
Buhr, Unteroffizier Helmuth	2 Staffel, P.O.W., 26-8-40
Christoph, Unteroffizier	4 Staffel, ♱ 7-9-40
Davids, Oberleutnant	III.Gruppe
Dilcher, Leutnant Walter	1 Staffel, ♱ 10-10-40
Dillger, Feldwebel Robert	1 Staffel, ♱ 24-10-40
Dürtmann, Felwebel	8 Staffel
Eitze, Oberleutnant Erich	Stab, II.Gruppe
Elbert, Gefreiter Wilhelm	9 Staffel
Ermecke, Leutnant	2 Staffel, ♱ 21-8-40
Ertl, Gefreiter	8 Staffel, ♱ 15-9-40
Fahrenbach, Unteroffizier Hans	3 Staffel
Faust, Gefreiter Kurt	1 Staffel, ♱ 24-10-40
Felimann, Gefreiter Hans	3 Staffel, P.O.W., 15-10-40
Fink, Oberst Johannes, ★ (20-6-40)	Geschw.Kdr.
Flemming, Unteroffizier	8 Staffel
Flisk, Unteroffizier	II.Gruppe
Fuchs, Major Adolf	Gr.Kdr., III.Gruppe
Furst, Obergefreiter Helmut	1 Staffel, ♱ 24-10-40
Glaser, Feldwebel	9 Staffel, ♱ 15-9-40
Gonzow, Oberleutnant	II.Gruppe
Grabner, Obergefreiter Herbert	Stab, ♱ 18-10-40
Greiner, Unteroffizier	4 Staffel, ♱ 7-9-40
Gröben, Oberleutnant von der	7 Staffel
Gussmann, Unteroffizier Rudolf	7 Staffel, P.O.W., 26-8-40
Gutzmann, Major Martin	Gr.Kdr., I.Gruppe, P.O.W., 26-8-40
Hafner, Oberfeldwebel	5 Staffel
Hänsten, Feldwebel Rudolf	7 Staffel, Missing 13-8-40
Hasse, Feldwebel	5 Staffel
Heiderich, Oberleutnant	7 Staffel, ♱ 26-8-40
Hellmers, Oberleutnant	Stab St.Kap.
Hertel, Oberleutnant Siegfried	2 Staffel, ♱ 26-8-40
Hirsch, Feldwebel	8 Staffel, P.O.W., 26-8-40
Hoffmann, Obergefreiter	II.Gruppe
Hoffmann, Gefreiter	9 Staffel
Hohenstädter, Feldwebel Willi	7 Staffel, P.O.W., 26-8-40
Holleck-Weitmann, Oberleutnant Hugo	8 Staffel
Holz, Obergefreiter Ernst	Stab, P.O.W., 13-8-40
Hoppe, Unteroffizier	9 Staffel, ♱ 15-9-40
Hörwick, Oberfeldwebel Anton ★ (8-8-44)	Staffel not known
Hüber, Unteroffizier	5 Staffel, ♱ 15-9-40
Hübner, Leutnant Johannes	5 Staffel, ♱ 11-9-40
Hunger, Leutnant Heinrich ★ (5-7-41)	Stab, ♱ 14-8-41
Illing, Unteroffizier Siegfried	7 Staffel, P.O.W., 26-8-40
Kindler, Oberleutnant Alfred ★ (10-10-42)	II.Gruppe
Kittmann, Oberleutnant Werner	8 Staffel, P.O.W., 15-9-40
Köhl, Flieger	II.Gruppe
Köhler, Gefreiter Heinz	8 Staffel
Konrad, Oberleutnant	3 Staffel
Knorky, Unteroffizier Frederick	III.Gruppe, P.O.W., 26-8-40
Kreipe, Major Werner	Gr.Kdr., III.Gruppe (until 13-8-40)
Kriegel, Feldwebel	5 Staffel
Krieger, Hauptmann Walter	3 Staffel, P.O.W., 10-7-40
Krieger, Leutnant Peter	7 Staffel, P.O.W., 26-8-40
Krummheuer, Unteroffizier	9 Staffel, ♱ 15-9-40
Kunze, Obergefreiter Karl	1 Staffel, ♱ 24-10-40
Kzienzyk, Unteroffizier	8 Staffel
Landenberger, Leutnant	II.Gruppe, ♱ 8-9-40
Landhorst, Leutnant	8 Staffel, ♱ 27-9-40
Langer, Oberfeldwebel	7 Staffel, Missing, 13-8-40
Langer, Unteroffizier Paul	8 Staffel, P.O.W., 15-9-40
Latz, Oberleutnant Ulrich	5 Staffel
Lenz, Unteroffizier	9 Staffel, ♱ 15-9-40
Lindemann, Hauptmann	6 Staffel
Lindemeier, Unteroffizier	8 Staffel
Lintz, Obergefreiter Friedrich	Stab, ♱ 18-10-40
Löhrer, Feldwebel	II.Gruppe
Lotter, Gefreiter	II.Gruppe, ♱ 8-9-40

Lunghard, Unteroffizier Theodor | 2 Staffel, P.O.W., 26-8-40
Maas, Gefreiter Kurt | 1 Staffel, ✝ 24-10-40
Matussek, Unteroffizier | II.Gruppe
Mechetzki, Hauptmann | St.Kap., II.Gruppe
Mehringer, Unteroffizier Willi | 7 Staffel, P.O.W., 13-8-40
Meyer, Unteroffizier Hans | 1 Staffel, ✝ 24-10-40
Mobius, Unteroffizier | 5 Staffel
Mollenbock, Leutnant | 3 Staffel, ✝ 16-8-40
Morch, Oberleutnant | 7 Staffel, Missing, 13-8-40
Müller, Oberleutnant | 7 Staffel, Missing, 13-8-40
Nigisch, Gefreiter | 5 Staffel, ✝ 3-9-40
Obermayer, Leutnant | 10 Staffel
Osinsky, Feldwebel | 3 Staffel, ✝ 10-7-40
Oswald, Oberleutnant Gerhard | Stab, P.O.W., 13-8-40
Outzmann, Major | Gr.Kdr., I Gruppe
Pilz, Gefreiter | 4 Staffel, ✝ 7-9-40
Reinische, Unteroffizier | 5 Staffel
Roch, Oberleutnant Hubert | 5 Staffel, ✝ 28-9-40
Röder, Obergefreiter | 2 Staffel, P.O.W., 26-8-40
Röwe, Oberleutnant | II. Gruppe
Rutkowski, Unteroffizier Hans | 3 Staffel
Sandmann, Gefreiter | 8 Staffel
Schadt, Gefreiter Ludwig | III.Gruppe, P.O.W., 26-8-40
Schaffer, Unteroffizier Heinrich | III.Gruppe, P.O.W., 26-8-40
Scheffel, Leutnant Gunther | 8 Staffel, ✝ 30-9-40
Schermann, Unteroffizier Wilhelm | 1 Staffel, ✝ 24-10-40
Schildt, Leutnant | 5 Staffel, ✝ 3-9-40
Schinz, Gefreiter Gunther | 9 Staffel, ✝ 24-10-40
Schlegel, Oberleutnent Heinz | II.Gruppe
Schmidt, Unteroffizier Ellert | 2 Staffel, 26-8-40
Schneider, Oberleutnant | II.Gruppe
Schneider, Gefreiter Gunther | 7 Staffel, P.O.W., 26-8-40
Schmölzer, Unteroffizier Ambros | 2 Staffel, P.O.W., 26-8-40
Schreiner, Gefreiter Adolf | 5 Staffel, ✝ 11-10-40
Schumacher, Unteroffizier | II.Gruppe
Schütze, Flieger | II.Gruppe, ✝ 8-9-40
Schweighart, Unteroffizier | 8 Staffel
Sehrt, Unteroffizier | 9 Staffel
Seidel, Oberleutnant | II.Gruppe
Selter, Unteroffizier | II.Gruppe, ✝ 8-9-40
Simon, Unteroffizier Willi | III.Gruppe, P.O.W., 26-8-40
Staib, Oberfähnrich | 9 Staffel, ✝ 15-9-40
Stamfer, Unteroffizier Josef | 8.Staffel, P.O.W., 15-9-40
Steudel, Leutnant Eberhard | Stab, ✝ 18-10-40
Steudel, Leutnant Josef | 8 Staffel
Strobel, Oberfeldwebel Paul, ★ (2-44) | II.Gruppe, ✝ 19-9-43
Swientsch, Unteroffizier | 5 Staffel, ✝ 3-9-40
Schweitring, Oberleutnant Rolf | 7 Staffel, ✝ 15-9-40
Thalman, Oberfeldwebel Werner | 3 Staffel, P.O.W., 10-7-40
Treuer, Unteroffizier | 4 Staffel, ✝ 7-9-40
Trost, Unteroffizier Ewald, ★ (4-44) | II. Gruppe
Trinkner, Unteroffizier Richard | 3 Staffel
Umkelmann, Feldwebel | 3 Staffe13-8-40
Vögel, Unteroffizier Georg | 7 Staffel, P.O.W., 13-8-40
Wachtel, Unteroffizier Gotthard | 8 Staffel
Waldmann, Oberfeldwebel Otto | 8 Staffel
Weitkus, Oberstleutnant Paul, ★ (18-9-41) | Gr.Kdr., II.Gruppe
Welf, Obergefreiter Wilhelm | 1 Staffel, ✝ 24-10-40
Winter, Unteroffizier Karl | 7 Staffel, P.O.W., 26-8-40
Winterfeldt, Hauptmann von | I.Gruppe, ✝ 22-8-40
Wittmann, Leutnant | 9 Staffel, ✝ 30-8-40
Zechner, Obergefreiter Willi | 5 Staffel, ✝ 11-10-40
Ziems, Oberleutnant | II.Grupp, ✝ 8-9-40
Zierer, Gefreiter | 9 Staffel

Note. Kreigsberichter Wolfgang Köhler was flying with 8./KG 2 on 15th September 1940 when he baled and and was made P.O.W. at Chatham, Kent.

KAMPFGESCHWADER 3
KG 3 (< Blitz-Geschwader >)

Long-range bomber *Geschwader* of II.*Fliegerkorps, Luftflotte 2*, equipped with Dornier Do 17Zs. Headquarters and I.*Gruppe* based at Le Culot, II.*Gruppe* at Antwerpe/Deune, and III.*Gruppe* at St. Trond. Unit Codes

5K. Commanded by Oberst Wolfgang Chamier-Glisczinski. This *Geschwader* was heavily committed to raids on British fighter airfields on 26th and 28th August, and in the big daylight raids of 7th and 15th September, II. and III. *Gruppen* suffering particularly heavy casualties on these days.

Bauer, Feldwebel | 8 Staffel
Becker-Ross, Oberleutnant Helmut | 5 Staffel, ✝ 15-9-40
Berghahn, Leutnant | 2 Staffel, ✝ 5-10-40
Berndt, Feldwebel | II.Gruppe
Blasche, Unteroffizier | II.Gruppe
Bock, Unteroffizier | II.Gruppe
Bormann, Flieger | 4 Staffel
Bott, Oberleutnant | II.Gruppe, ✝ 10-7-40
Brinkmann, Feldwebel | 5 Staffel
Brückmann, Flieger Anton | 6 Staffel, P.O.W., 28-8-40
Brückner, Oberfeldwebel | 5 Staffel, ✝ 15-9-40
Bulach, Oberfeldwebel | II.Gruppe
Burballa, Oberfeldwebel | 4 Staffel, ✝ 15-9-40
Burghardt, Gefreiter Artur | 6 Staffel, P.O.W., 28-8-40
Büttner, Gefreiter Walter | 8 Staffel
Chamier-Glisczinski, Oberst Wolfgang, ★(6-10-40) | Geschw.Kdr., ✝12-8-43
Dümler, Leutnant Kurt | 4 Staffel, ✝ 15-9-40
Eggert, Leutnant Karl | 7 Staffel, P.O.W., 26-8-40
Essmert, Feldwebel Willi | 7 Staffel, P.O.W., 26-8-40
Falke, Felfwebel | 5 Staffel
Fischer, Leutnant | I Gruppe
Franke, Feldwebel | 5 Staffel, 15-9-40
Friebel, Unteroffizier | 4 Staffel
Gabelmann, Oberstleutnant | Gr.Kdr., I Gruppe
Gahtz, Oberleutnant | II.Gruppe
Gailer, Gefreiter Willi | 6 Staffel, P.O.W., 28-8-40
Geissler, Oberleutnant Richard | 2 Staffel
Goertz, Feldwebel von | 4 Staffel
Gutat, Feldwebel | II.Gruppe
Hansburg, Unteroffizier | 4 Staffel, ✝ 15-9-40
Hansen, Feldwebel | 5Staffel, ✝ 15-9-40
Haupt, Unteroffizier Rudolf | 7 Staffel, P.O.W., 26-8-40
Hausdorf, Unteroffizier Harald | 1 Staffel, 15-9-40
Heese, Feldwebel Karl | 9 Staffel
Hilbrecht, Unteroffizier | 9 Staffel, ✝ 2-9-40
Höbel, Oberfeldwebel | 5 Staffel
Howind, Oberfeldwebel | 5 Staffel
Hubert, Feldwebel | Stab
Hühn, Gefreiter Hans | 7 Staffel, ✝ 26-8-40
Kleine, Oberfeldwebel | Stab, ✝ 7-9-40
Köhnke, Oberleutnant Otto, ★ (6-8-42) | I.Gruppe
Kostropetsche, Unteroffizier | II.Gruppe
Kringler, Leutnant | 6 Staffel, ✝ 15-8-40
Krüg, Leutnant Peter | 6 Staffel, P.O.W., 28-8-40
Krüger, Leutnant Helmut | 6 Staffel, ✝ 21-8-40
Kükens, Hauptmann | St.Kap., 6 Staffel, ✝ 8-9-40
Lange, Oberfeldwebel | II.Gruppe
Langenhain, Oberleutnant Adolf | 5 Staffel
Leitner, Leutnant | 5 Staffel
Lindmann, Hauptmann | 6 Staffel
Maskules, Unteroffizier | 4 Staffel, ✝ 15-9-40
Michaelis, Leutnant Herbert | 4 Staffel
Neumann, Gefreiter | II.Gruppe
Nickel, Feldwebel | II.Gruppe
Nitzsche, Felfwebel Rudi | 1 Staffel, ✝ 28-20-40
Otting, Hauptmann | Stab Staffelkapitân, ✝ 7-9-40
Passler, Feldwebel | 7 Staffel, ✝ 27-10-40
Pilger, Hauptmann | Gr.Kdr., II.Gruppe
Platen-Hallermund, Oberleutnant Graf von, | 3 Staffel, ✝ 28-8-40
Püttmann, Hauptmann Ernst | 5 Staffel, ✝ 15-9-40
Ramm, Unteroffizier | 7 Staffel, ✝ 26-8-40
Rathmann, Hauptmann | Gr.Kdr., III.Gruppe
Reinhard, Unteroffizier Helmut | 7 Staffel, ✝ 26-8-40
Rilling, Oberfeldwebel | 7 Staffel, ✝ 15-9-40
Ritzel, Unteroffizier Richard | 7 Staffel, ✝ 26-8-40
Rohr, Oberleutnant | 9 Staffel
Sachse, Leutnant | 7 Staffel, ✝ 26-8-40
Salomo, Feldwebel | 8 Staffel
Scharpkowski, Oberleutnant | I.Gruppe
Schierling, Feldwebel | 8 Staffel

Schild, Gefreiter	4 Staffel	Meierhofer, Unteroffizier	8 Staffel
Schonn, Unteroffizier	8 Staffel	Meissner, Hauptmann	*Gr.Kdr.*, I.Gruppe
Schopper, Leutnant	11 Gruppe	Meissner, Oberleutnant	*St.Kap.*, 8 Staffel, ✝ 26-8-40
Schrader, Oberleutnant	4 Staffel	Müller-Wernscheid, Unteroffizier	3 Staffel, ✝ 14-9-40
Schreiber, Feldwebel Alwin	1 Staffel, ✝ 28-10-40	Piontek, Unteroffizier Otto	7 Staffel, ✝ 27-10-40
Schröder, Leutnant	II.Gruppe, ✝ 10-7-40	Podbielski, Oberleutnant Friedrich	*St.Kap.*, 7 and 9 Staffeln
Schroff, Unteroffizier	8 Staffel	Preugscha, Obergefreiter	8 Staffel
Schulze, Leutnant Rudolf	9 Staffel, ✝ 2-10-40	Reitz, Unteroffizier	6 Staffel
Schwartz, Oberleutnant	*St.Kap.*, 6 Staffel	Rath, Oberstleutnant Hans-Joachim, ★ (9-5-42)	*Geschw.Kdr.*
Seidel, Feldwebel	9 Staffel	Rohloff, Hauptmann	*St.Kap.*, 9 Staffel, ✝ 7-7-40
Siegmund, Unteroffizier	6 Staffel, ✝ 21-8-40	Scholz, Gefreiter	8 Staffel
Sonntag, Unteroffizier	II.Gruppe	Schröder, Oberleutnant	6 Staffel, ✝ 6-9-40
Spring, Feldwebel	9 Staffel	Schubert, Oberleutnant-zur-See Johann	8 Staffel
Stolle, Oberfeldwebel	6 Staffel, ✝ 21-8-40	Steiner, Oberleutnant	II.Gruppe, ✝ 19-8-40
Ullrich, Oberleutnant	7 Staffel	Stiefelhagen, Oberfeldwebel Helmut	7 Staffel
Vogel, Feldwebel	4 Staffel, ✝ 15-9-40	Strickstrock, Unteroffizier Georg	1 Staffel, P.O.W., 26-7-40
Volkert, Unteroffizier	*Stab*	Töpfer, Unteroffizier	3 Staffel, ✝ 14-9-40
Vosshagen, Feldwebel Kurt	1 Staffel, P.O.W., 28-10-40	Wagner, Oberleutnant	9 Staffel
Walter, Leutnant	6 Staffel	Weber, Feldwebel Alfred	3 Staffel, P.O.W., 2-7-40
Wechmar, Oberstleutnant Freiherr von	*Gr.Kdr.*, I.Gruppe	Wick, Gefreiter	6 Staffel, ✝ 6-9-40
Weymar, Gefreiter	4 Staffel	Wolf, Unteroffizier	6 Staffel, ✝ 7-9-40
Wien, Unteroffizier	4 Staffel	Wolff, Major Doktor Gottlieb, ★ (1-43)	*Gr.Kdr.*, II.Gruppe
Wünsch, Feldwebel	II.Gruppe	Zeiss, Leutnant	I. Gruppe, ✝ 8-8-40
Zien, Leutnant	6 Staffel, ✝ 29-8-40	Ziegler, Leutnant	6 Staffel
Zimmermann, Feldwebel	5 Staffel		
Ziebursch, Flieger Josef	8 Staffel		

KAMPFGESCHWADER 4
(KG 4 (< General Wever>))

Long-range bomber *Geschwader* of IX.*Fliegerkorps*. Head-quarters at Soesterburg, Holland, commanded by Oberstleutnant Hans-Joachim Rath (Knight's Cross, 9-5-42). *Stabschwarm* and I.*Gruppe* based at Soesterburg with Heinkel He 111Hs; II.*Gruppe* based at Eindhoven with Heinkel He 111Hs, and III.*Gruppe* based at Schipol with Junkers Ju 88As. Unit Codes 5J. Employed continuously on raids against South-East England throughout the Battle of Britain.

Annis, Leutnant	7 Staffel, ✝ 27-8-40
Arnold, Leutnant	II.Gruppe, ✝ 10-9-40
Athens, Leutnant-zur-See von	7 Staffel
Beckmann, Gefreiter	6 Staffel
Blödorn, Hauptmann Erich, ★ (13-10-40)	*Gr.Kdr.*, III.Gruppe
Borchardt, Unteroffizier	8 Staffel
Camp, Oberfeldwebel	8 Staffel, 28-9-40
Dahlmann, Leutnant Kurt, ★ (24-1-45)	III.Gruppe
Draisbach, Oberfeldwebel Hermann	3 Staffel, P.O.W., 2-7-40
Ehrbach, Oberfeldwebel Werner	8 Staffel
Ernst, Oberfeldwebel Rudolf	3 Staffel, P.O.W., 2-7-40
Fommer, Unteroffizier Wilhelm	1 Staffel, ✝ 26-7-40
Gebser, Feldwebel	8 Staffel, ✝ 17-9-40
Geisler, Oberleutnant	9 Staffel
Grabke, Gefreiter Helmuth	1 Staffel, ✝ 26-7-40
Guldenberg, Unteroffizier	8 Staffel
Hähnel, Unteroffizier Gerhardt	1 Staffel, 26-7-40
Hansmeier, Obergefreiter	8 Staffel
Heier, Feldwebel Hans	7 Staffel
Herrmann, Oberleutnant Hajo, ★★★ (13-10-40, 2-8-43 and 23-1-44)	
	St.Kap., 7 Staffel (ex-KG 30)
Herold, Gefreiter Karl	8 Staffel
Hobe, Feldwebel	3 Staffel
Kell, Oberleutnant Hermann	3 Staffel
Kessler, Oberfeldwebel Hermann	1 Staffel, ✝ 26-7-40
Kiedrowski, Oberfeldwebel Karl	7 Staffel
Kieg, Obergefreiter	8 Staffel, ✝ 28-9-40
Klein, Unteroffizier	6 Staffel
Klotz, Oberleutnant	6 Staffel, ✝ 7-9-40
Knoll, Unteroffizier	6 Staffel
Koch, Oberleutnant Friedrich Wilhelm	3 Staffel, P.O.W., 2-7-40
Krauss, Obergefreiter	8 Staffel, ✝ 17-9-40
Lange, Leutnant Fritz	8 Staffel, ✝ 28-9-40
Marschardt, Gefreiter	8 Staffel
Marlwitz, Oberleutnant Dietrich	8 Staffel
Marten, Obergefreiter	6 Staffel, ✝ 6-9-40

KAMPFGESCHWADER 26
(KG 26 < *Löwen-Geschwader* >)

Long-range bomber *Geschwader* based at Stavanger, Norway, as part of *Luftflotte 5* with Heinkel He 111Hs. Unit Codes 1H. Isolated raids were carried out against the British Isles during July and early August, culminating in the attack of 15th August against targets in North-East England. Thereafter parts of the *Geschwader* were moved south to France and the Low Countries, suffering fairly heavy casualties during September.

Abenhausen, Oberleutnant	3 Staffel
Baltes, Leutnant	6 Staffel
Bartels, Unteroffizier	6 Staffel, ✝ 6-9-40
Bastin, Feldwebel Walter	3 Staffel, ✝ 26-10-40
Bertram, Oberleutnant	5 Staffel
Beer, Unteroffizier Heinz	9 Staffel, P.O.W., 17-7-40
Besser, Oberleutnant von	8 Staffel
Bischoff, Oberleutnant	4 Staffel, ✝ 6-9-40
Blasius, Unteroffizier	1 Staffel, ✝ 4-10-40
Bräutigam, Unteroffizier Willi	5 Staffel
Burk, Leutnant	8 Staffel
Busch, Major	*Gr. Kdr.*, I.Gruppe
Büttner, Feldwebel	1 Staffel
Denner, Unteroffizier Otto	7 Staffel, P.O.W., 9-8-40
Domes, Unteroffizier	I.Gruppe
Dreyer, Unteroffizier	I.Gruppe
Entrich, Gefreiter	5 Staffel
Ewertz, Feldwebel	4 Staffel
Fass, Unteroffizier	2 Staffel
Feinekat, Unteroffizier Fritz	7 Staffel, P.O.W., 9-8-40
Felleger, Gefreiter Josef	5 Staffel
Friedrich, Feldwebel	I.Gruppe
Fuchs, Oberstleutnant Robert, ★ (6-4-40)	*Geschw. Kdr.*
George, Feldwebel	I.Gruppe
Giess, Feldwebel	5 Staffel
Gutacker, Feldwebel	5 Staffel
Haertel, Feldwebel Willi	7 Staffel, P.O.W., 9-8-40
Handwerker, Feldwebel	4 Staffel
Haslache, Gefreiter	2 Staffel
Hauswald, Feldwebel	·3 Staffel
Heimbach, Gefreiter Kurt	9 Staffel, ✝ 17-7-40
Henningsen, Unteroffizier	4 Staffel
Herms, Unteroffizier	3 Staffel, ✝ 11-9-40
Hofmann, Unteroffizier	I.Gruppe
Hollmann, Oberleutnant Ottmar	2 Staffel, P.O.W., 15-8-40
Hoper, Feldwebel	4 Staffel
Horn, Feldwebel	2 Staffel, ✝ 11-9-40
Hübrig, Obergefreiter	4 Staffel, ✝ 6-9-40
Huck, Leutnant	9 Staffel, ✝ 12-7-40
Imhof, Oberleutnant Georg	3 Staffel, ✝ 26-10-40

Jabusch, Febwebel	1 Staffel
Jenreck, Gefreiter Werner	6 Staffel, P.O.W., 24-9-40
Jessen, Feldwebel Harald	2 Staffel
Karkos, Unteroffizier Gustav	7 Staffel, P.O.W., 9-8-40
Kaublau, Unteroffizier Willi	5 Staffel
Kisling, Gefreiter	4 Staffel
Koch, Oberleutnant	I.Gruppe
Kohlhopp, Unteroffizier	4 Staffel, ✝ 6-9-40
Kose, Leutnant Werner	1 Staffel, 28-9-40
Kramer, Oberfeldwebel	5 Staffel, ✝ 11-9-40
Kruger, Unteroffizier Heinz	I.Gruppe
Kuckelt, Oberleutnant	4 Staffel
Küne, Oberleutnant Helmut	II.Gruppe
Künstler, Hauptmann	*St.Kap.*, 1 Staffel
Lehmann, Unteroffizier Albert	II.Gruppe
Leibnitz, Gefreiter Heinrich	6 Staffel, P.O.W., 24-9-40
Lensch, Oberleutnant	1 Staffel, ✝ 11-9-40
Liedtke, Unteroffizier Harri	9 Staffel, ✝ 17-7-40
Lorenz, Oberleutnant Gerhard	9 Staffel, P.O.W., 17-7-40
Lossberg, Major Vikton von, ★ (17-10-41)	*Gr.Kdr.*, III.Gruppe
Lubke, Oberleutnant von	8 Staffel
Mahlmann, Unteroffizier	4 Staffel
Marenbach, Feldwebel	I.Gruppe
Markuse, Feldwebel	6 Staffel, ✝ 6-9-40
Meier, Gefreiter	6 Staffel, ✝ 6-9-40
Meusel, Unteroffizier	5 Staffel, ✝ 11-9-40
Niemeyer, Unteroffizier Karl	6 Staffel, P.O.W., 24-9-40
Ölerich, Leutnant	Erg.Staffel ✝ 23-9-40
Potenberg, Feldwebel	I.Gruppe
Prefzger (rank unknown)	2 Staffel, P.O.W., 15-7-40
Probst, Obergefreiter Heinrich	2 Staffel, P.O.W., 15-7-40
Radloff, Unteroffizier Ebhard	3 Staffel, ✝ 26-10-40
Reinhardt (rank unknown)	2 Staffel, ✝ 15-7-40
Renner, Leutnant	8 Staffel
Reinelt, Unteroffizier	1 Staffel, ✝ 4-10-40
Riedel, Oberleutnant	8 Staffel
Schachtbeck, Leutnant	2 Staffel, ✝ 6-9-40
Schäfer, Feldwebel	1 Staffel, ✝ 11-9-40
Schang, Unteroffizier	1 Staffel
Schmidt, Unteroffizier	1 Staffel
Schneider, Gefreiter	4 Staffel, ✝ 6-9-40
Schröder, Gefreiter	5 Staffel
Schwartz, Feldwebel	I.Gruppe
Schweizer, Unteroffizier	6 Staffel, ✝ 6-9-40
Sommer, Oberleutnant Karl	5 Staffel
Staffeldt, Oberfeldwebel	6 Staffel, ✝ 6-9-40
Stenzel, Unteroffizier	II.Gruppe
Stirnemann, Unteroffizier	I.Gruppe
Streubel. Leutnant Heinrich	I.Gruppe
Stut, Unteroffizier	4 Staffel, ✝ 6-9-40
Süssman, Oberfeldwebel	4 Staffel
Walter, Leutnant Kurt, ★ (18-5-43)	Staffel not known
Walz (rank not known)	2 Staffel, P.O.W., 15-7-40
Wanderer, Oberleutnant	5 Staffel, ✝ 3-9-40
Weinlich, Gefreiter Stephan	6 Staffel, P.O.W., 24-9-40
Weniger, Unteroffizier Hermann	3 Staffel, ✝ 26-10-40
Wesemann, Leutnant	5 Staffel
Westfalen, Feldwebel	3 Staffel, ✝ 11-9-40
Wilde, Feldwebel	II.Gruppe
Winter, Unteroffizier	1 Staffel, ✝ 4-10-40
Zähle, Gefreiter	3 Staffel, ✝ 11-9-40
Zingel, Leutnant Hans	1 Staffel, ✝ 4-10-40
Zobernig, Leutnant	5 Staffel, ✝ 3-9-40

KAMPFGESCHWADER 27
(KG 27 < *Boelcke* >)

Bomber *Geschwader* of *Fliegerkorps* IV, *Luftflotte 3*, equipped with Heinkel He 111H aircraft. Headquarters and I.*Gruppe* based at Tours, II.*Gruppe* at Dinard and Bourges, and III.*Gruppe* at Rennes. Unit Codes 1G (and occasionally 1K).

Bautz, Unteroffizier Ernst	I.Gruppe, ✝ 22-10-40
Beck, Feldwebel Wilhelm	Stab, 22-10-40
Behrendt, Oberst	*Geschw. Kdr.*

Bendrich, Oberfeldwebel Willi	*Stab* II.Gruppe
Bernd, Unteroffizier	8 Staffel, ✝ 13-9-40
Blumenthal, Unteroffizier Adolf	9 Staffel, P.O.W., 14-8-40
Böhle, Oberfeldwebel Hugo	II.Gruppe
Brehmer, Maj.i.G. Hans-Jurgen	II.Gruppe, P.O.W., 12-8-40
Buss, Oberleutnant	*Stab*, ✝ 17-7-40
Dubral, Felwebel Oscar	8 Staffel, P.O.W., 14-8-40
Eilms, Feldwebel Klaus	I.Gruppe
Elster, Oberfeldwebel	III.Gruppe, ✝ 13-9-40
Erfurth, Oberfeldwebel Friedrich	II.Gruppe
Fellinger, Hauptmann Josef	I.Gruppe
Flick, Unteroffizier Edo	9 Staffel, P.O.W., 14-8-40
Fock, Oberleutnant Horst	I.Gruppe
Forster, Unteroffizier Wilhelm	I.Gruppe, ✝ 22-10-40
Frey, Oberfeldwebel Herbert	*Stab* II.Gruppe, P.O.W., 12-8-40
Friele, Leutnant Fritz	1 Staffel, ✝ 9-10-40
Gebhardt, Feldwebel Rudolf	I.Gruppe
Georgi, Oberst	*Gesch. Kdr.*, ✝ 17-7-40
Ginzinger, Leutnant	I.Gruppe, ✝ 23-8-40
Gietz, Feldwebel Walter	8 Staffel, P.O.W., 14-8-40
Heiner, Feldwebel Engelbert, ★ (12-42)	9 Staffel
Hünerbein, Oberleutnant	III.Gruppe
Jannsen, Unteroffizier Ernst	I.Gruppe
Jennau, Unteroffizier Alfons	I.Gruppe, ✝ 22-10-40
Jug, Feldwebel Nikolaus	9 Staffel, P.O.W., 14-8-40
Knoblich, Feldwebel Franz	8 Staffel, Missing, 14-8-40
Köchy, Unteroffizier Hans	8 Staffel, P.O.W., 14-8-40
Kramwinckel, Feldwebel Max	III.Gruppe, ✝ 22-10-40
Kremm, Unteroffizier Josef	9 Staffel, P.O.W., 14-8-40
Kück, Oberfeldwebel Heinz	II.Gruppe
Kupsch, Gefreiter Kurt	9.Staffel, P.O.W., 14-8-40
Löhneng, Oberfeldwebel Gunther	*Stab* II.Gruppe, P.O.W., 12-8-40
Mahnke, Oberleutnant	I.Gruppe, ✝ 6-10-40
Moosbauer, Unteroffizier Hans	iII.Gruppe, ✝ 22-10-40
Neuziel, Leutnant Gerhard	*Gruppe not known*
Nonnemann, Unteroffizier	I Gruppe
Okuneck, Unteroffizier	III.Gruppe, ✝ 13-9-40
Oschinski, Oberfeldwebel Helmut	II.Gruppe
Pommerening, Oberleutnant	Stab
Ramstetter, Obergefreiter	9 Staffel, P.O.W., 14-8-40
Riedel, Hauptmann	III.Gruppe
Röder, Feldwebel Heinrich	8 Staffel, P.O.W., 14-8-40
Rother, Gefreiter Gerhardt	9 Staffel, P.O.W., 14-8-40
Schaum, Unteroffizier Walter	8 Staffel, ✝ 14-8-40
Schlesser, Unteroffizier	III.Gruppe
Schlichting, Major Friedrich-Karl	*Gr.Kdr.*, II.Gruppe, P.O.W., 12-8-40
Schmidt, Unteroffizier Erwin	III.Gruppe, ✝ 22-10-40
Schmiedfelden, Fahnrich Kurt	III.Gruppe, ✝ 22-10-40
Schrage, Unteroffizier Heinrich	8 Staffel, ✝ 14-8-40
Schwerb, Óbergefreiter	I.Gruppe
Sickmann, Oberleutnant Erduard	I.Gruppe, ✝ 17-10-40
Siebers, Unteroffizier	III.Gruppe
Siegel, Oberleutnant	III.Gruppe
Spazier, Unteroffizier	I.Gruppe
Stadel, Leutnant	I. Gruppe, ✝ 24-7-40
Sternberg, Major Freiherr Speck von	*Gr.Kdr.*, III.Gruppe, ✝ 22-10-40
Stössel, Oberleutnant	III.Gruppe
Sulzbach, Unteroffizier Kurt	9 Staffel, P.O.W., 14-8-40
Taussman, Unteroffizier Ernst	III.Gruppe, ✝ 22-10-40
Uhland, Leutnant	III.Gruppe
Uhlenschlager, Oberleutnant Ernst	9 Staffel, P.O.W., 14-8-40
Ulbrich, Major	I.Gruppe
Ullmann, Unteroffizier Gustav	8 Staffel, P.O.W., 14-8-40
Walpert, Obergefreiter	III.Gruppe
Walther, Oberleutnant Kurt	III.Gruppe, ✝ 22-10-40
Wappler, Oberleutnant Harry	III.Gruppe
Wiedenhoft, Leutnant	II.Gruppe
Wiesemann, Oberleutnant	III.Gruppe
Wiesemeyer, Feldwebel Tom	8 Staffel, Missing, 14-8-40
Wilhelm, Leutnant Wolfgang	I.Gruppe, ✝ 22-10-40
Wunderlich, Gefreiter Willi	*Stab*, I.Gruppe
Zobel, Oberartz Doktor	✝ 17-7-40

KAMPFGESCHWADER 30
(KG 30 < *Adler-Geschwader* >)

Bomber *Geschwader* of *Luftflotte 5* based at Aalborg, Denmark, during July and August with Junkers Ju 88As and Cs. After the daylight defeat of *Luftflotte 5* on 15th August, the *Geschwader* was temporarily withdrawn and re-deployed at Gilze-Rijen and Eindhoven, Holland, during September. Unit Codes 4D (occasionally used 4K).

Balt, Gefreiter	5 Staffel
Bauer, Gefreiter	7 Staffel, ✝ 3-10-40
Baumbach, Leutnant Werner, ★★★ (8-5-40, 14-7-41, 17-8-42)	5 Staffel
Baumgarten, Obergefreiter	8 Staffel, ✝ 9-9-40
Beck, Unteroffizier	Stab
Bendaren, Unteroffizier	4 Staffel
Bieger, Oberleutnant Otto	7 Staffel, 3-10-40
Böbel, Gefreiter	9 Staffel, ✝ 6-10-40
Brandmüller, Unteroffizier	5 Staffel
Bünker, Feldwebel	5 Staffel, ✝ 3-10-40
Buroth, Leutnant	8 Staffel
Diebler, Unteroffizier	II.Gruppe, ✝ 9-9-40
Doensch, Major Fritz, ★ (19-6-40)	Gr.Kdr., I.Gruppe
Fecht, Unteroffizier	II.Gruppe
Fuchs, Unteroffizier	9 Staffel
Fuss, Feldwebel	Stab
Gerard, Gefreiter	5 Staffel
Golnisch, Oberleutnant	II.Gruppe
Görth, Gefreiter	II.Gruppe
Hackbarth, Major	Gr.Kdr., III.Gruppe, ✝ 9-9-40
Hallert, Unteroffizier	II.Gruppe
Hamerla, Unteroffizier	II.Gruppe
Hass, Hauptmann Erich	**Gr.Kdr.**, II.Gruppe, ✝ 16-10-40
Heil, Oberleutnant	Stab
Heilmeier, Feldwebel	7 Staffel, ✝ 3-10-40
Herndeck, Gefreiter	7 Staffel, ✝ 3-10-40
Herrman, Oberleutnant Hajo, ★★★ (13-10-40, 2-8-43 and 23-1-44)	St.Kap., 7 Staffel
Hettinger, Unteroffizier	8 Staffel, ✝ 9-9-40
Holzmeier, Unteroffizier	9 Staffel
Jung, Feldwebel	8 Staffel
Kellewe, Hauptmann	Gr. Kdr., III.Gruppe
Kessels, Feldwebel Josei	Stab, II.Gruppe, ✝ 16-10-40
Kiessner, Leutnant	6 Staffel, ✝ 27-8-40
Kohler, Feldwebel Martin	5 Staffel
Koschella, Feldwebel	4 Staffel
Läge, Feldwebel	9 Staffel
Langsdorf, Hauptmann von	8 Staffel
Loebel, Oberstleutnant	Geschw. Kdr.
Manger, Oberfeldwebel	III.Gruppe
Meinhold, Leutnant	1 Staffel, ✝ 7-7-40
Menz, Unteroffizier Heinz	5 Staffel
Ortlepp, Oberfeldwebel	9 Staffel
Paustian, Unteroffizier	Stab
Petermann, Gefreiter	III.Gruppe, ✝ 9-9-40
Phel, Unteroffizier	4 Staffel
Pohling, Unteroffizier Gerhard	8 Staffel
Rachmann, Oberleutnant	III.Gruppe
Richter, Oberleutnant Justus	9 Staffel
Riede, Leutnant	7 Staffel
Röder, Leutnant	9 Staffel
Rodermund, Unteroffizier Alfred	8 Staffel
Rolf, Unteroffizier	II.Gruppe
Sawallisch, Unteroffizier	III.Gruppe, ✝ 9-9-40
Schulte-Matr, Oberfeldwebel Hans	8 Staffel
Stahl, Unteroffizier	II.Gruppe
Suhr, Feldwebel Günter	Stab, II.Gruppe, ✝ 16-10-40
Suppick, Gefreiter	1 Staffel
Symonski, Hauptmann von	Gr. Kdr., II.Gruppe, ✝ 8-10-40
Thies, Feldwebel Heinrich	5 Staffel
Vetter, Unteroffizier	8 Staffel
Wallenstein, Leutnant	1 Staffel, ✝ 7-7-40
Wilhenig, Feldwebel	4 Staffel
Wowereit, Feldwebel Wilhelm	8 Staffel

Note: *Luftwaffe* Kriegsberichter Kap. Anton Doppelfeld was killed with KG 30, 16-10-40

KAMPFGESCHWADER 40
(KG 40)

Long-range bomber-reconnaissance and maritime patrol unit equipped with Focke-Wulf Fw 200C Condor aircraft, based at Brest. Unit Codes F8.

Berghaus, Feldwebel Walter	I.Gruppe
Diesel, Leutnant Willi	5 Staffel, ✝ 21-9-40
Eschmann, Oberleutnant	Ausb. Staffel, ✝ 23-8-40
Geisse, Oberstleutnant	Gesch. Kdr.
Gruber, Feldwebel Fritz	I.Gruppe
Gressle, Gefreiter Walter	I.Gruppe
Jope, Hauptmann Bernhard, ★ (30-12-40)	2 Staffel
Köpplin, Feldwebel	Stab
Krüger, Reg. Rat. Doktor	I.Gruppe
Kulken, Feldwebel Herbert	2 Staffel, P.O.W., 20-7-40
Meier, Feldwebel	2 Staffel, ✝ 20-7-40
Meinhold, Leutnant-zur-See	Ausb. Staffel, ✝ 23-8-40
Mollenhausen, Oberleutnant	I.Gruppe
Nicolai, Feldwebel Karl	2 Staffel, P.O.W., 20-7-40
Schuldt, Oberleutnant Theo	I.Gruppe
Schwengke, Oberleutnant	Stab
Stesym, Hauptmann	I.Gruppe
Sturm, Met. Doktor	I.Gruppe
Zenke, Hauptmann	2 Staffel
Zraunig, Gefreiter	2 Staffel, ✝ 20-7-40

KAMPFGESCHWADER 51
(KG 51 < *Edelweiss* >)

Long-range bomber *Geschwader* of V.*Fliegerkorps*, equipped with Junkers Ju 88A aircraft. Headquarters at Paris-Orly, commanded by Oberst Doktor Johann Fisser (until 12th August; thereafter by Major Hans Bruno Schulz-Heyn). *Geschwader Stabschwarm* and I.*Gruppe* based at Paris-Orly until 1st August, thereafter at Melun-Villaroche; II.*Gruppe* at Étampes-Mondésir until 24th August 1940, thereafter at Paris-Orly; III.*Gruppe* at Étampes-Mondésir. Unit Codes 9K. Employed extensively throughout the Battle, particularly during September and October when the *Geschwader* suffered very heavy casualties. Unit establishment approximately 90 pilots and 280 aircrew members.

Altmann, Gefreiter	7.Staffel, ✝ 24-9-40
Andree, Gefreiter	Staffel not knowm, ✝ 25-9-40
Apfelbeck, Feldwebel Johannes	Geschw. Erg. Staffel, ✝ 20-10-40
Baader, Feldwebel	7 Staffel
Bachauer, Feldwebel	7 Staffel, ✝19-8-40
Baussart, Oberfeldwebel Armin	4 Staffel
Becher, Unteroffizier Josef	4 Staffel, ✝ 9-7-40
Bender, Unteroffizier Emil	7 Staffel, ✝ 27-9-40
Bein, Leutnant Fritz	II. Gruppe, ✝ 7-10-40
Besenbeck (rank not known)	Staffel not known
Berghhammer, Unteroffizier Josef	Staffel not known
Bigalke, Sonderführer	8 Staffel, ✝ 12-8-40
Bischoff, Unteroffizier Gerhard	7 Staffel, ✝ 4-7-40
Bittner, Gefreiter Hans	4 Staffel, ✝ 8-10-40
Böhmisch, Gefreiter	7 Staffel, ✝ 30-7-40
Breuker, Unteroffizier Heinz	1 Staffel, ✝ 15-9-40
Brünningsen, Feldwebel	7 Staffel, ✝ 27-9-40
Brustellin, Hauptmann	Gr. Kdr., Gruppe not known
Burmeister, Gefreiter Herbert	Staffel not known
Capesius, Leutnant	9 Staffel
Claer, Oberleutnant Helmut von	4 Staffel, ✝ 18-10-40
Conrad, Feldwebel	7 Staffel, ✝ 27-9-40
Czepik, Gefreiter Horst	3 Staffel, ✝ 12-8-40
Darjes, Oberleutnant Paul-Friedrich, ★ (14-10-42)	Staffel not known
Döttlinger, Leutnant Gottfried	4 Staffel, ✝ 8-10-40
Dürrschmidt, Gefreiter	I.Gruppe
Effler, Gefreiter	7 Staffel
Eimers, Feldwebel	7 Staffel, ✝ 24-9-40
Fabian, Oberleutnant Maximillian	1 Staffel, ✝ 21-10-40
Fischer, Unteroffizier	8 Staffel, 12-8-40
Fisser, Oberst Doktor Johann	Geschw. Kdr., ✝ 12-8-40
Flegel, Oberleutnant	6 Staffel, 12-8-40
Flöter, Unteroffizier Walter	3 Staffel, ✝ 12-8-40

Franke, Unteroffizier	9 Staffel
Freundl, Unteroffizier Hans	Staffel not known
Friedel, Feldwebel Erhard	Staffel not known
Geilenkirchen, Leutnant Hans	8 Staffel
Geyer, Obergefreiter Willi	Staffel not known
Gosch, Gefreiter Hans-Jurgen	Staffel not known
Graf, Oberleutnant	I.Gruppe, ✞ 12-8-40
Gravenreuth, Oberleutnant Ullrich von	1 Staffel, ✞ 27-9-40
Greiff, Hauptmann von	*Gr.Kdr.*, I.Gruppe, from 12-8-40
Gundlach, Feldwebel Otto	8 Staffel, ✞ 12-8-40
Gutberlet, Unteroffizier	9 Staffel, ✞ 12-9-40
Haag, Feldwebel	7 Staffel, ✞ 19-8-40
Haak, Unteroffizier Wilhelm	Staffel not known
Haberl, Leutnant Wilhelm	I.Gruppe
Hartmann, Unteroffizier	Staffel not known
Hauff, Gefreiter Arnold	9 Staffel, ✞ 28-10-40
Hausen, Unteroffizier Georg	Staffel not known
Heinrich, Leutnant	7 Staffel, ✞ 9-7-40
Heinig, Oberleutnant Günther	I.Gruppe, 1-10-40
Helms, Oberfeldwebel Hugo	4 Staffel
Henker, Unteroffizier Woldemar	3 Staffel, ✞ 19-9-40
Hennike, Unteroffizier Karl	2 Staffel, ✞ 12-9-40
Herich, Gefreiter	7 Staffel, ✞ 24-9-40
Heye, Oberleutnant Sigmund	II.Gruppe, ✞ 7-10-40
Hinterland, Unteroffizier Gustav	6 Staffel
Hirschfeld, Unteroffizier	I.Gruppe, ✞ 15-9-40
Hochstätter, Leutnant Heinrich	III.Gruppe, ✞ 12-8-40
Holzner, Unteroffizier Wilhelm	2 Staffel, ✞ 12-9-40
Israel, Gefreiter Kurt	7 Staffel, ✞ 27-9-40
Jedicke, Gefreiter Rudi	4 Staffel
Jorg, Feldwebel Wilhelm	7 Staffel, ✞ 30-7-40
Jung, Gefreiter	7 Staffel, ✞ 27-9-40
Kafka, Unteroffizier Karl	III.Gruppe, 10-10-40
Kaltenhauser, Feldwebel Alois	I.Gruppe, ✞ 1-10-40
Kastner, Unteroffizier Karl	4 Staffel, ✞ 12-8-40
Keffel, Oberfeldwebel Karl	8 Staffel, ✞ 12-8-40
Kesper, Oberleutnant Fritz	6 Staffel, ✞ 13-7-40
Kessel, Oberfeldwebel	4 Staffel, ✞ 12-8-40
Kienbauer, Gefreiter Erwin	7 Staffel, ✞ 27-9-40
Kirch, Unteroffizier Helmut	2 Staffel, ✞ 12-9-40
Kirchberger, Feldwebel Oskar	*Geschw. Erg. Staffel*
Kirchhoff, Oberleutnant Hans-Jurgen	9 Staffel, ✞ 18-8-40
Knoll, Gefreiter Leonhard	6 Staffel
Köhler, Gefreiter	2 Staffel, ✞ 12-9-40
Köhne, Gefreiter Diegbert	II.Gruppe, ✞ 8-10-40
König, Gefreiter Erich	9 Staffel, ✞ 28-10-40
König, Oberfeldwebel	II.Gruppe, ✞ 7-10-40
Krämer, Unteroffizier Ernst	9 Staffel, ✞ 28-10-40
Krell, Oberfeldwebel	II.Gruppe, ✞ 7-10-40
Küchle, Oberleutnant	Stab, III.Gruppe
Kühne, Gefreiter Siegfried	4 Staffel, ✞ 8-10-40
Kupfernägel, Unteroffizier Walter	4 Staffel, ✞ 15-9-40
Kurzer, Albert (rank not known)	Staffel not known; ✞ 6-10-40
Kurzweg, Feldwebel Emil	7 Staffel, ✞ 30-7-40
Kussin, Feldwebel Hans	I. Gruppe, ✞ 1-10-40
Lang, Feldwebel	8 Staffel
Lange, Oberlautnant Hans	8 Staffel, ✞ 12-8-40
Laube, Feldwebel Erich	6 Staffel
Lemke, Feldwebel Fritz	6 Staffel
Lokuschuss, Feldwebel	8 Staffel, ✞ 12-8-40
Luckhardt, Oberfeldwebel Heinrich	3 Staffel, ✞ 19-9-40
Lüderitz, Oberleutnant	Stab
Mader, Gefreiter Eusabius	8 Staffel
Maier, Leutnant Gustav	7 Staffel, ✞ 24-9-40
Maier, Unteroffizier	7 Staffel, ✞ 27-9-40
Marienfeld, Major Walter, ★ (27-11-41)	*Gr. Kdr.*, III.Gruppe
Märte, Feldwebel Heinrich	II.Gruppe, ✞ 18-10-40
Mathias, Oberleutnant	8 Staffel
Maurer, Unteroffizier	7 Staffel, ✞ 25-8-40
Meiser, Leutnant	Staffel not known. ✞ 25-9-40
Meissner, Unteroffizier Helmut	7 Staffel
Merker, Gerfreiter	4 Staffel
Metschuldt, Unteroffizier Richard	III.Gruppe
Moser, Feldwebel Johann	7 Staffel, ✞ 19-8-40
Muche, Feldwebel Helmut	I.Gruppe, ✞ 1-10-40
Müller, Feldwebel	7 Staffel
Nölken, Oberleutnant Wilhelm	7 Staffel, ✞ 12-8-40
Noetel, Gefreiter Siebo	Staffel not known. ✞ 12-8-40
Nowak, Unteroffizier Gottfried	Staffel not known. ✞ 12-8-40
Oschliess, Feldwebel Ewald	7 Staffel, ✞ 30-7-40
Paczinski, Feldwebel Fritz	1 Staffel, ✞ 30-9-40
Pagel, Oberleutnant Wolfgang	1 Staffel, ✞ 22-7-40
Pahl, Fahnrich	9 Staffel
Panitzki, Hauptmann	1 Staffel (*St.Kap.* from 12-8-40)
Penka, Gefreiter	I.Gruppe, ✞ 30-9-40
Pfaff, Gefreiter	7 Staffel, ✞ 25-8-40
Pötter, Leutnant Joachim	7 Staffel
Rath, Oberleutnant	*Stab*, III.Gruppe
Rattel, Oberfeldwebel Josef	3 Staffel, ✞ 12-7-40
Rechenberg, Oberleutnant Dieter	3 Staffel, ✞ 17-7-40
Reisach, Unteroffizier Hermann	*Geschw. Erg. Staffel,* ✞ 20-10-40
Reiser, Unteroffizier Heinrich	Staffel not known. ✞ 12-8-40
Richter, Leutnant Wilhelm	I.Gruppe, ✞ 15-9-40
Rieder, Oberleutnant	Staffel not known. ✞ 6-10-40
Röder, Grefeiter	I.Gruppe, ✞ 19-9-40
Roppert, Gefreiter	I.Gruppe, ✞ 30-9-40
Rosch, Unteroffizier Konrad	8 Staffel, ✞ 12-8-40
Rothhäuser, Gefreiter Friedrich	7 Staffel
Roy, Leutnant Walter	5 Staffel, ✞ 26-8-40
Ruckdeschel, Leutnant	I.Gruppe
Rückert, Flieger Emil	5 Staffel, ✞ 26-8-40
Rueba, Obergefreiter	9 Staffel, ✞ 12-9-40
Schachtner, Feldwebel Max	7 Staffel, ✞ 19-8-40
Sched, Leutnant	*Stab*
Schifferings, Oberleutnant Ernst	9 Staffel, ✞ 8-8-40
Schlegel, Oberleutnant	II.Gruppe
Scholz, Unteroffizier Max	1 Staffel, ✞ 21-9-40
Schrägel, Unteroffizier Albrecht	III.Gruppe, ✞ 10-10-40
Schubert, Unteroffizier Konrad	I.Gruppe, ✞ 15-9-40
Schulz, Unteroffizier	7 Staffel, ✞ 25-8-40
Schulze, Unteroffizier	8 Staffel
Schulze, Unteroffizier	Staffel not known. ✞ 24-8-40
Schulze-Heyn, Major Hans Bruno	*Gr.Kdr.*, I.Gruppe; *Geschw. Kdr.*, from 12-8-40
Schuss, Feldwebel	4 Staffel, ✞ 12-8-40
Schwärzler, Feldwebel Josef	Staffel not known. ✞ 16-8-40
Schweisgut, Leutnant	*Stab*, III.Gruppe
Semper, Unteroffizier Gerhard	4 Staffel, ✞ 8-10-40
Siedel, Leutnant Paul	8 Staffel, ✞ 12-8-40
Simon, Oberleutnant	7 Staffel
Sonntag, Leutnant Siegfried	4 Staffel, ✞ 18-10-40
Stadlbauer, Gefreiter Franz	I.Gruppe, ✞ 6-10-40
Stahr, Unteroffizier Alfred	4 Staffel, ✞ 12-8-40
Stangel, Feldwebel Sebastian	Staffel not known. ✞ 16-8-40
Stegmüller, Oberfeldwebel Anton	4 Staffel, ✞ 18-10-40
Stelzner, Gefreiter	II.Gruppe, ✞ 15-9-40
Stern, Oberleutnant	III.Gruppe
Steszyn, Hauptmann Roman	1 Staffel (✞ 20-7-40, with KG 40)
Storek, Obergefreiter Herbert	4 Staffel, ✞ 12-8-40
Torpzisseck, Feldwebel Bruno	7 Staffel, ✞ 12-10-40
Velten, Feldwebel	8 Staffel, ✞ 12-8-40
Vivanco, Oberleutnant Horst de	II.Gruppe, ✞ 15-9-40
Vogel, Feldwebel Kurt	II.Gruppe, ✞ 15-9-40
Vogel, Feldwebel Kurt	Staffel not known. ✞ 16-10-40
Wagner, Feldwebel Johann	3 Staffel, ✞ 9-10-40
Walter, Feldwebel Wilhelm	3 Staffel, ✞ 19-9-40
Weindl, Feldwebel	8 Staffel
Wildemuth, Oberleutnant	8 Staffel, ✞ 12-8-40
Winkler, Major	II.Gruppe
Wilhelm, Unteroffizier Ernst	1 Staffel, ✞ 21-10-40
Wöhler, Unteroffizier Fritz	2 Staffel, ✞ 12-9-40
Wolf, Gefreiter	7 Staffel
Wolff, Feldwebel Hans	III.Gruppe, ✞ 10-10-40
Zimmermann, Gefreiter Helmut	9 Staffel, ✞ 28-10-40

KAMPFGESCHWADER 53
(KG 53 < *Legion Cóndor* >)

Long-range bomber *Geschwader* of II.*Fliegerkorps*, equipped with Heinkel He 111Hs, based at Lille-Nord, Belgium. Unit Codes, A1.

Altaker, Leutnant	8 Staffel, ✝ 1-8-40
Altmann, Unteroffizier	I.Gruppe
Anger, Leutnant	III.Gruppe
Armbruster, Unteroffizier	III.Gruppe
Bansch, Leutnant Helmut	II.Gruppe
Bauer, Feldwebel	II.Gruppe
Baumeister, Feldwebel Peter	8 Staffel, P.O.W., 12-7-40
Behrands, Feldwebel	II.Gruppe
Benz, Feldwebel	*Stab*, ✝ 15-9-40
Bergmann, Unteroffizier	II.Gruppe
Bettert, Feldwebel	4 Staffel
Bickl, Unteroffizier	III.Gruppe
Böck, Leutnant Hermann	I.Gruppe
Bohmert, Leutnant	II.Gruppe
Bohn, Feldwebel	III.Gruppe, ✝ 5-9-40
Bolte, Feldwebel Hans	8 Staffel, P.O.W., 12-7-40
Breuer, Oberleutnant	II.Gruppe
Brock, Unteroffizier	4 Staffel, ✝ 30-8-40
Brocke, Oberleutnant Helmut von	8 Staffel, ✝ 12-7-40
Broderich, Feldwebel	III.Gruppe
Büchler, Oberleutnant Gerhard	3 Staffel
Buttler, Unteroffizier	II.Gruppe
Chutz, Unteroffizier	II.Gruppe
Cichi, Leutnant Hans	2 Staffel
Cionber, Feldwebel	Stab
Distler, Feldwebel Georg	7 Staffel, P.O.W., 30-8-40
Ditrich, Oberfeldwebel Thomas	5 Staffel, ✝ 30-8-40
Dörig, Feldwebel	III.Gruppe, ✝ 9-9-40
Döring, Leutnant Arnold, ★ (3-43)	9 Staffel
Eckert, Feldwebel	II.Gruppe, ✝ 30-8-40
Endorf, Feldwebel	III.Gruppe, ✝ 9-9-40
Engelhardt, Feldwebel Adolf	9 Staffel, P.O.W., 24-8-40
Fauerleber, Unteroffizier Adolf	5 Staffel, Missing, 30-8-40
Fellner, Feldwebel Andreas	5 Staffel, P.O.W., 30-8-40
Fischbach, Leutnant Ernst	7 Staffel, P.O.W., 30-8-40
Fischer, Obergefreiter	3 Staffel, ✝ 30-8-40
Franck, Unteroffizier	4.Staffel, ✝ 30-8-40
Fraas, Feldwebel Alfred	9 Staffel, P.O.W., 24-8-40
Fritz, Oberleutnant	I.Gruppe, ✝ 9-7-40
Gall, Unteroffizier Helmut	3 Staffel, Missing, 30-8-40
Geiger, Unteroffizier	Stab, ✝ 15-9-40
Gerding, Unteroffizier	I.Gruppe
Gleissner, Obergefreiter Erwin	III.Gruppe, ✝ 24-8-40
Gluck, Gefreiter Friedrich	6 Staffel, P.O.W., 30-8-40
Grassi, Feldwebel	II.Gruppe, ✝ 15-9-40
Gruber, Major Max	*Gr. Kdr.*, II.Gruppe, P.O.W., 15-9-40
Günther, Gefreiter	II.Gruppe
Haak, Gefreiter	III.Gruppe
Hanau, Leutnant Günther	2 Staffel
Hartmann, Feldwebel Karl	8 Staffel, P.O.W., 12-7-40
Hermans, Unteroffizier Herbert	9 Staffel, P.O.W., 24-8-40
Hoffmann, Gefreiter	II.Gruppe, 15-9-40
Honig, Flieger	I.Gruppe, ✝ 7-9-40
Hugenschütz, Unteroffizier Hugo	5 Staffel, Missing, 30-8-40
Huhn, Oberleutnant	III.Gruppe
Hummel, Feldwebel Alois	5 Staffel
Kauffmann, Major	*Gr.Kdr.*, I Gruppe
Kempgen, Feldwebel	I.Gruppe
Klapp, Gefreiter Albert	6 Staffel, P.O.W., 30-8-40
Kliffken, Leutnant	I.Gruppe, ✝ 28-7-40
Klitscher, Unteroffizier Hans	9 Staffel
Köhler, Gefreiter Hans-Georg	6 Staffel, P.O.W., 30-8-40 (Died later)
Kollmer, Oberleutnant	I.Gruppe, ✝ 9-7-40
König, Unteroffizier	II.Gruppe
Kraft, Oberfeldwebel Jakob	2 Staffel
Kramer, Unteroffizier Alfred	III.Gruppe, ✝ 24-8-40
Kreuzer, Unteroffizier	1 Staffel
Kühnheim, Feldwebel Johann-Erhard	3 Staffel, ✝ 30-8-40
Kupfer, Leutnant	III.Gruppe, ✝ 10-7-40
Kurzawski, Obergefreiter	I.Gruppe
Kusserow, Feldwebel Wilhelm	9 Staffel, P.O.W., 30-8-40
Lackner, Unteroffizier Oscar	9 Staffel, P.O.W., 24-8-40
Lange, Unteroffizier	II.Gruppe, ✝ 15-9-40
Leber, Leutnant	III.Gruppe
Lehner, Unteroffizier	3 Staffel, ✝ 15-9-40
Lenger, Unteroffizier	III.Gruppe
Lichtenhagen, Feldwebel	II.Gruppe
Lonicer, Hauptmann von	III.Gruppe
Lüdecke, Unteroffizier Harry	9 Staffel
Ludmann, Leutnant	II.Gruppe, ✝ 18-8-40
Lüttigen, Leutnant Willi	9 Staffel, P.O.W., 24-8-40
Mauer, Gefreiter Willi	9 Staffel, P.O.W., 24-8-40
Mayer, Feldwebel	II.Gruppe, ✝ 15-9-40
Mehringer, Gefreiter Albert	8 Staffel, P.O.W., 12-7-40
Meier, Unteroffizier	Stab, ✝ 15-9-40
Meinecke, Oberleutnant	III.Gruppe
Metzger, Oberfeldwebel Heinrich	9 Staffel
Möhlenhoff, Gefreiter	II.Gruppe
Müller, Oberleutnant Karl	2 Staffel, ✝ 22-10-40
Müller, Oberfeldwebel	I.Gruppe, ✝ 7-9-40
Nagel, Feldwebel	II.Gruppe, P.O.W., 15-9-40
Neumann, Hauptmann	5 Staffel, ✝ 28-8-40
Neumann, Obegefreiter	II.Gruppe, ✝ 7-9-40
Novotny, Gefreiter	III.Gruppe
Panzel, Oberfeldwebel Karl	9 Staffel
Petroll, Gefreiter	II.Gruppe
Pfeiffer, Hauptmann	*St.Kap.*, III.Gruppe
Pitzkar, Oberfeldwebel	II.Gruppe
Platzer, Unteroffizier Karl	9 Staffel, P.O.W. 24-8-40
Raschmer, Unteroffizier	6 Staffel
Richter, Gefreiter	3 Staffel
Riess, Gefreiter Fritz	7 Staffel, ✝ 30-8-40
Ritscherle, Major Karı	III.Gruppe, ✝ 24-8-40
Römpert, Unteroffizier	6 Staffel
Rosenberger, Unteroffizier	III.Gruppe
Rösler, Leutnant Wolf	3 Staffel, Missing, 30-8-40
Rutig, Unteroffizier	3 Staffel, ✝ 15-9-40
Sailer, Gefreiter	II.Gruppe, ✝ 15-9-40
Salvino, Flieger Erich	III.Gruppe, ✝ 24-8-40
Sam, Unteroffizier Adolf	3 Staffel, ✝ 30-8-40
Schaffner, Unteroffizier Gerhard	III.Gruppe, P.O.W., 24-8-40
Schall, Unteroffizier	6 Staffel
Schattka, Leutnant	I.Gruppe, ✝ 29-7-40
Schiedel, Gefreiter	4 Staffel, Missing, 30-8-40
Schirning, Oberleutnant Hans	II.Gruppe, P.O.W., 15-9-40
Schmidt, Unteroffizier Hans	9 Staffel, P.O.W., 15-9-40
Schmittborn, Oberfeldwebel	II.Gruppe, P.O.W., 15-9-40
Schweiger, Feldwebel	*Stab*, ✝ 15-9-40
Seddvig, Leutnant	8 Staffel, ✝ 1-8-40
Seidel, Oberleutnant Hans	1 Staffel
Sigger, Unteroffizier Florian	9 Staffel
Simon, Leutnant	4 Staffel, ✝ 28-8-40
Stahl, Oberst	*Geschw. Kdr.*
Stamminger, Gefreiter	3 Staffel
Steinberg, Feldwebel Fritz	5 Staffel
Stilp, Gefreiter	7 Staffel, ✝ 30-8-40
Stock, Feldwebel Kurt	6 Staffel, P.O.W., 30-8-40
Tamm, Major	*Gr. Kdr.*, II.Gruppe, ✝ 18-8-40
Tonn, Gefreiter Helmuth	8 Staffel, ✝ 12-7-40
Uhrich, Gefreiter	II.Gruppe
Wagner, Gefreiter	8 Staffel, ✝ 12-7-40
Wagner, Unteroffizier	6 Staffel
Waier, Feldwebel	III.Gruppe
Weber, Oberleutnant	I.Gruppe
Weber, Unteroffizier Werner	8 Staffel, ✝ 12-7-40
Weidner, Feldwebel	1 Staffel
Wenninger, Feldwebel	III Gruppe, ✝ 9-9-40
Wieck, Unteroffizier Otto	9 Staffel, P.O.W., 24-8-40
Winkler, Major	*Gr. Kdr.*, II.Gruppe
Winter, Oberfeldwebel	I.Gruppe
Winter, Oberleutnant Gerhard	9 Staffel, P.O.W., 24-8-40
Woldmann, Leutnant	III.Gruppe
Zickler, Oberfeldwebel	1 Staffel
Ziller, Oberfeldwebel	1 Staffel
Zilling, Unteroffizier	II.Gruppe

Zipse, Oberleutnant	III.Gruppe
Zittwitz, Unteroffizier Heinz	8 Staffel, † 12-7-40

Wiese, Leutnant Karl	II.Gruppe, † 16-9-40
Winkler, Oberleutnant Max	II.Gruppe
Zingel, Oberfeldwebel	I.Gruppe, † 8-9-40

KAMPFGESCHWADER 54
(KG 54 < *Totenkopf-Geschwader* >)

Long-range bomber *Geschwader* of Luftflotte 3, equipped with Junkers 88A aircraft, based at Evreux (Staff and I,Gruppe), and St. André-de-L'Eure (II.Gruppe). Unit Codes B3. Heavily committed throughout the Battle of Britain.

Bauer, Feldwebel	I.Gruppe
Bauer, Unteroffizier Ernst	I.Gruppe, † 17-9-40
Belz, Leutnant	III.Gruppe, † 4-7-40
Birkenstock, Oberleutnant	I.Gruppe
Bischoff, Unteroffizier Gerhard	4 Staffel, † 4-7-40
Böggemann, Unteroffizier Hans	I.Gruppe, † 18-10-40
Brehmer, Oberfeldwebel	II.Gruppe, † 7-9-40
Brisch, Hauptmann	I.Gruppe, † 8-9-40
Erdmann, Oberleutnant	I.Gruppe, † 13-8-40
Fachinger, Oberfeldwebel Willi	I.Gruppe, † 17-9-40
Feldmann, Flieger Karl	I.Gruppe
Fischer, Leutnant	II.Gruppe, † 10-9-40
Fischer, Feldwebel	II.Gruppe, † 19-9-40
Fortmann, Feldwebel Rudolf	6 Staffel, P.O.W., 16-7-40
Fredebeul. Oberleutnant	II.Gruppe
Ganslmayr, Leutnant Rudolf	I.Gruppe, † 17-9-40
Gerling, Oberleutnant	II.Gruppe, † 14-8-40
Gödecke, Feldwebel	II.Gruppe
Hasreiter, Gefreiter Johann	I.Gruppe
Henke, Hauptmann Willi	I.Gruppe, † 16-9-40
Herbert, Gefr. Helmut	6 Staffel, P.O.W., 16-7-40
Heydebreck, Hauptmann	*Gr. Kdr.,* I.Gruppe
Höhne, Oberstleutnant	*Geschw. Kdr.*
John, Oberleutnant	II.Gruppe, † 10-9-40
Kalucza, Feldwebel	II.Gruppe, † 7-9-40
Karwelat, Unteroffizier Heinz	4 Staffel, P.O.W., 4-7-40
Kiefer, Leutnant	II.Gruppe
Klinkmann, Unteroffizier August	I.Gruppe
Köster, Oberstleutnant,	*Gr. Kdr.,* II Gruppe
Krack, Unteroffizier Hermann	4 Staffel, † 4-7-40
Kudina, Flieger	I.Gruppe, † 8-9-40
Leonardi, Major	*Gr. Kdr.,* II.Gruppe, † 11-8-40
Liebernecht, Feldwebel	II.Gruppe
Lockowandt, Gefreiter Otto	I.Gruppe
Mainwald, Hauptmann	II.Gruppe
Männer, Gefreiter Franz	I.Gruppe, † 18-10-40
Marb, Gefreiter Otto	6 Staffel, † 16-7-40
Matzel, Oberfeldwebel Heinrich	I.Gruppe
Meissner, Unteroffizier Heinz	I.Gruppe
Meyer, Oberleutnant	I.Gruppe
Neumann, Gefreiter	II.Gruppe, † 19-9-40
Niessel, Gefreiter	6 Staffel, P.O.W., 13-8-40
Ofschonka, Feldwebel	I.Gruppe, † 8-9-40
Östermann, Oberleutnant	1 Staffel, † 13-8-40
Perleberg, Feldwebel	I.Gruppe
Pettau, Unteroffizier	II.Gruppe
Rattay, Unteroffizier	I.Gruppe, † 16-9-40
Rörig, Oberfeldwebel	II.Gruppe, † 19-9-40
Rosse, Oberleutnant	II.Gruppe
Schaden, Oberleutnant	II.Gruppe, † 11-8-40
Schauer, Unteroddizier	II.Gruppe, † 10-9-40
Schlake, Feldwebel	II.Gruppe
Schlössler, Unteroffizier Karl	I.Gruppe, † 17-9-40
Schmitz, Oberfeldwebel	II.Gruppe, † 7-9-40
Schott, Oberleutnant	II.Gruppe, † 11-8-40
Schrieber, Gefreiter Heinz	I.Gruppe, † 18-10-40
Schwenzfeier, Unteroffizier	II.Gruppe
Strauch, Hauptmann Wilhelm	II.Gruppe, † 13-8-40
Streitz, Unteroffizier Rudolf	I.Gruppe
Trenz, Gefreiter Alois	I.Gruppe, † 18-10-40
Vetter, Obergefreiter Herbert	6 Staffel, † 16-7-40
Weiler, Gefreiter	II.Gruppe, † 10-9-40
Welte, Oberleutnant	II.Gruppe
Wiegand, Oberleutnant	5 Staffel, † 7-9-40

KAMPFGESCHWADER 55
(KG 55 < *Greifen-Geschwader* >)

Long-range bomber *Geschwader* of V.*Fliegerkorps,* *Luftflotte 3,* equipped with Heinkel He 111H and P aircraft. Headquarters and III.*Gruppe* based at Villacoublay, I.*Gruppe* at Dreux and II.*Gruppe* at Chartres. Unit Codes G1.

Albert, Feldwebel	I.Gruppe, † 19-9-40
Altrichter, Unteroffizier	I.Gruppe, † 25-9-40
Barabas, Unteroffizier	*Stab,* † 30-9-40
Bauer, Gefreiter	II.Gruppe
Beck, Gefreiter	II.Gruppe, † 25-9-40
Biedmann, Gefreiter	II.Gruppe
Birkholz, Feldwebel	III.Gruppe, † 29-9-40
Boker, Unteroffizier Kurt	8 Staffel, P.O.W., 27-7-40
Brand, Hauptmann Helmut	II.Gruppe, † 25-9-40
Bröcker, Oberleutnant Hans	III.Gruppe, † 25-9-40
Brossler, Oberleutnant	*Stab,* † 14-8-40
Duren, Unteroffizier Hans	I.Gruppe, P.O.W., 26-8-40
Eggert, Unteroffizier	II.Gruppe
Eitner, Oberleutnant Bodo	*Stab,* † 26-1-40
Engel, Feldwebel	II.Gruppe
Ens, Feldwebel Ernst	8 Staffel, † 8-10-40
Ernstberger, Unteroffizier Johann	8 Staffel, † 8-10-40
Firchau, Unteroffizier	III.Gruppe, † 29-9-40
Flügge, Leutnant Ulrich	8 Staffel, † 8-10-40
Frank, Oberst i.G.	Ch.d.St.Lg. VIII, with KG 55, † 14-8-40
Gailk, Feldwebel Heinrich	II.Gruppe
Gass, Feldwebel	II.Gruppe, † 24-10-40
Geib, Gefreiter	II.Gruppe
Geiger, Unteroffizier	*Stab,* † 14-9-40
Geist, Flieger	I.Gruppe
Gerdsmeier, Feldwebel	II.Gruppe
Gers, Unteroffizier	I.Gruppe
Geyer, Obergefreiter	II.Gruppe
Gittler, Oberfeldwebel	II.Gruppe
Goliath, Unteroffizier	I.Gruppe, † 19-9-40
Göpel, Leutnant	I.Gruppe
Günther, Gefreiter	III.Gruppe, † 29-9-40
Haidt, Stabfeldwebel Heinrich	II.Gruppe
Hanft, Unteroffizier	III.Gruppe, † 25-9-40
Hansen, Leutnant Wolfgang	4 Staffel
Heiland, Leutnant Gerhard	II.Gruppe
Hennecke, Feldwebel Otto	4 Staffel, † 26-8-40
Herber, Unteroffizier Ernst	8 Staffel, † 8-10-40
Jerusel, Leutnant	III.Gruppe
Jesuiter, Oberfeldwebel	II.Gruppe, † 24-10-40
Jürges, Feldwebel	I.Gruppe
Kalina, Feldwebel Heinz	*Stab,* P.O.W., 12-7-40
Karbe, Oberleutnant	I.Gruppe
Kirschhoff, Oberfeldwebel	II.Gruppe, † 25-9-40
Kleinhanns, Oberleutnant Walther	*Stab,* † 12-7-40
Kless, Major Friedrich, ★ (14-10-40)	*Gr. Kdr.,* I.Gruppe
Knecht, Oberfeldwebel Fritz	*Stab,* P.O.W., 12-7-40
Köhler, Oberleutnant Hans	III.Gruppe
Korte, Major	*Gr. Kdr.,* I.Gruppe, and later *Geschw. Kdr.*
Kothke, Hauptmann Karl	I.Gruppe
Krenn, Oberleutnant Igo	I.Gruppe, P.O.W., 26-8-40
Kübler, Unteroffizier	II.Gruppe, † 30-9-40
Kühl, Major Ernst, ★★ (26-10-42 and 18-12-43)	*Stab*
Lachemaier, Major	*Gr. Kdr.,* II.Gruppe
Liebenstein, Tr.Arzt Dr. Freiherr von	II.Gruppe, † 14-8-40
Lippert, Feldwebel	III.Gruppe
Mankl, Feldwebel Josef	8 Staffel, P.O.W., 5-8-40
Marmer, Unteroffizier Fritz	4 Staffel, P.O.W., 26-8-40
Mertz, Unteroffizier	II.Gruppe, † 25-9-40
Metzger, Leutnant	II.Gruppe
Metzner, Feldwebel Theodor	8 Staffel, P.O.W., 27-7-40
Möhn, Feldwebel John	*Stab,* P.O.W., 12-7-40
Möller, Oberfeldwebel Werner	II.Gruppe

Morgenthal, Gefreiter	8 Staffel, P.O.W., 29-7-40
Morrack, Unteroffizier Helmut	I.Gruppe, P.O.W., 26-8-40
Mössner, Oberleutnant Hans	I.Gruppe
Müller, Oberfeldwebel Philipp	*Stab*, P.O.W., 12-7-40
Müller, Flieger Otto	I.Gruppe
Müller, Unteroffizier	2 Staffel, ✝ 11-7-40
Narres, Oberfeldwebel	II.Gruppe
Nedden, Oberleutnant	III.Gruppe
Nützel, Leutnant	III.Gruppe, ✝ 28-8-40
Oberhofer, Leutnant Franz	*Stab*, ✝ 26-10-40
Ostheimer, Gefreiter	8 Staffel, P.O.W., 29-7-40
Parei, Leutnant Hans	*Stab*, ✝ 14-9-40
Peterson, Obergefreiter	*Stab*, ✝ 14-9-40
Pewlik, Gefreiter Hans	8 Staffel, ✝ 8-10-40
Pöhl, Unteroffizier	I.Gruppe, ✝ 19-9-40
Reiter, Unteroffizier	I.Gruppe
Richter, Leutnant Gerhard, ★ (24-11-40)	III.Gruppe
Rockenhäusen, Leutnant Helmut	III.Gruppe, ✝ 13-9-40
Rösel, Gefreiter	II.Gruppe
Rudek, Gefreiter	II.Gruppe
Sabler, Hauptmann	II.Gruppe, ✝ 16-8-40
Scharps, Unteroffizier	III.Gruppe
Schlemell, Major	*Gr. Kdr.*, III.Gruppe
Schlink, Leutnant Friedrich	*Stab*, ✝ 14-9-40
Schlüter, Oberfeldwebel	2 Staffel, ✝ 11-7-40
Schneiders, Unteroffizier Willi	4 Staffel, P.O.W., 26-8-40
Schob, Unteroffizier	2 Staffel
Schocke, Obergefreiter	II.Gruppe, ✝ 30-9-40
Scholz, Oberleutnant Harry	III.Gruppe, ✝ 25-9-40
Schreck, Feldwebel Louis	I.Gruppe, P.O.W., 26-8-40
Schufft, Unteroffizier Oscar	4 Staffel, P.O.W., 26-8-40
Schweinhagen, Oberleutnant Siefried	2 Staffel, P.O.W., 11-7-40
Schweinitz, Oberleutnant Graf	2 Staffel
Slotosch, Oberfeldwebel Erich	2 Staffel, P.O.W., 11-7-40
Steiner, Feldwebel Herbert	2 Staffel, P.O.W., 11-7-40
Stoeckl, Oberst Alois	*Geschw. Kdr.*, ✝ 14-8-40
Strauss, Gefreiter	II.Gruppe
Theobald, Leutnant	III.Gruppe
Thümel, Gefreiter	I.Gruppe
Thurner, Leutnant Hans, ★★ (6-8-41 and 20-9-44)	*Staffel* not known
Trenkmann, Unteroffizier	I.Gruppe
Walter, Leutnant Klaus	4 Staffel, P.O.W., 26-8-40
Wamser, Oberleutnant Erich	II.Gruppe, ✝ 24-10-40
Wandfrei, Leutnant	II.Gruppe, ✝ 14-8-40
Wanger, Gefreiter	*Stab*, ✝ 14-9-40
Wastian, Gefreiter	2 Staffel
Weidner, Unteroffizier	III.Gruppe, ✝ 25-9-40
Weigel, Oberleutnant Gottfried	II.Gruppe, ✝ 25-9-40
Weissbach, Gefreiter	I.Gruppe
Westhaus, Oberleutnant	III.Gruppe, ✝ 19-7-40
Widmann, Unteroffizier	2 Staffel
Wieland, Oberleutnant	II.Gruppe
Wimmer, Flieger Sepp	4 Staffel, P.O.W., 26-8-40
Wittmer, Leutnant Heinrich, ★ (12-11-41)	*Staffel* not known
Witzkamp, Oberfeldwebel	II.Gruppe, ✝ 25-9-40
Wolf-Witte, Oberleutnant	III.Gruppe
Wrenski, Leutnant	III.Gruppe

KAMPFGESCHWADER 76
(KG 76)

Bomber *Geschwader* of I.*Fliegerkorps*, *Luftflotte 2*. Headquarters and Staff with Dornier Do 17s at Cormeilles-en-Vexin; I.*Gruppe* with Do 17s at Beauvais; II.*Gruppe* with Junkers Ju 88As at Creil, and III.*Gruppe* with Do 17s at Cormeilles. Unit Codes F1.

Agel, Unteroffizier	6.Staffel
Ahrends, Oberleutnant	9 Staffel, ✝ 18-8-40
Altenmüller, Oberleutnant	III.Gruppe, ✝ 4-10-40
Anameister, Unteroffizier	1 Staffel
Armbruster, Obergefreiter	1 Staffel
Bieseroth, Unteroffizier	II.Gruppe, ✝ 5-10-40
Böhme, Obergefreiter	9 Staffel, ✝ 15-9-40
Boss, Unteroffizier	II.Gruppe
Domenik, Oberleutnant	9 Staffel, ✝ 10-9-40

Donaubauer, Major i.G.	With 4 Staffel
Ebele, Unteroffizier Friedrich	7 Staffel, ✝ 27-10-40
Fahler, Feldwebel	II.Gruppe
Florian, Oberleutnant Martin	2 Staffel
Fritz, Unteroffizier Karl	7 Staffel, ✝ 27-10-40
Frölich, Oberstleutnant Stefan, ★ (4-7-40)	*Geschw. Kdr.*
Genth, Oberstleutnant	*Gr. Kdr.*, III.Gruppe, ✝ 29-7-40
Geyer, Unteroffizier	6 Staffel
Goschenhöfer, Unteroffizier	1 Staffel, ✝ 15-9-40
Graf, Gefreiter	II.Gruppe, ✝ 5-10-40
Grell, Leutnant	4 Staffel
Greza, Gefreiter	9 Staffel
Haenel, Unteroffizier	6 Staffel, ✝ 6-9-40
Heitmann, Unteroffizier	8 Staffel
Heitsch, Feldwebel	8 Staffel
Holdenriet, Gefreiter	9 Staffel, ✝ 15-9-40
Holzer, Oberleutnant Johann	II.Gruppe, ✝ 5-10-40
Hübel, Unteroffizier	1 Staffel, ✝ 15-9-40
Illg, Feldwebel Wilhelm-Friedrich, ★ (1-10-40)	9 Staffel, P.O.W., 1-9-40
Jöckel, Oberfeldwebel Richard	III.Gruppe, ✝ 25-10-40
Johannes, Unteroffizier Erich	7 Staffel
Karl, Unteroffizier Richard	7 Staffel, ✝ 27-10-40
Keck, Feldwebel	8 Staffel, ✝ 15-9-40
Kernbach, Leutnant	6 Staffel
Klepmeier, Leutnant	II.Gruppe
Kohn, Obergefreiter	6 Staffel, ✝ 6-9-40
Kolb, Feldwebel	II.Gruppe, ✝ 5-10-40
Kottusch, Gefreiter	9 Staffel, ✝ 15-9-40
Lamberty, Oberleutnant	9 Staffel
Lang, Oberfeldwebel	II.Gruppe
Leder, Leutnant	8 Staffel, ✝ 18-8-40
Lindeiner, Hauptmann	*Gr. Kdr.* I.Gruppe
Lommatzich, Oberleutnant	Stab
Maassen, Unteroffizier Mathias	9 Staffel, P.O.W., 1-9-40
Magin, Oberleutnant	9 Staffel, ✝ 18-8-40
Malter, Unteroffizier	9 Staffel, ✝ 15-9-40
Meister, Leutnant	III.Gruppe, ✝ 4-10-40
Mölinnus, Oberleutnant	6 Staffel
Möricke, Major	*Gr. Kdr.*, II.Gruppe, ✝ 24-8-40
Morr, Leutnant Fritz	III.Gruppe
Mroszinsky, Unteroffizier	III.Gruppe
Niebler, Feldwebel	3 Staffel, ✝ 15-9-40
Nier, Leutnant	4 Staffel
Nümber, Unteroffizier	9 Staffel
Osenow, Unteroffizier	8 Staffel, ✝ 15-9-40
Peters, Hauptmann	9 Staffel
Pfeiffer, Feldwebel	8 Staffel
Pohl, Feldwebel	III.Gruppe
Raab, Feldwebel	9 Staffel
Riesel, Gefreiter	6 Staffel
Roche, Feldwebel Erich	*Stab*, P.O.W., 7-9-40
Roth, Hauptmann	*St. Kap.*, 9 Staffel
Rupprecht; Unteroffizier	*Stab*, ✝ 7-9-40
Sauter, Feldwebel	8 Staffel
Schatz, Unteroffizier	3 Staffel, ✝ 15-9-40
Schmidt, Feldewebel Stephan	8 Staffel, ✝ 15-9-40
Schneider, Obergefreiter Gerhard	*Stab*, ✝ 7-9-40
Schneider, Oberfeldwebel Karl	*Stab*, ✝ 7-9-40
Schulte, Oberleutnant	*Stab*, II.Gruppe, ✝ 24-8-40
Schumacher, Feldwebel	6 Staffel
Sommer, Oberst Doktor	With 9 Staffel
Spiess, Gefreiter	9 Staffel, ✝ 1-9-40
Stodt, Oberleutnant	1 Staffel, ✝ 18-8-40
Stösser, Feldwebel Georg	III.Gruppe, ✝ 21-10-40
Stralendorf, Unteroffizier	9 Staffel, ✝ 10-9-40
Streit, Oberfeldwebel	9 Staffel
Teuffert, Feldwebel	9 Staffel
Wagner, Oberleutnant	6 Staffel
Wagner, Oberfahnrich	9 Staffel, ✝ 15-9-40
Wagner, Unteroffizier	III.Gruppe, ✝ 6-10-40
Wildhagen, Leutnant Heinz	III.Gruppe
Wilke, Oberleutnant Walter	3 Staffel
Wilpern, Obergefreiter Gustav	7 Staff, ✝ 27-10-40
Wissmann, Feldwebel	3 Staffel, ✝ 15-9-40
Wöhner, Feldwebel Heinrich	9 Staffel, P.O.W., 1-9-40
Zahn, Unteroffizier	8 Staffel

Zehbe, Oberleutnant Robert	1 Staffel, ✝ 15-9-40
Zremer, Feldwebel	3 Staffel

KAMPFGESCHWADER 77
(KG 77)

Bomber *Geschwader* equipped with Junkers Ju 88A aircraft. Not fully operational against the British Isles during July and August 1940, this unit was brought north to Laon, Neufchatel and Amiens during early September and suffered heavy casualties in raids on Southern England during the second half of that month. Unit Codes 3Z

Ackermann, Unteroffizier	2 Staffel
Adler, Feldwebel	*Stab*, II.Gruppe, ✝ 27-9-40
Baumann, Obergefreiter	8 Staffel
Berbecker, Oberleutnant Ernst	6 Staffel, ✝ 16-10-40
Bräutigam, Feldwebel	3 Staffel
Brendel, Oberfeldwebel	8 Staffel, ✝ 18-9-40
Brodbeck, Unteroffizier	*Stab*, II.Gruppe
Burkant, Feldwebel	9 Staffel
Burkhartd, Obergefreiter	5 Staffel
Büs, Hauptmann	*St. Kap.*, 5 Staffel, ✝ 29-8-40
Buschbeck, Gefreiter	8 Staffel
Carnet, Feldwebel Erich	II.Gruppe
Damerius, Unteroffizier	3 Staffel, ✝ 27-9-40
Damschen, Feldwebel	8 Staffel, ✝ 18-9-40
Dorawa, Unteroffizier	1 Staffel, ✝ 19-9-40
Eggert, Unteroffizier	8 Staffel, ✝ 18-9-40
Eichinger, Feldwebel	6 Staffel, ✝ 27-9-40
Einbrick, Gefreiter	3 Staffel
Etzold, Unteroffizier	1 Staffel
Fiebig, Oberleutnant Siegward	*Stab*
Föllinger, Gefreiter	8 Staffel
Friedel, Feldwebel	7 Staffel, ✝ 18-9-40
Fuchs, Oberleutnant Georg	8 Staffel, ✝ 18-9-40
Gallion, Oberleutnant Hans-Georg	8 Staffel, P.O.W., 3-7-40
Ganter, Unteroffizier	4 Staffel
Gebhardt, Unteroffizier	6 Staffel, ✝ 27-9-40
Gehring, Oberfeldwebel Heinz	6 Staffel, ✝ 29-10-40
Gillios, Oberleutnant	8 Staffel, ✝ 1-7-40
Gläseker, Unteroffizier	9 Staffel
Göbel, Oberfeldwebel	*Stab*
Görke, Oberfeldwebel	2 Staffel
Gorn, Feldwebel	8 Staffel
Graf, Feldwebel	9 Staffel
Grönke, Unteroffizier	5 Staffel
Gurnkrantz, Obergefreiter Fritz	II.Gruppe, ✝ 25-10-40
Hackmann, Obergefreiter	3 Staffel
Hartmann, Stabfeldwebel	3 Staffel
Hastrich, Unteroffizier	3 Staffel, ✝ 27-9-40
Hekers, Unteroffizier Wilhelm	III.Gruppe, ✝ 25-10-40
Herold, Unteroffizier	3 Staffel, ✝ 4-10-40
Hertlein, Unteroffizier	2 Staffel, ✝ 27-9-40
Himsel, Feldwebel	*Stab*, III.Gruppe
Hoffmann, Obergefreiter Erich	8 Staffel, ✝ 3-7-40
Hofmann, Obergefreiter Harmut	III.Gruppe, ✝ 25-10-40
Höhn, Oberfeldwebel Anton	II.Gruppe
Hollstein, Gefreiter Werner	III.Gruppe, ✝ 20-10-40
Hülsmann, Gefreiter	2 Staffel
Isensee, Unteroffizier	5 Staffel, ✝ 27-9-40
Jörn, Unteroffizier Ludvig	1 Staffel
Kapsch, Oberleutnant	I.Gruppe, ✝ 31-7-40
Kasing, Unteroffizier	3 Staffel, ✝ 27-9-40
Kissel, Feldwebel Erich	III.Gruppe, ✝ 23-10-40
Kless, Major Maxim	*Gr. Kdr.*, III.Gruppe, ✝ 18-9-40
Klinger, Unteroffizier Johann	1 Staffel
Köhn, Gefreiter	9 Staffel, ✝ 18-9-40
Kollmansmäger, Unteroffizier	1 Staffel
Krauss, Oberleutnant Otto	1 Staffel
Krebs, Flieger	2 Staffel, ✝ 27-9-40
Kretschmer, Feldwebel Erhard	II.Gruppe
Kretzschmann, Oberleutnant	2 Staffel
Kripmann, Feldwebel	8 Staffel, ✝ 18-9-40
Kuhn, Obergefreiter	5 Staffel, ✝ 27-9-40
Künkel, Unteroffizier	8 Staffel, ✝ 18-9-40
Kunz, Unteroffizier	1 Staffel
Kurz, Unteroffizier	9 Staffel, ✝ 18-9-40
Lauth, Oberleutnant Fritz	*Stab*, III.Gruppe, ✝ 18-9-40
Leppelt, Unteroffizier Ernst	*Stab*, III.Gruppe
Lesker, Gefreiter	9 Staffel, ✝ 18-9-40
Liebler, Oberleutnant Otto	*Stab*, III.Gruppe
Ludwig, Unteroffizier	3 Staffel
Lüschen, Hauptmann Friedrich	*Gr. Kdr.*, III.Gruppe
Lutze, Oberleutnant Karl-Heinz	*Stab*, II.Gruppe, ✝ 27-9-40
Marl, Feldwebel	5 Staffel
Menningmann, Unteroffizier	2 Staffel, ✝ 27-9-40
Merschen, Unteroffizier	3 Staffel
Meyer, Unteroffizier Josef	II.Gruppe
Möckel, Gefreiter	1 Staffel, ✝ 19-9-40
Möttig, Obergefreiter	4 Staffel
Müller, Oberfeldwebel Herbert	1 Staffel
Müller, Oberfeldwebel Robert	1 Staffel
Müller, Feldwebel Rudi	II.Gruppe
Neuweg, Gefreiter	8 Staffel, ✝ 18,9-40
Niederer, Feldwebel	5 Staffel, ✝ 27-9-40
Nölp, Feldwebel	4 Staffel
Nolte, Feldwebel	7 Staffel, ✝ 18-9-40
Oeser, Oberleutnant Friedrich	2 Staffel
Peltz, Oberleutnant Dietrich, ★★★ (14-10-40, 31-12-41,23-7-43)	II.Gruppe
Pfeiffer, Oberleutnant	III.Gruppe
Pflüger, Leutnant Walter	5 Staffel
Pirschan, Unteroffizier Kurt	III.Gruppe, ✝ 25-10-40
Precht, Feldwebe	3 Staffel, ✝ 27-9-40
Pröbst, Feldwebel	*Stab*, III.Gruppe
Reiner, Gefreiter	3 Staffel
Reinhardt, Gefreiter	5 Staffel, ✝ 27-9-40
Reiss, Oberleutnant Georg	9 Staffel, ✝ 16-10-40
Richter, Unteroffizier Erich	3 Staffel
Richter, Unteroffizier Gerhard	3 Staffel
Röder, Oberleutnant	I.Gruppe, ✝ 31-7-40
Rohne, Oberfeldwebel Herbert	*Stab*, III.Gruppe
Ruhlandt, Unteroffizier	3 Staffel
Ruthof, Feldwebel	*Stab*
Scheibner, Feldwebel	4 Staffel
Schmidt, Unteroffizier Gerhard	2 Staffel
Schmitt, Obergefreiter Walter	I.Gruppe
Scholz, Gefreiter	1 Staffel, ✝ 19-9-40
Schulz, Gefreiter	1 Staffel, ✝ 19-9-40
Schumann, Unteroffizier	2 Staffel
Seif, Oberleutnant Horst	6 Staffel, ✝ 27-9-40
Semerau, Oberfeldwebel	8 Staffel
Sergocke, Feldwebel	2 Staffel
Seiffert, Unteroffizier	*Stab*
Sonntag, Obergefreiter Ernst	1 Staffel
Spaar, Leuthant Walter	III.Gruppe
Stammnite, Unteroffizier	7 Staffel
Steiner, Oberleutnant	1 Staffel
Stier, Feldwebel	8 Staffel, ✝ 18-9-40
Strahl, Oberfeldwebel	1 Staffel
Tenholt, Unteroffizier	2 Staffel
Theilig, Unteroffizier Waldemar	8 Staffel, ✝ 3-7-40
Tiechtmayer, Gefreiter	5 Staffel
Treutmann, Gefreiter	8 Staffel
Tschentke, Gefreiter Wilhelm	II.Gruppe
Urban, Oberleutnant Heinz	3 Staffel, ✝ 21-9-40
Wagner, Leutnant Heinz	I.Gruppe, ✝ 28-10-40
Wahl, Feldwebel	9 Staffel, ✝ 18-9-40
Weber, Oberleutnant Hans-Ludwig	8 Staffel
Weidmüller, Unteroffizier	8 Staffel
Winkelmann, Unteroffizier	3 Staffel, ✝ 27-9-40
Winkelmann, Feldwebel	1 Staffel
Wursche, Feldwebel	7 Staffel, ✝ 18-9-40
Zabel, Gefreiter	1 Staffel
Zeller, Feldwebel	*Stab*, II.Gruppe, ✝ 27-9-40
Zetzsche, Hauptmann Günther	*St. Kap.*, 5 Staffel
Ziel, Oberleutnant Friedrich	5 Staffel, ✝ 27-9-40
Zimmer, Leutnant Josef	7 Staffel
Zinsmeister, Feldwebel	6 Staffel
Zott, Gefreiter	5 Staffel, ✝ 27-9-40

Note: Unteroffizier Smorlatzy, a *Sonderführer* of Lw.Kr.Ber.Kp.4, was killed in action over the British Isles whilst flying with KG 77 on 18-9-40.

Set, Leutnant-zur-See	2 Staffel, ✞ 21-7-40
Stelle, Oberleutnant-zur-See	2 Staffel, ✞ 26-9-40

KAMPFGRUPPE 100
(KGr. 100)

Navigational specialist and pathfinder unit equipped with Heinkel He 111Hs based at Vannes, Western France. Unit Codes 6N

Aschenbrenner, Hauptmann Friedrich	*Gr. Kdr.*
Begemann, Hauptmann Hans	1 Staffel, ✞ 20-10-40
Jürgens, Oberleutnant Gunter	1 Staffel, ✞ 20-10-40
Krische, Unteroffizier	1 Staffel
Nachtmann, Leutnant Heinz	*Staffel* not known. ✞ 25-10-40
Nilius, Unteroffizier Gerhard	1 Staffel, ✞ 20-10-40
Perkel, Gerfreiter	1 Staffel
Steiger, Unteroffizier Hans	1 Staffel
Stock, Unteroffizier	1 Staffel
Tomuschat, Feldwebel	1 Staffel
Zetzsche, Leutnant	*Stab*

KAMPFGRUPPE 126
(KGr. 126)

Previously a coastal reconnaissance unit, KGr. 126 was absorbed into the *Luftwaffe*'s strategic bombing force in mid-1940 and operated from several bases against Britain, equipped with Heinkel He 111H-4 and H-5 aircraft. Unit Codes 1T.

Blau, Gefreiter	1 Staffel
Drews, Leutnant-zur-See Hans	1 Staffel
Gläser, Unteroffizier Konrad	2 Staffel, ✞ 16-10-40
Granetz, Gefreiter Hans	2 Staffel
Greeven, Unteroffizier	1 Staffel
Grunewald, Leutnant-zur-See Günter	✞ 2-10-40
Günther, Feldwebel Heinz	2 Staffel, ✞ 17-10-40
Irrgang, Obergefreiter Hans	2 Staffel, ✞ 17-10-40
Kirchner, Gefreiter Robert	1 Staffel, ✞ 25-10-40
Löwe, Obergefreiter Walter	1 Staffel, ✞ 25-10-40
Mayer, Oberfahnrich Ernst	1 Staffel, ✞ 25-10-40
Mellin, Unteroffizier	1 Staffel
Mesche, Oberleutnant Paul	2 Staffel
Newald, Leutnant Kurt	2 Staffel
Plenert, Unteroffizier	✞ 2-10-40
Saal, Flieger	1 Staffel
Reith, Unteroffizier Hans	1 Staffel, ✞ 25-10-40
Schoder, Unteroffizier	2 Staffel
Schrader, Unteroffizier	2 Staffel
Schreyer, Leutnant-zur-See Kurt-Fritz	1 Staffel
Stender, Oberleutnant-zur-See Wilhelm	2 Staffel, ✞ 17-10-40
Tordik, Gefreiter Johann	2 Staffel, ✞ 16-10-40
Veit, Leutnant Friedrich	2 Staffel
Volkmar, Oberleutnant	3 Staffel, ✞ 16-8-40
Weger, Gefreiter	1 Staffel

KÜSTENFLIEGERGRUPPE 106
(Kü.Fl.Gr.106)

Coastal reconnaissance and maritime minelaying unit equipped with Heinkel He 115 and Dornier Do 18 aircraft, based at Norderney. Unit Codes M2

Arnim, Leutnant	3 Staffel
Brasch, Feldwebel	2 Staffel, ✞ 26-9-40
Brommen, Unteroffizier	3 Staffel
Geschke, Leutnant-zur-See	1 Staffel
Hennigsen, Gefreiter	3 Staffel
Heuveldorp, Oberleutnant	2 Staffel
Kahlfeld, Unteroffizier	2 Staffel
Kennengiesser, Hauptmann Hans	*St. Kap.*, 1 Staffel, ✞ 19-9-40
Kinzel, Leutnant-zur-See	3 Staffel
Kirchwehn, Obergefreiter	1 Staffel, ✞ 19-9-40
Lohse, Oberleutnant Joachim	1 Staffel, ✞ 19-9-40
Molis, Leutnant-zur-See	1 Staffel

KÜSTENFLIEGERGRUPPE 196
(Kü.Fl.Gr. 196)

Fleet reconnaissance and short-range coastal reconnaissance unit equipped with Arado Ar 196 floatplanes; *Staffeln* based at naval anchorages from Brest to Narvik, and single aircraft and crews detached with units of the German Navy at sea. Unit Codes 6W

Behrmann, Leutnant-zur-See	5 Staffel
Burk, Leutnant-zur-See	5 Staffel, ✞ 19-8-40
Eich, Oberfeldwebel Hans	1 Staffel
Hirschberg, Leutnant-zur-See	5 Staffel, ✞ 19-8-40
Kottwitz, Unteroffizier Willi	5 Staffel
Müller, Leutnant	5 Staffel, ✞ 30-7-40
Nowrat, Leutnant-zur-See	1 Staffel
Schlenker, Leutnant-zur-See	1 Staffel, ✞ 15-8-40
Stamp, Feldwebel Helmut	1 Staffel
Stelter, Leutnant	1 Staffel, ✞ 7-10-40
Thewaldt, Hauptmann Karl	*St. Kap.*, 5 Staffel, ✞ 17-10-40
Wiegmink, Hauptmann	1 Staffel

KÜSTENFLIEGERGRUPPE 406
(Kü.Fl.Gr. 406)

Maritime reconnaissance unit equipped with Dornier Do 18 flying boats based at Thiestadt, with detachments on Dutch, Belgian and French coasts. Unit Codes K6

Dietrich, Oberleutnant	3 Staffel
Logier, Leutnant-zur-See	3 Staffel, ✞ 2-9-40

KÜSTENFLIEGERGRUPPE 506
(Kü.Fl.Gr. 506)

Minelaying unit equipped with Heinkel He 115C floatplanes based at Trondheim and Stavanger, Norway. Unit Codes K6

Ballier, Oberleutnant-zur-See	3 Staffel, ✞ 3-8-40
Bergmann, Hauptmann Ernst-Wilhelm	3 Staffel, P.O.W., 16-9-40
Bierich, Oberleutnant-zur-See Richard	2 Staffel
Bock, Leutnant	1 Staffel
Ducoffre, Leutnant	1 Staffel
Fahn, Unteroffizier Hermann	2 Staffel
Hoffert, Oberfeldwebel	1 Staffel, ✞ 15-8-40
Kalinowski, Feldwebel Erich	3 Staffel, P.O.W., 16-9-40
Kemper, Leutnant-zur-See Karl-Heinz	1 Staffel
Kriependorf, Hauptmann Hans	3 Staffel, P.O.W., 16-9-40
Lenz, Oberleutnant-zur-See Gottfried	1 Staffel
Lucas, Oberleutnant Clemens	3 Staffel, P.O.W., 16-9-40
Lindner, Oberleutnant Karl	2 Staffel
Neuberg, Obergefreiter	1 Staffel
Raether, Oberleutnant-zur-See	3 Staffel, ✞ 29-8-40
Rentzsch, Major Wilhelm	1 Staffel
Richter, Leutnant-zur-See	3 Staffel, ✞ 1-8-40
Schmidt, Oberfeldwebel Josef	1 Staffel
Schroers, Unteroffizier Paul	1 Staffel, ✞ 15-8-40
Schweetke, Unteroffizier	1 Staffel
Starke, Leutnant-zur-See	3 Staffel
Tonne, Leutnant-zur-See Hans-Eberhardt	1 Staffel, P.O.W., 15-8-40

KÜSTENFLIEGERGRUPPE 606
(Kü.Fl.Gr.606)

Originally trained to attack coastal targets, this unit was based at Brest and took part in numerous raids against targets in the British Midlands from September onwards. Equipped almost exclusively with Dornier Do 17Z-3s. Unit Codes 7T

Arpert, Feldwebel Heinrich	1 Staffel

Blank, Oberleutnant-zur-See Erwin	2 Staffel, † 16-10-40
David, Unteroffizier	*Stab*
Dorfschmidt, Hauptgefreiter	*Stab*, † 3-10-40
Eiselt, Unteroffizier Kurt,	*Stab*
Fährmann, Gefreiter Rudolf	3 Staffel, † 16-10-40
Faupel, Feldwebel Heinrich	2 Staffel, † 16-10-40
Felber, Leutnant-zur-See Horst	2 Staffel, † 11-10-40
Fuchs, Unteroffizier	*Stab*, † 4-10-40
Göhlisch, Feldwebel Kurt	*Stab*
Harbou, Leutnant-zur-See Erich	† 9-10-40
Havemann, Leutnant-zur-See Heinz	3 Staffel, † 16-10-40
Hoferrichter, Obergefreiter Albert	*Stab*
Hölscher, Unteroffizier Karl	3 Staffel, † 16-10-40
Hoppmann, Gefreiter Walter	2 Staffel, † 11-10-40
Johannsen, Unteroffizier Heinz	1 Staffel, † 11-10-40
Krause, Leutnant-zur-See Jurgen von	1 Staffel
Krenzien, Leutnant-zur-See	2 Staffel
Krosigk, Oberleutnant-zur-See Eberhardt von	3 Staffel, † 21-9-40
Küttner, Unteroffizier Martin	1 Staffel, P.O.W., 21-10-40
Langer, Feldwebel Hans	† 9-10-40
Postel, Unteroffizier von	*Stab*
Rees, Leutnant-zur-See	1 Staffel
Richter, Oberleutnant Friedrich-Wilhelm	2 Staffel, † 11-10-40
Rübesam, Obergefreiter Albert	† 9-10-40
Saueracker, Leutnant-zur-See Martin	*Stab*
Schmidt, Leutnant-zur-See Max-Dieter	† 3-10-40
Schnacke, Obergefreiter Wilhelm	2 Staffel, † 16-10-40
Schörnich, Unteroffizier Fritz	1 Staffel, P.O.W., 21-10-40
Seidenstahl, Unteroffizier	*Stab*
Sibeth, Leutnant-zur-See	2 Staffel, † 14-9-40
Söcknitz, Unteroffizier Gerhard	3 Staffel, † 16-10-40
Starf, Feldwebel Hans	1 Staffel, P.O.W., 11-10-40
Steppat, Feldwebel Erhard	2 Staffel, † 16-10-40
Stirnar, Leutnant Walter	1 Staffel, P.O.W., 21-10-40
Stock, Leutnant-zur-See	2 Staffel
Sundermann, Obergefreiter Helmut	1 Staffel
Vetterl, Feldwebel Josef	1 Staffel
Vollbrecht, Leutnant-zur-See Paul	*Stab*
Weber, Unteroffizier Jürgen	2 Staffel
Weiss, Unteroffizier Heinrich	*Stab*
Wilm, Feldwebel	*Stab*, † 3-10-40
Wurdemann, Leutnant-zur-See Heinrich	1 Staffel, P.O.W., 21-10-40

KÜSTENFLIEGERGRUPPE 806 (Kü.Fl.Gr. 806)
KAMPFGRUPPE 806 (KGr. 806)

Originally a coastal bomber-reconnaissance unit, this became absorbed into *Luftflotte 3* as an orthodox bomber *Gruppe*, while retaining its nucleus of naval officers, Based at Nantes with detachments at Caen, and equipped with Junkers Ju 88As. Unit Codes M7

Baasch, Feldwebel	1 Staffel, P.O.W., 21-9-40
Bachmann, Unteroffizier Fritz	Stab
Brückmann, Oberleutnant Helmut	2 Staffel
Davidson, Leutnant-zur-See	Stab
Dresen, Unteroffizier	1 Staffel
Druschelka, Feldwebel	Stab
Erdmann, Feldwebel	Stab
Grunwald, Leutnant Günter	1 Staffel, P.O.W., 21-9-40
Jansen, Oberleutnant	Stab
Krüger, Feldwebel	1 Staffel, P.O.W., 21-9-40
Kunert, Feldwebel	Stab
Metzner, Oberleutnant-zur-See Otto	3 Staffel, † 25-10-40
Michael, Unteroffizier Harry	Stab
Müller, Obergefreiter Horst	Stab
Neumann, Oberleutnant Wilhelm	3 Staffel, † 25-10-40
Quedenau, Leutnant-zur-See	† 28-9-40
Reischerle, Oberleutnant-zur-See Günther	† 22-10-40
Schlegel, Leutnant-zur-See Herbert	2 Staffel, † 8-10-40
Schwengers, Hauptmann	1 Staffel, † 2-9-40
Sowade, Oberfeldwebel	1 Staffel
Springfeld, Gefreiter	1 Staffel
Strube, Feldwebel	1 Staffel, P.O.W., 21-9-40
Weigand, Unteroffizier	1 Staffel
Weth, Unteroffizier Helmuth	2 Staffel

KÜSTENFLIEGERGRUPPE 906
(Kü.Fl.Gr. 906)

Coastal minelaying unit equipped with Heinkel He 115Bs, based at Ijmuiden and Schellingwoude. Unit Codes 8L

Aldus, Leutnant-zur-See Otto	1 Staffel
Anderson, Leutnant-zur-See	3 Staffel
Biegel, Feldwebel Hans	2 Staffel
Bock, Unteroffizier	3 Staffel, † 2-9-40
Günther, Oberleutnant-zur-See Hans-Rolf	3 Staffel, † 2-10-40
Hildebrand, Oberleutnant-zur-See	3 Staffel, † 12-7-40
Kalkowski, Obergefreiter Ernst	2 Staffel
Kothe, Hauptmann Heinrich	1 Staffel
Krupp, Unteroffizier Wilhelm	2 Staffel
Meissner, Unteroffizier	1 Staffel
Neymeyr, Oberleutnant-zur-See Konrad	2 Staffel
Sack, Unteroffizier Erwin	2 Staffel
Steinert, Leutnant Doktor	3 Staffel, † 12-7-40

LEHRGESCHWADER 1
(LG 1)

Mixed unit mainly composed of former instructors and personnel of the pre-War Technical Development Flying Unit, deployed as operational within VIII *Fliegerkorps*, with Headquarters at Orléans/Bricy. I. and II.*Gruppen* were based at Orléans/Bricy, and III.*Gruppe* at Chateaudun, all with Junkers Ju 88 bombers. IV.(*Stuka*)/LG 1 was based in the Pas de Calais with Ju 87Bs, and V.(*Zerstörer*)/LG 1 flew Messerschmitt Bf 110s from Caen. Unit Codes L1

Adametz, Leutnant Hugo	14 Staffel
Annerl, Gefreiter Rudi	I.Gruppe
Battre, Unteroffizier Günter	III.Gruppe
Beck, Leutnant	V.Gruppe, † 13-8-40
Berchtold, Unteroffizier	15 Staffel, † 27-9-40
Bergsträsser, Feldwebel	I.Gruppe
Blasig, Hauptmann Arnulf, ★ (4-9-41)	*St.Kap.*, 10 Staffel
Borman, Major Ernst, ★★ (5-10-41 and 4-9-42)	*Gr. Kdr.*, III.Gruppe
Bossert, Gefreiter	I.Gruppe
Brandt, Oberfeldwebel Walter, ★ (24-3-43)	I.Gruppe
Brauchitsch, Hauptmann von	*Gr. Kdr.*, IV Gruppe
Braukmeier, Leutnant	14 Staffel
Bremser, Unteroffizier Karl	14 Staffel, † 4-9-40
Brügow, Unteroffizier	15 Staffel
Bruns, Feldwebel	13 Staffel, † 27-9-40
Bülowius, Oberst Alfred, ★ (4-7-40)	*Geschw. Kdr.*
Cramer, Major Heinz, ★ (18-9-40)	*Gr. Kdr.*, II.Gruppe
Debratz, Major,	*Gr. Kdr.*, II.Gruppe
Donner, Gefreiter Karl	III.Gruppe
Döpfer, Obergefreiter Karl	14 Staffel, P.O.W., 31-8-40
Döscher, Feldwebel Rudi	I. Gruppe
Ehrenfordt, Hauptmann	II.Gruppe, † 12-9-40
Eichorn, Leutnant Karl-Joachim	14 Staffel, P.O.W., 31-8-40
Eiselert, Leutnant	V.Gruppe, † 13-7-40
Forster, Unteroffizier	III.Gruppe
Furnwagner, Leutnant	11 Staffel
Gerigk, Unteroffizier	13 Staffel
Glienke, Oberleutnant	V.Gruppe
Gorisch, Leutnant Ernst	13 Stafel, † 15-9-40
Gottlob, Feldwebel Fritz	14 Staffel, † 31-8-40
Grafenreuth, Oberleutnant Ulrich von	*St. Kap.*, 15 Staffel, † 27-9-40
Gramling, Oberleutnant	10 Staffel
Gröwe, Unteroffizier	14 Staffel, † 31-8-40
Gröwel, Gefreiter	13 Staffel
Harzog, Leutnant	9 Staffel, † 7-8-40
Heinrich, Oberleutnant	I.Gruppe
Heinrich, Leutnant Otto	II.Gruppe, † 17-9-40
Helbig, Hauptmann Hans-Joachim ★★★ (24-10-40, 16-1-42 and 28-9-42)	*St. Kap.*, and *Gr. Kdr.*, IV.Gruppe
Heinz, Oberfeldwebel	*Stab*, I.Gruppe, † 29-9-40
Heyden, Feldwebel Werner	I.Gruppe, † 29-10-40
Hirsch, Oberleutnant	III.Gruppe, † 1-9-40
Hoffmann, Leutnant Ottfried	II.Gruppe, † 5-10-40

Hoffmann, Feldwebel Andreas	14 Staffel, ♱ 15-9-40
Hübner, Obergefreiter,	14 Staffel, 27-9-40
Jäckel, Unteroffizier Joachim	14 Staffel, P.O.W., 4-9-40
Jäckel, Feldwebel	15 Staffel, ♱ 31-8-40
Jahn, Gefreiter	II.Gruppe, ♱ 4-10-40
Junge, Oberleutnant Michael	14 Staffel, ♱ 4-9-40
Kanus, Major	Gr. Kdr., I.Gruppe, ♱ 8-9-40
Kern, Hauptmann Wilhelm	Gr. Kdr., I.Gruppe
Kirchbaur, Unteroffizier	II.Gruppe
Klemm, Gefreiter	14 Staffel
Köbert, Oberfeldwebel Rudolf	13 Staffel, P.O.W., 1-9-40
Koch, Unteroffizier	15 Staffel, ♱ 27-9-40
Körpke, Unteroffizier	V.Gruppe, ♱ 27-9-40
Kothe, Oberleutnant	11 Staffel, ♱ 28-7-40
Kramp, Unteroffizer	15 Staffel, ♱ 9-9-40
Kraus, Unteroffizier Franz	10 Staffel, ♱ 15-8-40
Krebitz,Leutnant	V.Gruppe
Krings, Feldwebe	III.Gruppe
Krischewski, Obergefreiter	14 Staffel, ♱ 4-9-40
Kross, Unteroffizier	II.Gruppe
Kuhn, Leutnant	12 Staffel
Külin, Gefreiter Stefan	III.Gruppe
Liensberger, Hauptmann	Gr. Kdr., V.Gruppe, ♱ 27-9-40
Lindemann, Feldwebel	14 Staffel, ♱ 29-9-40
Lorenz, Feldwebel	I Gruppe
Lorenz, Gefreiter	III.Gruppe, ♱ 27-9-40
Maltitz, Hauptmann von	I.Gruppe
Meinig, Feldwebel Werner	13 Staffel, P.O.W., 1-9-40
Meyer, Oberleutnant	Stab, ♱ 8-7-40
Müller, Oberleutnant	II.Gruppe
Müller, Oberleutnant	13 Staffel, ♱ 15-9-40
Münchenhagen, Hauptmann	10 Staffel
Neuenberg, Gefreiter	II.Gruppe, ♱ 5-10-40
Neumann, Unteroffizier	14 Staffel, ♱ 4-9-40
Osterried, Unteroffizier Karl	I Gruppe
Päckel, Oberleutnant Heinz	I.Gruppe, ♱ 17-10-40
Pfafflhuber, Unteroffizier	15 Staffel, ♱ 9-9-40
Pfanf, Leutnant	II.Gruppe
Pfeiffer, Obergefreiter Heinz	I.Gruppe, ♱ 17-10-40
Pohl, Oberleutnant	II.Gruppe
Reinhold, Feldwebel	15 Staffel
Rintelen, Leutnant Elmar	III.Gruppe, ♱ 24-9-40
Röhmer, Gefreiter Friedrich	III.Gruppe
Röhrung, Feldwebel	14 Staffel, ♱ 4-9-40
Rösler, Flieger	15 Staffel
Schaumann, Hauptmann	St. Kap., III.Gruppe
Schenplein, Hauptmann	III.Gruppe,♱ 13-8-40
Schlegel, Leutnant	12 Staffel, ♱ 8-10-40
Schlund, Oberfeldwebel Franz	IV.Gruppe
Schöffmann, Gefreiter	II.Gruppe, ♱ 4-10-40
Schultz, Feldwebel Franz	II.Gruppe
Sochting, Feldwebel	III.Gruppe
Sodemann, Oberleutnant Kurt	I.Gruppe
Sonneberg, Oberleutnant	II.Gruppe, ♱ 14-7-40
Speier, Unteroffizier	14 Staffel
Stahl, Leutnant	I.Gruppe
Steiner, Gefreiter	II.Gruppe, ♱ 5-10-40
Stief, Obergefreiter	14 Staffel
Strasser, Oberleutnant Richard	III.Gruppe
Stück, Gerfreiter	13 Staffel
Stützel, Oberfeldwebel	II.Gruppe
Suin de Boutemard, Oberleutnant	II.Gruppe
Swjetlik, Gefreiter	13 Staffel
Vanselow, Oberfahnrich	III.Gruppe
Vitende, Oberleutnant	II.Gruppe, ♱ 11-7-40
Wächtler, Unteroffizier	III.Gruppe, ♱ 27-9-40
Weber, Unteroffizier Hermann	10 Staffel, ♱ 15-8-40
Weckeisser, Oberleutnant Otto	15 Staffel
Weiske, Unteroffizier Heinz	I.Gruppe
Welz, Gerfreiter	13 Staffel
Werner, Leutnant	14 Staffel
Worbanger, Unteroffizier	II.Gruppe, ♱ 5-10-40
Wurm, Unteroffizier	III.Gruppe

LEHRGESCHWADER 2
(LG 2)

The second operational development *Geschwader*, LG 2 performed in several rôles throughout the Battle of Britain, including fighter-bombing (with Messerschmitt Bf 109E-7s), fighter escort (with Bf 109E-1s and E-4s) and photographic reconnaissance (7 *Staffel* with Messerschmitt Bf 110C-5s). Bases were Calais-Marck and Monchy-Breton. Unit codes were 3X (seldom if ever used before October 1940) on Bf 109s; L2 on Bf 110s.

Bühl, Oberleutnant Adolf	St. Kap., 1 Staffel
Claus, Oberleutnant Rudolf	II.Gruppe, ♱ 13-8-40
Dörffel, Oberleutnant Georg,★★ (21-8-41, 14-4-43)	St.Kap., 5 Staffel
Dörnbrack, Hauptmann Werner,★★ (21-8-41, 25-11-44)	St.Kap.,6 Staffel
Dürtgen, Leutnant	II.Gruppe
Ebeling, Unteroffizier Rudolf	7 Staffel, ♱ 20-10-40
Eberspächer, Leutnant Helmut, ★ (2-45)	7 Staffel
Eckert, Oberleutnant	7 Staffel, ♱ 2-10-40
Frank, Leutnant Heinz, ★★ (14-9-42, 12-1-43)	II.Gruppe
Gotting, Unteroffizier	I.Gruppe
Gottschalk, Feldwebel	II.Gruppe
Grote, Oberleutnant Horst, Freiherr, ★ (21-7-40)	4 Staffel
Harmeling, Oberfeldwebel	4 Staffel
Heckmeier, Unteroffizier	I.Gruppe, ♱ 11-9-40
Heyden, Feldwebel Werner	I.Gruppe, ♱ 29-10-40
Ihlefeld, Hauptmann Herbert, ★★★ (13-9-40, 27-6-41, 24-4-42)	
	Gr. Kdr., I.Gruppe
Klick, Unteroffizier	I.Gruppe
Lagois, Feldwebel Ehrenfried, ★ (4-44)	5 Staffel
Lemmerich, Oberleutnant Roland	7 Staffel, P.O.W., 20-10-40
Lenz, Leutnant Ludwig	Stab, I.Gruppe, ♱ 15-10-40
Ley, Unteroffizier	4 Staffel
Mairl, Unteroffizer Franz	3 Staffel, ♱ 20-10-40
Meyer, Leutnant Bruno	5 Staffel
Mörschel, Unteroffizier	4 Staffel
Nelson, Feldwebel	7 Staffel, ♱ 25-9-40
Pankratz, Feldwebel	6 Staffel
Perthes, Oberleutnant von	I.Gruppe, ♱ 31-8-40
Rank, Feldwebel Max	4 Staffel, ♱ 29-10-40
Schenk, Oberleutnant Benno von	St. Kap., 5 Staffel, ♱ 29-10-40
Stollnberger, Unteroffizier Hans, ★ (25-10-42)	II.Gruppe
Streibing, Unteroffizier	I.Gruppe
Striberny, Leutnant	3 Staffel
Thiem, Oberleutnant Egon. ★ (21-7-40)	St. Kap., 5 Staffel
Tritsch, Feldwebel Willi, ★ (1-43)	II.Gruppe
Trübenbach, Major Hans	Geschw. Kdr.
Weiss, Hauptmann Otto, ★★ (18-5-40, 2-1-42)	Gr. Kdr., II.Gruppe
Werdin, Oberleutnant	7 Staffel
Weyergang, Oberleutnant	7 Staffel, ♱ 25-9-40

STUKAGESCHWADER 1
(St.G 1)

Dive-bomber *Geschwader* of VIII.*Fliegerkorps* based during August 1940 at Angers with Junkers Ju 87B and R aircraft. I.*Gruppe*, operational in 1939-40 in Poland and France; II.*Gruppe*, formed on 6th July 1940 from III./St.G 51. III.*Gruppe*, formed 6th July 1940 from Träg.Gr. 186. Unit Codes A5 (some aircraft still carried 6G from III./St.G 51)

Aulehner, Gefreiter Max	5 Staffel
Bevernis, Oberfeldwebel Heinz, ★ (25-5-42)	7 Staffel
Bietmeyer, Obergefreiter Herbert	9 Staffel
Bischof, Feldwebel Emil	2 Staffel
Blumers, Oberleutnant Otto	9 Staffel
Boldt, Uneroffizier Martin	2 Staffel
Brück, Obergefreiter Georg	9 Staffel
Dilley, Hauptmann Bruno, ★★ (4-6-42, 12-1-43)	St. Kap., 3 Staffel
Druschel, Oberleutnant Alfred, ★★★ (21-8-41, 4-9-42, 20-2-43)	St.Kap.
Eppen, Oberleutnant Heinrich, ★ (5-7-41)	St.Kap., 1 Staffel
Erdmann, Feldwebel Bernhard	Stab, P.O.W., 25-7-40
Fick, Leutnant Ernst, ★ (2-10-42)	I.Gruppe
Fryer, Oberleutnant Tankred	Stab
Grossmann, Feldwebel Erich	Stab, P.O.W., 25-7-40
Hachtel, Feldwebel August, ★ (6-1-42)	4 Staffel

Hagan, Major Walter, ★★ (21-7-40, 17-2-42) *Geschw. Kdr.*
Hozzel, Major Paul-Werner, ★★ (8-5-40, 11-4-43) *Gr. Kdr.*, I.Gruppe
Karrach, Gefreiter Werner 5 Staffel
Kathe, Oberleutnant III.Gruppe, ✝ 28-8-40
Kaubisch, Unteroffizier Horst, ★★ (29-11-42, 25-6-44) II.Gruppe
Keil, Hauptmann Anton, ★ (19-8-40) *Gr.Kdr.*, II.Gruppe (ex.III./StG 51)
Koch, Gefreiter Willi 9 Staffel, ✝ 14-11-40
Lengenbrink, Unteroffizier Kurt *Stab*, ✝ 25-7-40
Mahlke, Hauptmann Helmut, ★ (16-7-41) *Gr. Kdr.*, III.Gruppe
Möbus, Leutnant Martin, ★★ (8-5-40, 27-4-44) I.Gruppe
Mühltaler, Leutnant III.Gruppe, ✝ 28-8-40
Müller, Unteroffizier Julius 9 Staffel
Nordmann, Leutnant Theodor, ★★★ (17-9-41, 17-3-43, 20-9-44) 8 Staffel
Osterreich, Unteroffizier Heinrich 9 Staffel
Ostmann, Oberleutnant II.Gruppe
Peppler, Oberleutnant *Stab*
Pytlik, Oberfeldwebel *Stab*
Roden, Leutnant II.Gruppe, ✝ 21-7-40
Saminarz, Obergefreiter Anton 9 Staffel
Schmidt, Obergefreiter Johann 9 Staffel
Schrepfer, Oberleutnant Karl, ★★ (19-6-42) II.Gruppe
Schütz, Unteroffizier Gerhard 9 Staffel

STUKAGESCHWADER 2
(St.G 2 < *Immelmann-Geschwader* >)

Dive-bomber *Geschwader* of VIII.*Fliegerkorps* based at St. Malo and Lannion during August 1940 with Junkers Ju 87B and R aircraft. Unit Codes T6

Banker, Leutnant III.Gruppe
Berndl, Feldwebel Alois, ★ (7-44) I.Gruppe
Bock, Feldwebel Albert, ★ (4-9-41) Staffel not known
Boerst, Oberleutnant Alwin, ★★★ (5-10-41, 30-11-42, 6-4-44) 3 Staffel
Brand, Feldwebel Hans-Joachim, ★ (12-43) 4 Staffel
Brücker, Oberleutnant Heinrich, ★ (22-6-41) *Gr. Kdr.*, III.Gruppe
Brücker, Oberleutnant Rolf 3 Staffel
Dinort, Major Oskar, ★★ (20-6-40, 14-7-41) *Geschw. Kdr.*
Enneccerus, Major Walter, ★ (21-7-40) *Gr. Kdr.*, II.Gruppe
Filius, Feldwebel Ernst, ★ (5-44) I.Gruppe
Freitag, Leutnant Bruno, ★ (5-10-41) 3 Staffel
Hamann, Oberleutnant III.Gruppe
Hamester, Oberleutnant Berhard, ★ (29-9-42) *St.Kap.*, 5 Staffel
Hitschold, Hauptmann Hubertus, ★★ (21-7-40, 31-12-41)
  Gr. Kdr., I.Gruppe
Jacob, Leutnant Eberhard, ★ (3-44) *Adj.*, II.Gruppe
Kühn, Leutnant III.Gruppe
Kupfer, Hauptmann Doktor Ernst, ★★★ (23-11-41, 12-1-43, 11-4-44)
  I.Gruppe
Lang, Leutnant Friedrich, ★★★ (23-11-41, 28-11-42, 4-7-44) I.Gruppe
Pekrun, Leutnant Dieter, ★ (22-6-41) Staffel not known
Plenzat, Feldwebel Kurt, ★★ (10-43, 27-1-45) 2 Staffel
Rosen, Leutnant von II.Gruppe
Schenkel, Leutnant *Stab*
Steen, Hauptmann Ernst-Siefried, ★ (17-10-41) Staffel not known

---

STUKAGESCHWADER 3
(St.G 3)

Dive-bomber *Geschwader* equipped with Junkers Ju 87Bs. Only I.*Gruppe* formed during summer 1940. Unit Codes S7

Braun, Leutnant Rudolf, ★ (14-6-41) 1 Staffel
Hofferick, Unteroffizier Ewald 3 Staffel
Imspringt, Unteroffizier Friedrich 3 Staffel
Krohn, Unteroffizier Fritz 3 Staffel
Kummer, Leutnant Walter 3 Staffel
Kusko, Oberleutnant *Stab*, ✝ 2-8-40
Morgenroth, Leutnant Eberhard
Müller, Oberleutnant I.Gruppe, ✝ 8-8-40
Sigel, Hauptmann Walter, ★★ (21-7-40, 3-9-42) I.Gruppe

STUKAGESCHWADER 51
(St.G 51)

Dive-bomber *Geschwader* with Junkers Ju 87Bs operational for a short period during the Battle of Britain. Headquarters base not known.

Hettinger, Feldwebel Franz, ★ (8-44) 1 Staffel
Naumann, Oberleutnant Helmut, ★ (22-6-41) I.Gruppe
Schwarze, Leutnant III.Gruppe

STUKAGESCHWADER 77
(St.G 77)

Dive-bomber *Geschwader* equipped with Junkers Ju 87B and R aircraft, based at and around Caen during August 1940. Withdrawn and dispersed to Argentan and Maltot during September. *Stabskette* flew Dornier Do 17Zs. Unit Codes (also used F1)

Amelung, Oberleutnant Heinz-Gunter, ★ (15-7-42) *St. Kap.*, 5 Staffel
Bode, Hauptmann Helmuth *Gr. Kdr.*, III.Gruppe
Bruck, Hauptmann Helmut, ★★ (4-9-41, 21-12-43) *Gr.Kdr.*, I.Gruppe
Dalwigk, Friedrich-Karl, Freiherr von und zu Lichtenfels *Gr.Kdr.*, I.Gruppe
Dann, Unteroffizier August 3 Staffel, ✝ 18-8-40
Dawedeit, Oberfeldwebel Herbert, ★ (3-44) 8 Staffel
Gläser, Leutnant Alexander, ★ (19-2-43) I.Gruppe
Grewe, Oberfeldwebel Josef, ★ (8-44) III.Gruppe
Henze, Leutnant Karl, ★★ (15-7-42, 6-6-44) *Adj.*, I.Gruppe
Hitz, Leutnant Günter III.Gruppe
Hörner, Flieger Siegfried 8 Staffel, ✝ 19-10-40
Huhn, Oberleutnant Kurt, ★ (4-43) II.Gruppe
Jakob, Oberleutnant Georg, ★ (27-4-42) *St.Kap.*, 2 Staffel
Kaiser, Gefreiter Alois 8 Staffel, ✝ 19-10-40
Kohl, Unteroffizier Erich 2 Staffel, ✝ 18-8-40
Meisel, Hauptmann I.Gruppe
Merenski, Oberleutnant II.Gruppe
Meuerer, Leutnant Josef 7 Staffel
Müller, Gefreiter Hans-Willi 8 Staffel, ✝ 19-10-40
Nowack, Gefreiter Bruno 8 Staffel, ✝ 19-10-40
Plewig, Hauptmann Waldemar, ★ (14-12-40)
  Gr. Kdr., II.Gruppe, P.O.W., 8-8-40
Pressler, Hauptmann Gustav, ★★ (4-2-42, 26-1-43) 4 Staffel
Sailer, Oberleutnant I.Gruppe
Schäffer, Oberleutnant Hans-Jakob 3 Staffel, ✝ 18-8-40
Scheffel, Oberleutnant Kurt I.Gruppe
Schmack, Hauptmann II.Gruppe
Schmidt, Oberleutnant I.Gruppe, ✝ 18-8-40
Schönborn-Weisenheid, Major Clemens, Graf von, ★ (21-7-40)
  Geschw. Kdr.
Sinn, Leutnant I.Gruppe
Sonntag, Oberleutnant II.Gruppe
Strecker, Oberleutnant *Stab*, ✝ 18-7-40
Wilhelm, Oberleutnant I.Gruppe

ZERSTÖRERGESCHWADER 2
(ZG 2)

Long-range fighter-destroyer *Geschwader* equipped with Messerschmitt Bf 110s under Jafu 3 in *Luftflotte* 3, transferred to *Luftflotte* 2 on 29th August 1940. Originally based at Tousée-le-Noble, Amiens and Guyancourt; later deployed to St. Aubin and Berck-sur-Mer. Unit Codes 3M (*Stab* and I.*Gruppe*) and A2 (II.*Gruppe*). The total aircrew establishment of this *Geschwader* during the Battle of Britain was 124 pilots and gunners.

Abert, Leutnant Hans Dietrich 1 Staffel, ✝ 7-9-40
Becker, Unteroffizier Siegfried 1 Staffel, P.O.W., 2-9-40
Beil, Feldwebel II.Gruppe, ✝ 2-9-40
Bendjus, Unteroffizier Heinz *Stab*, P.O.W., 4-9-40
Blume, Oberleutnant I.Gruppe, ✝ 1-9-40
Brede, Oberleutnant Willi 4 Staffel, P.O.W., 9-9-40
Brief, Obergefreiter Josef 1 Staffel, ✝ 25-8-40
Carl, Major *Gr. Kdr.*, II.Gruppe, ✝ 16-8-40
Dahnke, Unteroffizier Reinhold I.Gruppe, P.O.W.. 7-9-40
Deuke, Unteroffizier II.Gruppe
Dyroff, Unteroffizier II.Gruppe, ✝ 30-8-40
Eppen, Oberleutnant II.Gruppe
Fiez, Gefreiter Heinrich II.Gruppe, ✝ 7-9-40
Galla, Unteroffizier August II.Gruppe, ✝ 7-9-40
Giglhuber, Obergefreiter Otto I.Gruppe, P.O.W., 13-8-40
Gottschalk, Oberlautnant I.Gruppe
Götz, Oberleutnant Gerard 1 Staffel, P.O.W., 25-8-40
Granz, Oberleutnant Gerhard II.Gruppe, P.O.W., 7-9-40
Grasser, Oberleutnant Hartmann, ★★ (4-9-41, 31-8-43) II.Gruppe
Haupt, Unteroffizier Kurt 1 Staffel, P.O.W., 7-9-40
Heinlein, Hauptmann I.Gruppe, ✝ 28-9-40
Hensel, Oberleutnant *Stab*, ✝ 11-8-40
Heyder, Leutnant II.Gruppe
Hoffmann, Unteroffizier I.Gruppe
Hoffmann, Leutnant Werner, ★ (14-5-44) II.Gruppe
Hollekamp, Oberleutnant II.Gruppe, ✝ 16-8-40
Jess, Leutnant I.Gruppe
Kiel, Oberleutnant Johannes, ★ (18-3-42) I.Gruppe
Kislinger, Leutnant 3 Staffel, ✝ 7-9-40
Kling, Gefreiter I.Gruppe
Knapp, Unteroffizier II.Gruppe
Korn, Unteroffizier I.Gruppe, ✝ 3-9-40

Kulbel, Hauptmann	St.Kap., I.Gruppe, ✝ 12-8-40
Labusch, Unteroffizier Fritz	1 Staffel, ✝ 13-8-40
Lessman, Hauptmann Karl-Heinz	Gr.Kdr., II.Gruppe
Mescheden, Unteroffizier	II.Grupp, ✝ 7-9-40
Messner, Oberleutnant	I.Gruppe
Meyer, Leutnant	II.Gruppe, ✝ 24-8-40
Müller, Oberleutnant	I.Gruppe
Münchmeyer, Leutnant Wolf	I.Gruppe, P.O.W., 13-8-40
Öhl, Obergefreiter	II.Gruppe, ✝ 2-9-40
Ohligschläger, Hauptfeldwebel Friefrich	3 Staffel, ✝ 7-9-40
Ott, Major	Gr. Kdr., I.Gruppe, ✝ 11-8-40
Otterbach, Oberfeldwebel Ernst	3 Staffel, ✝ 7-9-40
Santoni, Unteroffizier	I.Gruppe
Schäffer, Oberleutnant Wilhelm	Stab, ✝ 4-9-40
Scharf, Unteroffizier Hans	II.Gruppe, ✝ 7-9-40
Schipper, Leutnant	I.Gruppe
Schockenhoff, Gefreiter	I.Gruppe
Schönemann, Leutnant	II.Gruppe, ✝ 7-9-40
Schuberth, Unteroffizier	I.Gruppe, ✝ 3-9-40
Schuldt, Hauptmann	II.Gruppe, ✝ 30-8-40
Schumichen, Unteroffizier Kurt	I.Gruppe, P.O.W., 13-8-40
Schurk, Feldwebel	4 Staffel, ✝ 16-8-40
Schutel, Feldwebel Willi	I.Gruppe, P.O.W., 7-9-40
Sosser, Gefreiter	I.Gruppe
Stix, Leutnant Carl	II.Gruppe, P.O.W., 7-9-40
Vollbracht, Oberstleutnant Friedrich, ★ (13-10-40)	Geschw. Kdr.
Wagenbreth, Feldwebel	I.Gruppe, ✝ 3-9-40
Weiler, Gefreiter	I.Gruppe
Wetsphal, Leutnant	I.Gruppe, ✝ 25-8-40
Winkler, Oberfeldwebel	I.Gruppe
Wöpzel, Obergefreiter Walter	1 Staffel, P.O.W., 25-8-40
Krüsphow, Unteroffizier Erwin	2 Staffel, P.O.W., 11-9-40
Kuhrich, Leutnant	III.Gruppe, ✝ 10-7-40
Lidtke, Gefreiter	III.Gruppe, ✝ 27-9-40
Lüdtke, Hauptmann	St.Kap., 4 Staffel
Lutter, Feldwebel Johannes	III.Gruppe
Mader, Leutnant	3 Staffel
Makrocki, Hauptmann Wilhelm, ★ (6-10-40)	Gr. Kdr., I.Gruppe
Manhard, Leutnant	6 Staffel
Mauer, Unteroffizier	II.Gruppe
Meyer, Leutnant Eduard, ★ (20-12-41)	I.Gruppe
Meyer, Oberfeldwebel Willi	8 Staffel, P.O.W., 10-7-40
Naumann, Leutnant Johannes, ★ (9-11-44)	III.Gruppe
Nechwatal, Gefreiter Karl	8 Staffel, P.O.W., 27-9-40
Neuss, Unteroffizier	I.Gruppe
Obermayer, Unteroffizier	III.Gruppe
Preuler, Unteroffizier Paul	III.Gruppe, P.O.W., 7-10-40
Proske, Oberleutnant	I.Gruppe
Radelmeier, Feldwebel	II.Gruppe, ✝ 11-9-40
Repik, Gefreiter	III.Gruppe, ✝ 7-10-40
Rettburg, Hauptmann Ralph von, ★ (14-6-41)	Gr. Kdr., II.Gruppe
Rochel, Oberfeldwebel Kurt	5 Staffel, P.O.W., 2-9-40
Rohde, Feldwebel	I.Gruppe
Romm, Oberleutnant Oskar, ★ (6-8-41)	St.Kap., 5 Staffel
Roth, Unteroffizier	Stab, ✝ 6-9-40
Schalk, Oberstleutnant Johann, ★ (5-9-40)	Gr. Kdr., III.Gruppe
Scharnhorst, Leutnant	I.Gruppe, ✝ 1-10-40
Scherer, Feldwebel	III.Gruppe
Schilling, Unteroffizier	II.Gruppe
Schmidt, Unteroffizier	I.Gruppe, ✝ 27-9-40
Schözler, Unteroffizier Willi	5 Staffel, P.O.W., 2-9-40
Schuhmacher, Gerfreiter	III.Gruppe, ✝ 25-9-40
Schupp, Unteroffizier Fritz	8 Staffel, P.O.W., 27-9-40
Schulze-Dickow, Leutnant Fritz, ★ (7-3-42)	III.Gruppe
Schumann, Gefreiter	.7 Staffel, ✝ 6-9-40
Schütz, Feldwebel Karl	2 Staffel, ✝ 2-9-40
Sengbusch, Obergefreiter	III.Gruppe, ✝ 29-10-40
Sidow, Leutnant Kurt	III.Gruppe, ✝ 7-10-40
Siegmund, Oberleutnant	III.Gruppe
Sommer, Leutnant Bodo	III.Gruppe, P.O.W., 7-10-40
Spiess, Hauptmann Wilhelm, ★★ (14-6-41, 5-4-42)	St.Kap., 1 Staffel
Stahl, Oberfeldwebel	III.Gruppe
Stüwe, Feldwebel Herbert	2 Staffel, P.O.W., 2-9-40
Thierfelder, Oberleutnant Werner, ★ (10-10-41)	St.Kap., II.Gruppe
Tipelt, Oberfeldwebel	I.Gruppe, ✝ 27-9-40
Ucker, Unteroffizier	7 Staffel, ✝ 3-9-40
Viertel, Oberleutnant	Stab
Volk, Leutnant	6 Staffel
Wehmeyer, Leutnant Alfred, ★ (4-9-42)	III.Gruppe

ZERSTÖRERGESCHWADER 26
(ZG 26 < Horst Wessel >)

Long-range fighter *Geschwader* of *Luftflotte 2* equipped with Messerschmitt Bf 110s. I.*Gruppe* based at Yvrench, II.*Gruppe* at Crecy, and III.*Gruppe* at Barley. Unit Codes varied considerably during the Battle of Britain, I.*Gruppe* normally using U8 and E8, while II. and III.*Gruppen* used 3U.

ZERSTÖRERGESCHWADER 76
(ZG 76)

Long-range fighter *Geschwader* equipped with Messerschmitt Bf 110Cs and Ds. Headquarters and III.*Gruppe* based at Laval, France; II.*Gruppe* at Abbeville-Yvrench, France. Both units part of IX.*Fliegerkorps, Luftflotte 2.* I.*Gruppe* based at Stavanger, Norway, as part of *Luftflotte 5.* Unit Codes M8 and 2N.

ZG 26

Baagoe, Oberleutnant Sophus, ★ (14-6-41)	III.Gruppe
Bachmann, Obergefreiter	III Gruppe, ✝ 7-10-40
Barschel, Oberleutnant Hans	III.Gruppe
Becker, Unteroffizier	8 Staffel
Bergen, Oberleutnant von	8 Staffel
Birkner, Oberleutnant	4 Staffel
Brinkmann, Feldwebel Hermann	2 Staffel, P.O.W., 11-9-40
Brossig, Unteroffizier	I.Gruppe, ✝ 27-9-40
Deissen, Unteroffizier Klaus	II.Gruppe, ✝ 27-9-40
Demmig, Gefreiter	III.Gruppe
Driews, Unteroffizier	6 Staffel
Ebben, Unteroffizier Willi	3 Staffel ✝ 13-8-40
Eckert, Gefreiter	9 Staffel
Eiberg, Unteroffizier	III.Gruppe, ✝ 26-9-40
Feder, Feldwebel	I.Gruppe
Franke, Unteroffizier Rudolf	6 Staffel, P.O.W., 30-8-40
Gensler, Oberfeldwebel	II.Gruppe
Grau, Feldwebel	7 Staffel
Grisslich, Oberleutnant Hubert	III.Gruppe
Häfner, Unteroffizier	II.Gruppe
Haugk, Feldwebel Helmut, ★ (21-12-42)	III.Gruppe
Heinrich, Unteroffizier Herbert	4 Staffel, ✝ 26-8-40
Heller, Oberfeldwebel Richard, ★ (21-8-41)	III.Gruppe
Helmut, Oberleutnant	6 Staffel, ✝ 18-8-40
Henken, Oberleutnant	II.Gruppe, ✝ 11-9-40
Hertzog, Oberfeldwebel	II.Gruppe
Hofman, Obergefreiter	II.Gruppe
Hoppe, Hauptmann	4 Staffel
Hubner, Unteroffizier Willi	6 Staffel, P.O.W., 30-8-40
Huth, Oberstleutnant Joachim-Friedrich, ★ (11-9-40)	Geschw. Kdr.
Jackstedt, Gefreiter	III.Gruppe
Junghans, Oberleutnant	9 Staffel
Kaminski, Oberleutnant Herbert, ★ (6-8-41)	2 Staffel
Kästner, Leutnant	6 Staffel
Kaufman, Feldwebel	7 Staffel
Kennel, Oberleutnant Karl, ★★ (9-43, 25-11-44)	4 Staffel
Kiehn, Unteroffizier	I.Gruppe, ✝ 6-9-40
Kirchof, Oberleutnant	3 Staffel
Klatt, Unteroffizier	I.Gruppe, ✝ 3-9-40
Kleiber, Unteroffizier	4 Staffel, ✝ 11-9-40
Klose, Unteroffizier	III.Gruppe
Kogler, Hauptmann	St.Kap., 1 Staffel, P.O.W., 11-8-40
Konopka, Leutnant	III.Gruppe, ✝ 26-9-40
Köspel, Leutnant Joachim	I.Gruppe

ZG 76

Albrecht, Leutnant Egon, ★ (3-43)	9 Staffel
Anthony, Oberfeldwebel Georg	II.Gruppe, ✝ 30-8-40
Bartmus, Unteroffizier	II.Gruppe, ✝ 27-9-40
Bierling, Unteroffizier Georg	III.Gruppe, ✝ 9-9-40
Bilek, Unteroffizier Richard	1 Staffel, P.O.W., 4-9-40
Borchers, Hauptmann Walter, ★ (27-7-44)	St.Kap., 5 Staffel
Bremer, Oberleutnant	I.Gruppe
Calame, Leutnant	II.Gruppe
Castell, Leutnant	III.Gruppe
Conde, Gefreiter Rudolf	II.Gruppe, ✝ 4-9-40
Daun, Oberfeldwebel	III.Gruppe, ✝ 4-9-40
Dickoré, Hauptmann	Gr. Kdr., III.Gruppe, ✝ 15-8-40
Drewes, Leutnant Martin, ★★ (?,?)	III.Gruppe
Eckardt, Oberleutnant Reinhold, ★ (30-8-41)	I.Gruppe
Eichborn, Oberleutnant Wilfred von	II.Gruppe
Eisenach, Leutnant Franz, ★ (11-44)	II.Gruppe
Falck, Hauptmann Wolfgang	2 Staffel
Florenz, Oberleutnant	III.Gruppe
Göring, Oberleutnant	III.Gruppe, P.O.W., 11-7-40
Grabmann, Oberstleutnant Walter, ★ (14-9-40)	Geschw. Kdr.
Groth, Hauptmann Erich	Gr. Kdr., II.Gruppe
Hahn, Leutnant	II.Gruppe
Herbert, Gefreiter	III.Gruppe
Hempel, Obergefreiter	III.Gruppe, ✝ 4-9-40
Helwig, Unteroffizier	III.Gruppe
Herget, Oberleutnant Wilhelm, ★★ (7-43, 11-4-44)	II.Gruppe
Hommel, Unteroffizier Georg	II.Gruppe, P.O.W., 4-9-40

Hoyen, Hauptmann Graf	*St.Kap.,* III.Gruppe, ✝ 12-8-40
Kadow, Oberleutnant Gerhard	III.Gruppe, P.O.W., 11-7-40
Kaeser, Unteroffizier	III.Gruppe
Kaldrack, Hauptmann Rolf, ★★ (2-11-40, 9-2-42)	*Gr. Kdr.,* III.Gruppe
Karella, Unteroffizier	III.Gruppe, ✝ 9-9-40
Ketling, Oberleutnant	1 Staffel
Knop, Oberleutnant	*Stab*
Kociok, Feldwebel Josef, ★ (6-43)	III.Gruppe
Köhler, Leutnant	3 Staffel, ✝ 15-8-40
Koops, Feldwebel Hermann	3 Gruppe, P.O.W., 9-9-40
Kubisch, Oberfeldwebel Walter, ★ (1-44)	I.Gruppe
Lemmer, Leutnant	II.Gruppe
Linke, Leutnant Lothar, ★ (9-43)	I.Gruppe
Loobes, Oberleutnant	*Adj.,* I.Gruppe, ✝ 15-6-40
Lutter, Leutnant Johannes, ★ (5-10-41)	III.Gruppe
Mayer, Unteroffizier	III.Gruppe
Miakich, Leutnant	III.Gruppe, ✝ 15-8-40
Michael, Unteroffizier Max	II.Gruppe, P.O.W., 4-9-40
Mirow, Unteroffizier	III.Gruppe
Münich, Oberleutnant Hans	III.Gruppe, P.O.W., 4-9-40
Nacke, Hauptmann Heinz, ★ (2-11-40)	*St.Kap.,* 6 Staffel
Nordmeyer, Unteroffizier Heinrich	II.Gruppe, P.O.W., 30-8-40
Ostermüncher, Feldwebel	III.Gruppe, ✝ 9-9-40
Peterburs, Oberfeldwebel Hans, ★ (12-42)	III.Gruppe
Piduhn, Oberleutnant Gunther	II.Gruppe, ✝ 4-9-40
Rätsch, Oberleutnant Kurt	III.Gruppe, ✝ 4-9-40
Reinecke, Hauptmann	I.Gruppe
Restmeyer, Hauptmann Werner	*Gr. Kdr.,* I.Gruppe, ✝ 15-8-40
Schiller, Oberleutnant Walter	I.Gruppe, P.O.W., 4-9-40
Schlaffer, Oberleutnant	*St.Kap.,* III.Gruppe
Schlotheim, Oberleutnant Freiherr, Ernst Hartmann von,	
	II.Gruppe, P.O.W., 4-9-40
Schmidt, Stabfeldwebel	II.Gruppe, ✝ 30-8-40
Schob, Oberfeldwebel Herbert, ★ (9-6-44)	I.Gruppe
Scholz, Gefreiter Helmut	III.Gruppe, P.O.W., 11-7-40
Schröder, Leutnant	III.Gruppe
Schuhmacher, Oberfeldwebel Leo, ★ (1-3-45)	2 Staffel
Schultis, Unteroffizier Wilhelm	1 Staffel, P.O.W., 4-9-40
Viedebant, Oberleutnant Helmut, ★ (1-43)	*St.Kap.,* III.Gruppe
Wagner, Hauptmann	II.Gruppe, ✝ 30-8-40
Walther, Leutnant Gerhard, ★ (4-44)	II.Gruppe
Wandel, Oberleutnant Joachim	*St.Kap.,* 2 Staffel
Weber, Oberleutnant Hermann	II.Gruppe, P.O.W., 4-9-40
Weiher, Unteroffizier	III.Gruppe, ✝ 9-9-40
Weissflog, Leutnant Erich, ★ (7-44)	II.Gruppe
Wien, Oberleutnant	II.Gruppe, ✝ 15-8-40
Winkler, Feldwebel Helmut	I.Gruppe, P.O.W., 4-9-40
Wrede, Oberleutnant	II.Gruppe, ✝ 2-9-40
Zimmermann, Gefreiter	III.Gruppe, ✝ 9-9-40

ERPROBUNGSGRUPPE 210
(Erpr.Gr. 210)

Activatedunder Hauptmann Walter Rubensdörffer on 10th July 1940 (and taking over the designation of a unit originally intended to conduct Service trials of the Messerschmitt Me 210), Erpr.Gr. 210 was initially located at Denain in *Luftflotte* 2. It later detached *Staffeln* elsewhere in Northern France for setpiece attacks. *Stab*, 1 and 2 *Staffeln* were equipped with Messerschmitt Bf 110Cs and Ds (including a small number of D-0s), 3 *Staffel* with Messerschmitt Bf 109Es. Stab pilots occasionally flew the single-seaters. The unit was constantly employed on difficult and hazardout attacks, and suffered heavily as a result. Total aircrew establishment was never more than 36 pilots and 24 gunners.

Ahrenheim, Hauptmann von	*Gr. Kdr.,* from c.5-10-40
Bäde, Unteroffizier Hans-Georg	2 Staffel
Bertram, Leutnant	*Stab*, ✝ 11-8-40
Beuel, Leutnant	1 Staffel, ✝ 15-8-40
Boltenstern, Hauptmann von	*Gr. Kdr.,* 15-8-40 until ✝ 4-9-40
Brinkmann, Leutnant	Staffel not known, ✝ 14-8-40
Brokop, Leutnant	2 Staffel, ✝ 4-8-40
Büttner, Feldwebel Otto	2 Staffel, ✝ 29-10-40
Dünsnig, Feldwebel	1 Staffel, ✝ 5-10-40
Ebner, Feldwebel Fritz	2 Staffel, P.O.W., 27-9-40
Ebert, Feldwebel	Staffel not known
Eherkercher, Feldwebel Richard	*Stab*, ✝ 15-8-40
Ernst, Gefreiter Edmund	1 Staffel, P.O.W., 6-9-40
Fallenbach, Oberleutnant	*Stab*, ✝ 25-7-40
Fiedler, Oberleutnant	*Adj.,* *Stab*, ✝ 15-8-40
Forgatsch, Oberleutnant Heinz, ★ (23-9-41)	Staffel not known
Gerold, Leutnant	1 Staffel, ✝ 29-7-40
Glaske, Feldwebel Ernst	2 Staffel, P.O.W., 31-8-40
Gorlich, Leutnant Johann	*Stab*
Habisch, Oberleutnant	2 Staffel
Hesse, Unteroffizier Werner	*Stab*

Hintze, Oberleutnant Otto, ★ (24-11-40)	*St.Kap.,* 3 Staffel,
	Gr.Kdr., c.15-9-40 until P.O.W., 29-10-40
Horst, Leutnant Ulrich von der	*Stab*
Hübner, Unteroffizier	1 Staffel
Kepptisch, Feldwebel Helmuth	1 Staffel, ✝ 5-10-40
Koch, Leutnant	*Tech.Off., Stab*
Kopf, Feldwebel Josef	*Stab*
Kowatsch, Unteroffizier Joachim	2 Staffel
Lutz, Hauptmann Martin, ★ (1-10-40)	Gr.Kdr., 4-9-40 until ✝ 27-9-40
Marx, Leutnant	3 Staffel
Marx, Oberfeldwebel	2 Staffel
Neumann, Unteroffizier Walter	1 Staffel, P.O.W., 17-11-40
Ortner, Leutnant	2 Staffel
Ollers, Obergefreiter	*Stab*
Pfeiffer, Oberleutnant Johannes, ★ (10-10-41)	
	Gruppenführer, 2-9-40 to 4-9-40
Rehkugler, Unteroffizier Kurt	Staffel not known
Richter, Feldwebe	1 Staffel, ✝ 27-9-40
Rössiger, Leutnant Wilhelm-Richard, ★ (1-10-40)	
	St.Kap., 2 Staffel, ✝ 27-9-40
Röbermacher, Obergefreiter Willi	2 Staffel
Rubensdörffer, Hauptmann Walter, ★ (19-8-40)	*Gr. Kdr.* until ✝ 15-8-40
Rüger, Unteroffizier Gerhard	1 Staffel, ✝ 6-9-40
Schenk, Oberleutnant Wolfgang, ★★ (14-8-41, 30-10-42)	
	St.Kap., Staffel not known
Schlichter, Flieger Hermann	*Stab*
Schmidt, Leutnant Gerhard	1 Staffel
Schneider, Feldwebel	*Stab*, ✝ 4-9-40
Schön, Unteroffizier Anton	1 Staffel, ✝ 27-9-40
Schrank, Gefreiter Ewald	2 Staffel, P.O.W., 14-8-40
Schweda, Obergefreiter Konrad	2 Staffel, ✝ 31-8-40
Stäler, Unteroffizier Eckhard	*Stab*
Steding, Unteroffizier	2 Staffel, ✝ 14-8-40
Stoff, Obergefreiter Karl	1 Staffel, P.O.W., 17-11-40
Ströbel, Unteroffizier Hans	2 Staffel
Tratt, Oberleutnant Eduard, ★★ (12-4-42, 22-2-44)	1 Staffel
Tröppel, Feldwebel	2 Staffel, ✝ 29-10-40
Valesi, Hauptmann	*St. Kap.,* 3 Staffel, ✝ 5-10-40
Weimann, Oberleutnant	Gruppenführer, 4-10-40 until ✝ 5-10-40
Zwick, Gefreiter Werner	2 Staffel, ✝ 27-9-40

JAGDGESCHWADER 2
(JG 2 < *Richthofen* >)

Single-seat fighter *Geschwader* of *Jagdfliegerführer 3*, equipped with Messerschmitt Bf 109Es. I. and II.*Gruppen* based at Beaumont-le-Roger, III.*Gruppe* based at Le Havre.

Bader, Unteroffizier Walter	I.Gruppe
Bauer, Oberleutnant Viktor, ★★ (30-7-41, 26-7-42)	*St. Kap.*
Bertram, Hauptmann Otto, ★ (28-10-40)	*Gr. Kdr.,* III.Gruppe
Bühlingen, Oberfeldwebel Kurt, ★★★ (4-9-41, 2-3-44, 14-8-44)	
	Staffel not known
Bülow-Bothkamp, Oberstleutnant Harry von, ★ (22-8-40)	*Geschw. Kdr.*
Dietrich, Gefreiter Karl	*Stab*, ✝ 29-10-40
Dilthey, Unteroffizier	4 Staffel
Dollinger, Unteroffizier	II.Gruppe
Fiby, Leutnant	*Stab*
Falting, Oberleutnant Walter	III.Gruppe, ✝ 18-10-40
Fricke, Oberleutnant	III.Gruppe, ✝ 11-8-40
Glomb, Unteroffizier	II.Gruppe
Gotz, Oberleutnant	I.Gruppe
Grüsech, Oberleutnant	I.Gruppe
Hahn, Oberleutnant Hans, ★★ (24-9-40, 14-8-41)	*St.Kap.,* 4 Staffel
Harbauer, Feldwebel	II.Gruppe, ✝ 30-8-40
Heimberg, Leutnant	II.Gruppe
Hellriegel, Felwebel Horst	I.Gruppe
Hippel, Unteroffizier Georg	III.Gruppe, ✝ 26-8-40
Hoffmann, Leutnant	8 Staffel
Krahl, Hauptmann Karl-Heinz, ★ (13-11-40)	*Gr. Kdr.,* I.Gruppe
Leie, Oberleutnant Erich, ★ (1-8-41)	3 Staffel
Lux, Obergefreiter	III.Gruppe
Macholds, Oberleutnant	*St.Kap.,* 7 Staffel
Melchert, Unteroffizier	II.Gruppe
Mix, Hauptmann Erich	*Gr. Kdr.,* III.Gruppe
Moekel, Oberleutnant	II.Gruppe
Moller, Oberleutnant	II.Gruppe
Müller, Oberleutnant	II.Gruppe
Pflanz, Oberleutnant Rudi	Tech. Off.
Pollach, Gefreiter Alois	II.Gruppe
Raithel, Hauptmann Johann, ★ (17-10-41)	*Gr. Kdr.,* Gruppe not known
Reih, Unteroffizier	III.Gruppe
Rempel, Oberleutnant	II.Gruppe, ✝ 11-8-40
Schäfer, Leutnant	III. Gruppe, ✝ 14-9-40
Schnell, Leutnant	II.Gruppe

Schimmelheller, Leutnant | 1 Staffel
Schuhmacher, Gefreiter | II.Gruppe
Seeger, Oberfeldwebel Günter | *Stab*
Siebold, Fähnrich Hans-Eduard | I.Gruppe, ✟ 18-10-40
Sponeck, Oberleutnant Hans-Kurt, Graf von | *Geschw. Adj.*
Stein, Unteroffizier von | II.Gruppe
Strümpel, Major Henning | I.Gruppe
Temme, Oberleutnant Paul | I.Gruppe
Wenger, Leutnant Leopold | 3 Staffel
Wick, Major Helmut, ★★ (27-8-40, 6-10-40)
Gr.Kdr., I.Gruppe and *Geschw. Kdr.*

JAGDGESCHWADER 3
(JG 3 < *Udet* >)

Single-seat fighter *Geschwader*, fully activated against Britain during mid-August 1940, equipped with Messerschmitt Bf 109Es, under *Jafu 2, Luftflotte 2*. Headquarters and II.*Gruppe* based at Samer (from 14th August), I.Gruppe at Colombert (from 21st August), and III.*Gruppe* at Desvres.

Achleitner, Leutnant | III.Gruppe
Balthasar, Hauptmann Wilhelm, ★★ (14-6-40, 2-7-41) *Gr.Kdr.*, III.Gruppe
Bauer, Feldwebel | 7 Staffel
Bauer, Oberfeldwebel Wilhelm | 8 Staffel
Beyer, Leutnant Franz, ★ (30-8-41) | III.Gruppe
Binder, Leutnant | I.Gruppe, ✟ 31-8-40
Bittenfeld, Feldwebel von | 1 Staffel
Boremski, Oberfeldwebel Eberhard von, ★ (3-5-42) | III.Gruppe
Buckolz, Oberleutnant Max, ★ (12-8-41) | I.Gruppe
Busch, Leutnant Wilhelm | *Stab*, I.Gruppe
Dahl, Oberleutnant Walther, ★★ (11-3-44, 1-2-45) | *Adj., Stab*
Elbing, Unteroffizier | 7 Staffel
Engfer, Feldwebel Siegfried, ★ (2-10-42) | III.Gruppe
Fahrian, Unteroffizier | 6 Staffel
Floorke, Oberleutnant | *Stab*, ✟ 28-8-40
Fonderen, Leutnant von | III.Gruppe, ✟ 18-8-40
Gericke, Unteroffizier | 4 Staffel, ✟ 28-8-40
Gessel, Oberfeldwebel | 1 Staffel
Gollob, Leutnant Gordon, ★★★★ (18-9-41, 26-10-41, 24-6-42, 30-8-42) | II.Gruppe
Götz, Oberfeldwebel Horst | 5 Staffel, ✟ 29-10-40
Grabow, Unteroffizier | 3 Staffel
Hahn, Hauptmann Hans von, ★ (9-7-41) | I.Gruppe
Hopp, Oberleutnant Willi | *Stab*, ✟ 23-9-40
Keller, Hauptmann Lothar von, ★ (9-7-41) | 2 Staffel
Kienitz, Hauptmann Walter | *Gr. Kdr.*, III.Gruppe
Klöber, Leutnant | 2 Staffel, ✟ 5-9-40
Lampskemper, Oberfeldwebel | 2 Staffel
Landry, Leutnant | I.Gruppe, ✟ 28-8-40
Larisch, Leutnant | 4 Staffel, ✟ 31-8-40
Loidolt, Oberleutnant | I.Gruppe
Lützow, Major Günther, ★★★ (18-9-40, 20-7-41, 11-10-41) | *Geschw. Kdr.*
Massman, Unteroffizier | 7 Staffel
Michalek, Leutnant Georg, ★ (4-11-41) | I.Gruppe
Müller, Hauptmann | *St. Kap.*, 4 Staffel
Müller, Oberfeldwebel | 4 Staffel
Müller, Leutnant Friedrich-Karl, ★★ (14-9-41, 23-9-42) Staffel not known
Oesau, Hauptmann Walter, ★★★ (20-8-40, 6-2-41, 15-7-41) | III.Gruppe
Olejnik, Leutnant Robert, ★ (27-7-41) | I.Gruppe
Pfeifer, Unteroffizier | III.Gruppe
Rau, Oberleutnant Helmut | I.Gruppe
Rech, Oberleutnant Horst | III.Gruppe
Reumschüssel, Oberleutnant Helmut | *St.Kap.*, 7 Staffel
Rungen, Gefreiter Hubert | 7 Staffel
Schmidt, Leutnant Winfrid, ★ (18-9-41) | III.Gruppe
Schnabel, Leutnant | 1 Staffel
Selle, Hauptmann Erich von | *Gr. Kdr.*, II.Gruppe
Schück, Gefreiter Walter | *Stab*
Schuller, Gefreiter | 6 Staffel
Sochatsky, Leutnant Kurt, ★ (12-8-41) | III.Gruppe
Stechmann, Feldwebel Hans, ★ (4-9-41) | III.Gruppe
Tiedtmann, Hauptmann | *St. Kap.*, 2 Staffel
Viek, Oberstleutnant Carl | *Geschw. Kdr.*
Vogt, Oberleutnant Werner | *St. Kap.*, 4 Staffel
Volmer, Feldwebel | 1 Staffel
Wedel, Oberstleutnant Hasso von | *Geschw. Kdr.*
Werra, Oberleutnant Franz von | *Gruppe Adj.*, II.Gruppe
Westerhof, Oberleutnant | 6 Staffel
Wipper, Oberleutnant | 4 Staffel, ✟ 28-8-40

JAGDGESCHWADER 26
(JG 26 < *Schlageter* >)

Single-seat fighter *Geschwader* of *Luftflotte 2*, equipped with Messerschmitt Bf 109Es, based in the Pas de Calais.

Adolph, Hauptmann Walter | II.Gruppe
Arp, Feldwebel Heinrich | 2 Staffel, ✟ 22-10-40
Bartels, Leutnant Werner | III.Gruppe, P.O.W., 24-8-40
Beese, Feldwebel | 9 Staffel
Beyer, Oberleutnant Georg | *Adj., Stab*, P.O.W., 28-8-40
Bickir, Gefreiter Karl | 7 Staffel, ✟ 6-9-40
Blüder, Unteroffizier Hans | 4 Staffel, ✟ 1-10-40
Blume, Leutnant Walter | III.Gruppe, P.O.W., 8-8-40
Bock, Unteroffizier | 7 Staffel, ✟ 17-9-40
Bode, Unteroffizier | 7 Staffel
Borris, Leutnant Karl, ★ (25-11-44) | 8 Staffel
Braun, Unteroffizier Ernst | 6 Staffel, P.O.W., 7-9-40
Burschgens, Hauptmann Josef | 7 Staffel, P.O.W., 1-9-40
Butterweck, Oberleutnant | 1 Staffel, ✟ 12-8-40
Christinnecke, Leutnant Hans | 7 Staffel, P.O.W., 6-9-40
Dahmer, Unteroffizier Hugo, ★ (1-8-41) | 6 Staffel
Dahne, Oberleutnant Kurt | *Adj., Stab*, ✟ 14-9-40
Ebbighausen, Hauptmann Karl | *Gr. Kdr.*, II.Gruppe, ✟ 16-8-40
Ebeling, Oberleutnant Heinz, ★ (5-11-40) | *St. Kap.*, 9 Staffel
Ebersberger, Oberleutnant Kurt | *St. Kap.*, 9 Staffel
Eberz, Feldwebel Bernhard | 9 Staffel, ✟ 25-7-40
Eichstädt, Oberleutnant Kurt | 5 Staffel, ✟ 25-10-40
Fischer, Hauptmann Kurt | *Gr. Kdr.*, I.Gruppe
Fronhöfer, Leutnant Willy | 9 Staffel, P.O.W., 31-8-40
Galland, Major Adolf, ★★★★ (1-8-40, 25-9-40, 21-6-41, 28-1-42)
Gr. Kdr., III.Gruppe, and *Geschw. Kdr.*
Gartner, Oberfeldwebel Josef | 8 Staffel, ✟ 25-10-40
Gotthardt, Major Handrick | *Geschw. Kdr.*
Grzymalla, Oberfeldwebel | 8 Staffel, ✟ 23-9-40
Hafer, Leutnant Ludwig | I.Gruppe, ✟ 31-8-40
Haferkorn, Unteroffizier Gottfried | 2 Staffel, ✟ 23-9-40
Haibock, Hauptmann Josef, ★ (9-6-44) | 9 Staffel
Hasselmann, Oberleutnant | *Adj., Stab*
Henrici, Obergefreiter Eberhard | *St. Kap.*, 1 Staffel
Heyer, Obergefreiter Werner, | 6 Staffel, ✟ 31-8-40
Holtey, Oberleutnant Hubertus, Freiherr von | *St. Kap.*, 1 Staffel
Holzapfel, Gefreiter Peter | 7 Staffel, ✟ 6-9-40
Hornatschek, Gefreiter Heinrich | 9 Staffel, ✟ 30-9-40
Hörnig, Oberleutnant Franz | *St. Kap.*, 1 Staffel
Jäckel, Oberfeldwebel Konrad | 8 Staffel, ✟ 29-10-40
Jennewein, Unteroffizier Josef, ★ (5-12-43) | 2 Staffel
Kaminski, Hauptmann Herbert | II.Gruppe
Kemen, Feldwebel Gerhard | 1 Staffel, P.O.W., 14-8-40
Kienzle, Major Walter | *Stab*, ✟ 30-9-40
Klar, Feldwebel | 7 Staffel, P.O.W., 31-8-40
Kosse, Oberleutnant Wolfgang | *St. Kap.*, 5 Staffel
Krug, Leutnant | *St. Kap.*, 4 Staffel
Küpper, Feldwebel Arnold | 8 Staffel, ✟ 23-9-40
Liebeck, Gefreiter Horst | 7 Staffel, P.O.W., 31-8-40
Losigkeit, Hauptmann Fritz, ★ (4-45) | *St. Kap.*, 2 Staffel
März, Leutnant Waldi | II.Gruppe
Mietusch, Oberlautnant Klaus, ★★ (26-3-44, 18-11-44) Staffel not known
Müller, Gefreiter Otto-Gunther | 5 Staffel, ✟ 5-10-40
Müller, Oberfeldwebel Wilhelm | 3 Staffel
Müller-Duhe, Leutnant Gerhard | 7 Staffel, ✟ 18-8-40
Müncheberg, Oberleutnant Joachim, ★★★ (14-9-40, 7-5-41, 9-9-42)
St. Kap., 7 Staffel
Noack, Hauptmann Erich | *Gr. Kdr.*, II.Gruppe, ✟ 6-7-40
Öhm, Oberleutnant Willi | 8 Staffel, ✟ 8-8-40
Perez, Unteroffizier Horst | 4 Staffel, ✟ 30-9-40
Philipp, Feldwebel Wilhelm, ★ (26-3-44) | 4 Staffel
Pingel, Hauptmann Rolf, ★ (14-9-40) | *Gr. Kdr.*, I.Gruppe
Priller, Oberleutnant Josef, ★★★ (19-10-40, 20-7-41, 2-7-44)
St. Kap., 6 Staffel
Regenauer, Leutnant Hans-Werner | 2 Staffel, P.O.W., 12-8-40
Ripke, Leutnant Hermann | 8 Staffel, ✟ 25-10-40
Roch, Leutnant Eckhardt | *Stab*, II.Gruppe, ✟ 3-9-40
Rothenberg, Oberleutnant | *Adj., Stab*
Schauff, Leutnant | III.Gruppe, ✟ 24-7-40
Schmid, Oberleutnant Johann, ★ (21-8-41) | 8 Staffel
Schneider, Oberleutnant Walter | *St. Kap.*, 6 Staffel
Schöpfel, Major Gerhard | *Gr. Kdr.*, III.Gruppe
Schür, Feldwebel Fritz | 3 Staffel, ✟ 28-9-40
Sprick, Oberleutnant Gustav, ★ (1-10-40) | 8 Staffel
Straub, Feldwebel | 7 Staffel, P.O.W., 28-8-40
Töpfer, Unteroffizier Kurt | 7 Staffel, ✟ 30-10-40

Treuberg, Oberfeldwebel Graf von | 1 Staffel, ✝ 29-8-40
Wemhöner, Unteroffizier Hans | 5 Staffel, P.O.W., 13-8-40
Wendt, Oberleutnant Kuno | *St. Kap.*, 8 Staffel
Wolf, Unteroffizier Hans, | I.Gruppe
Ziemans, Gefreiter Helmut | 7 Staffel, ✝ 30-9-40

JAGDGESCHWADER 27
(JG 27)

Single-seat fighter *Geschwader* of *Jafu 3* equipped with Messer-schmitt Bf 109Es. I.*Gruppe* based at Plumetot, II.*Gruppe* at Crépon and III.*Gruppe* at Carquebut. Commanded by Oberst Max Ibel until 14th October 1940, thereafter by Major Bernhard Woldenga. Heavily committed throughout the Battle of Britain.

Ackmann, Unteroffizier Erich | III.Gruppe, Missing, 26-8-40
Adolph, Oberlautnant Walter | *St.Kap.*, 5.Staffel until 9-40
Ahrens, Oberleutnant Werner | 1 Staffel, Missing, 15-9-40
Andres, Hauptmann Werner | *Gr.Kdr.*, II.Gruppe until 30-8-40
Ankum-Frank, Hauptmann Albrecht | *St.Kap.*, 5 Staffel until ✝ 2-8-40
Arnold, Feldwebel Ernst | 3 Staffel, P.O.W., 30-8-40
Axthelm, Oberleutnant Erwin | 3 Staffel, P.O.W., 30-8-40
Balthasar, Oberleutnant Wilhelm, ★ (2-7-41) | *St.Kap.*, 7 Staffel until 7-40
Bartsch, Fahnrich Lothar | 9 Staffel, P.O.W., 7-10-40
Becker, Oberleutnant Arno | *St.Kap.*, 8 Staffel, from 10-40
Bendert, Oberfeldwebel Karl-Heinz, ★ (1-43) | 5 Staffel
Bertram, Oberleutnant Hans | *Adj.*, 2 Staffel, ✝ 30-9-40
Beushausen, Oberfeldwebel Heinz | 3 Staffel, ✝ 20-7-40
Birkenbach, Leutnant Igor | 1 Staffel, ✝ 8-8-40
Blazytke, Feldwebel Franz | III.Gruppe
Bode, Oberleutnant Günther | *Stab.*, I.Gruppe, P.O.W., 10-9-40
Böer, Feldwebel Günther | 2 Staffel, Missing, 26-7-40
Born, Unteroffizier Karl Bern | 7 Staffel, ✝ 9-9-40
Börngen,Leutnant Ernst, ★ (3-8-44) | II.Gruppe
Bothfeld, Leutnant Karl-Heinz | 1 Staffel, ✝ 8-8-40
Braun, Feldwebel Erich | 5 Staffel, P.O.W., 6-9-40
Braune, Oberleutnant Erhard | *St.Kap.*, 7 Staffel, from 7-40
Busenkeil, Gefreiter Albert | 9 Staffel
Clauser, Unteroffizier Erich | 9 Staffel, Missing, 20-9-40
Daig, Oberlautnant Erwin | II.Gruppe, P.O.W., 9-9-40
Deicke, Oberleutnant Günther | *St.Kap.*, 8 Staffel, from 15-10-40
Dobislaw, Hauptmann Max | *St.Kap.*, 9 Staffel; *Gr.Kdr.*, III.Gruppe
Düllberg, Hauptmann Ernst | *St.Kap.*, 5 Staffel, from 15-8-40
Eilers, Oberfeldwebel Klaus | 3 Staffel
Elles, Gefreiter Franz | 2 Staffel
Fluder, Oberleutnant Emmerich | 5 Staffel
Framm, Oberleutnant Gert | *St.Kap.*, 2 Staffel
Freis, Oberfeldwebel Gotthard | 6 Staffel, Missing, 15-10-40
Freis, Feldwebel Konrad | 6 Staffel, ✝ 15-10-40
Frank, Hauptmann von | II.Gruppe, ✝ 1-8-40
Franzisket, Oberleutnant Ludwig, ★ (23-7-41) | I.Gruppe
Genske, Leutnant Günther | 1 Staffel, P.O.W., 7-9-40
Gerhard, Feldwebel Rudolf | 3 Staffel
Gerlach, Hauptmann Hans-Joachim | *St.Kap.*, 6 Staffel
Gissbach, Unteroffizier Ludwig | III.Gruppe, Missing., 8-8-40
Glöckner, Gefreiter Walter | 9 Staffel, P.O.W., 18-9-40
Gonschorrek, Unteroffizier Artur | 5 Staffel, P.O.W., 28-10-40
Halbach, Leutnant Heinz | 5 Staffel
Hammer, Unteroffizier | 4 Staffel, P.O.W., 30-9-40
Harting, Feldwebel Wilhelm | 3 Staffel
Hollweg, Oberleutnant Hermann | *St.Kap.*, 4 Staffel, until 1-9-40
Homuth, Oberleutnant Gerhard, ★ (14-6-41) | *St.Kap.*, 3 Staffel
Ibel, Oberst Max, ★ (22-8-40) | *Geschw. Kdr.* until 14-10-40
Janssen, Unteroffizier Ernst | 3 Staffel
John, Gefreiter Hans-Dieter | 5 Staffel, ✝ 27-9-40
Kaganeck, Oberleutnant Erbo Graf von | 9 Staffel, from 18-9-40
Kargl, Fahnrich Otto | III.Gruppe
Kirstein, Oberleutnant Karl-Heinz | III.Gruppe
Kohl, Leutnant Hermann | II.Gruppe
Kothmann, Leutnant Willi | 2 Staffel
Krafftschick, Oberleutnant Rudolf | 1 Staffel, P.O.W., 18-9-40
Krenzke, Oberfeldwebel Erich | 5 Staffel
Kriker, Leutnant Heinz | III.Gruppe, ✝ 21-7-40
Lackner, Unteroffizier Siegfried | 5 Staffel, Missing, 11-8-40
Lage, Unteroffizier Paul | 5 Staffel, ✝ 7-10-40
Lederer, Unteroffizier Paul | 5 Staffel, P.O.W., 7-10-40
Lehmann, Feldwebel Georg | III.Gruppe, ✝ 30-8-40
Linke, Unteroffizier Ulrich | 8 Staffel, Missing, 24-10-40
Lippert, Hauptmann Wolfgang | *Gr. Kdr.*, II.Gruppe, from 1-10-40
Menz, Unteroffizier Rüdiger | III.Gruppe, Missing, 11-8-40
Mitsdörfer, Leutnant Gerhard | 1 Staffel., P.O.W., 18-8-40
Morgenstern, Unteroffizier Wilhelm | 4 Staffel
Neumann, Major Eduard | *Gr. Kdr.*, I.Gruppe, from 21-7-40
Neumann, Oberleutnant Julius | 6 Staffel, P.O.W., 18-8-40
Neef, Unteroffizier Fritz | 1 Staffel

Nittmann, Unteroffizier Ernst | 1 Staffel, ✝ 6-9-40
Nolte, Unteroffizier Karl | 6 Staffel, ✝ 18-8-40
Pointer, Oberleutnant Anton | *St.Kap.*, 8 Staffel, 6-10-40 until 27-10-40
Poppek, Gefreiter Günther | 1 Staffel, ✝ 18-9-40
Preiser, Oberleutnant Karl | II.Gruppe
Rauwolf, Unteroffizier Georg | 6 Staffel, P.O.W., 9-9-40
Redlich, Hauptmann Karl-Wolfgang | *St.Kap.*, 1 Staffel
Rethfeldt, Gefreiter Werner | 9 Staffel
Riegel, Hauptmann Kurt | *Gr.Kdr.*, I.Gruppe, until Missing, 20-7-40
Rirchenbach, Leutnant | I.Gruppe
Rödel, Oberleutnant Gustav | *St.Kap.*, 4 Staffel, from 1-9-40
Roos, Oberleutnant Walter | *St.Kap.*, 5 Staffel
Rosenboom, Oberleutnant Hans-Volkert | III.Gruppe, ✝ 16-8-40
Sander, Oberleutnant Richard | 3 Staffel, ✝ 30-9-40
Sawallisch, Feldwebel Otto | 2 Staffel, Missing, 18-8-40
Scherer, Leutnant Ulrich | 3 Staffel
Scheidt, Unteroffizier Josef | 6 Staffel, ✝ 27-9-40
Schlichting, Hauptmann Joachim, ★ (14-12-40) | *Gr. Kdr.*, III.Gruppe
Schmidt, Leutnant Herbert | 6 Staffel, P.O.W., 30-9-40
Schüller, Oberleutnant Werner | 3 Staffel, P.O.W., 6-9-40
Schultz, Unteroffizier Edgar | 5 Staffel, Missing, 8-8-40
Schulz, Feldwebel Ernst | 9 Staffel, ✝ 18-9-40
Seyfert, Oberleutnant Werner, | *St.Kap.*, 6 Staffel
Sickmann, Oberleutnent Eduard | 3 Staffel, ✝ 17-10-40
Strobl, Leutnant Helmut | 5 Staffel, Missing, 5-9-40
Trümpelmann, Oberleutnant Martin | 1 Staffel, ✝ 18-8-40
Uebe, Unteroffizier Heinz | 6 Staffel
Wacker, Unteroffizier Paul | I.Gruppe
Walburger, Unteroffizier Andreas | 2 Staffel, P.O.W., 15-9-40
Wasserzier, Leutnant | I.Gruppe
Wels, Gefreiter Eugen | 3 Staffel, ✝ 17-10-40
Wiemann, Unteroffizier | 5 Staffel
Wilbert, Unteroffizier Paul | 6 Staffel, ✝ 16-8-40
Woldenga, Major Bernhard | *Geschw. Kdr.*, from 15-10-40
Zirkenbach, Leutnant Igor | I.Gruppe

JAGDGESCHWADER 51
(JG 51 < Mölders >)

Single-seat fighter *Geschwader* of *Jafu 2* equipped with Messerschmitt Bf 109Es, I. and II. *Gruppen* bassed at Wissant, and III.*Gruppe* based at St. Omer. (Note that the honour title *<Mölders>* was approved in 1942, after the death of Werner Mölders)

Asmus, Hauptmann Hans | *Stab*
Bär, Leutnant Heinrich, ★★★ (2-7-41, 14-8-41, 16-2-42) | I.Gruppe
Beckh, Hauptmann Friedrich, ★ (18-9-41) | *Stab*
Bildau, Leutnant | 7 Staffel
Birg, Feldwebel Leonhard | 7 Staffel
Böhm, Leutnant Johann | 4.Staffel, P.O.W., 8-7-40
Borchers, Leutnant Adolf, ★ (22-11-43) | Staffel not known
Brunk, Fahnrich Otto | 5 Staffel
Bübenhöfer, Feldwebel Karl | 3 Staffel
Canier, Leutnant Gerhard | 9 Staffel, ✝ 30-9-40
Eichele, Hauptmann | I.Gruppe, ✝ 28-7-40
Fleig, Leutnant Erwin, ★ (12-8-41) | 2 Staffel
Fözö, Hauptmann Josef, ★ (2-7-41) | *St.Kap.*, II.Gruppe
Gallowitsch, Leutnant Bernd, ★ (24-1-42) | IV.Gruppe
Garneth, Unteroffizier | 1 Staffel
Hoffmann, Oberfeldwebel Heinrich, ★★ (12-8-41, 19-10-410 | 12 Staffel
Hohagen, Oberleutnant Erich, ★ (5-10-41) | 4 Staffel
Höhn, Unteroffizier Erich | 4 Staffel
Hubel, Unteroffizier | 7 Staffel, ✝ 30-9-40
Huppertz, Leutnant Herbert, ★★ (30-8-41, 24-6-44) | II.Gruppe
John, Feldwebel Hans | 4 Staffel, ✝ 28-10-40
Joppien, Oberleutnant Hermann-Friedrich, ★★ (16-9-40, 23-4-41) | *Gr. Kdr.*, I.Gruppe
Kircheis, Oberleutnant | *Stab*
Klotz, Feldwebel | 9.Staffel, P.O.W., 15-9-40
Knittel, Leutnant Werner | II.Gruppe, ✝ 28-10-40
Koch, Unteroffizier | 9 Staffel
Kolbow, Leutnant Hans, ★ (27-7-41) | 6 Staffel
Koslowski, Feldwebel Willi | 7 Staffel
Kraft, Leutnant Heinrich, ★ (18-3-42) | I.Gruppe
Lange, Leutnant | III.Gruppe, ✝ 13-7-40
Lenz, Unteroffizier Alfred | 4 Staffel, ✝ 29-10-40
Leppla, Hauptmann Richard, ★ (27-7-41) | *St.Kap.*, 3 Staffel
Lessing, Leutnant | 3 Staffel, ✝ 18-8-40
Liegnitz, Oberleutnant | III.Gruppe
Limpert, Unteroffizier | 7 Staffel, ✝ 30-9-40
Mathes, Hauptmann Günther | II.Gruppe
Meudner, Feldwebel | 3 Staffel
Meyer, Leutnant Erich | 2 Staffel
Misalla, Unteroffizier Walter | 9 Staffel
Mölders, Oberleutnant Viktor | *St.Kap.*, 2 Staffel, P.O.W., 7-10-40

Mölders, Major Werner, ★★★★ (29-5-40, 21-9-40, 3-7-41, 16-7-41)
Geschw. Kdr. [✝ 22-11-41]
Müller, Fahnrich Kurt — 3 Staffel
Pitcairn, Hauptmann Douglas — 1 Staffel
Ruttkowski, Unteroffizier — 1 Staffel, ✝ 2-9-40
Siemer, Feldwebel — 8 Staffel, ✝ 11-9-40
Strohlein, Oberfeldwebel — 2 Staffel
Terry, Oberleutnant Ernst — Adj., I.Gruppe
Thorl, Leutnant — 1 Staffel
Tietzen, Hauptmann Horst, ★ (20-8-40) — St.Kap., 6 Staffel, ✝ 20-8-40
Tornow, Leutnant Heinrich — 4 Staffel, ✝ 29-10-40
Trautloft, Hauptmann Hannes, ★ (27-7-41) — Gr.Kdr., III.Gruppe
Triebel, Leutnant — II.Gruppe
Wehnelt, Leutnant — III.Gruppe
Werner, Gefreiter — 3 Staffel
Wiggers, Hauptmann — St.Kap., 2 Staffel, ✝ 11-9-40
Wilcke, Oberleutnant Wolf-Dietrich, ★★★ (6-8-41, 9-9-42, 23-12-42)
St.Kap., Staffel not known
Zurlage, Unteroffizier — 1 Staffel

JAGDGESCHWADER 52
(JG 52)

Single-seat fighter *Geschwader* of *Jafu 2* equipped with Messerschmitt Bf 109Es. Two *Gruppen* only; I.*Gruppe* based at Coquelles, and II.*Gruppe* at Peupligne, France.

Barkhorn, Oberleutnant Gerhard, ★★★ (23-8-42, 11-1-43, 2-3-44)
II.Gruppe
Beisswenger, Leutnant Hans, ★★ (9-5-42, 3-10-42) — II.Gruppe
Berthol, Leutnant Hans — Adj., I.Gruppe
Bielefeld, Oberleutnant — St.Kap., 7 Staffel, ✝ 25-7-40
Bielmaier, Feldwebel Ludwig — 5 Staffel
Boche, Feldwebel — 4 Staffel
Bott, Gefreiter Karl, — 2 Staffel
Dammers, Feldwebel Hans, ★ (23-8-42) — 9 Staffel
Denk, Oberfeldwebel Gustav — II.Gruppe
Dickfeld, Leutnant Adolf, ★★ (19-3-42, 18-5-42) — I.Gruppe
Eichel-Streiber, Leutnant Diethelm, ★ (5-44) — Staffel not known
Erlich, Oberleutnant — St.Kap., 8 Staffel, ✝ 24-7-40
Ewald, Hauptmann Wolfgang, ★ (12-42) — Gr. Kdr., I.Gruppe
Fermer, Oberleutnant — 7 Staffel, ✝ 24-7-40
Friedemann, Oberfeldwebel Walter — 6 Staffel, ✝ 20-10-40
Geist, Leutnant Hans — 4 Staffel
Gelhalsis, Leutnant — II.Gruppe
Geller, Leutnant — I.Gruppe
Grislawski, Feldwebel Alfred, ★★ (1-7-42, 11-4-44) — 9 Staffel
Hammerl, Feldwebel Karl, ★ (2-10-42) — 1 Staffel
Hoeckner, Leutnant Walter, ★ (6-4-44) — Staffel not known
Hoffmann, Feldwebel — 5 Staffel
Houwald, Hauptmann von, — Gr.Kdr., III.Gruppe, ✝ 24-7-40
Kaganeck, Leutnant Erbo, Graf von, ★★ (30-7-41, 26-10-41)
Later to JG 27
Keidel, Oberleutnant — St.Kap., 7 Staffel
Kind, Unteroffizier — 1 Staffel, ✝ 5-9-40
Köppen, Feldwebel Gerhard, ★★ (18-12-41, 27-2-42) — 7 Staffel
Leesmann Oberleutnant Karl-Heinz, ★ (23-7-41) — St.Kap., 2 Staffel
Mommert, Gefreiter — 4 Staffel
Öhlschläger, Leutnant — St.Kap., 1 Staffel
Schieverhöfer, Feldwebel Lothar — 3 Staffel
Schmidt, Leutnant — III.Gruppe
Steinhilper, Oberleutnant Ulrich — 3 Staffel
Steinhoff, Leutnant Johannes, ★★★ (30-8-41, 2-9-42, 28-7-44) — 4 Staffel
Strasser, Gefreiter — 6 Staffel
Treiber, Oberleutnant Karl — II.Gruppe, P.O.W., 27-9-40
Trübenbach, Major Hans — Geschw. Kdr.
Urlings, Feldwebel — I. Gruppe
Waller, Oberleutnant — 3 Staffel
Wolf, Unteroffizier — 3 Staffel

JAGDGESCHWADER 53
(JG 53 < *Pik As* >

Single-seat fighter *Geschwader* of *Jafu 3* equipped with Messerschmitt Bf 109Es. I.*Gruppe* based at Rennes, II.*Gruppe* at Dinan, and III.*Gruppe* at Sempy and Brest.

Adelwart, Unteroffizier — I.Gruppe, ✝ 8-9-40
Bauer, Oberleutnant — III.Gruppe, ✝ 1-9-40
Becker, Gefreiter Peter — 8 Staffel, ✝ 9-9-40
Below, Leutnant — III.Gruppe
Bennemann, Hauptmann Doktor Helmut, ★ (2-10-42) — Adj., I.Gruppe
Berg, Feldwebel Alfred — 4 Staffel
Berwanger, Leutnant — II.Gruppe

Bodendiek, Leutnant Erich — Gruppe not known
Bogel, Unteroffizier — II.Gruppe
Brändle, Oberleutnant Werner, ★★ (1-7-42, 28-8-42) — Staffel not known
Bretnütz, Hauptmann Heinz, ★ (22-10-40) — Gr.Kdr., II.Gruppe
Deutsch, Leutnant — 7 Staffel
Dodendiek, Leutnant Erich — 4 Staffel
Feldmann, Unteroffizier — 3 Staffel
Fiel, Oberleutnant Ludwig — 8 Staffel
Gehsla, Unteroffizier — 1 Staffel
Geiswinckler, Unteroffizier — 6 Staffel
Gottmann, Oberleutnant — III.Gruppe, ✝ 7-9-40
Götz, Oberfeldwebel Franz, ★ (30-9-42) — III.Gruppe
Harder, Hauptmann — Gr. Kdr., III.Gruppe, ✝ 12-8-40
Hase, Oberleutnant Julius — St.Kap., 3 Staffel, ✝ 15-9-40
Hempel, Feldwebel — 8 Staffel, ✝ 6-9-40
Höhnisch, Feldwebel — 1 Staffel
Karl, Unteroffizier — I.Gruppe
Kuhlmann, Oberfeldwebel — I.Gruppe
Kuhnert, Oberleutnant — St.Kap., III.Gruppe, ✝ 8-9-40
Lammer, Oberleutnant — 1 Staffel
Langer, Unteroffizier — 9 Staffel, ✝ 17-9-40
Liesendahl, Hauptmann Frank, ★ (25-9-42) — Staffel not known
Maculan, Hauptmann — II.Gruppe
Maltzahn, Major Günther , Freiherr von, ★★ (30-12-40, 24-7-41)
Geschw. Kdr.
Mayer, Hauptmann Hans-Karl, ★(3-9-40) — Gr.Kdr., I.Gruppe, ✝ 17-10-40
Merkeu, Gefreiter Adolf — II.Gruppe, ✝ 18-10-40
Müller, Oberfeldwebel Alfred — 1 Staffel
Ohly, Oberleutnant Hans — I.Gruppe
Pfannschmidt, Leutnant — II.Gruppe, ✝ 13-8-40
Poschenrieder, Unteroffizier — III.Gruppe
Radlick, Oberleutnant Walter — Stab, III.Gruppe, ✝ 2-10-40
Riegel, Oberleutnant — 3 Staffel
Roos, Leutnant — I.Gruppe
Rupp, Oberleutnant Walter — St.Kap., 3 Staffel
Schersand, Unteroffizier — I.Gruppe, ✝ 15-9-40
Schlitt, Unteroffizier Hermann — 4 Staffel
Schmidt, Feldwebel Hermann — 6 Staffel
Schulte, Unteroffizier — 7 Staffel
Schulz, Feldwebel — I.Gruppe
Schulz, Unteroffizier Karl — 6 Staffel
Schulz-Blank, Oberleutnant — II.Gruppe, ✝ 9-9-40
Seliger, Oberfeldwebel Herbert — 9 Staffel
Seufert, Oberfeldwebel Bernhard — 6 Staffel
Stoll, Oberleutnant Jakob — St.Kap., 9 Staffel
Strack, Oberfeldwebel Oskar — 1 Staffel
Stronk, Oberleutnant Siegfried — 8 Staffel, ✝ 2-10-40
Strasser, Leutnant — III.Gruppe
Tschopper, Feldwebel — 1 Staffel
Ursinus, Oberleutnant Werner — II.Gruppe
Vogel, Oberleutnant Richard — St.Kap., 4 Staffel
Witmeier, Oberleutnant — I.Gruppe
Zag, Gefreiter — 8 Staffel
Zweis, Leutnant Alfred — 1 Staffel

JAGDGESCHWADER 54
(JG 54 < *Grünherz* >)

Single-seat fighter *Geschwader* under *Jafu 2*, *Luftflotte 2*, equipped with Messerschmitt Bf 109Es. Headquarters at Cam-pagne, later at Guines; I. and III.*Gruppen* at Guines, and II. *Gruppe* at Hermalinghen.

Adameit, Leutnant Horst, ★★ (16-4-43, 2-3-44) — Gruppe not known
Behse, Unteroffizier — II.Gruppe, ✝ 5-9-40
Biber, Feldwebel — 1 Staffel
Bob, Leutnant Hans-Eckehard, ★ (7-3-41) — St.Kap., 9 Staffel
Bonin, Hauptmann Hubertus von, ★ (21-12-42) — Gr.Kdr., I.Gruppe
Braats, Unteroffizier — 9 Staffel, ✝ 30-9-40
Brixel, Feldwebel — Stab, ✝ 24-10-40
Broennle, Oberfeldwebel Herbert, ★ (14-3-43) — 4 Staffel
Chrobek, Major Bruno, ★ (4-7-40) — Gr.Kdr., I.Gruppe
Drewes, Oberleutnant — III.Gruppe
Eberle, Leutnant Josef — 9.Staffel, ✝ 9-10-40
Eckerle, Oberleutnant Franz, ★★ (18-9-41, 12-3-42) — St. Kap.
Elbers, Unteroffizier — 8 Staffel
Elsing, Oberleutnant — II.Gruppe, ✝ 2-9-40
Gorlach, Leutnant — 2 Staffel
Götz, Leutnant Hans, ★ (1-43) — 2 Staffel
Hahn, Oberleutnant Hans, ★★ (24-9-40, 14-8-41) — Also with JG 2
Hild, Oberleutnant — I.Gruppe
Höhne, Oberstleutnant Otto, ★ (5-9-40) — Geschw. Kdr.
Hotzelmann, Unteroffizier — I.Gruppe
Hrabak, Hauptmann Dietrich, ★★ (21-10-40, 25-11-43)
Gr.Kdr., II.Gruppe, from 30-8-40
Jowig, Feldwebel Adolf — 9 Staffel

Kempf, Feldwebel Karl, ★ (4-2-42) — III.Gruppe
Kleeman, Unteroffizier — II.Gruppe
Knippsheer, Oberfeldwebel — 3 Staffel, † 23-9-40
Lange, Oberleutnant Heinz, ★ (18-11-44) — III.Gruppe
Lignitz, Oberleutnant Arnold, ★ (5-11-40) — Gr.Kdr., III.Gruppe
Marks, Unteroffizier — 7 Staffel
Mettig, Major Martin — Geschw. Kdr.
Mütherick, Leutnant Hubert, ★ (6-8-41) — Staffel not known
Philipp, Oberleutnant Hans, ★★★ (22-10-40, 24-8-41, 12-3-43) — St.Kap., 4 Staffel
Rath, Oberleutnant Hans — II.Gruppe, P.O.W., 30-8-40
Rudorffer, Leutnant Erich, ★★ (1-5-41, 11-4-44) — Staffel not known
Schelcher, Oberleutnant — Stab, III.Gruppe, † 2-9-40
Schmöller-Halder, Oberleutnant Hans — I.Gruppe
Schnell, Leutnant Siegfried, ★★ (9-11-40, 9-7-41) — Staffel not known
Schön, Oberleutnant Anton — 8 Staffel, † 27-9-40
Schölz, Hauptmann — Gr.Kdr., III.Gruppe (from 6-9-40)
Schöttle, Feldwebel — I.Gruppe
Schweser, Feldwebel Fritz — 7 Staffel
Schypek, Oberleutnant Joachim — 5 Staffel
Seiler, Oberleutnant Reinhard, ★★ (20-12-41, 2-3-44) — St.Kap., 1 Staffel
Stegmann, Oberleutnant Hans — II.Gruppe
Trautloft, Oberleutnant Hannes, ★ (27-7-41) — Geschw. Kdr., from 25-8-40
Ultsch, Hauptmann — Gr.Kdr., III.Gruppe (until 6-9-40)
Wagner, Leutnant — 6 Staffel
Winterer, Hauptmann — Gr.Kdr., II.Gruppe (until 30-8-40)
Witt, Oberleutnant — 3 Staffel
Ziegler, Leutnant Rudolf — II.Gruppe
Zimmermann, Unteroffizier Arno — 7 Staffel

JAGDGESCHWADER 77
(JG 77)

Single-seat fighter *Geschwader* with Messerschmitt Bf 109Es, based in Scandinavia (Stavanger and Trondheim). From 25th August I./JG 77 formed the nucleus of the II.*Gruppe*, JG 51 and redeployed to St. Omer in the Pas de Calais. It is unlikely that all the pilots listed flew operations over Britain, but were undoubtedly in action against Fighter Command Blenheims over Norway during the Battle of Britain.

Arnoldy, Leutnant Arnold — II.Gruppe
Erick, Oberleutnant — 2 Staffel
Eschwerhaus, Leutnant Hein — 1 Staffel
Ettler, Feldwebel — I.Gruppe
Evers, Feldwebel — 1 Staffel, † 31-8-40
Fröba, Unteroffizier — 4 Staffel
Goltzsche, Oberfeldwebel — 1 Staffel
Hackl, Unteroffizier, ★★★ (27-5-42, 6-8-42, 9-7-44) — II.Gruppe
Hauck, Oberleutnant — I.Gruppe
Hentschel, Hauptmann — Gr.Kdr., II.Gruppe
Huy, Leutnant Wolf-Dietrich, ★★ (5-7-41, 17-3-42) — St.Kap., III.Gruppe
Isken, Feldwebel Eduard, ★ (14-1-45) — III.Gruppe
Janke, Hauptmann Johannes — Gr.Kdr., I.Gruppe
Kaiser, Oberfeldwebel Herbert, ★ (14-3-43) — III.Gruppe
Keck, Unteroffizier — 1 Staffel
Kind, Oberleutnant — 3 Staffel
Kramer, Feldwebel — 1 Staffel
Kunze, Oberleutnant Herbert — Adj., I.Gruppe, † 14-9-40
Leyerer, Oberleutnant Walter — 2 Staffel, † 29-9-40
Meizner, Unteroffizier — 3 Staffel
Niemeyer, Unteroffizier — II.Gruppe
Petrenko, Leutnant — 1 Staffel
Priebe, Oberleutnant — 2 Staffel
Raisinger, Gefreiter Karl — 3 Staffel
Setz, Leutnant Heinrich, ★★ (31-12-41, 23-6-42) — 4 Staffel
Still, Gefreiter — I.Gruppe, † 18-9-40
Weber, Oberleutnant — III.Gruppe
Wilhelm, Feldwebel Heinz — 3 Staffel
Winterfeldt, Oberleutnant Alexander von, ★ (5-7-41) — St.Kap., III.Gruppe
Woldenga, Oberleutnant Bernard, ★ (5-7-41) — St.Kap., Staffel not known

NACHTJAGDGESCHWADER 1
(NJG 1)

Home defence night fighter *Geschwader* activated at the end of August 1940 with Junkers Ju 88Cs, Messerschmitt Bf 109Es and Bf 110Cs and Ds. *Staffel* components detached to München, Könen, Ingolstadt, Lechfeld, Vlissingen and Handorf. Unit Codes G9

Berger, Oberleutnant — 1 Staffel
Bertram, Unteroffizier Karl — 7 Staffel, † 28-10-40
Bregand, Leutnant — II.Gruppe, † 29-8-40
Hoffmann, Unteroffizier Horst — 8 Staffel, † 21-10-40
Lorenz, Oberfeldwebel Kurt — 7 Staffel, † 28-10-40
Mangersdorf, Leutnant — Stab, † 15-10-40
Schmitz, Leutnant — 3 Staffel
Stillgried, Hauptmann Graf — Gr.Kdr., II.Gruppe, † 6-10-40
Walther, Oberleutnant Arno — St.Kap., 8 Staffel, † 21-10-40

NACHTJAGDGESCHWADER 2
(NJG 2)

Night intruder *Geschwader* activated early in September 1940 for night interdiction over Great Britain. Equipped with Junkers Ju 88C-2s, Dornier Do 17Zs and Messerschmitt Bf 110Ds, and based principally at Gilze-Rijen. Unit Codes R4 (and also 2A and 3M from previous component units)

Haberland, Gefreiter — 3 Staffel
Pahn, Feldwebel — 3 Staffel, † 16-9-40
Reinisch, Gefreiter — 3 Staffel
Schlicht, Feldwebel — 3 Staffel
Zimmermann, Oberleutnant Paul — 4 Staffel, † 17-10-40

SEENOTBEREICHSKOMMANDO:
Seenotflugkommandos and Staffeln

Air-sea rescue organisation with detached *Seenotflugkommandos* based on Norwegian, Danish, German, Dutch, Belgian and French coasts, equipped with Heinkel He 59s, Dornier Do 18s and, from October onwards, French Breguet 521 flying boats. Aircraft usually carried civil registration letters, e.g. D-ASUO

Anders, Unteroffizier Walter — Seenotflugkdo. 1, P.O.W., 9-7-40
Bachmeier, Unteroffizier K. — Seenotflugkdo. 3, † 26-10-40
Barbinger, Unteroffizier Helmut — Seenotflugkdo. 4, † 2-10-40
Beneke, Oberfeldwebel H. — Seenotflugkdo. 3
Börner, Leutnant-zur-See — Seenotflugkdo. 4, † 15-8-40
Brandt, Gefreiter — Seenorflugkdo. 4
Bridi, Feldwebel Nicolai — Seenotflugkdo. 2
Brodman, Leutnant — Seenotflugkdo. 3
Chudziak, Oberleutnant — Seenotflugkdo. 3
Fehske, Leutnant Hans-Joachim — Seenotflugkdo. 3
Fischer, Oberfereiter G. — Seenotflugkdo. 3
Fischer, Unteroffizier Helmuth — Seenotflugkdo. 2
Gräfe, Feldwebel K. — Seenotflugkdo. 3
Grimmig, Feldwebel R. — Seenotflugkdo. 3
Hilke, Leutnant Heinrich — Seenotflugkdo. 3, † 26-10-40
Hirschmann, Unteroffizier Karl — Seenotflugkdo. 2
Horr, Feldwebel — Seenotflugkdo. 4
Ielsen, Unteroffizier Ernst-Otto — Seenotflugkdo. 3
Jahnke, Leutnant — Seenotflugkdo. 2, † 19-8-40
Kämpf, Obergefreiter Karl — Seenotflugkdo. 2
Klintsche, Major Ulrich — Seenotflugkdo. 3
Kruse, Unteroffizier Friedrich — Seenotflugkdo. 1
Lange, Unteroffizier D. — Seenotflugkdo. 3
Maywald, Feldwebel Günther — Seenotflugkdo. 1; P.O.W., 9-7-40
Michels, Gefreiter W. — Seenotflugkdo. 3; † 26-10-40
Mietlin, Leutnant-zur-See — Seenotflugkdo. 2; † 27-8-40
Niess, Oberfeldwebel — Seenotflugkdo. 4
Philipp, Obergefreiter Erich — Seenotflugkdo. 3
Priebe, Obergefreiter H. — Seenotflugkdo. 3
Roddy, Oberfeldwebel — Seenotflugkdo. 3
Sandgaard, Leutnant — Seenotflugkdo. 3
Scheel, Leutnant Wilhelm — Seenotflugkdo. 1; † 28-10-40
Schiele, Unteroffizier Erich — Seenotflukdo. 1; P.O.W., 9-7-40
Schulz, Leutnant-zur-See Bernhard — Seenotflugkdo. 2
Sprenger, Leutnant-zur-See — Seenotflugkdo. 2
Stargnet, Unteroffizier — Seenotflugkdo. 2
Stelzner, Leutnant-zur-See Siegfried — Seenotflugkdo. 2
Stuckmann, Unteroffizier — Seenotflugkdo. 3
Unterhorst, Leutnant-zur-See — Seenotflugkdo. 1
Vogel, Oberleutnant Doktor Arnold von — Seenotflugkdo. 2
Waldheim, Unteroffizier W. — Seenotflugkdo. 3
Wischer, Unteroffizier Karl — Seenotflugkdo. 2
Wölke, Leutnant — Seenotflugkdo. 1

HAWKER HURRICANE I

Aircraft representative of the Battle of Britain

Aircraft 'B-Baker', P3144, of No. 32 (F) Squadron, Biggin Hill and Hawkinge, July 1940, as flown variously by Sqn. Ldr. John Worrall and Flt. Lt. Michael Crossley. It destroyed a Messerschmitt Bf 109E before it was itself shot down near Dover on 19th July while being flown by Sgt. G. Turner who was wounded.

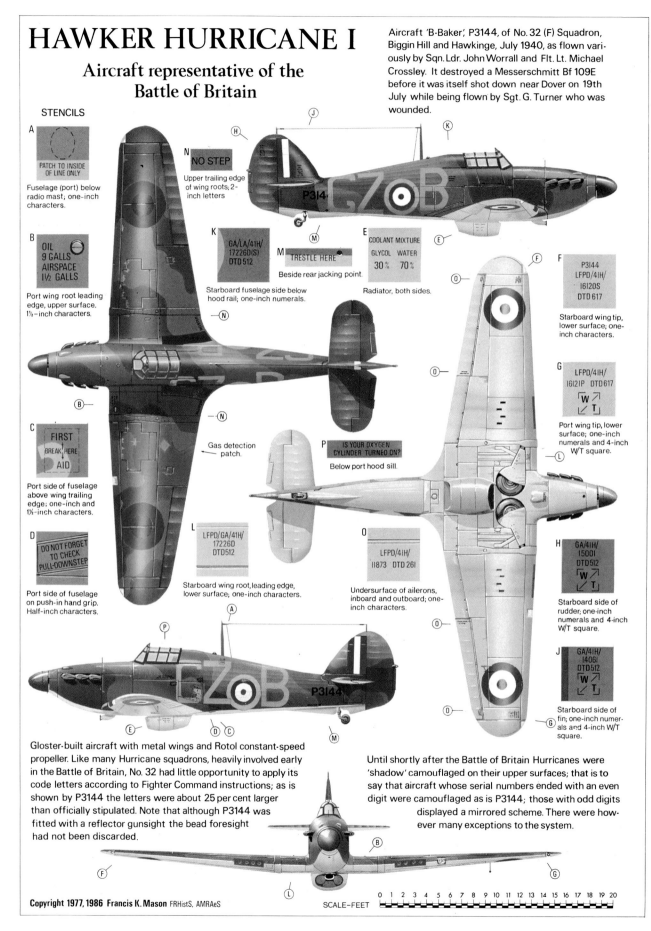

STENCILS

A — PATCH TO INSIDE OF LINE ONLY
Fuselage (port) below radio mast; one-inch characters.

B — OIL 9 GALLS AIRSPACE 1½ GALLS
Port wing root leading edge, upper surface. 1½-inch characters.

C — FIRST BREAK HERE AID
Port side of fuselage above wing trailing edge; one-inch and 1½-inch characters.

D — DO NOT FORGET TO CHECK PULL-DOWNSTEP
Port side of fuselage on push-in hand grip. Half-inch characters.

N — NO STEP
Upper trailing edge of wing roots; 2-inch letters.

K — GA/LA/41H/ 17226D(S) DTD 512
Starboard fuselage side below hood rail; one-inch numerals.

M — TRESTLE HERE
Beside rear jacking point.

E — COOLANT MIXTURE GLYCOL 30% WATER 70%
Radiator, both sides.

Gas detection patch.

P — IS YOUR OXYGEN CYLINDER TURNED ON?
Below port hood sill.

L — LFPD/GA/41H/ 17226D DTD512
Starboard wing root, leading edge, lower surface; one-inch characters.

O — LFPD/41H/ 11873 DTD 261
Undersurface of ailerons, inboard and outboard; one-inch characters.

F — P3144 LFPD/41H/ 16120S DTD 617
Starboard wing tip, lower surface; one-inch characters.

G — LFPD/41H/ 16121P DTD 617 W/T
Port wing tip, lower surface; one-inch numerals and 4-inch W/T square.

H — GA/41H/ 15001 DTD512 W/T
Starboard side of rudder; one-inch numerals and 4-inch W/T square.

J — GA/41H/ 14061 DTD512 W/T
Starboard side of fin; one-inch numerals and 4-inch W/T square.

Gloster-built aircraft with metal wings and Rotol constant-speed propeller. Like many Hurricane squadrons, heavily involved early in the Battle of Britain, No. 32 had little opportunity to apply its code letters according to Fighter Command instructions; as is shown by P3144 the letters were about 25 per cent larger than officially stipulated. Note that although P3144 was fitted with a reflector gunsight the bead foresight had not been discarded.

Until shortly after the Battle of Britain Hurricanes were 'shadow' camouflaged on their upper surfaces; that is to say that aircraft whose serial numbers ended with an even digit were camouflaged as is P3144; those with odd digits displayed a mirrored scheme. There were however many exceptions to the system.

SCALE-FEET 0 1 2 3 4 5 6 7 8 9 10 11 12 13 14 15 16 17 18 19 20

SUPERMARINE SPITFIRE I

Aircraft representative of the Battle of Britain

Late-standard Spitfire Mark I, built by Vickers-Armstrong (Supermarine) Ltd., X4559/EB-C of No. 41 (Fighter) Squadron, based at Hornchurch during September-October 1940. It was shot down by Messerschmitt Bf 109Es at Albourne, West Sussex, on 1st October; the pilot, Plt. Off. G.H. Bennions, D.F.C., baled out at Dunstalls Farm, severely wounded.

SCALE—FEET 0 1 2 3 4 5 6 7 8 9 10 11 12 13 14 15 16 17 18 19 20

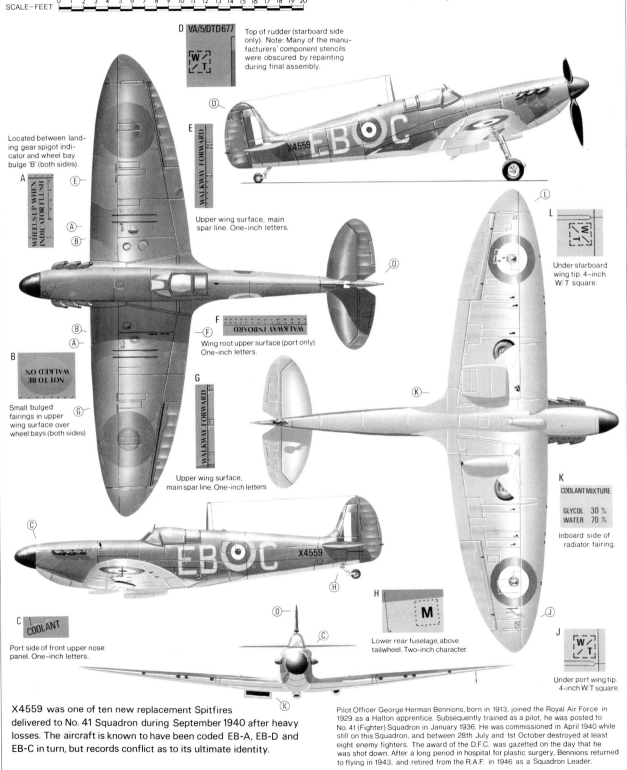

D VA/5/DTD677 — Top of rudder (starboard side only). Note: Many of the manufacturers' component stencils were obscured by repainting during final assembly.

A WHEELS UP WHEN INDICATOR FLUSH — Located between landing gear spigot indicator and wheel bay bulge 'B' (both sides).

E WALKWAY FORWARD — Upper wing surface, main spar line. One-inch letters.

B NOT TO BE WALKED ON — Small bulged fairings in upper wing surface over wheel bays (both sides)

F WALKWAY INBOARD — Wing root upper surface (port only). One-inch letters.

G WALKWAY FORWARD — Upper wing surface, main spar line. One-inch letters

L Under starboard wing tip. 4-inch W/T square.

K COOLANT MIXTURE — GLYCOL 30 % / WATER 70 % — Inboard side of radiator fairing.

C COOLANT — Port side of front upper nose panel. One-inch letters.

H M — Lower rear fuselage, above tailwheel. Two-inch character.

J Under port wing tip. 4-inch W/T square.

X4559 was one of ten new replacement Spitfires delivered to No. 41 Squadron during September 1940 after heavy losses. The aircraft is known to have been coded EB-A, EB-D and EB-C in turn, but records conflict as to its ultimate identity.

Pilot Officer George Herman Bennions, born in 1913, joined the Royal Air Force in 1929 as a Halton apprentice. Subsequently trained as a pilot, he was posted to No. 41 (Fighter) Squadron in January 1936. He was commissioned in April 1940 while still on this Squadron, and between 28th July and 1st October destroyed at least eight enemy fighters. The award of the D.F.C. was gazetted on the day that he was shot down. After a long period in hospital for plastic surgery, Bennions returned to flying in 1943, and retired from the R.A.F. in 1946 as a Squadron Leader.

Copyright 1975, 1990 Francis K. Mason FRHistS AMRAeS

APPENDIX C
THE AIRCRAFT OF THE BATTLE

HAWKER HURRICANE I

The Hawker Hurricane was the first operational R.A.F. aircraft capable of a top speed in excess of 300 miles per hour. The design of the Hurricane, directed by Sydney Camm, was the outcome of discussions with the Directorate of Technical Development towards the end of 1933, aimed at breaking the deadlocked biplane formula; in these discussions Camm proposed a monoplane, based otherwise on his successful Fury biplane formula, using the proposed new Rolls-Royce P.V.12 engine (later to beome the Merlin), and in time incorporating a retractable undercarriage. Originally, in concert with current armament requirements, a four gun battery was proposed; in 1934, however, with successful negotiations to licence-build the reliable Colt machine gun, it was deemed possible to mount an eight-gun battery in the wings, unrestricted by the propeller arc and thus dispensing with synchronising gear.

The first Fighter Command unit to receive Hurricanes was No. 111 (Fighter) Squadron, commanded by Squadron Leader John Gillan, based at Northolt before Christmas 1937; and it was the squadron's C.O. who flew one of the new fighters from Turnhouse, Edinburgh, to Northolt, London, at an average ground speed of 408.75 m.p.h.—a feat which earned the pilot the nickname "Downwind" Gillan for all time. Nos. 3 and 56 Squadrons were the next to take delivery and, by the outbreak of war a year later, 497 Hurricanes had been completed from an order book totalling more than 3,000 fighters. At about this time the Gloster Aircraft Company started sub-contract manufacture of the standard Mark I, which was now emerging from the factories with metal wings and three-blade variable-pitch propellers. One final refinement was adopted between the outbreak of war and the Battle of Britain; this was the Rotol constant speed propeller which, apart from enabling the pilot to select an optimum pitch for take-off, climb, cruise and combat (thereby bestowing a better performance under certain conditions), also prevented the engine from overspeeding in a dive.

A total of 1,715 Hurricanes flew with Fighter Command during the period of the Battle of Britain, far in excess of all other British fighters combined. Having entered service a year before the Spitfire, the Hurricane was "half a generation" older, and was inferior in terms of speed and climb. Be that as it may, it was at least as manœuvrable as the Spitfire and a much steadier gun platform—an attribute that probably accounted for the generally higher scores of Hurricane pilots during the Battle. It was an extremely robust aeroplane that was capable of sustaining fearsome combat damage before write-off; and, unlike the Spitfire, it was a go-anywhere, do-anything fighter by July 1940. Being of long-established construction, it could be serviced and repaired at almost any R.A.F. station in Britain—a vital asset during the Battle of Britain. If there was one characteristic of the Hurricane, criticised and feared by pilots, it was the speed with which the aircraft became engulfed in flames, once it had been set on fire in combat; there was no single reason why this should have been so, yet it cannot have been a coincidence that more pilots suffered the appalling effects of "Hurricane burns" than those of other fighters.

It is estimated that Hurricane pilots were credited with four-fifths of all enemy aircraft destroyed in the period July—October 1940. Indeed, by the end of the Second World War, the Hurricane was still well ahead of the Spitfire in terms of enemy aircraft (German, Italian and Japanese) destroyed.

Wing span: 40 ft. 0 in. *Length:* 31 ft. 4 in. *Height:* 13 ft . 1 in. *Wing area:* 258 sq. ft. *Powerplant:* One 1,030 h.p. Rolls-Royce Merlin III twelve-cylinder liquid-cooled engine. *Armament:* Eight 0.303-inch Browing machine guns mounted in the wings. *Maximum speed:* 328 m.p.h. at 20,000 feet. *Maximum range:* 505 miles. *Service ceiling:* 34,200 feet.

SUPERMARINE SPITFIRE I

The Spitfire, though far less numerous than the Hurricane during the Battle, has always attracted more public attention for a variety of reasons. Its long service life, which did not come to a close until well after the War, kept it in the public eye; its superb handling qualities engendered an almost idolatrous affection and confidence in its pilots; and its enormously photogenic appearance has assured it of immortality as, arguably, the most beautiful fighter aircraft ever built.

The immediate predecessor of the Spitfire was the Supermarine Type 224, designed to meet Specification F.7/30 by Reginald J. Mitchell, creator of the magnificent Supermarine seaplanes which won three successive Schneider Trophy contests. The Type 224 , with its gull wing and cumbersome "trousered" undercarriage, returned a thoroughly pedestrian performance, and Mitchell was justifiably disappointed with it, even before it flew. He began to design a new aircraft as a private venture, but the basic design was revised twice, first to incorporate the new P.V.12 (Merlin) engine and then an eight-gun battery, and the final design was accepted by the Air Ministry in January 1935. The prototype, *K5054*, powered by a 990-h.p. Merlin C, first flew on 5th March 1936; at the controls was Vickers' chief test pilot, J. "Mutt" Summers. (Vickers (Aviation) Ltd. had acquired the entire share capital of the Supermarine Company in 1928.)

The first order for 310 machines was placed on 3rd June 1936, requiring an enormous expansion of the Woolston factory and widespread sub-contracting. The following year another order was placed, for 200 aircraft; and in the same year Reginald Mitchell died at the tragically early age of 42. His successor as Supermarine's chief designer was Joseph Smith, who was to be responsible for the subsequent development of the Spitfire series. In April 1938 the Nuffield Organisation was awarded an order for 1,000 Spitfires to be built at a "shadow" plant planned for Castle Bromwich near Birmingham; and further orders in 1939 brought the number of aircraft on the order book to a total of 2,143 by the outbreak of war.

Between August and December 1938 No. 19 Squadron at Duxford was equipped with the Spitfire Mark I. By the outbreak of war nine squadrons were fully equipped, although only four were fully operational by day, and none by night; two others were in the process of taking deliveries. From the 78th aircraft onwards the original two-blade fixed-pitch wooden propeller was replaced by a three-blade, two-position de Havilland model; modifications introduced during 1939 included a domed cockpit canopy instead of the original flat-topped hood, and increased pilot protection. Problems were being encountered with the guns icing-up, and pilots complained that their canopies frosted over during descent from high altitude—a problem that was not fully solved until well into 1940. The 175th aircraft brought the introduction of the Merlin III engine, of similar output to that of the Merlin II (1,030 h.p.), but with a standardised shaft for de Havilland or Rotol propellers. The "A" type wing mounted eight 0.303-inch Browning machine guns; thirty aircraft with the type "B" wing, mounting four Browning machine guns and two 20-mm. Hispano cannon with 60 rounds per gun, were delivered to No. 19 Squadron for operational trials during the summer of 1940. Details of the shortcomings of these Spitfire Mark IBs may be found in the body of the text.

A total of 1,583 Spitfire Is was built. Deliveries of the Mark II (basically a Mk. I powered by a 1,175-h.p. Merlin XII) began in June 1940, but widespread re-equipment with the new version did not begin until the following winter, and it was the Mark I which took the Spitfire's main share of the fighting during the Battle of Britain; by July 7th nineteen Fighter Command Squadrons were fully equipped with the type, although twelve of these were not operational by night, and three others were subject to altitude restriction (though this was waived during August). Between June and early August 1940, all de Havilland propellers on Spitfire Is were converted to constant-speed units, and the resulting improvement in climb and ceiling paid handsome dividends during the Battle—particularly during the high-flying "*Jabo*" phase in October.

To many fighter pilots of 1940, frustrated by hours in a Tiger Moth or Master trainer, the Spitfire was the answer to a prayer. While less robust and forgiving than the Hurricane, and rather vulnerable to battle damage in certain areas, such as the "small" of the rear fuselage, the fighter more than made up for this weakness in terms of acceleration and manœuvrability.

Wing span: 36 ft. 11 in. *Length:* 29 ft. 11 in. *Height:* 12 ft. 3 in. *Wing area:* 242 sq. ft. *Powerplant*: One 1,030-h.p. Rolls-Royce Merlin III twelve-cylinder liquid-cooled engine. *Armament:* Eight 0.303-inch Browning machine guns mounted in the wings with 300 rounds per gun. *Maximum speed:* 355 m.p.h. at 19,000 feet. *Normal range:* 395 miles. *Service ceiling:* 31,900 feet.

BRISTOL BLENHEIM IF

The Bristol Type 135 cabin monoplane, designed by Frank Barnwell in 1933, attracted the attention of the Press baron Lord Rothermere who, in 1934, ordered a Mercury-powered version for his own use as part of a campaign to popularise commercial aviation. The aircraft first flew in April 1935, and soon caused great interest in Air Ministry circles on account of its high performance—its top speed of 307 m.p.h. being higher than any R.A.F. fighter in service—by a wide margin. Lord Rothermere presented the aircraft (named "Britain First") to the nation for evaluation as a bomber; and in 1936 the modified design was designated the Blenheim Mark I.

The type was ordered "off the drawing board", and the first deliveries to No. 114 Squadron began in March 1939. By the time of the Munich Crisis sixteen home-based bomber squadrons were equipped with the type. By then, however, the first of Germany's new bombers had also entered service and, with comparable performance and superior bomb-carrying and range capabilities, quickly rendered the Blenheim Mark I obsolescent. When war broke out in September 1939 seven home-based fighter squadrons had re-equipped or were re-equipping with the Blenheim IF, a fighter version with four extra 0.303-inch Browning machine guns in a ventral pack. As a day fighter the Mark IF was a failure, proving to be easy meat for single-engine interceptors, and casualties were high. Nevertheless, like the Defiant, it served as a useful interim night fighter during the Battle of Britain and early in the night *Blitz*, even though enemy bombers shot down were few. Its greatest value was, in effect, as an operational trainer for the Beaufighter. In one other respect, the Blenheim night fighter had a claim to fame: in the hands of No. 25 (Fighter) Squadron, it became the first aircraft in the world to carry aloft airborne interception radar, one flight of this Squadron being equipped with special Blenheim Is during the first six months of the War. And it was a radar-equipped Blenheim of the Fighter Interception Unit, based at Shoreham and Tangmere, that claimed the first-ever victim using the AI equipment at night (on 22nd/23 July 1940).

Wing span: 56 ft. 4 in. *Length:* 39 ft. 9 in. *Height:* 9 ft. 10 in. *Wing area:* 469 sq. ft. *Powerplant:* Two 840-h.p. Bristol Mercury VIII nine-cylinder air-cooled radial engines. *Armament:* One 0.303-inch Browning machine gun in the port wing, four 0.303-inch Browning machine guns in ventral fairing, and one 0.303-inch Vickers K machine gun in hydraulically-operated semi-retractable dorsal turret. *Maximum speed:* 285 m.p.h. at 15,000 feet. *Maximum range:* 1,125 miles. *Service ceiling:* 27,280 feet.

BOULTON PAUL DEFIANT I

The long period that elapsed between the first concept of the Defiant turret fighter and its operational acceptance seriously impaired its usefulness. That its concept was fatally flawed can easily be seen in retrospect, yet one wonders what was so attractive to the Air Ministry in an interceptor fighter that possessed no forward-firing armament, and one that was already hard pressed to out-manœuvre German bombers by the time it entered operational service. The delays in production, to some extent caused by enormous demand for the Merlin engine in other fighters, resulted in only three Defiants being delivered by the outbreak of war.

The first unit to equip with the type was No. 264 Squadron, which moved to Martlesham Heath in December 1939. Engine and hydraulic malfunctions caused a grounding order late in January 1940, but this was lifted the following month. The Defiant first entered combat in May, and achieved a somewhat patchy record. Against bombers, the Defiant's heavy dorsal armament was effective; and by operating mixed formations of Defiants and Hurricanes, the R.A.F. could exploit the superficial resemblance between the two types to confuse and entrap German fighters. However, the pedestrian speed performance of the Defiant proved a heavy handicap for the single-seater, and only in a brief moment of glory over Dunkirk was the Defiant able to achieve any

MESSERSCHMITT Bf 109E~1

German single~seat fighter as flown over the Channel Front in the Battle of Britain.

Aircraft flown by Major Adolf Galland while based in the Pas de Calais as Kommandeur, III. Gruppe, Jagdgeschwader 26 «Schlageter» in August 1940. One of the leading German fighter exponents, Galland was appointed Geschwader Kommodore, JG 26, on the 22nd of that month.

SCALE - FEET   0 1 2 3 4 5 6 7 8 9 10 11 12 13 14 15 16 17 18 19 20

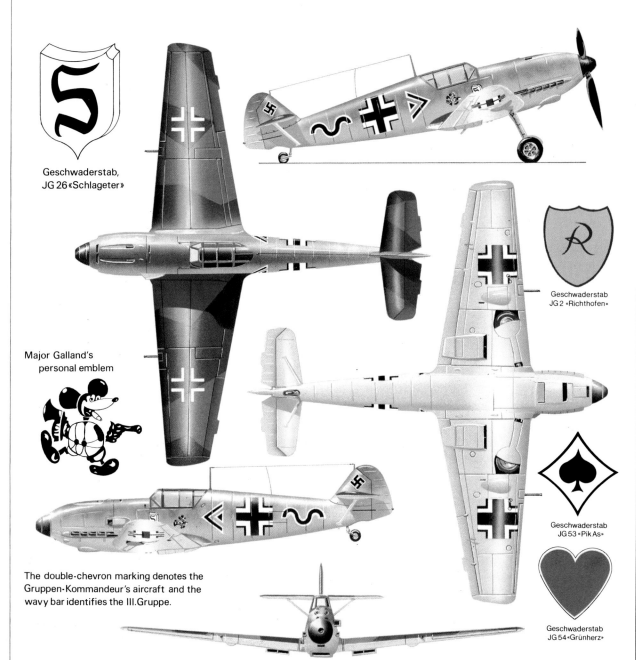

Geschwaderstab,
JG 26 «Schlageter»

Major Galland's
personal emblem

Geschwaderstab
JG 2 «Richthofen»

Geschwaderstab
JG 53 «Pik As»

Geschwaderstab
JG 54 «Grünherz»

The double-chevron marking denotes the Gruppen-Kommandeur's aircraft and the wavy bar identifies the III. Gruppe.

Produced in larger numbers than any other fighter in the Second World War, the Messerschmitt Bf 109 was the Luftwaffe's only single-seat fighter in the Battle of Britain. The "Emil" was at least a match for the Spitfire Mark I, and the E-1 variant was armed with two wing-mounted 20-mm cannon and two nose-mounted 7,9-mm machine guns.

Adolf Galland, born in 1912, had already shot down 17 Allied aircraft by 1st August 1940, the day on which he was awarded the Knight's Cross. He received the Oakleaves on 25th September, by which time his score had risen to 40. Galland was to become the youngest General in the German armed forces when he was appointed General of the Fighter Arm aged 30. By the end of the War he was the senior surviving holder of the Diamonds, and had shot down a total of 104 Allied aircraft – all of them in the West.

Copyright 1977, 1990 Francis K. Mason, FRHistS, AMRAeS

MESSERSCHMITT Bf 110C-4

German long-range escort fighter and fighter-bomber

Aircraft M8+CP, Wkr. Nr. 2089, of 6th Staffel, Zerstörergeschwader 76. II.Gruppe, known as the Haifisch (Shark) Gruppe, was caught by Spitfires of No.72 Squadron over Kent on 4th September 1940, losing three machines. M8+CP was shot down at 13.45 hrs. and crashed at Cowden, seven miles west of Tunbridge Wells. The pilot, Oberleutnant Günther Piduhn, and his gunner, Gefreiter Rudolf Conde, were both killed.

SCALE-FEET 0 1 2 3 4 5 6 7 8 9 10 11 12 13 14 15 16 17 18 19 20 21 22 23 24 25 26 27 28 29 30

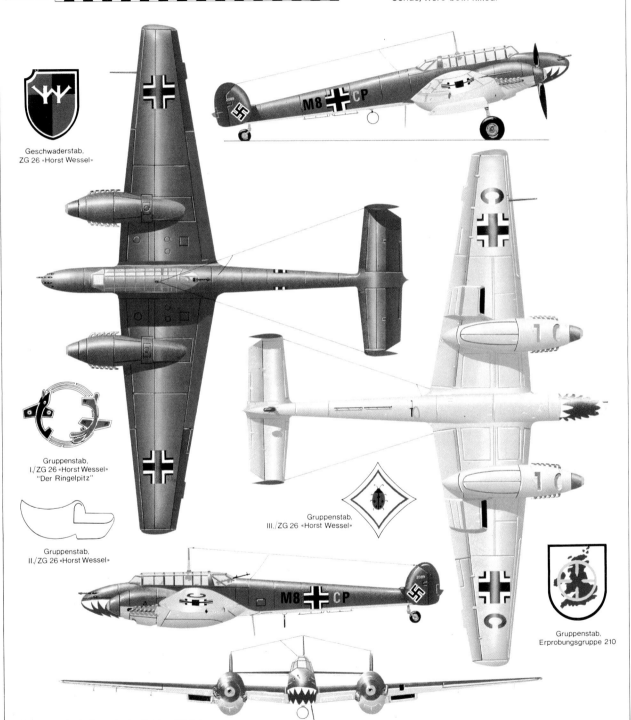

Geschwaderstab, ZG 26 «Horst Wessel»

Gruppenstab, I./ZG 26 «Horst Wessel» "Der Ringelpitz"

Gruppenstab, II./ZG 26 «Horst Wessel»

Gruppenstab, III./ZG 26 «Horst Wessel»

Gruppenstab, Erprobungsgruppe 210

Also extensively flown in the Battle of Britain was the Bf 110C-4/B fighter-bomber variant, which could carry up to 2,000 lb. of bombs externally under wings and fuselage.

Also shown above are the principal insignia of Zerstörergeschwader 26 «Horst Wessel» whose Bf 110s were heavily involved in operations against targets in South-West England in the latter stages of the Battle. Outstanding among other Bf 110 units in the summer of 1940 was Erprobungsgruppe 210, the brilliantly-led pathfinder/fighter-bomber Group whose insignia is also depicted above.

measure of success. These engagements were to be the downfall of the turret fighter for they suggested to the Air Ministry that the Defiant possessed combat superiority that did not in fact exist—once the German pilots came to realise just how vulnerable the British aircraft was. When the pilots of Messerschmitt 109s caught Defiants of their own—as occurred on 19th July 1940— they recognised them for what they were, and inflicted crippling losses. The technique of the pilot positioning himself with the gunner's field of fire in mind may have been feasible against slower bombers, but quite impossible in the whirl of a dogfight. Aircrew losses were high in Nos. 264 and 141 Squadrons, particularly when it was found that in an emergency a Defiant gunner had very little chance of escaping from his turret.

Wing span: 39 ft. 4 in. *Length:* 35 ft. 4 in. *Height:* 12. ft. 2 ins. *Wing area:* 250 sq. ft. *Powerplant::* One 1,030-h.p. Rolls-Royce Merlin III twelve-cylinder liquid-cooled engine. *Armament:* Four 0.303-inch Browning machine guns with 600 roungs per gun mounted in electrically-operated B.P. "A" Mark IID dorsal turret. *Maximum speed:* 304 m.p.h. at 17,000 feet. *Range:* 465 miles. *Service ceiling:* 30,350 feet.

BRISTOL BEAUFIGHTER I

The Beaufighter was the first high performance purpose-designed night fighter in the world, and such was the increasing tempo of combat aircraft design at the end of the 1930s that it is often forgotten just what an advance the Beaufighter represented. Its armament of four 20-mm. Hispano cannon and six 0.303-inch Browning machine guns was by far the heaviest carried aloft by an operational aircraft at the time of its combat debut in 1940. It was relatively fast and manœuvrable and, although it displayed a number of unpleasant tendencies—especially during take-off and landing—experienced Blenheim pilots found little difficulty in converting to the new aircraft.

The first Beaufighter to be taken on charge by an operational unit was *R2055*, delivered to the Fighter Interception Unit on 12th August, this aircraft being equipped soon after with A.I. Mark IV radar; however, not being fitted with I.F.F. equipment it was not permitted to fly patrols until early in September, by which time Beaufighters were beginning to appear with line squadrons. At first, each night fighter squadron received a single aircraft for conversion purposes but, as the weight of the night *Blitz* increased, calls were made to step up the rate of deliveries. Yet it was to be some time before crews could master the intricacies of the new radar, let alone apply the theory of the classroom to the reality of a dark night. And it was a long period of trial and error, during the last three months of 1940, that was to repay handsome dividends in a growing rate of night victories in 1941.

Most of the Beaufighters delivered to Fighter Command before the end of October 1940 carried only their cannon armament, the wing gun bays being ballasted; this was a precaution against a shortage of Browning machine guns for the all-important Hurricanes and Spitfires. No such shortage occurred and by mid-November all squadron Beaufighters were fully armed.

Wing span: 57 ft. 10 in. *Length:* 41 ft. 4 in. *Height:* 15 ft. 10 in. *Wing area:* 503 sq. ft. *Powerplant:* two 1,400-h.p. Bristol Hercules fourteen-cylinder sleeve-valve air-cooled engines. *Armament:* Four 20-mm. Hispano cannon in the fuselage nose, and six 0.303-inch Browning machine guns in the wings (four in the starboard wing, two in the port). *Maximum speed:* 321 m.p.h. at 15,800 feet. *Normal range:* 1,170 miles. *Service ceiling:* 26,500 feet.

GLOSTER GLADIATOR II

Numerically the least important day fighter in R.A.F. service during the Battle of Britain, the Gladiator was by 1940 an anachronistic survival from an earlier generation of fighter aircraft. It was, nevertheless, the immediate predecessor of the Hurricane and Spitfire in Fighter Command, so that most of the experienced British pilots in the Battle had first experienced the magic of a biplane fighter in the Gladiator (or its stablemate, the Gloster Gauntlet).

Gladiator biplanes constituted the mounts for the pilots of No. 247 Squadron during the Battle of Britain, being deployed at Roborough for the defence of Plymouth. Although the pilots flew constant patrols, frequently escorting in-bound convoys, they were seldom called into combat, and as far as is known did not claim any victories. In the North, No. 804 Squadron of the Fleet Air Arm flew Sea Gladiators from Hatston on dockyard defence patrols.

Wing span: 32 ft. 3 in. *Length:* 27 ft. 5 in. *Height:* 11 ft. 7 in. *Wing area:* 323 sq. ft. *Powerplant*: One 840-h.p. Bristol Mercury VIII.AS nine-cylinder air-cooled radial engine. *Armament:* Four 0.303-inch Browning machine guns, two mounted in the nose with 600 rounds per gun, and two mounted under the lower wings with 400 rounds per gun. *Maximum speed:* 257 m.p.h. at 14,600 feet. *Normal range:* 444 miles. *Service ceiling:* 33,500 feet.

MESSERSCHMITT Bf 109E-4

Designed by Willy Messerschmitt's *Bayerische Flugzeugwerke* team during 1934, and originally powered by a Rolls-Royce Kestrel V engine, the Bf 109 won a fighter competition at Travemünde in October 1935. It incorporated several features of the successful Bf 108 *Taifun* four-seater tourer, including leading edge slats and slotted flaps. The various high-lift devices countered the extremely high wing loading of 32 lb./sq. ft., the result of Messerschmitt's deliberate marrying of the smallest practicable airframe with the most powerful engine available. During the process of progressive development in the pre-War years the aircraft appeared in successively more powerful and heavier armed versions; and the Bf 109B and C models achieved great success in Spain with the *Legion Cóndor's* fighter unit, *Jagdgruppe 88*. Many of the *Luftwaffe's* most successful wartime fighter pilots received their operational blooding in Spain on the early Bf 109 models. When Germany invaded Poland on 1st September 1939 the 850 Bf 109E-1s available equipped twelve *Gruppen*. By August 1940 twenty-three *Gruppen* were in action on the Channel front, the E-3 version, which mounted two MG 17 machine guns in the nose, two in the wings, and an MG FF/M cannon firing through the spinner, being joined by the E-4; the latter and the E-7 were frequently employed as fighter-bombers to carry a 250-kilo bomb on fuselage crutches.

The various strengths and shortcomings of the Messerschmitt, the Hurricane and the Spitfire largely cancelled out in combat. The Hurricane's comparative weakness in acceleration was offset by its manœuvrability and strength. There was little to choose between the Spitfire and the Bf 109E (familiarly known in the *Luftwaffe* as the "Emil") between 12,000 and 17,000 feet, but above 20,000 feet the Messerschmitt was undoubtedly the better machine. It was extremely steady and stable, could be reefed round in high-g turns, and dived faster than either of its opponents. Control was rather heavy, and required more sheer physical effort from the pilot than its British contemporaries; and the high ground angle cut taxying visibility drastically. The weak, narrow track undercarriage and a powerful incipient swing on take-off and landing were the Bf 109's worst vices, and caused many accidents. Despite these faults, and the awkwardness of the cramped cockpit, the Messerschmitt was popular with pilots; throttle response was quick and clean, acceleration was brisk, the take-off short and steep, and low-speed handling characteristics were remarkable. The direct fuel injection was clearly superior to British carburettor feed, and prevented the engine from cutting when the aircraft was inverted.

The major drawback of the Bf 109 lay in its lack of range, and the lack of adequate fuel capacity prevented the fighter from operating north of the Thames on anything but a fleeting sortie; moreover, when called on to provide close escort for bomber formations, there were countless occasions when the Bf 109 pilots had to turn back before reaching the bombers' targets. On the other hand, when ordered to fly offensive sweeps over the southern counties, the "free chasing" Emils posed the most serious threat to the survival of Fighter Command.

Wing span: 32 ft. 4 in. *Length:* 28 ft. 8 in. *Height:* 11 ft. 2 in. *Wing area:* 174 sq. ft. *Powerplant:* One 1,150-h.p. Daimler Benz DB601A twelve-cylinder liquid-cooled engine. *Armament:* Two 7.9-mm. MG 17 machine guns in upper nose decking with 1,000 rounds per gun; two 20-mm. MG FF cannon in wings with 60 rounds per gun. *Maximum speed:* 357 m.p.h. at 12,300 feet. *Range:* 412 miles. *Service ceiling:* 36,000 feet.

MESSERSCHMITT BF 110C-4

The Messerschmitt Bf 110 *zerstörer*—"destroyer"—was the fruit of a development contract placed with Willy Messerschmitt's *Bayerische Flugzeugwerke* design bureau late in 1934. The *zerstörer* requirement called for an aircraft capable of both offensive and defensive rôles. As a long-range fighter it was intended to cut a path for the bombers through the enemy defences; as a defensive weapon it was to deny enemy bombers access to friendly airspace. In the former rôle it was to fail dismally, although it came to be used as a defensive night fighter with great success later in the War.

The first true operational version was the Bf 110C-1, which saw limited service as a ground attack machine in Poland in September 1939. Small numbers were also used during the invasion of Norway in April 1940; but the first confrontation with modern defensive fighters came in the following month, when some 350 aircraft of the type saw action during the invasion of France and the Low Countries. Losses were higher than had been expected; nevertheless, large numbers were committed to the daylight operations over Great Britain during the summer. Eight *Gruppen* of Bf 110Cs and Ds took part in the Battle, and by the close of 1940 the appalling losses suffered by these units finally convinced O.K.L of the folly of pitting the relatively sluggish *zerstörer* against a determined force of modern single-engine interceptors. The 110's defensive firepower and manœuvrability were wholly inadequate, while the maximum speed was impressive on paper but seldom realistic under combat conditions owing to very poor acceleration. Its presence in the combat area quickly became an unwelcome defensive liability for the over-stretched Bf 109E formations. It was a measure of this liability that, once committed to combat with nimble interceptors, the *zerstörer* formations frequently adopted a defensive circle—the so-called "circle of death"—a sterile manœuvre that firmly confounded their rôle of "cutting a path" through the defences. Intruder and setpiece operations generally fared little better than escort missions, with a few isolated exceptions. Perhaps the best exponents of the *zerstörer* were the pilots of *Erprobungsgruppe 210,* a well-trained and courageous unit which employed the Bf 110 in the fighter-bomber rôle under the protection of an autonomous *Staffel* of Emils.

The Bf 110C-4 differed from earlier models only in its improved MG FF cannon and a revised electrical system, which included Telefunken FuG 10 radio. A fighter-bomber modification with racks for two 250-kilo bombs was introduced under the designation Bf 110C-4/B.

Wing span: 53 ft. 5 in. *Length:* 39 ft. 8 in. *Height:* 11 ft. 6 in. *Wing area:* 413 sq. ft. *Powerplant:* Two 1,150-h.p. Daimler Benz DB601A twelve-cylinder liquid-cooled engines. *Armament:* Four 7.9-mm. MG 17 machine guns with 1,000 round per gun and two 20-mm. MG FF cannon with 180 rounds per gun in the nose; one rear-firing 7.9-mm. MG 15 machine gun with 750 rounds in the rear cockpit. *Maximum speed:* 349 m.p.h. at 22,960 feet. *Normal range:* 530 miles. *Service ceiling:* 32,000 feet.

HEINKEL He 111P-2

The Heinkel He 111P embodied the first major design changes in the He 111 bomber series, which had appeared in 1935. Designed by Siegfried and Walter Günther, supposedly as a fast mail and passenger aircraft for *Deutsche Lufthansa,* the He 111 prototype had provision for three gun positions and a 1,000-kilo bombload, and early production versions featured the conventional stepped cabin windscreen . The He 111B, D, E and F variants served with home-based *Gruppen* and with *Kampfgruppe 88* in Spain; the aircraft of the latter unit proved to be virtually immune to attack by the Republican fighters owing to their speed and, by contemporary standards, adequate defensive armament.

The P-series began to leave the production lines during 1938 with a new straight-tapered wing and a completely redesigned nose section and cockpit; extensively glazed and offset to starboard to improve pilot visibility, this new nose formed an unbroken projection of the fuselage contours, and was to beome the "trademark" of the He 111 throughout the War. Another new feature introduced in the P-series was the streamlined ventral gondola, which replaced the unsatisfactory and drag-producing retractable "dustbin" of the earlier models.

Units of He 111Ps saw action over Poland, but it was not until the Battle of France that a significant fighter defence was encoun-

HEINKEL He 111P-2

German four/five-crew heavy bomber flown extensively during 1940

Aircraft 5J+JP, Wkr. Nr. 3078, of the 6th Staffel, Kampfgeschwader 4 «General Wever», based at Eindhoven, Holland, under the command of Major Dr. Gottlieb Wolff (later awarded the Knight's Cross).

SCALE–FEET
0 2 4 6 8 10 12 14 16 18 20 22 24 26 28 30 32 34 36 38 40

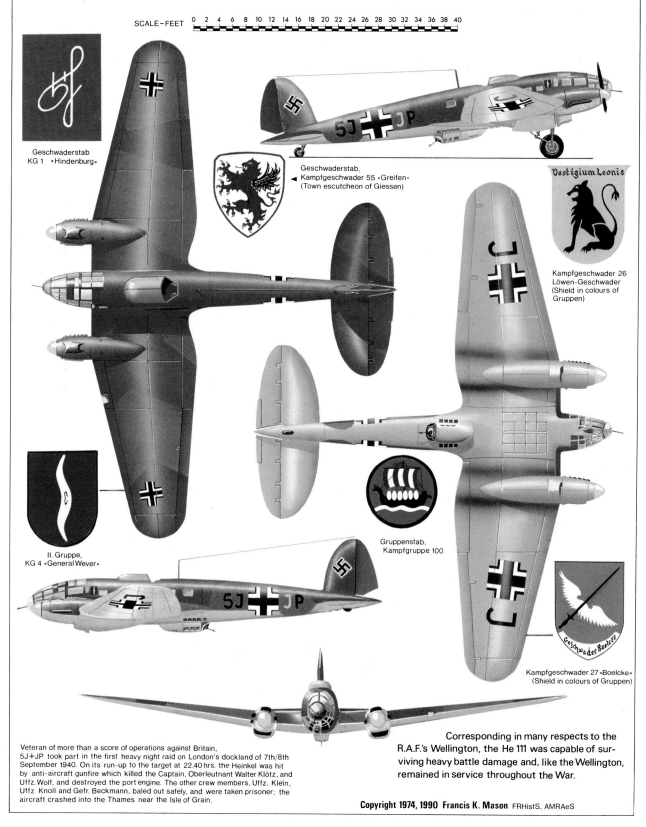

Geschwaderstab KG 1 «Hindenburg»

Geschwaderstab, Kampfgeschwader 55 «Greifen» (Town escutcheon of Giessen)

Vestigium Leonis

Kampfgeschwader 26 Löwen-Geschwader (Shield in colours of Gruppen)

II. Gruppe, KG 4 «General Wever»

Gruppenstab, Kampfgruppe 100

Kampfgeschwader 27 «Boelcke» (Shield in colours of Gruppen)

Veteran of more than a score of operations against Britain, 5J+JP took part in the first heavy night raid on London's dockland of 7th/8th September 1940. On its run-up to the target at 22.40 hrs. the Heinkel was hit by anti-aircraft gunfire which killed the Captain, Oberleutnant Walter Klötz, and Uffz. Wolf, and destroyed the port engine. The other crew members, Uffz. Klein, Uffz. Knoll and Gefr. Beckmann, baled out safely, and were taken prisoner; the aircraft crashed into the Thames near the Isle of Grain.

Corresponding in many respects to the R.A.F.'s Wellington, the He 111 was capable of surviving heavy battle damage and, like the Wellington, remained in service throughout the War.

Copyright 1974, 1990 Francis K. Mason FRHistS, AMRAeS

DORNIER Do 17Z~2

German four-crew medium bomber flown by Luftflotten 2 and 3 in the Battle of Britain and the night Blitz

Aircraft 3Z+GS of the 8th Staffel, Kampfgeschwader 77, shot down by ground defences over Kent on 1st July 1940, after being crippled by R.A.F. fighters. The bomber's Captain, Oberleutnant Gillios, was killed and his three crew members were posted Missing.

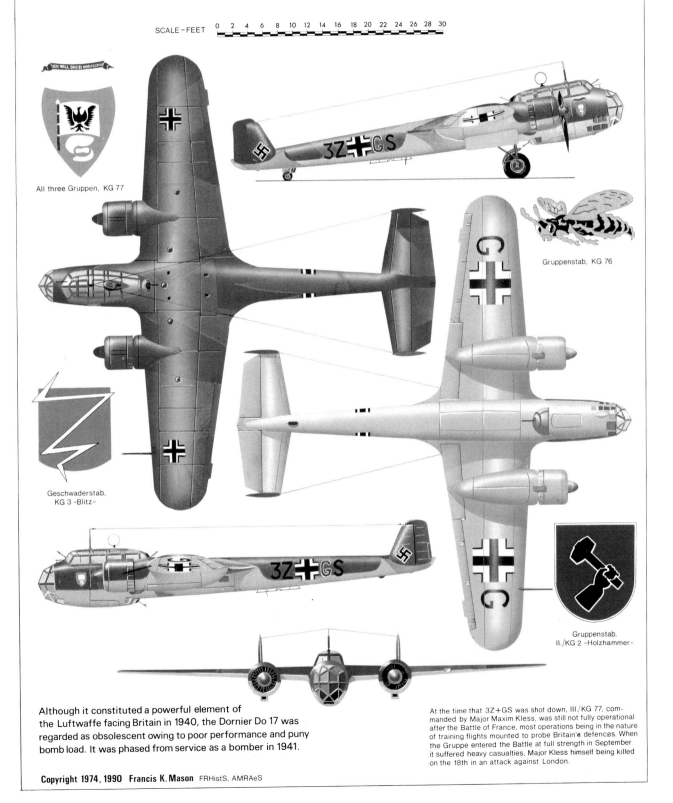

SCALE — FEET 0 2 4 6 8 10 12 14 16 18 20 22 24 26 28 30

ICH WILL DAS ES VOR. FECHRAN

All three Gruppen, KG 77

Gruppenstab, KG 76

Geschwaderstab, KG 3 «Blitz»

3Z+GS

Gruppenstab, II./KG 2 «Holzhammer»

Although it constituted a powerful element of the Luftwaffe facing Britain in 1940, the Dornier Do 17 was regarded as obsolescent owing to poor performance and puny bomb load. It was phased from service as a bomber in 1941.

At the time that 3Z+GS was shot down, III./KG 77, com-manded by Major Maxim Kless, was still not fully operational after the Battle of France, most operations being in the nature of training flights mounted to probe Britain's defences. When the Gruppe entered the Battle at full strength in September it suffered heavy casualties, Major Kless himself being killed on the 18th in an attack against London.

tered in combat. By the opening of the Battle of Britain progressive replacement by the new and improved He 111H was in hand, but He 111Ps were still in service with at least two *Kampfgeschwader*. In common with the early He 111H models, they suffered from inadequate firepower when challenged by British fighters. Shortly after the beginning of the night *Blitz* He 111s introduced a fixed MG 17 mounted in the extreme tail of the aircraft in a somewhat forlorn attempt to discourage attacks by night fighters from directly astern.

Wing span: 74 ft. 2 in. *Length:* 53 ft. 9 in. *Height:* 13 ft. 1 in. *Wing area:* 942.9 sq. ft. *Powerplant:* Two 1,100-h.p. Daimler Benz DB601A twelve-cylinder liquid-cooled engines. *Defensive armament:* Three 7.9-mm. MG 15 machine guns in nose, dorsal and ventral positions. *Bombload:* 4,414 lb. *Maximum speed:* 247 m.p.h. at 16,400 feet. *Maximum range:* 1,224 miles. *Service ceiling:* 26,250 feet.

DORNIER Do 17Z-2

Prominent member of the German bomber trio during the Battle of Britain, the Dornier Do 17 in its basic form had largely disappeared from front line units by the end of 1942, while its partners of 1940—the Heinkel He 111 and Junkers Ju 88—soldiered on until 1945. The Do 17 was originally designed as a fast passenger and mail transport for *Deutsche Lufthansa*'s European Express services, and the prototype made its maiden flight in the autumn of 1934. The slim fuselage was unsuitable for a passenger carrier, and the first three prototypes were mothballed. A new series of prototypes, resurrected as a *schnellbomber* project, was built and by 1937 Do 17E and F-series bombers and reconnaissance aircraft were entering service with the *Luftwaffe*.

Foreign observers were much impressed by the Dornier's showing at the Military Aircraft Competition, held in 1937 at Zurich; a specially prepared aircraft displayed a speed (248 m.p.h.) almost as fast as that of any foreign fighter at the meeting. Export sales to Yugoslavia followed in due course. The Do 17E and F served with *Kampfgruppe 33* and *Aufklärungsstaffel 88* respectively during the Spanish Civil War and, like the He 111s in Spain, they fared well against the Republicans' rather motley collection of fighters.

The major production variant was the Do 17Z, which appeared in 1939. The Dornier Do 17Z-2 was powered by 1,000-h.p. Bramo radials with two-stage supercharging, and could mount up to eight rifle-calibre machine guns. The new deepened nose section incorporated a rear-facing ventral position for a prone gunner; the bombload remained at 2,200 lb., and the maximum crew complement was increased to five (although the aircraft still seldom carried more than four). When war broke out in September 1939, 23 reconnaissance *Staffeln* were operating Do 17Ps, and nine *Gruppen* of *Kampfgeschwader 2, 3, 76* and 77 were equipped with Do 17Ms or Do 17Zs. *Kampfgeschwader 77* played a major part in the bombing of Warsaw, and all four *Geschwader* operated extensively during the battles of France and Britain.

As if aware of their vulnerability to determined attacked by the British fighters, operations by the Dornier crews were characterised by particularly tight formation keeping, and it was a feature of numerous raids that the Dorniers' crossfire was highly effective in limiting losses.

Wing span: 59 ft 1 in. *Length:* 52 ft. 0 in. *Height:* 14 ft. 11 in. *Wing area:* 592 sq. ft. *Powerplant:* Two 1,000-h.p. Bramo 323P nine-cylinder air-cooled engines. *Defensive armament:* Four to eight 7.9.-mm. MG 15 machine guns in front, rear and beam cockpit mountings and ventral position. *Bombload:* 2,200 lb. *Maximum speed:* 265 m.p.h. at 16,400 feet. *Normal range:* 745 miles. *Service ceiling:* 26,400 feet.

JUNKERS Ju 87B-2

The Junkers Ju 87B-2 was the main early production variant of the *Stuka* series, which had orginated in 1935 (*Stuka* for *Sturzkampfflugzeug* =dive-bomber). The Junkers design won a dive-bomber competition in mid-1936, and the first Ju 87A-1s were delivered to the *Luftwaffe* the following spring; in the summer they were issued to the newly-formed *Stukageschwader 163* "*Immelmann*". Three A-1s were sent to Spain in December 1937, and in 1939 several B-1s arrived in time to take part in the last weeks' fighting in the Civil War. They proved extremely successful as pinpoint bombers, and the Spanish terrain offered a host of worthwhile targets such as bridges, road junctions, and harbour installations. The B-series was larger, more powerful, better armed, and generally cleaner in outline than the original version; it went into production in 1938, and by the outbreak of war against Poland some 360 were in service.

In Poland and the West, the angular *Stuka* became a symbol of *blitzkrieg*; under conditions of almost complete air supremacy, the squadrons roamed ahead of the *panzer* columns as long-range artillery. They would drop into near-vertical dives over roads, railways, strongpoints and troop concentrations, doing as much damage to morale as to material. The aircraft's unique appearance and dramatic tactics had a profound psychological effect on even the most seasoned troops.

It was over Dunkirk that the *Stuka*'s reputation first suffered seriously; and in the opening weeks of the Battle of Britain the lesson was devastatingly repeated. Faced by a determined and modern fighter defence the Junkers was helpless; once separated from its Messerschmitt escort it was "easy meat" for the Hurricanes and Spitfires, and after a few weeks of serious losses the type was largely withdrawn from operations over Britain. There were a few isolated raids in November, but after the demonstration of its fatal limitations the *Stuka* was moved to areas where its specialised talents could be employed at less cost.

Wing span: 45 ft. 3 in. *Length:* 36 ft. 1 in. *Height:* 13 ft. 10 in. *Wing area:* 343 sq. ft. *Powerplant:* One 1,100-h.p. Junkers Jumo 211A-1 twelve-cylinder liquid-cooled engine. *Armament:* Two 7.9-mm. MG 17 machine guns in the wings, one 7.9-mm. MG 15 machine gun on a rear cockpit mounting. *Bombload:* One 1,100-lb. bomb carried on swinging crutch mounting under the fuselage, and four 110-lb. bombs under the wings. *Maximum speed:* 232 m.p.h. at 13,500 feet. *Range:* (1,100-lb. bombload), 370 miles. *Service ceiling:* 26,500 feet.

JUNKERS Ju 88A-1

The Junkers Ju 88 first flew in December 1936. It had been designed in response to a *Luftwaffe* fast bomber requirement announced by the R.L.M. the previous year, and was the brainchild of W.H. Evers and the American designer Al Gassner, who was working in Europe during 1935-36. The V-4 prototype introduced the characteristic ventral gondola and the blunt, glazed nose section built up from optically flat "beetle's eye" panels.

Tooling up for mass production and assembly at several dispersed plants began in 1938, and the first batch of ten pre-production Ju 88A-0 machines was delivered to the Service test unit *Erprobungskommando 88 i*n the spring of 1939. Some 60 Ju 88A-1s had been delivered by the end of 1939, and in August of that year *Erprobungskommando 88* was redesignated I./KG 25. The following month the unit was renamed as I. *Gruppe, Kampfgeschwader 30*, and it was to be KG 30"*Adler Geschwader*" which became the most famous of all Ju 88 units; in its ranks served several of the *Luftwaffe's* celebrated bomber pilots, including Hajo Herrmann and Walter Baumbach. During the Battle of Britain the Ju 88 served with KG 30, KG 51, KG 54, LG 1 and KGr.806; elements of KG 4, KG 76 and KG 77; and several *Aufklärungsgruppen.*

This most versatile of all German aircraft remained in service throughout the War, and distinguished itself in the rôles of dive bomber, level bomber, torpedo bomber, minelayer, day fighter, night fighter, intruder, reconnaissance aircraft, close support aircraft and, finally, flying bomb.

Wing span: 59 ft. 11 in. *Length:* 47 ft. 1 in. *Height:* 15 ft. 5 in. *Wing area:* 540 sq. ft. *Powerplant:* Two 1,200-h.p. Junkers Jumo 211B-1 twelve-cylinder liquid-cooled engines. *Defensive armament:* Three 7.9-mm. MG 15 machine guns in front and rear cockpit mountings and ventral gondola. *Bombload:* Normal load, 3,968 lb. carried on four underwing racks, plus small internal capacity. *Maximum speed:* 286 m.p.h. at 16.00 feet. *Range:* 1,553 miles. *Service ceiling:* 26,500 feet.

ARADO Ar 196A-3

An attractive and efficient twin-float seaplane, the Arado Ar 196 entered service in 1939 when the first production batch was assigned to Germany's principal warships as on-board reconnaissance aircraft. In service with merchant shipping raiders, their task was to search for likely victims beyond the horizon, and if necessary to attack the target's bridge and superstructure with its twin cannon armament to prevent wireless transmissions being broadcast that would compromise the raider's position.

The improved Ar 196A-3 version appeared in 1940 and was used primarily for coastal reconnaissance and patrol, although it possessed a light attack capability with small bombs carried under the wings. Several examples were encountered by pilots of Fighter Command, particularly over the western approaches to the English Channel on convoy and air-sea rescue reconnaissance sorties.

Wing span: 40 ft. 10 in. *Length:* 36 ft. 1 in. *Height:* 14 ft. 5 in. *Wing area:* 305 sq. ft. *Powerplant:* One 970-h.p. B.M.W. 132K nine-cylinder air-cooled engine. Armament: One 7.9-mm. MG 17 machine gun in the starboard side of the engine cowling, two 20-mm. MG FF cannon in the wings, and a single or twin 7.9.-mm. MG 15 machine gun on a rear cockpit mounting. *Bombload:* Two 110-lb. bombs carried on underwing racks. *Maximum speed:* 193 m.p.h. at 13,120 feet. *Range:* 670 miles. *Service ceiling:* 23,000 feet.

HEINKEL He 115B-1

The Heinkel He 115 twin-engine, twin-float seaplane was widely used in a number of rôles during the Battle of Britain, most notable of which was the mining of British estuaries and coastal waters. It first flew in 1936, and by the end of the War was adjudged one of the best floatplanes of any combatant nation. Deliveries commenced in 1937, and an export order to Norway was filled in 1939. The B-1 version was essentially similar to the first production model, and the majority produced in 1940 were adapted to accommodate a pair of acoustic sea mines.

In furtherance of the German policy of attempting to deny the British safe passage along the South and East Coasts, the Heinkel He 115s of *Küstenfliegergruppen 106, 506* and *906* were tasked with aerial mining the approaches to the River Thames, and to Iswich, Harwich, Great Yarmouth, Hull, Scarborough, the Firth of Forth and Aberdeen; between them these three *Gruppen* dropped slightly more than 800 mines during the period of the Battle, at a cost of eighteen aircraft and 76 airmen. Seven aircraft were lost from causes other than combat. The task of aerial mining was particularly hazardous in such shallow waters as the Thames Estuary as the German pilots were obliged to fly very low, not only to escape detection but to ensure accuracy of mining. On several occasions the mines exploded prematurely, fatally damaging the Heinkels.

(It should, however, be explained that the mining efforts of the three He 115 *Gruppen* constituted only about one third of all air mining by the *Luftwaffe* during the Battle of Britain, several *Gruppen* of He 111s and Ju 88s being allotted the task of sowing mines in the Bristol Channel and in the approaches to the Mersey, as well as off Dover, Portsmouth, Portland, Plymouth and the Clyde, this activity being stepped up during September and October.)

Wing span: 73 ft. 1 in. *Length:* 56 ft. 9 in. *Height:* 21 ft. 8 in. *Wing area:* 933 sq. ft. *Powerplant:* Two 970-h.p. B.M.W. 132K nine-cylinder air-cooled radial engines. *Defensive armament:* Two 7.9-mm. MG 15 machine guns in nose and rear cockpit mountings. *Bombload:* One 1,760-lb. torpedo and two 550-lb. bombs; one 2,028-lb. accoustic mine and two 550-lb. bombs; two 2,028-lb. accoustic mines. *Maximum speed:* 203 m.p.h. at 11,150 feet. *Range:* normal 1,300 miles; maximum 2,080 miles. *Service ceiling:* 17,000 feet.

JUNKERS Ju 87B-2

German dive bomber flown against R.A.F. and Royal Navy installations in Southern England during August 1940

Aircraft T6+JL (Wkr.Nr.0557) of 3.Staffel, Stukageschwader 2 «Immelmann», commanded by Hauptmann Hubertus Hitschold and based at Lannions and St. Malo, France, during the Battle of Britain.

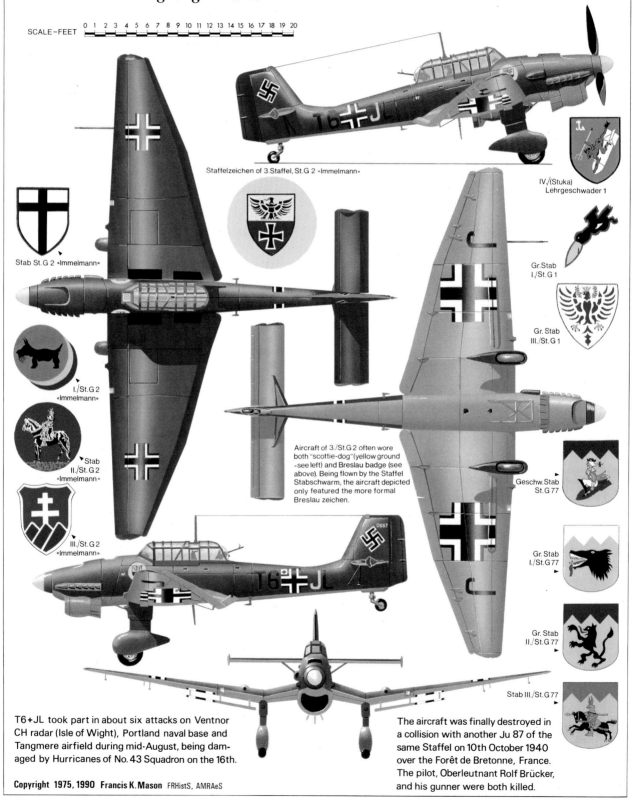

SCALE-FEET 0 1 2 3 4 5 6 7 8 9 10 11 12 13 14 15 16 17 18 19 20

Staffelzeichen of 3.Staffel, St.G 2 «Immelmann»

Stab St.G 2 «Immelmann»

I./St.G 2 «Immelmann»

Stab II./St.G 2 «Immelmann»

III./St.G 2 «Immelmann»

IV./(Stuka) Lehrgeschwader 1

Gr.Stab I./St.G 1

Gr.Stab III./St.G 1

Aircraft of 3./St.G 2 often wore both "scottie-dog" (yellow ground -see left) and Breslau badge (see above). Being flown by the Staffel Stabschwarm, the aircraft depicted only featured the more formal Breslau zeichen.

Geschw.Stab St.G 77

Gr.Stab I./St.G 77

Gr.Stab II./St.G 77

Stab III./St.G 77

T6+JL took part in about six attacks on Ventnor CH radar (Isle of Wight), Portland naval base and Tangmere airfield during mid-August, being damaged by Hurricanes of No. 43 Squadron on the 16th.

The aircraft was finally destroyed in a collision with another Ju 87 of the same Staffel on 10th October 1940 over the Forêt de Bretonne, France. The pilot, Oberleutnant Rolf Brücker, and his gunner were both killed.

Copyright 1975, 1990 Francis K. Mason FRHistS, AMRAeS

JUNKERS Ju 88A~1

German medium/dive bomber flown in the Battle of Britain and night Blitz, 1940

Aircraft 9K+DH (Wkr.Nr. 2063) of 1. Staffel, Kampfgeschwader 51 «Edelweiss», based at Mélun-Villaroche, France, under the command of Major Hans Bruno Schulz-Heyn in September 1940.

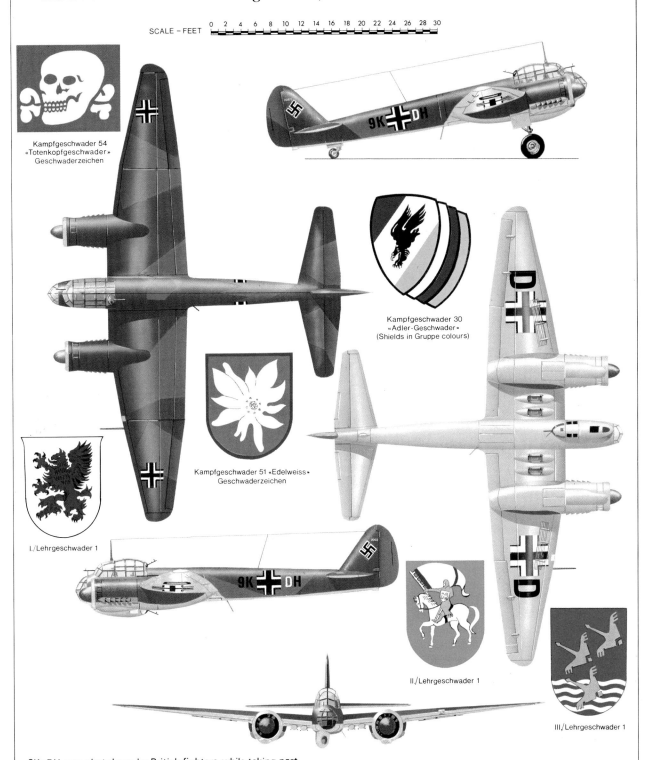

SCALE – FEET
0 2 4 6 8 10 12 14 16 18 20 22 24 26 28 30

Kampfgeschwader 54
«Totenkopfgeschwader»
Geschwaderzeichen

Kampfgeschwader 30
«Adler-Geschwader»
(Shields in Gruppe colours)

Kampfgeschwader 51 «Edelweiss»
Geschwaderzeichen

I./Lehrgeschwader 1

II./Lehrgeschwader 1

III./Lehrgeschwader 1

9K+DH was shot down by British fighters while taking part in a raid over South-East England on 30th September 1940. Three crewmen, Fw. Fritz Paczinski, Gefr. Peuka and Gefr. Roppert were killed; the fourth, Gefr. Eduard Dürrschmidt, was posted Missing.

Copyright 1975, 1990 Francis K. Mason FRHistS, AMRAeS

FOCKE-WULF Fw 200C-1

The Focke-Wulf Fw 200 Condor was designed as a trans-Atlantic airliner in 1936 in a bold bid to establish a regular air route to the Americas. However, although early aircraft performed some outstanding world flights, the inevitability of war encouraged the R.L.M. to investigate the possibility of adapting the aircraft for maritime reconnaissance duties, and this was assisted by work already carried out in response to a possible order for such an aircraft by Japan. The military version, the Fw 200C-1, entered production at Cottbus late in 1939 and, apart from a batch of six pre-production C-0s, deliveries of the C-1 commenced to I./KG 40 early in July 1940. These aircraft were employed in the long-range maritime reconnaisance and anti-shipping rôles flying a long over-sea route between Bordeaux-Merignac on the Brest peninsula and either Trondheim or Stavanger-Sola in Norway, this flight passing over the sea convoy routes off the Irish and Scottish coasts. By September the strength of I./KG 40 had increased, despite losses, to fifteen aircraft, and between 1st August and 30th September the *Gruppe* had accounted for more than 90,000 tons of Allied shipping. Its most spectacular success was the discovery and bombing of the Canadian Pacific liner, *Empress of Britain*, off the Irish coast on 26th October, the crippled vessel being sunk by a U-boat while attempts were being made to tow her to safety.

There is no doubt that the depredations of the Fw 200s caused much concern among British commanders (Churchill himself referred to them as "Focke-Wolves"), but the improving countermeasures taken during 1941 forced KG 40 to confine its activites to the shadowing of convoys rather than engaging in actual attacks, yet in so doing they became the "eyes" of the growing U-boat packs.

Apart from their constant long-distance patrolling, the Fw 200s of KG 40 are known to have participated in a number of bombing raids over Britain during the Battle, and on one occasion no fewer than three such aircraft were positively identified during a raid over the West Country. At least one other was shot down over Britain during the night Blitz.

Operating the Fw 200 under military conditions demanded considerable care and skill for the aircraft underwent relatively little strengthening to withstand combat stresses, and it was not until the arrival of the Fw 200C-3 in mid-1941 that any real effort was made to provide the strength necessary to withstand combat manœuvres at high all-up weights.

Wing span: 107 ft. 9.5 in. **Length:** 76 ft. 11.5 in. **Height:** 20 ft. 8 in. **Wing area:** 1,290 sq. ft. **Powerplant:** Four 830-h.p. B.M.W. 132H nine-cylinder air-cooled radial engines. **Defensive armament:** three 7.9-mm. MG 15 machine guns in forward and rear dorsal, and rear ventral positions, and one 20-mm. MG FF cannon in forward ventral position. **Bombload:** 2,750 lb. **Maximum speed:** approx. 230 m.p.h. at 16,000 feet. **Normal range:** 2,200 miles. **Service ceiling:** 19,000 feet.

DORNIER DO 215B-1

The Dornier Do 215 was evolved as an export version of the Dornier Do 17Z; the Do 215V1 and V2 demonstration prototypes were converted from pre-production Do 17Z-0s. Production of the Do 215A-1 with Daimler Benz DB601A in-line engines began in August 1939 in response to orders from Yugoslavia and Sweden. Before deliveries could begin, however, the aircraft were taken over by the *Luftwaffe* and modified as Do 215B-1 reconnaissance bombers, with mountings for three cameras. Relatively few were produced and during 1940 only *Aufklärungsgruppe Oberbefehlshaber der Luftwaffe* and one or two other *Staffeln* received the type. Being engaged on reconnaissance duties, such aircraft almost invariably operated singly over Britain.

However, on account of pre-War publicity given to the V1 and V2 demonstration prototypes, British Intelligence concluded that the Do 215 was entering widespread service with the *Luftwaffe*, replacing the familiar Do 17, and most aircraft recognition documents issued to Fighter Command during the early summer of 1940 referred only to the Do 215 bomber. For this reason almost every twin-engine Dornier claimed shot down by pilots of Fighter Command during July and August was referred to as a Do 215. In fact probably fewer than a dozen Do 215s were shot down in combat—the remainder being Do 17Ps and Zs.

Wing span: 59 ft. 1 in. **Length:** 52 ft. 0 in. **Height:** 14 ft. 11 in. **Wing area:** 592 sq. ft. **Powerplant:** Two 1,075-h.p. Daimler Benz DB 601A twelve-cylinder liquid-cooled engines. **Defensive armament:** Three to five 7.9-mm. MG 15 machine guns mounted singly in front, rear and beam cockpit positions and rear of ventral gondola. **Bombload:** 2,200 lb. **Maximum speed:** 292 m.p.h. at 16,400 feet. **Normal range:** 965 miles. **Service ceiling:** 31,170 feet.

HEINKEL He 59B-2

A large twin-engine, twin-float biplane, the Heinkel He 59 first flew in 1931 as a landplane but was subsequently developed as a seaplane, initially intended to perform the torpedo-bombing and maritime reconnaissance rôles in the still-clandestine *Luftwaffe*. By the mid-1930s the B-2 version was in production, incorporating nose and ventral gun positions, each mounting single machine guns; an unsual feature was the location of all fuel in the large floats.

The He 59 saw operational service with the *Legion Cóndor* early in the Spanish Civil War, being employed as a night bomber and for anti-shipping duties. By mid-1940 the B- and C-series aircraft were flown almost exclusively in the air-sea rescue and coastal reconnaissance rôles, although ten such aircraft participated in the assault on, and capture of the vital river bridge at Rotterdam during the German invasion of Holland in May that year. During the Battle of Britain Heinkel He 59s were frequently discovered flying in the vicinity of British coastal convoys, being marked with prominent Red Crosses. When it was suspected that these seaplanes were using their radio to disclose the presence of the convoys to *Luftwaffe* bombers, orders were given to British pilots for them to be destroyed. In the course of numerous such encounters, half a dozen He 59s were shot down and several others damaged; on only two occasions were the crews found to include medical staff, and all were crewed by fully operational military personnel. Heinkel He 59Bs and Cs equipped *Seenotflugkommando 1, 2, 3, 4* and *5*, as well as *Seenotzentrale Cherbourg* and *Seenotzentrale Boulogne*, and the average number of such aircraft on the strength of these units at any one time during the Battle of Britain totalled around 50.

Wing span: 77 ft. 9 in. *Length:* 57 ft. 1 in. *Height:* 23 ft. 3 .5 in. *Wing area:* 1,649 sq. ft. *Powerplant:* Two 660-h.p. B.M.W. VI 6.0 ZU twelve-cylinder air-cooled engines. *Defensive armament:* Three 7.9-mm. MG 15 machine guns in nose, dorsal and ventral positions. *Bombload:* 2,200-lb. or one torpedo. *Maximum speed:* 137 m.p.h. at sea level. *Maximum range:* 1,087 miles. *Service ceiling:* 11,480 feet.

DORNIER Do 18G-1

A descendant of the well-known family of Dornier *Wal* (Whale) flying boats of the 1920s and 1930s, the Do 18 was a twin-engine parasol monoplane employing stub-wing sponsons for on-water stability; the twin Junkers Jumo diesel engines were mounted on the centreline in tandem in a nacelle on top of the wing. Of graceful appearance, it had been in production for some years prior to the Second World War and in 1939 the Do 18G-series entered service with defensive armament increased to feature a large power-operated dorsal gun turret amidships.

Crewed by four or five men, the Do 18 served with *2.Staffel, Küstenfliegergruppe 106, 2.Staffel,* Kü.Fl.Gr.906, and all three *Staffeln* of Kü.Fl.Gr.406 during the Battle of France, but by the period of the Battle of Britain only 2./Kü.Fl.Gr.106 and 2./Kü.Fl.Gr.406 were still operational; between them these *Staffeln* flew a total of fifteen aircraft, of which two were encountered and shot down by Fighter Command pilots, and two by aircraft of the Fleet Air Arm. Like the Heinkel He 59, their primary task was air-sea rescue, but as far as is known they did not carry Red Cross markings and were also frequently employed in genuine maritime reconnaissance and shipping search duties. Later, however, with all armament removed, the Do 18N-1 was introduced exclusively for air-sea rescue and ambulance duties and were, from 1941 onwards, adorned with the Red Cross.

Wing span: 77 ft. 9 in. *Length:* 63 ft. 7 in. *Height:* 17 ft. 5 in. *Wing area:* 1,054 sq. ft. *Powerplant:* Two 88-h.p. Junkers Jumo 205D six-cylinder double-opposed liquid-cooled diesel engines. *Defensive armament:* One 13-mm. MG 131 heavy machine gun in the bow position, and one 20-mm. MG 151 20-mm. cannon in a midships power-operated turret. *Bombload:* 440 lb. *Maximum speed:* 165 m.p.h. at 6,560 feet. *Maximum range:* 2,175 miles. *Service ceiling:* 13,800 feet.

FIAT CR.42

The Fiat CR.42, a robust and highly manoeuvrable biplane fighter, entered series production late in 1939 under the Italian "Programme R" re-equipment plan. By the time of Italy's entry into the War in June 1940, some two dozen *squadrigli* had received the type, and it first entered combat during the last few days of the Battle of France.

As a largely political manoeuvre, Mussolini obtained Hitler's sanction to deploy aircraft of the *Regia Aeronautica* to Belgium to participate in the Battle of Britain. However, by the time the Italian force was considered to be fully operational the main daylight Battle was virtually over, and Fighter Command had recovered its strength. When Italian fighters and bombers made their belated appearance in daylight on 11th November off the coast near Harwich, they were met by a powerful force of Hurricanes and suffered fairly heavy losses—with the result that the adventure was not repeated, and the *Corpo Aereo Italiano* soon returned to the warmer and familiar skies of the Mediterranean.

Wing span: (Upper) 31 ft. 9.5 in.; (lower) 21 ft. 4 in. *Length:* 27 ft. 0 in. *Height:* 10 ft. 0 in. *Wing area:* 241.1 sq. ft. *Powerplant:* One 840-h.p. A.74 R.I.C.38 fourteen-cylinder air-cooled radial engine. *Armament:* One 12.7-mm. and one 7.7-mm. SAFAT machine guns in the upper fuselage nose decking, with 950 rounds of 7.7-mm. and 500 rounds of 12.7-mm. ammunition. *Maximum speed:* 274 m.p.h. at 20,000 feet. *Maximum range:* 485 miles. *Service ceiling:* 33,500 feet.

FIAT BR.20M

The Fiat BR.20M was an improved version of the BR.20 bomber first delivered to the *Regia Aeronautica* in September 1936. Twelve machines of the original version saw action during the Spanish Civil War, and 85 machines were exported to Japan in 1938. The M-version, with longer fuselage, cleaned-up nose and heavier defensive armament, appeared late in 1939.

By June 1940 four *Stormi* were operating a total of 162 BR.20s, of which a third were BR.20Ms. The type saw service in Southern France, Greece, North Africa and over Malta, and was generally similar in abilities to the Dornier Do 17. Although a rugged and steady aircraft, the BR.20 was not a success as a night bomber in 1940; the crews were inadequately trained for night navigation, and the aircraft were poorly equipped for instrument flying. Eighty such aircraft accompanied the *Corpo Aereo Italiano* in its brief deployment to Belgium at the end of the Battle of Britain, but did not impress the opposing pilots of R.A.F. Fighter Command.

Wing span: 70 ft. 8 in. *Length:* 55 ft 1 in. *Height:* 14 ft. 1 in. *Wing area:* 796.5 sq. ft. *Powerplant:* Two 1,000-h.p. A.80R.C.41 eighteen-cylinder air-cooled engines. *Defensive armament:* three or four 12.7-mm. SAFAT heavy machine guns in nose, ventral and dorsal positions. *Bombload:* 3,550 lb. *Maximum speed:* 267 m.p.h. at, 13,120 feet. *Maximum range:* 1,193 miles. *Service ceiling:* 24,935 feet.

APPENDIX D

THE LUFTWAFFE ORDER OF BATTLE

The Forces Facing Britain at 09.00 hrs., 13th August 1940 (Adler Tag)

LUFTFLOTTE 2 Headquarters, Brussels, Belgium. Commanded by Generalfeldmarschall Albert Kesselring. Bases in Holland, Belgium and Northern France.

I Fliegerkorps Headquarters, Beauvais, France. Commanded by Generaloberst Ulrich Grauert.

LONG-RANGE BOMBERS
Kampfgeschwader 1 Commanded by Oberstleutnant Exss.[1] Headquarters at Rosiéres-en-Santerre. *Stabsschwarm*, Heinkel He 111.
    I *Gruppe* Major Maier.[2] Based at Montdidier. Heinkel He 111.
    II *Gruppe* Oberstleutnant Benno Kosch. Based at Montdidier. Heinkel He 111
    III *Gruppe* Major Willibald Fanelsa. Based at Rosiéres-en-Santerre. Dornier Do 17.

Kampfgeschwader 76 Commanded by Oberstleutnant Stefan Frölich. Headquarters at Cormeilles-en-Vexin. *Stabsschwarm*, Dornier Do 17.
    I *Gruppe* Hauptmann Lindeiner. Based at Beauvais. Dornier Do 17.
    II *Gruppe* Major Möricke. Based at Creil. Junkers Ju 88.
    III *Gruppe* *Gruppenkommandeur* not known.[3] Based at Cormeilles-en-Vexin. Dornier Do 17.

LONG-RANGE RECONNAISSANCE
5 Staffel, Aufklärungsgruppe 122	Hauptmann Bohm. Based in Holland with Heinkel He 111 and Junkers Ju 88
4 Staffel, Aufklärungsgruppe 123	Based in Belgium with Heinkel He 111, Junkers Ju 88 and Messerschmitt Bf 110.

II Fliegerkorps Headquarters, Ghent, Belgium. Commanded by General Bruno Lörzer.

LONG-RANGE BOMBERS
Kampfgeschwader 2 Commanded by Oberst Johannes Fink. Headquarters at Arras. *Stabsschwarm*, Dornier Do 17.
    I *Gruppe* Major Gutzmann. Based at Epinoy. Dornier Do 17.
    II *Gruppe* Oberstleutnant Paul Weitkus. Based at Arras. Dornier Do 17.
    III *Gruppe* Major Werner Kreipe.[4] Based at Cambrai. Dornier Do 17.

Kampfgeschwader 3 Commanded by Oberst Wolfgang von Chamier-Glisczinski. Headquarters at Le Culot. *Stabsschwarm*, Dornier Do 17.
    I *Gruppe* Oberstleutnant Gabelmann. Based at Le Culot. Dornier Do 17.
    II *Gruppe* Hauptmann Pilger. Based at Antwerp/Deurne. Dornier Do 17.
    III *Gruppe* Hauptmann Rathmann. Based at St. Trond. Dornier Do 17.

Kampfgeschwader 53 Commande d by Oberst Stahl. Headquarters at Lille-Nord. *Stabsschwarm*, Heinkel He 111.
    I *Gruppe* Major Kauffmann. Based at Lille-Nord. Heinkel He 111.
    II *Gruppe* Major Winkler.[5] Based at Lille-Nord. Heinkel He 111.
    III *Gruppe* Major Edler von Braun. Based at Lille-Nord. Heinkel He 111.

DIVE-BOMBERS
II Gruppe, Stukageschwader 1	Hauptmann Anton Keil. Based in Pas de Calais. Junkers Ju 87..
IV(Stuka) Gruppe, Lehrgeschwader 1	Hauptmann von Brauchitsch. Based at Tramecourt. Junkers Ju 87.

FIGHTER-BOMBERS
Erprobungsgruppe 210   Commanded by Hauptmann Walter Rubensdörffer.[6] Based at Calais-Marck. Messerschmitt Bf 109 and 110
    1 *Staffel* Oberleutnant Martin Lutz. Bf 110.
    2 *Staffel* Oberleutnant Wilhelm-Richard Rössiger. Bf 110.
    3 *Staffel* Oberleutnant Otto Hintze. Bf 109.
II Gruppe, Lehrgeschwader 2   Hauptmann Otto Weiss. Based at St. Omer.

IX Fliegerdivision[7] Headquarters, Soesterberg, Holland. Commanded by Generalmajor Joachim Coeler.

Kampfgeschwader 4 Commanded by Oberstleutnant Hans-Joachim Rath. Headquarters Soesterberg. Stabsschwarm, Heinkel He111
    I *Gruppe* Hauptmann Meissner. Based at Soesterberg. Heinkel He 111.
    II *Gruppe* Major Dr. Gottlieb Wolff. Based at Eindhoven. Heinkel He 111.
    III *Gruppe* Hauptmann Erich Bloedorn. Based at Amsterdam/Schipol. Junkers Ju 88.
Kampfgruppe 100[8]	Hauptmann Friedrich-Carl Aschenbrenner. Based at Vannes, Britanny. Heinkel He 111;
Kampfgeschwader 40	Oberstleutnant Geiss. Based at Brest, Brittany. Focke-Wulfe Fw 200. (I.Gruppe only)
Kampfgruppe 126	Coastal detachments. Heinkel He 111.
Küstenfliegergruppe 106	Coastal detachments. Heinkel He 115 and Dornier Do 18.
3 Staffel, Aufklärungsgruppe 122	Oberstleutnant Fritz Koehler. Junkers Ju 88 and Heinkel He 111

[1] Later succeeded by Oberst Karl Angerstein.
[2] Killed in action, 4-9-40. Successor not known.
[3] The O.K.L. *8th Abteilung*. Order of Battle lists Oberstleutnant Genth as *Gruppenkommandeur*. He had however been killed on 27-7-40.
[4] Major Werner Kreipe was replaced by Major Adolf Fuchs on this day, 13-8-40.
[5] Major Winkler was replaced by Major Max Gruber, who was in turn captured on 15-9-40.
[6] Hauptmann Rubensdörffer was killed on 15-8-40. He was succeeded by Hauptmann von Boltenstern who was in turn killed on 4-9-40. Hauptmann Hartin Lutz then took command only to be killed on 27-9-40. Oberleutnant Werner Weimann took over acting command until he was killed on 5-10-40. It is believed that Hauptmann von Ahrenhein commanded the *Gruppe* until the end of the Battle.
[7] IX *Fliegerdivision* later became IX *Fliegerkorps*.
[8] *Kampfgruppe 100* was transferred to IV *Fliegerkorps* in *Luftflotte 3* w.e.f. 17-8-40.

Jagdfliegerführer 2 Headquarters, Wissant, North-east France. Commanded by Generalmajor Theodor Osterkamp. Fighter and destroyer forces in North-east France.

Jagdgeschwader 3 Commanded by Oberstleutnant Carl Viek.[1] Headquarters at Samer (from 14-8-40). *Stabsschwarm*, Messerschmitt Bf 109E.
  I *Gruppe*   Hauptmann Hans von Hahn. Based at Colombert. Messerschmitt Bf 109E.
  II *Gruppe*   Hauptmann Erich von Selle. Based at Samer (from 14-8-40)
  III *Gruppe*   Hauptmann Walter Kienitz.[2] Based at Desvres. Messerschmitt Bf 109E.

Jagdgeschwader 26 Commanded by Major Gotthard Handrick.[3] Headquarters at Audenbert. *Stabsschwarm*, Messerschmitt Bf 109E
  I *Gruppe*   Hauptmann Kurt Fischer.[4] Based at Audembert. Messerschmitt Bf 109E
  II *Gruppe*   Hauptmann Karl Ebbighausen.[5] Based at Marquise. Messerschmitt Bf 109E
  III *Gruppe*   Major Adolf Galland.[6] Based at Caffiers. Messerschmitt Bf 109E

Jagdgeschwader 51 Commanded by Major Werner Mölders (from 27-7-40). Headquarters at Wissant. *Stabsschwarm*, Messerschmitt Bf 109E
  I *Gruppe*   Hauptmann Hans-Heinrich Brustellin.[7] Based at Wissant. Messerschmitt Bf 109E.
  II *Gruppe*   Hauptmann Günther Matthes. Based at Wissant. Messerschmitt Bf 109E.
  III *Gruppe*   Major Hannes Trautloft.[8] Based at St. Omer. Messerschmitt Bf 109E.

Jagdgeschwader 52 Commanded by Major von Merhert.[9] Based at Coquelles. *Stabsschwarm*, Messerschmitt Bf 109F
  I *Gruppe*   Hauptmann Siegfried von Eschwege.[10] Based at Coquelles. Messerschmitt Bf 109E
  II *Gruppe*   Hauptmann von Kornatzki.[11] Based at Peuplingne. Messerschmitt Bf 109E

Jagdgeschwader 54 Commanded by Major Martin Mettig.[12] Headquarters at Campagne. *Stabsschwarm*, Messerschmitt Bf 109E
  I *Gruppe*   Hauptmann Hubertus von Bonin. Based at Guines. Messerschmitt Bf 109E
  II *Gruppe*   Hauptmann Winterer.[13] Based at Hermalinghen. Messerschmitt Bf 109E
  III *Gruppe*   Hauptmann Ultsch.[14] Based at Guines. Messerschmitt Bf 109E

I Gruppe, Lehrgeschwader 2 Commanded by Major Hans Trubenbach.[15] Based at Calais-Marck. Messerschmitt Bf 109E.

Zerstörergeschwader 26 Commanded by Oberstleutnant Joachim Huth. Headquarters at Lille. *Stabsschwarm*, Messerschmitt Bf 110.
  I *Gruppe*   Hauptmann Wilhelm Makrocki. Based at Yvrench. Messerschmitt Bf 110.
  II *Gruppe*   Hauptmann Ralph von Rettburg. Based at Crécy. Messerschmitt Bf 110.
  III *Gruppe*   Hauptmann Johann Schalk. Based at Barley. Messerschmitt Bf 110.

Zerstörergeschwader 76 Commanded by Major Walter Grabmann. Headquarters at Laval. *Stabsschwarm*, Messerschmitt Bf 110.
  II *Gruppe*   Hauptmann Max Groth. Based at Abbeville. Messerschmitt Bf 110.
  III *Gruppe*   Hauptmann Dickore.[16] Based at Laval. Messerschmitt Bf 110.

LUFTFLOTTE 3 Headquarters, Paris. Commanded by Generalfeldmarschall Hugo Sperrle. Bases in North and North-West France.

IV Fliegerkorps Rear Headquarters at Compeigne; forward Headquarters at Dinard. Commanded by General Kurt Pflugbeil.

LONG-RANGE BOMBERS
Lehrgeschwader 1 Commanded by Oberst Alfred Bülowius. Based at Orléans/Bricy. *Stabsschwarm*, Junkers Ju 88
  I *Gruppe*   Hauptmann Wilhelm Kern. Based at Orléans/Bricy. Junkers Ju 88.
  II *Gruppe*   Major Debratz. Based at Orléans/Bricy. Junkers Ju 88.
  III *Gruppe*   Major Dr. Ernst Bormann. Based at Chateaudun. Junkers Ju 88.

Kampfgeschwader 27 Commanded by Oberst Behrendt. Headquarters at Tours. *Stabsschwarm*, Heinkel He 111
  I *Gruppe*   Major Ulbrich. Based at Tours. Heinkel He 111.
  II *Gruppe*   Major Schlichting. Based at Dinard. Heinkel He 111.
  III *Gruppe*   Major Freiherr Speck von Sternberg. Based at Rennes. Heinkel He 111.

Stukageschwader 3 Command administration of the following echelons: *Stabsschwarm*, Dornier Do 17 and Heinkel He 111

Kampfgruppe 806   Based at Nantes. Junkers Ju 88.
3 Staffel, Aufklärungsgruppe 31   Based in Northern France. Messerschmitt Bf 110, Dornier Do 17 and Henschel Hs 126.

V Fliegerkorps Headquarters, Villacoublay, France. Commanded by Generalleutnant Robert Ritter von Greim.

LONG-RANGE BOMBERS
Kampfgeschwader 51 Commanded by Oberst Dr. Fisser. Headquarter at Orly. *Stabsschwarm*, Junkers Ju 88.
  I *Gruppe*   Major Schulz-Hein. Based at Melun. Junkers Ju 88.
  II *Gruppe*   Major Winkler. Based at Orly. Junkers Ju 88.
  III *Gruppe*   Major Walter Marienfeld. Based at Etampes. Junkers Ju 88.

Kampfgeschwader 54 Commanded by Oberstleutnant Höhne. Headquarters at Evreux. *Stabsschwarm*, Junkers Ju 88.
  I *Gruppe*   Hauptmann Heydebrock. Based at Evreux. Junkers Ju 88.
  II *Gruppe*   Oberstleutnant Köster. Based at St. André-de-l'Eure. Junkers Ju 88.

Kampfgeschwader 55 Commanded by Oberst Alois Stöckl.[17] Headquarters at Villacoublay. *Stabsschwarm*, Heinkel He 111.
  I *Gruppe*   Major Korte. Based at Dreux. Heinkel He 111.
  II *Gruppe*   Major von Lachemaier. Based at Chartres. Heinkel He 111.
  III *Gruppe*   Major Schlemell. Based at Villacoublay. Heinkel He 111.

---

[1] Later succeeded by Major Günther Lützow.
[2] Later succeeded by Hauptmann Wilhelm Balthasar.
[3] Succeeded by Major Adolf Galland on 21-8-40.
[4] Succeeded by Hauptmann Rolf Pingel on 21-8-40.
[5] Succeeded by Hauptmann Erich Bode on 17-8-40.
[6] Succeeded by Hauptmann Gerhard Schöpfel on 21-8-40.
[7] Later succeeded by Oberleutnant Hermann-Friedrich Joppien.
[8] Succeeded by Hauptmann Walter Oesau on 25-8-40.
[9] Later succeeded by Major Hans Trübenbach.

[10] Later succeeded by Hauptmann Wolfgang Ewald.
[11] Later succeeded by Hauptmann Ensslen. *Gruppe* withdrawn to Jever.
[12] Succeeded by Major Hannes Trautloft on 25-8-40.
[13] Succeeded by Hauptmann Dietrich Hrabak on 30-8-40.
[14] Succeeded by Hauptmann Scholz on 6-9-40.
[15] Later succeeded by Hauptmann Herbert Ihlefeld.
[16] Later succeeded by Hauptmann Kaldrack.
[17] Succeeded by Major Korte on 14-8-40; his appointment as *Gruppen-kommandeur*, I *Gruppe*, taken over by Major Friedrich Kless.

VIII Fliegerkorps Commanded by Generalmajor Dipl.-Ing. Wolfram Freiherr von Richthofen. Headquarters at Deauville.

DIVE-BOMBERS
Stukageschwader 1 Commanded by Major Hagen. Headquarters at Angers. *Stabsschwarm*, Dornier Do 17.
   I *Gruppe* Major Paul Hozzel. Based at Angers. Junkers Ju 87.
   III *Gruppe* Hauptmann Helmut Mahlke. Based at Angers. Junkers Ju 87.
Stukageschwader 2 Commanded by Major Oscar Dinort. Headquarters at St. Malo. *Stabsschwarm*, Dornier Do 17.
   I *Gruppe* Hauptmann Hubertus Hitschold. Based at St. Malo. Junkers Ju 87.
   II *Gruppe* Major Walter Enneccerus. Based at Lannion. Junkers Ju 87.

Stukageschwader 77 Commander by Major Clemens Graf von Schönborn. Headquarters at Caen. *Stabsschwarm*, Dornier Do 17.
   I *Gruppe* Hauptmann Friedrich-Karl Freiherr von Dalwigk zu Lichtenfels.[1] Based at Caen. Junkers Ju 87.
   II *Gruppe* Hauptmann Waldemar Plewig. Based at Caen. Junkers Ju 87.
   III *Gruppe* Hauptmann Helmut Bode. Based at Caen. Junkers Ju 87.

V (Zerstörer) Gruppe, Lehrgeschwader 1 Commanded by Hauptmann Liensberger. Based at Caen. Messerschmitt Bf 110.

RECONNAISSANCE
II Gruppe, Lehrgeschwader 2   Hauptmann Otto Weiss. Based at Boblingen, Germany. Dornier Do 17.
2 Staffel, Aufklärungsgruppe 11   Based in Le Bourget area. Messerschmitt Bf 110 and Dornier Do 17.
2 Staffel, Aufklärungsgruppe 123   Junkers Ju 88

Jagdfliegerführer 3 Headquarters, Cherbourg, Northern France. Commanded by Oberst Werner Junck. Fighters and destroyers Central Channel Front.

Jagdgeschwader 2 Commanded by Oberstleutnant Harry von Bülow.[2] Headquarters at Evreux. *Stabsschwarm*, Messerschmitt Bf 109E.
   I *Gruppe* Major Hennig Strumpell.[3] Based at Beaumont-le-Roger. Messerschmitt Bf 109.
   II *Gruppe* Major Schellmann.[4] Based at Beaumont-le-Roger. Messerschmitt Bf 109.
   III *Gruppe* Major Dr. Erich Mix.[5] Based at Le Havre. Messerschmitt Bf 109.

Jagdgeschwader 27 Commanded by Major Max Ibel. Headquarters at Cherbourg-West. *Stabsschwarm*, Messerschmitt Bf 109E
   I *Gruppe* Hauptmann Eduard Neumann. Based at Plumetot. Messerschmitt Bf 109E.
   II *Gruppe* Hauptmann Lippert. Based at Crépon. Messerschmitt Bf 109E.
   III *Gruppe* Hauptmann Joachim Schlichting.[6] Based at Carquebut. Messerschmitt Bf 109E.

Jagdgeschwader 53 Commanded by Major Hans-Jurgen Cramon-Taubadel. Headquarters at Cherbourg. *Stabsschwarm*, Messerschmitt Bf 109E
   I *Gruppe* Hauptmann Blumensaat.[7] Based at Rennes. Messerschmitt Bf 109E.
   II *Gruppe* Major Günther Freiherr von Maltzahn. Based at Dinan. Messerschmitt Bf 109E.
   III *Gruppe* Hauptmann Hans-Joachim Harder.[8] Based at Sempy and Brest. Messerschmitt Bf 109E.

Zerstörergeschwader 2 Commanded by Oberstleutnant Friedrich Vollbracht. Headquarters, Toussée-le-Noble. *Stabsschwarm*, Messerschmitt Bf 109E.
   I *Gruppe* Hauptmann Heinlein. Based at Amiens. Messerschmitt Bf 110.
   II *Gruppe* Major Carl.[9] Based at Guyancourt. Messerschmitt Bf 110.

LUFTFLOTTE 5 Headquarters, Stavanger, Norway. Commanded by Generaloberst Hans-Jürgen Stumpff. Bases in Norway and Denmark.

X Fliegerkorps Headquarters at Stavanger. Commanded by Generalleutnant Hans Geisler.

LONG-RANGE BOMBERS
Kampfgeschwader 26 Commanded by Oberstleutnant Robert Fuchs. Based at Stavanger. *Stabsschwarm*, Heinkel He 111.
   I *Gruppe* Major Busch. Based at Stavanger. Heinkel He 111.
   III *Gruppe* Major Viktor von Lossberg. Based at Stavanger. Heinkel He 111.

Kampfgeschwader 30 Commanded by Oberstleutnant Loebel. Based at Aalborg, Denmark. *Stabsschwarm*, Junkers Ju 88.
   I *Gruppe* Major Fritz Doensch. Based at Aalborg. Junkers Ju 88.
   III *Gruppe* Hauptmann Kellewe. Based at Aalborg. Junkers Ju 88.

LONG-RANGE FIGHTERS
Zerstörergeschwader 76 I *Gruppe.*   Hauptmann Werner Restemeyer. Based at Stavanger. Messerschmitt Bf 110.

SHORT-RANGE FIGHTERS
Jagdgeschwader 77 I *Gruppe.*   Hauptmann Hentschel. Based at Stavanger and Trondheim. Messerschmitt Bf 109E.

COASTAL RECONNAISSANCE AND MINELAYING
Küstenfliegergruppe 506   Based at Stavanger and Trondheim. Heinkel He 115.

LONG-RANGE RECONNAISSANCE
1 Staffel, Aufklärungsgruppe 120   Based at Stavanger. Heinkel He 111 and Junkers Ju 88.
1 Staffel, Aufklärungsgruppe 121   Based at Stavanger. Heinkel He 111 and Junkers Ju 88.
Aufklärungsgruppe 22   Dornier Do 17P based at Stavanger. Messerschmitt Bf 110 detached to Vlissingen.
Aufklärungesgruppe Ober-   Based at Stavanger. Dornier Do 215.
befehlshaber der Luftwaffe

---

[1] Hauptmann Von Dalwigk had been killed in action on 9th July but was still officially listed as missing. His name was therefore included in the Order of Battle as no successor had been appointed.
[2] Succeeded by Major Schellmann.
[3] Later succeeded by Major Helmut Wick.
[4] Succeeded by Hauptmann Griesert.

[5] Later succeeded by Hauptmann Otto Bertram.
[6] Later succeeded by Hauptmann Max Dobislav.
[7] Later succeeded by Hauptmann Hans Mayer.
[8] Later succeeded by Hauptmann Wolf-Dietrich Wilcke.
[9] Succeeded by Hauptmann Karl-Heinz Lessmann.

APPENDIX E

PRODUCTION, AVAILABILITY AND WASTAGE OF BRITISH FIGHTERS

Week ending	FIGHTER PRODUCTION				Total of these types	Total of all fighters	AIRCRAFT IN MAINTENANCE AND STORAGE UNITS[1]															
	Hurri-cane	Spit-fire	De-fiant	Beau-fighter			Hurricane				Spitfire				Defiant				Beaufighter			
							1	2	3	4	1	2	3	4	1	2	3	4	1	2	3	4
June	68	26	13	Nil	107	292	170	25	59	39	97	10	7	3	20	4	2	3	–	Nil	–	–
July	65	32	12	Nil	109	281	222	21	74	45	119	21	13	3	32	2	–	2	–	Nil	–	–
July	57	30	12	Nil	99	230	186	18	79	39	122	4	10	7	45	–	2	1	–	Nil	–	–
July	67	41	11	1	120	270	174	20	84	37	107	17	30	12	52	1	12	–	–	Nil		–
July	65	37	14	4	120	269	176	26	89	38	80	15	27	15	56	–	17	–	–	–	–	4
August	58	41	13	3	115	262	164	26	128	36	100	8	49	16	72	–	4	–	–	–	–	6
August	54	37	10	5	106	230	160	23	150	33	132	11	51	13	80	–	11	–	–	–	2	8
August	43	31	11	5	90	222	98	17	119	36	118	34	21	6	73	1	24	–	–	–	4	10
August	64	44	8	5	121	265	86	17	113	33	84	11	28	8	79	1	18	4	–	1	6	12
August	54	37	3	5	99	243	78	22	127	31	73	19	24	15	40	–	18	35	–	7	7	11
September	54	36	11	5	106	203	86	21	56	24	41	21	24	19	67	1	13	17	2	2	11	6
September	56	38	10	6	110	221	80	17	68	8	47	10	15	9	81	1	14	10	1	7	9	9
September	57	40	6	4	107	211	100	21	81	5	38	17	23	6	54	3	30	11	3	5	8	12
September	58	34	10	Nil	102	214	116	17	109	5	43	9	34	4	66	–	40	6	3	7	8	10
October	60	32	12	Nil	104	210	111	22	82	8	51	13	20	5	74	–	31	7	5	9	–	8
October	55	31	11	4	101	201	119	19	102	3	52	7	39	9	77	1	39	7	7	7	9	9
October	55	25	8	6	94	202	156	24	80	3	71	3	26	8	82	1	40	6	9	9	8	15
October	69	42	16	9	136	241	152	15	85	18	61	16	31	7	92	–	44	4	3	6	9	24
November	56	41	10	3	110	208	158	21	90	19	50	16	30	12	103	–	41	4	6	7	9	20

Returns submitted by Maintenance Units were submitted to Air Ministry corrected to the previous day, therefore all figures in these columns refer to the day previous to that shown in the hand column. The classification of aircraft in storage was as follows: Category 1, Ready for immediate issue at acceptable standard of preparation; Category 2, Estimated to be ready for within four days; Category 3, Under actual preparation for issue; Category 4, "Aircraft on ground, awaiting modification and/or spares."

WASTAGE OF BRITISH FIGHTERS

Week ending	Hurricane		Spitfire		Blenheim		Beaufighter		Defiant	
	Cat. 2	Cat. 3	Cat. 2	Cat. 3	Cat. 2	Cat. 3	Cat. 2	Cat. 3	Cat. 2	Cat. 3
6th July	3	4	1	5	–	2	–	–	–	–
13th July	6	22	6	15	1	–	–	–	2	–
20th July	5	13	5	6	–	4	–	–	1	6
27th July	3	12	8	14	2	–	–	–	–	–
3rd August	4	7	7	11	1	1	–	–	–	–
10th August	4	16	4	12	2	3	–	–	1	1
17th August	21	82	11	40	1	11	–	–	–	–
24th August	9	53	3	21	5	7	–	–	1	5
31st August	4	70	7	50	–	2	–	–	1	7
7th September	8	84	8	53	–	2	–	–	3	1
14th September	6	47	10	26	–	4	–	1	1	–
21st September	8	34	11	21	1	3	–	–	–	–
28th September	11	40	5	35	–	1	–	–	–	2
5th October	16	29	5	10	–	3	–	–	–	–
12th October	3	28	4	22	–	4	–	–	–	2
19th October	10	28	2	9	–	2	–	–	–	–
26th October	7	34	2	9	–	5	–	–	1	–
2nd November	9	16	2	14	1	–	–	1	–	–

APPENDIX F

TYPICAL BOMB PLOT

As a means of illustrating the scope and extent of damage inflicted upon British towns and cities by German bombs during the *Blitz*, a single typical example has been selected. The area shown was typical of the residential eastern suburbs of London, with streets lined with substantially-built Victorian terraced houses.

A total of five bombs fell in the area illustrated. A stick of three, each of approximately 100 pounds, and a single 500-kilo (1,100-lb.) bomb fell during the night of 28th September 1940. A single 2,000-lb. "land mine" (referred to as a Type GG bomb and in fact an adaptation of the hydrostatically or barometrically fused marine parachute mine) fell on the night of 15th/16th October, causing the deaths of thirteen people and rendering 2,000 homeless. Total demolition can be seen to extend over an area of approximately four acres. It is estimated that 470 of these "mines"—which were designed to have the greatest blast effect—were dropped on Britain between 7th and 31st December 1940, no less than 180 falling on Greater London.

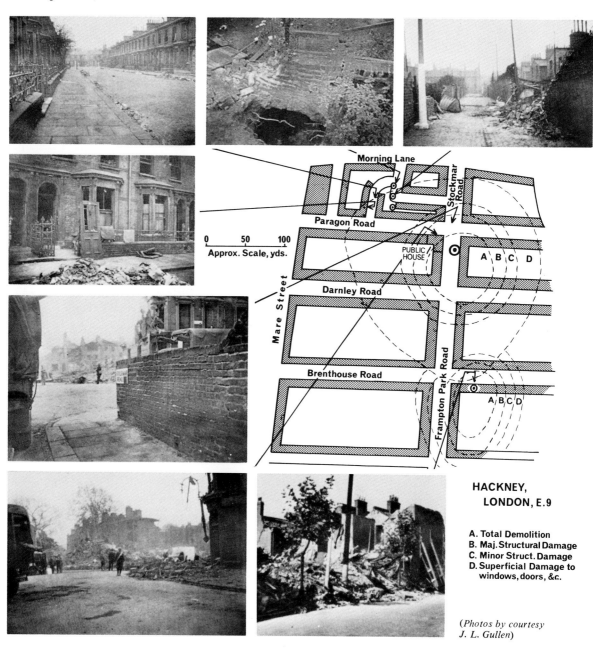

HACKNEY,
LONDON, E.9

A. Total Demolition
B. Maj. Structural Damage
C. Minor Struct. Damage
D. Superficial Damage to
   windows, doors, &c.

(*Photos by courtesy*
J. L. Gullen)

APPENDIX G

AWARDS OF THE VICTORIA CROSS AND GEORGE CROSS DURING THE BATTLE OF BRITAIN, THE BATTLE OF THE BARGES AND THE BLITZ

Extract from the Royal Warrant for the award of the Victoria Cross

"It is ordained that the Cross shall only be awarded for the most conspicuous bravery or some daring or pre-eminent act of valour or self-sacrifice or extreme devotion to duty in the presence of the enemy,"

1. Acting Seaman J.F. Mantle, V.C., R.N.	4th July 1940	Under direct enemy air attack he continued to operate an anti-aircraft gun aboard H.M.S. *Foyle Bank* in Portland Harbour though mortally wounded by a bomb which shattered his left leg.
2. Flight Lieutenant J.B. Nicolson, V.C., D.F.C., R.A.F.	16th August 1940	While on a defensive patrol near Southampton his aircraft was attacked and set on fire; though severely wounded and burned he remained in his aircraft long enough to continue his attack on an enemy aircraft before baling out.
3. Flight Lieutenant R.A.B. Learoyd, V.C., R.A.F.	12th August 1940	During a raid on the Dortmund-Ems Canal he flew his Hampden bomber down to 150 feet to drop his bombs under intense flak which had decimated his formation. His aircraft in tatters, he returned home safely.
4. Sergeant J. Hannah, V.C., R.A.F.	15th September 1940	At the age of eighteen he was wireless operator in a Hampden raiding barges at Antwerp. The aircraft was hit and set ablaze and two crew members baled out. Hannah attacked the fire with extinguishers and his log book, putting out the blaze and enabling his pilot to bring the almost wrecked aircraft home.

Extract from the Royal Warrant for the award of the George Cross

"It is ordained that the Cross shall be awarded only for acts of the greatest heroism or of the most conspicuous courage in circumstances of extreme danger, and that the Cross may be awarded posthumously."

(*Note:* The George Cross was instituted by King George VI on 24th September 1940; it replaced the Empire Gallantry Medal, previous recipients of which automatically become holders of the George Cross by Royal Warrant.)

1. Aircraftman V. Hollowday, G.C., R.A.F.	July and August	At Cranfield, Bedfordshire, he first extracted the pilot from a crashed and blazing aircraft, suffering severe burns to his hands, and secondly, at the moment of his return from hospital a month later, made three trips into a blazing aircraft to bring out three crew members despite exploding ammunition. Hollowday remarkably survived near-fatal burns.
2. T.H. Alderson, G.C.	15th, 20th and 23rd August 1940	At Bridlington, Yorkshire, as an A.R.P. Rescue Party Detachment Leader he on three occasions saved, repectively, one, eleven and five people trapped in buildings collapsed by bombs, in desperately prolonged and dangerous circumstances despite being unrecovered from severe bruising suffered in the first incident.
3. Lieutenant E.W. Reynolds, E.G.M., R.E.	17th August and 3rd September 1940	Twice, and without proper training, he defused clockwork time fuses from German 250-kilo bombs which had caused massive evacuation from council estates.
4. Lance Sergeant W.J. Button, E.G.M, R.E.	18th August 1940	One of three survivors of a party of eight under his charge who lost a digging race against a delayed-action bomb which had fallen in a built-up area.
5. 2nd Lieutenant E.E.A. Chetwynd Talbot, E.G.M., R.E.	24th/25th August 1940	At Loughor Railway Station, Glamorgan, he unearthed a delayed-action bomb and, being without training for dealing with an unfamiliar type of fuse, carried the bomb on his shoulder for 200 yards to a safe place for detonation.
6. Lieutenant W.L. Andrews, E.G.M., R.E.	26th August 1940	Survived with shock and minor injuries the explosion from about thirty-five yards of a bomb specially required for research when attempting to remove a spring-loaded fuse with a length of cord.
7. Squadron Leader E.L. Moxey, G.C.,	27th August 1940	After having repeatedly risked his life de-fusing delayed-action bombs on various R.A.F. airfields, he was killed at Biggin Hill whilst engaged in this work, aged 47.
8. 2nd Lieutenant B.S.T. Archer, G.C. R.E. (later Col., O.B.E., E.R.D.)	2nd September 1940	At Llandarcy, South Wales, he performed and survived the first successful de-fusing of a new type of bomb fitted with an anti-handling device (the ZUS 40) from a stick of four bombs in a blazing oil tank farm. During four and a half hours' work in tremendous heat, two of the three other bombs exploded.
9. A.G. Dolphin, G.C.	7th September 1940	At New Cross, London, this hospital porter protected a severely injured nurse who was trapped near a wall which was about to collapse. The wall collapsed. When rescuers eventually dug through the rubble they found the nurse alive, but Dolphin was dead.
10. Lieutenant R. Davies, G.C., R.E. 11. Sapper G.C. Wylie, G.C., R.E.	12th September 1940	St. Paul's Cathedral in the City of London was saved from a large unexploded bomb which was removed from the proximity of a blazing gas main and damaged electricity cables. Wylie had fitted the lifting harness at the bottom of a foul and dangerous 20-foot shaft, so that Lt. Davies was able to load the bomb on to a lorry and drive it alone through evacuated streets to Hackney Marshes for detonation.
12. A.D. Merriman, G.C., O.B.E.	11th September 1940	For numerous acts of great gallantry while de-fusing bombs as an Experimental Officer of the Department of Scientific Research, notably at Southampton where, in the bomb-bay of a crashed German bomber he de-fused ten bombs with delayed action fuses and anti-handling devices; and again (11th September) in Regent

Street, London, where he directed the steaming out of the main charge of a ticking bomb to reduce the force of the explosion.

13. Sergeant M. Gibson, G.C., R.E.	14th September 1940	He saved an important factory by de-fusing a bomb that was hissing, despite the explosion of a similar bomb close by during the operation.
14. H. Errington, G.C.	17th September 1940	At Shaftesbury Aveune, London, despite burns and shock he savedthe lives of two fellow Auxiliary Firemen, after a direct hit on a garage basement shelter had killed about twenty people. He refused to leave the building until he had freed his trapped colleagues.
15. R.T. Harris, G.C. (later Lt.Col., R.E.)	18th September	At Croydon, Surrey, he acted as an unofficial civilian bomb disposal officer when the Royal Engineers were overburdened by the number of de-fusing operations required. He several times disarmed highly sensitive bombs on his own initiative.
16. Lieutenant J.M.S. Patton, G.C., R.CAN.E.	21st September 1940	At Weybridge, Surrey, he towed on an improvised sled behind a truck a badly distorted delayed-action bomb which had fallen on the vital Hawker Aircraft factory. It exploded later in a nearby crater where Patton had placed it.
17. L.J. Miles, G.C.	21st/22nd September 1940	At Ilford, Essex, he warned people of an imminent explosion instead of taking cover himself. Although mortally wounded, Miles refused all medical aid and directed subsequent fire fighting operations on a fractured gas main until he died.
18. N. Tunna, G.C.	26th September 1940	At Birkenhead he prevented the almost certain explosion of an ammunition train in the marshalling yards by dislodging an ignited incendiary bomb which was jammed between two R.A.F. bomb and was heating the whole waggon to an explosive temperature.
19. Sub-Lieutenant W.H. Taylor, G.C. (later Lt. Cdr., R.N.R.)	26th September—7th October 1940	At R.A.F. Uxbridge, Middlesex, for a particularly hazardous piece of mine disposal.
20. Lt. Cdr. R.J.H. Ryan, G.C., R.N.	September—	For many acts of great gallantry in de-fusing parachute mines, including the first C-type at Clacton, and a mine in a canal at Hornchurch where the weapon threatened the important airfield. This intrepid pair from H.M.S. Vernon were finally killed by a mine dangling from the roof of a warehouse at Dagenham.
21. Chief Petty Officer R.V. Ellingworth G.C., R.N.	October 1940	
22. Sub-Lieutenant P.V. Danckwerts, G.C. R.N.V.R. (later M.B.E., and Professor,	September—October 1940	Without specialist training and not yet Commissioned six weeks, Danckwerts on his own initiative de-fused sixteen parachute mines in less than 48 hours in London, including one in which the detonating clock ran for 22 seconds, but then stopped.
23. Wg. Cdr. L.F. Sinclair, G.C., R.A.F. (later Air Vice-Marshal, K.C.B., C.B.E., D.S.O. AND BAR)	30th September 1940	At Wattisham, Suffolk, he ran into a crashed bomber after only two of the four bombs aboard had exploded, and dragged out the air gunner, who unfortunately subsequently died.
24. Section-Commander G.W. Inwood G.C., H.G.	15th/16th October 1940	At Bishop Road, Birmingham, this Home Guardsman succeeded in rescuing two unconscious people from the gas-filled cellar of a bombed house.Despite being nearly overcome, he insisted in making a further effort but collapsed and died in the attempt.
25. 2nd Lieutenant A.F. Campbell, G.C., R.E.	19th October 1940	The Triumph Engineering Company works in Chapel Road, Coventry and another vital factory had to be evacuated because of a delayed-action bomb. After eight hours of digging it proved impossible to de-fuse, so Campbell lifted it on to a lorry and lay with an ear to it to warn the driver to stop and and run if it stopped ticking. Campbell was killed with six others when it exploded at the disposal point.
26. Sub-Lieutenant J.M.C. Easton, G.C. R.N.V.R.	19th October 1940	After sixteen successful de-fusings, Easton had to run for his life at Clifton Street, East London, with Southwell when a C-type parachute mine's fuse started running. The mine exploded and destroyed six streets. The decapitated body of Southwell was found six weeks later. Despite a broken back and fractured skull, Easton miraculously survived, spent a year in plaster and eventually assumed command of a minesweeper.
28. Flight Lieutenant W.H. Charlton, G.C., R.A.F.	September—October 1940	This Officer was credited with de-fusing over 200 bombs on vital airfields, and was decorated for the sheer repetition of the awful risks he took day after day.
29. Acting Major H.J.L. Barefoot, G.C., R.E.	September—October 1940	This Officer was decorated for persistent courage in bomb and mine disposal, much of it of a desperately hazardous, pioneering nature.
30. Lieutenant R.S. Armitage G.C., R.N.V.R. (also awarded the George Medal in 1944)	September—October 1940	His tenth parachute mine blew up when he had only covered 30 yards since the clock started ticking. He was severely bruised and shaken but reported for duty the next day.
31. Sub-Lieutenant R.V. Moore, G.C., R.N.V.R. (later C.B.E.(civil))	September—October 1940	Despite a lack of training he de-fused five parachute mines and then tackled another, when its clock started to run. Instead of running for cover, Moore stayed on the job and just managed to get the fuse clear in the nick of time. The detonator exploded a few seconds later.
32. Sub-Lieutenant J.B.P. Miller, G.C., R.N.V.R.	Autumn 1940	This team worked on ten mines, and notably one in the Roding River, Barking Creek, one of London's main sewer outlets, which involved working in the foulest conditions and a lifting operation with a crane.
33. Able Seaman S.J. Tuckwell, G.C., R.N.		
34. Sub-Lieutenant J.H. Babington, G.C. R.N.V.R. (later O.B.E.)	1940	At Chatham, Kent, he had to tackle a bomb fitted with a probably-lethal anti-withdrawal device, at the bottom of a 16-foot pit. The withdrawal line broke so Babington went down the pit three times to remove the fuse before successfully directing the lifting of the bomb for removal and destruction.

APPENDIX H

GERMAN INTELLIGENCE APPRECIATION OF THE R.A.F. AND COMPARISON WITH CURRENT LUFTWAFFE STRENGTH

Oberkommando der Luftwaffe
16th July 1940.

Operations Staff IC

I. THE MILITARY VALUE OF THE R.A.F.

A. Strength and Equipment

1. *Fighter Formations*

With 50 fighter squadrons each having about 18 aircraft, there are 900 first line fighters available, of which about 675 (75 per cent) may be regarded as serviceable.

About 40 per cent of the fighters are Spitfires and about 60 per cent are Hurricanes. Of these types the Spitfire is regarded as the better.

In view of the combat performance and the fact that they are not yet equipped with cannon guns both types are inferior to the Bf 109, while the individual Bf 110 is inferior to skilfully handled Spitfires.

In addition to the above formations Blenheim squadrons are available for night fighter tasks as auxiliary heavy fighters and operate in cohesion with particularly intense searchlight defence.

2. *Bombing Formations*

Assuming the average squadron strength to be 20 aircraft, the 55 or 60 bomber squadrons contain about 1,150 first line bombers, of which about 860 (75 per cent) may be regarded as serviceable.

This strength is divided among four types of aircraft of various series, approximately as follows:

Hampden	400
Wellington	350
Whitley	300
Lochkeed Hudson	100

Comparison of these types shows that the Hampden has the best qualities as a bomber.

In addition, there is a large number of Blenheim bombers available. Most of these are in training schools but there are also some in operational units. However, in view of its performance, this type can no longer be considered a first line aircraft.

In comparison with German bombers, all these types have inadequate armour, and poor bomb-aiming equipment. However, they usually have strong defensive armament.

3. *Other Formations*

These include coastal formations equipped with Lockheed Hudsons (reconnaissance) and flying boats and various obsolescent types of aircraft—close reconnaissance and low-level attack aircraft designed for co-operation with the army.

These need not be taken into consideration in this report.

4. *Anti-Aircraft Artillery*

In view of the island's extreme vulnerability to air attack and the comparatively limited amount of modern equipment the number of heavy and light A.A. guns available (1,194 plus 1,114) is by no means adequate to ensure the protection of the island by ground defences.

The large number of efficient searchlights available (3,200) constitutes an advantageous factor in defence at night.

Only limited importance should be attributed to the numerous barrage balloons, as these can be used only at low altitudes (1,000 to 2,000 metres) owing to the medium wind velocities prevailing over the island. The balloons cannot be raised at all at appreciable wind velocities.

B. Personnel and Training

At present there are no difficulties regarding the number of men available.

From the outset the training is concentrated on the production of good pilots, and the great majority of the officers in particular are trained solely as such. By comparison tactical training is left far in the background. For this reason the R.A.F. has comparatively well-trained fighter pilots while the bomber crews are not up to modern tactical standards. This applies to the bomb-aimers in particular, most of whom are N.C.O.s and men with little service experience. Although there are deficiencies in equipment, the comparatively low standard in bombing accuracy may be attributed to this factor.

C. Airfields

In the ground organisation there is a considerable number of air-strips in the southern part of the island and in some areas in the north. However, only a limited number can be considered as operational airfields with modern maintenance and supply installations.

In general, the well-equipped operational airfields are used as take-off and landing bases, while the numerous smaller airfields located in the vicinity serve as alternative landing grounds and rest bases.

There is little strategic flexibility in operations as ground personnel are usually permanently stationed at home bases.

D. Supply Situation

1.   As regards aircraft, the R.A.F. is at present almost entirely dependent on home production. American deliveries will not make any important contribution before the beginning of 1941.

If deliveries arriving in Britain in the immediate future are supplemented by French orders these aircraft may be ready for operations by the autumn.

At present the British aircraft industry produces about 180 to 300 first line fighters and 140 first line bombers a month. In view of the present conditions relating to production (the appearance of raw material difficulties, the disruption or breakdown of production at factories owing to air attacks, the increased vulnerability to air attack owing to the fundamental reorganisation of the aircraft industry now in progress), it is believed that for the time being output will decrease rather than increase.

In the event of an intensification of air warfare it is expected that the present strength of the R.A.F. will fall, and this decline will be aggravated by the continued decrease in production.

2.   Unless an appreciable proportion of present stocks is destroyed, the fuel situation can be regarded as secure.

3.   *Bombs.* Bomb production is limited by the method of manufacture (cast casings). However, there will be no difficulty in the supplies of bombs so long as present stocks are not used and operations continue on a moderate scale. It is believed that these stocks will be adequate for intensive operations lasting several weeks.

Most of the bombs available are of medium calibre (112 and 224 kilogrammes), of which a large proportion are of an obsolete pattern with unfavourable ballistic qualities (bombs with fins).

E. Command

The Command at high level is inflexible in its organisation and strategy. As formations are rigidly attached to their home bases, command at medium level suffers mainly from operations being controlled in most cases by officers no longer accustomed to flying (station commanders). Command at low level is generally energetic but lacks tactical skill.

II. THE OPERATIONAL SCOPE OF THE R.A.F.

(a)   For its operations the R.A.F. has at its disposal an area of only 200 to 300 kilometres in depth. This corresponds approximately to an area the size of the Netherlands and Belgium.

There is little possibility of Ireland being used in the system of depth owing to the lack of ground organisation and the fact that once R.A.F. units have been transferred there they cannot restore their serviceability.

In contrast the *Luftwaffe* has at its disposal an area extending from Trondheim, across Heligoland Bay and along the North Sea and Channel coasts to Brest with a practically unlimited zone in depth.

(b)   In view of the inferiority of British fighters to German fighters, enemy bomber formations, even with fighter escort, are not capable of carrying out effective daylight attacks regularly, particularly as escort operations are in any case limited by the lack of long-range single-engine or heavy fighters.

The R.A.F. will therefore be obliged to limit its activity to night operations even in the advent of intensified air warfare. These operations will undoubtedly achieve a nuisance value but will in no way be decisive.

In contrast, the *Luftwaffe* is in a position to go over to decisive daylight operations owing to the inadequate air defences of the island.

CONCLUSION

The *Luftwaffe* is clearly superior to the R.A.F. as regards strength, equipment, training, command and location of bases. In the event of an intensification of air warfare the *Luftwaffe*, unlike the R.A.F., will be in a position in every respect to achieve a decisive effect this year if the time for the start of large-scale operations is set early enough to allow advantage to be taken of the months with relatively favourable weather conditions (July to the beginning of October).

APPENDIX I

SHIPS OF THE ROYAL NAVY LOST THROUGH ENEMY ACTION IN HOME WATERS BETWEEN 1st JULY AND 31st OCTOBER, 1940

H.M. Destroyers	*BRAZEN*	1,360 tons	20.7.40	Sunk by aircraft off Dover.
	CODRINGTON (flotilla leader)	1,540 tons	27.7.40	Bombed and sunk in Dover Harbour.
	WREN	1,120 tons	27.7.40	Bombed and sunk off Aldeburgh, Suffolk.
	DELIGHT	1,375 tons	29.7.40	Bombed and sunk off Portland.
	ESK	1,375 tons	1.9.40	Sunk by mine in the North Sea.*
	IVANHOE	1,370 tons	1.9.40	Sunk by mine in the North Sea.*
	VENETIA	1,090 tons	19.10.40	Sunk by mine in Thames Estuary.
	ACHERON	1,350 tons	17.12.40	Sunk by mine off the Isle of Wight.
H.M. Auxiliary Anti-Aircraft Ship	*FOYLE BANK* (requisitioned)	5,582 tons	4.7.40	Sunk by aircraft at Portland.
H.M. Netlayer	*KYLEMORE* (requisitioned)	319 tons	21.8.40	Sunk by aircraft at Harwich.
H.M. Minesweeper	*DUNDALK*	710 tons	16.10.40	Sunk by mine off Harwich.
H.M. Torpedo Boats	*No. 15*	18 tons	24.9.40	Sunk by mine in Thames Estuary.
	No. 106	—	16.10.40	Sunk by mine in Thames Estuary.
	No. 16	18 tons	31.10.40	Sunk by mine in Thames Estuary.
H.M. Trawlers	*CRESTFLOWER*	550 tons	19.7.40	Foundered after damage by aircraft off Portsmouth.
	FLEMING (requisitioned)	356 tons	24.7.40	Sunk by aircraft in Thames Estuary.
	KINGSTON GALENA	550 tons	24.7.40	Sunk by aircraft off Dover.
	RODINO (requisitioned)	230 tons	24.7.40	Sunk by aircraft off Dover.
	STAUNTON (requisitioned)	283 tons	28.7.40	Presumed blown up by magnetic mine in Thames Estuary.*
	CAPE FINISTERRE (requisitioned)	590 tons	2.8.40	Sunk by aircraft off Harwich.
	DRUMMER (requisitioned)	297 tons	4.8.40	Mined off Brightlingsea, Essex.
	OSWALDIAN (requisitioned)	260 tons	4.8.40	Mined in Bristol Channel.*
	RIVER CLYDE (requisitioned)	276 tons	5.8.40	Sunk by mine off Aldeburgh.
	PYROPE (requisitioned)	295 tons	12.8.40	Sunk by aircraft in Thames Estuary.
	TAMARISK	545 tons	12.8.40	Sunk by bombers in Thames Estuary.
	ELIZABETH ANGELA (requisitioned)	253 tons	13.8.40	Sunk by aircraft in Downs.
	RESPARKO (requisitioned)	248 tons	20.8.40	Sunk by aircraft at Falmouth.
	ROYALO (requisitioned)	248 tons	1.9.40	Sunk by mine off South Cornwall.
	DERVISH (requisitioned)	346 tons	9.9.40	Mined off Humber.
	LOCH INVER (requisitioned)	356 tons	24.9.40	Probably mined in Harwich area.*
	RECOIL (requisitioned)	344 tons	28.9.40	Lost on patrol, presumed mined, English Channel.*
	COMET (requisitioned)	301 tons	30.9.40	Sunk by mine off Falmouth.
	RESOLVO (requisitioned)	231 tons	12.10.40	Sunk by mine in Thames Estuary.
	LORD STAMP (requisitioned)	448 tons	14.10.40	Sunk by mine in English Channel.
	KINGSTON CAIRNGORM (requisitioned)	448 tons	18.10.40	Sunk by mine in English Channel.
	VELIA (requisitioned)	290 tons	19.10.40	Presumed mined in Harwich area.*
	WAVEFLOWER	550 tons	21.10.40	Mined off Aldeburgh.
	HICKORY	505 tons	22.10.40	Mined in English Channel.
	JOSEPH BUTTON (requisitioned)	290 tons	22.10.40	Mined off Aldeburgh.
	LORD INCHCAPE (requisitioned)	338 tons	25.10.40	Mined off Plymouth.* Subsequently salved.
H.M. Yachts	*WARRIOR II* (requisitioned)	1,124 tons	11.7.40	Sunk by aircraft off Portland.
	GULZAR (requisitioned)	197 tons	29.7.40	Sunk in air attack on Dover Harbour.
	AISHA (requisitioned)	117 tons	11.10.40	Believed mined in Thames Estuary.*
H.M. Mooring Vessel	*STEADY*	758 tons (deep)	17.7.40	Mined off Newhaven.*
H.M. Drifters	*DUTHIES* (requisitioned)	89 tons	25.10.40	Sunk by aircraft at Montrose.
	HARVEST GLEANER (requisitioned)	96 tons	28.10.40	Sunk by aircraft off East Coast.
H.M. Tanker	*WAR SEPOY*	5,574 tons	19.7.40	Damaged beyond repair by aircraft off Dover.
Special Service Vessel	*MINNIE DE LARINAGA*	5,046 tons	7–9.9.40	Total loss from air raids on London docks.

* Assumed sunk by air-sown mine.

APPENDIX J

AIR RAIDS ON GREAT BRITAIN, JULY – DECEMBER 1940

(a) Tonnage of Bombs dropped on British Targets

Target	High explosive (including land mines) Tons	Incendiary bombs Tons	No. of bombs
London	23,716	2,918	2,951,000
Liverpool and Merseyside	2,114	274	278,300
Birmingham	1,780	141	143,000
Coventry	965	231	234,700
Manchester	933	105	107,000
Bristol	360	112	113,500
Southampton	421	106	108,000
Plymouth	362	95	96,000
Airfields	1,710[1]	28	28,100
Other raids	4,303	211	205,000
Total	**36,664**	**4,221**	**4,264,600**

(b) Civilian Air Raid Casualties

Month	Men killed (injured)	Women killed (injured)	Children under 16 killed (injured)	Total killed (injured)
July	178 (227)	57 (77)	23 (17)	258 (321)
August	627 (711)	335 (448)	113 (102)	1,075 (1,261)
September	2,844 (4,405)	2,943 (3,807)	1,167 (2,403)	6,954 (10,615)
October	2,791 (4,228)	2,900 (3,750)	643 (717)	6,334 (8,695)
November	2,289 (3,493)	1,806 (2,251)	493 (458)	4,588 (6,202)
December	1,838 (2,962)	1,434 (1,775)	521 (307)	3,793 (5,044)
Total	**10,567 (16,026)**	**9,475 (12,108)**	**2,960 (4,004)**	**23,002 (32,138)**

(c) Principal Historic and Important Buildings Destroyed or Damaged by Air Attack, July–December 1940

Churches: Westminster Abbey; St. Paul's Cathedral; Canterbury Cathedral; Coventry Cathedral; Birmingham Cathedral; St. Martin-in-the-Fields; St. Clement Danes; St. Giles, Cripplegate; St. Swithin's, Cannon Street; St. Augustin, Watling Street; St. Boniface, Adler Street; St. Dunstan-in-the-East; St. Clement's, Eastcheap; Jewin Chapel; Dutch Church, Austin Friars; Swedish Church, Rotherhithe; St. Magnus the Martyr; St. Mary at Hill; St. Mary Woolnoth; St. Margarets, Westminster; Christ Church, Westminster Bridge Road; St. John's, Kensington; St. Mark's, Regent's Park; Islington Parish Church; St. Bride's, Fleet Street; St. Lawrence Jewry; St. Stephen, Coleman Street; Christ Church, Greyfriars; St. Leonard Foster; St. Mary, Aldermanbury; St. Andrew-by-the-Wardrobe; St. James's, Piccadilly; St. Leonard's Church, Streatham; Temple Church, Bristol.

Palaces: Buckingham Palace (damaged three times); Kensington Palace; Lambeth Palace; Eltham Palace.

Embassies: American (delayed action bomb removed); Japanese (evacuated); Swedish.

Newspaper Offices: "The Times"; Associated Press of America; "Daily Mail"; "Daily Express"; "Daily Herald"; "Daily Mirror"; "Daily Sketch"; "New Statesman and Nation"; "Daily Worker"; "Evening Standard"; London Offices of the "Glasgow Herald".

Other Buildings of Worldwide Interest: House of Lords; British Museum; Law Courts; Tate Gallery; Imperial War Museum; Somerset House; Wallace Collection; Burlington House; Windsor Castle; Tower of London; the Guildhall; Westminster Hall; Temple; Inner Temple Library; Coopers' Hall; Stationers' Hall; Saddlers' Hall; Barbers' Hall; Hall of the Society of the Apothecaries; Girdlers' Hall; Greenwich Observatory; Savile House, Eton College; Royal Hospital, Chelsea; Hogarth House; Holland House; Rednor House, Twickenham; the statue of Richard Cœur de Lion.

Public Places: Australia House; Bank of England (near); County Hall; Madame Tussaud's; National City Bank of New York; Public Record Office; South Africa House; University College Library; Yokohama Specie Bank; Y.M.C.A. Headquarters; The London Zoo; Leicester Town Hall; Salford Town Hall; Birmingham Town Hall; Argyle Theatre, Merseyside; the Birkenhead Arts Theatre; the Birmingham Art Gallery; the Royal College of Surgeons; Wimbledon Centre Court.

Hospitals: Charterhouse Clinic; Great Ormond Street; London Hospital; Queen Mary's Hospital; St. Bartholomew's Hospital; St. Thomas's; Swiss Relief Centre; St. Dunstan's Headquarters; Ford's Hospital, Coventry; American Ambulance Unit, Tunbridge Wells; St. Peter's Hospital, Bristol; Charing Cross Hospital.

Squares and Streets: Berkeley Square; Leicester Square; Kensington Square; Sloane Square; Smith Square; Berwick Market; Bond Street; Burlington Arcade; Bruton Street; Carnaby Street; Lambeth Walk; Maddox Street; Oxford Street; Park Lane; Piccadilly; Regent Street; Rotten Row; Royal Arcade; Birdcage Walk; Saville Row; Watling Street; Elephant and Castle; Newgate Street; Cheapside; Aldersgate; London Wall; St. Paul's Churchyard; Paternoster Row; Tower Hill; the Minories.

Stores: Austin Reed (Piccadilly); Bourne and Hollingsworth; Ford Showrooms, Regent Street; Gamage's, Cheapside; John Lewis; Peter Robinson's; Selfridge's.

Clubs: Arts (Dover Street); Carlton; Reform.

---

[1] Including fragmentation bombs.

APPENDIX K

GROUND DEFENCES

Disposition of Gun Defences—Battle of Britain

A.A. Division	Heavy Anti-Aircraft Gun Zone	11th July	21st August	11th September	9th October
4th Division (in conjunction with No. 12 Group, R.A.F.)	Barrow	Nil	Nil	8	8
	Birmingham	64	71	64	64
	Coventry	44	32	24	24
	Crewe	8	16	8	8
	Donnington	Nil	Nil	Nil	4
	Liverpool	52	56	58	76
	Manchester	20	20	20	20
	Ringway airfield	4	4	4	4
	Light A.A. guns	52	80	84	92
	A.A. machine guns	376	389	397	411
5th Division (in conjunction with No. 10 Group, R.A.F.)	Bramley	8	8	8	8
	Bristol	36	32	32	32
	Brockworth	36	24	24	24
	Brooklands	16	16	16	16
	Cardiff	12	26	26	30
	Falmouth	8	12	4	8
	Farnborough	Nil	Nil	8	4
	Holton Heath	8	8	8	8
	Milford Haven	Nil	Nil	4	4
	Newport	4	16	20	22
	Plymouth	18	46	26	24
	Portland	6	14	14	16
	Portsmouth	44	44	40	40
	Southampton	43	39	31	32
	Swansea	Nil	16	24	24
	Tangmere airfield	4	4	4	4
	Yeovil	Nil	4	4	4
	Light A.A. guns	136	181	190	184
	A.A. machine guns	560	547	553	521
6th Division (in conjunction with No. 11 Group, R.A.F.)	Biggin Hill airfield	4	4	8	8
	Dover	18	18	14	14
	Harwich	17	15	8	8
	Hawkinge airfield	7	7	7	7
	Ipswich	4	2	2	2
	Manston airfield	8	8	8	8
	Martlesham airfield	4	4	4	4
	North Weald airfield	4	4	8	8
	Rochford airfield	4	4	4	4
	Thames and Medway (N)	46	48	48	48
	Thames and Medway (S)	70	72	72	72
	West Malling airfield	2	2	2	2
	Light A.A. guns	101	133	141	145
	A.A. machine guns	437	415	397	443
1st Division (in conjunction with No. 11 Group, R.A.F.)	Hounslow	4	4	4	4
	Inner Artillery Zone, London	92	92	199	199
	Langley	28	28	28	28
	Stanmore	4	4	4	4
	Light A.A. guns	34	38	44	60
	A.A. machine guns	183	167	161	161

A.A. Division	Heavy Anti-Aircraft Gun Zone	11th July	21st August	11th September	9th October
2nd Division (in conjunction with No. 12 Group, R.A.F.)	Daventry	4	4	4	4
	Derby	40	40	32	32
	Duxford airfield	2	2	2	2
	Feltwell airfield	2	2	2	2
	Grantham	4	4	4	4
	Horsham St. Faith airfield	2	2	2	2
	Humber	38	38	26	26
	Leighton Buzzard	4	4	4	4
	Marham airfield	2	2	2	2
	Norwich	Nil	Nil	4	4
	Nottingham	16	16	16	16
	Scunthorpe	Nil	24	Nil	Nil
	Sheffield	23	27	27	28
	Wattisham airfield	4	4	4	4
	Watton airfield	2	2	2	2
	Mobile battery	8	8	Nil	Nil
	Light A.A. guns	82	78	82	82
	A.A. machine guns	788	765	835	839
7th Division (in conjunction with No. 13 Group, R.A.F.)	Acklington airfield	2	2	2	2
	Dishforth airfield	Nil	Nil	2	2
	Driffield airfield	4	4	Nil	Nil
	Leeds	20	20	20	22
	Linton airfield	4	4	4	4
	Teesside	30	30	30	30
	Thornaby airfield	4	4	4	Nil
	Topcliffe airfield	Nil	Nil	2	Nil
	Tyneside	54	50	50	46
	Mobile guns	Nil	Nil	Nil	Nil
	Light A.A. guns	50	62	55	55
	A.A. machine guns	321	270	277	263
3rd Division (in conjunction with No. 13 Group, R.A.F.)	Aberdeen	4	4	4	4
	Ardeer	8	8	8	8
	Belfast	7	7	7	12
	Castletown airfield	Nil	2	2	2
	Clydeside	28	27	34	40
	Kinloss airfield	2	2	2	2
	Kyle of Lochalsh	4	4	4	4
	Londonderry	Nil	Nil	4	4
	Lossiemouth airfield	2	2	2	2
	Scapa Flow	88	88	88	88
	Shetlands	12	12	12	12
	Wick airfield	4	2	2	2
	Light A.A. guns	119	122	132	132
	A.A. machine guns	368	378	367	375

Note: The heavy anti-aircraft guns listed above consisted in the main of 4·7-inch and 4-inch fixed (i.e. not mobile) gun installations; the light guns included 40-mm. Bofors, Vickers Mark VIII 2-pounder and 3-inch guns; the machine guns included 0·303-inch Lewis, 0·303-inch Bren and 20-mm. Hispano guns.

THE RADAR STATIONS OF GREAT BRITAIN—SEPTEMBER 1940

Fair Isle

W   X   Y   Z   V   W   X

Caitnip
Nether Button

B   C   D   E   A   B   C

Thrumster

Hillhead
Rosehearty
G   H   J   K   F   G   H
Doonies Hill
School Hill

St. Cyrus

M   N   O   Douglas Wood   L   M   N
P Anstruther

Cockburnspath
Drone Hill
R   S   T   U   Bamburgh   Q   R   S
Ottercops Moss   Cresswell

Shotton
W   X   Y   Z   V   W   X
Danby Beacon

Flambrough Hd.

B   C   D   E   A   Easington   B   C
Stenigot

Ingoldmels
West Beckham
G   H   J   K   F   G   Happisburgh
H
Stoke Holy Cross
Dunwich
High Street
M   N   O   P   L   M   Bawdsey N
Strumble Hd. Bromley   Walton
Haycastle St. Twynells
Warren   Canewdon

Foreness
Dunkirk   Dover
R   S   T   U   Trueleigh   Q   Rye R   S
Fairlight
Pevensey
Carnanton   Hawks Tor   Poling   Beachy Head
Worth   Ventnor
Rame Hd. W. Prawle Z   V   W   X
W   Drytree X   Y

10 0 10 20 30 40 50 60 70 80 90 100   STATUTE   ● C.H. STATIONS
MILES   ⊘ C.H.L. STATIONS

APPENDIX L

RESCUE OF AIRMEN FROM THE SEA DURING THE BATTLE OF BRITAIN

1. British Air/Sea Rescue Procedures

It was an extraordinary omission of logic that, prior to the Battle of Britain, no regular organisation existed for the rescue of ditched airmen from the seas which surrounded the island. In general, peacetime rescue arrangements continued in being during the early months of the War on a strictly *ad hoc* level. Aircraft alighting on the sea were searched for by aircraft from their own units and, if located, any nearby vessel was diverted to the area. When the War brought about a ban on W/T transmissions from civil airfields, heavy congestion of post office telephones often caused fatal delays in calling out the lifeboat service. Moreover the War also brought broadcasts to shipping by the G.P.O. to an end.

In March 1940 the Fighter Command Movements Liaison Section caused revised instructions to be issued introducing a new chain of communication for aircraft in distress over the sea. Such an aircraft transmitted a Mayday ("*m'aidez*") message which was passed by any R.A.F. unit receiving it to the Movements Liaison Section. Thence the message passed to the naval authorities, the appropriate reconnaissance Group of Coastal Command for action by air and/or marine craft, and to the Group Distress Area headquarters for action by the coastguards.

It was soon found that an unnecessary loss of life occurred when G.P.O. broadcasts to shipping could not be enlisted, and in June 1940 it was agreed that the saving of life was of greater importance than the possibility of giving information to the enemy. The G.P.O. W/T stations were therefore brought back into commission for rescue work. It is interesting to note that at this time there were still only fourteen high speed launches available round the coasts.

The intensity of air operations over the Channel during the early stages of the Battle focused the authorities' attention on the losses among airmen falling in the sea close to British shores. During the last 21 days of July well over 200 aircrew were killed or missing—most of them over the sea. As a result, at the end of July, Vice-Admiral Sir Bertram Ramsay (Vice-Admiral, Dover) and Air Vice-Marshal Keith Park organised a local rescue service with light naval craft, R.A.F. high-speed launches and some Lysander aircraft borrowed from Army Co-operation Command.

On 22nd August the Deputy Chief of the Air Staff, Air Vice-Marshal Arthur Harris, called a meeting at Air Ministry to discuss a draft organisation run by the high-speed launches of Coastal Command with the rescue functions of the Naval Auxiliary Patrol, and to place the R.A.F. rescue craft under the operational control of the local naval authorities. It was agreed that the R.A.F. should be responsible for organising the necessary air search and for informing the naval authorities of the area being searched. Thus nearly twelve months after the outbreak of war, the first steps were taken towards the formation of an organisation specifically allotted the task of sea rescue.

2. The German Air/Sea Rescue Organisation

In direct contrast to the Royal Air Force, the *Luftwaffe* possessed a fully established organisation for the recovery of its pilots and crews from the sea, an organisation which performed regular patrols over the North Sea from the outbreak of war with Britain, and which had been in existence as an integral part of the *Luftwaffe* for three years prior to 1939. During the Battle of Britain the *Seenotdienst* was extended to cover the English Channel, the operational echelons (*Seenotbereichkommando* and *Seenotflugkommando*) being established and detached along the German-occupied coast from the Brest peninsula to North Norway. Equipped principally with Heinkel He 59 floatplanes and Dornier Do 18 flying boats, the seaplanes were sometimes assisted by fast rescue launches, and carried three collapsible rubber boats, blankets, medical stores and portable two-way radio sets. They were frequently painted white and marked with Red Crosses, until representations were made to the Germans that the use of the Red Cross in this manner could not be countenanced.

The average strength of the five *Seenotflugkommando* operating during the Battle of Britain (excluding *Seenotzentrale Cherbourg* and *Seenotzentrale Boulogne*) provides an interesting comparison with the R.A.F.'s allocation of twelve Lysanders—which were not seaplanes in any case:

July 1944   33 Heinkel He 59; 1 Dornier Do 24
Aug. 1940   39 Heinkel He 59; 1 Dornier Do 24; 2 miscellaneous
Sept. 1940   41 Heinkel He 59; 2 Dornier Do 24; 3 Breguet 691
Oct. 1940   37 Heinkel He 59; 2 Dornier Do 24; 8 Breguet 691

One of the more interesting innovations of the German rescue services was the introduction of Sea Rescue Floats (inevitably nicknamed "lobster pots"); a number of these first appeared in October 1940, placed in position halfway across the English Channel. Very considerable care had been taken to equip these floats in every detail for the maintenance of life for any airman who might reach them. They were fitted with bunks for four men, blankets, clothing, food and water, distress signals and lamps. Apart from games of draughts and Halma, the Germans thoughtfully provided a wooden mallet and a supply of wooden pegs for hammering into holes made by machine gun attacks. The floats were 13 ft. long, 7 ft. 10 inches broad and 8 ft. 6 in. deep. The hull was surmounted by a conning tower, on which were painted prominent Red Crosses.

APPENDIX M

CONTEMPORARY EXAMINATION OF CRASHED GERMAN AIRCRAFT

Sometime early in October 1940 British Technical Intelligence began circulating reports detailing its findings in the course of examination of crashed German aircraft. Unfortunately it has not proved possible to trace the first eight batches of such reports, but the following is a summary of those examinations carried out between 10th and 31st October 1940. No attempt was made at the time to apportion credit for the enemy aircraft's destruction, either to a particular pilot or gun battery, but comparison with the October loss tables given in this book will, in many instances, confirm the claims made by Fighter Command pilots.

Report No. 4/65. Junkers Ju 88A-1

Crashed on 10-10-40 at about 04.00 hrs. in River Roach at Horseshoe Corner, Foulness Island. Map reference M.4211. Markings: 9K+HS (H black, outlined white). Aircraft made by Ju. *Flugzeug und Motorenwerke*, Dessau. WkrNr. 299 on fin. No other numbers could be found. Engines Jumo 211. Starboard engine WkrNr. 53367; port engine number not ascertainable. Cause of this crash could not be ascertained, and no evidence of .303 or A.A. strikes were found in the wreckage which was visible at low tide. Aircraft was completely wrecked after crew had baled out. The usual external and internal bomb racks were traced. Armour: Pilot's seat armoured as usual. The bottom of the rear upper gunner's seat armoured 9 mm. thick. Crew: 4, prisoners. Underside of aircraft crosses and swastika on fin blacked out. Owing to position of wreckage, no further details possible.

(The crew of this Ju 88 is believed to have been briefed to bomb Crewe—referred to in German records as Target No. 7119—and, in the absence of any evidence of bullet strikes, it must be assume that the aircraft suffered engine failure or became lost. From British records it appears that two of the crew members subsequently died of injuries sustained when baling out. See item No. 10 in the German loss tables for 9-10-40).

Report No. 4/67. Messerschmitt Bf 109E-7

Crashed on 12-10-40 at Chantry Farm, Hollingbourne. Map reference: R.2676. Markings not decipherable. One plate found in wreckage showed aircraft made by Ger. Fieseler, Cassel. Following fighter action, during which the pilot baled out, aircraft dived into ground. Engine is buried and aircraft totally wrecked. Pilot prisoner. Traces of 20-mm shell guns and two M.G.17s were found. No further details available.

(It transpired that this was the first Bf 109E-7 to be examined by the British, and a closer examination of the manufacturer's plate disclosed that this was the aircraft shot down by Stanford Tuck while flying with No. 92 Squadron. German records state that the pilot was killed, and it must be assumed that he died in captivity from wounds sustained.)

Report No. 4/68. Messerschmitt Bf 109E-7

Crashed on 12-10-40 at Bean's Hill, Harrietsham, near Maidstone. Map reference: R.3174. Markings not decipherable. One small plate showed aircraft or component made by

Erla, Leipzig. Following fighter action, during which pilot baled out, aircraft came down in flames and dived into ground. Engine buried. Traces of two 20-mm shell guns and two M.G.17s found. One piece of armour found—probably piece of cross-bulkhead. Pilot prisoner. No further details available.

(The loss of this aircraft was not mentioned in Luftwaffe records, but was clearly one of no fewer than four aircraft belonging to 2.Staffel, Lehrgewschwader 2, all of which fell over Kent and could therefore be confirmed by the British. It was later credited to Plt. Off. A. Ingle of No. 605 Squadron.)

Report No. 4/69. Messerschmitt Bf 109

Crashed on 12-10-40 at Weeke's Lane, West Brabourne, Ashford. Map reference: R.5361. Markings not decipherable. Cause of crash is presumed to be fighter action, as pilot baled out. Aircraft dived into ground, and engine and most of wreckage is buried in crater. Traces of two 20-mm shell guns, and two M.G. 17s found. No further details possible.

(Discovery of this crashed aircraft only followed after interrogation of the German pilot by A.D.I.(K), and also proved to be from 2./LG 2. Its destruction was officially credited to Plt. Off. P.W. Rabone (New Zealander) of No. 145 Squadron whose combat report tallied in respect of location.)

Report No. 4/70. Messerschmitt Bf 109E-3

Crashed on 12-10-40 at Chapel Holding, Small Hythe, Tenterden. Map reference: R.3349. Markings < I +. The horizontal vee and vertical bar consist of alternate black and white stripes of different thickness. Aircraft made by Erla, Leipzig. WkrNr. 969, reception date 11-4-39. Engine DB601, Nr. 60081, made by Daimler-Benz *Motorenwerke*, Genshagen, Teltow. Impossible to establish cause of forced landing from examination of aircraft. Pilot made very good belly landing. No sign of .303 strikes or A.A. fire, and engine does not appear to have overheated. Armour: usual cross bulkhead in fuselage. Head protection not found as cockpit cover had been jettisoned. Two 20-mm shell guns and two M.G.17s fitted; about 2,000 rounds of 7,9-mm and 100 rounds of 20-mm ammunition. No bomb gear fitted to this aircraft. Pilot prisoner.

(Fourth of the 2./LG 2 Bf 109s to be lost over Kent on this date, the reason for this aircraft's crash was never established, and no R.A.F. combat claim tallied in any respect; nor was British Intelligence able to obtain any information by interrogation

of the pilot, whose name was not disclosed except in Red Cross documents.)

Report No. 4/71. Messerschmitt Bf 109E-3

Crashed on 13-10-40 at Robert's Dane, Wye, Kent. Map reference: R.5264. Markings 1 + 7; the figures 1 and 7 are white with black edging. Nose and rudder yellow. Aircraft made by Erla, Leipzig. WkrNr. 860; reception date, 23-2-39. A second plate showed the name Kieler Leichtbau GmbH, Kiel-Hassee. Engine: DB601, Nr. 61721, made by Daimler-Benz *Motorenwerke*, Genshagen. Following fighter action, pilot made belly landing. Only seven or eight strikes in aircraft, but some of these in radiator, and engine overheated. Two 20-mm shell guns and two M.G.17s fitted. About 2,000 rounds of 7.9-mm and 100 rounds of 20-mm. ammunition in aircraft. Aircraft fitted with bomb release gear, but bomb rack could not be seen owing to position of aircraft. Armour: cross bulkhead in fuselage; no head protection found as cockpit cover had been jettisoned. Pilot prisoner.
(This aircraft was reported to be a Bf 109E-4, flown by Gefreiter Hubert Rungen, in German records; it was credited to Fg. Off. C.B.F. Kingcombe of No. 92 Squadron; see Item No. 9 of the German loss table for 13th October.)

Report No. 4/72. Heinkel He 111H-3

Crashed on 16-10-40 at 02.15 hrs at Cressey Farm, Hutton, near Brentwood. Map reference: M.0812. Markings not decipherable on wreckage, but papers showed 1T+LK. Airframe made by Allegemeine *Transportenlagen* Ges. Leipzig. WkrNr. 5709L. Reception Date, March 1940. Engines: Jumo 211. Cause of crash said to have been fighter action and aircraft dived into ground. Aircraft caught fire and an explosion followed, completely destroying aircraft. Four M.G.15s were traced. Portions of parachute mine shrouds were found burnt in wreckage, but no evidence of a mine rack could be found. Assisted take-off hook and take-off gear under pilot's seat traced with tail tripod. A steel cylinder, 6 ft. long and 7-inches diameter was fitted in the tail fairing of fuselage; this is damaged but is being further investigated. Armour: semi-circular bulkhead aft of the top rear gunner; shield for lower rear gunner and strips of armour on floor of gondola. Crew: Presumed four; two dead in wreckage and two prisoner.
(One of two He 111s to fall at or near Brentwood on this night, the destruction of this aircraft was not officially credited to a specific British pilot, although the evidence now seems to point conclusively to it being a bomber that was claimed as damaged by Plt. Off. Hughes in a Defiant of No. 264 Squadron—in addition to another He 111 claimed by him to have fallen at Brentwood 45 minutes earlier; see Item 18 in the German loss table for 16-10-40.)

Report No. 4/74. Messerschmitt Bf 109E-1

Crashed on 15-10-40 at Owls Castle Farm, Lamberhurst. Map reference: R.1054. Markings not decipherable, but rudder is yellow. Airframe made by Arado Warnemunde in 1939. Following fighter action, pilot baled out and aircraft dived into ground in flames. Four M.G.17s traced. Armour: cross bulkhead in fuselage; Also neck shield and curved head

protection. Pilot prisoner. No further details possible.
(This was the aircraft flown by Unteroffizier Erich Höhn of 4.Staffel, Jagdgeschwader 51, shot down by Sgt. R.H. Fokes of No. 92 Squadron at 12.05 hrs.; see Item No. 23 of the German loss table for 15th October.)

Report No. 4/75. Messerschmitt Bf 109E-1

Crashed on 15-10-40 at 12.30 hrs at Everton, near Lymington. Map reference: U.7314. Markings not decipherable. Engine DB601. Following fighter action, aircraft caught fire and pilot baled out at low altitude. Aircraft crashed and an explosion followed. Totally destroyed. Armament: three M.G.17s traced, but probably four fitted. Armour: cross bulkhead in fuselage traced but no head protection as cockpit cover jettisoned. Pilot prisoner.
(Equating the above report with that of A.D.I.(K) shows this aircraft to be that flown by Gefreiter Alois Pollach of II./JG 2, although it proved impossible to discover which of several likely R.A.F. pilots, probably of No. 145 Squadron, was responsible for shooting down the enemy fighter. See German loss table, Item 14, for 15th October.)

Report No. 3/105. Messerschmitt Bf 109

Crashed at 10.15 hrs on 15-10-40 at Sandwich, on the beach below high water mark. Map reference: R.8078. Markings 1 + 7, all in black. Orange nose and rudder; spinner red. Engine DB601. Following fighter action, during which aircraft was apparently hit in engine or radiator, pilot force landed at edge of sea. Armament: two 20-mm. cannon and two M.G.17s. Armour: could not be traced owing to position of crash. Camouflage: mottled dark grey and olive green. Pilot prisoner.
(German records indicate this as the aircraft flown by Ober-feldwebel Wilhelm Bauer who was shot down by Fg. Off R.C. Brown of No. 229 Squadron "east of Canterbury" at 10.15 hrs. See Iem No. 19 of the German loss table for 15th October. Bauer was made prisoner.)

Report No. 3/106. Messerschmitt Bf 109E-7

Crashed at Elham on 15-10-40. Map reference R.6163. During fighter action aircraft blew up in the air at a comparatively low altitude and wreckage was scattered over a wide area. No details as to armament, etc., can be given.
(One of eleven aircraft which crashed within four miles of Elham during the Battle of Britain, this is now known to be the Bf 109, flown by Leutnant Ludwig Lenz of Stab I./LG 2, shot down by Sergeant D.E. Kingaby of No. 92 Squadron. The combat opened some twenty miles to the north of the crash site, and continued southwards—the German pilot being buried at Hawkinge cemetary; see Item No. 11 of the German loss table for 15th October).

Report No. 3/107. Assumed Messerschmitt Bf 109

Crashed on 15-10-40 at Olantigh, near Wye. Map reference: R.5067. The cause of this crash is not known, but the aircraft dived into fairly soft ground at very high speed and the engine and complete airframe are buried. There is nothing left to indicate the type of aircraft. The pilot is said to be buried in the crater.

(As far as is known, the identity of this aircraft and its pilot was never firmly established as no entry in German records shows the name of a pilot not otherwise accounted for by British Intelligence and Red Cross records. It may therefore have been an aircraft always believed to have been shot down over the sea.)

Report No. 4/76. Junkers Ju 88A

Crashed on 16-10-40 at Bishops Stortford. Map reference: L.9240. Markings not decipherable. From plate found, aircraft made by Junkers *Flugzeug und Motorenwerke*, Dessau. Engines: Jumo 211B, made by Junkers, Dessau; (one engine WkrNr. 47751). The cause of crash is not known and no bullet holes were to be found in the wreckage. Aircraft dived into ground and disintegrated, and it is thought that a bomb or bombs exploded on impact. A large damaged external bomb rack was found, and is being further investigated. Three M.G.15s found; probably more in the wreckage. A few pieces of broken armour found. Remains of three bodies found; no evidence of fourth man.

(This proved to be the Junkers Ju 88A-5, Wkr.Nr. 0317:4D+DM of Stab II/KG 30, flown by the Gruppenkommandeur, Hauptmann Erich Hass, which is assumed to have suffered engine trouble and crashed with little warning for the crew; it was later established that the large bomb rack was stressed to carry a 1,000-kg. bomb. The aircraft on this occasion was indeed only carrying a three-man crew. See Item No. 7 of German loss table for 16th October.)

Report No. 4/77. Messerschmitt Bf 109E-4

Crashed on 15-10-40 at 13.00 hrs at Bowcombe Down, Isle of Wight. Map reference: U.8707. Markings: 8 (the 8 is yellow outlined in black). Cowling and rudder orange-yellow. Crest: a red "R" in script on a silver shield with red outline. On opposite side of fuselage a Mickey Mouse in singlets, shorts and boxing gloves. Airframe made by Erla, Leipzig. WkrNr. 1588. Reception date, 24-4-40. Engine: DB601A-1 made by Daimler-Benz, Genshagen, Teltow; WkrNr. 62879. Following fighter action, pilot made good belly landing. Only ten .303-inch strikes, all in port wing, but pilot states that petrol tank was hit. Armament: Two M.G.17s and two 20-mm cannon. About 1,800 rounds of 7,9-mm. ammunition salved. Armour: cross bulkhead in fuselage; head protection not found as cockpit cover was jettisoned. Pilot prisoner.

("Yellow 8" identifies this as the Emil-4 flown by Feldwebel Horst Hellriegel (confirmed by the Wkr.Nr. in German records, as well as by the Geschwader badge) of I./JG 2 which was shot down by Flt. Lt. A.H. Boyd of No. 145 Squadron. See Item No. 13 on the German loss table for 15th October.)

Report No. 4/78. Heinkel He 111

Crashed on 16-10-40 at 22.00 hrs. on foreshore at Shotley. Map reference M.7051. Markings not decipherable, but one plate found reads: (—) und See Leichtbau Ges., Kiel. WkrNr. 3510 June 1940. Engines: Jumo 211. Aircraft is said to have hit barrage balloon cable at 3,000 feet, dived into ground and burned. Armament: Four M.G.15s found, but more probably

in crater. Armour: Bulkhead 9-mm. traced and pilot's back shield; none other found. Auxiliary petrol tank fitted in place of port bomb cells. Auxiliary oil tank in bomb compartment gangway. Damaged mine-carrying gear found. Assisted take-off gear and cast iron tube 6 feet long by 7 inches diameter fitted in tail fairing of fuselage. Crew: Four killed.

(This He 111H-5, captained by the Kriegsmarine officer, Oberleutnant zur See Wilhelm Stender of 2.Staffel, Küstenfliegergruppe 126, did indeed strike a balloon cable in the Harwich/Felixstowe barrage; it was the first German bomber to be examined in which the tail grenade launcher was fitted—although the significance of the launching tube was not fully appreciated for a further week. See Item 8 in the German loss table for 17th October.)

Report No. 4/80. Dornier Do 17Z

Believed to have crashed at 00.01 hrs on 17-10-40 (not found until mid-day 17-10-40) at Masbury Ring, near Wells. Map reference: U.0468. Markings: 7T+HK (H in black, outlined red on wing tips. Crest: Grey and black eagle standing on projected map of England, attacking it with claws and beak; England marked in red with white cliffs, sapphire sea and pale blue sky. The whole outlined by black and white shield. Aircraft made by Dornierwerke Friedrichshafen. WkrNr. 2691: built 1939. Engines: Bramo built by Brandenburgischer *Motorenwerke*, Berlin Spandau. Cause of crash is unknown, but aircraft was heard circling in district, apparently with engine trouble. No bullet holes can be traced; aircraft is badly wrecked. Armament: Six M.G.15s found. Ten 50-kg. bombs lying near wreckage unexploded, fitted with No. 15 fuses and whistles. Armour: One piece found in wreckage, position not known. Crew: Four dead.

(According to local Observer Corps personnel this bomber in fact crashed at 23.50 hrs on the night of 16th/17th October. The Dornier was also captained by a naval officer, Oberleutnant zur See Erwin Blank of 2.Staffel, Küstenfliegergruppe 606, and a subsequent examination of the engines disclosed that one had suffered two .303-inch bullet strikes, but it has proved impossible to credit a particular night fighter pilot with this action. See Item 19 of the German loss table for 16th October.)

Report No. 3/108. Dornier Do 17Z

Crashed at 19.20 hrs. on 16-10-40 near Nantglynn, Denbigh. Map reference: J.4682. Markings not decipherable. Engines: Apparently Bramo, but only small pieces of engines seen. Following fighter action the aircraft dived into ground and bombs exploded on impact, scattering wreckage over wide area. Crew presumed to have been four from remains found. No further details possible. Traces of three M.G.15s found and a few fragments of armour.

(Third German bomber shot down on this night found to have been captained by a naval pilot, this time Leutnant zur See Heinz Havemann of 3.Staffel, Küstenfliegergruppe 606; once more no credit for this action can be attributed as no fewer than seven Blenheim pilots claimed to have fired on German bombers without apparent effect. See Item 20 in the German loss table for 16th October.)

Report No. 3/109. Messerschmitt Bf 109E-4

Crashed on 17-10-40 at Manston airfield at 15.45 hrs. Markings: 1 + (1 in yellow). Nose and tail orange, spinner yellow. The manufacturers' plates had been removed, but WkrNr. appears to be 1106, dated 1939. Engine: DB601A, made by Daimler-Benz, Genshagen, Teltow, WkrNr. 62150. Following fighter action, during which radiator was hit and engine overheated, the pilot made fair belly landing on the aerodrome. Armament: Two 20-mm. shell guns and two M.G.17s; one bomb rack suitable for 250-kg. bomb, and normal bomb gear fitted. Armour: Cross bulkhead in fuselage, but no head protection found as cockpit cover had been jettisoned. Pilot prisoner.

(This Emil, shot down by Fg. Off. D.A.P. McMullen of No. 222 Squadron, was being flown by Oberleutnant Walter Rupp, the St.Kap. of 3./JG 53, and is detailed as Item 21 of the German loss table of 17th October.)

Report No. 4/82. Messerschmitt Bf 109E-3

Crashed at 13.45 hrs. on 20-10-40 at Plumstead, Woolwich. Markings not decipherable. Yellow nose, rudder and spinner. Crest: Shield with blue eagle looking backwards. Aircraft made by B.F.W., WkrNr. 2780, date 1940. Following fighter action the aircraft apparently broke up in the air, crashed and is completely destroyed. There were several .303-inch strikes in all three propeller blades. Armament: Two 20-mm. shell guns and two M.G.17s. Camouflage: Dark green on top of wings with pale blue cloud effect running diagonally. Armour: pilot's head protection found without curved piece. Pilot killed.

(The Wkr.Nr. 2780 identifies this aircraft as being flown by Oberfeldwebel Walter Freidmann of 6./JG 52, shot down by Fg. Off. M.P. Brown of No. 41 Squadron; see Item No. 18 in German loss table for 20th October.)

Report No. 3/110. Messerschmitt Bf 109E-1

Crashed on 20-10-40 at Waldron, Sussex. Map reference: Q.9736. Markings not decipherable but fin and rudder yellow. Engine: DB601. Following fighter action, the pilot baled out and the aircraft dived into ground from high altitude, being completely destroyed. Armament: Four M.G.17s traced. The normal armour bulkhead in fuselage was found, but no head protection as it had been jettisoned. Pilot prisoner. Owing to the condition of the crash, no further details possible.

(From pilot interrogation it was established that this aircraft was flown by Feldwebel Heinz Wilhelm of 3.Staffel, Jagdgeschwader 77, and was shot down by Spitfires of No. 603 Squadron; a manufacturer's plate was recovered in 1984 confirming the Wkr.Nr. as 4007; see Item 21 in German loss table for 20-10-40.)

Report No. 3/111. Messerschmitt Bf 109E.

Crashed on 20-10-40 at North Fording, near New Romney. Map reference: R.4946. Markings not decipherable, but spinner is white. From plate found, aircraft made by Arado in 1939, WkrNr. 316. Engine: DB601A-1 built by Daimler-Benz, Genshagen; WkrNr. 61477. Following fighter action, aircraft made crashed belly landing. A number of .303-inch

strikes in aircraft, two of which had struck the rear side of petrol tank in the corner, coming out at front of tank and wounding the pilot in arm and leg. After crash the aircraft caught fire. Armament: Two 20-mm. shell guns and two M.G.17s. Armour: Usual cross bulkhead in fuselage, but head protection not fitted in this aircraft. Pilot, wounded, prisoner.

(Loss of this aircraft was not included in any traceable Luftwaffe records, and only circumstantial evidence suggests that the Messerschmitt was destroyed by No. 603 Squadron. Unfortunately the contemporary examination failed to establish whether or not the aircraft was equipped with a belly bomb rack. See Item No. 22 in the German loss table for 20th October.)

Report No. 3/112. Dornier Do 17Z

Crashed at 01.04 hrs on 21-10-40 at Ness Point, near Shotley. Map Reference: M.6930. Markings: 7T+AH ("A" outlined white). Crest: Eagle holding map of British Isles in claw. Tips of spinners white. Aircraft WkrNr. apparently 2783. Engines: Bramo 323. The cause of the crash is unknown, but two bullet strikes passed through the fuselage from below. Aircraft made good belly landing on mud and is half submerged in mud and water. Armament: Five M.G.15s found, but possibly six fitted. Armour: Pilot's rear armoured, but other armour not visible owing to mud. Two light metal streamlined bulges, one fitted each side of fuselahge abreast of pilot's position; these are quickly detachable and contain inflatable rubber buoys—presumably to give increased buoyancy in the event of a forced landing on water. The number of crew and their fate are unknown, but windows are broken and there are bloodstains in the aircraft.

(Subsequent investigation confirmed that this was the Dornier Do 17Z-3 of 1/Ku.Fl.Gr.606 whose crew baled out near Salisbury following an attack on Liverpool; the aircraft continued to fly eastwards and eventually made an unmanned belly landing 120 miles away on the foreshore near Shotley; see Luftwaffe loss table for 20th October, Item 9.)

Report No. 3/113. Messerschmitt Bf 109

Crashed on 20-10-40 at Mereworth Wood, near Maidstone. Map reference: R.0974. Markings undecipherable. Following fighter action, the pilot baled out and aircraft dived into the ground. From the size and type of crater, it appears that a bomb or bombs exploded on impact. Traces of two 20-mm. shell guns and two M.G.17s found. Pilot prisoner. No further details possible.

(Interrogation of the pilot, Feldwebel Adolf Jowig, suggested that the aircraft had been shot down by Spitfires of No. 603 Squadron and the recent discovery of a manufacturer's plate near the crash site contributes evidence to support this, although no eyewitness reported the time of the crash. See Item No. 20 in the German loss table for 20th October.)

Report No. 3/114. Messerschmitt Bf 109

Crashed on 20-10-40 at Lenham Heath at 10.00 hrs. Map reference: R.3569. Marking undecipherable. Engine: DB601. Following fighter action, the pilot baled out and the aircraft dived into the ground and disintegrated. Armament: Two 20-mm. shell guns and two M.G.17s. Bomb rack fitted for 250-

kg. bomb. The usual armour bulkhead was found, but no other armour traced. The pilot was killed—it is reported locally that his parachute harness broke.

(Only in 1988 it was established almost without doubt that this was the Messerschmitt Bf 109E (2059: "Yellow 8") flown by Unteroffizier Franz Mairl, shot down by Flt. Lt. A.A. McKellar of No. 605 Squadron. See Item No. 13 of the German loss table for 20th October).

Report No. 3/115. Messerschmitt Bf 110C-5

Crashed at 12.50 hrs. on 20-10-40 at Bockingford, Horsmonden. Map reference: R.1464. Markings: L2+MR ("M" in white); these markings had been painted over. Aircraft made by Gothaer *Waggonfabrik*. Engines: DB601. Following fighter action, the aircraft made a good belly landing and was set on fire by crew. There were numerous .303-inch strikes in parts of the fuselage and wings not burnt. Armament: Four M.G.17s in nose, and apparently one M.G.15 in rear upper position, but no shell guns fitted. Remains of camera and photographic equipment found in wreckage of fuselage in position unusually taken up by shell gun breeches. Armour: The usual armour plate fitted between the rear of the front machine guns and the pilot was missing, but several plates were found—apparently fitted as protection against rear attack; their position cannot be accurately determined. Crew: One prisoner, one dead.

(In due course, further examination of the remains of this reconnaissance Messerschmitt was to furnish information of considerable importance to British Intelligence. Interrogation of the pilot, Oberleutnant Roland Lemmerich, failed to disclose any information regarding the nature of his sortie or of his Unit, but it emerged that his gunner, Unteroffizier Rudolf Ebeling, had probably been mortally wounded in action, and that Lemmerich probably chose to force land in an attempt to save the man's life. It had been established that the British fighters involved were flown by Villa and Saunders of No. 92 Squadron. See Item No. 15 in the German loss table for 20th October.)

Report No. 3/116. Junkers Ju 88A-5

Crashed at 13.30 hrs. on 21-10-40 at New Milton. Map reference: U.6715. Identification markings are not clear. BK in black (which are probably old markings) appear in front of cross, followed by BH in white. Airframe made by *Norddeutsche* Dornierwerke; WkrNr. 8116 on fin. Engines: Jumo 211. Following fighter action the starboard engine was on fire and the aircraft made a crash landing and, with the exception of the tail unit, was extensively burnt. A number of .303-inch strikes from astern and the beam were found in the wreckage not burnt. Part of several machine guns were found, but their position is not known. A few plates of armour were found in the wreckage but their position cannot be determined. Three articles, 20 cm. long and 55 mm. diameter, fitted with stick at end and propeller in nose, were found in the wreckage; these appear to be grenades or some type of flare; they are being further examined and a report will follow. Crew of four killed.

(This aircraft, whose target was the Gloster aircraft factory at Brockworth, had been attacked by the Spitfires flown by

Howell and Hill of No. 609 Squadron. The Unit code markings, quoted in German records, were in fact 9K+BH, indicating the aircraft was from 1 Staffel, Kampfgeschwader 51, being flown by Oberleutnant Max Fabian. At the time, the R.A.F. was unaware of the existence of the A-5 variant of the Ju 88. See Item 5 of the German loss table for 21st October.)*

Report No. 4/84. Dornier Do 215B-1

Crashed at 12.35 hrs. on 24-10-40 near St. Neots. Map reference: L.6277. Markings L2-KS, all in black; spinners yellow. Airframe manufacturered by Dornier Werke, Friedrichshafen; WkrNr. 0060. Engines: DB601A-1, made by Daimler-Benz at *Werke 90*, Berlin Marienfelde; starboard engine WkrNr. 11674 (made 20-11-39); port engine WkrNr. 11689 (made 4-12-39). Following fighter action, during which both engine are said to have caught fire in the air, the crew baled out; the aircraft hit the ground at high speed in a shallow dive, scattering wreckage over a considerable area. A number of .303-inch strikes, coming from astern, found in pieces of wreckage. Five MG.15s found, but no armour plate could be traced. Fittings for two cameras found in rear bomb compartment, together with a quantity of film (35-cm across). Several components were marked "Do 17Z". Crew of four: three killed as they apparently baled out too low; one prisoner.

(This was one of fewer than half a dozen Do 215s examined by British Intelligence during the Battle of Britain, their service at that time being confined to the Aufklärungsgruppe Oberbefehlshaber der Luftwaffe. The enemy aircraft, caught alone in daylight over the English Midlands was attacked by at least six Hurricanes from two Squadrons, and stood little chance of survival. It was correctly identified by British Intelligence as being from the Unit's 3./Staffel. See Item 1 in German loss table for 24th October.)

Report No. 4/87. Messerschmitt Bf 109E-4

Crashed at 15.30 hrs on 22-10-40 at Littlestone. Map reference: R.5460. This aircraft broke up in the air and is believed to have exploded. The bulk of the wreckage fell in the sea, but the tail unit and part of a wing fell on land. The cause is believed to have been fighter action. No details can be given about this aircraft. Pilot killed.

(No attribution to an R.A.F. pilot for this combat victory has been possible as a number of conflicting claims were entered, possibly suggesting that several pilots attacked the same aircraft at slightly different times; the German pilot was Unteroffizier Heinrich Arp, flying 1124: "black 10" of 2./JG 26 <Schlageter>, and who was buried at Hawkinge cemetary. See Item No. 12 of the German loss table for 22nd October.)

(About ten crash reports covering investigations between 23rd and 26th October 1940 are missing from available records)

Report No. 4/96. Messerschmitt Bf 109E-7

Crashed at 12.30 hrs on 27-10-40 at Addington Court Farm, Addington. Map reference: Q.8383. Markings < - + (black with white outline). The manufacturer's name is not known, but the WkrNr. of the airframe is 4124. Engine presumably DB601. The cause of this crash is not certain, but is believed to have been fighter action, during which the pilot baled out. The aircraft dived into the ground at high speed; the engine is buried and the airframe entirely wrecked. Armour: fuselage cross bulkhead found; head protection found, but curved head shield not fitted. Owing to condition of crash no details are possible. Pilot prisoner.

(Flown by Leutnant Wilhelm Busch, Signals Officer of Stab I./ JG 3 <Udet>, this Emil-7 was shot down by Plt. Off. K.W. Mackenzie of No. 501 Squadron. See Item No. 17 in German loss table for 27th October.)

Report No. 4/97. Junkers Ju 88A-5.

Crashed at 18.10 hrs on 27-10-40 at Kirby Grindalythe, near Malton, Yorks. Map reference: A.3887. Markings 5J+ER ("E" in white). Crest: Flying bat on yellow crescent moon. Tips of spinners white. Airframe manufactured by Norddeutsche Dornier Werke under licence to Junkers in 1940. WkrNr. 1258. Engines: Jumo 211B, made by Junkers, Dessau (WkrNrs. 47853 and 62847). This aircraft is said to have been brought down by light A.A. fire, and the starboard engine was put out of action. Aircraft made good belly landing. Armament: Only four M.G.15s fitted as follows: two upper rear, one front nose and one lower rear. Armour: The usual protection fitted for pilot's seat and upper and lower rear gunners. Crew: Four; one dead and three prisoners.

(Apart from the fact that the crash report quotes an incorrect Wkr.Nr., which probably referred to a component rather than the aircraft itself (whose correct Wkr.Nr. was 6129), this event was well documented. Among the crew was Oberleutnant Friedrich Podbielski, Staffelkapitan of 7.Staffel, Kampfgeschwader 4, who was among those made prisoner. The aircraft, being in excellent condition, provided British Intelligence with its first good opportunity to study the A-5 version of the Ju 88. See Item No. 8 of the German loss table for 27th October.)

Report No. 3/123. Messerschmitt Bf 109E

Crashed on 27-10-40 at Hooks Wood, Lenham. Map reference: R3070. Markings not decipherable. Crash followed fighter action, during which pilot baled out. The aircraft dived into the ground at high speed and is almost completely buried. No details possible. Pilot prisoner.

(As far as is known no attempt was ever made to examine or recover this enemy fighter as its major components were considered to be wholly inaccessible, and only fairly small fragments—scattered far and wide—have ever been found; the aircraft could have been any one of about six Bf 109s that may have crashed in the area; as the pilot is said to have survived, this may be covered by Item No. 20, 21, 22, 23, 24 or 26 in the German loss table for 27th October.)

Report No. 3/124. Messerschmitt Bf 109E

Crashed at 09.45 hrs on 27-10-40 at Upstreet, near Canterbury. Map reference: R.6882. Markings not decipherable. The crash followed fighter action, during which the pilot baled out, and the aircraft dived into the ground at high speed and was almost completely buried. Traces of two shell guns found. The cockpit top cover with head protection and curved head shield was found some distance away from crash. A

plate on a small piece of wreckage carried the inscription *Bayerische Flugzeugwerke*. Pilot prisoner. No further details possible.

(The same remarks under Report No. 3/123 also apply in this instance.)

Report No. 3/125. Messerschmitt Bf 109E

Crashed at 15.15 hrs on 28-10-40 at Leybourne, near West Malling. Map Reference: R.1477. Markings not decipherable. Following fighter action, during which the pilot baled out, the aircraft dived into the ground and is almost entirely buried. A plate bears the name Arado Werke (but may refer only to a component). Traces of four M.G.17s found. Pilot taken prisoner. No further details possible.

(A manufacturer's plate was recovered at the position of the crash in September 1986 denoting the aircraft's WkrNr. as 4906, identifying the aircraft as a Bf 109E-8, "Black 2" of 5.Staffel, Jagdgeschwader 27, shot down by Stanford Tuck of No. 257 Sqn. south of Gravesend; the German pilot, Unteroffizier Artur Gonschorek, was taken prisoner.)

Report No. 3/126. Dornier Do 17Z

Crashed at 02.00 hrs on 28-10-40 at Boughton Malherbe, near Faversham. Map reference: R.3167. Markings: 5K+CH (all in black). Crest: A man's figure with cockatoo's head, carrying a bomb under the left arm and an owl on his right hand; all on a pale blue shield. A large pink horizontal stripe on the rudder. Airframe made by Dornier Werke, Friedrichshafen; WkrNr. 2544. Engines: Bramo 323. Plate on reduction gear housing showed Humboldt Deutz Motoren Reparatur Werke, Hamburg. This aircraft is reported to have been brought down by A.A. fire, and no 0.303-inch strikes are visible in the wreckage. The starboard engine, wing and rudder are badly oiled up; the aircraft crash landed and both engines broke off. Armament: Eight M.G.15s were found in the wreckage, but positions are not certain; a large amount of ammunition was also found. Armour: Pilot's seat armoured as usual; cross bulkhead behind crew's cockpit; roof on detachable cover armoured; and strips of armour below rear upper gunner's position. The forward bomb bay contained an extra self-sealing petrol tank. Crew: Four; two dead and two injured (one of the latter subsequently died).

(See Item 3 of Luftwaffe loss table, 28th October 1940. This was Feldwebel Kurt Vosshagen's Do 17Z-2 of 1.Staffel, Kampfgeschwader 3, three of whose crew were killed or succumbed to injuries. The aircraft crest described above has not been identified elsewhere, and must be assumed to be a personal insignia rather than that of the Staffel. The previous attribution of this aircraft's destruction to pilots of No. 17 Squadron was incorrect.)

Report No. 3/128. Messerschmitt Bf 109E-1

Crashed at 09.30 hrs on 27-10-40 near Lydd, Kent. Map reference: R.5239. Markings: 13+ ("13" in white, outlined black, the numeral being located on the fuselage forward of the windscreen, and the "+" halfway down fuselage in normal position). Rudder and nose yellow, spinner white. Crest: A white Dutch clog, edged in black with wings. Airframe made by Arado, Wkr.Nr. 3576. Engine: DB601A, built at Niedersachsiche Motoren Werke; WkrNr. 20195. Following fighter action, pilot made very good belly landing. Engine appears to have seized and had been hit by an incendiary cannon shell which had burnt all plug leads on the port side of the engine and had punctured the water jacket. There were a few .303-inch strikes in the port wing. Armament: Four 7,9-mm M.G.17s. Armour: Fuselage cross bulkhead and head protection with curved head shield. No ammunition appears to have been expended. The camouflage on the upper surface of the wings is darkish grey except for a triangle formed from wing root to trailing edge to a point halfway along leading edge; this triangle towards the fuselage is a dirty light blue; the fuselage is also dirty light blue dappled with grey. Pilot prisoner.

(The shooting down of this aircraft was officially credited to Fg. Off. W.H. Nelson, flying a Spitfire of No. 74 Squadron, although this is now discounted as there is no possibility of his having been flying a cannon-armed Spitfire; photographs taken at the time leave no doubt that the Messerschmitt had been hit by both 20-mm. and 0.303-inch ammunition and the circumstances of the combat remain a mystery. The German pilot, Unteroffizier Arno Zimmermann of 7./JG 54, was taken prisoner; Fg. Off. Nelson was to be killed four days later on 1-11-40. See Luftwaffe loss table, 27-10-40.)

Report No. 3/130. Messerschmitt Bf 109E-4

Crashed at 16.45 hrs on 28-10-40 at North Common, Chailey, East Sussex. Map reference: Q.8239. The cause of the crash is not known but is thought to have been from A.A. gunfire. The aircraft dived into the ground, was partly buried and burst into flames. The pilot had baled out and was made prisoner. Parts of the jettisoned hood were found some distance away and were covered with oil suggesting that the aircraft had been hit in the engine. No further details available.

(Pilot's name given as Feldwebel Alfred Berg, indicating that this was a Bf 109E-4, "White 3" of 4./JG 53, one of several Staffeln that flew free chase sorties over Sussex on the afternoon of 28th October. Berg was taken prisoner but vouchsafed no information on interrogation. See Luftwaffe loss table, Item 20, for 28th October 1940).

Report No. 4/99. Messerschmitt Bf 109E

Crashed at 14.20 hrs on 29-10-40 near Pluckley, west of Ashford. Map reference: R.5549. No identification markings traced. Cause of crash is presumed to have been fighter action; aircraft dived into ground at high speed and is almost entirely buried. Pilot baled out and taken prisoner. Some loose ammunition found, and armament appears to have been two 20-mm. shell guns and two M.G.17s. Owing to condition of crash, no further details possible.

(Pilot's name is corrupt in records, but approximates to Otto Brunk; Fhr. Brunk was reported missing on this day, flying a Bf 109E-4 ("Black 2") of 5./JG 52, said to have been shot down by Spitfires of No. 602 Squadron south of London "during the afternoon" of 29th October; he was taken prisoner. See Luftwaffe loss table, 29th October 1940).

Report No. 4/100. Messerschmitt Bf 109E-4

Crashed at 17.10 hrs on 28-10-40 at Fielding Land, Dymchurch. Map reference: R.5549. Markings not decipherable, but nose and tail (from pieces of cowling and fabric found) were yellow. Following fighter action, the aircraft dived into the ground and is almost completely buried. From ammunition found, the armament was probably two 20-mm. cannon and two M.G.17s. Pilot dead, buried in wreckage. No. further details possible.

(Plate recovered from vicinity of crash site in 1982 shows aircraft's WkrNr. to have been 5095, confirming that this Messerschmitt was the aircraft flown by Leutnant Werner Knittel, Adjutant of II.Gruppe, JG 51—although some other details appear conflicting. No attribution to an R.A.F. pilot has been possible. See Luftwaffe loss tables for 28th October 1940).

Report No. 4/101. Dornier Do 17Z

Crashed at 18.50 hrs on 27-10-40 in Holebrooke Creek on the River Stour. Map reference: M.6851. The cause of this crash was thought to have been A.A. fire, and the wreckage is covered by water, even at low tide. Pieces of wreckage have been salvaged and the wreck examined by a diver. A new type of bomb rack has been recovered; this rack has ten units and each unit appears capable of carrying eight small bombs. There is provision for electro-magnetic release but no Rheinmetall electric fusing gear. A second rack of this type has been seen in the wreckage. The rack that has been salved will be further investigated and reported on later. An engine cowling plate gives the manufacturer's name as Henschel *Flugzeugwerke*.

(It was established soon after this report was written that the Dornier was shot down by a Hurricane flown by Plt. Off. J.K. Ross of No. 17 Squadron. The German bomber had just previously attacked Martlesham Heath (whence No. 17 Squadron was operating) with a large number of small anti-personnel fragmentation bombs, this fact explaining the new type of bomb rack. Post-War examination of relics recovered from the site provided traces of the Dornier's Wkr.Nr., 1150, confirming that it was the aircraft flown by Unteroffizier Erich Johannes of III./KG 76—see Item 13 in the Luftwaffe loss table of 27th October 1940).

Report No. 4/102. Messerschmitt Bf 109E

Crashed at 17.10 hrs on 29-10-40 near Langham Hoe, Colchester. Map reference: M.4835. Markings: Δ+N (triangle black with white edge, and "N" white with black edge); crest, black and white Mickey Mouse holding axe in one hand and large pistol in the other, all on a yellow disc. (Old markings, which are still discernable, were DH+EJ). Cowling and rudder, yellow. Wing tips had been yellow, but now covered by green paint. Spinner has white tip and blue and white bands. Engine: DB601A-1 manufactured by Daimler-Benz, Werke 90, Berlin Marienfelde; WkrNr. 11820 dated 23-11-39. Following fighter action, during which the cooling system was hit and the engine overheated, the pilot made a fair belly landing.60-70 .303-inch strikes from astern are evenly distributed over the airframe, and each radiator has two strikes. Armament: Two 20-mm. shell guns and two

M.G.17s; no rounds had been fired from the shell guns and very few from the machine guns. Armour: Fuselage cross bulkhead; no head protection found as cockpit cover had been jettisoned. One external bomb rack under fuselage. Pilot made prisoner, slightly wounded.

(All evidence points to this being the aircraft of Ober-feldwebel Harmeling of 4./LG 2, one of the units detailed to cover a raid by Erpr.Gr.210 on North Weald, Essex. No attribution can be made with certainty as several Hurricane pilots claimed to have hit Bf 109s which broke away with glycol streams from punctured radiators, and no claims exactly match the time of crash within ten minutes or so. See Item 12 in Luftwaffe loss table for 29th October 1940).

Report No. 4/104. Messerschmitt Bf 109E

Crashed at 16.30 hrs. on 29-10-40 at Elham, north of Folkestone. Map reference: R.6263. Markings not decipherable. Airframe manufactured by Arado in 1940; WkrNr. 1363. Following fighter action, the pilot baled out and the aircraft dived smoking into the ground; completely wrecked and partly buried. Armament: Four M.G.17s traced. Armour: No information available. Pilot taken prisoner but no further details.

(This crash has always presented something of a mystery—unless the aircraft had been mistaken for one that had crashed on a previous date. The Luftwaffe records include no aircraft lost around this date whose Wkr.Nr. tallies, while the date, time and location suggests that the aircraft was from 9.Staffel, Jagdgeschwader 3—see following Report No. 4/105—however all pilots and aircraft flying on this day have been otherwise accounted for. As Intelligence records have consistently omitted the name of the pilot, reported captured, it has been impossible to identify either the German pilot or the R.A.F. pilot(s) involved).

Report No. 4/105. Messerschmitt Bf 109E-4

Crashed at 16.30 hrs on 29-10-40 at Wootton Cross Roads, near Shepherds Well, north of Folkestone. Map reference: R.6866. Markings: 5 + 1 (figures yellow, outlined black). Crest: On side of cockpit a red sea-horse on blue ground; on port side of cowling a double-headed battle-axe in black on white ground; on starboard side, in addition to battle-axe, the word "Erika". Airframe manufactured by Wiener Neustadter F.W. in 1940, Wkr.Nr. 5153. Engine: DB601A, made by Daimler-Benz at Genshagen, WkrNr. 60303. Following fighter action, aircraft made good belly landing in field. Eight to ten .303-inch strikes found in wings and fuselage, but oil radiator also probably hit, although this could not be verified owing to position of crash. Armament: Two 20-mm. shell guns and two M.G.17s; a large quantity of ammunition still unexpended. Armour: Fuselage cross bulkhead and head protection with curved head shield. Pilot made prisoner.

(Unlike the item referred to in the previous Report, no doubt exists about the circumstances surrounding this crash. The Bf 109E-4 "Yellow 5" was flown by Oberleutnant Egon Troha, St.Kap. of 5.Staffel, Jagdgeschwader 3—Item 21 in the Luftwaffe loss table for 29th October—and Marsland's combat film, examined by the Author, uniquely indicates the identity numerals on a Bf 109E, even though some records suggest he

claimed a Bf 110; no Bf 110 was lost by the Luftwaffe over Britain on this day.)

Report No. 4/106. Messerschmitt Bf 109E-4

Crashed at 17.15 hrs. on 29-10-40 at Tillingham, Essex. Map reference: M.4723. Markings not decipherable. Following fighter action, pilot baled out and aircraft dived into the ground, was buried and burnt out; engine buried deeply in soft ground, presumably a DB601. A few .303-inch strikes found in pieces of wreckage, but position not known. Armament: traces of one 20-mm. shell gun found, but nothing else. Pilot taken prisoner; no further details.

(This was the aircraft flown by Feldwebel Konrad Jäckel, "Black 1" of 8.Staffel, Jagdgeschwader 26, which was shot down by Kumiega and Hogg of No. 17 Squadron, although these pilots reported that their victim had crashed on Foulness—an understandable case of mistaken map-reading in the heat of combat; see Item 22 of the Luftwaffe loss table for 29th October 1940).

Report No. 4/107. Messerschmitt Bf 109E-4

Crashed at 16.55 hrs on 29-10-40 near Goldhanger, Essex. Map reference M.4723. Markings not decipherable. During fighter action the pilot baled out and the aircraft crashed and caught fire. Some .303-inch strikes found in the wreckage but position unknown. Armament: Traces of two M.G.17s and one 20-mm. shell gun found. Armour: Fuselage bulkhead traced and also pilot's head protection and curved shield. Pilot was wounded, but has since died.

(This aircraft was evidently sent to the North Weald area on a Free Chase in advance of Erpr.Gr.210's attack on the airfield, being the Bf 109E-4 flown by Oberleutnant Benno von Schenk, the St.Kap. of 5.Staffel, Lehrgeschwader 2; it was shot down by the Hurricane flown by Plt. Off. K.W. Mackenzie of No. 501 Squadron).

Report No. 4/108. Messerschmitt Bf 109E-1

Crashed at 17.15 hrs on 29-10-40 at Plummers Plain, Horsham, Sussex. Map reference: R.6448. Markings: White "5", outlined in red. Crest: On a light blue shield (with the corner broken off) a weeping, parrot-like bird with a long beak, and with a red umbrella under left wing; under the shield the words "Gott strafe England" in red. Airframe made by Arado, 19-9-40. WkrNr. 704 (as quoted). Engine: DB601. Following fighter action, the pilot attempted to land but hit obstruction posts in field; the aircraft broke up and caught fire. No bullet strikes found in the wreckage, but the pilot was badly wounded and has since died. Armament: Probably four M.G.17s, but only two found; also large amount of burnt 7,9-mm. ammunition; no trace of 20-mm. cannon or shells. Armour: fuselage bulkhead traced, but no head protection as cockpit cover had been jettisoned.

(This was the Bf 109E-1 flown by Unteroffizier Alfred Lenz of 4./JG 51, the only "White 5" reported missing by the Luftwaffe on this day, shot down by the Hurricane flown by Sergeant M. Maciejowski of No. 249 Squadron. The WkrNr. quoted above evidently referred to some component rather than the whole airframe as the correct number was 4828—one of a known batch of Arado-built Bf 109E-1s. See Item No.

26 in Luftwaffe loss table for 29th October).

Report No. 4/110. Messerschmitt Bf 109E-4

Crashed at 17.20 hrs on 29-10-40 at Langton Green, near Tunbridge Wells. Map reference: Q.9858. Markings: White "9", outlined in red. Crest: The same in previous report No. 4/108 above; nose painted yellow with dark green spinner. Engine: DB601, WkrNr. 61804. Following fighter action, the aircraft dived into the ground and disintegrated. A few .303-inch bullet strikes were traced in wings and fuselage. Armament: Two 20-mm. shell guns and two M.G.17s. Armour: Fuselage cross bulkhead found but no head protection as cockpit cover is missing. Pilot killed.

(An aircraft of the same Staffel as that in Report No. 4/108, this Bf 109E-4 was flown by Leutnant Heinrich Tornow, whose death was notified by the Red Cross. Being shot down at almost the same time as the previous aircraft, it seems likely that it too was shot down by a Hurricane pilot of No. 249 Squadron, but his identity has proved impossible to establish with certainty. See Item No. 25 in Luftwaffe loss table for 29th October).

Report No. 4/-?-. Heinkel He 111H-2

Aircraft crashed at 01.05 hrs on 29-10-40 in River Stour, one mile west of Parkstone. Map reference: M.6750. Markings not decipherable, but said to be Al+LT. The crew of this aircraft baled out and the aircraft dived vertically into soft mud near low water mark, and the wreckage caught fire. From a plate found, the airframe was made by Heinkel Werke, Oranienburg in April 1939. It is understood that the crew lost their way, thought they were over Holland and baled out.

(This Heinkel, of 9.Staffel, Kampfgeschwader 53, was Item 9 in the Luftwaffe loss table for 28th October; the unit codes were indeed Al+LT, the WkrNr. 5536. All five members of the N.C.O. crew were unhurt and made prisoner. The report number is evidently corrupt).

Report No. 4/111. Junkers Ju 88A-1

Crashed at 14.25 hrs at Stuntley, near Ely, on 30-10-40. Map reference: M.0397. Markings: L1+GS ("G" in black, outlined in white). Crest: On port side of nose a red griffin on white shield, and under this "R.8009/18". On starboard side three white swans on blue field, flying over sea. Spinners red. Engines: Jumo 211. Airframe made by *Allgemeine Transportanlagen*, Leipzig; WkrNr. 088-5008; reception date, February 1940. The cause of this crash has not yet been established, but the aircraft made a good belly landing. There are some .303-inch strikes evenly distributed, all from the rear, but none of these was vital. The starboard engine, however, appears to have seized up. Armament: The number of guns carried is not certain as all but one have been looted. The usual four external bomb racks are fitted, but one of these is stencilled in red on the fairing "1000 K"; this rack is being removed and investigated. Crew: Four; two baled out and two landed in aircraft, uninjured.

(Shot down by the Hurricanes of Fg. Off. R.G. Lewis and Sergeant V. Jicha (Czech) of No. 1 Squadron, this Junkers Ju 88 belonged to III.Gruppe, Lehrgeschwader 1, and is recorded as Item 7 in the Luftwaffe loss table for 30-10-40).

Report No. 4/112. Messerschmitt Bf 109E-4

Crashed at 11.40 hrs on 30-10-40 at Brook Farm, Marden. Map reference: R.1764. Markings not decipherable, other than a crest comprising a black "S" on a white shield. Airframe made by Wiener Neustadter F.W. in 1940. WkrNr. 5242. Following fighter action, the aircraft broke up in the air, the engine falling a considerable distance from the main wreckage, and not yet found. A large number of .303-inch strikes through the wing roots, petrol tank, and through starboard side of the back of pilot's seat, about 5 inches from the edge of the seat. Armament: Two 20-mm. shell guns and two M.G.17s traced and a large quantity of 7,9-mm ammunition in wreckage. Armour: Fuselage cross bulkhead fount; no verification of head protection as cockpit cover missing. Pilot killed.

(Unteroffizier Kurt Töpfer of 7./JG 26 <Schlageter> was the pilot of this Bf 109E-4 when it was shot down by Fg. Off. J.N. Mackenzie (New Zealander) of No. 41 Squadron. See Item No. 13 of the Luftwaffe loss table, 30th October 1940).

Report No. 3/131. Messerschmitt Bf 109E-4

Crashed at 16.05 hrs on 30-10-40 at Court Lodge Farm, East Farleigh. Map reference: R.1672. Markings: 1 + - (the "1" and bar in yellow, outlined in black); nose, rudder and fin yellow. Crest: Shield with red outline, divided into black and white triangles from a central point. Airframe made by Erla; acceptance date 3-1-40. WkrNr. 1474. Engine: DB601A-1 made by Daimler Benz, WkrNr. 61064. Following fighter action, during which the pilot was wounded, aircraft made good belly landing. Several .303-inch strikes in instrument panel and one in pilot's seat; one strike in starboard wing. Armament: Two 20-mm. shell guns and two M.G.17s. No ammunition had been expended. Armour: Cross bulkhead in fuselage; head protection found, but no curved head shield fitted. Pilot made prisoner.

(This aircraft was officially credited to Griffiths of No. 17 Squadron, but the time of crash does not tally with this pilot's combat report; it may therefore have been the Bf 109 claimed as only damaged by Fg. Off. D.A. Adams of No. 41 Squadron, whose time and place of combat tallies almost exactly; the German pilot was Gefreiter Schuller of 6./JG 3; see Item 12 of the German loss table for 30-10-40).

Report No. 3/132. Messerschmitt Bf 109E-4

Crashed at 14.00 hrs at Leylands, near Wrotham, on 30-10-40. Map reference: R.0781. Markings: - + (the bar in yellow, outlined black). Following fighter action, during which the pilot baled out, the aircraft dived into the ground and is entirely destroyed. Armament: Four M.G.17s, as far as has been ascertained. Armour: Cross bulkhead in fuselage, but no head protection found as cockpit cover is missing. Pilot, wounded, made prisoner. (From the wreckage it appears that this aircraft had been quite new.)

(The shooting down of this 6./JG 3 Bf 109, flown by Unteroffizier Fahrian, was credited to Czernin of No. 17 Squadron, even though the time of combat in his report does not tally; this is not a conclusive reason to believe that Czernin did not gain this victory as there is some doubt as to the accuracy of the time of crash reported by ground witnesses. After all, the

coincidence of two aircraft from the same Staffel apparently falling in the same area two hours apart is questionable to say the least.)

The above extracts are taken from a very large series of crash reports compiled following contemporary examination of fallen enemy aircraft. All were signed by Wing Commander J.A. Easton of A.I. 1(g). Easton was a Regular pilot who had specialised in enemy armament Intelligence and who controlled a number of crash investigation teams who, wherever possible, visited enemy crash sites to report on modifications being carried out by the Luftwaffe to its aircraft, particularly in the matters of guns, bomb loads and armour protection. The care also taken to investigate such features as aircraft markings, Works Numbers and manufacturers' plates may seem somewhat esoteric in the environment of deadly combat, but this Intelligence was to prove of the utmost importance. In due course, the equating of badges, markings and unit code letters with the results of enemy pilot interrogation, enabled the R.A.F. to compile a complete list of all Luftwaffe units, their code letters and badges, thereby providing the Allies with information of the enemy Air Force's deployment. A knowledge of Works Numbers of airframes and engines, together with dates of acceptance, gave fairly accurate information about the rates of production achieved by the German aircraft industry, and the location of factories which, in the fullness of time, became targets for British bombers.

The Author has been granted permission to visit almost all the above crash sites during the past twenty years (as well as more than 120 others), although few display obvious signs of aircraft remains. In a number of instances some relics have been recovered for display in local museums. However, recovery of such remains—which, technically, are the property of the Ministry of Defence—has become the subject of very tight restriction for obvious and entirely justifiable reason; after all, in some known instances it was never possible to recover the crew members' body, and the site has been declared a War Grave, and therefore hallowed ground. In other instances there are indications that explosives may remain and these can only be disturbed by qualified and authorised personnel. Apart from these obvious restrictions, imposed for reasons of public safety and an essential respect for the fallen, the majority of crash sites lie on private property and the due processes of law apply to trespass, so that the euphemism of "archaeology" cannot be justified. It is emphasised, therefore, that any examination of a crash site—whether for recovery of relics or a determination of cause of crash—should only be undertaken by a recognised and authorised body after all the statutory provisions have been completed to the satisfaction of the Ministry of Defence, the Home Office, the Local Authority and the owner of the land.

SELECTED BIBLIOGRAPHY

The First World War

Boyle, Andrew, *Trenchard*; Collins, London, 1962

Brett, R. Dallas, *The History of British Aviation, 1908-1914*; Hamilton, London, 1933

Bruce, J.M., *British Aeroplanes, 1914-1918*; Putnam, London, 1957

Bülow, Major Freiherr von, *Die Luftwacht*; Berlin, 1927

Fredette, Major Raymond, *The First Battle of Britain, 1917-1918*; Cassell, London, 1956

Gray, Peter, and Thetford, Owen, *German Aircraft of the First World War*; Putnam, London, 1957 *et seq.*

Haddow, G.W., and Grosz, P.M., *The German Giants*; Putnam, London, 1963

Hoeppner, von, *Deutschlands Krieg in der Luft*; Berlin, 1920.

Kerr, Rear-Admiral Mark, *Land, Sea and Air*; Longmans, Green, London, 1927

Penrose, Harald, *British Aviation: The Great War and Armistice*; Putnam, London, 1969

Between the Wars, 1918-1939

Air Ministry, *The Origins and Development of Operational Research in the Royal Air Force*, H.M.S.O., London, 1963

Barnes, C.H., *Bristol Aircraft since 1910*; Putnam, London, 1964

Burney, Sir Charles Dennistoun, *The World, the Air and the Future*; London, 1929

Cowie, Donald, *An Empire Prepared: A Study of the Defence Potentialities of Greater Britain*, Allen and Unwin, London, 1938

Gritzbach, Erich, *Hermann Göring: The Man and His Work*; Hurst and Blackett, London, 1939

Herlin, Hans, *Udet: A Man's Life*; Macdonald, London, 1960

Kennedy, Captain B., *Modern War Defence Reconstruction*; London, 1936

Kingston McCloughry, Wg. Cdr. E.J., *Winged Warfare*; Jonathan Cape, London, 1937

Liddell Hart, Captain B., *When Britain Goes to War*, London, 1935

Mason, Francis K., *Hawker Aircraft Since 1920*, Conway/Putnam, 1961 *et seq.*

Mitchell, Brig. Gen., William, *Winged Defence*; New York, 1925

Mowat, Charles L., *Britain Between the Wars, 1918-1940*; Methuen, London, 1955 *et seq.*

Poturzyn, Fischer von, *Luftmacht: Gegenwart und Zukunft im Ursteil des Auslandes*; Berlin, 1938.

Richmond, Admiral Sir Herbert, *Sea Power in the Modern World*; London, 1934.

Richmond, Admiral Sir Herbert, *National Policy and Naval Strength*; R.U.S.I. Lecture, February, 1923.

Rowan-Robinson, Maj.-Gen. H., *Imperial Defence a Problem in Four Dimensions*; Frederick Muller, London, 1938.

Slessor, J.C., *Air Power and the Armies*; London 1936

Stewart, Oliver, *Strategy and Tactics of Air Fighting*; London, 1925

Vauthier, Lieut.-Col., *Le Danger Aérien et l'Avenir de la Paix*; Paris, 1930

(Also *The Journal of the Royal Air Force College, Cranwell*, Volume I — Volume XIX No. 2 (Autumn 1939)

The Second World War: The Battle of Britain

Air Ministry, **The Battle of Britain**; H.M.S.O., 1941

Air Ministry, *The Rise and Fall of the German Air Force*; London, 1946

Apostolo, G., *No. 110, The Fiat BR.20*; Profile, Leatherhead, 1966

Barrymaine, Norman, *The Story of Peter Townsend*; Davies, London, 1958

Beedle, J., *No. 43 Squadron*; Beaumont, London, 1985

Bekker, Cajus, *Radar-Duel im Dunkel*; Oldenburg-Hamburg, Stalling Verlag, 1958

Bekker, Cajus, *The Luftwaffe War Diaries*; Macdonald, 1966

Bickers, Richard T., *Ginger Lacey, Fighter Pilot*; Robert Hale, London, 1962

Bishop, Edward, *The Guinea Pig Club*; Macmillan, London, 1963

Blackstone. G., *History of the British Fire Service*; Routledge, London, 1957

Bowyer, Michael, *No. 117, The Boulton Paul Defiant*; Profile, Leatherhead, 1966

Braham, Wg. Cdr. J.R.D., *Scramble*; Muller, London, 1961

Braybrooke, Keith, *Wingspan—A History of R.A.F. Debden*; Hart, Saffron Walden, 1956

Brickhill, Paul, *Reach for the Sky*; Collins, London, 1957

Brown, George, and Lavigne, Michel, *Canadian Wing Commanders*, Battleline, Langley, B.C., Canada

Carter, Ernest, *Railways in Wartime*; Muller, London, 1964.

Cattaneo, Dott. Ing. Gianni, *No. 16, The Fiat CR.42*; Profile, Leatherhead, 1965

Churchill, Winston, **The Second World War**, Vols. I and II; Cassell, London 1948 *et seq.*

Cluett, D., Bogle, J., and Learmonth, B., *Croydon Airport and the Battle of Britain*, Sutton Library, 1984.

Collier, Basil, *The Defence of the United Kingdom*, H.M.S.O.,

Selected Bibliography—*continued*
London, 1952

Collier, Basil, *Leader of the Few*; Jarrolds, London, 1957

Crook, Flt. Lt. D.M., *Spitfire Pilot*, Faber, London, 1942

Cynk, Jerzy, *History of the Polish Air Force, 1918-1968*, Osprey, London, 1972

Deere, Gp. Capt. A.C., *Nine Lives*, Hodder & Stoughton, London, 1959

Dierich, Wolfgang, *Kampfgeschwader 51 "Edelweiss": Eine Chronik aus Dokumenten und Berichten, 1937-1945*; Motorbuch Verlag, Stuttgart.

Dixon, J.L., *In All Things First: A History of No. 1 Squadron*, Orpington Press, 1954

Faircloth, N.W., *New Zealanders in the Battle of Britain*, Dept. of Internal Afairs, Wellington, New Zealand, 1950

Fielder, Arkady, *303 Squadron: The Story of a Polish Fighter Squadron with the R.A.F.*; Davies, London, 1942

Forell, Fritz von, *Mölders*; Sirius-Verlag, Salsburg, 1951

Forrester, L., *Fly for your Life: Story of Stanford Tuck*; Muller, 1956

Foster, Reginald, *Dover Front*; Secker & Warburg, London, 1941

Galland, Lieut. Gen. Adolf, *The First and the Last*; Methuen, London, 1955

Gibbs, Air Marshal Sir Gerald, *Survivor's Story*; Hutchinson, London, 1956

Halliday, Hugh, *No. 242 Squadron: The Canadian Years*; Ontario, Canada, 1981

Hanna, A.M., *Fighter Command Communications*; The Post Office Electrical Engineers' Journal, Vol. 38, Part 4

Hartley, A.B., *Unexploded Bomb*; Cassell, London, 1958

Hillary, Richard, *The Last Enemy*; Macmillan, London, 1942

Information, Ministry of, *Front Line, 1940-41: The Official Story of the Civil Defence of Britain*; H.M.S.O., London, 1942

Jackson, R., *Douglas Bader*, Barker, London, 1982

Julian, Marcel, *La Bataille d'Angleterre*; Presses de la Cité, Paris, 1965

Kennedy, A. Scott, *"Gin Ye Daur", No. 603 (City of Edinburgh) Fighter Squadron*; Pillams & Wilson, Edinburgh, 1943

Kent, Gp. Capt. J.A., *One of the Few*; Kimber, London, 1971

Kesselring, Generalfeldmarschall Albert, *Memoirs*; Kimber, London, 1953

Mackenzie, Wg. Cdr. K.W., *Hurricane Combat*; Kimber, 1987

Manvell, Roger, and Fraenkel, Heinrich, *Hermann Göring*; Heinemann, London, 1962

Mason, Francis K., *The Gloster Gladiator*, Macdonald, London, 1963

Mason, Francis K., *The Hawker Hurricane*, Aston, Bourne End, 1987

Mason, Francis K., and Turner, Michael, *Luftwaffe Aircraft*, Newnes, London, 1986

Mason, Francis K., *War in the Air*; Temple Press/Aerospace, London, 1985

Mouchotte, Gené, *Carnets de 1940—1943*; Flammarion, 1945 *et seq.*

Moulson, T., *The Flying Sword, The Story of No. 601 Squadron*; Macdonald, London, 1964

Moyes, P.J.R., *No. 41, The Supermarine Spitfire I and II*; Profile, Leatherhead, 1965

Obermeier, Enrst, *Die Ritterkreuzträger der Luftwaffe: Jagdflieger, 1939—1945*; Dieter Hoffmann, Mainz, 1966

Obermeier, Ernst, *Die Ritterkreuzträger der Luftwaffe: Stuka- und Schlachtflieger, 1939—1945*; Dieter Hoffmann, Mainz, 1976

Orange, Vincent, *Sir Keith Park*, Methuen, London, 1984

Orde, Capt. Cuthbert, *Pilots of Fighter Command*; Harrap, London, 1942

Osterkamp, General Theo, *Experiences as Jagdfliegerführer on the Channel Front*; Karlsruhe Collection, Hamburg

Park, Air Chief Marshal Sir Keith, *Background to the Blitz*; Hawker Siddeley Review, London, December 1951

Postan, M.M., *British War Production*; H.M.S.O., London, 1952

Price, Alfred, *Instruments of Darkness*; Kimber, London, 1967

Priller, Josef, *Geschichte eines Jagdgeschwaders, das JG 26 "Schlageter"*; Kurt Vowinckel Verlag, Heidelberg, 1956

Rawlings, J., *Fighter Squadrons of the R.A.F. and their Aircraft*, Macdonald, London, 1969 *et seq.*

Rawnsley, C.F., and Wright, Robert, *Night Fighter*; Collins, London, 1957

Reekie, *These and Other Things were Done*; Standard Telephones

Richards, Denis, *Royal Air Force, 1939—1945; Vol. I, The Fight at Odds*; H.M.S.O., London, 1953

Richey, Paul, *Fighter Pilot*, Batsford, London, 1941

Richthofen, General Baron von, *Personal Diary*; Karlsruhe Collection, Hamburg, 1941-44.

Ries, Karl, *Dora Kurfürst und rote, Books 1-3*; Dieter Hoffmann, Mainz, 1964 *et seq.*

Ries, Karl, *Markierungen und Tarnantriche der Luftwaffe im 2.Weltkrieg, Books 1-2*; Dieter Hoffmann, Mainz, 1963 *et seq.*

Ring, Hans, and Girbig, Werner, *Jagdgeschwader 27: Die Dokumentation über den Einsatz an allen Fronten, 1939—1945*; Motorbuch Verlag, Stuttgart, 1971

Rowe, A.P., *One Story of Radar*; Cambridge, 1948

Royal Canadian Air Force, *Among the Few; Canadian Airmen in the Battle of Britain*; Ottawa, 1948

Rüdel, Hans, *Stuka Pilot*; Transworld Publications, London, 1957

Seeman, Gerhard von, *Die Ritterkreuzträger, 1939—1945*; Podzun Verlag, Bad Nauheim, 1955

Shirer, William, *The Rise and Fall of the Third Reich*; Secker and Warburg, 1960

Shirer, William, *Berlin Diary*; Hamilton, London, 1941

Sutton, Barry, *The Way of a Pilot*, Macmillan, London, 1943

Sturtivant, R.C., *The Squadrons of the Fleet Air Arm*, Air Britain, Tonbridge, 1984

Swinton, Lord, *I Remember*; Hutchinson, London, 1948

Townsend, P., *Duel of Eagles*; Weidenfeld and Nicolson,

Selected Bibliography—*continued*
London, 1970

Vincent, Air Vice-Marshal S.F., ***Flying Fever***, Jarrolds, London, 1972

Walker, Oliver, ***Sailor Malan***; Cassell, London, 1953

Wallace, Graham, ***R.A.F. Biggin Hill***; Putnam, London, 1953

Watson-Watt, R., ***Three Steps to Victory***; Odhams, London, 1958

Weber, Dr. Theo, ***Die Luftschlacht um England***; Flugwelt Verlag, Wiesbaden, 1956

Wheatley, Ronald, ***Operation Sea Lion***; Oxford University Press, 1958

Williams, P., and Harrison, ***McIndoe's Army***; Pelham, London, 1979

Wood, Derek, and Dempster, Derek, ***The Narrow Margin***; Hutchinson, London, 1961 *et seq.*

Wright, Robert, ***Dowding and the Battle of Britain***; Macdonald, 1969.

Wykeham, Peter, ***Fighter Command***; Putnam, London, 1960

Wynn, K.G., ***Men of the Battle of Britain***, Gliddon, Norwich

INDEX

In the interests of space and to avoid tedious repetition, base airfields and personnel references included in the daily loss tables and repeated in the Orders of Battle and alphabetically-ordered Appendices are omitted from this Index.

McIndoe, Sir Archibald, *261 (footnote), 346*
McLean, Sqn. Ldr. (later Gp. Capt.) J.,
  O.B.E., D.F.C., *195 (footnote)*
McMullen, Fg. Off. (later Sqn. Ldr.) D.A.P.,
  D.F.C.✸✸, *110, 254*
McNab, Sqn. Ldr. (later Gp. Capt.), E.A.,
  O.B.E., D.F.C., R.C.A.F., *203 (footnote),
  243*
"Meacons", *148*
Measures, Flt. Lt. W.E.G., A.F.C., *112, 120*
Mechetski, Hptm., KG 2, *126*
Medway river, Kent, *148, 163, 197*
Medway towns, Kent, *126, 166, 222, 299,
  326*
Meissner, Hptm., KG 4, *163*
Memel, cession of, *54*
Mesopotamia, campaign in, *34*
Messerschmitt, Willi, *43, 48*
Messerschmitt Bf 109 aircraft: *48, 54, 71,
  77, 79, 81, 94, 96, 106-108, 111-113,
  116, 118, 123, 129, 138, 139, 141, 143,
  148, 150, 152, 153, 156, 159, 164, 166,
  169, 170, 178, 179, 187, 193, 214, 220,
  222, 239, 243, 246, 260, 268, 281, 288,
  291, 298, 315*
  armament, *48, 54,*
  Austrian production, *53, 54,*
  design and introduction, *48*
  in Spain, *53*
  production, September 1939, *54*
  see also Appendix C, *et passim*
Messerschmitt Bf 110 aircraft: *54, 79, 83,
  94, 96, 109, 116-118, 123, 124, 126, 129,
  133, 134, 141, 143, 169, 170, 178, 179,
  184, 188, 190, 196, 197, 199, 214, 219,
  226, 232, 243, 256, 268, 271, 281, 291,
  298, 305, 315, 340*
  production, September 1939, *54*
  see also Appendix C, *et passim*
Metz, France, airfield at, *81*
Meyer, Oblt., LG 1, *113*
Middlesbrough, Yorkshire, *200*
Middle Wallop airfield, Hampshire, *103,
  106, 109, 116, 123, 136, 143, 153, 170,
  178, 179, 190, 193, 204, 236, 238, 328*
  German target map of, *194*
Milan, Italy, air operations over, *273*
Milch, Generalfeldmarschall Erhard, *43-
  50, 54, 55, 73, 145*
Miles Master aircraft, *136*
Miller, Flt. Lt. R.R., *101,*
Millington, Plt. Off. W.H., D.F.C., *118*
Milne, Fg. Off. (later Wg. Cdr.) R.M.,
  D.F.C.✸, *116*
Mines, German air-dropped weapons, *134,
  141*
Ministry of Aircraft Production (M.A.P.),
  72, 93
Mitchell, Brig. Gen. William, *32*
Mitchell, Fg. Off. E.W., *113*
Mitchell, Plt. Off. G.T.M., *123*
Mitchell, Fg. Off. L.R.G., *137*
Mitchell, Reginald, *61-64, 73*
Mix, Hptm. Dr. Erich, *178*
Moberley, Fg. Off. G.E., *104*
Moerdijk bridge, Holland, *82*
Mölders, Oberstleutnant Werner, *114, 131,
  154*

Montgomery, Sqn. Ldr. D.H., *183*
Montrose airfield, Angus, *105, 136, 158,
  197 (footnote)*
Morane-Saulnier MS.406 aircraft, *81, 83*
Morgan, Flt. Lt. (later Wg. Cdr.) T.P. Dalton,
  D.S.O., O.B.E., D.F.C.✸, *128, 171*
Morris, Plt. Off. (later Wg. Cdr.) G.E., *146*
Morton, Fg. Off. (later Wg. Cdr.) J.S.,
  D.F.C.✸, *132, 135*
Mould, Sgt. (later Fg. Off.) E.A., *120*
Mudie, Plt. Off. M.R., *131*
Müller-Dühe, Ltn. Gerhard, *193, 203, 212*
Müncheberg, Oblt. Jochen, *193, 310*
Münchenhagen, Hptm., LG 1, *198*
Mungo-Park, Fg. Off. (later Flt. Lt.) J.C.,
  D.F.C.✸, *120*
Munich Crisis, 1938, *54, 73, 74, 75*
Murlis-Green, Capt. G.W., D.S.O.✸,
  M.C.✸✸, R.F.C., *22 (footnote), 25, 29
  (footnote), 92 (footnote)*
Mussolini, Benito, *47, 50, 193 (footnote)*

N
Namsos, Norway, *79*
Namur, France, *83*
Nancy, France, airfield at, *81*
Narvik, Norway, *79, 80*
National Government, 1931, *59*
National Physics Laboratory, Teddington,
  64, 67
*National Sozialistische Deutsche Arbeiter
  Partei, 44, 58*
Naujocks, Alfred, *77 (footnote)*
Naval Staff, German Imperial, *12, 14*
Navy, German Imperial, *13, 14*
Needles, air operations over, *134, 185*
Neissl, Gefr., KG 54, *189*
Netheravon airfield, Wiltshire, *36*
Neville, Sgt. W.J., *179*
Newall, Air Chief Marshal Sir Cyril (later
  Marshal of the Royal Air Force), G.C.B.,
  O.M., G.C.M.G., C.B.E., *59 (footnote)*
Newcastle-upon-Tyne, air operations over,
  200, 201
Newling, Plt. Off. M.A., D.F.C., *139*
Nicolson, Flt. Lt. (later Wg. Cdr.) J.B., V.C.,
  D.F.C., *213, 255 (footnote)*
Nieuwmunster, airfield at, *16*
Northcliffe, Lord, 1st Viscount, *28, 32 (foot-
  note)*
North Foreland, Kent, air operations over,
  112, 117, 118, 120, 126, 149, 183, 188
Northolt airfield, Middlesex, *18, 36, 64, 66,
  73, 109, 116, 137 (footnote), 147, 164,
  185, 255, 300, 320*
North Weald (Bassett) airfield, Essex, *26,
  36, 64, 66, 71, 116, 120, 126, 154, 189,
  198, 222, 235, 255, 257, 267, 270, 274,
  275, 289*
Norway, German operations against, 1940,
  78-80
Norwich, Norfolk, air operations over, *159,
  163, 164, 193, 258*
  German target document for, *176*
Nottingham, air operations over,

O
Observer Corps (later prefixed Royal), *20*

*(footnote), 25, 70, 71, 137, 141 (foot-
  note), 158, 166, 184, 188, 197, 205, 255,
  256, 261, 281, 287, 301, 324, 327*
Observer Corps Liaison Officer, duties of,
  71
Ochey, France, airfield at, *24 (footnote)*
Odhams printing works, Long Acre, London,
  27
Odiham airfield, Hampshire, *189, 204*
O.H.L. (*Oberste Heeresleitung*), *14, 15, 19,
  23, 29, 30*
O.K.L. (*Oberkommando der Luftwaffe*), *53,
  55, 82, 92, 125, 182, 188, 190, 199, 278,
  300, 301, 311, 321*
O.K.W. (*Oberkommando der Wehrmacht*),
  55, 87, 92, 94, 125, 133, 300
Old Meldrum, Aberdeenshire, *136*
"Olympic Ring" insignia, *190 (footnote)*
Operational Training Units (O.T.U.), *165,
  195, 218*
Operations Room, R.A.F. Fighter
  Command, *70*
Orfordness, Suffolk, *67, 68, 149*
Oslo-Fornebu, Norway, airfield at, *79*
Oslo-Kjeller, Norway, airfield at, *79*
Ostend, Belgium, *14, 15*
Osterkamp, Generalmajor Theo, *197, 227*
Ostfriesland, German warship, *32 (foot-
  note)*
Ostowicz, Fg. Off. A., *127*
Oswaldian, H.M. Trawler, *167 (footnote)*
Ott, Maj., ZG 2, *178, 179, 189*
Ottercops Moss CH radar station, *69, 200*
Outram, Lieut.-Col. H.W.S., C.B.E., *93*

P
Page, Plt. Off. (later Sqn. Ldr.) A.G., D.S.O.,
  D.F.C., *141*
Palli, Capt. N., *32 (footnote)*
Parabellum machine guns, *16*
Parachute and Cable (P.A.C.) defences, *219,
  220*
Paris Air Agreement, 1922, *43*
Park, Air Chief Marshal Sir Keith, G.C.B.,
  K.B.E., M.C., D.F.C., *76 (footnote), 85, 92,
  93, 109, 111, 112, 116-118, 120, 136,
  141, 143, 161, 163, 178, 184, 185, 199,
  220, 227, 235, 238, 240, 244, 247-248,
  254, 271, 281, 285, 288, 306, 316, 320,
  345*
Parnall, Fg. Off. D.G., *113*
Pas de Calais, France, air operations over,
  *108, 112, 116, 120, 129, 176, 190, 193,
  198, 203, 227, 230, 235, 240, 274, 305,
  312*
Paterson, Fg. Off. J.A., M.B.E., *148*
Pattinson, Air Cdre. L.A. (later Air Marshal
  Sir Lawrence), K.B.E., C.B., D.S.O., M.C.,
  64
Paul, Sub-Lieut. F. Dawson *102, 108, 111,
  121, 129, 150*
Pearce, Sgt. L.H.B., *121*
Pease, Fg. Off. A.P., *158*
Peel, Sqn. Ldr. (later Wg. Cdr.) J.R.A.,
  D.S.O., D.F.C., *110, 127, 136, 137, 163,
  170, 172, 195*
Pegge, Plt. Off. (later Sqn. Ldr.) C.O.J.,
  D.F.C.✸, *113*

Pemberton, Sqn. Ldr. D.A., D.F.C.,*147*
Pemberton-Billing, Noel, M.P., *17, 18, 19*
Pembrey airfield, Carmarthenshire,*121,145*
Peterhead, Aberdeenshire, *105, 132, 141*
Petworth, Sussex, *189*
Pevensey CH radar station, *69, 111, 183,*
257
Pflugbeil, General Kurt, *189*
Phillips, F/Sgt. N.T., *118*
Photographic Development Unit (P.D.U.),
108
Photographic Reconnaissance Unit(P.R.U.),
108 (footnote), 322
Pinkham, Sqn. Ldr. P.C., A.F.C., *103, 281*
Pitcairn, Hptm. Douglas, *166*
Pittman, Plt. Off. (later Sqn. Ldr.) G.E.,*126,*
203
Pixton, C. Howard, *21 (footnote)*
Plan D, War Contingency, *83*
Plymouth, Devon, air operations over, *109,*
124, 145-147, 154, 163, 244
Pohl, Admiral Hugo von, *13, 14*
Poland, German military operations against,
1939, *49, 77-78*
Polikarpov I-16 *Rata* aircraft, *53*
Poling CH radar station, *69, 146, 183, 221,*
222, 278
Polish Air Force (*Lotnictwo Wojskowe*), *77-*
78
    Squadrons:
    No. 1, *164*
    No. 42, *78*
    No. 111, *78*
Polish pilots in the R.A.F., *164, 165, 218*
Pond, F/Sgt. (later Sqn. Ldr.) A.H.D., A.F.C.,
123
Poplar, London, *18*
Porthcawl, Glamorgan, *148*
Porthtowan, Cornwall, *151*
Portishead Point, Somerset, *152*
Portland, Dorset, air operations over, *75,*
106, 116, 118, 123, 124, 127-129, 134,
139, 145, 150, 153, 157, 178, 179, 182,
185, 189, 190, 204, 239, 247
Portsmouth, Hampshire, air operations over,
109, 124, 145, 184, 185, 231, 233, 244,
292
Pour le Mérite, 131
Powell-Sheddon, Flt. Lt. (later Gp. Capt.)
G.ff., D.S.O., D.F.C., *147*
Prestwick, Ayrshire, *104, 145*
Proudman, Fg. Off. G.V., *108, 111*
PZL P.11 aircraft, *77*
PZL P.23 aircraft, *77*

Q

Queen's Island, Belfast; Short Bros. factory
at, *192*
Quill, Fg. Off. J.K., O.B.E., A.F.C., *185 (footnote)*
Quilter, Sir Cuthbert, Bt., *68*

R

Rabagliati, Flt. Lt. (later Wg. Cdr.) A.C.,
D.F.C.✳, *282*
Radar, Airborne Interception (A.I.)
equipment, *76, 146*
Radar, CH, raid reporting procedures on,

68-70
Radar, CHL, low-looking, *92*
Radar, introduction of, *67-69*
Radar, cover in 1940,
Radio Telephony, ground-to-air, *30, 67*
Radom, Polish airfield at, *77*
Ramming tactics, *121*
Rammkommando, Luftwaffe, 146 (footnote)
Ramsgate, Kent, air operations over, *118,*
183, 190, 234, 235, 378
Rathmann, Hptm., KG 3, *168, 203*
Raven, Plt. Off. A.L.B., *113*
Rechenberg, Oblt., KG 51, *135*
Red Cross Convention, *101, 118, 130*
Redhill, Surrey, A.A. Defence Centre, *26,*
278
Regia Aeronautica, 193 (footnote), 384
Reichsluftfahrtministerium (R.L.M.), *48,*
Reichswehr Ministerium, 42, 43, 49, 95
Reprisal raids on Germany, *32*
Restemeyer, Hptm. Werner, *200*
Rettberg, Hptm. Ralph von, *222*
Reynaud, Paul, French Prime Minister, *84*
Rhineland, German re-occupation of, *50,*
53,
Rhodes-Moorhouse, Fg. Off. W.H., *124,*
134
Rhodes-Moorhouse, 2nd Lieut. W.B., V.C.,
134 (footnote)
Richardson, Sqn. Ldr. (later Wg. Cdr.) W.A.,
138
Richthofen, Rittmeister Manfred Freiheer
von, *42 (footnote), 96*
Richthofen, Generalfeldmarschall Wolfram
Freiherr von, *42, 51, 83, 96, 170*
Richthofen Geschwader (1918), *47*
Richthofen Geschwader, JG 132 (1937), *48,*
Riddle, Fg. Off. (later Sqn. Ldr.) H.J., *124*
Riesenflugzeug (R-type) bombers, *15, 22,*
23, 24, 27, 29
Riesenflugzeugabteilung 500, 23
Riesenflugzeugabteilung 501, 13, 23, 24, 30
Ritchie, Plt. Off. (later Wg. Cdr.) I.S., *105,*
135
River Clyde, H.M. Trawler, *167 (footnote)*
Roberts, Wg. Cdr. (later Air Cdre.) D.N.,
C.B.E., A.F.C., *179, 190*
Robertson, Field Marshal Sir William, G.C.B.,
G.C.M.G., K.C.V.O., D.S.O., C.I.G.S., *19*
Robinson, Sgt. (later Flt. Ltn.) J., A.F.C., *154*
Robinson, Sqn. Ldr. (later Wg. Cdr.) M.,
C.B., A.F.C.✳,
Robinson, W.A., C.B., *28*
Robinson, Lieut. W. Leefe, V.C., *14, 106*
(footnote)
Roborough airfield, Devon, *147*
Rochester, Kent, *25,126,190,197,203,324*
Rochford airfield, Essex, *26, 115, 129, 198,*
249, 255, 270
Rogers, Capt. W.W., R.F.C., *25 (footnote)*
Rolls-Royce Condor engine, *38 (footnote)*
Rolls-Royce F.XI Kestrel engine,*38,39,48,*
49, 63
Rolls-Royce Goshawk engine, *62, 63,*
Rolls-Royce Ltd., *38, 40, 41, 72*
    factory at Crewe, *72,*
    factory at Glasgow, *72, 137-138*
Rolls-Royce P.V.12 Merlin engine, *63, 72*

Romilly, France, airfield at, *81*
Rootes Group, *72*
Rossiger, Hptm. Wilhelm, *183*
Rothermere, Lord, 1st Viscount, P.C.,*28,29,*
30, 71
Rotherfield, Sussex, air operations over,*206*
Rotterdam, Holland, *72*
Rowe, A.P., *67*
Royal Aero Club, *20 (footnote), 21 (foot-
note)*
Royal Air Force, foundation of, *19, 21, 27,*
28
Royal Air Force Groups:
    No. 2 (Bomber), *118*
    No. 10 (Fighter), *65, 92, 143, 153, 154,*
    157, 170, 178, 189, 235, 314
    No. 11 (Fighter), *65, 74, 76, 92, 93, 101,*
    106, 113, 116, 120, 123, 124, 132, 136,
    138, 150, 156, 194, 198, 199, 220, 229,
    242, 248, 314, 316
    No. 12 (Fighter), *65, 76, 92, 93, 235,*
    248, 256, 274, 314
    No. 13 (Fighter), *65, 92, 200*
Royal Air Force High Speed Flight,*40 (foot-
note)*
Royal Air Force Squadrons,
    No. 1, *25, 36, 37, 40, 61, 66, 81, 83, 84,*
    88, 147, 178, 198, 203, 213, 214, 257,
    274
    No. 3,*35,36,38,61,66,73,83,134,298*
    No. 12, *39,*
    No. 17, *35, 36, 38, 61, 66, 85, 87, 104,*
    118, 126, 179, 198, 203, 240, 274, 298,
    305, 385
    No. 19, *36, 40 (footnote), 61, 66, 73, 74,*
    76, 103, 109, 114, 161, 189 (footnote),
    203, 235, 274, 275, 281, 291
    No. 23, *36, 37, 40, 41, 58, 61, 66, 76,*
    No. 25, *34, 36, 40, 61, 66, 76, 197, 203,*
    254, 270, 275, 277, 320
    No. 29, *36, 61, 66, 76, 85, 100, 218, 252*
    No. 32, *36, 61, 66, 73, 88, 105, 107, 120,*
    121, 139, 141, 150, 166, 178, 193, 198,
    206, 211, 214, 240, 247
    No. 35, *18, 189*
    No. 39, *14, 29*
    No. 41,*36,61,65,66,74,113,152,154,*
    156, 197, 274, 291, 306, 323, 326
    No. 43, *36, 37, 40, 61, 66, 74, 75, 117,*
    127, 139, 141, 171, 178, 189, 190, 204,
    213, 221, 244, 256, 267, 270, 291
    No. 44, *20, 320*
    No. 46,*19,66,79,80,267,274,275,385*
    No. 50, *24*
    No. 54,*36,61,66,73,88,105,110,113-*
    115, 117, 118, 120, 129, 141, 148, 150,
    152, 178, 179, 198, 199, 211, 219, 249,
    254, 261, 262
    No. 56, *18, 19, 36, 37, 61, 66, 73, 105,*
    120, 121, 129, 132, 141, 150, 190, 198,
    214, 236, 250, 257, 267, 305, 343
    No. 61, *20,*
    No. 64, *65, 66, 102, 108, 111, 121, 129,*
    133 (footnote), 135, 139, 150, 167, 178,
    198, 211, 214, 220
    No. 65, *66, 73, 74, 108, 111, 113, 114,*
    118, 148, 150, 152, 165-166, 182, 183,
    185, 193, 198, 211, 224, 247